THE JOHNS HOPKINS GUIDE
TO LITERARY THEORY & CRITICISM

THE JOHNS HOPKINS GUIDE TO LITERARY THEORY & CRITICISM

Edited by Michael Groden and Martin Kreiswirth

THE JOHNS HOPKINS UNIVERSITY PRESS

Baltimore and London

This book has been brought to publication with the generous assistance of a subvention from the Centre for the Study of Theory and Criticism, the University of Western Ontario.

The Johns Hopkins University Press
2715 North Charles Street
Baltimore, Maryland 21218-4319
The Johns Hopkins Press Ltd., London

03 02 01 00 99 98 97 96 95 94
5 4 3

Library of Congress Cataloging-in-Publication Data

The Johns Hopkins guide to literary theory and criti-
   cism / edited by Michael Groden and Martin
   Kreiswirth.
         p.   cm.
      Includes bibliographical references (p.) and index.
      ISBN 0-8018-4560-2 (acid-free paper)
      1. Criticism—Bibliography.   I. Groden, Michael.
   II. Kreiswirth, Martin.
   Z6514.C97J64   1993
   [PN81]   93-12935
   016.809—dc20

A catalog record for this book is available
from the British Library.

FOREWORD

by Richard Macksey

The young Edward Gibbon, fresh from his Calvinist cure in Lausanne, published his first book, *Essai sur l'étude de la littérature,* in 1761. He had early learned, as he remarked near the end of his life, to be sententious. Thus he began this apprentice work with the observation: "L'Histoire des Empires est celle de la misère des hommes. L'Histoire des Sciences est celle de leur grandeur et de leur bonheur." The history of literary theory, a sprawling subset of the history of institutions, seems to fall somewhere between that of Empires and that of Sciences (or Knowledge), reflecting both the *splendeurs* and the *misères* of academic ambition. As the present *Guide* graphically illustrates, literary theory always bears the impress of larger political and cultural debates but also aspires, from Aristotle to Hans-Georg Gadamer or Jacques Derrida, toward a systematic statement of the principles and methods governing interpretation and evaluation. Inevitably tensions arise between the imperial claims of what the editors of the present work call the "underlying social, historical, or ideological interests and presuppositions" and the scientific quest for an objective and eternal system. It is perhaps the most striking paradox of contemporary critical theory that recent speculation on the side of "system" has been profoundly antitheoretical and antifoundational in character. A "hermeneutics of suspicion" with considerable theoretical subtlety challenges the Enlightenment legacies of positivism, progress, humanism, and rationalism. (Thus Richard Rorty portrays epistemology as a failed experiment in theorizing ultimate foundations, and philosophic critics as diverse as Gadamer, Derrida, Michel Foucault, and Jean-François Lyotard counterpose "universal questionability" to traditional philosophic universalism.) The vitality of this pervasive phenomenon underscores the timeliness and utility of a comprehensive survey of critical theory both before and after the great doubting.

The Johns Hopkins Guide to Literary Theory and Criticism necessarily reflects the agonistic concerns and polemical urgencies of its time, a *fin-de-siècle* era when the boundaries of critical theory and practice are particularly permeable to influences from other disciplines and cultural hegemonies. While recognizing the imperial character of the traditional claims of literary theory, the editors have also embraced the ambition of a scientific survey—the possibility of organizing in a single volume an overview of the major landmarks of criticism from classical antiquity to the present day (seen, it should be added, from a very specific, "postmodern" historical moment). In this latter ambition they join a history of guides, surveys, prolegomena, and handbooks from the Renaissance to the modern classroom.

Unlike influential reference works of earlier periods—say August Boeckh's posthumous *Encyklopädia* or René Wellek's and Austin Warren's *Theory of Literature*—this survey is presented not as a series of lectures or a master narrative but as an inventory of key critics and dominant "schools" organized under the oldest and simplest of principles, the alphabet. It is a considerable accomplishment to have faced the fearsome problems of selection and reduced the number of entries to 226. It is a comparable achievement, in the interests of what the editors call the "multivocal" and "inclusive," to have disciplined more than 200 contributors, by the nature of their trade both polemical and dilatory, into something like an investigative team observing common rules of exposition and citation. Their goal of inclusiveness is also reflected in the decision to include a substantial number of entries for theorists whose affiliation or discipline is not primarily literary studies— philosophers, political theorists, anthropologists, psychologists and psychiatrists. The disciplinary boundaries of the empire of criticism have always been notoriously unstable.

The editors have also included synoptic surveys of groups, schools, and movements (largely concentrated on contemporary practice) as well as some historical accounts of major national or ethnic bodies of criticism. All the entries are bound together by a system of internal and terminal cross-references, primary and secondary bibliographies, and a comprehensive set of indexes allowing the reader to pursue topics and figures throughout the volume.

By the nature of this organization, the *Guide* invites the reader to participate in the Shandean construction of multiple histories. Where he or she fails to find a significant critic or influential topic in the budget of entries, a trip to the apparatus will often reveal the missing element or connection. (A reader with a formalist bias, for example, will discover on consulting the indexes that apparently neglected figures from the American New Criticism are in fact discussed from several critical angles.) And like that most critical of novels, *Tristram Shandy,* the volume has no simple, unambiguous beginning or ending.

The editors have quite deliberately chosen to "foreshorten" their entries on twentieth-century critics. This is not a decision grounded in any muzzy notion of "scientific progress." Rather it is, as they confess, partially in deference to what they conceive as user needs, and partially because so much contemporary speculation in fact comprises fresh *rereadings* of critical ancestors—whether from antiquity (Plato, Aristotle, Longinus) or from more recent theoretical initiatives (Friedrich Nietzsche, Sigmund Freud, Karl Marx, Ferdinand de Saussure). This principle should, of course, invite the reader who begins with contemporary debates to make selective sorties into much earlier entries.

Although modern criticism like that of antecedent periods has seemed to flourish in a climate of continuing crisis (real or staged) and the polemical edges of the critics discussed in this volume are all too obvious, it may prove useful for the reader exploring this *Guide* to consider a few irenic observations about the issues that underlie this warfare. Simply put, despite the intrinsically polemical character of literary criticism, there is not quite so much disagreement among conflicting critical theorists as there might seem to be, if only the following metacritical tasks are faced: (a) the discrimination of the major critical *questions* that emerge from the polemical welter; (b) the situation of primary *subject* of study (whether it be the "work," text or context, creative pretext or postconstructive consequences); and (c) the patient discrimination of which critical *languages* or lexicons are being invoked. In the manner of Georges Perec's preliminaries to his *La Vie: mode d'emploi,* these few comments about the issues common to all modes of critical discourse may be taken as a sketchy "user's manual" for readers exploring this *Guide.*

While they skirt the truly difficult problems exposed within the volume, they can *grosso modo* offer some sense of direction and continuity to those just starting out. By the very nature of their limitations, these schematics can also suggest the complexity of the recurrent issues and the difficulty of navigating with only compass and map.

The recurrent critical questions seldom, of course, occur in isolation, but one reason for the total deafness of many critics to each other, even as they attend to the same text, is often that they are primarily concerned with addressing very different though equally complex problems. A preliminary—and admittedly partial—inventory of basic critical questions would include the following baker's dozen of queries directed to either textual parts or wholes:

1. *Ontological:* What is the literary work's nature and mode of existence? This question inevitably raises consequent questions about the philosophy of language and mimetic representation. The response may also involve the discrimination of strata in reading and implicate a number of the other critical questions noted below.

2. *Epistemological:* How can we "know" the work (or process); what is its "cognitive content," its kind of "truth" (or uncertainty)?

3. *Teleological:* What is the function and purpose of the work (or literature)—in, for example, the good society, the Marxist state, the constitution of gender, the ideal university?

4. *Archeological:* What is the source or origin of the work—in the individual or tradition, in the response of the person or society—and how can we describe its genesis?

5. *Descriptive:* What can be said formally about the intrinsic characteristics of the work itself—about (a) its phonetic aspects; (b) its semantics of either simple or complex units; (c) the relations of phonetics and semantics? This question is usually extended to include most semiotic, stylistic, and rhetorical analysis.

6. *Interpretive:* What can be said about the extrinsic relations of the work to the "real" world—about (a) thematics and (b) thesis statements? The labors of hermeneutics traditionally move from question 5 to question 6.

7. *Performative:* How can the critic reenact or "perform" the work in its richest sense? This approach

generally involves related questions about competency, "optimal" reading, and the critic's identification with the text. While in its simplest form this involves Ion's trade, combined with historical and cultural concerns, it can raise issues of reader's response accounts and cultural conditioning.

8. *Normative:* How is literature to be judged by the application of explicit or implicit standards, by criteria such as unity, complexity, originality, moral seriousness, and so on? The act of judging an individual work can also implicate normative issues such as the authority of artistic canons, traditions, hierarchies of genres, etc.

9. *Historical:* How can the work as an "event" be related to other events, artistic or otherwise? In contemporary practice, this is clearly one of the most complex and divisive questions; but taken simply, the principles of organization for an historical account may be any of the following: (a) *annalistic,* a simple chronological sequence of works, authors, or schools; (b) *organic,* integrating each text to a governing value, norm, convention, unit-idea, or analogue considered diachronically; (c) *dialectical,* introducing another level of necessity where the work is related to an underlying causal factor or factors, such as determining economic, social, political, linguistic, or psychological structures; (d) *narrative,* the construction of a coherent story (in the words of R. S. Crane, "a continuity of a sequence of distinct events connected causally by whatever individual men [sic] or groups of men, through a period of time, happened to do with respect to the element constituting the continuum of change"); this construction specifically involves selection and the discovery of "plots" and agents in the changing relationships between the author and his or her materials, forms, or objectives. This last version may include a history of artistic "kinds" as well as of devices, conventions, preoccupations, and uses—all implicating other questions in this budget.

10. *Cultural:* How may literary documents (and popular culture generally) illuminate our understanding of cultural groups, ethnic or gender interests, "marginalities," etc.? This is an approach, related to the question of history and of much recent currency, that shifts the focus of inquiry away from the institution of literature toward an account of these collective bodies. Against the formalist emphasis on the "work" as independent entity (implicit in the way many of the other questions in this budget are framed), the cultural question attends to calibrating issues such as the degrees of exclusion and inclusion, of domination and sufferance, of complicity and resistance in the social sphere. It also tends to extend the notion of textual well beyond traditional notions of "literature."

11. *Psychological:* This represents another complex question or congeries of questions that interrogates how the text is related to mind (feelings, ideas, obsessions, repressions). Apart from studying the representation of "psyches" or "types" within the work, this inquiry is usually directed toward two quite different aspects of the artistic process, one preconstructive and the other postconstructive, namely—

Genetic: How did the author's (or group's) mind operate in the creation and the shaping up of the work?

Affective: How does the mind of the reader or the audience respond to the work and contribute to its completion?

12. *Appreciative:* How does it grab you? The celebration of the work through the appreciative response of the critic is always in danger of lapsing into narcissism.

13. *Metacritical:* How does the critical work (a second-order object) reveal certain implicit or explicit critical assumptions, metaphysical presuppositions, and controlling methodologies in approaching the sphere, limits, and uses of art? Like the initial questions, this is in fact the domain of the philosopher.

Not all of these questions have at any given period been considered interesting, appropriate, or even decent, but clearly the choice of critical language and the vector of the critic's attention will in part be a function of which question or complex of questions is being valorized. And since not all texts respond equally generously to individual questions, the same matter of privilege may well help to determine the choice of text or canon (though for an ideal critic the text should probably dictate the question).

The fact remains, however, that in traversing the *Guide* a discrimination of the executive critical questions and of the relevant critical subject can go a long way in helping us to recognize significant continuities and change in theoretical postures.

Finally, the vexed problem of discriminating critical "languages" is far too complex to address in a brief liminal note. Each major critic shapes a discourse that inflects the language of the tribe with a special and privileged body of terms. Even more fundamentally, from the time of the *Cratylus,* the viscosity of language has been a daunting problem for philosophic criticism. In our own time, the antifoundationalist critics have attempted to turn this embarrassment into a critical asset. Thus, to take but the most familiar contemporary statement of this allegedly "happy fall" from absolutes into language ("the home of contingency"), Jacques Derrida has argued (in the strategic vocabulary of warfare):

> However the topic is considered, the problem of language has never been simply one problem among others. But never as much as at present has it invaded, as such, the global horizon of the most diverse researches and the most heterogeneous discourses, diverse and heterogeneous in their intention, method, and ideology. . . . An historico-metaphysical epoch must finally determine as language the totality of its problematic horizon. (*Of Grammatology,* 6)

If a formal consideration of the place of language in the definition of these conditions is beyond the scope of these remarks, at a more trivial level the reader can attend to the constantly changing contours of the critical lexicon. Writing of "critical games-

manship," I have elsewhere argued that in the lower reaches of academic criticism it is not so much a matter of pursuing an argument or exploring a text as invoking the right *words.* Schools and charters of critical privilege are, however, as the *Guide* can remind us, frequently dissolved or reorganized. While the central problems persist, the critical vocabularies can change with the rapidity of Parisian *haute couture.*

All this should serve to remind us of what was implicit in critical theory's long history of polemical disputation. Much that is original and insightful in genuine criticism depends upon the angry response to what is perceived as bad criticism—the mindless, repetitive, and pretentious. Put somewhat more cynically this dynamic could be stated as The First Law of Relativity: earlier schools of criticism are trivial (i.e., ridiculous); later schools are deliberately opaque (i.e., infuriating).

Against atrabilious comments such as these, the selectivity, range, and expository clarity of the *Guide* should serve as a timely antidote or *pharmakon.* The editors speak of their effort to suppress "programmatic bias." Every reader, turning the volume to local use, can supply this.

PREFACE

Over the course of the past two or three decades literary theory and criticism have come to play a central role in the academic study of the humanities and social sciences. The diverse, often apparently competing or incompatible approaches, perspectives, and modes of inquiry that flourish today under the generic label "theory" have brought most scholars to a welcome awareness of the importance of attending at least to methodological concerns in critical practice. Moreover, criticism as it is currently understood no longer confines itself to the study of literature: its discourses now extend well beyond literature to intersect with anthropology, philosophy, psychology, linguistics, political science, and much else besides, even as the objects of critical analysis by "literary" scholars encompass all forms of cultural production, literary and nonliterary.

Criticism still embraces exegesis, interpretation, and evaluation, as it has traditionally done, but today it often encroaches upon the territory of "theory," whether we characterize theory as discussion and debates about basic definitions, as the search for necessary and sufficient foundations for evaluating critical practice, or as the self-reflexive process of making explicit underlying social, historical, or ideological interests and presuppositions. The semantic boundaries between "theory" and "criticism" blur. We see the terms often used interchangeably. Frequently, however, they occur together to signal at once their overlapping as well as their divergent possible meanings, and this is the reason both appear in the title of this book.

There is a growing sense among specialists that a watershed has been reached in the great literary-theoretical adventure leading up to the present. The *Guide* is designed in part to assist with the necessary work of stock-taking and consolidation: if it helps to make accessible in clear and concise form a body of material that has become overwhelming, it will have achieved a large task indeed. We hope it will have a wide audience in the academy, not only of professors and graduate students in literary studies but also of many others working in adjacent fields that have been significantly influenced by recent developments in literary theory and criticism.

Intended for use by scholars as well as by students and others seriously interested but without specialized knowledge, the *Guide* endeavors to act as an informative, reliable introduction to the principal manifestations of this large and challenging area of inquiry. Our hope is that the *Guide* will answer most of the questions that occur to teachers, students, and others as they traverse the critical and theoretical landscape and that it will show them where to turn for instruction beyond the range of the *Guide* itself.

As evidence of the widespread interest in literary theory and criticism, there has been a proliferation of study aids, tools, and reference guides that either touch upon or deal extensively with the subject. Valuable as many of them are, these books—anthologies of primary texts, dictionaries, narrative surveys of one sort or another—nonetheless fail to offer readers an accessible means of establishing a context broad, deep, and flexible enough to engage directly the many definitional difficulties and discursive complexities that abound in literary theory and criticism.

The *Johns Hopkins Guide to Literary Theory and Criticism* is designed to furnish readers with the means to establish just such a context. Its chronological range extends from Plato and Aristotle to the present, with wide geographical and cultural coverage. In deference to the probable needs of the majority of potential users, however, we have concentrated on the vast outpouring of modern criticism and theoretical research. While thus deliberately foreshortened on the twentieth century, the *Guide* is decidedly historical in orientation: topics are weighted in terms of their importance in the field of literary studies, as seen from the vantage point of today and especially as pursued in North America, although allowances have naturally been made for unusually complex or technical subjects.

The *Guide* consists of 226 alphabetically arranged

entries on individual critics and theorists, critical and theoretical schools and movements, and the critical and theoretical innovations of specific countries and historical periods. It also treats figures who did not explicitly deal with, but who still deeply affected, literature, literary theory, or literary criticism, as well as figures and kinds of inquiry from other fields that have been shaped by or have themselves shaped literary theory and criticism. Each entry includes a selective primary and secondary bibliography, and there is extensive cross-referencing both within and at the conclusion of each entry. The indexes are designed to allow readers to locate substantive discussions of people and topics wherever they occur in the *Guide*. A complete list of entries immediately follows the last *Guide* entry. Given the multiplicity of access points provided—alphabetically arranged entries, ample cross-referencing, bibliographies, indexes—the reader should be able to make use of what the *Guide* offers in a variety of ways.

Mindful of the political, if not polemical, cast of contemporary literary studies, we face squarely the question of bias. Entry topics have been selected as objectively as possible, with the benefit of a great deal of outside advice, and we are convinced that the editorial contours of the volume do indeed accurately reflect the coverage and focus described above. In some cases, it must be said, individuals and topics became prominent only after we had fixed the list of entries, and so have not been included; to a smaller extent the final contents were limited by our ability to find appropriate contributors or by the ability of contributors to submit commissioned essays. But the guiding motive behind this project has been not to present the field through any one critical or theoretical avenue but to provide readers with informed access to the field.

The result is not, nor could it have been, wholly unobjectionable on this score, but whatever limitations may be attributed to the *Guide* reflect inevitable differences in editorial judgment and personal perspective, not programmatic bias. Although no principle of organizing information is altogether theoretically or ideologically innocent, we have attempted to make the *Guide* open and useful to all critical and theoretical purposes, to avoid imposing a theoretically prejudiced view of the whole.

Representing the combined effort of more than two hundred contributors, the book is multivocal and inclusive. As was the case with the selection of entry topics, the selection of contributors reflects the advice of hundreds of scholars and experts. We sought specialists who were able to place their subjects in the context of the larger intellectual environment, and ideally their entries provide reliable, accurate, and also interesting accounts in which their own positions neither dominate nor are obscured. We read and assessed all the completed entries, which were also appraised by external readers chosen by the publisher. Entries are all signed by their authors, and a complete list of the contributors precedes the indexes.

Using the *Guide*

To make the *Guide* as convenient to consult as possible, we have adopted throughout certain uniform conventions:

- Cross-references are indicated by SMALL CAPS, but only when the name or phrase exactly matches an entry title (for example, RENÈ DESCARTES is cross-referenced, while "Cartesian" is not).

- Parenthetical "see" references within entries and more general "see also" indications at the end of each entry direct readers to related discussions elsewhere in the volume.

- For an individual critic or theorist who was or is also a poet, novelist, or playwright, a cross-reference is provided only when he or she is considered as a critic-theorist (no cross-reference is provided, for example, when Johann Wolfgang von Goethe is discussed only as the author of *Faust*).

- A cross-reference is provided only at the first appearance in each entry of another entry title.

- Translations of non-English texts are by the entry authors unless a parenthetical reference points to a published translation listed in the bibliography.

- For non-English titles, we have tried to give both the original and an English translation in the entries and in the bibliographies, but complete consistency in this has eluded us.

- To save space in the references, we call attention to italics only where the author of an entry has introduced them into a quotation; where no indication follows italicized words in a quotation, the italics appear in the original text.

- Quotations are referenced in accordance with the system adopted by the Modern Language Association of America.

- Abbreviations are the conventional ones or are otherwise self-evident.

The bibliographies that appear immediately after the body of each entry offer selected lists of primary sources (first paragraph) and secondary ones (second paragraph). These bibliographies also include sources for quotations that appear in the entries, unless full references are given within the entry. Lists of entries and of contributors may be found immediately after the last *Guide* entry. The indexes that follow these lists reference names and topics treated at substantial length within one or more entries (we mean by "sub-stantial" a full paragraph or the equivalent). The indexes list names and topics that are not discussed so often that their inclusion would be meaningless. Names and topics in SMALL CAPS are themselves full entries. Finally, the indexes direct readers to entries by title.

Michael Groden and Martin Kreiswirth

ACKNOWLEDGMENTS

A project of this scope, magnitude, and duration could not have been brought to fruition without the help of many people and institutions. The Academic Development Fund of the University of Western Ontario provided seed money at the start. Throughout the project the University's Centre for the Study of Theory and Criticism provided substantial support. Needless to say, the *Guide* itself would not exist but for the efforts of the legion of contributors, who conscientiously and patiently wrote and sometimes rewrote their entries at our request. Along the way we consulted far more people than we can name; the list of entry topics evolved and mutated substantially under the pressure of this counsel and advice. We benefited greatly in addition from the numerous outside evaluators enlisted by the publisher to appraise completed entries.

We want to thank the student and research assistants who helped us in various important ways: Cameron Bailey, David Brooks, Jim Horton, Susan Jay, Andrew Johnson, Kinny Kreiswirth, Will McConnell, Karim Mamdani, Dan Mellamphy, Michelle Reynolds, Anand Thakkar, and Anita Utas. We are grateful to Eric Halpern, editor-in-chief at the Johns Hopkins University Press, for taking a chance on the book on the basis of only a short proposal and a few sample entries and for remaining supportive all the way, as well as to Joanne Allen, Theresa Donnelly, Li-Wen Huang, Kimberly Johnson, and Jacqueline Wehmueller, at the Press, for their support, advice, cooperation, patience, and expertise. Errors that remain in the book are our responsibility, but there would have been many more without the heroic copyediting labors of Joanne Allen. We also thank Vicki Mahaffey, Ted Mason, and Bonnie Scott for helping out at particularly urgent moments.

Finally, for continuing love and support of a distinctly nontheoretical nature, Michael Groden dedicates this book to Molly Peacock, and Martin Kreiswirth to Kinny, Aaron, Nathan, and Hannah Kreiswirth.

M.G. and M.K.

THE JOHNS HOPKINS GUIDE
TO LITERARY THEORY & CRITICISM

A

ABRAMS, M. H.

Meyer Howard Abrams (b. 1912) set the standard of critical authority for American literary studies for the quarter-century after World War II. Author of two magisterial syntheses of English Romantic thought, he has also been general and Romantic period editor of the most widely used college anthology of English literature *(The Norton Anthology of English Literature),* author of a popular *Glossary of Literary Terms,* promulgator of a generally accepted schema of orientations of critical theories, author of several influential essays on English Romanticism *(The Correspondent Breeze),* critic of criticism *(Doing Things with Texts),* and mentor of, among many other Romanticists, HAROLD BLOOM. Trained in the 1930s at Harvard in what Jonathan Arac has called the " 'Harvard' school of literary history" (77), Abrams studied with I. A. RICHARDS at Cambridge University in 1935, the year after Richards's *Coleridge on Imagination* appeared.

Abrams's 1940 dissertation, expanded and published in 1953 as *The Mirror and the Lamp: Romantic Theory and the Critical Tradition,* shares Richards's New Critical admiration for SAMUEL TAYLOR COLERIDGE's organicist theory, continues Irving Babbitt's New Humanist critique of WILLIAM WORDSWORTH's Romantic primitivism and irrationalism, and answers historian of ideas A. O. Lovejoy's skeptical "Discrimination of Romanticisms" with a single Romantic "expressive" orientation toward the poet. Abrams distinguishes that orientation from the mimetic orientation, which treats art as an imitation of aspects of the universe; the pragmatic orientation, which treats art as an attempt to affect its audience; and the objective orientation, which treats the relations of parts within the work of art itself. This scheme of orientations, simplified from the Chicago critic Richard McKeon's philosophical semantics, has been adopted in many anthologies and surveys of criticism as well as in James Kinneavy's *Theory of Discourse.* (See also CHICAGO CRITICS, HISTORY OF IDEAS, NEW CRITICISM, and NEW HUMANISM.)

In addition to demonstrating the ubiquity of the expressive orientation in Romantic critical prose, Abrams amplified a number of oppositions that define Romantic critical theory, most notably the opposition his title highlights between art as mimetic mirror and art as expressive lamp but also oppositions between organic and mechanical theories of mind and between science and poetry. He also documented the "varieties of Romantic theory" (chapters 5–6) within the unity of expressive poetics. Abrams's historical method treats Romantic texts from a variety of genres as sources of statements that illustrate the themes and topics of his own argument, subordinating their internal conflicts and various purposes to the establishment of a broad Romantic consensus that characterizes a distinctive Romantic age. *The Mirror and the Lamp* contributed to the legitimation of English Romanticism as a field of study and provided a model of erudition and authority to which many young scholars in the 1950s aspired (e.g., Thomas McFarland in Lipking). Like his friendly rival Earl Wasserman at Johns Hopkins, Abrams built at Cornell an unimpeachable career as a Jewish scholar of Romanticism in the then predominantly WASP profession of English on the foundation of thorough, unpolemical coverage of the field.

Nearly 20 years later, in *Natural Supernaturalism,* Abrams asserted a different thesis with similar authority. Arguing the continuity of Romantic with Christian and Neoplatonic thought, he replaced without comment the paradigmatic text of *The Mirror and the Lamp,* Wordsworth's "Preface to *Lyrical Ballads,*" with a new Romantic paradigm, Wordsworth's Prospectus to *The Recluse,* and treated it and other major works of English and German Romanticism as secular variations on the religious themes of "the fall, the redemption, and the emergence of a new earth which will constitute a restored paradise" (29). More ambitious than *The Mirror and the Lamp* in representing "Romantic thought and literature . . . [as] a decisive turn in Western culture" (14), *Natural Supernaturalism* asserted its magisterial authority to a dramatically different critical reception. J. HILLIS MILLER, in the wake of the 1966 Johns Hopkins conference on the Languages of Criticism and the Sciences of Man—the event that marked the arrival of DECONSTRUCTION in American criticism—challenged both the traditional scholarship Abrams exemplified and the metaphysical tradition he celebrated from the deconstructive perspectives of FRIEDRICH NIETZSCHE, JACQUES DERRIDA, and PAUL DE MAN. As the principal exemplar of humanist critical authority, Abrams has also drawn fire from New Historicist Romanticist Jerome McGann *(The Romantic Ideology)* (see also NEW HISTORICISM). Wayne Booth has analyzed Abrams's rhetoric and defended its authority *(Critical Understanding),* Jonathan Culler (in Lipking) has reread Abrams's analysis of figurative language in *The Mirror and the Lamp* as proto-deconstructionist, and Jonathan Arac has situated Abrams's work in its own cultural context. Abrams's elaboration of his humanist credo, his development of his theoretical principles, and his answers to these and other critics have been gathered in *Doing Things with Texts.*

Don Bialostosky

See also BRITISH THEORY AND CRITICISM: 3. ROMANTIC PERIOD AND EARLY NINETEENTH CENTURY, GERMAN THEORY AND CRITICISM: 2. ROMANTICISM, and HISTORICAL THEORY AND CRITICISM.

M. H. Abrams, *The Correspondent Breeze: Essays on English Romanticism* (1984), *Doing Things with Texts: Essays in Criticism and Critical Theory* (ed. Michael Fischer, 1989), *A Glossary of Literary Terms* (1957, 6th ed., 1993), *The Mirror and the Lamp: Romantic Theory and the Critical Tradition* (1953), *Natural Supernaturalism: Tradition and Revolution in Romantic Literature* (1971).

M. H. Abrams, Wayne C. Booth, and J. Hillis Miller, "The Limits of Critical Pluralism," *Critical Inquiry* 3 (1977); Jonathan Arac, *Critical Genealogies: Historical Situations for Postmodern Literary Studies* (1987); Wayne C. Booth, *Critical Understanding: The Powers and Limits of Pluralism* (1979); James L. Kinneavy, *A Theory of Discourse: The Aims of Discourse* (1971); Lawrence Lipking, ed., *High Romantic Argument: Essays for M. H. Abrams* (1981); Jerome J. McGann, *The Romantic Ideology: A Critical Investigation* (1983); J. Hillis Miller, "Tradition and Difference," *diacritics* 2 (1972).

ADORNO, THEODOR W.

Theodor W. Adorno (1903–69) began his intellectual career in Frankfurt and Vienna during the Weimar Republic, continued his work during the Hitler period in British and (often together with Max Horkheimer) American exile, and returned to West Germany after the war to reconstitute with Horkheimer the FRANKFURT SCHOOL of neo-Marxist "critical theory." A capacious European intellectual of universal interests, his writings address an astonishing variety of concerns and disciplines: phi-

losophy and sociology, psychology and social research, aesthetics, literary and music criticism, the philosophy and sociology of music. His essays in literary criticism form a relatively small part of his *oeuvre,* which sets forth a coherent philosophical position that must be briefly addressed through mention of some of his central works.

Dialectic of Enlightenment (1947) proposes an overarching philosophy of history based on the notion of the domination of nature, arguing that the Western world, impelled by the instinct of self-preservation, once overcame the terrors of nature through magic, myth, and finally the Enlightenment but that this cognitive and technological Enlightenment then reverted to myth and barbarism (the historical reference point is German fascism). Reason became instrumental and technocratic, and humans forgot their imbrication with the natural environment. The theme of the domination of nature, with nature conceived (as in Karl Marx) as both outer and "inner" nature, is thus combined with the Weberian motif of rationalization and "disenchantment" of the world to produce a "concept of Enlightenment" (the title of the first, programmatic chapter) that betrays its own original liberating impulse. The equivocation in this account, never explicit in the book, is its reliance on an emphatic or even utopian concept of "good" reason as the basis for its criticism of the insufficient, truncated reason of the Enlightenment.

Negative Dialectics (1966) addresses this truncation of plenitudinous reason on the cognitive level of (philosophical) concepts: insisting on the nonidentity of concept and object, of universal and particular, and evoking the danger that the former will subsume the latter, the book posits a number of philosophical polarities in order to work through in immanent criticism the inadequacies of conceptual opposites, and this by means of a dialectic that never results in synthesis or closure but insists on the continuing tension between concepts. The central term "nonidentity" (similar to JACQUES DERRIDA's *différance*), by evoking the fundamental disjunction between the concept and its purported referent, goads Adorno into philosophizing in "constellations" or "models," where the concepts and oppositions of traditional metaphysics (subject and object, the universal and the particular) are considered in the chiasmatic perspective of both their truth and their falsehood. Dialectic without closure, or "negative dialectics," based on the materialist assumption of the "priority of the object," thus becomes a never-ending effort to transcend by means of concepts the limitations of those concepts, circling about the ideal object: the individual, the specific, the nonidentical.

In its distrust of logical rigor or Cartesian clarity and distinctness, such thought clearly tends toward the aesthetic: the posthumously published fragment *Aesthetic Theory* (1970) addresses classical themes of aesthetics—the autonomy of the work of art and its status as sociohistorical phenomenon, the beauty of nature and of art, *schöner Schein* ("beautiful semblance")—in order to insist that philosophical aesthetics must come to grips with (not necessarily "beautiful") modernist art and its persistent negation of society, as part of social criticism's recurrent struggle to resist social conformity and mindless passivity in the postwar West. For Adorno, the paradigmatic innovation of modernist art was the atonal music of the Vienna school, led by Arnold Schönberg. In his *Philosophy of Modern Music* (1949), which juxtaposes Schönberg with Igor Stravinsky and founds a new discipline—the sociology of music—Adorno analyzes the composers' compositional techniques and argues both that atonal music represents the logical "immanent" development of musical material and that such development depicts precisely in its obstinate negativity the historical-philosophical course of the capitalist West in the twentieth century. All Adorno's writings reflect the dominance of the musical model in their compositional technique.

The preeminent challenge of Adorno's aesthetics of negativity, and of his writings on literature and music, is the Marxist project of relating not only themes but also technique—not only content but also the intricacies of artistic form—to general social and historical development, while avoiding the familiar dead ends of orthodox Marxist criticism. Great art is for Adorno an indispensable historical-philosophical sundial, illuminating aspects of social reality while irreconcilably criticizing and negating it. Philosophy or criticism, employing "The Essay as Form" (the opening essay of the collection *Notes to Literature*), interprets works (in the manner of WALTER BENJAMIN) as sudden allegorical flashes of historical truth, which criticism reconstructs by placing the philosophical concepts they elicit into a new constellation, from which the historical truth content of the works might emerge. The essay as form thus mediates between philosophy and art and partakes of both. Of particular interest to Adorno are the works of high modernism that have been such a bane for orthodox Marxism, which (as in GEORG LUKÁCS's analyses) has tended to favor referential realism (see KARL MARX AND FRIEDRICH ENGELS and MARXIST THEORY AND CRITICISM).

The essays "Extorted Reconciliation" and "Commitment" are typical: in the former, Adorno excoriates Lukács for his reductionist insistence on content to the exclusion of form and for his ahistorical sanctification of one particular literary form as forever appropriate for depiction of historical reality. The criticism of JEAN-PAUL SARTRE in "Commitment" forms part of Adorno's ongoing confrontation with existentialism (his usual target is MARTIN HEIDEGGER), the dominant philosophical movement when he was writing; here Adorno claims that in his plays Sartre exhibits his intention or thesis, the necessity for a "decision." Such completely subjective "decisionism" not only ignores the objective collectivity; the criterion of irrational "choice" would also be compatible on its own terms with a call for self-sacrifice exploitable by fascism. Adorno's critique of Bertolt Brecht in this essay is less satisfying than his warnings of the dangers of existentialism: so intent is he on rejecting a particular "content" or "doctrine" advanced by the work that he also ignores Brecht's own technical and formal innovations in drama. The antipode in drama to Sartre or Brecht is Samuel Beckett: in "Trying to Understand *Endgame*," Adorno defends Beckett from the labels "absurd" and "existentialist" and insists that after Auschwitz, culture is inextricably bound up with guilt, a culture embodied by Beckett's ashcans. The play shows what pathetic fragments of language and of individuality remain to truncated humans but contains no vision of reconciliation, insisting only on the negative.

Lyric poetry offers a greater challenge for historical or Marxist criticism than drama, and Adorno directly confronts it in "On Lyric Poetry and Society." The titular phenomena are juxtaposed in classical dialectical fashion: no poetry without spontaneity and individual experience but no individuality without universality and society. The great poet is the one who can surrender most completely to the most advanced demands of poetic language and as a result can produce poetry that exhibits the historical moment. The central historical moment is the decline of the "heroic" phase of bourgeois society and the emergence of mass capitalism in the mid-nineteenth century; and the poet of this transition is CHARLES BAUDELAIRE, the first modern poet, who thematizes antilyrical modern society. The essay explores this transition by interpreting two poems: an Eduard Mörike poem still contains elements of classicism and bourgeois humanism, albeit depicting them as transient and ephemeral, whereas a later poem by Stefan George exemplifies hermetic and refined withdrawal from crass commercialized society. Here Adorno attempts to rescue the hermeticism of aesthetes such as George or Hugo von Hofmannsthal (an essay in *Prisms* addresses their correspondence) as a negation of the literary marketplace, despite their aristocratic conservatism. It is a large burden to place on principles of aesthetic selection and exclusion—the alleged surrender to pure language—to claim that they constitute lyrical protest and negation and are thus amenable to Marxist criticism.

Other essays discuss high modernist prose: *Prisms* contains essays entitled "Valéry Proust Museum" and "Notes on Kafka," while *Notes to Literature* contains "Short Commentaries on Proust" and "The Artist as Deputy" (on PAUL VALÉRY's prose), where Adorno's procedure is on display. Marcel Proust's "involuntary memory" and Franz Kafka's opaque motifs and gestures embody artistic memory of the high price of reason and individuality and negate the inhumanity of their era. But Adorno does not limit himself to the critique of the liberal capitalist era and the modernist art it produced. One stimulating aspect of his literary essays is that they also confront premodern, "classical" literary works.

Here again, his task is great, for often he must rescue the authors from their (conservative) supporters and the corresponding reception history. An essay on Joseph Eichendorff emphasizes the allegorical nature of his apparently so mundane poetic images, viewing their immediacy as a false facade, a longing for fulfillment destined never to be reached. Where such drastic rescue is not necessary, as in the politically critical Heinrich Heine ("Heine the Wound"), Adorno shows an insensitivity similar to his blindness for Brecht's virtues. Two essays treat JOHANN WOLFGANG VON GOETHE. One, "On the Final Scene of *Faust*," employs concrete details to question the ultimate validity of the supposed mythical equality of the pact. A second seeks to rescue the classical humanism of Goethe's *Iphigenie* from decades of apolitical (and pedagogical) hypostatization. While "humanism" is the "intentional" thesis of the play, the achievement of reconciliation is illusory and forced; one easily forgets that the most humane figure is Thoas. The play's real achievement is formal: the subjugation of subjectivity, its autonomous realization in language. The play demonstrates the emptiness of heroic gestures but does so by the questionable means of aristocratic distance. Finally, one essay on a pre-modern writer discovers a modern after all: the essay "Parataxis" shows how FRIEDRICH HÖLDERLIN's use of this form in his late poems demonstrates the poet's suspicion of bounded discourse. He employs allegorical fragments (even historical names) in a sequence without logical connection, thereby transcending merely subjective intentionality by evoking free association of correspondences and inspiring memory, as in the late "Mnemosyne," which becomes an example of the "anamnesis of oppressed nature" called for in *Dialectic of Enlightenment*.

In all his essays, Adorno employs a procedure of jux-taposing fragments without hierarchy or synthesis. Each interpretive "vignette" is equal to the others, and together they constitute a new constellation. Such essays cannot be summarized, for they are not organized as "thesis" and "demonstration." In abruptly juxtaposing detailed observation with larger sociohistorical claims, they run the danger of arbitrariness. But that also results in their stimulating quality. Most stimulating is Adorno's tireless effort to read advanced works of literary modernism in a recognizably materialist and Marxist fashion, while having abandoned its customary but inapplicable categories, such as realism and reflection.

Michael T. Jones

See also FRANKFURT SCHOOL.

Theodor W. Adorno, *Ästhetische Theorie* (*Gesammelte Schriften*, vol. 7, ed. Gretel Adorno and Rolf Tiedemann, 1970, *Aesthetic Theory*, trans. C. Lenhardt, 1984), *Mahler: A Musical Physiognomy* (trans. Edmund Jephcott, 1992), *Negative Dialektik* (1966, *Negative Dialectics*, trans. E. B. Ashton, 1973), *Noten zur Literatur* (ed. Rolf Tiedemann, 2 vols., 1974, *Notes to Literature*, trans. Shierry Weber Nicholsen, 1991–92), *Philosophie der neuen Musik* (1949, 2d ed., 1958, *Philosophy of Modern Music*, trans. Anne G. Mitchell and Wesley V. Blomster, 1973), *Prismen: Kulturkritik und Gesellschaft* (1955, *Prisms*, trans. Samuel Weber and Shierry Weber, 1981); Theodor W. Adorno et al., *Aesthetics and Politics* (trans. Anna Bostock et al., 1977); Andrew Arato and Eike Gebhardt, eds., *The Essential Frankfurt School Reader* (1978); Max Horkheimer and Theodor W. Adorno, *Dialetik der Aufklärung: Philosophische Fragmente* (1947, *Dialectic of Enlightenment*, trans. John Cumming, 1972).

Seyla Benhabib, *Critique, Norm, and Utopia: A Study of the Foundations of Critical Theory* (1986); Susan Buck-Morss, *The Origin of Negative Dialectics: Theodor W. Adorno, Walter Benjamin, and the Frankfurt Institute* (1977); Paul Connerton, *The Tragedy of Enlightenment: An Essay on the Frankfurt School* (1980); Fredric Jameson, *Late Marxism: Adorno, or, The Persistence of the Dialectic* (1990), *Marxism and Form: Twentieth-Century Dialectical Theories of Literature* (1971); Martin Jay, *Adorno* (1984), *The Dialectical Imagination: A History of the Frankfurt School and the Institute of Social Research, 1923–1950* (1973), *Marxism and Totality: The Adventures of a Concept from Lukács to Habermas* (1984); Eugene Lunn, *Marxism and Modernism: A Historical Study of Lukács, Brecht, Benjamin, and Adorno* (1982); John O'Neill, ed., *On Critical Theory* (1976); Gillian Rose, *The Melancholy Science: An Introduction to the Thought of Theodor W. Adorno* (1978).

AFRICAN THEORY AND CRITICISM

African literary theory and criticism has emerged out of a discourse of nationalism/continentalism constituted in a political and cultural act of resistance. Ironically, the components of African nationalist ideology are often derived from the colonial-imperial discourse against which this nationalism struggles. Thus the language and representational framework within which African literary creation and criticism have evolved, to say nothing of the control of the book market, tends to be determined by the still largely dominant structures of colonial power.

The establishment of *Présence Africaine* as a literary journal and publishing house in Dakar and Paris under the patronage of Western intellectuals epitomizes the paradoxical relationship of African literature to Western influences. Ngugi wa Thiong'o (Kenya) asserts that

> the root cause of the African writer's predicament [is] historically explainable in terms of the colonial/racist encirclement and brutal suppression of African languages and cultures; that the African writer [is] himself part of the petty bourgeois class which has completely imbibed . . . western bourgeois education and cultures and the world outlook these carried. (*Writers* 57–58)

Since the writing and critical reception of the European-language African texts in the years preceding 1960 occurred under the tutelage of European and U.S. "promoters," indigenous African literary practice since then has vacillated between the rejection of and the fascination with Western structures. Critical apparatus and modes of reading and interpretation of African literatures continue to issue out of the Euro-American bloc. In "Out of Africa: Typologies of Nativism" (1988) Kwame Anthony Appiah (Ghana) postulates that "the language of empire—of center and periphery, identity and difference, the sovereign subject and her colonies—continues to structure the criticism and reception of African literature *in* Africa as elsewhere." Two opposing currents impede critical balance: "the emphasis on the demonisation of a dominant Europe producing and perpetuating a cultural margin called the Other"; and resistance, "the multiform varieties of individual and collective agency available to the African subject . . . the achievements and the possibilities of African writing" (175).

Given the multiplicity of linguistic, historical, cultural, racial, ethnic, gender, and national differentiations on the African continent, is it not perhaps more meaningful to speak of African *literatures* rather than African *literature?* Chinua Achebe (Nigeria) once wrote that "you cannot cram African literature into a small, neat definition. . . . I do not see African literature as one unit but as a group of associated units—in fact the sum total of all the national and ethnic literatures of Africa" (*Morning Yet on Creation Day*, 1975, 56).

Issues of national autonomy, language, ideology, and cultural politics are framed within external and internal hegemonies with considerable implication for African daily existence. There is consensus that the forging of a theory or theories of African literatures has to be generated by African textual practice and texts rather than by external hegemonic interest. In *Writers in Politics* (1981) Ngugi wa Thiong'o argues pointedly that cultural imperialism under colonialism was "part and parcel of the thorough system of economic exploitation and political oppression of the colonized peoples and [colonial] literature was an integral part of that system of oppression and genocide" (15). A dissident literature of struggle and cultural assertion that predates colonial invasion was consolidated under empire and continues, in the postindependence epoch, to combat neocolonial hegemony exercising itself through an indigenous elite groomed through colonial apprenticeship.

The development of a broadly African (or individual national) literary theory and practice is inseparable from the project of total decolonization. The *Cultural Charter for Africa* (1976), drawn up by the General Secretariat of the Organization of African Unity, articulates the conviction that "cultural domination led to the depersonalization of part of the African peoples, falsified their history, systematically disparaged and combated African values, and tried to replace progressively and officially, their languages by that of the colonizer." The *Charter* notes that

> culture constitutes for our people the surest means of overcoming our technological backwardness and the most efficient force of our victorious resistance to imperialist blackmail [, that] African culture is meaningless unless it plays a full part in the political and social liberation struggle, and in the rehabilitation and unification efforts and that there is no limit to the cultural development of a people. (2–4)

The intransigence of apartheid in South Africa bears out this pronouncement; it also contributes to the existence in one country of two literatures that do not speak to each other.

Colonization resulted in the linguistic and political division of Africa into zones based on European languages. For African writers and critics to insist on an identity based on colonial languages is to subscribe to the will to self-fragmentation. In *L'Idéologie dans la littérature négro-africaine d'expression française* (1986) Guy Ossito Midiohouan (Benin) suggests that behind the appellation "Francophone" lies the continued cooperation between African countries and France that is but a not-so-subtle cover for French imperialist ideology. "La Francophonie" is a purely ideological space, an immense mythic territory encompassing all the corners of the world where the French language is used (22). Even later (and probably well-intentioned) critical works such as Jonathan Ngaté's *Francophone African Fiction: Reading a Literary Tradition* (1988) and Christopher Miller's *Theories of Africans* (1990) pander to the supposed logic of a cultural-linguistic cartography.

In their controversial *Toward the Decolonization of African Literature* (1980), Chinweizu, Onwuchekwa Jemie, and Ihechukwu Madubuike raise the issue of defining the "Africanness" of a literary text, an issue already tackled in a 1962 conference of "African Writers of English Expression" at Makerere University College, Kampala, Uganda, with the theme "What Is African Literature?" Ngugi wa Thiong'o recalls that "the whole area of literature and audience, and hence of language as a determinant of both the national and class audience, did not really figure: the debate was more about the subject matter and the racial origins and geographical habitation of the writer" (*Decolonising* 6).

The language debate was first foregrounded by a Nigerian critic, Obiajunwa Wali, who in 1963 published a controversial article, "The Dead End of African Literature?" in which he observed that "African literature as now understood and practised is merely a minor appendage in the main stream of European literature. . . . The whole uncritical acceptance of English and French as the inevitable medium for educated African writing . . . has no chance of advancing African literature and culture" (*Transition* 10 [1963] 14). The elitist association of literature with academic education in European languages led Kwame Anthony Appiah to lament that "modern African writing" usually denotes what is taught in high schools all around the continent:

> The role of the colonial [and postcolonial] school in the reproduction of Western cultural hegemony is crucial to African criticism because of the intimate connection between the idea of criticism and the growth of literary pedagogy. . . . the role of literature, indeed, the formation of the concept, the institution of "literature," is indissoluble from pedagogy. ("Out of Africa" 156)

Albert Memmi (Tunisia) argues that even where bilingualism obtains, the mother tongue of the colonized gets "crushed" in the conflict of power with the colonizer:

> Colonial bilingualism is neither a purely bilingual situation in which an indigenous tongue coexists with a purist's language . . . nor a simple polyglot richness benefiting from an extra but relatively neuter alphabet. . . . [The colonized writer] incarnates a magnified vision of all the ambiguities and impossibilities of the colonized. (*The Colonizer and the Colonized*, 1967, 107–8)

Interestingly, the West and its adherents continue largely to ignore traditional oral literatures and written literatures in African languages.

Ngugi wa Thiong'o has been the foremost champion of writing in African languages as an extension of the historical cultural struggle between the national and the foreign. In language that echoes Amilcar Cabral's theme of "return to the source," Ngugi has submitted that "only by a return to the roots of our being in the languages and cultures and heroic histories of the Kenyan people can we rise up to the challenge of helping in the creation of a Kenyan patriotic national literature and culture" (*Writers* 65). "Orature," a term coined by Pius Zirimu (Uganda) to denote oral texts, constitutes the primary source of literary creativity in Africa. The privileging of (written) *literature* over *orature* is increasingly discredited in view of the continual flux between orality and literacy. In most of Africa orature already provides exemplary texts of resistance and discursive contest. Ngugi and Kwame Appiah concur in characterizing as Afro-European (Europhone) literature that literature written by Africans in European languages. Ngugi insists that "African literature can only be written in African languages . . . the languages of the African peasantry and working class, the major alliance of classes in each of our nationalities and the agency for the coming inevitable revolutionary break with neo-colonialism" (*Decolonising* 27). The intertextuality between orature and the printed text is a recurrent theme in literary debate and practice in African letters; witness, for instance, Mahamadou Kane's *Roman africain et tradition* (1982) and Ngugi wa Thiong'o's *Decolonising the Mind* (1986). This intertextuality becomes the nexus of resistance and self-empowerment: the appropriation of a certain specific Western set of tools—language, theories, textual practice—affords African literary practice a means by which to counter the alienating effects of Western assault.

Quite predictably, nativism, the idea that "true African independence requires a literature of one's own," that is, a literature or literatures in indigenous African languages, has been contested. The multiplicity of African languages, the limitation of the audience, and questions of orthography have been cited as impediments to the generation and continuity of literatures in African languages. Nevertheless, the identification of indigenous African languages with programs of effective decolonization has held sway, given that European languages were (and are) the synecdochical instrumentality for cultural hegemony. However, such a projection may sometimes assign a fetishlike character to a common language and a common ethnic or national provenance. In "Ideology or Pedagogy: The Linguistic Indigenization of African Literature," Al-Amin M. Mazrui posits that the equation of indigenous language(s) with national identity has no validity "without a concomitant struggle for the nation to determine its own politico-economic destiny" (*Race & Class* 28 [1986] 66). For Mazrui, the linguistic indigenization of African literature becomes meaningful and attains its greatest importance only in relation to the revolutionary function of literature.

"Negritude" has been a recurrent motif in the criticism of African literature, both internal and external. Paulin Hountondji (Benin), Stanislas Adotevi (Senegal), Félix Eboussi Boulaga (Cameroon), and Marcien Towa (Cameroon) are among those who have undertaken a serious critique of the movement and concepts of Negritude. The dividing line between French-speaking and English-speaking practitioners and critics of Negritude is more apparent than real: South African Ezekiel (Es'kia) Mphahlele in "The African Personality" sees no distinction between "the African personality" and Negritude, because "each concept involves the other. They merely began at different times in different historical circumstances. . . . Negritude claims the whole of the black world, the African Personality refers only to Africa" (*The African Image*, 1962, 67).

Negritude has been recognized broadly as a strategic moment and movement that had to be surpassed before the political kingdom could be reached. At a 1965 writers' conference, Sembène Ousmane (Senegal) acknowledged the historical strategic necessity of Negritude but disparaged the "African" essentialism inherent in certain definitions of Negritude, seeing no future in it "because negritude neither feeds the hungry nor builds roads" (Killam 149). Cheikh Hamidou Kane (Senegal) argued for the utility of Negritude as anti-imperialist discourse: "We had, at some point, to make ourselves felt, if we were ever to make ourselves known and refuse cultural or political assimilation, especially at a time when, politically speaking, we had no prospects of an early liberation" (Killam 152). But Negritude has been

faulted for often being complicit with the ethnocentric discourse of the West concerning Africa, confirming the West's stereotyping of Africa. Léopold Séder Senghor's typical opposition of "the negro" to "the European" constantly commits this blunder: "Classical European reason is analytical and makes use of the object. African reason is intuitive and participates in the object" (*Prose and Poetry*, 1965, 34).

Despite its limitations, Negritude construed itself, at least in part, as constructing a bridge between Africa and the black diaspora. In "Negritude," Senghor views Negritude as constituting "a weapon of defence and attack and inspiration" that, "instead of dividing and sterilizing, unified and made fertile" (*Prose* 99). In his *Cahier d'un retour au pays natal* [Notebook of a return to the native land], first published in 1938 and considered by many to be the pan-Negritude text par excellence, the Martinican poet Aimé Césaire projects the poet's role as that of a spokesperson for the inhabitants of

> this impossibly delicate tenuity separating one America from another; and these loins which secrete for Europe the hearty liquor of a Gulf Stream, and . . . Guadeloupe, split in two down its dorsal line and equal in poverty to us, Haiti where negritude rose for the first time and stated it believed in its humanity, and . . . Florida where the strangulation of a nigger is being completed, and Africa gigantically caterpillaring up to the Hispanic foot of Europe. (47)

In *Les Fondements de L'Africanité, ou Négritude et Arabité,* Senghor sees "Negritude" and "Arabness" as overlapping in the African context, rejecting the facile separation of the "Arab" from the "African": "I have often defined Africanity as the 'complementary symbiosis of the [cultural] values of Arabism and the values of Negritude.'" Senghor endeavors to demonstrate that "this symbiosis is achieved through métissage (mixing of races and ethnics) and through the convergences of Arab and Negro-African cultures" (10). Concerning the founding of the Organization of African Unity, for instance, Senghor points to the danger of an African identity conferred by the European imperial imagination. Writes Senghor: "To found a common organisation whose sole motive force is anti-colonialism is thus to build on shaky ground. The colonial past has characterised us only as Africans. We have much in common with all the other peoples of Asia and America" (9–10).

Ngugi wa Thiong'o, among others, has advocated the study of the global dimensions of the African diaspora, in particular "our essentially colonial situation, our struggle [to achieve] a kind of homecoming." In *Homecoming* (1972), Ngugi laments the utter neglect of Caribbean studies in African departments of literature. "We forget, or have been made to forget . . . that the West Indies has been very formative in Africa's political and literary consciousness: Marcus Garvey, C. L. R. James, George Padmore, Aimé Césaire, FRANTZ FANON: these are some of the most familiar names in Africa. Yet we ignore their work" (81). In addition, the ideological-cultural links between the peoples of Africa and Asia find their literary expression in *Lotus: Journal of Afro-Asian Literature*. The links binding the common political-cultural histories of Africa, Asia, and Latin America find common expression in terms such as "resistance," "commitment" (or "engagement"), and "solidarity." Within Africa itself, a literature of solidarity takes sides in the struggle against neo-colonialism. As Guy Ossito Midiohouan writes,

> The fact remains that on our continent neo-colonialism knows no borders—nor do hunger, poverty, totalitarianism. . . . Our role, today, should not be to cultivate our difference and legitimize borders but rather, as the writers themselves have done, it must be to assume responsibilities to confront our common reality and our common destiny. ("The Nation-Specific Approach to African Literature," in Harrow 3–4)

Marxist/socialist theoretical approaches, while broadly popular as anti-imperialist praxis, have been found unfit for articulating an African reality. For Chidi Amuta, the historical determination and theoretical orientation of Marxism renders it "impotent when it comes to the elaboration of societies, cultural manifestations and historical developments that did not form part of the cognitive universe of Marx and Engels" (*The Theory of African Literature: Implications for Practical Criticism*, 1975, 73–74).

If male writers and critics dominate the arena of writing, patriarchal attitudes also often influence the literary representation of women and the reception of women's writing and criticism (especially feminist). In the preface to Carole Boyce Davies and Anne Adams Graves's *Ngambika: Studies of Women in African Literature* (1986), Graves states the book's objective as an attempt "to redress the relative inattention to women in African literary scholarship." The essays in the text aspire to address "the absence of a feminine perspective or the stunted characterization of women," issues that are "as demanding of critical attention as is the more complete presentation of feminine presence" (vii). Molara Ogundipe-Leslie (Nigeria) shares these sentiments in "The Female Writer and Her Commitment," in which she posits the woman writer's major responsibilities as being "first to tell about being a woman; secondly to describe reality from a woman's view, a woman's perspective." Ogundipe-Leslie attributes some women writers' and/or

critics' lack of "[commitment] to their womanhood" to the successful intimidation of African women by men over the issue of women's liberation and feminism and to male ridicule, aggression, and backlash, which assign a stigma to the term "feminist" (*African Literature Today* 15 [1987] 5, 10–11).

Susan Z. Andrade also notes that "the [literary] history of African women has gone unnamed, its absence unnoticed." According to Andrade, African feminist criticism must build beyond "its historical links to white feminist and male cultural critics," with which it intersects ("Rewriting History, Motherhood, and Rebellion: Naming an African Women's Literary Tradition," *Research in African Literatures* 21 [1990] 91). Andrade, like an increasing number of women writers and critics, insists on an intertextual reading of women's narratives and on the intersection between race and gender, which is often elided in much Western feminist writing on Africa.

Gitahi Gititi

See also FRANTZ FANON, POSTCOLONIAL CULTURAL STUDIES, and WOLE SOYINKA.

Kwame Anthony Appiah, "Out of Africa: Typologies of Nativism," *Yale Journal of Criticism* 2 (1988); Frantz Fanon, *Les Damnés de la terre* (1961, *The Wretched of the Earth*, trans. Constance Farrington, 1976); Kimani Gecau, "Do Ethnic Languages Divide a Nation?" *African Perspectives* 2 (1978); Kenneth Harrow, Jonathan Ngaté, and Clarissa Zimra, eds., *Crisscrossing Boundaries in African Literatures* (1991); G. D. Killam, ed., *African Writers on African Writing* (1973); Locha Mateso, *La Littérature africaine et sa critique* (1986); Emmanuel Ngara, *Art and Ideology in the African Novel: A Study of the Influence of Marxism on African Writing* (1985), "The Role of the African Writer in National Liberation and Social Reconstruction," *Criticism and Ideology* (ed. K. Petersen, 1988); Ngugi wa Thiong'o, *Decolonising the Mind: The Politics of Language in African Literature* (1986), *Writers in Politics* (1981); Wole Soyinka, *Myth, Literature, and the African World* (1976).

Chinua Achebe, "African Literature as Celebration," *African Commentary: A Journal of People of African Descent* 1 (1989); Ayi Kwei Armah, "Masks and Marx: The Marxist Ethos vis-à-vis African Revolutionary Theory and Praxis," *Présence Africaine* 131 (1984); Albert Gérard, *African Language Literatures: An Introduction to the Literary History of Sub-Saharan Africa* (1981); Georg M. Gugelberger, *Marxism and African Literature* (1985); Russel G. Hamilton, "Lusophone Literature in Africa: Lusofonia, Africa, and Matters of Language and Letters," *Callaloo* 14 (1991), *Voices from an Empire: A History of Afro-Portuguese Liter-*

ature (1975); Janheinz Jahn, *Bibliography of Creative African Writing* (1971); Adeola James, ed., *In Their Own Voices: African Women Writers Talk* (1990); Eldred D. Jones, ed., *African Literature Today* 15 (1987, special issue on women); Penina Muhando Mlama, "Creating in the Mother-Tongue: The Challenges to the African Writer Today," *Research in African Literatures* 21 (1990); V. Y. Mudimbe, *The Invention of Africa: Gnosis, Philosophy, and the Order of Knowledge* (1988); Emmanuel Ngara and Andrew Morrison, ed., *Literature, Language, and the Nation* (1989); Ngugi wa Thiong'o, *Homecoming: Essays on African and Caribbean Literature, Culture, and Politics* (1972); Lewis Nkosi, *Tasks and Masks: Themes and Styles in African Literature* (1982); Emmanuel Obiechina, *Tradition and Society in the West African Novel* (1975); Isidore Okpewho, "Comparatism and Separatism in African Literature," *World Literature Today* 55 (1981); Sembène Ousmane, *Man Is Culture / L'Homme est culture* (Sixth Annual Hans Wolff Memorial Lecture, 1979); Wole Soyinka, "The Critic and Society: Barthes, Leftocracy, and Other Mythologies," *Black Literature and Literary Theory* (ed. Henry Louis Gates, Jr., 1984), "The Writer in a Modern African State," *The Writer in Modern Africa* (ed. Per Wastberg, 1968); Peter Sultzer, *Schwarze Intelligens: Ein literarisch-politischer Streifzug durch Süd-Afrika* (1955).

AFRICAN-AMERICAN THEORY AND CRITICISM

1. Harlem Renaissance to the Black Arts Movement

Perhaps *the* informing question in African-American literary criticism prior to the 1970s is the relation between the literary arts and developing conceptions of the nature of African-American culture. Many of the major critical texts from the first six decades of the twentieth century certainly advance our understanding of the nature of African-American literary production. Among these may be included Sterling Brown's *Negro in American Fiction* (1937), Hugh Gloster's *Negro Voices in American Fiction* (1948), and Robert Bone's *Negro Novel in America* (1958). For all the considerable value of their local insights, these works appear now to be methodologically outdated, relying too heavily on unreflective sociological or formalist perspectives. The best introduction to early African-American literary criticism is the pronouncements of writers themselves, rather than the critical surveys that sought to "interpret" African-American literature.

Grounded in a representationalist and moralistic "reading" of literature dependent on a Christian humanist ideology, African-American literary criticism early in the twentieth century found its accents in a vision of cultural formation not significantly different from that of major Victorian literary critics (see BRITISH THEORY AND CRITICISM: 4. VICTORIAN). The major venue for this early criticism of African-American literature was *Crisis*. This journal, the organ of the National Association for the Advancement of Colored People (NAACP), first appeared in 1910 under the editorial direction of W. E. B. DuBois, who did much of the early reviewing and literary commentary (assisted by William Stanley Braithewaite and Jessie Redmond Fauset).

The early editorial position of *Crisis* owed much to the political and social aims of the NAACP, particularly its emphasis on racial uplift and social development. Literature certainly needed to be beautiful, but it also needed to be utilitarian. Art properly considered was a merging of aesthetics and politics. In 1921 DuBois argued: "We want everything that is said about us to tell of the best and highest and noblest in us. We insist that our Art and Propaganda be one" ("Negro Art," *Crisis* 22 [1921] 55); and in 1926 he said, "All Art is propaganda and ever must be, despite the wailing of the purists" ("The Criteria of Negro Art," *Crisis* 32 [1926] 296). *Crisis* consistently attempted to contextualize literature as a tool in the struggle for political liberation, just as it emphasized the need for "Beauty," even to the point of characterizing "the great mission of the Negro to America and to the modern world" as "the development of Art and the appreciation of the Beautiful" (DuBois, "Truth and Beauty," *Crisis* 25 [1922] 7).

The fundamental defects of this early criticism in *Crisis* rose precisely from this attempt to mediate the opposition between an aesthetic conception of literature and an instrumental one. Repeatedly in the early numbers of the journal, casting literature as a source of aesthetic pleasure came into conflict with seeing the work of art as a tool in the liberation of the "race." In his review of Alain Locke's *New Negro*, DuBois himself tried to balance these two critical perspectives by wondering "if ever in this world in any renaissance there can be a search for disembodied beauty which is not really a passionate effort to do something tangible, accompanied and illumined and made holy by the vision of eternal beauty" ("Our Book Shelf," *Crisis* 31 [1926] 141). The DuBoisian critical position constantly foundered on the perceived conflict between a reading that emphasized beauty and one that emphasized propaganda, since the meaning of "truth" in the former tended to be idealized and in the latter tended to be pragmatic.

Complicating this problematic opposition was *Crisis*'s unqualified acceptance of a class-based interpretation of artistic production. From this perspective, art was clearly the province of the more "intelligent" and "advanced" classes. This view had its clearest immediate source in DuBois's well-known conviction in natural elites, "the talented tenth," articulated most explicitly in his *Souls of Black Folk* (1903, reprint, 1989). The question whether beauty or truth was paramount found itself complicated by antecedent questions concerning the nature of black culture; that is, who best represented "the Negro," the "advanced" class or those behind the "advanced" class?

Perhaps the most influential consideration of the problem of African-American culture during the Harlem Renaissance is Locke's *New Negro* (1925, reprint, 1992). In this anthology, Locke assembled the work of scholars and artists alike, by way of representing what he clearly saw as an emerging world historical phenomenon, the development of modern black culture. The list of contributors to this volume is impressive if only by dint of its scope. Aside from Locke himself, one finds DuBois, William Stanley Braithewaite, Countee Cullen, Jessie Fauset, Rudolph Fisher, E. Franklin Frazier, Melville Herskovitz, Langston Hughes, Zora Neale Hurston, Claude McKay, Jean Toomer, and Walter White, among others. Although this colloquy of voices cannot be said even to aim for unanimity, *The New Negro* nevertheless is motivated by certain common ideas, articulated in Locke's lead essay, "The New Negro."

In this essay, Locke attempts to outline what he sees as the critical transformation of mass black consciousness into a more heightened sense of itself as a "progressive" force (3). Rather than seeing the demographic shift northward of the black population following World War I as exclusively a response either to the extreme poverty in the South or to the racialist violence of the Ku Klux Klan, Locke casts this mass movement primarily within the context of an emerging affirmative sense of a "common consciousness" (7). In Locke's accents, what is occurring is "a deliberate flight not only from countryside to city, but from medieval to America to modern" (6).

Harlem, then, becomes a "race capital" for the black masses, not unlike "Dublin . . . for the New Ireland" (7). Although the new consciousness is not yet entirely full-blown in the masses, Locke insists on its inevitable maturity. In a modulation of DuBois's vision of the "talented tenth," the role of the "intelligentsia" is now somewhat diminished. "In a real sense it is the rank and file who are leading, and the leaders who are following" (7). Yet this emerging collective consciousness, for all its

nationalist implications, is not to be confused with separatism (here Locke's target is clearly Marcus Garvey). Rather, Locke sees this nationalism as "no limitation or reservation with respect to American life" (12), but rather as a constructive phase of development toward democracy, "American ideals progressively fulfilled and realized" (12), and an eclectic engagement with "white" culture. In his construction of the relation between the aspirations of African Americans and the future of American democracy Locke assuredly foreshadows Ralph Ellison, with his sense of democratic possibility, just as Locke's sense of a mediated nationalism anticipates some aspects of Richard Wright's thought, though without Wright's Marxist accents.

Although Locke's engagement of the question of African-American culture in *The New Negro* is perhaps the most well known, others considered the problem of culture too. In accents considerably different but not entirely unrelated to those of both DuBois in *Crisis* and Locke in *The New Negro,* George S. Schuyler's "The Negro-Art Hokum" took up the issue of African-American artistry in the *Nation* during the summer of 1926 (vol. 122). Schuyler's skepticism, clearly indicated by his title, found its source in a "historical" reading of cultural development, one that privileged the nation-state as the basis for cultural formation: "Negro art there has been, is, and will be among the numerous black nations of Africa; but to suggest the possibility of any such development among the ten million colored people in this republic is self-evident foolishness" (662). Citing a long list of "Negro" artists, including Claude McKay, Edward Wilmot Blyden, Alexander Pushkin, Paul Laurence Dunbar, James Weldon Johnson, and Charles Chesnutt, Schuyler continued, "All Negroes; yet their work shows the impress of nationality rather than race. They all reveal the psychology and culture of their environment—their color is incidental" (663).

The value of Schuyler's perspective is his insistence on bringing the idea of *culture* into relation with the idea of *race*. In doing so, he usefully problematizes both concepts by suggesting the possibility of a more fluid notion of identity (and cultural production) than simply the idea of *race* would allow. To that extent he anticipates Ralph Ellison's sense of the possibilities for African-American life within liberal democracy. Further, in his intent to see identity as rising from commingled sources, Schuyler also anticipates the similar dismantling of the idea of "race" undertaken by some postmodern commentators.

Unfortunately, Schuyler's analysis operates out of a largely underdeveloped conception of race, culture, and nationality. Revealingly, his analysis alternately separates and then conflates all three categories, whenever it proves convenient. Schuyler is assuredly aware of the limitations of a concept such as race, particularly when he construes the sources of theories of "racial" difference as being motivated by racialist or "Negrophobist" impulses (663). But having devalued the idea of color as a signifier of difference, Schuyler can only substitute in its place the idea of "nation," a conception here no less insubstantial. And although "The Negro-Art Hokum" tries to locate the source of human consciousness in some form of "history," largely the function of environmental forces, it can finally offer only an unapologetically classist reading of artistic creation. What passes for Negro art either is indistinguishable in all respects from other forms of "high" art (i.e., "it shows more or less evidence of European influence") or is the product of "the peasantry of the South," whose skin color is mere "coincidence" (662).

One of the more powerful voices rising in opposition to a class-based reading of literary imperatives belonged to Langston Hughes. Although *Crisis* published one of Hughes's first major poems, "The Negro Speaks of Rivers," in 1921, his early critical statements in particular proposed explicit revisions of African-American gentility. One week after the publication of Schuyler's "Negro-Art Hokum," Hughes responded in the *Nation* with a different reading of the problem of African-American art. In the issue of 23 June 1926 (vol. 122), Hughes's "The Negro Artist and the Racial Mountain" began by playing off of DuBois's conception of the double consciousness articulated early in the first chapter of *Souls of Black Folk* (5). The problem for the Negro artist from Hughes's perspective was not so much the balancing of African and American identities within this double consciousness as it was the emphasizing of a Negro cultural integrity out of which might rise an authentic conception of African-American art.

Standing in the way of this effort is the racial mountain—"the urge within the race toward whiteness, the desire to pour racial individuality into the mold of American standardization, and to be as little Negro and as much American as possible" (692)—a perspective adopted all too persistently by the black middle class, according to Hughes. The flight from race not only robs the Negro artist of his or her informing cultural perspective but also distances the artist from the most fertile source of material—working-class Negro life, a locus of cultural integrity Hughes felt was untouched by the urge toward whiteness and uninfected by a suspicion of "play" (the result of the bourgeois fetishization of work). Hughes emphasized the importance of jazz as an artistic influ-

ence because of its roots in working-class life and because it retained the integrity he saw as so crucial to the artist. "But jazz to me is one of the inherent expressions of Negro life in America: the eternal tom-tom beating in the Negro soul—the tom-tom of revolt against weariness in a white world, a world of subway trains, and work, work, work; the tom-tom of joy and laughter, and pain swallowed in a smile" (694). Hughes's insistence on the *legitimacy* of "racial" art (to say nothing of its *superiority*) prefigures not only Richard Wright's engagement with a nationalistic perspective on art (and to some extent Ralph Ellison's) but also that of the Black Arts movement of the 1960s.

Yet in many respects, both Hughes's championing of the qualities of lower-class black life and his excoriation of the black middle classes and their desire for an "Episcopal heaven" seem oversimplified and unreflective. The characterization of lower-class black life as playful, direct, unmediated, and somehow more natural than the world of work characteristic of the middle class is overly romantic at best and might be seen as a simple inversion of the traditional racist stereotype that figures African Americans psychologically as children. Both Richard Wright's subsequent criticism and that of the Black Arts movement 40 years later extend the idea of *nationalism*, but they also wrestle with the problem of how to define such an idea in a more problematic and complicated form.

In "Blueprint for Negro Writing" (*New Challenge* 2 [1937]) Wright tried to balance two different and competing claims regarding the relation of the artist to the community. Wright clearly had affinities for the nationalist position articulated by Hughes in "Negro Artist," though he was far too cognizant of the reality of racism and its effect on African Americans to allow for a valorizing of the idea of play. Further, the idea of Negro "playfulness" resonated precisely that persistent racism in Wright's ears. For instance, his chief criticism of Zora Neale Hurston's *Their Eyes Were Watching God* was that she "*voluntarily* continues in her novel the tradition that was *forced* upon the Negro in the theater, that is, the minstrel technique that makes the 'white folks' laugh" ("Between Laughter and Tears," *New Masses* 25 [1937] 25).

Despite his wariness of constructions of blackness that too readily conformed to stereotype, Wright nevertheless sought other grounds for a rehabilitated version of nationalism, for he was convinced of the integrity of African-American culture. "The nationalist character of the Negro people is unmistakable. Psychologically this nationalism is reflected in the whole of Negro culture, and especially in folklore" ("Blueprint" 56). Moreover, the searing experience of racism tended to fashion a collective experience that contributed heavily to the formation of a nationalist perspective (57) and, hence, a culture. This culture was transmitted by a whole range of speech acts within the black community, ensuring a consequent integrity and continuity. African-American writers played a significant role within the project of cultural transmission. At their best, black writers conceive of themselves as summary figures, encapsulating and communicating the entire historical range of African-American cultural life, "as though they in one life time had lived it themselves throughout all the long centuries" (63). Having gained this historical view, African-American writers may then "stand shoulder to shoulder with Negro workers in mood and outlook" (55). In Wright's view, this solidarity would go a long way toward lessening the distance between the masses and the typically middle-class literary artist.

Wright's nationalistic posture is complicated, if not vexed, by his allegiance to doctrinaire Marxism at this point in his life. Marxist class analysis reads history in a different fashion than does the racial and cultural analysis favored by the black nationalist. This is particularly important for Wright, since a nationalist analysis makes problematic the Marxist insistence on solidarity across racial lines. Wright tries to mediate these two competing perspectives by affirming African-American cultural integrity, yet at the same time warning against a "specious" nationalism. In the view advanced by Wright at this time, nationalism was not a final goal but rather an intermediate one. "Negro writers must accept the nationalist implications of their lives, not in order to encourage them, but in order to change and transcend them" (58). The primary job of the Negro artist remained the unmasking of previously hidden class conflict and the location of that conflict within the arena of economic oppression. This imperative required the artist to forsake a vision of literature either as primarily aesthetic or as a vehicle by which one might gain entrance into white society or petition that society for justice.

Yet in order to achieve this revisionist and revolutionary posture, Wright argues, the Negro writer needs to turn his or her attention to the material conditions of black life in America rather than to the conditions of white society. Such a shift requires a clear and unequivocal embrace of the proletarian perspective held by black laborers—who are freer from the bonds that hinder the black artist's necessary escape from bourgeois values. Not the least influential of these bourgeois values is the conception of the artist as an isolated individual. The collectivism implicit in Wright's sense of nationalistic imperative locates the act of writing as a publicly committed, socially conscious act. Two conditions make this synthesis finally very uneasy. Precisely how the writer makes the transition from a nationalist perspective focusing on African-American cultural life to a more full-fledged revolutionary solidarity remains unexpressed. Wright's insistence on this transition remains only a gesture. Further, Wright himself admits that to some considerable degree the nationalistic aspects of African-American culture are a function of segregation, which fosters "a warping way of life" (54). While this distortion clearly leads Wright to insist on the need to transcend nationalism, the affirmative aspects of this nationalism become vexed by virtue of their origins being located in segregation. African-American culture becomes positioned, then, less as a self-generating phenomenon and more as a function of a racist society. The central position of African-American lower-class life becomes even more ironic, given the consistent criticism throughout Wright's career that fiction revealed a completely underdeveloped knowledge of the full range of African-American life (see Langston Hughes, "The Need for Heroes," *Crisis* 48 [1941] 184).

In her review of Wright's *Uncle Tom's Children* (1938), Zora Neale Hurston took Wright to task precisely for this incompleteness. Praising Wright's capacities as a writer of fiction, Hurston then "wonders what he would have done had he dealt with plots that touched the broader and more fundamental phases of Negro life instead of confining himself to the spectacular" ("Stories of Conflict," reprint, *Richard Wright: The Critical Reception*, ed. John Reilly, 1978, 9). For Hurston, Wright's work tended to reduce African-American characters to being merely the product of racial animosities and thereby turned the work of art into little more than a chronicle of crime and outrage. Hurston's criticism antedates by at least two decades the similar attacks on Wright made by critics such as Nathan Scott and, more importantly, by novelists such as James Baldwin and Ralph Ellison.

Like Hurston, Baldwin sees profound limitations in naturalistic "protest" fiction, particularly of the sort practiced by Wright. The evolution of African-American fiction from a body of literature emphasizing uplift and affirmation to one emphasizing protest and degradation results finally in a highly reductive and monolithic form. What is worse, that fictional form fails to deliver on its promise. "The 'protest' novel, so far from being disturbing, is an accepted and comforting aspect of the American scene, ramifying that framework we believe to be so necessary. Whatever unsettling questions are raised are evanescent, titillating" ("Everybody's Protest Novel," 1949, *Price* 31). But even more problematic, the protest novel can mask, as it did for Wright from Baldwin's perspective, "an almost ineradicable self-hatred" and a fundamental ignorance of black life ("Alas, Poor Richard," 1961, *Price* 287, 285–86).

Eschewing the bankrupt form of the "protest novel," Baldwin hoped to construct a vision of fiction in which the work of art engaged the problems of race and democracy but then also somehow transcended them. For Baldwin, America itself was a kind of fiction in the process of the making—a text not fully cognizant of its own power or nature. Additionally, Baldwin saw literature constantly within the context of alienation and expatriation, in terms of both race and sexuality, even in America. There was no home for the black writer anywhere, at least insofar as Baldwin's vision was concerned. In spite of the younger writer's reproaches, Wright and Baldwin shared a similar view of the writer's fundamental alienation from both black and white American society; further, Baldwin's criticisms of Wright need to be seen within the context of a generational conflict, nearly Oedipal in its contours, for Baldwin's indebtedness to Wright was greater than he tended to acknowledge. Baldwin's distance from Ellison may be measured by the former's far less sanguine view of prospects in American society for blacks (writers and others) and homosexuals as well.

Ralph Ellison's most important contribution to African-American literary study is undoubtedly *Invisible Man* (1953), yet his contributions to African-American literary criticism have been only slightly less significant. His most important volumes of literary and cultural essays are *Shadow and Act* (1966) and *Going to the Territory* (1986), along with other occasional essays. Within the history of African-American literary criticism, Ellison's work may be seen as an attempt to reintroduce the work of literary art into the context of the national debate concerning democracy, specifically regarding the place of people of African descent within that discourse. In both the novel and his first volume of essays, Ellison tries to make race the defining issue for American democracy. The struggle for individual and collective freedom implied by the issue of race is the venue to be explored by the novel. The work of art, in this view, refuses to provide specific answers but instead is an arena for speculation, for investigation, for a complex meditation on the informing social conflict of the day.

The clearest statement of Ellison's critical intentions comes in his acceptance speech for the National Book Award, printed as "Brave Words for a Startling Occasion" in *Shadow and Act*. In that essay, Ellison tries to signify the distance between himself and other American writers, both black and white. Although Wright is not men-

tioned by name, his presence motivating this essay is unmistakable, for in "Brave Words" Ellison advances an unvarnished criticism of naturalism, envisioning "a fiction leaving sociology to the scientists" (113). Ellison would rather have the writer forsake the "final and unrelieved despair" (113) so characteristic of naturalism and embrace instead a more magical and expansive form of writing, the sort of prose more characteristic of late modernism or early POSTMODERNISM. In that kind of literature Ellison finds a more pronounced authorial intention to foreground the power of the work of art, over and against the power of an intractable experience.

Ellison continues this line of analysis in most of the other essays in *Shadow and Act*. Central to his critical position is the insistence on treating African-American art with the same sophistication used to examine other kinds of art, all by way of avoiding a reductivist sociological reading of the sort offered by Irving Howe in his "Black Boys and Native Sons" (1963, reprint, *The Decline of the New*, 1970). Yet while he emphasizes the necessity of engaging the text as text, and not simply as a sign of a particular political position, Ellison never removes the literary work of art from its cultural grounding. That is, the work of art is significant only insofar as it engages the central issues of the time. As one may readily see from "Twentieth-Century Fiction and the Black Mask of Humanity," how one handles the centering of African-American figures is less significant than the centering itself. Ellison reads the African-American fictional character (his central example is, naturally enough, Jim from Mark Twain's *Huckleberry Finn*) as signifying the informing drama of American cultural life, the conflict between the professed ideals of democracy and the real practice of slavery in its past and present forms. This role confers upon African-American characters an "irrepressible moral reality" (*Shadow and Act* 51).

Supporting this reading of the centrality of the African-American character and of the equivalent value of the novel to democracy is Ellison's attempt at the rehabilitation of liberalism, expressed most clearly in the epilogue to *Invisible Man* but implicit in all Ellison writes. His criticism and fiction may well be understood as themselves embodying the kind of paradox and ambiguity outlined in the pages of *Invisible Man*. On the one hand, Ellison was convinced that the "invisibility" of African Americans had specific historical causes, namely, racism and classism. But in advocating what Thomas Hill Schaub has termed a "psychologized Marxism" ("From Ranter to Writer: Ellison's *Invisible Man* and the New Liberalism," *American Fiction in the Cold War*, 1991, 111), Ellison's language seems of a piece with the liberalism of his time. This conflation tends to "universal-ize," "existentialize," and therefore "whiten" the condi-tion of African Americans, making it nearly identical with what might be called the "modern condition." Continuing the drift away from doctrinaire Marxism sig-naled by Wright in his later work and by others, Ellison sees a principle of freedom at work in liberalism, a prin-ciple worth saving, not only because it appears as a bul-wark against despair, but also because it leaves room to recognize "the invented character of identity and social institutions" (Schaub 109). Yet Ellison's affirmation of liberalism seems no less visionary and ephemeral than Wright's interest in Marxism and then existentialism, particularly since his language allows him to be con-structed as a liberal centrist, like Arthur Schlesinger. The simply asserted belief in the superiority of the principles of democracy over and against the practices done in the name of those principles (as in *Invisible Man*) proves a target far too inviting for later commentators, especially members of the Black Arts movement, who read Ellison's advocacy of democratic virtues as fundamentally naive and assuredly assimilationist.

The fundamental ideological basis for the Black Arts movement is its conviction in the reality of black nation-hood and its connection with the Black Power movement (Neal, "Black" 257). Equally informing is the antecedent recognition that racism is perhaps the most significant force in the current construction of African-American culture, a recognition that leads the Black Arts move-ment to venerate a figure such as Wright and particu-larly his *Native Son* (1940), a novel that seemed com-pletely conditioned by this ideological position. As a result of persistent racism, African Americans find them-selves alienated from white American culture (Baraka 114–15; Hoyt Fuller, "Towards a Black Aesthetic," Gayle 9). But unlike the DuBoisian trajectory as expressed in *Souls,* which required a synthesis of two different selves, or the trajectory inscribed by Ellison's sense of ambigu-ity, the theorists of the Black Arts movement held that a recognition of this fundamental alienation should lead the black artist to embrace a fervent nationalism, such as that advanced by Wright in one stage of his career, though Wright's revisions of that position are largely ignored. "Implicit in the Black Arts Movement is the idea that Black people, however dispersed, constitute a *nation* within the belly of white America" (Neal, "Black" 257). This nationalism finds itself voiced in such anthologies as Addison Gayle's *Black Aesthetic* or LeRoi Jones and Larry Neal's *Black Fire* (1968)—in many ways descendants of Locke's *New Negro* in their advocacy of nationalism.

The implications of this nationalism for the artist are profound and wide-ranging. This art, "from the people and for the people" (Karenga 33), must necessarily shape the contours of this black nation and reveal it to the world. The black artist's primary duty, then, "is to speak to the spiritual and cultural needs of Black people. There-fore, the main thrust of this new breed of contemporary writer is to confront the Black man's experience in the racist West" (Neal, "Black" 257). This imperative, an-swered by organizations such as the Black Arts Reper-toire School in 1964, inclined Black Arts criticism and theory to advance an instrumental view of literature specifically and all artistic production generally.

The emphasis on instrumentality makes Black Arts movement criticism inevitably evaluative. *Validity* be-comes a primary artistic criterion, indicated not so much by idealized *truth* as by political efficacy. "Black art, like everything else in the black community, must respond positively to the reality of revolution. . . . what is needed is an aesthetic, a black aesthetic, that is a criteria [*sic*] for judging the validity and/or the beauty of a work of art" (Karenga 31). In fact, Karenga's distinction becomes ephemeral, since the *valid* readily subsumes the *beau-tiful.* The motive forces behind validity are two: the need to represent the truth concerning the black community and the need to "reflect and support the Black revolu-tion" (31) rather than simply "protest" conditions as in previous schools of African-American literature (Neal, "Black" 258; Hoyt Fuller, "The New Black Literature: Pro-test or Affirmation," Gayle 335).

In the criticism produced by the Black Arts move-ment, validity is approached by constructing a form of art that is "functional, collective and committing or committed" (Karenga 32), one that immerses itself in the concrete particulars of black life rather than in "abstrac-tions" (Neal, "Black" 260). But perhaps the most impor-tant means toward this artistic vision is the attempt to create a separate "symbolism, mythology, critique, and iconology" consistent with the ideological position of nationalism (Neal, "Black" 257; see also Fuller, "New Black Literature" 327–28).

Everything rises from this commitment to a black world, to paraphrase Imamu Amiri Baraka's poem "Black-Art." All aesthetic choices derive from the centering of a black audience and a black artist operating in a black world—from the choice of aesthetic materials to prob-lems of evaluation and judgment. Black Arts movement poetry, fiction, drama, and criticism all point toward the visionary goal of the reformation of African-American consciousness. As Don L. Lee has it in his poem "The New Integrationist," "We seek the integration of Negroes with black people."

But read at 30 years' remove, and even if there is no compelling evidence that the social conditions that form the basis of the movement have changed profoundly, the literary criticism (as opposed to the political analysis) of the Black Arts movement nevertheless seems in many respects hopelessly dated and profoundly romanticized (this latter particularly critical for a movement priding itself on an unflinching realism). In fact, a realism *is* there in the movement's willingness to expose the degrading conditions of some parts of black life. Yet the visionary character of the Black Arts movement inclines it to advance a vision of "blackness" that is fundamentally essentialized, monolithic, and ahistorical, so that rather than standing in opposition to the West, the movement too often employs categories of analysis rooted firmly in Western sociocultural perspectives (especially but not exclusively the homophobia and sexism of the fiction, poetry, and prose characteristic of the Black Arts movement). In fact, the sexism of the Black Arts movement, its tendency to figure political power in the language of male potency (sexual and otherwise), gives a motive force to the feminist revisions of African-American critical discourse common since the 1980s. Prominent among the people producing these revisions are artists, critics, and theorists who conceive of Hurston as a far more suitable ancestor than Wright.

We return, then, to the relation between various conceptions of African-American "national" identity and literary production. What the history of early African-American literary criticism reveals is how problematic a foundation "nationalism" is, since the term seems to be much more of a variable signifier than those who use it intend. By implicitly unpacking the idea of nationalism, the theoretical revisions occasioned in the 1970s and 1980s by feminism (African-American and otherwise), postmodern literary criticism (generally considered), and contemporary versions of cultural criticism move African-American literary criticism into a generally much more fruitful realm of discourse than it had enjoyed in earlier decades.

Theodore O. Mason, Jr.

Houston Baker, "Discovering America: Generational Shifts, Afro-American Literary Criticism, and the Study of Expressive Culture," *Blues, Ideology, and Afro-American Literature: A Vernacular Theory* (1984); James Baldwin, *The Price of the Ticket: Collected Nonfiction, 1948–1985* (1985); Imamu Amiri Baraka, *Home: Social Essays* (1966); Dexter Fisher and Robert Stepto, eds., *Afro-American Literature: The Reconstruction of Instruction* (1979); Addison Gayle,

ed., *The Black Aesthetic* (1972); Stephen Henderson, *Understanding the New Black Poetry: Black Speech and Black Music as Poetic References* (1973); Zora Neale Hurston, *I Love Myself When I Am Laughing* (ed. Alice Walker, 1979); Ron Karenga, "Black Cultural Nationalism" (Gayle); Don L. Lee, "Toward a Definition: Black Poetry of the Sixties (after Leroi Jones)" (Gayle); Larry Neal, "The Black Arts Movement" (1968, Gayle), "Some Reflections on the Black Aesthetic" (1968, Gayle); J. Saunders Redding, *A Scholar's Conscience: Selected Writings of J. Saunders Redding, 1942–1977* (ed. Faith Berry, 1992), *To Make a Poet Black* (1939); Richard Wright, "Literature of the Negro in the United States," *White Man, Listen!* (1957).

2. 1977 and After

Two major developments have marked the history of African-American theory and criticism since 1977: the appearance of more theoretically grounded approaches to African-American literary production (aiming in part to establish an African-American literary tradition) and the emergence of a vigorously feminist African-American literary theory and criticism. In their own fashion these movements extended some of the central characteristics of earlier aspects of African-American literary theory and criticism. For instance, the consciously literary and theoretical readings of African-American literature found an appropriate forebear in the motivation for Ralph Ellison's literary essays. Versions of African-American feminism traced a clear line of descent from the self-positioning of Zora Neale Hurston. More generally, the movements toward theory and toward African-American literary feminism attempted to draw the contours of a distinctive literary practice, much as the essays of W. E. B. DuBois, Langston Hughes, Richard Wright, and Ellison had earlier in the century.

The best-known impetus for the inclination toward more consciously literary and theoretically based analyses of African-American literature was the seminar on "Afro-American Literature and Course Design" held at Yale University in June 1977. Funded by both the Modern Language Association of America and the National Endowment for the Humanities, the seminar was led by Robert Stepto and had its print incarnation as *Afro-American Literature: The Reconstruction of Instruction* (1978), edited by Stepto and Dexter Fisher. Embodied in the volume's title was the seminar's intention to revise significantly pedagogy and (by implication) research in the field.

The field of African-American criticism required reconstruction because it had become dominated by fundamentally ideological or sociological methodologies that tended toward the naively reductive. As Stepto wrote in his introductory essay, "Teaching Afro-American Literature," the contemporary fashion of teaching and thinking about African-American literature was "antiquated" by and large because African-American literature was yet conceived by many as merely "an agreeable entree to black history, sociology, and politics" (*Reconstruction* 9). This reduction occurred for a number of reasons, not the least of which was the tendency of the critic to fetishize the "racial" content of the work of art, rather than make certain that African-American literature was "taught as literature" (23). Henry Louis Gates, Jr., in his "Preface to Blackness: Text and Pretext," revoiced and extended this sentiment by decentering a consideration of "blackness . . . [as] a material object or an event" (67) and turning the critic's "attention to the nature of black figurative language, to the nature of black narrative forms, to the history and theory of Afro-American literary criticism, to the fundamental unity and form of content, and to the arbitrary relations between the sign and its referent" (68). The decentering of simplistic sociological approaches to literature meant, in the words of Robert Hemenway, another contributor, a "concentration . . . on the aesthetic forms, linguistic constructions, and imaginative patterns" of African-American literature (123). The idea of an African-American literary tradition remained important to all the contributors to this volume; however, tradition was to be established not by the "race" of the author, for instance, but rather by a consideration of *intertextuality*. Fundamentally, *The Reconstruction of Instruction* took as its primary aim the outlining of what forms that intertextuality might take in both theory and practice.

Needless to say, this advocacy of reconstruction has its significant opponents. Perhaps the foremost weakness of this collection was its apparent reinstitution of literary criteria at the expense of political ones. To those taking an instrumental view of the content of the work of art, *Reconstruction of Instruction* seemed to reinvoke "art for art's sake" rather than constructing art as a weapon in a social and political struggle for liberation (protestations of the reconstructors notwithstanding). Further, the theoretical language adopted by many of the contributors seemed to some unnecessarily inflated and ultimately elitist. Finally, the critics of *Reconstruction* saw both the volume and the general movement it indicated as attacking the fundamentally reflectionist ethos of earlier criticism upon which this instrumental reading of literature was based.

The emphasis on language use owed much to the

criticism of Ellison, who earlier had insisted on the distinction between sociology and literature in "Brave Words for a Startling Occasion" (*Shadow and Act*, 1964, 113). The emphasis on language continued in the criticism produced by the two most important theorists of African-American literature in the period, Henry Louis Gates, Jr., who was a contributor to *Reconstruction*, and Houston Baker, Jr.

At times Gates and Baker could be seen as antagonists in a developing contest over the direction of African-American letters. This impression was supported by Gates's early contention that Baker's work seemed to emphasize the extraliterary, that his "criticism teaches us more about his attitude toward being black in white America than it does about black literature" (Stepto and Fisher 65). Yet over time their apparent opposition became bracketed by their growing agreement about many, though certainly not all, of the principles articulated in *Reconstruction*, for example, that African-American literary criticism required some sort of reform and that formal consideration of literature was not at all necessarily apolitical or antipolitical. The critical positions of Baker and Gates developed an affinity for each other, proving it useful to imagine them as inscribing a dialectic.

Of the two, Gates's critical position began with the closest connections with traditional academic "high theory." His "Criticism in the Jungle" (in *Black Literature and Literary Theory*, 1984) was an obvious homage to GEOFFREY H. HARTMAN's *Criticism in the Wilderness*. In this early piece, Gates attempted to lay out a theoretical basis for the initial development of an African-American literary canon and for the study of African-American literature as a form of language use rather than as a form of unmediated social practice. "The challenge of black literary criticism is to derive principles of literary criticism from the black tradition itself, as defined in the idiom of critical theory but also in the idiom which constitutes the 'language of blackness,' the signifyin(g) difference which makes the black tradition our very own" (8). The development of an African-American tradition by means of a "synthesis" of African-American vernacular and the language of theory was further articulated in *"Race," Writing, and Difference* (1986) and was given fullest expression in *The Signifying Monkey* (1988) and *Figures in Black: Words, Signs, and the "Racial" Self* (1987). "Signifyin(g)" is both a linguistic process, the vernacular improvising on formal critical speech by way of a "double-voicedness," and a metaphor indicating a larger cultural practice (*Signifying* 44–51).

In this view, the significant motives driving Gates's paradigm were therefore three: 1) the need to reform the study of African-American literature; 2) the positioning of this reform as an explicit "signifyin(g)" revision of dominant critical theory; and 3) the development of a culturally specific theory of African-American literature and literary criticism. All three of these ideas were resident in Gates's writings from the very first, but over time his work tended to emphasize the third over and against the other two. Having "signified" on "high academic theory" (and in doing so, cleared the field), Gates moved on to a revised form of criticism, evidenced by his conclusion to "Authority, (White) Power and the (Black) Critic: Or, It's All Greek to Me": "Now we must, at last, don the empowering mask of blackness and talk *that* talk, the language of black difference" (*Cultural Critique* 7 [1987] 46).

Gates's critics regularly and mistakenly castigated him for a kind of cultural transgression, as though an emphasis on the literary necessitated the neglect of politics (see Barbara Christian, "The Race for Theory," *Cultural Critique* 6 [1987]; and Baxter Miller, "Baptized Infidel: Play and Critical Legacy," *Black American Literature Forum* 21 [1987]). This error resulted from reinscribing the dominant opposition between the literary and the social, or the aesthetic and the political. A more useful way of considering Gates would be to see his insistence on a distinctive African-American theory as a political act, or at least as an act with affirmative political consequences. The critic who "signified" moved from being simply a trickster figure to being something more in the way of a culture worker in a field with nationalist overtones.

The career of Houston Baker ran parallel to that of Gates, though in a somewhat opposite direction. The trajectory of Baker's work, from the early *Long Black Song* (1972), through *Blues, Ideology, and Afro-American Literature* (1984), to *Workings of the Spirit: The Poetics of Afro-American Women's Writing* (1991), revealed this relation to Gates's *oeuvre*. While Gates could be seen as moving from theory toward literary nationalism (to put it crudely), Baker could be seen as moving from a profoundly nationalistic cultural base toward a revision of that position complicated by an engagement with language and with theory. Consequently, by the end of the period in question, both Gates and Baker, for all their differences, early and late, could be seen as occupying relatively similar positions.

In his early work, such as *Long Black Song,* Baker took as his chief task the defining of African-American literature within a cultural setting. In "Completely Well," for instance, he tried to outline the contours of a distinctly African-American notion of culture based on the idea of the whole life of a people. "One does not worship, dis-

play, or teach culture; one acknowledges it as a whole way of life grounded in the past, and one necessarily lives a culture" (*Long* 1). He juxtaposed this version of culture with a more Victorian or Arnoldian vision that fetishized the best products of the best classes (see MATTHEW ARNOLD). Baker continued this interest in African-American cultural formation in *Blues, Ideology, and Afro-American Literature, Modernism and the Harlem Renaissance* (1987), and *Afro-American Poetics: Revisions of Harlem and the Black Aesthetic* (1988). The central aim of all these works was to establish a connection between the African-American cultural past and current African-American discursive and cultural practice. Significantly, over time Baker's focus grew to be more and more on language use and its relation to culture, rather than on an idea of culture apart from language use. Such a shift he indicated explicitly in "Discovering America: Generational Shifts, Afro-American Literary Criticism, and the Study of Expressive Culture," in which he distanced himself from the "race and superstructure" criticism and "romantic Marxism" of the early Black Arts movement (*Blues* 81), even as he retained and revised their emphasis on cultural anthropology (105). Such a revision was also indicated by a concomitant movement away from an early concept such as "repudiation," in which black culture was marked by a rejection of things "white" (*Long* 13), to a critical recognition of the "hybridity" inherent in cultural forms. This recognition of hybridity was indicated in part by Baker's engagement with Euro-American literary and cultural theory, for instance in his "signifyin(g)" on Gaston Bachelard's *Poetics of Space* in *Workings of the Spirit,* to choose but one example. Undoubtedly, Baker had articulated serious reservations about "reconstructionist" approaches to African-American literature (*Blues* 90 ff.). Those articulations notwithstanding, his work shows the imprint of much reconstructionist thinking, just as the criticism by Gates, for instance, shows the influence of Baker's work.

The theoretical debates occasioned by the various reconsiderations of the Black Arts movement were mirrored by another and potentially more significant development, the foregrounding of gender and its relation to an African-American literary tradition. Just as the new generation of African-American theorists have claimed Ellison as one of their precursors, particularly in his opposition to sociological approaches and to the naturalism of Wright, so too have the recent generation of African-American feminist critics looked to the past for significant progenitors, and they found one in the figure of Zora Neale Hurston. And just as the opposition between Ellison and Wright seemed informing for the theorists, so too was the opposition between Hurston and Wright for the feminist critics after 1977. Hurston's feminist-centered fiction, for instance, with its emphasis on female intersubjectivity, contrasted with Wright's emphasis on the construction of an embattled masculinity within a racist environment. The opposition between Wright and Hurston became figured as an opposition between a feminist and a patriarchal tradition in African-American letters, only marginally less damaging than the white hegemonic tradition itself. Giving impetus to this view of the development of African-American literary feminism was the publication of two volumes by Alice Walker. Her edition of writings by Hurston, *I Love Myself When I Am Laughing,* concluded with "Looking for Zora," an account of her discovery of Hurston's grave, an event marking "times when greater disciplines are born" (313). Hurston's discovery became a metonym for the archaeological act of another form of reconstruction, the recovery of an African-American women's literary and cultural tradition. Walker explicitly continued this enterprise in her *In Search of Our Mothers' Gardens: Womanist Prose* (1983). This volume's title essay meditates on the question, "What did it mean for a black woman to be an artist in our grandmothers' time? In our great-grandmothers' day?" (233). By drawing connections back to Hurston and earlier, Walker hoped to establish a historical trajectory of the African-American woman's expressive creativity.

To establish this trajectory required not simply a distancing from the masculinist writing of Wright, for instance, or of some of the more prominent authors of the Black Arts movement; it also required an equivalent distancing from white academic feminism and toward what Walker would call "womanist" writing. This break was explicitly signaled by two essays in Elaine Showalter's *The New Feminist Criticism: Essays on Women, Literature, and Theory* (1985). In "Toward a Black Feminist Criticism," Barbara Smith pointed to the general invisibility of black women writers generally (and black lesbian writers specifically) and called for a counteracting mode of criticism

> in this country that would open up the space needed for the exploration of Black women's lives and the creation of consciously Black woman–identified art. At the same time a redefinition of the goals and strategies of the white feminist movement would lead to much-needed change in the focus and content of what is now generally accepted as women's culture. (169)

Smith furthered this claim by advancing the fundamentally "lesbian" nature of African-American women's writ-

ing by way of its general opposition to white patriarchy (175). In a companion essay, "New Directions for Black Feminist Criticism," Deborah McDowell took exception to the representation of the inherent "lesbian" qualities of African-American women's writing, conceiving of Smith's argument as reductive, even as she agreed with Smith's general call for a more intimate focus on literature by and about African-American women. McDowell's concentration on language use (reminiscent of *Reconstruction*) inclined her away from what she took to be the potential for a dangerous essentialism and led her to assert the possibility of some linguistic similarities between African-American women's and men's writing.

> Whether Black feminist criticism will or should remain a separatist enterprise is a debatable point. Black feminist critics ought to move from this issue to consider the specific language of Black women's literature, to describe the ways Black women writers employ literary devices in a distinct way, and to compare the way Black women writers create their own mythic structures. (196)

The period since 1977 has witnessed the publication of a number of works furthering the general aims outlined by Smith and McDowell. Toni Cade Bambara's *The Black Woman: An Anthology* (1970) was one slightly earlier precursor to this movement. Later anthologies include Roseann P. Bell, Bettye J. Parker, and Beverly Guy-Sheftall's *Sturdy Black Bridges: Visions of Black Women in Literature* (1979), Barbara Smith's *All the Women Are White, All the Blacks Are Men, But Some of Us Are Brave: Black Women's Studies* (1982) and *Home Girls: A Black Feminist Anthology* (1982), Marjorie Pryse and Hortense Spillers's *Conjuring: Black Women, Fiction, and Literary Tradition* (1985), Joanne M. Braxton and Andrée McLaughlin's *Wild Women in the Whirlwind* (1990), and Henry Louis Gates's *Reading Black, Reading Feminist* (1990). Each of these volumes undertook, in Braxton's words, "an exploration of intertextuality, not only within Black female literary tradition, but also within the Black and female experience which has given rise to this tradition" (*Wild Women* xxiv).

Like any critical movement, however, African-American literary feminism could not be construed as being made out of whole cloth into a seamless garment. Rather it was a center of oppositional thought frequently more problematic than not. For instance, Smith's claim that African-American women's writing was inherently (even if not explicitly or intentionally) lesbian ("Black Feminist" 175 ff.) assuredly threatened to create more problems than it solved, not only by way of reductivism, but also as it seemed ironically to marginalize literature focusing on explicitly eroticized relations between women. Conversely, texts such as Smith's own *Home Girls* or Audre Lorde's *Sister Outsider* (1984), with their important assertion of lesbian difference made even more problematic, if not impossible, a stable and uniform representation of African-American woman as oppositional other.

Another complicating factor in the development of African-American literary feminism proved to be its positioning inside the academy, a locale consistently pictured as antithetical to any significant concentration on African-American women's expressivity. Hazel Carby's influential *Reconstructing Womanhood* (1987) advocated "that black feminist criticism be regarded as a problem, not a solution, as a sign that should be interrogated, a locus of contradictions. Black feminist criticism has its source and its primary motivation in academic legitimation, placement within a framework of bourgeois humanistic discourse" (15). While there was considerable room to quarrel with Carby's absolute identification of African-American feminist criticism with bourgeois humanism, there was also no doubt that the contradictions within the genealogy of African-American feminist discourse—such as the self-confirming and tautological assumption of the existence of a tradition prior to the investigations that might establish the nature of that tradition or African-American feminist criticism's inclination to rely on traditional forms of literary analysis—needed to be engaged. Carby's work complicated matters further by interrogating the neglect of middle-class African-American writers such as Jessie Fauset and Nella Larsen, a neglect attributable to the romanticization of "the folk" and to the construction of African-American identity as fundamentally rural (175).

Perhaps most influentially complicating of all was the work of bell hooks (Gloria Watkins). Her *Talking Back: Thinking Feminist, Thinking Black* (1979), *Feminist Theory: From Margin to Center* (1984), and *Yearning: Race, Gender, and Cultural Politics* (1990) constituted a project designed not only to engage the construction of an African-American feminist discursive practice but also to make that practice more attuned to questions of class and postmodern critical practice as well. In "Feminist Theory: A Radical Agenda" she advanced the theorizing activity as indispensable to a feminist practice (in direct opposition to Barbara Christian) and located the animus against theory as a form of anti-intellectualism (*Talking Back* 38–39). hooks's interest in theory and her inclination to pursue the value of postmodern ideas such as the "decentered subject" moved her to construct a postmodern attack on essentialism within African-American feminist discourse, even as she centered the significance of African-American women's experiences and was equally critical of the shortcomings of POSTMODERNISM. For hooks, the margin became an arena of possibility where "one develops critical thinking and critical consciousness, as one invents new, alternative habits of being, and resists from that marginal space of difference inwardly defined" (*Yearning* 15). This movement had the obvious effect of centering the margin, even while critically combating overly stable notions of identity, much in the same fashion as did Carby's work. In the same vein, too, hooks also saw the value in interrogating the relation between African-American literary feminism and the academy.

By the end of the 1980s, the critical and theoretical concerns regarding the nature of African-American literary discourse remained for the most part unresolved. Even if it was clear that postmodernism and academic feminism had value for a consideration of African-American literature, the nature and the extent of that value were not at all clear. Equally unclear was the relation between the ideology of the academy and the scholarly consideration of African-American discursive practice. Assuredly clear, however, was that African-American literary criticism and theory promised considerable intellectual richness, in addition to fruitful controversy, with implications for the general study of literature as well.

Theodore O. Mason, Jr.

Molefi Kete Asante, *The Afrocentric Idea* (1987); Houston A. Baker, Jr., "Belief, Theory, and Blues: Notes for a Post-Structuralist Criticism of Afro-American Literature," *Belief vs. Theory in Black American Literary Criticism* (ed. Joe Weixlmann and Chester J. Fontenot, 1986), *Blues, Ideology, and Afro-American Literature: A Vernacular Theory* (1984), "In Dubious Battle," *New Literary History* 18 (1987), *The Journey Back: Issues in Black Literature and Criticism* (1980), *Long Black Song: Essays in Black American Literature and Culture* (1972), *Singers of Daybreak: Studies in Black American Literature* (1974); Houston A. Baker, Jr., and Patricia Redmond, eds., *Afro-American Literary Study in the 1990s* (1989); Joseph Beam, ed., *In the Life: A Black Gay Anthology* (1986); Joanne M. Braxton and Andrée Nicola McLaughlin, eds., *Wild Women in the Whirlwind: Afra-American Culture and the Contemporary Literary Renaissance* (1990); Hazel Carby, *Reconstructing Womanhood: The Emergence of the Afro-American Woman Novelist* (1987); Barbara Christian, *Black Feminist Criticism* (1985); Michael Cooke, *Afro-American Literature in* the Twentieth Century: The Achievement of Intimacy (1984); Mari Evans, ed., Black Women Writers (1950–1980): A Critical Evaluation (1984); Henry Louis Gates, Jr., "Authority, (White) Power and the (Black) Critic: Or, It's All Greek to Me," Cultural Critique 7 (1987), Black Literature and Literary Theory (1984), The Signifying Monkey: A Theory of Afro-American Literary Criticism (1988), "'What's Love Got to Do With It?': Critical Theory, Integrity, and the Black Idiom," New Literary History 18 (1987); bell hooks, Yearning: Race, Gender, and Cultural Politics (1990); Zora Neale Hurston, I Love Myself When I Am Laughing . . . And Then Again When I Am Looking Mean and Impressive: A Zora Neale Hurston Reader (ed. Alice Walker, 1979); Joyce A. Joyce, "The Black Canon: Reconstructing Black American Literary Criticism," New Literary History 18 (1987), "'Who the Cap Fit': Unconsciousness and Unconscionableness in the Criticism of Houston A. Baker and Henry Louis Gates Jr.," New Literary History 18 (1987); Deborah McDowell, "New Directions for Black Feminist Criticism," The New Feminist Criticism: Essays on Women, Literature, and Theory (ed. Elaine Showalter, 1985); Theodore O. Mason, Jr., "Between the Populist and the Scientist: Ideology and Power in Recent Afro-American Literary Criticism or, 'The Dozens' as Scholarship," Callaloo 11 (1988); R. Baxter Miller, ed., Black American Literature and Humanism (1981); Toni Morrison, "Unspeakable Things Unspoken: The Afro-American Presence in American Literature," Michigan Quarterly Review 28 (1989); Barbara Smith, "Toward a Black Feminist Criticism" (Showalter); Valerie Smith, Self-Discovery and Authority in Afro-American Narrative (1987); Robert Stepto, From Behind the Veil: A Study of Afro-American Narrative (1979); Alice Walker, In Search of Our Mothers' Gardens: Womanist Prose (1983); Susan Willis, Specifying: Black Women Writing the American Experience (1987).

AMERICAN THEORY AND CRITICISM: NINETEENTH CENTURY

Nineteenth-century American writers produced a considerable range of theory and criticism. While some published essays and books explicitly devoted to the subject, many others inserted important statements within explanatory prefaces and works now deemed canonical. Fired by the prospect of shaping the literary traditions of a new nation, the American Romantics tended to issue pronouncements about fundamentals, for example, the role of the artist in expressing, even creating, a national identity. Henry David Thoreau and Walt Whitman advocated distinctly American expression supported by Romantic-transcendentalist theories of organicism articulated by RALPH WALDO EMERSON. Nathaniel Hawthorne and Herman Melville justified an indigenous romance fiction to plumb the depths of the human heart. Later in the century, the realists, most notably William Dean Howells, promoted European realism modified by national and ethical concerns. Romantics and realists alike responded to foreign theories (British, German, and French), as well as to national ambitions. The result is a hybrid tradition, at once derivative and indigenous, that continues to influence current literary theory, criticism, and practice.

American Romantics, like their British and European predecessors, sought to revitalize concepts of self, nature, and society in a climate of intellectual skepticism. According to G. W. F. HEGEL in his Aesthetics: Lectures on Fine Art (1835, trans. T. M. Knox, 2 vols., 1975), the Enlightenment "intellect made God into a mere ens rationis" and "believed no longer in the appearance of his spirit in concrete reality" (1:507). In reaction to this "supreme renunciation, the renunciation of knowing nothing of God" (1:508), the Romantic imagination had "for its substantial content the reconciliation of God with the world" and the "satisfaction of the heart" so that the "Ideal" might be "completely at home" in the world (1:530). American writers were introduced to German ideas by British Romantics, especially WILLIAM WORDSWORTH, SAMUEL TAYLOR COLERIDGE, and Thomas Carlyle. Twenty years after Edward Tyrell Channing charged Americans to rely upon the "indignant freedom" of "genius" to create a distinctly American literature ("On Models in Literature," North American Review, 1816), Ralph Waldo Emerson drew on British critical theory to provide a philosophical ground for a spiritualized American genius commensurate with American nature and history.

A brief discussion of Emerson's critical theory is necessary here, since it influenced other American writers profoundly. Emerson in Nature (1836) combines Wordsworth's aesthetics of nature ("Preface to Lyrical Ballads," 1800), Coleridge's theory of the imagination (Biographia Literaria, 1817), and Carlyle's ideas concerning "Natural Supernaturalism" (Sartor Resartus, 1832–33) to empower the American self. Particularly in the chapter "Language," Emerson formulates his idea of "radical correspondence" between the Carlylian Me and Not Me (1:29). As Carlyle explains in "Natural Supernaturalism" and "Symbols," the self finds its home in the world by recognizing the "Miracle" of ordinary experience in nature, by perceiving nature to be "one vast Symbol of God" (*Sartor* 255, 220). Accordingly, Emerson asserts that since "words are signs of natural facts" and "particular natural facts are symbols of particular spiritual facts," a kind of "picturesque" language of verbal hieroglyphics can "pierce" the "rotten diction" of hollow convention and "fasten words again to things" (1:25, 29). Complemented by a Coleridgean primary imagination, which perceives the spiritual ground of Wordsworthian nature, this transcendental naming enables the American poet to establish "an original relation to the universe" in literature (1:3). In "The American Scholar" (1837) Emerson advises young Americans to ignore "the courtly muses of Europe" (1:114). In place of artificial genres and mechanical techniques, the true artist relies on a creative imagination whose works are as organic as the productions of nature: Whitman's *Leaves of Grass* (1855) derives from "metrical laws" and "buds from them as unerringly and loosely as lilacs or roses" (*Prose Works* 2:440); Thoreau's *Week on the Concord and Merrimack Rivers* (1849) traces the flow of the rivers, and *Walden* (1854) follows the cycle of the seasons; Hawthorne's "tales and essays" in *Mosses from an Old Manse* (1849) are "flowers" that have "blossomed" from the writer's "heart and mind" (10:34); Melville's chapters in *Moby-Dick* (1851) "grow" like "branches" (ch. 63).

Although Whitman was not the first of Emerson's disciples, he remained closest in spirit, hoping to find in himself the redemptive poet whom Emerson, like John the Baptist, had prophesied. Emerson called America "a poem in our eyes" and predicted that America's "ample geography" would "not wait long for meters" (3:38). In the 1855 preface to his life's work, *Leaves of Grass,* Whitman declares no less an intention than to pen "the great psalm of the republic" (2:437). He agrees with Emerson that the "United States themselves are essentially the greatest poem" (2:434). Whitman's most distinctively Emersonian tenet, one that Emerson had learned from Carlyle, is the correspondence between the Me and the Not Me. As a "seer" who is "complete in himself," the Whitmanian poet can "indicate the path between reality" and the people's "souls" (2:439). In a later preface, "A Backward Glance O'er Travelled Roads" (1888), Whitman expresses full assurance that in his forthright effort to "put *a Person,* a human being (myself, in the latter half of the Nineteenth Century, in America) on record," he also expresses the fundamental identity of his nation (2:731). In "Democratic Vistas" (1871) Whitman insists in a note that "all interest culminates in the field of persons" (2:392), and in the central text he maintains that "personalism" constitutes the "compensating balance wheel of the successful working machinery of aggregate

America" (2:391–92). The essential self, the "American stock personality, with literatures and arts for outlets," Whitman hopes, will redeem a commercial America that remains "canker'd, crude, superstitious and rotten," an America that in his view is inhabited increasingly by "a mob of fashionably dress'd speculators and vulgarians" (2:369). As Leo Marx has shown in *The Machine in the Garden* (1964), such concerns are typical of those nineteenth-century writers who anguished over the fate of the soul in an age of science, mechanics, and commercialism.

Whitman's more distinct contribution to poetics lies in his revolutionary form and manner. In his essays he aligns himself with monumental bards of the past but distinguishes himself from traditional expression. In a mood of largess in "Democratic Vistas," he praises the great works of "Old and New testament, Homer, Aeschelus, PLATO, Juvenal, etc." (2:406). After all, as he puts it in "A Backward Glance," "Herder taught to the young Goethe, that really great poetry is always (like the Homeric or Biblical canticles) the result of a national spirit, and not the privilege of a polish'd and select few" (2:731–32). In "Democratic Vistas," Whitman would discover in his personality, as the bards of old had done, "national, original archetypes in literature" (2:405). But Whitman is different. For one thing, he employs "the dialect of common sense," as he explains in the 1855 preface (2:457). Although he admires the "English language," which "befriends the grand American expression," he emphasizes what is "brawny enough and limber and full enough" in colloquial speech (2:456). Also, he strives for a Romantic's version of realism; that is, he rejects all "which distorts honest shapes or which creates unearthly beings or places or contingencies" (2:450). He believes that "the attributes of the poets of the kosmos concentre in the real body and soul" and reflect "the superiority of genuineness over all fiction and romance" (2:450–51). His version of "Natural Supernaturalism" frees poets from constraints of genre and convention. Like Thoreau, Whitman finds "works most beautiful without ornament" (2:451). And Whitman rejects both the formal and sentimental aims of EDGAR ALLAN POE and the didactic aims of the conventional fireside poets: "The poetic quality is not marshalled by rhyme or uniformity or abstract addresses to things nor in melancholy complaints or good precepts" (2:439–40). Relying on his own free form in the spirit of the epic bards, Whitman strives to "vocalize the vastness" (1877 preface, 2:472).

Henry David Thoreau, who graduated from Harvard in 1837, may have heard Emerson deliver "The American Scholar." In any case, growing up in Concord, Massachusetts, as Emerson's protégé, Thoreau embraced Emerson's idea that poetic language could link the divine in the self with the divine in nature. But Thoreau's rigorous, independent mind converted Emerson's transcendentalism into a theory of writing as a mode of life, what MARTIN HEIDEGGER in 1951 would call "building" and "dwelling," the "manner in which mortals are on earth" ("Building Dwelling Thinking," *Poetry* 148). Anticipating Heidegger, Thoreau insisted that the true artist establishes an original relation to the universe by dwelling in a certain way, a way reflected by form and style. Like Whitman, Thoreau distinguished himself from Emerson by attending to ordinary, brawny experience. It is no accident that Thoreau's best-known book, *Walden* (1854), is subtitled *Life in the Woods* and that the locus of his thought is, as he writes, "a house which I had built myself" (325). In *Sartor Resartus,* Carlyle points out that since "man is guided and commanded" by "Symbols," "Not a Hut he builds but is the visible embodiment of a Thought" (220). Thoreau links the constructive element of thought and writing with natural, organic *activity,* thereby seeking to resolve distinctions between the natural and the artificial in his work. In his *Journal,* he likens the form of his first book, *A Week on the Concord and Merrimack Rivers,* to a "hypaethral" (open) temple. *A Week* is an "unroofed book" admitting the aroma of the "fields and woods" and the "ether" of the sky (274–75). Again, his language looks forward to that of Heidegger, who celebrates "the Open" and calls "language" the "precinct *(templum),* that is, the house of Being," which constitutes a gathering of earth, sky, humans, and gods ("What Are Poets For?" *Poetry* 106, 132; "The Thing," *Poetry* 179–81).

Thoreau speculates in *Walden* that "if men constructed their dwellings with their own hands . . . the poetic faculty would be universally developed, as birds universally sing when they are so engaged" (359). He took seriously what Carlyle called "those 'architectural ideas' which . . . lurk at the bottom of all Modes" and which "lead to important revolutions" (*Sartor* 271). In *American Renaissance* (1941), F. O. Matthiessen explains that Thoreau's unjustified attack in *Walden* on sculptor Horatio Greenough's proclivity for "architectural ornament" registers Thoreau's supersensitive concern for organic form and authentic style (150–54). Despite the obvious rhetorical flourishes and careful organization in *Walden,* Thoreau nominally rejects any artist who "strains after effect in the style of his dwelling" and who labors on ornamentation that is "literally hollow." To introduce "ornaments of style in literature" is to empty writing of significance (*Walden* 358–60).

For Thoreau, writing should exactly parallel character. He articulates this idea most fully in his essay "Thomas Carlyle and His Works" (1847). Because he saw Carlyle as the "usher" of "what philosophy and criticism the nineteenth century had to offer" after Coleridge's death (223), the essay deserves special emphasis. Thoreau praises Carlyle as "a strong and finished workman in his craft," a workman who, like SAMUEL JOHNSON, "makes the literary class respectable" (224). "Eminently colloquial," Carlyle's style captures "the rhythms and cadences of conversation endlessly repeated," so that the "written answer[s] to the spoken word, and the spoken word to a fresh and pertinent thought in the mind" (226). As Thoreau stresses, a true style results in the very language that the transcendentalists wished to employ: "Nature is ransacked, and all the resorts and purlieus of humanity are taxed, to furnish the fittest symbol for [Carlyle's] thought. He does not go to the dictionary" (227). The ideal style reconciles self, landscape, and community, as Thoreau indicates in a powerful image of physical conquest paralleling the violence of backwoods settlement. An authentic style "tries the back-stitch and side-hug with it [the subject], and downs it again—scalps it, draws and quarters it, hangs it in chains, and leaves it to the winds and dogs" (231). Although his classicism leads him to advise Carlyle and others to temper "mannerism" (239), Thoreau's ideas about "originality of style" and "emancipating the language" (232) forecast the American vernacular of writers such as Mark Twain, William Faulkner, and Ernest Hemingway.

In his lengthiest preface, "The Old Manse" (1846), Nathaniel Hawthorne explicitly locates the "Abode" of his imaginative life not in the "speculative extravagances" of transcendental theory but in "the system of human society" (10:25). Neither primitive nature nor transcendental self-reflection counts as much for Hawthorne as does historical consciousness. Although he admires Thoreau's "strange faculty of finding what the Indians have left behind," Hawthorne asserts that the Manse is freighted with cultural heritage "worth a thousand wigwams" (10:11); the Manse has seen New England's ministerial, revolutionary, and domestic history. Also, while Hawthorne identifies Emerson as "a poet of deep beauty and austere tenderness," Hawthorne claims to seek "nothing from him as a philosopher" (10:31). In actual fact, Hawthorne ironically employs Emerson's theories of symbolism and organicism to defend a creative life anchored primarily in American history rather than American nature. The Manse, where Emerson himself had once resided, becomes a "symbol" of the "institutions that had grown out of the heart of mankind" (10:26). For

Hawthorne, American history and institutions are, after all, no less organic than American nature and the life of the mind. His theory of the American romance establishes an original relation to the "domestic circle," the local "tradition," and the regional history that provide the substance of his characters' inner lives (10:3–4). Influenced as much by Scottish association philosophy as by Romantic transcendentalism, Hawthorne suggests that fiction requires historical associations of locale, activity, and sensation: "For myself the book [*Mosses from an Old Manse*] will always retain one charm—as reminding me of the river, with its delightful solitudes, and of the avenue, the garden, and the orchard, and especially, the dear old Manse [where] I wrote" (10:34–35). Richard Brodhead has masterfully demonstrated in *The School of Hawthorne* (1986) just how Hawthorne's connections between psychology, experience, locale, and tradition have informed the work of later American writers as diverse as William Dean Howells, Sarah Orne Jewett, HENRY JAMES, William Faulkner, and Flannery O'Connor. Hawthorne, Brodhead comments, "pulls disparate writing into a continuous and coherent line" (9).

It is in "The Custom House," the introduction to *The Scarlet Letter* (1850), that Hawthorne precisely defines the nature of romance fiction. More philosophical than Sir Walter Scott's historical novel-romances, Hawthorne's work presents a "neutral territory," a fictive region "somewhere between the real world and fairy land, where the Actual and the Imaginary may meet, and each imbue itself with the nature of the other" (1:35–36). As scholars have pointed out more recently, the neutral territory of Hawthorne's work is also a meeting place of masculine and feminine sexuality (Carton 208–16).

To bring this region of "strangeness" to life, the writer requires special conditions (1:35–36). Worn by the ordinary business of daily life, the writer's "imagination" becomes a "tarnished mirror" displaying "characters of the narrative" with the "rigidity of dead corpses" (1:33–34). These "fixed" characters recall Coleridge's description of mere objects as "essentially fixed and dead" when they are manipulated by the mechanical "fancy" rather than enlivened by the creative "secondary imagination" (*Biographia* 1:202). To repair the damaged imagination, the artist induces a dream state not unlike the state between sleeping and waking that another American romancer, Edgar Allan Poe, identifies in "Marginalia" (1846) as a source of "psychal impressions" (89). Imagining himself at rest but awake "late at night," Hawthorne observes objects illuminated by "moonlight," or the "cold" light of the intellect, and by "coal-fire," the "warmer light" of the "heart." Then, placing objective reality "one

remove further," he describes a "looking-glass" that presents "a repetition of all the gleam and shadow of the picture," a repetition "nearer to the imaginative" (1:34–37). The imagination, like a mirror, composes external objects and interior reflections into a single world of fiction, a unity that only the romance can provide. Nevertheless, the imagination is not self-sufficient. The inspiration for the romance—for "Hester Prynne's story"—originates in two kinds of writing, both historically grounded: the antiquated "documents" of a "private nature" and the symbolic "letter A," which has "some deep meaning in it, most worthy of interpretation" (1:31–32). In his fabrication about discovering these artifacts, Hawthorne conveys an important idea: writing itself is as potent an origin for significant experience as nature is. While Emerson and the transcendentalists locate their inspirations and symbols in nature, Hawthorne locates his inspirations and symbols in texts. Texts link the present with the past and the future, and they represent the dream lives—the "private nature"—of writers. Thus, Hawthorne's romance balances reality and imagination, intellect and emotion, masculinity and femininity, past and present.

Excited by the literary nationalism of Evert Duyckinck's Young America group, inspired by the transcendentalists' reverence for "genius," and awed by Hawthorne's expressive power, Herman Melville amplified the American Romantic theory of the 1840s and 1850s. His most important review, "Hawthorne and His Mosses" (1850), crystallizes his radical concept of the romance. At the outset of the review, Melville endorses Hawthorne's suggestion that an adequate appreciation of another writer's works requires psychological identification with the other writer. Mirroring as much as possible the situational origin of *Mosses*, Melville places himself imaginatively in a "papered chamber in a fine old farmhouse, a mile from any other dwelling" (535). This identification accomplished, the critic Melville advances to his central assertions about what it takes to produce a grand national literature: an acquaintance with "suffering" that underlies a "boundless sympathy with all forms of being"; a "deep intellect, which drops down into the universe like a plummet"; a "great power of blackness" or "sense of Innate Depravity and Original Sin, from whose visitations . . . no deeply thinking mind is always and wholly free"; a willingness "to fail in originality" rather than "succeed in imitation" (540–42). These characteristics, as Richard Brodhead, Rowland A. Sherrill (*The Prophetic Melville: Experience, Transcendence, and Tragedy*, 1979), and others have argued, raise authorship to the status of prophecy—what Melville calls the "Great Art of Telling the Truth" (542). Soon after writing the review, which helped to inaugurate a friendship with Hawthorne, Melville practiced his theory in *Moby-Dick* (1851), which is "Inscribed" to Hawthorne's "Genius."

After 1851, both Hawthorne's and Melville's comments about authorship signal declining confidence in the authority of their craft. In prefaces to *The Blithedale Romance* (1852) and *The Marble Faun* (1860), Hawthorne emphasizes two weaknesses of the romance. First, he exposes a rift between art and experience, imagination and reality. In the *Blithedale* preface he calls his characters mere "creatures of his brain," fictions engaging in "phantasmagorical antics" (3:1). Second, he argues that American romancers struggle unsuccessfully for a "foothold between fiction and reality" because America possesses so little history. Because of the immediacy and materialism of American life, readers readily perceive the "pasteboard" of the romancer's "compositions" (3:2). In his preface to *The Marble Faun* he magnifies the problem with a list of America's cultural deficiencies: "no shadow, no antiquity, no mystery, no picturesque and gloomy wrong, nor anything but commonplace prosperity, in broad and simple daylight" (4:3). Melville's negations are even more pronounced. In *Pierre* (1852), Melville not only satirizes the commercialism and puffery that increasingly attended literary nationalism but also empties the writer's personality of interior significance, as the following passage about Pierre's self-discovery through authorship suggests: "By vast pains we mine into the pyramid; . . . with joy we espy the sarcophagus; but we lift the lid—and no body is there!— appallingly vacant as vast is the soul of a man!" (9:397). By the time of *Clarel* (1876), a Gargantuan anti-epic poem, Melville hints that all artistic form is necessary but empty superstructure. As his character Rolfe explains in an architectural metaphor typical of Melville, "Art," like a building, provides "ordered form" that shelters human beings from "Nature's terror" but returns only an "echo" to those who seek interior meanings (*Clarel: A Poem*, ed. Walter E. Bezanson, 1960, 248). Edgar Dryden observes in *Melville's Thematics of Form* (1968) that Melville practices a "metaphysics of emptiness" (216). However, the later Melville does believe it worthwhile to write as "a counterpoise to the exorbitant hopefulness, juvenile and shallow, that makes such a bluster in these days" (*Log* 2:788–89).

With the erosion of Romantic convictions and the end of the Civil War came a decided change in the dominant expectations concerning literary representation. RENÉ WELLEK points out that "the practice of close observation and realistic techniques in local-color fiction,

Western humor, and even the sentimental novel was widespread" long before the "theory of realism was imported from Europe" (*History* 4:206). America's chief theorist of realism, William Dean Howells, eventually articulated a coherent Americanized theory of realism in *Criticism and Fiction* (1891), a compilation of pronouncements gathered from his "Editor's Study" essays in *Harper's Monthly* (January 1886–May 1891). But as early as 1867, Howells expressed a realist's expectations in practical criticism appearing in the *Atlantic Monthly*. Taking aim at Melville's *Battle-Pieces and Aspects of the War* (1866) in a review for February 1867, Howells finds Melville's poetry indicative of "the negative virtues of originality in such a degree that it not only reminds you of no poetry you have read, but of no life you have known." Significantly, neither of the primary Romantic gifts— "originality" and "genius"—rescues Melville from censure, because from Howells's perspective, Melville represents "events" only "as realistically as one can to whom they have presented themselves as dreams." In *The Confidence-Man* (1857), Melville had directly challenged realists who require "severe fidelity to real life" by insisting that "it is with fiction as with religion; it should present another world, and yet one to which we feel the tie" (12:244). However, in reviewing *Battle-Pieces,* which in fact includes much realistic detail, Howells crystallizes the new perspective: Melville's "pictures" of the war, however "good," possess a "heroic quality of remoteness, separating our weak human feelings from them by trackless distances." Calling for the death of the "ideal grasshopper" in *Criticism and Fiction,* Howells assured major preoccupation with verisimilitude—the "real grasshopper" (12). In *Crumbling Idols* (1894), Hamlin Garland espouses a theory of "veritism," advocating a regional literature based on "passion for truth and for individual expression" (35, 21), and in "A Plea for Romantic Fiction" (1901), Frank Norris defends not Romanticism but naturalism, a more earthy realism of passion, abnormality, and violence.

In one important respect Howells and many of his disciples kept faith with American Romantics: most of the new writers continued to promote literary nationalism. Howells in *Criticism and Fiction* urges "born Americans" to court the "muse 'Americanus'" and to ensure that characters speak "true American" (137). Donald Pizer clarifies Howells's use of the "environmental determinism" of the French literary historian HIPPOLYTE TAINE and the "evolutionary science" of social Darwinists, such as Herbert Spencer, to promote American fiction (*Realism* 72). In light of environmental and evolutionary theories, the relative absence of tragedy and sexuality in American novels proves for Howells the high state of American culture. Howells explains that American realism lacks the tragic intensity of "Dostoievsky's novel, *The Crime and the Punishment,*" because America has surpassed Russia in evolutionary development; thus, Hawthorne's earlier criticism of a cultural landscape devoid of "shadows and inequalities in our broad level of prosperity" seems wrongheaded (128). For Howells, depicting other than "the smiling aspects of life" is "as false and mistaken in its way as dealing in American fiction with certain nudities which Latin peoples find edifying" (*Criticism* 128). Repeatedly he champions the "commonplace" of American prosperity and morality in the novel as appropriate to the high level of American culture (128–29). While his squeamishness and ethnocentrism have diminished Howells's critical authority during the twentieth century, his usual willingness to judge each work by "its class, its function, and its character" rather than by the critic's "personal" bias has contributed to the modern preference for objective criticism (33). In addition, his ideas about the ethical dimensions of fiction, especially his condemnation of "novels that merely tickle our prejudices and lull our judgment," have influenced current ethical critics such as Wayne C. Booth.

John Allison

See also BRITISH THEORY AND CRITICISM: 3. RO-MANTIC PERIOD AND EARLY NINETEENTH CENTURY and 4. VICTORIAN, RALPH WALDO EMERSON, and FICTION THEORY AND CRITICISM: 2. NINETEENTH-CENTURY BRITISH AND AMERICAN.

Edward Bank, ed., *American Romanticism: A Shape for Fiction* (1969); Thomas Carlyle, *Sartor Resartus: The Life and Opinions of Herr Teufelsdrockh* (1833, ed. Charles Frederick Harrold, 1976); Samuel Taylor Coleridge, *Biographia Literaria* (1817, ed. J. Showcross, 2 vols., 1907); Ralph Waldo Emerson, *The Complete Works of Ralph Waldo Emerson* (ed. Edward Waldo Emerson, 10 vols., 1903–4), *Emerson's Literary Criticism* (ed. E. W. Carlson, 1979); Hamlin Garland, *Crumbling Idols* (1894); Nathaniel Hawthorne, *The Centenary Edition of the Works of Nathaniel Hawthorne* (ed. William Charvat et al., 18 vols. to date, 1962–); William Dean Howells, *Criticism and Fiction* (1891), *Editor's Study* (ed. James W. Simpson, 1983), *Literary Friends and Acquaintances* (1900, ed. David F. Hiatt and Edwin H. Cady, 1968); Henry James, *Literary Criticism* (ed. Leon Edel, 2 vols., 1984); Herman Melville, "Hawthorne and His Mosses," *Moby-Dick* (1851, ed. Harrison Hayford and Hershel Parker, 1967), *The Letters of Herman Melville* (ed. Merrell R. Davis and William H. Gilman, 1960), *The Melville Log: A Documentary Life of Herman Melville, With a Supplementary Chapter* (ed. Jay Leyda, 2 vols., 1969), *Works* (Standard Edition, 16 vols., 1963); Frank Norris, *The Literary Criticism of Frank Norris* (ed. Donald Pizer, 1964); Edgar Allan Poe, "Marginalia," *The Complete Works of Edgar Allan Poe* (ed. James A. Harrison, 1902); Robert E. Spiller, ed., *The American Literary Revolution, 1783–1837* (1967); Floyd Stovall, *The Development of American Literary Criticism* (1955); Henry David Thoreau, *The Writings of Henry David Thoreau* (Walden Edition, 20 vols., 1906); Walt Whitman, *Prose Works 1892* (ed. Floyd Stovall, 2 vols., 1963).

George J. Becker, "Modern Realism as a Literary Movement," *Documents of Modern Literary Realism* (ed. Becker, 1963); Michael Davitt Bell, *The Development of American Romance: The Sacrifice of Relation* (1980); Warner Berthoff, *The Ferment of Realism: American Literature, 1884–1919* (1965); Richard H. Brodhead, *Hawthorne, Melville, and the Novel* (1976), *The School of Hawthorne* (1986); Lawrence Buell, *Literary Transcendentalism: Style and Vision in the American Renaissance* (1973), *New England Literary Culture: From Revolution through Renaissance* (1986); Edwin H. Cady, *The Light of Common Day: Realism in American Fiction* (1971); Evan Carton, " 'A Daughter of the Puritans' and Her Old Master: Hawthorne, Una, and the Sexuality of Romance," *Daughters and Fathers* (ed. Lynda E. Boose and Betty S. Flowers, 1989); Stanley Cavell, *In Quest of the Ordinary: Lines of Skepticism and Romanticism* (1988); Leon Chai, *The Romantic Foundations of the American Renaissance* (1987); William Charvat, *The Profession of Authorship in America, 1800–1870* (1968); Ann Douglas, *The Feminization of American Culture* (1977); Robert P. Falk, *The Victorian Mode in American Fiction, 1865–1885* (1965); G. W. F. Hegel, *Vorlesungen über die Aesthetik* (ed. H. G. Hotho, 1835, rev. ed., 1842, *Sämmtliche Werke*, ed. Hermann Glockner, 3d ed., 1949–59, vols. 12–14, *Hegel's Aesthetics: Lectures on Fine Art*, trans. T. M. Knox, 2 vols., 1975); Martin Heidegger, *Poetry, Language, Thought* (trans. Albert Hofstadter, 1971); Leo Marx, *The Machine in the Garden: Technology and the Pastoral Ideal in America* (1964); F. O. Matthiessen, *American Renaissance: Art and Expression in the Age of Emerson and Whitman* (1941); Perry Miller, *The Raven and the Whale: The War of Words and Wits in the Era of Poe and Melville* (1956); Donald Pizer, *Realism and Naturalism in Nineteenth-Century American Literature* (rev. ed., 1984); Robert E. Spiller et al., *Literary History of the United States* (1960); Eric J. Sundquist, *American Realism: New Essays* (1982); Jane P. Tompkins, *Sensational Designs: The Cultural Work of American Fiction, 1790–1860* (1985); Robert Weisbuch, *Atlantic Double-Cross: American Literature and British Influence in the Age of Emerson* (1986); René Wellek, *A History of Modern Criticism: 1750–1950*, vol. 4, *The Later Nineteenth Century* (1965).

ANTHROPOLOGICAL THEORY AND CRITICISM

There is no one clearly defined anthropological criticism, but anthropology, traditionally defined as "the study of man," has made its impact felt in literary criticism in multiple ways through the twentieth century. The rise of comparative evolutionary anthropology in the last third of the nineteenth century, initiated with E. B. Tylor's *Primitive Culture* in 1871 and culminating with James G. Frazer's *The Golden Bough* (published in various versions from 1890 through 1922), provided literary criticism with its first strong anthropological impact.

Influenced most strongly by James Frazer, the CAMBRIDGE RITUALISTS, or Hellenists, most notably Jane Harrison, Gilbert Murray, and F. M. Cornford, applied then-current anthropological notions to the study of the classics. Following an evolutionary framework, the Hellenists held that classical religion and, significantly, art had their origins in primitive ritual. The civilized myth and literature of high Greek culture was evolved from vital primitive rituals that reflected primal mystical ways of thinking: the pantheons of humanlike gods, for instance, developed out of the tribal and totemic worship of animals and plants and, before that, the even more elemental and less anthropomorphic fire or lightning. The ur-ritual was that of the conquest of life over death as reflected in the annual change of the seasons, and it was this agon that gave birth to the chants and gestures that later developed, in evolutionary fashion, into poetry and drama.

In works such as Harrison's *Themis* (1912) and Cornford's *Origin of Attic Comedy* (1914), the Cambridge Ritualists most strongly advanced their arguments on the primitivist-ritualist nature of Greek art. Murray and Cornford in particular emphasized the ritual origins of Greek drama, seeing in both tragedy and comedy the survival of five or six primitive stages—in the case of tragedy, the contest itself, the sacrificial death, the messenger announcing the death, the lamentation, and the resurrection. This eminently anthropological approach revitalized the study of the classics and soon made its way into the analysis of modern literatures. Murray's 1914 lecture "Hamlet and Orestes" marks the first application of the ritualist approach to nonclassical material through a comparative study of the ritual beginnings of Greek and Shakespearean drama, and this was followed by Jessie Weston's *From Ritual to Romance,* the 1920 study of the Grail romances as civilized versions of fertility rites. (T. S. ELIOT cited Weston's study, along with *The Golden Bough,* as a prime influence on *The Waste Land*.) In the 1920s, as Stanley Edgar Hyman notes, the influence of the ritualist approach spread to Northern epic poetry, fairy tales, and folk drama; and in the 1930s Lord Raglan's influential book *The Hero* (1936) considered the ritual patternings of the hero figure in literary and nonliterary materials alike, while William Troy began his ritual studies of modernist authors, such as D. H. LAWRENCE and F. Scott Fitzgerald (Stanley Edgar Hyman in Vickery, *Myth* 50–51).

Modernist literary creation of course was galvanized by the anthropology of Frazer, Tylor, and other comparativists, as John Vickery and others have well documented in their treatments of the high modernist art of W. B. Yeats, James Joyce, Eliot, Ezra Pound, Virginia Woolf, and Lawrence. And yet modernist criticism also was significantly affected. Pound and Eliot in particular borrowed from comparative anthropology in several important areas. The comparative method itself became an enabling tool in the critical articulation of modernist organization and technique: most notable is Eliot's conception in "*Ulysses,* Order, and Myth" of the "mythical method" that, "in manipulating a continuous parallel between contemporaneity and antiquity," takes "a step toward making the modern world possible for art" (177–78). Also, "primitive mentality" (as borrowed by Eliot from Lucien Lévy-Bruhl) and "blood consciousness" (as loosely borrowed by Lawrence from Frazer and Harrison) became very significant critical terms for meditations upon the nature of the modern literary artist. Finally, the very rhetorical authority of the modern literary and social critic was significantly augmented by the breadth of the comparative anthropologist's reach and the profusion of sources within that figure's grasp.

It is utterly significant that Eliot's celebration of Frazer in his notes to *The Waste Land* and in his review of *Ulysses* falls within a year of the publication of Bronislaw Malinowski's *Argonauts of the Western Pacific* (1922), the model for the emerging anthropological monograph, a kind of study based upon participant observation and dismissive of the evolutionary method and comparative organization of the armchair anthropologist (Manganaro 19). Modernist art and criticism found evolutionary comparative anthropology more enabling than the new ethnography's emphasis upon societal function within the *particular* culture, and in general the Anglo-American functionalist monograph did not exert significant influence upon Anglo-American criticism of the first half of the twentieth century. And yet the push for a tough, unimpressionistic, and even scientific criticism by professional critics such as Eliot and I. A. RICHARDS roughly parallels the increasing professionalization of the discipline of anthropology as shaped by Malinowski and others after him. And in a general sense NEW CRITICISM's insistence, from the 1930s through the 1960s, upon a noncomparative analysis of the discrete literary text, an approach shorn from loose historical and biographical considerations, exhibits an important parallel to the standard monograph of mid-century cultural anthropology.

In the 1950s and early 1960s, however, New Criticism faced a formidable challenge in MYTH THEORY AND CRITICISM. What John Vickery in 1966 called "the critical shift in the last decade or so from rhetoric to myth" (*Myth* xi) signaled a need for criticism to move beyond the restrained and relatively objective explication of single texts to the sustained and even passionate meditation upon the larger mythic patternings of the human mind that produce ritual, myth, legend, romance, and ultimately literature. Indeed, much of the rhetorical power of myth criticism lay not just in a claim to erect or preserve a literary or cultural tradition (as did New Criticism) but in the feeling that it was participating vitally in a pan-disciplinary effort, often combining the "findings" of anthropology (Frazer), mythology (Ernst Cassirer), and psychology (C. G. Jung primarily but SIGMUND FREUD as well) to get at the ways that humanity makes meaning. Nowhere is this clearer than in the immense success of an inaugural work of myth criticism, Joseph Campbell's 1949 *Hero with a Thousand Faces*.

But of course the anthropological sources for this criticism were quite skewed, and their findings often considered defunct. Myth critics such as Campbell, Philip Wheelwright, Stanley Edgar Hyman, Richard Chase, and NORTHROP FRYE implemented certain Frazerian and Cambridge Ritualist assumptions that had been put into question by anthropologists, classicists, and mythologists years before. Many myth critics, for example, celebrated the recurrence of Frazer's scapegoat figure in literary creation long after anthropological research effectively disproved its existence in real cultures. And as Richard Hardin has shown, while much substantial drama criticism, such as that by Francis Fergusson and C. L. Barber, was enabled by the ritualist turn, works such as Fergusson's influential *Idea of a Theater* (1949) depended heavily upon, and significantly perpetuated, the oversimplified Cambridge Ritualist notion that "Greek tragedy originated in primitive Greek ritual, with the corollary that other forms of drama, perhaps all drama, had such roots" (Hardin 847).

Myth criticism reached the height of its status in the work of Northrop Frye, whose *Anatomy of Criticism* (1957) attempted a comprehensive classification of literature into four narrative categories (comic, tragic, romantic, ironic) that corresponded to four *mythoi* (spring, summer, autumn, winter). Like Hyman, Campbell, and other myth critics, Frye was heavily dependent upon ritualist assumptions. As complex and qualifying as his arguments on literary creation and genre can become, essentially he lays over literature a simplified evolutionary grid on which ritual evolves into myth, which evolves into literature. *Anatomy* represents the height of myth criticism's authority because of Frye's sheer comprehensive aim and supposed "scientific" method, but crucial to its success, as Frye realized, was the ability to obscure its dependence upon the Cambridge Ritualist argument that ritual chronologically precedes myth and literature. "It does not matter two pins to the literary critic whether such a ritual [the "content of naive drama" as reconstructed in *The Golden Bough*] had any historical existence or not," Frye notes in *Anatomy*. "The *literary* relation of ritual to drama . . . is a relation of content to form only, not one of source to derivation" (109).

Criticism dependent upon Cambridge Ritualist assumptions faded with the 1960s, though one still encounters the occasional essay on the dying god as it operates in the work of some author or movement. But vital criticism implementing ritual as a social phenomenon or organizing principle of literature has since surfaced: one prominent example is RENÉ GIRARD's *Violence and the Sacred* (1972), which proposes sacrifice as a mediation by which humans have regulated what is otherwise uncontrollable violence. In general, ritual as an anthropological concept has remained attractive to the literary critic precisely because it represents, according to Francesco Loriggio, a powerfully primal example of "socially manifested behavior" (39). The focus upon that behavior by anthropologists, resulting in "a study of ceremonies, of acts that are at once socialized and archaic in nature" (39), appeals to literary criticism's inexorable urge toward the social and pragmatic in the broadest sense and certainly has generally influenced literary critical theorizing upon concepts of collectivity, performance, and the materiality of language.

It is no surprise, then, that there has existed since the inception of MARXIST THEORY AND CRITICISM a strong yet complicated series of links between anthropology, literary criticism, and Marxism. In *The German Ideology* KARL MARX AND FRIEDRICH ENGELS themselves state that "language *is* practical consciousness . . . language, like consciousness, only arises from the need, the necessity, of intercourse with other men" (*Marx-Engels Reader*, ed. Robert C. Tucker, 2d ed., 1978, 158). This innately anthropological stress on the inherent socialness of language use parallels in fundamental ways early anthropological notions of collectivity, such as in Émile Durkheim's *Elementary Forms of the Religious Life* (1912), and will reverberate in M. M. BAKHTIN's important notion of language as social utterance and in turn will enable the criticism of theorists as various as KENNETH BURKE and RAYMOND WILLIAMS.

But perhaps the most explicit use of anthropological notions of collectivity in Marxist literary criticism can be found in the work of British critics Christopher Caudwell and George Thomson. Both Caudwell's *Illusion and Reality* (1937) and Thomson's *Aeschylus and Athens* (1941) theorize upon the development of modern social formations, from the ritualistic to the religious to the secular, in a manner that derives directly from Cambridge Ritualist notions of the evolution of primitive society. Caudwell argues for the practical and communal purpose of poetry as both a distillation and a projection of group experience in ways that strongly depend upon Durkheim and Jane Harrison. Thomson also borrows from the ritualism of Harrison in the Marxist effort toward cultural critique. Thomson views catharsis, for example, as an effort at aesthetic socialization that can be turned toward social formation. Drawing from anthropological accounts of collective frenzy, Thomson notes the "subversive" side of the cathartic process, asserting that "the artist leads his fellow men into a world of fantasy where they find release, thus asserting the refusal of the human consciousness to acquiesce in its environment, and by this means there is collected a store of energy, which flows back into the real world and transforms fantasy into fact" (360).

At the same time, but on the other side of the channel, the College of Sociology, composed of GEORGES BATAILLE, Roger Caillois, Michel Leiris, and others, was similarly concerned with anthropological accounts of primitive collectivity and their potential for revitalizing modern society. Like the British Marxists, the College relied upon evolutionary conceptions of savage solidarity, explicitly influenced by Marcel Mauss but, as Michèle Richman has shown, owing a great debt to Durkheim's important *Elementary Forms of the Religious Life*. Between 1937 and 1939, the College met with the explicit aim of forming a "moral community" that would attempt to revive the "sacred" within everyday life through collective energies. The participants, themselves creative artists, critics, and intellectuals, produced an interdisciplinary pool of writings that, though not always explicitly in the realm of literary criticism, had a significant impact upon later critical writings: Bataille's notion of expenditure within primitive societies (as derived from Marcel Mauss's reflection upon potlatch in *The Gift*) was ex-

tended by Jean Baudrillard in *The Mirror of Production,* and his notion of transgression, in all its complex forms, has a significant connection to later radical critics such as MICHEL FOUCAULT, ROLAND BARTHES, and JACQUES DERRIDA, as James Clifford has shown (*Predicament* 127).

Anglo-American anthropologists from the beginning professed "literary" affiliations: note Frazer's flamboyantly literary style (vacillating between "grand" and "plain" styles of writing) and Malinowski's own authorial identifications—W. H. R. Rivers is "the Rider Haggard of Anthropology," Malinowski once wrote, "I shall be the Conrad!" And yet the links between literary pursuit and anthropological endeavor in France were much stronger, less attenuated. As Clifford demonstrates, French ethnographic experimentation in the 1920s, especially as manifested in the College, was directly affiliated with the artistic avant-garde: Michel Leiris, for example, was a member of the Mission Dakr-Djibouti (1932), an ethnographic expedition that spent almost two years in Africa. The almost seamless relation between anthropological experience and literary experimentation produced what Clifford terms "ethnographic surrealism," in which cultural encounter in all the delight of its tension and juxtaposition approximates surrealist collage.

The undecidability and incompleteness of ethnographic surrealism, as typified in the College and fostered by Mauss, had a significant impact upon DECONSTRUCTION, but STRUCTURALISM is also indebted to Mauss and his disciples. CLAUDE LÉVI-STRAUSS's tribute to Mauss's "constant striving toward the fundamental," his ability to "hit the bedrock" of social phenomena ("French Sociology" 527) suggests Mauss as a formative influence upon structural thought. Now, as Clifford notes, Lévi-Strauss overplays the connection, portraying Mauss as a kind of "protostructuralist" (*Predicament* 128), and clearly Lévi-Straussian structuralism, with its emphasis upon getting at the essential truth of culture by grasping the underlying structural relation of that culture's terms, is indebted much more directly to the structural linguistics of FERDINAND DE SAUSSURE and N. S. Troubetskoy.

More important here, though, is not the origin of Lévi-Straussian anthropological structuralism so much as the debt of structural literary criticism to Lévi-Strauss. Jonathan Culler has pointed out the possible limitations of Lévi-Straussian structural analysis for literary criticism (53–54); still, Lévi-Strauss, especially in texts such as *The Elementary Structures of Kinship* (1949), *Structural Anthropology* (1958), and *The Raw and the Cooked* (1964), decodes the myths of exotic societies in ways more compelling to literary criticism than much structural linguistic interpretation. Lévi-Strauss's identification with literary criticism is also due to his co-authoring, with ROMAN JAKOBSON, of the inaugural tour de force of structuralist criticism, the analysis of CHARLES BAUDE-LAIRE's poem "Les Chats." Lastly, as James Boon has illustrated, Lévi-Strauss's adoption by the literary-minded is indebted not only to his own literary style and organization (especially as illustrated in *Tristes Tropique* [1955]) but to an important message that runs throughout his work, namely, that both artists and students of culture construct significance out of "texts," whether cultural or literary. In this respect Lévi-Strauss's study of "savage" tribes and minds had a formidable impact upon deconstructionist criticism.

In America, the textual or discursive nature of anthropological interpretation has been most visibly advanced by anthropologists Clifford Geertz and Victor Turner. In books such as *The Interpretation of Culture* (1973) and *Local Knowledge* (1983), Geertz has theorized upon and practiced an anthropology that is essentially semiotic, approaching cultural phenomena as a system of signs to be read by the anthropologist as culture reader. His *Works and Lives* (1988) makes the claim that anthropology is essentially rhetorical and hence the best anthropologists are those that persuade us through their writing of the viability of their other-cultural experience. In works such as *Dramas, Fields, and Metaphors* (1974) and *From Ritual to Theatre* (1982), Turner approaches culture as essentially performance, sketching cultural activity in metaphoric and specifically dramatistic terms. Both Geertz and Turner, like Lévi-Strauss, have enabled the literary analysis of culture by collapsing several distinctions: between culture in general and aesthetic practice, between anthropological and literary interpretation, and between ethnography and the literary text as written products.

The publication of the influential critical anthology *Writing Culture* (1982) marked a fairly dramatic departure from previous anthropological writing. Following in the legacy of Lévi-Strauss, Geertz, and Turner, the contributors to this volume (which include its editors, James Clifford and George E. Marcus) emphasize the "poetics," the writerly nature of anthropological pursuit, but they also persistently assert the "politics" of anthropology as an institutional endeavor. Influenced by the recent critical and social theory on power relations (as in the work of Foucault), colonialist discourse (especially EDWARD W. SAID's 1978 *Orientalism*), and postmodernist theory (of JEAN-FRANÇOIS LYOTARD and FREDRIC JAMESON, among others), the contributors to *Writing Culture* seriously indict anthropology as a politi-cal activity while also celebrating its potential as an exercise in otherness and as a powerful tool of cultural critique. Clifford's own *Predicament of Culture* (1988) and Marcus and Michael Fischer's *Anthropology as Cultural Critique* (1986) also significantly advanced these arguments.

The new interpretive anthropology, especially as typified in *Writing Culture,* has met with some criticism on several grounds: its sometimes naive affiliations to 1960s radical ideology, its insufficient consideration of feminist concerns, and its historically narrow focus upon modern ethnography. The lack of a feminist viewpoint may be the most telling absence, but since *Writing Culture* much feminist anthropological theory has emerged to augment and challenge interpretive anthropology of the 1980s and 1990s, for example, Trinh T. Minh-Ha's *When the Moon Waxes Red* (1991) and Micaela di Leonardo's collection *Gender at the Crossroads of Knowledge* (1991). The deep involvement of this new anthropological writing with postmodernist, colonialist, and feminist theory illustrates the extent to which disciplinary boundaries are breaking down, or at the least, loosening, so that literary criticism necessarily entails the interpretation of culture, while anthropology necessarily means the reading of a discourse (anthropology's increasing involvement in the theoretical and curricular reconfiguration known as CULTURAL STUDIES is testimony to this development). The immediate future of "anthropology" in literary criticism may be less a matter of the influence of anthropological theory and more a matter of shared discursive and societal concerns.

Marc Manganaro

See also ARCHETYPAL THEORY AND CRITICISM, CAMBRIDGE RITUALISTS, NORTHROP FRYE, CLAUDE LÉVI-STRAUSS, MYTH THEORY AND CRITICISM, and STRUCTURALISM.

Joseph Campbell, *The Hero with a Thousand Faces* (1949); Christopher Caudwell, *Illusion and Reality: A Study of the Sources of Poetry* (1937); F. M. Cornford, *The Origin of Attic Comedy* (1914); Émile Durkheim, *The Elementary Forms of the Religious Life* (1912, trans. Joseph Wood Swain, 1965); T. S. Eliot, "*Ulysses,* Order, and Myth" (1923, *Selected Prose,* ed. Frank Kermode, 1975); Francis Fergusson, *The Idea of a Theater* (1949); James G. Frazer, *The Golden Bough: A Study in Magic and Religion* (2 vols., 1890, 3d ed., 12 vols., 1907–15); Northrop Frye, *Anatomy of Criticism: Four Essays* (1957); Clifford Geertz, *The Interpretation of Cultures* (1973), *Works and Lives: The Anthropologist as Author* (1988); René Girard, *La Violence et la sacré* (1972,

Violence and the Sacred, trans. Patrick Gregory, 1977); Jane Harrison, *Themis* (1912); Denis Hollier, ed., *The College of Sociology* (1979, trans. Betsy Wing, 1988); Micaela di Leonardo, ed., *Gender at the Crossroads of Knowledge: Feminist Anthropology in the Postmodern Era* (1991); Claude Lévi-Strauss, *The Elementary Structures of Kinship* (1949, ed. and trans. James Harle Bell et al., 1969); Marcel Mauss, *The Gift: Forms and Functions of Exchange in Archaic Societies* (1925, trans. Ian Cunnison, 1954); Lord Raglan, *The Hero: A Study of Tradition, Myth, and Drama* (1936); George Thomson, *Aeschylus and Athens: A Study in the Social Origins of Drama* (1941); Victor Turner, *Dramas, Fields, and Metaphors: Symbolic Action in Human Society* (1974).

James Boon, *From Symbolism to Structuralism: Lévi-Strauss in a Literary Tradition* (1972); James Clifford, *The Predicament of Culture: Twentieth-Century Ethnography, Literature, and Art* (1988); James Clifford and George E. Marcus, eds., *Writing Culture: The Poetics and Politics of Ethnography* (1986); Jonathan Culler, *Structuralist Poetics: Structuralism, Linguistics, and the Study of Literature* (1975); Richard Hardin, " 'Ritual' in Recent Criticism: The Elusive Sense of Community," *PMLA* 98 (1983); Stanley Edgar Hyman, "The Ritual View of Myth and the Mythic" (Vickery, *Myth*); Claude Lévi-Strauss, "French Sociology," *Twentieth Century Sociology* (ed. Georges Gurvitch and Wilbert Moore, 1945); Francesco Loriggio, "Anthropology, Literary Theory, and the Traditions of Modernism," *Modernist Anthropology: From Fieldwork to Text* (ed. Marc Manganaro, 1990); Marc Manganaro, *Myth, Rhetoric, and the Voice of Authority: A Critique of Frazer, Eliot, Frye, and Campbell* (1992); George Marcus and Michael M. J. Fischer, *Anthropology as Cultural Critique: An Experimental Moment in the Human Sciences* (1986); Michèle H. Richman, *Reading Georges Bataille: Beyond the Gift* (1982); John Vickery, *The Literary Impact of "The Golden Bough"* (1973); John Vickery, ed., *Myth and Literature: Contemporary Theory and Practice* (1966).

ARABIC THEORY AND CRITICISM

Classical criticism and theory. The Arabic literary tradition has preserved critical statements that are as old as Arabic literature itself. The earliest critical remarks form part of the anecdotal heritage ascribed either to the poets themselves or to some important persons in Arab history. (The adjective "Arab" here is used to refer to the people, while "Arabic" refers to the language, and "Arabian" refers to the Arabian peninsula only.) These early critical remarks are primarily impressions and based on taste; they did not develop systematically for a long period of time, mainly because of the oral nature of the society. In some cases one can discern a synthetic and generalizing attitude. Overall impressions, not reasoned arguments, are expressed; feelings about poetry are offered in a language that is very similar, if not identical, to that of poetry itself. In other instances we see concrete critiques of the misuse of language or of imagery. But all of this is generally an instrument to compare poets with each other and to judge the merits of each ('Abbās 13 ff.; Ibrāhīm 19–58; Sallām 1:74 ff.). This is because of the special position attained by poets in pre-Islamic society, where the more prominent (e.g., al-Nābighah al-Dhubyānī) "chaired" meetings that took place in the large markets and judged poets and poetry during the four months of peace each year in which it was prohibited to fight among tribes, a custom that provided the opportunity for trade, festivals, sporting competitions, gambling, drinking, and the recital or singing of poetry. (Because most of the pre-Islamic and classical Arabic literary output that had a privileged status in Arab-Islamic culture was in verse form, the concept "poetry" can be safely used to refer to literature altogether. Prose never attained a status comparable to that of poetry, not even in the twentieth century; theories of prose were generally derived from those about poetry—the literary was the poetic.)

The impact of Islam on Arabic literature and literary criticism was vast. One issue that remains puzzling is how literature not only survived the attacks of the Koran and Prophet Muḥammad but also flourished and attained a status as high as or even higher than it had prior to Islam. Poetry was also able to negotiate for itself a space within society that was for a long period relatively free of religious coercion or interference. Such outstanding critics as al-Aṣmaʿī (d. c. 830), Ibn Jinnī (d. 1001), al-Ṣūlī (d. 946), and al-Qāḍī al-Jurjānī (d. 1001) could state that great poetry was associated with unbelief and that the religious attitude only weakened poetry (examples of this were some poets who converted to Islam during the times of the Prophet but whose poetry after conversion was considered inferior to their poetry before it). These critics were not marginal, and some were authorities on Islamic law and jurisprudence. For the most part, however, criticism remained a marginal activity of grammarians, philologists, or hermeneuts. Only in the ninth century did criticism start to attain an autonomous status as a legitimate intellectual and scholarly activity, and by the tenth century it developed into an institution that had a privileged status even vis-à-vis poetry itself.

But literary theory and criticism bore the pangs and scars of its birth, and for this reason it is important to understand how literary criticism developed in its earlier stages.

Arabic pre-Islamic and early Islamic poetry was transmitted orally. This explains why only recent pre-Islamic poetry was known during the period of collection and recording that began around the beginning of the eighth century. Organized literary-critical activity had its origins within the context of collecting this poetry. Different transmitters gave different versions of a poem, thereby leading to a controversy concerning its correct wording. Criticism was thus from the beginning text-centered, philological, and grammatical (see PHILOLOGY). The philological and grammatical activities were also related to religious issues. One of the results of the rise of competing and conflicting religious and social groups within Islam was conflicting interpretations of the holy text, the Koran. Pre-Islamic poetry functioned in this respect as the most important linguistic and semantic frame of reference for the interpretation of the Koranic text. The knowledge of poetry was an integral part of the knowledge of language and grammar that was the basis for Islamic hermeneutics. And naturally, these fields were studied jointly. The study of literature started within such a context. There was little to say about the nature of poetry or literary theory within such a paradigm.

By the end of the eighth century the civilizing process within the Islamic empire made its impact felt on almost all aspects of life. The urbanization of the Arabs in the new and old cities of the empire turned the Bedouin element into a small minority. This was a part of the larger process in the Abbasid period by which the empire became a multiethnic and multicultural society, which witnessed the full development of the state and its institutions. The interaction with other, more developed civilizations—Persian, Byzantine, Greek, Indian, and Eastern Christian—accompanied by the quick adoption of Islam by large numbers of the non-Arab population, many of whom soon made Arabic their language of expression due to the Arabization of state records, made it imperative for the Arabs and Muslims to preserve their traditions, especially as they still retained power as the ruling elite. It was within the eighth century that literacy and literate culture developed, including the concept of the book, that of *adab* (which in modern Arabic means "literature" but at this time covered what we now call the humanities), and the new and more differentiated concepts of the intellectual, the *kātib* (the professional writer in a court), and the poet.

This period paved the way for the institutionalization of literary criticism as an autonomous activity independent of yet in apposition to philology, grammar, rhetoric, theology, and so on. During this period the concepts and terms of criticism (i.e., its discursive formation) took shape. The principles of Arabic prosody took on their authoritative form in the studies of al-Khalīl ibn Aḥmad (718–86). Following him, literary-critical terms used by philologists and early critics were mostly derived from Bedouin life—especially such terms as those for "tent," "camel," and "horse"—which shows the close association of critical studies with early Arabic poetry ('Abbās 27). A "theory" of genres of Arabic poetry was also developed in terms of the "aims" or "objectives" (*funūn* or *aghrāḍ*) of poetry. Because lyrical poetry was the only kind of Arabic poetry, genre theory was based on content or subject matter rather than on form. In its initial stage there were four genres of poetry: panegyric (*rithā'*), invective (*hijā'*), love (*ghazal*), and vainglorious (*fakhr*) poetry. These later became five by the addition of the elegy (*rithā'*) and then six by that of descriptive (*waṣf*) poetry. This theory of genre remained dominant until the nineteenth century, although some critics attempted to add new themes (or "aims") or to divide old genres, such as love poetry, into two or more categories. A theory of genre for prose had to wait until the tenth century.

The main characteristics of Arabic literary criticism until the beginning of the ninth century can be summarized as follows. Criticism was dependent on taste, which was thought to become refined by the quantitative knowledge of poetry. Literary criticism was anecdotal and segmental; that is, it was centered on a line or a small number of lines of poetry and not on the whole poem. One cannot discern any attempt to work out general criteria for the understanding and interpretation of poetry other than basic grammatical and philological ones. Last but not least, criticism was generally concerned with the problem of innovation as well as that of the models of excellence, which were considered to be mainly the older pre-Islamic poetry.

By the ninth century the influence of the native philosophical traditions, especially those of the Mu'tazilites (a group of rationalists in Islamic theology) and that of Greek philosophy, especially ARISTOTLE, came to be felt in all fields of intellectual activity. Although these factors provided some of the impulses behind the development of criticism during those two centuries, the changes in sensibility and in literary production were the driving force behind the rise of critical practice and theory. Innovative poets such as Abu Nuwās (762–813) and Bashshār (714–84) were a challenge to the critical activity of early critic-grammarian-philologists, but the battle surrounding Abu Tammām (796–843) and al-Buḥturī (821–79), which was in many ways a battle between two conceptions of poetry, lasted for many decades but was later "forgotten" with the rise of the new challenge of al-Mutanabbī (915–65), arguably the greatest of all Arab poets.

The first attempts to develop a systematic study of poetry started around the end of the ninth century, and by the tenth century the study of poetry became a prestigious activity to which whole treatises and books could be devoted. It is impossible to attempt to provide a comprehensive history of classical Arabic criticism. Instead we will discuss some of the basic problems that were at the center of critical activities.

The problem of the old and the new was one of the earliest issues in Arabic criticism. But recent research shows that critics were not generally proponents of the old against the new, as Reynold Nicholson, Ṭaha Ḥusayn, and Muḥammad Mandūr, among others, maintained. Many critics sided with the new, while many who sided with the old either neglected or were explicitly critical of some older pre-Islamic poetry, although a few were grammarians and philologists, such as Ibn Jinnī. But the issue of the old and the new soon turned into a battle between the proponents of Abu Tammām and his opponents, who thought highly of al-Buḥturī. Both stuck to the classical meter, yet Abu Tammām's poetry contained a new type of metaphoric language and placed much emphasis on technique (ṣan'ah), while that of al-Buḥturī was nearer to the old conventions but was considered more natural (maṭbū'). The competition between these poets is responsible for the development of a new and important genre of criticism called *al-muwāzanah,* "comparison," as seen in the writings of al-Ṣulī (d. 946) and al-Āmidī (d. 980). This battle as well, and the one to follow it around al-Mutanabbī (al-Qāḍī al-Jurjānī [d. 1001], al-Ḥātimī [d. 998], ibn Wakī' [d. 1002], and ibn Jinnī [d. 1001]), was instrumental in shifting the emphasis of criticism to the meticulous analysis of poetry, especially its imagery and metaphors, and to demonstrations of the influence of one poet over the other. Influence, however, was conceived in negative terms and dubbed as theft (sariqāt). But most critics related influence to the relationship between form and content (al-lafẓ wa-al-ma'nā).

Despite resorting to this dichotomy, all critics now paid more attention to form. There were probably two root theories for approaching this problem. One had its origins with al-Jāḥiẓ (d. 868), who was a Mu'tazilite and who said that meanings or contents were readily available in every walk of life but what really mattered in literature was form or composition. Others, such as ibn

Qutaybah (d. 889), gave equal status to both and developed a four-part taxonomy based upon good and bad meaning and good and bad form. Many critics, such as ibn Ṭabāṭabā (d. 933) and ibn Rashīq (d. 1063), attempted to look at meaning and form as inseparable but were not successful because they started by acknowledging the two as separate entities. The most ingenious attempt at resolving this dichotomy was that of 'Abd al-Qāhir al-Jurjānī (d. 1078). Although the germs of his attempt can be found in al-Jāḥiẓ, his theory of composition (naẓm) gave expression to the idea that although meanings are available to every eye and mind, there is another, more sophisticated and higher level of meaning that is present only in composition. Any composition is a creation of meaning, and every single detail or change in composition necessarily entails a change in meaning or content ('Abbās 419–38 and Abu Deeb).

The issue of the unity of the poem and/or the independence of each line was never conceived of in the Western Romantic parameters of organic unity. Although many critics pointed to the possible independence of the lines, most critics looked at the poem as a unit. Despite the different "aims" or themes of single parts of the poem, critics emphasized the importance of the transition (ḥusn al-takhalluṣ) from one theme to another. One can also find the poem compared to the human body, and the lines to its different organs (al-Ḥātimī and Ibn Rashīq), which is a possible Aristotelian influence.

Contrary to many academic and popular conceptions, especially in the West, Islam had little direct impact on the development of literary production, with the exception of religious (especially Sufi) and ascetic poetry. Although some critics associated good poetry with ethical or religious ideals, the more dominant tendency among critics was to dissociate poetry from religion or morals. Many scholars also rejected the idea of judging the poetry by the poet's behavior or beliefs. This was a double strategy for preserving the high status of pre-Islamic poetry and for defending the greatest poets of the language, many of whom were known for their irreligious or heretic beliefs and practices ('Umar ibn Abī Rabī'ah, Abu Nuwās, and al-Mutanabbī, to name only a few).

Another central problem for literary critics was the relationship between poetry and truth. Here one can discern two main trends. The first followed the native tradition of the Mu'tazilites, which emphasized the importance of truth. Ibn Ṭabāṭabā, for example, emphasized the truth of imagery, the poet's feelings, and the poem itself as prerequisites for good poetry. This was part and parcel of his theory of symmetrical harmony as the basis of beauty, according to which truth is what achieves the harmony, which in turn constitutes the beauty of the poem. This view was accepted by later critics such as 'Abd al-Qāhir al-Jurjānī, who revised it to accommodate imagination, although the latter was ranked second in matters of excellence.

The second trend was influenced by Aristotelian poetic theory as it was interpreted by the Arabs, namely, as a part of the Organon, or the books of logic. Qudāmah's (d. 948) position provides an extreme example of associating poetry with lies: he described the best poetry as that which is richest in lies. That attitude was also common among many critics who were not influenced by the Aristotelian, or logical, school. Only the philosophers, and following them, Ḥāzim, were able to resolve the issue of truth and poetry in a convincing manner.

Philosophers and poetic theory. Following the late Alexandrian school, Arab philosophers considered the *Poetics* an essay on method like all the other logical books of Aristotle. Yet, since method itself was a "faculty" without "content," like all sciences of the Organon, it would lead to a "contentless" theory of poetry, or as O. B. Hardison called it, a "context theory" of poetics (Preminger et al. 342). Because each logical faculty "was supposed to be distinguished from the others by its use of a unique logical device, the inclusion of *Poetics* in the Organon shifted emphasis from 'imitation,' the key term in the Greek poetics, to the 'device' which differentiates poetry from its sister faculties" (342). This special logical device in poetry came to be called the "poetic syllogism" or "syllogismus imaginativus" (342; Walzer 131). This was the starting point for Arab-Islamic philosophers, but they could not treat poetry as contentless or as only a logical faculty.

Al-Fārābī (d. 950) reinterpreted the late Alexandrian Aristotle by trying to reconnect poetics with grammar and by emphasizing poetry's function in society. We can observe a clear shift of emphasis from his early conception of poetic statements as completely false to a later conception of poetry based upon imitation and meter. He insisted that meter alone does not produce poetry, but imitation without meter produces what he called "poetic discourse" *(qawl shi'rīy)*. He subsumed the method of poetic creation under the concept of imitation and the process of reception under the concept of *takhyīl*, "imaginative representation." *Takhyīl* meant invoking in the minds of listeners the image of something itself or the image of something in something else, the goal being to stimulate the listener to do the thing imagined, since people tend to follow their imagination or opinion rather than their reason. On the other hand, al-Fārābī subsumed the concept of poetic text (diction and the sciences of

meter and rhyme) under linguistics. The concept of poetic syllogism, being the central concept, was the connecting thread that explained imitation (poetic production) and its function and therefore could be considered the essence of poetry. Al-Fārābī classified poets into three groups: those with a natural disposition, who are not syllogizing in the real sense; the syllogizing poets; and those who imitate. Despite his great attachment to logic, he could not but reiterate the traditional Arabic attitude that "the best poetry is that which is natural."

Ibn Sīnā (980–1037), known as Avicenna in the West, defined poetry as imaginatively representational discourse consisting of rhythmic and equipoised locutions, which among the Arabs are also rhymed. Yet the central point for the logician is that poetry is imaginatively representational discourse. Whether poetry was true or false became marginal, as mimetic activity in poetry aimed at *takhyīl*, "invoking images and moving to action," based on *ta'jīb*, "invoking wonder or surprise." The importance of Greek poetry, according to Ibn Sīnā, was that it had a "civil purpose," that is, a social aim and function. Arabic poetry, on the other hand, had one of two functions, or both, namely, *ta'jīb* and a civil purpose. The civil purpose could be deliberational, disputational, or epideictic, all of which are common to poetry and rhetoric. While rhetoric employed means of persuasion, poetry used imaginative representation. Ibn Sīnā saw poetry as both imaginatively representational and metrical, but he added that one can have discourses that are prosaic but imaginatively representational and others that are metrical but not imaginatively representational. Neither of these was poetry. Imitation, according to him, can have one of two aims, either amelioration *(taḥsīn)* or depreciation *(taqbīḥ)*, and it is a way of learning and providing pleasure *(ladhdhah)* to the soul. Ibn Sīnā pointed out that the Greeks had imitated actions and states only, while the Arabs imitated persons *(dhawāt)* in addition to actions and states. What is clear from these and other remarks is how conscious Ibn Sīnā was of the problem of cultural and literary differences between the Greeks and the Arabs.

Ibn Sīnā developed these points in his psychological theory, within which he tried to explain the processes of mimesis by shifting the emphasis toward what he called *takhayyul,* that is, the process of using the imagination proper and the active imagination to produce likenesses of things. While memory recollects images and meanings apprehended in the past within a temporal context, *takhayyul* recollects them without associating them with their temporal context. Poetic composition is the product of the activity of the imagination under the supervision of reason, thereby combining the active and the deliberative imagination. Ibn Sīnā thus introduced the psychological aspects to poetic composition and connected them with the process of reception, which was basically worked out by al-Fārābī. But Ibn Sīnā added the important concept of *ta'jīb* ("invoking wonder or surprise") and added pleasure as a central function of poetry. The difference between the civil purpose Ibn Sīnā identified with Greek poetry and the "intersubjective validity" of poetry associated with Arabic was that because the subject is the linchpin of poetic activity, Arabic poetry is intersubjective in the sense that it depends on generating a community of feeling between subjects (Kemal, *Poetics*). In this way psychology became central in the processes of poetic production and reception and in determining the functions of poetry, namely, learning, pleasure, and intersubjective community of feeling.

Ibn Rushd (1126–98), known as Averroës in the West, shifted the emphasis from the psychological to the logical by concentrating on the poetic text and its logical structure. His emphasis was on *muḥākāt* and *tashbīh*, "mimesis" and "comparison," which is nearer to al-Fārābī's conception. He emphasized the mechanisms, rather than the processes, of constructing images in the language of poetry. He defined the imaginatively representational arts that effect *takhyīl* as three: melody, meter, and mimetic discourses. He divided poetic discourses, by which he meant similes and metaphors, into three classes: amelioration, depreciation, and correspondence. But Ibn Rushd's main thrust was to work out a theory of image-making (mimesis) that would explain poetic and figurative language in poetry. He attempted unsuccessfully to develop a typology of figurative language based on such an understanding of mimesis because his interest remained philosophical and logical, and his aim was to defend rationality as governing poetic processes and mechanisms rather than to explain them in their own right and in their specific manifestations.

What can be discerned from the work of philosophers are a gradual shift of emphasis that facilitated the development of a relatively comprehensive theory of poetry (production, text, reception) more suitable to Arabic poetry and a shift from associating poetry with lies or falsehood to that of associating it with imaginative representation *(takhyīl)*. Yet these shifts were not enough to produce a theory of Arabic literature based on the concepts developed by philosophers, as their object was not poetry but philosophy.

Ḥāzim al-Qarṭājannī (1211–85) represents the nexus at which the two traditions, the native and the revised Aristotelian, met. Through a complex process the two quite

distinct traditions now began to draw nearer to each other under the pressure of poetry itself, on the one hand, and the necessity for theory building and systematization on the other. Ḥāzim, himself a poet, utilized the Arabic Aristotelian tradition, especially al-Fārābī and Ibn Sīnā, and the native tradition of literary criticism. He looked at poetry from three different yet complementary perspectives, considering it as an act of *takhayyul* ("creation"), *takhyīl* ("reception"), and *muḥākāt* ("poetic text").

Ḥāzim defined poetic discourses as those that "are based on imaginative representation and in which there is imitation . . . whether their premises are apodeictic, argumentative or rhetorical; certain, generally known or assumed" (67; cf. Cantarino 210). He defined poetry as "rhythmic and rhymed discourse" with the "function of making attractive or repugnant to the human spirit whatever it aims at making so" (71; cf. Cantarino 214). And elsewhere he said that "poetry is imaginatively representational and metrical discourse, characterized in Arabic by the inclusion of rhyme. The imaginatively representational premises it combines, whether objectively truthful or false, have as their only condition, in so far as they are poetry, imaginative representation" (89; cf. Cantarino 218).

The production of poetry is performed by the poet, and a person becomes a poet through the combination of three external factors with three internal ones. The external factors are the atmosphere or environment, the acquisition of the instruments of composition (i.e., the science of wording and concepts), and the external stimuli. The internal ones are the retentive faculty *(ḥāfiẓah)*, which stores and organizes images; the discriminatory faculty *(mā'izah)*; and the artistic faculty, or craftsmanship. According to Ḥāzim, if the three internal factors are present, the person has a good propensity to produce poetry (40–43).

The determining factor of poetry is imaginative representation, which is found in poetry in

> four aspects: in the poetic concept, the composition, the wording, and the rhythm. In relation to poetry, imaginative representation is divided into two types: necessary imaginative representation, and the other which is not necessary but imperative and well-liked for its being a complement to the necessary and an aid in arousing the soul to the pursuit of or avoidance of the intended object. (89; cf. Cantarino 218)

The necessary elements are the "poetic concepts from the standpoint of their wording. The imperative and well-liked ones are the words in themselves—style, meter, and composition" (89; cf. Cantarino 218–19).

Poetry's function is *takhyīl*, by which Ḥāzim meant the invoking of images in the mind of the listener and which became associated with the concept of arousing wonder:

> Imaginative representational discourse is rarely devoid of arousing wonder; it seems that wonder accompanies imaginatively representational discourses, ranging between the minimal and the maximal. Arousing wonder in imaginatively representational discourses is achieved either through . . . imitating the thing and its imaginative representation . . . or that which is imitated being of the strange things themselves. If wonder is achieved through having both these aspects, this is the ultimate objective of arousing wonder. This will move the soul powerfully. (al-Qarṭājannī 127)

In developing the concept of *muḥākāt* (the mechanisms of image-making), Ḥāzim mentioned three types: amelioration, depreciation, and correspondence. Based on the basic assumption regarding these types, he developed a typology of figures of speech that is comprehensive and logical. This typology was derived, not from general laws, but from the study of poetry itself, as the "laws of poetry" should be derived from the study of "poetry and no other art." His typology of figurative language is one of the most exhaustive in Arabic literary criticism. The important thing is that Ḥāzim was able to synthesize both traditions to produce the most comprehensive concepts for the analysis of Arabic poetry, situated within a well-knit and logically developed theoretical framework. Thus, despite the fact that the Aristotelian tradition was not readily or easily accepted, it helped produce one of the most monumental works in Arabic literary criticism and theory.

Modern criticism.   The period from the fourteenth to the nineteenth centuries was characterized by general stagnation and decline in all aspects of cultural, social, and economic life in the Arab world. But the increasing influence of the West beginning in the latter part of the nineteenth century brought with it a modern renaissance in literary studies. Most of the literary criticism produced in the last century has been derivative, either from classical Arabic models or from European ones. Battles raged, and still rage, over how to interpret the literary and the critical traditions. But the real challenge to criticism was again the developments in Arabic literature itself, especially the rise of the new poetry, which started to deviate from, then broke away from, the classical models, both metrically and in sensibility, and the rise of new genres, such as the novel and drama, which quickly acquired a central position in modern Arabic literature.

Until the 1950s, a strong conservative trend was seen in the resuscitation of tradition and the following of traditional poetic rules. Another trend was to reinterpret literary traditions according to modern Western rationality. This second trend was generally influenced by the work of Orientalists, led by such figures as the Egyptian Ṭaha Ḥusayn (1889–1973). A third trend, influenced by Western (especially English) Romanticism, emphasized the individuality of the poet and the centrality of imagination. This trend was basically associated with three groups in modern Romantic Arabic poetry, the émigré poets (e.g., Jibran) and the Diwān and Apollo groups in Egypt (the last two included poets who revolted against the neoclassical Arabic poetry of the late nineteenth and early twentieth centuries; both groups were influenced by European, especially English Romantic, poetry [see Brugman]). A prominent figure was the Egyptian al-ʿAqqād (1889–1964), who emphasized the psychological aspects of poetic and literary production. A fourth trend was the social trend, as exemplified in the work of another Egyptian, Salamah Mūsā (1888–1958).

Looking at the decades since the 1950s, the traditionalists are still strongly represented in academic criticism, while the Romantic trend is almost dead. Although the social trend remains alive in different forms—mild socialist in the cases of Egyptians Luwīs ʿAwad (1915–91) and Muḥammad Mandūr (1907–65), Marxist–socialist realist in the case of the early criticism of the Egyptian Maḥmūd Amīn al-ʿĀlim, or more open to recent debates in the case of the younger generation of Marxists—the most prominent and productive trends in the decades since the 1950s have been associated with the modernist movements in Arabic poetry. The Syrio-Lebanese poet and critic Adūnīs (b. 1930) launched a critical project to reread the classical poetic tradition in order to justify his own formidable poetic production. But the project turned into one of the most fascinating critical appropriations of tradition and the reworking of literary historical and critical concepts. On the other hand, Kamāl Abū Dīb's (b. 1942) structuralist project, which in many ways runs in tandem with Adūnīs's (see STRUCTURALISM), emphasized the meticulous reading of texts and the reworking and reinterpretation of classical critical writings with the objective of producing a new Arabic poetic theory that revises even its most "sacred" aspects, such as prosody. Despite all these and other mostly academic enterprises, contemporary criticism in the Arab world remains basically derivative. It also still lags behind the great achievements of Arabic writers and poets.

Walid Hamarneh

Iḥsān 'Abbās, *Tārīkh al-Naqd al-Adabī 'Ind al-'Arab* (1971); Ilfat Kamāl 'Abd al-'Azīz, *Naẓarīyāt al-Shi'r 'Ind al-Falāsifah al-Muslimīn* (1984); Kamal Abu Deeb, *al-Jurjānī's Theory of Poetic Imagery* (1979); Adānīs, *An Introduction to Arab Poetics* (trans. Catherine Cobham, 1990); Mansour Ajami, *The Alchemy of Glory: The Dialectic of Truthfulness and Untruthfulness in Medieval Arabic Literary Criticism* (1988), *The Neckveins of Winter: The Controversy over Natural and Artificial Poetry in Medieval Arabic Literary Criticism* (1984); 'Abd al-Rahmān Badawī, *Arisṭūṭālīs: Fann al-Shi'r* (1953); Deborah Black, *Logic and Aristotle's Rhetoric and Poetics in Medieval Arabic Philosophy* (1990); J. Brugman, *An Introduction to the History of Modern Arabic Literature in Egypt* (1984); Charles Butterworth, trans., *Averroes Middle Commentary on Aristotle's Poetics* (1986); Vincente Cantarino, *Arabic Poetics in the Golden Age* (1975); Ismail Dahiyat, trans., *Avicenna's Commentary on the Poetics of Aristotle* (1974); Walid Hamarneh, "The Reception of Aristotle's Theory of Poetry in the Arab-Islamic Mediaeval Thought," *Poetics East and West* (ed. Milena Doleželová-Velingerová, 1990); O. B. Hardison, "The Place of Averroes' Commentary on the *Poetics* in the History of Medieval Criticism," *Medieval and Renaissance Studies* 4 (1968); Wolfhart Heinrichs, *Arabische Dichtung und griechische Poetik* (1969), "Die antike Verknüpfung von Phantasie und Dichtung bei den Arabern," *Zeitschrift der deutschen morgenländischen Gesellschaft* 128 (1978); Ṭāha Aḥmad Ibrāhīm, *Tārīkh al-Naqd al-Adabī 'Ind al-'Arab* (1974); Salim Kemal, "Arabic Poetics and Aristotle's Poetics," *British Journal of Aesthetics* 26 (1986), *The Poetics of al-Farabi and Avicenna* (1991); Muḥammad Mandūr, *al-Naqd al-Manhajī 'Ind al-'Arab* (1969); Alex Preminger et al., eds., *Classical and Medieval Literary Criticism* (1974); Ḥāzim al-Qarṭājannī, *Minhāj al-Bulaghā' wa Sirāj al-Udabā'* (1966); Muḥammad Zaghlūl Sallām, *Tārīkh al-Naqd al-'Arabī* (2 vols., 1964); Gregor Schoeler, *Einige Grundprobleme der autochthonen und der arabischen Literaturtheorie* (1975), "Der poetische Syllogismus: Ein Beitrag zum Verständnis der 'logischen' Poetik der Araber," *Zeitschrift der deutschen morgenländischen Gesellschaft* 133 (1983); Jābir Aḥmad 'Uṣfūr, *Mafhūm al-Shi'r* (1978), *al-Ṣurah al-Fannīyah fī al-Turāth al-Naqdī wal-Balāghī* (1974); Richard Walzer, *Greek into Arabic: Essays on Islamic Philosophy* (1962).

ARCHETYPAL THEORY AND CRITICISM

Archetypal theory and criticism, although often used synonymously with MYTH THEORY AND CRITICISM, has a distinct history and process. The term "archetype" can be traced to PLATO (*arche*, "original"; *typos*, "form"), but the concept gained currency in twentieth-century literary theory and criticism through the work of the Swiss founder of analytical psychology, C. G. Jung (1875–1961). Jung's *Psychology of the Unconscious* (1916, B. M. Hinkle's translation of the 1911–12 *Wandlungen und Symbole der Libido*) appeared in English one year after publication of the concluding volume with bibliography of the third edition of J. G. Frazer's *The Golden Bough: A Study in Magic and Religion* (2 vols., 1890, 3d ed., 12 vols., 1911–15). Frazer's and Jung's texts formed the basis of two allied but ultimately different courses of influence on literary history.

Jung most frequently used "myth" (or "mythologem") for the narrative expression, "on the ethnological level" (*Collected* 9, pt. 1: 67), of the "archetypes," which he described as patterns of psychic energy originating in the collective unconscious and finding their "most common and most normal" manifestation in dreams (8:287). Thus criticism evolving from his work is more accurately named "archetypal" and is quite distinct from "myth" criticism.

For Jung, "archetype is an explanatory paraphrase of the Platonic *eidos*" (9, pt. 1: 4), but he distinguishes his concept and use of the term from that of philosophical idealism as being more empirical and less metaphysical, though most of his "empirical" data were dreams. In addition, he modified and extended his concept over the many decades of his professional life, often insisting that "archetype" named a process, a perspective, and not a content, although this flexibility was lost through the codifying, nominalizing tendencies of his followers.

At mid-century, Canadian critic NORTHROP FRYE (1912–91) introduced new distinctions in literary criticism between myth and archetype. For Frye, as William K. Wimsatt and Cleanth Brooks put it, "archetype, borrowed from Jung, means a primordial image, a part of the collective unconscious, the psychic residue of numberless experiences of the same kind, and thus part of the inherited response-pattern of the race" (*Literary Criticism* 709). Frye frequently acknowledged his debt to Jung, accepted some of Jung's specifically named archetypes—"persona and anima and counsellor and shadow"—and referred to his theory as Jungian criticism (*Anatomy* 291), a practice subsequently followed in some handbooks of literary terms and histories of literary criticism, including one edited by Frye himself, which obscured crucial differences and contributed to the confusion in terminology reigning today (see C. Hugh Holman and William Harmon, *A Handbook to Literature,* 5th ed., 1986; and Northrop Frye, Sheridan Baker, and George Perkins, *The Harper Handbook to Literature,* 1985). Frye, however, notably in *Anatomy of Criticism,* essentially redefined and relocated archetype on grounds that would remove him unequivocally from the ranks of "Jungian" critics by severing the connection between archetype and depth psychology: "This emphasis on impersonal content has been developed by Jung and his school, where the communicability of archetypes is accounted for by a theory of a collective unconscious—an unnecessary hypothesis in literary criticism, so far as I can judge" (111–12). Frye, then, first misinterprets Jungian theory by insisting on a Lamarckian view of genetic transmission of archetypes, which Jung explicitly rejected, and later settles on a concept of "archetype" as a literary occurrence per se, an exclusively intertextual recurring phenomenon resembling a convention (99).

On a general level, Jung's and Frye's theorizings about archetypes, however labeled, overlap, and boundaries are elusive, but in the disciplines of literature the two schools have largely ignored each other's work. Myth criticism grew in part as a reaction to the formalism of NEW CRITICISM, while archetypal criticism based on Jung was never linked with any academic tradition and remained organically bound to its roots in depth psychology: the individual and collective psyche, dreams, and the analytic process. Further, myth critics, aligned with writers in comparative anthropology and philosophy, are said to include Frazer, Jessie Weston, Leslie Fiedler, Ernst Cassirer, CLAUDE LÉVI-STRAUSS, Richard Chase, Joseph Campbell, Philip Wheelwright, and Francis Fergusson. But Wheelwright, for example, barely mentions Jung (*The Burning Fountain,* 1954), and he, Fergusson, and others often owe more to SIGMUND FREUD, Ernest Jones, *Oedipus Rex,* and the Oedipus complex than to anything taken from Jung. Indeed, myth criticism seems singularly unaffected by any of the archetypal theorists who have remained faithful to the origins and traditions of depth, especially analytical, psychology—James Hillman, Henri Corbin, Gilbert Durand, Rafael Lopez-Pedraza, Evangelos Christou. This article, then, treats the only form of literary theory and criticism consistent with and derived directly from the psychological principles advanced by Jung. Other forms previously labeled "Jungian" are here subsumed under the term "archetypal" because whatever their immediate specific focus, these forms operate on a set of assumptions derived from Jung and accept the depth-psychological structure posited by Jung. Further, Jung termed his own theory "analytical psychology," as it is still known especially in Europe, but Jungian thought is more commonly referred to today in all disciplines as "archetypal psychology."

The first systematic application of Jung's ideas to literature was made in 1934 by Maud Bodkin in *Archetypal Patterns in Poetry:* "An attempt is here made to bring psychological analysis and reflection to bear upon the imaginative experience communicated by great poetry, and to examine those forms or patterns in which the universal forces of our nature there find objectification" (vii). This book established the priority of interest in the archetypal over the mythological.

The next significant development in archetypal theory that affected literary studies grew out of the effort made by U.S.-born, Zurich-trained analyst James Hillman (b. 1924) "to move beyond clinical inquiry within the consulting room of psychotherapy" to formulate archetypal theory as a multidisciplinary field (*Archetypal* 1). Hillman invokes Henri Corbin (1903–78), French scholar, philosopher, and mystic known for his work on Islam, as the "second father" of archetypal psychology. As Hillman puts it, Corbin's insight that Jung's "mundus archetypalis" is also the "mundus imaginalis" that corresponds to the Islamic "alam al-mithl" (3) was an early move toward "a reappraisal of psychology itself as an activity of *poesis*" (24). Hillman also discovers archetypal precursors in Neoplatonism, Heraclitus, Plotinus, Proclus, Marsilio Ficino, and GIAMBATTISTA VICO. In *Re-Visioning Psychology,* the published text of his 1972 Yale Terry Lectures (the same lecture series Jung gave in 1937), Hillman locates the archetypal neither "in the physiology of the brain, the structure of language, the organization of society, nor the analysis of behavior, but in the processes of imagination" (xi).

Archetypal theory then took shape principally in the multidisciplinary journal refounded by Hillman in 1970 in Zurich, *Spring: An Annual of Archetypal Psychology and Jungian Thought.* According to Hillman, that discourse was anticipated by Evangelos Christou's *Logos of the Soul* (1963) and extended in religion (David L. Miller's *New Polytheism,* 1974), philosophy (Edward Casey's *Imagining: A Phenomenological Study,* 1976), mythology (Rafael Lopez-Pedraza's *Hermes and His Children,* 1977), psycholinguistics (Paul Kugler's *Alchemy of Discourse: An Archetypal Approach to Language,* 1982), and the theory of analysis (Patricia Berry's *Echo's Subtle Body,* 1982).

These archetypalists, focusing on the imaginal and making central the concept that in English they call

"soul," assert their kinship with SEMIOTICS and STRUC-
TURALISM but maintain an insistent focus on psychoid
phenomena, which they characterize as meaningful.
Their discourse is conducted in poetic language; that is,
their notions of "soul-making" come from the Romantics, especially WILLIAM BLAKE and John Keats. "By speaking of soul as a primary *metaphor,* rather than defining
soul substantively and attempting to derive its ontological status from empirical demonstration or theological
(metaphysical) argument, archetypal psychology recognizes that psychic reality is inextricably involved with
rhetoric" (Hillman, *Archetypal* 19).

This burgeoning theoretical movement and the generally unsatisfying nature of so much early "Jungian
literary criticism" are both linked to the problematic
nature of Jung's own writing on literature, which comprises a handful of essays: "The Type Problem in Poetry,"
"On the Relation of Analytical Psychology to Poetry,"
"Psychology and Literature," "*Ulysses:* A Monologue,"
and "Is There a Freudian Type of Poetry?" These essays
reveal Jung's lack of awareness as a reader despite his
sense that they "may show how ideas that play a considerable role in my work can be applied to literary material" (*Collected* 15:109n). They also attest to his self-con-
fessed lack of interest in literature: "I feel not naturally
drawn to what one calls literature, but I am strangely
attracted by genuine fiction, i.e., fantastical invention"
(*Letters* 1:509). This explains his fascination with a text
like Rider Haggard's novel *She: The History of an Adventure* (1886–87), with its unmediated representation of the
"anima." As Jung himself noted: "Literary products of
highly dubious merit are often of the greatest interest to
the psychologist" (*Collected* 15:87–88). Jung was also more
preoccupied with dreams and fantasies, because he saw
them as exclusively (purely) products of the unconscious,
in contrast to literature, which he oddly believed, citing
Joyce's *Ulysses* as an example, was created "in the full
light of consciousness" (15:123).

Issues of genre, period, and language were ignored or
subjected to gross generalization as Jung searched for
universals in texts as disparate as the fourth-century
Shepherd of Hermas, the *Divine Comedy,* Francesco Colon-
na's *Hypnerotomachia Poliphili* (1499), E. T. A. Hoffman's
tales, Pierre Benoit's *L'Atlantide* (1919–20), and Henry
Wadsworth Longfellow's "Hiawatha," as well as works by
Carl Spitteler and William Blake. But the great literary
text for Jung's life and work was Johann Wolfgang von
Goethe's *Faust,* not because of its literary qualities but
because he sensed that the drama expressed his own
personal myth (*Letters* 1:309–10). Further, the text offered
confirmation (and poetic representation) of the only

direct contribution Jung made to literary theory: a distinction between "psychological" and "visionary" texts
(*Collected* 15:89–90). This heuristic distinction was
formed, however, solely on psychobiographical grounds:
Did the text originate in, and remain principally shaped
by, the author's experience of consciousness and the
personal unconscious or his or her experience at the
level of the archetypal collective unconscious? And con-
comitantly, on which of these levels was the reader affected? Confirmation of this theory was Jung's reading
of *Faust:* part 1 was "psychological"; part 2, "visionary."

Thus Jungian theory provided no clear avenue of access for those outside of psychology, and orthodox Jung-
ians were left with little in the way of models for the
psychological analysis of literature. Many fell prey to
Jung's idiosyncrasies as a reader, ranging widely and
naively over genres, periods, and languages in search of
the universal archetypes, while sweeping aside culture-
and text-specific problems, ignoring their own role in
the act of reading and basing critical evaluation solely
on a text's contribution to the advancement of the
reader's individuation process, a kind of literature-as-
therapy standard. This way of proceeding had the effect
of putting, and keeping, archetypal criticism on the margins of academic discourse and outside the boundaries
of traditional academic disciplines and departments.

Bettina Knapp's 1984 effort at an authoritative demonstration of archetypal literary criticism exemplified
this pattern. Her *Jungian Approach to Literature* attempts
to cover the Finnish epic *The Kalevala,* the Persian Atar's
The Conference of the Birds, and texts by Euripides, Wol-
fram von Eschenbach, Michel de Montaigne, Pierre Corneille, Goethe, Novalis, Rabbi ben Simhah Nachman,
and W. B. Yeats. And despite frequently perceptive readings, the work is marred by the characteristic limitless
expansionism and psychological utilitarianism of her
interpretive scheme.

Given this background, it is not surprising to find in a
1976 essay entitled "Jungian Psychology in Criticism:
Theoretical Problems" the statement that "no purely
Jungian criticism of literature has yet appeared" (Baird
22). But Jos van Meurs's critically annotated 1988 bibliography, *Jungian Literary Criticism, 1920–1980,* effectively
challenges this claim. Despite his deliberately selective
focus on critical works written in English on literary
texts that are, for the most part, also written in English,
van Meurs, with the early assistance of John Kidd, has
collected 902 entries, of which he identifies slightly over
80 as valid and valuable literary criticism.

While acknowledging the grave weaknesses of much
Jungian writing on literature as "unsubtle and rigid ap-

plication of preconceived psychological notions and schemes" resulting in "particularly ill-judged or distorted readings," van Meurs still finds that "sensitively, flexibly and cautiously used, Jungian psychological theory may stimulate illuminating literary interpretations" (14–15). The critical annotations are astute and, given their brevity, surprisingly thorough and suggestive. Van Meurs also does a service by resurrecting successful but neglected early studies, such as Elizabeth Drew's of T. S. Eliot (1949), and discovering value even in reductionist and impressionistic studies, such as June Singer's of Blake. He notes that Singer's *Unholy Bible: A Psychological Interpretation of William Blake* (1970), though oversimplified in its psychobiographical approach and its treatment of characters as psychological projections of the author, does make original use in a literary context of such Jungian techniques of dream interpretation as "amplification" and of such fantasy-evoking procedures as "active imagination."

Van Meurs's bibliography conveys the great variety of Jungian writings on literature even within one language, the increasingly recognized potential for further development and use of Jung's ideas, and the growth in numbers of literary scholars falling under the influence of Jung. A few names form a core of writers in English (including many Canadians)—Martin Bickman, Albert Gelpi, Elliott Gose, Evelyn Hinz, Henry Murray, Barton L. St. Armand, Harold Schechter, and William Stein—though no single figure has attracted the attention of academic literary specialists, and no persistent commonalities fuse into a recognizable school critics who draw on Jung's theories. To date, the British *Journal of Analytical Psychology* and the retitled American *Spring: A Journal of Archetype and Culture* are the best resources for archetypal criticism of literature and the arts even though only a small percentage of their published articles treat such topics.

Thus, with the archetypal theorists multiplying across disciplines on the one hand and the clinically practicing followers serving as (generally inadequate) critics on the other, archetypal literary theory and criticism flourished in two independent streams in the 1960s and 1970s. From the theorists, dissertations, articles, and books, often traditionally academic in orientation, appeared; the productions of the practitioners are chronicled and critiqued in van Meurs's bibliography. And the 1980s saw a new, suggestive, and controversial direction in archetypal studies of literature: the feminist. With some of its advocates supported through early publication of their work in the journal *Spring,* feminist archetypal theory and criticism of literature and the arts emerged full-

blown in three texts: Annis Pratt's *Archetypal Patterns in Women's Fiction* (1981), which self-consciously evoked and critiqued Maud Bodkin's 1934 text; Estella Lauter's *Women as Mythmakers: Poetry and Visual Art by Twentieth Century Women* (1984); and Estella Lauter and Carol Schreier Rupprecht's *Feminist Archetypal Theory: Interdisciplinary Re-Visions of Jungian Thought* (1985). This last text explicitly named the movement and demonstrated its appropriation of archetypal theory for feminist ends in aesthetics, analysis, art, and religion, as well as in literature.

Feminist archetypal theory, proceeding inductively, restored Jung's original emphasis on the fluid, dynamic nature of the archetype, drawing on earlier feminist theory as well as the work of Jungian Erich Neumann to reject absolutist, ahistorical, essentialist, and transcendentalist misinterpretations. Thus "archetype" is recognized as the "tendency to form and reform images in relation to certain kinds of repeated experience," which may vary in individual cultures, authors, and readers (Lauter and Rupprecht 13–14). Considered according to this definition, the concept becomes a useful tool for literary analysis that explores the synthesis of the universal and the particular, seeks to define the parameters of social construction of gender, and attempts to construct theories of language, of the imaginal, and of meaning that take gender into account.

Ironically, as in the feminist revisioning of explicitly male-biased Jungian theory, the rise in the 1980s of READER-RESPONSE THEORY AND CRITICISM and the impetus for canon revision have begun to contribute to a revaluation of Jung as a source of literary study. New theoretical approaches appear to legitimize orthodox Jungian ways of reading, sanction Jung's range of literary preferences from *She* to *Faust,* and support his highly affective reaction to *Ulysses,* which he himself identified (positively) as a "subjective confession" (15:109n). And new theories increasingly give credence to the requirement, historically asserted by Jungian readers, that each text elicit a personal, affective, and not "merely intellectual" response. Even French feminist JULIA KRISTEVA has been brought to praise a Jungian contribution to feminist discourse on the maternal: recognition that the Catholic church's change of signification in the assumption of the Virgin Mary to include her human body represented a major shift in attitude toward female corporality (113). In addition, many powerfully heuristic Jungian concepts, such as "synchronicity," have yet to be tested in literary contexts.

Archetypal criticism, then, construed as that derived from Jung's theory and practice of archetypal (analytical) psychology, is a fledgling and much misconstrued field of inquiry with significant but still unrealized potential for the study of literature and of aesthetics in general. Two publishing events at the beginning of the 1990s in the United States may signal the coming of age of this kind of archetypal criticism through its convergence with postmodern critical thought, along with a commensurate insistence on its roots in the depth psychology of Jung: the reissue of Morris Philipson's 1963 *Outline of a Jungian Aesthetic* and the appearance of Karin Barnaby and Pellegrino D'Acerino's multidisciplinary, multicultural collection of essays, *C. G. Jung and the Humanities: Toward a Hermeneutics of Culture.*

Carol Schreier Rupprecht

See also ANTHROPOLOGICAL THEORY AND CRITICISM, FEMINIST THEORY AND CRITICISM, NORTHROP FRYE, and MYTH THEORY AND CRITICISM.

James Hillman, *Archetypal Psychology: A Brief Account* (1983), *Re-Visioning Psychology* (1975); C. G. Jung, *Collected Works* (ed. Herbert Read, Michael Fordham, and Gerhard Adler, 20 vols., 1953–79), *Letters* (trans. R. F. C. Hull, 2 vols., 1973–75).

James Baird, "Jungian Psychology in Criticism: Theoretical Problems," *Literary Criticism and Psychology* (ed. Joseph P. Strelka, 1976); Karin Barnaby and Pellegrino D'Acerino, eds., *C. G. Jung and the Humanities: Toward a Hermeneutics of Culture* (1990); Martin Bickman, *The Unsounded Centre: Jungian Studies in American Romanticism* (1980); Maud Bodkin, *Archetypal Patterns in Poetry: Psychological Studies in Imagination* (1934); Northrop Frye, *Anatomy of Criticism: Four Essays* (1957); Albert Gelpi, *The Tenth Muse: The Psyche of the American Poet* (1975); Naomi Goldenberg, "Archetypal Theory after Jung," *Spring* (1975); Julia Kristeva, "Stabat Mater" (1977, *The Kristeva Reader,* ed. Toril Moi, trans. Léon S. Roudiez, 1986); Estella Lauter and Carol Schreier Rupprecht, *Feminist Archetypal Theory: Interdisciplinary Re-Visions of Jungian Thought* (1985); Erich Neumann, *Art and the Creative Unconscious: Four Essays* (trans. Ralph Manheim, 1974); Morris Philipson, *Outline of a Jungian Aesthetic* (1963, reprint, 1991); Annis Pratt et al., *Archetypal Patterns in Women's Fiction* (1981); Jos van Meurs and John Kidd, *Jungian Literary Criticism, 1920–1980: An Annotated Critical Bibliography of Works in English (with a Selection of Titles after 1980)* (1988); William K. Wimsatt, Jr., and Cleanth Brooks, *Literary Criticism: A Short History* (1957).

ARISTOTLE

Aristotle (384–322 B.C.E.), the son of a physician, was the student of PLATO from approximately 367 B.C.E. until his mentor's death in 348/347. After carrying on philosophical and scientific investigations elsewhere in the Greek world and serving as the tutor to Alexander the Great, he returned to Athens in 335 B.C.E. to found the Lyceum, a major philosophical center, which he used as his base for prolific investigations into many areas of philosophy. Much of Aristotle's published work, including all his carefully written and polished essays, has disappeared. The studies that have survived, including the *Poetics,* have come down to us in a fragmented form, which suggests that they may be lecture notes (of Aristotle himself or of a student attending his lectures), outlines for future works to be published, or summaries of already published works. There has long been speculation that the original *Poetics* comprised two books, our extant *Poetics* and a lost second book that supposedly dealt with comedy and/or *katharsis.* No firm evidence for the existence of this second book has been adduced, but Richard Janko has argued that evidence for its content can be recovered. Our knowledge of the text of the *Poetics* depends principally on a manuscript of the tenth or eleventh century and a second manuscript dating from the fourteenth century. These sources are supplemented by a thirteenth-century Latin translation of the text by William of Moerbeke, a tenth-century Arabic translation, and a fragment of an earlier Syriac translation.

On a number of subjects Aristotle developed positions that significantly differed from those of his teacher. We very clearly note this profound difference of opinion with Plato and, indeed, observe the overt correction of his erstwhile master in Aristotle's literary and aesthetic theories. As is well known, Plato's negative view of art stems from, first, his view that its essential character as *mimesis* forces upon it a profound ontological alienation from true reality and, second, his observation that artistic mimesis addresses itself essentially to the emotional, rather than the intellectual, aspect of the human psyche and thus dangerously subverts the character of both the individual and the state.

The principal source of our knowledge of Aristotle's aesthetic and literary theory is the *Poetics,* but important supplementary information is found in other treatises, chiefly the *Rhetoric,* the *Politics,* and the *Nicomachean Ethics.* As expressed in these works, Aristotelian aesthetics directly contradicts Plato's negative view of art by establishing a potent intellectual role for artistic mimesis. For Aristotle, mimesis describes a process involving the use by different art forms of different means of representation, different manners of communicating that representation to an audience, and different levels of moral and ethical behavior as objects of the artistic representation. Thus Aristotle distinguishes between tragedy and comedy essentially on the basis of the fact that the former represents "noble" or "morally good" agents, while the latter portrays "ignoble" or "morally defective" characters. All forms of mimesis, however, including tragedy and comedy, come into existence because of a fundamental intellectual impulse felt by all human beings. In the *Metaphysics* Aristotle describes this impulse as humanity's "desire to know," and in chapter 4 of the *Poetics* he identifies it with the essential pleasure we human beings find in all mimesis, the pleasure of "learning and inference." In chapter 14, moreover, Aristotle states that the tragic poet must provide pleasure from pity and fear through mimesis, thus alerting us again to the intellectual pleasure generated by tragic mimesis. In chapter 9 he asserts that poetry "is more philosophical and more significant than history" because its goal is the representation of that which is universal, while history has the expression of the particular as its object. In this emphasis on the intellectual and philosophical dimensions of mimesis, Aristotle directly contradicts Plato's derogation of art as an inferior appeal to human emotions.

Aristotle's main focus in the *Poetics* is on the genre of tragedy, but he also makes important comments on comedy and epic. His fundamental theoretical stipulations about the essential nature of mimesis must apply to all genres of literature (tragedy, comedy, epic, etc.) and all other forms of mimesis (music, dance, painting, sculpture, etc.). These basic stipulations are that mimesis is fundamental to our nature as human beings, that human beings are the most imitative of all creatures, that first learning experiences take place through mimesis, and that all human beings take pleasure in mimesis because all find "learning and inference" essentially pleasant. Since the focus of the *Poetics* is mainly on literary mimesis, it is necessary for us to concentrate on Aristotle's understanding of the way this aspect of mimetic activity leads to the intellectual pleasure he assigns to art.

Aristotle specifies that the function of literary mimesis is to represent a complete and unified action consisting of a beginning, middle, and end linked by necessary and probable causes. The magnitude of such a work is to be such as may easily be held in the memory and yet remain quite clear to an audience. If the beginning, middle, and end of an action are clearly and persuasively motivated, the conditions will be present for "learning and inference" to occur (ch. 4). What could interfere with the accomplishment of this goal are "simple" and "episodic" plots, the former occurring without reversal of fortune *(peripeteia)* and recognition of some unknown person or fact *(anagnorisis)* and the latter occurring when the sequence of episodes fails to obey the laws of necessity and probability. To serve the goal of persuasive lucidity, both reversal and recognition must arise naturally out of the structure of the plot because, as Aristotle says, "it makes a great difference if something happens because of something else or merely after it" (ch. 10).

According to Aristotle, the emotions represented and evoked in tragedy are pity and fear. He defines pity as the emotion we feel toward someone who has suffered undeserved misfortune, and fear as the emotion we feel when we realize that the one who suffers this misfortune is someone like ourselves. Now, pity and fear, when we experience them in actual life, are painful feelings, but when they occur in tragic mimesis they are integrated into a structure that has the production of intellectual pleasure as its goal. Aristotle connects the effective evocation of pity and fear to the nature of the *hamartia,* the tragic mistake or flaw, attributed to the protagonist.

Pity and fear arise only when someone who is very much like ourselves, that is, neither unqualifiedly virtuous nor deeply flawed, falls from happiness to misery because of a hamartia or even a great hamartia. Earlier disputes about the meaning of "hamartia" in this context in the *Poetics* have given way to an evolving interpretive consensus. It was not uncommon formerly to identify Aristotelian hamartia with a "moral flaw" and to attempt to find in the plot of Sophocles' *Oedipus Tyrannus* justification for this view. Some critics in the past have identified Oedipus's hamartia as his violent anger. Thus Philip Whaley Harsh comments that "the preeminently good and just man does not fly into a fury when a carriage crowds him from the road, and he does not commit murder indiscriminately even when he is lashed by the driver" (48). Perceptive interpretations of that play (Sophocles himself provides an eloquent defense of Oedipus in the *Oedipus at Colonus*) and of the term "hamartia," however, offer a persuasive refutation of this view. Kurt von Fritz represents this line of thinking when he argues persuasively that no blame can attach to Oedipus for defending himself against an attack by a party of strangers in an isolated locale where no other protection was available. It now seems clear that since the protagonist of Aristotle's "best tragedy," the tragedy of pity and fear, must be a "good" *(spoudaios)* human being, the required hamartia must be some kind of intellectual mistake that cannot subvert the dignity of someone "like ourselves." D. W. Lucas defines it as "the blindness which is part of the human condition" (307), and P. van Braam describes it as "the insufficiency of the human mind to cope with the mysterious complex of the world" (271).

The key term, and the most controversial one, in Aristotle's theory of artistic mimesis is *katharsis*. The term has fascinated and troubled scholars at least since the sixteenth century, and the abundant interpretive literature on the concept continues to increase. Three major lines of interpretation emerge, representing the medical, moral, and cognitive views of *katharsis*.

The medical interpretation, deriving most influentially from the work of Jacob Bernays, bases itself on Aristotle's use of *katharsis* in the *Politics* (1341b36–1342a16) to describe a process through which music effects a medical cure by purging a pathological excess of emotion. Bernays assumed that precisely this type of therapeutic *katharsis* takes place in tragedy. According to this interpretation, the audience must be assumed to suffer from an excess of pity and fear, to seek a remedy for this excess through the homeopathic cure afforded by exposure to additional pity and fear in tragedy, and to experience pleasure because of the relief felt when the cure has been achieved. There are obvious difficulties with such an interpretation, which requires that artistic mimesis be identified with a therapeutic process. There is no evidence in the *Poetics* to support the view that the essential goal of mimesis is therapeutic; indeed, there is very strong evidence leading to a quite different conclusion.

The interpretation of *katharsis* as a form of moral purification is identified with the great German dramatist and critic G. E. LESSING, whose view, often combined with aspects of the purgation theory, has influenced a number of subsequent critics. This interpretation is based on a passage in the *Nicomachean Ethics* (1106b16–23) that asserts that our goal must be to experience emotions virtuously, that is, in accordance with the proper mean between excess and deficiency. The purgation theory views pity and fear as pathological states that must be removed, while the purification interpretation makes the experiencing of these emotions in the proper amount and way a sign of virtue. The idea of *katharsis* as purification in this moral sense, like purgation, has no supporting evidence in the text of the *Poetics*.

It is only when we turn to the cognitive interpretation of *katharsis* that we find explicit supporting evidence in the *Poetics*. This evidence has been most fully explored by Kurt von Fritz, Pedro Laín Entralgo, and Leon Golden. First, we recall the important passage in chapter 4 (1448b4–17), where Aristotle tells us that mime-

sis is by nature a part of human experience from childhood on, that it is the basis of our first learning experiences, and that all human beings derive pleasure from it. This pleasure does not derive from the nature of the object represented in the mimesis, for as Aristotle says, we take pleasure in *imitated* objects such as "despised wild animals and corpses," which would cause us pain if we saw them in reality. For Aristotle, the pleasure arising from mimesis is the pleasure of learning and inference, which "is not only most pleasant to philosophers" but pleasant to all others as well, though in a more limited way. Aristotle further supports the cognitive nature and goals of mimesis when he attributes to poetry in chapter 9 a philosophical dimension arising from its capacity to express universals rather than particulars. In chapter 14 (1453b8–14) he tells us that "it is necessary for the poet to provide pleasure from pity and fear through mimesis" and so once again calls attention to the cognitive function of mimesis, whose essential pleasure we know to be "learning and inference."

The theme of *katharsis* as a cognitive process is very much a product of twentieth-century thought about this concept. Translations denoting "purgation" and "purification" dominate the interpretations of *katharsis* from the sixteenth century to the end of the nineteenth century, which Ingram Bywater collected in an appendix to his important edition of the *Poetics*. Donald Keesey, in his 1979 survey of twentieth-century interpretations of *katharsis*, notes the appearance of various nuances of "clarification" in more recent analysis. Matthias Luserke, in his anthology of nineteenth- and twentieth-century documents relating to the interpretation of *katharsis*, includes two essays advocating the "clarification" theory of *katharsis* in a "pure" or modified form. The cognitive view of *katharsis* is now gaining momentum as an alternative to the traditional interpretations of "purgation" and "purification."

Gerald Else, although he never accepted an intellectual interpretation of *katharsis*, opened up the way for such an interpretation by his sharp attack on the purgation theory. He called attention to the fact that such a theory "presupposes that we come to the tragic drama (unconsciously, if you will) as patients to be cured, relieved, restored to psychic health. But there is not a word to support this in the *Poetics*, not a hint that the end of drama is to cure or alleviate pathological states" (440). Else, in his turn, defined *katharsis* as "the purification of the tragic act by the demonstration that its motive was not *miaron* [morally polluted]" (439). As a consequence of such a determination the audience is permitted to experience pity for the tragic hero. In spite of Else's reluctance to accept an interpretation of *katharsis* as "clarification," his view does require *katharsis* to be based on some form of cognitive process, since the judgment that an act was not morally polluted must begin with the intellectual analysis of the circumstances under which the act was performed.

The cognitive view of *katharsis* is supported both by the analysis of the internal argument of the *Poetics* and by arguments based on the way words are used in ancient and modern psychotherapy. Both Pedro Laín Entralgo, a historian of ancient medicine, and Bennett Simon, a practicing psychiatrist, offer us a persuasive insight into the way words in literary contexts affect an audience. Laín Entralgo notes that in the mind of the spectator at a tragedy there is a "deep demand for expression and clarification of the human destiny" (230), and he notes that any emotional and somatic pleasure felt in tragedy is a secondary resultant of a primary intellectual pleasure. In regard to such emotional and somatic pleasure he says, "Previous to it and determining its genesis were and had to be those [pleasures] pertaining to the good order of the soul, both of affective character (having to do with the thymos) and of intellective nature (concerning dianoia)" (236). Simon argues that

> tragedy should bring some altered and new sense of what one is and who he is in relation to those around him . . . the audience acquires a new sense of the possibilities in being human and in coming to terms with the forces that are more powerful than any one individual. In therapy we also expect an enlarged view of the possibilities that are open in relationships to the self and others. Thus good therapy and good theater have in common a set of inner processes. (144)

Simon, however, correctly understands, as the defenders of the purgation theory of *katharsis* do not, the essential difference between therapy and aesthetics. He notes that "theater is not, and was not for the Greeks, primarily intended to be therapy for especially disturbed or distressed people. It was expected to provide a certain form of pleasure, even in Greek culture, and was an integral part of the *paideia* (education in the broadest sense) of each Athenian" (144–45). It is only—and this is a matter of very great importance—the verbal triggering of intellectual and emotional responses that the two processes share in common.

Evidence for the interpretation of *katharsis* as "intellectual clarification" based on the internal argument of the *Poetics* has been presented by Leon Golden, Martha Nussbaum, and Christian Wagner, who have suggested ways of expanding or modifying this interpretation. Nussbaum argues for *katharsis* as "clarification," but a clarification that does not depend exclusively on the intellect but could be generated by emotion as well. Wagner maintains that the clarification involved in tragedy is limited to ethical issues.

While the principal subject of the *Poetics* is tragedy, important comments are also made in the work about comedy and, to a lesser extent, about epic. As mentioned above, there has long been speculation about the existence of a lost second book of the *Poetics* dealing with Aristotle's theory of comedy. In the absence of that book, if it ever existed, scholars have had recourse to two sources as a basis for establishing Aristotle's views about the nature of comedy. One of these is the *Tractatus Coislinianus*, a treatise contained in an early tenth-century manuscript whose value and authenticity have been subjected to strong scholarly disagreement. Bywater called it a "sorry fabrication" and cited Bernays's view of it as a travesty (xxii). Janko has defended its value as a source for Aristotelian comic theory. The other source is the *Poetics* itself and other indisputably genuine Aristotelian texts that provide us with enough reliable data to permit us to reconstruct most, if not all, of Aristotle's theory of comedy.

We must first recall that for Aristotle all forms of mimesis, including tragic and comic mimesis, have as their goal the evocation of intellectual pleasure. Thus, comic mimesis must meet all of the stringent requirements set forth for tragic mimesis in terms of the persuasive lucidity that is the necessary prerequisite for the climactic experience of "learning and inference" required of all mimesis. Tragedy, we have been told, aims at the *katharsis* of pity and fear and thus must represent the actions of "good" or "noble" (in a moral or ethical sense) human beings. Comedy, Aristotle tells us, represents the opposite kind of character, which we can designate as "base" or "ignoble." Moreover, comedy represents such characters, not

> in regard to every kind of vice, but in regard to the ridiculous, a subdivision of the general category of moral and physical deformity. For the ridiculous is some error and deformity which is not painful or destructive—the example which immediately comes to mind is the comic mask which is ugly and distorted but which does not cause pain. (*Poetics* ch. 5)

We can learn a great deal about the nature of the "base" characters represented in comedy from the discussion of human vices and virtues in the *Nicomachean Ethics*. Thus, a great deal of what we must know about the means, objects, and manner of comic mimesis is provided to us by available, authentic Aristotelian texts. What these texts do not provide is a discussion of the emotions, analogous to pity and fear in tragedy, that are aroused in comedy.

What we do know with certainty is that the emotion or emotions aroused in comedy must be related to the representation of "base" human beings involved in action designated by Aristotle as "ridiculous" and thus must be opposed in some way to the emotions evoked by the "noble" characters represented in tragedy. On the basis of this authentically Aristotelian view of the nature of comedy and tragedy, we can at least speculate reasonably about the emotions evoked in comedy. Since for Aristotle tragedy and comedy are directly opposed to each other in terms of the character and action they represent, we may ask whether Aristotle anywhere designates the emotion that is opposed to pity and fear. Here we do have information that could help us in developing a hypothesis about comic emotion. In the *Rhetoric* Aristotle addresses the question of pity and its opposed emotional experience. He states there that the direct opposite of pity is what may be called "righteous indignation" *(nemesan),* which is a feeling of pain at undeserved good fortune in the same way that pity is a feeling of pain at undeserved misfortune. Edward M. Cope analyzes the concept of righteous indignation (expressed by the Greek terms *nemesan* and *nemesis*) as follows:

> According to Aristotle's definition of nemesis "a feeling of pain at undeserved good fortune" it represents the "righteous indignation" arising from a sense of the claims of justice and desert, which is aroused in us by the contemplation of success without merit, and a consequent pleasure in the punishment of one who is thus undeservedly prosperous. (2:108)

We can say that both Old Comedy and New Comedy provide significant instances of "base" characters behaving in a ridiculous manner and achieving, at least temporarily, undeserved success. At the end of the comedy these characters regularly meet with deserved punishment. Thus the idea of righteous indignation alluded to in the *Rhetoric* as the opposite of pity does bear a clear relationship to the action of comedy. Calling attention to this suggestive idea, however, is probably as far as we should go in our speculation on Aristotle's view of the comic emotions.

In the final chapter of the *Poetics* Aristotle compares tragedy and epic, both of which represent "noble" characters. He notes that tragedy contains all of the elements in epic and additional ones unique to itself. The most important way, however, in which tragedy differs from, and is superior to, epic is in its much more compact structure. Aristotle sees the much greater length of epic, with its main plot and subplots, as an impediment to the lucid and persuasive unfolding of the poem's theme. He judges tragedy to be superior because its carefully orchestrated incidents, bound together from beginning to middle to end by psychological and aesthetic necessity and probability, achieve tragedy's mimetic goal more effectively than is possible for epic, with its looser and more cumbrous structure. Here again, at the end of the *Poetics,* Aristotle reveals the central role cognitive pleasure plays in his aesthetic theory.

Aristotle has exerted a large and enduring influence on literary criticism and aesthetic theory. New translations and new interpretations of his work in this area regularly appear. In part these new contributions continue interpretive disagreements that have existed for centuries, but recent scholarship has also been moving toward the resolution of some longstanding controversies and the deeper illumination of others. We can be certain that in changing aesthetic landscapes, where the expectations for criticism may undergo radical transformations, the voice of Aristotle will always be heard, asserting authoritatively that the critic's essential duty is to investigate the way the organic structure of a work of art leads us to a universalizing epiphany involving the highest human pleasure, the pleasure of learning and inference about significant human actions.

Leon Golden

See also CHICAGO CRITICS, CLASSICAL THEORY AND CRITICISM, DRAMA THEORY, MEDIEVAL THEORY AND CRITICISM, and RENAISSANCE THEORY AND CRITICISM.

Samuel Henry Butcher, *Aristotle's Theory of Poetry and Fine Art, with a Critical Text and Translation of the "Poetics"* (1902); Ingram Bywater, *Aristotle on the Art of Poetry* (1909); Lane Cooper, *An Aristotelian Theory of Comedy* (1922), *Aristotle on the Art of Poetry* (1947); Edward M. Cope and John Edwin Sandys, *The Rhetoric of Aristotle, with an adaptation of the "Poetics" and a Translation of the "Tractatus Coislinianus"* (3 vols., 1877, reprint, 1988); Roselyne Dupont-Roc and Jean Lallot, *Aristote: La Poétique* (1980); Gerald Frank Else, *Aristotle's "Poetics": The Argument* (1957); Leon Golden and O. B. Hardison, Jr., *Aristotle's Poetics: A Translation and Commentary for Students of Literature* (1981); D. W. Lucas, *Aristotle: "Poetics"* (1968).

P. van Braam, "Aristotle's Use of Hamartia" *Classical Quarterly* 6 (1912); R. D. Dawe, "Some Reflections on *Ate* and *Hamartia,*" *Harvard Studies in Classical Philology* 72 (1967); Gerald Frank Else, *Plato and Aristotle on Poetry* (1986); Kurt von Fritz, *Antike und moderne Tragödie* (1962);

Leon Golden, "Aristotle on Comedy," *Journal of Aesthetics and Art Criticism* 42 (1984), "Catharsis," *Transactions of the American Philological Association* 93 (1962), "The Clarification Theory of Katharsis," *Hermes* 104 (1976), "Comic Pleasure," *Hermes* 115 (1987); Stephen Halliwell, *Aristotle's "Poetics"* (1986); Philip Whaley Harsh, "Hamartia Again," *Transactions of the American Philological Association* 76 (1945); Malcolm Heath, "Aristotelian Comedy," *Classical Quarterly* 39 (1989), *The Poetics of Greek Tragedy* (1987); Richard Janko, *Aristotle on Comedy: Towards a Reconstruction of Poetics II* (1984); Donald Keesey, "On Some Recent Interpretations of Catharsis," *The Classical World* 72 (1979); Pedro Laín Entralgo, *The Therapy of the Word in Classical Antiquity* (1970); Jonathan Lear, "Katharsis," *Phronesis* 33 (1988); Matthias Luserke, *Die Aristotelische Katharsis* (1991); Richard P. McKeon, "Literary Criticism and the Concept of Imitation in Antiquity," *Critics and Criticism: Ancient and Modern* (ed. R. S. Crane, 1952); Martha C. Nussbaum, *The Fragility of Goodness* (1986); Bennett Simon, *Mind and Madness in Ancient Greece* (1978); Richard Sorabji, *Necessity, Cause, and Blame: Perspectives on Aristotle's Theory* (1980); Christian Wagner, "'Katharsis' in der aristotelischen Tragödiendefinition," *Grazer Beiträge* 11 (1984).

ARNOLD, MATTHEW

In the preface to his selection from SAMUEL JOHNSON's *Lives of the Poets,* Matthew Arnold (1822–88) identifies Johnson as a central point of reference for the study of English literature. He says that Johnson provides "a fixed and thoroughly known centre of departure and return" (*Complete* 8:310). Arnold frequently disagreed with Johnson, especially about poetry, the one subject nearest to his own heart. In rising above these disagreements to acknowledge the quality of authority in Johnson's criticism, Arnold himself displays that authority of critical judgment that has helped to render him the single most important modern successor to Johnson as a critical center. Even now, when criticism is vastly more abundant than ever before, and when the institutional structure of academic literary study has helped to give various contemporary critics exceptional power and prominence, Arnold is quoted, paraphrased, and referred to perhaps more often than any other figure. His status as a pervasive cultural presence, at least within the culture of criticism, is in this respect parallel to that of Shakespeare. Arnold's distinctive phrases and formulas—"the grand style," "the modern spirit," "the best that has been known and thought," "to see the object as in itself it really is," "the function of criticism at the present time," "sweet-

ness and light," "sweet reasonableness," "Hebraism and Hellenism," "culture and anarchy," "doing as one likes," "the best self," "high seriousness," "a criticism of life"— are commonplace idioms even among those who could not identify their source. He is often opposed, sometimes mocked, and by those critics whose historical perspective stops short with our own generation he is usually taken as merely the personification of a now antiquated and thoroughly discredited "humanism." At the highest level of contemporary criticism, he remains the critic who is most to be reckoned with. His formulations serve either as rallying points or as standards in opposition to which one must establish one's own position.

Why is Arnold so important as a living historical presence in critical thought? There are, I think, five main reasons: his disinterested temper, the quality of his literary intelligence, the scope of his studies, his fully elaborated claim for the authority of a central Western tradition, and the deep coherence of his cultural theory.

The word "disinterested," as used in such phrases as "a disinterested effort to learn and propagate the best that is known and thought in the world" (3:282), is now the most violently disputed word in the Arnoldian lexicon. Marxist and New Historical critical ideology, for example, make a good deal of epistemological heavy weather over this term (see MARXIST THEORY AND CRITICISM and NEW HISTORICISM). Arnold himself had the tact to avoid philosophical wrangling, and what he himself means by *disinterested* he vindicates through his own critical performance. To be disinterested is to participate in a common cultural tradition or a common body politic, and it is to evince a genuine, generous appreciation for what is truly excellent within these forms of common experience. To be generous in this way is to embody one's "best self," and it is from the perspective of this best self that the disinterested critic passes judgment on all specific social and intellectual issues.

Like Johnson, Arnold unites his generosity of temper with a literary intelligence of the very first quality. Through his critical studies, he gives access to an extraordinarily diverse and comprehensive range of cultural experience and to the finest tonalities within that experience. He campaigned constantly for a common European culture that would include a knowledge of the classical languages and literatures, the major European literatures, and the findings of modern science and scholarship. He located the eighteenth-century writers—"classics of our prose" (9:181)—firmly within the range of modern cultural experience, and though he harbored serious reservations about the intellectual quality of English Romanticism, his essays on William Wordsworth, Lord Byron, and John Keats did much to establish their canonical status. He was among the most forceful proponents for the "free play of the mind upon all subjects" (3:268), but he was at the same time one of the most distinguished voices of cultural conservation. More than any other writer, he established "culture," and especially literature, as an object of the highest veneration among civilized people. He was the first major critic in English to invest poetry with sacral status, but he also did more than any other critic to transform critical prose into a genuinely creative medium. He isolated the quality of "high seriousness" as a "touchstone" for poetic excellence (9:185, 168), and in his prose he established a standard of genial, urbane wit that has not been surpassed. The central unifying ideal of his thought is the "harmonious expansion of *all* the powers which make the beauty and worth of human nature" (5:94), and in his own work he exemplified this ideal.

The New Historicist challenge to Arnoldian disinterestedness centers on the charge that Arnold's own judgments and values, though presented as objective and universal, actually reflect and reinforce his quite specific "interests" as a European male of the upper middle class. Arnold's own analysis of social class and of his position as an intellectual within the English class structure was shrewd and unillusioned, but it is quite true that he invoked "right reason" or "reason and the will of God" (5:156, 92) as a sanction for all his own specific judgments. In this respect, he remains pre-Darwinian, premodern, and neoclassical. Unlike the neoclassical theorists, however, he envisioned cultural values as essentially historical and developmental, unfolding over time and articulating certain possibilities of style or thought within a necessary organic sequence. Like many mid-Victorians, including George Eliot and JOHN STUART MILL, he believed that the historical progression of culture was tending toward the realization of human "perfection," if not in his own generation, then perhaps in the next or the one after that. Darwin has rendered all such teleological doctrines obsolete, but one can still preserve from Arnold's historical vision the idea that the works of Western culture embody a central tradition of human development, and indeed it is this idea that is now the object of so much animus among the various forms of multiculturalism.

The final reason for Arnold's preeminent significance as a critic is that he understood the necessity of system. T. S ELIOT, F. R. LEAVIS, and many who have followed them have treated Arnold as an exemplar of a theoretically amorphous literary "sensibility." In opposition to

this view, I would argue that the effectiveness of Arnold's prose depends fundamentally on the profound consistency of his thought. His formulations could not have gained the currency they have if they were merely felicitous phrases. Each individual formulation derives much of its power from the whole network of such formulations, and this network provides a firm conceptual frame for the celebrated grace and poise of his prose. Arnold's own intellectual temper, his own literary sensibility, and the whole range of his cultural experience are fully theorized in a critical system that includes and coordinates analytic schemes of the human faculties, of literary genres and the forms of intellectual activity, of European ethnography, of the four elements, or "powers," of civilization (knowledge, beauty, manners, and conduct), of political and social order, and of the main phases of Western cultural history. After his early period of despairing confusion, most fully explored in his drama *Empedocles on Etna* (1852), he actively engaged in the pursuit of what he called "an intellectual deliverance" from spiritual distress (1:19). The deliverance that he fashioned for himself was precisely the theory of culture developed through and reflected in his critical essays. His identity as a critic is commensurate and coterminous with his cultural theory.

The coherence of Arnold's thought has been obscured in some measure by his method of composition, the diversity of his topics, and the course of his intellectual development. Most of what he wrote was in essay form, designed for publication in journals like the *Cornhill* and the *Fortnightly Review*. Even his most celebrated "book," *Culture and Anarchy*, was originally a series of journal essays. The subjects of the essays in Arnold's collections are, on the surface, heterogeneous—poets and prose writers from several languages, ancient and modern philosophers, political issues, religious controversies, historical periods, and cultural institutions—and even the titles of the collections, titles such as *Essays in Criticism* and *Mixed Essays*, suggest a casual, impressionistic criticism. In fact, throughout his study of these diverse topics, Arnold is continuously articulating a unified cultural theory; however, his critical career, after the early period of his poetry, passes through three distinct phases: a phase that begins with "On the Modern Element in Literature" in 1857 and culminates with *Culture and Anarchy* in 1868; a decade in which his preoccupation with religious topics results in works such as *Literature and Dogma* (1873) and *God and the Bible* (1875); and finally a decade in which he returns to literary and social topics.

Arnold's most theoretically constructive phase is that of the early essays culminating in *Culture and Anarchy*. During this phase, he seeks to strike a balance between the "Hebraic" moral consciousness and the "Hellenic" critical intelligence, but the dominant force within his own critical system is Hellenism. In the phase of his religious studies, he gives a primary emphasis to moral consciousness. Within his scheme of the human faculties, religion and poetry both affiliate themselves with the "heart and imagination" rather than with "the senses and the understanding" (3:225, 223). In order to preserve the "poetry" of traditional religion while discarding its dogma, he redefines religion as "morality touched by emotion" (6:176). This line of thought leads him ultimately to establish poetry proper as the medium of modern spiritual experience. In his final decade, he elaborates and applies the cultural theory he had developed in the 1860s, but he also expresses a new, deeper regard for Romantic poetry, especially the poetry of Wordsworth.

In order to illustrate Arnold's position as a constant point of reference within criticism, we can focus on one salient issue: the relative status of imaginative literature and literary criticism. This issue will also serve to illustrate the way in which Arnold's authority often remains in force even while being explicitly deprecated. The ruling authority in the age of NEW CRITICISM was T. S. Eliot, and Eliot's conception of his own role as a critic not only of literature but of "culture" is crucially dependent on Arnold's definitions of the functions of criticism. In conformity with his dictum that the great writer does not "borrow" ideas but rather "steals" them, Eliot expresses his indebtedness largely by disparaging Arnold and concealing, as much as possible, the derivative character of many of his own conceptions. Eliot's essay "The Function of Criticism" is essentially a pastiche of Arnoldian formulations—some acknowledged, some not—and in this essay Eliot chides Arnold for distinguishing "too bluntly" between "creative" and "critical" work (29, 30). Eliot says that Arnold "overlooks the capital importance of criticism in the work of creation itself." This is a whopper. In "The Function of Criticism at the Present Time," the very essay from which Eliot takes his title, Arnold declares that "the creation of a modern poet, to be worth much, implies a great critical effort behind it; else it must be a comparatively poor, barren, and short-lived affair. This is why Byron's poetry had so little endurance in it, and Goethe's so much" (3:261–62). Arnold hoped that the critical work done by his own generation would serve as the catalyst for a new phase of imaginative literature, and in vindication of this hope we can note that his own criticism had a major impact on the work of writers such as WALTER PATER, OSCAR WILDE, George Eliot, HENRY JAMES, Thomas Hardy, and even, by way of GEORGE SANTAYANA, WALLACE STEVENS. While empha-

sizing the inherent superiority of imaginative literature—especially poetry—Arnold argues that criticism too can be "creative." He declares that if it is "sincere, simple, flexible, ardent, ever widening its knowledge," then criticism "may have, in no contemptible measure, a joyful sense of creative activity" (3:285).

As is often the case with convenient misrepresentations, Eliot's version of what Arnold said has now in some measure supplanted what Arnold actually said. In a recent book of interviews with prominent critics, Imre Salusinszky remarks that "the main subject within criticism seems always to have been 'The Function of Criticism,' and one could construct a brief history of the field simply by tracing the sequence of major essays bearing that title" (1). Salusinszky himself then quotes and approves Eliot's declaration that Arnold overlooks the importance of criticism in the work of creation itself (2). So also GEOFFREY H. HARTMAN, following Eliot, maintains that "the Arnoldian Concordat . . . assigns to criticism a specific, delimited sphere distinct from the creative" (6). In order to claim originality in assigning a creative function to criticism itself, Hartman must tacitly acquiesce in Eliot's misrepresentation of Arnold's own position.

Arnold's pervasive influence realizes itself not only at the first level, through direct references such as those in the "function-of-criticism" titular tradition, but also at a second level through the medium of those critics who have taken him as a primary source. In order to illustrate Arnold's presence at this second level of influence, we can consider the case of HAROLD BLOOM, a critic who expresses a lofty disdain for Arnold. As one of the leading contemporary Freudian critics, Bloom is, as he himself acknowledges, a successor to LIONEL TRILLING, and Trilling in his own day was, next to Eliot, the most important successor to Arnold in the field of general cultural criticism. Trilling's first major work was his critical biography of Arnold, a study that is still widely regarded—rightly—as among the best appreciative critiques of Arnold. As an alternative to the lineage of critical authority descending from Arnold, Bloom affiliates himself with Walter Pater, Oscar Wilde, and NORTHROP FRYE (Salusinszky 55, 62, 63). As already noted, Pater and Wilde themselves both respond directly to Arnold, and indeed much of Pater's work is so heavily dependent on Arnold that it could fairly be characterized as derivative. Northrop Frye, now widely considered the most important critical theorist of this century, contributes to the "function-of-criticism" titular tradition, and in *The Critical Path*, one of his most expansive efforts to articulate a general theory of cultural history, Frye explicitly engages Arnold and develops his own views as a modification of the terms defined by Arnold. Thus, despite his efforts to relegate Arnold to marginal status, Bloom is inescapably encircled by Arnoldian influences at the second level. The multitudes of lesser critics influenced primarily by Bloom would receive Arnold's influence at yet a third level, though often only in the negativistic phase of Bloom's repressions and evasions, that is, with little sense of the positive authority from which Bloom seeks to escape.

To offer one final illustration of Arnold's pervasive, inescapable presence within contemporary criticism, we may note that Bloom himself, in an apparently unconscious fashion, rises to the first level of Arnoldian influence by drawing directly from Arnold for one of his own largest formulations. Bloom poses the question, "What is the larger subject of which the study of poetic influence is only a part?" His answer is "the deep split" in "Western culture" between "the fact that its religion and its morality are Hebraic-Christian, and its cognition and aesthetics—and therefore its dominant imaginative forms—are Greek" (Salusinszky 68). In other words, the two basic elements of Western culture are, as Arnold explained at some length, Hebraism and Hellenism. This curious instance of an unwilling and apparently unconscious theoretical dependence on Arnold should suggest how much authority Arnold still has within contemporary criticism. Arnold has this kind of authority because he defines the central issues in our cultural tradition and because his judgments about this tradition display a justness of understanding possible only to the greatest critics.

Joseph Carroll

See also BRITISH THEORY AND CRITICISM: 4. VICTORIAN.

Matthew Arnold, *The Complete Prose Works of Matthew Arnold* (ed. R. H. Super, 11 vols., 1960–77), *The Letters of Matthew Arnold, 1848–1888* (ed. George W. E. Russell, 2 vols., 1895), *The Letters of Matthew Arnold to Arthur Hugh Clough* (ed. Howard Foster Lowry, 1932), *The Note-Books of Matthew Arnold* (ed. Howard Foster Lowry, Karl Young, and Waldo Hilary Dunn, 1952), *The Poems of Matthew Arnold* (ed. Kenneth Allott, 2d ed., ed. Miriam Allott, 1979), *Unpublished Letters of Matthew Arnold* (ed. Arnold Whitridge, 1923).

Joseph Carroll, *The Cultural Theory of Matthew Arnold* (1982); David J. DeLaura, "Arnold and Carlyle," *PMLA* 79 (1964), *Hebrew and Hellene in Victorian England: Newman, Arnold, and Pater* (1969); T. S. Eliot, "The Function of Criticism," *Selected Essays* (1932, 3d ed., 1950); Northrop Frye, *The Critical Path: An Essay on the Social Context of Literary Criticism* (1971); Geoffrey H. Hartman, *Criticism in the Wilderness: The Study of Literature Today* (1980); Henry James, "Matthew Arnold," *Literary Criticism: Essays on Literature, American Writers, English Writers* (ed. Leon Edel and Mark Wilson, 1984); F. R. Leavis, "Arnold as Critic," *Scrutiny* 7 (1938); William Robbins, *The Ethical Idealism of Matthew Arnold* (1959); Imre Salusinszky, *Criticism in Society: Interviews with Jacques Derrida, Northrop Frye, Harold Bloom, Geoffrey Hartman, Frank Kermode, Edward Said, Barbara Johnson, Frank Lentricchia, and J. Hillis Miller* (1987); Lionel Trilling, *Matthew Arnold* (1939).

ART THEORY

While the term "art theory" may well have been employed from the Renaissance through the Enlightenment as a means of validating certain philosophical practices of art, art historians in the second half of this century have become particularly uncomfortable with its implications. For when the phrase is applied to their own scholarly enterprise, it suggests that the history of art is an interpretive activity rather than an empirical practice. The internal debates of the 1980s between traditional and revisionist, or "new," art histories have been waged precisely over this epistemological point. The issue is a complex one, involving the history of the discipline, its gender and class biases, its origins in certain elitist institutions, its resistances to other modes of disciplinary inquiry, and its internal divisions over what constitutes the story of art as advanced in its standard histories.

For centuries, literary historians based their discussion of texts in some part upon theories of imitation and concepts of periodicity borrowed from the general discussion of the visual arts. Lately, however, contemporary literary critics appear to look with bemused superciliousness upon what seem to them to be antiquated theoretical models in art history proper. While most of the other humanities have been engaged in critical self-reflection and metahistorical commentary for several decades, art history has lagged behind for several historically legitimate reasons: its newness as a distinct discipline; the discovery, authentication, and classifying of objects that had first to be accomplished; and the aesthetic status of the objects themselves, a status that resulted in the preference given to description over interpretation in the visual arts. Consequently, most art historical studies in this century have fallen into the prevalent modes of stylistic analysis, iconographic readings, and historical documentation.

Beginning around 1980, scholars began to speak of a

"crisis" in the discipline. No longer secure with the idea of empirical research, an insecurity sparked in large part by poststructuralist critiques in literary criticism, historians of art began to speak of "theory" as that something which was ideologically opposed to "history." At stake seemed to be the conception of Art as such. The crisis mentality eventuated in a hardening of positions: those scholars who long had an investment in positivistic pursuits proudly reasserted their role as "historians" and became outspoken in their dismissal of extra-artistic analyses, particularly those that paraded their origins in psychoanalysis, feminism, SEMIOTICS, and Marxism. On the other side, the self-proclaimed "new" art historians (read "theoreticians") descried the politically invested, what they called the conservatively capitalist, motives of academically entrenched art historians, particularly in England and the United States. Two book titles from the middle of the 1980s, *The End of the History of Art?* (Hans Belting, 1983, trans., 1987) and *The End of Art Theory* (Victor Burgin, 1986) suggest that the result of the controversy raging in a discipline long unaccustomed to attack was that feelings of crisis had turned into self-aggrandizing visions of the apocalypse. Matters became a little less strident as the 1980s ended, and it seems possible to map the historical evolution of the disciplinary changes and attempt a brief overview of the variety of theoretical positions that have come to animate the field.

In its modern origins, art history certainly engaged theoretical issues. The noted founders of the discipline in its German *Kunstwissenschaft* phase were all involved with principles of interpretation. Jacob Burckhardt, Edwin Panofsky, Alois Riegl, Aby Warburg, and Heinrich Wölfflin, to name only an illustrious few, may have been in fundamental disagreement about the central issue in art historical interpretation—why and how styles of art come into being and then pass away again—but not one avoided explanations for the process on the ground that theorizing was something extrinsic to the study of art as art. All in fact offered grand Hegelian schemes to account for the diachronous process at work, and if their focus on the objects (as well as the objects themselves) differed, their primary commitment to interpretation never faltered.

For these early analysts, "theory" would be the term assigned to the mode of explanation, and more often than not, the argument underlying the historical evidence had to do with the cause of stylistic change and whether it could be attributed to factors intrinsic to the history of images or whether the explanation for transformation should be sought in the cultural world that surrounded their production. The points were rarely argued apart from specific historical examples; in fact, it is usually from the complex of talk on individual artists or works or periods or genres that a contemporary historiographer has to extract something that can be called the "theory."

Jacob Burckhardt initiated the study of art in its sociohistorical context. Although his 1855 *Cicerone* can certainly assume its place in histories of art based upon the revered principles of connoisseurship, he intended his 1860 *Civilization of the Renaissance* to be a cultural and historical prologue to his analysis of Renaissance imagery. He isolated certain motivating themes evident in literature, ethics, politics, and so on—the development of selfhood, the return to the classics, the sense of the past, the tyranny of statehood—to account for the changing subject matter of Renaissance art. Arguing from the theoretical point of view of a distant observer, Burckhardt claimed that art was always a product of its time and could only be historically understood if it was mapped against a larger panorama of cultural, social, and especially literary meaning.

Riegl and Wölfflin had a decidedly different notion of context. More interested in the intrinsic circumstances in which art is generated, their works can be read as theoretically invested in discovering "hidden" principles at work in the history of form, a history hermetically sealed off from other cultural and intellectual expressions. In *Classic Art* (1899) and *Principles of Art History* (1915), for example, Heinrich Wölfflin was intent upon detecting the laws of stylistic change that mandate the evolution of form as it metamorphoses from one style to another. He developed five pairs of opposing optical modalities that he hoped would morphologically account for the changing eye of perception. Using the minor arts, particularly those rooted in ornamental expression, Alois Riegl formulated the concept of the *Kunstwollen* to account for the history of art in terms of changing modes of spatial perception. In *Stilfragen* (1893) and *Spätromische Kunstindustrie* (1901), he elaborated a will-to-form based upon his version of what came to be Saussurean linguistics. Both thinkers helped to undermine the question of hierarchy and value in the history of art. Since all art participates equally in the laws of historical determinism, there are no lesser artists, no lesser arts, no lesser civilizations.

Erwin Panofsky, on the other hand, has been accused of being elitist and ethnocentric. His art histories center upon the highpoints of Western civilization, particularly Gothic France and Renaissance Italy, and the principles he deduced for artistic expression there became the template for evaluating art for all times and all places. Yet Aby Warburg, while returning regularly to his beloved Florence, also journeyed to the American Southwest to study Indian culture and spent much time in Italian studies investigating popular engravings, astrological symbolism, contemporary literary journals, and other sources that might seem extrinsic to mainstream art history (*Gesammelte Schriften*, ed. Gertrud Bing, 1932).

In a number of mostly unpublished essays as well as in the organization of his famed institute in Hamburg and London, Warburg developed, and Panofsky then refined, the practice of iconology. If any method can be said to constitute a theory of art, then iconology would have to be recognized as the paradigmatic theory underpinning all critical histories in this century (see in this regard W. J. T. Mitchell's *Iconology: Image, Text, Ideology,* 1986).

Parenthetically acknowledged, however, must be a vehement counterpractice in twentieth-century art studies: formalist aesthetics and its attendant commitment to the principles of connoisseurship. While not a theory per se, formalism nonetheless constitutes the primary locale of art appreciation in the United States and was responsible not only for the critical response to modern art (e.g., Clement Greenberg's emphasis on "flatness" as the primary virtue of avant-garde painting [*Collected Essays,* ed. John O'Brian, 2 vols., 1986]) but also for the organization of American museums and academic departments. Its practice is dependent upon the trained eye of the connoisseur, a commitment to certain aesthetic standards, and an inclination to exclude works of art, modes of interpretation, and classes of artists who do not conform to a preconceived canon of values.

While it did not arise in deliberate opposition to this formalist sensibility, iconology addressed itself to very different sorts of problems and can therefore be more explicitly seen as presaging postmodern sensibilities. Panofsky's preface to *Studies in Iconology* (1939) distinguishes three levels of investigation and employs Leonardo's *Last Supper* as a pictorial demonstration of the method at work. The pre-iconographic level depends upon practical experience and interprets primary subject matter as distinct from its historical and textual embodiments (e.g., the universal recognition of thirteen men seated at a table laden with food). The iconographic level, which has everything to do with literary precedents, "reads" the pre-iconographic level in tandem with the texts that it illuminates; that is, it identifies its subject matter by recourse to the Gospel story (word here always preceding image). An iconological analysis, the third level, represents "iconography turned interpretive." The art historian

deciphers the painting as a cultural document, expressive of the "essential tendencies of the human mind" as they are crystallized into a particular historical, personal, and cultural moment. Here the *Last Supper* is not only a testimony to the artist's idiosyncratic genius but also the "supreme" embodiment of Renaissance ideas and ideals. Panofsky put this method to work in many well-regarded essays and texts, among them *Gothic Architecture and Scholasticism* (1951), *Early Netherlandish Painting* (1953), *Meaning in the Visual Arts* (1955), and *Renaissance and Renascences in Western Art* (1960). His emphasis on the conventionality of artistic expression has been interestingly paralleled in the representational theories of the philosopher Nelson Goodman (*Languages of Art,* 1976).

Ernst Gombrich has been for a long time the heir apparent to Warburg's ideals and Panofsky's monumental erudition. His theoretical career, however, is split into halves. A scholar of the Renaissance, Gombrich's early writings further extend the iconological method. In *Symbolic Images* (published in volume form in 1972, but essays written during the 1940s and early 1950s) and *Norm and Form* (published in 1966, with most of the essays being from the 1950s), he isolates a theme in Renaissance imagery, discovers its antique and medieval precedents in art and especially literature, and then charts its changing symbolism across time in order to arrive at a pictorial index of Renaissance cultural values. In *Art and Illusion* (1961) and *Meditations on a Hobby Horse* (1963), however, his focus is decisively different. The earlier book, which has had a significant impact on all fields of the humanities, discusses the role of convention in artistic production and makes the claim not only that the beholder's share in the reading of images is crucial but also that perception is always already conditioned by expectations. Relying on both Gestalt psychology (as does Rudolf Arnheim) and Popperian notions of falsifiability, the book effectively initiated a revolution in thinking about the relativity of vision.

This once radical text has itself been subject to the charge of conservatism from several quarters, the most cogent of which comes from the recent work of Norman Bryson. In *Vision and Painting* (1983), Bryson claims that the great problem with Gombrich's work is that he views art as the record of a perception rather than as the site for the production of a sign. One of the few art historians in the past decade who has not remained oblivious to semiotic thinking (Meyer Schapiro being a much earlier exception), Bryson appropriates concepts from ROLAND BARTHES, JACQUES LACAN, and FERDINAND DE SAUSSURE to argue that art in no simple-minded way reflects reality but is instead engaged in the active production of a universe of meaning. It is itself a signifying system actively involved with other systems of signification, particularly those of the social world of which it is a part. In works such as *Word and Image* (1981) and *Tradition and Desire* (1984), Bryson has effectively compelled art history to confront semiotics and begin to interrogate the relationship between discursive and visual aspects of both literature and art. Similarly, the work of the literary critic Mieke Bal has turned to the domain of "reading images." Together Bal and Bryson have co-authored "Semiotics and Art History" (1991), an essay that is most useful for all scholars engaged with issues of both verbal and visual representation.

Challenges to the reigning canon of art historical thinking have also come from more intradisciplinary directions than semiotics. Svetlana Alpers has been insistent upon reformulating the theoretical principles by which we characterize the art of the North. In *The Art of Describing* (1983) and *Rembrandt's Enterprise* (1988), she insists upon the essentially visual culture of the North as distinct from the textual culture of the Italian Renaissance and therefore demanding of different "readings" than the traditional iconological method can give it. Her 1972 essay with Paul Alpers, "'Ut Pictura Poesis'? Criticism in Literary Studies and Art History," was one of the first attempts within the discipline to come to terms with modes of analysis at work in literary criticism. Michael Baxandall, an influential Warburg scholar, has for the past two decades (in *Painting and Experience in Fifteenth-Century Italy*, 1972; *The Limewood Sculptors of Renaissance Germany*, 1980; and *Patterns of Intention*, 1985) been intent upon deciphering visual images in terms of all the conventions that might structure the consciousness of people living in a certain period, from barrel-gauging skills to Newtonian color theory.

Also necessary to mention is the traditional intersection of art theory and philosophy. The relationship has existed since the Renaissance. In its contemporary form, analytic philosophers such as Arthur Danto (*The Transfiguration of the Commonplace*, 1981; *The Philosophical Disenfranchisement of Art*, 1986) and Richard Wollheim (*Art and Its Objects*, 1980) speak directly to the criteria of artistic cognition. Worth noting in this context also is the evolution of phenomenological perception from MARTIN HEIDEGGER and Merleau-Ponty to the recent controversial work of the prominent art historian Michael Fried, who in *Absorption and Theatricality: Painting and Beholder in the Age of Diderot* (1980) temptingly argues for a recognition of the bodily involvement (or its lack) between the spectator and the artist and the insistent physicality of the painted image (see PHENOMENOLOGY).

In a different vein altogether, art history has sporadically and idiosyncratically flirted with Marxism. Works by Frederick Antal (*Florentine Painting and Its Social Background*, 1948) and Arnold Hauser (*The Sociology of Art*, 1974, trans., 1982) for many years exemplified the insights that a social history of a period or a style or an artist can bring to the discipline. Since the 1970s, however, essays by T. J. Clark (*Image of the People*, 1973; *The Absolute Bourgeois*, 1973; *Painting of Modern Life*, 1985), Thomas Crow (*Painters and Public Life in Eighteenth Century Paris*, 1985), Keith Moxey (*Peasants, Warriors, and Wives*, 1989), and Janet Wolff (*The Social Production of Art*, 1981) have done for art history what Terry Eagleton did for literary criticism. In their studies of the conditions of production and the public for whom works of art were intended, they have reanimated the field of social criticism and demonstrated a lively irreverence for the petrified concepts of formalists and iconographers alike. (See KARL MARX AND FRIEDRICH ENGELS and MARXIST THEORY AND CRITICISM.)

Perhaps nothing, however, has shaken the very foundations of the discipline as much as the feminist criticism of the 1970s and 1980s. In 1971 Linda Nochlin asked the provocative question, "Why Have There Been No Great Women Artists?" (*Art News* 69 [1971]) and rooted her discussion in institutional expectations about the nature of artistic achievement. Ten years later in *Old Mistresses: Women, Art, and Ideology* (1981), Rozsika Parker and Griselda Pollock pushed the position further by arguing that only an analysis of women's historical position could account for the ideological suppression of female artistic sensibilities.

The so-called second generation of feminist art critics no longer attempts to insert the female producer into a canon of male creative values but instead uses the processes of her exclusion to question the motives and value of the discipline as such. Borrowing from Marxist ideology critiques, Pollock's *Vision and Difference* (1988) contends that the only viable conceptual framework for the study of women's artistic history is one that emphasizes the ways in which gender differences are socially constructed. While indebted to poststructuralist French feminist thinkers such as JULIA KRISTEVA (who also wrote several important essays in art theory, such as "Motherhood According to Giovanni Bellini," *Desire in Language: A Semiotic Approach to Literature and Art*, ed. Leon S. Roudiez, 1980), contemporary English-speaking feminists such as Pollock, Lisa Tickner (*The Spectacle of Women: Imagery of the Suffrage Campaign, 1907–1914*, 1988), Eunice Lipton (*Looking Into Degas: Uneasy Images of Women and Modern Life*, 1988), Carol Duncan ("Virility and Domination in Early Twentieth Century Vanguard Painting," *Feminism and Art History: Questioning the Litany,* ed. Norma Broude and Mary Garrard, 1982), and Jacqueline Rose tend to focus on the articulation of sexual difference rather than on a definition of a specific female artistic sensibility. They simultaneously restore a certain power to images, for they emphasize that art is as capable of constituting ideology as it is of reflecting it—a political commitment that goes way beyond the mission of art history proposed by either the formalist tradition or the iconological method. (See FEMINIST THEORY AND CRITICISM.)

Recent discussions about the nature of visuality, the differentiation of modes of looking, and the specific identity of the viewing subject—debates that come together under the term "gaze"—are deeply influenced by insights primarily developed within feminist literary studies, and particularly within film criticism, originating with Laura Mulvey's 1975 essay on "Visual Pleasure and Narrative Cinema" and continuing through Jacqueline Rose's *Sexuality in the Field of Vision* (1986) and Kaja Silverman's *Male Subjectivity at the Margins* (1992). As a recently emerged discipline, film studies has endorsed perspectives traditionally marginalized within both literary and art criticism. The most important perspective that needs mentioning is psychoanalysis (Freudian and Lacanian), a mode of inquiry that, as a theory and as a therapeutic practice, is itself an example of the interaction between word and image, particularly as it concerns ideas about visual subjectivity. Film's relation to the verbal dimension, through the spoken word but also through the narrative dimension, has contributed considerably to the bridging of the gap between visual and verbal art. (See FILM THEORY and PSYCHOANALYTIC THEORY AND CRITICISM: 3. THE POST-LACANIANS.)

From tangential directions in literary studies come NARRATOLOGY and RECEPTION THEORY. Starting with Barthes's *S/Z* (1970, trans., 1974), visual narratologists, such as Mieke Bal, examine the ways in which different narrative agents account for the lack of unification of visual subjects. Like semiotics, this view of narrative implies that the act of looking at a painting is always a dynamic process. Reception theory has had its greatest impact in German art theory. Scholars such as Wolfgang Kemp adhere to the notion that a work of art only functions as a work of art when it is concretized on a particular historical horizon.

Literary critics seem recently to have discovered for art historians the idea that the domain of the visual is not limited to images, let alone to the objects traditionally studied as art. If in the last couple of decades many well-known literary thinkers have turned toward the study of visual art, such a development does not imply a move away from literature, but rather stands for an acknowledgment of the many aspects images and verbal artifacts, in spite of their differences, share. Inversely, the traditional disciplinary approaches in art history have not always been able to address those aspects in images that may be called discursive: narrative strategies, propositional content, the dynamic interaction between image and viewer. Through the work of JACQUES DERRIDA, we have come to see how the histories of discourses on art link themselves inextricably to concerns and interests that lie outside the privileged domain of aesthetic comprehension and its framing sensibility. In *The Truth in Painting* (1978, trans., 1987), he calls attention to the ways in which notions of value, beauty, form, subject matter, and even the "truth" of history itself are preconditioned by our Western philosophical legacy, a tradition of textuality that has itself always been subject to the dislocating forces at work in the production of language.

Clearly, art history is no longer an empirical and monographic study of monuments, artists, styles, periods, and so on. The "new" art history, in the process of foregrounding the theoretical (as opposed to empirical) commitments of its founders, is now focusing on the history, context, and politics of visual interpretation. It interrogates gender boundaries and the unequal power distribution they encourage. It examines the distinction between the so-called high and popular cultures and their attendant artistic expressions. It engages in a dialogue between art forms in an effort to overcome the privileging of either the word or the image. In short, the general deconstructionist debates in the humanities that are engaging scholars across disciplinary boundaries into more general discussions of cultural critique are also informing contemporary art theory. The relations between the arts, the process of figuring forth physical images, the interaction between theory and critical practice, the investigation of the social embedding and historicity of vision, are all serving to question the object of art's traditional status as a "still" image. The issue has become less how history can serve art than how art can serve theory (and history) as a basis of cultural and social criticism.

Michael Ann Holly

Svetlana Alpers, *The Art of Describing* (1983), *Rembrandt's Enterprise* (1988); Svetlana Alpers and Paul Alpers, " 'Ut Pictura Poesis'? Criticism in Literary Studies and Art History," *New Literary History* 3 (1972); Mieke Bal, *Reading*

'Rembrandt': Beyond the Word/Image Opposition (1991); Mieke Bal and Norman Bryson, "Semiotics and Art History," *Art Bulletin* 73 (1991); Michael Baxandall, *The Limewood Sculptors of Renaissance Germany* (1980), *Painting and Experience in Fifteenth-Century Italy* (1972), *Patterns of Intention* (1985); Norman Bryson, *Tradition and Desire* (1984), *Vision and Painting: The Logic of the Gaze* (1983), *Word and Image* (1981); Jacob Burckhardt, *The Civilization of the Renaissance in Italy* (1860, trans. S. G. C. Middlemore, 1958); T. J. Clark, *The Absolute Bourgeois* (1973), *Image of the People* (1973), *Painting of Modern Life* (1985); Thomas Crow, *Painters and Public Life in Eighteenth Century Paris* (1985); Jacques Derrida, *La Vérité en peinture* (1978, *The Truth in Painting*, trans. Geoff Bennington and Ian McLeod, 1987); Michael Fried, *Absorption and Theatricality: Painting and Beholder in the Age of Diderot* (1980); Ernst Gombrich, *Art and Illusion: A Study in the Psychology of Pictorial Representation* (1961, 4th ed., 1972), *Meditations on a Hobby Horse* (1963); Michael Ann Holly, *Panofsky and the Foundations of Art History* (1984); Wolfgang Kemp, "Death at Work: A Case Study on Constitutive Blanks in Nineteenth Century Painting," *Representations* 10 (1985); W. J. T. Mitchell, *Iconology: Image, Text, Ideology* (1986); Keith Moxey, *Peasants, Warriors, and Wives: Popular Imagery in the Reformation* (1989), "Semiotics and the Social History of Art," *New Literary History* 27 (1991); Laura Mulvey, "Visual Pleasure and Narrative Cinema" (1975), *Visual and Other Pleasures* (1989); Erwin Panofsky, *Studies in Iconology* (1939); Rozsika Parker and Griselda Pollock, *Old Mistresses: Women, Art, and Ideology* (1981); Griselda Pollock, *Vision and Difference: Femininity, Feminism, and Histories of Art* (1988); Kaja Silverman, *Male Subjectivity at the Margins* (1992); Janet Wolff, *The Social Production of Art* (1981); Heinrich Wölfflin, *Classic Art: An Introduction to the Italian Renaissance* (1899, trans. Peter Murray and Linda Murray, 1952), *Principles of Art History* (1915).

AUDEN, W. H.

The British-born Wystan Hugh Auden (1907–73) read, owned, and distributed copies of SIGMUND FREUD's writings when he was at Gresham's School, Norfolk, in his eighteenth year. His interest in psychoanalysis persisted after he went up to Oxford in 1925 but received its greatest fillip in Berlin in 1928, when he met John Layard, who had been a patient of the American psychologist Homer Lane. Through Layard, Auden became familiar with the theories not only of Lane but also of Georg Groddeck. In these thinkers, as in Freud and D. H. LAWRENCE, with whom he was already familiar, he found what Humphrey Carpenter has called "a positive doctrine of psychological liberation" (89), which left a lasting mark on his personal life as well as on his poetry and criticism.

In his Oxford years Auden had also read KARL MARX AND FRIEDRICH ENGELS, whose political and economic theories he readily assimilated within the framework of Freudian psychology as he understood it. In 1935 he was able to argue that Marx and Freud were both "right": "As long as civilisation remains as it is, the number of patients the psychologist can cure are very few, and as soon as socialism attains power, it must learn to direct its own interior energy and will need the psychologist" (*English* 341). Auden was never orthodox in either his Freudianism or his Marxism and moved on to consider other ideologies as the basis for his life and art. The most notable—and most durable—of these was Christianity, to which he was reconverted in 1940, shortly after he had settled in New York. In *Auden's Apologies for Poetry*, Lucy McDiarmid has argued that in the 10 or 15 years after that date, and in part because of the commitment to "ultimate value" that Auden's conversion required, "every major poem and every major essay [became] a *retractatio*, a statement of art's frivolity, vanity, and guilt" (x). Auden had in fact never maintained an unqualified belief in the serious, direct usefulness of art, not even during his most Freudian, most Marxist phases. The relationship he saw between art and life, complex and attenuated before his conversion, merely became more difficult and more oblique after 1940. Some connection persisting, however, psychology and society continued as important themes in his work and thought.

Auden was 25 when he published his first extended statement of poetic theory, an essay called "Writing: or the pattern between people." The ideas explored in this work, as Edward Mendelson has observed, are strikingly premature; we encounter "aspects of a late Romantic theory of language, brought to a crisis by modernism, and agonized over by the young Auden a generation before Derrida and Lacan" (*Early* 21). For Auden, language as a referential tool is a product of humanity's emergence from what JACQUES LACAN, also thinking with Freud, would later call the "imaginary" state, in which subject and object are not clearly distinguished, into self-consciousness: "At some time or other in human history [individuals] began to feel, I am I and you are not I" (*English* 303). Language arises out of a need to bridge the gap thus created, and "what the bridge carries, i.e., what the speaker gives and the listener receives, we call the *meaning* of words" (304). We are thus in the Lacanian realm of the "symbolic," of unstable signifiers, in which "most of the power of words comes from their *not* being like what they stand for" (305). Auden explicitly rejects linguistic theories of "presence": words originate in a sense of difference between subject and object, and their relation to the things they signify is also always one of difference. In a much later essay, "The Virgin and The Dynamo" (1962), Auden writes that only in a magical world (characterized by "a consciousness of the self as self-contained, as embracing all that it is aware of in a unity of experiencing") would "the image of an object, the emotion it aroused and the word signifying it [be] all identical" (*Dyer's* 65–66).

We do not inhabit such a world, and Auden does not especially mourn the fact—neither in 1962 nor in the "Writing" essay 30 years earlier. Despite its concern with the origins of language, that early piece comes to concentrate on language not as an index of our lost subjective innocence but as a device of potentially great social utility. "When we read a book," Auden writes, "it is as if we were with a person" (*English* 310). Words, which originate in the need to construct a social bridge, can in themselves and in their written form provide lessons in human interaction. Thus, "you must use your knowledge of people to guide you when reading books, and your knowledge of books to guide you when living with people" (311). By 1962, and the second essay called "Writing," Auden has invested language and its use with an ethical value, and after labeling "solipsist subjectivity" a "modern peril," he goes on to note that "however esoteric a poem may be, the fact that all its words have meanings which can be looked up in a dictionary makes it testify to the existence of other people" (*Dyer's* 23). That testimony validates the entire poetic enterprise, or to adapt a word very common in Auden's vocabulary of the 1960s, it makes even the most formalist exercise in some measure an act of "love." To speak or to write at all is an acknowledgment of one's estrangement from the world and the "other," but it is also a protest against that condition. The injunction, issued in the face of imperfection, is, "You shall love your crooked neighbour / With your crooked heart" (*Collected* 115), as much guidance for writing as for living. In "Squares and Oblongs," an essay of 1957, we find Auden treating words *as* people, as in his argument that "the writing of a short poem is a more democratic process than the writing of a long one" (177). And then in his conclusion to "The Virgin and The Dynamo" comes the expected step: the notion that poems are verbal "communities," that "every poem . . . is an attempt to present an analogy to that paradisal state in which Freedom and Law, System and Order are united in harmony" (*Dyer's* 71).

Given this ongoing stress on language and literature as phenomena with social origins, analogues, and responsibilities, it is not surprising that Auden came to be associated in the 1930s with theories of political "engagement." However, his position on this matter has been greatly distorted. Perhaps because the difference between language and its objects lay at the base of all his thinking about poetry, Auden was always skeptical of the direct efficacy of literature in the realm of political practice. In 1939 the death of W. B. Yeats brought from him at least two clear statements on this point. One is, "Poetry makes nothing happen" (*Collected* 197), the well-known line from his elegy for the poet, and the other is from a less known piece, an essay called "The Public v. the Late Mr. William Butler Yeats," in which Auden writes that "art is a product of history, not a cause" (*English* 393). This comes at the end of his supposedly "engaged" phase, admittedly, but the same note had been sounded much earlier. In 1935, in the introduction to his anthology *The Poet's Tongue*, we find Auden answering "moral or political" propagandists as follows: "Poetry is not concerned with telling people what to do, but with extending our knowledge of good and evil, perhaps making the necessity for action more urgent and its nature more clear, but only leading us to the point where it is possible for us to make a rational and moral choice" (ix). In the same year, he argues that the task of art is identical to that of psychology: "not to tell people how to behave, but by drawing their attention to what the impersonal unconscious is trying to tell them, and by increasing their knowledge of good and evil, to render them better able to choose, to become increasingly morally responsible for their destiny" (*English* 340–41). Precisely how a poem might produce a social effect is thus clearly a matter for explanation, not by practical politicians ("propagandists"), but by psychoanalysts.

Central to Auden's thinking on this issue is the idea, already alluded to, that in dealing with a text we are dealing with a "person." Auden encourages us as critics to approach a work initially with the question, "What kind of a guy inhabits this poem?" (*Dyer's* 51), but this does not imply a naive belief in the "presence" of the author. In "Squares and Oblongs" he writes that "a poem is a pseudo-person" (175), which makes clear that the speaking subject implied by the text is a *constructed* subject, at least partly a product of the "verbal contraption" (*Dyer's* 50) on the page. This idea—that the "person" we encounter in a poem is construed and construable from nowhere but its linguistic surface—is stressed by Auden's further suggestion that such a person is like "an image in a mirror" ("Squares" 175). The comparison is crucial for a number of reasons, the suggestion that language constitutes its own "reality" being perhaps the principal one. In essays of the late 1950s and 1960s, and in poems such as "Words" (1956), Auden commonly talks of the independent power of language itself, of how the "final poetic order of a poem is the outcome of a dialectical struggle" between the feelings and intentions of the poet and "the verbal system" ("Squares" 175). In arguing that the system is as much the "author" of a poem as the poet, Auden shows his premature affinity with STRUC-TURALISM and poststructuralist thought.

The analogy between text and mirror is also important for what it implies about the status of the reader, and of the text vis-à-vis the reader. Stan Smith has noted that the comparison negotiates "the doubleness of the text, which is both a historical product . . . and yet a discourse that floats free of its origins" (4). When we encounter a poem, that "guy" who "inhabits" it and whose experiences are its subject is in part a reflection of ourselves, or rather the poet is the product of *another* "dialectical struggle," this time between ourselves and the linguistic contraption before us. The poet's experiences, insofar as they feel "real" to us, are nobody's but our own. The distinguishing peculiarity of the whole situation is that the contents of the poem (the words as well as what they are taken to stand for) are imputed to a subjectivity other than that of the reader (Smith 5 and ch. 1); invited to do so by the text, the reader projects some aspect of himself or herself onto the "speaker" and then relates to it as an "other," something liable to conscious examination and even judgment. In this sense poetry can do what Auden argued it should do: not "tell people how to behave" but provide an occasion for scrutinizing the self and the promptings of the "impersonal unconscious," the ultimate aim being to make informed choice the prelude to action.

Although Auden's position on the nature and function of literature altered considerably over the course of his relatively long career, the questions outlined above proved to be of enduring interest. While he moved quite rapidly beyond his initial preoccupation with our dissociation from subjective unity, difference (between "I" and "Thou," sign and referent, vision and reality) can be discerned throughout his career as a goad in his poetic thought and practice. Increasingly, the broader social ramifications of "difference" came to absorb him, and so the rather precious theoretical, linguistic, and psychoanalytical subjects of his poems and essays gave way to a more pragmatic concern with "community" and "society," less as metaphors for poetic unity than as human phenomena.

Patrick Deane

W. H. Auden, *Collected Poems* (ed. Edward Mendelson, 1976), *The Dyer's Hand* (1968), *The English Auden* (ed. Edward Mendelson, 1977), "Squares and Oblongs," *Language: An Enquiry into Its Meaning and Function* (ed. Ruth Nanda Anshen, 1957); W. H. Auden, ed., *The Poet's Tongue* (1935).

Humphrey Carpenter, *W. H. Auden: A Biography* (1981); Lucy McDiarmid, *Auden's Apologies for Poetry* (1990); Edward Mendelson, *Early Auden* (1981); Stan Smith, *W. H. Auden* (1985).

AUERBACH, ERICH

Ranked with Ernst Robert Curtius and Leo Spitzer as one of the great exponents of the German philological tradition, Erich Auerbach (1892–1957) is best known today for his magisterial survey of the representation of reality in Western literature, *Mimesis* (1946). In this work, as well as in his earlier book on Dante, his later study of European literature in late antiquity, and the essays collected in *Scenes from the Drama of European Literature,* Auerbach refined the techniques of close philological and stylistic analysis. (See PHILOLOGY and STYLISTICS.) Unlike Spitzer, who forged an aesthetic program out of an attention to precise linguistic detail, or Curtius, who set out to identify and chronicle the *topoi* that expressed the habits of expression for antiquity and the Middle Ages, Auerbach proposed a history of culture through the study of styles. Building on the work of his teacher, Eduard Norden, and strongly influenced by the historicism of GIAMBATTISTA VICO and the idealism of G. W. F. HEGEL, Auerbach claimed to have described the changing patterns of literary reality. His work, while not explicitly theoretical, has implications for a theory of historical understanding and the conception of style itself. As he put it in *Literary Language and Its Public,* "my purpose is always to write history" (20)—a claim that may have motivated the sweep of his critical attention (from Homer to Virginia Woolf) and that has more recently been the focus of a variety of scholarly critiques of his enterprise.

Born in Berlin, Auerbach took a degree in law before turning to the study of Romance literature. His doctorate in 1921 was soon followed by his appointment as Ordinarius University Professor at Marburg (1929), the same year he published *Dante als Dichter der irdischen Welt.* He left Nazi Germany in 1936, traveling to Istanbul, where he taught at Istanbul State University until 1947. There he wrote the studies collected in *Mimesis,* as well as an introductory handbook of Romance philology and many reviews. From 1947 he taught at several American universities, concluding his career at Yale, where he was Sterling Professor at the time of his death.

Auerbach's importance for modern criticism rests on a set of terms and oppositions he developed to explain the workings of literary allegory and the transformations of the classical doctrine of style in Western Christian literature. Under the term *figura*—defined in the essay of that title (1938) and developed in the opening chapters of *Mimesis*—Auerbach defined a view of reality, at work in Christian thought and biblical narrative, whereby one historical personage or event prefigures or signifies a second, later one. The latter will, effectively, fulfill the former such that while the two remain distinct historical realities, their full significance is to be sought in the figural relationship between them. Developing this concept from the hermeneutics of ST. AUGUSTINE and the exegetics of the fathers, Auerbach deploys it most effectively (and with the greatest subsequent critical impact) in his reading of Dante. As he puts it in the "Farinata and Cavalcante" chapter of *Mimesis,* it is the "figural realism" of the Christian Middle Ages "which dominates Dante's view" and which grounds his literary style in the aesthetic and historical consciousness of his time (196).

If his interest in figural understanding bespeaks a sensitivity to Christian manipulations of Old Testament history, then it is Auerbach's concern with what he labels *sermo humilis* that encapsulates his view of the Christian response to classical literary style. Broadly speaking, it is the concept of the separation of styles (drawn from ARISTOTLE and later Roman rhetorical theory [see CLASSICAL THEORY AND CRITICISM: 2. RHETORIC]) that motivates Auerbach's generic interests. In the parabolic language of the New Testament, the sermons of the fathers, or the stories of the saints, Auerbach finds an apparently low or humble diction pressed into the service of transcendent spirituality. Again developing an argument of Augustine's—here, on the power of the Christian word stripped of the trappings of classical eloquence—Auerbach sees the progress of late antique and medieval literature as moving inexorably toward the synthesis of the humble and the sublime.

While Auerbach's primary influence on North American scholarship has been in medieval studies, more recently his projects have been the focus of a renewed interest in the nature of historical understanding, the sociology of criticism, the methods of historicism, and the ideologies of the academy. His debts to Vico have been brought out to show his understanding of the interrelatedness of poetry, history, philology, and philosophy. The presence of Hegel in his work has been noted, at times critically, as contributing to the teleological flavor of *Mimesis* in particular. While Auerbach rarely theorized explicitly about the implications of his philological method (save for the first chapter of *Dante als Dichter der irdischen Welt* and the late essays "Philologie der Weltliteratur" and "Epilegomena zu Mimesis"), recent critics have abstracted from his works a governing conception of literary history itself as a kind of narrative enterprise. What had been criticized in early reviews as the aesthetic qualities of Auerbach's work—its *Feingefühl* rather than its *Methode*—have now been seen as participating in a larger synthesis of poetry and history that he inherited from Vico and bequeathed to a later generation of Romance scholars.

Seth Lerer

See also GERMAN THEORY AND CRITICISM: 4. TWENTIETH CENTURY TO 1968.

Erich Auerbach, *Dante als Dichter der irdischen Welt* (1929, *Dante, Poet of the Secular World,* trans. Ralph Manheim, 1961), "Epilegomena zu Mimesis," *Romanische Forschungen* 65 (1953), "Figura" (1938, *Scenes from the Drama of European Literature,* trans. Ralph Manheim, 1959), *Introduction aux études de philologie romane* (1949, *Introduction to Romance Languages and Literature,* trans. Guy Daniels, 1961), *Literatursprache und Publikum in der lateinischen Spätantike und im Mittelalter* (1958, *Literary Language and Its Public in Late Latin Antiquity and in the Middle Ages,* trans. Ralph Manheim, 1965), *Mimesis: Dargestellte Wirklichkeit in der abendländischen Literatur* (1946, *Mimesis: The Representation of Reality in Western Literature,* trans. Willard R. Trask, 1953), "Philologie der Weltliteratur" (1952, "Philology and *Weltliteratur*," trans. Edward Said and Marie Said, *Centennial Review* 13 [1969]).

Timothy Bahti, "Auerbach's *Mimesis*: Figural Structure and Historical Narrative," *After Strange Texts: The Role of Theory in the Study of Literature* (ed. Gregory S. Jay and David L. Miller, 1985), "Vico, Auerbach, and Literary History," *Philological Quarterly* 60 (1981); Paul A. Bové, *Intellectuals in Power: A Genealogy of Critical Humanism* (1986); Luiz Costa-Lima, "Erich Auerbach: History and Metahistory," *New Literary History* 19 (1988); Thomas M. DePietro, "Literary Criticism as History: The Example of Auerbach's *Mimesis,*" *Clio* 8 (1979); Klaus Gronau, *Literarische Form und gesellschaftliche Entwicklung: Erich Auerbachs Beitrag zur Theorie und Methodologie der Literaturgeschichte* (1979); W. Wolfgang Holdheim, "Auerbach's *Mimesis*: Aesthetics as Historical Understanding," *Clio* 10 (1981); Carl Landauer, "*Mimesis* and Erich Auerbach's Self-Mythologizing," *German Studies Review* 11 (1988);

Ralph Manheim, "Bibliography of the Writings of Erich Auerbach," *Literary Language and Its Public in Late Latin Antiquity and in the Middle Ages* (1965).

ST. AUGUSTINE

Renowned theologian and controversialist of late antiquity, Augustine (C.E. 354–430) was born in the Numidian town of Thagaste. He lived in North Africa and Italy and died in Hippo as Vandals laid siege to that city. During his lifetime he witnessed the military chaos and social transformations of the western Roman Empire in decline. Prolific dogmatist that he was, Augustine made no small impact on the shifting consciousness of his age; as the author of numerous treatises and as a highly influential bishop, he helped shape the cultural and political traditions of late antiquity and the Middle Ages. His influence as a theologian, a philosopher of language, and an autobiographer is still felt in the present century (see LINGUISTICS AND LANGUAGE).

Augustine's personal history mirrors the ideological upheavals of his day, as his autobiographical *Confessions* attests. In that book he describes his upbringing by a militantly Christian mother, his education in the Latin classics, his youthful errancy, and his conversion to Christianity at the age of 32. He details the phases of his training and professional life as a rhetorician—phases marked by flirtations with Ciceronian Stoicism, Manicheism, and Neoplatonism (see CLASSICAL THEORY AND CRITICISM: 2. RHETORIC). He later rejected each of these philosophical positions, together with his career as a rhetorician, which he deemed an inappropriate use of his intellect and his human capacity for language. After his conversion he redirected his rhetorical skills and flair for debate toward the challenges of biblical exegesis and toward the eradication of rival interpretations of Scripture and Christian practice, views that he tended to construe as heretical.

Ever one to separate the sheep from the goats, Augustine distinguished between two societies, the heavenly and earthly, in his *City of God (De civitate dei),* a work of monumental importance to the theology and political thought of the Middle Ages, the Renaissance, and the Reformation. Members of the City of God are pilgrims on earth, where they find themselves among the vain and idolatrous denizens of the earthly city. In this comprehensive attack on pagan culture, Augustine sets forth an austere predestinarian theology, in which, according to the inscrutable will of God, some individuals are saved and others damned (15.1). Not surprisingly, Augustine's theory of the two cities was adapted frequently by rulers, theologians, and intellectuals over the next millennium in order to justify various political enterprises.

Another view promulgated by the *City of God* and other of Augustine's works was the condemnation of secular writing, particularly poetic and theatrical representations, which he called *fabula* (6.5). Since such *fabula,* or fictions, consist of falsehoods—concerning, for example, the immoral exploits of the pagan gods—Augustine advised that Christians eschew them completely. This view of poetic fiction as false and therefore problematic or dangerous remained influential in Western culture for the next thousand years.

Despite his attacks on secular poetry, Augustine remained in many ways a theoretician of rhetoric and of language. Of particular interest to contemporary literary critics is his theory of signs, the foundation of medieval semiology and the precursor to many modern debates on language and SEMIOTICS. In the *Confessions,* Augustinian epistemology—how one knows and experiences God, the ultimate reality—is thoroughly bound up with questions of language—how ineffable theological mysteries can be understood and articulated via the inadequate medium of human speech. Augustine imagines an abyss between a timeless, transcendent realm of God and the fallen, contingent world of humankind, yet that abyss is bridged, he writes, by Christ, the Word made flesh (10.43, 11.29). Interestingly, Augustine's solution to the problem of knowing God is specifically a linguistic one, insofar as the logos, the creative word of God incarnated in the historical presence of Christ, renders the will and power of God at least partly intelligible to the temporal world. Nevertheless, Augustine yearns for a transverbal future in the next life, when humankind will finally know God without the mediation of language, "not in part, not darkly, not through a glass, but wholly, clearly, and face to face" ("non ex parte, non in aenigmate, non per speculum, sed ex toto, in manifestatione, facie ad faciem" [12.13]).

In *On Christian Doctrine (De doctrina christiana),* a handbook demonstrating the procedures for the proper extraction and dissemination of biblical meaning, Augustine asserts that the chief requirement for the interpretation of Scripture is a divinely inspired charity, or Christian love, on the part of the reader (1.40.44, 2.7.10). Charity does not render the meanings of Scripture wholly transparent, however. The act of reading evokes the predicament of postlapsarian humankind continually confronted with linguistic ambiguity. Such ambiguity arises in part from the nature of signs *(signa),* often unknown or obscure, but necessarily pointing toward something beyond themselves and demanding interpretation. Augustine says that signs can be natural (unintentional signs such as smoke, indicating fire) or conventional (intentional signs, including language, that humans and animals use to communicate).

Scriptural signs, belonging to the second category, are either literal *(signa propria)* or figurative *(signa translata)*. *Signa propria* are words that convey literally, while *signa translata* would include persons or situations with a symbolic content (for example, the biblical story of Abraham and Isaac represents an Old Testament historical event, as well as the passion of Christ). PHILOLOGY, the "knowledge of languages" *(linguarum notitia),* helps clarify the former; and history and other sciences, the "knowledge of things" *(rerum notitia),* the latter. With these forms of knowledge, along with charity, the reader can partially cross the divide separating the binary categories of reality—words and things, the figural and the literal, the temporal and the eternal. Augustine's hermeneutics, dependent on divine charity, aims at reverence more than mastery. It draws, he says, "the kernels from the husk" (3.12.18), thereby providing an accurate though necessarily incomplete understanding of scriptural truth.

In *On the Teacher (De magistro),* a dialogue between Augustine and his son Adeodatus on language and teaching, Augustine further elaborates the connections between his semiotics and his Christology. In a discussion of scriptural interpretation, Augustine contends that signs do not in themselves provide knowledge but rather the occasion for remembering what one already knows. The degree of one's illumination depends on Christ, the interior teacher, whose interventions make possible such remembrance or sometimes, in the case of the unbeliever, a new, rather than remembered, knowledge of God.

Augustine's writings about language include two other influential treatises: *On Dialectic (De dialectica),* in part an analysis of language and intentionality, which relegates linguistic ambiguity not to words themselves but to the varying and multiple intentions of their users; and *On the Trinity (De trinitate),* where Augustine compares his epistemology to the figure *aenigma,* that hybrid of simile and riddle. By studying *aenigmata* such as the human soul, which in its own structure mirrors the Trinitarian form of the divinity, one can gain a valid though admittedly partial understanding of the nature of God.

Augustine's thought is of considerable relevance to twentieth-century critical theory, if only because his works insist that epistemology cannot be separated from a theory of language. Augustine's writings also suggest that the notion of the instability or inadequacy of the linguistic sign is by no means a modern one. Augustine stresses that the knowledge of nonsensible realities is always problematic and approximate at best, though he argues that the human predicament of unknowing will be overcome in the next life, where the saved can encounter God/Truth "face to face."

The conflicts between Augustinian thought and contemporary theory should not be underestimated, however. Various poststructuralist schools—DECONSTRUCTION, feminisms, and Marxisms, for example—would tend to view Augustine's work as a *locus classicus* of the metaphysics of presence, within which notions of logocentrism, patriarchal privilege, and class difference are exalted. Yet the angst-ridden Augustine of the *Confessions,* the Augustine who insists on reading *per speculum in aenigmate,* through a glass darkly, remains for many a prototype of modern critical consciousness.

Dolora Wojciehowski

St. Augustine, *City of God* (trans. Gerald G. Walsh, 1958), *Confessions* (trans. R. S. Pine-Coffin, 1961), *Of True Religion* (trans. J. H. S. Burleigh, 1959), *On Christian Doctrine* (trans. D. W. Robertson, Jr., 1958), *Sancti Aurelii Augustini . . . opera omnia, Patrologiae cursus completus series latina,* vols. 32–46 (ed. J. P. Migne, 1841–42), *The Teacher; The Free Choice of the Will; Grace and Free Will* (trans. Robert Russell, 1968), *The Trinity* (trans. Stephen McKenna, 1963), *Works,* vols. 1–8, *A Select Library of Nicene and Post-Nicene Fathers* (1st ser., 1886).

Roy Battenhouse, ed., *A Companion to the Study of St. Augustine* (1955); Peter Brown, *Augustine of Hippo: A Biography* (1967); Kenneth Burke, *The Rhetoric of Religion: Studies in Logology* (1961); Marcia Colish, *The Mirror of Language: A Study in the Medieval Theory of Knowledge* (1968, rev. ed., 1983); Pierre-Paul Courcelle, *Recherches sur les Confessions de Saint Augustin* (1950, 2d ed., 1968); Margaret Ferguson, "Saint Augustine's Region of Unlikeness: The Crossing of Exile and Language," *Georgia Review* 29 (1975); Geoffrey Galt Harpham, "The Fertile World: Augustine's Ascetics of Interpretation," *Criticism* 28 (1986); Richard McKeon, "Rhetoric in the Middle Ages," *Speculum* 17 (1942); R. A. Markus, *Augustine: A Collection of Critical Essays* (1972); Joseph Mazzeo, "St. Augustine's Rhetoric of Silence: Truth vs. Eloquence and Things vs. Signs," *Renaissance and Seventeenth-Century Studies* (1964); James O'Donnell, *St. Augustine* (1985); Elaine Pagels, *Adam, Eve, and the Serpent* (1988); Armand Strubel, " 'Allegoria in factis' et 'Allegoria in verbis,' " *Poétique* 23 (1975); Tzvetan Todorov, *Théories du symbole* (1977, *Theories of the Symbol,* trans. Catherine Porter, 1982); Eugene Vance, *Marvelous Signals: Poetics and Sign Theory in the Middle Ages* (1986).

AUSTRALIAN THEORY AND CRITICISM

Australia has produced no single critic or theorist of international stature, nor has it developed a distinct school of criticism or theory. In the past, Australian readers generally looked to international critics for commentary on literature from abroad and for critical theory. This is not to say that Australians neglected to write about literature; they wrote mainly about British and classical literature until after World War II, when books from the United States, South America, and Europe became more accessible. At that time the audience for homegrown work was limited, considering the scarcity of Australian-based journals and the fact that most Australians would rather read an overseas critic. Since 1945 the situation has changed as the nation has moved toward establishing its own cultural identity. Yet current Australian criticism on European and American writing tends to be imitative. The poet-critic Chris Wallace-Crabbe (b. 1934) observed, in an essay he ironically titled "Among the Front Runners," that Australian intellectuals have always considered themselves isolated, not "front runners," for they have long believed—and still do to an extent—that "new ideas are being worried into shape elsewhere and are only slowly filtering through" to their remote country (55).

Admitting to Australia's relative marginalization in the international picture, this discussion will focus for the most part on criticism of the national literature. I will also examine briefly the development of criticism on writing in English from countries other than Great Britain and the United States. In both areas the critics have had no authorities to imitate, no fixed canon to revere, no tradition to honor.

The pioneer figures in criticism on Australian literature were not academics, for only in the late 1950s did the country's literature finally gain reluctant admission into the universities. Throughout the nineteenth century and well into the twentieth, critical writing considered worthy of the academy addressed literature from overseas, for the professors, many of them born and trained in Great Britain, held Australian writing in contempt and branded those interested in it as second-rate. Journalists in many cases, sometimes poets, novelists, or playwrights—these were the early critics who took seriously a national literature that most Australians either ignored or considered inferior, even though it started to flourish not many years after the first European settlement in 1788.

This fragile critical tradition was initiated in 1856 when Frederick Sinnett (1830–66) published in the *Journal of Australasia* what literary historians consider the first critical essay on Australian literature. Calling his article "The Fiction Fields of Australia," Sinnett addresses the question that has long prevailed: How Australian should the literature be? Sinnett commented that too often the fiction resembled travel accounts, and he proposed that it move to more universal concerns. By the end of the century, though, the nationalism that Sinnett feared had come to dominate. The writers and critics of the late 1800s envisioned a literature distinguished by its Australianness. Such cultural chauvinism found a voice in the *Bulletin,* established in 1880 and long a prime determiner of the course the national literature was to take. The newspaper's literary "red page" promoted writing by and for Australians about Australian life, especially life lived in the bush, and eschewed what the editors considered "internationalism."

Ironically, it was a critic from the United States, C. Hartley Grattan (1902–80), who placed Australian writing within a world context when he published "Australian Literature" in a 1927 issue of an American journal, the *Bookman;* a year later the slightly revised essay appeared as a University of Washington chapbook. Grattan's evaluation remains an important work in a then scantily documented tradition. He saw much to praise but decried Australians' apathy toward their own literature. For the next 50 years Grattan maintained his interest in Australian writing, continued to write about it, formed friendships with writers, and promoted their books abroad.

Two other important figures during this pre–World War II period were Vance Palmer (1885-1959) and his wife Nettie (1885-1964). They called for a strong literary nationalism that would return to the values of the 1890s, that is, the revelation of national consciousness through literature. The Palmers and their circle considered the work of writers such as Henry Lawson, Joseph Furphy, and Bernard O'Dowd as the true expression of the Australian spirit and the Arnoldian touchstone for all Australian writing. In novels, plays, and poetry, adherents to the Palmer school attempted to put this theory into practice; but their work, both critical and creative, has generally fallen into obscurity. John Barnes concludes in his 1979 article "The Time was Never Ripe" that the aspirations of the Palmers and their group faded as Australian literature evolved into something vastly different from what they had envisioned. Since her death, however, Nettie Palmer has been rescued from oblivion, her work reissued and reconsidered as more forward-looking than it was originally thought to be.

The late 1930s produced another kind of literary nationalism when a critical school called the Jindyworobaks emerged. Taking their name from an Aboriginal word meaning "to annex" or "to join," the Jindyworobaks were inspired in part by P. R. Stephenson's *Foundation of Culture in Australia* (1936), which called for a distinctively Australian art that would draw from the spirit of the land. The movement's leader, Rex Ingamells (1913–55), expressed the goal in his manifesto, *Conditional Culture* (1938), to set Australian art free from "alien influences" (37). Supposedly embracing Aboriginal culture along with everything else truly Australian, the Anglo-Celtic Jindyworobaks wrote poetry for the most part and regularly published anthologies. By the early 1950s the movement had run its course, especially in face of the "alien influences" that were not only steadily encroaching but also finding a receptive audience.

Strident opposition to such cultural isolationism became the battle cry of a journal called *Angry Penguins,* published from 1940 to 1946. Edited by John Reed (1901–81) and Max Harris (b. 1921), this short-lived publication paraded its modernism and internationalism. Attempting to connect Australian writers to their European counterparts, namely, those in the modernist movement, *Angry Penguins* fell into disgrace when it published poems purportedly written by Ern Malley, represented as an insurance salesman and mechanic who had just died. Although they were thought to have been contributed by Malley's sister, the poems in truth were a hoax, written and submitted by two Australian poets, James McAuley (1917–76) and Harold Stewart (b. 1916), who had set out to undermine *Angry Penguins* because they believed that modernist writing had no place in the Australian tradition.

Australian literary historians, who have written extensively about the "Ern Malley Affair," argue that it blighted the literature's development at an important juncture. The latter-day observers see the literary scandal—so bizarre that it brought Australian criticism its first overseas attention—as an embarrassment to the internationalists and a triumph for the traditionalists. In the long run, though, the victory had a hollow ring, for Australian history was plotting against cultural isolationism. Even during the two decades before World War II, Australia had started to emerge from its physical and cultural cocoon; after 1945 it moved swiftly away from a colonial past into a surer, more independent future that would affect all aspects of Australian culture, including criticism.

One critical work that marks this change is A. A. Phillips's (1900–1985) essay "The Cultural Cringe," published in a 1950 issue of the arts journal *Meanjin.* Calling for neither a national nor an international literature, Phillips simply urges Australians not to draw comparisons when reading their own literature by unconsciously asking what a cultivated English reader would think of it. He proposes that this "cringe" cripples the writer because it affects the Australian reader's responsiveness and therefore hampers critical judgment.

Was the critical stance that Australian literature must concern itself only with Australianness—so firmly taken by the *Bulletin* editors, revived by the Palmer group, reinforced in another way by the Jindyworobaks, then promoted by the Ern Malley tricksters—an undetected "cultural cringe"? Was the literature unsuited for the international arena? Should it be protected? Must it remain forever at home, concerned solely with things Australian? Would it ever meet the approval of the imaginary English reader? It can be conjectured that Phillips's essay on the "cringe" served as a watershed in this critical dilemma. He may well have defined the unspoken fear of interiority thus far held by both writers and critics. So the question how Australian the literature should be became largely irrelevant. To a great extent, though, the writers and not the critics led this revolution. By the 1960s the writers no longer felt compelled to "Write Australian," as novelist Michael Wilding (b. 1942) titled a 1971 article. Another author, Murray Bail (b. 1941), noted in the introduction to *The Faber Book of Contemporary Australian Short Stories* (1988) that Australian writers have forgotten about "place" in favor of "intellectual, emotional, stylistic" concerns (xvii).

Still, as most of the writers and some critics accepted this altered view, others in the Australian literary-critical establishment longed for the past. A notable example of the traditionalists' refusal either to understand or to accept what was astir occurred when many of them rejected, even ridiculed, the work of Patrick White (1912–90) during the 1950s and 1960s, while he received acclaim abroad and was to be awarded the Nobel prize in 1973. Though not all critics at home found White's modernist novels offensively un-Australian, many saw his metaphysical use of Australian materials and his fictional forays abroad as a threat to the realist tradition they admired and considered superior. Even today White's work is not universally accepted in Australian critical circles. Another internationally recognized Australian novelist, Christina Stead (1902–83), had been largely ignored as well; after all, she rarely set her fiction in Australia. The Nobel Academy's recognition of an Australian writer and Stead's belated but overwhelming success abroad showed that Australian literature could be judged first-rate by world standards. It need no longer be protected. And banished was the English reader whose approval had been sought.

By the late 1960s most critics were catching up with their writers. An important step toward this recognition had already taken place in 1940, when a journal of the arts, *Meanjin,* started publication. Although not focusing entirely on Australian writing, *Meanjin* tirelessly promoted the national literature—sometimes it must have seemed in vain—by publishing both criticism and creative work by Australians; its diligence certainly has been and continues to be invaluable to the development of Australian critical studies. Another important journal was founded in 1963, *Australian Literary Studies,* the first scholarly journal devoted exclusively to Australian literature; still in publication, it now has an international circulation. By this time Australian literature courses were well established in the universities. In 1977 the Association for the Study of Australian Literature was organized; it consists primarily of academics involved in the teaching of Australian literature, but its membership includes journalistic critics, writers, publishers, editors, and overseas scholars as well. In 1973 the Literature Board, an arm of the government's Australia Council, was formed to oversee funding of writers and critics, to promote Australian literature at home and abroad, and to subsidize publications, both creative and critical.

As Australia enters its third century of European settlement, its critical project matures. For one thing, while in the past most of the effort was directed toward Anglo-Celtic writing, critics are now attending to the literature of the Aborigines, who were on the land 40,000 years before the Europeans' arrival. They had developed a sophisticated oral literature, now supplemented by a written literature in English. And as Australia turns more multicultural in population and outlook, there is a developing critical awareness of a heretofore almost invisible body of immigrant writing. Women writers and the way literature depicts women are also receiving lively critical attention. Thus, Australian literary history, like that of many countries, is in the process of being rewritten to include the work of what many consider minorities too long ignored or marginalized.

Other critics are approaching Australian literature as part of what once was called "Commonwealth literature," now more accurately termed "international writing in English." They are placing Australian writing, formerly considered an isolated appendage to British literature, into a world context. Some Australian literary scholars view this movement with suspicion, arguing that the nation's literature should be treated independently. The practitioners in this emergent field—generally called

"postcolonial discourse"—are a diverse group coming from the old Commonwealth countries as well as Europe and the United States. But one of the internationally recognized works to appear thus far on postcolonial discourse, *The Empire Writes Back* (1989), was written by three Australians. Possibly, then, Australian critics are at last making an international mark—not on their country's own literature but on the wealth of writing that has in common a colonial background.

Robert Ross

See also CANADIAN THEORY AND CRITICISM and POSTCOLONIAL CULTURAL STUDIES.

Antipodes (ed. Robert Ross, 1987–); Bill Ashcroft, Gareth Griffiths, and Helen Tiffin, *The Empire Writes Back: Theory and Practice in Post-Colonial Literatures* (1989); *Australian and New Zealand Studies in Canada* (ed. Thomas E. Tausky, 1989–); *Australian Literary Studies* (ed. L. T. Hergenhan, 1963–); John Barnes, "The Time Was Never Ripe: Some Reflections on Literary Nationalism," *Westerly* 4 (1979); John Barnes, ed., *The Writer in Australia* (1969); John Docker, *In a Critical Condition: Reading Australian Literature* (1984); R. D. FitzGerald, "Nationalism and Internationalism," *Southerly* 27 (1967); C. Hartley Grattan, "Australian Literature," *Bookman* 67 (1928, reprinted in *Antipodes* 2 [1988]); H. M. Green, *A History of Australian Literature* (2 vols., 1961, rev. ed., 1984); Laurie Hergenhan, ed., *The Penguin New Literary History of Australia* (1988); A. D. Hope, "A. D. Hope Reflects on the Advent of an Australian Literature," *London Review of Books* (September 4, 1986); Grahame Johnston, ed., *Australian Literary Criticism* (1962); Brian Kiernan, "Bibliographical Spectrum: What Is Australian Literature?" *Review of National Literatures* 11 (1982), *Criticism* (1974); Leonie Kramer, ed., *The Oxford History of Australian Literature* (1981); *Meanjin* (ed. Jenny Lee, 1940–); Patrick Morgan, "The Misuse of Australian Literature," *Quadrant* 11 (1967); A. A. Phillips, "The Cultural Cringe," *Meanjin* 9 (1950); Robert L. Ross, *Australian Literary Criticism—1945–1988: An Annotated Bibliography* (1989), "The Recurring Conflicts in Australian Literary Criticism since 1945," *Australian and New Zealand Studies in Canada* 1 (1989); Clement Semmler, ed., *Twentieth Century Australian Literary Criticism* (1967); Frederick Sinnett, "The Fiction Fields of Australia" (1856, Barnes, *The Writer in Australia*); Chris Wallace-Crabbe, "Among the Front Runners: Intellectuals and Australian Literature," *Melbourne or the Bush: Essays on Australian Literature and Society* (1974); *Westerly* (ed. Bruce Bennett, 1963–); Michael Wilding, "Write Australian," *Journal of Commonwealth Literature* 6 (1971).

BACON, FRANCIS

Francis Bacon (1561–1626) was neither a theorist nor a critic of literature, but literary theory, criticism, and history were within the purview of his assessment of the state of the arts and sciences in his time and of his project for their advancement. Because that assessment and project have been powerful in shaping the modern world, they have also crucially shaped the place of literature and the enterprises that study it. Bacon's remarks on poetry and the imagination are brief and scattered (see Levin for a summary), but they have been influential and controversial, and they remain pregnant with unexplored possibilities. Though he is perhaps best known in this context for deprecating poetry in favor of science or philosophy, he also projected an enterprise of literary history in the widest sense, located imagination in a crucial place between the faculties of reason and will, anticipated an aesthetic approach to poetry, appreciated poetry's special power to reveal the workings of the passions, and called for an art of critical judgment that arguably could be taken to anticipate postmodern criticism (see Gillespie). His influence on BEN JONSON, John Donne, John Milton, JOHN DRYDEN, Abraham Cowley, GIAMBATTISTA VICO, WILLIAM WORDSWORTH, SAMUEL TAYLOR COLERIDGE, PERCY BYSSHE SHELLEY, WILLIAM HAZLITT, John Keats, RALPH WALDO EMERSON, Walt Whitman, KARL MARX AND FRIEDRICH ENGELS, and Bertolt Brecht, among others, has been documented (see Sessions).

The tradition of Francis Bacon's works in twentieth-century Anglo-American literary theory and criticism, however, is not continuous. Although his *Advancement of Learning* figured among the texts published at the beginning of the century to give academic literary study a history and theory, the terms of the mid-century New Critical consensus relegated Bacon to the margins. In the New Critical hierarchical oppositions between literature and science, aesthesis and praxis, poetry and rhetoric, atemporality and history, intrinsic and extrinsic, unity and diversity, individual and social, Bacon was inevitably associated with the latter and lower terms.

The New Critical tradition and system codified, for example, by MURRAY KRIEGER in *Theory of Criticism* (1976) leaves Bacon out of account altogether and derives itself from Renaissance roots in SIR PHILIP SIDNEY's *Defence of Poetry*; this tradition prefers Sidney's epideictic exaltation of poetry over history and philosophy to Bacon's deliberative placements of poetry, literary history, and the art of critical judgment among the other arts and sciences he set out to appreciate and advance. (See NEW CRITICISM.)

In the 1970s and 1980s, challenges to and reversals of these New Critical priorities opened the way to rehabilitation of Bacon and renovation of his works. His innovation in Renaissance dialectic (Jardine), his restructuring of classical rhetoric (Cogan), and his enactment of a paradoxical modernity (Whitney) have received sympathetic and intelligent attention, but discussions of the implications of his work for literary criticism and theory were only beginning to go beyond earlier debates over whether Bacon was a friend or an enemy to poetry.

Among the topics still pregnant with unexplored implications for critical theory and practice is Bacon's definition of "literary history" as "a just story of learning, containing the antiquities and originals of knowledges, their sects, their inventions, their traditions, their diverse administrations and managings, their flourishings, their oppositions, decays, depressions, oblivions, removes, with the causes and occasions of them, and all other events concerning learning, throughout the ages of the world" (*Advancement* bk. 2, ch. 1, par. 2), a definition congenial to the growing interest in the institutional histories of academic disciplines and to the attempt to move beyond narrow aesthetic definitions of the "literary." Equally interesting is his omission of "literary philosophy" as a discipline parallel to literary history, as well as his decision not to call for a science concerned with imagination, coordinate with the extant sciences of the reason and the will. These disciplines, ghostly anticipations of modern literary theory and aesthetics, would have been logical developments of his terms but were not developed in part because Bacon imagined that poetry and imagination in his time required no additional cultivation or study. The subsequent triumph of the scientific project Bacon advocated may require moderns to revise his judgment that there is no "deficience" in our society's cultivation of poetry and imagination (*Advancement* bk. 2, ch. 4, par. 5) and to reevaluate his judgments of the human faculties most in need of cultivation and the cultural projects most in need of funding. But in reconsidering his map of the intellectual world and reevaluating his judgments of the relative cultivation of its various domains, they would be engaged in his practical and humane deliberations about the vitality of the arts and sciences and their serviceability to the ends of liberating all humanity from ignorance, want, and oppression, not just in a celebration of the superiority of poetic or literary knowing to all other kinds of knowledge.

Bacon's specific judgments, then, are open to challenge in the light of changes in the relative cultivation of the faculties and the relative dominance of some arts and sciences over others that his own enterprise has helped to bring about. Shelley, who greatly admired Bacon, recognized this and urged a cultivation of imagination at the expense of the overdeveloped calculating understanding *(Defence of Poetry),* whereas Bacon had urged the disciplining of both imagination and reason by historical attention to matters of fact. New Historicist critics may be returning to Bacon's sense of the urgency of such historical knowledge in the face of what they see as the overindulged imagination and impractical theoretical speculation that has characterized their critical predecessors (see NEW HISTORICISM).

The lapsed Baconian tradition in literary criticism and theory may be reviving on the Baconian premise that "the images of men's wits and knowledge remain in books, exempted from the wrong of time, and capable of perpetual renovation. Neither are they fitly to be called images, because they generate still, and cast their seeds in the minds of others, provoking and causing infinite actions and opinions in succeeding ages" (*Advancement* bk. 1, ch. 8, par. 6).

Don Bialostosky

Francis Bacon, *The Advancement of Learning* (1605, ed. G. W. Kitchin, 1973), *The Works of Francis Bacon* (7 vols., 1857–74, ed. James Spedding, R. L. Ellis, and D. D. Heath, 1968).

Marc Cogan, "Rhetoric and Action in Francis Bacon," *Philosophy and Rhetoric* 14 (1981); Gerald Gillespie, "Scientific Discourse and Postmodernity: Francis Bacon and the Empirical Birth of 'Revision,'" *Boundary 2* 7 (1979); D. G. James, *The Dream of Learning* (1951); Thomas Jameson, *Francis Bacon: Criticism and the Modern World* (1954); Lisa Jardine, *Francis Bacon: Discovery and the Arts of Discourse* (1974); Harry Levin, "Bacon's Poetics," *Renaissance Rereadings: Intertext and Context* (ed. Maryanne Cline Horowitz, Anne J. Cruz, and Wendy A. Furman, 1988); Timothy J. Reiss, *The Discourse of Modernism* (1982); Paolo Rossi, "Baconianism," *Dictionary of the History of Ideas,* vol. 1 (1973); William A. Sessions, "Recent Studies in Francis Bacon," *English Literary Renaissance* 3 (1987); Brian Vickers, *Essential Articles for the Study of Francis Bacon* (1968), *Francis Bacon* (1978); Charles Whitney, *Francis Bacon and Modernity* (1986).

BAKHTIN, M. M.

Mikhail Mikhailovich Bakhtin (1895–1975) was arguably the most original and yet the most misunderstood Russian thinker of the twentieth century. By Soviet standards, his life was not especially eventful. He earned a degree in classics (a lifelong interest) and PHILOLOGY at Petrograd University (1913–18). To avoid the hardships of the Russian Civil War, he moved to Nevel and later to Vitebsk, where his study circle included Valentin Voloshinov and Pavel Medvedev. There he married, and the couple returned to Leningrad in 1924. Afflicted by a bone disease, and lacking proper political credentials, he was unable to find stable employment. In 1929 he was arrested, apparently for alleged participation in the underground Russian Orthodox church, and sentenced to 10 years in the Solovetsky Islands camp (tantamount to a death sentence). He managed to get the sentence commuted to six years' internal exile in Kazakhstan, where he worked as a collective farm bookkeeper and at other odd jobs.

Bakhtin's first professional appointment came in 1936 when he was hired by the Mordovia State Teachers College in Saransk to teach Russian and world literature. But rumors of the purges led him to resign and seek the safety of still greater obscurity in an even less visible town, where he remained until he returned to teach at Saransk after World War II. His obscurity was such that when interest in his work revived in the 1950s, his admirers were amazed to discover that he was still alive. A miraculous survivor from the 1920s, he became a cult figure. He was allowed to revise and expand the only major work of his to have been published, his book on Dostoevsky (1929), in 1963 and to publish his book on Rabelais in 1965. In 1975 and 1979 large collections of his writings from various periods appeared in Russian; his important essay "Toward a Philosophy of the Act" was published in 1986. Because Bakhtin's executors, who control his archives, have not been especially informative, it is impossible to be sure what the archives still contain.

Reception of Bakhtin's writings in both Russia and the West has been unusually complicated and politicized, thus impeding an understanding of his work. In the Soviet Union, the cult of Bakhtin led to strained attempts (in which the executors have participated) to recruit him as an ally in various intellectual battles. In the United States, the first book to attract attention was *Rabelais and His World,* which is the least representative of his thought as a whole but which became the glass through which subsequently translated writings were read. Although he was a severe critic of formalism and STRUCTURALISM, Jakobsonians claimed him without qualification for their camp (see ROMAN JAKOBSON and RUSSIAN FORMALISM); despite his withering comments on Marxism, Marxists have done the same (see MARXIST THEORY AND CRITICISM); poststructuralists seeking to appropriate him have also tended to overlook those passages where Bakhtin seems to be most unsympathetic with such an ethos. The attempt to see him as an essentially religious thinker, as some Slavists and others have proposed, has some basis but has probably been exaggerated.

Perhaps the most hotly argued question concerns the "disputed texts." In 1970 the Soviet semiotician Vyacheslav Ivanov declared that the principal works of Voloshinov and Medvedev had in fact been written by Bakhtin. The works in question included articles and three books, Voloshinov's *Marxism and the Philosophy of Language* and *Freudianism: A Critical Sketch* and Medvedev's *The Formal Method in Literary Scholarship.* Ivanov offered no evidence to substantiate his assertions. The Soviet copyright agency, VAAP, prepared a document asserting that Bakhtin was the author, but Bakhtin refused to sign it. The issue was further complicated by the usual politics; by a kind of "biographical imperialism" on the part of Bakhtin's admirers; and by the fact that works by Bakhtin could now be published in the Soviet Union, whereas works by Voloshinov and Medvedev, who had not been rehabilitated, could not, thus making it advantageous to attribute their works to him. Bakhtin remained silent on the question. The evidence for his authorship has consisted largely of highly ambiguous anecdotes. 'Glasnost' has not changed that situation.

In the West, the issue became entangled with the question of "Bakhtin and Marxism" inasmuch as Voloshinov's and Medvedev's works are avowedly Marxist.

Some who argued for Bakhtin's authorship concluded that the Marxism of the Voloshinov and Medvedev books was mere window dressing, others that Bakhtin must have been a Marxist. The authors of the present article first assumed Bakhtin's authorship but later switched sides. We believe (1) that the disputed texts were written by Voloshinov and Medvedev; (2) that the Marxism of the books is not window dressing but sincere, as well as highly sophisticated; (3) that Voloshinov and Medvedev produced what might be called "monologizations" of Bakhtin's ideas; and (4) that Bakhtin was himself influenced by these monologizations and Marxifications. His work had previously lacked a significant sociological dimension, and he responded to the challenge of his friends with his own non-Marxist sociology of literature, which is one of his most durable contributions to theory.

Despite his popularity, the ethos of Bakhtin's work is quite at odds with current American trends. One might look at his work as a series of models designed to show that creativity and ethical responsibility, his two most recurrent concerns, are meaningful and real. Beginning with his earliest writings, he attacks "theoretism"—the explanation of human behavior in terms of an abstract system of norms—as inevitably impoverishing the real complexity of life, as eliminating the meaningfulness of moral decisions, and as reducing creativity to mere discovery. He was hostile to all "instantiation" models—Saussurean, formalist, structuralist, Freudian, Marxist, or in principle any other—which understand particular acts *(parole)* as mere instantiations of timeless norms *(langue)* (see SIGMUND FREUD, PSYCHOANALYTIC THEORY AND CRITICISM, and FERDINAND DE SAUSSURE). Such models think away "the eventness" of events and lead to an underappreciation of the richness of daily life and particular actions. He insisted that relativism has the same effects; thus, he continually opposed the assumption, so common in modern thought, that knowledge to be real must be a system capable in principle of explaining anything. Relativists accept this view of knowledge but simply deny that such firmly grounded systems are possible. Bakhtin felt that such systems were unnecessary and turned instead to a rich understanding of the complex forms of everyday social life.

Three global concepts reappear in Bakhtin's various attempts to approach his recurrent concerns. In various formulations and combinations, these global concepts inform most of his work. One, for which the term "prosaics" might be used, involves both a view of the world and an approach to literature. As a view of the world, prosaics is suspicious of explanatory systems (of theoretism); it also suggests that the most important events in life are not the grand, dramatic, or catastrophic but the apparently small and prosaic ones of everyday life. When these ideas are important to Bakhtin, they contribute to his many insights about the value of tradition and lend a strong antirevolutionary aura to his writing. As developed in "Discourse in the Novel" (in *Dialogic Imagination*) and other writings, prosaics (as opposed to poetics) is an approach to novels and related forms of prose that takes them on their own terms. Since the ethos of novels is a prosaic world-view, the two senses of prosaics are closely connected.

Bakhtin strongly believed that criticism of novels in terms borrowed from poetics tends to miss just what is most distinctive about them. For example, the richness of poetic language (the trope) is essentially different from that of the novel (dialogized heteroglossia). Other constituent features of novels, such as their special sense of temporality and psychology, have also been missed because they were approached in terms set by poetics.

Bakhtin used the term "unfinalizability" for his second global concept. The best-known formulation of it occurs in his Dostoevsky book: "Nothing conclusive has yet taken place in the world, the ultimate word of the world and about the world has not yet been spoken, the world is open and free, everything is still in the future and will always be in the future" (*Problems* 166). It leads to a view of people as always making themselves and as always able to render untrue any "finalizing" definition. So long as they live, people have a "loophole." The recognition of each person's unfinalizability, the capacity for "surprisingness," is central to Bakhtin's ethics. He came to view the novel as the genre that understands people in just this correct way, for in the novel, no matter how many categories are applied to a character, whether physical, social, or even psychological, something is always left over—a "surplus of humanness" (*Dialogic* 37). Unrealized "potential" makes one human. Part of Bakhtin's hostility to the tenor of modern psychology—Freud, Pavlov—derives from its lack of appreciation of this surplus. That, according to Bakhtin, was what Dostoevsky meant by his startling assertion that he was not a psychologist (*Problems* 60).

Dialogue is Bakhtin's third global concept. The term has many meanings in his work. As a global concept, it refers to a concept of "truth" as a conversation rather than a series of propositions. Whereas some truths are monologic—i.e., they can be stated by a single person and in a single voice—others require at least two interacting consciousnesses and are therefore essentially dialogic in nature. Dialectics is supremely monologic and

must not be confused with dialogue: "Dialogue and dialectics. Take a dialogue and remove the voices (the partitioning of voices), remove the intonations (emotional and individualizing ones), carve out abstract concepts and judgments from living words and responses, [then] cram everything into one abstract consciousness—and that's how you get dialectics" (*Speech* 147).

When applied to language, "dialogue" has at least two principal meanings. First, it indicates that language is essentially a matter of utterances rather than of sentences; and utterances are by their nature dialogic in that listeners (or readers), real and potential, shape the utterance from the outset. In this sense, all language is dialogic; there are no monologic utterances. But a second sense of "dialogic language" does allow for monologic utterances. Some (but not all) speech and writing makes the foregrounding of interacting voices the essential "task."

These global concepts interact variously in Bakhtin's works of different periods. In his earliest studies, he had not yet discovered the importance of language as a problem, nor had he singled out the novel as the most important literary genre. Written in a Kantian or neo-Kantian vein, these works—"Art and Responsibility," "Author and Hero" (both in *Art and Answerability*), and "Toward a Philosophy of the Act"—explore the relation of self to other and of aesthetics to ethics. Each person, Bakhtin argues, enjoys a "surplus of vision" with respect to each other person; I can see things about you (the sky that frames you, the way you look when you are not self-conscious) that you cannot see about yourself, and you have the same surplus with respect to me. I can form a finalizing image of you, which you then incorporate into your sense of self but which you experience from within, that is, as something you can interrogate and overcome. These writings are characterized by remarkably perceptive passages on the phenomenology of dreams and fantasy, on the sense of experience from within and from without, and on mirrors and self-image, as well as by a strong argument that theoretism is inadequate for understanding ethics, which can never be reduced to a set of rules.

Bakhtin's critique of Russian formalism in his 1924 essay "The Problem of Content" (in *Art and Answerability*) marks the transition to his second period. *Problems of Dostoevsky's Poetics* contains two main lines of argument, one concerning Bakhtin's theory of "polyphony" and the other outlining his dialogic approach to language. "Polyphony" refers to a form of writing, which he claims Dostoevsky invented, that establishes a new relation of author to hero. Bakhtin had earlier believed that authors necessarily enjoy an "essential surplus" of vision with respect to their heroes (*Problems* 73). Indeed, not only do they have the same sort of surplus we have with respect to each other but they know in advance other essential information inaccessible to the hero, for example, his or her experiences later in life. The author knows, as no person knows about him- or herself, the whole sweep of the hero's life. And what this means is that even authors who want to write novels demonstrating human freedom are implicitly contradicted by the very form in which they write. Dostoevsky found a way to overcome this obstacle, to write about free people who are really represented as free. To do so, he had to surrender his essential surplus of vision and place himself on the same level as his heroes, which is to say, to know about them at any given moment no more than would be possible for the heroes themselves (or other characters) to know. This surrender of knowledge makes it possible for the author to argue with his heroes as equals, and in fact Dostoevsky's own ideological views often lose out in these arguments. What is most important, polyphonic authors write in such a way that the characters may surprise them. Of course, many authors find that their characters behave in unanticipated ways, but such surprise is accidental to their design and may be concealed in a later draft. Such surprise is essential to polyphony, which would not be polyphony without it. Polyphony, in short, is a theory of the creative process. It is also a theory of ethics, because it treats people as truly unfinalizable.

In outlining his dialogic approach to language, Bakhtin places the greatest emphasis on utterances in which two voices are meant to be heard as interacting, what Bakhtin calls "double-voiced words." Here he outlines a theory of stylization (the two voices are felt to be in agreement) and parody (the voices are felt to be in disagreement); it is important to recognize that for Bakhtin agreement is as much a dialogic relation as disagreement. Both of these types of double-voicing are passive, because the second voice we detect (e.g., the parodic target) is not felt to be resisting the impulse of the first voice. But such resistance is present in other utterances, which are Bakhtin's main concern. He describes numerous types of "active double-voiced words," most notably his discussion of "the word with a loophole," which incorporates from within an assertion, the provocation of its denial, and a hostile reaction to that denial, potentially infinitely.

Bakhtin's third period, which extends from the 1930s to the 1950s, introduces new concerns into his work, including the sociology of culture, the theory of genres,

and the prosaic approach to the novel. He pursued two distinct lines of thought during these years, and so we distinguish a period 3A from a period 3B. On the one hand, he combined his three global concepts, his concerns with ethics and creativity, and his new interest in sociology and the novel to produce what appear to be his most durable contributions: "Discourse in the Novel," "Forms of Time and of the Chronotope in the Novel," and "From the Prehistory of Novelistic Discourse" (all in *Dialogic*). There was also his book on Goethe (*The Bildungsroman and Its Significance in the History of Realism*), of which only a few tantalizing drafts or fragments remain (period 3A; in *Speech*). On the other hand, he played with the possibility of taking one global concept—unfinalizability—to an extreme, at which point he would jettison the other two (period 3B).

The 3A writings develop a theory of genre, which Bakhtin extended in his fourth period. Initially under Medvedev's influence, he described genres neither as sets of conventions nor as hierarchies of devices but as ways of seeing the world. These habits of vision have accumulated over centuries and represented a sort of sedimented wisdom, "congealed" experience in interpreting and evaluating the world. Each is characterized by a "form-shaping ideology"; for example, the form-shaping ideology of polyphony is the "dialogic sense of truth." Criticism can "transcribe" a genre's form-shaping ideology into propositional form, but such transcription, though helpful as a first step, nevertheless usually involves significant loss. Bakhtin contends that genres, as special forms of thinking, have often made the greatest contributions to human thought, which intellectual historians tend to overlook until (usually weaker) transcriptions appear in expository form.

Bakhtin's first approach to the novel (in "Discourse in the Novel" and "Prehistory") deals with its form-shaping ideology in terms of a special understanding of language that combines dialogue with a new concept, heteroglossia. Language is said to be composed of countless *languages,* each the product of a particular kind of experience (e.g., of a profession, ethnic group, social class, generation, region) and each with its own way of understanding and evaluating the world (analogous to a genre). Again, it is not formal markers (dialects) but senses of experience that are important. We all participate in numerous "languages of heteroglossia," each of which claims a privileged view of a certain aspect of experience. But we all also experience the competition of these languages. We come to view one aspect of experience, which we are accustomed to treat in one "language," through the "eyes" of another. A little dialogue of world-views is set up: "dialogized heteroglossia." When this happens, it is no longer possible for languages to be "naive," that is, to presume that there is no other way for their usual realm of experience to be understood.

Novelistic language works by extending (developing the potentials of) dialogized heteroglossia and producing new and complex forms of dialogue among languages. In so doing, it creates a "Galilean" language consciousness (*Dialogic* 366), the sense that there are many "languages of truth" in unending dialogue with each other and with experience. Bakhtin also argues that consciousness is essentially novelistic in this way. That is, consciousness is inner speech, and inner speech is the orchestration of the dialogic, heteroglot voices that we have heard. Where a Freudian would subvert simplistic notions of consciousness through a model of the unconscious, Bakhtin (like Tolstoy, Vygotsky, and other Russian thinkers) turns instead to a much more complex view of consciousness according to which the contents of consciousness are essentially social, because inner speech is outer dialogues we have learned to perform in our heads.

In "Chronotope" and "Bildungsroman" Bakhtin also approached the novel in terms of its special sense of space (understood as social) and time (understood as historical), that is, in terms of its chronotope. Different genres imagine the relation of social context, history, individual agency, and ethical responsibility in different ways, which may never be explicitly articulated but which are embodied in their various "form-shaping ideologies." Thus, in several ancient genres that Bakhtin discusses, social context tends to be mere background, and selfhood is understood either as fixed or as developing along a predetermined path that context may obstruct or clear but not essentially shape. Bakhtin discusses the chronotopes of numerous genres throughout literary history. He sees the novelistic chronotope as closest to "real historical time" and Goethe as the one who made the crucial chronotopic discoveries that led to the novel. The novel views people, each with a surplus of humanness, constantly making themselves in surprising ways, and sees social context as actively (though not exhaustively) affecting that process of making. Or to put the point differently, in the novel both the individual and society undergo real (and unfinalizable) becoming. Each kind of becoming impinges on the other in an open prosaic dialogue.

The carnival writings of period 3B celebrate pure antinomianism, describe carnival as purely liberating, and redescribe the novel as the "carnivalized" genre, that is, as purely parodic. *Rabelais and His World* and the fram-

ing sections of "Epic and Novel" exemplify this line of thinking, which in its extreme form Bakhtin apparently considered a dead end and abandoned. (Writings on Rabelais, carnival, and Menippean satire from periods 3A and 4 are quite different in tone.)

In his final period, Bakhtin once again produced a synthesis of his three global concepts, deepened his theories of language and genre, returned to ethical and broadly philosophical themes of his first period, and extended his ideas to the humanities generally. To this period belong the greatly revised edition of the Dostoevsky book (with its new and lengthy fourth chapter on Menippean satire and "genre memory"), his notes "Toward a Reworking of the Dostoevsky Book" (translated as an appendix to *Problems of Dostoevsky's Poetics*), and several short essays or sets of notes, including "Response to a Question from the *Novy Mir* Editorial Staff," "The Problem of Speech Genres," "The Problem of the Text," "From Notes Made in 1970–71," and "Toward a Methodology for the Human Sciences" (all in *Speech*). Perhaps most notable is his theory of interpretation (see esp. "Response to a Question"), which is strikingly at odds with current American theory. Bakhtin distinguishes three broad types of interpretation. In "enclosure within the epoch," the interpreter tries, as far as possible, to see the world in terms set by the other period or culture. The benefit is that the interpreter comes to appreciate another view of the world; nonetheless, the interpreter does nothing significant with that appreciation. Still worse is "modernization and distortion": interpreters simply read into the text the concerns and values of their own epoch, which are assumed to be especially wise or privileged. Here we see how Bakhtin differs both from those modern theorists who assume that this interpretation is the only one and from those who pillage other cultures only for those themes useful for debates set by current American politics. Bakhtin would have viewed such exercises as the cultivation of a purely spurious otherness. Both "enclosure within the epoch" and "modernization and distortion" recognize only one side of a potential dialogue. But the best approach, "creative understanding," recognizes the otherness of the other without giving up one's own "outsideness"; one creates a special sort of dialogue with the other. As in all true dialogues, the result is likely to be the creation of insights that neither side had separately; in other words, each side realizes the "potentials" of the other in a way neither could have foreseen. The concept of potential, an especially important one for Bakhtin, also allowed him to rethink the concept of intentionality, for works may contain potentials put there by the author, who may realize their richness but may not comprehend specific insights to which they might lead. The theory also contains a theory of literary value according to which works really are, in an important sense, intrinsically great: great works contain great potential. It is perhaps in his last period that the radical difference between Bakhtin and many of his current admirers is most apparent.

Gary Saul Morson and Caryl Emerson

See also LINGUISTICS AND LANGUAGE and RUSSIAN FORMALISM.

M. M. Bakhtin, *Art and Answerability: Early Philosophical Essays* (ed. Michael Holquist and Vadim Liapunov, trans. Vadim Liapunov, 1990), *The Dialogic Imagination: Four Essays* (ed. Michael Holquist, trans. Caryl Emerson and Michael Holquist, 1981), *Estetika slovesnogo tvorchestva* [The aesthetics of verbal creation] (ed. S. G. Bocharov, 1979), "K filosofii postupka" [Toward a philosophy of the act], *Filosofiia i sotsiologiia nauki i tekhniki* (1986), Prefaces to Tolstoy, *Rethinking Bakhtin: Extensions and Challenges* (ed. Gary Saul Morson and Caryl Emerson), *Problems of Dostoevsky's Poetics* (1929, 2d ed., 1963, ed. and trans. Caryl Emerson, 1984), *Rabelais and His World* (1965 [wr. 1946], trans. Helene Iswolsky, 1968), *Speech Genres and Other Late Essays* (trans. Vern W. McGee, ed. Caryl Emerson and Michael Holquist, 1986), *Voprosy literatury i estetiki: Issledovaniia raznykh let* [Questions of literature and esthetics: research of various years] (1975); P. N. Medvedev, *The Formal Method in Literary Scholarship: A Critical Introduction to Sociological Poetics* (1928, trans. Albert J. Wehrle, 1978), *V laboratorii pisatelia* [In the writer's laboratory] (1971); V. Voloshinov, *Freudianism: A Critical Sketch* (1927, trans. I. R. Titunik, ed. I. R. Titunik and Neil H. Bruss, 1976), *Marksizm i filosofiia iazyka* (1929, *Marxism and the Philosophy of Language,* trans. Ladislav Matejka and I. R. Titunik, 1973).

Wayne C. Booth, Introduction to Bakhtin's *Problems;* Katerina Clark and Michael Holquist, *Mikhail Bakhtin* (1984); "Forum on Baxtin," *Slavic and East European Journal* 30 (Spring 1985); Michael Holquist, "The Politics of Representation," *Allegory and Representation* (ed. Stephen J. Greenblatt, 1982); Viach. Vs. Ivanov, "The Significance of M. M. Bakhtin's Ideas on Sign, Utterance, and Dialogue for Modern Semiotics," *Semiotics and Structuralism: Readings from the Soviet Union* (ed. Henryk Baran, 1976); Gary Saul Morson, ed., *Bakhtin: Essays and Dialogues on His Work* (1986); Gary Saul Morson and Caryl Emerson, *Mikhail Bakhtin: Creation of a Prosaics* (1990); Gary Saul Morson and Caryl Emerson, eds., *Rethinking Bakhtin: Extensions and Challenges* (1989); I. R. Titunik, "Baxtin &/or Volosinov &/or Medvedev: Dialogue &/or Doubletalk," *Language and Literary Theory* (ed. Benjamin A. Stolz, I. R. Titunik, and Lubomir Dolozel, 1984); Tzvetan Todorov, *Mikhail Bakhtine: Le Principe dialogique* (1981, *Mikhail Bakhtin: The Dialogical Principle,* trans. Wlad Godzich, 1984).

BARTHES, ROLAND

Roland Barthes (1915–80) and JEAN-PAUL SARTRE died within one month of each other, Barthes in March and Sartre in April 1980, and though they represent two different and conflicting generations of French intellectuals, their wide-ranging influence can be compared and, indeed, shown to overlap. Both Barthes and Sartre have fascinated wide audiences while constantly shifting in the theories they invented and propounded, and both have been "writers" in everything they published, even when they pretended to be producing pure theory. But whereas the philosopher Sartre's reputation, despite his obvious flaws, seems beyond dispute, Barthes, with his flippant dandyism, urbane skepticism, and epicurean sensibility, has run the risk of limiting his contribution to literary theory to that of a gifted dilettante writing in the tradition of Michel de Montaigne and André Gide; such is the picture offered to the American public by, for instance, SUSAN SONTAG, who pictures a virtuoso of the essay, one who should not be taken too seriously as a theoretician of literary studies. On the contrary, a retrospective overview would tend to stress, along with his finesse and versatility, the impressive depth and systematic consistency of a huge critical work that, to a great extent, has molded our contemporary understanding of textuality.

Whereas Sartre's entire *oeuvre* has been identified with the label "existentialism," Barthes was eager to promote his French brand of STRUCTURALISM for only a few years before he rejected most of its methodological assumptions. Such a label proves extremely misleading in Barthes's case because of its technical slant and its persistent blindness to diachrony. The first way to approach the logic of textuality at work in Barthes's writings is to get a clear idea of the various trends he found himself engaged in, and several periods can be distinguished. His numerous essays and books, written over 25 years from the 1950s to the 1970s (some published posthumously in the 1980s), have taught a whole generation "how to read" (to quote EZRA POUND) and have accompanied that generation through increasingly rapid changes in theory. Besides, even though he retained a set of favorite concepts, Barthes's own swiftness of mind rendered these concepts mobile and capable of important shifts in meaning; for example, the term "writing" underwent momentous modifications from *Writing Degree Zero* (1953, trans., 1967) to the last essays. Indeed, despite the sometimes willful variations, a systematic concern with "writing" has remained Barthes's most distinguished contribution to literary studies.

Of the four phases in Barthes's critical career that may be roughly sketched, the first corresponds to a meditation on History, always written with a capital *H*. This meditation takes a double form: an almost psychoanalytical analysis (in the Bachelardian mode) of the work of Jules Michelet, the great poet of history (*Michelet,* 1954, trans., 1987), which considerably anticipates a later concern for the body of language and the body of the author; and a systematic study of the concepts of language, style, and writing in *Writing Degree Zero.* As Barthes recalled his beginnings in his "Inaugural Lecture, Collège de France" (1978, trans., 1982), he started his career by combining the influences of Sartre, Bertolt Brecht, and FERDINAND DE SAUSSURE (*Barthes Reader* 471). In a way, *Writing Degree Zero* is a kind of answer to Sartre's *What Is Literature?* since it opposes to a Marxist analysis of committed literature the notion "writing." In Barthes's delineation, three instances are brought into play: language, the general code of signs never to be directly modified by literature; style, relevant to each writer as a kind of idiolect, determined by his or her private history, closer to his or her body than to the history of forms; and writing, which transcends individual styles and appears as both the locus of freedom, since different writers can opt for different writings, and the locus of social determinism, since a writing can be "bourgeois" or "revolutionary." Barthes here clears the ground for his subsequent research, which would be a history of writing, a history of literary language that is never reduced to the history of language or to the history of styles but instead explores the historicity of the signs of literature. The modern period, initiated by GUSTAVE FLAUBERT and Stéphane Mallarmé, has announced the end of classical writing; thereafter, literature has turned into a problematics of pure language. Hence, the concept of "writing degree zero," exemplified by writers such as Albert Camus or the novelists of the *nouveau roman:* an attempt to create a neutral literary style deprived of all traditional markers that heralds an encounter with language as such, while stressing the gap between language and the world.

Such a gap is not to be dialectically overcome, as in Sartre's analysis of content, for Barthes is primarily interested in literary form: literature is not communication, as phenomenology would have it, but language. Literature is a form-making activity, not just one particular case of social communication. This remains one of the fundamental tenets of Barthesian theory. It is from this standpoint that he engages in a systematic criticism of the illusions pertaining to the naturalization of form. When form is taken for content, History is reduced to Nature, production reverts to ideological consumption, and myth covers all facts with an illusory transparent gauze. This denial of History corresponds to the world of myth. Barthes's well-known "readings" of contemporary myths still follow in the path of Sartrean anger at the self-deluding tactics of contemporary ideology, but with a Brechtian edge: as in Brecht's epic theater, the critical outlook must create a distance from which the audience can judge and understand instead of passively identifying with people or events. Barthes's positing of such an active function for the reader immediately met with a fierce resistance from the academics. His provocative and at times offhand thematic treatment of Racine in *Racine* (1963, trans., 1964) sparked off a controversy with Raymond Picard that eventually turned into a replay of the seventeenth- and eighteenth-century Quarrel between the Ancients and the Moderns (see also *Criticism and Truth,* 1966, trans., 1987). By the end of the 1960s it was clear that the Moderns had won the day and had completely redefined the map of contemporary literary studies in France, even if the academics remained somewhat skeptical.

The originality of Barthes's approach is more clearly apparent in the second phase of his career, in which the main object of inquiry is the mythology of everyday life in the context of a general analysis of codes. This originality lies in the linking of Brecht's distanciation with the linguistic analysis of RUSSIAN FORMALISM and of ROMAN JAKOBSON, for if the gap between signifier and referent has a critical function—that of questioning evidences that are taken for granted and of destroying the habitual link we tend to establish between Nature and Culture— this gap is constitutive of poetic language as such. Literary language is intransitive; it functions in a realm of its own, independent of any reference to reality. Denotation is merely the lure whereby language attempts to hide the interplay of connotations that constitutes its codes.

> Denotation is not the first meaning, but pretends to be so; under this illusion, it is ultimately no more than *last* of the connotations (the one which seems both to establish and to close the reading), the superior myth by which the text pretends to return to the nature of language, to language as nature. (*S/Z* [trans.] 9)

This is a later summary of the whole drift of this period, characterized by multitudinous attempts to apply SEMI-OTICS to various fields (theater, advertisements, photography, film, fashion, media at large).

The second phase thus deploys a linguistic strategy in order to engage with the universe of signification, and in this second moment Barthes indeed appears as the founder of French semiology, even though he often deferentially quotes CLAUDE LÉVI-STRAUSS or Saussure. The first text to find immediate acclaim was *Mythologies* (1957, trans., 1972 and 1979), a witty exploration of contemporary idols and clichés in which Barthes's rigor and subtlety found their proper object, followed by a short theoretical introduction to semiology. Myth is defined as a "semiological system" in the fashion of Saussure, who had heralded the birth of semiology as the general science of signs. Myth is made up of the three Saussurean components—signifier, signified, and sign—but it is a secondary system in which what is a sign in the first system becomes a signifier. Hence, the scheme, later to be exploited for the analysis of fashion (115):

	1. Signifier	2. Signified	
Language	3. Sign		
	I. SIGNIFIER	II. SIGNIFIED	
MYTH	III. SIGN		

Language becomes the object of a metalanguage that connotation keeps redoubling. The arbitrary nature of the linguistic sign receives a purely cultural motivation in the mythological system. The polemic edge and the theoretical foundation attack the same distortion of faked motivation: Barthes finds himself "sickened" by the recourse to a "false nature" of language that condones all sorts of ideological exploitations: "This nausea is like the one I feel before the arts which refuse to choose between *physis* and *antiphysis,* using the first as an ideal and the second as an economy. Ethically, it is quite low to wish to play on these two levels at once" (126 n. 7). The bogey to destroy is always the irrepressible ghost of a naturalization of signs. In this battle, a scientific outlook never precludes the ethical position, and indeed it is no surprise to witness an increasing "ethical" preoccupation in Barthes's writings, even if the values he praises are not those of conventional morality.

Myth is the direct inversion of poetry: myth transforms a meaning into form, whereas poetry is a regressive semiological system that aims at reaching the meaning of things themselves. In such a general view, the former analysis of *Writing Degree Zero* had been only "a

mythology of literary language" that "defined writing as the signifier of literary myth" (*Mythologies* [trans.] 134), and "the subversion of writing was the radical act by which a number of writers have attempted to reject Literature as a mythical system" (135). This remained Barthes's basic motive when he approached the experimental writing of Philippe Sollers in *Writer Sollers* (1979, trans., 1987). Yet for a time Barthes also seemed to believe in the possibility of a science valid for all possible narratives, and he displayed his skill at adroit synthesis in "Introduction to the Structural Analysis of Narratives" (1966, trans. in *Image-Music-Text,* 1977), where he manages to combine the approaches of Algirdas Julien Greimas, Claude Bremond, Vladimir Propp, Jakobson, and Russian Formalism by distinguishing between the level of functions (such as "request," "aid," and "punishment" in the logic of the plot), the level of actions (characters are "actants" in a literary praxis that questions the status of subjectivity), and the level of narration (or discourse, implying a narrator and an addressee).

An even more systematic treatment of semiology is provided in the two essays *Elements of Semiology* (1964, trans., 1967) and *The Fashion System* (1967, trans., 1983): fashion, for instance, is treated not in the sociological mode one could have expected but instead as "written fashion," and the corpus is limited to the chronicles of a couple of women's magazines. Louis Hjelmslev, André Martinet, and N. S. Troubetskoy relay Saussure and Sartre to produce a vertiginous nesting of signifying systems (in which *E* stands for "plane of the expression" and *C,* "plane of the content") (*Fashion* 293):

4. The analyst's metalanguage	E	C			
3. Rhetorical system		E		C	
2. Terminological system		E	C		
1. Vestimentary code			E	C	

Nevertheless, the conclusion of the brilliant if rather heuristic analysis opens out onto a reiterated assertion of death: the eternal present of fashion rhetorics supposes a repression of its own futility, therefore of its death-haunted mutability, whereas "the semiologist is a man who expresses his future death in the very terms in which he has named and understood the world" (294).

Barthes's decision to focus on written or described fashion may correspond to a reversal of priorities. Whereas Saussure believed that linguistics was only a part of a wider science of signs (semiology), Barthes tends to think that semiology is only a part of the science of linguistics: human language is not merely a model, a pattern of meaning, but its real foundation. If everything is always caught up in the nets of a discourse already spoken by other subjects, it is only another step to JACQUES LACAN's formula that "there is no metalanguage." This emphasis on a discourse already spoken may describe the move to a third phase in Barthes's career, a phase in which a scientific language is not abandoned but remultiplied, pluralized, in order to reach beyond the object (such as text or myth or fashion) to the activity that produces it as such (textuality as textualization).

This third phase corresponds to the primacy of the notion of text over that of signifying system. The influence of the avant-garde represented by the *Tel Quel* movement becomes more conspicuous, and Barthes abandons semiology as a rigid scientific discourse in order to promote a new science, that of the production of signs. The key publication of this period is probably *S/Z* (1970, trans., 1974), an exhaustive reading of Balzac's story "Sarrasine." This virtuoso analysis of one short "classical" text shows the story's endless riches, thereby managing to undo a strict opposition between classicism and modernity. The essay stresses plurality and combines all possible semiological approaches, finally reading like a musical score and creating a work of art of its own kind. Its insights also owe a lot to JULIA KRISTEVA's influential collection of essays *Séméiotiké* (1969). Central to an approach to the story is the notion of textuality understood as a weaving of codes: "*text, fabric, braid:* the same thing" (*S/Z* [trans.] 160). In this braiding of textures, Barthes distinguishes five codes—corresponding to sequences of actions or behavioral patterns (proairetic codes), to the disclosure of the truth (hermeneutic codes), to descriptions of significant features (semic codes), to quotations from scientific or cultural models (cultural codes), and to the symbolic architecture of language (symbolic codes).

The text is defined as the productive progression through codes: "The five codes create a kind of network, a *topos* through which the entire text passes (or rather, in passing, becomes a text)" (20). In an earlier essay, "The Death of the Author" (1968, trans. in *Image-Music-Text,* 1977), which took its cue from an ambiguous sentence in "Sarrasine," textuality is defined as an interplay of codes that negates any origin: "Writing is the destruction of every voice, of every point of origin. Writing is that neutral, composite, oblique space where our subject slips away, the negative where all identity is lost, starting with the very identity of the body writing" (*Image* 142). And the essay tantalizingly concludes with the reader's new active role: "The birth of the reader must be at the cost of the death of the Author" (148).

When Barthes visited Japan, he himself became that ideal reader facing a writing that covers the world in order to cover up for the absence of the Author. Japan is the happy utopia of a country in which everything is sign. But signs do not refer; they only exhibit their fictive, indeed fabricated, nature. What underpins the Japanese semiology is therefore the void at the center expressed by the haiku or Zen Buddhism. The whiteness or blankness of the satori is a mystical equivalent of what Barthes is looking for in systems of signs. Writing exposes the emptiness of speech and merely points to the world. Japan is the necessary healing (and disturbing) experience of a culture that has done away with any naturalization of signs. *Empire of Signs* (1970, trans., 1982) shows the influence of JACQUES DERRIDA's powerful meditation on writing as the ruin of presence and of origin; a gloss to a reproduction of a beautiful calligraphy merely enumerates "Rain, Seed, Dissemination. Weaving, Tissue, Text. Writing" (*L'Empire* 14; not in *Empire*).

Japan also opens up a space of erotic enjoyment of signs; it is, in fact, in his study of Japan that the very important motif "pleasure" first appears in Barthes's texts. The "erotic grace" of hypercodified attitudes in Japanese plays, for instance, calls for its European equivalent, and Barthes finds it in the Marquis de Sade's seemingly boring descriptions of sexual orgies and perversions, in Ignatius Loyola's mental exercises teaching the soul to approach God, or again in Charles Fourier's ritualized catalogs of passions. *Sade, Fourier, Loyola* (1971, trans., 1976) continues the semiological approach to textuality but resolutely centers around three deviant writers who are all "logothetic" because they stand out as "founders of languages," precisely because they intrepidly systematize a strategy of excess, an excess that becomes identical with writing as such (*Sade* [trans.] 3). The introduction to the work coins for the first time the expression "the pleasure of the Text" and states that "the text is an object of pleasure" (7). This linkage is taken up in the slim, elegant collection of maxims and aphorisms entitled *The Pleasure of the Text* (1973, trans., 1975), which closes off this third phase of Barthes's *oeuvre*. Instead of asking, What do we know about texts? Barthes now asks only, How do we enjoy texts?

Barthes rewrites a distinction elaborated earlier in *S/Z* between "writerly" *(scriptible)* and "readerly" *(lisible)* texts (*S/Z* 10, trans. 4), or between texts that merely obey a logic of passive consumption and texts that stimulate the reader's active participation, as an opposition between textual *plaisir* and textual *jouissance. Jouissance* calls up a violent, climactic bliss closer to loss, death, fragmentation, and the disruptive rapture experienced when transgressing limits, whereas *plaisir* simply hints at an easygoing enjoyment, more stable in its reenactment of cultural codes. Lacan's terminology proves helpful in a strategy that aims not so much at discrediting pleasure in favor of a higher, sublimated type of enjoyment as at creating a critical vocabulary capable of concretely describing the effect of words on bodies and, conversely, of bodies on words. The modern text *de jouissance* may often be boring, tedious, and repetitive, yet it concentrates energy and strikes the innermost core of the reading/writing subject; thus, we are not left with a purely subjective process, for "this body of bliss [*jouissance*] is also *my historical subject*" (*Pleasure* 62), even if this subject belongs to an empty space of History.

The wish to connect the most particular and the most historical from the point of view of a body at work through language was bound to take into account Barthes's own subjectivity as a whole, and this is why he accepted the commission, from the series that published his *Michelet,* of a double signature in the writing of one of the most stimulating works of autobiographical criticism ever written, *Roland Barthes by Roland Barthes* (1975, trans., 1977). Not only could Barthes not resist the challenge of his publisher but he was irresistibly driven to a piece of writing that would do justice to all his changes, moves, and coinings, while constituting a sort of ideogram of the self, a self that would be more than just the old personality. The book opens with a tantalizing disclaimer in the position of an epigraph: "It must all be considered as if spoken by a character in a novel."

The last phase of Barthes's literary career, which he himself called the period of his "moralities," is perhaps the most haunting, for nowhere does he come closer to becoming a novelist in his own right. But whereas another gifted semiotician, UMBERTO ECO, was able to write two best-selling novels, Barthes's fiction, which would have been strongly autobiographical and basically Proustian, as several remarks of *Roland Barthes* and *Camera Lucida* (1980, trans., 1981) show, has to remain unwritten—another token that only silence approaches the disappearance of the Author and the blank space of living enunciation. The couple "enunciation/enounced" is indeed one of the last conceptual doublets that Barthes set to work, and he did it with the utmost consistency.

In this last period, however, no pretense of scientificity hinders the direct encounter with cultural and literary signs, which are organically related to the body of their "scriptor." The closest Barthes comes to writing pure fiction is in *A Lover's Discourse* (1977, trans., 1978), which opts for a "dramatic" method of presentation by varying the voices and blending quotations, personal remarks, and subtle generalizations. (Indeed the text has often been performed on stage as a theatrical play for voices.) The fictive character who enounces all the utterances is an archetypal lover—at times Johann Wolfgang von Goethe's Werther, at times Barthes himself—who comments on the ineluctable solitude of love.

The increasingly sentimental drift of these last works is counterbalanced by the sweeping and majestic summary of Barthes's beliefs about theory in the "Inaugural Lecture" (1978), the discourse pronounced when he was elected to the Collège de France, the crowning of his academic career. Enunciation is alluded to as the exposure of the subject's absence to himself or herself, semiotics become a DECONSTRUCTION of linguistics, and the main adversary is the power of language seen as a totalitarian structure: language, according to one daring formula, is always fascistic (*Barthes Reader* 461). Literature condenses all the forces of resistance to such a reactionary power, thanks to its hedonistic capacity for transforming knowledge into play, pleasure, and enjoyment. Barthes sees himself as Hans Castorp in Thomas Mann's *Magic Mountain* and finally claims his hope of achieving a possible wisdom, a *sapientia* linking knowledge and taste, in short, a whole *art de vivre.*

Camera Lucida, Barthes's last book before the many posthumous collections of essays, is a very moving autobiographical disclosure of his love for his mother under the guise of a study of photography that recants all previous semiological approaches. Whereas in many former essays Barthes had stressed the artificial nature of such a medium and its ideological power, he now identifies photography as pure reference; it immediately bespeaks a past presence, and its ultimate signifier is the death and absence of the loved mother. Photography is akin to a haiku poem and forces one to stare directly at reality. The last conceptual couple invented by Barthes opposes *studium,* scientific approach, ultimately boring and missing the main point, and *punctum,* the point or small detail that catches the eye of the beholder (*Camera* 26–27); this dualism justifies an apparently subjective selection of photographs all chosen and lovingly described because of some minor but revealing element that varies from picture to picture. This Zen-like meditation on the illusions of Appearance and the triumph of Death is a fitting testament to Barthes as a Writer of an almost magical power of analysis and utterance.

Jean-Michel Rabaté

See also FRENCH THEORY AND CRITICISM: 5. 1945–1968 AND 6. 1968 AND AFTER, RUSSIAN FORMALISM, JEAN-PAUL SARTRE, FERDINAND DE SAUSSURE, SEMIOTICS, and STRUCTURALISM.

Roland Barthes, *L'Aventure sémiotique* (1985, *The Semiotic Challenge,* trans. Richard Howard, 1988), *A Barthes Reader* (ed. Susan Sontag, 1982), *Le Bruissement de la langue* (1984, *The Rustle of Language,* trans. Richard Howard, 1986), *La Chambre claire: Note sur la photographie* (1980, *Camera Lucida: Reflections on Photography,* trans. Richard Howard, 1981), *Critique et vérité* (1966, *Criticism and Truth,* ed. and trans. Katherine Pilcher Keuneman, 1987), *Le Degré zéro de l'écriture* (1953, *Writing Degree Zero,* trans. Annette Lavers and Colin Smith, 1967), "Éléments de sémiologie" (1964, *Elements of Semiology,* trans. Annette Lavers and Colin Smith, 1967), *L'Empire des signes* (1970, *Empire of Signs,* trans. Richard Howard, 1982), *Essais critiques* (1964, *Critical Essays,* trans. Richard Howard, 1972), *Fragments d'un discours amoureux* (1977, *A Lover's Discourse: Fragments,* trans. Richard Howard, 1978), *Le Grain de la voix: Entretiens, 1962-1980* (1981, *The Grain of the Voice: Interviews, 1962-1980,* trans. Linda Coverdale, 1985), *Image-Music-Text* (ed. and trans. Stephen Heath, 1977), *Leçon* (1977, "Inaugural Lecture, Collège de France," trans. Richard Howard, *A Barthes Reader*), *Michelet par lui-même* (1954, *Michelet,* trans. Richard Howard, 1987), *Mythologies* (1957, *Mythologies,* ed. and trans. Annette Lavers, 1972, *The Eiffel Tower and Other Mythologies,* trans. Richard Howard, 1979), *Nouveaux essais critiques* (1972, *New Critical Essays,* trans. Richard Howard, 1980), *L'Obvie et l'obtus: Essais critiques III* (1982, *The Responsibility of Forms: Critical Essays on Music, Art, and Representation,* trans. Richard Howard, 1985), *Le Plaisir du texte* (1973, *The Pleasure of the Text,* trans. Richard Miller, 1975), *Roland Barthes par Roland Barthes* (1975, *Roland Barthes by Roland Barthes,* trans. Richard Howard, 1977), *Sade, Fourier, Loyola* (1971, *Sade/Fourier/Loyola,* trans. Richard Miller, 1976), *Sollers écrivain* (1979, *Writer Sollers,* trans. Philip Thody, 1987), *Sur Racine* (1963, *On Racine,* trans. Richard Howard, 1964), *Système de la mode* (1967, *The Fashion System,* trans. Matthew Ward and Richard Howard, 1983), *S/Z* (1970, *S/Z,* trans. Richard Miller, 1974).

Contardo Calligaris et al., *Prétexte, Roland Barthes* (1978); Louis-Jean Calvet, *Roland Barthes* (1990); *Communications* 36 (1982, special issue on Barthes); Jonathan Culler, *Barthes* (1983); Sanford Freedman and Carole Anne Taylor, *Roland Barthes: A Bibliographical Reader's Guide* (1983); Stephen Heath, *Le Vertige du déplacement: Lecture de Barthes* (1974); Vincent Jouve, *La Littérature selon Roland Barthes* (1986); Annette Lavers, *Roland Barthes: Structuralism and After* (1982); Patrizia Lombardo, *The Three Paradoxes of Roland Barthes* (1989); Michael Moriarty, *Roland Barthes* (1991); *Poétique* 47 (1981, special issue on Barthes); Susan Sontag, "Writing Itself: On Roland Barthes" *(A Barthes Reader);* Philip Thody, *Roland Barthes:*

A Conservative Estimate (1977); Steven Ungar, *Roland Barthes: The Professor of Desire* (1983); Steven Ungar and Betty R. McGraw, eds., *Signs in Culture: Roland Barthes Today* (1989); Mary Wiseman, *The Ecstasies of Roland Barthes* (1989).

BATAILLE, GEORGES

Within the history of the avant-garde in France, few twentieth-century writers have left a more far-reaching legacy than has Georges Bataille (1897–1962). Librarian, libertine, radical thinker, author of erotic fictions—Bataille, in life and in writing, traversed disparate institutions, identities, and discourses. He was a trained paleologist and archivist and worked for 20 years at the Bibliothèque Nationale; in 1951 he was named conservator of the Bibliothèque Municipale at Orléans, a position he held until a few months before his death. But in his twenties Bataille rejected the Catholicism that had perhaps to some degree influenced his initial choice of career, and he began to take an active part in the Parisian avant-garde literary scene. Objecting to what he saw as the aestheticism and potential sentimentality of the surrealists, he rapidly became André Breton's most forceful antagonist of the intellectual ultraleft. After the war, as founding editor of the journal *Critique* and author of transgressively "philosophical" books—*L'Expérience intérieure* (1943), *Le Coupable* (1944), *Sur Nietzsche* (1945), *La Part maudite* (1947)—Bataille emerged as a visible alternative to JEAN PAUL SARTRE and existentialism; he was to become, posthumously, an exemplary figure for the next generation of avant-garde writers centered around *Tel Quel.* Throughout his life Bataille inspired friendships, journals, and societies, among these latter the short-lived antifascist political group Contre-Attaque (1935–36), the influential Collège de Sociologie, and the journal *Acéphale* and the secret society by the same name (1936–39). Bataille's friendship with MAURICE BLANCHOT has acquired legendary status and has become a touchstone for French post-Heideggerian discussions of friendship and community (see, e.g., Nancy); one might also recall here, in order to suggest among other things his remarkable intellectual range, Bataille's intimacy at one point or another in his life with Roger Caillois, René Char, Pierre Klossowski, Alexandre Kojève, JACQUES LACAN, Michel Leiris, André Masson, and Pablo Picasso.

Bataille's work transgresses disciplines and genres so frequently and so radically that capsule accounts of his *oeuvre* are forced to commit themselves to particularly misleading abstractions. One can say that his thought consists in a meditation on, and performance of, "transgression"; however, such a project is necessarily antimeditative and nonphilosophical, committed to a principled, violent specificity. Bataille's erotic fictions *(Histoire de l'oeil, Madame Edwarda),* for instance, are in important (and often quite explicit) ways as "theoretical" as his writings on society, economics, and history are "fictional." Such generic transgressions in no way depend on a facile appeal to the irrational; they occur as aspects of a rigorous critique that, in its philosophical register, frequently appears as an appropriation and disarticulation of certain Hegelian themes. For G. W. F. HEGEL—as anthropologized by Bataille's friend and teacher, Kojève—humans and History come into being through humanity's deathlike power to negate what exists, via consciousness (the power of abstraction) and labor. Bataille, drawing on FRIEDRICH NIETZSCHE (and on SIGMUND FREUD, Stéphane Mallarmé, the Marquis de Sade), will insist on the disruptive, excessive character of this negative power. All philosophical, social, and psychological sublimations (language, consciousness, social forms, genital sexuality, etc.) are inhabited by an excess that at once makes sublimation possible and threatens its stability. In the terms Bataille proposes in "The Notion of Expenditure" *(Visions* 116–29) and elaborates in *La Part maudite,* any "restricted economy"—any putatively closed, reciprocal system, such as an identity, a concept or structure, marketplace, ecosystem, and so on—produces more than it can account for. Any restricted economy is fractured by its own unacknowledged excess, and in seeking to maintain itself it will, against its own logic, crave expenditure and loss (hence Bataille's interest in sacrifice and automutilation). This is to say that any restricted economy is situable in a "general economy" irreducible to proper conceptualization.

Thus Bataille, like Blanchot, is frequently cited as a precursor for much of what Anglo-American criticism calls "French theory." JACQUES DERRIDA and MICHEL FOUCAULT have documented their investment in Bataille in various texts, while libidinal theorists such as Gilles Deleuze and JEAN-FRANÇOIS LYOTARD and post-Marxist sociologists such as Jean Baudrillard have pursued Bataillean themes (eroticism, transgression, expenditure) even more explicitly. Bataille's influence on contemporary critical thought would thus be difficult to overestimate. But in the wake of such influential mediations he has been more often received than read, particularly in the English-speaking world: the term "general economy," for instance, has entered the Anglo-American critical lexicon through paths circuitous enough that it is often employed with little sense of its history or import.

Marc Redfield

See also FRENCH THEORY AND CRITICISM: 5. 1945–1968 and 6. 1968 AND AFTER.

Georges Bataille, *Oeuvres complètes* (12 vols., 1970–88), *L'Érotisme* (1957, *Oeuvres* 10, *Death and Sensuality: A Study of Eroticism and the Taboo,* trans. Mary Dalwood, 1962), *L'Expérience intérieure* (1943, *Oeuvres* 5, *Inner Experience,* trans. Leslie Anne Boldt, 1988), *La Littérature et le mal* (1957, *Oeuvres* 9, *Literature and Evil,* trans. A. Hamilton, 1973), *Visions of Excess: Selected Writings, 1927–1939* (trans. and ed. Allan Stoekl, 1985).

L'Arc 32, 44 (1967, 1971, special issues on Bataille); *Critique* 195/196 (1963, special issue on Bataille); Jacques Derrida, "From Restricted to General Economy: A Hegelianism without Reserve," *L'Écriture et la différence* (1967, *Writing and Difference,* trans. Alan Bass, 1978); Michel Foucault, "A Preface to Transgression," *Language, Counter-Memory, Practice: Selected Essays and Interviews* (ed. Donald F. Bouchard, trans. Donald F. Bouchard and Sherry Simon, 1977); Jane Gallop, *Intersections: A Reading of Sade with Bataille, Blanchot, and Klossowski* (1981); Denis Hollier, *Against Architecture: The Writings of Georges Bataille* (trans. Betsy Wing, 1989); Joseph Libertson, "Excess and Imminence: Transgression in Bataille," *MLN* 92 (1977), *Proximity: Levinas, Blanchot, Bataille, and Communication* (1982); Jean-Luc Nancy, *La Communauté désoeuvrée* (1986); Michèle H. Richman, *Reading Georges Bataille: Beyond the Gift* (1982); Jean-Paul Sartre, "Un Nouveau Mystique," *Situations I* (1947); Steven Shaviro, *Passion and Excess: Blanchot, Bataille, and Literary Theory* (1990); *Stanford French Review* 12 (1988, special issue on Bataille); Allan Stoekl, *Politics, Writing, Mutilation: The Cases of Blanchot, Bataille, Roussel, Leiris, and Ponge* (1985); *Yale French Studies: On Bataille* 78 (1990).

BAUDELAIRE, CHARLES

Charles Baudelaire (1821–67) is above all celebrated as a poet and practitioner of double consciousness, incarnating two intertwined natures. As flowers and evil play against each other in his poetry—the naked and the adorned, the female and the male, the religious and the damned—in his life also he was occupied with a Venus Blanche and a Venus Noire. The way in which his theory and practice interpenetrate each other is itself characteristic of his approach. This Baudelairean imagination, as it works and plays itself out, is a mixture of the erotic and the standoffish, the idealistic and the cynical, the feminine and the masculine. The tension between two opposite poles informs Baudelaire's entire theory, as it does his writing.

One of his major contributions to the literature of theoretical poetics is at once a theory of ambivalent analogy and an analogous embodiment of that theory. It is his meditation upon the "thyrse," that strange stick with a vine wrapping around it, the symbol of medicine and of communication. The female ornament visibly twines around the male baton, as poetry around prose, and their love affair is itself the best example of a prose poem as a theory, erotically visualized. Seldom do we find in French literature an image so useful for all purposes and so memorable.

The theory, like the poem, aims for a flexibility that the image of the thyrse embodies: "Straight line and arabesque, intention and expression, will most rigorous, language most flexible, with a variety of means leading to one end, omnipotent and indivisible amalgam of genius," he addresses it, remarking that no one could separate its elements (*Oeuvres* 1:336). Just so with Baudelaire's own inseparably double nature, uniting the masculine and the feminine: the "Confessions préliminaires" insist upon the "penetrating feminine way" of the author (1:447). Baudelaire's theoretical writings are based exactly upon this flexibility of the double sensitivity.

The genius of each writer is his own precise sensibility; Baudelaire's own was intense. It was—no less than his theories and his practice—a masterpiece of entwining, for the synesthesia he advocated and exemplified in his noted sonnet "Correspondances" (1:11) has to do with feel and smell and sight all mingling in a delighted and mystical confusion, as dizzying as in the poem "Harmonie du soir," a testimony to the ecstatic and yet languorous spinning of the senses. With its combining, penetrating, insinuating power, this synesthesia achieves a commanding presence, even in its metaphoric ambivalence about motion and hesitation, meeting and textual stress, enables a prose deeply poetic and apt to seize the passing phenomena in flight.

After Gautier's use of *la modernité* in 1855, it becomes Baudelaire's key term, indicating the sense of the fleeting and of the ambivalent life about him in its appealing transitoriness. The painter of modern life, in whatever genre, will thus be characterized by an ability to make an intelligent sketch of what is passing ("Le Peintre de la vie moderne," 2:674). Of Constantin Guys, Baudelaire says: "Ainsi il va, il court, il cherche" ("Thus he goes, runs, seeks"). The modern is restless.

But in all the fleeting it does not renounce depth. For it is in correspondence with what is beyond, above, behind, below it. Swedenborg furnishes the underlying philosophy of the vertical and horizontal correspondences between sky and ground, sense and sense, and this long wandering in a forest recalls both Dante's *Inferno* and Góngora's baroque footsteps. Nevertheless, it is always a matter of not forgetting the present (2:696).

Baudelaire's imaginer, like the later surrealist adventurer in the center of a twisting tornado of senses, is a *homo duplex* par excellence, attracted to God and Satan with the same intensity as to poetry and prose, passionate about the high and low, about the powerful use of oppositions, far before the surrealists who made of those contrasts their own theories. His *Journaux intimes* and *Ecrits sur l'art* all tell the same story, of an exacerbated personality whose creative imagination tended toward the idea of art for art's sake but whose politics often drew him the other way, toward a democratic art and life, against the sterility of the nonuseful. Even when he leaned toward the nonutility of art, he still was to believe that *good art* had always a moral.

As for beauty, he clung firmly to the notion of its irregularity, its bizarre nature, its mingling of the absolute and the temporary. These were stimuli to the imagination, that way of knowing, that supreme power of intelligence, which proceeded largely by analogy, and by correspondence. What it discovered by those procedures was the symbolic, based on the phenomena in nature that most adequately represented the state of the poet's soul. Thus once more the abstract and the concrete are mingled, with the vision leading from inside to out, and vice versa, in the double nature of the poet, who continues to long for a language expressive without a fault, a language that will take him past the breaking of the human voice, as he laments in his "Cloche fêlée" (2:71). This aesthetic nostalgia itself, represented by his poem about the swan, "Le Cygne" (1:85), is to be read also, and significantly, as later in Stéphane Mallarmé's, through its homonym "Le Signe," or the sign. The swan is, like the poet, both one and the other thing, always ambivalent, longing always for some other home. Poetic theory, and the sign as analogical presence, has to take into account the exiled poet's continual analogical longing for escape ("No matter where, out of this world").

The poet is to be above all a high-strung creature of nerves, excited by the senses to a peak of imaginative enthusiasm that can be read as spiritual excess or as the height of the artistic temperament par excellence. Baudelaire the poet, like the artists he lauded in "The Painter of Modern Life," was a hero of intensity. "I maintain that inspiration is related to *cerebral congestion,* and that every sublime thought is accompanied by a nervous shock of varying strength, which reverberates even in the cerebellum" (2:690). His double sensitivity, partaking of both genders, is allied in that fashion with the defense of cosmetics against the "abominable naturalness" of the female face. The face Baudelaire presents is that of a "dandy"—putting on the power of art, finding its supreme strength through the efforts of the senses and their symbols. The human brain is able to reform the dullness of nature by "making it up" (2:716), putting a new face on it. That face is the face of the modern.

Everything found in Baudelaire's critical, theoretical, and textual world can be stated as if it were a refinding. The odd and persistent perfume of nostalgia (as in the poems of "Spleen") pervades his aesthetic theories and his modernist consciousness. Finally, finding and loss are inseparably linked in his meditations and in his practice: each true paradise, he was wont to say, is a paradise we have already lost. But what Baudelaire knew how to see, and helped his successors to see, was the possibility of a poetry based not upon the stable but upon the fleeting, resounding as a sustained elegy of the passerby; what he found about him, in painting and in the street, was what he was to call the modern. What he founded was an undying sense of its importance.

Mary Ann Caws

Charles Baudelaire, *Oeuvres complètes* (ed. Claude Pichois, 2 vols., 1975), "Le Peintre de la vie moderne" (1863, *L'Art romantique*, 1868, *The Painter of Modern Life and Other Essays,* trans. and ed. Jonathan Mayne, 1964).

Leo Bersani, *Baudelaire and Freud* (1977); Mary Ann Caws and Hermine Riffaterre, eds., *The Prose Poem in France* (1983); Robert Greer Cohn, "A Poetry-Prose Cross" (Caws and Riffaterre); Margaret Gilman, "Imagination Enthroned: Baudelaire," *The Idea of Poetry in France: From Houdar de la Motte to Baudelaire* (1958); Barbara Johnson, "Disfiguring Poetic Language" (Caws and Riffaterre), "Poetry and Its Double: Two *Invitations au voyage,*" *A World of Difference* (1987); Roger Shattuck, "Vibratory Organism: *Crise de prose*" (Caws and Riffaterre).

BEAUVOIR, SIMONE DE

Simone de Beauvoir (1908–86) was born in Paris and lived, during her childhood, on the Boulevard Raspail and the Rue de Rennes. Her parents sent her to study at Catholic schools, the prestigious Cours Désir, and the Institut Sainte-Marie in Neuilly. She graduated from these institutions just at the time when educational reforms in France gave women equal access to the *baccalauréat* examination, enabling them to attend universities. Simone

de Beauvoir attended the École Normale Supérieure and in 1929 became a candidate for the *agrégation de philosophie,* a competitive postgraduate examination for lycée and university teaching positions, along with CLAUDE LÉVI-STRAUSS, Maurice Merleau-Ponty, and JEAN-PAUL SARTRE. She studied and succeeded at the *agrégation* at the same time as Sartre, with whom she began a lifelong love and partnership. Through dialogue and mutual influence, Beauvoir and Sartre developed existentialism, a philosophy that concerned the exercise of human freedom in a world where existence has no transcendent purpose or essence to give it meaning.

As existentialists, both Beauvoir and Sartre defined a human as that being whose being is not to be. They clarified this paradoxical definition by means of the important distinction between "Being-for-itself," which is conscious, and "Being-in-itself," which is unconscious and superfluous; they showed how consciousness implies a Being other than itself that enables the For-itself to be at once a revelation, negation, desire, and choice of Being only because it *is not* Being. Although Beauvoir and Sartre agreed in defining human beings in terms of what they lacked, Sartre was more pessimistic in describing the "useless passion" of human beings and the anguish, despair, and nausea they experience.

Beauvoir found in human lack the promise of imaginative possibilities. In *The Ethics of Ambiguity* she argued that humans must choose themselves as a lack and assume the responsibility of their ambiguous situation. This means first of all that they should reject authorities and absolutes and create meaning through ethical acts. Against the charge that existentialism results in nihilism, Beauvoir countered that "if God does not exist, man's faults are inexpiable" (16). She explored the kind of here-and-now accountability an existentialist ethics would imply and argued that humans must choose freedom as their chief end both for themselves and for others. In defining an existentialist ethics, Beauvoir found the me-other relation just as irreducible as the subject-object relation. Her focus on human interrelations distinguishes her existentialist ethics from the more psychoanalytic reflective ethics Sartre evolved. Although she was later critical of *The Ethics of Ambiguity,* her reflections on morality in this work significantly presage her subsequent efforts to understand structures of oppression and to commit herself to political struggles. As co-founder and one of the principal editors of the journal *Les Temps modernes,* she helped shape the political and cultural awareness of French intellectuals for more than 40 years.

Beauvoir described herself as a literary writer rather than a philosophical one. Concerned with concrete experience, Beauvoir valued fiction as a mode of communication that most fully conveyed lived realities. In addition to her numerous philosophical and autobiographical works, she wrote one play, two collections of short stories, and five novels. Of the novels, the most celebrated is *The Mandarins,* which won her the Prix Goncourt in 1954. Although Beauvoir did not write extensively about literary theory, in her essay "Littérature et métaphysique" [Literature and metaphysics] she reflected on what it means for literature to be philosophical and on the relationship between the novel and metaphysics. She agreed with those who oppose philosophical literature on the grounds that a novel should not be translatable into abstract concepts or reducible to formulas. She argued that the meaning of a novel cannot be detached from it, no more than a smile can be detached from a face: in some respects, the meaning of a novel, like the meaning of objects around us, always exceeds and escapes its readers. And not only does it escape the readers, it also escapes the author, despite the author's original intentions. In the act of writing a novel, a writer discovers new ideas, confronts unforeseen problems, and enriches her or his original design. For the author, the novel is a spiritual adventure, the end of which is recognized with astonishment.

Yet, for Beauvoir, the main reason why authors of philosophical novels should not begin with an a priori theory or formula has to do with the nature of metaphysics. Metaphysics is not first of all a system: it is an attitude philosophers take by placing their total being up against the totality of the world. Even PLATO, who believed the world was but a mistaken shadow of an eternal Idea, began by describing the movement toward this Idea in terms of human reality and the sensible world. Beauvoir's emphasis on metaphysics as discoverable through lived experience reflects the debt existentialism owes to PHENOMENOLOGY, a philosophy that stressed the observation of phenomena and a return to the things themselves. This emphasis also underscores the existentialist idea that existence precedes essence and that the temporal and the historical are the matter from which meanings and essences are created. Thus, for Beauvoir, the temporal lived-through quality of literature is well suited to engage or reflect the metaphysical process. The philosophical novel discovers the thickness, opacity, and rich ambiguity of the world.

Although Beauvoir contributed, in a limited way, to a theory of the philosophical novel, she continues to have relevance to literary theory largely because of her trailblazing study on the existential situation of woman, *The Second Sex.* In this work, Beauvoir argued that prevailing concepts of "the feminine" are not natural to women but have instead imprisoned women and held them in a status secondary to men. Following G. W. F. HEGEL, who in *Phenomenology of Spirit* (1807) analyzed a master-slave relationship as one in which a consciousness sets itself up as essential in hostile opposition to an "Other," Beauvoir showed in her Introduction to *The Second Sex* how man defines woman as relative and subordinate to him and not in herself. She also examined women's complicity in accepting the status of objectified "Other" and argued that social, legal, and economic inequalities worked against women's ability to claim their position as autonomous subjects. Notably, these inequalities also affected the ability of female writers to achieve the genius of male writers. Beauvoir wrote:

> As VIRGINIA WOOLF has made us see, Jane Austen, the Brontë sisters, George Eliot, have had to expend so much energy negatively in order to free themselves from outward restraints that they arrive somewhat out of breath at the stage from which masculine writers of great scope take their departure. (709)

Yet, Beauvoir's well-known claim that "one is not born, but rather becomes, a woman" (267), while indicative of the existentialist's refusal to accept ready-made essences, has seemed extreme to some. French literary theorists of the 1970s and 1980s, such as HÉLÈNE CIXOUS, LUCE IRIGARAY, and JULIA KRISTEVA, have argued instead that it is in women's difference, understood in poststructuralist terms, that women may find the source of liberation from a phallocentric discourse.

Before she died in 1986, Beauvoir responded unsympathetically to Cixous's notion of an *écriture féminine.* In agreement with Beauvoir, some feminists have warned that the emphasis on woman's difference, either as an essentializing concept or as a political category, forestalls the dissolution of the binary oppositions between "men" and "women" and inhibits cultural innovation. Beauvoir's suggestion that women have no natural necessity or essence is one that philosopher Judith Butler finds promising, and she reminds us that for Beauvoir, "to choose a gender is to interpret received gender norms in a way that reproduces and organizes them anew" (131). For Beauvoir, "existing" one's body becomes a concrete way of politicizing the personal and opens the possibility that we can transform cultural institutions. Butler's reminder echoes Beauvoir's admonishment in the conclusion to *The Second Sex:* "Let us not forget that our lack of imagination always depopulates the future" (730).

Susan R. Carlton

See also FEMINIST THEORY AND CRITICISM and JEAN-PAUL SARTRE.

Simone de Beauvoir, *Le Deuxième Sexe* (1949, *The Second Sex,* trans. H. M. Parshley, 1953, reprint, 1989), "Littérature et métaphysique" (1946, *L'Existentialisme et la sagesse des nations,* 1963), *Les Mandarins* (1954, *The Mandarins,* trans. Leonard M. Friedman, 1960), *Pour une morale de l'ambiguité* (1947, *The Ethics of Ambiguity,* trans. Bernard Frechtman, 1948).

Jeffner Allen and Iris Marion Young, eds., *The Thinking Muse: Feminism and Modern French Philosophy* (1989); Deirdre Bair, *Simone de Beauvoir: A Biography* (1990); Joy Bennet and Gabriella Hochmann, *Simone de Beauvoir: An Annotated Bibliography* (1988); Judith Butler, "Variations on Sex and Gender: Beauvoir, Wittig, and Foucault," *Feminism as Critique* (ed. Seyla Benhabib and Drucilla Cornell, 1988); Mary Evans, *Simone de Beauvoir: A Feminist Mandarin* (1985); Terry Keefe, *Simone de Beauvoir: A Study of Her Writings* (1983); Toril Moi, *Feminist Theory and Simone de Beauvoir* (1990), *Sexual/Textual Politics: Feminist Literary Theory* (1985); Judith Okely, *Simone de Beauvoir: A Re-reading* (1986); Alice Schwarzer, *After "The Second Sex": Conversations with Simone de Beauvoir* (trans. Marianne Howarth, 1984); Anne Whitmarsh, *Simone de Beauvoir and the Limits of Commitment* (1981); Hélène Vivienne Wenzel, ed., *Simone de Beauvoir: Witness to a Century, Yale French Studies* 72 (1986).

BENJAMIN, WALTER

A principal preoccupation of the theory and criticism of Walter Benjamin (1892–1940) is criticism itself. For Benjamin, in its broadest sense critique means that nothing can simply be taken as given. Any text or artifact always demands something more, exceeds itself, in a movement that structures not only literature and culture but also history itself.

As early as his dissertation, *Der Begriff der Kunstkritik in der deutschen Romantik* [The concept of aesthetic criticism in German Romanticism] (1920), Benjamin explored the notion of critique as *Ergänzung* ("fulfillment," "completion"), claiming with the Romantics (primarily Friedrich Schlegel) that critique was immanent to the movement of art itself and thus less something contingent to art than its necessary supplement. There would be no art without critique, not because critique has priority over art but because the artifact is itself unfinished, already critical from the start. In an essay on JOHANN WOLFGANG VON GOETHE's *Elective Affinities* (1922) that Hugo von Hofmannsthal called "epoch-making," Benjamin insisted on the difference between critique and commentary, the former concerned with "truth content," the latter with "subject matter." Against the tradition of monumentalizing biography that dominated Goethe criticism, Benjamin saw the work's history as a "funeral pyre," at which the commentator could study the wood and ashes, while the critic "is concerned only with the enigma of the flame itself, . . . the truth whose living flame goes on burning over the heavy logs of the past and the light ashes of life gone by" (quoted in *Illuminations* 4–5).

Benjamin investigated this enigmatic historicity of critique in a series of early essays on language, notably "Über die Sprache überhaupt und über die Sprache des Menschen" (1916, "On Language as Such and the Language of Man," *Reflections*) and "Die Aufgabe des Übersetzers" (1923, "The Task of the Translator," *Illuminations*). He outlined a theory of language that questioned the "bourgeois" notion of a merely goal-directed practice of communication or representation (*Reflections* 324). Translation, insofar as it is a relation between one language and another, exemplified for Benjamin a mode of critique to the extent that it resists imitating the original and instead reveals what in that original cannot become fixed but remains in motion or incomplete (*Illuminations* 72–73). As in "Zur Kritik der Gewalt" (1921, "Critique of Violence," *Reflections*), Benjamin here suspends thinking in an economy of ends and means (the transmission of information for and between subjects) and tries instead to understand the sheer materiality—of language, historical survival, violence—that makes possible and renders precarious the institutions of culture, politics, and economics.

The arcane corpus of German baroque drama, the *Trauerspiel,* furnished the occasion for a more pointedly materialist criticism in *Der Ursprung des deutschen Trauerspiel* (1928, *The Origin of the German Mourning Play,* 1977). Rejected as a thesis by the University of Frankfurt, the text articulated a curiously Platonic epistemology of criticism with a reflection on the materiality of "things" and of language. Departing from the Idealist promotion of the organic and totalizing symbol, Benjamin rehabilitated the discontinuous and arbitrary model of allegory, together with a theory of critique as "mortification" (*Origin* 182).

During the composition of the *Trauerspiel* book, Benjamin began to engage Marxist theory and practice, primarily in a reading of Marx and GEORG LUKÁCS. Having met THEODOR W. ADORNO in 1923, he later became affiliated with the Institute for Social Research (the FRANKFURT SCHOOL), publishing some of his most important essays in its journal and becoming a member in 1935. He cultivated connections with agitprop theater and leftist intellectual culture generally, and in the winter of 1926–27 he journeyed to Moscow with Asja Lacis, wondering whether he should join the Communist party. This intense political engagement pushed Benjamin to new thinking about the relation of theory and critique, exemplified in his promise that his *Moskauer Tagebuch* (1980, trans., 1986) "will be devoid of all theory. . . . I want to write a description of Moscow at the present moment in which 'all factuality is already theory'" (132). (See also MARXIST THEORY AND CRITICISM.)

During the same period Benjamin, a Jew born in Berlin, studied Hebrew and considered leaving Germany to teach in Jerusalem with Gershom Scholem but decided against it. Without academic employment, he wrote extensively for German newspapers and magazines well into the 1930s. He published reviews, autobiographical texts, literary studies (notably "Surrealism" and essays on Bertolt Brecht and Franz Kafka), studies of cities, and hybrid works of social commentary and cultural theory, such as the aphoristic *Einbahnstrasse* (1928, *One-Way Street*, 1979). He insisted, thematically and formally, that only "fools lament the decay of criticism. For its day is long past. . . . What, in the end, makes advertisements so superior to criticism? Not what the moving red neon sign says—but the fiery pool reflecting it in the asphalt" (*Reflections* 85–86).

At the same time that he was writing for newspapers and journals, Benjamin was constantly at work on the Arcades project, a vast assemblage of quotation and commentary on Paris, CHARLES BAUDELAIRE, architecture, Marx, and commodity culture of the nineteenth century. This work, along with separate studies on Baudelaire and "Paris, die Hauptstadt des XIX Jahrhunderts" ("Paris, Capital of the 19th Century," *Reflections*), scrutinized the new media of reproduction and representation and explored the implications of "technical reproducibility" in film and photography for an understanding of aesthetics in general and the task of criticism. In "Die Kunstwerk im Zeitalter seiner technischen Reproduzierbarkeit" (1935, "The Work of Art in the Age of Mechanical Reproduction," *Illuminations*) and "Eduard Fuchs, der Sammler und der Historiker" (1937, "Eduard Fuchs, Collector and Historian," *One-Way*) Benjamin demonstrated the necessity of reading aesthetics and politics together in a method derived from the dialectical materialism of KARL MARX AND FRIEDRICH ENGELS, yet transformed by his own heterodox vision of history (in its resistance to narrative) and his special attention to allegory as a structuring principle of language and history. His work on Baudelaire and the Arcades, despite its unfinished

state, offers one of the most powerful examples of an engaged critique, joining close reading, informed historical study, and a philosophically rigorous thinking of representation and its technologies—articulations that remain one of the principal burdens for the future of literary theory and criticism.

Ian Balfour and Thomas Keenan

See also FRANKFURT SCHOOL and GERMAN THEORY AND CRITICISM: 4. TWENTIETH CENTURY TO 1968.

Walter Benjamin, "Central Park" (trans. Lloyd Spencer with Mark Harrington, in Smith, *Thinking Through Benjamin*), *Charles Baudelaire: Ein Lyriker im Zeitalter des Hochkapitalismus* (1955, *Charles Baudelaire: A Lyric Poet in the Era of High Capitalism*, trans. Harry Zohn, 1973), *Einbahnstrasse* (1955, *One-Way Street and Other Writings*, trans. Edmund Jephcott and Kingsley Shorter, 1979), *Gesammelte Schriften* (ed. Rolf Tiedemann and Hermann Schweppenhäuser, 7 vols. to date, 1974–, trans. forthcoming), *Illuminations* (ed. Hannah Arendt, trans. Harry Zohn, 1968), *Moskauer Tagebuch* (1980, *Moscow Diary*, ed. Gary Smith, trans. Richard Sieburth, 1986), "N [Theoretics of Knowledge; Theory of Progress]" (trans. Leigh Hafrey and Richard Sieburth, in Smith, *Thinking Through Benjamin*), *Reflections: Essays, Aphorisms, Autobiographical Writings* (ed. Peter Demetz, trans. Edmund Jephcott, 1978), *Der Ursprung des deutschen Trauerspiels* (1928, ed. Rolf Tiedemann, 1963, *The Origin of German Tragic Drama*, trans. John Osborne, 1977), *Versuche über Brecht* (1966, *Understanding Brecht*, trans. Anna Bostock, 1973).

Paul de Man, "Conclusions: Walter Benjamin's 'The Task of the Translator,'" *The Resistance to Theory* (1986); Terry Eagleton, *Walter Benjamin, or Towards a Radical Criticism* (1981); Michael Jennings, *Dialectical Images: Walter Benjamin's Theory of Literary Criticism* (1987); Rainer Nägele, ed., *Benjamin's Ground: New Readings of Walter Benjamin* (1988); *New German Critique* 17, 34, 39, 48 (1979, 1985, 1986, 1989, special issues on Benjamin); Gary Smith, ed., *On Walter Benjamin* (1988), *Thinking Through Benjamin* (1989).

BENVENISTE, ÉMILE

Émile Benveniste (1902–76) was a disciple of Antoine Meillet and held the chair of comparative grammar at the Collège de France from 1937 until his death. Although his thought was much influenced by Saussurean linguistics, the theories of communication and reference he developed were quite distinct from those of FERDINAND DE SAUSSURE.

Benveniste published very extensively: his complete bibliography comprises some 18 volumes and almost 300 articles (Moïnfar). Many of his contributions have had a major impact on literary theorists, especially in NAR-RATOLOGY, and on French theorists, such as Gérard Genette, ROLAND BARTHES, and Tzvetan Todorov, in particular. His influence in related fields has been considerable, especially in work on poetry (Michael Riffaterre) and on autobiography and first-person narration (Jean Rousset, Philippe Lejeune). Though Benveniste's range is extremely broad, including his interests in Indo-European linguistics, the part of his work that has most influenced linguists, semioticians, literary theorists, and speech-act theorists is his research in general linguistics, representative selections of which are included in the two volumes of the *Problèmes de linguistique générale* (1966, 1974), only the first of which has been translated into English.

The two volumes gather his key essays in general linguistics that appeared in 1939–64 and 1965–72, respectively. Three Benveniste dichotomies have been particularly influential: I/non-I *(je/non-je)*; story/discourse *(histoire/discours)*; and semiotic/semantic *(sémiotique/sémantique)*. The essays in volume 1 dealing with the link between the use of personal pronouns and subjective versus objective utterance have had a marked impact on literary theory. The first and second persons singular *(je, tu)* are confined to the subjective mode that Benveniste calls "discourse" *(discours)* and contrast with the use of the third person *(il)*, the non-person that characterizes "story" *(histoire)*. The status of *je* and *tu* is contingent solely on the utterances in which they are used. The third person is not really a "person" at all, since the *il*, just as it is defined in Arabic linguistics, is "the one who is absent."

The essential characteristic of "I" and "you" is the possible interchange between them, "I" becoming "you" and vice versa. This is not possible between the third and any other person. The use of *je* entails an utterance involving a speaker and an utterance about the same speaker. Similarly, two characteristics mark off the use of the first and second persons: personalization and subjectivity.

In a related study ("La Nature des pronoms"), Benveniste focuses on the problem of deixis and reference. The referent of *je* and *tu* is necessarily new each time either is used. Contrary to other signs in language, the first and second persons can have no referents outside of the particular speech events in which they occur. Demonstratives such as "this" *(ce*, etc.) and adverbs such as "here" *(ici)*, "now" *(maintenant)*, "today" *(aujourd'hui)*, "yesterday" *(hier)*, and "tomorrow" *(demain)* belong to the same category of deictic terms whose referents are restricted to their context of utterance.

Benveniste shows (in "De la subjectivité dans le langage") that there is no concept of *je* to which all instances of *je* can refer. The first- and second-person pronouns thus escape the normal rule that all signs in language refer to fixed concepts (signifieds). *Je* can refer only to the speech act in which it is used and in which it designates the speaker.

To this crucial problem of subjectivity in language Benveniste relates his well-known distinction between story *(histoire)* and discourse *(discours)*. "Historical" utterances are defined as those that relate events that occurred in the past, without the speaker intervening in the narrative. The historian will thus never have recourse to the first person or to other deictics such as "here" and "now"; the third person is mandatory in such situations.

This objective mode of language requires the use of the third person together with the preterite *(passé simple)*, imperfect, or pluperfect. It precludes the use of the present, future, or present perfect. It is contrasted with the subjective mode, with its use of the first person and the present or present perfect tense, which can be defined as a speech act that presupposes a speaker and an addressee and the speaker's intention to influence the addressee in some way. The subjective mode includes all types of spoken discourse, from trivial conversation to elaborate political speeches, as well as various types of texts that reproduce spoken discourse, such as letters, memoirs, and plays. Discourse makes free use of all three personal pronouns—*je, tu, il*—together with any tense except the preterite. The imperfect tense is common to both modes.

For Benveniste, tense is thus as significant a discursive marker as the personal pronouns. He considers the use of the present, future, and present perfect incompatible with "historical" utterance (by which he means works of history as well as narrative in which past events are recounted impersonally), since they would be alien to the historian's mission of objectivity and detachment.

Benveniste's crucial distinctions between *histoire* and *discours;* objective and subjective utterance; and the use of, on the one hand, the first or second person and, on the other hand, the third person can be linked to ROMAN JAKOBSON's functions of language, specifically to the referential versus the emotive functions. Benveniste's dichotomy provided the basis for a grammar of narrative modes that has been developed by many narratologists, starting with Gérard Genette.

Benveniste's key concept of discourse is expanded in volume 2, in a chapter entitled "Sémiologie de la langue," in which he shows how language, for him the principal semiological channel, consists of two distinct modes: the semiotic (peculiar to the sign) and the semantic (peculiar to discourse). The semiotic mode is concerned with isolated units of language, that is, words, considered out of context and without reference when they offer themselves for possible use. The semantic mode is based on the sentence and thus entails reference. As the realm of the speech act, it is linked to the universe of discourse.

Benveniste's contribution to the theory of communication is crucial. His distinction between semiotics and semantics aimed to complement Saussure's definition of the sign, which was in fact a closed concept, offering no bridge between the sign and its use in discourse, or between the sign and the world of which it forms part.

Michael Issacharoff

See also LINGUISTICS AND LANGUAGE.

Émile Benveniste, *Problèmes de linguistique générale,* vol. 1 (1966, *Problems in General Linguistics,* trans. Mary Elizabeth Meek, 1971), vol. 2 (1974, "Sémiologie de la langue" [ch. 3], "The Semiology of Language," trans. Genette Ashby and Adelaide Russo, in Lotringer and Gora).

Roland Barthes, "Introduction à l'analyse structurale du récit," *Communications* 8 (1966, "Introduction to the Structural Analysis of Narratives," *Image-Music-Text,* ed. and trans. Stephen Heath, 1977), *S/Z* (1970, *S/Z,* trans. Richard Miller, 1974); Gérard Genette, *Figures III* (1972, *Narrative Discourse: An Essay in Method,* trans. Jane E. Lewin, 1980), "Frontières du récit," *Figures II* (1969, "Frontiers of Narrative," trans. Alan Sheridan, *Figures of Literary Discourse,* 1982), *Nouveau discours du récit* (1983, *Narrative Discourse Revisited,* trans. Jane E. Lewin, 1988); Philippe Lejeune, *Je est un autre: L'Autobiographie de la littérature aux médias* (1980), *Le Pacte autobiographique* (1975, *On Autobiography,* ed. Paul J. Eakin, trans. Katherine Leary, 1989); Sylvère Lotringer and Thomas Gora, eds., *Polyphonic Linguistics: The Many Voices of Émile Benveniste* (*Semiotica* 33, special suppl., 1981); M. D. Moïnfar, "Bibliographie des travaux d'É. Benveniste," *Mélanges linguistiques offerts à Émile Benveniste* (1975); Michael Riffaterre, *Essais de stylistique structurale* (1971), *Semiotics of Poetry* (1978), *Text Production* (trans. Terese Lyons, 1983); Jean Rousset, *Narcisse romancier: Essai sur la première personne dans le roman* (1973, rev. ed., 1986); Ferdinand de Saussure, *Cours de linguistique générale* (1916, *Course in General Linguistics,* trans. Roy Harris, 1983); Tzvetan Todorov, *Poétique de la prose* (1971, *The Poetics of Prose,* trans. Richard Howard, 1977).

BIBLICAL THEORY AND CRITICISM

1. Midrash and Medieval Commentary

The text of the Old Testament, known by the acronym *Tanakh*—for Torah, *Nevi'im* (Prophets), and *Ketuvim* (Writings)—for centuries has been subjected to critical scrutiny by Jewish scholars. Rabbinic authorities in late antiquity (tannaim, from the time of the Mishnah; amoraim, from the time of the Talmud) developed some of the best-known and most influential forms of traditional interpretive theories of the text of the Bible. The contributions of these scholars have been preserved in numerous volumes of midrash compilations and in the Talmud (the definitive compilation of rabbinic laws, legends, and interpretation from the first to the sixth century).

The Hebrew word *midrash* means "interpretation." It most commonly refers to 1) classic compilations of Bible interpretation in early rabbinism (the first six centuries C.E.), 2) some of the major interpretive styles associated with those compilations, and 3) some types of contemporary interpretations of texts (of Scripture or of fiction) that bear resemblances to the classic rabbinic modes.

Classical rabbinic midrash is a complex and diverse sort of writing compiled and written over a period that spans several centuries and fills many discrete volumes. Midrash most frequently takes the form of a commentary to biblical verses. There are also brief but sometimes complex narrative segments embedded in midrash compilations.

Midrash emphasizes national themes, dwells on religious themes and theological issues, and bears barely concealed moralistic and political messages. In contrast to the biblical text it seeks to illuminate, it contains few of the major themes of literature and verse: it is rarely interested in human stories of love or hate, war or peace, loyalty or duplicity, or in the personal struggles of individuals in a society of open choices. It is a theological genre; nearly all the messages of rabbinic midrash are rigorously controlled within structured religious schemata. Consequently, scholars have yet to apply extensively the general methods of literary criticism to the corpus of midrash texts. More groundwork is now under way employing current literary theory to illuminate the meanings of midrash.

The fact that midrash traditions "do not seem to involve the privileged pairing of a signifier with a specific set of signifieds . . . has rendered midrash . . . fascinating to some recent literary critics" (Boyarin viii). Indeed, some critics view the methods of midrash as an early process of deconstructing a text and use the term to describe more recent techniques of interpretation. Nevertheless, contemporary theorists mold the term "midrash" according to their own needs and stop short of inquiring into its diverse implications in late-antique rabbinism.

The privilege of rabbinic authority is central to the concept of midrash. Implied in the classical uses of the term is the notion that the results of interpretations of the sacred texts are themselves in some sense sacred. The early rabbis voiced this when they suggested that their writings constituted an oral Torah tradition that had been given to Moses at the revelation at Mount Sinai along with the text of the Israelite written Torah. The notion of a dual Torah signifies that the authority of the text and of the interpretation are correlative.

Many works of classical rabbinic exegesis share common strategies with regard to interpreting the texts of the Bible. Midrash tends to atomize a canonical text and to associate with each segment one or more interpretive remarks. These may be alternate or contradictory explanations, expansions, or even entirely independent traditions.

In the early scholarship of the nineteenth century, authors tended to search for the specific unifying features of the genre "midrash." They frequently assumed that they could identify and distill the exact rules of midrash and thereby describe a unified paradigm of rabbinic interpretive principles. These efforts did not extend to defining the essence and function of midrash. The features and rules they catalogued were in fact either too general to be meaningful or, in some cases, incorrect and misleading. The study of midrash improved and accelerated in the 1980s. Recent research in the field builds on novel and more modern paradigms of inquiry.

It is useful to provide some examples to illustrate the progress in midrash scholarship. Earlier scholarship commonly asserted that midrash falls into two content-specific categories: *halakhic* (legal) and *aggadic* (homiletical). To be sure, since many of the texts of *Tanakh* can be categorized as either legal or nonlegal, there appears to be some strong basis for this distinction. However, the validity of this dichotomy derives from an allegorical-philosophical polemic frequently associated with Maimonides and his successors within medieval rabbinism. By contrast, more modern approaches investigate the hermeneutical moves or motives of the various rabbinic compilers who used midrash techniques in their compositions.

Early twentieth-century scholarship frequently invoked the distinction between styles of exegesis—*peshat,* "plain meaning," and *derash,* "fanciful interpretation"— to define the nature of midrash and its later derivatives in medieval rabbinic Bible commentaries. This division was first articulated by the rabbis themselves. Of course, many midrash moves do fall into the categories "literal" and "imaginative." Nevertheless, this differentiation confines the focus to the microexegetical moves of the processes. Current research attempts to provide a more substantial window into the larger intent of exegete/compiler/author of midrash or of commentary.

Recent scholarship on the subject of midrash insists that because rabbinic Judaism was not a monolithic movement, we ought not limit the academic exploration of midrash to searching for independent principles of Jewish hermeneutics. Instead, we now ought to consider how each of its major works of interpretation contributes its own substantive methods of text study. Each author or compiler, it is argued, responds in some way to his particular inner dynamic and to his social and historical circumstance. Unfortunately, little is known of the lives of the authors and compilers of the midrash books. What can be retrieved inductively from the texts themselves demonstrates a diversity of both style and substance within the various works. The work of Jacob Neusner and his students embodies various productive functional approaches to text found in the classic midrash compilations.

Neusner identifies three trends in classical rabbinic Bible interpretation: exegetical, propositional, and narrative. In the classic work *Sifra,* the tannaitic midrash to Leviticus, and in *Sifré to Numbers* Neusner finds the interpretation to be a form of exegesis yielding propositions. The discourse of such texts is sustained by the anchoring of each of the brief excurses to a successive verse in the text of Torah. The second form of midrash interpretation starts with propositions and yields exegeses. From the texts of *Genesis Rabbah, Leviticus Rabbah,* and *Pesiqta derab Kahana* we can easily observe the "overriding themes and recurrent tensions that precipitated Bible interpretation among their authorships" (Neusner viii). *The Fathers according to Rabbi Nathan* exemplifies a third trend, the narrative task of midrash, which extends and rewrites the themes and stories of the canonical text.

Among the classic works of rabbinic midrash, the *Tannaitic Midrashim,* those that cite the rabbis of the Mishnah, include *Mekhilta Attributed to Rabbi Ishmael* on Exodus 12:1–23:19, *Sifra* for Leviticus, *Sifré to Numbers,* and *Sifré to Deuteronomy.* These are generally thought to have been completed by 400 C.E. *Mekhilta* has been described as a scriptural encyclopedia joining together propositions engendered by the biblical text. By contrast, other early midrash compilations have been found to set forth an agendum of questions and to proceed to answer the questions through their discourses.

Sifra sets its distinctive approach by adhering to a three-pronged polemical inquiry. The compilers asserted that all taxonomy must derive from scriptural classifications. They presented these discussions in a dialectical form of discourse. They also undertook to recast the rabbinic, oral Torah in the context of the original, written Torah. For this aim they utilized the citation form of expression. They finally sought to revise the Torah itself and did so through their use of commentary forms.

The earlier *rabbah* midrash compilations are thought to have been completed in the fourth and fifth centuries. *Genesis Rabbah* makes a coherent claim that the origins of the world and of the tribes of Israel reveal God's plan and portend for the future of Israel's salvation. Neusner argues that this midrash book was issued as a response to historical trends, most likely to the conversion of Constantine and the legalization of Christianity in the Roman Empire. Accordingly, narratives such as that of Jacob's struggle with Esau are turned into accounts of the strife between Israel and Rome. Rabbinic commentators in this work use verses from the Torah to write about the history and destiny of Israel.

The later *rabbah* midrash compilations are said to derive from the sixth and seventh centuries. *Ruth Rabbah* makes clear through its comments that opposite entities may be united under God's will. The editors of this book dealt with the issues of Gentiles becoming Jews and the distinction between men and women. The proposition that from a Moabite woman comes the Israelite messiah is repeatedly conveyed by means of a symbolic vocabulary of verbal images embedded in the midrash materials. *Song of Songs Rabbah* understands the biblical text as a metaphor for the love of God for Israel. The compilation furnishes us with listlike comments that systematically connect the poetry of the *Song* with the symbols of rabbinism. Thus, this work forms for us a discourse, not of narrative or of polemics or propositions, but rather of the symbolism that defines the religion. These latter two compilations make crucial theological claims in the distinct rhetoric of the rabbis.

It used to be thought that the methods of midrash analysis are largely replicated in the Talmud of the Land of Israel and in the Babylonian Talmud, but this view has largely been refined or refuted. Neusner found that Mishnah rarely engages in scriptural exegesis. The Talmud of the Land of Israel does engage in scriptural investiga-

tion, mainly assuming that Mishnah needs support for the purposes of its authority and a scriptural basis for its norms. Thus, the new view links oral and written Torah in accord with the theological point of reference of the editors of that latter corpus. In contrast, extensive studies show that the Babylonian Talmud builds equally on the texts of the oral Torah, the Mishnah, and on verses of the written Torah, Scripture.

Much later, during the Middle Ages, Jewish scholars developed several different types of biblical criticism. These derived from diverse sources: the traditions of conventional rabbinic exegesis; medieval mystical traditions within Judaism; and grammatical, syntactical, and other critical advances of the Middle Ages. Many of the commentaries and expositions of that period are eclectic mixtures of these strands of interpretation.

Scholarship has come to argue that it is not sufficient to describe the growth of Bible criticism in the Middle Ages in terms of the clash between the literal and homiletical interpretations of Scripture. Rather, as is the case for earlier midrash, it is more urgent to examine the materials in a broader cultural context. Hence, we now seek to determine how medieval rabbis transformed and extended earlier rabbinic midrash into a commentary form of exegesis, how they melded it together with newer mystical speculations on the Torah, and how they integrated into their glosses and expositions the fruits of linguistic explorations and discoveries.

The paradigmatic master of medieval rabbinic commentary was Rashi (Rabbi Solomon ben Isaac, 1040–1105), a scholar from the north of France. While he is often credited with the move to "literal commentary" in medieval times, even a cursory study of his commentaries reveals how indebted he was to the rabbinic exegesis of the earlier classical compilations. With Rashi we witness the mature development of a new paradigm of interpretation. He delicately balances his interpretations between gloss and exposition. He picks at and edits the earlier midrash materials and weaves together with them into his commentary the results of new discoveries, such as philology and grammar. His main proposition is hardly radical within rabbinism. He accepts that there is one whole Torah of Moses consisting of the oral and written traditions and texts. In his commentaries he accomplished the nearly seamless integration of the basics of both bodies of tradition.

During the Middle Ages, especially in the tenth century, the new methods of the lower criticism of the Hebrew text make their way into medieval interpretation. These derived mainly from the authorities in Spain: Menahem ben Jacob ibn Saruq, Dunash ben Labrat, Judah ben Hayyuj, Jonah ibn Janah. The eclectic commentaries of Abraham ibn Ezra (1090–1164) are sometimes depicted as indications of the beginnings of more independent and radical critical examinations of the canonical text. Ibn Ezra appears to move more freely away from the standard theological postulates of rabbinic interpretation and to treat the text of the Torah as more of an independent entity. The so-called synthetic commentaries of David Kimhi (1160–1235) and Nahmanides (1195–1270) range farther from the received traditions of earlier midrash compilations. Nahmanides wrote a more expositional commentary and frequently interjected mystical references and allusions.

Some important Jewish interpretation did not adhere to or derive from the paradigmatic styles or agenda of midrash. The early Hellenistic allegory of Philo of Alexandria (b. c. 10 B.C.E.), for instance, is seen by some as a precursor of rabbinic midrash that represents a distinctive Hellenistic Jewish cultural context dealing in its way with the same authoritative texts. Philo's allegory exemplifies the application of Hellenistic techniques to the Greek translation of the Torah. Another collection of exegetical texts, the Dead Sea Pesharim from Qumran (first century B.C.E.), contains examples of an apocalyptic Jewish group's interpretations of the Prophets out of their view of messianic eschatology. These materials are for the most part disjointed from prior and later Jewish biblical interpretation.

A less radical disjuncture can be identified in medieval Jewish thought. Some leading medieval rationalists deemphasized the fruits of the midrash and Aggadah and lauded at its expense the processes of philosophical analysis. Maimonides's (1135–1204) philosophical allegory in the *Guide for the Perplexed* is seen by some critics as an illustration of the process of cloaking semiesoteric philosophical precepts in interpretive garb to be passed on to the newly initiated disciple. Some Maimonideans saw philosophy as inimical to the process of midrash.

Tzvee Zahavy

Daniel Boyarin, *Intertextuality and the Reading of Midrash* (1990); Roger Brooks, *The Spirit of the Ten Commandments: Shattering the Myth of Rabbinic Legalism* (1990); Jose Faur, *Golden Doves with Silver Dots: Semiotics and Textuality in Rabbinic Tradition* (1986); Michael Fishbane, *Biblical Interpretation in Ancient Israel* (1985); Moshe Greenberg, *Parshanut ha-Mikra ha-yehudit: Pirke mavo* (1983); David Halivni, *Peshat and Derash: Plain and Applied Meaning in Rabbinic Exegesis* (1991); Barry Holtz, ed., *Back to the Sources: Reading Classical Jewish Texts* (1984); James L. Kugel, *In Potiphar's House: The Interpretive Life of Biblical Texts* (1990); James L. Kugel and Rowan A. Greer, *Early Biblical Interpretation* (1986); Ezra Zion Melamed, *Mefarshe ha-Mikra: Darkehem ve-shitotehem* (1975); Jacob Neusner, *The Midrash: An Introduction* (1990); Gary Porton, "Midrash" (*Anchor Bible Dictionary*, vol. 4, 1992), *Understanding Rabbinic Midrash* (1985); J. W. Rogerson and Werner G. Jeanrond, "Interpretation, History of" (*Anchor Bible Dictionary*, vol. 3, 1992); M. H. Segal, *Parsanut HaMiqra* (1952); David Stern, *Parables in Midrash: Narrative and Exegesis in Rabbinic Literature* (1991); Burton L. Visotzky, "Hermeneutics, Early Rabbinic" (*Anchor Bible Dictionary*, vol. 2, 1992), *Reading the Book: Making the Bible a Timeless Text* (1991).

2. Modern Criticism

Coeval with the revitalization of literary theory that took place in America in the late 1960s and early 1970s, the term "biblical criticism" began to command for scholars and practitioners of literary study almost as wide a semantic field as it did for nearly two centuries in Germany, where, under the rubric "documentary hypothesis," it referred (and continues to refer) to the multiplicity of compositional schools said to make up the Judeo-Christian Old Testament. The advent of theory brought with it a heightened concern for the dynamics of critical reading. And as the discussion of these dynamics (and in general of the "hypothesis of textuality") made its way increasingly into the study of other cultural monuments, it was probably inevitable that this concern would show up in biblical study as well.

The conjunction may be more than fortuitous. There may be a deeper affinity, even an intimacy, between biblical Scripture and literary texts of which such a conjunction is only the outermost expression, an affinity that has escaped the purview of most scholars, although secretly animating each domain throughout their history, and yet deserves our attention if we are to understand either of them more fully. The unearthing of this affinity, however, may not be easy, and most of the ways in which the project is currently pursued may prove more of an obstacle to that understanding than an aid. Modern "biblical criticism," for example, conceived and constructed along the lines of "Shakespeare criticism" or "classical criticism," as one more subject for literary analysis, may be a misnomer in a number of important ways. Where Kantian aesthetics presumes a fundamental gulf between its own domain and that of the object of its critical attention, an object rendered passive, if inspired, before this appreciative and meaning-oriented gaze, Hebraic biblical reading makes no such assumptions.

In the first place, the individual biblical reader is never independent of the long tradition of exegetical commentary—Talmudic, midrashic, kabbalistic, rabbinic, and so on—in which Scripture and its reading are embedded. Second, the center of critical gravity in biblical interpretation is never the reader at all but the text and the divine encounter whose traces it bears (and before which the individual reader is something like the "site of an instruction"). Third, the goal of biblical interpretation is never to identify the "meaning" of Scripture, the fitting or revelatory understandings by which a heterogeneous scriptural presentation may be rendered unified and coherent beyond contradiction or conflict, but rather to show how by virtue of an identifiable Toradic commentary (which is given in advance and which is available via the above exegetical traditions) what appears outside Torah is in fact within. And finally, the reading or commentary that proceeds in this fashion does so not by the synchronic representational analysis to which since PLATO we have become accustomed in the West but by a diachronic, "prophetic," or "anti-idolatrous" account consonant with biblical revelation itself.

"Biblical reading" or "biblical commentary" would therefore appear more reflective of this inner Hebraic teaching or instruction. But "biblical" is no less laden with difficulty than "criticism." In a Western European context, "biblical" inevitably suggests "Judeo-Christian." But no such scriptures exist for Jews. Although the words of the Old Testament may at times appear identical with the Hebrew Torah (although even here there are discrepancies), there is no Jewish Old Testament, if only because there is no New Testament. The Bible, the Torah, the teaching *(torah)* or instruction or commandments *(mitzvot)* given by God through Moses at Sinai to the community of Israel is all there is. All the rest, as the sages say, is commentary. The very word "Bible," deriving from the Greek *ta biblia* and meaning "books" or "the books," has no correlative in Hebrew, where *mikra, tanakh,* and *torah* refer to the same body of writings but are deemed indissolubly linked to their divine author.

Would not, then, *"Torah* reading" or *"Toradic* commentary" satisfy at least the linguistic components of the comparison? As soon as we consider the parameters of our subject matter, new difficulties arise. The Torah for Judaism is indisputably the central document for which all other collections—Talmudic, midrashic, kabbalistic, rabbinic, and so on—are properly regarded as supplements or extensions. At the same time, since what the Torah teaches is the way what appears novel is in fact a part of the creative "blueprint," such exegetical traditions may also be said to be the register of traditions already contained within Torah, and consequently this supplementary Torah, which is said to register the oral teachings, has come to be regarded historically within Judaism as containing as much divine authority as the written. According to an ancient midrashic tradition, the entirety of Torah—both oral and written—was given to Moses during the forty days of his sojourn on Sinai.

And if the external parameters are fluid, easy distinctions regarding internal parameters are no less quickly confounded. For if we take, for example, the text commonly referred to as Torah—the *Chumash,* the Pentateuch, the five books of Moses—we note that the whole Torah can be said to be contained within only one portion of that book, within the chapters in Exodus *(shemoth)* and Deuteronomy *(davarim)* where the Ten Commandments are given. Similarly, the whole of the Ten Commandments may be said to be contained within the first commandment, the whole of the first commandment within the first word of that commandment—*anochi,* "I," God's self-reference. And within some more esoteric traditions, the whole of that first word *anochi* is itself said to be contained within the first letter of that word, the aleph, indeed even within the first stroke undertaken by a scribe to produce in writing that aleph (composed as it is of an upright *yod,* an inclined *vav,* and another upright *yod*), *yod* being of course itself the first letter of the name of God, YHVH. And if the *Chumash,* with which we began, is taken already to contain the vast plethora of Toradic commentaries to which we have already referred, and that conglomerate itself said to contain already the world (of which it is the "blueprint"), then the entire world may be said to be contained within the initial *yod* by which the aleph is constructed. The fantasy concocted by Jorge Luis Borges by which the entirety of the world's knowledge is contained in the "Aleph" observable in the basement of the house of the narrator's professional rival in Buenos Aires is compatible with the deepest structures of kabbalistic understanding.

The clothing of Torah, then, within such modern Kantian phenomenological garb (to use a kabbalistic metaphor) risks fashioning an object that neither resembles other objects nor reflects anything like the self-understanding of the tradition from which it comes. Such dangers have not, of course, inhibited readers from aligning this ancient text within a wide variety of alien strategies, and as the beginning of an attempt to map an account of Torah reading that is answerable to Hebraic origins (i.e., one in which, in the language of Emmanuel Levinas, the Hebraic is translated into Greek), it might be helpful to survey current practice.

In the modern context, we may broadly distinguish two readings, those that accept and extend the New Critical, humanistic, historical perspective and those that resist or reject it. Mainstream Christian institutions, for example, continue to read the Hebrew Bible much as they have for nearly two thousand years—as indissolubly linked to the New Testament (and especially to the gospel of Jesus of Nazareth), whether mediated by church authority or developed by individual textual experiences informed by a tradition of such reformist reading. The fundamental insufficiency of an Old Testament of wrath and violence before a triumphant new covenant of mercy and love, conceived either theologically or historically, remains a cornerstone of Christian biblical interpretation.

Far from rejecting such a distinction, Jewish readings recognize it as preeminently Toradic and regard its appropriation by Christian or other communities at the expense of Jewish sources to be episodes in a long history of irony and persecution. Long before Christianity, Judaism regarded its scripture as the Word of God—given to Moses at Sinai on behalf of Israel as a set of teachings or commandments designed to enable the human community to live in harmony with God's creative plans. Unlike Christianity, however, Judaism regards Torah as sufficient to this task. Beyond the wide variety of modern styles of observance, including not only the three major orthodox, conservative, and reform styles but the multifarious older and alternative variants (Hasidic, reconstructionist, secular humanist, egalitarian, etc.), the sine qua non of modern Jewish life remains the distinction between Jewish and non-Jewish modalities of being and reading conceived in these terms, a history particularly intensified for Jews by experiences during the years 1933–45 (see, e.g., Geoffrey Hartman's *Bitburg in Moral and Political Perspective*).

Before one community that rejects Torah in favor of an alternative and incarnate revelation yet to come and another that appears to outsiders to globalize its propositions to the exclusion of non-Toradic texts, a third position developed that identified both strategies as doctrinal, dogmatic, or theological—in short, subjective—and opted instead for a more demonstrable, "documentary," objective approach. Born within the context of critical philosophy, which detaches a sovereign subject from the object of his or her attention and detaches both from the interference of any extrahuman authority, modern biblical criticism, the *Wissenschaft des Judentums* as practiced in Germany since the end of the eighteenth century, would thus appear as a kind of Protestantism without divinity.

Scholars continue to debate whether the "documentary hypothesis" should be traced to medieval philosophers such as Joseph Ibn Kaspi, who were interested in the multiple names for God; to renegade seventeenth-century rationalists such as Baruch Spinoza, who thought Scripture could be studied scientifically; or to a series of late-eighteenth- and nineteenth-century researchers, among them Jean Astruc, Johann G. Eichhorn, W. M. L. De Wette, Herman Hupfeld, K. H. Graf, Bernhard Duhm, and Julius Wellhausen (whose work is often cited as representing this group at its most characteristic), who carried out, largely within the German university, an analysis of the sources and conditions from which Old Testament documents derive. But all agree upon attributing the heterogeneity of scriptural presentation to principally four or more scriptural segments (labeled variously J, E, P, and D) in accordance with a given document's distinctive use of the name for God (J or "Jahwist" where the Tetragrammaton (YHVH) is employed, E or "Elohist" where the word *elohim* is used), its inclusion of ritual or cultic material in place of other narrative styles (P or "Priestly"), its approach to legal matters (D or "Deuteronomic"), and so on. (For accounts of this tradition and method see Umberto Cassuto, *The Documentary Hypothesis and the Composition of the Pentateuch* [1959, trans. Israel Abrahams, 1961]; Herbert F. Hahn, *The Old Testament in Modern Research* [1970]; and Moshe Weinfeld's "Biblical Criticism" in Cohen and Mendes-Flohr. For an example see Wellhausen's *Geschichte Israels* [2 vols., 1878, *Prolegomena to the History of Israel,* trans. J. Sutherland Black and Allan Menzies, 1885, reprint, 1957].)

The success of this "historical-critical" approach in isolating a document (or set of documents) from the more dogmatic constraints of earlier expositors was enormous. An explosion of interest in what came to be called "biblical criticism" was evident in all arenas of critical philosophy. But the very sources of its success could also be perceived as its greatest liability, and more recent views deriving equally from the Kantian revolution in critical philosophy have set aside the success of the historical approach in favor of what might be deemed "biblical aesthetics." Attempting to avoid such earlier doctrinal constraints (more recent views could argue), the historical-critical approach erred in the other extreme: it avoided reading the textual dynamics of Torah at all. The more the "documentary hypothesis" was confirmed, the more it was corrected and corroborated by similar research being conducted in neighboring disciplines—anthropology, sociology, archaeology, linguistics, the history of ancient Near Eastern religions, and so on—the more in fact these sources, contexts, and consequences were available to be substituted for a close reading of the text itself.

And in light of the historical upheavals of the first half of the twentieth century, it is hardly to be wondered (these newer views could further observe) that the humanist faith of these nineteenth-century researchers was perceived as naive and inadequate. A loss of confidence in the separability of belief from structure consequent of this modern turmoil threw the historical approach into disarray, and the current hyperactive interest in what appears to be at once a return to theology and a new turn to the dynamics of close critical reading is the result. Parallels for such a development in the study of modern English and European literatures, which reoriented itself away from PHILOLOGY before World War II toward NEW CRITICISM after, or even in the study of other ancient literatures (study of the classics, for example, underwent similar alterations at a slower pace) of course abound.

The work of Robert Alter is especially important in this regard. In a powerful book on biblical narrative (1981), Alter suggested that the formalist approach developed by the New Critics for the study of seventeenth-century metaphysical poetry might productively be applied to biblical Scripture. Quite apart from questions about compositional origins or limitations (which motivated older commentators, for example, E. A. Speiser in his "Genesis" in the *Anchor Bible,* 1964), one had now, Alter argued, to ask more difficult "literary" questions about how such admittedly disparate compositional traditions could be perceived as "going together." In 1985 Alter extended his consideration to biblical poetics, and together with Frank Kermode, who had written widely on the relation between narrative and religious scripture himself, as in *The Genesis of Secrecy: On the Interpretation of Narrative* (1979), he compiled *The Literary Guide to the Bible* (1987), which gathered essays on all books of the Judeo-Christian Old and New testaments. With these publications, the literary study of the Bible was off to a running start. Other critics, more visibly influenced by Continental theory, began undertaking projects of a more hybrid and experimental nature. GEOFFREY H. HARTMAN, for example, whose own work in English Romanticism had previously become embroiled in post-structuralist debates, against some opposition organized a session at the English Institute at Harvard in the early 1980s to which he brought scholars and critics from literature and Near Eastern (and religious) studies departments (including Alter, Michael Fishbane, Herbert Marks, and Leslie Brisman), and biblical study was quickly projected into the maelstrom of theoretical debate. Hart-

man's own essay was published in Budick and Hartman's *Midrash and Literature* (1986).

In the wake of these events, the study of the Bible within both of these literary and theoretical orientations has quickly expanded. In 1987 David Damrosch applied some of the recent theoretical discussions of narrative to the older historical-critical approach (see also Daniel Boyarin's *Intertextuality and the Reading of Midrash,* 1990). New conferences and subsequent collections have also become more frequent. Regina Schwartz describes her collection of essays deriving from a conference she directed (*The Book and the Text: The Bible and Literary Theory,* 1990) as "complementary" to the project of Alter and Kermode, including theoretical currents that their "literary" guide explicitly excludes. Jacob Rosenblatt and Joseph Sitterson published a collection of essays from a 1989 conference at Georgetown University in which the question of aesthetic unity and its relation to biblical reading was placed center stage (*"Not in Heaven": Coherence and Complexity in Biblical Narrative,* 1991), and a volume edited by Stephen Prickett in 1991 undertakes the ambitious task of tracing in a series of essays the history of biblical interpretation.

Amid this flurry of new approaches, older scholars and critics long known for their work in other domains of literary criticism now attracted attention for their biblical study. NORTHROP FRYE's argument for a typological literary reading in *The Great Code* (1983) garnered new interest, and in 1990 Frye completed a second volume (*Words with Power*) on the same subject matter. HAROLD BLOOM, who had long identified his theory of poetic influence with Jewish mystical sources (see *Kabbalah and Criticism,* 1975) but had concerned himself thematically with English Romantic and modernist poetry, published a series of investigations of documentary authorship from a postmodernist perspective; examples are his introduction to the 1982 reprint of Martin Buber's *On the Bible: Eighteen Studies* (ed. Nahum N. Glatzer, 1968), his review of the Alter and Kermode anthology ("Literature As the Bible," *New York Review of Books,* March 1988), and his introductions to his Chelsea House collections of critical essays, *Genesis* (1986), *Exodus* (1987), and *The Bible* (1987). With David Rosenberg, Bloom produced *The Book of J* (1991), in which he develops at length his arguments about biblical authorship and produces a version of the "J" document.

Formalist, poststructuralist, neoreligious, and neo-historical critical approaches aside, writing about the Bible within literary studies has come from other quarters as well. Younger scholars, such as Susan Handelman, have begun to trace more systematically the intersection between Judaic and poststructuralist interpretation. And some of the practitioners of structuralist or deconstructionist approaches have themselves written in this area. ROLAND BARTHES's "Wrestling with the Angel" (in *Image-Music-Text*, 1977, and Bloom's anthology *Genesis*), for example, might be contrasted with Hartman's discussion of the same text, Genesis 32:22–32 (see also Alfred M. Johnson Jr.'s collection, *Structuralism and Biblical Hermeneutics*, 1979). Feminist readings of the Bible have been plentiful if at times unconventional, as in Mieke Bal's reading of love stories (*Lethal Love: Feminist Literary Readings of Biblical Love Stories*, 1987) and the Book of Judges (*Death and Dissymmetry*, 1988).

JACQUES DERRIDA's scattered remarks on biblical and theological texts have attracted increasing attention. For example, his philosophic and literary critiques of Edmond Jabès and Emmanuel Levinas turn upon biblical and more broadly Hebraic themes in those writers (see, e.g., "Edmond Jabès and the Question of the Book" and "Violence and Metaphysics," both in *Writing and Difference*, 1967, trans., 1978). For an example of Jabès's own poetic critical output see the multivolume *Book of Questions* (1963–65, trans., 1976–77).

Concomitant with this activity, researchers in Near Eastern (or religious) studies trained by an older generation (e.g., Nahum Sarna and Jacob Neusner, for whom "biblical criticism" retained its more European sense) began to engage more boldly hermeneutical pursuits. Thus, for example, the hermeneutics studies of Michael Fishbane, the poetics studies of James Kugel, David Stern's studies of midrash and interpretation, and Phyllis Trible's studies of biblical sexuality and terror. (For an interesting collection contrasting Jewish and Christian approaches to interpretation see Frederick Greenspahn's *Scripture in the Jewish and Christian Traditions: Authority, Interpretation, Relevance*, 1982.) Similarly in Israel, where scholars such as Martin Noth, Umberto Cassuto, Gershom Scholem, and Yehezkel Kaufmann were once unquestioningly revered, new more critical studies have begun to appear. Meir Sternberg's *The Poetics of Biblical Narrative* (1985) develops the potential for looking at biblical texts with the methodological apparatus once reserved for the novel, and Moshe Idel's *Kabbalah* (1988) attempts to remedy the limitations he feels have been imposed upon our appreciation of the Jewish mystical tradition by studying aspects that, in his view, Scholem left out.

In France, the work of André Neher and Emmanuel Levinas merits singular attention. Neher's analysis of the story of Cain and Abel, which was later included in his general study of silence in the biblical and modern contexts (*The Exile of the Word: From the Silence of the Bible to the Silence of Auschwitz*, 1970, trans., 1981), has been extraordinarily influential. And Levinas's "Talmudic lessons" have become the centerpiece of the yearly meetings of the Colloques des intellectuels juifs de langue française (see, e.g., *Nine Talmudic Readings* and *Difficult Freedom*. For an account of this group as part of the larger context of modern French Jewry see Judith Friedlander's *Vilna on the Seine: Jewish Intellectuals in France since 1968*, 1990). Levinas's work is especially important to the changing status of biblical study in France. Developed in a powerful series of books and essays (as in *Totality and Infinity* and *Otherwise than Being*), his central philosophic thesis—the radical otherness or alterity of transcendence to the traditional ontological terms in which, within the practice of Platonic philosophy, transcendence has customarily been thought—translates the notion of the law of anti-idolatry, an idea that in turn powerfully informs discussions of Torah in a number of religious-studies contexts and as such is likely to prove decisive in their future contact. (A selection of texts from the Colloques is available in Sandor Goodhart and Suzanne Stewart's *"We Will Do and We Will Hear."*)

Finally, a few other researchers who continue to interest themselves in the intersections between biblical texts and contemporary theoretical concerns deserve special mention. One of the most powerful instances of modern biblical criticism has emerged from the work of RENÉ GIRARD, a Frenchman working in America largely on texts in literature, cultural anthropology, and psychoanalysis. His volumes on the European novel and on the relation between violence and the sacred in primitive communities have attracted a large international following (see *Deceit, Desire, and the Novel* and *Violence and the Sacred*). More recently, Girard has turned his attention to origins of his own disclosures, identifying the possibility of understanding the scapegoating mechanisms he finds at the origin of cultural order in the biblical critique of sacrifice in the Hebrew Bible and Christian gospel. Raymund Schwager, S.J., has developed the implications of Girard's biblical reading for Christian thought (*Must There Be Scapegoats? Violence and Redemption in the Bible*, trans. Maria L. Assad, 1987), and Sandor Goodhart has developed their implications for the reading of Jewish texts (*Sacrificing Commentary*). PAUL RICOEUR's analysis of biblical time is reflected in *Essays on Biblical Interpretation* (ed. Lewis S. Mudge, 1980). Bernard-Henri Lévy's much maligned *Testament of God* (1979, trans., 1980), which studies the relation between contemporary politics and biblical reading, may prove more important than originally imagined. And MAURICE BLANCHOT's writings on religious themes, which have begun only recently to be translated (e.g., *The Infinite Conversation*, 1969, trans., 1992), have powerfully influenced French critical writing, including Derrida's, for a number of years and deserve closer study.

The energy currently devoted to biblical study in literary-critical practice is, in short, enormous (a keyword search for items under both "bible and criticism" and "bible and interpretation" in a major research library yields more than 3,800 volumes since 1970 alone!). And annotated bibliographies such as Mark Powell's *The Bible and Modern Literary Criticism* are the order of the day. On the other hand, it is far from clear that all this energy is of the same kind. In the immediate postwar period in the United States, in which New Criticism flourished, the relation between literary study and the Higher Criticism (which for SAMUEL TAYLOR COLERIDGE and even MATTHEW ARNOLD was still a complicated and sensitive one) had lost much of its charge, and biblical study was consigned to elucidating the historical background of the canonic figures of imaginative literature in the West—DANTE ALIGHIERI, William Shakespeare, John Milton—or, more broadly, the human condition at large. ERICH AUERBACH's opening chapter in *Mimesis* (1946, trans., 1953), in which he contrasts the externalized style of Homer with the more internalized style of Hebraic Scripture, is a good example. And Herbert Schneidau's *Sacred Discontent: The Bible and Western Tradition* (1977) reflects the kind of humanistic cultural-studies context into which biblical thinking could be projected when it was considered an object of discussion at all. The notable exception is the work of KENNETH BURKE, whose concern with logology and rhetoric (as in *The Rhetoric of Religion*, 1963) predates much later interest, but Burke's "eccentricity" (in the eyes of his peers) only confirms this general claim.

The advent of Continental theory in the late 1960s and early 1970s in America certainly shifted things around a great deal. But are we sure that the changes wrought by the advent of theory are as thorough as we have imagined them to be? The more we reflect upon Jewish experience from 1933 to 1945, and the more we come to think of the Holocaust less as a takeover by hostile forces from the outside than as the monstrous extremity of a perspective endemic to European Romantic thought itself, the more mythic and naively self-serving such humanistic and historical accounts of our past begin to appear. And as a result, the more we may need to rethink current critical practices that are based upon those accounts.

In other words, I would suggest that the gravest threat to biblical study in the early 1990s appears to issue less from the refusal to read Torah at all (which is the charge aesthetic accounts level against older approaches) than from the urge to read it in ways that repeat and act out older humanist and historicist patterns, with all their limitations, in a post-Holocaust setting. To what extent, we need to ask ourselves, do we remain responsible in our current reading to both our own experiences and those of the texts we read (and of which they are both the concrete reflection and a commentary)? Is the literary approach of Alter and Kermode significantly different finally, for example, from the methodology of New Critics? And if New Criticism is deemed to be an extension of nineteenth-century humanist thought, what implications does that claim entail for current "literary" biblical approaches? On the other hand, is the structuralist and poststructuralist perspective urged upon us by other critics (which concerns itself with the vagaries of "textuality") any less a displacement of inner biblical reading than the historical-critical approach to which it so vehemently, and often systematically, opposes itself (see, e.g., Mieke Bal's *Death and Dissymmetry*)? Poststructuralism has undoubtedly done away with the subject and the object and in general the primacy of consciousness in favor of language, and that is a great achievement. But is the representational understanding of language that has emerged in the wake of Heideggerian thinking, upon which it so often relies, any less "Greek," finally, any less a suppression of the "prophetic," and consequently of the biblical and the Hebraic, than the Kantian cognitive and aesthetic traditions it supplants?

To read Torah, in other words, as dogma, as document, or in accord with even the most sophisticated techniques of current literary-critical or aesthetic practice is identically to presume and preserve a gulf between our own experience and that of the text before us, to remove us from the very Hebraic biblical assumptions we have presumably undertaken this project to apprehend, and thereby to bar ourselves from the very encounter or meeting such "inner Biblical exegesis" or teaching (to use Michael Fishbane's phrase) has to offer us. The affinity between biblical Scripture and literature may be apprehendable less within the cognitive or aesthetic models by which we customarily pursue it than within the inner critical reading common to both, whose subject is ironically such misreading itself, and which we commonly repudiate and reenact. In the shadow of the death camps and the rendering unexpectedly visible of a secret equation between humanism, historicism, and murder, such an encounter would seem especially urgent, and its refusal especially costly.

Sandor Goodhart

See bibliographies in ERICH AUERBACH, ROLAND BARTHES, MAURICE BLANCHOT, HAROLD BLOOM, KENNETH BURKE, JACQUES DERRIDA, NORTHROP FRYE, and RENÉ GIRARD for texts by those writers.

Robert Alter, *The Art of Biblical Narrative* (1981), *The Art of Biblical Poetry* (1985); Robert Alter and Frank Kermode, eds., *The Literary Guide to the Bible* (1987); Mieke Bal, *Death and Dissymmetry: The Politics of Coherence in the Book of Judges* (1988); Leslie Brisman, *The Voice of Jacob: On the Composition of Genesis* (1990); Sanford Budick and Geoffrey H. Hartman, eds., *Midrash and Literature* (1986); Arthur Cohen and Paul Mendes-Flohr, eds., *Contemporary Jewish Religious Thought* (1988); David Damrosch, *The Narrative Covenant: Transformation of Genre in the Growth of Biblical Literature* (1987); Michael Fishbane, *Biblical Interpretation in Ancient Israel* (1985), *The Garments of Torah: Essays in Biblical Hermeneutics* (1989); Sandor Goodhart, *Sacrificing Commentary: Reading the End of Literature* (1993); Sandor Goodhart and Suzanne Stewart, eds., *"We Will Do and We Will Hear": Biblical Reading in France* (1994); Susan Handelman, *The Slayers of Moses: The Emergence of Rabbinic Interpretation in Modern Literary Theory* (1982); Geoffrey H. Hartman, ed., *Bitburg in Moral and Political Perspective* (1986); Moshe Idel, *Kabbalah: New Perspectives* (1988); Edmond Jabès, *Le Livre des questions* (3 vols., 1963–65, *The Book of Questions,* trans. Rosemarie Waldrop, 3 vols. in 2, 1976–77); James Kugel, *Early Biblical Interpretation* (1986), *The Idea of Biblical Poetry: Parallelism and Its History* (1981), *In Potiphar's House: The Interpretative Life of Biblical Texts* (1990); Emmanuel Levinas, *Autrement qu'être: ou, Au-delà de l'essence* (1974, 2d ed., 1978, *Otherwise than Being: or, Beyond Essence,* trans. Alphonso Lingis, 1981), *Difficile liberté: Essais sur le judaisme* (1963, 3d ed., 1984, *Difficult Freedom: Essays in Judaism,* trans. Sean Hand, 1990), *Quatres lectures talmudiques* and *Du Sacré au saint: Cinq nouvelles lectures talmudiques* (1968, 1977, *Nine Talmudic Readings,* trans. Annette Aronowicz, 1990), *Totalité et infini: Essai sur l'exteriorité* (1961, *Totality and Infinity: An Essay on Exteriority,* trans. Alphonso Lingis, 1969); Bernard-Henri Lévy, *Le Testament de Dieu* (1979, *The Testament of God,* trans. George Holoch, 1980); André Neher, *L'Exil de la parole, du silence biblique au silence d'Auschwitz* (1970, *The Exile of the Word: From the Silence of the Bible to the Silence of Auschwitz,* trans. David Maisel, 1981); Mark Powell, *The Bible and Modern Literary Criticism: A Critical Assessment and Annotated Bibliography* (1992); Stephen Prickett, ed., *Reading the Text: Biblical Criticism and Literary Theory* (1991); David Stern, *Midrash and Parable* (1988); Meir Sternberg, *The Poetics of Biblical Narrative: Ideological Literature and the Drama of Reading* (1985); Phyllis Trible, *God and the Rhetoric of Sexuality* (1978), *Texts of Terror: Literary Feminist Readings of Biblical Narratives* (1984).

BLACKMUR, R. P.

Richard Palmer Blackmur (1904–65) grew up in Boston, and although he never received a university degree, he was shaped by the intellectual environment of Harvard and Cambridge, Massachusetts. Since he came to maturity in the *anni mirabiles* of modernism, 1921–25, he was instinctively in touch with the best in contemporary writing, and his position as an editor of *Hound and Horn* (1928–30) drew him to the center of the American literary scene. A fine poet himself, Blackmur brought to his literary criticism a practical understanding of how writers think and feel.

Blackmur began to write criticism at precisely the time when "close reading" became the dominant mode of literary analysis, and his essays of 1930–34 (collected in *The Double Agent*) are models of the genre. His early critical method may be seen as a fusion of 1) T. S. ELIOT's practice of never generalizing without a text at hand, 2) HENRY JAMES's gift for delicate moral and aesthetic discriminations, and 3) WILLIAM EMPSON's demonstration (in *Seven Types of Ambiguity,* 1930) that the theories of I. A. RICHARDS could be transformed into an intricate procedure for linguistic analysis that teases out the paradoxes and nuances of poetic discourse. Blackmur was especially influenced by Richards's clinical analyses (in *Practical Criticism,* 1929) of the act of reading and by the distinction Richards draws between the determined "statements" of science and the open "pseudostatements" of poetry. In many ways Blackmur shared the same assumptions about the instability of language found in later deconstructionist criticism, but with the crucial difference that he felt that these contradictory linguistic signals could be partially controlled by the "rational imagination" of the writer and reader.

One might say that Blackmur was uniquely equipped to handle the poets of his age, since his critical sensibility had been shaped by the same forces that underlay their methods, and it is not surprising that his criticism of the 1930s contains the definitive—and enduring—early assessments of the art of W. B. Yeats, Ezra Pound, Eliot, Wallace Stevens, E. E. Cummings, and Marianne Moore. In each case Blackmur's analysis is based upon scrupulous research (which always lies beneath the surface) and an admirable grasp of each writer's distinctive "voice." His form of critical attack varies from author to author, emphasizing linguistic effects in the case of Stevens and Cummings, the use of myth and magic in Yeats, the problem of poetry and belief in Eliot. In every instance Blackmur strikes so close to the essential qualities of the writer that his early essays remain authoritative and exciting after nearly half a century. No critic of the 1930s, save Pound and Eliot, has worn so well.

After the early 1940s, when Blackmur gave up his career as an independent man of letters and accepted a teaching position at Princeton, his criticism gradually became engaged with wider cultural and intellectual interests. His essays of the 1940s on Henry James still display the keen interest in language that marks his early criticism, but they are also concerned with the social and moral dimensions of James's imagination. Like the later Eliot, Blackmur became more interested in general problems of literature and culture (although without Eliot's doctrinal emphasis), and in his later years he concentrated on the European novel, believing with James (in the preface to *The Ambassadors*) that the novel is "the most independent, most elastic, most prodigious of literary forms." In these studies he is concerned with the ways in which cultural assumptions determine literary forms and with the nature of literature as a social institution. NEW CRITICISM, with its emphasis on close reading of individual "poetic" passages, had always been weakest when confronted with the larger architecture (and the more explicit social concerns) of the novel. In his work on Henry James and in *Eleven Essays in the European Novel* Blackmur took up the challenge of moving beyond formal analysis to a consideration of the moral dramas embodied in fiction. In many ways his concerns in these essays are those of his contemporary LIONEL TRILLING, although Blackmur's point of view is less ideological. His aim was to uncover the writer's fundamental (and often conflicted) assumptions about how behavior is represented in language.

The essay was Blackmur's chosen form, but throughout his career he labored on a critical biography of Henry Adams, whose skeptical spirit appealed to his deepest emotions and beliefs. Published in an edited version 15 years after his death, *Henry Adams* (and especially the chapter "King Richard's Prison Song") reveals in moving detail Blackmur's ability to penetrate, and reinvoke in highly charged language, the thoughts and feelings of another writer.

Although R. P. Blackmur played a major role in shaping modern American literary criticism, his greatest achievement lay (as he would have wished) in his impact on American poetry. A generation of poets—among them Randall Jarrell, Robert Lowell, Delmore Schwartz, and John Berryman—was deeply influenced in style and sensibility by the example of his criticism. Speaking of an obscure review that Blackmur published in *Poetry* magazine in May 1935, Berryman said flatly that it "changed my life." Later Berryman wove part of that review into his poetic tribute to Blackmur, "Olympus" (*Love & Fame*, 1970, 18). Appropriately, Blackmur's words are set up as what they were: poetry.

In my serpentine researches
I came on a book review in *Poetry*
which began, with sublime assurance,
a comprehensive air of majesty,

'The art of poetry
is amply distinguished from the manufacture of verse
by the animating presence in the poetry
of a fresh idiom: language

so twisted & posed in a form
that it not only expresses the matter in hand
but adds to the stock of available reality.'
I was never altogether the same man after *that*.

A. *Walton Litz*

R. P. Blackmur, *The Double Agent: Essays in Craft and Elucidation* (1935), *Eleven Essays in the European Novel* (1964), *The Expense of Greatness* (1940), *Henry Adams* (ed. Veronica A. Makowsky, 1980), *Language as Gesture: Essays in Poetry* (1952, *Form and Value in Modern Poetry*, 1957, selections), *The Lion and the Honeycomb: Essays in Solicitude and Critique* (1955), *Outsider at the Heart of Things: Essays by R. P. Blackmur* (ed. James T. Jones, 1989), *A Primer of Ignorance* (ed. Joseph Frank, 1967), *Selected Essays* (ed. Denis Donoghue, 1986), *Studies in Henry James* (ed. Veronica A. Makowsky, 1983).

Robert Boyers, *R. P. Blackmur: Poet-Critic: Towards a View of Poetic Objects* (1980); Edward T. Cone, with Joseph Frank and Edmund Keeley, eds., *The Legacy of R. P. Blackmur: Essays, Memoirs, Texts* (1987); Joseph Frank, "R. P. Blackmur: The Later Phase," *The Widening Gyre: Crisis and Mastery in Modern Literature* (1963); Russell Fraser, *A Mingled Yarn: The Life of R. P. Blackmur* (1981); Stanley Edgar Hyman, *The Armed Vision: A Study in the Methods of Modern Literary Criticism* (1948, rev. ed., 1955); James T. Jones, *Wayward Skeptic: The Theories of R. P. Blackmur* (1986); René Wellek, *A History of Modern Criticism: 1750–1950*, vol. 6, *American Criticism, 1900–1950* (1986).

BLAKE, WILLIAM

The saturation of William Blake (1757–1827), an engraver by trade, in the practice and history of painting and printmaking grounded a preoccupation with style, vision, and reproduction. Confronting the alienating imperatives toward standardization and specialization in London's late-eighteenth-century publishing industry, Blake countered that culture by authoring, calligraphing, illustrating, singeing, etching, printing, binding, and publishing his own work. Such strength of commitment compounded with the haunting psychocultural "myth-mash" drama of his "giant forms" in a composite art form that was the subject of the early work of a number of theoretically inclined critics, for example, Hazard Adams (*William Blake,* 1963), HAROLD BLOOM (*Blake's Apocalypse,* 1965), NORTHROP FRYE (*Fearful Symmetry,* 1947), and E. D. Hirsch (*Innocence and Experience,* 1964).

Blake's scattered critical formulations reflect largely his training in the visual arts; they are difficult to reconcile with each other and, especially, with his literary practice and its many strategies for dissemination (unusual punctuation, puns, variant "copies" of a given title). His recurrent emphasis on "line" may be contrasted with the then dominant "finished" style of engraving, whose pretension to mime in monochrome tone, color, and shadow required decomposing the image into a tedious system of tiny cross-hatchings or dots and lozenges; the polished style of Augustan poetry, with its code of diction and allusion, made for Blake a kind of literary analog. In the labored mediation that such style demands, Blake saw the illusion underlying any attempt to represent external nature (or historical acts); drawing directly on the copperplate, he argued, offers an unmediated line from the beholder to the artist's insight into the artificial nature of reality ("Mental Things are alone Real," *Poetry* 565). Only a firm and determinate line establishes the individual identities or minute particulars in which "the Infinite alone resides" (205). On the other hand, the "bounding line" entails the loss of other possibilities inherent in realized form, so that only by the institution of "contrary" identities (e.g., text and design) can Blake ensure "progression" (34).

In the 1790s Blake urged "energy" and "an improvement of sensual enjoyment" (39; e.g., greater pleasure in reading); after 1800 he favored "mental fight" and a vision of redemptive imagination that taps a heritage of Christian radicalism. From the perspective of energy he inaugurated the Romantic revaluation of Milton as "a true Poet and of the Devils party without knowing it" (35), and then in *Milton, a Poem* he developed his reading into a new type of epic. Blake's complex psychological model gives large play to sexual drive and to repression as it unfolds in the ongoing strife of old Urizen ("horizon"/"your-eyes-in"/"your reason," etc.) and inspiring Los ("loss"/"Sol" [Apollos]), of male Zoas and female Emanations. "The stubborn structure of the language" is Los's building (183). Blake's emphasis on individual identity is engaged on one side by a concern with prideful "selfhood" and on the other by the conclusion that "we are not Individuals but States: Combinations of Individuals" (131). The "true" or "Real Man" appears in or as "Poetic Genius" (1–2) or "Imagination / (Which is the Divine Body of the Lord Jesus, blessed for ever)" (148).

Blake confronts literary theory with a semiotics that stresses how significance can be found in every particular—not least in the "Revelation in the Litteral Expression" (143)—a psychology that highlights the role of the perceiver, a deconstructive dialectic that vibrates with awareness of how form and frame are at once indispensable and intolerably limiting, and the moving instance of a half-century's daily care about making a difference: "I must Create a System, or be enslav'd by another Mans" (153).

Nelson Hilton

William Blake, *The Complete Poetry and Prose of William Blake* (ed. David V. Erdman, rev. ed., 1982), *The Illuminated Blake* (annotated by David V. Erdman, 1974), *The Paintings and Drawings of William Blake* (ed. Martin Butlin, 1981).

Hazard Adams, ed., *Critical Essays on William Blake* (1991); G. E. Bentley, Jr., *Blake Books: Annotated Catalogues of William Blake's Writings* (1977), *Blake Records* (1969); David V. Erdman, *Blake: Prophet against Empire* (rev. ed., 1969); Robert N. Essick, *William Blake, Printmaker* (1980); Northrop Frye, *Fearful Symmetry: A Study of William Blake* (1947); Nelson Hilton, *Essential Articles for the Study of William Blake, 1970–1984* (1986); Nelson Hilton and Thomas A. Vogler, eds., *Unnam'd Forms: Blake and Textuality* (1986); Edward Larrissy, *William Blake* (1985); Dan Miller, Mark Bracher, and Donald Ault, eds., *Critical Paths: Blake and the Argument of Method* (1987); W. J. T. Mitchell, *Blake's Composite Art: A Study of the Illuminated Poetry* (1978).

BLANCHOT, MAURICE

The fiction and philosophical-literary essays of Maurice Blanchot (b. 1907) form one of the most elusive *oeuvres* in modern French letters. A principled recluse, Blanchot has avoided interviews, photographs, and academic affiliations; public knowledge of his life consists of a handful of minor anecdotes and of inferences built around the appearance of his books and essays. In the mid-1930s Blanchot contributed articles to right-wing journals, most notably to the Maurassian periodical *Combat*. During the German occupation his political views changed radically, and since the end of the war he has been a disembodied but unambiguous presence on the left, a co-signer (and rumor has it, the author) of the "Declaration of the 121" (1960), a call to resist French intervention in Algeria. Blanchot's political turn coincided with the inauguration of a literary project that was to help shape French literary modernity. His novels and *récits* (*Thomas l'obscur*, 1941; *Aminadab*, 1942; *L'Arrêt de mort*, 1948) arguably number among the most significant contributions to twentieth-century French literature. Meanwhile, his review of Jean Paulhan's *Les Fleurs de Tarbes*, "Comment la littérature est-elle possible?" (1941), opened theoretical questions that were to achieve definitive formulation a few years later in "La Littérature et le droit à la mort" (*La Part du feu*, 1949), and in the collection of essays bearing the title *L'Espace littéraire* (1955). After the war, and until the early 1970s, Blanchot published regularly in journals such as *Critique* and *La Nouvelle Revue française* and periodically assembled the better part of these essays into books (*Le Livre à venir*, 1959; *L'Entretien infini*, 1969; *L'Amitié*, 1971).

The topical book review served as the vehicle for Blanchot's thought throughout most of his career, and his late work has explored other genres evocative of contingency or incompletion: the fragment in *L'Écriture du désastre* (1980) and gestures of dialogue or commemoration in *La Communauté inavouable* (1983) and *Michel Foucault tel que je l'imagine* (1986). Blanchot's loyalty to occasional forms is consonant with his understanding of "literary space," as is his double engagement with fiction and criticism, a dichotomy that his *oeuvre* at once maintains and subverts: the fictions are "philosophical," and the essays possess a "literary" quality that is in no way gratuitous but derives from the very tenacity with which they pursue their object. "Literary space," for Blanchot, is the locus of an anonymous, unmasterable, unspeakable experience; and his patient attention to this experience imparts to his own writing a curious difficulty. More than one critic has remarked that reading Blanchot "differs from all other reading experiences" (de Man 62). His prose is at once limpid and opaque: classically pure, seamlessly articulated, yet inhabited by an obscurity resulting from a thought held at the limit of its own possibility.

Blanchot's work frequently takes the form of a meditation inspired by one of a select number of exemplary writers (Friedrich Hölderlin, Franz Kafka, Stéphane Mal-

larmé, Rainer Maria Rilke, the Marquis de Sade) and often articulates itself thematically as a critique of dialectical and existential thought. He is not recorded as having attended Alexandre Kojève's influential seminar on G. W. F. HEGEL's *Phenomenology*, but his work resembles that of a number of Kojève's *auditeurs assidus* (GEORGES BATAILLE, JACQUES LACAN, Raymond Queneau) in the intensity with which it examines a relatively narrow spectrum of Hegelian themes and metaphors: work, death, consciousness, history. For Hegel, particularly as mediated by Kojève, humanity and consciousness come into being as action, with action defined as an essentially positive power of negation. The negation of natural desire (i.e., the willingness to risk death) produces humans as self-consciousness, the negation of particularity produces the concept, and so on. Blanchot intervenes at the level of the dialectical mechanism itself, suggesting that the positivity of negation conceals a fundamental neutrality and passivity. Death, the engine of the dialectic, harbors a more absolute death; action masks a more radical passivity. The approach of "literary space" registers the proximity of this irrecuperable death (Blanchot's terms vary: other metaphors that characterize literary space include "the neutral," *desoeuvrement*, "the outside," "essential solitude," and "the other night"). Literature, in its ontological inessentiality, cannot be mastered by a concept or a desire; literature names the unthinkable burden of what Blanchot in a counter-Heideggerian formulation calls "being *as dissimulation*: dissimulation itself" (*Espace* 343). The predicament of the writer, for Blanchot, is that of Orpheus, who loses the object of his desire in the moment of turning toward it and simultaneously loses his own identity in the anonymity and nonpresence of "literary space." To write is to submit to an inexhaustible exhaustion, an endless dissolution of the "I" that cannot even be known as such: the writer betrays the literary experience in remaining true to it, producing an *oeuvre* by remaining blind to its necessary failure. The *oeuvre*, similarly, dissimulates as aesthetic unity its essential contingency and incompletion.

The focus of Blanchot's later work has tended to shift from literature to ethics and politics, returning to such public concerns at the far side of three decades of literary reviewing. His *oeuvre* can certainly be described as "literary" both in his own terms and following common parlance, but it is perhaps worth emphasizing that Blanchot's understanding of literature was always at the farthest remove from academic formalism. Not only does literature, in Blanchot's sense, always involve a turning away from literature, but this turning away has empirical and existential as well as ontological dimensions: historical contingencies of production and dissemination participate in the (de)formation of the *oeuvre;* furthermore, for all its impossibility and inessentiality, the literary is nonetheless an *experience.* The literary, in other words, participates in a much wider communicational predicament. In a late text, when Blanchot describes "dissimulation" as the "effect of the disaster" (*Écriture* 16), he displaces a privileged term but retains the logic of its formulation. The extermination camps are the disaster of history: they are the realized nightmare of an aesthetic and utilitarian ideology that, unwilling to confront its own impossibility, transforms this impossibility into horror. In response, Blanchot pursues the elusive ontologies of friendship, conversation, and community, intersubjective themes that repeat, in a text like *La Communauté inavouable,* some of the characteristic detours of the "literary" experience. The community, like literary space, is "unavowable" and impossible, founded on the anonymity of an endless, impersonal death rather than on the redemptive generality of Hegelian negation or Christian sacrifice. The possibility of ethics, meanwhile, turns out to reside not merely in the self's recognition of the Other but in the self's being "put into question by the Other to the point of not being able to respond except by a limitless responsibility" (*Communauté* 73).

Blanchot's importance for a certain element in contemporary criticism would be hard to overestimate, but it is also hard to assess. Although his essays are in many ways foreign to the academic institution and its discourses, few critics writing at the intersection of philosophy and criticism in postwar France have failed to pay homage to Blanchot, and if anything, his *oeuvre* has struck many serious commentators as being uncannily, disempoweringly infectious. Critics as different as JEAN STAROBINSKI and MICHEL FOUCAULT have noted their inability to move from paraphrase or repetition to a genuine exegesis of Blanchot's work. The careful circularity with which JACQUES DERRIDA and post-Heideggerian philosophers such as Philippe Lacoue-Labarthe and Jean-Luc Nancy approach his *oeuvre* constitutes a similar, more elaborate act of homage. In the Anglophone world, Blanchot has remained a somewhat esoteric figure, though through the mediation of PAUL DE MAN's rather different tone and vocabulary, certain aspects of Blanchot's reflection on literature have haunted readers with little or no firsthand knowledge of his work.

Marc Redfield

See also FRENCH THEORY AND CRITICISM: 5. 1945–1968 and 6. 1968 AND AFTER.

Maurice Blanchot, *La Communauté inavouable* (1983, *The Unavowable Community,* trans. Pierre Joris, 1988), *L'Écriture du désastre* (1980, *The Writing of the Disaster,* trans. Ann Smock, 1986), *L'Entretien infini* (1969, *The Infinite Conversation,* trans. Susan Hanson, 1992), *L'Espace littéraire* (1955, *The Space of Literature,* trans. Ann Smock, 1982), *The Gaze of Orpheus and Other Literary Essays* (ed. P. Adams Sitney, trans. Lydia Davis, 1981), *La Pas au-delà* (1973, *The Step Not Beyond,* trans. Lycette Nelson, 1992), *The Siren's Song: Selected Essays of Maurice Blanchot* (ed. Gabriel Jospovici, trans. Sacha Rabinovitch, 1982).

Françoise Collin, *Maurice Blanchot et la question de l'écriture* (1986); *Critique* 229 (1966, special issue on Blanchot); Paul de Man, "Impersonality in the Criticism of Maurice Blanchot," *Blindness and Insight: Essays in the Rhetoric of Contemporary Criticism* (1971); Jacques Derrida, *Parages* (1986, including "Pas" ["Pas I" appeared in *Gramma* 3/4] and essays translated as "The Law of Genre," trans. Avital Ronell, *Glyph* 7 [1980], "Living On: Border Lines," trans. James Hulbert, Harold Bloom et al., *Deconstruction and Criticism,* 1979, and "TITLE [to be specified]," trans. Tom Conley, *Sub-Stance* 31 [1981]); *L'Esprit Créateur* 24.3 (1984, special issue on Blanchot); Michel Foucault, *La Pensée du dehors* (1986, trans. with Blanchot's *Michel Foucault tel que je l'imagine,* 1986, in *Maurice Blanchot: The Thought from Outside / Michel Foucault as I Imagine Him,* trans. Brian Massumi and Jeffrey Mehlman, 1987); *Gramma* 3/4 (1976, special issue on Blanchot); Emmanuel Levinas, *Sur Maurice Blanchot* (1975); Joseph Libertson, *Proximity: Levinas, Blanchot, Bataille, and Communication* (1982); Jeffrey Mehlman, "Blanchot at *Combat*: Of Literature and Terror," *MLN* 95 (1980); Steven Shaviro, *Passion and Excess: Blanchot, Bataille, and Literary Theory* (1990); *Sub-Stance* 14 (1977, special issue on Blanchot).

BLOOM, HAROLD

Harold Bloom (b. 1930) earned his bachelor of arts degree at Cornell in 1951 and his doctorate from Yale, where he has taught since 1955. He is the author of 19 books, editor of over 30 anthologies, and general editor of the 6 Chelsea House literary criticism series, for which he prepared over 350 introductions. Like his theory of poetic relations, Bloom's literary career can be divided into early and later phases in agonistic relationship with one another and specified further in terms of the different literary antagonists—from 1954 to 1967 with T. S. ELIOT and the New Critics' Anglo-Catholic orthodoxy (see NEW CRITICISM) and then subsequently with JACQUES DERRIDA and the Yale school of DECONSTRUCTION—with whom Bloom struggled. He was manifestly engaged in battles on other fronts as well. The academic revolts of the student counterculture in the late 1960s provided an explicit historical referent for his notion of intergenerational rivalry, and the counterculture's overvaluation of the Romantic imagination's power to effect social change induced Bloom's reevaluation of Romanticism and repression.

From 1957 until 1963 Bloom joined NORTHROP FRYE in a literary campaign against the poetic tradition established by Eliot. He wrote a trilogy of books on Romantic poetry—*Shelley's Mythmaking* (1959), *The Visionary Company* (1961), and *Blake's Apocalypse* (1963)—that reaffirmed the importance of Milton and the visionary company of British Romanticism and proposed a mythopoetics of Romanticism founded upon the centrality of the Blakean Imagination. Understood as a process whereby natural phenomena were transmuted into figures of poetic thought, the Romantic imagination resulted in a spatial conquest of external nature (the Imagination Naturalized) and a visionary counter to a New Critical orthodoxy's opposition to Romanticism. But in the summer of 1967 Bloom wrote an interpretive poem entitled "The Covering Cherub or Poetic Influence" wherein he drastically revised his understanding of the Blakean Imagination as a repression of his precursor John Milton's influence and as a figurative cancellation rather than a temporal fulfillment of Milton's vision. (See also WILLIAM BLAKE and PERCY BYSSHE SHELLEY.)

Because Bloom had previously aspired to internalize the Blakean Imagination as his critical identity, "The Covering Cherub" eventuated a massive shift in Bloom's interpretive allegiances displayed first in *Yeats* (1970), a magisterial reading of W. B. Yeats's complex literary career. As a poet who had himself written a critical commentary on Blake's theory of the Imagination and who straddled the Romantic and modernist periods, Yeats became for Bloom an ideal figure to distinguish his later project from his earlier work. Upon explaining Yeats's later poetry as a repression of his earlier imaginative efforts, Bloom disassociated his understanding of the Imagination's workings from the Greek *logos* (a word referring to power to gather into order) and correlated it with the Hebrew *davhar* (a "word-event" meaning the drawing out of a repressed thing). In *Yeats* the Imagination represented an inclusive figurative process correlating a drive to become original together with tropological defenses against that drive, as well as a temporal medium whereby the tropological defenses against it facilitated the return of the originary drive.

Since his 1970 critical reading of Yeats's poetry, Bloom

has been following his own reading of psychoanalysis to elaborate a psychopoetics of the entire Western literary tradition that replaced Blake's Imagination with FRIEDRICH NIETZSCHE's will to power as its key trope and posited the contest for temporal priority of later (post-Enlightenment) and precursor poets as its central problematic. Underwriting the paradigmatic shift from *The Visionary Company* (1961) to *The Anxiety of Influence* (1973) was Bloom's redescription of the Blakean Imagination as a medium of psychic repression whereby such primary sources as the Hebrew Bible, Homer, William Shakespeare, and Milton were reconfigured as if secondary to the contemporary poet's imaginative needs. Previous exercises in influence study depended upon a topographical model of reallocatable poetic images, distributed more or less equally within "canonical" poems, each part of which expressively totalized the entelechy of the entire tradition. But Bloom now understood this cognitive map of interchangeable organic wholes to be criticism's repression of poetry's will to overcome time's anteriority.

In the wake of this re-cognition, Bloom proposed an understanding of the site of poetic production as the work of an extensive but necessarily split subject: a poet who aspired to a complete understanding of the poem's literal significance and a critic who aspired to evade the death drive in which literality inheres. Because poetry happens at the crossroads where the poet's repression of a precursor (into criticism's significance) intersects with a critic's sublimation of the death drive (into poetry's "lies against time"), each poem must consequently be understood as an "inter-poem," an overdetermined anxiety conjoining poet, poetry, precursor, and critic together with the need endlessly to renegotiate their relationship.

Bloom calls the crossroads where criticism's sublimation intersects with poetry's repression of belatedness the "Scene of Instruction," which is important for the persistent stretching of the mental space out of which it is (re)produced. Here the demand upon the critic for an adequate description of the poetics of belatedness results in an utterly original critical lexicon. As Bloom evokes the revisionary ratios out of which poetry originates, the critic's theoretical earliness becomes a function of the poet's belatedness. The names Bloom calls these primordial forces—"clinamen," "tessera," "kenosis," "daemonization," "askesis," "apophrades"—themselves instantiate a convergence of Greek with Hebraic gnosticism, two archaic sources of the Western literary tradition. As originative energies, these names designate not specific referents but ongoing performative powers whose significance for Bloom's theory of psychopoetics becomes recognizable only in the revisions into the rhetorical (irony, synecdoche, metonymy, hyperbole, metaphor, transumption) and psychological (reaction-formation, reversal, regression, repression, introjection, and projection) equivalents that Bloom claims they authorize:

> As tropes of contraction or limitation, irony withdraws meaning through a dialectical interplay of presence and absence (clinamen), metonymy reduces meaning through an emptying-out that is a kind of reification (kenosis), metaphor curtails meaning through the endless perspectivizing of dualism, of inside-outside dichotomies (askesis). As tropes of restitution or representation, synecdoche enlarges from part to whole (tessera); hyperbole heightens (daemonization); metalepsis overcomes temporality by a substitution of earliness for lateness (apophrades). (*Map* 95)

Never the selfsame but always in transit, the composite origin—in rhetoric, psychology, history, philosophy, cosmology—of these psychopoetic forces renders any (mis)reading of them less important than the precursor text upon which they are projected. In the revisionist itinerary he tracked, Bloom displaced the following succession of textual backdrops: his own earlier mythopoetics of Romanticism (*The Anxiety of Influence,* 1973); Northrop Frye's *Anatomy of Criticism* (*A Map of Misreading,* 1975); Blake's theory of the Imagination (*Kabbalah and Criticism,* 1975; *Poetry and Repression,* 1976); Derrida's "Scene of Writing" (*Figures of Capable Imagination,* 1976); SIGMUND FREUD's "magic writing pad" (*Agon,* 1982; *The Breaking of the Vessels,* 1982).

Providing a local context for Bloom's ongoing self-revision were his Yale colleagues GEOFFREY H. HARTMAN and J. HILLIS MILLER, whose turn in the 1970s to deconstruction and the formation of the "Yale school" was partly the result of PAUL DE MAN's influence. De Man's revisionist readings of the Nietzschean will to power and its rhetorical effects provided the strongest counter to Bloom's theory of misprision. In a review of *The Anxiety of Influence,* de Man redescribed Bloom's theory of intergenerational rivalry as itself a metaphor for a reader's anxious encounter with a text the status of whose rhetoricity—as a system of tropes or a mode of persuasion—remained undecidable. Bloom claimed in response that poetry constituted an *art* (rather than a system) of persuasion, whose misprisions consequently could be understood as either "the process by which the meanings of intentionality trope down to the mere significances of language" (*Wallace Stevens* 394) or "the process by which the significance of language can be transformed or troped upward into the meaningful world of our Will-to-Power over time and its henchman, language" (394–95).

The latter formulation enabled Bloom to "transume" deconstruction and the work of his colleagues in the Yale school as a belated reading of his own criticism. Bloom having become earlier than the latest form of postmodernity, other forms of postmodernist criticism perforce repress his critical contemporaneity. Having thus become both contemporaneous and anterior, Bloom returned in *Ruin the Sacred Truths* (1989) to his original topic, the poetic imagination. Having interpreted the entire post-Enlightenment tradition, from Blake and the Romantics to Franz Kafka and Freud, as a process akin to the secondary repression of primary drives, Bloom went on to a new project that entailed the construction of a critical medium capable of enabling the return of these primary sources. The Hebrew Bible, Homer, Shakespeare, and Milton, Bloom explained, constituted modes of representations out ahead of any interpretive power to contain them and therefore predicted Blake's theory of the Imagination and Freud's theory of repression as more or less equivalent gestures of interpretive accommodation. Then in *The Book of J* (1991) Bloom fashioned his muse, the "J writer," as a figure constructed out of his theory, that is, a woman engaged in competition with a male rival, and thereby inherited the Western literary tradition as if from himself. By way of the same gesture Bloom transumed the feminist reaction to the male patriarchal tradition by transforming a feminist into the muse for the patriarchal tradition. Impersonating the Poetic Imagination as well as the interpretive powers through which it is necessarily repressed, Bloom, in his project, can finally be said to have constructed a critical medium whereby the Imagination could become identical with the most primordial of originary drives—the will to mastery over the true.

Donald E. Pease

Harold Bloom, *Agon: Towards a Theory of Revisionism* (1982), *The American Religion: The Emergence of the Post-Christian Nation* (1992), *The Anxiety of Influence: A Theory of Poetry* (1973), *Blake's Apocalypse: A Study in Poetic Argument* (1963), *The Book of J* (1991), *The Breaking of the Vessels* (1982), *Figures of Capable Imagination* (1976), *Kabbalah and Criticism* (1975), *A Map of Misreading* (1975), *Poetry and Repression: Revisionism from Blake to Stevens* (1976), *The Ringers in the Tower: Studies in Romantic Tradition* (1971), *Ruin the Sacred Truths: Poetry and Belief from the Bible to the Present* (1989), *Shelley's Mythmaking* (1959), *The Visionary Company: A Reading of English Romantic*

Poetry (1961, rev. ed., 1971), *Wallace Stevens: The Poems of Our Climate* (1976), *Yeats* (1970); Harold Bloom, ed., *Ralph Waldo Emerson: Modern Critical Views* (1985).

M. H. Abrams, "How to Do Things with Texts," *Partisan Review* 46 (1979); Jonathan Arac, *Critical Genealogies: Historical Situations for Postmodern Literary Studies* (1987); Paul A. Bové, *Destructive Poetics: Heidegger and Modern American Poetry* (1987); Peter de Bolla, *Harold Bloom: Towards Historical Rhetorics* (1988); Paul de Man, Review of *The Anxiety of Influence, Blindness and Insight: Essays in the Rhetoric of Contemporary Criticism* (rev. ed., 1983); David Fite, *Harold Bloom: The Rhetoric of Romantic Vision* (1985); Geoffrey H. Hartman, "The Sacred Jungle 1: Carlyle, Eliot, Bloom," *Criticism in the Wilderness: The Study of Literature Today* (1980); Frank Lentricchia, "Harold Bloom: The Spirit of Revenge," *After the New Criticism* (1980); Daniel T. O'Hara, "The Genius of Irony: Nietzsche in Bloom," *Romance of Interpretation: Visionary Criticism from Pater to de Man* (1985); Louis A. Renza, "Influence," *Critical Terms for Literary Study* (ed. Frank Lentricchia and Thomas McLaughlin, 1990); Ann Wordsworth, "An Art That Will Not Abandon the Self to Language: Bloom, Tennyson, and the Blind World of the Wish," *Untying the Text* (ed. Robert Young, 1981).

BLOOMSBURY GROUP

Desmond MacCarthy's claim that there "is little in common between the work of Lytton Strachey, VIRGINIA WOOLF, Clive Bell, David Garnett, Roger Fry, Maynard Keynes, Leonard Woolf, Vanessa Bell, Duncan Grant, E. M. Forster" (*Memories* 172) is a useful starting point. It provides the necessary names, his own included, and raises the crucial issue of the nature of the group. Some have made stronger claims for Bloomsbury, especially Forster, who once described it "as the only genuine *movement* in English civilization" (Rosenbaum, *Bloomsbury Group* 25), but MacCarthy's comment that they "were neither a movement, nor a push, but only a group of old friends" (172) is closer to the way most of these "old friends" saw their relationship. "We were and always remained," in Leonard Woolf's estimation, "primarily and fundamentally a group of friends. . . . We had no common theory, system or principles which we wanted to commit the world to" (*Beginning* 23–25). Clive Bell's answer to his own rhetorical question, "But did such an entity exist? All one can truthfully say is this. A dozen friends" (Rosenbaum, *Bloomsbury* 87), sums up the Bloomsbury view of itself.

Bloomsbury's insistence on seeing itself as only a "group of friends" is indeed one of its defining traits. But the Bloomsbury group is based on more than friendship. One can, for example, identify specific aesthetic and ethical concerns that link the most important literary figures on Desmond MacCarthy's list: E. M. Forster (1879–1970), Lytton Strachey (1880–1932), and Virginia Woolf (1882–1941). These concerns have their primary formulation in aesthetic terms in the theoretical writings of Roger Fry (1866–1934) and Clive Bell (1881–1964). A full account of Bloomsbury would involve consideration of the economic theory of Keynes, the political activity of Leonard Woolf, and the painting of Vanessa Bell and Duncan Grant. In this discussion, however, only those writings that deal with aesthetic and literary theory will be examined. (See also VIRGINIA WOOLF and, for Woolf's and E. M. Forster's theories of fiction, FICTION THEORY AND CRITICISM: 3. EARLY TWENTIETH-CENTURY BRITISH AND AMERICAN.)

Although Forster's word "movement" may be too emphatic, Bloomsbury's shared literary history, as S. P. Rosenbaum has documented, reveals far more coherence than the disclaimers of Leonard Woolf and MacCarthy suggest. With the word "civilization" Forster pointed to what RAYMOND WILLIAMS describes as "the centrality [for Bloomsbury] of shared values of personal affection and aesthetic enjoyment" (45–46). However, for Williams this is a problematic notion in an argument that sees "the true organizing value of the group . . . [as] the unobstructed expression of the civilized individual" (61).

Because the most important Bloomsbury texts belong to the second and third decades of the twentieth century, Bloomsbury theory and practice need to be seen both as part of and as a response to high modernism. Bloomsbury's emphasis on the private, the personal, and the domestic offered an alternative to the heroic modernism of James Joyce, Ezra Pound, and Wyndham Lewis. Perry Meisel sees Bloomsbury practice as a critique of modernism: "the Bloomsbury design of replacing modernist ideals in all their registers with the real structures of desire that produce them as ideological defences" (191). In its formalist aspect, however, Bloomsbury participated directly in the modernist polemic.

The terms in which its aesthetic theory is stated derive from A. C. Bradley's 1901 Oxford lecture, "Poetry for Poetry's Sake." For Bradley, the poem was an "end in itself," possessing "intrinsic value" (4). Form and content are inseparable. Like painting and music, poetry can be neither paraphrased nor translated. What the reader apprehends in a poem, according to Bradley, "may be called indifferently an expressed meaning or a significant form" (19), using a phrase that was to have a long afterlife in twentieth-century ART THEORY.

Bradley did not argue, as the aesthetes of the previous century had done, that art was the end of life, only that it was one kind of human good whose value should not be determined by reference to another. Similarly, Roger Fry in "An Essay on Aesthetics" (1909) placed art in another realm "separated from actual life by the absence of responsive action" (*Vision* 20). For Fry, the work of art was "an expression of emotions regarded as ends in themselves" (29), the object of artistic vision "exist[ing] . . . for no other purpose than to be seen" (25). The emphasis on the absoluteness of the object is related to Fry's discovery of Cézanne. In the preface to the catalog of the second post-impressionist exhibition (1912; Fry had organized the first exhibition, in 1910, as well), he argued that the aim of the post-impressionists was "to express by pictorial and plastic form certain spiritual experiences" (237). They did not "seek to imitate form but to create form" (239; just as in Bradley's terms, poets do not "decorate the mere 'matter' with a mere 'form', but . . . produce a new content-form" [31]).

Clive Bell's *Art* (1914) was also directly inspired by these exhibitions. It was originally to have been part of a longer work, "The New Renaissance," which was to trace the history of "contemporary art, thought and social organization . . . from earliest times to the present" (*Civilization* 9). Some of that material appeared in considerably revised form in *Civilization* (1928) with a dedicatory letter to Virginia Woolf describing its genesis. The 1928 text, however, is very different from the formalist manifesto of 1914, where Bradley's phrase "significant form" reappears as the answer to the question, "What quality is shared by all objects that provoke our aesthetic emotions?" (*Art* 8). Bell acknowledged the subjectivity of this formulation but argued that "we have no other means of recognizing a work of art than our feeling for it" (9). What he sought was a way of linking the viewer's emotions with the artist's—a certain arrangement moves us "because it expresses the emotions of its creator" (49)— but he was uneasy with a formulation that suggested that significant form was "the expression of a peculiar emotion felt for reality" (100). He did nonetheless attempt to link aesthetics and ethics. Thus, the claim that "art is above morals" meant "all art is moral . . . because works of art are immediate means to good" (20). Such a claim derives directly from G. E. Moore, the Cambridge philosopher, whose *Principia Ethica* (1903), emphasizing "personal affection and the appreciation of what is beautiful in Art or Nature [as] good in themselves" (188), was probably the single most influential text in the forma-

tion of the Bloomsbury intellectual outlook. Here Bell was using Moore to refute Tolstoy's "What Is Art?" with its emphasis, in Bell's phrasing, on art's "power of promoting good actions" (*Art* 114). Fry also made a similar criticism, but he saw the importance of Tolstoy's claim that art need have no necessary connection with what is beautiful in nature as marking "the beginning of fruitful speculation in aesthetic" (*Vision* 292).

The issues of representation and reference involved both Fry and Bell in speculating on the relationship among the various arts. Bell felt that "if a representative form has value, it is as form, not as representation" (*Art* 25). He used music as an example of an art form that is purely nonrepresentational and reprehended the tendency (shared by himself) to hear "the galloping of horses . . . the laughing of demons" (32), possibly alluding to Forster's depiction in *Howards End* (1910) of Helen listening to the "goblin walking quietly over the universe" (30) in Beethoven's Fifth Symphony. Although Bell argued that literature, unlike music, is not a pure art form—it is by definition intellectual—he assumed in *Proust* (1928) that the literary text could be submitted to formal analysis. Proust's time masses were seen as similar to the impressionist's space masses, for example. But in Bell's view, Proust was primarily a psychologist and thus failed the test of significant form: "He gives us little or nothing that life would not give if only we could press life hard enough" (57).

Fry also argued in "Some Questions in Esthetics" (1926) that "few novelists ever conceived of the novel as a single perfectly organic esthetic whole" (*Transformations* 7). But he was more willing than Bell to concede that "an absolutely pure work of art has never been created" (3), although the distinction between pure and impure (following a similar distinction made by Bradley about poetry [Bradley 23, 30]) remained a useful hypothesis. Fry's writing is on the whole of more interest to literary theory than Bell's, for Fry maintained the applicability of his approach to all art. "In all cases our reaction to works of art is a reaction to a relation and not to sensations or objects or persons or events" (*Transformations* 3). Thus, for example, what is essential in great tragedy is "not the emotional intensity of the events portrayed, but the vivid sense of the inevitability of their unfolding, the significance of the curve of crescendo and diminuendo" (10). Similarly, pleasure in a "first-rate novel" does not lie in the recognition of reality; rather, the pleasure "consists in the recognition of inevitable sequences" (*Artist* 288).

It was Charles Mauron in *The Nature of Beauty in Art and Literature* (1925, trans., 1927) who provided Fry with the analogy that helped him formulate the relationship among the arts: "What analogue in literature shall we give to volume? . . . As the painter creates a spatial being, the writer creates a psychological being" (66–67), or, in Fry's version, "psychological volume" (*Transformations* 9). This phrase, even more than "significant form," is crucial for Bloomsbury literary theory and practice. It has considerable explanatory power for Virginia Woolf's creation of character, for example, and it may lie behind Forster's distinction between round and flat in *Aspects of the Novel* (1927; see also Hutcheon). Mauron is an important figure for the linking of the aesthetic and the psychological or the formal and the representational in Bloomsbury theory. His works include *Mallarmé l'obscur, L'Inconscient dans l'oeuvre et la vie de Racine, Psychocritique du genre comique, Le Dernier Baudelaire,* and, in English, the two texts that were translated by Roger Fry. As much a psychological critic as an aesthetician, however, Mauron did not follow Fry to his purely formal conclusions. In *Aesthetics and Psychology* (trans. 1935), Mauron asked how "purely formal combinations [can] suddenly open to us . . . a kingdom our consciousness never reaches in real life" (27). He also found Fry's musical analogies misleading, for "in the plastic arts, as in poetry, the zero from which the artist starts is not, as in music, pure chance, but a certain preexistent organization of the world, which he will have to destroy in order to create new combinations" (79). For Mauron, the referent neither disappears nor becomes merely a function of aesthetic design. This is obvious in his literary criticism, where, as Linda Hutcheon suggests, "even at his most formalistic, Mauron . . . could not underestimate the role of meaning or representation in literature; what he would do was displace the *locus* of both form and signification from the conscious to the unconscious" (39).

As a result of Mauron's influence, the formalist position in Fry's later writing was considerably modified to allow for an expanded emphasis on the artist's emotions: "The contemplative artist is also an adventurer, a discoverer of the emotions and the mysterious significance of his own experiences in front of nature" (*French* 205–6). Fry and Mauron converge in Forster's critical writing. Both were friends; both helped him look at pictures. Although Forster shared certain of Fry's formalist assumptions concerning organic unity, especially as these were mediated by Mauron, all his literary criticism from the early essay "Inspiration" (1913) to *Aspects of the Novel* (1927, dedicated to Mauron) to the 1949 essay "Art for Art's Sake" reveals his ambivalence toward formalism.

In "Anonymity" (1925), Forster assumed the formalist premise of organic unity. The poem is "a universe that only answers to its own laws, . . . [it] internally coheres,

. . . a poem is absolute" (*Two Cheers* 81). Twenty-four years later, in "Art for Art's Sake," he repeated the statement with an interesting qualification: "A work of art—whatever else it may be—is a self-contained entity, with a life of its own imposed on it by its creator. It has internal order. It may have external form" (88; the use of "may" marks the distance between Forster's position and Fry's and Bell's). But "order" in Forster's vocabulary is not simply a technical term; it implies both a social critique and a metaphysics. Art, for example, is offered as "the one orderly product which our muddling race has produced, . . . the lighthouse which cannot be hidden" (90). It is the product of a creative state to which criticism has essentially no access; it is "rooted in the underside of the mind" ("Inspiration," *Albergo* 121). Forster several times compared the creative process to letting "a bucket down into the subconscious" ("Anonymity," "The Raison d'être of Criticism in the Arts"). Criticism, by contrast, "does not conceive in sleep, or know what it has said [only] after it has said it" (*Two Cheers* 112). The best that a critic can be is a kind of secular priest who wants to pass on his or her experience, the "glow derived from the central fire" (104). But it is the works of art that are finally empowering insofar as they can "make minor artists out of those who have felt their power" (104), for art can transform "the person who encounters it towards the condition of the person who created it" (113). Literature in this argument is impersonal and anonymous for both writer and reader. Reading thus belongs to the creative rather than the critical faculty. Although Forster repeatedly insisted on the gulf between the creative and critical states, in his own practice the distinction became blurred. He seems to have required it for what one may call his theory of the nontheoretical, an aspect of the same eclecticism that S. P. Rosenbaum suggests is both the form and substance of *Aspects of the Novel,* thus making it "an anti-critical work of criticism" (*"Aspects"* 68).

This same ambivalence marked Forster's writing on music. In "The C Minor of This Life" (1941), he attempted to identify the essential qualities of different keys in much the same way that Fry had tried to classify the properties of colors. He acknowledged in "Not Listening to Music" (1939) that the best music was "untainted by reference" but that it was nevertheless not abstract. What he listened for was "something which [was] neither an aesthetic pattern nor a sermon" (*Two Cheers* 124), but he was unable to define that "something" more precisely. In terms of structure, Forster's position was relatively formalist; in terms of response—the activity that was of greater interest to him—his stance, like Mauron's, was psychological and impressionistic.

"Psychological" and "impressionistic" also describe Strachey's writing—biographical, historical, and literary. In the essay "A Sidelight on Frederick the Great" he praised the book under review because it was "entirely personal and psychological. . . . The historian neglects Oliver Cromwell's warts; but it is just such queer details of physiognomy that the amateur of human nature delights in" (*Biographical* 106–7). But the historian is not an anecdotist, for "his first duty . . . is to be an artist," and he accomplishes this through his power of interpretation, for "uninterpreted truth is as useless as buried gold; and art is the great interpreter" (*Spectatorial* 13). The clearest statement of his revisionary project for biography occurs in the preface to *Eminent Victorians* (1918) and is illustrated in the four biographies that follow. His method will be to "shoot a sudden, revealing searchlight into obscure recesses" and, using a metaphor that Forster was to pick up, to "row out over that great ocean of material, and lower down into it, here and there, a little bucket" (*Eminent* vii). Although Strachey does not describe his methods in the language of Fry and Mauron, it is precisely through the manipulation of "psychological volumes" that he "elucidate[d] certain fragments of the truth" (viii) in his unmasking and remaking of the Victorian past both here and in *Queen Victoria* (1921). Indeed, his sense of his biographical subject is very close to Fry's and Bell's view of the artist's object and to Forster's view of the atemporality of the literary text. For Strachey, "human beings . . . have a value which is independent of any temporal processes—which is eternal, and must be felt for its own sake" (*Eminent* viii).

One other relatively minor Bloomsbury literary figure turns up on most lists, the journalist and critic Desmond MacCarthy (1877–1952). He is remembered today chiefly for his drama criticism, especially of Shaw's Court Theatre plays (*The Court Theatre*, 1907); for his interest in Ibsen, Proust, and *War and Peace* (literary tastes shared by all Bloomsbury); and for the criticism he wrote under the signature "Affable Hawk." He was literary editor of the *New Statesman* and, from 1928 to 1952, chief book reviewer for the *Sunday Times*. He appears in memoir after memoir more for his contribution to "the general social climate of Bloomsbury," in Quentin Bell's phrase, than for his literary accomplishment.

In Bloomsbury writing, the letter, the lecture, the essay, the story all turn into each other; they are all textualizations of voice. But Bloomsbury not only wrote conversation as an art; it practiced it as well. Virginia Woolf not only talked about painting but she composed a dinner party as one would a still life in order to talk with Walter Sickert about his painting and then imag-

ined that conversation as an essay ("Walter Sickert"). This crossing of generic boundaries is also related to the problematizing of gender—in biographical writing in Strachey's *Elizabeth and Essex*, for example, and, in the mode of fantasy, in Forster's short fiction and Woolf's *Orlando*. In Woolf's *A Room of One's Own* and *Three Guineas*, this generic revisionism is part of a feminist challenge to traditional modes of writing and their implicit ideology. Although the Bloomsbury label describes no single literary theory, the writing of the Bloomsbury group has implications for many of the developments of twentieth-century criticism, from formalism and Anglo-American NEW CRITICISM to theories of biography, narrative, gender, and genre.

Judith Scherer Herz

See also FICTION THEORY AND CRITICISM: 3. EARLY TWENTIETH-CENTURY BRITISH AND AMERICAN and VIRGINIA WOOLF.

Clive Bell, *Art* (1914), *Civilization* (1928), *Proust* (1928), *Since Cézanne* (1922); A. C. Bradley, "Poetry for Poetry's Sake," *Oxford Lectures on Poetry* (1909); E. M. Forster, *Abinger Harvest* (1936), *"Albergo Empedocle" and Other Writings* (1971), *"Aspects of the Novel" and Related Writings* (Abinger Edition, vol. 12, ed. Oliver Stallybrass, 1974), *Collected Tales* (1947), *Howards End* (Abinger Edition, vol. 4, ed. Oliver Stallybrass, 1973), *The Longest Journey* (Abinger Edition, vol. 2, ed. Elizabeth Heine, 1984), *Two Cheers for Democracy* (Abinger Edition, vol. 11, ed. Oliver Stallybrass, 1972); Roger Fry, *The Artist and Psycho-analysis* (1924), *Cézanne: A Study of His Development* (1966), *French, Flemish, and British Art* (1951), *Last Lectures* (1939), *Transformations* (1927), *Vision and Design* (1920); Desmond MacCarthy, *The Court Theatre: A Commentary and Criticism* (1907), *Criticism* (1932), *Memories* (1953); Charles Mauron, *Aesthetics and Psychology* (trans. Roger Fry, 1935), *The Nature of Beauty in Art and Literature* (trans. Roger Fry and Katherine John, 1927); G. E. Moore, *Principia Ethica* (1959); Lytton Strachey, *Biographical Essays* (1948), *Elizabeth and Essex* (1928), *Eminent Victorians* (1918), *Literary Essays* (1948), *Queen Victoria* (1921), *Spectatorial Essays* (1964); Leonard Woolf, *Beginning Again: An Autobiography of the Years 1911–1918* (1964), *Sowing: An Autobiography of the Years 1880–1904* (1960); Virginia Woolf, *Orlando* (1928), *Roger Fry: A Biography* (1940), *A Room of One's Own* (1929), *Three Guineas* (1938).

Peter Allen, *The Cambridge Apostles: The Early Years* (1978); Quentin Bell, *Bloomsbury* (1968); Mary Ann Caws, *Women of Bloomsbury* (1990); David Cecil, *Desmond MacCarthy: The Man and His Writings* (1984); David Dowling,

Bloomsbury Aesthetics and the Novels of Forster and Woolf (1985); Leon Edel, *Bloomsbury: A House of Lions* (1979); P. N. Furbank, *E. M. Forster: A Life* (2 vols., 1977–78), "Forster and 'Bloomsbury' Prose," *E. M. Forster: A Human Exploration: Centenary Essays* (ed. G. K. Das and John Beer, 1979); David Gadd, *The Loving Friends: A Portrait of Bloomsbury* (1974); Angelica Garnett, *Deceived with Kindness: A Bloomsbury Childhood* (1984); Michael Holroyd, *Lytton Strachey: A Biography* (1971); Linda Hutcheon, *Formalism and the Freudian Aesthetic: The Example of Charles Mauron* (1984); Samuel Hynes, *The Edwardian Turn of Mind* (1968); J. K. Johnstone, *The Bloomsbury Group: A Study of E. M. Forster, Lytton Strachey, Virginia Woolf, and Their Circle* (1954); Donald A. Laing, *Clive Bell: An Annotated Bibliography of the Published Writings* (1983), *Roger Fry: An Annotated Bibliography of the Published Writings* (1979); Paul Levy, *G. E. Moore and the Cambridge Apostles* (1979); Perry Meisel, *The Myth of the Modern: A Study in British Literature and Criticism after 1850* (1987); S. P. Rosenbaum, "*Aspects of the Novel* and Literary History," *E. M. Forster: Centenary Revaluations* (ed. Judith Scherer Herz and Robert K. Martin, 1982), *Edwardian Bloomsbury* (1993), *Victorian Bloomsbury: The Early Literary History of the Bloomsbury Group* (1987); S. P. Rosenbaum, ed., *The Bloomsbury Group: A Collection of Memoirs, Commentary, and Criticism* (1975); Richard Shone, *Bloomsbury Portraits: Vanessa Bell, Duncan Grant, and Their Circle* (1976); Frances Spalding, *Roger Fry: Art and Life* (1980); Raymond Williams, "The Significance of 'Bloomsbury' as a Social and Cultural Group," *Keynes and the Bloomsbury Group* (ed. Derek Crabtree and A. P. Thirwell, 1980).

BOCCACCIO, GIOVANNI

The historical importance of Giovanni Boccaccio (1313–75) as a literary theorist and critic lies not so much in the originality of his thinking as in his civic-spirited mediation between Dantean (scholastic) and Petrarchan (proto-humanist) cultures.

Born at Certaldo, Boccaccio lived in Florence until the age of 13, when he joined his father at the Florentine merchant colony at Naples. There he trained as an apprentice merchant before switching to the study of canon law at the Neapolitan Studio. Returning to Florence in 1341, he became a vigorous supporter of the republican regime and served during the next thirty years as, *inter alia*, ambassador to emperor and pope, overseer of mercenary troops, and advisor to the bishop of Florence. He wrote his *Decameron* immediately after the catastrophic Black Death of 1348. By the time he first met Petrarch (1350), he was the undisputed leader of Florentine literary culture. Under Petrarch's influence, he turned increasingly away from vernacular fiction in favor of Latin encyclopedism. He took lessons in Greek, solicited translations from Greek texts, and in 1360 successfully worked to establish at Florence the first chair of Greek in non-Byzantine Europe. In 1373 the citizens of Florence chose him to give the world's first *lecturae Dantis*, probably the first lecture series ever dedicated to the exposition of a European vernacular text. He died at Certaldo in 1375 (Branca).

When Boccaccio visited Petrarch at Padua in 1351, he was disturbed to discover that Petrarch possessed no copy of Dante's *Comedy*. Petrarch's tortuous justification of this in *Familiares* 21:15 only moved Boccaccio to greater efforts as a Dantean apologist. The first of the three versions of his *Trattatello in laude di Dante* [Short treatise in praise of Dante] (c. 1351–55) survives in an autograph manuscript, where it accompanies the *Vita Nuova*, the *Comedy*, and fifteen Dantean canzoni and so functions like the introduction to a modern critical edition. Modeled to some extent on the Virgilian biographies of Servius and Donatus and borrowing from medieval saints' lives, the *Trattatello* celebrates Dante as poet-hero. It also explores the relationship of poetry to theology and makes the claim (adapted from Petrarch) that "theology is nothing other than a poetry of God" (*Medieval* 455, 498).

In his public lectures on Dante (1373), Boccaccio joins the tradition of commentators who since Dante's death in 1321 had transferred the exegetical techniques of scholasticism from the analysis of Scripture to the exposition of Dante's Italian *Comedy*. These Italian *Esposizioni* open with an *accessus*, which follows the traditional four-part structuring of the scholastic "Aristotelian prologue" (Minnis 28–29). Boccaccio then considers first the literal and then the allegorical sense of each canto; the work ends incomplete at *Inferno* 17.

Boccaccio evidently shared Dante's conviction that a great vernacular poem might be taken as seriously as any Latin text. The new humanist championing of *Latinitas* did, however, induce Boccaccio to inquire why Dante wrote in Italian (*Medieval* 518–19). Petrarch, in *Familiares* 21:15, had censured Dante for laying sacred truths open to the gaze of the unlearned multitude. Boccaccio's Italian lectures on Dante's Italian poem met with similar criticisms from Florentine humanists. When he fell ill and was unable to continue lecturing, the elderly Boccaccio lost his nerve: his sickness, he said, had been sent from heaven to punish his presumption.

Boccaccio's most influential scholarly work is his *Ge-*

nealogia Deorum Gentilium. This massive encyclopedia assembles classical myths and legends from a great range of scattered texts and proposes to analyze them by following the familiar fourfold distinction of sacred hermeneutics among literal, allegorical, moral, and anagogical senses. Boccaccio does not adhere rigidly to the scheme he proposes in 1:3. He makes strenuous use of etymology in analyzing the meaning of classical names: Orpheus, for example, means "aurea phone," "the sweet voice of eloquence" (*On Poetry* xxvi). The last two books of this work mount an impassioned defense of poetry: the arguments of *Genealogia* 14 and 15 were to circulate widely in Italy and form an important precedent for SIR PHILIP SIDNEY's *Defence of Poesy.* Poetry is seen as "a sort of fervid and exquisite invention" that "proceeds from the bosom of God" (39). Poetry is not to be classified under grammar, as it was for earlier medieval theorists: grammar and all the liberal arts are to be seen as disciplines that serve poetry as their superior (*Medieval* 387). Fiction is defined as "a form of discourse, which, under guise of invention, illustrates or proves an idea; and, as its superficial aspect is removed, the meaning of the author is clear" (*On Poetry* 48). To condemn fictions is to call God a liar, since both the Holy Spirit and "Christ, the very God . . . , have uttered fictions" (50). Poetry, like theology, protects sacred truths from the eyes of the vulgar and makes "truths which would otherwise cheapen by exposure the object of strong intellectual effort and various interpretation" (60). Thus, if philosophy is the keenest investigator of truth, poetry is "its most faithful guardian, protecting it as she does beneath the veil of her art" (84).

Boccaccio's *Genealogia,* like his other encyclopedic works, is designed to fortify and encourage the efforts of the literary interpreter as well as the poet: if you wish "to appreciate poetry, and unwind its difficult involutions, . . . you must read, you must persevere, you must sit up nights, you must inquire, and exert the utmost power of your mind" (62). Whereas Petrarch was notoriously unwilling to share or circulate his scholarly works, Boccaccio, like Dante in his *Convivio,* was much more generous with his labors: if poetry was to help regenerate civic life, the truths of poetry must be rendered more accessible to people of good will. These differing visions of the social functions of humanist culture that divide Boccaccio from Petrarch reflect differing political choices: Boccaccio remained loyal to the broad-based, participatory polity of republican Florence, whereas Petrarch chose to serve northern Italian despots. Although he remained on friendly terms with Petrarch, Boccaccio found it deplorable that Petrarch's talents should be employed to legitimize the brutal acts of tyrannical regimes.

David Wallace

See also MEDIEVAL THEORY AND CRITICISM.

Giovanni Boccaccio, *Boccaccio on Poetry: Being the Preface and Fourteenth and Fifteenth Books of Boccaccio's "Genealogia Deorum Gentilium"* (trans. Charles G. Osgood, 1956), *Tutte le opere di Giovanni Boccaccio* (ed. Vittore Branca et al., 9 vols. to date, 1964–); *Medieval Literary Theory and Criticism, c. 1100–c. 1375: The Commentary-Tradition* (ed. A. J. Minnis and A. B. Scott, with David Wallace, 1988); Francesco Petrarca, *Rerum familiarum libri* (trans. Aldo S. Bernardo, 3 vols., 1981–85).

Vittore Branca, *Boccaccio: The Man and His Works* (trans. Richard Monges, 1976); A. J. Minnis, *Medieval Theory of Authorship: Scholastic Literary Attitudes in the Later Middle Ages* (1984, 2d ed., 1988).

BOILEAU-DESPRÉAUX, NICOLAS

Nicolas Boileau-Despréaux (1636–1711), poet, satirist, and literary critic, is cited most often as the arbiter of the aesthetics of French classicism. His positions on poetry, the genres, and particular authors are scattered throughout his *Satires* and *Epîtres;* they are found as well in his *Réflexions sur Longin* and his preface to the 1701 edition of his works, but *L'Art poétique* offers the most complete and the most enduring statement of his poetics. While modeled on HORACE's *Ars Poetica* and borrowing freely from ARISTOTLE, this poem represents mainly a synthesis of conventions that already governed literary production during Boileau's time. It includes as well a few of his personal prejudices regarding certain authors, genres, and periods. *L'Art poétique* not only passes sure judgment on specific works of literature as it prescribes the essential requirements for the art of fine writing; Boileau aspires to provide in the poem itself a demonstration of its principal doctrine: the duty of poetry to at once please and instruct. Written in finely honed verse, enlivened with humorous anecdotes and witty remarks, not only does it set forth the rules of good writing but it purports to illustrate them as well. The aphoristic nature of Boileau's verses lent to their ready transformation into a handy pedagogical text upon which generations of French schoolchildren have been raised, thus transmitting since the seventeenth century an aesthetic of classical expression to which writers aspire or against which they revolt but which none of them ignore.

Boileau was born into a family of well-established clerks. Parisian and bourgeois by birth, he privileged wit and common sense in his writing. Although he was trained in theology and then in the law, neither profession suited him. A modest inheritance permitted him to devote himself to literature. He is regarded as the first of a new breed, the professional writer, although he wrote at a transitional stage when writing bore all the marks of a vocation susceptible of translation into a career but was still enmeshed in patronage systems and not yet viable as a means of making a living. Further, throughout the seventeenth century the profession's constituency modeled itself on the titled elite instead of forging a more commercial identity.

Noted for his sharp tongue, Boileau ventured opinions on all the writers of his day, attacking particularly the *précieux* and the *galants* for what he condemned as their stilted circumlocutions, out of line with his program favoring clear and simple language. He was markedly misogynistic at a time when women were influential contributors in the world of literature (see his *Satire X*). He dismissed the entire novel genre and only belatedly commented on the epistolary, because these two were understood as feminine in his time. His pronouncements on works of his contemporaries contributed significantly to the shaping of the classical canon, as it has come to be known. Challenged to produce a more positive statement on his guiding aesthetics than his habitual caustic criticisms, he produced *L'Art poétique,* reading it aloud to his friends, continually refining it before and subsequent to its publication in 1674. In 1677, along with Jean Racine, he was appointed historiographer to Louis XIV (see FRENCH THEORY AND CRITICISM: I. SEVENTEENTH CENTURY). In 1684 he was received as a member of the Académie française. But he was primarily a townsperson, frequenting *salons* and literary circles, happier in his more independent role as critic and satirist than in any official (and hence indebted) capacity.

He was a major partisan of the ancients in the Quarrel between the Ancients and the Moderns, arguing conservatively that the ancients had long since achieved excellence; the most he and his contemporaries might aspire to was effective imitation of them. Further, he was scornful of the Jesuits' practice of casuistry. To their accommodating ambiguity he preferred the rigorous morality and exacting language of Jansenism. His authoritarian vision of literature reflects the absolutist spirit of Louis XIV's reign in positing a single standard of absolute beauty that all writers must industriously strive to meet.

L'Art poétique, a didactic poem, represents the summary of his reflections on the art of writing and sketches out his own highly valuative history of literature. Organized in four cantos, it is addressed not so much to scholars, dismissed as a pedantic lot, as to the more sociable amateurs of literature, to the elite literati of his day. It includes not only recommendations for forms of literature worthy of personal investment but specific prescriptions for the professional character of the writer. The first and final cantos address the would-be poet (who is presumed to be male), adjuring him to be certain that writing is in fact his calling, to know his particular talent and to practice only that genre to which he is suited, to privilege reason over style and content, and above all to aim to please the reader. Poetry is not merely a gift of genius, according to Boileau; genius is necessary but must be coupled with discipline, and writing is enfigured more as a craft to be learned than as a matter of inspiration. In order to produce a masterpiece, the writer must continually refine, polish, and edit his text; he must submit his writing to a rigorous censor whose judgment he respects and will heed. Since there is nothing new to be said, all depends on how it is said, and proper wording is a matter of work. The vocation of poet also exacts a standard of personal comportment: the poet must be virtuous, sociable, and loyal to his friends, and this standard is to translate into only moral examples in his writing. He must write only for glory, not for gain, although Boileau is not insensitive to the dilemma this may present.

Woven into these recommendations is a history of French poetry that clearly privileges seventeenth-century classical standards: Boileau recognized as exemplary the talent of certain poets (François Villon, Clément Marot) for their plain-spoken style, and he condemned others, in particular Pierre de Ronsard, for indulging excessively in neologisms and complicated turns of phrase. He singularly praised François de Malherbe for standardizing the rules of syntax and verse and for restoring the French language to the state of purity it purportedly enjoyed prior to its sixteenth-century enslavement to Italian fashion. This can be understood retrospectively as one of many forms of the nationalism that manifested itself as absolutist France established cultural hegemony in Europe while charting and consolidating its territorial domain.

Boileau proceeds to offer a running history and description of the minor genres with judgments in passing on various practitioners of these forms, recommending imitation of such models as Theocritus, Virgil, and Juvenal (all from a distant world of unsurpassed glory to which France could afford to compare itself) and avoidance of vulgarity in even the less noble forms of poetry.

In the same vein, Boileau defines and pronounces on the great genres—tragedy, the epic poem, and comedy—requiring that they remain above all distinct from one another (a rigidity against which the Romantics would revolt in their invention of the *drame*) (see FRENCH THEORY AND CRITICISM: 2. EIGHTEENTH CENTURY). His tenets for tragedy are largely based on Aristotle's, but Boileau's innovation is to justify the unities of action, time, and place from the perspective of reception. An audience captive in the physical space of the theater for a designated length of time, focused on one spectacle, expects the internal dynamics of the play to conform to its own situation. Plausibility, based on the norm, is more important than the truth, and the conventions governing polite society, propriety, determine what is acceptable material for the stage and what must be repressed or merely reported. Boileau insists on grandeur of character for the hero and clear treatment of the tragic flaw that occasions his downfall. The tragedian must depict the nuances that render his characters powerful individuals, at once believable and real, not merely copies modeled on some notion of himself or an empty formula of heroism.

As for the epic poem, the marvelous is the governing principle. Here, consistent with his nationalistic tendencies and his desire to contribute to the legitimation of the French state, Boileau cites classical mythology, as opposed to Christian imagery, as appropriate ornamentation for the genre. He thus at once dismisses the Italian models, such as Torquato Tasso, as inadequate and advocates a stance of admiring cultural competition with the classical world.

With regard to comedy, Boileau insists on attention to human nature and the importance of observation for capturing the characteristics of the different ages of man. He bans obscenity and buffoonery from the stage, vaunting the merit of comedy of character (e.g., Molière's *Le Misanthrope*) over vulgar slapstick.

The poem ends in praise of Louis XIV as patron of the arts and with an apology for Boileau's own negative talent, best suited to satire and criticism. *L'Art poétique* does not investigate in any depth the key concepts reason, imitation, nature, plausibility, and beauty, which inform the doctrine of classicism, although it refers to all of them. Rather, it offers an entertaining synthesis of the prevailing aesthetics of the time in formulaic and eminently quotable fashion. Boileau claims that the ultimate criterion of the value of a work is public consensus;

thus, while he does not hesitate to pronounce on the writers of his day as well as those of the past, he insists that the real fate of their works is posterity's to decide.

Boileau also translated LONGINUS's treatise *On the Sublime,* from which he derived his notion of the *je ne sais quoi* that distinguishes the truly great work of art or isolates the moment of greatness in a piece. This phrase was much in circulation among the seventeenth-century arbiters of taste and surfaces regularly as an attempt to explain attraction for persons or works of art. The fact that this latter-day "sublime" defies definition, as the term so much as states, hints at the arbitrary manner in which it could be deployed by the gatekeepers of the republic of letters to admit a selected elite of writers and to exclude others deemed unworthy. This indefinable quality is vaguely characterized by Boileau as one of extreme simplicity, more easily felt than described, consisting in the perfect coincidence of true thoughts and correct expression.

Michèle Longino Farrell

See also FRENCH THEORY AND CRITICISM: 1. SEVENTEENTH CENTURY.

Nicolas Boileau-Despréaux, *The Art of Poetry: The Poetical Treatises of Horace, Vida, and Boileau* (ed. Albert S. Cook, trans. Francis Howes, Christopher Pitt, and Sir William Soames, 1926), *Oeuvres complètes* (ed. Charles Boudhors, 7 vols., 1934–43), *Oeuvres complètes* (ed. Françoise Escal, 1966), *Oeuvres diverses du Sr. Boileau Despréaux* (1701), *Selections from Boileau* (ed. Oscar Kuhns, 1908).

Bernard Beugnot and Roger Zuber, *Boileau: Visages anciens, visages nouveaux, 1665–1970* (1973); Jules Brody, *Boileau and Longinus* (1958); Robert Corum, "Paris's Barrier: Boileau's *Satire VI,*" *Papers on French Seventeenth-Century Literature* 9 (1982); Marc Fumaroli, ed., *Critique et création littéraires en France au XVIIe siècle* (1977); Paul Joret, *Nicolas Boileau-Despréaux: Révolutionnaire et conformiste* (1989); Joseph Pineau, *L'Univers satirique de Boileau: L'Ardeur, la grâce et la loi* (1990); Gordon Pocock, *Boileau and the Nature of Neo-Classicism* (1980); Susan W. Tiefenbrun, "Boileau and His Friendly Enemy: A Poetics of Satiric Criticism," *MLN* 91 (1976); Alain Viala, *Naissance de l'écrivain: Sociologie de la littérature à l'âge classique* (1985); Allen Wood, "The Régent du Parnasse and Vraisemblance," *French Forum* 3 (1978).

BRITISH THEORY AND CRITICISM

1. Early Eighteenth Century

Literary criticism developed in the early eighteenth century as part of a broader cultural discourse that included moral philosophy, politics, aesthetics, science, and economics. For critics otherwise as different as Alexander Pope (1688–1744), Joseph Addison (1672–1719), and Anthony Ashley Cooper, the third earl of Shaftesbury (1671–1713), the study of literature offered a means to promote the moral education of its readers; however, what that education entailed varied from critic to critic. Although the first half of the eighteenth century is often termed the "neoclassical" or "Augustan" age for its fascination with championing the moral and literary models of ancient Greece and Rome, the criticism of the period was ultimately less concerned with establishing rules of literary composition based on classical precedent than with promoting literature as a standard of civilized taste to which all educated men and women could look for guidance. In this respect, criticism from the time of JOHN DRYDEN to the death of Pope was concerned primarily with moral—and sociopolitical—issues rather than with establishing methodological procedures or analyzing individual texts.

Debates among eighteenth-century critics, particularly the "Battle of the Books" between the so-called ancients and moderns, should be seen within the context of the changing conditions of publication and the professionalization of criticism. During the early eighteenth century the reading public became increasingly large and diverse. Prior to 1700, literary critics, such as Dryden and the playwright William Congreve (1670–1729), perceived themselves as writing primarily for an educated elite. "Poetry," Congreve says, "is sacred to the Good and Great," that is, to those who are morally and socially privileged (392). But by 1709, when Richard Steele (1672–1729) and Addison began the triweekly paper the *Tatler,* criticism assumed the ideological function of promoting civilized values among a wide and diverse readership, including tradespeople, women, and readers in the country. For Addison and Steele, literary journalism offered a way to promote values of educated taste, good breeding, refinement, and decorum among the middle classes, who previously had been excluded or ignored by critical formulations that made literature the domain of "the Good and Great." For Addison and Steele, particularly in their second paper, the *Spectator* (1711–12, 1714), criticism provided a means to mediate potentially

divisive conflicts between the middle and upper classes; the language of "taste" and "refinement" offered the opportunity to forge what Terry Eagleton calls a "historical alliance" between bourgeois conceptions of virtue and propriety and aristocratic principles of birth and honor (10–11). This yoking of morality and manners testifies to the cultural importance that criticism assumed in the early eighteenth century. The appreciation of literature, at least according to Addison and Steele, became a way to bring together potentially antagonistic elements of society by emphasizing the shared principles and values that support the union of art and morality.

To the extent that critics in the early eighteenth century shared an ideal vision of literature as a means of moral education, their critical vocabulary of order, stability, and virtue may seem consistent. But this common vocabulary cannot mask the debates that raged about what its terms—"wit," "judgment," and "nature," among others—can and should mean. As James William Johnson argues, neoclassicism in the eighteenth century was not a doctrine but a series of attempts to explore and to resolve the internal contradictions that arose from efforts to model English critical and literary practice on the examples of the ancients. As Johnson notes, eighteenth-century neoclassicists were frequently devout Christians who celebrated pagan writers as authorities on morality as well as art. Also, they promoted the cultural and political example of the Roman Empire as a model for England's own "Augustan" age, yet they took as their heroes defenders of the Roman republic, including Cato (the subject of a popular tragedy by Addison performed in 1713) and Cicero (xi). If these problems resist simple solutions, they should focus our attention on the ideological and cultural implications of neoclassical rhetoric.

Precisely because criticism was viewed in the eighteenth century as part of larger moral and political discourses, controversies about literary tastes and aesthetic principles reveal often fundamentally different assumptions about the values and practices of English society. As the debates between Pope and John Dennis (1657–1734) illustrate, criticism often seemed to its contemporaries little more than invective. But the no-holds-barred rhetoric of the era reveals the intense passions unleashed by an ongoing struggle for a common vocabulary. What was at stake in early eighteenth-century criticism was competing views of civilization, history, and social order as well as of wit and the efficacy of the Aristotelian "rules": the antagonists in the debate were, on the one hand, those critics and philosophers who saw English civilization progressing toward new conceptions of individualism and economic prosperity founded upon the accumulation of capital and, on the other, those who resisted such changes and saw in eighteenth-century British culture a fall from classical ideals of morality, prudence, and moderation. This confrontation between the moderns and the ancients was, however, immensely complicated and involved multiple loyalties on the part of its participants. In some respects, it was less a battle of diametrically opposed intellectual camps than a struggle to define the moral value of a civilized, literary education.

On one level, the battle between the ancients and the moderns centered on the question whether the classical unities of time, place, and action—the "rules"—should be followed rigorously or be subordinated to the writer's imagination. But its implications are much larger. Dennis identified the neoclassical unities with the moral purpose of art. In *The Impartial Critick* (1693) he declared that the "rules of *Aristotle* are nothing but Nature and Good Sence reduc'd to a Method" (1:39), and in *The Grounds of Criticism in Poetry* (1704) he argued that "if the End of Poetry be to instruct and reform the World, that is, to bring Mankind from Irregularity, Extravagance, and Confusion, to Rule and Order" (1:335), then the rules were essential to this purpose. Similarly, Charles Gildon (1665–1724) in *The Complete Art of Poetry* (1718) maintained that art is "Nature reduc'd to Form" (1:94). Other critics, however, including Addison, Leonard Welsted (1688–1747), and Henry Felton (1679–1740), disagreed, arguing for a flexibility in applying the rules. Dennis's argument, as he makes explicit in *A Large Account of the Taste in Poetry* (1702), is based on the need for a strict adherence to authority, given the decline in the quality of theater audiences (and by implication of all consumers of literature) since the reign of Charles II (1660–85). Whereas in those days "a considerable part of an Audience had those Parts, that Education and that Application which were requisit[e] for the judging of Poetry . . . there are [in the early eighteenth century] three sorts of People now in our Audiences, who have had no education at all": "younger Brothers, Gentlemen born, who have been kept at home, by reason of the pressure of the Taxes"; war profiteers, "who from a state of obscurity, and perhaps of misery, have risen to a condition of distinction and plenty"; and "a considerable number of Foreigners" (1:291, 293). All three categories of unqualified spectators are products of England's unpopular involvement in a series of wars on the Continent that Dennis, a staunch Tory, opposed. In this regard, "judging Poetry" is a sociopolitical as well as a critical act, one of the skills that gentlemen of "Parts" and "Education" must acquire. For Dennis, the rules are not simply formal principles of composition but part of the structure of cultural authority—moral, political, and theological as well as literary—that informs his vision of an ordered society.

On another level, critical conflicts about whether the rules guided or hindered the artistic imagination were manifestations of efforts to define the individual's relationship to both artistic and social convention. In his *Essay Concerning Human Understanding* (1690), John Locke (1632–1704) held that ideas formed from sensory impressions constitute the only legitimate basis for a theory of knowledge or language. Although language may be a socially contrived system, it is arbitrary and contractual. Only the individual's ideas, which Locke discusses as though they were personal possessions, can be represented, and knowledge therefore is also the product of each individual's sensory experience. The individual, in Locke's philosophy, becomes paradoxically both isolated and free from the sorts of social determinations that underlie contemporary critical debates about the representation of a transhistorical and unchanging Nature. Shaftesbury, a former pupil of Locke's, perceived the threat to the established social order that Locke's view posed and sought to bring the imaginative faculty within the bounds of aristocratic views of an ordered, stable, and hierarchical society. "To *philosophize,*" Shaftesbury maintains, "is but To carry *Good-Breeding* a step higher. For the accomplishment of Breeding is, To learn whatever is *decent* in Company, or *beautiful* in Arts: and the Sum of Philosophy is, to learn what is *just* in Society, and *beautiful* in Nature, and the Order of the World" (3:161). In seeking to counter the individualistic emphases in Locke's *Essay,* Shaftesbury creates a unified vision of art, morality, philosophy, and social stability that emphasizes the creative power of the imagination, what he calls "enthusiasm." His aestheticized view of an ordered and harmonious world influenced a number of contemporaries, including Addison and Steele, and subsequent critics, among them SAMUEL TAYLOR COLERIDGE.

In contrast to Locke, Shaftesbury, and Addison, the Tory satirists, particularly Pope and Jonathan Swift (1667–1745), sought to preserve classical ideals of civilization and viewed most modern innovations—from the verse of their political enemies to the scholarship of Richard Bentley (1662–1742), who argued that many ancient texts were corrupt or spurious—as a threat to the classical idea of civilization the ancients represented. For Pope and Swift, history was a process of corruption and decay, a fall from ancient virtues to the degenerate standards they repeatedly associated with the Whig prime minister, Horace Walpole. The role of literature is to recall society to sanity and stability, often through satiric attacks on literary and political enemies, as in Pope's poem *The Dunciad* (1728, rev. ed., 1743), a savage satire of writers who in one way or another abandoned neoclassical ideals. Similarly, the function of criticism is to guide readers to establish sound principles of aesthetic judgment that will reunite morality and art. Unlike Shaftesbury, however, Pope's view was Christian as well as classical; his stance, like Swift's, was that of the isolated moralist who recognized the corruption of his age and used satire as his weapon both to attack vice and to point the way toward a restoration of virtue.

Pope's critical principles are fully articulated in his *Essay on Criticism* (1711), a work that implicitly rejects Lockean accounts of language and society in favor of an aesthetic that seeks to define the relationships between the imagination and social convention. Despite his poem's title, Pope's chief theoretical interest lies in defining "wit," a problematic term for English critics since the seventeenth century. In the years prior to writing his essay, Pope was engaged in revising the poems of the aging playwright William Wycherley (1640–1716). Wycherley, the leading dramatist of the 1670s and still a considerable literary figure in the early eighteenth century, resisted Pope's efforts to regularize his verse, disparaging "method" in favor of an unfettered wit. In responding to Wycherley, Pope developed a sophisticated argument for wit as a mediating force between the imagination and poetic convention that is fully laid out in the *Essay* (Hooker 46–50). Pope defines wit as "Nature to advantage dress'd, / What oft was thought, but ne'er so well express'd" (ll. 297–98). Wit is the individual's imaginative recreation of general human experience, his or her unique expression of nature's "clear, unchanged, and universal Light" (l. 71). Pope's description of the relationship between individual imagination and literary conventions steers carefully between Lockean individualism and the reliance on the rules by critics such as Dennis, who offer "dull receipts how poems may be made" (l. 115). For Pope, the rules were "discover'd, not devised"; they are "Nature still, but Nature methodized" (ll. 88–89). To explicate these lines, Pope uses a political image: "Nature, like Liberty, is but restrain'd / By the same laws which first herself ordain'd" (ll. 90–91). Nature, then, functions in the poem as both an absolute standard against which all literary works must be judged and a kind of contractual entity that acts as a regulative force on art. Later in the poem, Pope argues that "Nature and Homer [are] the same" (l. 135). This identification underlies the values of neoclassicism. Homer and ancient civilization in general are idealized as representations of a golden age in which poets had seemingly an unmediated access to nature. For modern writers, art becomes a recreative as well as a creative endeavor, an attempt to embody the principles that the ancients had known and used to "methodize" Nature, to represent it as fully as possible.

Pope's *Essay on Criticism,* then, can be read as a polemical piece that is intended less to establish guidelines for critics than to identify the moral and cultural significance of criticism. Criticism, for Pope, was crucial to the literary culture of his time because it regulated the relationships between imagination and convention; it functioned ideally not as a form of detraction but as a means to encode those neoclassical values that will establish the importance of literature in creating a moral and ordered society. In this regard, Pope recognized that neoclassical values, literary and political, represented idealized visions of art and society. The ancients, for him, were both historical figures and deliberately idealized extensions of the union of art and nature. Because Pope and his contemporaries could not reconcile the contradictions of a Christian and mercantilist society's taking a pagan empire as its standard of political and moral value, they sought to transcend these tensions by aestheticizing them, by seeking a set of principles that would allow society to be defined—and judged—in the same way as a work of art. In this respect, the metaphors of harmony and order that figure prominently in eighteenth-century criticism represent efforts to transcend the complexities and contradictions of historical experience, to escape to the kind of idealism that is evident in Shaftesbury's works and is satirized by Swift in book four of *Gulliver's Travels.* The fact that the early eighteenth century generally is considered the great age of English satire suggests the extent to which Pope, Swift, and their contemporaries recognized and sought to overcome the discrepancies between neoclassical ideals and the corruption of their age. In this regard, the criticism of the period 1700–1740 represents the other side of the satiric impulse: a series of attempts to legislate rather than ridicule the corruption of the times out of existence.

Robert Markley

Donald F. Bond, ed., *The Spectator* (5 vols., 1965); Gerald Wester Chapman, ed., *Literary Criticism in England, 1660–1800* (1966); William Congreve, *The Complete Plays of William Congreve* (ed. Herbert Davis, 1967); John Dennis, *The Critical Works of John Dennis* (ed. Edward Niles Hooker, 2 vols., 1939–43); W. H. Durham, ed., *Critical Essays of the Eighteenth Century, 1700–1725* (1915); Charles Gildon, *The Complete Art of Poetry* (1718, 2 vols., facs.

reprint, 1970); John Locke, *An Essay Concerning Human Understanding* (1690, ed. Peter H. Nidditch, 1975); Alexander Pope, *The Poems of Alexander Pope* (ed. John Butt et al., 11 vols., 1939–69); Anthony Ashley Cooper, third earl of Shaftesbury, *Characteristicks of Men, Manners, Opinions, Times* (6th ed., 3 vols., 1737–38); J. E. Spingarn, ed., *Critical Essays of the Seventeenth Century* (3 vols., 1908–9).

Edward A. Bloom, Lillian D. Bloom, and Edmund Leites, *Educating the Audience: Addison, Steele, and Eighteenth-Century Culture* (1984); Leopold Damrosch, "The Significance of Addison's Criticism," *Studies in English Literature 1500–1900* 19 (1979); Bonamy Dobree, *English Literature in the Early Eighteenth Century, 1700–1740* (1959); Terry Eagleton, *The Function of Criticism: From the Spectator to Post-Structuralism* (1984); James Engell, *Forming the Critical Mind: Dryden to Coleridge* (1989); Edward Niles Hooker, "Pope on Wit: The Essay on Criticism" (*Eighteenth Century Literature: Modern Essays in Criticism,* ed. James L. Clifford, 1959); James William Johnson, *The Formation of English Neo-Classical Thought* (1967); Robert L. Montgomery, *Terms of Response: Language and Audience in Seventeenth- and Eighteenth-Century Theory* (1992); David B. Morris, "Civilized Reading: The Act of Judgment in *An Essay on Criticism*" (*The Art of Alexander Pope,* ed. Howard Erskine-Hill and Anne Smith, 1979); Irene Simon, "Art and Nature in Early Eighteenth-Century Criticism," *English Studies* 60 (1979); H. T. Swedenberg, Jr., "Rules and English Critics of the Epic, 1650–1800," *Studies in Philology* 35 (1938); Dabney Townsend, "Shaftesbury's Aesthetic Theory," *Journal of Aesthetics and Art Criticism* 41 (1982); David Wheeler, "John Dennis and the Religious Sublime," *College Language Association Journal* 30 (1986).

2. Late Eighteenth Century

In the second half of the eighteenth century, literary criticism turned away from the predominantly neoclassical thought of a previous generation, shifting from a vision of literature as a standard of civilized taste to one based on individual experience. Social change, such as the growth of the reading public, which was increasingly bourgeois (rather than aristocratic), profoundly influenced literary production during the later eighteenth century. While criticism itself became a more specialized discipline, it was produced by a host of professional critics who catered to the expanding reading public and appealed to the general audience rather than the educated elite. In place of the stress on the "civilized" standard of classical learning, late-eighteenth-century criticism drew many of its tenets from individual experience,

as reflected in its frequently psychological approach. During this time, the emphasis on the public and moral function of literature faded; the injunction to "please and instruct" shifted away from didacticism and focused almost completely on the sources of pleasure in poetry. While unwilling to abandon neoclassicism completely, critics began to move away from the ideals of order, refinement, and decorum, searching instead for new sources of aesthetic pleasure and new criteria for genius. Formalism, characterized most vividly by those dramatic "rules" championed by French critics such as NICOLAS BOILEAU-DESPRÉAUX and René le Bossu, was generally rejected in favor of a new focus on sensibility and psychology. Discussions of literature and the arts began to center on a series of new topics: poetic originality, reevaluation of "primitive" literature, the sublime, and the picturesque. As a topic of criticism, the sublime would come to dominate aesthetic theory. Often referred to as "pre-Romantic," the critics of the later eighteenth century developed issues that were to become the foundation for criticism in the Romantic period.

Few critics ignored these new developments, and few completely abandoned the standards of reason and universal truth so important to the previous generation. At one end of the spectrum, conservative critics such as SAMUEL JOHNSON and philosopher DAVID HUME incorporated some elements of contemporary criticism into their arguments. *Four Dissertations,* Hume's most widely read literary criticism, expresses his interest in universal nature and refinement, as well as his distrust of irregularity, all topics popular with critics in the early decades of the eighteenth century. Nonetheless, Hume is skeptical about such popular neoclassical issues as literary rules (see "Of Tragedy") and rules for defining taste (see "Of the Standard of Taste"). The most important critic of this period, Samuel Johnson, was also closely attuned to the familiar precepts stressing the imitation of nature and the dual function of literature to please and instruct. Yet, despite the conservatism of these ideas, Johnson also firmly rejects the notion of literary rules on psychological grounds, arguing that the popular concept of dramatic "unities" is based on a false notion of verisimilitude: requiring a play's action to conform to a single day and a single place is an unnecessary and artificial constraint, since "the truth is, that the spectators are always in their senses, and know, from the first act to the last, that the stage is only a stage, and that the players are only players" (7:77). In the end, "a play, written with nice observation of critical rules," becomes nothing more than "an elaborate curiosity" (7:80). Later, in *The Lives of the Poets,* Johnson uses the increasingly familiar terms of originality and sympathy as the bases for his judgment of the poets of his generation.

One of the most prominent developments in mid-century criticism was the increased emphasis on literary originality, reflecting a corresponding shift toward the individual and away from the standards of classical education. It was assumed that in order to be considered an original, a writer should rely upon him- or herself, using for a model only nature, not the works of other writers. While earlier critics had sanctioned imitation, both of nature and of other writers, by mid-century the sense of the term was largely pejorative, a literary endeavor akin to mere transcription. Imitation, particularly of other writers, was regarded merely as servile copying. The topic became a central focus in the works of critics such as Edward Young, William Duff, and Joseph and Thomas Warton. The growing interest in originality and its relationship to genius was sparked largely by Young's *Conjectures on Original Composition* (1759). Young argues that originality is a prime criterion for genius and that those who imitate can claim no more than "good understanding." While originals benefit mankind by "extend[ing] the republic of letters" (6), imitations only duplicate that which is original; they cannot improve it. In Young's eyes, imitation can even be harmful both because of its artificiality and because it causes learning to stagnate. It encourages writers to "think little and write much" (20). Shakespeare, writing purely from his heart, without the learning that dulled even Milton's genius, is the great original of English literature. In contrast, Alexander Pope, the greatest poet of the previous age, forfeits the title of genius because he was too willing to imitate, too inclined to refine and polish "what oft was thought, but ne'er so well expressed" (Pope, *Essay on Criticism*, 1711, l. 298).

While not all critics accepted Young's argument (his friend Joseph Warton thought he had gone too far), most agreed that originality should be a major criterion for judging literature and concurred with Johnson's Imlac, who claimed that "no man was ever great by imitation" (16:41). Originality becomes a standard by which most writers are judged, as in Johnson's "Life of Milton," where his final assessment of *Paradise Lost* is dependent on the poem's originality: "[It] is not the greatest of heroic poems, only because it is not the first" (*Johnson as Critic* 298).

The emphasis on originality points to a larger reassessment of the sources and judgment of art, linking originality inversely with the rise of Western civilization. Following Young's lead, critics such as William Duff (*An Essay on Original Genius,* 1767) argue that original poetic genius is displayed most vigorously in early periods of society and that it rarely appears to any high degree in civilized life, because the uncultivated poet is closer to nature, and the imagination less fettered. Using criteria much stricter than those of Young, Duff identifies Shakespeare, long known for his failure to imitate classical form, as the only modern writer who can be seen as original. "Refinement," a term with positive connotations for critics in the early part of the century, here becomes a sign of human falling away from the purer emotions and more vivid imagination of the primitive. By idealizing the primitive as the source of originality and genius, Duff rejects the underpinnings of neoclassic critical tenets and leads the way for both the redefinition of what constitutes literature and the establishment of a new literary canon based on native English works, paralleling the popular interest in working-class poets such as Robert Burns.

Examined in its larger context, late-eighteenth-century criticism can be seen as following the tide of British nationalism that swept the country in the second half of the century. Rejecting the values of a previous generation that had looked to Greece and Rome for its models, critics now turned to native English poets, in particular Chaucer, Spenser, and Shakespeare, as examples of poetic genius. Much of this criticism can be characterized by its reevaluation of earlier, nonclassical literature. Thomas Warton, for example, absolves Spenser's *Fairie Queene* from earlier critics' charge that it did not follow the rules dictating unity in an epic. He stresses instead the importance of considering the age in which a literary work was written and notes with approval that Spenser wrote rapidly out of strong feeling, a trait that engages the reader's affections more strongly than would a regular but emotionless epic. This emotional power Warton ties to the remote age in which Spenser wrote, before the obsession with rules and classical form had vitiated the primitive power of native English literature.

Interest in medieval and Renaissance literature grew as critics looked at the past, particularly the English past, not as a barbaric and unrefined age but as a time when writers were closer to poetic inspiration. "Primitivism" became a means of reclaiming an English literary tradition, and it influenced even critics with close ties to traditional neoclassic criticism, such as Richard Hurd, who looked back nostalgically to medieval romance and legend. In *Letters on Chivalry and Romance* (1762) Hurd suggests that the "Gothic barbarism" of the Middle Ages was uniquely poetical, its superstitions and fantasies more "awakening to the imagination" (48) than even the mythology that preceded Homer. Hurd's suggestion that Augustan theorists had gone too far in their adherence to classical texts sets up a replacement of traditional classical models with the irregular, enchanting, and sublime "fancies" of so-called primitive poets. This nostalgia for a golden age of poetry and genius is widely reflected in the work of late-eighteenth-century poets, artists, and architects, many of whom used the past to evoke a sense of grandeur and mystery, particularly by the gothic revival in architecture and the steadily growing popularity of the gothic novel.

Akin to the interest in the primitive was the concept of the sublime, associated by Hurd and others with non-classical literature and itself the focus of much aesthetic theory. The term originated in LONGINUS's third-century treatise *On the Sublime,* a work long familiar to critics but most often cited in discussions of style. By the later eighteenth century, critics used the term increasingly to discuss a state of intense, awe-struck emotion. Predicated upon the individual response, the sublime, with its language of sensibility, is related to what social historian Lawrence Stone, in *The Family, Sex, and Marriage in England, 1500–1800* (1977), has termed the growth of "affective individualism." The catalyst for much of the interest in the sublime was EDMUND BURKE's *Philosophical Enquiry into the Origin of Our Ideas of the Sublime and the Beautiful* (1757). Burke discusses general concepts of the sublime in nature and in art but devotes a sizable section of his treatise to an examination of the sublime in poetry. His study focuses on the emotional impact of the sublime, characterized by its power, obscurity, darkness, and vastness of scale and its excitation of pain, terror, and awe. "The passion caused by the great and sublime in *nature* . . . is astonishment . . . it anticipates our reasonings, and hurries us on by an irresistible force" (53). For Burke and his contemporaries, the sublime incorporates those emotional and irrational elements of art that tended to be absent from or less emphasized in neoclassical art. In contrast, the qualities of the beautiful are smallness, smoothness, and delicacy. It is comprehensible where the sublime is incomprehensible, and the emotional response it excites is love, not awe. Burke finds Milton's *Paradise Lost,* in particular the scenes in hell, illustrative of sublimity, whereas the smooth versification and compact heroic couplets practiced by Pope and his contemporaries neatly illustrates Burke's concept of the beautiful.

Most criticism in the second half of the eighteenth century incorporated some discussion of the sublime, a change of focus that led to a conception of poetry different from that popular at the beginning of the century. One notable example, Joseph Warton's *Essay on the Genius and Writings of Pope* (1756), articulates a new defini-tion of poetry, one that separates poetry from morality and emphasizes the primal role of imagination in the creation of literature. Warton argues that "the sublime and the pathetic are the two chief nerves of all genuine poesy" (Chapman 204). He delineates four categories of poets based on this assumption: 1) sublime and pathetic poets; 2) poets with noble talents for moral, ethical, and panegyrical poetry; 3) writers of wit with a talent for describing familiar life, although not the "higher scenes of poetry"; and 4) mere versifiers (Chapman 204–5). Only three English poets fall into the category of sublime and pathetic poetic genius: Spenser, Shakespeare, and Milton. Pope falls short because of what Warton perceives as his lack of pathos and because he rarely introduces the sublime into his poetry. Pope's poems, while brilliant, are too regular and too even to qualify as "genuine poetry." Warton's brother and fellow critic Thomas Warton indirectly accuses his Augustan predecessors of a lack of sensibility by locating poetic genius in an age before satire, "that bane of the sublime" (2:111), became a popular genre.

The search for new sources of aesthetic pleasure also appears in the interest in the "picturesque," a term that would become increasingly popular in the late eighteenth and early nineteenth centuries. Writers such as William Gilpin ("On Picturesque Beauty," 1792) and Sir Uvedale Price (*An Essay on the Picturesque,* 1794) sought to define a quality somewhere between the sublime and the beautiful, something characterized by "ruggedness," "ruin," and "the destruction of symmetry" (83). The picturesque inspired neither the astonishment of the sublime nor the simple pleasure of the beautiful but instead curiosity, "an effect which, though less splendid and powerful, has a more general influence" (98). The term became synonymous with ruined abbeys and overgrown, rustic landscapes. Like the interest in the sublime, the interest in the picturesque represents a search for aesthetic pleasure outside of the realm of social art, in particular apart from the social world of satire.

Perhaps the most effective summary of late-eighteenth-century criticism can be seen in the writings of Sir Joshua Reynolds. Reynolds, the foremost English painter of his day, delivered a series of fifteen lectures to students at the Royal Academy of Art between the years 1769 and 1790. While Reynolds may not be a strictly original thinker, his *Discourses* provide a valuable record of popular thought; typical of many late-eighteenth-century critics, Reynolds possessed a strong neoclassical background, which became more and more infused with the new ideas current in literary theory. While his earlier discourses examine topics familiar to Augustan critics—

the imitation of nature and the importance of reason and judgment in the creation of art—the later discourses focus more and more on issues such as the primacy of imagination and feeling. Reynolds's discussion of Renaissance artists illustrates this progression. In discourse 5 (1773) he compares the talents of Raphael, characterized by taste, fancy, and proper judgment, with those of Michelangelo, noted for his genius and imagination, the creator of ideas both vast and sublime, and finds the artists equally gifted. By discourse 15 (1790) this balance no longer exists, as Reynolds concludes the *Discourses* with praise of Michelangelo as the emblem of genius, energy, and the sublime. Here Reynolds, like most of his contemporaries, considers these characteristics more artistic than those of Raphael, who is seen, not coincidentally, as the embodiment of the values lauded by critics and writers a generation before.

The last years of the eighteenth century produced a variety of experimental approaches to literature focusing on issues such as character analysis and the process of poetic creation. Most of these works were strongly influenced by John Locke's theories of the human mind, in particular the association of ideas. Locke argued that thought processes in the mind operate by association, one thought leading to a whole spectrum of loosely related thoughts, rather than by simple logical progression. Unlike earlier critics such as Shaftesbury, who rejected Locke's individualistic emphasis as a critical tool, writers in the last decades of the eighteenth century promoted individual response as a necessary part of criticism. One notable example of Locke's influence on literary criticism appears in *An Essay on the Dramatic Character of Sir John Falstaff* (1777), Maurice Morgann's book-length study of Shakespeare's character. Based in part on Locke's principle of associations, Morgann's *Essay* stresses the importance of impressions ("the *Impression* is the *Fact*" [146]), as well as how literature consists of a series of impressions that create a whole. This assumption implies that simply examining literature on a rational level distorts it; it must be felt as well as understood. Morgann's *Essay*, which ranges far beyond Falstaff himself, develops what would later be called the concept of organic unity, the sensation of wholeness or roundness that arises from a variety of disparate elements. Other critics applied the principle of association to aesthetic theory (Archibald Alison, *Essays on the Nature and Principles of Taste,* 1790) and to the process of composition as manifested in Shakespeare's image clusters (Walter Whiter, *A Specimen of a Commentary on Shakespeare,* 1794). Like Morgann, both Alison and Whiter base their work on the concept of associative imagination. Alison attributes the emotional effect of literature to the train of images it excites, and Whiter traces specific patterns of association at work in the imagery of Shakespeare.

By the 1790s, then, little remained of the staunch emphasis on order and the classics that had characterized criticism in the late seventeenth and early eighteenth centuries. Most discussions of literature focused on individual experience, emphasizing sensibility rather than restraint and finding irregularity a virtue rather than a vice. For critics in the later eighteenth century, the glorification of classical learning and refinement, so important to a preceding generation, had become sterile, and the ideal of an ordered, harmonious, and ultimately aristocratic society had become an anachronism. The late-eighteenth-century critics, with their interest in originality, the sublime, and the primitive, coupled with their incorporation of British nationalism, appealed to a larger, increasingly bourgeois, general readership. The appeal to a common reader helped define the criticism of this transitional age, linking seemingly disparate elements with a focus on individualism rather than social consensus.

Jean I. Marsden

Edmund Burke, *A Philosophical Enquiry into the Origin of Our Ideas of the Sublime and the Beautiful* (1757, ed. Adam Phillips, 1990); Gerald Wester Chapman, ed., *Literary Criticism in England, 1660–1800* (1966); David Hume, *Essays Moral, Political, and Literary* (ed. Eugene F. Miller, 1963); Richard Hurd, *Letters on Chivalry and Romance* (1762, ed. Hoyt Trowbridge, 1963); Samuel Johnson, *The Yale Edition of the Works of Samuel Johnson* (ed. Allen T. Hazen and John Middendorf, 16 vols. to date, 1958–), *Johnson as Critic* (ed. John Wain, 1973); Maurice Morgann, *An Essay on the Dramatic Character of Sir John Falstaff* (1777, ed. Daniel A. Fineman, 1972); Sir Uvedale Price, *On the Picturesque: With an Essay on the Origin of Taste, and Much Original Matter* (1794, ed. Sir Thomas Dick Lauder, 1842); Sir Joshua Reynolds, *Discourses on Art* (1769–90, ed. Robert R. Wark, 1975); Thomas Warton, *Observations on the Faery Queen of Spenser* (1754); Walter Whiter, *A Specimen of a Commentary on Shakespeare* (1794, ed. Alan Over and Mary Bell, 1964); Edward Young, *Conjectures on Original Composition* (1759, ed. Stephen Cornfold, 1989).

Walter Jackson Bate, *The Burden of the Past and the English Poet* (1970), *From Classic to Romantic: Premises of Taste in Eighteenth-Century England* (1961); James Engell, *Forming the Critical Mind: Dryden to Coleridge* (1989); Walter John Hipple, Jr., *The Beautiful, the Sublime, and the Picturesque in Eighteenth-Century British Aesthetic Theory*

(1957); Thomas McFarland, *Originality and Imagination* (1985); Marjorie Hope Nicolson, *Mountain Gloom and Mountain Glory: The Development of the Aesthetics of the Infinite* (1959); Douglas Lane Patey, *Probability and Literary Form: Philosophic Theory and Literary Practice in the Augustan Age* (1984); Ernest L. Tuveson, *The Imagination as a Means of Grace: Locke and the Aesthetics of Romanticism* (1960); Thomas Weiskel, *The Romantic Sublime: Studies in the Structure and Psychology of Transcendence* (1976).

3. Romantic Period and Early Nineteenth Century

In 1832, at the end of what is now called the Romantic age, SAMUEL TAYLOR COLERIDGE described "three silent revolutions in England: 1. When the Professions fell off from the Church; 2. When Literature fell off from the Professions; 3. When the Press fell off from Literature" (*Table Talk* 1:285). These fallings were, so to speak, "revolutions" within the revolution—the larger revolution of capitalist modernity from the seventeenth to the early nineteenth century. To Coleridge and other Romantic theorists, the emergence of the "professions," "literature," and the "press" mirrored the political revolutions of England (1642), the North American colonies (1775), and France (1789). In his "Preface to *Lyrical Ballads*" of 1800, WILLIAM WORDSWORTH had similarly proposed a transformation of poetry that would correspond to the "revolutions not of literature alone, but likewise of society itself" (121). Such thinking presupposed an already formed separation between the categories of politics and literature by the end of the eighteenth century. The Romantics were not the first to separate literature from politics, but they were the first to confront self-consciously the modern separation between these realms and to attempt to mediate it.

Few assessments of European modernity were more critical or more sweeping than FRIEDRICH SCHILLER's contrast between the "polypoid character of the Greek states, in which every individual enjoyed an independent existence but could, when need arose, grow into the whole organism" of social life, and the "mechanical kind of collective life," composed of "innumerable but lifeless parts" characteristic of European modernity. Like Coleridge and PERCY BYSSHE SHELLEY in England, Schiller pointed to the division of labor, institutions, and knowledges that was gradually shattering all forms of the universal, the capacity of man and woman to grasp the totality of their own purposes and acts. "State

and church, laws and customs, were now torn asunder; enjoyment was divorced from labor, the means from the end, the effort from the reward." The human being, who was now "everlastingly chained to a single little fragment of the whole," had become himself a "fragment": "nothing more than the imprint of his occupation or of his specialized knowledge" (35). This perspective became the paradoxical foundation of the Romantic theorist's claim for "Culture," an attempt to reinstitute the shattered universals by means of literature, symbol, the aesthetic, and reimaginations of mind and self (Abrams; Williams).

For Schiller, Wordsworth, and many other European liberals the year of the Terror (1793–94 in the French Revolution) came to signify a crisis in the relation between the political will and the social body, reason and nature, form and sensuousness (Eagleton 113–19). In this sense it also disclosed a crisis in criticism: if literature speaks to the audiences of civil society, to whom does criticism speak? By 1800 British literary and aesthetic theory would begin to talk about politics and social order *indirectly,* by way of allegory instead of direct address. Coleridge wrote in a letter of 1800 that his planned "Essay on the Elements of Poetry . . . would in reality be a *disguised* System of Morals & Politics" (*Collected Letters* 632). Something of this political allegorizing informed a great many Romantic arguments, making literary criticism a discourse on politics by other means.

Literary history has commonly recognized Wordsworth's preface of 1800 as the first text of English Romantic criticism, but Wordsworth was hardly alone, in the last years of the eighteenth century, in making the attempt to confront the political and cultural crisis of Europe in the 1790s with claims for new, transformative kinds of cultural production. Three years before the appearance of the preface, William Godwin (1757–1836) and Joanna Baillie (1762–1851) had each attempted to rethink the progressive political ideas and rhetorics of the radical Enlightenment within the complicating genres of narrative and dramatic representation. Baillie, a Scottish playwright and poet, appealed in her "Introductory Discourse" to *Plays on the Passions* (1798) to an analytic, revisionist mode of tragedy that would reconstruct the tragic, "tyrannical passions" from the little, unremembered gestures of everyday life. A rare example of female literary theory in this period, Baillie's "Discourse" was an ideological critique of tragedy's claim to represent a universal human nature, which she countered by tracing the human passions through their genealogy from domestic life to the torrential, officially "tragic" visitations in which (to put it more simply than

Baillie does) angry educated men flog and humiliate women, children, and finally one another, as surrogates for themselves. By displacing tragedy from the realm of the state to the domestic spheres of civil society, Baillie also tried to make the latter, gender-defined arena a basis for criticizing the public world, where, in traditional tragedy, the "tragic passions" had been made to appear transhistorical rather than specifically masculine and contextually linked to the larger "tyranny" of England's own *ancien régime*. In this way, Baillie's theory of tragedy was less an attempt to privatize and domesticate formerly public and political controversy than an effort to rethink the mode of dramatic representation as a discourse capable of making explicit the political restaging of private life.

Meanwhile, Godwin's essay "Of History and Romance" (1797) began to rethink the English novel as an inquiry into the private, secretive, and politically formative moments of individual lives. This unpublished essay belonged to Godwin's larger campaign, conducted in *The Enquirer* (1797), to build a progressive British intelligentsia through literary, educational, and canon-organizing means, since it was becoming clear in the late 1790s that British radical discourse was now failing to be sustained by the community of radical discussion and dissent (Philp). In "Of History and Romance" Godwin took up old and unresolved problems of modern fictional narrative, the problems of truth, skepticism, fiction, and virtue that belong to the early history and institutionalizing of the English novel (McKeon). Here Godwin grasped earlier conservative arguments for the novel's self-conscious removal from historical truth or progressive political aims as a new opportunity for progressive discourse. He proposed the novel as a mode of investigation into the secret folds and darkened closets of its characters' otherwise public lives, aiming to uncover the hidden truth behind universal history's ideological commitment to a law-governed history that will happen the same way in the future as it has happened in the past.

Seventeen years before Walter Scott's *Waverley*, Godwin imagined a historical novel capable of rivaling Enlightenment historiography as a mode of truth-telling. Yet he also recognized, near the end of a sophisticated argument on narrative epistemologies, that his case for the progressive historical romancer threatened to reintroduce the figure of a divine artificer into what had been meant as a wholly secular and highly skeptical argument for narrative knowledge. In the only materialist conclusion drawn by a Romantic critical thinker, Godwin averted that quasi-theological outcome by referring both historiography and novel-writing to the unfinished narratives of natural history being told by modern English science.

The year 1797–98 was a crucial turning point for British criticism, however; Godwin's brilliant meditation on the politics of historical romance never saw print in the projected second volume of *The Enquirer*. Instead, T. J. Mathias's (1754–1835) *Pursuits of Literature,* published in parts from 1794 to 1798, became one of the most widely read books of literary reflection in the early 1800s. Mathias's book was one-tenth "satirical poem," nine-tenths literary and political criticism loaded into a byzantine system of footnotes. Published alongside Thomas Malthus's *Essay on Population* (1798) and the periodical essay *The Anti-Jacobin* (1797–98), Mathias's *Pursuits* was read as a kind of Malthusian poetics, a manual of British literary population-politics for the nineteenth century. England's literary intellectuals read and loathed Mathias, as they did Malthus, for saying too crudely and publicly what many now had come to suspect privately: "Literature, well or ill conducted, is the great engine by which all civilized States must ultimately be supported or overthrown" (244). "Our peasantry," Mathias insisted, "now read the *Rights of Man* on mountains and moors. . . . Our *unsexed* female writers now instruct, or confuse, us and themselves in the labyrinth of politics, or turn us wild with Gallic frenzy." The surge of political and sexual frenzy animating Mathias's own critical prose spilled over in pages devoted to denouncing M. G. Lewis's *The Monk*—"lewd and systematic seduction"—and Godwin's *Enquirer,* which Mathias read as the cultural extension of *Political Justice* (244–53, 388–97). Much maligned by those young literary intellectuals who had said it was "Bliss to be alive" at the dawn of the French Revolution, Mathias's book indeed helped furnish the social and political *topoi* of English Romantic criticism for the next generation. Often, what Mathias announced none too subtly in 1797 would henceforth travel within the political allegories of Romantic criticism, or as Coleridge put it, "a *disguised* system of Morals & Politics" (*Collected Letters* 632).

Wordsworth's 1800 preface was written against some of Mathias's own antagonists—Gothic fiction and its female readerships, the Enlightenment politics of Thomas Paine and Godwin. Yet from 1800 to 1815 the preface was often greeted as itself an "experiment" in Jacobin poetics, seeming to promote the "real language of men" as a demotic, quasi-political standard of public verse. Unlike Godwin, Baillie, or even Mathias before him, Wordsworth had in fact broken with political theory as a framework for literary theory. WILLIAM HAZLITT, who seemed to admire Wordsworth's demotic poetics in *The Spirit of* the *Age* (1825), also suspected the deep ambivalence of Wordsworth's "levelling Muse." "The secret of the Jacobin poetry and the anti-Jacobin politics of this writer are the same," Hazlitt charged in 1816; "his lyrical poetry was a cant of humanity about the commonest people to level the great with the small; and his political poetry is a cant of loyalty to level Bonaparte with kings and hereditary imbecility" (7:144). In the contradiction between Wordsworth's "lyrical poetry" and his "political poetry," Hazlitt understood how Wordsworth had deepened rather than healed the separation between civil society and the state, how he had reproduced within his own texts the division between literature and politics Wordsworth's preface had promised to overcome.

Coleridge also changed his mind about Wordsworth's proposal to remodel the "real language" of civil society by means of poetry. By 1817 Coleridge was redefining the powers of poetry, "derived from reflection on the acts of the mind itself" (*Biographia* 2:54), so that they would resonate with Schiller's sense that the aesthetic "play drive" works reflexively on the conscious will embodied in the national state. This is why Coleridge, unlike Wordsworth, increasingly devoted his writing to institutional theory and historical accounts of the ways literature had "fallen" from the church, the professions, and the public discourse of the press. In *The Statesman's Manual* (1816), the *Friend* (1818), and *On the Constitution of Church and State* (1830) Coleridge completed a long, complex meditation on the transmission of symbolic meanings from a special body of intellectuals (or "clerisy") to the lay publics of civil society. Coleridge's theory formed yet another allegorical account of how literature, by means of criticism or symbolic interpretation, might restabilize the fractural, highly unstable relation of the British state to the social groups and classes of the early nineteenth century. Hence, Coleridge's works of political and institutional theory formed essential armatures to the more visibly "literary" theory of the *Biographia Literaria* (1817) and the literary lectures of 1808–19 (Klancher; Leask).

Coleridge therefore understood the emerging British culture industry—the realm of book publication, the periodical press, and the new scientific and literary lecturing institutions—as a crucial arena of political and social definition. These cultural institutions were demarcating the new reading audiences of the nineteenth century, and Coleridge's acute sense of the commodification of British reading and writing often sharpened the difference between a commercially organized and an institutionally directed form of the national culture. In *The Statesman's Manual* he complained: "I would that

the greater part of our publications could be thus *directed,* each to its appropriate class of Readers" (*Lay Sermons* 36), a plea made to an audience of economically and culturally distinguished readers whom Coleridge believed should themselves begin assuming such directive institutional powers. Yet Hazlitt, writing in the *Edinburgh Review,* replied to the *Statesman's Manual* with a question: "Do not publications generally find their way there, without a *direction?*" (16:105n). Hazlitt assumed a coherent, market-organized world of cultural communication that had no need of "direction" from above but instead was proving to be a substantial basis for criticizing the institutions of state and church. In this way, Hazlitt allied himself with the cultural marketplace in order to fend off the larger counterrevolution that had been launched in England since the coming of *The Anti-Jacobin* (1797–98) and Godwin's abortive effort to remake a progressive British intelligentsia in those critical years.

Hazlitt's own critical career was generally secured by the periodical industry, his essays appearing in the liberal *Examiner,* the *Yellow Dwarf,* the *New Monthly Magazine,* or the *Edinburgh Review,* and by the newly built world of the scientific and literary lecturing institutions, where Hazlitt delivered his series of talks later published as *Lectures on the English Poets* and other programs at the Surrey and Russell institutions for an audience of Quakers and Dissenters. This is one reason why we do not find bitter criticism of the commercialization of British culture in Hazlitt's writing as we find it in Coleridge's; the emerging culture industry seems rather to have been a foundation for Hazlitt's liberal distinction between political matters for the public realm and aesthetic matters for the private realm. In his essays on art, for instance, Hazlitt discredited the public English art institutions (all state-sponsored in this period) while enlarging the pleasures of personal aesthetic contemplation (Barrell). Hazlitt's unyielding reproaches to the British state, or to the Romantic conservative critics who would connive with it in their aesthetics, were matched in his critical practice by a defense of private aesthetic responses that distinguished "common" or "vulgar" from sensitive, discriminating tastes. The latter were not only separate from but a guarantee against the incursions of political and public institutional authority, but they fit wholly into what Hazlitt saw as the diverse mechanisms and protections of the cultural marketplace.

This is also why Hazlitt's canonizing activity was inimical to Coleridge's Romantic allegorizing of politics in poetics and his secularizing of sacred meanings in symbolic interpretation. Hazlitt's collection *Select British*

Poets (1824) belonged to the market-driven canonizing process that had stimulated British cultural selectivity since the landmark *Becket v. Donaldson* copyright decision of 1774; it joined such earlier anthologies as John Bell's *Poets of Great Britain* (1776–82), Vicesimus Knox's *Elegant Extracts* (1784), Robert Anderson's *Poets of Great Britain* (1792–95), Alexander Chalmers's *Works of the English Poets* (1810), and Anna Barbauld's *British Novelists* (1810) (Bonnell; Patey). His *Lectures on the English Poets* as well as his lectures on the English comic writers or the characters of Shakespeare's plays can be read as intricate commentaries on an emerging British literary canon selected and circulated by these economically rather than theologically inspired procedures.

Such canon-shaping, which today appears to us laden with claims to institutional authority, was important to Romantic liberals such as Hazlitt as a guarantee against the arbitrary authority of European monarchs and state-empowered institutions. Hence to the liberal imagination, England's literary markets served as well as Napoleon's public museums to secure poems, plays, or paintings from the aristocracy's political will. As Hazlitt would write of his first astonishing visit to the Louvre in 1802: "Art, no longer a bondswoman [to European kings, was now herself] seated on a throne, and her sons were kings. . . . Those masterpieces were the true handwriting on the wall, which told the great and mighty of the earth that their empire was passed away" (13:212). The birth of a modern aesthetic canon in the extinction of Europe's *ancien régime* implied that the older privileges of personal distinction were now being transferred, by means of the collection of masterpieces, to the spectators and readers who learned how best to read them. Thus, anyone excluded from the rights conferred by aristocratic birth and title could now point to the new collections of painting, poetry, or plays and retort, as Hazlitt imagined himself saying in the Louvre, "Look around! These are my inheritance; this is the class to which *I* belong!" (13:212). Hazlitt's criticism often bore the mark of this personalized, sublimated aristocratism of "taste" exercised by the aesthetically educated self who was otherwise a democrat in matters of public life and political right.

In the early 1800s, then, there emerged not one but at least two very different Romantic aesthetics, both predicated on the common problem of the relation of civil society to the state, yet diverging in their critical methods and cultural visions. Coleridge's philosophical and theologically inflected aesthetic, which established the protocols of a "symbolic" reading of canonically defined texts (from the Bible to Shakespeare and Milton), compelled Romantic criticism to supplement the function of state and church in an hour of the English rulers' woeful incapacity to unify the social and intellectual whole. Hence his aesthetic competed against the market-organized canonizing process and the rise of new cultural institutions, such as the scientific and literary lecturing institutions where Coleridge began his own career as Romantic cultural critic and which he nonetheless renounced as "Theo-mammonist," perversions of divine and poetic transmission into commercial and ideological reproduction (Klancher 179–83).

In response to Schiller's hope that aesthetic theory would work toward restoration of the common, collective life against the fragmenting force of capitalist modernity, Romantic theory in the early nineteenth century could only develop rival aesthetic programs, canonizing protocols, or critical agendas. Modern-day Romantic criticism has been more generally influenced by the "culture-and-society" tradition of politically allegorical critical theory, descending from Schiller, Coleridge, and Wordsworth, than by the Romantic criticism that descends through the marketplace canonizing tradition represented by Hazlitt, Francis Jeffrey, or Leigh Hunt. For the latter, politics became one thing, and aesthetics another. Yet both critical practices have defined the meaning of "Romantic" in the history of criticism and literature, practices that entered into the day-to-day cultural divisions of the later nineteenth and twentieth centuries.

Jon Klancher

See also SAMUEL TAYLOR COLERIDGE, WILLIAM HAZLITT, and WILLIAM WORDSWORTH.

Joanna Baillie, "Introductory Discourse," *A Series of Plays . . .* (1798); Anna Barbauld, "On the Origin and Progress of Novel-Writing," *British Novelists* (ed. Barbauld, 1810); David Bromwich, ed., *Romantic Critical Essays* (1987); Samuel Taylor Coleridge, *Biographia Literaria* (*Collected Works*, vol. 7, pts. 1–2, ed. James Engell and W. Jackson Bate, 2 vols., 1983), *Collected Letters*, vol. 1 (ed. Earl Leslie Griggs, 1956), *Lay Sermons* (*Collected Works*, vol. 6, ed. R. J. White, 1972), *Lectures, 1808–1819: On Literature* (*Collected Works*, vol. 5, pts. 1–2, ed. Reginald Foakes, 2 vols., 1987), *Table Talk* (*Collected Works*, vol. 14, pts. 1–2, ed. Carl Woodring, 2 vols., 1990); William Godwin, *The Enquirer: Reflections on Education, Manners, and Literature* (1797, reprint, 1965), "Of History and Romance," appendix D in *Caleb Williams, or Things as They Are* (ed. Maurice Hindle, 1988); William Hazlitt, *The Collected Works of William Hazlitt* (ed. P. P. Howe, 21 vols., 1930–34); Francis

Jeffrey, *Contributions to the 'Edinburgh Review'* (4 vols., 1854); T. J. Mathias, *The Pursuits of Literature: A Satirical Poem in Four Dialogues with Notes* (1797–98, reprint, 1808); Friedrich Schiller, *On the Aesthetic Education of Man* (ed. Elizabeth M. Wilkinson and L. A. Willoughby, 1967); Percy Bysshe Shelley, "A Defence of Poetry," *Shelley's Poetry and Prose: Authoritative Texts, Criticism* (ed. Donald H. Reiman and Sharon B. Powers, 1977); William Wordsworth, *The Prose Works of William Wordsworth,* vol. 1 (ed. W. J. B. Owen and J. W. Smyser, 1974).

M. H. Abrams, *The Mirror and the Lamp* (1953); John Barrell, *The Political Theory of Painting from Reynolds to Hazlitt: "The Body of the Public"* (1986); Thomas Bonnell, "Bookselling and Canon-Making: The Trade Rivalry over the English Poets, 1776–1783," *Studies in Eighteenth Century Culture* 19 (1989); Marilyn Butler and Mark Philp, "Introduction," *Collected Writings of William Godwin* (7 vols., 1991); Terry Eagleton, *The Ideology of the Aesthetic* (1990); Paul Hamilton, *Coleridge's Poetics* (1983); John Kinnaird, *William Hazlitt: Critic of Power* (1978); Jon Klancher, "Transmission Failure," *Theoretical Issues in Literary History* (ed. David Perkins, 1991); Nigel Leask, *The Politics of Imagination in Coleridge's Critical Thought* (1988); Jerome J. McGann, *The Romantic Ideology* (1983); Michael McKeon, *The Origins of the English Novel, 1600–1740* (1987); Douglas Lane Patey, "The Eighteenth Century Invents the Canon," *Modern Language Studies* 18 (1988); Mark Philp, *Godwin's Political Justice* (1986); Raymond Williams, *Culture and Society, 1780–1950* (1958).

4. Victorian

Victorian literary theory, sometimes dismissed as a hinterland, is a remarkably diverse and productive field. Of the four lines of theorizing identified by the philosopher of art Francis Sparshott in *Theory of the Arts* (1982)—the classical, expressive, oracular, and purist lines—Victorian theory has original contributions to make to all but the first. Its theological and Hegelian alignments, as well as its later doctrine of art for art's sake, also anticipate important developments in twentieth-century HERMENEUTICS and formalism.

The most important British critics of the 1830s are Thomas Carlyle (1795–1881), a representative of the oracular line of theorizing, which venerates the poet as an involuntary channel of communication with higher powers, and three expressive critics, Arthur Hallam (1811–33), W. J. Fox (1786–1864), and JOHN STUART MILL (1806–73). In an influential theory of poetic empathy, published in 1831 in *The Englishman's Magazine*, Hallam praises poets of sensation such as Percy Bysshe Shelley,

John Keats, and Alfred, Lord Tennyson for their remarkable ability to find in the "colors . . . sounds, and movements" of external nature the signature of "innumerable shades of fine emotion," which are too subtle for conceptual language to express (850, 856). In a *Westminster Review* article earlier in 1831 on Tennyson's *Poems, Chiefly Lyrical* (1830), Fox argues that the poet can best concentrate his energies by sketching his relation to a desolate landscape or to some ruined paradise, as in Tennyson's "Mariana" or "Oenone." Insisting that the sensory correlatives of feeling, like music, can convey complexities of meaning and subtly nuanced moods for which no dictionary words exist, Hallam is the prophet of a symbolist aesthetic later endorsed by W. B. Yeats. Fox, on the other hand, writes as a disciple of James Mill. Just as Joseph Addison is liberated by John Locke's theory of the ideality of the secondary qualities, according to which sounds and colors are truly a poem of the perceiver's creation, so Fox is liberated by the penetrating power conferred on the mind by the empirical psychology of James Mill's treatise *Analysis of the Phenomena of the Human Mind,* published two years earlier, in 1829. Since Fox's poet dramatizes each interior landscape through projection, and since Hallam's poet internalizes each picture, they tend to converge on common ground. Despite their different starting points, both critics anticipate modern psychological theories of introjection and projection, and both are agreed that poets must find in some external object the focus or medium of their truest self-expression.

Like Fox and Hallam, John Stuart Mill also subscribes to an expressive theory of art. But he is always ready to inhibit theory and quicken truth in pursuit of the wider premise, the more inclusive synthesis. His earliest articles on poetry, which he published in 1833, try to vindicate the poet against Jeremy Bentham's charge that because poetry is fictitious and untrue, it is a dangerous enemy of utilitarianism. The failure to see that poets use language in ways beyond the scope of traditional description in order to express and refine emotion and to do things with words is also the failure to which J. L. Austin draws attention when trying to extricate from descriptive statements the kind of utterance he calls "performative" (see SPEECH ACTS). To distinguish between poetry and rhetoric, Mill also insists that in poetic language there is no direct address: as OSCAR WILDE observed of WALTER PATER when he lectured, Mill's poet is overheard rather than heard. The oracle speaks in a state of rapt self-communion.

The other most innovative theorist of the 1830s, Thomas Carlyle, holds that a great poet such as DANTE

ALIGHIERI or William Shakespeare is an autonomous source of power, not reducible to anything in the world that may stimulate him. Since only the unconscious is healthy, Carlyle paradoxically concludes in "The Poet as Hero" that in writing allegory in *The Divine Comedy,* Dante, like any sincere poet, did not, in the precise sense of the phrase, know what he was doing. Does Carlyle's unselfconscious poet create a genuine novelty? Or does he merely manifest some higher antecedent power of which he is unconscious? If truth lies outside of consciousness, perhaps the answer does not matter. Because creative artists are a mystery, even to themselves, why should they not be willing to ascribe their creation of novelty to an equally mysterious higher source?

Carlyle also deserves to be remembered for his contribution to SEMIOTICS in his chapter on symbols in *Sartor Resartus.* Anticipating CHARLES SANDERS PEIRCE'S notion of an icon and of a sign that requires a more developed sign to interpret it, Carlyle argues that only intrinsic symbols exhaust their subject and that they cannot be analyzed. Only extrinsic symbols can be analyzed, and like the ritual naming by the herald at the coronation of George IV, they tend to trivialize their subject. The life of Christ, Carlyle argues, was once authentically symbolic, and intrinsically so, just as the original Last Supper was a symbolic performance of the utmost daring and genius. But if we try too hard or self-consciously to invent a rite or make our life an allegory, it will become instead a mere piece of theater. Like David Friedrich Strauss's notion that myth is *unconscious* invention, lives that become allegories are unconsciously symbolic. When we try to invent a symbol, like the festivals in honor of a supreme being in *The French Revolution,* we discover that an authentic intrinsic symbol can never be legislated; it has to be believed into being, by faith and civic love. The harder Carlyle tries to explain intrinsic symbols, the less intelligible they become: all intrinsic symbols require other symbols, or what Peirce calls "interpretants," to explain them.

One of the most original critical theorists of the late 1830s and the 1840s is John Keble (1792–1866). Though a psychological and expressive critic, Keble continues to honor the classical precept that literature is mimetic, or an imitation of nature, long after that doctrine has ceased to deserve his theoretical respect. Few passages in Victorian criticism are more revealing than the one in which Keble casually equates Aristotelian imitation with his own antithetical expressive doctrines. "It would seem," Keble says in an 1838 review of John Gibson Lockhart's *Memoirs of the Life of Sir Walter Scott,* "that the analogical applications of the word 'poetry' coincide well enough with Aristotle's notion of it, as consisting chiefly in Imitation or Expression" (435). Yet in his *Praelectiones Academicae* (1832–41), better known in its English translation as *Oxford Lectures on Poetry,* as well as in his review of *Scott,* Keble argues, contrary to ARISTOTLE, that all epic and dramatic genres are displacements of the poet's lyric impulse. Thus Virgil's epic the *Aeneid* is said to disguise a pastoral yearning, indulged most directly in the *Georgics.* Fed by unconscious sources, "Virgil's master passion" for pastoral celebration is so artfully veiled in his epic poem that it is preserved by being disguised, by *not* being named directly. Keble's originality consists in his taking a familiar theological doctrine, the Tractarian theory of reserve, and transplanting it to the psychology of poetic composition, where it anticipates Freudian theories of displacement.

In other essays, however, Keble asserts that great poetry exists only as a fallout from religion. In tract 89 of *Tracts for the Times,* "On the Mysticism Attributed to the Early Fathers of the Church" (1840), Keble argues as a brilliantly conservative critic, insisting that the unity of Scripture is the expressive evidence of divine power. By "mysticism" Keble means the typological interpretation of Scripture that allows a reader to discern a resemblance between Old Testament types and their New Testament antitypes. As God's grammar or code, biblical typology is more than a mere set of "poetical associations" chosen at will by individual interpreters. But this is not to say that hermeneutics properly conceived and practiced is a univocal decoding of God's meaning. Because every figural analogy merely approximates, like any analogy, the unnameable essence of what it tries to name, Keble uses his doctrine of reserve to keep intact the mystery of indefinition.

Benjamin Jowett's influential essay "On the Interpretation of Scripture" (1860) develops a far more liberal theory of biblical interpretation than Keble's. Asserting that readers should be able to recover a biblical author's original intentions and the effects the meaning had on the "hearers or readers who first received it," Jowett (1817–93) assails as anachronistic and dangerous the typological methods of biblical interpretation revived by Keble and Newman. But Jowett's appeal for unprejudiced reading, however plain and straightforward, assumes a zero degree of literacy that is illusory in theory and unattainable in critical practice. The real problem with Jowett's hermeneutics is its attempt to assess an author's original intention. As twentieth-century critics of the "intentional fallacy" have argued, an intention that has not already been realized and made accessible to an intelligent reader can never in practice be recovered. In what sense, then, can it qualify as an intention at all? If Jowett wants to call an unrealized intention an intention, he is free to do so. But it seems to be of doubtful authority and of no interpretive use.

Outside Keble's writings, the most innovative critical theories of the 1840s are to be found in JOHN RUSKIN's *Modern Painters,* especially in his commentaries on the imagination, which contain the most important contribution to their subject since SAMUEL TAYLOR COLERIDGE. Ruskin (1819–1900) identifies three forms in which the imagination operates. Achieving the *integritas* that St. Thomas Aquinas associates with the aesthetic object, the "imagination penetrative" is the faculty most consistently displayed by Ruskin's first and highest order of poets. In 1846 Ruskin insists upon this faculty "as the highest intellectual power of man" (4:251): he associates it with Dante and Shakespeare, whom ten years later he places in the highest rank of poets, among those who "feel strongly, think strongly, and see truly" (5:209). Their art is the product of educated innocence, an art that is "naturalist, because studied from nature," but also "ideal, because . . . mentally arranged in a certain manner" (5:113).

Once Ruskin's poet has been initiated into the mysteries of a thing's existence, using the imagination penetrative to expose the wonder of the thing and to present it as an imaginative whole, the poet may then proceed to combine a number of such wholes into new and harmonious arrangements. Corresponding to the *consonantia,* or harmony, of Aquinas's aesthetic object, the arrangement of sensory wholes is the function of Ruskin's "imagination associative." What is expressed in art by the imagination associative is usually something self-effacing and elusive, something just out of sight, which the artist can merely point toward or intimate. Though Ruskin is baffled to explain its operation, he takes this uncanny power of intimation (a power E. S. Dallas will later ascribe to its unconscious manner of working) to be the chief hallmark of the imagination associative.

When a poet such as John Milton or Shelley is prophetically inspired and begins to "see in a sort untruly, because what [he] see[s] is inconceivably above [him]" (5:209), he may approximate what Aquinas calls the radiance, or *claritas,* of oracular vision. The poet then exhibits the faculty Ruskin calls the "imagination contemplative." But because Ruskin, as a Victorian, has more in common with Keble or Pater than with Dante or John Bunyan, he has a keener sense than his medieval and Renaissance predecessors that the mystery of life and its arts does not allow the poet to fix or assign one meaning only to each visible type of the spiritual world. The imagination contemplative of Ruskin's poet has all the hallmarks of a true allegorical symbolism except one. Its symbols are untranslatable, because unlike the goat or wolf of conventional allegory, they lack an assigned connotation.

The 1850s mark the emergence of MATTHEW ARNOLD's early criticism, which staunchly opposes the dominantly expressive criticism of contemporaries such as David Masson and Sydney Dobell. One twentieth-century critic, R. G. Cox, argues that Arnold's neoclassical criticism is simply the best-known example of an anti-Romantic "minority tradition" running through the first half of the Victorian period. More recently, Antony H. Harrison has tried to elucidate the "literary politics" surrounding Arnold's preface to his *Poems* of 1853, which endorses an overtly Aristotelian theory of poetry that consistently misreads Aristotle by substituting an inward, psychological action for an outward, dramatic one. Arnold (1822–88) is covertly attacking his rival, Alexander Smith, a member of the so-called Spasmodic school of Byronic and Shelleyan imitators, and is trying to purge from his own poetry, partly for political reasons, all traces of Spasmodic influence. Arnold's conservative aesthetic must be seen as a response to the political radicalism of the Spasmodic poets and, like his essays on the Romantic poets, to his own complex and changing reactions to the cockney Keats.

David Masson (1822–1907), the reviewer whom Arnold misquotes in his 1853 preface and the author of important critical pieces collected in *Essays Biographical and Critical* (1856), draws attention to distinctive Spasmodic features of language that help distinguish poetical ideas from scientific ones. Masson repeats IMMANUEL KANT's teaching that whereas scientific understanding translates sensory facts into concepts, the poet's imagination is effective, not in duplicating nature, but in creating a second and stronger nature. It replaces the open-ended orderliness of nature with an orderliness that is closed, repeatable, and intensive. Masson's arresting word for this process is the imagination's capacity to "secrete" fictitious circumstance (431).

The rhapsodic, visionary writing that Masson's essays are best designed to analyze is also the subject of an important essay, "The Nature of Poetry" (1857), by the Spasmodic poet and critic Sydney Dobell (1824–74). Shrewdly noting that there is often a phenomenal difference between an aesthetic idea or feeling and its metaphoric equivalent, Dobell criticizes the many-breasted Hindu goddess for being too similar to the fertility she is meant to represent. By contrast, Bertel Thorwaldsen's celebrated statue of night, which makes an observer experience a black and shapeless void, is sculpted out of white marble. To explain the paradox, Dobell develops his theory of substitution. Instead of saying "I love," a poet will call up in his imagination some beautiful object, such as a rose, and then find for the object some equivalent in words. The poet's metaphoric equivalents, what Dobell calls his "homotypes," are related to each other, not in the way types are related to their biblical antitypes, and not in the way an algebraic sign is related to an unknown quantity, but in the way atoms are joined together to form the beautiful structure of a crystal.

The most ambitious work of literary theory to appear in the 1860s is E. S. Dallas's monumental two-volume study, *The Gay Science* (1866). Arguing that only the paradox of unconscious thought can explain the difference between the imagination of a Homer and the genius of an Aristotle, Dallas (1822–79) claims that both are automatic but only the former is an involuntary or unconscious process. Dallas believes there are two tests the critic can conduct to determine whether the poet's mind has indeed been operating imaginatively "in the dusk of unconsciousness" (1:265). A poet who has been composing imaginatively (i.e., in an involuntary or unconscious manner) will discern resemblances rather than differences. And that poet will also "assert the resemblance of wholes to wholes" (1:269). Dallas's theory of the unconscious has important antecedents in German criticism, especially in F. W. J. Schelling (see GERMAN THEORY AND CRITICISM: 2. ROMANTICISM). But in Victorian Britain the idea of unconscious and automatic mental processes, though applied by Carlyle in his essay "Characteristics" to mental health in general, does not assume a crucial role until Dallas offers what he takes to be a new theory of imagination, that "Proteus of the mind," which has been identified with all the human faculties—memory, passion, reason—and which has proved as a result "the despair of metaphysics" (1:179).

Dallas's earlier and more modest monograph, *Poetics: An Essay on Poetry* (1852), deserves to be known for the ingenious theory of genres it proposes. That theory, which praises the drama as the culminating genre of nineteenth-century literature, may be hard to understand until we grasp its connection with G. W. F. HEGEL's theory of an evolution of symbolic, classical, and romantic genres. When Dallas calls the lyric and visionary genres of poetry the dominant mode of Eastern, primitive art, he is alluding, like Hegel in his posthumously published *Philosophy of Fine Art,* to the lyric art of the Psalmist. Having used the genres of lyric poetry to describe the divine poetry of the ancients, Dallas must equate the dominantly religious art of the nineteenth

century, which he finds comparably sublime, with a different genre. When he speaks of dramatic art as a religious, Romantic form, embodying hope and the impulse to worship, Dallas is thinking, not of Shakespeare or Greek drama, but of Robert Browning's dramatic monologues and of lyrics of "saving faith" written by devotional poets such as Christina Rossetti.

One of Dallas's most original insights is that the transformation of classical epic into Hebrew lyric and then into modern Romantic and Christian forms of art is accompanied by a corresponding change in the poet's use of pronouns. In classical literature the poet describes persons and things: the third-person pronoun dominates. By contrast, the sublime lyric poetry of the Psalms is a poetry of first-person pronouns. Only in nineteenth-century poetry, which is a literature of dramatic intimacy and empathy, does the "you" enter. Anticipating T. S. ELIOT's argument in "The Three Voices of Poetry," Dallas distinguishes the first-person voice of lyric and the third-person voice of drama proper from "the familiar you-and-me style" of genres such as the monologue, which uses first- and second-person pronouns to dramatize a speaker's efforts to empathize with his or her auditor.

The last three decades of the nineteenth century mark the ascendancy of a far-reaching Hegelian legacy in Victorian criticism, one that is already discernible, as we have seen, in Dallas's theory of genres. Among major critics, Walter Pater (1839–94) shows Hegel's influence most clearly. Pater manages to formalize Hegel in subtler but no less radical ways than he manages to formalize Plato in *Plato and Platonism* (1893). In the most Hegelian of his critical writings, the essay on J. J. Winckelmann (1867), Pater draws upon Hegel's theory of a symbolic, a classical, and a romantic cycle of art, each phase aligned with a particular art form. "As the mind itself has had an historical development," Pater observes, "one form of art, by the very limitations of its material, may be more adequate than another for the expression of any one phase of that development" (1:210). Few pronouncements could be more Hegelian. And yet there is nothing in Pater's statement to rule out a relativism quite alien to Hegel's theory of progressive aesthetic change. Unlike Hegel, who sees in the progress of the arts a secure evolution toward an eventual victory of Absolute Spirit, when art will perfect itself by turning into dialectic, Pater sees a progressive attenuation of spirit. He actually reverses Hegel's strategy. Instead of freeing a spiritual *content* from a material *form,* which is the process Hegel analyzes, Pater praises art for freeing a highly refined and attenuated *form* from the bondage of any impure *content* or contaminating *message*. Pater keeps altering the teleological drift of Hegel's aesthetic doctrines by assimilating life to art, subordinating the spiritual content of Romantic art to the subtleties and refinements of the art form itself.

In his essay "The Philosophy of Art" (1883), W. P. Ker (1855–1923), a more scholarly interpreter than Pater, is torn between conflicting reactions to Hegel's theories. Should the critic use poems for their educative value, subordinating art to the claims of some absolute spirit that is asserted to be the ground of art's efficacy? Or must each poem be studied as an end in itself? A chief tenet of Hegel's theory is that art is an education, that it exists for the sake of something higher. Ideally, poetry is absorbed at last into philosophic vision. But Ker, like Pater, always wants to honor the integrity of each work of art. Ker criticizes Hegel for failing to see that though art is educational, it is not necessarily "an education for some end different from art" (166). Is poetry's transformation into science or philosophy a consummation devoutly to be wished? Or does poetry educate by a nonutilitarian but valuable deployment of the cognitive faculties, in abstraction from any practical context?

The second possibility is the one preferred by Oscar Wilde (1856–1900), who allows art to occupy a spiritual territory segregated from the everyday world. The claim of purist art to be holier or more sacred than other activities is not supported by any moral or metaphysical claim. Indeed the artist as such is said to have no "ethical sympathies" (230). Purist art has its priest, rite, church, and congregation but no god. It is endotelic, never merely a means to some external end. The absence of teleology is even celebrated as a virtue: "All art is quite useless," Wilde says in the preface to *The Picture of Dorian Gray* (1890). Its value is its very pointlessness. Like later formalists, Wilde knows at first hand how a despotic moral or theological consciousness can inhibit the creative faculties. To defend the poet against a censorious superego, Wilde revels in the paradox that the "morality of art" consists wholly "in the perfect use of an imperfect medium." "An ethical sympathy in an artist is an unpardonable mannerism of style" (230).

Wilde's celebration of art's inutility and reduced ambition remains, however, a Victorian aberration. Unlike the pursuit of virtue or a liberal education, the pursuit of literary theory in Victorian Britain is seldom regarded as its own reward. It is not the autonomous study that specialists laboring in a more Alexandrian age have tried to make it. To understand Victorian literary theory, we must study it in the context of nineteenth-century hermeneutics, for example, or philosophies of history, science, and religion. As G. B. Tennyson says in *Victorian Devotional Poetry: The Tractarian Mode* (1981), these disciplines do not "grow in alien soils." In the Victorian period, "they are branches of the same tree" (61).

W. David Shaw

Matthew Arnold, *The Complete Prose Works* (ed. R. H. Super, 11 vols., 1960–77); Thomas Carlyle, *The Works of Thomas Carlyle* (ed. H. D. Traill, 30 vols., 1898–1901); E. S. Dallas, *The Gay Science* (2 vols., 1866), *Poetics: An Essay on Poetry* (1852); W. S. Fox, Review of Alfred, Lord Tennyson, *Poems, Chiefly Lyrical* (1830, reprint, Isobel Armstrong, *Victorian Scrutinies: Reviews of Poetry, 1830–1870*, 1972); Arthur Hallam, "On Some of the Characteristics of Modern Poetry" (1831, reprint, *Victorian Poetry and Poetics*, ed. Walter E. Houghton and G. Robert Stange, 2d ed., 1968); G. W. F. Hegel, *Philosophy of Fine Art: Introduction* (trans. Bernard Bosanquet, 1886); Benjamin Jowett, "On the Interpretation of Scripture" (*Essays and Reviews*, 1860); John Keble, *Keble's Lectures on Poetry, 1832–1841* (trans. E. K. Francis, 2 vols., 1912), "On the Mysticism Attributed to the Early Fathers of the Church" (tract 89, *Tracts for the Times*, 1833–41), Review of John Gibson Lockhart, *Life of Sir Walter Scott, British Critic and Quarterly Theological Review* (1838); W. P. Ker, "The Philosophy of Art," *Essays in Philosophical Criticism* (1883, ed. Andrew Seth and R. B. Haldane, 1971); G. H. Lewes, *The Principles of Success in Literature* (1865); David Masson, Review of E. S. Dallas's *Poetics* and Alexander Smith's *Poems, North British Review* 19 (1853); J. S. Mill, *Collected Works of John Stuart Mill*, vol. 1, *Autobiography and Literary Essays* (ed. John M. Robson and Jack Stillinger, 1981); J. H. Newman, "Poetry, with Reference to Aristotle's Poetics" (1829, reprint, *Essays Critical and Historical*, 1871); Walter Pater, "Winckelmann" and "Style," *The Works of Walter Pater*, vols. 1 and 5 (1910); Coventry Patmore, *Principle in Art, Religio Poetae, and Other Essays* (1889); John Ruskin, *The Works of John Ruskin* (ed. E. T. Cook and Alexander Wedderburn, 39 vols., 1903–12); Robert Louis Stevenson, "On Some Technical Elements of Style" (1885, reprint, *English Prose of the Victorian Era*, ed. C. F. Harrold and W. D. Templeman, 1938); Oscar Wilde, *Literary Criticism of Oscar Wilde* (ed. Stanley Weintraub, 1968).

Patricia M. Ball, *The Science of Aspects: The Changing Role of Fact in the Work of Coleridge, Ruskin, and Hopkins* (1971); R. G. Cox, "Victorian Criticism of Poetry: The Minority Tradition," *Scrutiny* 18 (1951); Antony H. Harrison, *Victorian Poets and Romantic Poems: Intertextuality and Ideology* (1989); George P. Landow, *The Aesthetic and Critical Theories of John Ruskin* (1971); Robert Preyer, "Sydney Dobell and the Victorian Epic," *University of Toronto Quarterly* 30 (1961); Alba H. Warren, *English Poetic Theory, 1825–1865* (1950).

5. Symbolism

Symbolism, an aesthetic movement devoted primarily to discovering the true nature of poetry, originated in France in the latter half of the nineteenth century. CHARLES BAUDELAIRE and Stéphane Mallarmé, the central figures in the theory and practice of symbolism in France, developed EDGAR ALLAN POE's major premise about the poetic principle—that poetry is an evocation of eternal states through the discrete image or symbol—into a program for purifying poetry of the nonpoetic. The artists we classify as Symbolists aimed at purifying their art of all that was nonessential (some, such as Villiers de l'Isle Adam, were dramatists; a few, such as J. K. Huysmans, were novelists). Symbolist poets such as Paul Verlaine and Arthur Rimbaud, for example, rejected both the superficial rhetoric of argument and discussion and the dense notation of description and narration, all things that had obscured the true nature of poetry, in favor of the severe purity of a symbolic lyricism. The Symbolist poem was necessarily short, evocative, and mysterious.

Symbolism was introduced into the English-speaking world by Verlaine's friend Arthur Symons (1865–1945). In *The Symbolist Movement in Literature* (1899) Symons argues that symbolism is the essence of language and literature: our first words were symbolic, and all truly imaginative writers have been symbolists. Symbolism became a conscious movement in the late nineteenth century as a necessary reaction against the dense, descriptive method of the naturalistic school of ÉMILE ZOLA and others. The Symbolists restored purity to the arts, Symons maintains, by suggesting rather than saying, by evoking through symbols rather than submitting to the "old bondage of rhetoric, the old bondage of exteriority" (5) and describing through the logic of argument or the record of details. Symbols both reveal and conceal: they blend the visible and the invisible, the particular and the universal, the finite and the infinite. Symbols communicate indirectly: concrete images, such as the rose or the cross, summon up emotional and intellectual associations that cannot be precisely numbered or named.

The Symbolist method focuses on these internal associations and frees poetic language from the restraints of logical sequence or referential accuracy. This "liberty," as Symons calls it, from the governing principles of common discourse restores the "authentic speech" of

mystery to literature. "Start with an enigma, and then withdraw the key to the enigma" (72), Symons counsels those who would approach the Symbolist method. Often this insistence on mystery leads to a dark obscurity of language, especially with a symbol system in which the correspondences between the concrete term and its multiple associations seem private to the artist. Many of the writers Symons discusses, however, draw their symbols from traditional sources of hermetic or occult doctrine, like the Rosicrucian symbol system Villiers weaves into the fabric of his *Axel*. The true sources of Symbolism, Symons concludes, lie in ancient systems of mysticism, and the true purpose of the movement was to evoke the presence of the infinite and confirm the possibility of immortality through the associative network of symbols, ancient and modern.

Symons's presentation of the method and mysteries of the French Symbolists exerted a profound influence on the new generation of writers in English. T. S. ELIOT acknowledged this influence when he said in 1930: "I myself owe Mr. Symons a great debt: but for having read his book I should not . . . have begun to read Verlaine; and but for reading Verlaine, I should not have heard of Corbière" (Symons xv). Symons himself was influenced and directed in his understanding of Symbolism by the poet he described as the "chief representative of that movement in our country" (xix) and to whom he dedicated his book, W. B. Yeats (1865–1939). Although Yeats was deeply impressed by Villiers's *Axel,* which he saw in 1894, he derived his Symbolist principles from his studies in magic and Irish mythology and from his pioneering study (with Edwin Ellis, 1891) of the prophetic books of WILLIAM BLAKE, a poet he regarded as the preeminent Symbolist. Yeats made his major theoretical statements on the method of Symbolism in a series of essays written from 1896 to 1903 collected under the title *Ideas of Good and Evil* (a title borrowed from Blake).

In an essay on PERCY BYSSHE SHELLEY, another of his Symbolist precursors, Yeats argues that "there is for every man some one scene, some one adventure, some one picture that is the image of his secret life, for wisdom first speaks in images" (*Essays* 95). If the man or woman is a true poet, then his or her particular image (for Shelley a boat drifting down a river between towered hills and toward a distant star) blends into a universal and invisible order. "An image that has transcended particular time and place becomes," Yeats writes, "a symbol, passes beyond death, as it were, and becomes a living soul" (80). Although he maintains that "it is only by ancient symbols . . . that any highly subjective art can escape from the barrenness and shallowness of a too conscious arrangement, into the abundance and depth of Nature" (87), he finally makes no distinction between what he calls "inherent symbols and arbitrary symbols" in his essay "Magic" (49). Both species of symbol, traditional and private, evoke the presence of the infinite, or what Yeats calls the Great Mind and Great Memory. The borders of our field of awareness, Yeats declares, are not closed, and our individual mind can become part of this larger consciousness only through the network of symbols. Neither metaphor nor allegory can fulfill this poetic principle: Symbolism alone evokes the richness of the Great Mind and Memory.

This Memory, which transcends and connects each individual mind, provided Symbolism with a theory or explanation of both the process of writing and the experience of reading. The Memory was evoked through the medium of certain conditions of consciousness, moments of trance, contemplation, or "the moment when we are both asleep and awake" (*Essays* 159), moments prolonged in the rapt attention of reading. "So I think," Yeats argued in "The Symbolism of Poetry," a crucial essay from *Ideas of Good and Evil,* "that in the making and in the understanding of a work of art, and the more easily if it is full of patterns and symbols and music, we are lured to the threshold of sleep" (160). In this threshold or medial state, produced by a rapt attention to the rhythm of the work, the reader joins the artist in the work of evocative creation. "The purpose of rhythm," Yeats maintains, "is to prolong the moment of contemplation, the moment when we are both asleep and awake, which is the one moment of creation" (159). In this prolonged moment, making and understanding, the production and reception of the text, are joined and created through the intersubjective Memory.

In his poetry, in his making, Yeats was, as PAUL DE MAN has noted (153–62), a Symbolist from the beginning. Before he had any experience of the French writers, he worked in the Symbolist method, evoking in his early poetry (*The Rose,* 1893) the rose and cross of the Rosicrucian symbol system he afterwards saw enacted in Villiers's *Axel.* Later he sought for a more arbitrary symbolism, for a system of images available in his direct experience of contemporary Ireland that could become the symbolic vehicle of the Great Memory. The violence and meanness as well as the heroism and extravagance of Irish life provided him occasionally with symbols that balanced his lifelong interest in the esoteric symbols of the occult. With his purchase of a ruined tower in the west of Ireland, he finally found a symbol both arbitrary and inherent, both particular to his secret life and universal within the ancient occult traditions. This tower,

an image of hermetic wisdom made a symbol through long usage in Milton, Shelley, and others, inspired much of Yeats's best poetry in *The Tower* (1928) and later volumes. The occult disciplines, which were, in Yeats's view, ancient systems for evoking the Great Memory through the manipulation of symbols, remained his deepest inspiration and exerted a profound influence on *Per Amica Silentia Lunae,* his mystical-poetic statement of 1917 (now in *Mythologies*), and on *A Vision,* his cosmological system completed first in 1925 and then in 1937. For Yeats, as for Symons, the true meaning of Symbolism lay in the mystical evocation of infinitude.

Although Symbolism influenced other major writers of the twentieth century in very different ways—WALLACE STEVENS, for example, discovered there a precursor to his secular and euphonic metapoetry—the Symbolist image of the poet pursuing the essence of poetry into mystic solitude remained dominant. This image informed the two most influential critical studies of Symbolism in English: EDMUND WILSON's *Axel's Castle* (1931), a study centered on the consequences of Yeats's fascination with Villiers's drama, and Frank Kermode's *Romantic Image* (1957), an analysis of several of Yeats's key symbols (the dancer and the tree).

Murray McArthur

See also STÉPHANE MALLARMÉ AND FRENCH SYMBOLISM.

Arthur Symons, *The Symbolist Movement in Literature* (1899, rev. ed., 1908, 1919, intro. Richard Ellmann, 1958); Philippe Auguste Villiers de l'Isle Adam, *Axel* (trans. June Guicharnaud, 1970); W. B. Yeats, *Essays and Introductions* (1961), *Mythologies* (1959), *A Vision* (1925, rev. ed., 1937).

Paul De Man, "Image and Emblem in Yeats," *The Rhetoric of Romanticism* (1984); Frank Kermode, *Romantic Image* (1957); Giorgio Melchiori, *The Whole Mystery of Art: Pattern into Poetry in the Work of W. B. Yeats* (1960); David Perkins, *A History of Modern Poetry: From the 1890s to the High Modernist Mode* (1976); Edmund Wilson, *Axel's Castle: A Study in the Imaginative Literature of 1870–1930* (1931).

BURKE, EDMUND

A Philosophical Enquiry into the Origin of our Ideas of the Sublime and Beautiful, by Edmund Burke (1729–97), was the early, revolutionary work of an author who went down in history as both a politician and the arch-theorist of anti-Jacobin conservatism (*Reflections on the Revolution in France,* 1790). Yet the *Enquiry*—begun in the

1740s, published in 1757, and revised in 1759—became one of the most popular eighteenth-century treatises on aesthetics. Its originality does not consist so much in its approach to the aesthetic problem, essentially a psychological one, with its origins in John Locke, nor in its "Introduction on Taste," added in the second edition. In this discussion, intervening in a debate that was in full swing both in England and in France (as in Alexander Gerard's *An Essay on Taste*, 1759, which includes English translations of texts on the issue by Voltaire, Jean-Baptiste Le Rond d'Alembert, and the baron de Montesquieu), Burke draws conclusions developed over the course of the whole *Enquiry* in order to demonstrate the universality of taste, which he characterizes, not at the level of judgment as DAVID HUME had done ("Of the Standard of Taste," 1757), but at the level of sensibility. The *Enquiry*'s originality lies in its redefinition of the concepts of the sublime and, not less significantly, of the beautiful.

From the time of NICOLAS BOILEAU-DESPRÉAUX's translation of LONGINUS's *Peri Hupsous* (1674), the sublime had offered itself—in England much more than in France—"as a justifiable category into which could be grouped the stronger emotions and the more irrational elements of art," which were at variance with the neoclassic system (Monk 85). By doing so, it had played an important role in the progressive erosion of the values traditionally associated with artistic beauty (order, regularity, symmetry). This erosion culminates in Burke, who both ties together all the many reflections on the sublime developed during the first decades of the century and introduces new and major elements that would make his *Enquiry* (translated into French in 1765 and into German in 1773) extremely influential throughout Europe in the later evolution of taste and culture. At the end of the century, Burke is the single author cited by IMMANUEL KANT in "Analytic of the Sublime," in his *Critique of Judgement* (1790).

The first new element introduced by Burke, and the most consequential, is the emphasis on terror and its causes: obscurity, power, infinity, and so on. Longinus had defined terror as a passion that was not sublime, and Boileau had not even thought it worthy of mention. In Joseph Addison the astonishment traditionally identified with the effect produced by the sublime—a sublime that in "The Pleasures of the Imagination" (*Spectator*, nos. 411–21, 1712) had already been conclusively displaced from the realms of rhetoric and poetry, in which Longinus and Boileau had restricted it, to the natural world—had been interpreted as "delightful stillness." Reechoing Addison, John Baillie had spoken of "a solemn sedateness," explicitly contrasting the sublime with terror (*An*

Essay on the Sublime, 1747). Thus Thomas Gray, prefiguring William Wordsworth, invested the humble churchyard in his *Elegy* (1751) with the sublime: "And all the air a solemn stillness holds." On the other hand, John Dennis had pointed out that terror was the specific passion produced by that source par excellence of the sublime that is God (the Miltonic God)—and not only God but also nature in its most angst-ridden and threatening aspects (*The Grounds of Criticism in Poetry*, 1704). In the 1730s and 1740s, poets such as James Thomson, David Mallet, and Richard Savage had amply drawn on these aspects (earthquakes, volcanoes, sea storms, wild beasts, etc.), and there is no doubt that their works, together with those of the so-called graveyard poets (e.g., Robert Blair and Edward Young), exercised a deep influence on the young Burke.

Without actually quoting Dennis, Burke appropriates his identification of both the sublime and the pathetic (denied by Longinus and Addison) in his thesis that terror is "the ruling principle" (54), "the common stock of every thing that is sublime" (59). Unlike beauty, which pertains to the passions concerning "society," the sublime pertains to the passions concerning "self-preservation." As Dennis had already stated, whatever terrorizes threatens the existence of the individual—at the same moment in which the individual places himself or herself at a safe distance from it. Thus, the sublime becomes (imaginatively) linked to death: whatever appears sublime evokes death and causes a presentiment of its effects, without, however, putting the life of the individual in jeopardy. From this link between the sublime and death, Burke adds, there derives a particular type of pleasure, not a *positive pleasure* but, we can say along with Kant, a *negative pleasure,* which Burke calls "delight" and which (like tragic pleasure, from which it descends) is inherent in the distance separating the terrorized subject from the terrorizing object.

In part 4 of the *Enquiry*, however, Burke modifies this view. Investigating the "efficient causes" of the sublime and the beautiful (which Addison had refrained from doing) and resorting to contemporary physiology (which was a step beyond Lockean psychology), Burke attributes terror to a tension of the nerves. Such tension distances the organism from that state of "indifference" that is the normal condition of life and that Jean Baptiste Du Bos in his *Réflexions critiques sur la poësie et sur la peinture* (1719, trans., 1748) had called "ennui," decrying it as even worse than pain. Exactly because of this stimulation of the nerves and consequently of the passions, terror is pleasing. As a result, Burke's "delight" is no longer here the relief that subjects feel when they discover themselves at a distance from the object that, threatening them with death, terrorizes them. Instead, it is the thrill felt as they draw near to it; in other words, as they masochistically approach death. Not only terror but also pain itself (as long as it is not excessive) delights. As tension, moreover, terror and pain become precisely like lust, as Burke depicts it—"rapturous and violent" (37). Therefore, whatever excites in the sublime is the presence—the evocation—not only of death but of an *eroticized* death. Thanatos has transformed itself into Eros.

The parabola of the beautiful is the symmetrical inverse of the parabola of the sublime (their general opposition had already been stated by Akenside, radicalizing Addison's distinction). If the connection of beauty and love is traditional, Burke's configuration of it as a withdrawal of the libido (as SIGMUND FREUD might have said) is original and far-reaching. Animals, Burke argues, are promiscuous because, unaware of beauty, they do not know love. Human beings, in contrast, have a sense of beauty, and therefore love replaces lust: transformed into sentiment, eros becomes "tenderness and affection" (39) ending up in contemplation (83). In other words, love is a socialization of lust: beauty represses the libido and, by sublimating it in love, channels it into forms compatible with society and morality. At the same time, love is also defined as a relaxation of the nerves, "an inward sense of melting and languor," and such languor takes on clearly mortuary characteristics: "The head reclines something on one side; the eyelids are more closed than usual . . . the mouth is a little opened, and the breath drawn slowly . . . the whole body is composed, and the hands fall idly to the sides" (135). Withdrawing from eros its libidinous components, beauty generates an endearment that is bloodless pathos, tender emotion, and agony. Love turns to "a species of melancholy" (112) from which if there derives a pleasure, it is a pleasurelike dissolution hardly distinguishable from death—from a death that is languid rather than tense, "beautiful" rather than "sublime." Eros, in short, has transformed itself into Thanatos.

At the limit of their parabolas, the sublime and the beautiful have changed roles, and each can be placed under the sign of the other. But the two signs are really one and the same sign. The polarization of the beautiful and the sublime is removed in Death, which is the guiding star of Burke's whole enquiry—"frenzied" death on one side, "melancholy" death on the other. This is tantamount to gothicism *versus* sentimentalism, or better still, to gothicism *and* sentimentalism. The coordinates of sensibility and of culture in the second half of the eighteenth century, after the waning of classicism, are all present. For decades, Burke's not-so-juvenile *Enquiry* would serve as a reservoir of *topoi,* images, and effects.

Now, what is death but *loss of self?* This is perhaps Burke's major point of originality in the modern history of the sublime. For Longinus and for the line that ran from Boileau to Baillie, the sublime was a *potentiation* of the self; for Burke, on the contrary, it is a *de-potentiation.* In the experience of sublimity the self "shrinks" and suffers "annihilation" in the face of what exceeds it (63). The passion of the sublime is the passion of being submitted (103), vanquished—to a point of (near) disintegration. The delight that accompanies it is the thrill of such a disintegration. Doubtless this delight is bound up with the (residual) survival of the self and exists only insofar as the self does not disappear, but it is constituted by the *intimation* of—the (unconscious) desire for—its disappearance. This process of delight is analogous to the experience of the beautiful. In form antithetical to that of terror, along the axis of languor rather than tension, the self experiences the love beauty arouses in it as a process of decline and dissolution. Here too the movement is one of loss, by way of dissolution rather than oppression and disintegration. As for art, set between the extremes of the beautiful and the sublime, it "plays on" the effacing of the self up to the limit of the survival of subjectivity that is the limit of its capacity to (continue to) exist.

At the end of the century, Kant's *Critique of Judgment* would be the firmest and most rigorous reply to the radical conclusions of the *Enquiry*—and to everything that descended from it. In his discussion of the sublime Kant would not deny the vertigo experienced by the self but would subsume it to the interior of a movement that, in the end, reaffirms and indeed exalts the Self. In opposition to Burke, Kant would come back to the "noble passions" of Longinus, thus humanistically reproposing the idea of Art as the expression of full and sovereign Subjectivity (humans as rational and moral beings), not the expression of a dissipated subjectivity that only longs to lose itself into Otherness. Classicism yet again, that of Kant. On the other hand, Wordsworth's Romanticism and his "egotistical sublime," in which the mind "expands" to match itself to the object and the self preserves its own integrity—indeed, aggrandizes its own capacity—through what Neil Hertz calls the "identification with the blocking agent" (53), would also be a rejection not only of Burke's (or the gothicists') terror but of his (and their) whole conception of the sublime. After Kant and Wordsworth, however, in G. W. F. HEGEL and ARTHUR SCHOPENHAUER, as well as, later on, in Freud's death instinct, it would be once again the Burkean sublime (no less than his beautiful, as in late-nineteenth-century art) that would tacitly come to the fore and project itself, precisely as the experience of an ego that aspires to self-annihilation (not necessarily by way of terror), into a large part of modernity and postmodernity. Σίβυλλα τί θέλεις; ἀποθανεῖν θέλω ("Sybil, what do you want? I want to die"). This well-known epigraph to T. S. Eliot's *The Waste Land,* epitomizing the crisis of faith in Human-as-Subject that emerged at the end of the nineteenth century and is still with us, might serve as a reminder that Burke's analysis of literature and art as embodying human discontent with the "indifference" of the "normal" self, world, and history has not yet finished intriguing us.

Giuseppe Sertoli

See also BRITISH THEORY AND CRITICISM: 1. EARLY EIGHTEENTH CENTURY and 2. LATE EIGHTEENTH CENTURY and LONGINUS.

Edmund Burke, *A Philosophical Enquiry into the Origin of our Ideas of the Sublime and Beautiful* (1757, ed. Adam Phillips, 1990).

Peter De Bolla, *The Discourse of the Sublime* (1989); Frances Ferguson, "Legislating the Sublime," *Studies in Eighteenth Century British Art and Aesthetics* (ed. Ralph Cohen, 1985), "The Sublime of Edmund Burke, or the Bathos of Experience," *Glyph* 8 (1981); Clara I. Gandy and Peter J. Stanlis, *Edmund Burke: A Bibliography of Secondary Studies to 1982* (1983); Neil Hertz, *The End of the Line: Essays on Psychoanalysis and the Sublime* (1985); Walter John Hipple, Jr., *The Beautiful, the Sublime, and the Picturesque in Eighteenth-Century British Aesthetic Theory* (1957); Samuel Holt Monk, *The Sublime: A Study of Critical Theories in Eighteenth-Century England* (1935, 2d ed., 1961); David B. Morris, *The Religious Sublime* (1972); Marjorie Hope Nicolson, *Mountain Gloom and Mountain Glory: The Development of the Aesthetics of the Infinite* (1959); Murray Roston, *Changing Perspectives in Literature and the Visual Arts* (1990); *The Sublime and the Beautiful: Reconsiderations,* special issue, *New Literary History* 16 (1985); Thomas Weiskel, *The Romantic Sublime: Studies in the Structure and Psychology of Transcendence* (1976).

BURKE, KENNETH

Kenneth Burke (b. 1897) is one of the most unorthodox, challenging, and theoretically sophisticated American-born literary critics of the twentieth century. He began writing fiction and criticism in Greenwich Village in the early 1920s (his friends there included William Carlos Williams, Hart Crane, Malcolm Cowley, and E. E. Cummings) and proceeded to produce a body of criticism and theory that has spanned some 67 years. That criticism has often reflected Burke's engagement with emerging critical "schools"—in the 1930s Marxism and psychoanalysis, in the 1940s NEW CRITICISM, in the 1950s rhetorical criticism—but it evolved in a more fundamental way out of Burke's ambitious attempt to investigate on his own terms both how language operates in literary and other discourses as "symbolic action" and how interpretive systems attempt to account for the motives that determine such action. Pursuing the former he evolved a scheme for analyzing the network of motives he felt could be isolated in any text (a mode of analysis he called "Dramatism"), and pursuing the latter he created a rich if disparate series of meditations on critical theory, or what he called "the criticism of criticism."

Burke's work as a theorist of literature and criticism is all the more impressive in that he had little formal training. He was born in Pittsburgh, Pennsylvania. As a high school student he became intensely interested in European and modern literature, and by the time he graduated he had decided on writing as a vocation. He studied briefly at Ohio State University (1916) and at Columbia (1917–18), dropping out of Columbia, where he had been studying philosophy and the classics, in the winter of 1918. With some financial help from his father, he was able to make his way in New York, putting together an income from reviewing, translating, and editing (he was an assistant editor for *The Dial* in the early 1920s), as well as from the sale of his short stories and essays. By 1932 he had published three books, a collection of his stories (*The White Oxen and Other Stories,* 1924), a novel (*Towards a Better Life,* 1932), and his first book of criticism (*Counter-Statement,* 1931). The stories and the novel sold poorly, and by 1933 he decided to devote his full attention to criticism.

Burke completed three more books in the 1930s. Both *Permanence and Change* (1935) and *Attitudes toward History* (1937) reflected his intellectual engagement with Marxism (though sympathetic with the political aims of many popular-front groups, he refrained from becoming active in any of them), while *The Philosophy of Literary Form* (1941) collected much of the literary criticism and theory he had written during the decade. In 1937 he was invited to lecture on literary criticism at the New School for Social Research. From 1943 through 1961 he taught part-time at Bennington College in Vermont. While at Bennington he wrote *A Grammar of Motives* (1945) and *A Rhetoric of Motives* (1950). Burke completed the manuscript for a third book on motives (to be called "A Symbolic of Motives") but he has not had it published. Instead, he published another book on rhetoric,

The Rhetoric of Religion: Studies in Logology (1961), and a collection of his lectures and essays in literary criticism, *Language as Symbolic Action* (1966).

The scope and complexity of Burke's work as a literary critic makes generalizations difficult. However, from the early essays on literary form in *Counter-Statement* through his work on motives and on language as symbolic action, his criticism has essentially been rhetorical in its orientation. The theory of form in *Counter-Statement,* for example, holds that form in a literary work is a function of the author's attempt to move or affect the reader in some specific way. "Form in literature," he writes, "is an arousing and fulfillment of desires" (124). It is equated, in fact, with the "psychology of the audience" or reader because it reflects "the creation of an appetite in the mind of the auditor, and the adequate satisfying of that appetite" (31). Although *Permanence and Change* is primarily a book about interpretive systems, it closes with the insistence that the rhetorician's vocabulary of tropes is ready-made to "describe the specific patterns of human behavior" as they surface in both art and social life, since both are bound up in a "problem of appeal" (264).

By the 1940s, Burke's interest in rhetoric and his interest in the analysis of a literary work's internal form (the preoccupation of many of the essays in *The Philosophy of Literary Form*) merge in the development of a system of textual or discursive analysis in *A Grammar of Motives* that he calls "Dramatism." Dramatistic analyses are aimed at understanding "what is involved, when we say what people are doing and why they are doing it" (xv). Dramatism posits five terms necessary for any complete analysis of motive. Burke calls these terms, collectively, his Pentad: "act," what was done; "scene," when or where it was done; "agent," who did it; "agency," how the agent did it; and "purpose," why something was done. These terms, taken together, are meant to provide a critical vocabulary for isolating motivation in any text or discourse. They provide something like what structuralist critics would call "deep structure," since Burke's position is that all discourse is structured around a deployment of these terms. *Every* narrative act, in his view, is motivated by some aspect of the scene, the agent, an agency, a purpose, or some combination of one or more of them (and stressing the role of a particular term over the others will produce a specific interpretation of the text). The Pentad is complemented by a similar analytical scheme presented in an essay at the end of *A Grammar of Motives,* "The Four Master Tropes." The four master tropes, for Burke, are "metaphor, metonymy, synecdoche, and irony." He treats them much as he treats

the terms of his Pentad; that is, he focuses on their role in discovering and articulating "the truth" (503). Burke puts the phrase "the truth" in quotation marks because he wants to stress how these tropes actually *construct* (rather than reflect) what we take to be "truth" or "reality." For example, speaking of metaphor, he writes that "language develops by metaphorical extension, in borrowing words from the realm of the corporeal, visible, tangible and applying them by analogy to the realm of the incorporeal, invisible, intangible; then in the course of time, the original corporeal reference is forgotten, and only the incorporeal, metaphorical extension survives" (506). A textual analysis based on an examination of these four master tropes will trace these extensions, borrowings and forgettings, focusing on how the terms are deployed to make an argument or construct a narrative.

These methods for the formal analysis of texts are linked to rhetoric (as appeal and persuasion) in *A Rhetoric of Motives,* where Burke attempts to reclaim rhetoric as a tool for literary criticism. He argues that literature always attempts to persuade "to *attitude*" and that "the notion of persuasion to *attitude* would permit the application of rhetorical terms to purely *poetic* structures" (50). Burke's attempt to reclaim rhetoric, his Aristotelian interest in both drama and writing as a cathartic act, and his appropriation of both SIGMUND FREUD and Karl Marx, distinguish his "formalism" from that of New Criticism (see KARL MARX AND FRIEDRICH ENGELS). Throughout his career, Burke has viewed a close structural analysis of literary texts as one step in a comprehensive treatment that must always take into account biographical, historical, political, and ideological elements as well. While "the ability to treat of form is always the major test of a critical method" (*Rhetoric of Motives* 162), "the very thoroughness of the critic's attempt to discuss the poem exclusively" in formal terms "should help us realize the points at which the poem requires analysis not just in terms of Poetics, but . . . as the product of a citizen and taxpayer" (*Language* 38).

Burke would question the distinction between practice and theory, but it is important to emphasize that over and above his practical criticism of literary texts he has always been preoccupied with critical theory, or the criticism of criticism. Most of his books deal extensively with systems of interpretation and analysis, be they literary-critical, philosophical, Marxian, Freudian, or rhetorical in their orientation. Early in his career Burke's writings pushed beyond the conventions of literary criticism because his central concern became the attempt to understand what motivates interpretive behavior. In fact, in *Permanence and Change* Burke insists that what distinguishes humans from other organisms is our ability to go "beyond the criticism of experience to a criticism of criticism. We not only interpret the character of events . . . we may also interpret our interpretations" (6). This comprehensive view of the critical process helps explain why Burke developed less into a literary critic or literary theorist than into a *critical theorist*. Expanding his analysis of literary language and the forms of its interpretation into an investigation of philosophical, political, and psychological language and the forms of *their* interpretation, Burke produced an interdisciplinary body of work that is not simply literary criticism but a criticism of the discursive behavior of myriad cultural languages. Within that context the literary criticism he produced is remarkable for its precision, daring, and theoretical rigor. But what most sets him apart from other American critics of his generation is his attempt to understand literature and its criticism within the context of an ambitious and sophisticated analysis of the relationship between structures of language and structures of power in a host of cultural discourses. His interest in structure came from his conviction that the aims of any discourse are embedded in its formal principles, and his focus on power came from his interest in the *effect* of cultural discourses as they seek to change individual attitudes and behavior.

Paul Jay

Kenneth Burke, *Attitudes toward History* (2 vols., 1937), *Counter-Statement* (1931), *A Grammar of Motives* (1945), *Language as Symbolic Action: Essays on Life, Literature, and Method* (1966), *Permanence and Change: An Anatomy of Purpose* (1936), *The Philosophy of Literary Form: Studies in Symbolic Action* (1941), *A Rhetoric of Motives* (1950), *The Rhetoric of Religion: Studies in Logology* (1961), *Terms for Order and Perspectives by Incongruity* (ed. Stanley Edgar Hyman, 1964), *Towards a Better Life, Being a Series of Epistles or Declamations* (1932).

Bernard I. Duffey, "Reality as Language: Kenneth Burke's Theory of Poetry," *Western Review* 12 (1948); Armin Paul Frank, *Kenneth Burke* (1969); Greig E. Henderson, *Kenneth Burke: Literature and Language as Symbolic Action* (1988); Stanley Edgar Hyman, "Kenneth Burke and the Criticism of Symbolic Action," *The Armed Vision: A Study in the Methods of Modern Literary Criticism* (1948, rev. ed., 1955); Fredric Jameson, "The Symbolic Inference; or, Kenneth Burke and Ideological Analysis," *Critical Inquiry* 4 (1978); Paul Jay, "Kenneth Burke," *Dictionary of Literary Biography*, vol. 63, *American Critics, 1920–1955* (1988), "Kenneth Burke and the Motives of Rhetoric," *American Literary History* 1 (1989); Frank Lentricchia, *Criticism and Social Change* (1984); William Rueckert, *Critical Responses to Kenneth Burke: 1924-1966* (1969), *Kenneth Burke and the Drama of Human Relations* (1963); Herbert Simons and Trevor Melia, eds., *The Legacy of Kenneth Burke* (1989); Samuel Southwell, *Kenneth Burke and Martin Heidegger: With a Note against Deconstructionism* (1987); Hayden White and Margaret Brose, eds., *Representing Kenneth Burke: Selected Papers from the English Institute* (1982).

CAMBRIDGE RITUALISTS

Both "Cambridge Ritualists" and "Cambridge school of anthropology" have been used to refer to the writers Jane E. Harrison (1850–1928), Gilbert Murray (1866–1957), Francis M. Cornford (1874–1943), and Arthur B. Cook (1868–1952). Included with them but himself only a temporary ritualist and never a member of any group is James G. Frazer (1854–1941). Frazer was the only anthropologist; the others were classicists alert to the relevance of the new science of anthropology to their field. Classical studies were then identified with a well-worn PHILOLOGY and badly in need of revitalization. Credit must be given to Jane Harrison as the catalyst around whom both the new ideas and the members of the group came together. But the success of the group was also due to the complementary nature of the members' interests. Harrison began as a historian of ancient art; Murray was interested in Greek literature, especially drama; Cornford was a classical philosopher; and Cook was interested in archaeology. What brought them together was the study of religion. Christianity as a revelatory and dogmatic theology had been in crisis for some time. The high and low criticism of the Bible, Charles Lyell's geological record of the Earth's age, and Charles Darwin's theory of evolution made the revelatory authority, the literal acceptance of any holy book, seem ever more naive and preposterous. In Matthew Arnold's words, "Our religion has materialised itself in the fact, in the supposed fact; it has attached its emotion to the fact, and now the fact is failing it" ("The Study of Poetry," *Complete Prose Works,* ed. R. H. Super, 1973, 9:161).

Religion needed a new foundation, an origin more in line with the dominant evolutionary perspective and the new historical awareness that codified systems of belief had existed and changed over a great span of time. The reassurance that sectarian religions provide for their believers—that they alone are the true children of God, created in His image, and so on—was shattered when confronted with the fossil record, comparative anatomy, the phylum hierarchy, and the indifference of aeons with-

out human presence. Not only did religion need a more believable explanation but the traditional values it had supported also needed an alternative rationale. The Cambridge group alleviated both of these problems. The ritual basis of religion was not original with them—only its application to Greek religion and art. By going behind the Homeric gods and providing a more believable origin for Greek religion and culture, they also could provide some reassurance regarding Western values, which, after all, go back to Greek culture as a prime source.

The Cambridge group pursued the origins not only of religion but of literature and art as well. They felt that literature could best be understood as an evolutionary development from a primitive ritualism. This ritualism celebrated (acted out) the victory of the force of life over that of death as seen preeminently in the alternation of the seasons. This basic agon, said the Cambridge group, lies at the origin of Greek drama and dithyrambic poetry. The widespread and profound reaction of humans to the cycle of summer and winter, the alternation of day and night, the coming and going of generations, the birth and death of vegetation, culminated in the personification of an Eniautos-daimon, or "Year Spirit." Later the Eniautos-daimon was to emerge in manifold variations as the dying and resurrecting God. This movement from the unconscious and inarticulate (ritual) to the articulate (myth, drama, poetry) was to fascinate artists and literary theorists throughout the coming century.

The entry of anthropology into classical studies, specifically through the ritualistic approach to religion, can be dated from around 1890, when Robertson Smith's *Religion of the Semites* (1889), Jane Harrison's *Mythology and Monuments of Ancient Athens* (1890), and James G. Frazer's two-volume edition of *The Golden Bough* (1890) appeared. Frazer was to go on expanding his work to three volumes in 1900 and twelve volumes by 1915, and he even added *Aftermath: A Supplement to "The Golden Bough"* in 1936. Frazer synthesized a vast amount of diverse material in his effort to eschew the supernatural and give a naturalized history of human spirituality. He perceived connections between early Near Eastern religions, the folk customs of central Europe, and contemporary anthropological findings about primitive beliefs in Australia, Africa, and Polynesia. Never leaving his study for field trips, Frazer used the reports of others to weave a history of human emergence from the dark prehistorical ages into the dawn of recorded time.

Frazer's view of human destiny was evolutionary and progressive, as was the Cambridge school's in general. Human mental functioning, like that of the organic world, evolved from simpler forms such as magic to more complicated forms such as religion and science. Frazer believed that the human mind was identical in all people (psychic unity) but that its functioning had to go through the three stages listed above—magic, religion, science—and that some cultures had progressed faster than others. His motive in writing *The Golden Bough* was that of an enlightened rationalist who wanted to attack Christianity as a superstitious survival impeding the progress of science. He did so by deriving religion from an earlier psychological stage in which shamans, using magical practices of homeopathy (like produces like) and contagion (things or persons once in contact can later influence each other), increased life and fertility and warded off death and barrenness. As human thought progressed from magical practices to religion, these earlier shamans became priest-kings, supposedly endowed with divine powers. These kings became identified with nature's life force, whose seasonal pattern emerged in the many myths of dying and resurrecting gods—Adonis, Attis, Osiris, and Dionysus. The striking similarity of another variant—Jesus as the Christ with his attendant rite of Holy Communion—Frazer discreetly allowed his readers to perceive and to draw their own conclusions.

For the Cambridge Ritualists all these myths were interpreted as variations on the Eniautos-daimon, whose rites were celebrated annually at agricultural festivals. Impressed with the scope and amount of material that Frazer had amassed on dying and reviving gods, Jane Harrison, Gilbert Murray, and F. M. Cornford, primarily during the period 1900-1915, sought to link up Greek religion and literature, especially drama, to prehistoric fertility rites. Unlike Frazer, the Cambridge group were not interested in explaining myths by how primitives thought, but by what they did.

Jane Harrison agreed with Robertson Smith that the study of ancient religion must begin with ritual and traditional usage. Greek religion did not begin with the Olympian gods described by Homer and Hesiod. In her *Prolegomena* (1903), she investigated three of the most important Greek festivals and found that underneath a superficial linkage with Olympian gods, their true origin had to do with appeasement, purification, and fertility. In *Themis* (1912), she began to relate ritual to drama. Drama, she pointed out, is derived from *drômenon,* literally "to do or accomplish." Borrowing from Émile Durkheim the notion of "imitative rites," she described how primitive people reenact whatever makes them feel intensely—birth, adolescence, marriage, death. When such emotion is socialized and made collective, it becomes objectified and permanent. The motives for imitative rites are either commemorative or anticipatory, *re-done* or *pre-done,* and in their socially active representation on the way to being religious and artistic. Art and religion both spring from unsatisfied desire that is acted out. This process of projection, of deification, is helped greatly by our storytelling instinct. We hear much of the pathos of Dionysus, which, of course, is primarily the pathos or suffering of his worshipers. They, too, have acted out the initiation rite of Second Birth, have endured the death that issues in transformation. But once desire has been projected into a life history, into the Twice-Born god, it tends to consolidate into a personality, to crystallize and clear itself of its original inarticulate longing and vagueness. It clarifies itself in image and story.

The achievement of Greek religion and its contribution to civilization, as Jane Harrison put it in *Mythology,* is that the Greeks started with the same religious material as other races, "with fear of the unseen, with fetish worship, with unsatisfied desire, and out of this vague and crude material they fashioned their Immortals, such as Hermes . . . Demeter . . . Apollo, Dionysus, Zeus" (xx). Before the appearance of these gods, with their distinct personalities, nameless powers operated in the shadows. The Greeks in their mythology, art, and philosophy created beautiful images out of their ignorant desire and expelled fear. When we come to the Olympic gods of Hesiod and Homer, sacrifice has become a banquet, a sharing, a celebration. We hear little about fasting, purification, and atonement, with its often bloody scapegoating. It was a victory of Hellenism over barbarism, of humanity over savagery. For a time, the Olympians expurgated the old rites, brought order to the older chaos, and tended to the new social needs of the city-state. Ultimately they failed, but according to Gilbert Murray, the movement from *Urdummheit* ("primitive stupidity") to Olympian religion can provide a parallel to bolster hopes that modern men and women can shift from dogmatic Christian superstition to a higher level of spirituality. If the Greeks can fashion beautiful art and literature out of unmentionable beginnings, from "the beastly devices of the Heathen," then the goal of the modern humanist, "whether he has a Friend behind Phenomena or not," is "to raise life to some higher level and redeem the world from its misery" (*Myths* 3).

This process of spiritualization is wondrously evident in Greek art and literature, especially drama. Gilbert Murray, in an "Excursus on the Ritual Forms Preserved in Greek Tragedy" (appended to Harrison's *Themis*), and F. M. Cornford, in *The Origin of Attic Comedy* (1914), persuasively derive Greek tragedy and comedy from the fertility rites of the Year Spirit. It is the form of the ritual more than its content that still shows through today. Condensing Murray, we can outline the sequence of an Eniautos celebration as follows: 1) an agon, or contest: the old year against the new, life versus death, summer versus winter, light versus darkness; 2) a pathos, generally a ritual or sacrificial death, in which Adonis or Attis is slain, the Pharmakos stoned, Osiris, Dionysus, Pentheus, Orpheus, Hippolytus torn to pieces (the sparagmos); 3) the announcement of this death by a messenger, for it usually is not shown (the news comes that Pan the Great, Tammuz, Adonis, Osiris, is dead, and the dead body is often brought in on a bier); 4) a threnos, or lamentation; 5) possibly, an anagnorisis, or recognition, of the slain and mutilated Daimon; and finally, 6) his resurrection or theophany ("Excursus" 344). These six elements can be traced quite clearly in Greek tragedy, says Murray. For example, *The Bacchae* of Euripides contains 1) a long agon in which Dionysus pleads with Pentheus in vain but then exerts his Bacchic influence and conquers him and then the two go up the mountain; 2) the pathos and sparagmos of Pentheus narrated by 3) a messenger; 4) an elaborate threnos in the midst of which comes the collection of fragments of Pentheus's body and 5) his recognition by Agave; and 6) the epiphany of Dionysus. When we remember that Pentheus is only another form of Dionysus himself, "we can see that the *Bacchae* is simply the old *sacer ludus* itself. The daimon is fought against, torn to pieces, announced as dead, wept for, collected and recognized, and revealed in his new divine life" (346). The pattern is even more visible in Aristophanic Old Comedy, where ritual combat, death, and resurrection and the sacred marriage may still be glimpsed under the diverse topical activities. Gilbert Murray went on to urge literary parallels of ritual and myth patterns in Shakespeare's *Hamlet* (an Orestes figure), medieval liturgical drama, and the mummers' pantomime.

The influence of Frazer and the Cambridge Ritualists in those areas where they did most of their work, that is, in classical Greek culture, primitive religion, and folklore, has been mostly superseded by later psychological and anthropological research. However, in the field of literary criticism their influence, though diluted, has continued, even though formalism replaced the evolutionary genetic paradigm basic to the ritualist approach. In the main current of MYTH THEORY AND CRITICISM, that of Joseph Campbell (Jungian), NORTHROP FRYE, and CLAUDE LÉVI-STRAUSS, the underlying pattern of the Year Spirit, with its conflict and reconciliation of opposites derived from the vegetative cycle of life and death, summer and winter, food and famine, fertility and barrenness, has remained firmly in place. Gone, of course, is the evolutionary historical development, with its progressive optimism. In its stead now operates a timeless formalism through which the psyche constructs its world. Rather than using early myth and ritual to establish the origin of literature, these later myth theorists saw that Frazer and the Cambridge Ritualists had revealed, perhaps unknowingly, how the creative psyche operated. Diverse as these later myth theorists were in their description of how the unconscious or imagination functioned, whether they spoke in terms of compensatory self-realization, equilibritive reconciliations, or laws of identity and analogy, their lineage or parentage back to the Eniautos pattern is visible and indubitable. In the meantime, creative writers, suffering from a deracinated Christian tradition, toiled to provide their own subjective foundation to replace obsolete authority. Ritual pattern and its mythic accompaniment gave their artistic works a reverberative dimension not otherwise possible. It became a central feature in the writings of W. B. Yeats, T. S. Eliot, James Joyce, D. H. Lawrence, and Thomas Mann and more recently in the postmodern questing of John Barth, Thomas Pynchon, Robert Coover, Donald Barthelme, and writer–film director Peter Greenaway.

While used parodistically and ironically by the latter group of writers, myth has continued to serve as a positive resource for both literary writers and theorists. With the turn against universalizing abstractions and the insistence on cognition that is particular, embodied, and situated, the ritual basis of myth has once again become attractive as a more inclusive approach for human imaginative response to existence. The recent upsurge of interest in the Cambridge Ritualists, as well as the fact that *The Golden Bough* celebrated its hundredth anniversary in 1990 (it has been in print as a popular one-volume paperback since 1963, a phenomenal publishing record for a scholarly work), forces one to conclude that the staying power of ritual and myth resides in communication channels that not only formed ancient cultures but remain useful and meaningful when communicating experiences of today.

Vernon Gras

See also ARCHETYPAL THEORY AND CRITICISM and MYTH THEORY AND CRITICISM.

Arthur B. Cook, *Zeus: A Study in Ancient Religion* (3 vols., 1914–40); F. M. Cornford, *From Religion to Philosophy* (1912), *The Origin of Attic Comedy* (1914), *Thucydides Mythhistoricus* (1907); James G. Frazer, *The Golden Bough: A Study in Magic and Religion* (2 vols., 1890, 3d ed., 12 vols., 1911–15, abridged ed., 1 vol., 1922); Jane E. Harrison, *"Epilegomena to the Study of Greek Religion" and "Themis"* (1921 and 1913, reprint, 2 vols. in 1, 1962), *Mythology* (1924), *Prolegomena to the Study of Greek Religion* (1903); Gilbert Murray, *The Classical Tradition in Poetry* (1927), *Euripides and His Age* (1913), "Excursus on the Ritual Forms Preserved in Greek Tragedy" (appendix to Harrison, *Themis*), *Five Stages of Greek Religion* (1925, 3d ed., 1951), *Myths and Ethics; or, Humanism and the World's Need* (1944).

Robert Ackerman, *The Myth and Ritual School: J. G. Frazer and the Cambridge Ritualists* (1991); Shelley Arlen, *The Cambridge Ritualists: An Annotated Bibliography of the Works By and About Jane Harrison, Gilbert Murray, Francis Cornford, and Arthur Cook* (1990); Walter Burkert, *Structure and History in Greek Mythology and Ritual* (1979); William M. Calder III, ed., *The Cambridge Ritualists Reconsidered* (1991); William G. Doty, *Mythography: The Study of Myths and Rituals* (1986); Edward Evans-Pritchard, *Theories of Primitive Religion* (1965); Colin Falck, *Myth, Truth, and Literature* (1989); Joseph Fontenrose, *The Ritual Theory of Myth* (1966); Clifford Geertz, *The Interpretation of Cultures* (1973); Vernon Gras, "Myth and the Reconciliation of Opposites: Jung and Lévi-Strauss," *Journal of the History of Ideas* 42 (1981); G. S. Kirk, *Myth: Its Meaning and Functions in Ancient and Other Cultures* (1970); Sandra Peacock, *Jane Ellen Harrison: The Mask and the Self* (1988); Robert A. Segal, "The Myth-Ritualist Theory of Religion," *Journal for the Scientific Study of Religion* 19 (1980); Jessie Stewart, ed., *Jane Harrison: A Portrait from Letters* (1959); H. S. Versnel, "What's Sauce for the Goose is Sauce for the Gander: Myth and Ritual, Old and New," *Approaches to Greek Mythology* (ed. Lowell Edmunds, 1989); John Vickery, *The Literary Impact of "The Golden Bough"* (1973); Francis West, *Gilbert Murray: A Life* (1984); Jessie L. Weston, *From Ritual to Romance* (1920).

CANADIAN THEORY AND CRITICISM

1. English

Since its beginnings in the mid-nineteenth century, anglophone Canadian literary criticism has been visible primarily as a criticism of Canadian literature, often being closely tied to the project of defining a national culture and often proposing narratives of growth—Canada as the child of Britain, Canada as the young giant—that invoked the narrative assumptions of political and literary history. While Anglophone Canadian critics have participated in the criticism of other literatures, most—NORTHROP FRYE and MARSHALL MCLUHAN being notable exceptions—have done so within the transnational critical discourses and practices associated with those literatures. Since World War II, Anglophone Canadian literary critics have also done substantial work in the theorizing of comparative literary studies and of Commonwealth and postcolonial literatures (Dorsinville, New, Goldie), although for the most part Canadian criticism, often uncomfortably aware of the complex web of intertextuality that ties Canadian texts to others in English, has resisted the incorporation of Canadian writing within these categories.

Nineteenth-century Canadian criticism devoted itself mostly to attempting to sort out relationships between Anglophone Canadian writing and universal literary values, the political utility of a distinct national culture, the prestige of British literature, the specificities of the Canadian landscape, the materialist preoccupations of a pioneer society, and the presence within Canada of the introspective French-language culture of Quebec and without of the powerful new culture of the United States. Although universities had been established in parts of Canada as early as 1797, the critics were nearly all professionals—journalists, newspaper editors, clergymen—without academic affiliation. Journalist and politician Thomas D'Arcy McGee, writing in 1857, outlined several issues that would become leitmotifs in the literature over the next century: the country had no mythology; its people were "plain," "matter-of-fact," and nonliterary; they were also "strongly imbued with the . . . feelings . . . of the old country." Here he also made the first argument for a multicultural Canada, which might transcend "British sentiment" by "the acknowledgement of all elements . . . the recognition of all nationalities in one idea and in one name" (Daymond and Monkman 42–43). In 1858 McGee articulated a fourth concept that would recur in

Canadian criticism: "Every country, every nationality, every people, must create and foster a National Literature, if it is their wish to preserve a distinct individuality from other nations" (43). Throughout the century and into the next this nationalist emphasis often became part of an attempt to construct the literature of English Canada as Canadian literature, and the French literature of Quebec as marginal but potentially disruptive of national cohesion.

The two major critical formulations of the nineteenth century, the introductions to Edward Hartley Dewart's anthology of Anglophone Canadian poetry, *Selections from Canadian Poets* (1864), and to William Douw Lighthall's anthology, *Songs of the Great Dominion* (1889), disagreed strongly over the relevance of "universal standards" to Canadian culture. Dewart reiterated the nationalist principle that a "national literature is an essential element in the formation of national character" (ix) and deplored colonial attitudes that "cling" to the "honoured names" of the "Old Country" (xiv). His arguments in favor of a Canadian literature, however, were expressed in terms of transcendent, usually British, values—"truths which find their highest embodiment in poetry" (x), "a Milton or a Shakespeare [who may] arise among us" (xv). His rhetoric alternated between celebrating independence and celebrating Canadian texts for resembling the poetry of other nations. His notes on individual poets emphasized their transnational legitimacy: various poets were "intensely human" (xvii), had "Miltonic stateliness," displayed "strong human sympathy," "simple and graphic truthfulness," "sympathy with humanity" (xviii). In Lighthall's introduction, Dewart's attempt to negotiate between Canadian specificity and universal value became an openly declared dichotomy between the local and the literary, with "poems whose merit lies in perfection of finish" being passed over in favor of a poetry that "illustrates the country and its life *in a distinctive way*" (xxxiv). In the place of universal values Lighthall called on a romanticized Canadian geography—"great Niagara falling," "towering snow-capped Rockies," "hoary Laurentians"—to be the legitimizer of the texts that address it (xxi–xxii).

In the prefaces, manifestoes, and handbooks that followed in the next century, as university-based critics began developing Canadian literature as an academic field, the quarrel between theories that saw Canadian writing as elaborating and extending a universal literature and those that saw it as specifically Canadian became an internal conflict within the critical texts themselves. Critics such as Archibald MacMechan (*Headwaters of Canadian Literature,* 1924), J. D. Logan and D. G. French (*Highways of Canadian Literature,* 1924), Lionel Stevenson

(*Appraisals of Canadian Literature,* 1926), Lorne Pierce (*Outline of Canadian Literature,* 1927), and V. B. Rhodenizer (*Handbook of Canadian Literature,* 1930) argued the specificity of Canadian literature while simultaneously claiming its participation in universal norms. These studies frequently raised questions about who could be a "Canadian author," argued that Canadian writing was the product of specific "historic conditions" (Rhodenizer 11), and proposed that a unique Canadian landscape had left distinguishing marks on Canadian texts, while also arguing that Canadian authors could claim legitimacy only through favorable comparison with British authors and through participation in what Stevenson termed "the outstanding achievements of human thought and genius everywhere" (4). They employed geographic and landscape metaphors in their constructions of the literature, while arguing also for "cosmopolitan breadth" (MacMechan 237).

With the emergence of modernist theory and criticism in the writing of A. J. M. Smith and E. K. Brown, the critical task turned away from seeking the distinctly Canadian within international norms and toward evaluating Canadian texts by "timeless" standards. Influenced by T. S. ELIOT, NEW CRITICISM, and a residual Arnoldian discourse (see MATTHEW ARNOLD), evident in Canada from Dewart through MacMechan, in which literature safeguarded longstanding cultural values, these critics sought not an indigenous literature but a context-free "pure" literature written by Canadians. As Smith wrote in his introduction to *The Book of Canadian Poetry* (1943), "The emphasis . . . is not upon literary history or social background but on the poetry itself" (3). Both Brown and Smith developed dichotomies between the cosmopolitan and the provincial, which enabled them to praise high art and disparage nationalism and regionalism, while also occasionally praising "localism" for having evoked "timeless" significances. Smith's preference for cosmopolitan standards was given a Leavisite twist in the 1950s and 1960s by the British-born George Woodcock (see F. R. LEAVIS), who founded the first periodical of Canadian criticism, *Canadian Literature,* in 1959 and whose extremely influential studies of Canadian writing, *Odysseus Ever Returning* (1970) and *Northern Spring* (1987), represented it as a regional variant of a humanistic universal text.

The widely known attack on A. J. M. Smith by small-press publisher and critic John Sutherland, in the introduction to his polemic poetry anthology *Other Canadians* (1947), questioned Smith's preference for the "cosmopolitan" rather than the cosmopolitan-parochial dichotomy itself. Sutherland attacked Smith by reconfiguring his dichotomy in a number of ways: as a middle-class oppression of working-class language and politics, as a colonialist dismissal of things North American, and as a British resentment of U.S. cultural influence. For Sutherland, although almost all Canadian writing to date had been "colonial," the elements for an indigenous literature were available in the "common" language of the working class, in U.S. literary models, and in a "rapport between . . . poetry and the environment" (16). Sutherland's intervention led to a sustained attempt by Louis Dudek to theorize Canadian literature in terms of an opposition between a particularist, indigenous tradition (which he linked both with realist and naturalist fiction and with the imagism and ideogrammic method of Ezra Pound) and a cosmopolitan mythopoetic tradition (which sought transcendent universal values). Within the second category he would eventually include the global communications theories of Marshall McLuhan and the archetypal criticism of Northrop Frye. Paradoxically, however, like Lighthall and Stevenson before him, he continued to use the sort of universals he opposed to legitimate the particularism he endorsed, for example, accusing both Frye's archetypal system and McLuhan's media theories of ignoring the particular qualities of art objects, devaluing "masterpieces" and encouraging barbarism.

Ironically, Frye's Canadian criticism, particularly his conclusion to the 1965 *Literary History of Canada*, produced under the general editorship of Carl F. Klinck, set Canadian writing apart from his general theory, proposing that this writing was more "a part of Canadian life than . . . a part of an autonomous world of literature" (822). Instead of reading Canadian literary texts (which both he and Klinck understood more broadly than did many of the Leavis-influenced contributors to the *Literary History*) through the system of his *Anatomy,* Frye read them for symbols that he understood as metaphoric constructions of Canadian experience. While his mythopoetic criticism of Canadian literature indeed, as Dudek charged, constructed normative generalizations that took little account of the idiosyncrasies of individual texts, it nevertheless did attend to particularities of Canadian history and geography. In a rhetoric much different from the celebratory rhetoric of Lighthall, he similarly invoked the Canadian landscape to endorse a "Laurentian" theory of an enveloping Canadian geography and propose his "garrison mentality" theory of the Canadian response to nature. Frye's exempting of Canadian literature from both his own "autonomous world of literature" and "evaluative criticism" and his "topocentric" readings of Canadian texts (Leon Surette, "Here Is Us:

The Topocentrism of Canadian Literary Criticism," *Canadian Poetry: Studies, Documents, Reviews* 10 [1982]) opened the way for the descriptive methodologies of various nationalist scholars who came quickly to be known within Canada as the "thematic critics."

The major works of the thematic critics were D. G. Jones's *Butterfly on Rock* (1970), Margaret Atwood's *Survival* (1973), John Moss's *Patterns of Isolation: In English-Canadian Fiction* (1974), and Laurence Ricou's regional study *Vertical Man / Horizontal World: Man and Landscape in Canadian Prairie Fiction* (1973). In this criticism, literary texts served almost exclusively as indicators of national psychology, as "the dreams and nightmares of a people" (Jones 4). The "dreams" were usually expressed in the same landscape metaphors—snow, cabins, winter, tragic animals—through which earlier critics had also tried to define a distinct national literature. The "people" of these dreams were a homogeneous Anglophone Canadian constituency, unmarked by regional, class, ethnic, or gender difference, and could be represented by a single national figure: Atwood's "survival," Moss's "isolation," Frye's "garrison," or Jones's butterfly. Closely tied to thematic criticism were two bipolar Anglophone-Francophone Canadian comparative models that were proposed in the late 1960s and early 1970s—the doubled-single-identity model of Ronald Sutherland's *Second Image* (1971) and the unity-in-slight-divergence model of *Ellipse,* a journal founded in 1971 by D. G. Jones and several colleagues. Here too a single figure or paradigm was proposed for an essentially homogeneous literature.

Until this period in Canadian criticism, preoccupation with universal legitimacy and/or national distinctiveness had kept critics from considering cultural or linguistic questions and from developing theories of historicity, positionality, relativity, or context. Growing resistance throughout the 1970s to both the thematic criticism and the humanist criticism of Woodcock, however, saw the emergence not only of critics who desired a return to evaluative criticism (Cude, Keith, McLulich) and of others who urged a STRUCTURALISM purged of the normative insistences of thematic criticism (Russell Brown, Dixon and Cameron) but also of those who called for more textually grounded criticism (Davey, "Surviving the Paraphrase"); for diachronic, phenomenological approaches that acknowledged both the text's and the reader's position in history and community (Davey, "Surviving the Paraphrase"; Lee; Mandel); for deconstructive readings that exposed ideological gaps and contradictions (Godard, "Other Fictions"; Kroetsch) or that explored contradiction as aesthetic structure (Irvine, Scobie); for criticism that acknowledged the reader's role in the production of meaning (Heidenreich, Hutcheon) or investigated the role of cultural institutions and publishing structures in literary production (Davey, *Reading;* Forsyth). As Barbara Godard has noted, the idiosyncratic development of twentieth-century Canadian criticism from the modified New Criticism of A. J. M. Smith to the thematic criticism of Frye, Jones, Atwood, and Moss, without benefit of phenomenology or structuralism, led in the 1970s and early 1980s to the almost simultaneous introduction of PHENOMENOLOGY, SEMIOTICS, READER-RESPONSE THEORY AND CRITICISM, NARRATOLOGY, discourse theory (see DISCOURSE: 2. DISCOURSE THE-ORY), DECONSTRUCTION, and feminist deconstruction (see FEMINIST THEORY AND CRITICISM: 3. POSTSTRUC-TURALIST FEMINISMS), often all under such banners as "the new new criticism" or "post-structuralism" and often with peculiar combinations of methodology (Godard, "Structuralism/Post-Structuralism"). In Canada, phenomenology emerged as a critique of the quasi-structuralism of Frye, rather than preceding structuralism as it had in Europe; semiotics, Godard suggests, has been "the successor to structuralism" (37); and deconstruction, rather than being instituted, as elsewhere, as a challenge to the implicit metaphysics of phenomenology, has evolved from the diachronic and positional emphases of phenomenology. The latter two methodologies have been particularly evident in the writing of poet-critics such as Eli Mandel, George Bowering, Robert Kroetsch, Frank Davey, Stephen Scobie, and Steve Mc-Caffery.

Perhaps because of the highly fragmented condition of Canadian culture in the 1980s and 1990s, in which constructions of region, gender, ethnicity, and language have outweighed any construction of a unified national state, recent Canadian criticism has tended to build more on European understandings of feminist and deconstructionist theory than on American ones and to prefer implicitly political and conflictual theories of literature over ostensibly apolitical ones. Among the more powerful book-length criticisms of this kind have been in feminist studies the anthologies *AMazing Space* (ed. Shirley Neuman and Smaro Kamboureli, 1986) and *Gynocritics* (ed. Barbara Godard, 1987), in comparative literature E. D. Blodgett's *Configuration* (1982) and Philip Stratford's *All the Polarities* (1986), and in new constructions of English-Canadian literature Steve McCaffery's *North of Intention* (1986), Linda Hutcheon's *The Canadian Postmodern* (1988), and Smaro Kamboureli's *The Contemporary Canadian Long Poem: At the Edge of Genre* (1991). In Hutcheon's case, she has extended her political and dialogical understand-

ings of Canadian textuality into her theorizing of international literature (*A Poetics of Postmodernism,* 1988; *The Politics of Postmodernism,* 1989).

Frank Davey

E. K. Brown, *On Canadian Poetry* (1943); Russell Brown, "Critic, Culture, Text: Beyond Thematics," *Essays on Canadian Writing* 11 (1978); Wilfrid Cude, *A Due Sense of Difference: An Evaluative Approach to Canadian Literature* (1980); Frank Davey, *Reading Canadian Reading* (1988), "Surviving the Paraphrase," *Canadian Literature* 70 (1976, reprint, *Surviving the Paraphrase,* 1983); Douglas M. Daymond and Leslie G. Monkman, *Towards a Canadian Literature: Essays, Editorials, and Manifestos* (1984); Michael Dixon and Barry Cameron, "Introduction: Mandatory Subversive Manifesto: Canadian Criticism vs. Literary Criticism," *Studies in Canadian Literature* 2 (1977); Max Dorsinville, *Caliban without Prospero: Essay on Quebec and Black Literature* (1974); Louis Dudek, *Selected Essays and Criticism* (1978); Louise Forsyth, "La Critique au feminin: Vers de nouveaux lieux communs," *Parlons-en / Talking Together* (1981); Barbara Godard, "Epi(pro)logue: In Pursuit of the Long Poem," *Open Letter* 6 (1985), "Other Fictions: Robert Kroetsch's Criticism," *Open Letter* 5 (1984), "Structuralism/Post-Structuralism: Language, Reality, and Canadian Literature," *Future Indicative: Literary Theory and Canadian Literature* (ed. John Moss, 1987); Terry Goldie, *Fear and Temptation: The Image of the Indigene in Canadian, Australian, and New Zealand Literatures* (1989); Rosmarin Heidenreich, *The Postwar Novel in Canada: Narrative Patterns and Reader Response* (1989); Linda Hutcheon, *Narcissistic Narrative* (1980); Lorna Irvine, *Sub/Versions* (1986); W. J. Keith, *Canadian Literature in English* (1985); Robert Kroetsch, *Essays* (ed. Frank Davey and bpNichol, *Open Letter* 5 [1983]); Dennis Lee, *Savage Fields* (1977); Thomas D'Arcy McGee, "A Canadian Literature" (1857, reprint, Daymond and Monkman), "Protection for Canadian Literature," (1858, reprint, Daymond and Monkman); T. D. McLulich, *Between Europe and America: The Canadian Tradition in Fiction* (1988); Eli Mandel, *Another Time* (1977); W. H. New, *Among Worlds: An Introduction to Modern Commonwealth and South African Fiction* (1985); Stephen Scobie, *bpNichol: What History Teaches* (1984); A. J. M. Smith, *Towards a View of Canadian Letters: Selected Critical Essays* (1973).

2. French

Since the expansion of the universities in the 1960s, there has been a steady stream of Canadian criticism in

French devoted to various aspects of the literature of France, particularly studies of individual writers, and a more intermittent flow of critical works on other literatures, sometimes in a comparative perspective. However, this engagement with world literature, with few exceptions and until very recently, has been relatively untheorized and has had little impact on larger international debates. In fact, after a long period of academic neglect, university critics since the 1960s have tended to see as their most urgent task the description and interpretation of a national corpus, thereby accepting, although on very different terms and conditions, the traditional mission of French-Canadian criticism, which since the nineteenth century has been the constitution and promotion of a national literature.

There was no extended literary criticism of any significance in French Canada before the twentieth century. This is not to say that what occasional criticism there was had little impact or did not constitute a coherent ideological, if not literary, vision; on the contrary, writing about literature in the nineteenth century was at first formally normative, along the lines of French classicism, then evangelically prescriptive, tending—particularly after 1860, as the Catholic church strengthened its grip on cultural production and consumption, weaning the reading public away from the relatively liberal values of the early and mid-century—to subjugate literary concerns to the problems of nation building. The prime task of the essayist or reviewer or preface writer was to argue the inappropriateness of works imported from France (and elsewhere) to a Canadian context and to promote, by contrast, domestic models of verisimilitude founded on the simple, wholesome, and conservative values of an agrarian, Catholic community. Literature, for a critic such as Henri-Raymond Casgrain ("Le Mouvement littéraire au Canada," *Le Foyer canadien,* 1866), was to be a faithful reflection of the day-to-day life of a pious people; to write *about* literature was to be a defender of the faith and an implacable critic of those forms suspected of embodying the postrevolutionary (and therefore immoral) values of the godless, urban society across the Atlantic. In practice, this strategy came perilously close to a denial of literature as such, as indigenous productions were rhetorically withdrawn from the prevailing literary system and assimilated to nonliterary discursive formations more easily policed by the arbiters of public morality. If a novel was not a novel but a slice of (suitably sanitized) life, it could be placed under the tutelage of other social institutions and legitimated according to criteria derived from outside the dominant (transnational) literary paradigms of the period. The nationalist

discourse of Casgrain and his even more dogmatic followers (Adolphe-Basile Routhier, Jules-Paul Tardivel, Thomas Chapais) thus worked fairly consistently against any significant autonomization of the literary sphere.

These strictures were to be taken up and developed in the early twentieth century by French Canada's first literary critic, Monseignor Camille Roy, for whom literature, ineluctably "croyante et canadienne," was to be pressed into the service of the nation. A literary historian of the French school (Ferdinand Brunetière, Émile Faguet, Gustave Lanson) who used the methods of his mentors to confine Canadian literature within a national ghetto isolated from France and from the modern world in general, Roy produced the first edition of his *Manuel d'histoire de la littérature canadienne-française* in 1918. By virtue of his own standing as well as through the work of disciples such as Maurice Hébert and the literary historian Séraphin Marion, his influence would continue to be felt for several decades, although his nationalist orthodoxy did not go completely unchallenged. Dissenting voices were to be heard quite early in the day, such as those of Marcel Dugas and Louis Dantin, two critics-in-exile (in Paris and Boston, respectively) who appealed to more "universal" (i.e., modern and aesthetic) values in the judgment of art and who detected in Roy's program of "Canadianization" the symptoms of a national inferiority complex. Their writings constituted the first real breach in the monolithic edifice of French-Canadian critical discourse and set in motion the slow process of autonomization and modernization of literature within that community. Dantin's aesthetic positions, in particular, would influence a number of younger writers, such as his friend and disciple Alfred DesRochers, whose *Paragraphes* appeared in 1931, while another of Roy's detractors, Albert Pelletier, would take a more independent, if less subtle, line, finding Dantin's (French) preoccupation with form a little too refined for his own (Canadian) taste. Such divisions between (literary) form and (social) content were at the heart of French Canada's own version of the Quarrel between the Ancients and the Moderns, a quarrel which started at the beginning of the century and ran well into the 1930s and which brought into conflict "regionalists" and "exoticists." In effect, the slow modernization of French-Canadian literary-critical discourse that took place between the two world wars was inseparable from a process not only of secularization but also of denationalization.

Further signs of pluralizing pressure would come in the 1930s and 1940s from within the Catholic fold—from Roy's own camp, so to speak—which would produce the young generation of *La Relève,* a review founded in 1934 and renamed, in 1941, *La Nouvelle Relève.* The members of this group, such as Robert Charbonneau and Jean Le Moyne, along with such contemporaries as Roger Duhamel and Guy Sylvestre, professed a progressive Catholicism in which the confining tendencies of Camille Roy's nationalism were countered by a real desire for engagement with the modern world and modern literary concerns, particularly those of their French counterparts. It was this generation that would attempt to overcome the historical separation of form and content by constructing the literary work, not as an ideological vehicle, but as an integrated whole to be analyzed and appreciated as such. A similarly nonprescriptive view of literature would be developed after World War II by the group surrounding another review, *Cité libre,* founded in 1950 and, although still Catholic, taking an anti-Duplessis, antinationalist position. (This was the period of systematic repression known as the Great Darkness of Quebec politics, the age of Maurice Duplessis, who, as leader of the Union Nationale, was premier from 1936 to 1939 and from 1944 until his death in 1959, the year another influential review was founded, significantly entitled *Liberté.*) The secularizing tendency continued to make steady gains in Quebec criticism throughout the 1940s and 1950s, without encouragement from church or state, though with the support of a gradually changing cultural infrastructure, particularly in the world of journalism, where such critics as Clément Lockquell, René Garneau, and Pierre de Grandpré first made their mark.

Two names stand out among the newspaper critics of the 1950s and 1960s: Jean Éthier-Blais (*Signets,* 1967–73), whose aesthetic individualism was in the mold of a Dugas or a Dantin; and Gilles Marcotte, more eclectic and more socially minded, whose landmark collections brought together first his own pieces, in *Une Littérature qui se fait* (1962), and then those of twelve other critics, in *Présence de la critique* (1966). Apart from the intrinsic quality of their literary reviews and essays, these two critics are interesting for the trajectories taken in their professional lives, which saw them build an academic career on a base in journalism. Such a transition would become representative of a generation and was itself a reflection of the transformation of public life and institutions during the Quiet Revolution of the 1960s, a period of rapid modernization and liberalization that followed the death of Duplessis and saw the universities become, for the first time in Quebec, a place of social critique and contestation in which the national literature could be studied with the same seriousness and rigor as that of France.

The founding of *Parti pris* in 1963 signaled the rise, on the left, of a new generation and a new project of nation-

alization—Marxist rather than Thomist this time and applied to Quebec rather than to French Canada—articulated within a discourse of decolonization derived from JEAN-PAUL SARTRE, FRANTZ FANON, Albert Memmi, and Jacques Berque. Right across the political spectrum but especially in left-nationalist circles, the 1960s saw an enormous increase in the volume of writing about literature, an increase that did not slow when *Parti pris* ceased to publish in 1968, by which time most of those associated with the review had found positions within the university or college systems and had access to such scholarly journals as *Études françaises* (founded in 1965), *Voix et images du pays* (1967), and *Études littéraires* (1968). The shift from journalistic criticism to longer scholarly studies went hand in hand with the discovery and importation of modern French critical methods, in the first instance phenomenological, then structuralist, though for the most part thematically rather than formally oriented. The earlier essays collected in *L'Instance critique, 1961–1973* by André Brochu, one of the founders of *Parti pris,* are exemplary in this respect, with their strong emphasis on interpretation and thematic structure; the later, retrospective pieces, however, betray two sources of concern, or even anxiety. One is the perennial problem of the relation between literary criticism and revolutionary politics: what exactly is the status of a criticism that espouses a nationalist politics but refuses to reduce every work of literature to an expression of what it is to be colonized? The other has to do with the fact that the theoretical models adopted by the *Parti pris* generation were so soon displaced in France by the epistemological revolution that took place in the late 1960s: how does one cope with JACQUES DERRIDA, MICHEL FOUCAULT, and JACQUES LACAN when one is still coming to terms with Sartre and Fanon? These apparently quite different questions were in fact closely linked and would continue to be relevant, in slightly divergent forms, throughout the 1970s and 1980s.

The most striking feature of these two decades was the steady proliferation of critical methodologies, as academic critics continued the arduous and sometimes frustrating process of theoretical modernization. With the importation of French STRUCTURALISM at the end of the 1960s came an interest in poetics and formalist NARRATOLOGY, both the narrative SEMIOTICS of Algirdas Julien Greimas, Vladimir Propp, and Claude Bremond and, what was most influential, Gérard Genette's brand of narrative discourse analysis. This interest probably peaked in the late 1970s, and it has since become both more pragmatic and more successfully integrated with other approaches, as has been the case with literary semiotics in general, which, with its principal patrons—ROLAND BARTHES, Tzvetan Todorov, UMBERTO ECO, JULIA KRISTEVA—was most visible in Quebec between 1975 and 1985. It would be misleading, however, to discuss any of these methodologies without pointing out that in Quebec they have frequently been used in conjunction with, or as part of, a more general sociological approach applied to a national corpus produced in particular social conditions.

Sociological approaches to literature, in the most general sense of reading literature as the historical product of a given society, have always had currency in French Canada, but the first attempts to produce a methodologically explicit sociocriticism, loosely inspired by the work of Lucien Goldmann in France, came in the pioneering studies of sociologist Jean-Charles Falardeau (*Notre société et son roman* [1967]; *Imaginaire social et littérature* [1974]) and in Gilles Marcotte's more textually sophisticated analyses in *Le Roman à l'imparfait* (1976). Marcotte would go on in subsequent books to refine his own brand of fluid and methodologically unobtrusive sociocriticism, while another major line of thinking, reflecting the influence of M. M. BAKHTIN, was being developed in the writings of André Belleau. Both Belleau and Marcotte contributed significantly to what was arguably the most important critical development in the 1980s: the analysis of both the literary institution (Maurice Lemire) and the institution (Lucie Robert)—or, in a variant, the constitution (Bernard Andrès)—of the literary. Important advances were made in this respect by research teams working at Laval University, under the direction of Maurice Lemire and Denis Saint-Jacques, on the constitution of the literary field in Quebec (CRELIQ), and at the University of Sherbrooke, under the direction of Richard Giguère and Jacques Michon, on problems of literary reception and publishing (GRELQ). In both cases, but to varying degrees according to individual projects, the single most important theoretical influence has been the work of French sociologist Pierre Bourdieu. Andrès's critical study, on the other hand, owes more to Foucault's archaeology, while Robert, in an unusual and stimulating departure from the norms of critical discourse in Quebec, ranges much further afield, finding inspiration, for example, in Anglo-German traditions, not only in JÜRGEN HABERMAS and earlier members of the FRANKFURT SCHOOL but also in RAYMOND WILLIAMS, Terry Eagleton, and other British Marxists. Also important at the end of the 1980s were the emergent fields of social discourse analysis (Marc Angenot) and sociosemiotics (Javier García-Méndez, Michel van Schendel), both of which looked beyond a narrowly defined national corpus to engage variously with larger theoretical issues, foreign literatures, and nonliterary texts (see also DISCOURSE: I. DISCOURSE ANALYSIS).

Other strains of academic criticism have transplanted less well in Quebec. DECONSTRUCTION, for example, is remarkable for its relative invisibility, though there are signs that some of its more important lessons have been learned and assimilated. (It is significant that in the "Index-thesaurus, 1967–1987" to *Voix et images,* a scholarly journal devoted solely to the literature of Quebec, deconstruction does not even figure in the inventory of critical approaches used.) PSYCHOANALYTIC THEORY AND CRITICISM, derived initially from SIGMUND FREUD and Charles Mauron (as in the essays of Gérard Bessette and André Vanasse) and more recently from Lacan, has fared somewhat better, although it would be difficult to claim that it has had a major impact on literary studies in Quebec, where theories of the subject have not seemed an urgent priority. On the other hand, it might be argued that the main fruit of psychoanalytic thinking, as of deconstruction, has been precisely in its theorizing of a split and gendered subject as taken up and developed in FEMINIST THEORY AND CRITICISM, perhaps best exemplified by Patricia Smart's *Écrire dans la maison du père* (1988), which draws not only on the work of such French feminists as LUCE IRIGARAY but also on a broad Anglophone feminist culture. Creative writers such as Louky Bersianik, Nicole Brossard, Madeleine Gagnon, Suzanne Lamy, and France Théoret have also been active in theorizing their own feminist writing practices, often referred to as *écriture au féminin,* "writing in the feminine." Some have argued the need for a corresponding *critique au féminin,* "criticism in the feminine," that would avoid the reduction of writing to feminist theory by placing the emphasis on individual texts, thereby allowing theory to be revitalized and replenished by dialectical interaction with new readings.

In recent years a double lament has been heard concerning theory. On the one hand, a disenchantment in certain quarters with the increasing specialization of literary studies and their vocabulary has led to nostalgic calls for a return to a more literary (or writerly) criticism, less driven by theory and by the peculiar economies of academic discourse. On the other hand, a number of those who have been associated with particular theoretical approaches have publicly regretted the fact that more than two decades of working with imported methodologies have not led to the elaboration of any significant body of literary theory in Quebec. Both of these complaints should be seen against the background of the historical debate around the status and function of the national literature. For example, if it is true that there has been little theoretical innovation in Quebec, this is at least in part due to the fact that the constitution and promotion of the national corpus has consistently taken precedence over more purely theoretical projects, even during the 1970s and 1980s. (The five-volume *Dictionnaire des oeuvres littéraires du Québec* is but one monument amongst many to the exceptional success of Quebec university research in this domain.) Thus, it might be argued that one of the primary functions of the critical methodologies imported from France in the 1960s and 1970s was to bestow some of the prestige of the parent literature upon a domestic corpus composed of texts that could be shown to be rich enough, from a literary point of view, to sustain and benefit from such sophisticated methods of analysis. Such a move had the added advantage of definitively removing Quebec literary production from the ghetto of "content" to which it had been assigned in the nineteenth century, and of making it fully "literary" by recognizing its formal dimension *as literature*. Legitimated by the (imaginary) gaze of French theory, Quebec literature was at last free to become itself, which allowed critics in the late 1980s and early 1990s (Andrès, García-Méndez, Simom Harel, Pierre Nepveu) to start looking at other issues and other cultures.

Anthony Purdy

Bernard Andrès, *Écrire le Québec: De la contrainte à la contrariété: Essai sur la constitution des lettres* (1990); Marc Angenot, *1889: Un État du discours social* (1989); André Belleau, *Le Romancier fictif* (1980), *Surprendre les voix* (1986); Louky Bersianik et al., *La Théorie un dimanche* (1988); André Brochu, *L'Instance critique, 1961–1973* (1974); Louis Dantin, *Gloses critiques* (1931, 2d ed., 1935); Marcel Dugas, *Apologies* (1919), *Littérature canadienne: Aperçus* (1929); Javier García-Méndez, *La Dimension hylique du roman* (1990); Simon Harel, *Le Voleur de parcours: Identité et cosmopolitisme dans la littérature québécoise contemporaine* (1989); Maurice Lemire, ed., *L'Institution littéraire* (1986); Gilles Marcotte, *Une Littérature qui se fait* (1962), *Le Roman à l'imparfait* (1976); Gilles Marcotte, ed., *Présence de la critique* (1966); Clément Moisan and Denis Saint-Jacques, eds., "L'Autonomisation de la littérature," *Études littéraires* 20 (1987); Pierre Nepveu, *L'Écologie du réel: Mort et naissance de la littérature québécoise contemporaine* (1988); Lucie Robert, *L'Institution du littéraire au Québec* (1989); Camille Roy, *Manuel d'histoire de la littérature canadienne-française* (1918); Patricia Smart, *Écrire dans la maison du père: L'Émergence du féminin dans la tradition littéraire du Québec* (1988); Michel van Schendel, "L'Idéologème est un quasi-argument," *Texte* 5–6 (1986–87).

Jacques Allard, *Traverses de la critique littéraire au Québec* (1991); André Belleau, "La Démarche sociocritique au Québec," *Voix et images* 8 (1983); E. D. Blodgett and A. G. Purdy, eds., *Problems of Literary Reception / Problèmes de réception littéraire* (1988); *Dictionnaire des oeuvres littéraires du Québec* (5 vols., 1978–87); David M. Hayne, ed., "La Critique littéraire," *Revue d'histoire littéraire du Québec et du Canada français* 14 (1987); Annette Hayward and Agnès Whitfield, eds., *Critique et littérature québécoise* (1992); Pierre Hébert, ed., "L'Age de la critique, 1920–1940," *Voix et images* 50 (1992); Larry Shouldice, *Contemporary Quebec Criticism* (1979); Robert Vigneault, "La critique Littéraire" (*Le Québécois et sa littérature*, ed. René Dionne, 1984).

CARIBBEAN THEORY AND CRITICISM

Due to the economic and sociopolitical fragmentation that constitutes the legacy of four European colonial powers in the Caribbean region, the most urgent theoretical and practical issue in Caribbean literary and cultural studies remains the articulation of a discourse on Caribbeanness. Following Albert Gérard, A. James Arnold argues that a comparative approach to Caribbean literature and its history has been inhibited by intellectual Balkanization and the concomitant lack of a cross-cultural historiography of the region ("Caribbean" 39). In *La isla que se repite: El Caribe y la perspectiva posmoderna* (1989), Antonio Benítez Rojo puts the matter succinctly: "How can one even begin to talk about Caribbean literature when its very existence is in question?" (xxx–xxxi). While hardly anyone would still take seriously Trinidadian novelist V. S. Naipaul's claim that "nothing was created in the West Indies" (*The Middle Passage*, 1962), the question of a transnational cultural identity continues to loom large in a region troubled by the failure of political unification and regarded by many of its major writers as an utterly desolate cultural landscape. According to St. Lucian poet-playwright Derek Walcott and Barbadian novelist George Lamming, Caribbean culture had to be created out of nothing.

Since the 1930s many Caribbean writers and theorists, notably C. L. R. James (Trinidad), Alejo Carpentier (Cuba), Aimé Césaire (Martinique), Edward Kamau Brathwaite (Barbados), Roberto Fernández Retamar (Cuba), Wilson Harris (Guyana), and Edouard Glissant (Martinique), have challenged the Caribbean's supposed lack of an indigenous history and a distinctive cultural tradition or identity. Caribbean cultural-literary history became the object of spirited debates when several local journals were launched in the 1940s, among them Frank Collymore's *Bim* (Barbados, 1942), Edna Manley's *Focus* (Jamaica, 1943), A. J. Seymour's *Kyk-over-al* (Guyana, 1945), Aimé Césaire's *Tropiques* (Martinique, 1941), and the University of the West Indies's *Caribbean Quarterly* (1949). *Casa de las Américas* was added to the list after Cuba's revolution. In "Caribbean Critics" (1969), Brathwaite defends the idea of a Caribbean culture "different from, though not exclusive of Europe" that exists as "a complex of voices and patterns held together by geography, political force and social interaction" (*Roots* 114). In *Contradictory Omens* (1974) he situates the Caribbean outside of "classic" (North American and African) plural paradigms, insisting on "interculturation" or creolization as "the tentative cultural norm of the society. Yet this norm, because of the complex historical factors involved in making it . . . is not whole or hard, but cracked, fragmented, ambivalent, not certain of itself" (5–7, 25). In order "to see the fragments/whole," Brathwaite believes, "the culture of [the] ex-African majority [has to be accepted] as the paradigm and norm for the entire society" (30).

This pan-Africanism made Brathwaite a principal heir to Caribbean Negritude at a time when many denounced its cultural separatism. It has informed much of his poetic and critical practice since his return from Ghana in 1962, most notably the poetry of his *Arrivants* trilogy (1973) and "The African Presence in Caribbean Literature" (1974), in which he attributes the distinctiveness of Caribbean writing to its African "survivals." The more recent *History of the Voice* (1984), in turn, outlines a vernacular aesthetic for Caribbean poetry that seems more consistent with Brathwaite's previous emphasis on creolization.

Brathwaite's Afrocentrism, shared by historian–social theorist C. L. R. James ("From Toussaint L'Ouverture to Fidel Castro," 1963), found one of its most ardent critics in Derek Walcott, whose first book of poems, *In a Green Night* (1962), had established him as the foremost poet of the West Indies. Walcott's resistance to the idea that the Caribbean's salvation lay in Africa was influenced by FRANTZ FANON's critique of Negritude in *Black Skin, White Masks* (1952) and *The Wretched of the Earth* (1961). Vehemently opposed to a reduction of Caribbean literature's identity to the "shallowness of racial despair," Walcott ridiculed the intellectual embrace of Africa as the facile romanticism of "reactionaries in dashikis" celebrating "another treachery" ("Twilight" 21, 27, 8), insisting that "my memory cannot summon any filial love"

("Muse" 27). That the Black Power movement, which had reached the islands in the late 1960s, provided a context in which Brathwaite's ideas were received positively only fueled Walcott's fire: "For the Colonial artist the enemy . . . was those who had elected themselves as protectors of the people, . . . who cried out that black was beautiful . . . without explaining what they meant by beauty" ("Twilight" 35).

At the center of the controversy about Caribbean cultural history in the 1970s was the unresolved issue of ethnic particularism. Significant in this context is that the various movements of "black consciousness" that have emerged in different parts of the Caribbean since the beginning of the twentieth century were invariably inspired by foreign intrusion (Arnold, "Caribbean" 42). While the Afro-Antillean "movement" that began to flourish in Cuba and Puerto Rico in the late 1920s also profited from the literary production of the Harlem Renaissance, it was mainly a response on the part of predominantly white local elites to U.S. military and political interference in Hispanic Caribbean affairs after the Spanish-Cuban-American War (1896–98). The almost simultaneous rise of Haitian *indigénisme*, another ideology of national consciousness centered around journals such as *Les Griots* and *La Revue indigène*, can be attributed to the invasion of the U.S. marines in 1915. Francophone Caribbean Negritude, with *Tropiques* as its focal point, was partly a response to the racism of the French army that occupied Martinique and Guadeloupe from 1940 to 1943. The presence of the Shell petroleum refinery in Aruba prompted Dutch-Caribbean publications such as Frank Martinus Arion's *Stemmen uit Afrika* (1957). Kenneth Ramchand suggests that the presence of U.S. military personnel in Trinidad during World War II had similar effects ("West Indian Literary History," 1988), while Ian Smart relates the popularity of Garveyism in Panama and Costa Rica to the construction of the Panama Canal and the labor policies of the United Fruit Company. Emphasizing the large Jamaican and Haitian emigrant populations in both countries, Smart proposes a revised canon of pan-Caribbean literature to include Central American writers of Caribbean descent (*Central American Writers of Caribbean Origin,* 1984).

Despite these similarities, the relations of each of these literary phenomena both to the notion of a national literature and to the idea of Caribbeanness are different enough to arouse suspicion about theoretical shortcuts such as Janheinz Jahn's construct "neo-African literature" (1968) and the more recent "Afro-Caribbean literature." For instance, to see *poesía afroantillana* and the ideology of *mestizaje/transculturación* it promoted as a

Hispanic Caribbean manifestation of Negritude is no less problematic than to conflate Césaire's Negritude with Jacques Roumain's Haitian indigenism or even with Léopold Sédar Senghor's black essentialism. At the same time, it is also true that some of the principal intellectual sources of Césaire's Negritude, a neologism he coined in a 1935 essay in *L'Étudiant noir* (Paris), were the same ones that inspired the *negrista* writings of Puerto Rican poet Luis Palés Matos and of the Cubans Nicolás Guillén and Alejo Carpentier: Oswald Spengler's *The Decline of the West* (1918–21) and Leo Frobenius's ethnographic work on Africa, disseminated in Latin America by JOSÉ ORTEGA Y GASSET's *Revista de Occidente*.

Césaire's reputation as a spokesman for the worldwide decolonization of black cultures is based largely on his "Negritude epic" *Return to My Native Land,* first published in 1939 and reissued twice after Césaire's "discovery" by surrealist André Breton in 1941. While Césaire's name tends to be associated primarily with Marxism, his early writings on poetics, notably "Poetry and Cognition" (*Tropiques,* 1945), combine a strong interest in ethnography and psychoanalysis with the metaphysics of FRIEDRICH NIETZSCHE. While Césaire gradually moved away from the Jungian notion of a collective racial unconscious and began to historicize the earlier premises of his Negritude, he did not altogether abandon his belief in its transcendent qualities. "Culture and Colonization," delivered at the First International Congress of Negro Writers and Artists in Paris (1956) only months before Césaire's spectacular break with the French Communist party (*Lettre à Maurice Thorez,* 1956), distinguishes between "national culture" and "civilization," arguing that important elements of African civilization are maintained even after the destruction of a specific African culture and claiming for all colonized blacks the right to preserve their African legacy. This, like the equation of racism and colonialism in *Discourse on Colonialism* (1955), points to a Marxism modified by the requirements of cultural specificity. Such local specificity is encoded in the neologism *marronner* (from the Spanish *cimarrón,* "runaway slave"), which Césaire coined in his poem "Response to Depestre, Haitian Poet" (1955) to defend his surrealist poetic practice against critical realism.

Since the 1950s and 1960s, African and Caribbean Marxist critics have opposed Negritude's utopianism and cultural separatism. Calls for the deracialization of all cultural claims began with Fanon and have since been repeated by writers as different as Walcott, Lamming, WOLE SOYINKA, and (esp. in *Bonjour et adieu à la négritude,* 1986) René Depestre. But the ideological critique of Negritude notwithstanding, certain aspects of Césaire's poetics of decolonization, notably his critique of the Cartesian ego, proved valuable even to some of his critics. For Césaire, the self is not an individual agent but a site of collective articulation and regeneration. This idea of the decentered subject preoccupied with the unresolved contradictions of the group unconscious influenced the theme of psychic dispossession in Fanon's *Black Skin* and has more recently been elaborated in the work of Edouard Glissant and Guyana's 1987 literary laureate, Wilson Harris. That Michael Dash, translator of Glissant's critical writings (*Caribbean Discourse,* 1989), would render "une poétique de la Relation" as "a cross-cultural poetics" already suggests affinities between Glissant's notions of *métissage* (synchronic relations within and across cultures) and *antillanité* and Harris's ongoing re-visions of Caribbean and New World identities from the essays collected in *Tradition, the Writer and Society* (1967) and *Explorations* (1981) to *The Womb of Space* (1983).

The starting point for both Glissant and Harris is the demythification of the self (including that of the author) and an emphasis on the structuring potential of the collective unconscious. "What . . . is remarkable about the West Indian in depth," Harris writes, "is a sense of subtle links, the series of subtle and nebulous links which are latent within him, the latent ground of old and new personalities" (*Tradition* 28). What is the Caribbean, Glissant asks, other than "a multiple series of relationships" (*Caribbean* 139)? The need to unmask language and literary conventions leads both novelists to attack literary realism's pretensions of "total" representation: "Political radicalism is merely a fashionable attitude unless it is accompanied by profound insights into the experimental nature of the arts and sciences" (*Tradition* 46). Their respective critiques of mimesis also encompass Western historiography's systematization of the world through ethnocultural hierarchies and chronology. Glissant calls this history "a highly functional fantasy of the West" from which even Marxism is not exempt. "History," according to Glissant, "is fissured by histories," eclipsed voices that Caribbean literature must gather together in what Harris, in *The Infinite Rehearsal* (1987), calls "an impossible quest for wholeness." Both Glissant's and Harris's writings mark "a significant departure from the Caribbean's fixation with prelapsarian innocence" (Glissant, *Caribbean* xii), of which Walcott's Adamic proclivities are but one instance (see "Twilight" 7).

Even those who disagreed with Harris's condemnation of West Indian "protest" fiction's conventionality, most notably C. L. R. James, whose *Black Jacobins* (1938) Harris praised (*Tradition* 45), were struck by his views on language. James admits that "Harris, grappling with a

West Indian problem, had arrived at conclusions that dealt with the problem of language as a whole in the world at large" (Harris, *Tradition* 71–72). That problem, clearly, is the postcolonial world's search for linguistic authenticity. Critical of Creole as a vehicle for such authenticity, Glissant warns against a simple return to orality and folklore to escape baroque excesses that, like Caliban's cursing, attempt to compensate for alleged linguistic inadequacies. Instead, Glissant, much like Harris, turns to painting and sculpture for an alternative metalanguage, a poetics of incompleteness through which, Harris claims, communion and community (what he calls *coniunctio* in *Womb*) become possible again as a "privileged rehearsal pointing to unsuspected facets and the reemergence of forgotten perspectives in the cross-cultural and the universal imagination" (*Infinite* vii). For both Harris and Glissant, this idea of a "rehearsal" is best articulated in the figure and phenomenon of carnival, an exemplary Caribbean space whose creative disorder, or "primordial chaos," provides an escape from the plantation society. Like Octavio Paz's *fiesta* (see *The Labyrinth of Solitude*, 1959), carnival is conceived as a permanent revolution, a ceaseless metamorphosis that displaces the idea of Genesis: "Composite peoples, that is, those who could not deny or mask their hybrid composition, . . . do not 'need' the idea of Genesis, because they do not need the myth of pure lineage" (Glissant, *Caribbean* 141).

Chaos and carnival also play a major role in Benítez Rojo's *La isla que se repite* (*The Repeating Island*, 1989), whose "rereading" of the Caribbean avails itself of chaos theory to reveal "shared dynamics" within the "historiographic turbulence and ethnologic and linguistic noise" that characterize the Caribbean as a "cultural meta-archipelago" without center and boundaries (iv–v). Following Gilles Deleuze and Félix Guattari, Benítez Rojo proposes the notion of a "Caribbean machine" (naval, military, commercial, bureaucratic, political, legal, religious) that "repeats" itself in the form of the plantation (ix). Poised against this are "traditional" Caribbean "performances" of displacement (music, dance, sports) whose "carnivalesque catharsis" escapes from and neutralizes the plantation's excesses through an "antiapocalyptic" desire for nonviolence. Benítez Rojo's suggestion that "Caribbean texts are fugitive by nature" (xxxii) also echoes Césaire's poetics of *marronner*.

Despite *Isla*'s indebtedness to Deleuze and Guattari, RENÉ GIRARD, ROLAND BARTHES, and M. M. BAKHTIN, Benítez Rojo cautions that "poststructuralism, which corresponds to postindustrialism . . . , cannot altogether explain Caribbean discourse, which has much of the pre-modern in it" (xxx). Traditional culture in the Carib-

bean, he explains, refers to "an interplay of supersyncretic signifieds whose principal 'centers' are located in preindustrial Europe, in the aboriginal subsoil, in sub-Saharan Africa, and in certain island and coastal areas of tropical Asia" (xxvii). These "supersyncretisms" (such as *mestizaje*) are the opposite of syntheses: they signify "a concentration of differences" in which binary oppositions "dissolve in differential equations without resolution" (xxxiv). Ultimately, then, Benítez Rojo's conclusions are quite similar to those at which Harris and Glissant arrive in their cross-cultural poetics: that it is "impossible to assume a stable identity for the Caribbean—what can be reconstructed is the possibility for being 'in a certain way' [*de cierta manera*] in the midst of the noise and fury of chaos" (xxxv).

The indeterminate carnivalesque space of *de cierta manera*, whose regenerative potential Benítez Rojo identifies as "powerfully feminine" (xxxviii), combines Harris's notion of "infinite rehearsals" in the "womb of space" with Glissant's "poetics of the recognition of diversity" (*Caribbean* 251). It also points to a highly problematic aspect of the Caribbean discourse thus en-gendered: its tendency to exclude women as cultural producers while at the same time appropriating their "regenerative" powers. If the significance of race in Caribbean literature remains an open question, gender dynamics have barely been addressed.

Critical work on Caribbean women writers, sponsored in some not entirely unproblematic measure by the fairly recent impact of Western European and Euro-American feminisms, is still, in many ways, in its infancy. Overall, gender differences and sexuality as topics within Caribbean literature have received far less attention than race, and theoretical approaches to the race-gender nexus are rare. There is, however, a growing number of studies on Caribbean women, ranging from investigations of race and gender stereotypes in the work of male writers to the inscriptions of identity in the novels, poetry, and drama written by Caribbean women. Two ground-breaking collections of Caribbean feminist criticism were published in 1990: Selwyn Cudjoe's *Caribbean Women Writers: Essays from the First International Conference* (held in 1988 at Wellesley College) and Carole Boyce Davies and Elaine Savory Fido's *Out of the Kumbla: Caribbean Women and Literature*. Both volumes are significant attempts at acknowledging the diversity of Caribbean women's writing. Even though their primary focus remains on the English-speaking West Indies, both collections also include essays on Dutch and Hispanic Caribbean literature, two areas in which little serious critical work has been done to date (see Phaf, "Caribbean Imagination" 1988).

Kumbla laments the lack of "sufficient excitement and passion about feminist issues . . . in Caribbean intellectual and activist circles. . . . Too often, feminism is seen as a social science/development issue" or dismissed as a European import (ix–xi, 15). Whereas its editors and most of its contributors find a convergence of African-American womanist and Euro(American)-feminist perspectives congenial to the multicultural reality of the Caribbean, Sylvia Wynter, in her "Afterword," challenges such "paradoxical" alliances on the basis of Western feminism's complicitousness with a Eurocentric "patriarchal" discourse of "civic humanism" (355–57). Wynter's rereading of *The Tempest* goes "beyond" both Miranda's and Caliban's "meanings." It differs significantly from previous revisions of the Prospero-Caliban paradigm— from Fanon's *Black Skin* to Césaire's *Tempest* (1968–69) and Fernández Retamar's "Caliban" (1971)—in its call for an "alternative sexual-erotic model of desire" (360) to be derived from the "demonic" ground of Caliban's absent mate. For Wynter, the current womanist/feminist phase in Caribbean criticism is but a transition toward a radically new epistemology. Wynter's essay is certainly one of the most provocative contributions to Caribbean feminist criticism, but, as Kathleen Balutansky notes in "Naming Caribbean Women Writers" (1990), it remains caught up in an old dilemma: whether or not to privilege racial oppression over sexism. The process of confronting this volatile issue is perhaps a "rehearsal" of a different kind, one that will no doubt redraw the boundaries of Caribbean literary and critical discourse.

Vera M. Kutzinski

See also AFRICAN-AMERICAN THEORY AND CRITICISM, FEMINIST THEORY AND CRITICISM, and MARXIST THEORY AND CRITICISM.

Edward Baugh, ed., *Critics on Caribbean Literature* (1978); Antonio Benítez Rojo, *La isla que se repite: El Caribe y la perspectiva posmoderna* (1989); Edward Kamau Brathwaite, "The African Presence in Caribbean Literature" *(Roots), Contradictory Omens: Cultural Diversity and Integration in the Caribbean* (1974), *History of the Voice: The Development of Nation Language in Anglophone Caribbean Poetry* (1984), *Roots: Essay* (1986); Aimé Césaire, *Discours sur le colonialisme* (1955, *Discourse on Colonialism*, trans. Joan Pinkham, 1972), "Poésie et connaissance," *Aimé Césaire, l'homme et l'oeuvre* (by Lilyan Kesteloot and Barthélemy Kotchy, 1973); Selwyn R. Cudjoe, ed., *Caribbean Women Writers: Essays from the First International Conference* (1990); Carole Boyce Davies and Elaine Savory Fido, eds., *Out of the Kumbla: Caribbean Women and Literature* (1990); René Depestre, *Bonjour et adieu à la négritude* (1980); Roberto Fernández Retamar, *Caliban* (1989); Edouard Glissant, *Le Discours Antillais* (1981, *Caribbean Discourse: Selected Essays,* trans. J. Michael Dash, 1989); Wilson Harris, *Explorations: A Selection of Talks and Articles, 1966–1981* (ed. Hena Maes-Jelinek, 1981), *The Infinite Rehearsal* (1987), *Tradition, the Writer, and Society: Critical Essays* (1967), *The Womb of Space: The Cross-Cultural Imagination* (1983); C. L. R. James, "From Toussaint L'Ouverture to Fidel Castro," *The Black Jacobins: Toussaint L'Ouverture and the San Domingo Revolution* (2d ed., 1963); George Lamming, *The Pleasures of Exile* (1960); Derek Walcott, "The Muse of History," *Is Massa Day Dead? Black Moods in the Caribbean* (ed. Orde Coombs, 1974, reprint, Baugh), "What the Twilight Says: An Overture," *Dream on Monkey Mountain and Other Plays* (1970); Sylvia Wynter, "Beyond Miranda's Meanings: Un/silencing the 'Demonic Ground' of Caliban's 'Woman'" (Davies and Fido).

A. James Arnold, "Caribbean Literature / Comparative Literature," *Mélanges offerts à Albert Gérard: Semper aliquid novi: Littérature comparée et littératures d'Afrique* (ed. Janos Riesz and Alain Richard, 1990), *Modernism and Negritude: The Poetry and Poetics of Aimé Césaire* (1981); Kathleen M. Balutansky, "Naming Caribbean Women Writers: A Review Essay," *Callaloo* 13 (1990); Maryse Condé, *La Parole des femmes: Essai sur des romancières des Antilles de langage français* (1979); Gabriel R. Coulthard, *Race and Colour in Caribbean Literature* (1962); J. Michael Dash, "The World and the Word: French Caribbean Writing in the Twentieth Century," *Callaloo* 11 (1988); Albert Gérard, "Problématique d'une histoire littéraire du monde caraïbe," *Revue de littérature comparée* 1 (1988); Roberto González Echevarría, "Literature of the Hispanic Caribbean," *Latin American Literary Review* 8 (1978); Janheinz Jahn, *A History of Neo-African Literature: Writing in Two Continents* (1968); C. L. R. James, *Wilson Harris: A Philosophical Approach* (1965); Monica Mansour, *La Poesía negrista* (1973); Sandra Pouchet Paquet, *The Novels of George Lamming* (1982); Ineke Phaf, "Caribbean Imagination and Nation Building in Antillean and Surinamese Literature," *Callaloo* 11 (1988); Ana Pizarro, "Reflections in the Historiography of Caribbean Literature," *Callaloo* 11 (1988); Kenneth Ramchand, "West Indian Literary History: Literariness, Orality, and Periodization," *Callaloo* 11 (1988), *The West Indian Novel and Its Background* (1970); Ian Smart, *Central American Writers of West Indian Origin: A New Hispanic Literature* (1984); Patrick Taylor, *The Narrative of Liberation: Perspectives on Afro-Caribbean Literature, Popular Culture, and Politics* (1989).

CHICAGO CRITICS

In 1937, John Crowe Ransom claimed that if the fledgling movement "for the erection of intelligent standards of criticism" were to succeed, "the credit would probably belong to Professor Ronald S. Crane, of the University of Chicago, more than to any other man. He is the first of the great professors to have advocated it as a major policy for departments of English. It is possible that he will have made some important academic history" ("Criticism Inc.").

Chicago criticism can be said to begin in 1935 with "History versus Criticism in the Study of Literature" (Crane, *Idea* 2:3–24), the article in which Crane (1886–1967) rejects the privileged position hitherto given to history in the study of literature and transfers it to criticism (explication and theory). Crane had previously established himself as a mainline philologist, historian of ideas, and bibliographer. "History versus Criticism" thus marked an important change for Crane, one that coincided with the arrival at Chicago of the philosopher Richard McKeon (1900–1985). McKeon's commitment to philosophic pluralism and his reading of ARISTOTLE (see "Literary Criticism and the Concept of Imitation in Antiquity," 1936; "The Philosophic Bases of Art and Criticism," 1943–44; and "Aristotle's Conception of Language and the Arts of Language," 1946–47, all in *Critics and Criticism: Ancient and Modern*, 1952) provided the stimulus for the more literary theorizing of Crane and Elder Olson (1909–92), the two most articulate proponents of what came to be known as Chicago criticism. The sense of a collective school was firmly entrenched with the publication of *Critics and Criticism* by the first generation of Chicago critics: Crane, W. R. Keast (b. 1914), McKeon, Norman Maclean (1902–90), Olson, and Bernard Weinberg (1909–73).

By 1952 it was clear that while Crane and his colleagues continued to share with Ransom and the other New Critics a belief in the centrality of textual analysis in literary study, they had significant disagreements about the best way to perform that analysis based on differing theories of literature and literary language. After a decade of hostile polemics, and in the wake of the enormous popularity of the New Critics, Ransom wrote of the failure of the Chicago critics to realize their promise, a failure he attributed to their decision to use Aristotle's *Poetics* as a "hand book" rather than tackle "the hard questions" for themselves ("Humanism at Chicago"). For Ransom, the Chicago critics had abandoned their place in the critical vanguard to join the forces of reaction. To put it another way, having failed in their challenge to the developing New Critical hegemony of the 1940s and 1950s, the Chicago critics remained at the margins of the dominant critical discourse of their time.

Ransom was probably right to attribute the failure of the Chicago critics to win wide support to their Aristotelian "hand book." He was wrong, however, to assume that it was the *Poetics* that contributed most to Chicago criticism, since Aristotle's analysis of literary texts was less important than his general method of inquiry. What Aristotle offered them was, as David H. Richter puts it, "a method similar to that of science. . . . [T]he critical aims of the Chicago School included the attainment of power through the successful search for objective truth" (732). PAUL DE MAN describes the Chicago critics as a group like the more recent reception theorists of the Constance school, made up of "a liberal association of scholars, informally united by methodological concerns that allow for considerable diversity. . . ." "The concerns of such groups," he argues, "are methodological rather than, as in the case of the New Criticism or the FRANKFURT SCHOOL, cultural and ideological" (*The Resistance to Theory*, 1986, 54). It is hardly surprising, then, that these "displaced scientists," as Richter calls them, failed to win the kind of support given to the New Critics, that far more inspirational group of "disappointed priests seeking in literature for a new Word to replace the one the world had lost."

Chicago critics focused on critical methods for the study of literature, both their own and other critics', both past and present, and on the application of those methods to particular works. Their efforts shared a desire to introduce more rigor and precision into critical discourse. Olson's observation that "criticism in our time is a sort of Tower of Babel" is almost commonplace in twentieth-century criticism. What follows for him is not commonplace: "Moreover, it is not merely a linguistic but also a methodological Babel; yet, in the very pursuit of this analogy, it is well to remember that at Babel men did not begin to talk nonsense; they merely began to talk what *seemed* like nonsense to their fellows. A statement is not false merely because it is unintelligible; though it will have to be made intelligible before we can say whether it is true" (*Critics* 546). To make it intelligible requires, in Crane's words, "a general critique of literary criticism . . . such as might yield objective criteria for interpreting the diversities and oppositions among critics and for judging the comparative merits of rival critical schools" (*Critics* 5). Such "objectivity" is possible only when the "basic principles" (Olson's "semantic orientation") and "methods" (Olson's "propositional structures," "truth value," and "principles of validation") (Crane,

Languages 31; Olson, *On Value* 337) are understood. Crane concludes that if the critic understands a number of alternative systems, "critical approaches of the most diverse sorts can coexist without implying either contradiction or inconsistency" (*Languages* 31); or, in Olson's terms, "once the subject of the arts has been described in these systems, it determines the solutions of all artistic problems" (*On Value* 353). "The moral," Crane argues, "is surely that we ought to have at our command, collectively at least, as many different critical methods as there are distinguishable major aspects in the construction, appreciation, and use of literary works" (*Languages* 192). Such calls for critical pluralism form a recurring theme in Chicago criticism.

Chicago pluralism is but one of several critical alternatives. Olson points to three others, all of which reject the pluralistic view that "true interpretation is impossible when one system is examined in terms of another, as is true refutation when the refutative arguments are systematically different from those against which they are directed." Each of Olson's alternatives fails to meet his interpretive standards: "Dogmatism holds the truth of a single position and the falsity, in some degree at least, of all others; syncretism holds the partial falsity of all; skepticism the total falsity of all" (*Critics* 547). The interest in critical methodologies resulted in a number of pluralistic readings in the history of criticism. *Critics and Criticism* includes essays on Aristotle (by McKeon), LONGINUS (Olson), medieval poetics and rhetoric (McKeon), Robortello and Castelvetro (Weinberg), English neoclassical criticism (Crane), SAMUEL JOHNSON (Keast), and eighteenth-century theories of the lyric (Maclean). Other important work includes Olson on Aristotle and Reynolds, and Weinberg's introduction to his *Critical Prefaces of the French Renaissance* and his two-volume *History of Literary Criticism in the Italian Renaissance*. The similar Chicago pattern is found throughout these essays: first the principles and methods of the criticism under discussion are determined, and then they are used to provide the basis for evaluating its strengths and weaknesses.

When the Chicago critics apply the same approach to the criticism of their contemporaries, the result is predictably more polemical and more contentious, often characterized by a stronger impatience with sloppy, dogmatic, or skeptical thinking. Criticism based on universal philosophic systems (from G. W. F. HEGEL and KARL MARX AND FRIEDRICH ENGELS to SIGMUND FREUD and JEAN-PAUL SARTRE) is a special object of distrust in Chicago criticism, but the Chicago critics' most extensive critique is reserved for the New Critics, whose exclusive concern with figurative language and irony they thought was limiting and reductive. The essays in *Critics and Criticism* on I. A. RICHARDS (by Crane), WILLIAM EMPSON (Olson), Cleanth Brooks (Crane), Robert B. Heilman (Keast), and Robert Penn Warren (Olson) represent the core of the Chicago critique of New Criticism.

The pluralism of the Chicago critics developed along with a special, though not exclusive, interest in the *poetic* method of Aristotle (who remains a "dogmatic" critic for Olson [*On Value* 347]), for Aristotle offers the most useful antecedent for their special version of formalism. In Crane's words, "He grasped the distinctive nature of poetic works as *synola*, or concrete artistic wholes, and made available, though only in outline sketch, hypotheses and analytical devices for defining literally and inductively, and with a maximum degree of differentiation, the multiple causes operative in the construction of poetic wholes of various kinds and the criteria of excellence appropriate to each" (*Critics* 17). Much of the theoretical and practical criticism of the Chicago school consists in fleshing out the Aristotelian skeleton as they have reconstructed it. Their choice of Aristotle is thus "pragmatic"; their Aristotle differs from others': "It may not, indeed, except in a general way, be Aristotle at all!" (*Critics* 12, 17); but it nevertheless provides a useful methodological basis for further critical inquiry. "Neo-Aristotelian" is thus a more accurate label for their work than "Aristotelian."

Two of the concepts the Chicago critics return to repeatedly, namely, form and genre, developed from their reading of Aristotle. Literary works are imitations, objects made for the sake of their own power and beauty. Literary form becomes a "principle of construction, from which [the artist] infers, however instantaneously, what he must do in constituting and ordering the parts" (Crane, *Idea* 2:57). The task for the critic becomes one of reconstructing those parts as the author originally must have constructed them consciously or unconsciously, in order, logically, to create the whole work under discussion. The intentionalism of the Chicago critics, then, follows from their acceptance of Aristotelian mimesis.

Their Aristotelian concepts of form and genre follow naturally from their more general principles of form. Literary forms are "species of works, inductively known, and differentiated, more or less sharply, in terms of their artistic elements and principles of construction" (Crane, *Idea* 2:59). Genre for the Chicago critics is always a heuristic concept; attribution of membership in a generic class is conjectural, not prescriptive. Falsifiability remains a consistent requirement for hypotheses in literary studies. One of the more controversial consequences of their assumption that literary meaning is to be found in the (generic) intention of the text is that like Aristotle, they subordinate the function of literary language to the larger structure of the work as a whole: "The words must be explained in terms of something else, not the poem in terms of the words; and further, a principle must be a principle of something other than itself; hence the words cannot be a principle of their own arrangements" (Olson, *On Value* 13).

The Chicago focus on genre and method does not preclude an interest in historical analysis. The various studies of literary critics produced by Chicago critics form the basis for a history of criticism. And many of their genre studies—Olson on comedy and tragedy, Maclean on the lyric, Crane on eighteenth-century literature—are developed around hypotheses of historical change. Literary history for Crane is exemplified in a "narrative-causal" history of forms, a concept he explains in his "Critical and Historical Principles of Literary History" (in *Idea*).

PRACTICAL CRITICISM is rarely noticed in considerations of the Chicago critics as a group, although many of their books and articles are well known to specialists and frequently anthologized. Particularly influential have been Crane's essays "Suggestions toward a Genealogy of the 'Man of Feeling,' " "The Houyhnhnms, the Yahoos, and the History of Ideas" (both in *Idea*), and "The Concept of Plot and the Plot of *Tom Jones*" (in *Critics*); Olson's books on tragedy, comedy, and Dylan Thomas, as well as his essays "Rhetoric and the Appreciation of Pope" and "Hamlet and the Hermeneutics of Drama" (both in *On Value*); and Weinberg's books on Racine and symbolism. As their subjects and titles indicate, Chicago critics rarely neglect theoretical concerns, even in so-called practical criticism.

The concerns of the Chicago critics have been developed by a second and third generation, many but not all of whom studied at Chicago. It is not surprising that as more and more critics apply Chicago methods to an ever larger number of critical questions and an ever-expanding canon, it becomes increasingly difficult to find shared conclusions. The general trend, influenced largely by Wayne C. Booth, has been from poetics to RHETORIC and from an almost exclusive focus on text to an increasing interest in both author and reader (Sheldon Sacks and Ralph W. Rader playing a large role). More recent Chicago criticism has redefined pluralism (Booth and Walter Davis), broken down relatively rigid, mutually exclusive generic categories (Rader, Booth), and heightened the intentionalism always inherent in the constructionist model (Sacks, Rader). A partial list of more recent Chicago critics includes: Booth, Norman Friedman, Paul Goodman, Homer Goldberg, Phillip Harth, Arthur Heiserman, Walter J. Hipple, Gwin J. Kolb, Richard Levin, Robert Marsh, Moody E. Prior, Rader, Edward W. Rosenheim, Sacks, Mary Doyle Springer, Douglas H. White, and Austin M. Wright (the second generation); and Janet E. Aikins, James L. Battersby, Don Bialostosky, Michael M. Boardman, Walter A. Davis, Barbara Foley, Elizabeth Langland, Zahava K. McKeon, James S. Malek, James Phelan, Peter J. Rabinowitz, David H. Richter, Adena Rosmarin, and Howard D. Weinbrot (the third generation).

Brian Corman

See also ARISTOTLE and NEW CRITICISM.

Wayne C. Booth, *Critical Understanding: The Powers and Limits of Pluralism* (1979), *The Rhetoric of Fiction* (1961, 2d ed., 1983); R. S. Crane, *The Idea of the Humanities and Other Essays Critical and Historical* (2 vols., 1967), *The Languages of Criticism and the Structure of Poetry* (1953); R. S. Crane, ed., *Critics and Criticism: Ancient and Modern* (1952); Walter A. Davis, *The Act of Interpretation: A Critique of Literary Reason* (1978); Elder Olson, *On Value Judgments in the Arts and Other Essays* (1976), *Tragedy and the Theory of Drama* (1961); Ralph W. Rader, "Defoe, Richardson, Joyce, and the Concept of Form in the Novel," *Autobiography, Biography, and the Novel* (1973), "From Richardson to Austen: 'Johnson's Rule' and the Development of the Eighteenth-Century Novel of Moral Action," *Johnson and His Age* (ed. James Engell, 1984); Sheldon Sacks, *Fiction and the Shape of Belief: A Study of Henry Fielding, with Glances at Swift, Johnson, and Richardson* (1964).

Wayne C. Booth, "Between Two Generations: The Heritage of the Chicago School," *Profession 82* (1982); Kenneth Burke, *A Grammar of Motives* (1945); Gerald Graff, *Professing Literature: An Institutional History* (1987); Vincent B. Leitch, *American Literary Criticism from the Thirties to the Eighties* (1988); Richard McKeon, "Criticism and the Liberal Arts: The Chicago School of Criticism," *Profession 82* (1982); John Crowe Ransom, "Humanism at Chicago," *Kenyon Review* 14 (1952), *The World's Body* (1938); David H. Richter, ed., *The Critical Tradition: Classic Texts and Contemporary Trends* (1989); Hoyt Trowbridge, "Aristotle and the 'New Criticism,' " *Sewanee Review* 52 (1944); Eliseo Vivas, "The Neo-Aristotelians of Chicago," *Sewanee Review* 61 (1953); René Wellek, *A History of Modern Criticism: 1750–1950*, vol. 6, *American Criticism, 1900–1950* (1986); William K. Wimsatt, Jr., *The Verbal Icon: Studies in the Meaning of Poetry* (1954).

CHINESE THEORY AND CRITICISM

1. Pre-Modern Theories of Poetry

Poetry enjoyed a unique prestige in traditional China. The great poets were culture heroes, and every cultivated person was expected to be able to compose poetry. The ability to write fluently was closely linked with and significant of self-cultivation, Confucian and otherwise, and therefore appropriately tested on the great imperial examinations. Poetry was composed in great quantities—over 40,000 poems survive from the Tang dynasty (618–907) alone—and it generated a proportionate amount of criticism and discussion.

There are nevertheless difficulties in discussing the history of traditional Chinese poetic criticism and theory. The language of criticism was allusive and metaphorical, and critics combined a passion for key terms with an almost total disinterest in the problems of their definition. Instead, writers on literature assumed a complex web of continuities and analogies between and within the natural and social/cultural worlds that worked to subvert and evade analytic distinctions. Moreover, most discussions of poetry and its nature took place in the contexts of essays, letters, or obiter dicta about particular poems or couplets; full-scale, integral works of theory were the exception rather than the rule. Indeed, there is no term in Chinese strictly analogous to "theory," with its implications of the systematic presentation of an organizing structure. When we speak of theories of poetry in traditional China, then, it must be understood that we are typically discussing largely tacit models or systems reconstructed from characteristic vocabularies and discursive strategies rather than synoptic models analytically presented.

Nor is there any single word in Chinese that exactly translates the English term "poetry." Perhaps the term most prominent in early discussions of poetry and literature generally was *wen*, which referred to "patterned" (i.e., rhymed) or literary language, or to writing generally, but also to the patterns or markings on natural objects, to the received high cultural tradition, and to the pattern or order of the cosmos. Writers on poetry and literature, such as Liu Xie (c. 465–523), took advantage of this broad range of reference to assert the integral continuity between the generative order of the cosmos and the creative powers of the literary artist, as well as the cosmic and historical significance of poetry and writing generally.

If *wen* referred to both poetry and much more than poetry, the other term important in early discussions of poetry had a narrower extension than the English term. In Warring States (403–221 B.C.E.) and Han (202 B.C.E.–C.E. 220) texts, *shi* referred to the Odes, that is, to the ancient song works collected together and canonized as the *Shijing* [Odes classic], probably compiled around the sixth century B.C.E.. The discussions that arose concerning the reading and interpretations of this canonical text generated perhaps the most influential theory of poetry in traditional China. This view of poetry was summed up in the paronomastic definition *Shi yan zhi* ("The Odes [or "poetry"] articulate the *zhi*"), the latter term encompassing some of the same territory as the English "intention," "aim," or even the Heideggerian "project" *(Entwurf)*. This well-known formula was taken to assert the hermeneutical integrity of the Odes and of poetry generally: by expressing the emotional reactions of their historical authors, the Odes inscribed and preserved for later generations both the personalities of their authors and the social worlds that moved them to song. While the influential *Maoshi xu* [Preface to Mao's Odes], written around the early first century C.E., and much of subsequent *Shijing* scholarship focused on the Odes as indexes to the historical moments in which they were made, later discussions of lyric poetry tended to view the poem as the inscription of the personality and of the literal, historical experiences of its author. At the same time, because the responses inscribed in the Odes were paradigmatically normative ones, those texts had the power to effect the moral transformation both of their individual readers and of society as a whole. The belief that poetry and literature generally had powerful pragmatic powers—and thus an important moral and political dimension—continued as a mainstay of traditional criticism over the next 20 centuries and survives today.

The most important poetic genre in traditional China, the *shi*, or "lyric," first appeared as a popular form as early as the second century B.C.E.; but it was not until the very end of the Han and the long period of political disunion known as the Six Dynasties period (222–589) that the form fully matured. This development stimulated a great efflorescence of poetic theory and criticism. The earliest surviving example from this first golden age of poetic theory and criticism comes from the hand of Cao Pei (187–226, Emperor Wen of the Wei dynasty), a leading figure in the circle of court poets in whose hands the genre was perfected. In his short treatise *Lun wen* [On literature] Cao gives prescriptive descriptions of several genres, including the lyric, maintains that the function of literature is to make its author known to subsequent generations, and emphasizes the paramount importance of *qi* ("vital breath," "energy") in literary composition. In his essay, Cao demonstrates a number of features characteristic of much later Chinese writing on poetry: a taste for the evaluation and ranking of other writers, a strongly practical interest in instructing the aspirant poet, and a conviction of the cosmic and historical significance of literature.

The *Wenfu* [Rhapsody on literature], by Lu Ji (261-303), is known both for the ideas it develops and as a masterpiece of Chinese literature. Although Lu, like Cao Pei, offers brief descriptions of a number of genres as well as of poetic defects, his great theme is the process of inspiration and composition, in particular the intuitive communion that, achieved, makes the poet the vehicle of and spokesman for the workings of the *dao,* or "Way."

The period from the fourth through the sixth century witnessed a rapid development in the formal sophistication of the lyric, and critics played an important role in this process. Perhaps the most important was Shen Yue (441-513), who specified "Eight Defects" for poets to avoid. His theory (as well as his poetry) excited controversy in his own day and thereafter as well, but the attention he paid to prosody and diction was to characterize much of Tang poetry.

Shen became known not only for his prosodic rules but also for his elegant, often erotic poetry in the so-called palace style *(gongti shi).* Palace poetry, like the ornate, florid parallel prose style *(pianti wen),* with which it was often linked, raised anew issues first discussed centuries before in connection with the *fu,* or "rhapsody," most notably how to reconcile the pleasures of poetry with the didactic/pragmatic mission envisioned for literature by, say, the *Maoshi xu.* These issues came to a head in the circles surrounding the Liang (502-56) court. On the one side, representing the poetic avant-garde, were Shen Yue and Xiao Gang (503-51), a member of the Liang ruling house. In the anthology he commissioned, the *Yutai xinyong* [New songs from the jade terrace], and in a number of letters, Xiao Gang rejected the ideas that literature was a development of the Confucian canon and that it need serve any pragmatic end; for him, it was simply the expression of unrestrained feeling. These views were opposed by a number of more traditional critics, including Zhong Hong (c. 465-518) and Xiao Tong (501-31), the elder brother of Xiao Gang and heir apparent to the Liang throne from 506 to 531. Like Xiao Gang, Zhong Hong and Xiao Tong were anthologists, and their views on poetry were often developed in the context of discussions of the rankings of particular writers and of the literary history of the past centuries. Although Zhong's anthology does not survive, an ac-

companying essay known to posterity as the *Shipin* [Poets evaluated] does. The essay comments upon and ranks some 122 poets from the third through the sixth century; it is our major source for the history of the reception of poetry during the Six Dynasties period. Xiao Tong's anthology, the *Wen Xuan* [Literary writings selected], was an early attempt to classify the entire literary tradition in terms of a system of genres. It is, after the Odes, the most important anthology in Chinese literary history, and it defined Six Dynasties poetry and literature for generations. Both the anthology itself and Xiao Tong's preface to it reflect his essentially traditionalist view of literature and poetry.

The most important and most influential work to come from this period was the *Wenxin diaolong* (translated as *The Literary Mind and the Carving of Dragons,* 1959), by Liu Xie (c. 465-523). The *Wenxin* is the great exception to the general rule that full-length works of literary theory and criticism were not written in traditional China. Organized into 50 short chapters, the work begins by linking literature with the Way *(dao)* of the cosmos and with the Confucian classics *(jing)* that are its canonical expression; indeed, all the 36 genres that Liu surveys in the first half of the book are ultimately derived from and to be judged against one or another of the classics. In the second half of his work, Liu treats a number of topics, some largely technical ("the carving of dragons"), such as phonetics, parallelism, allusion, and the like; others having to do with the personal and psychological sources of literature ("the literary mind"). While acknowledging the importance of rhetorical technique, Liu Xie insists throughout on the importance of an authentic and energizing emotional and moral origin for literature within the psyche of the writer. In this respect, and in his classicism, Liu Xie is part of a conservative reaction against the excesses of the florid and decadent style advocated by Shen Yue and Xiao Gang—this even though Liu's own work is itself a masterpiece of the parallel prose style.

In the Sui and early Tang, the conservative reaction to the Six Dynasties style in poetry was consolidated under the banner of *fugu,* "return to antiquity." *Fugu* poetics saw a close link between literary style and moral character, ranging on one side formal perfection and moral excess and on the other an austere and rugged style that was taken to represent a muscular and politically involved Confucianism. Although *fugu* critics preferred always to see themselves as the champions of an embattled and marginalized tradition, in fact *fugu* ideals became a kind of orthodoxy in the Tang, advocated by poets working in a host of different styles. Perhaps its most well-known advocates were Meng Jiao (751–814) and Han Yu (768–824).

The Tang dynasty was the great age of the lyric, but no work of commensurate theory or criticism survives. Nevertheless, there were a number of important works. Wang Changling (c. 690–c. 756), himself a major poet, anticipated many of the features and themes characteristic of later writing on poetry: the fondness for Buddhist metaphors, the interest in the interrelations between the external scene *(jing)* and the poet's psychology, and the loose, disjointed style characteristic of later *shihua*, "remarks on poetry." The monk Jiaoran (730–99) was also interested in a poetry that achieved true self-expression through the description of a scene, and this poetry was again described in Buddhist terms. Perhaps the most influential of the Tang writers on poetry was Sikong Tu (837–908). His *Ershisi shipin* [Twenty-four moods of poetry] comprises 24 poems in the archaic four-syllable meter of the Odes, each presenting a poetic mood or effect in evocative, often metaphorical language.

Although the disposition to describe the development of later Chinese literature into *pai*, "schools" or "factions," has probably been exaggerated, it is true that literary thought in the later Imperial period was preoccupied with questions concerning authority, tradition, filiation, and orthodoxy. The problematic was given influential expression in the *Canglang shihua* [Remarks on poetry by the recluse of Canglang], by Yan Yu (fl. c. 1200). Much has been made of Yan Yu's equation of poetry with Chan (Japanese Zen), but his theory probably owed as much to Song Neo-Confucianism as it did to Buddhism. In any event, for Yan Yu, poetry was not just significant of self-cultivation; the practice of poetry was itself a means to self-cultivation. Yan Yu advises the aspirant poet to immerse himself or herself in an intensive study of the orthodox tradition, that is, the poetry of the Han and Wei periods or of the High Tang (c. 715–65), although not that of the Mid Tang (c. 765–835) or Late Tang (c. 835–907). If the student poet thoroughly internalizes the great tradition, the poetry he or she creates will reenact the great poetry of the past: it will embody or rather gesture beyond itself to essentially ineffable principles or intentions *(yi)*. Such poetry may be a spontaneous and essentially artless product (as with the poetry of the Han and Wei), or it may be the product of careful study under a master possessed of the authentic received tradition; that is, it may be the product of enlightenment *(wu)*. Since the poetry of the High Tang was made in the latter fashion, it is naturally the best model for an aspirant poet who is embarked on a course of self-cultivation and study. Thus, even as Yan Yu's theory

aims ultimately at a wholly "natural" poetry, one that has transcended artifice and imitation, it paradoxically insists that such poetry can only be the product of the very extremity of artifice and imitation.

Yan Yu's ideas deeply influenced the theory and criticism of the Ming dynasty, as well as Qing dynasty thinkers such as Wang Shizhen (1634–1711). In the twentieth century, however, more attention has been paid to a line of thinkers who defined themselves in opposition to the poetics of orthodoxy and whose best-known representatives were members of the so-called Gongan school. Yuan Hongdao (1568–1610) argued against imitation and vehemently rejected the idea that the poetry of some eras is superior to that of others, arguing in effect for a radical revaluation of the received view of the poetic tradition. He discounted the poetry of the High Tang and championed that of the Song and Yuan, long despised by "orthodox" critics. Above all, he insisted that poetry must be authentic self-expression unconstrained by concerns about poetic form or decorum. In the Qing, Yuan Mei echoed much of the Gongan school's view and went further in insisting (in contradistinction to generations of moralizing and expurgating critics) that love poetry did not reflect badly on the character of its creators.

In the twentieth century, the theory and criticism of traditional Chinese poetry has been deeply influenced by Western ideas. At the same time, the characteristic vocabularies and concerns of the traditional criticism still survive in the commentaries and exegeses of traditional poetry, which are so widely published and read. Traditional literary thought also plays an important role in the attempts by such thinkers as James J. Y. Liu and Stephen Owen to establish a synthesis of traditional Chinese and modern Western views.

Steven Van Zoeren

Fan Wenlan, ed., *Wenxin diaolong* (1958, *The Literary Mind and the Carving of Dragons: A Study of Thought and Pattern in Chinese Literature,* trans. Vincent Yu-chung Shih, 1959); Guo Shaoyu, ed., *Canglang shihua jiaoshi* (1962), *Zhongguo lidai wenlun xuan* (1979); Stephen Owen, trans., *Readings in Chinese Literary Thought* (1992); Siu-kit Wong, trans., *Early Chinese Literary Criticism* (1983).

E. Bruce Brooks, "A Geometry of the *Shr Pin*," *Wen-lin: Studies in the Chinese Humanities* (ed. Chow Tse-tsung, 1968); Achilles Fang, "Rhymeprose on Literature: The *Wen-fu* of Lu Chi (A.D. 261–333)," *Studies in Chinese Literature* (ed. John L. Bishop, 1966); Donald Gibbs, "Notes on the Wind: The Term 'Feng' in Chinese Literary Criticism," *Transition and Permanence: Chinese History and*

Culture (ed. David C. Buxbaum and Fritz Mote, 1972); Guo Shaoyu, *Zhongguo wenxue piping shi* (1948); James R. Hightower, "Literary Criticism through the Six Dynasties," *Topics in Chinese Literature* (rev. ed., 1962), "The Wen-hsüan and Genre Theory," *Studies in Chinese Literature* (ed. Bishop); David Knechtges, *The Han Rhapsody: A Study of the Fu of Yang Hsiung (53 B.C.–A.D. 18)* (1976); James J. Y. Liu, *Chinese Theories of Literature* (1975); Lo Genzi, *Zhongguo wenxue piping shi* (1947); Richard John Lynn, "Orthodoxy and Enlightenment: Wang Shih-chen's Theory of Poetry and Its Antecedents," *The Unfolding of Neo-Confucianism* (ed. William Theodore DeBary, 1975); David McMullen, "Historical and Literary Theory in Mid-Eighth Century," *Perspectives on the T'ang* (ed. Arthur F. Wright and Denis Twitchett, 1973); Stephen Owen, *Traditional Chinese Poetry and Poetics: Omen of the World* (1985); Adele Austin Rickett, "The Personality of the Chinese Critic," *The Personality of the Critic* (ed. Joseph P. Strelka, 1973); Adele Austin Rickett, ed., *Chinese Approaches to Literature from Confucius to Liang Ch'i-ch'ao* (1978); Steven Van Zoeren, "The Preface to Mao's Odes," *Poetry and Personality: Reading, Exegesis, and Hermeneutics in Traditional China* (1991); Zhu Dongrun, *Zhongguo wenxue piping shi dagang* (1959).

2. Pre-Modern Theories of Fiction and Drama

Chinese theories of drama and the novel were systematically formulated only in the seventeenth century, while the theories of other Chinese arts—poetry, music, calligraphy, and painting—were already firmly established many centuries earlier. This tardy arrival can be explained historically by the late development of the two literary genres themselves: following long and complex formative processes, Chinese drama emerged as a full-fledged form only in the twelfth century, and the novel in the fourteenth century.

Some of the essential components of Chinese drama—music, dance, poetry, songs, acrobatic acts, symbolic masks, costumes, systems of gestures, as well as dramatic dialogue itself—had origins in the ritual performances and theatrical shows of earlier stages of Chinese culture. A fully formed Chinese musical drama was able to emerge only much later, after the short stories and the oral narratives from the preceding six centuries had developed the narrative themes essential for the creation of a dramatic plot. Equally important for the final shaping of the early musical drama were some of the artistically advanced forms of professional storytelling from the

eleventh and twelfth centuries: they provided models for composing suites of rhymed and sung arias, the most essential parts of a Chinese dramatic text.

The Chinese novel underwent a similar development over several centuries by the gradual addition of narrative components from historiography, mythology, and legends and by the integration of structural and thematic elements from professional oral storytelling and early dramatic forms. Recent scholarship has, moreover, revived a previous thesis that the structure of both drama and the novel was shaped according to a specific model: the *bagu wen,* or "eight-legged essay," a major genre of literary prose that flourished from the fourteenth to the early twentieth century and was composed according to the principle of strict parallelism. In the pre-modern period, dramas and novels were printed from wooden blocks to produce cheap as well as lavish, large-format editions, both frequently furnished with woodcut illustrations. The prints were sold commercially to a wide-ranging audience, including well-to-do scholars and upper-class women, as well as less prosperous lower-class officials, merchants, shopkeepers, and students.

Chinese drama and the novel developed from common sources; in fact, traditional Chinese scholars often considered these two genres as a single category, fictional narrative. Their critical discourses therefore often addressed issues that were common to the two genres during a particular period. In the formative stage of criticism, before the seventeenth century, works on drama preceded those on the novel owing to the earlier rise of drama and to the fact that drama included sung lyrics, which as a poetic genre became the object of scholarly appreciation. The early treatises on drama written in the fourteenth century deal with the theory and practice of singing, such as *Chang lun* [On singing] by Zhi'an from Yannan, or with prescribed rules for tones and rhymes in arias, such as *Tai he zheng yin pu* [A formulary for the correct sounds of great harmony] by Zhu Quan (1378–1448). By far the most important treatise from the early period is *Zhongyuan yin yun* [Sounds and rhymes of the central plains], written in 1324 by Zhou Deqing (c. 1270–after 1324). This work became one of the most significant contributions to studies of the phonetic development of the Chinese language. Zhou recognized the changes in the phonological systems of northern and southern dialects. Moreover, he set a standard in phonology on the basis of the northern dialect and thus strengthened contemporary moves to establish the northern dialect as a countrywide norm for Chinese literary language.

The fourteenth-century treatises, which discussed predominantly technical matters of dramas' sung lyrics *(qu),* were modeled on handbooks of poetic composition. With the arrival of fiction criticism at the end of the fifteenth century, and particularly in the sixteenth century, this format gradually changed. Discussions of fiction were conveyed in various prefatory materials, postscripts, analyses, and running commentaries to particular works. This practice had been previously established in treatises on philosophical and historical texts, as well as in exegeses of Chinese art. It was introduced into the study of fiction by Liu Chenweng (1232–97), who added his terse annotations into the text of *Shishuo xinyu* [New account of tales of the world], a fifth-century anthology of brief anecdotes, remarks, and noteworthy conversations. Traditional Chinese criticism of fiction and drama appeared mainly as commentaries *(pingdian)* on individual texts, a reason why later, more developed discourses on fiction often underestimated the traditional criticism's theoretical value. It has recently been pointed out, however, that the close attachment of Chinese critical discourses to a particular text gives much insight into conceptual differences between Western and Chinese literary thought. While Western theoretical treatises draw from particular texts only to exemplify deductive arguments, in the Chinese cultural tradition the principal method of theoretical thinking is inductive, grounded in the investigation of a specific text and leading to issues of a more general and theoretical nature. The inductive method was also at work in essays and miscellaneous notes *(biji),* in which several well-known scholars conveyed their observations on drama and fiction, among other topics.

The earliest known example of fiction criticism is the 1494 preface to the fourteenth-century novel *Sanguo zhi tongsu yanyi* (translated as *Popular Romance of the Three Kingdoms).* Because this novel drew extensively on historical records, Yong Yuzi, the author of the preface, set out to distinguish between historiography and the historical novel, arguing that while historiography follows the facts of reality, the novel unravels the meaning of the historical process. In the sixteenth century, many critics addressed the emancipation of fiction from historiography, because historical novels during that period represented the mainstream of Chinese fiction.

The most influential ideas on literature, however, were spelled out by the unorthodox and controversial thinker Li Zhi (1527–1602). Li Zhi's literary discussions appear in two collections of essays, letters, and poems—*Fenshu* [A book to be burned] (1590) and *Cangshu* [A book to be hidden away] (1599)—as well as in his (putative) commentary on the fourteenth-century novel *Shuihu zhuan* (1592?, *Water Margin,* trans. J. H. Jackson,

1937). He wrote under the influence of sixteenth-century neo-Confucian thought, which stressed the role of introspection and intuition in the individual's cognitive process. His fundamental literary ideas are contained in his well-known essay "Tongxin shuo" [Childlike mind/ heart], included in *Fenshu.* In a period when technical brilliance was greatly valued, Li Zhi argued that only spontaneity and genuine sentiment can produce great literature. And in reaction to the prevalent view that literary masterworks were created only in antiquity, he pointed out that particular eras throughout history had produced their own outstanding genres and works.

Li Zhi's inclusion of drama among these genres and his explicit citation of the thirteenth-century romantic drama *Xixiang ji (Romance of the Western Chamber,* trans. S. I. Hsiung, 1936) and the novel *Water Margin* are the first attempts to include drama and the novel, the two new genres struggling for recognition, in the literary canon. His emphasis on genuine sentiment also led him, in his preface to *Water Margin,* to view the act of writing of this work as the author's outburst of indignation and frustration. In another essay, he advocated the vivid depiction of fictional characters *(chuan shen),* a concept transferred from the theory of painting. In the essay "Za shuo" [Miscellanea], also included in *Fenshu,* while commenting on three well-known dramas of the day, he delineated the differences between art—the outcome of natural spontaneity—and craft—the outcome of technical virtuosity. Li Zhi also recognized, however, the didactic value of the novel *Water Margin* because its heroes were, to him, the embodiments of important moral virtues, and he emphasized that the author's own moral outlook should be projected in a novel's characters and plot.

Li Zhi's ideas had a far-reaching impact on his contemporary literary scene. Drama criticism became involved in a heated debate between two groups: one, led by the dramatist Shen Jing (1553–1610), defended the strict adherence of dramatic lyrics to the poetic canon, while the other, led by the playwright Tang Xianzu (1550–1617), prized expression of sentiment over strict musical and prosodic norms. What is more important, Li Zhi's notion of the natural succession of dominant genres became a critical commonplace and stirred scholarly interest in hitherto neglected folk and popular texts. Some scholars, notably Yuan Hongdao (1568–1610), went so far as to claim folk songs to be of higher value than the poetry of the literati because of the songs' plain diction and genuine sentiment. Others, such as Xu Wei (1521–93) in his collection of random notes *Nanci xulu* [Account of the southern style of drama] (1557?), revealed that *nanxi,* the southern-style drama, which acquired a highly regarded artistic sophistication in the fourteenth century, actually originated from late-twelfth-century ballads "of the alleys" and popular variety shows. Investigations into the genealogy and typology of fiction also brought to light evolutionary transformations in fiction, linked to the changing social status of fiction writers. Thus Hu Yingling (1551–1602), a renowned critic of poetry, observed in his 1584 *Shaoshi shanfang bicong* [Notes from the studio of (Master) Shaoshi] that after the Tang (607–907), fiction declined as it came to be written by boorish schoolmasters instead of refined literati.

In the seventeenth century drama and fiction criticism followed two routes. In the first two decades criticism was concerned with the genres' various relationships to culture and society, high as well as popular. In this period, issues of appropriate language and rhetoric—intelligibility and cultivation—became central. From the 1640s on, however, the artistic elevation of fiction and drama became dominant issues.

The early seventeenth-century treatises on drama turned to the problem of the interrelation between *ya,* "elegance and refinement," and *su,* "vulgarity and commonness." In *Qu pin* [Ranking of the dramas], Lu Tiancheng still evaluated rustic dramas as "wanting." Yet with scholarly interest shifting from the musical to the verbal components of drama, including the spoken dialogue sections, the dramatists cum critics, such as Qi Baojia (1602–45), expected a successful dramatist to transmute the vulgar into the refined and to write neither pompous nor coarse dialogues. Ling Mengchu (1580–1644), better known as a short story writer but also an accomplished playwright and critic of southern drama, relished the use of plain, direct language because it represented the object truthfully, whereas ornate language obscured and falsified it (see his 1624 *Nan yin san lai* [Three kinds of southern sound]). Wang Jide (d. c. 1624) in his *Qu lu* [Rules of songs], published in 1624, argued for clarity and comprehensibility in the spoken dramatic parts in order to accommodate a changing audience, including not only literati and high-class women but also men, young and old, from the villages.

In fiction criticism, a highly original concept of literary and linguistic integration was expounded by Feng Menglong (1574–1646), the well-known collector, fiction writer, playwright, drama critic, and publisher of the day. In the introductions to his three collections of short stories published in the 1620s he clarified the didactic potential of fiction seen in the communicability of its language "attuned to the common ear," as well as in its affective power—both eminently suitable for the dis-

semination of moral values among commoners. His aim to create socially engaged literature catering to a wide audience is perhaps best expressed in the preface to his work of fictionalized history *Xin lieguo zhi* [A new history of the states] (after 1627), where he praised the narrative "for allowing the uneducated to share in the knowledge of the learned" *(ya su gong shang).*

From the 1640s to the end of the century critical discussions of the novel and drama turned commonly to artistic concerns. Following contemporary trends in art criticism, where systematic but fairly routine analyses attempted to reinvigorate the stagnant art of the day, several writer-critics devised new analytical methods and concepts drawn from neo-Confucian epistemology and organismic understanding of the universe, as well as from the established theories of the arts, particularly poetry, the eight-legged essay, and painting.

The seminal theoretical works on the novel during this period were written by Jin Shengtan (1610–61), Mao Zonggang (1632–1709?) with his father Mao Lun (b. c. 1610), and Zhang Zhupo (1670–98), all active in the cultural center of the day, the lower region of the Yangzi River. Jin Shengtan is usually credited with the newly devised critical apparatus that was also used, with adaptations, by the Maos and Zhang. As before, their discussions were directly attached to texts of particular novels, Jin Shengtan's in his 1641 edition of *Shuihu zhuan (Water Margin),* the Maos' in the 1679 edition of *Sanguo zhi yanyi (Romance of the Three Kingdoms,* trans. C. H. Brewitt-Taylor, 1925), and Zhang Zhupo's in his 1695 edition of *Jin ping mei (Golden Lotus,* trans. Clement Egerton, 1939, rev. ed., 1972). But the seventeenth-century scholars organized their various forms of critical discourse—prefatory material, guides on methods of reading *(dufa),* pre-chapter discussions, and interlinear or upper-margin commentaries—topically, moving from general and theoretical issues to more detailed and practical ones, with strong emphasis on the interrelation between individual parts and between parts and the whole.

This systematic and comprehensive treatment of particular novels led to the emergence of a general theory of the novel made up of three indivisible parts: discussion of the creative process, close textual analysis of the artistic features of a particular text, and an examination of reader reception. The creative process of the novelist, termed "the maker of the text," includes two related stages: a cognitive stage, during which the author investigates reality or experiences it emotionally; and a creative stage, during which the author transforms the observed phenomena into artistic paradigms. The writer thus approaches the artistic task with a premeditated overall design and is therefore likened to a tailor, chess player, builder of a house, or gardener. The thrust of Jin's, the Maos', and Zhang's textual analyses rests on the thesis that a novel is a finely constructed whole, in the Maos' and Zhang's term, a "structure" *(jiegou),* made up of components—themes, episodes, characters, sentences, words—that mutually resonate on both the syntagmatic and paradigmatic levels of the text, endowing it with rhythmical dynamism and dramatic tension. The novel is thus a highly complex organization of a stratified character with multiple relationships whose patterns are set up at the text's beginning by a small unit (e.g., a prologue or the first chapter) that is repeated, with textual variations, in larger units throughout the whole text.

In response to the thematic diversity of the analyzed novels, the four scholars had different explanations for the relationship between the story and the *fabula* of the text. Jin Shengtan was not interested in the real-life stories *(xingshi)* of the large number of outlaws who people these novels. What was most important was the pursuit of the "divine principle" *(shen li)* that organizes and unifies the text, and this he found in parallelism. Zhang Zhupo likewise warns that the effect of the real in the novel is deceptive, because it leads to misinterpretations: in this way, the novel becomes mere pornography. He argues instead that this novel of "mundane passions" *(shi qing)*—*Golden Lotus*—which describes the rise and fall of a rich merchant's large household, should be understood as an artistic expression of the natural transmutation from "hot" *(re)* to "cold" *(leng).* By analogy with the transitory character of this natural phenomenon, the reader should also understand the transitory character of human passions. To the Maos, however, the close relation between the authentic events in China's third-century history and their artistic elaboration in the novel is a virtue. They call the novel a "naturally made text" *(ziran zhi wen),* because the development of the history of the Three Kingdoms as well as of the novel's plot parallels the structure of nature in one unifying aspect, cyclical change.

Observing that young people as well as sophisticated literati read *Water Margin* for its surface story rather than for its complex artistry, Jin Shengtan introduced into the critical apparatus "guides on the methods of reading" *(dufa),* fashioned along the methods of reading Confucian classics elaborated by the neo-Confucian philosopher Zhu Xi (1130–1200). In *dufa* the scholars explained specific narrative techniques *(fa)* and other artistic methods used in the novels in order to stress that the text should be studied *(du)* in order to be understood. The process of reading was thus interpreted as a cognitive activity that should lead the reader to self-cultivation.

The efforts of Jin, the Maos, and Zhang were clearly orchestrated toward the artistic elevation of the novel and its transformation into an art form by literati and for literati. To meet this goal, the Maos and especially Jin extensively rearranged and partly rewrote the old, vulgar *(su)* editions in accordance with their theoretical tenets. It seems also to be no accident that Zhang Zhupo chose the later of two sixteenth-century editions of *Golden Lotus* because it no longer exhibited the embarrassing residua of the novel's oral origins and because the new arrangement of the first chapter suited better his tenet that the opening has a modeling function for the whole novel.

Given the close relationship between the critical pronouncements and the artistically upgraded texts of the novels, it is possible to observe that the treatises themselves underwent a substantial transformation. The critical works were now altered into auto-communicative discourses in which the theoreticians, particularly Jin and Zhang, identified themselves with their respective novels' authors, whom they endowed with identifiable fictional personae but who in fact were little known or entirely unknown historical figures. Thus, Jin and Zhang actually commented on their own creative methods and found critical commentary a fitting medium in which to express their own views or sentiments. These new directions were well in tune with the growing individualism and subjectivism that came to characterize China's seventeenth-century art.

The seventeenth-century theory of drama evolved along lines similar to the lines along which the theory of the novel developed: in the foreground was the analysis of artistic features, and the more abstract theory was formulated in conjunction with the critic's artistic practice. Jin Shengtan's critical commentary on the drama *Romance of the Western Chamber,* for which he used the same critical apparatus as he used for the study of the novel, aimed at a refinement of the vulgar thirteenth-century drama. Jin strove to bring the romantic drama within the confines of propriety by cutting out parts he considered raw and bawdy in the original and by refining its language; he treated it not as a play to be performed to a popular audience but as a literary text destined for a sophisticated reader.

This approach was radically altered by Li Yu (1610/11–80), a brilliant fiction writer, playwright, and producer of his own plays. His two chapters on drama and staging, included among other aesthetic deliberations in his 1671 *Xian qing ou ji* [Casual expressions of idle feeling], constitute the most original treatment the genre received in pre-modern times. Li Yu upset the traditional priorities by proclaiming himself to be no authority on the prosody of aria-writing (music is, for him, a technical matter) and by beginning his treatise with plot construction *(jiegou)*. Other innovations can be seen in Li Yu's emphasis on speech (which should follow certain prosodic rules) and in his concern with dramatic training and performance.

It was generally thought that Li Yu's critical works on the novel were limited to a preface and comments on the novel *The Romance of the Three Kingdoms,* but a recent attribution to him of the erotic novel *Rou putuan* (c. 1659, *The Prayer Mat of Flesh,* trans. Richard Martin, 1963) expands the sphere of his innovative ideas, since the commentaries inserted into this text appear to be his own. By this new narrative strategy, the old implicit duality of the narrator and author has been replaced by the explicit duality of author-narrator and critic. A similar device was used by the novelist Chen Chen (1616?–66?) in his novel *Shuihu hou zhuan* [Continuation of *Water Margin*] (1664), but the artistic results are different. Chen created a fictionalized persona of the author-narrator in order to express freely his own political ideas, while the persona of the critic explains, à la Jin Shengtan, the art of the novel. In contrast, Li Yu created a fictionalized self-persona in order to create a witty dialogue between the author and the critic, who not only comment on narrative methods and imagery but also take pleasure in mocking the author's craft.

The last significant contribution to seventeenth-century drama theories are the essay, prefaces, postscripts, and commentaries written by another brilliant playwright, Kong Shangren (1648–1718), to his well-known drama *Taohua shan* (1699, *The Peach Blossom Fan,* trans. Chen Shih-hsiang and Harold Acton, 1976). There he discussed the historicity of his drama; its parallel themes of love and the fate of the nation; the artistic structure, grounded in the reciprocal relations of its parts; and the correlation between spoken and sung parts.

The noticeable decline in the critical discussions of drama during the eighteenth and nineteenth centuries is usually explained by the rise of regional drama, the most elemental form of theater in China, which was unattractive to scholars. Still, the modern researcher on Chinese theater will find the handbook for actors *Liyuan yuan* [The origins of Pear Garden], written about 1819 but published in 1917, an invaluable document, because it is the only work before 1900 that describes the performing aspects of drama.

A certain stagnation of fiction criticism in the same period is probably due to other cultural changes. In the wake of literary inquisitions, launched by the first emperors of the newly enthroned Manchu dynasty (1644–1911), numerous novels and dramas were banned as seditious propaganda, and the contemptuous attitude toward fiction already given expression in certain orthodox Confucian scholars' works began to gather strength. Nevertheless, a number of critical works discussed important as well as lesser-known novels written from the sixteenth century on. Among them should be cited at least those that have appeared, in part, in excellent English translations: The Woxian caotan discourses (1803, in Rolston) on the eighteenth-century masterwork *Rulin waishi* (*The Scholars,* trans. Yang Hsien-yi and Gladys Yang, 1957); Liu Yiming's critical work (1808) on the sixteenth-century fantastic novel *Xiyou ji* ([The journey to the West], partially translated as *Monkey* by Arthur Waley, 1942); and Zhang Xinzhi's commentaries (1850) on the eighteenth-century *Honglou meng* (*Dream of the Red Chamber,* trans. Chi-Chen Wang, 1958), which is generally viewed as artistically the most successful traditional Chinese novel.

From the 1930s on, however, another critical work on the *Dream of the Red Chamber* (known as the "Zhiyanzhai [Red Ink Studio] Commentary" in one version of the manuscript dated 1754 but published only in 1928) became a cause célèbre in Chinese literary scholarship because the still-unidentified commentators were intimate friends or relatives of the novel's author, who apparently changed the manuscript versions of his novel on the critics' advice. It appears that most of the critical works written after the seventeenth century did not bring any major contribution to the theory of fiction because they followed, with some adaptations, the format and concepts established in the seventeenth century. The cultivation of the theory had, however, a strong impact on the rapid development of the novel in the seventeenth century and its artistic advancement in the eighteenth.

During the first decade of the twentieth century, theories of drama and the novel underwent a major transformation, deeply affected by a general drive for a fundamental reorientation of the whole concept of literature. This demand came from outside the cultural sphere. China's bitter conflicts with the West and its waning wealth and power brought about a deep national crisis that the politicians sought to solve by a pragmatic solution: use the techniques of the West, but preserve China's essence. Literature and its edifying role then once again became a central issue, but this time there was a pronounced willingness to look for models outside China and to break traditional norms. Upon the observation that in the West fiction occupied a high position in literary study, a large number of Chinese intellectuals conceded that fiction—embracing the novel, the short story, drama, and the storyteller's oral narrative—was the paramount literary genre. The reasons for this claim, however, varied vastly from critic to critic.

Yan Fu (1853–1921), Xia Zengyou (1865–1924), and primarily Liang Qichao (1873–1929) advocated the didactic function of fiction because they believed that fiction was capable of transforming the whole nation. They took this idea from the fundamental tenet of orthodox Confucian aesthetics that "literature conveys Dao," but they explained that what makes fiction superior to the Confucian classics is its ample, comprehensible language and its power to affect readers emotionally. To explain this power, Liang Qichao adopted several concepts from Buddhism and formulated a sophisticated theory of reception in which he explained the process of reading as a cognitive activity culminating in the reader's emulation of the fictional hero. He saw fiction as the effective medium for transforming the mind of the people and, ultimately, the whole nation. Dissatisfied with what he called the "poisonous" ideas in the Chinese novel, he called for a "revolution of fiction" and for the creation of "new fiction" that would disseminate democratic thought.

Liang Qichao's theory was inspired by the Japanese concept of "political fiction," which flourished during the modernizing of Japan in the 1870s and was inspired, in turn, by the writing of Edward Bulwer-Lytton and Benjamin Disraeli in England. Elements from Chinese and foreign cultural traditions were reconciled also in Wang Guowei's rather different theories. Wang Guowei (1877–1927), one of the most erudite and versatile Chinese thinkers of his time, was an avid student of IMMANUEL KANT, ARTHUR SCHOPENHAUER, and FRIEDRICH NIETZSCHE in his youth, and he revitalized Chinese theories of the novel through Western philosophical aesthetics.

Since Chinese dramas and novels usually culminate in a reconciliatory denouement, Schopenhauer's concept of tragedy (in his 1819 *Die Welt als Wille und Vorstellung*) as the highest form of literary art was a provocative inspiration for a Chinese scholar. In 1904 Wang wrote a brilliant study, *"Honglou meng" pinglun* [A critique of *Dream of the Red Chamber*], where he used Schopenhauer's concept of tragedy as a basis for concluding that this Chinese novel has no artistic equal. According to Wang, the truth that humanity bears responsibility for its own suffering is conveyed in essence in the opening chapter of the novel, where the mythological Stone expresses his will *(yu)* to be transformed into a human

being despite the bleak prospect of lifetime suffering. It is therefore no coincidence, says Wang, that no character in the novel affirms the will to live without ordeal and that numerous characters commit suicide to be released from this will. In the end, however, argues Wang, Bayyu—the incarnate Stone and the novel's protagonist—arrives through his own travail at a spiritual awakening that enables him to be released from suffering by his pursuit of asceticism.

Through an acceptance of Western philosophy, Wang freed himself from the negative view of the novel and drama promulgated by orthodox Confucianism, and from 1908 to 1912 he included in his researches the early Chinese drama and the musical forms of storyteller narratives. He collected an enormous number of historical materials on these subjects, laying foundations for modern studies in these fields. In his last work on drama, *Song Yuan xiqi kao* [On Song and Yuan drama] (1912), he identified seven celebrated Chinese plays as tragedies, although he had earlier lamented the lack of a Chinese tragic drama.

Huang Moxi (1869?–1914?) is the least-known theoretician of fiction in this transitional period, despite the striking proximity of his ideas to the modern Western understanding of literary art. He published his views in the inaugural issue of the magazine *Xiaoshuo lin* [Forest of fiction] (1907). In contradistinction to many of his contemporaries, he regarded fiction not as a vehicle of ideology but as an artistic construct: the writer draws the material from the actual world, but it is the artistic drive that urges the artist to create. The fictional work results, therefore, from the artist's imagination, but its composition has specific, often imperceptible, artistic norms that are frequently grounded in parallelism, as, he pointed out, in the *bagu wen* essays. The reader's reception of a fictional work is thus different from his or her reception of a nonfictional (e.g., philosophical) work, and the role of fiction in society is not didactic but aesthetic. In 1907 Huang Moxi invoked G. W. F. HEGEL's philosophy to support his requirement that fiction be able to satisfy aesthetic needs, but little is known about his knowledge of other Western thinkers.

By the middle of the second decade of the twentieth century, however, Huang's pioneering speculations shared the fate of those of the many brilliant Chinese critics and theoreticians of fiction and drama from the preceding centuries. Although Jin Shengtan's and the Maos' editions of *Water Margin* and the *Romance of the Three Kingdoms* became canonized and widely read in the modern period, pushing the older recensions into oblivion, their theoretical work seems to have been totally forgotten during this period. Zhang Zhupo's and Li Yu's studies met a similar fate following the ban and physical destruction of Zhang Zhupo's critical edition of *Golden Lotus* and Li Yu's literary studies during various literary inquisitions. The treatises of Jin Shengtan, the Maos, and Li Yu were rediscovered in the 1920s, while Zhang Zhupo reemerged only in the 1970s. The discovery of the critical texts by these major seventeenth-century scholars did not, however, warrant an immediate recognition of their drive toward the creation of an autochthonous theory of fiction and drama. Since their writings were, at best, taken as mere philological commentaries to particular literary works, even preeminent Chinese scholars did not find it appropriate to include their works in the histories of pre-modern China's literary thought. Only in the last three decades of the twentieth century, when their critical texts were once again published, have Chinese scholars and Western Sinologists begun to recognize the theoretical importance of these critics' work. Thus traditional Chinese theories of drama and the novel will finally be accorded their place in the canon of Chinese aesthetics.

Milena Doleželová-Velingerová

Huang Lin and Han Tongwen, eds., *Zhongguo lidai xiaoshuo lunzhu xuan* [A selection of traditional Chinese discourses on fiction] (2 vols., 1982–85); *Ming Qing xiaoshuo xuba xuan* [A selection of prefaces and postscripts to Ming and Qing fiction] (ed., Dalian Tushuguan Cankaobu, 1983); *Zhongguo gudian xiqu lunzhu jicheng* [A compendium of classical Chinese discourses on drama] (10 vols., 1959).

C. D. Alison Bailey, "The Mediating Eye: Mao Lun, Mao Zonggang, and the Reading of *Sanguo zhi yanyi*" (Ph.D. diss., U. of Toronto, 1990); Jean-François Billeter, *Li Zhi, philosophe maudit (1527–1602)* (1979); Duncan M. Campbell, "The Techniques of Narrative: Mao Tsung-kang (fl. 1661) and *The Romance of the Three Kingdoms*," *Tamkang Review* 16 (1986); Milena Doleželová-Velingerová, C. D. Alison Bailey, and Hua L. Wu, *Seventeenth-Century Chinese Theories of the Novel* (forthcoming); Patrick Hanan, *The Chinese Vernacular Short Story* (1981), *The Invention of Li Yu* (1988); Robert E. Hegel, *The Novel in Seventeenth-Century China* (1981); C. T. Hsia, "Yen Fu and Liang Ch'i-ch'au as Advocates of New Fiction" (Rickett); Bauzhen Huang, Cai Zhongxiang, and Cheng Fuwang, *Ahongguo wenxue lilun shi* [A history of Chinese literary criticism], vols. 3 and 4 (1987); Andrew H. Plaks, ed., *Chinese Narrative: Critical and Theoretical Essays* (1977), *The Four Masterworks of the Ming Novel: Ssu ta ch'i shu* (1987); Adele A. Rickett, ed., *Chinese Approaches to Literature from Confucius to Liang Ch'i-ch'ao* (1978); Boris L. Riftin, "Teorija kitajskoj dramy (XII–naealo XVII vv.)" [Theory of Chinese drama (from the twelfth to the early seventeenth century)], *Problemy literatury i estetiki v stranax Vostoka* (1964); David L. Rolston, ed., *How to Read the Chinese Novel* (1990); David T. Roy, "Chang Chu-p'o's Commentary on the *Chin P'ing Mei*," *Chinese Narrative: Critical and Theoretical Essays* (1977); Dieter Tschanz, "Ein illegitimes Genre: Zu den Auseinandersetzungen um die fiktionale Literatur in niederer Literatursprache im vormodernen China, 1550–1750: Eine Dokumentation" (Ph.D. diss., U. of Zurich, 1990); John C. Y. Wang, "The *Chih-yen Chai Commentary* and the *Dream of the Red Chamber*: A Literary Study" (Rickett), *Chin Sheng-t'an* (1972); Wang Xianpei and Zhou Weimin, *Ming Qing xiaoshuo lilun piping shi* [A history of Ming and Qing fiction theory and criticism] (1988); Hua L. Wu, "Jin Shengtan (1608–1661): A Founder of a Traditional Chinese Theory of the Novel" (Ph.D. diss., U. of Toronto, 1993).

3. Twentieth Century

The twentieth century has been a time of unprecedented tumult in China, intellectually, politically, and socially. For a variety of reasons, literature and theories of literature in particular have at most times been close to the center of intellectual and political contention in modern China, the theories at once being shaped by their times as well as contributing substantially to various visions of what the new China was to become. It is often difficult, in fact, to tell where literary theory ends and social and political theorizing begins. Perhaps the most remarkable thing about the mainstream of literary criticism in China after the late 1910s is the extent to which it has consciously been engaged in an iconoclastic project designed to overturn what it perceives as the pernicious legacy of traditional literary practice and literary ideas. The set of these departures from past practice is conventionally named after a particularly influential ·student demonstration that took place on May 4, 1919. What has come to be called the May Fourth Movement (also known as the New Culture Movement) signifies all the reforms undertaken in China from as early as 1915 through the early 1920s and, by implication at least, the full range of reformist and revolutionary initiatives that have marked modern Chinese thought as a whole.

At least up until the mid-1980s there was a convenient narrative of the development of theories of literature in China after May Fourth that had wide currency in China. The story dates back to 1917, when Hu Shi's (1891–1962) first calls for a literature composed in the vernacular language were published in the Beijing magazine *New Youth,* edited by Chen Duxiu (1879–1942). From the official perspective, literary theory in this period was a tale of the development of a realism that has become ever more consonant with the scientific view of reality espoused by the Marxist perspective of the Community party. In this view, the various left-wing deviations, such as the anti-rightist movement of the late 1950s and the Cultural Revolution of the late 1960s, represent merely temporary interruptions in this account of continuous progress. It is clear that Party and governmental coercion contributed substantially to the widespread circulation of this view. It is, however, remarkable how even oppositional writers and literary intellectuals tended to produce a narrative that was very similar to the official version in those brief periods when it was possible to advance a critique of orthodox literary thought. The only real difference was that the dissenters tended to regard the Party and/or Marxist ideology as the primary impediments to the progress toward the realization of realism.

This version of the progression of literary thought obviously occludes many of its more interesting developments. But there was significant compliance by the main body of modern Chinese critics and authors, later enforced by the official organs of the Left after 1930 and, from 1949 until about 1985, by the government itself. This story does, therefore, tell us more about the general direction of modern Chinese literary theory than any other account could. But we cannot forget that this discourse was never as absolute as it depicted itself to be, and it is rather poor at accounting for both the specifics of the literature produced and the complexities of the theory itself. Thus, in the years after 1985, as the official discourse rapidly lost its ability to persuade, features of literary thought that had been so carefully excluded by the official story have begun to come to light. The fact remains, however, that probably the most notable thing about literary theory in modern China is the extent to which the official version of literary thought, or something very much like it, maintained its influence, not just in criticism, but as guide to the creation of literary work. Given the politically interested orthodoxy that resulted, modern Chinese literary theory has tended in the main to be uninspiring, eventually an impediment rather than an encouragement to literary innovation.

Many of the ideas about literature that May Fourth represented to itself as its own discoveries had in fact been prefigured in the last fifteen years of the Qing dynasty, a period that began after China's 1895 defeat at the hands of Japan. The stunning evidence of the smaller country's rapid modernization stimulated a new generation of Chinese intellectuals to look to Japan for ways to adapt to the pressures exerted by the imperialist West. This process of adaptation was understood as being emblematized more than anything else by a new willingness to appropriate Western ideas concerning social structure and culture. Among the more resonant ideas adapted at the time was the notion of literature *(wenxue)* as a general and autonomous field of inquiry extending over a number of written genres, replacing the focus on the rhetoric of specific genres that had characterized the study of writing in the post–Song dynasty period. Within this new and comprehensive field of literature two ideas surfaced in the late Qing that were to exert vast influence for the rest of the century: that literary forms evolved through time and that a new and effective vernacular literature would be required to bring a broader spectrum of people into a revitalized polity. The critic Liang Qichao (1837–1929) is most prominently associated with the latter, or popularization, trend.

In the final years of the empire, however, for all the pressure to create new popular forms, writers held to the cultural primacy of the traditional elite literary (or classical) language that for over two thousand years had been regarded as the sole vehicle for serious literary expression. If anything, the literary style was accorded an even higher value in these years, as scholars such as Liu Shipei (1884–1919) and Zhang Binglin (1868–1936) seized upon the old language as a "national essence" that would remain as that ultimate signifier of Chineseness when so much else was being remolded using explicitly Western models. There was thus a two-tiered model for literary creativity at the end of the Qing: a vernacular suitable for the novels and meant to bring the semieducated into political and cultural life, and a continuation of the old literary language for works written by and for the educated.

Since there was so much precedent for it, the call for adoption of the vernacular language per se did not create much of a stir when it was first published in *New Youth* in 1917. Hu Shi, Chen Duxiu, Liu Fu (1891–1934), Qian Xuantong (1887–1939), and the other advocates of language reform, however, insisted upon taking the further step of championing the vernacular as the universal Chinese written language. In other words, the proponents of reform held that the vernacular was no longer to be simply a tool for educating the masses; it was also to be the means of written communication for everyone, from the very learned to those with only a rudimentary education. By stressing the radicalism of their advocacy, those who proposed this idea at once drew attention to their project and established a position from which they felt they could open the floodgates for the wholesale emulation of a wide variety of Western literary ideas. Chen Duxiu in 1917 wrote: "I do not mind being an enemy of all old-fashioned scholars in the country and raising to great heights the banner of 'the Army of Literary Revolution' . . . Destroy aristocratic literature which is nothing but literary chiseling and flattery" ("On Literary Revolution," *Sources of Chinese Tradition,* ed. William Theodore DeBary, 2 vols., 1960, 2:162).

The other principal feature of modern criticism dating back to the late Qing that received renewed impetus after May Fourth was the setting of literary history on an evolutionary track. Reformers and revolutionaries alike based their thinking on the notion that all literary genres and ideas are part of a universal historical process. Evolutionary theory was probably the most influential of the ideologies imported into China after 1895 and would prove to be the most tenacious. Its initial appeal lay in its apparent guarantee that even backward China would eventually catch up with the modern West. The disadvantage of this theory as borrowed from such thinkers as Thomas Henry Huxley and Herbert Spencer, however, lay in the social Darwinian aspect of a code that also guaranteed that some social formations would fail to meet the test and were thus bound to expire. This brought with it the fear that the backwardness evident in Chinese society and culture foretold eventual doom for the Chinese nation as a whole. "Madman's Diary," a story written in the vernacular by Lu Xun (pen name of Zhou Shuren, 1881–1936) and published in 1918, represented the Darwinist thesis with great force. This and other of Lu Xun's stories from this early period thus became almost universally regarded as essential theoretical guides to the creation of literature in the years after 1920.

From the Chinese perspective, then, the anxiety at the heart of the evolutionary scheme was that China was behind the "world standard" so evidently set by the advanced Western powers. Some sort of extraordinary effort was thus required of all facets of Chinese culture and society to catch up to this standard. Evolutionary thought found its literary counterpart in the sequence of literary terms "classical-romantic-realism-naturalism," set out by Chen Duxiu as early as 1915, a scheme that dominated literary thought in the early May Fourth years. In this formula Chinese literature was seen as frozen somewhere between classicism and romanticism, and realism thus became the "logical" goal of the most influential segment of Chinese critical opinion from May Fourth even into the 1980s. In such a context, however, for all the attempts to equate it with simple representation of ordinary life, realism was also seen as just beyond reach. It

also seemed to require a radical suspension of old rules if it was to be brought into being.

One of the principal needs of the iconoclast literary movement was to differentiate the legacy of the past from the needs of the present so as to create the perception of need for radical change. Such advocates of cultural reform as Fu Sinian (1896–1950) and Zhou Zuoren (1885–1967), Lu Xun's brother, in the period between 1918 and 1920 took a step beyond mere promotion of the vernacular by finding the problems they saw in all Chinese humanistic discourse to be more fundamental than any such surface phenomenon as linguistic expression. In articles such as "Humane Literature" and "Literature of the Common People" by Zhou and "Vernacular Literature and Psychological Reform" by Fu, Chinese culture was diagnosed as being marked by a fundamental lack of seriousness, with the result that writing and thinking had become frozen into unproductive stereotypes. The vision of an airtight past impinging upon any possibility of natural evolution created the intellectual need for a complete transformation of literary ideology.

Negating the past was the easy part of May Fourth literary theory: the various factions largely agreed on the nature of the problem. Far more difficult was the task of constructing a set of ideas that would meet the needs of the modern age. A number of groups sprang up advocating different notions of change. The Society for Literary Research was founded at the end of 1920 and included such eminent critics and writers as Guo Shaoyu (1893–1984), Shen Yanbing, better known as Mao Dun (1896–1981), Wang Tongzhao (1897–1957), Ye Shaojun (1894–1988), Zheng Zhenduo (1898–1958), and Zhou Zuoren. They set as their task the careful scrutiny of Western literary ideas. Since they took as part of their task the need to avoid the irrelevancy to actual life that they assumed to be the essence of traditional literature, the rhetoric of engagement they adopted had much in common with theories of realism and naturalism that they were translating from foreign languages. Thus, while none of their official manifestoes advocated realism or naturalism, their common advocacy of "literature for life," combined with the fact that many of the prominent members of the society advocated realism and/or naturalism, led to the easy assumption among the literate public that the society stood for realism.

Meanwhile, another group of young Chinese writers, this one based principally in Japan, established themselves as the Creation Society. Members of this association had come to the conclusion that the need for self-expression was more important than any careful attempt to match literature to social needs. Founded in July 1921, the society included Cheng Fangwu (1897–1984), Guo Moruo (1892–1978), Tian Han (1898–1968), Yu Dafu (1896–1945), and Zhang Ziping (1893–?). A good deal of superficial sloganeering on the virtues of romantic self-expression masked the fact that the Creation Society shared many ideas with the Society for Literary Research. Principal among these common ideas was a disgust with the Neo-Confucian idea of *wen yi zai dao,* "literature as the vehicle of the way." Both groups took this phrase as the embodiment of the Confucian didacticism they saw as having been so damaging to literary expression of all sorts. Nonetheless, by 1923 a positive loathing had sprung up between the two groups, a foretaste of the personal antagonism that came to mark literary debate in modern China.

Aside from a few rather poorly reasoned attacks, traditional men of letters were never able to launch a concerted response to the May Fourth critique. For all the apparent unanimity with which these new, European ideas were used as clubs for beating traditional ideas about literature and practices of writing, there was one notable effort to resuscitate classicism. Ironically enough, this steadfast defense of the values of tradition was launched by a group of scholars most of whom had received their training in the United States, many from the neoclassicist Irving Babbitt at Harvard (see NEW HUMANISM). Founded by Hu Xiansu (1893–1968), Mei Guangdi (1890–1945), and Wu Mi (b. 1894) in 1922, *Xueheng* [Critical review] attacked what it saw as the fashion for disparaging literature written in the classical language. Its defense of classical values met with little response beyond overt hostility in the iconoclastic atmosphere of the 1920s, however, and the journal soon expired.

The Bolshevik revolution in Russia had from the beginning been attractive to Chinese intellectuals. As the 1920s drew on, this attraction became both stronger and more concrete, what with Soviet advisors in China assisting a reorganized Guomindang (Nationalist Party) as well as providing ideological backing for a newly founded Chinese Communist party. Many of the most prominent literary reformers, such as Chen Duxiu and Mao Dun, became involved in organizing the new party, and literary thinkers in general were increasingly intrigued by the vision of social meliorism that Marxism offered. Marxism came to play a large role in the transformation of Chinese politics in the years between 1925 and 1927, when the newly militant Guomindang set about its military campaign to unify China under its own rule. The Marxian view of history fitted neatly into the evolutionary pattern that already had such deep roots in modern Chinese thought and explained to many how the events

then in progress were to unfold. The conversion of so many of the more prominent members of the Creation Society to Marxism in these years is but the most striking evidence of Marxism's broadening allure.

If anything, the violent expulsion of the Communists from their alliance with the Guomindang in 1927 increased the currency of Marxist ideas among Chinese writers and instantiated a general antipathy to the new ruling party among intellectuals. A new generation of young critics such as Qian Xingcun, also known as A Ying (1900–1977), led an assault on selected writers and ideas of the May Fourth period. Qian selected as his target Lu Xun, the brilliant writer whose stories were so influential. Qian's accusation that Lu Xun had been mired in anachronistic portraits of traditional ways clearly stung a writer who had been universally considered a pungently innovative voice only a few years before. That Lu Xun responded by immersing himself in a study of Marxism and Marxist literary theory was characteristic of the period.

Most of those involved in this squabbling among dissident writers were not happy that energy was being expended in this fashion. Neither were those responsible for cultural policy within the Communist party, and by the end of 1929 a number of the feuding voices agreed to work together. This led to the founding, in February 1930, of the League of Left-Wing Writers, a group that soon included such people as Ding Ling (1904–85), Feng Xuefeng (1903–76), Guo Moruo, Hu Feng (1902–85), Lu Xun, Mao Dun, Qian Xingcun, Qu Qiubai (1899–1935), Tian Han, Yu Dafu, and Zhou Yang (1908–89). As the two most prominent writers, Lu Xun and Mao Dun played leading roles as spokespersons for what the Party clearly regarded as an organization existing primarily to propagate its ideas about how literature should serve the purposes of the revolution. In the years that followed the founding of the league, Lu Xun and Qu Qiubai (a former Party leader) were to issue forth with numerous brilliantly written polemics in support of league policy. These polemics were devoted predominantly to promoting writing for a mass audience through more popular themes and writing styles and adhering to the Party's notion of "proletarian revolution." There were various attempts by independent critics in the years between 1927 and 1937 to establish theories of writing separate from Party policy. Whether these efforts called for a focus on aesthetics, continued attention to Western theory, or simply alternative voices, the league critics were generally able to portray all such initiatives as elitist attempts to recuperate the days when the educated communicated with one another in their own inaccessible literary language.

When another war with Japan ensued in 1937, then, the literary community was already habituated to calls to support efforts of political and social mobilization. Once again in alliance with the Guomindang, the Communist party now had a broader platform from which to propagate its ideas about literature. While the Guomindang proved unable to present a compelling message, the Communists effectively built upon their expanding territorial base and patriotic appeals to amplify certain ideas first broached by Qu Qiubai. One of the first calls Mao Zedong (1893–1976) made was for a reinvigoration of national forms at the expense of ideas about literary theories imported during the May Fourth period. In advocating this repudiation of May Fourth ideology, Mao was clearly following Qu's perception that May Fourth vernacular represented a "new classical language" because it had incorporated elements of Western syntax and a whole set of neologisms. Mao's invocation of this argument caused much consternation among veteran critics, including such leftist stalwarts as Mao Dun and Hu Feng, a follower of Lu Xun, by then deceased.

Mao Zedong's most decisive move into literary criticism came with his talks at the so-called Yan'an Conference on Literature and Art of May 1942. He sought on this occasion to give a definitive shape to literary activity in those regions controlled by the Communists. More than anything else, Mao broke down the notion of literary universals into class-specific attributes. All writing had to become conscious of the fact that it was aimed at a particular audience. In this way Mao reinstated the distinction between a literature for the intellectual elite and one for the ordinary people. And by stressing the fact of wartime exigency, he set forth the notion that mobilizing the masses had to take priority. He also established a distinction between the literature of critique, appropriate to zones controlled by the Guomindang, and a literature intent upon extolling the achievements of the workers, peasants, and soldiers and, by implication, the party that spoke in their name. It is perhaps needless to add that he sought to establish the latter in those areas of China under Communist control.

With the coming to power of the Communist party in 1949, the "Talks at the Yan'an Conference" became official policy, or more properly, the "Talks" became the official justification for complete Party dictation in literary matters. Anyone who tried to resist this dictation, as Hu Feng did in the early 1950s, was ruthlessly crushed through massive campaigns of denunciation that pointedly included the dissenting writer or critic's close associates. The 20 years after 1949 thus witnessed an ever-tightening grip of Maoist ideas in the literary arena. This mode of treating the literary world achieved an extreme in the Cultural Revolution, which reached a crescendo in 1966–69 that saw virtually all modern Chinese writers and their works banished as having been part of a nefarious campaign to restore the old order. The sole exception among veteran writers was Lu Xun, whose writings had been rendered politically correct by swaddling them in an expanse of Maoist exegesis.

With Mao's death in 1976, those who had been in charge of the radical policies of the Cultural Revolution were soon brought down. The campaign against the Maoist legacy that ensued enlisted literature most prominently in its ranks. Notions of critical realism that Maoist literary theory had for years tried to transmute into various formulas for representing the inevitability of progression into Marxism suddenly came back in full force. After reaching a peak in the early spring of 1979, the liberalization engendered by this critique was abruptly reined in by the Party. While the next decade was marked by alternating liberalizations and Party crackdowns on dissent, the overall trend was toward diminution of intellectual control. After 1985, in particular, literary criticism seems to have regained a life of its own, with a renewed appetite for trying out a variety of theories, some borrowed, such as modernism, and some domestic, such as the "seeking roots" movement of 1985.

The years before 1989 were replete with new ventures and experimentation in all sectors of literary life. Characteristically, Liu Zaifu (b. 1941), a high official in the literary wing of the Academy of Social Sciences, sought to revive the notion of authorial subjectivity that had been anathema to Party literary policy for over 40 years. While the Tiananmen incident on June 4, 1989, certainly brought on a wave of political repression, literary criticism seems to have been allowed to continue much in the same direction it had taken since 1985. The years since 1989 have seen a discourse on literature that has become more like that of the West, as the theories that have circulated in North America and Europe since the late 1960s are translated into Chinese and naturalized into domestic literary theory. Most recently, however, Chinese literary criticism has taken on a reflexive tone, once again taking up the question of its relationship with literary events outside China. The issue of how the particular literary theories and practices of China fit into the literary "universals" of the rest of the world, a matter so bedeviled by political overdetermination through the years since May Fourth, has once again come to the surface.

Theodore Huters

Beijing daxue et al., eds., *Wenxue yundong shiliao xuan* [A selection of historical materials on the literary movement] (5 vols., 1979); John Berninghausen and Ted Huters, eds., *Revolutionary Literature in China: An Anthology* (1976); Howard Goldblatt, ed., *Chinese Literature for the 1980s: The Fourth Congress of Writers and Artists* (1982); Bonnie S. McDougall, *Mao Zedong's "Talks at the Yan'an Conference on Literature and Art"* (1980); Zhao Jiabi, ed., *Zhongguo xin wenxue daxi* [A comprehensive anthology of China's new literature], vols. 1–2, 10 (1936).

Marston Anderson, *The Limits of Realism: Chinese Fiction in the Revolutionary Period* (1990); Chow Tse-tsung, *The May Fourth Movement: Intellectual Revolution in Modern China* (1960); Marián Gálik, *The Genesis of Modern Chinese Literary Criticism* (1980), *Mao Tun [Mao Dun] and Modern Chinese Literary Criticism* (1969), *Milestones in Sino-Western Literary Confrontation (1898–1979)* (1986); C. T. Hsia, *A History of Modern Chinese Fiction* (1961, 2d ed., 1971); Leo Ou-fan Lee, ed., *Lu Xun and His Legacy* (1985); Bonnie S. McDougall, *The Introduction of Western Literary Theories into Modern China, 1919–1925* (1971); Paul Pickowicz, *Marxist Literary Thought in China: The Influence of Ch'ü Ch'iu-bai [Qu Qiubai]* (1981); David Pollard, *A Chinese Look at Literature: The Literary Values of Chou Tso-jen [Zhou Zuoren] in Relation to the Tradition* (1973); Jaroslav Prusek, *The Lyrical and the Epic: Studies of Modern Chinese Literature* (1980); Yi Chu Wang, *Chinese Intellectuals and the West, 1872–1949* (1966).

CHOMSKY, NOAM

Avram Noam Chomsky (b. 1928) was born in Philadelphia. As a student at the University of Pennsylvania he studied mathematics, philosophy, and linguistics. In the early 1950s he pursued research in linguistics as a junior fellow at Harvard, where ROMAN JAKOBSON was then teaching, and since 1955 he has held various posts at the Massachusetts Institute of Technology. Since the early 1960s his influence within the field of linguistics has been unrivaled by any other living scholar. He has also become known to a wider public through his writings on political issues.

Chomsky's linguistic thought has its roots in structuralism, in the broadest sense of that term. ("Structuralist" linguistics, in this broad sense, includes but must be distinguished from the more narrowly conceived "structural" linguistics of his immediate American predecessors, to which Chomsky was opposed. It also must be distinguished from the STRUCTURALISM that derives primarily from the work of FERDINAND DE

SAUSSURE.) Structuralism in linguistics rests on the proposition that underlying the observable phenomena of language there are discrete, determinate entities analyzable as systems of correlations between "forms" and "meanings." Structuralists differ in terms of the ontological status they ascribe to linguistic systems: one must distinguish "psychologistic" from "nonpsychologistic" forms of structuralism. Psychologistic structuralists suppose that in analyzing linguistic systems they are investigating some aspect of the *realia* of linguistic behavior. That is because they take linguistic behavior (i.e., the use of language) to be primarily a matter of implementing such a system. Nonpsychologistic structuralists make no such assumption. Saussure was a psychologistic structuralist: the Saussurean *langue* is an idiosynchronic system of signs held to exist in the collective mind of a linguistic community, among whose members communication is possible in virtue of their shared knowledge of the system. In contrast, in the versions of structuralism subsequently espoused in a North American tradition whose most prominent exponents are Leonard Bloomfield (1887–1949) and Zellig Harris (b. 1909), linguistic form (but not meaning) is analyzed in terms of units identified at various descriptive "levels" (phonemes, morphemes, etc.), without consideration of whether or in what sense the units are "real" for the human beings whose language is under analysis. Chomsky, who was a pupil of Harris, may be seen as having re-psychologized structuralist linguistics.

The domain within which Harris wields his analytic procedures is a corpus of attested utterances taken, for purposes of the analysis, as representing the whole language. The result is a set of statements about the distribution of the different classes of unit contained in the corpus. Chomsky's first step was to invert Harris's procedures by treating these distributional statements as *rules* governing the synthesis or prediction of utterances. That is, instead of saying, for example, that a corpus of English phrases such as "the dog," "a cat," and "some chickens" shows that a class of items called "determiners" *(a, some, the)* can appear immediately before a class of items called "nouns" *(cat, chickens, dog),* Chomsky would say that application of a rule NP → Det N (i.e., a Noun Phrase may consist of a Determinator followed by a Noun) generates an *indefinitely large number* of well-formed English noun phrases. This reversal of the direction in which linguistic description proceeds opened the way to an analogy between the linguist's task in drawing up the set of rules that would generate the infinitely large set of utterances (sentences) of which a language consists and the child's task in learning that language. The child's task is clearly not to acquire a fixed corpus of utterances, but it might conceivably be a matter of acquiring a set of principles (generative rules) enabling him or her to produce and understand indefinitely many utterances. Thus Chomsky's generative grammar was from the outset linked to a theory of language acquisition; and structuralist linguistics was once again concerned with the relationship between languages and their speaker-hearers.

In Chomsky's earliest writings the key elements of a generative grammar were a set of "phrase-structure rules" and a set of "transformational rules." Simple active declarative sentences ("fish swim," "lions eat meat," "the dog chased the rabbit") were treated as basic and, very roughly speaking, were generated by phrase-structure rules alone. So "fish swim" is a sentence consisting of a noun phrase (NP) and a verb phrase (VP). The NP, in turn, consists of a noun ("fish"); the VP, of a verb ("swim"). Sentences related to these in being versions that are negative, interrogative, passive, and so on (e.g., "fish don't swim," "do lions eat meat?" "the rabbit was chased by the dog"), were derived from the output of the phrase-structure rules (the "deep structure") by transformations that altered the phrase structure in various ways. As the title of Chomsky's first book, *Syntactic Structures* (1957), suggests, the emphasis was on syntax (as opposed to phonology or semantics), and this has remained his main concern ever since. Chomsky's detailed ideas about syntactic theory have changed radically over the years: suffice it to say that the main trend has been to elaborate the scope and complexity of the phrase-structure rules at the expense of the transformations.

Of more general import is the way that interest in the speaker's mental representation of language has latterly come to eclipse the description of "languages" altogether. The objective is now to understand the structure of the language faculty, that is, the function-specific mental "organ" that the child brings with him into the world, which, given appropriate environmental stimuli, "grows" to reach a "steady state" envisaged as underlying mature native-speaker control of a natural language. But a natural language itself is an institutionalized cultural product determined by many factors besides its speakers' language organs. Chomsky has abandoned his stipulative definition of a language as "the set of sentences generated by the rules of a (mentally represented) grammar"; instead, he recognizes that what he claims to be mentally represented—and what he is primarily interested in—is by no means congruent with what we ordinarily call a language.

Chomsky himself has said little or nothing about literature or about how his theorizing might be relevant to its study. He has frequently stressed what he calls the creative aspect of language use, but he means by this, for instance, that although the English-speaking reader has very probably never encountered this particular sentence before, it poses no problem of interpretation. That is, his or her grammar recognizes it as syntactically well formed and assigns it an unproblematic semantic "reading." "Creativity," in this sense, is simply a corollary of the fact that the rules of a grammar generate infinitely many sentences. But Chomsky has nothing to say about genuinely innovative uses of language—creativity that consists in going beyond what is generated by the rules—ultimately, perhaps, because radical innovation calls into question the fundamental structuralist tenets of the enterprise. Anyone who thinks (or thought) of English as a fixed structure specifiable, in advance of any particular use of it, by a determinate set of rules can only say of, for example, *Finnegans Wake* that it is not written in English.

Not that literary theory has not been influenced by Chomskyan linguistics. On the contrary, it has given rise to such studies as generative metrics and generative STYLISTICS, for example. However, it is fair to say that such extensions of his thought have never had the benefit of Chomsky's personal involvement, that they derive their inspiration from stages in his intellectual odyssey now in the past, and that their connection with his linguistics, which is mainly a matter of taking over terminology and descriptive formalisms, is at best tangential. *Au fond* Chomsky is concerned to elucidate (one aspect of) the biological basis for all language use. The creation of works of literary art requires that biological basis but in that respect is no different from the many other purposes for which we deploy our linguistic capacities.

Nigel Love

See also LINGUISTICS AND LANGUAGE.

Noam Chomsky, *Aspects of the Theory of Syntax* (1965), *Cartesian Linguistics: A Chapter in the History of Rationalist Thought* (1966), *Current Issues in Linguistic Theory* (1964), *Knowledge of Language: Its Nature, Origin, and Use* (1986), *Language and Mind* (1968, rev. ed., 1972), *Language and Problems of Knowledge: The Managua Lectures* (1988), *Language and Responsibility* (1979), *Rules and Representations* (1980), *Syntactic Structures* (1957); Noam Chomsky and Morris Halle, *The Sound Pattern of English* (1968); Massimo Piattelli-Palmarini, ed., *Language and Learning: The Debate between Jean Piaget and Noam Chomsky* (1980).

George L. Dillon, *Language Processing and the Reading of Literature* (1973); Stanley Fish, "What Is Stylistics and Why Are They Saying Such Terrible Things about It?" *Approaches to Poetics* (ed. Seymour B. Chatman, 1973); Roger Fowler, "Style and the Concept of Deep Structure," *Journal of Literary Semantics* 1 (1972); Morris Halle and Samuel J. Keyser, *English Stress: Its Form, Its Growth, and Its Role in Verse* (1971); Zellig S. Harris, *Methods in Structural Linguistics* (1951); Richard Ohmann, "Generative Grammars and the Concept of Literary Style," *Word* 20 (1964); Robert W. Rieber, ed., *Dialogues on the Psychology of Language and Thought* (1983); James Thorne, "Generative Grammars and Stylistic Analysis," *New Horizons in Linguistics* (ed. John Lyons, 1970).

CIXOUS, HÉLÈNE

Hélène Cixous (b. 1937), whose formidable production includes 23 volumes of poems, 6 of essays, 5 historical plays, and a number of articles, is best known in America for "The Laugh of the Medusa" and *The Newly Born Woman*. In France, however, she has been a far more politicized and controversial figure, as was evident in May 1968 when she emerged as a radical academic in the "revolutionary" university of Vincennes, a theorist writing for the Women's Press, and an avant-garde fiction writer. Through her own innovative reading and writing, she tries to dismantle patriarchal authority in the academy, including the institution of cultural criticism and theory. She attacks the binary system to which logocentrism subjects thought in the Western world and questions the solidarity between logocentrism and phallocentrism that posits woman as the repressed and ensures the system's functioning.

The focus of Cixous's discourse is *écriture féminine* ("feminine writing"), a project begun in the middle 1970s when Cixous, LUCE IRIGARAY, JULIA KRISTEVA, and Catherine Clément, among others, began reading texts in the particular contexts of women's experience. Their general strategy, at odds with biologically based readings of SIGMUND FREUD, reflected a notion of femininity and feminine writing based not on a "given" essence of male and female characteristics but on culturally achieved conventions, such as "openness" in feminine texts as a lack of repressive patterning. This theorizing, pursued in the politicized French atmosphere during DECONSTRUCTION and cultural revolution, prompted questions about how "writing" deploys power, how to read a feminine (nonpatriarchal) text, and, with even greater urgency, what the "feminine" is.

In *La Venue à l'écriture*, perhaps her most strongly Derridean text, Cixous challenges the boundaries between theory and fiction and projects *écriture féminine* as not necessarily writing by a woman but writing also practiced by male authors such as Jean Genet and James Joyce. "Laugh of the Medusa" and "Castration or Decapitation?" present Cixous's case for the reading of feminine writing against psychoanalysis. In "Laugh" she describes how writing is structured by a "sexual opposition" favoring men, one that "has always worked for man's profit to the point of reducing writing . . . to his laws" (883). Writing is constituted in a "discourse" of relations social, political, and linguistic in makeup, and these relations are characterized in a masculine or feminine "economy." In this model, patterns of linearity and exclusion (patriarchal "logic") require a strict hierarchical organization of (sexual) difference in discourse and give a "grossly exaggerated" view of the "sexual opposition" actually inherent to language (879).

But it is in the apocalyptic scenario that she envisions as preparatory to the *venue à l'écriture* of woman that Cixous makes her mark:

> When the "repressed" of their culture and their society returns, it's an explosive, *utterly* destructive, staggering return, with a force never yet unleashed and equal to the most forbidding of suppressions. For when the Phallic period comes to an end, women will have been either annihilated or borne up to the highest and most violent incandescence. ("Laugh" 886)

Cixous is aware of the difficulties of envisioning a writing practice that cannot be theorized and whose existence is scanty. She notes how in France the only inscriptions of the feminine can be found in the work of Marguerite Duras and Colette and in Genet's *Pompes funèbres*. Cixous claims woman's privileged relationship with the voice as a result of her being never far from "mother. . . . There is always within her at least a little of that good mother's milk. She writes in white ink" ("Laugh" 881). But she refuses to conceive of the effects of the past as irremovable, and when she speaks of women's writing—or, as she later said in *Illa*, of women's search for a *langue maternelle*—she speaks in the future tense: she sets out, not to say what it is, but to speak "about *what it will do*" (875). The exclusion of women from writing (and speaking) is linked to the fact that the Western history of writing is synonymous with the history of reasoning and with the separation of the body from the text. The body entering the text disrupts the masculine economy of superimposed linearity and tyranny: the feminine is the "overflow" of "luminous torrents" ("Laugh" 876), a margin of "excess" eroticism and free-play not directly attributable to the fixed hierarchies of masculinity.

The "openness" of such writing is evident in Cixous's own style both in fictional texts such as *Souffles* (1975) and *Angst* (1977) and in "Laugh," as when she writes that "we the precocious, we the repressed of culture, our lovely mouths gagged with pollen, our wind knocked out of us, we the labyrinths, the ladders, the trampled spaces, the bevies—we are black and we are beautiful" ("Laugh" 878). In such language Cixous forces exposition into poetic association and controls the "excess" of imagery through repetition and nonlinear accretions. VIRGINIA WOOLF contrasts such writing to "male," "shadowed," or violently imposed writing. This is Kristeva's conception, too, of *jouissance,* the poetic discourse "beyond" the masculine text of reason and order. For Cixous, Woolf, and Kristeva, there is the key assumption that the feminine economy of excess does not need re-creation, to be made anew, because it persists in the margins and gaps (as the repressed, the unconscious) of male-dominated culture. As a characteristically deconstructive reader, she understands texts as built upon a system of cultural contradictions, especially concerning values. In her reading she strives to focus on those contradictions and then to find the channels of "excess" and violation, accidents of meaning and perversities of signification, through which texts inscribe a feminine writing that goes beyond and escapes the masculine economy of texts.

Cixous's post-Lacanian discourse, however, has also been indicted for supporting patriarchal and psychoanalytic norms. Ann Rosalind Jones and others have charged that underlying Cixous's feminine economy, her sophistication in articulating it notwithstanding, is the assumption of an "essential" femininity in texts, the identifiable quality that allows feminine discourse to be named as such in relation to Oedipus, the essential quality of "openness" that allows a text to resist external control and the superimposition of closed Oedipal patterns. More recently, however, other critics have come to her rescue. Christiane Makward has emphasized Cixous's production as creative writer and has argued that while most of her readers are determined to neglect her creative work and to see "Laugh of the Medusa" as encapsulating her thinking, Cixous's work continues to change: "Medusa has been classified, petrified, sentenced, guilty of biologism, guilty of essentialism, of utopianism. . . . But she does not laugh, she is not listening, she just is not there" (2). Anu Aneja has suggested that the case against *écriture féminine* results from a desire "to locate *l'écriture féminine* within a definite category, a desire to co-opt into a literary theory that which always exceeds it" (195). Aneja's

observations place Cixous's discourse in relation to the Eastern doctrine of nonduality: "Cixous' proposed depersonalization, like that of the ancient east, desires to put something back into an incomplete and mechanical life, a life lived without passion or intensity" (198–99). This view clarifies the trajectory of Cixous's most recent work, which has moved away, as Cixous herself claims, from "work on the ego" (Jardine and Menke 236).

Recently at work in the theater, Cixous sees *Portrait de Dora* (1976) as marking the beginnings of her theatrical career. Focusing on "what Freud did not understand and all that Dora didn't know" (Franke, "Interview" 173), this piece was not written as a play (like *Le Nom d'Oedipe: Chant du corps interdit* [1978], which was a libretto for an opera). She wrote about Dora in her novel *Portrait du soleil* in 1973 and in *The Newly Born Woman* (1975) and finally wrote the play for staging at the Théâtre d'Orsay in Paris in 1976. Her first play written for the Théâtre du Soleil, *L'Histoire terrible mais inachevée de Norodom Sihanouk, roi du Cambodge* (1985), is "an epic way of approaching reality" (Franke, "Interview" 155), and it reflects her recent involvement in the history of Cambodia in relation to her ongoing concern with the discourse of love. *L'Indiade ou l'Inde de leurs rêves* (1978), which she takes to be her philosophical text (164), is about the India-Pakistan partition of 1946 and "the paradoxes of fidelity."

In the theater Cixous has found a new freedom from her own voice and from the self. She claims that the theater allows her to "step out of [her] own language, and borrow the poorest of languages" (166), to forget Hélène Cixous, French intellectual, and become a peasant woman. Time is not artificially elongated in the theater as it is in fiction, she argues, and the theater, therefore, is better equipped to capture a precise moment in human destiny (170)—for Cixous, the theater's highest achievement over fiction. In her plays she considers most poignant the pauses that she imposes on events, scenes that stop history and become the moments, political and personal, when "we interrogate ourselves and we say our fear and our indecision" (152).

Chiara Briganti and Robert Con Davis

Hélène Cixous, "Castration or Decapitation?" (trans. Annette Kuhn, *Signs* 7 [1981]), "The Character of 'Character'" (trans. Keith Cohen, *New Literary History* 5 [1974]), *"Coming to Writing" and Other Essays* (ed. Deborah Jensen, trans. Sarah Cornell, Deborah Jensen, Ann Liddle, and Susan Sellers, 1991), *Illa* (1980), *Readings: The Poetics of Blanchot, Joyce, Kafka, Kleist, Lispector, and Tsvetayeva* (trans. Verena A. Conley, 1991), "Le Rire de la Méduse" (1975, "The Laugh of the Medusa," trans. Keith Cohen and Paula Cohen, *Signs* 1 [1976]), *Vivre l'Orange* (bilingual ed., trans. Ann Liddle and Sarah Cornell, 1979); Hélène Cixous and Catherine Clément, *La Jeune née* (1975, *The Newly Born Woman,* trans. Betsy Wing, 1986); Hélène Cixous, Madeleine Gagnon, and Annie Leclerc, *La Venue à l'écriture* (1977); Catherine Anne Franke, "Interview with Hélène Cixous," *Qui parle* 3 (1989).

Anu Aneja, "The Mystic Aspect of *L'Écriture féminine:* Hélène Cixous' *Vivre l'Orange,*" *Qui parle* 3 (1989); Verena A. Conley, *Hélène Cixous: Writing the Feminine* (1984), *Hélène Cixous* (1992); Robert Con Davis, "Woman as Oppositional Reader: Cixous on Discourse," *Gender in the Classroom: Power and Pedagogy* (ed. Susan L. Gabriel and Isaiah Smithson, 1990); Jean-Joseph Goux, *Freud, Marx: Economie et symbolique* (1973); Elizabeth A. Grosz, "Lacan and Feminism," *Jacques Lacan: A Feminist Introduction* (1990); Alice Jardine, *Gynesis: Configurations of Woman and Modernity* (1985); Alice Jardine and Anne Menke, "The Politics of Tradition: Placing Women in French Literature," *Yale French Studies* 75 (1988); Sarah Kofman, *L'Enfance de l'art: Une Interprétation de l'esthétique freudienne* (1970, *The Childhood of Art: An Interpretation of Freud's Aesthetics,* trans. Winifred Woodhull, 1988); Christiane Makward, "Hélène Cixous and the Myth of 'Feminine Writing,' or 'Hélène in Theoryland'" (1990); Toril Moi, *Sexual/Textual Politics: Feminist Literary Theory* (1985); Elaine Showalter, ed., *The New Feminist Criticism: Essays on Women, Literature, and Theory* (1985); Gayatri Chakravorty Spivak, *In Other Worlds: Essays in Cultural Politics* (1987).

CLASSICAL THEORY AND CRITICISM

1. Greek

It is in the work of PLATO and ARISTOTLE that we find the most influential contribution of Greek thought to the history of literary theory. Plato provocatively challenged the most fundamental axioms by which artists justify their existence, and in response to his mentor, Aristotle fashioned a defense of mimetic art that continues to have a significant influence on the analysis and teaching of literary works. Both of these great thinkers, however, adapted for their own aesthetic theories currents of thought that had evolved in Greek culture over a considerable period of time.

The earliest commentaries we have on the nature of poetry and poets are fragmentary and often indirect allusions in the work of the preclassical poets and philosophers. Their comments 1) affirm the role of divine inspiration in validating the poet's wisdom and art; 2) attest to the emotional impact, pleasurable or otherwise, of poetry on an audience and warn about the capacity of words to deceive; and 3) recognize the power of the poet to preserve fame and glory for humankind. At *Iliad* 2.484–92 Homer (c. eighth century B.C.E.) addresses the muses as the indispensable source of all the real knowledge poets have; the philosopher Democritus (565–470 B.C.E.) concurs in assigning divine inspiration as the source of Homer's poetic achievement; Hesiod (c. 700 B.C.E.) asserts in his opening hymn to the Muses that they know how to tell many lies that resemble the truth but also how to tell the truth itself (*Theogony* 27–28); and Pindar (518–438 B.C.E.) states in *Olympian* 2.83–85 that there are sharp arrows in his poetic quiver that offer illumination to those who understand. In the *Odyssey* 1.325–59 the bard's tale of the disastrous return of the Achaeans from Troy causes Penelope to break into tears and ask him to stop his song. Telemachus, however, advises his mother that poets are not to blame for the tragedies that befall humanity and that they must be permitted to tell the stories of great events, which all wish to hear. Theognis (c. sixth or fifth century B.C.E.) in a preserved fragment asserts that his poetry will keep the memory of Cyrnus alive forever, and Pindar (*Nemean* 7.20–22) announces that glorious deeds such as those of Odysseus are remembered only because of the eloquent songs of poets such as Homer. The Sophist and teacher of rhetoric Gorgias of Leontini (c. 483–c. 376 B.C.E.) in an extant work in defense of Helen notes the power words have to evoke every kind of emotion and to propagate every kind of idea, true or false.

Homer, Aristotle tells us, shaped the evolution of subsequent Greek literature by influencing the development of the important genres tragedy and comedy. In the *Iliad* and *Odyssey* he presented the noble characters and actions that are required for tragedy, and the plots of a number of fifth-century dramas reflect Homeric themes. Because of dignity, courage, and nobility, coupled with a fallibility that leads to suffering, Achilles is a prototype of the later tragic heroes who fall from happiness to misery and evoke pity and fear through a significant judgment (hamartia). Also in these poems, and in the lost *Margites,* Homer transcended mere invective (although a considerable number of insults still appear in the text) to raise comedy to the level of the dramatic representation of the ridiculous such as we find in Hera's seduction of Zeus in book 14 of the *Iliad* or in the tragicomic episodes associated with Paris. These incidents could be models for Aristotle's brief but penetrating analysis of comedy as a genre aimed at representing the ridiculous, a concept defined as an error or ugliness that does not cause pain (*Poetics* 1449a32–37). In the *Republic*, however, Plato bans Homer from his ideal state because of his vivid depiction of scenes of divine immorality and human baseness and denounces comedy as a demoralizing force in society. Here a major conflict arises over the right of artists to depict the world as they see it, or as it may actually be, if their representations conflict with moral standards held in a society. The content of the Homeric epics offers no difficulty to Aristotle, but he faults the expansive narrative structure of epic, which, in contrast with the compact, unified form of tragedy, dilutes its meaning and effect.

It is Aristophanes (c. 457–c. 385 B.C.E.) who most clearly focuses on the two canons—one moral and ethical and the other aesthetic—that play such central roles in the subsequent history of literary criticism. In *Clouds* (423 B.C.E.) he addresses the disintegrating moral fiber of his native city by attacking what he believes to be the causal subversive forces of that disintegration: sophistry, science, imperialism, war, the excessive freedom and tolerance of the city of Athens, and the new literary movements of that city represented most blatantly by Euripides. The terminal breakdown in the relationship between the older and younger generations is vividly illustrated by the debate over the literary merits of the poets of the previous and contemporary generations. The old man Strepsiades asks his son to entertain his guests with selections from the works of Simonides and Aeschylus, the favored poets of his youth, which praise virtue, heroism, and patriotism. His son, Pheidippides, is outraged by the old-fashioned themes of these poets, who to his generation are the greatest of bores, and insists on reciting a passage from a typical play of Euripides, the literary hero of his generation, which describes an incestuous relationship between a brother and a sister. The argument that ensues between father and son leads to the son's beating his father for his inability to appreciate current literary taste and demonstrating, by the logic he has learned from Socrates, that he also has the right to whip his mother. That causes a rebellion on the part of his father, who returns to the values of his youth and destroys Socrates's school, which symbolizes the immorality of the new learning and art.

In *Frogs* (405 B.C.E.) Aristophanes provides an extended thematic and stylistic evaluation of the work of Aeschylus and Euripides that culminates in the assertion of a moral canon for judging works of art. The play begins with the comic adventures of Dionysus, who travels to Hades to accord to the two dead tragedians the privilege of competing for the right to return to an Athens now devoid of any great tragic poets. In the second half of the play Aeschylus and Euripides engage in a vigorous debate over the moral and stylistic values of each other's work. In regard to stylistic matters each attacks the other's language and meter. Euripides alludes to the pompous and obscure diction of his predecessor in contrast to the simpler and much more accessible style of his own work. Aeschylus defends himself on the grounds that he must use a grand style suitable to the great patriotic and heroic themes of his work, while Euripides, enamored as he is of the debased and seamier side of life, embraces a fully appropriate pedestrian diction. Each skillfully finds fault with the flaws of the other's metrical schemes.

The deeper issue separating them, and the one that is the focal point of the play, is the role of poetry and the poet in society. For Aeschylus the poet's task is to teach virtue and elevate the thoughts and feelings of humankind by providing examples of heroic and patriotic achievements. He denounces Euripides for abandoning such themes and instead portraying tales of seduction and incest. In his own defense Euripides demands to know whether he has not been faithful to the truth in relating these stories of human degradation. Aeschylus responds that the stories may be true but that the poet's task is to suppress comment about what is debased in the human condition and articulate only that which is ennobling. For Aeschylus, the poet is essentially a *teacher* who must communicate only what is good and virtuous. For Euripides, whatever is true is the proper subject matter of the poet, who bears no responsibility for serving the moral or ethical agenda of a culture. Aeschylus speaks for the political and ethical outlook of Aristophanes, and so he, of course, wins the verbal duel with Euripides. In the end the god of the underworld sends him back to earth to teach virtue to a society on the verge of moral and military collapse.

The principal concern of the great historian Thucydides (c. 460–c. 400 B.C.E.) is the art and science of historiography, but his views on this subject also relate to central issues in literary theory and criticism. Thucydides sees historical events as the particular manifestations of the universal and unchanging principles of human nature. For this reason he can claim that his study of the Peloponnesian War will forever remain a valuable reference work on the role of power in the relationship between states. The speeches that he attributes to political and military leaders, and that play such an important role in his work, are carefully wrought works of fiction.

It was not possible for him to have an actual record of what was said, but on the basis of the situation and the parties involved, he created orations and dialogues that fully illustrate the Aristotelian standard of necessity and probability in expressing action, character, and thought. Moreover, there is good reason to believe that Thucydides imposed upon his narrative an interpretative structure related to, and very likely derived from, literary tragedy. The immediate linking of Pericles's proud glorification of Athens in his funeral oration with the devastating physical and moral consequences of the great plague, the contemplation of genocide by Athens at Mytilene and the vicious imposition of it at Melos, and the arrogant confidence with which the Sicilian expedition was undertaken and the abject defeat in which it ended suggest the nearly proverbial pattern of tragic action, which requires a movement (as in Sophocles's *Antigone*) from hybris (arrogance) to ate (mad violence) and then to nemesis (vengeance).

Thucydides differs radically from the type of historian who is criticized by Aristotle in chapter 9 of the *Poetics* for excessive concern with particular events. On the contrary, he shares with artists the philosophical impulse to transcend the particular and express the universal. His invented speeches and thematic suggestion of the inevitable tragedy of human history achieve a distillation of the truth at the universal level, which Aristotle claims as the province of great art.

Out of this matrix of early and fragmentary aesthetic thought arose the much more comprehensive and profound views of art that we find in Plato and Aristotle. The cognitive inspiration of the muses that is hailed by the first poets evolves in Aristotle's *Poetics* into the process of learning and inference (*manthanein kai syllogizesthai*, 1448b16) that is the essential purpose and pleasure of all artistic mimesis. Moreover, if *katharsis* means "clarification" rather than "purgation," as some scholars have argued, then this important but enigmatic term will turn out to have a direct relationship to the knowledge Homer, Hesiod, and Pindar insisted was communicated to poets by the muses. Although Plato warns against the naive identification of mimesis with reality, he also recognizes that artistic mimesis yields knowledge, as we see from the abundant use in his work of artistically fashioned myth and dialogue to gain insight into reality.

In Plato's aesthetic theory the issue of the moral and ethical content of mimetic art, which was raised by Aristophanes, becomes a central theme. Plato argues for the banishment of Homer and the tragic and comic poets because their portrayal of immoral and debased behavior on the part of both gods and human beings and their evocation of intense emotion in poetry undermine the discipline with which the good citizen must meet all of life's exigencies. Like Aeschylus in *Frogs,* he sees the poet's mission as that of a moral guide. Aristotle stands much more directly in the tradition of Homer, Thucydides, and Euripides (both the historical Euripides and Aristophanes's creation in *Frogs*) in affirming the poet's obligation to express universal realities independent of the moral implications of those realities.

The most significant contributions to Greek literary theory outside of Plato and Aristotle are to be found in the era that preceded them, when the groundwork was laid for their influential contributions. After Plato and Aristotle we have only two significant names to mention: Theophrastus (370–288/85 B.C.E.), Aristotle's successor as head of the Lyceum, whose work on rhetoric, poetry, and style we know only from later fragmentary references; and *Demetrius: On Style,* a handbook of uncertain authorship and date (from the third to the first century B.C.E. has been conjectured) that surveys and illustrates four principal literary and rhetorical styles.

The concerns of classical Greek criticism were broad and inclusive. Its significant contributions ranged from profound analysis of the source and goal of artistic achievement to close examination of the structure and style of works of art.

Leon Golden

See also ARISTOTLE and PLATO.

Demetrius: On Style (ed. W. Rhys Roberts, 1902); Hesiod, *Theogony* (ed. M. L. West, 1966), *Theogony and Works and Days* (trans. M. L. West, 1988), *Works and Days* (ed. M. L. West, 1978); Homer, *Homeri Opera,* vols. 1–2, *Iliad* (ed. D. B. Monro and T. W. Allen, 3d ed., 1920), *Homeri Opera,* vols. 3–4, *Odyssey* (ed. T. W. Allen, 2d ed., 1917–19), *The Iliad of Homer* (trans. Richmond Lattimore, 1951), *The Odyssey of Homer* (trans. Richmond Lattimore, 1965); G. Lanata, ed., *Poetica pre-Platonica* (1963); Pindar, *The Odes of Pindar* (trans. Richmond Lattimore, 1947), *Pindari Carmina* (ed. A. Turyn, 1952); A. Preminger, O. B. Hardison, and K. Kerrane, eds., *Classical and Medieval Literary Criticism* (1974); D. A. Russell and M. Winterbottom, eds., *Ancient Literary Criticism* (1972, rev. ed., 1989).

M. Fuhrmann, *Einführung in die antike Dichtungstheorie* (1973); G. M. A. Grube, *The Greek and Roman Critics* (1965); R. Harriott, *Poetry and Criticism before Plato* (1969); D. A. Russell, *Criticism in Antiquity* (1981); George B. Walsh, *The Varieties of Enchantment* (1984).

2. Rhetoric

While the art of rhetoric is often said to have originated in Sicily about 476 B.C.E. with the teaching of Corax and his pupil Tisias, the beginning of its prominence in Greco-Roman culture, including its influence on poetic theory, may fairly be dated with the opening of Gorgias's school of rhetoric in Athens (c. 431 B.C.E.). Defending in his sophistic encomium *Helen* the irresistible power of discourse, and especially poetic discourse, to arouse emotion and thus control the opinions *(doxai)* of an audience, Gorgias not only teaches the strategies of style that effect persuasion—antithesis, alliteration, and parallelism—but practices these strategies in his own oratory. Both precepts and practice are criticized by his student Isocrates (436–338 B.C.E.), who rejects this technical approach in favor of a more ethical and political grounding for rhetoric.

Privileging conjecture about matters of public interest over more exact knowledge about less useful subjects (*Antidosis* 271; *Helen* 4–5), Isocrates elevates political discourse above both the more private, more specialized legal discourse and the less practical, even trivialized, sophistic encomium (*Antidosis* 269). A person of practical wisdom who judges soundly in the majority of cases, the Isocratean orator combines native ability, practice—including imitation—and the rules of art (*Against the Sophists* 10; *Antidosis* 189). Although these rules assist orators in choosing, arranging, and ornamenting their arguments, rhetoric, like politics and ethics, ultimately subordinates hard and fast rules to a flexible measure designed to accommodate particular circumstance (*Against the Sophists* 12, 13, 16–17).

PLATO (429–347 B.C.E.) shares Isocrates' project of examining rhetoric in the context of moral philosophy but comes to very different conclusions. While the Isocratean rhetor *is* a philosopher, defined as someone of good character and practical wisdom, Plato's rhetorician, like his poet (*Republic* 595a ff.), does not even practice an art. On the contrary, this public speaker, as depicted by Socrates in the *Gorgias* and the *Phaedrus,* is someone with a knack whose subject is not politics but the mere semblance *(eidolon)* of politics and whose task is not to enlighten but merely to gratify an audience (*Gorgias* 462c, 463d).

The current state of the so-called art, according to Socrates, confirms this view (*Phaedrus* 266c–267e). While neglecting the first principles of persuasion, contemporary rhetoricians, including Thrasymachus, Theodorus, and Gorgias, emphasize the technical aspects of rhetoric—the individual parts of an oration, particular strategies of style, the workings of the emotions or probability. A true art of rhetoric, by contrast, must be grounded in dialectic and psychology (*Phaedrus* 271a–b). Like the dialectician, the orator must discover the similarity in dissimilar things and generality in the particular instance (261e, 265d, 266b, 277b–c); and if oratory is to lead human souls from opinion to knowledge, it must apply the dialectical method to the kinds of souls that make up its audience (273d–e).

The oldest extant analytical treatment of the art, and maybe the first, the *Rhetoric* of ARISTOTLE (384–322 B.C.E.) not only addresses Plato's charges but looks to satisfy his prescriptions. In opposition to his teacher, Aristotle begins by authorizing rhetoric (as he had poetics) as an art in its own right, capable of rationalizing the methods and causes of persuasion (1.1.1, 1.2.1; cf. 1.1.14). In full agreement with Plato, on the other hand, Aristotle defines rhetoric as a combination of dialectic and politics (1.2.7; cf. 1.1.1) and further identifies rhetorical argument, or *logos,* with the procedure of negotiating between particular instances and generalities, either inductively by example or deductively by enthymeme (1.2.9). But *logos,* the focus of the first book of the *Rhetoric,* is only one of the three principal forms of rhetorical proof (1.2.2). The other two—*ethos,* or character, and *pathos,* or emotion—as the double focus of the second book, also answer to Plato's call in the *Phaedrus* by investigating the psychological makeup of both the speaker and the audience.

In addition to grounding his art in dialectic and psychology, Aristotle also agrees with Plato on the inadequacy of the work of his predecessors. Whereas they attend exclusively to emotional appeal, he both shifts the emphasis to argumentation and its topics (1.1.3–4) and reassesses the role of the emotions in the ethical and political activity of making judgments (2.1.8). Whereas they employ probability to exploit the inherent susceptibility of the human mind to deception (2.24.11; cf. *Phaedrus* 273b–c), he employs it, as an instrument of dialectical argument, to accommodate the inherent unpredictability of human affairs (1.2.12–14). Whereas they concentrate on forensic oratory, one of the three kinds with epideictic and deliberative (1.3.1–3), he, like Isocrates before him, privileges deliberative or political oratory (1.1.10). Whereas they often treat exclusively the more technical elements of the art, such as the parts of the speech (1.1.9) or the strategies of style, he covers only in the third book both style *(lexis)* and, more briefly, arrangement *(taxis).*

Furthermore, Aristotle's treatment of style, addressing poetry as well as oratory, is fundamentally philosophical. At its center are metaphor and the theory of the mean. While metaphor, like the dialectic at the core of rhetorical argument, works to discover the similarity in dissimilar things (3.11.5), style worthy of approval is style that aims at appropriateness, often a mean, analogous to the mean in ethics (*Nicomachean Ethics* 2.6.10–14), between the extremes of obscurity and bland transparency (*Rhetoric* 3.2.1–3, 3.5.1, 3.7.1–5; cf. *Poetics* 1457b ff.). And the same principle of appropriateness informs the treatment of arrangement, with its simplified bipartite plan of statement and proof, subject to elaboration as the occasion demands (3.13.1–4).

During the roughly 250 years between Aristotle's *Rhetoric* and Cicero's *De Inventione* (c. 87 B.C.E.) the center of rhetorical activity shifts from Athens to Rome. Meanwhile, rhetorical pedagogy, with its proliferation of technical manuals, replaces rhetorical theory. In spite of this proliferation, no handbooks remain in anything but fragmentary form, with the exception of the *Rhetorica ad Alexandrum,* nearly contemporary with Aristotle's *Rhetoric,* and the pseudo-Ciceronian *Rhetorica ad Herennium* (c. 90 B.C.E.), contemporary with Cicero's early work on invention and especially influential throughout the Middle Ages. Even from the fragmentary evidence, however, the outlines of a tradition emerge.

One of the features of this tradition is the influence of Hermagoras (late second century B.C.E.), whose so-called *status* system, designed to locate the questionable issue in any controversy, becomes the basis of the first of the five activities of rhetoric: invention *(heuresis, inventio),* or the finding of arguments (*Ad Herennium* 1.2.3; *De Inventione* 1.7.9–1.11.16). The other four are arrangement *(taxis, dispositio),* style *(lexis, elocutio),* delivery *(hypokrisis, actio),* and memory *(mneme, memoria).* Another feature, one to which the breakdown of rhetoric into five activities attests, is a tendency toward classification. This process is evident, for instance, in the treatment of the parts of an oration, expanded from Aristotle's two to six, including introduction, statement of facts, division, proof, refutation, and conclusion (*Ad Herennium* 1.3.4; *De Inventione* 1.14.19).

The tendency toward classification similarly affects treatments of style, now defined in terms of *characters* and *virtues.* Whereas Aristotle had proclaimed moderation a virtue of style more generally, his successors transform this stylistic mean into one of the three characters of style, the moderate or middle, distinguished from the other two—the high, or grand, and low, or plain—by its intention, its level of verbal ornament, including its use of figures, and the complexity of its sentence structure (*Ad Herennium* 4.8.11). The virtues of style, meantime,

are fixed at four: clarity, appropriateness, purity, and ornamentation (*Orator* 79; cf. *Ad Herennium* 4.12.17), although the Stoics add brevity as a fifth (see Diogenes Laertius, 7.59). And figures, now classified as pertaining either to thought or to speech, are regularly incorporated into these discussions of style (*Ad Herennium* 4.13.18–4.60.69).

By the first century B.C.E., moreover, some of the most important rhetorical treatises address almost exclusively matters of style. Demetrius's *On Style* adds to the familiar three characters a fourth: the forceful, characterized by obscurity and abruptness and the figures that create these effects (5.240 ff.). Dionysius of Halicarnassus (late first century B.C.E.), whose *On the Ancient Orators* and *On Literary Composition* help to fill in the details of Augustan literary theory, also commends forcefulness and so characterizes the oratory of Demosthenes (cf. LONGINUS 12.3–5), while Lysias and Isocrates serve as models of the plain and middle styles, respectively; and in the *Brutus* and the *Orator* (both 46 B.C.E.) Cicero himself participates in the contemporary debate over competing styles, with the *Orator* setting the distinctions of the *Brutus* between the plainer Attic and the more ornate Asian within the broader context of the three stylistic characters (*Brutus* 291, 325; *Orator* 28, 69–74). This focus on style equally characterizes the development of poetic theory, by this time almost exclusively dependent on rhetorical principles (see HORACE).

In this first-century context of increasing classification and concentration on style, Cicero's *De Oratore* (55 B.C.E.) stands outside the mainstream. In a dialogue reminiscent of the *Phaedrus* (1.7.28), Cicero has his interlocutors, Crassus and Antonius, debate once again the place of moral philosophy in the rhetorical art. The orator, Cicero would seem to agree with Crassus, must know more than the technical elements of his art; he must strive to repair the divorce initiated by Socrates between wisdom and eloquence (1.14.63, 3.15.57 ff.; cf. *Orator* 12–13).

Quintilian's *Institutio Oratoria* (c. C.E. 95) reformulates this Ciceronian program for the Roman world of the first century C.E., now a principate rather than a republic, where rhetoric forms the backbone of the curriculum and declamation, the principal means of practical training. Following not only Cicero but Isocrates and Aristotle, Quintilian preserves many of the traditional organizing principles of the art, including its division into five activities (3.3.1 ff.), into three kinds of oratory (3.4.1 ff.), into the parts of an oration (4.1.1 ff.), into the virtues of style (8.1.1), and into figures of thought and speech (9.1.1 ff.). What is more important, Quintilian reaffirms the ethical and logical foundations of rhetoric. His orator is a man of good character, a *vir bonus,* who combines sound thinking with eloquent speaking (12.1.1 ff.; cf. 2.15.37).

Quintilian's best-known contemporaries share his concern both with the relation of rhetoric to philosophy and with the political and social causes of its decline (see *Institutio Oratoria* 8.6.76; cf. Longinus 44.1–11). Before him, Seneca the Younger (c. 4 B.C.E.–C.E. 65)—whose father, Seneca the Elder (55 B.C.E.–C.E. 37), compiled a handbook of declamatory exercises—rejects the Ciceronian grand style for the philosophical plain style as a truer reflection of character. The deterioration of style, including its excessive refinement, Seneca attributes in turn to a widespread moral decay that pervades learning generally (*Epistulae Morales* 38.1, 75.4–5, 88.1 ff., 114.1 ff.). In his *Dialogus de oratoribus,* Tacitus (c. C.E. 55–117) expresses some of the same concerns. His principal interlocutors, Maternus and Aper, debate not only the current role of rhetoric in public life but the very usefulness of political involvement. While reassessing the interaction between ethics and style, their debate sharpens the contrast between the antique style of oratory, appropriate to the affairs of a republic, and the modern, with its qualities of abruptness and indirection, on the one hand, and excessive, even poetical, ornamentation, on the other (20.4–5).

Between the second and fourth centuries, rhetoric remains at the very center of Western culture. Philosophers, orators, and historians—among them Suetonius (c. 69–160), Fronto (?100–?166), Lucian (c. 115–c. 200), and Philostratus (fl. c. 210)—continue to reflect on its theory and practice. Because of the continuing centrality of rhetoric to the traditional program of education, moreover, pedagogical manuals in the form of both rhetorical *artes* and *progymnasmata* (rules and exercises for composition) not only proliferate but continue to exert their influence on poetic theory and practice. Best known among the latter are those of Hermogenes (fl. 161–80) and Aphthonius (315–?). In addition, the fathers of the church, including Tertullian, Ambrose, Jerome, and ST. AUGUSTINE, accommodate classical rhetoric to the demands of a Christian discourse. While this accommodation helps to preserve for the centuries that follow select elements of classical rhetoric, it is not until the fifteenth and sixteenth centuries that the so-called humanists reinvigorate with the power of their own aspirations the rhetorical ideals of Cicero and Quintilian.

Kathy Eden

See also LINGUISTICS AND LANGUAGE, MEDIEVAL THEORY AND CRITICISM, and RHETORIC.

Aphthonius, "The Progymnasmata of Aphthonius in Translation" (trans. Raymond Nadeau, *Speech Monographs* 19 [1952]); Aristotle, *Rhetoric* (trans. George A. Kennedy, 1991); Cicero, *Brutus* (trans. G. L. Hendrickson, 1939), *Orator* (trans. H. M. Hubbell, 1939), *De Inventione; De Optimo Genere Oratorum; Topica* (trans. H. M. Hubbell, 1949), *De Oratore, Book III; De Fato; Paradoxa Stoicorum; Partitiones Oratoriae* (trans. H. Rackham, 1942), *Rhetorica ad Herennium* (sometimes attributed to Cicero, trans. Harry Caplan, 1954); Demetrius, *On Style* (trans. D. C. Innes, *Ancient Literary Criticism: The Principal Texts in Translation,* ed. D. A. Russell and M. Winterbottom, 1972); Diogenes Laertius, *Lives of Eminent Philosophers* (ed. H. S. Long, 2 vols., 1964, trans. R. D. Hicks, 1925, rev. ed., 1931); Dionysius of Halicarnassus, *On Literary Composition* (trans. W. Rhys Roberts, 1910); Longinus, *On the Sublime* (ed. D. A. Russell, 1964, *On Sublimity,* trans. D. A. Russell, 1965); Isocrates, *Works* (3 vols., trans. George Norlin and Larue Van Hook, 1928); Plato, *Gorgias* (trans. Terence Irwin, 1979), *Phaedrus* (trans. R. Hackforth, *The Collected Dialogues,* ed. Edith Hamilton and Huntington Cairns, 1961); Quintilian, *Institutio Oratoria* (4 vols., trans. H. E. Butler, 1920); Seneca the Elder, *Controversiae; Suasoriae* (2 vols., ed. and trans. Michael Winterbottom, 1974); Seneca the Younger, *Epistulae Morales* (3 vols., trans. Richard M. Gummere, 1919); Tacitus, *Dialogue of Orators* (trans. M. Winterbottom, *Ancient Literary Criticism,* ed. D. A. Russell and M. Winterbottom, 1972).

Stanley Frederick Bonner, *Roman Declamation in the Late Republic and Early Empire* (1949); Thomas Cole, *The Origins of Rhetoric in Ancient Greece* (1991); Richard L. Enos, "The Classical Period," *Historical Rhetoric: An Annotated Bibliography of Selected Sources in English* (ed. Winifred B. Horner, 1980); Keith V. Erickson, ed., *Aristotle: The Classical Heritage of Rhetoric* (1974); Elaine Fantham, "Imitation and Decline: Rhetorical Theory and Practice in the First Century after Christ," *Classical Philology* 73 (1978); G. M. A. Grube, *The Greek and Roman Critics* (1965); George Lincoln Hendrickson, "The Origin and Meaning of the Ancient Characters of Style," *American Journal of Philology* 26 (1905); David S. Kaufer, "The Influence of Plato's Developing Psychology on His Views of Rhetoric," *Quarterly Journal of Speech* 64 (1978); George A. Kennedy, *The Art of Persuasion in Greece* (1963), *The Art of Rhetoric in the Roman World* (1972); Heinrich Lausberg, *Handbuch der literarischen Rhetorik* (2 vols., 1960); Henri-Irenee Marrou, *A History of Education in Antiquity* (trans. George Lamb, 1964); Raymond Nadeau, "Classical Systems of Stases in Greek: Hermagoras to Hermogenes,"

Greek, Roman, and Byzantine Studies 2 (1959); Friedrich Solmsen, "The Aristotelian Tradition in Ancient Rhetoric," *American Journal of Philology* 62 (1941), "Aristotle and Cicero on the Orator's Playing upon Feelings," *Classical Philology* 33 (1938).

COLERIDGE, SAMUEL TAYLOR

In "My First Acquaintance with Poets," WILLIAM HAZLITT offers a description of his former mentor, Samuel Taylor Coleridge (1772–1834), which he cannot resist turning from humorous to critical purposes.

His forehead was broad and high, light as if built of ivory, with large projecting eyebrows, and his eyes rolling beneath them like a sea with darkened lustre. . . . His mouth was gross, voluptuous, open, eloquent, his chin good-humoured and round; but his nose, the rudder of the face, the index of the will, was small, feeble, nothing—like what he has done. (17:109)

Hazlitt, Coleridge's main competitor for preeminence among the English critics of the Romantic period, attained while still in his twenties the literary and political values that he would defend throughout his life. Coleridge, for his part, had a mind always in flux. He was eclectic, a polymath, irresolute, distracted, and undisciplined. His eloquence kept him in conversation and away from his desk; his interests overtook one another with astonishing rapidity; those intellectual tasks that he did attend to were frequently stopgaps to keep him from larger and more ambitious projects such as the philosophical epic provisionally entitled "The Brook" and the august synthesis of Christian doctrine and German idealism that Coleridge thought of, portentously and therefore inhibitingly, as the magnum opus. He failed to complete these two projects and most of the dozens of others that he sketched out in his bulging notebooks. The ever-guilty Coleridge would often have agreed with Hazlitt's sour assessment of his career. Yet the achievement that Hazlitt derided as "nothing," and that was a source of continual shame for Coleridge himself, has, perhaps more than that of any writer since, worked to shape Anglo-American literary criticism.

Central to that achievement were Coleridge's ideas about the imagination, which reach a point of concentration in the often-cited passage from chapter 13 of the *Biographia Literaria:*

The IMAGINATION then I consider either as primary, or secondary. The primary IMAGINATION I hold to be the living Power and prime Agent of all human Perception,

and as a repetition in the finite mind of the eternal act of creation in the infinite I AM. The secondary I consider as an echo of the former, co-existing with the conscious will, yet still as identical with the primary in the *kind* of its agency, and differing only in *degree,* and in the *mode* of its operation. It dissolves, diffuses, dissipates, in order to re-create; or where this process is rendered impossible, yet still at all events it struggles to idealize and to unify. It is essentially *vital,* even as all objects (*as* objects) are essentially fixed and dead. (1:304)

The passage illustrates a number of the key tendencies in Coleridge's thinking. There is, first of all, the attempt to synthesize the Romantic faith in poetic creation with the tenets of orthodox Christianity. (Among the six major Romantic poets, Coleridge was the only one who sustained conventional religious beliefs.) The actions of the secondary, or poetic, imagination are modeled on those of the primary, human imagination, the faculty that gives form to immediate sense perceptions. It is with the primary imagination that a human being repeats, and in repeating gives thanks for, the ongoing act of creation by which God, as ST. AUGUSTINE and others affirmed, perpetuates the being of the world. To love something, Augustine thought, is actively to will its existence and thus to experience at one remove the supreme creator's joy in creation.

Coleridge proposes that poetic invention takes this pious activity one step further. The poetic imagination is continuous in kind, different only in mode and degree from the actions of the pious (and commonplace) mind. In saying as much, Coleridge seeks both to exalt and to constrain the Romantic shaping power: it is God-like but subordinate. He seems to arrive at a comprehensive synthesis, the state in which he wished all of his thinking to culminate. It was this addiction to comprehensive knowledge and inclusive conceptual models that John Keats had in mind when he wrote in the letter on negative capability that Coleridge "would let go by a fine isolated verisimilitude caught from the Penetralium of mystery, from being incapable of remaining content with half knowledge" (1:193–94).

Yet in the *Biographia* passage on imagination, another tendency in Coleridge's thought is active as well. For this "pious" secondary imagination possesses a rather violent will to disruption. "It dissolves, diffuses, dissipates." That is to say, the poetic imagination is prone to turn against what is given to it by the "infinite I AM." It finds created nature inadequate to its desires for fresh and vitalizing experience. This visionary restlessness is, presumably, the condition of the Ancient Mariner, at least until he is chastened and becomes an apostle of the primary imagination:

"He prayeth best, who loveth best
All things both great and small;
For the dear God who loveth us,
He made and loveth all."

(*Poetical* 1:209)

Despite the Mariner's piety, which is in many ways Coleridge's, "The Rime of the Ancient Mariner," the imagination passage in the *Biographia,* and numerous other moments in Coleridge's poetry and prose betray an allegiance to powers of mind at odds with Christian humility.

In many ways, Coleridge was what mid-twentieth-century Anglo-American literary criticism took him to be, a lover of organic cohesion and perfect synthesis, harmony in all things social and poetic. But his attraction to fertile and impious disorder is also large. His thinking, particularly as it is recorded in his notebooks, pays frequent heed to the multiplicity of human perspectives, to the complexity and divergence (sometimes the near chaos) of sensory perceptions, and to the humanly uncontrollable energies of words. This sort of awareness may have been augmented by Coleridge's use of opium, which was habitual from about his twenty-fifth year, but it also stemmed from his intellectual disposition. Despite Keats's observation to the contrary, Coleridge was rarely willing to shut out phenomena, even when they challenged his strongest aspirations for conceptual synthesis.

Other disparities also infuse Coleridge's criticism. Although he claimed to trust in God for spiritual guidance, he at times affirmed a subjective idealism so radical that it left the poet-perceiver with no resources to rely on but his own. Coleridge's profession in the last sentence of the passage above, contrasting the potential vitality of the imagination with objects in the world, which are, by their nature, fixed and dead, heaps an enormous burden on the human subject. If experience is not always vital, there is only one's own corruption to blame. This harsh gospel is one of the subjects of the great ode "Dejection": "I may not hope from outward forms to win / The passion and the life, whose fountains are within" (*Poetical* 1:365). In saying as much, Coleridge subtly upbraids his friend, collaborator, and competitor WILLIAM WORDSWORTH, who for the most part insisted on a reciprocity between mind and nature in which we "half create" and half perceive. "Dejection" answers the first four stanzas of the "Intimations" ode by arguing that Wordsworth's faith in nature is a mystification. "We receive but what we give, / And in our life alone does Nature live" (1:365). Again one sees Coleridge's mind divided: his piety harkens back to the tradition of Jeremy Taylor, of whose theology and prose style he thought highly; his individualism, so radical that it touches the borders of solipsism, reaches forward to RALPH WALDO EMERSON.

The many tensions that inform Coleridge's thinking are manifest in his critical style, a style largely both unprecedented and unimitated. The passage on the poetic imagination is more lucid and available than most of Coleridge's speculative writing, which tends, even when it is celebrating the "esemplastic" (that is, unifying) powers of the mind, to be unfocused in its argument and irregular in rhythm, clotted and sprawling by turns. "His style," Hazlitt writes,

is not succinct, but incumbered with a train of words and images that have no practical, and only a possible relation to one another—that add to its stateliness, but impede its march. One of his sentences winds its 'forlorn way obscure' over the page like a patriarchal procession with camels laden, wreathed turbans, household wealth, the whole riches of the author's mind poured out upon the barren waste of his subject. The palm-tree spreads its sterile branches overhead, and the land of promise is seen in the distance. (12:15)

The confidently direct prose of Hazlitt himself, and of SAMUEL JOHNSON, Coleridge's great eighteenth-century predecessor, signifies among other things the writers' faith in the solidity of their own egos and in their very active powers of judgment. Coleridge, forecasting in some ways the postmodern experience of liminal subjectivity, sustained no such faith.

The imagination passage resounds with the conceptual terminology of German idealism, and part of Coleridge's distinction as a critic, as well as some of the scandal that still surrounds his name, arises from his involvement with German philosophy. The extent and significance of Coleridge's plagiarism has been debated by scholars since Thomas De Quincey, himself an accomplished borrower, published an expose in *Tait's Magazine* a couple of weeks after Coleridge's death. Coleridge copied from the work of IMMANUEL KANT, F. W. J. Schelling, and A. W. Schlegel. Whether this copying resulted from psychoneuroses, indolence, or an overrich memory is uncertain. What is certain, and more significant, is that Coleridge brought philosophical concerns to English literary criticism, where before they had been in little evidence.

On the opening page of the *Biographia,* Coleridge states as one of the book's goals "the application of the rules, deduced from philosophical principles, to poetry and criticism." RENÉ WELLEK writes that "Coleridge differs from almost all preceding English writers by his claim to an epistemology and metaphysics from which he derives his aesthetics and finally his literary theory and critical principles" (2:158). Johnson and Hazlitt generally invoked a commonsense British empiricism when they bothered to think about philosophy at all: their criticism was experiential, frequently journalistic, and aimed at the common reader.

Coleridge introduces England to a relatively new form of criticism when he refuses the view that philosophy and poetry are natural antagonists, a view that goes back at least to PLATO. Poetry, for Coleridge, becomes a source for fresh insight into philosophical perplexities, and, too, poetry becomes a fit object for philosophical generalities such as the one distinguishing between primary and secondary imaginations. Among Coleridge's contemporaries there was no little resistance to the injection of philosophy into literary criticism. At the opening of *Don Juan* (which Jerome McGann has argued was written in part as a response to the *Biographia*), Byron ridicules Coleridge's speculative pretensions:

> And Coleridge, too, has lately taken wing,
> But, like a hawk encumber'd with his hood,
> Explaining metaphysics to the nation—
> I wish he would explain his Explanation.
> (*Complete Poetical Works,*
> ed. Jerome J. McGann, vol. 5, 1986, 3)

Clearly Coleridge had raised the stakes in literary-critical writing beyond Byron's sense of due proportion. After Coleridge, criticism is a genre in which one can entertain—or demystify—questions of ultimate importance. After Coleridge, too, criticism has license to be abstract and difficult. It can become the province of an elite. Byron, a proud man but a popular writer, had reason to disparage such developments, as have others. Whatever the justice of their criticisms, it is worth remembering that Coleridge's commitment to unconfined speculation, to philosophy, and to an elite audience did a great deal to lay the groundwork for academic literary criticism in its current (elitist, sophisticated, speculative) form.

At the center of Coleridge's intellectual concerns was a problem bequeathed to him chiefly by Kant: the nature of the relations between the human subject and his or her objects of perception. Kant had posited a necessary gap between the experiencing subject and the thing in itself, the noumenon. Perception gave access to phenomena, entities mediated and accordingly transformed by the senses and the mental faculties, but not to objects

in their authentic being. Encountering this rift in RENÉ DESCARTES and Kant, and being disposed, at least overtly, against all unnecessary dualisms, Coleridge sought a solution within literature. To Coleridge the longed-for synthesis of subject and object took place through the exercise of the poetic imagination. Thus it was the poet who created harmony where the philosophers had been forced to acknowledge an alienating gap. "No man," Coleridge wrote in the *Biographia*, "was ever yet a great poet, without being at the same time a profound philosopher" (2:25-26).

Coleridge associated the synthesizing power of the poetic mind with the symbol, which he affirmed at the expense of allegory. In a well-known passage from *The Statesman's Manual* he observes that

> a Symbol is characterized by a translucence of the Special in the Individual or of the General in the Especial or of the Universal in the General. Above all by the translucence of the Eternal through and in the Temporal. It always partakes of the Reality which it renders intelligible; and while it enunciates the whole, abides itself as a living part in that Unity, of which it is the representative. (30)

The symbol proceeds from, and gives the reader access to, a God's-eye view of experience. It generates universal knowledge, knowledge not conditioned by a particular historical or personal position, and dissolves the boundaries between subject and object. Thus it satisfies both the spirit, which longs for unity, and the intellect questing for truth. Allegory, on the other hand, is a mere picture language: one interprets allegory exclusively with the understanding. It is a mechanical device, provoking an estranging automatism of response. Yet, as PAUL DE MAN observes, Coleridge is not willing to sustain the notion that allegory and symbol are simple antipodes: at a certain point his definitions of the two begin to blur (192-93). A seeker after clarity, Coleridge frequently found instability, uncertainty, complexities that no conceptual scheme, no matter how well-developed, could quite contain.

Consumed by the problem of dualism, Coleridge was accordingly fascinated by the power that, as he saw it, dissolved opposition, the power of poetic genius. By the time Coleridge wrote his most influential criticism, he had designated himself a failure as a poet, yet he believed that his early experience gave him special insight: "Like the ostrich, I cannot fly, yet I have wings that give me the feeling of flight" (*Biographia* 1:xlvii). To Coleridge, the archetype of all geniuses was Shakespeare, in whose work he found what he took to be the four "characteristics of poetic genius in general." Shakespeare provides the "sense of musical delight"; exhibits the power of annulling his own identity and entering into the minds and spirits of others; modifies all poetic perceptions by submitting them to one or another "predominant passion," thus giving his imagery "a human and intellectual life"; and exhibits "depth and energy of thought." For all of its variety, Shakespeare's mind is also a splendid unity: "He becomes all things, yet for ever remaining himself" (*Biographia* 2:19–28). Despite the promise these observations hold as principles for the comprehensive criticism of Shakespeare's plays, one must note that Coleridge's actual Shakespeare criticism tends to be limited to character studies, of which the remarks on Hamlet (whose delays Coleridge associated with an overdeveloped intellect not, presumably, unlike his own) have been the most influential.

Wordsworth's poetic genius was, Coleridge thought, undeniable and yet far from Shakespeare's apogee. Coleridge believed (rather surprisingly, perhaps) that Wordsworth's poetry lacked empathy: Wordsworth can feel *for* others but not *with* them. But Wordsworth's virtues are many: his poems possess an "austere purity of language," a purity proven by the fact that they will not suffer paraphrase "without injury to the meaning." His poetic sentiments are fresh and are gleaned not chiefly from reading but from sane observation of nature. (One recalls Robert Frost's remark that poetry ought to contain what is common in life and rare in books.) His poetic figures, moreover, are frequently of unusual beauty; his images possess "the perfect truth of nature" (*Biographia* 2:142–59).

Coleridge's major contention with Wordsworth is over the questions of poetic diction and the appropriate subject matter for poetry, and the dispute is not so minor or arbitrary as it might first seem. Coleridge is critical of Wordsworth's view that at least at the moment when he is writing, the true language of poetry is the language of simple persons leading simple lives, the language of rustics, and that country people are the best subject for poetry because they exhibit the essential passions of the heart in a way that more sophisticated figures do not. Coleridge argues at some length that rustic diction is too limited for poetry and that country people as they actually exist lack the scope and refinement of character that can make them representative, rather than merely particular, figures. Coleridge claims that his bias is Aristotelian: he looks to poetry for the ideal, which Wordsworth, despite his doctrines, actually provides in his best work.

Overtly, Coleridge's objective is to point out the gap between Wordsworth's aesthetic doctrines and his actual achievements. But there are other stakes in the controversy as well. Hazlitt, in his brilliant lecture on his poetic contemporaries, had associated Romantic poetry with the French Revolution: it was a leveling poetry demanding that "all was to be natural and new" and that "nothing that was established was to be tolerated" (5:161–62). Coleridge's turn against simplicity in poetic diction and subject matter should probably be understood as a turn against the populist allegiances of early Romantic poetry, his own included. The argument with Wordsworth's "Preface to *Lyrical Ballads,*" then, qualifies as an effort to change the political image of Romanticism. For if Romantic art really had little to do with the people per se, then it could not be associated with the Revolution, or with threats to the established order.

It is probably not coincidental that in 1817, the year Coleridge brought out the *Biographia,* he published his Second *Lay Sermon,* which the title page says is "Addressed to the Higher and Middle Classes." (*The Statesman's Manual,* published a year before, addresses itself exclusively to the higher orders.) Literary culture, Coleridge suggests, ought henceforth to be the property of an elite, a select group from the upper and middle orders, who will attempt to improve society from above. Coleridge's turn to conservative elitism was significant enough to inform the thinking of MATTHEW ARNOLD and T. S. ELIOT, as well as today's antidemotic culture of academic criticism.

In fact, I have maintained here that Coleridge has had a role in shaping almost every aspect of contemporary academic criticism. Yet there are reasons to doubt such a judgment. The last significant manifestation of the grand synthesizing urge Coleridge endorsed was probably NORTHROP FRYE's *Anatomy of Criticism,* published in 1957. Since that time, the deconstructive movement has compelled almost every literary critic to doubt his or her attractions to organic thought. Paul de Man's 1969 essay "The Rhetoric of Temporality" has been influential in its claim to expose the theological residues in Coleridge's aesthetics of the symbol. In that essay, too, de Man took steps to rehabilitate allegory, claiming that it is a representational mode that defers meaning indefinitely and puts the interpreter in contact with an "authentically temporal predicament." De Man's conception of allegory (which bears strong resemblance to JACQUES DERRIDA's "writing") has, for many, come to define the experience of reading overall, and in ways that Coleridge would have emphatically disliked.

Coleridge's faith in genius has also been undermined. Critics at present frequently argue that "great" literary works may derive at least some of their status from appealing to the interests of socially dominant groups: that they are, in other words, wish-fulfillments of the master classes. Then, too, many critics now believe that the creation (or production) of major literary works is less dependent on the powers of this or that individual than it is a function of cultural circumstances and the ripeness of a particular genre. All art, many now conceive, is socially produced.

But no matter how much the consensus of contemporary literary criticism departs from Coleridge, it continues to focus on the questions that mattered to him, even as it has come to ignore many of the issues that absorbed Johnson and Hazlitt. Questions about the provenance of the literary work, the nature of the poetic image, the tensions between words and their referents, the social utility of criticism, the function of intellectual elites, the relations between poetry and philosophy, and the existence of a properly literary language are all, in a certain sense, Coleridgean questions. Even in disagreeing with Coleridge, critics often have recourse to terms he introduced or redefined. It is also probably the case that Coleridge's peculiar personality has, however subtly, helped to shape many critical personalities after him: his vast curiosity, his speculative disposition, his attractions to nuance and to the minutiae of learning, along with the odd combination of timidity and daring that informs his writing, manifest themselves frequently in critics who have followed him. Coleridge is, for the Anglo-American academic critic, an inescapable presence. Anyone who wishes to undermine that presence must first understand how much of Coleridge he or she already contains.

Mark Edmundson

See also BRITISH THEORY AND CRITICISM: 3. ROMANTIC PERIOD AND EARLY NINETEENTH CENTURY, GERMAN THEORY AND CRITICISM: 2. ROMANTICISM, WILLIAM HAZLITT, PRACTICAL CRITICISM, and WILLIAM WORDSWORTH.

Samuel Taylor Coleridge, *Biographia Literaria* (*Collected Works*, vol. 7, pts. 1–2, ed. James Engell and W. Jackson Bate, 2 vols., 1983), *Coleridge's Miscellaneous Criticism* (ed. Thomas M. Raysor, 1936), *Coleridge's Shakespearean Criticism* (ed. Thomas M. Raysor, 2 vols., 1930), *Collected Letters of Samuel Taylor Coleridge* (ed. Earl Leslie Griggs, 6 vols., 1956–71), *The Complete Poetical Works of Samuel Taylor Coleridge* (ed. Ernest Hartley Coleridge, 2 vols., 1912), *Essays on His Times* (*Collected Works*, vol. 3, pts. 1–3, ed. David V. Erdman, 3 vols., 1978), *Inquiring*

Spirit: A New Presentation of Coleridge from His Published and Unpublished Prose Writings (ed. Kathleen Coburn, 1979), *Lay Sermons* (*Collected Works*, vol. 6, ed. R. J. White, 1972), *Marginalia* (*Collected Works*, vol. 12, pts. 1–3 to date, ed. George Whalley and A. J. Jackson, 1980–).

Owen Barfield, *What Coleridge Thought* (1971); Walter Jackson Bate, *Coleridge* (1968); Marilyn Butler, "The Rise of the Man of Letters," *Romantics, Rebels, and Reactionaries: English Literature and Its Background, 1760–1830* (1981); Jerome C. Christensen, *Coleridge's Blessed Machine of Language* (1981); James Engell, *The Creative Imagination: Enlightenment to Romanticism* (1981); William Hazlitt, *The Complete Works of William Hazlitt* (ed. P. P. Howe, 21 vols., 1930–34); Richard Holmes, *Coleridge: Early Visions* (1989); John Keats, *The Letters of John Keats: 1814–1821* (ed. Hyder Edward Rollins, 2 vols., 1958); Thomas McFarland, *Coleridge and the Pantheist Tradition* (1969); Jerome J. McGann, "The *Biographia Literaria* and the Contentions of English Romanticism," *Coleridge's "Biographia Literaria": Text and Meaning* (ed. Frederick Burwick, 1989); I. A. Richards, *Coleridge on Imagination* (1934); E. P. Thompson, "Disenchantment or Default? A Lay Sermon," *Power and Consciousness* (ed. Conor Cruise O'Brien and William Dean Vanech, 1969); René Wellek, *A History of Modern Criticism: 1750–1950*, vol. 2, *The Romantic Age* (1955); Kathleen M. Wheeler, *Sources, Processes, and Methods in Coleridge's Biographia Literaria* (1980).

CROCE, BENEDETTO

Benedetto Croce (1866–1952), for decades Italy's exemplar of the essential link between intellect and conscience, was born in the Abruzzi hills, the elder son of an ancient and wealthy Neapolitan family. Around 1892, he came under the influence of Antonio Labriola, professor of ethics at Rome, and despite qualms about the impracticality of a career devoted to mere learning, he pursued the study of philosophy for the rest of his life. In 1895, influenced by Labriola, he became attracted to Marxism and connected himself with European socialist movements, but in the course of his investigation of Marx and his intellectual roots, he developed a critique of Marxism (1900) that one may suspect cured him of his commitment. Although he was initially trained in positivism, the predominant doctrine at the time of his education, and found German philosophy ridiculously abstract, Croce was drawn to Hegelian idealism. In 1902 he published the *Estetica come scienza dell' espressione e linguistica generale* (*Aesthetic as Science of Expression and General Linguistic*), which remains his most significant production and was the foundation of his later works on logic, ethics, and history. During the first half of the twentieth century, he was a patriot and an outspoken foe of fascism, attacked by Mussolini's gangs but too renowned to be silenced. After World War II, Croce became one of the main architects of the postwar Italian constitution but refused offers to become head of the government or president of the republic. Nearly 80, he became minister of education briefly before returning to private life as a professor of history and philosophy. A severe stroke in 1950 slowed his apparently inexhaustible production of publications, but Croce continued to read and to dictate his essays until his death in 1952.

Croce was perhaps the most important philosopher of the twentieth century to occupy himself with problems of pure aesthetics. His approach is one usually termed neo-idealist; his aesthetic derives principally from earlier idealists such as G. W. F. HEGEL, although it corrects Hegel's tendency to view art as a declining spiritual field that will be superseded by transcendental philosophy. But Hegel's notion that art furnishes "the sensuous semblance of the idea" (quoted in Richter 343) is not far removed from Croce's concept of the "lyrical intuition." For Croce, art is a form of knowledge; and while reason gives us knowledge of the universal, our intuition gives us knowledge of the particular. Works of art are "lyrical" or "pure" intuitions because they are immaterial. Unlike the intuition that gives us knowledge of the phenomenal world, they are entirely constructed by the mind, rather than adapted by the mind from matter. They are also pure because they are ideal, untainted by contingency.

Croce essentially identifies intuition with expression: one is a complex of feeling and thought, while the other is the image that derives from it, but for Croce they are the interior and exterior views of the same thing. Logically, we cannot have an intuition without a corresponding expression; that would be like talking about a poem inside us that we are incapable of writing down. People do talk that way from time to time, of course, but others are entitled to doubt whether the poem is really there. The reason we may think we have intuitions that we cannot express is that most of our intuitions (like our memories) are vague and cloudy; when we come to actualize them, we realize this and put the fault down to poor technique. What differentiates artists from the rest of us is that artists' intuitions are clearer than ours and become clearer still in the process of expression.

Given Croce's idealism, the third factor in the artistic process, communication, is relatively insignificant. If intuition and expression exist in the artist's mind, then the work of art exists; its actualization as matter, as words on paper or paint on canvas, is a comparatively trivial issue and one that, for Croce, has nothing to do with aesthetics as such. In Croce's aesthetic the poem comes into existence when the poet silently recites its words, the painting when the artist has fully visualized it, the song when the composer has heard its melody in his or her head. Communication is crucial, of course, to the appreciation of the work of art by anyone other than the artist. And here technique becomes important. For the audience, the process works backwards: we move from the actualization to the expression until we have apprehended the lyrical intuition with which the artist began.

It is important to recall that these three steps are presented in a *logical,* but not necessarily a *temporal,* order. Croce is not under the illusion that a work comes into being full-blown in the artist's head and only then is transferred to some material form. Poets have their drafts, and painters their sketches, and Croce is well aware that artists constantly refine and reshape their work, that they move, in his terms, from the act of expression to that of communication and back again.

One consequence of Croce's theory is that the beauty of nature, of human beings as well as of landscapes, becomes difficult to explain unless one is willing (as Croce himself is not) to posit a divine creator given to actualizing lyrical intuitions. For Croce the sense of natural beauty is not prior to but rather derivative of the sense of art. This may not seem historically likely.

As a pure complex of thought and feeling, Croce's lyrical intuition is insusceptible to categorizing of any sort. Therefore, genre distinctions such as those between comedy and tragedy or between lyric, epic, and drama are for Croce purely accidental, since they depend on the material form chosen for the actualization of the intuition. As categories, they may be necessary to librarians and useful to rationalistic literary critics, but in terms of the aesthetic question of our immediate experience of art, they are meaningless.

Even more obviously, art is not any of the rational sciences: philosophy, history, natural science, or rhetoric. Hegel may have felt that it was the destiny of literature to be superseded by philosophy, just as Pythagoras felt that music would become mathematics, but for the post-Hegelian Croce, the pursuit of the universal and the pursuit of "unreflective intuition" are entirely different and incompatible aims.

It may be less clear why Croce insists that art has nothing to do with the "play of the imagination" or the provocation of "pleasure" or "immediacy of feeling."

Here one must tread warily. The imagination is indeed the faculty that produces lyrical intuitions, but that faculty in art is not at play, as it is in a daydream, but at work, operating according to a disciplined framework. Pleasure is a by-product of art, not its essential function. And while feeling is surely one of the essential components of the lyrical intuition, the emotions of art operate at second hand: they are contemplated rather than experienced directly, as poet-critics from WILLIAM WORDS-WORTH to T. S. ELIOT have insisted.

Croce's mode of criticism follows from his premise that works of art are the unique mental products of an individual artist. The critic should merely assist the audience in seeing the integrity and clarity of the individual work of art. As Croce says in "Aesthetica in Nuce,"

> There is really no other way than to follow out the individualizing method to the very end: to treat works of art not in relation to social history but as being each one a world in itself, each one, in its hour, receiving the inflow of the whole of history, transfigured and elevated by the power of fancy into the individuality of the work of art which is a creation, not a reflection, and a monument, not a document. (*Philosophy—Poetry—History* 239; in Richter 462)

In his critical practice, Croce follows a broadly humanistic tradition by indicating the lines of force and of feeling that inform a given work. He is impressionistic in the best sense. Croce's own critical studies, including those of DANTE ALIGHIERI, Lodovico Ariosto, and Torquato Tasso, are still widely influential in Italy today.

David H. Richter

See also ITALIAN THEORY AND CRITICISM: 2. TWENTIETH CENTURY.

Benedetto Croce, *Ariosto, Shakespeare e Corneille* (1920, *Ariosto, Shakespeare, and Corneille*, trans. Douglas Ainslie, 1920), *Estetica come scienza dell' espressione e linguistica generale* (1902, *Aesthetic as Science of Expression and General Linguistic*, trans. Douglas Ainslie, 1953), *Filosofia, poesia, storia* (1951, *Philosophy—Poetry—History: An Anthology of Essays*, trans. Cecil Sprigge, 1966), *La Poesia di Dante* (1921, *The Poetry of Dante*, trans. Douglas Ainslie, 1922), *Problemi di estetica: E contributi alla storia dell' estetica italiana* (1910).

M. E. Brown, *Neo-Idealist Aesthetics: Croce—Gentile—Collingwood* (1966); H. Wildon Carr, *The Philosophy of Benedetto Croce: The Problem of Art and History* (1917); Paolo D'Angelo, *L'estetica di Benedetto Croce* (1982); Angelo De Gennaro, *The Philosophy of Benedetto Croce: An Introduction* (1961); Gian Napoleone Giordano Orsini, *Benedetto Croce: Philosopher of Art and Literary Critic* (1961); L. M. Palmer and H. S. Harris, eds., *Thought, Action, and Intuition as a Symposium on the Philosophy of Benedetto Croce* (1975); David H. Richter, ed., *The Critical Tradition: Classic Texts and Contemporary Trends* (1989); Cecil Sprigge, *Benedetto Croce: Man and Thinker* (1952); Edward Wasiolek, "Croce and Contextualist Criticism," *Modern Philology* 57 (1959); René Wellek, *Four Critics: Croce, Valéry, Lukács, and Ingarden* (1981), *A History of Modern Criticism: 1750–1950*, vol. 8, *French, Italian, and Spanish Criticism, 1900–1950* (1993).

CULTURAL STUDIES

1. United Kingdom

While the field of literary studies from its inception took as its exclusive object of interest the literary canon, cultural studies has generally been concerned with what is left over, *popular* or mass culture—newspapers, magazines, radio, film, television, popular song, and so on—following especially RAYMOND WILLIAMS's argument in *Culture and Society: 1780–1950* (1958) that a proper study of culture should be concerned with not just part but the whole of cultural production. However, in the later 1970s and 1980s cultural studies began to respond to developments of STRUCTURALISM and poststructuralism, with the result that the binary opposition between high and popular culture has been increasingly challenged. As Antony Easthope has argued in *Literary into Cultural Studies*, a sense of cultural studies has emerged that takes the works of both high and mass culture together as its purview (considering them as "texts," "discursive practices," or "signifying practices"). In Britain these changes followed particularly from the initiatives worked through in the early 1970s in the area of FILM THEORY by Stephen Heath, Colin MacCabe, Jacqueline Rose, and others associated with the journal *Screen*, initiatives that soon became influential in other academic fields—in art history, literary studies proper, and musicology, as well as in the social sciences, historical studies, and social psychology (see Antony Easthope, *British Post-Structuralism since 1968*, 1988).

The *Screen* project set out to theorize "the encounter of Marxism and psychoanalysis on the terrain of semiotics" (Heath, *"Jaws"* 201). In doing so it relied heavily on Louis Althusser's essay "Ideology and Ideological States Apparatuses" (see MARXIST THEORY AND CRITICISM: 2. STRUC-

TURALIST MARXISM), which in turn rests on JACQUES LACAN's psychoanalytic account of how the infant identifies itself in the mirror stage. Looking in a mirror, though it is never more than my likeness, I see the image reflected there as myself and *misrecognize* my identity in it ("it's me") ("The Mirror Stage," *Ecrits,* 1966, *Ecrits: A Selection,* trans. Alan Sheridan, 1977). Similarly, since I must be somewhere, I live out constituted social roles and identities as though I had freely chosen them. For Althusser it is the crucial work of ideology to "interpellate" or "hail" individuals as subjects, constructing people to act as if they were free agents. This analysis was developed by film theory and subsequently in cultural studies as an account of ideology not (in traditional terms) as content but rather as the operation of a text or group of texts, how they might work to provide a position for the reader. This theorization of *subject position* owes a lot to the writing of JULIA KRISTEVA (esp. *La Révolution du langue poétique: L'Avante-garde à la fin du XIXe siècle, Lautremont et Mallarmé,* 1974, *Revolution in Poetic Language,* trans. Margaret Waller, 1984), with the difference that while she writes of the subject as positioned within history, *Screen,* following Althusser's conception of ideology as acting to interpellate the subject, analyzed the subject as an effect of the text.

Colin MacCabe, for example, in a 1974 essay, "Realism and the Cinema: Notes on Some Brechtian Theses," aims to analyze what he calls "the classic realist text," as exemplified in both the nineteenth-century novel and traditional Hollywood. While all texts consist of a bundle of different discourses, in the classic realist text—so MacCabe proposes—discourses are composed in a hierarchy "defined in terms of an empirical notion of truth" (34). This hierarchy corresponds to that between an object language and a metalanguage, between discourse in which a sentence is *used* and a higher order or metalanguage in which that sentence might be cited or discussed. In MacCabe's example (one more controversial than he meant it to be), a passage from George Eliot's *Middlemarch* is described to show that what the characters "in" the novel say to each other constitutes an object language set off in quotation marks, while the passages without inverted commas, the narration, seems able to stand outside dialogue as a metalanguage and explain it as it cannot explain itself. In classic realist cinema what is said has the function of object language, while what the camera *shows* us performs as a metalanguage, revealing the truth about word and action. From this textual strategy two related consequences follow. One is that the metalanguage can present itself to the reader as unwritten, immaterial, a transparent window onto what is rep-

resented; another is that the reader (or viewer) is situated as though outside and looking on: "The classic realist text ensures the position of the subject in a relation of dominant specularity" (39). The position of dominant specularity could be seen as confirming the Cartesian (see RENÉ DESCARTES) or transcendental ego promoted in bourgeois culture, so that against the realist text, the modernist text, by subverting the imaginary security of the subject, potentially might act as a radical intervention (see Colin MacCabe, *James Joyce and the Revolution of the Word,* 1978). And the position of dominant specularity arguably is also a gendered position.

Laura Mulvey's essay "Visual Pleasure and Narrative Cinema," first published in *Screen* in 1975, has effectively founded a whole body of feminist scholarship concerned with cinema, painting, and the gendering of the gaze (see FILM THEORY). Picking up the work of Juliet Mitchell in her book of 1974, *Psychoanalysis and Feminism,* Mulvey draws on psychoanalysis to examine areas of ideology and gender that operate below the level of conscious intention. Conventional Hollywood cinema organizes the possibilities of the gaze into a particular structure of binary opposition, so that "active," "male," and "sexual looking" are gathered on one side, while "passive," "female," and "identification" are gathered on the other: "The determining male gaze projects its phantasy on to the female figure which is styled accordingly" (19). A whole regime of representation is summed up in Mulvey's sidehead: "Woman as image, man as bearer of the look." This analysis has been contested, even by Mulvey herself ("Afterthoughts"), but it has formed a framework for other important work, including Liz Cowie's essay "Fantasia" (*m/f* 9 [1984]), Jacqueline Rose's *Sexuality in the Field of Vision* (1986), Griselda Pollock's work in art history, *Vision and Difference: Femininity, Feminism, and Histories of Art* (1988), and Mary Ann Doane's book on "women's weepies," *The Desire to Desire: The Woman's Film of the 1940s* (1987).

Analysis of the ideological effect of a text in terms of the subject position it offers to its reader was soon taken over from work on the cinema into other areas of cultural studies, for example in 1978 in Judith Williamson's *Decoding Advertisements: Ideology and Meaning in Advertising.* It also entered literary studies, notably with Catherine Belsey's widely influential book, *Critical Practice* (1980), which acknowledges that it has drawn "very freely on recent work on film in *Screen* magazine" (69), and art history, with Norman Bryson's *Vision and Painting: The Logic of the Gaze* (1983). However, as far as cultural studies—or a reconstituted and less supinely canonical literary studies—was concerned, a profound theoretical obstacle lay in the path of these new initiatives, one acutely summarized by Stuart Hall, then head of the Centre for Contemporary Cultural Studies at the University of Birmingham. In an essay entitled "Cultural Studies: The Two Paradigms" (1980), reviewing work from the previous 20 years, Hall defines the two prevailing traditions in cultural studies as "culturalist" and "structuralist." The former, based on the work of Raymond Williams and the liberal humanist inheritance, conceives the human subject (whether individual or collective) as freely able to make up meanings for itself and rework social institutions, while the latter, deriving from structuralism and poststructuralism, envisages the subject as an identity or position determined within social and ideological structures of which he or she is an effect. Hall notes but fails to arbitrate between these two views, not least because they point to opposed and probably incompatible sets of assumptions. A culturalist study of signifying practice, affirming the active intervention of individuals and groups within history, gives prominence to the empirical subject, the "actual" reader of the text rereading and reworking it as an event in a social and historical process, while a structuralist-poststructuralist study in contrast, preoccupied with the social and textual structures that individuals live out, would analyze the text or a group of texts in terms of the position it provided to its reader (one which he or she might or might not actually take up).

Within cultural studies a determined and noble attempt to reconcile culturalism and structuralism, the actively experiencing reader with the constituted and positioned reader, was made by the Open University "Popular Culture" course, which ran from 1982 to 1987 and was taken by over 5,000 students. Sponsored by Tony Bennett and involving almost 50 teachers, this course drew on ANTONIO GRAMSCI's concept of hegemony as an explicit means to integrate culturalism and structuralism. It is argued that hegemony specifies that relations between ruling and subordinate blocs are *negotiated* and that therefore the concept encompasses a theoretical reconciliation between the imposed structures of the dominant ideology and an active cultural expression by the dominated class (see Bennett, Mercer, and Woollacott, *Popular Culture and Social Relations*). However, it is likely that this view misunderstands Hall's argument in the "Two Paradigms" essay. Bennett and his co-authors are thinking of a relationship between two blocs within the social formation, while Hall is talking about different conceptions and explanatory accounts of the social formation *as a whole*. As is well argued by William Ray in *Literary Meaning: From Phenomenology to Deconstruction* (1984), probably no total conceptualization is able to theorize together in a coherent whole both meaning as *event* (the process of meaning stressed by culturalism) and meaning as it arises from *structure* (the organization of the signifiers). If Ray is correct, there will always be a disjunction between the empirical subject and the subject as positioned by the text, between the act of reading and the text read, neither of which can be set aside in any study of culture, whether it stresses the sociological or the semiological, the social formation or the signifying practice.

That issue and the unfolding of the debate around cultural studies in the 1980s have had enormous consequences for the future of literary studies. As the theory wars of the 1970s and 1980s have worn themselves out, academic concern in the humanities increasingly has moved from theoretical generalities to how the new kinds of paradigms for textual analysis might be applied in practice across the variety of literary and non-literary texts. Though this view is certainly not accepted universally, it is integral to the new paradigms that the canon of traditional texts on which literary studies had been founded could no longer claim automatic privilege. Terry Eagleton, for example, in his enormously influential book *Literary Theory: An Introduction* (1983) argued that textual analysis should be directed at a "whole field of practices rather than just those sometimes rather obscurely labelled literature'" (205). Whether named "discursive practice," "signifying practice," or "cultural studies," a widened version of literary study is now rapidly coming to encompass areas previously designated as "media" or "communication studies" to examine contemporary film, television, advertising, and the popular press alongside works of the literary canon. In the United Kingdom the polytechnics, because of their different relation to the academy, have already widely embraced combined literary and cultural studies courses, and such work is now being instituted as well at a number of university centers—at Sussex, Cardiff, Southampton, Nottingham, and Lancaster (but notably not at the traditionally hegemonic institutions Oxford and Cambridge). In Canada and Australia growing interest in a combined literary-cultural study is gathering pace, and in the United States new forms of curriculum are already in operation at such universities as Duke, Syracuse, and Carnegie-Mellon. I would argue that the future of literary studies lies with a rethought cultural studies, one that perhaps would aim to hold the balance between culturalism and structuralism in a mode more appropriate to the study of signifying practices than of the historical formation, and so holding in the background some of the sociohistorical concern with which cultural studies began and concentrating more (but not exclusively) on textuality and modes of analysis appropriate to that.

Antony Easthope

Louis Althusser, "Ideology and Ideological State Apparatuses" (1970, *Lenin and Philosophy and Other Essays,* trans. Ben Brewster, 1971); Catherine Belsey, *Critical Practice* (1980); Tony Bennett, Colin Mercer, and Janet Woollacott, *Popular Culture and Social Relations* (1986); Tony Bennett et al., "Popular Culture" (Open University Course U203, 1981); Patrick Brantlinger, *Crusoe's Footprints: Cultural Studies in Britain and America* (1990); Terry Eagleton, *Literary Theory: An Introduction* (1983); Antony Easthope, *Literary into Cultural Studies* (1991); Antony Easthope and Kate McGowan, eds., *A Cultural Studies Reader: Texts and Textuality* (1992); John Fiske, *Understanding Popular Culture* (1989); Lawrence Grossberg, Carey Nelson, and Paula Treichler, eds., *Cultural Studies* (1992); Stuart Hall, "Cultural Studies: The Two Paradigms," *Media, Culture, and Society* 2 (1980, reprint, *Culture, Ideology, and Social Process,* ed. Tony Bennett et al., 1981), "The Emergence of Cultural Studies and the Crisis of the Humanities," *October* 53 (1990); Stephen Heath, "*Jaws,* Ideology, and Film Theory," *Popular Television and Film* (ed. Tony Bennett et al., 1981), *Questions of Cinema* (1981); Colin MacCabe, "Realism and the Cinema: Notes on Some Brechtian Theses," *Theoretical Essays: Film, Linguistics, Literature* (1985); Laura Mulvey, "Afterthoughts on 'Visual Pleasure and Narrative Cinema' inspired by King Vidor's *Duel in the Sun* (1946)" (1981, *Visual and Other Pleasures,* 1989), "Visual Pleasure and Narrative Cinema" (1975, *Visual and Other Pleasures,* 1989); Morag Shiach, *Discourse on Popular Culture: Class, Gender, History in Cultural Analysis* (1989); Graeme Turner, *British Cultural Studies: An Introduction* (1990).

2. United States

Cultural studies emerged as a distinctive academic discipline in the English-speaking world between the 1960s and the 1990s as part of the broad shift in universities to new kinds of interdisciplinary analysis. Parallel to contemporaneous developments in ethnic studies and women's studies, programs in cultural studies, which often originated as units of English or communications departments, tended to be institutionalized as centers and institutes rather than as departments. What most readily distinguished cultural studies from mainline literary studies were new and different objects of study and modes of

inquiry. In addition, cultural studies both reflected and propounded a cultural politics opposed to the belletrism and formalism characteristic of postwar academic literary studies in the Anglophone world. Typically, adherents of cultural studies conceived themselves—and were conceived by others—as being in opposition to the reigning establishment of university disciplines and values.

Among the objects of study commonly examined in programs of cultural studies were such wildly diverse "discourses" as advertising, art, architecture, urban folklore, movies, fashion, popular literary genres (thrillers, romances, Westerns, science fiction), photography, music, magazines, youth subcultures, student texts, theories of criticism, theater, radio, women's literature, television, and working-class literature. Against the regnant exclusive focus on aesthetic masterpieces of canonized high literature, advocates of cultural studies characteristically advanced the claims of "low," popular, and mass cultures. (In this work they followed in the wake of the earlier FRANKFURT SCHOOL scholars and the NEW YORK INTELLECTUALS, among others, who pioneered modes of cultural inquiry from the 1930s to the 1960s.) During the postmodern period the arts and activities to be found in the ordinary shopping mall appeared as worthy of serious study and analysis as the artifacts and artworks enthroned in the traditional monumental museum. Potentially, the whole spectrum of cultural objects, practices, and texts constituting a society provided the materials of cultural studies. In the event that belletristic literature was examined from the perspective of cultural studies, the emphasis was invariably put on literature as communal event or document with social, historical, and political roots and ramifications. In short, the work of "literature" was not treated as an autonomous aesthetic icon separable from its conditions of production, distribution, and consumption—quite the contrary.

The modes of inquiry employed in cultural studies included not only established survey techniques, field interviews, textual explications, and researches into sociohistorical backgrounds but also and especially institutional and ideological analyses. For scholars of cultural studies institutional analysis entailed a conception of institutions as productive agencies that both constituted and disseminated knowledge and belief by means of systematic practices and conventions affecting cultural discourses. For example, studies of present-day popular romances examined the practices of publishing companies and bookstores in shaping and maintaining the rules of the romance genre as well as in packaging and promoting ongoing avalanches of "successful" (re)productions of the form. Since institutions overlap, an investigation into one frequently leads to a second. In the case of romance, a scrutiny of the genre's powerful presence in television soap operas and women's magazines links together publishers, booksellers, television programmers, and magazine editors. To generalize, networks of institutions play crucial roles in creating, conditioning, and commodifying cultural works. As such, the application of institutional analysis is central to the enterprise of cultural studies.

Whereas institutional analysis is focused on the material means and methods employed by institutions involved in the circulation of cultural objects and texts, ideological analysis is given over to examining the ideas, feelings, beliefs, and representations embodied in and promulgated by the artifacts and practices of a culture. Obviously, institutional and ideological analysis overlap. For instance, Richard Ohmann in *English in America* (1976) depicted the institution of English studies as a disseminator not only of the skills of analysis, organization, and fluency but of the "attitudes" of detachment, caution, and cooperation, all of which aid the smooth operation of modern capitalist societies. Because the objects, texts, and institutions of a culture create and convey ideology, the use of ideological analysis is fundamental to the work of cultural studies, which invariably seeks to investigate the ideological dimensions and forces of cultural works.

Characteristic of cultural studies in English-speaking universities is a leftist political orientation rooted variously in Marxist, non-Marxist, and post-Marxist socialist intellectual traditions all critical of the aestheticism, formalism, anti-historicism, and apoliticism common among the dominant postwar methods of academic literary criticism. Advocates of cultural studies regularly apply to the analysis of cultural materials insights from contemporary anthropology (esp. ethnography), economics, history, media studies, political theory, and sociology. Not surprisingly, the twin habits of isolating and of monumentalizing the arts and humanities are anathema to adherents of cultural studies. To sacralize is to deracinate and mummify. Cultural studies seeks to analyze and assess the social roots, the institutional relays, and the ideological ramifications of communal events, organizations, and artifacts. Such a project predisposes analysts to intervene actively in arenas of cultural struggle. The conservative role of the traditional intellectual as disinterested connoisseur and custodian of culture is widely regarded as suspect and unworthy by proponents of cultural studies.

The most well-known academic program in cultural studies in Anglophone countries exists at the Centre (lately Department) for Contemporary Cultural Studies (CCCS), which was established at the University of Birmingham in England in 1964 under the directorship of Richard Hoggart. Initially part of the Department of English, the Centre became independent in 1972 during the directorship of Stuart Hall, whose term lasted from 1969 to 1979. Previously, Hall was the inaugural editor of Britain's *New Left Review*. It was during the 1970s that over 60 Stencilled Papers and 10 issues of the journal *Working Papers in Cultural Studies* (founded in 1971) were brought out. This journal was absorbed into a CCCS-Hutchinson Company book series that published in the closing years of the decade the collectively edited *Resistance through Rituals: Youth Sub-Cultures in Post-War Britain* (1976), *On Ideology* (1978), *Women Take Issue* (1978), *Working Class Culture* (1979), and especially *Culture, Media, Language: Working Papers in Cultural Studies, 1972–79* (1980), which amounted to a CCCS reader, complete with an introductory account of the Centre by Stuart Hall. At the peak of this pioneering period in the 1970s, the Centre had 5 faculty members and 40 graduate students. By decade's end other university programs in cultural studies were set up in England, primarily at polytechnical institutes. With the founding in England of the Cultural Studies Association in 1984, the whole contemporary movement toward establishing cultural studies in the academy attained a significant moment of maturation.

During the mid-1980s the then director and longtime member of the Birmingham Centre, Richard Johnson, had occasion to publish in the United States a landmark manifesto, "What Is Cultural Studies Anyway?" which, following Hall, observed that two distinct methodological branches of cultural studies had developed at the Centre. The "culturalist" line, derived from sociology, anthropology, and social history and influenced by the work of RAYMOND WILLIAMS and E. P. Thompson, regarded a culture as a whole way of life and struggle accessible through detailed concrete (empirical) descriptions that captured the unities or homologies of commonplace cultural forms and material life. The "(post)structuralist" line, indebted to linguistics, literary criticism, and semiotic theory and especially attentive to the work of Louis Althusser (see MARXIST THEORY AND CRITICISM: 2. STRUCTURALIST MARXISM), ROLAND BARTHES, and MICHEL FOUCAULT, conceived of cultural forms as semiautonomous inaugurating "discourses" susceptible to rhetorical and/or semiological analyses of cognitive constitutions and ideological effects. While the members of the former group preferred to research, for instance, oral histories, realistic fictions, and working-class texts, seeking to pinpoint and portray private social "experience," the latter group analyzed avant-garde or literary texts and practices, attempting to uncover underlying constitutive communal codes and conventions of representation. One especially influential American study blending culturalism and poststructuralism was EDWARD W. SAID's *Orientalism* (1978), which depicted the history of Western research on the Near East as a massive disciplinary discourse structuring and dominating the Orient in a consistently racist, sexist, and imperialistic way that bore little relation to actual human experience.

In the United States widespread academic interest in cultural studies flowered particularly during the 1980s and 1990s, primarily among university intellectuals and critics on the left. In addition to pioneering programs being established, new journals appeared, for example, *Cultural Critique, Differences, Representations* and *Social Text.* The editors of *Cultural Critique,* founded in 1985 at the University of Minnesota, declared their representative objects of study to be "received values, institutions, practices, and discourses in terms of their economic, political, social, and aesthetic genealogies, constitutions, and effects" (*Cultural Critique* 1 [1985]: 5). Regarding preferred disciplinary modes of inquiry, they singled out a "broad terrain of cultural interpretation that is currently defined by the conjuncture of literary, philosophical, anthropological, and sociological studies, of Marxist, feminist, psychoanalytic, and poststructuralist methods" (6). On the advisory board of the journal were leading American and British Marxists, nonsectarian leftists, and feminists. In the North American setting, cultural studies aspired to be a new discipline but served as an unstable meeting point for various interdisciplinary feminists, Marxists, literary and media critics, postmodern theorists, social semioticians, rhetoricians, fine arts specialists, and sociologists and historians of culture.

During the 1980s, one of the more influential American literary proponents of cultural studies was the liberal Robert Scholes, who in *Textual Power* (1985) argued that "we must stop 'teaching literature' and start 'studying texts.' Our rebuilt apparatus must be devoted to textual studies. . . . Our favorite works of literature need not be lost in this new enterprise, but the exclusivity of literature as a category must be discarded. All kinds of texts, visual as well as verbal, polemical as well as seductive, must be taken as the occasions for further textuality. And textual studies must be pushed beyond the discrete boundaries of the page and the book into the institutional practices and social structures" (16–17). Over a period of 10 years, Scholes had moved from an apolitical and belletristic STRUCTURALISM to an increasingly political "textual" (cultural) studies steeped in (post)struc-

turalist thought, as revealed in his trilogy *Structuralism in Literature: An Introduction* (1974), *Semiotics and Interpretation* (1982), and *Textual Power* (1985). Typical of some other American university intellectuals advocating cultural studies in the 1980s, Robert Scholes evidently had little knowledge of the pioneering work done by the British school in the 1970s.

What most American literary intellectuals in the post-Vietnam decade knew about British views of cultural studies came mainly from the influential last chapter of Terry Eagleton's highly popular text *Literary Theory* (1983) or occasionally from Dick Hebdige's *Subculture: The Meaning of Style* (1979) or sometimes from Janet Batsleer and others' *Rewriting English: Cultural Politics of Gender and Class* (1985), the latter two of which were works from the CCCS that gained limited notoriety in the United States. Cast in a poststructuralist mode and indebted to the Centre's earlier *Resistance through Rituals,* Hebdige's book, for example, illustrated how the spectacular styles of postwar subcultures of English working-class youths, particularly teddy boys, mods, rockers, skinheads, and punks, challenged obliquely social consensus, normalization, ideology, and hegemony, functioning through displacement as symbolic forms of dissent and resistance. "Style," in Hebdige's formulation, consisted of special disruptive combinations of dress, argot, music, and dance, often "adapted" by white youths from marginal black groups such as the Rastafarians and frequently subjected to cooption and mainstreaming by being turned into products for mass markets. As a scholar of cultural studies, Hebdige conceived "style" to be a complex material and aesthetic ensemble rooted in specifiable historical and socioeconomic contexts, possessing demonstrable semiotic values and ideological valences, all potentially subject to diffusion, routinization, and commodification by means of the agencies and institutions of established societies. From the vantage point of cultural studies, the aesthetic and the social, innovation and history, the avant-garde and the lower-class, creative words and common gripes, disco and assembly line, nestled together inseparably and inevitably.

It was not surprising that in the closing years of the 1980s a new journal, *Cultural Studies,* was launched under the guidance of an international editorial collective with the explicit goal of fostering "developments in the area worldwide, putting academics, researchers, students and practitioners in different countries and from diverse intellectual traditions in touch with each other and each other's work" (1 [1987]: flyleaf). What this emergent internationalization indicated was the increasing expansion of research interest and commitment among university intellectuals and scholars to the work of cultural studies. At the same time, cultural studies scholars stepped up work on postcolonial cultures, focusing on deracinated subaltern subjects, heterodox traditions, and hybrid regimes scattered across the globe. Near the end of the century the diffusion of cultural studies appeared headed for increasing diversification into multiple branches and modes.

Vincent B. Leitch

Janet Batsleer et al., *Rewriting English: Cultural Politics of Gender and Class* (1985); *Cultural Studies and New Historicism,* special issue, *Journal of the Midwest Modern Language Association* 24 (1991); Terry Eagleton, "Conclusion: Political Criticism," *Literary Theory: An Introduction* (1983); Michel Foucault, *La Volonté de savoir* (1976, *The History of Sexuality, Vol. 1: An Introduction,* trans. Robert Hurley, 1978); Henry Giroux et al., "The Need for Cultural Studies: Resisting Intellectuals and Oppositional Public Spheres," *Dalhousie Review* 64 (1984); Lawrence Grossberg, "The Circulation of Cultural Studies," *Critical Studies in Mass Communication* 6 (1989), "Cultural Studies Revisited and Revised," *Communications in Transition: Issues and Debates in Current Research* (ed. Mary S. Mander, 1983), "The Formation of Cultural Studies: An American in Birmingham," *Strategies* 2 (1989), "History, Politics, and Postmodernism: Stuart Hall and Cultural Studies," *Journal of Communication Inquiry* 10 (1986, special issue on Stuart Hall); Lawrence Grossberg, Carey Nelson, and Paula Treichler, eds., *Cultural Studies* (1992); Stuart Hall, "Cultural Studies: The Two Paradigms," *Media, Culture, and Society* 2 (1980, reprint, *Culture, Ideology, and Social Process,* ed. Tony Bennett et al., 1981); Stuart Hall et al., *Culture, Media, Language: Working Papers in Cultural Studies, 1972–79* (1980); Richard Johnson, "What Is Cultural Studies Anyway?" *Social Text* 16 (1986–87); Vincent B. Leitch, "Cultural Criticism," *New Princeton Encyclopedia of Poetry and Poetics* (3d ed., ed. Alex Preminger and T. V. F. Brogan, 1993), *Cultural Criticism, Literary Theory, Poststructuralism* (1992), "Leftist Criticism from the 1960s to the 1980s," *American Literary Criticism from the Thirties to the Eighties* (1988); Cary Nelson and Lawrence Grossberg, eds., *Marxism and the Interpretation of Culture* (1988); Richard Ohmann, *English in America: A Radical View of the Profession* (1976); Jeffrey M. Peck, "Advanced Literary Study as Cultural Study: A Redefinition of the Discipline," *Profession 85* (1985); Edward W. Said, *Orientalism* (1978); Robert Scholes, *Textual Power: Literary Theory and the Teaching of English* (1985); Gayatri Chakravorty Spivak, *In Other Worlds: Essays in Cultural Politics* (1987); Graeme Turner, *British Cultural Studies: An Introduction* (1990); Hayden White, *Tropics of Discourse: Essays in Cultural Criticism* (1978); Raymond Williams, *Culture and Society, 1780–1950* (1958).

DANTE ALIGHIERI

"Modern" literary criticism and theory can be said to begin with Dante Alighieri (1265–1321) and his work. For the first time in Western culture, a nonclassical writer successfully established himself not only as an *auctor* but also, and more significantly, as a vernacular *auctor*, the match of the great Greek and Latin poets (see, e.g., *Inferno,* canto 4). As a result, Dante's extensive interest in matters of literary criticism and history was primarily aimed at explaining and justifying the enormity of his claims and the attendant "experimental" quality of his own writings. "A constant feature of Dante's personality is . . . the way in which technical reflection constantly appears alongside poetry" (Contini 4) in an ever more sophisticated act of auto-elucidation, a procedure that per se represents an important new direction in the history of exegesis. The extent of the poet's success can be gauged by the fact that in Italy the *Comedy* (c. 1307–21) almost immediately inspired an imposing tradition of commentary and discussion on a par with that normally reserved for classical authors. As the poet had hoped and planned, his contemporaries recognized and confirmed his "authoritativeness." Benvenuto da Imola (c. 1330–88), the most important of his fourteenth-century *lectores,* openly stated that Dante was the greatest of all poets (1:8).

Dante was born into a noble Florentine family and died, a political exile, in Ravenna. He lived during a period of cultural and social transition, and his *oeuvre* both reflects the tensions of his time and exploits the possibilities offered by the shifts in ideology. Dante was always fascinated by new ideas, and his major works—the *Vita Nuova* (c. 1292–94), the *Convivio* (c. 1304–7), the *De vulgari eloquentia* (c. 1305–7), the *Commedia,* and the *Monarchia* (c. 1316–18)—constitute significant original developments in the history of literature. They are united by similar "summative" designs that reflect Dante's attempts to come to terms with the totality and variety of his world. They also share a deeply ethical, not to say religious, viewpoint, which endows them with strong didactic qualities. The problem facing Dante of how most

effectively to present his "encyclopedic" concerns, and thereby of how to influence his audience, while at the same time accounting for his ideological and formal innovations ensured that all his writings were characterized by a common fascination with literary matters. Dante thus addressed most of the key critical issues of his day, ranging from the social and personal functions of literature to its contacts with SEMIOTICS, education, and aesthetics, and from the differences between divine and human writing to linguistic history.

Poetry and poetics were indissolubly linked in Dante's mind, as is immediately clear from the fact that two of his works, the *Vita Nuova* and the *Convivio,* are both closely modeled on the structures of critical texts, in particular on those of the glossed poetic manuscript. The former is an account of the protagonist's divinely sanctioned exemplary love for Beatrice. It is recounted via a mixture of verse, which seemingly was written first and provides the immediate record of his feelings, and prose, which was added later and analyzes the formal organization of the poems according to the exegetical conventions of the *divisio textus* and clarifies their "deeper" meaning (ch. 1). Similarly, the *Convivio,* which Dante repeatedly labeled a *comento* and which has overt links with the *accessus ad auctores,* was planned as a philosophical summa built around a literal and doctrinal allegorical "reading" of fourteen of his canzoni. (Dante in fact abandoned the treatise after writing the introduction and analyzing just three of the poems.) By applying to his vernacular poetry interpretive schemes that conventionally had been restricted to scriptural and classical texts, Dante both highlighted the prestige of his "contemporary" writings and provided recognizable exegetical means with which their *novitas* could be appreciated.

It was a hallmark of Dante's critical self-reflection always to assess the originality of his works in relation to the tradition. Without such a point of reference, the danger existed that his *oeuvre* would be "uninterpretable," something Dante considered to be a major fault (*Vita Nuova* ch. 25). Thus, the poet structured the *Vita Nuova* in such a way as to present an idealized picture of the development of the youthful Italian vernacular love lyric, which reaches its apogee in his own "religious" poetry in praise of Beatrice. In the *prosimetrum,* Dante also implicitly examined the romance erotic tradition as a whole (Picone) and, at the same time, highlighted once again the superiority of his own art, since the source of its inspiration was not earthly desire but Christian *caritas.* From this perspective, the *Vita Nuova* is a summa of both a national and an international literary culture. In his other works, too, Dante incorporated and judged the practices of classical and medieval writers in order to underline their weaknesses, while putting forward his own writings as examples of how their limitations might be overcome (Barolini; Contini 33–62, 69–111; Hollander, *Il Virgilio*). Yet, despite his reservations, the poet was always careful to recognize the achievements of his fellow artists and the debts he owed them (it is enough to think of the prominence he gave Virgil in the *Commedia*). Ultimately, another of Dante's successes was to have revitalized the concepts of *imitatio* and *aemulatio* (the rigidly hierarchical rhetorical doctrine of strict creative dependence on, and limited independence from, the literary techniques of one's models).

Dante was intent on becoming not simply an *auctor* but the *auctor* par excellence, and "his self-promotion was inextricably intertwined with the promotion of the Italian language" (Minnis, Scott, and Wallace 374). In the *Vita Nuova* he conventionally acknowledged the superiority of Latin writers over vernacular ones and claimed that the *volgare* should only be used when writing about love, so that women could understand the poetry addressed to them. However, he also challenged his own claims from within the book, first, by granting the label *poeta,* until then the exclusive property of classical *auctores,* to vernacular writers, and, then, by discussing in his prose biographical and literary matters that went beyond the narrow confines of the erotic. In the *Convivio* this initial challenge to Latin culture became much more sustained. Although on the surface Dante continued to recognize the preeminence of Latin "on account of its nobility, virtue and beauty" (1.5.7), there is no longer even the hint in the treatise that the vernacular should be restricted in its *materia.* Indeed, Dante so stresses its communicative power that he concludes his discussion by prophesying the vernacular's imminent victory over Latin (1.13.12).

The *De vulgari eloquentia* takes the positions of the previous two works to their logical conclusion: not only can *poetae vulgares* talk about the same things the poets of antiquity talked about but they can actually do this in a language that is "nobler" than Latin, since it is older,

universal, and natural (1.1.4). Ostensibly a rhetorical manual giving instruction on how to compose in the vulgar tongue, in reality the treatise is an "encyclopedic" survey of language that touches, *inter alia,* on linguistic history, the lessons of the *genera dicendi* (whose efficacy Dante strongly supports), metrics, the Italian dialects, and ethics. In particular, it continues the analysis of the romance literary tradition begun in the *Vita Nuova* and attempts to establish that the "illustrious vernacular," the refined supraregional form of Italian that had primarily been used by Dante himself, was the most effective language for the writing of vernacular verse.

Despite undoubted and important elements of continuity, what separates Dante's critical thinking in his three early works from that in the *Commedia* is the latter's much greater radicalism. When he composed his masterpiece, the poet rejected many of the traditional assumptions about literature that had structured his previous writings. Thus, he openly revealed the superiority of his great epic poem in relation even to the foremost classical authors. He rejected the conventions of the *genera dicendi* (that artificial hierarchy of *auctoritates,* subject matter, style, and language on which all thinking on literature had stood at least from the time of ARISTOTLE); he claimed instead that since his poem was divinely inspired and bore God's message for the reform of humanity, it was modeled on the all-embracing stylistic and thematic interests of God's two "books": the universe and the Bible. Since the *Commedia* has no overt formal links with the ordinary conventions of exegesis, Dante introduced into the poem a highly sophisticated internal system of self-reflective critical allusion that is closely tied to the development of the action and to its poetic representation. Many episodes not only describe events in the afterlife but also raise metaliterary issues. For instance, Dante organized several cantos in such a way as to reveal the poem's unique dependence on the structures of fourfold scriptural allegory (Barański, "La lezione"). Although in book 2 of the *Convivio,* after conventionally examining the fundamental differences between secular and biblical allegory (2.1.2–8), Dante had already hinted that his works could on occasion be interpreted according to the latter exegetical scheme (2.1.15), he had also been extremely careful to assert that in general his canzoni needed to be considered according to the traditional twofold "senses" of the "allegory of the poets" (2.1.4). In the *Commedia,* on the other hand, no such caveats are forthcoming.

Given the audacious nature of Dante's claim, supplementary evidence for the *Commedia*'s links with the *allegoria in factis* has been sought in the so-called "Epistle to

Cangrande" (7–8). Although a majority of scholars continue to believe that the letter was written by Dante, much argument has been accumulated in recent years against its authenticity. In fact, its discussion of the poem's allegory, rather than supporting the *Commedia*'s contacts with the Bible, implies that it should be read according to the twofold model of the *allegoria in verbis;* similarly, its general presentation of the *Commedia* offers no sense of the poem's uniqueness. The letter treats Dante's "sacred poem" as if it were any work of fiction with an ethically useful message—an approach typical of the most basic trends in medieval criticism. The epistle is a fairly ordinary *commentarium* (Barański, "Comedia"), an unexceptional part of that rich debate that characterized Dante's fourteenth-century reception, a debate whose greatest merit was to have confirmed the possibility and the desirability of a hermeneutics of vernacular writing. Moreover, it was a debate of such stature that it attracted the attention of both the principal intellectual figures of the century: Petrarch (1304–74) with considerable reluctance and GIOVANNI BOCCACCIO with avid enthusiasm. The *Commedia* stimulated an extraordinarily detailed exegesis of its "literal" meaning and of its allegorical "senses" (Minnis, Scott, and Wallace 439–519); at the same time, however, few of the commentators were prepared to accept Dante's claim to be writing according to the conventions of scriptural allegory, just as none, with the exception of Benvenuto, were willing to analyze the implications of his unconventional formal "experimentation." More crucially, Dante and his poem also became directly implicated in key current critical questions: the relative standing of Latin and the vernacular, the role of the poet, and the relationship between poetry and theology. It thus seems appropriate that the poet who first theorized and demonstrated the value of vernacular writing should have continued to this day to be an obligatory point of reference in most major critical discussions of literature.

Zygmunt G. Barański

See also MEDIEVAL THEORY AND CRITICISM.

Dante Alighieri, *The Banquet* (trans. Christopher Ryan, 1989), *Dante's Lyric Poetry* (ed. and trans. Kenelm Foster and Patrick Boyde, 2 vols., 1967), *De vulgari eloquentia* (trans. A. G. Ferrers Howell, 1973), *La Divina Commedia* (ed. Natalino Sapegno, 3 vols., 1955, 3d ed., 1985), *The Divine Comedy* (trans. John D. Sinclair, 3 vols., 1961), *Dantis Alagherii Epistolae: The Letters of Dante* (ed. and trans. Paget Toynbee, 2d ed., 1920), *Opere minori* (2 vols., 1979–88), *La Vita Nuova* (trans. Mark Musa, 1962); Benvenuti de

Rambaldis de Imola, *Comentum super Dantis Aldigherij Comoediam* (ed. J. P. Lacaita, 5 vols., 1887).

Zygmunt Barański, "Comedia: Notes on Dante, the Epistle to Cangrande, and Medieval Comedy," *Lectura Dantis* 8 (1991), "Dante's (Anti-) Rhetoric: Notes on the Poetics of the Commedia," *Moving in Measure: Essays Presented to Brian Moloney* (ed. Judith Bryce and Doug Thompson, 1989), "La lezione esegetica di *Inferno* I: Allegoria, storia e letteratura nella Commedia," *Dante e le forme dell'allegoresi* (ed. Michelangelo Picone, 1987); Teodolinda Barolini, *Dante's Poets* (1984); Gianfranco Contini, *Un'idea di Dante* (1976); Robert Hollander, *Allegory in Dante's "Commedia"* (1969), *Il Virgilio dantesco* (1983); Francesco Mazzoni, "L'Epistola a Cangrande," *Atti della Accademia Nazionale dei Lincei. Classe di Scienze morali, storiche e filologiche,* 8th ser., 10 (1955); Pier Vincenzo Mengaldo, *Linguistica e retorica di Dante* (1978); A. J. Minnis, A. B. Scott, and David Wallace, eds., *Medieval Literary Theory and Criticism, c. 1100–c. 1375* (1988); Jean Pépin, *Dante et la tradition de l'allégorie* (1970); Michelangelo Picone, *"Vita Nuova" e tradizione romanza* (1979); Bruno Sandkühler, *Die frühen Dantekommentare und ihr Verhältnis zur mittelalterlichen Kommentartradition* (1967).

DECONSTRUCTION

"Deconstruction" is the name given to a radical and wide-ranging development in the human sciences, especially philosophy and literary criticism, initiated by the French philosopher Jacques Derrida in a series of highly influential books published in the late 1960s and early 1970s, including (in translation): *Of Grammatology, Writing and Difference, Speech and Phenomena, Margins of Philosophy,* and *Dissemination.* "Deconstruction," Derrida's coinage, has subsequently become synonymous with a particular method of textual analysis and philosophical argument involving the close reading of works of literature, philosophy, psychoanalysis, linguistics, and anthropology to reveal logical or rhetorical incompatibilities between the explicit and implicit planes of discourse in a text and to demonstrate by means of a range of critical techniques how these incompatibilities are disguised and assimilated by the text. In one of its typical analytical procedures, a deconstructive reading focuses on binary oppositions within a text, first, to show how those oppositions are structured hierarchically; second, to overturn that hierarchy temporarily, as if to make the text say the opposite of what it appeared to say initially; and third, to displace and reassert both terms of the opposition within a nonhierarchical relationship of "difference."

Both historically and methodologically, deconstruction as a form of critical reading is related to the advent of poststructuralism. In addition to influences from FRIEDRICH NIETZSCHE and MARTIN HEIDEGGER, several of its key concepts are derived from the structural linguistics of FERDINAND DE SAUSSURE's *Course in General Linguistics* (1916), which inaugurated STRUCTURALISM by postulating such ideas about language as the arbitrary nature of the linguistic sign; the division of the sign into *signifier* (the spoken or written word) and *signified* (the mental concept); the notion of linguistic value as a function of "difference" or noncoincidence rather than of correspondence or nomenclature; and the adumbration of SEMIOTICS or semiology (see CHARLES SANDERS PEIRCE), the study of signs and their mechanisms of signification. By grounding his theory in the arbitrary nature of the sign, Saussure affirmed that there is no intrinsic, organic, or "motivated" reason for signifying a particular concept by means of a particular word; the meaning of a word is arbitrary but agreed upon by social convention. Hence words acquire value or identity not through any natural correspondence between signifier and signified but through each word's opposition to every other word within a system of interdependence in which both signifiers and signifieds are defined in terms of what they are not, that is, in terms of a simultaneous linguistic presence and absence, or what Saussure calls "difference" (*Course in General Linguistics,* trans. Wade Baskin, 1959, 111–22).

The concept of difference is crucial to Derrida, who uses it to "deconstruct" Western philosophy, which he argues is founded on a theory of "presence," in which metaphysical notions such as truth, being, and reality are determined in their relation to an ontological center, essence, origin *(archè),* or end *(telos)* that represses absence and difference for the sake of metaphysical stability. The best-kept secret of Western metaphysics is thus the historical repression of difference through a philosophical vocabulary that favors presence in the form of voice, consciousness, and subjectivity. Derrida calls this philosophy "logocentrism" or "phonocentrism" in that it is based on a belief in a *logos* or *phonè,* a self-present word constituted not by difference but by presence (*Writing and Difference* 278–82). Logocentrism, for Derrida, represents Western culture's sentimental desire for a natural or Adamic language whose authority is guaranteed by a divine, transcendental signified. On the surface, language seems unwilling to face up to its human arbitrariness, yet on closer inspection it also appears to call attention to its differential structure: language at once posits and retracts its own desire for presence.

Derrida's deconstructive method proceeds by means of slow and ingeniously detailed close readings of texts, focusing on those points where a binary opposition (e.g., signifier/signified, presence/absence, nature/culture, literal/figural, outside/inside), a line of argument, or even a single word breaks down to reveal radical incongruities in the logic or rhetoric. Unlike ambiguity, irony, or paradox, these incompatibilities cannot be harmonized in the service of textual "unity" or "integrity," terms that for Derrida would be synonymous with "self-presence." Instead, the contradictions expose the text to the force of its own difference, its displacement from a univocal center of meaning. They show that what a text says and how it says it do not converge but simultaneously strive toward and defer convergence. Deconstruction always reveals difference within unity.

One of Derrida's clearest examples of a deconstructive reading concerns the relation between speech and writing in Saussure's *Course (Of Grammatology* 27–73). Whereas Saussure, as "phonocentric" linguist, favors speech as the proper object of linguistic investigation, rather than writing as a secondary representation or even disguise of speech, he is forced to acknowledge the dangerous, usurping power of writing over speech (*Course* 24–31). Derrida approaches this problem, first, by confirming historically the priority of voice over the letter: speech is immediate, self-present, and authentic in that it is uttered by a speaker who hears and understands himself or herself in the moment of speaking; by contrast, writing is the copy of speech and is therefore derivative, marginal, and delayed. But having outlined a speech/writing hierarchy in this way, Derrida shows how Saussure's text inverts the hierarchy, giving priority to writing over speech. The inversion of the hierarchy constitutes one-half of a deconstruction; Derrida completes the procedure by showing how *in Saussure's own terms* both speech and writing are subsumed into a larger linguistic field in which all language, spoken and written, is constituted by difference rather than hierarchy. Thus those inferior, secondary qualities attributed to writing (temporal delay, spatial distance from a speaker) are seen to inhabit speech itself; difference has been there, too, all along.

The privileging of speech and the repression of writing represent for Derrida a fundamental aspect of the logocentric history of Western culture. In order to deconstruct this hierarchical tradition of presence, Derrida elaborates Saussure's notion of linguistic difference to create what he calls *différance,* spelled with an *a* (*Speech and Phenomena* 129–60). (In French there is no phonetic difference between *différence* and *différance;* the difference, seen and not heard, thus reveals in writing something speech does not have.) *Différance* retains its Saussurean structuralist connotation of noncoincidence—as well as its meanings of deferring in time / differing in space—but Derrida expands the concept to include the whole field of signs. This field he names *écriture,* or "writing," not in the literal sense of graphic script but in the figural sense of writing as any system inhabited by differance. The study of writing, which he calls "grammatology," is the science of differance itself, involving the analysis of the play of terms within a closed semiotic system in which each term acquires value only through its opposition to the other terms. "Play," another name for differance, is Derrida's word for the interpenetration of terms—that is, how each sign simultaneously confers and derives meaning with respect to other signs, so that any given sign is tacitly implied in another as a "trace" or an effect of linguistic interdependence (*Speech and Phenomena* 154–58; *Writing and Difference* 292).

The concept of a linguistic system—for example, a text—structured by difference raises questions concerning referentiality, meaning, and representation in language. Instead of resting assured in the ability of the sign to embody meaning, or to refer simply and directly to an object existing in the outside world, a deconstructive interpreter such as Derrida affirms that there is nothing "outside" the text and that meaning and reference must be constituted from within the system as functions of difference (*Of Grammatology* 158). Referentiality is not denied so much as it is problematized: if signs acquire linguistic value only insofar as they are opposed to and differentiated from other signs, then a word's "reference" must necessarily take into account its own difference. Thus what a word is "about" is partly itself, in its very "aboutness." This idea is analogous to the phenomenological concept of "intentionality" or directedness, by which one means that consciousness is always conscious "of" something present to but different from consciousness itself. Deconstruction turns reference into self-reference, avoiding the misunderstanding that meaning is created by directedness from words to things rather than from words to words in an "intertextual" play or semiosis. Linguistic representation, in this view, becomes less a mimesis of the world than a self-representation in which rhetorical operations at once repress and foreground themselves, creating an illusion of referentiality that veils an abyss of words.

Critics of deconstruction have tended to address two polarized issues. The first issue, in a sense superficial, is

Derrida's prose style, a challenging, allusive, witty, even literary style—it has been compared to the style of James Joyce, and Derrida himself has written on Joyce—that some readers feel is "mere wordplay," ingenious in its puns and other tropes but also obfuscating and resistant to comprehension. Derrida's prose may dazzle, critics say, but it does not enlighten, preferring instead to indulge in jargon, rhetorical games, and overly subtle metaphysical conceits. Against such a criticism it is possible to argue that Derrida's style, difficulties of English translation notwithstanding, is a deliberate and strategic expression of his theory: there is nothing "mere" or trivial about wordplay; on the contrary, "play" is what constitutes words themselves, what gives them linguistic value in their very difference. While such a counterargument is unlikely to convince some critics, or to succeed in justifying a genuinely demanding style, it is nevertheless an argument implicit in Derrida's own work.

The second issue is much deeper than surface style. If language, metaphysics, and consciousness really are structured by difference, then there can be no solid foundation, no fixed point of reference, no authority or certainty, either ontological or interpretive. Everything can be "put in question," that is, viewed as arbitrary, free-floating elements in a closed system of "writing," with the result that previously settled assumptions of stability and coherence, both in words and in things, become radically shaken, even, as a number of critics have claimed, to the point of nihilism. Again, it is possible to counter this charge, as some of Derrida's followers have done, by showing that deconstruction seeks not to destroy meaning but to expose the production of meaning as an arbitrary effect of writing. The exposure of this arbitrariness is most apparent at those points where a text's explicit statement is incompatible with its implicit principles of logic or rhetoric.

These two main criticisms, when viewed together, form a paradoxical hierarchy of surface and depth that can itself be deconstructed. According to normal logic, it is puzzling that something as superficial as mere wordplay could strike so deeply to the root of Western metaphysics. But according to the logic of paradox, or to use a trope appropriated by deconstructive terminology, the "aporia," the hierarchical opposition of surface and depth, in which depth is valorized over surface, the ground over the figure, seems to be inverted and then deconstructed in such a way that surface interpenetrates ground, thus constituting a relationship of difference rather than of discrete self-presence. Superficiality appears to inhabit the very depths of language.

Despite these and other resistances to deconstruction, Derrida's impact on critical thought, as evidenced in the pages of scholarly journals and books, has been significant and extensive. As part of a general poststructuralist tendency to move language to the forefront of discussion—that is, to rethink both word and world from the point of view of textuality—deconstruction has had a vital influence in multidisciplinary studies involving feminism, theology, psychoanalysis, Marxism, anthropology, and linguistics. As a method of literary criticism, however, deconstruction first became identified largely with the work of certain critics at Yale University—GEOFFREY H. HARTMAN, J. HILLIS MILLER, and PAUL DE MAN—though these critics have responded to Derrida in markedly different ways.

Hartman's engagement with deconstruction can be seen most obviously in terms of style, though Hartman would quickly remind readers that the question of style is also the question of method. In its own method, Hartman's style operates largely on the level of the signifier in a punning, associative manner that incorporates both learned allusion and verbal cliché, always calling attention to questions of language and forcing the reader to recognize that texts are also intertexts. In this way Hartman attempts to reclaim for interpretation a sense of literary history—classical, Romantic, and modern.

In the preface to *Deconstruction and Criticism,* Hartman describes himself as barely a deconstructor (ix), but his recent work on William Wordsworth, for example, is thoroughly informed by poststructuralist ideas about the priority of the signifier over the signified, the textualization of consciousness, and the rhetoric of form. Yet the question of style always seems uppermost in Hartman's mind, whether in discussions of Derrida, Wordsworth, or Shakespeare. In his most theoretical moments Hartman remains text-oriented, committed to explicating but moreover to interrogating the text, as well as critical commentary on it. To some extent this orientation accounts both for the appearance that he is not a systematic deconstructor and for his longstanding interest in the practice of interpretation—including his recent involvement with Midrashic commentary—as a legitimate and independent, though not autotelic, form of writing. Interpretation, for Hartman, must always be a reflective act, a "consciousness of self" (*Wordsworth's Poetry* 17) raised to critical pitch in order to question and to problematize this turning of the mind upon itself. The interpreter must be located in time and history and culture, but never entirely outside language. As an answer to the art of literature, Hartman's continuing effort is to develop for criticism a responsible style.

J. Hillis Miller enters deconstruction through language

itself, the "groundless ground" of words that offers an illusion of presence and reference only for them to be swallowed up in an abyss of difference. Miller repeatedly uses the concept of an abyss structure, or *mise en abyme,* to suggest the possibility of infinite play in language, the endless substitution of one sign for another (*Deconstruction and Criticism* 232). The expression *mise en abyme,* taken from heraldry via André Gide and used strategically by Derrida, denotes the repetition-in-miniature of a whole within itself, as in the example of a painting within a painting. In such a model, repetition has, as Derrida would say, "always already" taken place: the regression is synchronic, at once originary and teleological. No matter where the regression halts, there will always be the traces of past and future repetitions.

Miller sees such a theory as part of a "tradition of difference" working within and against a "tradition of presence" ("Tradition and Difference"). Deconstruction works "within" logocentrism because it cannot exist "outside" it; there is nothing outside a logocentric metaphysic in Western culture, no such thing as a deconstructive metaphysic: deconstruction stands in interdependent relation to logocentrism even as one sign does to another in Saussurean linguistics. Every presence in language, Miller argues, can be deconstructed and exposed as difference, shown to be based on a baseless fabric of words, not a real metaphysical ground. Whether the key to the abyss in a text is a semantic ambiguity, a double-faced etymology, or a tropological deviance, it is in any event a linguistic problem, a question of language as such. The critic's function is to face that problem, not to attempt to solve or neutralize it, but to recognize the abyss as an inherent feature of an arbitrary and differential system of language.

In this sense, deconstruction for Miller is not a method of analysis that a critic "applies" to a text. It is something that the text has already done to itself. Every text is always already deconstructed. What the critic does, then, is repeat the text in his or her analysis, that is, repeat its rhetorical operations, its linguistic maneuvers, its very difference. Deconstruction, Miller claims, is just good close reading (*Deconstruction and Criticism* 230). Such a statement has two implications, the first of which has already been noted: deconstruction is less an applied method than an intrinsic habit of language; second, all texts, not just some texts or some periods of literature, can be deconstructed. If play, difference, the abyss, and the trace, for example, are the "essence" of language, then there is no theoretical reason why all discourse—literary and nonliterary, Romantic and modern—should not be subject to the radical forces of "writing."

While Miller is often regarded as the spokesperson for Yale deconstruction in that he has attempted in his writing, in conferences, and in panel discussions and interviews to explain deconstruction and defend it against charges of hermeneutical anarchy and nihilism, Paul de Man, by contrast, is a deconstructor who makes no apology for either his method or its startling results. De Man's interest is in the operation of rhetorical figures, and his essays often focus on a single trope—metaphor, prosopopoeia, apostrophe, or metonymy—as a means of opening up a text to its "allegory of reading," by which de Man means the text's reflexive awareness of itself as a system of rhetorical figures. Allegory, de Man argues, belongs to a "rhetoric of temporality" (*Blindness and Insight* 187–228) in which signs repeat other signs and in that repetition signify their difference. Reading is an act that critics perform vis-à-vis texts but also something that texts perform on themselves in those moments when they declare and at the same time dispute their status as language.

De Man's method of textual analysis resembles Derrida's in its recurrent effort to uncover hierarchical oppositions within texts and to reveal the linguistic and philosophical grounds upon which those hierarchies are built. Such a method, called a "critique," seeks to make explicit what is implicit, assumed, repressed, or contradicted in a text. Thus de Man is less concerned to explicate theme than to show how rhetoric is "thematized," that is, how the literal or narrative level of a text may repeat its figural substructure. Stylistically, however, de Man is far from Derrida: puns, multilingual resonances, and other rhetorical flourishes do not play a significant role in de Man's prose, which by contrast is sedate and analytical.

Deconstruction for de Man involves the careful drawing out of those moments when what a text says seems at odds with the rhetoric in which it says it. Such moments are examples of what de Man calls "undecidability" or "unreadability," when questions of epistemology are suspended within rhetoric and ways of knowing are dependent on ways of saying. The figure for such an impasse is the aporia, or textual doubt, involving the mutual assertion and negation of opposing systems of logic or rhetoric. In an aporia, nothing can be harmonized, nor can it be wholly canceled; any figure in question oscillates between contrary poles of discourse. For example, a text may lay claim to a certain figure of rhetoric—metaphor, perhaps—but if one reads carefully, de Man suggests, one will find that the privileged term or figure is part of a rhetorical hierarchy that depends on the repression of an opposing term—say, metonymy (*Allegories of Reading* 13–16). But the repression can never be complete; indeed, the moment of deconstruction will be precisely that instant when the return of the repressed figure occurs and the most striking metaphorical identifications are revealed to depend on metonymic contiguities. Metaphor and metonymy neither simply assert nor automatically cancel each other; they interinvolve themselves in a simultaneous affirmation and negation of their rhetorical authority. All texts, literary or critical, go on forever saying and unsaying their own language.

In the initial stages of deconstruction, from 1966 through the early 1980s, the Yale critics exerted the chief influence on the development of deconstructive criticism. Since then, however, deconstruction has not been confined to any one school or group of critics, though many of today's leading deconstructors do trace their critical affiliations back to the Yale school, as former students or otherwise. Not unexpectedly (nor unproblematically), this second phase of deconstruction can be described as *applied* deconstruction, or "deconstruction and *x*"—deconstruction and feminism, deconstruction and psychoanalysis, deconstruction and Marxism, and so on. In each case the insights and techniques of deconstructive reading are transferred to another field of the human sciences, sometimes with very fruitful results. (For whatever reasons, the reverse cross-fertilization—for example, a psychoanalytic or feminist reading of deconstruction—has not occurred to the same extent.) A further distinction might be made between criticism *on* deconstruction and deconstructive criticism: many articles and books have been published to explain or to market deconstruction, but these, obviously, are not necessarily the same as a deconstructive criticism. Indeed, as Rodolphe Gasché has written in "Deconstruction as Criticism," even much of what passes for deconstructive criticism is not really deconstructive (*Glyph* 6 [1979]). Among poststructuralist literary critics writing in the later 1980s and 1990s, those most closely identified with the practice of deconstruction overwhelmingly show the influence of Derrida in the spirit of their criticism but the impact of de Man in their technique.

The best-known second-generation deconstructor is undoubtedly Barbara Johnson, whose two books *The Critical Difference: Essays in the Contemporary Rhetoric of Reading* (1980) and *A World of Difference* (1987), along with her translations of Derrida, quickly became regarded as classics of deconstructive criticism. Deeply influenced by de Man's teaching, Johnson brilliantly adapted his mode of dismantling texts through close readings of their rhetorical operations. Her analyses of ROLAND BARTHES, Herman Melville, EDGAR ALLAN POE, JACQUES

LACAN, and Derrida are dramatically ingenious and original and stand as excellent models of deconstructive readings. In her second book, however, she modifies the strict literary focus of her method to include questions of gender, race, canonicity, and the institutionalization of academic criticism. Johnson takes deconstruction, and theory generally, out of the realm of critical abstraction to apply it to political concerns: feminist literature, African-American writing, and polemics and patriarchy in criticism. For Johnson, deconstruction is not just a technique of reading literary texts but an attitude toward a whole field of signs, an entire world composed of textual, sexual, and racial difference.

Johnson's later work thus may be viewed as the second stage of deconstruction, as its applied rather than purely theoretical mode, or simply as what Johnson calls the "consequences of theory." While such a binary opposition between abstraction and application, or between theory and practice, is itself suspicious to a deconstructor, it is a distinction that Johnson herself makes. Of course, applied deconstruction is always already at work in any deconstructive reading, no matter what the text; however, what differentiates deconstructive criticism of the 1980s and 1990s from its earlier rhetorical and phenomenological types is the target or context, now more likely to be "political" in some sense. While deconstruction has always been either implicitly or explicitly concerned with problems in the history of Western philosophy and culture, and therefore necessarily with ethical and political issues, critics such as Johnson address these concerns of the "real world" (always written in ironic quotation marks) directly and self-consciously, with the full complement of deconstructive techniques at their disposal.

Attempts to discuss deconstruction in connection with Marxism and NEW HISTORICISM have been made by critics such as Marjorie Levinson, Andrew Parker ("Between Dialectics and Deconstruction: Derrida and the Reading of Marx," *After Strange Texts: The Role of Theory in the Study of Literature,* ed. Gregory S. Jay and David L. Miller, 1985), Michael Ryan (*Marxism and Deconstruction,* 1982), and GAYATRI CHAKRAVORTY SPIVAK ("Speculation on Reading Marx: After Reading Derrida," *Post-Structuralism and the Question of History,* ed. Derek Attridge, Geoff Bennington, and Robert Young, 1987). The marriage has not been particularly fruitful; not surprisingly, deconstruction and Marxism have been seen as oxymoronic bedfellows, and critics inevitably tend to privilege one methodology over the other. While Ryan argues that deconstruction "put[s] the very possibility of a totalistic [i.e., Marxist] reading into question" ("Political Criti-

cism," *Contemporary Literary Theory,* ed. G. Douglas Atkins and Laura Morrow, 1989, 204), many critics have tried to find common ground. Levinson, for example, envisions a "deconstructive materialism" that would employ shared aspects of Marxism and deconstruction (*Wordsworth's Great Period Poems: Four Essays,* 1986, 10), yet her readings clearly privilege the materialism over the deconstruction. Spivak has brought her knowledge of deconstruction (she translated Derrida's *De la grammatologie* into English) to bear on feminist and cultural studies, particularly issues in colonialism and phallocentrism (see "Displacement and the Discourse of Woman," *Displacement: Derrida and After,* ed. Mark Krupnick, 1983; and "Poststructuralism, Marginality, Postcoloniality, and Value," *Literary Theory Today,* ed. Peter Collier and Helga Geyer-Ryan, 1990). As her essays demonstrate, deconstruction and Marxism can intersect profitably, though not entirely rigorously, in the analysis of hierarchies, oppositions, and power structures, about which the two methodologies may yet have something to teach each other. A genuine dialogue between them remains to be achieved, however. The same must be said for the engagement of deconstruction and new historicism: insofar as the ground of history, as constructed by new historicists, carries with it, as Derrida would say, "the theme of a final repression of difference" (*Speech and Phenomena* 141), the engagement remains unproductive. Parker suggests that rather than taking sides on Marx versus Derrida, or on history versus difference, critics need to maintain the differences, "both to discourage the premature assimilation of the one to the other as well as to mitigate the increasing hostility displayed by advocates of each 'opposing' mode" ("'Taking Sides' (On History): Derrida Re-Marx," *diacritics* 11 [Fall 1981]: 72).

Not all second-generation deconstructive criticism is politically inclined, and examples of readings that use deconstruction in relation to literary history and rhetoric are still the most numerous. Cynthia Chase and Carol Jacobs, for example, two practitioners of deconstruction in the rhetorical mode, clearly show the influence of de Man in their readings of English and European texts in which literary or tropological self-consciousness leads to "the insistence in each text that it stage its own critical performance" (Jacobs, *Uncontainable Romanticism: Shelley, Brontë, Kleist,* 1989, ix). Thus figures of self-reflexivity, scenes of reading, and the aporia are prominent here in analyses that focus on interpretation and its textual thematizations. Chase, like de Man or Derrida, often scrutinizes a particular rhetorical trope or figure— prosopopoeia or personification, for example—for what it reveals about the rhetorical conditions of meaning (see Chase, *Decomposing Figures: Rhetorical Readings in the Romantic Tradition*, 1986).

In a related vein, Timothy Bahti ("Figures of Interpretation, The Interpretation of Figures: A Reading of Wordsworth's 'Dream of the Arab,'" *Studies in Romanticism* 18 [1979]), David L. Clark ("Monstrous Reading: *The Martyrology* after de Man," *Studies in Canadian Literature* 15.2 [1990]), and Andrzej Warminski (*Readings in Interpretation: Hölderlin, Hegel, Heidegger*, 1987) have produced deconstructive readings of British, Continental, and Canadian literary and philosophical texts whose rhetoric problematizes conventional understandings of interpretation. Still others who have theorized about deconstruction but who are not, ultimately, deconstructors themselves would include Tilottama Rajan, whose work on Romanticism and reading has historicized deconstruction and poststructuralism by placing them within the perspective of a hermeneutics of indeterminacy (*The Supplement of Reading: Figures of Understanding in Romantic Theory and Practice*, 1990); and Gregory L. Ulmer, whose "applied grammatology" has "turn[ed] attention away from an exclusive concern with deconstruction" toward the fields of pedagogy and performance (*Applied Grammatology: Post[e]-Pedagogy from Jacques Derrida to Joseph Beuys*, 1985, x).

On the interface between psychoanalysis and deconstruction, critics such as Shoshana Felman and Stephen W. Melville, reading Derrida's work "as in large measure an extension of psychoanalysis into the history of philosophy" (Melville, *Philosophy beside Itself: On Deconstruction and Modernism*, 1986, 84), have with the help of Lacan mounted poststructuralist psychoanalytic readings of both literary and nonliterary texts. Felman's work exhibits a brilliant combination of psychoanalysis and deconstruction in her insistent "interpretation of difference" and her Lacanian-Derridean "analysis of the signifier as opposed to an analysis of the signified" (*Jacques Lacan and the Adventure of Insight: Psychoanalysis in Contemporary Culture*, 1987, 43, 44). Much of Derrida's work has been an explicit dialogue with SIGMUND FREUD (and some of it a mute dialogue with Lacan); his essay "Freud and the Scene of Writing" (*Writing and Difference* 196–231) and his book *The Post Card* amply show the possibilities of a deconstructive psychoanalysis.

As it now stands, deconstructive criticism is literally and figuratively all over the map. As a result, some hard-line deconstructors have complained that over time deconstruction has lost its original radical impact, that it has been neutralized or eclectically diluted by less rigorous techniques of reading. Paradoxically, others maintain that it is still nihilistic, without respect for meaning,

history, or truth. While early fears that deconstruction would destroy the academy by questioning Western values have proved to be unfounded, there is no denying that deconstruction has undergone considerable changes in focus and application over its relatively brief development. The turning outward by some deconstructors from literary matters to political issues and current events can be construed, in the context of late-twentieth-century attacks on theory, as an attempt to make deconstruction "relevant," to demonstrate the practical or social benefits of deconstruction as part of a larger defense of theory. At the same time it is inevitable that certain aspects of deconstruction—whether its vocabulary, ideas, or procedures—will be appropriated by other disciplines and thus transmuted into new forms of reading.

Unquestionably, the work of the Yale critics and, subsequently, that of a younger generation of critical readers has helped to legitimate and popularize deconstruction as a form of literary criticism, but their efforts have done more than promote a fashionable style of thought and writing. Deconstruction has forced critics to reexamine their philosophical assumptions and to rethink their own language. What is more, the products of such reconsiderations have been often brilliant insights and new understandings of specific texts by JEAN-JACQUES ROUSSEAU, Sigmund Freud, CLAUDE LÉVI-STRAUSS, WILLIAM WORDSWORTH, PERCY BYSSHE SHELLEY, Charles Dickens, Marcel Proust, and W. B. Yeats, among others, as well as a radically different understanding of textuality and the philosophy of language generally. Deconstructive criticism has brought an intellectual rigor to the reading of texts, not just by questioning previous readings but by questioning reading itself. As the initiator of deconstruction, Jacques Derrida has begun a project that, in taking language, arbitrary and differential, as its medium and focus, continues to engage a striking array of topics, from philosophy to psychoanalysis to contemporary architecture, that have implications for virtually all aspects of human activity—culture, discourse, science. After nearly three decades of productive theory and practice, deconstruction remains one of the most significant developments in twentieth-century critical thought.

J. Douglas Kneale

See also JACQUES DERRIDA, FRENCH THEORY AND CRITICISM: 5. 1945–1968 and 6. 1968 AND AFTER, and SPEECH ACTS.

Harold Bloom et al., *Deconstruction and Criticism* (1979); Paul de Man, *Allegories of Reading: Figural Language in Rousseau, Nietzsche, Rilke, and Proust* (1979), *Blind-*

ness and Insight: Essays in the Rhetoric of Contemporary Criticism (2d ed., 1983); Jacques Derrida, *Acts of Literature* (ed. Derek Attridge, 1992), *La Carte postale: De Socrate à Freud et au-delà* (1980, *The Post Card: From Socrates to Freud and Beyond,* trans. Alan Bass, 1987), *De la grammatologie* (1967, *Of Grammatology,* trans. Gayatri Chakravorty Spivak, 1976), *A Derrida Reader: Between the Blinds* (ed. Peggy Kamuf, 1991), *La Dissémination* (1972, *Dissemination,* trans. Barbara Johnson, 1981), *L'Écriture et la différence* (1967, *Writing and Difference,* trans. Alan Bass, 1978), *Marges de la philosophie* (1972, *Margins of Philosophy,* trans. Alan Bass, 1982), *Positions* (1972, *Positions,* trans. Alan Bass, 1981), *La Voix et la phénomène: Introduction au problème du signe dans la phénoménologie* (1967, *Speech and Phenomena, and Other Essays on Husserl's Theory of Signs,* trans. David B. Allison, 1973); Geoffrey H. Hartman, *Criticism in the Wilderness: The Study of Literature Today* (1980), *Saving the Text: Literature/Derrida/Philosophy* (1981), *Wordsworth's Poetry, 1787–1814* (1964); J. Hillis Miller, "The Critic as Host" (Bloom et al.), *The Linguistic Moment: From Wordsworth to Stevens* (1985).

Thomas J. J. Altizer et al., *Deconstruction and Theology* (1982); Jonathan Arac, Wlad Godzich, and Wallace Martin, eds., *The Yale Critics: Deconstruction in America* (1983); Jonathan Arac and Barbara Johnson, eds., *Consequences of Theory* (1991); Jonathan Culler, *On Deconstruction: Theory and Criticism after Structuralism* (1982); Robert Con Davis and Ronald Schleifer, eds., *Rhetoric and Form: Deconstruction at Yale* (1985); Terry Eagleton, *Literary Theory: An Introduction* (1983); Josué V. Harari, ed., *Textual Strategies: Perspectives in Post-Structuralist Criticism* (1979); Irene E. Harvey, *Derrida and the Economy of Différance* (1986); J. Douglas Kneale, *Monumental Writing: Aspects of Rhetoric in Wordsworth's Poetry* (1988); Vincent B. Leitch, *Deconstructive Criticism: An Advanced Introduction* (1983); Frank Lentricchia, *After the New Criticism* (1980); Christopher Norris, *Deconstruction and the Interests of Theory* (1988), *Deconstruction: Theory and Practice* (1982), *The Deconstructive Turn: Essays in the Rhetoric of Philosophy* (1983), *Derrida* (1987), *Paul de Man: Deconstruction and the Critique of Aesthetic Ideology* (1988); Hugh Silverman, ed., *Derrida and Deconstruction* (1989).

DELLA VOLPE, GALVANO

Galvano della Volpe (1895–1968) was born in Imola, Romagna, to a conservative aristocratic family. After teaching in various *licei* (high schools) in Romagna and then at his alma mater, the University of Bologna (1929), he obtained a chair in the history of philosophy at the University of Messina, where he was to spend the rest of his academic career as a somewhat isolated figure (he commuted from Rome to Messina for ten days a month). As an academic philosopher he contributed to the major fields of his discipline: logic, politics, ethics, and aesthetics. His philosophic positions, however, underwent revolutionary changes. Starting as an idealist but soon criticizing the "actualism" of Giovanni Gentile (the most prominent idealist to be associated with Italy's fascist regime), he was soon exposed, because of the historical bent of his research, to other schools of thought: he published a study of DAVID HUME's empiricism *(La filosofia dell'esperienza di Davide Hume)* in 1933 and in the next ten years turned to pragmatism, existentialism, and the work of FRIEDRICH NIETZSCHE. This period prepared his transition to Marxism on a theoretical level, made possible on the practical level by the allied occupation of Sicily in 1943. The following year he became a member of the Italian Communist party. Della Volpe's interest in aesthetics developed with his philosophical maturation and can best be understood in this context; his *Critica del gusto* has perhaps remained his best-known work, partly because it has not met with as much challenge from the philosophical "technocrats" and their established "schools" as his work in other fields, partly because it showed the originality of his methodological approach to the Marxian tradition (which is certainly not limited to his work on aesthetics) in its brightest light. Despite the recognition for this work, della Volpe never gave rise to a clear "school" of criticism (in the sense of a number of scholars who identify with and/or are frequently subsumed under a particular label or category), although some of his followers are sometimes known as his "school," and his most prominent pupils did not devote themselves to the field of aesthetics. The importance of his arguments and of his use of a materialist methodology within the Marxian tradition is, however, inversely proportional to his "popular recognition."

Della Volpe's return to what he considered some of the most basic questions of logic, epistemology, and methodology and the examination of some of the great struggles of the history of philosophy (ARISTOTLE versus PLATO, Galileo versus scholasticism, IMMANUEL KANT versus G. W. Leibniz, and Karl Marx versus G. W. F. HEGEL [*Opere* 3:139 ff., 4:283 ff.]) were the first steps in the transformation of his own philosophic praxis, overcoming idealist hypostasis and dogma (see also KARL MARX AND FRIEDRICH ENGELS). To some extent della Volpe had already attempted to reconcile the contrasting principles of the "dialectic of opposites" (of reason) and the "dialectic of distinct entities" (of idealized matter), as represented by Gentile and BENEDETTO CROCE, at the outset of his career (1:7, 34–38), but it was only after his introduction to historical materialism that a satisfactory "synthesis of heterogeneous entities" or "tauto-heterologic identity" could take shape (4:418 ff.).

The above-mentioned "synthesis" allows della Volpe to unify the achievements of both philosophical traditions: that of *reason* coinciding roughly with the recognition of the necessity of meaningful conceptual relations (unity, deduction, contradiction) and that of *matter* with the recognition of the distinct and discrete nature of reality and our experience of it (multiplicity, induction, noncontradiction). It follows that scientific cognition requires the circular (concrete-abstract-concrete [4:458, 464–65, 470–79 ff.]) process of testing hypotheses by experiment, that is, "reason" with "matter" (praxis). The use of historical "determinate abstractions" (in della Volpe's conception *determinate* abstractions are the opposite of *idealist* abstraction, in that the chain of abstractions can always be controlled and verified, the meaning generated by the *process* of abstraction can be followed back to its origins in empirical reality [see 4:418 ff.]) was della Volpe's answer to idealist abstraction, where idea and reality are improperly mediated, giving rise to vicious circles and hypostases in the logical argument. His interest in logic and gnosiology found its crowning achievement in *Logica come scienza positiva* (1950, 2d ed., 1956, ed. Ignazio Ambrosio, 1969), where he elaborates "the specific logic of a specific object" (for della Volpe this follows from his conception of "determinate abstractions": each field of scientific inquiry should rationally be limited by material or empirical properties of this field; the resulting chain of abstractions, hypotheses, theories, and sciences will thus be shaped by the object of inquiry). He also applied this methodological approach in working through the contradictions of opposing traditions in the realm of ethics and politics. The development of socialism out of bourgeois individualism (and its legal implications) was his principal concern, and the result was *Rousseau e Marx* (1957, 4th ed., 1964).

Finally della Volpe extended his scientific method to the realm of aesthetics, countering the Romantic tradition by emphasizing the cognitive aspects of art rather than the fantastic. The resulting summa is *Critica del gusto* (1960, 3d ed., 1966). To explain the specific characteristics of literature, della Volpe employs structuralist theories of language, including its "glossematic" elaboration in the work of Hjelmslev ("glossematic" was the term Louis Hjelmslev used to describe his own linguistic theory, and by extension it came to designate this particular school of Danish structuralism; the emphasis in

Hjelmslev's theory is on the "internal relations" of language, and it excludes any consideration of the "substance" of expression and content as opposed to its "form" [see esp. 6:221–25]). Poetic language is thereby qualified as *polysemous* (plurality of meaning is intentional and constructed), in contrast with everyday language, which is *ambiguous* (plurality of meaning can be either accidental or intentional; this level of language is that from which the *polysemous* and the *unequivocal* abstract), and scientific language, which is *unequivocal* (any plurality of meaning is intentionally avoided; language is constructed and valued for its lack of ambiguity) (6:91 ff.). The resulting meaning of an artistic work is "organically contextual," whereas that of a scientific work is "omnicontextual." To better understand the formal characteristics of the literary text, the interpreter prepares a "critical paraphrase" of the content and compares the original with it (6:138 and esp. 146 ff.). Following logically from della Volpe's concern with the cognitive aspect of art is his emphasis on the *translatability* of poetry across *natural languages*.

Della Volpe then develops his methodological approach to include other artistic media, consciously continuing in the tradition of G. E. LESSING's *Laokoon* but transforming it in the nonprescriptive context of historical materialism. Because of the specific characteristics of each medium, della Volpe in this case underscores the fundamental *untranslatability* of a work's *effects* across *media*. He applies the term *genere* (the Italian noun can be translated either as "genre" or, the meaning emphasized in this case, as "genus") to specific material media, while criticizing its current usage referring to classifications *within* a medium, which he would rather define as (epistemologically nonessential) "species" (6:179–80).

The lack of an adequate philosophy of language and concept formation weakens the basis of his method, not only in aesthetics but most fundamentally in logic. Alternately describing the relation of language to thought as analogous to the distinction between form and content or to that between means and end (6:79 ff. and 158–59), ignoring problems of the relation of reference to semantics, and overlooking the implications of language as a human product are some of the defects imputable to his reliance on structuralism and its formal idealist tendencies. Obliviousness to other social functions of artistic media (literature, architecture) or to the number, power, and combination of senses they affect is not only curious in a thinker for whom the problem of sensation provided the break with idealism; it also weakens his distinction of the literary from the nonliterary, and of the cognitive from the sensory aspects of artistic experience. Characteristically, della Volpe recognized some of these flaws himself in his last article on art, " 'Linguaggio' e ideologia nel film" (1968), focusing on the application of the linguistic model to other media and the relation of art to ideology.

The epistemological and methodological focus of his research led Galvano della Volpe to criticize idealist interpretations of Marx in literary theory and criticism as well as elsewhere. He first attacked GEORG LUKÁCS's Hegelianism (5:72 ff.) and later the idealist-historicist tradition of Italian Marxism that was partly derived from the work of ANTONIO GRAMSCI (5:52–55 ff., 6:11–12, 40), whereas he occasionally used Gramsci's own *practical* criticism as a model. This concern for the materialist, scientific nature of Marx's research has led several critics to compare della Volpe's Marxism with that of another academic philosopher, Louis Althusser. While both are concerned with Marxism as science, Althusser's work is more structuralist and concentrates on the relation of art to ideology. What is more, della Volpe explicitly dissociated himself from Althusser in his analysis of the evolution of Marx's relation to Hegel (6:430). (See MARX-IST THEORY AND CRITICISM: 2. STRUCTURALIST MARX-ISM.) Della Volpe's major concern is instead to abstract the methodological kernel of Marx's scientific praxis, enabling others to apply it, thereby independently expanding and testing the Marxian scientific tradition itself. This was his main legacy to some of his followers, sometimes known as his "school"—Ignazio Ambrogio, Umberto Cerroni, Lucio Colletti, Nicolao Merker, Alessandro Mazzone, Armando Plebe, Mario Rossi, and Carlo Violi.

Mark W. Epstein

See also ITALIAN THEORY AND CRITICISM: 2. TWENTIETH CENTURY.

Galvano Della Volpe, *Critique of Taste* (trans. M. Caesar, 1978), *Opere* (ed. Ignazio Ambrogio, 6 vols., 1972–73), "Settling Accounts with the Russian Formalists," *New Left Review* 113–14 (1979).

Massimo Alcaro, *Dellavolpismo e nuova sinistra* (1977); Nicola Badaloni, *Il marxismo italiano degli anni sessanta* (1971); David Forgacs, "The Aesthetics of Galvano Della Volpe," *New Left Review* 117 (1979); John Fraser, *An Introduction to the Thought of Galvano della Volpe* (1977); Riccardo Guastini, "Astrazione determinata e formazione economico-sociale," *Il marxismo italiano degli anni sessanta e la formazione teorico-politica delle nuove generazioni* (1972); Mario Montano, "On the Methodology of Determinate Abstraction," *Telos* 7 (1971); Carlo Natali,

"Galvano della Volpe e il principio di non-contraddizione," *Rivista critica di storia della filosofia* 36 (1981); Giuseppe Prestipino, *La controversia estetica nel marxismo* (1974); Mario Rossi, "Galvano della Volpe: Dalla gnoseologia critica alla logica storica," *Critica marxista* 6 (1968); Carlo Violi, *Galvano della Volpe: Testi e studi (1922–1977)* (1978).

DE MAN, PAUL

Paul de Man (1919–83) was born in Antwerp, Belgium, and died in New Haven, Connecticut. He strongly influenced literary criticism and the emergence of "theory," first through his teaching at Cornell (1960–66), Johns Hopkins (1967–70), and Yale (1970–83) and then, beginning in the 1970s, through his writings, which came to be associated with DECONSTRUCTION but might best be characterized as "rhetorical reading." De Man's work focuses on reading as it arises from the rhetorical character of any text: its possibility of having a figural as well as a literal meaning. Like JACQUES DERRIDA's, de Man's work brings to the fore questions of language; he writes that "the advent of theory . . . occurs with the introduction of linguistic terminology in the metalanguage about literature," when historical and aesthetic considerations give place to linguistic ones (*Resistance* 8). These considerations include the manner in which the text relates to the extralinguistic, by way of its referentiality and by way of nonsemantic or noncognitive dimensions (mechanical elements such as grammar)—for de Man the performative dimension of language. De Man's writing examines the disparity and conflict between the cognition or statement and the performance of a text. RHETORIC, for de Man, pertains both to a system of tropes and to persuasion and SPEECH ACTS. Rhetorical reading is a practice of reading attentive to their disparity, to the tension between a text's figures and its "grammar," between a text's statements and its process or occurrence, or, most broadly, to "a non-convergence of 'meaning' with the devices that produce 'meaning' " (*Allegories* 7; *Resistance* 66).

De Man's work is poststructuralist in the sense that it refutes the reduction of texts to their code, structure, or "grammar" and at the same time "deconstructs" texts' rhetoric by revealing the tropological structures (such as metaphor or chiasmus) behind texts' presumed intentions. It departs from the philosophical tradition within which literature is subsumed under the category of the aesthetic, grasped as the phenomenalization or sensible presentation of a meaning; instead, the noncognitive, material dimension of language is conceived as interfering with the establishment of phenomenal cognition. For de Man, literature or texts—works or configurations that as signifying structures require reading—undo claims of authority, claims based on assumptions of the continuity of form with meaning and the possibility of totalizing a structure and, in a dominant philosophical tradition, on the category of the aesthetic or the continuity between perception and knowledge supposed to be guaranteed and exemplified by works of art. As an undoing and critique of these assumptions and others that his later writings call "the aesthetic ideology," de Man's work is a kind of ideology critique, a kind starting from the premise that "one could approach the problems of ideology and by extension the problems of politics only on the basis of critical-linguistic analysis, which had to be done in its own terms, in the medium of language" (*Resistance* 121).

In 1987 it was discovered that de Man's earliest writings include 180 book reviews and short articles on cultural topics from 1940 to 1942 for *Le Soir* and *Het Vlaamsche Land,* newspapers in Brussels that had been taken over by collaborators after the German invasion of Belgium. One of these articles, "Les Juifs dans la littérature actuelle" (*Wartime Journalism* 45), uses the language of anti-Semitism to argue that the Jews have not corrupted European literature but that it has remained healthy. Not surprisingly, the discovery provoked considerable debate—"the de Man Affair"—about the significance of this article, with its repellent statements, and about the relation of de Man's youthful journalism to his mature work (see Chase, *diacritics;* Hamacher, Hertz, and Keenan; Herman, Humbeck, and Lernout; "On Jacques Derrida's 'Paul de Man's War'"; and "Paul de Man Colloquium"). In addition to reflections on the specificity of national character and of the literature of France and Germany, the articles include praise for the Dreyfusard Charles Péguy and other writers disapproved of by the Nazis (such as French surrealist poets) and argue for the autonomy of literature and literary history in defense against the demand that art and literature serve the "totalitarian revolution." To the extent that these writings from a collaborationist press also contain still-current clichés about literature and criticism, such as the organic development of literature, its incarnation of eternal values, and its direct expression of transcendent truths, their discovery confirms the necessity and importance of the critique of "aesthetic ideology" and organicist conceptions of art carried out through deconstruction, rhetorical reading, and related practices of ideology critique.

A distinctive feature of de Man's essays from 1953 through 1983 is the status they accord to literature or the literary as the undoer of ideological mystifications. Ideology is "the confusion of linguistic with natural reality, of reference with phenomenalism" (*Resistance* 11); literature, as we acknowledge when we speak of "fiction," assumes the divergence between sign and meaning. For de Man, literature is identified with the rhetoricity of a text rather than with its being less discursive than other forms of writing. In de Man's first book, *Blindness and Insight,* "literature" appears as a kind of language "privileged" in the sense that it is language not blind to its own statement: "any text that implicitly or explicitly signifies its own rhetorical mode and prefigures its own misunderstanding as the correlative of its rhetorical nature" (136). (It is to JEAN-JACQUES ROUSSEAU's texts, "On the Origin of Inequality" as well as *La Nouvelle Héloïse,* that de Man is ascribing this capacity.) *Allegories of Reading* focuses on the literary or rhetorical as the impossibility of deciding on sheerly linguistic grounds alone between a literal and a figurative meaning of a text, and thus emphasis shifts from the text's cognition of its rhetorical mode to a noncognitive performative dimension of the text that interferes with its understanding or knowledge. The crucial characteristic of a text that literary texts suppose is that it posits realities rather than simply revealing given realities. Thus literature has the critical power of disclosing the unreliability of linguistic artifacts that are passed off by the dominant ideology as truthful representations of the world (Richard Klein, "De Man's Resistances," in Hamacher, Hertz, and Keenan). A text does *not* have the power of closing off its performance or reading, of existing as self-knowledge or self-reflection, for it begins in a linguistic positing, which cannot be derived, which does not signify, although it is the presupposition for any communicable meaning (Hans Jost Frey, "Undecidability," in "The Lesson of Paul de Man" 132).

This nonsemantic dimension of discourse is stressed, as the materiality of language, or "inscription," in de Man's late essays in *The Resistance to Theory.* "Everyday" and "literary" language are finally inseparable because the deictic and representational function of both—the function of cognition—derive from the illegitimate power without authority of a *figure,* the figure whereby the materiality of language gets confused with and conferred on meanings, on signifieds, and ultimately on things, which thereby acquire their phenomenality, their illusory presence. Thus rhetorical reading does not deny (as is sometimes supposed) the existence of referents or the referential function of language; rather, it challenges the "authority" of that linguistic function "as a model for natural or phenomenal cognition" (11). The "fictional narratives" in which such authority is assumed, in which the modeling of language and the world on one another is taken for granted, are ideologies, or "fictional narratives [whose] impact upon the world may well be all too strong for comfort" (rather than texts being not part of the world or of reality). Reading responsive to language as literature—to its positing of its realities rather than mirroring phenomenal givens and to the conflict between the material, nonsemantic, noncognitive dimension of the referential function and the intentional or figural dimension of phenomenal cognition—is thus "a powerful and indispensable tool in the unmasking of ideological aberrations," de Man argues, even as "the linguistics of literariness is . . . a determining factor in accounting for their occurrence" (11).

An earlier phase in de Man's work, in which the main categories of criticism are consciousness, intentionality, and temporality, can be distinguished from a later one, in which the major categories are linguistic and rhetorical: symbol, allegory, irony, metaphor, metonymy, prosopopoeia, catachresis, and the distinction between the performative and constative functions of language. An influential transitional work is the 1969 essay "The Rhetoric of Temporality," where, reexamining the supposed shift from allegorical to symbolic diction in late-eighteenth-century poetry, de Man challenges the assumed superiority of symbol to allegory, since the latter "designates primarily a distance in relation to its own origin" and thus locates the subject in a world in which "time is the originary constitutive category," preventing its illusory self-coincidence or identification with a natural world (*Blindness* 207). *Allegories of Reading* (1979) uses the same term, "allegory," to describe the second- or third-order narratives about the conditions of signification that follow from the impossibility of closing off the reading of a text in a deconstruction of that text's figures, since the deconstruction produces a certain negative knowledge but does not gain control over the rhetoric of its own discourse. The second half of this book, on the *Social Contract* and other works of Rousseau, uses linguistic categories and the analysis of speech acts to analyze the structure of political institutions, such as property, the national state, and statutory law. De Man examines, for instance, how the interplay of grammar and reference is played out in the legal text, in the discrepancy between the law as radically general (in its formulation) and necessarily particular (in its application); and how the tension between the constative and performative functions of language is played out in the differentiation between the state as system and as executive power.

Raised throughout de Man's work are questions of history, including the conditions of literary history and texts' impingement on historical events. One way the issue is engaged is through the theorization of narrative, as in essays on GEORG LUKACS's *Theory of the Novel,* FRIEDRICH NIETZSCHE's *Birth of Tragedy,* and autobiography. De Man's own chief contribution to literary history is the revaluation of early Romanticism as the decisive, not yet superseded moment of the modern period. Essays written between 1956 and 1983 gathered in *The Rhetoric of Romanticism* read FRIEDRICH HÖLDERLIN, Rousseau, WILLIAM WORDSWORTH, PERCY BYSSHE SHELLEY, W. B. Yeats, CHARLES BAUDELAIRE, and Heinrich von Kleist; complementary to them are rhetorical readings of texts of IMMANUEL KANT, FRIEDRICH SCHILLER, and G. W. F. HEGEL gathered in *Aesthetic Ideology,* focused on the concept of the sublime and on the function and status of the category of the aesthetic. The concept of materiality that emerges through these readings is connected by de Man with the concept of history as irreversible occurrence. Close consideration of the category of the aesthetic in Kant and Hegel and of a literary text staging the Schillerian notions of "aesthetic education" and the "aesthetic state" (Kleist's "On the Marionette Theater") leads de Man to diagnose and indict, as a fundamental strategy of the aesthetic ideology he links with the totalitarian state, "aesthetic formalization": the aesthetification, as a satisfying, recognizable *form,* of the formal, mechanical, arbitrary, and contradictory processes of language. His counterproposal to the conception of the work as a fully formal system is that of a reading process in which the formal and referential aspects of language are continually in conflict and at stake. Questions of history thus merge with questions of the structure and role of institutions and specifically of the institution of teaching.

Cynthia Chase

Paul de Man, *Aesthetic Ideology* (ed. Andrzej Warminski, 1992), *Allegories of Reading: Figural Language in Rousseau, Nietzsche, Rilke, and Proust* (1979), *Blindness and Insight: Essays in the Rhetoric of Contemporary Criticism* (1971, 2d ed., 1983), *Critical Writings, 1953–1978* (ed. Lindsay Waters, 1989), *The Resistance to Theory* (1986), *The Rhetoric of Romanticism* (1984), *Romanticism and Contemporary Criticism: The Gauss Seminars and Other Papers* (ed. E. S. Burt, Kevin Newmark, and Andrzej Warminski, 1992), *Wartime Journalism, 1939–43* (ed. Werner Hamacher, Neil Hertz, and Tom Keenan, 1988).

Cathy Caruth and Deborah Esch, eds., *Reviewing Deconstruction* (1992); Cynthia Chase, "Giving a Face to a

Name," *Decomposing Figures: Rhetorical Readings in the Romantic Tradition* (1986); Cynthia Chase, ed., *diacritics* 20.3 (1990, special issue on de Man); Jacques Derrida, "Like the Sound of the Sea Deep within a Shell: Paul de Man's War," *Critical Inquiry* 14 (1988), *Memoires: For Paul de Man* (1986); Wlad Godzich and Lindsay Waters, eds., *Reading de Man Reading* (1989); Werner Hamacher, Neil Hertz, and Tom Keenan, eds., *Responses: On Paul de Man's Wartime Journalism* (1989); Luc Herman, Kris Humbeck, and Geert Lernout, eds., *(Dis)continuities: Essays on Paul de Man* (1989); Fredric Jameson, "Immanence and Nominalism in Postmodern Theoretical Discourse," *Postmodernism, or the Cultural Logic of Late Capitalism* (1991); Tom Keenan, "Bibliography of Texts by Paul de Man," *Yale French Studies* 69 (1985, also in de Man, *Resistance to Theory*); *The Lesson of Paul de Man,* special issue, *Yale French Studies* 69 (1985); Christopher Norris, *Paul de Man: Deconstruction and the Critique of Aesthetic Ideology* (1988); "On Jacques Derrida's 'Paul de Man's War,'" *Critical Inquiry* 15 (1989); "Paul de Man Colloquium," *Colloquium Helveticum: Cahiers suisses de littérature générale et comparée* 11/12 (1990); William Ray, "Paul de Man: The Irony of Deconstruction / The Deconstruction of Irony," *Literary Meaning: From Phenomenology to Deconstruction* (1984); Marc Redfield, "Humanizing de Man," *diacritics* 19.2 (1989); Michael Sprinker, "Politics and Language: Paul de Man and the Permanence of Ideology," *Imaginary Relations: Aesthetics and Ideology in the Theory of Historical Materialism* (1987).

DERRIDA, JACQUES

The difficulty of introducing a major contemporary philosopher such as Jacques Derrida (b. 1930) in a reference work presenting central issues of literary criticism is double, and this danger, this hesitation on the threshold, has already been systematically thematized in the writings of the philosopher himself. First, there is the danger of oversimplifying, of pigeonholing, of reducing, of defining artificial boundaries, when facing a movement of thought that constantly evolves so as deliberately to defeat and baffle all preordained categories. Then, there is the danger of being merely mimetic, of just repeating strategies and gestures that have been identified with a signature, with an author (and may well have been anticipated by other writers), and that tend to be singular, unrepeatable, yet endowed with universal validity. However, the possibility of bypassing such an initial aporia exists, and it consists in considering the fundamentally affirmative nature of Derrida's

thought and writing rather than in stressing the "playful" or "negative" element of his textual practices.

This affirmative aspect seems to be confirmed by the more recent writings of the philosopher, who has engaged with new fields such as law, ethics, politics, architecture, and teaching as an institution, while moving some distance from the early misconceptions brought about by a very enthusiastic reception of his theses in some North American universities in the late 1970s. Derrida has strongly objected to the interpretations of DECONSTRUCTION (a term he still accepts as his own coining and invention) that see it as a purely destructive notion of criticism, deploying an almost nihilistic critique of all institutions, hierarchies, and values. He has remarked that "deconstruction is not negative," adding in an interview that the term he used was meant to translate MARTIN HEIDEGGER's notions of *Abbau* and *Destruction,* concepts that also are not negative. Deconstruction is "not destructive, not having the purpose of dissolving, distracting or subtracting elements in order to reveal an internal essence. It asks questions about the essence, about the presence, indeed about this interior/exterior, phenomenon/appearance schema" (*French Philosophers* 96–97). Even if these remarks beg the question of what deconstruction is or does, they point to a gesture that hesitates between the assertive and the interrogative. And they show that being basically exploited by literary critics, Derrida's concepts should be seen less as tools than as landmarks in a philosophical meditation on the essence of literature. Therefore, there cannot be anything such as a "Derridean criticism," nor should one be on the lookout for a positive notion of "grammatology" if by "grammatology" one understands a new "science of writing" meant to replace the ancient metaphysical "logocentrism." Indeed, we shall have to understand why no "grammatology" is possible and why such an impossibility nevertheless liberates incalculable critical energies.

A second type of commonplace current among exegetes of "deconstruction" consists in stressing that the movement triggered by Derrida blurs all distinctions between philosophy and literature. Even if this may well be the case, one will be wise enough to follow Rodolphe Gasché's caveat and lay the stress on the strict philosophical training of the author. Derrida is best seen as a philosopher who poses philosophical questions to texts, wherever they come from, and to textuality as such. This should prevent the facile exploitation of his theories in the field of literary criticism by critics untrained in the reading of the often difficult texts he alludes to, from PLATO to Heidegger, for instance.

Indeed, one can note that Derrida's earliest theoretical project consisted in an investigation of "the ideality of the literary object" in the late 1950s. The vocabulary bears the mark of what remains Derrida's major philosophical tradition, namely, PHENOMENOLOGY. He will soon find in Edmund Husserl's *Origin of Geometry* a similar approach to another type of ideality, the ideality of science. Just as Husserl studies the conditions of possibility of ideal objects and situates them within language, intersubjectivity, a communal world humanized by a ground and a horizon, Derrida will later meditate on the conditions of possibility of literature. And just as Husserl occupies a paradoxical position, refusing the positivism of objectivist science as well as a blind empiricism extolling facts over theories, Derrida will attempt to go deeper, toward "origins," determining the proper depth of archaeological excavations. Derrida's major "family"—it is rather a matter of "style" in the development of philosophical argumentation—remains that of phenomenology, starting with Husserl and Heidegger, JEAN-PAUL SARTRE and Maurice Merleau-Ponty, although caught up within psychology and the trivialization of Heideggerianism dubbed as existentialism, to tie up more closely with thinkers and writers as closely associated and as creative as MAURICE BLANCHOT and Emmanuel Levinas. But what prevents the neat inscription of Derrida in the games philosophers play with each other—Husserl is "overtaken" by Heidegger, who in his turn is "overtaken" by Derrida—is that he stands firmly at the crossroads between phenomenology and what used to be called STRUCTURALISM in Europe during the 1960s: a diffuse movement of thought ranging between human sciences and linguistics, linking anthropology, psychoanalysis, SEMIOTICS, mythology, and sociology. Rather than to the major exponents of the movement, with whom Derrida kept discussing crucial concepts, such as JACQUES LACAN, CLAUDE LÉVI-STRAUSS, ROLAND BARTHES, and MICHEL FOUCAULT, one should merely point to the writings of the linguist who inspired them all, FERDINAND DE SAUSSURE.

Most structuralists took their cue from Saussure's system, endorsing his ideas about the prevalence of synchrony over diachrony, the arbitrary nature of the link between signifier and signified, the conception of language as a system made up of differential tokens. By a kind of oversimplification, one might say that Derrida uses this theory of the sign—a purely diacritical mark, made up of absence, since in language there are "only differences," according to Saussure—to criticize Husserl and Heidegger, while bringing the phenomenological inquiry to bear on the foundations (or lack of foundation) of structuralist scientism, thus forcing two very different traditions to grind ceaselessly against each other. Or perhaps, by an even bolder structural homology, one might say that Derrida has taken up Heidegger's critique of all language theories that would attempt to bypass a certain type of HERMENEUTICS, showing how they remain trapped up in pure instrumental approaches, but has changed the ground of Heideggerian foundational criticism: instead of attacking the recurrent metaphysical blindness to ontological difference (to the fact that we forget Being inasmuch as we reduce beings to being-present, to presences or to presence as such), Derrida locates the differential hinge in the always unsteady relationship between language and trace. This blind spot in a tradition as old as philosophy itself (and "philosophy" is a term that can never be detached from its Greek, and specifically post-Platonic, context) takes the familiar name "writing," although one should not identify writing with its historical or cultural manifestations. Instead, one should be aware of the "ideality" proper to writing, an ideality that constantly crosses the boundaries between idea and matter, between transcendental questioning of a priori conditions and the factual account of empirical realizations.

Thus Derrida can easily show how Husserl meets considerable difficulties as soon as he tries to ground the tradition necessary to the preservation of mathematical truths in a concept of consciousness defined by an intentionality of meaning, ultimately identical to the capacity of "hearing oneself speak," and point at the same time to Saussure's strange overrating of speech phenomena and parallel dismissing of writing, seen as a mere tool bringing confusions. Both commonsense evidence and a tradition dating back to Plato tend to pin consciousness down to a form of vocalization of the self, to a living voice proving its validity and permanence by being always at hand and identical to itself. Against this alleged evidence, Derrida stresses writing, not as a tool or concept, but as an experience, and this recognition of writing implies the disquieting fact that one leaves a trace that can survive without the presence of its author, without being corroborated by the living agency of its original inscription.

Writing leads to a deeper understanding of origins and of the paradoxes clustering around the notion of "presence" (which is never "condemned" as such; on the contrary). Writing implies in itself the capacity of an endless repetition deprived of any fixed standard of authorization, therefore an ambivalent knot of death and survival. Writing is a trace that cannot be present here and there without having already divided itself, since it always refers back to another being, to another trace. The fold between Being and beings described by Heideggerian hermeneutics is thus reinscribed as the operation of an "original trace," with the added difference that it rules out any belief in an absolute, pristine origin. Inscription, instead of engendering a meaning vested in a paternal authority, recontextualizes everything that would hold a claim to uniqueness and oneness. Any reader of Derrida will have recognized the motif underlying countless readings of classical and less classical authors, including Plato and JEAN-JACQUES ROUSSEAU, Lévi-Strauss and Antonin Artaud, SIGMUND FREUD and PAUL VALÉRY.

The complex strategies of reading elaborated by Derrida actually take a lot of time and space, deliberately resist summary, and entail a complete and varying scenography. One may note the constant shifting back and forth between philosophers, poets, and novelists. It is not only that one would find in literature what remains lacking in philosophy, the awareness of the opacity of signs, the deeper insight into the metaphorical nature of language being too often obscured by the philosophical wish to hit on absolute truths. Indeed, the first two magazines with which Derrida associated himself at the beginning of his "public" career, *Critique* and *Tel Quel,* had been dominated by personalities who refused a strict dichotomy between literary and philosophical endeavors, GEORGES BATAILLE and Philippe Sollers. Varied and multiple as they are, Derrida's literary authors all fall under three rough headings: the Romantics (in a vague sense), where Rousseau, PERCY BYSSHE SHELLEY, and CHARLES BAUDELAIRE figure prominently; the post-Symbolists, with Valéry and Stéphane Mallarmé (see STÉPHANE MALLARMÉ AND FRENCH SYMBOLISM); and the "Moderns," among whom one could distinguish a purely Jewish tradition with Franz Kafka, Edmond Jabès, and Paul Célan, and an avant-gardist mode, with James Joyce, Artaud, Bataille, Sollers, Francis Ponge, and Jean Genet (the last 10 names would in fact make up the entire *Tel Quelian* canon), with a special mention for Blanchot because of the proximity of his own status as author of novels, narratives, and literary essays. Most of these writers teach something about writing, Mallarmé and Joyce having been granted the privilege of a direct anti-Platonic practice of writing in the early essays, while the later books stress the generosity of Célan over Joyce's infinitely cunning calculations and take Baudelaire's prose poems as an excellent antidote to Marcel Mauss's ingenuous theory of the "gift." However, it is not certain that they have more to "teach" than, say, FRIEDRICH NIETZSCHE, Freud, or Heidegger (as Lacan could say of poets who show the way to analysts and thinkers), or even than Plato himself—the founder of metaphysics being the first to find himself in the "double bind" to which is condemned a thinker who rejects writing yet expresses himself almost exclusively in the mode of literary dialogue, and in the name of another philosopher, Socrates, who did not write.

One could roughly oppose a first moment in Derrida's strategies when he aimed at showing how a text always subverts or exceeds the author's intended meaning thanks to a complex functioning of metaphors, tensions, or distortions between layers of sense owing to an unperceived linguistic instability typical of textuality in general, and a second moment when the notions of "undecidability" and "incalculability" run counter to the economic metaphors still implied by the first approach. The first moment would be distinguished by the often misconstrued notion that there is "nothing outside the text"—*pas de hors-texte*—(*Grammatology* 58), the second by a stress on critical gestures themselves, with an ethical or political questioning of boundaries and global economies of meaning. The first moment stresses a continuously plural language—"one must speak several languages and produce several texts at once" (*Margins* 135); the second would consider the endless autobiographical task of unveiling and confession implied by any writing ("Circonfession"). The first moment would thus naturally select *Finnegans Wake* as a model of a perpetually self-deconstructing literary object, whereas the second would take Joyce to task for having programmed everything in advance, for having engineered an encyclopedic memory of culture, including the hubristic desire to calculate undecidability itself, and opt rather for Molly Bloom's more naive "yes" to life at the end of *Ulysses* (see "Two Words for Joyce" and "Ulysses Gramophone: Hear say yes in Joyce" in *Acts of Literature*).

But throughout this progression in the constitution of a general aesthetics of paradoxes and transgression of accepted limits, Derrida sticks to a few critical tenets. One is that no hermeneutics of literature is possible. The criticism of Jean-Pierre Richard's thematic readings in the "Double Session" has often been documented and clearly provides a major reading of Mallarmé. The long argument with thematicism leads to the replacement of polysemy by "dissemination," not only because of the lability of themes, neither signifiers nor ideas, too slippery to be identified before they merge into one another, but most of all because no critical metalanguage can free itself from the pervasive metaphoricity of the text. Terms as crucial as the Mallarméan "fan," which keeps closing and opening, function both as metaphor and metonymy of the fold by which the text ceaselessly re-marks itself (*Dissemination* 250–59).

The later confrontation with Hans-Georg Gadamer reveals that there has been no compromise with current versions of post-Heideggerian hermeneutics. It would take too much space to compare the various readings of Célan and Mallarmé by Gadamer and Derrida to list everything that opposes them. When Gadamer concludes a reading of Mallarmé's *Salut* with the statement that "both dimensions of meaning can be carried out as the same melodious gesture of language and in the same unity of discourse" (*Dialogue* 45–46), one could hardly be further from Derrida's constant contention that no single "plane of discourse" can be established, that the metaphors always clash violently and dangerously in a poem, and, fundamentally, that any writer attempts to achieve the impossible by leaving the trace of an absolute singularity. Thus, Célan's poetry becomes entirely paradigmatic, with its difficult relation to the language in which it is written (German, the language of the Nazi oppressors); its short, cryptic utterances; and its multilayered games with traditions, allusions, and personal contexts. In "Shibboleth" as in "*Fors:* The Anglish Words of Nicolas Abraham and Maria Torok" (the introduction to Abraham and Torok's *The Wolf Man's Magic Word*) one would find the same "anasemic" poetics: literature always hides the crypt of a dead body and attempts to let it survive by inscribing the disordered letters—filtered by multiple and perverse language-games—in a signature. In this sense, one could speak of an approach very close to the radical psychoanalysis invented by Abraham and Torok, not so far even from certain of Lacan's formulas ("to love means to give what one hasn't got"), while staunchly opposing the neo-Hegelianism of Lacan's system (see "Pour l'amour de Lacan").

The central questions of these poetics become indissociable from the new philosophical problematics of Derrida's recent writings: What is an event? Under which conditions is it possible? How can a poem be given if giving must entail the abolition of exchange (nothing must be expected from it, otherwise giving becomes bartering)? What is a signature? What is a name in a text? How can the title be distinguished form the name of the author and from the content of the text? How far and how long can one play on an author's name (the French poet Francis Ponge's name thus turns into "sponge" and many other "things" alluding to his own poetic corpus)? What is a "corpus"? These problems still imply the strategy of "double b(l)inds" and "vicious performatives" invented in order to destroy John Searle's hasty reappropriation of Austinian theories of SPEECH ACTS, while

hesitating between broad recontextualizations (within large institutions defining areas of supposed competence) and extremely precise issues posed by untranslatable idioms. Yet as soon as one "translates" a proper name, the gesture may trigger off a violent style of punning, as when, in "Limited Inc a b c . . . ," Searle's name is deftly turned into the French abbreviation "Sarl" (*Société à responsabilité limitée*, "Society with Limited Responsibility" [*Limited Inc* 36]).

The wish to come closer to an untranslatable idiom implies a more "writerly" style; indeed, after *Glas*, a very baroque piece of writing that proves that "doing things with words" is possible, Derrida's concerns seem to expand so as to include anthropological or psychoanalytical issues such as incorporation, introjection, fetishism, mourning, eating, and sexual difference, broaching at times religious themes such as baptism, the Eucharist, circumcision, alliance, and negative theology, without excluding a strong political commitment, taking sides on very contemporary issues (Derrida was for instance arrested in Prague in 1981 because of his active support for dissident intellectuals), such as the end of Communist regimes in Eastern Europe, the foundation of the American constitution, the Gulf War, the insane calculations involved by the threat of nuclear war, the concept of a new Europe, and so on. These multiple activities, involving countless texts on painting, architecture, and drawing as well, finally place him in the French tradition of the committed intellectual, as exemplified by Sartre or Foucault, never loath to plan a state reform of philosophy teaching or to launch an institution such as the groundbreaking Collège de Philosophie in Paris.

In view of this committed stance, can we speak with Christopher Norris (Gasché is more reserved; see 157–58) of Derrida as a neo-Kantian, propounding a more sophisticated and updated version of transcendental criticism? To be sure, in a recent interview in the *Magazine littéraire* Derrida insists that deconstruction must continue a dialogue with post-Kantian critique. Criticism supposes, after IMMANUEL KANT, KARL MARX AND FRIEDRICH ENGELS, and the whole Enlightenment, a judgment between two terms in a situation of crisis. If it refuses alternatives set by binary logics or dialectics, deconstruction does not attempt a "criticism of criticism" but aims at thinking the same process from another side, linked to the genealogy of judgment, of will, of consciousness: the decidability of truth criteria cannot be reached by a blindness to the aporias of undecidability. Deconstruction therefore strives to let appear the affirmative (not positive) movement presupposed by any criticism. This has consequences for politics—the politics of a different Europe to be thought anew in *The Other Heading*—as well as for the intelligence of an intellectual heritage dominated by German philosophy and its mystique of the *Geist* ("spirit"). Derrida's mixture of innate skepticism and Jewish faith in the written word could be evoked by Joyce's tortuous praise of Stephen Dedalus: "It had better be stated here and now at the outset that the perverted transcendentalism to which Mr. S. Dedalus' (Div. Scep.) contentions would appear to prove him pretty badly addicted runs directly counter to accepted scientific methods. Science, it cannot be too often repeated, deals with tangible phenomena" (*Ulysses*, 1922, ed. Hans Walter Gabler, 1984, ch. 14, ll. 1223–26). Derrida's persistent interrogation of the foundational and thus impossible act of "giving" makes us want to probe behind the reassuring existence (and etymology) of all phenomenal "givens" or "data."

Thus, in a recent text Derrida seems to recant even his antiphonological stance when he answers the question "What is poetry?" by saying that poetry can be defined by a desire to "learn by heart." This is no falling back into naive immediacy, however. To learn by heart is the only chance of an "embodiment" of letters in a subject: "Eat, drink, swallow my letter, carry it, keep it in you, like the law of a writing transformed into your body: *writing as such*," this would be the lesson or "fable" conveyed by any poem that *gives* itself entirely, in the familiar Mallarméan gesture of legacy (Ferraris 240). This poetical and subjective text about poetry is rather typical of Derrida's recent mode of confessional writing: he writes about his own desire to incorporate letters thanks to poems that have relinquished their Heideggerian pretensions, their claim to let language (or truth) speak. No pathos of creation, a pure passivity, deprived of either quotations or title, yet bearing witness to the "passion of the singular mark," a "signature rehearsing its own disappearance." Derrida has to conclude a little wistfully, however, that such an account finally rules out any question in the form of "What is ———?" since as soon as this is asked, not only does metaphysics hold its sway again but the form of the question heralds in itself the birth of prose.

Jean-Michel Rabaté

See also DECONSTRUCTION and FRENCH THEORY AND CRITICISM: 5. 1945–1968 and 6. 1968 AND AFTER.

Geoffrey Bennington and Jacques Derrida, *Jacques Derrida* (1991); Jacques Derrida, *Acts of Literature* (ed. Derek Attridge, 1992), *L'Autre Cap* (1990, *The Other Heading: Reflection on Today's Europe*, trans. Pascal-Anne Brault

and Michael B. Naas, 1992), "Circonfession," *Jacques Derrida* (Bennington and Derrida), *De la grammatologie* (1967, *Of Grammatology*, trans. Gayatri Chakravorty Spivak, 1976), *De l'esprit: Heidegger et la question* (1987, *Of Spirit: Heidegger and the Question*, trans. Geoffrey Bennington and Rachel Bowlby, 1989), *A Derrida Reader: Between the Blinds* (ed. Peggy Kamuf, 1990), *La Dissémination* (1972, *Dissemination*, trans. Barbara Johnson, 1981), *Donner le temps: I. La Fausse Monnaie* (1991, *Given Time: I. Counterfeit Money*, trans. Peggy Kamuf, 1992), *L'Écriture et la différence* (1967, *Writing and Difference*, trans. Alan Bass, 1978), "Fors: Les Mots anglés de Nicolas Abraham et Maria Torok," foreword to *Cryptonomie: Le Verbier de l'homme aux loups*, by Abraham and Torok (1976, "Fors: The Anglish Words of Nicolas Abraham and Maria Torok," trans. Barbara Johnson, foreword to *The Wolf Man's Magic Word: A Cryptonymy*, by Abraham and Torok, 1986), *Glas* (1974, trans. John Leavey and Richard Rand, 1986), *Limited Inc* (trans. Samuel Weber, Jeffrey Mehlman, and Alan Bass, 1988), *Marges de la philosophie* (1972, *Margins of Philosophy*, trans. Alan Bass, 1982), *Parages* (1986), "Pour l'amour de Lacan," *Lacan avec les Philosophes* (1991), *Schibboleth: Pour Paul Célan* (1986, "Shibboleth," trans. Joshua Wilner, in *Midrash and Literature*, ed. Geoffrey H. Hartman and Sanford Budick, 1986), *Ulysse Gramophone: Deux mots pour Joyce* (1987, "Two Words for Joyce" and "Ulysses Gramophone: Hear say yes in Joyce," *Acts of Literature*, ed. Attridge, 1992), *La Vérité en peinture* (1978, *The Truth in Painting*, trans. Geoffrey Bennington and Ian McLeod, 1987).

François Ewald, "Une 'folie' doit veiller sur la pensée" (interview with Derrida), *Magazine littéraire* 286 (1991); Maurizio Ferraris, *Postille a Derrida: Con due scritti di Jacques Derrida* (1987); Rodolphe Gasché, *The Tain of the Mirror: Derrida and the Philosophy of Reflection* (1986); Diane P. Michelfelder and Richard E. Palmer, *Dialogue and Deconstruction: The Gadamer-Derrida Encounter* (1989); Raoul Mortley, *French Philosophers in Conversation: Derrida, Irigaray, Levinas, Le Doeuff, Schneider, Serres* (1990); Christopher Norris, *Derrida* (1987); William R. Schultz and Lewis L. B. Fried, *Jacques Derrida: An Annotated Primary and Secondary Bibliography* (1992); David Wood, ed., *Derrida: A Critical Reader* (1992).

DE SANCTIS, FRANCESCO

Francesco De Sanctis (1817–83) is one of the pivotal figures of nineteenth-century Italian intellectual history. An activist member of the generation that witnessed the 1848 revolution, the Bourbon reaction to it, and the making of the Italian sovereign state, he contributed seminally to Italian public and intellectual life in areas ranging from the ministry of education to publications on aesthetics, literary history, cultural history, and literary criticism. After training in law he taught, for a decade or so, critical philology (the study of language in the context of political history, literary history, philosophy, grammar, and rhetoric) at a private school in Naples. His participation in the 1848 revolution as a supporter of the leftist liberal Mazzinians led to his three-year incarceration by the Bourbon reaction and to his exile in Turin and Zurich, where he lectured on Italian literature and culture. After his return to Naples in 1860 he was involved in a series of activities. He published a major newspaper involved in progressive reform politics, *L'Italia;* helped organize a liberal opposition party; and held high public offices and influential university chairs. He served as governor of his native province of Avellino, minister of education in the Cavour government, and chair of comparative literature at the University of Naples. Most of his addresses, essays, and publications dealing with cultural literacy; aesthetic, literary, and cultural theory; and the making of a national literature were written in the period 1860–83. Among these are *Saggi critici* (1869), *Saggio critico sul Petrarca* (1869), and his most important work, *Storia della letteratura Italiana* (1870–71, *History of Italian Literature*).

Born in southern Italy and working there by choice for emancipatory social and political causes, De Sanctis was one of those militant intellectuals who were conscious of the underprivileged status, underdevelopment, and undereducation of the South. Part of his educational program as politician and influential intellectual was thus to demand secularized public education for all those people who traditionally had been denied access to literacy and culture. He defined freedom as access to cultural literacy by all social classes. By the same token, his understanding of culture, literature, and art is based on the notion that a culture does not mean ipso facto high culture. To the extent that a poet is not only a poet but also a citizen, philosopher, and person of religious convictions, a human being who lives in a specific historical moment and a specific society, true art will address the diversity of social practices and beliefs while simultaneously unifying that content in a specific form. The essence of art is in the form united with the content.

The form-content problematic inherited from the Hegelian tradition in particular and from Romantic aesthetics in general does not, however, in De Sanctis lead to the primacy of the content or the idea, as in G. W. F. HEGEL's aesthetics. Rather, De Sanctis posits the primacy of the form. While he agrees with Hegel that artistic forms and genres are tied to a specific historical moment in that forms live in and with a content, he contends against Hegel that forms transcend history. The end of art does not arrive. While the content is subject to the politics, culture, and society of a specific moment in history, the form itself is immortal. What he suggests, therefore, on the one hand, is a methodological procedure to examine the single form of the poetic work separate from its historical context. On the other hand, he opts for a simultaneous understanding of the unity of form and content as a structure that lives and functions in the context of a philosophy of art, a history of a nation, a history of customs, passions, tendencies, languages, opinions, and thoughts. His notion of *critica* ("critical theory") thus contains both an aesthetic validation of the intrinsic form and the historical contextualization of that form. Universality and historicity become one in De Sanctis's critical theory.

History of Italian Literature exemplifies quite well the type of applied criticism that he postulates in his aesthetics. His theory understands the history of literature as a history of single authors who, by living in a specific historical moment, artistically recreate a reality of a multiclass collective attempting to solidify and unify a nation in one culture. Thus, he outlines and evaluates the various epochs of Italian literary history according to the forces that either shaped or impeded the trajectory toward a national culture. In that scheme, for instance, Torquato Tasso, or as he calls him, "Guiccardini's man," stands as the representative of a political and moral resignation accompanying a socioeconomic crisis, and figures such as Bernardino Telesio, Giordano Bruno, Tommaso Campanella, Paolo Sarpi, Galileo Galilei, and GIAMBATTISTA VICO are the "new scientists" envisaging a future of greater freedoms and autonomies in which life, art, and science will become one. The desideratum of the unity of art, science, and life is the master key of De Sanctis's theory, wherein art stands for the production of many diverse forms of knowledge, life for the various social practices carrying a nation, and science for the way in which a society intelligently and democratically organizes its relations of power and runs its affairs. De Sanctis left a legacy many Italian intellectuals were subsequently eager to claim, among them no less a figure than ANTONIO GRAMSCI.

Renate Holub

Francesco De Sanctis, *Autobiografia, critica e politica* (1924), *La crisi del romanticismo* (1972), *Giacomo Leopardi* (ed. Enrico Ghidetti, 1983), *Storia della letteratura Italiana*

(2 vols., 1870–71, *History of Italian Literature,* trans. Joan Redfern, 1959), *Scelta di scritti critici* (ed. Gianfranco Contini, 1959).

Michele Cantandella, *Francesco De Sanctis: Immagini e ambiente* (1984); Bruno Luis Carpineti, *Francesco De Sanctis y la critica literaria* (1981); Dante Della Terza, "La Storia della letteratura italiana: Premesse erudite e verifiche ideologiche" and "Francesco De Sanctis: Gli itinerari della storia," *Letteratura italiana,* vol. 4, *L'Interpretazione* (1985); Enzo Noé Girardi, *Manzoni, De Sanctis, Croce e altri studi di storia della critica italiana* (1986); Sergio Landucci, *Cultura e ideologia in Francesco De Sanctis* (1977); Nicola Longo, *Il ritorno del De Sanctis: Storia, ideologia, mistificazione* (1980); Fortunato Matarrese, *Goethe e De Sanctis* (1975); Carlo Muscetta, *Studi sul De Sanctis e altri scritti di storia della critica* (1980); Francesco Nicolosi, *Verga tra De Sanctis e Zola* (1986); Antonio Prete, *Il realismo di De Sanctis* (1970); Mechthild Westhoff, *Schiller e De Sanctis* (1977).

DESCARTES, RENÉ

Born to a family of the small nobility in La Haye (France), René Descartes (1596–1650) was educated at the Jesuit college of La Flèche and trained in the scholastic tradition predominant at the time. Though he seems to have read widely in classical philosophy and literature, he was, by his own account, more interested in the exact sciences—mathematics, geometry, and physics—than in philosophy. Because of the religious institutions' strict control over what could be published in most disciplines, of Galileo's forced abjuration, which is said to have had a profound effect on Descartes, and of his desire to avoid the social obligations of the French court, Descartes remained most of his mature life in the more tolerant Netherlands. He died in Stockholm, shortly after being summoned there by Queen Christina to help organize a scientific academy.

Descartes's statements on literature as such are rare and always subordinate to his philosophical concerns. His quest for a language that would convey philosophical ideas and propositions as unambiguously as mathematics is consistent with his distrust of literary language and rhetoric. He saw as detrimental and ultimately debilitating literature's capacity for creating the illusion of reality and truth. A passage from the *Discourse on Method* summarizes this mistrust:

Fables make one imagine many events possible which in reality are not so, and even the most accurate of histories, if they do not exactly misrepresent or exaggerate the value of things in order to render them more worthy of being read, at least omit in them all the circumstances which are basest and least notable; and from this fact it follows that what is retained is not portrayed as it really is, and that those who regulate their conduct by examples which they derive from such a source, are liable to fall into the extravagances of the knights-errant of Romance, and form projects beyond their power of performance. (*Philosophical Works* 1:84–85)

In philosophy's use of language, truth must have its own implacable force of persuasion, inseparable as it is, in Descartes's vision, from clarity and intelligibility.

For all their apparent conservatism, such pronouncements should not detract from Descartes's primordial role in reshaping modern critical thought. With Descartes, the subject can no longer be considered as contingent and hence irrelevant to the content of philosophy. Although his radical shift in philosophy did not have immediate effects on literature and literary theory, its pervasive influence cannot be ignored, especially as it is first through a stylistic device that Descartes distinguishes himself most strikingly from previous philosophy. His constant reference to himself, to his intellectual autobiography, grants the "I" in his texts unprecedented prominence in philosophical writing. Culminating as it does in the *cogito* argument ("I think, therefore I am"; I cannot doubt that I am, as that very doubt proves that I am), this emphasis on the self cannot be read simply as apologetic explanation but has to be understood as part of Descartes's strategy as he shifts the center of gravity in science and philosophy from the object of knowledge to the subject. By presenting the *cogito* argument as at once exemplary of methodical thought and as the beginning of true science, Descartes seeks to undermine the all-encompassing philosophical authority of the Aristotelian school and its reliance on unyielding sets of axioms, categories, and rules of procedure (see ARISTOTLE).

Philosophy begins for Descartes with absolute doubt, with the questioning of all knowledge and even of ordinary perception, in order that the individual subject might rebuild knowledge on firmer ground by the methodical search for principles as clear and distinct as mathematical propositions or as the *cogito* argument. Since all thinking individuals are capable of arriving at the *cogito,* they can—as Descartes attempts to do—attain certain knowledge of themselves (their bodies, their passions), of the world and its laws, and, ultimately, of the universe.

Yet Descartes's own description of the universe is presented under the guise of a fable, in order, as he explains elsewhere, to disarm potential detractors. Similarly, several of his statements in his correspondence and in responses to his objectors reveal an attention to style so acute that his expressed distrust of literature might itself be reread as rhetorical. But it is precisely in these dealings with the questions, the actual and potential misunderstandings of his readers, that Descartes becomes most clearly aware of the position of the subject in knowledge. Resituating the subject in philosophy, as Descartes does, inescapably increases the risk of ambiguity in communication. Ironically, ignoring literature's capacity for exploiting language's infinite potential for ambiguity forces Descartes to constantly redefine and reformulate what he sees as the same ideas. In this redefinition, his own recourse to literary and rhetorical devices appears as an attempt to overcome the contradictory role language plays in at once partially allowing and partially obstructing the objectification of knowledge between subjects. Modern critical theory insofar as it has inherited Descartes's resituating of the subject also has inherited an acute awareness of the crisis in language that it entails.

Gabriel Moyal

René Descartes, *Oeuvres de Descartes* (ed. Charles Adam and Paul Tannery, 13 vols., 1974–76), *Oeuvres philosophiques* (ed. Ferdinand Alquié, 3 vols., 1963–73), *Philosophical Letters* (ed. and trans. Anthony Kenny, 1970), *The Philosophical Works of Descartes* (2 vols., trans. E. S. Haldane and G. R. T. Ross, 1973).

Jean-François Bordron, *Descartes: Recherches sur les contraintes sémiotiques de la pensée discursive* (1987); Pierre-Alain Cahné, *Un Autre Descartes: Le Philosophe et son langage* (1980); Hiram Caton, *The Origin of Subjectivity: An Essay on Descartes* (1973); Dalia Judovitz, *Subjectivity and Representation in Descartes: The Origins of Modernity* (1988); Sarah Kofman, "Descartes Entrapped" (trans. Kathryn Aschheim, *Who Comes after the Subject?* ed. Eduardo Cadava, Peter Connor, and Jean-Luc Nancy, 1991); Jonathan Rée, *Philosophical Tales: An Essay on Philosophy and Literature* (1987); Timothy J. Reiss, *The Discourse of Modernism* (1982); Charles Taylor, *Sources of the Self: The Making of the Modern Identity* (1989).

DEWEY, JOHN

John Dewey (1859–1952) is probably the greatest of American pragmatist philosophers and certainly the most influential for cultural criticism and aesthetics. His voluminous writings cover all the major philosophical disciplines, and among his primary themes are naturalism, instrumentalism, experience and experimentation, and an antifoundationalist historicism that sees philosophical problems as the reflection of real practical problems that emerge through social and scientific change. Apart from his eminence as a professional philosopher, Dewey was also an important public figure, a controversial educational reformer, and an outspoken supporter of the labor movement and other progressive causes. Not only his ethics and politics but also his epistemology and philosophy of science were deeply imbued with a commitment to participatory democracy and the openness of inquiry.

I shall concentrate here on Dewey's aesthetics as represented primarily in *Art as Experience* (1934), which, however, involves much more than aesthetics as traditionally conceived. Though Dewey's aesthetics initially aroused much interest among artists and critics as well as philosophers, it was, in academic circles, totally eclipsed by analytic philosophy of art, which by and large dismissed Dewey's aesthetic theory as "a hodge-podge of conflicting methods and undisciplined speculations" (Isenberg 128). Deweyan aesthetics is best portrayed by contrast to analytic aesthetics, and it contains many of the major themes of contemporary Continental theory that analytic philosophy either ignores or repudiates.

One of the most central features of Dewey's aesthetics is its naturalism. The first chapter of *Art as Experience* is entitled "The Live Creature," and it and all the subsequent chapters are dedicated to grounding aesthetics in the natural needs, constitution, and activities of the embodied human organism. Dewey aims at "recovering the continuity of esthetic experience with normal processes of living" (16). Esthetic understanding must start with and never forget the roots of art and beauty in the "basic vital functions," the "biological commonplaces" people share with "bird and beast" (19–20). For Dewey, all art is the product of interaction between the living organism and its environment, an undergoing and a doing that involves a reorganization of energies, actions, and materials. Though human arts have become more spiritualized, "the organic substratum remains as the quickening and deep foundation," the sustaining source of the emotional energies of art, which make it so enhancive to life (30–31, 85). This essential physiological stratum is not confined to the artist. The perceiver, too, must engage his or her natural feelings and energies as well as his or her physiological sensory motor responses in order to appreciate art, which for Dewey amounts to reconstituting something as art in aesthetic experience (60, 103–4).

In contrast, the major thrust of analytic aesthetics is sharply opposed to naturalizing art and its aesthetic value. G. E. Moore established this attitude with his doctrine of the naturalistic fallacy, a fallacy that "has been quite as commonly committed with regard to beauty as with regard to good" (*Principia* 201). Aesthetic qualities must not be identified with natural ones and are not even reducible or logically entailed by them.

Part of Dewey's naturalism is to insist that art's aim "is to serve the whole creature in his unified vitality," a "live creature" demanding natural satisfactions (*Art* 122). This stands in sharp contrast to the extreme emphasis on disinterestedness that analytic aesthetics inherited from IMMANUEL KANT. This emphasis goes beyond the mere Moorean point that beauty, like good, is a purely intrinsic value or end in itself that can only be misconceived as a means. There is the further characterization of art as something essentially defined by its noninstrumentality and gratuitousness. The underlying motive for such analytic attempts to purify art from any functionality was not to denigrate it as worthlessly useless but to place its worth apart from and above the realm of instrumental value and natural satisfactions. However noble the intention, this attitude portrayed aesthetic experience as eviscerate and socially irrelevant. No wonder theorists have turned to FRIEDRICH NIETZSCHE, GEORGES BATAILLE, and MICHEL FOUCAULT for recognition of the bodily factors and desires involved in the aesthetic, just as they turn to Continental Marxian theories for greater appreciation of art's historico-political and socioeconomic determinants and instrumental power.

But these very themes can be found in Dewey. Though no less devoted than the analysts to defending the aesthetic and to proving its infungible worth, Dewey did so by insisting on art's great but *global* instrumental value. For anything to have human value, it must in some way serve the needs and enhance the life and development of the human organism in coping with its environing world. The mistake of the Kantian tradition was to assume that since art had no specific, identifiable function that it could perform better than anything else, it could only be defended as being beyond use and function. Dewey's important corrective is to argue that art's special function and value lie not in any specialized, particular end but in satisfying the live creature in a more global way, by serving a variety of ends, and most important, by enhancing our immediate experience, which invigorates

and vitalizes us, thus aiding our achievement of whatever further ends we pursue. Not only does the work song sung in the harvest fields provide the harvesters with a satisfying aesthetic experience but its zest carries over into their work and invigorates and enhances it. The same can be said for works of high art. They are not merely tools for generating aesthetic experience: they modify and enhance perception and communication; they energize and inspire because aesthetic experience is always spilling over and getting integrated into our other activities, enhancing and deepening them.

Dewey's recognition of the global functionality of art is related to another view in which he seems to differ sharply from analytic philosophers—the philosophical primacy and centrality of art and the aesthetic. For Dewey, the aesthetic experience is the "experience in which the whole creature is alive" and most alive (33; see also 24–25, 109). "To esthetic experience, then, the philosopher must go to understand what experience is" (278). While Dewey saw art as the qualitative measure of any society (347), analytic philosophers saw science as the ideal and paradigm of human achievement. And analytic aesthetics, at least initially, was largely an attempt to apply the logically rigorous and precise methods of scientific philosophy to the wayward and woolly realm of art. Yet Dewey, appreciative as he was of scientific method and progress, could not help but regard scientific experience as thinner than art. For art engages more of the human organism in a more meaningful and immediate way (90–91, 126, 278), including the higher complexities of thinking: "The production of a work of genuine art probably demands more intelligence than does most of the so-called thinking that goes on among those who pride themselves on being 'intellectuals'" (52). He therefore held "that art—the mode of activity that is charged with meanings capable of immediately enjoyed possession—is the complete culmination of nature, and that 'science' is properly a handmaiden that conducts natural events to this happy issue" (*Experience* 358).

Dewey tries to deconstruct the traditional privileging opposition of science over art not only by reversing the privilege but by denying that there is any rigid dichotomy or opposition between the two. He insists that "science is an art," for "esthetic quality . . . may inhere in scientific work," and both enterprises perform the same essential function of helping us order and cope with experience (*Experience* 358; *Art* 33, 125–26, 202). Like JACQUES DERRIDA's idea of the general text, Dewey's central continuity thesis was aimed at breaking the stranglehold of entrenched dualisms and rigid disciplinary distinctions that stifle creative thought and fragment both individual experience and social life. He sought to connect aspects of human experience and activity that had been divided by specialized, compartmentalizing thought and then more brutally sundered by specialist, departmentalizing institutions in which such fragmented disciplinary thinking is reinscribed and reinforced (Shusterman 12–17, 46–55). In these ways he also anticipates THEODOR W. ADORNO and Foucault.

Dewey's aesthetic naturalism, aimed at "recovering the continuity of esthetic experience with normal processes of living," is part of his attempt to break the stifling hold of "the compartmental conception of fine art," that old and institutionally entrenched philosophical ideology of the aesthetic that sharply distinguishes art from real life and remits it "to a separate realm"—the museum, the theater, and the concert hall (Art 9, 14). But Dewey's aesthetics of continuity and holism not only undermines the art/science and art/life dichotomies but also insists on the fundamental continuity of a host of traditional binary notions and genre distinctions whose long-assumed oppositional contrast has structured so much of philosophical aesthetics: form/content, fine/practical art, high/popular culture, spatial/temporal arts, artist/audience, to name but a few.

Analytic aesthetics, pursued under the ideal of science, thus tended to shirk issues of evaluation and reform. The aim was to analyze and clarify the established concepts and practices of art criticism, not to revise them; to give a true account of our concept of art, not to change it. In vivid contrast, Deweyan aesthetics is interested not in truth for truth's sake but in achieving richer and more satisfying experience. For Dewey's pragmatism, *experience,* not *truth,* is the final standard. The ultimate aim of all enquiry, scientific or aesthetic, is not knowledge itself but better experience or experienced value, and Dewey insists on "the immediacy of aesthetic experience" and its experienced value (123). From this follows his view of the supremacy of the aesthetic: art's "immediately enjoyed," active experience is "the complete culmination of nature," for which truth or science serves as an auxiliary "handmaiden" (*Experience* 358). It also follows that aesthetic values cannot be permanently fixed by aesthetic theory or criticism but must be continually tested and may be overturned by the tribunal of changing experience.

A more dramatic and radical consequence of this experiential standard is that our aesthetic concepts, including the concept of art itself, are revealed as mere instruments that need to be challenged and revised when they fail to provide the best experience. This can account for Dewey's obvious attempt to direct his aesthetic the-

ory at radically reforming our concepts of art and the aesthetic. Dewey deplores the dominant elitist tradition of fine art, which he attacks under the labels of "the museum conception of art" and "the esoteric idea of fine art" (*Art* 12, 90). The prime motive for his opposition to the spiritualized sequestration of art was not ontological considerations of naturalistic continuity and emergence. Rather, the motive was the instrumental aim of improving our immediate experience through a sociocultural transformation in which art would be richer and more satisfying to more people because it would be closer to their most vital interests and better integrated into their lives. The compartmentalization and spiritualization of art as an elevated "separate realm" set "upon a remote pedestal," divorced from the materials and aims of all other human effort, has removed art from the daily experience of most of us and thus has impoverished the esthetic quality of our lives (9–16).

But more than art suffers from its spiritualized sequestration; nor was this compartmentalization established simply by and for aesthetes to secure and purify their pleasures. The idea of art and the aesthetic as a separate realm distinguished by its freedom, imagination, and pleasure has as its underlying correlative the dismal assumption that ordinary life is necessarily one of joyless, unimaginative coercion. This provides the powers and institutions structuring our everyday life with the best excuse for their increasingly brutal indifference to natural human needs for the pleasures of beauty and imaginative freedom. These are to be sought, not in real life, but in fine art, an escape that gives temporary relief. Art becomes, in Dewey's mordant phrase, "the beauty parlor of civilization" (339), covering with an opulent aesthetic surface its ugly horrors and brutalities, which, for Dewey, include class snobbery and capitalism's profit-seeking oppression and alienation of labor. Modern socioeconomic forces have so divided between joyless "externally enforced labor" and free enjoyment and between production and consumption that the "chasm between ordinary and esthetic experience," art and real life, has become theoretically convincing (15–16, 285). Thus, for Dewey, not only art but philosophical theories about art are significantly shaped by "extraneous" socioeconomic conditions, so our concept of art needs to be reformed as part and parcel of the reform of society that has so constituted it.

I conclude with Dewey's perhaps most central aesthetic theme: the privileging of aesthetic experience over the material object that ordinary, reified thinking identifies (and then commodifies and fetishizes) as the work of art. For Dewey the essence and value of art is not in such artifacts but in the dynamic and developing experiential activity through which they are created and perceived. He therefore distinguishes between the "art product" and "the actual work of art [which] is what the product does with and in experience" (9). Dewey's emphasis on art as experience stands in sharp opposition to analytic philosophy's suspicion of aesthetic experience, which it typically regarded as too elusive, variable, and psychologistic to serve as the center of philosophy of art. Analytic philosophy instead privileged art's objects, and it expended enormous efforts in trying to fix the precise criteria for identifying the same object in its various manifestations (e.g., authentic copies and performances) and for individuating it from other objects and inauthentic manifestations (e.g., forgeries).

Dewey thus anticipates poststructuralism in attacking the notion of the artwork as a fully fixed, self-sufficient, and inviolable object and in insisting on the active role and openness of aesthetic perception as a creative practice that reconstitutes aesthetic meaning. The poststructuralist move from closed work to open textual practice was prefigured in Dewey's move from a closed artistic product to open transformative aesthetic experience. But Dewey seems more moderate than most poststructuralists in his rejection of traditional ideas of unity and structure. While he repudiates for both ontological and aesthetic reasons the notions of structural fixity and reification, he advocates flexible stabilities and durable unities through change, asserting that such relative stabilities and unities are necessary ingredients for the fashioning of a satisfying life and for fruitful social action.

Pragmatism has recently been revived in literary theory through the writings of STANLEY FISH and RICHARD RORTY. But neither of them pays attention to Dewey's aesthetics, and indeed they present theories that are un-Deweyan in their disembodied "textualism" and elitist professionalism. Though some of Dewey's aesthetic ideas and judgments may be dated, his work still represents the best point of departure for progressive pragmatist literary theory and aesthetics.

Richard Shusterman

John Dewey, *Art as Experience* (1934), *Democracy and Education* (1916), *Ethics* (1932), *Experience and Nature* (1929), *Liberalism and Social Action* (1935), *Logic: The Theory of Inquiry* (1938), *Philosophy and Civilization* (1931), *The Public and Its Problems* (1927), *The Quest for Certainty* (1929), *Reconstruction in Philosophy* (1948).

Richard Bernstein, *John Dewey* (1966); Arnold Isenberg, "Analytical Philosophy and the Study of Art," *Journal of Aesthetics and Art Criticism* 46 (1987); G. E. Moore, *Principia Ethica* (1959); Richard Rorty, *Consequences of Pragmatism (Essays: 1972–1980)* (1982); Richard Shusterman, *Pragmatist Aesthetics: Living Beauty, Rethinking Art* (1992); Cornel West, *The American Evasion of Philosophy* (1989); Robert Westbrook, *John Dewey and American Democracy* (1991).

DISCOURSE

1. Discourse Analysis

For many years, discourse analysis was less an explicit "theory" than a practical and empirical approach for supporting fieldwork on relatively little-recorded languages and cultures (see, e.g., Grimes, Longacre, Malinowski, Pike). One domain of early work that attracted notice in general and humanistic circles was the cross-cultural study of stories and narratives (e.g., CLAUDE LÉVI-STRAUSS, *Anthropologie Structurale [Structural Anthropology]*). Major concerns later on included the discourse of schooling and education (Sinclair and Coulthard, Stubbs, Widdowson) and, with a sociological turn, the organization of conversation (Sacks, Schegloff, and Jefferson).

These practical and empirical emphases fostered some variance with the "theoretical linguistics" postulating a dichotomy between language and discourse (e.g., *langue* versus *parole* for FERDINAND DE SAUSSURE, "competence" versus "performance" for NOAM CHOMSKY). The project of abstracting "language" away from the cultural and social contexts in which it appears as a human phenomenon seemed attractive on theoretical grounds, especially for an emergent science like linguistics, but the consensus today is that this project is unrealistic. The rising pressure upon theory and method to resituate language in these contexts accounts for the explosive interest in discourse analysis, a field that from its very beginnings has implicitly or explicitly maintained the unity of language as both structure and event, both knowledge and action, both system and process, both potential and actual (Firth, Halliday, Hartmann, Pike).

In the 1970s, discourse analysis became a convergence point for a number of trends: "text linguistics" on the European continent; "functional" or "systemic linguistics" in Czechoslovakia, Britain, and Australia; "cognitive linguistics," "critical linguistics," "ethnography of communication," ethnomethodology, and the STRUCTURALISM, poststructuralism, DECONSTRUCTION, and feminism emanating from France; along with SEMIOTICS and cognitive science, both convergence points in their own right. This drift has made it possible, indeed essential, to contemplate discourse from multiple viewpoints: linguistic, philosophical, cognitive, social, anthropological, literary, historical, political, and ideological. Admittedly, essaying to do so makes us keenly aware of how multifarious and complex discourse transactions can be. Our best guarantee that we can ultimately make sense of all this is that they generally succeed in social practice. The task of discourse analysis is to describe the systematic organization and intersubjectivity that enable the success.

Accordingly, theories and models are being developed on numerous fronts: for the syntactical contours and the large-scale ("global") coherence of discourse; for the interactive performance of discourse actions, or "SPEECH ACTS"; for the plans, goals, and strategies of discourse participants; for the interface of meaning or significance with culture, ideology, personality, gender, and emotion; for the roles and relations of power or solidarity among participants or institutions in discourse.

The notion of "discourse" itself has been commensurately expanded. Besides being the standard designation for a recorded sequence of utterances (Longacre, Pike) or of "texts" (Beaugrande and Dressler), "discourse" may designate elaborate complexes all the way up to a definite order of concepts (Hindess and Hirst) or the entire practice and communication within a social institution (e.g., MICHEL FOUCAULT, *L'Archéologie du savoir [The Archeology of Knowledge]; Language, Counter-Memory, Practice*). Such is the diversity that one can find two "introductions" to discourse analysis with no overlap at all (see Coulthard; Macdonnell).

Still, discourse analysis does manifest some general and consistent principles, which might be formulated as follows:

1. *A "discourse" is not merely a linguistic unit, but a unit of human action, interaction, communication, and cognition.* The habit of identifying the "discourse" with its recorded (usually written) language trace, though deeply entrenched, must be transcended.

2. *The source of data should be naturally occurring discourses rather than isolated brief examples invented by investigators.* Having established the importance of context, we must discard the convenient fiction of "context-free" words or sentences. Such items are merely transposed by our citation into a different context, and we should inquire how we may be changing their significance, for example, concealing constraints or mystifying institutional commitments.

3. *Discourse analysis should balance analytic with synthetic viewpoints.* The traditional methods of discovering "linguistic units" and "constituents" by segmenting discourse should be more evenly correlated with methods that focus on how discourses are assembled and how the various units or aspects contribute to a constellation of mutual relevance (Beaugrande).

4. *A discourse is not a static, idealized, or totalized unity of words and significances, but a dynamic field of interests, engagements, tensions, conflicts, and contradictions.* This field in turn reflects the organization of society and its institutions and the roles and power structures inherent therein (Fowler et al., Wodak et al.).

5. *A discourse or discourse domain should not be isolated from others but be seen in its mutual relevance to them.* To appreciate the nature and problems of a domain such as "technical language," we should not reduce it to its incidental features, such as lists of special terms or tables of formulas. We must inquire how it functions within the general acquisition of knowledge through discourse and how it could function more effectively for wider participation.

6. *Discourse analysis should continually reflect upon its own procedures.* Given the unmanageably large and diverse range of data, each project must be selective and focused and so should declare and justify its motives in terms of epistemological interests. The discourse of science itself should be examined (Gilbert and Mulkay), as should that of specific fields such as anthropology (Geertz).

7. *Discourse analysis obliges the investigator to engage and reengage with discourse.* The idealized separation of subject from object, or investigator from data, is not feasible here. Since one's involvement in the data and one's commitments and priorities cannot be eliminated, they can be profitably made a further object of reflection: on how the discourse being analyzed correlates with the discourse of the analysis.

8. *Discourse analysis is rich and expansive rather than formalized and reductive.* Discourse cannot be adequately analyzed with a fixed algorithm for reifying it into a configuration of formal symbols. Instead, the analysis should pursue the relevance of a discourse in any direction and to any degree needed in order to grasp its status within social practices, such as in news reporting (Dijk) or psychotherapy (Labov and Fanshel, Wodak).

9. *To master its issues and problems, discourse analysis must adopt an encompassing interdisciplinary perspective.* In the past, interdisciplinarity has too often been restricted to programmatic statements of intent; we are now filling in the content of such programs with a cred-

itable body of results. Hence, discourse analysis should be, not one more Kuhnian battleground for warring "paradigms," but a domain for cooperation and integration among alternative paradigms (see THOMAS S. KUHN).

10. *Discourse analysis should interact with institutions and groups both inside and outside the academy to pursue urgent issues and problems.* We cannot assume that our current methods address all the most pressing issues. Instead, we should periodically take stock of and adapt our methods to more issues, such as the discourse of politicians about the nuclear arms race (Chilton et al.) or the discourse of judges and defendants in courtrooms (Atkinson and Drew, Leodolter).

11. *The highest goals of discourse analysis are to support the freedom of access to knowledge through discourse and to help in revealing and rebalancing communicative power structures.* Following the lead of "critical linguistics" (Dijk, Fowler et al., Mey), this thesis has now been widely acknowledged. Special attention has been devoted to geopolitical problems such as public policy, colonialism, racism, and sexism, which, though restricted by laws and statutes, persist at deeper levels in discourse, not merely through lexical choices, but through background assumptions, hierarchical structuring, rights of turn-taking, and so on.

12. *The demanding tasks facing us today call for an explicit, coherent research plan.* Past trends have been unduly dependent on personal or institutional commitments and decisions. Now that a global dispersion of discourse study is under way, larger projects seem feasible, provided that scholars can interact over long distances and shorter intervals.

The future of discourse analysis will depend to no small degree on whether principles such as these can be fully implemented and suitable frameworks and resources provided for research. The prospects seem especially favorable for interaction between discourse analysis and literary studies, a field in which the notion of discourse is being generally recognized as a foundational problem. The principles just enumerated readily invoke some ongoing trends as well as some future desiderata:

1. The traditional philological, formalistic, or New Critical focus on the literary text as language has been complemented by a concern for literary action, interaction, communication, and cognition, though so far (inspired by French scholars such as Foucault) more from a philosophical than a sociological or psychological orientation (see also NEW CRITICISM and PHILOLOGY).

2. The literary texts taken as objects of study are almost never invented by the investigator. Yet their "natural occurrence" requires specific conditions and conventions that need to be more clearly formulated and understood (Schmidt). Further groundwork is now being supplied by literary journals with an empirical outlook, such as *Poetics* and *Empirical Studies in the Arts*.

3. Recent trends show a more even balance between the analytic tactics of "close reading" or "text exegesis" and synthetic models of literary "production" and "reception" (Jauss) (see RECEPTION THEORY).

4. The traditional harmonizing, or "totalizing," tendencies of literary criticism have been offset by widening probes of literary discourse as a field of interests, engagements, and conflicts, including the estrangement from the putative "real world" of the reader (Iser) (see READER-RESPONSE THEORY AND CRITICISM).

5. Scholars reveal a renewed willingness to resituate literature, long isolated as a privileged preserve set above other discourse or even in opposition to it, among the plurality of social and ideological discourses of its own time and ours (Fowler; HAYDEN WHITE, *Metahistory: The Historical Imagination in Nineteenth-Century Europe, Tropics of Discourse;* FREDRIC JAMESON, *The Political Unconscious*).

6. The enterprise of reflecting upon procedures is at the very heart of the prestigious "literary theory" movement (see Beaugrande, *Critical Discourse*), though the theorizing is sometimes obscure about its goals.

7. The fastidious reaching for ultimate, tidy closure of the "meaning" of the literary work has been yielding to an open-ended readiness to engage and reengage the work, notably in J. HILLIS MILLER's appropriation of "deconstruction" ("Deconstructing the Deconstructors" in *Theory Then and Now*). The individual work itself is viewed as an "intertextual weaving" of other discourses (GEOFFREY H. HARTMAN, *Saving the Text*).

8. The expectation that analysis should be rich and expansive was only rarely suppressed in literary studies by the kind of strict "scientism" we have seen in some schools of linguistics. The brief "structuralist" turn to narrow linguistic method has long since swerved toward the wide-ranging "poststructuralist" revision (both trends documented by Harari).

9. The value of an encompassing interdisciplinary perspective on literature is no longer seriously contested today, and joint projects are commonplace, for example, between the Psychological Institute of the Hungarian Academy of Science and the American Council of Learned Societies (results edited by Martindale).

10. Shifts of focus outside the academy are still regrettably rare, but promising signs can be seen in some recent detailed investigations of the reading public and the literary publishing industry, as presented at the first

symposium of the International Society for the Empirical Study of Literature in 1987 (Schmidt, ed.).

11. The freedom of access to the unique experiences literature affords is still not a firmly established goal, due to the elitist disdain for naive readers. But discourse analysis has shown the processing of quite ordinary discourse to be enormously sophisticated and the supposed naiveté of nonelite readers to be an illusion.

12. Literary theory has been replete with calls for an explicit, coherent research plan. So far, progress has been slowed by the idiosyncratic and self-indulgent communicative strategies of some conspicuous theorists, who seem less concerned with any such plan than with the enhancement of their personal prestige. Here, the paradigm of discourse analysis, which addresses issues of such complexity that unplanned research would remain ineffectual, could act as a model.

The problems facing both discourse analysis and literary studies in the coming years are obviously enormous, but a concerted interaction between the two would surely improve the prospects for significant advances on both sides.

Robert de Beaugrande

See also LINGUISTICS AND LANGUAGE and SPEECH ACTS.

See bibliographies in MICHEL FOUCAULT, GEOFFREY H. HARTMAN, FREDRIC JAMESON, CLAUDE LÉVI-STRAUSS, J. HILLIS MILLER, and HAYDEN WHITE for texts by those writers.

John Atkinson and Paul Drew, *Order in Court: The Organization of Verbal Interaction in Judicial Settings* (1979); Robert de Beaugrande, *Critical Discourse: A Survey of Contemporary Literary Theorists* (1988), *Text, Discourse, and Process* (1980), *Text Production* (1984); Robert de Beaugrande and Wolfgang Dressler, *Introduction to Text Linguistics* (1981), "A New Introduction to the Study of Text and Discourse" (forthcoming); Paul Chilton, ed., *Language and the Nuclear Arms Debate: Nukespeak Today* (1985); Malcolm Coulthard, *An Introduction to Discourse Analysis* (1985); Teun van Dijk, *News as Discourse* (1988); Teun van Dijk, ed., *Discourse Analysis: Psychological Aspects* (1986), *Handbook of Discourse Analysis* (1985); John Rupert Firth, *Papers in Linguistics, 1934–1951* (1957); Roger Fowler, *Literature as Social Discourse: The Practice of Linguistic Criticism* (1981); Roger Fowler, Robert Hodge, Gunther Kress, and Tony Trew, *Language and Control* (1979); Clifford Geertz, *Works and Lives: The Anthropologist as Author* (1988); Nigel Gilbert and Michael Mulkay, *Opening Pandora's Box: A Sociological Analysis of Scientists' Discourse* (1984); Joseph Grimes, *The Thread of Discourse* (1975); Michael Halliday, *Introduction to Functional Grammar* (1985); Josué V. Harari, ed., *Structuralists and Structuralism: A Selected Bibliography of French Contemporary Thought* (1971), *Textual Strategies: Perspectives in Post-Structuralist Criticism* (1979); Peter Hartmann, *Theorie der Sprachwissenschaft* (1963); Barry Hindess and Paul Hirst, *Modes of Production and Social Formation* (1977); Wolfgang Iser, *Der Akt des Lesens: Theorie ästhetischer Wirkung* (1976, *The Act of Reading: A Theory of Aesthetic Response,* trans. Iser, 1978), *Der implizite Leser: Kommunikationsformen des Romans von Bunyan bis Beckett* (1972, *The Implied Reader: Patterns of Communication in Prose Fiction from Bunyan to Beckett,* trans. Iser, 1974); Hans Robert Jauss, *Ästhetische Erfahrung und literarische Hermeneutik* (1982, *Aesthetic Experience and Literary Hermeneutics,* trans. Michael Shaw, 1982), *Toward an Aesthetic of Reception* (1982); William Labov and David Fanshel, *Therapeutic Discourse* (1977); Ruth Leodolter, *Das Sprachverhalten von Angeklagten bei Gericht* (1975); Robert Longacre, *An Anatomy of Speech Notions* (1976), *Grammar of Discourse* (1983); Diane Macdonnell, *Theories of Discourse: An Introduction* (1986); Bronislaw Malinowski, "The Problem of Meaning in Primitive Languages," *The Meaning of Meaning* (by C. K. Ogden and I. A. Richards, 1923); Colin Martindale, ed., *Psychological Approaches to the Study of Literary Narratives* (1988); Jacob L. Mey, *Whose Language? A Study in Linguistic Pragmatics* (1985); Kenneth Lee Pike, *Language in Relation to a Unified Theory of the Structure of Human Behavior* (1967); Harvey Sacks, Emmanuel Schegloff, and Gail Jefferson, "A Simplest Systematics for the Organization of Turntaking for Conversation," *Language* 50 (1974); Siegfried J. Schmidt, *Foundations for the Empirical Study of Literature: Components of a Basic Theory* (1982); Siegfried J. Schmidt, ed., *Aspects of the Empirical Study of Art and Media,* special issue, *Poetics* 18 (1989); John McHardy Sinclair and Malcolm Coulthard, *Toward an Analysis of Discourse* (1975); Michael Stubbs, *Discourse Analysis* (1983); Henry Widdowson, *Explorations in Applied Linguistics* (1979); Ruth Wodak, *Language Behavior in Therapy Groups* (1986); Ruth Wodak et al., *Language, Power, and Ideology* (1989).

2. Discourse Theory

Discourse theorists take discourse, rather than language, as their domain in part because of difficulties with the latter term. The standard definition of "language" in linguistics (a set of units and the rules for combining them to make well-formed sentences) treats language as invariant over domains, occasions, speakers, and purposes; other traditional uses of language do specify for some particulars (the language of the courtroom, insurance policies, advertising, Satan in book 1 of *Paradise Lost,* this document), but even these uses share with linguistics a tendency to analyze texts (or transcriptions of speech) in terms of patterns of choices, to objectivize in terms of words and structures. Discourse, for discourse theory, is not sets of formally identified structures but a type of social action. Discourse theory criticizes theories of SPEECH ACTS for their focus on the acts of individual agents speaking without social determination or constraint.

Because of this orientation toward social action, discourse theory also distinguishes itself sharply from philosophical concerns with the truth of statements and the validity of arguments, substituting a concern for conditions under which one can be judged to have made a serious, sound, true, important, authoritative statement. This program is clearly sketched by MICHEL FOUCAULT in *The Archaelogy of Knowledge* and very concisely in his lecture to the Collège de France ("The Discourse of Language") appended to the *Archaelogy.* Foucault speaks of "rules" of discourse, but it is widely agreed that the conditions under which one can make serious, authoritative statements include material and social institutions and practices. A theory of discourse therefore implies a theory of society, most particularly a theory of power, legitimacy, and authority. Moreover, since society can to a very large extent be viewed as the sum of discourses, there is a tendency in discourse theory, particularly in its French varieties, for discourse to merge into praxis, undermining the commonsense ("Anglo-Saxon") distinction between talking and doing.

Broadly construed, discourse theory draws insights and support from three intellectual traditions: HERMENEUTICS, social construction and ethnography, and the analysis of power of the political Left. The tradition of hermeneutics as transmitted by Hans-Georg Gadamer and JÜRGEN HABERMAS (and THOMAS S. KUHN) emphasizes that every discourse takes place within a shared horizon of preunderstanding (or "lifeworld") that cannot be fully or explicitly formulated. No discourse can be completely self-grounded, and the ability to function as a participant cannot be acquired wholly from a book, but arises from initiation and experience. Relevant concepts here include the notions of discourse community and "culture" (in one sense) (see CULTURAL STUDIES).

A second major source for discourse theory is the vein of ethnography and social theory that is concerned with the offering and validating of accounts of cultural practices, including the writings of Clifford Geertz, Erving Goffman, and a host of others supporting the general program of symbolic interaction or social construction (see ANTHROPOLOGICAL THEORY AND CRITICISM). These approaches typically seek to "make strange" or denaturalize or make visible rules and practices underlying various institutions and transactions. They share with hermeneutics a sense of the rootedness of discourse in particular social forms and practices and tend to foreground the uncertain status of the analyst as an outsider and the potential artificiality of accounts of insider understanding. Pierre Bourdieu in *Outline of a Theory of Practice* emphasizes that practical knowledge and action are rooted in a habitus that resists theorizing or systematization in terms of abstract, "underlying" principles, including those of economic interest. Though Bourdieu is perhaps best known as a social theorist and researcher, one of his research sites is academic discourse, upon the French version of which he has much of interest to say in *Reproduction in Education, Society, and Culture* and *Homo Academicus.* He speaks, for example, of acquiring not only language but socially constituted attitudes toward language and so can refer to "bourgeois language," which, *nota bene,* is acquired as a habitus by growing up bourgeois, not by explicit, schooled instruction.

Discourse as a mode of power, which in late capitalist societies means the enactment and legitimation of inequality, is the special emphasis of Marxists such as Louis Althusser, Michel Pêcheux, and FREDRIC JAMESON. These Marxist writers have stimulated new interest in V. N. Voloshinov's *Marxism and the Philosophy of Language* (1929) and the more general view of discourse as embodying the conflicting values and stances of different groups found in M. M. BAKHTIN's "Discourse in the Novel." Discourse as a mode of concealing and perpetuating inequality and of regulating behavior is a theme also of such non-Marxist advocates of resistance to discursive regulation as Foucault and feminists focusing on the silencing and marginalizing effects of hegemonic discourses. Since theorizing itself is an activity not untinged by hegemonic aspirations, feminists such as HÉLÈNE CIXOUS adopt the devices of myth, contradiction, and hyperbole and could be said to refuse to do theory at all. (For critical reviews of feminist theories, see Cameron and Moi.)

In addition, most of the very large amount of work on language in institutional settings (medical, legal, educational, media) explores the intertwining of discourse and historical-material fact, either through the shaping and maintaining of the "client" (pupil) role or through the management and manipulation of mass audiences.

So much of discourse theory is oriented toward unmasking, debunking, and raising our consciousness about the ways current discourses serve power that one sympathizes with Foucault's suggestion that it reflects intellectuals' uneasiness, embarrassment, or fear of power, which has as much a creative, positive aspect as it does an exclusionary, silencing one. That observation, made late in his life, remains to be fully assimilated into discourse theory.

George L. Dillon

Louis Althusser, *Lenin and Philosophy and Other Essays* (trans. Ben Brewster, 1971); M. M. Bakhtin, "Discourse in the Novel," *The Dialogic Imagination: Four Essays* (ed. Michael Holquist, 1981); Pierre Bourdieu, *Esquisse d'une théorie de la pratique, précédé de trois études d'ethnologie kabyle* (1972, *Outline of a Theory of Practice,* trans. Richard Nice, 1977), *Homo Academicus* (1984, *Homo Academicus,* trans. Peter Collier, 1988); Pierre Bourdieu and Jean-Claude Passeron, *La Reproduction: Éléments pour une théorie du système d'enseignement* (1970, *Reproduction in Education, Society, and Culture,* trans. Richard Nice, 1977); Hélène Cixous, "Le Rire de la Méduse" (1975, "The Laugh of the Medusa," trans. Keith Cohen and Paula Cohen, *Signs* 1 [1976]); Michel Foucault, *L'Archéology du savoir* (1969, *The Archaeology of Knowledge,* trans. A. M. Sheridan Smith, 1972), "Truth and Power," *Power/Knowledge: Selected Interviews and Other Writings, 1972–1977* (ed. and trans. Colin Gordon, 1980); Hans-Georg Gadamer, *Wahrheit und Methode: Grundzüge einer philosophischen Hermeneutik* (1960, 5th ed., *Gesammelte Werke,* vol. 1, ed. J. C. B. Mohr, 1986, *Truth and Method,* ed. and trans. Garrett Burden and John Cumming, 1975, 2d ed., trans. rev. Joel Weinsheimer and Donald G. Marshall, 1989); Jürgen Habermas, *Theorie des kommunikativen Handelns,* vol. 1, *Handlungsrationalität und gesellschaftliche Rationalisierung* (1981, *The Theory of Communicative Action,* vol. 1, *Reason and the Rationalization of Society,* trans. Thomas McCarthy, 1983); Fredric Jameson, *The Political Unconscious: Narrative as a Socially Symbolic Act* (1981); Michel Pêcheux, *Les Vérités de la Palice* (1975, *Language, Semantics, and Ideology,* trans. Harbans Nagpal, 1982); V. N. Voloshinov, *Marksizm i filosofiia iazyka* (1929, *Marxism and the Philosophy of Language,* trans. Ladislav Matejka and I. R. Titunik, 1973).

Deborah Cameron, *Feminism and Linguistic Theory* (1985); Diane Macdonnell, *Theories of Discourse: An Introduction* (1986); Toril Moi, *Sexual/Textual Politics: Feminist Literary Theory* (1985).

DRAMA THEORY

ARISTOTLE's *Poetics,* the first major text of Western drama theory, defined the terms of much subsequent discussion. Unlike such classical Eastern theoretical works on drama as the Sanskrit *Natyasastra* or Zeami's writings on Nō, it makes only minor passing observations on the physical realization of the dramatic text, thus establishing an orientation essentially unchanged until the past century. Aristotle considers both the nature of tragedy (an idealized imitation of human action) and its function (the catharsis of such emotions as pity and fear). This argument for the psycho/social benefit of catharsis may have been at least partly in response to PLATO's distrust of art as a stimulus to the passions and as an inferior imitation of the world of appearance. The other most influential classical theorist was HORACE, whose *Art of Poetry* contains specific formal directions and the often quoted double aim of poetry, to delight and to instruct. During the medieval period, when the classic theatrical tradition was lost, such writers as DANTE ALIGHIERI considered the terms "tragedy" and "comedy" only as descriptive of various poetic genres, tragedies showing dark conclusions and comedies, happy ones, usually the result of good or evil moral choices by the characters.

Early Renaissance theorists were again aware of drama as an art involved with performance, though they followed Aristotle in foregrounding the creation, form, and purpose of the written text. The authority of Aristotle was supplemented by Horace and others, since the general theoretical approach was a regularizing one, seeing the classical tradition as essentially univocal. Yet the Renaissance itself developed many conflicting interpretations of classical thought. Perhaps the most widely held position was that moral utility should be the primary end of poetry, though Ludovico Castelvetro gave preference to pleasure. The traditional genres comedy and tragedy were generally accepted, though Giambattista Guarini and others championed a variety of new mixed genres, such as the pastoral tragicomedy. The concept of verisimilitude, requiring the drama to resemble life, was almost universally accepted but variously interpreted. The champions of mixed genres, anticipating certain Romantic arguments, looked to specific and perhaps idiosyncratic reality, while the more common view was that the reality should be more general or idealized. Closely related to verisimilitude was the concept of decorum, suggesting that dramatic characters should act and speak according to the expectations of their particular class, sex, and social position. Perhaps the best-known

Renaissance concerns dealt with the "three unities"—time (depiction of events within a single day or less), place (a single setting or a few closely adjacent ones), and action (avoidance of subplots). These unities were widely attributed to Aristotle, but in fact they were essentially defined by Italian theorists. (See RENAISSANCE THEORY AND CRITICISM.)

These major precepts—verisimilitude, decorum, moral purpose, the unities—in the late fifteenth century spread to Spain, France, and England, where they were developed by such theorists as Francisco Cascales, Vauquelin de la Fresnaye, and SIR PHILIP SIDNEY. In each of these countries a successful popular theater was developing in ignorance or in defiance of most such precepts, providing a pragmatic base for the countermovement of Romantic theory in the nineteenth century. In France, however, both theorists and major dramatists after the 1630 triumph of Pierre Corneille's *Le Cid* generally accepted and elaborated the major tenets of Italian Renaissance theory, and the distinction of Corneille, Jean Baptiste Poquelin Molière, and Jean Racine, reinforced by the political and cultural dominance of France during the seventeenth and eighteenth centuries, ensured the European dominance of this theoretical orientation.

The common eighteenth-century vision of the universe as rational and benevolent was naturally reflected in its theory, and drama was almost universally regarded as both participating in and reflecting this moral order. This resulted in an important reorientation of attitude toward the traditional dramatic genres. Renaissance theorists had provided a moral function for the laughter of comedy, as a weapon of ridicule for the correction of social deviation, but the moral function of tragedy was less clear. Eighteenth-century theory returned to an attitude closer to the medieval distinctions, comedy depicting the happiness resulting from good actions and tragedy the sufferings resulting from evil ones. This doctrine of suitable rewards, called "poetic justice" by John Dennis in England, became so widely accepted that even the major plays of Shakespeare were reworked to bring their endings into harmony with it. A new kind of comedy, the sentimental, was developed to conform to this new concern, and soon after there developed a new serious form, the middle-class drama, since the sufferings of the kings and heroes of traditional tragedy were considered too remote to serve as the most effective negative examples for the bourgeois public of this period. The theory and practice of this type of drama were developed by George Lillo in England, G. E. LESSING in Germany, and Denis Diderot in France.

Although JEAN-JACQUES ROUSSEAU shared Plato's distrust of the theater as an institution of illusion and falsehood, his influence on this art has been enormous. In general, his championing of nature over culture and emotion over reason provided key elements of subsequent Romantic theory and practice, and more specifically, his celebration of populist theater and of unmediated performance became major concerns in twentieth-century theater. The basic elements of Romantic dramatic theory were evolved in Germany at the end of the eighteenth century, reaching their fullest expression in the writings of FRIEDRICH SCHILLER and August W. Schlegel. These were in turn taken into Italy by GERMAINE DE STAËL and Schlegel, into France by Staël and Stendhal, and into England by SAMUEL TAYLOR COLERIDGE.

Romantic theory frequently defined itself in opposition to classicism, and thus much attention was given to defiance of the traditional unities and to the conscious mixture of genres. Victor Hugo and Coleridge felt that such a mixture not only presented a truer picture of experienced reality but, what is more important, suggested through the clash of contrary elements a deeper and more mysterious reality beyond everyday appearance. The dialectic consciousness so typical of Romantic thought owes much to IMMANUEL KANT, whose wedge between human consciousness and the absolute was reflected in Schiller's freedom and necessity, JOHANN WOLFGANG VON GOETHE's destiny and will, and an infinite series of subsequent dualities. Romantic theorists also rejected the classical emphasis on the general and the typical, exalting individual poetic insight and expression and the individual work of art organized not according to general rules but according to its own inner dynamic, called "organic unity."

Although the Romantic theorists rejected the rigid genre distinctions of French neoclassicism, they by no means renounced such concepts as tragedy and comedy. On the contrary, German theorists in particular provided penetrating analyses of tragedy. Despite considerable individual differences, these analyses may be generally divided into two groups according to their attitude toward Romantic dualism. Some theorists, such as Schlegel, G. W. F. HEGEL, and FRIEDRICH NIETZSCHE, hypothesized that tragedy could function to bridge the gap between human consciousness and the absolute, or at least to hold these in a creative tension. Others, such as Friedrich Schleiermacher and ARTHUR SCHOPENHAUER, felt that tragedy's function was to reveal the unbridgeability of the gap.

Dramatic genre itself was viewed dialectically, so that Hegel and Hugo considered drama as a synthesis, a modern form fusing the earlier objective poetry of the epic with the subjective of the lyric. Such historical orientation is in itself more Romantic than classic, since classicism presumed an aesthetic world of stable values, unaffected by circumstance. This orientation remained central to the realists of the later nineteenth century, though in many other respects they defined themselves in opposition to the Romantics. Analysis of the historical situation of a work fitted in very well with the scientific spirit of early realists such as HIPPOLYTE TAINE and ÉMILE ZOLA and may also be seen in the minor but highly influential comments of KARL MARX AND FRIEDRICH ENGELS on historical drama.

Realism turned away from the metaphysical concerns of Romanticism to seek an apparently objective presentation of observed reality. Its familiarity and accessibility were so attractive to nineteenth-century audiences that it became in effect the new classicism, against which a whole series of new, more subjective and abstract Romanticisms would react. The first such reaction was Symbolism, whose participants, rejecting the surface concerns of realism, looked back to the German Romantic tradition and its interest in a hidden deeper reality. Richard Wagner was a key source, in the spirituality of his concerns and in his interest in an artwork synthesizing all means of expression. Symbolism also encouraged, in theorists such as Gordon Craig, the first attempts to establish a theory of theater as an art based on sensual impressions, opposed to drama, a literary art. (See also BRITISH THEORY AND CRITICISM: 5. SYMBOLISM and STÉPHANE MALLARMÉ AND FRENCH SYMBOLISM.)

The first avant-garde reaction to realism in the twentieth century was futurism, founded by Tommaso Marinetti, a movement that stressed speed, technology, and the rejection of all established forms and works. Despite its anarchic flavor, futurism prepared the way for an important tradition of twentieth-century art, from Dada to contemporary performance art, which stresses the immediate and attempts to deny or subvert normal discursive language and even representation and theatricality itself.

In the early twentieth century, most theorists approached drama in a much less radical way. Despite inevitable overlap and blending, one might consider their work as of three general types—social, metaphysical, and formal. The theorists interested in the political, social, or economic background of the drama or dramatist usually favored realism and included such champions of the didactic drama as George Bernard Shaw. This orientation owed much to Marx and the tradition of the Russian civic critics as well as to the positivists such

as Taine, who stressed the importance of a work's historical situation. The metaphysical or aesthetic theorists, like the Symbolists, saw the drama as a means of contacting a normally hidden deeper reality. The theories of C. G. Jung (see ARCHETYPAL THEORY AND CRITICISM) and SIGMUND FREUD provided new inspiration for such theory, and the unconscious or subconscious assumed a theoretical position similar to the Romantic Dionysian or Geist.

The conflict between social and metaphysical theory, in various guises, has fueled much debate in dramatic theory of the twentieth century. Early surrealism was clearly metaphysical in orientation, inspiring Artaud, whose rejection of discursive language echoes certain Symbolist concerns and whose quest for the turbulent heart of existence recalls German Romanticism. The early German expressionists also felt that drama could reveal the hidden side of the human psyche, though expressionists also became concerned with politics and society, unquestionably influencing both the theory and the practice of Bertolt Brecht, the century's best-known representative of social theory. Brecht situated his "epic" theater in opposition to the "dramatic" or "Aristotelian" theater, though in fact his more immediate target was the nineteenth-century bourgeois theater, which Brecht, like Wagner and Marx, saw as a commodity serving the apparatus of the existing social structure. Unlike Wagner, however, Brecht called for a drama whose elements were not blended but disjunctive, presenting reality as unpredictable and thus alterable.

A third approach, formal criticism, dates back to Aristotle, but it received new impetus in the late nineteenth century, when scientific analysis was applied not only to playwriting by naturalists such as Zola but to play analysis by theorists such as Gustav Freytag, who sought to discover the "rules" of dramatic structure by empirical analysis of the great dramas. Structural and social theories of drama have until very recently almost totally dominated dramatic theory in England and America, where Anglo-Saxon pragmatism and empiricism have tended to discourage metaphysical speculation. Perhaps the two most influential theoretical schools in America in the mid-twentieth century, NEW CRITICISM and the neo-Aristotelian CHICAGO CRITICS, consciously excluded from the analyses of drama both social circumstances and metaphysics.

Thus it is not surprising that modern American and English critics have devoted particular attention to such formal matters as analysis of traditional dramatic genres, particularly tragedy. Although such European theorists as GEORG LUKÁCS and WALTER BENJAMIN produced major works discussing the disappearance of tragedy in modern times, they were particularly concerned with exploring the social and metaphysical backgrounds of this phenomenon. Something of their sense of modern alienation may be found in Joseph Wood Krutch's and George Steiner's pronouncements of the death of this genre, but most of the many English-language articles and books in the mid-twentieth century dealing with tragedy dealt with the genre largely on formal terms. More recently, similar but less extensive attention has been accorded the mixed form of the dark, grotesque, or tragic comedy, thought by many to be a more appropriate vehicle for expressing the modern human condition.

During the 1950s and 1960s new support appeared for each of these critical orientations. Eugène Ionesco and other leaders of a new experimental theater in France provided both drama and theory that was metaphysical in orientation. The political unrest in the latter part of this period, with the rising black consciousness in America, stimulated a new interest in socially and politically engaged theory. Finally, also in the late 1960s, ROLAND BARTHES and UMBERTO ECO wrote seminal essays reviving an interest in the application of semiotic analysis to drama and theater, a project begun in Prague in the 1930s but little developed after that decade (see PRAGUE SCHOOL STRUCTURALISM and SEMIOTICS).

During the 1970s semiotic theorists explored the signifying dynamics of dramatic and stage texts, but subsequently Marco de Marinis, André Helbo, and others moved from an interest in the production of signs to a concern with their reception and processing, thus approaching the interests of *Rezeptionsaesthetik* (see RECEPTION THEORY). At the same time, semiotic analysis itself was challenged by phenomenological theorists and related theorists of performance such as Bert States and Richard Foreman, who suggested that semiotics, with its assumption of an absent signified, ignored or gave inadequate attention to the fact of presence in theater. Poststructuralist theorists such as Herbert Blau or JEAN-FRANÇOIS LYOTARD have also attempted to qualify or dismantle the structuralist/semiotic enterprise by emphasizing the displacement, the disjunctures, and the libidinal flows that work against the structural codification of texts, an enterprise aided by the neo-Freudian theories of JACQUES LACAN.

During the 1980s other, more directly ideological methodologies also gained prominence. Although extremely varied in the work of individual theorists, these approaches have been generally grouped under three headings: British cultural materialism; its close cousin American NEW HISTORICISM; and the very broad international field of FEMINIST THEORY AND CRITICISM. The term and the general approach of cultural materialism comes from the later work of RAYMOND WILLIAMS, who has applied a basically Marxist study of social dynamics to a wide range of cultural phenomena, including the drama. The American New Historicists, led by Stephen Greenblatt, have been influenced more by the French poststructuralists and by MICHEL FOUCAULT, leading them to give particular attention to concerns of power, authority, and subversion at work in the originary conditions of dramatic texts. Feminist theory has been far more diverse than cultural materialism or New Historicism, but in drama three major approaches have been often proposed: liberal, seeking to give women, past and present, opportunity to be judged fairly by the same artistic standards as men; radical, seeking a feminist counteraesthetic, with its own standards; and materialist, exploring the sociocultural dynamic that establishes and directs gender conditions in general. Closely related to the second of these has been the work of certain French feminists, such as HÉLÈNE CIXOUS, who has sought a feminist writing that in its playfulness and avoidance of closure has much in common with the concerns of poststructuralism. Clearly, Marxist, psychoanalytic, and poststructuralist concerns, all major forces in contemporary theory, have each contributed importantly to the heteroglossia of contemporary feminist theory.

Marvin Carlson

See also CULTURAL STUDIES: I. UNITED KINGDOM and SEMIOTICS.

Antonin Artaud, *The Theatre and Its Double* (1938, trans. M. C. Richards, 1958); Roland Barthes, *Essais critiques* (1964, *Critical Essays*, trans. Richard Howard, 1972); Walter Benjamin, *Der Ursprung des deutschen Trauerspiels* (1928, ed. Rolf Tiedemann, 1963, *The Origin of German Tragic Drama*, trans. John Osborne, 1977); Herbert Blau, *The Eye of Prey* (1987); Bertolt Brecht, *Schriften zum Theater* (1957, *Brecht on Theatre: The Development of an Aesthetic,* ed. and trans. John Willett, 1964); Sue-Ellen Case, *Feminism and Theatre* (1988); Lodovico Castelvetro, *Poetica d'Aristotele vulgarizzata e sposta* (2 vols., 1978–79); Hélène Cixous, "Aller à la mer" (1977, trans. Barbara Kerslake, *Modern Drama* 27 [1984]); John Dennis, *Critical Works* (ed. Edward Niles Hooker, 2 vols., 1939–43); Denis Diderot, *Diderot's Writings on the Theatre* (ed. F. C. Green, 1978); Umberto Eco, "Semiotics of Theatrical Performance," *The Drama Review* 21 (1977); Erika Fischer-Lichte, *The Semiotics of Theater* (trans. Jeremy Gaines and Doris L.

Jones, 1992); Gustav Freytag, *Technique of the Drama* (1863, ed. Elias J. MacEwan, 1896); Stephen J. Greenblatt, *Renaissance Self-Fashioning: From More to Shakespeare* (1980); Victor Hugo, *Dramas* (trans. I. G. Burnham, 10 vols., 1895–96); Eugène Ionesco, *Notes and Counter-notes* (1962, trans. Donald Watson, 1964); Georg Lukács, "The Sociology of Modern Drama" (1909, abr. trans. Lee Baxandell, *Tulane Drama Review* 9 [1965]); Jean-François Lyotard, "Le Dent, la paume," *Les Dispotifs pulsionnels* (1973); August W. Schlegel, *Über dramatische Kunst und Litteratur* (2 vols., 1809–11, *A Course of Lectures on Dramatic Art and Literature,* 1817, trans. John Black, rev. A. J. W. Morrison, 1846); George Bernard Shaw, *Shaw on Theatre* (ed. E. J. West, 1958); Richard Wagner, *Prose Works* (trans. William Ashton Ellis, 8 vols., 1893–99); Raymond Williams, *Marxism and Literature* (1978).

Marvin Carlson, *Theories of the Theatre* (1984); Barrett Clark, *European Theories of the Drama* (1965); Bernard F. Dukore, *Dramatic Theory and Criticism: Greeks to Grotowski* (1974).

DRYDEN, JOHN

John Dryden (1631–1700) carried out a significant critical project, the understanding of which has generally remained within the lines laid down in SAMUEL JOHNSON's essay, which divided Dryden's work into the "general or [the] occasional," identified as the necessary and true as opposed to the contingent and corrupt. "In his general precepts, which depend upon the nature of things, and the structure of the human mind, he may doubtless be safely recommended to the confidence of the reader; but his occasional and particular positions were sometimes interested, sometimes negligent, and sometimes capricious" (Johnson, *Lives* 1:227). Attention being directed to the codification of Dryden's opinion within the terms of this opposition, critical discourse on Dryden has consisted largely in separating Dryden's principles from his own contingent failures to adhere to those principles.

The thematic elements of Dryden's criticism—ancients versus moderns, French neoclassicism versus English practice, rhyme versus blank verse, lexical usage versus prescription, probability versus poetic justice, universal value versus the spirit of the age, and so on—have been codified concisely by W. K. Wimsatt and Cleanth Brooks (*Literary Criticism* 196–217) and painstakingly by Robert Hume *(Dryden's Criticism).* This activity of paraphrase and selection in the interest of establishing an organic corpus of Dryden's principles ignores the extent to which Dryden insisted that the principles by which both general and occasional criticism should be judged should form an organic whole, the mind of a critic. To attend to Drydenic principles is to miss the significance of the force of Dryden's criticism as an event that centered literary criticism in the critic's opinion or response. That is to say, Dryden initiated the blurring of the division of general theory from occasional appreciation that came to define the literary-critical activity. And he did this by recasting the framework of criticism in terms of a critic's consistency with his own perceptions of the literary work: the subjective critical consciousness is the resolutely organic point of intersection of the human mind with the objects of nature. While earlier critics would have grounded their projects in terms of either formal consistency with regard to the precepts of classical authority or contentual unity with revealed scriptural truth, Dryden organizes concern for both the objective truth of the artwork (the instruction of content) and the subjective appreciation of it (the delight of form) around a notion of correspondence that is organic rather than formal. His negotiation with the neoclassical terms of BEN JONSON and Pierre Corneille is thus in no way faithful to earlier conceptions of the division of form and content.

The insistence upon critical subjectivity is thus accompanied by an understanding of the artwork as the organic product of a parallel subjectivity. While neoclassicism attended to both form and content, instruction and delight, it conceived their coming together at a purely formal level, with poetic imitation as the site of a correspondence between the two distinct functions (see SIR PHILIP SIDNEY's *Defence of Poetry*). However, in Dryden's criticism, lifelikeness as the criterion of poetic imitation or verisimilitude is replaced by a notion of *liveliness* (Wimsatt and Brooks reveal the extent to which their thought is in thrall to Dryden by treating liveliness and verisimilitude as synonymous [186]). Lisideius, in "An Essay of Dramatick Poesie," defines the criterion of the judgment of poetic merit, "when he was to make a judgement of what others writ: that he conceiv'd a Play ought to be, *A just and lively Image of Human Nature, representing its Passions and Humours, and the Changes of Fortune to which it is subject; for the Delight and Instruction of Mankind*" (*Works* 17:15). Poetic imitation is not merely an issue of formal correspondence but one of just *and lively* correspondence to life. Liveliness introduces to the notion of formal or objective correspondence (mimetic justice) the idea of a fusion or unity of form and content in an organic correspondence of the artwork to forms of life, whether subjective or objective. The rigid distinction of thought from expression is now brought into an organic unity in the appropriation of the artwork by consciousness, which determines both the moment of reading and the moment of writing. This definition is a guide for both critical judgment and composition, which are rarely distinguished in the formulation of Drydenic prescriptions: criticism is no longer simply propaedeutic in regard to composition, as in the Renaissance manuals such as that of Puttenham; rather, reading and composition are structured in parallel as moments of literary inwardness or interiority (see RENAISSANCE THEORY AND CRITICISM).

The redescription of poetic imitation as organic correspondence produces a new definition of "literary inwardness" as the grounds of both composition and criticism. This is apparent in Dryden's critical account of Shakespeare in the "Essay," which Johnson hailed as a "perpetual model of encomiastic criticism" (*Lives* 1:226). Neander ("New Man," usually taken to be a self-portrait) says that Shakespeare

> was the man who of all Modern, and perhaps Ancient Poets, had the largest and most comprehensive soul. All the Images of Nature were still present to him, and he drew them not laboriously, but luckily: when he describes any thing, you more than see it, you feel it too. Those who accuse him to have wanted learning, give him the greater commendation: he was naturally learn'd; he needed not the spectacles of Books to read Nature; he look'd inwards, and found her there. I cannot say he is every where alike; were he so, I should do him injury to compare him with the greatest of Mankind. (*Works* 17:55)

Reading and writing, criticism and composition, are one activity for Dryden: there is no friction between the two sides of the one operation. Writing is not a laborious work, an exterior operation, but the practice of an inwardness, the felicity of a subject. Nature and psychology are fused as the organic being of the literary subject. Correspondence to organic nature (instructive poetic verisimilitude) is united with a psychologism of the delighted reader, who is directly addressed by the critic as by the text, the use of the second person marking the absence of spectacles. A psychology of response offers to form the possibility of delighting by organic correspondence rather than by mere technical rigor; like nature, poetic technique can be lively as well as just, in that "you more than see it, you feel it too." The apparent innocence and colloquial tone of this statement mark it as the commencement of the informal treatment of form that was the forgetting of RHETORIC and the beginning of appreciative literary criticism. The poet's art is no

longer an external operation but a function of inwardness that corresponds to the interiority of a reader's response. Reading is responding, the turning of the exteriority of a text (a visible public image) into the interiority of a personal response (a raw private feel). Decorum becomes a matter of psychological satisfaction (realism and decency) rather than a strictly formal constraint. Instruction and delight are thus brought together by the poet in the unification of content (the facts of Nature) and form (the values of psychological response) as an organic whole. The criterion by which the effectiveness of this fusion is judged is Shakespeare's achieved subjective self-identity, his capacity to be himself. Instead of instruction or delight, we have the singular criterion of adequacy to self—he is not everywhere alike. According to Dryden, the criterion of literary judgment is the poet's adequacy to self, the correspondence of his work to his inner perception of Nature in the first instance and the correspondence to that inwardness across his *oeuvre* in the second. This was, of course, precisely the criterion by which Johnson was to judge Dryden.

Dryden's importance can be measured in the terms of Johnson's criticism of him for being "by no means constant to himself" (*Lives* 1:227). The literary critic is judged, not in terms of constancy to classical authority (with regard to form) or scriptural truth (with regard to content), but in terms of *self-consistency*. Dryden's legacy determines the site of literary-critical activity as the subjective interiority or inwardness of the critic.

Literary excellence thus becomes a function of interiority: the mark of literary achievement is that it establishes its own ground as *equal to itself*:

> Yet give me leave to say thus much, without injury to their Ashes, that not onely we shall never equal them, but they could never equal themselves, were they to rise and write again. We acknowledge them our Fathers in wit, but they have ruined their Estates themselves before they came to their childrens hands. . . . This therefore will be a good Argument to us either not to write at all, or to attempt some other way. (*Works* 17:74–75)

Since aesthetic value is organically self-defining by analogy with subjective individuality, the regulatory criterion belongs to the artwork, not to criticism.

Thus, in Dryden's work criticism becomes appreciative rather than prescriptive, descriptive rather than definitive. In the discussion of contemporary poetry with which the "Essay of Dramatick Poesie" begins, all four interlocutors concur in Crites's attack on the twin extremes of rhetorical elaboration and neoclassical restraint. The judgment of the virtue of poetic imitation no longer consists in a separate consideration of form (manner) and content (matter) as the distinct poles of the understanding of a literary object. In that literary value is situated by Dryden as inherently singular and interior, it is ultimately unassailable by any external technology of reading, whether Renaissance rhetoric or neoclassical regulation. The presence of technical forms of analysis in Dryden's criticism never functions authoritatively. The basis of poetic discrimination is the subjective appreciation of the artwork in terms of an opposition of lively inwardness (organic unity of form and content) to dead exteriority (the failure to fuse form and content organically). That dead exteriority can be produced either by the "wresting and torturing" of formal rhetorical excess or by the "want of imagination" of the excess of contentual restraint (*Works* 17:10–11).

Dryden's regulation of literary appreciation by analogy with a description of subjectivity as self-identity raises a problem for criticism, in that the distance of interpretive activity from the text becomes a threat to the literary interiority it serves to delineate. The problem of the distance of interpretation may be stated as follows: if we seek to justify our readings by appeal to a textual interiority (the text as a thing in itself), then how can we ever say anything about a text that does not either repeat that interiority in a less proper form or transgress it? Either interpretation is different from the text and betrays the inwardness that is the origin of textual value, or it is not, in which case it is not interpretation but repetition. Now that the text is a primary organic unity, how is criticism to partake of that inwardness? How can criticism overcome its inevitable secondariness? This fear animates Dryden's attacks on the Restoration as an age of criticism, a calumny that might seem strange in someone responsible for much of that critical output. It underlies the rank inaccuracy of such statements about himself as, "For I am as little apt to defend my own Errours, as to find those of other Poets. Only observe, that the great Censors of Wit and Poetry, either produce nothing of their own, or what is more ridiculous than any thing they reprehend" ("Preface to Tyrannic Love," *Works* 10:111).

The vast majority of Dryden's critical writing takes place in prefaces to literary works. This is not a purely aleatory choice of the space of critical activity but the location of the work of criticism in a problematic relation to the inwardness of the literary text, at once part of that interiority and not part of it, both inside the work and outside it. The problematic of the preface is the difficult site of literary criticism as a secondary activity with the goal of appreciating the primacy of literary texts. The space of the preface articulates the problem of critical distance established by Dryden:

> The writing of Prefaces to Plays was probably invented by some very ambitious Poet, who never thought he had done enough: Perhaps by some Ape of the *French* Eloquence, who uses to make a business of a Letter of gallantry, an examen of a Farce; and in short, a great pomp and ostentation of words on every trifle. This is certainly the talent of that Nation, and ought not to be invaded by any other. They do that out of gayety which would be an imposition upon us.
>
> We may satisfie our selves with surmounting them in the Scene, and safely leave them those trappings of writing, and flourishes of the Pen, with which they adorn the borders of their plays, and which are indeed no more than good Landskips to a very indifferent Picture. I must proceed no farther in this argument, lest I run my self beyond my excuse for writing this. ("Preface to *The Tempest*," *Works* 10:1)

The problem of criticism as secondary or as prefatory establishes the discipline of the field of textuality as structured through bordering, by limits and boundaries. The excess of interpretive or prefatory work over the text itself, by its very excess, implies a lack on the part of the text, a "not-having-done-enough." Exceeding the borders of the text in this way is, moreover, a specific characteristic of the French. Dryden marks interpretation as foreign precisely in order that it may be given its own place, its own interiority. However, the native spontaneity of interpretation is to be, for itself, foreign: the native attribute of French gaiety is for it to lie over the border, to be an excessive efflorescence. French critical activity, in its overt recognition of itself as a formal technology of reading, is not just foreign to the text, it is foreign to itself.

Dryden thus implies the possibility of a kind of critical reading that, in being native to itself in the sense for which he praised Shakespeare, would not be foreign or secondary to the text itself, not parasitic. For English criticism to keep its proper place, it should not invade the French, should not cross the frontier. And since the place of French criticism is defined by a textual boundary, between play and margin, picture and frame, then the proper place of English criticism is, by analogy, on the other side of that border, on the side of textual interiority. English criticism would thus escape the supplementary logic of secondariness that doomed it to diminish textual interiority by its excess over it. It would represent a noninvasive reading of the interior of the text. This is not merely a question of writing literature rather than criticizing it, for as Dryden recognizes, he is writing a preface himself. The point is that his prefatory addition to the "scene" in some sense will not transgress the borders of that scene, will remain native to the literary text that it interprets. The interpretive activity of the native as opposed to the foreign critic consists in the recognition of textual interiority *in its own terms*. And this recognition is made possible by the disposition of an organic psychology of critical response as analogous to the organic interiority that it has been Dryden's business to ascribe to literary texts.

T. S. ELIOT praised Dryden for being the first critic to pay attention to "the native element" in literature and the language (*Use* 24). Johnson called him the "Father of English Criticism" (*Lives* 1:225). The importance of this immensely prolific writer, poet, playwright, critic, laureate, and hack journalist does not lie solely in the attention to English letters, which his literary-critical successors imply, but in the paying of attention to a native element in reading, in the siring of an idea of criticism as not foreign to the text.

Bill Readings

See also BRITISH THEORY AND CRITICISM: 1. EARLY EIGHTEENTH CENTURY and 2. LATE EIGHTEENTH CENTURY and FRENCH THEORY AND CRITICISM: 1. SEVENTEENTH CENTURY.

John Dryden, *Of Dramatic Poesy and Other Critical Essays* (ed. George Watson, 2 vols., 1962), *Works* (ed. Edward Niles Hooker, H. T. Swedenberg, Jr., Earl Miner, Alan Roper, Vinton A. Dearing, and George Robert Guffey et al., 20 vols. to date, 1956–).

Thomas Docherty, "The Impossibility of Authenticity," *On Modern Authority: The Theory and Condition of Writing, 1500 to the Present Day* (1987); T. S. Eliot, "Introduction" and "The Age of Dryden," *The Use of Poetry and the Use of Criticism* (1933); Robert Hume, *Dryden's Criticism* (1970); Samuel Johnson, "John Dryden," *Lives of the English Poets,* vol. 1 (ed. L. Archer Hind, 1925); Bill Readings, "Why Is Theory Foreign?" *Theory between the Disciplines: Authority/Vision/Politics* (ed. Martin Kreiswirth and Mark A. Cheetham, 1990); John Wilmot, earl of Rochester, "An Allusion to Horace, The Tenth Satyr of the First Book," *Complete Poems* (ed. David M. Vieth, 1968); William K. Wimsatt, Jr., and Cleanth Brooks, *Literary Criticism: A Short History* (1957).

ECO, UMBERTO

The critical activities of Umberto Eco (b. 1932) are remarkably varied. He has written extensively on medieval aesthetics, James Joyce, the nature of the open work, forms of mass communication and culture, SEMIOTICS, and theories of reception. He has also written two novels, *The Name of the Rose* (1980) and *Foucault's Pendulum* (1988). This eclecticism is reflected by Eco's diverse professional interests. In addition to holding the chair of semiotics at the University of Bologna, he has been a regular contributor to numerous Italian newspapers and magazines, among them *Il giorno, La stampa,* the *Corriere della sera, La repubblica, L'espresso,* and *Il manifesto.* Between 1954 and 1959 Eco was editor for cultural programs at the Radiotelevisione Italiana (RAI). Moreover, he has been at the forefront of a number of avant-garde organizations in Italy, notably the Gruppo 63. As one might expect, these interests are often mutually informing; his work in semiotics, for example, complements his cultural criticism and novels. In addition to his direct involvement in these activities, Eco has assumed the role of a kind of cultural historian, documenting the vicissitudes of various critical movements and cultural trends, not to mention his own earlier formulations and engagements. In this respect he exemplifies the engaged intellectual that he himself has often discussed. As he puts it in the preface to *Travels in Hyperreality* (1986), "My way of being involved in politics consists of telling others how I see daily life, political events, sometimes the way I look at a movie. I believe that it is my job as a scholar and a citizen to show how we are surrounded by 'messages,' products of political power, of economic power, of the entertainment industry and the revolution industry, and to say that we must know how to analyze and criticize them" (xi). Eco has managed to address a larger audience through his journalism and novels without suffering any decline in scholarly output.

Eco's first book grew out of his dissertation, which explored problems of aesthetics in St. Thomas Aquinas's works. The critique of the aesthetics of BENEDETTO CROCE that underlies his second book, *Opera aperta* (1962), arose partly from this earlier interest in medieval aesthetics. *The Open Work* constitutes Eco's first attempt to engage issues related to contemporary works of art. It builds on many of the ideas formulated by Luigi Pareyson, one of Eco's philosophy professors at the University of Turin. Eco, quoting Henri Pousseur, defines the "open" work as one that "produces in the interpreter acts of conscious freedom, putting him at the center of a net of inexhaustible relations among which he inserts his own form" (4). Eco's study, which examines Joyce, Alexander Calder, Karlheinz Stockhausen, Pousseur, and other contemporary and near-contemporary artists, opposes this concept to the traditional closed work, which allows the reader or viewer far less choice in interpretation. The categories are ideal—no work can be completely open or closed—but they function well in making distinctions between different kinds of art. What is more important, adopting the proper attitude toward an open work has political and social ramifications: the open work denies conventional views of the world, replacing them with a sense of its discontinuity, disorder, and dissonance. Eco considers the alienation attendant on this realization as beneficial, since from this feeling of crisis, one may derive a new way of seeing, feeling, and understanding a social order in which traditional relationships have been shattered.

Eco's next two books, *Diario minimo* (1963) and *Apocalittici e integrati* (1964), are characteristic of his ongoing analysis of mass culture, a project that has become increasingly prominent for him. Each work consists of a collection of essays on popular forms of entertainment and contemporary issues. As in *The Open Work,* he is concerned with uncovering the ideologies informing works of art and the type of engagement that they demand, but the focus of the later books is considerably broader. The title *Apocalittici e integrati* refers to two different attitudes toward mass culture: that of the "apocalyptic" intellectual, who believes that mass media have irretrievably debased culture and who responds by withdrawing in disgust from the public sphere; and that of the "integrated" intellectual, whose wholesale acceptance and celebration of mass culture is largely unexamined. Eco locates the implicit question underlying these two attitudes—is mass culture good or bad?—and reformulates it, asking instead, "When the present situation of an industrial society makes mass communication a fact, what can be done to render these means of communication capable of transmitting cultural values?" (47). Given that mass culture is ubiquitous and inescapable, Eco argues that our efforts ought to focus on ensuring that it mediates positive values, and not the illusory, consolatory, oversimplified, and static values of kitsch. For Eco, the burden of such responsibilities falls on the intellectual, who ought to accept the fact of mass culture and to intervene when possible. But aside from this general summons to acceptance and intervention, Eco makes no further recommendations. The rest of the book is devoted to an examination of the ideological implications of different forms of popular entertainment (comic strips, novels, television, songs). It is important to note that while *Apocalittici e integrati* lays the theoretical foundation for the analysis of mass culture, it never discusses the practical problems involved in intervention. This is an issue to which Eco returns in *The Name of the Rose,* a work that in many ways seeks to provide the kind of culturally responsible entertainment called for in *Apocalittici e integrati.*

At the end of his theoretical treatment of mass culture in *Apocalittici e integrati,* Eco makes what in retrospect is a wryly proleptic comment: "I believe that there can be a novel intended at once as a work of entertainment, a consumer item, and as an aesthetically valid work capable of providing original, not kitsch, values" (53–54). This double intention seems to fit his best-selling novel very well. Couched as a mystery in a fourteenth-century monastery, replete with grizzly (or witty) murders, sprinkled with a generous dose of Latinate obscurity, offering historical accuracy for the plausibility hounds in the audience, hinting at less than celestial relations between the monks, and providing a steamy sexual encounter for the narrator, the novel features many of the tricks of the potboiler trade. But alongside these devices, Eco presents William of Baskerville, whose views, though carefully attuned to the historical moment, are reminiscent of some of Eco's earlier pronouncements and whose function in the novel parallels that which Eco has set out for the engaged intellectual in society. William offers us the spectacle of the intellectual in confrontation with the mass culture of his own day, and his remarks on the people (whom he calls with a wonderfully bifurcated attitude, "the simple") serve to remind us of the difficulties in and importance of this confrontation.

Between *Diario minimo* and *Apocalittici e integrati,* Eco

became acquainted with the main currents of STRUCTURALISM and semiotics. His main contribution in this area consists of a critique of certain tenets espoused by CLAUDE LÉVI-STRAUSS. Eco distinguishes between methodological and ontological conceptions of structure, between the use of projections and constructions and the claim of Lévi-Strauss's brand of structural anthropology to the discovery of existing, even transcendent, structures in reality. Eco's disagreement with such claims is documented in great detail in *La struttura assente* (1968).

It is instructive to compare Eco's earlier and later involvement in structuralism. For example, his analysis of Ian Fleming's James Bond novels (1979) consists primarily in decoding recurring narrative structures. However, a later essay such as "*Casablanca:* Cult Movies and Intertextual Collage" (1986) focuses on the audience's shifting apprehension of a variety of implied clichés. Eco's emphasis has turned from the sign to the dynamics of reception—a concern that can be traced in his short study of Alphonse Allais's *Un Drame bien parisien* (1979). In this essay Eco self-consciously problematizes the open/closed dichotomy explored in *The Open Work.* His personal involvement with structuralism follows the trajectory of the movement itself: like many recent scholars, Eco can be seen to be participating in the general critique of the sign prevalent in poststructuralist thought. His initial enthusiasm for structuralist approaches to narrative gave way to a series of articles in which he explored the limits of the linguistic model of interpretation. However, unlike many purely literary critics, Eco has never used the language of crisis in his discussions of the limits of structuralism and semiotics. He has always viewed such systems as tools.

Neither Eco's cultural criticism nor his work on semiotics has escaped criticism. Scholars have commented on his penchant for broad, synthesizing generalizations and his tendency to stress similarities at the expense of differences. Many of his essays give the lie to this assessment, but it must be admitted that his project as engaged intellectual leaves him open to such "apocalyptic" assessments on the whole. Moreover, his "methodological" view of conceptual systems (and of structure generally) as "tools" remains largely unexamined in his own work. This is the inevitable price of maintaining an interventionist cultural position that seeks to address many audiences while evaluating the role of the intellectual in society.

Deborah Parker

See also SEMIOTICS and STRUCTURALISM.

Umberto Eco, *Apocalittici e integrati* (1964), *Art and Beauty in the Middle Ages* (1959, trans. Hugh Bredin, 1988), *Il costume di casa* (1973), *Dalla periferia dell'impero* (1977), *Diario minimo* (1963), *Le forme del contenuto* (1971), *Il nome della rosa* (1980, *The Name of the Rose,* trans. William Weaver, 1983), *Opera aperta* (1962, *The Open Work,* trans. Anna Cancogni, 1989, including essays from a variety of sources), *Il pendulo di Foucault* (1988, *Foucault's Pendulum,* trans. William Weaver, 1989), *Postille a "Il nome della rosa"* (1983, *Postscript to "The Name of the Rose,"* trans. William Weaver, 1984), *Il problema estetico in San Tommaso* (1956, *The Aesthetics of Thomas Aquinas,* trans. Hugh Bredin, 1988), *The Role of the Reader: Explorations in the Semiotics of Texts* (1979), *Il segno* (1971), *Semiotics and the Philosophy of Language* (1984), *La struttura assente* (1968), *Il superuomo di massa* (1976), *A Theory of Semiotics* (1976), *Travels in Hyperreality* (trans. William Weaver, 1986); Umberto Eco with Richard Rorty, Jonathan Culler, and Christine Brooke-Rose, *Interpretation and Overinterpretation* (ed. Stefan Collini, 1992).

Nanni Balestrini, ed., *Gruppo 63: Il romanzo sperimentale* (1966); Theresa Coletti, *Naming the Rose: Medieval Signs and Modern Theory* (1988); Teresa de Lauretis, *Umberto Eco* (1981); Renato Giovannoli, ed., *Saggi su Il nome della rosa* (1985); M. Thomas Inge, ed., *Naming the Rose: Essays on Eco's "The Name of the Rose"* (1988); David Robey, "Umberto Eco," *Writers and Society in Contemporary Italy* (ed. Michael Caesar and Peter Hainsworth, 1986); Marco Santambrogio and Patrizia Violi, eds., *Umberto Eco* (1988); Christopher Wagstaff, "The Neo-avantgarde," *Writers and Society in Contemporary Italy* (ed. Michael Caesar and Peter Hainsworth, 1986).

ELIOT, T. S.

Thomas Stearns Eliot (1888–1965) has described his criticism as a "by-product" of his "private poetry-workshop" and as "a prolongation of the thinking that went into the formation of my own verse" (*On Poetry* 117). These devaluations minimize his status as a critical theorist, and his early references to himself as a poetical practitioner also suggest that theory is permissible only to the extent necessary to dispense the poetic prescription. In due course the poetical practitioner becomes the Man of Letters, but even the later description suggests an Arnoldian assumption of office as the voice of the humanities rather than a claim to have articulated an anatomy or system. Eliot indeed places himself implicitly in the JOHN DRYDEN–SAMUEL JOHNSON–MATTHEW ARNOLD

succession of poet-critics, pointing out that only poets can write authentically about poetry (129). The observation, like the first one quoted, tends to treat criticism as primarily an annotation of the creative enterprise. Finally, we have Eliot's dismissive reference to "a few notorious phrases" of his "which have had a truly embarrassing success in the world" (117). It is notable that the reference is to "phrases" rather than to "ideas" or "generalizations." The suggestion that even as an apparent theorist, Eliot's contribution is to the rhetoric rather than the structure of theory is one that deserves further consideration.

Eliot's own remarks strongly advise us to treat his criticism as embedded in and nourished by the literary situation that it endeavors to move forward, as seeking to reconsider the canon in order to align it with contemporary interests. It is in fact their capacity to reorder the inheritance that has given those notorious phrases some of their embarrassing success. But the notorious phrases may also have exercised some of their persuasiveness because they are connected to each other in ways that are more than rhetorical and because rising as they do out of individual author studies, they seem to offer a solid and lasting connection between literary "facts" and a potential structure of understanding. It is time to examine the more crucial of these phrases.

"Tradition and the Individual Talent" (1917) can be read as indicating how the canon may change. The "literature of Europe from Homer" and within it the literature of England has a "simultaneous existence" and "composes a simultaneous order" (*Selected Essays* 14). The geo-historical restriction should not be brushed aside. Twenty years later Eliot's titles continue to refer to the Man of Letters and the Future of Europe and to Virgil and the Christian World. The simultaneous European order changes, but only slightly, when "the new (the really new) work of art" is admitted to membership (5). The change is evolutionary, a matter of seating arrangements, quite different from MICHEL FOUCAULT's epistemic fissures or HAROLD BLOOM's swerving from a past that the strong successor must re-form in his image. Eliot's almost invocatory deference to a simultaneous order out of history strongly underlines the impersonality of the tradition, and the poet's mind can then be treated as correspondingly impersonal, a catalytic chamber for a process that is independent of the contents of that mind.

In "The Metaphysical Poets" (1921) Eliot proceeds to characterize the canon, and the characterization is predictably historical. The simultaneous order is seen in relation to an ideal configuration from which poetry has lapsed and which it must now seek to reconstitute. Something has happened to the mind of England between the time of Lord Herbert of Cherbury and that of Robert Browning. For John Donne, thought was an experience, immediate as the odor of a rose. The intellect was at the tips of the senses. Falling in love, reading Spinoza, the sound of a typewriter, and the smell of cooking came together in the poetic experience (*Selected Essays* 247). Marvell ("Andrew Marvell," 1921) could create an alliance of levity and seriousness in which the components strengthened rather than threatened each other (252). On the other hand, John Milton ("Milton I," 1936, *On Poetry* 162) had to be read first for the sound and then for the sense. A dissociation of sensibility had taken place, and modern poetry had to reinstate the original integrity by forcing and, if necessary, dislocating language into meaning (*Selected Essays* 248). The suggestion that the history of English poetry from Milton onwards is the history of deviation from a mainstream now re-recognized has been immensely influential even though its effects have been largely circumvented by reinterpreting devalued or excluded authors such as Milton and Alfred, Lord Tennyson, so that they once again become admissible into the mainstream. The prescriptive force of the canon is increased by underlining its essential characteristics, so that the participation of a would-be entrant is determined by the extent to which the institution's requirements are satisfied. Since Eliot's characterizations are predominantly stylistic, they both sustain NEW CRITICISM and reinforce its claim of ideological neutrality.

The "objective correlative" may be the most notorious of Eliot's embarrassingly successful phrases. It is put forward in "Hamlet and His Problems" (1919, *Selected Essays* 124). At the risk of excessively simplifying a very large body of elucidation, we can say that Eliot argues that there is a verbal formula for any given state of emotion that when found and used will evoke that state and no other. We are in fact being offered a decisively representational view of language in which an unmistakable relationship is claimed between the sign and the state. Though not in the manner of ROLAND BARTHES or Foucault, Eliot's view does call for the effacement of the author both in his articulation of this concept and in his description of the manner in which tradition enters contemporaneity. The author is merely the agency through which the infallible sign comes into being. The critic's concern is with the sign and with the one right reading that the sign dictates rather than with the sign's sponsor or catalyst.

Tradition for Eliot is not (as with Bloom) a dramatic narrative of encounters with the past nor (as with NORTHROP FRYE) the shaping presence of basic forms of the imagination through the mutations of history and genre. The canon is composed by the literary profession in accordance with that profession's constitutive principles. "The 'greatness' of literature," Eliot observes, "cannot be determined solely by literary standards," but "whether it is literature or not can be determined only by literary standards" ("Religion and Literature," *Essays Ancient* 93). It is not wholly enlightening to argue that only the privileged and self-constituted world of literature can draw a distinction between literature and non-literature, but Eliot's sense of the profession as a kind of closed shop contributes to the academy's sense of solidarity, of collective engagement in a common pursuit.

The impersonal tradition; the aesthetically dominated, ideologically neutral canon, constituted by the profession rather than by the author; the poem as an act of unification bringing together otherwise disparate elements; the work of literature as a verbal icon, a unique realization pointing to the one right reading—all these propositions strongly support New Criticism, providing it with several of its foundational principles. Eliot does not put himself forward as a systematic critic, and his crucial generalizations are usually delivered as the climax of consideration of a specific literary problem. But these generalizations also seem to issue from presuppositions that are structurally cogent. They arm a generation with critical authority and a conceptual rhetoric because they are offered not simply by a scholar-critic but by the most individual and powerful poetic voice of its era.

High modernism could be vehement in its repudiation of the Romantics, and Eliot's view that PERCY BYSSHE SHELLEY's philosophy was not sufficiently respectable intellectually to command a willing suspension of disbelief (*Use* 95–97) is part of an antipathy now past. Spinoza, the typewriter, and the smell of cooking maximize the incongruity in what SAMUEL TAYLOR COLERIDGE called "the balance or reconciliation of opposite or discordant qualities," but the main proposition and its distinctive consequence (cointensification and not merely coexistence) are fully anticipated in the peroration to *Biographia Literaria,* chapter 14.

Eliot's later criticism moves cautiously away from his earlier work. The most significant revision is "Milton II" (1947, *On Poetry*), which is generally read as a recantation of "Milton I," though the extent and even the reality of the recantation can be debated. More important is the reinstatement of personality as a shaping force, particularly in a major poet's accomplishment. The work of a "great poet" is united "by one significant, consistent and developing personality" ("John Ford," 1932, *Selected Essays*). The superiority of W. B. Yeats's later poetry to his earlier lies in the fuller expression of personality within it ("Yeats," 1940, *On Poetry*). Collateral with this reinstatement is Eliot's growing interest in the overall identity of a writer's *oeuvre*. "The whole of Shakespeare's work is *one* poem," and George Herbert's poetry is "definitely an oeuvre to be studied entire" (*Selected Essays* 179; *Spectator* 148 [1932]: 360–61). Accompanying the reinstatement of personality is a more personal note in Eliot's criticism, carried up even into the title of a late essay, "What Dante Means to Me" (1950, *To Criticize*). "The Frontiers of Criticism" and "The Three Voices of Poetry" *(On Poetry)* contain disclosures of much interest to students of Eliot, for example, on the notes to *The Waste Land* (121) and on the "yellow fog" in "The Love Song of J. Alfred Prufrock" (125–26). It is a practice begun in *The Use of Poetry and the Use of Criticism,* where Eliot draws attention to the extraordinary fascination certain images held for him (148).

Eliot's lasting concern with the problems of poetic drama is developed in "The Three Voices of Poetry" (1953) and "Poetry and Drama" (1951). To bring poetry closer to the rhythms and language of speech is a commitment shared by Eliot, Yeats, and EZRA POUND and universalized in a later essay by Eliot. "Every revolution in poetry is apt to be, and sometimes to announce itself to be a return to common speech" ("The Music of Poetry," 1942, *On Poetry* 23). In drama the commitment involves writing for a popular theater and also writing for the educated imagination—an achievement of the Shakespearean moment that requires a frame of discourse less fissured than the one within which Eliot found himself. Yeats takes the opposite course, writing for an elitist theater in which the "depths of the mind" are sounded by a premeditated withdrawal from the "pushing world" of the popular stage.

Some of Eliot's most telling observations on language are to be found in his poetry, notably in *Four Quartets.* The proposition that every state of mind has its unique verbal representation can lead to the proposition that the sign should efface itself in the presence of the signified, that the verbal icon is important not finally as itself but for what it points at ("Rudyard Kipling," *On Poetry* 265). In Eliot's poetry, language struggles from a condition of inarticulateness to a threshold where it can approach the total presence, which is also its own extinction. It falls away inevitably in order to reconstitute itself as language. In the end language can point not to any finality but only to its continuing effort to proceed beyond itself in seeking that finality. That effort gives it its meaning and purpose as language.

Four Quartets is a poem that reflects formally on its own poetics to the extent of having specific places in its recurrent structure (sections 2 and 5) allotted to its self-examination. Since the character of the poem's self-scrutiny depends on the point reached in its progress, these recurrent investigations open the poem up to modern critical movements in which understanding is made contingent on the perspective in which it is installed. Eliot's status has waned since the passing of the New Critical era. Its retrieval will depend on the extent to which the self-revising nature of his poetry is read so as to counter the absolutes that are implicit in his criticism and also asserted more categorically in the dogmatic prose of his religious and cultural statements.

Balachandra Rajan

T. S. Eliot, *After Strange Gods* (1934), *Essays Ancient and Modern* (1936), *The Idea of a Christian Society* (1939), *Knowledge and Experience in the Philosophy of F. H. Bradley* (1964), *Notes towards the Definition of Culture* (1948), *On Poetry and Poets* (1957), *Selected Essays* (1932, 3d ed., 1950), *Selected Prose* (ed. Frank Kermode, 1975), *To Criticize the Critic* (1965), *The Use of Poetry and the Use of Criticism* (1933).

Mowbray Allan, *T. S. Eliot's Impersonal Theory of Poetry* (1974); Sean Lucy, *T. S. Eliot and the Idea of Tradition* (1960); F. O. Matthiessen, *The Achievement of T. S. Eliot* (1935, 3d ed., 1958); Jeffrey M. Perl, *Scepticism and Modern Enmity: Before and After Eliot* (1989); Richard Shusterman, *T. S. Eliot and the Philosophy of Criticism* (1987).

EMERSON, RALPH WALDO

After hearing Ralph Waldo Emerson (1803–82) lecture, Herman Melville described him as "this Plato who talks thro' his nose." As Melville perceived, Emerson's eclectic brand of idealism most deeply characterizes his writing. Influenced at the outset of his career primarily by SAMUEL TAYLOR COLERIDGE, Thomas Carlyle, JOHANN WOLFGANG VON GOETHE, and Emanuel Swedenborg, and through them by German idealism, especially IMMANUEL KANT, Emerson forged an American Romanticism, called transcendentalism by his countrymen, that emphasized creativity as a channel for divine inspiration. However, Melville also recognized a more daring, radical side to Emerson when he commented on his lyceum performance, "I love all men who *dive*." Emerson pio-

neered a fiercely independent tradition in American letters that stressed the visionary, prophetic voice and the
organic, open form.

During his lifetime he powerfully influenced major
writers such as Henry David Thoreau, MARGARET FUL-
LER, Walt Whitman, and Emily Dickinson. He inspired
William James's pragmatism, and KENNETH BURKE acknowledges a debt to him. Theodore Dreiser, Robert
Frost, Wallace Stevens, and Ralph Ellison are among the
many major American writers who have testified to Emerson's influence on their art. Indeed, many critics characterize Emerson as the most significant American writer
and the wellspring of American modernism.

Born into an important ministerial family in Boston,
Emerson in a very real sense inherited his role of cultural
spokesperson. He studied for the ministry at Harvard
Divinity School and became the minister of the prestigious Boston Second Church, where Cotton Mather
had preached. However, he was forced to resign from his
pulpit after, acting on his developing sense of authentic
worship, he refused to perform the Eucharist. He soon
embarked on a highly successful lifelong career as a lecturer and essayist. Although he saw his role as that of a
spiritual rather than a social reformer (a role for which
he felt temperamentally unsuited) and was thus slow to
publicly espouse the cause of slaves, women, and Native
Americans, he ultimately did speak out publicly in advocacy of these oppressed groups.

With the publication of *Nature* (1836), Emerson first
announced his credo of idealism and self-reliance. His
speeches "The American Scholar" (1837) and "The Divinity School Address" (1838) first thrust him into public
consciousness, as he dared to challenge Harvard's Unitarian orthodoxy. Banned from Harvard for decades because he undercut the Unitarian reliance on rational
explanations of faith with his assertion of the divinity
within, in later years Emerson lectured at the university
and served as an overseer, during which time the university was liberalized in accordance with the tenor of his
ideas.

In addition to *Nature* and the addresses cited above,
Emerson is best known for *Essays* (*First Series,* 1841; *Second Series,* 1844), especially "Self-Reliance," the complex
"Circles," "The Oversoul," "The Poet," and the dark essay
many commentators feel is his masterpiece, "Experience," which was written after the death in 1842 of Waldo,
the beloved first child of his second marriage. *Representative Men* (1850) and *English Traits* (1856) are also important, if less orphic, texts. Many scholars, however, came
to claim that his journals, published beginning in the
1960s, were Emerson's greatest accomplishment. His

habits of composition for his essays argue persuasively
for this view. Emerson began to keep his journal when
he was 17 and continued it for most of his life. His essays
are quarried out of the journals, often first passing
through an intermediate state in his lectures. And this
accounts for the sometimes discontinuous effect of his
prose, although he once said that he had deliberately
deleted transitions between thoughts so that the reader
would be more challenged by his ideas. The Emerson of
the journals is a more complex being, one whose conflicts and doubts, often expunged from the essays, are
voiced, as recent critical studies by Evelyn Barish, Julie
Ellison, and Barbara Packer have argued.

Toward the end of his life Emerson's powers of mind
failed, but he never lost his sense of humor. After glanc-
ing through some of his writings, he commented that
the writer seemed to have only a few ideas and that his
writings suffered from the repetition of them. Throughout his work, he argues that the source of "Power" is "the
divinity in man." Thus what Emerson calls "self-reliance" is actually premised on the transformation of the
self into a conduit to the "Over-Soul," or inner godhead.
He believed in "Compensation," that Nature was infused
with divine justice. For all evil and good deeds, Nature
would "compensate" humanity in kind. Under the influence of Swedenborg and the English Romantics, Emerson argued that Nature itself was a hieroglyphic text that
would yield to the inspired observer the truths of his or
her own nature. For the idealist Emerson, and this is
what irked many of his contemporaries, "evil" was but a
stage in the evolution of the "good."

No simple catalog of Emerson's core ideas can do
justice to the energy of his writing, however. As Stephen
Whicher has said, Emerson was a "poet of ideas." Careful
readers of Emerson's writing discover a complex consciousness, marked by what Whicher calls "a shifting,
complex dialectic of opposites" or "a living multiplicity," one in which Emerson assumes personae to create a
dramatic dialogue of ideas. The suggestiveness of his
thought anticipates some of the theories proposed by
contemporary cultural critics. HAROLD BLOOM's theory
of the "anxiety of influence" is indebted to Emerson. In
"The American Scholar" Emerson notes, "Genius is always
sufficiently the enemy of genius by over-influence" (*Complete* 1:91). In "Circles" he foreshadows one of MICHEL
FOUCAULT's leading ideas:

> Much more obviously is history and the state of the
> world at one time directly dependent on the intellec-
> tual classification then existing in the minds of men.
> The things which are dear to men at this hour are so on
> account of the ideas which have emerged on their men-

tal horizon, and which cause the present order of things, as a tree bears its apples. (2:310)

Emerson's world-view at times is akin to JACQUES DERRIDA's: "The natural world may be conceived of as a system of concentric circles, and we now and then detect slight dislocations which apprise us that this surface on which we now stand is not fixed, but sliding" (2:313–14). In "The Poet" his ideas anticipate Kenneth Burke's: "Words are also actions, and actions are a kind of words" (3:8). READER-RESPONSE THEORY AND CRITICISM was anticipated in, if not directly influenced by, Emerson's notions that "one must be an inventor to read well" and that "there is then creative reading as well as creative writing."

Emerson's role in current critical debate is a complex one. Influential American critics Harold Bloom and Richard Poirier and the American philosophers Stanley Cavell, RICHARD RORTY, and Cornel West claim an Emersonian lineage, although they appropriate his ideas to different ends; some poststructuralist critics decry his intuitionism and belletristic lack of theoretical grounding, while John Michael and Eric Cheyfitz have written poststructuralist appreciations of Emerson. Feminist critics, such as David Leverenz and Judith Fetterly, take Emerson to task for invocations of "Power" and "self-reliance" as inscriptions of masculine ideology, while other feminists celebrate him for championing Margaret Fuller and for his endorsement of equal rights for women. Marxist critics have condemned what seems to them Emerson's optimistic celebration of the progress of the American capitalist spirit, yet Myra Jehlen and Carolyn Porter have written sympathetically of the potential within Emerson's work for an examination of the construction of ideology.

Ultimately Emerson stands for resistance against system building and for a radical openness to the promptings of one's own native intelligence. His project is deeply antipathetic to the tenor of much of contemporary theory because his writing argues for a human center, a "soul," traversed by the influxes of transcendent wisdom.

Neal Tolchin

See also AMERICAN THEORY AND CRITICISM: NINETEENTH CENTURY.

Ralph Waldo Emerson, *The Collected Works of Ralph Waldo Emerson* (ed. Robert Spiller et al., 4 vols. to date, 1971–), *The Complete Works of Ralph Waldo Emerson* (ed. Edward Waldo Emerson, 12 vols., 1903–4), *The Early Lectures of Ralph Waldo Emerson* (ed. Stephen Whicher et al., 3 vols., 1959–72), *Journals and Miscellaneous Notebooks of Ralph Waldo Emerson* (ed. William Gilman et al., 16 vols., 1960–82), *The Letters of Ralph Waldo Emerson* (ed. Ralph L. Rusk, 6 vols., 1939).

Gay Wilson Allen, *Waldo Emerson: A Biography* (1981); Evelyn Barish, *Emerson: The Roots of Prophecy* (1989); Harold Bloom, ed., *Ralph Waldo Emerson: Modern Critical Views* (1985); Eric Cheyfitz, *The Trans-Parent: Sexual Politics in the Language of Emerson* (1981); Julie Ellison, *Emerson's Romantic Style* (1984); F. O. Mathiessen, *American Renaissance: Art and Expression in the Age of Emerson and Whitman* (1941); Joel Myerson, ed., *The Transcendentalists: A Review of Research and Criticism* (1984); Barbara Packer, *Emerson's Fall* (1982); Carolyn Porter, *Seeing and Being: The Plight of the Participant-Observer in Emerson, James, Adams, Faulkner* (1981); Ann C. Rose, *Transcendentalism as a Social Movement, 1830–1850* (1981); Stephen E. Whicher, *Freedom and Fate: An Inner Life of Ralph Waldo Emerson* (1953).

EMPSON, WILLIAM

William Empson (1906–84) was born into the landed gentry of Yorkshire and attended Magdalene College, Cambridge (1925–29), where he won firsts in both mathematics and English. Empson's director of studies at Cambridge was I. A. RICHARDS, who had just published *Principles of Literary Criticism* (1924) and was writing *Practical Criticism* (1929). Richards explained the origin of Empson's first major work, *Seven Types of Ambiguity* (1930): "At about his third visit he brought up the games of interpretation which Laura Riding and Robert Graves had been playing [in *A Survey of Modernist Poetry*, 1927] with the unpunctuated form of 'The expense of spirit in a waste of shame.' Taking the sonnet as a conjuror takes his hat, he produced an endless swarm of lively rabbits from it and ended by 'You could do that with any poetry, couldn't you?' This was a Godsend to a Director of Studies, so I said, 'You'd better go off and do it, hadn't you?'"

Empson's close readings in *Seven Types* of Gerard Manley Hopkins's "The Windhover," George Herbert's "The Sacrifice," and many other short works and passages eventually made it one of the seminal texts of twentieth-century criticism. With this stunning debut as a critic, Empson legitimized ambiguity as a positive quality of literary texts without giving up authorial intention, and this achievement made him a powerful force in modern theory. Critics quickly protested, however, that his focus on short texts slighted the complete work; that he ignored the relations among poetry, history, and ideology; that the human needs satisfied by poetry were lost in intricate formalist explication; that his approach valued ambiguity too highly as a measure of merit; and that he detected ambiguities too easily.

Empson defended his method twenty years later in "The Verbal Analysis" (in *Argufying*), explaining that for him analysis is a valuable function of criticism, that he begins with an intuitive sense of the worth of a work and proceeds to study its complexities, and that lack of complexity is not necessarily a bad thing in a text. Moreover, he supported the authority of the author's mind, asserting that whenever a reader fails to make sense of a text, then it is the reader's own fault and not the author's. Consequently, Empson scorns theories that dismiss the writer's intentions because they deny "spontaneous contact" with the author's mind ("Intentional" 435).

Although he defends the author's intention repeatedly, in "Verbal Analysis" and elsewhere, Empson's stress on multiple meanings has also made him look like an anti-intentionalist. Thus when PAUL DE MAN says of Empson's first type of ambiguity that "it deploys the initial experience into an infinity of associated experiences that spring from it" (235), it is easy to see how Empson clearly enriched the practice of NEW CRITICISM. But Christopher Norris compares Empson to de Man in Empson's resisting "any premature retreat to a ground of aesthetic reconciliation where opposites can peacefully coexist within a structure of irony, paradox, etc." ("Some Versions of Rhetoric" 199), justly dissociating Empson from the verbal icon and ontological criticism of the New Critics. And John Haffenden states that "on a loose sheet of notes Empson sometime noted, without comment but surely in dumbfounded disbelief, that [E. D.] Hirsch [Jr.] considered him an 'anti-intentionalist'" (*Argufying* 58).

The seven essays in *Some Versions of Pastoral* (1935) depart from the method of *Seven Types* by analyzing whole, longer works (e.g., *The Beggar's Opera* and *Alice in Wonderland*) in a broad context, by discussing topics of class and society in "Proletarian Literature," and by applying Freudian psychology in the *Alice* essay. Empson does not define "pastoral" directly, but the mode apparently dissolves the complex in the simple and mitigates the differences between social classes. When Empson comments in the essay on "Marvell's Garden" that one of the assumptions about pastoral is "that you can say everything about complex people by a complete consideration of simple people" (137), he is saying something close to WILLIAM WORDSWORTH's declaration about the value of rustic life in the "Preface to *Lyrical Ballads.*"

The essays in *Some Versions* are stimulating and original, and probably they were written "under the aegis of Marxism," as de Man asserts (240), but exactly what stance Empson takes toward Marxism is not clear. Norris finds "many statements which would seem politically suspect or evasive from a Marxist viewpoint" but does not think *Some Versions* can be read as "some kind of cryptic anti-Marxist tract" ("Some Versions of Rhetoric" 211). And Haffenden does not even mention Marx in his remarks on *Some Versions* in *Argufying*.

In *The Structure of Complex Words* (1951) Empson responds to Richards's teachings on the emotive power of language. Empson accepts that words carry feeling, but he argues that in Richards's formulation the feelings conveyed by words get separated from the sense of the words. In an autobiographical note published in 1955, Empson explains his thesis: "Roughly, the moral is that a developing society decides practical questions more by the way it interprets words it thinks obvious and traditional than by its official statements of current dogma" (Kunitz 307). This argument produces such essays as "Wit in the *Essay on Criticism*," "Honest in *Othello*," and "The English Dog." Many of these pieces sparkle, combining the talent for language analysis demonstrated in *Seven Types* with the attention to social and psychological themes of *Some Versions,* and the three appendixes on "Theories of Value" make such points as his faith in what he calls "naive realism."

Empson's lifelong preoccupation with freeing the canon from the grip of Christian and symbolist readings appears most strikingly in *Milton's God* (1961). Empson's rationalism comes alive vividly in his hatred of the Christian God and invigorates *Milton's God* at the same time that it shapes what most critics consider a perverse argument: that "the poem is not good in spite of but because of its moral confusions, which ought to be clear in your mind when you are feeling its power" (13). *Milton's God* is a problematic book, difficult to assess, but it argues theological issues with more vigor and more originality than is usually found in literary criticism.

Three volumes of essays, all published posthumously, collect many of Empson's scattered reviews and other, longer pieces. The title *Using Biography* (1984) reflects Empson's affirmation of the value of biography and of heeding authorial intention. The eleven essays range over many topics. In *"Ulysses:* Joyce's Intentions" Empson rejects all arguments that Joyce ever relented in his antipathy to the church, and in *"Tom Jones"* he provides an inspired reading of Tom's noble nature.

Essays on Shakespeare (1986) reprints seven bristly essays that often show Empson in a polemical mood. *Hamlet, Macbeth,* and *A Midsummer Night's Dream* get separate discussions, as do the Globe Theatre, the narrative poems, Falstaff, and symbol-searching in the plays. In "Falstaff" Empson takes on J. Dover Wilson for "preaching at us about his Medieval Vice and his Ideal King" (57) and trying to explain away the "pathetic description" of Falstaff's death and thereby justify the "modern royalist" in his respect for Hal. In "The Globe Theatre" Empson defends reconstruction of Elizabethan stage practices by inference, finding in certain critics' rejection of "insight and intuition and what not" evidence that "the Wimsatt Law, which says a reader may never understand the intention of an author, has been at its fell work here too" (158).

John Haffenden has collected 600 pages of Empson's shorter pieces in *Argufying: Essays on Literature and Culture* (1987). The long sections "Literary Interpretation: The Language Machine," "Moderns and Contemporaries," "Cultural Perspectives: Ethics and Aesthetics, East and West," and others capture Empson's many interests.

In his last long study, *Faustus and the Censor* (1987), Empson contends that both the A and B versions of Christopher Marlowe's play show evidence of ecclesiastical censorship; for the censor, Faustus would have had to suffer for his overreaching, and Empson asserts that the original play held out the possibility of Faustus's escape. *Faustus and the Censor* is a bold book, prejudiced but well-informed and canny.

Finally, Empson's work as a poet should be acknowledged. His poems are difficult to explicate, but the best, such as "Missing Dates," are powerful and piercing. The 1962 edition of the *Collected Poems* includes all of the *Poems* (1935) and the works in *The Gathering Storm* (1940). The critic and the poet are one in sensibility, and several of the poems continue to be anthologized.

As Haffenden notes, Empson "always deprecated the importance of proclaiming a theory, a code of critical practice" (*Argufying* 5). But his close readings in *Seven Types* and *Complex Words* are models of explication, even if their theoretical apparatus have not been easily applied by other critics. His definition of "pastoral" has not been taken up by others, nor have many agreed with the arguments in *Milton's God;* but whatever his approach or his thesis, his numerous insights have always been bracing. His campaign to de-Christianize and desymbolize masterpieces such as *The Rime of the Ancient Mariner* has had

few followers but has provided a loyal opposition for those critics he judged too pious. Scholars give him ample attention in histories of literary criticism (see, e.g., the generous and perceptive discussion of his criticism in Patrick Parrinder's *Authors and Authority,* 1991), and his spirited and intelligent commentaries will enliven literary criticism for some time.

Frank Day

William Empson, *Argufying: Essays on Literature and Culture* (ed. John Haffenden, 1987), *Collected Poems* (1962), *Essays on Shakespeare* (1986), *Faustus and the Censor* (1987), "The Intentional Fallacy, Again," *Essays in Criticism* 23 (1972), *Milton's God* (1961), *Seven Types of Ambiguity* (1930, rev. ed., 1947), *Some Versions of Pastoral* (1935), *The Structure of Complex Words* (1951), *Using Biography* (1984).

Paul Alpers, "Empson on Pastoral," *New Literary History* 10 (1978); Cleanth Brooks, "Empson's Criticism," *"Accent" Anthology: Selections from "Accent," a Quarterly of New Literature, 1940–1945* (ed. Kerker Quinn and Charles Shattuck, 1946); Frank Day, *Sir William Empson: An Annotated Bibliography* (1984); Paul de Man, "The Dead-End of Formalist Criticism," *Blindness and Insight: Essays in the Rhetoric of Contemporary Criticism* (1971); Paul H. Fry, *William Empson: Prophet against Sacrifice* (1991); Roma Gill, ed., *William Empson: The Man and His Work* (1974); Stanley Edgar Hyman, "William Empson and Categorical Criticism," *The Armed Vision: A Study in the Methods of Modern Literary Criticism* (1948, rev. ed., 1955); Hugh Kenner, "Alice in Empsonland" (1952, *Gnomon: Essays on Contemporary Literature,* 1958); Stanley Kunitz, ed., *Twentieth Century Authors, First Supplement: A Biographical Dictionary of Modern Literature* (1955); Christopher Norris, "Some Versions of Rhetoric: Empson and de Man," *Rhetoric and Form: Deconstruction at Yale* (ed. Robert Con Davis and Ronald Schleifer, 1985), *William Empson and the Philosophy of Literary Criticism* (1978); Patrick Parrinder, *Authors and Authority: English and American Criticism, 1750–1990* (1991); John Crowe Ransom, "Mr. Empson's Muddles," *Southern Review* 4 (1938–39); I. A. Richards, "William Empson," *Furioso* 1.3 (1940, unpag. suppl.); Roger Sale, "The Achievement of William Empson," *Modern Heroism* (1973).

F

FANON, FRANTZ

Frantz Fanon (1925–61) was born on the Caribbean island of Martinique. He went to France as a young man to study medicine, specializing in psychiatry. He practiced in France for a few years before leaving to serve in Algeria as a practicing psychiatrist in the French colonial administration of North Africa. The Algerian revolutionary war of independence, one of the bitterest anticolonial wars of the twentieth century, broke out during the period of Fanon's service there. And Fanon's psychiatric work enabled him to observe the colonial system at the point of its most violent and neurotic contradictions. In the event, Fanon resigned from the colonial administrative and medical service and went over to the Algerian revolutionaries, becoming one of their most eloquent and effective spokespersons. From this point on Fanon's writings took on their decisive mix of penetrating analyses of colonialism, fervent advocacy of revolt, and apocalyptic visions of the reconstitution of humans and society.

This may be one reason why some of Fanon's books, especially *Black Skin, White Masks, Studies in a Dying Colonialism,* and *The Wretched of the Earth,* became primers and manifestoes for Third World national liberation movements and why the emancipatory promptings of these books have also been embraced by militants and activists of racial, ethnic, and national minorities in the "First World" in North America and Europe, such as the black struggles in the United States in the 1960s, the autonomist struggles in Puerto Rico and Quebec, and the nationalists of Northern Ireland.

Beyond the evocative power of Fanon's work for such mass movements, his writings have been of great interest for critics and theorists of the new national literatures of Africa, parts of Asia, and the Caribbean, as well as for cultural critics of oppositional movements of women and minorities in North America and Europe. In this particular regard, Fanon's theory of the stages in the evolution of the literature of all colonized peoples has been widely applied, often rather schematically. According to this theory, the first stage in the emergence of the "national literatures" of the colonized world, which Fanon describes as a "derivative," "imitative" stage, is a stage of apprenticeship to the traditions and models of the colonizing countries. The second stage is characterized by the rejection of the authority and dominance of the colonizers' paradigms and traditions and, simultaneously, a nostalgia for the indigenous, autochthonous traditions of the colonized. The third and final stage in this process is for Fanon a "fighting" stage that produces a genuinely revolutionary literature, a people's literature that forges new forms and themes closer to the movement to end colonial rule and to construct a genuinely democratic and egalitarian postcolonial culture. Another perceived salience of Fanon's work for contemporary critical theory lies in the ways his writings seemed to prefigure current theoretical obsessions with issues such as subject formation, otherness, and alterity; identity politics; and the centrality of psychoanalytic and linguistic paradigms for literary and cultural studies.

Given the fact that Fanon is only one name among the group of classical theorists of revolutionary decolonization in this century, a group that includes such important figures as C. L. R. James, Mahatma Gandhi, Aimé Césaire, Jose Mariategui, Amilcar Cabral, and Malcolm X, it becomes pertinent to frame the problematic of Fanon's influence in terms of the question, What factors in his work make him so distinctive within the broad field of classical theorists of decolonization that he seems so enduring, so topical for our own current theoretical discourses?

To begin to address this question, we might consider the crucial fact that although Fanon has entered twentieth-century intellectual history as patron and prophet of Third World national liberation movements and one of the major theorists of decolonization, he started writing as an *evolué,* as indeed a French patriot who, despite his brilliant, penetrating critique of the colonial system, nonetheless saw himself as a Frenchman, an *assimilé* into French culture and the intellectual legacy of Western civilization.

Under the rather unique system of French colonialism, the colonies were considered "overseas departments" of a single empire whose metropolitan heartland was France. And in accordance with this policy, the class of "evolved" elites of these "overseas departments" could aspire to full citizenship in the French republic, could indeed become scions of the professional-administrative, intellectual, or artistic establishments of France. With his education, professional training, and intellectual gifts, Fanon belonged to the small circle of "black Frenchmen" who rose to this level of assimilation into French culture and civilization and began to powerfully assail the system from within. This "critique from within" that inaugurated Fanon's writings enabled him to so totalize his paradigms of the colonial order that his theoretical purview has found convincing applicability in a wide variety of colonial contexts and spaces.

Three particular inscriptions of Fanon's analysis of race, culture, and colonialism in *Black Skin, White Masks,* his first published book, are pertinent to this point. First, Fanon shifted the analysis of colonialism away from the political and economic factors emphasized by other theorists of decolonization to an emphasis on psycho-analytic and phenomenological factors. This enabled him to plumb the depths of subjectivity in the construc-tion of the colonizer and the colonized as *racialized* sub-jects and to thereby indicate the differential paths of the neuroses generated by colonial domination: inferioriza-tion and delusions on the part of the colonized, phobias and anxieties on the part of the colonizer. Second, Fanon insisted throughout this book and his subsequent writ-ings that the psychoanalytic categories, though crucial, were not enough to explicate the colonial system, that racism was not a mere psychic aberration or mental quirk but belonged in a total structure that involved economic exploitation, political disenfranchisement, and cultural imposition through the vast, signifying sys-tems of culture: language, novels, films, folklore and ethnology, scientific discourses, and popular culture. And third, Hegelian phenomenology weighed heavily on Fanon at this stage of his thought, for the transcen-dence and liberation he envisaged embraced both the colonizer and the colonized in an appropriately *deraci-nated* French culture and civilization. At this stage of his work Fanon wanted, in his own words, to break with both "the great white error" and the "great black mirage."

Once Fanon moved to Algeria, once he gave up his *assimilé* interpellation and joined the colonized in their desperate, bitter struggles *in* the colonies, he turned his gaze totally away from the colonizers. But in his writings Fanon continued to be extraordinarily careful not to move too quickly or too easily from the dialectical opera-tions of colonial domination to anticolonial nationalist resistance. Recent debates over Fanon's work miss the mark in placing the central tension of the Fanonian *oeuvre* on the issue whether his theory privileged Mani-chean, polarized opposition between colonizer and colonized or, conversely, exposed the futility of such binary demarcations of identity and community. A care-ful reading of Fanon's writings would reveal that he in fact moved back and forth between these two poles, sometimes fitfully and haphazardly but quite often (and I would argue mostly) as a heuristic tactic to apprehend the colonial dialectic both at moments of centered, consolidated, and brutal rigidities and at moments of flux, of the play of energies, forces, and desires that ex-ceed the conscious, intelligible, and rational inten-tionalities of the actors in the agon of colonization and resistance.

The central tension of Fanon's work thus lies else-where. It lies in the fact that his revolutionary fervor and partisan identifications did not always sit well with the unbounded, irrepressible energy of his intellect. The drama of this tension achieves an instructive poignancy in three particular facets of his work. First, though he ultimately cast his lot with the colonized, with "the wretched of the earth," this solidarity with the disen-franchised and inferiorized of the colonial order was tempered by a rigorously dialectical, nonvoluntaristic keenness to historical and social processes. Some of his forebodings on the problems, dilemmas, and false starts that would plague the postindependence new nations created from the colonies have proved remarkably pre-scient. Second, though Fanon's work, no doubt influ-enced by his psychiatric training, is imbued with an acute awareness of the play of neurotic, irrational drives and the preponderant role of fantasy in culture and soci-ety, he was an ultrarationalist who believed in the power of logic and persuasion. And third, while Fanon worked for a disciplined revolutionary movement and became a spokesperson for its set objectives and program, his mode of radical, innovative cultural analysis ranged across disparate disciplines and domains: from psychia-try, psychoanalysis, and philosophy to economic theory, literature, and popular culture; and from linguistic, aes-thetic, and ethical investigations to uncovering the play of sexuality, the affects of the body, and the dispositions of the psyche. Given this range and complexity of Fanon's work, his continuing relevance for cultural studies, espe-cially in contested social and political spaces, seems sol-idly assured.

Biodun Jeyifo

See also AFRICAN THEORY AND CRITICISM and POST-COLONIAL CULTURAL STUDIES.

Frantz Fanon, *L'An V de la révolution algérienne* (1952, *Studies in a Dying Colonialism*, trans. Haakon Chevalier, 1965), *Les Damnés de la terre* (1961, *The Wretched of the Earth*, trans. Constance Farrington, 1963), *Peau noire, masques blancs* (1952, *Black Skin, White Masks*, trans. Charles Lan Markmann, 1967, reprint, 1986), *Pour la révolution africaine* (1964, *Toward the African Revolution*, trans. Haakon Chevalier, 1967).

Homi Bhabba, "Remembering Fanon: Self, Psyche, and the Colonial Condition," foreword to *Black Skin, White Masks* (1986); Hussein Abdulahi Bulhan, *Frantz Fanon and the Psychology of Oppression* (1985); David Caute, *Frantz Fanon* (1970); Jeffrey Louis Decker, "Terrorism (Un)Veiled: Frantz Fanon and the Women of Algeria," *Cultural Critique* 17 (1990–91); Henry Louis Gates, Jr., "Critical Fanonism," *Critical Inquiry* 17 (1991); Peter Geismar, *Fanon* (1971); Irene L. Gendzier, *Frantz Fanon: A Critical Study* (1974); Albert Memmi, *The Colonizer and the Colonized* (1967); Benita Parry, "Problems in Current Theories of Colonial Discourse," *Oxford Literary Review* 9 (1987); Barbara Marie Perinbam, *Holy Violence, The Revolutionary Thought of Frantz Fanon: An Intellectual Biography* (1982); Renate Zahar, *Kolonialismus und Entfremdung: Zur politischen Theorie Frantz Fanons* (1969, *Colonialism and Alienation: Concerning Frantz Fanon's Political Theory*, trans. Willfried F. Feuser, 1974).

FEMINIST THEORY AND CRITICISM

1. 1963–1972

Anglo-American feminist theory and criticism today are indebted to earlier literary scholarship on women, but the main impetus for this work came from the Women's Liberation movement. In both the United States and Britain, this feminism emerged during the 1960s as a result of social change. Legislation, such as the Equal Pay Act (1963) in the United States and the Abortion Act (1967) in Britain, made women's issues a subject of widespread discussion. Movements—the Civil Rights and New Left movements in the United States, the trade unionist and Marxist movements in Britain—provided the concepts and methods that women used to develop their own analyses, as well as the events that brought them together.

American women's expectations were raised in 1961 when President John F. Kennedy established a Commis-sion on the Status of Women, which, together with state commissions, made women's issues the subject of congressional review and legislation. But when changes were slow in coming, Betty Friedan and others saw the need for a Civil Rights organization to speak on behalf of women and founded the National Organization for Women (NOW) in 1966. Its members were primarily white, middle-class, and professional women; its structure hierarchical; and its politics liberal feminist. It sought reforms—equality for women in education, employment, and legal status. Objecting to its liberalism, Ti-Grace Atkinson and others broke away in 1968 to form one of the first radical feminist groups. These groups, by contrast, analyzed patriarchy, the system that oppressed women, and made the public aware of this oppression through zap actions, demonstrations, and campaigns.

Meanwhile, feminism was also stirring in the Civil Rights and New Left movements. Teaching black children in a Mississippi freedom school during 1964, Florence Howe acquired a critical view of received knowledge and a pedagogy of empowerment. Later, however, as a founder of women's studies, she needed more than these tools. "Looking back," she wrote, "I can see that a social movement is helpful, if not essential, to the process" of change ("Women" 150). At the same time, angered by sexism in the Civil Rights movement, Mary King and Casey Hayden wrote two position papers, "Women in the Movement" and "Sex and Caste," which were read by members of the Student Non-Violent Coordinating Committee (SNCC) and the Students for a Democratic Society (SDS). Influenced by these papers, women organized workshops on their own issues at the SDS conferences in 1965 and 1967.

From 1967 to 1969, radical and leftist feminist groups formed in Chicago, New York, Boston, Seattle, San Francisco, and Washington, D.C. To avoid reproducing structures of domination, the New York Radical Feminists wanted to build a mass movement by proliferating "leaderless/structureless groups of no more than 15" members ("Organizing Principles of the New York Radical Feminists," *Notes from Second* 120; see also Jo Freeman, "The Tyranny of Structurelessness," *Berkeley Journal of Sociology* 17 [1972–73]). New groups proliferated when existing ones split over ideological or political matters or when they grew too large to sustain a participatory structure. This growth was called development by fission, a metaphor that conveyed the energy of a movement intent on changing both consciousness and society.

Consciousness-raising, a method used to initiate such change, took place in small groups where women could aggregate their personal experiences, generalize from them, and think critically about male supremacy. At its best, the process synthesized analysis and action. Kathie Sarachild (Amatniek), an early proponent, explained that "our feelings [about our experiences as women] will lead us to our theory, our theory to our action, our feelings about that action to new theory and then to new action" ("A Program for Feminist 'Consciousness Raising,'" *Notes from Second* 78). Necessarily emphasizing the similarities among women—the categorical oppression they suffered and their common interest in opposing it—the process constituted, at once, a sex class, as it was called, and a feminist consciousness about it. The educational purpose of consciousness-raising was to show women that personal problems had social causes and therefore political solutions. The organizational purpose was to separate women from leftist politics and bourgeois male-centered households in order to integrate them as an independent women's movement.

The movement itself, like its members, required analysis. Indeed, as Atkinson recognized, "without a programmatic analysis, the 'women's movement'" would be running blind; it would have no map, only action. She concluded that in 1969 "the most radical *action* that any woman or group of women could take was a feminist analysis" ("Radical Feminism," *Notes from Second* 33). The programmatic analysis never appeared, but from this matrix of personal experience and collective action, radical feminists developed analyses of sexual politics. Many such analyses appeared in a series—*Notes from the First Year: Women's Liberation* (1968), *Notes from the Second Year: Women's Liberation* (1970), and *Notes from the Third Year: Women's Liberation* (1971)—and were reprinted in *Radical Feminism* (1973). Among the influential pieces are Carol Hanisch's "The Personal Is Political," Pat Mainardi's "The Politics of Housework," Anne Koedt's "The Myth of the Vaginal Orgasm," and Radicalesbian's "The Woman Identified Woman."

In Britain, the political origins of the Women's Liberation movement can be located in the Campaign for Nuclear Disarmament during the late 1950s and early 1960s, the resurgence of Marxism in the 1960s, and trade unionism in Hull, Dagenham, and London. In 1968 a few socialist women's groups formed. By 1970 there were women's groups in England, Scotland, Southern Ireland, and Wales. Those in London confederated as the London Women's Liberation Workshop, which eventually had over 70 member groups. The movement was loosely connected by the National Women's Liberation Conferences convened annually throughout the 1970s. The first one, held in 1970 at Oxford, made four demands: equal pay for equal work; educational and employment opportunities; free contraception and abortion on demand; and free 24-hour child care *(The Body Politic)*.

British feminists also engaged in consciousness-raising and public action, but they were, by and large, socialist (not radical) feminists who produced analyses of class and gender. Their work appeared in the London Women's Liberation Workshop's *Shrew* (1968–78), *Socialist Woman* (1969–72), the Maoist *Women's Liberation* (1970–75), the National Coordinating Committee's *Women's Struggle* (1970–77), the Marxist-feminist *Red Flag* (1972–80), and *Spare Rib* (1972–), the first commercially successful feminist magazine.

In both countries, sociopolitical concerns, not academic subjects, organized the early feminist anthologies. The liberal *Women's Liberation: Blueprint for the Future* (1970) had sections on women's struggle; sex roles; women and law, education, and the arts; and current movement writings. The radical *Sisterhood Is Powerful: An Anthology of Writing from the Women's Liberation Movement* (1970) featured articles on women's oppression, changing consciousness, emerging feminist ideologies, and protest. *The Body Politic: Women's Liberation in Britain* (1972) added to such issues as work and family accounts of women's groups and campaigns. Typically, these anthologies mixed genres; literary and journalistic pieces appeared alongside personal narratives and position papers, which were short, forceful, and often collectively authored political statements.

Two anthologies marked important departures from movement analysis. The stories and essays in Toni Cade's *The Black Woman: An Anthology* (1970) highlighted the inadequacies of single-oppression analysis. Kay Lindsey's "The Black Woman as Woman," Frances Beale's "Double Jeopardy: To Be Black and Female," and Cade's "On the Issue of Roles" showed black women marginalized, according to Lindsey, by a black movement "concerned with the liberation of Blacks as a class" and a feminist movement "concerned with the oppression of women as a class" (85). The analogy between racism and sexism, made by white feminists, only obscured the particular situations of black women, who were exploited racially, sexually, and economically.

Although *Woman in Sexist Society: Studies in Power and Powerlessness* (1971) continued the focus on movement themes, it included the new academic feminist work in the United States. Seventeen of the 33 contributors were academics, and most became leading academic theorists during the 1970s. Among the landmark essays in this anthology are Wendy Martin's "Seduced and Abandoned in the New World: The Image of Woman in American Fiction," Linda Nochlin's "Why Are There No Great

Women Artists?" and Naomi Weisstein's "Psychology Constructs the Female." Delving into the politics of representation, they examined the institutional preconditions for the production of both female images and their makers.

In addition to and distinct from movement analysis, cultural theory was an important influence on women's liberation and later on feminist literary theory and criticism. The women who did cultural theory were academically trained, if not employed, and drew on academic literatures as well as sociopolitical issues. They investigated women's oppression multiperspectively—through the lenses of several disciplines, of past and present, of social and psychological manifestations.

SIMONE DE BEAUVOIR's *The Second Sex* (1949, trans., 1953) is an academic study that examines women from the perspectives of biology, psychoanalysis, and historical materialism; traces their history from nomadic to twentieth-century Western culture; reviews their treatment by five literary authors; and analyzes their situations in contemporary life. Beauvoir insisted on the relative yet hierarchical structure of gender in Western culture. Woman, she wrote, "is defined and differentiated with reference to man and not he with reference to her. . . . He is the Subject, he is the Absolute—she is the Other" (xvi). The alterity of woman was an effect of androcentrism: "The categories in which men think of the world are established *from their point of view, as absolute. . . .* A mystery for man, woman is considered to be mysterious in essence" (257). Beauvoir concluded that "one is not born, but rather becomes, a woman" (267), a being whose body and "relation to the world are modified through the action of others than herself" (725). Women will achieve liberation only through their own agency or "positive action [in] human society" (678).

A decade later, Betty Friedan's *The Feminine Mystique* (1963) analyzed the situation of middle- and upper-class women in the United States. Friedan also noticed the relationality of gender—men acted in the world and women retreated to the home, men were empowered and women infantilized—and argued that women suffered "a stunting or evasion of growth that is perpetuated by the feminine mystique" (77). This mystique was a complaisant femininity that made women economically, intellectually, and emotionally dependent upon husbands. Friedan's analysis was liberal in focusing on the identities of privileged women but also radical in criticizing the liberal institutions—Freudian psychoanalysis, functionalist social science, sex-differentiated education, consumerism—that supported complementary sex roles.

Juliet Mitchell's "Women: The Longest Revolution" (1966) examined the treatment of women's oppression in socialist theory. Charles Fourier, KARL MARX AND FRIEDRICH ENGELS, and August Bebel were economistic in linking women's subordination to the family and private property; since they made women's oppression "an adjunct to socialist theory, not structurally integrated into it" (15), this theory could not readily be used to understand women's condition. Instead, Mitchell proposed that women's condition was always overdetermined by four structures: production, reproduction, sexuality, and socialization. Feminist analysis should denaturalize the latter structures as Marxism had denaturalized production.

Shulamith Firestone's *The Dialectic of Sex: The Case for Feminist Revolution* (1970) combined Beauvoir's critiques of Freudian psychoanalysis and historical materialism with analyses of such cultural themes as romance. Her approach was markedly integrative at a time when many leftists saw no connection between the classism or racism they opposed and women's oppression. Instead of analogizing from race to sex, as some feminists had done, she declared that "racism is a sexual phenomenon" (122) and examined the relations of both categories in terms of a nuclear family engaged in Oedipal dramas and capitalist transactions. Though problematically subsuming one oppression under another, Firestone pointed up the need for a psychosocial synthesis.

Mitchell's earlier analysis of women's oppression was elaborated for *Woman's Estate* (1971), which also contained a history of the 1960s movements and an account of the women's liberation movements in several nations. The elaboration drew on empirical data, socialist and psychoanalytic theory, liberal sociology, and the work of American feminists. It anticipated a project that Mitchell and many other feminists would undertake during the 1970s and 1980s: the rehabilitation of psychoanalytic theory in order to understand women's oppression.

While the work of these four writers was organized around the dual nature of oppression, its social and psychological aspects, Kate Millett's *Sexual Politics* (1970) consisted of "equal parts of literary and cultural criticism" (xii) verging toward political theory. Defining sexual politics as the "arrangements whereby one group of persons is controlled by another" (23), she analyzed the politics—ideological, biological, social, economic, educational, religious, psychological, and physical—that maintained the system of patriarchy. Even more controversial than her cultural criticism was her literary criticism. She devoted chapters to D. H. LAWRENCE, Henry Miller, and Norman Mailer, who mythologized a machismo "cornered by the threat of a second sexual revo- lution" (335), and to Jean Genet, who saw how women and homosexuals challenged the heterosexual catego- ries. For her radical analysis, Millett was attacked in both popular and academic reviews. They accused her of scholarly improprieties and reviled her *ad feminam.* *Time* dubbed her the "Mao Tse-tung of Women's Libera- tion," and Norman Mailer described her as an acolyte killer with a sawed-off shotgun ("The Prisoner of Sex" [*Harper's,* March 1971]). Her criticism was threatening because it was so powerful: it crossed many bound- aries—between disciplines, between cultural domains, between academic and trade readers—thereby effec- tively revealing the pervasiveness of women's oppres- sion in Western cultures. Millett was a movement activ- ist and doctoral student when she wrote this book as a dissertation.

The early feminist literary critics were, like Millett, women on the margins of the academy. As graduate stu- dents and adjunct faculty, often with movement experi- ence, they wrote the first academic papers and taught the first women's studies courses. Their enterprise was supported throughout the 1970s by the Modern Lan- guage Association of America's (MLA) Commission on the Status of Women, whose members monitored the status of women, organized forums at the annual con- ventions, and edited *Female Studies,* a series of syllabi and resources. Whereas the women's liberation journals had integrated theory and criticism into the political struggle, special issues of *College English* in 1971 and 1972 published academic work on women's literature and status. Soon new academic journals—*Feminist Studies* (1972), *Mary Wollstonecraft Newsletter* (1972; retitled *Women and Literature* in 1975), and *Women's Studies* (1972)—encouraged the development of distinctively academic theory and criticism. At first this work drew from earlier Anglo-American scholarship on such sub- jects as the *querelle des femmes,* the learned ladies of the Renaissance, and the female novelists.

Katharine M. Rogers extended the tradition of *querelle* scholarship in *The Troublesome Helpmate: A History of Misogyny in Literature* (1966). Rogers defined "misogyny" as direct and indirect "expressions of hatred, fear, or contempt of womankind" (xii). Her study revealed its pervasiveness in every genre (epics, lyrics, tragedies, novels, tracts, sermons, manuals) and every period from the biblical to the contemporary. Similarly, Eva Figes's *Patriarchal Attitudes* (1970) maintained that patriarchal attitudes toward women, though they were transmuted, survived intellectual change. In a critique of European thinkers (G. W. F. HEGEL, ARTHUR SCHOPENHAUER,

Johann Gottlieb Fichte, FRIEDRICH NIETZSCHE, and Otto Weininger), she explored the connections between will and sexual domination, sexism and racism, the cate- gorical absolutism of German philosophy and the pol- itics of the Third Reich.

With much-admired wit, Mary Ellmann's *Thinking About Women* (1968) subsumed misogynous expression under the larger subject of the sexual analogies that organized thinking about literature. "Books by women," she observed, "are treated as though they themselves were women, and criticism embarks, at its happiest, upon an intellectual measuring of busts and hips" (29). With regard to readers, "the working rule is simple, basic: there must always be two literatures like two pub- lic toilets, one for Men and one for Women" (32). Rela- tionality was also the rule in characterization: "Women tend to be not merely what men are not, but what the individual speaker is not, and even what he is not *at any given moment*" (70). In style, authority and prophecy marked the masculine voice; wit and irony, both self- deprecating, marked the feminine one. Pursuing these hints, Josephine Donovan noted that nineteenth-century women writers had "to deal with a stylistic tradition" so "alien to their own way of thinking" that they might as well have written "in a foreign language" ("Feminist Style Criticism," *Images* 341). But a close stylistic analysis of Jane Austen, George Eliot, Kate Chopin, VIRGINIA WOOLF, and Dorothy Richardson left Donovan wonder- ing whether "there is a female 'mind'" and whether "there is or ought to be a feminine style tradition appro- priate" to it (341).

Many early studies surveyed the images of women in male-authored texts, censuring those that seemed to be inaccurate reflections of women's lives. Subsequently these studies were disparaged for their naiveté about representation, a criticism not entirely on the mark. Although some of the essays in *Images of Women in Fic- tion: Feminist Perspectives* (1972) catalogued images, oth- ers investigated their use in socializing women to femi- ninity. The investigation, as Florence Howe pointed out, led feminists to ask other "questions about the nature and purpose of literature" ("Feminism and Literature," *Images* 267) and to realize that whereas literature usually served a conservative purpose, it might also serve a femi- nist purpose. "We read," she announced, "to change ourselves and others" (268).

The gender conventions that controlled these images also operated formally. If they dictated character and plot, Marcia R. Lieberman observed, then they were "a structural element of the novel" ("Sexism and the Dou- ble Standard in Literature," *Images* 333). By changing the sex of protagonists in typical plots, Joanna Russ demonstrated that the conventions of gender, character, and plot were related: "A young girl in Minnesota finds her womanhood by killing a bear," and "A young man who unwisely puts success in business before his personal fulfillment loses his masculinity and ends up as a neurotic, lonely eunuch" ("What Can a Heroine Do? Or Why Women Can't Write," *Images* 3). Ellen Morgan speculated more particularly about adapting the Bildungsroman so that it might present women's struggle with institutionalized sexism and "their progress toward the goal of full personhood" ("Humanbecoming: Form and Focus in the Neo-Feminist Novel," *Images* 185).

Studies of female authorship were published earlier in this century by, for instance, M. Phillips and W. S. Tomkinson (*English Women in Life and Letters,* 1926), Joyce Horner ("The English Women Novelists and Their Connection with the Feminist Movement [1688–1797]," 1929–30), and B. G. MacCarthy (*The Female Pen,* 1946–47). As a bridge between these and feminist studies, Hazel Mews's *Frail Vessels: Woman's Role in Women's Novels from Fanny Burney to George Eliot* (1969) sketched a women's tradition in the British novel. The connections she found among a dozen novelists included their examination of women's experiences, their "pressing need to examine their own role" (199), and their presentation of female subjectivity from a female perspective. Breaking with New Critical strictures against "extrinsic" criticism, Mews contextualized the novels in women's socioeconomic circumstances and their authors' personal histories. Without this break, gender could not have become a category for understanding authorial tradition and textual reception.

Taking a historical approach, Elaine Showalter contended that women writers had been forcibly alienated from their experiences. Nineteenth-century women, she found, were prohibited from writing what did not correspond to femininity and were reviled for doing so. Twentieth-century women were trivialized for their portrayal of female experience, while male writers were admired for "their ruthless appropriation of life for their art" ("Women Writers and the Female Experience," *Radical Feminism* 400). Howe explained the contradiction: "Traditionally, a man's life is his work; a woman's life is her man. That a woman's life might have connections with her work is a revolutionary idea in that it might—indeed, must—lead her to examine and question her place as woman in the social order" ("Feminism," *Images* 254).

The contradiction between female life and authorship was the subject of papers given by two prominent American women writers—Tillie Olsen and Adrienne Rich—at a 1971 forum sponsored by the MLA Commission on the Status of Women and later published in *College English* (1972). Olsen enumerated the experiences that prevented women from writing ("Women Who Are Writers in Our Century: One Out of Twelve," *Silences*) and movingly recounted the obstacles to her own creativity. Raising four children, working at a job, and keeping house, she wrote in snatches during bus rides from work or in "the deep night hours for as long as I could stay awake" ("Silences: When Writers Don't Write," *Images* 110). Significantly, her first publishable work began with her experience: "I stand here ironing . . ." (110). Rich also adverted to her own experiences: she was a daughter writing for her father, a poet learning her craft from male poets, a mother jotting fragments while her children napped, a woman who thought the choice was between love and egotism. "Re-vision," she argued, the act of seeing text and life "with fresh eyes," was more than a feminist critical method; it was "an act of survival" (18). A radical feminist literary criticism would take the text as a clue to "how we have been living," "how our language has trapped as well as liberated us," and "how we can begin to see—and therefore live—afresh" (18). The point was "not to pass on a [patriarchal] tradition but to break its hold over us" (19).

Extending Ellmann's work, several studies detailed the reception of female-authored texts. The tumultuous reception accorded *Jane Eyre* was owing to its presentation of female passion and independence, thus making the sex of the author paramount in assessing it. "Many critics," Showalter reported, "bluntly admitted that they thought the book was a masterpiece if written by a man, shocking or disgusting if written by a woman" ("Women Writers and the Double Standard," *Woman in Sexist Society* 341). Carol Ohmann discovered that reviewers who assumed *Wuthering Heights* was male-authored attributed power, originality, and clarity to it, while those who knew it was female-authored considered it an interesting addition to the tradition of women's novels in England. Ohmann found "considerable correlation between what readers assume or know the sex of the writer to be and what they actually see, or neglect to see, in 'his' or her work" ("Emily Brontë in the Hands of Male Critics," *College English* 909).

Feminist critics evaluated modern critical approaches with the same attention to contextualization. Fraya Katz-Stoker faulted formalism for allowing critics "to study literature as a privately created world completely independent of its social and political context" ("The Other Criticism: Feminism vs. Formalism," *Images* 321). For formalist critics, "the words *literature, poetry,* and *art* conjure up images of bubbles floating in a cloudless, Platonic sky" (316). "Feminist criticism," Katz-Stoker declared, "is a materialist approach to literature which attempts to do away with the formalist illusion that literature is somehow divorced from the rest of reality." The grotesqueness of that reality "cannot be corrected until it is perceived" (326).

Lillian S. Robinson and Lise Vogel criticized both formalism and HISTORY OF IDEAS. Formalism placed "an overriding emphasis on the autonomy of the work of art and its formal characteristics, on the permanence of modal change, and on the independence of critical judgment" ("Modernism and History," *Images* 278). History of ideas perpetuated the unexamined assumptions "that *if* art has a race, it is white; *if* it has a sex, it is male; *if* it has a class, it is the ruling one" (279). They objected that these modes disqualified female, black, and working-class people from participation in high culture and also disqualified other forms of culture as culture. By situating excellence in artworks and success in artists and critics, they supported bourgeois individualism and interests.

Mapping the new feminist criticism, Annis Pratt identified four tasks: rediscovering women's works, "judging the formal aspects of texts" ("The New Feminist Criticism," *College English* 873), understanding what literature reveals about women and men in socioeconomic contexts, and describing "the psycho-mythological development of the female individual in literature" (877). Noting that Pratt had only compounded the bourgeois modes of bibliographical, textual, contextual (or sociological), and archetypal criticism, Robinson argued that feminist criticism ought to be alienated from them. Otherwise, feminist criticism would be trapped by contradictory judgments—a sexist work as well-crafted but ideologically repellent or a feminist work as "historically useful" but "artistically flawed" ("Dwelling in Decencies: Radical Criticism and the Feminist Perspective," *College English* 888). "Feminist criticism" should be "criticism with a Cause. . . . It must be ideological and moral criticism; it must be revolutionary" (879). It must ask of literature and criticism whose interests they serve.

Concluding her essay, Robinson took a position that in retrospect marked a turning point in feminist theory: "I am not terribly interested in whether feminism becomes a respectable part of academic criticism; I am very much concerned that feminist critics become a useful part of the women's movement. . . . In our struggle for liberation, Marx's note about philosophers may apply to critics as well: that up to now they have only interpreted the world and the real point is to change it" (889). Her

words appeared in 1971, a pivotal moment when the movement analyses and cultural theories of the 1960s began to give way to the academic criticism of the 1970s. As Alice Echols remarked in a recent history of this period, the focus of feminism shifted from oppositional struggle to female culture, from political activism to intellectual inquiry, from integrative categories to differential ones. The development of a brilliant and diverse body of feminist literary theory and criticism during the 1970s and 1980s was made possible by an academic institutionalization and specialization that, however, separated feminist inquiry from social change.

Ellen Messer-Davidow

Simone de Beauvoir, *Le Deuxième Sexe* (1949, *The Second Sex,* trans. H. M. Parshley, 1953); *The Black Woman: An Anthology* (ed. Toni Cade, 1970); *The Body Politic: Women's Liberation in Britain* (ed. Micheline Wandor, 1972); *College English* 32 (May 1971, special issue on women in the profession); *Conditions of Illusion* (ed. Feminist Books Collective, 1974); Mary Ellmann, *Thinking About Women* (1968); Eva Figes, *Patriarchal Attitudes* (1970); Shulamith Firestone, *The Dialectic of Sex: The Case for Feminist Revolution* (1970); Betty Friedan, *The Feminine Mystique* (1963); *Images of Women in Fiction: Feminist Perspectives* (ed. Susan Koppelman Cornillon, 1972, rev. ed., 1973); *Liberation Now! Writings from the Women's Liberation Movement* (ed. Deborah Babcox and Madeline Belkin, 1971); Hazel Mews, *Frail Vessels: Woman's Role in Women's Novels from Fanny Burney to George Eliot* (1969); Kate Millett, *Sexual Politics* (1970); *Notes from the First Year: Women's Liberation* (ed. New York Radical Women, 1968); *Notes from the Second Year: Women's Liberation* (ed. Shulamith Firestone, 1970); *Notes from the Third Year: Women's Liberation* (ed. Anne Koedt, 1971); Tillie Olsen, *Silences* (1978); *Radical Feminism* (ed. Anne Koedt, Ellen Levine, and Anita Rapone, 1973); Adrienne Rich, "When We Dead Awaken: Writing as Re-Vision," *On Lies, Secrets, and Silence* (1979); Katharine M. Rogers, *The Troublesome Helpmate: A History of Misogyny in Literature* (1966); *Sisterhood Is Powerful: An Anthology of Writing from the Women's Liberation Movement* (ed. Robin Morgan, 1970); *Woman in Sexist Society: Studies in Power and Powerlessness* (ed. Vivian Gornick and Barbara K. Moran, 1971); *Women's Liberation: Blueprint for the Future* (ed. Sookie Stambler, 1970).

Ti-Grace Atkinson, *Amazon Odyssey* (1974); David Bouchier, *The Feminist Challenge: The Movement for Women's Liberation in Britain and the USA* (1983); Susan Brownmiller, "Sisterhood Is Powerful" (*Women's Libera-*

tion, ed. Stambler); Marlene Dixon, "Why Women's Liberation?" *Ramparts* 8 (December 1969); David Doughan and Denise Sanchez, *Feminist Periodicals, 1855–1984: An Annotated Critical Bibliography of British, Irish, Commonwealth, and International Titles* (1987); Alice Echols, *Daring To Be Bad: Radical Feminism in America, 1967–1975* (1989); Sara Evans, *Personal Politics: The Roots of Women's Liberation in the Civil Rights Movement and the New Left* (1979); *Female Studies* 1–10 (1970–75); Jo Freeman, *The Politics of Women's Liberation: A Case Study of an Emerging Social Movement and Its Relation to the Policy Process* (1975); Judith Hole and Ellen Levine, *Rebirth of Feminism* (1971); Florence Howe, "Women and the Power to Change," *Women and the Power to Change* (ed. Howe, 1975); Juliet Mitchell, *Woman's Estate* (1971), "Women: The Longest Revolution," *New Left Review* 40 (1966); Sue O'Sullivan, "Passionate Beginnings: Ideological Politics, 1969–72," *Feminist Review* 11 (1982); Sheila Rowbotham, *The Past Is Before Us: Feminism in Action since the 1960s* (1989).

2. Anglo-American Feminisms

Women's experience as encountered in female fictional characters, the reactions of women readers, and the careers, techniques, and topics of women writers was the focus of the most accessible feminist criticism in the United States and Britain by the mid-1970s. A goal became the detection and further cultivation of a women's tradition in literature. Originally opposed to theory as male-inflected, scholars engaged in these projects have gradually acknowledged and cultivated it.

Initially, feminist critics of this group had part-time, adjunct, or assistant-professor status in academic institutions, and they turned their activism toward the formation of the women's studies programs that now exist in most U.S. universities. By the early 1990s, institutions that had been slow to start women's studies programs were recruiting feminist scholars at the top level. Feminists Florence Howe and Catharine R. Stimpson had been elected to the presidency of the Modern Language Association of America, Phyllis Franklin had become executive director, and Women's Studies in Language and Literature had developed into the third-largest division in the organization and a major force in its programming.

The process of recovering neglected work by women writers was greatly assisted by feminist reprinting houses, such as the Feminist Press in the United States and Virago Press and the Women's Press in Britain. Founded by Florence Howe, the Feminist Press published its first

book in 1972 and regularly offers work that recovers marginal cultural subjects—the working class, race—and 1930s texts. Howe reaffirms experientially centered feminist study in her introduction to *Tradition and the Talents of Women*, a 1991 collection that includes the borderline geopolitics of Chicanas and disperses work on lesbian and black women's experience into various categories. Howe prefers strategically to argue a singular tradition of women, because she is "convinced that to imagine a series of separate, 'monumental' traditions is only to establish (or to continue) a hierarchy among them, in which the traditional white male canon would survive dominant" (13).

Feminist periodicals such as *Signs, Feminist Studies, Women's Studies Quarterly, Women and Literature,* and *Chrysalis* have provided a forum for feminist theoretical discussion. Founded in 1975 by Catharine Stimpson, *Signs* set out to publish "the new scholarship about women" as "a means to the end of an accurate understanding of men and women, of sex and gender, of large patterns of human behavior, institutions, ideologies and art." In the experiential vein, it wanted its audience to be able to "fix and grasp a sense of the totality of women's lives and the realities of which they have been a part" (*Signs* 1 [1975]: v). It has also published landmark French feminist work in translation. In its second number, Elaine Showalter presented a review essay on feminist scholarship in literature that moved into the project of a separate women's tradition. *Signs* declared itself interdisciplinary. Theoretical borrowing from history, sociology, and psychology has remained crucial to literary study. *Signs* publishes special numbers and debates on emerging issues, such as lesbian identification, and the uses of Nancy Chodorow's *The Reproduction of Mothering: Psychoanalysis and the Sociology of Gender* (1978) in theoretical revision of the mother (vol. 6). Chodorow's post-Freudian theory reconstructs the Oedipal crisis for men and women, and its continuing post-Oedipal mother/daughter relation has served the theorizing of women's traditions. The first issue of *Signs* contained historian Carroll Smith-Rosenberg's "Female World of Love and Ritual," which relies on women's correspondence to recover a tradition of "long-lived, intimate, loving friendship between two women" (1) and all-female rituals and customs as focal events of nineteenth-century American women's lives.

VIRGINIA WOOLF offered the most important literary-critical model to feminists interested in recovering the experience of women writers. Now a standard text, *A Room of One's Own* (1929) gives an account of the frustrations that a fictional female researcher must go through to arrive at a theory of women and fiction. Gender bias hampers her access to the resources of the university, and historical and imaginative male accounts of woman, whether distorted by anger or by the imagination, fail history and experience. Woolf imagines historical woman writers in their social contexts and searches out the sources of the bitterness she reads in their works. Jane Marcus has been the most active editor of feminist Woolf collections. In *Art and Anger,* Marcus identifies her own training as American NEW CRITICISM and intellectual history and attributes what theory she exhibits to "the texts under discussion in relation to their historical context, as well as to a problematizing of the issue of reading by gender gained from reading Virginia Woolf's fiction" (xiii). She identifies Woolf as a socialist feminist and has collected work on her mystical aspect, women in her contexts, and BLOOMSBURY GROUP misogyny, revising views expressed in the family biography by Quentin Bell. In "Still Practice, A/Wrested Alphabet" (in *Art and Anger*), Marcus resists the contemporary hierarchy that privileges language-centered DECONSTRUCTION. She argues for the importance of studying the production of a literary work in process and identifies with the mythos of Penelope "the tradition of *making* the art object," rooted in daily experience, as a feminine aesthetic. Like Lillian Robinson in *Sex, Class, and Culture,* Marcus asserts the importance of Woolf's radical feminist work *Three Guineas.*

The importance of female experience is marked in the significantly titled collection *The Authority of Experience* (1977), edited by Arlyn Diamond and Lee R. Edwards. Although they collected their essays "practically and intuitively," the editors found that theory was emerging. They saw "concern with society's beliefs about the nature and function of women in the world" as the concern of feminists and brought "personally felt reality" to the fore as a criterion. Their authors examined art as "the product of a particular cultural milieu, sometimes embodying a society's most deeply held convictions, sometimes questioning these values, sometimes disguising an artist's own ambivalence with regard to these matters" (ix–x). Unlike in subsequent studies by Ellen Moers and Elaine Showalter, there was a balance between male and female writers. Geoffrey Chaucer, William Shakespeare, and Samuel Richardson come off well in rendering the historical experience of women through their female characters. The Diamond and Edwards collection is an early example of the importance of anthologies and collections to the development of feminist theory, enriching the sense of women's experience of specific historical periods and new genre traditions. Diverse examples

are *Shakespeare's Sisters: Feminist Essays in Women Poets,* edited by Sandra M. Gilbert and Susan Gubar (1979); *Women Reading Women's Writing,* edited by Sue Roe (1987); *The Private Self: Theory and Practice of Women's Autobiographical Writings,* edited by Shari Benstock (1988); *The Voyage In: Fictions of Female Development,* edited by Elizabeth Abel, Marianne Hirsch, and Elizabeth Langland (1983); *Arms and the Woman: War, Gender, and Literary Representation,* edited by Helen M. Cooper, Adrienne Auslander Munich, and Susan Merrill Squier (1987); *Breaking the Sequence: Women's Experimental Fiction,* edited by Ellen G. Friedman and Miriam Fuchs (1989); and *The Gender of Modernism: A Critical Anthology,* edited by Bonnie Kime Scott (1990). Among the theoretical collections incorporating diverse practices, see *The Poetics of Gender,* edited by Nancy K. Miller (1986); *Feminist Issues in Literary Scholarship,* edited by Shari Benstock (1987); and *The New Feminist Criticism: Essays in Women, Literature, and Theory* (1985) and *Speaking of Gender* (1989), both edited by Elaine Showalter.

Judith Fetterley wrote on Hemingway for the Diamond and Edwards collection. Her book *The Resisting Reader* (1978) considers the writing of additional male writers from Washington Irving to Norman Mailer, including canonized figures such as Faulkner, Fitzgerald, Hemingway, and James. Fetterley discusses the loss and mental confusion of the "immasculated" woman reader, forced to identify against herself with male characters, whose essential experience is betrayal by the female, and forced to see women characters scapegoated and killed off in the typical scenarios. Against this politics of male empowerment, Fetterley offers the female reader the power of naming what is real, in terms of her own experience. Fetterley's strategy for re-vision of the reading process for women was inspired by ADRIENNE RICH and Kate Millett and has been further theorized by Patrocinio Schweickart, who suggests the importance of establishing the subject-object relations between the female reader and the text. Fetterley's representation of American literature as a "masculine wilderness" and of America as a female to be discovered and conquered is resonant with Annette Kolodny's *The Lay of the Land* (1975) and with the ecofeminism of Susan Griffin (*Woman and Nature,* 1978). Studies of James Joyce can represent the continuing analysis of male writers. Joyce was credited with a degree of cultural realism in representing the familial, vocational, and artistic experiences of women characters (*Women in Joyce,* ed. Suzette Henke and Elaine Unkeless, 1982, and *Joyce and Feminism,* by Bonnie Kime Scott, 1984). By the late 1980s Joycean feminist analysis favored psychoanalytic and French feminist approaches (see PSYCHOANALYTIC THEORY AND CRITICISM: 3. THE POST-LACANIANS).

Marginal development of a female countercanon posed a challenge to the central literary canon and contributed to a questioning of canonicity itself. Nina Baym's *Women's Fiction: A Guide to Novels by and about Women in America, 1820–1870* (1978), for example, introduces an alternate tradition of trivialized women writers. Her essay "Melodramas of Beset Manhood: How Theories of American Fiction Exclude Women Authors" encourages a reexamination of criteria of greatness, noting the masculine limitation of concepts such as that of America as a nation and the myth of individual opportunity in the wilderness. Lillian S. Robinson's "Treason Our Text: Feminist Challenges to the Literary Canon" questions limitations of both old masculinist and new feminist canons. Feminists also tested the adequacy of periodization based exclusively on male literary production and introduced gender as a factor in genre. Annette Kolodny introduced the concept of a coded language of a female subculture in "A Map for Rereading," its title a reaction to the narrow literary culture defined in HAROLD BLOOM's *A Map of Misreading.*

"Gynocritics" is the name Elaine Showalter has given to those critics who wish "to construct a female framework for the analysis of women's literature, to develop new models based on the study of female experience, rather than to adapt male models and theories" ("Toward a Feminist Poetics," *New Feminist Criticism* 131). In a series of essays, Showalter is increasingly willing to talk about various schools of feminist theory. She finds the social theory of subcultures useful to gynocriticism in "Feminist Theory in the Wilderness." In "Critical Cross-Dressing," she is skeptical about the ability of prominent male critics (Jonathan Culler and Terry Eagleton, in particular) to turn feminist as readers without surrendering "paternal privileges." What she fears is that "instead of breaking out of patriarchal bounds," they will merely compete with women, failing to acknowledge women's feminist contributions (143). She includes feminist aesthetics and French feminism in the introduction to her edited collection *The New Feminist Criticism* and begins talking more about men through the category of gender in her later edited collection *Speaking of Gender.*

Feminist freedom from male theory was a goal for Showalter, but its accomplishment remains problematic in critiques of gynocritics' practices. There are traces of Freudianism and traditional literary categories in work by Ellen Moers and by Sandra M. Gilbert and Susan Gubar. Toril Moi places Showalter in a humanist tradition. For Moi, the empirical methods and close textual analysis of gynocritics links them to the male practice of New Criticism, though their construction of female social history certainly mitigates this. The extensive archival work of Showalter, Baym, Marcus, and Gilbert and Gubar, by their own admission, applies skills learned in traditional graduate study (see Marcus's "Storming the Toolshed" in *Art and Anger*). Annette Kolodny has advocated a "playful pluralism" for feminist theory and practice ("Dancing through the Minefield"), a model that excited objections from GAYATRI CHAKRAVORTY SPIVAK, whose juxtaposition of feminism with Marxism, psychoanalysis, and deconstruction discloses some perils. Further discussion by Judith Kegan Gardner offered a political model of several schools of feminist criticism: liberal, socialist, and radical. The radical views of lesbians and black critics had been neglected in the pluralist concept and indeed in much of the 1970s feminist criticism. Myra Jehlen found the self-contained gynocritical position problematic. If, like Archimedes, the feminist would shift the world, she must position her fulcrum on male ground—she cannot work from a totally female stance. In "Archimedes and the Paradox of Feminist Criticism," Jehlen advocates attending to confrontations along the long border contingent to dominant male traditions, achieving "radical comparativism." Jehlen's isolation of politics from aesthetics in literature was regarded as suspect by Moi, although both critics attend to unconscious ideology.

By the late 1970s, major female-centered studies had begun to appear. In *Literary Women* (1976), Ellen Moers expresses the intention not to impose doctrine on women writers—an attitude that resembles Showalter's in its distrust of theory. She presents a practical, living history of women writers from the eighteenth century through the twentieth, attempting to shape it with their concerns and language. The account features new anecdotal details and minute observations from manuscript sources, selected for their relevance to women's unique experiences. Many of the categories she uses to discuss the history and tradition of women writers in the first half of her study are derived from traditional period and genre studies: "The Epic Age," "Traditions, Individual Talent," "Realism," and "Gothic." In the second half, she sets out to familiarize readers with literary feminism, a heroic structure for the female "voice" in literature that she calls "heroinism." Her categories of heroinism incorporate characters in roles of loving, performing, and educating. Her discussion of female erotic landscape emerges from an introduction of SIGMUND FREUD's sexual dream symbols, assessing male bias that goes back to the naming of female anatomy (vagina = scabbard). This introduction of metaphors of the female body finds a response in French feminist theory, with LUCE IRIGARAY's "two lips" of the female body and HÉLÈNE CIXOUS's concept of writing in mother's milk.

Showalter's landmark work, *A Literature of Their Own* (1977), constructs a history of British women novelists' literary subculture in three phases, designated as feminine (1840–80), feminist (1880–1920), and female (continuing since 1920, with a new phase beginning in 1960). Showalter's dates are not to be taken rigidly; they overlap, and multiple phases can be seen in a single writer. Critical of the practice of selecting only great figures for analysis, in an appendix she lists 213 women writers with "sociological" data, writers who provide diversity and generational links. She also avoids concepts of female imagination, preferring to look at the ways "the self-awareness of the woman writer has translated itself into a literary form in a specific place and time-span" and to trace this self-awareness within the tradition (12). Her "feminine" phase includes intense, compact, symbolic fiction that used "innovative and covert ways to dramatize the inner life" (27–28), as well as "an all-inclusive female realism" that was "a broad, socially informed exploration of the daily lives and values of women within the family and the community" (29). "Feminists" confronted Victorian sexual stereotypes, produced socialistic theories of women's relationships to work, class, and the family, and entertained an "all-out war of the sexes" (29). Some writers fantasized sexual separatism in Amazonian or suffragette communities. Early parts of the "female" phase of self-exploration are seen by Showalter as carrying "the double legacy of feminine self-hatred and feminist withdrawal" (33). It polarized sexuality, but the female sensibility moved from sacred to self-destructive and paradoxically failed to confront the female body. The concept of androgyny, explored from the Greeks to Bloomsbury in male as well as female authors by Carolyn Heilbrun (*Toward a Recognition of Androgyny*, 1973), comes under attack as an escapist "flight" in Showalter's controversial handling of Woolf (263–97), a position that echoes the attacks of Queenie Leavis and F. R. LEAVIS's *Scrutiny*. The phase of the female novelists since 1960 operates in Freudian and Marxist contexts and for the first time accepts anger and sexuality as "sources of female creative power" (35).

Sandra Gilbert and Susan Gubar have theorized the position of woman and the literary imagination in the nineteenth century (*The Madwoman in the Attic*, 1979) and the twentieth (*No Man's Land*, 2 vols., 1987–89) and offer a large selection of women authors who conform to their paradigms in their edition of *The Norton Anthology*

of Literature by Women (1985). Their approach includes historical references to the material, social, and gendered conditions of authors' lives; to literary canons and archives; and to popular movements and artifacts—typical strengths of American feminist theory. Like Showalter and Moers, they detect historical stages of a female literary tradition, but they ground these in male comparisons and frequently make their points through metaphors and puns, as seen in their titles. According to them, for early nineteenth-century women writers the dominant vision of literary creativity was paternal. Women had to cope further with male fantasies of the female. These fantasies come in angelic and monstrous versions and were imposed as literary models. The madwoman or monster repeatedly created by women writers is the author's double, expressing her anxiety, rage, and "schizophrenia of authorship" (*Madwoman* 78). They detect asymmetrical male and female responses to the rise of female literary power. Women have emerged from their liminal position in the attic to wage the battle between the sexes.

In *The War of the Words*, volume 1 of *No Man's Land*, which offers numerous studies of male authors, the battle is manifested in tropes of erotic dueling, the advent of the "no-man" to replace the virile man, and plots of males defeating alarming forms of female sexuality through a theology of the phallus, mutilations, rapes, and campaigns against the mothers of "castrated" sons. Women begin to have literary reactions to preceding female writers, sometimes arriving at parodic or comic treatments, as well as serious and positive ones. Gilbert and Gubar's collection of stereotypes and misogynistic plot types that progress through the decades is reminiscent of Kate Millett's *Sexual Politics* (1970). Women writers express belligerence less directly and render characters who are victorious through duplicity, subterfuge, or luck. The suffragist movement gives the early century metaphors of militarism and sacrifice. Modernist women offer private triumphs. Later women writers respond to male backlash with nightmares of defeat or dreams of triumphant women warriors. Volume 2, *Sexchanges*, sustains the model of sex war refined into the consideration of sexchanges: "The sexes battle because sex roles change, but when the sexes battle, sex itself (that is eroticism) changes" (xi). Major changes include the rebellion against the feminization of the American woman, powerful roles assumed by women in World War I, varied lesbian arrangements, and transvestism. A more tortured experience of women in war emerges in Cooper, Munich, and Squier's essay collection *Arms and the Woman*.

Two theoretical models in Gilbert and Gubar are

worthy of mention. Their concept "anxiety of author-ship," used perhaps too broadly to describe nineteenth-century women writers—like Harold Bloom's male-applied term "anxiety of influence"—derives from Freud's psychosexual paradigm of the Oedipus complex. If women follow a normative female resolution of the Oedipus complex, the father (the male literary tradition) becomes the object of female desire, and the pre-Oedipal desire for the mother (or her literature) is renounced. Twentieth-century women writers have the option of the "affiliation complex," which allows them to "adopt" literary mothers and to escape the male "belatedness," or the "anxiety of influence" theorized by Bloom, which is in effect a biological imperative for literary descent from an originatory father. Normative resolution of the Oedipus complex may leave women anxious about the fragility of paternal power, worried about usurping paternal primacy, and fearful of male vengeance. Non-normative Freudian resolutions of the Oedipus complex offer advantages to authors such as GERTRUDE STEIN. The resulting "masculinist complex" grants autonomy, a new maternal relation, and the creative option of male mimicry—a departure from Freud's negative judgment.

Gilbert and Gubar also implicate fantasies in theory, *The War of the Words* focusing on linguistic fantasies, and *Sexchanges* on fantasy identifications. The feminist linguistic fantasy grants an intuitive primacy in language acquisition to the mother rather than to the father, a more powerful position than the male-associated symbolic language and social contract of JULIA KRISTEVA's post-Lacanian analysis. Proceeding from Woolf's remarks on women's language, Gilbert and Gubar suggest that women fantasize a revision not of women's language but of women's relation to language. They would overturn male sentencing—the sentence as definitive—in judgment, decree, or interdiction. They see agonistic oral competitiveness and the acquisition of a privileged, priestly language, as theorized by Walter Ong, as a male fertility rite, resisting vernacular and controlling mother tongue. Modernist men such as EZRA POUND, D. H. LAWRENCE, James Joyce, and T. S. ELIOT and the deconstructionist theory of JACQUES DERRIDA have mystified, claimed, or transformed mother tongue, so as to retain priestly authority. *Sexchanges* begins with *fin de siècle* myths of popular culture that have also interested Nina Auerbach *(Woman and the Demon)* and Elaine Showalter *(Sexual Anarchy)*. Increasingly, women writers find enabling fantasies and roles—Sappho as a predecessor, Aphrodite as an erotic authority, and transvestism as metaphor. In the same sexchanges, men express loss and failure. We must ask whether Gilbert and Gubar estab-

lish the victory of a woman's tradition or another myth. Were there not larger cultural projects, including the problematics of a binary conflict between the sexes? These questions arise in postmodern feminist discussions.

Bonnie Kime Scott

See also ADRIENNE RICH.

Elizabeth Abel, Marianne Hirsch, and Elizabeth Langland, eds., *The Voyage In: Fictions of Female Development* (1983); Nina Auerbach, *Woman and the Demon* (1982); Nina Baym, "Melodramas of Beset Manhood: How Theories of American Fiction Exclude Women Authors," 1981, *New Feminist Criticism* (ed. Showalter), *Women's Fiction: A Guide to Novels by and about Women in America: 1820–1870* (1978); Helen M. Cooper, Adrienne Auslander Munich, and Susan Merrill Squier, eds., *Arms and the Woman: War, Gender, and Literary Representation* (1987); Arlyn Diamond and Lee R. Edwards, eds., *The Authority of Experience* (1977); Josephine Donovan, ed., *Feminist Literary Criticism: Explorations in Theory* (1976); Rachel Blau DuPlessis, *Writing beyond the Ending: Narrative Strategies of Twentieth-Century Women Writers* (1985); Hester Eisenstein, *Contemporary Feminist Thought* (1984); *Feminist Readings: French Texts / American Contexts,* special issue, *Yale French Studies* 62 (1981); *Feminist Theory,* special issue, *Signs* 7 (1982); Judith Fetterley, *The Resisting Reader: A Feminist Approach to American Fiction* (1978); Jane Gallop, *Around 1981: Academic Feminist Literary Theory* (1992); Judith Kegan Gardner et al., "An Interchange on Feminist Criticism: On 'Dancing through the Minefield,'" *Feminist Studies* 8 (1982); Sandra M. Gilbert and Susan Gubar, *The Madwoman in the Attic: The Woman Writer and the Nineteenth-Century Literary Imagination* (1979), *No Man's Land: The Place of the Woman Writer in the Twentieth Century* (vol. 1, *The War of the Words,* 1987; vol. 2, *Sexchanges,* 1989); Sandra M. Gilbert and Susan Gubar, eds., *The Norton Anthology of Literature by Women: The Tradition in English* (1985); Susan Griffin, *Woman and Nature: The Roaring Inside Her* (1978); Carolyn Heilbrun, *Toward a Recognition of Androgyny* (1973); Florence Howe, ed., *Tradition and the Talents of Women* (1991); Mary Jacobus, ed., *Women Writing and Writing about Women* (1979); Myra Jehlen, "Archimedes and the Paradox of Feminist Criticism," *Signs* 6 (1981); Sydney Janet Kaplan, "Varieties of Feminist Criticism," *Making a Difference: Feminist Literary Criticism* (ed. Gayle Greene and Coppelia Kahn, 1985); Annette Kolodny, "Dancing through the Minefield: Some Observations on the Theory, Practice, and Politics of Feminist Literary Criticism," *Femi-*

nist Studies 6 (1980), *The Lay of the Land: Metaphor as Experience and History in American Life and Letters* (1975), "A Map for Rereading: or, Gender and the Interpretation of Literary Texts," 1980, *New Feminist Criticism* (ed. Showalter); *The Lesbian Issue,* special issue, *Signs* 9 (1984); Jane Marcus, *Art and Anger* (1988); Ellen Moers, *Literary Women: The Great Writers* (1976); Toril Moi, *Sexual/Textual Politics: Feminist Literary Theory* (1985); Adrienne Rich, *On Lies, Secrets, and Silence: Selected Prose, 1966–1978* (1979); Lillian Robinson, *Sex, Class, and Culture* (1978), "Treason Our Text: Feminist Challenges to the Literary Canon," 1983, *New Feminist Criticism* (ed. Showalter); Patrocinio P. Schweickart, "Reading Ourselves: Toward a Feminist Theory of Reading," *Gender and Reading* (ed. Schweickart and Elizabeth Flynn, 1986); Elaine Showalter, "Critical Cross-Dressing: Male Feminists and the Woman of the Year," *Raritan* 3 (1983), "Literary Criticism: A Review Essay," *Signs* 1 (1975), *A Literature of Their Own: British Women Novelists from Brontë to Lessing* (1977), *Sexual Anarchy: Gender and Culture at the Fin de Siècle* (1990); Elaine Showalter, ed., *The New Feminist Criticism: Essays on Women, Literature, and Theory* (1985), *Speaking of Gender* (1989); Carroll Smith-Rosenberg, "The Female World of Love and Ritual," *Signs* 1 (1975); Dale Spender, *Man Made Language* (1980); Gayatri Chakravorty Spivak, "Feminism and Critical Theory," *In Other Worlds: Essays in Cultural Politics* (1987); Catharine R. Stimpson, *Where the Meanings Are* (1988); *Within and Without: Women, Gender, and Theory,* special issue, *Signs* 12 (1987); *Women—Sex and Sexuality,* special issue, *Signs* 5 (1980).

3. Poststructuralist Feminisms

"The question of gender is a question of language." This statement is Barbara Johnson's (*World* 37), and her succinct formulation of the relationship between gender and language does much to characterize the approach of a group of feminists who draw upon the discourses of poststructuralism. This feminist work takes as its starting point the premise that gender difference dwells in language rather than in the referent, that there is nothing "natural" about gender itself. In placing their emphasis on language, however, these feminists are not suggesting a sort of linguistic or poetic retreat into a world made only of words. Rather, language intervenes so that "materiality" is not taken to be a self-evident category, and language itself is understood as radically marked by the materiality of gender. The poststructuralist focus on language thus raises fundamental questions that extend beyond matters of usage. The understanding of writing and the body as sites where the

material and the linguistic intersect requires the interrogation of woman as a category of gender or sex.

Contesting patriarchal discourse. Questioning the political and ethical grounds of language, the poststructuralist feminists considered here share a common opponent in patriarchal discourse, a feature that emerges in their readings of literature, philosophy, history, and psychoanalysis. This is not to suggest that they all counter or even define patriarchal discourse in the same way. If, as HÉLÈNE CIXOUS suggests, "it has become rather urgent to question this solidarity between logocentrism and phallocentrism—bringing to light the fate dealt to woman," how one might go about such questioning is a point of dispute (*Newly* 65).

According to LUCE IRIGARAY, we cannot simply step outside of phallogocentrism so as suddenly to write and think in ways completely free of the rules of patriarchy, for language and discourse are themselves inscribed with those rules. Instead, we have to work like a virus from within patriarchal discourses to infect and radically change them, thus "leaving open the possibility of a different language" (*This Sex* 80). Not surprisingly, then, the discourses of philosophy and psychoanalysis have become prime "hosts" for Irigaray's work. As she explains, "Unless we limit ourselves naively—or perhaps strategically—to some kind of limited or marginal issues, it is indeed precisely philosophical discourse that we have to challenge, and *disrupt* inasmuch as this discourse sets forth the law for all others, inasmuch as it constitutes the discourse on discourse" (74). In posing this challenge, Irigaray hopes to expose the ways in which patriarchal discourses are politically determined and disrupt altogether the power structures they hold in place. With this goal in mind, Irigaray has sought to disrupt the discourses of SIGMUND FREUD and PLATO (*Speculum of the Other Woman*), JACQUES LACAN and KARL MARX AND FRIEDRICH ENGELS (*This Sex Which Is Not One*), MARTIN HEIDEGGER (*L'Oubli*), FRIEDRICH NIETZSCHE (*Amante marine*), and Baruch Spinoza and Emmanuel Levinas (*Éthique*), to name only a few.

Similar political interventions have been made by Catherine Clément both in her study of opera (*Opera, or the Undoing of Woman*) and in her consideration of the sorceress and the hysteric (*The Newly Born Woman*); by Michèle Le Doeuff in her interrogation of the role of lack and the place of knowledge acquisition in Western philosophy (*L'Imaginaire philosophique*); by Barbara Johnson in her readings of literature and DECONSTRUCTION (*The Critical Difference* and *A World of Difference*); by JULIA KRISTEVA in her numerous works on linguistics, psychoanalysis, and literature (*Revolution in Poetic Language, De-*

sire in Language, Powers of Horror, Tales of Love, and *Black Sun*); and by GAYATRI CHAKRAVORTY SPIVAK in her analyses of the relationship between philosophy, Marxism, deconstruction, and subaltern studies *(In Other Worlds).*

Some poststructuralist feminists, however, have preferred to develop an alternative to patriarchal discourse in place of the strategy of subversive rewriting. Monique Wittig attempts to create completely new, nonphallogocentric discourses in her fictional works *Les Guérillères* (1969, trans. David LeVay, 1971), *L'Opoponax* (1969, *The Opoponax,* trans. H. Weaver, 1976), and *Le Corps lesbien* (1973, *The Lesbian Body,* trans. David LeVay, 1975). As a counter to the heterosexual, patriarchal social contract, Wittig proposes a structural change in language that will destroy the categories of gender and sex. Frequently this change takes the form of experimentation with pronouns and nouns, which she calls the "lesbianization of language" because, as she explains, "lesbian is the only concept I know of which is beyond the categories of sex" ("One Is Not" 53).

Cixous's work might seem similar to Wittig's in that she also engages in a political project designed to create an alternative, nonphallogocentric discourse. Like Wittig, Cixous turns to fiction *(Angst, Illa, Souffles)* and is concerned with "getting rid of words like 'feminine' and 'masculine,' 'femininity' and 'masculinity,' even 'man' and 'woman'" ("Exchange" 129). Yet upon closer examination, Cixous's work radically differs from Wittig's. First, Cixous relies heavily upon psychoanalysis and Derridean deconstruction, which are anathema to Wittig. Second, Cixous goes on to develop what she calls "feminine writing" *(écriture féminine),* envisaged in terms of bisexuality rather than Wittig's "lesbianization." For Cixous, the space of feminine writing cannot be theorized or defined, enclosed or encoded ("Laugh of the Medusa," trans. Keith Cohen and Paula Cohen, *New French Feminisms,* ed. Marks and de Courtivron, 253). It can, however, be understood as "the ideal harmony, reached by few, [which] would be genital, assembling everything and being capable of generosity, of spending" ("Exchange" 131). Feminine writing is also the province of metaphor, not limited to written words and possibly taking the form of "writing by the voice," a harmonic *écriture féminine* metaphorized as writing in mother's milk or the uterus *(Illa* 208, *Newly).* Although her metaphors here are maternal, are biologically the province of women, according to Cixous neither biological women nor men need be condemned to the space of phallogocentrism. Cixous understands feminine writing as a bisexual political act that holds open "the very possibility of change" ("Laugh" 249).

Cixous has engaged the literary texts of James Joyce, Edgar Allan Poe, and Clarice Lispector in these terms *(L'Exil de James Joyce, ou, l'art du remplacement* [translated into English as *The Exile of James Joyce], Prénoms de personne, Vivre l'orange / To Live the Orange);* deconstructed Greek, Latin, and Egyptian mythology *(Illa, Le Livre de Promethea, La);* and taken up specific instances of political struggle that place feminist concerns in larger cultural and historical perspectives (the plays *L'Histoire terrible mais inachevée de Norodom Sihanouk roi du Cambodge* and *L'Indiade ou l'Inde de leurs rêves).* Her practice of *écriture féminine* is not, however, without its detractors. Wittig attacks it for what she believes is its complicity with heterosexual, bourgeois capitalism (the distinction between bisexuality and lesbianization is significant). Hélène Wenzel argues that it "perpetuates and recreates long-held stereotypes and myths about woman as natural, sexual, biological, and corporal by celebrating essences" (272).

Writing (and) the body.   Whether the emphasis is on alternative writing or subversive rewriting, what is at stake in this feminist attention to language is the relationship between the twin materialities of writing and the body. This is perhaps most obvious in Cixous's work, which specifically stresses the importance of the connection. Cixous exhorts women to write through their bodies in order to make "the huge resources of the unconscious" burst out *(Newly* 94–97). In a rather different move, Irigaray turns to the female body in order to develop an account of woman's pleasure that does not privilege sight. Irigaray argues that all accounts of bodily pleasure have traditionally been dominated by the scopophilic drive of male pleasure described by psychoanalysis. Deemphasizing the role played by visual pleasure, which is by definition primarily patriarchal, Irigaray goes so far as to argue that "woman takes more pleasure from touching than from looking" *(This Sex* 26). Woman's pleasure, for which the language of psychoanalysis is inadequate, is fluid, tactile, and, what is most important, plural: "Woman has sex organs more or less everywhere" (28). It must be noted that Irigaray's use of anatomical analogies to describe feminine pleasure (and thus to reinterpret the phallogocentric discourse of philosophy and psychoanalysis) leaves her open to charges of essentialism. Yet it is also possible to think of her work as turning to biological metaphors and images of woman already prevalent in Western discourse in order to produce a new discourse that does not *see* sexual difference as a question of pure anatomical difference.

Irigaray's political move away from vision is not, however, borne out in work by other psychoanalytically informed feminists. First, if Irigaray identifies masculine pleasure as primarily visual (as would film theorist Laura Mulvey), Teresa de Lauretis attempts to reclaim visual pleasure for the female spectator. Drawing on the work of Lacan and on the discourse of FILM THEORY, de Lauretis argues that "narrative and visual pleasure need and should not be thought of as the exclusive property of dominant codes, serving solely the purposes of 'oppression'" (*Alice* 68). Second, if Irigaray calls for a return to the tactile, an emphasis that falls on touching the body, Kaja Silverman stresses the subversive quality of women's voice. In her examination of film, Silverman argues that "the female voice has enormous conceptual and discursive range once it is freed from its claustral confinement within the female body" (*Acoustic* 186).

There are even harsher counters to Irigaray's and Cixous's approaches to the body. Wittig believes that Cixous and Irigaray fetishize the body and do not take into account that the body is only part of the total subject. Ann Rosalind Jones takes a different view of the problem when she points out that "it is possible to argue that the French feminists make of the female body too unproblematically pleasurable and totalized an entity" (254).

Leaving these objections aside, it would be impossible to discuss the poststructuralist feminists' engagement with writing and the body without looking at how it has led to a revalorization of the mother, or more precisely, of the maternal body. Poststructuralist feminism recognizes that the figure of the mother has a particularly overdetermined relationship with writing and the body. This "valorization of the maternal," as Domna Stanton points out, "marks a decisive break with the existentialism of *The Second Sex,* wherein SIMONE DE BEAUVOIR stressed the oppressiveness of motherhood" (160). For both Cixous and Irigaray, the mother is an important affirmative figure. Cixous first metaphorizes the mother as a figural product of language, then both valorizes and defetishizes the mother so as to remove her from the patriarchal structures of the family ("Laugh," *Souffles*). Similarly, Irigaray stresses the inextricability of women and mothers. "When we are women," says Irigaray, "we are always mothers" (*Éthique* 27). Although Irigaray makes this statement in her work devoted to ethics, she has also devoted two short texts to the mother-daughter relationship ("And the One Does Not Stir without the Other" and *Le Corps à corps avec la mère*). An even stronger example of the valorization of the maternal is found in the work of Barbara Johnson, who stresses that it is important to recognize and valorize the fact that anyone, regardless of gender, can write from the maternal position (*A World of Difference*).

Julia Kristeva, unlike Cixous, Johnson, or Irigaray, worries about the absolute rejection or acceptance of motherhood. Along these lines, Kristeva urges us to focus on a complex question:

> How can an enquiry into the nature of motherhood lead to a better understanding of the part played in love by the woman, a role no longer that of a virgin for ever promised to the third person, God, but that of a real woman whose essentially polymorphic sexuality will sooner or later have to deal with a man, a woman, or a child? (Moi, *French* 116)

This is a question that Kristeva herself has addressed in psychoanalytically informed works such as *Tales of Love* and "Motherhood according to Giovanni Bellini" (*Desire in Language*). But Kristeva's approach is not without its critics. Susan Suleiman, for instance, generally questions the psychoanalytic framework *tout court* as adequate for the analysis of mother's writing.

Sex and gender. The poststructuralist feminist attention to language and materiality, which has given rise to a renewed concern for the maternal, has also provoked an extended debate over the meanings of "gender" and "sexual difference." Joan Scott usefully explains that gender denotes "a rejection of the biological determinism implicit in the use of such terms as 'sex' and 'sexual difference'" (28). Teresa de Lauretis puts this even more strongly when she argues that "sexual difference constrains feminist critical thought within the conceptual frame of a universal sex opposition," which makes it difficult, if not impossible, to articulate differences among and within women (*Technologies* 2). De Lauretis prefers to privilege the term "gender," which for her is not only a "classificatory term" in grammar but also "a representation of a relation" that is an ongoing social "construction" (3–5). Trinh Minh-ha similarly argues that the "notion of gender is pertinent to feminism as far as it denounces certain fundamental attitudes of imperialism and as long as it remains unsettled and unsettling" (*Woman* 113). Trinh, however, notably registers more reservations about gender than does de Lauretis; she warns that "gender, reduced to a sex-determined behavior, serves to promote inequality" (14).

Wittig takes this reservation even further and calls for the destruction of gender and sex altogether. She understands gender to be "the linguistic index of the political opposition between the sexes and of the domination of women," while sex is a political and philosophical category "that founds society as heterosexual" ("Mark" 64, "Category" 66). That is to say, within language women are marked by gender, and within society they are marked by sex. As a way of eluding this patriarchal economy of heterosexual exchange, Wittig appeals to a lesbianization of language.

Cixous takes a still different approach. Rather than focusing on the distinction between "gender" and "sexual difference" per se, she concentrates on the way sexual difference "becomes most clearly perceived at the level of *jouissance,* inasmuch as a woman's instinctual economy cannot be identified by a man or referred to the masculine economy" (*Newly* 82). And in turn, according to Cixous, the best way to engage with these different economies is through recourse to a theory of bisexuality.

By privileging bisexuality, Cixous could be doing nothing more than returning us to the binary oppositions of phallogocentric sexual difference, of male and female. That is certainly what Julia Kristeva maintains when she argues that bisexuality, no matter what qualifications accompany the term, always privileges "the totality of one of the sexes and thus [effaces] difference" (*Kristeva Reader* 209). Despite such objections, Cixous insists that bisexuality is a notion meant to call attention to the multiplicity of possible sites for desire and pleasure (*Newly,* "Laugh"). That is to say, bisexuality "doesn't annul differences but stirs them up, pursues them, increases their number" ("Laugh" 254). In this respect, Cixous's position lines up with JACQUES DERRIDA's belief in the possibility of "the multiplicity of sexually marked voices" ("Choreographies" 76).

While these poststructuralist feminists have brought us a long way, the most complex analysis of the distinction between gender and sex belongs to Judith Butler. She contends that "gender is not to culture as sex is to nature" (7). Rather, gender as a discursive element gives rise to a belief in a prediscursive, natural sex. That is to say, sex is retrospectively produced through our understanding of gender, so that in a sense gender comes before sex (7). Butler argues that in light of this counterintuitive situation, we should deconstruct the "gender fables [that] establish and circulate the misnomer of natural facts" and recognize that "it becomes impossible to separate out 'gender' from the political and cultural intersections in which it is invariably produced and maintained" (xiii, 3). Gender thus "proves to be performative." That is to say, "gender is always a doing, though not a doing by a subject who might be said to preexist the deed" (25).

The question of woman. In the wake of this dispersal of gender positions and the disruption of the economy of phallogocentric discourse, poststructuralist feminists have formulated significantly different answers to the

question, What is woman? Kristeva contends that the question simply cannot be answered; there is no such thing as "woman" (*New French,* ed. Marks and de Courtivron, 137). For Kristeva, the subject is always in process, a series of identities held accountable only to an arbitrary imposition of the law of the father; and as a way to keep open as many subject positions as possible, she favors "a concept of femininity which would take as many forms as there are women" (Moi, *French* 114).

Other poststructuralist feminists have echoed Kristeva's words. Although she takes her distance from Kristeva on some counts, Drucilla Cornell argues as Kristeva does that there is no essential woman, no possibility of sharing experience based on a common female nature (26). According to Cornell, "woman 'is' only in language, which means that her 'reality' can never be separated from the metaphors and fictions in which she is presented" (18). Similarly, Denise Riley emphasizes both plurality and identity when she contends that " 'women' is indeed an unstable category," while at the same time "to be named as a woman can be the precondition for some kinds of solidarity" (5, 99). Judith Butler takes Riley's argument a step further when she reminds us that even the plural form "women" is always incomplete and permanently a contested site of meaning. "Women" exist in relation to a matrix of differences such that "it would be wrong to assume in advance that there is a category of 'women' that simply needs to be filled in with various components of race, class, age, ethnicity, and sexuality in order to become complete" (15).

By contrast, Wittig sees nothing positive in either "woman" or "women." For her, "woman" is "the equivalent of *slave*" and only has meaning in heterosexual systems of thought and economics, in which women are defined in terms of their reproductive function ("Mark" 70). This leads Wittig to conclude that "lesbians are not women" but rather are the undivided "I" of the total subject ("Straight" 110). Irigaray takes a similarly skeptical view, arguing that "woman" is man's creation, a masquerade of femininity: "In our social order, women are 'products' used and exchanged by men. Their status is that of merchandise, 'commodities'" (*This Sex* 84). For Irigaray, woman has always been merely the *means* by which male sexual identity is confirmed, really a nonsex represented in an economy of "hom(m)osexualité," of men *(homme)* and identity or sameness *(homo).* Thus, Irigaray goes so far as to conclude that the question itself is really the wrong one:

> They should not put it, then, in the form "What is woman?" but rather, repeating / interpreting the way in which, within discourse, the feminine finds itself

defined as lack, deficiency, or as imitation and negative image of the subject, they should signify that with respect to this logic a *disruptive excess* is possible on the feminine side. (78)

Instead of creating a theory of woman, Irigaray wants "to secure a place for the feminine within sexual difference" where "the feminine cannot signify itself in any proper meaning, proper name, or concept, not even that of woman" (156). Thus, her refusal to answer the question, What is woman? can be understood as a refusal to reproduce the phallogocentric system, which keeps in place the same oppressive language and systems of representation.

Politics and ethics.   Given all the differences among the poststructuralist feminists that have been raised thus far, none has been more divisive than the division between the *political* argument about the oppression of women in society (e.g., Christine Delphy, Monique Wittig, and the journal *Questions féministes*) and the *psychoanalytic* argument about the role of gender difference in the psychic construction of the individual (e.g., Hélène Cixous, Luce Irigaray, Michèle Montrelay, and Antoinette Fouque). This split reached perhaps its most controversial moment in the French group Psychanalyse et Politique (Psych et Po), under the leadership of the psychoanalyst Antoinette Fouque. In their defense of psychoanalysis, the members of Psych et Po derided feminism for its interest in obtaining power for women within the terms of the patriarchy. Taking a more radical course, Psych et Po even went so far as to register the trademark "MLF" (Mouvement de la Libération des Femmes) for their publishing company, des femmes.

After the late 1970s, the Psych et Po group seems to have run its course, although a feminist concern for psychoanalysis and politics certainly remains. In fact, there is an increasing interest among poststructuralist feminists to bring together these two discourses. For some, such as Jacqueline Rose, the importance of deconstruction is that it serves as a hinge between the political and psychoanalytical positions in order to produce a feminist ethics.

Cixous puts the feminist concern for ethics most simply when she says, "For me, there is only ethics" ("Exchange" 138). Irigaray expands this position when she argues that to bring about the needed revolution in thought and ethics, "we must constitute a place that could be inhabited by each sex, body or flesh. This supposes a memory of the past and a hope for the future, bridging the present, and confounding the mirror-symmetry that annihilates the difference of identity" (Moi,

French 128). For Kristeva as well, the question of femininity is above all else ethical. She makes the important clarification that when she speaks of ethics she is not advocating a return to moral philosophy. Far from it: "In the event, contrary to moral philosophy, this ethics displays its own degree of *jouissance:* it is concerned both with what it can and cannot demonstrate, with sense and non-sense, with what is and is not given by the thesis, with truth and whatever resists it" (Moi, *French* 115).

The importance of ethics for feminism is that it allows us to think the social and the psychic, the questions of the political and of the subject, beside each other. As Drucilla Cornell puts it, "It is only if we see the inevitable intertwinement of justice, politics, and utopian possibility in feminism, that we can understand the promise and the necessity for the affirmation of the feminine, even if as a transition, as a threshold" (20). The ethical intervenes for deconstructive feminism as the condition of thought outside the determinations of patriarchal discourse (for which ethics would only be moral philosophy). The ethical, then, is invoked, much as *écriture féminine* is, as the site of an exploratory thought for which neither the self nor the field of the political is a fixed entity—what happens once the personal is the political, and the political is personal.

Diane Elam

See also HÉLÈNE CIXOUS, LUCE IRIGARAY, JULIA KRISTEVA, and PSYCHOANALYTIC THEORY AND CRITICISM: 3. THE POST-LACANIANS.

See bibliographies in HÉLÈNE CIXOUS, LUCE IRIGARAY, and JULIA KRISTEVA for texts by those writers.

Elizabeth Abel, ed., *Writing and Sexual Difference* (1982); Rosi Braidotti, *Patterns of Dissonance* (trans. Elizabeth Guild, 1991); Teresa Brennan, ed., *Between Feminism and Psychoanalysis* (1989); Judith Butler, *Gender Trouble* (1990); Catherine Clément, *L'Opéra, ou la défaite des femmes* (1979, Opera, or the Undoing of Women, trans. Betsy Wing, 1988); Drucilla Cornell, *Beyond Accommodation: Ethical Feminism, Deconstruction, and the Law* (1991); Teresa De Lauretis, *Alice Doesn't: Feminism, Semiotics, Cinema* (1984), *Technologies of Gender: Essays on Theory, Film, and Fiction* (1987); Christine Delphy, *Close to Home* (ed. and trans. Diana Leonard, 1984); Jacques Derrida and Christie V. McDonald, "Choreographies," *diacritics* 12 (1982); Mary Ann Doane, *The Desire to Desire: The Woman's Film of the 1940s* (1987); Claire Duchen, *Feminism in France: From May '68 to Mitterrand* (1986); Jane Gallop, *The Daughter's Seduction: Feminism and Psychoanalysis* (1982); Alice Jardine, *Gynesis: Configurations of*

Woman and Modernity (1985); Alice A. Jardine and Hester Eisenstein, eds., *The Future of Difference* (1980); Barbara Johnson, *The Critical Difference* (1980), *A World of Difference* (1987); Ann Rosalind Jones, "Writing the Body: Toward an Understanding of *L'Écriture féminine*," *Feminist Studies* 7 (1981); Dorothy Kaufmann-McCall, "Politics of Difference: The Women's Movement in France from May 1968 to Mitterrand," *Signs* 9 (1983); Sarah Kofman, *L'Énigme de la femme: La Femme dans les textes de Freud* (1980, *The Enigma of Woman*, trans. Catherine Porter, 1985), *Le Respect des femmes* (1982); Michèle Le Doeuff, "Cheveux longs, idées courtes," *L'Imaginaire philosophique* (1980, "Women and Philosophy," trans. Debbie Pope, in Moi, *French Feminist Thought*); Eugénie Lemoine-Luccioni, *Partage des femmes* (1974, *The Dividing of Women, or Women's Lot,* trans. Marie-Laure Davenport and Marie-Christine Réguir, 1987); Elaine Marks and Isabelle de Courtivron, eds., *New French Feminisms: An Anthology* (1980); Nancy K. Miller, ed., *The Poetics of Gender* (1986); Toril Moi, *Sexual/Textual Politics: Feminist Literary Theory* (1985); Toril Moi, ed., *French Feminist Thought: A Reader* (1987); Michèle Montrelay, *L'Ombre et le nom: Sur la féminité* (1977); Laura Mulvey, "Visual Pleasure and Narrative Cinema" (1975, *Visual and Other Pleasures,* 1989); Linda J. Nicholson, ed., *Feminism/Postmodernism* (1990); Denise Riley, *Am I That Name? Feminism and the Category of "Women" in History* (1988); Jacqueline Rose, *Sexuality in the Field of Vision* (1986); Joan Wallach Scott, *Gender and the Politics of History* (1988); Susan Sellers, *Language and Sexual Difference: Feminist Writing in France* (1991); Kaja Silverman, *The Acoustic Mirror: The Female Voice in Psychoanalysis and Cinema* (1988); Gayatri Chakravorty Spivak, "Displacement and the Discourse of Woman," *Displacement: Derrida and After* (ed. Mark Krupnick, 1983), *In Other Worlds: Essays in Cultural Politics* (1987); Domna Stanton, "Difference on Trial: A Critique of the Maternal Metaphor in Cixous, Irigaray, and Kristeva," *The Poetics of Gender* (ed. Miller); Susan Rubin Suleiman, "On Maternal Splitting: A Propos of Mary Gordon's *Men and Angels*," *Signs* 14 (1988); Trinh T. Minh-ha, *When the Moon Waxes Red: Representation and Cultural Politics* (1991), *Woman, Native, Other* (1989); Hélène Vivienne Wenzel, "The Text as Body/Politics: An Appreciation of Monique Wittig's Writings in Context," *Feminist Studies* 7 (1981); Monique Wittig, "The Category of Sex," *Feminist Issues* 2 (1982), "The Mark of Gender," *The Poetics of Gender* (ed. Miller), "One Is Not Born a Woman," *Feminist Issues* 1 (1981), "On the Social Contract," *Feminist Issues* 9 (1989), "The Straight Mind," *Feminist Issues* 1 (1980).

4. Materialist Feminisms

Although feminists and socialists have engaged in continuous conversations since the nineteenth century, those crosscurrents within literary theory that might be designated "materialist feminisms" have their origins in the late 1960s with various attempts to synthesize feminist politics with Marxist analyses. Early work on this projected alliance directed itself, not to questions of literary criticism and theory, but to the problem of bringing feminist questions of gender and sexuality into some form of strategic dialogue with class analysis. In keeping with subsequent developments within the women's movement, the materialist feminist problematic has extended to questions of race; nationality or ethnicity; lesbianism and sexuality; cultural identity, including religion; and the very definition of power. Conversations and disagreements among English-language writers framing a materialist feminist analysis in the United States and the United Kingdom sometimes acknowledge the influence of French feminists such as Christine Delphy and Monique Wittig but have yet to engage fully with the critiques of Marxist theory being constructed by feminists working in other international locations.

The very term "materialist feminisms" proves contentious, since there has been little general consensus whether women's interests can, or indeed should, be addressed in terms of traditional socialist and Marxist formulas. In the United Kingdom, Juliet Mitchell's groundbreaking essay "Women: The Longest Revolution" (1966), which she expanded to book length in *Woman's Estate* (1971), initiated the revision of traditional Marxist accounts by analyzing the position of women in terms not only of relations of production and private property but also of psychoanalytically based theories of sexuality and gender. Michèle Barrett's highly influential *Women's Oppression Today* (1980) insists that the way forward for feminists will necessarily involve direct engagement with and transformation of Marxist class analysis. In their editorial to the final issue of the important U.K. journal *m/f* (1978–86), Parveen Adams and Elizabeth Cowie adopt a more extreme position, stating, "As socialist-feminists we were opposed to the much discussed union of Marxism and feminism" and sought instead "to problematise the notion of sexual difference itself" through a fundamental critique of psychoanalytic categories (3). These differences should be understood as both intellectual and representative of a specific context of partisan disputes within the British Left. The situation differs in the United States, where, largely working outside the pressures of party politics but constrained by the memory of Joseph McCarthy, feminists as diverse as Lise Vogel, Zillah Eisenstein, Nancy Hartsock, and Donna Haraway identify themselves as "socialist feminists," thereby distinguishing their work from that of radical and liberal feminists, who contend that women's oppression will end with the achievement of women's power, or women's equality, within existing capitalist societies, positions strangely like the traditional Marxist view that women's oppression would end once women entered into production.

The importance of these critical positions and developments for feminist literary theory and criticism arises from their foundations in political theory, psychoanalysis, and sociology rather than from traditional literary concerns with questions of canon, form, genre, author, and *oeuvre*. Materialist feminist literary critics focus instead on key problems in language, history, ideology, determination, subjectivity, and agency from the basic perspective of a critique of the gendered character of class and race relations under international capitalism.

The significance of Juliet Mitchell's work for feminist literary theory is indirect yet fundamental. Initially trained as a literary scholar, Mitchell focuses on questions concerning the family and child rearing by means of a feminist critique of psychoanalytic theories of sexual development largely based upon a literary-critical examination of texts within the Freudian and Marxist canons. Mitchell's project, continued in her influential *Psychoanalysis and Feminism* (1974) and *Women: The Longest Revolution* (1984), which reprints her 1966 essay alongside exemplary studies of literary texts, has been to inflect feminist politics with insights from Marxism and psychoanalysis. With Jacqueline Rose (in their edition of JACQUES LACAN's *Feminine Sexuality: Jacques Lacan and the "école freudienne,"* 1982), she has continued the engagement between the psychoanalytic theories of Lacan and materialist feminist thinking in Britain (see Rosalind Coward and John Ellis, *Language and Materialism: Developments in Semiology and the Theory of the Subject,* 1977). Working from the Freudian principle that "the fate of the adult personality can be largely decided in the initial months of life" and the Marxist principle of dialectical materialism that "human society is, and always will be, full of contradictions" (*Woman's Estate* 118, 90), Mitchell has recently criticized "the voluntarist underestimation of the great difficulty of psychic change," since, she argues, "the best-cared for child has a caretaker who has grown up with problems—this will always be the case. And these problems will be transmitted in an uneven way" (McRobbie 87). Mitchell's consistent emphasis upon reading critically Marxist, Freudian, and

Lacanian discourses on sexuality and socialization leads to questions of ideology and literary representation that are of considerable importance for such feminist literary studies as Jacqueline Rose's *Sexuality in the Field of Vision* (1986) and Jane Gallop's *The Daughter's Seduction: Feminism and Psychoanalysis* (1982), which takes *Psychoanalysis and Feminism* as its "point of departure" (xiii).

For a sociologist of knowledge like Michèle Barrett, literary questions are contingent rather than central. Her treatment of ideology in *Women's Oppression Today,* however, has been highly influential among feminist literary theorists. According to Barrett, the political urgencies of women's liberation bear directly on the need for a feminist analysis of "culture," and it is here that the problematic relationship of Marxism and feminism engages questions important to literary theory, in particular questions of aesthetics, subjectivity, and ideology. In "Feminism and the Definition of Cultural Politics," her 1980 lecture to the Communist University of London, Barrett addresses three issues of direct importance to materialist feminist literary theory: 1) the indeterminacy of artistic and literary meaning, 2) the relationship between women's art and feminist art, and 3) the problem of judging aesthetic value and pleasure. Following RAYMOND WILLIAMS, Barrett focuses on the literary problem of "signification," the "systems of signs . . . through which meaning is constructed, represented, consumed and reproduced" (38). Artistic and literary meanings are determinable but not fixed, since meaning "may depend on who is reading or receiving . . . and how they do so" (39). This is not an argument for total indeterminacy, however, since for Barrett every work does carry a "dominant, or preferred, reading" (42) that limits the range of possible meanings. Barrett regards literary texts, art objects, and dramatic performances as marked by inner contradictions that cannot easily be adjudicated by reference to the artist's life or intentions. While agreeing with Rosalind Coward that women's art is not necessarily feminist, since feminism "is an alignment of political interests and not a shared female experience" (42), Barrett is reluctant to follow Coward and abandon female experience entirely. She does, however, argue that feminist political interests are not necessarily served by the recovery of women's past artistic achievements or even by self-proclaimed feminist artworks like Judy Chicago's *The Dinner Party.*

Barrett approaches the question how we distinguish cultural production in general from "art" within the framework of a historical materialist critique of ideology: "It is only the degradation of work under capitalist relations of production, including the degree to which workers have been stripped of mental control over their labour, that makes us perceive such a huge gulf between work and what we call 'creative' work" (48–49). Arguing that feminists ignore the dual question of aesthetic value and pleasure to their peril, Barrett finds the traditional assumption that value judgments can and should be made a highly suspicious assumption for feminist politics, since such judgments about "value" invariably tend to reinforce the values of the dominant classes as apparently natural and universal.

Barrett's materialist aesthetics seeks to democratize the relation between the producer and the consumer of art. Skills, though socially defined, are not innate but acquired and therefore improvable, while the imaginative rendering of social life in works of art and literature is typically foreclosed in much feminist criticism by an undue emphasis upon the work's content as unmediated representation. Barrett emphasizes the active role of the viewer/reader and suggests that there is no intrinsic merit in avant-garde forms; nor are the pleasures to be obtained from politically "regressive" art forms (TV soap operas, romances) to be rejected by feminists out of hand. Not only, she contends, can the feminist desire to reject the sexism of dominant cultural productions and to establish feminist alternatives prevent us from understanding our desires but the energy directed at developing alternatives might be used to develop "strategies directed at more fundamental changes" (56). Politics comes first for Barrett, since literature and art help constitute social life but do not determine it: "Cultural politics, and feminist art, are important precisely because we are not the helpless victims of oppressive ideology. We take some responsibility for the cultural meaning of gender and it is up to us all to change it" (58).

If for Barrett questions of literature, art, and aesthetic pleasure are important but not determining—there remain those "more fundamental changes" to be worked out—for Rosalind Coward, Catherine Belsey, Toril Moi, and Cora Kaplan the critical study of literary texts is of primary importance to the development and enunciation of a feminist politics firmly committed to socialism. In *Patriarchal Precedents* (1983), Coward critically historicizes from a feminist perspective the various disciplines within which sexual relations have traditionally been studied. For Coward, Lacan's observation that the unconscious is structured like a language provides the basis for a materialist feminist approach to SEMIOTICS that addresses how different forms of popular culture help construct gendered social subjects in ways that perpetuate oppressive social relations (see *Female Desire,* 1984). Belsey's *Critical Practice* (1980) argues that "the recurrent

suppression of the role of language" in traditional literary criticism is an ideological move by which the " 'correct' reading" of a text installs the reader as "transcendent subject addressed by an autonomous and authoritative author" (55). Belsey develops this bringing together of Lacanian and Althusserian theories of the subject in *The Subject of Tragedy* (1987), which rereads English Renaissance drama from a materialist feminist perspective, arguing that the emergence of liberal ideologies during the capitalist era has required the "interpellation" of women as, in part, willing subjects of their own oppression in relation to a normative and universal male Self. This critique of liberal humanism emphasizes the political importance of history, as well as the need for readings of literary texts against the grain of their ideological commitments. Preferring VIRGINIA WOOLF's modernist DECONSTRUCTION of the unitary self and the critique of the subject found in the French poststructuralists, Moi's *Sexual/Textual Politics* (1985) challenges the humanist presuppositions informing the influential feminist literary criticism of Elaine Showalter, Sandra Gilbert and Susan Gubar, Annette Kolodny, and Myra Jehlen. In their antisexist focus on female authors and readers, Moi contends, feminist literary critics adopt what Marcia Holly calls a "noncontradictory perception of the world" (Moi 10) that mystifies rather than disables patriarchal assumptions by positing for itself a place outside ideology. Celebrating women writers and readers as such reinscribes the unitary self and thereby begs the political questions of agency and resistance, "of how it is that some women manage to counter patriarchal strategies despite the odds stacked against them" (64). The primacy of such political concerns defined the project of the U.K. Marxist-Feminist Literary Collective (1976–78/79), which, Kaplan explains, explored "the contradictions and difficulties of working collectively in a field that prized the individual and original insight above any other," causing members to confront "how hard it was to 'let go' of a private property in ideas and language" (63). In Kaplan's work, and in that of Mary Jacobus and Penny Boumelha, the collective's interest "in developing a Marxist feminist analysis of literature" (61) continues, producing class-sensitive critiques of sexual ideology in various literary texts of the postindustrial era (in contrast to Belsey's focus on the literature of the early capitalist period).

Kaplan writes that her experience in the collective enabled her to overcome her fear of "theory," an antipathy that persists among the U.S. feminist literary critics Moi examines. Not all U.S. feminist critics, however, share this fear. Critiques of the disciplines of literary history and criticism from a class- as well as gender-conscious perspective have been undertaken by Lillian Robinson (*Sex, Class, and Culture,* 1978) and Jane Marcus ("The Asylums of Antaeus: Women, War, and Madness—Is There a Feminist Fetishism?" *The New Historicism,* ed. H. Aram Veeser, 1989). Gayle Rubin's much-cited essay, "The Traffic in Women" (1975), remains a useful reading of KARL MARX AND FRIEDRICH ENGELS, CLAUDE LÉVI-STRAUSS, and Lacan in the interests of rethinking the sex-gender system within social relations. Pioneering articles by Ann Rosalind Jones ("Writing the Body: Toward an Understanding of *l'écriture féminine,*" *Feminist Studies* 7 [1981]) and Biddy Martin ("Feminism, Criticism, and Foucault," *New German Critique* 27 [1982]) brought French feminism and Foucauldian theory to bear upon feminist criticism in the United States, while in 1981 Judith Newton's *Women, Power, and Subversion: Social Strategies in Women's Fiction, 1780–1860* raised questions concerning the class character of gender ideology for literary historians (see also subsequent work by Nancy Armstrong, Catherine Gallagher, and Mary Poovey). Written with Deborah Rosenfelt, Newton's 1985 introduction to *Feminist Criticism and Social Change* enthusiastically proclaims the emergence of "materialist feminist criticism" in a collection that reprints important studies by, among others, Barrett, Belsey, Jones, and the editors. In challenging the increasing institutional influence of liberal feminism in the later 1980s, the theoretical perspective of the introduction privileges literature over politics, thereby reversing the emphasis of many of its contributors. This is most evident in the selection and discussion of European Marxist feminists who address cultural issues pertaining to literature and the silence over important U.S. contributors to the Marxist feminist problematic working in political science (Zillah Eisenstein, Nancy Hartsock), sociology (Lise Vogel), economics (Heidi Hartmann), philosophy (Marilyn Frye, Alison Jaggar), and legal theory (Catharine MacKinnon).

Some of the most important U.S. contributions to materialist feminist criticism have come from socialists and feminists working directly with the interrelated literary problems of sexuality, racial difference, the politics of language, and postcoloniality, questions barely addressed by U.K. materialist feminists. The autobiographical essays by Elly Bulkin, Minnie Bruce Pratt, and Barbara Smith (*Yours in Struggle: Three Feminist Perspectives on Anti-Semitism and Racism,* 1984) and recent literary studies by Biddy Martin ("Lesbian Identity and Autobiographical Difference[s]," *Life/Lines: Theorizing Women's Autobiography,* ed. Bella Brodzki and Celeste Schenck,

1988), Katie King ("Audre Lorde's Lacquered Layerings: The Lesbian Bar as a Site of Literary Production," *Cultural Studies* 2 [1988]), and other lesbian feminists have fundamentally challenged the heterosexist biases and presuppositions of both capitalist ideology and socialist critique. Donna Haraway's influential "Manifesto for Cyborgs: Science, Technology, and Socialist Feminism in the 1980s" (*Socialist Review* 80 [1985]), reprinted with other essays in *Simians, Cyborgs, and Women* (1991), explores how recent developments in the technologies of the body destabilize not only gender categories but also the unity of self and body, with a view to constructing a socialist-feminist mythology of the future. Her *Primate Visions: Gender, Race, and Nature in the World of Modern Science* (1989) analyzes the interconnections of gender and racial ideologies within the history of primatology as a representative twentieth-century science. From *Ain't I a Woman: Black Women and Feminism* (1981) through *Feminist Theory: From Margin to Center* (1984) and *Yearning: Race, Gender, and Cultural Politics* (1990), bell hooks (Gloria Watkins) documents how the history of class and race blindness among U.S. feminists continues to affect the work of feminist scholars and cultural critics. Valerie Smith ("Gender and Afro-Americanist Literary Theory and Criticism," *Speaking of Gender,* ed. Elaine Showalter, 1989) analyzes the institutional pressures toward commodification that specifically affect African-American feminist critics. From the perspective of Derridean deconstruction, the essays in GAYATRI CHAKRAVORTY SPIVAK's *In Other Worlds* (1987) and the interviews in *The Post-Colonial Critic: Interviews, Strategies, Dialogues* (ed. Sarah Harasym, 1990) emphasize the complicities and dangerous instabilities of "class," "gender," and "race" among the analytical languages needed to negotiate a global politics that will destabilize the continuing logic of capitalism in the contemporary postcolonial era. Also working from a poststructuralist problematic, Hortense Spillers argues that African-American women writers, and women generally, are betrayed by liberal feminist literary critics who rely on master narratives that reinscribe legitimacy crises based on patriarchal and imperialist myths of Oedipal anxiety ("A Hateful Passion," 1983; "Mama's Baby, Papa's Maybe," 1987). Barbara Harlow's *Resistance Literature* (1987) examines literary texts from West Asia, Africa, and South and Central America from a race-conscious materialist feminist perspective. Not all race-sensitive U.S. feminist critics have been sympathetic to recent developments in literary theory, however; Barbara Christian (whose work is included by Newton and Rosenfelt) has raised her influential voice against "theory," by which she means poststructuralism, in "The Race for Theory" (1987; *Gender and Theory,* ed. Linda Kauffman, 1989).

Materialist feminist critics in the United Kingdom and the United States have contributed significantly to FILM THEORY, semiotics, and the study of popular culture, though work in these fields has often developed independently of socialist politics and outside of traditional Marxist analytical categories. A co-editor of and contributor to the important collection of essays *Feminism and Materialism* (1978), Annette Kuhn has subsequently developed theories of feminist film production and criticism that focus on questions of representation, ideology, and sexuality (*Women's Pictures: Feminism and Cinema,* 1982; *The Power of the Image: Essays on Representation and Sexuality,* 1985). In *The Subject of Semiotics* (1983), Kaja Silverman draws heavily on critical readings of Althusserian Marxism and the work of Foucault to examine problems in film theory, ideology, and aesthetic pleasure from a feminist perspective, as does Teresa de Lauretis in *Alice Doesn't: Feminism, Semiotics, Cinema* (1984) and *Technologies of Gender* (1987). Tania Modleski's important *Loving with a Vengeance* (1982), which employs a class-conscious feminist critique of psychoanalysis to explore subject formation in mass-market romances, Gothics, and soap operas aimed at female audiences; Terry Lovell's *Pictures of Reality: Aesthetics, Politics, and Pleasure* (1982) and *Consuming Fiction* (1987); Janice Radway's ethnographic *Reading the Romance: Women, Patriarchy, and Popular Literature* (1984); and Meaghan Morris's *The Pirate's Fiancée: Feminism, Reading, Postmodernism* (1988) have helped open up the study of popular genres to politically sophisticated feminist analysis. Although little concerned with literary or filmic texts, Diane Macdonnell's *Theories of Discourse: An Introduction* (1986) offers a lucid Marxist and feminist introduction to Louis Althusser, Michel Foucault, and Michel Pêcheux. Janet Wolff's *The Social Production of Art* (1981) and *Feminine Sentences: Essays on Women and Culture* (1990) and Rita Felski's *Beyond Feminist Aesthetics: Feminist Literature and Social Change* (1989) provide rigorous arguments for the inseparability of any effective feminist cultural politics from social analysis. Important materialist feminist essays in theory, film studies, semiotics, and popular culture can be found in the U.K. journals *Feminist Review, I&C* (formerly *Ideology and Consciousness*), *LTP, m/f, New Left Review, Oxford Literary Review, Red Letters,* and *Screen* and the U.S. journals *Camera Obscura, Cultural Critique, enclitic, Feminist Issues, Feminist Studies, Genders, Jump Cut, Signs,* and *Socialist Review.*

While feminist theorists such as Kuhn, de Lauretis, Modleski, Silverman, and Morris are critical of the unitary self of liberal feminism and insist on the materiality of signifying practices (such as film and mass fiction) in the ideological construction of gender, their concern with gender and subjectivity all but abandons the basic materialist questions of history, class, and the economic that variously remain crucial in Mitchell, Barrett, Coward, Belsey, Kaplan, Haraway, Felski, King, Lovell, Martin, Spivak, Spillers, and Wolff. It may be that the conversations, to use King's term, of the 1970s and early 1980s attempting to bring feminism into dialogue with Marxism are over, doomed from the start. But in Barrett's concern with the aesthetic, ideological, and class bases of women's oppression; in Belsey's and Kaplan's analyses of the historical constructions of female subjectivity in literary texts by and about women; in Martin's and King's theoretical examinations of lesbianism and sexuality; in Spivak's materialist-deconstructionist readings of the global texts of postcoloniality via *Capital;* in Spillers's critique of Judeo-Christian, Oedipal, imperialist historiography; and in Haraway's excavations of the ideology of what we so often mistake for "nature" or scientific "truth," many important questions raised by those conversations continue to generate new problems demanding the attention of feminists engaged in the construction of a leftist theory and practice of literary criticism.

Donna Landry and Gerald MacLean

See also AFRICAN-AMERICAN THEORY AND CRITICISM, GAY THEORY AND CRITICISM: 1. GAY MALE and 2. LESBIAN, and MARXIST THEORY AND CRITICISM: 2. STRUCTURALIST MARXISM.

Parveen Adams and Elizabeth Cowie, "The Last Issue between Us," *m/f* 11/12 (1986); Michèle Barrett, "Feminism and the Definition of Cultural Politics," *Feminism, Culture, and Politics* (ed. Rosalind Brunt and Caroline Rowan, 1982), *Women's Oppression Today: Problems in Marxist Feminist Analysis* (1980, rev. ed., *Women's Oppression Today: The Marxist/Feminist Encounter,* 1988); Catherine Belsey, *Critical Practice* (1980), *The Subject of Tragedy: Identity and Difference in Renaissance Drama* (1987); Rosalind Coward, *Female Desire: Women's Sexuality Today* (1984); Teresa de Lauretis, *Technologies of Gender: Essays on Theory, Film, and Fiction* (1987); Donna J. Haraway, *Simians, Cyborgs, and Women: The Reinvention of Nature* (1991); Cora Kaplan, *Sea Changes: Culture and Feminism* (1986); Annette Kuhn and AnnMarie Wolpe, eds., *Feminism and Materialism: Women and Modes of Production* (1978); Angela McRobbie, "An Interview with Juliet

Mitchell," *New Left Review* 170 (1988); Juliet Mitchell, *Psychoanalysis and Feminism* (1974), *Woman's Estate* (1971), "Women: The Longest Revolution," *New Left Review* 40 (1966), *Women: The Longest Revolution* (1984); Tania Modleski, *Loving with a Vengeance: Mass-Produced Fantasies for Women* (1982); Toril Moi, *Sexual/Textual Politics: Feminist Literary Theory* (1985); Judith Newton and Deborah Rosenfelt, eds., *Feminist Criticism and Social Change: Sex, Class, and Race in Literature and Culture* (1985); Gayle Rubin, "The Traffic in Women: Notes on the 'Political Economy' of Sex," *Toward an Anthropology of Women* (ed. Rayna R. Reiter, 1975); Hortense J. Spillers, "A Hateful Passion, a Lost Love," *Feminist Studies* 9 (1983), "Mama's Baby, Papa's Maybe: An American Grammar Book," *diacritics* 17 (1987); Gayatri Chakravorty Spivak, *In Other Worlds: Essays in Cultural Politics* (1987).

FICTION THEORY AND CRITICISM

1. Seventeenth- and Eighteenth-Century British

Seventeenth- and early eighteenth-century English readers had plenty of fiction to choose from, but authors (and critics) had no clear theoretical scheme or stable nomenclature for this diverse body of narrative. Most critical discussion of fiction occurs in short prefaces, which are perhaps booksellers' promotions as much as authors' defenses but are clearly reflections of a widespread feeling that fiction, precisely because it gives so much pleasure, is morally suspect and culturally retrograde. Such rationalizing points, as well, to the increasing popularity of a new and not clearly understood kind of fiction. In prefaces attached to fictional works that claimed serious moral purpose, two opposing terms recur: "true history" and "romance." Writers of romance in the late seventeenth century tend to justify their work by echoing Renaissance commonplaces derived from ARISTOTLE's *Poetics* that history is limited to the factual, while romance, in the words of Roger Boyle (1621–79), author of *Parthenissa, A Romance* (1655), "affords a larger field for instruction and invention" (Barnett 4). Boyle's defense of romance invokes an opposition between the moral effects of historical veracity and fictional arrangement that persists to the end of the eighteenth century. For Boyle, "tis not the truth of a wise counsel or ingenious design which invites men to an imitation thereof but the rationality and probability of it, whether it be real or imaginary" (4). But for the great majority of

defenders of fiction until the mid-eighteenth century, literal, historical truth gives narrative a moral efficacy and authority that overtly fictional instances, no matter how cogent, cannot match.

Aphra Behn (1640–89), for example, begins *Oroonoko; or The Royal Slave* (1678) by insisting that Oroonoko is no "feign'd Hero whose Life and Fortunes Fancy may manage at the Poet's Pleasure" (129). Behn asks the reader to believe that her novel is largely an eyewitness account, supplemented by the personal testimony of the hero himself. In part, truth claims such as Behn's respond to a traditional suspicion of fiction as a lie that may give pleasure but not moral instruction. But such insistence on documentary veracity may also have grown out of the hunger of a growing literate public for "news," information about a world conceived as an expanding accumulation of facts and data whose significance and validity lay precisely in their literal and particularized truth rather than in that generalized moral validity that an earlier consciousness thought of as a justification for fiction.

The early eighteenth century produced a flood of topical journalism: broadsides and pamphlets that offered accounts of sensational crimes and domestic violence, somewhat longer lives of notorious criminals, including pirates and highwaymen, and many accounts of travels to exotic places. The advertised appeal of this material was its rare or unusual singularity and its accompanying realistic probability. The preface to Daniel Defoe's (1661–1731) *Robinson Crusoe* (1719) is the most prominent fictional instance of this substantially new double claim. Crusoe is a "private Man" whose adventures are "worth making Publick," says the preface, because of its "Wonders . . . the Life of one Man being scarce capable of greater Variety" (3). In spite of the book's phenomenal popularity, Defoe thought it necessary to have Crusoe himself affirm in the preface to the sequel, *The Farther Adventures of Robinson Crusoe* (1719), that the book was not a "romance" and that "all the Endeavours of envious People . . . to search it for Errors in Geography, Inconsistency in the Relation, and Contradictions in the Fact, have proved abortive, and as impotent as malicious" (258). In 1720, when Defoe issued his *Serious Reflections during the Life and Surprising Adventures of Robinson Crusoe,* he again denied in the face of "the envious and ill-disposed Part of the World" that his book was a romance and insisted again that it was "all historical and true in Fact" (259, 260).

To the confusion of later readers, Crusoe claims that this "real Life of eight and twenty Years, spent in the most wandring desolate and afflicting Circumstances that ever Man went through" (261), is also allegorical, a moral parable. Robinson Crusoe says his story recommends and illustrates certain moral virtues—Patience, Application, Resolution—but Daniel Defoe affirms that Crusoe's story is an allegory of his own life. Take all the narrative's incidents, the preface declares as Defoe slips into a revealing inconsistency, and "there's not a Circumstance in the imaginary Story, but has its just Allusion to a real Story" (261), the life of "a Man alive, and well known too, the Actions of whose Life are the just Subject of these Volumes" (259–60).

Ultimately incoherent, Defoe's preface points to his instinctive grasp of what early eighteenth-century fiction seems to have implied for its readers, if not for its critics. Fiction such as *Robinson Crusoe* tries to balance its intensely exotic particularity against a unifying, generalized moral pattern. Defoe's fantastic, if oblique, claim that the novel is also an allegory of his own life is an insightful confusion, since the novel in its later manifestations will often reveal its origins in an author's experiences as a projection of authorial personality. In eighteenth-century critical speculation, such insights are rare and indeed forbidden by the general moral purposes thought proper to fiction.

Defoe's three prefaces underline the lingering defensiveness of narrative perceived by its critics as merely a popular and degraded modern version of romance. That many readers eagerly consumed books like Defoe's is evident from the alarm voiced by critics and moralists through the century. Charles Gildon (1665–1721), an irascible pamphleteer and political enemy of Defoe's, complained bitterly that "there is not an old Woman that can go to the Price of it, but buys thy Life and Adventures, and leaves it as a Legacy, with the *Pilgrim's Progress,* the *Practice of Piety,* and *God's Revenge against Murther,* to her Posterity" (Defoe, *Robinson Crusoe* 280). Two years later, Defoe began the preface to *Moll Flanders* (1722) by noting that "the World is so taken up of late with Novels and Romances, that it will be hard for a private History to be taken for genuine" (3). In their cultivation of documentary authenticity and in their studied formlessness, mimicking the randomness of everyday life, Defoe's novels are pseudo-autobiographies and thus project a positive dread of overt fictionality. Of course, they also offer readers the pleasures of vicarious identification with improbably resilient and extravagantly successful characters, who are to that extent manifestly fictional individuals.

Some practitioners in the early years of the eighteenth century tried to make a virtue of fiction's evolution from older, aristocratic romance to the demotic briskness of novels, as they were beginning to be called. In his preface to *Incognita: Or, Love and Duty Reconciled: A Novel* (1692), William Congreve (1670–1729) distinguished novels from romances by the distinctively modest pleasure they offered, that "more familiar nature" that delighted "with accidents and odd events, but not such as are wholly unusual or unpresidented, such which not being so distant from our belief bring also the pleasure nearer us" (Barnett 18). In the same vein, Mary Delarivier Manley's (1663–1724) preface to *The Secret History of Queen Zarah and the Zarazians* (1705) finds that "little Histories" of the sort she offers in her collection of scandalous anecdotes about Sarah, duchess of Marlborough, have banished the enormous seventeenth-century French romances, which had enjoyed considerable popularity in England after the Restoration. Manley says that her short pieces suit the impetuous humor of the English, who "have naturally no taste for long-winded performances, for they have no sooner begun a book but they desire to see the end of it" (22). In place of complicated and manifestly unreal romance, Manley promises a readable and undemanding story produced by a moderate realism whereby the "fabulous adventures" of the "ancient Romances" are replaced by "passions, virtues or vices, which resemble humanity" (24). The reader, she explains, is inspired "with curiosity and a certain impatient desire to see the end of the accidents" (24). But even as she underscores the reader's excited involvement, Manley affirms the conventional didactic purposes of narrative to recommend virtue and discourage vice. In practice, what Manley's scandal chronicles (including her popular *Secret Memoirs and Manners of several Persons of Quality, of Both Sexes from the New Atalantis,* 1709) offer is sensationalized "news" about prominent politicians. She admits as much in her preface, where she notes that virtue and vice are exemplified by inspiration and engagement rather than by "moral reflections, maxims, and sentences," which are "more proper in discourses for instructions than in Historical Novels" (26).

In Manley's fiction, didactic clarity is consistently buried by an avalanche of sexual fantasy and emotional melodrama, qualities purveyed in large quantities through the 1720s and 1730s by the amatory novella, whose most prolific producer was Manley's successor, Eliza Haywood (1693–1756). In her dedication to *The Fatal Secret, or Constancy in Distress* (1724), Haywood defiantly makes a virtue out of her disadvantages as a woman writer and in the process points ahead to a recurring emphasis in mid-century criticism of fiction. As a woman, Haywood is "depriv'd of those Advantages of Education which the other Sex enjoy," and she can write only about love, "that which Nature is not negligent to

teach us." The female novelist requires no literary training and "no general Conversation, no Application; a
shady Grove and purling Stream are all Things that's
necessary to give us an Idea of the tender Passion." Experienced professional that she was, Haywood may not
have been entirely serious in this preface, but her claims
appeal to a conception of the novelist as essentially
artless and therefore powerful. Twenty-five years later, in
Tom Jones (1749), Henry Fielding (1707–54) registered his
annoyance with such an approach to narrative as he
contemplated the "romances and novels with which the
world abounds" and remarked that for their composition "nothing is necessary but paper, pens, and ink, with
the manual capacity of using them" (bk. 9, ch. 1).

From the opening pages of *Tom Jones,* Fielding's
reader is offered an entity that requires more than pen-
manship to produce; his novel is an elaborately constructed and self-consciously literary artifact, what its
author had earlier called, in the preface to *Joseph Andrews*
(1742), a "comic epic-poem in prose." In that preface and
in the various introductory chapters in *Tom Jones,* Fielding outlines the eighteenth century's most explicit theory of fiction, a theory with two related emphases.
Although he claims originality and sets himself up in
Tom Jones as "the founder of a new province of writing"
(bk. 2, ch. 1), Fielding insists that he is maintaining continuity with the ancient literary genres. His chief justification for fiction is that like classical literature, it
offers a knowledge of human nature conceived as universal and uniform, recurrent through superficial historical changes. But all his novels also strive for a
sociohistorical comprehensiveness, and there is something of an implicit tension between his theory and
practice, between the generalizing, ahistorical moral-
psychological assertions of his theory and his novels'
comprehensive and particularized historical ambitions.
In *Joseph Andrews* and especially in *Tom Jones,* Fielding
employs an authoritative narrator who steers readers
through this central ambiguity; but his scattered theoretical remarks point to his sense of a deep instability
in his theory of fiction.

But Fielding's novels, with their built-in critical theory of fiction, establish one main tradition of English
fiction: the broadly comprehensive narrative that places
the protagonist's career against a panoramic social back-
drop. Fielding's less cerebral major rival, Tobias Smollett
(1721–71), offered in the dedication to *Ferdinand, Count
Fathom* (1753) a working definition that describes this
major strand of eighteenth-century novelistic practice
and treats its problems as essentially artistic and structural:

A Novel is a large diffused picture, comprehending the
characters of life, disposed in different groups, and
exhibited in various attitudes, for the purposes of an
uniform plan, and general occurrence, to which every
individuals figure is subservient. But his plan cannot
be executed with propriety, probability or success,
without a principal personage to attract the attention,
untie the incidents, unwind the clue of the labyrinth,
and at last close the scene by virtue of his own importance. (Barnett 65)

Like Hogarth's paintings, Fielding's and Smollett's novels seek to render contemporary life in its disorderly
plenitude but also to resolve it into artistic and moral
pattern. Their contemporaries tended to focus on their
novels' realism and to worry that it blurred moral distinctions. In *Rambler* essay number 4, published in
March 1750, the year after the great success of *Tom Jones*
and of Smollett's *Roderick Random,* SAMUEL JOHNSON
(1709–84) admired the didactic effectiveness of "these
familiar histories," which in their realism "convey the
knowledge of vice and virtue with more efficacy than
axioms and definitions" (Barnett 69). Johnson identified
the chief audience of fiction as "the young, the ignorant,
and the idle" and stressed the moral dangers in its
"power of example," which can "take possession of the
memory by a kind of violence and produce effects
almost without the intervention of the will" (69). So
Johnson counseled a restrained fictional representation
that encouraged virtue and depicted vice only in order
to "raise hatred [of it] by the malignity of its practices
and contempt by the meanness of its stratagems."

Johnson's warnings are eloquent testimony to what
he and his contemporaries saw as the disturbing power
of a new kind of fiction, and his denunciation of Fielding's novels and his praise of Samuel Richardson's (1689–
1761) in conversations with his biographer, James Boswell,
articulate a theory of two opposing fictional models.
Richardson, says Johnson, drew "characters of nature,"
whereas Fielding's are "characters only of manners"
(Boswell 2:49), superficial and limited to outward sociohistorical accidents. When Boswell countered this disparagement by saying that Fielding drew "very natural
pictures of human life," Johnson replied that Fielding
depicted "low life" and that "there is more knowledge of
the heart in one letter of Richardson's than in all *Tom
Jones*" (2:174). Richardson's originality, for Johnson and
others, lay in fact beyond the didactic purposes both
critics and novelists cherished. The "nature" Richardson
uniquely represented for Johnson was a psychological
intensity and moral complexity that Fielding and Smollett necessarily slighted in favor of social and moral

breadth. In 1778 Frances Burney (1752–1840), in the preface to her first novel, *Evelina,* tried to balance these concepts, describing her book as an attempt "to draw characters from nature, though not from life, and to mark the manners of the times" (Barnett 139). Characters worth paying attention to, she implies, are drawn from a "nature" that is somehow separate from "manners," which are implicitly a surface reality to be rendered by the novelist in order to be corrected by the revelation of the natural.

But this "nature" that fiction sought to represent presented serious problems for the regulated moralism Johnson championed. In spite of his heavily didactic intentions, Richardson found that many readers were morally confused by his depiction of his saintly heroine and rakish villain, Clarissa and Lovelace. Richardson's characters enact a struggle for dominance over each other as much as an exemplary battle between vice and virtue, and his first readers tended to stray from the neatness of his didactic model, drawn to Lovelace or suspicious of Clarissa's motives. Hoping to curb what he saw as wayward reading, Richardson revised the novel to make the moral contrast stronger and clearer, fighting against the essential drift of his genius for representing "nature." As part of this same revision of his novel in the face of many readers' demands for a happy ending, Richardson made elaborate literary claims for *Clarissa,* adding to the 1751 fourth edition a postscript that justified the novel (and its violation of poetic justice with the death of Clarissa) in terms of neoclassical literary theory as a new kind of Christian tragedy. Partly Richardson's defensive self-consciousness as a non-learned writer, such a claim points as well to his alarming experience of his own fiction's forceful rendering of the will to power of individual personalities. But finally in his postscript, Richardson bases his defense of *Clarissa,* of its inordinate length and its epistolary form, on the "necessity to be very circumstantial and minute in order to preserve and maintain that air of probability which is necessary to be maintained in a Story designed to represent real life" (bk. 4, 564).

Realistic innovation is, in fact, the sine qua non for all eighteenth-century appraisal of fiction, and in spite of his dismay over his readers' misinterpretations, Richardson does not waver in his commitment to evoking what turns out to be a disturbing and ambiguous truth. Romance and its remote improbabilities, many critic-novelists insist, must be banished, an insistence that points to the unsettling persistence of romance, both in the continued popularity of traditional romances into the late eighteenth century and in the emergence of the "Gothic" novel just after the middle of the century. Thus Horace Walpole (1717–97) noted in the preface to the second edition of his pioneering Gothic novel, *The Castle of Otranto* (1765), that modern "romance" had "by a strict adherence to common life" repressed "the powers of fancy" (Barnett 113). Walpole's attempt was to "conduct the mortal agents in his drama according to the rules of probability" (114). One might say that all eighteenth-century criticism of fiction consists in a similar project to reconcile a powerful and persistent appetite in readers for the amoral pleasures of romance with the moral-historical imperatives summed up in realism and probability that are its corrective opposites.

It is therefore fitting that the first book-length critical treatise on fiction in the eighteenth century should be Clara Reeve's (1729–1807) *Progress of Romance* (1785). Presented as a series of colloquies among three friends, the book proposes, in the words of Reeve's mouthpiece, Euphrasia, "to trace Romance to its Origin, to follow its progress . . . to shew how the modern Novel sprung up out of its ruins" (8). Euphrasia presents a well-informed defense and literary history of romance that describes its origins in epic poetry and its early manifestation in the Greek romances of antiquity, its medieval flowering, and its decadence in seventeenth-century French heroic romance. Reeve offers this exact history of romance in order to establish it as the essential ground for the modern novel but also to distinguish the two as clearly as possible and to mark the crucial differences for those who would confound the two in order to disparage the novel. "The Romance is an heroic fable, which treats of fabulous persons and things.—The Novel is a picture of real life and manners, and of the times in which it is written" (111). What the novel can uniquely do is to "represent every scene, in so easy and natural a manner, and to make them appear so probable, as to deceive us into a persuasion (at least while we are reading) that all is real, until we are affected by the joys of distresses, of the persons in the story, as if they were our own" (111). Reeve's dialogue thus articulates and seeks to reconcile the opposition between romance and the novel that shapes eighteenth-century critical discussion of fiction. For Reeve the novel is not a repudiation but an evolution from romance; its involving realism and immediacy mark the novel as distinct, but romance at its best inculcated "principles of virtue and honour" and deserves respect and preservation.

John J. Richetti

See also BRITISH THEORY AND CRITICISM: 1. EARLY EIGHTEENTH CENTURY and 2. LATE EIGHTEENTH CENTURY.

George L. Barnett, ed., *Eighteenth-Century British Novelists on the Novel* (1968); Aphra Behn, *The Works of Aphra Behn* (ed. Montague Summers, 1915); James Boswell, *Boswell's Life of Johnson* (ed. George Birkbeck Hill, 6 vols., 1887, rev. L. F. Powell, 1934–50); Daniel Defoe, *Moll Flanders* (ed. Edward Kelly, 1973), *Robinson Crusoe* (ed. Michael Shinagel, 1975); Henry Fielding, *Joseph Andrews* (ed. Martin Battestin, 1967), *Tom Jones* (ed. Martin Battestin, 1975); Charles Gildon, *The Life and Strange Surprizing Adventures of Mr. D—— De F——* (1719); Clara Reeve, *The Progress of Romance* (1785); Samuel Richardson, *Clarissa* (ed. John Butt, 1962).

J. M. Armistead, ed., *The First English Novelists: Essays in Understanding* (1985); Lennard Davis, *Factual Fictions: The Origins of the English Novel* (1983); J. Paul Hunter, *Before Novels: The Cultural Contexts of Eighteenth-Century Fiction* (1990); Michael McKeon, *The Origins of the Novel, 1600–1740* (1987); Thomas E. Maresca, *Epic to Novel* (1974); Ronald Paulson, *Satire and the Novel in Eighteenth-Century England* (1967); John J. Richetti, *Popular Fiction before Richardson: Narrative Patterns, 1700–1739* (1969); Sheldon Sacks, *Fiction and the Shape of Belief* (1964); Paul Salzman, *English Prose Fiction, 1558–1700* (1985); Ian Watt, *The Rise of the Novel: Studies in Defoe, Richardson, and Fielding* (1957).

2. Nineteenth-Century British and American

For more than half of the twentieth century literary criticism treated the nineteenth century's realist and naturalist fiction as an antitheoretical project, self-evident in aim and form. But what Tzvetan Todorov says about "the fantastic," an innovative mode in the nineteenth century—that it "initiated its own theory" (154)—may well apply to all nineteenth-century modes.

The theory underpinning Walter Scott's practice of historical novel-writing determines the content and form of three succeeding generations of novelists. A restatement of Scott's theory is therefore in order. To renew the scope and wonder of epic in an age skeptical of marvels and heroism, Scott made the plausibilities of modern history epic's new content. "Modern" history meant for Scott the long revolution (beginning with the Reformation, nascent capitalism, and global imperialism) of forms of life that are modern because they are anti-authoritarian, egalitarian, rationally self-interested, and bureaucratic and hence revolt against the glamour of ancient forms, which are heroic, patriarchal, tribal, hierarchic, and capricious. History and reality are grasped by Scott as multicultural revolutionary conflicts between different social orders. Since these conflicts affect

all the elements of a populace, Scott chose to center his stories on unknown or anonymous persons, representatives of the demos, who, even as they make history, suffer it and do not mark it with their names. Formal innovations follow from this content. To show that cultural revolutions take place in long-drawn, mediated ways and in terms of a social totality composed of small, intricate, ever-ramifying relations, narrative extends itself, eschewing immediate conflict and climax. Heroic characters, illustrated by world-historical figures, are pushed to the margins of representation. They are replaced by ordinary, mediocre persons, whose lack of unique specificity enables them to stand for collective aspects of the social orders in conflict. In such examples, form mimes content. But Scott's intention was also to use form to explain content. As a typical Russian heir of Scott, Nikolay Chernishevsky writes in 1853: "The relation of art to life is that of history. . . . the first task of history is to reproduce life; the second . . . to explain" (Becker 75). Scott's realism forms history so as to explain it as a series of self-contradictions in the unfolding of sequential social orders: the social past contains the social practices of the future; revolutionary modernity is informed by incoherent practices that sometimes derive from the past, sometimes gestate the future. As a result of these contradictions, Scott shows that the partisan ideologies of conflicting cultures are unstable, wavering, and compromised. The purity and self-containment of different modes of historical life are illusory.

Scott's interest in historical self-contradiction may have derived from his self-contradictory commitment of fiction to the cause of historical truth. He may have come to theoretical terms with the paradox by giving romance a conscious place in his historical realism. Using "romance" to name what is improbable, uncanny, and marvelous, Scott suggests the relative nature of the thing: what is real or probable at one moment of history appears romantic and improbable in the next, and vice versa. Moreover, Scott sees the continuing human invention of history as an eternal Viconian romance. The upshot of Scott's blurring of the boundaries between reality and romance, between history and imagination, was a handing on to his successors of a productive instability in novelistic theory and practice. Romance understood as a wavering, compromising mediator between opposing definitions of reality, on the one hand, and of imaginative fabrication, on the other, was able to abet the realist project. For other writers, as we will see, the compromise symptomized the inherently impossible match of fact with fiction.

The first innovation carried out by such immediate

successors of Scott as James Fenimore Cooper, Honoré de Balzac, George Sand, and Benjamin Disraeli was to make historical realism contemporary. They undertook to treat the present social order as itself history. Scott's voiceless and dispossessed subjects of the historical past become in the younger novelists the modern urban and rural proletariat, along with domestic workers, slaves, serfs, outcasts, and all those who had the least voice in terms of public power, including women and children. Scott's conflicts of cultures across time were redefined as the contemporary conflicts between the economic and ethical orders of "two nations": the middle class and the working class. An engagement with industrial capital, speculative finance, and commodity markets entered the realist's explanatory and formal intentions. The self-contradictions of the social totality, especially between its post-1789 egalitarianism and its meanly exploitative economics, became the representational focus. KARL MARX AND FRIEDRICH ENGELS looked to the representational and explanatory practices of the new historical realists, to Balzac's especially, as models for *Capital*'s theory of the world.

In shifting their attention from past social contradictions to immediate ones, the realists confronted new demands and strains on the attempt to fuse the novelist's with the historian's vocation. The alienating lawlessness of capitalistic order implicated the novelists themselves in speculation and commodification. Balzac (in *Lost Illusions*, 1837) and Dickens (in *Our Mutual Friend*, 1864) dramatize themselves, their writing, and their novels' structures as identical with nefarious economic forms of life. Having thereby admitted the loss of the historical novelist's disinterested distance in relation to the past, the novelists attempted to find ways to exculpate and to escape their complicity with the oppressive side of modernity. The legacy of romance in realism was enlisted as both an intensifier of realism and a facilitating medium for the novelist's impartial and yet critical address to social actuality. Harriet Beecher Stowe attributed to romance her advocacy of the slave's moral and political claims. She identified romance with "every craving for nobler . . . being than that which closes like a prison-house around us." Intensifying realism, "romance anoints" ordinary vision for Stowe, so that it can "see what poems . . . lie around us in the daily walk of life" (600). Dickens in his preface to *Bleak House* (1852) asserted that dwelling on "the romantic side of familiar things" frees the novelist to reveal and to analyze the social order's hidden interdependencies, which are otherwise masked by modern economic chaos and moral poverty and by the novelist's own proximity to them.

The theory of realism also became practical protest, an attempt to make the creative writer of novels literally a legislator. As if to supplement the representation and enfranchisement of hitherto unacknowledged lives in their novels, Edward Bulwer-Lytton, Disraeli (whose English Reform Bill of 1867 universalized male suffrage), Alessandro Manzoni, Victor Hugo, and Eugène Sue all captured legislative office. (The novelist Anthony Trollope was obsessed by his failed bid for a parliamentary seat.) Stowe's and Ivan Turgenev's novels were said to have caused the emancipation of American slaves and Russian serfs. In these legislative ambitions, the young heirs of historical realism attempted to fuse their individual authorship and their accurate as well as their imaginative visions of the world with collective political practices. But just as the novelists found it difficult to escape complicity with modern capitalist production, so the realist endeavor to enact the totality of social relations by merging novel-writing with collective action could not escape suspicions. On the one hand, the idea of the novelist-as-legislator was perhaps merely a romance in the most delusive sense, and the unity of collective action was perhaps only available as a formal possibility of narrative rather than an actual possibility of politics. On the other hand, perhaps the genuine source of social value and hope lay not in any group action but in the sphere of individualism.

Like romance, individualism played an equivocal role in the fortunes of realism's practice of its theory. Novels by and about women illustrate its double-sided effect. In light of Scott's relation to anonymity, his epic expanse ironically seemed to foreclose the already muted individual and domestic voices in women's fictions, which had exemplified the confines of propriety and "a prudential morality of private life" (Ferris 93). But domestic fiction also broke its confines by picturing the mutual impacts of private and public realms. Scott and Turgenev were influenced by Maria Edgeworth's novels (1800–1834). *Castle Rackrent*'s domestic servant–narrator intimately expresses, as well as registers, the thrust of modern English rule and economics on Irish tradition. Jane Austen's novels in part refer the difficulties her heroines experience to the new social mobility created by the Napoleonic wars. In Lady Morgan's *The Wild Irish Girl* (1806) the final compromise between Irish and Anglo-Irish cultures set the pattern for the endings of Scott's novels. Mary Shelley's *Frankenstein* (1816) blended domesticity-centered realism with the marvelous and the uncanny in order to criticize the domestic middle-class family as the seedbed of monsters. Similarly, George Sand's novels of the 1830s explored the monstrous tyranny of domestic patriarchy, with the result that Sand moved in the 1840s to partisanship with the urban and rural proletariat.

In *Uncle Tom's Cabin* Stowe exhibited the continuity of domestic privacy with male individualism's production of oppressive historical and economic disorder. Stowe's realism brought into question the categories of "the individual" and "the domestic" by seeing them as the social constructs of an era of commodification. Nevertheless, at one and the same time *Uncle Tom's Cabin*'s desire to abolish slavery was inspired by dedication to the rights of slaves as individuals! We expect historical realism to exhibit cultural self-contradictions, but it is unclear whether Stowe's work and the work of similar writers leaves the phenomenon of the individual unexamined by historical accounting. Lady Morgan's "On the Origin and Progress of Fictitious History" (1820) insists on the novel form's commitment to "essential individuality and transcendent emotions" and on its distrust of "concrete representations of social and cultural life" (Ferris 128). In a retrospective 1842 preface to *Indiana* (1831) Sand asserted that she has been seeking "to solve this insoluble problem: the method of reconciling the welfare and the dignity of individuals oppressed by . . . society without modifying society itself." A Victorian version of Sand's dilemma appears in the novels of Charlotte and Emily Brontë, which continue to make individualism a privileged center of realistic observation and representation and present even self-abnegating duty and repression as a new form of intensely felt selfhood. Romance shows itself here, this time in the reassignment of Byron's sadomasochistic intensity of will to female figures whose individuation and selfhood are the allies of revolutionary impulses. Whether or not such individualism acted as a stumbling block for realism's aim to merge critical individual consciousness with collective consciousness remains an open question.

Out of such open questions in realist theory, novelists were inspired to humble Scott's aims, or to subvert realism altogether and to institute new forms of fiction. The three love stories in George Eliot's historical-realist *Middlemarch* (1872) remain discontinuous vis-à-vis the others, the uniqueness of each resistant to theories of their shared historical representativeness and determination. In Eliot the incommensurability of nominally similar lives suggests an inherent structural impossibility in the attempt to represent historical totality. A modified realism, ironic about its aim, thus comes into being. As in Eliot, it is found in George Gissing's work in the 1880s and 1890s, which criticizes both the realist's and the Marxist's trust in seeing character as historically and

sociologically typical. During the same period William Dean Howells's passionate realism is accompanied by the wry admission, as in *A Hazard of New Fortunes* (1890), that even the most liberated, collective-minded literary theories and practices will inevitably extrude or kill off some vital social element of their production.

Alongside of these modesty-inspired revisions of realism, one finds the growth of fully antagonistic responses. Already in the 1840s Thackeray's fiction theorized the vain factitiousness of claims to construct full-scale pictures of the world; and Thackeray went on to theorize history not as a changing multicultural conflict but as eternally repetitious Oedipal psychodrama. Perhaps the most corrosive doubts about realism are Hawthorne's. Scott had blurred the distinction between reality and romance to suggest a new way of knowing more, and not less, about history. In Hawthorne's novels the blur introduces a wavering uncertainty into every narrative and referential component. Surprisingly, meanings thereby proliferate rather than shrink. But so evanescently fluid do meanings and their narrative constituents become in Hawthorne that they erode knowledge and certainty, even about what is happening in Hawthorne's stories. Ironically in the light of the Hawthornesque inspiration of Howells's and HENRY JAMES's realism, Hawthorne's romance profoundly unsettles realist theory's trust in fact, in fiction, and in their merger.

The vivid appearance, simultaneous with realism's, of alternative nineteenth-century theories and modes of fiction (even within the careers of realists themselves) may result from realism's theoretical liabilities. Hawthorne's use of romance allies him with the fantastic. This genre, whose exemplars extend from the work of E. T. A. Hoffmann (d. 1822) to James's *Turn of the Screw* (1898), "question[s] . . . the existence of an irreducible opposition between the real and the unreal" (Todorov 167) and leaves the representation and the reader without a foothold in either realm. Another possible reflex of the troubles of realism might be symptomized in the rise of detective fiction. Invented by Balzac, Dickens, Edgar Allan Poe, Hugo, Wilkie Collins, Émile Gaboriau, and Arthur Conan Doyle, the detective figure's policing of mystery, his marvelous capacity to survey disparate facts and to gather them into an uncanny pattern of total comprehension, typifies—and perhaps parodies—the explanatory surveillance and, even more, the arguably unacknowledged titanic will of the "disinterested" realist.

Because realism after Scott tended to ally itself with liberal or radical collective political agendas, the question of the politics inherent in the fictional practices that modify or subvert realisms inevitably arises. Since

GEORG LUKÁCS's *Historical Novel* (1937), these political tendencies have preoccupied our criticism. Following Marx's contention in *The Eighteenth Brumaire of Louis Bonaparte* that, at least especially after the failure of the revolutions of 1848, literary intellectuals remain inherently apologists for their class of origin, Lukács argued that artistic innovations in realism after the mid-century—the disruption of unifying awareness, the growing emphasis on formal and analytic indeterminacies—expressed, if only unconsciously, reactionary bourgeois politics, complicit with the rise of monopoly capital and the resurgence of imperialism. Among novelists whose work has served as an arena of contention about these matters is Herman Melville. Appearing to change one theory and practice of fiction for another in each of his works, Melville's career begins by fusing romance and realism in his books about sailors and South Seas imperialism and culminates in the romantic realism of the great industrial novel *Moby Dick* (1852); but thereafter, Melville exhibits a gamut of doubts about realism (and everything else). It has been argued that since Melville's desires for formal innovations appear early on, they represent a major philosophical shift in understanding the nature of language and meaning, irrespective of political intention. But the quirkiness has also been connected on the one hand to an American cultural nationalism, an assertion of freedom from European norms of reality and form, and on the other hand sometimes to his growing hatred of American politics and economics, sometimes to his complicity with what he hated, and sometimes to his idea of an artistic individualism that transcends political conditions. It should be noted that Melville exhibits an impatience with representations in general, perhaps because of an idea of culture too utopian for embodiment; a similar explanation has been given for English discontents with realism (see Gallagher).

Almost as a relief-bringing response to the gathering uncertainties about fiction's program, naturalism arose in France, at once reviving and refocusing realism's aims. Fiction's alliance with history now made way for its alliance with science, especially with the Darwinian science of evolution and with Herbert Spencer's science of sociology. Fiction was reborn as a way of seeing a new cultural conflict: that between historical artifice and all the objects of natural science, between the human construction of society and the construction of humanity by biology. The indeterminacies of the latter-day realisms gave way to the new novelistic sense of individual and social determination by environment. The theory of the novel passed under the influence of the evolutionary determinist HIPPOLYTE TAINE. In 1872 Henry James

summed up Taine's work, noting that it already had "been reiterated to satiety," as expressing "the theory that 'virtue and vice are products, like vitriol and sugar,' and that art, literature and conduct are the result of forces which differ from those of the physical world only in being less easily ascertainable" (1843).

One of the first formal differences resulting from the shift from realism to naturalism lay in the transformation of "character" into "temperament." In contrast to the realist character's expressive conjunction of socially unique and socially typical traits, the naturalist "temperament" is more obscure, imponderably biophysical rather than historically intelligible. In the preface to *Thérèse Raquin* (1867), naturalism's muse ÉMILE ZOLA wrote that he had chosen for his characters "people . . . dominated by their nerves and blood, without free will, drawn into action . . . by the . . . inexorable laws of their physical nature . . . human animals, nothing more" (22). In spite of this choice of subjects, however, the novelist forms his work, not as a brute, but as a scientist. "The novel has become a general inquiry into nature and man," Zola wrote in 1880. "We are the culmination of investigation." Zola insisted that determinism was not fatalism. The naturalist, "the experimental novelist," diminishes indeterminism, but "we disengage the determinism of human and social phenomena so that we may one day control and direct them" (Becker 181). Zola extends the explanatory and liberating intentions of realism. And in joining forces with Charles Darwin and Spencer, naturalism put itself, again like realism in its pride, on the side of progressive improvements in adaptation and intelligence. In Spencer's emphasis, moreover, evolutionary progress moved from "incoherent homogeneity to coherent heterogeneity" (Pizer 90), so that the representation of totality need not be a pursuit of formal or explanatory unity.

But naturalism's claim to reconcile animals and explanations, sciences and arts, was no less stable theoretically than realism's claim to reconcile reality and romance. Robert Louis Stevenson's *Dr. Jekyll and Mr. Hyde* (1886) is perhaps a narrativized theory of naturalism's self-contradictious split between reason and bestiality. The contradictions unfold in naturalism's politics and its demands on form. Naturalism's scientific basis, antiauthoritatively egalitarian and analytic, appears at first, no less than realism, to complement Marxist analysis. The industrial class conflicts in Zola's *Germinal* (1885) are explained in Marxist terms in the text itself, by Etienne, the text's hero. Yet the narrative distances itself from Etienne; it suggests that Etienne's Marxism may be one of his inherited debilities as the child of promiscuous alcoholics. What if Marxism is itself a narcotic, a whim of reason, founded on an environmental chance—a science by chance? The effect of the suggestion in this instance is the suspicion that the experimental novelist's program is also caprice, is not disinterested objectivity but yet another assertion of the will to power. Here one sees the confluence (partly intended, partly not) of naturalism with ARTHUR SCHOPENHAUER's and FRIEDRICH NIETZSCHE's ideas that all representations, and science itself, are the products of will rather than truth. A theory of the world ruled by chance is encapsulated in Thomas Hardy's English version of naturalism. And just as the determining role of arbitrary chance subverts naturalism's science, so the idea of an environing brutality subverts naturalism's progressivism. Cynically treated, naturalism facilitates the portrayal of non-Western natives as "human animals, nothing more" (Zola 22), and justifies the superior force of imperializing brutes. It has been argued that such an application of naturalism provides the theory of Rudyard Kipling's and Joseph Conrad's fiction.

An offshoot of naturalism is another new mode, literary impressionism, which treats "science" skeptically but continues to focus on temperament and to evoke the human animal's immediate sensation of life. Artists such as Kipling and Conrad wanted, in the words of Conrad's preface to "The Nigger of the 'Narcissus'" (1897), "above all to make you see." The object of vision, still in line with Scott's, is "solidarity" with "the obscure lives of the bewildered, the simple, and the voiceless." But solidarity melts to a mere privileged moment in "the remorseless rush of time"; substance becomes shadow: "the aim of art . . . like life itself is . . . obscured by mists. It is not in the clear logic of a triumphant conclusion, it is not in the unveiling of one of those heartless secrets which are called The Laws of Nature" (xxvii–xxviii). Impressionism may be able to capture the local color of an evolutionary moment, but to do so it must submit narrative structure to an erosion of all abstractions, including form's. At the level of form, the self-contradiction of *this* theory is poignant. "The worker in prose" is committed "to make you hear, to make you feel" by "the power of the written word," that is, by the manipulation of an artificial medium, distant from sensation, and by effects produced not by chance but by exacting calculation.

Exhausted by the self-contradictory purposes of novel-writing in the nineteenth century, Leo Tolstoy turned against his own achievements in realism, condemned the amorality of naturalism, and—in the face of political injustice—questioned the need for art altogether in "What Is Art?" (1897–98). The younger heirs of realism and naturalism were more resilient. H. G. Wells, seizing on impressionism as a prime exhibit of the way even "raw sensation" is an artificial invention, turned the naturalist match between science and fiction into science fiction. Wells projected the styles and forms of realism and naturalism anew as the elements of pure romance. Frank Norris's *McTeague* (1899) presents characters who are seen simultaneously or alternately through naturalist and realist lenses. The hero is now a brute by nature—and now by second nature, by the way culture has brutalized him. Indeed, *McTeague* is structured as a debate between realist and naturalist theories and explanations of the world; its form results from a wavering between theories of fiction. Walter Benn Michaels has shown how this wavering refers to contemporary debates about whether gold gives money and markets a "real" and "natural" source of wealth and value. These debates are analogues to realism's and naturalism's reference to reality and nature as the source of fiction's value. Norris's practice of theory denies exclusive reality or nature to either side of the debate. Hence his worship of Zola, ringing with echoes now of Scott and now of Hawthorne, endorses paradox: Zola's naturalism, he says, "is a form of romanticism, not an inner circle of realism" (1108), because "accuracy is realism and Truth romanticism" (1141).

Norris's work shows the relative rather than the absolute differences between theoretical paradigms that inspired the last century's novelists. A glance at one last theory—art for art's sake—suggests that its difference from others is less absolute than first appears. The idea of fiction primarily referring neither to history nor to nature but to itself—to literary form and to language—derives from EDGAR ALLAN POE. In his review of Hawthorne's tales (1842) and in "The Philosophy of Composition" (1845) Poe implicitly attacked realism for its mimicry of the extended mediations of social life. Short prose forms are superior to novels, Poe argued, because they enable "unity of effect or impression" (571) or of tone and because, pace the novel, they alone attain "totality." Although realists and naturalists borrowed the form, especially to convey a sense of realistic locale, the concentrated artifice necessitated by "unity of effect" became a value for the "art" novel. Manzoni had produced a classic historical fiction in 1828, but in *On the Historical Novel* (1850) he rejected the form. He argued that art must produce belief by way of "the verisimilar," an ideal aesthetic unity, which is destroyed by mixing art and history in a futile longing for ancient epic. "The verisimilar once offered and accepted as such becomes a truth that is altogether different from the real, but one that the mind perceives forever" (71).

Another historical realism that turned against itself, toward a version of Manzoni's ideal, was GUSTAVE FLAUBERT's. In the course of working on *Madame Bovary* (1851–57) Flaubert's dedication to absolute and impersonal objectivity led him to exalt "style, form, the indefinable Beautiful *resulting from the conception itself.*" By 1876 he was telling George Sand, "I hate what is conventionally called realism" (Becker 96). Yet we also find high aesthetic practices that are not at odds with realism and its century-long sociological and political ambitions. George Meredith, OSCAR WILDE, and Stevenson complicated the divorce between art's truth and the world's, in a way that again blurs boundaries. Meredith's *Egoist* (1879) exhibited and cherished its own artifice, as much as any postmodern metafiction, but it also pursued a feminist agenda. In Wilde's *Picture of Dorian Gray* (1890) it is a fantastic magic that holds the novel's uses of aestheticism, historical realism, and naturalism in separate compartments. The climax of the tale is the collapse of the separation, the blending of the genres and of what they stand for. Stevenson, no less than Wilde a formalist aesthete, theorizes his novels as imitations of others', pure exercises in intertextual style. Yet Stevenson exhibits the compatibility of such a theory with progressive radicalism. In *In the South Seas* (1896) and *A Footnote to History* (1892), the aesthete enlists realist and naturalist versions of history to document Western imperialism in the Pacific, and to intervene against it. Stevenson's practice of theory reminds us that aesthetic preoccupations were not incompatible with political ones and that realism and naturalism were not merely masks of the status quo.

Robert L. Caserio

See also AMERICAN THEORY AND CRITICISM: NINETEENTH CENTURY, BRITISH THEORY AND CRITICISM: 4. VICTORIAN, and HENRY JAMES.

George J. Becker, ed., *Documents of Modern Literary Realism* (1963); Joseph Conrad, *The Nigger of the "Narcissus," Typhoon, Amy Foster, Falk, To-morrow* (1978); Henry James, *Literary Criticism: French Writers; Other European Writers; Prefaces to the New York Edition* (ed. Leon Edel and Mark Wilson, 1984); Alessandro Manzoni, *On the Historical Novel* (trans. Sandra Bermann, 1984); Frank Norris, *Novels and Essays* (1986); Edgar Allan Poe, *Essays and Reviews* (1984); George Sand, *The Masterpieces of George Sand*, vol. 1 (trans. George Burnham Ives, 1900); Leo Tolstoy, *What Is Art? and Essays on Art* (1962); Émile Zola, *Thérèse Raquin* (trans. Leonard Tancock, 1962).

Marius Bewley, *The Eccentric Design: Form in the Clas-sic American Novel* (1957); Patrick Brantlinger, *Rule of Darkness: British Literature and Imperialism, 1830–1914* (1988); Richard H. Brodhead, *The School of Hawthorne* (1986); Gillian Brown, *Domestic Individualism: Imagining Self in Nineteenth-Century America* (1990); Charles Feidelson, Jr., *Symbolism and American Literature* (1953); Ina Ferris, *The Achievement of Literary Authority: Gender, History, and the Waverley Novels* (1991); Michael Fried, *Realism, Writing, Disfiguration: On Thomas Eakins and Stephen Crane* (1987); Catherine Gallagher, *The Industrial Reformation of English Fiction: Social Discourse and Narrative Form, 1832–1867* (1985); Howard Horwitz, *By the Law of Nature: Form and Value in Nineteenth-Century America* (1991); John Kucich, *Excess and Restraint in the Novels of Charles Dickens* (1981), *Repression in Victorian Fiction: Charlotte Brontë, George Eliot, and Charles Dickens* (1987); George Levine, *The Realistic Imagination* (1981); Georg Lukács, *The Historical Novel* (trans. Hannah Mitchell and Stanley Mitchell, 1983); Walter Benn Michaels, *The Gold Standard and the Logic of Naturalism: American Literature at the Turn of the Century* (1987); Robert Newsom, *Dickens on the Romantic Side of Familiar Things: Bleak House and the Novel Tradition* (1977); Sandy Petrey, *Realism and Revolution: Balzac, Stendhal, Zola, and the Performances of History* (1988); Donald Pizer, *Realism and Naturalism in Nineteenth-Century American Literature* (1966); John Robert Reed, *Victorian Will* (1989); Michael Paul Rogin, *Subversive Genealogy: The Politics and Art of Herman Melville* (1983); Naomi Schor, *Breaking the Chain: Women, Theory, and French Realist Fiction* (1985); Eric Sundquist, *Home as Found: Authority and Genealogy in Nineteenth-Century Literature* (1979); Darko Suvin, *Victorian Science Fiction in the UK: The Discourses of Knowledge and of Power* (1983); Richard Terdiman, *Discourse/Counter-Discourse: The Theory and Practice of Symbolic Resistance in Nineteenth-Century France* (1985); Tzvetan Todorov, *The Fantastic: A Structural Approach to a Literary Genre* (trans. Richard Howard, 1973).

3. Early Twentieth-Century British and American

Fiction writing had evolved far enough by the first decades of the twentieth century to allow EZRA POUND to badger other poets with his declaration that "poetry must be *as well written as prose*" (*Selected Letters of Ezra Pound, 1907–1941*, ed. D. D. Paige, 1950, 48), and F. R. LEAVIS could declare that "the poetic and creative strength of the English language [has gone] into prose fiction" (*D. H. Lawrence: Novelist*, 1955, 18). For much of the period, however, the theory and criticism of fiction lagged behind; as late as 1949 RENÉ WELLEK and Austin Warren claimed that "literary theory and criticism concerned with the novel are much inferior in both quantity and quality to theory and criticism of poetry" (*Theory of Literature*, 1949, 3d ed., 1962, 212). But by the 1970s and 1980s Anglo-American theory of fiction had progressed from a period of relative infancy (its birth coming in 1884, the date of HENRY JAMES's "The Art of Fiction") into a sophisticated enterprise that was the equal of the theory and criticism of the other literary arts.

In the early years of the century, Anglo-American considerations of fiction remained for the most part resolutely antitheoretical. Contemporaneous theoretical approaches to fiction in other languages, such as RUSSIAN FORMALISM and the work in its wake of Vladimir Propp and M. M. BAKHTIN, went almost entirely unnoticed in Anglo-American circles. The broad move in the late 1960s and 1970s from theories of the novel to theories of narrative, or NARRATOLOGY, coincided not just with the developments in STRUCTURALISM and poststructuralism in France and elsewhere in Europe but also with the rediscovery of these earlier theoretical considerations of fiction and narrative and their introduction into Anglo-American discourse.

The early years of the century can be termed "post-Jamesian," since James's example in his essays and reviews, and especially in his 1907–9 prefaces to the New York Edition of his novels, permanently changed the form and terms of the discourse on fiction. In "The Art of Fiction" and especially in the later prefaces James spoke as a major writer reflecting on the novel. After him, the debates about realism and romance, realism and naturalism, fiction and fact, and art and science that dominated much of the nineteenth century shifted to new grounds, roughly contained in the dichotomy variously demarcated as between content and form, subject matter and technique, or life and art. Following James's "art of fiction," discussions of the genre highlighted the "craft," "technique," "method," or "structure" of fiction as much as its content, relation to reality, or "life."

Among his many contributions to the theory of fiction, James not only highlighted but also problematized the relationship between life and art. Stating on the one hand that "the only reason for the existence of a novel is that it does attempt to represent life" ("Art of Fiction," *Literary Criticism: Essays* 46), he argued on the other that "we must grant the artist his subject, his idea, his *donnée*" (56) and that the only demand on a novel is that it be "interesting" (49). He modified the requirement that "art represents life" by his description of a novel as "a

personal, a direct impression of life" (50). This impression has moral as well as aesthetic implications: "the moral sense and the artistic sense lie very near together" in that "the deepest quality of a work of art will always be the quality of the mind of the producer" (63–64). In light of statements such as these, fiction theory from the first decades of the century can be seen as a series of statements by other novelist-critics on the distinction between art and life, which James highlighted but left ambiguous. Not surprisingly, each novelist advocates a kind of novel that strikingly resembles the ones that he or she actually produced.

Joseph Conrad and Ford Madox Ford extend the impressionist tendencies in James's theories. Conrad emphasizes both the fictional world-making capacities of the novelist ("Every novelist must begin by creating for himself a world, great or little, in which he can honestly believe" [*On Fiction* 79]) and also the novelist's power and need to create an impression in the reader. In his best-known discussion of fiction, the preface to *The Nigger of the "Narcissus"* (1897), he writes, "My task . . . is, by the power of the written word to make you hear, to make you feel—it is, before all, to make you see" (162). A reader's recognition of a truth in the fiction can come only after the impression has been successfully created. The novelist will more likely succeed if the possibilities of meaning are multiple, if the work "acquires a symbolic character" ("A work of art is very seldom limited to one exclusive meaning and not necessarily tending to a definite conclusion" [36]), and the rhetorical possibilities for a successful novelist are unlimited ("Give me the right word and the right accent and I will move the world" [118]). For Ford in both "On Impressionism" (1914) and *Joseph Conrad: A Personal Remembrance* (1924), impressionism means distinguishing between "a sort of rounded, annotated record of a set of circumstances" and "the record of the impression of a moment"; proper art is "the impression, not the corrected chronicle" (*Critical* 41), because the impression is "the general effect that life makes on mankind," and a novel should create a similar general effect (72).

For D. H. LAWRENCE in such essays as "Surgery for the Novel—or a Bomb" (1923) and "Morality and the Novel" (1925), James's linking of the quality of the artist's impression of life with "the moral sense" comes to the fore. In "Morality and the Novel" Lawrence emphasizes the "relation," the "for ever trembling and changing *balance*" between "man and the circumambient universe, at the living moment" (*Selected* 108, 109); morality "is the trembling instability of the balance" (110). The universe to be represented in novels is not a matter of external details; for Lawrence those details are just "existence." Done right ("if the novelist keeps his thumb out of the pan" and, rather than trying to pin things down, emphasizes relations), "the novel can help us to live, as nothing else can" (113). In "Surgery for the Novel" Lawrence claims that much recent fiction, such as that of James Joyce, Marcel Proust, or Dorothy Richardson, treats self-consciousness in so much obsessive detail that "you feel you are sewed inside a wool mattress that is being slowly shaken up, and you are turning to wool along with the rest of the woolliness" (115). Lawrence advocates instead a novel that will "have the courage to tackle new propositions without using abstractions" and will "present us with new, really new feelings, a whole line of new emotion, which will get us out of the emotional rut" (118).

VIRGINIA WOOLF also maps out a new direction for the novel and in doing so posits another set of relationships between art and life. In "Modern Fiction" (1919) and "Mr. Bennett and Mrs. Brown" (1924) she contrasts two groups of writers, the Edwardians (H. G. Wells, Arnold Bennett, John Galsworthy) and the Georgians (E. M. Forster, Lawrence, Lytton Strachey, Joyce, T. S. ELIOT [*Collected* 1:320]). The Edwardians, whom she calls "materialists" (2:104), give us only superficial external details and not inner experience. In "Modern Fiction" she asks, "Is life like this? Must novels be like this?" (2:106) and describes the proper content of fiction:

> Life is not a series of gig-lamps symmetrically arranged; life is a luminous halo, a semi-transparent envelope surrounding us from the beginning of consciousness to the end. Is it not the task of the novelist to convey this varying, this unknown and uncircumscribed spirit, whatever aberration or complexity it may display, with as little mixture of the alien and external as possible? (2:106)

As for Lawrence, access to this "spirit" involves attention to emotion not previously depicted in fiction, here a willingness to depict "the dark places of psychology" (2:108), as Russian writers such as Anton Chekhov have done. "Mr. Bennett and Mrs. Brown" focuses more directly on characterization. "In or about December, 1910, human character changed," Woolf claims (1:320), but Bennett and the other Edwardians go on as if nothing is different. Woolf recounts observing an elderly couple (whom she names Mrs. Brown and Mr. Smith) on a train and claims that if Bennett were to write about Mrs. Brown, he would offer nothing more than external information about her appearance and surroundings: "He is trying to hypnotize us into the belief that, because

he has made a house, there must be a person living there" (1:330). By ignoring inner life, the Edwardians have never looked at Mrs. Brown, "never at life, never at human nature" (1:330), and novelists must look inside for the modern novel to develop.

By the late 1910s and 1920s the ongoing critical and theoretical discourse about fiction that Lawrence and Woolf joined was developing in light of not only novelists such as James, Conrad, Joyce, Richardson, Ford, and themselves (and, soon, Ernest Hemingway, F. Scott Fitzgerald, William Faulkner, and many others) but also an expanding body of theoretical writings. Fiction theory was now just as likely to appear in books and articles as in essays, reviews, and prefaces and was written by critics and scholars as well as practicing novelists. Most of the theories attempted to negotiate James's problematical distinction between art and life, although as both Wallace Martin (20) and Daniel Schwarz (4) note, no one else achieved James's balance between the two poles, and the theories can be classified (with only some distortion) as emphasizing primarily either "art" or "life." If, as some critics claimed, an orthodoxy began to congeal during this period, it was on the art-craft-method-technique side.

The two most prominent theorists on the "art" side were Percy Lubbock and Joseph Warren Beach. Lubbock, "more Jamesian than James" according to Mark Schorer in the preface to the 1957 reprint of *The Craft of Fiction* (1921), codifies James's unsystematic statements about fictional technique into a book demonstrating that the novel attains full artistic status only in the Jamesian variety, with its preference for showing over telling, dramatized scene over pictured incident, and a fictional point of view filtered through a center of consciousness (third-person narration but limited to the perceptions and impressions of one character) rather than first-person or omniscient third-person narration. The aesthetic that Lubbock builds up—the novel approaching drama while retaining the filter of a single perceiving consciousness—includes an unobtrusive storyteller or narrator and the dramatization of the central consciousness as well as the story's events (the author "keeps a certain hold upon the narrator *as an object*" [259], and so *The Ambassadors* . . . is a story which is seen from one man's point of view, and yet a story in which that point of view is itself a matter for the reader to confront and to watch constructively" [170]). Ultimately, Lubbock's controlling assumption about the superiority of the Jamesian center-of-consciousness technique leads to his notorious summary statement (probably the best-known sentence from *The Craft of Fiction*), "The whole intricate question of method, in the craft of fiction, I take to be governed by the question of the point of view—the question of the relation in which the narrator stands to the story" (251).

Around the same time as the British Lubbock, the American Joseph Warren Beach produced book-length analyses of James's novels (*The Method of Henry James,* 1918) and the modern novel (*The Twentieth Century Novel: Studies in Technique,* 1932). Despite Beach's frequent disclaimers in the latter book—he is outlining only a history of the development of fictional technique, the preferences of his day might seem obsolete in the future, much of value may have been lost as technical sophistication increased—there is a strong teleological pattern to his history. For instance, Sir Walter Scott's narrative intrusions in the 1818 *Heart of Midlothian* directing the reader's thoughts and feelings are "great offenses" against fictional art (18), and Beach's chapter called "Exit Author" describes not only a historical development but a major artistic advance as well.

A second group of critics moved away from James's fiction and theory—with its emphasis on "craft," "technique," or "method" at the expense of content—as a model. In *Aspects of the Novel* (1927), the best-known book on fiction from the period, E. M. Forster is deliberately far less systematic than Lubbock; hence the title "aspects," which eschews "principles and systems" (15) and is "unscientific and vague, because it leaves the maximum of freedom" (16). "Aspects" is also far less prescriptive, since for Forster "method" means not the specific question of point of view—unlike Lubbock, he claims that "a novelist can shift his viewpoint if it comes off" (56)—but rather "the power of the writer to bounce the reader into accepting what he says" (78–79).

A few of Forster's formulations served for many years as the standard Anglo-American vocabulary. For example, he distinguishes "story" ("a narrative of events arranged in their time-sequence": "The king died and then the queen died") and "plot" ("also a narrative of events, the emphasis falling on causality": "The king died, and then the queen died of grief" (86). This crucial distinction parallels but has been refined by the Russian Formalists' *fabula* and *sjužet,* ÉMILE BENVENISTE's *histoire* and *discours,* Gérard Genette's *histoire* and *récit,* and Seymour Chatman's "story" and "discourse." Also, Forster's distinction between "flat" and "round" characters became widely known: flat, static characters "are constructed round a single idea or quality" (47), and "a novel that is at all complex often requires flat people as well as round" (49); round characters must be sufficiently developed to be "capable of surprising in a convincing way" (54). The flexibility of Forster's positions, which can

praise rather than condemn Scott because, despite his technical limitations, "he could tell a story" (32), is one of his most appealing features. But his loose terminology and his refusal to theorize, both of which prompted Woolf to ask, "What is this 'Life' that keeps on cropping up so mysteriously and complacently in books about fiction?" (*Collected* 2:53), sufficiently typifies the general level of discourse about fiction to indicate why Wellek and Warren could talk about the relative poverty of fictional theory as late as 1949.

A second attempt to move beyond the Jamesian view of the novel is Edwin Muir's *The Structure of the Novel* (1928). Like Forster, Muir tries to create "rough and ready" categories (7) that permit equal consideration of all kinds of novels. Muir contrasts the dramatic and character novels, and he introduces a subclass of the dramatic novel, the chronicle. Each category features its own kind of plots and characters: expansive plot for the character novel, intensive for the dramatic (59); an imaginative world in space for the character novel, in time for the dramatic (62–63). Muir's openness is mitigated by his view of the chronicle, with its "accidental" and "arbitrary" events (109), as "the ruling convention of the novel at present" but not as the place where "the most striking achievements of the contemporary novel lie" (115).

T. S. Eliot did not address the theory of the novel directly, but his 1923 review of Joyce's *Ulysses* ("*Ulysses,* Order, and Myth") opened up important issues for fiction theory in a different post-Jamesian direction. In arguing that Joyce took a "step toward making the modern world possible for art" by replacing the "narrative method" with the "mythical method," which Eliot described as "manipulating a continuous parallel between contemporaneity and antiquity" (*Selected Prose,* ed. Frank Kermode, 1975, 177–78), he linked modernist art, exemplified especially by *Ulysses* and his own *The Waste Land,* with methods that transcended the specific medium of poetry or prose fiction. (See also MODERNIST THEORY AND CRITICISM.) With Joyce and Proust among his examples and using symbolism rather than myth, EDMUND WILSON made a parallel argument in *Axel's Castle: A Study of the Imaginative Literature of 1870–1930* (1931). Eliot's approach was extended in an influential essay from the mid-1940s, Joseph Frank's "Spatial Form in Modern Literature" (1945), which discusses "the spatialization of form in the novel" (*Widening* 15) in Joyce, Djuna Barnes, and other writers. For Frank, "modern art is non-naturalistic," and so "we can say that it is moving in the direction of increased spatiality" (57), attempting "to remove all traces of time-value" (57) by "maintain-

[ing] a continual juxtaposition between aspects of the past and the present so that both are fused in one comprehensive view" (59). Modernist writers, he argues, are "engaged in transmuting the time world of history into the timeless world of myth" (60).

A final group of critics from this period, descendants more of Lawrence than of James, emphasize the "life" of fiction over the techniques used to render that life. Most prominent in this group is F. R. Leavis, who argues in *The Great Tradition: George Eliot, Henry James, Joseph Conrad* (1948) for a canon of great novels based on "the human awareness they promote; awareness of the possibilities of life" (2). In accord with MATTHEW ARNOLD's claim that literature is a "criticism of life," Leavis's values are based on "a vital capacity for experience, a kind of reverent openness before life, and a marked moral intensity" (9); he sees no "discrepancy" between the "technical ('aesthetic') intensity" and the "actual moral and human" depth of the subject (13), and there is an "organic principle determining, informing, and controlling" the structure "into a vital whole" (25). Leavis's canon of novelists in the "great tradition" numbers only five: Eliot, Conrad, James, Jane Austen, and Lawrence (in the 1970 *Dickens the Novelist,* co-authored with Q. D. Leavis, he elevated Charles Dickens into the canon). Leavis has often been criticized for his unduly restrictive canon, and his particular readings have sometimes been controversial, but through his readings he demonstrated that novels could be successfully analyzed as closely as poetry.

Leavis is the first of the major critics discussed so far who was not also a practicing novelist, and his criticism is concerned as much with teaching fiction as with the ongoing critical discourse. In both areas, he is part of the main movement from the decades beginning with the 1930s. Analyzing fiction was never a prime objective of NEW CRITICISM, but four years after the enormously influential *Understanding Poetry,* Cleanth Brooks and Robert Penn Warren published the companion textbook *Understanding Fiction* (1943), and in 1950 Caroline Gordon and Allen Tate produced *The House of Fiction.* As with poetry, Brooks and Warren emphasize organic unity in fiction. Like James—"A novel is a living thing, all one and continuous, like any other organism, and in proportion as it lives will it be found, I think, that in each of the parts there is something of each of the other parts" (*Literary Criticism: Essays* 54)—but even more like SAMUEL TAYLOR COLERIDGE, Brooks and Warren stress the "organic relation" among a work of fiction's characterization, action, and meaning (or moral) (viii). A sophisticated fiction reader's satisfaction depends upon "the total structure, upon a set of organic relationships, upon the

logic of the whole" (x). A work of fiction for Brooks and Warren is successful the more it approaches a poem by John Donne or Eliot, and certain short stories—with a fruitful tension between elements and with an impersonal form of narration—come closest to this ideal. Because of this model, early New Critical analyses of full-length novels tended to be less successful than those of some short stories or poetry.

The most successful applications of New Critical principles to fiction come from Mark Schorer and Dorothy Van Ghent. In "Technique as Discovery" (1948) Schorer argues that "the difference between content, or experience, and achieved content, or art, is technique" (*World* 3). Considering two basic elements of "technique," language and point of view (5), he argues that "technique alone objectifies the materials of art; hence technique alone evaluates those materials" (9); it is "not only that technique *contains* intellectual and moral implications, but that it *discovers* them" (10). In "Fiction and the 'Analogical Matrix'" (1949) Schorer considers the patterns of metaphor in three novels to argue that, for example, Austen's "images of the counting house" (44) in *Persuasion* help to create the sense of the novel as being "about marriage as a market, and about the female as marketable" (28). Van Ghent, in *The English Novel: Form and Function* (1953), offers a book-length analysis of 18 particular novels. Sustained by the principle that "the sound novel . . . has to hang together as one thing" (6), she relates form and content via a Jamesian argument that "we judge a novel . . . by the cogency and illuminative quality of the view of life that it affords," a view she describes as "the idea embodied in [the novel's] cosmology" (7).

By the 1950s the study of fiction had grown into a full-scale enterprise. Studies based on particular approaches and studies of specific categories of fiction appeared, along with books and articles on individual novelists and historical periods. Only some of these studies can be mentioned here. One group, emphasizing the reality depicted in novels, comes down more on the side of content than of form in the old Jamesian dichotomy. Arnold Kettle's loosely Marxist *Introduction to the English Novel: Defoe to the Present* (1951, rev. ed., 1967), for example, distinguishes between "life" and "pattern" (or "form") but insists that pattern and form are not only aesthetic terms: "Pattern is not something narrowly 'aesthetic'" (14), and "'form' is important only in so far as it enhances significance; and it will enhance significance just in so far as it bears a real relation to . . . the aspect of life that is being conveyed. But form is not *in itself* significant; the central core of any novel is what it has to say about life" (15). A later Marxist study, RAYMOND WILLIAMS's *The English Novel from Dickens to Lawrence* (1971), treats novelists who "in very different ways, found the common forms that mattered, in response to a new and varied but still common experience" (10), an experience that Williams describes as "the exploration of community: the substance and meaning of community" (11). Influential non-Marxist arguments for fiction's relationship to reality include ERICH AUERBACH's *Mimesis* (1946), which was translated into English in 1953, and Lionel Trilling's 1948 lecture "Manners, Morals, and the Novel" (included in Trilling's *Liberal Imagination,* 1950). Auerbach's monumental study of "the interpretation of reality through literary representation or 'imitation'" (554) from Homer through the modern novel presents an increasingly pessimistic view of literature in terms of the life it represents: the method of much modern fiction, Auerbach claims, "which dissolves reality into multiple and multivalent reflections of consciousness," is "a symptom of the confusion and helplessness" of the age and "a mirror of the decline of our world" (551). For Trilling, the novel represents "manners," which he defines as "a culture's hum and buzz of implication" (194); he argues that "our attitude toward manners is the expression of a particular conception of reality" (195). As the commitment to "our particular idea of reality" increases, the "interest in manners" decreases (203–4). For Trilling, "moral realism," "the perception of the dangers of the moral life itself" (206–7), can counter this commitment; and the novel is the best vehicle for moral realism, since the novel's "greatness and its practical usefulness lay in its unremitting work of involving the reader himself in the moral life, inviting him to put his own motives under examination, suggesting that reality is not as his conventional education has led him to see it" (209). Finally, in "The Concept of Plot and the Plot of *Tom Jones*" (1950), the best-known work of fiction theory by the first-generation CHICAGO CRITICS, R. S. Crane expands the idea of "plot" from a formal issue to one involving morality along lines similar to those of Trilling's concept. For Crane, plot, which has "a power to affect our opinions and emotions in a certain way," is "not simply a means . . . but rather the final end which everything in the work, if that is to be felt as a whole, must be made, directly or indirectly, to serve" (*Critics* 621, 622).

Emphasis on fiction's relation to reality also informs one of the most influential historical-critical studies from the period, Ian Watt's *The Rise of the Novel: Studies in Defoe, Richardson, and Fielding* (1957). Watt offers an account of the growth of the novel in terms of what he calls "formal realism," a term that includes "the premise

. . . that the novel is a full and authentic report of human experience" involving "details which are presented through a more largely referential use of language than is common in other literary forms" (32). In the next decade, W. J. Harvey in *Character and the Novel* (1965) applied a theory of mimesis, rather than one of artistic autonomy (11), to study the by-then-unfashionable topic of fictional characters.

By the 1950s and 1960s fiction's depiction of inner human experience was widely considered. As elsewhere, some of the studies emphasize the mimetic representation, others the techniques. In *The Modern Psychological Novel* (1955, rev. ed., 1961) Leon Edel considers "the stream-of-consciousness and interior monologue novel" and deals with both "the literary representation of thought in its flowing and evanescent state" and "the representation within consciousness of sensory experience" (v). Other books to consider these kinds of novels include Robert Humphrey's *Stream of Consciousness in the Modern Novel* (1954) and Melvin J. Friedman's *Stream of Consciousness: A Study of Literary Method* (1955). Simon O. Lesser's *Fiction and the Unconscious* (1957) utilizes Freudian psychoanalysis to discuss "some of the urgent needs which cause us to read" and "some of the basic characteristics of fiction which enable it to satisfy those needs" (9); his book deals as much with the reading process as with novels themselves (see also PSYCHOANALYTIC THEORY AND CRITICISM: 2. RECONCEPTUALIZING FREUD).

A few other books from these decades should be mentioned. E. K. Brown and David Lodge discuss technical issues, rhythm in Brown's case and language in Lodge's, with similar starting points. In *Rhythm in the Novel* (1950) Brown extends one of Forster's "aspects"; for Brown, rhythm is "repetition with variation" (7) and can involve repetitions of words, symbols, and what Brown calls "the interweaving theme" (63). Lodge, arguing in *Language of Fiction: Essays in Criticism and Verbal Analysis of the English Novel* (1966) that New Critical techniques had not yet been effectively applied to fiction, offers detailed verbal analyses of the language of several novels with verbal repetition as his focus. In two book-length essays on fiction, *The Sense of an Ending: Studies in the Theory of Fiction* (1967) and *The Genesis of Secrecy: On the Interpretation of Narrative* (1979), Frank Kermode looks at particular, related issues—how, trying to make sense of our lives while "in the middest" of them, we "need fictive concords with origins and ends, such as give meaning to lives and to poems" (*Sense* 7), and our need to interpret narratives, even though we are inevitably excluded from a narrative's "secrets," a process Kermode summarizes as "the forces that make interpretation necessary and virtually impossible" (*Genesis* 125). Finally, in a series of original and provocative books on modernist writers that began in the 1950s (including studies of Joyce, Samuel Beckett, and other novelists)—a list that includes *Dublin's Joyce* (1956), *Samuel Beckett* (1961, 2d ed., 1968), *Flaubert, Joyce, and Beckett: The Stoic Comedians* (1962), *The Pound Era* (1971), *A Homemade World: The American Modernist Writers* (1974), *Joyce's Voices* (1978), *A Colder Eye: The Modern Irish Writers* (1983), *A Sinking Island: The Modern English Writers* (1988), and many other books—Hugh Kenner, while disdaining theoretical overviews and generalizations, offers critical studies of modernist fiction that in their content and their own form continue Pound's project of "making it new."

By these decades, some critics began to see the concerns of much fiction criticism and theory—the dichotomy between art and life, the formal elements of fiction, the aesthetics of the modernist novel—as excessively limited. Several studies tried to open up the discussion by treating the novel as only one possibility within the broader field of narrative. For example, NORTHROP FRYE's *Anatomy of Criticism* (1957) includes a chapter on "Specific Continuous Forms (Prose Fiction)"; here, Frye sees "four chief strands binding" prose fiction together "from the point of view of form": "novel, confession, anatomy, and romance" (312). A decade later, in *The Nature of Narrative* (1966), Robert Scholes and Robert Kellogg treat many of the standard topics in studies of fiction—meaning, character, plot, point of view—in terms of a continuity between oral narrative and the modern novel: "We hope to put the novel in its place, to view the nature of narrative and the Western narrative tradition whole, seeing the novel as only one of a number of narrative possibilities" (3).

The most influential book from the 1960s, and a full-scale theory of fiction despite its avowedly antitheoretical position, is Wayne C. Booth's *Rhetoric of Fiction* (1961, 2d ed., 1983; see also CHICAGO CRITICS). At least two of this book's main concepts have become standard terms in the critical discourse on fiction: the "implied author" (71), which Booth describes as the author's "second self" (67), "an ideal, literary, created version of the real man" (75); and the distinction between "reliable" and "unreliable" narrators (158–59) based on the degree of "distance" (155) between the narrator and the implied author.

Rhetoric for Booth involves the "resources available to the writer . . . as he tries, consciously or unconsciously, to impose his fictional world upon the reader" (xiii). Such an imposition is inevitable, since "the author cannot choose to avoid rhetoric; he can choose only the kind of rhetoric he will employ" (149). From this as-

sumption, Booth attacks several prevailing post-Jamesian "rules": a novel should show and not tell; the author should be objective; to be pure, a novel should not try to affect its audience. If, as Booth claims, objectivity is both impossible and undesirable, the intrusive narrators of eighteenth- and nineteenth-century novels are marks, not of an inferior technique, but of one possible kind of rhetoric among many. *The Rhetoric of Fiction* inspired renewed interest in the technical aspects of pre-twentieth-century fiction and greater sophistication in discussions of such novels.

Booth's concept of the implied author carries strong theoretical implications. The implied author represents the text's norms and values and satisfies "the reader's need to know where, in the world of values, he stands— that is, to know where the author *wants* him to stand" (73). Thus, through successfully employed rhetoric the text imposes its intention on its "implied reader" (138; see also GERMAN THEORY AND CRITICISM: 5. CONTEMPORARY and RECEPTION THEORY for considerations of Wolfgang Iser's adaptation of this idea); the implied author embodying the work's norms and values serves as a check on the possibly unbridled relativism of reader response.

The most controversial aspect of *The Rhetoric of Fiction* has been its treatment of morality. "An author has an obligation to be as clear about his moral position as he possibly can be," Booth argues (389). He finds Joyce's *Portrait of the Artist as a Young Man,* like much modern fiction, faulty because "whatever intelligence Joyce postulates in his reader . . . will not be sufficient for precise inference of a pattern of judgments" about Stephen Dedalus; as a result, "we simply cannot avoid the conclusion that to some extent the book itself is at fault, regardless of its great virtues" (335).

By the 1970s and 1980s, Anglo-American theories of fiction were for the most part supplanted by international and interdisciplinary theories of narrative, or narratology, but the issues traditional fiction theory raised had become part of every major approach to literature, from feminist, Marxist, and psychoanalytic theories and criticisms to POSTMODERNISM and NEW HISTORICISM. Far from being the poor relatives of theories of poetry, theories of fiction began to become equated more and more with theories of literature itself.

Michael Groden

See also BLOOMSBURY GROUP, HENRY JAMES, D. H. LAWRENCE, F. R. LEAVIS, NARRATOLOGY, NEW CRITICISM, and VIRGINIA WOOLF.

Erich Auerbach, *Mimesis: Dargestellte Wirklichkeit in der abendländischen Literatur* (1946, *Mimesis: The Representation of Reality in Western Literature,* trans. Willard R. Trask, 1953); Joseph Warren Beach, *The Twentieth Century Novel: Studies in Technique* (1932); Wayne C. Booth, *The Rhetoric of Fiction* (1961, 2d ed., 1983); Cleanth Brooks and Robert Penn Warren, *Understanding Fiction* (1943); Joseph Conrad, *Joseph Conrad on Fiction* (ed. Walter F. Wright, 1964); R. S. Crane, ed., *Critics and Criticism: Ancient and Modern* (1952); Leon Edel, *The Modern Psychological Novel* (1955, rev. ed., 1961, reprint, 1964); Ford Madox Ford, *Critical Writings of Ford Madox Ford* (ed. Frank MacShane, 1964); E. M. Forster, *"Aspects of the Novel" and Related Writings* (1927, ed. Oliver Stallybrass, 1974): Joseph Frank, *The Widening Gyre: Crisis and Mastery in Modern Literature* (1963); Northrop Frye, *Anatomy of Criticism: Four Essays* (1957); Michael J. Hoffman and Patrick D. Murphy, eds., *Essentials of the Theory of Fiction* (1988); Henry James, *Literary Criticism: Essays on Literature; American Writers; English Writers* (ed. Leon Edel and Mark Wilson, 1984), *Literary Criticism: French Writers; Other European Writers; Prefaces to the New York Edition* (ed. Leon Edel and Mark Wilson, 1984); Frank Kermode, *The Genesis of Secrecy: On the Interpretation of Narrative* (1979), *The Sense of an Ending: Studies in the Theory of Fiction* (1967); Arnold Kettle, *An Introduction to the English Novel: Defoe to the Present* (2 vols., 1951, rev. ed., 1967, reprint, 2 vols. in 1, 1968); D. H. Lawrence, *Selected Literary Criticism* (ed. Anthony Beal, 1955); F. R. Leavis, *The Great Tradition: George Eliot, Henry James, Joseph Conrad* (1948); Percy Lubbock, *The Craft of Fiction* (1921, reprint, 1957); Wallace Martin, *Recent Theories of Narrative* (1986); Edwin Muir, *The Structure of the Novel* (1928); Robert Scholes and Robert Kellogg, *The Nature of Narrative* (1966); Mark Schorer, *The World We Imagine: Selected Essays* (1968); Daniel R. Schwarz, *The Humanistic Heritage: Critical Theories of the English Novel from James to Hillis Miller* (1986); Philip Stevick, ed., *The Theory of the Novel* (1967); Lionel Trilling, *The Liberal Imagination: Essays on Literature and Society* (1950, reprint, 1978); Dorothy Van Ghent, *The English Novel: Form and Function* (1953); Ian Watt, *The Rise of the Novel: Studies in Defoe, Richardson, and Fielding* (1957); Raymond Williams, *The English Novel from Dickens to Lawrence* (1971); Virginia Woolf, *Collected Essays* (ed. Leonard Woolf, 4 vols., 1966).

FILM THEORY

Because of the relative newness of the film medium compared with other art forms—Thomas Edison's Kinetoscope peephole machines were first open to the public in New York City only in 1894, and the Lumière brothers first projected their short *actualités* to a paying audience in a cafe in Paris in 1895—film theory and criticism are dependent on a limited number of major texts, and the lines of their discourse can easily be traced up to the point when STRUCTURALISM and poststructuralism had their profound effect on cultural history in general. From that point on, especially with the expansion of film departments and faculties at institutions of higher learning, film theory and criticism proliferated at a rapid rate, and film journals became as much a place for heated debate on the issues of art and aesthetics as the learned journals were for essays on literature. Much of the discourse on cinema from the start is concerned with fictional narrative films, an emphasis that parallels the vast popularity of such works compared with the more limited and specialized appeal of the documentary and avant-garde film.

For the first 20 years of motion pictures, film writing was largely descriptive and sometimes evaluative, but with the rise of the feature film, theory took its first pronounced steps with the appearance of two pioneer texts in English, Vachel Lindsay's *The Art of the Moving Picture* in 1915 (rev. ed., 1922) and Hugo Münsterberg's *The Photoplay: A Psychological Study* in 1916. Both of these works, the first by a poet and the second by a psychologist, consider this new medium in the context of other art forms. But whereas Lindsay is content to draw parallels between film and such other arts as architecture, sculpture, and poetry, Münsterberg goes much further in arguing for the unique properties of cinema by focusing in the first part of his work on the psychological responses of the viewer and in the second on the aesthetic properties of film as a mental creation. For him, film, by being freed from the constraints of real time and space as well as causality, is capable of being constructed with the free play of the viewer's mental life.

In relating the world depicted on the screen to the actual world and in demonstrating film's capacity to reformulate time and space to create the mental process of the imagination, Münsterberg was implicitly introducing a critical issue that would be the focus of much of the theoretical discussion of cinema for the next 40 years, namely, the tension between realism and formalism. The relationship between reality and film art was certainly a major issue in the eruption of criticism that began in

France about the same time, often touching upon theoretical issues. Heralded in his own country as the creator of French film criticism and eventually to become a leading force among the "impressionist" filmmakers, Louis Delluc, whose various writings from journals and newspapers were published in two collections, *Cinéma et cie* in 1919 and *Photogénie* in 1920, used the term *photogénie* to suggest film's capacity to present the real world as something newly seen, to depict the beauty of reality and make us comprehend the things of our world. Much in sympathy with these views was Riccioto Canudo, the Italian-born French critic whose writings were collected in *L'Usine aux images* in 1926 and who argued that cinema must go beyond realism and imagistically express the filmmaker's emotions as well as characters' psychology and even their unconscious. Jean Epstein, also on the verge of becoming a major "impressionist" filmmaker, published in 1921 *Bonjour cinéma,* in which he claimed that cinema abstracts, generalizes, and presents an idea of a form, while the viewer's eyes distill and perceive an idea of the idea of the form that is on the screen. (See Abel for essays by Delluc, Canudo, and Epstein.)

Most of these early theoreticians show a clear predilection toward the formalist possibilities of cinema, and certainly formalism is the underpinning of the montage theory expounded by the great Russian filmmakers starting in the 1920s. In the midst of a busy filmmaking career, Lev Kuleshov began to publish essays in 1917 and books in 1929 outlining his theory of montage, which had received its impetus from the practice of American filmmakers, especially D. W. Griffith. The term "Kuleshov effect" has passed into cinematic language to describe what for Kuleshov was the inherent magic of the film medium itself, the creation of meaning, significance, and emotional impact by relating and juxtaposing individual shots, resulting in a context that was not inherent in any of the single pieces of film but was a product of the editing itself. His pupil V. I. Pudovkin began writing the two manuals that together were to become the book *Film Technique* when he was working on his motion picture *Mother* in 1926. In this book he explores his own variation of montage, what Sergei Eisenstein referred to as "linkage," in which shots are unobtrusively linked together so that they continuously and naturally flow along with the film's narrative line, but he also pushes theoretical discourse further with his discussion of filmic space and time, dimensions created by the editing process itself and distinct from any space and time known in external reality.

Different from Pudovkin's concept of linkage editing is Eisenstein's "collision" theory of montage, in which the dramatic and dialectical juxtaposition of shots produces a kind of attraction to one another that makes the significance or meaning of their synthesis explode upon the viewer. Whereas Kuleshov had demonstrated how two juxtaposed shots could create a produced context not inherent in the individual images, Eisenstein went beyond his mentor in both his writing and films to show how the two images could be synthesized in the mind of the viewer to create a single totality and perception, even to create a level of thought or cognition beyond the realistic images. In an astonishing array of writings (see especially the book published in English as *Film Form,* which brings together twelve of his best essays written between 1928 and 1945), we can witness Eisenstein pushing beyond the relationships of individual shots in montage to search out the very form of film sequences and the entire film itself, exploring the ways in which shots are drawn to dominant and subsidiary lines or codes.

The formalist bent in early film theory was clearly a product of the silent film: cinema was divorced from the real world by the lack of natural sound (the typical musical accompaniment actually widened the gulf), and most of the artistic emphasis was on the *mise en scène.* It was for this reason that Rudolf Arnheim could argue in his book published in Germany in 1933 as *Film as Art* (the same title was used for a collection of his writings published in English in 1957 that included part of the original work) that the new dimension of sound was the death toll of film as an art form. Arnheim, a Gestalt psychologist and art critic, sees the very unreality of cinema as its greatest asset and the plasticity of its image as its major claim to art. In the Hungarian-born Béla Balázs's *Theory of the Film* (first published in the Soviet Union in 1945 as *The Art of Cinema*), however, we find ourselves at a transitional point where film is celebrated as both formalistic and realistic. Balázs may argue that technique must shape the raw material of nature into art, but at the same time he stresses that the filmmaker must never take us away from the natural and that a technique such as the closeup, so brilliantly employed in silent film, has the capacity to reveal to us what happens beneath appearances.

In the essays of André Bazin written in France in the late 1940s and the 1950s (published as *Qu'est-ce que le cinéma* in four volumes from 1958 to 1965 and in English as *What Is Cinema?* in two volumes in 1967 and 1971), we have an impressive blend of realist criticism and theory. Bazin found Kuleshov's and Eisenstein's emphasis on montage antithetical to the realistic possibilities of cinema, creating instead an illusory reality that is a product of the interaction of shots and not a reflection of the world photographed. He praised the American directors Orson Welles and William Wyler for emphasizing the individual image itself and what each reveals of reality (not the relationship of images), an emphasis largely absent in cinema since the silent films of Erich Von Stroheim and F. W. Murnau. Through the techniques of deep focus and the long take, Welles and Wyler present space and time as continuous and whole, as they appear in external reality, so that viewers are forced to immerse themselves in the image and select for themselves what to see. One of the founders of the important French film journal *Cahiers du cinéma,* Bazin influenced the criticism of such figures as François Truffaut, Jean-Luc Godard, Claude Chabrol, Eric Rohmer, and Jacques Rivette, who wrote for the journal. His emphasis on the individual image, his analysis of the single motion picture in the context of film genre, and his appreciation of the personal and the unique in the achievement of each film artist also had an impact on the new-wave films the five critics went on to direct. But it is basically Bazin's shrewd and perceptive appreciation of film, his ability to respond to the nuances of each work, his discerning eye for style and form, and his telling use of details and techniques as the source for his concepts that have survived as a model for future writers of film criticism.

Along with Bazin, Siegfried Kracauer must be recognized as one of the two major advocates of realist cinema. The title of his major theoretical text, *Theory of Film: The Redemption of Physical Reality* (1960), indicates the direction of his argument: the fictional films that most fulfill the potential of the filmic medium are those that least distort or remove the audience from the world as we know it, but those films also have the capacity to make us rediscover the real world, to expand our vision of it. The philosopher Stanley Cavell has also written on cinematic realism, in *The World Viewed: Reflections on the Ontology of Film* (1971, rev. ed., 1979). Cavell describes film as satisfying our desire to see the world unseen but, at the same time, as presenting a world that seems more natural than reality because, already drawn from fantasy, it relieves us from private fantasy and its responsibilities and also because, though not a dream, it awakens us from withdrawing into our longings deeper inside of us. Jean Mitry's two-volume *Esthétique et psychologie du cinéma* (1963–65) is an impressive and scholarly work that seeks to reconcile the formalist and realist camps by recognizing that the images of film are composed of analogues of people, places, and objects that exist in the real world but that the art of film orders this world, imposes on it significance and meaning. In this sense Mitry bases his

theory on the simple phenomenological truth that reality is known only through the perceiving mind: what we ourselves perceive on the screen is always the product of the filmmaker's own perceptions of reality, and the filmmaker's perceptions are conveyed through such techniques of cinema as montage.

The auteur school of criticism—suggested by François Truffaut in his essay "A Certain Tendency in French Cinema," which appeared in *Cahiers du cinéma* in January 1954 (trans. in Nichols, vol. 2); given substance by him and the other critics mentioned above who wrote for *Cahiers;* and popularized in English by Andrew Sarris in his essay "Notes on the Auteur Theory in 1962" (1962–63, in Mast, Cohen, and Braudy)—had great importance for a period of time. This critical approach gave major significance to the director, whose personal vision and style were now seen as the controlling force in a film, even a film made in Hollywood within the obstacles of the studio system. Auteur criticism sought to give to the director the same legitimacy as that given to the author of a novel, and to the film the same legitimacy as that given to literature itself. Indeed, it is mainly through auteur criticism that literary criticism and film criticism merge.

On the other hand, genre theory and criticism, which made considerable strides during the same period of time, sought to recognize and legitimate the very popular nature of film, especially as a product of the Hollywood studio system, and to identify and explain what was similar in a group of works from director to director. Although individual directors might be cited for their abilities in certain genres or for their innovations or personal stamp within the tradition, much genre theory and criticism was based on the connection between these works and their audiences and sought to explain the social and cultural needs of the viewer. Genre theory and criticism was itself the most profitable location for adopting the new emphasis on structuralism, which was having such a profound effect on cultural criticism during the late 1960s and the 1970s: Hollywood offered a large number of similar films with repeatable elements in each genre, which made these works the inevitable source for studies in cine-structuralism. The binary oppositions and structures explored in these studies may seem to be too superficial to suggest the deep structures that CLAUDE LÉVI-STRAUSS had propounded in myths from "primitive" cultures or in his treatment of the Oedipus myth, but a work such as Jim Kitses's *Horizons West* (1969) is able to establish a basic structural and thematic dialectic in the Western and also to show the individual contributions of specific directors within this context. Peter Wollen's discussions of Howard Hawks and John Ford in *Signs and Meaning in the Cinema* (1969, rev. ed., 1972) also uses genre in its auteur-structuralist approach to develop thematic structures and tensions in the films of these two directors.

Lévi-Strauss's discussion of FERDINAND DE SAUSSURE's SEMIOTICS left a great imprint on film theory and set off a train of argument that itself was to stay relevant even in the period of poststructuralism. The most important early work in this context was Christian Metz's *Film Language: A Semiotics of Cinema* (published in France as the first volume of *Essais sur la signification au cinéma* in 1968 and in English in 1974). Metz's major concern is to demonstrate the way films signify meaning through semiotic codes, especially *specialized* codes unique to the cinema, such as the eight arrangements of shots possible in a narrative sequence, which he outlines as the "grande syntagmatique." Such a code may seem compelling theoretically, but in actuality it had little applicability or function in relation to specific films.

It was the "second semiotics," a term employed for a series of theoretical texts based upon a combination of semiotics, Althusserian Marxism, and Lacanian post-Freudianism, that was to be the dominant theoretical discourse for almost two decades (see MARXIST THEORY AND CRITICISM: 2. STRUCTURALIST MARXISM and JACQUES LACAN). We are discussing here a filmic discourse that received considerable impetus from the politicization of theory and criticism from the late 1960s on in the French journals *Cinéthique* and *Cahiers du cinéma* and in the British publication *Screen*. This filmic discourse eventually became a strong force among a group of film teachers at American universities and in the professional journals for which they wrote. The impulse of the second semiotics was to identify and then deconstruct the ideological structures and codes of capitalistic society evident or, more often, implied in commercial narrative cinema and to tie this ideological focus in with Lacanian psychoanalytical theory about the child's early developmental stages, especially the mirror stage, to which we regress on some level when viewing the images on the screen—recreated within us in the imaginary, a feeling of oneness and self first developed in us when we viewed our reflections in a mirror during early childhood, but now actually shaped by the film's ideology. Jean-Louis Baudry's "Ideological Effects of the Basic Cinematic Apparatus" (1970) was the first of his several essays on the subject that were to influence Metz's further development and popularization of these ideas in the four texts he wrote between 1973 and 1976, published together as *The Imaginary Signifier* (1977, trans., 1982). Lacan's concept of *suture*, earlier introduced to film the-

ory in Jean-Pierre Oudart's essay "La suture," which appeared in *Cahiers du cinéma* (1969) and in English in *Screen* (trans. Kari Hamet, 1977–78), was to become the source of much debate on the recreation of the imaginary and subject positioning, on the way we impose unity on such techniques of narrative film as point-of-view editing, match cutting, and eye-line matching, and on the way such techniques impose unity upon us. Two 1981 books, both collections of related essays that present a provocative synthesis of ideology, psychoanalysis, and film technique, are Stephen Heath's *Questions of Cinema* and Bill Nichols's *Ideology and the Image*. Mention should also be made of Peter Brunette and David Wills's *Screen/Play: Derrida and Film Theory*, published in 1989, one of the few attempts to apply to film the ideas of the French philosopher JACQUES DERRIDA that already had played such a major role in literary theory.

Feminist film theory and criticism has also been a vigorous and influential school, one that has had a great impact on the teaching of film. Early texts in this area offer a straightforward critical approach in which the various stereotypes of women in film are traced and analyzed as products of a patriarchal society and culture, but feminist criticism has also become very much involved with the Althusserian, Lacanian, and semiotic approaches of poststructuralist film theory in its attempt to understand sexual differentiation within the narrative and textual codes of the film as well as within the viewing process itself. An important initial step in this feminist dialogue was made by Pam Cook and Claire Johnston in the mid-1970s with a series of essays for the Edinburgh Film Festival and the British Film Institute (see especially their essays on Raoul Walsh and Dorothy Arzner published in Penley). Cook and Johnston argue for the importance of analyzing classic Hollywood films from a theoretical perspective to understand the role of women and women's desire in these films. Within the Hollywood film, these critics sought to find ruptures, places where repressed female desire erupts and disturbs the patriarchal text.

Laura Mulvey's important essay "Visual Pleasure and Narrative Cinema" (1975) described the image of woman in the Hollywood cinema as the passive object for the active male gaze. But the pleasure of the male gaze is threatened by the woman's representation as a signifier of castration. Mulvey describes two unconscious responses of the male to alleviate his fear of castration, the first a process of sadistic voyeurism, which denigrates the woman, and the second a process of "fetishistic scopophilia," which overvalues the woman's physical appearance. In response to this focus on male pleasure and desire, Mulvey herself in "Afterthoughts on 'Visual Pleasure and Narrative Cinema' Inspired by King Vidor's *Duel in the Sun*" (1981), Kaja Silverman in "Dis-Embodying the Female Voice" (1984), and Mary Ann Doane in "Film and the Masquerade: Theorizing the Female Spectator" (1985) all consider, from a psychoanalytic perspective, the pressures and problems brought upon the female viewer by films structured for the male gaze and forbidding any positive identification with the female characters.

For Gaylin Studlar, however, sexual differentiation and patriarchy need not play a role in spectatorship, nor need the viewing experience be limited to Oedipal responses. Basing the theoretical argument of her book *In The Realm of Pleasure: Von Sternberg, Dietrich, and the Masochistic Aesthetic* on *Masochism: An Interpretation of Coldness and Cruelty* (Gilles Deleuze's study of the novels of Leopold von Sacher-Masoch), Studlar seeks to demonstrate, through the Von Sternberg–Dietrich films, a masochistic aesthetic that arises from the woman in the film creating visual pleasure in both male and female viewers by eliciting their unconscious identification with and desire for the pre-Oedipal mother of the child's oral stage. The cinema apparatus's suggestion of the dream screen, the representation of the maternal breast, evokes within the viewer archaic visual pleasures.

In the early 1990s, film theory and criticism seem to be at an impasse. A number of recent essays and books, notably Noël Carroll's *Mystifying Movies: Fads and Fallacies in Contemporary Film Theory* and David Bordwell's *Making Meaning: Inference and Rhetoric in the Interpretation of Cinema,* have argued that much of post-1970 criticism and theory has taken us further and further away from understanding film and the viewer's actual response to the images on the screen. Common criticisms of contemporary film theory argue that Lacanian post-Freudianism is ultimately itself an unprovable abstraction applicable to cinema only as a seemingly remote analogy and that Althusser's ideology has made theory and criticism into social and political tracts.

One response to the psychoanalytic-Marxist approach has been a greater emphasis on film form and technique. What is striking about this response is its reliance on literary concepts and its examination of what takes place on the screen in the context of the viewer's reactions—the creation of a type of film NARRATOLOGY that includes an important dose of viewer-response analysis. Edward Branigan's *Point of View in the Cinema: A Theory of Narration and Subjectivity in Classical Film* (1984) often uses the vocabulary and concepts of literary narratology to discuss filmic narrative texts but does so to achieve a detailed analysis of the ways film techniques create various types of subjectivity on the screen and subjective responses in the viewer. Branigan's mentor, David Bordwell, published in 1985 *Narration in the Fiction Film,* in which he develops a narrative theory that takes into account the spectator's perception and cognition. In addition to employing a constructivist theory of psychology, Bordwell leans heavily on the literary theory of the Russian Formalists, especially their notions *sjužet* and *fabula.* In *Flashback in Film: Memory and History* (1989), Maureen Turim uses Gérard Genette's and ROLAND BARTHES's structuralist and semiotic approaches to narrative textuality as the underpinning for her own theory of the flashback in film. She also refers to Derridean DECONSTRUCTION as a context for her discussion.

Although the recent emphasis on film history is also part of a retreat from past theory, such works themselves may employ theory, such as, for example, *The Classic Hollywood Cinema: Film Style and Mode of Production to 1960,* by David Bordwell, Janet Staiger, and Kristin Thompson. Published in 1985, this impressive and detailed study of four decades of Hollywood films is not averse to using genre theory and narratological concepts, especially those from the Russian Formalists. Historical changes and developments, however, ought themselves to be a consideration in film theory, as they are in Gilles Deleuze's *Cinema 1: The Movement-Image* and *Cinema 2: The Time-Image,* which use the writings of Henri Bergson and CHARLES SANDERS PEIRCE as springboards for a theoretical and philosophical study of the dominance of the movement-image in classical cinema and that of the time-image in cinema after World War II. It is still too early to know the impact these complex and richly documented volumes, published in French in 1983 and 1985 and in English in 1986 and 1989, respectively, will have on future film studies.

It is also impossible during this period of reconsideration to guess the future course of film theory and criticism in general. Psychological analysis of what takes place on the screen and in the audience both as individuals and as a group still seems a profitable way to proceed, but it needs to be cognizant of the insights of feminist writings and should not rely only on the works of Freud and Lacan, and social and cultural coding remains an important issue, especially if shorn of polemics and preconceptions. Theorists and critics still have much to say on the nature of filmic representation and film as art by further examining film form, technique, and style, but they must get beyond the terminology and concepts of literary narratology. The interface of technology and art in the cinema, which has only begun to be explored, offers the possibility of theoretical ramifications that could change our way of thinking about film both as a medium and as a cultural and social phenomenon. Through such investigations, we may come closer to understanding the unique properties of film and the medium's impact on viewers and to achieving the language for cinematic discourse that theoreticians and critics began to search for three-quarters of a century ago.

Ira Konigsberg

Richard Abel, *French Film Theory and Criticism: A History/Anthology, 1907–1939* (1988); Rudolf Arnheim, *Film as Art* (1933–38, partly pub. in English, 1957); Béla Balázs, *Theory of the Film: Character and Growth of a New Art* (1945, trans. Edith Bone, 1970); Jean-Louis Baudry, "Ideological Effects of the Basic Cinematographic Apparatus" (1970, trans. Alan Williams, 1974–75, in Mast, Cohen, and Braudy; Nichols, vol. 2 [rev.]; Rosen [rev.]); André Bazin, *What Is Cinema?* (4 vols., 1958–65, ed. and trans. Hugh Gray, 2 vols., 1967–71); David Bordwell, *Making Meaning: Inference and Rhetoric in the Interpretation of Cinema* (1989), *Narration in the Fiction Film* (1985); David Bordwell, Janet Staiger, and Kristin Thompson, *The Classical Hollywood Cinema: Film Style and Mode of Production to 1960* (1985); Edward R. Branigan, *Point of View in the Cinema* (1984); Noël Carroll, *Mystifying Movies: Fads and Fallacies in Contemporary Film Theory* (1988); Gilles Deleuze, *Cinéma 1: L'Image-mouvement* (1983, *Cinema 1: The Movement-Image,* trans. Hugh Tomlinson and Barbara Habberjam, 1986), *Cinéma 2: L'Image-temps* (1985, *Cinema 2: The Time-Image,* trans. Hugh Tomlinson and Robert Galeta, 1989); Mary Ann Doane, "Film and the Masquerade: Theorizing the Female Spectator" *Screen* 23 (1982, in Mast, Cohen, and Braudy); Sergei Eisenstein, *Film Form: Essays in Film Theory* (ed. and trans. Jay Leyda, 1949); Stephen Heath, *Questions of Cinema* (1981); Jim Kitses, *Horizons West* (1969); Siegfried Kracauer, *Theory of Film: The Redemption of Physical Reality* (1960); Lev Kuleshov, *Kuleshov on Film: Writings by Lev Kuleshov* (ed. and trans. Ronald Levaco, 1974); Christian Metz, *Film Language: A Semiotics of the Cinema* (1971, trans. Michael Taylor, 1974), *The Imaginary Signifier: Psychoanalysis and the Cinema* (1977, trans. Celia Britton, Annwyl Williams, Ben Brewster, and Alfred Guzzetti, 1982); Jean Mitry, *Esthétique et psychologie du cinéma* (2 vols., 1963–65); Laura Mulvey, "Afterthoughts on 'Visual Pleasure and Narrative Cinema' Inspired by King Vidor's *Duel in the Sun* (1946)" (1981, *Visual and Other Pleasures,* 1989), "Visual Pleasure and Narrative Cinema" (1975, *Visual and Other Pleasures,* 1989; in Mast, Cohen, and Braudy; Nichols, vol. 2; Rosen); Hugo Münsterberg, *The Film: A Psychological Study* (1916); Bill Nichols, *Ideology and the Image* (1981); Constance Penley, ed., *Feminism and Film Theory* (1988); V. I. Pudovkin, *"Film Technique" and "Film Acting": The Cinema Writings of V. I. Pudovkin* (1926–34, 2 vols., trans. Ivor Montague, 1929–37, reprint, 2 vols. in 1, 1954); Kaja Silverman, "Disembodying the Female Voice: Irigaray, Experimental Feminist Cinema, and Femininity," *The Acoustic Mirror: The Female Voice in Psychoanalysis and Cinema,* (1988); Gaylin Studlar, *In the Realm of Pleasure: Von Sternberg, Dietrich, and the Masochistic Aesthetic* (1988); Maureen Turim, *Flashbacks in Film: Memory and History* (1989); Peter Wollen, *Signs and Meaning in the Cinema* (1969, 3d ed., 1972).

Robert C. Allen and Douglas Gomery, *Film History: Theory and Practice* (1985); J. Dudley Andrew, *Concepts in Film Theory* (1984), *The Major Film Theories: An Introduction* (1976); Noël Carroll, *Philosophical Problems of Classical Film Theory* (1988); Teresa de Lauretis and Stephen Heath, eds., *The Cinematic Apparatus* (1980); Gerald Mast, Marshall Cohen, and Leo Braudy, eds., *Film Theory and Criticism: Introductory Readings* (1974, 4th ed., 1992); Bill Nichols, ed., *Movies and Methods* (2 vols., 1976–85); Philip Rosen, ed., *Narrative, Apparatus, Ideology: A Film Theory Reader* (1986); Elisabeth Weis and John Belton, *Film Sound: Theory and Practice* (1985).

FISH, STANLEY

Stanley Fish (b. 1938) is one of the best-known contemporary literary theorists on the American scene, known less for developing a new interpretive method or a new mode of theoretical discourse than for his ability to develop many such innovations, only to move beyond them in rapid succession. Fish is a controversial figure, widely imitated yet widely criticized. There is less disagreement over the clarity and power of his writing, as he is probably the clearest writer at work in contemporary literary theory.

After an initial book based on his dissertation with few theoretical implications, *John Skelton's Poetry* (1965), Fish quickly attained prominence as a literary theorist with the publication of his second book, *Surprised by Sin: The Reader in "Paradise Lost"* (1967). Romantic poets such as William Blake and PERCY BYSSHE SHELLEY had suggested that Satan was the hero, not the villain, of *Paradise Lost,* and the possibility of this "Satanic reading" of the poem is only one indication of the inconsistencies in style, tone, and genre that can be found in *Paradise Lost.*

The central thesis of *Surprised by Sin* is that these inconsistencies have a pattern, which is that the reader, like Adam, falls into error or sin and then is brought up short. The reader of *Paradise Lost* reenacts and experiences the fall and ultimate redemption of humanity as he or she reads. This reading of Milton's poem conflicted, of course, with a central principle of NEW CRITICISM, the affective fallacy, which argued that the meaning of a work of literature was not to be confused with its effect on a reader. And in the years after the publication of *Surprised by Sin,* Fish went on to argue that what had at first seemed a peculiarity of Milton's work was in fact characteristic of all literature. Reader-response criticism, to use Fish's term for his theory or method of reading, argues that reading is a temporal phenomenon and that writers depend upon this in several significant ways. Texts are constructed with dilemmas, changes in direction, and false starts of the kind analyzed in *Surprised by Sin,* and the meaning of such texts is in our experience of these phenomena, not simply some final, spatialized, or thematized resolution of them. The meaning of a literary work, in short, is the work a reader does while reading it.

This is a simple but powerful (or perhaps powerful because simple) model of reading, the power of which is best indicated by the fact that within a few years reader-response criticism had become sufficiently influential that the affective fallacy was itself considered a fallacy. But what gave the reader's experience its shape and nature? Reader-response criticism proposed simply to describe the reader's experience, but what was the status of that description or the cause of the experience it described? There are potentially two different answers to this question, one text-centered, stressing how the text itself creates the reader's experience, and the other reader-centered, stressing the reader's role in creating meaning. Fish's work immediately subsequent to the initial definition of reader-response criticism in "Literature in the Reader: Affective Stylistics" (1970) moved first in a text-centered, then in a reader-centered direction, until finally his work moved beyond the limits of anything usefully called reader-response criticism.

The text-centered direction is most fully represented by Fish's third book, *Self-consuming Artifacts: The Experience of Seventeenth-Century Literature* (1972). The thesis of this study is that the works studied, primarily seventeenth-century works of English prose such as FRANCIS BACON's *Essays* and Robert Burton's *Anatomy of Melancholy,* have a similar structure, which we might today call self-deconstructing. They begin by adumbrating a proposition or view of the world that they end by rejecting.

Again, structure or form in these works is dialectical and multivocal, not unified and one-dimensional. It seems clear enough in *Self-consuming Artifacts* that they were designed to be that way, which makes the multiplicity of the reader's experience—now seen to be controlled by the text—more apparent than real. But this conflicts with the multiplicity of our experience of literature; the range of actual response to any work of literature seems too multifarious to be designed.

Fish subsequently realized that the reader's response he had purported to describe in *Surprised by Sin* and *Self-consuming Artifacts* was really a response he had been prescribing. Reader-response criticism, far from being a pure description of reading, was simply a system for generating meaning. But this is true of all theories: they create meaning by prescribing in advance what will count as meaningful in a text. Readers—not texts—make meanings, and they do so by virtue of the theories or beliefs about meaning and about texts that they hold to be true. This new formulation, which quickly became known as the theory of interpretive communities, replaces the individual reader of reader-response criticism by a community of readers sharing a set of interpretive strategies in common.

In 1980 Fish collected his theoretical essays of the 1970s in his fifth book, *Is There a Text in This Class? The Authority of Interpretive Communities.* (A book on George Herbert, *The Living Temple,* had appeared in 1978.) These essays, beginning with "Literature in the Reader" but tracing his shift in such essays as "Interpreting the Variorum" away from reader-response criticism toward the theory of interpretive communities, consolidated his position as one of the most influential and most cited theorists of his time, influential despite—or perhaps because of—his refusal to settle on a fixed position or stance. The dynamic quality Fish once ascribed to reading was by now a property of his work *on* reading and interpretation. *Is There a Text in This Class?* is a wide-ranging collection, with essays on topics as diverse as STYLISTICS and the application of theories of SPEECH ACTS to Shakespeare's *Coriolanus.* The most sustained section is a group of four lectures that gave the book its title. These lectures, the most extended exposition of the theory of interpretive communities, answer the question in the title with both a no and a yes. No, there is no text if by that one means an unchanging entity with a fixed meaning; yes, there is a text because every interpretive community fixes and defines the meaning of the text it reads and, in a sense, writes.

The years subsequent to *Is There a Text in This Class?* have seen further changes and new directions in Fish's work, though he has not moved beyond the theory of interpretive communities as that theory moves beyond reader-response criticism. The essays of the 1980s were collected in his sixth book, *Doing What Comes Naturally: Change, Rhetoric, and the Practice of Theory in Literary and Legal Studies,* and where they move beyond restating and clarifying his already established positions, they show three important directions to the new work: the defense of professionalism in literary studies; the extension of interpretive theory into legal theory; and antifoundationalism and the critique of the possibility of theory.

Fish's work was from the first criticized for the power over the text it gave the reader, but *Is There a Text in This Class?* made it clear that not all readers are equally powerful. Criticism for Fish is a mode by which certain powerful readers persuade others of the nature and meaning of the text they are reading. This view has in turn been attacked for the power it assigns to "professional interpreters," to literary critics, but Fish argues in several essays in *Doing What Comes Naturally* that such antiprofessional arguments are themselves forms of professionalism. In Fish's view, one can no more escape professionalism, a commitment to a certain version of academic practice, than one can escape membership in an interpretive community, a commitment to a certain way of reading.

What lies behind Fish's vigorous defense of the profession of modern literary studies may partially be growing interest in a far better organized and more self-confident profession, the legal profession. As recently as 1970, though statutory interpretation was an important aspect of legal studies, and interpretation of literary works an important aspect of literary studies, few legal theorists sought illumination in literary theory, or vice versa. That has changed, as the law and literature movement—as it is sometimes called—has sought to connect these two fields of study and domains of human action. Stanley Fish has been the key player in this from the literary side, but though the net effect of his interest in legal theory has been to connect the fields of literary and legal theory, he has tended to argue against the kinds of connections being made between the two by such prominent legal theorists as Ronald Dworkin and Roberto Ungar. In different ways, Dworkin and Ungar seek in literary theory a theory of interpretation that can direct legal practitioners in their acts of interpretation. This is what Fish has repeatedly argued cannot be done.

Theory, according to Fish, has no consequences in the sense that it cannot direct practice by providing a general account of interpretation and meaning. This was a claim made at the end of *Is There a Text in This Class?*

and Fish, intensifying that claim across the 1980s, has argued in several essays collected in *Doing What Comes Naturally* that theory itself is an impossibility and should disappear. Fish's argument to this effect was quickly seconded in Steven Knapp and Walter Benn Michaels's "Against Theory," and these critics are often seen as forming with Fish a "neo-pragmatist" movement placing a higher value on practice over theory. But this position seems caught up in a number of contradictions. Fish's critique of theory is itself a piece of theory, a general account that seeks to direct practice, so it seems caught in a vicious circle. Moreover, the consistent thing for Fish to do, having recommended that we stop doing theory, would be to follow his own advice and return from theory to the domain of "practice," something he has through the early 1990s shown no signs of doing. But, of course, Fish's evolving positions have fruitfully embraced contraries and contradictions before, and we can be sure that Fish will revise the positions marked out in *Doing What Comes Naturally* in future articles and books that will in turn undergo revision.

Reed Way Dasenbrock

See also READER-RESPONSE THEORY AND CRITICISM and VALUE THEORY.

Stanley Fish, *Doing What Comes Naturally: Change, Rhetoric, and the Practice of Theory in Literary and Legal Studies* (1989), *Is There a Text in This Class? The Authority of Interpretive Communities* (1980), *John Skelton's Poetry* (1965), *The Living Temple: George Herbert and Catechizing* (1978), *Self-consuming Artifacts: The Experience of Seventeenth-Century Literature* (1972), *Surprised by Sin: The Reader in "Paradise Lost"* (1967, 2d ed., 1971).

Jonathan Culler, "Stanley Fish and the Righting of the Reader," *The Pursuit of Signs: Semiotics, Literature, Deconstruction* (1981); Reed Way Dasenbrock, "Do We Write the Text We Read?" *College English* 53 (1991); Gerald Graff, "Interpretation on Tlon: A Response to Stanley Fish," *New Literary History* 17 (1985); Thomas Kent, "Interpretation and Triangulation: A Davidsonian Critique of Reader-oriented Literary Theory," *Literary Theory after Davidson* (ed. Reed Way Dasenbrock, 1992); Steven Knapp and Walter Benn Michaels, "Against Theory" (1982, *Against Theory: Literary Studies and the New Pragmatism,* ed. W. J. T. Mitchell, 1985); Jules David Law, "Uncertain Grounds: Wittgenstein and the New Pragmatism," *New Literary History* 19 (1988); Steven Mailloux, *Interpretive Conventions: The Reader in the Study of American Fiction* (1982); Mary Louise Pratt, "Interpretive Strategies / Strategic Interpretations: On Anglo-American Reader Response Criticism," *Boundary 2* 11 (1982–83); Robert Scholes, "Who Cares about the Text?" *Textual Power: Literary Theory and the Teaching of English* (1985).

FLAUBERT, GUSTAVE

Gustave Flaubert (1821–80) remains one of the most important French novelists of the nineteenth century. Although he is most often associated with the realist and naturalist movements because of his desire for authorial objectivity, his works are not so easily classified. His masterpiece, *Madame Bovary* (1857), is indeed a stylistic exercise in which Flaubert attempted to eliminate all authorial visibility, yet the novel manifests the influence of virtually all of the various literary movements of the period, most notably the Romanticism whose "feminine phrases" Flaubert professed to despise (*Correspondance* 1:210). Instead, he advocates a doctrine of impersonality, which he sees as "the sign of Strength" (2:466). Unlike the Romantics, who sought to continually redefine the inner self, Flaubert aspired to a "grasp of the non-self and a representation of the world" (Poulet 15). Flaubert's vision of the world is, then, one that grows out of the Romantic tradition and is modified by his fundamental desire to let the text speak for itself.

Flaubert was born in Rouen, where his father was chief of surgery at the city hospital. It was in his youth in this provincial city that Flaubert developed his hatred of all that was "bourgeois," an appellation that had less to do with social class than with a limited, empty, bigoted view of the world. After studying law briefly in Paris, Flaubert was stricken in 1844 by the first of many nervous attacks that allowed him to withdraw from public life and devote himself to his writing. He had by that point formulated a rather pessimistic view of life, and thus his retreat from society caused him no great hardship. He spent the rest of his life in Croisset, outside Rouen, writing some of the most remarkable novels of his time: *L'Éducation sentimentale* (1846), *La Tentation de Saint Antoine* (1848), *Madame Bovary* (1857), *Salammbô* (1872), later versions of *L'Éducation sentimentale* (1869) and *La Tentation de Saint Antoine* (1874), and the unfinished *Bouvard et Pécuchet*. In addition, his *Trois contes* (1877) includes the celebrated short story "Un Coeur simple."

Although Flaubert left no definitive statement on literary theory, his correspondence allows us a view of the development of his aesthetic that might not be possible in a theoretical text. Through the late 1840s and early 1850s he wrote regularly of his attempts to depersonalize his works, championing "Form" as the only way to find "Truth" and "the Idea" (*Correspondance* 2:91). When he set out to write his "book about nothing" (2:31), *Madame Bovary,* he intended to eliminate all external elements, leaving nothing but style itself. The foundation of this aesthetic rests on his well-known declaration: "An author in his book must be like God in the universe, present everywhere and visible nowhere" (2:204). The more visible the author, the weaker the work.

Art, according to Flaubert, was moving toward a purity in which the subject would be virtually invisible, leaving style free to be an absolute "manner of seeing things" (2:229). Over the centuries, form had become freer, leaving behind all rule and measure. The epic had given way to the novel, poetry to prose. There was no longer any orthodoxy, and form was as free as the will of its creator. It is not surprising that Flaubert is seen by some as a precursor of the French "new novel" of the 1950s and that we have seen the publication of a collection of essays entitled *Flaubert and Postmodernism.* It could be argued, however, that his novels do not follow the precepts he espoused and should not be called postmodern works.

In 1856, after five years of work during which he expressed his desire to write a "book about nothing," Flaubert finished *Madame Bovary.* While the novel is certainly a monument to style, Flaubert realized that his aspirations toward complete impersonality were unrealistic. "I have always sinned that way; I have always put myself into everything that I have written" (*Correspondance* 2:127). At times during the writing of *Madame Bovary,* he became so emotionally involved in his heroine's fate that he fell ill. This novel about a young, romantic woman trapped in the despised "bourgeois" world not only spoke of Flaubert's romantic side but aroused enough passion in society to have the book brought to trial on morals charges.

Flaubert reinforced the realistic vision he attempted to create by his ingenious use of the *style indirect libre,* a stylistic device that enabled him to express a character's thoughts or words without directly identifying their source (of the many renderings of the term *style indirect libre,* two of the most common are "free indirect style" and "represented discourse" [Porter 1]). The first person is avoided, no quotation marks are used, and no verb tells us that the character is thinking or speaking. Only through context and style do we see that the objective narrator has turned the text over to the character for the moment.

Flaubert alternates the supposed objective account of the third person narrator's voice with the subjective experience of a character moving through the world.

The former is presented as a given that is in itself unproblematic for narrator and reader; the latter involves an individual's perception and misperception. The gap between the two gives rise to the familiar Flaubertian irony. (D. Porter 374)

This irony helped bring Flaubert a measure of critical acceptance during his lifetime.

Flaubertian criticism has varied widely over the years but can generally be broken down into three overlapping stages. Traditionally, Flaubert was seen as a realist; then, as criticism became more thematic, he was considered an idealist; and finally, structuralist and poststructuralist criticism have judged him to be an "indeterminist, a writer who resists conclusions" (Porter 2). Overriding mere, and sometimes simplistic, classifications is Flaubert's influence on writers of his time and on those who came after him. His unswerving search for the *mot juste* "called into question the notion that made literature a communication between author and reader" (Culler 13). Without the reassuring guidance of an ever-present narrator/author, the reader was presented with a new challenge. Authors of the last hundred years have continued Flaubert's legacy by giving the reader ever more leeway with which to interpret a work of fiction.

William VanderWolk

See also FRENCH THEORY AND CRITICISM: 3. NINETEENTH CENTURY.

Gustave Flaubert, *Correspondance* (ed. Jean Bruneau, 3 vols., 1973–91); *Oeuvres complètes* (2 vols., 1964).

Benjamin Bart, *Flaubert* (1967); Harold Bloom, ed., *Gustave Flaubert's "Madame Bovary": Modern Critical Interpretations* (1987); Geneviève Bollème, *La Leçon de Flaubert* (1964); Victor Brombert, *The Novels of Flaubert: A Study of Themes and Techniques* (1966); Jean Bruneau, *Les Débuts littéraires de Gustave Flaubert* (1962); Charles Carlut, ed., *Essais sur Flaubert* (1979); Jonathan Culler, *Flaubert: The Uses of Uncertainty* (1974); Eugenio Donato, *The Script of Decadence: Essays on the Fictions of Flaubert and the Poetics of Romanticism* (1991); Eric Gans, *Madame Bovary: The End of Romance* (1989); Gérard Genette, "Silences de Flaubert," *Figures I* (1966); Robert Griffin, *Rape of the Lock: Flaubert's Mythic Realism* (1988); Herbert Lottman, *Flaubert: A Biography* (1989); Dennis Porter, "Flaubert and the Difficulty of Reading," *Nineteenth-Century French Studies* 12 (1984); Laurence M. Porter, ed., *Critical Essays on Gustave Flaubert* (1986); Georges Poulet, "Flaubert," *Critical Essays* (Porter); Vaheed K. Ramazani, *The Free Indirect Mode: Flaubert and the Poetics of Irony* (1989); Jean-Pierre Richard, "La Création de la forme chez Flaubert," *Littérature et sensation* (1954); David Roe, *Gustave Flaubert* (1989); Naomi Schor and Henry F. Majewski, eds., *Flaubert and Postmodernism* (1984); Richard Terdiman, *The Dialectics of Isolation* (1976); Steven Ullman, *Style in the French Novel* (1957).

FOUCAULT, MICHEL

Michel Foucault (1926–84) took *licences* from the École Normale in both philosophy and psychology and spent several years observing in hospitals and writing about mental illness. In the mid-1950s he went abroad to teach first in Sweden, then in Poland, where he wrote his first major work, *Madness and Civilization* (1961). In 1970 he was awarded a chair in the history of systems of thought at the prestigious Collège de France, a post he held until his death. Although briefly associated with the French Communist party in the 1940s, Foucault did not actively participate in politics until after the events of May 1968. In the 1950s and early 1960s his work was associated with an emerging critique of psychology and medical practice in general that came to be known as the anti-psychiatry movement. With R. D. Laing in England and eventually Félix Guattari in France as the most prominent members, anti-psychiatry exposed hidden levels of domination in the practices and discourse of what appeared to be a humane science.

Beginning in the mid-1960s Foucault's interests turned to STRUCTURALISM, a relatively new intellectual trend that opposed "philosophies of consciousness" such as existentialism, PHENOMENOLOGY, and humanist forms of Marxism and psychoanalysis. The tendency of structuralism to reject the vantage point of the author or subject in favor of that of the text or object may be found in Foucault's *Order of Things* (1966) and *The Archaeology of Knowledge* (1969).

The political upheaval of May 1968 had profound impact on all French intellectuals. Structuralists were compelled to rethink their rejection of the subject; Marxists and socialists in general could no longer base their critique on the unique suffering of the working class nor limit its scope purely to capitalism as a mode of production (Poster; Smart, *Foucault, Marxism*). Foucault's work reflected this change in intellectual mood: *Discipline and Punish* (1975) argued the imbrication of power with discourse and uncovered a new dimension of domination in modern society, "technologies of power." Volume 1 of *The History of Sexuality* (1976) rejected the Freudian-Marxist analysis of repressed libido in favor of a focus on the normalizing effects of discourses on sex. During these years Foucault participated in political movements concerned with the reform of prisons and gay liberation. His work and politics reflected a shift in radical movements to groups and concerns outside the traditional working class.

But the promised further volumes of *The History of Sexuality* did not immediately appear. They were published in 1984 in the urgent months after Foucault knew he was seriously ill. In the eight years from 1976 to 1984 his thinking underwent still another change. Without abandoning the political and epistemologically radical stance of the concept of discourse/practice, he moved on to a concern for the way subjects constitute themselves through these discourse/practices. In volumes 2 and 3, his emphasis shifted from the theme of sex to the theme of the constitution of the self in the "truth" of discourse. When he died, Foucault left behind manuscripts from volume 4, which was to cover the confessional of the medieval period.

Foucault's writing has had a remarkable reception in the humanities in the English-speaking world, especially by literary theorists. During the 1970s and 1980s his books were read as part of the general interest in French poststructuralism, a term that includes such disparate figures as JACQUES DERRIDA, JEAN-FRANÇOIS LYOTARD, Gilles Deleuze, JACQUES LACAN, ROLAND BARTHES, and Jean Baudrillard. These writers are connected more by their rejection of certain features of structuralism than by any positive intellectual commonality. Foucault has had as great an impact as has any of these figures, perhaps ranking second only to Derrida.

As we have seen, his writing embraced several distinct positions in the course of his career, and the implications of his theoretical work for literary criticism vary considerably depending upon which period of his writings the critic considers primary. Attention to *Madness and Civilization* leads to a reading of texts for silences and exclusions; *The Order of Things* suggests a search for *épistèmes*—unconscious, regulating structures that limit what can be written in any epoch; *Discipline and Punish* encourages a more political reading, one that stresses the power effects of discourse; volumes 2 and 3 of *The History of Sexuality* sensitize the critic to the textual problematic of self-constitution.

Given this diversity of interpretive strategies, it is nonetheless fair to say that the major theoretical tendency of Foucault's work is to regard the literary text as part of a larger framework of texts, institutions, and practices. The two most important examples of criticism associated with Foucault's ideas, those of EDWARD W. SAID *(Orientalism)* and Stephen Greenblatt, are stunning examples of this kind of reading. Like other poststructuralists, Foucault urges the critic to complicate the interpretation, to reject the turn to the author's intention as the court of last resort, to look in the text for articulated hierarchies of value and meaning, above all to trace filiations of inter- and extratextuality, to draw connections between the given text and others, between the text and the intellectual and material context. Foucauldian readings are sensitive to the political impact of the text and the political unconscious behind the text, informing its statements and shaping its lines of enunciation.

Foucault has been a reluctant theorist, one unwilling to elaborate univocal concepts. Systematic theory opposes the interpretive strategy of this poststructuralist because it participates in a logic of representation. The concept is a sign that is "adequate" to the object ("reality"). The concept presupposes a transparency to language, one that allows words to represent things, to stand in their place, without introducing distortion. In addition, the concept empowers the rational subject as one who stands above and outside the representation, its creator and lord. Foucault opposes the concept because it implies the representationality of language and the rationality of the subject. In place of conceptual theories he has offered two methodological innovations: archaeology and genealogy.

Archaeology is a synchronic analysis of what Foucault calls the statements or enunciations in any discourse. Every discourse contains "rules of formation" that limit and shape what may be said. These rules of formation are not at the disposal of the author but come into play as the text is composed, out of phase with the consciousness of the writer. Archaeological analysis may be thought of as an elaboration of the figure of the *épistème,* which Foucault employed so effectively in *The Order of Things.* It may also be thought of as a sort of structuralist analysis, one that uncovers complexities within texts. The archaeological method, after all, was developed before Foucault turned to the problems of practice and power.

Genealogy is a diachronic method, one that attempts to reconstruct the origins and development of discourses by showing their rootedness in a field of forces. Genealogy is a Nietzschean effort to develop a critical method that undermines all absolute grounds, that demonstrates the origins of things only in relation to and in contest with other things. Genealogy disallows pure beginnings, those historical formations that deny their historicity by naturalizing themselves, absolutizing themselves, grounding themselves in some transcendent principle. From the vantage point of those who hold to absolute principles, genealogy appears as nihilist, relativist, amoral. Hubert Dreyfus and Paul Rabinow argue more convincingly that together with archaeology, genealogy constitutes "an analytic of finitude," one that undercuts metaphysical pretensions, overblown notions of reason's ability to ground discourse, but not ethical action in the best sense of the term.

The archaeological-genealogical method is best designed to explore the interplay between discourse and practice. As an interpretive strategy it is far less purely textual than SEMIOTICS or DECONSTRUCTION. Unlike the work of Derrida and Barthes, Foucault's work is difficult for writers inured to NEW CRITICISM. Deconstruction and semiotics, claims to the contrary notwithstanding, are formalist enterprises, ones carried out comfortably without ever investigating the context. Foucault, on the contrary, rejects the haven of the text, literary or otherwise, on the grounds that the disciplines that have developed in the course of the past two centuries around such texts are themselves part of the problem that needs to be analyzed. For Foucault, disciplines such as language are not neutral tools or containers serving the pursuit of truth without interference. A major issue for interpretation is precisely the way disciplines constitute "rules of formation" for the regulation of discourse. And with regard to the disciplines of literary criticism, the first "move" has been to denigrate or place into obscurity the role of the discipline as context of discourse. In this sense New Criticism and deconstruction constitute a continuous line of development: in the one case, a disciplinary strategy of formalism and aestheticism; in the other case, a movement of subversion of hierarchies. Yet in both cases the traditional apparatus of textuality is affirmed and the sanctity of the kinds of things done under the rubric of literary criticism is reinforced.

Foucauldian criticism looks different from earlier forms of criticism. For better or worse, literary and nonliterary texts are placed on the same plane, subjected to the same analytic tools, and interrogated in relation to the same contextual landscapes. However, to give the impression of a monolithic Foucauldian strategy with regard to literary texts would seriously distort the picture. In *This Is Not a Pipe* (1973), *Raymond Roussel* (1963), and other essays, Foucault reveals another side to his treatment of the literary text and the theoretical issues that derive from the question of aesthetics (Carroll).

It is more than likely that Foucault's impact on literary criticism will take shape as a renewed form of Marxist interpretation, perhaps along lines recently developed by NEW HISTORICISM. Foucault shares with the latter group an aversion to theory, in his case involving the paradox that he was read, in the United States at least, primarily as a theorist. Foucault's hostility to theory leads to several difficulties for those who attempt to practice his strategies of reading. First, Foucault's texts betray a continual shifting of the position of the author. Only in his late essays (such as "What Is Enlightenment?" in *Foucault Reader*) did he come to affirm the need for the writer to take responsibility for the act of writing by constituting him- or herself through writing in critical antagonism to the present. Second, Foucault's later works lead in the direction of a critique of the way discourse constitutes the self in "truth," but they fail to provide the criterion by which to distinguish the discursive effects of Foucault's own texts from those that confirm structures of domination. Finally, Foucault is unable adequately to justify his choice of topics, such as sex, prisons, and so forth. In "What Is Enlightenment?" he weakly contends that topics receive the "generality" of import from their historical repetition. The choice of the writer's topic is thereby divorced from his or her "responsibility" to take a critical stance toward the present, to strive for reflexivity by situating one's own project firmly in the context of the present conjuncture.

Mark Poster

See also DISCOURSE: 2. DISCOURSE THEORY and FRENCH THEORY AND CRITICISM: 5. 1945–1968 and 6. 1968 AND AFTER.

Michel Foucault, *L'Archéologie du savoir* (1969, *L'Ordre du discours,* 1971, *The Archaeology of Knowledge and the Discourse on Language,* trans. A. M. Sheridan-Smith, 1972), *Ceci n'est pas une pipe* (1973, *This Is Not a Pipe,* trans. James Harkness, 1983), *Folie et déraison: Histoire de la folie à l'âge classique* (1961, *Madness and Civilization: A History of Insanity in the Age of Reason,* trans. Richard Howard, 1965), *The Foucault Reader* (ed. Paul Rabinow, 1984), *Language, Counter-Memory, Practice: Selected Essays and Interviews* (ed. Donald F. Bouchard, trans. Bouchard and Sherry Simon, 1977), *Les Mots et les choses* (1966, *The Order of Things: An Archaeology of the Human Sciences,* 1970), *Naissance de la clinique: Une Archéologie du regard médical* (1963, rev. ed., 1972, *The Birth of the Clinic: An Archaeology of Medical Perception,* trans. A. M. Sheridan Smith, 1973), *Power/Knowledge: Selected Interviews and Other Writings, 1972–1977* (ed. Colin Gordon, 1980), "Qu'est-ce qu'un auteur?" (1969, "What Is an Author?" *Language, Counter-Memory, Practice*), *Raymond Roussel* (1963, *Death and the Labyrinth: The World of Raymond Roussel,* trans. Charles Ruas, 1986), *Le Souci de soi* (1984, *The History of Sexuality,* vol. 3, *The Care of the Self,* trans. Robert Hurley, 1986),

Surveiller et punir (1975, *Discipline and Punish: The Birth of the Prison,* trans. Alan Sheridan, 1977), *L'Usage des plaisirs* (1984, *The History of Sexuality,* vol. 2, *The Use of Pleasure,* trans. Robert Hurley, 1986), *La Volonté de savoir* (1976, *The History of Sexuality,* vol. 1, *An Introduction,* trans. Robert Hurley, 1978).

David Carroll, *Paraesthetics: Foucault, Lyotard, Derrida* (1987); Michael Clark, *Michel Foucault, an Annotated Bibliography: Tool Kit for a New Age* (1983); Mark Cousins and Athar Hussain, *Michel Foucault* (1984); Gilles Deleuze, *Foucault* (1986, *Foucault,* ed. and trans. Sean Hand, 1988); Hubert L. Dreyfus and Paul Rabinow, *Michel Foucault: Beyond Structuralism and Hermeneutics* (1982); Simon During, *Foucault and Literature: Towards a Genealogy of Writing* (1992); Didier Eribon, *Michel Foucault* (1989, trans. Betsy Wing, 1991); Stephen J. Greenblatt, *Renaissance Self-fashioning: From More to Shakespeare* (1980); David Couzens Hoy, ed., *Foucault: A Critical Reader* (1986); Charles Lemert and Garth Gillan, *Michel Foucault: Social Theory as Transgression* (1982); J. G. Merquior, *Foucault* (2d ed., 1991); James Miller, *The Passion of Michel Foucault* (1993); Mark Poster, *Foucault, Marxism, and History: Mode of Production versus Mode of Information* (1984); John Rajchman, *Michel Foucault: The Freedom of Philosophy* (1985); Edward W. Said, *Orientalism* (1978), "Travelling Theory" (1982, *The World, the Text, and the Critic,* 1983); Barry Smart, *Foucault, Marxism, and Critique* (1983), *Michel Foucault* (1985).

FRANKFURT SCHOOL

The name Frankfurt School has been used generally to denote a diverse body of neo-Marxian social theory, beginning with the founding of the Institut für Sozialforschung (Institute for Social Research) on February 3, 1923, at the University of Frankfurt, and continuing to the present day. More specifically, perhaps, the name refers to a smaller group of scholars in exile after 1933 who tried to elaborate a "critical theory" of society. The independent institute was conceived by Felix J. Weil, along with his fellow students Max Horkheimer and Friedrich Pollock, and endowed initially by his father Hermann Weil, a grain merchant. Early members of the institute included Horkheimer, Pollock, Leo Lowenthal, Carl Grünberg (its first director), Henryk Grossmann, Karl August Wittfogel, Franz Borkenau, and Julian Gumperz. The institute's research was to be grounded in nondogmatic Marxian thought, critical of existing society yet yielding, in Grünberg's words, "only relative, historically conditioned meaning" (Jay, *Dialectical* 11). The

elaboration of this perspective would be central to the theory of the Frankfurt School throughout its evolution. (Much of the factual information in this and the following paragraphs has been taken from Jay's invaluable history of the Institute for Social Research and the Frankfurt School [see also Held].)

Horkheimer became director of the institute in 1931 and remained its guiding force into the 1950s. THEODOR W. ADORNO was attached to the institute in the late 1920s, joining officially only in 1938 and becoming co-director in 1955. Herbert Marcuse joined in 1932. Erich Fromm, Karl Landauer (director of the Frankfurt Psychoanalytic Institute), Franz Neumann, Otto Kirchheimer, A. R. L. Gurland, Paul Massing, Paul Lazarsfeld, and Mirra Komarovsky, among many others, were affiliated with the institute in the 1930s; Fromm had severed his ties by the end of the decade. WALTER BENJAMIN, though linked more closely to individuals such as Adorno than to the institute itself, depended on its funding in the late 1930s. The Institute for Social Research fled Germany with Hitler's rise to power in 1933 and worked for a time from offices in Geneva, London, and Paris.

In 1936 the institute found a new home at Columbia University in New York, where it also had links to Lazarsfeld's Radio Research Project at Princeton. Throughout the 1930s the *Zeitschrift für Sozialforschung* was the institute's main organ of publication. Horkheimer and Adorno moved to Los Angeles in the 1940s. In its investigations of prejudice in the 1940s (co-sponsored by the American Jewish Committee), the institute worked with the Berkeley Public Opinion Study Group in collaborative efforts that included Bruno Bettelheim, Morris Janowitz, Nathan Ackerman, and others. These investigations in fact resulted in a series of publications under the heading *Studies in Prejudice,* with Horkheimer and Samuel H. Flowerman as general editors. The institute returned to Frankfurt in 1950 with Horkheimer, Adorno, and Pollock, though many of its members—Marcuse, Lowenthal, Kirchheimer, and Neumann among them—resigned and accepted positions in American universities. A "second generation" of Frankfurt School theory began to develop in the 1960s, with JÜRGEN HABERMAS as the leading figure; it included Alfred Schmidt, Oskar Negt, Albrecht Wellmer, and Karl-Otto Apel.

Economically and politically, the Frankfurt School's beginnings were rooted in the troubles of Germany's Weimar years. While in most cases its early members were the assimilated sons of middle- and upper middle-class Jewish families, the economic conflicts of postwar German society fueled revolutionary hopes. The goal of the institute's founders, however, was in many ways a form of Marxism that did not depend for its validity upon the imminent collapse of obviously damaged capitalist relations. More orthodox theses of the increasing impoverishment of the working class had already been questioned by figures such as Eduard Bernstein and Rosa Luxemburg, though Bernstein's revisionist Marxism would itself be rejected by institute members. One could claim that it was the apparent betrayal of proletarian aspirations by the Social Democratic party, the failure of the German revolution, and the splintering of more radical opposition that, in combination, prompted an interest in new theoretical work. The gap between theoretical reflection and practical politics would continue to grow as conditions in Europe worsened and prospects for positive change evaporated. There was a fairly wide spectrum of opinion, however. Adorno was never much interested in political activism, and his skepticism only deepened with time. Marcuse's early political involvement would survive dormant periods and surface again in the 1960s. Several early members—Wittfogel, Borkenau, and Gumperz—belonged to the Communist party. In spite of its members' refusal of conventional academic positions, the Frankfurt School remained a research-oriented enterprise independent of overt political affiliations. One of Habermas's goals has been to realign Frankfurt School theory in a more practical, though decidedly reformist, relation to political life.

Intellectually, the Frankfurt School drew on diverse but related traditions of philosophy and social thought. Many of these can be traced back to G. W. F. HEGEL's dialectical phenomenology, the leftist (or "critical") Hegelianism of the 1840s, and Karl Marx's dialectical materialism. But other strains of thought were equally important. IMMANUEL KANT's aesthetics played a crucial role in Adorno's thinking. Though generally criticized, Wilhelm Dilthey's notions of the "human sciences" and his *Lebensphilosophie* embodied for Horkheimer at least a resistance to more utilitarian demands from society and orthodox Marxism alike. FRIEDRICH NIETZSCHE's revaluation of morality and his meditations on the inescapable link between knowledge and interests (reflected later in the title of one of Habermas's works) would become epistemological cruxes. Skeptical both of metaphysical truth and of an evolving proletariat's role as the motor of history, the Frankfurt School would struggle with and against Nietzsche's reduction of knowledge to power throughout its existence. The ideas of SIGMUND FREUD, especially the late social psychology, were perhaps the most challenging addition to more traditional Marxian thought. Freud influenced not only Fromm and Marcuse but also Adorno and Horkheimer with his notions of

projection, sadomasochism, the importance of familial relations, matriarchal versus patriarchal values, and the repressive nature of bourgeois tolerance and, above all perhaps, via his tragic vision of civilization.

Remaining closer to the institute's beginning ideas were Max Weber and GEORG LUKÁCS. Weber's analysis of economic and social rationalization in the development of capitalism (especially as applied to twentieth-century monopolism) was basic, even if lacking a larger critical perspective. In *History and Class Consciousness,* Lukács developed a theory of social rationalization in conjunction with a notion of reification taken from Marx's analysis of the fetishism of commodities. It was this synthesis—a synthesis Habermas was later to reject (see *Theory of Communicative Action,* vol. 1, ch. 4)—that proved especially crucial in the development of critical theory. (Lukács had himself been present at a conference on Marxism organized by Felix Weil in 1922 that prefigured the formation of the institute a year later.)

In addition to these scholarly influences, there were the more subtle contexts of home and culture. Made up largely of secular German-Jewish intellectuals (Benjamin would reveal a more complex relation to his religious background), the Frankfurt School eventually found itself at a turning point in European history. Its early members appear to have showed only a passing concern with their Jewishness or with anti-Semitism; it was not until 1939 that the institute began to address such questions directly, and they became central to research done in the following two decades. Though marginalized by the institute before the Nazi triumph, anti-Semitism would come to exemplify basic flaws in traditional humanism's faith in progressive reason.

"Critical theory" was the operative term for the dialectical social criticism that provided the intellectual glue, such as it existed, for the Frankfurt School after 1933. Horkheimer, Adorno, and Marcuse were to play the major roles in its subsequent development, though Pollock, Lowenthal, and Fromm also made significant contributions. Broadly, critical theory can be understood as a sustained reflection on the dialectical relation between reason and freedom. Following Lukács, critical theory rejected the Kantian distinction between formal and substantive reason (between reason as means and reason as necessarily embodying certain ends) because such a distinction in fact promoted the "instrumental" character of thought. Likewise, the theory would treat Hegel (as well as Marx) dialectically: it would attempt to reveal and account for the discrepancies between Hegel's formal methods (the recognition and sublation of determinant contradiction) and Hegel's substantive claims (the necessary unfolding of reason in history toward freedom).

In many ways, it appears that the struggle was with the Enlightenment itself. Critical theory wished simultaneously to preserve the notion that reason served radical human emancipation but to reject all claims of any preestablished harmony between formal (instrumental) rationality and liberation. Orthodox Marxism itself would be questioned to the extent that it surreptitiously invoked such harmony, leading to either quietism or totalitarian blindness. But critical theory maintained this position at heavy cost. It was never able to articulate positively any but the vaguest notions of what "substantive" reason and "true" freedom would be; nor could it explain how to achieve them objectively. The theory had abandoned the more overt totalizations of Hegel and traditional Marxism as inadequate and stultifying. But it was then caught in a dizzying shuttle between the theoretical-practical need for a reconciled totality and the constant anxiety that in the falsely disenchanted worlds of capitalism and communism alike, Hegel's dictum— "Das Wahre ist das Ganze" ("The true is the whole")— could only mean mass deception. Adorno's later response, "The whole is the false," bluntly summarized a perspective that had been present in much of critical theory all along (*Minima Moralia: Reflections* 50). At the same time, such a perspective demanded a renewed concern for individual existence, a concern eradicated by both totalitarian communism and administered capitalism. This desire to preserve theoretical reflection equally from bureaucratic destruction and from the chimera of commodified "individualism" would be especially central to Adorno's aesthetics, musical theory, and literary criticism.

One could perhaps point to five motifs running through critical theory—with the added proviso that these motifs developed dynamically over some four decades and never achieved structural stability. First was the reinterpretation of Marxian social science in light of the growing discrepancies between dialectical materialism as theory and as practice. This meant the rejection of any simple totalization of history, of more mechanical relations of reflection between cultural superstructure and economic base, and of the proletariat as the necessary subject-object of historical progress (see especially the early Horkheimer and Pollock here). While class struggle was never denied, it lost its place of centrality amid the larger pressures of monopolization and rationalization. Such a perspective also entailed arguments, such as those between Pollock and Neumann in the 1940s, over the specific relation of capitalism to Nazism. In response to

more orthodox views, Horkheimer and others proposed a dialectical social theory whose changing categories would be responsive to present historical conditions but which (especially in its early forms) would still depend on nonrelativized axioms aimed at the reconciliation of social contradiction (see, e.g., Horkheimer's "On the Problem of Truth," in Arato and Gebhardt).

Second was the critique of the value-free claims and instrumental vision of positivist and pragmatist sociology. That is, social research must be "critical" and engaged, for the claims of scientific neutrality and practical expediency inevitably served to justify adaptation to existing conditions (see, e.g., Horkheimer's "Traditional and Critical Theory," in *Critical Theory*). While there was an accommodation with empirical research methods during the institute's time in America in the 1940s, especially concerning the family, prejudice, and authoritarianism, a deeply rooted skepticism toward positivist sociology remained. Habermas has attempted to reestablish ties between the "critical" and "positivist" sociological traditions.

Third, critical theory tried to address the social and psychological grounds of modern authoritarianism. This was largely pursued through attempts to bridge the gap between Freud and Marx, though distinctly non-Freudian, socially based studies of authority, less directly tied to critical theory, were produced at the same time (for an example of the latter, see Neumann). On the one hand, this meant investigating (sometimes through empirical devices such as questionnaires and clinical interviews) the relation between the structure and the stability of social groupings such as the family, the formation of prejudice, and fascist proclivities (see Adorno et al., *The Authoritarian Personality,* and the institute's *Studien über Autorität und Familie*). Such research attempted to evaluate, through the use of quantified scales, the psychic structure of tendencies such as ethnocentrism, anti-Semitism, and politico-economic ideology. On the other hand, Fromm and Marcuse used Freudian psychology to provide an alternative view of social hegemony, one that is related to but quite distinct from that found in Lukács and ANTONIO GRAMSCI. Fromm's identification of a link between the merely formal (Kantian) aspect of bourgeois tolerance and the adaptive purposes of orthodox psychoanalysis prefigured Marcuse's later elaboration of a specifically "repressive" tolerance in late capitalist societies (see Marcuse, "Repressive Tolerance," in *Critique*).

Fourth, as already noted, Enlightenment rationality was itself reevaluated. This motif derived from Lukács's early work on reification and from Freud's theories of the necessity of psychic repression in the development of human culture. In the 1940s Adorno and Horkheimer would raise the possibility, already expressed by Nietzsche, that Enlightened thought implicitly contained an ascetic drive toward domination: reason by turns liberated humanity through the ability to demystify and control a mythicized natural world and subjugated humanity in the newly mystified imperative to dominate nature (including human nature) at all costs (see Adorno with Horkheimer). In a sense, critical theory came to raise a Kantian question in Marxian terms: how to treat human beings and human reason, not as instruments to further pregiven or formally bracketed ends, but as substantive ends in themselves. In Adorno's late work, the philosophical drive toward concept-reality identity would itself represent an instrumental danger to be dialectically negated (see *Negative*).

Finally, there was the relation between critical theory and aesthetics. This has perhaps been the most salient motif for literary criticism. While for many members of the Frankfurt School the aesthetic was peripheral to the larger aims of social research, for a few—Adorno, Benjamin, Lowenthal—it was more central. Indeed, the importance of aesthetic judgment for social theory can be traced back to Kant, FRIEDRICH SCHILLER, Dilthey, Nietzsche, and Lukács. Lukács had made what might be called the paradigmatic observation that in extending the idea of aesthetic harmony beyond its formal conditions to the realm of human freedom, Schiller simultaneously recognized the destructive nature of bourgeois society and pointed toward its reconciliation in thought (though only in thought).

For Adorno, the aesthetic represented perhaps the last remaining "refuge for mimetic behavior" (*Aesthetic* 79), that is, for the preservation of reason on other than instrumental grounds. Viewed through Kant and Marx, art held out a *promesse de bonheur* abandoned and resented by alienated bourgeois society. His early musical studies with Alban Berg further motivated Adorno's support for modernist aesthetics: "The modernity of art lies in its mimetic relation to a petrified and alienated reality. This, and not the denial of that mute reality, is what makes art speak" (*Aesthetic* 31). Thus, a more straightforward interpretation of the ideological tendency of a work of art is doomed to be inadequate in an age grown too cynical to imagine any release from social alienation. The utopian promise of the work of art is embodied, rather, in its vain striving after an autonomy and coherence that is necessarily impossible if the work is true to the divisive, conflict-ridden society producing it. "Transcendent" (ideological) criticism must then be balanced by an "immanent" (formal) critique of those contradic-tions internal to the work itself (see "Cultural Criticism and Society," in *Prisms*).

Adorno's sense of a dialectic between ideological and formal properties has greatly influenced contemporary Marxian literary criticism (see esp. FREDRIC JAMESON's interpretation of narrative). Texts such as *Prisms* and *Noten zur Literatur* reveal Adorno's rigorously antisystematic, discipline-crossing, and constantly self-reflexive method of reading, one that reappears in the criticism of figures such as SUSAN SONTAG and EDWARD W. SAID. Adorno's writings have also had a direct impact on debates over mass culture and POSTMODERNISM. Together in the 1940s, Adorno and Horkheimer elaborated a notion of the "culture industry" in modern capitalism. Extending Lukács's theory of reification as rationalization, they focused on the organization of culture, entertainment, and leisure as instruments of social hegemony (see Adorno, "The Culture Industry: Enlightenment as Mass Deception," in *Dialectic*). In this project, their work anticipated motifs in Louis Althusser, MICHEL FOUCAULT, and Jean Baudrillard and revealed a new interest in processes of consumption as well as of production.

Benjamin's aesthetics were on the one hand far more directly tied to material conditions of production and reception than were Adorno's (see "The Author as Producer," in *Reflections*). His attention to urban life, technological reproduction, cinema, and Bertolt Brecht's epic theater punctured older myths of aesthetic "aura," which for Benjamin only served fascist goals in modern society (see *Illuminations*). On the other hand, Benjamin was himself no stranger to nostalgia, and there was a messianic quality in his thought that surpassed Schiller's romantic aesthetics. Benjamin's essays on Nikolai Leskov, CHARLES BAUDELAIRE, and Franz Kafka have influenced contemporary reassessments of the novel and of modernism, and his essays on translation and on history (see *Illuminations*) have had a wide currency within postmodernism. Following PAUL DE MAN, some have also claimed that his early work on the *Trauerspiel* and allegory anticipated certain ideas in deconstructive criticism.

Lowenthal did perhaps the most to develop a practical and scholarly sociology of literature. His interest in popular culture especially was quite opposed to Adorno's rejection of it and looked forward to later trends in sociological and historicist criticism (see *Literature, Popular Culture, and Society*). Though less stylistically self-conscious than Adorno, Lowenthal similarly attempted to relate formal technique to social relations. In essays on Fyodor Dostoevsky, Henrik Ibsen, and Knut Hamsun published in the *Zeitschrift* during the 1930s, Lowenthal examined ideological tendencies not only in literature but also in the popular and critical reception of it (see *Literature and the Image of Man* for versions of some of these essays). Like Benjamin, Lowenthal experimented with a mode of criticism that stressed the need to investigate the popular consumption of the work of art, a mode that would be further developed only decades later.

The work of Jürgen Habermas represents both a continuation of and a reaction against previous "critical theory." In his early work, Habermas returned to the fundamental relation of reason to freedom in the philosophical tradition he inherited, where Nietzsche became a pivotal, and largely destructive, force (see *Knowledge and Human Interests*). Habermas would later designate the wrong turn in the development of critical theory as the importation of Nietzschean thought in the late 1930s (see *The Philosophical Discourse of Modernity*). Habermas's interests expanded for a time toward systems theory and toward a more Weberian understanding of social rationalization. Not only was modernized social organization necessary in efficiently promoting the material quality of life but it actually resisted totalitarian control. The danger lay in the extension of managerial values to a noninstitutionalized life-world. In his later work, Habermas has elaborated a theory of "communicative action," which rejects the "philosophy of consciousness" presupposed by earlier critical theory in favor of the implicit formal constraints on consciousness assumed by intersubjective communication (see *The Theory of Communicative Action*). Throughout, Habermas has maintained a more accepting view of modernity, in stark contrast to many of his predecessors.

With its depth and range, the Frankfurt School represents a unique experiment in collaborative theory and research concerning modern Western society. At the same time, its failure to make more explicit the relation of theory to political practice and its tendency to retreat to philosophical or aesthetic reflection have been widely criticized (see, e.g., Habermas, Kolakowski, Tar, and Lichtheim). Lukács complained in the 1960s (in terms echoed by Habermas) that thinkers like Adorno, no less than the existentialists Adorno denounced in *The Jargon of Authenticity,* had retreated to "Grand Hotel Abyss." Likewise, empirical sociology has generally found little in critical theory worth preserving. But it is hard to imagine, given the grand scope of Frankfurt School aims, what would have constituted success. Moreover, for someone like Adorno, profound failure (in the great work of art, for example) was generally more worthy of attention than a false or trivial victory. In the philosopher, the crude wish to be "right" was already counterproductive: "When philosophers, who are well known to have diffi-

culty keeping silent, engage in conversation, they should try always to lose the argument, but in such a way as to convict their opponent of untruth" (*Minima Moralia: Reflections* 70). It is the provocative quality of such observations that gives much Frankfurt School theory a continuing relevance today.

Vincent P. Pecora

See also THEODOR W. ADORNO, WALTER BENJAMIN, SIGMUND FREUD, JÜRGEN HABERMAS, KARL MARX AND FRIEDRICH ENGELS, and MARXIST THEORY AND CRITICISM.

See bibliographies in entires on THEODOR W. ADORNO, WALTER BENJAMIN, and JÜRGEN HABERMAS for other texts by these writers.

Theodor W. Adorno, *Dissonanzen: Einleitung in die Musiksoziologie* (1973, *Introduction to the Sociology of Music,* 1976), *Drei Studien zu Hegel: Aspekte, Erfahrungsgehalt, Skoteinos oder Wie zu lesen sei* (1963), *Gesammelte Schriften* (1970–), *Minima Moralia: Reflexionen aus dem beschrädigten Leben* (1951, *Minima Moralia: Reflections from Damaged Life,* trans. E. F. N. Jephcott, 1974), *Zur Metakritik der Erkenntnistheorie* (1970, *Against Epistemology,* trans. W. Domingo, 1982); Theodor W. Adorno, with Else Frenkel-Brunswik, Daniel J. Levinson, and R. Nevitt Sanford, *The Authoritarian Personality* (1950); Theodor W. Adorno et al., *Aesthetics and Politics* (trans. Anna Bostock et al., 1986); Karl-Otto Apel, *Transformation der Philosophie* (1973, *Towards a Transformation of Philosophy,* trans. Glyn Adey and David Frisby, 1980); Andrew Arato and Eike Gebhardt, eds., *The Essential Frankfurt School Reader* (1978); Walter Benjamin, *Der Begriff der Kunstkritik in der deutschen Romantik* (1973), *Illuminationen* (ed. Siegfried Unseld, 1961), *Illuminations* (ed. Hannah Arendt, trans. Harry Zohn, 1968, not a translation of *Illuminationen*); Erich Fromm, *Escape from Freedom* (1941); Jürgen Habermas, *Erkenntnis und Interesse* (1968, *Knowledge and Human Interests,* trans. Jeremy J. Shapiro, 1972), *Nachmetaphysisches Denken: Philosophische Aufsatze* (1988); Max Horkheimer, *Eclipse of Reason* (1947), *Kritische Theorie* (ed. Alfred Schmidt, 2 vols., 1968, *Critical Theory,* partial trans. Matthew J. O'Connell et al., 1972), *Zur Kritik der instrumentellen Vernunft* (1967, *Critique of Instrumental Reason,* trans. Matthew J. O'Connell et al., 1974); Institute for Social Research, *Archiv für die Geschichte des Sozialismus und der Arbeiterbewegung* 1–15 (1910–30), *Studien über Autorität und Familie* (1936), *Studies in Philosophy and Social Science* 8.3–9.3 (1939–41), *Zeitschrift für Sozialforschung* 1–8.2 (1932–39); Leo Lowenthal, *Literature and the Image of Man* (1957), *Literature, Popular Culture, and Society* (1961); Herbert Marcuse, *Counterrevolution and Revolt* (1972), *Eros and Civilization* (1955), *An Essay on Liberation* (1969), *Kultur und Gesellschaft* (2 vols., 1979), *Negations: Essays in Critical Theory* (trans. Jeremy J. Shapiro, 1968), *One-Dimensional Man: Studies in the Ideology of Advanced Industrial Society* (1964); Herbert Marcuse, with Robert P. Wolff and Barrington Moore, Jr., *A Critique of Pure Tolerance* (1965); Franz Neumann, *Behemoth: The Structure and Practice of National Socialism, 1933–1944* (rev. ed., 1944); Albrecht Wellmer, *Critical Theory of Society* (1971).

Seyla Benhabib, *Critique, Norm, and Utopia: A Study of the Foundations of Critical Theory* (1986); Susan Buck-Morss, *The Origin of Negative Dialectics: Theodor W. Adorno, Walter Benjamin, and the Frankfurt Institute* (1977); Peter Dews, *Logics of Disintegration: Post-Structuralist Thought and the Claims of Critical Theory* (1987); Hans-Magnus Enzensberger, *The Consciousness Industry* (1974); George Friedman, *The Political Philosophy of the Frankfurt School* (1981); Raymond Geuss, *The Idea of a Critical Theory: Habermas and the Frankfurt School* (1981); David Held, *Introduction to Critical Theory: Horkheimer to Habermas* (1980); Fredric Jameson, *Late Marxism: Adorno, or, the Persistence of the Dialectic* (1990), *Marxism and Form: Twentieth-Century Dialectical Theories of Literature* (1971); Martin Jay, *Adorno* (1984), *The Dialectical Imagination: A History of the Frankfurt School and the Institute of Social Research, 1923–1950* (1973); Leszek Kolokowski, *Main Currents of Marxism* (1978); George Lichtheim, *From Marx to Hegel* (1971); Thomas McCarthy, *The Critical Theory of Jürgen Habermas* (1978); Zoltan Tar, *The Frankfurt School: The Critical Theories of Max Horkheimer and Theodor Adorno* (1977).

FRENCH THEORY AND CRITICISM

1. Seventeenth Century

Literary criticism in seventeenth-century France barely resembled any of its modern forms, although by the end of the century literature was established as an autonomous field of endeavor and the writer as a professional, even if one whose prestige was shaky. To speak of "French" literary criticism is even more problematic, for criticism was but one restricted aspect of a much broader context of human enquiry and activity, the *res literaria* inherited from antiquity and the Renaissance and sometimes called the republic of letters or, more recently, the age of eloquence. As Marc Fumaroli has stated, "Age of

eloquence, age of rhetoric—the seventeenth century witnesses the birth of *belles-lettres,* but it is not yet the age of literature" (*L'Age* 31).

Our idea of literature is linked, as Fumaroli points out, to the printed word, and it leaves out what was still highly important in the age of eloquence, the spoken word, the harangue, the orator's "actions" or gestures and body language, and also the art of conversation. All these were aspects of eloquence, the archetype of which was the classical orator personified at this time by Cicero, in whose person philosophy and eloquence were one, uniting nature to art, rhetoric, and the rules governing eloquence, expression, and gesture. (See also CLASSICAL THEORY AND CRITICISM: 2. RHETORIC.) The inheritors of this grand tradition of eloquence at the beginning of the seventeenth century were not so much writers and poets in our sense of the word as the magistrates and advocates of the higher courts of law, the most prestigious of which was the Parlement de Paris, which sat in the Palais de Justice. These magistrates and advocates were men of learning, eloquence, and letters who were generally Gallican in orientation and thus concerned with a French as against a Latin eloquence and opposed to such other centers of culture as the court and the Jesuits.

While MAURICE BLANCHOT may have introduced the notion of literary space into modern critical theory, it is significant that a similar expression was used in the seventeenth century to characterize the French *res literaria* that was then taking form. In his *Nouvelle allégorique; ou Histoire des derniers troubles arrivés au royaume d'Eloquence* (1658), Antoine Furetière delineates three spaces, or *pays:* the kingdom of Rhetoric, ruled by Queen Eloquence; the kingdom of Pedantry, governed by Galimatia, king of pedants; and the Lands of Printing, unsafe grounds given over to various forms of untrustworthy traffickers. Also used sometimes to outline the geography of the world of eloquence or letters in the making was another image, the Temple of Taste atop Mount Parnassus. This image set up a standard of taste, since those who had reached the top and been admitted into the temple came to be models of emulation for those still at the foot of the mountain, in the land of Eloquence. Furetière, in his land of Eloquence, might have distinguished between two opposed camps, namely, the Jesuits and Jansenists, as variations on religious eloquence. The existence of a land of Pedantry points to the role of schools, the university, and the various Jesuit *collèges* in the formation of literature, as well as the Latin culture, all of which had to be overcome before an autonomous French literature could be formed.

Although vernacular literature in verse and prose had been written since the Middle Ages, and French poetry had flourished in the Renaissance along with the prose of François Rabelais, John Calvin, and Michel de Montaigne, the prestige of the classical orator was high enough to overshadow the vernacular literature. The world of learning and its prestige stood with the Latin tradition and the erudites of the Renaissance, which meant the men of learning of the church and the *palais*. The *palais* was a place of learning, erudition, and culture, and it was opposed to a newer cultural center, the more worldly court, which was inclined to luxury, fine manners, music, theater, poetry, and art. The learned men of the church tended to look at the court as a center of frivolity and ignorance, where one spoke an elegant but insubstantial French, and a world of glitter that hid an underlying emptiness and uncertainty. The Jesuits who returned to France in the early seventeenth century were another important cultural power and an important factor in the rivalry between the court and the *palais*. They remained faithful to Latin, but they adapted the teaching of literature and eloquence to suit the court rather than the erudites of the *palais* and the learned men in the Renaissance tradition. Their education, and the ideas they had of education and of the educated man, gave more weight to elegance than to the austere learning of the humanist tradition. This policy unintentionally resulted in a turn of mind that eventually went beyond their own aims and became an important factor in the creation first of French literature and later of the Enlightenment.

What came to be known as *belles-lettres* and then French literature arose out of the various rivalries of the *palais* (with its Gallican orientation and opposition to the centralizing power of the state), the court, and the Jesuits. At issue was who would create the language of public discourse and determine its use. The development of this struggle of opposed rhetorics may be roughly divided into three periods or generations, although these are not always clearly delineated. The first period, lasting from the end of the sixteenth century to the 1630s, was a period dominated by Cardinal Richelieu and the establishment of a centralizing state. The new Académie française became an instrument of the state at this time, while a model for poetry was found in François de Malherbe and for prose writing in Jean-Louis Guez de Balzac, and an authority for literary theory in Jean Chapelain.

The second period corresponds roughly to the time between the foundation of the Académie in 1635 and the publication of NICOLAS BOILEAU-DESPRÉAUX's *Art poétique* in 1674. This period saw a consolidation of the gains of French at the expense of the prestige of Latin, a discussion of the qualities and characteristic of French and by extension of purism in the language, and the establishment of a standard of taste in literature. The question of whose eloquence to adopt was settled by a compromise between the court and the *palais,* that is, between elegance and learning, or the language of the court and the forms of classical literature.

The third period may be associated with the *Querelle des anciens et des modernes* (Quarrel between the Ancients and the Moderns). Literature had gained a certain degree of autonomy, and there were more professional writers than before, but the newly independent literature now took account no longer of the old traditional world of erudition, associated, often unjustly, with the pedants, but rather of the new science and Cartesianism. Whereas Boileau and Father Dominique Bouhours may be considered representative figures of the second period, Bernard le Bovier de Fontenelle (1657–1757) is a representative of the third. But the Abbé Jean-Baptiste Du Bos (1670–1742) is an equally significant figure. It is significant that his *Réflexions critiques sur la poésie et sur la peinture,* published in 1719, contains *réflections* and not an *art poétique* or a *rhétorique*. The book moves beyond those forms into what will later be called aesthetics. As for Fontenelle, it is significant that he began as a poet and playwright and ended as a writer on science and as secretary of the Académie des sciences. We are, in other words, past the age of eloquence.

The literary criticism of the period, what might be called the *pays de la critique,* reflected the grand questions at issue between the contending cultural centers. What was at stake, aside from the control of discourse, was the town, the well-to-do literate and somewhat learned bourgeoisie, and also, most important, the women of the better-off circles of the capital. The Académie française had spawned other *académies* in the provinces, and in Paris, the example of the marquise de Rambouillet and her *Hôtel* blue room, where she received poets, writers, and the polished people of the world of court and town, inspired other women to open *salons,* where people met for conversation, discussions of books and plays, or society games. Literary criticism thus began with the Académie and these *salons*. When in 1637 the Académie was asked to judge whether Pierre Corneille's *Le Cid* answered to the rules set forth in ARISTOTLE's *Poetics,* one form of criticism began. Chapelain had, however, preceded this judgment in his preface to Cavaliere Marino's *Adone,* and soon other people would write in other forms on questions related to style and rules that paralleled the conversations and questions raised in the *salons.*

An excellent example of the questions raised in what we may consider literary criticism are the writings of the Jesuit Father Dominique Bouhours (1628–1702), such as *Entretiens d'Ariste et d'Eugène* (1677), *De la manière de bien penser dans les ouvrages de l'esprit* (1687), and his various books on the French language, including *Remarques et doutes sur la langue française* (1674). The questions were concerned with what makes for quality in literature and in effect what marks literature off from other forms of writing: what is the *je ne sais quoi?* what is *bel esprit?* what are the *agréments?* what is delicacy? what makes for a true image in prose as opposed to something that only appears to be clear? what is true beauty in a passage of prose or poetry as against false beauty? These questions are raised in elegant conversations with examples at the ready from French, Spanish, and Italian literature as well as from Latin. Criticism thus meant not only knowing the so-called rules of rhetoric but knowing how to read and to acquire a standard of taste, that is, a criterion of judgment based on literary qualities rather than on truths or rules from outside literature itself.

But since criticism also meant learning how to read, related questions were involved, such as what books to read and, further, for whom to write. These questions could not be separated, since criticism was involved with establishing a criterion of taste. Thus, an early form of criticism was the *bibliothèque,* or "library," in effect a bibliography directed at readers and at those who would build up a library. Early examples are Charles Sorel's *Bibliothèque française* (1664), in effect a survey of books written in French, and his later *De la connoisance des bons livres* (1671), which sets up a standard of taste. Unlike the poetics, these *bibliothèques* did not take the form of learned treatises but of bibliographies that introduced the reader to the world of books, discussed the merits of certain works, and held up others for emulation or as examples of good prose. Adrien Baillet's *Jugements des savants sur les ouvrages des auteurs,* seven quarto volumes written in the seventeenth century and published from 1722 to 1730, not only surveys the world of the book, outlines a hierarchy of values and genres, and classifies the world of knowledge but also asks the pertinent questions, what makes a good book? what are the implications of writing? and even, what are the characteristics of authors?

The result of all these endeavors to create a language and a modern secular literature worthy of the ancients was French classicism and its complementary ideal readers, the *honnête homme* and lady of court and town—

prototypes of the figure VIRGINIA WOOLF would later address as the common reader—who might be learned but would never show off that learning, who might know how to write but would not be a professional. One thinks of François, duc de la Rochefoucault's *Maximes,* Madame de La Fayette's novels, Charles de Marquetel de Saint-Evremond, or the moralist Jean de La Bruyère, just as in England one may think of Sir William Temple rather than of the professional writer Jonathan Swift, or of Lord Chesterfield rather than of SAMUEL JOHNSON. For such gentlemen writers there was no distinction between writing and criticism, writing and reflection, conversation and thought, elegance and learning, or between pleasure and instruction, writing and morality, literature and dignity.

While Boileau is invariably associated with French classicism, along with the other three greats—Corneille, Jean Baptiste Poquelin Molière, Jean Racine—thereby making up a cliché fit for the old manuals of French literature, one must not forget that this image is a false and very partial one indeed. Nor must one associate French classicism with academicism or with adherence to and judgment by the so-called rules, in particular the three unities of time, place, and action, which were also made prominent in manuals. French classicism was the result of not only a struggle among the various forces mentioned here but also a struggle against the other modern literatures enjoying great prestige at the time, such as Italian and Spanish, which in effect means a struggle against the baroque. There was a time when no one thought to look for baroque literature in France. This is no longer the case, and examples of baroque poetry are now seen to have abounded in the reign of Louis XIII and Richelieu. The questions raised by taste, the insistence on clarity, and the suspicion of Jesuit imagery and ornamentation all implied a disciplining of the imagination that came to form French classicism, with its insistence on order, sobriety, regularity, clarity, self-discipline, and a balance between art and nature. The true poetics of French classicism is thus not really an Aristotelian poetics adapted to modern conditions, a pedantic set of rules, but is rather to be sought in LONGINUS's *On the Sublime,* which stresses the necessity of genius, inspiration, and therefore nature over the mere knowledge and application of the rules of rhetoric, and in Boileau.

The familiar doctrine that art is an imitation of nature implies something quite different from what it seems at first sight to mean. To imitate is not to copy. And the nature referred to here is not the external nature visible to the eye of an observer but ideal or general nature, as

Sir Joshua Reynolds later used the term. (See also BRITISH THEORY AND CRITICISM: 2. LATE EIGHTEENTH CENTURY.) *Belle nature* is the poet's or painter's idea of nature, closer to perfection than any physical, empirical nature, so that in the end a work of art, be it poem or painting, is an invention, a representation of the poet's or painter's idea but elaborated within the limits of the entire world of the arts and of the governing conditions of the time. French classicism thus supposes a tension between art and nature, convention and invention, tradition and the modern, the rules of art and rhetoric and the individual genius, wit, or imagination of poet, painter, or musician. Thus, Corneille is not Lope de Vega, Racine is not Euripides, Molière is not Plautus, and Boileau is not HORACE. Literary manuals may have called Boileau the legislator of Parnassus, and Corneille may have argued about the rules of Aristotle with his critics as if he were a lawyer disputing the interpretation of a statute. But while one generally admitted that rules existed, at the century's end the determining factor in the establishment of a canon and the judgment of the merits of a work of literature (or *belles-lettres*) was taste or discernment, inseparable from another ideal, the *honnête homme,* who, as the chevalier de Méré defined him, "ne se pique de rien," was above pedantic quarrels.

The penchant for controversy inherent in the contending cultures of the seventeenth century—the rivalries between *palais* and court, Jesuits and *parlementaires,* worldliness and Jansenism—was resolved in the creation of a language, discourse, and literature that was thought worthy of a great court and a great king as well as of the muses and judges established on Parnassus.

R. G. Saisselin

See also NICOLAS BOILEAU-DESPRÉAUX.
Abbé François Hédelin d'Aubignac, *La Pratique du théâtre* (1657); Jean Barbier d'Aucour, *Sentimens de Cléante sur les Entretiens d'Ariste et d'Eugène* (1671); Nicolas Boileau-Despréaux, *L'Art poétique* (1674, *Oeuvres complètes,* ed. Charles Boudhors, vol. 2, 1939, *The Art of Poetry: The Poetical Treatises of Horace, Vida, and Boileau,* ed., Albert S. Cook, trans. Francis Howes, Christopher Pitt, and Sir William Soames, 1926); Dominique Bouhours, *De la manière de bien penser dans les ouvrages d'esprit* (1687), *Les Entretiens d'Ariste et d'Eugène* (1671); Marguerite Buffet, *Nouvelles observations sur la langue française, avec les éloges des illustres savantes tant anciennes que modernes* (1668); Abbé Jean-Baptiste Dubos, *Réflexions critiques sur la poésie et sur la peinture* (1719); Antoine Furetière, *Nouvelle allégoriques; ou Histoire des derniers*

troubles arrivés au royaume d'Eloquence (1658); Gabriel Gueret, *La Guerre des auteurs anciens et modernes* (1671), *Le Parnasse réformé* (1667); Pierre-Daniel Huet, *Traité de l'origine des romans* (1669); François de La Mothe le Vayer, *Considérations sur l'éloquence française de ce temps* (1638); Guérin de La Pinelière, *Le Parnasse ou la critique des poètes* (1638); Gabriel Naudé, *Advis pour dresser une bibliothèque* (1627, *Advice on Establishing a Library,* trans. W. H. Alexander, John S. Gildersleeve, Harold A. Small, Thompson Webb, Jr., and John Evelyn, 1950); Abbé d'Pierre Joseph Thoulier d'Olivet, *Histoire de l'Académie française depuis 1652 jusqu'à 1700* (1730); René Rapin, *Réflexions sur la poétique d'Aristote et sur les ouvrages des poètes anciens et modernes* (1675); Charles Sorel, *De la connoissance des bons livres: ou, Examen de plusieurs auteurs* (1671); sieur de Claude Charles Guyonnet Vertron, *La Nouvelle Pandore ou les femmes illustres du siècle de Louis le Grand* (2 vols., 1698).

Antoine Adam, *Histoire de la littérature française au XVIIe siècle* (4 vols., 1948); Centre National de Recherche Scientifique, *Critique et création littéraires en France au XVIIe siècle* (1977); Claude Cristin, *Aux origines de l'histoire littéraire* (1973); Joan De Jean, *Tender Geographies: Women and the Origins of the Novel in France* (1991); Marc Fumaroli, *L'Âge de l'éloquence: Rhétorique et "res literaria" de la Renaissance au seuil de l'époque classique* (1980); Marc Fumaroli, ed., *Le Statut de la littérature: Mélanges offerts à Paul Bénichou* (1982); Elizabeth C. Goldsmith, *Exclusive Conversations: The Art of Interaction in Seventeenth-Century France* (1988); Erica Harth, *Ideology and Culture in Seventeenth-Century France* (1983); Jean Mesnard, ed., *Destins et enjeux du XVIIe siècle* (1985); Michael Moriarty, *Taste and Ideology in Seventeenth-Century France* (1988); Orest A. Ranum, *Artisans of Glory: Writers and Historical Thought in Seventeenth-Century France* (1980); Timothy J. Reiss, *The Meaning of Literature* (1992); Jean Rousset, *La Littérature de l'âge baroque en France: Circé et la paon* (1954); Remy G. Saisselin, *The Rule of Reason and the Ruses of the Heart: A Philosophical Dictionary of Classical French Criticism, Critics, and Aesthetic Issues* (1970); Domna C. Stanton, "The Fiction of Préciosité and the Fear of Women," *Yale French Studies* 62 (1981); Jean Tortel, *Le Préclassicisme française* (1952); Alain Viala, *Naissance de l'écrivain: Sociologie de la littérature à l'âge classique* (1985).

2. Eighteenth Century

The authority of French classicism tended to limit the range of technical and doctrinal innovation, especially in traditional genres, such as tragedy and epic poetry. "Classical doctrine," as René Bray has called it, had been based upon a series of compromises: between allegiance to Greco-Latin models and contemporary notions of decorum *(bienséance),* between the desire to impose rules and the demands of individual genius, and, in general terms, between tradition and reason. Yet long before the death of Louis XIV (1638–1715), these fragile compromises began to break down, as the hierarchical structure of the Old Regime itself unwillingly yielded to the forces of modernization. The authority of ancient models was gradually undermined by the desire to imitate "nature," while universal aesthetic criteria gave way to the relativist notion of *taste.*

The beginnings of this protracted struggle may be located as early as the 1630s, with the quarrel over the use of pagan gods in Christian epic. Advocates of a specifically Christian form of epic poetry, such as Desmarets de Saint-Sorlin, had been led to argue against blind allegiance to the conventions of pagan literature. The conflict continued in the years 1683–1719, in the *Querelle des anciens et des modernes* (Quarrel between the Ancients and the Moderns). Charles Perrault, author of the well-known *Tales,* launched the first phase of this controversy in 1687, when he delivered to the Académie française a speech (in verse) entitled "The Century of Louis the Great." In this text, he maintained that since modern authors were incomparably more learned than ancient ones, they must necessarily surpass them; and that thanks to the protection of the Sun King, the greatest authors of his age were the equals of the ancients. In response, Jean de La Fontaine (in his *Epistle to Huet*) asserted his belief in the enduring superiority of the ancients as artistic models. In 1688 Bernard Le Bovier de Fontenelle joined the fray with his *Digression on the Ancients and the Moderns,* in which he took a resolutely "modern" position: humanity was in its childhood in ancient times, but it has finally reached adulthood; now the human mind can capitalize upon the inheritance of its youthful imagination and, with the superior reasoning capacity *(lumières)* of adults, can surpass the achievement of the ancients. Jean de La Bruyère and NICOLAS BOILEAU-DESPRÉAUX gave their support to the ancients, though, and the first phase of this quarrel came to an end in 1700 with the public reconciliation of Perrault and Boileau.

The second phase was initiated by Mme Dacier's scrupulously faithful prose translation of the *Iliad* (1711), to which Antoine Houdar de La Motte (who not only did not know Greek but did not care to) responded with an expurgated and elegant rendering in French verse. In the *Lettre sur les occupations de l'Académie* (1716) and *Dialogues sur l'éloquence* (1718), François Fénelon took the somewhat paradoxical position of defending his admiration for the ancients in terms of the relativity of taste. The last significant contribution to the quarrel was made by abbé Jean-Baptiste Dubos, in his *Réflexions critiques sur la poésie et sur la peinture* (1719). While taking a moderate position in the polemic, Dubos proposed two important new ideas: that the heart (and not reason) is the ultimate judge of the beautiful and that artistic genius has no need to imitate models. Throughout the rest of the eighteenth century, critics would continue to debate questions that had been raised by the Quarrel between the Ancients and the Moderns. Yet regardless of their position in the polemic, nearly all writers shared the modern belief that beauty is relative to time and place, that it can only be judged by taste, and, therefore, that new forms of beauty may be invented.

A decline in the authority of objective standards, and the concomitant promotion of subjectivity, is illustrated in contemporary discussions of the novel and autobiography. In the prefaces to numerous novels, from *Gil Blas* (1715) and *Le Diable Boiteux* (1726) of Alain René Lesage to *Manon Lescaut* (1731) of abbé Prévost and the *Egarements du coeur et de l'esprit* (1736) of Prosper Crébillon, authors proposed abandoning the conventions of romance (exotic places, fantastic adventures, etc.) and telling more plausible or "natural" stories, that is, tales that related the experience of individuals in contemporary society. In similar fashion, JEAN-JACQUES ROUSSEAU saw the originality of his posthumous *Confessions* in the unprecedented *absence* of a model and in the absolute uniqueness of his life: "I have resolved on an enterprise which has no precedent, and which, once complete, will have no imitator. My purpose is to display to my kind a portrait in every way true to nature, and the man I shall portray will be myself" (*Confessions* 17; *Oeuvres* 1:5). Whereas ST. AUGUSTINE had relied upon the exemplary value of his *Confessions,* their capacity to convey universal truths about the nature of human life, Rousseau assumed that nothing could be more valuable than the account of his unique, individual experience.

Knowledge of that experience would soon require "sensibility," the capacity to sympathize with individual experience and to convey that sympathy to one's readers. Thus Denis Diderot, in his *Eulogy of Richardson* (1761), wrote: "Oh men, come learn from Richardson to reconcile yourselves with the evils of life; come, we shall cry together over the unhappy characters of his fictions, and we shall say, 'If fortune should overwhelm us, at least decent folk will cry over us'" (*Oeuvres* 30). For most of the century, however, such attempts to grant legitimacy to the novel in terms of its potential for realism or moral good were drowned out by a chorus of aesthetic and moral condemnation. The novel had no place in the traditional hierarchy of genres and was attacked in the name of good taste as either excessively realistic or implausible: in any case, the genre was still considered irremediably vulgar, meant to be read by women, chambermaids, lackeys, and other persons of dubious rational capacities. In addition to this aesthetic criticism, the novel was also subject to moral condemnation. For even when novelists were not supporters of the *philosophes,* it seemed that the very logic of the genre would lead them to espouse causes—such as hedonism, individualism, and indecent realism—that were anathema to traditional morality. What Georges May has called the "dilemma of the novel" in the eighteenth century is perhaps best formulated by the two prefaces Rousseau composed to his extraordinary epistolary novel, *Julie, ou la Nouvelle Héloïse* (1761). His typically severe judgment of the genre in the shorter preface—"Great cities must have spectacles, and corrupt peoples have novels"; "Never did a chaste girl read a novel" (*Julie* 3, 4)—makes it all the more difficult for Rousseau to justify his own contribution to it. Yet he maintains, with obvious discomfort, that while most people are already too corrupt to be affected by novels and others are too pure to even consider reading one, there remain a few persons, such as Jean-Jacques Rousseau, who "are not above the frailties of humanity, who do not immediately show virtue in Heaven, out of the reach of men, but who bring men to love virtue by first portraying it as less austere, and then from the midst of vice can lead them imperceptibly to it" (*Julie* 255–56).

Related changes were taking place in the realm of dramatic theory. Tragedy remained the most prestigious genre, although it had clearly lost its relevance for audiences. Voltaire, for example, was an unconditional admirer of Jean Racine, yet he sensed the necessity of making tragedy more interesting by making it more novelistic. In the *Dissertation sur la tragédie,* which preceded his *Sémiramis* (1748), he advocated the elimination of onstage seats so that the audience (not to mention the actors) would not be distracted from the splendor of tragic performance. On the one hand, the very idea of such a reform (which was finally put into effect in 1759) implied that tragedy had lost the religious, sacrificial dimension that it still retained at the time of Racine, that it had become simply another form of more or less convincing, but secular, fiction. On the other hand, Voltaire's proposal betrayed the anticlerical *philosophe's* paradoxical desire to take the place of the priest and transform the theater into a medium of enlightened propaganda.

Nowhere was this philosophical design upon theater more evident than in the theoretical writings of Diderot. The aristocratic perspective of classical doctrine in France had consigned members of the third estate to the realm of comedy. In his *Commentaries on "The Natural Son"* (1757) and *Discourse on Dramatic Poetry* (1758), Diderot laid the theoretical basis for a new genre that would be located between tragedy and comedy and would finally provide for serious representation of the bourgeoisie. The "serious" genre was meant to be bourgeois, not only because it concerned itself with private matters rather than affairs of state but because its hero would be shown in the intimacy of the nuclear family. Diderot suggested portraying professions or family situations ("conditions") rather than the supposedly universal "characters" of classical comedy, replacing verse with prose, eliminating onstage seats, as well as relying more upon visual (rather than verbal) effects. He also associated the sudden reversals of fortune, or *coups de théâtre,* of classical theater with the arbitrariness and shifting alliances of feudal society and urged that these devices be replaced by a pause in the action, or tableau. And while the proper effect of tragedy, according to ARISTOTLE, was to produce a catharsis of pity and fear, Diderot in the *Discourse* called for the serious genre, or *drame,* to elicit "the sweet pleasure of being moved and shedding tears" (*Oeuvres* 189).

In typically paradoxical fashion, Diderot thought that this sentimental effect was more likely to be achieved by a cerebral, detached style of acting. According to *The Actor's Paradox* (1770), great actors are persons who have completely mastered the technique of imitating emotions yet themselves feel nothing. They have none of the "sensibility" that in Diderot's view constitutes the common ground of humanity, but for that very reason they are able to move their audience to tears. What is proper to a great actress, her paradox, is that nothing, not even humanity, is properly hers.

Diderot's ideas about the "serious genre" were later developed by Pierre Caron de Beaumarchais, in the *Essai sur le genre dramatique sérieux* (1767) and *Lettre moderne sur la chute et la critique du "Barbier de Séville"* (1775). Starting from the assumption that the source of theatrical pleasure lies in the spectator's identification with the hero, he maintained that the portrayal of aristocratic characters in the classical repertory actually undermined the audience's ability to be moved by the action and draw moral conclusions from it. Only by having the illusion of seeing herself in the heroine's situation, argued Beaumarchais, would the spectator be moved to tears and to moral action. In terms of performance style, this reliance upon realistic illusion would require the *drame* to dispense with verse and all other signs of artifice.

His essays *Du théâtre* (1773) and *Nouvel Examen de la tragédie française* (1778) put Louis-Sébastien Mercier (1740–1814) among the most important theorists of this new genre. In Mercier's view, the time had come for French dramatists to repudiate the classical tradition of Pierre Corneille (after *The Cid*), Racine, and Voltaire, with its artificial distinctions, affected tone, and antiquated models. In its place he proposed reviving the more "natural" and flexible style of foreigners, such as William Shakespeare, Lope de Vega, and Carlo Goldoni, and writing plays inspired by one's own times and better suited to a contemporary audience: "Greek tragedies belonged to the Greeks; and should we not be so bold as to have our own theater, to paint our fellow men, to be moved and concerned with them?" (*Du théâtre*, ch. 8). For Mercier, the function of the *drame* was to give the people the social and moral education that no one else was willing to provide. Art became propaganda.

A similar concern for the welfare of the people had led Rousseau, in his *Letter to M. d'Alembert on the Theater* (1758), to call for the elimination of theater as such. Theater, he contended, encourages the audience to sympathize with fictional suffering instead of addressing real social problems; in addition, he insisted, by making people pay to be admitted, French classical theater only aggravates social inequalities. Rousseau therefore proposed doing away with theater entirely and allowing popular "festivals" to emerge spontaneously from the rhythms of everyday life: "Let the spectators become an entertainment to themselves; make them actors themselves; do it so that each sees and loves himself in the others so that all will be better united" (*Politics* 126). Although clearly lacking in spontaneity, the open-air Revolutionary festivals (culminating with the Festival of the Supreme Being on June 8, 1794) at least partially fulfilled Rousseau's antitheatrical program. Most Revolutionary theater, however, dealt more conventionally with contemporary political issues, in a way that would have been closer to Mercier's ideal of theater, had characters such as Brutus and Caesar not conjured up the spirits of the Greco-Latin past.

Jay L. Caplan

Pierre Caron de Beaumarchais, *Essai sur le genre dramatique sérieux* (1767) and *Lettre moderne sur la chute et la critique du "Barbier de Séville"* (1775), in *Théâtre complet* (1957); Anne Lefebvre Dacier, *Des causes de la corruption de goust* (1714), *Madame Dacier's Remarks upon Mr. Pope's Account of Homer, Prefixed to His Translation of the Iliad* (trans. Mr. Parnell, 1724); Denis Diderot, *Diderot's Selected Writings* (ed. Lester G. Crocker, 1966), *Oeuvres esthétiques* (1968); Jean-Baptiste Dubos, abbé, *Réflexions critiques sur la poésie et la peinture* (1719); Bernard Le Bovier de Fontenelle, *A Digression on the Ancients and the Moderns: The Continental Model: Selected French Critical Essays of the Seventeenth Century in English Translation* (ed. Scott Elledge and Donald Schier, 1960), *Poésies pastorales, avec un traité sur la nature de l'eglogue et une digression sur les anciens et les modernes* (1688); Louis Sébastien Mercier, *Du Théâtre, ou nouvel essai sur l'art dramatique* (1773, reprint, 1973); Charles Perrault, *Parallèle des anciens et des modernes en ce qui regarde les arts et les sciences: Dialogues; avec le poème du siècle de Louis le Grand et une épître en vers sur le génie* (1692, reprint, 1971); Jean-Jacques Rousseau, *a M. d'Alembert sur son article "Geneve" et particulierrement sur le projet d'établir un théâtre de comédie en cette ville* (1758, *Politics and the Arts: Letter to M. d'Alembert on the Theater*, trans. Allan Bloom, 1960), *Les Confessions de J. J. Rousseau: Oeuvres complètes* (1959, *The Confessions of Jean-Jacques Rousseau*, trans. J. M. Cohen, 1953), *Julie, ou la Nouvelle Héloïse* (1761, ed. René Pomeau, 1960, *Eloisa, or a Series of Original Letters,* trans. William Kenrick, 2 vols., 1803, reprint, 1989); Voltaire (François-Marie Arouet), *Le Théâtre de Voltaire* (2 vols., 1967).

René Bray, *Formation de la doctrine classique* (1966); Scott Bryson, *The Chastised Stage* (1990); Gianni Celati, *Finzioni occidentali* (1975); Henri Coulet, *Le Roman jusqu'à la Révolution* (1967); Denis Hollier, ed., *A New History of French Literature* (1989); Marie-Hélène Huet, *Rehearsing the Revolution: The Staging of Marat's Death* (1982); Georges May, *Le Dilemme du roman au XVIIIe siècle* (1963); Peter Szondi, "Tableau and Coup de théâtre: On the Social Psychology of Diderot's Bourgeois Tragedy," *On Textual Understanding and Other Essays* (trans. Harvey Mendelsohn, 1986); Philippe Van Tieghem, *Les Grandes Doctrines littéraires en France* (1946).

3. Nineteenth Century

Literary thought in France at the turn of the nineteenth century remained deeply marked by the memory of the Revolution. Still affected by the jolts of that great historical crisis, French society seemed to be deeply divided into two camps, each striving to promote a literature representing its own aspirations. One side was represented by a group of ideologues inspired by Pierre-Louis Ginguené (1748–1807), the founder of *La Décade,* a "political, philosophical and literary journal" that existed from 1794 to 1807, and by Georges Cabanis (1757–1808) and

Claude Fauriel (1772–1844). The other side was made up of the followers of Louis de Fontanes (1757–1821), appointed education minister by Napoleon and co-founder with Jean-François de Laharpe (1739–1803) of the *Mercure*.

Acknowledging the break the Revolution had imposed on French society, *La Décade* endorsed the continuity of the ideals of the Enlightenment and called for the coming into being of a literature that was broader in scope, free from the monopoly of a privileged class and of the need to represent the absolutist values of the *ancien régime*. For these ideologues, beauty is to be sought no longer in its conformity to eternal and general rules derived from the immutable ideals proffered by the ancients but rather in the psychological effect produced on readers' imagination, reason, and emotions. Subsequently, in his "Letter to Mr. T . . . . on the Poems of Homer" (1800), Cabanis developed the concept that beauty in the *Iliad* and the *Odyssey* depended less on the realization of an ideal form of the epic than on the concrete impression (admiration, identification) produced on the minds of the Greeks. He also maintained that a "poetics of the arts" must be founded theoretically, in this case on a positivist theory of the senses. *La Décade* had favorably hailed the reissuing of Etienne Bonnot de Condillac's works in 1797 and the publication of Denis Diderot's works by J. A. Naigeon in 1798. In 1810 Fauriel submitted a translation of Jens Baggesen's *Partheneid*. In his preface he attacked the definition of "genre" founded on formal similarities, deemed by him to be superficial and incomplete, and proposed a new definition based on various psychological effects likely to be produced. According to Fauriel, there would be "as many kinds of poetic compositions" as there were ways of affecting the reader's mind. The relationship between literature and a theory of the senses was highlighted once more.

In opposition to this reform-minded critical movement there arose the current of thought represented by the *Mercure*, to which Laharpe, author of the *Lycée, or Cours de littérature ancienne et moderne* (24 vols., 1799–1805), and Fontanes added a retrograde orientation by advocating a return to the pure classicism of the seventeenth century, against the disciples of the philosophers and the influence of sensualism. Concerned with restoring the practice of oral, improvised criticism of the *salons*, Joseph Joubert (1754–1824) defended the need to distinguish between "erroneous thinking" (JEAN-JACQUES ROUSSEAU, Denis Diderot, Voltaire) and "correct thinking" (Pierre Corneille, Molière, Jean de La Bruyère). Julien Louis Geoffroy (1743–1814), author of a *Cours de littérature dramatique* (1819–20) and from November

1800 editor of the *Année littéraire,* also became associated with the denunciation of modern principles and with the restoration of classical values. He defended the idea that the rules of poetry and eloquence are as immutable as the nature upon which they are founded and that such was the spirit of the arts in the time of Louis XIV, particularly toward the end of his reign, when the clergy held the most power. In his eyes the position of the ideologues, who inherited the atheistic and barbaric philosophy of the eighteenth century, was wrong.

When *De la littérature considérée dans ses rapports avec les institutions sociales* appeared in 1800, GERMAINE DE STAËL (1766–1817) was first thought to adhere to the ideologues' position. Indeed, from them she derived the theme of *perfectibility,* the concept of thought enrichment and of the continuing progress of civilizations. To put the product of thought—literature—and the content of civilizations in touch with one another was to recognize the influence of religion, mores, and laws on literature and, reciprocally, the latter's influence on all institutions. It also necessarily meant calling classical universality into question and postulating the rise, with time, of deeply divergent literatures, influenced by variations in climate, in accordance with Montesquieu's argument, extended here to the field of letters. According to Staël, under the influence of Christianity, the literatures of the north would therefore have achieved primacy over those of the south, since they were more apt to express the melancholy inherent in the new religion as well as its need for what is infinite.

François-René de Chateaubriand (1768–1848), despite his friendship with Fontanes and the hostility he never ceased to show toward the philosophy of the Enlightenment and the ideologues, developed this same theme in his *Génie du christianisme* (1802). The final outcome of progress would have to be found within the French Revolution, in the sense that the latter supplied literature with new topics of inspiration and the chance to express a whole new range of feelings. Yet it is particularly in *De l'Allemagne* (1814) that we see the most vigorous representation of Staël's contribution to literary theory. It contains both a criticism of classical literature as being irrelevant to the institutions of modern times and a defense and illustration of Romantic literature as being well-established in Germany and the only one subject to progress, by way of its national essence and its deeply rooted ties to the soil, religion, and history of European civilizations. For the north-south opposition expounded in *De la littérature* there was substituted the classicist-Romantic antithesis illustrated by paganism and Christianity, antiquity and the Middle Ages, and Greco-Roman institutions and chivalry. Under the influence of August Wilhelm Schlegel (1767–1845) in particular, Staël established a criticism founded on diversity, concerned with describing the characteristics of masterpieces, their qualities more than their flaws, with particular care to safeguard the freedom of genius (see GERMAN THEORY AND CRITICISM: 1. STURM UND DRANG / WEIMAR CLASSICISM and 2. ROMANTICISM). This concept is important in that it introduced the notion of historicity in literature, thereby laying the foundations for a genuine criticism. Once one ceases to believe in the immutability of human nature and in the unchanging nature of beauty, the work of art is henceforth called upon to represent the metamorphoses of an ever-changing and diverse humanity, while criticism, far from confining itself to a role of censure and supervision, is assigned the responsibility of revealing the degree of originality of each work, of presenting it as a phenomenon in its causes and effects, in its relationships to one human being, one milieu, and one moment in time.

The influence of Germaine de Staël's ideas was considerable, and CHARLES AUGUSTIN SAINTE-BEUVE (1804–69) was extremely sensitive to them. In Sainte-Beuve one finds especially a criticism of understanding that attempts to be open to all aspects of originality and is anxious to search for all new forms of talent, all the while remaining sensitive to avant-garde movements and serving the cause of Romantic literature. While his failings as a poet and novelist may have led him to fall back on the station of critic, Sainte-Beuve attempted to make criticism a poetic act, as can be seen in the way he produced and refined the art of the literary portrait. Although creative and poetic, his criticism remained above all biographical, claiming to depict the writer as much as the subject matter, in accordance with the new ideas that viewed a work no longer as a reflection of an immutable ideal but as the faithful expression of a creative individuality. The next step was to attempt to know the person and the personality that gave the work its stamp of originality. From 1838 onwards, after teaching in Lausanne, Sainte-Beuve began to yearn for the creation of a literary science, or to be more exact, a "literary natural history," the primary classifying principle of which would be the establishment of categories of thought. Henceforth the critical method would proceed in stages: it would focus on individuals in order to link them to kindred minds. For Sainte-Beuve, to know a writer was to situate him or her at different moments: within his or her race and educational background, within the group to which he or she belonged both in the hour of success and at the time of decline, and after his or her death, by study

through disciples and opponents. Here we detect the risk of succumbing to the temptation of globalizing. Sainte-Beuve, however, was only too aware of the vanity of such a scientific endeavor, and for several reasons. Even if this "science of minds" could come into being, it would always remain an art that would require the hand of a skillful artist. Moreover, Sainte-Beuve believed in the "individuality of talent and genius," in the mystery of the creative act, which no method, no matter how perfected, could ever explain completely. Later on, under the protection of the Second Empire, he reverted to the classical principles of moderation, order, and good taste. Swapping his old Romantic ideal for a stand more lenient toward the bourgeois order, he eventually more and more favored this "judgment from a viewpoint of station and indulgence" imposed upon him by external circumstances and proprieties.

Among the more typical representatives of the dogmatic tendency, we should first mention Désiré Nisard (1806–83), who, wishing to defend the classical legacy at all costs, kept a closed mind to the literature of his time, an "evil time" in his eyes, marked by all-too-easy infatuations, unbridled individualism, and the loss of all moral sense. In addition, he endowed his intransigently moralistic judgments with the so-called objectivity of an exact science. In the *Journal des Débats,* Saint-Marc Girardin (1801–73) upheld a similar viewpoint by turning good taste into an instrument in the service of moral order. Gustave Planche (1808–57), the influential critic of the *Revue des deux-mondes,* was also a severe judge of Romantic literature, which he saw as practicing a superficial kind of realism, almost a materialism, at the expense of a psychological reality that would in every case and time be true to itself. Valorizing a spiritualist concept of human nature, he saw in criticism the chance to uphold the unity of beauty, truth, and goodness. In an article dated January 1, 1835, Planche, after citing every false form of criticism (commercial, indifferent, witty, scholarly, school-of-thought), defined true criticism as "strict, vigilant, impartial, subjective in nature but not in its attacks . . . a dialectical invention, as daring, painstaking, and individualistic as poetic invention itself" (2:322). Although his opinions here tied in with those of Sainte-Beuve, Planche nevertheless was less sensitive to the literature of his time and showed a definite inclination for a classicism rooted in the cult of the past.

In the face of such confining and, more often than not, moralistic dogmatism, the writers' reaction was one of defiance: they aired their thoughts by claiming to be critics themselves. As early as in the preface to his *Orientales* (1829), Victor Hugo stated that "it is not up to the critic to ask for explanations; nor is it for the poet to give them. Art cannot be limited, handcuffed or gagged. . . . The poet is free. Let us try to see things through his eyes" (*Oeuvres poétiques*, 4 vols., 1964, 1:577). Théophile Gautier, in his preface to *Mademoiselle de Maupin* (1835), condemned critics for their narrow-mindedness, while on various occasions Honoré de Balzac (*Monographie de la presse parisienne* [1843], *Lettres sur la littérature* [1840], *La Muse du département* [1843], *Illusions perdues* [1837–43]) denounced a destructive and sterile state of criticism that, while ever bent on destroying "reputations, never quite manages to make one for itself" and was opportunistic and incapable of seeing things from the artist's point of view. As for CHARLES BAUDELAIRE, he stated in the *Salon de 1846* that "in order for it to be sound, which is the grounds for its existence, criticism needs to be partial, passionate, political, in other words positioned from an exclusive point of view, yet from one which opens up the widest horizon" (600). Romantic writers therefore presented a notion of criticism devoid of moral precepts and preoccupied solely with doing justice to the requirements of Art.

In the second half of the century, the history of criticism remained under the sway of the positivist debate. While paying tribute to Sainte-Beuve, whom he called above all the promoter of psychology in the field of criticism, HIPPOLYTE TAINE (1828–93) nevertheless recognized the need to acknowledge the role of analysis vis-à-vis description and of intelligence vis-à-vis imagination. Taine looked at literary criticism as a philosopher. His admiration for Spinoza and G. W. F. HEGEL led him to see both the logicality and the organicism of science. It was on the basis of this meeting of logic and biology that in his works of criticism he developed an ideal of scientific exactness to which he professed to systematically submit all phenomena. In his eyes, literary works were simply phenomena among others. His literary criticism covered the years 1852–94: *Essai sur les fables de La Fontaine* (1852), republished in 1861 under the title *La Fontaine et ses fables;* the *Essai sur Tite-Live* (1855); *Histoire de la littérature anglaise* (1856–63); *Essais, Nouveaux essais,* and *Derniers essais de critique et d'histoire* (1858, 1865, 1894). Concerned with uncovering the psychological traits of a writer or a nation, Taine inevitably simplified the painstaking questioning that guided Sainte-Beuve in his inquiries. As a result, Taine did not show much inclination to grasp the nuances or development of a literary personality as it unfolds in his or her works. He remained first and foremost a thinker in search of an all-embracing formula that could epitomize the dominant characteristics of any mind. For him, the first responsibility of a critic was to identify "the governing attribute" which could be applied, either to an individual, a nation or a civilization. The governing attribute, a classificatory principle, amounts to a transposition of the logician's "essence." In his preface to the second edition of *Essais de critique et d'histoire* (1866), Taine described it as a "psychological, dominating, and persistent condition" (ix), characteristic of an author and through which he or she represents the surrounding world. Livy would then be an orator turned historian, Stendhal a superior mind, George Sand an idealist artist, Jean Racine a monarchist poet with the reasoning of an orator, Diderot an erupting volcano. Each formula being the result of an induction, it is seen as a focal point from which a work of criticism can evolve through deduction, by bringing out factors that are determined by race (taken in the sense of national spirit) and circumstances of time and place. Taking Jean de La Fontaine as model, Taine attempted to demonstrate that fables are equivalent to "summary of a century" and that the more a poet "is drawn into his art, the more he is drawn into the spirit of his century and of his race" (*Essai* 344).

Taine's theory of criticism gave rise to controversies at the time. In *Mes haines* (1866) and *Le Roman expérimental* (1880), ÉMILE ZOLA (1840–1902) revealed his admiration for the man he called "the leader of our criticism." Later, in *Une Campagne* (1882), he admitted to having reservations about an endeavor that was deemed too systematic and was a product of critical juggling. Ferdinand Brunetière (1849–1906), who made a name for himself first by his virulent attacks on naturalism (*Le Roman naturaliste,* 1883), claimed to follow Taine inasmuch as the latter likened the study of literature to the procedures of natural science. But in the *Evolution des genres* (1890) he reproached Taine for neglecting aesthetics and "treating masterpieces like archival documents." While disinclined to believe in the possibility of scientific criticism, Brunetière nevertheless remained convinced of the need for objective criticism intended to explain, classify, and evaluate literary works. Edmond Scherer (1815–89), a former clergyman and a Genevan follower of Sainte-Beuve, opposed Taine's views and emphasized their contradictions from the point of view of theory and practice. According to Scherer, the governing attribute, inductive by definition, was used by Taine above all as an axiom from which he "draws the conclusions he believes to be therein contained." Perceived along these lines, it would reduce the psychological processes of an artist to a hollow mechanistic description. As for the theory of milieu, Scherer considered it too general and abstract and thus alien to literature itself.

Taine, however, remained one of the initiators of French criticism in the last third of the nineteenth century. His influence, though negligible by today's standards, which condemn such dogmatism and such a simplistic concept of science, made itself felt in the rising wave of enthusiasm for a thorough development of the scientific approach. Émile Hennequin (1858–88), following Taine, founded "esthopsychology," which he defined as "the science of the work of art as sign" (22), displaying aesthetic, psychological, and social characteristics. Mistrusting the excessive importance ascribed to biographical, hereditary, and environmental influences, Hennequin overturned Sainte-Beuve's viewpoint as well as Taine's. "It is from the scrutiny of the work alone that the critic will have to discover the clues necessary for the study of the author's thought" (65). The work thus ceases to be a pretext and becomes a diffuser of meanings instead.

For Ernest Renan (1823–92), in whose eyes "humanity alone is worthy of admiration . . . only the scientist has the right to admire" (*L'Avenir de la science*, 1890 [wr. 1848], 295). Criticism should be historical and scholarly first, capable of reconstructing the truth of any work, that is, capable of assessing the way it bears witness to its time, and should then proceed by empathy with the desire to detect the coming into being of reality behind the artistic representation. "Beauty is to be found in man and things, not in the way we speak of them" (188). From this perspective the distance between reality and beauty is abolished: in its manifestation of the successive aspects of universal dynamism, reality is always beautiful, with a beauty under whose spell the critic, in his or her capacity as attentive spectator, is bound to fall. This method leads to amateurishness, to impressionism such as that illustrated in the *Journal* of the brothers Edmond and Jules de Goncourt (1887), and to the total subjectivism of Anatole France, for whom "the worth of criticism lies only in the critic and the more personal it is, the more interesting it is bound to be" (*La Vie littéraire*, 1886–93, 491). Reacting simultaneously against dogmatic criticism and scientific criticism, the impressionistic option saw in the critic a reader more refined than others, a reader who read for his or her own pleasure and derived pleasure from relating that enjoyment. The Romantic spirit, with its continuing concern for variety and freedom, appears behind this interplay of subjectivism.

In its theoretic debate on literature, the nineteenth century was a century of synthesis and conflict. Many critical options came into being that were at times complementary but most often conflicting and that, in different ways, reiterated what was ideologically and aesthetically at stake. In contrast with judgmental criticism, which favored conservative and classical value, there emerged a criticism of diversity, devoted to understanding the specificity of works, people, and their times. When positivism replaced the Romantic spirit, the insistence on diversity persisted, but at the cost of being bound by the stability of a system made up of networks of rules and classificatory grids. Once turned scholar, the critic often had difficulties resisting the temptations of dogmatism. Once marginalized, both originality and individuality were able to regain their status only within the context of the impressionistic discourse.

A second controversy that pervaded the century opposed practitioners of external criticism, represented by Sainte-Beuve and Taine, to practitioners of a criticism that took greater account of the works themselves, of whom Hennequin and Brunetière are fairly good examples. No one better expressed this preoccupation, which continues to haunt and fuel the debate in contemporary literary criticism and theory, than did GUSTAVE FLAUBERT in his letter to George Sand dated February 2, 1869:

> In Laharpe's time, we were considered grammarians; in the days of Sainte-Beuve and Taine, historians. When can one ever be an artist, simply an artist intently concerned with a work in itself? The conditions under which a work is produced, the causes that brought it into existence, are subjected to the most minute analysis; but what of its *inherent* poetics? of its sources? its composition and style? (*Oeuvres complètes*, vol. 10, 1930, 8)

Roland Le Huenen

See also CHARLES AUGUSTIN SAINTE-BEUVE and GERMAINE DE STAËL.

Charles Baudelaire, *Oeuvres* (1951); Ferdinand Brunetière, *L'Évolution des genres dans l'histoire de la littérature* (1890), *Le Roman naturaliste* (1883); Anatole France, *Oeuvres complètes illustrés*, vol. 6 (1926); Émile Hennequin, *La Critique scientifique* (1888); Gustave Planche, *Portraits littéraires* (2 vols., 3d ed., 1852); Ernest Renan, *L'Avenir de la science* (1890); Charles Augustin Sainte-Beuve, *Oeuvres: Premiers lundis, portraits littéraires, portraits de femmes* (2 vols., ed. Maxime Leroy, 1956–60); Germaine de Staël, *De l'Allemagne* (5 vols., ed. Jean de Pange and Simone Balayé, 1959–60), *De la littérature* (ed. Paul Van Tieghem, 1959); Hippolyte Taine, *Essais de critique et d'histoire* (6th ed., 1892), *Essai sur les fables de La Fontaine* (1852), *Introduction à l'histoire de la littérature anglaise* (1863).

Roger Fayolle, *La Critique littéraire* (1964); Raphael Molho, *La Critique littéraire en France au XIXème siècle* (1963); Pierre Moreau, *La Critique littéraire en France* (1960); Georges Poulet, "La Pensée critique de Mme de Staël," *La*

Conscience critique (1971); René Wellek, *A History of Modern Criticism: 1750–1950,* vol. 2, *The Romantic Age* (1955), vol. 3, *The Age of Transition* (1965), vol. 4, *The Later Nineteenth Century* (1965).

4. Early Twentieth Century

Among the main currents of twentieth-century French thought as a poetics is a tradition of *poésie critique,* that combination of critical and creative poetics still alive and well. It is in some sense at the other pole from such criticism as that of Gustave Lanson, a clear and learned commentary that reads as prose to this poetry of criticism, the former sure of sources, of the influences of epoch and place, enabling the celebrated method of *explication de texte,* or the careful unfolding in great detail of the meaning seen to be, precisely, contained in and coextensive with the form of the text. One of the best examples here would be the readings by Jean-Pierre Richard in his *Microlectures.*

On the other side is a trembling of multiple meanings fluctuating with the reading, and a reliance on image and the high passion that marks poetic criticism as poetry. Just as Paul Eluard in the time of the surrealists was prone to speak of "Les Frères voyants," or the fraternity of artists, such poets as René Char and the younger Yves Bonnefoy carried on that inspiration of the visual and verbal combined; both had been associated with the surrealist movement in their youth, with its self-definition as a lyric comportment and its zeal for spontaneity. Bonnefoy continues to examine the problematics of naming and placing in poetic creation, in the strong line of aesthetician poets from CHARLES BAUDELAIRE to Stéphane Mallarmé (see STÉPHANE MALLARMÉ AND FRENCH SYMBOLISM). Several younger poets remain equally attached to this aesthetic tradition, among them Jacques Dupin, Michel Deguy, Claude Esteban, and Jacques Garelli.

From the modern point of view, taken by many readers and students of the aesthetic, a remarkable number of things literary and aesthetic begin in France with Marcel Proust. So will this brief essay on the creative and critical poetics of the *writers* of the twentieth century in France. Bergotte, the artist figure in Marcel Proust's *À la recherche du temps perdu,* gets up from his sickbed to see Johannes Vermeer's *View of Delft,* which is on loan to an exhibit, specifically a little piece of yellow wall in that painting that he could not remember. He is taken mortally ill in front of that little yellow wall as represented, and dies, but all that night in the windows of the bookstores the wings of the opened books he has created keep watch (*Recherche* 3:186–88; *Remembrance* 3:184–86). The

scene stirs the imagination. Here theory, like art, begins with the detail seen and recapturing some whole. For Proust, the recapturing of the moments lost is what art is about, and it is the task and genius of the artist to recreate voluntarily a work through the medium of whose miraculous instants and whole unity the past can be recaptured. This is what art strives after; it is its salvation and ours.

But those instants can also be recaptured in an involuntary memory through moments in which an accident brings back by a sort of miracle that same sense of the unity of all things. A madeleine dipped in tea, some uneven paving stone in the street one might stumble over, the sharp crease of the linen of a napkin—these "accidents" and their miraculous gift are the involuntary discovery that all art aims after. If we cannot summon these instants, we can try to reexperience them, in words after actions, as best we can. Proust celebrates the power of returning more powerfully than any other: his return to the same place, the same sight, the same hawthorns, for example, as he tries to recapture the original experience is the model for the project of his epic novel.

Proust places himself at first in the tradition of the aesthetic, that is, in the tradition of JOHN RUSKIN and WALTER PATER. His recall of the tradition, like his focus on reexperience and return, gives an impulse to the theoreticians of repetition, such as Gérard Genette, whose own reading of Proust and Proust's reading (*Figures III*) carries on the celebration of place and the appropriate ability to remember, to focus, and to cherish the recall. Genette is himself a powerful teacher of reading whose analysis of baroque poetry, with its inversions, makes us see the latter differently. From the beginning of the century, then, it is Proust who teaches us about reading and self and solitude; the essays of the "Days of Reading" section of *Pleasures and Days* (1896) are *journées de lecture* that have had lasting resonance in later criticism, leading, for example, straight to VIRGINIA WOOLF's essays on reading and libraries.

Proust points the way to the merging of theory and criticism so clearly embodied in the work of PAUL VALÉRY, followed by all the critics and creators under discussion here. Valéry's meditations on the thought of Leonardo da Vinci and on thought itself, in *Monsieur Teste* and in his notebooks *Tel Quel,* have continued to read with their original relevance. His aphoristic style sends us back to Pascal, while his sparkling essays and reflections on prosody, music, architecture, and the dance—as exemplified in his singularly sinuous *Dialogues* (themselves a kind of dance), in his essays *Variétés,* and in his superb

Degas danse dessin—are of a high order of poetic consciousness. This consciousness observes itself seeing and structuring its world even as it celebrates the tension between the irrational moment of inspiration and the construction that follows the rational and formal building of the poem. Valéry was to claim that his own poems were primarily generated by a rhythm he heard inside himself rather than from any subject matter.

It was around the intricate involvement of the mind with its own methods and power of structuration that Valéry's essays turned, the "universal mind" of Leonardo da Vinci being his chief prototype. *Monsieur Teste* and his *Introduction à la méthode de Léonard de Vinci* display, for the reader's full consciousness of Valéry's admiration of mind, this startling analysis of one great mind seen by another. Of a classical bent, his essays treat the poem and every work of art as a mental "act"—we think of WALLACE STEVENS's "the poem of . . . the act of the mind" ("Of Modern Poetry," *Collected Poems*, 1954, 240), and indeed Valéry's own greatest poems, such as "Le Cimetière marin" and "La Jeune Parque," themselves embody this working out of poetry as mental construction. His master was Stéphane Mallarmé, the difficult and most modern of all theoreticians, the nineteenth-century master of Symbolism, who, in his obsessions with the crisis of the poetic spirit, with the possibilities of elisions and suggestion and of multiple meanings, seems the most twentieth-century of all thinkers.

Paul Claudel, Valéry's contemporary in the post-Symbolist era, demonstrates, in his "Traité de la connaissance du monde et de soi-même" (*co-naissance,* literally, "be born with"), the essential mental act by which being born and knowing are knitted together. *The Eye Listens (L'Oeil écoute)* is the title of his other group of writings on art, mingling the senses and what they bring, like a latter-day Baudelairean sensitivity to correspondences.

When Max Jacob and Pierre Reverdy, along with Guillaume Apollinaire and Blaise Cendrars, are seen as the theoreticians and practitioners of cubism, it is because of their connection with the cubist painters; any text, any object in their hands, is glimpsed from all sides, in all its aspects. They all exist simultaneously, thus the alliance with the movement called simultanism or *Nunism,* "now-ism." Such poems as Apollinaire's "Zone" and Cendrars's "Dix-neuf poèmes élastiques" show the range and shifting of a modernist sensibility as well as any other statement might: they serve as manifestoes of this new kind of vision. Cendrars's epic poem "Prose du transsibérien et de la petite Jehanne de France" as it was illustrated by Sonia Delaunay is the most highly colored

manifestation of the simultanist philosophy. Even as it crosses the great spaces of the mind, it remains constant in its evocation of the local: "Blaise, tell me, are we far from Montmartre?" the little prostitute with him asks as they go further away (*Selected Writings* 179). One poem is worth a thousand theorizing words here: the sensibility is anchored in detail of image and context. The poem, says Reverdy, has to be *situated*.

Reverdy is equally responsible for the most celebrated surrealist theory besides that of convulsive beauty, that is, the faith that when two things are sharply brought together from two radically different realms, the shock of their confrontation will illuminate anything in calling range. This theory was picked up by the leonine ex-dadaist André Breton, the founder of the surrealist movement, which closely succeeds dadaism (itself a movement under the leadership of Tristan Tzara that showed the same passion for extremes and is said to have committed suicide in 1923), "the point where the *yes* and the *no* meet, not solemnly in the castles of human philosophies, but very simply on street corners like dogs and grasshoppers" (Tzara, *Sept manifestes Dada* 14). When Breton took up this willing confrontation and merging of elements, dream and the daylight real world pouring into each other as in the scientific experiment of communicating vessels *(Les Vases communicants),* the conception became the theory of the sublime point, in which death and life, up and down, would show no separation. To his baby daughter, subject of the last chapter of *L'Amour fou,* he is able to show this point, showing her also that he could not dwell in it (*Mad Love* 114). Convulsive beauty itself is founded on an extreme shock akin to hysteria and to that madness of passion that lies at the heart of surrealist aesthetics but was, all the same, hedged in by a certain prudence. Nadja, the real-life and temporary textual heroine of surrealist madness, about whom Breton writes a long prose poem of a book bearing her name (*Nadja,* 1928), is finally confined to an institution, and Breton, her erstwhile admirer, is bored by her, attracted by another, and inclined to lay down rules for a surrealism that Robert Desnos, once a member of the movement, will call a church with a pope who is Breton. That passion for enthusiasm, both literary and personal, that willing latter-day romanticism, was shared by the philosopher who is most closely associated with surrealism, Gaston Bachelard. In his books on the elements and on the poetics of space and on phenomenological aesthetics, Bachelard gave a rationale for the combination of the real and the imaginary that surrealism advocated. Bachelard's heritage, that of Jean-Pierre Richard and Georges Poulet and the GENEVA

SCHOOL, is a phenomenology at once vividly pragmatic and lucidly verbal.

The word "pragmatic" could also define the singularly effective teachings of ROLAND BARTHES, whose critical acumen directed itself toward fields as widely diverse as systems of fashion, of mythologizing, and of the written, spoken, and visual languages of art, photography, and music, as well as of literature. Barthes's *Essais critiques* and his other essays have taught us all how to see. Even the sinuous brilliance of JACQUES DERRIDA could be defined as, in one sense, pragmatic: the most influential philosopher and critic of the twentieth century in France (and perhaps even more influential in America), he, like Barthes, is in the tradition of persuasive teachers as major thinkers. Derridean thought is everywhere fertile and fertilizing; in literature, art, architecture, and film, his originality is matched only by the warmth of his personal style. The ways in which Barthes and Derrida force us to reexamine our first notions of text and textuality, of thought and vision, are ways more constructive, in the true sense of the term, than deconstructive, in the pejorative sense. Such appellations as DECONSTRUCTION are useful for the moment, but their criticism—as vivid in its style as that other *poésie critique* I began with, and in its own way as poetic—soars in its influence and its teaching beyond that and all appellations: these are the major thinkers of our epoch. As they teach us the limitations of our thought and our texts, and also their extensions, so the historians and theoreticians of art are themselves refusing absolute knowledge. In his influential book *Devant l'image,* Georges Didi-Huberman denounces our certainty of knowing and urges us to contemplate the possibility of our not knowing. Freed from "the net of knowing" (15), our consciousnesses are open to multiple guessings and self-suggestions.

One poet-thinker deserves a special place at the end for what he represents and for his influential personality. As the inheritor of a mystic tradition that merges with the Mallarméan tradition of the book, Edmond Jabès emerges from a perspective that is totally other. His reading, thought, and vision are more closely allied with that of Max Jacob, the Kaballah, and the Jewish tradition. He stands as the most troubling questioner of language and poetics, of the book of the book: in his *Livre des questions,* that Book of Questions and all that follows it, he brings his own exile from Egypt and, in a sense, the world into the presence of language. Jacques Derrida, one of the first to salute the profound quest and questions of Jabès, speaking of Deguy as the poet of joining, of likening, of gathering, speaks also (as does Gérard Genette in his *Seuils,* or *Thresholds*) of this kind of poem/poetics that opens the way to something, welcomes something, holds out something, calls something into being.

To sum up, we might say of the poetic criticism and critical poetry/poetics of the French twentieth century as it is seen here that it has as its purpose the naming, the calling of something, such as language, into its fullest being. It holds forth some hope of presence. Starting with that little patch of yellow, in a canvas upon another wall, it opens out.

Mary Ann Caws

See also PAUL VALÉRY.

Guillaume Apollinaire, *Apollinaire on Art: Essays and Reviews* (ed. LeRoy C. Breunig, 1972), *Oeuvres en prose complètes* (ed. Michel Decaudin, 1991); Roland Barthes, *Essais critiques* (1964, *Critical Essays,* trans. Richard Howard, 1972), *Image-Music-Text* (ed. and trans. Stephen Heath, 1977), *Le Plaisir du texte* (1973, *The Pleasure of the Text,* trans. Richard Miller, 1975), *S/Z* (1970, *S/Z,* trans. Richard Miller, 1974); Geoff Bennington and Jacques Derrida, *Jacques Derrida* (1991); Yves Bonnefoy, *The Act and the Place of Poetry: Selected Essays* (ed. John T. Naughton, 1989), *Le Nuage rouge: Essais sur la poétique* (1977); André Breton, *L'Amour fou* (1937, *Mad Love,* trans. Mary Ann Caws, 1980), *Ouevres complètes* (ed. Marguerite Bonnet, 1988), *Les Vases communicants* (1932, *Communicating Vessels,* trans. Mary Ann Caws and Geoffrey Harris, 1990); Blaise Cendrars, *Selected Writings of Blaise Cendrars* (ed. Walter Albert, 1962); René Char, *Oeuvres complètes* (1983); Paul Claudel, *Oeuvres en prose* (1965); Michel Deguy, *Actes* (1966), *Figurations: Poèmes—propositions—études* (1969); Jacques Derrida, *La Dissémination* (1972, *Dissemination,* trans. Barbara Johnson, 1981), *L'Écriture et la différence* (1967, *Writing and Difference,* trans. Alan Bass, 1978), *La Vérité en peinture* (1978, *The Truth in Painting,* trans. Geoff Bennington and Ian McLeod, 1987); Georges Didi-Huberman, *Devant l'image* (1990); Paul Eluard, *Oeuvres complètes,* vol. 2 (ed. Marcelle Dumas and Lucien Schéler, 1968); Gérard Genette, *Figures I, II, III* (1966–72); Edmond Jabès, *The Book of Dialogue* (trans. Rosmarie Waldrop, 1987), *The Book of Resemblances* (trans. Rosmarie Waldrop, 1990), *The Book of Shares* (trans. Rosmarie Waldrop, 1989); Marcel Proust, *À la recherche du temps perdu* (1913–27, rev. ed., 1954, *Remembrance of Things Past,* trans. C. K. Scott Moncrieff, Terence Kilmartin, and Andreas Mayor, 3 vols., 1981), *Contre Sainte-Beuve, précédé de Pastiches et mélanges, et suivi de Essais et articles* (ed. Pierre Clarac, 1971), *On Art and Literature, 1896–1919* (ed. and trans. Sylvia Townsend Warner, 1958); Pierre Reverdy, *Cette emo-*

tion appelée poésie: Écrits sur la poésie (1974); Jean-Pierre Richard, *Microlectures* (2 vols., 1979–84); Tristan Tzara, *Sept manifestes Dada, lampisteries* (*Seven Dada Manifestos and Lampisteries,* trans. Barbara Wright, 1977); Paul Valéry, *The Art of Poetry* (1958), *Degas danse dessin* (1938, reprint, 1983), *Selected Writings of Valéry* (trans. Louise Varèse, 1950).

Anna Balakian, *Surrealism: The Road to the Absolute* (1970); Philippe Boyer, *Le Petit Pan de mur jaune: Sur Proust* (1987); Mary Ann Caws, *The Poetry of Dada and Surrealism* (1970), *Yves Bonnefoy* (1984); Mary Ann Caws and Eugene Nicole, eds., *Reading Proust Now* (1990); Antoine Compagnon, *Proust entre deux siècles* (1989); David R. Ellison, *The Reading of Marcel Proust* (1984); Eric Gould, ed., *Edmond Jabès: The Sin of the Book* (1985); Jean Hytier, *The Poetics of Paul Valéry* (trans. Richard Howard, 1966); Rosalind Krauss, *The Originality of the Avant-Garde and Other Modernist Myths* (1985); James R. Lawler, *The Language of French Symbolism* (1969), *The Poet as Analyst: Essays on Paul Valéry* (1974); John T. Naughton, *The Poetics of Yves Bonnefoy* (1984); Christopher Norris, *Derrida* (1987); John K. Simon, ed., *Modern French Criticism: From Proust and Valéry to Structuralism* (1972); Richard Stamelman and Mary Ann Caws, eds., *Écrire le livre: Autour d'Edmond Jabès: Colloque de Cérisy* (1989).

5. 1945–1968

Since contemporary French theory traverses many fields and approaches, one should not be surprised that it eludes synthesis. However, even if a tightly organized synthesis is not possible, students of contemporary French thought are necessarily required to draw on G. W. F. HEGEL, KARL MARX AND FRIEDRICH ENGELS, FRIEDRICH NIETZSCHE, Edmund Husserl, SIGMUND FREUD, FERDINAND DE SAUSSURE, MARTIN HEIDEGGER, CLAUDE LÉVI-STRAUSS, and JEAN-PAUL SARTRE as basic reference points. Those who have recognized the important contributions of recent French theory have themselves mapped out new fields of critical inquiry based on the path-breaking works of writers such as MICHEL FOUCAULT, JACQUES DERRIDA, LUCE IRIGARAY, JACQUES LACAN, Jean Baudrillard, and JULIA KRISTEVA. The works of these and other contemporary French thinkers inform theories of the subject, reading and writing practices, and cultural as well as literary studies at the close of the twentieth century. Although French contemporary theory as we know it emerged as if full-blown in the 1960s, it reflected a profound rediscovery of intellectual currents that predated World War II as well as their reworking by a very young generation of intellectuals who were using struc-

turalist approaches to link figures as diverse as the Marquis de Sade, Hegel, Marx, and Freud.

To a large extent, theorists such as GEORGES BATAILLE and Lacan had already forged these links prior to the 1960s, Lacan in an aggressively structuralist mode. However, the younger generation, including Philippe Sollers, Jean-Louis Baudry, Foucault, Kristeva, and Derrida, had taken such analyses further by applying them to a number of fields and projects that argued for a more profound paradigm shift in intellectual history than had been thought plausible before. Whereas Bataille, MAURICE BLANCHOT, Lacan, Lévi-Strauss, ROMAN JAKOBSON, and Alain Robbe-Grillet had gone a long way toward demystifying the Cartesian notion of the subject by means of anthropological, phenomenological, psychoanalytic, linguistic, and even existential analyses (see RENÉ DESCARTES), the younger generation of theorists during the 1960s synthesized and hybridized many of these approaches in order to radically redefine not only the work of major intellectual precursors (JEAN-JACQUES ROUSSEAU, Freud, Heidegger, Husserl) but entire historical periods and institutional histories. What makes this period especially exciting is the fact that most of the younger intellectuals produced brilliant analyses without as yet having a well-defined sense of where they were headed as a group. Although in retrospect we can talk about STRUCTURALISM or poststructuralism, it is evident that during the 1960s almost every major book or essay had the effect of redefining and opening up entirely new ways of thinking that had been unimaginable in the 1950s.

Given time, of course, we have become familiar with many antecedents. For example, Lacan's publication of the *Écrits* in 1966 was largely an object lesson in intellectual history, given that most of the essays were developed in the decade prior to what some have called the new learning. Yet, even the *Écrits* had the force of yet another new and path-breaking text on the cutting edge of everything that was theoretically being conceptualized at the time. Lévi-Strauss's *La Pensée sauvage* (*The Savage Mind*) and *Mythologiques* (4 vols., *The Raw and the Cooked, From Honey to Ashes, The Origin of Table Manners, The Naked Man*), which were, again, rooted in work of the 1950s and even earlier, had a very similar impact, as did translation and republication of many essays by Jakobson stretching back to the 1920s or the discovery of the astonishing work of M. M. BAKHTIN that predated World War II. Developed in the years prior to the 1960s, then, the theories of these writers were read and recognized as if a lost continent of thought had suddenly been discovered.

Literary analysis, which had been important for figures such as Bataille, Blanchot, Lacan, Jakobson, and Lévi-Strauss, played a major role in the development of French thought in the 1960s, as can be seen in the journal *Tel Quel,* begun in the first year of the decade under the direction of a young novelist, Philippe Sollers. In many respects, *Tel Quel* could be considered the single most important French periodical of the second half of the twentieth century, since under its auspices contemporary French theory as we know it today was brought into being. Although many of its regular contributors have not become well known abroad (e.g., Dominique Desanti, Jacqueline Risset, Pierre Rottenberg, Jean Thibaudeau, Denis Roche), *Tel Quel* staged the intellectual context within which the writings of Foucault, Derrida, ROLAND BARTHES, Lacan, Kristeva, Sollers, and Gilles Deleuze could be understood on a large scale and as a highly diversified intellectual movement whose force was to overturn Sartrean existentialism and the various intellectual affiliations associated with it.

An important and often overlooked prelude to this displacement is the conflict between Sartrean *littérature engagée* and the *nouveaux romanciers,* whose major proponents in the 1950s were the novelist Robbe-Grillet and the literary critic Barthes. While Sartre in "Why Write?" argues that the literary work is essentially writing *for an other* that affirms or negates various relations with the world, Robbe-Grillet was arguing that the logic of writing could not be reduced to the reliable judgment of a real or implied author or to the real conditions of the world as such. In "Authors and Writers," Barthes argues that language should not be reduced to a vehicle or instrument for the "writer," who is a "transitive" individual for whom writing is merely a means of communication. The "author," in contrast, "is the only man, by definition, to lose his own structure and that of the world in the structure of language" (*Critical* 145). In a sentence indebted to the thinking of both Robbe-Grillet and Blanchot, Barthes notes,

> By identifying himself with language, the author loses all claim to truth, for language is precisely that structure whose very goal (at least historically, since the Sophists), once it is no longer rigorously transitive, is to neutralize the true and the false. But what he obviously gains is the power to disturb the world, to afford it the dizzying spectacle of *praxis* without sanction. This is why it is absurd to ask an author for "commitment." (146)

Such thinking about literary texts had direct antecedents in the wartime criticism and fiction of Blanchot, which deemphasized the subject as an active agency of change, even though there were strong suggestions of willed negativity. In "Le Silence de Mallarmé," Stéphane Mallarmé is praised as follows:

> One could say that Mallarmé, by an extraordinary effort of asceticism, has opened an abyss in himself where his conscience, in the very place it loses itself, survives itself and takes solitude in a pure despondency. Ceaselessly detached without exception to all that happens, he is as a hero of emptiness, and the night he broaches reduces it to an indefinite refusal of whatever might be—the designation even of spirit. (119)

"Le Silence de Mallarmé" is reminiscent of Sartrean negation (*le Néant* is explicitly mentioned), and the title of the essay reminds one of *Exercise du silence,* the title of a Brussels publication in which Sartre published parts of his wartime journal. Yet even though the titles connote resistance, in Blanchot the subject simply disappears and utterly disavows itself of the presence with which it might make any sort of claim, a disappearance Sartre could have viewed as existentially negative or counteractive. Mallarmé simply subtracts himself from the world, a subtraction whose political resonances in Blanchot mark a defaulting on the French fascist notion of spirit.

Mention of Blanchot is crucial in considering not only the history of a French avant-garde debate with *littérature engagée* that preceded the 1950s but a political division as well, since, unlike Sartre, Blanchot inclined to the right before World War II and had an ambiguous political identity during the Occupation. In fact, critics such as Jeffrey Mehlman have pointed out on a number of occasions that the intellectual movement associated with *Tel Quel* thinking had numerous affinities with French intellectuals who before and during the war had not unambiguously sided against fascism. Even a philosopher as guarded as Emmanuel Levinas has suggested parallels between DECONSTRUCTION, associated in its early days with *Tel Quel,* and the kind of defeatism that he believed was characteristic of those who came to accept, rather than reject, the occupation of France. However, *Tel Quel* had taken pains to advance itself as a leftist theoretical movement insofar as it was exploring the possibilities of a structuralist Marxism, which it sought to apply to a number of fields, including linguistic and psychoanalytic theory (see MARXIST THEORY AND CRITICISM: 2. STRUCTURALIST MARXISM).

One was left to puzzle, then, the extent to which the leftist slant was used to repatriate a number of intellectuals who before the 1960s were relatively isolated, obscure, and, in some people's eyes, politically objectionable. This rehabilitation extended even to figures such as

Louis-Ferdinand Céline and Ezra Pound, who were exonerated on the basis of the new literary and leftist critical dispensation. If we consider that this dispensation depended upon the work of Jewish theorists such as Jakobson and Lévi-Strauss, who were exiled from Europe during the war, we discover a very curious in-mixing in which various intellectual, social, and political backgrounds were being overlooked in order to make common cause.

Such a collapsing of difference was reflected, as well, in the hybridization and crossing over between disciplines such as linguistics, psychoanalysis, literary criticism, history, social theory, anthropology, and philosophy. And here once more common cause was the result, as fairly incompatible figures such as Saussure and Freud or Marx and Heidegger were being revised in order that theoretical linkage could be achieved. Overall, such violations of difference were viewed as liberating insofar as they produced sensationalistic theoretical advances that would become fundamental for a future generation of humanists in not only France but also the United States. No doubt, the role that literary theory played in the various conceptual mutations of the period was not slight.

It is often forgotten that Foucault, who published in *Tel Quel* and started to emerge as a major thinker in the early 1960s, was himself an excellent literary critic whose early book, *Raymond Roussel,* discusses discursive multilevels, false bottoms, embedding, mistaken conjunctions, anti-textualities, metagrams, self-generated sentences, cryptograms, reversed images, coincidences, fragmented spaces, and seriality. In short, *Raymond Roussel* could be read both as a commentary on the practices of the "New Novel" written before its advent in the 1950s and as a prototypical text anticipating studies such as *L'Archéologie du savoir (The Archeology of Knowledge).* Already in *Naissance de la clinique (The Birth of the Clinic)* Foucault looks at eighteenth-century medicine in a way quite reminiscent of the Roussel book in that he defines medical knowledge according to the "regularities" and "mappings" of discourse and how they create orders that do not, in fact, coincide. As in the Roussel study, Foucault stresses the orders of discourse that pertain to visible and invisible phenomena, and he once more stresses the role of secrecy in relationship to writing. Foucault also notes how the temporality and spatiality of the clinic is at odds with a practice of medical writing whose system has little tolerance for these clinical axes. What in Roussel was viewed as "non-coincidence" and the development of a writing whose "surface" negates space and time is now discovered in the medical writing of the eighteenth century.

Les Mots et les choses (The Order of Things) similarly applies literary-critical and linguistic paradigms borrowed from structuralism, though with the aim of defining historical *epistémès.* Although Foucault's descriptions of the Middle Ages and the Renaissance do not withstand close archival scrutiny (the periods are much more heterogeneous than Foucault suggests), they succeed in demonstrating how discursive and cultural practices determine and are determined by shifting assumptions about signification that are not always in phase when one looks at culture synchronically, even if, overall, they make up a general *epistémè* or dominant conceptual paradigm. That this view, so important today for American NEW HISTORICISM, is traceable back to the study of an avant-garde writer such as Roussel suggests the extent to which Foucault transgressed the disciplinary differences between literary and historical analyses.

The application of literary-critical practices to social or historical phenomena was already well established in Paris by such thinkers as Bataille, Roger Caillois, and WALTER BENJAMIN during the 1930s. But more relevant is the work of Barthes, whose *Mythologies* brings into relationship very acute aesthetic sensibilities with the ability to improvise with semiological categories derived from linguistics. In *Roland Barthes: The Professor of Desire,* Steven Ungar notes that "instead of concentrating on the objective forms of [popular myths], Barthes analyzes how they are produced, circulated, and exchanged—in other words, how myths manipulate the processes of meaning in order to create what purport to reflect collective conceptions of reality and 'human nature.'" Such a project, he says, exposes "the objective forms of alienation promoting class division" (21). Barthes, in other words, shares some basic concerns with French existential Marxists. However, Barthes's mode of analysis depends largely upon a rare sensibility to grasp inferences and details in a way characteristic of literary and art critics. Barthes notes, for example, that advertising images are doubly coded in that they replace the representation of actual social conditions with false stereotypes that appeal to our conscience by means of an identification with nature, the way "things are." Barthes also demonstrates how cultural events are secondary or even tertiary modeling systems whose deep structure could be explained through linguistic and semiotic categories. Barthes's *Système de la mode (The Fashion System)* anticipated slightly Jean Baudrillard's *Le Système des objets* and the studies that followed.

Indeed, by the latter half of the 1960s a common question for many *Tel Quel* intellectuals was how to think of language as a mode of production within Freudian, Marxist, and Saussurean contexts. Unlike Barthes, who used SEMIOTICS somewhat impressionistically, Kristeva, Jean-Louis Baudry, and Jean-Joseph Goux attempted to rigorously integrate Marx, Freud, and Saussure into a hierarchical theory of textual production that sometimes resembled the kind of linguistic analyses done by figures such as NOAM CHOMSKY.

Goux, who went furthest in terms of linking economy to linguistics, attempted to develop his work primarily in relation to Marxist thought. And for those who have wondered about the road not taken by Derrida in the late 1960s, when Marxism awaited him with open arms, Goux's "Marx et l'inscription du travail" of 1968 provides a rare glimpse of how Derrida's *De la grammatologie (Of Grammatology)* was viewed by his Marxist contemporaries of 1967. Goux argues that Derrida had shown how systems of meaning (speech) were indifferent to the ways in which signs are produced (writing). Hence, the concrete labor of producing signs needed to be seen in terms of Derridean "traces" accompanying a system of meaning in which the difference between production (writing) and circulation (exchange, value, meaning) is effaced in bourgeois culture (201).

Julia Kristeva's "La Sémiologie: Science critique et/ou critique de la science" ("Semiotics: A Critical Science and/or a Critique of Science," *Kristeva Reader*) is exactly contemporary with Goux's piece and makes a similar case; however, Kristeva is more sensitive to the literary contexts of thinking about writing as a mode of labor and as a means of production. She, too, writes that one ought to "adopt the term writing when it is a matter of a text seen in terms of production, in order to differentiate the concept of 'literature' from 'speech.'" According to Kristeva, writing is not mimetic but performative; the literature of writers such as James Joyce, Mallarmé, Roussel, and the comte de Lautréamont is not reducible to representation and can only be considered in terms of its semiological practices of productivity. Like Goux, Kristeva argues that

> the semiology of productivity accentuates the alterity of its object by means of relating to a (representable and representative) object of exchange which touches on the exact sciences. At the same time, it accentuates the overthrowing of scientific terminology and orients us towards that other scene of work before value, a scene which we can hardly see today without difficulty. (91)

(It should be noted that the articles by Goux and Kristeva did not originally appear in the journal *Tel Quel* but were published in *La Nouvelle Critique*. In 1968 these essays

were showcased in a collection of essays, put together by *Tel Quel* and called *Théorie d'ensemble*, that were considered representative of the best of the *Tel Quel* movement.) Kristeva, too, argues that the problematic of exchange concerns the establishment of reified representations, whereas the problematic of labor concerns a performance that is not translatable into reified terms. In Kristeva's later work the distinction between semiotic and symbolic will replace that between labor and exchange, and as is well known, the semiotic will be associated with the feminine, while the symbolic will be associated with the masculine.

Often overlooked is that by this time Kristeva, only in her mid-twenties, already had considerable influence on her immediate circle. Jean-Louis Houdebine, for example, was a Marxist critic whose conception of language and textuality was almost entirely indebted to Kristeva's intertextual and transformational understanding of semiotics. And Goux also appears to have been influenced by her. However, in Goux, and already to some extent in Kristeva herself, the influence of Derrida's notions of *écriture* and "trace" were quite perceptible in the wake of the simultaneous publication in 1967 of Derrida's *De la grammatologie, L'Écriture et la différence (Writing and Difference)*, and *La Voix et le phénomène (Speech and Phenomena)*.

Clearly, the *Tel Quel* group, of which Derrida was a part, saw *De la grammatologie* as a preface to a major work on Marx and Lenin. *De la grammatologie*, after all, mounts a devastating critique of the assumptions of presence that were latent in an inherently metaphysical approach to considering language, and to a large extent, Kristeva and others had already been addressing this question by means of privileging the semiotic over the symbolic. Unlike Derrida, however, these *Tel Quel* critics did not see the philosophical implications of their approach in a very broad historical sense. For their sights were too narrowly trained on, first, developing formal semiotic methods of analysis and, second, reinventing Marxism-Leninism. Because Derrida was not too interested in either of these two ventures, he could engage intellectual history in a much broader and more effective manner even while he left himself free to attack the very people whom the *Tel Quel* critics held in high esteem: the father of semiotics, Saussure, and that most virtuosic practitioner of semiotics, Lévi-Strauss. If *De la grammatologie* is an attack on the metaphysics of eighteenth-century language theory, it is just as much a disassembling of the rationales for putting one's trust in the semiotic adventure.

In fact, *Tel Quel*'s interest in semiotics extended back

to a general interest in RUSSIAN FORMALISM, that is, poetic and narrative theory, which Kristeva and others were hoping to merge with semio-linguistic approaches pioneered by Jakobson, Louis Hjelmslev, Chomsky, Lévi-Strauss, and ÉMILE BENVENISTE. However, within the *Tel Quel* group there were also theorists who, like Barthes, could be conversant in semiotics while at the same time subordinating that study to formal structural analyses, and so these theorists were linked to a sort of literary criticism not so far removed from the American NEW CRITICISM. Jean Ricardou, for example, was a formalist critic whose main interest was the *nouveau roman*. Although he was familiar with semiotics and structuralism, his work of the period focuses largely on literary devices or strategies that were the stock in trade of novelists such as Robbe-Grillet, Michel Butor, and Claude Simon.

Tzvetan Todorov's readings of Henry James in *Poétique de la prose (Poetics of Prose)* were, like Anglo-American readings, concerned with metatextuality. Todorov's earlier writings also develop Kristeva's notion of the intertext by considering the code or interpretant formed by means of an identification of predicates. In medieval romance the following schema is typical: the sun illuminates; Christ illuminates; the sun therefore signifies Christ. By means of such simple predication, narrative descriptions in which terms such as "sun" occur can be linked to prefabricated religious intertexts. Todorov's assertion that emphasis upon predication deemphasized agency mirrors the general slant of structuralist poetics away from subject-centered analyses.

Gérard Genette, also closely affiliated with *Tel Quel*, published a number of essays under the title *Figures* which similarly focused on literary language as a complex interrelation of multiple structures or signifying processes that constitute rather than merely imitate the referent. One of Genette's major accomplishments is overturning the mimesis-diegesis hierarchy in which showing is considered superior to telling. Here Wayne Booth's *Rhetoric of Fiction* (1961, 2d ed., 1983) was one of Genette's immediate concerns, and the fact that Genette was willing to converse with a Chicago literary critic as opposed to a Swiss linguist such as Saussure indicated a willingness to enter a literary-critical arena. (See CHICAGO CRITICS and FICTION A THEORY AND CRITICISM: 3. EARLY TWENTIETH-CENTURY BRITISH AMD AMERICAN.) To some extent, the overturning of the distinction between showing and telling has some resonances with the overturning of the distinction between voice and writing in Derrida's *De la grammatologie*. But Genette's overturning is not radical in that Genette is not interested in dismantling much of received philosophical tradition. In fact, his aim is not to

utterly scrap all narrative theory but rather to reformulate it and provide us with a more reliable and more accurate analytical vocabulary.

Whereas Kristeva's semiotic analyses are beyond the competency of most language and literature professors, Genette's methods and terminology are accessible and user-friendly. Whereas Barthes proliferated numerous semiological distinctions and approaches that were always quite experimental in that they had a short life span in his *oeuvre* as a whole, Genette has attempted to build a systematic approach to considering narrative meant to replace the familiar categories set forth, for example, in E. M. Forster's *Aspects of the Novel* (1927). In general, Genette and other structuralist critics (Claude Bremond, Michael Riffaterre, Philippe Hamon, Laurent Jenny, Paul Zumthor) made plausible the Russian Formalist assumption that we should not read according to what Riffaterre has called a mimetic fallacy, in which words transparently reflect a priori referents. Hence, notions such as character, point of view, or setting should be thought of on the order not of things but of verbal structures, constituted by means of highly artificial systems of signification that produce meanings that only appear to imitate the life-world (the reality effect). During the 1970s structuralist literary criticism would become influential abroad, its most visible critics being Genette, Todorov, and Riffaterre, the latter of whom developed a powerful theory of intertext as interpretant, which has had much influence in Anglo-American universities.

One could say that overall we have been considering what ought to be called the first phase of an intellectual revolution in France that would carry over strongly into the 1970s and beyond. In the second phase, Anglo-American academies would increasingly become major audiences for new developments in what became known as "French theory."

Herman Rapaport

See also ROLAND BARTHES, CLAUDE LÉVI-STRAUSS, JEAN-PAUL SARTRE, FERDINAND DE SAUSSURE, and STRUCTURALISM. [For assistance I wish to thank my research assistant, Elayne Zalis, and also my colleague Steven Ungar.]

See bibliographies in ROLAND BARTHES, JACQUES DERRIDA, MICHEL FOUCAULT, JULIA KRISTEVA, JACQUES LACAN, and CLAUDE LÉVI-STRAUSS for texts by those writers.

Jean Baudrillard, *Le Système des objets* (1968); Jean-Louis Baudry, *Les Images* (1963), *Personnes* (1967); Maurice

Blanchot, "Le Silence de Mallarmé," *Faux pas* (1943); Claude Bremond, *Logique du récit* (1973); Roger Caillois, "La Hiérarchie des êtres," *Les Volontaires* 5 (1939); Michel Foucault et al., *Théorie d'ensemble* (1968); Gérard Genette, *Figures* (3 vols., 1966–72); Jean-Joseph Goux, "Marx et l'inscription du travail" (Foucault et al.); Philippe Hamon, *Texte et idéologie* (1984); Roman Jakobson, *Questions de poétique* (1973); Laurent Jenny, *La Terreur et les signes* (1982); Emmanuel Levinas, "Tout autrement," *L'Arc* 54 (1973); Jeffrey Mehlman, *Legacies: Of Anti-Semitism in France* (1983); Jean Ricardou, *Problèmes du nouveau roman* (1967); Michael Riffaterre, *Semiotics of Poetry* (1978); Alain Robbe-Grillet, *Pour un nouveau roman* (1963, *For a New Novel: Essays on Fiction,* trans. Richard Howard, 1965); Jean-Paul Sartre, *Qu'est-ce que la littérature?* (1946, *What Is Literature?* trans. Bernard Frechtman, 1949, *"What Is Literature?" and Other Essays,* trans. Frechtman, 1988); Philippe Sollers, *Logiques* (1968), *Paradis* (1981); Tzvetan Todorov, *Poétique de la prose* (1971, *Poetics of Prose,* trans. Richard Howard, 1977); Steven Ungar, *Roland Barthes: The Professor of Desire* (1983); Paul Zumthor, *Introduction à la poésie orale* (1983, *Oral Poetry: An Introduction,* trans. Kathryn Murphy-Judy, 1990).

6. 1968 and After

In France, May 1968 marked an important historical moment insofar as students and workers were striking in solidarity to bring the French government down. For many intellectuals this time was reminiscent of the Paris Commune, roughly a century earlier. Oddly, however, the Communist party was less revolutionary during this time than the non-Party Left, which encouraged free self-expression. In terms of the journal *Tel Quel,* this meant a green light for the conviction that through the invention of new practices of writing (semiotics, writing, grammatology) the modes of signifying production would be changed and social revolution would transpire within the very transformation of the French language itself. For some of the followers of JACQUES LACAN, the liberation and transformation of language was directly tied to the conviction that the unconscious is structured like a language and that therefore we have to allow the unconscious to be heard and to have its effect on rigid, authoritarian, and ultimately bourgeois forms of expression.

Although it is inaccurate to say that contemporary French feminism had its inception in the events of May 1968, those events were significant in convincing people that the time had come for social revolution and that reconsidering the status of women was integral to this

process. Significant in the ongoing history of French feminism was the formation, in 1968, of Psychanalyse et Politique (Psych et Po), which founded the well-known publishing house Éditions des femmes. Monique Wittig's fictional work *Les Guérillères,* published in 1969, not only reflected a very strongly defined lesbian feminist orientation but also developed an anti-essentialist orientation toward language that undermined stable subject positions. Somewhat later, feminist writers would begin exploring what has become known as *écriture feminine.* Such writing refers specifically to a mode of semiotic production, in the Kristevean sense, that is inseparable from how unconscious processes affect somatic conditions that are particular to the female gender. Such a definition draws from *Tel Quel's* linkage of Marxism with SIGMUND FREUD, in which *écriture* represents a form of labor whose material conditions pertain to the body, the drives, and the unconscious. Such writing practices suggest on a theoretical level that, in fact, one ought not to forget the possibility that gender introduces yet another set of complex questions pertaining to "difference" that have to be considered alongside the Derridean critique of binarism at the semiotic level advanced in the essay "La Différance" ("Différance"). (See FEMINIST THEORY AND CRITICISM: 3. POSTSTRUCTURALIST FEMINISMS.)

Given the heterogeneity of *Tel Quel* and the emergence of thinkers from within its ranks who by 1970 had become strong intellectual leaders in their own right, it is not surprising that the group had begun to split apart. Already by 1968 Jean Pierre Faye, a radical leftist critic, began the Change group and criticized *Tel Quel* for being too linguistically oriented and too much in sympathy with right-wing ideologies (i.e. JACQUES DERRIDA's Heideggerianism). The enthusiasm of May 1968 affected many *Tel Quel* contributors by suggesting that one ought to produce a more political, more revolutionary theory, hence impelling the group to embrace Leninism and, via Philippe Sollers and JULIA KRISTEVA, Maoism. By 1970 *Tel Quel's* published quarrels were not only with Faye and the Change group but more broadly with the French Communist party (this is a main motivating factor in the journal's fascination with Maoist thought), the Union des écrivains, and the Comité d'action led by Marguerite Duras and MAURICE BLANCHOT. By June 1971 *Tel Quel* had made a decided commitment to Maoist thought—some of its members would later recant—marked by Maria Antonietta Macciocchi's *De la Chine* (*Daily Life in Revolutionary China,* originally published in Italian) and underscored in 1974 by Julia Kristeva's *Des Chinoises (About Chinese Women),* published, incidentally, by Éditions des femmes. The purpose of Kristeva's text was to consider how woman was being defined according to a non-Western, non-phallogocentric culture in which practices of inscription, particularly those of Maoist writings, were aligned against the logocentric and phonocentric traditions of the West. Of no small interest is how Kristeva used Lacanian psychoanalysis as an interpretant for figuring China in terms of Maoist thought.

By 1970 Derrida had already left *Tel Quel,* an event marked by his very important interviews with Kristeva, Jean-Louis Houdebine, Guy Scarpetta, and Henri Ronse, later published as *Positions.* Among the major issues raised in the interviews were why Derrida rejected *Tel Quel*'s materialist interpretation of grammatology, his closeness to Heideggerian thinking, and his rejection of Lacan. On all of these issues, Derrida was at odds with the *Tel Quel* group, which was beginning to suspect that Derrida was politically much more conservative than had been generally assumed.

During the 1970s, Derrida would become closely associated with a group of sympathetic colleagues whose most prominent figures included Jean-Luc Nancy, Philippe Lacoue-Labarthe, Sarah Kofman, and JEAN-FRANÇOIS LYOTARD. A newly formed press, Éditions Galilée, would become a prominent venue for publications by Derrida and his group. Although Lacan was never affiliated with *Tel Quel,* he became an important theoretical presence. Sollers's writings became increasingly influenced by Lacan, and during the decade Kristeva participated in Lacan's seminars.

Although a full workup of Lacan's career is not possible here, it should be said that his life's work falls into roughly four phases: a relatively conservative French psychiatric phase that flirts with psychoanalysis and surrealism before World War II; a stormy renegade phase in the 1950s, when he brought Husserlian, Hegelian, Saussurean, Heideggerian, Jakobsonian, and Lévi-Straussian thought to bear on Freud; an Olympian phase in the 1960s and early 1970s, when he had successfully founded his own École Freudienne and started to develop mathematical and logical models that built on his earlier teachings; and a somewhat waning phase in the late 1970s, when, even from the perspective of already esoteric teachings, he drifted into maddening inscrutability and turned the reins over to his son-in-law, Jacques-Alain Miller. Essentially, Lacan was an existential psychologist who radicalized JEAN-PAUL SARTRE's disassembly of Cartesianism by transferring Sartre's central insights into contexts Sartre was unable to negotiate, structuralist linguistics and anthropology being the

most important. Lacan's genius was that he could plausibly ground such intellectual acrobatics in Freudian psychology, not to mention in highly insightful clinical experiences. Unlike Derrida, Lacan was an acolyte of the spoken word and developed a great reputation as a teacher long before he became widely known for his writings. Only after the publication of *Écrits* did he enjoy a celebrated notoriety on an international scale.

Sherry Turkle has written at length of the many political uses to which Lacanian psychology was put in the 1960s and after. Lacan's idea that the unconscious is structured like a language appealed to the *Tel Quel* critics because it opened the way for a materialist interpretation, the kind embraced by feminists of the Psych et Po group. His semio-linguistic analyses not only "decenter" the Cartesian subject but also address the modes of linguistic production with an attention to gender difference. His argument that the "phallus" is just a signifier whose meaning is divided between two incommensurable sexualities opens the way for an anthropological understanding of gender that escapes patriarchal essentialism. Problematic for feminists, however, was that even if Lacan deconstituted phallogocentrism, he nevertheless made many comments that could be construed as misogynistic (for example, that he knew woman's desire better than any woman). Furthermore, even if he is exceptional in not having looked upon homosexuality as a pathology at a time when this was not the dominant view, his psychoanalysis nevertheless presupposes a nuclear triadic relation between father, mother, and child. What he called the Law of the Father is always operative, even in female homosexuality. In fact, to foreclose on this law would be to enter what Lacan terms psychosis. As David Macey has pointed out, much of Lacan's thinking about women relates to his earliest phase as a psychiatrist—the days of the notorious Papin sisters, maids whose foreclosure of the father principle led to their crime of ritualistically dismembering a mother and her daughter.

In 1974 LUCE IRIGARAY, a linguist and psychoanalyst, published a breakaway study entitled *Speculum de l'autre femme (Speculum of the Other Woman),* in which, as a Lacanian analyst, she turned against Freud the father and, by implication, Lacan. Like the surrealists of the 1920s, Irigaray embraced hysteria not as a malady but as another way of thinking that the West had systematically suppressed, though in a manner that carried the traces of hysteria's irrationality within itself. In *Tel Quel*'s terms, the semiotic is effaced in the symbolic, although its traces can be detected in the very place of its repression. The link between hysteria and the feminine is significant, then, in the way Irigaray analyzes its semiotic trace-work in the writings of influential male thinkers: PLATO, ARISTOTLE, RENÉ DESCARTES, Freud. It is this trace- or out-work in male discourse that in *Speculum* constitutes woman as Other. Woman is not to be considered a reified Other but rather understood as an arche-trace and, as such, unrepresentable and, as Irigaray says, unrealized. Woman is "cryptic" insofar as she is encrypted in an ontological paradigm within which she cannot occur except as a trace whose presence can only be detected as an irrational symptom in a foreign body. Even though Irigaray's work is meant to depart from Lacanianism, her thesis still conforms to Lacan's saying that "for man woman is a symptom." In *Ce sexe qui n'en est pas un (This Sex Which Is Not One)* Irigaray argues that physiologically woman's body has consequences for expression that impact on a phallocentric discourse. This thesis champions an *écriture feminine* in which woman's writing is necessarily a writing of the body (physiology and one's consciousness of that physiology as gendered). This argument, too, stems from Lacan's topological models in which psychology is configured geometrically in terms of "bodies." Whereas Lacan avoided literalizing these topological spaces in terms of male and female physiology, Irigaray argues for a materialization of gender that reintroduces essentialist and empirical assumptions that Lacan had struggled very hard to avoid.

HÉLÈNE CIXOUS, a literary critic, writer of fiction, and dramatist, shares Irigaray's sense that Freudian psychoanalysis is yet another institution that sanctioned violence against women. Cixous's dramatization of the Dora case is a terrible indictment of Freud. Her fiction, in general, has been exemplary of a lyrical prose that attempts to write the feminine body according to a materiality of the signifier reminiscent of 1960s writing at *Tel Quel* (e.g., Sollers's *Nombres*). In 1975 Cixous collaborated with Catherine Clément to write *La Jeune née (The Newly-Born Woman)*. Clément, one of Lacan's most devoted seminarians and perhaps his clearest expositor, contributes an essay on sorcery and hysteria in which the question of abjection and the female body is raised in order to speak about repression, transgression, and revolution. In particular, hysteria and witchcraft are seen in historical terms as linked to the feminine, exposing the unrepresentable, dredging up abjection, and heightening castration anxiety. Clément uses this perception to attack the Lacanian belief that woman, as hysteric, presents her mystery to an other because she believes that this will lead to a meaningful relationship, when, in fact, all she is doing is obviating the very object

by means of which a proper (sexual) relationship can be established. The hysteric or witch, Clément believes, returns the repressed in such a way that we have to think entirely outside of these Lacanian parameters. In "Sorties," Cixous uses the strategy of overturning prejudicial oppositions in order to create a systemic revaluation of hierarchical structures. The distinction between logos and writing, therefore, is akin to distinctions such as those between male and female, master and slave, son and father. The influence of Derrida's "La Pharmacie de Platon" ("Plato's Pharmacy") is strong. Whereas Clément shows the historical condition of woman viewed from the side of patriarchy, Cixous writes from the side of the Other and, in so doing, considers a body that is not definable in masculine terms, since this body is not logocentric but is typified by polymorphous intensities that do not necessarily converge. Here, too, the question of woman as lack is relevant in that for *l'écriture feminine* lack is reinscribed as what Derrida in "La Différance" called *espacement,* which is to say, a process of differentiating that breaks with the law of contradiction. Along these lines Cixous discusses what Marguerite Duras had explored in her India cycle and particularly in *Le Ravissement de Lol V. Stein (The Ravishing of Lol Stein),* where she used the phrase *le mot trou* ("the hole word") to characterize Lol's discourse.

Whereas feminists had explored the surrealist model of hysteria as a theoretical model for contemporary feminism, Gilles Deleuze and Félix Guattari rediscovered a surrealist passion for psychotic experience. In *Anti-Oedipe: Capitalisme et schizophrénie (Anti-Oedipus: Capitalism and Schizophrenia),* they reinvent schizophrenia as a new cultural paradigm that would develop a libidinal notion of capitalist economy whose logic is made up of "flows" that serve to de-territorialize and re-territorialize not only geographical but psychical boundaries (one is reminded of Salvador Dali's soft watches). One of the most important points of *Anti-Oedipe* is that capitalist production relies on "anti-production," or the violent undoing of codes, lack amid overabundance, increased illiteracy amid increases in knowledge, or what some Marxists call dis-accumulation. In *Mille plateaux (A Thousand Plateaus),* the second volume of the Capitalism and Schizophrenia project, Deleuze and Guattari develop the notion of deterritorialization in terms of rhizomes, molecules, nomads, stratoanalyses, black holes, particle physics—in short, a theoretical plasma of highly diverse analogies crisscrossing all the so-called disciplines and traversing First, Second, and Third World cultures. Central to the notion of a "thousand plateaus" are all the possible assemblages formed in both the organic and inorganic spheres and how they defy Western categories of thought inherited from the ancient Greeks.

Guattari, whose work is less well known than Deleuze's, has written a number of independent studies that focus on molecularization. In *La Révolution moléculaire (Molecular Revolution: Psychiatry and Politics)* and *L'Inconscient machinique,* for example, it is evident that Guattari was responsible for developing the biological, geological, and cosmic analogies that radiate throughout *Mille plateaux* and that he was especially interested in modes of counter- or antiproduction within highly organized structures. Guattari's antipsychiatric bias has led him to develop schizophrenia as a model for explaining phenomena on a more or less global order. More recently, Guattari has published *Cartographies schizoanalytiques* and *Les Trois Écologies.*

Deleuze, who is one of the most dazzling and prolific among the French theorists, published his first book, *Empirisme et subjectivité (Empiricism and Subjectivity),* in 1953 and has been considering radical subjectivities ever since. He has published two books on FRIEDRICH NIETZSCHE, two on Baruch Spinoza, and two on Henri Bergson. He has also published book-length studies of IMMANUEL KANT, Gottfried Wilhelm Leibniz, and Marcel Proust. All these books merit considerable commentary. In addition, in the late 1960s he published what are perhaps his two most outstanding volumes, *Logique du sens (The Logic of Sense)* and *Différence et répétition. Logique du sens* consists of short chapters in which Deleuze pioneers the notion of *schizanalyse* by means of reading Lewis Carroll, Antonin Artaud, and Pierre Klossowski, as well as figures such as Daniel Defoe and Lucretius. The book maps out not only notions such as the body without organs, the disorganization and reorganization of libidinal zones, the traversal of surfaces, pathological models of replication, the dismantling of Oedipus, and modes of antiproduction—all of major significance to the capitalism-and-schizophrenia project—but also the central concerns of Deleuze's very significant contribution to film studies, *Cinéma I: L'Image mouvement (The Movement-Image)* and *Cinéma II: L'Image-temps (The Time-Image).* In *Logique du sens* Deleuze writes:

> The first effect of Others is that around each object that I perceive or each idea that I think there is the organization of a marginal world, a mantle or background where other objects and other ideas may come forth in accordance with laws of transition which regulate the passage from one to another. I regard an object, then I divert my attention, letting it fall into the background. (305)

The cinema studies of the 1980s expand on this passage by interrogating what is marginal to the image and what has fallen into its background. Deleuze argues that cinema studies has erred in assuming a presence of the image as perceptual event, a presence that effaces the fading or dissolution of the image according to a logic of time that plays havoc with a metaphysical or presenced understanding of film as a totalized unity that can be categorically split up into thinglike appearances.

Another major thinker who uses scientific analogies is Michel Serres. One of the most lyrical and most erudite of all contemporary French critics, Serres became well known for analyzing the aberrant or catastrophic nature of complex systems of referenceless exchange. Serres was not a Marxist but a communications or information theorist. Having a rare grasp of the rigors of many fields, among them mathematics, physics, biology, history, literary criticism, and art history, Serres published five books on communications theory and culture under the general title *Hermès* and a number of other books on topics such as Jules Verne, ÉMILE ZOLA, Vittore Carpaccio, and the cybernetic notion of parasitism. Serres argues that communication is determined by chance and is not, strictly speaking, a reversible process. Meaning is determined by the unpredictable interruption of non-meaning, parasitic intrusions that ultimately become nodal points for new signifying systems. Serres is interested in processes of regulation, transformation, repetition, contradiction, disruption, undecidability, and genesis. Many of Derrida's systems critiques are paralleled by Serres's writings in the 1960s on mathematics, Descartes, and Leibnitz in the first *Hermès* volume, entitled *La Communication. Le Parasite (The Parasite)* is perhaps Serres's most ambitious study. The parasite marks for him the limit where formality and randomness become quite undecidable and open onto a "fuzzy logic": "Between yes and no, between zero and one, an infinite number of values appear, and thus an infinite number of answers" (57). The parasite demonstrates how scientific models allow us to step beyond a merely binary logic of communication in order to consider literature in terms of fuzzy sets in which dialectic is overcome by a stochastic fraying of differences.

While Serres implicitly relates to the scientific interests of Deleuze and Guattari, Jean Baudrillard inclines to their economic interests. Unlike Deleuze and Guattari, however, Baudrillard is tied much more to figures such as ROLAND BARTHES, MICHEL FOUCAULT, Jean-Joseph Goux, and even Lacan. Like his *Tel Quel* contemporaries, Baudrillard tried once more to fuse Marxism with FERDINAND DE SAUSSURE and Freud. *Le Système des objets* suggests that bourgeois objects are part of a symbolic economy with linguistic features and that consumption is linked to the performance of this language. In *Le Miroir de la production (The Mirror of Production)* Baudrillard notes that in First World countries the chief economic modes of production have shifted from fabricating material goods to producing symbolic codes of exchange. Baudrillard well anticipates the age of the personal computer, the fax machine, the cellular telephone, and the videocamcorder by suggesting that First World countries were shifting away from traditional heavy industry to the production of semiology, that is, communication. In *L'Échange symbolique et la mort,* he follows Deleuze and Lyotard in arguing that the symbolic orders of capitalist production have no absolute anchorage point or reference and that their value fluctuates erratically as they are hastily exchanged back and forth throughout the culture. These symbolic orders are predicated, not on reality, but on hyperreal or imaginary constructions of what any given symbolic system constitutes as real for it. The problem, Baudrillard says, is that these symbolic systems are modeled on other symbolic systems and hence have no grounding in real material reference. His sense is that eventually the processes of symbolic exchange will collapse into their absent center of reference.

In the 1980s Baudrillard wrote *Simulation et simulacres (Simulacra and Simulations),* in which he applies his previous theories to the media and cultural forms in general. He argues that we live in a simulation society and that our consciousness is formed by performing processes of symbolic exchange that are always on the verge of crashing. In recent years he has published *Cool Memories,* a commentary on postmodern culture in America that chronicles instantiations of his previous theories, and *La Transparence du mal,* a kind of postmodern *Mythologies* in the manner of Barthes. In *La Transparence* Baudrillard argues that Westerners live in a state of radical agnosticism. We are just as agnostic about sex and the economy as we are about God. As a result, everything tends toward complete "indifference," the only appropriate attitude in a world where beliefs no longer refer to anything that has the force of a universally held truth. We live in a world where everyone has suddenly become marginal, at once utterly insignificant and utterly unique. Unlike Foucault and Louis Althusser, Baudrillard is very indebted to Lacanian psychoanalysis and to a Deleuzian notion of simulation. An important part of Baudrillard's work, however, has been a moralistic disapproval of mass culture. Whereas Deleuze and Guattari celebrate the rhizome, Baudrillard appears suspicious and wary of a postmodern condition that produces a collective surface composed of simulations that feign difference. For Baudrillard, we are at the antipodes of the High Middle Ages. Whereas DANTE ALIGHIERI's culture was at the extreme of hierarchical structuring, in which moral judgment is overdetermined, we are approaching the extreme of flattened structuring, in which moral judgment has no place.

As the decade of the 1970s closed, many of the intellectuals associated with *Tel Quel* during the 1960s had achieved great distinction as major thinkers. Derrida, Foucault, Barthes, Kristeva, Deleuze, Serres, Baudrillard, Lyotard, Irigaray, and Cixous had almost become institutions in their own right. By the late 1970s Derrida's major work was being translated into English, though long before that he had had a strong influence on critical theorists in England and America. His books *Glas, Signéponge,* and *La Vérité en peinture (The Truth in Painting)* demonstrate a willingness to radically redefine not only the content but also the look of critical texts. *Glas's* double columns (one on G. W. F. HEGEL, the other on Jean Genet), with intercolumnar fragments, and its aggressive use of quotation represents a high point in his willingness to experiment with the semiotics of the book. Foucault's numerous interviews and his *Archéologie du savoir (Archeology of Knowledge), Surveiller et punir: Naissance de la prison (Discipline and Punish: The Birth of the Prison),* and *Histoire de la sexualité (History of Sexuality)* had especial impact in Anglo-American universities, where his thinking about power and institutionality kept remnants of countercultural thinking alive. Because Foucault's work often centered on victims—the insane, the criminal, the sexually misunderstood—his work, for all its structuralist indebtedness, invited a recuperation of the social subject that English and American scholars have found necessary in order to link with their own traditions. Hence the rise of NEW HISTORICISM. Kristeva's *La Révolution du langage poétique (Revolution in Poetic Language), Polylogue,* and *Pouvoirs de l'horreur (Powers of Horror)* mark a decisive shift from semio-Marxism to post-Lacanian psychoanalytical analyses. Having become a practicing analyst by the end of the 1970s, she advanced a path-breaking notion of abjection, which she has since followed up with a study on depression *(Soleil noir: Dépression et mélancolie [Black Sun: Depression and Melancholia]).* Anglo-American feminists, wary of Kristeva's allegiance to Lacan, have studied these texts with much intensity beginning in the early 1980s. Similarly, the work of Baudrillard and Deleuze had to wait for recognition abroad, which finally came in their case thanks to the concern with POSTMODERNISM.

One must bear in mind that ever since the late 1970s

there has been very little interest outside of French departments in the younger generations of French intellectuals who have moved away from what one might call the *Tel Quelism* of the 1960s, what some of the younger people in France have called *la pensée soixante-huit*. For example, toward the close of the 1970s, when the Nouveaux Philosophes, such as André Glucksmann *(Les Maîtres penseurs [The Master Thinkers])* and Bernard-Henri Lévy *(La Barbarie à visage humain [Barbarism with a Human Face])*, came to prominence, they were given the cold shoulder abroad, even though they rightly foresaw the breakup of the Soviet Union and predicted the liberal Left's lurch to an intolerant politics. Also during this time a number of young French philosophers began to show considerable annoyance with *la pensée soixante-huit* by turning to pragmatism. Analytic philosophy and not the existential phenomenological heritage became privileged.

Clément Rosset's work of the 1970s on the "real" was already decisive for a certain philosophical turn away from the structuralist's notion that reality is a "language effect." For Rosset the real is composed of singular objects that point to nothing other than "aspects of the real." In *L'Objet singulier* Rosset explains that the singular object's uniqueness precedes its becoming unusual, strange, or *l'idiot*. The object is not unique because it is unusual; it is unusual insofar as it is unique. Rosset was intrigued by the idea that the more real an object is, the less identifiable it is. In other words, the singularity or uniqueness of an object distances it from any discourse that would put it into a categorical (i.e., imaginary) relationship with any other object. The object's resistance to analysis is what guarantees its value as resonant and mysterious, affirmative and dubious. Rosset's inquiry into how comedy addresses the real concerns the "absurdity" that is latent in the uniqueness of all things. In *Le Philosophe et les sortilèges* Rosset argues that thinkers such as Bataille, Derrida, and Lacan have appealed to an exorcism of the real by invoking that which is always "other" or "elsewhere." Rosset irreverently argues that the notions of "evil" in Bataille, of the "arche-trace" in Derrida, and of "lack" in Lacan are part of a philosophical magic trick that grounds the spectral in a kind of backhanded positivism. "This is . . . the eternal privilege of charlatans: not only to speak, as the etymology of the word suggests, but above all to succeed in speaking *of nothing*" (8).

Like Rosset, Jacques Bouveresse is a philosopher who has been highly critical of the so-called *pensée soixante-huit*. In *Le Philosophe chez les autophages* Bouveresse draws support from figures such as Manfred Frank, Peter Sloterdijk, Peter Geach, Karl Popper, and RICHARD RORTY in order to question what *real* philosophers are supposed to be talking about when they undertake philosophical research. The thinkers of 1968, Bouveresse argues, have catapulted philosophy into a postphilosophical moment where "revolutionary phraseologies" have been subject to automatization thanks to structuralism's bracketing of the *cogito*. Citing Manfred Frank's *Das Sagbare und das Unsagbare*, Bouveresse agrees with the Heidelberg school that the "subject"'s being difficult to locate (as in, presumably, the works of Foucault) does not mean that individuals have not worked collectively to achieve some aim. Structuralism, according to Bouveresse, conveniently dispatches the individual into the dustbin of intellectual history so that it can develop poetic styles of writing that cumulatively build up responses to diverse questions that are not specifically philosophical at all. Bouveresse also attacks the "corporatist mentality" of academicians for whom philosophy is merely a careerist enterprise. Bouveresse's plea has been for a less self-aggrandizing role for philosophers and a return to more restricted and "properly" philosophical topics of inquiry. Like Rosset, he condemns the "irrationalism" of his philosophical contemporaries and declares a return to rationalist inquiry.

Although close to Rosset and Bouveresse in some respects, Vincent Descombes has not been overtly hostile to the thinkers who rose to prominence during the 1960s. His *Le Même et l'autre (Modern French Philosophy)* is a very astute reading of French intellectual history since 1933. In the earlier *L'Inconscient malgré lui* Descombes explores what is not said or given in the disjunction of enunciation and the enunciated. Following Lacanian theory, Descombes argues that the unconscious is the unsaid that accompanies every enunciation, an unsaid not necessarily known to the speaker but detectable nonetheless. The unconscious is not what the speaker does not want to express; it is what the speaker does not know how to express, what expresses itself despite the speaker. The non-said is discussed in various terms, among them secrecy, interdiction, the abject. In *Grammaire d'objets* Descombes touches on a number of issues close to Rosset and turns toward analytical philosophy, particularly to LUDWIG WITTGENSTEIN. Philosophical grammar, Descombes cautions, is not reducible to linguistics or to any other universal grammar. And in studying the "object," Descombes explores various grammatical implications that are raised in a number of different disciplinary contexts, for example, linguistics, the Kantian transcendental deduction, ontology, phenomenology, semiotics, and literature. In part, the purpose of his study is to show the logical and grammatical incongruity of defining the object as one traverses various fields of inquiry. Descombes has also written a book on Proust entitled *Proust: Philosophie du roman*. He reads *À la recherche du temps perdu* as an impure text that brings into relation various rhetorical constructions that vitiate the literary-critical argument that Proust's act of narration comprises a *récit pur*. Proust's text, in other words, resembles the "object" discussed in *Grammaire d'objets*.

While those who have been turning away from poststructuralism have been concerned with objects, grammatical relationships, the real, and rationality, intellectuals affiliated with DECONSTRUCTION have become interested in these questions with respect to postmodernity and the sublime. As if to mirror those who have turned to analytical philosophy, these intellectuals have abandoned Hegel for Kant, a turn that is quite striking, given French intellectual history and critical thought of the 1960s. Derrida himself was making the turn in the 1970s in *La Vérité en peinture*. But Lyotard has really been the key figure. He has published a large number of studies touching on Kant and in particular on postmodernity and the sublime. A very prolific and difficult critic whose *Discours, figure* and *Économie libidinale (Libidinal Economy)* demonstrate strong *Tel Quelist* concerns (Lyotard has also attempted to negotiate the relationships between Marx, Saussure, and Freud), his texts of the 1980s have been extremely influential. In *La Condition postmoderne (The Postmodern Condition)*, *Le Postmoderne expliqué aux enfants (The Postmodern Explained)*, *Le Différend (The Differend)*, *L'Enthousiasme*, *L'Inhumain*, and *Leçons sur l'analytique du sublime* he shows how the fracturing of a subject produces limits that have negative or sublime effects.

Lyotard's argument is extremely complex and covers the various trajectories of all the recent studies he has published, but one way of organizing the major ideas is by beginning with his argument in *La Condition postmoderne* that we have entered a period in which there are no master narratives and that this fact underscores our postmodernity. Lyotard's interest in Kant's *Critique of Judgement* relates to the insight that even in Kant a master narrative cannot be produced and that the faculties, far from being actual mental structures, are merely names that organize an archipelago of phrase regimes that obey the logic of the "differend" in *Le Différend*, except that in the context of Kant that differend bears on the notion of the sublime and its relationship to what Kant calls enthusiasm. The differend is that unstable site of language wherein something cannot be put into phrases. Silence is the trait of this phraseological *retrait*

(the trace that manifests itself in its own retreat). In Kant, "enthusiasm" is a term that is deconstructed at the moment that it is called upon to mark incompatible phrase regimes, one in which enthusiasm manifests itself as the pleasure of making rational sense out of something and another in which enthusiasm represents that negativity associated with the sublime.

The larger context for this discussion concerns what Lyotard calls the inhuman, namely, the dismantling of a universal subject in the name of whom societies seek liberty, freedom, and justice for all. In *Le Différend* the name Auschwitz stands for a postmodern condition in which the universal subject has been subject to the differend, the suspension of liberty, freedom, and justice for certain people and a racially motivated enthusiasm for genocide. The implication suggests that thinkers such as JÜRGEN HABERMAS are incorrect with respect to their understanding of reason and the public sphere in the Enlightenment. Moreover, Lyotard is suggesting that the "postmodern condition" is itself not a determinate historical break but a *différend* that situates itself across a number of historical contexts.

Like many other French intellectuals, Lyotard has been at the center of the recent controversy concerning MARTIN HEIDEGGER's past and the revelations that have suggested that his allegiance with National Socialism was much stronger than he had admitted. Emmanuel Levinas, MAURICE BLANCHOT, Jean-Luc Nancy, Philippe Lacoue-Labarthe, Michel Deguy, Pierre Bourdieu, Gianni Vattimo, and Derrida himself have been drawn into the controversy over how to evaluate Heidegger in relation to his politics. Then, too, Derrida has been drawn into the debate over PAUL DE MAN's collaborationist writings in Belgium during World War II. Derrida's *Mémoires pour Paul de Man (Mémoires: for Paul de Man)*, an homage to de Man which appeared prior to the disclosure, put him very much on the defensive after de Man's collaborationist articles were republished and interpreted by many critics.

In Anglo-American academic institutions these controversies have only helped critics to restore a subject-centered discourse in which individualism (pragmatism, the politics of direct action) is tempered with a populism that has sometimes advanced itself as a deconstructed (i.e., polyvalent) notion of *Volk*—race, gender, ethnicity. Given the Anglo-American adoption of a Foucauldian *epistémè*, such thinking about *Volk* has run the risk of being subsumed under the aegis of essentialism and a subject-centered theory concerning power to which literary study has been subordinated. Whereas for the avant-garde or modernist critic, the literary work stood out as a radical breaker of paradigms, for postdeconstructionist critics it has functioned more in the manner of an accomplice to a dominant political view. Whereas for Derrida the poetry of Francis Ponge advances radical formal structures that defy institutionalized logics, for American New Historicists and culture critics literary texts are often seen as anecdotal and positioned within a general cultural or *Volk*-ish weave within which they assert politically interested valencies.

In fact, in the wake of what we might loosely call the Anglo-American deconstruction of deconstruction, we discover that in the 1990s there is a return to the socius as a guarantor of meaning, though it is a socius characterized by factionalized group identities—the proliferation of unassimilable subalternities. Literature can no longer be thought of as the expression of common aspirations and values that characterize those individuals who transcend their local *Volk*-ish differences. Rather, literature has become representative of ethnic, racial, or nativist interests that refuse assimilation or compromise. Just as the dismantling of the Soviet Union has given way to renewed nationalist and *Volk*-ish agendas, the dismantling of Western metaphysics by contemporary French theorists has similarly created an opportunity for a return to the privileging of nativism, ethnicity, and race by critics such as Barbara Johnson, Trinh T. Minh-ha, Gloria Anzaldúa, and Lucy Lippard. However anti-essentialist their rhetoric, there can be little doubt that nativist voices such as Trinh's "spider woman" (the voice of the Native American Indian) or Anzaldúa's La Raza (the voice of a racially and ethnically defined people on both sides of the Mexican-American border) become the ground upon which the legacies of French theory risk being metaphysically recuperated and essentialistically recovered in the name of the marginal subject.

Herman Rapaport

See also HÉLÈNE CIXOUS, JACQUES DERRIDA, FEMINIST THEORY AND CRITICISM: 3. POSTSTRUCTURALIST FEMINISMS, LUCE IRIGARAY, JULIA KRISTEVA, JACQUES LACAN, JEAN-FRANÇOIS LYOTARD, MARXIST THEORY AND CRITICISM: 2. STRUCTURALIST MARXISM, and PSYCHOANALYTIC THEORY AND CRITICISM: 3. THE POSTLACANIANS. [For assistance I wish to thank my research assistant, Elayne Zalis, and also my colleague Steven Ungar.]

See bibliographies in ROLAND BARTHES, MAURICE BLANCHOT, HÉLÈNE CIXOUS, JACQUES DERRIDA, MICHEL FOUCAULT, LUCE IRIGARAY, JULIA KRISTEVA, JACQUES LACAN, and JEAN-FRANÇOIS LYOTARD for texts by those writers.

Gloria Anzaldúa, "How to Tame a Wild Tongue," *Out There: Marginalization and Contemporary Cultures* (ed. Russell Ferguson et al. 1990); Georges Bataille, *Oeuvres complètes* (12 vols., 1970–88); Jean Baudrillard, *Cool Memories* (1987, trans. Chris Turner, 1990), *L'Échange symbolique et la mort* (1976), *Le Miroir de la production* (1973, *The Mirror of Production,* trans. Mark Poster, 1975), *Simulacres et simulation* (1980, *Simulacra and Simulations,* trans. Paul Foss, Paul Patton, and Philip Beitchman, 1983), *Le Système des objets* (1968), *La Transparence du mal* (1990); Walter Benjamin, *Das Passagen-Werk* (ed. Rolf Tiedemann, 1982); Pierre Bourdieu, *La Distinction: Critique sociale de jugement* (1979, *Distinction: A Social Critique of the Judgement of Taste,* trans. Richard Nice, 1984); Jacques Bouveresse, *Le Philosophie chez les autophages* (1984); Michel Deguy, *Oui dire* (1966); Gilles Deleuze, *Le Bergsonisme* (1966, *Bergsonism,* trans. Hugh Tomlinson and Barbara Habberjam, 1988), *Cinéma 1: L'Image-mouvement* (1983, *Cinema 1: The Movement-Image,* trans. Hugh Tomlinson and Barbara Habberjam, 1986), *Cinéma 2: L'Image-temps* (1985, *Cinema 2: The Time-Image,* trans. Hugh Tomlinson and Robert Galeta, 1989), *Différence et répétition* (1968), *The Deleuze Reader* (ed. Constantin V. Boudas, 1992), *Empirisme et subjectivité* (1953, *Empiricism and Subjectivity: An Essay on Hume's Theory of Human Nature,* trans. Constantin V. Boundas, 1991), *Logique du sens* (1969, *The Logic of Sense,* trans. Mark Lester with Charles Stivale, 1990), *Marcel Proust et les signes* (1964, *Proust and Signs,* trans. Richard Howard, 1972); Gilles Deleuze and Félix Guattari, *L'Anti-Oedipe: Capitalisme et schizophrénie* (1972, *Anti-Oedipus: Capitalism and Schizophrenia,* trans. Robert Hurley, Mark Seem, and Helen R. Lane, 1983), *Mille plateaux* (1980, *A Thousand Plateaus: Capitalism and Schizophrenia,* trans. Brian Massumi, 1987); Vincent Descombes, *Grammaire d'objets en tous genres* (1983, *Objects of All Sorts: A Philosophical Grammar,* trans. Lorna Scott-Fox and Jeremy Harding, 1986), *L'Inconscient malgré lui* (1977), *Le Même et l'autre* (1979, *Modern French Philosophy,* trans. Lorna Scott-Fox and Jeremy Harding, 1980), *Proust: philosophie du roman* (1987); Marguerite Duras, *L'Amour* (1971), *India Song* (1973, trans. Barbara Bray, 1976), *Le Ravissement de Lol V. Stein* (1964, *The Ravishing of Lol Stein,* trans. Richard Seaver, 1966), *Le Vice-Consul* (1965, *The Vice-Consul,* trans. Eileen Ellenbogen, 1968); Manfred Frank, *Das Sagbare und das Unsagbare: Studien zur neuesten französischen Hermeneutik und Texttheorie* (1980); Mike Gann, *Baudrillard: Critical and Fatal Theory* (1991), *Baudrillard's Bestiary: Baudrillard and Culture* (1991); André Glucksmann, *Les Maîtres penseurs* (1977,

The Master Thinkers, trans. Brian Pearce, 1980); Félix Guattari, *L'Inconscient machinique* (1979), *La Révolution moléculaire* (1977, *Molecular Revolution: Psychiatry and Politics,* trans. Rosemary Sheed, 1984); Barbara Johnson, *A World of Difference* (1987); Philippe Lacoue-Labarthe, *Le Sujet de la philosophie* (1979, *The Subject of Philosophy,* ed. Thomas Trezise, trans. Tresize et al., 1993); Bernard-Henri Levy, *La Barbarie à visage humain* (1977, *Barbarism with a Human Face,* trans. George Holoch, 1979); Lucy Lippard, *Mixed Blessings* (1990); Maria Antonietta Macciocchi, *De la Chine* (1972, *Daily Life in Revolutionary China,* 1972, in Italian in 1971); David Macey, *Lacan in Contexts* (1988); Jean-Luc Nancy, *La Remarque spéculative* (1973); Clément Rosset, *L'Objet singulier* (1979), *Le Philosophe et les sortilèges* (1985); Michel Serres, *Esthétiques sur Carpaccio* (1975), *Feux et signaux de brume: Zola* (1975), *Hermès I: La Communication* (1968), *Hermès II: L'Interférence* (1972), *Hermès III: La Traduction* (1974), *Hermès IV: La Distribution* (1977), *Hermès V: Le Passage du nord-ouest* (1980), *Hermes: Literature, Science, Philosophy* (ed. Josué V. Harari and David F. Bell, 1982), *Jouvences sur Jules Verne* (1974), *Le Parasite* (1980, *The Parasite,* trans. Lawrence R. Schehr, 1982); Philippe Sollers, *Logiques* (1968), *Paradis* (1981); Trinh T. Minh-ha, *Woman, Native, Other* (1989); Sherry Turkle, *Psychoanalytic Politics: Jacques Lacan and Freud's French Revolution* (1978, 2d ed., 1992); Monique Wittig, *Le Corps lesbien* (1973, *The Lesbian Body,* trans. David LeVay, 1975), *Les Guérillères* (1969, trans. David LeVay, 1971).

FREUD, SIGMUND

Sigmund Freud (1856–1939) was not a literary theorist, but he was the important thinker of whom W. H. AUDEN could write: "to us he is no more a person / now but a whole climate of opinion / under whom we conduct our different lives" ("In Memory of Sigmund Freud [d. Sept. 1939]," *Collected Poems,* ed. Edward Mendelson, 1976, 217). The Viennese neuropathologist and subsequent founder of psychoanalysis saw himself as the systematic, scientific explorer of the human unconscious and, indeed, was embarrassed by the misunderstanding of André Breton and the surrealists, who wanted to make him into an apologist for the irrational. Of course, epistemologists, logicians, semanticists, linguists, and philosophers of language, not to mention psychologists and physicians, have all attacked Freud's pretensions to science, but his own belief in the objective and scientific validity of his work was unshakable. For this reason, though an avid reader of literature, Freud felt nervous about how his

early case histories might be perceived: they read like short stories and therefore might seem to lack the stamp of serious science. The impact and significance of Freud's work have obviously extended far beyond the narrowly scientific. No consideration of his place in contemporary cultural thinking can ignore the fact that his theories—such as those of infantile sexuality—changed forever humanity's confidence in its mastery and control of the self.

Although Freud was not in any way a deliberate aesthetic theorist, he did leave his mark on both literature and critical theory through his general psychoanalytic framework and also his specific turning to art to show that the range of applicability of psychoanalysis extended beyond dreams and neurosis to even the highest cultural achievements. Freud had always been interested in literature. Although in his "Contribution to a Questionnaire on Reading" he listed the works of Copernicus and Charles Darwin under the heading "most significant books," he also ranked the poems and plays of Homer, Sophocles, Johann Wolfgang von Goethe, and William Shakespeare under "most magnificent works" (9:245–47). These, it should be noted, were the works that had provided him with his best illustrations of psychoanalytic theories.

In 1912 Freud founded *Imago,* a journal of applied psychoanalysis, for he wanted to extend his insights from the individual to his or her interaction with the collective—in religion, aesthetics, mythology, philology, law, and so on. Freud also invited nonmedical people (Otto Rank, Hanns Sachs, Theodor Reik) to join the Vienna Association. Today the consequences for literary theory of Freud's fertile interdisciplinary efforts can be traced in Norman Kiell's two extensive bibliographies, *Psychoanalysis, Psychology, and Literature* (2d ed., 1982, and suppl., 1990) and *Psychiatry and Psychology in the Visual Arts and Aesthetics* (1965), as well as in the bibliographies printed in the journal *Literature and Psychology.*

Freud was admittedly generous in attributing to the artist the role of precursor of psychoanalysis in his or her insights into the unconscious, be it in prefiguring the significance of dreams, fetishism, repression and childhood eroticism, parapraxes, the object choice in love, the uncanny, the roles of Eros, daydreams, or almost anything else. Artists' sensitive perception of the hidden indicates that in their knowledge of the human mind "they are far in advance of us everyday people, for they draw upon sources which we have not yet opened up for science" (9:8). That "not yet" is both interesting and significant. Sarah Kofman has shown how Freud's reading of Wilhelm Jensen's *Gradiva* develops from admiration for the author's insights to astonishment that he could possibly have prefigured Freud's own findings. In other words, Freud elevated Jensen's work to the status of a case study and yet, at the same time, undercut his achievement by pointing out that *Gradiva* only described and did not explain: *that* task was left to Freud. And, in fact, Jensen could have had no idea how significant his descriptions would prove, he claimed.

Whatever Freud's own ambivalence about the relation of literature and literary criticism to psychoanalysis, Freudian literary critics since have shown the concerns and processes of interpretation the two share: meaning and hermeneutic method, symbolism and stylistic deviation, discourse and narrative. In addition, at least five areas of Freud's "implied" aesthetic are of special interest to literary theory. The first and most central is the primacy of the unconscious to theories of creativity and culture. There are obvious implications of such a view for, second, the theory of reception (aesthetic pleasure) and, third, the theory of interpretation. The fourth area is the relationship between the artist and the work, the psyche and the productions of its sublimation. And the final area is a methodological one, for Freud's comments both on art and on psychoanalysis in general suggest a number of possible literary-critical models for applied psychoanalysis.

Whether we believe that in writing on art Freud wanted only to verify his interpretation of neurotic symptoms, dreams, jokes, and parapraxes or that his ambition was actually to create an entire theory of culture, in either case Freud saw in all cultural and psychic phenomena the same source: the unconscious. This meant that the same principles (e.g., repression and the economy of psychic expenditure) operated and the same mechanisms (condensation, displacement, symbolization, etc.) were brought into play. Freud did not, of course, discover the unconscious, but he might be said to have posited the general psychic structural principles and contents of the unconscious mind. He argued that despite individual variants, the unconscious has universal laws. Otto Rank and Hanns Sachs later described the Freudian unconscious in terms that make its relevance to literary theory obvious: it is

> that part of the mental life which, bent upon immediate gain of pleasure, will not submit to adaptation to reality. So far, then, as human mental activity had to deal exclusively with reality and its domination, nothing could be started with the unconscious. But in all those fields where a diversion from reality was allowed the mind, where phantasy might stir its wings, its field of application was assured. (32)

It is from this point of view that Freudian literary theory has based its belief in the primacy of the unconscious in aesthetic production.

Since the unconscious is essentially and radically asocial, it can instigate the creation of cultural phenomena only by sublimation, that is, only when the sexual aim of the libido is turned into a cultural one via the mediation of the ego. For Freud, this displaced libido is actually more than just animal instinct, and its sublimation is a complex process of repression and transformation of these unconscious drives into something more acceptable to society. Sublimation, in other words, has the power to transform individual unconscious fantasy into universal art—a kind of legalized fantasy, halfway between a wish-frustrating reality and a wish-fulfilling world of imagination: "Art is a conventionally accepted reality in which, thanks to artistic illusion, symbols and substitutes are able to provoke real emotions" (13:188). Freud saw art as a path linking fantasy and reality (16:375–77). But this made art into a kind of alternative to *neurosis* rather than unrepressed, unconscious sexual drives; the artist "can transform his phantasies into artistic creations instead of into symptoms" (11:50) and by this linking path of art regain contact with reality. Art is social and public; neurosis is asocial and private. For Freud, the artist, always seen as male, was "in rudiments an introvert, not far removed from neurosis" (16:376), a man who was oppressed by excessively powerful instinctual needs for honor, power, wealth, fame, and the love of women but lacked the means of achieving satisfaction. This was where sublimation came into play: fantasy, the substitute satisfaction of all people, became the reserve, the psychic realm free from the reality principle.

This central Freudian tenet, as expressed in the 1916–17 *Introductory Lectures in Psycho-Analysis,* was first expounded in 1908 in an important paper entitled "Creative Writers and Day-dreaming." The artist was the one who could work out the overly personal (and therefore repellent) in his daydreams in order to let others enjoy them too. The "origin from proscribed sources" of the daydreams was hidden, for the artist possessed "the mysterious power of shaping some particular material until it has become a faithful image of his phantasy" (16:376). Therefore, others could derive consolation from their own unconscious depths, which had been inaccessible until this pleasure-yield lifted the repression. So, the artist managed to achieve *through* fantasy what he had wished for *in* fantasy: the fruits of success (see also 13:187).

In suggesting nonrational origins for art, Freud was in a sense only reworking a version of the old tradition of the divinely inspired poet. Philosophers and art theorists have often turned to some such theory of the imagination to explain overdetermined meaning, obsessive repetition, and any apparent disorder in art—gaps, contradictions, and so on. Psychoanalysis had posited the theory of the unconscious to explain those discontinuities in consciousness such as dreams and parapraxes.

But the artist, in Freud's view, was also like a daydreamer because he could objectify the subjective into a public, socially acceptable form—art—instead of turning it into private neurotic symptoms. This analogy allowed Freud to suggest that fantasies called art could therefore be interpreted by means of the methods of dream analysis. Freud had made an early and very strong commitment to the value of such analysis. "The interpretation of dreams," he emphasized, "is the royal road to a knowledge of the unconscious activities of the mind" (5:608). Writers, Freud duly noted, have always granted dreams great significance. His study of the dreams in Jensen's *Gradiva* corroborated his own clinical findings about the structures, mechanisms, and interpretations of dreams, and Freud was not surprised:

> The author no doubt proceeds differently [from the psychoanalyst]. He directs his attention to the unconscious in his own mind, he listens to its possible developments and lends them artistic expression instead of suppressing them by conscious criticism. Thus he experiences from himself what we learn from others— the laws which the activities of this unconscious must obey. (9:92)

Works of art, therefore, support Freud's theories; artists are "valuable allies and their evidence is to be prized highly" (9:8). But the artist's fantasy involves more than daydreaming or hallucinatory wish-fulfillment and its reworking into a shareable form. Here Freud turned to children's fantasies in play for an added analogy, for play involves control and mastery as much as fantasy. The hero of every story, then, the one who controls, is an embodiment of the ego, the part of the psyche whose role it is to master both reality and the unconscious. Daydreams, wrote Freud in summary,

> are the raw material of poetic production, for the creative writer uses his day-dreams, with certain remodellings, disguises and omissions, to construct the situations which he introduces into his short stories, his novels or his plays. The hero of the day-dreams is always the subject himself, either directly or by an obvious identification with someone else. (15:99)

Many questions can be raised at this point regarding Freud's choice of analog for art and artistic creation. Dreams, for Freud, had no aesthetic value per se. Where

did this aesthetic value in art lie? It was not in its form, which was seen only as a disguise or as a bribe of forepleasure. Daydreams and dreams are private and relatively formless on the surface; art is social and formal. This does not mean, of course, that they cannot fulfill the same functions for the psyche; that is, both can act as safety valves. Nor does this difference necessarily negate the similarity in latent structures and mechanisms, as the laws of the unconscious are said to be universal ones. The main objection, and the obvious one, to the use of dreams as a model for art is that it reduces art to a psychological framework for something else. A certain part of the history of psychoanalytic literary criticism would seem to bear out the view that the dream model has led only to facile, if attractive, formulations of the creative process. The ego psychologists were the ones to question most radically the adequacy of the concept of sublimation. Even more recently, psychologists working directly with artists have questioned even the primacy of the unconscious in creativity. The nonlogical primary processes of the unconscious, they argue, do not resemble the conscious elaboration that results in works of art. In other words, art resembles, if anything, the patient's *narration* of his or her dream, not the dream itself, as ÉMILE BENVENISTE had also argued from a linguistic point of view. The repressed elements of the unconscious may exert influence, but alone they cannot account for novelty, aesthetic form, artistic conventions, or, given their discontinuity, the humanist assertion of the essential organic unity of both art and the subject. This, of course, is where poststructuralists such as JACQUES DERRIDA have been able to play with Freud's model to challenge such assertions.

Freud's mechanisms of dreamwork—condensation, displacement, symbolization—mediating between preconscious censorship and unconscious desire, obviously resemble the processes of metonymy, metaphor, and symbol in poetry, but the actual equation of the two does not necessarily logically follow. Like works of art, those dreams, slips of the tongue and pen, jokes, and neurotic symptoms are all overdetermined; that is, they are capable of being interpreted in more than one way. Freud attributed this overdetermination in dreams to an element of dreamwork that he called "secondary revision." This is still not conscious aesthetic elaboration, though, for meanings are hidden and not intended for communication. This may be true of parapraxes and neurotic symptoms, but surely jokes share with works of art the desire to communicate precisely their overdetermined ambiguities. But for Freud, jokework was like dreamwork (8:54), and both provided analogies for art.

Freud argued that the overt, conscious order of art arose logically but from unconscious premises. The "much abused privilege of conscious activity" seemed to him to serve only to conceal what was truly important, and he concluded: "We are probably inclined greatly to over-estimate the conscious character of intellectual and artistic production" (5:613). What interested Freud was the deep unconscious structures that art shares with myth and religion as well as with dreams. The manifest individuality of the work was less significant for him than its latent universality.

Freud's theory of the unconscious as the root of artistic creativity held certain implications not only for the production of art but also for the theory of its reception. Given the belief in psychic universality, the pleasure that the viewer or reader derives from art must be directly linked to that of its creator:

Kindly nature has given the artist the ability to express his most secret mental impulses, which are hidden even from himself, by means of the works that he creates; and these works have a powerful effect on others who are strangers to the artist, and who are themselves unaware of the source of their emotion. (11:107)

As early as *The Interpretation of Dreams* (1900), Freud had seen the universality of safely released repression as the key to the continuing impact of works such as *Oedipus Rex* and *Hamlet*. The artist's disguised and objectified presentation of his unconscious fantasy in the form of art caused a yield of pleasure so great that repression was lifted and the audience could "derive consolation and alleviation" (16:376). In other words, there is a release and gratification (by fantasy) of unconscious desires common to both writer and audience. Therefore, to study creativity is automatically to study reception.

Nothing is arbitrary in art—or in any of the other manifestations of unconscious psychic processes. Or so Freud claimed. His determinism is clear in his assigning of meaning to all verbal ambiguities and seeming incongruities, be they in jokes, dreams, parapraxes, or works of art. There are obviously implications of this determinism for the interpretation of art, as well as for the response to it. If we accept a manifest-latent structure for all the productions of the unconscious, the task of the analyst—literary or psychological—becomes one of divining secret and concealed meanings. For Freud, this task entailed paying attention to the small, seemingly unimportant detail, which is then assumed to have significance (13:222, 229). His interpretation of the *Moses* of Michelangelo, for instance, centers on the attitude of the statue's right hand and the position of the Tables of the

Law. Unlike most traditional interpretations, which see Moses' pose as that at the inception of action, Freud's presents the statue as a representation of the remains of a completed action. Freud attributes this obvious deviation from the usual view of Moses, that is, that he does not break the tablets, to Michelangelo's inner motives in his relations with Julius II, whose tomb this statue was to adorn. But as several generations of commentators have asked since then, by what criteria are we to judge the validity of Freud's interpretation?

The same question has been posed regarding Freud's dream interpretations. Freud was a wily defender of his own views: contradictions were shown to be apparent, not real, and negatives were claimed, in actual fact, to conceal positives. In dream analysis, Freud used a mixture of free association and symbol decoding (5:360). It was not that dream symbols had a fixed, known meaning but rather that dreams used existent symbols to escape censorship and allow "representability" of the repressed. And some symbols did seem to have universal meanings, he argued. In addition, most dream symbols seemed to represent people, parts of the body, or activities invested with erotic interest. But given Freud's theories of repressed infantile desire, they could hardly do otherwise. The circularity of Freud's hermeneutic theory has, needless to say, not gone unnoticed.

Since Freud believed in the universality of these symbols, he felt justified in applying the laws of the unconscious, which he learned from the dreams of living patients, to the creative works of dead artists. In his study *Leonardo da Vinci and a Memory of His Childhood* (1910), he went beyond an interpretation of a particular work to investigate and pronounce upon the psyche of the artist himself. In his writings on Goethe and Fyodor Dostoevsky, Freud worked more in the opposite direction, interpreting works in the light of psychological details gleaned from the lives of the writers. In either case, the artist was cast in the role of the analysand, and the critic in that of the analyst. Yet, earlier, the artist was also credited with the insights of the analyst himself. This question involves the last major part of Freud's "implied" aesthetic. Aside from the dreamwork concept, at least three possible investigative models implied in Freud's writings theoretically could prove useful to literary theory and criticism: the model of the analytic situation, the image of archeology that Freud loved so dearly, and the technique of superimposition of examples to yield common factors.

In the first case, if the character was seen as manifesting the symptoms of a real neurotic person, the artist was credited with prefiguring Freud's own clinical findings. The author was a proto-analyst; the character, his patient. This shows Freud's ambivalence about the value of art: art could be a theoretical model to validate psychoanalysis to the public at large and yet also be reduced to little more than an illustration (rather than a confirmation) of Freud's version of psychic truth. Lady Macbeth could become only another example of one of "those wrecked by success," a character type Freud met constantly in his clinical practice (14:318–24). Ibsen's *Rosmersholm* could be reduced to "the greatest work of art of the class that treats of this common phantasy in girls" (331).

Freud, however, also suggested another investigative model for analysis. The psychoanalyst's task was said to be like the archeologist's, rather than the artist's, though his or her object of study was more complex. In both cases, fragments had to be discovered and pieced together. A seemingly insignificant detail—e.g., the position of Michelangelo's *Moses'* right hand—might prove to be the key to reconstituting the whole form of the work of art and its probable context. In dream analysis, this reconstruction of latent meaning was the product of a series of successive decodings and unravelings—a model used by many psychoanalytic theorists since. The problem is that despite Freud's theory of universality, any such reconstitution can only be hypothetical, and the evidence for this might lie, for example, in the many very different psychoanalytic readings offered since Freud for a text such as *Hamlet* or *Oedipus Rex*.

The third and final theoretical model of investigation that Freud suggested was not a model so much as a method. The method is one we would now call intertextual in the sense that it involved superimposing various manifest versions of a literary (or mythic) structure in order to let the latent common denominators show through. This was Freud's method in "The Theme of the Three Caskets," and it was used by French critic Charles Mauron as the basis for his theory of *psychocritique* (see BLOOMSBURY GROUP).

Although it is no doubt true that no complete and coherent aesthetic system could be derived from Freud's writings, these five aspects of his theory and practice suggest that Jack Spector's conclusion to his study of Freud's aesthetic is rather reductive: "Psychoanalysis as a technique has contributed little to the field of aesthetics, but as a technique it has had a most significant—and often stimulating—impact on some of the art and literature of this century" (164). Even the most unsympathetic observer would have to admit, I suspect, that at the very least Freud gave to literary theory a new vocabulary with which to discuss the functioning of the psyche and per-

haps the imagination and that this addition opened up potential new significance for literary symbolism but also for our concept of literature at large (see Skura). Recently the renewed interest in Freud has come from rereadings of his psychoanalytic and aesthetic theories in terms of structural linguistics (JACQUES LACAN) or feminism. For many feminist theorists, the Freudian unconscious is seen as a repository of the structural relations of patriarchy. Yet, even given the fact that Freud was a male, socialized into nineteenth-century ideas about women, his work is also being examined by other feminists, such as Juliet Mitchell and Teresa de Lauretis, to see what can be salvaged. That there are today almost as many kinds of Freudian literary theory as there are Freudian literary theorists is certainly a potentially disabling pluralism that points to fundamental ambiguities and a radical subjectivity in Freud's work. But it also bears witness to the fecundity of that work and its interest for aesthetic theory.

Linda Hutcheon

Sigmund Freud, *The Standard Edition of the Complete Psychological Works of Sigmund Freud* (ed. James Strachey, trans. Strachey et al., 24 vols., 1953–74).

Émile Benveniste, "Remarks on the Function of Language in Freudian Theory," *Problems in General Linguistics* (1966, trans. Mary Elizabeth Meek, 1971); Teresa de Lauretis, *Alice Doesn't: Feminism, Semiotics, Cinema* (1984); Jacques Derrida, *L'Écriture et la différence* (1967, *Writing and Difference,* trans. Alan Bass, 1978); Sarah Kofman, *L'Enfance de l'art: Une Interprétation de l'esthétique freudienne* (1970, *The Childhood of Art: An Interpretation of Freud's Aesthetics,* trans. Winifred Woodhull, 1988); Jean Laplanche and J.-B. Pontalis, *Vocabulaire de la psychanalyse* (1967, *The Language of Psycho-Analysis,* trans. Donald Nicholson-Smith, 1973); Charles Mauron, *Des métaphores obsédantes au mythe personnel: Introduction à la psychocritique* (1962); Juliet Mitchell, *Psychoanalysis and Feminism* (1974); Otto Rank and Hanns Sachs, "The Significance of Psychoanalysis for the Humanities," *Psychoanalysis as an Art and a Science: A Symposium* (ed. Rank et al., 1968); Paul Ricoeur, *De l'interprétation: Essai sur Freud* (1965, *Freud and Philosophy: An Essay on Interpretation,* trans. Denis Savage, 1970); Alan Roland, ed., *Psychoanalysis, Creativity, and Literature: A French-American Inquiry* (1978); Meredith Anne Skura, *The Literary Uses of the Psychoanalytic Process* (1981); Jack J. Spector, *The Aesthetics of Freud: A Study in Psychoanalysis and Art* (1973); Elizabeth E. Wright, *Psychoanalytic Criticism: Theory in Practice* (1984).

FRYE, NORTHROP

Northrop Frye (1912–91) was born in Sherbrooke, Quebec, and received his early education in Moncton, New Brunswick. He studied English and philosophy at Victoria College, University of Toronto, and then, after studying theology, was ordained a minister in the United Church of Canada in 1936. After a short period of pastoral work in Saskatchewan, he proceeded on scholarship to Merton College, Oxford, to study English. He returned to Canada in 1939 and was appointed to the Department of English in Victoria College, where he subsequently served as chair, then as principal, and finally in 1978 as chancellor of Victoria University. In 1967 he became the first University Professor of the University of Toronto, a position he held until his death.

As a young professor, Frye was influenced by the structures in the works of Sir James Frazer and Oswald Spengler, though he was repelled by many of their concepts. He was also working on a campus where many colleagues were engaged in constructing encyclopedic, interdisciplinary studies: Charles N. Cochrane and Eric Havelock in classics, Harold Innis in political economy, and MARSHALL MCLUHAN in English. When Frye began to publish, particularly in *Canadian Forum* (a political and literary magazine of Social Democratic slant which he later edited), he showed encyclopedic interests as well, writing as frequently on music, the visual arts, and political matters as on literary topics. From 1942 on, he composed many versions of his book on WILLIAM BLAKE; in 1947, *Fearful Symmetry* appeared, twenty years after his interest in Blake was first aroused. In a 1986 review of PAUL DE MAN's *Rhetoric of Romanticism,* Frye observes that "most Romantic-centred critics have one figure that they use as a Virgilian guide through its contradictory mazes, and for de Man that figure is Rousseau" (52). For Frye, that figure is Blake. At the end of "The Survival of Eros in Poetry," there is a transcript of questions addressed to Frye in 1983, including one asking whether his critical theory is Romantic, to which Frye replies, "Oh, it's entirely Romantic, yes." He goes on to agree that his theory probably differs little from Blake's, "because I've learned everything I know from Blake" (32). In *The Great Code* (1982), he states that what he learned from Blake, medieval exegetes, and "certain forms of Reformed commentary" (xvii) was how to read the Bible typologically and how to adapt the medieval fourfold interpretation of the Bible to poetic texts, so that his debts to Blake and the Bible are one: "In a sense all my critical work beginning with a study of Blake published in 1947, and formulated ten years later in *Anatomy of Criticism,* has revolved around the Bible" (xiv).

In clarifying Blake's poetry, Frye was intent upon helping readers to recover "a lost art of reading poetry" (*Fearful* 11), an art that depends upon counterpointing narratives and metaphors. "The contrapuntal symbolism of the Renaissance fell out of favour" (164) in the Augustan age, to be rediscovered by the Romantic poets. What the reader may learn of counterpoint from Blake is "that all poetry is allegorical" (9) and that major writers such as William Shakespeare and John Milton "require [of their readers] something of the allusive agility that the reading of Blake demands" (374). Such adroitness in analogical reading develops the reader's ability to understand polysemous meaning, as medieval and Renaissance audiences did. He or she will read any literary work first in terms of its linear units of narrative, then in terms of its spatial structure of imagery, then in relation to those structures in other works of the same genre, and so on to the structures of the literary universe itself. Such recurrent units are what Frye calls the archetypes of literature. As Tzvetan Todorov argues in *Literature and Its Theorists,* for Frye "every text is a palimpsest" (91), and "all textuality is intertextuality" (96).

Frye reads Blake's poetry as organized on one myth (i.e., for Frye, one narrative), a reworking of the biblical one of creation, fall, redemption, and apocalypse, and juxtaposes that temporal narrative with the spatial paradigm of Blake's images on four levels: a redeemed apocalyptic world, a level of unfallen Nature accessible to the mind, a fallen world of time and space, and a demonic world of isolation. This model of narrative and imagery (ARISTOTLE's *mythos* and *dianoia*) becomes the center for the structure of all Frye's subsequent work, developed in varying degrees but always present, whether in particular studies of Shakespeare, Charles Dickens, or Wallace Stevens or in general studies of critical theory. The hero's quest down through the levels of the fourfold world and back up becomes the radical narrative that he explores thoroughly in his works on romance, most schematically in *The Secular Scripture* (1976). His theory of a historical development of literary modes as a series of displacements of the hero as god originates in his exposition of the seven stages of Albion in *The Four Zoas.* Frye modulates that sequence into GIAMBATTISTA VICO's four stages—stories of gods, aristocratic heroes, and the people, followed by a *ricorso* through chaos back to the beginning—to arrive at the five stages of the development of modes in Western literature in the first essay of *Anatomy of Criticism:* myth, romance, high mimetic, low mimetic, irony.

In such works as *A Study of English Romanticism* (1968) and *The Critical Path* (1971), Frye finds Blake's patterns in other Romantic poets, through whose works a mythology, or cluster of narratives, shifts the focus from the traditionally objective God and Nature to constructs of the human imagination that are the organizing forms of the culture and civilization in which we live. The pivotal age for the modern world, then, is the Romantic period, because its poets stopped projecting their own creative powers outward and began recalling those powers into the human imagination. The narrative quest in literature since the Romantic period has therefore been an internal one. The influence of OSCAR WILDE's criticism on these conceptions is evident early and is repeatedly acknowledged throughout Frye's career, as in *Creation and Recreation* (1980), in which he describes Wilde as "one of our few genuinely prophetic writers" (5).

After *Fearful Symmetry,* Frye extended his study of myth to literature as a whole. He published preliminary articles that were later collected in *Fables of Identity* (1963); the full argument appeared in *Anatomy of Criticism* in 1957. In *Anatomy* Frye argues that criticism, like any science, should be developed descriptively and that value judgments, though inevitably made by critics in the process of exploring their ideas, should not be the basis of the structure of poetics. Many critics, among them HAROLD BLOOM, GEOFFREY H. HARTMAN, Frank Lentricchia, MURRAY KRIEGER, and Todorov have described the appearance of *Anatomy* as revolutionary, because Frye rejected the subordination of literary criticism to any other conceptual framework: "Criticism, rather, is to art what history is to action and philosophy to wisdom: a verbal imitation of a human productive power which in itself does not speak" (*Anatomy* 12). Similarly, he also broke the newly ascendant New Critics' isolation of individual works from each other and ended their denigration of Romantic theories of poetry and the imagination, while incorporating into his treatment of rhetorical criticism their emphasis on close reading of the figural structures of texts (see NEW CRITICISM). Among others, A. Walton Litz, Ian Balfour, Daniel O'Hara, and Krieger have also argued that this revolution made possible such later ones as STRUCTURALISM and DECONSTRUCTION as well as the renewed interest in PHENOMENOLOGY and HERMENEUTICS. Frye, however, sees these later movements as incomplete, because they "still seem only incidentally interested in literature itself and in what it does or can do for people" (*Spiritus* 106). It is nonetheless true that one of Frye's objectives in *Anatomy* is to bring together as many possible critical approaches and methods as he can. Todorov insists that this syncretizing tendency does not lead to relativism, but that "rather than being a priori obligation, truth becomes the common

horizon of a dialogue where different truths come into contact; it is what makes such dialogue possible" (101–2). On the other hand, in *Critical Understanding* Wayne Booth speaks for others as well as for himself in describing Frye's claims to pluralism as illusory and in asserting that Frye, like all "intelligent monists" (16), is not, as he suggests, accommodating all critical positions but affirming the ultimate truth of his own.

Frye defines the genre that gives its title to *Anatomy* in his discussion of the four forms of continuous prose fiction as the one that "relies on the free play of intellectual fancy . . . present[ing] us with a vision of the world in terms of a single intellectual pattern" (310). The vision in this instance is from the perspective of the total structure of criticism. If the first essay is temporal, the second is spatial in its patterning of the symbol (for Frye, the basic literary unit) on the medieval four levels of interpretation. The first level is split between the descriptive sign, which moves centrifugally outward to other areas of discourse, and the symbol as motif, which moves centripetally into the language of literature. Then the symbol is treated as image, which includes formal or rhetorical analyses; next the symbol is treated generically in terms of its place as archetype; finally, on the anagogic level, the symbol is revealed as a microcosm of the literary universe itself. In the third essay, Frye explores the variations of the pregeneric *mythoi* of comedy, romance, tragedy, and irony or satire on a wheel of the parallel seasons beginning with spring; these *mythoi* lie behind all narratives. Frye also elaborates the archetypal imagery that embodies Aristotle's *dianoia,* the meaning of those myths from apocalyptic at the top of the wheel to demonic at the bottom. In the fourth essay, he writes on genre both in poetry and in prose. In the "Tentative Conclusion," he widens the reference of his anatomy to all verbal structures, to a verbal universe beyond the literary one (352–53).

Many critics have been uneasy with what they have taken to be the static nature of the paradigms Frye elaborates and their isolation from the world of Becoming. In *After the New Criticism,* for instance, Lentricchia states that "Frye's entire literary universe (the 'real structure') stands isolated in its autonomous space, the river of time running far distantly beneath it" (15). Yet Frye strives to energize his model with such words as "counterpoints," "resonates," "drive," and "desire"; he conceives this model to be both diachronic and synchronous at the same time: "The *mythos* is the *dianoia* in movement; the *dianoia* is the *mythos* in stasis" (83). Frye varies this statement again and again in later writings, as in "Cycle and Apocalypse in *Finnegans Wake*" (1987): "And yet Vico's cyclical conception of historical process is really a vision of time within a spatial metaphor, and Bruno's conception of the identity of polarized opposites is a spatialized subject-object confrontation dissolving back into a temporal flux" (18).

Only the individual, mentally awakened reader can hold these tensions in the energy of his or her imagination, the imagination that is described as the source of all energy in Frye's essay on IMMANUEL KANT, "Literature as a Critique of Pure Reason" (1983). Frye resists a social resolution in a synthesis of the contending opposites: "An older, and perhaps wiser philosophical tradition [than the Hegelian-Marxist one] tells us that the synthesis in fact never comes into existence and that antithesis or tension of opposites is the only form in which [the ideal society] can exist" (*Critical* 168). A fitting emblem of Frye's model is the gyroscope (seemingly static when revolving most rapidly), the title and central metaphor of a play by the Canadian playwright James Reaney that is organized in Frye's narratives, images, and metaphors. Todorov uses a similar metaphor, the Viconian spiral, in describing Frye's method; Frye himself has repeatedly used Jerome Bruner's spiral curriculum to characterize his own circling back to restate earlier positions and to develop them further by doing so.

Indeed, Bruner's theory is important in Frye's working out of his own thoughts on the social function of literary criticism, particularly in *The Critical Path*. What criticism can do is awaken students to successive levels of awareness of the mythology that lies behind the ideology in which their society indoctrinates them. A society must have myths of concern, Frye concedes, but a myth of freedom is equally needed if its citizens are to perceive these myths as archetypes, not stereotypes. Education, then, is the source of social freedom, and the universities are the dynamo of education. It is in this area that MATTHEW ARNOLD's influence may be discerned, especially in his concept of the four powers of conduct, beauty, truth, and social life and manners. From the 1960s on, Frye used public lectures and the media to extend education in mythology to a wider audience; he campaigned relentlessly to demystify criticism and to bring it to the largest possible number of people. The lectures in *The Educated Imagination* (1963) were first delivered as Canadian Broadcasting Corporation radio lectures; between 1968 and 1977 Frye served as a member of the Canadian Radio-Television and Telecommunication Commission, the regulatory and policy-making body for broadcasting. Balfour, in the fifth chapter of his study of Frye, gives the fullest account of Frye's function as interpreter between writer and audience in his reviews of Canadian writing over the decades of his career. Two collections of those reviews and essays are *The Bush Garden* (1971) and *Divisions on a Ground* (1982).

After Frye's death, the novelist Margaret Atwood was quoted as saying that his greatest influence on Canadian writers was in his having treated writing as a serious occupation. His doing so was especially important in the decade of the 1950s, when he reported on the year's work in poetry for the annual "Letters in Canada" section of the *University of Toronto Quarterly.* His analyses are detailed and encouraging, while never failing to urge the development of greater skills in technique. In his "Conclusion" to the revised edition of *Literary History of Canada,* published in 1976, he celebrates what he calls the new professionalism of Canadian poets, referring to the advance in technique and craftsmanship that had resulted from the deepening awareness on the part of Canadian writers that structure and content are one and that the constructive power of the mind that unites them is the imagination. Frye's own writing on Canadian literature had much to do with this increasing professionalism.

Frye's first "Conclusion" to *Literary History of Canada* (1965) notes that the survey by many hands is a cultural history, and much of his essay is dedicated to defining Canadian culture by contrasting it to the American. Whereas Americans have proceeded deductively from the eighteenth-century a priori ideas of their Revolution, Canadians, whose loyalist forebears rejected that revolution, have moved inductively and expediently through their subsequent experience. That experience has been of nineteenth-century sophisticated ideas being thought out in the setting of the vast emptiness of an often terrifying and primitive nature. Frye argues that the result has been that Canadians have been forced to ask not Who am I? but Where is here? and to develop technology in transportation and communication to provide a vocabulary and grammar in which to answer that question. Out of this use of conceptual and rhetorical language to express that technology have come the theories of Innis and McLuhan. But Frye argues that the early Canadian preoccupation with formulating, asserting, and defending social and moral values created a garrison mentality in the literary mind that operated on the level of the conceptual rather than the poetic and thus revealed its origin in history rather than in myth. Consequently, Frye sees the coming to maturity of Canadian poets and novelists as a result of their moving back from history and argument to the more primitive metaphorical mode of thinking. "Literature is conscious mythology" becomes a refrain in this essay, as he insists that a mature literature presents an autonomous world of the imagination that gives readers a place from which to see their actual world. Recovering this power to think metaphorically opens the gates of the garrison mentality and frees writers and readers alike from conformist assertions. Only then does writing cease to be a rhetorical contest and become what he calls it in his second "Conclusion," an expression of play, which is, for Frye, the highest form of the serious. Ever the optimist, Frye found in the Canadian literature of the last few decades a steadily increasing playfulness.

Frye returns to his beginning in *The Great Code* (1982), as he counterpoints once more his theories of narrative, language and metaphor, typology, and polysemous interpretation in a detailed study of the Bible. The form of *The Great Code* is itself an emblem of Frye's criticism. The two testaments are reflected in the binary structure of the book, "The Order of Words" and "The Order of Types." The first part moves through chapters on language, myth, metaphor, and typology; the second part explores the same topics in reverse order. The result is, as Frye notes, a structure of double mirrors reflecting each other rather than any "outside." So, in narrative, the types in one testament become the antitypes in the second, the continuity of the myth of the whole Bible being U-shaped. The quest of descent and ascent is the pattern of romance that Frye has so frequently discussed, and yet again it is the reader who becomes the hero of that romance in search of identity. And it is typical of Frye that the quest ends in the mode of comedy, the mode of freedom, renewal, and joy. Balfour is as precise as he is witty in entitling his chapter on this work "The Great Coda: The Bible and Literature."

Words with Power (1990) is a companion to *The Great Code* in which Frye parallels the way in which the Bible "is held together by an inner core of mythical and metaphorical structure" (102) with the way in which Western literature is constructed. It is, Frye states, "something of a successor also to the much earlier *Anatomy of Criticism* (1957). In fact, it is to a considerable extent a summing up and restatement of my critical views" (xii). Whereas in *Anatomy* Frye defended the integrity of criticism in relation to literature, he now resists the attack on the integrity of literature by critics who fail to address the total coherence of the body of criticism and yield to "the popularity of rather aimless paradoxes that take us from 'everything is text' to 'nothing is text' and back again" (xix). Frye continues to find the coherence of criticism and of literature in the mythology at the center of every society. For Western societies, the first and fullest expression of that mythology is the Bible. In every verbal

utterance, Frye postulates five linguistic modes, though differing in degrees and developing in history. The descriptive mode of science is the latest, preceded by the conceptual mode of history and philosophy, the rhetorical mode of ideology, and the imaginative mode of the poetic. Beyond the imaginative is a fifth linguistic mode, which Frye calls the kerygmatic and for which he suggests prophetic and metaliterary as synonyms.

The title of his last work is adapted from Luke's description of how Jesus' parabolic preaching at Capernaum was received by his auditors: "His word was with power" (4:32). Such power is of the imaginative mode, which does not address auditors/readers directly nor compel their belief but presents them with hypothetical poetic models. These models embody their primary concerns, their desires for food and drink, sex, property, and freedom of movement; they are condensations of myth and metaphor in an autonomous poetic world (148). Movement outward to other linguistic modes involves displacement. First, the pure metaphor becomes metonymic in the rhetorical mode, made to stand for secondary concerns such as patriotism or religious belief in a social environment. Rhetoric, used in the poetic mode to ornament, becomes a means of persuasion to compel belief in some ideology; for Frye, "an ideology is applied mythology" (23). *Mythos* is displaced further and is more fully subordinated to the authority of *logos* in the conceptual mode, in which a dialectic forces the separation of subject and object. History and philosophy are the expressions in argument and logic of this dialectic. Now it is the structures of logic that compel belief, though Frye argues that behind them may still be discerned myth and metaphor. The last linguistic mode to strengthen the dominance of *logos* is the descriptive, which scientists use to compel belief in facts.

Frye consistently differentiates his criticism from that of most critics by defining it as a criticism of metaphor, as opposed to the criticism of concept practiced by historians of ideas, Marxists, structuralists, and followers of JACQUES DERRIDA. These other critics have their function in exploring the displacements of the poetic into the other three linguistic modes, but they are also inadequate because they accept the subordination of *mythos* to *logos*, of the unity of myth and metaphor to the dialectic of subject and object in history, philosophy, and science. This subordination dates from PLATO and Aristotle, and Frye finds it still dominant in Western culture (33). The Romantics attempted to reverse this relationship and to exalt *mythos* over *logos* once again; Frye endeavors to extend their enterprise in order to help readers perceive behind all verbal structures those myths and metaphors that may be found in their pure state as "two aspects of one identity" (71) only in literature. In responding to this pure model with heightened consciousness, readers may experience an epiphany going beyond the imaginative to the kerygmatic mode. Those who have criticized Frye as being antihistorical are answered by his insistence that it is only when readers dehistoricize experience that they escape the cycles of history and "become what they see" (84), transforming the poetic model into a model to live by, an existential metaphor, for "literature is a technique of meditation, in the widest and most flexible sense" (96).

In part 2 of *Words with Power,* Frye describes the model constructed out of counter-historical myth and counter-logical metaphor as the *axis mundi.* The model is the familiar fourfold one, and Frye traces one metaphor, an expression of one primary concern, for each level: mountain for freedom of movement, garden for sex, cave for food and drink, and furnace for property. Each is worked out from a central biblical example and explored through other examples from Western literature.

Frye's influence was, as Litz has argued, sweeping in the decade following the publication of *Anatomy,* and it has remained strong, as is evident in the huge number of entries in Robert Denham's bibliography. It is true that other critical schools have developed, and Frye himself was aware that some of their proponents have argued that his influence is over: "I am often described as someone who is now in the past and whose reputation has collapsed. But I don't think I'm any further down skid row than the deconstructionists" (Cayley 33). So long as readers focus on the literary structure itself, Frye will surely continue to be useful to them; and it is readers, and not other critics, that Frye always strove to reach. It is thus entirely fitting that his last publication should be *The Double Vision* (1991), consisting as it does of reworkings of public lectures in which he presents "a shorter and more accessible version of the longer books, *The Great Code* and *Words with Power"* (xvii).

Richard Stingle

See also RHETORIC.

Northrop Frye, *Anatomy of Criticism: Four Essays* (1957), *The Bush Garden: Essays on the Canadian Imagination* (1971), "Conclusion," *Literary History of Canada* (ed. Carl F. Klinck, 1965, 2d ed., vol. 3, 1976), *Creation and Recreation* (1980), *The Critical Path: An Essay on the Social Context of Literary Criticism* (1971), "Cycle and Apocalypse in *Finnegans Wake," Vico and Joyce* (ed. Donald Phillip Verene, 1987), *Divisions on a Ground: Essays on Canadian*

Culture (1982), *The Double Vision: Language and Meaning in Religion* (1991), *The Educated Imagination* (1963), *Fables of Identity: Studies in Poetic Mythology* (1963), *Fearful Symmetry: A Study of William Blake* (1947), *The Great Code: The Bible and Literature* (1982), "In the earth, or in the air?" review of Paul de Man, *The Rhetoric of Romanticism, Times Literary Supplement* (17 January 1986), "Literature as a Critique of Pure Reason," *Descant 40* 14 (1983), *Reading the World: Selected Writings, 1935–1976* (ed. Robert D. Denham, 1990), *The Secular Scripture: A Study of the Structure of Romance* (1976), *Spiritus Mundi: Essays on Literature, Myth, and Society* (1976), *A Study of English Romanticism* (1968), "The Survival of Eros in Poetry," *Romanticism and Contemporary Criticism* (ed. Morris Eaves and Michael Fischer, 1986), *A World in a Grain of Sand: Twenty-two Interviews with Northrop Frye* (ed. Robert D. Denham, 1991), *Words with Power: Being a Second Study of the Bible and Literature* (1990).

Ian Balfour, *Northrop Frye* (1988); Wayne C. Booth, *Critical Understanding: The Powers and Limits of Pluralism* (1979); David Cayley, "Inside Mythology: Northrop Frye Talks with David Cayley," *Idler* 32 (1991); David Cook, *Northrop Frye: A Vision of the New World* (1985); Eleanor Cook et al., eds., *Centre and Labyrinth: Essays in Honour of Northrop Frye* (1983); Robert D. Denham, *Northrop Frye: An Annotated Bibliography of Primary and Secondary Sources* (1987), *Northrop Frye and Critical Method* (1978); Robert D. Denham and Thomas Willard, eds., *Visionary Poetics: Essays on Northrop Frye's Criticism* (1991); A. C. Hamilton, *Northrop Frye: Anatomy of His Criticism* (1990); Murray Krieger, ed., *Northrop Frye in Modern Criticism: Selected Papers from the English Institute* (1966); Alvin A. Lee, "Towards a Language of Love and Freedom: Frye Deciphers the Great Code," *English Studies in Canada* 12 (1986); Frank Lentricchia, *After the New Criticism* (1980); A. Walton Litz, "Literary Criticism," *Harvard Guide to Contemporary American Writing* (ed. Daniel Hoffman, 1979); Tzvetan Todorov, *Critique de la critique* (1984, *Literature and Its Theorists: A Personal View of Twentieth-Century Criticism,* trans. Catherine Porter, 1987).

FULLER, MARGARET

Margaret Fuller (1810–50) achieved distinction, and some notoriety, on many scores—as feminist, transcendentalist, literary critic, editor, translator, journalist, and, finally, revolutionary participant in the Risorgimento, the Italian national revival that culminated in the unification of Italy in 1870. One of the most influential figures of the American renaissance, Fuller is best known today as the author of the first major feminist treatise published in the United States, *Woman in the Nineteenth Century* (1845), a work in which transcendentalist philosophy and literary-historical analysis support Fuller's argument for radical political and social change.

Before the publication of this hortatory document championing the rights of the enslaved—a group including white middle-class women of privilege such as Fuller herself, as well as African-American men and women who were legally slaves—Fuller served as the first editor of the transcendentalist journal *Dial*. During her editorship (1840–42), Fuller established her reputation as a leading literary critic. Her writings for the *Dial,* notably "A Short Essay on Critics" (1840) and "Goethe" (1841), adhere to Romantic tenets of the artist as godlike and of the critic as mediator between the human and the divine: "The maker is divine; the critic sees this divine, but brings it down to humanity by the analytic process" (*Margaret Fuller, American Romantic* 69). Fuller's most important contribution to the *Dial* was "The Great Lawsuit: Man versus Men, Woman versus Women" (1843), which she expanded two years later as *Woman in the Nineteenth Century.*

After completing "The Great Lawsuit," Fuller traveled to the Great Lakes region. *Summer on the Lakes, in 1843* (1844), which derives from this journey, combines travel narrative, cultural critique, Bildungsroman, meditation, and poetry to create Fuller's "poetic impression" of her exterior and interior journey. As a historical document of Fuller's travels, *Summer* foregrounds the "broken and degraded condition" of the Indians (153), the frontierswoman's "unfitness" for her lot (38), and the westward-bound colonizer's tendency to view the land and its Native American inhabitants as "objects" to exploit. As spiritual autobiography, *Summer* shows Fuller's outward journey as central to her personal and cultural enlightenment, particularly as she came to learn of the traditions and character of "the first-born of the soil," against whom "our people and our government have sinned alike" (114). Writers were among these sinners, as Fuller makes clear in her criticism of Washington Irving's portrayal of Native Americans as "academic figures only" (21). Sensitive to the inadequacy of "white" accounts of Native Americans, Fuller perceived that she was also unqualified to write of "the subjugated race," which she believed was "fated to perish" (144, 120). Instead, she saw that her task as writer was to record the degradation of women of her time and to encourage them to seek their rightful "share of the human inheritance" (111). Holding that "the observations of women upon the position of woman are always more valuable than those of men,"

Fuller discovered in *Summer* her most compelling subject (110).

Fuller's evolution as cultural critic is also evident in her many reviews and essays, first in the *Dial* and later in Horace Greeley's progressive *New York Tribune,* on American and European writers. In addition to praising Herman Melville, RALPH WALDO EMERSON, and EDGAR ALLAN POE, Fuller commended Charles Brockden Brown, Frederick Douglass, Lydia Maria Child, and Lydia Huntley Sigourney, the latter of whom scholars have only newly included in the American literary canon. Yet Fuller qualified her view of this canon in her pivotal essay "American Literature: Its Position in the Present Time, and Prospects for the Future" (1846). Looking back to Emerson's "American Scholar" (1836) and anticipating Whitman's preface to the 1855 edition of *Leaves of Grass,* Fuller judged that her native literary scene lacked a distinctively American "original idea" (*Margaret Fuller, American Romantic* 229).

Despite efforts in behalf of this national literature, Fuller turned to Europe for both literary and personal models, finding her best models in Elizabeth Barrett Browning and George Sand. Fuller was to meet these women and other luminaries, male and female, during the European tour she began in 1846. While traveling abroad, she continued to report on social and political topics for Greeley's daily and thus may have been the first American foreign correspondent.

In an 1847 letter, Fuller wrote to Emerson of the value of this European experience: "I find how true was the lure that always drew me towards Europe. . . . Had I only come ten years earlier! Now my life must be a failure, so much strength has been wasted on abstractions" (*Letters* 4:315). Her major work, *Woman in the Nineteenth Century,* makes clear that prior to her European travels, Fuller had wearied of transcendentalist abstractions.

Central to *Woman* is Fuller's belief in the redemptive power of "das Ewig-Weibliche," Goethe's eternal feminine. Holding with Goethe that the "peculiar secret" of "the feminine principle" could save man's soul, Fuller espoused spiritual values to argue for feminist goals. The mystical basis of Fuller's world-view is displayed in many passages emphasizing the transcendentalist belief in self-culture or self-cultivation, which affirmed the individual's right to free and continuing self-development. Fuller was confident that were women granted the possibility for self-cultivation, "a ravishing harmony of the spheres would ensue" (37). Fuller's idealism is checked by the dehumanizing reality she finds in the lives women lead. In seeing that abused wives, enslaved women, and prostitutes share a common plight, Fuller demonstrates that for most women of her day, self-cultivation is an illusory goal. Too many "arbitrary barriers" and "bad institutions" block woman's progress. Drawing upon the examples of the American and French revolutions, Fuller reasons that social and political reforms are required for woman to fulfill her promise: "We would have every arbitrary barrier thrown down. We would have every path laid open to Woman as freely as to Man. . . . There is but one law for souls" (37). It should be noted that Fuller envisions the ideas of "Man" and "Woman" in androgynous terms: "Male and female represent the two sides of the great radical dualism. But, in fact, they are perpetually passing into one another. There is no wholly masculine man, no purely feminine woman" (115–16). As long as society limits women's self-expression, Fuller maintains, they should practice another transcendentalist ideal, self-reliance: "I believe that, at present, women are the best helpers of one another" (172).

To urge women to action, Fuller refers to notable women from antiquity through the early nineteenth century who have advanced the idea of Woman. Her efforts to examine woman's place in literature and society reveal that Fuller's critical stance presages that of twentieth-century revisionist critics, most notably VIRGINIA WOOLF. Indeed, Fuller's own place in literary history is now being reassessed, yet the tribute to Fuller in the landmark *History of Woman Suffrage* (1881) remains fitting: "Margaret Fuller possessed more influence upon the thought of America, than any woman previous to her time." Like the editors of the *History*—Elizabeth Cady Stanton, Susan B. Anthony, and Matilda Joslyn Gage—the twentieth-century reader finds in Fuller's life and writing persuasive argument for "a vindication of women's right to think."

Clare Colquitt

See also AMERICAN THEORY AND CRITICISM: NINE-TEENTH CENTURY.

Margaret Fuller, *The Letters of Margaret Fuller* (ed. Robert N. Hudspeth, 5 vols., 1983–88), *Life Without and Life Within; or, Reviews, Narratives, Essays, and Poems* (1860, facs. reprint, 1970), *Margaret Fuller, American Romantic: A Selection from Her Writings and Correspondence* (ed. Perry Miller, 1963), *Papers on Literature and Art* (1846, facs. reprint, 1972), *Summer on the Lakes, in 1843* (1844, facs. reprint, 1991), *Woman in the Nineteenth Century* (1845, facs. reprint, 1971), *The Writings of Margaret Fuller* (ed. Mason Wade, 1941).

Margaret Vanderhaar Allen, *The Achievement of Margaret Fuller* (1979); Paula Blanchard, *Margaret Fuller: From Transcendentalism to Revolution* (1978); Bell Gale Chevigny, *The Woman and the Myth: Margaret Fuller's Life and Writings* (1976); Joel Myerson, ed., *Critical Essays on Margaret Fuller* (1980), *Margaret Fuller: A Descriptive Bibliography* (1978), *Margaret Fuller: An Annotated Secondary Bibliography* (1977); Marie Mitchell Olesen Urbanski, *Margaret Fuller's "Woman in the Nineteenth Century": A Literary Study of Form and Content, of Sources and Influence* (1980).

GAY THEORY AND CRITICISM

1. Gay Male

Gay male criticism is the most recent of the critical/ theoretical discourses to emerge from the "liberation" movements—New Left, anti–Vietnam War, counter-culture, black, and feminist—of the 1960s and early 1970s. When "in 1969, lesbian and gay street people, Puerto Rican drag queens, and bar gays fought back against a routine police raid at the Stonewall Tavern in New York City" (Gary Kinsman, *The Regulation of Desire: Sexuality in Canada*, 1987, 179), the incident, usually referred to as the catalyst of the gay liberation movement, also became a mythic point of origin and return for gay critique. Members of the new movement resisted oppression by police, psychiatrists, clerics, and others, but in ways that looked to a cultural, social, and political renovation that would change the conditions of personal existence generally. In *Homosexual Oppression and Liberation* (1971), Dennis Altman, an Australian writer living in the United States, describes gay liberation as "a process whereby homosexuals seek to come to terms with themselves and through self-affirmation commence on the path towards human liberation" (217). Although in this context "liberation" connotes the undoing of gender categories themselves, insofar as the movement did achieve visibility during the 1970s, it prompted the very different experience of gay self-definition as an individual and subcultural identity (Steven Epstein, "Gay Politics, Ethnic Identity: The Limits of Social Constructionism," *Socialist Review* 93–94 [1987] 17–19; Robert A. Padgug, "Gay Villain, Gay Hero: Homosexuality and the Social Construction of AIDS," Peiss, Simmons, and Padgug, 302–3).

The Stonewall Rebellion implies the prior history of male homosexual existence in the United States since the end of World War II. After the war, returning veterans and other young men whose wartime mobilization had permitted homosexual experimentation and self-discovery gathered in subcultures in cities such as New York, San Francisco, and Los Angeles. John D'Emi-

lio has argued that one unanticipated consequence of public persecution of homosexuals during the cold war was a growing self-awareness and group cohesion among gays ("The Homosexual Menace: The Politics of Sexuality in Cold War America," Peiss, Simmons, and Padgug, 237). Essays in physical culture magazines recalled the names of earlier polemicists such as Walt Whitman and Edward Carpenter, and expressions of camp taste in the arts and the mass media diffused gay sensibility more widely (Bruce Boone, "Gay Language as Political Praxis: The Poetry of Frank O'Hara," *Social Text* 1 [1979]). Although within the negative conditions of the time gay expressions were often marked by homophobia, as in the plays of Tennessee Williams (John M. Clum, "'Something Cloudy, Something Clear': Homophobic Discourse in Tennessee Williams," *South Atlantic Quarterly* 88 [1989]), writers such as Gore Vidal in *The City and the Pillar* (1948), James Baldwin in *Giovanni's Room* (1956), and others dealt openly with sexual and emotional relations between men. Vidal's novel provoked a sensation.

In the early 1960s, three of the leading figures of pop art were gay: Jasper Johns, Robert Rauschenberg, and Andy Warhol. Andrew Ross has argued that the emergence of pop presented the first major challenge to the high taste advocated by the alienated (male) intellectual elite centered in New York City. As SUSAN SONTAG observes in "Notes on 'Camp'" (1964, *Against Interpretation and Other Essays*, 1966), valorization of the vulgar and the popular was usually colored by a gay outlook (Moon, "Flaming Closets"). During the same decade, as a result of Supreme Court decisions, visual and written representations of sexual practices between men became widely available for the first time, usually in the form of pornography. Working-class writers such as the Chicano-American writer John Rechy, author of *City of Night* (1963), produced sexually explicit fiction. And on the East Coast gay activists began to resist discrimination in more overt and explicitly political fashion (John D'Emilio, *Sexual Politics, Sexual Communities: The Making of a Homosexual Minority in the United States: 1940–1970*, 1983, 5). All this activity—economic, political, high and mass cultural—took place before Stonewall.

In England, already in the late nineteenth century, Edward Carpenter, along with WALTER PATER, John Addington Symonds, and OSCAR WILDE, had established a diverse, highly self-conscious set of strategies for articulating homosexual existence and critiquing dominant norms. Symonds's death in 1893, Pater's in 1894, and the three Wilde trials of 1895 brought about an abrupt hiatus. Nonetheless, the ascendancy of the BLOOMSBURY GROUP between the wars made elite "queer" culture, personified in such diverse figures as E. M. Forster, Lytton Strachey, John Maynard Keynes, and, in a younger generation, W .H. AUDEN, Christopher Isherwood, and Stephen Spender, highly influential (see Andrew Hodges and David Hutter, *With Downcast Gays: Aspects of Homosexual Self-Oppression,* 2d ed., 1979). Alan Sinfield has argued that cross-class sexual contacts among homosexuals during and after the war "undermined the affiliations and barriers upon which" this culture depended for relative security from prosecution (*Literature, Politics, and Culture in Postwar Britain,* 1989, 66). Sinfield has gone on to conduct a major study of the micropolitics of homosexual identity formation in relation to the prominence of closeted homosexuals in the London theater scene between the 1930s and the mid-1960s ("Closet Dramas: Homosexual Representation and Class in Postwar British Theater," *Genders* 9 [1990]). The staging of John Osborne's drama about Colonel Alfred Redl, *A Patriot for Me,* at the Royal Court Theatre in 1965 and limited decriminalization of sexual activities between men in the Sexual Offences Act of 1967 opened possibilities of overt gay culture in England.

The points of departure of the special gay issue of *College English* in 1974 were the assertion of a fixed homosexual identity and the reclamation of a specifically homosexual literary tradition, a process that has continued to engage a number of gay critics (Louie Crew and Rictor Norton, "The Homophobic Imagination: An Editorial," *College English* 36 [1974]; Summers). Robert Martin's *The Homosexual Tradition in American Poetry* (1979) "considers the extent to which an author's awareness of himself as a homosexual has affected how and what he wrote" (xv). Writing in a line of critics that includes Carpenter, F. O. Matthiessen, and Newton Arvin, Martin also draws upon the politics of gay liberation in affirming the connections between "adhesiveness," Walt Whitman's term for male-male desire (Michael Lynch, " 'Here Is Adhesiveness': From Friendship to Homosexuality," *Victorian Studies* 29 [1985]), and his commitment to democratic and egalitarian values (David Bergman, "F. O. Matthiessen: The Critic as Homosexual," *Raritan* 9 [1990]). In *Hero, Captain, and Stranger*

(1986), Martin rewrites the preoccupation with male relations that Leslie A. Fiedler emphasized in the preface to *Love and Death in the American Novel* (1960, rev. ed., 1966), where Fiedler laments "the failure of the American fictionist to deal with adult heterosexual love and his consequent obsession with death, incest and innocent homosexuality" (xi). Martin focuses on Herman Melville's effort, in his novels of the South Seas, to celebrate emotional and sexual ties between men across lines of color in texts that contest "the subordination of women by men, of colored nations by white, and of nature by law" (x; see also Joseph Allen Boone, *Tradition Counter Tradition: Love and the Form of Fiction,* 1987, ch. 5). Since the publication of Martin's first book, the place of "manly friendship" in Whitman's work has been widely discussed, most recently in books by M. Jimmie Killingsworth (*Whitman's Poetry of the Body: Sexuality, Politics, and the Text,* 1989) and Michael Moon (*Disseminating Whitman: Revision and Corporeality in "Leaves of Grass,"* 1991).

In the 1980s, gay criticism followed principally one of two lines: either feminist theory or Foucauldian analysis, based especially on the distinction that MICHEL FOUCAULT draws in volume 1 of *The History of Sexuality* (1976) between the sodomite, defined in relation to transgressive sexual acts, and the homosexual, defined as "a singular nature" (43) (see also FEMINIST THEORY AND CRITICISM). Although writers have also drawn on Foucault's emphasis in *The Use of Pleasure* on an "aesthetics of existence" (12), a hermeneutics of the self based on consideration in texts by ancient writers of the connections between a range of male-male sexual practices and the structure of personal relations and self-awareness, attention has focused principally on questions of category: What is a sodomite? a homosexual? a gay? There now exists a wide range of materials dealing with the construction of the sodomite in theological and juridical discourses prior to the nineteenth century (e.g., Kent Gerard and Gert Hekma, eds., *The Pursuit of Sodomy: Male Homosexuality in Renaissance and Enlightenment Europe,* 1989; G. S. Rousseau, "The Pursuit of Homosexuality in the Eighteenth Century: 'Utterly Confused Category' and/or Rich Repository?" *Eighteenth-Century Life* 9 [1985]; Guide Ruggiero, *The Boundaries of Eros: Sex, Crime, and Sexuality in Renaissance Venice,* 1985; Randolph Trumbach, "The Birth of the Queen: Sodomy and the Emergence of Gender Equality in Modern Culture, 1660–1750," Duberman, Vicinus, and Chauncey). In addition, and despite arguments to the contrary (John Boswell, "Revolutions, Universals, and Sexual Categories," *Salmagundi* 58–59 [1982–83], rev. in Duberman,

Vicinus, and Chauncey), there is a consensus that the term "homosexual" should be restricted to meanings that derive from late-nineteenth-century legal and medical language (Ed Cohen, "Writing Gone Wilde: Homoerotic Desire in the Closet of Representation," *PMLA* 102 [1987], and "Legislating the Norm: From Sodomy to Gross Indecency," *South Atlantic Quarterly* 88 [1989] 210–211). As for the term "gay," though historians such as John Boswell use it to refer to men in ancient or medieval times who enjoyed sexual and emotional ties with other men (*Christianity* 42–43), the specific weighting of the word with reference to contemporary gay liberation suggests using that term too in a time-specific way.

Discussion has also focused on "the age-old difficulty, for our societies, of integrating these two phenomena—different phenomena at that—of the inversion of sexual roles and intercourse between individuals of the same sex" (Foucault, *Use* 18. See also George Chauncey, "From Sexual Inversion to Homosexuality: Medicine and the Changing Conceptualization of Female Deviance," *Salmagundi* 58–59 [1982–83]; and Craft). In revisionary masculine discourses, fascination with "becoming-woman" (Dellamora chs. 4, 7) touches on the contradictory relationship between male writing and the representation of lesbian desire (Lillian Faderman, *Surpassing the Love of Men: Romantic Friendship and Love between Women from the Sixteenth Century to the Present,* 1981, 43–45; Isabelle de Courtivron, "Weak Men and Fatal Women: The Sand Image," Stambolian and Marks; Joan DeJean, *Fictions of Sappho: 1546–1937,* 1989; Silverman; Jack Undank, "Diderot's 'Unnatural' Acts: Lessons from the Convent," *French Forum* 11 [1986]). Gay theory also has significant points of contact with the critique of masculinity within men's studies (Lee, Garrigan, and Connell; Ross; Schwenger; Mark Selzer, "The Naturalist Machine," *Sex, Politics, and Science in the Nineteenth-Century Novel,* ed. Ruth Bernard Yeazell, 1986).

In gay historiography, books by Alan Bray and John Boswell continue to be important. A century earlier, Greek studies had been a major locus of sexual politics in France and Germany and also at Oxford. Beginning with the publication of K. J. Dover's *Greek Homosexuality* in 1978, Greek pederasty has received significant renewed attention, most notably in the writing of David Halperin (see also John J. Winkler, *The Constraints of Desire: The Anthropology of Sex and Gender in Ancient Greece,* 1990). Again reviving a subject pertinent to earlier writers such as Pater and Forster, Arthur Evans (*The God of Ecstasy: Sex-Roles and the Madness of Dionysos,* 1988) has considered the myth and rituals of Dionysus in relation to desire between men (see also Bernard Sergent, *Homosex-*

uality in Greek Myth, trans. Arthur Goldhammer, 1986). Renaissance studies have provided a significant site of discussions of male-male desire (Gregory W. Bredbeck, "Milton's Ganymede: Negotiations of Homoerotic Tradition in *Paradise Regained*," *PMLA* 106 [1991]; Fineman; Goldberg; Stephen Orgel, "Nobody's Perfect: Or Why Did the English Stage Take Boys for Women," *South Atlantic Quarterly* 88 [1989]; Joseph Pequigney, *Such Is My Love: A Study of Shakespeare's Sonnets,* 1985; Saslow; Bruce R. Smith, *Homosexual Desire in Shakespeare's England: A Cultural Poetics,* 1991). Louis Crompton's *Byron and Greek Love* (1985) is a prime source of historical material for the nineteenth century. Jeffrey Weeks, in a number of works, has been the most important medium for transmitting a constructionist view of the sexual subject as well as for the history of homosexuality in Great Britain in connection with the history of women and the emergent discourses of late-nineteenth-century sexology. The *fin de siècle* has provided an especially rich moment for reflection on subjects of male-male desire, whether the men considered be termed "homosexual" or "heterosexual" (Bartlett; Cohen, "Writing Gone Wilde"; Christopher Craft, "Alias Bunbury: Desire and Termination in *The Importance of Being Earnest*," *Representations* 31 [1990]; Richard Dellamora, *Apocalyptic Overtures,* 1993; Jonathan Dollimore, "Different Desires: Subjectivity and Transgression in Wilde and Gide," *Genders* 2 [1988]; Linda Dowling, "The Decadent and the New Woman in the 1890's," *Nineteenth Century Fiction* 33 [1978]; Wayne Koestenbaum, *Double Talk: The Erotics of Male Literary Collaboration,* 1989, and "Wilde's Hard Labor and the Birth of Gay Reading," Boone and Cadden; Michael Moon, "Sexuality and Visual Terrorism in *The Wings of the Dove*," *Criticism* 28 [1986]; Reade; Elaine Showalter, *Sexual Anarchy: Gender and Culture at the fin de siècle,* 1990). Wayne Koestenbaum has produced a study of T. S. Eliot's collaboration with Ezra Pound on *The Waste Land* that demonstrates the centrality of homoerotic/homophobic bonding within Anglo-American modernism (*Double Talk,* ch. 4).

A main aim of gay translation, anthologizing, and criticism since the 1970s has been to direct attention to non-Anglophone writers such as C. P. Cavafy, Jean Genet, Frederico García Lorca, and Yukio Mishima, among others. Publication of Stambolian and Marks's *Homosexualities and French Literature* (1979) signaled the importance of the French literary tradition, in which expressions of male-male desire have been central to advanced writing since as early as the 1830s (Apter; J. E. Rivers, *Proust and the Art of Love: The Aesthetics of Sexuality in the Life, Times, and Art of Marcel Proust,* 1980). Moreover, poststructuralist theory in writers other than Foucault, such as ROLAND BARTHES, Gilles Deleuze, and Félix Guattari, has opened possibilities for gay criticism (Guattari, "A Liberation of Desire," Stambolian and Marks). The work of Richard Howard—as poet, translator, lecturer, critic, and friend—has been especially significant in suffusing gay high culture with a Barthesian delight in a desire that, "caught in the serious 'play' of representation, imagining and mimicking a self and other selves, exposes not merely its limits, ideologies, and evasions, but the astonishing scope and flexibility of its—what shall I call them?—unnatural, preternatural, blessedly unconventional, sympathies" (Undank, "Diderot's 'Unnatural' Acts" 163). In the field of reader-response theory, Ross Chambers has shown how ironic effects can suggest different desires to a reader or group of readers in opposition, wittingly or unwittingly, to the values of the dominant culture (*Room for Maneuver: Reading [the] Oppositional [in] Narrative,* 1991, 32).

Kate Millett in *Sexual Politics* (1970) devoted her final chapter to the work of Jean Genet because of "the emphasis given in his plays to the theme of sexual oppression and the necessity, in any radical program, for its eradication" (xii). ADRIENNE RICH, in contrast, has said: "In defining and describing lesbian existence I would hope to move toward a dissociation of lesbian from male homosexual values and allegiances" ("Compulsory Heterosexuality and Lesbian Existence," 1980, *The "Signs" Reader: Women, Gender and Scholarship,* ed. Elizabeth Abel and Emily K. Abel, 1983, 158). The two comments indicate something of both the affinities and the tensions that have existed between gay male and feminist and/or lesbian critique in the past two decades (Craig Owens, "Outlaws: Gay Men in Feminism," *Men in Feminism,* ed. Alice Jardine and Paul Smith, 1987), though Teresa de Lauretis *(Queer Theory)* has recently demonstrated the possibility of collaborative work between lesbian and gay theorists. Feminists such as Rich herself, moreover, as well as Elaine Showalter *(Speaking),* de Lauretis ("Sexual Indifference and Lesbian Representation," *Theatre Journal* 40 [1988]), Alice A. Jardine (*Gynesis: Configurations of Woman and Modernity,* 1985), and Monique Wittig ("The Straight Mind," *Feminist Issues* 1 [1980]), have exercised influence in particular areas within gay criticism. Eve Kosofsky Sedgwick's *Between Men* (1985), which demonstrates the triangulation in realist fiction of male attraction/repulsion across the body of a woman, remains the most influential single text. Sedgwick has devised a model of antihomophobic critique that emphasizes the "double bind" within the construction of the middle-class male subject:

Because the paths of male entitlement, especially in the nineteenth century, required certain intense male bonds that were not readily distinguishable from the most reprobated bonds, an endemic and ineradicable state of what I am calling male homosexual panic became the normal condition of male heterosexual entitlement. (*Epistemology* 185)

By showing the place of homophobia in the structure of normal gender relations, she has in effect moved homophobia, and with it male homosexuality, from the periphery of feminist discussions of the cultural construction of gender to a place near the center.

Epistemology of the Closet (1990) focuses on "the self-ignorance that this regime constitutively enforces" (186). As a critical instrument in analyzing texts whose sexual charge is indicated by gaps, silences, and symptomatic turns of phrase, Sedgwick's emphasis on operations of unknowing works to defamiliarize familiar texts in sharply illuminating ways. In the epistemology of the closet, silence is as important as speech. As Foucault writes, "There is no binary division to be made between what one says and what one does not say; we must try to determine the different ways of not saying such things. . . . There is not one but many silences, and they are an integral part of the strategies that underlie and permeate discourses" (quoted in Sedgwick, *Epistemology* 3; see also D. A. Miller, *The Novel and the Police,* 1988).

If Foucauldian analysis and the concept of the homosocial continuum undermine the confidence in a unitary homosexual subject that first-phase gay criticism relied on, those responses that draw on feminist theory of subject-position and feminist DECONSTRUCTION subvert notions of a fixed subject in other ways. In deconstructive approaches, homosexuality and "the homosexual" are deployed as privileged signifiers of difference (Joseph A. Boone, "Mappings of Male Desire in Durrell's *Alexandria Quartet," South Atlantic Quarterly* 88 [1989] 74–75). Drawing upon the work of both Foucault and JACQUES DERRIDA, Lee Edelman offers two definitions of what he refers to as "homographesis": on the one hand, the "inscription of the homosexual within a tropology that produces him in constitutive relation to inscription" (194), and on the other, "the putting into writing—and therefore the putting into the realm of difference—of the sameness, the similitude, of the metaphors of identity that the graphesis of homosexuality historically deconstructs" (195–96).

Recently, attention has begun to be directed to the experience of persons of color both in Great Britain and the United States and in other countries (Beam; Boffin and Gupta; Duberman, Vicinus, and Chauncey). Film has also received attention (Richard Dyer, *Now You See It: Studies on Lesbian and Gay Film,* 1990), and issues of representation in the visual arts have come to the fore on account of the 1990 controversy over Robert Mapplethorpe's photography (Carole S. Vance, "Misunderstanding Obscenity," *Art in America* 78 [1990]). During the 1980s, articles in *Screen* and special issues of *October* and *differences,* as well as books such as Simon Watney's *Policing Desire* (1987), have focused on the political implications of representation within AIDS discourses (Leo Bersani, "Is the Rectum a Grave?" Crimp; Boffin and Gupta; Douglas Crimp, "Mourning and Militancy," *October* 51 [1989]; Sander L. Gilman, "AIDS and Syphilis: The Iconography of Disease," Crimp; Donna J. Haraway, "The Biopolitics of Postmodern Bodies: Determinations of Self in Immune System Discourse," *differences* 1 [1989]; Padgug, "Gay Villain, Gay Hero"). While the politics of AIDS has put gays and their allies on the defensive, they have also shown remarkable resilience (Douglas Crimp and Adam Rolston, *AIDS Demographics,* 1990).

Emphasis in current writing on what Joseph Allen Boone refers to as "a flux of libidinous desire" ("Mappings" 77) carries a reminder of the centrality of bodies and their pleasures in the movement that provided gay criticism with its impetus. Even in a period of severe stress, gay criticism continues to entail what Andrew Ross refers to as a "liberatory imagination which sets the agenda of radical democracy beyond liberal pragmatism in pursuit of claims, actions, rights, desires, pleasures, and thoughts that are often still considered too illegitimate to be recognized as political" (177). In "post-AIDS" culture (Ed Cohen, "Are We (Not) What We Are Becoming? 'Gay' 'Identity,' 'Gay Studies,' and the Disciplining of Knowledge," Boone and Cadden, 161), gay theory in the early 1990s adopted the sobriquet "queer theory," whether that term expands, in problematical fashion, to mean the ensemble of antihegemonic theories of perversion or whether it signals, as it does in de Lauretis's *Queer Theory: Lesbian and Gay Sexualities,* affirmation

> that gay sexuality in its specific female and male cultural or subcultural forms acts as an agency of social process whose mode of functioning is both interactive and yet resistant, both participatory and yet distinct, claiming at once equality and difference, demanding political representation while insisting on its material and historical specificity. (iii)

Richard Dellamora

Emily S. Apter, *André Gide and the Codes of Homotextuality* (1987); Neil Bartlett, *Who Was That Man? A Present for Mr Oscar Wilde* (1988); Joseph Beam, ed., *In the Life: A Black Gay Anthology* (1986); Tessa Boffin and Sunil Gupta, *Ecstatic Antibodies: Resisting the AIDS Mythology* (1990); Joseph Allen Boone and Michael Cadden, eds., *Engendering Men: The Question of Male Feminist Criticism* (1990); John Boswell, *Christianity, Social Tolerance, and Homosexuality: Gay People in Western Europe from the Beginning of the Christian Era to the Fourteenth Century* (1980); Alan Bray, *Homosexuality in Renaissance England* (1982); Christopher Craft, " 'Kiss Me with Those Red Lips': Gender and Inversion in Bram Stoker's *Dracula,*" *Representations* 8 (1984, reprint, Showalter, *Speaking*); Douglas Crimp, ed., *AIDS: Cultural Analysis, Cultural Activism* (1988); Louis Crompton, *Byron and Greek Love: Homophobia in Nineteenth-Century England* (1985); Teresa de Lauretis, ed., *Queer Theory: Lesbian and Gay Sexualities* (1991); Richard Dellamora, *Masculine Desire: The Sexual Politics of Victorian Aestheticism* (1990); Martin Duberman, Martha Vicinus, and George Chauncey, Jr., eds., *Hidden from History: Reclaiming the Gay and Lesbian Past* (1989); Lee Edelman, "Homographesis," *Yale Journal of Criticism* 3 (1989); Joel Fineman, *Shakespeare's Perjured Eye: The Invention of Poetic Subjectivity in the Sonnets* (1986); Michel Foucault, *L'Usage des plaisirs* (1984, *The History of Sexuality, Vol. 2: The Use of Pleasure,* trans. Robert Hurley, 1986), *La Volonté de savoir* (1976, *The History of Sexuality, Vol. 1: An Introduction,* trans. Robert Hurley, 1978); Jonathan Goldberg, *Voice Terminal Echo: Postmodernism and English Renaissance Texts* (1986); David M. Halperin, *One Hundred Years of Homosexuality and Other Essays on Greek Love* (1990); John Lee, Tim Garrigan, and Bob Connell, "Toward a New Sociology of Masculinity," *Theory and Society* 14 (1985); Robert K. Martin, *Hero, Captain, and Stranger: Male Friendship, Social Critique, and Literary Form in the Sea Novels of Herman Melville* (1986), *The Homosexual Tradition in American Poetry* (1979); Michael Moon, "Flaming Closets," *October* 51 (1989); Kathy Peiss, Christina Simmons, and Robert A. Padgug, eds., *Passion and Power: Sexuality in History* (1989); Brian Reade, ed., *Sexual Heretics: Male Homosexuality in English Literature from 1850 to 1900* (1970); Andrew Ross, *No Respect: Intellectuals and Popular Culture* (1989); James M. Saslow, *Ganymede in the Renaissance: Homosexuality in Art and Society* (1986); Peter Schwenger, *Phallic Critiques: Masculinity and Twentieth-Century Literature* (1984); Eve Kosofsky Sedgwick, *Between Men: English Literature and Male Homosocial Desire* (1985), *Epistemology of the Closet* (1990); Elaine Showalter, ed., *Speaking of Gender* (1989); Kaja Silverman, *Male Subjectivity at the Margins* (1992); George Stambolian and Elaine Marks, eds., *Homosexualities and French Literature: Cultural Contexts, Critical Texts* (1979); Simon Stern, "Lesbian and Gay Studies: A Selective Bibliography," *Yale*

Journal of Criticism 3 (1989); Claude Summers, *Gay Fictions, Wilde to Stonewall: Studies in a Male Homosexual Literary Tradition* (1990); Simon Watney, *Policing Desire: Pornography, AIDS, and the Media* (1987); Jeffrey Weeks, *Coming Out: Homosexual Politics in Britain, from the Nineteenth Century to the Present* (1977), *Sex, Politics, and Society: The Regulation of Sexuality since 1800* (1981), *Sexuality and Its Discontents: Meanings, Myths, and Modern Sexualities* (1985).

2. Lesbian

At the beginning of the 1970s, the height of the many liberation movements that had emerged during the previous decade, a scholar interested in lesbian issues and images in literature could have turned to only two reference works: Jeannette Foster's privately printed 1956 study, *Sex-Variant Women in Literature,* and the compendious bibliography collected by Barbara Grier (under the pseudonym Gene Damon), *The Lesbian in Literature.* This situation would change dramatically, as social, cultural, and political forces began to supplant NEW CRITICISM with the politically grounded theories found in African-American, feminist, Marxist, gay male, and lesbian criticism.

The origins of lesbian criticism lie specifically in the political theory and movement of lesbian feminism, itself the outgrowth of the women's liberation and gay liberation movements. Impatient with the homophobia of heterosexual women and the sexism of gay men, lesbians created new groups and organizations, typically named "radicalesbians" or "lesbian liberation." They also shaped the theoretical position of lesbian feminism. The Radicalesbians collective, for example, crystallized a metaphorical definition of the lesbian as "the rage of all women" in their manifesto, "The Woman-Identified Woman" (1970). Jill Johnston electrified the emerging generation of radical lesbian feminists with her outrageous ideas and Steinian prose in *Lesbian Nation* (1973). These early writers articulated the position that lesbianism frees women from the constraints and oppressions of patriarchy, making it possible for lesbians to serve as role models for all women. As Johnston put it, "Feminism at heart is a massive complaint. Lesbianism is the solution" (166).

Some participants in the new movement developed an even more rigorous critique of heterosexuality that came to be known as lesbian separatism. Separatist theory proposed that lesbianism was a political more than sexual identity and that abandoning heterosexuality was a prerequisite to destroying male supremacy. Accordingly, separation from heterosexual women, all men, and even nonseparatist lesbians was seen as a political necessity. Theory generated practice: throughout the 1970s, separatist living collectives, newspapers and journals, and alternative institutions proliferated. Although the majority of lesbians then, as now, did not identify themselves with the theoretical rigidity of lesbian separatism, most made use of some of their institutions, and many lived a de facto separatist lifestyle.

Lesbian literary theory initially developed within this context of feminism and separatism. That is, lesbian (feminist) criticism constituted itself as a stream of thought separate from either heterosexual feminist or gay male thought, although related to some extent to the former. Most, although not all, lesbian feminist critics identified along the axis of gender (female/male or feminine/masculine) rather than that of sexuality (homosexuality/bisexuality/heterosexuality). It would be over a decade before significant numbers of lesbian critics developed theoretical and institutional connections to gay male critics.

The feminist-separatist (in the pragmatic if not always theoretical sense of the term) school of lesbian criticism grew rapidly during the 1970s, spurred on by the growth of a vigorous political-cultural movement, the establishment of lesbian and feminist journals and publishers (including such alternative presses as the Naiad Press, Spinsters/Aunt Lute, Spinsters Ink, and the Women's Press), the growth of women's studies programs, and the advance of lesbian fiction and poetry, the authors of which—particularly Judy Grahn, Audre Lorde, and ADRIENNE RICH—were often critics and theorists themselves. Much of this work moved easily between the boundaries of community and campus, which were far more permeable than they since have become. For example, the earliest compilations of lesbian literary theory were found in special issues of *Margins,* a small press journal, and *Sinister Wisdom,* a lesbian journal with wide community readership. Lesbian panels at the meetings of the Modern Language Association of America attracted hundreds of women in and outside academia, and one set of papers was published later in *Sinister Wisdom.*

Early theoretical constructions can be seen, first, as attempts to deconstruct the deviance model of lesbianism, in which lesbians were portrayed as unnatural, monstrous, "unsexed" creatures or pathetic victims of biology, and replace it with one stressing the normality, indeed desirability, of the lesbian choice. Adrienne Rich, for example, in her influential essay "Compulsory Heterosexuality and Lesbian Existence" (1979), coined the term "lesbian continuum" to describe what she saw as similarities, not differences, among various expressions of love between women. Female friendship, familial relationships, partnership, commitment, and sexuality all exist along the same continuum. Her conceptual framework (along with the historical scholarship of Carroll Smith-Rosenberg) became invaluable to the critics and scholars of the late 1970s and early 1980s. Perhaps the most important work to emerge from this period was Lillian Faderman's *Surpassing the Love of Men* (1979), a study of what she called "romantic friendship" in the lives and works of French, British, and American writers from the Renaissance to the present. Faderman argued that deep, committed, sensual relationships between women were not stigmatized until late in the nineteenth century, when a combination of factors resulted in the modern concept of the lesbian as social and sexual deviant. Faderman made no clear distinction between sexual and nonsexual relationships between women, a distinction that would become much more important in the decade to come.

Lesbian critics of this period also attempted to develop a perspective on cultural creativity that grew out of the particularity of lesbian experience. As contested as definitions of that particularity might be—what lesbianism means and who can be claimed for it was and continues to be an arena for intense debate—this notion of lesbian perspective, often identified as a view from the margins of patriarchal society, unified much of the lesbian criticism of the 1970s. One might say that the basic insight of lesbian critical theory was that the particularity of lesbian experience leads the writer to express her unique lesbian perspective in her texts and leads the reader-critic to see and therefore decipher these encodings of lesbian experience. Lesbian critics attempted to establish a tradition of overt and coded lesbian texts that would extend further the metaphors of vision and voice: to render lesbians visible in a society that had hitherto refused to notice them, to counter silence with lesbian speech. Armed with such theoretical notions, individual critics turned to canonical writers of the Western literary tradition, producing original and illuminating readings of the lives and works of such writers as Emily Dickinson, GERTRUDE STEIN, Natalie Barney, Renée Vivien, Radclyffe Hall, Willa Cather, and VIRGINIA WOOLF (see Cook, Jay, Marks, O'Brien, and Stimpson).

Less attention was paid initially to writers of color, since the lesbian movement then, as now, was predominately white. Some important work has appeared on figures of the Harlem Renaissance (see Hull). And the most influential and admired piece of lesbian criticism by far, Barbara Smith's "Toward a Black Feminist Criticism" (1977; originally published in *Conditions,* another community-based literary journal), contains a much-debated lesbian reading of Toni Morrison's *Sula.* In many ways, Smith's provocative essay marks a turning point not only for African-American feminist criticism but also for lesbian and feminist criticism in general. Numerous lesbians of color have followed Smith's lead, while, heeding their analyses, white lesbians have increasingly addressed the complex connections between race, class, gender, and sexuality (see Allen, Anzaldúa, Gomez, Moraga, and Shockley).

"Classic" lesbian theory, then, proceeded from a set of assumptions: that one could (with difficulty perhaps) define a category called lesbian; that lesbians shared certain experiences and concepts; and that discursive practices—literary texts, critical analyses, political theories—proceed from lived experience. The critical debates of the 1980s called many of these assumptions into question. Experience, authenticity, voice, writer, even "lesbian" itself—all have been scrutinized, qualified, and sometimes abandoned by theorists trained in DECONSTRUCTION and poststructuralist modes of analysis. Social construction theory, although a greater influence on historians than literary critics, also questions the validity of positing any kind of essentialist, universal, or transhistorical identity such as "lesbian." Furthermore, the criticisms raised by women of color caused white lesbian and feminist theorists to join them in completely reconceptualizing the nature of identity and the subject. Finally, these developments have been accompanied by a growing interest in gay and lesbian theory as a category of analysis, especially as gay male critics have increasingly incorporated feminist theory into their work. In gay and lesbian studies, lesbians are linked to gay men along the axis of sexuality, rather than being linked to heterosexual women along the axis of gender. This is obviously a shift from the 1970s notion of lesbianism as a variation, privileged or not, of female experience or identity.

Hence, by the late 1980s, lesbian critical theory had begun to engage strenuously in the critical transformations that have rendered the established notions of lesbian identity, history, and culture both unstable and problematic. On the one hand, many critics continue to envision lesbian existence and textuality as ontologically separate from that of gay men; they continue to work within a lesbian "perspective" and "tradition." They are less likely to be influenced by poststructuralism, except, perhaps, by the works of Francophone writers Monique Wittig and Nicole Brossard. They manifest the Anglo-American virtues of close reading, historical scholarship, and interest in links between life and text. But they no longer assume that literature is an unmediated expression of the author's inner truths; to that extent, all lesbian criticism has been influenced for the better by deconstruction. Instead, these critics attempt to deconstruct the lesbian as a unified, essentialist being and reconstruct her as a metaphor or subject position. In these formulations, the lesbian most often represents a disruptive space or subject position within the discourses of patriarchy. To that extent, this critical position, as found, for example, in many of the original essays collected in *Lesbian Texts and Contexts: Radical Revisions* (ed. Karla Jay and Joanne Glasgow, 1990), the first published anthology of lesbian criticism, maintains clear ties to the theoretical position developed by lesbian feminists in the 1970s.

A number of other critics, on the other hand, challenge the central notions of lesbian feminism, although they do not necessarily reject the idea of lesbianism as a category in itself. Feminist-separatist lesbian theory posited lesbianism as a quintessentially female condition and consequently rejected the traditional stereotypes of the "masculine," highly sexualized lesbian as a patriarchal construction too often internalized by "inauthentic" lesbians. The "true" lesbian, recognizing her woman-identification, would reject all vestiges of patriarchal thought, sexuality, power, and role-playing. By the end of the 1970s this orthodoxy had generated its own opposite position, and lesbians were openly, if acrimoniously, debating sexuality, power, and gender roles. Theorists have articulated a "sex-radical" position that reemphasizes the sexual specificity of lesbianism, in contrast to the gender inclusiveness of earlier lesbian feminism. In addition, butch-femme role-playing, both historical and contemporary, has become an especially rich topic for discussions of lesbian self-presentation in literature, film, theater, and performance art. Esther Newton, for example, argues that the mythic figure of the "mannish lesbian" permitted early twentieth-century women to embrace explicit sexuality as part of their self-definition as lesbians. For Sue-Ellen Case, the butch-femme couple is the lesbian, or feminist, subject position par excellence. Less centered on lesbian *expression* than on lesbian *representation,* these critics offer provocative new ways to conceptualize identity, subjectivity, gender, and the lesbian body.

Finally, several other contemporary critics raise yet another set of questions about the tenets of traditional lesbian feminism. Some of these critics, although not all, developed their political and theoretical identities in

the 1980s rather than the 1970s and are more closely connected to gay male theory and politics than to classic lesbian feminism. They are likely to use deconstructive, psychoanalytic, and poststructuralist theories and methodologies. They may be instrumental in developing gay and lesbian studies programs or what is coming to be called "queer theory," and like Diana Fuss, they are critical of lesbian feminist tendencies to erase gay men from its theoretical framework. Like the previous group of critics, they are skeptical of the tendency within lesbian feminist theory to essentialize lesbian existence, to construct a unitary lesbian identity, and to privilege certain varieties of lesbian behavior over others. Instead, they offer an anti-essentialist, rigorously historicized construction of lesbianism along the axes of gender and sexuality, and often of race and class as well. Biddy Martin's work on lesbian autobiography, for example, offers a notion of lesbianism that "unsettles" the boundaries around identity, thus opening it up to differences (103). In this way, the lesbian becomes one manifestation of what Teresa de Lauretis calls the "ec-centric" subject, not a unique and special category in a world marked exclusively by gender dualism.

As the 1990s progress, we find particularly rich and fruitful debates ongoing among lesbian critics and theorists over the nature of self, community, gender, and sexuality. We can also note the growing presence of lesbian and gay theory in literary criticism overall. The collision of poststructuralist theories, postmodern texts, changing political realities, and increasing academic respectability with the traditional ideas of lesbian feminism is producing a continuous reevaluation and reconceptualization of the meaning of lesbian identity, writing, and theory. Lesbian criticism can only be the better for that.

Bonnie Zimmerman

See also FEMINIST THEORY AND CRITICISM.

Paula Gunn Allen, *The Sacred Hoop: Recovering the Feminine in American Indian Traditions* (1986); Gloria Anzaldúa, *Borderlands / La Frontera: The New Mestiza* (1987); Nicole Brossard, *The Aerial Letter* (trans. Marlene Wildeman, 1988); Judith Butler, *Gender Trouble: Feminism and the Subversion of Identity* (1990); Mary Carruthers, "The Re-Vision of the Muse: Adrienne Rich, Audre Lorde, Judy Grahn, Olga Broumas," *Hudson Review* 36 (1983); Sue-Ellen Case, "Towards a Butch-Femme Aesthetic," *Making a Spectacle: Feminist Essays on Contemporary Women's Theatre* (ed. Lynda Hart, 1989); Blanche Wiesen Cook, "'Women Alone Stir My Imagination':

Lesbianism and the Cultural Tradition," *Signs* 4 (1979); Gene Damon [Barbara Grier], Jan Watson, and Robin Jordan, *The Lesbian in Literature: A Bibliography* (1967, 2d ed., 1975); Teresa de Lauretis, "Eccentric Subjects: Feminist Theory and Historical Consciousness," *Feminist Studies* 16 (1990); Teresa de Lauretis, ed., *Queer Theory: Lesbian and Gay Sexualities* (1991); Lillian Faderman, *Odd Girls and Twilight Lovers: A History of Lesbian Life in Twentieth-Century America* (1992), *Surpassing the Love of Men: Romantic Friendship and Love between Women from the Sixteenth Century to the Present* (1981); Marilyn Farwell, "Toward a Definition of the Lesbian Literary Imagination," *Signs* 14 (1988); Jeannette H. Foster, *Sex Variant Women in Literature* (1956, reprint, 1985); Diana Fuss, *Essentially Speaking: Feminism, Nature, and Difference* (1989); Jewelle Gomez, "Imagine a Lesbian . . . A Black Lesbian . . . ," *Trivia: A Journal of Ideas* 12 (1988); Judy Grahn, *The Highest Apple: Sappho and the Lesbian Poetic Tradition* (1985); Bertha Harris, "*What We Mean to Say:* Notes toward Defining the Nature of Lesbian Literature," *Heresies* 3 (1977); Gloria T. Hull, *Color, Sex, and Poetry: Three Writers of the Harlem Renaissance* (1987); Karla Jay, *The Amazon and the Page: Natalie Clifford Barney and Renée Vivien* (1988); Karla Jay and Joanne Glasgow, eds., *Lesbian Texts and Contexts: Radical Revisions* (1990); Jill Johnston, *Lesbian Nation: The Feminist Solution* (1973); Elaine Marks, "Lesbian Intertextuality," *Homosexualities and French Literature: Cultural Contexts, Critical Texts* (ed. George Stambolian and Elaine Marks, 1979); Biddy Martin, "Lesbian Identity and Autobiographical Difference[s]," *Life/Lines: Theorizing Women's Autobiography* (ed. Bella Brodzki and Celeste Schenck, 1988); Cherrie Moraga, *Loving in the War Years* (1983); Esther Newton, "The Mythic Mannish Lesbian: Radclyffe Hall and the New Woman," *Signs* 9 (1984); Sharon O'Brien, "'The Thing Not Named': Willa Cather as a Lesbian Writer," *Signs* 9 (1984); Radicalesbians, "The Woman-identified Woman," *Radical Feminism* (ed. Anne Koedt, Ellen Levine, and Anita Rapone, 1973); Adrienne Rich, "Compulsory Heterosexuality and Lesbian Existence," *The Signs Reader: Women, Gender, and Scholarship* (ed. Elizabeth Abel and Emily K. Abel, 1983); Judith Roof, *A Lure of Knowledge: Lesbian Sexuality and Theory* (1991); Ann Allen Shockley, "The Black Lesbian in American Literature: An Overview," *Conditions: Five* 2 (1979); Barbara Smith, "Toward a Black Feminist Criticism," *Conditions: Two* 1 (1977); Carroll Smith-Rosenberg, "The Female World of Love and Ritual," *Signs* 1 (1975); Catharine R. Stimpson, "Zero Degree Deviancy: The Lesbian Novel in English," *Critical Inquiry* 8 (1981); Monique Wittig, "One Is Not Born a Woman," *Feminist Issues* 1 (1981); "Paradigm," *Homosexualities and French Literature* (ed. Stambolian and Marks); Bonnie Zimmerman, *The Safe Sea of Women: Lesbian Fiction, 1969–1989* (1990), "What Has Never Been: An Overview of Lesbian Feminist Criticism," *Feminist Studies* 7 (1981).

GENEVA SCHOOL

"True criticism is creation," Marcel Raymond wrote, "a recasting of the work of art, more conscious than the original and more transparent" (*Sel* 36). The convictions Raymond expresses in this definition of the task of the critic are those that brought together, not in the form of an exclusive commitment but in the name of elective affinities, Raymond himself, Albert Béguin, and Georges Poulet, as well as, in the second generation, Jean Rousset, Jean-Pierre Richard, and JEAN STAROBINSKI. The Geneva critics give primacy to the literary text, whose themes and figures they attempt to articulate in their critical writing. This textual approach enables them to seize a particular consciousness, the creative impulse or certain expressive patterns at work in the writings of an author or in a group of texts. They do not share a method or a theory, but rather a particular response to literature that engages them in the activity of interpretation.

For the École de Genève, reading is a vocation, and criticism begins as an intimate encounter with the text, where the reader surrenders to the subjective consciousness alive in the work. Critical writing is a response to the summons of the work and a form of creation; it is of the domain of HERMENEUTICS: "The work experiences itself in me. It finds in me its significance," writes Poulet ("Phénoménologie" 23). The desire to make the literary text the source and origin of their own critical discourse is the main characteristic of the Geneva critics. This became the enabling gesture: they could in this way avoid the biographical fallacy (while still acknowledging the presence of the author) as well as the simple historical approaches of the kind that French criticism, in the wake of Gustave Lanson, was still pursuing in the 1950s. Moreover, since the text appears to them as form and content inextricably bound (even though, as we shall see later, the emphasis may vary), their criticism was destined to go beyond the philological studies or the tracing of sources on which French academic criticism was founded (see PHILOLOGY).

The acknowledged masters are to be found outside institutional literary criticism, among philosophers (Wilhelm Dilthey, Henri Bergson, the phenomenologists), in *La Nouvelle Revue française* (Jacques Rivière,

Charles du Bos, Ramon Fernandez), and preeminently in one writer, Marcel Proust. The narrator's critical pronouncement in *À la recherche du temps perdu* that what one finds in a great artist is "one work, or rather, refracted across different media, one same beauty that they bring to the world" (ed. Pierre Clarac and André Ferré, 3 vols., 1954, 3:375) seems to resonate like a leitmotif in the works of the Geneva critics, provided, however, that we replace "beauty" by such concepts as "consciousness" (Poulet), "spirituality" (Béguin), or "obsession" (Richard).

For the Geneva critics, the literary text embodies one individual way of making sense, through writing, of the self and the world. Their critical project ultimately consists in pursuing across the whole *oeuvre* of an author (books, diaries, letters, fragments) the particular vision that creates the work. When it defines writing as the mark of a subjective consciousness, the Geneva school is still responding to Proust, for whom "style is a question of vision" and "the revelation of the qualitative difference there is in the way in which the world appears to each of us" (3:895). Thus PAUL DE MAN (who, like J. HILLIS MILLER and Shoshana Felman, was influenced in his early work by the Geneva school) argued that one must look for "what there is that is specific, particular, singular in each work. When one sees what nobody else has seen, one holds the singularity of the work, which will lead to the interpretation of its intentionality" (in Poulet et al., *Chemins* 101).

Yet, in spite of the primacy given to the text and the importance of aesthetic appreciation, the critics of the Geneva school have always insisted that their work brings them back to the consciousness, the *subject* in whom writing originates. Thus their larger claims: that they are tracing in their criticism the significant moments of a history of the imagination, of feelings, and of consciousness in the modern era. In this history, they bring to the foreground, in their writings as well as in their teaching, a number of names: Michel de Montaigne, Blaise Pascal, JEAN-JACQUES ROUSSEAU, Gérard de Nerval, CHARLES BAUDELAIRE, Henri Frederic Amiel, Marcel Proust.

To understand why all the critics of the Geneva school would acknowledge their commitment to these authors (while showing themselves reluctant to defend common doctrines, methods, or theories) involves a detour. In his book *Jean-Jacques Rousseau: La Quête de soi et la rêverie,* Raymond explores the significance of the phrase *rêver à la suisse,* current in the mid-eighteenth century. *Rêver à la suisse,* "to dream the Swiss way," to dream "Switzerland," he explains, is to be in the position of the lonely Swiss soldier exiled from home, lost in seeming nothingness (*rêver* was for a long time synonymous with vacuity of mind and lack of activity). Yet, as dreaming and daydreaming acquired positive values, this expression took on the meaning of a self-reflective activity: lacking thought, memory, or sensation, the mind knows nothing but the intimate sense of its own existence and discovers, to use Rousseau's phrase, "le sentiment de l'existence." In this moment of recentering, where the individual awakens to his or her "interiority," Raymond and his followers recognize the birth of modern consciousness, of the modern subject. Rousseau's "Cinquième Promenade," which recounts precisely this revelation and about which the Geneva critics have written so much, appears thus to be a founding text for the Geneva school.

The sense of exhilaration perceptible in Raymond's study suggests that his scholarly work has led him to another kind of recognition: the solitary soldier *rêvant à la suisse* has become the emblem of the Geneva school's critical concerns. The exile from some original moment or country (Rousseau, Nerval, Proust), the retreat and the reflective absorption in the self (Montaigne, Pascal, Rousseau, Amiel), the power of daydreams and dreams to bring about knowledge (Nerval, Baudelaire)—these are some of the fundamental themes of their criticism. Moreover, the Geneva critics could identify in this figure a tradition of contemplation and interiority born in their (metaphoric) country whose exponents had been not only Rousseau but Benjamin Constant, Etienne Pivert de Senancour, Amiel, and Charles-Ferdinand Ramuz. In 1956, at a time when the notion of a Geneva school was gradually being defined, Poulet wrote to Raymond: "All my life has been enriched by the presence of a peripheral reality and by the contemplation, from a distance, of a central country, which I only visited at long intervals. This central country always appeared to me to be situated around the Lake of Geneva, and not on the banks of the Meuse or the Seine" (*Correspondance* 15).

In this same text Raymond sketches a third notion: in its progress from nothingness to the sense of existence, consciousness must ultimately go back to the perception of the Other. As Starobinski remembers in a moving tribute to Raymond, he and his colleagues learned from their master to encounter poetry as the creative power of writing, as that which only can mend the division between self and the world. The Geneva critics, de Man declared, wish "to substitute for the unhappiness of consciousness the happiness of the work" ("substituer à ce malheur de la conscience le bonheur de l'oeuvre," in Poulet et al., *Chemins* 124). The phrase is ambiguous in a revealing way: the saving power *(le bonheur)* of the work belongs both to the original creation and to the critical writing. Richard's sensuous prose, the carefully delineated motions and rhythms that convey the thinking of Poulet, the clear reflective style of a Starobinski or Rousset, or the poetry of Raymond's and Béguin's prose—born in empathy—all reveal the ultimate convergence of criticism and literature, as exemplified in the work of the Geneva school.

With its faith in language and the conviction that the subject, and preeminently the poet, is able to speak him- or herself through language, the Geneva school opposes itself clearly to STRUCTURALISM and to DECONSTRUCTION, whose instruments it helped to shape. Indeed, one finds in deconstruction the same attention to writing and the same inclination to isolate the text from history in order to focus on the production of meanings. But whereas deconstruction unweaves the text in order to reveal the thread of language, the impulse of the Geneva critics goes the other way, attempting to show how language conjures up presence and meaning, even on the verge of madness, solipsism, or silence, as in the case of Nerval, Rousseau, and Stéphane Mallarmé (see STÉPHANE MALLARMÉ AND FRENCH SYMBOLISM).

The Geneva critics shared a number of persuasions and interests. They were bound by friendships (see, e.g., the correspondence between Raymond and Poulet, or between Béguin and Raymond) and the sense of a community centered at the University of Geneva (which at times had to extend to Zurich, Basel, Paris, Nice, Edinburgh, and even the Johns Hopkins University in Baltimore, where both Poulet and Starobinski taught). However, they all developed not only concerns but also a style of their own; it is thus important to define the work of each in its singularity.

With *De Baudelaire au surréalisme,* published in 1933, Marcel Raymond (1897–1981) inaugurated a new mode and a new epoch in French criticism. All the Geneva critics have recognized, often in the form of a first book, their debt to this remarkable study: as a history of modern poetry and a reflection on the essence of poetry as a *"vital* operation" (12), it provides not only original approaches to literature but also unique responsibilities for the critic.

"The poet's task is to shake man, to make him take heart in the presence of life and of the universe, while putting him in touch permanently with the irrational" (395–96). Turned toward meaning, looking inward (the acknowledged influence is that of Bergson's notion of a "connaissance du dedans"), the critic, with a generous attitude toward the text and a privileged ability to respond to the images and symbols of the poem, partakes

of the visionary power of poetic language. The seduction of Raymond's critical approach stems from the fact that it relies on, and even encourages, a motion of aesthetic appreciation and identification. It also establishes criticism as an autonomous activity, independent from the pragmatic, scientific, or political realms.

It is precisely this ability to define the subject beyond historical, political, and psychological determinations, as pure untainted consciousness, that Raymond recognizes in the autobiographical writings of Rousseau. He has thus remained the authoritative interpreter as well as the exemplary editor of the "intimate works" of Rousseau (the Pléiade edition, which he established in collaboration with Bernard Gagnebin, is a masterful work of erudition and commentary).

Albert Béguin's doctoral dissertation, published as a book in 1937, represents a direct response to the teachings of Raymond and to the lesson in criticism of *De Baudelaire au surréalisme.* Indeed, in his *L'Âme romantique et le Rêve,* Béguin (1901–57) probes into the depths of German Romanticism (see GERMAN THEORY AND CRITICISM: 2. ROMANTICISM) to demonstrate how, in their willingness to let dream and daydream direct their writing, the Romantics have led the way to a particular form of knowledge. The poetry of an E. T. A. Hoffmann, a Novalis, or a Jean-Paul embodies truth—spiritual, ontological—in the form of myth; it acts as a revelation: "Words have a truly magical power, which enables them to seize that reality which cannot be grasped through the intellectual faculties" (400). Less interested in the formal aspects of the literary text than Raymond, Béguin emphasizes, particularly in his book on Nerval, how in and through writing the existential (personal) and the mythical (spiritual) aspects of human existence can be brought together.

One perceives in Béguin's work an urgency, a tragic note quite different from Raymond's subdued lyricism. Béguin came back deeply puzzled and anguished from Germany, where he had spent five years (1929–34) teaching and writing his thesis on German Romanticism. In the revealing last chapter of his *Âme romantique,* he asserts forcefully that the absorption in the world of dreams and the nostalgia for a golden age and a happy origin can only become meaningful when they lead back to a sharper vision of the real world. Béguin's work as an editor of *Les Cahiers du Rhône* and *Esprit* (following his conversion to Catholicism in 1940), as well as his writings on Georges Bernanos, Paul Claudel, and Ramuz and his involvement in Resistance activities in the Second World War testify to his conviction that "we are totally engaged in history; meditating on the power of imagination can no longer be a form of free play, nor the satisfaction of mere intellectual curiosity" (*Création et destinée* 1:184).

The "where am I?" that resonates across the work of Georges Poulet (1902–91) is a philosophical question, and the logical consequence of the encounter between a reader and a text as he conceives it. This emphasis on the act or phenomenology of reading distinguishes him among the Geneva school critics; it also constitutes the lasting, although often unacknowledged, ground of his influences on subsequent critical theories. A keen expounder of the Geneva school criticism (though only by intellectual affiliation, for he never taught at the University of Geneva) he appears to be, together with Starobinski, its most idiosyncratic and most challenging representative.

Poulet has written articles and books not only on a large variety of French authors but also on English, German and American literature. Each new reading of an author produces new insights, new reflections, a further "turn of the screw" in a critical thinking that never wants to find a resting point. Thus, for instance, Poulet's different writings on Proust weave an illuminating, complex, and sometimes contradictory critical interpretation of the Proustian *oeuvre*. The critic relies meanwhile on a movement of abstraction from the objective content of the text, reaching beyond the themes, images, and existential patterns so as to "seize the thinking consciousness [*la pensée pensante*] of each of [his] authors in the absence of the objects that they have given themselves" (*Correspondance* 199).

One particular motif seems to lie at the source of his own work, which he phrases in temporal terms: "The time of the work of art is the motion through which the work moves from a state where it has no shape and no duration, to a state where it acquires form and duration. This then is a *genetic* motion, deeply subjective, and experienced from the inside" (*Le Point* 40). The critical gesture thus aims at seizing the writing in its originating moment, where Poulet does not place experience, sensations, or objects (unlike most members of the Geneva school, he wants to refute phenomenology), but a *cogito* (the Cartesian notion resonates across his work). This *cogito* appears as the simultaneous articulation of thought and consciousness; it coincides with the writing. It may express itself as a recognition of time, as Poulet shows in his monumental *Études sur le temps humain*, of space (*L'Espace proustien*), of indeterminacy (*La Pensée indéterminée*), or of a metaphor that patterns our minds (*Les métamorphoses du cercle*), but the same critical imperative remains: to trace writing back beyond the forms it

takes and the representation it offers and to show the point where language in literature works against referentiality.

In his preface to Jean-Pierre Richard's first book, *Littérature et sensation,* Poulet reveals how for his fellow critic writing originates in the body. He identifies the pattern of Richard's critical work as a motion that recedes from the images to the sensations, in order to "seize the act through which the mind, coming to terms with its body and that of the others, unites with its object in order to constitute itself as subject" (10). Indeed, in his work on GUSTAVE FLAUBERT, Nerval, Baudelaire, and Mallarmé, Richard (b. 1922) represents writing as a privileged form of experience: it enables the author's objective and subjective worlds to merge in the creation of a mental universe, "un imaginaire."

To compare Mallarmé in Poulet's criticism (where the poet is shown as striving to achieve a state of pure virtuality and subjectivity through the abolition of reality) with the writer who emerges from Richard's monumental study of the "museum of the Mallarméan imagination" (19), *L'Univers imaginaire de Mallarmé,* is to be confronted with the full scope of the Geneva school's critical approaches. While Richard also studies consciousness, he probes into its depth with the conviction that subjectivity not only is reflective but "manifests itself as well in sensations, feelings, daydreams" (17). When read as a "vast, self-echoing poem," even Mallarmé's *oeuvre* can be shown to originate in the flesh. Not surprisingly, Richard's more recent studies, which focus on the obsessional figures and "the logic of the senses" (38) that speak in the writer's text, reveal an allegiance to psychoanalysis.

No member of the Geneva school has shown a greater awareness of the hidden assumptions and difficulties of the textual approach than Jean Rousset (b. 1910). He reminds us that "the best we can achieve is to convey our *present* experience of the lasting grounds of imagination that get transmitted to us in the life of forms" (*L'Intérieur* 8). Like Starobinski, Rousset shows an acute awareness, perceptible even in the cautious style of his *essais critiques,* that in literary criticism the epistemological separation of the perceiving subject from the object of study is always difficult to achieve, for identification is a necessary condition of reading. He knows too that when the critic concentrates on the formal aspects of the text (Rousset is naturally reluctant to use the word "structure"), he always runs the risk of emptying these forms of their subjective contents.

Rousset's writings thus reveal an exemplary critical lucidity combined with a remarkable ability to respond to the formal determinations inherent in a particular genre or form. He maintains a careful equipoise between formal analysis and thematic criticism, which he applies sometimes to genres (e.g., epistolary novels), to a period (see his early, groundbreaking study of the baroque imagination), to figures such as Don Juan or Narcissus, and to individual authors. He is thus able to demonstrate how, in the words of PAUL VALÉRY, "the form itself yields ideas" (quoted in *Forme* vii).

"Nous étudions la parole qui cherche à annuler l'arbitraire du signe," writes Rousseau ("We study those utterances that aim at abolishing the arbitrariness of the sign," in Poulet et al., *Chemins* 112). This may well be the best definition of the imperative that lies at the source of the criticism of the Geneva school. That these words find their echo not only in the work but in the recent critical pronouncements of a third generation of critics attached to Geneva (Lucien Dällenbach, John E. Jackson, Michel Jeanneret, Laurent Jenny) suggests that the tradition is kept alive.

Evelyne Ender

See also PHENOMENOLOGY and JEAN STAROBINSKI.

Albert Béguin, *L'Âme romantique et le Rêve: Essai sur le romantisme allemand et la poésie française* (1939, rev. ed., 1956), *Création et destinée: Essais de critique littéraire* (2 vols., ed. Pierre Grotzer, 1973–74), *Gérard de Nerval* (1945, rev. ed., 1956); Georges Poulet, *La Conscience critique* (1969), *L'Espace proustien* (1963, *Proustian Space,* trans. Elliott Coleman, 1977), *Études sur le temps humain* (1949, *Studies in Human Time,* trans. Elliott Coleman, 1956), *Les Métamorphoses du cercle* (1961, *The Metamorphoses of the Circle,* trans. Carley Dawson and Elliott Coleman, 1966), *La Pensée indéterminée* (3 vols., 1985–90), "Phénoménologie de la conscience critique," *Quatre conférences sur la "Nouvelle Critique"* (1968), "Phenomenology of Reading," trans. Richard Macksey, *New Literary History* 1 (1969), *La Poésie éclatée: Baudelaire/Rimbaud* (1980, *Exploding Poetry: Baudelaire/Rimbaud,* trans. Françoise Meltzer, 1984), *Le Point de départ, Études sur le temps humain* 3 (1964); Georges Poulet et al., *Les Chemins actuels de la critique* (1967); Marcel Raymond, *De Baudelaire au surréalisme* (1933, rev. ed., 1986, *From Baudelaire to Surrealism,* trans. G.M., 1949), *Être et dire* (1970), *Jean-Jacques Rousseau: La Quête de soi et la rêverie* (1962, rev. ed., 1986), *La Sel et la cendre* (1970); Marcel Raymond and Georges Poulet, *Correspondance, 1950–77* (ed. Pierre Grotzer, 1981); Jean-Pierre Richard, *Littérature et sensation* (1954), *Proust et le monde sensible* (1974), *L'Univers imaginaire de Mallarmé* (1961); Jean Rousset, *Forme et signification: Essais sur les*

structures littéraires de Corneille à Claudel* (1962), *L'Intérieur et l'extérieur: Essais sur la poésie et le théâtre au XVIIème siècle* (1968), *La Littérature de l'âge baroque en France* (1953), *Le Mythe de Don Juan* (1976).

Paul de Man, "The Literary Self as Origin: The Work of Georges Poulet," *Blindness and Insight: Essays in the Rhetoric of Contemporary Criticism* (1971, 2d ed., 1983); Jacques Derrida, "Force et signification," *L'Écriture et la différence* (1967, "Force and Signification," *Writing and Difference,* trans. Alan Bass, 1978); Sarah Lawall, *Critic of Consciousness: The Existential Structures of Literature* (1968); Richard Macksey, "The Consciousness of the Critic: Georges Poulet and the Reader's Share," *Velocities of Change* (1974); J. Hillis Miller, "The Geneva School: The Criticism of Marcel Raymond, Albert Béguin, Georges Poulet, Jean-Pierre Richard, et Jean Starobinski," *Theory Now and Then* (1991).

GERMAN THEORY AND CRITICISM

1. Sturm Und Drang / Weimar Classicism

In the 1760s and early 1770s the literary movement commonly called Sturm und Drang (literally, "Storm and Stress") developed new modes of critical, theoretical, and artistic discourse that mark the beginning of literary and philosophical idealism in Germany. Both Weimar classicism, which evolved out of Sturm und Drang, and German Romanticism, which followed Weimar classicism at the turn of the century, extended the aesthetic, critical, and political potential already evident in the new modes of discourse. Ultimately this attempt to revolutionize poetic practice and aesthetic theory has its critical and theoretical roots in the eighteenth-century cultivation of sentiment, or what G. E. LESSING (1729–81) called *Empfindsamkeit.* Alexander Gottlieb Baumgarten (1714–62) in Germany and Johann Jacob Bodmer (1698–1783) and Johann Jacob Breitinger (1701–76) in Switzerland all reveal in their critical and theoretical writing this growing concern with aesthetics, with the subjective factors involved in the production and reception of art. Yet like Lessing, they never fully question the dominance of moral over aesthetic concerns.

With the advent of Sturm und Drang, however, this situation changed. A relatively small group of intellectuals that included Johann Georg Hamann (1730–88), Heinrich Wilhelm von Gerstenberg (1737–1823), Jakob Michael Reinhold Lenz (1751–92), Johann Gottfried von

Herder (1744-1803), JOHANN WOLFGANG VON GOETHE (1749-1832), and FRIEDRICH SCHILLER (1759-1805) began to experiment with new modes of theoretical and critical as well as poetic, dramatic, and fictional discourse. Because traditional distinctions between different types of discourse began to break down, through the dissociation of aesthetic and moral concerns or the interpenetration of literary and philosophical discourse, these new modes of discourse also made new models of interpretive practice necessary.

The dissociation of moral and aesthetic norms is already evident in Hamann's "Aesthetica in nuce: Eine Rhapsodie in Kabbalistischer Prose" (1762, "Aesthetica in nuce: A Rhapsody in Cabbalistic Prose"), an aphoristic, metaphorical, and highly idiosyncratic expression of the author's thoughts on the nature of poetic language and beauty. When Hamann asserts that "poetic language is the mother tongue of the human race" (Loewenthal 121) he also claims that language use reveals the speaker's subjectivity precisely because it is always to some extent poetic. But it is Hamann's own rhapsodic style that, by revealing his subjectivity during the act of writing, supplements his theoretical claims for a new type of interpretive practice. The implications of this new mode of critical discourse for the interpretive relations between writers, readers, and critics is particularly evident in two of Hamann's shorter articles, "Schriftsteller und Kunstkritiker" and "Leser und Kunstkritiker." If criticism wishes to make authors understandable to readers, it can no longer approach art in terms of preestablished rules but must uncover the hidden aesthetic relationship between art and creator (Loewenthal 148).

This "hermeneutic potential" inherent in the relationship between form and content became the focus of literary criticism during the period of German idealism. Herder, perhaps the most important Sturm und Drang theoretician and critic, went much farther than Hamann in his use of it as a critical tool. In his early criticism—for example, *Fragmente über die neuere deutsche Litteratur* [Fragments on modern German literature] (1767) and *Kritische Wälder* [Critical forests] (1769)—he uses the way language functions as an expression of mental, cultural, and historical circumstances to supplement interpretation (*Frühe* 209 ff., 288 ff.).

Instead of discriminating between good and bad art as a means of cultivating proper taste in aesthetic judgment, as in the Enlightenment, the goal of criticism was now to understand and explain a work of art as a means of enhancing individual or collective self-awareness. Particularly through an analysis of the idiosyncratic nature of language—idioms *(Idiotismen)*, rhythms, images, concepts—critics sought to enhance the reader's understanding of the aesthetic or cultural functions of art (*Frühe* 186, 189, 193 f.). Critical response to Goethe's *Die Leiden des jungen Werther* (1773, *Sorrows of Young Werther*), certainly the most controversial Sturm und Drang work, indicates how traditional Enlightenment criticism was no longer able to cope with this provocative shift in the relationship between morality and aesthetics. Only Lenz in his review of the novel recognized the necessity for judging *Werther* aesthetically in terms of conflicting cultural demands and not morally with respect to socially acceptable norms (Lenz, Mandelkow). The Shakespearean criticism of Sturm und Drang also provides insight into the aesthetic and cultural functions of literature. Not only Goethe, whose play *Götz von Berlichingen* reveals the impact of reading Shakespeare, but also Herder, Lenz, and Gerstenberg attempted to account for the complexities of Shakespearean drama. Like Goethe's essay on the Strasbourg Cathedral ("Von deutscher Baukunst," 1773, "On German Architecture"), which rejects the "uncharacteristic" ideals of French classicism and well-proportioned architecture, these essays are paradigmatic examples of how criticism could view art as an expression of a people and a time. At the same time, the cultural impact of art must be a product of the same interaction between individual and cultural environment involved in the creative act. The unity of time, place, and action typical of Greek drama and French classicism, these "shackles of the imagination," as Goethe calls them in his essay "Zum Schäkespears Tag" (1771, "On Shakespeare's Day," *Werke* 12:225), are absent in Shakespeare. Instead, it is the freedom with which he presents the conflict between "the individuality of the self" and the "necessity of the whole" that determines the "natural" form of his plays (225).

For many members of the Sturm und Drang movement, the potential effects of art are connected with a complex dialectical process of cultural change that involves history, language, and consciousness. This is especially true for Herder, as it would be later for G. W. F. HEGEL (1770-1831). Herder outlined this conception of historical and cultural evolution first in *Auch eine Philosophie der Gerschichte zur Bildung der Menschheit* [Yet another philosophy of history for the education of mankind] (1774), then extended it to include the humanistic ideals of Weimar classicism in *Ideen zur Philosophie der Geschichte der Menschheit* [1784-91, Reflections on the philosophy of the history of mankind] written under Goethe's influence while at Weimar. Not only did these historical writings help to establish historiography as an academic discipline but they also had a direct impact on

Friedrich Schleiermacher (1768–1834) and the development of literary and philosophical hermeneutics (see HERMENEUTICS: I. NINETEENTH CENTURY). By insisting that every culture has its own virtues and values and should not be judged by the standards of other cultures, least of all one's own, Herder's historical and cultural relativism makes interpretation and understanding absolutely essential cultural activities. Since cultural change occurs through the dialectical interaction of all the different parts of a culture evolving in a natural way (Herder, *Sämtliche* 5:509, 588), individuals can neither fully control nor predict this development through the use of reason but are subject to it in ways that prevent them from seeing it (5:505 ff.). This is where both art and criticism acquire important cultural functions as the interpreters of form.

Although Herder's early criticism reflects this interest, it is in such works as "Über die Würkung der Dichtkunst auf die Sitten der Völker in alten und neuen Zeiten" [1798, On the effect of poetry on the customs of peoples in old and new times] and *Vom Geist der ebräischen Poesie* [1782–83, On the spirit of Hebrew poertry] that he demonstrates how poetry and indeed all modes of literature not only are products and stimulators of this dialectic but can also provide insights into its workings. Form, whether a cultural or an artistic product of this dialectic, becomes the means by which reality can be known.

Herder's writings on language and consciousness also reflect parallel developments in literary theory and criticism. His "Über den Ursprung der Sprache" [Essay on the origin of language] (1770), on a topic that fascinated many eighteenth-century thinkers, reveals his critical disagreement with the then new philosophy of language prevalent in Britain and France (Denis Diderot [1713–84], JEAN-JACQUES ROUSSEAU [1712–88]). Herder's fundamental insight lay in connecting the development of language with the development of consciousness *(Besonnenheit)*. If language use involves all human intellectual and emotional powers, then it is a necessary medium for human consciousness and communication that cannot exist apart from its cultural context *(Frühe* 717, 722). This view makes language the mediator between the world of the senses and the world of the imagination: "The ability to use language *(Der Sinn zur Sprache)* has become our mediating and combinatory sense: we are creatures of language *(Sprachgeschöpfe)*" (Pascal 222). Since language regulates, much as Novalis would later claim, the relationship of individuals as thinking, feeling, and creative beings to their environment, literature itself acquires a mediating psychological and cultural function.

Even more significant was the new conception of human subjectivity that began to emerge during Sturm und Drang. The interdependence of mind and matter, idealism and materialism, implied by this mediating function of language privileged a new conception of mind and imagination that facilitated the development of new modes of poetic discourse. Herder's essentially Romantic notion of genius as a "total personality" involving all human capabilities, which he developed in *Übers Erkennen und Empfinder in der menschlichen Seele* [1774–78, On experiencing the human soul], is indicative of this new conception of subjectivity and represents an advance over the common eighteenth-century differentiation of the soul into relatively separate and distinct faculties. The interdependence of mind and matter, mind and medium, now became the focus of both literary and critical discourse.

Like Sturm und Drang, Weimar classicism is a literary movement and should be viewed as a part of the broader cultural transformation known as German idealism. Goethe and Schiller were the major figures, although Herder as well as Christoph Martin Wieland (1735–87) and Karl Philip Moritz (1757–93), professor of aesthetics in Berlin and a close friend of Goethe's, were also influential. The term "classicism," which did not come into use until the nineteenth century, is often somewhat misleading, since neither Goethe nor Schiller viewed their own literary or critical discourse as "classicist," although they certainly relied on classical sources and ideals in some of their works. Designating the period as "classic" *(Die deutsche Klassik),* on the other hand, reflects in part the desire to possess a national literature on a par with those of England and France. In his essay "Literarischer Sansculottismus" (1795, "Literary Sanscullotism"), written in response to complaints about the state of German letters, Goethe rejects this desire for a classic literature because it originates in situations of social unrest that actually disrupt cultural productivity. Instead, he points to the already considerable achievements of German literary culture, which had accomplished so much without the necessity of a social and political revolution.

As for Goethe's ideas on what, despite classical overtones, is still a discourse of idealism or Romanticism, they are best formulated in an essay he wrote for Wieland's *Teutsche Merkur:* "Einfache Nachahmung der Natur, Manier, Stil" (1789, "Simple Imitation of Nature, Manner, and Style," *Goethe on Art* 21). According to Goethe, artistic beauty does not depend on stylization or idealization of dualities, but on the dynamic balance between the real and the ideal, the particular and the general. The dominance of one over the other, form over content, leads to a loss of naturalness and natural beauty. Style, in turn, is determined by the dynamic relationship between the real and the ideal, with "simple imitation of nature" and "manner" representing stages in the development of art (21 ff.). In the parallel piece to "Simple Imitation," "Der Sammler und die Seinigen" (1799, "The Collector and His Circle"), Goethe focuses on the single creative act (33 ff.). Once again he distinguishes between a series of stages: representation of an individual object, conception of the genus or generic idea, and, what seems to be the final stage, the attainment of the divine. But it is only when the artist looks back once again, as it were, that complex art appears to unite the seemingly incompatible elements, a realist orientation that favors general truths, laws, ideas, and ideals and an idealist orientation in which the allegorical, the symbolical, the abstract predominates (60 ff.). It is this union of counteracting tendencies, of classic and Romantic, real and ideal, that defines the literary and critical discourse of Weimar classicism and German idealism.

But even when Goethe and Schiller strove for a "classical" mode of presentation, this "classicism" was still very distant from the neoclassical norms of the French Enlightenment. In fact, it was Schiller who rightly called *Iphigenie auf Tauris* (1787, *Iphigenie on Taurus*), which had perhaps benefited most from Goethe's encounter with classical antiquity, "astonishingly modern and un-Greek." This is even more true of *Wilhelm Meisters Lehrjahre* (1795–96, *Wilhelm Meister's Apprenticeship*), along with Moritz's *Anton Reiser* (1785–90) one of the early German Bildungsromans dealing with contemporary life. This quintessential product of German idealism had such an enormous impact on the period, and not just on literature or literary theory and criticism, that Friedrich Schlegel (1772–1829) put it on a par with the French Revolution and Johann Gottlieb Fichte's *Die Grundlage der gesammten Wissenschaftslehre* (1794–95, *Foundations of the Entire Theory of Knowledge*) as one of the tendencies of the age (Athenaeum Fragment 216, *Schriften* 95–96). For Goethe, here as elsewhere, the author's task is to be both realistic and symbolic, to make inner truth or natural law "visible" through its manner of presentation.

Despite the efforts of Goethe, Schiller, and Herder in Weimar during the 1780s, it was IMMANUEL KANT's (1724–1801) *Kritik der Urteilskraft* (1790, *Critique of Judgement*), together with his *Kritik der reinen Vernunft* (1781, 2d ed., 1787, *Critique of Pure Reason*), that accelerated the theoretical development of German Romanticism. Particularly noteworthy is his influence on Schiller's aesthetic theory and, through Schiller, on philosophical idealism and the Romantic writers. The beautiful, the central concept in Kant's aesthetics, is a subjective form of experience constituting what he calls aesthetic judgment. An object is felt to be beautiful when the imagination, and not scientific knowledge (understanding or pure reason) or moral judgment (practical reason), initiates the free play of an individual's capabilities. Because beauty no longer depends on external criteria, but on the interplay *(Zusammenspiel)* of different cognitive functions (sensual or formal and conceptual) that produces pleasure, art is genuine only if it is autonomous. Kant's description of this free play as "purposiveness without purpose" *(Zweckmäßigkeit ohne Zweck)* caused much confusion, although as Hans-Georg Gadamer points out in *Wahrheit und Methode (Truth and Method)*, Kant was concerned with "dependent" as well as with "pure" beauty (*Truth* 44 ff.).

Herder unfortunately misunderstood Kant and in *Kalligone* (1800) attacked him for what he felt Kant had left out: the historical, the cultural, the complete psychological dimension. Schiller too feels that there are significant differences between his and Kant's aesthetic theory, which he describes in the so-called "Kallias" letters as "sensual-objective" versus "subjective-rational" (see Schiller to Körner, January 25, 1793, *Schillers Briefe*, ed. Erwin Streitfeld and Viktor Žmegač, 1983, 196). But despite substantial differences, the aesthetic autonomy Kant claims for art, insofar as it involves both the beauty of form as well as the constraints of conceptual thought or ideas, does bring all our emotional and cognitive powers into play. In fact, it is the very indeterminacy of the relations between these different cognitive functions that produces the aesthetic effect in the recipient. The Pandora's box of aesthetic theory and critical practice had finally been opened.

Schiller's response to Kant's aesthetics helped to fuel the transition from the classical idealism of Weimar to the more esoteric Romanticism of Jena, Heidelberg, and Berlin. In a number of influential works written during the 1790s, including *Über die ästhetische Erziehung des Menschen in eine Reihe von Briefen* (1795, *On the Aesthetic Education of Man, in a Series of Letters*) and *Über naive und sentimentalische Dichtung* (1795, *On Naive and Sentimental Poetry*), Schiller develops a more culturally oriented conception of idealist art and aesthetic autonomy. The harmonic ideal Schiller often strove for is still evident in "Über das Erhabene" (1793, "On the Sublime"), where the perfection of human nature depends upon the complete unity of duty and inclination: moral actions become beautiful when there is an absence of conflict between reason and sensuality and sublime when the sensual is freely subordinated to the rational (*Werke* 5:215 ff.). His preface to *Die Braut von Messina* (1803, *The Bride of Messina*), "Über den Gebrauch der Chors in der Tragödie" ("On the

Uses of the Chorus in Tragedy"), reveals even more clearly the aesthetic aims of this mode of classical idealism.

In the *Aesthetic Education of Man,* however, Schiller moved away from this harmonic ideal to a more Romantic conception of art that stresses the "alienated" relationship between individual and society and the cultural function of literature as a dialectical response to this alienation. In many ways, this essay is less a reaction against Kant than a response to the cultural alienation and the use of both realistic and allegorical modes in Goethe's *Wilhelm Meister.* For Schiller, as for Goethe, individuals retain their identity while their environment constantly changes only by changing and remaining unchanged, by adapting to ever-changing social and cultural conditions. Art thus becomes an instrument of aesthetic education that helps individuals cope with their increasing cultural autonomy by making them aware of the necessary interplay *(Spieltrieb)* between material and formal drives *(Stofftrieb and Formtrieb).* This alienated relationship between physical and human nature, classicism and Romanticism, is also at the basis of the distinction between "naive" and "sentimental" in *On Naive and Sentimental Poetry.* Here we find Schiller again trying to come to terms with the cultural function of art. The naive poet, in harmony with his surrounding environment, depicts reality as it is; the sentimental poet, no longer in harmony with nature, is a poet of ideas who raises reality to the ideal. Schiller, however, also distinguishes between different modes of sentimental art— satire, elegy, and idyll—each of which is defined by the artist's "subjective" response to particular relationships between the real and the ideal.

For Schiller, then, as for Goethe, art represents both a response to and, through the possibility of aesthetic education, a potential means of coping with the progressive alienation of intellectual and cultural life. In their reliance on both classical and Romantic modes to create an aesthetic world that would counter the oppressive nature of the real world and provide insight into its possible transformation, both must have felt that solutions to social and cultural problems were infinitely more complex and fundamental than had generally been recognized.

Steven Gillies

See also JOHANN WOLFGANG VON GOETHE, IMMANUEL KANT, and FRIEDRICH SCHILLER.

Johann Wolfgang von Goethe, *Essays on Art and Literature (Goethe's Collected Works,* vol. 3, ed. John Gearey, trans. Ellen von Nardroff and Ernest H. von Nardroff, 1986), *Goethe on Art* (ed. and trans. John Gage, 1980), *Werke* (ed. Erich Trunz et al., 10th ed., 1981); Johann Georg Hamann, *Hamann's Socratische Memorabilia* (ed. and trans. James C. O'Flaherty, 1967); Johann Gottfried von Herder, *Frühe Schriften: 1764–1772* (ed. Ulrich Gaier, 1988), *Herder on Social and Political Culture* (ed. and trans F. M. Barnard, 1969), *Outlines of a Philosophy of the History of Man* (trans. T. O. Churchill, 1800, reprint, 1966), *Sämtliche Werke* (ed. B. Suphan, 33 vols., 1877–1913); Friedrich Hölderlin, *Essays and Letters on Theory* (ed. and trans. Thomas Pfau, 1988), *Sämtliche Werke,* vol. 4 (ed. Friedrich Beiner, 1961); Immanuel Kant, *Kritik der reinen Vernunft* (1781, 2d ed., 1787, *Critique of Pure Reason,* trans. Norman Kemp Smith, 1965), *Kritik der Urteilskraft* (1790, *Critique of Judgement,* trans. James Creed Meredith, 1952); J. M. R. Lenz, *Briefe über die Moralität der "Leiden des jungen Werther"* (ed. L. Schmitz-Kallenberg, 1918); Erich Loewenthal, ed., *Sturm und Drang: Kritische Schriften* (1963); Karl Mandelkow, ed., *Goethe im Urteil seiner Kritiker,* vol. 1, *1773–1832* (1975); H. B. Nisbet, ed., *German Aesthetic and Literary Criticism: Winckelmann, Lessing, Hamann, Herder, Schiller, Goethe* (1986); Friedrich Schiller, *Ausgewählte Werke* (ed. Ernst Müller, 1954), *"Naive and Sentimental Poetry" and "On the Sublime": Two Essays* (trans. Julias A. Elias, 1966), *On the Aesthetic Education of Man, in a Series of Letters* (ed. and trans. Elizabeth M. Wilkinson and L. A. Willoughby, 1967); Friedrich Schlegel, *"Lucinde" and the "Fragments"* (trans. Peter Firchou, 1971), *Schriften und Fragmente* (ed. Ernst Behler, 1956); Karl Erwin Solger, *Vier Gespräche uber das Schöne und die Kunst* (ed. W. Henckmann, 1971).

Marshall Brown, *Preromanticism* (1991); Donald W. Crawford, *Kant's Aesthetic Theory* (1974); James Engell, *The Creative Imagination: Enlightenment to Romanticism* (1981); Hans-Georg Gadamer, *Wahrheit und Methode: Grundzüge einer philosophischen Hermeneutik* (1960, 5th ed., *Gesammelte Werke,* vol. 1, ed. J. C. B. Mohr, 1986, *Truth and Method,* trans. Garrett Barden and John Cumming, 1975, 2d ed., trans. rev. Joel Weinsheimer and Donald G. Marshall, 1989); Alexander Gillies, *Herder* (1945); Peter Uwe Hohendahl, *A History of German Literary Criticism, 1730–1980* (1988); Novalis, *Schriften* (ed. Richard Samuel, 1960); Roy Pascal, *The German Sturm und Drang* (1953); René Wellek, *A History of Modern Criticism: 1750–1950,* vol. 1, *The Later Eighteenth Century* (1955).

2. Romanticism

The literary theory and criticism of the Romantic movement in Germany, with a broader base than either Sturm und Drang or Weimar classicism, represents a further development of positions already in evidence since the 1760s and 1770s. For Heinrich Heine, adapting in book 1 of *Die romantische Schule* G. W. F. HEGEL's pronouncement about the end of art, Romanticism is simply the first phase in a period of idealist art, the "Kunstperiode," which began with JOHANN WOLFGANG VON GOETHE's birth and would end with his death. The break with the Enlightenment and with rationalism in general, however, is more extensive in Romanticism, although the antirationalistic tendencies of the period should not be overemphasized. Aesthetic theory and literary criticism, particularly during the early phases of the Romantic movement in Tübingen, Heidelberg, Berlin, and Jena, now reveal the strong influence of idealist philosophy: of IMMANUEL KANT's *Kritik der Urteilskraft (Critique of Judgement),* Johann Gottlieb Fichte's subjective idealism in *Die Grundlage der gesammten Wissenschaftslehre* (1794–95, *Foundations of the Entire Theory of Knowledge*), and F. W. J. Schelling's "Naturphilosophie" and "Identität-philosophie" (as well as somewhat later his *System des transcendentalen Idealismus* [1800, *System of Transcendental Idealism*] and *Die Philosophie der Kunst* [lectures 1801–4, pub. 1859, *The Philosophy of Art*]). Within a short span of time, from 1797 to 1800, Romantic writers laid the foundations for a new conception of art (e.g. Schelling, Hegel, and FRIEDRICH HÖLDERLIN in "Das Älteste Systemprogram des deutschen Idealismus" ["The Oldest System-Program of German Idealism," Frank and Kurz, and Pfau, *Essays and Letters on Theory*]) and for a new mode of writing that would combine literary, critical, and theoretical discourse (e.g., the fragments of Freidrich Schlegel or Novalis).

Because of its flexibility as a medium for both literary and aesthetic criticism, as well as poetic and philosophical expression, this new mode of poetic prose became the dominant mode of discourse, requiring not only greater participation by the reader in the critical and hermeneutic process but also a greater degree of aesthetic sensibility. This mixture of poetic, critical, and philosophical modes also led to the development of such highly poetic, theoretical novels as Hölderlin's *Hyperion,* with its explicit reflection on the nature of poetic discourse, Friedrich Schlegel's *Lucinde,* and Novalis's *Heinrich von Ofterdingen.*

Because this new mode of literary, critical, and theoretical discourse represents a radical break not only with Enlightenment poetics but also with literary and critical tradition in general, Friedrich Schlegel in his early critical essay "Über das Studium der griechischen Poesie" (1797, "On the Study of Greek Poetry") approached the problem that had fascinated so many eighteenth-century writers—the *Querelle des anciens et*

des modernes—no longer in terms of classical ideals and objectivity, as had Johann Gottfried Herder and FRIEDRICH SCHILLER, but in terms of a discourse of Romanticism that is now both objective and subjective. Schlegel's historical approach, adapted from Herder, led him to criticize neoclassical poetics for being too imitative of classical models and to praise modern poetry for its new *synthesis* of classical and modern that dissociates subjectivity from its imbeddedness in textuality as well as cultural reality. His opposition of old to new, as Hans Robert Jauss suggests, is thus more than a model of epochal change; it also represents a step toward a more thoroughly Romantic theory of art as a dissociative mode of aesthetic communication.

This fundamental aesthetic reorientation, for Manfred Frank one of the defining aspects of Romanticism, made it possible to use as well as write about discourse as a means of gaining insight into the contradictory nature of human existence (*Einführung in die frühromantische* 289 ff., 297 ff.). Humor, irony, wit, allegory, fragmentation—all are potential ways of revealing as well as dealing with existential contradictions, the counteracting forces by which individuals shape reality and by which they are in turn shaped. Fragments were the mode both Schlegel and Novalis favored most for developing their new poetics of Romanticism, in part because they required the active participation of the reader in the new poetic and aesthetic theories, in part because fragmentation reflects the fragmentary nature of existence (see Lacoue-Labarthe and Nancy 39 ff.; and Wheeler 10). Herder had made frequent use of this mode (as had Georg Christoph Lichtenberg, Hamann, and Johann Caspar Lavater before him), but it was Schlegel who first used fragments to approach discourse as process: as a product of social and cultural as well as psychological forces, and as a progressive moment in history.

The *Fragmente aus dem "Lyceum"* (1797, *Lyceum or Critical Fragments*) and the *Fragmente aus dem "Athenäum"* (1798, *Athenaeum Fragments*), together with Schlegel's fragmentary novel *Lucinde* (1799), became a model for this new mode of literature that was both systematic and nonsystematic, classic and Romantic: "It is equally deadly for the mind to have a system and to have none" is Schlegel's assessment in Athenaeum Fragment 53. Despite what seems to be a general lack of coherence, these aphoristic fragments, as Schlegel mentions in a letter to his brother, August Wilhelm, are in fact connected with one another (March 6, 1798). This unsystematic system, which the reader must reconstruct, becomes a paradigm for Romantic discourse in general. Novalis's best-known collection of fragments, which he described as *Blüthen-*

staub, "pollen" (1798, *Schriften* 3:301), convey in their radical fragmentariness the wholeness of his vision. Since all existence, all thoughts and actions, even life and death, are interconnected within a totality that can never be conceived of as such, the way fragments split apart existence actually reveals how interconnected everything is. By engaging readers in the hermeneutic activity of interpreting these hidden connections, the Romantic fragment involves them in the reconstruction of this totality. Life itself becomes a "colossal novel," real and at the same time fictional, fragmentary and yet also interconnected.

Irony, for Schlegel a combination of wit and allegory, is closely connected with this function of the fragment as a means of generating insight into the contradictory nature of reality. For Schlegel, "irony is a form of paradox" that involves a dual awareness of polarities that are not necessarily reconcilable: *savoir vivre* and "scientific spirit," "natural philosophy" and "philosophy of art," the "absolute" and the "relative," "the impossibility and the necessity of complete communication" (Lyceum Fragment 108, *Schriften* 87). What makes this insoluble conflict ironic is the way actions, decisions, and desires are counteracted by tendencies of which individuals are aware but over which they do not have complete control.

In Athenaeum Fragment 238 Schlegel describes this new form of discourse that was evolving as "transcendental poesie" *(Transzendentalpoesie):* "There is a kind of poetry whose essence lies in the relation between the ideal and the real, and which therefore, by analogy to philosophical jargon, should be called transcendental poetry" (*Schriften* 98). This modern poetic language combines "artistic reflection" and "self-reflection" with "transcendental raw materials" and a "theory of poetic creativity." Transcendental poetry is "Poesie" and "Poesie der Poesie" because poetic language as a medium itself becomes the focus of poetic reflection ("to represent oneself in every representation"). "Romantic poetry," as Schlegel says in the well-known Fragment 116, "is a progressive universal poetry," a mode of Romantic discourse "suspended" between "poetry and prose, inspiration and criticism, the language of art and the language of nature." In his "magic idealism" Novalis goes even further than Schlegel by making the relations between matter and mind reciprocal: "The world is a universal trope of the mind"; thoughts can be turned into things, things into thoughts, because of the way imagination links and at the same time dissociates perceptual and conceptual modes of thought.

An aesthetic orientation becomes enormously important for an individual's intellectual and cultural develop-ment, given this growing need to comprehend the hidden interdependence of subject and object or mind and medium and to cope with the often disparate realms of human existence. This is the principal reason why hermeneutics, the understanding and interpretation of literature and art, became an essential part of Schlegel's literary criticism and why in Schlegel's view literary criticism should also play a role in this educational process. This demand for a "total understanding" of literature that stresses both text and context is highly reminiscent of Herder and foreshadows Friedrich Schleiermacher's contributions to the development of literary hermeneutics as a discipline in the nineteenth century (see HERMENEUTICS: I. NINETEENTH CENTURY).

It also represents a response to what Schlegel called the "progressive, universal poetry" of Romantic discourse (Athenaeum Fragment 116, *Schriften* 93). In his articles on G. E. LESSING and Georg Forster, for example, he strove to achieve a socially relevant literary criticism that viewed literature not as isolated texts but as part of an ongoing process of cultural development. This meant grasping the author's mind as a whole, as he did in his article on Forster, or as part of a cultural context, as he did in his Lessing article, which, despite its polemic nature and its often inaccurate assessment of his writings, views Lessing as a precursor of his own critical practice and as a progressive, cosmopolitan, and on the whole enlightened critic of both the public and private spheres. His best-known essay, a critique of Goethe's *Wilhelm Meister,* is a masterful hermeneutic analysis of that work. For Schlegel, *Wilhelm Meister* initiated a new era of "objective poetry," though objective no longer meant classical, but a new mixture of subjective perspective and realistic representation of social details so typical of German Romanticism. By focusing on *Bildung,* an individual's process of intellectual self-development, Goethe was able to combine both fictional realism and symbolism.

Bildung, however, is a problematical concept in *Wilhelm Meister,* not least because it is connected with radical indeterminacy in the form of individual and cultural autonomy. Because the indeterminacy that results from this autonomy extends to all aspects of existence, including literature and criticism, *Bildung* in the sense of self-cultivation and self-development becomes an absolutely essential means of coping with this new reality. Within the discourse of Romanticism this means that the dissociation of moral from aesthetic concerns, of subject from object, mind from medium, increases resistance to understanding at the same time that it demands a greater effort of interpretation (Wheeler 13 ff.). Yet the impact of this new sense of *Bildung* extended beyond the limits of Romantic discourse to encompass a new conception of aesthetic discourse. The lectures August Wilhelm Schlegel gave in Berlin (*Über schöne Litteratur und Kunst,* 1802–4, *On Beautiful Literature and Art*) and in Vienna (*Über dramatische Kunst und Litteratur,* 1808, *On Dramatic Art and Literature*), for example, became well-known throughout Europe as the attempt on the part of German Romanticism to place literature and criticism within the larger context of individual and cultural self-development. Despite Karl Solger's view in *Erwin* (1816) that Schlegel's approach does not adequately reflect Romanticism, Schlegel's reliance on philosophical aesthetics and a genetic theory of poetry reveals a refined use of the formal, historical, and aesthetic methods first developed during the Sturm und Drang movement (Schelling often drew on Schlegel's lectures for examples he could use in his aesthetic writings).

Stimulated by Wilhelm von Humboldt's work in linguistics but also by Hamann, Herder, and the other Romantics, Schlegel explores the relations between language, cultural reality, and poetics. The sensitivity he brings to bear on poetic subjectivity and language as a medium of communication is always accompanied by an awareness of the cultural and historical context in which they are imbedded. Solger, however, was convinced that Schlegel and others did not properly understand the specific nature of aesthetic discourse. In *Erwin* he sets out in four fictional dialogues to link theory and criticism in a way that would make literary discourse hermeneutically more accessible. As in THEODOR W. ADORNO's *Ästhetischer Theorie* (1970, *Aesthetic Theory*) art is enigmatic, an "unstable synthesis" of the eternal and the temporal "that devolves into contradictions" (Solger 255). Not only does Solger view art as a mediator between contradictory aspects of human consciousness and existence, between reason and understanding, the eternal and the temporal, but his conception of art also transforms beauty into a dialectical phenomenon that contains or presupposes its opposite. This transformation of the concept of beauty, traces of which can be found in the writings of his close friend Johann Ludwig Tieck, already points toward the possibility of an "Ästhetic des Häßlichen" and "eine nicht mehr schöne Kunst." If art was to play a role in intellectual development, then it would do so by extending the realm of the aesthetic (see Wheeler 20 f., 127 ff.).

This connection between *Bildung* and aesthetic sensibility is also evident in the title of Jean Paul Richter's *Vorschule der Ästhetik* (1804, 2d ed., 1813, *School for Aesthetics*), intended as a primer for those seeking an aesthetic orientation and one of the early systematic approaches to literary criticism and theory in German Romanticism. This work on literary theory and practical criticism reflects the fundamental concern many Romantic writers had with discourse and the problem of *Darstellung* ("mode of presentation"). Jean Paul combines theory and practice in a creative, poetic manner ("horn of Oberon"), reminiscent in many ways of Romantic prose and intended to be a counterweight to more traditional, academic approaches ("horn of Astolfos") (*Vorschule,* preface to 2d ed., sec. 9). This figurative style fulfills his requirement that criticism be both poetic and philosophical. True poetry is situated between the "poetic materialists," a "copybook of nature," and the "poetic nihilists," the "haphazard painter" who "paints the ethereal in the ethereal with the ethereal" (sec. 3). As "a second world in this world" true poetry is a "beautiful imitation of nature" in which subject and object, the real and the ideal, interact as if they were in a "double mirror" (secs. 1, 4). The result is a "new nature" in which imagination *(Phantasie),* as the "elementary spirit of all the other powers" (wit and humor, the comic and the ridiculous, the ironic and the satiric), supplants beauty as the main criterion of aesthetic judgment (secs. 2, 8). Like Solger, Jean Paul is making the transition here to a new aesthetic.

Humor, however, is by far the most important mode in Jean Paul's poetic theory as well as in his novelistic practice; it also represents his most significant contribution to Romantic theory and criticism. As a type of "reverse sublime" (sec. 31), humor negates the limitations of empirical reality (the finite) by juxtaposing this reality with the world of abstract ideas and ideals, providing insight into this hidden dialectic and freeing the self temporarily from the limitations of existence (sec. 33). Like irony and wit, in other words, humor represents a way of coping with contradiction. Since humor makes these limitations tolerable by revealing how unimportant they often really are, "humoristic subjectivity" as an aesthetic orientation (sec. 34) is able to overcome the discrepancy between the real and the ideal, the "pain" and the "grandeur" of existence (sec. 33). This definition of humor comes very close to the Romantic conception of irony or other aesthetic modes as a procedure *(Verfahrensweise)* that provides insight into the contradictory nature of existence by stimulating a dual awareness of the counteracting processes involved.

Within the discourse of Romanticism, then, aesthetic insight represents the highest form of consciousness as well as artistic achievement. There are many reasons for this, but perhaps the most significant is the role imagination plays in all types of creative activity, including the creation of, as well as the response to, art. This is particularly evident in Schelling's *System of Transcendental Idealism,* in his essay "Über das Verhältniß der bildenen Künste zu der Natur" (1807, "Concerning the Relationship of the Plastic Arts to Nature"), and in his work on mythology. Mediating between subjective human nature and the objective world of the senses, the realm of the real and the realm of the ideal, imagination is what makes the cultural and psychological development of consciousness and self-consciousness possible. This is the reason Schelling privileged art within his system of philosophy and imagination within his conception of art. Since art is that mode of imaginative activity that through artistic or aesthetic intuition *(Dichtungsvermögen)* best reveals the dialectical unity of subjective and objective processes, it contains the greatest power or potential *(Potenz)* for developing consciousness. Because of this power to generate insight, Schelling accords to art a vital epistemological function it did not have in eighteenth-century poetic theory and to the systematic study of art, its historical interpretation, criticism, and theory, the task of exploring this epistemological potential.

Hegel too accords art a prominent place in his philosophical system, though it represents (together with religion and philosophy) only one potential means of gaining insight. His *Vorlesungen über die Ästhetik* (1835, rev. ed., 1842, *Aesthetics: Lectures on Fine Art*) explore the dialectical development of the absolute Spirit as a process in which the subjective spirit becomes conscious of itself. This developmental view of art can also be found in his *Phänomenologie des Geistes* (1806, *Phenomenology of the Spirit*) and generally reflects at this early stage both Schiller's and Schelling's influence. Art is a presentation, not a representation, of absolute spirit, an abstract entity that, whether individual or cultural, defies exact definition. This is why Hegel in the introduction to the *Lectures on Fine Art* stresses, as did Kant, the latent indeterminacy in the sensuous appearance of the Idea, an indeterminacy that makes potentially accessible not only the relationship between the reflective clarity of rational thought and the plasticity of sensual representation but also the horizon of creative intuitions and cultural values that motivate this relationship. Just as art differentiates the absolute identity of subject and object (Hölderlin's initial insight, which Schelling, Hegel, and Solger pursued in different ways), so the resulting indeterminacy, as Charles Taylor suggests, becomes a key to unlocking the dialectic (127 ff.). If art always contains traces of the horizon from which it sets itself off—emerging as it does within the context of older art forms—then different types or stages of art will depend on the dialectic inherent in the way they reveal this new horizon or absolute spirit in and through the mode of presentation. Despite his negative reaction to the contemporary discourse of Romanticism (which Schelling, Solger, or the other Romantics did not share), Hegel's historical approach to the modernity inherent in art nonetheless contributed to the development of modern criticism and theory.

Steven Gillies

See also G. W. F. HEGEL and HERMENEUTICS: 1. NINETEENTH CENTURY.

Heinrich Heine, *Die romantische Schule* (1835, ed. Manfred Windfuhr, 1979, *The Romantic School and Other Essays,* ed. Robert Holub and Jost Hermand, 1985); G. W. F. Hegel, *Vorlesungen über die Ästhetik* (1835, rev. ed., 1842, *Hegel's Aesthetics: Lectures on Fine Arts,* trans. T. M. Knox, 2 vols., 1975); Friedrich Hölderlin, *Friedrich Hölderlin: Essays and Letters on Theory* (ed. and trans. Thomas Pfau, 1988), *Hyperion: or, The Hermit in Greece* (trans. Willard R. Trask, 1965); Novalis [Friedrich von Hardenberg], *Schriften* (5 vols., ed. Paul Kluckhohn and Richard Samuel, 1960–88); Jean Paul Richter, *Vorschule der Ästhetik* (1804, ed. Wolfgang Henckmann, 1990, *Horn of Oberon: Jean Paul Richter's School for Aesthetics,* trans. Margaret R. Hale, 1973); F. W. J. Schelling, *Ausgewählte Schriften* (ed. Manfred Frank, 1985), "Concerning the Relationship of the Plastic Arts to Nature" (trans. Michael Bullock, *The True Voice of Feeling: Studies in English Romantic Poetry,* ed. Herbert Reed, 1968), *The Philosophy of Art* (trans. Douglas Stott, 1989); Friedrich Schiller, *Ausgewählte Werke* (ed. Ernst Müller, 1954); August Wilhelm Schlegel, *Vorlesungen über dramatische Kunst und Litteratur* (1808, *Course of Lectures on Dramatic Art and Literature,* trans. J. Black, 1815, rev. ed., 1846); Friedrich Schlegel, *Dialogue on Poetry* (trans. Ernst Behler and R. Struc, 1968), *"Lucinde" and the "Fragments"* (trans. Peter Firchou, 1971), *Schriften und Fragmente* (ed. Ernst Behler, 1956); David Simpson, ed., *German Aesthetic and Literary Criticism: Kant, Fichte, Schelling, Schopenhauer, Hegel* (1989); Karl Solger, *Erwin, Vier Gespräche über das Schöne und die Kunst* (ed. W. Henckmann, 1971); Kathleen Wheeler, ed., *German Aesthetic and Literary Criticism: The Romantic Ironists and Goethe* (1981).

Theodor Adorno, *Ästhetische Theorie* (ed. Gretel Adorno and Rolf Tiedemann, 1970, *Aesthetic Theory,* trans. C. Lenhardt, 1984); Ernst Behler and Jochen Hörisch, eds., *Die Aktualität der Frühromantik* (1987); Marshall Brown, *The Shape of German Romanticism* (1979); Manfred Frank, *Einführung in die frühromantische Ästhetik*

(1989), *Einführung in Schellings Philosophie* (1985); Manfred Frank and Gerhard Kurz, eds., *Materialien zu Schellings philosophischen Anfängen* (1975); Peter Uwe Hohendahl, *A History of German Literary Criticism, 1730–1980* (1988); Hans Robert Jauss, "Schlegels und Schillers Replik auf die 'Querelle des Anciens et des Modernes,'" *Literaturgeschichte als Provokation* (1970); Phillipe Lacoue-Labarthe and Jean-Luc Nancy, *L'Absolu littéraire: Théorie de la littérature du romantisme allemand* (1978, *The Literary Absolute: The Theory of Literature in German Romanticism*, trans. Philip Barnard and Cheryl Lester, 1988); Wolfgang Preisendanz, *Humor als dichterische Einbildungskraft: Studien zur Erzählkunst des poetischen Realismus* (1963, 2d ed., 1976), "Zur Poetik der deutschen Romantik," *Die deutsche Romantik* (ed. Hans Steffen, 1967); Charles Taylor, *Hegel* (1975); René Wellek, *A History of Modern Criticism: 1750–1950*, vol. 1, *The Later Eighteenth Century* (1955).

3. Nineteenth Century

The Napoleonic era and the rise of nationalism during the wars of liberation awakened hopes for liberal reform and social modernization in Germany; however, those hopes were quickly met by a series of repressive measures. The Karlsbad Decrees of 1819 introduced strict control of the universities as well as a complex system of censorship. In 1835 an additional law banned the writings of the Young German group, expressly including authors such as Heinrich Heine (1797–1856) and Carl Gutzkow (1811–78). Yet the net effect of political repression was to shift oppositional engagement from immediate political activity into the literary public sphere, thereby accelerating the politicization of literary criticism. As early as 1820, the seminal Romantic critic Friedrich Schlegel (1772–1829), cooperating with the restorationist forces in Austria, complained of the increasing partisanship in his essay "Signatur des Zeitalters" [Signature of the age]. During the decades prior to the revolution of March 1848, literary criticism became a vehicle for political dispute and an increasingly trenchant social criticism, in a process leading from the Romantics' elevation of the critical enterprise as a "poetry of poetry" to the leftist Hegelian agenda for revolutionary change. "Prose is a weapon," writes Ludolf Wienbarg (1802–72), "and we have to sharpen it" (Witte 73).

The literary criticism of the Young Germans responded to the ambiguous legacies of the Romantics and of JOHANN WOLFGANG VON GOETHE. The early Romantic conceptualizations of criticism as the completion of the work of art (rather than merely its description, analysis, or documentation) bequeathed to critical writers a license

to proceed beyond a given text to the presumably more urgent issues of politics. The progressive infinity of Romantic irony is thereby transformed into a sequential relationship between literary work and critical act, corresponding to the general sense of historical transition and, in Heine's *Romantische Schule* (1835, "The Romantic School"), the "end of the Wolfgang-Goethe age of art." Criticism surpasses the text, just as the Young Germans surpass Goethe; thus Heine: "The principle of the Goethean age, the idea of art is passing away, a new age with a new principle arises, and, how curious! . . . it commences with an insurrection against Goethe" (Witte 69). Such emphatic historicization of literature pervades contemporary criticism and theory, although the specific evaluations of history and the modalities of literature vary considerably. Schlegel's *Geschichte der alten und neuen Literatur* (1815, *Lectures on the History of Literature, Ancient and Modern*, 1818), initially presented as lectures to an aristocratic public in Vienna, mobilizes national literary history against the threat posed by the French Revolution, while simultaneously introducing history as a medium for reflection on literature. While the Young Germans rejected Schlegel's reactionary sentiments, they radicalized his historicism by insisting on the intervention of literature in political processes; thus G. E. LESSING and FRIEDRICH SCHILLER, cast as models of activism, are played out against Goethe, viewed, at best, as the apolitical author par excellence, at worst, by Ludwig Börne (1786–1837), as the obsequious "servant of despots." With the suppression of the Young Germans after 1835, a functional separation of public criticism and academic literary history began to emerge, as evidenced by the publication of Georg Gottfried Gervinus's *Geschichte der poetischen National-Literatur der Deutschen* [History of the poetic national literature of the Germans] (1835–42). A professor of history at the University of Göttingen, Gervinus (1805–83) insists on the separation of aesthetic criticism from history, which becomes a historicophilosophical narrative of national development from the Reformation to the present with its hopes for imminent change.

Opposing the conservative Romantic effort to impose "national value" through canonic choices, the Young Germans drew on the Romantic privileging of criticism to become, in Börne's words, "the great masters of criticism." Their criticism entailed an insistent subjectivity, an evaluative preference for prose, and a cultivation of wit, understood not as romantic fantasy but as a guarantor of civil liberty. Above all, criticism meant a rejection of aesthetic autonomy in the name of an operative political writing. The results included state suppression and a conservative campaign against the Young Germans, denounced as "sansculottes," "Francophiles," and "Jews."

Hegel's *Lectures on Aesthetics* were published posthumously in 1835–38 and certainly left a mark on Gervinus's literary history, but the leftist Hegelian positions of the 1840s took shape primarily through a critical reception of the *Philosophy of Right*. For the young Karl Marx (1818–83), Hegel has too quickly dissolved the contradictions between individual and general interests into the state as the putative guarantor of rationality. Civil society does not, however, allow for such a harmonious resolution of competing interests, since, as Marx argues, it is based on private property and capitalism, which presume the constant reassertion of class differences and a concomitant violence. In contrast to both the romantic imagination of a unified nation and the Young German assumption of a unified public as the addressee of its polemics, Marx underscores the divisiveness of a society of alienation, understood as the structural separation of the worker from the products of labor, individuals from each other, and humanity from nature. Alienation is presumed to generate necessary misunderstandings of the social condition, labeled "ideology," which is subject to criticism, modeled on the contemporary critique of religion by Ludwig Feuerbach (1804–72). Because Marx insists on the centrality of production to the social condition, his historiographical narrative of historical materialism entails a succession of "modes of production"—feudalism, capitalism, socialism—each marked by the "class struggles" between social groups defined by their relationship to the organization of labor.

Neither specific literary judgments nor general literary theory ever constituted the central concern of KARL MARX AND FRIEDRICH ENGELS. Yet the articulation of Marxist literary theory in the twentieth century could recur to Marx for several reasons. Heir to the cultural polemics of the Young Germans, he punctuates his political-economic and historical writings with references to literature, classical and contemporary. In addition, various issues grouped around the critique of ideology have direct ramifications for literary-critical projects. One of the most crucial is the image of a causal relationship between material experience and cognitive structures: "The sum total of these relations of production constitutes the economic structure of society, the real foundation, on which rises a legal and political superstructure and to which correspond definite forms of social consciousness. The mode of production of material life conditions the social, political and intellectual life process in general. It is not the consciousness of men that determines their being, but, on the contrary, their

social being that determines their consciousness" (Marx and Engels 85). Treated as a superstructural consequence of a materialist base, literature appears to be relegated to a secondary status, opening Marxist criticism to the accusation of reductionism. Yet the late Engels takes pains repeatedly to underscore the active role literature and other ideological formations play in social processes. Literature is most active, however, when it is least tendentious and when the subjective allegiances of the author recede behind the objectivity of aesthetic depiction. "The tendency must spring forth from the situation and the action itself, without explicit attention called to it; the writer is not obliged to offer to the reader the future historical solution of the social conflicts he depicts" (114). The logical uncoupling of authorial opinion from the cognitive validity of the text becomes even more extreme in comments on Goethe and Honoré de Balzac, where Marx and Engels defend the insights embedded in the literary works precisely despite the denigrated opinions of the writers as evidenced in other sources. Conversely, presumably correct political opinions did not necessarily lead to critical approbation. Measured against the engagement of the 1830s, this rudimentary Marxist criticism was more radical in its understanding of class conflict, while at the same time prepared to make apparently more conservative canonic choices.

During the nineteenth century, Marxist criticism was, of course, excluded from the universities and the established press, restricted instead to the organs of the socialist workers' movement. The central exponent, Franz Mehring (1846–1919), began to contribute to the Social Democratic press after the relaxation of the restrictive Anti-Socialist Laws in 1890. Mehring's work includes a continuous attack on the monarchistic celebration of the ruling Hohenzollern dynasty that pervaded Wilhelmine culture; a particularly extensive critique of such royalist and nationalist literary historiography in his *Lessing-Legende* (1893, *The Lessing Legend*, 1938), a revisionist account of eighteenth-century German literature; and his critical analyses of the theater of naturalism, in which he skeptically examined the claims of naturalism to represent the working class. Mehring's reticence with regard to naturalism could draw on Marx's rejection of tendentiousness and anticipated subsequent resistance to prescriptive programs for a "proletarian culture."

In the wake of the defeat of the 1848 revolution, literary production, and with it the erstwhile prominence of criticism, sank dramatically. A realist taste gained currency, especially through the *Grenzboten*, edited by Julian Schmidt (1818–86), but it was initially less a fundamental transformation of theory that took place than a revalorization of the connection between literature and history. Criticism ceased to represent an intervention into historical processes in the interest of radical change. For "it is not revolutions that build the progress of humanity but what lies outside them: science, which researches the law of nature, and art in the broad sense, which reigns over nature and forces her to serve the human will. Both are as bourgeois as they could possibly be" (Hohendahl, *History* 259). Art contributes to human progress not through activism but through the transfigurative idealization of a still inadequate reality. A rejection of the social-critical literature of the previous decades as fragmentary, false, and ultimately immoral ensues. This conservative inversion of Hegelian historicism is especially salient in the case of Robert Prutz (1816–72), editor of *Deutsches Museum,* a key journal of the postrevolutionary period.

The tradition of politicized literary criticism was further subverted by the commercialization of the press, which gradually transformed the critic into an employee rather than a representative advocate of a rational public. Moreover, the mass press addressed an increasingly heterogeneous public, and the critic could no longer presume a uniform cultural literacy within the readership. Earlier conventions of rational argument ceded ground to a literary journalism of feuilletonism, separated from other political concerns in an isolated section of the press and characterized by a subjective impressionism and relativism, renouncing the possibility of any objective claims. In the theater criticism of Theodor Fontane (1819–98) in the *Vossische Zeitung,* feuilletonism allowed the critic to draw implicit connections between literature and society, without, however, insisting on significant political consequences. Elsewhere this subjectivism appeared to supplant all issues of import with entertaining style and therefore participated affirmatively in the development of the modern culture industry. Karl Kraus (1874–1936), the Viennese cultural critic and editor of *Die Fackel,* focused on this trivialization of journalistic language (for which he blamed Heine), making it responsible for many of the social ills of the modern age. Subjectivist criticism culminated in the theater reviews of Alfred Kerr (1867–1948), who, treating his own prose and person as of equal status with the works, eventually provoked attacks from Kraus as well as Bertolt Brecht (1898–1956), who treated Kerr as the exponent of a "culinary criticism" of passive consumption.

Initially in opposition to the commercialized culture of the empire, the naturalist movement emerged during the 1880s as a first phase of the historical avant-garde.

Its literary-critical claims mixed nationalism, directed against a perceived French cultural hegemony, especially in the *Kritische Waffengänge* of Heinrich (1855–1906) and Julius Hart (1859–1930), with calls for more emphatically realistic treatments of social issues in *Die Gesellschaft* and the *Freie Bühne für modernes Leben* (later *Neue Rundschau*). A related theory for a rapprochement between literature and the natural sciences was articulated by Wilhelm Bölsche (1861–1939) in *Die naturwissenschaftlichen Grundlagen der Poesie* [The natural scientific bases of poetry] (1887). While the naturalists appealed polemically to the folk or the nation, a competing position developed in the circle around the poet Stefan George (1868–1933), whose journal, *Blätter für die Kunst,* cultivated a symbolist aestheticism and a hermetic isolation from the mass public.

Literary historiography after 1848 continued to treat literary history as corollary to an unfolding national teleology, with, however, considerable modifications of Gervinus's radicalism, leading gradually to an acceptance of the status quo. This evisceration of Hegelian progressivism prepared the ground for the methodological positivism of Wilhelm Scherer (1841–86) after the founding of the empire in 1871. No longer viewed as the development of an idea through time, literary history turned to an examination of factual connections of inheritance, biography, and experience. The tension between this natural-scientific conceptualization and the specific exigencies of cultural material is at the center of the work of Wilhelm Dilthey (1833–1911), whose studies of Novalis, Lessing, and Goethe in *Das Erlebnis und die Dichtung* [Poetry and lived experience] (1906) initiated the early twentieth-century movement *Geistesgeschichte.* Reasserting the status of hermeneutic understanding against a merely explanatory positivism, Dilthey also rejected the teleology of earlier historicism, viewing a studied epoch as a closed unit with no evident connection to the present, thereby precluding any critical agenda.

Two seminal thinkers outside of the centers of literary activity have profoundly influenced twentieth-century literary theory. FRIEDRICH NIETZSCHE (1844–1900) vigorously criticized the culture of the empire and the liberal bourgeoisie. In *Die Geburt der Tragödie* (1872, *The Birth of Tragedy,* 1909), an account of classical Greek drama, Nietzsche examines the dialectic between an Apollonian optimism of a principle of individuation and a prior Dionysian pessimism. Tragedy has its origins in the dithyrambic song of the chorus, which implies a pejorative judgment on later dramatic forms of realism and passive spectatorship, as well as on the enlightenment project of Socrates. Nietzsche's recovery of a mythic precondition for culture is echoed in the psychoanalytic theory of SIGMUND FREUD (1856–1939), whose work is replete with literary references (notably to Heine), despite its scientific and medical aspirations. The *locus classicus* of psychoanalytic literary criticism is in the fifth chapter of *Die Traumdeutung* (1900, *The Interpretation of Dreams,* 1913), where Freud examines *Oedipus* and *Hamlet* in the light of the "Oedipal complex," the antagonism of the son toward the father due to a desire for the mother. While other central categories of psychoanalysis have been appropriated by subsequent literary theory (e.g., displacement, melancholy, transference), Freud addressed various literary topics directly in writings such as "Delusions and Dreams in Jensen's *Gradiva*" (1907), "The Theme of the Three Caskets" (1913), "The Uncanny" (1919), and "Dostoevsky and Parricide" (1928).

Russell A. Berman

See also HERMENEUTICS and KARL MARX AND FRIEDRICH ENGELS.

Wilhelm Bölsche, *Die naturwissenschaftlichen Grundlagen der Poesie* (1887, ed. Johannes J. Braakenburg, 1976); Manfred Brauneck and Christine Muller, *Naturalismus: Manifeste und Dokumente zur deutschen Literatur, 1880–1900* (1987); Max Bucher et al., eds., *Realismus und Gründerzeit: Manifeste und Dokumente zur deutschen Literatur, 1848–1880* (1975–81); Wilhelm Dilthey, *Das Erlebnis und die Dichtung* (1906), *Poetry and Experience* (ed. Rudolf A. Makkreel and Frithjof Rodi, 1985); Georg Gervinus, *Shakespeare Commentaries* (1883); Heinrich Heine, "Die romantische Schule" (1885, *Sämtliche Werke,* ed. Manfred Windfuhr, vol. 8, 1979, "The Romantic School," trans. Helen Mustard, 1973, *"The Romantic School" and Other Essays,* ed. Jost Hermand and Robert Holub, 1985); Karl Kraus, *No Compromise: Selected Writings of Karl Kraus* (ed. Frederick Ungar, 1977); Karl Marx and Friedrich Engels, *Karl Marx and Friedrich Engels on Literature and Art* (ed. Lee Baxandall and Stefan Morawski, 1973); Franz Mehring, *Die Lessing-Legende* (1893, *The Lessing Legend,* abr. trans. A. S. Grogan, 1938); Friedrich Schlegel, *Dialogue on Poetry and Literary Aphorisms* (1968), *Geschichte der alten und neuen Litteratur* (1815, *Lectures on the History of Literature, Ancient and Modern,* 1859); Wulf Wulfing, *Junges Deutschland: Texte, Kontext, Abbildungen* (1976).

Russell A. Berman, *Between Fontane and Tucholsky: Literary Criticism and the Public Sphere in Imperial Germany* (1983); Peter Uwe Hohendahl, *Building a National Literature: The Case of Germany, 1830–1870* (1985, trans. Renate Baron Franciscono, 1989), *The Institution of Criticism* (1982); Peter Uwe Hohendahl, ed., *A History of German Literary Criticism, 1730–1980* (1988); Siegbert Prawer, *Karl Marx and World Literature* (1976); Jeffrey Sammons, *Heinrich Heine: A Modern Biography* (1979); Hartmut Steinecke, *Literaturkritik des jungen Deutschlands* (1982); Bernd Witte, "Literaturtheorie, Literaturkritik, und Literaturgeschichte," *Deutsche Literatur: Eine Sozialgeschichte,* vol. 6 (ed. Witte, 1980).

4. Twentieth Century to 1968

Early twentieth-century German criticism continues the strong tradition of nineteenth-century historicism. Beginning with Johann Gottfried von Herder's advocacy of cultural relativism and his rejection of restrictive neoclassical normative attitudes to literature, and later acquiring the consciously nationalistic character given it by figures of the late Romantic movement such as the brothers Grimm, German literary scholarship was by the late nineteenth century firmly committed to a genetic approach to literature. The achievements of the German philological tradition had given it great prestige and influence outside Germany, and since *Germanistik* as a discipline had always been associated with the idea of the unity of the Germanic peoples, the national unification that occurred in the late nineteenth century strengthened the domestic position of this tradition still further. Toward the end of the century it took on a rather self-consciously scientific character, and a stress on factual accuracy above all else arose that was parallel to Leopold von Ranke's dictum in historiography, *wie es eigentlich gewesen* ("how things really were"). Wilhelm Scherer (1841–86) had been the leading exponent of this view, but it was soon challenged by Wilhelm Dilthey (1833–1911), who set out a view of humanistic scholarship that was to be enormously influential; it laid the basis for the most pervasive and most characteristically German view of criticism of the first half of the twentieth century (see also HERMENEUTICS: 1. NINETEENTH CENTURY).

Dilthey argued that in the humanities what was important was not to establish causes in the succession of historical facts but rather to focus on the coherence and interdependence of phenomena existing at the same time. In this way he shifted the emphasis in the study of cultural phenomena away from antecedent causes and toward how cultural phenomena were part of a whole cultural situation existing at a particular time. This, he argued, required from the humanist empathy, imaginative interpretation, and judgment rather than scientific observation; its procedure was not the linear deductive method of science but the circular process of moving from the individual cultural event to the whole situation, and back again. The logic of Dilthey's distinction was faulty, relying as it did on vulgar prejudice about scientific method; imagination and interpretation are as necessary a part of scientific inquiry as factual accuracy is a part of humanistic study, and the movement from whole to part and back again is also characteristic of both. But Dilthey's argument was enormously influential, and it set the stage for the standpoint in the theory of criticism that was to be predominant in German criticism for many decades to come: *Geistesgeschichte,* the study of literature as a manifestation of the spirit of its age. The most monumental work of this kind was the four-volume *Geist der Goethezeit* [The spirit of the age of Goethe] (1923–57) by Hermann August Korff (1882–1963), which sees the essence of the 80-year period of JOHANN WOLFGANG VON GOETHE's life as first a contrast between, then a synthesis of, rationalism and irrationalism.

Geistesgeschichte provided the intellectual framework for the majority of prominent critics of this time. The young Ernst Cassirer's (1874–1945) first important work, *Freiheit und Form* [Freedom and form] (1918) was subtitled *Studien zur deutschen Geistesgeschichte,* and the most prestigious critic of the era, Friedrich Gundolf (1880–1931), contributed to the genre with his major work, *Shakespeare und der deutsche Geist* [Shakespeare and the German mind] (1911). As these two examples show, *Geistesgeschichte* in practice was quite likely to deal not just with the spirit of the times but also with the spirit of a people—the German people—over time. The common objection to *Geistesgeschichte* is that the search for *the* spirit of the time leads to single-factor, reductive analysis of all the diverse phenomena that make up an era, to unproven assumptions of a more integrated situation than is the case, to ideas so general that they could be applied to most other ages, and to unrealistic notions of the nature of individuality and originality. For example, Korff's leading ideas, "rationalism" and "irrationalism," distorted more than they explained when applied rigidly to all the products of an epoch.

The actual consequence of the demand for a more overtly interpretive history than the fact-obsessed Scherer had practiced was thus the reverse of what Dilthey had intended: less, rather than more, empathy for the concrete character of the historical situation. But from a broader perspective, what was remarkable about Dilthey's apparent challenge to the nineteenth-century historical tradition was that its success resulted in more continuity than change. The notion that literature was to be seen primarily as a historical document and manifestation of its time was really consistent with a historical tradition that was now in effect given a new form, a new rationale,

and new life, at precisely the time when far more decisive reactions against historicism were occurring outside Germany. In England and America NEW CRITICISM and in Eastern Europe RUSSIAN FORMALISM and PRAGUE SCHOOL STRUCTURALISM were beginning to treat literature as a distinctive phenomenon rather than as simply one more piece of historical evidence among others. This movement was clearly parallel to the new emphasis on analytical thinking in the turn from historical philology to structural linguistics with FERDINAND DE SAUSSURE and to the development of analytic philosophy in reaction to speculative metaphysics. German scholarship had been preeminent in all of these fields in the nineteenth century, and it is therefore perhaps not surprising that German scholars were not in the forefront of the reactions against the older attitudes when they came and that in the particular case of literary criticism the predominant German reaction to the past preserved rather than rejected its essentials.

Although *Geistesgeschichte* was the dominant mode of German criticism at this time, a more fundamental reaction against historicism was seen in the work of a small group of scholars whose contributions to literary analysis could on occasion show a degree of intellectual penetration that might have been hard to match in anything then going on outside Germany. Foremost among these was Oskar Walzel (1864–1944). Early in his career Walzel had taken on the task of finishing the literary history that Scherer had left unfinished at his death, but in the new preface to the completed work Walzel noted firmly that he had arrived at principles different from those employed by Scherer. In his 1924 essay "Vom Wesen des dichterischen Kunstwerks" [On the nature of the literary work of art] he was more explicit about the prevailing climate in German criticism. The current situation in Germany, he complained, was such that anyone who investigated literary structure was immediately written off as a mere formalist, even if the guiding principle was that the way to grasp the deepest meaning *(Gehalt)* of a literary work was through attention to its structure *(Gestalt)*. It was significant that here Walzel was reaching back to the terminology of the aesthetics of German classicism, which predated the historicism of the Romantic movement, and that he avoided the simpler terms "form" and "content" *(Inhalt),* the point being that the former could more easily be seen as a purely ornamental and external phenomenon separable from meaning, while the latter was too easily isolable from the context of a literary structure by the genetic critic, who could then find in it the undifferentiated historical material that was sought. Walzel's two books *Das Wort-*

kunstwerk [The verbal work of art] (1926) and *Gehalt und Gestalt im Kunstwerk des Dichters* [Meaning and structure in the poetic work of art] (1929) remain classics of their kind.

Robert Petsch (1875–1945) and Emil Ermatinger (1873–1953) were notable contemporaries of Walzel's whose work took a similar direction. Ermatinger argued against the prevailing historicism in his *Das dichterische Kunstwerk* [The poetic work of art] (1921), as did Petsch in his important 1930 essay "Die Analyse des Dichtwerks" [The analysis of the poetic work], that the critic's focus should not be on the precise origin of the various pieces of common experience that the poet had used in his work, but rather on what had been done with them by the unique creative talent of the writer. *Das literarische Kunstwerk* (1931, *The Literary Work of Art*), by the Polish philosopher Roman Ingarden, was another in the series of similarly titled books that analyzed the specific character of literature, this time from a more consciously logical and philosophical standpoint. The attempts by Ermatinger and Walzel to treat the whole range of theoretical problems of literary criticism made their works the only forerunners of the much later *Theory of Literature* by RENÉ WELLEK and Austin Warren (1949). Leo Spitzer's (1887–1960) two-volume *Stilstudien* (1928) is an important early attempt to use linguistic and philological information for interpretive purposes rather than as an end in itself. Käthe Friedemann made a remarkable contribution to narrative theory in *Die Rolle des Erzählers in der Epik* [The role of the narrator in the epic] (1910). Friedemann's major insights made almost no impact on her contemporaries but were to become the basis of modern thought about narrative many decades later. Arguing against a current view that narration should be "objective," that is, that it should present events so that the reader sees and judges them for himself or herself, she suggested that it was precisely characteristic of this genre that all events were presented through the consciousness of a narrator; consequently, narrative point of view was important for all narrative, and not just in the case of first-person narrators. Friedemann grasped the importance of the logical distinction between the author and narrator many decades before it became accepted generally and worked out its implications with great skill. The epic narrator, she said, is not the author who in writing is committing indiscretions about himself and others, disguised to a greater or lesser extent, which genetic critics never tire of trying to hunt down and uncover, but a figure existing entirely within the story who sees, feels, and evaluates all that is presented to us.

In the 1930s the advent of National Socialism had both immediate and long-term effects upon the character of German literary criticism. The immediate effect was to reinforce the more conservative aspects of the German critical scene and to entrench even more firmly the nineteenth-century conception of *Germanistik,* inherited from German Romanticism, as the historical study of the national past. *Geistesgeschichte* gained ground, while the developments associated with Walzel tended to fade, and this meant that the gulf between German- and English-language literary scholarship grew wider still. The even more important long-term effect was a diminution of the vitality and originality of the field that was felt for many decades; since the Nazi period, new perspectives in German criticism have been more likely to come from scholars who were in various senses "outsiders": from émigré scholars such as Leo Spitzer and ERICH AUERBACH, who left Germany altogether; from German-speaking Germanists who were not German nationals, such as the Swiss Emil Staiger or the Hungarian GEORG LUKÁCS; from foreign critics of German literature, such as E. M. Wilkinson; from German critics who were not Germanists but students of English or Romance literatures, such as Ernst Robert Curtius, Wolfgang Iser, Hans Robert Jauss, or Robert Weimann—in which group Spitzer and Auerbach could also be included. Even Wolfgang Kayser wrote his major theoretical work while living and working in Portugal. The Nazi era had in effect fostered an isolation from intellectual developments outside Germany that set back the clock in *Germanistik* within Germany. That the quintessentially German critical ideology of *Geistesgeschichte,* with its emphasis on the national past and the national spirit, was congenial to National Socialism was shown when its foremost practitioner, Hermann August Korff, jubilantly dated the third volume of his *Geist der Goethezeit* "Leipzig, am Tage der Einnahme von Paris, 14. Juni 1940" ("Leipzig, on the day Paris was taken, June 14, 1940"), and dedicated it "to the heroes of our struggle for freedom," an enduring stain on his monumental study; he attempted to remove the stain by omitting the dedication in the postwar reprint, which he assured his readers was an exact reprint of the first edition.

Not surprisingly, Marxist criticism made little impact on the German literary scene in the first half of the twentieth century. Georg Lukács (1885–1971), though a Hungarian, was the most noticeable Marxist presence in German criticism. Lukács published many of his major works in German, beginning with his *Die Theorie des Romans* (1920, *Theory of the Novel*) and including the important collection of essays *Deutsche Realisten des neun-*

zehnten Jahrhunderts [German realists of the nineteenth century] (1951). His Marxist criticism was consistent and orthodox: it located literature in the historical process as theorized by Marxism, with emphasis on class struggle. For him, "realism" meant faithfulness to the historical process so viewed. His *Geschichte und Klassenbewußtsein* (1923, *History and Class Consciousness*) profoundly influenced WALTER BENJAMIN (1892–1940), who as a result turned to Marxism after early interests in the language theory, mysticism, and myth of Novalis and J. G. Hamann. Benjamin now rejected both the aestheticism of the "George-Kreis" and Walzel's influence, which had been important in his early work. Largely ignored in his own time, Benjamin was rediscovered by THEODOR W. ADORNO, who published some of his work in 1955. Benjamin's Marxist writings had a considerable impact on younger scholars beginning in the late 1960s. Similarly, the short-lived FRANKFURT SCHOOL had comparatively little influence on the German criticism of its time but became influential in the later period.

The most important critic of the immediate postwar period was Emil Staiger (b. 1908), who worked in Zurich. Staiger's first major work was *Die Zeit als Einbildungskraft des Dichters* [The era as the imagination of the poet] (1939), wherein he set out a critical position from which, as he later correctly insisted, he never departed. As critical theory, it was virtually Dilthey's standpoint: the nature of the time determined poetic imagination, and it was to be captured by an imaginative empathy, which was necessary because of the gulf between the critic's era and that of the poet. Staiger excelled not as a theorist but rather as a brilliant reader and interpreter of literature, and it was as such that he was influential. Because of his preeminence as an interpreter, Staiger was later attacked (especially by left-wing critics) as one who relied on the critic's own inspiration almost in New Critical fashion, to the detriment of historical context. But this was a misconception, as is shown by Staiger's *Die Kunst der Interpretation* [The art of interpretation] (1951), which included a vitriolic polemic against any reading of poetry that was not biographical and historical: it was, he said, "sheer arrogance" to read poetry in such a way.

The most important theorist of the postwar period was Wolfgang Kayser (1906–59), whose 1948 treatise *Das sprachliche Kunstwerk* [The linguistic work of art] was exceptional in its erudition and in the breadth of its outlook. Kayser was able to draw upon scholarship in virtually all the European languages. Although it was more narrowly concerned with the analysis of literary texts than was Wellek and Warren's *Theory of Literature*, Kayser's book was the nearest equivalent to that work in

Germany at the time. Unlike Staiger, Kayser excelled in both the theory and the practice of criticism: his essay on Kleist as narrator has remained the most influential single piece of criticism on that subject for over 30 years.

Two landmark works of criticism that appeared during this time are *Mimesis* (1946, *Mimesis*), by Erich Auerbach (1892–1957), and *Europäische Literatur und lateinisches Mittelalter* (1948, *European Literature and the Latin Middle Ages*), by Ernst Robert Curtius (1886–1956). These are in some ways parallel cases: both were quickly translated into English and became enduring classics of world literary scholarship (something of a rarity for German literary scholarship at the time); both were written during World War II and first published just after it in Switzerland; both took a European rather than a German approach to literature, and neither author was a Germanist; and both were at odds with the Nazi government, Auerbach having been dismissed from his post for racial reasons, while Curtius had warned of its dangers in his 1932 pamphlet *Deutscher Geist in Gefahr* [The German mind endangered]. Of the two, Auerbach has been the more influential in the English-speaking world. His criticism is eclectic in the best sense, but even as it combines close reading of texts with reflection both on the author's circumstances and on the larger sociohistorical context, it retains a unified purpose: to show how literature draws us into asking fundamental questions about the human condition.

The two decades following World War II brought a gradual change in German criticism. These years saw a slow growth of *Einzelinterpretation* ("interpretation of individual texts") relative to other forms of criticism, but for the most part this development was not accompanied by the change in theoretical stance that had been its basis elsewhere. Most examples of *Einzelinterpretation* still situated themselves firmly in a biographical and historical context. Even when adapting to the critical climate that had been created by developments taking place outside Germany, then, German critics largely continued in their traditional biographical and historical orientation. The influence of New Critical theory (as opposed to practice) was slight, as can be seen from the fact that none of the major theoretical works of the New Critics was translated into German, and few references to them can be found in German scholarship of the time, until (and with the sole exception of) the 1959 translation of Wellek and Warren's *Theory of Literature*, which, however, met with hostile reviews.

The years 1967–68 constituted a turning point. The coming of age of the post-Nazi generation and world unrest over the Vietnam war combined with perennial dissatisfaction over the extreme conservatism of German universities to produce an upheaval that had marked effects on literary criticism and theory, chief among which was the greatly increased influence of Marxist criticism.

John M. Ellis and Evelyn W. Asher

See also THEODOR W. ADORNO, WALTER BENJAMIN, FRANKFURT SCHOOL, and GEORG LUKÁCS.

Erich Auerbach, *Mimesis: Dargestellte Wirklichkeit in der abendländischen Literatur* (1946, *Mimesis: The Representation of Reality in Western Literature,* trans. Willard R. Trask, 1953); Walter Benjamin, *Gesammelte Schriften* (ed. Rolf Tiedemann and Hermann Schweppenhäuser, 12 vols., 1972–80); Ernst Cassirer, *Freiheit und Form: Studien zur deutschen Geistesgeschichte* (1918), *Zur Logik der Kulturwissenschaften* (1942, *The Logic of the Humanities,* trans. Clarence Smith Howe, 1961); Ernst Robert Curtius, *Europäische Literatur und lateinisches Mittelalter* (1948, *European Literature and the Latin Middle Ages,* trans. Willard Trask, 1953); Wilhelm Dilthey, *Einleitung in die Geisteswissenschaften* (1883), *Das Erlebnis und die Dichtung* (1906), *Poetry and Experience* (ed. Rudolf A. Makkreel and Frithjof Rodi, 1985); Emil Ermatinger, *Das dichterische Kunstwerk* (1921); Emil Ermatinger, ed., *Philosophie der Literaturwissenschaft* (1930); Käthe Friedemann, *Die Rolle des Erzählers in der Epik* (1910); Friedrich Gundolf, *Shakespeare und der deutsche Geist* (1911); Roman Ingarden, *Das literarische Kunstwerk* (1931, *The Literary Work of Art,* trans. George B. Grabowicz, 1973); Wolfgang Kayser, *Das sprachliche Kunstwerk* (1948); Hermann August Korff, *Geist der Goethezeit* (4 vols., 1923–57); Georg Lukács, *Deutsche Realisten des 19. Jahrhunderts* (1951), *Geschichte und Klassenbewußtsein* (1923, *History and Class Consciousness,* trans. Rodney Livingstone, 1971), *Die Theorie des Romans* (1920, *The Theory of the Novel,* trans. Anna Bostock, 1971), *A történelmi regény* (1947, *Der historische Roman,* 1955, *The Historical Novel,* trans. Hannah Mitchell and Stanley Mitchell, 1962); Robert Petsch, *Gehalt und Form* (1925); Wilhelm Scherer, *Geschichte der deutschen Literatur* (1884, *A History of German Literature,* trans. Max Müller, 1899, 2d ed. by Scherer and Oskar Walzel, 1918); Emil Staiger, *Grundbegriffe der Poetik* (1946), *Die Kunst der Interpretation* (1951), *Die Zeit als Einbildungskraft des Dichters* (1939); Oskar Walzel, *Gehalt und Gestalt im Kunstwerk des Dichters* (1923), *Das Wortkunstwerk* (1926).

5. Contemporary

The years 1967–68 introduced significant change in German theory and criticism. In the previous 20 years German criticism had increasingly absorbed the work-centered *(werkimmanent)* practice of criticism prevalent elsewhere, without, however, abandoning its traditional biographical and historical concerns. Now several social forces combined to produce a major upheaval. The post-Nazi generation had matured, and its potential for anger over the fascist national past was heightened by world unrest over the Vietnam War: consequently, a new radicalism was now added to the longstanding dissatisfaction with the conservatism of German universities. A draft of new laws to govern the operation of universities written by progressive scholars and students at the Free University of Berlin in 1967 called for the universities to prepare students not only for professional posts but also "for their responsibility in society." Not surprisingly, the most noticeable change in German criticism was a greatly increased emphasis on political and social relevance in general and on Marxism in particular. What had previously been a static situation in German criticism now became a lively debate, and the general view was that a *Methodenpluralismus* had pushed aside the older orthodoxy. From a broader perspective, however, the German debate was still visibly restricted by the peculiar character of the German social and political climate. At a time when French thought, especially DECONSTRUCTION, was making a considerable impact in the English-speaking world, it aroused little attention in Germany. Similarly, German academic criticism was far less affected by feminism than was criticism in other countries, and the post-1968 role of SEMIOTICS in German criticism was much what it had previously been, that is, one limited to a marginal presence of the rather rigid "signals" approach of *Kommunikationsforschung* ("communications research").

The most noticeable result of these developments was a marked increase in criticism written from a decidedly left-wing viewpoint. It denounced the recent past in German criticism as empty formalism and ahistorical aestheticism, which it viewed as politically reactionary and by implication linked to the fascist catastrophe of the national past. But this was a misreading of German history: since the Romantic movement, German nationalism had always been linked with historicism, and *Geistesgeschichte,* with its emphasis on the national spirit and the national past, had been far more congenial to Nazism than the more broadly humanist perspective of Walzel's reprise of JOHANN WOLFGANG VON GOETHE's classical aesthetics. It would have been truer to say that recent criticism in Germany had always been concerned with historical context but that until now this concern had not been socially activist in nature.

The beginning of the contemporary theoretical debate on the relation of text to historical context emerged in reactions against the work of Hans-Georg Gadamer (b. 1900), whose major work, *Wahrheit und Methode (Truth and Method)*, was published in 1960. Following MARTIN HEIDEGGER, Gadamer insisted that historical objectivity is merely an illusion, for our judgment is conditioned by our necessarily limited historical perspective, or to use his word, *Horizont* ("horizon"). Because this horizon is steadily shifting, the interpretation of a text involves *Horizontverschmelzung*, the imaginative merging of the interpreter's horizon with that of the text. (Gadamer refers to this as hermeneutics.) This new reading will in turn be superseded, since a work's "meaning" is generated by the ongoing dialogue between past and ever-changing present. To recognize the contingency of our interpretation and its transitoriness is not, however, by any means to despair, for historical truth manifests itself in the persistence of works, institutions, and mores through time, that is, through "the tradition." Gadamer posits tradition as the basis of all our understanding yet as itself beyond rational comprehension: "Tradition has a justification that lies beyond rational grounding" (*Truth* 281). Critical inquiry serves the tradition by purging from the past those elements that now appear to have been merely local. In turn, since we are borne along by the stream of common tradition, we can come to recognize in ourselves and the works of our time those prejudices that are local and eccentric and distinguish them from those that are ratified by the tradition.

The conservative implications of Gadamer's investing tradition with such enormous authority generated a vigorous attack from the Left. Gadamer's sharpest critic has been his former student JÜRGEN HABERMAS. Influenced by the FRANKFURT SCHOOL's analysis of the subtle compulsion exercised by a society's structure, Habermas takes Gadamer to task for failing to recognize that language and culture can also be instruments of repression. Gadamer's blithe acceptance of the cultural status quo leaves no room for a radically adversarial critique. For Gadamer, tradition may be gradually modified but never seriously questioned or even disrupted.

Habermas's position was reinforced by the rediscovery and popularization in the 1960s and 1970s of the works of GEORG LUKÁCS (1885–1971), WALTER BENJAMIN (1892–1940), and two prominent members of the Frankfurt School, THEODOR W. ADORNO (1903–69) and Max Horkheimer (1895–1973). For Lukács, now seen as the more conservative Marxist, literary works are the unconscious reflection (*Widerspiegelung*) of contradictions inherent in "late capitalistic society." Literature for Lukács has a redeeming and possibly even a comforting function, precisely because it pits an imagined totality against a torn, capitalistic world. Yet, by concentrating too much on the work of art as "product," he underestimates, if he does not neglect, its power as a constituent factor in "forming" reality, that is, its power as "producer." Adorno, on the other hand, takes more seriously Karl Marx's exhortation to "ruthless criticism of all that exists" (Marx to Arnold Ruge, September 1843, trans. Jack Cohen, in Karl Marx and Friedrich Engels, *Collected Works*, vol. 3, 1975, 142) and therefore in his *Ästhetische Theorie* (1970, *Aesthetic Theory*) criticizes this failing in Lukács's theory (see also KARL MARX AND FRIEDRICH ENGELS). For him, text may not only reflect society but also deliberately negate it. In fact, the quality and extent of the negation of society (which for Adorno is almost always bourgeois society) in a work of art becomes the sole criterion of its value. A consensus on the exact nature of the relationship between economic base and artistic superstructure has remained as elusive for Marxists in Germany as it has elsewhere.

While growth in the scope of sociopolitical criticism has been the most striking feature of contemporary German criticism, the most important theoretical innovation has been RECEPTION THEORY (*Rezeptionsästhetik*). Two different though complementary strands of this theory were developed by Hans Robert Jauss and Wolfgang Iser, whose fields of study were French and English literature, respectively. Jauss, who was the first to call for a theory of reception in his provocative lecture at Constance, "Was heißt und zu welchem Ende studiert man Literaturgeschichte?" (1967, "Literary History as a Challenge to Literary Theory"), is primarily concerned with the development of a new, socially conscious literary history, while Iser's aim in his seminal work "Die Appellstruktur der Texte" (1970, "Indeterminacy and the Reader's Response in Prose Fiction") is to analyze the process of reading in the interaction of reader and text.

Criticizing formalism for its narrow preoccupation with aesthetic value and Marxism for its equally limiting insistence on defining aesthetic worth solely in terms of social function, Jauss strives in his own system to move beyond the limits of these opposing theories, without, however, sacrificing their central concerns: aesthetics and history. He proposes a linking of history and literature by extending the formalist notion of the evolutionary nature of all systems developed first by ROMAN JAKOBSON and Iurii Tynianov to social as well as literary history:

If on the one hand literary evolution can be comprehended within the historical change of systems, and on the other hand pragmatic history can be comprehended within the processlike linkage of social conditions, must it not then also be possible to place the "literary series" and the "non-literary series" into such a relation that comprehends the relationship between literature and history without forcing literature, at the expense of its character as art, into a function of mere copying or commentary? (Jauss, "Literary History" 18)

Positioning the reader at the crucial junction of text and time, Jauss hopes to lay the foundation for a literary history that reveals not only the interconnectedness of literary texts but also their effect on society, that is, their role in shaping and reshaping the consciousness of a multitude of readers. In actual literary analysis Jauss proposes moving synchronically as well as diachronically. He would examine the public responses to a "great work" by comparing them with the reception of other works popular at the same time and try, by means of a method borrowed from STRUCTURALISM and RUSSIAN FORMALISM, to isolate those aesthetic features and "devices" of the text that because of their novelty (here an aesthetic quality) can be said to have a mind- (or "horizon"-) expanding effect on the reader. Thus, Jauss views features that differ significantly from the "norm" and explode the traditional "horizon of expectations" as a kind of Darwinian mutation, capable of propelling literary history forward. Literature thus has for Jauss a socially formative function, while its aesthetic value is determined primarily by its challenge to tradition.

Although it would seem that for Jauss reader and text, past and present, stand in a dialectical relationship, when his system of thought is examined more closely, it cannot altogether escape the charge of reductionism usually associated with the two theories it has tried to supplant. His giving priority to the reader and consumption rather than to the author and production might be interpreted as redressing the disturbance in the balance between the two that results from the heavy emphasis placed on the latter by Marxist critics. But as Robert Weimann, of the former German Democratic Republic, points out in rebuttal, Jauss's system falls into subjectivism by making the consciousnesses of individual readers—even his groups are just class-indeterminate collections of individuals, Weimann argues—the determiners of history as the individuals respond to the literary text. As Weimann persuasively remarks, Jauss supplies no overarching principle for evaluating and judging either text or response. (Weimann offered his own alternative to Jauss in *Structure and Society in Literary History*, 1976.)

In time, Jauss himself became aware of the theoretical shortcomings of his system, and by shifting his emphasis from literary *reception* to *aesthetic experience* he tried to come to terms with them in his subsequent works, especially in his essay "Kleine Apologie der äesthetischen Erfahrung" (1972, *Aesthetic Experience and Literary Hermeneutics*).

Whereas Jauss was concerned primarily with the role of literature in history and society, Iser attempts to define and analyze what has generally been taken for granted: the processes of reading and meaning-formation by the reader. Iser sees reception theory as the continuation of structuralism and thus begins by treating the work as an as-yet-undetermined structure incorporating various literary devices. Like the Russian Formalists, Iser sees textual devices as stimulating the reader to generate meaning by filling in "blanks" or "gaps," as Iser calls them (*Act* 8–9, 167–70). But while these devices bring about a reaction, the *particular type* of reaction and the kind of tension arising between reader and text depends on all the experiential factors that have contributed to the formation of each individual reader's unique horizon. Meaning for Iser is generated by an interaction between reader and text that ultimately transcends both, belonging neither completely to the text nor to the individual reader. By speaking of a reader as "implicit" in the text, he hopes to avoid the problems involved in looking at actual individuals, but in so doing he opens himself to the same criticism made against Jauss, that of reducing the reader to an extension of the text. In his attempt to describe the reading process and deal with the text as a "living event" (*Act* 127–29), Iser elaborates Roman Ingarden's phenomenological model of reading by introducing a profusion of terms and phrases often borrowed from other systems ("repertoire," "strategies," "blanks," "vacancies," "primary" and "secondary negations," "wandering viewpoint," etc.), which sometimes illuminate but often obscure what he is doing.

Iser's view of reading presupposes, of course, a reader sufficiently open-minded to submit his or her own "horizon" to the challenge of a text, a text not nearly as devoid of inherent meaning or intent as Iser's theory requires. It is this very contradiction between the theoretical assumption and the actual result of Iser's system that has been the source of criticism for some and of admiration for others. His restatement in modern theoretical guise of what is in many ways a traditional view of the function of literature (reading as a form of self-realization) has had an impact in the German secondary school system, where his theory of criticism has been influential in the restructuring of the literature curriculum.

The reunification of Germany in 1990 has created a situation of mutual excitement and distrust among critics of both East and West, as it has more generally for the two populations concerned. If the critics of the former German Democratic Republic are not just to imitate those of the Federal Republic of Germany but to engage in productive cross-fertilization, their task will be to take what can be salvaged from Marxist literary theory in the face of communism's decay and reconcile it with the generally more conservative thought of the West in a way that does not abandon their common concerns. If the outcome is fruitful, the stimulus to new thought could lead German theory and criticism to regain the prominence it enjoyed in the earlier part of the century.

Evelyn W. Asher and John M. Ellis

See also JÜRGEN HABERMAS, HERMENEUTICS, READER-RESPONSE THEORY AND CRITICISM, and RECEPTION THEORY.

Theodor Adorno, *Ästhetische Theorie* (1970, *Gesammelte Schriften,* vol. 7, *Aesthetic Theory,* trans. C. Lenhardt, 1984), *Negative Dialektik* (1966, *Negative Dialectics,* trans. E. B. Ashton, 1973); Hans-Georg Gadamer, *Wahrheit und Methode: Grundzüge einer philosophischen Hermeneutik* (1960, 5th ed., *Gesammelte Werke,* vol. 1, ed. J. C. B. Mohr, 1986, *Truth and Method,* trans. Garrett Barden and John Cumming, 1975, 2d ed., trans. rev. Joel Weinsheimer and Donald G. Marshall, 1989); Jürgen Habermas, *Erkenntnis und Interesse* (1968, *Knowledge and Human Interests,* trans. Jeremy Shapiro, 1972), "Der hermeneutische Ansatz," *Zur Logik der Sozialwissenschaften* (1970, "A Review of Gadamer's *Truth and Method,*" *Understanding and Social Inquiry,* ed. and trans. Fred R. Dallmayr and Thomas A. McCarthy, 1977), *Theorie des kommunikativen Handelns* (2 vols., 1981, *Theory of Communicative Action,* trans. Thomas McCarthy, 1983–87); Wolfgang Iser, *Der Akt des Lesens: Theorie ästhetischer Wirkung* (1976, *The Act of Reading: A Theory of Aesthetic Response,* trans. Iser, 1978), "Die Appellstruktur der Texte: Unbestimmtheit als Wirkungsbedingung literarischer Prosa" (1970, *Rezeptionsästhetik, Theorie und Praxis,* ed. Rainer Warning, 1975, "Indeterminacy and the Reader's Response in Prose Fiction," *Aspects of Narrative,* ed. J. Hillis Miller, 1971); Hans Robert Jauss, *Ästhetische Erfahrung und literarische Hermeneutik* (1982, *Aesthetic Experience and Literary Hermeneutics,* trans. Michael Shaw, 1982), "Was heißt und zu welchem Ende studiert man Literaturgeschichte?" (1967, *Literaturgeschichte als Provokation,* 1970, "Literary History as a Challenge to Literary Theory," *Toward an Aesthetics of Reception,* trans. Timothy Bahti, 1982); Georg Lukács, *Geschichte und Klas-* *senbewusstsein: Studien über marxistische Dialektik* (1924, *History and Class Consciousness: Studies in Marxist Dialectics,* trans. Rodney Livingstone, 1971); Robert Weimann, "'Reception Aesthetics' and the Crisis in Literary History," trans. Charles Spencer, *Clio* 5 (1975, reprint, *Structure and Society in Literary History: Studies in the History and Theory of Historical Criticism,* 1976).

GIRARD, RENÉ

René Noël Girard (b. 1923), the son of the local archivist in Avignon, trained to enter his father's career, attaining the status of *archiviste-paléographe* at the École de chartes. After the war he came to the United States, where he studied medieval French history, literature, and culture. He has taught in departments of modern languages, comparative literature, and English, and in 1982 he assumed the Andrew B. Hammond Chair of French at Stanford University.

His work in the 1950s was concerned with the moral dilemmas of existentialist writers and focused upon such figures as JEAN-PAUL SARTRE, Albert Camus, and André Malraux. His interest shifted in the early 1960s from literature and philosophy to anthropology and psychoanalysis, and he became increasingly associated with the intellectual currents identified in North America as STRUCTURALISM and poststructuralism and linked with such figures as CLAUDE LÉVI-STRAUSS, ROLAND BARTHES, JACQUES LACAN, JACQUES DERRIDA, and MICHEL FOUCAULT. Since the late 1970s he has worked increasingly in the field of religious studies, where his work, in particular his theories of scapegoating, violence, and mimetic desire, has acquired a wide international renown.

Girard's first major book, *Mensonge romantique et vérité romanesque* (1961, *Deceit, Desire, and the Novel*), proposes that the phenomenon of desire in the writers of the great European narrative tradition is imitative or appropriative in origin rather than spontaneous or need-based. The major characters of Miguel de Cervantes, Stendhal, Gustave Flaubert, Fyodor Dostoevsky, and Marcel Proust (whose work he studies) borrow their desires from others, whom we as readers may identify as their "mediators" or "models." The books of these writers record the discovery of the "mimetic" nature of this phenomenon and disclose (to us and sometimes to the characters themselves) the romantic lie that hitherto concealed and enabled it.

In *La Violence et le sacré* (1972, *Violence and the Sacred*) Girard expands this literary insight into an account of cultural order at large. Turning to those monumental texts by which our culture has interrogated its own boundaries—Greek tragedy, the plays of William Shakespeare, and Freudian psychoanalysis, for example—Girard suggests that modern culture can experience what he describes as "runaway" mimetic desire because it lacks the protections that customarily inform communities classified by anthropologists as "primitive." Employing the philosophic language of difference utilized by French ethnologists (e.g., by Lévi-Strauss) and the concept of the primacy of the sacred to social order popularized by Émile Durkheim, Marcel Mauss, and others, Girard argues that within the primitive religious community, the sacred is itself violence that is effectively sequestered from human contact. Violence is likewise the sacred deviated from its safely transcendental locus and come down to wreak havoc upon inhabitants of the city.

Sacrifice, in these terms, becomes the mechanism by which the distinction between the two conditions—the peace before and the violence after—is sustained or reestablished. In a "sacrificial crisis" (*Violence and the Sacred* 39), in which the distinctions that would normally ensure harmony suddenly destroy it, human beings become, through their reciprocal attempts at establishing the original sacred conditions, in effect violent "enemy twins" (55–67). At this point, the collective substitution of a unique surrogate victim for the individual each "enemy twin" dreams of "sacrificing" can "miraculously" restore order, and Girard postulates that similar structurative paroxysms once both destroyed and enabled the community itself.

Toward the end of the 1970s, Girard began to probe a question raised at the conclusion of *Violence and the Sacred:* How is it possible that we moderns, who are fully aware of this founding mechanism, are not destroyed by it? Given, in Girard's view, the thorough reliance within the primitive universe upon both the scapegoat mechanism and its mystification, how is it possible that we can both articulate its conditions and live to tell about it?

The answer for Girard, expressed in *Des choses cachées depuis la fondation du monde* (1977, *Things Hidden since the Foundation of the World*), is the Christian gospel. The evangelical text, in particular the texts of the persecution and passion of Jesus, demystifies the mechanism of sacrificial violence and its founding effects. Appearing as the pivotal moment of a revelatory process that began, in Girard's view, with the Hebrew Torah, the Gospel formulates globally the internal discussion that Jesus conducts with members of his own community. Do you not see what you are doing? Jesus asks them. You say that

had you been there (at the event of the stoning of the prophets), you would not have participated. But in making that claim, in putting yourself at a sacred remove from those who stoned the prophets, you do the same thing. You stone the prophets once again. Moreover, those who come after you will (in my name) repeat your violent and differentiating gesture, calling themselves "Christians" and you "Jews." Historical Christianity, in Girard's view, is thoroughly permeated by such sacrificial misunderstandings of the gospel's revelatory anti-sacrificial message.

In other book-length publications on Job, medieval texts of persecution, and most recently Shakespeare, as well as in numerous essays, both collected and uncollected, Girard has continued to elaborate these literary, anthropological, psychological, and religious ideas, and his theories have attracted interest from a wide variety of disciplines—from the fields of political and economic theory, thermodynamic theory, and dance, for example. His work has inspired numerous colloquia, *homage* editions of journals, and most recently a traveling "Colloquium on Violence and Religion."

How might Girard's ideas apply to the study of literature? What Girard describes is not so much a method of reading literature as literature's method of reading us. The task that confronts the reader of Girard's writing is not to formulate a critical method that can be extracted from his works and applied to a text under literary-critical discussion but rather to allow his discussions of scapegoating violence or imitative desire to disrupt our most deeply held assumptions about subjects, objects, and the texts that contain them, even as those same assumptions, as Girard suggests, constitute already the subject matter of our most revered classical exemplars and even though in our sacrificial interpretation of their writings we continue to expel and suppress such powerfully "deconstructive" readings.

Sandor Goodhart

René Girard, *Le Bouc émissaire* (1982, *The Scapegoat*, trans. Yvonne Freccero, 1986), *Des choses cachées depuis la fondation du monde* (1978, *Things Hidden since the Foundation of the World*, trans. Stephen Bann and Michael Metteer, 1987), *Mensonge romantique et vérité romanesque* (1961, *Deceit, Desire, and the Novel: Self and Other in Literary Structure*, trans. Yvonne Freccero, 1966), *La Route antique des hommes pervers* (1985, *Job, the Victim of His People*, trans. Yvonne Freccero, 1987), *A Theater of Envy: William Shakespeare* (1991), *"To Double Business Bound": Essays on Literature, Mimesis, and Anthropology* (1978), *La*

Violence et la sacré (1972, *Violence and the Sacred,* trans. Patrick Gregory, 1977).

Michel DeGuy and Jean-Pierre Dupuy, eds., *René Girard et le problème du mal* (1982); Paul Dumouchel, ed., *Violence et vérité: Autour de René Girard* (1985, partial trans., *Violence and Truth: On the Work of René Girard,* ed. and trans. Dumouchel, 1988); Robert Hamerton-Kelley, ed., *Violent Origins: Walter Burkert, René Girard, and Jonathan Z. Smith on Ritual Killing and Cultural Formation* (1987); Alphonse Juilland, ed., *To Honor René Girard* (1986); Paisley Livingston, *Models of Desire: René Girard and the Psychology of Mimesis* (1992); Paisley Livingston, ed., *Disorder and Order* (1984); Andrew McKenna, *Violence and Difference: Girard, Derrida, and Deconstruction* (1992); Raymund Schwager, S.J., *Must There Be Scapegoats? Violence and Redemption in the Bible* (trans. Maria L. Assad, 1987).

GOETHE, JOHANN WOLFGANG VON

CHARLES AUGUSTIN SAINTE-BEUVE called Johann Wolfgang von Goethe (1749–1832) "the greatest critic of all ages," and MATTHEW ARNOLD termed him "the supreme critic," yet as late as 1955, RENÉ WELLEK could still complain that there existed "no systematic discussion of [Goethe's] literary criticism" (201). There are many good reasons why this should be so. Goethe seems not to have been interested in a systematic theory of literature. The same "fear of abstraction" that had led him to develop an alternative scientific method seems to have informed his work as a literary critic. Many of his most important theoretical pronouncements are obiter dicta scattered throughout minor essays, reviews, and conversations recorded by others. Some are presented in a dialogic form that refuses to reveal which of several positions, if any, is to be privileged. The majority refer to art generally rather than literature per se. Goethe also changed his mind, or seemed to, several times in the course of his long life. Thus, in order to speak of Goethe's "literary theory," one must not only assemble widely scattered comments but also remember their original contexts and beware of elevating passing remarks into fundamental theoretical axioms (Koopmann 30).

Clearly, the extent to which one can and should generalize from such unsystematic comments is questionable, yet Goethe's heirs have not hesitated to read their own ideological programs (German classicism, *Bildung,* dialectical method) into his writings, whereas Goethe himself sought to promulgate nothing of the sort. Among the worst culprits in this program of ideological recruitment are the *Geistesgeschichtler,* a school of German intellectual historians that was widely influential during the first half of the twentieth century, who went so far as to read Goethe's entire literary *oeuvre* as an extended allegory of a philosophical system. Ernst Robert Curtius, for example, sees Goethe's view of literature as a Hegelian "phenomenology of human existence" (52). Yet not only do such historians fail to respect the particularity of Goethe's theoretical pronouncements; the *Geistesgeschichtler* (and also, surprisingly, the German *textimmanent* school, or New Critics) fail to respect the "literariness" of his literary works by reading texts such as the discussion of *Hamlet* in *Wilhelm Meister's Apprenticeship,* as well as Goethe's drama *Torquato Tasso,* as pronouncements on literary theory (see, e.g., Curtius 32 and Wellek 204 ff.).

More recently, and not surprisingly, several studies have been published that seek to recruit Goethe as a progenitor of contemporary literary schools. Some, such as Benjamin Bennett's and other vaguely poststructuralist attempts to co-opt him, are wild and completely alien to the spirit of Goethe's work. Others, such as the arguments offered in Karl Fink and Max Baeumer's collection *Goethe as a Critic of Literature* that Goethe must be seen as having anticipated *Rezeptionsästhetik* (RECEPTION THEORY) or READER-RESPONSE THEORY AND CRITICISM, deserve to be taken far more seriously but remain ultimately unconvincing. Goethe rejected emphatically any concession to the psychology of the audience, asking in a review of Johann Georg Sulzer, "What does the gaping audience matter?" and arguing in his essay "On Harsh Judgements" that "the true artist must ignore his public, just as the teacher disregards the whims of his children, the physician the desires of his patients, the judge the passions of the litigating parties" (Wellek 203, 216).

Just as it has been claimed that Goethe's contribution can be resolved into one or another programmatic philosophy or reduced to an anticipation of contemporary schools, so it has also been argued that Goethe merely gave fuller and more elegant expression to ideas that had been initially formulated earlier in the eighteenth century. Helmut Koopmann, for example, contends that central ideas of German classicism such as verisimilitude *(Wahrscheinlichkeit),* aesthetic freedom, and the shift from a genre-based to a conceptually based aesthetics had been enunciated by Johann Christoph Gottsched as early as 1730 (33 ff.; see also GERMAN THEORY AND CRITICISM: I. STURM UND DRANG / WEIMAR CLASSICISM). Indeed, Koopmann goes so far as to view both Goethe and his friend and collaborator FRIEDRICH SCHILLER as mere "dilettantes," as "in a sense constructive collectors" (40).

This is certainly far too harsh a judgment, for Koopmann himself sees Goethe and Schiller as having raised philosophical demands on the critic to hitherto unprecedented levels, while resisting successfully the general decline of criticism into mere reviewing and *Geschmacksrichterei,* or "pronouncements on taste" (see also Curtius). My own contention is that Goethe contributed new, important, and influential ideas to the field of literary theory, the most important of which are original reflections on genre, the distinction between allegory and symbol, and the notion of *Weltliteratur,* or "world literature."

Goethe's development as a literary theorist, like his development as an artist, divides easily into three distinct phases. The first, conventionally termed his Sturm und Drang (or proto-Romantic) phase, can be seen as commencing with his speech "Zum Schäkespears Tag," composed in 1771 at the age of 22, and ending with his abrupt departure for Italy in 1786. Inspired by Johann Gottfried von Herder, Goethe rejects neoclassicism root and branch: his patron saints are Ossian and, above all, William Shakespeare. In this phase, Goethe develops no systematic literary theory; indeed, he rejects theory as "blocking the way to true enjoyment." The one and only touchstone of great art is the true "feeling" provided by "the fulfilled moment"; the artist who can create the "inner form" that bears such feeling is a genius. Goethe's concept of "inner form" was borrowed from Anthony Ashley Cooper, third earl of Shaftesbury, via Herder (see BRITISH THEORY AND CRITICISM: I. EARLY EIGHTEENTH CENTURY) but also has roots in Pietism and the hermetic tradition generally. Goethe comes closest to a systematic presentation of his view of literature during this phase in his reviews in *Frankfurter Gelehrte Anzeigen* written from 1772 to 1773 (*Gedenkausgabe* 14: passim; *Werke* 12:15–21). Wellek captures their spirit well when he claims, "They are all either satirical squibs or lyrical meditations rather than critical analyses. They all assert his dislike of the rationalistic, rococo civilization around him, and contrast the artificial with the natural and genuine, the greatness of the past with the littleness of the present" (203–4). One important theoretical distinction does emerge from these early reviews, however: that between "productive" criticism, in which empathy helps the poet to emerge from the poem, and the poem from the poet; and "genetic criticism," which seeks to interpret literary works in the light of their historical contexts.

Despite the attractions of youthful vitality and radicality in Goethe's early pronouncements on literature, it is only in the middle period of his career, the "classical" phase inaugurated by his journey to Italy (1786–88), that Goethe emerges as a mature critic. Wellek is surely right in seeing this phase not as a mere restatement of traditional neoclassicism but rather as an original synthesis of neoclassical elements and Goethe's own, earlier Sturm und Drang positions, whereby the work of art is seen as manifesting the very laws of nature's own unity, and the poet's subjectivity is seen as a privileged mode of access to that lawfulness. Goethe attempts to distinguish this more penetrating mimesis from crude imitation and projected subjectivity in his essay "Simple Imitation of Nature, Manner, Style" of 1789 (*Goethe on Art* 21–24).

Goethe's central theoretical preoccupation in this middle period is, however, the question of genre. The earliest evidence of his thinking on this issue is an essay of 1797, co-authored by Schiller, entitled "On Epic and Dramatic Poetry" (*Gedenkausgabe* 14:367–70; *Werke* 12:249–51), in which the differences between the epic and the drama are defined in terms of past and present action, active and suffering protagonists, outward- and inward-directedness, and rhapsodic and mimetic representation, respectively. While respecting the historical particularity of the texts they consider, Goethe's critical and theoretical pronouncements in this middle phase generally attempt (in typically neoclassical fashion) to articulate distinctions with a claim to universal validity and to insist on generic purity. Genre is also a central focus in Goethe's extensive correspondence with Schiller, an extraordinary window on the creative process in which two great authors respond to drafts of each other's works in progress and debate larger questions of literary theory.

Goethe eventually comes to view genres as rather like biological species, terming them "natural forms of poetry" (*Naturformen der Dichtung*) in his "Notes and Essays on the *West-Eastern Divan*" of 1819 (*Werke* 2:126–267). He contends that there are only three genuine genres, "that which narrates clearly, that which is enthusiastically excited, and that which is personally acting: epic, lyric, and drama" (187). Here he allows that genres can "work together or separately," arranges them around a circle (reminiscent of his color circle), and exhorts his fellow critics to fill in the intermediate forms until the circumference is full. These forms are to be understood neither as historical exemplars nor as traditional neoclassical categories but as structural "types." This latter aspect bears a striking resemblance to contemporary genre theories such as NORTHROP FRYE's or Paul Hernadi's.

Goethe's concept of genre as naturally or psychologically "given" a priori would prove tremendously influential: the fundamental triadic structure of his *Naturformen* continued to dominate German genre theory until well into the 1950s in variations such as Wilhelm

Dilthey's "forms of literary experience" *(Erlebnisformen der Dichtung),* applied to literature by critics such as Rudolf Unger and Wilhelm Wundt, and the theories of Karl Viëtor, Robert Petsch, and Emil Staiger (see HERMENEUTICS: I. NINETEENTH CENTURY and GERMAN THEORY AND CRITICISM: 4. TWENTIETH CENTURY TO 1968). Ironically, of Goethe's literary texts, what proved most influential were his novels, which, of course, are not legitimate *Naturformen,* but only impure admixtures at best.

Many of Goethe's most important theoretical texts of the middle period were originally published in, or intended for, his journal *The Propylaea* (1798–1800), among them the introduction to the first volume *(Goethe on Art* 3–16), "The Collector and His Circle" (31–72), and the unpublished sketches "On Dilettantism," co-authored with Schiller *(Gedenkausgabe* 14:179–85; *Werke* 12:239–44). As promised in his introduction, all of these essays "relate particularly to visual art and the arts in general" *(Goethe on Art* 6) and contain little or nothing on literature as such. "Literary Sansculottism," which appeared in 1795 in Schiller's journal *The Horae,* is a scathing response to an article that lamented Germany's lack of "classic national authors." Goethe argues that such authors arise only when a unified nation is caught up in the throes of great upheavals and that the price for obtaining them is not one he would be willing to pay. Goethe's classical phase can be seen as concluding with the publication in 1813 of the essay "Shakespeare and More Shakespeare" *(Gedenkausgabe* 14:755–69; *Werke* 12:287–98), Goethe's contribution to the *Querelle des anciens et des modernes,* in which he develops an elaborate and uncharacteristically schematic typology of binary qualities (heroic/romantic, real/ideal, necessary/free, should/would) associated with the ancient and the modern.

Historically, the literary theory of Goethe's classical period has remained the focus of interest. However, it is in the third phase of his career (roughly 1814–32) that Goethe first conceives, or gives definitive expression to, his most original and most important contributions to literary theory, namely, his deliberations on symbol and allegory and the concept of "world literature."

Wellek has accorded Goethe the honor of having been "the first to draw the distinction between symbol and allegory in the modern way" (210). The earliest evidence of Goethe's working on this problem dates from a return to his native city of Frankfurt in 1797: a treatise begun in that year, and eventually published in 1799, entitled "On the Subjects of the Plastic Arts" (appendix to Adams). However, Goethe's theory of allegory and symbolism is fully elaborated only in the third period, chiefly in his *Maxims and Reflections* of 1822 *(Werke* 12:365–547).

Prior to Goethe, "symbol" and "allegory" were functionally interchangeable terms (Adams 47). Goethe relegates much that had previously been termed "symbolism" to the "allegorical" and privileges the symbolic as the poetic power that is able not merely to refer to the universal but actually to embody it in the particular. He enunciates this distinction clearly in number 751 of his *Maxims and Reflections:*

> It makes all the difference whether the poet seeks the particular for the universal or sees the universal in the particular. Out of the former mode arises allegory, where the particular serves only as an instance, an example of the universal; the latter, however, is really the nature of poetry: it speaks forth a particular, without thinking of the universal or pointing to it. (*Werke* 12:471)

Indeed, the symbolic is able to generate the universal out of the particular "as the seed generates the plant or the poem such interpretations as we make of it. This is the sense in which the particular *contains*" (Adams 19). Thus Goethe's claim that "true symbolism is where the particular represents the more universal, not as dream and shadow, but rather as a living-fleeting [*lebendig-augenblicklich*] revelation of the inscrutable." The allegorical, on the other hand, "destroys the interest in the representation itself and drives the spirit back into itself, so to speak, and removes from its eyes what is actually represented" (*Werke* 12:471), draining out "the precious individuality of things in the process" (Adams 57). Goethe's 1799 article was already enough to impress his contemporaries greatly and served as the basis and direct inspiration for important theoretical deliberations on allegory and symbolism by Romantic critics and philosophers such as the brothers August Wilhelm and Friedrich Schlegel, F. W. J. Schelling, and, indirectly, SAMUEL TAYLOR COLERIDGE.

As he continued to study Western writers and discovered the literature of the Near East and, eventually, the Orient, Goethe's classicism broadened in his later years into a rich and sympathetic literary cosmopolitanism that led him to speak of a "world literature." This term was actually coined by Goethe, although he means by it something rather different from our contemporary notion "comparative literature." For Goethe, world literature is an evolutionary process whereby the various national literatures will gradually, through countless individual encounters and "corporate actions," unite in a grand synthesis (perhaps reminiscent of Northrop Frye's structuralist notion of an "order of words"). He sees the approaching epoch of "world literature" as an opportunity for authors "to look beyond their own surroundings" and thereby avoid "pedantic arrogance," as an opportunity for mutual support and correction, and as a development that everyone must now work to accelerate. And yet, even here Goethe cannot abandon the idea that the Greeks stand alone and unchallenged as a literary ideal (*Gedenkausgabe* 24:227–32, 260–62).

Aside from his theories regarding allegory and symbolism, Goethe's direct influence on the subsequent history of literary criticism and theory has been slight, chiefly the problematical morphological school (see Neubauer), which was in any case inspired more by Goethe's scientific works than by his literary pronouncements. His indirect influence, however, has arguably been vast, with Goethean elements discernible in the archetypal and structural theories of critics such as SIGMUND FREUD, C. G. Jung (see ARCHETYPAL THEORY AND CRITICISM), André Jolles, Vladimir Propp (see RUSSIAN FORMALISM), Frye, and perhaps even STRUCTURALISM generally (see Schneider).

Frederick Amrine

See also BRITISH THEORY AND CRITICISM: I. EARLY EIGHTEENTH CENTURY and GERMAN THEORY AND CRITICISM: I. STURM UND DRANG / WEIMAR CLASSICISM and 2. ROMANTICISM.

Johann Wolfgang von Goethe, *Der Briefwechsel zwischen Schiller und Goethe* (ed. Emil Staiger, 1966), *Conversations of Goethe with Eckermann and Soret* (trans. John Oxenford, 2 vols., rev. ed., 1883), *Correspondence between Schiller and Goethe* (trans. L. Dora Schmitz, 2 vols., 1877–98), *Essays on Art and Literature* (ed. John Gearey, trans. Ellen von Nardroff and Ernest H. von Nardroff, 1986), *Gedenkausgabe der Werke, Briefe und Gespräche* (ed. Peter Boerner, 24 vols., 1948–64), *Goethe on Art* (ed. and trans. John Gage, 1980), *Goethes Werke* (ed. Erich Trunz, 14 vols., 1948–60).

Hazard Adams, *Philosophy of the Literary Symbolic* (1983); Wilfried Barner, Eberhard Lämmert, and Norbert Oellers, eds., *Unser Commercium: Goethes und Schillers Literaturpolitik* (1984); Benjamin Bennett, *Goethe's Theory of Poetry: "Faust" and the Regeneration of Language* (1986); Ernst Robert Curtius, "Goethe als Kritiker" (1948, *Kritische Essays zur Europäischen Literatur,* 1950); Karl J. Fink and Max L. Baeumer, eds., *Goethe as a Critic of Literature* (1984); Helmut Koopmann, "Zur Entwicklung der literaturtheoretischen Position in der Klassik," *Deutsche Literatur zur Zeit der Klassik* (ed. Karl Otto Conrady, 1977); John Neubauer, "Morphological Poetics?" *Style* 22 (1988); Mark A. Schneider, "Goethe and the Structuralist Tradition," *Studies in Romanticism* 18 (1979); Fritz Strich, *Goethe*

und die Weltliteratur (2d ed., 1946, *Goethe and World Literature,* trans. C. A. M. Sym, 1949); René Wellek, "Goethe," *A History of Modern Criticism: 1750–1950,* vol. 1, *The Later Eighteenth Century* (1955); Joachim Wohlleben, *Goethe als Journalist und Essayist* (1981).

GRAMSCI, ANTONIO

Antonio Gramsci (1891–1937) was born in Ales, a village in southern Sardinia. Although intellectually precocious, he was not a healthy child: a serious fall at the age of four and an early disease caused him to be dwarfed and hunchbacked in later life. Financial difficulties beset Gramsci's family over the entire period of his schooling, but in 1911 a special fellowship permitted him to leave Sardinia to study at the University of Turin. While in Turin, he read literature, linguistics, and philosophy and began writing journalism. He became actively interested in socialism and in labor organizations during this period, and in 1921, following the difficulties encountered by the factory councils he had helped organize in the Turin automobile plants and elsewhere, he joined with a nucleus of socialist revolutionaries in splitting from the socialists and founding the Italian Communist party, the Partito Comunista d'Italia (PCI). In 1922 Gramsci traveled to Moscow as the PCI's representative to the executive council of the International, where he discussed revolutionary strategy with Vladimir Lenin and where he met his future wife, Julka Schucht. While outside Italy, Gramsci was elected to the Italian house of deputies (a post that, owing to parliamentary immunity, permitted him to re-enter Italy despite an arrest warrant that had been issued for him by the fascist government on account of his political activities). On November 8, 1926, however, Mussolini revoked all parliamentary immunity, and Gramsci was arrested and confined to the Regina Coeli Prison in Rome. He spent most of the rest of his life imprisoned in Turi on the outskirts of Bari in southern Italy. Due to seriously failing health, he was transferred to a special prison clinic at Formia in December 1933, and a while later, because of arteriosclerosis and pulmonary tuberculosis, he was moved to another clinic, the Quisisana in Rome, where he died of a cerebral hemorrhage.

In the arena of literary theory, Gramsci's primary contribution concerns the evaluation of culture, and in particular the crucial social role that culture is seen to play when construed from Gramsci's distinctively post-Marxian, early twentieth-century perspective. Although he published a good deal of material before his incarceration in the mid-1920s, primarily articles written for the newspapers and journals with which he was associated in Turin, such as *L'Ordine Nuovo* and *Avanti!,* and although there do exist significant differences between his early and later thought (especially in regard to BENEDETTO CROCE's influence and to Gramsci's view of Italy as a backward or an advanced economic society), the lasting contribution of Gramsci's sociopolitical and cultural writings is constituted by the massive collection known as *Quaderni del carcere,* the roughly 30 "prison notebooks" written between 1929 and 1935 primarily in Turi di Bari. For the most part it is on the basis of this body of work that Gramsci's theoretical contribution should be assessed.

Gramsci conceives of both literature within culture and culture within society in terms of his characteristic set of sociopolitical categories: hegemony, ideology, and the division between civil society and political society. From Gramsci's point of view, culture does not function as a mere reflection of the economic base; but if culture is not regarded as utterly contingent, neither is it envisioned as being a totally separate entity with its own internal group of mediating base-superstructure relations, as is the case in some competing social analyses. It is important to note that while Gramsci thus rejects both standard Marxist reflection theory (explicit in Georgi Plekhanov, implicit in much of GEORG LUKÁCS and Lucien Goldmann) and the Althusserian sort of mystification at work in current theories of parallel realms (in which each sociocultural category would have its own internal relations of base to superstructure), he never abandons the Marxian infrastructure-superstructure schema. Rather, he recasts the underlying notion of reflection, in which the vital economic base generates its masked and/or obfuscating reflective superstructure, by changing the nature of the relationship from one of *reflection* to one of *reciprocity.* It is this theoretical conception of mutually reciprocal forces that gives culture its authentic power in Gramsci's thought even as his thought retains, *grosso modo,* the traditional Marxist framework.

This assessment of the overall significance that Gramsci's work holds for literary theory should be complemented by consideration of two somewhat more specific issues: his rigorous historicism and his concern for popular, as opposed to elite, culture. In its openly historicist slant, Gramsci's work demonstrates his penchant for adopting other thinkers' critical categories and terminology (in this regard, those of Croce, Lenin, Vincenzo Cuoco, and Georges Sorel) as well as his eventual reworking of these prior concepts to his own ends. Gramsci's interest in cultural history also encompasses the history of folklore, as the cultural expression of Italy's subaltern classes, and it does so in such a forthright way that Gramsci may be seen as the modern father of the sociology of literature and culture in Italy. This combination of popular and historical studies is evident, too, in his examination of the phenomenon of "national-popular" literature, which he finds signally lacking in modern Italy.

Given the breadth of Gramsci's historicist perspective, his concept of the process of domination and oppression within human society, including cultural factors, is complex yet consistent. A social class dominates by attaining hegemony in civil as well as in political society, through the multilayered construction of a *blocco storico,* or "historical block," of social power. The dominating class, often made up of historically contingent alliances, such as that between the aristocracy and the church in Gramsci's own region of southern Italy, diffuses its ideologically motivated view of the world of human society, but it is important to see that in Gramsci's estimation ideology is not so much false consciousness as a distorted vision of what is in fact the historical truth of a particular social situation. Ideology, whether expressed in the form of political orations, sermons from the pulpit, or such popular literary forms as song and folklore, is thus construed as being an object of interpretation and understanding rather than of denigration. Indeed, one of the tasks of "the philosophy of praxis" (the term Gramsci adopted in his notebooks for historical materialism, in part to avoid the watchful eye of the prison censors) is to explain both the roots and the ramifications of the historical development of currently operative ideologies.

It is at this point that literature enters most directly into the Gramscian framework. As acts of social expression, at once individual and communal, the various forms of literature take part in a unique way, distinct even in comparison with the other arts, in the struggle for hegemony that makes up each modern society. On a different plane, criticism, too, can be seen to join in this struggle either explicitly or implicitly, through idealist evasion (such as in the writings of Croce) or through attempted sociocultural engagement (such as in the work of one of the often acknowledged models for Gramsci's own critical practice, FRANCESCO DE SANCTIS). In the more advanced countries of the West, in which social revolutions will most likely come from a gradual and thoroughgoing "war of position" rather than from a violent and immediate "war of movement," culture in general and literature in particular can come to play a key role both in countering existing hegemonies and in establishing new ones. This is true in Gramsci's thought not only because of the notion of reciprocity between base and superstructure but also because of Gramsci's genuine respect for the power of culture—and for the *potential* future benefits offered by the revolutionary contributions of "organic-collective" intellectuals—in all human endeavors.

At times in the notebooks, Gramsci's analysis of individual authors and their works becomes considerably detailed. Despite this closer focus, however, Gramsci's characteristic view of literary expression as a creative act, as a form of voluntary praxis, remains unchanged. The forces of hegemony are in various ways the historical object of fictional representation, but with greater or lesser degrees of awareness in each separate work. Gramsci repeatedly castigates those writers (the many offspring of Padre Bresciani, an author singled out for attack by De Sanctis) who in attempting to represent the truth of everyday life only manage to reproduce their own socioreligious and cultural prejudices, which is to say, most often those of the church and the dominant bourgeoisie. In a different vein, Gramsci's ambivalence concerning Luigi Pirandello's works carries over from his earlier writings, though in the notebooks Pirandello is lauded for introducing the shock of dialectics into the theater and for being at one and the same time Sicilian, Italian, and European. DANTE ALIGHIERI, too, though even more so, is the object of extended admiring discussion in Gramsci's well-known treatment of canto 10 of the *Inferno*. The futurists, on the other hand, are treated with an acerbity bordering on disdain primarily for their immaturity and their distinctly non-"national-popular" character. There are also, dispersed here and there, commentaries on the other arts (the "collective" nature of architecture, the immediate force of music) and on the future of Italian literature (which, to fulfill its potential, must set its roots in what Gramsci terms the rich "humus" of popular culture [*Quaderni* 1822]). Of all Gramsci's comments on art, however, perhaps the most fascinatingly suggestive, given the period in which he wrote, are contained in those few passages in which he links the immediate *and* collective effects of music and oratory with, first, the theater as melodrama and, second, the cinema as, at least *in potentia*, the genuine *romanzo popolare*, or popular novel, of the West's cultural future (1677, 1821, 2122, 2195).

The writings contained in Gramsci's notebooks were not widely diffused until well after the fall of Italian fascism. Initial arrangements to smuggle the notebooks out of Italy following his death were made in 1937 by Gramsci's sister-in-law, Tatjana Schucht, yet they did not arrive in Moscow until almost exactly a year later. At roughly the same time, Palmiro Togliatti (a charter member, along with Gramsci, of the Italian Communist party) received copies to read while in exile in Spain. But owing to an extent to the massive editorial enterprise required to prepare Gramsci's writings for publication, the works written during the period of his incarceration did not begin to appear until the late 1940s, the letters in 1947 and the notebooks in 1948. Since their publication, the principal controversy surrounding Gramsci's prison works has had to do with whether his thinking is truly revolutionary in a strict Marxian sense. The various ways in which this question has been approached over the decades following the 1940s have often reflected internal divisions within the Italian Communist party as well as within the Italian Left overall; but, that aside, the continuing vitality of Gramsci's writings is due to the fact that the central issue of the relation between culture and social change, to which his thought repeatedly returned, is still, in the West, at best unresolved. Even beyond the most naively optimistic formulations of the members of the 1960s avant-garde in Italy, for whom a new culture would have inevitably led to a new society, the force of Gramsci's lesson and the undeniable challenge of his thought remain as powerful and as pressing today as ever in the past. It should be noted that part of this same problematic and this same challenge have also played major roles in the thought of those English and American critics and theorists on whom Gramsci's works have had the most direct influence, among them Terry Eagleton, Stanley Aronowitz, FREDRIC JAMESON, and EDWARD W. SAID.

Gregory L. Lucente

See also ITALIAN THEORY AND CRITICISM: 2. TWENTIETH CENTURY and MARXIST THEORY AND CRITICISM.

Antonio Gramsci, *Letteratura e vita nazionale* (*Quaderni del carcere*, ed. Felice Platone, vol. 5, 1950), *Letters from Prison* (ed. and trans. Lynne Lawner, 1973, selections), *Quaderni del carcere* (ed. Valentino Gerratana, 4 vols., 1975), *Selections from Cultural Writings* (ed. David Forgacs and Geoffrey Nowell-Smith, trans. William Boelhower, 1985), *Selections from the Political Writings: 1910–1920* (ed. Quintin Hoare, trans. John Mathews, 1977), *Selections from the Political Writings: 1921–1926* (ed. and trans. Quintin Hoare, 1978), *Selections from the Prison Notebooks of Antonio Gramsci* (ed. and trans. Quintin Hoare and Geoffrey Nowell-Smith, 1971).

Walter L. Adamson, *Hegemony and Revolution: A Study of Antonio Gramsci's Political and Cultural Theory* (1980); Alberto Asor Rosa, *Scrittori e popolo: Il populismo nella letteratura italiana contemporanea* (1965); Nicola Badaloni,

Il marxismo di Gramsci: Dal mito alla ricomposizione politica (1975); Norberto Bobbio, *Gramsci e la concezione della società civile* (1976); Martin Clark, *Antonio Gramsci and the Revolution That Failed* (1977); Robert S. Dombroski, *Antonio Gramsci* (1989), "Ideology, Hegemony, and Literature: Some Reflections on Gramsci," *Forum Italicum* 23 (1989); *Egemonia e democrazia: Gramsci e la questione comunista nel debattito di Mondoperaio* (preface by Federico Coen, 1977); Joseph Femia, *Gramsci's Political Thought: Hegemony, Consciousness, and the Revolutionary Process* (1981); Giuseppe Fiori, *Vita di Antonio Gramsci* (1966); Renate Holub, *Antonio Gramsci: Beyond Marxism and Postmodernism* (1992); James Joll, *Gramsci* (1977); Gregory L. Lucente, "Yesterday, Today, Tomorrow: Notes on Gramsci's Theory of Literature and Culture," *Forum Italicum* 23 (1989); Maria Antonietta Macciocchi, *Per Gramsci* (1974); Chantal Mouffe, ed., *Gramsci and Marxist Theory* (1979); Thomas Nemeth, *Gramsci's Philosophy: A Critical Study* (1980); Pietro Rossi, ed., *Gramsci e la cultural contemporanea: Atti del convegno internazionale di studi gramsciani tenuto a Cagliari il 23–27 aprile 1967* (2 vols., 1969–70); Paolo Spriano, *Antonio Gramsci and the Party: The Prison Years* (trans. John Fraser, 1979).

HABERMAS, JÜRGEN

Jürgen Habermas (b. 1929) has been the most important intellectual in Germany since the early 1960s. A prolific member of the second generation of the FRANKFURT SCHOOL, he has contributed seminally to German public life in fields ranging from sociology to philosophy and political science. From 1949 to 1954 he attended the universities of Göttingen and Bonn, receiving his doctorate in philosophy with a dissertation on F. W. J. Schelling. Although his education was rather traditional, in the mid-1950s he became acquainted with central works in the Marxist tradition. His interest in critical theory led him in 1956 to Frankfurt, where he became an assistant to THEODOR W. ADORNO at the Institute for Social Research. After teaching in Heidelberg and Frankfurt, he became director of the Max Planck Institute for Research into the Living Conditions of the Scientific-Technical World in 1971. In 1983 he returned to Frankfurt as a professor in the Department of Philosophy.

Habermas's interdisciplinary research has touched on matters important to students of literature at several points. Perhaps his most influential work for literary studies in Germany was the book *Strukturwandel der Öffentlichkeit* (1962, *The Structural Transformation of the Public Sphere*). The "public sphere" is a realm in which opinions are exchanged between private persons unconstrained (ideally) by external pressures. Theoretically open to all citizens and founded in the family, it is the place where something approaching public opinion is formed. It should be distinguished both from the state, which represents official power, and from the economic structures of civil society as a whole. Its function is actually to mediate between society and state; it is the arena in which the public organizes itself, formulates public opinion, and expresses its desires vis-à-vis the government.

Habermas's discussion makes clear that the public sphere is not a given for every type of society; nor does it possess a fixed status. The Middle Ages had no public sphere in the sense in which Habermas defines it, but rather a sphere of representation of feudal authority. Only in the eighteenth century, with the breakdown of religious hegemony and the rise of the middle class, does a public sphere emerge. The liberal model of the public sphere, in which private individuals and interests regulate public authority and in which property owners speak for humanity, is eventually transformed during the nineteenth and twentieth centuries into a realm in which the activities of reasoning and the formulation of public opinion are superseded by mass consumption and publicity.

Habermas's hypothesis of a "literary public sphere" as an anticipation of the political public sphere found tremendous resonance among literary critics in Germany during the late 1960s and early 1970s. Particularly provocative were the notion of the commodification of art in the eighteenth century and the discussion of the various institutions in which art and criticism occurred (coffeehouses, moral weeklies). Habermas also made important observations on the rise of new genres, pointing out that the publication of correspondence as a literary form and the emergence of the psychological novel are reactions to a restructuring of the relationship between author, text, and reader. Intimacy as a matter for public scrutiny in fictional works depends on and fosters the legitimation of the public utterance of private opinions.

Habermas's debate with the ontological tradition of HERMENEUTICS, represented by Hans-Georg Gadamer, also has implications for literary theory. Although he agreed with the necessity for historicization, he objected primarily to the political implications contained in Gadamer's affirmation of "authority," "tradition," and "the classical." Habermas criticizes the conservative nature of Gadamer's dialogical stance because of its nonreflexive affirmation of tradition. In order for emancipation to occur, we must possess the ability to reflect upon and to reject pernicious or regressive aspects of our heritage. Connected with this, Habermas believes that Gadamer's hermeneutics excludes precisely the social moment inherent in all linguistic interchange. Although Habermas, unlike MICHEL FOUCAULT, posits in his later work communication free from domination as a regulative principle, he nonetheless takes Gadamer to task for ignoring the place of power and hegemony in dialogue.

Habermas's work during the 1980s, in particular *Der philosophische Diskurs der Moderne* (1985, *The Philosophical Discourse of Modernity*), thrust him into the center of controversy concerning the concepts of modernity and postmodernity. Opposing JEAN-FRANÇOIS LYOTARD's notion of the postmodern condition, Habermas contends that modernity poses for us a task that must still be completed. Habermas's notion of modernity stems from the tradition of German idealism, in particular from G. W. F. HEGEL, who posited subjectivity as the key for comprehending the modern world (see also GERMAN THEORY AND CRITICISM: 1. STURM UND DRANG / WEIMAR CLASSICISM and 2. ROMANTICISM). The constellation between modernity, consciousness, and rationality that crystallized in his philosophy had three distinct fates in post-Hegelian thought. The progressive neo-Hegelians, such as Karl Marx, operating with a more modest notion of reason, continued the project of modernity. The new conservatives, who reduced reason (*Vernunft*) to understanding (*Verstand*) and affirmed scientistic notions of rationality, jettisoned any critical element in the project. The young conservative faction, which draws its inspiration from FRIEDRICH NIETZSCHE and includes most adherents to poststructuralism, abandons reason altogether and falls into nihilism or anarchy. Habermas's contention is therefore that those who feel that they have gone beyond the project of modernity are deceiving themselves. There is no escape from the problems raised by subjectivity and enlightenment, only a continuation, a trivialization, or a pseudoradicalization of the initial premises.

Habermas's own solution to the project of modernity involves a return to a path abandoned early in Hegel's writings. He posits intersubjectivity as a way to avoid the dilemmas inherent in the "philosophy of consciousness." Instead of proceeding from the isolated subject confronting the objective world, Habermas opts for a model that considers human beings in dialogue with each other to be the foundation for emancipatory social thought. By differentiating between instrumental reason, which has unfortunately achieved hegemony in the modern world, and communicative reason, which has the potential to transform societies into genuine democracies, Habermas can retain a critical edge to reflections on modernity while explicating a positive program for change. In his magnum opus, *Theorie des kommunikativen Handelns* (1981, *The Theory of Communicative Action*), Habermas develops his views on communicative rationality in the endeavor to rethink the original project of critical theory along intersubjective lines. His criticism of postmodernity is thus an outgrowth of a larger philosophical view that affirms the Enlightenment principles of emancipation and progress, while refusing to abandon the critical potential of modernity.

Robert C. Holub

See also FRANKFURT SCHOOL, GERMAN THEORY AND CRITICISM: 4. TWENTIETH CENTURY TO 1968 and 5. CONTEMPORARY, and HERMENEUTICS: 2. TWENTIETH CENTURY.

Karl-Otto Apel et al., *Hermeneutik und Ideologiekritik* (1971); Jürgen Habermas, *Der philosophische Diskurs der Moderne* (1985, *The Philosophical Discourse of Modernity*, trans. Frederick Lawrence, 1987), *Strukturwandel der Öffentlichkeit: Untersuchen zu einer Kategorie der bürgerlichen Gesellschaft* (1962, *The Structural Transformation of the Public Sphere: An Inquiry into a Category of Bourgeois Society*, trans. Thomas Burger, 1989), *Theorie des kommunikativen Handelns* (2 vols., 1981, *The Theory of Communicative Action*, trans. Thomas McCarthy, 1983–87).

Richard J. Bernstein, ed., *Habermas and Modernity* (1985); Raymond Guess, *The Idea of a Critical Theory: Habermas and the Frankfurt School* (1981); David Held, *Introduction to Critical Theory: Horkheimer to Habermas* (1980); Robert C. Holub, *Jürgen Habermas: Critic in the Public Sphere* (1991); David Ingram, *Habermas and the Dialectic of Reason* (1987); Thomas McCarthy, *The Critical Theory of Jürgen Habermas* (1978); David M. Rassmussen, *Reading Habermas* (1990); Tom Rockmore, *Habermas on Historical Materialism* (1989); Rick Rodrick, *Habermas and the Foundations of Critical Theory* (1986); John B. Thompson and David Held, eds., *Habermas: Critical Debates* (1982); Stephen White, *The Recent Work of Jürgen Habermas: Reason, Justice, and Modernity* (1988).

HARTMAN, GEOFFREY H.

A major voice in contemporary criticism, Geoffrey H. Hartman (b. 1929) has played a leading role in the invigoration of Romantic studies. Shuttling effectively between theory and practice, he is an influential advocate of a renewed practical criticism at once philosophical and speculative, experimental and artful, and cognizant of its social and cultural responsibilities. No matter what his subject—William Wordsworth or JACQUES DERRIDA, André Malraux or Alfred Hitchcock, "the fate of reading" or "the Jewish imagination"—Hartman shows "the dependence of mind on text" (*Saving* xv). In the words of one recent commentator, "His criticism is the most *realistic* record we have of what literate reading is like" (Fry

200). Whether, as another commentator has claimed, Hartman "represents the future of the profession" of literary studies (O'Hara 114), in him PRACTICAL CRITICISM shows signs of growing up.

Trained as a comparatist at Yale, Hartman has long been associated with Continental modes of criticism and, in the 1970s and 1980s, as a member of the "Yale school," with DECONSTRUCTION. He cannot, however, be identified with any particular theoretical position. Though in his early work he focused on the "consciousness of consciousness" displayed in literary texts, he recognized the impossibility of going "beyond formalism." And though he has devoted an admiring book to Derrida (*Saving the Text*) and contributed to the "manifesto" published as *Deconstruction and Criticism* (Harold Bloom et al., 1979) on occasion Hartman writes against this influential movement. At the same time, however, pointing to the work of "a controversial array of writers active in America since about 1955," in which he must be included, Hartman claims that "the *practice* of deconstruction was forged in America, even if the *theory* had to await Derrida" (*Easy* 190). Individualistic and dialectical, Hartman cannot be pinned down or categorized, except perhaps as *sui generis*.

The object of the proto-deconstructive effort he describes was, he says, "to create a more dialectical and open view" of how literature works (*Easy* 190). Influenced as much by his lifelong fascination with Wordsworth as by his reading in philosophy, Hartman has always exhibited just such open and dialectical thinking. Aware of the interimplications of conflicting notions, and practicing a "negative HERMENEUTICS" not unlike Keats's understanding of "negative capability," Hartman reveals a certain generosity as he resists either/or "solutions." Looking through texts, over which he lovingly broods, and at large philosophical and theoretical issues, from the beginning Hartman has practiced a criticism distinct from explication, which he describes as "puerile, or at most pedagogic," critics having forgotten "its merely preparatory function, that it stands to a mature criticism as pastoral to epic" (*Beyond* 57).

Borrowing from while modifying a variety of theoretical positions, Hartman exhibits an impurity by no means indicative of confusion or lack of rigor. On the contrary, the deliberate impurity marks a maturity, for one does not sense when reading Hartman, as one does when reading more systematic critics, that "texts are being processed through a pre-determined schema—and roughly forced to yield up their meanings" (Handelman 203). The "mix" in Hartman's thinking indicates not just an openness but also a resistance, no doubt deriving from his childhood experience (he fled his native Germany at the age of nine to avoid Hitler's persecution of Jews), to the "purity perplex" that he believes is "a more basic category than presence" (*Criticism* 147). Hartman believes, too, that "we have succumbed to our innate purity perplex," that we now conceive of the practical too narrowly, isolating (and insulating) criticism from theory and from history, philosophy, law, psychoanalysis, religion, as well as from society (292, 287). Hartman's own work specifically addresses the need for "an unservile, an enlarged and mature, criticism, neither afraid of theory nor overestimating it" (4). What he writes of his "personal and macaronic procedure" in *Criticism in the Wilderness* applies to much of his work: he shuttles between formal ideas in critical theory and analyses of individual poems (5).

Enlarging the scope of criticism, Hartman confronts head-on the question of its status vis-à-vis literature, to which it has traditionally been secondary and subservient. Probably Hartman's most controversial position concerns the "creative" nature of criticism. His claim derives, at least in part, from the dialectical recognition that "the circle of understanding" is encompassing both interpreter and text, which Hartman describes as engaged in a symbiotic relationship. A considerable burden thus devolves upon the reader, who must recognize, receive, and respond to the extraordinary language-event that constitutes the great literary work. How to respond to a text's "call" is the issue, and so the question of style is raised: "How can the critic respond to the extraordinary language-event and still maintain a prose of the center?" (*Criticism* 157). Once critics try to find an "answerable style," their work "crosses over." Hartman maintains, in fact, that criticism is "within literature, not outside of it looking in," the critical essay at its best an "intellectual poem":

> The situation of the discourse we name *criticism* is, therefore, no different from that of any other. If this recognition implies a reversal, then it is the master-servant relation between criticism and creation that is being overturned in favor of what Wordsworth, describing the interaction of nature and mind, called "mutual domination" or "interchangeable supremacy." (*Criticism* 1, 195–96, 259)

Hartman practices what he advocates, his own essays being experimental and demanding, his style mixed and variable, his language anything but tempered. Like the work of THEODOR W. ADORNO, ROLAND BARTHES, WALTER BENJAMIN, and Derrida, which, in its mixture of the philosophic and the practical, has given the form "more intellectual and creative space," Hartman's essays cross over, at least some of them, into literature (*Criticism* 257, 175).

With characteristic balance, Hartman has managed to avoid the Charybdis menacing those who escape the Scylla of "plain style" criticism: his is not an aesthetic but a richly cultural criticism. Since his *André Malraux* (1960), in fact, Hartman's criticism has rarely failed to carry political implications, and recently he has been more direct, especially in addressing various issues related to Judaism and the Holocaust, most notably in his edited volume *Bitburg in Moral and Political Perspective*. Hartman brings to such vital issues the perspective of the humanities, understood as making available "delay time" necessary for "hermeneutic reflection" (*Easy* 172, 187), which disables "the one-dimensional, progressive claims of conqueror or would-be conqueror" and so "subverts the very idea of winning" (*Criticism* 75). Humanists are crucial to society because they "will not easily sacrifice anything to anything else: they take their time, and ponder—often elaborately—whether a new step does not entail an exclusion rather than an advantageous change or transformation" (*Criticism* 300): an apt description of Hartman's own practical—and grown-up—criticism.

G. Douglas Atkins

See also DECONSTRUCTION.

Geoffrey H. Hartman, *André Malraux* (1960), *Beyond Formalism: Literary Essays, 1958–1970* (1970), *Criticism in the Wilderness: The Study of Literature Today* (1980), *Easy Pieces* (1985), *The Fate of Reading and Other Essays* (1975), *Minor Prophecies: The Literary Essay in the Culture Wars* (1991), *Saving the Text: Literature/Derrida/Philosophy* (1981), *The Unmediated Vision: An Interpretation of Wordsworth, Hopkins, Rilke, and Valéry* (1954), *The Unremarkable Wordsworth* (1987), *Wordsworth's Poetry, 1787–1814* (1964).

G. Douglas Atkins, "Dehellenizing Literary Criticism" and "Reader-Responsibility Criticism: The Recent Work of Geoffrey Hartman," *Reading Deconstruction / Deconstructive Reading* (1983), *Geoffrey Hartman: Criticism as Answerable Style* (1990), "Geoffrey H. Hartman," *Modern American Critics since 1955* (ed. Gregory S. Jay, *Dictionary of Literary Biography*, vol. 67, 1988); Paul H. Fry, *The Reach of Criticism: Method and Perception in Literary Theory* (1983); Susan A. Handelman, review of *Criticism in the Wilderness*, *Wordsworth Circle* 12 (1981); Robert Moynihan, *A Recent Imagining: Interviews with Harold Bloom, Geoffrey Hartman, J. Hillis Miller, Paul de Man* (1986); Daniel T. O'Hara, "Afterwords: Geoffrey Hartman on the Critic's

Desire for Representation," *The Romance of Interpretation: Visionary Criticism from Pater to de Man* (1985); Imre Salusinszky, *Criticism in Society: Interviews with Jacques Derrida, Northrop Frye, Harold Bloom, Geoffrey Hartman, Frank Kermode, Edward Said, Barbara Johnson, Frank Lentricchia, and J. Hillis Miller* (1987); Helen Vendler, "Critical Models," *New Yorker* (May 3, 1982).

HAZLITT, WILLIAM

"At the outset of life . . . our imagination has a body to it": so wrote William Hazlitt (1778–1831), with his genius for aphorism, in "My First Acquaintance with Poets" (1823). That autobiographical essay relates two experiences that shaped the body of his own imagination in 1798 (17:116). The first occurred in January, when, himself the son of a Dissenting minister from Shropshire and preparing for the Dissenting ministry, he met SAMUEL TAYLOR COLERIDGE, who had come to Shrewsbury to take charge of the Unitarian congregation. "That my understanding . . . found a language to express itself," he acknowledged, "I owe to Coleridge" (107). The second occurred when Hazlitt visited Coleridge and WILLIAM WORDSWORTH in Somerset that June. There, amid three weeks of intense conversation, Hazlitt heard them read from the volume of poetry they were preparing, *Lyrical Ballads* "and the sense of a new style and a new spirit in poetry came over me" (117). But impressive as these events undoubtedly were, there were still larger forces at work on the body of Hazlitt's imagination, as he makes clear in "On the Feeling of Immortality in Youth" (1827): "I set out in life with the French Revolution, and that event had considerable influence on my early feelings" (17:196–97).

Between 1798 and 1827, in becoming one of the most lively and trenchant cultural critics ever to write in English, Hazlitt never failed to imagine those he wrote about, or to see himself, as inhabitants of a world in which social forces shaped subjectivity. The new "style" and "spirit" of contemporary literature remained prominent in his selection of topics, and as his long, late work on *The Life of Napoleon* (1828–30) attests, his sense of the political world continued until the end to be defined by the issues of the Revolution. That those who wrote about the Revolution often tended to discuss it in terms of abstractions such as "political justice" and "the rights of man" did not make its consequences any less materially felt. Interestingly, when Hazlitt moved in 1802 to Paris, where he lived for ten years, he attempted to pursue a career as a painter. He would later call his political sketches in *The Spirit of the Age* (1825) a "gallery" of portraits, and one of his important contributions to English critical terminology—the notion of "gusto"—had to do precisely with a capacity for apprehending things in their concreteness: "Gusto in art is power or passion defining any object" (4:77).

Not that Hazlitt had no taste for abstract speculation. At the time he met the poets, Hazlitt was reading such empiricists as DAVID HUME and thinking his way through a work of moral philosophy that he published in 1805 as *An Essay on the Principles of Human Action*. In the *Essay*, which adumbrated critical positions that would later prove both inimical to Wordsworth and influential for John Keats, Hazlitt extended the skeptical argument about personal identity in the direction of William Godwin's doctrine of benevolence. He developed a strong analogy between what separates us from others and what separates us from our own future selves in order to suggest that we may be theoretically as disinterested in our own future affairs as we are in the affairs of others (and, conversely, as interested in others as in our own future selves). "Interest," in its many interconnected senses, would indeed remain a crucial notion for many of Hazlitt's critical studies. His best work couples an appreciation for aesthetic power with analyses of how such power served *political* power and how it resisted it. A good discussion of imagination in service to power can be found in Hazlitt's mordant *Letter to William Gifford* (1819), whom he called "the Government Critic . . . the invisible link that connects literature with the police" (9:13). A good discussion of its resistance to power appears in "On Poetry in General," one of the *Lectures on the English Poets* (1818).

Both of these last pieces belong to the period of Hazlitt's finest writing. True, some of the later success is adumbrated in his early essays published under the title *The Eloquence of the British Senate* (1807), especially in the telling account of the style of Burke. After 1812, however, Hazlitt took the critical essay to a level it had never reached before and—as if to confirm his view that "the arts are not progressive"—arguably has not approached since. The immediate impetus to this new phase of Hazlitt's work was Leigh Hunt's 1812 suggestion that they together publish a series of pieces in Hunt's *Examiner* "in the manner of the periodical Essayists, the Spectator and Tatler." Hazlitt devoted a full lecture to "the Periodical Essayists" in his *Lectures on the English Comic Writers* (1819), and what he says about their work tells much about his. Theirs, he says, is

> that sort of writing which . . . consists in applying the talents and resources of the mind to all that mixed

mass of human affairs, which, though not included under the head of any regular art, science, or profession, falls under the cognizance of the writer, and "comes home to the business and bosoms of men." . . . It does not deal in sweeping clauses of proscriptions and anathema, but in nice distinctions and liberal constructions. It makes up its general accounts from details, its few theories from many facts. It does not try to prove all black or all white as it wishes, but lays on the intermediate colours. (6:91–92)

What Hazlitt found in Richard Steele and Joseph Addison—ultimately in Montaigne—was a critical mode answerable to the empiricism of the Humean moral philosophy to which he had committed himself, and it became the critical mode of his own best writing. We must look to Hazlitt, not for a critical system, but for a body of "nice distinctions" and "liberal constructions" as capacious as any critical imagination has had to offer.

Hazlitt's philosophical orientation makes his relation to Coleridge a matter of special interest in the history of English criticism, for Hume's empiricism was one of the prominent targets of Coleridge's influential theorizing. Hazlitt's acknowledgment that Coleridge gave him the language in which to express himself suggests that while Hazlitt's practical work may not be governed by an aprioristic theory of poetry or imagination, it was carried out in the light of what such a theory might be and do. In perhaps his best-known work, *The Spirit of the Age*, certain notions such as "contradiction" and "character," as well as "the spirit of the age" itself, achieve a quasi-technical status. The essays gain force both from the idealist philosophical associations carried by those terms and from the refusal to allow these associations to realize the expectations they raise. No identifiable "spirit of the age" emerges from the "contemporary portraits" assembled in that volume, and no resolute pattern emerges from what Hazlitt calls the "spirit of contradiction," which is kept constantly in play. Hazlitt's essays frequently defeat expectations of consistency by disrespecting the distinction between persons and principles. For any literary portrait he painted, and especially for those in *The Spirit of the Age*, he achieved an astonishing fusion of what eighteenth-century criticism held apart under the paired rubrics "moral" and "poetical" characters. Hazlitt's observations led him to look for an author's characteristic weaknesses in the same areas as his distinctive strengths: Coleridge's ability to see all sides of a question goes hand in hand with his incapacity for action, Wordsworth's "hebetude of intellect" with his strength of sympathy.

This view of character finds expression in some extraordinary prose transitions, as in the essay on Walter Scott, where lavish praise becomes savage condemnation in the space of a single paragraph. On the other hand, the surprising transition is a device of wide application in Hazlitt's writings. To explain his use of it, he mentions having noticed that by comparison with his literary treatment of his favorite topics, his conversations about them "took a much wider range, and branched off into a number of indirect and collateral questions, which were not strictly connected with the original view of the subject." To "combine these two styles, the *literary* and the *conversational*," thus seemed "to promise a greater variety and richness, and perhaps a greater sincerity, than could be attained by a more precise and scholastic method." The issue of style is indeed prominent in most of Hazlitt's best criticism, and sincerity is one of its avowed criteria. Hazlitt stands among the best early essayists in not attempting to construct a particularized persona. The staccato sequence of unconjoined clauses marks another feature of this style, and since, as he said, an editor abhors an ellipsis, it was a feature that had to be fought for. Together with the conversational unpredictability and the penchant for apparently irrelevant (and often misquoted) allusion, this feature of Hazlitt's writing enabled him to claim for himself what he saw in his hero Montaigne: "the courage to say as an author what he felt as man" (6:92). His prose became an object of clubby, nostalgic admiration for later writers such as Robert Louis Stevenson ("We are all of us fine fellows, but none of us writes like Hazlitt" [quoted in Bromwich 3]), but it was a great obstacle to many of Hazlitt's contemporaries and was taken by hostile critics as an index of his political and intellectual anarchism. Hazlitt courted such charges in sentences that enacted what they described: "Every word should be a blow; every thought should instantly grapple with its fellow" (12:10). Not the least part of his critical legacy, Hazlitt's style attempted, for all it was worth, to guard the power of what he wrote, and wrote about, against appropriation by what he called the "tyrants" and the "toad-eaters" alike.

James K. Chandler

See also BRITISH THEORY AND CRITICISM: I. EARLY EIGHTEENTH CENTURY, 2. LATE EIGHTEENTH CENTURY, and 3. ROMANTIC PERIOD AND EARLY NINETEENTH CENTURY.

William Hazlitt, *Complete Works of William Hazlitt* (ed. P. P. Howe, 21 vols., 1930–34).

Herschel Baker, *William Hazlitt* (1962); David Bromwich, *Hazlitt: The Mind of a Critic* (1983); Mary Jacobus, "The Art of Managing Books: Romantic Prose and the Writing of the Past," *Romanticism and Language* (ed. Arden Reed, 1984); Stanley Jones, *Hazlitt: A Life, from Winterslow to Frith Street* (1989); John Kinnaird, *William Hazlitt: Critic of Power* (1978); Thomas McFarland, *Romantic Cruxes: English Essayists and the Spirit of the Age* (1987); John Nabholtz, *"My reader my fellow labourer": A Study of English Romantic Prose* (1986); Roy Park, *Hazlitt and the Spirit of the Age: Abstraction and Critical Theory* (1971); Ralph M. Wardle, *Hazlitt* (1971).

HEGEL, G. W. F.

Georg Wilhelm Friedrich Hegel's (1770–1831) most important contribution to literary criticism consists in the concepts he developed to combat the philosophical tradition shaped by RENÉ DESCARTES and John Locke. Despite their differences, these philosophers created an atmosphere in which the fundamental task of philosophy was to make secure the possibility of true representations and lawful generalizations. Johann Gottlieb Fichte offered a coherent alternative, insisting that this emphasis on representation could not account for or direct the dynamic forces that produced the representations and adapted them to specific centers of consciousness. Yet Fichte could do little more than replace atomistic propositions by an atomistic subjective idealism, incapable of forging social bonds for those dynamic centers. While a philosophy concentrating on description cannot handle the desires underlying its acts, a philosophy emphasizing subjective desire seems trapped in a kaleidoscopic PHENOMENOLOGY unable to deal with causes or establish communal values.

Hegel saw himself as resolving these contradictions by showing how subjective being could only fulfill itself if it managed to develop for all experience the relation between legislative subject and lawful objectivity that IMMANUEL KANT had theorized for a rational morality. In order to understand the fundamental structure of human experience, the being for itself of self-reflexive activity must grasp its own concrete place within an overall rational scheme—not Descartes's or Kant's static rationality but one that itself gradually reveals its capacity to integrate spirit and substance. Spirit would take the form of dynamic lawfulness within experience, and substance would take on its full concreteness as the elemental relational features giving the law material existence. But consciousness could only grasp the full intricacy of that conjunction by pursuing a dialectical form of thinking: reason becomes manifest through our grasp of the development that emerges as self-consciousness struggles to find terms that give it substance, then finds itself surpassing and hence negating what had allowed it to know certain things about itself. In this dialectical method, no longer bound to the atemporal structures of traditional logic and epistemology, "truth" becomes a predicate to be used only with quotation marks. The task of philosophy is to position truth claims within specific modes of thinking, to dramatize the limitations each mode reveals over time, and to show how subsequent acts of spirit are capable of negating, preserving, and sublating those limited perspectives so that the reflexive mind can appreciate the more comprehensive positions that become available as spirit works beyond its own fullest self-expressions.

Suppose, for example, that one asks whether the claims of Stoicism are true. Section 4 of Hegel's *Phenomenology of Spirit* (1807) argues that we cannot answer the question by treating Stoic arguments as discrete propositions that one tests against experience. Rather, one must understand the role they have played in shaping what we understand experience to be. One must position Stoicism against the contradictions that it tried to reconcile, and one must understand its disseminating role in provoking philosophical stances that build upon what it discloses. Our specific analysis must begin by recognizing that the first effort to postulate a philosophical ethic derives from the collapse of heroic culture and the need to find alternative ways to secure people's efforts to be known as creators of meaning for their individual lives. The hero could win that meaning by conquest: standing over his victim, the successful warrior allowed him his life on the condition that he accept the conqueror's authority and become his slave. But the first of many ironies makes its appearance on Hegel's historical stage: what good is affirmation from a slave? So the warrior must continually seek new victims. It proves to be the slaves who create a stable social order because renouncing the quest for heroic individuality allows them to win a mode of collective identity based on the forms their labor creates for nature. Those forms provide enduring reflections of the meanings humans create, and they exemplify the social bonds those meanings could establish. Stoicism, then, emerges as the spirit's way of incorporating that lesson for reflective consciousness. Heroic struggle becomes possible once more, but against the self rather than against other persons. And in that struggle the hero seeks not to develop a specific identity but to align with a sense of deeper possible universalizing identities projected by the abstracting power of thought.

These possibilities also produce severe problems that eventually disperse the forces of individualism and universalization Stoic philosophy managed to reconcile, forcing them to seek higher-level integrations. For the price of that universalization is the loss of the difference that continues to define the particular conditions that agents encounter. Stoicism then dialectically generates skepticism, because skepticism consists precisely in the sense that thinking is not bound to particular contexts and hence is free to revel in its own boundless intricacy. In skepticism the individual can once again claim a distinctive subjective life for itself, but only in the guise of an indeterminacy that accompanies this revel of abstractions freed from any single controlling context. From the point of view of the skeptic, Stoicism is correct in its recognition of the power thought has, but it appears foolish in attempting to subordinate the individual to a universal that in fact is only one of thought's possible moments.

This freedom, however, soon discloses a third dialectical twist that leads the reflective mind beyond skepticism to the unhappy consciousness characterizing early Christian thought. Here the skeptic's liberated "I" turns on itself in disgust as it recognizes the enormous gulf between what the abstracting power of thought could provide and its own petty, contingent manipulations of that power. Yet the fact that self-consciousness can register that gulf shows that it is capable of identifying with the sublimities of thought leading far beyond the casual indeterminacy cultivated within skepticism. The self once again feels the power of the universal lodged within, but that power remains terrifyingly alien, since the self experiences itself only as the victim of that power, abject over the gulf between the human and the transcendental. So the unhappy consciousness internalizes within one state of mind both Stoic respect for law and skepticism's ungroundedness. The very powers that distinguish it also mock it and force it to turn, with a mix of fealty and rebelliousness, toward a god whom it can only posit as its absolute other. Yet it is only by experiencing these contradictions that the spirit can enter, and the reflective mind take on, the next major step in spirit's unfolding, a step where reason appears as a mediating force (made concrete in Christ) allowing the individual to align with the abstracting powers of thought because they provide types that can be appropriated for the individual's own situations.

It takes Hegel's *Phenomenology* several more complex dialectical movements in order to show how this spirit becomes fully articulate in, and as, substance, making itself more determinate and God less alien. For an abstract rendering of the specific principles at work within that dialectic we must turn to Hegel's work on logic, best represented in part I of his *Encyclopedia of the Philosophical Sciences* (1830). Here he argues that there can be a logic not only for discrete assertions (things already fixed within thought) but also for processes by which spirit gives order to its own relational energies. Then, for the application of these logical principles to particular dialectical processes we must turn to his posthumously published lectures on philosophy, history, and the fine arts, as well as to his work on the ideal relations between the individual and the collective comprising his *Philosophy of Right* (1821). But for now we must rely on our one example of this interpreting of the "truth" of Stoicism as our basis for understanding Hegel's four most important contributions to literary theory: his rendering of how reflexive activity takes on expressive force, his treatment of artworks as distinctive embodiments of that force, his way of taking those embodiments as representative for historical contexts, and his overall model of how attention to expressive desires gives purpose and direction to the study of cultures.

Hegel's model of reflective activity is central to the arts and to literary criticism because it makes clear the limitations of those approaches that concentrate only on mimetic relations between work and world. For Hegel, expressive acts not only represent worlds but also constitute modes of intelligibility and emotional intensity for those worlds. Thus, these acts are also in constant tension with established principles of representation, at once negating them and opening a way for significant originality. These expressions call attention to productive energies within spirit not yet realized within public forms, and they provide material for new public forms that mediate the very differences generating them by showing how and why the differences can be said to make a difference.

How Hegelian thinking influences theory in the arts will depend on how we understand the way the mind comes to handle these differences. If we stress his work on logic, dialectical thinking becomes a vehicle for demonstrating how particulars can serve as "concrete universals" that we grasp in terms of their relation to an underlying structure they help establish. That approach has its most pronounced relation to literary criticism in the model of tradition that T. S. ELIOT developed from F. H. Bradley's idealism: significant works of art both depend on and transform a single tradition and thereby make articulate a common, complexly figured image of human needs, desires, and powers. At the other pole, the relentless ironies of historical development in the *Phenomenology* lead thinkers from ARTHUR SCHOPENHAUER

to WALTER BENJAMIN and JEAN-PAUL SARTRE to PAUL DE MAN and JACQUES DERRIDA to stress the constant slippage within the dialectic. From this perspective the very effort to posit encompassing wholes necessarily distorts particulars, inaugurating compensatory slippages and compensations that make interpretation seem the positing of endless substitutes for an unrecoverable original. And the critic's claim to knowledge then seems little more than an effort to escape those ironies, an effort doomed by its own evasion of the interpreter's place within the chain of historical determinants.

Hegel's *Aesthetics: Lectures on Fine Arts* (1835) had a quite different influence, because in it he concentrated on positive articulations of spirit in its different historical efforts to mediate between subject and object and between the sensuous and the ideal. In preclassical, or "symbolic," art, spirit sought a space it could set against the tyranny of sense, so the art emphasized the power to set its own internal meaning against appearances, for example, in the pyramids. With classical art the emphasis shifts to celebrating the integration of spirit with sensuous matter, preeminently in the idealized bodies of fifth-century Greek sculpture. Finally, "Romantic" art achieves a state at once subjective and universal, subjective because it calls on modes of being that cannot be captured within appearance, yet universal because it establishes its own forming energies as a transpersonal content. In such art self-consciousness becomes not the end but the medium, which then only philosophy can make fully articulate.

Hegel's triad generated three basic critical orientations. Probably his most important influence was on Stéphane Mallarmé, who developed a poetics in which the forming energies might tease the mind out of its sensuous attachments and then serve as the new sensuous content, a poetics fundamental to the development of modernist abstraction. Second, thinkers such as Wilhelm Dilthey and BENEDETTO CROCE focused less on any one stage in Hegel's model than on the overall sense of how art provides distinctive sensuous representations expressing the deepest spiritual experience of a culture (see HERMENEUTICS: I. NINETEENTH CENTURY). And finally, art historians, led by Henri Focillon and Heinrich Wölfflin, developed an internal history of art on much the same principles by treating forms themselves as dialectically emerging, reaching their full expressive power, and becoming subject to myriad transformations as internal contradictions and external pressures built up.

Each of these models concentrates on specific expressive forces, as if one could build theory from within

Hegel's concrete analyses. But it is also possible to shape theoretical concerns in relation to the most general levels of Hegel's thinking, where he works out the internal demands that drive the entire dialectical process and thus enable him to attribute meaning for his present to a history that otherwise becomes only a mausoleum of failed belief systems. For theorists, those concerns provide means of speculating on how we might understand general cultural and moral forces sustained and organized by the range of works of art we study. The sharpest use of Hegel in this regard comes from those who attempted to turn on its head what they saw as Hegel's metaphysical evasion of real historical forces. Yet those criticisms masked the degree to which these thinkers differed from the main line of European historicism, because they had taken enough of Hegel to develop other, equally problematic general motivational and evaluative schema for locating directions within history. Even though Karl Marx bitterly criticized Hegel's idealism, he projected his own version of metaphysics in his proposals for a teleology within history making class struggle the primary interpretive category for understanding social change (see KARL MARX AND FRIEDRICH ENGELS). And while the FRANKFURT SCHOOL thinkers escaped the more determinist aspects of Marx, they relied on an ill-defined and watered-down version of Hegelian rationality in order to sanction their mandarin attitudes toward popular culture and the evils of commodification. By now, one must add, thinkers like Charles Taylor have managed to keep Hegel's dialectical scope without miming his metaphysics as they draw out how the past defines possibilities for the present and even for probable futures.

Hegel's model of rationality as the unfolding of an ultimate identity between subject and object can no longer serve as a plausible foundation for that historical work. But some of the most important twentieth-century literary criticism takes from that account a sense of how our desires involve concerns for identity and how these concerns open complex interconnected levels allowing us intricate identifications with social groups. Here Hegel's most important heritage is his case for understanding human agents as driven less by instinct or social forces than by the desire to find meanings for their experiences and thus to identify themselves in terms of the meanings they can establish. On that basis JACQUES LACAN has reinterpreted the entire Freudian story, and GEORG LUKÁCS managed to make the ideal of subjects defining themselves as concrete universals a basic criterion for setting socially conscious and effective art against the "abstract particularity" cultivated in modernist aesthetics. Recent criticism has also used Hegel's example to investigate aspects of artistic expression that involve levels of meaning not available to the agent but that also do not invite the specific biographical contexts invoked by the Freudian unconscious. FREDRIC JAMESON seeks utopian desires within those aspects of fiction that seem to carry intense investments but yet are not quite fully articulated in their specific social environment. Imagination must find means of giving desire social forms, but it must do so within the limits the social order imposes. Therefore, Jameson seeks those traces within socially constructed desires that connect to other texts, and this can be said to reveal a shared political unconscious within those overt forms. And this unconscious then provides a contemporary version of spirit establishing directions for social labor. Pushing the same ideas to more idealist conclusions, NORTHROP FRYE finds in the patterns that expressive desires take for the imagination not only an index of the goals for civilizing work but also a fundamental locus for forging identifications that extend beyond the limitations shaping particular forms of social life. What for Hegel was a reason within history giving it form may have to be for the late twentieth century only an imaginary glimpse of bonds that make ideal worlds necessary counterparts to divisive empirical realities.

However, as Hegel dissipates into the many Hegels generated by our scholarship, we also must return to the Hegel who saw each identification as misidentification, each social bond a trap for the spirit that is initially enlarged by it. Then we have two options. We can use this sense of each particular imaginative position as deeply unstable to reject, with thinkers such as JEAN-FRANÇOIS LYOTARD and Gilles Deleuze, the entire edifice of idealization that seeks deeper structures and potential identities within the author's struggles, or we can make that realization itself the basis for recognizing how these frustrations reveal shared needs and desires by which to direct future labors.

Charles Altieri

G. W. F. Hegel, *Aesthetics: Lectures on Fine Art* (trans. T. M. Knox, 2 vols., 1975), *Early Theological Writings* (trans. T. M. Knox, 2 vols., 1948), *Encyclopedia of the Philosophical Sciences* (3d ed., 1830, pt. 1, *Hegel's Logic*, trans. William Wallace, 1975; pt. 2, *Hegel's Philosophy of Mind*, trans. William Wallace, 1971; pt. 3, *Hegel's Philosophy of Nature*, trans. A. V. Miller), *Hegel on the Arts: Selections from G. W. F. Hegel's "Aesthetics, or the Philosophy of Fine Art"* (ed. Henry Paolucci, 1979), *Hegel on Tragedy* (ed. Henry Paolucci and Anne Paolucci, 1962), *Hegel: Selections* (ed. Jacob Loewenberg, 1929), *Lectures on the Philosophy of*

History (trans. J. Sibtree, 1956), *Phenomenology of Spirit* (trans. A. V. Miller, 1977), *Philosophy of Right* (trans. T. M. Knox, 1942), *Sämtliche Werke* (ed. Hermann Glockner, 26 vols., 1927–40, 3d ed., 1949–59).

Shlomo Avineri, *Hegel's Theory of the Modern State* (1972); Stephen Bungay, *Beauty and Truth: A Study of Hegel's Aesthetic* (1984); Benedetto Croce, *Ciò che è vivo e ciò che è morte della filosofia di Hegel* (1907, 3d ed., 1912, *What Is Living and What Is Dead of the Philosophy of Hegel,* trans. Douglas Ainslie, 1915); Jacques Derrida, *L'Écriture et la différence* (1967, *Writing and Difference,* trans. Alan Bass, 1978), *Glas* (1974, *Glas,* trans. John P. Leavey, Jr., and Richard Rand, 1986); John N. Findlay, *Hegel: A Re-examination* (1958); Martin Heidegger, *Hegel's Concept of Experience* (1970); Jean Hippolyte, *Genesis and Structure of Hegel's Phenomenology of Spirit* (trans. Samuel Cherniak and John Heckman, 1974); Alexandre Kojève, *Introduction to the Reading of Hegel* (ed. Allan Bloom, trans. James II. Nichols, Jr., 1969); Georg Lukács, *Der junge Hegel: Über die Beziehungen von Dialektik und Ökonomie* (1948, *The Young Hegel: Studies in the Relations between Dialectics and Economics,* trans. Rodney Livingstone, 1975), *Marxism and Human Liberation: Essays on History, Culture, and Revolution* (ed. Epifanio San Juan, Jr., 1973); Alasdair MacIntyre, ed., *Hegel: A Collection of Critical Essays* (1972); Stephen Priest, ed., *Hegel's Critique of Kant* (1987); Stanley Rosen, *G. W. F. Hegel: An Introduction to the Science of Wisdom* (1974); Josiah Royce, *Lectures on Modern Idealism* (1919); Judith N. Shklar, *Freedom and Independence: A Study of the Political Ideas of Hegel's Phenomenology of Mind* (1976); Charles Taylor, *Hegel* (1975).

HEIDEGGER, MARTIN

The early philosophical career of Martin Heidegger (1889–1976), culminating in the publication of *Sein und Zeit* (1927, *Being and Time*), is dominated by Gottfried Wilhelm Leibniz's old question, Why is there something rather than nothing? Heidegger's idea is that the philosophical tradition has lost the sense of this question. Being, like Nothing, is an empty category. There are no conditions in which it makes sense to speak of it. It is not a philosophical problem, unless it is just the problem of the copula, the "is." The history of philosophy, or of ontology or metaphysics, is, Heidegger likes to say, the history of the "forgetfulness of being."

There is also a sense, however, in which Being is not forgotten at all but is, rather, always already understood, and this understanding is what characterizes our relationship with the world around us, our being-in-the-

world. It is this fundamental, pre-theoretical understanding that Heidegger tries to clarify in *Being and Time* by means of a phenomenological analysis of our everydayness, that is, a descriptive account of how it is with us, what it is like, in our everyday world. Heidegger's idea is that our relationship with the world is not one of knowing; that is, it does not consist in having things in view. The world is not made of objects present before us or before our conceptual gaze. We belong to the world, are in it and involved with it. We are not spectators at a passing show. Rather, things surround us—they are what Heidegger calls "ready-at-hand"—and our relation to them is one of practical familiarity, or knowing what they are for, rather than one of theoretical interest, or knowing what they are as such. Philosophy quarrels over the existence of the world, but what matters to us is not the existence of the world but our ontological involvement with it.

Heidegger's word for us in *Being and Time* is *Dasein,* "Being-there," which does not mean we ourselves but rather where we find ourselves. Against the subjectivist tradition of picturing an individual as an ego or self, a thinking subject or transcendental unity of apperception, a mind or a consciousness, Heidegger characterizes us in terms of our historicality and belongingness, our situatedness, our finitude or temporality. We are historicized beings. Transcendence, seeing the world from God's point of view, is closed to us. So we can never, for example, bring ourselves before ourselves as objects. That is, we can never conceptualize or objectify ourselves or see ourselves either from the outside or from the inside out; rather, we encounter ourselves in our temporality in a strange way. In section 40 of *Being and Time* Heidegger says that it is "in anxiety [that] Dasein gets brought before itself through its own being" (228). In anxiety our being makes itself felt as that which threatens to withhold itself from us. In anxiety the question of being is brought home as a question of most urgent concern.

Most commentators think that the question of being remained dominant for Heidegger until the end of his life, but after *Being and Time* his reflections on this and other formal philosophical subjects came to be mediated extensively by questions of language, technology, poetry, and thinking. Moreover, his own writings, mainly lectures and addresses, became increasingly fragmented and obscure. Never a systematic thinker, Heidegger moved further and further away from the propositional style of philosophic discourse, so that many do not regard his later writings as having anything to do with philosophy at all. Frequently his writings are free commentaries on poetic texts and the fragments of pre-Socratic thinkers. No longer simply a critic of philosophical reasoning, Heidegger seemed to have abandoned Reason altogether. Crucial to his turn away from rigorous philosophy was his study of FRIEDRICH NIETZSCHE during the 1930s and his increasing absorption in the poetry of FRIEDRICH HÖLDERLIN. The meaning of this turn is complicated further by his undoubted fascism, which involved him with the Nazis during the most critical period of his philosophical development. In light of this involvement, many commentators see Heidegger as aestheticizing philosophy, shrouding it in a mysticism that isolates it from historical and cultural reality. Others see Heidegger as a primary influence in the postmodern critique of rationality, particularly in his characterization of a technocratic culture so dominated by ideologies of totalization and control that the freedom of what is wayward and singular, strange or different, is no longer thinkable (see POSTMODERNISM). It is not clear that these two interpretations of Heidegger are entirely opposed to one another; nor is it clear that they exclude other readings. Heidegger's thinking is always shifting, heterogeneous, and open-ended. It is resistant to final interpretations.

Of all Heidegger's ideas, the most important for criticism and theory is his reformulation and critique of the Romantic idea that art is foundational for human culture. What sort of culture? In his writings immediately following *Being and Time,* the emphasis seems nationalistic and consistent with Nazi ideology. His later writings suggest that art is foundational for a culture free from the constraints of instrumental reason, bureaucratic control, and systematic hierarchies, but the social and political implications of Heidegger's thinking with respect to art and culture remain far from clear. What is clear is that his conception of art is ontological rather than formal and aesthetic. In "The Origin of the Work of Art" (1933–34), he says that the work of the work of art, its truth, is to open up a world, a human dwelling place. The work is no longer reducible to a product of subjective expression or the object of aesthetic contemplation. It is less an object than an event that sets us free from what is merely timeless and fixed, inserts us into history, situates us together in an ongoing world. However, Heidegger is not interested in laws that make it possible for art to work in this way; rather, he seems to be attracted to the strangeness and irreducibility of art. The task of art is to set up a world, but the work does not belong to the world it establishes. The work belongs to the earth, which constitutes something like the absolute horizon of the world, the limit that determines the world's historicality and

finitude. Heidegger emphasizes the density and strangeness of the work of art, its refusal of every effort we make to grasp it conceptually and to reduce it to its essence. The work opens a clearing in the density of the forest; it lightens a place within the darkness of what withholds itself. But it belongs to density and darkness; the work opens the world but proves uncontainable within it. Hence the ontological peculiarity of the work of art, which is always excessive with respect to human history and culture.

"All art," Heidegger says, "is essentially poetry" (*Poetry* 72). "Poetry" here is *Dichtung* rather than *Poesie;* that is, it is a primordial naming rather than the art of making verses.

> The poet names the gods and names all things in that which they are. This naming does not consist in merely something already known being supplied with a name; it is rather that when the poet speaks the essential word, the existent is by this naming nominated as what it is. So it becomes known *as* existent. Poetry is the establishing of being by means of the word. (*Existence* 281)

Poetry here is a sort of world-making. The poet is an Orphic singer who brings things into being for the first time. However, the poet bears an ambiguous relation to the world that poetry establishes. The brightness of being, Heidegger says, "drives the poet into the dark" (*Existence* 285). There is no place for the poet in the world; the poet always dwells apart. In his later writings, Heidegger becomes increasingly absorbed in the nature of this "apartness" *(Abgeschiedenheit)*.

In "The End of Philosophy and the Task of Thinking" (1972), Heidegger says that the history of philosophy has come to an end, not in the sense that philosophy is now over and done with, but in the sense that it can no longer undergo any internal changes and still remain philosophy. In our present age systematic rationality has become dominant and can be displaced only at the cost of philosophy itself. But systematic rationality, Heidegger says, is not thinking. The question of thinking remains open. In his later writings, Heidegger is interested in what thinking can learn from that which philosophy excludes as foreign to its nature; above all, this means, What can thinking learn from poetry *(Dichten)?* Heidegger works through this question in his later writings collected in *On the Way to Language* (1959). Systematic philosophy seeks to bring language, and therefore all that language brings into the open, under the rule of logic and the construction of concepts. With poetry it is far otherwise. In an essay entitled "The Word" (1957), Heidegger says that "the poet renounces having words under his control" (*On the Way* 147). Poetry is the letting go of language. Poetry is release *(Gelassenheit)*. For Heidegger, poetry is no longer a discursive practice governed by a poetics or a kind of speaking that can be compared with other uses of language but rather a listening that picks up on the speaking that language speaks *(Die Sprache spricht)*. But what is this speaking?

The speaking of language is an event *(Ereignis)* that Heidegger calls the worlding of the world. This is no longer understood as a process of world-making over which the poet presides. It is rather a movement of the concealment and disclosure of things into which poetry lets itself go. Perhaps in a dialogue of poetry and thinking we can learn what it would be for thinking to let itself go in similar fashion. Certainly it would mean the abandonment of philosophy as the practice of conceptual reasoning and the reduction to logical form. And certainly this might entail the ancient risk of madness. What would it be for thinking to expose itself to poetry? Heidegger's answer to this question is perhaps not very different from PLATO's. But unlike Plato, Heidegger imagines the thinker staying with, instead of banishing, the poet, as if it were only in the nearness of poetry, in the freedom of its company, that thinking could occur. Thinking in this case would resemble listening more than it would reasoning, responsiveness more than assertiveness. So the question would no longer be, What does thinking try to grasp, to affirm or deny, to know? but, What calls for thinking? This question seems to replace the question of Being in Heidegger's later work. The sense of this question has been developed in striking ways by the American philosopher Stanley Cavell in his writings on RALPH WALDO EMERSON and LUDWIG WITTGENSTEIN.

Although it seems to be generally accepted that Heidegger's philosophy is an important part of the conceptual background of our current intellectual situation, the bulk of his writings remain largely unstudied except among specialists in Continental philosophy. For many literary critics and theorists, he is more interesting for his involvement with National Socialism than for his writings on poetry and language.

Gerald L. Bruns

Martin Heidegger, *Basic Writings* (ed. David Farrell Krell, 1977), *Erläuterungen zu Hölderlins Dichtung* (1951), "Hölderlin and the Essence of Poetry" and "Remembrance of the Poet" (trans. Douglas Scott, *Existence and Being*, 1949), *Holzwege* (1950), *Nietzsche* (1961, 4 vols., trans. David Farrell Krell, 1979), *Poetry, Language, Thought* (trans. Albert Hofstadter, 1971), *The Question Concerning Technology and Other Essays* (trans. William Lovitt, 1977), *Sein und Zeit* (1927, *Being and Time*, trans. John Macquarrie and Edward Robinson, 1962), *Unterwegs zur Sprache* (1959, *On the Way to Language*, trans. Peter D. Hertz, 1971), *Was heisst Denken?* (1961, *What Is Called Thinking?* trans. J. Glenn Gray, 1968), *Zur Sache des Denkens* (1969, *On Time and Being*, trans. Joan Stambaugh, 1972).

Robert Bernasconi, *The Question of Language in Heidegger's History of Being* (1985); Gerald L. Bruns, *Heidegger's Estrangements: Language, Truth, and Poetry in the Later Writings* (1989); Stanley Cavell, "Thinking of Emerson" and "An Emerson Mood," *The Senses of Walden* (1972, rev. ed., 1981); Jacques Derrida, *De l'esprit: Heidegger et la question* (1987, *Of Spirit: Heidegger and the Question*, trans. Geoffrey Bennington and Rachel Bowlby, 1989); Véronique Fóti, *Heidegger and the Poets: Poiesis, Sophia, Techne* (1992); Christopher Fynsk, *Heidegger: Thought and Historicity* (1986); Philippe Lacoue-Labarthe, *Heidegger, Art, and Politics: The Fiction of the Political* (1987, trans. Chris Turner, 1990); Hugo Ott, *Martin Heidegger: Unterwegs zur seiner Biographie* (1988); Otto Pöggeler, *Philosophie und Politik bei Heidegger* (1972); Herman Rapaport, *Heidegger and Derrida: Reflections on Time and Language* (1989); Andrzej Warminski, *Readings in Interpretation: Hölderlin, Hegel, Heidegger* (1987); Richard Wolin, ed., *The Heidegger Controversy: A Critical Reader* (1991).

HERMENEUTICS

1. Nineteenth Century

Hermeneutics, as opposed to exegesis, is the theory, rather than the practice, of interpretation. Initially concerned with how we interpret texts, hermeneutics in the nineteenth century becomes the theory of understanding itself, dealing with texts only as one example of the *event* of understanding between persons. Developed originally as a biblical discipline, it begins with the problem of a distance between text and reader that renders meaning opaque. But beginning in the late eighteenth century, when Johann Gottfried Herder introduces an awareness of cultural relativism, and when the expansion of hermeneutics to the study of secular scriptures changes the understanding not only of the classics but also of the Bible as text, this distance comes to be seen in cultural and historical rather than theological terms. Despite the impediment of cultural and historical differences between author and reader, nineteenth-century hermeneutics often has as an ideal the recovery of the text's "true" meaning. Twentieth-century theorists see such differences as constitutive of a text whose meaning is culturally variable. However, we must be wary of drawing too rigid a line between Romantic and modern hermeneutics, not only because the notion of a fixed meaning still has adherents today but also because many of the ideas of such major contemporary theorists as Hans-Georg Gadamer and PAUL RICOEUR are explicitly or embryonically present in their precursors.

Before the nineteenth century, interpretation is identified with textual exegesis as a process that yields a single valid meaning. The methods for arriving at that meaning are increasingly those of classical PHILOLOGY. Thus, for J. A. Ernesti, in his hermeneutical manual of 1761, the only criteria are the use of words, the historical circumstances governing their use, and the author's intention. For F. A. Wolf (1759–1824), whose work already points to the less narrowly linguistic definition of philology provided by his student Philip August Boeckh (1785–1867), meaning is established through the three stages of grammatical, historical, and philosophical interpretation: the study of the text in terms of the language, in terms of historical and biographical facts, and in terms of its ideas. According to Wolf, hermeneutics tries to "grasp the written or even spoken thoughts of an author as he would have them be grasped" (293). But meaning is not always equated with original meaning. J. S. Semler and G. E. LESSING see interpretation as a form of "demythologizing" that understands the spirit behind the work and translates it into modern (i.e., rational) terms. Conceding that interpretation is to some degree historical, these men nevertheless preserve the idea of an objective meaning by stopping history at their own period. Enlightenment hermeneutics is scientific, concerned with the text and its contexts rather than the interpreter or author, and committed to an objective though not necessarily original meaning.

Romantic hermeneutics introduces two far-reaching shifts whose full force has not been felt till now: an interest in the act of interpretation and an awareness of its historicity. With Friedrich Ast (1778–1841) and more influentially Friedrich Schleiermacher (1768–1834), philological hermeneutics is subsumed into "philosophical" hermeneutics, which is concerned less with establishing textual meaning than with the acts of understanding for which the text is an occasion. The dwindling authority of philology is most evident in the work of Ast, who replaces Wolf's philosophical interpretation with spiritual (geistig) interpretation: a Romantic version of the anagogic level in allegorical exegesis, which understands the text in relation to the spirit of the age as part of a world-historical totality. In addition to a methodology outlining the levels of interpretation, Ast also provides a philosophy of understanding based on F. W. J. Schelling's (1775–1854) philosophy of identity. Although he is more concerned with philology than Ast, Schleiermacher, too, moves in a metatheoretical direction, by insisting that particular rules of interpretation must be founded on a general theory of how we understand. The result is a shift of interest from validity in interpretation to the phenomenology of reading and the subjectivities of reader and author.

Because Schleiermacher's hermeneutics was developed over a long period of time (1805–32) in lectures never codified into books, we must be cautious about reading him too reductively. The traditional view is provided by Wilhelm Dilthey (1833–1911), whose biography of Schleiermacher traces the influence on him of JOHANN WOLFGANG VON GOETHE's research on organisms whose parts cohere within a living whole and places him in the context of a post-Kantian belief in the human capacity to understand wholeness from within instead of explaining it discursively. In Schleiermacher's well-known account of understanding, "grammatical" interpretation, which approaches the text in terms of the meaning of particular words, must be complemented by "psychological" interpretation, which is a projection into the creative process and the subjectivity of the author. The two approaches are interdependent, because by itself the philological dissection of the work is merely dry, while the phenomenological intuition of it as a product of the author's consciousness is mystical and unscholarly. The paradox of the "hermeneutic circle" is that we cannot truly understand the text's structural and linguistic parts except in the light of the whole, and yet we can only know the whole as it is expressed in its parts. Schleiermacher translates hermeneutics into distinctly Romantic terms, by emphasizing that interpretation must grasp the inner form of the text, what SAMUEL TAYLOR COLERIDGE calls the "essence" as distinct from the mere copyable "form" (Biographia Literaria, ed. J. Shawcross, 2 vols., 1954, 2:255). As Dilthey represents him, Schleiermacher's contribution to modern hermeneutics lies in his raising hermeneutics from a technical discipline to a form of humanistic interchange. Although the lives of other people are given us only in external forms such as actions and writings, the existence of a common substratum of human nature allows us to grasp "the distinct individuality of another" from within by translating external signs "from our own lives," in a version of what biblical hermeneutics describes as "applicative" reading

(Dilthey, *Selected* 247–48). Thus hermeneutics is not just an education in reading texts but a means of overcoming cultural distance and broadening our horizons.

But the Schleiermacher represented by Dilthey also serves modern theorists as a polemical point of contrast. He is distinctly Romantic in assuming that cultural interchange involves a simple identity between author and reader and that meaning is fixed by the author's intention. He assumes, moreover, a certain inadequacy in written texts, overcome through understanding as translinguistic contact between individuals. Were we to read only the 1819 *Compendium*, this view might seem accurate. But the "Academy Addresses" of 1825 and the untranslated final lectures also disclose tendencies that place Schleiermacher closer to his modern opponents than they might think. For one thing, his account of psychological interpretation grows steadily more complex, as it comes to include the analysis of "underlying" and "collateral" thoughts not fully articulated in the text (*Hermeneutik und Kritik* 159). The relationship of these "secondary" strands of thought to "leading" trains of thought is seen as one of complication as well as enrichment (*Hermeneutics* 154). Understanding thus becomes the grasping of a process rather than an original intention. Although Schleiermacher differs from Gadamer in subordinating reader to author, his awareness that the author is a highly complex entity, constituted through discourse with others, complicates the use of the author to limit the meaning of the text and is not inconsistent with a hermeneutics that allows for different readings. As important in disestablishing originary meaning is Schleiermacher's concept of "divinatory" or "prophetic" interpretation, which is mentioned in the *Compendium*, where a distinction between "divinatory" and "historical" reading intersects the major division between grammatical (objective) and psychological (subjective) interpretation. At the psychological level, for instance, "subjective-historical" reading *reconstructs* the author's intention; but "subjective-divinatory" reading *projects* a meaning not yet expressed in the text, thus allowing Schleiermacher to make his often-cited statement that the reader understands the text better than the author does. Divination clearly complicates any substantialist notion of the text as containing a single meaning and allows for the difference between the text and future readers explored by Gadamer.

The idea of divinatory interpretation is further developed by Schelling in the introduction to *The Ages of the World*, as well as by G. W. F. HEGEL (1770–1831), who consolidates the second major shift brought about by Romantic hermeneutics, toward an awareness of inter-

pretation as historically changing. Although he is concerned with the understanding of Being rather than with that of texts, Hegel is crucial in beginning the expansion of literary hermeneutics into a general hermeneutics concerned with all products of the human spirit that underlies the very different work of Dilthey and Ricoeur. In both *The Phenomenology of Mind* (1807) and the lectures on aesthetics given between 1823 and 1829, Hegel uses methods drawn from hermeneutics to read the text of intellectual history and the history of the arts. He deepens a grammatical reading that yields only a discontinuous succession of forms and events through a psychological reading that sees cultural forms as part of a teleologically unfolding whole. In other words, he breaks the hermeneutic circle at the level of history. He argues that individual historical moments can only be understood in the light of the entire history of Spirit, just as earlier theorists had argued that parts of the text must be read in the light of the whole and that the text itself must be placed in the author's canon. As distinct from his precursors, however, Hegel historicizes meaning. Moreover, historical study is no longer reconstructive nor even (as for Semler) the enlightened rereading of the past by the present; it is the opening of past and present to the future. Hegel thus prepares the way for Marxists such as FREDRIC JAMESON, who describes himself as restoring to the understanding of history a "hermeneutic" dimension evaporated from it by Althusserian structuralism (Jameson, *The Political Unconscious: Narrative as a Socially Symbolic Act*, 1981, 21). Jameson uses the term "hermeneutics" figuratively, to imply the understanding of surface phenomena that seem "unreadable" (to borrow PAUL DE MAN's word), so that these phenomena refer us to a deeper (but unknowable) necessity that binds them together.

But if Hegel abandons the philological reading of cultural forms in terms of their original significance, he also closes the process of interpretation by substituting teleological for original meaning. This pattern of anticipation and deflection also marks the relation to modern hermeneutics of Dilthey, often mistakenly identified with Schleiermacher. Writing at the turn of the century, Dilthey continues the Romantic interest in historicity, but without Hegel's interest in the metaphysical or Schleiermacher's in the psychological. He broadens the field of hermeneutics from the study of texts to the study of "life-expressions," anticipating the collapse of disciplinary boundaries that occurs in SEMIOTICS. Cultural forms are recognized as historical, but Dilthey does not anthropomorphize history by positing behind it a Spirit with which the interpreter can make contact. Correspondingly, in the study of texts, he is not interested in contact with the author and defines the inner form grasped by hermeneutics as a "mental structure" (*Essence* 34) created by "the processes in the poet's mind . . . yet separable from them" (*Pattern* 70). That Dilthey's very modernity makes him less akin than Schleiermacher to contemporary theorists of indeterminacy in meaning is, however, apparent if we recognize his approach as a "structural hermeneutics." He is hermeneutic in stressing the lived experience in cultural expressions rather than reducing experience to a system of semiotic exchange. But the inner meaning of signs is described through terms such as "structure" and "system," and hermeneutics as far as he is concerned traces recurrent patterns in life expressions so as to classify them rather than to disclose their irreducible complexity. This tendency to close meaning is repeated in Dilthey's hermeneutics of history. Rejecting both empirical history and a metaphysics of history that ascribes to it a total meaning, Dilthey practices a historicized Kantianism. He constructs a nonteleological but still global narrative of world-views, a classification but not an eschatology.

In conclusion, we can divide nineteenth-century hermeneutics into two phases, of which the earlier is the more radical. In its "Romantic" phase it opens the way to the contemporary awareness of indeterminacy, by seeing meaning as a historical or psychological process rather than as a finished product. Although the earlier theorists close this process by conceiving of it teleologically, this phase culminates in the work of SØREN KIERKEGAARD (1813–55), who retains the Romantic interest in subjectivity while placing closure and teleology under erasure. Thus *The Concept of Irony* (submitted as a dissertation in 1841) attempts a hermeneutics of the ironic or self-deconstructing text, only to frame its project within the very mode it is investigating. In *Point of View for My Work as an Author,* Kierkegaard crosses the threshold separating hermeneutics from READER-RESPONSE THEORY AND CRITICISM: he provides a retrospective interpretation of his canon, only to deconstruct his own authority by suggesting that the author is no more than a reader. In its "modern" phase, by contrast, nineteenth-century hermeneutics becomes more conservative. In the narrower field of biblical hermeneutics D. F. Strauss (1808–74) returns to the aporias within and between the gospels that initially stimulated Schleiermacher's work. But where his predecessor was interested in the indeterminacies of the processes behind texts, Strauss is more concerned with how interpretation is *determined* by a series of interpretive communities. In the wider field of the hermeneutics of understanding, Dilthey similarly abandons

metaphysical closure, but only to embrace a historical STRUCTURALISM, in which interpretation *places* life-expressions rather than allowing them to be *displaced* in the dialogue between past and present.

Tilottama Rajan

See also GERMAN THEORY AND CRITICISM: 1. STURM UND DRANG / WEIMAR CLASSICISM, 2. ROMANTICISM, and 3. NINETEENTH CENTURY.

Friedrich Ast, *Grundlinien der Grammatik, Hermeneutik und Kritik* (1808); August Boeckh, *Enzyklopädie und Methodologie der philologischen Wissenschaften* (ed. E. Bratuscheck, 2d ed., 1886, *On Interpretation and Criticism,* ed. and partial trans. John Paul Pritchard, 1968); Wilhelm Dilthey, *Die Entstehung der Hermeneutik* (1900, *Gesammelte Schriften,* vol. 5, 1958), *The Essence of Philosophy* (1907, trans. Stephen A. Emery and William T. Emery, 1954), *Das Leben Schleiermachers* (1870, *Gesammelte Schriften,* vols. 13–14, 1967), *Pattern and Meaning in History: Thoughts on History and Society* (ed. and trans. H. P. Rickman, 1961), *Selected Writings* (ed. and trans. H. P. Rickman, 1976); G. W. F. Hegel, *Phänomenologie des Geistes, Sämmtliche Werke* (ed. Hermann Glockner, 1927–40, 3d ed., 1949–59, vol. 2, *The Phenomenology of Mind,* trans. J. B. Baillie, rev. ed., 1931), *Vorlesungen über die Aesthetik* (ed. H. G. Hotho, 1835, rev. ed., 1842, *Sämmtliche Werke,* vols. 12–14, *Hegel's Aesthetics: Lectures on Fine Art,* trans. T. M. Knox, 2 vols., 1975); Søren Kierkegaard, *The Point of View for My Work as an Author* (1848, trans. Walter Lowrie, 1962), *The Concept of Irony* (trans. Lee M. Capel, 1966); Kurt Mueller-Vollmer, ed., *The Hermeneutics Reader: Texts of the German Tradition from the Enlightenment to the Present* (1985); F. W. J. Schelling, *Die Weltalter, Sämmtliche Werke* (ed. K. F. A. Schelling, 1861, pt. 1, vol. 8, *The Ages of the World,* trans. F. de Wolfe Bolman, 1946); F. D. E. Schleiermacher, *Hermeneutik* (ed. Heinz Kimmerle, 1959, *Hermeneutics: The Handwritten Manuscripts,* trans. James Duke and Jack Forstman, 1977), *Hermeneutik und Kritik mit besonderer Beziehung auf das Neue Testament* (ed. Friedrich Lücke, *Sämmtliche Werke,* 1868, pt. 1, vol. 2); David Friedrich Strauss, *Das Leben Jesu für das deutsche Volk bearbeitet* (1864, *The Life of Jesus, critically examined,* trans. George Eliot, ed. Peter C. Hodgson, 1972); F. A. Wolf, *Vorlesung über die Enzyklopädie der Altertumswissenschaft* (ed. J. D. Gürtler, 1831).

Julie Ellison, *Delicate Subjects: Romanticism, Gender, and the Ethics of Understanding* (1990); Hans Frei, *The Eclipse of Biblical Narrative: A Study in Eighteenth and Nineteenth Century Hermeneutics* (1974); Hans-Georg Gadamer, "Hegel and Heidegger," *Hegel's Dialectic: Five*

Hermeneutical Studies (trans. Christopher Smith, 1976); Roy Howard, *Three Faces of Hermeneutics: An Introduction to Current Theories of Understanding* (1982); Rudolf Makkreel, *Dilthey: Philosopher of the Human Studies* (1975); Richard E. Palmer, *Hermeneutics: Interpretation Theory in Schleiermacher, Dilthey, Heidegger, and Gadamer* (1969); Tilottama Rajan, *The Supplement of Reading: Figures of Understanding in Romantic Theory and Practice* (1990); William V. Spanos, "Heidegger, Kierkegaard, and the Hermeneutic Circle: Towards a Postmodern Theory of Interpretation as Dis-closure," *Martin Heidegger and the Question of Literature* (ed. Spanos et al., 1979); Peter Szondi, "Schleiermacher's Hermeneutics Today," *On Textual Understanding and Other Essays* (trans. Harvey Mendelsohn, 1986); Tzvetan Todorov, *Symbolisme et interprétation* (1978, *Symbolism and Interpretation,* trans. Catherine Porter, 1982).

2. Twentieth Century

In the twentieth century, the central innovation in hermeneutics is associated with the work of MARTIN HEIDEGGER (1889–1976) and his student Hans-Georg Gadamer (b. 1900). The general shift they advocated can be summarized in three areas. First, in contrast to the tradition since at least the Enlightenment, hermeneutics no longer concerns itself exclusively with the understanding and interpretation of written documents or speech. Second, unlike in Romantic hermeneutic theory from Friedrich Schleiermacher to Wilhelm Dilthey, the aim of understanding is not focused on the communication with or the psychology of another person. Third, the hermeneutics of Heidegger and Gadamer explores a realm that is prior to or more fundamental than Dilthey's separation of the natural sciences from the human sciences. Twentieth-century hermeneutics takes leave of the epistemological arena in which previous theories of understanding operated and moves into the area of "fundamental ontology," to use Heidegger's phrase. This means that understanding is not to be conceived transitively; we are not concerned with understanding something. Rather understanding is grasped as our way of being-in-the-world, as the fundamental way we exist prior to any cognition or intellectual activity. Ontological hermeneutics thus replaces the question of understanding as knowledge about the world with the question of being-in-the-world.

Heidegger's essential contribution to hermeneutic theory occurs in *Being and Time.* Indeed, he conceives of the phenomenology of *Dasein* as a fundamentally hermeneutic task. For him, understanding is something that exists prior to cognition. Its essence does not entail grasping the present situation but, rather, projection *(Entwurf)* into the future. It has to do with the grasping of *Dasein*'s own potentiality-for-Being, the Being-possible that is essential for the structure of *Dasein.* Thus, hermeneutics encompasses two aspects in Heidegger's thought. On the one hand, understanding designates the existentially prior order of *Dasein,* and, on the other, interpretation involves the possibility of Being belonging to *Dasein.* For Heidegger, interpretation is always grounded in something we have in advance, in a fore-having *(Vorhabe);* in something we see in advance, in a fore-sight *(Vorsicht);* and in something we grasp in advance, in a fore-conception *(Vorgriff).* This is another way of saying that we do not come to any object or text innocent of all presuppositions; we are always already filled with the primordial understanding Heidegger assigns to all *Dasein.* To understand a text in Heidegger's sense involves, not ferreting out some meaning placed there by the author, but rather unfolding the possibility of Being indicated by the text. And interpretation entails, not throwing a "signification" on a text or placing a value on it, but clarifying the involvement that is disclosed in our always prior understanding of the world.

Gadamer's magnum opus, *Truth and Method,* is an explication and continuation of Heidegger's thought. Gadamer is primarily concerned with the pernicious association of truth with the natural sciences in the modern age. His general thesis is that the experimental method hailed by the natural sciences since the seventeenth century is not the sole path to truth. The "and" in his title is thus disjunctive rather than connective. By contrast, Gadamer proposes a more fundamental level of truth identified with hermeneutic reflection. Against the tendency of natural science to ignore the primordial scope of understanding, Gadamer proposes hermeneutics as both a corrective and a metacritical orientation that would oversee all methodological endeavor. He is interested in explaining understanding as a universal category, conceived as the essence of our being-in-the-world.

To show how we have arrived at our present situation and to facilitate the recovery of former notions of truth and understanding, Gadamer embeds two parallel narratives in his book. The first tells the story of the Western philosophical tradition in the form of a fall from grace and a possible future redemption from this fallen state. In some pre-Cartesian time the scientific method had not yet come to dominate the notion of truth. Subject and object, being and thinking, were not yet radically severed from each other. But with the advent of Cartesian dualism the alienation of Western human beings became the cornerstone of Western philosophy. IMMANUEL KANT's *Critique of Pure Reason* is the most important philosophical document in this tradition, since he supplies the most ingenious epistemological apology for the natural sciences. Opposed to this tradition is the sphere of art. Gadamer's claim is that art has been systematically excluded from the sphere of truth by the hegemonic discourse of the natural sciences. In his critique of aesthetic consciousness he therefore seeks to recuperate this tradition for hermeneutics. Particularly important is the notion of play or game *(Spiel)*, which has the potential to overcome the subject/object dichotomy. In a game we give ourselves over to a set of rules beyond any individual subjectivity. We do not confront the game as an object but rather participate in it as an event. And in this participation the subject is itself transformed. Our relationship to art is analogous: we do not confront the artwork as a subject cognating an object; instead, we participate in the game that constitutes genuine art and are ourselves transformed. Indeed, for Gadamer play is the truth and essence of authentic art.

The second narrative has to do with the hermeneutic tradition. For Gadamer the origins of hermeneutics are intimately linked with the concern for discovering the correct sense of texts; hermeneutics seeks to reveal original meaning, whether the texts it treats are from the religious or the secular tradition. If the activity of legal interpretation is added to these two traditions, then we can see why pre-Romantic hermeneutics is presented in terms of a threefold power: *subtilitas intelligendi* (understanding), *subtilitas explicandi* (explication), and *subtilitas applicandi* (application). Gadamer's thesis is that hermeneutics abandons its original task. Starting with Schleiermacher, hermeneutics becomes associated with recapturing psychological states. Even when it had significant insights into the nature of understanding, nineteenth-century hermeneutics falls back onto a subject/object dichotomy informed by methodological thinking. A turning point is reached with Heidegger's critique of Edmund Husserl's PHENOMENOLOGY. In opening the ontological question, Heidegger did not seek a radical grounding of philosophy itself, as Husserl has done, or a foundation for the human sciences, which was Dilthey's project. Rather, in his fundamental ontology the whole idea of grounding itself experiences a total revision. His thesis, that Being is itself time, introduces a fundamental historicality into hermeneutic thought and allows history to become a productive force in understanding rather than an obstacle.

Gadamer integrates Heidegger's historicity of *Dasein* in his discussion of prejudice *(Vorurteil)*, a provocative

rephrasing of the Heideggerian structure of preunderstanding. One's necessary situatedness, consisting of "prejudices" and preconceptions brought to any text or encounter with another, is a fundamental aspect of hermeneutic understanding. Unlike in previous hermeneutic theory, the historicality of the interpreter is not a barrier to comprehension. A truly hermeneutic thinking must take into account its own historicality *(die eigene Geschichtlichkeit mitdenken)*. It is only a "proper hermeneutics" when it demonstrates the effectivity *(Wirkung)* of history within understanding itself. Accordingly, Gadamer calls this type of hermeneutics effective history *(Wirkungsgeschichte)*. With this notion Gadamer is not promoting a new type of method that would take influence and impact into account. Rather, he is calling for a new type of consciousness, "effective-historical consciousness" *(wirkungsgeschichtliches Bewußtsein)*, which would recognize what is already occurring when we encounter documents from the past. It encompasses the inevitable hermeneutic situation that occurs whenever we enter into a dialogue with the past. As such, effective-historical consciousness is intimately linked with Gadamer's notion of the horizon. Drawn from phenomenological theory, "horizon" describes and defines our situatedness in the world. It is not a closed or fixed structure but something that changes as we do. The act of understanding is conceived as a fusion of one's own horizon with the historical horizon *(Horizontverschmelzung)*.

In Germany the ontological conception of hermeneutics has been challenged most forcefully by JÜRGEN HABERMAS (b. 1929). Habermas agrees with Gadamer's notion of language as an open structure and finds himself allied with him in the struggle against positivistic tendencies in the social sciences. He contends, however, that Gadamer has gone too far in separating method from truth. Method, he points out, is part of our heritage as well and cannot be neatly separated out from effective-historical consciousness. By contrast, Habermas seeks a linking of the empirical and the analytical from the natural sciences with hermeneutics procedures. His more severe objections to Gadamer, however, concern a perceived ideological bias in Gadamer's work. Like many critics, he takes strong exception to Gadamer's anti-Enlightenment polemics with regard to prejudice, authority, and tradition. According to Habermas, Gadamer's championing of the prejudices handed down by tradition denies our ability to reflect upon these prejudices and to reject them. Agents appear as passive recipients caught in the endless stream of their heritage. What Habermas wants is a critical dimension in hermeneutic thought, one that would enable us to carry out a critique of ideology *(Ideologiekritik)* without sacrificing the notion of historicality.

The chief challenge to Gadamer in the United States has come from more conservative quarters. Unlike Habermas, E. D. Hirsch (b. 1928) has objected to Gadamer's reliance on historicality, since it relativizes meaning and calls into question a valid standard for interpretation. Indeed, Hirsch's main concern is to establish the existence of a timeless validity for interpretation. His first task is therefore to account for the empirical fact that different epochs and different critics interpret the same work differently. He does this by establishing two levels on which we relate to texts. The first he labels "meaning" or "verbal meaning." It is invariable; it is the concern of interpretation; and the faculty that governs it is understanding. The second level Hirsch calls "significance." This level may vary according to the age or the author, although it is not arbitrary. It is defined by the relationship of verbal meaning to something outside this meaning. The task Hirsch assigns to criticism is to determine significance in texts. The faculty we exercise in doing criticism is judgment. The empirically observable variety of commentary on literary works is thus attributable to differences in significance. Meaning in Hirsch's model remains determinate.

Hirsch's second task is to find a valid standard against which to measure this determinate meaning. Opposing the New Critical intentional fallacy as well as Gadamer's claim that meaning always surpasses the intention of the author, Hirsch returns to older psychological models in maintaining that only authorial intent supplies a valid criterion for meaning. Validity for him is a relationship of correspondence: a valid interpretation is one that corresponds to the meaning represented by the text. Rejecting all variants of semantic autonomy, he contends in an argument influenced by phenomenology that meaning is invariably an affair of consciousness. Thus, meaning must be associated with one of the two consciousnesses that come into contact with the text, that of the author or that of the reader. Hirsch believes, however, that if we take the reader's consciousness as our standard, we sacrifice any yardstick for measuring validity, since there are invariably many readers for every text. Hirsch's strongest defense of authorial intent therefore rests on the simple fact that it alone offers us a genuinely discriminating norm against which to compare various interpretations.

The various conflicts in theories of interpretation from the twentieth century have been mediated most successfully by PAUL RICOEUR (b. 1913). His phenomenological hermeneutics has often been involved with reconciling rival claims to priority. He has successfully shown how apparently exclusive branches of philosophy are dependent on each other. In discussing the relationship between STRUCTURALISM or phenomenology and hermeneutics, he demonstrates that each remains the presupposition of the other. Perhaps most original in his own work is his theory of symbolism. For Ricoeur, language stands at the center of any interpretive theory. But not every linguistic artifact calls for the application of hermeneutics. Hermeneutics is needed only in those instances in which there exists a surplus of meaning, or when multivocal expressions are employed. Ricoeur identifies such occurrences with symbolism, which he defines as any structure of signification in which a direct, primary, literal meaning designates, in addition, another meaning that is indirect, secondary, and figurative and can be apprehended only through the first. The task of interpretation is thus limited to dealing with symbols. It is the mode of thought that deciphers the hidden meaning in the apparent meaning or that unfolds the levels of meaning implied in the literal meaning.

In Ricoeur's view, theories of interpretation can be divided into two categories. The first type, associated with the work of the German theologian Rudolf Bultmann, attributes to hermeneutics the function of recapturing or recollecting meaning. This hermeneutics of faith or hermeneutics of the sacred seeks to make manifest or to restore a meaning, understood as a message, a proclamation, or a kerygma. It tries to make sense of what was once understood but has become obscure because of distantiation. Opposed to this religiously tinged hermeneutics of the sacred is a hermeneutics of suspicion. Identified in particular with the work of KARL MARX AND FRIEDRICH ENGELS, FRIEDRICH NIETZSCHE, and SIGMUND FREUD, this model of interpretation tears away masks and reveals false consciousness. It distrusts the word and therefore attempts to go below the surface to disclose some more authentic realm of meaning. But even these two distinct branches of hermeneutics are ultimately united by Ricoeur. In a brilliant analysis of Freud's work he shows how symbols function both to disguise our desires and to reveal a dialectic of self-consciousness. Thus, the two hermeneutics are themselves only aspects of a larger cultural process.

Two postwar German contributors to hermeneutic theory, Peter Szondi (1929–71) and Manfred Frank (b. 1945), have also applied a strategy of mediation in their work. Both Szondi and Frank, however, have been most productive in bringing together recent French thought, particularly structuralism and poststructuralism, and German hermeneutics through the work of Schleiermacher.

For Szondi, whose goal was to develop a philological hermeneutics, Schleiermacher is relevant because of his emphasis on a material theory of interpretation. In contrast to most of his contemporaries, who saw words and language as a mere vehicle for the transmission of ideas, Schleiermacher stressed the constraints imposed by genre, poetic form, and the letter. His insistence on the letter makes him for Szondi a forerunner to various brands of poststructuralism and suggests a basic compatibility between French and German theory.

Frank's work has confronted Gadamer's hermeneutics with poststructuralist tendencies, especially with DECONSTRUCTION. In terms of the history of philosophy, he points out that poststructuralism and hermeneutics confront the essential problems of modern thought: the absence of transcendental values and the questioning of subjectivity. They have diverged most significantly with regard to their evaluation of the possibility of an authentic dialogic situation. Relying on Schleiermacher's hermeneutical theory, Frank develops the notion of dialogue as both an individual and a general activity *(individuelles Allgemeines)*. Understanding could not occur without a shared, supra-individual code. But it would also be impossible without the individual construction and actualizing of that code. Deconstruction and hermeneutics are most compatible, however, when they affirm the insurmountable asymmetry of encounters between speaking subjects. Unlike some of the wilder poststructuralists, Frank does not feel that asymmetry opens the floodgates to arbitrariness. Hypotheses made by one partner in a dialogue, he points out, are always motivated, and in this sense they can also be called upon for (relative) accountability. But versions of hermeneutics and poststructuralism can be reconciled only by limiting the infinite play of signification while at the same time maintaining the impossibility of determinacy.

Robert C. Holub

See also GERMAN THEORY AND CRITICISM: 4. TWENTIETH CENTURY TO 1968, JÜRGEN HABERMAS, and MARTIN HEIDEGGER.

Manfred Frank, *Das individuelle Allgemeine: Textstrukturierung und -interpretation nach Schleiermacher* (1977); Hans-Georg Gadamer, *Wahrheit und Methode: Grundzüge einer philosophischen Hermeneutik* (1960, 5th ed., *Gesammelte Werke,* vol. 1, ed. J. C. B. Mohr, 1986, *Truth and Method,* trans. Garrett Barden and John Cumming, 1975, 2d ed., trans. rev. Joel Weinsheimer and Donald G. Marshall, 1989); Jürgen Habermas, "Der hermeneutische Ansatz," *Zur Logik der Sozialwissenschaften* (1967, "A Review of Gadamer's *Truth and Method,*" *Understanding and Social Inquiry,* ed. Fred R. Dallmayr and Thomas A. McCarthy, 1977), "Der Universalitätsanspruch der Hermeneutik," *Hermeneutik und Dialektik* (ed. Conrad Kramer and Reiner Wiehl, 1970, "The Hermeneutic Claim to Universality," *Contemporary Hermeneutics: Hermeneutics as Method, Philosophy, and Critique,* ed. Josef Bleicher, 1980); Martin Heidegger, *Sein und Zeit* (1927, *Being and Time,* trans. John Macquarrie and Edward Robinson, 1962); E. D. Hirsch, Jr., *Validity in Interpretation* (1967); Paul Ricoeur, *Le Conflit des interprétations: Essais d'hérméneutique* (1969, *The Conflict of Interpretations: Essays in Hermeneutics,* trans. Don Ihde, 1974), *De l'interprétation: Essai sur Freud* (1965, *Freud and Philosophy: An Essay on Interpretation,* trans. Denis Savage, 1970); Peter Szondi, *Einführung in die literarische Hermeneutik* (ed. Jean Bollack and Helen Stierlin, 1975), *On Textual Understanding and Other Essays* (trans. Harvey Mendelsohn, 1986).

Josef Bleicher, *Contemporary Hermeneutics: Hermeneutics as Method, Philosophy, and Critique* (1980); Roy J. Howard, *Three Faces of Hermeneutics: An Introduction to Current Theories of Understanding* (1982); David Couzens Hoy, *The Critical Circle: Literature, History, and Philosophical Hermeneutics* (1978); Diane P. Michelfelder and Richard E. Palmer, eds., *Dialogue and Deconstruction* (1989); Kurt Müller-Vollmer, ed., *The Hermeneutics Reader: Texts of the German Tradition from the Enlightenment to the Present* (1985); Gayle L. Ormiston and Alan D. Schrift, eds., *The Hermeneutic Tradition: From Ast to Ricoeur* (1990); Richard E. Palmer, *Hermeneutics: Interpretation Theory in Schleiermacher, Dilthey, Heidegger, and Gadamer* (1969); T. K. Seung, *Semiotics and Thematics in Hermeneutics* (1982); Gary Shapiro and Alan Sica, eds., *Hermeneutics: Questions and Prospects* (1984); John B. Thompson, *Critical Hermeneutics: A Study in the Thought of Paul Ricoeur and Jürgen Habermas* (1981); Georgia Warnke, *Gadamer: Hermeneutics, Tradition, and Reason* (1987); Joel C. Weinsheimer, *Gadamer's Hermeneutics: A Reading of "Truth and Method"* (1985).

HISTORICAL THEORY AND CRITICISM

Historical theory and criticism embraces not only the theory and practice of literary historiographical representation but also other types of criticism that, often without acknowledgment, presuppose a historical ground or adopt historical methods in an ad hoc fashion. Very frequently, what is called literary criticism, particularly as it was institutionalized in the nineteenth century and even up to the late twentieth century, is based on historical principles.

ARISTOTLE commented on the origins of tragedy, Quintilian reviewed the history of oratory, and bibliographies and collections of books studied together existed in antiquity and in the Middle Ages. Yet a genuine literary or art history, finding continuity and change amid documents and data, was not possible until the growth of the historical sense in the Renaissance. Giorgio Vasari's *Lives of the Artists* (1550), comprising over 150 biographies, towers above all Renaissance literary and art histories. It was no mere grouping of separate lives but an attempt to trace the progress of Italian art from Giotto to the age of Michelangelo, to establish the concept of a period (three of them for 1300–1550), and to distinguish one period from another. Despite Vasari's example, the art history and literary history of the next two centuries were dominated by antiquarianism and chronologism.

The theory of modern historical criticism begins in the Enlightenment. Responding to the scientific revolution of the previous century, GIAMBATTISTA VICO divided mathematics and physics from the humanities and what are now called the social sciences and stipulated by his *verum factum* principle that one can fully know only what one has made, namely, the products of language, civil institutions, and culture. In his *New Science* (1725) he argued that the closest knowledge of a thing lay in the study of its origins; outlined a concept of poetic logic by which one could grasp imaginatively the myths, customs, and fables of primitive cultures; and presented a theory of cultural development. Neither theology, philosophy, nor mathematics was the science of sciences: it was the "new science"—"history"—understood in Vichian terms. In his *History of Ancient Art* (1764) Johann Joachim Winckelmann studied "the origin, growth, change, and decline of classical art together with the different styles of various nations, times, and artists," including Etruscan, Oriental, Greek, and Roman art. Though he surveyed "outward conditions," he undermined his relativizing initiative in maintaining the neoclassical doctrine that Greek art is timeless and normative and in urging its imitation. Nevertheless, his definition of Greek art in terms of "noble simplicity and tranquil grandeur" distinguished the classical ideal from postclassical tendencies, thereby establishing one of the two polarities and prompting the need to define the other (quoted in Winckelmann, *Reflections on the Imitation of Greek Works in Painting and Sculpture*, 1987, xvii, 33).

In England, the Homeric studies of Thomas Blackwell (1735) and Robert Wood (1769) sought to link the epic poet to the character of the times. Blackwell enumerated "a *concource* of *natural* causes" that "conspired to produce and cultivate that mighty genius": climate, geography, phase of cultural and linguistic development, Homer's "being born poor, and living a stroling indigent Bard" (quoted in Mayo 50). In his pioneering *History of English Poetry* (1774–81) Thomas Warton explored the changing fortunes of various genres from the Middle Ages to the sixteenth century in terms of primitive and sophisticated art. SAMUEL JOHNSON joined the narrative of a life, a critical analysis of the works, and a study of the poet's mind and character in his *Lives of the Poets* (1779–81), virtually creating the genre of literary biography. He also pondered writing a "History of Criticism . . . from Aristotle to the present age" (Walter Jackson Bate, *Samuel Johnson*, 1977, 532).

Although Johann Gottfried von Herder was not willing to abandon artistic universality or German nationalism, he was too much of a historical relativist to take the art of any one society as normative. He criticized Winckelmann for valuing Greek over Egyptian art when he did not take into account their vast cultural and environmental differences. Herder showed his appreciation for these difficulties in his treatment of the Arab influence on Provençal poetry. His historical method posited two basic assumptions: "that the literary standards of one nation cannot apply directly to the work of another" and "that in the same nation standards must vary from period to period" (Miller 7). In his *Ideas on the Philosophy of History* (1784–91) he drew analogies from organic nature and pressed for the investigation of physical, social, and moral contexts to depict the progressive development of national character. In his view, literature *(Volkspoesie)* is the product of an entire people striving to express itself, and though he himself believed that each nation contributed to the overarching ideal of universal art, his writings were subsequently appropriated to support national literary history. In response to Winckelmann, he located the beginnings of the modern artistic spirit in the Middle Ages and considered the *Roman* (a mixed genre of broad, variegated content, including philosophy) to be the quintessentially modern genre.

Both the theory and the practice of literary history expanded in the wake of the French Revolution and German idealist philosophy. G. W. F. HEGEL defined *Geist* as the collective energies of mind and feeling that produce the *Zeitgeist,* or spirit of the age, and he conceived of the history of art in three movements illustrating the dialectical progression of *Geist:* oriental, in which matter overcomes the plastic expression of the idea; classical, in which the idea and its embodiment are in perfect equilibrium; and Romantic or modern, in which the idea, freed from subjugation, cannot be adequately expressed in material form. August von Schlegel's *Lectures on Dramatic Art and Literature* (1809–11) developed Herder's notion of the two categories of Western art, classical and postclassical (conditioned by Christianity and mainly "northern") for which the word "Romantic" became the preferred term. His goal was to trace "the origin and spirit of the *romantic* in the history of art." In his formulation, the classic represents formal unity, natural harmony, objectivity, distinctness, the finite, and "enjoyment"; the Romantic signifies incompleteness, subjectivity, "internal discord," indistinctness, infinity, and "desire," idealism and melancholy being the chief characteristics of Romantic poetry (25–27). The Romantic outlook on historical writing stressed the organic nature of change, process rather than mere product. GERMAINE DE STAËL adopted the distinction between classic and Romantic in her influential *De L'Allemagne* (1810, *On Germany*).

Friedrich von Schlegel set these historical categories on firmer theoretical ground. His sociologically oriented *Lectures on the History of Literature* (1815) examine not only European languages but also Hebrew, Persian, and Sanskrit, thereby extending the range of comparative literary studies. Yet he advised against comparing poems of different ages and countries, preferring that they be compared with other works produced in their own time and country. He called for the study of the "national recollections" of a whole people, which are most fully revealed in literature, broadly defined and including poetry, fiction, philosophy, history, "eloquence and wit." Literature contains "the epitome of all intellectual capabilities and progressive improvements of mankind." For Schlegel, the modern spirit in literature reveals itself best in the novel combining the poetic and the prosaic; philosophy, criticism, and inspiration; and irony. Beyond the histories of individual nations, he applied his organicist principle to the effect that literature is "a great, completely coherent and evenly organized whole, comprehending in its unity many worlds of art and itself forming a peculiar work of art" (7–10). This is the Romantic ideal of totality, as in Hegel's formulation that the true is the whole, and Schlegel heralded a "universal progressive poetry" (quoted in Wellek, *Discriminations* 29). "The national consciousness, expressing itself in works of narrative and illustration, is *History*." The stage was set for the major achievements of nineteenth-century narrative literary history.

The unifying ideal of these works—the essence of nineteenth-century historicism—was that the key to reality and truth lay in the continuous unfolding of history. They were founded on a few key organizational premises: "an initial situation from which the change proceeds"; "a final situation in which the first situation eventuates and which contrasts with the first in kind, quality, or amount"; "a continuing matter which undergoes change"; and "a moving cause, or convergence of moving causes" (Crane 33). The subject matter might be an idea (the sublime), a technique (English prose rhythm), a tradition (that of "wit"), a school (the Pléiade), a reputation (Ossian), a genre or subgenre, the "mind" of a nation or race. The principal subject was treated like a hero in a plot (birth, struggle to prominence, defeat of an older generation); emplotments were of three basic types, "rise, decline, and rise and decline" (Perkins, *Is Literary* 39). The works as a whole were characterized by a strong teleological drive. Representative narrative histories of the national stamp are Georg Gottfried Gervinus's *History of the Poetic National Literature of the Germans* (1835–42), Julian Schmidt's *History of German Literature since the Death of Lessing* (1861), FRANCESCO DE SANCTIS's *History of Italian Literature* (1870–71), Wilhelm Scherer's *History of German Literature* (1883), and Gustave Lanson's *Histoire de la littérature française* (1894). Taking a "scientific view," Georg Brandes considered literary criticism to be "the history of the soul," and his supranational and comparatist *Main Currents in Nineteenth Century Literature* (1872–90) traces "the outlines of a psychology" of the period 1800–1850, its thesis being "the gradual fading away and disappearance of the ideas and feelings of the preceding century, and the return of the idea of progress" (*Main* 1:vii).

In the mid-nineteenth century literary historians began searching among the social and natural sciences for models and analogies, for instance, Comtean positivism, JOHN STUART MILL's atomistic psychology, or Charles Darwin's evolutionary biology. CHARLES AUGUSTIN SAINTE-BEUVE borrowed scientific analogies of a general nature in his historical and biographical criticism. His subtle, probing works cannot be pigeonholed. "I analyze, I botanize, I am a naturalist of minds," he said (quoted in Bate 490), and he counseled that "one cannot take too many methods or hints to know a man; he is another thing than pure spirit" (Bate 499). For Victorian literary history RENÉ WELLEK proposes four main categories: the scientific and static, the scientific and dynamic, the idealistic and static, and the idealistic and dynamic (*Discriminations* 153). Henry Hallam's *Introduction to the Literature of Europe* (1837–39) is atomistic and cyclical, starting at 1500 and beginning again at 50-year intervals. In his *History of English Literature* (1863–64) HIPPOLYTE TAINE set forth a deterministic explanation of literary works with three principal causes (race, moment, and milieu); these are the "externals," which lead to a center, the "genuine man," "that mass of faculties and feelings which are the inner man" (*History* 1:7). His dictum "Vice and virtue are products, like vitriol and sugar" (1:11) is a chemical analogy. He chose England as if he were a scientist preparing an experiment: England had a long and continuous tradition that could be traced developmentally and up to the present, in vivo as well as in vitro. Other national literatures were rejected for one reason or another. Latin literature had too weak a start, Germany had a two-hundred-year interruption, Italy and Spain declined after the seventeenth century. A Frenchman might lack the requisite objectivity in writing the history of his own nation. The Darwinian influence can be seen in the work of Taine's pupil Ferdinand Brunetière. In *L'Évolution des genres dans l'histoire de la littérature* (1890) he treated a literary genre as if it were a genus of nature, noting its origin, rise, and fall and situating a work of art at its appropriate place on the curve.

Some literary historians produced works in several categories. Leslie Stephen's *History of English Thought in the Eighteenth Century* (1876) adapts an idealist viewpoint to describe the rise of agnosticism, while his *English Literature and Society in the Eighteenth Century* (1904) is deterministic, sociological, and "scientific": literature is the "noise of the wheels of history" (quoted in Wellek, *Discriminations* 155). An example of the idealistic and dynamic category is W. J. Courthope's six-volume *History of English Poetry* (1895–1910), which finds "the unity of the subject precisely where the political historian looks for it, namely, in the life of the nation as a whole," and which uses "the facts of political and social history as keys to the poet's meaning" (1:xv). Courthope wanted to uncover the "almost imperceptible gradations" of linguistic and metrical advance: "By this means the transition of imagination from mediæval to modern times will appear much less abrupt and mysterious than we have been accustomed to consider it" (1:xxii). George Saintsbury's *Short History of English Literature* (1898), *History of Criticism* (1906), and *History of English Prose Rhythm* (1912) are at once erudite and impressionistic, and occasionally idiosyncratic in their judgments. Obviously many literary histories were eclectic in their methodology and fell between categories.

Among the shortcomings of nineteenth-century narrative histories were the imbalance between the space given to the individual work of art and the background materials required to "explain" it. Too little attention

was given to analysis of the work itself and to questions of literary merit. Often enough, works were submerged by their contexts and causes, which were in a sense infinite (philological, psychological, social, moral, economic, political). David Masson's seven-volume "life and times" biography of Milton (1881) was heavily weighted toward the times; in his review James Russell Lowell complained that Milton had been reduced to "a speck on the enormous canvas" (251). The problem of multiplicity of contexts and the consequences involved in choosing among them was addressed by Johann Gustav Droysen in *Historik* (1857–82), which anticipates BENEDETTO CROCE. Droysen accepted the fact that a historian's ideological biases, often unexamined and arbitrary, came into play and predetermined the investigation. He showed how the historian could use this knowledge to advantage and mapped the different rhetorics of historical representation.

Inevitably, large-scale narrative history sank beneath its own weight and fell from favor. Literary historians chose ever-smaller areas of investigation, though with a wider attention to the variety of causal contexts. As Louis Cazamian said in his and Émile Legouis's *History of English Literature* (1924), the "field of literature" needed to be widened to comprehend "philosophy, theology, and the wider results of the sciences" (1971 ed., xxi). Whatever their shortcomings, many narrative literary histories were brilliantly conceived and immensely readable, and perhaps these are the reasons why the genre has not ceased to be written.

In the last quarter of the nineteenth century the weaknesses and failings of the whole historicist enterprise were exposed by FRIEDRICH NIETZSCHE, Wilhelm Dilthey, and Croce. Although Nietzsche's *Birth of Tragedy* (1872) also falls in the category of narrative literary history, he attacked historical criticism in the second of his *Untimely Meditations*, "On the Advantages and Disadvantages of History for Life." Nietzsche argued, not without irony, against history because the preoccupation with the past tended to relativize all knowledge, weigh down individual effort, and sap the vigor "for life." The past must be "forgotten" in some sense if anything new was to be done.

Dilthey also objected to the positivist domination of history and formulated a theory of *Geisteswissenschaften,* or "human sciences," comprising the social and humanistic sciences, which differed from the natural sciences in their interpretive approach. According to his method of *Geistesgeschichte,* material and cultural (i.e., natural) forces join in the creation of the unifying mind or spirit of a period. The critic must come into contact with the

Erlebnis ("lived experience") of a writer, a hermeneutical recapturing, or "re-experiencing," of the past that requires not only intellect but imagination and empathy. The biographical essay becomes one of Dilthey's preferred kinds of practical criticism: "Understanding the totality of an individual's existence and describing its nature in its historical milieu is a high point of historical writing. . . . Here one appreciates the will of a person in the course of his life and destiny in his dignity as an end in itself" (*Introduction* 37). *Das Erlebnis und die Dichtung* (1906) illustrates his method in studies of G. E. LESSING, JOHANN WOLFGANG VON GOETHE, Novalis, and FRIEDRICH HÖLDERLIN.

Like Dilthey, though from a very different point of view, Benedetto Croce offered a critique of historicism that takes place within the historicist tradition itself. In *Estetica* (1902) Croce, who began his career as a historian of the theater and memorials of Naples, attacked dry positivist historicism and sociological criticism for dissolving the essential quality of the literary work, its "intuition," into myriad causes (psychology, society, race, other literary works). He objected strongly to the organization of literary history on the basis of genres, schools, rhetorical tropes, meters, sophisticated versus folk poetry, the sublime, and so on. These were "pseudo-concepts," useful labels perhaps for a given purpose but essentially arbitrary designations standing between reader and text. Moreover, none of these "pseudo-concepts" could help decide a case between "poetry" and "nonpoetry": "All the books dealing with classification and systems of the arts could be burned without any loss whatever." Croce argued on behalf of the presentness and particularity of the "intuition"; what is past is made present and vital in the act of judgment and narration: "Every true history is contemporary history" (*Aesthetic as Science of Expression and General Linguistic,* 1902, trans. Douglas Ainslie, 1953, 114; *History* 11). His goal was to bring about a cultural renewal in which the traditional humanistic subjects, history and poetry, might once again play their central educative role and a new form of literary history would replace historicism. Croce's critique was one of the first salvos in the idealist attack on science and positivism that continued well into the twentieth century. Aestheticism itself contributed to the disparagement of science and the revival of the idea of the genius, wholly exceptional, inexplicable, "above" an age.

In the twentieth century literary history lost the theoretical high ground in the academy. Modernism, NEW CRITICISM, RUSSIAN FORMALISM, *nouvelle critique*—all have an antihistoricist bias, posit the autonomy of the

work of art, and focus on structural and formal qualities. At the same time, though the age of criticism had succeeded the age of historicism, literary history remained the most common activity within literary studies. Formalist and psychological approaches to a work of art are often found to lean on historical premises or to require a historically determined fact to build a case. As for narrative literary history, the errors and lessons of the nineteenth century were not in vain, and the achievements of modern historical scholarship are characterized by an awareness of the intellectual and rhetorical problems involved in their production.

Twentieth-century literary history offers a variety of models. One of the most common is a dialectical structure in which the main subject oscillates between two poles. In Cazamian's history, long a standard work, phases of reason and intelligence (the classical) alternate with phases of imagination and feeling (Romantic). The dialectic of J. Livingston Lowes's *Convention and Revolt in Poetry* (1919) is apparent from its title. The same writer's *Road to Xanadu: A Study in the Ways of the Imagination* (1927) is an exhaustive source study of Samuel Taylor Coleridge's "Rime of the Ancient Mariner" and "Kubla Khan." In another model the literary historian depicts a "time of troubles" or "babble-like era of confusion—a time of transition from a purer past to a repurified future" (LaCapra 99). R. S. Crane and David Perkins each argue on behalf of "immanentist" theories that study the processes of change from a viewpoint within a tradition. Writers are compared and contrasted with predecessors and successors, and newness and difference are valued. Examples are Brunetière, the Russian Formalists, W. Jackson Bate's *Burden of the Past and the English Poet* (1970), HAROLD BLOOM's *Anxiety of Influence* (1973) and *The Map of Misreading* (1975), and Perkins's *History of Modern Poetry* (2 vols., 1976–87), but Vasari's *Lives* also has an immanentist theme. Some of the finest modern literary histories mix history, narrative, and criticism, selecting their contexts as particular works of art suggest them: F. O. Matthiessen's *American Renaissance: Art and Expression in the Age of Emerson and Whitman* (1941), with its attempt to portray the *Geist* of transcendentalism; Douglas Bush's *English Literature in the Earlier Seventeenth Century, 1600–1660* (1945); and *A Literary History of England,* ed. Albert C. Baugh (1948). The period has also produced major literary biographies in Leon Edel on HENRY JAMES, Richard Ellmann on James Joyce and OSCAR WILDE, and W. Jackson Bate on John Keats and Samuel Johnson.

In the era of POSTMODERNISM the theory of literary history has again received serious attention in MICHEL FOUCAULT, HAYDEN WHITE, and NEW HISTORICISM.

Postmodern literary histories flout the conventions of historical narrative and display the gaps, differences, discontinuities, crossing (without touching) patterns, not in the hope of capturing the essence of reality, but with the intention of showing that reality has no single essence. The avowedly "postmodern" *Columbia Literary History of the United States* (1988), which has 66 writers, "acknowledges diversity, complexity, and contradiction by making them structural principles, and it forgoes closure as well as consensus." "No longer is it possible, or desirable," the editor claims, "to formulate an image of continuity" (xiii, xxi). The encyclopedic idea has replaced historical narration. New Historicism situates the text at the center of intense contextualization, a single episode being examined from multiple perspectives. This runs the risk of overcontextualization, loss of the larger picture, and failure to account for the dynamics of historical change (see LaCapra).

In his skeptical *Is Literary History Possible?* (1992) Perkins reviews the theory and practice of literary history and comments on the "insurmountable contradictions in organizing, structuring, and presenting the subject" and "the always unsuccessful attempt of every literary history to explain the development of literature that it describes." At the same time, he defends both the writing and the reading of literary history, maintaining that objectivity is not an all-or-nothing affair. Literary history must not "surrender the ideal of objective knowledge," for without it "the otherness of the past would entirely deliquesce in endless subjective and ideological reappropriations" (ix, 185). His humanistic position, skeptical of system and classification, shows one way through the antihistoricism and skepticism of the present, while remaining aware of the pitfalls that have beset historical criticism in the past.

John Paul Russo

See also M. H. ABRAMS, BENEDETTO CROCE, and HIPPOLYTE TAINE.

Walter Jackson Bate, ed., *Criticism: The Major Texts* (1952, rev. ed., 1970, prefaces published separately as *Prefaces to Criticism,* 1959); Sacvan Bercovitch, ed., *Reconstructing American Literary History* (1986); Georg Brandes, *Hovedstrømninger: Det 19de aarhundredes litteratur* (6 vols., 1872–90, *Main Currents in Nineteenth Century Literature,* trans. Diana White and Mary Morison, 1901–5); Douglas Bush, "Literary History and Literary Criticism," *Literary History and Literary Criticism* (ed. Leon Edel et al., 1964); Peter Carafiol, *The American Ideal: Literary History as a Worldly Activity* (1991); Bainard Cowan and Joseph G. Kronick, eds., *Theorizing American Literature: Hegel, the Sign, and History* (1991); Ronald S. Crane, *Critical and Historical Principles of Literary History* (1971); Benedetto Croce, *La Poesia* (1936, 6th ed., 1963, *Benedetto Croce's Poetry and Literature: An Introduction to Its Criticism and History,* trans. Giovanni Gullace, 1981), *Teoria e storia della storiografia* (1917, 2d ed., 1919, *History: Its Theory and Practice,* trans. Douglas Ainslie, 1921); Philip Damon, ed., *Literary Criticism and Historical Understanding* (1967); Wilhelm Dilthey, *Introduction to the Human Sciences: An Attempt to Lay a Foundation for the Study of Society and History* (1883, trans. Ramon J. Betanzos, 1988), *Poetry and Experience, Selected Works,* vol. 5 (ed. Rudolf A. Makkreel and Frithjof Rodi, 1985); Emory Elliott et al., eds., *Columbia Literary History of the United States* (1988); Michel Foucault, *Les Mots et les choses* (1966, *The Order of Things: An Archeology of the Human Sciences,* trans. Alan Sheridan, 1970); Giovanni Getto, *Storia delle storie letterarie* (1942); John G. Grumley, *History and Totality: Radical Historicism from Hegel to Foucault* (1989); Giovanni Gullace, *Taine and Brunetière on Criticism* (1982); G. W. F. Hegel, *The Introduction to Hegel's Philosophy of Fine Art* (trans. Bernard Bosenquet, 1905); Peter Uwe Hohendahl, *Building a National Literature: The Case of Germany, 1830–1870* (1985, trans. Renate Baron Franciscono, 1989); J. R. de J. Jackson, *Historical Criticism and Meaning of Texts* (1989); Hans Robert Jauss, *Toward an Aesthetic of Reception* (trans. Timothy Bahti, 1982); Reinhart Koselleck, *Futures Past: On the Semantics of Historical Time* (1979, trans. Keith Tribe, 1985); Dominick LaCapra, *History and Criticism* (1985); Émile Legouis and Louis Cazamian, *Histoire de la littérature anglaise* (1924, *History of English Literature,* trans. Helen Douglas Irvine, 2 vols., 1926–27, rev. ed., 1 vol., 1930, rev. ed., 1971); James Russell Lowell, *Among My Books* (1904); Jerome J. McGann, *The Beauty of Inflections: Literary Investigations in Historical Method and Theory* (1985); Robert S. Mayo, *Herder and the Beginnings of Comparative Literature* (1969); G. M. Miller, *The Historical Point of View in English Literary Criticism from 1570–1770* (1913); David Perkins, *Is Literary History Possible?* (1992); David Perkins, ed., *Theoretical Issues in Literary History* (1990); Paul Ricoeur, *Temps et récit* (3 vols., 1983–85, *Time and Narrative,* vols. 1–2, trans. Kathleen McLaughlin and David Pellauer, 1984–85, vol. 3, trans. Kathleen Blamey and David Pellauer, 1988); Richard Ruland, *The Rediscovery of American Literature: Premises of Critical Taste, 1900–1940* (1967); August von Schlegel, *Über dramatische Kunst und Litteratur* (2 vols., 1809–11, *A Course of Lectures on Dramatic Art and Literature,* 1817, trans. John Black, rev. A. J. W. Morrison, 1846); Friedrich von Schlegel, *Geschichte der alten und neuen Litteratur* (1815, *Lectures on the History of Liter-*

ature, Ancient and Modern, 1859); Hippolyte Taine, *Histoire de la littérature anglaise* (4 vols., 1863–64, *History of English Literature,* trans. H. van Laun, 2 vols., 1872, rev. ed., 8 vols., 1897); H. Aram Veeser, ed., *The New Historicism* (1989); Giambattista Vico, *The New Science* (1725, 3d ed., 1744, trans. Thomas Goddard Bergin and Max Harold Fisch, 1948, rev. ed., 1968); Robert Weimann, *Structure and Society in Literary History: Studies in the History and Theory of Historical Criticism* (1976); René Wellek, *Discriminations: Further Concepts of Criticism* (1970), *A History of Modern Criticism, 1750–1950* (8 vols., 1955–93); Hayden White, *The Content of the Form: Narrative Discourse and Historical Representation* (1987), *Metahistory: The Historical Imagination in Nineteenth-Century Europe* (1973).

HISTORY OF IDEAS

Construed most broadly, the history of ideas is at least as old as ARISTOTLE's account in book 1 of *Metaphysics* of pre-Socratic speculation about "nature" *(phusis).* The historian of the history of ideas, in describing a conceptual approach to intellectual history, would have to review many subsequent developments, such as the rise and exfoliation of "universal histories" from Polybius to GIAMBATTISTA VICO, IMMANUEL KANT, and F. W. J. Schelling. This inventory would also include various nineteenth-century discussions of *Zeitgeist, Denkstil,* and world-view, as well as the work of later historiographers, from Émile Meyerson, R. G. Collingwood, and Ernst Cassirer to the current *Begriffsgeschichte* tradition descending from Wilhelm Dilthey's historicism (see HERMENEUTICS: I. NINETEENTH CENTURY).

For the literary critic, however, the history of ideas is inevitably and most intimately associated with the movement initiated in the twentieth century by Arthur O. Lovejoy (1873–1962) and his associates at the Johns Hopkins University. Lovejoy was the dominant force in its early history and energetically raised in his writings most of the methodological issues that have continued to inspire debate. His friend and colleague George Boas spoke of him as "Reason-in-Action." Very briefly put, the history of ideas in the Lovejovian sense involves an interdisciplinary approach to the identification and tracing of certain "unit-ideas" as they find expression in a wide range of cultural fields from philosophic systems to literature, the other arts, the sciences, and social thought. Lovejoy, who combined the powers of critical philosophy with vast historical scholarship in a manner unrivaled in his generation, certainly never claimed to have a patent on the term "history of ideas" or its appli-

cation, and he would have been the first to acknowledge that his own historiographic method depends in a specific way on his epistemological views, not shared by all of his fellow workers. While he could be a fierce controversialist and a great drawer of distinctions who never displayed any tolerance for imprecision, he did not pretend to have established a "school" in the sense of strict methodological rules or a canon of received texts. The history of ideas as an institution is customarily dated from the organization of a "club" for critical exchange, the History of Ideas Club, founded at Johns Hopkins by Lovejoy, Boas, and Gilbert Chinard during 1922–23. They were joined in monthly meetings by colleagues from the literary, classical studies, history of medicine, and history departments, as well as from political science, economics, biology, physics, chemistry, and medicine. The club sponsored occasional publications, notably Lovejoy's *Essays in the History of Ideas,* a Festschrift collection, *Studies in Intellectual History,* and the essay collection *Forerunners of Darwin.*

In 1940 Lovejoy and his associates founded the *Journal of the History of Ideas* with the announced purpose of casting a wide net for studies in intellectual history extending (then and now) well beyond the classical version of the eponymous method. (Following a familiar pattern of academic development, a *Newsletter* was established in 1955 for the orthodox.) During the 1960s the history of ideas, quite broadly conceived, served as the rationale for a number of new degree programs (e.g., at Brandeis University and the University of California at Santa Cruz) and for an experiment in graduate adult education that began at Johns Hopkins and has spread to more than fifty other institutions (often in the form of nondenominational, interdisciplinary "liberal arts" degrees). In 1973 the publication of the five-volume *Dictionary of the History of Ideas,* which examined in detail 317 "selected pivotal ideas," marked another stage in the institutional history of the movement.

The paradigm work for scholarship in the history of ideas is Lovejoy's *The Great Chain of Being: A Study in the History of an Idea,* delivered in 1933 as the William James Lectures at Harvard and published in 1936. (What remains his most important contribution to philosophy, *The Revolt against Dualism: An Inquiry Concerning the Existence of Ideas,* a powerful defense of epistemological dualism against the reigning varieties of monism, had been published in 1930.) Tracing with great erudition the related ideas of plenitude, continuity, and gradation from PLATO to the early nineteenth century, Lovejoy in *The Great Chain* moves freely across traditional disciplinary, period, linguistic, and genre boundaries on the trail of the "single pervasive complex of ideas" embodied in the title. He prefaces the book by commenting that "the phrase which I have taken for the title was long one of the most famous in the vocabulary of Occidental philosophy, science, and reflective poetry" (vii). For over two millennia the phrase constituted "one of the half-dozen most potent and persistent presuppositions in Western thought." In following the ramifications of this term as the descriptive name for the universe, Lovejoy argues that its history reveals both "a certain conception of the nature of God" and its conjunction with "another [conception] to which it was in latent opposition—an opposition which eventually became overt." This, in barest outline, is the historical narrative and dialectical development that Lovejoy proposes.

Although he was a mature scholar in his sixties when this book appeared, the origins of Lovejoy's method and a number of his leading topics can, in fact, be found in some of his earlier publications, notably his work on the dialectic of Giordano Bruno and Baruch Spinoza (1904), "The Thirteen Pragmatisms" (1908), "Kant and the English Platonists" (1908), and "On the Discrimination of Romanticisms" (1924), this last essay still a cautionary text for literary historians. In his earlier works Lovejoy displayed his talents as a master anatomist, dissecting received notions into their often contradictory components and disambiguating intellectual confusions. But it was *The Great Chain* that for nonphilosophic readers first revealed on a broad canvas Lovejoy's method at work. Although he would shift emphases and refine distinctions in the years that followed, the first chapter of this book ("The Study of the History of Ideas") offers an appropriate point of departure for any discussion of Lovejoy's historiography. The method proposed has several distinctive characteristics: since it draws evidence from a wide range of cultural domains, it must be broadly interdisciplinary in its approach; since it also proposes to cover a vast historical terrain, it encourages cooperative scholarship that enlists specialized knowledge in a larger task; and in its search for intelligibility it asserts the need to isolate a characteristically migratory, elemental object of study, an element that can combine with others into more complex intellectual systems. The last principle is at once the most distinctive and the most contentious part of the program. In one sense of the word, Lovejoy was a vigorously *analytic* philosopher, impatient with ambiguities and intent on making distinctions (witness the "thirteen pragmatisms") that would resolve semantic muddles. The very term "idea" for the object of study seems, in the multiplicity of its uses, an invitation to a mind like Lovejoy's to make preliminary distinctions.

Lovejoy begins *The Great Chain* by noting that "the history of ideas," for him, means "something at once more specific and less restricted than the history of philosophy. It is differentiated primarily by the character of the units with which it concerns itself." His procedure "cuts into the hard-and-fast individual systems and, for its own purposes, breaks them into unit-ideas" (3). The term "unit-idea" thus identifies the object of study, the constitutive element of all the larger systems, creeds, and isms that traditionally engage the historian of philosophy or of intellectual life generally. More complex conceptions and doctrines, "compounds" which he held to be unstable "aggregates," must be analyzed into these elemental and persisting units. Lovejoy seems to suggest that these unit-ideas are finite in number and persistent through time, a position closely related to his own epistemological dualism. He is therefore unwilling to speak of the "originality" of these basic units and asserts instead that "most philosophic systems are original or distinctive rather in their patterns than in their components" (3). The question also arises whether a unit-idea in isolation from its various contexts and compounds can be said to have any "history" at all.

However useful his analytic process for resolving complex doctrines into their constitutive elements, Lovejoy's emphasis on this anatomizing process tends to foreground continuity over discontinuity, since "the seeming novelty of many a system is due solely to the novelty of the application or arrangement of the old elements which enter into it" (4). (One could, of course, conceive of a very different kind of intellectual history that would attend primarily to the "patterning," to the recomposition of the constituents and to the *dis*continuities in the narrative.) Since his focus of study is on the unit-ideas as "the primary and persistent or recurrent dynamic units of the history of thought" (7), Lovejoy is generally less concerned with the question or questions to which a given system is responding or with its motivating force than he is with its content. Even aside from this bias toward the continuous narrative at the expense of the originality of any given formulation, there are also some basic semantic difficulties with the term "unit-idea." As he made clear in subsequent polemical exchanges, Lovejoy is surely not unaware of these difficulties, and he clearly recognizes, for instance, the "dangers" of the chemical analogy he uses (from which he draws his metaphorics of "elements," "unstable compounds," and "affinities").

In the pages of *The Great Chain* (7–15) that immediately follow the initial programmatic statement, Lovejoy gives a typology and examples of different kinds of unit-ideas. Most are in form quite different from classic philosophical propositions and are of the following types: implicit or incompletely explicit assumptions, or "more or less unconscious mental habits"; "dialectical motives"; types of "metaphysical pathos"; "sacred words or phrases of a period or movement"; and, more explicitly, specific propositions or principles (e.g., "the Great Chain"). Two of these types described by Lovejoy are especially useful to anyone attempting to account for the nonrational substrate in intellectual history: the "dialectical motives," which are the mental tics that form the characteristic turns of reasoning or assumptions of an individual, school, or even generation; and "metaphysical pathos," which is Lovejoy's term for the emotional "charge" of certain words and phrases. It is also worth remarking that the examples given are not abstract formulations but are already "cases" deeply embedded in their human and historical contexts. The class of these "embedded" unit-ideas, at least as we find them represented in human subjects and texts, obviously contains a number of genera, including those of a nonrational and nonexplicit character. This concern with embeddedness further argues that ideas in context are often mediated or occluded and not the fixed, abstract, and unchanging entities that the chemical analogy might suggest. Lovejoy subsequently made some revisions to his list, moving to include more explicitly philosophical formulations, but he did not banish these nonrational factors affecting thought. Thus, in "The Historiography of Ideas" (1938) he gives the following instances: "types of categories, thoughts concerning particular aspects of common experience, implicit or explicit presuppositions, sacred formulas and catchwords, specific philosophic theorems, or the larger hypotheses, generalizations or methodological assumptions of various sciences" (*Essays* 9).

Later, in the preface to *Essays in the History of Ideas* (1948), Lovejoy underscores three important aspects of the recurrent phenomena he proposes to study: "the presence and influence of the same presuppositions or other operative 'ideas' in very diverse provinces of thought and in different periods"; "the role of the semantic transitions and confusions, of shifts and of ambiguities in the meanings of terms, in the history of thought and of taste"; and "the internal tensions or waverings in the mind of almost every individual writer— sometimes discernible even in a single writing or on a single page—arising from conflicting ideas or incongruous propensities of feeling or taste, to which, so to say, he is susceptible" (xiii–xvii). Innovation for Lovejoy is largely a matter of the "recombination" of his basic elements of thought, but cultural change is brought about

by two rather different forces: "the logical pressure of ideas," working against the "tensions" and "ambiguities" he identifies, and "the individual propensities of feeling, taste, and temperament, which tend to inform both thought and action."

Lovejoy sees his unit-ideas as migratory and promiscuous in their passage through human culture. This means that the historian of ideas must also range widely in the search and be prepared to spend considerable effort in disentangling any given idea from the ambiguities it has acquired over time as well as from the all-too-human contexts in which it finds local expression. In 1938 Lovejoy drew up a budget of a dozen fields in which the historian of ideas could expect to practice, but philosophy (including recent heterodoxies), political thought, and literature still remain the most popular terrain. Linguistic issues also remain central, but the original "semantic" focus has been largely displaced by semiotic and hermeneutic concerns. For Lovejoy the various provinces and disciplinary fields in his list were not conceived of as discrete and exclusionary; the historian of ideas was expected to frequent many if not all of them in pursuing a major project.

While the influence of history of ideas was felt in the United States and, to some extent, in Britain, in the Francophone world intellectual history followed rather a different course. What is there still called *histoire des idées* is often not very different from academic source study at the beginning of this century. On the other hand, Gaston Bachelard's "elemental" studies of literary imagery and the "criticism of identification" associated with the so-called GENEVA SCHOOL, including Marcel Raymond, Georges Poulet, Albert Béguin, and JEAN STAROBINSKI, attended less to *idées* than to *pensées,* the shifting mental states and the *prise de conscience* of the author. (Poulet, for instance, is more concerned with the concepts we think *with* than the things we think about.) The Italian aesthetician GALVANO DELLA VOLPE in his benchmark study of the history of taste has drawn freely on the work of the historians of ideas. In Germany, which has the longest and most academically established tradition of philosophical approaches to intellectual history, there are several rival versions of conceptional history in the generation after Dilthey, notably Friedrich Meinecke's *Ideengeschichte* and the more recent work of Erich Rothacker in collaboration with Hans-Georg Gadamer and Joaquim Ritter in the *Archiv für Begriffsgeschichte* (1955–) and the *Historisches Wörterbuch der Philosophie* (1972–). One other German development, although more purely philological in its address, bears mention as an exploration of the commonplaces, "sacred words and phrases," and dominant tropes that fascinated Lovejoy: Ernst Robert Curtius's magisterial study of the continuity of *topoi* (including the "aurea catena Homeri"), *Europäische Literatur und lateinisches Mittelalter* (1948, *European Literature and the Latin Middle Ages,* 1953).

The practical literary applications of the history of ideas have been extremely various, ranging from local precisions about the use of period terms, movements, influence, and reception to extended intertextual studies of dominant ideas, *topoi,* metaphors, and themes in both canonical and popular literature. Literary historians, for instance, have learned some caution from the historians of ideas in talking about familiar isms, as in Romanticism (which Lovejoy preferred to use in the plural) and the Renaissance (Erwin Panofsky took a hard look at the idea of "Renaissance[s]"). Literary studies of certain periods have contracted special debts to the history of ideas. Renaissance scholars have continued to mine conceptual veins such as cosmic harmony, fortune, fate and chance, humanism, Machiavellianism, microcosm, mythography, and *virtù.* Many second-generation studies in the history of ideas have not been confined to individual periods but have pursued unit-ideas over larger tracts of time; limiting myself to publications from Johns Hopkins, examples include Albert Hammond's *Ideas of Substance,* Roy Harvey Pearce's *Savages of America: A Study of the Indian and the Idea of Civilization,* and Delbert Hillers's *Covenant: The History of a Biblical Idea.*

Maurice Merleau-Ponty remarked that there is no philosopher without a shadow; the same could be said for any significant critical method. In fact, the vitality and persistence of the history of ideas in the twentieth century could perhaps best be measured by its ability to stimulate fruitful objections. We can consider only a few cases here. (In "Lovejoy's *The Great Chain of Being* after Fifty Years" [1987] Daniel J. Wilson has given a very useful summary of the major attacks and counterattacks attending the history of this central book.) At the most trivial level, some of the objections have come from the custodians of disciplinary or textual preserves. Early and late, there has also been a resistance to the history of ideas from the ranks of formalist literary critics of various persuasions. And not surprisingly, in view of the vast sweep of Lovejoy's narrative, there has been skirmishing over the years involving Lovejoy's specific textual interpretations. In general, however, Lovejoy's far-ranging scholarship has stood the test of time remarkably well.

More instructive are the objections raised to the history of ideas on general methodological grounds. For example, one of the earliest attacks on Lovejoy's methods came from his colleague at Johns Hopkins, Leo Spitzer (1944), who opposes what he calls the "analytical kind of 'History of Ideas'" to his own "synthetic" version of *Geistesgeschichte.* Taking the alleged recurrence in contemporary Nazi doctrine of three unit-ideas that Lovejoy had identified in German Romanticism—*Ganzheit, Streben,* and *Eigentümlichkeit* ("holism or organicism, dynamism or voluntarism, diversificationism" [191])—Spitzer argues against what he holds to be "an abstract idea that survives in history from generation to generation" and that is "detachable from . . . the spiritual climate which nourished it." He claims that his own "synthetic" method allows the historian to comprehend the "totality of features of a given period or movement," the *Begriffsfeld* seen "as a unity" (202). (See also STYLISTICS.) Second, Maurice Mandelbaum contributed in 1965 a more reasoned and sympathetic assessment of Lovejoy's contribution in a provocative essay that is still of capital importance for understanding the history of ideas and its methodological assumptions. He proposes a modification of Lovejoy's method of "stress[ing] . . . the continuity of the unit ideas" (37) to account for two related but different kinds of unit-ideas: a distinction between *continuing ideas,* which have a long "unitary history" that can be fruitfully traced backward in time, and *recurrent ideas,* "which human beings are apt to entertain on many different occasions, quite independently of whether or not others had previously entertained them" (38). Third, Louis O. Mink (1968), returning to the vexed "analytic chemistry" analogy at the beginning of *The Great Chain,* questions what he sees as a tendency to treat "[unit-]ideas as if they were things," that is, in their "elemental" form as timeless and unchanging. He argues that Lovejoy's history depends upon two functions, "a doctrine of elements and a doctrine of forces," with the latter accounting for change, while the unit-ideas or constants "cannot be said to have a history at all." Fourth, among the newer European historiographers, MICHEL FOUCAULT throughout his career was tireless in his attacks on what he called "the history of ideas" (which included practices at times far removed from the Lovejoy tradition); see especially the chapter "Archaeology and the History of Ideas" in *L'Archéologie du savoir* (1969, trans., 1972). Because his own earliest work owes certain debts precisely to this tradition, there is a tone of personal urgency in some of the protests. Despite the many programmatic differences, there remain certain similarities between Foucault's practices and those of his adversary: both he and Lovejoy were committed to a vigorously cross-disciplinary approach; both identified and studied the profound break in thought separating the Enlightenment from the Romantic era; both were more interested in the constraints on thought at any given period than in its unimpeded "flow"; and both were in their different ways antiformalists in their approach to texts (or to use Foucault's term, "monuments"). Finally, in a later and basically sympathetic critique, Thomas Bredsdorff, after again identifying some of the difficulties inherent in the term "idea" itself, attempts to rescue Lovejoy and his method from the consequences of his own idealism and the constraints of his historical moment. He concludes by restating the fresh relevance of a revisionist history of ideas.

This account of the fortunes of the history of ideas, which has had a remarkably long life as a mode of scholarly inquiry, might well conclude with a few words about enduring problems and some opportunities for renewed investigations. The historiographic problems are real and include the need to reexamine the underlying issues of the status of "ideas," causality and influence, the presence of real discontinuities or "paradigm shifts," as well as the old questions of meaning and value (these last being of special interest to literary critics). The opportunities are equally various and include the use of the history of ideas to analyze issues that have arisen since the 1970s in the study of gender, ethnicity, canon formation, the "new cultural history," and notions of professionalism and disciplinarity in the sociology of knowledge.

Richard Macksey

George Boas, "A. O. Lovejoy: Reason-in-Action," *American Scholar* 29 (1960), *Essays on Primitivism and Related Ideas in the Middle Ages* (1948), *The History of Ideas: An Introduction* (1969), *Vox Populi: Essays in the History of an Idea* (1969); George Boas and Arthur O. Lovejoy, *Primitivism and Related Ideas in Antiquity* (1935); George Boas et al., *Studies in Intellectual History* (1953); Thomas Bredsdorff, "Lovejoy's Idea of 'Idea'," *New Literary History* 8 (1977); R. S. Crane, "Philosophy, Literature, and the History of Ideas," *The Idea of the Humanities and Other Essays Critical and Historical* (1967); Galvano Della Volpe, *Critica del Gusto* (1963, *Critique of Taste,* trans. M. Caesar, 1978); Michel Foucault, *L'Archéologie du savoir* (1969, *The Archaeology of Knowledge,* trans. A. M. Sheridan Smith, 1972); Bentley Glass, Owsei Temkin, and William L. Straus, Jr., eds., *Forerunners of Darwin: 1745–1859* (1959, 2d ed., 1968); Albert Hammond, *Ideas about Substance* (1969); Delbert R. Hillers, *Covenant: The History of a Biblical Idea* (1969); Donald R. Kelley, ed., *The History of Ideas: Canon and Variations* (1990); Simo Knuuttila, ed., *Reforging the Great Chain of Being: Studies of the History of Modal Theories*

(1981); Nils B. Kvastad, "Semantics in the Methodology of the History of Ideas," *Journal of the History of Ideas* 38 (1977); Arthur O. Lovejoy, *Essays in the History of Ideas* (1948), *The Great Chain of Being: A Study in the History of an Idea* (1936); Richard Macksey, "The History of Ideas Club," *Johns Hopkins Magazine* 14 (1962); Maurice Mandelbaum, "The History of Ideas, Intellectual History, and the History of Philosophy," *History and Theory, Beiheft* 5 (1965); J. A. Mazzeo, ed., *Reason and the Imagination: Studies in the History of Ideas* (1962); Louis O. Mink, "Change and Causality in the History of Ideas," *Eighteenth-Century Studies* 2 (1968); Francis Oakley, *Omnipotence, Covenant, and Order: An Excursion in the History of Ideas from Abelard to Leibniz* (1984); Roy Harvey Pearce, *The Savages of America: A Study of the Indian and the Idea of Civilization* (1953, 2d ed., 1965); Melvin Richter, "*Begriffsgeschichte* and the History of Ideas," *Journal of the History of Ideas* 48 (1987); Erich Rothacker, "Das 'Begriffsgeschichtliche Wörterbuch der Philosophie,'" *Zeitschrift für philosophische Forschung* 6 (1951); Quentin Skinner, "Meaning and Understanding in the History of Ideas," *History and Theory* 8 (1969); Leo Spitzer, "*Geistesgeschichte* vs. History of Ideas as Applied to Hitlerism," *Journal of the History of Ideas* 5 (1944, with Lovejoy's "Reply to Professor Spitzer"); Owsei Temkin, "The Historiography of Ideas in Medicine," *The Double Face of Janus* (1977); Philip P. Wiener, ed., *Dictionary of the History of Ideas: Studies of Selected Pivotal Ideas* (5 vols., 1973); Daniel J. Wilson, *Arthur O. Lovejoy: An Annotatedibliography* (1982), *Arthur O. Lovejoy and the Quest for Intelligibility* (1980), "Lovejoy's *The Great Chain of Being* after Fifty Years," *Journal of the History of Ideas* 48 (1987).

HÖLDERLIN, FRIEDRICH

In contrast to his contemporary FRIEDRICH SCHILLER and his fellow seminarians G. W. F. HEGEL and F. W. J. Schelling, Friedrich Hölderlin (1770–1843) had little influence on poetic theory in his own lifetime. During his erratic career, which effectively ended in 1806, when he was confined as clinically insane, he published only the novel *Hyperion,* some translations of Sophocles, and a few poems. Nevertheless, *Hyperion* reflects and recasts the aesthetic ideas of the period between classicism and Romanticism and constitutes a significant innovation in the genre of Romantic autobiography. A novel in which the protagonist, Hyperion, recounts his spiritual development in letters to his friend Bellarmin, *Hyperion* is related to the epistolary novel of the Sturm und Drang (JOHANN WOLFGANG VON GOETHE's *Die Leiden des jungen Werther [Sorrows of Young Werther]*), the Bildungs-roman (Goethe's *Wilhelm Meisters Lehrjahre [Wilhelm Meister's Apprenticeship]*), and the Romantic autobiography of the poetic mind (William Wordsworth's *Prelude*) (see GERMAN THEORY AND CRITICISM: I. STURM UND DRANG / WEIMAR CLASSICISM). Yet its distinction from these forms may be defined in terms of the interdependence of action and narration, whereby Hyperion's character develops through the process of critical reflection on his own history in a way that is motivated and legitimated by the events of that history. The events, in turn, are shaped into a continuity through the narrative process; the episodes of Hyperion's life come to be seen as necessary approaches to and deviations from the goal of Beauty, conceived of as an ultimate unity between the soul, nature, and the divine. In the forewords that he published with successive versions of *Hyperion*, Hölderlin characterizes this process in theoretical terms as the "eccentric path" that human consciousness must travel in order to realize the ideal of *hen kai pan,* the identity of the individual with the whole, a unity that is only apprehended in the Heraclitean realization that "the One differs in itself."

In the context of eighteenth-century philosophy and German idealism, *Hyperion* has been read as a critique of IMMANUEL KANT, JEAN-JACQUES ROUSSEAU, and Enlightenment ideals (Christoph Jamme), a critical response to Johann Gottlieb Fichte's dialectic of spirit and nature, or "I" and "not-I," and an assimilation of Friedrich Heinrich Jacobi's essay on Spinozan pantheism and Schiller's ideal of the "beautiful soul" (Richard Unger). These philosophers, along with PLATO, are the major influences on Hölderlin's attempts to work out a poetic theory, mainly in a series of unfinished essays known as the "Homburg writings" (1798–1800) and in the brief commentaries that accompany his translations of *Oedipus Tyrannus* and *Antigone*. In the most extensive of the Homburg fragments, "Über die Verfahrungsweise des poetischen Geistes" ("On the Process of the Poetic Spirit"), Hölderlin describes the poetic spirit as subject to the opposed forces of identity (or coexistence) and difference (or individuality, temporality, representation). The poetic process culminates in a recognition that these two drives exist in a state of "harmonious opposition," which operates within the poetic spirit and within the material or content of poetry as well as between spirit and material. By comprehending the struggle between subjectivity and objectivity, or between the spirit as an undifferentiated whole and its constant drive for expression in individual objects, the poet achieves a suspension (but also an intensified perception) of con-

traries in what Hölderlin calls the "resting points and principal moments" of the poem.

The state of harmonious opposition, which derives from both the pre-Socratic (Empedoclean and Heraclitean) conception of a cosmos governed by opposed forces and from Kantian epistemology, is also a historical moment for Hölderlin. The opposed influences of subjectivity and nature on history are a major subject of Hölderlin's elegies and odes, and the prose fragment "Das Werden im Vergehen" ("Becoming in Dissolution") postulates that Being reveals itself only in a state of becoming, in the dissolution of or transition from an existing world order. The moment of historical representation is analogous to the moment of linguistic or poetic signification in being an expression of the eternal in the individual.

In terms of poetic theory, the dialectic of "On the Process of the Poetic Spirit" is sublimated in some of the Homburg fragments into a threefold structure. The third term is formed through the interaction of the first two (spirit and material) and is variously called the poem's "meaning" or the "metaphor" (in the etymological sense of transition). This triadic structure gives rise to a theory of genres according to which the forms of lyric, epic, and tragedy are determined, respectively, by naive, heroic, and ideal "tones." The dialectic of opposed forces, which is never absent from Hölderlin's poetry or his critical prose, returns in his stipulation that the character of a poetic work is determined not only by its "ground tone" *(Grundstimmung)* but by its manifestation of an opposing tone as appearance or "artistic character" *(Kunstkarakter).* Given the perpetual tendency of one tone toward another, Hölderlin's complex generic scheme is known as the "interchange of tones" *(Wechsel der Töne).*

Hölderlin's influence on German thought has been far-reaching, beginning with a generation of younger Romantic poets in the 1820s, who, like Rainer Maria Rilke and Stefan George three-quarters of a century later, regarded him as the prophet of a new poetic revelation, and passing over into philosophy through FRIEDRICH NIETZSCHE (whose concept of the *Übermensch* was influenced by Hölderlin's tragic hero Empedocles) and especially MARTIN HEIDEGGER, for whom Hölderlin's poetry is a paradigm of the revelation of Being in language. Hölderlin's direct influence on literary theory came much later, beginning with the turn to his theoretical writings in the 1960s by Lawrence Ryan (the first to undertake a systematic study of the *Wechsel der Töne*), Ulrich Gaier (who argues for the influence of Swabian Pietism on Hölderlin's poetic theory), and Michael Konrad and Fred Lönker (both of whom analyze the Homburg writings in a philosophical context). Recent discoveries of previously unknown writings by Hölderlin have led to reinterpretations of his place in the history of German idealism, especially his relationship to Hegel and his critique of Fichte, as well as to his adoption by Continental philosophy as a forerunner of DECONSTRUCTION. The notes first published in 1961 under the title "Urtheil und Seyn" ("Judgement and Being") are regarded as a key document in the development of German idealism by Dieter Henrich and Hans-Jürgen Gawoll, while Andrzej Warminski, deconstructing previous interpretations, uses "Judgement and Being" to demonstrate the paradox inherent in self-consciousness and the impossibility of saying "I."

Contemporary theorists have focused attention on a few late and notoriously difficult texts that contain Hölderlin's response to the eighteenth-century *Querelle des anciens et des modernes*. In a letter to his friend Casimir Ulrich Böhlendorff (December 4, 1801), Hölderlin characterizes the relationship between modern Hesperian poets and the ancient Greeks as a chiasmic one. The Greeks, to whom "holy pathos" is natural, are for that very reason less able to manifest it and have become masters of Hesperian "sobriety" instead; conversely, Hesperian poetry manifests the foreign quality of pathos more easily than its inborn sobriety, since "the free use of that which is one's own is the most difficult." In these observations Hölderlin approaches a profound critique of eighteenth-century classicism and its aesthetics of mimesis, since he begins to represent Greek art as a historical moment, one that may be acknowledged and "learned" without being imitated. In a second letter to Böhlendorff and in correspondence with his publisher Friedrich Wilmans he goes a step further, predicting the birth of a new Hesperian poetry: "We . . . are beginning once more to sing nationally and naturally, in a truly original way."

Understanding why Hölderlin sees his participation in the development of modern poetry precisely in terms of translating Greek tragedy is only one of many challenges posed by his late work. In the essay "Grund zum Empedokles" ("Ground for Empedocles"), Hölderlin describes tragedy as arising out of a profound inwardness that can only express itself through its opposite, so that subjectivity is sublimated into a profoundly effective objectivity, and the two contraries reach their highest reconciliation in the moment of most intense contradiction. The "Notes" Hölderlin wrote to accompany his translations of Sophocles propose a rigorous methodology for keeping these contrary drives in check, a "lawful calculus" *(gesetzlicher Kalkül)* exemplified in Sophoclean tragedy by a thematic interruption or caesura that keeps the parts of the drama in balance. All Hölderlin's writings on poetic theory are also fragments of a philosophical system, and in these late texts he moves from poetics into theories of tragedy, history, and modernity. Warminski's reading of Hölderlin's theoretical prose as a record of the subject's recognition of itself in the other and of the representation of representation, along with Philippe Lacoue-Labarthe's focus on Hölderlin's theory of tragedy as a deconstruction of the same speculative or dialectical philosophy that it seems to elaborate, are indications of the increasing significance of Hölderlinian poetics and poetic theory for poststructuralist thought.

Angela Esterhammer

Johann Christian Friedrich Hölderlin, *Friedrich Hölderlin: Essays and Letters on Theory* (ed. and trans. Thomas Pfau, 1988), "On the Process of the Poetic Mind," trans. Ralph R. Read III, *German Romantic Criticism* (ed. A. Leslie Willson, 1982), "On Tragedy: 'Notes on the Oedipus' and 'Notes on the Antigone,'" trans. Jeremy Adler, *Comparative Criticism* 5 (1983), *Sämtliche Werke* (ed. Friedrich Beissner, 8 vols., 1946–85), *Sämtliche Werke* (Frankfurter Ausgabe, ed. D. E. Sattler, 1975–).

Ulrich Gaier, *Der gesetzliche Kalkül: Hölderlins Dichtungslehre* (1962); Michael Konrad, *Hölderlins Philosophie im Grundriß: Analytisch-kritischer Kommentar zu Hölderlins Aufsatzfragment "Über die Verfahrungsweise des poetischen Geistes"* (1967); Philippe Lacoue-Labarthe, "The Caesura of the Speculative," trans. Robert Eisenhauer, and "Hölderlin and the Greeks," trans. Judi Olson, *Typography: Mimesis, Philosophy, Politics* (ed. Christopher Fynsk, 1989); Fred Lönker, *Welt in der Welt: Eine Untersuchung zu Hölderlins "Verfahrungsweise des poetischen Geistes"* (1989); Lawrence J. Ryan, *Hölderlins Lehre vom Wechsel der Töne* (1960); Peter Szondi, "Hölderlin's Overcoming of Classicism," trans. Timothy Bahti, *Comparative Criticism* 5 (1983), *Hölderlin-Studien* (1967), *Poetik und Geschichtsphilosophie II* (1974); Andrzej Warminski, "Hölderlin in France," *Studies in Romanticism* 22 (1983), *Readings in Interpretation: Hölderlin, Hegel, Heidegger* (1987).

HORACE

As an influence on European criticism and literary theory Horace (65–8 B.C.E) has been second only to ARISTOTLE, even superseding him when "correctness" and craftsmanship become dominant concerns. Horace is cited by Isidore of Seville in the seventh century and by DANTE

ALIGHIERI in the fourteenth. Renaissance theorists read Aristotle through the eyes of Horace, and his doctrines were spread during the sixteenth century by Girolama Vida and Francesco Robortello in Italy, Joachim du Bellay and Pierre de Ronsard in France, and SIR PHILIP SIDNEY in England. Through later critics such as NICOLAS BOILEAU-DESPRÉAUX, Horatian ideas, joined awkwardly with those of Aristotle, dominated neoclassical criticism well into the eighteenth century. Phrases like *in medias res* (the beginning of narrative in the middle of events) have had a life of their own and occur as echoes in drama and central themes in later theory.

Quintus Horatius Flaccus was the son of a former slave turned auctioneer. He was carefully educated in Rome and Athens. As a military tribune under Brutus in the Republican army Horace underwent the rout at Philippi in 42 B.C.E. He was granted amnesty but returned home to find his father dead and his farm confiscated. From 41 B.C.E. to 38 B.C.E. he worked in a lucrative and important government clerkship until Varius and Virgil, already known as poets, arranged an interview for him with Maecenas, the rich, cultivated, dissolute, and shrewd intimate of the emperor Augustus. Maecenas's support for the poet included the gift of a farm in the Sabine country near Rome and a welcome to the highest political and literary circles. In his will Maecenas commended Horace to the care of the emperor, but Horace died in the same year as his patron and was buried beside him.

Variable fortune followed by security and recognition prompted the amiable pragmatism and ironic social insight of Horace's lyric and satiric verse. His praise of Sabine privacy is only a reflex of his satisfaction with his patron's social circle, whose atmosphere is reflected in the style of his *Epistles* and *Satires,* called by the poet *sermones,* or "conversations."

Two of the three relevant "literary" *Satires* defend satire as a genre. Horace's first book of *Epistles* comments on the hostile reception of his *Odes* and his decision to abandon lyric verse. The second book of *Epistles* contains a literary letter to Augustus and one to Florus. A third and possibly later epistle, now known as the *Ars Poetica,* is Horace's most important critical statement.

Although they display the concern with diction that runs through all of Horace's literary writings, the *Fourth* and *Tenth Satires* are less concerned with criticism than with self-presentation: Horace as the plausible Roman, modest, prudent, candidly self-interested, denying that his shrewd exposure of folly and vice makes him a radical or police informer. The *Fourth Satire* attributes personal invective in Lucilius (?180–?102 B.C.E.) to the imitation of Greek dramatists such as Aristophanes, but after praising his predecessor's wit and social judgment, he condemns his diffuseness and poor craftsmanship. The *Tenth Satire* defends this criticism of Lucilius, advising brevity, variety, understatement, and above all careful revision. The *First Satire* of book 2 is a dialogue in which Horace, charged with satiric sharpness, asks an old lawyer for advice. After telling Horace to lie low or to praise Augustus, Trebatius declares Horace clear of the charges when the poet claims that his satires are appreciated by the emperor.

In the epistle "To Maecenas" (1.19), Horace condemns the critics of his *Odes,* claiming that he was the first to Romanize the Greek meters of Archilochus and Alcaeus and refusing to buy popular approval with dinners or even to stoop to literary argument. The epistle "To Augustus" (2.1, apparently written on request) begins with praise of the emperor and condemnation of those who laud only ancient Roman works, neglecting the modern. It is true, writes Horace, that the Greeks were naturally artists, as the Romans are businessmen. Now, however, all Rome writes poetry, which, if it is unpolished, still has civilizing and moral uses. Crude early Roman verse evolved through imitating Greek drama, though the poets failed to revise tragic works sufficiently and underestimated the difficulties of comedy. Even though the current Roman stage is all spectacle and empty applause, Horace urges Augustus to reward Roman poets as Alexander rewarded the Greeks, and as the emperor now rewards Varius and Virgil. Finally, Horace declares his own talent inadequate to portray the emperor's greatness. In the second epistle "To Julius Florus" (2.2), Horace apologizes for no longer writing poetry: he is tired, distracted, too soft for the difficult labor of enriching the language.

Horace's influence rests on the work first called by Quintilian the *Ars Poetica.* The title is defensible, since the poem resembles the old handbook *artes* in its practical emphasis, yet the title is misleading to modern readers, who expect an *Ars Poetica* to be both comprehensive and extensively theoretical. *De Arte Poetica,* as it should properly be called, is pragmatic in defining the social aims and effects of poetry and in heaping together traditional doctrines and technical rules of thumb. Its apparent lack of formal organization results in part from Horace's limited theory of poetry, from his use of the *sermo* ("conversational") mode, and from his apparently greater interest in creating images or vivifying phrases that make poetry out of abstractions than in the abstractions themselves.

De Arte opens with a grotesque image exemplifying the disunity and indecorum of bad poetic invention; it closes with a grotesque image of a lunatic poet. Within this hoop the 476 lines of the poem are without clear system. C. O. Brink takes lines 1–40 as introductory, 41–118 as concerned with style *(poema)*, 119–294 with content *(poesis)*, and everything later as concerned with the poet *(ad poetam)*. This division reflects the belief that Horace followed the tripartite scheme of Neoptolemus, a Hellenistic critic, whose separation of form and content was attacked by Philodemus, the Epicurean philosopher-poet at whose school in Naples Virgil had studied. Neoptolemus is at best an elusive figure, reconstructed from Philodemus's mutilated text and, perilously, from *De Arte* itself, though his influence on Horace is attested to by the third-century commentator Porphyrio.

Although Horace is trying to domesticate Greek ideas about narrative and dramatic poetry as Cicero had done for prose in *De Oratore,* no model can fully account for *De Arte.* Even to label it "Aristotelian" is misleading. To search *De Arte* for Aristotle's concepts of the mimesis of action (i.e., change of fortune), hamartia (reversal and recognition), or catharsis is to search in vain. Horace's idea of imitating models (ll. 128–35) is Hellenistic, and his idea of imitation as verisimilitude (153–78, 317–18) is perennial; neither is particularly Aristotelian. Horace's wit and verbal precision are as important as his omissions and emphases. For example, Horace says little about the kinds of poetry he wrote himself, though treating epic, drama, and, oddly at length, the satyr play. Scholars have had difficulty with this last emphasis and with the many transitionless leaps of subject (e.g. at l. 391), though Horace clearly lingers over opportunities for descriptive or satirical verses such as those about the Four Ages of Man (158–78) or the lunatic poet (453–76). Perhaps, as Frischer argues, *De Arte* was a satire on the impossibility of composing a true *ars poetica;* perhaps it was a friendly warning on the difficulties of a literary vocation.

Despite its social and literary insights and its charming digressions, *De Arte* can seem disappointingly miscellaneous and bland, apparently depending heavily on the commonplaces of Greek rhetorical handbooks and traditional moral criticism. Almost all the 41 propositions that Fabricius culled from *De Arte* in 1560 could have been found in popular sources.

For all that, it was through the formulations of Horace that some of the most frequently voiced ideas entered the mainstream of criticism. Among them was the concept of the vital role of literature in the evolution of language. In a particularly striking passage comparing language to the seasonal growth and decay of forests (48–72), Horace notes the sad but inevitable loss of once charming turns of speech and argues for the poet's right to renew the common language with verbal inventions, always, however, subjecting himself to the rule of usage.

Another idea taken up by later critics is the phrase *ut pictura poesis.* Some pictures are best viewed at a distance, some close up. Horace suggests by analogy that literary works on a grand scale demand a critical perspective that accommodates flaws that would be condemned in a short poem. The phrase and the idea have led as much to mischief in fanciful theories relating to the arts (such as the argument that poetry should be like a painting) as to insight.

More significant are Horace's remarks on subject matter and formalization. For all his insistence on unity and coherence, content and form are distinguishable categories in his criticism. Horace holds that content, subject matter, is primary, and that when the subject is well chosen—within the writer's powers and acceptable to audiences that typically value morality over invention—then expressiveness and proper organization will follow (38–43, 310). What audiences want are moral tales adorned with commonplaces; they want "profit" with their "delight" (319–22, 332–35, 343–46).

Horace's attitudes toward the formal aspects of poetry accord with his conservative views of subject matter. Contrary to his own practice (even in *De Arte*), he counsels observance of the purity of genres (99–113) and of the distinctions between comic and tragic diction and insists also on mimetic representation and decorum. The idea of decorum, an appropriate harmony of person, speech, and act, seems now artificial, contradicted by the inconsistencies of experience. Yet for Horace the aim of both representation and decorum is verisimilitude, an "imitation of life." Both poet and performer must aim at accuracy in the representation of youth and age (161–76) and propriety in the depiction of social status and social relationships. No wonder that in *De Arte* the correlatives of artistic failure are the grotesque and bizarre. For both writer and actor, however, the test of the resemblance of their work to reality lies in their ability to actually feel the emotions they are representing.

Later criticism found much to repeat and reflect on in *De Arte:* Horace's concern with diction; his insistence on the need for harmony and unity in the parts of a work as well as in the elements constituting each part; his ideas on intellectual control and order, on putting important things first; and his recurrent statements of the importance of decorum in the presentation of dramatic character and of long-term revision and polish became maxims of criticism well into the eighteenth century. His arguments for poetic freedom in coining words but only moderate use of it; for the observance of traditions of genre, meter, and legendary character; for mixing the true and the untrue in invention; for the relativity of viewpoint in interpretation *(ut pictura poesis);* and above all for the political and moral uses of poetry and poets (391 ff.) underlay much of European criticism prior to the Romantic era.

In many ways *De Arte* is a critical reprise for the *Satires* and the *Epistles.* It gives us the nexus of Horatian attitudes: nostalgia for the older Roman virtues; regret that art, that great civilizing force, comes naturally to Greeks, as does, alas, business to Romans; a commitment to the common sense, hard work, and social propriety that are Roman second nature—with all these translated into an insistence on poetry as a long, difficult craft and on the fierce ridicule awaiting irrationality and incoherence in poetry and poet alike.

Sheldon Zitner

See also CLASSICAL THEORY AND CRITICISM.

Horace, *Ars Poetica* (ed. Friedrich Klingner, 1939), *Horace on Poetry* (ed. Charles Oscar Brink, 3 vols., 1963–82), *Horace: Satires and Epistles* (ed. Niall Rudd, 1989).

David Armstrong, *Horace* (1989); K. Buechner, "Das Poetische in der Ars Poetica des Horaz," *Studieren zur romantische Literatur* 10 (1980); Robert Bolgar, *The Classical Heritage and Its Beneficiaries* (1954); Bernard Frischer, *Shifting Paradigms* (1991); Caroline Godd, *Horace in the English Literature of the Eighteenth Century* (1967); Barbara K. Gold, ed., *Literary and Artistic Patronage in Ancient Rome* (1982); G. M. A. Grube, *The Greek and Roman Critics* (1965); Marvin T. Herrick, *The Fusion of Horatian and Aristotelian Literary Criticism, 1531–1555* (1946); Eduard Norden, *Kleine Schriften zum klassischen Altertum* (1966); D. A. Russell, *Ancient Literary Criticism: The Principal Texts in New Translations* (1972), *Criticism in Antiquity* (1981); J. Wesley Trimpi, "Horace's 'ut pictura poesis': The Argument for Stylistic Decorum," *Traditio* 34 (1979).

HUME, DAVID

David Hume (1711–76), best known as author of *A Treatise of Human Nature* (1739–40), *Philosophical Essays concerning Human Understanding* (1748), *An Enquiry concerning the Principles of Morals* (1751), *The History of England* (1754–62), and the posthumously published *Dialogues concerning Natural Religion* (1779), was a Scot born in Edinburgh. His analytical intelligence and skepticism joined with a temperamental preference for the consolations of common sense and ordinary life. He was both gregarious and a man apart.

Hume's specific judgments of literature were conventional for his time. He liked Joseph Addison but disliked John Bunyan. He liked Thomas Otway's tragedies and did not much like John Dryden's comedies. In his essay "Of Eloquence," he credited Edmund Waller with a "cultivated genius" for poetry (106). The conventionality of these judgments contrasts with the originality of his aesthetic theory, as reflected especially in the essay "Of the Standard of Taste" (1757). This essay attempts to explain the contradictory sentiments of critics "with regard to beauty and deformity of all kinds," while common sense nonetheless denies "an equality of genius and elegance between Ogilby and Milton, or Bunyan and Addison" (227, 230–31).

Hume regarded a priori reasoning about rules of composition as unacceptable, and he doubted the moral usefulness of literature. "Of the Standard of Taste" thus embraces empiricism but faces its unsettling consequences. In its antiformalism, its emphasis on the consensual, and its consequent claim that survival counts as an index of aesthetic value, Hume's argument resembles SAMUEL JOHNSON's in "Preface to Shakespeare" (1765). In his implicit denial of ethical considerations, however, Hume differs sharply from Johnson.

The rules of composition, says Hume, are no more than empirical observations concerning "what has been universally found to please in all countries and in all ages" (231). Homer is admired by all, and "delicacy of taste" rests on principles established by "the uniform consent and experience of nations and ages" (237). Despite this empirical emphasis on the test of time, Hume stakes his argument for a standard of taste on those educated critics who establish and transmit judgments of aesthetic value.

The qualifications of such critics include delicacy of judgment, constant practice, the habit of making comparisons, freedom from prejudice, and good sense. And yet, Hume observes anxiously, "where are such critics to be found? By what marks are they to be known?" These questions are "embarrassing," and Hume retreats. When doubts occur, we can only "acknowledge a true and decisive standard to exist somewhere" (241).

The circularity of the argument implies, against Hume's design, that the true and decisive standard may exist only in the fact that Homer, for example, has survived. If so, locating the standard of taste is ultimately not difficult. While philosophical and theological systems pass in and out of fashion, "just expressions of passion and nature" receive public applause "for ever" (242).

But even this claim Hume puts in question by recognizing, in himself and others, a preference for "the particular manners and opinions of our age and country" (243). The eighteenth-century armchair philosopher in Hume admits to being uncomfortable with the "simplicity of ancient manners" or the spectacle of "princesses carrying water from the spring, and kings and heroes dressing their own victuals" (245). If, as he says, the purpose of eloquence is to persuade, of history to instruct, and of poetry to please—and only to please—he concedes that not every age will be equally pleased with even the greatest poets. The dilemma is the same one that Johnson addressed in "Preface to Shakespeare" (1765) when he described the purpose of poetry as "to instruct by pleasing" (7:67), while nonetheless giving a largely empirical account of aesthetic value.

Hume argues his claim that a true standard of taste must exist by analogy to sensory experience. Someone in a fever is a bad judge of flavors, and someone with jaundice a bad judge of colors, but someone in health will see what is regarded as "true and real colour, even while colour is allowed to be merely a phantasm of the senses" (234). This analogy between sensation and aesthetic judgment underlay other contemporary treatises on aesthetic taste, such as Alexander Gerard, *Essay on Taste* (1759). It influenced EDMUND BURKE's *Philosophical Enquiry into . . . the Sublime and Beautiful* (1756). And it illustrates the subjectivist turn of British aesthetic theory in the later eighteenth century.

Of Hume's other writings on literary theory, the most significant is "Of Tragedy" (1757), an essay intended to account for pleasure in the experience of tragedy. The analogy between sensation and aesthetic response enters into Hume's description of the very problem he sets out to solve. Spectators, he says, "never are so happy as when they employ tears, sobs, and cries, to give vent to their sorrow, and relieve their heart, swoln with the tenderest sympathy and compassion" (217). Conceiving aesthetic judgment as a matter of "taste," Hume also conceives aesthetic response as immediate rather than reflective. In this concern with immediacy he anticipates aspects of READER-RESPONSE THEORY AND CRITICISM. At the same time, he underscores values of his own time that depend on the moral standing assigned to sympathy and compassion.

W. B. Carnochan

See also BRITISH THEORY AND CRITICISM: 2. LATE EIGHTEENTH CENTURY.

David Hume, *Essays Moral, Political, and Literary* (ed. Eugene F. Miller, 1963); Samuel Johnson, *Johnson on Shakespeare* (ed. Arthur Sherbo, *Yale Edition of the Works of Samuel Johnson*, vol. 7, 1968).

Oliver Brunet, *Philosophie et esthétique chez David Hume* (1965); Noël Carroll, "Hume's Standard of Taste," *Journal of Aesthetics and Art Criticism* 43 (1984–85); Ralph Cohen, "David Hume's Experimental Method and the Theory of Taste," *ELH* 25 (1958); Marcus Hester, "Hume on Principles and Perceptual Ability," *Journal of Aesthetics and Art Criticism* 37 (1978–79); Peter Jones, "Hume's Aesthetics Reassessed," *Philosophical Quarterly* 26 (1976); Peter Kivy, "Hume's Neighbor's Wife: An Essay on the Evolution of Hume's Aesthetics," *British Journal of Aesthetics* 23 (1983), "Hume's Standard of Taste: Breaking the Circle," *British Journal of Aesthetics* 7 (1967); Carolyn W. Korsmeyer, "Hume and the Foundations of Taste," *Journal of Aesthetics and Art Criticism* 35 (1976–77); Ernest Mossner, *The Life of David Hume* (2d ed., 1980); Harold Osborne, "Hume's Standard and the Diversity of Aesthetic Taste," *British Journal of Aesthetics* 7 (1967); Mary Carman Rose, "The Importance of Hume in Western Aesthetics," *British Journal of Aesthetics* 16 (1976); Steven Sverdlik, "Hume's Key and Aesthetic Rationality," *Journal of Aesthetics and Art Criticism* 45 (1986–87); Jeffrey Wieand, "Hume's Two Standards of Taste," *Philosophical Quarterly* 34 (1984).

INDIAN THEORY
AND CRITICISM

The Western tradition of literary theory and criticism essentially derives from the Greeks, and there is a sense in which PLATO, ARISTOTLE, and LONGINUS mark out positions and debates that are still being played out today. At a moment when we are questioning the sufficiency of such Western critical methods to make sense of the plethora of literatures produced by the world's cultures, it may be useful to remind ourselves that other equally ancient classical critical traditions exist. There is an unbroken line of literary theory and criticism in Indian culture that goes back at least as far as the Western tradition. Indian criticism constitutes an important and largely untapped resource for literary theorists, as the Indian tradition in important respects assigns a more central role to literature than the Greek tradition does.

While explicit literary theory in India can be traced as far back as the fourth century B.C.E., placing Indian critical theory at the same time as Aristotle and Plato, there is much discussion of poetic and literary practice in the *Vedas*, which developed over the period 1500 B.C.E. –500 B.C.E. In India, literary theory and criticism was never isolated simply as an area of philosophy; the practice and appreciation of literature was deeply woven into religion and daily life. While Plato argued in *The Republic* that the social role of the poet was not beneficial, *Ayurveda*, the science of Indian medicine, believed that a perfectly structured couplet by its rhythms could literally clean the air and heal the sick. We know this perfect couplet today as the *mantra*, literally "verse." Sanskrit poetry has to be in the precise meter of the *sloka*, comparable to the heroic couplet, to be able to speak to the hearer. The Vedic Aryans therefore worshipped Vach, the goddess of speech or holy word (De Bary et al. 5–6). Like the Greeks, Indian critics developed a formalistic system of rules of grammar and structure that were meant to shape literary works, but great emphasis was also laid on the meaning and essence of words. This became the literary-critical tenet of *rasadhvani*. In contrast to Plato's

desire to expel poets and poetry from his republic, poetry in India was meant to lead individuals to live their lives according to religious and didactic purposes, creating not just an Aristotelian "purgation of emotions" and liberation for an individual but a wider, political liberation for all of society. Society would then be freed from bad *ama*, or "ill will" and "feelings that generate bad *karma*," causing individuals to live in greater harmony with each other. This essay outlines the various systems that aimed at creating and defining this liberatory purpose in literature through either form or content.

The three major critical texts that form the basis of Sanskrit critical theory are Bharata's *Natyasastra* (second century C.E.), Anandavardhana's *Dhvanyaloka*, which was the foundation of the *dhvani* school of criticism, and Bhartrhari's theory of *rasa* in the *Satakas*, the last two dating to about C.E. 800. I shall discuss these works in the order in which the three genres—poetry, drama, and literary criticism—developed. Interestingly, these works asked questions that sound surprisingly contemporary. For example, a major question concerned whether "authority" rested with the poet or with the critic, that is, in the text or in the interpretation. In his major critical treatise, *Dhvanyaloka*, Anandavardhana concluded that "in the infinite world of literature, the poet is the creator, and the world changes itself so as to conform to the standard of his pleasure" (Sarma 6). According to Anandavardhana, *kavirao* ("poet") is equated with *Prajapati* ("Creator"). The poet creates the world the reader sees or experiences. Thus, Anandavardhana also jostled with the issue of the role of the poet, his social responsibility, and whether social problems are an appropriate subject for literature. For Anandavardhana, "life imitated art"; hence the role of the poet is not just that of the "unacknowledged legislator of the world"—as PERCY BYSSHE SHELLEY stated (*Shelley's Critical Prose*, ed. Bruce R. McElderry, Jr., 1967, 36)—not just that of someone who speaks for the world, but that of someone who shapes social values and morality. The idea of *sahrdaya* ("proper critic"), "one who is in sympathy with the poet's heart," is a concept that Western critics from I. A. RICHARDS through F. R. LEAVIS to STANLEY FISH have struggled with. In the

Indian tradition, a critic is the sympathetic interpreter of the poet's works.

But why interpretation? Why does a community that reads the works of its own writers need interpretation? How does the reader read, and what is the role of criticism? Indian philosophers and priests attempted to answer these questions in terms of the didactic purpose of literature as liberation. As we shall see, *rasadhvani* approximated closely to the Indian view of life, detachment from emotions that would cause bad *karma,* purgation of harmful emotions, and the subsequent road to *moksha,* "liberation." Twentieth-century critics such as K. R. Srinivasa Iyengar and Kuppuswami Sastriar (both South Indians, the latter being the major Tamil interpreter of Sanskrit literary criticism) have brought about a revival of the *rasadhvani* schools of criticism. Similarly, Bengali writers such as Rabindranath Tagore were greatly influenced by the didactic purpose of literature that *rasadhvani* critics advocated.

To understand how these critical theories developed, we need to look briefly at the development of Indian literature. The *Rig Veda* is considered the earliest extant poem in the Indo-European language family and is dated anywhere between 2500 B.C.E. and 600 B.C.E. It does, however, make reference to *kavya,* "stanzaic forms," or poetry, that existed before the *Rig Veda* itself. The word *gatha,* referring to Zoroastrian religious verses that are sung, also occurs frequently in the *Rig Veda.* Valmiki, the author of the *Ramayana,* is considered the first poet, but as we shall see, Valmiki is also considered the first exponent of poetic form. The period between 600–500 B.C.E. and C.E. 200 is labeled the epic period by Sarvepalli Radhakrishnan (the first president of the postcolonial Republic of India and the most prolific scholar of Indian philosophy and critical theory) because it saw the development of the great epics, the *Ramayana* and the *Mahabharata* (Radhakrishnan and Moore xviii). According to Radhakrishnan, the *Bhagavad Gita,* which is a part of the *Mahabharata,* ranks as the most *authoritative* text in Indian philosophical literature because it is considered to have been divinely revealed and because it apparently was noted down as it was revealed and therefore was not merely transmitted orally. In the *Gita,* Krishna and Arjuna philosophize about the role of the poet. The responsibility of maintaining order in the world is on the shoulders of the poet-sage, such as Janaka, for ordinary mortals tend to imitate the role model as portrayed by Janaka. Thus it is the poets who set the standards for the world to follow.

The period of Indian philosophy that spans more than a millennium from the early Christian centuries until the seventeenth century C.E. is considered the *sutra* period, or the period of treatises upon the religious and literary texts. It was this period that saw the rise of the many schools of literary criticism and interpretation. Radhakrishnan calls this the scholastic period of Indian philosophy, and it was in this period that interpretation became important. Sanskrit is the language in which the *Vedas* are written, and because the *Vedas* are the basis of the all-Indian Hindu tradition, all of India's religious, philosophical, literary, and critical literature was written in Sanskrit. Sanskrit served as a lingua franca across regional boundaries but predominantly for the learned, upper classes and the Brahmins, who made up the priestly class. The Brahmins then interpreted the religious, literary, and critical texts for local individuals by using the indigenous languages.

While Sanskrit remained the language of religion in the south, local versions of the religious literature began to emerge in order to meet the needs of the South Indian people, who spoke predominantly Tamil or Telugu. It was not until the breakup of the Brahminical tradition in about the seventh century C.E. (Embree 228–29) that literary religious hymns emerged in Tamil. The Indian-English writer R. K. Narayan's version of the *Ramayana* is based on the Tamil version by the poet Kamban in the eleventh century. Tamil literary criticism remained rooted in the classical Sanskrit critical tenets, however, as is evidenced by the continuance (even in the 1900s) of *Dhvanyaloka* criticism by Kuppuswami Sastri in Madras.

Early Indian criticism was "ritual interpretation" of the *Vedas,* which were the religious texts. Such ritual interpretation consisted in the analysis of philosophical and grammatical categories, such as the use of the simile, which was expounded upon in the *Nirutka* of Yasaka, or in applying to a text the grammatical categories of Panini's grammar. This critical method, which consisted in the analysis of grammar, style, and stanzaic regularity, was called a *sastra,* or "science." Panini's *Sabdanusasana* [Science of *sabda,* or "words"] and the *Astadhyayi* [Eight chapters of grammatical rules] (Winternitz 422) are perhaps the oldest extant grammars, dated by various scholars to about the beginning of the Christian era. *Alankara sastra* is "critical science," which emanated from Panini's grammar and was dogmatic and rule-governed about figures of speech in poetry. The word *alankara* means "ornament" (Dimock 120), and as in Western rhetorical theory, this critical science consisted of rules for figurative speech, for example, for *rupaka* ("simile"), *utpreksa* ("metaphor"), *atisya* ("hyperbole"), and *kavya* ("stanzaic forms"). As Edwin Gerow has noted in his chapter "Poetics of Stanzaic Poetry," in *The Literature of India:*

Alankara criticism passes over almost without comment the entire range of issues that center around the origin of the individual poem, its context, its appreciation, and its authorship. It does not aim at judgement of individual literary works or at a theory of their origin. (Dimock 126)

The idea of criticism as a science is rooted in the centuries-old Indian belief that *vyakarana,* "grammar," is the basis of all education and science. Rules were to be learned by rote, as were declensions and conjugations, as a means of developing discipline of the mind.

Patanjali, whose work is ascribed to the second century B.C.E., believed that a child must study grammar for the first twelve years; in fact, before studying any science, one must prepare for it by studying grammar for twelve years (see Winternitz 420). Since grammar lay the foundation of all other study, a series of rule-governed disciplines arose, each of which had categories and classifications to be learned by heart. These disciplines were *arthasastra,* a grammar of government or political science; *rasa-sastra,* the science of meaning or interpretation specifically for poetry, that is, literary criticism; *natyasastra,* the science of drama or dramaturgy; and *sangitasastra,* the science of music or musicology. Each was further broken down; for instance, musicology was divided into *jatilaksana* ("theory"), *atodya* (the "study of musical instruments"), *susira* ("song"), *tala* ("measure"), and *dhruva* ("rhythm").

Poetry was most governed by the *alankara,* the rules of critical science; but since poetry existed before criticism, it in itself was generative of that criticism. Critics in the last few centuries B.C.E. believed that any association of word and memory having a special quality generates *kavya.* The creation of mnemonic rhymes was considered essential to poetry. Poetry was considered as having two qualities: *alankara,* here loosely translated to mean "formal qualities"; and *guna,* or "meaning" and "essence."

According to the *Alankara sastra,* form has as much to do with creating the *sphota,* the "feeling evoked by a poem," as the *sphota* has to do with creating meaning. Tradition has it that Valmiki, the sage wandering in the forest, heard a pair of Kaunca birds mating. When the male of that pair was shot down by a hunter, Valmiki heard the grieving of the female bird, which was metrically so perfect that Valmiki himself expressed her grief in the form of a perfect couplet. Ever since then Valmiki is considered the father of Sanskrit poetry as well as of poetic criticism. The appropriate *vibhav,* "cause," in this case grief, gives rise to the *anubhav,* "effect," which in turn gives rise to perfect rhythmic expression. Valmiki, the author of the *Ramayana,* which is contemporaneous

with the *Mahabharata* and belongs to the epic period, thus became the first poet to proclaim a critical tenet (see Sankaran 5–7).

Drama developed later in India than in Greece. Bharata's *Natyasastra* [Science of drama], written about the second century C.E., not only lay down rules governing the creation of drama but also prepared the way for developing the theories of *rasa,* "meaning" or "essence." Lee Siegel provides the following explanation in his important book on comedy in Indian drama:

Playing upon the literal meaning of *rasa,* "flavor" or "taste," [Bharata] used the gastronomic metaphor to explain the dynamics of the aesthetic experiences. Just as the basic ingredient in a dish, when seasoned with secondary ingredients and spices, yields a particular flavor which the gourmet can savor with pleasure, so the basic emotion in a play, story, or poem, when seasoned with secondary emotions, rhetorical spices, verbal herbs, and tropological condiments, yields a sentiment which the connoisseur can appreciate in enjoyment. Love yields the amorous sentiment, courage the heroic mode. (7–8)

Thus Bharata provided formulas for producing the corresponding sentiments in the audience—recipes similar to Aristotle's definition of "tragedy" and "comedy" but corresponding mostly with the means to produce homeostasis or balance in an audience by having the audience identify with certain *rasas.*

It is in the idea that literature is meant to cause a purgation of emotions and create a homeostasis in the audience that Indian criticism most approximates Aristotle's theory of tragedy. This idea, though, is drawn from Indian philosophy and religious emphasis on liberation and freedom from bad *karma.* All literature is supposed to generate the feeling of *moksha* ("liberation"). Literature, more particularly drama or tragedy, must cause the purgation of the emotions of *satva* ("happiness"), *rajas* ("anger"), and *tamas* ("ignorance" or "laziness") so as to free the soul from the body.

Bharata divided up the *Natyasastra* into *hasya-rasa* ("comedy") and *karuna-rasa* ("tragedy"). The effect of drama can be obtained through, first, *vibhava,* the conditions provoking a specific emotion in the audience, which are controlled by *alambana-vibhava,* or identification with a person, as in Aristotle's dictum of identification with the fall of a great man, and *uddipana-vibhava,* the circumstances causing the emotion to be evoked, as in the role of fate, pride, ambition, and so on; second, *anubhava,* or the technicalities of dramaturgy, gesture, expression, and so on; and third, *vyabhicari,* the buildup toward the dominant emotion, or as Aristotle would put it, the climax and subsequent catharsis. S. N. Dasgupta says that the theory of *rasa*

> is based on a particular view of psychology which holds that our personality is constituted, both towards its motivation and intellection, of a few primary emotions which lie deep in the subconscious or unconscious strata of our being. These primary emotions are the amorous, the ludicrous, the pathetic, the heroic, the passionate, the fearful, the nauseating, the wondrous. (37)

Each of these, however, can be classified under the three primary emotions—*satva, rajas, tamas.* In freeing the audiences of these emotions, dramaturgy functions rather like *karma yoga,* or the "yoga of good deeds."

The other major dramaturgist is Dandin. His poetics, entitled *Kavyadarsa,* dated to the eighth century C.E. (He also wrote the first prose romance, *Dasa Kumara-carita.*) He, too, emphasized the *gunas,* or emotions generated by the "excellence of arrangement" (Mishra 202). Thus he attempted to bring *rasas* together with *alankaras.*

Literary criticism in India resulted from the historical developments in poetry and drama. It was Anandavardhana who, in writing the *Dhvanyaloka,* first explicitly developed a systematic literary criticism. This was the beginning of a formal literary criticism as opposed to the critical criteria that were generated alongside poetry and drama by the pronouncements of poets and dramatists. Anandavardhana, poet laureate of the court of Avantivaranan (C.E. 855–85), the king of Kashmir, turned to the centuries-old theory of *dhvani* and for the first time succeeded in establishing that *dhvani,* "sense as suggested by the form," is the soul of poetry (Banerji 13). He chose to oppose the *rasa* theorists by going back to the emphasis on words laid by the grammarians, or *Alankarikas,* exponents of the *Alankara* school of criticism. Mishra describes the theory of *dhvani* as follows:

> The theory of Dhvani was based on the *Sphotavada* of grammarians who held that the *sphota* is the permanent capacity of words to signify their imports and is manifested by the experience of the last sound of a word combined with the impressions of the experiences of the previous ones. The formulation of the doctrine of *sphota* was made in order to determine the significative seat of a word and the *Alankarikas* concerned themselves first with this grammatico-philosophical problem about the relation of a word to its connotation in order to get support, strong and confirmatory for their theory. (209)

Anandavardhana then ruled form over content and felt that the best poetry, especially dramatic poetry, suggested not only meaning but also poetic form.

To the *alankaras* Anandavardhana added *slesa,* "rules that governed the stylistic choices" of homonyms, synonyms, and so on. *Slesa* can be considered roughly equivalent to rules for parsing and metrical analysis. Two types of *slesas* are *sabdaslesa,* "word play" or "word sound," and *arthaslesa,* "meaning and sense." The closest analogy to this in Western terms is, perhaps, Robert Frost's theory of "getting the sound of sense" (*Poetry and Prose,* ed. Edward Connery Lathem and Lawrance Thompson, 1972, 261).

In light of contemporary Western critical theory, there is a very interesting twist to the theories of Anandavardhana. For him, *vyanjana,* "revelation," is an important characteristic of poetry. But the revelation rests in the heart of the "hearer," that is, the reader. In other words, *readers make meaning.* To make this move to the reader, Anandavardhana turned to the grammarians. According to Mukunda Madhava Sharma, "The grammarians do not recognize any suggestive function of the expressive words but they hold that the syllables that we hear suggest an eternal and complete word within the heart of the hearer, which is called *sphota* and which alone is associated with meaning" (35). Therefore, if a poet follows the correct rules for combining sounds and words, meaning will follow from the *sphota* that exists within the reader.

Rasadhvani, then, became the critical tenet of currency following the 41 literary-critical commentaries written by Abhinavagupta (dated variously between the ninth and eleventh centuries C.E.) on the *Dhvanyaloka* and the *Natyasastra.* With the commentaries of Abhinavagupta, the emergence of the *rasadhvani* school was finally complete. This school of criticism recognizes the importance of both *rasa* and *dhvani* as critical principles that influence and permeate a creative work. *Rasadhvani* can be summed up simply in Aristotle's language as a theory that believed in both "language embellished with each kind of artistic ornament, the several kinds being found in separate parts of the play; in the form of action," and also in emotions (and their role in the aesthetic experience), which "through pity and fear effect the proper purgation of emotions" (61). It is in this sense that Indian criticism is closest to that of the Greeks, and it is also here that it begins possibly via influences to pick up on Plato's rejection of poets.

With the *rasadhvani* theory, the *reader* becomes the central focus of literary criticism. The aim of *kavya* is to give pleasure, but this pleasure must not bind the soul to the body. Thus, the idea of *aucitya,* "content," becomes important. According to Anandavardhana, as well as to Bharata, "poetry must not propagate deplorable ideas"

(Sharma 252), must not cause attachment or bad *karma*, and must aim at liberation as "the highest goal of human life." Anandavardhana's definition of the *santarasa* is very similar to Aristotle's idea of *katharsis:* "excess of bliss on account of loss of desires." *Aucitya* is properly translated as "propriety" or "appropriateness," which is linked to *vakrokti*, "technical ability with words," with the emphasis on *anumana*, "inference." Ksemendra, a Kashmiri writer who lived about the eleventh century and who helps us date the commentaries of Abhinava Gupta, who lived just before him, wrote in his *Aucitya-vicara-carca* that "whatever is improper detracts from *rasa* and is to be avoided" (Banerji 417). It is from this that the usual association of the *rasa* theory as didacticism or moral criticism is made.

While *aucitya* is greatly elaborated on by these later critics, the word actually occurs first in Anandavardhana's *Dhvanyaloka*. Anandavardhana feels that *aucitya,* the "soul of poetry," is the result of *rasa-dhvani* (Raghvan 115)—this is the only mention of *rasa* and *dhvani* together. Thus, in Anandavardhana, as in all earlier Indian criticism, the effect literature has on the reader is of prime importance.

What is interesting about the emphasis on readers is that the public was

> expected to possess a certain amount of theoretical knowledge [communicated by the Brahmin priests as they taught the religion and interpreted the literature]; for the *rasika* or *Sahrdaya* [the "proper critic"] is a man of taste. The true appreciators of poetry must be, according to the conception of the Sanskrit theorists, not only well read and wise and initiated into the intricacies of theoretic requirements, but also possessed of fine instincts of aesthetic enjoyment. The poet naturally liked to produce an impression that he had observed all the rules, traditions, and expectations of such an audience; for the ultimate test of poetry is laid down as consisting in the appreciation of the *Sahrdaya*. (De 43)

Rasadhvani is the basic foundation of Indian critical theory. Earlier criticism leads up to it, and later criticism simply elaborates on it. Some later Sanskrit critics include Mammta, who lived close to the end of the eleventh century, Visvanatha, and Jagannatha Pandita. Visvanatha's *Sahityadarpana*, dated to about the fourteenth century, draws together all the earlier critical tenets emphasizing *lakshana*, "the characteristic of a work," essentially an analysis of theme or content; *alankara;* and *riti,* "style."

This essentially Sanskrit tenet of *rasadhvani* had a major exponent in the South Indian Tamil critic Kuppuswami Sastri. In 1919 he presented 20 lectures at Madras University on the methods and materials of literary criticism in Sanskrit, making frequent comparisons between the traditional *sastras* and the criticism of JOHN DRYDEN, SAMUEL JOHNSON, and SAMUEL TAYLOR COLERIDGE. His student V. Raghvan did much to promote Sanskrit literary criticism in South India.

Lee Siegel, in *Laughing Matters,* points out that so many of the ancient critical and theoretical principles have been handed down and kept current that they are absorbed by contemporary Indian writers and critics, whether working in indigenous Indian languages or in English, almost by osmosis. Thus these ancient critical tenets have a curious currency even today. In fact, Siegel's entire discussion of wordplay and punning draws a line from the ancient *alankarikas* through couplets about Krishna to the work of the contemporary Indian-English writer R. K. Narayan and that of his brother, the cartoonist R. K. Laxman. Siegel's discussion shows the power of a tradition that has been learned by osmosis, passed around, and handed down for centuries.

S. Radhakrishnan notes that "after the sixteenth century India in philosophy and criticism lost its dynamic spirit":

> First the Muslims and then the British assumed control of the country, not only physically but also in the realm of thought. The Muslims undermined Aryan culture and thought as far as possible, and the British in their time did as much as they could to belittle the thought of traditional India. For a long time, the English-educated Indians were apparently ashamed of their own philosophical tradition, and it became the mark of intelligence as well as expediency to be as European and as English in thought and life as possible. (Radhakrishnan and Moore xxi)

These historical trends are of course reflected in the literature and critical practice of India since the sixteenth century. With Emperor Akbar on the throne, Persian poetry and Persian and Islamic critical practice became the norm. Persian couplets influenced by Islamic antirepresentational traditions tended toward the abstract. Love for God in the Sufi tradition became the subject of poetry. Yet the *doha*, the poetic rhyming riddle as developed by Kabir, had its roots in the Hindu tradition of the "perfect" *sloka*, the perfectly rhyming heroic couplet. The Muslims also brought with them a tradition of *baedbazi*, a kind of Shakespearean rhetorical retort—an Indian form of stichomythia. Hyperbole and verbosity characterized poetry, while the function of satire was reserved only for the court jester, the *qawal*. Islamic tradition put an end to drama.

Verbosity and the florid Persian style merged with the

European traditions to produce a pseudo-Tennysonian literature in English written by Indians such as Raja Rammohun Roy and Aru and Toru Dutt. By the beginning of the twentieth century, a new development in Indian literature was beginning to call for a reexamination of the indigenous critical tradition. This development, a twentieth-century phenomenon, was the increasing production of literature in English by Indians. Early South Indian critics such as K. R. Srinivasa Iyengar and C. D. Narasimhaiah, educated at Cambridge, where their teachers included F. R. Leavis, sought to apply European standards to a literature that increasingly defied judgment by those standards. Indian writing, it appeared, failed to use English "properly." It seemed to these critics that writers such as Narayan, Raja Rao, and Mulk Raj Anand did not write in what they considered to be "good English." And yet they were increasingly being read abroad and championed by the E. M. Forsters and Graham Greenes that these critics held in great esteem. And so the questions began to arise, How should new Indian writing in English be judged? What yardstick should be applied?

K. R. Srinivasa Iyengar, in his landmark assessment of this literature, *Indian Writing in English,* attempted to turn to HIPPOLYTE TAINE's formula of race, moment, and milieu. And yet with the emergence of a literature that is both Western and Indian but is even more permeated with Indianness, the question of a return to the *rasadhvani* criticism is becoming increasingly urgent. In a reversal of his previous position, which was based on European standards, Narasimhaiah has established at Mysore University in South India a critical school called *Dhvanyaloka.* In response to new theoretical and Marxist approaches to what are increasingly coming to be called the new literatures in English, nationalist critics ask whether Indians must even import their radicalism from the West. Does it not make more sense, for example, to see a writer such as Salman Rushdie in the Indian tradition of wordplay and the Islamic tradition of a *qawal* than to see him as a post-Joycean, postmodern Marxist spokesperson for an oppressed other—an "other" that has, ironically, vehemently rejected him? What constitutes the Indianness of a writer such as Rushdie or Anita Desai, who is albeit a mixture of East and West? What Indian critical and theoretical positions have these writers absorbed by osmosis? A new Indian literary theory needs to be forged to suit the multicultural Indian context of the newer literatures, whether those of the vernaculars or in English.

Feroza Jussawalla

Aristotle, *Poetics* (trans. S. H. Butcher, 1894, 4th ed., 1911, reprint, 1961); Sures Chandra Banerji, *A Companion to Sanskrit Literature* (1971); Bhartrhari, *The Satakas* (ed. and trans. J. M. Kennedy, n.d.); S. N. Dasgupta, "The Theory of Rasa" (Raghavan and Nagendra); S. K. De, *Sanskrit Poetics* (1960); William Theodore de Bary et al., eds., *Sources of Indian Tradition,* vol. 1 (1958, rev. Ainslie T. Embree, 1988); Edward C. Dimock, ed., *The Literatures of India: An Introduction* (1974); R. C. Dwivedi, *Principles of Literary Criticism in Sanskrit* (1969); Ainslie T. Embree, *The Hindu Tradition* (1966); K. R. Srinivasa Iyengar, *Indian Writing in English* (1962, 2d ed., 1973); Feroza Jussawalla, *Family Quarrels: Towards a Criticism of Indian Writing in English* (1985); P. V. Kane, *History of Sanskrit Poetics* (1971); Hari Ram Mishra, *The Theory of Rasa in Sanskrit Drama* (1964); R. K. Narayan, *The Ramayana: A Shortened Modern Prose Version of the Indian Epic* (1972); S. Radhakrishnan and Charles Moore, eds., *A Source Book in Indian Philosophy* (1957); V. Raghavan and Nagendra, *An Introduction to Indian Poetics* (1970); A. Sankaran, *Some Aspects of Literary Criticism in Sanskrit or the Theories of Rasa and Dhvani* (1926); D. S. Sarma, *Literary Criticism in Sanskrit and English* (1950); Mukunda Madhava Sharma, *The Dhvani Theory in Sanskrit Poetics* (1968); Lee Siegel, *Laughing Matters: Comic Tradition in India* (1987); Moriz Winternitz, *History of Indian Literature* (trans. Subhadratha Jha, 3 vols., 1967).

IRIGARAY, LUCE

Associated with feminism and psychoanalysis, Luce Irigaray is a remarkable cultural theorist best known for her work published in France through the 1970s. Psychoanalyst, linguist, and philosopher, Irigaray is concerned, particularly in *Speculum of the Other Woman* (1974, trans., 1985) and *This Sex Which Is Not One* (1977, trans., 1987), with exposing how Western discourse has effaced woman as the specular image of man. By contrast, Irigaray carefully eschews enclosing her own ideas as "theory" to avoid an essentialism that will support patriarchalism. Accordingly, *Speculum,* which caused her expulsion from psychoanalytic and academic circles, "has no beginning or end . . . [and] confounds the linearity of an outline, the teleology of discourse, within which there is no possible place for the 'feminine,' except the traditional place of the repressed, the censured" (*This Sex* 68).

This major text of the 1970s—which precedes her critiques of MARTIN HEIDEGGER in *L'Oubli,* FRIEDRICH NIETZSCHE in *Amante marine,* and Baruch Spinoza and Emmanuel Lévinas in *Ethique*—takes its title from the curved mirror of feminine self-examination (a mirror folded back on itself) as opposed to the flat mirror, which privileges the relation of man to other men and excludes the feminine. The book "begins" with a DECONSTRUC- TION of SIGMUND FREUD's "Femininity" and "ends" with PLATO, traversing history backwards and ending at the beginning with a decentering of male discourse in Western philosophy and a transformation of Plato's cave into the mother's womb. The substituting of the curved for the flat mirror challenges psychoanalysis's attempt to despoil woman of "all valid, valuable images of her sex/organs, her body" (*Speculum* 55), condemning her to psychosis or hysteria for lack "of a valid signifier for her 'first' desire and for her sex/organs" (*Speculum* 55).

Speculum foregrounds Irigaray's preoccupation with the "sexual indifference that underlies the truth of any science, the logic of every discourse" (*This Sex* 69). Thus conceptualizing female sexuality within masculine pa- rameters, psychoanalysis, for example, cannot say any- thing about woman and her pleasure and cannot account for woman, for the "dark continent," and enacts a con- tradiction in relation to her. Psychoanalysis denies the specificity of female sexuality, as in Freud's contention that "the little girl is therefore a little man" who envies the possession of the penis and whose attachment to the mother must end in hate. Irigaray responds to the male conception of woman by becoming a "living mirror" and by replacing the loss of specularization with an "in- cendiary blaze" while maintaining woman's plurality (*Speculum* 197).

Irigaray returns to Freud repeatedly to reiterate the fact of psychoanalysis's blindness to female sexuality. Haunted by Freud as it elaborates important themes in *Speculum, This Sex* presents all the difficulties of break- ing with tradition and yet enacts some of the disruptions it considers necessary to create the interstices in which woman's voice can be heard. In this way, Irigaray sug- gests the reading of literary texts in the manner that she writes them, as a critique of the underlying masculine economy of texts, as a critique of the male underpinning of the very idea of texts. To this end, as a reader Irigaray explores textual representations of female "fluid" me- chanics—images and metaphors of plurality, polysemy, malleability, and dynamism—and of male "solid" me- chanics—images and representations of unity, mono- logism, intractability, and fixity. These coordinates in many ways mark off her interests as a reader of texts. The title *This Sex Which Is Not One* even summarizes the thesis that a woman's sex *is not* one within the psycho- analytic framework, which only valorizes the masculine, and is not *one* in Irigaray's book either, where it is multiple.

And as psychoanalysis fails to investigate its own his- torical determinants, so any attempt to explore female sexuality cannot inscribe itself within Western discourse, simply reflecting it as if a flat mirror, but must operate radically to reinterpret Western discourse, a reinterpreta- tion as critique that concerns not only science and politi- cal economy but particularly language. Given that lan- guage is laid out according to masculine parameters, how does one speak (as) woman? The masculine dimen- sion of culture has maintained mastery over discourse by producing "a syntax of . . . discursive logic" that is "always . . . a means of masculine self-affection, or mas- culine self-production or re-production, or self-genera- tion or self-representation, . . . whereas the 'other' syn- tax, the one that would make feminine 'self-affection' possible, is [always] lacking, repressed, censured" (*This Sex* 132). *Speculum,* with its defiance of chronology and closure, and "When Our Lips Speak Together," the last section in *This Sex,* emphasizing plurality, proximity, and difference perceived as resemblance to another woman rather than to a masculine standard, strive to make feminine self-affection possible.

Irigaray calls attention to psychoanalysis's effacement of the uterus, the vulva, the lips, the breasts, the unmen- tionable menstrual blood, and capitalizes on the plurality of female genitals to construct her idea of woman's syn- tax, therein fashioning her own version of Freud's noto- rious dictum "anatomy is destiny" to indicate that women have "sex organs more or less everywhere." Woman en- joys a more diffuse, plural pleasure, and as a result, " 'she' is indefinitely other in herself" (*This Sex* 28), lead- ing back once again to *Speculum of the Other Woman.* Female sexuality is always in excess, everywhere at once, and a language that writes the body defies closure and resists interpretive mastery. In a culture that numbers everything by units—"the *one* of form, of the individual, of the (male) sexual organ, of the proper name, of the proper meaning"—she is an enigma, for "she is neither one nor two"; "she has no 'proper' name, and her sexual organ, which is not *one* organ, is counted as *none*" (*This Sex* 26). In a woman's syntax, "there would no longer be either subject or object, 'oneness' would no longer be privileged, there would no longer be proper meaning, proper names, proper attributes" (134).

Given the role played by hysteria in the development of psychoanalysis and the interest expressed by feminists in Freud's hysterics, Irigaray necessarily must address the presumed coincidence of the discourse of woman and the hysteric, a coincidence that JULIA KRISTEVA ac- cepts as a given and HÉLÈNE CIXOUS tends to glorify but that Irigaray casts as the failure to speak. The hysteric is caught between silence and mimicry, repressed desire and a language that belongs to the father. The hysteric's ludic mimicry is not free, as Cixous would have it, but controlled and subject to repressive interpretation. It is necessary, then, to find a continuity between "that speech of desire—which at present can only be identified in the forms of symptoms and pathology—and a language, including a verbal language" (137), while granting that the hysteric may be the victim of a patriarchal maneuver to erase and repress her relationship to a kind of origin.

Irigaray believes that theory and practice are never separate, that they intersect in the field of analysis. Here, too, she shows her interest in deconstructing hierarchical relations such as those Cixous relies on. Arguing that male sexuality is scopophilic and questioning the privileging of the merely visible and of the "proper meaning," she is convinced of the need to strip the analyst of the screen of "benevolent neutrality" behind which he protects himself. She intends to produce a "woman-analysis" in which to listen to and interpret the unconscious in order to deconstruct hierarchical relations, both concerning sexual difference and the relationship between analyst and analysand. While the analytic scene advocated by Freud and JACQUES LACAN involves a silent analyst and an analysand whose speech is ultimately silenced, Irigaray's analysis proposes a dialogue where difference is allowed to emerge and where a restaging of transferences runs parallel to the restaging of differences that she advocates for all of Western discourse. The analyst must no longer interpret the analysand but must attempt "a restaging [of] *both* transferences" (*This Sex* 148). Her ultimate goal is not isolation but rather to find a possibility of nonhierarchical articulation between the sexes, so that women will not always have to say with Antigone, "Between her and him, nothing can ever be said" (155), but, "Speaking (as) woman would, among other things, permit women to speak *to* men" (136).

Chiara Briganti and Robert Con Davis

See also FEMINIST THEORY AND CRITICISM: 3. POST-STRUCTURALIST FEMINISMS and FRENCH THEORY AND CRITICISM: 6. 1968 AND AFTER.

Luce Irigaray, *Amante marine de Friedrich Nietzsche* (1979), "And One Doesn't Stir without the Other," *Signs* 7 (1981), *Ce Sexe qui n'en est pas un* (1977, *This Sex Which Is Not One*, trans. Catherine Porter with Carolyn Burke, 1985), *Le Corps-à-corps avec la mère* (1981), "The Fecundity of the Caress," *Face-to-Face with Levinas* (ed. Ralph A. Cohen, 1986), "For Centuries We've Been Living in the Mother-Son Relation. . . ," *Hecate* 9 (1983), "Is the Subject of Science Sexed?" *Cultural Critique* 1 (1985), *L'Oubli de l'air chez Martin Heidegger* (1983), *Speculum de l'autre femme* (1974, *Speculum of the Other Woman*, trans. Gillian C. Gill, 1985), "Women's Exile: Interview with Luce Irigaray," *Ideology and Consciousness* 1 (1977).

Carolyn Burke, "Irigaray through the Looking Glass," *Feminist Studies* 7 (Summer 1981); Judith Butler, "Subjects of Sex/Gender/Desire," *Gender Trouble: Feminism and the Subversion of Identity* (1990); Diana Fuss, "Luce Irigaray's Language of Essence," *Essentially Speaking: Feminism, Nature, and Difference* (1989); Elizabeth Gross, "Philosophy, Subjectivity, and the Body: Kristeva and Irigaray," *Feminist Challenges: Social and Political Theory* (ed. Carole Pateman and Elizabeth Gross, 1986); Elizabeth A. Grosz, "Lacan and Feminism," *Jacques Lacan: A Feminist Introduction* (1990); Alice Jardine, *Gynesis: Configurations of Woman and Modernity* (1985); Toril Moi, *Sexual/Textual Politics: Feminist Literary Theory* (1985); Monique Plaza, "'Phallomorphic Power' and the Psychology of 'Woman,'" *Ideology and Consciousness* 4 (1978), "That Sex Which Is Not One," *Language, Sexuality, and Subversion* (ed. P. Foss and Meaghan Morris, 1978); Kaja Silverman, "Disembodying the Female Voice: Irigaray, Experimental Feminist Cinema, and Femininity," *The Acoustic Mirror: The Female Voice in Psychoanalysis and Cinema* (1988); Margaret Whitford, *Luce Irigaray: Philosophy in the Feminine* (1991), "Rereading Irigaray," *Between Feminism and Psychoanalysis* (ed. Teresa Brennan, 1989).

ITALIAN THEORY AND CRITICISM

1. Romanticism

Romanticism became an issue in Italy on January 1, 1816, with the publication of a short article by GERMAINE DE STAËL—"Sulla maniera e la utilità delle traduzioni" [On the manner and usefulness of translations]—in the journal *La biblioteca italiana* in Milan. It was shortly after the conclusion of the Congress of Vienna, and Milan, which had been a lively center of Enlightenment culture in the prerevolutionary period, was now newly restored to Austrian rule after the Napoleonic interlude.

Habsburg-dominated Lombardy-Venetia was but one of several political units on the Italian peninsula. Not only was Italy politically disunited (the Kingdom of Italy would come into being only in 1861) but much of it was ruled by foreign sovereigns. The recently ended Napoleonic domination had first generated and then thwarted nationalist aspirations, especially among northern intellectuals and entrepreneurs. If nascent Italian political nationalism was bound to be in a state of disorientation in 1816, cultural nationalism, and therefore the potential appeal of the Romantic message, was even more problematic. It would have been very difficult to identify an Italian *Volksgeist* in a country where popular culture was extremely fragmented, even at the overtly linguistic level. There was no such thing as a spoken Italian language. Italians spoke in local languages (the so-called dialects), which were considerably different from each other and often mutually incomprehensible. On the other hand, a strong national tradition with a distinguished and powerful history existed at the level of the literary language, a rigidly codified medium, especially in the lyrical tradition.

In Italy, then, it was the classicist tradition that embodied the national culture, such as it was. This meant that a nationalist ideology could have developed along classicist lines, and in fact some convergence between classicism and nationalism did take place. But the battle lines came to be seen as pitting Romantic patriots against classicist Austrian lackeys.

Staël attacked Italian traditional literature on the grounds that it was based on pointless erudition and concerned merely with producing empty words. She exhorted Italians to let in the winds of change from over the Alps: a familiarization with contemporary European (largely German and English) literary products would jolt Italians into creating a modern literature of their own, one inspired by imagination *(fantasia)* and natural spontaneity, which would then appeal to readers' hearts. Here, then, was a foreigner trying to appeal to a group of progressive intellectuals ruled by a foreign (Germanic) power, proposing that they imitate foreign (Nordic) models. The first response to her article took up precisely these contradictions and was thus emblematic of a possible development of a nationalist renewal along anti-Romantic lines. In April 1816 the *Biblioteca italiana* carried an article entitled "'Un Italiano' risponde al discorso della Staël" ["An Italian" replies to Staël's essay]. The author was Pietro Giordani, one of the leading Italian classicists. Giordani's piece is fascinating precisely because it attacks Romanticism through the use of arguments, and indeed terminology, that are at least partially of a Romantic nature. He accepts Staël's criticism of the ideological and emotional bankruptcy of traditional Italian literature, especially of the lyrical tradition, but rejects the notion that the situation can be put right through the imitation of foreign models. This is because a valid Italian literature can spring only from Italian culture. This he defines in terms of language, history, climate, and imagination.

It was Ludovico Di Breme, in *Intorno all'ingiustizia di alcuni giudizi letterari italiani* [On the injustice of some Italian literary judgments], published in Milan as an independent broadsheet in June 1816, who made it possible for Romanticism to become the banner of patriotic intellectuals. He achieved this quite simply by "rewriting" Italian cultural history along lines that were to establish a lasting canon. He carved out a line of national identity linking contemporary Italians, whom he defined as being of "Southern or Romantic stock," to the great figures of the past—Petrarch, DANTE ALIGHIERI, Torquato Tasso, Lodovico Ariosto—whom he even called "luxuriantly romantic." Out of this Italian, and therefore southern and Romantic, enclave, he excluded precisely those Renaissance intellectuals who had laid the foundations of the classicist tradition. He lumped these together as "exiles from Byzantium" who had contaminated the national heritage with empty erudition and imitation.

And so an Italian Romantic movement was born. It was to be short-lived. As the decade advanced, its members became more and more involved with anti-Austrian political conspiracies. The show trials following the failed coups of 1820–21 de facto decapitated the leadership of the movement, and the heavy Austrian repression that ensued forced the patriotic groups to reassess the situation and to find new ways of conducting their ideological and cultural battle.

The most cogent theoretical statement of a specifically Italian Romanticism had been Giovanni Berchet's *Lettera semi-seria* [Half-serious letter], published in Milan as a pamphlet in December 1816. Through a judicious amalgamation and modification of German Romantic theories and those of GIAMBATTISTA VICO, Berchet comes to propound a literature addressed essentially to the developing middle classes. He theorizes a threefold division of humans into "Hottentots," "Parisians," and "the people" *(popolo)*. The use of the term "Hottentots" to designate that section of humanity whose "imagination" and "heart" are so inert as to make them almost completely insensitive to poetry is but one further sign of the ingrained, if unconscious, Eurocentric racism of Western culture. Berchet's "Parisians," on the other hand, are those who have reached such intellectual refinements that they have lost the capacity to respond with imagination and heart. The "people" are the group in between, made up of those who have enough education and leisure to be able to think and read but who have not gone so far as to lose their capacity to respond emotionally. These are the members of the reading public to whom poets must address their art, and it is in this sense that true poetry is popular poetry *(poesia popolare)*.

Berchet also believed, in common with Di Breme and many European Romantics, that classical poetry and Romantic poetry are eternal rather than historically determined categories, the former stemming from the imitation of models and therefore producing "dead poetry" *(poesia dei morti),* the latter springing from the "interrogation of nature" and therefore producing "live poetry" *(poesia del vivi).* In this way the great poets of the past come to be "in a sense Romantics."

Shortly before their demise, the Milanese Romantic group produced their own journal, *Il Conciliatore* (the *Conciliator*). The journal lasted for about a year (September 1818–October 1819), during which time it published a lively mixture of contributions ranging over foreign and Italian literature, arts and crafts, commerce and industry, social issues, and even the latest agricultural machinery.

The two giants of Italian nineteenth-century literature, Alessandro Manzoni and Giacomo Leopardi, were either negative or cautious toward Romanticism in their overt pronouncements. In 1823 Manzoni (*Lettera sul romanticismo* [Letter on Romanticism]) thought that Romanticism was dead, and a good thing too, if by Romanticism one meant "that abominable mixture of witches and ghosts." He was a Milanese, had lived in Milan throughout the years of Romanticism, and had been friendly with the protagonists of the movement, but he had never actually committed himself to their cause. Now that the movement was disbanded, he found himself in agreement with the critical aspects of their theories—the condemnation of the incessant use of classical mythology, of the unconditional imitation of classical writers, and of normative rules such as that of the dramatic unities. About their constructive suggestions he was far less sure; indeed he thought that they were none too sure themselves. When he wrote the *Lettera,* his only overt statement on Romanticism, Manzoni had just completed the first draft of *I promessi sposi (The Betrothed).* The very fact of writing a novel, arguably the first modern Italian novel, implied an adherence to, or at least a willingness to engage in dialogue with, Romantic ideas. And indeed the whole drift of Manzoni's literary career, with its concern to uncover the hidden patches of history and communicate with a wide readership rather than with a narrow circle of fellow writers, was in itself a sign that Romanticism had not been in vain. He was not averse even to dabbling with the Gothic, in spite of his scathing condemnation of the "abominable mixture of witches, etc."

The poetry of Giacomo Leopardi, with its celebration of the inner life of the individual and of the individual's rebellion against artificial constraints, falls into line with much of European Romantic poetry. And many would argue that his invention of a truly new poetic language makes him ipso facto a Romantic. And yet Leopardi, even more than Manzoni, always stood apart from the dominant Romantic culture. He defended the classicist tradition's use of mythology in 1818 in his *Discorso di un italiano intorno alla poesia romantica* [An Italian's discourse over Romantic poetry] and certainly never embraced the Romantic exaltation of the "popular" in all its various understandings.

If one looks at the development of Italian culture during the course of the nineteenth century, it is difficult to avoid the conclusion that the impact of Romanticism was becoming stronger and stronger. More and more novels, especially historical novels, were being written, as was poetry that tried to shake off the classicist heritage. Perhaps above all, the relationship between writer and readers was changing, in the direction of a literature written for public consumption rather than for professional intellectuals. But problematic aspects persisted, not least the ones linked to the continuing linguistic disunity of Italians and to the sheer weight of the classicist tradition. And even though Romanticism came to be seen as the positive, and then as the dominant, side, it is useful to keep in mind a revisionist interpretation such as that of Sebastiano Timpanaro, who understands Romanticism as a "particular movement which gathered together the majority, but not the totality of intellectuals . . . and which therefore found itself opposed by different approaches, different groups, which were overtly anti-Romantic, and which attempted to give different responses to the crisis of early nineteenth-century society."

Verina R. Jones

Febo Allevi, *Testi di poetica romantica (1803–1826)* (1960); Egidio Bellorini, ed., *Discussioni e polemiche sul romanticismo (1816–1826)* (2 vols., 1975); Aldo Borlenghi, ed., *La polemica sul romanticismo* (1968); Vittore Branca, ed., *Il Conciliatore* (3 vols., 1948–54); Carlo Calcaterra, ed., *I manifesti romantici del 1816 e gli scritti principali del Conciliatore sul romanticismo* (1979); Fernando Figurelli, ed., *La prima teorizzazione della poetica romantica in Italia* (1973); Giacomo Leopardi, *Discorso di un italiano intorno alla poesia romantica* (ed. Ettore Mazzali, 1957); Alessandro Manzoni, "Lettera sul romanticismo," *Tutte le opere,* vol. 5 (ed. Alberto Chiari and Fausto Ghisalberti, 1991).

Vittore Branca and Tibor Kardos, eds., *Il romanticismo* (1968); Domenico Consoli, *Critici romantici* (1979); Benedetto Croce, "Romanticismo," *Storia d'Europa nel secolo XIX* (1932, "The Romantic Movement," *History of Europe in the Nineteenth Century*, trans. Henry Furst, 1965); Mario Fubini, *Romanticismo italiano: Saggi di storia della critica e della letteratura* (1965); Attilio Marinari, "Classicismo, romanticismo e liberalismo nell'età della Restaurazione," *La letteratura italiana: Storia e testi*, vol. 7 (1977); Mario Puppo, *Poetica e critica del romanticismo* (1973), *Poetica e cultura del romanticismo* (1963), *Il romanticismo* (1975); Sebastiano Timpanaro, *Classicismo e illuminismo nell'otto-cento italiano* (1965); René Wellek, "The Italian Critics," *A History of Modern Criticism: 1750–1950*, vol. 2, *The Romantic Age* (1955).

2. Twentieth Century

The history of Italian literary theory and criticism in the twentieth century can be written, for the pre–World War II period especially, as a series of attempts to grasp and develop, or to critique and overcome, the thought and influence of BENEDETTO CROCE (1866–1952). Although he hated and seldom used the word, the "structure" of Croce's immanent Spirit gave it impressive range and legitimizing power. In a way, it can be said that he adapted G. W. F. HEGEL to IMMANUEL KANT: stop the Absolute Spirit from its spiraling through history and rest it on a fixed, "olympic" architecture, balancing it atop four basic categories, namely, the aesthetic, the logical, the economic and ethical, and the historical. This also permitted the adaptation of a dualist scheme: art and philosophy were the idealized, pure disciplines of which the economic, the pragmatic, the lived everydayness that go into the making of history were but the concrete aspect and evidence.

Croce's fundamental aesthetic principles can be summarized as follows: art is an autonomous spiritual category; it falls under the sphere of theory; it is constituted by images and intuitions uncontaminated by intellectual, moral, practical, or material concerns. In other words, art does not distinguish, is not analytical, and cannot be philosophical, being pure fantasy. In the work of art, intuition and expression coincide. But this does not mean that Croce's aesthetic was irreducibly abstract, for as an erudite historian he placed great importance on concrete philological research and documentation, and he was a thoroughly militant critic. The polemic over verism, which held that art had to attain a maximum level of impersonality, reaching a sort of perfect mimesis with the unfolding of everyday reality, compelled Croce to consider whether, on the contrary, it was art that was necessarily personal, unique, the expression of one single individual's emotion or vision, and as such in tune with a representation of a pure form or spirit. In this view, naturalistic and realistic writing tend to lose aesthetic power and consistency, and it is lyric poetry that is enthroned as queen of the arts, Euterpe replacing Calliope.

Croce studied most intensively the seventeenth and nineteenth centuries, times during which the arts both raised the tension of individual expression and self-assertiveness and also introduced a more psychological time scale. During these centuries we see the emergence of subjectivity as it attempts to be more scientific and secular. But the *Grund* is: there is one unrepeatable human life, with its own specific, unique voice. In the *Logic* (1909) Croce gives a fuller exposition of his epistemology: thought and knowledge can in fact be linked, but the "method" of reasoning, the discourse of interpretation, proceeds by artfully written syllogisms. Philosophy explains art, phenomena, indeed reality itself, by using concepts that can be organized according to the laws of induction and deduction. Yet philosophy is not reality. In the later, more readable version of 1912, the *Breviario di estetica*, Croce reiterates that art is an a priori synthesis of feeling *(sentimento)* and intuition that has turned into a full, complete representation.

From this brief sketch of the premises, we expect several corollaries to follow. There is no "content" to look for in an artwork. Art expresses the sentiments of its author. Poets cannot be compared, as each is unique. Translation is impossible; it is only a pedagogical necessity. The responsibility of the interpreter is to capture "the mood or state of being *(stato d'animo)* of its author." Finally, since all arts aspire to the purity of the lyrical, understood as the *vox anima*, the question arises whether it is at all possible to write literary history or a history of literature, for in the background Clio demands to be heard. The problem is the following: if we try to write a literary history, we are doing no more than tracing a map that is fundamentally conceptual, a philosophical enterprise, and we would be treating individual works of art as if they were laboratory objects or logical constructs. This has no bearing on aesthetics, for it is a logical problem; in principle we should not even call it literary history, but the philosophy of art, as the aesthetic category is one and universal. As a result, Croce would only write "monographs."

But history, as it turns out, is of the four probably the most problematic cornerstone in Croce's edifice of Spirit. In Croce's thought and in that of three generations of scholars, critics, and historians, the notion and understanding of history certainly underwent the greatest amount of development, in a sense forcing Croce to make occasional modifications to his aesthetic in order to be coherent. It must be remembered that the aristocratic, secular liberalism that underlies his thought was badly shaken by World War I, then a decade later again by the rise of fascism. In the early stages, history was identified with aesthetics, insofar as what can represent a concrete individual person is a pure form. In this conception, not only distinctions such as those between what is real and what is not are illogical; time and space themselves are thought to be incidental, contingent: they are "ingredients" of Spirit, Croce argued, and not "ordering" principles. There can be no history of the expressions of Spirit, because history is spirit in the making. By the 1920s Croce's absolute idealism identified history with the philosophy of history. In the 1930s this was further elaborated into an even broader ontology wherein historicism became the truth of humanism, serving as the foundation of culture, legitimizing its claim to being *human,* and, finally, motivating the claim that history is the need of and search for *freedom.*

But the fundamental separation between the two categories, between that of art or the aesthetic and that of thought or the logical (or scientific), remained. It could only be bridged by a third faculty, that of judgment. To even begin to think about what history is one must acknowledge the necessity of linking spirit to individual, or as Croce states in the first paragraph of the 1902 *Aesthetics,* fantasy and intellect, the individual object with the universal one, the single things and the relations among them. As a result, in evaluating a work of art we undertake two separate and yet interconnected pursuits: we reconstruct the personality of the author, and we characterize the "moment" in which the work happened in terms of whether it achieved the a priori synthesis of intuition and expression. Insofar as art is a special event, and the expression of human genius, we do a critique of taste. The fact that the earlier, pivotal notion of art as individual lyrical expression was later altered to become art as cosmic expression only proves that history was to become the necessary common ground to both art and philosophy. In the later stages of Croce's thought, in short, the poem expresses no longer solely an individual contingent reality but an entire universe.

According to Mario Puppo (*La critica letteraria del novecento,* 1985), the monographic conception of history is not the exasperated manifestation of an individualistic notion of the work of art, celebrating the author as model or authority against some hierarchy, but rather, and almost to the contrary, historiographical research focused on the work itself, on its unity and uniqueness. Critical judgment for Croce is, at one and the same time, philosophical (because it seeks to establish an intellectual mediation), aesthetic (because it speaks to the values of the work), and historical (because it is the locus where the two coincide). And yet, owing to his conception of spirit, Croce ultimately believed that there was no substantial difference between the critic and the artist, for what obtains at most is a distinction of degree, not of originality and authenticity. One may overhear here echoes of JOHANN WOLFGANG VON GOETHE, PERCY BYSSHE SHELLEY, and even OSCAR WILDE, as well as an uncanny hermeneutic predisposition.

Through his journal *La Critica,* begun in 1903, and subsequently through the industrious editorship of authors from abroad as well as from less-traveled corners of the Italian cultural grid, Croce intervened in all sectors of critical and theoretical discourse. Marxism and sociology were banned early on from any aesthetic and literary evaluation, so much so that there later developed a sort of "leftist idealism" or "idealistic materialism." This can be perceived already in ANTONIO GRAMSCI and will be variously developed in the work of literary historians such as Natalino Sapegno (whose "comment" to *The Divine Comedy* has been studied in Italian high schools for over 40 years) and, since the 1960s, Giuseppe Petronio.

Idealist-historicist principles underlie also the crucial and influential work of the Indo-European linguist Giacomo Devoto, whose criticism did have the advantage of focusing on the *parole,* although the background assumption concerning the *langue* was that it consisted of four aspects, the literary or controlled, the habitual, the expressive, and the technical (*Studi di stilistica,* 1950). This reproduces Croce's later scheme in *La poesia* (1936), wherein artistic expression is said to be—or is interpretable according to the categories—sentimental or immediate, poetic, prosastic, and oratorical. Devoto's criticism and linguistics pulled more toward Karl Vossler and Leo Spitzer, very important interlocutors on the Italian scene, than toward FERDINAND DE SAUSSURE, for whose influence we must wait until the 1950s. On the same horizon we find the stylistic contributions of Cesare De Lollis and, later, Aldo Schiaffini. These critics adapted the Crocean paradigm to account for aspects that had been left undetermined and therefore dangling. Although in different ways, both sought to explain also the meaning of "tradition." De Lollis explored how "passions" go into the making of the work of art (though, strictly speaking, he used no psychological metalanguage), suggesting that the purpose of literary study is not to (re)exhume a text for its own sake but rather to respond to it in a general way, keeping in sight the individual workings of a text in relation to any and all possible connections with other cultures and writers. Moreover, when doing criticism, we seek not only the "manner" or the *how* of our reading, which is a mediating factor, but also the "purpose" or the *why* of the investigation, which is an ontological consideration. Schiaffini instead sought the "fusion" between the inherited literary patrimony and the poem itself. The post–World War II stylistic criticism of Mario Fubini (*Critica e poesia*, 1956) can also be read in this light.

Other versions or motivated rejections of Crocean thought came from Giuseppe Antonio Borgese, Adriano Tilgher, and Renato Serra, all of whom were, strictly speaking, aestheticians or what would later be called cultural critics rather than philologists or literary historians. Serra in particular has been rehabilitated most recently by Ezio Raimondi and others for his approach to the text, which borders on what would come to be called "reading." But by and large, these critics cannot be understood outside the Crocean horizon. Art has no real purpose besides that of becoming itself, Croce had decreed; it does not relate to empirical reality, neither ontologically nor cognitively. Its pure state is by definition unrelated to anything, including the materials that went into it. This blocked out large areas of culture, experimentation, and all avant-garde art.

Positivistic philology in the tradition of Adolfo Bartoli at the end of the nineteenth century and Vittorio Rossi at the beginning of the twentieth was strongly opposed to these dogmatic principles, but the historicist-idealist credo penetrated academia nevertheless. According to Giuseppe Petronio (*Teorie e realtà della storiografia italiana*, 1981, xlix), one can follow the rising influence and hegemony of an abstracting or "totalitarian idealism" (a phrase used in Borgese's 1913 reaction to Croce when the former took over the editorship of *La cultura*) by reading sequentially the several books titled *History of Italian Literature* adopted in the formative, pre-university curricula written by G. A. Cesareo (1908), Eugenio Donadoni (1923), Attilio Momigliano (1933–35), Natalino Sapegno (1936–47), Mario Sansone (1938), and Francesco Flora (1940). On another front, that of literary genres, criticism made little progress, as genres were condemned theoretically by Croce. Naturalism was seen as too obviously grounded upon a logical or conceptual framework or nonaesthetic principle, and this grounding prevented it from becoming pure individual coincidence of expression and intuition. "Decadentism" was interpreted as the crisis of dissociation and close to art for art's sake. The historical avant-gardes, beginning with the *scapigliatura* and on through futurism and its epigones, were not even allowed within shouting distance of the pantheon of Poetry.

Croce, moreover, is responsible for revaluing and relaunching the critical method of FRANCESCO DE SANCTIS, to whom in fact most of the above-mentioned critics later also turned in various guises. But in Croce's version the importance of De Sanctis lies primarily in the latter's having thematized the problem of history through literature, which he did by proposing an aesthetic of literature as made up of individual forms of a pure form that is somehow also capable of being dynamic, of "progressing" through factual historical time. But after fleshing most of Hegel out of the greatest nineteenth-century Italian critic, Croce reiterated that the work of art was autogenetic and absolutely individual; thus it was the passion, the commitment, and the notion of pure form in De Sanctis that remained of value, not his reading of Italian literary history. Against De Sanctis, Croce argued that it was mistaken to read the history of Italian literature as saying anything about Italy's concrete development in other areas, because art is art; it does not matter whether it is upper- or lower-class, Italian or non-Italian, political or moral or scientific. As a matter of fact, extreme emphasis on "content" is anathema to pure expression and ultimately irrelevant to critical evaluation.

"Back to De Sanctis" was also in part the call to arms of one of the most important critics who came to prominence in the period between the two World Wars, Luigi Russo (*Problemi di metodo critico*, 1950). Sensitive to the value-oriented and yet formal readings of a Giosuè Carducci, and trained at the school of the great DANTE ALIGHIERI scholar Michele Barbi (see, e.g., his *La nuova filologia e l'edizione dei nostri scrittori da Dante a Manzoni*, 1938, reprint, 1977), Russo gave more relevance to *context*, to the lived experience somehow referred to in the work, as well as to the specificity of the literary phenomenon. His readings rejected the use and imposition of any one method, and he stayed away from closed unitary ideologies. His approach is more historical and less aesthetic than Croce's, as it points toward what might be called a genealogy of effects, and ultimately discloses an intentional and/or ethical finality of the work that paved the way for the (re)discovery of poetics as an integral element of interpretation. Criticism is understood here as a dialectical activity in which the poem and what is being said about the poem, the many poetics that grow around it, interact and can be reciprocally enlightening. By becoming a "poetics," criticism cannot be made absolutely "systematic" or, worse, "universal," insofar as each reading was for Russo essentially an experiment, a hypothesis, and a metacritical exercise (*La critica letteraria contemporanea*, 1967, 643), as well as a conscientious intervention in the cultural debate.

Russo's Croceanism was leftist, so to speak, somewhat closer to Gramsci's, for he ultimately questioned not the theory but the method, not the aesthetic principles per se but the actual reading, the use of historical information, and the notion of what constitutes judgment. For Gramsci, who admired and respected Croce's thought, interpretation must take place in the context of ideological struggle and in terms of the role and function of the critic as crucial cultural mediator. Thus a break in Croce's circle is effected. Likewise Russo, who also shared most of Croce's tenets on art, breaks through the fiction of pure philosophy: interpretation is always impure, he argues, it is intrinsically unstable, as it is also in part a self-clarification set in motion by the complex and uncanny emergence of those "flowers," the artworks, that grow in the "hecatomb of history."

In the mid-1930s the notion of poetics emerges as a major concept for literary theory and aesthetic interpretation. Besides that of Russo, we can identify at least three influential versions. First we have Walter Binni, whose *La poetica del decadentismo* (1936) valorizes the literary context, including the author's own writings on art, and is predisposed to a social role of art while staying away from the sociology of art. Second is the final map of Croce's system, *La poesia* (1936), which while still holding pure poetry to be the "mother tongue," a "conversation with God," and an eternal and necessary spiritual category now introduces a new category, namely, that of literature, understood as "one aspect of civilization and education, similar to courtesy and etiquette," a civilizing institution, a mentor and a force, a "conversation with men." The difference between poetry and literature (i.e., prose) foreshadows many post–World War II debates on the status of poetry vis-à-vis the other verbal arts, especially in STRUCTURALISM and HERMENEUTICS.

At this point comes the first philosophically informed alternative to Crocean interpretation, and the third version of poetics, Luciano Anceschi's *Autonomia ed eteronomia dell'arte* (1936, reprint, 1976), which proposes a phenomenological aesthetic and methodology capable of reading the shifts and effects of the dialectic between thought and art, theory and praxis, art as social and historical and art as autonomous and eternal. In this book one also finds the seeds of what in later years Anceschi will develop as the phenomenology of poetics (see his *Le istituzioni della poesia*, 1968, and *Le poetiche del novecento in Italia*, 1974). From this perspective, the ideas contained in a work are an integral and key aspect for its understanding, as are those expressed in a "critical" mode, as when, for example, an artist jots down notes on how to proceed with a given work in progress. Anceschi

thus introduces terms such as "implicit" and "explicit poetics" when considering the work; on the interpreter's side, notions such as the horizon of comprehension and the referents of signification calibrate the assessments. On this terrain, moreover, Anceschi develops the notion of "institution(s) of criticism," which can be thought of as stylemes, representative metaphors, or the tenets of a school or movement and which create, for critic and artist alike, a common field of references, a more localized or regional ontology, or a recognizable historical horizon. With the founding of his journal *Il verri* in 1956, Anceschi also spurred the birth in the early 1960s of the last true avant-gardes in Italy, the Novissimi for poetry and Gruppo 63 for prose. Finally, mention should be made, for the period between 1920 and 1940, of Massimo Bontempelli's *novecentismo*, which argued for a practical, professional approach to the writing arts, going so far as to advocate unionization independent of ideological and aesthetic preferences, in order to reach and respond to a real and contemporary public, not one idealized or situated in the deep past (*L'avventura novecentista*, 1974).

In the post–World War II period we can perceive in the culture as a whole a conceptual shift from the theoretical to the methodical and to praxis, from metaphysics to epistemology, so to speak. The 1950s were marked by the explosion of the long-suppressed Marxist verb, the issues of realism, of commitment, of being able to finally reach the people, the new commodified urban mass. But these years were also marked by the frenetic activity of "importing" the new metalanguages from the rest of Europe and elsewhere that 20 years of fascism had more or less successfully kept out of the country. Practitioners of the Italian version of *Stilkritik* and historical linguistics, such as Benvenuto Terracini (*Analisi stilistica: Teoria, storia, problemi*, 1966), Domenico De Robertis, and Gianfranco Contini (*Varianti e altra linguistica [1938–1968]*, 1979), were quick to school themselves in the new structural linguistics and were, moreover, open to the various structuralisms, not only the more glorified one from Paris but, even before that, those from the schools of Moscow, Prague, Copenhagen, and later Tartu, as well as to American figures such as Leonard Bloomfield, Edward Sapir, Charles Morris, and NOAM CHOMSKY (see also MOSCOW-TARTU SCHOOL and PRAGUE SCHOOL STRUCTURALISM). Contini in particular developed the "critique of variants," which opened up inquiry to the process of text construction, amplifying and fine-tuning both the philological responsibility of the critic and the idealistic and nominalist premises of his own aesthetic.

The 1960s were witness to a true "structuralist decade," and we can point to the work of Cesare Segre (*Semiotica filologica*, 1979), Maria Corti (*Principi della comunicazione letteraria*, 1976; *Introduction to Literary Semiotics*, 1978; *La felicità mentale*, 1983), and d'Arco Silvio Avalle (*Principi di critica testuale*, 1972) for crucial contributions, especially at the level of textual analyses. In the 1970s one can refer to Gianluigi Beccaria, Stefano Agosti (*Il testo poetico*, 1972), and Angelo Marchese (*Metodi e prove strutturali*, 1974) for representative cases of a ROMAN JAKOBSON–inspired criticism that relies on Jakobson's five functions of language. Poetry is here understood as simply one of the functions that can be emphasized during the transmission of the message, in short, poetry as *écart* from a given code or paradigm, fleshing out the work of all extratextual referents connected with Jakobson's conative, phatic, metalinguistic, and emotive aspects. Segre in particular has consistently and influentially held that a literary history as such is impossible, that what we can aspire to is a history of literary techniques focused on structure, a mapping of the shifts in literariness, and accounts of the strategies of communication within reformulated Saussurean premises (*Time and Structure*, 1983). One major difficulty of this position is that it does not emphasize the reader, or the receiver of the message. However, in his latest work Segre has altered his views somewhat in order to vindicate the crucial nature of the phenomenology of the reading act, integrating insights from Russian semiotics concerning literature as a "field" and as "model of the world" (*Introduction to the Analysis of the Literary Text*, 1988). In the 1980s a newer generation of critics, including Costanzo di Gerolamo and Franco Brioschi (see their *Elementi di teoria letteraria*, 1984) and in particular Marcello Pagnini, have instead elaborated the pragmatic aspect of text construction and reception, sensitive to insights coming from sociology, SEMIOTICS, and *Rezeptionsaesthetik* (see RECEPTION THEORY); in a way they stand for what is most fruitful and interesting at the moment.

Semiotic perspectives were introduced in Italy in the 1950s primarily by logicians and philosophers of language. Among them was Ferruccio Rossi-Landi, who edited, translated, and wrote a book on Charles Morris in 1957. Rossi-Landi would subsequently call on semiotics to answer questions concerning the procedures, analogies, and transactions of ideology and economics. Among the insights useful to literary study is the homological method employed to read economics in linguistic terms and to consider sign behavior as subject to the processes of production, exchange, and consumption much as an economic entity is. In this perspective, stock phrases or "ordinary language" can become also meta-

critical, and "common speech" is in fact a technical term and conceptual referent in Rossi-Landi's work (*Between Signs and Non-Signs*, 1992).

The main influence for structuralism and semiotics alike, however, came through the anthropology of CLAUDE LÉVI-STRAUSS and the semiology of ROLAND BARTHES. Among the fruits of such an encounter were the introduction of NARRATOLOGY, UMBERTO ECO's early writings on mystery novels and mass culture, and much-needed scientific rigor in literary analysis. By 1975, however, Eco had overcome the aporias and abstractions of a semiology based on the Saussurean model and shifted to a more Aristotelian model, counterpoising communication and signification, relating the possibilities of the code to the modes of sign production, and finally making John Locke, CHARLES SANDERS PEIRCE, and Charles Morris the three main modern precursors of the discipline. Semiotics now treated art as an "ideolect" and aspired to become the general science of culture. In the 1980s Italian semiotics shifted the emphasis to sign reception, moving from the text qua text to the codes of the receiver, and to the systems of signs that preexist sign production. In this area one ought to look at the work of Gianfranco Bettetini (*Produzione del senso e messa in scena*, 1975), Alberto Abruzzese, Mauro Wolf, Omar Calabrese, Ugo Volli, Patrizia Magli, Augusto Ponzio, and Paolo Fabbri. Yet while semiotics became the adopted methodology in areas such as cinema studies (see FILM THEORY), architecture, mass media studies, and so on, in literary study it was less successful than structuralism (where at most, especially in the case of the students of Segre and Corti, the two are combined).

Marxist thought did not really enter the literary scene until the late 1940s, when circulation of leftist literature was again permitted, Antonio Gramsci's *Notebooks* were published, and GEORG LUKÁCS was translated. Although he also believed in the autonomy of art, Gramsci paid much more attention to the interpretations given to art in specific periods or conditions, in this being true to his materialist conception of history. In this view, the critics, or more broadly the "intellectuals," assume the status of a social category that is necessarily involved in all stages of cultural exchange. Intellectuals are the bearers of culture and shapers of education and therefore are responsible for the culture's appropriate mediation and transmission of values. Because there is always the danger that the intellectual will turn into a spokesperson for this or that regime or group, the true critical objective is to correlate functionally the historical and epistemological values of the aesthetic artifact with the specific aspects of its form, that is, with the expressive instruments through which it came to be realized and mediated and is uniquely distinguishable.

Apart from the ideological-political call to "commitment"—which made for lively debates among members of the various currents from the mid-1950s through the 1970s—we have here the theoretical premises for a Marxist aesthetic and criticism that was most fully developed by GALVANO DELLA VOLPE in his *Critica del gusto* (1960, 3d ed., 1966, *Critique of Taste*). In his view, it is form that leads to thought, as it arises from the problem of the construction of meaning; content, in contrast, leads us back to the image, as it arises from the cognitive-sensorial domain. Diametrically opposite to Croce's aesthetic and ontology, Della Volpe was also moving away from the influential Lukácsian current, which in its dualistic premises and specular realism still prevented a fuller appreciation of the avant-garde and such writers as James Joyce, Franz Kafka, and Marcel Proust.

Della Volpe successfully integrated Marxism with structuralism and contributed to broadening the horizons of both. In fact, the concrete historical situations of both writer and reader require that we consider reference, effect, and the sphere of interaction. Della Volpe argued that whether we deal with prose, poetry, or dialogue, language is the common denominator of all human undertaking. We can therefore distinguish between literary discourse, which is polysemous and, like all art, subject to subsequent interpretations; scientific discourse, which is univocal and universal, perfectly translatable (think of formulas); and common speech, which is ambiguous and unstable, even the most habitual environment requiring during communication the constant monitoring of a host of other factors in order to determine for each utterance in what sense a given expression is to be understood. This criticism, which was more influential at the theoretical than at the practical level, places a premium on semantics, on the meanings the artistic forms generate, and finally on the references variously coded or interspersed in a work, its "organic contextuality." Thus poetry can no longer be conveniently suspended in the realm of a pure expression devoid of ideas; rather, it participates actively in the interpretation and construction of values. The opposition between art and science is misconstrued, according to Della Volpe. Both require imagination, thought, and processes of realization; the means of expression, the specific language used, changes, but the truth content is the same if the truth be one.

Among the most original and influential Marxist critics are Alberto Asor Rosa (*Scrittori e popolo,* 1964), Carlo Salinari (*La questione del realismo,* 1960), Gianni Scalia (*Critica, letteratura e ideologia,* 1968), Edoardo Sanguineti (*Ideologia e linguaggio,* 1970), Pier Paolo Pasolini (*Empirismo eretico,* 1972, *Heretical Empiricism,* trans. Ben Lawton and Louise K. Barnett, 1988; and *Passione e ideologia,* 1960), Franco Fortini (*Verifica dei poteri,* 1965), and Romano Luperini (*Il Novecento,* vol. 2, 1982). Asor Rosa in particular has been engaged in demystifying Gramsci's notion of popular (or populist) literature and in conceiving of Italian literary history in terms of two major blocks, one extending from the origins to the seventeenth century and another, triggered by the rise of bourgeois culture, capitalism, and the concomitant decline of Italian society in Europe, from the seventeenth century on (see *Letteratura italiana,* ed. Asor Rosa, 9 vols., 1982–87). This by way of explaining the feeling of "unrelatedness" or "non-appurtenance" in much modern Italian literature.

Psychological and PSYCHOANALYTIC THEORY AND CRITICISM arrived relatively late on the scene, but by the mid-1960s both SIGMUND FREUD and JACQUES LACAN were amply discussed and tested on specific texts. Among the critics who practiced a structuralist literary psychoanalysis, often on non-Italian texts, are Michel David (*La psicanalisi nella cultura italiana,* 1966), Francesco Orlando (*Lettura freudiana della "Phèdre"* and *Per una teoria freudiana della letteratura,* 1971, 1973, *Toward a Freudian Theory of Literature,* trans. Charmaine Lee, 1978), Giuliano Gramigna, Mario Lavagetto, and Stefano Agosti (*Modelli psicoanalitici e teorie del testo,* 1987). Critics who developed a literary-philosophical perspective on Freudian thought include the early Franco Rella and Giuseppe Sertoli. Perhaps more important and more subterranean has been the influence, especially in the 1950s, of C. G. Jung, as we perceive in the criticism of Giacomo Debenedetti (*Il romanzo italiano,* 1971), Furio Jesi (*Letteratura e mito,* 1968), and the young Edoardo Sanguineti (see ARCHETYPAL THEORY AND CRITICISM).

Despite the activity of several collectives that published their own journals, such as *dwf, memoria,* and most recently *diotima,* Italian FEMINIST THEORY AND CRITICISM never really took off, in the sense that it never gained a strong foothold in the universities. Well informed and constantly translating their French and American counterparts, Italian feminist critics have suffered from too close association with specific political or theoretical currents or were mired in broader social problems.

In the Italian panorama the sociology of literature is one thing, studied by sociologists and not terribly empirical, and the sociology of criticism is another, a terrain guarded by educators, editors, and publishers. "Sociological criticism" has been a primary pursuit of Marxists of all stripes, and after Gramsci and Lukács we perceive, especially through the 1960s and into the 1970s, the growing relevance of Lucien Goldmann, WALTER BENJAMIN, and the FRANKFURT SCHOOL. On another front, as in the work of Alberto Abruzzese, the social aspect of literature has been studied with reference to other sociosemiotic systems, such as television, newspapers, and special print events. On yet a third front, there have been many fine studies on the "influence" a particular work or author has had on the ideas and taste of his or her time and society, as well as on the politics of publishing, for instance, by Gianpaolo Vené, Walter Pedullà (*La letteratura del benessere,* 1973; *L'estrema funzione,* 1975), and Gian Carlo Ferretti (*Letteratura e ideologia,* 1964; *Il mercato delle lettere,* 1979). Although sociological criticism has been interested in the aesthetics of reception and in the work of Hans Robert Jauss in particular (see RECEPTION THEORY), most writings in this area tend to be informative (and only occasionally theoretical) rather than, strictly speaking, textual.

It should be noted that given the specific cultural history of Italy, much criticism appears on the pages of nonspecialized publications, from the cultural pages of major daily newspapers to the review sections of weeklies, partisan journals, and endless encounters in nonacademic spaces. Especially important has been the criticism of the writers themselves, who have often gathered their interventions in volumes that have later been discussed and dissected by professional critics and have typically influenced younger writers as much as have the works themselves. These writer-critics include Carlo Emilio Gadda, Elio Vittorini (*Diario in pubblico,* 1957), Alberto Moravia (*L'uomo come fine,* 1964), Italo Calvino (*The Uses of Literature,* 1989), Umberto Eco, Alberto Arbasino, Alfredo Giuliani, and others.

Until the late 1970s, RHETORIC was confined to traditional philological and historiographic reconstructions (see HISTORICAL THEORY AND CRITICISM and PHILOLOGY). After that time, with the introduction of Chaim Perelman, Gérard Genette, Max Bense, and Groupe μ and in conjunction with developments in STYLISTICS on the one hand and PHENOMENOLOGY on the other, new proposals began to emerge. Important in this sector are the studies of Ezio Raimondi and his school at the University of Bologna, which focus on the relationship between poetics and rhetoric and most recently hermeneutics (see Raimondi, *Ermeneutica e commento,* 1990). The philosopher Giulio Preti rekindled the discussion of how rhetoric and logic are really not so different (*Retorica e logica,* 1968), and he has been echoed in this by Marcello Pera (*Scienza e retorica,* 1991). Renato Barilli's conceptual *Rhetoric* (1979, trans., 1989) supersedes Barthes's

semiological model, while Giovanni Bottiroli (*Retorica della creatività,* 1987) breaks through structuralist limitations and addresses the issue of the creativity of texts. Working from the United States, and impressively going beyond structuralist, rationalist, and semiotic approaches to the rhetorical, Paolo Valesio brings in both philosophical and theological reconsiderations, exploring the *figura* and the dilemma of silence (*Novantiqua: Rhetoric as a Contemporary Theory,* 1980). Another Italian expatriate, Ernesto Grassi, who spent most of his adult life in Germany, instead brought Heideggerian thought to a rethinking of metaphor and the essence of poetry. Coupled to his own rediscovery of GIAMBATTISTA VICO, Grassi initiated a revival and reappreciation of the literary insights of Italian humanism in particular and the creative act in general (*Rhetoric as Philosophy,* 1980). Lastly, although Bice Mortara Garavelli's very useful manual (*Manuale di retorica,* 1988) is still basically in the tradition of Heinrich Lausberg and *Textlinguistik,* we should turn to Armand Plebe and Pietro Emanuele's manual by the same name (also 1988) if we want finally to place the rhetorical on a par with the philosophical, for here the focus is on invention (both conceptual and, strictly speaking, linguistic) rather than on elocution, with important consequences for literary study and interpretation. This is particularly significant at a time when some branches of philosophy and literary theory, in Italy as well as elsewhere, are redirecting their sights on the rhetorical constitution of all human constructs, both critical and creative.

Finally, and ironically for a country whose literary culture has always been politically sensitive, there is very little in the way of critical readings that focus on issues of race, gender, or ethnicity in literature. Moreover, there is a dearth of research on "minor" literatures, and whereas studies on writings in dialect are showing signs of growth, there is next to nothing, for instance, on theory and literature by Italians outside of Italy and what that might mean to more canonical forms of theorizing. This extends also to the relationship between literature and religion, and literature and science. Carlo Dionisotti's attempt to introduce geography, or "geopolitics," into literary study (*Geografia e storia della letteratura italiana,* 1967) has not had a following, except, perhaps, outside of Italy.

One last note: in the past few years many philosophers—and not just hermeneuticians and aestheticians, but philosophers of language and of science as well—and even critics have turned to literature for help in either understanding or solving some riddles or issues. This has often had an effect on their thinking, and in some cases their writing, which is neither scientific-philosophical nor literary but both at the same time. Ultimately, it appears, critical thought is facing the seduction and the horror of creation head-on. I do not mean only those critics who have written novels—such as Eco, Corti, and Valesio, who raise a host of problems concerning roles, styles, and social categorizations—but also texts produced by such diverse figures as Aldo Gargani, Giorgio Agamben, Giampiero Comolli, Raffaele Perrotta, Franco Rella, Guido Ceronetti, and a few others. These latter figures produce amorphous, borderline texts, still to be studied and described but certainly likely to raise even newer questions concerning genres, reference, meaning, and the relationship between thought, language, and reality.

Peter Carravetta

See also BENEDETTO CROCE, GALVANO DELLA VOLPE, FRANCESCO DE SANCTIS, UMBERTO ECO, and ANTONIO GRAMSCI.

Andrea Battistini and Ezio Raimondi, "Retoriche e poetiche dominanti," *Letturatura italiana*, vol. 3 (ed. Asor Rosa, 1984); Gianfranco Bettetini and Francesco Casetti, "Semiotics in Italy," *The Semiotic Sphere* (ed. Thomas A. Sebeok and J. Umiker-Sebeok, 1986); Filippo Bettini and Mirko Bevilacqua, eds., *Marxismo e critica letteraria in Italia* (1978); Walter Binni, *Poetica, critica e storia letteraria* (1963, 2d ed., 1964); Peter Carravetta, "Postmodern Chronicles," *Annali d'Italianistica* 9 (1991); Ottavio Cecchi and Enrico Ghidetti, eds., *Fare storia della letteratura* (1986), *Sette modi di fare critica* (1983); Remo Ceserani, *Raccontare la letteratura* (1990); Maria Corti and Cesare Segre, eds., *I metodi attuali della critica in Italia* (1970); Benedetto Croce, *Aesthetic as Science of Expression and General Linguistics* (1902, trans. Douglas Ainslie, 1953), *La poesia* (1936, 6th ed., 1963, *Benedetto Croce's Poetry and Literature: An Introduction to Its Criticism and History,* trans. Giovanni Gullace, 1981); Costanzo Di Girolamo, *Critica della letterarietà* (1978); Costanzo Di Girolamo, Alfonso Berardinelli, and Franco Brioschi, *La ragione critica: Prospettive nello studio della letteratura* (1986); Umberto Eco, *The Limits of Interpretation* (1989), *Opera aperta* (1962, *The Open Work,* trans. Anna Cancogni, 1989), *The Role of the Reader* (1979), *A Theory of Semiotics* (1975); Gilberto Finzi, *L'utopia letteraria* (1973); Antonio Gramsci, *Selections from Cultural Writings* (1986); Ernesto Grassi, *Rhetoric as Philosophy* (1980); Furio Jesi, *Letteratura e mito* (1968); Guido Lucchini, *Le origini della scuola storica* (1990); Romano Luperini, "Criticism in Contemporary Italy," *Rethinking Marxism* (1992); Filiberto Menna, *Critica della critica* (1980); Luciano Nanni, ed., *Identità della critica* (1991); Giorgio Pasquali, *Storia della tradizione e critica del testo* (1934, 2d ed., 1962); Santini Ritter, Lea Raimondi, and Ezio Raimondi, eds., *Retorica e critica letteraria* (1978).

JAKOBSON, ROMAN

Roman Jakobson (1896–1982), who in both literary studies and in linguistics was an exceptionally prolific scholar
with broad interests spanning such fields as phonology,
PHILOLOGY, Slavic literature and folklore, general linguistics, aesthetics, comparative mythology, avant-garde
painting, poetry, and comparative metrics, has had an
outstanding impact on literary theory, especially in SE-
MIOTICS and discourse analysis, as well as in many other
fields that do not concern us here, such as social anthropology and psychoanalysis. Born in Moscow in 1896, he
was co-founder of the Moscow Linguistic Circle (1915)
and the Prague Linguistic Circle (1926). Following the
Nazi invasion of Czechoslovakia in 1941, he fled to the
United States via Scandinavia. From 1942 to 1946 he taught
at the École Libre des Hautes Études, a Free French university hosted by the New School for Social Research in
New York, where he met CLAUDE LÉVI-STRAUSS, on whose
work he was to have a profound influence. Subsequently
he was professor at Columbia, Harvard, and M.I.T.

It would be absurd to attempt to summarize in a few
words the considerable impact Jakobson's work has had
in all the literary and linguistic fields to which he contributed. For some idea of the scope of this impact, the
reader should consult Armstrong and Schooneveld's *Roman Jakobson: Echoes of His Scholarship*. Additional insight
into the nature of Jakobson's contribution to poetics,
folklore, metrics, phonology, time and space in language
and literature, grammar and poetry, and semiotics can
be gleaned from the extended interview with Krystyna
Pomorska in the Jakobson-Pomorska *Dialogues*.

Applications of Jakobson's concepts to literary analysis have been too numerous to list exhaustively. The
bibliography appended, however, includes representative
items. In the rest of this entry I focus on the two essays
that have had the most profound and exceptionally long-
lasting impact on literary theory and criticism.

Jakobson's model of the functions of language, which
integrates Karl Bühler's tripartite system (emotive, conative, and referential) and Bronislaw Malinowski's concept of phatic communion, has had a decisive influence

on literary theorists for the last 30 years. He writes in
"Linguistics and Poetics: Closing Statement" that all acts
of communication, be they written or oral, are contingent
on six constituent elements:

CONTEXT
MESSAGE
ADDRESSER . . . . . ADDRESSEE
CONTACT
CODE

A message is sent by an addresser to an addressee. For
this to occur, the addresser and addressee must use a
common code, a physical channel, or contact, and the
same frame of reference, or context. (Though Jakobson
stipulates that by "context" he means "referent," the
term is confusing, since it could be mistakenly construed
as pointing to the circumstances of utterance rather than
to what the message is about.) Each of the constituent
elements of the communicative act has a corresponding
function; thus:

REFERENTIAL
POETIC
EMOTIVE   PHATIC   CONATIVE
METALINGUAL

Focused on the addresser (or sender), that is, on the first
person, the emotive function reflects the speaker's attitude to the topic of his or her discourse. As we shall see,
the emotive function can be linked to ÉMILE BENVENISTE's
concept of *discours* (discourse). The conative function is
centered on the second person, the addressee (or receiver). The most explicit instance is illustrated by two
grammatical categories—the vocative and the imperative—neither of which is subject to the true/false criterion of declarative utterances.

The four other functions concern the message sent.
The referential function can be equated with the cognitive use of language, which privileges the informa-
tional content of an utterance, virtually eliminating the
focus on the speaker or on the addressee. The referential
function can be linked to Benveniste's concept of *récit*

(story) as opposed to discourse, which entails the presence of a self-conscious narrator. The poetic function (which should not be confused with poetic discourse) valorizes the signifier, foregrounding what might be called the decorative or aesthetic function of language, in Jakobson's words, the message for its own sake, thereby deemphasizing (though not necessarily eliminating) the referential function. The metalingual function is focused on the verbal code itself, that is, on language speaking of itself, its purpose being to clarify the manner in which the verbal code is used. Finally, the phatic function is centered on the channel used and thus on the contact between speaker and addressee.

Literary examples of Jakobson's functions of language are easy to locate. The emotive function is to be found especially in lyric poetry or in introspective (first-person) narrative. The conative function is well illustrated by Michel Butor's novel *La Modification,* which is written entirely in the second person, or by Carlos Fuentes's *The Death of Artemio Cruz,* sections of which are likewise written in the second person. Examples of the poetic function abound in dadaist and surrealist poetry. Instances of the phatic function are to be found in the opening scene of Eugène Ionesco's *Bald Soprano* and in many scenes of Harold Pinter's early plays. The metalingual function is often the principal focus of stage directions, whose express purpose is to clarify the dialogue and the delivery intended by the dramatist. Finally, the referential function is dominant in naturalist fiction by such authors as Émile Zola and Guy de Maupassant.

Despite the apparent simplicity of Jakobson's model of communication, his "Closing Statement" has had a marked influence on literary STRUCTURALISM and semiotics. Perhaps almost as influential have been his study of metaphor and metonymy (published a few years earlier), "Two Aspects of Language and Two Types of Aphasic Disturbances," and his concept of poetics itself. The essay, as its title indicates, makes a suggestive use of aphasia as methodological frame, and despite its brevity, it has had a very widespread impact, especially on research in the aesthetics and philosophy of metaphor. Jakobson's point, and it seems convincing, is that we can learn as much from linguistic communication when it breaks down or is impaired as when it functions normally. The focus of the essay is the manner in which aphasia affects oral expression, particularly figurative expression. For Jakobson, in this instance adopting FERDINAND DE SAUSSURE's distinction, there are two complementary yet radically opposed uses of language: selection and combination. Selection, or substitution, which is a metalingual operation, is equated with similarity or the metaphoric

use of language, whereas combination is shown to be identical to contiguity, that is, to the metonymic function. He demonstrates how in aphasia one or, in extreme cases, both of these speech functions are impaired. Aphasic impairment thus affects either the similarity (or metaphoric) function or the contiguity (or metonymic) function. Aphasics who have a problem with selection have to rely on context, which enables them to react in continuing a conversation rather than beginning one. This type of aphasic usually has difficulty with synonyms or with similar circumlocutions. Jakobson observes that an aphasic who has an impaired similarity function falls back on the contiguity function. The latter can likewise be impaired. When this occurs, the syntactic frame of the patient's sentences collapses. Coordination and grammatical subordination are eliminated. Jakobson posits that while the variant types of aphasia are numerous, what is common to all of them is the impairment of the faculty of selection or the impairment of the faculty of combination and contextualization.

Jakobson suggests that his distinction between metaphoric and metonymic can help categorize not only various modes of literary discourse but also other art forms. Thus, for example, if the metaphoric mode predominates in Romanticism and symbolism, the metonymic mode prevails in realism. In painting and film, the metonymic is central, particularly in film, which makes liberal use of synecdochic closeups. (For the purposes of this discussion, Jakobson places synecdoche and metonymy in the same category, in contrast to metaphor.) For Jakobson, the distinction between metaphor and metonymy is crucial. Of course, both modes entail substitution of one term for another, but the fundamental difference lies in the fact that metaphor entails a transfer of meaning between normally unrelated domains, whereas metonymy utilizes a term that is a property of the key word or is related to it contiguously.

Michel Le Guern, in an important essay (1973) based on Jakobson's distinction between metaphor and metonymy, develops Jakobson's highly condensed presentation, showing how the central thesis is far more persuasive than it may appear. There are, for example, good reasons for placing metonymy and synecdoche in contrast to metaphor, especially when it is realized that whereas metaphor entails a transfer of sense, metonymy and synecdoche entail a transfer of reference. In other words, reference is the key to the distinction between metaphor and metonymy. The metonymic relationship obtains between extralinguistic entities, that is, between objects, and is in no way contingent on the language used to express such a relationship. Metonymy and synecdoche entail a transfer of reference and the use of ellipsis. Metaphor (i.e., live metaphor as opposed to clichés that have lost their figurative force) is necessarily perceived as incongruous or surprising, at first apparently not compatible semantically with its context. The metonymic pole is thus essentially a referential process, located beyond language, while the metaphoric pole is semantic and consequently intralinguistic.

Jakobson's essay has acquired a somewhat unusual afterlife for a piece of theoretical writing. It is not common for theory to be turned into fiction, but this is precisely the use to which David Lodge puts the essay in *Nice Work* (1988), a novel that even offers a discussion of Jakobson's theory of metaphor and metonymy.

Michael Issacharoff

See also PRAGUE SCHOOL STRUCTURALISM, SEMIOTICS, and STRUCTURALISM.

Roman Jakobson, "Aphasia as a Linguistic Topic," *Selected Writings*, vol. 2 (1971), "Linguistics and Poetics: Closing Statement," *Style in Language* (ed. Thomas Sebeok, 1960), *Questions de poétique* (1973), "Two Aspects of Language and Two Types of Aphasic Disturbances," *Fundamentals of Language* (by Jakobson and Morris Halle, 1956), *Verbal Art, Verbal Sign, Verbal Time* (ed. Krystyna Pomorska and Stephen Rudy, 1985); Roman Jakobson and Krystyna Pomorska, *Dialogues* (1983).

Daniel Armstrong and Cornelis H. van Schooneveld, eds., *Roman Jakobson: Echoes of His Scholarship* (1977); Christine Brooke-Rose, *A Structural Analysis of Pound's "Usura Canto": Jakobson's Method Extended and Applied to Free Verse* (1976); Karl Bühler, "Axiomatization of the Language Sciences," *Karl Bühler: Semiotic Foundations of Language Theory* (by Robert E. Innis, 1982), *Sprachtheorie: Die Darstellungfunktion der Sprache* (1934); Jonathan Culler, *Structuralist Poetics: Structuralism, Linguistics, and the Study of Literature* (1975); Algirdas Julien Greimas, "L'Actualité du saussurisme," *Le Français moderne* 24 (1956); Catherine Kerbrat-Orecchioni, *L'Énonciation: De la subjectivité dans le langage* (1980); Michel Le Guern, *Sémantique de la métaphore et de la métonymie* (1973); David Lodge, *The Modes of Modern Writing: Metaphor, Metonymy, and the Typology of Modern Literature* (1977); Bronislaw Malinowski, "The Problem of Meaning in Primitive Languages," *The Meaning of Meaning* (by C. K. Ogden and I. A. Richards, 1923); Krystyna Pomorska, "Poetics of Prose" (Jakobson, *Verbal Art*); Paul Ricoeur, *La Métaphore vive* (1975, *The Rule of Metaphor: Multidisciplinary Studies of the Creation of Meaning in Language*, trans. Robert Czerny with Kathleen McLaughlin and John Costello, 1977); Michael Riffaterre,

Semiotics of Poetry (1978); Ferdinand de Saussure, *Cours de linguistique générale* (1916, *Course in General Linguistics*, trans. Roy Harris, 1983); Tzvetan Todorov, *Poétique de la prose* (1971, *The Poetics of Prose*, trans. Richard Howard, 1977); Linda Waugh, "The Poetic Function and the Nature of Language" (Jakobson, *Verbal Art*), *Roman Jakobson's Science of Language* (1976).

JAMES, HENRY

Henry James (1843–1916), known primarily as a major writer of fiction, was the son of Henry James, a somewhat eccentric student of social and religious thought, and the brother of William James, the eminent philosopher and psychologist. In the 1860s James began to submit reviews to the *North American Review,* edited by James Russell Lowell and Charles Eliot Norton, to the *Atlantic,* and to the *Nation.* Even after he began to devote himself to creative writing, he no less steadily produced literary essays and reviews, as well as criticism of art and the theater. James spent a great deal of his mature life in England and on the Continent, and his literary criticism, particularly his book reviewing, reflects his cosmopolitanism: for American magazine editors, James was an expert on English and European fiction; for English editors, he was called on for his expatriate American perspective. In the late 1890s he contributed both "London Notes" to *Harper's Weekly* and "American Letters" to the British periodical *Literature.*

In 1878 James published his first book of critical essays, *French Poets and Novelists,* and in 1879 his only full-length critical study, *Hawthorne,* which was commissioned by Macmillan for their English Men of Letters series. He assembled three more volumes of his criticism himself: *Partial Portraits* (1888), *Essays in London and Elsewhere* (1893), and *Notes on Novelists* (1914). Unlike the reviews, which James did not collect for republication (although some were republished during his lifetime in *Views and Reviews,* ed. LeRoy Phillips, 1908), the essays in these volumes tend to deal with theoretical discussions of literature, particularly of prose fiction, and focus typically on an author's career (e.g., "Anthony Trollope," "Alphonse Daudet") or on more expansive and general topics that James began to explore during the 1880s (e.g., "The Art of Fiction," "The Science of Criticism"). Practically all of James's nearly 300 literary essays and reviews have been republished in the two volumes of the Library of America edition of his *Literary Criticism* (1984).

Although many of James's central concerns remain constant throughout his critical career, his voluminous output can be usefully divided, with both formal and chronological warrant, into two categories: 1) reviews, which are fundamentally evaluative, oriented toward the book consumer, and associated with a mass medium such as the press; and 2) critical essays, which are more interpretive, analytical, and theoretical, directed toward a disinterested enrichment of culture generally, and are associated with the literary or academic world. James himself saw true criticism as of a different order than reviewing: in "The Science of Criticism" (1891) he noted that "the conditions of contemporary journalism" in England and America had "engendered the practice of 'reviewing'—a practice that in general has nothing in common with the art of criticism." This type of spurious "literary conduct" is merely part of the commercial apparatus that magazines, like trains, use to keep all the "seats" occupied so that the advertised journey can begin (*Essays* 95).

The critical act, for James, must first of all be a disinterested and dignified search for "truth," for "life." Like MATTHEW ARNOLD, one of his earliest critical models, James saw criticism as a means of making "truth generally accessible"; "it does not busy itself with consequences" but "takes *high ground,* which is the ground of theory" (717). Unlike the vulgar, "off-hand" productions of his English contemporaries, James's reviews self-consciously attempt to rise above practical matters of "rough-and-ready" evaluation (96–97) and achieve detached discrimination, analysis, and appreciation, the qualities that he felt characterized both Arnold and CHARLES AUGUSTIN SAINTE-BEUVE, another early critical model.

But the reviews, while exhibiting some of the speculative rigor, range, and concern for literary form and technique that came to distinguish the singular and, with regard to the novel, even revolutionary nature of James's criticism generally, remained on the whole decidedly more dogmatic and conventional than the later essays. They were, as well, much more concerned with taking an overtly moral stance, one that assumes, to some degree, an accepted, "external" standard of conduct. James would argue in "The Art of Fiction" and in other essays of that period that fiction should not, and indeed constitutionally could not, express a "conscious moral purpose": "how (a novel being a picture) [can] a picture . . . be either moral or immoral?" (62). But many of his reviews, especially those dealing with the French naturalists, strongly condemn what was felt to be a "depraved," "unclean," or "grotesque" moral atmosphere. Here, too, James seemed to be unconcerned with what later became one of his central critical principles— granting "the artist his subject, his idea, his *donnée*" (56). Charles Baudelaire, James noted, "was the victim of a

grotesque illusion": he "tried to make fine verses on ignoble subjects"; "thinking" readers would find "the beauty perverted by the ugliness" and ultimately "avert" their "heads" (*French* 158). Reviews such as these were what provoked EZRA POUND to comment that James's early critical program was based upon "a desire to square all things to the ethical standards of a Salem mid-week Unitarian prayer meeting" (299).

These kinds of pronouncements, however, are virtually absent from the later critical essays. Beginning with "The Art of Fiction" in 1884—the great turning point in James's critical career—his moral attitudes, like his critical perspective in general, became infinitely more complex, refined, and analytical. This absolutely central critical pronouncement not only constitutes the true entry into his own criticism—the discovery of his subject, critical language, and aesthetic goals—but also marks a change in the very kind of critical activity he engaged in. After this article, James turned from reviewing to essay writing and, consequently, began to look toward a new audience and a new relationship between himself and that audience. Now he wanted not simply to evaluate and judge individual works of fiction for the consumer but to engage in a more ambitious project, the creation of a new consumer, a new reader for fiction, one who might be convinced of the seriousness of prose fiction as an art form and be attuned to the technical strategies of its presentation. This is the kind of reader James wanted for his own novels and, *a fortiori,* for serious novels in general. Before the appearance of "The Art of Fiction," James wrote approximately 200 reviews almost entirely on individual works. During this same period he wrote about 20 essays (including his book on *Hawthorne*) on more expansive topics, literary figures, schools, or movements. After its appearance he wrote only six reviews but published almost 100 critical essays, including the 18 prefaces to the collected New York Edition of his novels (1907–9). It was in these essays and prefaces that James voiced his major aesthetic, critical, and theoretical concerns.

"The Art of Fiction" (published in September 1884) is both a model for and epitome of James's entire critical enterprise. Because of its almost global scope, seen in its ambitiously "comprehensive" title, encompassing the "high ground" of both "art" and "fiction," it introduces more of James's major critical ideas than any other work. Because of its crucially transitional place in James's development, it provides a synthesis of 20 years of inchoate and desultory thoughts about fiction and fiction writing and transforms them into a group of interrelated principles upon which most of his later criticism rests.

Although some commentators on James's criticism, such as R. P. BLACKMUR, see the collected prefaces as James's attempt to present a kind of poetics for the novel, this function seems more adequately served by "The Art of Fiction." Even though this essay was originally written as a rebuttal to Walter Besant's somewhat simplistic lecture of the same title (delivered in April and published in May 1884) and thus is organized more polemically than systematically, and even though it does not extensively explore some issues that are important for James's theories, most notably "point of view," "The Art of Fiction" does offer an extremely comprehensive theoretical grounding for the novel, providing, if not a poetics, at least a necessary first step that would make such a poetics possible, including an examination of the value of speculating on this subject in the first place.

In his very first critical article, written in 1864, when he was 21, James (somewhat precociously) complained: "We had long regretted the absence of any critical treatise upon fiction" (*Essays* 1196). Twenty years later James begins "The Art of Fiction," his attempt in some degree to fill this gap, by calling again for this kind of inquiry. Art, he notes, lives upon "Discussion, suggestion, formulation . . . upon the exchange of views"; artistic achievement "is a delightful spectacle, but the theory too is interesting." James felt that of all the arts, the novel, and particularly the English novel, needed this kind of critical attention; it needed "a theory, a conviction, a consciousness of itself behind it" (44–45). Without this type of self-reflexive analysis, examination, and commentary, the novel would never achieve the stature of a true art form; "it must take itself seriously for the public to take it so" (45).

And taking the novel (and, consequently, theoretical discussion of the novel) seriously is perhaps *the* foundational premise of James's criticism of fiction; everything else—his ideas about form, consciousness, point of view, the proper reader, and so on—depend upon this. For James, the novel is indeed the ultimate art form and should be accorded a position in the culture commensurate with this fact, including a body of criticism worthy of the form. By first calling attention to the need for, and then providing, a serious, learned, and analytical examination of the novel in "The Art of Fiction," James was able to advance his position by a kind of double strategy; he demonstrated the genre's significance and power by presenting cogent arguments against his contemporaries' naive view of it as entertainment and/or moral instruction, while at the same time he offered the essay itself as an example of precisely the kind of critical commentary that the novel as an art form warranted.

The novel's chief strength and importance as a genre, James argues, derive from its unparalleled freedom; there cannot be rules of composition "applied *a priori*" (49). It has only two fundamental requirements: 1) it must "attempt to represent life," and 2) it must "be interesting" (46, 49). These conditions are repeated, in various forms, in other essays and in the prefaces (e.g., *French* 130, 242, 1044) and have been interpreted, singly and in conjunction, in diverse and sometimes contradictory ways. On the one hand, James appears to be a "realist," and many critics have labeled him so: he seems to be calling on the novel to provide a faithful imitation, or mimesis, of the external world. On the other hand, James uses "represent" and not "imitate," which seems to imply (as do many of his other pronouncements) a reordering or rearrangement of the stuff of life; this kind of restructuring process seems to be suggested by the requirement of making the work "interesting," by giving it shape or form dependent upon some projected notion of the reader's response. Consequently, there are also those who label him a "formalist." James's criticism of other writers has similarly been seen as stemming from principles designated either as realist, for example, when he judges a work primarily by the morality of its content, or formalist, when he evaluates a work essentially by its aesthetic structure.

As critics such as James E. Miller have noted, however, James is in truth neither a formalist nor a realist but, in some sense, both together. He attempts to establish a group of related critical principles that work dialectically between these poles—as he similarly does between the formal poles of realism and romance, or French naturalism and English moralism. James was wary of labels and applied the same first condition of freedom to the critical as well as to the artistic sensibility. He constantly questions and probes the basic terms of the critical discussion—"life," "represent," "interest," and, further, "experience," "reality," "form," "plot"—so that his formulations and reformulations of central premises remain in a kind of interactive suspension.

In "The Art of Fiction," for example, he enriches his notion of the genre by subtly expanding its basic requirements: "A novel is in its broadest definition a personal, a direct impression of life: that, to begin with, constitutes its value" (*Essays* 50). Here the representational act is seen as a *personal impression;* what the novelist offers, then, is not external "reality" or "life" but a mental construction (an "impression") of it. For James, life is "all inclusion and confusion"; art is "all discrimination and selection" (*French* 1138). Taking an essentially neo-Kantian position, he thus does not emphasize a single, apprehensible reality, external to the perceiver, but rather sees reality in the interrelation of the individual consciousness with the world outside of it. Jamesian reality is dynamic and multiple: "Humanity is immense, and reality has a myriad forms" (*Essays* 52). And each individual consciousness has a determining role to play in creating it, for art as well as for life: "I am perfectly aware that to say the object of a novel is to represent life does not bring the question to a point so fine as to be uncomfortable for any one. . . . For, after all, may not people differ infinitely as to what constitutes life—what constitutes representation?" (*French* 242).

Placing consciousness as the center of both life and art marks an almost revolutionary break from the conventional realism of his contemporaries and connects James, as many have noted, with modernist and phenomenological modes of thought. "Internalizing" reality, bringing it into the experiencing acts of an individual's consciousness, is a radical move and, as James was fully aware, requires a total readjustment of basic fictional and critical principles. For James, then, the novel need not be limited to the existing conventions of representation but can discover fresh means to deal with "the immense sensibility" of experience (*Essays* 52). Action, for instance, need no longer be seen exclusively in terms of external "adventures" or "incidents"; and "character," the experiencing subject, naturally receives new prominence. Indeed, character seems to subsume incident: "What is character but the determination of incident?" James asks. "What is incident but the illustration of character? . . . It is an incident for a woman to stand up with her hand resting on a table and look out at you in a certain way; or if it be not an incident I think it will be hard to say what it is. At the same time it is an expression of character" (55). Similarly, the novel need not limit itself to the description of physical events: "A psychological reason is, to my imagination, an object adorably pictorial" (61). And traditional plot may be replaced by "subjective adventures" or "dramas of consciousness."

This kind of openness to the novel's formal potentialities for representing the full range of experience, including "inner" experience, is emphasized in almost all of James's critical, theoretical, and pragmatic statements. In the prefaces, for example, James spends a great deal of time analyzing the practical question of "point of view," speculating on the kinds of relationship—in terms of knowledge, vantage point, voice, and grammatical person—that exist between the narrator, the subject, and the conditions of narration. Although codified into nor-

mative rules by his immediate followers, most notably Percy Lubbock (*The Craft of Fiction*, 1921) and Joseph Warren Beach (*The Twentieth Century Novel: Studies in Technique*, 1932), point of view for James was simply the most effective method for keeping the narrative focus squarely upon the character's consciousness, where, of course, he felt the "*leading* interest" of the novel must lie (see, e.g., *French* 1088-96). James's emphasis on "dramatic" methods of presentation, on the importance of "scene," on the relationship between "scene" and "picture" and between what was later termed "telling" and "showing" (see 1170-71, 1317-18), was made similarly prescriptive by later critics. Like point of view, though, these compositional strategies are, for James, features of what he terms "rendering" or "execution"; they are choices of method determined solely by the writer's artistic sensibility. They are, as well, the primary focus of the critic's analysis and evaluation (as he demonstrates in his criticism both of others and of himself—in the prefaces); but they are decidedly not a priori rules of narrative construction.

For James, the only formal requirement of the novel is simply that it have form. Without form, a novel is not a work of art and therefore, James's somewhat circular argument goes, not a novel. His well-known criticism of Leo Tolstoy's, Alexandre Dumas's, and William Makepeace Thackeray's "loose baggy monsters" is based on his sense that they have no aesthetic structure; rather than being intentionally organized as "premeditated art," they appear to partake of the "inclusion and confusion" of life itself, "with their queer elements of the accidental and the arbitrary" (1107). If a novel is valuable as the product of a selective and discriminating consciousness, the structural manifestation of that consciousness—the work's form—determines that value: "There is life and life, and as waste is only life sacrificed and thereby prevented from 'counting,' I delight in a deep-breathing economy and an organic form" (1107-8). Novelistic form, James is one of the first to point out, is not different from artistic form in general; it is all-embracing. Despite what many of his contemporaries—Besant, for example—believe, there is no separation between a work of fiction's "subject" and "treatment": "The story and the novel, the idea and the form, are the needle and thread, and I never heard of a guild of tailors who recommended the use of the thread without the needle or the needle without the thread" (*Essays* 60). To realize fully how radical are the kinds of claims James was making here, one must remember that these pronouncements on the identity of the novel's subject and form were written in 1884, practically 40 years before RUSSIAN FORMALISM would address similar issues and almost 60 years before NEW CRITICISM would approach fiction with its own brand of formalism.

Perhaps even more original, however, is James's insistence on the relationship between fictional form and morality. Unlike his own early reviews, in which he seemed to insist that there were immoral subjects regardless of treatment, and unlike his French contemporaries, who he felt saw absolutely no relationship between morality and art (see, e.g., *French* 1013–14), the essays and prefaces subtly demonstrate that morality in the novel stems not from consciously implanted "ideas" but from the whole cast of the artist's informing consciousness. The overall temper of the author's mind, the fineness and openness of his or her perceptions, determines the web of relationships in the text that come to be perceived by the reader as its moral dimension. It is almost, it seems, as if James sees the moral sense as a kind of unconscious pressure that underlies conscious formal decisions: "There is one point at which the moral sense and the artistic sense lie very near together; that is in the light of the very obvious truth that the deepest quality of a work of art will always be the quality of the mind of the producer" (*Essays* 63–64).

This moral sense, moreover, works by aesthetic, not propositional or didactic, means, and it works by a kind of expansion, not limitation, of the reader's sensibility and sympathy: "The success of a work of art, to my mind, may be measured by the degree to which it produces a certain illusion; that illusion makes it appear to us for the time that we have lived another life—that we have had a miraculous enlargement of experience" (*French* 242). And the novel, because of its own unparalleled freedom, can accomplish this better than any other art form: the novel "can do simply everything, and that is its strength and its life. Its plasticity, its elasticity are infinite" (*Essays* 105).

While James deals with many important questions of literary theory generally (the function of criticism, the role of consciousness, etc.), his unique contribution to criticism and his legacy must be seen in his attempt to accord the novel its proper status in the culture, to move it from entertainment to art. He not only introduced a remarkably broad and comprehensive set of first principles but also offered a body of critical texts that show these principles in action and constitute models for their application. He established, as well, the importance of analytically examining the genre's formal achievements, a kind of activity that before James, if done at all, would have been directed toward poetry or drama. And finally, and perhaps most subtly, through his own example as a reader—of his own fiction (in the prefaces) as well as of others'—he created the kind of reader the fictional art form required and thus provided the novel with the necessary groundwork to make it "what the French call *discutable*" (44).

Martin Kreiswirth

See also FICTION THEORY AND CRITICISM: 3. EARLY TWENTIETH-CENTURY BRITISH AND AMERICAN.

Henry James, *Literary Criticism: Essays on Literature; American Writers; English Writers* (ed. Leon Edel and Mark Wilson, 1984), *Literary Criticism: French Writers; Other European Writers; Prefaces to the New York Edition* (ed. Leon Edel and Mark Wilson, 1984).

Paul B. Armstrong, *The Phenomenology of Henry James* (1983); Richard P. Blackmur, Introduction to *The Art of the Novel: Critical Prefaces,* by Henry James (1934); Sharon Cameron, *Thinking in Henry James* (1989); Sara S. Chapman, *Henry James's Portrait of the Writer as Hero* (1990); Sarah B. Daugherty, *The Literary Criticism of Henry James* (1981); Jonathan Freedman, *Professions of Taste: Henry James, British Aestheticism, and Commodity Culture* (1990); John Goode, "The Art of Fiction: Walter Besant and Henry James," *Tradition and Tolerance in Nineteenth-Century Fiction* (ed. David Howard, John Lucas, and John Goode, 1966); Vivien Jones, *James the Critic* (1985); Susanne Kappeler, *Writing and Reading in Henry James* (1980); Walter R. McDonald, "Inconsistencies in Henry James's Aesthetics," *Texas Studies in Language and Literature* 10 (1969); J. Hillis Miller, *The Ethics of Reading* (1987); James E. Miller, Jr., "Henry James in Reality," *Critical Inquiry* 2 (1976), *Theory of Fiction: Henry James* (1972); Ezra Pound, "Henry James," *Literary Essays of Ezra Pound* (ed. T. S. Eliot, 1954); Morris Roberts, *Henry James's Criticism* (1929); John Carlos Rowe, *The Theoretical Dimensions of Henry James* (1984); David Seed, "The Narrator in James' Criticism," *Philological Quarterly* 60 (1981); Mark Spilka, "Henry James and Walter Besant: 'The Art of Fiction' Controversy," *Novel* 6 (1973); William Veeder, "Image as Argument: Henry James and the Style of Criticism," *Henry James Review* 6 (1985); William Veeder and Susan Griffin, *The Art of Criticism: Henry James on the Theory and Practice of Fiction* (1986); René Wellek, "Henry James," *A History of Modern Criticism: 1750–1950,* vol. 4, *The Later Nineteenth Century* (1965).

JAMESON, FREDRIC

Fredric Jameson (b. 1934) is generally considered to be one of the foremost contemporary Marxist literary critics writing in English. He has published a wide range of works analyzing literary and cultural texts and developing his own neo-Marxist theoretical position. In addition, Jameson has produced a large number of texts criticizing opposing theoretical positions. A prolific writer, he has assimilated an astonishing number of theoretical discourses into his project and has intervened in many contemporary debates while analyzing a diversity of cultural texts, ranging from the novel to video.

In his first published book Jameson analyzed the literary theory and production of JEAN-PAUL SARTRE. Written as a doctoral dissertation at Yale University, *Sartre: The Origins of a Style* (1961) was influenced by Jameson's teacher ERICH AUERBACH and by the STYLISTICS associated with Leo Spitzer and focused on Sartre's style, narrative structures, values, and vision of the world. The book is devoid of the Marxian categories and political readings characteristic of Jameson's later work, but read in the context of the stifling conformism and banal business society of the 1950s, Jameson's subject matter (Sartre) and his intricate literary-theoretical writing style (already the notorious Jamesonian sentences appear full-blown) can be seen as revealing an attempt to create himself as a critical intellectual against the conformist currents of the epoch. One also sees him already turning against the literary establishment, against the dominant modes of literary criticism. All Jameson's works constitute critical interventions against the hegemonic forms of literary criticism and modes of thought regnant in the Anglo-American world.

After intense study of Marxian literary theory in the 1960s, when he was influenced by the New Left and antiwar movement, Jameson published *Marxism and Form,* which introduced a tradition of dialectical neo-Marxist literary theory to the English-speaking world (1970). Since articulating and critiquing the structuralist project in *The Prison-House of Language* (1972), Jameson has concentrated on developing his own literary and cultural theory in works such as *Fables of Aggression: Wyndham Lewis, the Modernist as Fascist* (1979), *The Political Unconscious: Narrative as a Socially Symbolic Act* (1981), and *Postmodernism, or, The Cultural Logic of Late Capitalism* (1991). He has also published three volumes of essays—*The Ideologies of Theory* (vol. 1, *Situations of Theory,* and vol. 2, *Syntax of History,* both 1988) and *Signatures of the Visible* (1991), which collects some essays on film and visual culture—as well as a book on

THEODOR W. ADORNO, *Late Marxism* (1990), and a second book on film, *The Geopolitical Aesthetic* (1992).

No early/late dichotomy in Jameson's publications presents itself as a viable hermeneutical device for interpreting his works as a whole, other than the obvious distinction between his pre-Marxian text *Sartre* and his later writings. Rather, what is striking are the remarkable *continuities* in Jameson's works. One can pick up his articles or books from the early 1970s through the late 1980s and discover strong similarities in their concerns, style, and politics. Indeed, one gets the feeling in reading Jameson's two-volume collection of essays that they could have all been written yesterday, or in the recent past. Yet, as Jameson notes in the introduction to these essays, there is a fundamental shift of emphasis in his works that he describes as

> a shift from the vertical to the horizontal: from an interest in the multiple dimensions and levels of a text to the multiple interweavings of an only fitfully readable (or writable) narrative; from problems of interpretation to problems of historiography; from the attempt to talk about the *sentence* to the (equally impossible) attempt to talk about *modes of production.* (*Ideologies* 1:xxix)

In other words, Jameson's focus has shifted from a vertical emphasis on the many dimensions of a text—its ideological, psychoanalytic, formal, mythic-symbolical levels—which require a sophisticated and multivalent practice of reading, to a horizontal emphasis on the ways texts are inserted into historical sequences and on how history enters and helps constitute texts. Yet this shift in emphasis also points to continuities in Jameson's work, for from the late 1960s to the 1990s he has privileged the historical dimension of texts and historical readings, bringing his critical practice into the slaughterhouse of history, moving critical discourse from the ivory tower of academia and the prison-house of language to the vicissitudes and contingencies of that field for which the term "history" serves as marker.

One therefore reads Jameson as a (still open) totality, as a relatively unified theoretical project in which the various texts provide parts of a whole. Jameson has characteristically appropriated into his theory a wide range of positions, from STRUCTURALISM to poststructuralism and from psychoanalysis to POSTMODERNISM, producing a highly eclectic and original brand of Marxian literary and cultural theory. Marxism remains the master narrative of Jameson's corpus, a narrative that utilizes a dual hermeneutic of ideology and utopia to criticize the ideological components of cultural texts, while setting forth their utopian dimension, and that helps produce criticism of existing society and visions of a better world. Influenced by Marxist theorist Ernst Bloch, Jameson thus has developed a hermeneutical and utopian version of Marxian cultural theory. (See KARL MARX AND FRIEDRICH ENGELS, and MARXIST THEORY AND CRITICISM.)

Jameson's first three major books and most of his early articles involve the effort to develop a literary criticism that cuts against the dominant formalist and conservative models of NEW CRITICISM and the academic Anglo-American establishment. *Marxism and Form* can be read as an introduction to the new versions of Hegelian Marxism that began to appear in Europe and the United States in the late 1960s and early 1970s. Yet as Jameson presents some of the basic positions of Adorno, WALTER BENJAMIN, Herbert Marcuse, Bloch, GEORG LUKÁCS, and Sartre, one finds his own concepts and positions emerging from the analyses. In particular, he makes clear his attraction both to Lukácsian literary theory and to his version of Hegelian Marxism, an allegiance that remains with Jameson in his later works.

Lukács's work on realism and on the historical novel strongly influenced Jameson's way of seeing and situating literature. While Jameson never accepted Lukács's polemics against modernism, he appropriated key Lukácsian categories, such as reification, to describe the fate of culture in contemporary capitalism. The Hegelian markers of Jameson's work include the contextualizing of cultural texts in history, the broad historical periodizing, and the use of Hegelian categories. Dialectical criticism involves the attempt to synthesize competing positions and methods into a more comprehensive theory, as Jameson does in *The Prison-House of Language,* where he incorporates elements of French structuralism and SEMIOTICS, as well as RUSSIAN FORMALISM, into his theory. In *The Political Unconscious* he draws on a wide range of theories, applying them to concrete readings that relate texts to their historical and cultural context, analyze the "political unconscious" of the texts, and depict both ideological and utopian moments of texts.

Dialectical criticism for Jameson also involves thinking that reflexively analyzes categories and methods, while carrying out concrete analyses and inquiries. Categories articulate historical content and thus must be read in terms of the historical environment out of which they emerge. For Jameson, dialectical criticism thus involves thinking that reflects on categories and procedures, while engaging in specific concrete studies; relational and historical thinking, which contextualizes the object of study in its historical environment; utopian thinking, which compares the existing reality with possible alternatives and finds utopian hope in literature,

philosophy, and other cultural texts; and totalizing, synthesizing thinking, which provides a systematic framework for cultural studies and a theory of history within which dialectical criticism can operate. All these aspects are operative throughout Jameson's work, the totalizing element coming more prominently (and controversially) to the fore as his work evolved.

During the 1970s Jameson published a series of theoretical inquiries and many more diverse cultural studies. One begins to encounter the characteristic range of interests and depth of penetration in his studies of science fiction, film, magical narratives, painting, and both realist and modernist literature. One also encounters articles concerning Marxian cultural politics, imperialism, Palestinian liberation, Marxian teaching methods, and the revitalization of the Left. Many of the key essays have been collected in *The Ideologies of Theory,* which provide the laboratory for the theoretical project worked out in *The Political Unconscious* and *Fables of Aggression.* These texts, along with his essays collected in *Postmodernism,* should be read together as inseparable parts of a multilevel theory of the interconnections between the history of literary form, modes of subjectivity, and stages of capitalism.

Jameson's theoretical synthesis is presented most systematically in *The Political Unconscious.* The text contains an articulation of Jameson's literary method, a systematic inventory of the history of literary forms, and a hidden history of the forms and modes of subjectivity itself, as it traverses through the field of culture and experience. Jameson boldly attempts to establish Marxian literary criticism as the most all-inclusive and comprehensive theoretical framework as he incorporates a disparate set of competing approaches into his model. He provides an overview of the history of the development of literary form and concludes with articulation of a "double hermeneutic" of ideology and utopia—which critiques ideology while preserving utopian moments—as the properly Marxian method of interpretation.

Jameson employs a Lukács-inspired historical narrative to tell how cultural texts contain a "political unconscious," buried narratives and social experiences, which require sophisticated literary hermeneutics in order to be deciphered. One particular narrative of *The Political Unconscious* concerns, in Jameson's striking phrase, "the construction of the bourgeois subject in emergent capitalism and its schizophrenic disintegration in our own time" (9). Key stages in the odyssey of the disintegrating bourgeois subjectivity are articulated in George Gissing, Joseph Conrad, and Wyndham Lewis, a story that will find its culmination in Jameson's account of postmodernism.

Indeed, Jameson's studies on postmodernism are a logical resultant of his theoretical project. He presented his first analysis of the defining features of postmodern culture in an essay "Postmodernism and Consumer Society" (a 1982 lecture), published in Hal Foster's collection *The Anti-Aesthetic* (1983). Eventually, he synthesized and elaborated his emerging analysis in the article "Postmodernism, or the Cultural Logic of Late Capitalism," which more systematically interprets postmodernism in terms of the Marxian theory of capitalism and as a new "cultural dominant" (*Postmodernism* 1 ff., slightly expanded from the essay by the same name).

Within his analysis, Jameson situates postmodern culture in the framework of a theory of stages of society—based on a neo-Marxian model of stages of capitalist development—and argues that postmodernism is part of a new stage of capitalism. Every theory of postmodernism, he claims, contains an implicit periodization of history and "an implicitly or explicitly political stance on the nature of multinational capitalism today" (*Postmodernism* 3). Following Ernest Mandel's periodization in his book *Late Capitalism* (1975), Jameson claims that "there have been three fundamental moments in capitalism, each one marking a dialectical expansion over the previous stage. These are market capitalism, the monopoly stage or the stage of imperialism, and our own, wrongly called postindustrial, but what might better be termed multinational, capital" (35). To these forms of society correspond the cultural forms realism, modernism, and postmodernism.

The important essay "The Existence of Italy" (in *Signatures of the Visible*) further develops this problematic, as does the conclusion to *Postmodernism*. Jameson emerges as a synthetic and eclectic Marxian cultural theorist who attempts to preserve and develop the Marxian theory, while analyzing the politics and utopian moments of a stunning diversity of cultural texts. His work expands literary analysis to include popular culture, architecture, theory, and other texts and thus can be seen as part of the movement toward CULTURAL STUDIES as a replacement for canonical literary studies.

Douglas Kellner

See also MARXIST THEORY AND CRITICISM: 2. STRUCTURALIST MARXISM and POSTMODERNISM.

Fredric Jameson, *Fables of Aggression: Wyndham Lewis, the Modernist as Fascist* (1979), *The Geopolitical Aesthetic: Cinema and Space in the World System* (1992), *The Ideologies of Theory*: vol. 1, *Situations of Theory*, vol. 2, *Syntax of History* (1988), *Late Marxism: Adorno, or, the Persistence of the Dialectic* (1990), *Marxism and Form: Twentieth-Century Dialectical Theories of Literature* (1971), *The Political Unconscious: Narrative as a Socially Symbolic Act* (1981), "Postmodernism, or the Cultural Logic of Late Capitalism," *New Left Review* 146 (1984), *Postmodernism, or the Cultural Logic of Late Capitalism* (1991), *The Prison-House of Language: A Critical Account of Structuralism and Russian Formalism* (1972), *Sartre: The Origins of a Style* (1961), *Signatures of the Visible* (1990).

Steven Best and Douglas Kellner, *Postmodern Theory: Critical Interrogations* (1991); *Critical Exchange* 14 (1983, special issue on Jameson); *diacritics* 12 (1982, special issue on Jameson); William C. Dowling, *Jameson, Althusser, Marx: An Introduction to "The Political Unconscious"* (1984); Hal Foster, ed., *The Anti-Aesthetic: Essays on Postmodern Culture* (1983); Douglas Kellner, ed., *Postmodernism/Jameson/Critique* (1989); *New Orleans Review* 11 (1984, special issue on Jameson); Michael Sprinker, *Imaginary Relations: Aesthetics and Ideology in the Theory of Historical Materialism* (1987).

JAPANESE THEORY AND CRITICISM

Literary criticism in Japan has a history extending over more than ten centuries. Most of those who contributed to its development were not philosophers or rhetoricians but poets, novelists, and playwrights who were actively engaged in creative writing. Consequently their thoughts on literature tended to be unsystematic yet rich in pragmatic wisdom, which helped their colleagues working in the same genre. Professional critics finally emerged in the twentieth century, but their writings focus on the creative process, too. For ideas and terms, the Japanese often resorted to Buddhism and CHINESE THEORY AND CRITICISM until the late nineteenth century and to Western literature and aesthetics thereafter. In doing so they had to modify what they borrowed and make it workable within their literary conventions, and that effort sometimes led to critical concepts uniquely their own. Insofar as literature occupied a high place in Japanese society, literary criticism functioned as an important determinant of the cultural climate in each age.

The Ten Thousand Leaves (*Man'yōshū*, eighth century), the earliest anthology of Japanese verse, already shows evidence that poets thought seriously about their craft. The headnote "Allegorical Poem," for instance, indicates the conscious use of allegory for a literary device, while the prefatory note "Pouring Forth My Emotion" suggests the germ of an expressive theory of poetry. Those ideas, originally imported from China, were gradually transformed so as to fit Japanese reality. The first major work to show that attempt is Ki no Tsurayuki's preface to the anthology *Kokin Wakashū* (905). Fully aware that the poetry of his country was largely lyrical, Tsurayuki stressed the importance of spontaneity in composition and harmony between emotion and words, comparing the creative process to the growth of a tree, from the germination of the seed to the eventual blossoming and bearing of fruit. Poets in the succeeding generations amplified the theory in various ways, but when Japan became torn with civil wars in the twelfth century, this type of lyrical expressionism began to give way to idealistic aestheticism, which encouraged poets to create unearthly beauty by means of language. Thus Fujiwara no Shunzei (1114–1204) cultivated such poetic ideals as *aware* ("pathos") and *yūgen* ("mystery and depth"), reflecting his pessimistic view of contemporary society, as well as his longing for the golden age that had long passed. His son Teika (1162–1241) went farther in this direction and advocated a type of poetry embodying even more ethereal beauty, which he called *en*. Essays written by them and their followers point toward a symbolic theory of poetry that aims to capture mysterious beauty lying far beyond physical reality.

Criticism of fiction had a later start. The first notable attempt to comment on the nature of prose narrative was made by Murasaki Shikibu (978–1016) in a chapter of her celebrated novel, *The Tale of Genji (Genji monogatari)*. Using the novel's hero for her mouthpiece, she put forward the view that a good tale is just as valuable as a book of history, because it embodies imaginative truth, and just as edifying as a religious parable, because it helps the reader to distinguish between good and evil. Her argument went unnoticed for some centuries, since it was subtly woven into the texture of the novel. But *The Tale of Genji* itself stimulated many readers to make critical comments and thereby helped the development of fiction criticism. Prominent among these readers was an unidentified noblewoman who wrote *Mumyō zōshi* (*The Nameless Booklet*, 1196–1202) and recorded her impressionistic appraisals of characters and events described in *The Tale of Genji* and other tales she had read.

In the meantime, two new developments in poetry had given rise to new types of criticism. One was the increasing popularity of poetry contests, which promoted practical and valuational criticism. At poetry contests, usually refereed by a prestigious poet of the time, verses written by different poets on the same topic would be paired and judged. Sometimes a participating poet dis-

satisfied with the judgment wrote a protest, thereby starting a lively literary controversy and helping to identify critical problems. The other new poetic development was the emergence of *renga* (linked poetry), in which two or more poets would contribute verses to the making of a single poetic sequence. Inevitably rules had to be invented to ensure coherence among sequential verses, and that prompted discussions on problems of structural unity. Various methods of linking two verses, such as "explicative linking," "allusive linking," and "linking through unusual association," were discussed by master poets for the benefit of those who studied under them. Some of those discussions, written by such poets as Nijō Yoshimoto (1320–88), Shinkei (1406–75), and Sōgi (1421–1502), remain valuable documents that explore problems of poetic structure.

Critical writings on drama finally began to appear in the fourteenth century, when the *nō* attained maturity as a theatrical art. Chief among them are treatises written by actor-playwrights Zeami (1363–1443) and Zenchiku (1405–70?), who wanted to hand down the secrets of their craft to their heirs. Zeami's theory of acting centered around three basic principles: imitation, by which he meant representation of essences rather than surface mimicry; *yūgen*, elegant beauty with underlying implications of mystery and depth; and "the sublime," the highest type of theatrical effect, which he suggested by means of the image of the sun shining brightly at midnight. His treatise on playwriting stressed the use of a three-part structure called *jo-ha-kyū* (introduction-development-finale), a structure borrowed from a style of Chinese court music. Zenchiku, Zeami's son-in-law, tried to integrate the art of the *nō* with Buddhism. In his view, a *nō* performance of the highest quality would produce an effect as transparent and tasteless as water, yet inclusive of all the colors and tastes on earth—an effect not unlike the Buddhist concept of the void.

With the rise of the merchant class in the seventeenth century, literary thinking became more earthly and humanistic. Chikamatsu Monzaemon (1653–1724), who wrote plays for the *kabuki* and puppet theater, reportedly made a statement implying that a high dramatic tension could be created if the play's main character was torn between love and social obligation. In his last years Matsuo Bashō (1644–94), a prominent *haiku* poet, taught that poets should aim at creating *karumi* ("lightness"), a mood arising from detached observations of imperfect human nature revealed in ordinary life. The novelist Takizawa Bakin (1767–1848) took a more moralistic view of literature, saying that the writer's aim lay "simply in presenting truth about human feelings so as to promote virtue." Other writers of popular fiction in the seventeenth and eighteenth centuries tried to produce ambiences of *sui* ("pure essence") and *iki* ("high spirit"), both designating varieties of urbane, chic beauty admired by affluent dilettantes of the merchant class.

The seventeenth century also saw the rise of *kokugaku* ("national learning"), a type of classicism advanced by a group of scholars who wanted to elucidate and advance Japan's cultural identity. Their profound interest in classics promoted historical linguistics, which in turn helped to encourage intensive textual studies. They annotated such books as *The Ten Thousand Leaves* and *The Tale of Genji* with a degree of exacting scholarship never known before. Their penchant for primitive culture also led to an emphasis on the role of emotion in creative writing. Ardent nationalists, they rejected the rationalism of Chinese philosophers and valued free expression of the inmost heart in both life and literature. Thus in the poetics of Kamo no Mabuchi (1697–1769), a major *kokugaku* scholar, the central principles were *makoto* ("truthfulness") and *masuraoburi* ("manliness"), the former designating artless expression of feelings unhampered by intellect and the latter indicating the vigorous, stout heart of a primitive man that spontaneously vents itself in a simple, rhythmical language. Mabuchi's theory was significantly modified by his disciple, Motoori Norinaga (1730–1801), who considered basic human nature to be more effeminate. In formulating his own theory, Norinaga replaced *masuraoburi* by *mono no aware* ("pathos of things"), an empathic appreciation of ephemeral beauty manifest in nature and human life. This and other *kokugaku* theories of literature had the effect of restoring emotion to a prominent place in Japanese literary criticism.

European literature and thinking began to flow into Japan in the late nineteenth century, as the new government that came into power in 1868 adopted the policy of modernizing the country by importing Western civilization. The Japanese were impressed, above all, by European writers' greater effort toward verisimilitude. Thus many of those who wrote on literature in early modern Japan came to stress Western-type realism. The most influential among them was Tsubouchi Shōyō (1859–1935), a novelist and translator of Shakespeare, who in his book *Shōsetsu shinzui* [The essence of the novel] (1885–86) asserted that the main aim of the novel was to bare truths about human nature and the ways of the world. The poet Masaoka Shiki (1867–1902) wanted to apply realism to traditional Japanese poetry such as *haiku* and eventually formulated the principle of *shasei* ("sketch from life"). Some of his followers, such as Kawahigashi

Hekigodō (1873–1937), stretched the principle to an extreme and began to advocate the writing of *haiku* in free style, arguing that any arbitrary attempt to mold a poem into a fixed syllable pattern would compromise the poet's aim of copying his subject faithfully. Their ideas of poetry foreshadowed the theory of free verse.

Among the various types of realism, the naturalistic variety had the greatest appeal to the Japanese in the early twentieth century. Consequently the main current of literary criticism developed along that line, although the notion of naturalism inevitably came to assume a distinctly native color. Partly due to the traditional penchant for harmony with nature, and partly due to the underdeveloped idea of the self in Japan at the time, critics who advocated naturalism emphasized the importance of the writer's merging with nature and grasping its life from within rather than presenting a biological or economic force for a theme. This line of thinking was articulated most eloquently by Shimamura Hōgetsu (1871–1918), who saw the main aim of naturalism to be to destroy all the abstract—"unnatural"—doctrines of the modern age and show life as it is naturally lived. His theory was welcomed in contemporary Japan. Under the rubric "naturalism," stories that differed little from fragments of diaries appeared in great numbers and received high critical acclaim.

Other Western ideas did continue to reach Japan, the number rapidly increasing in the 1920s. Aestheticism, surrealism, Imagism, and dadaism all found ardent followers there, albeit temporarily in most instances. The theory that had the greatest impact on practicing poets and writers was Marxism, but it produced few great works of literature or literary criticism. More fruitful was European symbolism, which had been introduced earlier and in the late 1920s became a motivating force for a literary movement called *shin kankaku shugi* ("neo-sensualism"). Led by the novelist Yokomitsu Riichi (1898–1947), the group advocated reaching for ultimate truth through sensory, nonintellectual perception and presenting it through symbolic language. Also inspired by European symbolism, the poet Hagiwara Sakutarō (1886–1942) came to view poetry as a metaphysical expression of universal human nostalgia for an existential homeland and eventually developed this into a poetic theory in his book *Shi no genri* [The principles of poetry] (1928). Common to both these theorists is their awareness that traditional Japanese literature is rich in its own type of symbolism and that the European variety can be integrated into the literary language of Japan easily and in a meaningful way. The most influential critic of the mid-century, Kobayashi Hideo (1902–83), kept himself aloof from most of the literary movements of his time, relying largely on his own considerable critical instinct and literary sensibility in approaching a writer or a work. Primarily an impressionistic critic, he probed deep into himself in search of the source that responded to a given literary work, and through that source he tried to reach for the fountainhead of the writer's creative imagination. Because he worked mainly in modern literature, his writings inevitably focused on the existential anxiety that haunted the minds of both himself and the writer who was his subject. Thus in his later years he turned his attention more to the writer's life and times, and he came to write biographical criticism in a manner reminiscent of CHARLES AUGUSTIN SAINTE-BEUVE. His psychological insights and highly polished style remained intact from the earlier years, making his essays almost as inspiring as poems or stories of the highest order. With Kobayashi, Japanese literary criticism for the first time became a branch of creative writing.

Some of Kobayashi's contemporaries who were more theoretically inclined endeavored to reinterpret the aesthetic ideals of traditional Japanese literature in the light of Western aesthetics. Watsuji Tetsurō (1889–1960), for instance, analyzed *mono no aware* by using a philological method learned from European scholars. Kuki Shūzō (1888–1941) examined the concept of *iki* from the viewpoint of an expert in German PHENOMENOLOGY. The most ambitious attempt along this line was made by Ōnishi Yoshinori (1888–1959), another specialist in German philosophy, who built his own elaborate aesthetic system incorporating both Japanese and Western ideas of art. In his system, the traditional Japanese concept of *yūgen*, for example, is organically related to Western ideas of the sublime and the tragic. Sublime beauty, according to Ōnishi, comes into existence when one perceives physical or metaphorical greatness in nature or human life. When one has a sense of greatness about one's own capability and dares to confront the great power of nature, there emerges the beauty of the tragic. On the other hand, when one has a modest view of oneself and sees nothing but mysterious darkness in nature, there appears the beauty of *yūgen*. Ōnishi's aesthetic system, criticized by some as being too arbitrary, nevertheless was a significant step toward establishing universal standards applicable to both Eastern and Western art.

Internationalism can be seen even in the works of nationalistic writers and critics who gained power during the years leading to World War II. The very name of their group, *Nihon rōman-ha* (Japanese Romantics), echoes German Romantics, under whose influence their movement began. Their leader, Yasuda Yojūrō (b. 1910), scrutinized contemporary literature by utilizing F. W. J. Schelling's idea of Romantic irony. Also like the German Romantics, he was dedicated to the preservation of the native tradition and wrote a number of essays on the uniqueness of Japanese culture. As the war intensified, however, his romantic search for Japanese identity gradually dissolved into the general trend of ultranationalism.

Japan's defeat in World War II brought chaos to the contemporary literary scene, inducing many men of letters to turn to Marxism for a framework with which to reshape their thoughts. Some of them, however, were painfully aware of the failure of left-wing literature a decade earlier, and they insisted on the independence of literature from Marxism or any other dogma. In 1946 they founded a magazine called *Kindai bungaku* [Modern literature], which soon became a leading critical voice in the postwar era. Among the critics associated with the magazine, Hirano Ken (1907–78) was especially interested in a predicament common to autobiographical novelists and formulated a theory of Japanese *ich-roman*. Haniya Yutaka (b. 1910) envisioned what he called a "literature of impossibility," basing the vision on his anarchical view of the cosmos. Yamamuro Shizuka (b. 1906), an admirer of Albert Schweitzer and Rabindranath Tagore, introduced a humanitarian viewpoint to Japanese literary criticism. Those and other critics who wrote for *Kindai bungaku* prepared fertile soil for radically new literature to germinate, as it did, in the postwar period.

As the gloom of the war and its aftermath gradually lifted, works of critics outside of the *Kindai bungaku* group became more conspicuous. Most prominent among them was Nakamura Mitsuo (1901–88), who viewed modern Japanese fiction as part of *Weltliteratur* and examined it from a comparative standpoint. Yamamoto Kenkichi (1907–88), under the influence of NEW CRITICISM, analyzed works of classical Japanese poetry with an unprecedented degree of sophistication and skill. Katō Shūichi (b. 1919), who taught at European and Canadian universities for years, wrote many critical essays as well as a history of Japanese literature from a perspective that synthesizes both Chinese and European concepts. Saeki Shōichi (b. 1922), a scholar in modern American literature, has tried to combine a biographical approach with New Criticism and has set up a new method of analysis for Japanese literature, which is generally bent toward autobiography. The works of those independent critics became increasingly more influential as Japan proceeded with its economic recovery and Marxism rapidly lost its appeal.

Some writers known primarily as poets or novelists

have also contributed to the evolution of critical thoughts in recent times. Itō Sei (1905–69), who began his literary career as a lyric poet, later came to formulate an imaginative theory of the novel based on his original view of the "life-force" and social order. Yoshimoto Takaaki (b. 1924), a free-verse poet, has written provocative criticism from various viewpoints, ranging from that of a Buddhist, to a Christian's, to a linguist's. The novelist Mishima Yukio (1925–70) was more consistent in his stance, his unique philosophy of action underlying most of his critical works. His *Sun and Steel* (*Taiyō to tetsu*, 1968) eloquently expounds that philosophy and makes clear literature's place in it.

Literary criticism in Japan in the 1980s has been faced with the task of discovering ways to incorporate recent Western theories, such as those based on SEMIOTICS, STRUCTURALISM, and DECONSTRUCTION. Major works of ROLAND BARTHES, ROMAN JAKOBSON, JACQUES LACAN, and JACQUES DERRIDA were translated into Japanese in the 1970s, and their ideas and terminology began to be used by some radical critics. One example is *Natsume Sōseki ron* [A study of Natsume Sōseki] (1978), by Hasumi Shigehiko (b. 1936), which, despite its title, assumes that the well-known Japanese novelist did not write to express himself but merely drew upon an immense preexistent dictionary of language and culture. Another example is *Toshi kūkan no naka no bungaku* [Literature within city space] (1982), by Maeda Ai (1932–87), which tries to interpret modern Japanese fiction in terms of linguistic and cultural signs that lie hidden in its background descriptions. These and other similar studies, however, remain only a small minority isolated from the main corpus of contemporary literary criticism. A large majority of critics, ever aware that their literary tradition has been dominated by a confessional type of writing, continue to harbor serious misgivings about the usefulness of approaches that minimize the role of the author. It will be interesting to observe how those Western theories will fare in Japan in the years to come, for they are facing a stringent test as to their universal validity.

Makoto Ueda

Hasumi Shigehiko, *Natsume Sōseki ron* (1978); Shūichi Katō, *Nihon bungakushi josetsu* (2 vols., 1975–80, *A History of Japanese Literature,* trans. David Chibbett and Don Sanderson, 3 vols., 1979–83); Kobayashi Hideo, *Kobayashi Hideo zenshu* (12 vols., 1967–68); Maeda Ai, *Toshi kūkan no naka no bungaku* (1982); Yukio Mishima, *Taiyō to tetsu* (1968, *Sun and Steel,* trans. John Bester, 1970); Murasaki Shikibu, *Genji monogatari* (c. 1015, 2 vols., 1958–63, *The Tale of Genji,* trans. Edward Seidensticker, 1976); Nakamura Mitsuo, *Nihon no kindai shōsetsu* (1964, *Japanese Fiction in the Meiji Era,* trans. Donald L. Philippi, 1966); Ryusaku Tsunoda et al., eds., *Sources of Japanese Tradition* (1958); Ki no Tsurayaki, "Kino Preface," *Kokin Wakashū* (980, reprint, 1958, *Kokin Wakashū,* trans. Helen Craig McCullough, 1985); Yoshida Seiichi et al., eds., *Kindai bungaku hyōron taikei* (10 vols., 1971–75); Zeami, *Nōgakuron shū* (1961, *On the Art of the Nō Drama: The Major Treatises of Zeami,* trans. J. Thomas Rimer and Yamazaki Masakazu, 1984).

Robert H. Brower and Earl Miner, *Japanese Court Poetry* (1961); Hisamatsu Sen'ichi, *Nihon bungaku hyōronshi* (5 vols., 1936–51), *The Vocabulary of Japanese Literary Aesthetics* (1963); Donald Keene, *Dawn to the West: Japanese Literature of the Modern Era,* vol. 2, *Poetry, Drama, Criticism* (1984); Jin'ichi Konishi, *Nihon bungeishi,* vol. 1 (1985, *A History of Japanese Literature,* vol. 1, *The Archaic and Ancient Ages,* ed. Earl Miner, trans. Aileen Gatten and Nicholas Teele, 1984); William R. LaFleur, *The Karma of Words: Buddhism and the Literary Arts in Medieval Japan* (1983); Earl Miner et al., *The Princeton Companion to Classical Japanese Literature* (1985); J. Thomas Rimer, *Culture and Identity: Japanese Intellectuals during the Interwar Years* (1990); Makoto Ueda, *Literary and Art Theories in Japan* (1967); Seiichi Yoshida, *Kindai bunoei hyōronshi* (2 vols., 1975–77).

JOHNSON, SAMUEL

Samuel Johnson (1709–84), who was such a dominant literary figure in the second half of the eighteenth century that the period has sometimes been called the Age of Johnson, lived most of his adult life in London. Until the crown granted him a pension in 1763, he had to support himself by his literary activity, including major projects such as the *Dictionary of the English Language* (1755) and his edition of the plays of Shakespeare (1765), as well as periodical essay series such as the *Rambler* (1750–52) and the *Idler* (1758–60), other separate publications such as the poem *The Vanity of Human Wishes* (1749) and the tale *Rasselas* (1759), and miscellaneous writing, mainly for a variety of periodicals. His last major literary project was the series *Lives of the Poets* (1779–81).

In his 92d *Rambler* essay Johnson states that "criticism reduces those regions of literature under the dominion of science, which have hitherto known only the anarchy of ignorance, the caprices of fancy, and the tyranny of prescription" (*Yale* 4:122). For him, the business of criticism is reasoned literary judgment. It may involve, as he remarked in his "Life of Dryden," "general precepts, which depend upon the nature of things and the structure of the human mind" (*Lives* 1:413) or "occasional and particular positions" that concern individual works and grow from the sort of piece he is writing (see JOHN DRYDEN). Most of Johnson's criticism is directed to particular literary works and problems, and one of its most striking features is the intensity of his response to individual works, but his judgments are based on a set of coherent underlying principles emerging in general pronouncements that illuminate the particular occasion.

In the analysis of Johnson's criticism offered here, a summary statement of Johnson's critical "system" as it may be deduced from his various writings (for he nowhere codifies it himself) will be followed by a more detailed discussion of certain points and the illustration of his criticism at work in his writing on Shakespeare. Though Johnson's remarks on particular works and writers may be what is remembered most, the underlying principles are remarkably consistent throughout his career from his early journalistic writing in the 1730s and 1740s to the *Lives of the Poets* in the 1780s.

For Johnson the end of all writing is to instruct. This implies a necessary relationship between writer and reader. The end of poetry is to instruct by pleasing. The subjects of writing are nature and life: the writer must know and understand both the natural and moral worlds in order to imitate them and teach about them; the reader must recognize and respond to the imitation. From this response the writer's success may be judged. Thus Johnson keeps coming back to the test of the "common reader" and always allows an appeal from the laws of criticism to nature itself.

In Johnson's view, then, art teaches through giving pleasure. He explores the sources of this pleasure often. They are somewhat paradoxical. On the one hand, pleasure comes from the reader's response of recognition—recognition of just representations of general nature, recognition of the truth of the imitation—and from the sympathy or fellow feeling that the reader is stimulated to feel with the imaginative creation. But, and it is a large but, this imaginative response must be distinguished from a response to actuality. The reader is conscious of the fact of fiction, and his or her response consists in bringing realities to mind. The response to reality itself would be different and might not be pleasurable. On the other hand, pleasure comes from variety and from the recognition of the truly new—not the novelty of unnatural fantasy and the heresies of paradox but the newness of a fresh vision of the truth of nature. In Johnson's view, a writer can never achieve true greatness by mere imitation of previous literature, however accomplished that imitation.

The author, in addition to creating pleasure through manipulations of language, teaches, persuades, and moves; the author can excite sympathy and confer honor. Authorial activity, while central, is always directed beyond the writer to the reader. What Johnson is most frequently getting at in his use of the term "general" is this capacity for communication through stimulating recognition in the reader. Thus, an equally important element in Johnson's model of the literary transaction is the reader's response to the literary text. When Johnson comes to examine specific literary kinds such as pastoral and comedy or codified principles such as the "unities," he assesses them in terms of their relation to nature and to real human imaginative response.

Johnson views truth and nature as for the most part uniform across place and time. However, he recognizes that human manners and societies change as do languages and the associations of words. Thus, he sees the need for a historically based criticism. Furthermore, he recognizes that all judgment is comparative. We recognize merit by a comparison with what we know to be meritorious. We gain our sense of what humanity can do by examining what humanity has done. In judging the particular beauties and faults of a composition or a writer and in assessing proprieties, then, we must be aware of the many relativities involved, as well as of the absolutes. Both literature and life are complex and gain much of their interest from their complexity.

Some of the elements in this schema of Johnson's critical attitudes need amplification. In his last *Rambler* paper, he says that criticism "is only to be ranked among the subordinate and instrumental arts." But he continues: "Arbitrary decision and general exclamation I have carefully avoided, by asserting nothing without a reason, and establishing all my principles of judgment on unalterable and evident truth" (*Yale* 5:319). Many years later, in calling Dryden "the father of English criticism," he described him as "the writer who first taught us to determine upon principles the merit of composition" (*Lives* 1:410). For Johnson, then, the critic is ultimately a judge, but a judge who understands thoroughly the laws or principles of writing and bases his judgments on this knowledge and who, rather than merely asserting his own authority, respects the judgments of other informed readers, especially when they are recurrent.

In the "Preface to Shakespeare" Johnson states that "the end of writing is to instruct; the end of poetry is to instruct by pleasing" (*Yale* 7:67). This assertion implies a conception fundamental to Johnson's critical thought.

Though works of literature may well be viewed as products of the characteristic genius of their authors, they are fundamentally transactions between writer and reader. At point after point in his critical writing Johnson insists that works must please their readers to hold them. In the "Life of Dryden," for example, he says, "Works of imagination excel by their allurement and delight; by their power of attracting and detaining the attention. That book is good in vain which the reader throws away" (*Lives* 1:454). It is this capacity to hold the attention and teach through giving pleasure, then, that discriminates belles-lettres from other kinds of writing. The pleasure, furthermore, is to be discovered especially in large effects and the general tenor of a work rather than in particular small details.

Before analyzing how this pleasure operates, we must examine Johnson's views on the subjects of such writing, the material with which an author works. A certain pairing, "nature" and "life," is pervasive in his criticism. The pairing occurs several times in reference to Shakespeare, for example in the "Proposals for an Edition": "It is the great excellence of Shakespeare, that he drew his scenes from nature, and from life" (*Yale* 7:53). And it appears, as well, in various essays on other writers (see, e.g., "Life of Cowley," *Lives* 1:19; "Life of Dryden," *Lives* 1:410; *Rambler* no. 36, *Yale* 3:197). The most memorable, though not the clearest, occurrence is in the "Preface" itself: "Shakespeare is above all writers, at least above all modern writers, the poet of nature; the poet that holds up to his readers a faithful mirrour of manners and of life" (*Yale* 7:62). These ideas are elaborated upon in Imlac's dissertation on poetry in chapter 10 of *Rasselas*. "Nature" is the subject of poetry. It involves the whole perceptible world created by God. Men and women are to be the poet's audience, and to communicate effectively with them the poet must know all the modes of life. The poet must also have analyzed the nature of the human condition and the workings of the human mind and must ultimately teach human beings the truth about the natural and moral world they inhabit and in the process move and involve them. Thus, in Imlac's words, "He must write as the interpreter of nature, and the legislator of mankind" (16:27).

The reader's pleasurable response includes for Johnson involvement, recognition, and surprise. Ideally the reader will be stimulated to an act of sympathy by which he or she enters vicariously into the experience of the other lives represented in the work, bringing his or her own experience to bear on an understanding of theirs. As Johnson points out in *Rambler* no. 60, such an experience is an essential part of our response to biography,

but it operates in fiction, in feigned lives and histories, as well. Much of the basic pleasure given by poetic writing is that of recognition, the "general power of gratifying every mind by recalling its conceptions," which Johnson mentions in *Rambler* no. 36 (3:197). As Imlac says, the poet "is to exhibit in his portraits of nature such prominent and striking features, as recall the original to every mind" (16:26). At the same time, as Johnson points out in the "Life of Cowley," "the pleasures of the mind imply something sudden and unexpected" (*Lives* 1:59). Alexander Pope's *Rape of the Lock,* for example, exhibits "the two most engaging powers of an author: new things are made familiar, and familiar things are made new" (3:233). Furthermore, as Johnson notes in the "Life of Butler" as well as in the "Preface to Shakespeare," "the great source of pleasure is variety. Uniformity must tire at last, though it be uniformity of excellence. We love to expect; and, when expectation is disappointed or gratified, we want to be again expecting" (*Lives* 1:212). This need for variety is gratified as much by the skillful distribution of the parts of a work as by diverse subject matter.

But the pleasures of recognition and the elevation of the mind by grand conceptions are brought about by what Johnson refers to as "generality." It is important to recognize that Johnson is not using here a Neoplatonic ontological conception, as W. K. Wimsatt and some others have asserted, but is, rather, employing Lockean epistemology, language theory, and psychology. The details have been elucidated by Jean Hagstrum, Donald Greene, and William Edinger, among others. The concept involves no contradictions in Johnson's thought; when properly understood, it is perfectly consistent. The "general" in this sense does not negate the value of particulars, especially psychological particulars. In Lockean thought the general idea is built up from particulars. Reality always resides in the particulars, not, as in Platonic thought, in the general (see PLATO). The general stands for the many rather than the one. It is arrived at by a process of abstraction, of omitting irrelevant parts of a complex idea. By leaving out what is too limiting, too specific, too particularly of only one time or place, we arrive at something that many can recognize by projecting onto it the specifics of their own experience. For John Locke, we communicate by means of generals such as this. For Johnson, this is the mode as well of literary communication and literary pleasure. But in addition there is a "grandeur of generality" (*Lives* 1:45), a stretch given to the mind and imagination by the extent and number of conceptions that can sometimes be recognized in the generalized statement or image.

In the end, it is to the standard of the response of the common reader that Johnson appeals in questions of literary judgment. Only this can take into full account human complexity and eliminate the dangers of partial and prejudiced judgment. One of the fullest statements appears in the "Life of Gray":

> In the character of his *Elegy* I rejoice to concur with the common reader; for by the common sense of readers uncorrupted with literary prejudices, after all the refinements of subtilty and the dogmatism of learning, must be finally decided all claim to poetical honours. The *Church-yard* abounds with images which find a mirrour in every mind, and with sentiments to which every bosom returns an echo. (3:441)

Despite the consistency of his critical principles, Johnson's criticism is also very sensitive to the special circumstances of its origin. He unashamedly wrote to earn money. The forms in which he wrote were those demanded by the occasion, and what he wrote was adapted to what was appropriate for that form. Johnson was willing to recirculate work already on hand, and sometimes this work may seem out of place in its new setting; but when composing he was keenly sensitive to what was appropriate to his present occasion. A reader approaching Johnson's criticism needs to cultivate an understanding of the demands set by each kind of piece that he wrote—prefaces, dedications, lives, notes, reviews, and separate essays. The reader also needs, if possible, to develop some sense of the context of literary discussion Johnson is joining, for although the particular topics he treats may be largely determined by this context, he is often much less explicit than a modern scholar would be about providing references to orient his reader in the controversy. His Shakespeare criticism provides a good example of most of these observations. While we are liable to find anywhere in it those gnomic statements that grow out of a full knowledge of literature and life, without a proper sense of the whole piece in which they occur we will not have a true idea of the weight Johnson intended them to have.

His first substantial piece of Shakespeare criticism was the *Miscellaneous Observations on the Tragedy of Macbeth* (1745). Here he was exhibiting his capabilities as a prospective editor, and the notes he provides rather self-consciously display skills in interpretation founded on knowledge of historical and cultural background, on knowledge of old linguistic meanings, on sharp criticism of the work of previous editors and emenders such as Lewis Theobald, as well as on a demonstration of his own skill at making sense from a corrupt text.

Copyright difficulties prevented Johnson from undertaking the edition he projected in 1745, but after the publication of his *Dictionary* in 1755, he once more proposed an edition, in 1756, which finally appeared in 1765. The principles remain those first outlined, and the edition is a kind of encyclopedia of Johnson's critical skills (imperfect though the execution may be in relation to the editorial vision he enunciated). The essential view of Shakespeare does not change from his earlier writings on the subject, but the context and function of statements do. In addition, the annotation gives many examples of the way he went about reading particular passages, and the general observations at the end of the text of each play illustrate how he formed his judgments of particular works.

It is especially in the "Preface to Shakespeare" that we can see Johnson working with general critical principles. Statements from this piece are so often quoted in isolation that an examination of its nature as a preface may be useful. It has a clear and rational underlying structure, though Johnson has been at pains to give it a smooth surface through the skillful use of the art of transition.

The purpose of the preface is to introduce an author and an edition, and its principal parts reflect this dual intention. Somewhat more than the first half is concerned with the judging of Shakespeare and his accomplishment (*Yale* 7:59–91). The rest deals with the editing of Shakespeare, its history and practice (91–113). In judging Shakespeare Johnson is concerned with both excellencies and faults. Rational criticism must give due weight to both and must discriminate real from merely imputed faults. The first part of the preface begins with an analysis of the general problem of why old writings should be reverenced (59–61). The analysis grounds the whole discussion of Shakespeare in an understanding of the human situation and human nature. Johnson demonstrates that the accepted fact—that the dead are praised and antiquity is honored—has a real justification, and from the argument emerges the reasoned basis for one of his central critical principles: reliance on the long-continued judgment of many readers even against the theoretical objections of critics. It is from this line of argument that one of Johnson's most noted critical sentences emerges: "Nothing can please many, and please long, but just representations of general nature" (61).

The generalized introduction, then, leads Johnson into an examination of Shakespeare's characteristic excellencies as a poet of nature and life (61–71). The observations here are cast in general terms suitable to a preface; detailed and particularized observations occur in the notes to individual plays. The central theme in this part of the preface is summed up by Johnson thus: "This therefore is the praise of Shakespeare, that his drama is the mirrour of life" (65). Readers derive pleasure and instruction from such writing through their recognition of the credibility of the imitation. From this position Johnson argues against the neoclassical detractors of Shakespeare, showing that their "rules"—such as those requiring that characters be adapted to particulars of time and social stature and that comic and tragic scenes not occur in the same play—are only valid insofar as they foster the general and overriding ends of writing and of poetry; a critic should always be willing to reassess such rules on the basis of the experience of life. "There is always an appeal open from criticism to nature" (67).

The preface then moves to a consideration of Shakespeare's faults, a necessary balance to the discussion of his particular merits (71–74). In the enumeration of them Johnson characteristically begins with a moral one, moves to faults in the large design of the plays, and ends with mere verbal and stylistic objections, such as to Shakespeare's fascination with puns. Johnson follows this part of his discussion too with a refutation of other critics (74–81). Shakespeare had been charged with the fault of neglecting the "unities" of time, place, and action. Again by an analysis of the nature of dramatic illusion and an audience's imaginative experience, Johnson refutes magisterially a persistent critical dogma. Many of his arguments had been anticipated, but his is the final memorable statement on the subject.

Having considered the general merits and faults of his writer, Johnson now sets that writer in context. In the long section that closes this first half of the preface (81–91), he attempts to judge Shakespeare in relation to his age with respect to his sources, his learning or lack of it, his lack of social position and the advantages that go with it for judging certain kinds of human behavior, and his verse.

The second half of the preface is concerned with the duties of an editor as they grow out of Shakespeare's attitude to his own works, his lack of care to provide an accurate text for posterity. As an editor whose author has been edited many times before, Johnson must take into account the work of his predecessors and must let his readers know how he himself will treat problems of text and annotation. First, he undertakes a critical survey of the history of Shakespearean editing and textual criticism up to his own time (91–101). He next sets out the editorial practice and rationale of his own edition (101–10). Finally, he makes a brief assessment of his own

achievement in the edition and offers some advice on how the new reader may best approach Shakespeare (110–13). It is this last, of course, that the new reader should now be prepared intelligently to do.

Many of the things pointed out in this analysis will seem familiar as examples of "neoclassical" criticism. Whether that term has very much real use is today in question. However, if we seek to characterize Johnson's criticism in general terms, it clearly has certain things in common with the dominant critical attitudes and formulations of its own century and of the preceding two centuries as well as with criticism from classical antiquity. We see in the "Preface to Shakespeare" the treatment of an author in terms of an assessment of beauties and faults, the assumption that art both teaches and delights and that it is the imitation of nature, and thought about literature in terms of certain recognized genres such as tragedy and comedy. We also see some attention given to "rules" of writing that critics have formulated and to a sense of appropriateness or decorum as one of the elements producing literary effect. At the same time it is apparent that while Johnson thinks about literature within the broad framework provided by such criticism, he is always ready to question and rethink any of its assumptions. Such rethinking of the dogmas of criticism takes place on the basis of his broad knowledge of lived experience and his own fresh analysis of the nature of a reader's response to particular works. He is constantly trying to reduce any categorization he touches to an understanding of its true essentials. Thus in *Rambler* nos. 36 and 37 pastoral is seen not as a collection of conventions and artificial constructions but, on the perfectly neoclassical grounds of appealing to Virgil's example, as "a poem in which any action or passion is represented by its effects upon a country life" (*Yale* 3:201), a definition that would embrace William Wordsworth as well as Pope.

Johnson's attitude toward literature is in a certain sense rhetorical, as is the attitude of most writers and critics of his time, in that he sees literature not so much as the expression of an individual (though he *is* interested in the mind of genius) but as an act of communication or, in the broadest sense, persuasion. As W. R. Keast has pointed out, the emphasis in Johnson's critical system falls on the writer and reader rather than on the work in the middle or the subject matter to which it has reference. In his criticism Johnson's interest is not in expounding the structure of particular works but in illuminating and judging the work of authors in communicating with readers. The refinement, development, and understanding of such communication depends on knowledge of the workings of the human mind. Johnson relies to a large extent on the psychological theories of Locke, and in this emphasis he is again typical of a trend in thought about literature during the eighteenth century. It may be seen as early as Joseph Addison, who, Johnson said, at his best "founds art on the base of nature, and draws the principles of invention from dispositions inherent in the mind of man" (*Lives* 2:148). It continues in many later "philosophical" critics, including EDMUND BURKE, DAVID HUME, and Lord Kames. Burke's treatment of the sublime and the beautiful was one of the few pieces of contemporary criticism that demonstrably had a significant influence on Johnson. Johnson is also "Lockean" in the way he tests the truth of propositions more against the experience of reality than for internal consistency within previously formulated systems (though there is some of this too). While Johnson starts with the fundamental categories and structures of the old critical systems, he tests and uses them according to the standards of the new ways of thought. For example, it is not really true, as is sometimes asserted, that Johnson is unconcerned with genre, but he insists on referring the recognized genres back to a base in real experience. Likewise, in the "Preface to Shakespeare" we find him upholding tragicomedy as closer to the experience of reality, though tragedy and comedy are in the traditional "Aristotelian" criticism exclusive categories (see ARISTOTLE). In this as in other ways, Johnson is perhaps the first great modern English critic.

The Johnson that has been presented here may seem strange to some—to those who retain an image of Johnson as "the Great Cham of Literature," as the sort of critic who flies by his intuitions and his sensibility alone, as the memorable enunciator of one blind prejudice after another, or as the great neoclassical literary dictator. Unfortunately, appealing though many of these images may be, they cannot be supported very well by Johnson's writings. Scholars since around 1950 have put together a different image of a critic sensitive and intuitive, very much of his time, but rational, principled, and consistent. On some points Johnson's ideas certainly changed or grew over time. The "sublime" has been mentioned; "poetic justice" might be mentioned as well. And doubtless there are some inconsistencies in Johnson's criticism. But anyone who is tempted to accuse Johnson of inconsistency in critical principles would be well advised first to examine his or her own interpretations very carefully to be certain that the assumption is not based on a misunderstanding of Johnson. Regularly one part of his criticism will illuminate another, even though the writings are occasional, even ephemeral. Literary activity is

in the end for Johnson a humanistic social activity, and its theory must be constantly reassessed on the basis of an analysis of life experience. This, along with the combination of strong and considered underlying principle, intense and lively response, and a talent for pungent statement, makes Johnson a critic whose work is alive— one who can be argued with and who can still teach something about literature and life, and in whose writings can always be found something new.

James Woodruff

See also BRITISH THEORY AND CRITICISM: I. EARLY EIGHTEENTH CENTURY and 2. LATE EIGHTEENTH CENTURY.

Allen T. Hazen, *Samuel Johnson's Prefaces and Dedications* (1937); Samuel Johnson, *A Dictionary of the English Language* (2 vols., 1755, rev. ed., 1773), *Early Biographical Writings of Dr Johnson* (ed. J. D. Fleeman, 1973; see esp. lives of Savage, Browne, Ascham), *Lives of the Poets* (1779–81, orig. titled *Prefaces, Biographical and Critical, to the Works of the English Poets,* ed. G. B. Hill, 3 vols., 1905), *Poems* (ed. D. N. Smith and E. L. McAdam, 2d ed., 1974), *Works* (9 vols., 1825), *Yale Edition of the Works of Samuel Johnson* (gen. eds. Allen T. Hazen and John Middendorf, 1958–: vol. 2, ed. W. J. Bate, John M. Bullitt, and L. F. Powell, *Idler and Adventurer* [see esp. *Idler* nos. 25, 36, 40, 59–61, 63, 65–66, 68–70, 77, 84–85, 90–91, 102; *Adventurer* nos. 58, 85, 92, 95, 115, 137–38]; vols. 3–5, ed. W. J. Bate and Albrecht B. Strauss, *Rambler* [see esp. nos. 3–4, 14, 16, 21–23, 27, 36–37, 60, 88, 90–94, 96, 106, 121–22, 125, 136–37, 139–40, 143, 145–46, 152, 156, 158, 163, 168, 180, 208]; vols. 7–8, ed. Arthur Sherbo, *Johnson on Shakespeare;* vol. 16, ed. Gwin J. Kolb, *Rasselas, and Other Tales*); "Samuel Johnson," *New Cambridge Bibliography of English Literature,* vol. 2 (ed. George Watson, 1971).

Walter Jackson Bate, *The Achievement of Samuel Johnson* (1955); James L. Battersby, *Rational Praise and Natural Lamentation: Johnson, Lycidas, and Principles of Criticism* (1980); Leopold Damrosch, Jr., *The Uses of Johnson's Criticism* (1976); William Edinger, *Samuel Johnson and Poetic Style* (1977); Donald Greene, *Samuel Johnson* (1970); Jean H. Hagstrum, *Samuel Johnson's Literary Criticism* (1967); W. R. Keast, "The Theoretical Foundations of Johnson's Criticism," *Critics and Criticism: Ancient and Modern* (ed. R. S. Crane, 1952); R. D. Stock, *Samuel Johnson and Neoclassical Dramatic Theory: The Intellectual Context of the "Preface to Shakespeare"* (1973); William K. Wimsatt, Jr., "The Neo-Classic Universal: Samuel Johnson," *Literary Criticism: A Short History* (by Wimsatt and Cleanth Brooks, 1957).

JONSON, BEN

Ben Jonson (c. 1572–1637) is best known as a poet and a playwright, a rival of William Shakespeare on stage and John Donne in verse, and a model for Restoration comedy and the neoclassical poetic tradition of the seventeenth and eighteenth centuries. He was one of the leading scholars of his day, having translated both ARISTOTLE and HORACE into English, written a grammar of English in Latin, and accumulated one of the largest personal libraries in England. He was also, for a time, the most prominent literary force in the court masque, a theatrical form of central political importance.

Jonson's reputation as a critic stems from three sources: his practice, in which he championed the neoclassical virtues of imitation, proportion, and restraint; his personal influence on an entire generation of younger poets; and his recorded critical pronouncements. The latter are, for a major critic, surprisingly scarce, confined to an aphoristic collection of observations and notes titled *Timber, or Discoveries,* a collection of conversations recorded by Sir William Drummond, and various prologues and epistles he routinely attached to his poems and plays.

Much of Jonson's stated neoclassicism centers on the Horatian imitation of literary models. In contrast to his predecessor SIR PHILIP SIDNEY, who emphasized the creative power of the artist, Jonson argued for the long and careful study of earlier writers. The artists as well as the art were to be imitated: Jonson also espoused the Horatian *vir bonus* argument that to be a good poet it is first necessary to be a good person, an accomplishment attainable through hard work, reflection, and restraint. Training in letters became a path to wisdom and virtue, and an argument for the social position of the poet as advisor to those in power.

While the idea of literary merit based on acquired knowledge involved issues of class mobility for Jonson (he had apprenticed as a bricklayer and was largely self-taught), it also had clear formal consequences: he took particular aim at his rival Shakespeare, who was already becoming revered as a "natural talent" (see JOHN DRYDEN's later *Essay of Dramatic Poesy*) for his alleged aversion to revision. In the prologue to *Every Man In His Humour* he attacked those very freedoms with time and plot that characterize much of Shakespeare's work, arguing instead for adherence to the disciplined unities popularized by Julius Caesar Scaliger's Aristotelian revival (Dryden later argued that Jonson, in fulfilling these requirements most exactly, had written the perfect play). The formalism and apparent conservatism of these arguments, however, should not obscure the complexity of Jonson's position. Recent criticism has demonstrated the links between Jonson's neoclassical poetic processes and more radical aspects of the formation of Renaissance subjectivity, and his patterning of a more "literate" poetic and dramatic practice placed him at the forefront of his times.

Jonson's conscious formalism also coexisted in a complex relationship with his impulse toward social realism, his desire to write in "language such as men do use," and to present characters that, while based on "humours" or types, presented a far greater range of social classes than did those of most of his contemporaries. Jonson's drama also invariably evokes not only the organizing powers of art but the more anarchic tendencies of a reality that it could never fully control. It is, finally, the tension between these two aspects of his medium—the formal, constructive, and institutional on the one hand and the representational, realistic, and social on the other—that informs much of his work.

In this respect, Jonson's plays are perhaps his least understood but most enduring critical legacy, since within them are found not only parodic commentaries on all the major Renaissance critical movements but a relentless investigation of the interplay between representational institutions and their greater social context. *Volpone* (1607) offered a parodic critique of Renaissance expressionism in which the elaborately constructed illusions of an upper-class authority figure are eventually usurped by his servant, who represents both the institutional forces of his medium (language and the institutions of theatrical production) and the emergent middle class that was coming to control them. *Epicoene* (1609), in which a tragic and monologic hero is defeated by a younger generation of witty conversationalists more in touch with the shifting relation between action and power, documented the development of drama from tragedy into New Comedy (a transition later central to FRIEDRICH NIETZSCHE), in which the autonomy of character gave way to a more explicitly elaborated plot. By stressing the importance of plot as a predictive and proto-scientific device, the play documented the changing sense of time in the Renaissance and the pedagogical function of drama within it and paralleled as well the political entrenchment of the parliamentary bourgeoisie against a reactionary elite, as idealist aesthetic notions were shown to give way before the practical imperatives of a more Aristotelian vision of structure. The dismantling of the idealist notions of identity was foregrounded by the play's central device, an elaborate pun based on Renaissance all-male acting conventions and sexual ambiguity.

The further dismantling of both naturalistic notions

of identity and traditional dramatic structure was finally pursued in *The Alchemist* (1610) and *Bartholomew Fair* (1614). *The Alchemist* investigated the relation of representational structure to the creation of value (the metaphor of alchemy itself) and its complicity in a kind of Althusserian replication of social power. Even the aesthetics of formalism appeared as a projection of social function and power, and drama itself was presented as essentially nonaesthetic and functional. In *Bartholomew Fair* dramatic conventions themselves fell open to attack in an image of social life in which representation occurs at every level without a validating center. In the puppet show that concludes the play, actors and the larger notions of character and identity are categorically identified as pure markers in a system of social practice determined by local transients of power.

These plays are perhaps unique in their relentless self-consciousness of the very representational process in which they are engaged: where Shakespeare consistently pulled back to reaffirm the illusory process that stabilized his art, Jonson resolutely worked for its critical self-exposure. Jonson's investigation, in this respect, was inherently more dangerous. In working through the stages of Renaissance drama, he arrived at the logic of his drama's own dissolution: if dramatic representation was finally without "content" and came neither from the moral imperatives of the author nor from the aesthetic functions of the theater but rather from the reorganization of social and representational categories, then drama, in fulfilling its function, left itself very little to say. Jonson's later plays, while further investigating these and other themes, were less commercially successful, and Jonson, who had once known the heights of fame and power, died in poverty.

The value of Jonson's commitment to this extremely ambitious combination of theory and practice lay not, perhaps, in its conclusions but in its method, which established a kind of relentless investigation in which the final contradictions of one play or poem formed the basis for the next. Through this method Jonson's works uncovered much of the underlying structure of representation in the Renaissance and provided an account not only of the development of nearly all the theoretical positions of his time but of their relation to the larger representational order in which they occurred. The linking of such theoretical positions to the development of Jonson's own media (theater and the emerging poetic medium of print) and to the shifting social context of the Renaissance points to the social and historical roots of both representational modes and critical thought. Criticism, the twentieth century has come to argue, is, like art, a mode of social production and not the simple reflection of an idealist truth. For Jonson, the realization of this position was the work of a lifetime.

R. L. Kesler

See also RENAISSANCE THEORY AND CRITICISM.

Ben Jonson, *Ben Jonson* (ed. C. H. Herford, Percy Simpson, and Evelyn Simpson, 11 vols., 1925–52), *Ben Jonson's Literary Criticism* (ed. James D. Redwine, 1970).

Jonas A. Barish, *Ben Jonson and the Language of Prose Comedy* (1960); Alvin B. Kernan, "Introduction," Ben Jonson, *Volpone* (ed. Kernan, 1962); Lionel Charles Knights, *Drama and Society in the Age of Jonson* (1937); Stephen Orgel, *The Illusion of Power: Political Theater in the English Renaissance* (1975); Don E. Wayne, *Penshurst: the Semiotics of Place and the Poetics of History* (1984); Peter Womack, *Ben Jonson* (1986).

KANT, IMMANUEL

Immanuel Kant (1724–1804) began his career in mathematics and natural science (physics) at the University of Königsberg and at 31 published a treatise on the origin of the universe but turned to philosophy when he was appointed to a university chair in metaphysics and logic. Through his lectures, Kant gained a reputation as the leading intellect in Germany. Philosophically, Kant was the heir equally of the modern subjectivism of RENÉ DESCARTES and of JEAN-JACQUES ROUSSEAU's sensibility for the moral law; his concept of the nature of a philosophical critique deepens in many ways the principles of method outlined in the *Discourse on Method* by Descartes, and his elaboration of the principles of practical reason sharpens the moral critique made by Rousseau. He was at the same time one of the most important predecessors of G. W. F. HEGEL, whose much-discussed criticism of him marks the beginning of Kant's controversial philosophical reception.

Within the eighteenth century, Kant was a pivotal figure. He is regarded as a paragon of Enlightenment rationalism who set in place for later generations of literary critics a series of presuppositions about the autonomy of artworks, while his commitment to the ideals of freedom, to the notion of things-in-themselves, and to the concept of genius positions him squarely within the idealist branch of Romanticism. Today, Kant is recognized as the author of three of the most important works of modern philosophy: the *Critique of Pure Reason,* which deals with the possibility and limits of our knowledge of the external world; the *Critique of Practical Reason,* which discusses moral judgment; and the *Critique of Judgement,* which combines the "Critique of Aesthetic Judgement" and the "Critique of Teleological Judgement" in what is recognized as the first modern treatise on aesthetics. Because of its seminal position with regard to idealist aesthetics, many of the beliefs at work in the modes of discourse that dominated criticism up to and including the work of the New Critics can be traced to Kant's third critique. Central to all three critiques, as they are to Kant's mature work in general, are the beliefs that reason can test and recognize its own limits and that the implementation of a philosophical critique in which we submit even our deepest beliefs to critical examination can save us from various forms of illusion, including the skepticism and dogmatism prevalent in Kant's own day. Thus Kant begins the *Critique of Pure Reason* with a call to allow reason

> to undertake anew the most difficult of all its tasks, namely, that of self-knowledge, and to institute a tribunal which will assure to reason its lawful claims, and dismiss all groundless pretensions, not by despotic decrees, but in accordance with its own eternal and unalterable laws. (A, xi–xii)

At the same time, Kant recognizes that deceptions and illusions are themselves the products of reason, that is, of reason attempting to transgress its legitimate bounds:

> Human reason has this particular fate that in one species of its knowledge it is burdened by questions which, as prescribed by the very nature of reason itself, it is not able to ignore, but which, as transcending all its powers, it is also not able to answer. (A, vii)

Accordingly, Kant views his primary task, and construes the nature of the philosophical critique, as delimiting the proper bounds of reason.

Kant's concern with skeptical doubts concerning our knowledge of the external world was prompted by the work of Gottfried Wilhelm Leibnitz and DAVID HUME. Leibnitz had argued from a rationalist perspective that human understanding contains within it certain principles that enable us to form a complete and accurate description of the world as if from a perspectiveless stance; Hume, by contrast, had argued on empiricist grounds that reason must operate through ideas and that all ideas must be acquired through the senses. Kant regarded Leibnitz's rationalism and Hume's skepticism as wrong in equal measure: the one allowed knowledge only from a "pure" stance, one that could correspond to no actual observer; the other denied the possibility of metaphysics altogether in favor of a skeptical empiricism. Kant's response to these positions constituted what is often described as a "Copernican turn" in philosophy, entailing a reversal of the relationship between the knowing subject and the possible objects of knowledge. Whereas most philosophers had assumed that knowledge could be achieved only if we could succeed in matching our mental concepts to a world of independent, objective facts, Kant argued that we can legitimately claim knowledge of the external world by bringing that world in line with the categories of our understanding. Indeed, Kant devotes a major portion of the first critique (the "Transcendental Analytic") to a discussion of the categories through which we are able to synthesize or construct a world. Thus, while some critics (e.g., Strawson) choose to stress the objectivist interpretation of Kant, it is by the same token true that Kant deepens the subjective tendency in philosophy marked out by Descartes. For Descartes, it is the foundational principle of thought itself, the *cogito,* that serves as a rational bulwark against the threat of skepticism; for Kant, it is the transcendental ego, the locus of the synthetic operations referred to above, that performs this function.

Throughout his work in epistemology, morals, and aesthetics, Kant accepted the fact that there may arise paradoxes or antinomies created by the operations of reason itself. These are a primary source of deception and illusion. For example, we can describe nature as a realm of regular, lawful experience as confirmed by its conformity to rules and by our ability to synthesize experience into a coherent whole. Yet this understanding of the lawfulness of nature flies in the face of our fundamental beliefs about human agents as capable of originating actions free from external constraints, hence as giving rise to changes spontaneously. Kant's solution to this and similar antinomies was made possible by recourse to the hypothesis that there exist "two worlds," the one a realm of phenomena (appearances), the other a realm of noumena, or things-in-themselves. Because Kant held that both of these realms exist, he is known both as an empirical realist and a transcendental idealist; an accurate account of his philosophy cannot separate the two.

Many critics share the opinion that the most troubling aspect of Kant's thought lies precisely in the claim that things-in-themselves are knowable by the understanding but remain inaccessible to the operations of reason, which must proceed by sense impressions. There exists a similar resistance to Kant's conception of the human subject as divided between two worlds, one in which we are determined and another in which we are free. Recent speculative work has attempted to identify strategies to reconcile this breach by recourse to aesthetics. Indeed, Kant's own aesthetic theory attempts to repair the split between the realms of sense and understanding gener-

ated by his earlier work. Thus Kant begins the *Critique of Judgement* by recognizing, in an attempt to overcome, the division between the sensible and supersensible worlds:

> Between the realm of the natural concept, as the sensible, and the realm of the concept of freedom, as the supersensible, there is a great gulf fixed, so that it is not possible to pass from the former to the latter (by means of the theoretical employment of reason), just as if they were so many separate worlds, the first of which is powerless to exercise influence on the second. (14)

Kant's *Critique of Judgement* influenced a number of his immediate successors, including FRIEDRICH SCHILLER, who saw it as offering a possible solution to the social disintegration and political divisions of the modern age. According to this interpretation, the *Critique of Judgement* shows that Kant himself could not rest content with the differentiations between sense and understanding, necessity and freedom, nature and mind, implicit in the earlier critiques, because he perceived these distinctions as an expression of the dichotomies inherent in modern life. Schiller follows Kant's example insofar as he is able to think of art as a means to achieve harmony in society. He expects aesthetic experience to produce a total revolution of "the whole made perception." And yet this project remains incomplete insofar as the aesthetic remains an autonomous realm, a form of pure appearance isolated from all other dimensions of reality.

Indeed, many of the ideas in the *Critique of Judgement* have been taken, implicitly or explicitly, as sources for the belief that artworks, including works of literature, are autonomous cultural forms and must be examined without reference to the social, historical, and political interests that gather around them. The thesis of the autonomy of art was a guiding, if often unarticulated, premise of the work of Anglo-American New Critics as well as of Continental stylisticians. While both NEW CRITICISM and STYLISTICS may be placed within a history of idealist aesthetics that is far broader than Kant, it was Kant who first formulated the fundamental principles relating to the analysis and judgment of works of art. When Kant considers the special circumstances that obtain when we form judgments about a painting, a novel, or a play, he argues that we must not take an interest in the object as if it in fact existed. "A judgment on the beautiful which is tinged with the slightest interest," Kant writes, "is very partial and not a pure judgment of taste. One must not be in the least prepossessed in favour of the real existence of the thing, but must preserve complete indifference in this respect" (43). Instead, what is required of us in aesthetic judgments is that we maintain a relationship of disinterestedness, or aesthetic distance, to the work in question. Kant understands taste not in any empirical or historical sense but from a transcendental point of view.

Recognizing some of the difficulties inherent in Kant's conception of disinterested pleasure and of judgments of taste—both of which are fundamentally aligned to the aesthetic category of the beautiful—some recent theorists have tended to emphasize that portion of Kant's aesthetics that deals with the sublime. Whereas the beautiful represents the coincidence or harmony of the imagination and the understanding, the pleasure we associate with the sublime derives from representations that allow us to see some dimension of our own inadequacy; specifically, these reveal the inability of the imagination to represent ideas that can nonetheless be conceived and, indeed, "the mere capacity of thinking which evidences a faculty of mind transcending every standard of sense" (98). For instance, we can have an idea of what the world as a totality is, but we are unable to show any successful example of it; similarly, we are able to think of something as absolutely great but remain unable to find satisfactory representations for it. Insofar as the sublime allows us to present what is, strictly speaking, unpresentable, and in so doing to confirm that it exists, it has been elevated by thinkers such as JEAN-FRANÇOIS LYOTARD to a principle of postmodern thought. For Lyotard, the postmodern is that which, like the Kantian sublime, "puts forward the unpresentable in presentation itself; that which denies itself the solace of good [read "beautiful"] forms, . . . that which searches for new presentations, not in order to enjoy them but in order to impart a stronger sense of the unpresentable" (*The Postmodern Condition: A Report on Knowledge,* trans. Geoff Bennington and Brian Massumi, 1984, 81). Under this conception, the postmodern thinker-artist is a descendant of Kant's genius, albeit a descendant who no longer makes reference to nature or reason, as Kant did. Kant was the first to see the paradox that while art cannot itself produce the rules by which its products may be generated, nothing can be called art for which there is not some preceding rule. Kant resolved this antinomy in the *Critique of Judgement* by claiming that *"nature in the individual* . . . must give the rule to art, i.e., fine art is only possible as a product of genius" (168, emphasis added).

It must at the same time be said that exclusive emphasis on the sublime destroys Kant's interest in the faculty of taste as a means by which we are able to form valid judgments in the absence of preexisting (or a priori) concepts. Thus, some recent thinkers have attempted to restore Kant's project of a rational critique while at the same time seeking to avoid the disadvantages that follow from a concept of the knowing subject cut off from the objects of its knowledge and from the community of other like-minded subjects. JÜRGEN HABERMAS's theory of communicative action, which may be located in this vein, is heavily dependent on the premises of the Kantian critique, while positing intersubjective norms as part of the basic competencies and expectations attributable to all speakers who take part in discourse. To be sure, the Habermassian project has in turn met with strenuous objections, many of these from French or French-influenced poststructuralist thinkers who see in both Habermas and Kant an attempt to posit rational ideals on the basis of our membership in a "universal community of mankind" (or, in the case of Habermas, in a universal speech-community). They argue that these claims are illegitimate and serve only to strengthen the political hold of a Eurocentric discourse.

In these and other ways Kant stands among the figures currently at the center of the literary-philosophical debate over aesthetic judgment, the nature of modernity, the culture of the Enlightenment, and their relationship to postmodernism. According to Kant, citizens of the Enlightenment must take up HORACE's maxim and exercise the courage of reason *(sapere aude!)*. Only this will allow our release from our "self-incurred tutelage" (*Foundations* 85). Modernity is for Kant a historical epoch characterized by enlightenment insofar as this means the attainment of independence (autonomy) and maturity through the use of reason. In order for reason to accomplish its task, however, the citizens of the Enlightenment require freedom. Indeed, Kant's understanding of reason is that it is essentially free. Thus in the *Critique of Practical Reason* Kant claims that freedom is "the keystone of the whole architecture of the system of pure reason and even of speculative reason" (3) and seeks to derive all our other concepts, including those of the highest things, such as God and immortality, from it. These are not themselves the prior conditions of the moral law but are instead derived from it: they are "conditions of the necessary object of a will which is determined by this law" (4). And in the *Foundations of the Metaphysics of Morals* (1785), Kant insists that "nothing . . . can possibly be conceived which could be called good without qualification except a *good will*" (9). In so saying, Kant reveals that his critical rationalism and metaphysical idealism rest on a concept of the will as sovereign and free and that this constitutes the "ungrounded ground" of his philosophical system.

Anthony J. Cascardi

Immanuel Kant, *The Conflict of the Faculties* (trans. Mary J. Gregor, 1979), *Critique of Judgement* (1790, trans. James Creed Meredith, 1952), *Critique of Practical Reason* (1788, trans. Lewis White Beck, 1956), *Critique of Pure Reason* (1st ed. [A], 1781, 2d ed. [B], 1787, trans. Norman Kemp Smith, 1965), *Foundations of the Metaphysics of Morals and What Is Enlightenment?* (1785, trans. Lewis White Beck, 1959).

Anthony J. Cascardi, "From the Sublime to the Natural: Romantic Responses to Kant," *Literature and the Question of Philosophy* (ed. Cascardi, 1987); Ernst Cassirer, *Rousseau, Kant, Goethe: Two Essays* (trans. James Gutmann, Paul Oskar Kristeller, and John Herman Randall, Jr., 1945); Ted Cohen and Paul Guyer, eds., *Essays in Kant's Aesthetics* (1982); Francis X. J. Coleman, *The Harmony of Reason: A Study of Kant's Aesthetics* (1974); David Cook, "The Last Days of Liberalism," *The Postmodern Scene: Excremental Culture and Hyper-Aesthetics* (ed. Arthur Kroker and David Cook, 1986); Donald W. Crawford, *Kant's Aesthetic Theory* (1974); Gilles Deleuze, *Kant's Critical Philosophy: The Doctrine of the Faculties* (trans. Hugh Tomlinson and Barbara Habberjam, 1984); Gilles Deleuze, *La Philosophie critique de Kant* (1963, *Kant's Critical Philosophy: The Doctrine of the Faculties,* trans. Hugh Tomlinson and Barbara Habberjam, 1984); Terry Eagleton, "The Kantian Imaginary," *The Ideology of the Aesthetic* (1990); James Engell, *The Creative Imagination: Enlightenment to Romanticism* (1981); Paul Guyer, *Kant and the Claims of Taste* (1979); Jürgen Habermas, "Hegel's Critique of Kant," *Knowledge and Human Interests* (trans. Jeremy J. Shapiro, 1971); Martin Heidegger, *Kant and the Problem of Metaphysics* (trans. James S. Churchill, 1962); Philippe Lacoue-Labarthe and Jean-Luc Nancy, *The Literary Absolute* (trans. Philip Barnard and Cheryl Lester, 1988); Stanley Rosen, "Transcendental Ambiguity: The Rhetoric of Enlightenment," *Hermeneutics as Politics* (1987); P. F. Strawson, *The Bounds of Sense* (1966); Barry Stroud, "Kant and Skepticism," *The Skeptical Tradition* (ed. Myles Burnyeat, 1983); T. E. Wilkerson, *Kant's Critique of Pure Reason: A Commentary for Students* (1976).

KIERKEGAARD, SØREN

Scarcely known in the nineteenth century outside of Scandinavia, Søren Kierkegaard (1813–55) came to occupy an imposing place in almost every area of twentieth-century thought. Philosophy, theology, psychology, cultural criticism, and various currents of literary studies have drawn on his writings. Along with Ludwig Feuerbach, Karl Marx, and ARTHUR SCHOPENHAUER, he is often credited with the dismantling of the Hegelian tradition, and in conjunction with FRIEDRICH NIETZSCHE he has been represented, most notably by Karl Jaspers, as a founder of existentialism (see G. W. F. HEGEL and KARL MARX AND FRIEDRICH ENGELS). Kierkegaard's religious writings have been an ineluctable presence in both Christian and non-Christian religious thought. In their early work LUDWIG WITTGENSTEIN, GEORG LUKÁCS, MARTIN HEIDEGGER, and WALTER BENJAMIN all drew on Kierkegaardian themes. His impact on literature has been broad enough to include writers as different as Franz Kafka, JEAN-PAUL SARTRE, and Isak Dinesen. Although Kierkegaard's writings on aesthetics have often been considered as little more than elaborations of Hegelian paradigms, his contribution to Henrik Ibsen's idea of modern theater and Georg Brandes's work on literary realism is considerable. Recent poststructuralist studies have brought his concept of repetition to bear on a complex of issues explored in the work of MAURICE BLANCHOT, Gilles Deleuze, and JACQUES DERRIDA. Kierkegaard's treatment of irony has also contributed to a reevaluation of Romantic irony in recent work in rhetorical theory.

Kierkegaard, who rarely ventured far from Copenhagen, wrote his earliest work in close association with the influential group of writers and actors who gathered around Johan Ludvig Heiberg, one of the luminaries of the "golden age" in Danish literature. Although he was never quite accepted into this circle, Kierkegaard's first book, a lengthy and acerbic attack on Hans Christian Anderson as a novelist, was conceived as a contribution to Heiberg's journal of aesthetic criticism. In this early work Kierkegaard introduced the key notion of a "life-view" as a comprehensive vision of human existence whose function is to sustain an author throughout the difficult process of representing distress and thereby relieve him of unwarranted and aesthetically unpleasant sentimentality. In his master's dissertation, *On the Concept of Irony*, Kierkegaard examines in depth one possible life-view, Socratic irony as a standpoint from which to view mundane existence in its entirety. Since irony cannot present itself directly, Socrates' life has to be deciphered from its various literary and philosophical representations. Irony turns out to be that life-view that brings to light absolute, subjective negativity; its culmination is a view of an incomprehensible death, the singularity of which corresponds to the singularity of Socrates's life. The difficulty, then, is to conceptualize the singularity characteristic of irony, a difficulty made all the more apparent by the reemergence of the concept of irony in German Romanticism. Friedrich Schlegel, Johann Ludwig Tieck, and Karl Solger, according to Kierkegaard, are not engaged in the renewal of Socratic irony; rather, their ironic texts are instances of an inability to master irony as a standpoint. "Mastered irony," then, denotes that life-view that recognizes the nullity of each particular artistic work but is nevertheless able to sustain such nullification on the basis of a unified artistic subjectivity. Whether the thesis of mastery in a master's thesis should itself be read ironically has always puzzled commentators on this youthful work, especially when the very effort to decipher Socrates runs counter to his specific standpoint.

Each of the aesthetic fragments that make up the first part of *Either/Or,* Kierkegaard's first pseudonymous book and the beginning of his so-called authorship, can be seen as further developments of his conception of irony. Since the aesthete, whose characteristic indecisiveness occupies the center of attention throughout the work, has absolved himself of all ethical and religious ties, he encounters nothing but figurations and shadows of himself. And these figurations make up the fragments of the first, "aesthetic" part of the work. The loss of all transcendental validity leaves its traces in the aesthete's various moods—melancholia, anxiety, sudden enthusiasm, boredom. The aesthetic stage thus emerges in Kierkegaard's writing as the sphere of pure immanence. "The Diary of the Seducer," the last section of the first part and perhaps Kierkegaard's best-known text, is a study of a relentless yet seemingly passionless seduction that discloses the link between the ironic standpoint and aestheticism: the seduction takes place on the condition that the seduced one—and it is never clear precisely who is seducer and who seduced—no longer knows what is being said, and this hovering in language gives the seducer both a peculiar power and a distinct pleasure. The singularity of the act, which distinguishes seduction from marriage, gives rise to renewed seductions, and so the complete image of the aesthetic "sphere" is one in which the seducer is forced to seduce again and again.

Kierkegaard's decision to break off his engagement to Regine Olsen gives shape to much of his writing. It has also given rise to countless speculations on his true motivations and on its ramifications for his pseudonymous authorship in general. In the second part of *Either/Or* one finds a lengthy argument for the "aesthetic validity" of marriage. Although the argument itself is significant to the extent that it is an unexpected reflection on the relation between Kantian ethics and aesthetics, there seems to be little recognition of the radical nihilism to which the aesthete has been driven in the first part through the pursuit of aesthetic pleasure (see IMMANUEL

KANT). What the pseudonymous author demonstrates in his explication of the imperative "Choose yourself!" is that aestheticism, whose culmination is seduction, discloses repetition and at the same time makes authentic repetition impossible. For the *same one* cannot be seduced twice. Repetition thereafter becomes a leading concept throughout Kierkegaard's writings. Unlike Hegelian supercession or sublation *(Aufhebung),* repetition has nothing to do with the act of comprehension; it is therefore only a singularity—a miracle, an individual—that partakes of repetition, and repetition is precisely singularization, the paradigmatic examples of which are Abraham's lonely journey on the way to sacrifice Isaac and Job's isolation from his community.

In *Repetition* and *Fear and Trembling* Kierkegaard explores the relation of repetition to marriage, on the one hand, and to faith, on the other. The pseudonymous author of *Fear and Trembling* finds Abraham's situation so singular that he is compelled to write ever more incomprehensible accounts of Abraham's journey. In contrast to the tragic hero, whose situation is defined by the work of supercession, the "knight" of faith does not heed a universal claim and cannot clarify his action in direct communication. He thus appears to be struck dumb. The knight abandons everything, and yet he has faith that he can receive everything back. For his faith consists in the knowledge that in God all things are possible. Such a suspension of tragic paradigms makes every temporal account of an action, hence every narrative, into an ever-changing allegorical representation whose significance defies explication and whose figures are anything but exempla of ethical conduct rewarded and vicious action punished.

In *Stages on Life's Way,* the opening section of which is a reworking of PLATO's *Symposium,* a new pseudonym represents the dialectical unity of the tragic and comic as the highest achievement. It is not, however, a literary achievement but rather the inception of authentic "existence." For such existence is the paradoxical redoubling wherein an essentially contradictory and hence "comic" inwardness everywhere appears tragic. Humor then emerges in the *Concluding Unscientific Postscript* as the life-view that marks the border between ethics and the paradoxical movement of faith. The "comic" contradiction between inwardness and expression does not open up a view of absolute subjective negativity—an apparently meaningless death; on the contrary, it now designates the site of a rebirth. In the introductory pages of *Concluding Unscientific Postscript* a pseudonym explains why existence has no choice but to communicate itself indirectly. Pseudonymous fragmentation corresponds to the redoubling of thought, first as the reflection that draws on the universality of conceptual language and then as that paradoxical inwardness that renounces universality for the sake of its own authentic, that is, "subjective," self. Since, however, aesthetics itself functions as a surpassed stage on life's way, Kierkegaard's enormous pseudonymous production, which he himself puts under the category of the aesthetic, achieves a kind of vertiginous ambiguity. Not only has it invited the most diverse interpretive efforts but it drew Kierkegaard himself into ever more urgent attempts to explain to posterity precisely what he intended to do and what these peculiar texts are supposed to mean.

After Kierkegaard abandoned his pseudonymous authorship and began a so-called second authorship, in which he sought to liquidate the stratified layers of Christendom, he nevertheless continued to discuss aesthetic and literary issues. His controversy with a satirical journal over the publication of his image occasioned numerous attempts to evaluate the place of the literary in a world dominated by a phantom press and a spectral public. In *A Literary Review* Kierkegaard undertakes an exhaustive analysis of a novel entitled *Two Ages,* the last work of Fru Gyllembourg, Heiberg's mother. On the basis of this analysis, the aim of which is to show the reflection of two ages in their respective domestic relations, Kierkegaard produces a tableau of the present age; not surprisingly, two characteristics of the aesthetic sphere—apathetic indecisiveness and reflective abstraction—are shown to be its basic features. In the present age, the press and its anonymous reviewers tend to overshadow the works under review, and they thereby make writing itself into an anonymous, entirely "public" specter. Although Kierkegaard insists that *A Literary Review* is in service of *Two Ages,* it is hardly an accident that its polemical critique of the present age has vastly overshadowed the novel itself. As a review that virtually rewrites the entire novel, Kierkegaard's text not only denounces but also enacts the predicament of the literary in the present age. His subsequent remarks on this predicament are vitiated by the same ambiguity, for he never ceases to call for a restoration of authority while at the same time renouncing all authority of his own, indeed even his own authority to call for a restoration of authority. He thereby locates a certain emptiness in the very concept of authority in modernity, and it is the highly polemical exploration of this emptiness in contemporary Christendom, not abstract musings on existential "nothingness," that occupies his attention in the last phase of his effort, as he writes in the unpaginated appendix to *Concluding Unscientific Postscript,* "to read solo the original text of the individual . . . to read it through once more, if possible in a more heartfelt way."

Peter Fenves

Søren Kierkegaard, *The Concept of Anxiety* (1844, ed. and trans. Reidar Thomte and Albert B. Anderson, 1980), *The Concept of Irony with Continual Reference to Socrates* (1841, trans. Howard V. Hong and Edna H. Hong, 1989), *Concluding Unscientific Postscript* (1846, trans. David Swenson and Walter Lowrie, 1941), *The Crisis and a Crisis in the Life of an Actress* (1848, trans. Stephen Crites, 1967), *Early Polemical Writings* (ed. and trans. Julia Watson, 1990), *Either/Or* (1843, trans. Howard V. Hong and Edna H. Hong, 1987), *Fear and Trembling—Repetition* (1843, trans. Howard V. Hong and Edna H. Hong, 1983), *Kierkegaard's Attack on "Christendom"* (1845–55, trans. Walter Lowrie, 1968), *On Authority and Revelation, The Book on Adler* (1846–47, trans. Walter Lowrie, 1955), *Philosophical Fragments—Johannes Climacus* (1844, trans. Howard V. Hong and Edna H. Hong, 1985), *The Point of View for My Work as an Author* (1848, trans. Walter Lowrie, 1962), *Stages on Life's Way* (1845, trans. Howard V. Hong and Edna H. Hong, 1988), *Two Ages: The Age of Revolution and the Present Age, A Literary Review* (1846, trans. Howard V. Hong and Edna H. Hong, 1978).

Theodor W. Adorno, *Kierkegaard: Construction of the Aesthetic* (1966, trans. Robert Hullot-Kentor, 1989); Sylviane Agacinski, *Aparté: Conceptions and Deaths of Søren Kierkegaard* (1977, trans. Kevin Newmark, 1988); Pat Bigelow, *Kierkegaard and the Problem of Writing* (1988); Henning Fenger, *Kierkegaard: The Myths and Their Origin* (trans. George C. Schoolfield, 1980); Alastair Hannay, *Kierkegaard* (1982); Ralph Harper, *The Seventh Solitude* (1967); Louis Mackey, *Kierkegaard: A Kind of Poet* (1971); John Vignaux Smyth, *The Question of Eros* (1986); Henry Sussman, *The Hegelian Aftermath* (1982); Mark Taylor, *Kierkegaard's Pseudonymous Authorship* (1975); Michael Theunissen and Wilfried Greve, eds., *Materialen zur Philosophie Søren Kierkegaards* (1979); Josiah Thompson, ed., *Kierkegaard: A Collection of Essays* (1972); Jean Wahl, *Études kierkegaardiennes* (1938).

KRIEGER, MURRAY

Murray Krieger (b. 1923) has been writing about and contributing to contemporary theory since 1956, long before theory became a popular topic in North American literary studies. As co-founder of the influential School of Criticism and Theory and its first director (from 1976 to 1981, at the University of California at Irvine and then at Northwestern University) and as founding director of the University of California Humanities Research Institute (established in 1987), he has been an important figure in institutionalizing the study of theory within American universities.

In *Arts on the Level: The Fall of the Elite Object* (1981) Krieger laments recent theorizing that refuses to distinguish between literature and other forms of discourse. His allegiance in this respect is with RUSSIAN FORMALISM and NEW CRITICISM, schools for which literary language was different in kind from ordinary language and for which the literary work was a unique object of contemplation. The tenacity with which Krieger has defended literature against "leveling" tendencies that he finds in both MARXIST THEORY AND CRITICISM and DECONSTRUCTION has resulted in charges of social elitism (Frank Lentricchia) and belatedness (Grant Webster). The charge of social elitism rests insecurely on the assumption that an argument concerning differences among texts and discursive realms conceals a belief in differences among people and social groups. It must be acknowledged, however, that Krieger may have invited such criticism when he suggested social origins in the seventeenth-century Levelers for the textual leveling he decries (*Arts on the Level* 5 n. 1).

The notion of Krieger's belatedness does scant justice to his ongoing responsiveness to contemporary developments in theory. His first book, *The New Apologists for Poetry* (1956), attempted to correct formalism along more logically rigorous lines; *The Tragic Vision* (1960), a study of various late-nineteenth- and twentieth-century narratives, responded to the existential anxiety of its time while calling for a "thematic" criticism that moves beyond formalism; *A Window to Criticism* (1964), a study of Shakespeare's sonnets, also attempted to move beyond formalism by wedding it to history, a move that Krieger called "contextualism" and that he further defined in the essays collected in *The Play and Place of Criticism* (1967); *Poetic Presence and Illusion* (1979) and *Words about Words about Words* (1988) have responded to the challenges of poststructural and Marxist criticisms. *A Reopening of Closure: Organicism against Itself* (1989) employs insights derived from deconstruction to argue that the organic tradition contained within itself tendencies that would open the closed structures we associate with it.

And yet Krieger has remained faithful to a vision of the primary and unique status of the literary work and has resisted attempts to empty literature of the "presence" of a signified or to elevate criticism to the level of literature. The theories of Eliseo Vivas, particularly his

definition of the poem's "subsistent," "insistent," and "existent" aspect, strongly influenced the historicism of *Window to Criticism,* and Leo Spitzer, Sigurd Burckhardt, ERICH AUERBACH, and Rosalie Colie (especially in her theory of metaphor) have also been important influences. But Krieger's system has continued to evolve and recenter itself, incorporating what he finds most compelling in recent theoretical developments, including PHENOMENOLOGY and RECEPTION THEORY. A study of this evolving system is therefore a study in microcosm of developments in critical theory during the second half of the twentieth century.

But Krieger's concern has been as much with the history of literary theory as with its present forms, and he has been a strong advocate of the teaching of this history in the university curriculum. *Theory of Criticism* (1976) is his attempt to "establish the theoretical tradition" (ix) and to offer a theory describing the dynamics of the tradition's evolution. Krieger is candid about the fact that any attempt at canon formation (in the critical canon as well as the literary canon) may embody an invisible agenda, and he warns us that he "may very well have conceived the tradition eccentrically, so that it would appear to lead toward my extensions" (179). In keeping with his attitude toward his own work—his extensions—Krieger sees the major texts of the theoretical tradition as being in crucial ways unfinished. This is because there is a "necessary conflict between literary experience and literary theory, which leads to a conflict in the critic between his sensibility and his system" (x). Furthermore, Krieger believes that each critic who struggles to articulate a new insight is nonetheless bound by an inherited discourse with built-in assumptions and limitations, creating something like a deconstructive fault line within the critical text; an example would be ARISTOTLE's inability to escape entirely the mimetic assumptions inherited from PLATO.

The agon Krieger narrates in this book is one in which formalism, the hero, does battle down the centuries with the villainous mimesis—"imitation theory is the enemy" (67). The tradition this story establishes is a conservative one; Karl Marx is entirely absent, and SIGMUND FREUD and FRIEDRICH NIETZSCHE receive only the most passing mention (see also KARL MARX AND FRIEDRICH ENGELS). On the other hand, the book offers assessments of PAUL DE MAN and JACQUES DERRIDA, both of whom he disagrees with over the question of presence. *The New Apologists for Poetry* was Krieger's only previous book devoted exclusively to theory, and *Theory of Criticism* can be compared with it as a measure of the evolution of Krieger's thought during the 20 intervening years. What moves him significantly beyond the formalism of the past are his claims for the phenomenological presence of the poem, as opposed to the more literally conceived "objective" presence of New Criticism, and for an anthropological dimension to aesthetic studies. With these claims Krieger shifts emphasis from the poetic object of formalism to the way the poem operates within culture as a projection of the desires of readers.

These departures from formalism are clarified in "An Apology for Poetics" and in the colloquy conducted on this position paper at the University of Konstanz in 1982, both printed in *Words about Words about Words*. It is the play and place of desire in Krieger's system that accounts for his insistence on the fictional or "as if" status of critical formulations, and his concern with critical fictions aligns him with Frank Kermode, particularly *The Sense of an Ending*. Krieger argues, for instance, that despite what theory will "prove" about absence, we are constitutionally and culturally driven to treat the poem "as if" it embodied presence. Indeed, his willingness to accept paradox is one of the most central characteristics of his work, suggested in titles such as *Poetic Presence and Illusion* and "Both Sides Now." While critics such as Joel Weinsheimer have complained that Krieger disregards logical consistency, others argue that Krieger's dualistic formulations mirror developments in scientific and mathematical thought and are therefore an advanced form of logic appropriate to the complexities of the phenomenon being described (see James Huffman's analysis in *Murray Krieger and Contemporary Critical Theory*, ed. Bruce Henricksen).

In *A Reopening of Closure* Krieger argues the paradoxical claim "for the literary text as at once aesthetic and anthropological" (79). He asserts that literature's power lies in its ability to subvert dominant ideologies, and in this regard Krieger aligns himself with the likes of EDWARD W. SAID and THEODOR W. ADORNO. At the same time, however, Krieger complains about today's "hegemony of historical reduction that seeks to govern current theory" (79). Thus, once again, Krieger demonstrates his ability to absorb what is crucial in recent theory without succumbing to mere fashion or critical opportunism.

Bruce Henricksen

Murray Krieger, *Arts on the Level: The Fall of the Elite Object* (1981), *The Classic Vision: The Retreat from Extremity in Modern Literature* (1971), *Ekphrasis: The Illusion of the Natural Sign* (1992), *The New Apologists for Poetry* (1956), *The Play and Place of Criticism* (1967), *Poetic Presence and Illusion: Essays in Critical History and Theory* (1979), *A Reopening of Closure: Organicism against Itself* (1989), *Theory of Criticism: A Tradition and Its System* (1976), *The Tragic Vision: Variations on a Theme in Literary Interpretation* (1960), *A Window to Criticism: Shakespeare's Sonnets and Modern Poetics* (1964), *Words about Words about Words: Theory, Criticism, and the Literary Text* (1988).

William J. Free, "Murray Krieger and the Place of Poetry," *Georgia Review* 22 (1968); Gerald Graff, "Tongue-in-Cheek Humanism: A Response to Murray Krieger," *ADE Bulletin* 69 (1981); Bruce Henricksen, ed., *Murray Krieger and Contemporary Critical Theory* (1986); Terri B. Joseph, "Murray Krieger as Pre- and Post-Deconstructionist," *New Orleans Review* 12 (1985); Donald M. Kartiganer, "The Criticism of Murray Krieger: The Expansions of Contextualism," *Boundary 2* 2 (1974); Vincent B. Leitch, *American Literary Criticism from the Thirties to the Eighties* (1988); Frank Lentricchia, *After the New Criticism* (1980); Wesley Morris, "The Critic's Responsibility 'To' and 'For,'" *Western Humanities Review* 31 (1977), *Toward a New Historicism* (1972); Gwen Raaberg, "*Ekphrasis* and the Temporal/Spatial Metaphor in Murray Krieger's Critical Theory," *New Orleans Review* 12 (1985); Grant Webster, *The Republic of Letters: A History of Postwar American Literary Opinion* (1979); Joel Weinsheimer, "On Going Home Again: New Criticism Revisited," *PTL: A Journal of Descriptive Poetics and Theory of Literature* 3 (1977).

KRISTEVA, JULIA

Born in Bulgaria in 1941, Julia Kristeva went to Paris in 1966 to finish her dissertation on French literature; there she worked with ROLAND BARTHES and Lucien Goldmann. By 1979 she had also completed her training in psychoanalysis. Her analytic practice has a significant influence on her writing of the 1980s. *Tales of Love* (1983) and *Black Sun* (1987), for example, include transcripts from her analytic sessions.

In her early writing—*Séméiotiké: Recherches pour une sémanalyse* (1969), *Le Texte du roman* (1970), *La Révolution du langage poétique* (1974), *Polylogue* (1977)—Kristeva is concerned to bring the speaking body back into PHENOMENOLOGY and linguistics. In *Revolution in Poetic Language* she says that "our philosophies of Language, embodiments of the Idea, are nothing more than the thoughts of archivists, archaeologists, and necrophiliacs" (13). In order to counteract what she sees as the necrophilia of phenomenology and structural linguistics, which study a dead or silent body, Kristeva develops a new science that she calls "semanalysis." She describes semanalysis as a combination of semiology (or SEMIOT-ICS), which starts with FERDINAND DE SAUSSURE, and psychoanalysis, which starts with SIGMUND FREUD. Unlike traditional linguistics, semanalysis addresses an element that is beyond, heterogeneous to, language, Freud's other scene. This other scene, however, challenges the very possibility of science. Semanalysis, in order to avoid the necrophilia of other theories of language, must always question its own presuppositions and uncover, record, and deny its own ideological gestures (*Semeiotiké* 78–79).

With semanalysis, Kristeva attempts to bring the speaking body, complete with drives, back into language. She does this in two ways. First, she argues that the logic of signification is already present in the material body. Within Lacanian psychoanalytic theory, signification is the result of a separation, a lack, which begins in the mirror stage and is completed through castration. JACQUES LACAN explains that this separation necessitates the demand that turns need into desire. While Kristeva works within the Lacanian framework, she criticizes Lacan for overlooking processes that take place prior to the mirror stage.

In *Revolution in Poetic Language* she argues that a logic of material rejection is already operating within the body prior to the onset of signification (17). For example, anality is a process of rejection and separation that prefigures the separation that gives rise to signification. In anality excess leads to separation: too much matter is expelled. And although it is a privation, it is pleasurable. For Kristeva, the entrance into language is not just the result of lack and castration. Rather, pleasure and excess, as well as lack, motivate the move into language. Kristeva suggests that more people would be psychotic and refuse to leave the safe haven of the maternal body if the entrance into language were motivated solely by threats and lack.

Birth is another example where separation is inherent in the body. As Kristeva points out in *Powers of Horror,* one body is violently separated from another in birth (10). In the maternal body excess gives rise to separation. The maternal body not only embodies a separation that is material but also harbors a regulation that is prior to the mirror stage. The maternal body regulates the availability of the breast, among other things. This maternal regulation operates as a law before the Law. The maternal law prefigures and sets up the paternal Law, which, within traditional psychoanalytic theory, forces the child into language and sociality.

The second way in which Kristeva brings the speaking body back to language is by maintaining that bodily drives make their way into language. One of Kristeva's

major contributions to literary theory is her distinction between two heterogeneous elements in signification: the semiotic and the symbolic. Within Kristeva's writings "semiotic" *(le sémiotique)* becomes a technical term which she distinguishes from "semiotics" *(la sémiotique).* The semiotic elements within the signifying process are the drives as they discharge within language. This drive discharge is associated with rhythm and tone. The semiotic is this subterranean element of meaning within signification that does not signify.

The symbolic, on the other hand, is the element of meaning within signification that does signify. The symbolic is associated with syntax or grammar and with the ability to take a position or make a judgment that syntax engenders. The threshold of the symbolic is what Kristeva calls the "thetic" phase, which emerges out of the mirror stage (*Revolution* 49). There is a breaking, a rejection, already within the body that becomes, at a certain threshold, the thetic break. The thetic break is the point at which the subject takes up a position, an identification.

The semiotic gives rise to, and challenges, the symbolic. Kristeva describes the relation between the semiotic and the symbolic as a dialectic oscillation. Without the symbolic we have only delirium or nature, while without the semiotic, language would be completely empty, if not impossible. We would have no reason to speak if it were not for the semiotic drive force. So this oscillation between the semiotic and the symbolic is productive and necessary. It is the oscillation between rejection and stasis, found already within the material body, that produces the speaking subject.

Kristeva's own writing seems to be governed by this logic of oscillation between symbolic identity and semiotic rejection or difference. *Revolution in Poetic Language* and *Powers of Horror* are focused on material maternal rejection, which prefigures signification and sets up the logic of rejection. *Tales of Love* and *Black Sun* are focused on primary narcissism, which prefigures all subsequent identity and sets up the logic of repetition. And *Strangers to Ourselves* (1989) and *Lettre ouverte à Harlem Désir* (1990) are focused on rejection or difference within identity.

Kristeva is concerned with discourses that break identity. She examines crises in signification, places where identity breaks down. She analyzes the extremes of language, the before and after of language, the child's acquisition of language, and the psychotic's loss of language. Three of her models for discourses that challenge identity are Poetry, Maternity, and Psychoanalysis. Poetry, first of all, points to the signifying process qua process. Its attention to sounds and rhythms in language points to the semiotic element in signification, out of which the symbolic and any subject position come. This pointing reactivates the semiotic within language. It reactivates semiotic drives and thereby puts the unified subject in process/on trial.

The maternal body is the very embodiment of the subject in process/on trial. It cannot be neatly divided into subject and object. It is the embodiment of alterity within. Maternity is the most powerful model of alterity within because it exists at the heart of the social and the species. In *Tales of Love* Kristeva uses the maternal body as a model for an outlaw ethics, what she calls "herethics" (263). This ethics binds the subject to the other through love and not through Law.

Like poetry and maternity, psychoanalysis points to alterity or difference within the subject's identity and thereby puts the subject on trial. In *Black Sun* Kristeva says that while literature (as well as religion) is merely an antidepressant, psychoanalysis is a counterdepressant. Psychoanalysis elaborates the semiotic even while discharging it and thereby treats the cause of repression and not just the symptoms. Psychoanalysis is concerned with elaborating semiotic alterity within the subject, the Unconscious as the Other within the subject. Just as Kristeva brings the speaking body back into language by putting language in the body, she brings the subject into the place of the other by putting the other in the subject. Just as the pattern and logic of language are already found within the body, the pattern and logic of alterity are already found within the subject.

In *Strangers to Ourselves* Kristeva emphasizes the ethical and political implications of postulating that the social relation is interior to the psyche. We can now imagine an ethics, such as herethics, that does not merely legislate a relation between a subject and others. We can imagine ethics as an outgrowth of the logic of the psyche. When we learn to embrace the return of the repressed/ the foreigner within ourselves, then we learn to live with, and love, others.

Kelly Oliver

See also FEMINIST THEORY AND CRITICISM: 3. POST-STRUCTURALIST FEMINISMS, FRENCH THEORY AND CRITICISM: 5. 1945–1968 and 6. 1968 AND AFTER, and PSYCHOANALYTIC THEORY AND CRITICISM: 3. THE POST-LACANIANS.

Julia Kristeva, *Au commencement était l'amour: Psychanalyse et foi* (1985, *In the Beginning Was Love: Psychoanalysis and Faith,* trans. Arthur Goldhammer, 1987), *Étrangers à nous-mêmes* (1989, *Strangers to Ourselves,* trans. Leon Roudiez, 1991), *Histoires d'amour* (1983, *Tales of Love,* trans. Leon Roudiez, 1987), *The Kristeva Reader* (ed. Toril Moi, 1986), *Le Langage, cet inconnu: Une Initiation à la linguistique* (1981, *Language: The Unknown: An Initiation into Linguistics,* trans. Anne M. Menke, 1989), *Lettre ouverte à Harlem Désir* (1990), *Polylogue* (1977, partial trans., *Desire in Language: A Semiotic Approach to Literature and Art,* trans. Thomas Gora, Alice Jardine, and Leon Roudiez, 1980), *Pouvoirs de l'horreur* (1980, *Powers of Horror,* trans. Leon Roudiez, 1982), *La Révolution du langage poétique: L'Avant-garde à la fin du XIXe siècle, Lautréamont et Mallarmé* (1974, *Revolution in Poetic Language,* trans. Margaret Waller, 1984), *Les Samouraïs* (1990, *The Samurai: A Novel,* trans. Barbara Bray, 1992), *Séméiotiké: Recherches pour une sémanalyse* (1969), *Soleil noir: Dépression et mélancolie* (1987, *Black Sun: Depression and Melancholy,* trans. Leon Roudiez, 1989), *Le Texte du roman: Approche sémiologique d'une structure discursive transformationelle* (1970).

Judith Butler, "The Body Politics of Julia Kristeva," *Hypatia* 3 (1989); John Fletcher and Andrew Benjamin, eds., *Abjection, Melancholia, and Love* (1990); Jane Gallop, *The Daughter's Seduction: Feminism and Psychoanalysis* (1982); Elizabeth A. Grosz, *Sexual Subversions: Three French Feminisms* (1989); Alice Jardine, "Opaque Texts and Transparent Contexts: The Political Difference of Julia Kristeva" (*The Poetics of Gender,* ed. Nancy K. Miller, 1986); Ann Rosalind Jones, "Julia Kristeva on Femininity: The Limits of a Semiotic Politics," *Feminist Review* 18 (1984); John Lechte, *Julia Kristeva* (1990); Toril Moi, *Sexual/Textual Politics: Feminist Literary Theory* (1985); Kelly Oliver, *Unraveling the Double-bind: Julia Kristeva's Theory of the Subject on Trial* (1992); Jacqueline Rose, "Julia Kristeva: Take Two," *Sexuality in the Field of Vision* (1986); Ewa Ziarek, "At the Limits of Discourse: Heterogeneity, Alterity, and the Maternal Body in Kristeva's Thought," *Hypatia* 7 (1992).

KUHN, THOMAS S.

Thomas S. Kuhn (b. 1922) was educated at Harvard as a physicist. He has been Laurance S. Rockefeller Professor of Philosophy at the Massachusetts Institute of Technology since 1983. Although he has done theoretical work in physics, his reputation is as a historian and philosopher of science whose most influential work is *The Structure of Scientific Revolutions* (1962).

Kuhn's importance to the practice of literary criticism is tangential but of genuine interest and significance. For the most part, he is invoked in literary contexts in connection with the term "paradigm," a term he, in turn, borrowed from linguistics and prosody. In

The Structure of Scientific Revolutions he defined "paradigms" as "accepted examples of actual scientific practice—examples which include law, theory, application, and instrumentation together—[that] provide models from which spring particular coherent traditions of scientific research" (10). The essence of his argument—a highly radical and controversial one within the history of science—is that the natural sciences are typically governed by such a paradigm for lengthy periods and that scientific development tends to be a sudden global theoretical and intellectual change, which he calls a "paradigm shift." Examples of such shifts are the changes that followed such paradigmatic achievements as Aristotle's *Physica,* Sir Isaac Newton's *Principia,* and Charles Lyell's *Geology.*

Literary scholars will recognize in this model of theoretical change the standard "historicist" model of cultural change. Cultural historians have routinely divided the past into "periods," which are seen to share features that distinguish them from both earlier and later ones. This habit goes back to the nineteenth-century invention of the Renaissance and the Dark Ages. At its strongest, such a view of cultural history argues that different cultural periods are radically incommensurable, that we can no longer truly understand the ancient world, the Middle Ages, or even the 1920s. Similarly, Kuhn argues that scientific theories on either side of a "paradigm shift" are incommensurable, by which he means, not that two or more paradigms cannot be conceived by the same mind, but rather that the mind must oscillate between them sequentially. A helpful analogy might be the case of the bilingual who, although perfectly competent in, say, English and French, must shift between languages to avoid uttering an incomprehensible Franglais.

Kuhn himself is quite explicit about the filiation of his own theories from the "historicist" views sketched above. In the preface to *The Structure of Scientific Revolutions* he acknowledges an intellectual debt to Alexandre Koyré's *Études Galiléenes,* to A. O. Lovejoy's *Great Chain of Being,* and, what is more surprising, to Benjamin Lee Whorf's "speculations about the effect of language on world view" (vi). A passage from the 1970 "Postscript" to *The Structure of Scientific Revolutions* identifies his position and relation to cultural historians succinctly:

> To the extent that the book portrays scientific development as a succession of tradition-bound periods punctuated by non-cumulative breaks, its theses are undoubtedly of wide applicability. But they should be, for they are borrowed from other fields. Historians of literature, of music, of the arts, of political development, and of many other human activities have long described their

subjects in the same way. Periodizations in terms of revolutionary breaks in style, taste, and institutional structure have been among their standard tools. If I have been original with respect to concepts like these, it has mainly been by applying them to the sciences, fields which had been widely thought to develop in a different way. (208)

Kuhn quite clearly draws inspiration from sources that assume some degree of projection in our view of the world, a projection that European PHENOMENOLOGY calls "reflexivity" and that Donald Davidson calls "the dogma of a dualism of scheme and reality" (198). Karl Popper, the principal critic of such notions of cultural and cognitive relativity—and redoubtable critic of historicism—was quick to attack Kuhn for his temerity in challenging the *positive* character of scientific language. Popper has been supported by other powerful voices, such as those of Davidson and Stephen Toulmin. Kuhn has responded to the assault on his historicist views, most accessibly in the "Postscript" (1969) appended to the Japanese translation of *The Structure of Scientific Revolutions* and to the 1970 English-language reissue.

The "Postscript" makes an important refinement to the concept of paradigm. Kuhn acknowledges that he had used it in two distinct senses: first, to stand for "the entire constellation of beliefs, values, techniques, and so on shared by the members of a given community," and second, "for one sort of element in that constellation, the concrete puzzle-solutions which . . . can replace explicit rules as a basis for the solution of the remaining puzzles of normal science" (175). The second sense conforms to that employed in linguistics and prosody, and to Michael Polanyi's well-known notion of "tacit knowing" (*Personal Knowledge,* 1964), while the first conforms to the historicist notion of a culture as an entity having spatial and temporal boundaries like those of a biological organism.

Kuhn's importance to literary studies in the last quarter of the twentieth century is that his prestige and that of his followers can be used to legitimate the historical study of literature against the structuralist insistence on synchronic study as the only legitimate and "scientific" mode. He represents a response from within analytic philosophy to the positivist and physics-based model of serious academic study—most prominently articulated in Karl Popper's *Poverty of Historicism* (1957)—which has long frightened the humane disciplines. However, the Kuhnian contribution to the resistance to antihistorical, "synchronic" models for the humane studies has been overshadowed by that of his European avatars, particularly MICHEL FOUCAULT. Foucault, rather than Kuhn, is the inspiration behind American NEW HISTORICISM as represented by Frank Lentricchia and Stephen Greenblatt. An indication of the slightness of Kuhn's influence in American literary criticism is the fact that Lentricchia makes no reference to him in his seminal work, *After the New Criticism.* FREDRIC JAMESON is another American historicist (inspired by the FRANKFURT SCHOOL rather than by Foucault) whose one extended reference to Kuhn in *The Prison-House of Language* misrepresents him as a "Structuralist."

Despite the absence of any substantive impact on literary criticism, the terms "paradigm" and "paradigm shift" have become canonized in literary-critical vocabulary. Moreover, it is through Kuhn, it seems, that the term "historicism" has been purged of the strong negative values with which Popper invested it in *The Poverty of Historicism.* Lentricchia and RICHARD RORTY, for example, identify their arguments as "historicist" without any sense of embarrassment.

Kuhn himself has not branched out into literary or cultural history except in the 1969 essay "Comment on the Relations of Science and Art" (in *The Essential Tension*), in which he suggests that his approach to the problem of theoretical change in science might be applicable to the problem of style in the arts. He there describes that approach as "ethological or sociological," that is, one that considers the social and professional utility of shared ideas and modes of procedure as opposed to an exclusive focus on their descriptive or generative effectiveness or on their truth. Such a contribution, while welcome support from the "other" culture, is unlikely to generate very much excitement in literary circles. Kuhn is an "old" Lovejoyan historicist, not a "new" one on the Foucauldian model. His antagonists are hard-nosed positive realists such as Popper and Davidson, who stoutly believe in the possibility of "an unmediated touch with the familiar objects whose antics make our sentences and opinions true or false" (Davidson 198). On the other hand, Kuhn is not as close to European phenomenological priorization of "schema" as Richard Rorty implies by endorsing, more or less in Kuhn's name, a revisionist philosophical tradition comprising JOHN DEWEY, LUDWIG WITTGENSTEIN, and MARTIN HEIDEGGER in place of the more orthodox canon of Gottlob Frege, Bertrand Russell, and Rudolf Carnap (5).

Leon Surette

See also HISTORY OF IDEAS.

Thomas S. Kuhn, *The Copernican Revolution: Planetary Astronomy in the Development of Western Thought* (1957), *The Essential Tension: Selected Studies in Scientific Tradition and Change* (1977), *The Structure of Scientific Revolutions* (1962, 2d ed., 1970).

Barry Barnes, "Thomas Kuhn," *The Return of Grand Theory in the Human Sciences* (ed. Quentin Skinner, 1985); D. G. Cedarbaum, "Paradigms," *Studies in the History and Philosophy of Science* 14 (1983); Donald Davidson, "On the Very Idea of a Conceptual Schema" (1974, *Inquiries into Truth and Interpretation*, 1984); Imre Latakos and Alan Musgrave, eds., *Criticism and the Growth of Knowledge* (1970, containing a critique by Karl Popper, "Normal Science and Its Dangers," and a defense by Kuhn, "Reflections on my Critics"); Andrew Ortony, ed., *Metaphor and Thought* (1979); Richard Rorty, *Philosophy and the Mirror of Nature* (1979).

LACAN, JACQUES

Jacques Marie Émile Lacan (1901–81) trained as a medical doctor at the Faculté de médecine de Paris and worked extensively with patients suffering from what psychiatrists called "automatism" or *délires à deux*. This condition led people to believe that their speech or writing was governed by an unseen but omnipotent force beyond their control. Often coupled with severe personality disorders and a history of familial conflict, the symptoms of automatism resembled certain aspects of the cases then being studied by the nascent psychoanalytic movement in France, and Lacan pursued this connection between psychiatric medicine and psychoanalysis in his thesis for the *doctorat d'état* in psychiatry, *De la psychose paranoïaque dans ses rapports avec la personnalité* (1932). Over the next 50 years, this combination of extensive clinical practice with speculative theoretical argument continued to distinguish what Lacan described as his "return to Freud." Through extended close readings of Freud's texts and his own clinical practice, Lacan expanded the field of psychoanalysis to include insights from philosophy, linguistics, literature, and, finally, mathematics. Although he sometimes explicitly discussed literature, his importance for literary theory and criticism derives primarily from his more general speculations on language, the subject, and sexuality. By the time of his death, Lacan was one of the most prominent and most controversial intellectual figures in the world, and his work had influenced the academic study of literature and film as well as the theoretical discourse and clinical practice of psychoanalysis.

Lacan's career is often divided into four stages. From 1926 to 1953 his work evolved from the conventional psychiatric practice of the time to incorporate many psychoanalytic concepts into the clinical diagnosis and treatment of patients. His earliest publications consist of brief case studies, but beginning in the late 1930s he began publishing a number of articles that focus on the importance of the "mirror stage" in the development of a child's sense of self during the first two years of life. Drawing upon the work of the French psychologist Henri Wallon and others, such as J. M. Baldwin, Charlotte Bühler, and Otto Rank, Lacan argued that the child's emergent sense of self was always formed in reference to some "other." That other could be the child's own image in a mirror, a sibling or friend, or any number of alternative models with which the child associated itself according to what Freud had termed narcissistic identification.

Rather than being the first step toward the formation of a healthy and stable ego, the mirror stage in Lacan's account is the origin of a fundamental alienation in the individual's sense of self. Because that self is oriented in the "fictional direction" of an other who is perceived as omnipotent and thus as a potential rival to the self, the ego that emerges from this stage inevitably bears within it a hostility or "aggressivity" that threatens the very stability attributed to it. Lacan therefore concluded that human identity is formed only within an intersubjective context in which alienation and aggressivity are the norm rather than aberrations.

Lacan's insistence on the *méconnaissance,* or misperception, at the heart of the ego controverted the therapeutic pretensions of ego psychology, which conceived of the ego as the origin and basis of psychic stability and which was endorsed by most of the International Psycho-Analytical Association (IPA). Tension between Lacan and the IPA increased until 1953, when he broke with the IPA and formed his own group, the Société française de psychanalytique (SFP). At the first meeting of this group, in Rome that year, Lacan presented his paper "Fonction et champ de la parole et du langage en psychanalyse," which quickly became known as the manifesto of the new society, the "Discourse of Rome" (*Écrits* 30–113).

Lacan argued that speech and, more generally, language were central to psychoanalytic practice and to any theoretical conclusions that might be extrapolated from it. He rejected the tendency to treat psychoanalysis as a subspecialty of biology and neurology and instead turned toward Saussurean linguistics and Hegelian philosophical traditions for his theoretical vocabulary. (See G. W. F. HEGEL and FERDINAND DE SAUSSURE.) Coupled with Lacan's bitter and sarcastic characterization of the ego as the seat of neurosis rather than the source of psychic integration, this emphasis on the symbolic organization of human experience staked out a radically new territory for psychoanalytic inquiry, one that Lacan claimed had been discovered by Freud but obscured by his followers.

The charge that psychoanalysts had abandoned the founding texts of their profession exacerbated tensions between the IPA and the SFP until Lacan left the group in 1963 to form another organization, the École Freudienne de Paris (EFP). This third turn in his career began in a series of lectures conducted under the aegis of the École Pratique des Hautes Etudes. There, Lacan continued his close readings of Freud's texts, but he now began to introduce a number of terms and concepts not found in Freud's own work. These new seminars were broader in scope and were addressed to a more diverse audience than the analysts and psychiatrists who had attended the earlier seminars at Saint Anne's Hospital. Lacan made few concessions to his new audience, but by the time his selected essays appeared as *Écrits* in 1966, his seminars were drawing huge crowds, and he was the object of an intense if often bemused scrutiny by the popular media. The press associated him with "structuralists" such as JACQUES DERRIDA, CLAUDE LÉVI-STRAUSS, and MICHEL FOUCAULT, and along with other members of this group, Lacan was often criticized for the hermetic difficulty of his style, his open disdain for the autonomous *cogito* of traditional humanism, and his utter disregard for orthodox European Marxism (see STRUCTURALISM).

Lacan's standing among psychoanalysts during this period became increasingly vexed as well, since the training methods of the EFP departed drastically from the more conventional training of new analysts sanctioned by the IPA. Within the EFP itself, many of the practicing analysts were concerned about what they perceived as the increasingly theoretical and academic emphasis of Lacan's work. That concern was heightened by the founding of a department of psychoanalysis at the University of Paris at Vincennes in 1969, which Lacan hoped would lend a new, scientific rigor to psychoanalysis by integrating linguistics, logic, and especially the mathematical field of topology in psychoanalytic training. Lacan appointed himself "Scientific Director" at Vincennes in 1974 and began this program in earnest.

During this last stage of his career, Lacan began working toward a "meta-theory" of psychoanalysis that would recast his earlier insights in the more precise language of mathematics. Faced with an often bewildering array of topological figures, such as the Borromean knot, however, even many of Lacan's followers complained that his arguments had grown arcane and opaque and were increasingly irrelevant to clinical practice. He responded

by dissolving the EFP and founding yet another association, the École de la Cause Freudienne, over which he presided until his death.

Lacan's emphasis on the symbolic constitution of human subjectivity in his seminal essay "The Function and Field of Speech in Psychoanalysis" echoes the work of MARTIN HEIDEGGER and, more broadly, that of Hegel, especially as interpreted by Alexander Kojève in his enormously influential lectures on Hegel's *Phenomenology of Spirit*. Nevertheless, Lacan maintained that Freud himself had demonstrated the importance of symbolic relations in our lives, and he insisted that his emphasis on speech and language was in fact a "return to Freud," with direct consequences for analytic practice. Lacan proposed two fundamental principles for that practice: the short session and what he called the "analyst's abstention." These strategies are both designed to undercut the subject's tendency to identify with the analyst as the ideal form of subjectivity and to attribute an independent objectivity to the "reality" perceived by the subject through the lens of that identification. Lacan agrees that such moments are essential to transference, which is crucial to the analytic experience. He argues, however, that contrary to accepted practice, the analyst must thwart these imaginary relations, because they constitute an "empty" speech, which sustains the illusion of a coherent ego modeled on the imaginary other to which that speech is addressed. Abruptly terminating the analytic session at unpredictable moments short of the usual hour frustrates the subject's attempt to sustain the illusions in which he is already alienated. What is even more important, it discloses a "full" speech, which more accurately reflects the subject's relation to the symbolic order and orients the subject toward another "Other," written with a capital O, whose true alterity is undisguised.

Shortening the session in this way "punctuates" the subject's speech and reveals the dialectical character of the intersubjective context. It forces patients to deal with the analyst as truly other to the field of the subject's discourse, not simply as a reflection of their own fantasies. Lacan therefore insists that the analyst must "abstain" from the role of an ideal ego or imaginary other despite the patient's efforts to address the analyst as such. Resisting that expectation forces the subject to recognize the difference between the "I" who speaks and the idealized ego that is projected onto the analyst but that in fact is derived from the subject's own narcissistic desire for omnipotence. Moreover, because the subject's sense of self also depends on the way the subject represents the world and his or her place in it—what Lacan calls the "reality" of the subject's experience—the analyst's abstention also marks the boundary between the symbolic order of the subject's speech and what lies beyond it and resists incorporation into the symbolic. Lacan calls this "remainder" the "real" to distinguish it from the reality represented through the subject's discourse. Together, the terms "symbolic," "imaginary," and "real" indicate three "elementary registers" of human experience that Lacan claims to have distinguished for the first time in psychoanalysis.

These issues occupied Lacan for the rest of his career. In the decade following the "Discourse of Rome," he devoted his seminars and most of his writing to theoretical elaborations on the role of the symbolic in Freud's own work. Focusing on topics such as the ego, transference, psychosis, the death drive, repression, and sexuality, Lacan argued that Freud had understood the linguistic nature of human psychology but that he had simply lacked the Saussurean vocabulary necessary to articulate it. In Freud's analysis of Daniel Paul Schreber's case, for example, Freud had argued that Schreber's psychotic delusions were actually a defense against latent homosexual desires, but in Lacan's interpretation Schreber's delusions stem from the "foreclosure" of a "primordial signifier," the Name-of-the-Father. Schreber's fantasies about being the wife of God are attributed to his inability to assume a position in the symbolic order of language, and Schreber's auditory hallucinations are described as imaginary manifestations of the symbolic functions that he lacks.

This revision in Freud's theory of psychosis reflects Lacan's broader interests in the symbolic basis of Oedipal sexuality and even of the unconscious. In *Les Psychoses: Seminar III*, Lacan claims that the Saussurean distinction between the signifier and the signified enables us to see that the unconscious is "structured like a language" (187). It is governed entirely by the order of the signifier rather than by some autonomous realm of repressed desire and instinctual urges. Even sexual identity is determined by the subject's relation to the signifier, Lacan says, and not by some innate, biological predisposition. For Lacan, what Freud described as the Oedipal phase is actually a moment in which the individual faces the option of accepting or rejecting the signifier in the place of the object or the imaginary other. Although Freud called this signifier the phallus, its primary characteristic is not its status as a biological organ that one may or may not possess. Rather, this primordial signifier possesses the fundamental property of being separable from the object it represents. Freud identified this possibility as "castration," but Lacan claims that it is simply the functional

principle that enables the signifier to appear as such. Sexuality and, more generally, personal identity is thus not biologically determined but instead constructed through one's relation to the symbolic order. The phallus, for example, is described by Lacan as "the privileged signifier of that mark in which the role of the logos is joined with the advent of desire" (*Écrits* 287).

Most of Lacan's work from this period traces the connections between specific properties of the signifier and their effects in human experience. In his seminars on EDGAR ALLAN POE's "Purloined Letter," he claims that the entire structure of intersubjective relations is determined not by the individuals involved but by the way those individuals "model their very being on the moment of the signifying chain which traverses them. If what Freud discovered and rediscovers with a perpetually increasing sense of shock has a meaning, it is that the displacement of the signifier determines the subjects in their acts" (60). This displacement is possible, Lacan says, because the signifier is entirely autonomous from the signified. The link between them, which we ordinarily think of as "meaning," is merely an effect of the signifier itself and its relation to other signifiers in the signifying chain.

In "The Insistence of the Letter in the Unconscious, or Reason since Freud," Lacan describes the way that effect comes about. Drawing upon ROMAN JAKOBSON's distinction between two poles of language, metaphor and metonymy, Lacan claims that these functions can account for our sense that language somehow contains meaning when there is in fact an absolute barrier between the signifier and the signified, or between the symbolic and the real. Meaning never "consists" in language, Lacan says; it "insists" in the chain of signifiers as one supplants the other metonymically, deferring and so "always anticipat[ing] meaning by unfolding its dimension before it" (*Écrits* 153). The only reason that language seems to "mean" in the usual sense is that the displaced signifiers tend to function as the signified in Saussure's model do. Subsequent signifiers merely refer back to earlier ones, and it is this retrospective "reference" that sustains the *effect* of reference in the absence of a referent or an actual signified (152–54).

Lacan describes this effect as the "creative spark" of metaphor, and he claims that it constitutes the site of human subjectivity and the "radical heteronomy that Freud's discovery shows gaping within man" (172). Lacan goes on to observe that subjectivity has been traditionally understood as a juncture between words and things and thus as situated on the bar between the signifier and the signified, the border between language and the world.

But that border, Lacan argues, is nowhere, or at least it was nowhere until Freud discovered the unconscious. Read through Saussure's influence and Lacan's emphasis on the absolute autonomy of the signifier, Freud's discovery thus installs a radical "lack-of-being" in the subject's relation to the object and to the self that catches the subject "in the rails of metonymy," "eternally stretching forth towards the *desire for something else*" (167).

This something else is the "*objet a*," which might be simply defined as the object of desire as such. Lacan argues that the psychoanalytic discovery of the unconscious reveals a subject constituted in relation to an Other it cannot know and oriented toward an object that it can never possess. This "splitting," which Freud called the *Ichspaltung*, is brought about by the subject's entry into the symbolic, and it supersedes (or at least supplants) the imaginary unity derived through identification with the other. In place of that identification arises a more complex relation to the symbolic Other. Introduced in the "Discourse of Rome," the "Other" comes to designate any number of concepts for Lacan: death, the symbolic father, the role of the analyst, the locus of speech, the unconscious. These designations are not simply interchangeable, but they are all characterized by what Jacques-Alain Miller has called "their dimension of exteriority and . . . their determinant function in relation to the subject" (623). The "*objet a*" is *dissimulé* in this Other, Lacan claims, and consequently "the desire of man is the desire of the Other" in the sense that desire is both "for" the Other and also experienced as the Other's desire.

Invoking neologisms, slogans, and complex diagrams and graphs, Lacan's exposition of Freud's work grew increasingly difficult and, some analysts felt, idiosyncratic. During the years 1964–73, Lacan's departure from conventional psychoanalysis became even more apparent as a uniquely Lacanian discourse gradually supplanted the traditional Freudian terms and formulations of his earlier work. Among the terms Lacan introduced to psychoanalytic discourse during these years, one of the most influential was *jouissance*. He describes *jouissance* as an experience of pleasure ordinarily associated with sexual climax, and its prominence in his work echoes the importance of sexuality to ordinary Freudian psychoanalysis. For Lacan, however, *jouissance* discloses an intricate interdependence between sexuality and the symbolic that subordinates the body to the law of the signifier. Because the position of any subject vis-à-vis the symbolic is marked by a lack or what Lacan calls a "fading" before the object of desire, relations between the sexes are always structured according to some missing or third

element that makes the relation, strictly speaking, "impossible." Thus Lacan claims flatly in *Le Séminaire livre XX: Encore* that there is no such thing as sexual relations. This impossibility lifts the significance of sexual pleasure from the biological realm of satisfaction to the level of *jouissance,* and Lacan now claimed that it relegates woman to the symbolic status of a *pas-tout,* literally a "not-all" or lack that "does not derive from the body but results form the logical exigency of speech [*parole*]" (15). "Woman" as a general category exists, Lacan says, only as that which is excluded from the symbolic order, and a man relates to woman only as the missing "*objet a*," a phantasm of wholeness or totality.

Lacan's revisionary reading of Freudian sexuality antagonized many analysts as well as feminists outside the psychoanalytic community. His argument attacks the essentialist strain of feminism that proposes the feminine as a privileged realm free from cultural determination in general. Feminists sympathetic to Lacan claimed that his argument exposes the cultural ground of women's oppression and thus at least provides a point from which that subordination can be contested. Feminists hostile to Lacan argued, however, that he has simply replicated the phallocentric character of traditional Freudianism, substituting symbolic determination for biological destiny and universalizing what are in fact historically specific social values and practices. From this point of view, the Lacanian symbolic thus appears as simply one more explanation of why women must keep to the place assigned them by conventional psychoanalysis, which is no place at all.

The issue of femininity and relations between the sexes appears frequently in Lacan's work throughout the early 1970s, but by the end of *Encore* his attention had shifted to a more abstract concern: the mathematical field of topology and the figure of the Borromean knot. Drawing upon the triad he had introduced 30 years earlier, Lacan once again reconceived the primary issues of psychoanalysis in terms of the real, the symbolic, and the imaginary. But this time, he cast their relations in the language of topology and "mathemes" rather than Saussurean linguistics. "La mathématisation seule atteint à un réel," he claimed, and from 1974 to his death in 1981 he explored the intricate intersections among his three registers through a proliferating series of knots and even more complicated topological figures, such as the Klein bottle and the torus. Praised by some as strikingly innovative and precise formulations, and denounced by others as self-indulgent, senile ramblings, Lacan's last turn split his followers yet again, this time into those who would pursue the "mathematization" of psychoanalysis as a step toward scientific rigor and those who would reject it as a misleading attempt to found a "meta-theory" that ignores the more concrete and useful work of the *Écrits*. This split continues to divide Lacanians and has resulted in an often bewildering congeries of organizations and movements devoted to Lacan's work.

Michael P. Clark

See also FEMINIST THEORY AND CRITICISM: 3. POST-STRUCTURALIST FEMINISMS and 4. MATERIALIST FEMINISMS, FRENCH THEORY AND CRITICISM: 6. 1968 AND AFTER, and PSYCHOANALYTIC THEORY AND CRITICISM: 3. THE POST-LACANIANS.

Jacques Lacan, *De la psychose paranoïaque dans ses rapports avec la personnalité* (1932, reprint, 1975), *Écrits* (1966, *Ecrits: A Selection*, trans. Alan Sheridan, 1977), *Les Écrits techniques de Freud: Seminar I, 1953-54* (ed. Jacques-Alain Miller, 1975, *Freud's Papers on Technique, 1953-1954*, trans. John Forrester, 1988), *L'Éthique de la psychanalyse: Seminar VII, 1959-60* (1986), *Le Moi dans la théorie de Freud et dans la technique de la psychanalyse: Seminar II, 1954-55* (ed. Jacques-Alain Miller, 1978, *The Ego in Freud's Theory and in the Technique of Psychoanalysis, 1954-55*, trans. Sylvana Tomaselli, 1988), *Les Psychoses: Seminar III, 1955-56* (ed. Jacques-Alain Miller, 1981), *Les Quatre Concepts fondamentaux de la psychanalyse: Seminar XI, 1964* (ed. Jacques-Alain Miller, *The Four Fundamental Concepts of Psychoanalysis,* trans. Alan Sheridan, 1977), *Le Séminaire livre XX: Encore* (ed. Jacques-Alain Miller, 1975), "Seminar on 'The Purloined Letter,'" trans. Jeffrey Mehlman, *Yale French Studies* 48 (1972), *Télévision* (1974, *Television,* ed. Joan Copjec, trans. Denis Hollier, Rosalind Krauss, and Annette Michelson, 1990).

Malcolm Bowie, *Lacan* (1991); Michael Clark, *Jacques Lacan: An Annotated Bibliography* (2 vols., 1988); Robert Con Davis, *The Fictional Father: Lacanian Readings of the Text* (1981); Shoshana Felman, *Jacques Lacan and the Adventure of Insight: Psychoanalysis in Contemporary Culture* (1987); Jane Gallop, *Reading Lacan* (1985); Jonathan Scott Lee, *Jacques Lacan* (1990); Anika Lemaire, *Jacques Lacan* (1970, trans. David Macey, 1977); Jacques-Alain Miller, "Jacques Lacan: 1901-81," *Psychoanalysis and Contemporary Thought* 7 (1984), *L'Excommunication* (*Ornicar?* 8, suppl., 1977), *La Scission de 1953* (*Ornicar?* 7, suppl., 1976); John P. Muller and William J. Richardson, *Lacan and Language: A Reader's Guide to "Ecrits"* (1982); Ellie Ragland-Sullivan, *Jacques Lacan and the Philosophy of Psychoanalysis* (1986); Madan Sarup, *Jacques Lacan* (1992); Joseph H. Smith and William Kerrigan, eds., *Interpreting Lacan* (1983); Anthony Wilden, *The Language of the Self: The Function of Language in Psychoanalysis* (1968, reprint as Jacques Lacan, *Speech and Language in Psychoanalysis,* trans. Wilden, 1984).

LATIN AMERICAN THEORY AND CRITICISM

Trying to delineate the progression of theoretical and critical thought in Latin America is like trying to embroider one of those Chilean *arpilleras* in which the composite designs formed by sewing together multicolored bits of fabric tell a story. Each of the two dozen Latin American countries fought its own battles and evolved in its own unique way. However, in spite of the important differences among these nations, the single most important unifying factor remains the testimonial nature of Latin American literary and critical activity, both resolutely territorial in spirit and in purpose. Roberto González Echevarría has observed that in Latin America, criticism is far from being on an equal with creative writing. Indeed, the evolution of critical thought is more readily traced in the literary works themselves, since it is rarely constituted in specifically theoretical writings. However, even though criticism in Latin America is largely derivative, it is itself inscribed in the process of "transculturation" (Ortiz; Rama), which means that ideas and strategies are reformulated in view of the Latin American reality. These considerations and the inescapable constraints of a short essay have largely determined the present account. Given that the evolution of literary ideas is a continuous process dependent upon the interrelatedness of a multitude of factors, the following chronological categorization based on literary currents will chart this evolution in view of the volume and diversity of the material at hand. Thus, four great periods emerge: Romantic, modernist/realist, avant-garde/Americanist, and contemporary.

The Romantic period. The end of the colonial period in Latin America, during the nineteenth century, coincides with the emergence of a narrative of Romantic inspiration that attempts to elucidate the complex post-independence reality. Jean Franco observes that while in Europe Romanticism appears in the wake of the Industrial Revolution, in Latin America it corresponds to the continent's period of underdevelopment (97). Romantic narrative and poetry of this period contain the seeds of the most important themes in Latin American critical thought. They reveal the new nations' awareness of a basic duality in their configurations, a rift dating back to the time when the European conquerors violated the aboriginal civilizations. Thus, postindependence writings attest to an essential need for reconciliation between two conflicting terms: Europe and America, or civilization and barbarism. Emblematic of this hybrid culture, *Facundo: Civilización y barbarie* [Facundo: civilization and barbarism] (1845) by the Argentinian Domingo Faustino Sarmiento, is a combination of Romantic fictional narrative and political essay whose profound significance can be seen as extending to the rest of the continent. Sarmiento's reflections on key sociopolitical and cultural issues are at the root of an ongoing intellectual debate that continues to occupy critics today.

Sarmiento's compatriot Esteban Echeverría (1805–51) develops a literary program in the preface to his verse narrative *La cautiva* (1837) and in his essay "Fondo y forma de la obras de imaginación." He celebrates the spiritual richness of the national patrimony and its potential role in the development of a national literature. His nouvelle *El matadero* (1838) epitomizes *costumbrismo*, a literary tendency born from an attempt to transmit veridical events from a Romantic perspective. Noé Jitrik describes *costumbrismo* as a realist aesthetic predating the emergence of realism in Europe in which the grouping of realist elements anchors a solid Romantic framework ("Forma y significación en *El Matadero* de Esteban Echeverría," *El fuego de la especie*, 1971). Like most Latin American writers of this period, Echeverría and the participants of the Argentinian Salón Literario of 1837 find in Romanticism an aesthetics capable of conveying political and social criticism. In the same country, *Amalia* (1851) by José Mármol (1817–71) offers a powerful denunciation of the tyrannical regime of Manuel de Rosas.

The Venezuelan-born Andrés Bello (1781–1865) and the Chilean Francisco Bilbao (1823–65), as well as José María Mora (1794–1850) in Mexico, shared with Sarmiento the Americanist view that the emancipated nations should seek cultural freedom from Europe. However, paradoxically, their Americanist ideal does not take into consideration the aboriginal population; on the contrary, they do not hesitate to proclaim their negative attitude toward the latter. In Brazil, the same abrupt juxtaposition of civilization and barbarism appears a few years after the abolition of slavery in Euclides da Cunha's *Os sertões* (1902, *Rebellion in the Backlands*). In Peru, Manuel González Prada (1848–1918) develops an indigenist philosophy in which he dismisses notions about the inferiority of the aboriginal races. In *Horas de lucha* he examines literary matters in close relationship with the cultural renewal of Peru, stating that political emancipation goes hand in hand with linguistic freedom: language should express the American mentality, its tastes, and its milieu. His energetic prose exemplifies the kind of writing he advocates: clear, spontaneous, and dynamic, free from florid turns and archaisms, in short, as fresh and original as the American continent. In Ecuador, Juan Montalvo (1832–89), a liberal who opposed the tyranny of García Moreno, advocates a moralistic humanist philosophy that is present in his *Capítulos que se le olvidaron a Cervantes* (1895).

The Cuban José María Heredia (1803–39) wrote Romantic poetry, drama, and criticism and translated Pierre Jean de Béranger, Johann Wolfgang von Goethe, James Fenimore Cooper, and André Marie Chénier while in exile in Mexico. Four volumes of the review *Miscelánea* (1829–32) contain Heredia's principal literary conceptions and attest to his commitment to the literary and cultural development of his country. A Cuban poet of the next generation, José Martí (1853–95), a fervent admirer of RALPH WALDO EMERSON, saw the potential in literature to advance the cause of justice and independence for the subjugated nations. "Nuestra America" substantiates Martí's conception of language as the repository of positive human values. This view goes hand in hand with his fervent commitment to freedom and his belief in the integration of all the races within a nation.

The modernist/realist period.   The term *modernismo* was first used by the Nicaraguan poet Rubén Darío in "La literatura en Centroamérica," which appeared in the *Revista de artes y letras* in Chile in 1887. A brief manifesto published in 1894 articulates the innovative principles of *modernismo*: a combination of the aesthetic notions inherited from Europe—Parnassianism, or art for art's sake, and Symbolism (see STÉPHANE MALLARMÉ AND FRENCH SYMBOLISM)—with authentically American components—nativism, the promotion of New World subjects for literary representation. Nowadays, the term is used to designate both the movement, which flourished between approximately 1880 and 1920, and the aesthetic criticism it generated. The appearance of *modernismo* coincided with a period of economic expansion and with the arrival of a mass of European working-class immigrants in countries such as Argentina, Chile, Uruguay, and Mexico. Amid the prosperity there emerged an elitist mentality imbued with *fin de siècle* French artistic and cultural tastes. Contrary to this tendency, the Uruguayan José Enrique Rodó (1871–1917) figures prominently among modernist critics who advocated the supremacy of classical and Renaissance learning. His influential essay *Ariel* (1900) was instrumental in promoting the kind of rapprochement between Latin Europe and Latin

America propounded by the followers of Rubén Darío. The French-born Argentinian critic Paul Groussac (1848–1929), an admirer of Michel de Montaigne, William Shakespeare, and HIPPOLYTE TAINE, consistently promotes the intellectually refined attitude toward literature characteristic of the *modernistas*. Groussac dismisses Romanticism as "childish" and unrealistic. Throughout Latin America, artists and critics alike embraced Darío's poetics: a language acclimatized to the exuberant Latin American scene, diverse in form and exquisitely refined in style.

In Mexico, Gutiérrez Nájera's "El arte y el materialismo" (1876) studies the influence of the various literary tendencies—European and nativist—grouped under *modernismo*. Mariano Azuela's writings (journalistic and fictional), inspired by the spirit of the Mexican Revolution, denounce positivist ideals. His novel *Los de abajo* (1915, *The Underdogs*), the first social realist novel in Latin America, effectively juxtaposes the values of cosmopolitan intellectuals and peasants from the countryside.

The *modernista* tendency was promoted in other Latin American countries mainly through literary articles published in reviews. The writings of critics such as the Bolivian Ricardo Jaimes Freyre (1868–1933), Darío's most faithful disciple; the Dominicans Max and Pedro Henríquez Ureña, and Gastón F. Deligne; the Puerto Rican Eugenio María de Hostos; the Venezuelan Rufino Blanco Fombona; the Peruvian Ventura García Calderón; and the Costa Rican Ricardo Fernández Guardia all contributed to the advancement of Latin American *modernismo*. In Brazil, the critical works of Machado de Assís reveal the classical stamp of the great poet, playwright, and novelist. Néstor Vítor's (1868–1932) *A hora* (1900), *Farias Brito* (1917), and *Cartas a gente nova* (1924) typify the naturalist-Parnassian-Symbolist criticism of this period (in Brazil, the term *modernismo* refers to the subsequent period). As Claude Hulet says, Vítor "unhesitatingly believed in the things of the spirit, inveighed against everything smacking of the prosaic, and was ever the champion of art over matter" (2:236). Silvio Romero (1851–1914) writes on Romanticism in Brazil, a theme that figures prominently in his *História da literatura brasileira* (1888) and in *Evoluçao do lirismo brasileiro* (1905). José Veríssimo (1857–1916) adopts the same aesthetic approach in his *História da literatura brasileira* (1916).

The avant-garde/Americanist period. The avant-garde/Americanist period, a period of artistic renewal, is marked by a quest for authenticity in the artistic portrayal of Latin American mores, nature, myths, and society. Pedro Henríquez Ureña's *Seis ensayos en busca de nuestra expres-* *sion* (1926) eloquently expresses this endeavor. Eduardo Mallea's *História de una pasión argentina* (1935) and Ezequiel Martínez Estrada's *Radiografía de la Pampa* (1933), *La cabeza de Goliat* (1940), and *Los invariantes históricos en el Facundo* (1947) also give ample evidence of this tendency. Ricardo Rojas's essay *Eurindia* (1924) validates indigenist and historico-folkloric considerations in art from a historical perspective. Similarly, *La raza cósmica* (1925), by the Mexican José Vasconcelos, and *Creación de una pedagogía nacional,* by the Bolivian Franz Tamayo, assert the telluric approach to literature. In the same vein, *La vorágine* (1924, *The Vortex*), by the Colombian José Eustasio Rivera, argues that the Amazonian jungle contains in its wilderness and its mystery the past and the future of Latin America. The Venezuelan Rómulo Gallegos's (1884–1969) novel *Doña Bárbara* (1929) offers a new perspective on the original Latin American conflict, civilization versus barbarism, by vividly portraying, for the time, the ascending bourgeoisie.

In the cosmopolitan climate of the 1920s in Argentina, Angel Battistessa emerges as the pioneer theorizer of comparative literature. Inspired by the universalist humanist European tradition, Battistessa seeks verifiable (rather than analogical) textual correspondences between Latin American and European literature. He is one of the precursors of the notion that literary influence signifies active re-creation rather than passive emulation, as exemplified by his "Güiraldes y Laforgue."

The 1920s saw the evolution of the São Paulo–born Brazilian modernist movement, contemporary with the avant-garde current in the rest of the continent. Mario de Andrade's theoretical manifesto *Pau-Brasil* (1924) considers the question of the foreign versus the autochthonous in Brazilian art. A member of the Verde-Amarelo movement, which supported a purely nationalist art, Paulo Prado denounces the heterogeneity of Brazil's artistic expression in his "Portrait of Brazil" (1928). Regionalism appeared in the northern city of Recife and generated, as had the Gaúcho movement of Rio Grande do Sul in the late 1920s, a mixture of aesthetic and militant criticism. Gilberto Freire's proclamation *Casa grande e senzala* (1933, *The Masters and the Slaves*) sums up the regionalist view. Antônio de Alcantara Machado (1901–35) also wrote pro-regionalist dramatic criticism. However, in the 1950s, under the influence of NEW CRITICISM, Afrânio Coutinho's (b. 1911) *Correntes cruzadas* (1952) and *Da crítica e da nova crítica* (1957) promote the theories of this movement with an emphasis on distinctions between ORALITY AND LITERACY. His criticism is influenced by BENEDETTO CROCE and Leo Spitzer (see STYLISTICS). In general, after World War II, Latin American criticism preserves its historical imprint but abandons its hitherto chiefly aesthetic bias in favor of an approach based to some degree on RUSSIAN FORMALISM.

The contemporary period. Another fundamental issue that recurs in Latin American critical and creative writing is the profound sense of isolation and separateness that, in Gerald Martin's view, marks the "abandonment of Europeanized minds in Mestizo bodies, the sense of living nowhere and of living outside of history" (18). In his essay *El laberinto de la soledad* (1950, *The Labyrinth of Solitude: Life and Thought in Mexico*), the Mexican Octavio Paz proposes a metaphysical interpretation of this phenomenon. On the other hand, *El pensamiento latinoamericano* (1965), by Leopoldo Zea, a supporter of Paz's appeal for the integration of Latin America in the world, provides a Hegelian interpretation of the evolution of Latin American thought (see G. W. F. HEGEL). In Brazil, José Guilherme Merquior (1941–91) takes up the ideas of Herbert Marcuse, THEODOR W. ADORNO, and WALTER BENJAMIN in *Arte e sociedade* (1969), while Haroldo (b. 1929) and Augusto (b. 1931) de Campos adhere to a theoretical model based on STRUCTURALISM.

Jorge Luis Borges's (1899–1986) particular blend of short story and ARTHUR SCHOPENHAUER–inspired criticism had a powerful influence on the literary development of Latin America. Paradoxically, this occurred in spite of his distant attitude toward revolutionary social doctrines. The reason for his pivotal role may be, as Gerald Martin writes, that Borges "supplied the sense of precision and structure which permitted the intertextual systematization of . . . culture and the creation of . . . Latin American literature" (152). Following in Borges's footsteps, the Argentinian Julio Cortázar (1914–84) has contributed to the definition of the vigorous Latin American version of the short story.

Yet, because of the resounding success of the Latin American novel after 1960, criticism during this period has largely concentrated on this genre, in all its diverse forms. In 1967, in a series of interviews with Alejo Carpentier, Borges, and Miguel Angel Asturias published in *Into the Mainstream* (1967), Luis Harss traced the origins of the new fiction to the end of the *modernista* period. Cortázar figures prominently among the writers whose aesthetic pursuits are one with their political preoccupations. His Marxist humanist ideal is clearly stated in "Acerca de la situación del intelectual latinoamericano" in *Ultimo Round* (1969) and in his "Literatura en la revolución y revolución en la literatura," a response to the accusation that his literature was not truly committed to the Latin American cause of political and cultural emancipation. These allegations, by the Cuban Oscar Collazos

in his "La encrucijada del lenguaje," appeared in *Marcha* (special issue on Cortázar). In their theoretical writings, the Paraguayan Augusto Roa Bastos (b. 1917; see "Imagen y perspectivas de la narrativa latinoamericana actual") and the Peruvian Mario Vargas Llosa (b. 1936; see "Luzbel, Europa y otras conspiraciones") adopt a position similar to Cortázar's and defend the autonomy of literature, while recognizing the importance of its role within the sociopolitical sphere. In *La nueva novela hispanoamericana* (1969) the Mexican Carlos Fuentes (b. 1928) engages in a critique of the Latin American novel from a broad historical perspective. In later writings, he emphasizes the dialogical, open-ended dimension of the genre in terms derived from M. M. BAKHTIN.

In *De Sarmiento a Cortázar* (1971) the Argentinian David Viñas engages in a kind of Marxist form of "parricide" (see Rodríguez Monegal, *El juicio*). This critical approach has been deemed fundamentally patriarchal and contingent by Roberto González Echevarría. Mindful of the pitfalls of rhetoric in criticism, González Echevarría underlines the crucial role of critical language and calls for a functional approach that takes into account linguistic, discursive, Derridean, and semiotic perspectives in an attempt to undertake the monumental task of forging a Latin American literary tradition.

In roughly one and a half centuries of postindependence history, literary criticism and theory in Latin America have echoed the momentous transformations and ramifications of the original sociocultural conflict, that is, civilization versus barbarism. Unquestionably, theoretical and critical inspiration and legitimation derived from European models have always been at work. But a close look at the landmarks of this area's continuing cultural evolution shows how much Latin America's own impetuous critical self-awareness, along with its desire to articulate a distinctive indigenous reality, have always been at the root of its manifold transformations.

Mónica Lebron

José María Arguedas, "No soy un aculturado" (1968, appendix to *El zorro de arriba y el zorro de abajo*, 1971); Machado de Assis, *Crítica literária: Obras completas* (1957); Angel J. Battistessa, "Güiraldes y Laforgue," *Nosotros* 16 (1942), "Tradición temática y revolución expresiva," *Boletín de la Academia Argentina de letras* 26 (1961); Jorge Luis Borges, *The Spanish Language in South America: A Literary Problem* (1964); Alejo Carpentier, *Tientos y diferencias* (1966); Afrânio Coutinho, *Crítica e poética* (1968); Carlos Fuentes, *Myself with Others: Selected Essays* (1989), *La nueva novela hispanoamericana* (1969); Luis Harss, *Into the Mainstream* (1967); Pedro Henríquez Ureña, *Literary Currents in Hispanic America* (1945); *Marcha* (1987, special issue on Julio Cortázar); Fernando Ortiz, "The Social Phenomenon of 'Transculturation' and Its Importance," *Cuban Counterpoint* (1947); Angel Rama, *Transculturación narrativa en América Latina* (1982); Mario Vargas Llosa, "Algo mas sobre la novela latinoamericana," *El Urogallo* 1 (1970), "En torno a la novela latinoamericana," *Teoría de la novela* (ed. German Guillón and Agnes Guillón, 1975).

Salvador Bacarisse, ed., *Contemporary Latin American Fiction* (1980); Leslie Bethell, *Cambridge History of Latin America* (1985); Alfredo Bosi, *História concisa da literatura brasileira* (1979); César Fernández Moreno, *América Latina en su literatura* (1972); Jean Franco, *Spanish American Literature since Independence* (1973); Roberto González Echevarría, *Isla a su vuelo fugitiva: Ensayos críticos sobre literatura hispanoamericana* (1983), *The Voice of the Masters: Writing and Authority in Modern Latin American Literature* (1986); Claude L. Hulet, *Brazilian Literature* (3 vols., 1974–75); Alceu Amoroso Lima, *A crítica literária no Brasil* (1952); Gerald Martin, *Journeys through the Labyrinth* (1989); Françoise Pérus, *Historia y crítica literaria: El realismo social y la crisis de la dominación oligárquica* (1982); Emir Rodríguez Monegal, *El boom de la novela latinoamericana* (1973), *El juicio de los parricidas* (1956); Kessel Schwartz, *A New History of Latin American Fiction* (2 vols., 1971); Leopoldo Zea, *El pensamiento latinoamericano* (1976); Alberto Zum Felde, *Indice crítico de la literatura hispanoamericana* (2 vols., 1954–59).

LAWRENCE, D. H.

David Herbert Lawrence (1885–1930) produced great quantities of polemical prose during the last decade and a half of his life, dispersing it throughout his fictions, in his letters, and in book reviews, literary essays, and monograph-length critical and philosophical studies. The most significant of these texts include *Studies in Classic American Literature* (1924); "Study of Thomas Hardy," published posthumously in *Phoenix;* several essays on the novel, including "Why the Novel Matters," "Surgery for the Novel—or a Bomb," and "Morality and the Novel"; an important piece entitled "Pornography and Obscenity"; the politico-philosophical essays in *Reflections on the Death of a Porcupine;* the quasi-psychoanalytic texts "Fantasia of the Unconscious" and "Psychoanalysis and the Unconscious"; a series of essays on sexual politics called "A Propos of *Lady Chatterley's Lover*"; and the quasi-mystical text *Apocalypse.*

Lawrence articulates in his art a vitalistic metaphysics, obliquely and partially derived from FRIEDRICH NIETZSCHE and SIGMUND FREUD, that in his essays produces a revisionary tool for criticizing social and cultural forces that attenuate animal vitality, repress sexuality, or thwart individual potentiality and power. By making organic "quickness" a chief category of value, Lawrence's literary and cultural criticism relies on an essentialism with an atavistic ground that allows him to penetrate novelistic themes below their level of social representation in order to explore the ontology of human and animal interaction in terms of sexuality, mutability, mortality, power, perception, and sensation. As a result, his critical discourse, like the novelistic, violates traditional generic boundaries and produces intellectually bastardized texts relegated to the far margins of the modern critical canon.

Like many of his contemporaries, Lawrence was interested in occult symbolism and theosophy as a source of primitive theology, and because he subsequently expressed the life force in the tropes of spirit and the supernatural, F. R. LEAVIS and other modern critics tended to regard him as a deeply religious writer whose animistic fervor revivified modern spirituality. Lawrence's vitalism had political ramifications as well; since it was a form of natural power, its excessive potency in particular individuals (of human and other species) made it threatening to society and invited attenuation and repression. The antidemocratic polemic of much of his prose and the proto-fascist themes of mastery and aggression in the later fictions and essays reflect Lawrence's Nietzschean repulsion by mass humanity and herd mentality. His individualism, however, rarely takes social form except as potent leadership or potent mastery (to be distinguished from "bullying," domination, or subjugation produced by forces other than personal potency) and must not be confused with the social self-actualizations that result in ambition, success, or control.

Because Lawrence's concept of identity is organic, the development of the subject manifests itself in fluidity and multiplicity of form. For this reason, sexuality becomes the central metaphor in Lawrence's psychology, a trope that inflects the style of his critical discourse with *energia* rather than logic. Lawrence thus not only justifies the salutary function of sexuality in literature as theme, character motivation, and poetic inspiration but in "Introduction to These Paintings" rewrites English literary history as deformed and scarred by the dread of the body that is introduced along with syphilis at the time of the Renaissance. "And so I am certain that *some* of Shakespeare's father-murder complex, *some* of Hamlet's horror of his mother, of his uncle, of all old men came from the feeling that fathers may transmit syphilis, or syphilis-consequences, to children" (*Phoenix* 555). Because novelists themselves suffer from socialization and repression, Lawrence's critical dictum is to trust the tale, not the artist (*Studies* 9). He read and reviewed widely, and much of his literary criticism takes the form of producing a vitalistic counterreading of the text against the author's ostensible moral intention: a moral psychoanalysis that uncovers the unconscious, passionate quick of the novel betrayed and repressed by the author's conscious judgment. For example, Lawrence chastises writers such as Thomas Hardy and Leo Tolstoy, who, he argues, defile their own passionate impulses when in their emplotted judgments they side with social law against the primitive nature of their characters.

Lawrence's criticism is thus performative, and because his vitalism belongs to no traditional discourse, he continually invents rhetorical voices and figurations in his essays. His rhetoric in the critical prose is opinionated, partisan, and emotional, and he thereby eschews the marks of rationality. The aggressive tone, which critics often find hectoring and sarcastic, is intended as an exercise of courage and potency rather than as an instrument of coercive persuasion. Lawrence's tropes for literary events take a variety of organic forms in his essays in order to personify poetic and novelistic practice in vital figures. In *Studies in Classic American Literature* the old European self-consciousness, which must be discarded in favor of the new, primitive, American sensibility, is figured as an old snakeskin that must be sloughed off (55–56). The characters of John Galsworthy behave, to Lawrence, like urban dogs in heat, while those of Hardy appear like verdant vegetation, "bursting suddenly out of bud and taking a wild flight into flower" (*Phoenix* 410). Lawrence tropes the novel itself, in "Surgery for the Novel—or a Bomb," according to the ages of humanity to make the modern novel a case of self-conscious adolescent arrested development (*Phoenix* 518). Lawrence's primitive revaluations of English, American, and Continental literature, delivered in the tropes and rhetoric of what might be called a libidinal style, make a uniquely modern contribution to literary criticism that, teleologically, stands in marked contrast to the poetic theories of his modern American contemporaries, T. S. ELIOT and EZRA POUND.

Margot Norris

D. H. Lawrence, *Apocalypse* (1932), *Phoenix: The Posthumous Papers* (ed. Edward McDonald, 1936), *Phoenix II: Uncollected, Unpublished, and Other Prose Works* (ed. Warren Roberts and Harry T. Moore, 1968), *"Psychoanalysis and the Unconscious"* and *"Fantasia of the Unconscious"* (1921), *Reflections on the Death of a Porcupine* (1925), *Selected Literary Criticism* (ed. Anthony Beal, 1955), *Studies in Classic American Literature* (1924).

Harold Bloom, ed., *D. H. Lawrence: Modern Critical Views* (1986); Roger Ebbatson, *Lawrence and the Nature Tradition: A Theme in English Fiction, 1859–1914* (1980); David J. Gordon, *D. H. Lawrence as Literary Critic* (1966); John B. Humma, "D. H. Lawrence as Friedrich Nietzsche," *Philological Quarterly* 53 (1974); Frank Kermode, *D. H. Lawrence* (1973); Colin Milton, *Lawrence and Nietzsche: A Study in Influence* (1987); George J. Zytaruk, "The Doctrine of Individuality: D. H. Lawrence's 'Metaphysic,'" *D. H. Lawrence: A Centenary Consideration* (ed. Peter Balbert and Phillip L. Marcus, 1985).

LEAVIS, F. R.

Frank Raymond Leavis (1895–1978) is one of the most important and controversial figures in twentieth-century British literary criticism. Apart from war service and several visiting professorships, which he accepted after his retirement in 1962, he spent virtually his whole life in Cambridge, without being granted the recognition he believed he deserved. He was a probationary faculty lecturer from 1927 to 1931 and was finally appointed fellow of Downing College and an assistant university lecturer in 1936; but for much of his early life he was dependent on insecure part-time teaching, and at 40 he had not had a salaried post for several years. In 1929 he married Queenie Dorothy Roth, author of the seminal sociological study, *Fiction and the Reading Public*. From 1932 to 1953 Leavis was chief editor of the journal *Scrutiny*, which published most of his work prior to its appearance in book form. *Scrutiny* was co-founded by a group of impecunious research students and was commercially unsuccessful, but its contributors saw themselves, Leavis later said, as "the essential Cambridge in spite of Cambridge." The journal combined an intense concern with literature and morality with the practical criticism of I. A. RICHARDS and aimed to discredit what it perceived as the amateur belletrism characterizing English studies at the turn of the century. This warfare was later to be reproduced in Leavis's campaign against the metropolitan literary culture symbolized by the Sunday newspapers. Though his role as cultural critic assumed greater importance in the post-*Scrutiny* years, at least in his own eyes, no neat periodization of his work is possible, for the later writings elaborate on themes clearly articulated at the beginning of his career.

Of Leavis's more exclusively "literary" works, the pioneer was *New Bearings on English Poetry* (1932), which helped to establish the reputations of T. S. Eliot, Ezra Pound, and Gerard Manley Hopkins. It opposes the nineteenth-century conception of the poetical as sensuous and expressive, substituting for it "wit, play of intellect, stress of cerebral muscle" (14); in attacking Victorian poetry for having lost touch with the thought of its age, it highlights the achievement of the modern poet, who represents "the most conscious point of the race in his time" (16). *Revaluation* (1936) changed the face of the English poetic canon, judging writers by reference to standards implicit in a "line of wit" derived from the Metaphysicals. Milton studies, in particular, took a long time to recover from the charge that Milton had effectively "forgotten the English language" (56). In *The Great Tradition* (1948) Leavis carried out a more drastic winnowing of the fictional canon, nominating only Jane Austen, George Eliot, Henry James, Joseph Conrad, and D. H. Lawrence as truly great practitioners for having promoted "awareness of the possibilities of life" (10). The apparent denigration of Dickens, whose genius was said to be "that of a great entertainer" (p. 30), was later redressed in *Dickens the Novelist* (1970), co-authored with Q. D. Leavis. In *D. H. Lawrence: Novelist* (1955) Leavis enlarged his case for Lawrence as the greatest creative writer of his age—a championing that, together with a somewhat unexpected rediscovery of William Blake, heralded Leavis's swing from the urbane to the prophetic in later life.

Leavis's literary criticism is therefore manifestly and purposely evaluative, and the criteria he employs are at once consistent and infamously vague. Technical originality is lauded in *The Great Tradition* only insofar as it subserves a "reverent openness before life" (18), and it is the "interests of life" (16) that are identified as the genuine moral preoccupation of the creative writer and critic alike. These interests apparently entail such things as individuality, spontaneity, and authenticity in personal relations, but more often they are characterized negatively by all that is antagonistic to them in the modern world. Literature is privileged because the prized qualities are there infused into a rich and subtle use of the living language and thereby made available to subsequent generations. Leavis's reluctance to articulate his critical presuppositions more openly was the cause of a celebrated exchange with RENÉ WELLEK in *Scrutiny* in 1937: Wellek argued that such presuppositions generated aesthetic preferences and that Leavis's devaluation of certain Romantic conceptions had been impelled by a merely implicit realist philosophy; somewhat missing this point,

Leavis replied by asserting the absolute distinction between philosophy and literary criticism and the irrelevance of a philosophical approach to a discipline that dealt in concrete responses to the complex experiences embodied in literary language.

Leavis's broader cultural preoccupation was consistently with the perceived dangers of "technologico-Benthamite" civilization. The influential early pamphlet *Mass Civilization and Minority Culture* (1930) stressed the unprecedented character of the machine age and castigated its corollary leveling-down effects in areas such as the press, film, and literature. The susceptibility of the majority to such standardizing trends meant that it devolved upon a small, independent-minded minority to maintain the cultural tradition and resuscitate for present needs the best human experience of the past. The elitism implicit in this stance is one of the most common sources of opposition to Leavis. Another is the idea of the "organic community," in which work and life were a harmonious totality and which has been supplanted by postindustrial forms of mechanized and alienated labor. Although Leavis claimed that his concern with village craftspersons had been misrepresented (e.g., in *Culture and Environment,* 1933), his treatment of this historical alternative to modern society has an undeniably mythic dimension.

In *Education and the University* (1943) and *English Literature in Our Time and the University* (1969) Leavis advanced the thesis that the university, and within it preeminently the English school, had the opportunity and duty to become a center of consciousness for society and that the educated elite it produced might exert an influence disproportionate to its numbers in countering the "blind drive onward of material and mechanical development" (*Education* 16). Despite these ambitions, it seems clear now that the kind of sensibility Leavis sought to train would always find itself on the defensive, though the increasingly impassioned militancy of his own stand may have obscured this fact. In a notorious polemic, "Two Cultures? The Significance of C. P. Snow" (1962, a response to Snow's 1959 Rede Lecture), Leavis excoriated the crassly materialistic vision of the future he attributed to Snow and appealed instead to a collaborative-creative "third realm" (neither private nor public, more a world of shared significances and values) exemplified in the study of literature. But the community thus invoked was, as Leavis was to recognize bitterly after the collapse of *Scrutiny,* no more than potential; and as RAYMOND WILLIAMS has argued, it always fell far short of the transformation of common culture that might offer genuine social hope (see CULTURAL STUDIES: I. UNITED KING-

DOM). *Nor Shall My Sword* (1972), which reprinted "Two Cultures?" along with other essays, is a painfully eloquent elaboration of its argument.

Always an uncomfortable and discomforting presence in the academic world, arousing deep hostility to his style and manner as much as to his message, Leavis, along with his contribution to English studies, was for a time fashionably derided. It is now becoming possible to assess more objectively the transformations he wrought in critical practice and theory (despite his own aversion to "theory" as such), and he has also won qualified admiration from the Left for the scale and courage of his cultural interventionism. His influence on teaching, particularly at the secondary level in Britain, has also been immense.

Robin Jarvis

F. R. Leavis, *D. H. Lawrence: Novelist* (1955), *Education and the University: A Sketch for an "English School"* (1943, 2d ed., 1948), *English Literature in Our Time and the University* (1969), *The Great Tradition: George Eliot, Henry James, Joseph Conrad* (1948), *The Living Principle: "English" as a Discipline of Thought* (1975), *Mass Civilization and Minority Culture* (1930), *New Bearings in English Poetry: A Study of the Contemporary Situation* (1932, 2d ed., 1950), *Nor Shall My Sword: Discourses on Pluralism, Compassion, and Social Hope* (1972), *Revaluation: Tradition and Development in English Poetry* (1936); F. R. Leavis and Denys Thompson, *Culture and Environment: The Training of Critical Awareness* (1933).

Michael Bell, *F. R. Leavis* (1988); R. P. Bilan, *The Literary Criticism of F. R. Leavis* (1979); Ronald Hayman, *Leavis* (1976); M. B. Kinch, William Baker, and John Kimber, *F. R. and Q. D. Leavis: An Annotated Bibliography* (1989); Francis Mulhern, *The Moment of "Scrutiny"* (1979); *New Universities Quarterly* 30 (1975, special issue on Leavis); P. J. M. Robertson, *The Leavises on Fiction: An Historic Partnership* (1981); Anne Samson, *F. R. Leavis* (1992); William Walsh, *F. R. Leavis* (1980).

LESSING, G. E.

Gotthold Ephraim Lessing (1729–81) inaugurated a new period in the history of German literary theory and criticism. For the first time in this tradition, criticism was liberated from its determination as a manual for the production of poetry and traditional philological text-criticism and became overtly political. Lessing's practical criticism, which brought the study of sources (both literary texts and examples from the "plastic" arts) and the interpretation of terms to a new level of precision, was designed to reach the broader public and incite critical debate concerning important literary, cultural, and political issues within and outside of academic circles. His literary theory made the decisive contribution of providing a semiotic theory of the arts and rendering the philosophical aesthetics of Alexander Baumgarten and Georg Friedrich Meier more concrete and exact. It also made specific recommendations for the advancement of German literature.

Against Johann Christoph Gottsched's "rule" poetics, which remained indebted to rhetorical tradition, Lessing argued in the seventeenth letter of the *Briefe, die neueste Literatur betreffend* (1759) that German critics should not impose the French model of the theater on German drama; the English model of Shakespeare, being much closer to the German mode of thought, ought to serve as the model for the German stage. By adopting Shakespeare as the model for German drama, Lessing effectively revolutionized the German theater. His reinterpretation of key terms and phrases of ARISTOTLE's *Poetics*, especially the notions of fear and pity, was to prove decisive for the development of the modern German drama. In letter 63 of the *Briefe*, and in the section 89 of the *Hamburgische Dramaturgie* (1767), he placed poetry above history and argued, as Aristotle had done, that poetry is at once more philosophical and more useful than history because of its universality and that historical material must be appropriated and molded for the purpose of dramatic effect.

For Lessing, genre, its requirements and limitations, is of utmost importance, but instead of delivering a prescriptive theory, Lessing intended to provoke and motivate his readers by providing precise arguments and soliciting a response from them. His "system," however, was anything but rigid. In section 95 of the *Hamburgische Dramaturgie* he insisted that the function of criticism was to produce critique and critical readers:

> I remind my reader that these sheets are meant to contain nothing less than a dramatic system. I am therefore not required to resolve all the difficulties that I create. My thoughts might cohere less and less, indeed, they might seem to be contradictory; if only they are thoughts with which the readers find material to think for themselves. Here, I simply want to distribute *fermenta cognitionis*. (*Sämtliche Schriften* 10:187–88)

Departing from rhetoric and from the "rule" poetics of Gottsched and the Swiss critics Johann Jakob Bodmer and Johann Jakob Breitinger, Lessing emphasizes the importance of taste *(Geschmack)*. In the preface to the *Hamburgische Dramaturgie*, he defines true taste as the more universal taste that extends beyond single works and genres and is able to form and inform educated judgments concerning aesthetic objects of any kind. It is restricted alone by the law of genre in that it does not expect more from a specific work than it can produce according to its kind. The true critic, according to Lessing, does not deduce a set of abstract "rules" from taste but rather "educates" his or her taste according to the laws that the nature of the object exhibits: "The true critic does not conclude rules from his own taste, but has rather formed his taste according to the 'rules' that the nature of the matter demands" (Mayer 183). Good taste requires historical knowledge of the genre. In section 95 of the *Dramaturgie,* Lessing follows Denis Diderot in his critique of the use of older verse forms in tragedy. He argues historically: because the figures in Greek tragedy discourse in a *public* forum, in accordance with societal position and status, there is a justifiable demand for the rhetorical use of language apt to the rhetorical situation. With the privatization of discourse in modernity, where characters speak as historical individuals within the confines of "private" spaces, rigid use of verse is no longer necessary: "But we moderns who have gotten rid of the chorus and allow our characters to speak for the most part between four walls; what cause do we have in spite of this to let them speak this decorous contrived, rhetorical language?" (*Sämtliche Schriften* 10:30). As his essay "How the Ancients represented death. An Investigation" (1769) demonstrates, Lessing's criticism recognizes the historical chasm between the ancients and the moderns and reflects a heightened awareness of the practical consequences of this knowledge for the theory of taste, genre, and the historical context of language.

The scholarship on Lessing's literary criticism and theory of literature is, however, far from unified. While one critic has recently claimed that Lessing exemplifies the shift in which "a sensualistic aesthetics of effect triumphed over rhetorical rules and classicistic 'rule' poetics" (Berghahn 49), another has identified Lessing's theory as primarily *aesthetic,* not concerned with "tactics for achieving successful performances" (Wellbery 69). Some scholars have argued that Lessing advocates the Enlightenment notion of the public sphere *(Öffentlichkeit)* as it is discussed by JÜRGEN HABERMAS, while others have insisted on the radical irony in Lessing's writing that implies the rupture of the very concept of a homogeneous public sphere (Burgard). While David Wellbery's pathbreaking study of *Laocoon* (1984) claims that Lessing's aesthetics is a "representational" and semiotic the-

ory, having nothing to do with the hermeneutic approach to texts that emerges decisively at the end of the eighteenth century, other recent work has traced the hermeneutic and rhetorical dimensions of Lessing's literary criticism and theory (Jacobs, Knodt, Leventhal). There is still a great deal of controversy concerning Lessing's relation to rhetoric, the so-called genius-aesthetics of the 1770s, and how his criticism is to be positioned with regard to Romanticism. Incontrovertible is his status as the primary literary theorist and critic of the German Enlightenment.

Lessing's most important contribution to the history of literary *theory* is his *Laocoon: An Essay on the Limits of Painting and Poetry* (1766). In recent years there has been a dramatic increase in critical scholarship on Lessing and literary theory focused on this single work. As Tzvetan Todorov pointed out, Lessing prefigures modern theorists such as Jan Mukarovsky and ROMAN JAKOBSON by seeking to identify the semiotic specificity of poetic language. In *Laocoon,* his theories concerning the relationship between semiotics, represented objects and their specific ontology, and the mode of representation achieve their most precise formulation. Karlheinz Stierle has observed that Lessing's *Laocoon* issues in a transformation in aesthetic discourse by departing from the dominant aesthetics of imitation (mimesis) and focusing instead on the aesthetic qualities of the semiotic media themselves, specifically the types of signs utilized by the various arts (38). By grasping language as an arbitrary sign system, and by radically distinguishing the task of the critic from that of the philologist or philosopher, Lessing created the discipline of modern literary criticism in Germany and initiated the commonplace modern doctrine of aesthetic autonomy. For him, the work of art and judgment concerning the work are emancipated from the artwork's function within the narrowly defined political spheres of the court and the church. Rather than being restricted to the function of works within these sites, the critic is interested in mediating between the work of art, the historical system of works and genre, and the public, understood not as an academic elite but as all educated individuals who participate in public debate.

Lessing's use of image, rhetorical devices, and allusions in his criticism to provoke the self-reflection and critical understanding of the reader not only fulfilled the performative function of activating a critical sensibility but also served a more global political purpose. Lessing often deliberately circumlocuted his intended opponent—other critics such as Christian Adolf Klotz, the church, and the state—by utilizing figural language. His sharp polemics reached a wide audience, and it can be argued that he intentionally sought to be censored in order to expose the intersection of church and state authority. It was the "lively, dramatic and dialogical spirit" (Schlegel 50) of Lessing's criticism and theory, his familiar and conversational tone, his rigorous and incisive argumentation, and the clarity of his reasoning that had a profound influence on JOHANN WOLFGANG VON GOETHE, Friedrich Schlegel, and later critics and made him one of the great stylists of modern essayistic writing.

Robert Leventhal

See also GERMAN THEORY AND CRITICISM: 1. STURM UND DRANG / WEIMAR CLASSICISM and 2. ROMANTICISM.

Gotthold Ephraim Lessing, *Briefe, die neueste Literatur betreffend* (1974), *Laocoon: An Essay on the Limits of Painting and Poetry* (1766, trans. E. McCormick, 1982), *Sämtliche Schriften* (ed. Karl Lachmann and Franz Muncker, 3d ed., 1924); Friedrich Schlegel, "Lessings Gedanken und Meinungen," *Kritische Friedrich Schlegel Ausgabe,* vol. 3 (ed. Ernst Behler, 1958).

Klaus Berghahn, "From Classicist to Classical Literary Theory, 1730–1806," *A History of German Literary Criticism* (ed. Peter Uwe Hohendahl, 1988); Joachim Birke, "Der junge Lessing als Kritiker Gottscheds," *Euphorion* 62 (1968); Klaus Bohnen, *Geist und Buchstabe: Zum Prinzip des kritischen Verfahrens in Lessings literaturästhetischen und theologischen Schriften* (1974); Peter Burgard, "Schlangenbiß und Schrei: Rhetorische Strategie und ästhetisches Programm in *Laokoon*," *Streitkultur: Strategien des Überzeugens im Werk Lessings* (ed. W. Mauser, 1992); Gunter Gebauer, ed., *Das Laokoon-Projekt: Pläne einer semiotischen Ästhetik* (1984); Carol Jacobs, "The Critical Performance of Lessing's *Laokoon*," *MLN* 102 (1987); Eva Knodt, *Negative Philosophie und dialogische Kritik: Zur Struktur poetischer Theorie bei Lessing und Herder* (1989); Robert Leventhal, "Körper-Tod-Schrift: Zur rhetorischen Umschreibung bei Lessing," *Streitkultur: Strategien des Überzeugens im Werk Lessings* (ed. W. Mauser, 1992), "The Parable as Performance: Interpretation, Cultural Transmission, and Political Strategy in Lessing's *Nathan*," *German Quarterly* 61 (1988); Hans Mayer, *Deutsche Literaturkritik,* vol. 1, *Von Lessing bis Hegel, 1730–1830* (ed. Mayer, 1978); Peter Michelsen, "Der Kritiker des Details: Lessing in den Briefen über die neueste Literatur betreffend," *Wolfenbüttler Studien zur Aufklärung* 2 (1975); Horst Steinmetz, "G. E. Lessing: Über die Aktualität eines umstrittenen Kritikers," *Lessing in heutiger Sicht* (ed. E. Harris and R. Schade, 1977); "Der Kritiker Lessing: Zur Form und Methode der *Hamburgischen Dramaturgie*," *Neophilologus* 52 (1968); Karlheinz Stierle, "Das bequeme Verhältnis: Lessings *Laokoon*

und die Entdeckung des ästhetischen Mediums" (Gebauer); Tzvetan Todorov, "Esthétique et sémiotique au XVIIIe siècle," *Critique* 29 (1973); David Wellbery, *Lessing's "Laokoon": Semiotics and Aesthetics in the Age of Reason* (1984).

LÉVI-STRAUSS, CLAUDE

The leading figure in post–World War II French ethnology, Claude Lévi-Strauss (b. 1908) adapted approaches from linguistics, Durkheimian sociology, and several schools of anthropology to analyze comparative kinship and marriage, ritual practice, mythologies, and the interrelation of semantic, aesthetic, and economic values of nonliterate societies. *Anthropologie structurale (Structural Anthropology)* was the title given to two widely influential volumes of essays on cross-cultural method and theory. Lévi-Strauss was particularly inspired by FERDINAND DE SAUSSURE's semiology, ROMAN JAKOBSON's poetics, and both mathematical and musical theories of "internal properties" of any system of signification. His influential ideas about *pensée sauvage*—undomesticated, differential thought codes, which he contrasted to conformist regulations of centralized state administrations—helped consolidate the movement designated STRUCTURALISM throughout the social and literary sciences. Literary theorists and critics of various schools and interests have eclectically drawn from his work on myth, communication, and methodology.

After fieldwork experiences in Amazonia (1935–39) and wartime expatriation from France at the New School for Social Research in New York (1942–45), Lévi-Strauss joined the Musée de l'homme and later the École Pratique des Hautes Etudes. In 1959 he received the first chair of social anthropology at the Collège de France, and in 1973 he was voted a member of the Académie française. Educated in philosophy, learned in literature, masterful in encyclopedic ethnology, aggressive in polemic, and brimming with preferences and prejudices in all the arts, Lévi-Strauss became for his colleagues and followers a bona fide savant. He was seen as somewhat less significant by the intellectual vanguard after the political developments of 1968 and was branded as logocentric by critics turning to DECONSTRUCTION in the 1970s and 1980s. Lévi-Strauss nevertheless remained very prominent, as he continued producing ambitious analyses in a virtuoso prose saturated with details of remote human evidence and flavored with pastiches of many styles of rumination on human nature and culture. His corpus helped restore intellectual verve and reflexive rhetoric to anthropological-cum-philosophical argument and critique.

Lévi-Strauss's formation, fieldwork, and travels are intricately recalled in *Tristes tropiques* (1955, trans., 1973), a narrative of professional awakening, whose complex style echoes both Amerindian mythic devices and moments from European literary history. *De près et de loin* (1988, *Conversations with Claude Lévi-Strauss*) looks back over accomplishments, ironies, and incongruities of his illustrious career; he revisits important debates with JEAN-PAUL SARTRE concerning the salience of historical consciousness and reiterates misgivings about phenomenological, existentialist, and functionalist approaches insensitive to variational structures of human experience informed by the ethnographic record.

Lévi-Strauss's views of marriage exchange as regulated social arrangements positively asserted to back up negative incest taboos (brother-sister, parent-child, etc.) have been particularly influential. He approached not just marriage systems but all cultural classifications as representations of desired communication (periodicities, reciprocities, cycles, and circulations) posited against those contradictions and transgressions elaborated in myths of incest, unanswered riddles, and unspoken questions. Various critics, however, have found aspects of power, gender, political strategy, and individual endeavor inadequately addressed in his work.

Perhaps the most general critical debate has concerned the nature of "universals" sometimes invoked in Lévi-Strauss's programmatic essays and of "dialectics" often inscribed in his actual analyses. Some commentators have declared him a roundabout, Enlightenment logician of totalized order; others have considered him a dialectician who decoded meanings of social divisions in contexts ignored by theories of superstructure restricted to dramatically antagonistic historical classes. Lévi-Strauss's clearest statement on such issues was offered in 1972, after he completed his four-volume magnum opus, *Mythologiques*:

> The difference [in my approach] from a Hegelian outlook lies in the fact that instead of coming from nowhere as the philosopher's writ (or maybe inspired by a hasty flight over a few centuries of a local past history), these specific constraints of the human mind are inductively found . . . by making a minute study of . . . the particular ideology of many different cultures. Besides, they are not given once and for all, as a kind of key which from now on and in the psychoanalyst's fashion, may open all the locks. We rather follow in the path of the linguists well aware that all grammars exhibit common properties or that, in the long run, uni-

versals of language may be reached. But linguists are also aware that the logical system made up of these systems will be much poorer than each particular grammar and never replace them. They also know that since the study of language in general and of the particular languages which have existed or still exist is an endless task, their common properties will never become encapsulated in a final set of rules. If and when universals are reached, their framework will remain open so that new determinations can be adduced while earlier ones may be enlarged or corrected. (*Structuralism and Ecology* 7)

Many critics pointed out Lévi-Strauss's relative neglect of historical process and his overreliance on Saussurean notions of *langue/parole* and synchrony/diachrony in theories of structure as relational differences. But one should not forget his active rejection of historical consciousness, linear sequencing, and developmental schemes. Many formats, elaborate digressions, and winking asides in Lévi-Strauss's most memorial arguments, particularly in *The Savage Mind* and "The Structural Study of Myth," challenged epistemologies of historicism, questioned cause-effect explanation, and carnivalized chronology as a mode of authoritative order. Moreover, three of his methodological trademarks were to metaphorize metonymies (and vice versa); to pulverize plot (i.e., assert narrative "harmony" over "melody"); and to use allusive alliteration (*Tristes tropiques, Le Cru et le cuit*) as a way of suggesting his model of variation: repetitions plus difference.

Much of the aptly designated "structuralist controversy" restricted itself to abstract issues of theory and method. These quarrels conveyed little of the actual experience of reading Lévi-Strauss's dauntingly orchestrated texts. A typical section of *Mythologiques II, Du meil aux cendres (From Honey to Ashes)*, provides a telling example. The section first outlines South American myths of the origin of cultivated plants that are sometimes endowed with speech. It then reviews long-term evidence of the utterly unstatic quality of tribal codes: such Indian languages as Nambikwara and Machiguenga, for example, demonstrate creative plasticity by self-consciously distorting terms, playing with muttering, altering consonants, inventing slang, and indulging in interlingual "osmosis" when unmaking and remaking words. Next come ethnographic details of meaningful sounds (flutes, rattles, whistles, speech, cries, taps) and myths of communication modes between gods and humans, humans and plants, women and men, and allies and enemies. From these Lévi-Strauss distills a general theme, a formula, and a crystalline diagram (320–33, esp. 328).

The theme here, that "music supplements language, which is always in danger of becoming incomprehensible if it is spoken over too great a distance" (326), leads to the tricky, vital formula: "a melodic phrase is a metaphor of speech" (328). (Unfortunately, the English translation here renders *discours* as "speech," also used to translate *parole*, contrasted to song [*chant*] and signal [*signal*] on the diagram; *discours* and *parole* cannot be merged in Lévi-Strauss's model.) The force of his formula is that "metaphor" (versus metonymy) stands to discourse as "melodic phrasing" (versus harmony) stands to music. This provocative, general analogy vibrates with implications for different arts of message-making, including both the specific myths under investigation and the *Mythologiques* investigating them. Finally, the diagram: called "the structure of the acoustic code," it is redescribed as a prism whose "four diagonals form two isosceles tetrahedra which interpenetrate" (332). In this vintage Lévi-Straussian twist, parallel and oblique relations are shown among indigenous categories of song, speech, and signal. These include styles of insulting, courtly, confused, and whistled "language"; signalings by name, epithet, tapping, and again whistling; and variant instrumentations of flute, drum, gourd, and shell rattle. The lush cross-connections key to a local, Amazonian organology that meticulously opposes drums to diverse, jangling noises from rattles made of nutshells or animals' hooves, used in dances to imitate ambiguous buzzing sounds of dragonflies, wasps, and hornets.

Readers of Lévi-Strauss tolerant of copious ethnographic details found that his demonstrations eventually wound back to Marcel Proust's *petite phrase mélodique*—a leitmotif *of* leitmotifs involved at the finale of *Mythologiques,* as Wagner and Debussy were saluted in the overture. Such are the simultaneities of Lévi-Strauss's texts, whose endlessly challenging pages both disclose and reinscribe reticulations of riddled communication. According to the theatrically oracular endings of his major books, diverse cultural *sciences concrètes* (including his own "myth of mythology") have been left in and as the wake of a humankind doomed, no doubt, to *Dämmerung.*

James A. Boon

Claude Lévi-Strauss, *Anthropologie structurale* (1958, *Structural Anthropology,* trans. Claire Jacobson and Brooke Grundfest Schoepf, 1963), *Anthropologie structurale deux* (1973, *Structural Anthropology, Vol. II,* trans. M. Layton, 1976), *Histoire de lynx* (1991), *Mythologiques I–IV* (trans. John Weightman and Doreen Weightman: *Le Cru et le cuit,* 1964, *The Raw and the Cooked,* 1969; *Du meil aux cendres,* 1966, *From Honey to Ashes,* 1973; *L'Origine des manières de table,* 1968, *The Origin of Table Manners,* 1978; *L'Homme nu,* 1971, *The Naked Man,* 1981), *Paroles donnés* (1984, *Anthropology and Myth: Lectures, 1951–1982,* trans. Roy Willis, 1987), *La Pensée sauvage* (1962, *The Savage Mind,* 1966), *La Potière jalouse* (1985, *The Jealous Potter,* trans. Bénédicte Chorier, 1988), *Le Regard éloigne* (1983, *The View from Afar,* trans. Joachim Neugroschel and Phoebe Hoss, 1985), *Structuralism and Ecology* (1972), *Les Structures élémentaires de la parenté* (1949, *The Elementary Structures of Kinship,* ed. Rodney Needham, trans. J. H. Bell, J. R. von Sturmer, and Rodney Needham, 1969), *Le Totemisme aujourdhui* (1962, *Totemism,* trans. Rodney Needham, 1963), *Tristes tropiques* (1955, trans. John Weightman and Doreen Weightman, 1973), *La Voie des masques* (1972, *The Way of the Masks,* trans. Sylvia Modelski, 1982); Claude Lévi-Strauss and Didier Eribon, *De près et de loin* (1988, *Conversations with Claude Lévi-Strauss,* trans. Paula Wissing, 1991).

Raymond Bellour and Catherine Clément, eds., *Claude Lévi-Strauss* (1979); James A. Boon, *From Symbolism to Structuralism: Lévi-Strauss in a Literary Tradition* (1972), *Other Tribes, Other Scribes: Symbolic Anthropology in the Comparative Study of Cultures, Histories, Religions, and Texts* (1982), "The Reticulated Corpus of Claude Lévi-Strauss," *The Philosophy of Discourse: The Rhetorical Turn in Twentieth-Century Thought,* vol. 2 (ed. Chip Sills and George H. Jensen, 1992); Terence Hawkes, *Structuralism and Semiotics* (1977); Michel Izard and Pierre Smith, eds., *Le Fonction symbolique* (1979, *Between Belief and Transgression: Structuralist Essays in Religion, History, and Myth* (trans. John Leavitt, 1982); Edmund Leach, *Claude Lévi-Strauss* (1970, rev. ed., 1974); Edmund Leach, ed., *The Structural Study of Myth and Totemism* (1967); Richard Macksey and Eugenio Donato, eds., *The Structuralist Controversy: The Languages of Criticism and the Sciences of Man* (1970); Ino Rossi, *The Logic of Culture: Advances in Structural Theory and Methods* (1982); Ino Rossi, ed., *Structural Sociology* (1982).

LINGUISTICS AND LANGUAGE

The extensive field covered by the category "linguistics and language" is historically split in the West on an issue that might be summed up in terms of whether the category is to be understood as hypotactic or paratactic: whether "language" is contained in or controlled by "linguistics" (hypotaxis, "language as defined by linguistics"—the mainstream view) or whether the two stand alongside each other with a rift in between (parataxis,

"language as opposed to linguistics"—various oppositional views).

Linguistics begins in classical antiquity, in the philo-
sophical/theological tradition from PLATO and ARIS-
TOTLE to ST. AUGUSTINE, as a will to mastery over what
Plato calls *doxa,* or "opinion" (what people say) and
what Augustine calls "fleshly" speech (words produced
by the mouth for the ears). Plato is still divided on the
desirable extent of this control: in the *Phaedrus,* for example, he has Socrates prefer living speech to writing,
because writing alienates language users from memory
(274b–276a); and while he explores this opposition to
writing *in* writing, he does so in dialogue form, clinging
mimetically to the interactional structure of living speech.
By *On Christian Doctrine* (C.E. 427), Augustine is advancing writing over speech because it is more visual and
more stable and thus more like the divine *Logos;* and
Platonist though he is, he is imitating not Platonic dialogue but the logical or *logos*-like discourse of Aristotle,
purged of mimetic interchange. Real speech, what people actually say to each other, is ideologically threatening to Plato and Augustine, for similar reasons: to Plato
because real or "doxic" speech is centrifugal, because it
flees the philosophical "center" of truth toward which
all discourse should be aimed; to Augustine because it is
carnal, generated by and for deathly bodies given over to
Satan and thus (as for Plato) disinclined to strive toward
the pure, single, stable *Logos.*

Linguistics is developed, one might argue, especially
in its founding document, *On Christian Doctrine,* in order
to consolidate a methodological defense against this
ideological threat: to subordinate language to the *Logos*
or logic and to exclude all insubordinate language (real
speech in particular) as not really language at all and
therefore beyond the analytical pale. Hence the clash
that has characterized the study of language since classical antiquity. For the Platonic-Augustinian tradition, followed in our century by FERDINAND DE SAUSSURE,
ROMAN JAKOBSON, Leonard Bloomfield, Louis Hjelmslev,
J. R. Firth, NOAM CHOMSKY, ÉMILE BENVENISTE, and
the entire linguistic mainstream, "language" is to be
defined as that stable (because ideal) systemic "core"
that is susceptible to linguistic formalizations (Saussure's
langue, Chomsky's "competence"); everything else is
mere "speech" (Saussure's *parole*), which is not language
but the mere "performance" (Chomsky's Platonic copy-
term) of true ("ideal") language. For various counterhegemonic traditions, by contrast, "language" is to be
defined precisely as speech, as what people say to each
other in real-life situations; everything else, everything
linguists call "language," is a Platonic fantasy of pure

transcendental structure. (For a useful history of linguistics, see Harris and Taylor.)

This rift has led to a situation in our time where two
groups—"linguists" and an unnamed and disunified
group of oppositional scholars—study language with few
or no methodological or terminological bridges in between and rarely recognize each other as "legitimate"
students of language. (The symmetry in that description
is, however, misleading. While both groups may resist
each other's legitimacy, one group is clearly validated by
the dominant ideology in Western thought in relation
to its legitimate object of inquiry, language: "linguists."
Typically, therefore, counterhegemonic students of language angrily and anxiously *deny* the legitimacy of linguistics, while hegemonic linguists calmly *ignore* the
legitimacy of oppositional language studies.)

Linguistics is torn, as any discipline is, by internal
disagreements: structuralists versus transformational-
generativists, prescriptivists versus descriptivists, empiricists versus rationalists, formalists (phonologists,
morphologists, syntacticians, semanticians, textlinguists)
versus contextualists (sociolinguists, psycholinguists,
geolinguists, social semioticians, pragmaticians, discourse analysts). Far more powerfully than its opponents, however, linguistics is united by an abstract formalist methodology that remains directly indebted to
Plato, Aristotle, and Augustine and therefore remains
ideologically "correct" in Western thought. Twentieth-
century linguists all share the assumption that the study
of transcendental "form" or "structure" is more scientific and therefore more valuable than the study of what
this or that individual says or writes to this or that other
individual in this or that situation. Thus, for the various
linguistic "contextualists," for example, the primary aim
is not to explore the complexity of what happens in
specific language-use contexts but to delineate the transcendental forms or structures governing *all* contexts, or
context "types": the semiotic structures regulating the
use of language in various societies or social subgroups
(see M. A. K. Halliday, *Language as Social Semiotic: The
Social Interpretation of Language and Meaning,* 1978), the
types of pragmatic relations between signs and various
"typical" (methodologically idealized) interpreters in
"typical" speech-use situations (see Stephen Levinson,
Pragmatics, 1983), and so on.

Lacking ideological validation, the other group lacks
ideological and methodological unity as well. For convenience, four different oppositional approaches might be
identified, focused around four revolutionary thinkers:
Wilhelm von Humboldt and Romanticism, M. M. BAKHTIN
and socio-ideological dialogism, LUDWIG WITTGEN-

STEIN and ordinary language philosophy, and KENNETH BURKE and dramatism. (A fifth might be traced from Sigmund Freud's *Interpretation of Dreams*, 1900; *Psychopathology of Everyday Life*, 1901; and *Jokes and Their Relation to the Unconscious*, 1905 [see PSYCHOANALYTIC THEORY AND CRITICISM: 1. TRADITIONAL FREUDIAN CRITICISM] to object-relations studies of introjected voices or to JACQUES LACAN. For a sixth, see SPEECH ACTS; there are others.)

The Romantic tradition in language studies runs from Humboldt in the early nineteenth century to BENEDETTO CROCE and Karl Vossler in the early twentieth; it is identified by V. N. Voloshinov in *Marxism and the Philosophy of Language* (1930) as "subjectivist," in opposition to the mainstream "objectivist" tradition. Here, to use Humboldt's terms, primary emphasis is placed not on inert objectivized "outer form" but on culturally specific but creative subjective "inner form." This theory was to lead to various kinds of linguistic chauvinism, including Romantic folkloristics (the search for the inner linguistic form of a nation in its fairy tales and folk poetry) and Romantic philology (which posited a single ethnic origin for all Indian and European languages, a quasi-biblical fantasy that the Nazis were to appropriate by locating the original "Indo-Europeans" or "Aryans" in blond Scandinavia). Tempered by the American pragmatism of RALPH WALDO EMERSON and CHARLES SANDERS PEIRCE, it would lead to the radical subjectivism of William James in the "Stream of Thought" chapter of *Principles of Psychology* (1890): for James the meaning of a word was a "single pulse of subjectivity, a single psychosis, feeling, or state of mind" (1:278), "an altogether specific affection of our mind" (1:253). Inner form remains inner but is cut loose from the collectivizing effect of a *Volk*, a people, a community, and becomes an ever-changing flow. Uneasily tied to Platonic-Augustinian formalism, it would lead to Noam Chomsky's transformational-generative linguistics, which affirms Humboldtian creativity but splits it down the middle, valorizing it positively in the "ideal" speaker as generative "competence" and negatively in real speakers as deviant "performance" (see *Aspects*, ch. 1).

Probably the most influential Romantic linguist in our century, however, was MARTIN HEIDEGGER, who transformed the creative inner form of language into a messianic "speaking" of language that is potentially redemptive. Heidegger deconstructs the mainstream linguistic view that language is an activity performed by the autonomous human subject, the individual speaker's expression or pushing out of an internal idea, arguing instead that "it is language that first brings man about, brings him into existence" (192) and that "man speaks in that he responds to language" (210). The progeny of this Romantic mysticism has been legion, and the legion has largely been French. Jacques Lacan and JACQUES DERRIDA use Heidegger to read Saussure against the grain, Lacan arguing that the "signifier effects the advent of the signified" (233), that is, that the sign generates meaning, the psychoanalytical transference/countertransference dialogue controls the sickness, language speaks us; and Derrida, less hopefully, that "the movement of signs defers the moment of encountering the thing itself" (138), that is, that the sign divides meaning, perpetuates and exacerbates the split or the fold Heidegger postulated between the speaking of language and the responsive hearing of human speakers. MICHEL FOUCAULT politicizes Heidegger's mysticism, seeing in the "speaking" of language the replication of discourses of power: for Foucault, what speaks us, what subjects us (in Louis Althusser's pun), what constitutes us as human speakers, is no mystical Being but social power, hegemony, ideology. "I am supposing," Foucault writes in "The Discourse on Language," "that in every society the production of discourse is at once controlled, selected, organised and redistributed according to a number of procedures, whose role is to avert its powers and its dangers, to cope with chance events, to evade its ponderous, awesome materiality" (216).

While the Marxist V. N. Voloshinov dismisses Romantic linguistics as little more than the decadent liberal bourgeois mirror image of mainstream linguistics, it is clear that the socio-ideological dialogism he and his non-Marxist friend and teacher Mikhail Bakhtin developed in their writings in the 1920s and 1930s is itself a brilliant extension of the Romantic tradition (most proximately of Martin Buber's dialogism in *I and Thou*, 1922), an extension, in fact, that anticipates Foucault's analyses of the discourse of power. Largely focused around Voloshinov's *Marxism and the Philosophy of Language* and Bakhtin's "Discourse in the Novel" (1934–35), this approach stresses the ideological saturation of language, its embeddedness in ongoing dialogical uses of language both in society ("ideology") and in each individual's head ("internal dialogism"). For Bakhtin, discourse is never either purely objective, as it is for the mainstream linguistic tradition, or purely subjective, as it is for the Romantics; it is always ideologically dialogized, bringing collective ideological structures and tonalizations into each individual's speech and individual accents into collective ideology, speaker into listener and listener into speaker in a continuous recycling of personally and socially accented or inflected words.

Bakhtin stresses the groundedness of all speaking *between* speaker and listener in the dialogical interchange that mediates between them and generates out of that mediation community. If language speaks us, it speaks us as social, as internally and externally dialogized; it "double-voices" us, and we each other, as (inter)active, participatory, transformative events in an ongoing exchange. (See Gary Saul Morson and Caryl Emerson, *Mikhail Bakhtin: Creation of a Prosaics,* 1990; and the essays by Emerson, Stewart, and Holquist in Morson, ed., *Bakhtin: Essays and Dialogues on His Work,* 1986.)

A third oppositional "linguistics" in the twentieth century has formed around the late work of Ludwig Wittgenstein, most particularly his *Philosophical Investigations* (1953). Wittgenstein's late "ordinary language" philosophy is often summed up by his principle that "the meaning of a word is its use in the language" (sec. 43), which detranscendentalizes "meaning" by recognizing its contextual contingency, its situational plasticity, and making that plasticity (rather than transcendental stability) methodologically primary (see Garth Hallett, S. J., *Wittgenstein's Definition of Meaning as Use,* 1967). This principle removes the need for classic linguistic dualisms such as "normal" versus "deviant" meanings (there are no "norms" outside fluctuating linguistic use) and "ordinary" versus "special" language (all language is ordinary, even poetic, oneiric, and schizophasic discourse, because all language is situationally contingent) (see Stanley Cavell, "Must We Mean What We Say?" *Must We Mean What We Say? A Book of Essays,* 1969; and Stanley Fish, "How Ordinary Is Ordinary Language?" *Is There a Text in This Class? The Authority of Interpretive Communities,* 1980). But Wittgenstein's assault on the petrified edifices of mainstream linguistics goes much further than this. His theory of language games points toward J. L. Austin's speech-act theory, according to which "to say something is to do something" (12), and his relativistic conception of those games as never stable or unified but loosely related or connected or overlapping through what he calls "family resemblances" undermines mainstream assumptions positing a stable transcendental "essence" of language. He breaks down the traditional emphasis on static, abstract linguistic "rules" by exploring the psychosocial complexities of "following a rule" and "being guided" (see Herman Parret, "Regularities, Rules, and Strategies," *Journal of Pragmatics* 8 [1984]).

Wittgenstein has inspired, directly or indirectly, most of the fiercest attacks on mainstream linguistics in our day (for explicitly Wittgensteinian attacks, see Ian Robinson, *The New Grammarians' Funeral: A Critique of Noam Chomsky's Linguistics,* 1975, and G. P. Baker and P. M. S.

Hacker, *Language, Sense, and Nonsense: A Critical Investigation into Modern Theories of Language,* 1984; for attacks in an implicitly Wittgensteinian spirit, see Terence Moore and Christine Carling, *Understanding Language: Toward a Post-Chomskyan Linguistics,* 1982, and Roy Harris, *The Language-Makers,* 1980, and *The Language Myth,* 1981). Geoffrey Sampson's "empiricist" attacks on Chomsky's rationalism seem ideologically more indebted to John Locke than to Ludwig Wittgenstein, but his Lockean empiricism is more commonsensical (based on ordinary-language use) than scientist.

A fourth oppositional "linguistics" can be found in the works of the American philosopher Kenneth Burke. Burke's quirky, eclectic thought is difficult to summarize, but his organizing linguistic principles are presented in summary form in the introductory chapter to *A Rhetoric of Religion: Studies in Logology,* the practice of tracing etymologies and other historical narratives ideologically, so that the *Logos,* or transcendental Word of God, for example, becomes logic or transcendental Form or Reason but continues to awaken the same respect in Western thinkers; and "dramatism," the notion that all action (including the act of theorizing, doing linguistics for example) is dramatically or symbolically or emotionally motivated, so that the linguist who says speech is not language is "dramatistically" saying "Thou shalt not study speech" (see William Wasserstrom, "Kenneth Burke, 'Logology,' and the Tribal No," *Representing Kenneth Burke,* ed. Hayden White and Margaret Brose, 1982). Burke is steeped in the ancient discipline of RHETORIC, which he attempts to unearth from under logicalizing conceptions of it as figurative ornamentation or enthymemic formalism: for Burke, as for the pre-Socratic Sophists or Cicero (see CLASSICAL THEORY AND CRITICISM: 2. RHETORIC), rhetoric is situationally contingent persuasion (see Michael Leff, "Burke's Ciceronianism," *The Legacy of Kenneth Burke,* ed. Herbert W. Simons and Trevor Melia, 1989). He discusses the contingent persuasion in terms of "identification," the process of at once (for persuasive purposes) making yourself one with another person and remaining separate from him or her:

> One need not scrutinize the concept of "identification" very sharply to see, implied in it at every turn, its ironic counterpart: division. Rhetoric is concerned with the state of Babel after the Fall. Its contribution to a "sociology of knowledge" must often carry us far into the lugubrious regions of malice and the lie. (*Rhetoric of Motives* 23)

These regions, along with the entire region of "fallen" (i.e., "real") human communication, have been excluded from the purview of mainstream linguistics precisely because they are "lugubrious," because they are not simple and pure and ideal. Burke demands that we stare human reality, including the reality of real language use, in the face. (For more detailed explorations of these four oppositional approaches to the study of language, see Robinson.)

Since literary texts typically deal more in the local, the human, the fleshly, or the imagistic than in the universal, the transcendental, the abstract, or the mathematical, it is not surprising that these oppositional traditions in language studies have proved far more productive for literary criticism than mainstream linguistics; indeed, two of the "revolutionary linguists," Bakhtin and Burke, are themselves literary critics of note. If, from these various oppositional points of view, linguistics is a form of systematized hostility toward language, it is equally hostile toward literature: language conceived as real human speech, what people really say (and write) to each other, is alien to linguistics but the very stuff of which literature is made.

(There is, in fact, a worldwide schism between linguists and literary critics, the former tending toward the "hard" methodologies of the social sciences, the latter toward the "soft" methodologies of the humanities; the former scorning the latter as impressionistic, the latter scorning the former as scientistic. In the United States, this schism has taken the institutional form of token linguists on English faculties and token quantitative analyses of literary texts in linguistics departments. In Europe and elsewhere, linguists and literary critics tend to be more evenly split in language departments, and pitched battles between linguist and literary critic are often fought over specific faculty appointments.)

As a result, there are far more Jamesian, Heideggerian, Lacanian, Derridean, Foucauldian, Bakhtinian, Wittgensteinian, and Burkean literary critics and theorists than, say, Saussureans or Chomskyans—too many of the former to list. It is not only that the various oppositional approaches to language are more amenable to the study of literature but also that the study of literature is more amenable to an oppositional approach to language. Indeed, the study of literature often seems to be a breeding ground for oppositional approaches to language. In these circumstances it is often difficult, and in any case largely unnecessary, to distinguish innovative theories of literature from theories of language. Are Mikhail Bakhtin and Kenneth Burke literary critics who also write about language, or counterhegemonic linguists who also write about literature, or—the usual solution—"philosophers" who write about both?

Still, mainstream linguistic theories have been applied to the study of literature both by literary critics interested in linguistics and by linguists interested in literature. The latter group has been concerned primarily to assimilate literary studies to linguistic methodologies, hence also to assimilate the literary text to stable abstract forms amenable to linguistic description (see, e.g., Geoffrey N. Leech, *A Linguistic Guide to English Poetry,* 1969; and Roger Fowler, *Linguistic Criticism,* 1986, and *Literature as Social Discourse: The Practice of Linguistic Criticism,* 1981). The computational study of literature, or quantitative STYLISTICS, is an extreme form of this approach (see Robert L. Oakman, *Computer Methods for Literary Research,* 1984). The former group, literary critics interested in linguistics, is methodologically more eclectic, largely because it has tended to plunder linguistics for specific methods and incidental insights, often with indifference toward or even a systematic deconstruction of the hegemonic assumptions on which the linguistic analysis was originally predicated. (For examples and further discussion, see ÉMILE BENVENISTE, NOAM CHOMSKY, DECONSTRUCTION, JACQUES DERRIDA, JULIA KRISTEVA, JACQUES LACAN, FERDINAND DE SAUSSURE, SEMIOTICS, and SPEECH ACTS.)

One of the most interesting trends in contemporary language study, often neglected in discussions of language and linguistics, is the nondiscriminatory usage movement, or what has been branded by its opponents as leftist language hygiene, the imposition of "politically correct" forms on "natural" usage (see, e.g., Mary Vetterling-Braggin, ed., *Sexist Language: A Modern Philosophical Analysis,* 1981; and Francine Wattman Frank and Paula A. Treichler, eds., *Language, Gender, and Professional Writing: Theoretical Approaches and Guidelines for Nonsexist Usage,* 1989). Given the normative antiprescriptivism of mainstream linguistics, the prescriptive thrust of the campaigns against sexist, racist, classist, ageist, and other discriminatory usage has aroused a good deal of ire among conservatives, who insist that generic "he," "man," and "mankind," for example, are ideologically "neutral," that they are just examples of the way the English language happens to work, not part of a concerted program to exclude or denigrate women. The argument is that people who employ such usages in their speech are not sexist; they are simply adhering to the rules of "correct" or "standard" English. The flaw in this argument is evident in the implicit assumption that discriminatory usage is "normal," new nondiscriminatory usage therefore "deviant": the "antiprescriptivism" of so-called descriptive linguistics only prohibits overt prescriptions, overt attempts to force people to use or avoid certain words or phrases. Covertly, descriptive linguistics remains prescriptive in its hegemonic refusal to "describe" (or even, in extreme cases, to recognize the existence of) any usage that lies outside a "standard" rule-governed linguistic system (any local or idiolectal usage, all speech, all linguistic innovation, oneiric and other irrational discourse, etc.). Thus, linguistic "descriptivism" authorizes a conservative tolerance for the status quo and resistance to all change; and it protects this conservatism by refusing to recognize that language is ever ideologically charged. Language, in this line of thinking, is simply a formal sign system, not a repository and instrument of social power relations and attitudes. Feminist linguists in particular are beginning to dislodge this hegemonic set of assumptions, both in their specific social programs—the eradication of sexist discourse—and in their attempts to forge a new linguistic "descriptivism," attentive to the ideological saturation of language, and thus also of all language users (see, e.g., Kristeva; and Eleanor Kuykendall, "Feminist Linguistics in Philosophy," in Vetterling-Braggin).

It may be, in fact, that mainstream linguistics is already being "corrupted" or "contaminated" by the oppositional forces it has long excluded from serious study, that as more and more feminists and masculists and gay men and lesbians and black activists and Marxists become linguists and retain (and infect their scholarship with) their commitments to ideological awareness and social change, the mystificatory Platonism of mainstream linguistics is already eroding and will continue increasingly to erode. Formal linguists who deny the centrifugal complexity and ideological saturation of local usage are quickly becoming a beleaguered minority among twentieth-century students of language; and it may be that as the more holistically minded majority gradually expand their sphere of methodological influence, the schisms between hegemonic and counterhegemonic linguists will increasingly be resolved in a new and broader linguistics, a linguistics that is attentive to all the complexities of language use.

Douglas Robinson

See also RHETORIC.

St. Augustine, *On Christian Doctrine* (427, trans. D. W. Robertson, Jr., 1958); J. L. Austin, *How to Do Things with Words* (1962, ed. J. O. Urmson and Marina Sbisà, 2d ed., 1975); Mikhail Bakhtin, "Discourse in the Novel" (1934–35, trans. Caryl Emerson and Michael Holquist, *The Dialogic Imagination: Four Essays*, ed. Holquist, 1981); Kenneth Burke, *A Rhetoric of Motives* (1950), *The Rhetoric of Reli-*gion: *Studies in Logology* (1961); Noam Chomsky, *Aspects of the Theory of Syntax* (1965), *Syntactic Structures* (1957); Jacques Derrida, "Différance," *La Voix et la phénomène: Introduction au problème du signe dans la phénoménologie* (1967, *Speech and Phenomena, and Other Essays on Husserl's Theory of Signs,* trans. David B. Allison, 1973); Michel Foucault, "L'Ordre du discours" (1970, "The Discourse on Language," trans. A. M. Sheridan Smith, *The Archeology of Knowledge and The Discourse on Language,* 1972); Roy Harris and Talbot J. Taylor, *Landmarks in Linguistic Thought: The Western Tradition from Socrates to Saussure* (1989); Martin Heidegger, "Language" (trans. Albert Hofstadter, 1950, *Poetry, Language, Thought,* 1971); Wilhelm von Humboldt, *On Language: The Diversity of Human Language-Structure and Its Influence on the Mental Development of Mankind* (1836, trans. Peter Heath, 1988); William James, *The Principles of Psychology* (1890, 2 vols., 1908); Julia Kristeva, *Desire in Language: A Semiotic Approach to Literature and Art* (ed. Leon S. Roudiez, trans. Thomas Gora, Alice Jardine, and Roudiez, 1980), *La Révolution du langage poétique: L'Avant-garde à la fin du XIXe siècle, Lautréamont et Mallarmé* (1974, *Revolution in Poetic Language,* trans. Margaret Waller, 1984); Jacques Lacan, "The Direction of the Treatment and the Principles of Its Power" (1958, *Écrits,* 1966, *Écrits: A Selection,* trans. Alan Sheridan, 1977); Plato, *Phaedrus* (trans. R. Hackforth, *The Collected Dialogues of Plato,* ed. Edith Hamilton and Huntington Cairns, 1961, rev. ed., 1980); Douglas Robinson, *The Translator's Turn* (1991); Geoffrey Sampson, *Forms of Language* (1975), *Liberty and Language* (1979), *Making Sense* (1980); Ferdinand de Saussure, *Course in General Linguistics* (1916, trans. Roy Harris, 1983); Mary Vetterling-Braggin, ed., *Sexist Language: A Modern Philosophical Analysis* (1981); V. N. Voloshinov, *Marksizm i filosofiia iazyka* (1929, *Marxism and the Philosophy of Language,* trans. Ladislav Matejka and I. R. Titunik, 1973); Ludwig Wittgenstein, *Philosophical Investigations* (trans. G. E. M. Anscombe, 1953, 3d ed., 1967).

LONGINUS

The treatise *Peri Hupsous,* traditionally rendered in English as "On the Sublime," occupies a position unique in the history of literary criticism. It is the sole surviving work of its author, who is known by convention as Longinus but whose very name is in doubt. There is, in fact, no ancient reference to the tractate or sign of its influence, so its history effectively begins possibly a millennium and a half later with the Basel publication by Francisco Robertello in 1554 of the tenth-century manuscript known as the Codex Parisinus (or Parisiensis) 2036, or the Paris MS. Furthermore, there is no consensus regarding its date, which from the Renaissance until quite recently was commonly given as the third century C.E., although on the basis of internal evidence most scholars have reached an uneasy agreement that it is a work of the first century. About the genius of the author and the abiding fascination of his solitary work there has always been considerably more unanimity, however different the uses to which it has been enlisted.

Among the literary criticism of classical antiquity, Longinus's text also stands alone in its tone, technique, and "temperature." For those accustomed to the lecture notes of ARISTOTLE's *Poetics,* the handbooks of the rhetoricians (see CLASSICAL THEORY AND CRITICISM: 2. RHETORIC), or even the urbanity of HORACE, a personal encounter with Longinus—his brilliant citations, close readings, and rapid transitions—can be a shock; for some, those who find in him a displaced contemporary, this can be the "shock of recognition." Part of this effect is a function of Longinus's own style, which on occasion mimetically rises to vie with the styles of authors whom he admires. Thus it was a commonplace of his neoclassical readers, beginning with NICOLAS BOILEAU-DESPRÉAUX, to say that Longinus was himself a prime instance of the quality he celebrates: a writer, in Alexander Pope's formulation, "Whose *own* Example strengthens all his Laws, / And *Is himself* that great *Sublime* he draws" ("An Essay on Criticism," 1711, *The Poems of Alexander Pope,* vol. 1, ed. E. Audra and Aubrey Williams, 1961, ll. 679–80). A generation later, Edward Gibbon wondered in his journal "which is most sublime, Homer's Battle of the Gods, or Longinus's apostrophe . . . upon it" (October 3, 1762, *Journal to January 28, 1763,* ed. D. M. Low, 1929, 155–56). Like the sublime itself, however, this effect is a matter of passages and fragments, a transitory brilliance, since, as a sober modern commentator has observed, the writing of Longinus can be characterized as "at one moment rising to passion, at another collapsing in self-parody" (Walsh 252).

The *Peri Hupsous* also differs in other remarkable ways from the concerns and methods of surviving rhetorical treatises. Its style, range of reference, power of explication, and reversals of conventional oppositions all clearly set it apart from more pedestrian treatments of diction or regional rhetorical effects. Nor does the work observe the conventional genre boundaries. In his citations and comparisons Longinus moves with freedom across prose and verse, with examples drawn from oratory, epic and lyric poetry, drama, history, and philosophy. The discussion of the sublime may also be taken as the first significant example of the comparative spirit at work: Longinus compares style and effect across the linguistic frontier that normally confined Greek critics, comparing the language of Demosthenes and Cicero and citing Hebrew Scripture in apposition to Homer.

The textual history of the *Peri Hupsous* is relatively simple. Of the eleven manuscripts, the tenth-century Paris codex, which also contains portions of Aristotle's *Problemata,* is the eldest and incontestably the best. (The other manuscripts are much later—from the fifteenth and sixteenth centuries—and at least eight clearly descend from the first.) Unhappily, the Paris codex bears a number of grievous wounds; missing leaves at seven points in the manuscript total more than a thousand lines. Since several of these lacunae occur at critical points in the argument, the "silences" of the treatise, inviting readers' imaginative extrapolations, have been almost as influential in the work's reception as what Longinus actually does say. On the question of authorship, the Paris codex does not shed much light, although it does account for several of the earlier, fanciful attributions. The manuscript gives the author as "Dionysius Longinus," with a space between the two names; in the table of contents this is repeated with a scribal insertion in another hand of "or" between the names. Consequently, the work was early attributed either to Cassius Longinus, the third-century rhetorician and ill-fated counselor of Queen Zenobia, or to the influential Augustan rhetorician Dionysus of Halicarnassus. On the basis of internal historical evidence and, in the latter case, style and precept, both attributions fail to command any credibility. (More recently, noting the author's familiarity with the Hebrew Scripture and Philodemus of Gadara as well as some lexical clues, attempts have been made to associate him with the milieu of Philo Judaeus, who according to this argument may be the "certain philosopher" engaged in the last chapter. To attribute the work to a Hellenized Jew at least has the virtue of beginning to explain the pervasiveness of the author's metaphorics of light—in the manner of Philo—and the resonance of his striking citation in the ninth chapter of the Creation lines from Genesis 1. [See Philo's *On the Account of the World's Creation Given by Moses.*])

The title of the work demands some commentary. *Peri Hupsous,* "on elevation" or "on sublimity," clearly is not intended as a discussion of "the high style" in the tradition common to many ancient critics of a rhetoric of stylistic gradation (e.g., High, Middle, and Low). In fact, some of the most striking examples cited by Longinus are precisely cases of the "plain style." He is concerned, rather, with certain distinctions of conception and expression, with the sources and effects achieving a state of elevation that he calls "transport" (*ekstasis*, in the quite literal sense of being "carried outside" oneself). This sublimity is a quality not easily stabilized, since Longinus variously associates it with the inspired author, the "excited" text itself, and the impact transmitted to the audience. What is clear throughout the work, however, is that the consequences of *hupsos* are irresistible and lend themselves to a rhetoric of astonishment *(ekplexis)* and domination.

Like so many works of literary criticism, Longinus's treatise begins with a polemical issue. In the first few sentences, addressed to his "studious young friend," Posthumius Terentianus, the author takes exception to an earlier treatment of his subject by Caecilius of Calacte, noting its inadequacies in method and literary judgment. After observing that his predecessor's treatment was "too trivial" *(tapeinoteron)* for the subject at hand, Longinus identifies a more fundamental defect: that Caecilius has "failed to grasp the main points" and offers too little of the "usefulness" *(orpheleia)* that it is the critic's duty to supply. The statement that "we should examine whether any of my observations are useful [*khresimon*] to men in public life [*politikoi andres*]" would seem to suggest a rhetorical or even forensic context for what follows, although as D. A. Russell observes in his 1964 edition, *politikos* is a word of many nuances. At all events, superficially it establishes a fairly conventional rhetorical goal against which much of the rest of the treatise (and its examples) will struggle. Thus, almost immediately, in his definition of sublimity as "a certain excellence and distinction in expression," Longinus begins to subvert the oratorical focus by adding that *hupsos* is the sole "source" from which "the greatest poets and historians have acquired their preeminence and won for themselves an eternity of fame." Moving to pragmatics, he suggests the moral and psychological bases of his subject and departs further from the rhetorical model with the assertion that "the effect of elevated language is not to persuade the hearers, but to entrance them; and at all times, and in every way, what transports us with wonder [*ekplexis*] is more telling [*aei kratei*] than what merely persuades or gratifies us." Arguing, moreover, that a single phrase can reveal genius, he contrasts the normal concerns of rhetorical composition (inventive skill, the proper order and disposition of material), which must be developed "by slow degrees" throughout the "whole texture" of the work, with the "well-timed stroke of sublimity [that] scatters everything before it like a thunderbolt and in a flash reveals the full power of the speaker over his audience." The second chapter proceeds to the question whether there is "an art [*tekhnē*] of the sublime." This introduces the recurrent tension between nature/genius and culture/craft that plays through the treatise.

Chapters 3–5 consider the various defects that militate against the achievement of *hupsos:* first, tumidity or bombast, "the most difficult to guard against," "a desire to outdo the sublime"; second, puerility, "the complete antithesis of grandeur," "a thought that is pedantically elaborated until it tails off into frigidity"; and third, false sentiment [*parenthyrsus*], "misplaced, hollow emotionalism where emotion is not called for," or "immoderate passion where restraint is what is needed." Longinus concludes that all these defects arise from a common cause: the contemporary craze for novelty of thought.

Chapters 6 and 7 are devoted to identifying some marks of the "true" *hupselon* (introducing a new tension between the true and false sublime). The true sublime by means of "some innate power" "uplifts our souls." The power of sublimity is transmitted to the audience: "we are filled with a proud exaltation and a sense of vaunting joy, just as though we had ourselves produced what we had heard." Furthermore, the true sublime survives the tests of use and of universality: it can "stand up to repeated examination"; and it is both irresistible and memorable, pleasing "all men at all times" *(semper ubique).*

Chapter 8 is crucial for the deployment of Longinus's argument [*pragmatikon*]. He lists the five sources of the *hupsos,* all of which "have as a common foundation the command of language." They proceed more or less temporally from the initial conception to final synthesis. The first two are, as Longinus observes, largely a matter of natural or innate talents, while the last three sources fall within the domain of art or craft [*tekhnē*]. The sources are: the ability to conceive great thoughts; the stimulus of powerful and inspired emotion; the appropriate formation of certain kinds of rhetorical figures of thought and of speech; nobility of diction, including the proper choice of words and handling of metaphor; and composition, that is, word order, rhythm, and euphony, in a suitably elevated manner. The rest of the chapter sketches how Longinus plans to proceed with the rest of his treatise. Chapters 9–15 are devoted to the first two sources of sublimity, the initial one now described as "nobility of the soul."

In the tenth chapter Longinus proposes another route to the *hupsos,* through the selection and organization of material. Here the set-piece is Sappho's *phainetai moi* ode (which has been preserved through Longinus's text). Dealing with a private, nonheroic lyric and an emotion that carries the speaker to the brink of death, he explores the drama of the "undoing" of the poet's body in the very act that "embodies" the poem in the selection and fusion of the emotions. The entire experience of her "scattered body" is thus recuperated in the unity of the effect on the audience. Chapters 11 and 12 deal with "amplification," "language that invests the subject with grandeur," which Longinus finds ineffective without a sense of the whole and the element of sublimity, and in chapters 13 and 14 he discusses imitation as a means to the *hupsos*. Chapter 15 concludes this section on high thinking and high feeling with a discussion of *phantasía*, imagery and the power of the imagination, in both the orator and the poet.

The discussion of figurative language [*skhemata*] occupies the largest section of the surviving part of the text, chapters 16–29. The tropes considered, a very partial list compared with ordinary rhetorical manuals, are nearly all related to grammatical abnormalities or perturbations of the verb. The section begins with the analysis of a successful figure, the adjuration of the "Marathon oath" in the *De Corona* of Demosthenes (which had surfaced at the end of the preceding section). Faced with the crushing defeat at Chaeronea, Demosthenes deflects his audience's attention to "those who stood the shock at Marathon." As Neil Hertz has observed, Longinus strategically courts danger along with the orator: by making Demosthenes' technique explicit, the critic comes close to turning the effect (the conflation of victory and defeat) into a sublime conjuring trick. The figures discussed in the remaining chapters in the section—rhetorical questions, asyndeton (the omission, for effect, of conjunctions), polysyndeton (a multiplying of conjunctions), hyperbaton (transposition of words out of normal order), and polyptoton (repetition of words in different syntactic inflections)—all work because they express *emotion.*

The fourth source of sublimity, nobility of diction, is discussed in chapters 30–38 (along with a well-known digression on flawed masterpieces). In chapter 30, introducing the proper choice of diction, the point is made that "thought and diction are . . . mutually interdependent," and returning to a familiar metaphor, words properly used "are the light of thought." Chapters 33–36 constitute an extended digression on the superiority of works of "flawed genius" over those of "flawless mediocrity" before the treatise returns to the general topic of the fourth source with a discussion of comparisons and similes. The fifth source of the sublime, composition or the disposition of material, concerns word order, rhythm, and euphony and is covered in chapters 39–42. Chapter 43, which deals with low and undignified ex-

pression, seems to stand outside the general plan of the treatise.

Chapter 44, the final one, is a brief essay on the "decay of eloquence" and its causes, a favorite topic of first-century authors from the rhetoricians to Petronius. Longinus casts this chapter in the form of a dialogue with "a certain philosopher" who finds the causes in political despotism and universal peace. Longinus characteristically advances more "personal" reasons for the decline: moral decay of individuals, enslavement to the love of pleasure and gain, a pervasive "materialism." He proposes to "move on to the next problem, that is, the emotions, which I have previously promised to treat as the main topic of a separate work, for they seem to me to share a place in literature generally, and especially in the sublime." At this point the manuscript breaks off in the last of its several lacunae.

While there are no surviving references to the *Peri Hupsous* in the classical West nor any other voice that sounds remotely like his, there are some interesting parallels to his enterprise in a remarkable prose poem on "the art of letters" written several centuries later in China, during the early Tsin dynasty, by the maverick poet, scholar, and reluctant warrior Lu Chi [Lu Ji]. His *Wen Fu* (302 C.E.) is a sustained reflection on the creative sources and discipline of great writing. Like Longinus, he draws eloquently on the poetry of his predecessors, turning with "strong feeling" from the book to the process of writing. And he too recognizes the paradox of the literary critic, who must sustain his discussion in the same medium (and often at the same level) as the authors he is citing. While Lu Chi stresses reason rather than transport in the poetic process, he insists that an author cannot achieve mastery in the art of writing unless he has both a great conception [*yi**] and intense emotions [*ch'ing**].

As already noted, one of the strange distinctions of Longinus has been his extraordinary power to elicit responses from very different readers holding very different critical assumptions. The neoclassical critics praised his judicial and rhetorical address, his judgment and his "laws." The generation of SAMUEL TAYLOR COLERIDGE found in him a champion of "intensity" and self-constituting expression. In the twentieth century, Elder Olson, a latter-day Aristotelian and one of the CHICAGO CRITICS, has reconstructed Longinus's "argument" to square it with the more orderly procedures of the *Poetics,* while in the 1980s Longinus was rediscovered as a profoundly subversive reader of a deconstructive sort (as in Neil Hertz's reading) or a forerunner of enunciation theory (as in Suzanne Guerlac's).

We can only sketch here in briefest outline the trajectory of Longinian reception. (Tracing the variations on the theme of the sublime from the eighteenth century to such late-twentieth-century critics as Thomas Weiskel and Frances Ferguson would alone require an ambitious essay.) In the midst of the Renaissance debates about Aristotle's *Poetics*, Horace's *Ars Poetica*, revived Platonism, and the "Quarrels," Longinus was a slow starter. Robertello's 1554 *editio princeps* was followed in the next year by a more reliable edition from Manutius in Venice; this was supplemented by an influential Geneva edition from Franciscus Porta in 1569. Eventually, Longinus began to pass from the hands of scholarly humanists to those of more general readers. A Latin translation was published in 1612 by Gabriel de Petra, and the first English translation, by John Hall, was published in 1652.

The appearance in 1674 of Boileau's preface to and translation of the *Peri Hupsous* (published in the same volume as his own *Art poétique*) marked a major turn in the treatise's reception. Boileau obviously recognized certain affinities of tone and precept in Longinus, and he managed to translate these effectively not only into his version of the *Peri Hupsous* but into his own poetry and criticism as well. In response to issues raised by other scholars, he revised and supplemented the *Remarques* that were originally attached to the translation. The more informal *Réflexions critiques sur quelques passages du rhéteur Longin,* which he published much later in two installments (1694 and 1713), are more loosely connected to the text but display considerable sympathy with its salient points. Both Longinus and Boileau in their discussions of the poetic process shuttled comfortably back and forth between cause and effect. Boileau saw pleasure and not transport as the aim of his own poetry, and he was abstract and judicial at precisely the points where Longinus was concrete and demonstrative. But by practice as well as precept Boileau shaped the neoclassical version of Longinus, who was more rhetorician than enthusiast.

JOHN DRYDEN as poet-critic carried this image into English criticism, where many Longinian aphorisms became community property. In the next generation, Pope retailed a number of these in his *Essay on Criticism* (1711) and in addition to praising Longinus produced a witty and malicious contemporary satire in the guise of a parody of the *Peri Hupsous*—his *Peri Bathous: or Martinus Scriblerus, His Treatise of the Art of Sinking in Poetry* (1728). Another Augustan of somewhat weightier gait, John Dennis, was parodically known as "Sir Tremendous Longinus" for his Longinian attitudes: an essentially conservative critic in many respects, he still preached that the

emotions are primary, genius and passion are innate, figurative discourse is the "natural Language of the Passions," and so on (see *The Advancement and Reformation of Modern Poetry*, 1701, and *The Grounds of Criticism in Poetry*, 1704). Later in the century, Bishop Lowth, in his *Lectures on the Sacred Poetry of the Hebrews* (1753, delivered 1741–50), championed the notion of "poetry" as the heightened language of emotion. Again, "new rhetoricians" such as Hugh Blair also identified with the Longinian notion that poetic discourse imitates and evokes the passions. Discourses on genius and originality also reverted to the dictum "Sublimity is the echo of a noble mind." (M. H. ABRAMS in *The Mirror and the Lamp* has traced the roots of Romantic expressive theories to a number of eighteenth-century lamp-lighting Longinians.) The general drift through the century was from a "rhetorical," pragmatic Longinus to an "expressive," greatsouled one.

Perhaps the most important eighteenth-century issue derived from the *Peri Bathous* is the opposition of the beautiful and the sublime, which concerned thinkers from EDMUND BURKE to IMMANUEL KANT. This is a large topic that must be pursued elsewhere; Frances Ferguson gives a provocative survey of both the empirical (Burke) and transcendental (Kant) lines of development and demonstrates how the issue of the sublime informs much contemporary critical debate.

The English Romantics, who inherited the earlier drift toward an expressive aesthetic, recognized in Longinus certain affinities, largely focused on the "criterion of intensity," which assumed that the highest quality of style invests only a *brief passage* (as in EDGAR ALLAN POE); that the *fragment* bursts on the auditor with the effect of intensity, shock, and illumination; and that we recognize the sublime not analytically but through the experience of transport [*ekstasis*]. John Keats struck the characteristic note when he wrote in a letter that "the excellence of every Art is its intensity" (December 21, 1817, *The Letters of John Keats, 1814–1821,* ed. Hyder Edward Rollins, 2 vols., 1958, 1:192). Among the Victorians the trace of Longinus is harder to discern, but he clearly anticipates MATTHEW ARNOLD's qualitative "touchstones" and many of WALTER PATER's remarks on style. In the twentieth century, readers with an eye for such things have noted some family resemblances between Longinus and critics as different as M. M. BAKHTIN and WALTER BENJAMIN.

HAROLD BLOOM has identified SIGMUND FREUD as "the last great theorist" of the sublime mode and, linking it to narcissism and repression, proclaims Freud's essay on "Das Unheimliche" (1919) "the only major contribution that the twentieth century has made to the aesthetics of the Sublime" (101). Bloom, himself a major Longinian revisionary of our time, identifies strongly with a canon of "personalist critics" descending in an Oedipal line from the *Peri Hupsous,* but he reserves for Freud a central place in the dynamics of influence, repression, and "crossings."

Over the past four centuries Longinus's text has thus found echoes in many critics and readers; that these echoes have not been identical is but one function of the complexity (some would say the duplicity) of his argument. It is also a gauge, *semper ubique,* of its author's genius to stimulate the minds and move the passions of his readers.

Richard Macksey

See also NICOLAS BOILEAU-DESPRÉAUX, BRITISH THEORY AND CRITICISM: 2. LATE EIGHTEENTH CENTURY, EDMUND BURKE, and CLASSICAL THEORY AND CRITICISM: 2. RHETORIC.

Longinus, *Del sublime* (ed. C. M. Mazzucchi, 1992), *On Sublimity* (trans. D. A. Russell, 1965), *On the Sublime* (trans. W. Rhys Roberts, 1899, 2d ed., 1907), *On the Sublime* (ed. D. A. Russell, 1964).

M. H. Abrams, *The Mirror and the Lamp: Romantic Theory and the Critical Tradition* (1953); J. W. H. Atkins, *Literary Criticism in Antiquity: A Sketch of Its Development,* vol. 2, *Graeco-Roman* (1934); Harold Bloom, *Agon: Towards a Theory of Revisionism* (1982); Paul Crowther, *The Kantian Sublime: From Morality to Art* (1989); Frances Ferguson, *Solitude and the Sublime* (1992); Paul H. Fry, *The Reach of Criticism: Method and Perception in Literary Theory* (1983); G. M. A. Grube, *The Greek and Roman Critics* (1965); Suzanne Guerlac, "Longinus and the Subject of the Sublime," *New Literary History* 16 (1985), "The Sublime in Theory," *MLN* 106 (1991); Neil Hertz, "A Reading of Longinus," *The End of the Line: Essays on Psychoanalysis and the Sublime* (1985); Murray Krieger, *Ekphrasis: The Illusion of the Natural Sign* (1992); Demetrio St. Marin, *Bibliography of the "Essay on the Sublime"* (1967); Samuel H. Monk, *The Sublime: A Study of Critical Theories in Eighteenth-Century England* (1935); *The Sublime and the Beautiful: Reconsiderations,* special issue, *New Literary History* 16 (1985); Elder Olson, "The Argument of Longinus' 'On the Sublime,'" *Critics and Criticism: Ancient and Modern* (ed. R. S. Crane, 1952); Allen Tate, "Longinus," *Lectures in Criticism* (ed. Elliott Coleman, 1949); George B. Walsh, "Sublime Method: Longinus on Language and Imitation," *Classical Antiquity* 7 (1988); Thomas Weiskel, *The Romantic Sublime: Studies in the Structure and Psychology of Transcendence* (1976).

LUKÁCS, GEORG

Georg Lukács (1885–1971) was a politically committed thinker with a lifelong talent for aligning himself with small, oppositional, and inevitably doomed political factions. By contrast, his aesthetic, critical, political, and philosophical writings have had a marked and often decisive effect on Western Marxist and post-Marxist critical theory. The FRANKFURT SCHOOL, genetic STRUCTURALISM, and more indirectly, poststructuralism and cultural materialism are all considerably in his debt.

Lukács attended Budapest University, where he joined radical intellectuals in bringing education and theater to the workers, and between 1909 and 1917 he studied in Berlin and Heidelberg. Here his work was influenced by George Simmel, Heinrich Rickert, Wilhelm Dilthey, Emil Lask, Erwin Szabó, Georges Sorel, Max Weber, G. W. F. HEGEL, and KARL MARX AND FRIEDRICH ENGELS. In these years, Lukács wrote (in German) his best known pre-Marxist works, *Soul and Form* (1911) and *The Theory of the Novel* (1916), as well as the posthumously published *Heidelberger Äesthetik,* and he laid the foundation for his *Literatursoziologie.*

Diverse though they are in philosophical affiliation, Lukács's principal pre-Marxist works all explore aspects of a schema he outlined in *History of the Development of Modern Drama* (1907): "Economic and cultural relations—world view—Form (in the artist as an a priori of creation)—Life as Formed   Public (here again the causal sequence: world view—economic and cultural relations)." In *Soul and Form* he examines the ways in which genres ("a priori forms") transform life into art ("Life as Formed") and why traditional forms are incompatible with modern life. In *History of the Development of Modern Drama* and in *Theory of the Novel* he considers literary form as an expression of a world-view or ideology that grows out of economic and cultural relations or out of the writer's experience of them, and he tries to show why different literary forms grow up in different periods of social development. And in the *Heidelberger Äesthetik* he is concerned with, among other things, the way literary form acts as "the bearer of adequate communication" between writer and public, while permitting "normative misunderstandings" in the reception of works.

In 1918 Lukács joined the Hungarian Soviet, serving during its short life as minister of culture and education and almost immediately becoming deputy leader of the Party's "left Communist opposition," later known as the Landler faction. In exile in Vienna during the 1920s, he drafted the controversial Blum Theses, which argued for soviet-based democracy in the Party, and wrote *History* and Class Consciousness (1923). History and Class Consciousness assumed that the proletarian revolution was "on the agenda of world history" and used "the standpoint of the proletariat" for a far-reaching critique of the reification of bourgeois society and of positivist science. Reification means that "a relation between people takes on the character of a thing, and thus acquires a phantom objectivity" (83). Well before the rediscovery of Marx's Economic and Philosophical Manuscripts of 1844, this book elaborated the Hegelian dimension of Marxism and made alienation a central category of analysis. And in a period when what revisionists saw as economism prevailed, it insisted that by puncturing the false consciousness of the proletariat and raising critical consciousness, theory could produce revolutionary practice and become a material force capable of transforming society. History and Class Consciousness was attacked by the Party; the Blum Theses were ignominiously rejected; and in 1929 Lukács was obliged to practice self-criticism. But the book became a seminal text for European left-wing intellectuals. Lukács's more orthodox book on Lenin, which Gareth Stedman-Jones has described as "a classical expression of the materialist conception of the socialist revolution" (54), has not had the same impact.

During the 1930s and the war years, most of which he spent in Russia, Lukács worked for the Popular Front against Fascism and intervened in a heated debate in the Communist party about the form and function of proletarian literature. Against the Proletcult line (which became Party Orthodoxy), which held that literature is a class product and an instrument in the hands of the dominant class that must be used, under Party directives, for the organization and education of the masses, Lukács argued (with Trotsky and the Russian Association of Proletarian Writers) that literature provides critical understanding of underlying social and historical processes by revealing hidden causalities and inherent contradictions. Attacking the crude tendentiousness, the stereotyped characters, and the "reportage" he thought socialist realism shared with naturalism, Lukács urged proletarian writers to learn from bourgeois realists such as Walter Scott, Honoré de Balzac, Leo Tolstoy, and Thomas Mann to portray society critically by showing typical characters wrestling with social conflicts during historical periods of transition. Lukács is perhaps most widely associated today with his advocacy of critical realism and his attacks on socialist realism, naturalism, modernism, and stream-of-consciousness techniques in Studies in European Realism (1930s), The Historical Novel (1937), Essays on Realism (1948), Realism in Our Time (1958), and Solzhenitsyn (1964).

Lukács has been widely criticized for having "refused the way of the martyr" and for having submitted to Stalinism. At the same time, careful examination of such writings as The Young Hegel (1938), Goethe and His Age (1945), and The Destruction of Reason (1946–49), which Lukács described as "theoretical masquerades," shows that during the period of Stalinism, he was practicing veiled writing and painfully examining his Marxist premises. His defense of Marxism after the war in his polemic with JEAN-PAUL SARTRE, Existentialisme ou Marxisme (1948), suggests that he had decided to remain faithful to Marxism because he saw it as the only alternative to fascism and to ideological and historical nihilism and because he could still justify Marxist theoretical work to himself by the hope that, as he wrote in The Young Hegel, "once the realm of ideas has been revolutionized, reality cannot hold out" (506).

Lukács returned to Hungary in 1945 in the wake of the Red Army. While Matthias Rakosi, Stalin's pupil and emissary, was courting the country, Lukács was a member of the Hungarian Academy of Sciences and professor of aesthetics and philosophy at Budapest University. During 1949, when Rakosi Stalinized Hungary, the "Lukács debate," in which Lukács was attacked by key Party officials for his democratic and humanist views and for his theory of realism, served to underline the turnabout in political and cultural policy. With Imre Nagy and the Petofi Circle, Lukács opposed Rakosi and prepared the Hungarian Revolution of 1956, during which he served as Nagy's minister of culture and as a member of the Party's central committee. After the suppression of the Hungarian Revolution, Lukács was deported to Rumania and expelled from the Communist party, to be reinstated before his death. In these years, Lukács worked on a vast, systematic Marxist aesthetic, Die Eigenart des Ästhetischen [The specificity of the aesthetic] (1963), and on a multivolume Marxist ontology, Zur Ontologie des gesellschaftlichen Seins [Toward an ontology of social being] (1971), neither of which he managed to complete. These works have been entirely ignored in the West.

Despite continuities, Lukács's writings are not all of a piece, and the theoretical impact of his work has varied according to which of his writings have been appropriated. In some of his pre-Marxist works and in History and Class Consciousness, Lukács used Simmel's notion of abstract sociological form to establish correspondences between the "economic forms of society," its "cultural forms," its "forms of expression," and its literary forms and to show that the same ideology or world-view manifests itself in different ways in all strata of social life. This homological approach was adopted by some members of the Frankfurt School and by genetic structuralism and was still being used, to some effect, by Marxist "ideology critics," such as Terry Eagleton, in the 1970s.

In the same works, Lukács argued that the objectification of all aspects of production, its alienation from producers, the reification of social relations, the quantification and depersonalization of culture, and the rational calculation practiced by bureaucracy subject individuals in capitalist society to systems of relations that seem to operate according to their own laws, independently of anyone's will or control. He also criticized positivist social and natural science for "uncritically" accepting "the nature of the object" as given and for reflecting "the manner in which data immediately present themselves" (*History* 7) and thus for accepting the status quo and acting as an apologist for capitalist society. Elaborated by the Frankfurt School into an analysis of advanced capitalism and into a critique of instrumental reason, and later translated into a theory of language, this view of society as an impersonal, reified system operating independently of individuals and subjecting them to its constraints has dominated poststructuralism and the recent "return to history."

Although he is often identified with the Marxist theory of reflection, Lukács never subscribed to that theory as it is generally understood. He believed that knowledge of objective reality is possible, but only if it goes beyond the reflection of immediate reality (which for him characterizes positivist science and descriptive naturalist literature). He argued that mimesis is not photographic and that "to go beyond this immediacy can only mean the genesis, the creation of the object" (*History* 155). Lukács emphasized the active role of the subject both in constructing knowledge of the real world and in transforming objective circumstances. He argued that theory has a radical, transformative role to play in society and in history. And after the failure of the Hungarian Revolution, he argued that creative intellectual work is the only form of work that enables workers to overcome their alienation from themselves, from their world, and from other people. In many of these respects, Lukács prefigures poststructuralism and cultural materialism.

Lukács never believed that the critic's role is to elucidate the "real meaning" of literary works. In *Soul and Form* he argued that the critic uses literature to ask ultimate questions about life. In his Marxist essays he used the concept of "doing it without knowing it" to make novels say what he wanted them to say rather than what their authors might have been supposed to be saying.

And in his late aesthetic he fictioned a history of the development and separation of art, science, magic, and religion from primitive human labor as an act of "combative humanism," to show that humanity always makes itself. Lukács must have been among the first critics this century to have said "Too bad for the facts."

Bertolt Brecht, with whom Lukács had several confrontations, criticized the "utopian and idealistic element" in his work. Methodologically, this utopian and idealistic element manifested itself in Lukács's emphasis on totality and in his insistence that realist literature constructs a coherent, nonalienated human world by relating everything back to man and by creating meaningful connections between people and things and between interiority and exteriority. It also manifested itself, as Mihailo Markovic has pointed out, in Lukács's tendency to construe "ought" as if to some extent it already is, as well as in his tendency to show ideals as end products of existing trends. But Lukács was not completely simpleminded about his ideal of wholeness. He argued, much as Pierre Macherey and Etienne Balibar argued after him, that realist fictions measure the real against an ideal that is "always and never there in reality" in such a way as to show the limits and deficiencies of extant ideologies and modes of being. And he looked to literary and theoretical demonstrations that all aspects of the social totality interrelate to mend what he perceived to be the principal evils of society in his time: fragmentation, alienation, overspecialization, and anomie.

Whether we want to admit it or not, the interrelationship of all aspects of culture and history remains the presupposition of all interdisciplinary and intertextual approaches that "transgress" boundaries, indicate differential relations, and give us an overall picture of the pervasiveness of dominant patterns of language and thought. And utopianism of one sort or another has become inseparable from left-wing thought since communism failed to realize the Marxist dream of the good society even in one country: one has only to think of Ernest Bloch, WALTER BENJAMIN, THEODOR W. ADORNO, and Max Horkheimer and of the more plural, decentered, and "incommensurable" utopias of French poststructuralism and cultural materialism.

No seminal thinker has been attacked more than Lukács, both by those in the Party whose bad faith he showed up and by those who fed off his ideas and were ashamed to own it. Criticism of Lukács has become a cheap shot. It would be fairer to remember Lukács as a thinker who found that he was obliged to "give up political activity and concentrate on ideological impact" and for whom every essay was "the first step towards a never-to-be-achieved revolution."

Eve Tavor Bannet

See also KARL MARX AND FRIEDRICH ENGELS and MARXIST THEORY AND CRITICISM.

Georg Lukács, *Essays über Realismus* (1948, *Essays on Realism,* ed. Rodney Livingstone, trans. David Fernbach, 1981), *Geschichte und Klassenbewusstein: Studien über Marxistische Dialektik* (1923, *History and Class Consciousness,* trans. Rodney Livingstone, 1971), *Gespräche mit Georg Lukács* (1967, *Conversations with Lukács,* ed. Theo Pinkus, trans. Hans Heinz Holz, Leo Kofler, and Wolfgang Abendroth, 1975), *Goethe und seine Zeit* (1947, *Goethe and His Age,* trans. Robert Anchor, 1968), *Der junge Hegel* (1948, *The Young Hegel,* trans. Rodney Livingstone, 1976), *Labour* (trans. David Fernbach, 1980), *Political Writings, 1919–29: "The Question of Parliamentarianism" and Other Essays* (ed. Rodney Livingstone, trans. Michael McColgan, 1972), *Record of a Life: An Autobiographical Sketch* (ed. Istvan Eörssi, trans. Rodney Livingstone, 1983), *Die Seele und die Formen* (1911, *Soul and Form,* trans. Anna Bostock, 1974), *Solzhenitsyn* (1969, trans. William David Graf, 1970), *Studies in European Realism* (trans. Edith Bone, 1950), *Die Theorie des Romans* (1916, *Theory of the Novel,* trans. Anna Bostock, 1971), *A történelmi regeny* (1947, *Der historische Roman,* 1955, *The Historical Novel,* trans. Hannah Mitchell and Stanley Mitchell, 1962), *Wider den missverstandenen Realismus* (1958, *Realism in Our Time: Literature and the Class Struggle,* trans. John Mander and Necke Mander, 1964), *"Writer and Critic" and Other Essays* (trans. Arthur D. Kahn, 1970), *Die Zerstörung der Vernunft* (1954, *The Destruction of Reason,* trans. Peter Palmer, 1981).

Andrew Arato and Paul Breines, *The Young Lukács and the Origins of Western Marxism* (1979); J. M. Bernstein, *The Philosophy of the Novel: Lukács, Marxism, and the Dialectics of Form* (1984); Lucien Goldmann, *Lukács and Heidegger* (trans. William Q. Boelhower, 1977); Agnes Heller, ed., *Lukács Reappraised* (1983); Fredric Jameson, *Marxism and Form: Twentieth-Century Dialectical Theories of Literature* (1971); François H. Lapointe, *Georg Lukács and His Critics: An International Bibliography with Annotations, 1910–1982* (1983); George Lichtheim, *George Lukács* (1970); Michel Löwy, *Georg Lukács: From Romanticism to Bolshevism* (trans. Patrick Camiller, 1979); Istvan Meszaros, *Lukács' Concept of Dialectic* (1972); David Pike, *Lukács and Brecht* (1985); Tom Rockmore, ed., *Lukács Today: Essays in Marxist Philosophy* (1988); Gareth Stedman-Jones, "The Marxism of the Young Lukács," *Western Marxism: A Critical Reader* (1978); Eve Tavor, "Art and Alienation: Lukács' Late Aesthetic," *Orbis Litterarum* 37 (1982).

LYOTARD, JEAN-FRANÇOIS

Jean-François Lyotard (b. 1922) has produced a series of writings on philosophy, politics, and aesthetics that are remarkable for their engagement with DECONSTRUCTION, psychoanalysis, and Marxism. Lyotard's *oeuvre* may be characterized as a struggle with the problem of discourse, whether in contradistinction to vision, or as the field of philosophical, aesthetic, and political experimentation, or as the site of a discussion of the problem of justice with enormous ramifications for the justice of all discourse studies.

Phenomenology (*La Phénoménologie,* 1954, trans. Brian Beakley, 1991) is the product of an early discipleship of Maurice Merleau-Ponty, a discipleship that perhaps determines Lyotard's concern with perceptual as well as discursive aesthetics and his abiding interest in the avantgarde's refiguration of the two. A discussion of the next 17 years, which Lyotard spent on the fringes of heterodox Marxism, may be found in *Peregrinations* (1988). *Discours, figure* (1971), Lyotard's longest work, is an attempt to consider post-Saussurean orthodoxies in an analysis of the aesthetics of difference that underlay all "deconstructive" thought. The book sets up a series of oppositions, of which the master trope appears to be the paradoxical positive deployment of difference in opposition to opposition. Within this framework, the irreducible difference of the figural is opposed to the reductive systematic divisions of the textual or discursive. This is at one level an important corrective to a certain form of textualism derived from the structural linguistics of FERDINAND DE SAUSSURE, which sought to ignore reference by reducing it to an effect of the tabular system of oppositions that constitute the structuralist account of language. Lyotard, in a series of plausible analogies (to optics, modernist painting, psychoanalysis, etc.), insists that language also activates a vertical function of designation that is heterogeneous to signification and cannot be reduced to an effect of the horizontal system of opposed linguistic terms, but relies on the difference of the referent from the system, on the opacity of the sign rather than the transparency of the signifier (see LINGUISTICS AND LANGUAGE and STRUCTURALISM).

However, Lyotard is not engaged in any simple return to the reality of things, since the density of objects, which exceeds the flatness of textual space, itself inhabits what he calls "figural space." The density of things is not a reality opposed to the artificiality of texts, since things escape textuality not by virtue of a real identity, which texts do not possess, but insofar as their difference cannot be reduced to a simple set of conceptual oppositions (e.g., that of the sensory real to the textual fiction) such as texts are able to signify through the oppositional structuring of linguistic terms. Despite appearances, the book is not so much a defense of the figural against the real as it is a deconstruction of the analysis of signification that forms the basis of the early work of deconstructive thinkers such as PAUL DE MAN and JACQUES DERRIDA. The work of the book is thus to move from the analysis of oppositions to their deconstruction. Its force lies in the disruption of the binary oppositions that it identifies, in a constant finding of the incommensurate presence of the figural in the textual, and vice versa.

Économie libidinale (1974) and *Des dispositifs pulsionnels* (1973) represent Lyotard's assault on the three most powerful models of critical practice in the 1970s—the Lacanian model of desire as lack, Marxist dialectics, and the semiotic analysis of signification—in an attempt to produce an affirmative model of the economy of signification and of politics and to rebut the charge of nihilism so often leveled at poststructuralist thought. These works are at times a satirical meditation upon the question of how the work of undermining humanist conventions performed by "deconstruction" might prove more than merely the theoretical negation of the empirical, a question that itself troubles the place of theory. (See JACQUES LACAN, MARXIST THEORY AND CRITICISM, and SEMIOTICS.)

The importance of the experimental in Lyotard's work may be gauged from the two extended accounts he has provided of the routes discourse might take to move beyond the limitations of metaphysics—the terrorism of truth—without itself falling into the complacency of a metalanguage, without claiming to offer a modular theory that would seek to guarantee itself by appeal to a supra-discursive reality. He has named these two potentialities the "postmodern" and the "pagan": each attempts to challenge the metanarratives of modernism and to reorganize knowledge as a series or patchwork of "little narratives," which make no claim to finality, which do not seek to put an end to narration. In *Instructions païennes* (1977) and *Rudiments païens: Genre dissertatif* (1977) he supplies an analysis of narrative, and in *The Postmodern Condition* (1979, trans., 1984) and *Le Postmoderne expliqué aux enfants* (1986) he provides an account of epistemic production that relates directly to the problem of the grounding of critical discourse. These works attempt to break with the model of theory as providing a meta- or "grand" narrative for the study of discourse, to work through the paradox of a theoretical denial of theory. Attention in this respect should also be

lent to Lyotard's own literary experiments in *The Pacific Wall* (1979, trans., 1990) and *Récits tremblants* (1977), as well as to his writings on various contemporary artists, such as *Que peindre?* (1987). (See POSTMODERNISM.)

Lyotard's more recent works, *Just Gaming* (1979, trans., 1985), *The Differend* (1988), and *Heidegger and "the jews"* (*Heidegger et "les juifs,"* 1988, trans. Andreas Michel and Mark S. Roberts, 1990), rephrase the problem of the subject and the praxis of experimentation in terms of ethics, in an attack on a mimetic theory of justice, to open what is potentially the most fruitful contemporary field of speculation on the problem of discourse. The refusal of a mimetic theory of justice or of representation has the most far-reaching implications for the politics of interpretation. How are we to do justice to texts after Auschwitz has introduced a horror that exceeds representation, that must be neither forgotten nor remembered (represented to consciousness as one more event among others)? The justice of an interpretation thus depends upon the rethinking of reading as a singular ethical-political act (a kind of rewriting) rather than as an attempt to mirror the text read. As readers, we write after rather than about texts, seeking to link phrases to them that will best testify to their irrepresentable difference, the singularity of their demand to be read, their differend.

Bill Readings

See also FRENCH THEORY AND CRITICISM: 6. 1968 AND AFTER.

Jean-François Lyotard, *La Condition postmoderne: Rapport sur le savoir* (1979, *The Postmodern Condition: A Report on Knowledge,* trans. Geoff Bennington and Brian Massumi, 1984), *La Différend* (1983, *The Differend: Phrases in Dispute,* trans. G. Van den Abbeele, 1988), *Discours, figure* (1971), *Économie libidinale* (1974, *Libidinal Economy,* trans. Iain Hamilton Grant, 1992), *L'Inhumain: Causeries sur le temps* (1988, *The Inhuman: Reflections on Time,* trans. Geoff Bennington and Rachel Bowlby, 1991), *The Lyotard Reader* (ed. Andrew Benjamin, 1989), *Peregrinations: Law, Form, Event* (1988), *Political Writings* (trans. Bill Readings with Kevin Paul Geiman, 1993), *Le Postmoderne expliqué aux enfants* (1986, *The Postmodern Explained,* ed. and trans. Julien Pesaris and Morgan Thomas, trans. Pesaris et al., 1992), *Que peindre? Adami Arakawa Buren* (2 vols., 1987); Jean-François Lyotard and Jean-Loup Thébaud, *Au juste: Conversations* (1979, *Just Gaming,* trans. Wlad Godzich, 1985); Jean-François Lyotard et al., *La Faculté de Juger* (1985).

L'Arc 64 (1984, special issue on Lyotard); Andrew Benjamin, ed., *Judging Lyotard* (1992); Geoffrey Bennington, "Lyotard: From Discourse and Figure to Experimentation and Event," *Paragraph* 6 (1985), *Lyotard: Writing the Event* (1988); David Carroll, *Paraesthetics: Foucault, Lyotard, Derrida* (1987); *diacritics* 14 (1984, special issue on Lyotard); Bill Readings, "The Deconstruction of Politics," *Reading de Man Reading* (ed. Lindsay Waters and Wlad Godzich, 1989), *Introducing Lyotard: Art and Politics* (1991); Maureen Turim, "Desire in Art and Politics: The Theories of J.-F. Lyotard," *Camera Obscura* 12 (1984).

M

McLUHAN, MARSHALL

Herbert Marshall McLuhan (1911–80) spent most of his career as a professor of English literature at the University of Toronto, where he established the Centre for Culture and Technology, a center still operative after his death. His reputation was established by *The Gutenberg Galaxy* (1962) and *Understanding Media* (1964), both books arguing that Western civilization had reached a watershed in the twentieth century as profound as that of the Renaissance itself. In this "epochal" analysis of historical process McLuhan's voice was one among many in the 1960s, and it was swallowed up in the popular cultural movement. McLuhan has come to be remembered mostly as part of that movement. Both the movement and McLuhan have in the late 1980s experienced something of a revival in the academy.

In fact, although he permitted himself to be carried along in its wake, McLuhan did not belong to the counterculture movement of the 1960s. His sources were literary modernism, the Cambridge of F. R. LEAVIS (McLuhan received his doctorate from Cambridge), NEW CRITICISM (esp. Cleanth Brooks), and, more remotely, German idealistic historiography and the notion of *Zeitgeist*. He took a very strong historicist position, asserting that "the 'civilized' man is—whether crude or stupid—a man of strong visual bias in his entire culture, a bias derived from only one source, the phonetic alphabet" (*Gutenberg* 108). He contrasted the visual bias of what he called alphabetic man to the "aural" (or later "tactile") bias of nonalphabetic man and maintained that the electronic twentieth century was returning to those archaic cognitive modes: "The visual makes for the explicit, the uniform, and the sequential in painting, in poetry, in logic, history. The non-literate modes are implicit, simultaneous, and discontinuous, whether in the primitive past or the electronic present" (*Gutenberg* 57).

McLuhan represents a North American strain of cultural relativism deriving most particularly from Edward Sapir and Harold Innis. Innis was a University of Toronto political economist whose *Bias of Communication* (1951) discriminated between the temporal bias of Egyptian culture (exemplified by its concentration of monumental sepulchers) and the spatial bias of European culture (exemplified by colonization and the technology of travel). Innis's contribution was the perception that cultural biases, or "fore-structures," can be "read off" the technology of a society. Sapir's influence came to McLuhan through the anthropologist E. S. Carpenter (the two edited *Explorations* collaboratively). Carpenter's principal "discovery" was the indifference of the Eskimo to spatial orientation, which he argued was a consequence of orality and a relatively featureless visual environment. Edward Sapir (who worked for ten years in Ottawa for the National Museum of Canada) had observed that distinct linguistic communities possessed distinct and incommensurable cognitive realms. Carpenter merely extended that relativistic and reflexive principle to spatial orientation. These two men gave McLuhan his touchstones for cultural analysis: technology of communication (alphabetic writing, print, and the electronic media) and cognitive organization founded upon either visual/spatial organization (linear, sequential, and perspectival), on the one hand, or auditory organization (spherical, simultaneous, and immanent), on the other. His association of the latter with both prealphabetic orality and the postprint electronic age achieved a folding of the archaic into the avant-garde—an anachronistic move that anticipated some features of poststructuralism.

During his heyday McLuhan was perceived as a cultural relativist or historicist in the manner of Lucien Lévy-Bruhl (*Les Fonctions mentales dans les sociétés inférieures,* 1910), Oswald Spengler (*Untergang des Abenlandes,* 1918), and T. S. ELIOT ("The Metaphysical Poets," 1921). Like them, he adopted an epochal view of history, identifying cultural watersheds and placing one relatively close to the present. What marks McLuhan apart from these thinkers—as well as from FRIEDRICH NIETZSCHE and MARTIN HEIDEGGER—is his location of the cause of cultural change in technology rather than in general culture, religion, epistemology, ideology, or history itself. He maintained that the technology of linguistic inscription generated profound cultural shifts by altering the "sensory balance":

If a technology is introduced either from within or from without a culture, and if it gives new stress or ascendancy to one or another of our senses, the ratio among all of our senses is altered. . . . Tribal, non-literate man, living under the intense stress on auditory organization of all experience, is, as it were, entranced. (*Gutenberg* 24)

This remark contains the essence of McLuhan's originality: the notion that cognitive processes themselves reflect the processing properties of our sensory organs, particularly of the two symbolic organs, the ear and the eye.

McLuhan's special subject was print, more than the larger issue of alphabetization. He argued that the invention of moveable type greatly accelerated and intensified the kinds of cultural and cognitive changes already begun in Greece with the perfection of the alphabet. Print greatly simplified the alphabetic sign, permitting the complete divorce of eye and ear in the phenomenon of silent reading. Consequences of print culture included the decline of dialogue that Walter J. Ong had already documented (*Ramus: Method and the Decay of Dialogue,* 1958). Individualism, democracy, Protestantism, capitalism, and nationalism are all said to be consequences of the distancing medium of print. Clearly McLuhan claimed too much for a single factor in cultural change, but his "probes" have had some enduring effect on historiography. A major study investigating the defensibility of McLuhan's sweeping claims for print is Elizabeth L. Eisenstein's *The Printing Press as an Agent of Change* (1979), but she documents only social, professional, and pedagogic effects, avoiding the more controversial claim of cognitive effects.

McLuhan's strong claims for the consequences of print and the alphabet are a mirror image of JACQUES DERRIDA's argument a decade later for the priority of writing over speech. Where McLuhan saw alphabetization as destroying the tribal world of dialogue and face-to-face contact, Derrida sees the Christian privileging of the spoken over the written word as generating a "logocentrism," to which he attributes the same centralizing, hegemonic properties that McLuhan attributes to print culture.

McLuhan's popular fame rested on his prophecy that the age of print was coming to its close. In *Understanding Media* he argued that radio and the phonograph had given Western culture back its ear and would inevitably produce a cognitive shift back toward sphericality, simultaneity, and participation—toward "cool" values as opposed to the "hot" values of the print culture. These terms were borrowed from the world of jazz. "Cool"

meant easygoing, impersonal, dispassionate, abstract, and slow tempo, while "hot" meant involved, ego-centered, passionate, sensuous, and fast tempo. McLuhan adopted "cool" to mean nonsubjective, or "tribal." To be cool was to be submerged in a social and cultural collectivity. Electronic mass media like radio and television qualified as cool partly because networks were anonymous corporations representing no point of view. Print media were hot because they were fragmented (McLuhan read the front page as a mosaic) and represented "points of view" or editorial biases.

McLuhan's principal exemplars of the new culture were the works of James Joyce and Ezra Pound, in which linearity, sequentiality, and external point of view were suppressed, and the intellectual and moral principles of the counterculture, according to which participation, simultaneity, and sphericality were practiced in a perception of the world as a "global village" (McLuhan's phrase), where everyone's business was everyone else's responsibility. His attitude to the counterculture of the 1960s, however, remained ambivalent. Like his audience, he was somewhat seduced by the perception that he could explain the tremendous social, political, and cultural turmoil of post–World War II Europe and America, but unlike Timothy Leary he did not embrace the counterculture.

Few have followed McLuhan very far on his strongest claim: that the privileging of the eye in the technology of writing and printing brought about a broad cultural and cognitive shift typified by Western logic, philosophy, and science and contrasted to the tribal or primitive world. However, he found some support in the precedent work of Walter J. Ong, Milman Parry, and Albert A. Lord (whose *Singer of Tales* was published just two years before *Gutenberg Galaxy*) and a contemporaneous ally in Eric A. Havelock's *Preface to Plato* (1963). Although these scholars represent a common approach to cultural history, they worked independently of one another and did not form any sort of school.

Television proved to be something of an Achilles heel for McLuhan. In order to maintain his theory that the electronic age would reconstitute the archaic world of orality, he had to incorporate television into his oral and acoustic cognitive model. Unhappily, although television was like radio in that it was an electronic mass medium, it was inescapably visual. McLuhan was driven to argue that the television image, because of its poor resolution, paradoxically reinforced oral values. To cover the difficulty presented by television, he began to contrast visual values to "tactile" ones instead of to oral or auditory ones. "Tactility" became his label for everything previously attached to the acoustic, and it was confusingly attributed to visible artifacts that had poor resolution and no vanishing point and that privileged color over chiaroscuro and projection, such as mosaics and the television image. This later stage of his development is represented in the collaborative work *Through the Vanishing Point* (with Harley Parker, 1968).

There are also affinities between McLuhan's style of cultural commentary and those of the roughly contemporaneous essays of ROLAND BARTHES (esp. those collected in English in *Mythologies* and *The Eiffel Tower*) in that it involved "reading off" the tacit message of apparently nonsymbolic cultural phenomena. For example, McLuhan explained the popularity of the Volkswagen "Beetle" by pointing to the intimacy of its "wrap-around" space, an intimacy allegedly much desired by cool, post-print, electronic man. His prose style was also highly gnomic and playful (both linguistically and typographically), like that of Barthes, Derrida, and their disciples. However, McLuhan's style is derived from Joyce and Pound rather than directly from Nietzsche and Stéphane Mallarmé.

McLuhan has not been blessed with any prominent disciple, nor has his work founded a school of criticism such as that which grew out of the work of his colleague at the University of Toronto, NORTHROP FRYE.

Leon Surette

See also ORALITY AND LITERACY.

Marshall McLuhan, *The Gutenberg Galaxy: The Making of Typographic Man* (1962), *The Interior Landscape: The Literary Criticism of Marshall McLuhan* (ed. Eugene McNamara, 1969), *Letters of Marshall McLuhan* (ed. Matie Molinari, 1987), *The Mechanical Bride: Folklore of Industrial Man* (1951), *Understanding Media: The Extensions of Man* (1964); Marshall McLuhan, with E. S. Carpenter, *Explorations in Communication: An Anthology* (1960); Marshall McLuhan, with Harley Parker, *From Cliché to Archetype* (1970), *Through the Vanishing Point* (1968).

John Fekete, *The Critical Twilight: Explorations in the Ideology of Anglo-American Literary Theory from Eliot to McLuhan* (1977); Arthur Kroker, *Technology and the Canadian Mind* (1984); Philip Marchand, *Marshall McLuhan: The Medium and the Messenger* (1989); Jonathan Miller, *McLuhan* (1971); Raymond B. Rosenthal, *McLuhan: Pro and Con* (1968); George Sanderson and Frank MacDonald, *Marshall McLuhan: The Man and His Message* (1989); Gerald E. Stearn, ed., *McLuhan: Hot & Cool* (1967).

MALLARMÉ, STÉPHANE, AND FRENCH SYMBOLISM

It is no accident that references to the literary ideas and example of Stéphane Mallarmé (1842–98) abound in contemporary literary criticism and theory. The great French poet's notoriously refined aestheticism and fervent devotion to language led him to expound a view of literature and literary meaning that profoundly influenced the modernist avant-garde from Symbolism through surrealism and on into postmodern cultural theory. Mallarmé's firm belief in the self-sufficiency and self-referentiality of literary language, to which his own eccentric, stylistically innovative poetry and prose attested, came to fruition most dramatically in the STRUCTURALISM and poststructuralism of the 1960s and 1970s in France. Mallarmé was a favorite of both ROLAND BARTHES and MICHEL FOUCAULT, whose own stylistic achievements compared favorably with his. The controversial French psychoanalyst JACQUES LACAN frequently invoked Mallarmé, and what many took to be the obscurantist style of the former was attributed in no small part to the latter's influence. One of JACQUES DERRIDA's most influential essays, "The Double Session," is a deconstructionist reading of Mallarmé's brief prose fragment "Mimique." In her early work, JULIA KRISTEVA upheld Mallarmé, along with the comte de Lautréamont (1846–70), as an exemplary figure in the development of a subversive modernist "revolution" in poetic language.

As a result of the immediate influence of these and other theorists, a new generation of critics on both sides of the Atlantic has returned to Mallarmé, producing an impressive array of books and essays that increasingly present him as a vital force in a postmodern literary culture reverberating, a full century later, with his enigmatic pronouncements. In a very real sense, Mallarmé's influence remains greater today than it was in his own lifetime, limited as it was to a small, devoted circle of friends and admirers.

Stéphane Mallarmé was a relatively obscure English teacher employed by a series of lycées. His evenings were devoted largely to poetry, typically sonnets and other short poems but also the prose poem genre he, along with Arthur Rimbaud (1854–91), inherited from CHARLES BAUDELAIRE (1821–67) and continued to refine. Mallarmé also produced critical treatises and even brought out, single-handedly, a women's fashion magazine *(La Dernière Mode)* during the period of 1874–75. With the exception of his voluminous correspondence, his complete works comprise a single substantial volume in the standard Pléiade edition. Regarded since his death as one of the greatest poets in the French language, Mallarmé is remembered for a handful of poems marked by uncommon beauty, intelligence, and often baffling linguistic complexity.

After years of teaching in lycées throughout France, Mallarmé secured a position in Paris and moved his family there in 1871. He gradually befriended a circle of prominent fellow poets, such as Paul Verlaine (1844–96) and, much later in his life, PAUL VALÉRY (1871–1945), as well as the painters Edouard Manet (1832–83), Edgar Degas (1834–1917), Berthe Morisot (1841–95), James McNeill Whistler (1834–1903), and Odilon Redon (1840–1916). In the last years of his life, Mallarmé and his friends formed the habit of gathering at the poet's home each Tuesday evening for discussions, or perhaps one should say monologues, wherein Mallarmé would hold forth, omnipresent cigarette in hand, on the aesthetic topics that most concerned him. Much of what we know of these *Mardis* was recounted by Valéry. The ideas Mallarmé expressed to his friends, in conversation and in letters, on the subject of poetry and aesthetics in general were to have a profound impact on *fin-de-siècle* French culture, particularly on the artistic movement known as Symbolism.

Both representing and transcending the limits of French Symbolism, Mallarmé can be seen as one of the most significant figures in a process of transition in the modern development of poetic meaning and the role of the poet. "Symbolism," a suspiciously tidy label for a host of complex and contradictory aesthetic tendencies, yokes together the successive attempts of Baudelaire, Mallarmé, Rimbaud, and Verlaine to redefine the poetic task, previously viewed as one of conveying powerful emotional states or of crafting art as an end in itself, as one of forging a separate symbolic reality by means of densely coded subtle sensations perceptible only to a select readership uncompromised by the banality of bourgeois tastes.

The Symbolists reacted against the *l'art pour l'art* emphasis of the so-called "Parnassian" school of the mid-nineteenth century, as well as against positivism and literary naturalism, in favor of impressionistic, contemplative preoccupation with powerful symbols and their effects on consciousness. Baudelaire's poetry was the first to explore these often private symbols, selected for their ability to produce what he would call "synaesthesia," or the tendency for one sensory experience (such as a color) to evoke another (such as a sound) related with it. With this goal in mind, he sought to broaden the scope of metaphoric and metonymic language in order

to elevate sensory experience to the level of intellect, fueling it yet remaining separate. Whatever the enduring power or aesthetic appeal of the symbols, however, Baudelaire's poetry still remains close to the late Romantic, subjective sensibilities that produced it.

As Symbolism continued to develop in French poetry, the personal, subjective stance of the poet could nevertheless be glimpsed through the forest of symbols that proliferated around it. Of all the poets who worked within the Symbolist tradition inaugurated by Baudelaire, Mallarmé appears to have devoted the greatest energy to populating a symbolic universe whose inhabitants bore few obvious traces of their poetic creator. Perhaps this is why many critics and historians of French Symbolism regard him as the Symbolist *par excellence,* for all of Symbolism's diverse tendencies. In recent years, as preoccupation with symbols has given way to analysis of linguistic signs and multiple effects of signification, poststructuralist fascination with and emphasis on Mallarmé has changed the way we view Symbolism. Whereas earlier generations of critics mined Mallarmé's *oeuvre* for telltale symbols that offered clues to his personal and poetic preoccupations, poststructuralist approaches have explored the dense textuality of Mallarmé's writings in order to advance a poetics of literary signification.

Where Baudelaire had been content to generate poetic symbols that retained an obvious link to his personality, Mallarmé, beginning with the very poem in which he rendered homage to Baudelaire ("Le Tombeau de Charles Baudelaire"), expressed the wish for his own poetic "death," in terms of suppressing his personal voice in favor of a sacrificial opening up to language. Mallarmé's symbolism was thoroughly rooted in language. He believed in the pure essence of words and a poetic ideal of such dazzling immediacy that words need serve no referential purpose beyond their placement in the text. His frequent expression of this poetic credo cannot fail to spark a knowing response in readers steeped in postmodern literary theory, and yet his was a thoroughly classical view, harking back to PLATO's vision, discussed in the dialogue *Cratylus,* of the absolute unity of language with the real objects it would designate.

In his most ambitious and experimental writings, Mallarmé created an intensely visual, nonreferential style that, for all its "Cratylan" idealism, appears to anticipate recent concepts of the "materiality" of the signified, in need of no validation outside the text. Nearly a century before DECONSTRUCTION would refuse any reality beyond the text, Mallarmé was to declare that "tout, au monde, existe pour aboutir à un livre" ("everything in the world exists in order to end up in a book"), one of many such Mallarméan statements that encourage a cult-ish fetishization of the literary work of art.

After 1866, very near the time of "Le Tombeau de Charles Baudelaire," Mallarmé, at work on his great poem *Hérodiade,* saw his poetic task as one of breaking from the Parnassian emphasis on representation of objects and moving toward a poetic language that could portray the effects of objects on the poet's consciousness. In his words: "Peindre, non la chose, mais l'effet qu'elle pro-duit." What recent critical emphasis on language or dis-course helps us to appreciate is the extent to which Mal-larmé's creative labors led him to a poetics of language's effects per se. He came to feel that it was his poetic responsibility to "yield the initiative to the words" *(céder l'initiative aux mots).* While he may have articulated this view out of his belief in the power of words to contain true meaning, for the contemporary critic his move ap-pears to solicit the multiple, even contradictory effects of literary signification, especially as it becomes rather pointless, if not impossible, to declare with any degree of certainty what Mallarmé's own most challenging texts may "mean."

Increasingly Mallarmé's poems, such as the late poems "Prose pour Des Esseintes" and the boldly experimental "Un Coup de dés," refer not to a representable world or to the poet's own consciousness but to themselves, or most radically to the act of writing and the unstable character of black marks on white page—what Rimbaud had designated *l'alchimie du verbe* ("the alchemy of the word"). Moreover, Mallarmé, for all his faith in the in-herent immediacy of poetic meaning, forced a radical separation between the aural, bardic sense of poetry and the silent arrangement of marks on the page that con-stitutes the written poem. In "Un Coup de dés" [A roll of the dice], the work that preoccupied Mallarmé during the last years of his life, the bizarre configuration of the words of the poem on the page mimic both the roll of dice across a table *and* the reader, regularly turning pages, in the act of reading. The poem has become a visual artifact, albeit an unstable one. For these reasons, it has been better elucidated by recent critics preoccupied with the multiple effects of written language than by earlier practitioners of NEW CRITICISM, who treated the poem as a complete, stable entity.

Paul Valéry, discussing his regular attendance at the legendary Mallarméan *Mardis,* remarked that Mallarmé spoke and acted as if he himself had invented language. Mallarmé's strong convictions and ideas about language dominate his later poetry, beginning, according to Rob-ert Greer Cohn, with his "first truly hermetic poem," "Ses purs ongles très haut dédiant leur onyx," or the

"Sonnet in *yx.*" Published in 1887 (although incubating since the 1860s), this sonnet would appear at first glance to be "about" his lover's attractive fingernails, yet the rhyme scheme that makes use of words ending in *yx* (e.g., "onyx" and the strangely non-French "ptyx") allows the verbal play to take over, so that the poet's fascination with stubborn consonant sounds displaces the represen-tational function of poetic language. Indeed, Mallarmé had begun to declare open rebellion against mimetic language and representation per se. This preoccupation with consonants was also a feature of his *Les Mots anglais* (1877), one of the prose works of this dedicated Anglo-phile. Using the phrase introduced by Roland Barthes, we would say today that the "Sonnet in *yx*" is a *scriptible* (writerly) text, its unprecedented material elements in-viting us to remake it playfully in the act of reading.

In "Prose pour Des Esseintes" (1885), words that would appear to designate objects are metamorphosed into hy-brid forms that could only be found in the silent play of language within consciousness. Thus "irises" merge with "ideas" to form *iridées,* a new kind of linguistic way sta-tion located somewhere between the world of flowers and the world of ideas. In his essay "Crisis in Poetry," Mallarmé seemed to pen a kind of poetic manifesto, one that contained the celebrated proclamation "Je dis: une fleur! . . . l'absente de tous bouquets" ("I say: a flower! . . . the one absent from every bouquet"). Much as his *iridées* are objects found only in poetic language, Mallarmé seems here to refer to an effect unique to the act of reading, the only way to glimpse or savor a flower *l'ab-sente de tous bouquets* of our accustomed daily experience.

Viewed from the perspective of recent textual criti-cism, this becomes a way of stating that literature pro-vides sensory experiences that are distinct from, yet no less real than, lived human experience. One thinks per-haps of René Magritte's realistic painting of a pipe, with its paradoxical caption *Ceci n'est pas une pipe* (which translates as "This is not a pipe"), a blunt and startling reminder of the distinction between "reality" and repre-sentation. Or it may be analogous to the paradoxes of Lacanian psychoanalysis, where language can only im-perfectly serve to express frustrated desire for the unat-tainable object. Even more recently, the flower able to bloom only within a reader's consciousness must seem to be a manifestation of the Derridean "trace," the de-layed detonation that can only occur beyond the hear-ing range of an ethereal presence.

In poem after poem, Mallarmé's fascination with sky, foam, lace, or fog seems metaphorically to express a sense of the impermanence of language, its tendency to dissolve or be transformed into new elements. Edmund

Jabès (1912–91), a contemporary French poet who expressed his considerable debt to Mallarmé, remarked that he used to wonder why the words in a book did not get all jumbled up during the night while the book was closed. This seemingly whimsical observation conveys rather neatly Mallarmé's own fascination with language that is as delicate and impermanent as foam settling onto a beach.

Such willingness to view written language in this way helps to explain the importance of Mallarmé for contemporary critical theory, especially the work of Jacques Derrida and the deconstructionist criticism he has inspired. Those convinced by Derridean advocacy of "writing" in opposition to speech and presence, with the many textual operations that are seen as undercutting or subverting linear narrative, stable meanings, and ethereal control, are tempted to view Mallarmé as a poststructuralist *avant la lettre*. Recently, this has also been true of new FEMINIST THEORY AND CRITICISM, as the search for an alternative feminist written discourse has emerged. Such a discourse is viewed by some feminist theorists as necessarily in opposition to what is seen as a patriarchal ideology of authorial mastery and fixed meanings. One of the critical strategies for exposing this has been metaphorically to equate the female body with a celebration of the open-ended textuality of writing, as opposed to the "phallic" would-be mastery of male authorship. Mallarmé has been cited as a masculine writer who nevertheless evolved a differently gendered approach to writing more in keeping with a would-be feminist alternative. Whatever the merits of these or other contemporary uses of Mallarmé, it is safe to say that he has come into his own during the late twentieth century.

James A. Winders

See also BRITISH THEORY AND CRITICISM: 5. SYMBOLISM.

Stéphane Mallarmé, *Mallarmé: Prose Poems, Essays, and Letters* (ed. Bradford Cook, 1956), *Oeuvres complètes* (ed. Henri Mondor and G. Jean-Aubry, 1945), *Selected Letters of Stéphane Mallarmé* (ed. and trans. Rosemary Lloyd, 1988), *Selected Poetry and Prose* (ed. Mary Ann Caws, 1982).

Maria L. Assad, *La Fiction et la mort dans l'oeuvre de Stéphane Mallarmé* (1987); Harold Bloom, ed., *Stéphane Mallarmé: Modern Critical Views* (1987); Malcolm Bowie, *Mallarmé and the Art of Being Difficult* (1978); Steven M. Cassedy, *The Flight from Eden: The Origins of Modern Literary Criticism and Theory* (1990); Robert Greer Cohn, "Mallarmé on Derrida," *French Review* 61 (1988), *Toward the Poems of Mallarmé: Expanded Edition* (1980); Jacques

Derrida, "The Double Session," *Dissemination* (trans. Barbara Johnson, 1981); Roger Dragonetti, *Un Fantôme dans le kiosque: Mallarmé et l'esthétique du quotidien* (1992); Gérard Genette, "Au défaut des langues," *Mimologique: Voyage en Cratylie* (1976); Barbara Johnson, "Mallarmé as Mother: A Preliminary Sketch," *Denver Quarterly* 18 (1984); Julia Kristeva, *La Révolution du langage poétique: L'Avantgarde à la fin du XIXe siècle: Lautréamont et Mallarmé* (1974, *Revolution in Poetic Language,* trans. Margaret Waller, 1984); Virginia A. La Charité, *The Dynamics of Space: Mallarmé's "Un Coup de dés jamais n'abolira le hasard"* (1987); Jean-Pierre Lecercle, *Mallarmé et la mode* (1989); Mary Lydon, "Skirting the Issue: Mallarmé, Proust, and Symbolism," *Yale French Studies* 74 (1988); Kevin Newmark, "Beneath the Lace: Mallarmé, the State, and the Foundation of Letters," *Yale French Studies* 77 (1990); Marshall C. Olds, *Desire Seeking Expression: Mallarmé's Prose pour des esseintes* (1983); Laurence M. Porter, "Mallarmé's Disappearing Muse," *The Crisis of French Symbolism* (1990); Jean-Michel Rabaté, " 'Rien n'aura eu lieu que le lieu': Mallarmé and Postmodernism," *Writing the Future* (ed. David Wood, 1990); Deirdre A. Reynolds, "Mallarmé et la transformation esthétique du langage, à l'exemple de 'Ses purs ongles,'" *French Forum* 15 (1990); Donald Rice and Peter Schofer, "Mallarmé's Clown," *Rhetorical Poetics: Theory and Practice of Figural and Symbolic Reading in Modern French Literature* (ed. Donald Rice and Peter Schofer, 1983); Frederic C. St. Aubyn, *Stéphane Mallarmé* (rev. ed., 1987); Nathaniel Wing, *The Limits of Narrative: Essays on Baudelaire, Flaubert, Rimbaud, and Mallarmé* (1986); *Yale French Studies* 54 (1977, special issue on Mallarmé).

MARX, KARL, AND FRIEDRICH ENGELS

Marxism is commonly associated with politics or political economy. Since many people subscribe to what in the Marxist tradition would be described as a "reified" concept of culture (i.e., a definition according to which literature could have little to do with politics or economics), it can come as a surprise to discover how much attention Marxist theorists have devoted to literature and art. The collected writings of Marx and Engels on literature and art fill two large volumes in the standard German edition, and references to and quotes from literary works abound in all their writings, whatever the subject.

Marxism, the result of the lifelong collaboration of Karl Marx (1818–83) and Friedrich Engels (1820–95), has been variously described as an economic theory, a revolutionary theory, a philosophy of history, and a sociology of capitalism. In recent years, however, it has emerged through the influence of such twentieth-century "Western Marxists" as ANTONIO GRAMSCI, GEORG LUKÁCS, Louis Althusser, RAYMOND WILLIAMS, FREDRIC JAMESON, and Terry Eagleton as an ambitious and comprehensive cultural theory, one that can account for literary creation or aesthetics in relation to capitalist production and consumption, understood always in relation to history. Indeed, insistence on history, on recognizing that social and cultural reality should always be regarded in process, has been one of the most enduring themes of Marxist theory. It would not be possible to claim that Marxism constitutes a theory of literature as such. Moreover, much of the applicability of Marxism to literature and criticism has been demonstrated only relatively recently. Therefore, even in an introductory essay on the origins of Marxist aesthetics and critical theory it will be necessary to refer occasionally to more recent work.

Another vital point to make about Marxism is that it is a thoroughgoing materialism, interpreting human social and historical experience as an encounter with the material realities of the physical world out of which culture has evolved. Culture is inseparable from language, and recent Marxist theorists, engaging advanced linguistic and literary theories, have increasingly come to view language as "material" in a textual sense. Marx in particular developed his critique of capitalism in terms of sensuous human interaction with the natural, material world, of which productive labor was but one example. Marx's theories were by no means limited to political economy. More broadly, Marxism, treating myriad topics and historical examples, became a comprehensive cultural criticism, one as capable of addressing aesthetic questions as it would be of examining political and economic theories. "Ideology" as defined by Marx, Engels, and later Marxists (who increasingly locate ideology in language) is one of the most useful concepts available for linking these seemingly separate spheres.

Marx and Engels viewed the capitalist mode of production as one highly adept at securing its legitimation through the habitual patterns of thought encouraged by the social structures it fostered, such as the division of labor peculiar to the factory system but replicated throughout bourgeois social institutions. "Ideology" would refer to the sum total of the writings, speeches, teachings, pronouncements, beliefs, and opinions that assert the naturalness and desirability of such structures and social practices. Marx and Engels first set forth their concept of ideology in *The German Ideology* (1845), a polemical work

aimed at the neo-Hegelian philosophical school. In it, they attributed the "ruling ideas" of any given historical period to that age's dominant class, but their explanation of the workings of ideology moved beyond simplistic assertions of cause-and-effect relationships between power and ideas, or some one-to-one correspondence between economic forces and cultural trends.

Marx and Engels inherited the Napoleonic sense of ideology as confusion or distraction from the practical realities of everyday life, as opposed to the later use of "ideologies" (still common today) to refer to specific political views or agendas. In *The German Ideology* they began to transform the meaning of "ideology" more toward the sense of "false consciousness," a way of misunderstanding the world and our place in it. What is most important, they suggest the inescapable nature of ideology, that is, that it refers to that which we just do not see, comprehend, or anticipate as we confront the world.

Later Marxist theory expanded this notion (indeed, the phrase "Marxist conception of ideology" invokes a tradition that extends for more than a century after Marx) to examine the ways authors unconsciously reproduce the prevailing ideology of their time. As the word "unconsciously" reminds us, many twentieth-century Marxists have incorporated the insights of Freudian psychoanalysis into their social theory (see SIGMUND FREUD). For literature, the influence of Louis Althusser has been most decisive for the refinement of the concept of ideology found in the work of such recent Marxist aestheticians as Pierre Macherey and Eagleton (see MARXIST THEORY AND CRITICISM: 2. STRUCTURALIST MARXISM). The view that ideology is inescapably present (in fact "inscribed") in any text has been enormously productive for recent Marxist criticism, as well as for much FEMINIST THEORY AND CRITICISM and PSYCHOANALYTIC THEORY AND CRITICISM.

One of Marxism's most original contributions to social and cultural theory has been the concept of "relations" *(Verhältnisse)*, the insistence that nothing in social life can be regarded in static isolation, but must be viewed in mediation *(Vermittlung)* with other social phenomena and forces. To speak about the "worker" is thus to speak also about the employer, about social classes and class conflict, and about behavior, morality, consciousness, and so on. Any one thing or object thus exists within unseen complex networks of social relations. But the English "relations" fails to convey the diachronic, active character of the German *Verhältnisse*. Social relations must, according to Marx and Engels, be understood in dynamic historical process: nothing ever just "is" any more than it exists in isolation from other phenomena. Rather, everything in human societies is in the process of becoming transformed according to an internal dialectical process of negation and synthesis, best summed up by the Hegelian concept of *Aufhebung* (meaning both "canceling" and "conserving") (see G. W. F. HEGEL).

The multiple ways human beings, under capitalism, are alienated from each other, from their own natural characteristics and qualities, and from the products of their labor and creative achievements are subjected to detailed analysis in Marx's early writings. Capitalism produces objects that stand over against (the German *Gegenstand* makes this especially vivid and forceful) the human beings who have become alienated from them and who, and this is important, increasingly fail to recognize them as products of their labor, thus forgetting their history. In volume 1 of *Das Kapital (Capital)*, Marx developed his theoretical examination of the "commodity" at length. "Commodity" was preferable to "product" for Marx, once it referred to the multiple tendencies under capitalism to present the product of alienated industrial labor as something automatic or given, as if it had dropped from the sky so that the capitalist could discover it. Through advertising, especially, the commodity then becomes "fetishized," or made to seem independent from the labor process that produced it. The twentieth-century Hungarian Marxist aesthetician Georg Lukács was the first to develop these insights of Marx into a broad indictment of the multiple tendencies toward "reification" under capitalism, or the tendency to reduce complex historical processes involving human agency to objects or things. It seems significant that a Marxist thinker of a particularly literary bent would be the one to explore this theme.

Marxist criticism means to strike at the heart of the familiar habit of regarding "art" and "literature" as separate, or given, human cultural spheres or domains, since they are understood within internally self-transforming networks of social relations that certainly include the economy or politics. Marxist cultural theory, accordingly, is able to account for the social character of literature as well as consciousness, form, taste, literary history, and tradition. Although literature and art were not the central preoccupations of early Marxism, most of the fundamental themes and concerns of what would come to be known as Marxist literary criticism and theory were present in some form in the writings of Marx and Engels, including opposition to the ways capitalism mystifies the role of the author as well as the literary "product"; the complex relationship between literature and society (not to be reduced to a one-to-one, or reflectionist, rela-

tionship); and, closely related to the previous two, the ideological character of literature, including the ideological effects of the very notion of literature.

Stylistically, the very writings of Marx and Engels can be called "literary." Marx in particular was a brilliant German prose innovator, capable of exploiting that language's propensity for coining new noun forms to maximum effect. Moreover, Marx's writings are sprinkled with literary references and, often, lengthy passages quoted from such authors as Aeschylus, Sophocles, William Shakespeare, and Johann Wolfgang von Goethe. In a section of his *Economic and Philosophic Manuscripts of 1844* devoted to the alienating power of money, Marx reproduces a lengthy passage from Shakespeare's *Timon of Athens* to make his point. What is perhaps most significant, the writings of Marx and Engels defy conventional categorization, a fact of immediate interest in the critical climate that emerged in the 1970s and 1980s, wherein even the notion of literature itself was increasingly subsumed within a more broadly conceived notion of writing.

It is significant that *Die heilige Familie* (1845, *The Holy Family*), the first collaborative work by Marx and Engels, was devoted in part to literary criticism. Engels was more inclined, relatively speaking, toward historical and anthropological writing. Marx was relatively more literary in his enthusiasms, and he was indeed a prodigious reader. As a young man he wrote Romantic poetry, much in keeping with the German philosophic idealism that prevailed in his native Prussia during the early nineteenth century. As a philosophy student he worked on the pre-Socratic Greeks and also gained a lifelong love for the great tragic playwrights, particularly Aeschylus, with whose Prometheus he strongly identified. According to the testimony of his daughter Eleanor, Marx venerated Homer, Shakespeare, Honoré de Balzac, and Walter Scott and would often recite or read aloud to his family from those authors. According to his son-in-law Paul Lafargue, Marx planned, though he did not live to attempt, a comprehensive study of Balzac's *La Comédie humaine*.

Marx's love of literature did not prevent his being sharply critical of the role that bourgeois ideology played in severing intellectual and cultural activities conceptually from the material forces and processes that shape them. The refusal to assent to such abstraction never fails to scandalize anti-Marxists. One of their most persistent criticisms of Marxism has been that it is deterministic, reducing human cultural achievement to the mere "effects" of economic forces or "modes of production." Engels made a point, however, of preferring "conditioning" to "determining," and the reality of his and

Marx's treatment of such topics is much subtler and more complex than anti-Marxists have cared to admit. Marx and Engels did develop a way of theorizing society that distinguished between a material "base" (i.e., the mode of production, or underlying system of economic forces and relations) and a "superstructure" composed of social institutions such as the family, education, religion, politics, and art. But what served Marx and Engels as a convenient schematism was taken much more seriously and dogmatically by later Marxists, particularly in the Soviet Union. This habit of thought, which Lenin himself denounced as "economist," did indeed set up a one-to-one relationship between base and superstructure, with the base, so to speak, "pulling the strings." In literary criticism and theory, this meant a way of reading literary works that sought to demonstrate their economic and social determinants. Marx and Engels only occasionally wrote on literary matters, but when they did, they avoided the crude determinism of which they have sometimes been accused. They demonstrated a sophisticated appreciation and understanding of literature, even as they considered it in relation to other, more obviously "Marxist" topics, such as economic forces or revolutionary politics. Literary critics and theorists of today are increasingly able to appreciate that Marx and Engels were able to handle literary topics well, not in spite of, but *as a result of,* their attention to these "other" concerns. Late-twentieth-century Western Marxism, from the so-called FRANKFURT SCHOOL to the recent work of Jameson, has developed an even stronger (some might argue exclusive) emphasis on aesthetic experience and has increasingly defined itself as cultural criticism.

In the words of the Yugoslav Marxist theorist Gajo Petrovic, Marx saw literature as a "universal-creative, self-creative activity by which man transforms and creates his world and himself" (Prawer 405). Thus it is important to realize that Marx's love of literature did not reproduce the mystical romantic notion of the suffering artistic genius who managed miraculously to produce inspired art. Rather, literary creation for Marx was a particular type of the "sensuous human activity" to which his ongoing discussion of the labor process was devoted. For his part, Engels described art as a highly "mediated" cultural product that could nevertheless be traced to some kind of material base. On such insights were the later cultural theories of Gramsci founded, and more recently semiological critics have expanded the meaning of "material" to include the components or "signifiers" of language itself.

The Marxist critique of bourgeois ideology encompasses the commodity abstracted unnaturally from the social relations of production that generated it and the *objet d'art* treated as a timeless cultural commodity surrounded by its aura of aesthetic refinement. Marx and Engels saw the writer as a worker, even if a highly specialized type. What post-Romantic ideology would ignore, namely, that the writer works for a type of capitalist known as a publisher, they made central to their conception of literature. The writer's labor is alienated, in Marxist terminology, to the degree that payment must be involved and surplus value is expropriated by the publisher as profit. Whereas some students of Marxism, particularly those influenced by Althusser, emphasize the idea of a break between the early writings of Marx, where aesthetic and philosophical themes are emphasized, and later, more "scientific" texts devoted to a critical analysis of the capitalist system, it can certainly be demonstrated that Marx's early work (c. 1843–45) complements and anticipates the mature (c. 1857–83) *Capital.*

From the perspective of later Marxist criticism, including that of Lukács, we can see more easily how Marx's theory of the commodity can be applied to literature. Marxism refuses the Romantic-idealist literary mystique whereby literary creation is all bound up with notions of artistic genius and inspiration, insisting instead on a materialist recognition of the writer's relationship to the publisher and the market. The Marxist critique of "reification" also rejects the austere formalism of NEW CRITICISM and other methods that would locate literary works in some ahistorical realm, refusing, from a Marxist point of view, to acknowledge texts as historical and social products. The literary work must never be reduced to an object, however allegedly pure and perfect according to extreme literary formalists. Recent Marxist critics have argued as well that the very concept of literature has been reified, illustrating the tendency toward compartmentalization and the intellectual division of labor in capitalist society. In the conventional, that is, bourgeois capitalist, view, literature is cut off as a cultural category from political life and therefore can have nothing to do qua literature with politics. Crudely, this characterizes the mainstream "humanist" view of literature, which sees Marxist criticism as guilty, in trying to demonstrate the temporal, social relations that tie literature to our world, of reductionism, or, more specifically for the Marxist tradition, of "reflectionism," that is, assuming that a literary work mirrors its society or that an author speaks automatically for a single class position. A reflectionist criticism would be one that searches a text for clear signs of the political sensibility that formed it and for the duplication through the text of the exact societal structures and ideological errors that gave rise to its authorship.

Such a simplistic and one-dimensional approach has long been abandoned by Marxist criticism, and it is certainly absent from the works of Marx and Engels, yet detractors continue to employ this caricature of a criticism they believe uniquely to be guilty of the sin of "politicizing" literary interpretation. Their own categories and procedures they believe to be politically neutral. From a Marxist point of view, the methods and assumptions of bourgeois critics and aestheticians can easily be shown to provide elaborate support for very specific social relations of capitalism, and the didacticism of which they accuse their Marxist counterparts is finally an eloquent commentary on their own rigidity. Of course, in the 1930s and 1940s, Stalinist "socialist realism" insisted on sentimentalized, heavily didactic works that would put literature in the service of the class struggle. An examination of the specific instances in which Marx and Engels commented upon literary works will reveal that they did not commit the error of reflectionism and that they would not have sanctioned socialist realism. They did not assume that writers were mere mouthpieces for class bias, and they understood the complicated, contradictory ideological effects that often resulted in literature, whatever the author's intention or purpose.

In their most sustained piece of literary analysis, Marx and Engels demonstrated that good fiction does not necessarily result from ideologically "correct" authorial intentions. French writer Eugène Sue's *Les Mystères de Paris,* a *roman feuilleton,* or serially appearing novel (1842–43), that delighted Parisian readers during its gradual appearance, was a work that, from a socialist realist perspective, Marx and Engels "should" have liked. The author's sympathies with workers are made abundantly clear, and the novel gives way near the end to sustained impassioned preaching on their behalf. But it is obvious from their criticism that they found it banal and distasteful.

Their reaction to the novel and its wild popularity occupies the last part of their polemical work *The Holy Family.* This text was primarily devoted to a critique of the speculative idealism practiced by the neo-Hegelian philosopher Bruno Bauer and his circle. Part of their condemnation of these philosophers was that in their hands the intellectual rigor and power of Hegelian thought had degenerated into precisely the kind of cheapened romantic sentimentality exemplified by Sue's novel.

In *The Holy Family* Marx and Engels examine at some length the seductive appeal of Sue's text, including the

way Sue is able to gratify the reader's "baser instincts" while fostering the illusion of noble, uplifting sentiment. The author's professed political sentiments should not be taken at face value. To Sue, who had somewhat suspect political intentions, Marx and Engels contrast Balzac, who was able to produce politically significant fiction in spite of his self-proclaimed monarchist leanings. In this way, Marx and Engels demonstrate a realization that the text may well accomplish something other than what an author might have intended for its readers.

Nothing could be more disastrous, according to Marx and Engels, than an author's use of characters as mere vehicles for specific political ideologies. Engels especially condemned *Franz von Sickingen* (1859), the historical drama by their great political rival Ferdinand Lassalle, for the one-dimensionality of characters designed as mouthpieces for political positions. In a telling assessment of Goethe, Engels expressed admiration for the literary work that expresses its time while at the same time transcending its limitations. This is indeed a far cry from reflectionism. One cannot help but note here that in expressing a preference for literature that "transcends" and that continues to yield new readings, Marx and Engels still clung to a somewhat privileged position for literature from which such later Marxist critics as Raymond Williams have pulled away. And yet, in their insistence on a view of literature that would not separate it from other productive human activities or from history itself, as well as in the subtle sophistication of many of their critical writings, they inaugurated a rich critical tradition that has included Williams, Lukács, and a host of other influential twentieth-century theorists.

James A. Winders

See also MARXIST THEORY AND CRITICISM.

Karl Marx and Friedrich Engels, *Die heilige Familie und Schriften von Marx von Anfang 1844 bis Anfang 1845: Marx/Engels Gesamtausgabe: Erste Abteilung, Band 3* (1970, *The Holy Family or Critique of Cultural Criticism, Collected Works, Volume 4: Marx and Engels: 1844–45,* 1975), *Marx and Engels on Literature and Art* (ed. Lee Baxandall and Stefan Marawski, 1973), *The Marx-Engels Reader* (2d ed., ed. Robert C. Tucker, 1978), *Über Kunst und Literatur: In Zwei Bänden* (ed. Manfred Kliem, 1967–68).

Tony Bennett, *Outside Literature* (1990); George Bisztray, *Marxist Models of Literary Realism* (1978); Terry Eagleton, *Criticism and Ideology: A Study in Marxist Literary Theory* (1976), *Ideology: An Introduction* (1991), *The Ideology of the Aesthetic* (1990), "Marxism and the Future of

Criticism," *Writing the Future* (ed. David Wood, 1990), *Marxism and Literary Criticism* (1976), "Two Approaches in the Sociology of Literature," *Critical Inquiry* 14 (1988); John Frow, *Marxism and Literary History* (1986); Philip Goldstein, *The Politics of Literary Theory: An Introduction to Marxist Criticism* (1990); Fredric Jameson, *Marxism and Form: Twentieth-Century Dialectical Theories of Literature* (1971), *The Political Unconscious: Narrative as a Socially Symbolic Act* (1981), *Postmodernism, or the Cultural Logic of Late Capitalism* (1991); Georg Lukács, *History and Class Consciousness: Studies in Marxist Dialectics* (1971); Cary Nelson and Lawrence Grossberg, eds., *Marxism and the Interpretation of Culture* (1988); Bertell Ollman, *Alienation: Marx's Conception of Man in Capitalist Society* (2d ed., 1978); S. S. Prawer, *Karl Marx and World Literature* (1978); Paul N. Siegel, "The Style of *The Communist Manifesto*," *Science and Society* 46 (1982); Raymond Williams, *Marxism and Literature* (1977).

MARXIST THEORY AND CRITICISM

1. Classical Marxism

KARL MARX AND FRIEDRICH ENGELS produced no systematic theory of literature or art. Nor has the subsequent history of Marxist aesthetics comprised the cumulative unfolding of a uniform perspective; rather, it has emerged, aptly, as a series of responses to concrete political exigencies. While these responses have sometimes collided, they achieve a dynamic and expansive coherence (rather than the static coherence of a finished system) through both a general overlap of political motivation and the persistent reworking of a core of predispositions about literature and art deriving from Marx and Engels themselves. These predispositions include:

1. The rejection, following G. W. F. HEGEL, of the notion of "identity" and a consequent denial of the view that any object, including literature, can somehow exist independently. The aesthetic corollary of this is that literature can only be understood in the fullness of its *relations* with ideology, class, and economic substructure.
2. The view that the so-called objective world is actually a progressive construction out of collective human subjectivity. What passes as truth, then, is not eternal but institutionally created. "Private property," for example, is a bourgeois reification of an abstract category; it does not necessarily possess eternal validity. Language itself, as Marx said in *The German Ideology*,

must be understood not as a self-sufficient system but as social practice (*Marx-Engels Reader* 158).
3. The understanding of art itself as a commodity, sharing with other commodities an entry into material relations of production. If, as Marx said, human beings produce themselves through labor, artistic production can be viewed as a branch of production in general.
4. A focus on the connections between class struggle as the inner dynamic of history and literature as the ideologically refracted site of such struggle. This has sometimes gone hand in hand with prescriptions for literature as an ideological ancillary to the aims and results of political revolution.

To these predispositions could be added, for example, Engels's comments on "typicality," recommending that art should express what is typical about a class or peculiar historical trends (Solomon 67–68). One might also include the problem raised by Engels's granting a "relative autonomy" to art, his comments that art can transcend its ideological genesis and that superstructural elements are determined only in the "last instance" by economic relations (*Correspondence* 475–77). In the general introduction to the *Grundrisse*, Marx too acknowledges, in speaking of the arts, and in particular of Greek art, that "it is well known that certain periods of their flowering are out of all proportion to the general development of society, hence also to the material foundation, the skeletal structure as it were, of its organization" (*Marx-Engels Reader* 245). What, then, is the connection between art and the material base into which its constituting relations extend? Given the inconclusive and sometimes ambiguous nature of Marx's and Engels's scattered comments on art, the proposed solutions to such dilemmas have been as various as the political soils on which they were sown.

As Europe witnessed a widespread nascence of socialist political parties in the later nineteenth century, together with the impact of Marxism on sociology, anthropology, history, and political science, the first generation of Marxist intellectuals included the influential Italian Antonio Labriola (1843–1904), who emphasized the highly mediated connection between economic conditions and artistic products and the causal potential of such products in subsequent economic and superstructural developments. Another star in the firmament of early Marxist theory was Franz Mehring (1846–1919), who, along with Rosa Luxemburg and others, founded the German Communist party in 1918. His writings included the first authoritative biography of Marx, *Karl Marx: The Story of His Life* (1918) and *The Lessing-Legend* (1892–93), which both applied Marxist categories to the analysis of major German literary figures and brought these within the reach of working-class readers. Mehring attempted to situate Marxist thought and aesthetics in necessary relation to the preceding classical German tradition. Another German, Karl Kautsky (1854–1938), was a propagandist for the Social Democratic party and founded in 1883 the prestigious Marxist journal *Die neue Zeit,* a forum for the elaboration of Marx's economic and political thought. In his *Foundations of Christianity* (1908) Kautsky showed how religious ideas are tied to the levels of artistic and industrial maturity allowed by a particular economic substructure.

Georgi Plekhanov (1856–1918), the "father of Russian Marxism," was a founder of the Russian Social Democratic Party. His writings include *Fundamental Problems of Marxism* (1908), *Art and Social Life* (1912), and some shorter pieces, such as *The Role of the Individual in History* (1898). In the last of these he argues that gifted individuals in history, such as Napoleon, appear only wherever social conditions facilitate their development: every talent that acts as a social force is the product of social relations. In *Art and Social Life* Plekhanov notes that an "art for art's sake" tendency arises "where the artist is in disaccord with his social environment" (172). A "utilitarian" attitude, viewing art as promoting social betterment, "arises . . . wherever a mutual sympathy exists between the individuals more or less actively interested in artistic creation and some considerable part of society" (172). Another area in which Plekhanov pioneered a Marxist standpoint was the significance of "play," whereby human beings pursue an activity not for its usefulness but simply for pleasure. This subject was later taken up by Herbert Marcuse. A striking figure in the Marxist canon was Rosa Luxemburg (1871–1919), whose contribution to Marxist economics was profound. However, she was anxious to preserve an aesthetic dimension for art, a recalcitrance to what she saw as reductive theoretical analysis.

Vladimir Ilyich Lenin (1870–1924) occupied a central role not only in the revolution of 1917 but also in the unfolding of Marxist aesthetics toward a more politically interventionist stance. Lenin's most controversial piece is his "Party Organization and Party Literature" (1905), which, along with certain comments of Marx and Engels, was later misleadingly claimed to authorize socialist realism. But hostile, non-Marxist critics have also misinterpreted Lenin's essay, viewing it as an attempt to repress free creativity in literature. This interpretation overlooks both the context of the essay and its arguments. Written shortly after the general strike of October 1905, it belongs to a politically volatile period in which the

work of revolution was far from complete, as Lenin emphasizes: "While tsarism is *no longer* strong enough to defeat the revolution, the revolution is *not yet* strong enough to defeat tsarism" (*On Literature and Art* 23). Moreover, free speech and a free press, as Lenin points out, did not in any case exist. It can come as no surprise, then, when Lenin insists that literature "must become *part* of the common cause of the proletariat, 'a cog and screw' of one single great Social-Democratic mechanism" (23). Lenin is well aware that art cannot be "subject to mechanical adjustment or levelling, to the rule of the majority over the minority" (24). But he is not prescribing partisanship *(partynost)* for all literature: only for literature that claims to be Party literature. He grants that freedom "of speech and the press must be complete" (25). What he is suggesting is that "freedom of association" must also be complete: the Party reserves the right to circumscribe the ideological boundaries of writing conducted under its banner. Lenin also points out that in bourgeois society the writer cherishes but an illusory freedom: "The freedom of the bourgeois writer . . . is simply masked . . . dependence on the money-bag, on corruption, on prostitution" (26). Writers imagine themselves to be free but are actually "prisoners of bourgeois-shopkeeper literary relations," dependent upon an entire prescriptive network of commercial relations and interests (24–25). This echoes Marx's comment that the "first freedom of the press consists in not being a trade" (*On Freedom of the Press and Censorship,* trans. Saul K. Padover, 1974, 41). In contrast, the free literature that Lenin desires "will be *openly* linked to the proletariat." Also underscoring Lenin's arguments is his recognition that literature "cannot . . . be an individual undertaking," as liberal-bourgeois individualism would have us believe (*On Literature and Art* 23).

Lenin's articles on Tolstoy (1908–11) exemplify through their detailed analyses both the political urgency informing Lenin's aesthetic approach and his ability to explain the circumstances limiting the potential partisanship of great writers. According to Lenin, the contradictions in Tolstoy's works—for example, his "merciless criticism of capitalist exploitation," his denunciation of "poverty, degradation and misery among the working masses" as against his "crackpot preaching of . . . 'resist not evil' with violence," and his preaching of a reformed religion—mirror the contradictory conditions of the revolutionary peasantry (*Collected Works* 15:205). Tolstoy's misguided renunciation of politics reflect the "pent-up hatred, the ripened striving for a better lot, the desire to get rid of the past—and also the immature dreaming, the political inexperience, and the revolutionary flabbiness" characterizing the peasantry (15:208). But while Tolstoy's doctrines are "certainly utopian," Lenin is able to call them "socialistic" and to hail Tolstoy's portrayal of the epoch of revolution as "a step forward in the artistic development of humanity as a whole" (16:325). Lenin's methodological insights are equally interesting: the contradictions in Tolstoy can *only* be apprehended from the standpoint of the class that led the struggle for freedom during the revolution (16:325). This point helps to put into perspective some of Lenin's earlier comments on "Party literature": not only is it impossible to write as an individual, but, equally, "individual" acts of reading and interpreting are conducted within parameters dictated by class interests. At a deeper level, Lenin's approach to aesthetic value, embracing as it does the totality of historical circumstances including class, preceding literary traditions and relation to political exigency, can be seen to derive from his acknowledgment, in his *Philosophical Notebooks,* of the dialectical character of Marxism, which insists on viewing any "individual" entity in its necessary historical connection with what is universal.

The early debates on art during and after the revolutionary period in Russia focused on questions such as the degree of Party control over the arts, the appropriate stance toward the bourgeois cultural legacy, and the imperative to clarify the connections between the political and the aesthetic. A related question was the possibility of creating a proletarian culture. The other major protagonist in the Russian Revolution, Leon Trotsky (1879–1940), played a crucial role in these debates. His works include *Lenin* (1924), *History of the Russian Revolution* (1932), and *The Revolution Betrayed* (1937), as well as his renowned *Literature and Revolution* (1924). Trotsky, already exiled in 1900 and 1905 for his revolutionary activities, was finally ousted by Joseph Stalin in the struggle for leadership following Lenin's death in 1924. He continued, in exile, to oppose Stalin's regime until his murder in 1940. In *Literature and Revolution* (1924) Trotsky stressed that only in some domains can the Party offer direct leadership; the "domain of art is not one in which the party is called upon to command. It can and must protect and help it, but it can only lead it indirectly" (*Trotsky on Literature and Art* 56). But just as Lenin's views on this topic have been misread, so Trotsky's claims for freedom of art have been subject to misprision. He states quite clearly that what is needed is "a watchful revolutionary censorship, and a broad and flexible policy in the field of art" (58). What is important for Trotsky is that the limits of such censorship be defined very clearly: he is against "the liberal principle of *laissez faire* and *laissez passer,* even in the field of art" (58). Hence

Trotsky cannot be accused of indifference to the ideological threats posed by reactionary literature and ideas, although in a 1938 manifesto, *Towards a Free Revolutionary Art,* drawn up in collaboration with André Breton, Trotsky urges a "complete freedom for art" (119), while acknowledging that all true art is revolutionary in nature. The latter position evolved in reaction to what Trotsky calls Stalin's "police patrol spirit" (115–21).

In *Literature and Revolution* Trotsky also urges that the Party give "its confidence" to what he calls "literary fellow-travelers," those non-Party writers sympathetic to the revolution. Behind this lies Trotsky's insistence that the proletariat "cannot begin the construction of a new culture without . . . assimilating the . . . old cultures" (*Trotsky on Literature and Art* 59). Given the proletariat's need for a continuity of creative tradition, it currently realizes this continuity indirectly, through the creative activity of the sector of the bourgeois intelligentsia that gravitates toward the proletariat. In the same work, Trotsky addresses the question whether proletarian culture is possible. To Trotsky, the question is "formless," because not only will the energy of the proletariat be consumed primarily in the acquisition of power but, as it succeeds, it "will be more and more dissolved into a socialist community and will free itself from its class characteristics and thus cease to be a proletariat. . . . The proletariat acquires power for the purpose of doing away forever with class culture and to make way for human culture" (42). Other aspects of Trotsky's approach to aesthetics are exemplified in his *Class and Art.* There Trotsky suggests that art has "its own laws of development" and that there is no guarantee of an organic link between artistic creativity and class interests. Moreover, such creativity "lags behind" the spirit of a class and is not subject to conscious influence. Trotsky maintains that certain great writers, such as Dante, Shakespeare, and Goethe, appeal to us precisely because they transcend the limitations of their class outlook (Solomon 194–96).

The call to create a proletarian culture was the originating theme of Proletkult, a left-wing group of writers whose foremost ideologist was A. A. Bogdanov (1873–1928). This group, opposed by the Bolshevik leadership, insisted on art as a weapon in class struggle and rejected all bourgeois art. Also active in the debates of this period were the formalists and the futurists, notably the critic Osip Brik, whose term "social command" embodied the ideal of interventionist art, and the poet Vladimir Mayakovsky, who wrote an influential pamphlet "How Are Verses Made?" The formalists and futurists, as well as the radical constructivist El Lissitsky (1890–1941), found a common platform in the journal *LEF* (Russian acronym for the Left Front of Art). The formalists, focusing on artistic forms and techniques on the basis of linguistic studies, had arisen in pre-revolutionary Russia but now saw their opposition to traditional art as a political gesture, allying them somewhat with the revolution. All these groups were attacked by the most prominent Soviet theoreticians, such as Trotsky, Nikolai Bukharin (1888–1937), Anatoly Lunacharsky (1875–1933), and Alexander Voronsky (1884–1943), who decried the attempt to break completely with the past and what they saw as a reductive denial of the social and cognitive aspects of art. V. N. Voloshinov later attempted to harmonize the two sides of the debate—formal linguistic and sociological analysis—by treating language itself as the supreme ideological phenomenon (see M . M . BAKHTIN). A further group was the Association of Proletarian Writers (known by the Russian acronym VAPP, later RAPP), which insisted on Communist literary hegemony.

The Communist party's attitude toward art in this period was epiphenomenal of its economic policy. A resolution of 1925 voiced the Party's refusal to sanction any one literary faction. This reflected the New Economic Policy (NEP) of a limited free-market economy. The period of the first Five Year Plan (1928–32) saw a more or less voluntary return to a more committed artistic posture, and during the second Five Year Plan (1932–36) this commitment was crystallized in the formation of a Writer's Union. The first congress of this union in 1934, featuring speeches by Maxim Gorki and Bukharin, officially adopted socialist realism, as defined influentially by A. A. Zhdanov (1896–1948). Aptly dubbed "Stalin's cultural thug" by Terry Eagleton, it was Zhdanov whose proscriptive shadow thenceforward fell over Soviet cultural affairs. Although Bukharin's speech at the congress had attempted a synthesis of formalist and sociological attitudes, premised on his view that the word is a microcosm of history, Bukharin was eventually to fall from his position as leading theoretician of the Party: his trial and execution, stemming from his political and economic differences with Stalin, were also symptomatic of the atmosphere in which formalism soon became a sin once more. Bukharin had called for socialist realism to portray reality not "as it is" but rather as it exists in socialistic imagination. Zhdanov defined socialist realism as the depiction of "reality in its revolutionary development." The "truthfulness . . . of the artistic portrayal," he went on to say, "should be combined with . . . ideological remolding" (12). But as several commentators have pointed out, despite the calls for socialist realism to express social values as embodied in the movement of history (rather than embracing a static naturalism), the actual aesthetic adopted was largely a return to nineteenth-century realist techniques infused with a socialist content.

Socialist realism had a considerable impact outside the Soviet Union and received its most articulate and powerful theoretical expression in the work of the Hungarian philosopher GEORG LUKÁCS (1885–1971), whose notion of realism conflicted with that of Bertolt Brecht (1898–1956). Their debate could be regarded as a collision between two personalities, or between a writer (Brecht) and a critic (Lukács), since their "definitions" of socialist realism overlap in crucial ways, a fact that is often ignored. According to Lukács, modern capitalist society is riven by contradictions, by chasms between universal and particular, intelligible and sensible, part and whole. The realist artist expresses a vision of the possible totality embracing these contradictions, a totality achieved by embodying what is "typical" about various historical movements. For example, an individual character might enshrine an entire complex of historical forces. But Brecht, in his notebooks, also equates realism with the ability to capture the "typical" or "historically significant." Realists, says Brecht, identify the contradictions in human relationships, as well as their enabling conditions. Socialist realists, moreover, view reality from the viewpoint of the proletariat. Brecht adds that realist art battles false views of reality, thereby facilitating correct views (109). Perhaps the conflict between the two thinkers is rooted in Lukács's (arguably Stalinist-inspired) aversion to modernist and experimental art on the grounds that the ontological image of humanity they portrayed was fragmented, decadent, and politically impotent. In the 1930s, Brecht's work was viewed as tainted, though later he was received into the ranks of Marxist aestheticians. In contrast, Brecht's experimentalism was crucial to his attempts to combine theory and practice in a Marxist aesthetic. Contrasting dramatic theater (which follows ARISTOTLE's guidelines) with his own "epic" theater, Brecht avers that the audience's capacity for action must be roused and that far from undergoing catharsis, the audience must be forced to make decisions, partly by its standard expectations' being disappointed, a procedure Brecht called "the alienation effect" (91). The action on stage must also implicitly point to other, alternative versions of itself. Far from being sterile, the disputes between Lukács and Brecht display the multidimensional potential of any concept approached from Marxist viewpoints, as well as the inevitable grounding of those viewpoints in political circumstances.

M. A. R. Habib

See also GEORG LUKÁCS and KARL MARX AND FRIEDRICH ENGELS.

Bertolt Brecht, *Schriften zum Theater* (1957, *Brecht on Theatre: The Development of an Aesthetic,* ed. and trans. John Willett, 1964); V. I. Lenin, *Collected Works* (46 vols., 1960–70, 1978), *On Literature and Art* (1970), *Selected Works* (1971); Karl Marx, *Selected Writings* (ed. David McLellan, 1977); Karl Marx and Friedrich Engels, *The Correspondence of Marx and Engels, 1846–1895: A Selection with Commentary and Notes* (ed. and trans. Dona Torr, n.d.), *The Marx-Engels Reader* (2d ed., ed. Robert C. Tucker, 1978), *On Literature and Art* (1978); George V. Plekhanov, *Art and Social Life* (1970); Maynard Solomon, ed., *Marxism and Art: Essays Classic and Contemporary* (1973); Leon Trotsky, *The Basic Writings of Trotsky* (ed. Irving Howe, 1965), *Leon Trotsky on Literature and Art* (ed. Paul N. Siegel, 1970); A. A. Zhdanov, *Essays on Literature, Philosophy, and Music* (1950).

Louis Althusser, *Lenin and Philosophy and Other Essays* (trans. Ben Brewster, 1971); Chris Bullock and David Peck, *Guide to Marxist Literary Criticism* (1980); Peter Demetz, *Marx, Engels, and the Poets: Origins of Marxist Literary Criticism* (trans. J. L. Sammons, 1967); Terry Eagleton, *Marxism and Literary Criticism* (1976); Dave Laing, *The Marxist Theory of Art: An Introductory Survey* (1978); Cliff Slaughter, *Marxism, Ideology, and Literature* (1980); Robert H. Stacy, *Russian Literary Criticism: A Short History* (1974); Raymond Williams, *Marxism and Literature* (1977).

2. Structuralist Marxism

Karl Marx's mature writing from *A Contribution to the Criticism of Political Economy* (1859) through the first edition of *Capital* (1867) offers to analyze social and economic relations as systems and structures that follow scientific laws. In Marx's vocabulary, a distinction is drawn between the "forces" and "relations" of economic production on the one hand, and class contradiction and human oppression on the other. The first terms are structural, the second historical and humanistic. These distinct lines of inquiry between economic theory and the history of the human subject have never been completely resolved in Marxism. Different Marxist schools have placed the emphasis on scientific structures or on concrete political struggle and strategy.

In the period after World War II, primarily in France, the theoretical divisions within the Marxist tradition were reawakened with the emergence of STRUCTURALISM and poststructuralism. Structuralism challenged the humanism and historicism of the social sciences of anthropology, psychology, and linguistics. With a curious twist, however, it sometimes did so in the name of Marxism. CLAUDE LÉVI-STRAUSS, calling himself a Marxist, challenged the remnants of Hegelian dialectics in JEAN-PAUL SARTRE's existential-humanist project. JACQUES LACAN rewrote Freudian psychoanalysis in terms of the structural principles of Saussurean linguistics. MICHEL FOUCAULT radically questioned the assumption that history is progressive and whether, indeed, the so-called human sciences had a real object of knowledge in the first place. Structuralism, in favoring structure over subject, synchronic over diachronic analysis, opened old divisions in Marxism itself.

The specific structuralist challenge within Marxism made its debut in the work of Louis Althusser in his two most important books: *Pour Marx,* a collection of his essays written between 1960 and 1965, and *Lire le "Capital,"* co-authored with Etienne Balibar and based on a series of seminars on Marx's writings; both books were published in 1965. Althusser was professor of philosophy at the École Normale in Paris, where he taught alongside the most influential French structuralists of the 1960s. Critics of Althusser have incorrectly seen his work as a simple combination of structuralism and Marxism. But certainly his most radical insights into the writings of KARL MARX AND FRIEDRICH ENGELS overlap with the anthropological work of Lévi-Strauss, Lacanian psychoanalysis, and Foucault's historical analysis of the social control exercised within different humanistic disciplines. Althusser in fact cites them approvingly in his own writings. The deeper question that Althusser poses for contemporary Marxist thought is whether the concerns of the structuralists, who challenge the veracity of lived experience and the general empiricism of the human sciences, is compatible with Marxism's commitment to political criticism and practical social activity. For Althusser, structuralism does not alter Marxism but, rather, provides the opportunity to reawaken the original spirit of Marx's later writings, especially *Capital,* which already contains and surpasses the structuralist attack on humanism and empiricism. According to Althusser, Marx himself had to overcome the humanistic concerns of his earlier writings, as in *The Economic and Philosophical Manuscripts of 1844* or *The German Ideology,* in order to develop what was truly original and revolutionary about the scientific laws of production and their relation to cultural history.

The fate of Althusserian Marxism in the last 25 years has been closely bound up with acceptance or rejection of Althusser's revisionary reading of *Capital* as setting the stage for a truly scientific understanding of the entire concept of "production" as the transformative law of all social activity, from the most material economic activity to the cultural practices of literature, law, and family life, which Althusser has dubbed the "functions" of the "Ideological State Apparatuses." In some of Althusser's most sophisticated followers, such as Pierre Macherey in France and, first among Anglophone Marxists, FREDRIC JAMESON, the Althusserian in-depth analysis of the concept of production has made it possible to see literary works in a radically different way: as the products of symbolic production and ideological conflict rather than the creative expressions of humanistically defined authors or a direct reflection of the writer's historical context with special reference to class. Others, such as Terry Eagleton, have gone through an intense engagement with Althusserian thinking only to return to a less theoretical agenda that would place the emphasis, once again, on the immediate political issues of writers' and readers' lived experience of class contradiction.

On what basis does Althusser separate scientific Marxism from humanistic Marxism? How does his reading of *Capital* contribute to literary theory, specifically literature's ideological function? How have Althusserian concepts shaped the kinds of questions posed by such Marxist critics as Macherey, Jameson, and Eagleton? In spite of their differences with regard to Althusser and structuralism in general, they all share in the effort to de-idealize the value and meaning of literary works without falling into reductive biographical or historical interpretations of specific literary works. These questions take us back to Althusser's vexing analysis of the concept of production and his revisionary reading of Marx.

For Althusser, the Marxist concept of production contains the most revolutionary aspects of the entire theory. It defies analysis and understanding within the narrowly "classical" theories of economics, psychology, and epistemology which immediately preceded it and which it attempts to surpass completely. Classical writers would include empiricists such as John Locke and economists such as Adam Smith and David Ricardo. Classical concepts would include a definition of human needs in order to analyze the value of economic commodities, feelings of alienation as the base for political awareness, and theory as an intellectual reflection upon practice. To the extent that we are still held by these classical notions, we fail to grasp the revolutionary philosophical significance of Marxism, or we treat it very narrowly as one economic doctrine centered upon the relations between capital, labor, and exchange value. In *Lire le "Capital"* Althusser does not attempt to compare directly Smith's

definition of "labor" with Marx's. Instead, he asks what sorts of assumptions are hidden in the very "appearance" of the terms of inquiry. To stand back from a given set of economic practices in order to analyze them objectively already begs the question what shapes the nature of the given in the first place. Productive activity is present at all levels of philosophical inquiry, in the construction of objects of analysis, in the perspective of the human inquirer, and in the concept of theorization as itself an activity that is collectively produced. To paraphrase Althusser, the first object of knowledge is already an ideological product, a transformation of the real, or a *Verarbeitung* ("labour of transformation" [*Reading* 42]).

But "production" should not be read loosely as a synonym for "bias" or as a shallow definition of "ideology." Althusser is attempting to get at the radical proposition that production, in a very specific Marxist sense, permeates and mediates the texture of reality, that there is no such thing as a nonproblematic, nonideological mode of scientific inquiry into the functions and structure of social divisions and cultural institutions. Pushed to their rigorous end, transformative actions that alter and shape the texture of social existence encompass what we ordinarily think of as being a human subject.

At a very sophisticated level of theoretical debate, Althusser distinguishes Marx's contribution to the concept of production from the tradition of Hegelianism on one side and from pure structuralism on the other. Hegelianism had already put forward the total mediation of the given world to the critical, ever-developing human subject. If production were synonymous with mediation, there would be nothing philosophically new in Marxism. Althusser's writings would fit into Marx's own characterization of his relationship to Hegel as the inversion of dialectical idealism into dialectical materialism. But for Althusser, the difference between Hegel and Marx lies precisely in Marx's realization that the process of mediation could never be completed in the name of the human subject, that reality and subjectivity never reach a state of identity, as they are meant to in Hegelian logic. The forces of production perform the transformations of the world and its multiple articulations. Production is the underlying real base of culture, but it can only be apprehended through the filter of ideology. (The subject's inability to reach a perfect grasp of the real conditions of its identity is one of the points at which Althusserian Marxism and Lacanian psychoanalysis converge.) The burden of Marxist analysis, therefore, becomes the effort to determine or specify with ever greater precision the nature of productive activity without ever being able to put it into the terminology of appearances or conscious reflections. That terminology would harken back to the earlier Hegelian phenomenological project. The forces of production generate effects within the organization, or a *Gliederung* ("articulated combination" [*Reading* 48]) of society as a whole, in its institutions, such as the church and the legal system, and in its aesthetic products. But these effects are not direct results or expressions or appearances of the same forces of production. In fact, in a manner that is nonreductive when compared with other interpretations of Marx, Althusser asserts that art, theology, literature, and family life need to be determined according to their own laws of production, which are not governed by or identical to the laws of production, in the ordinary sense, of goods and commodities (see the important essay entitled "Ideology and Ideological State Apparatuses"). The inevitable gap between the real base of production and its ideologically inflected apprehension brings Althusser into proximity with the discourse of the structuralists.

Structuralism provides Althusser with a terminology for analyzing ideological and symbolic modes of apprehending production without having to resort to the classical lexicon. Without directly supporting the Marxist concept of labor as radical transformative actions upon nature and our own human identity, structuralism, from a strictly linguistic angle, puts into question the link between appearance and meaning, subject/object epistemology with its accompanying metaphors of mimetic or reflective representations of the world, and indeed the entire aesthetic terminology of formalism, organic unity, and the objectlike stability of given works of literature.

For some Marxists, such as Perry Anderson, structuralism should be kept at arm's length because it poses the greatest danger Marxism has had to meet in our time, greater even than the disgrace of Stalinism, the weakening of Eurocommunism, and the collapse of solidarity among the international labor organizations in Latin American and developing nations. The concern over structuralism may seem out of place in the context of such world-historical events, but that is exactly how Anderson, examining the fortunes of Marxism today, sees it. Anderson's assault on structuralist forms of Marxism as developed by Althusser and Jameson is important to consider at this juncture, for it recognizes that the future of Marxism is linked to genuinely philosophical problems. It would be easy, in the vituperative manner of E. P. Thompson, to dismiss almost any philosophical reading of Marx as a merely intellectual preoccupation, but Anderson's rejection of structuralism looks deeper into the radical rethinking of aesthetic, expressive, linguistic activity, which challenges the priority of the concept of labor in Marxist social analysis. For Althusser, structuralism and Marxism converge because there is no going back to a direct critique of the state or the family or the distribution of wealth. Each object of critique must be determined in a postclassical mode before it can be invoked. Anderson brings forward the crucial issue for Marxism today: in the long run, will an extremely sophisticated theory of production kill Marxism by turning it into something like HERMENEUTICS or SEMIOTICS? Or is a postclassical, posthumanist analysis of what determines things such as literature and ideology a means of giving Marxism a new lease on life, especially by taking it past vulgar materialism and empiricism?

The answer to these questions takes on very specific rather than global formulations in Macherey, Jameson, and Eagleton. Each writer has understood very well the consequence of Althusser's critique of appearance and reflective models of understanding. If production does not take on a straightforward ideological expression, then it must be determined through its theoretical problematic and its symptomatic mode (*Reading* 25). The problematic poses for critical analysis the inevitable gaps and absent explanations of ideology and thus seeks out the structure and conditions of production. The quality of the determination, which I repeat is never finalized, is what gives the method point and substance. And that is where its philosophical significance must remain. This lack of analytical closure and immediate result must remain unsatisfying for orthodox Marxism; indeed, even within revisionary Marxism it seems to defy the ongoing debate about the need for "totalizable" explanations of historical events (see Jay). In the first instance, however, Althusserian Marxism has led to a set of remarkable insights into literary production, and it has succeeded in determining ideological structures within literary texts. As an indisputably powerful determination of the literary, Althusserian Marxism goes beyond the mere application of Marxist tenets to literary texts. The concept of production reshapes the terms of inquiry into literature. The questions that remain are whether this new determination of literary/ideological production will alter our concept of verbal activity in a lasting way, and if so, whether it will be powerful enough to change the way we view the family, the state, and the educational system. The specific interpretations of Althusser in Macherey, Jameson, and Eagleton belong in the context of these questions.

Pierre Macherey's *Pour une théorie de la production littéraire*, published in 1966 (trans. 1978), was written during the most intense phase of Althusser's own theoretical development. The book is written in a spirit of active collaboration with Althusser. In the theoretical portion of the book, primarily its first part, Macherey follows many of the same lines of inquiry that Althusser does, rejecting all classical approaches to the study of literature that are based in empiricism, formalism, and humanism. Like Althusser on economic appearances, Macherey begins by examining the notion of the literary text as a fixed, stable object for analysis. What gives rise to this appearance of literature in the first place? And if uncritically accepted, does it not commit literary criticism to a host of fallacious procedures? Criticism becomes the "consumption" of a "mysteriously" (because already given) literary object. In one of his densest but most important statements, Macherey advocates an analysis of literature based on structure but one that cannot be mistaken for mere form or derived from a special category of authorship:

> The problem . . . is that of the structure . . . from which the work derives, its determinateness. But the notion of structure is misleading in so far as it pretends to show us . . . its intelligible image. . . . If we are to make sense of the concept of structure it must be with the recognition that structure is neither a property of the object nor a feature of its representation: the work does not derive from the unity of an [authorial] intention which permeates it, nor from its conformity to an autonomous model. (*Theory* 40)

The link between structure and determinateness is all-important. Macherey bypasses all surface qualities of a literary work that could be confused with mere formalism. Structure, the final shape of a narrative or poem or tale, determines the ideological matrix of the author's culture. Labor, for Macherey (and unacceptably for Anderson), is the actual effort to reach a structure by wrestling with ideological material. Structure is not in any way external to the meaning of a literary work; it is immanent in the work itself. It cuts deeper into the culture than traditional (Aristotelian) literary terms such as plot or genre, and it cannot be related to the culture at large by the trope of structure as a mirror of reality. Honoré de Balzac, for example, does not mirror Paris; he fictionalizes Paris as a complex system of relations (57). The meaning of Parisian images is in the Balzacian labor of drawing connections, in the gaze and pursuit of objects out of which Balzac determines the conditions of city life. By contrast, when Lenin himself attempts to give a strict Marxist reading of Leo Tolstoy's nostalgia for the peasant, he fails (115–29). Lenin's historically sophisticated analysis of false class complicity between the aristocracy and the peasantry is not matched by an equal sophistication in untangling Tolstoy's writings, because

Lenin continues to talk about Tolstoy's writings in terms of reflecting and expressing contradictory social conditions against a fixed yardstick of true or false class consciousness. From that theoretical perspective, Tolstoy's ideology consists in falsely admiring the peasant from the perspective of the aristocrat. But Macherey looks for contradiction at the ground level of what determines the production of Tolstoy's narrative in the first place. The historical deficiencies of Tolstoy's novels arise from deficiencies within the ideological material that Tolstoy is working upon and shaping in determinate form for analysis. Macherey's approach takes us back to the detailed investigation of the silences, gaps, and absences within the structure of Tolstoy's writings. Macherey avoids a reductive frontal assault on the validity of the single author's point of view, a validity predicated on a simplistic notion of texts as expressions of ideological bias.

Fredric Jameson is probably the most important Anglophone Marxist literary critic since World War II. His work has engaged and attempted to absorb into Marxism every major intellectual movement since the war: existentialism, structuralism, psychoanalysis, the new waves of literature and film from developing nations, and most recently feminism and POSTMODERNISM. His contribution to the school of Althusserian analysis, however, is located in his important theoretical work, *The Political Unconscious*, published in 1981. Like Macherey's book, Jameson's comprises a lengthy theoretical first chapter followed by specific interpretations of different writers and their ideological value (Balzac, George Gissing, and Joseph Conrad). Jameson's theoretical chapter takes for granted the contribution of Althusser and Macherey to literary theory. It assumes a critique of Althusser's "expressive causality" (or Hegelianism [see 28]) and a method based on the specification of the literary text's ideological "symptoms" (33). But at the same time Jameson adds a new dimension to the structuralist Marxist project. His main contribution lies with the dialectical features of textual structure, or what he calls his effort to reformulate the "coordination between a semiotic and a dialectical method" (83).

The Althusserian reading of Marx on production shifts critical theory away from empirical causes and subject-based definitions of ideology; Macherey develops the theory further in the direction of the structural definition of ideology. Jameson takes this structure and gives it a thoroughly dialectical treatment. He follows Macherey's approach to Balzac in looking for an ideological structure in literature rather than a direct relation of contradiction between author and social context. But the symptoms and structure undergo dynamic modification.

Jameson maps contradictions and oppositions through different levels of textual organization, often in the form of Greimassian narratological rectangles and allegorical levels of meaning. Almost any unit of textual meaning, from style to point of view to characterization, can be put into a dialectical process of constant transformation; and these transformations, in turn, become maps of contradictory but connected levels of ideology. (See NARRATOLOGY.) The revolutionary import of Jameson's method is best seen in its handling of specific examples, such as the image of the sea in Conrad's novels or the creation of objects of desire in Balzac's supposedly realistic descriptions (see 154–69 and 230–35). Jameson's dialectical semiotics does not challenge any fundamental Marxist principles. For all its sophistication, his method remains rooted in the belief that we are in a historical period of oppression and that literature is one form of aspiration to a better life ahead. Jameson's work will remain of central importance as long as modern and postmodern forms of expression and aesthetics support these beliefs and aspirations.

Terry Eagleton's copious and diverse output of criticism has established him as one of the most recognized Anglophone Marxist critics of the last twenty years, but his engagement with the work of Althusser and Macherey is found primarily in one book, *Criticism and Ideology*, published in 1976. In contrast to Jameson, Eagleton has not remained committed to the development of structuralist Marxism in subsequent writings. In fact, his work in the early 1990s on the ideology of the aesthetic indicates a return to such topics as affect, sense-experience, and the control of the human body and would seem to indicate a rejection of the whole direction of Althusserian thought. Eagleton is as well versed as Jameson in a wide range of literary theories, and he has written numerous books of literary and cultural criticism. But his writing is consistently marked by dissatisfaction with the role of the academic Marxist and with the entire institutionalization of literary study. In the mid-1970s the work of Althusser and Macherey seemed to fit well with Eagleton's general assault on the empirical tradition of English "lit. crit." In his later work, however, the scholastic style of the Althusserian school has proven to be incompatible with his demand for concrete judgments upon the ideological value of specific writers and critics. Eagleton's turn toward and then away from Althusser and Macherey does have theoretical significance, but unlike Jameson's, it is not found in an effort to rework Althusser from within. *Criticism and Ideology* emphasizes the importance of Althusser's work as a break with a simple cause-and-effect model of economics

and literature. Eagleton, perhaps out of his own frustration with applied Marxism, draws a distinction between the "history of criticism" and the "science of the history of criticism" (20–21) and finds in Althusser and Macherey support for literature as product obeying its own signifying practices. But by the same token, he already expresses a discomfort, which will grow stronger, with the lack of immediate application of this insight. He attacks Althusser and Macherey for their "mysterious" linkage of history, ideology, and literature (84). Althusser and Macherey help us to understand what is wrong with vulgar Marxism, but their lack of explicit guidelines remains, for Eagleton, a fatal weakness.

Theoretically, Eagleton is unable to break out of the circle of immediacy versus structure, authenticity versus disengagement. I think that the force of his criticism against the Althusserian school must be distinguished from the reasons he gives to back it. It becomes clear that Eagleton, in comparison with Althusser on passages from Marx, or Macherey on passages from Tolstoy, or Jameson on passages from Balzac, is skeptical from the outset about the possibility of achieving radical insights into ideology through the close reading of a text. He is outside structuralist Marxism from the beginning because the transformations of the theory occur, for him, against larger, underdetermined values and principles. His commentary on specific writers immediately reaches for a high level of generalization above the plane of textual analysis. For that reason, his protests against the scholasticism of Althusser indicate a bias against the whole idea of an immanent form of criticism. Critics who are against the entire idea of close reading can hardly find consolation in Althusser's suggestion that we read Marx as if he were writing like Spinoza. But for readers today Eagleton does have a point. His dissatisfaction with Althusser raises as many theoretical problems as it hopes to settle, but he is certainly right in his claim that the writings of structuralist Marxists lack a certain expressive range, that the depth of the analysis always seems cramped in its articulation. The strongest challenge to structuralist Marxism may come not from the high ground of theory but from other movements that, since the 1960s, have put the question of ideology into multiple forms, movements such as feminism and ethnic studies. The determination of ideology is all-important for the study of race and gender, but the multiplicity of the determination cannot be captured in the generic vocabulary that is a noticeable feature of structuralist Marxism.

Gary Wihl

See also G. W. F. HEGEL and STRUCTURALISM.

Louis Althusser, "Ideology and Ideological State Apparatuses" (1970, *Lenin and Philosophy and Other Essays,* trans. Ben Brewster, 1971), *Pour Marx* (1965, *For Marx,* trans. Ben Brewster, 1969); Louis Althusser and Etienne Balibar, *Lire le "Capital"* (1965, *Reading "Capital,"* trans. Ben Brewster, 1970); Terry Eagleton, *Criticism and Ideology: A Study in Marxist Literary Theory* (1976), *The Ideology of the Aesthetic* (1990); Fredric Jameson, *The Political Unconscious: Narrative as a Socially Symbolic Act* (1981), *The Prison-House of Language: A Critical Account of Structuralism and Russian Formalism* (1972); Pierre Macherey, *Pour une théorie de la production littéraire* (1966, *A Theory of Literary Production,* trans. Geoffrey Wall, 1978).

Perry Anderson, *In the Tracks of Historical Materialism* (1983); Ted Benton, *The Rise and Fall of Structural Marxism* (1984); Alex Callinicos, *Althusser's Marxism* (1976); William Dowling, *Jameson, Althusser, Marx: An Introduction to "The Political Unconscious"* (1984); Gregory Elliott, *Althusser: The Detour of Theory* (1987); Susan James, "Louis Althusser," *The Return of Grand Theory in the Human Sciences* (ed. Quentin Skinner, 1985); Martin Jay, "Louis Althusser and the Structuralist Reading of Marx," *Marxism and Totality: The Adventures of a Concept from Lukács to Habermas* (1984); James H. Kavanaugh, "Marxism's Althusser: Towards a Politics of Literary Theory," *diacritics* 12 (1982); Dominick LaCapra, "Marxism in the Textual Maelstrom: Fredric Jameson's *The Political Unconscious,*" *Rethinking Intellectual History* (1983); E. P. Thompson, "The Poverty of Theory or An Orrery of Errors," *The Poverty of Theory and Other Essays* (1978).

MEDIEVAL THEORY AND CRITICISM

Literary theory in the Middle Ages is not one theory or one tradition. The diverse critical systems and practices of the Middle Ages represent different attempts, over the course of a millennium (approximately the fifth century through the fifteenth century), to assimilate the theoretical traditions inherited from antiquity and the early church with new social, institutional, and intellectual developments. The single consistent theme of medieval literary theory is that of *translatio studii,* the carrying over of ancient learning through reading and commentary. The traditional elements that form the bases of medieval critical attitudes can be divided roughly into four strains: the tradition of Neoplatonism, especially as mediated through early Christian hermeneutics; the re-

ception of ARISTOTLE, which has two phases: early medieval treatments of Aristotle's logic and language theory and late medieval receptions of a more complete picture of Aristotelian science; a tradition of prescriptive poetics, which traces itself back to HORACE, Ciceronian rhetoric, and classical grammatical teaching on style (see CLASSICAL THEORY AND CRITICISM: 2. RHETORIC); and methods of textual exegesis (gloss, commentary, and prologues to the authors), known as *enarratio poetarum,* "exposition of the poets," derived from the techniques of textual commentary practiced by the ancient grammarians and revised throughout the Middle Ages for expositions of the Bible and curricular texts.

These strains overlap, of course, in terms of both their theoretical implications and their historical influence. What is most important, the technique of *enarratio poetarum* was the basic critical methodology underlying all approaches to texts, as it was the foundation of the art of grammar, the first of the liberal arts, which included literary analysis of the ancient poets along with study of language. The various historical strains inform both sacred and secular hermeneutics; and sacred and secular, in turn, inform each other, despite the distinctions medieval theorists drew between the reading of the Bible and the reading of secular or pagan authors.

The Neoplatonist tradition survived, and was continually revived throughout the Middle Ages, in a variety of theoretical and theological positions on literature. Neoplatonism is a legacy of late antiquity. Its major exponents were Plotinus (third century C. E.) and his disciple and literary executor, Porphyry. The Neoplatonists offer a spiritual interpretation of the material world, a doctrine of the ascendence of the human soul toward some contact with an immutable universe or a transcendent Unity that confers meaning on the visible world. The writings of Proclus (c. 410) apply this philosophical system to literary criticism: Proclus argues that poetry, proceeding from the various faculties of the soul, can have a divine, visionary capacity and as such must express its truths through allegory or enigma.

Proclus's writings were not translated into Latin and so had only an indirect influence on the Christian West. But such critical principles were transmitted to the Latin Middle Ages in the work of Macrobius (c. 400), Fulgentius (c. 500–600), and Boethius (480–524). These three writers bring into perspective the continuing importance of PLATO's *Timaeus* (available to the Latin West in Chalcidius's translation): in the cosmology of the *Timaeus,* the human world is a microcosm of a transcendent order of Being, and the materiality of the world renders that higher order partially intelligible to our senses. This cosmography could also be applied, in textual criticism, to a justification of fable or fiction as a container of philosophical or moral truth.

Macrobius's influential *Commentary on the Dream of Scipio* articulates these critical assumptions. The *Commentary* (based on a section of Cicero's *De re publica,* which is extant only in fragments) begins with a distinction between kinds of fictions: those that are merely a pleasant pastime (and can thus be relegated to the nursery) and those that serve a higher purpose by illustrating or expressing serious philosophical ideas. Of this latter kind of fiction the most important is the "fabulous narration" *(narratio fabulosa),* which is the proper provenance of philosophical discourse, as exemplified in Plato's texts (e.g., the use of myth in the *Republic*). The "fabulous narration" appropriate to philosophers will be "an honest idea of sacred truths hidden under a pious veil of fictions" (*sacrarum rerum notio sub pio figmentorum velamine honestis* [1.2.11]). The "pious fiction" works by "clothing" the philosophical truth in the "dress" of story: plot and character are devised as vehicles of ideas. This practice is tied to a cosmological principle: Nature (personified in feminine terms) protects her own secrets from common view by enveloping them in mysterious garments, thereby revealing her truths only to those of select intelligence. Macrobius's idea of *fabula* is a *locus classicus* for medieval theories of allegory as both a mode of reading and a style of writing.

Fulgentius develops this critical principle of allegory into a consistent methodology. Two of Fulgentius's works—the *Exposition of the Content of Virgil According to Moral Philosophy* and the *Mythologies*—offer important models of *allegoresis,* that is, the allegorical interpretation of a given text. In the *Exposition of the Content of Virgil* Fulgentius reads the *Aeneid* as a human pilgrimage from birth to adulthood, from ignorance and error to wisdom and virtue, seeing the narrative action of each book of the *Aeneid* as an allegory for each stage of this process: the shipwreck stands for birth, Dido's funeral pyre stands for the self-consuming flames of adolescent passion, the descent to the underworld in book 6 stands for the penetration of the mysteries of knowledge through philosophy and experience, and so on throughout Virgil's text. The medieval tradition of allegorical interpretation of myth also owes much to Boethius's *Consolation of Philosophy,* which, along with Virgil's *Aeneid,* was a central curricular text throughout the Middle Ages. In its embodiment of key themes from the *Timaeus* (e.g., bk. 3, verse 9) and in its use of myth to illustrate philosophical doctrine, the *Consolation* exemplified the poetic principle of *fabula* and expounded the assumptions of the allegorical method.

Much Neoplatonist criticism centers on the idea of the "great poet," such as Virgil, whose work could be read encyclopedically, as a repository of mystical, prophetic, and philosophical truths. For later medieval schoolmen, this mode of allegorical exposition was not just an exegetical technique but a powerful hermeneutics of recuperation, a justification for reading the fictions of pagan poets: the pagan poets could be accommodated within the Christian *imperium* because of the ulterior truths their fictions could be found to contain. This idea is most forcefully expressed by a number of academics and literati associated with the schools of Chartres and Orléans in the twelfth century: Thierry of Chartres, William of Conches, Bernardus Silvestris, Alain de Lille, and Arnulf of Orléans. These writers developed the method of allegorical exposition into an art: in William of Conches's commentaries on Plato's *Timaeus* and Boethius's *Consolation of Philosophy,* in Bernardus Silvestris's exposition of the *Aeneid* and of Martianus Capella's *Marriage of Mercury and Philology,* and in Alain de Lille's two allegorical poems, *The Plaint of Nature* and *The Anticlaudianus,* the guiding assumption is that poetry and poetic figures can render a transcendent order of divine harmony accessible to human senses (Wetherbee 4–5, 16–18).

Among these writers, Macrobius's term *fabula* is generally replaced with the word *integumentum* ("cloak," "veil," or "covering"), which is used strictly in reference to the fictive garb of pagan or secular writings; it is distinguished from *allegoria,* which refers to the literal level of Holy Scripture as something that is true in and of itself but that also contains ulterior spiritual truths. The poetic fictions or *integumenta* of the pagan poets (Virgil, Ovid, Lucan, Statius) have no truth in themselves, but exist to convey philosophical themes. One of the most elaborate realizations of this principle is the commentary on the first six books of the *Aeneid* attributed to Bernardus Silvestris, which owes much to Fulgentius's commentary but goes far beyond its source to articulate a coherent theory of polyvalent reading. These twelfth-century allegorists exert considerable influence on later vernacular literary culture: they establish a norm of allegorical writing that we can trace, for example, in Jean de Meun, DANTE ALIGHIERI, and even Geoffrey Chaucer; and they legitimize poetic metaphor as an intellectual access to truth.

Sacred hermeneutics is also indebted to Neoplatonist thought. ST. AUGUSTINE's synthesis of Neoplatonism, Pauline doctrines of the sign, and Stoic and Aristotelian theories of language produced an essentially verbal conceptual framework for reading material reality (Colish 34–35). In Augustine's semiotics, all the things of this world are signs to lead us to a knowledge of God (*On the Trinity* 6.10.12). This Pauline notion of the world as a book is echoed and refined throughout the Middle Ages. John Scotus Eriugena (b. c. 810) reinforces this principle through a tradition of Christian Neoplatonism in his commentary on *The Celestial Hierarchy* of the Pseudo-Dionysius. Through Eriugena's translations, the works of the Pseudo-Dionysius became important sources for later medieval theories of the symbol, especially of analogical signification. We find these themes in the school of mystical theology associated with the monastery of St. Victor in the twelfth century, exemplified in the principles of textual criticism set forth in Hugh of St. Victor's instructional work, the *Didascalicon,* as well as in Hugh's own commentaries on the Pseudo-Dionysius. Neoplatonist thought also underlies Franciscan theories of textuality, enunciated in academic theology in the writings of Bonaventure (1221–74) and disseminated through the humbler but wider channels of vernacular preaching. Neoplatonism forges links between Christian and secular hermeneutics, as we see in the familiar verses of Alain de Lille: "Every creature in the world is like a book and a picture and a mirror for us" (*Patrologia latina* 210, col. 579).

This theory of signs produced a technique of biblical exegesis. In *On Christian Doctrine* Augustine sets forth a program of reading and preaching, *lectio* and *praedicatio,* which represent two faces, hermeneutical and rhetorical, of the same coin—study of the Bible—and which formed the staple of monastic activity through the Middle Ages. The commonplace of removing the kernels from the shells (3.12.18) is a point of departure for a theory of reading figuratively rather than just literally, especially to bring the Old Testament into a kind of prophetic accord with the incarnational truths of the New Testament. But reading figuratively does not just mean analyzing verbal tropes: it means recognizing the symbolic value of *things* (material realities and events), what Augustine calls "transposed signs" (2.13.20). Thus in *On the Trinity* Augustine says that allegory is found not in words but in historical events themselves (15.9.15).

The problem of how to resolve the difference between allegory as a verbal trope and allegory as a symbolic event was defined more precisely in a treatise by the English monk Bede (673–735), *Concerning Figures and Tropes.* In this treatise Bede strives to substitute the scriptural text for the pagan authors to exemplify the use of figures of speech, thus imitating the pedagogy of

Augustine and Jerome. Bede introduces the terms *allegoria in factis* and *allegoria in verbis* ("allegory in facts" and "allegory in words"). *Allegoria in factis* designates multiple levels of significance in the events of sacred history: it is an extralinguistic symbolism produced by two events within the economy of salvation (thus Abraham's two sons represent the two covenants). *Allegoria in verbis* designates a metaphorical text: it refers to a spiritual reality (e.g., the root, branch, and fruit, respectively, stand for the race of David, the Virgin, and Christ), but the allegory is simply a rhetorical trope, a product of human invention, and bears only a contingent resemblance to spiritual truths (Strubel 347–53).

The theory of *allegoria in factis* was elaborated into such systems as the three or four levels of scriptural exposition (literal or historical, moral or tropological, allegorical or the church on earth, anagogical or the spiritual afterlife), which expound the text in terms of theological categories (Hugh of St. Victor, *Didascalicon* 5.2 and 6.3–5). But we even see this fourfold exposition applied to Dante's *Commedia,* in the *Epistle to Can Grande.* This system of reading facts allegorically, that is, imposing on them the value of verbal signs, is also reflected in the mystical exegesis of Bernard of Clairvaux (1090–1153), whose distinction between a "carnal" (human) and a spiritual response to Christ expresses itself as a theoretical distinction between a carnal (or literal) and a spiritual mode of reading the content of Scripture (*Sermons on the Song of Songs*).

The reception of Aristotle in the Latin West begins with Boethius's Latin translations of Aristotle's *Categories* and *On Interpretation,* along with his translation and exposition of Porphyry's *Isagoge,* which was an introduction to Aristotle's logic. Boethius's transmission of Aristotelian texts was important not just for logical studies but for study of language and language theory. Indeed, all the elements of the medieval trivium—grammar, rhetoric, and dialectic—were "language sciences": grammar was the science concerned with description of linguistic systems and with analysis of literary texts; rhetoric was the art of eloquence, or production of discourse; and dialectic (sometimes equated with all of logic) was the study of rational argumentation, of discovering arguments and evaluating propositions. Thus each science was concerned, in its own way, with theories of discourse, signification, and interpretation, and the legacy of Aristotelian logic was central to medieval discussions of verbal meaning.

This Aristotelian tradition of the language sciences was carried forward by the grammarians Donatus (fourth century) and Priscian (sixth century) and by encyclopedists such as Martianus Capella (fifth century) and Isidore of Seville (seventh century), all of whom were transitional figures from antiquity to the Middle Ages: their work helped to preserve classical learning within early European Christian culture after the fall of Rome in the fifth century and the breakdown of the Roman civic institutions that had supported education in the empire. Donatus, Priscian, and the early medieval encyclopedists reflect the influence of Aristotelian (and Stoic) language theory in their teaching of grammar: linguistic signification is divided into spoken sounds, mental experience, letters (utterance that can be written), and the actual things to which signs refer. Of more importance for the history of criticism, early medieval grammatical study carries forward Aristotle's concern for the semantic principles that underlie interpretation of nonliteral discourse, although the grammatical treatment of tropes and figures (at least in this early period) is fairly programmatic and descriptive.

In the early twelfth century, the recovery of Aristotle's other logical texts—*Prior Analytics, Posterior Analytics, Topics,* and *Sophistical Refutations*—contributed to the emergence of a new kind of grammatical study, theoretical and speculative in its orientation, concerned with philosophical investigations of language, syntax, and semantics. This form of language theory became a key issue in the study of logic in late medieval universities: we see these scholastic concerns with the logical categories of language in the "speculative" grammarians, or *modistae,* of the thirteenth century and in the nominalist controversies, especially the work of William Ockham (c. 1285–c. 1349), in the fourteenth century. Such academic debates are also reflected in some vernacular poetry of the later Middle Ages, for example, in Chaucer's *House of Fame,* in *Piers Plowman,* and in the works of the *Gawain*-poet, which raise sophisticated questions about the relationship of signs to reality (Irvine, "Medieval").

The reception of Aristotle in the Latin West has another phase, one that is very important for the history of literary theory: the transmission of Aristotelian texts and thought through Arab scholarship. The Arabs had access to a considerable body of Greek philosophical texts in Syriac translations made around the fifth century. After Aristotle's logical texts were translated into Arabic during the eighth and ninth centuries, Arab scholars began to systematize Aristotelian epistemology and theories of science, producing commentaries and encyclopedic studies. These studies proved very influential in the Latin West.

One of the earliest and most important of these theoretical treatises is the *Catalogue of the Sciences,* by Al-Farabi (c. 870–950). In this work, Al-Farabi categorized Aristotle's logical texts according to a scheme Arab scholars had inherited from late Greek commentators: to these logical texts, known collectively as the Organon, Al-Farabi added Aristotle's *Rhetoric* and *Poetics.* The texts of the Organon represent "instrumental" sciences, that is, tools or techniques of analysis rather than subject matter or content: the tradition of classifying the *Rhetoric* and the *Poetics* among the instrumental sciences of logic led to a definition of the arts of rhetoric and poetry in terms of logical method or technique rather than in terms of content or material (Hardison, "Place," 59–60). Al-Farabi's treatise was twice translated into Latin during the twelfth century, and it was the source for an important compendium, *On the Division of the Sciences,* by Dominicus Gundissalinus (fl. 1125–50). Gundissalinus's treatise shows the implications of placing Aristotle's *Rhetoric* and *Poetics* in the Organon: he turns them into texts on logic. The parts of logic correspond to the eight texts of the Organon, and each part of logic is distinguished by its purpose and its particular syllogistic device. The purpose of rhetoric is persuasion, and its device is the enthymeme; the purpose of poetics is imaginative (figurative) representation, and its logical device is the "imaginative syllogism" (Gundissalinus 73–76). On this view, then, poetry becomes a branch of logic.

The major figure in the transmission of Aristotle's *Poetics* to the Latin West is the Arab philosopher Averroes (Ibn Rushd, 1120–98) (see also ARABIC THEORY AND CRITICISM). Averroes produced some 38 commentaries on all of Aristotle's major works, nearly half of which were translated into Latin during the thirteenth century. His commentary on the *Poetics* was an attempt to reconcile the principles of Aristotle's literary criticism with the literary practice of Arab culture. He modifies Aristotle's criticism to accord with the terms of Arabic and Hispano-Arabic poetry. Two themes that emerge in Averroes's commentary are that poetry is a branch of logic (derived from the tradition of Al-Farabi) and that poetry is an art of praise and blame. The theory of poetry as a branch of logic is used to explain Aristotle's idea of imitation: poetry is image-making and uses the devices of simile, metaphor, and analogy as logical instruments of comparison. The theory of poetry as a form of praise and blame was really a borrowing from rhetoric, where epideictic (speeches of praise or blame) is one of the three genres of oratory. According to Averroes, praise and blame constitute the two major poetic genres. Averroes developed this theory of poetry out of Aristotle's suggestion (*Poetics* ch. 4) that poetry originated in the genres of invective and panegyric. The commentary by Averroes was translated into Latin in 1256 by Hermannus Aleman- nus and had much wider circulation than the transla- tion of the *Poetics* itself by William of Moerbeke in 1278.

The work of Averroes, together with earlier Arab schol- arship on Aristotelian science, had considerable influ- ence on theories of poetry in the Latin West. The idea that poetry is a branch of logic was developed in scholas- tic philosophy in the wake of Aristotelian studies at the universities of Paris and Oxford. In the classification of the sciences proposed by Thomas Aquinas (c. 1224–74), poetry is seen as a part of "inventive logic," along with dialectic and rhetoric. The purpose of poetic (the sacred poetry of the Bible) is estimation through representa- tion: poetic comparison *(similitudo)* is the basic device of poetry, and in terms of its approximation to truth, poetry is ranked just above the most fallacious form of logic, sophistic (Dahan 179; McKeon 23–24). For Aquinas, as for Roger Bacon (c. 1220–c. 1292), poetic as a part of logic can also be identified with moral philosophy: po- etry can teach ethics through the logical device of exam- ple and becomes a form of "moral logic," an instrument of moral philosophy along with rhetoric.

But for Aquinas's older contemporary Albertus Mag- nus (c. 1200–1280), poetic and rhetoric are sciences of language to be associated not with logic but with prac- tical action: poetry moves people to action and in this way is to be associated with ethics (Dahan 182–85). This idea that poetry is a form of moral philosophy and leads to action by teaching ethics through example can be traced to the tradition of Al-Farabi and Averroes. Gun- dissalinus offers a view along these lines: while he places Aristotle's *Poetics* among the logical texts of the Organon, he also classifies poetry as a part of the science of elo- quence, which is a branch of "civil" or human science (Gundissalinus 16), that is, a practical science, as Aris- totle would have called it (*Nicomachean Ethics* bk. 6), a branch of knowledge dealing with human actions, eth- ics, and society. Poetry concerns human actions because it delights and instructs in knowledge and in morals. This classification of poetry is easily assimilated to the praise-and-blame theory as presented in Averroes.

Such a view of poetry is a critical commonplace, for example, in medieval interpretations of pagan literature (analogous to the Horatian formula of poetry as instruc- tion and delight, which was well known in the Middle Ages): medieval commentaries on Ovid typically explain Ovid's moral intention as that of exemplifying chaste love by condemning foolish or unchaste love (which was a useful justification for Ovid's scurrilous verse). In the late thirteenth century, Giles of Rome (d. 1316) dis-

cusses ethics as something that can only be taught in an "approximate" way, through figurative representations and examples of moral actions (*De regimine principum* 1.1.1): this treatment of ethics uses the very terms that are applied to theoretical definitions of poetry in scholastic Aristotelianism. Dante's classification of poetry as a form of ethical persuasion that attracts readers through its beauty and leads them to moral enlightenment (*Con- vivio* bk. 2) can also be associated with the Averroistic tradition (see Allen 3–66). The praise-and-blame theory of poetry was even applied to Dante's own *Commedia* in a fourteenth-century commentary on Dante's work by Benvenuto Da Imola (1375).

The medieval tradition of prescriptive poetics, that is, guides to the writing (as opposed to just the criticism) of poetry, is a product of a historical synthesis of classical poetics, rhetoric, and teaching on style. Horace's *Art of Poetry* and Ciceronian rhetorical texts were prescriptive guides to composition. Classical teaching on style was of a prescriptive order (i.e., aimed at the production of new texts) when taught by the rhetoricians, as in the case of the list of figures and tropes given in book 4 of the pseudo-Ciceronian *Rhetorica ad Herennium;* but when the same body of information on style was presented in grammatical teaching, in the form of *enarratio poetarum,* such as the exhaustive commentary on the *Aeneid* by the fourth-century grammarian Servius, or even the list of figures and tropes in book 3 of Donatus's *Ars maior,* it took on a descriptive character, because grammarians directed their instruction to analysis and description of given texts, not to production of new texts.

The *Art of Poetry* combines the analytical stance of *enarratio poetarum* with the productive stance of rhetor- ical precept: it is a guide to producing new texts through mastery of the principles of criticism (Murphy, *Rhetoric* 29–35). The *Art of Poetry*, along with Cicero's *On Invention* and the anonymous *Rhetorica ad Herennium,* long attrib- uted to Cicero, were widely studied (and commented on) throughout the Middle Ages. The medieval schools continued the classical practice of *enarratio poetarum,* and Horace's text was valuable for teaching the classical poetry that formed a good part of the arts curriculum. Moreover, its doctrine that poetry gives both instruction and delight (ll. 333–44) provided an ethical justification for poetry, which could be readily assimilated into a broader picture of the ethical function of poetry, where ethics involves not just moral instruction but a striving for well-being (Olson 19–38, 90–115).

These traditions of rhetoric, poetic, and grammar found their distinctly medieval expression in a number of Latin *artes poetriae* ("arts of poetry") written by teachers of grammar between 1175 and 1280: Matthew of Vendôme's *Ars versificatoria;* Geoffrey of Vinsauf's *Poetria nova* and *Documentum de modo et arte dictandi et versificandi;* Gervase of Melkley's *Ars versificaria;* John of Garland's *Parisiana poetria;* and Eberhard the German's *Laborintus* (Murphy, *Rhetoric* 135–93). These *artes* represent a synthesis of the Horatian and Ciceronian traditions with the grammatical study of style and the grammatical practice of *enarratio poetarum.* They are prescriptive guides to composition, in the manner of Horace's poetic and Cicero's rhetoric: some of these *artes* (those of Matthew of Vendôme, Geoffrey of Vinsauf, and John of Garland) use the vocabulary and systems of technical Ciceronian rhetoric, discussing invention, disposition, and style; the *artes* by Gervase of Melkley and Eberhard the German focus mainly on style, tropes, and versification, in the manner of ancient and medieval grammarians; John of Garland and Gervase of Melkley also discuss prose and prose rhythms. These *artes poetriae* also employ the critical methodology of *enarratio poetarum* by devoting attention to analysis of given texts, whether of pagan Latin authors from the school curriculum or of texts composed by the author of the *ars* for the purposes of illustration (e.g., the exemplary poems Geoffrey of Vinsauf composed for the *Poetria nova*).

The influence of Horace is especially notable in the *artes* of Matthew of Vendôme and Geoffrey of Vinsauf, which elaborate the fundamental Horatian principle of stylistic decorum. Geoffrey's *Poetria nova* may have been intended, as its title suggests, to be a new *Art of Poetry,* not so much to replace as to complement the "old" *poetria* of Horace, refining Horatian precepts for a medieval audience: whatever its intention, the *Poetria nova* was one of the most popular and successful of these *artes.* Matthew's *Ars versificatoria* and Geoffrey's *Documentum,* which may have been intended as elementary pedagogical guides, both cite Horace's advice on imitation (*AP* ll. 119–35), that it is of greater difficulty (and according to Matthew and Geoffrey, of greater merit) to treat a traditional and familiar subject in a way that is new than to invent matter that has never before received literary expression. Such precepts harmonized with the orientation of medieval poetic theory and practice (both Latin and vernacular), which, in the spirit of *translatio studii,* gave priority to inherited materials that carried the authority of tradition; poetic ingenuity was directed at discovering new ways of presenting traditional matter, and such ingenuity was seen to best advantage in skillful deployment of conventional forms and themes. In the *artes poetriae,* and in medieval poetic practice, invention (rhetorical *inventio*) is the choice of subject matter from

available and traditional topics: the real burden of poetic skill falls on the presentation and reshaping of traditional themes and texts through the techniques of description, amplification, and abbreviation. These are the chief concerns of the *artes poetriae:* discussions of style are directed to amplification and abbreviation of inherited textual sources; and the theory of narrative arrangement (rhetorical *dispositio*) is largely concerned with the questions of natural order (i.e., beginning at the beginning) as opposed to various forms of artificial order. In sum, these texts apply the conceptual tools of technical rhetoric to the task, derived from *enarratio poetarum,* of reading, reevaluating, and transforming traditional materials (Copeland 158–78).

Vernacular writers also produced a number of arts of poetry aimed at codifying and hence authorizing vernacular poetic practice. Dante's *On Eloquence in the Vernacular* (1304–9) is the best-known of these. While written in Latin, it is a justification for vernacular poetry: it proceeds from a theoretical history of language and of linguistic difference (based on the myth of Babel), to a survey of Italian dialects (as well as of French and Provençal) and their comparative merits as languages of poetry in order to establish an ideal ("illustrious") literary vernacular, and then to prescriptive considerations, of a very technical order, about the *desiderata* of poetic genre, meter, and style. In its theoretical considerations of language and in its critiques of contemporary verse the influence of the grammatical tradition is visible; in its strongly prescriptive stance its debt to the Ciceronian rhetorical tradition is also clear. The Old Provençal *Las Leys d'amors* ("The Laws of Poetry," 1328–37, revised 1355–56, and existing in various other versions), originally compiled by Guilhem Molinier, was part of an effort that began in Toulouse in 1323 to encourage the continuation of Provençal poetry, in the tradition of the troubadours, after the Albigensian Crusade. It is a comprehensive guide to phonetics, dialects, poetic genres, metrics, grammar, rhetoric, and the tradition of Provençal verse itself.

In 1392 Eustache Deschamps (c. 1346–c. 1406), one of the most celebrated of fourteenth-century northern French poets, the younger contemporary of Guillaume de Machaut and exact contemporary of Chaucer, wrote a remarkable theoretical and prescriptive work called *L'Art de Dictier et de fere chançons.* Deschamps begins with an account of the traditional seven liberal arts—grammar, logic, rhetoric, geometry, arithmetic, astronomy, and music. The last of these, music, he divides into two kinds: "artificial music," by which he means musical sounds or melody, and "natural music," by which he means poetry, the "music of metrical speech." Here we find one of the most significant historical references to the deep relationship between music and lyric poetry, so fundamental to medieval poetic composition and performance. Under "natural music" Deschamps offers a technical account of the *formes fixes* of medieval French lyric poetry. He defines music, and hence "natural music" (poetry), as a form of healthful, therapeutic refreshment, thus distantly echoing the Horatian doctrine of poetry as delight and edification.

Medieval methods of textual exegesis derive from the classical grammatical tradition of *enarratio poetarum:* the foremost exemplars for medieval exegetical practice are late classical encyclopedic commentaries on pagan poets and patristic exegesis of the Bible. Medieval exegesis of sacred and secular texts takes basically two forms: the gloss, which could be interlinear or marginal and was generally restricted to elucidation of individual words and phrases; and the commentary, or *expositio,* which was originally marginal but could also be produced or copied as a freestanding, continuous commentary. Gloss and commentary were not afterthoughts to the text; rather, they were integral to the experience of reading any authoritative text, and the manuscript page was organized to allow room for the copying of traditional commentaries. The production of commentary itself was part of the process of teaching, copying, and transmission of curricular texts in the schools, and a given commentary on a major curricular text—such as Boethius's *Consolation,* Virgil's *Aeneid,* or the Psalms—is more often than not the cumulative record of many generations and even centuries of gloss and commentary on that text. The very best example of this is the *Glossa ordinaria,* the most important commentary (interlinear and marginal) on the Bible in the Middle Ages, the origins of which are now associated with Anselm of Laon (d. 1117); it was still being compiled in the mid-twelfth century. In its standard form the *Glossa ordinaria* is the product of several generations of schoolmen (Smalley 46–66).

The interchange between biblical and secular exegesis is best seen in the tradition of prologues to the authors, *accessus ad auctores* (Minnis, *Authorship*). Academic prologues to the authors originated in commentaries by late classical grammarians: in manuscripts of Servius's commentary on the *Aeneid* we find exegetical introductions to Virgil's text covering such topics as the life of the poet, the quality of the poem, the intention of the poet, the number and order of the books, and the poem's meaning. This basic prologue paradigm was reshaped and revised in a number of ways during the Middle Ages. What is most important, this paradigm was borrowed from commentary on secular authors of the arts curriculum to be applied to exegesis of sacred Scripture.

This transference of a technique from secular to sacred commentary was accomplished by the twelfth century. In twelfth-century biblical and secular commentary the prologue took the following form: title, name of the author, intention of the author, matter *(materia)* of the book, mode of treatment *(modus tractandi),* order of the book, value or utility *(utilitas)* of the book, and the branch of knowledge to which the book belongs *(cui parti philosophiae supponitur).* The heading "intention" was valuable for justifying pagan poetry: if the exegete could assert that the intention of Ovid or Horace was moral edification, this solved the question of the "utility" of the text and also assigned the text to the branch of philosophy known as ethics. It also provided an answer to the question of style or *modus tractandi,* for the technical analysis of form, genre, and versification could be directed to the moral purpose of the work, to teach by example, to teach by censure (as in the case of satire), or to teach through delight (as in the case of the lyric meters of Boethius's *Consolation*).

Conrad of Hirsau's *Dialogue on the Authors* (c. 1100–1150) incorporates the standard *accessus* formulas on the ancient poets into a continuous essay on the pagan and Christian curricular authors. In biblical exegesis, the prologue heading *modus tractandi* encouraged attention to the stylistic character of biblical texts, often discussed in terms borrowed from commentary on secular authors (e.g., the poetic mode of the Psalms). But more generally, twelfth-century discussions of biblical *modus tractandi* entailed allegorical readings of the spiritual sense of the text.

The full-scale recovery and revaluation of Aristotelian science in the twelfth-century schools transformed literary-critical attitudes and exegetical methods. This transformation is reflected in the emergence of a new prologue form that enabled a broader range of theoretical discussion. The new prologue, used for both secular and scriptural authors, was based on Aristotelian theories of causality (derived from the *Physics* and *Metaphysics*): the "Aristotelian prologue" considers the text under the headings of efficient cause (author), material cause (subject matter), formal cause (literary form, *forma tractandi*), and final cause (intention, purpose, or utility). This prologue scheme, and the scientific assumptions that lay behind it, focused attention on certain issues that earlier exegesis had tended to sidestep. For biblical exegetes it encouraged sophisticated discussions of authorial role and of literary form.

The Aristotelian model of degrees of causality allowed

exegetes to distinguish various levels of authorial control. The authorship (or "efficient cause") of a biblical text could be double *(duplex causa efficiens):* God is the primary efficient cause, and the individual human author (e.g., David, Solomon, Luke) is the secondary or instrumental cause. Once the divine authority of sacred Scripture was designated, the exegete could concentrate on the human author behind the text and on the material forms of textuality—rhetoric, affect, form, structure—that are the products of human agency. The concern with the human author led, in thirteenth- and fourteenth-century biblical exegesis, to precise distinctions between kinds of authorial roles: author, commentator, compiler, scribe. Here the human authors of Scripture might be regarded as scribes in relation to God, the primary cause or author, but as authors to their human readers; by the same token, a commentator on Scripture, such as Peter Lombard (c. 1100–1160), might be regarded by his later readers and beneficiaries as an author.

In paying attention to the human authors of Scripture, commentators intended to describe the way that human writing can give certain access to divine meaning. But they also focused attention on textual and historical issues. Pagan and secular poetry had long occupied an inferior position because it was only the product of human agency: it had no claim to divine authority. But when biblical exegetes developed an interpretive system that could accommodate the human author and human-produced rhetoric, this opened a door to appreciation of human authorship on its own terms and thus to more flexible critical reception of secular and pagan authors. This in turn had important implications for medieval literary activity. Latin and vernacular writers began to apply the fourfold Aristotelian prologue to introduce their own texts and thus to define their own authorial status in relation to their texts. Vernacular writers such as Geoffrey Chaucer and John Gower exploited the scholastic theory of authorial roles to delineate their particular relationships to literary tradition (Copeland 179–220; Minnis, *Authorship* 168–210).

The most systematic application of scholastic terminology to vernacular poetry is found in the tradition of Dante commentary, beginning with the *Epistle to Can Grande,* which is traditionally attributed to Dante himself. In *Can Grande* the *Commedia* is analyzed according to standard *accessus* topics. The *forma tractandi* of the poem is poetic, fictive, descriptive, digressive, and metaphorical—terms deriving from scholastic discussions of the affective quality of theology; but the *forma tractandi* also consists in definition, division, proof, refutation, and exemplification, which are scholastic terms for the

ratiocinative sciences. In other words, Dante's poetics are defined in the terms of both human and divine sciences (Minnis, *Authorship* 118–59; Sandkühler 16–46). Guido da Pisa's commentary on the *Commedia* (1328–33) also uses this twofold poetic to describe Dante's poem. In addition, Guido also applies the Aristotelian prologue form to the *Commedia,* as did Pietro Alighieri in his commentary on the *Commedia* (three recensions, 1340–58): Pietro exploits the Aristotelian format to focus on formal and rhetorical considerations rather than on the spiritual truths contained in the allegories. The scholastic accommodation of the human author and of the *modus poeticus* thus provided a critical model both for exegetical theory and for contemporary poetic production.

Rita Copeland

See also ARABIC THEORY AND CRITICISM, ST. AUGUSTINE, GIOVANNI BOCCACCIO, DANTE ALIGHIERI, and PHILOLOGY.

Alain de Lille [Alanus di Insulis], *De planctu naturae* (ed. Nikolaus M. Häring, 1978, trans. James J. Sheridan, 1980); Boethius, *The Theological Tractates and the Consolation of Philosophy* (trans. H. F. Stewart, 1973); Edmond Faral, ed., *Les Arts poétiques du XIIe et du XIIIe siécle: Recherches et documents sur la technique littéraire du moyen âge* (1924); Dominicus Gundissalinus, *De divisione philosophiae* (ed. Ludwig Baur, 1903); Robert S. Haller, ed. and trans., *Literary Criticism of Dante Alighieri* (1973); O. B. Hardison, Jr., et al., eds., *Medieval Literary Criticism: Translations and Interpretations* (1974); Hugh of St. Victor, *Didascalicon* (ed. C. H. Buttimer, 1939, trans. Jerome Taylor, 1961); Isidore of Seville, *Etymologiae sive Origines* (ed. W. M. Lindsay, 2 vols., 1911); Macrobius, *Commentarii in somnium Scipionis* (ed. James Willis, 1970, trans. William H. Stahl, 1952); A. J. Minnis, A. B. Scott, with David Wallace, eds., *Medieval Literary Theory and Criticism, c. 1100–c. 1375: The Commentary Tradition* (1988); James J. Murphy, ed., *Three Medieval Rhetorical Arts* (1971); Bernardus Silvestris, *The Commentary on the First Six Books of the Aeneid Commonly Attributed to Bernardus Silvestris* (ed. Julian Ward Jones and Elizabeth Frances Jones, 1977, trans. Earl G. Schreiber and Thomas E. Maresca, 1979).

Judson Allen, *The Ethical Poetic of the Middle Ages* (1982); Marcia L. Colish, *The Mirror of Language: A Study in the Medieval Theory of Knowledge* (1968, rev. ed., 1983); Rita Copeland, *Rhetoric, Hermeneutics, and Translation in the Middle Ages: Academic Traditions and Vernacular Texts* (1991); Gilbert Dahan, "Notes et textes sur la poétique au moyen âge," *Archives d'histoire doctrinale et littéraire du moyen âge* 47 (1980); Peter Dronke, *Fabula: Explorations into the Uses of Myth in Medieval Platonism* (1974); O. B. Hardison, Jr., "The Place of Averroes' Commentary on the *Poetics* in the History of Medieval Criticism," *Medieval and Renaissance Studies* (ed. John Lievsay, 1970); Martin Irvine, "A Guide to the Sources of Medieval Theories of Interpretation, Signs, and the Arts of Discourse: Aristotle to Ockham," *Semiotica* 63 (1987), "Medieval Grammatical Theory and Chaucer's *House of Fame*," *Speculum* 60 (1985); H. A. Kelly, "Aristotle-Averroes-Alemannus on Tragedy: The Influence of the *Poetics* on the Latin Middle Ages," *Viator* 10 (1979); Robert Lamberton, *Homer the Theologian: Neoplatonist Allegorical Reading and the Growth of the Epic Tradition* (1986); Richard McKeon, "Rhetoric in the Middle Ages," *Critics and Criticism: Ancient and Modern* (ed. R. S. Crane, 1952); A. J. Minnis, *Medieval Theory of Authorship: Scholastic Literary Attitudes in the Later Middle Ages* (1984); James J. Murphy, *Rhetoric in the Middle Ages: A History of Rhetorical Theory from St. Augustine to the Renaissance* (1974); Glending Olson, *Literature as Recreation in the Later Middle Ages* (1982); D. W. Robertson, *A Preface to Chaucer: Studies in Medieval Perspectives* (1962); Bruno Sandkühler, *Die frühen Dantekommentare und ihr Verhältnis zur mittelalterlichen Kommentartradition* (1967); Beryl Smalley, *The Study of the Bible in the Middle Ages* (1952); Armand Strubel, "*Allegoria in factis* et *allegoria in verbis*," *Poétique* 23 (1975); Winthrop Wetherbee, *Platonism and Poetry in the Twelfth Century: The Literary Influence of the School of Chartres* (1972).

MILL, JOHN STUART

John Stuart Mill (1806–73) is an original critical thinker, whose contribution to poetic theory has been underestimated partly because some of his most innovative ideas lie buried in essays not explicitly devoted to poetics and partly because his most celebrated statements about poetry are not his most original. Mill's well-known antithesis "Eloquence is heard, poetry is overheard" (1:348), for example, is now seen as a mere Romantic commonplace that has helped perpetuate the myth that Mill is wed to a private, narrowly emotive theory of poetry. Equally misleading is Mill's assertion that poetic utterances about lions that look like statements made by naturalists "intent on stating the truth, the whole truth, and nothing but the truth" (347) are not designed to state the truth at all. It is too often assumed that in making this claim Mill is merely anticipating I. A. RICHARDS's overly simple distinction between scientific statements and the emotive utterances of the poet, whose sentences consist of "pseudo-statements."

In fact, Mill is never entirely happy with the distinction he draws between science's descriptive language and the emotive language of poetry. His real originality as a literary theorist lies in efforts to extend the meaning of the prize word "truth" so that it includes versions of the world that can still be judged as right or wrong but by different, though no less exacting, criteria than those the philosopher applies to a logical intuition or to a hypothesis in science. Mill's originality resides, not in his anticipation of Richards's problematic doctrine of the poet's "pseudo-statements," but in his anticipation of two doctrines that have exercised a far more pervasive influence on modern theory: I am referring to ROMAN JAKOBSON's distinction between metaphoric and metonymic methods of associating ideas and to J. L. Austin's important distinction between constative and performative discourse (see SPEECH ACTS).

The mistake of construing as descriptions of lions utterances that record the reactions of an observer is the mistake of two modes of discourse, one referential, framed on the empirical model of truth by correspondence, and the other emotive. The failure to see that poets use language in ways beyond the scope of traditional description, in order to evince emotion, is the same failure to which Austin draws attention when trying to extricate from "constative" or "locutionary" statements, which describe or report events, the kind of utterance he calls "performative" (those that "do" things). Mill's axiom in an 1833 essay that poetry is "the expression or utterance of feeling" (384) leads him to ascribe to poetry two features of language that Austin ascribes to all performative speech. In the first place, both are activities, mental performances. Poetry expresses, Mill says, "state(s) of awe, wonder, or terror" (347). When William Wordsworth's heart fills with pleasure and he joins the daffodils in a sacramental dance, his elated diction gives a verdict or estimate of the daffodils' worth. In celebrating his ability to renew felicity now and in the future, the poet's use of language has less in common with a botanical description of flowers and trees than with the words used in christening ships and making wagers. A second characteristic of both poetic and performative speech is that neither can be said to advance a strictly "true or false" proposition. Or as Austin whimsically insists, when propounding his "doctrine of the *Infelicities*" (14), the poet is not judged by true or false criteria; what the poet says will be evaluated as more or less happy or apt.

For the distinction between two methods of compounding ideas, one by temporal and spatial connection and the other by synchronous association, Mill is indebted to his father, James Mill. And he owes to James Martineau's articles on Joseph Priestly, the first of which appeared in the same number of the *Monthly Repository* (January–April 1833) as Mill's essay "What Is Poetry?" the specific application of his father's distinction to the poet's synchronous and the scientist's successive methods of associating their ideas. When Mill says the poet compounds his ideas under the influence of dominant feelings, under emotions of awe or terror, for example, which allows him to substitute one idea for another, he is anticipating, without in any way influencing, Jakobson's influential distinction between metonymic combination of ideas and metaphoric substitution of them. If only scientific knowledge is genuine, then all education is education by metonymy. But poets want to substitute their ideas synchronously. Unpredictable breaks in logic and abrupt shifts from one idea to another allow them to celebrate the sovereignty of their ideas over the temporal and spatial connections of the scientist. The poet shows what it means to think in and be educated by metaphor.

Earlier empiricists such as John Locke and DAVID HUME deplore the process of synchronous association, because it may so transform present sensations that they lose all correspondence to their sequence in nature. But Mill commends these changes. If the feelings the poet associates correspond to no sensation he is conscious of mirroring, they continue to be logically valid intuitions only if they are inferences in disguise. And feelings can be inferences in disguise only if they correspond to sensations once registered on the mirror of the mind but now forgotten or obscured. Although the mind's unconscious memory is not a faculty that Locke or Hume recognizes, it is of central importance to the autobiographical poetry of Wordsworth or Alfred Lord Tennyson, whom Mill admired. The faculty of unconscious memory helps Mill explain how the emotional associations of his poet, which are founded on feeling and effective memory, are not an exception to empirical laws. Even when claiming that the poet's function is to describe, not the lion, but the emotions it evokes, Mill is unwilling to eliminate the lion altogether, because he is reluctant to discard a correspondence theory of truth. Mill is always in pursuit of a theory that can do justice to poetic genius without forcing him to abandon the empirical basis of his theory.

On utilitarian premises, poetry would seem to be feigned history, as it was for FRANCIS BACON. If this is so, then how is Mill to reconcile an empirical theory of knowledge with anything but the narrowest empirical conception of poetic truth? An answer can be found not only in Mill's theory of the poet's synchronous associations and intuitive inferences but also in Mill's doctrine of ends. In book 6 of his *Logic*, he argues that art is ultimately a source of knowledge, for the artist's high vocation is to discern and proclaim the ends we should pursue, then relinquish to science the task of determining how to reach them.

Mill's doctrine of ends is anticipated in a letter to Thomas Carlyle dated July 5, 1833. The letter assigns to the poet the persuasive function of making truth impressive to those who already know it. As Mill explains in a passage that anticipates John Henry Newman's distinction between real and notional assent, "The artist's is the higher part, for by him alone is real *knowledge* of such truths conveyed." It must be possible, says Mill, in a sentence that could have found its way into Newman's "Essay in Aid of a Grammar of Assent," to "convince" the logician "who never could *know* the intuitive truths . . . that they are even very *probable,* and that he may have faith in them when higher natures than his own affirm that they are truths" (12:163).

In the last chapter of the *Logic,* however, Mill takes one crucial step beyond this position. "The only one of the premises . . . which Art supplies, is the original major premise, which asserts that the statement of the given end is desirable. Science then lends to Art the proposition . . . that the performance of certain actions will attain the end" (8:944–45). In the letter to Carlyle, truth resides with the logician alone. In order to be moved by the poet, the reader must have an antecedent faith in what he says. In the *Logic,* by contrast, the artist's intuitions are the antecedent conditional of truth. The antithesis of art is no longer the truth or falsehood of logical inquiry, but the meaninglessness of a world from which human purpose has been banished. Until Mill's artist has intuited humanity's ends, there is no intelligible world for his logician or scientist to study.

W. David Shaw

See also BRITISH THEORY AND CRITICISM: 4. VICTORIAN.

John Stuart Mill, *Autobiography and Literary Essays* (*Collected Works of John Stuart Mill,* vol. 1, ed. John M. Robson and Jack Stillinger, 1981), *The Earlier Letters of John Stuart Mill, 1812–1848* (*Collected Works,* vols. 12–13, ed. John M. Robson and Francis E. Mineka, 1962), *System of Logic: Ratiocinative and Inductive* (*Collected Works,* vols. 7–8, ed. John M. Robson and R. F. McRae, 1974).

M. H. Abrams, *The Mirror and the Lamp: Romantic Theory and the Critical Tradition* (1953); Edward Alexander, "The Utility Of Poetry," *Matthew Arnold and John Stuart Mill* (1965); J. L. Austin, *How to Do Things with Words* (1962, ed. J. O. Urmson and Marina Sbisà, 2d ed., 1975); Walter J. Ong, "J. S. Mill's Pariah Poet," *Philological Quarterly* 29 (1950); J. M. Robson, "J. S. Mill's Theory of Poetry," *Mill: A Collection of Critical Essays* (ed. J. B. Schneewind, 1969), "Literary Essays," *Collected Works of John Stuart Mill,* vol. 1 (1981); W. David Shaw, *The Lucid Veil: Poetic Truth in the Victorian Age* (1987); Alba H. Warren, *English Poetic Theory, 1825–1865* (1950).

MILLER, J. HILLIS

Joseph Hillis Miller (b. 1928) first distinguished himself as a Victorian critic. His inaugural work on Charles Dickens (*Charles Dickens: The World of His Novels,* 1958) remains a landmark in the field. Although he has continued to ground his research in that area, it is mainly as a literary theorist, linked first with the GENEVA SCHOOL and later with the deconstructive critics of the "Yale school" (see DECONSTRUCTION), that Miller has come to occupy a place at the forefront of American literary criticism.

Although formative influences such as those of Georges Poulet's phenomenology and KENNETH BURKE's sociosymbolism are often noted, Miller's early work already reveals his particular concern with the way poetic language and rhetoric undermine—deconstruct—all cognitive claims to understanding. Early in his study of Dickens Miller informs readers that "the words of the work are themselves the primary datum" (x). Also evident in this book is a pattern of dialectical destructuring that, put schematically, might be understood as "Not A, but B; not B, but A." For example, in describing the essential relationship between Pip and Magwitch in *Great Expectations* Miller writes: "By choosing his servitude to Magwitch, Pip transforms it into freedom. . . . For Dickens, as for Kierkegaard, the self can only affirm itself through self-sacrifice. . . . Only the mutually self-denying, self-creating relationship of love succeeds, whereas the active assertion of will and the passive hope of great expectations both fail" (276). Miller is frequently drawn, throughout his writings, to this curious form of *repetition* whereby the truth asserts itself as other, as the word repeats the world, or as one destroys the "meaning" of the text in the very act of understanding.

In Miller's next two books this dialectic is applied to a historical overview of the continued presence of an absent God in post-Romantic literature. For the Victorian writers discussed in *The Disappearance of God* (1963), this takes the form of a frustrating and liberating interplay between mediacy and immediacy where, as in the case of Thomas De Quincey's debilitating fascination with digressions and details, the divine object is perpetually omnipresent and yet nowhere at all. For Matthew Arnold, "the empty phrases [e.g., "the absolute beauty and fitness of things"] are a way of keeping the void open after the disappearance of God" (265), while for Gerard Manley Hopkins, the poet's "almost unique sense of the immanence of God in nature and in the human soul" (324) leads first to a renunciation of his poetry as Satanic and finally to a moment of redemptive grace totally concomitant with this failure. *Poets of Reality* (1965) turns its attention to more modern writers (W. B. Yeats, T. S. Eliot, Wallace Stevens, William Carlos Williams, Joseph Conrad, Dylan Thomas), who, in contrast, have attempted to ground their transcendental visions in the here and now. Perhaps Miller feels most at home with Stevens, whose musings on "the nothing which is not there, and the nothing which is" so closely mirror Miller's own philosophical approach to criticism. Through a series of "fluid transformations" Stevens's work unfolds before us as a literal world of metaphorical transformations in which every object is capable of becoming every other and "impermanence is the only permanence in this flat world of circulating colored surfaces" (230).

In 1976 Miller published two important articles that argue for the necessity of viewing criticism from deconstructionist perspectives. He uses "Ariadne's Thread" as a model for the critical paradox of *constructing* a textual labyrinth at the same time as one is fashioning an escape from the same. In place of the logocentric narrative *line* that would slay the monster, reveal the Truth, reward the reader, and so on, Miller substitutes a Möbius strip of doubling inversions that join as well as separate Theseus, Ariadne, Dionysus, Phaedra, JOHN RUSKIN, FRIEDRICH NIETZSCHE, and others in a labyrinth of meanings that emerges from our attempt to understand the meaning of the labyrinth. In "Stevens' Rock and Criticism as Cure, II" (1976, reprint, *Theory Now and Then*) Miller similarly distinguishes "canny" (nondeconstructive) from "uncanny" critics on the basis of the latters' "labyrinthine attempt to escape from the labyrinth of words." One touchstone for critics of the "Yale school" such as JACQUES DERRIDA, PAUL DE MAN, and Miller is to avoid an "Apollonian" cure for the problematics of reading if such a cure would exclude a "Dionysian" immersion in the multiple meanings of the text.

Miller left Johns Hopkins University for Yale in 1972, and after the move he published *Fiction and Repetition* (1982) and *The Linguistic Moment* (1985). Although he discusses, for the most part, the same pantheon of English and American writers as before, his concerns are more overtly theoretical, and his attention to language, particularly figuration, more pronounced. *Fiction and Repetition* distinguishes between a kind of repetition that emphasizes unity and one that emphasizes difference, the latter being, in a very real sense, no repetition at all, not least because it must repeat the first type as well as deviate from it. The oscillation between the two means, for Miller's interpretation of WALTER BENJAMIN'S interpretation of Marcel Proust, an emptying of either, which produces the meaning of each. This *catachrestic* model (Miller's leading trope) is deftly applied to Conrad's Lord Jim's "confidence in this illusory image of himself which is the source of his inability to confront the truth about himself" (29), to the impressive array of critics who have "covered up" the meaning of Emily Brontë's *Wuthering Heights* in the very act of understanding it, and to Virginia Woolf's miming of the past in *Between the Acts* in order to subvert it, as well as numerous other examples.

Although Miller's fascination with language and temporality is nothing new, the influence of his Yale colleague de Man is strongly felt in *The Linguistic Moment,* where the "pure word" *(reine Wort)* of Benjamin that emerges from the caesurae of language is elided with Nietzsche's notion of the "moment" *(Augenblick)* as a necessary catachresis of eternity ("Postface"): "The moment is, so to speak, its own image. It is haunted by itself as if it were its own uncanny *revenant*" (432). Similarly, Wallace Stevens is viewed as having reversed as well as returned to ARISTOTLE's original notion of metaphor as a foreignness at the ground of things ("That which momentously declares / Itself not to be I and yet / Must be"), while Matthew Arnold's attempts to cancel out ("anathematize") his poem on Empedocles turn out to be indistinguishable from statements of that text's true importance.

Between his arrival at the University of California, Irvine, in 1986 and 1992 Miller published eight books, two of which bring together a number of important, previously uncollected essays. Without departing from the concerns of his previous work, he nonetheless incorporates, in *The Ethics of Reading* and *Versions of Pygmalion,* a "second Critique," intended to defend the "political correctness" of his and other deconstructors' methodology. Miller rejects the obvious (and fallacious) referential approach, which would look to what is actually said or done in literature for moral guidance. He instead posits a more fundamental figurative model of the "ethics of reading" whereby we respond ethically as "good readers" of literature precisely because there is no

literal reason or ground on which to do so. Miller begins by analyzing IMMANUEL KANT's need for a person who represents the "as if" of respect *(Achtung)* and the Law but turns out to be more figurative than literal. In the following chapter, de Man's notion of "ethicity" is taken as a corrective for all those who would confidently assert a less aberrant notion of the "truth": "we can never understand why we cannot read our own epistemological wisdom clearly enough to avoid making ethical statements or telling ethical stories that are contradicted, undermined, and disqualified by that wisdom" (56).

Versions of Pygmalion continues this concern with the "ethics of reading" but returns the emphasis to language, this time to the figure of prosopopoeia (personification) as a model of the figurative way we read life into texts, ourselves (the ultimate personification), or life itself. Like the above-mentioned "ethical stories," we are inevitably driven to read into the text a Galatea who is not there. But, unlike Pygmalion, we can refuse to embrace our own interpretations and so move from an aesthetical level to an ethical one. The two apparently unrelated halves of MAURICE BLANCHOT's *Death Sentence* are thus seen as a model of the way literature both constructs and destructs—deconstructs—meaning, thereby ensuring ethical responsibility.

Such impressive publications might lead one to suspect otherwise, but Miller's service to the profession has been equally extraordinary. A tireless supporter of students, colleagues, and ideas, he was president of the Modern Language Association of America in 1986 and has contributed to countless committees, seminars, and organizations. In the wake of revelations in the 1980s about de Man's wartime activities, Miller devoted much time to defending his former colleague, and deconstruction in general, against charges of political *in*correctness. Whatever the fate of deconstructive criticism (Miller insists that overly insistent claims of its demise might be read as signs of continued vitality), Miller's voluminous output of books demonstrates the inexhaustibility of his heroic (or better, unheroic) refusal to cut the Ariadnean thread of literature's labyrinthine logic.

Paul Gordon

See also DECONSTRUCTION, PAUL DE MAN, and GENEVA SCHOOL.

J. Hillis Miller, "Ariadne's Thread: Repetition and the Narrative Line," *Critical Inquiry* 3 (1976), *Ariadne's Thread: Story Lines* (1992), *Charles Dickens: The World of His Novels* (1958), *The Disappearance of God: Five Nineteenth-Century Writers* (1963), "Dismembering and Disremembering in

Nietzsche's 'On Truth and Lies in a Non-Moral Sense,' " *Boundary 2* 9 (1981), *The Ethics of Reading: Kant, de Man, Eliot, Trollope, James, and Benjamin* (1987), *Fiction and Repetition: Seven English Novels* (1982), "The Figure in the Carpet," *Poetics Today* 1 (1980), *The Form of Victorian Fiction: Thackeray, Dickens, Trollope, George Eliot, Meredith, and Hardy* (1968), "The Geneva School: The Criticism of Marcel Raymond, Albert Béguin, Georges Poulet, Jean Rousset, Jean-Pierre Richard, and Jean Starowbinski" (1972, *Theory Then and Now*), *Hawthorne and History: Defacing It* (1991), *Illustration* (1992), "J. Hillis Miller and His Critics—A Reply," *PMLA* 103 (1988), *The Linguistic Moment: From Wordsworth to Stevens* (1985), "Marxism and Deconstruction," *Genre* 17 (1984), *Poets of Reality: Six Twentieth-Century Writers* (1965), *Theory Then and Now* (1991), *Thomas Hardy: Distance and Desire* (1970), *Tropes, Parables, Performatives: Essays on Twentieth-Century Literature* (1991), *Versions of Pygmalion* (1990), *Victorian Subjects* (1991).

Art Berman, "Deconstruction in America," *From the New Criticism to Deconstruction: The Reception of Structuralism and Post-Structuralism* (1988); Jonathan Culler, "Introduction," *On Deconstruction: Theory and Criticism after Structuralism* (1982); Sarah Lawall, "J. Hillis Miller," *Critics of Consciousness: The Existential Structures of Literature* (1968); Frank Lentricchia, "Versions of Phenomenology," *After the New Criticism* (1980); Christopher Norris, "Aesthetic Ideology and the Ethics of Reading: Miller and de Man," *Paul de Man* (1988); Imre Salusinszky, *Criticism in Society: Interviews with Jacques Derrida, Northrop Frye, Harold Bloom, Geoffrey Hartman, Frank Kermode, Edward Said, Barbara Johnson, Frank Lentricchia, and J. Hillis Miller* (1987).

MODERNIST THEORY AND CRITICISM

"Modernist" is a term most often used in literary studies to refer to an experimental, avant-garde style of writing prevalent between World War I and World War II, although it is sometimes applied more generally to the entire range of divergent tendencies within a longer period, from the 1890s to the present. Modernism is an international movement, erupting in different countries at different times; in fact, one characteristic of modernism is its transgression of national and generic boundaries. My main focus here, however, is on English-language modernism. As a historically descriptive term, then, "modernism" is misleading not only because of its vary-

ing applications (to the historical period or to a highly organized style characteristic of some but not all writers of the period) but also because it is typically more evaluative than descriptive. In its positive sense, "modernism" signals a revolutionary break from established orthodoxies, a celebration of the present, and an experimental investigation into the future. As a negative value, "modernism" has connoted an incoherent, even opportunistic heterodoxy, an avoidance of the discipline of tradition. This critical overtone has sounded periodically since the eighteenth century, from the time that Jonathan Swift, in *A Tale of a Tub* (1704), lampooned the "modernists" as those who would eschew the study of the ancients through the late-nineteenth-century reform movement in the Catholic church, which was labeled "modernist" and condemned as the "synthesis of all the heresies" in the papal encyclical *Pascendi* of Pope Pius X (1907). It is interesting to note that in the recent debates over modernism versus POSTMODERNISM, the characteristic unorthodoxy of modernism has been displaced onto the postmodern; in a motivated reversal, modernism is characterized as the corrupt, canonized orthodoxy (identified, misleadingly, with the NEW CRITICISM attributed to T. S. ELIOT, among others), with postmodernism as its experimental offshoot.

The project of identifying a modernist criticism and theory is vexed not only by the imprecision and contradictory overtones of the word "modernist" but also by the category "theory." Certainly many modernist writers wrote criticism: VIRGINIA WOOLF published hundreds of essays and reviews; W. B. Yeats's most important literary criticism has been collected in *Essays and Introductions* (see BRITISH THEORY AND CRITICISM: 5. SYMBOLISM); EZRA POUND's voluminous criticism is well known for its informality and directness; Eliot was as important a critic, especially in his later years, as he was a poet. But the most interesting theoretical dimension of modernist writing is not always explicitly presented as either criticism or theory but is instantiated in the writing itself; the theory can be deduced, however controversially, from the practice.

One axiom of modernist theory that was importantly articulated by T. E. Hulme in "Romanticism and Classicism" (1913–14, posthumously published in *Speculations*, 1924) is an acceptance of limits that are identified with classicism. Hulme argues: "The classical poet never forgets this finiteness, this limit of man. He remembers always that he is mixed up with earth. He may jump, but he always returns back; he never flies away into the circumambient gas" (120). The classical style, Hulme states, is carefully crafted, characterized by accurate description and a cheerful "dry hardness" (126). He asserts that "it is essential to prove that beauty may be in small, dry things" (131); Hulme's preference is for the visual and the concrete over the general and abstract, for freshness of idiom, for the vital complexities that are "intensive" rather than extensive (139).

Hulme's sounding of the note of classical style as one that is local, limited, intensive, and fresh resonates widely through the work of other modernist writers. Pound's dictum "Make it New," Eliot's objective correlative ("Hamlet," 1919, *Selected Prose* 48), James Joyce's epiphanies, Woolf's moments of being, and the explosive power of the concrete image celebrated in Imagism are all instances of a "classical" technique, a preference for the local and well-defined over the infinite. In *Dubliners*, Joyce defined the sickness of modern life as paralysis, a loss of local control, and he set about designing his fiction in a way that requires the reader to understand its individual, local parts before the whole can assume a meaningful shape.

The classical style is characteristic of much, but not all, modernist writing (D. H. Lawrence's work being one well-known exception). However, the classical theory begins to bifurcate, producing political implications that are diametrically opposed, when the insistence on finitude is applied to the individual. Both groups of classical writers accepted the view that the individual is limited, but one group, which included Woolf, Joyce, and Yeats, began to develop a theory of supplemental "selves" that points toward a celebration of diversity as antidote to individual limitation. In *Mrs. Dalloway*, Woolf has Clarissa propose a theory that she is many things and many people, "so that to know her, or any one, one must seek out the people who completed them" (1925, reprint, 1981, 52–53). Yeats worked out an analogous idea in his theory of the anti-self in "Per Amica Silentia Lunae" (1917), a notion that each individual is implicit in his or her opposite, which eventuated in the complex theory of interlocking personality types outlined in *A Vision* (1925, rev. ed., 1937). In *Ulysses* (1922), Joyce also pursues the idea that the self is luxuriously heterogeneous, a heterogeneity brought to the surface by multiple encounters with difference. He makes his hero an apostate Jew who is defined on either extreme by a "spoiled priest" and an adulterous woman, and in these slippages between limited individuals he celebrates such limits, such insufficiencies, as conditions of communal possibility. As Stephen Dedalus explains in the library, the varied world represents the potential scope of a disunited selfdom: "Every life is many days, day after day. We walk through ourselves, meeting robbers, ghosts, giants, old men,

young men, wives, widows, brothers-in-love, but always meeting ourselves" (*Ulysses*, 1922, ed. Hans Walter Gabler, 1984, chap. 9, ll. 1044–46).

The same recognition of the limitation of the individual produced in other modernist writers an insistence on strict, authoritarian regulation of the individual, the germ of fascist tendencies for which the movement became notorious. Hulme again articulates the premises of this position: "Man is an extraordinarily fixed and limited animal whose nature is absolutely constant. It is only by tradition and organisation that anything decent can be got out of him" (116). He speaks of liberty and revolution as essentially negative things, citing the French Revolution as evidence that when you remove the restraints on individuals, what emerges is their destructiveness and greed. Like Eliot, Hulme appreciated religion for its power to control human depravity through traditional order.

The problem with controlling "human depravity" through institutional restrictions is that the controlling "order" tends to legislate sameness, so that some orders of existence are seen as preferable to—less depraved than—others. And this is where the seams of "classical" modernist theory split: not over the limited nature of humanity, but over the question of the value of difference. The split was a jagged one; some writers, such as Pound, could cultivate difference in their writing and denounce it in society (as he did in his infamous radio broadcasts of the 1930s). The different premium accorded to ethnic, social, religious, and sexual differences by writers who agreed on the limited nature of the individual, however, explains how the offensive tirades of Wyndham Lewis and the brilliant feminism of Woolf, the anti-Semitic propaganda of Pound and the Jewish hero of Joyce's *Ulysses* could stem from the same "classical" root.

In a period that was to culminate in World War II, racism was an inevitably controversial issue. The related cause of feminism was also hotly debated during the period, since women had only been granted suffrage after World War I (1920 in the United States, 1928 in Great Britain). Woolf, in *A Room of One's Own*, details clearly and unpolemically the historical and material restrictions on women that prevented them from full participation in artistic and professional life. Her best illustration of the greater circumstantial constraints on women is her invention of a wonderfully gifted sister for Shakespeare named Judith, his counterpart in everything but freedom and opportunity. Woolf outlines what would have happened to this young girl if she had wanted to act in London, as her brother did; she sketches in the ridicule to which she would have been subjected, the ease with which more experienced men could have taken advantage of her, and the passion with which, upon finding herself with child, she would have killed herself: "Who shall measure the heat and violence of the poet's heart when caught and tangled in a woman's body?" (1929, reprint, 1981, 48). Woolf's main argument is that women need space—a room of their own—and economic freedom (a fixed income) for their hitherto pinched genius to flourish.

Finally, no discussion of modernist criticism and theory is complete without an account of the collapse of plot and its replacement by intertextual allusion and the "stream of consciousness." In a much-cited review of Joyce's *Ulysses* called *"Ulysses,* Order and Myth" (1923) Eliot argued that developments in ethnology and psychology, and Sir James Frazer's *The Golden Bough,* had made it possible to replace the narrative method with what he called the "mythical method," which was first adumbrated by Yeats (see CAMBRIDGE RITUALISTS). The mythical method works not through narrative but through allusion to different mythical narratives that, when fleshed out and juxtaposed, illuminate both the text in which they appear and each other in surprising and often revisionary ways. For example, Yeats's early poetry worked to contextualize his hopeless love for Maud Gonne within the competing and mutually reinforcing contexts of Greek myth (Helen of Troy) and Celtic myth (Deirdre of the Sorrows; the magic of the Sidhe). In *Ulysses,* the main mythic parallels are the *Odyssey* and *Hamlet,* although individual episodes are further complicated by allusions to other intersecting narratives, historical, fictional, or mythic. Eliot's *The Waste Land* provides the densest illustration of the mythical method, where the range of allusion includes a variety of Christian, Greek, occult, Scandinavian, Judaic, and Buddhist references, as well as allusions to music, drama, literature, and history (see MYTH THEORY AND CRITICISM).

Eliot chose to highlight myth as the key to modernist stylistics, but actually myth was just one category of narrative accessed through allusion; one might say that all kinds of narratives were situated behind the page, identifiable only through "tags" in the text, and that the interplay between these narratives produces a submerged commentary on it that imitates the pressure of the cultural unconscious (in narrativized form) on any individual performance. The stream-of-consciousness technique is yet another way of drawing the reader's attention from conscious, deliberate, intentionalized discourse to the pressure of the unsaid on the said, of the repressed on the expressed. The apparent randomness of associative thought prompts the reader to question the submerged "logic" of connection, to listen for the unconscious poetry of repressed desire. This attention to the unknown as the shadow of the known is reversed in Joyce's *Finnegans Wake,* in which it is the known that is obscured by the highly organized distortions of language and history as processed by the unconscious mind and the "mudmound" of the past. It is no surprise, in light of this sensitivity to the muted voice of the unconscious in the literature of the period, that another great modernist theorist was SIGMUND FREUD.

In fact, the opposing political tendencies of modernist writers bear a significant relationship to their different attitudes toward the unconscious. Bounded by the eruption of two world wars, the modernist period can be read as a historical enactment of the tension between FRIEDRICH NIETZSCHE's Apollonian and Dionysian forces. The Dionysian power of the unconscious was making itself felt, and the writers who sought to contain or deny it through the Apollonian power of civic or religious authority were, like Pentheus in the *Bacchae,* torn apart. Others sought to express the creative potential of the unconscious, its capacity to unify without homogenization, to proliferate via division, and it is the writing of this group that is most animated by the zest of manifold contradictions. As Yeats wrote near the end of his career in the voice of a crazed old woman,

> 'Fair and foul are near of kin,
> And fair needs foul,' I cried.
> 'My friends are gone, but that's a truth
> Nor grave nor bed denied,
> Learned in bodily lowliness
> And in the heart's pride.
>
> 'A woman can be proud and stiff
> When on Love intent;
> But love has pitched his mansion in
> The place of excrement;
> For nothing can be sole or whole
> That has not been rent.'

> ("Crazy Jane Talks with the Bishop," *Collected Poems of W. B. Yeats: A New Edition,* ed. Richard J. Finneran, 1983, rev. ed., 1989, 259–60)

Vicki Mahaffey

See bibliographies in T. S. ELIOT, EZRA POUND, and VIRGINIA WOOLF for additional texts by those writers.

T. S. Eliot, *"Ulysses,* Order, and Myth" (1923, reprinted in *Selected Prose of T. S. Eliot,* ed. Frank Kermode, 1975);

T. E. Hulme, *Speculations: Essays on Humanism and the Philosophy of Art* (ed. Herbert Read, 1924, 2d ed., 1936); Wyndham Lewis, *Time and Western Man* (1927); Lawrence I. Lipking and A. Walton Litz, eds., *Modern Literary Criticism, 1900–1970* (1972); Virginia Woolf, *A Room of One's Own* (1929, reprint, 1981); W. B. Yeats, *Essays and Introductions* (1961), *Mythologies* (1959).

Malcolm Bradbury and James McFarlane, eds., *Modernism: 1890 1930* (1976); Hugh Kenner, *The Pound Era* (1971); Frank Kermode, *Romantic Image* (1957); Michael H. Levenson, *A Genealogy of Modernism: A Study of English Literary Doctrine, 1908–1922* (1984); Sanford Schwartz, *The Matrix of Modernism: Pound, Eliot, and Early Twentieth-Century Thought* (1985); Vincent Sherry, *Ezra Pound, Wyndham Lewis, and Radical Modernism* (1993).

MOSCOW-TARTU SCHOOL

The Moscow-Tartu school (MTS) is a group of Soviet linguists (including Valerii Ivanov, Isaak Revzin, Vladimir Toporov), folklorists (Eleazar Meletinskij, Dmitri Segal), Orientalists (Aleksandr Piatigorskij, Boris Ogibenin), and literary scholars (including Jurij Levin, Jurij Lotman, Boris Uspenskij) who, since about 1960, have developed in close cooperation a set of comprehensive, semiotically oriented theories of literature, the text, myth and folklore, cinema, theater, and cultural systems in general, dealing with their systematic-structural, typological, and historical-dynamic regularities and mechanisms. The original members of the school, as well as a second generation of scholars, are currently active in both the former Soviet Union and the West. Four periods can be distinguished in the school's history: the first years, 1958–64, which saw the introduction of mathematical, cybernetic, and linguistic models into cultural studies, mostly on the programmatic level; 1964–70, the intensive development of semiotic models for particular cultural systems; 1970–73, formulation of global models of culture and of cultural universals; and the years since 1973, refinement of the details of cultural theory and applications to the history and typology of Russian literature and culture.

The school's work, especially in the literary field, is based on structuralist linguistics, classical SEMIOTICS (Charles Morris, CHARLES SANDERS PEIRCE), information and communication theory, systems theory, RUSSIAN FORMALISM and FILM THEORY of the 1920s (Sergey Eisenstein), PRAGUE SCHOOL STRUCTURALISM, and some elements of M. M. BAKHTIN's writings. A logical reconstruction of the group's mode of theorizing reveals four levels

of abstraction and generalization. At the outset, a set of quasi-formal concepts is assumed, including model, dynamic system, (in)variant, hierarchy, binary opposition and equivalence, sign, expression and content, function, code, message, information, and communication. The first step of theorizing proper envisages the development of a unified semiotic metalanguage in terms of which one then proceeds to formulate theories, models, and typologies for a culture and cultural texts in general, that is, a semiotics of culture. As a second step, and using the same theoretical vocabulary, models, and theories, specialized semiotic sciences are established for specific cultural spheres (cinema, myth, literature), bringing out what is specific to each as well as what they share with culture as a whole. Finally, descriptive models, based on the previous two stages, are set up for individual historical formations or phenomena: an artistic period or school, the *oeuvre* of an author, or an individual work. The MTS thus reveals a high degree of methodological self-awareness and a clear tendency toward the formulation of a hierarchically integrated science of culture. At the center of attention are always the mechanisms of meaning formation and transformation, meaning being seen as a relative-contrastive phenomenon. Formal and pragmatic factors are considered primarily with respect to their semantic contribution.

Culture is defined in MTS as a collective semiotic mechanism for the production, circulation, processing, and storage of information. It is both a collective memory and a program for the generation of new messages. It regulates human behavior and how humans project structuredness upon the world. Culture can be seen as the totality of nonhereditary information and as the means of its organization and preservation. At each time, a culture constitutes a system of systems that stand in relations of complex interdependence. It is a hierarchical totality of all individual signifying systems, each with its own internal structure and relative independence. Culture is hence both a unitary system and a union of relatively autonomous semiotic formations. General semiotics of culture studies the mechanisms of unity of a culture, the interrelations of the diverse semiotic systems within it, and the contribution of each of them to the whole. As a first stage, it seeks to formulate universals of culture, that is, the basic elements, structures, and mechanisms of human culture, that apply to it as a whole as well as to each of its subsystems. Since cultures are inherently dynamic and enormously variable in space and time, such universals must be formal and abstract, formulated in response to basic questions about the demarcation of culture from the extracultural, the specific role of each sign system, and the interrelations between sign systems, such as hierarchy, borrowing, and conflict. Basic pairs of oppositions for the description of components of culture include their systemic or extrasystemic status, their ambivalence or univocity with regard to their context, the distinction between core elements (maximum rigidity) and peripheral ones (disorganization), essential or superfluous in terms of the system and translatable or not into another code or subsystem.

Central theses about the structure and mechanisms of culture include the following: The culture-extracultural boundary and the hierarchical organization of culture are different for each culture and period. Within culture as a whole and within any of its subsystems internal variety (heterogeneity, options, alternatives, two or more concurrent structural principles in a state of tension and conflict) must exist at each time to maintain informativeness. A culture can exist only if it contains at least two semiotic systems or means of modeling reality, such as words and pictures. Each culture requires extracultural areas, peripheral ones, and deviations from its norms, which act as essential reservoirs for the next stage of its development. Different cultural subsystems reveal different degrees of organization and complexity and change at different rates and in different directions. Central mechanisms of cultural change include rehierarchization of subsystems, information, and values; change of place between center and periphery; redistribution of functions among subsystems; increase in systemic differentiation and complexity; incorporation of extrasystemic elements and the exclusion of codes or texts from cultural memory.

Because of the difference in their underlying codes, full intertranslatability between different cultural subsystems and between different stages of the same subsystem is impossible; incomplete communication, misinterpretation, and reinterpretation are part of the nature of culture. All cultures manifest a tension between homeostatic and dynamic tendencies. Novelty, diversity, and the proliferation of relatively independent subsystems are in conflict with the desire for uniformity and unification, for regarding the entirety of culture as a homogeneous whole with rigid, stable organization. Without diversity culture ossifies (no self-renewal); without some homogeneity and cohesiveness cultural communication becomes impossible. Beyond a certain degree of inner diversity, each culture produces a metacomponent: a unifying self-image or interpretation of itself and its past, a simplifying universal normative model that gives it overall orientation, hierarchical self-regulation, and

stability, but at the price of oversimplification and imposed uniformity. Being a tool of self-organization, it is never an objective reflection of the actual cultural situation.

Cultural typology is the contrastive study of the basic semiotic assumptions and global categorizations of reality embraced by different cultures. In MTS this typology is formulated in terms of binary oppositions. Thus, a culture may tend toward autonomization of the sign (free play or ritual) or toward its semantization, postulating a one-to-one relation between sign and reality. It may regard the expression-content relation in its own system as essential or as merely conventional and may posit itself as the only possible or correct culture or, conversely, acknowledge a plurality of different cultures. A culture's orientation may be toward absolutization of its current state, or it may adopt an ideology of innovation and change. It may define as its foundation a set of texts or a set or rules, while nonculture may be equated with nature, chaos, the nonsemiotic sphere, or alien cultures. One could also compare cultures in terms of the number, nature, and interrelations of the signifying systems of which they consist. When comparing world models, a topological vocabulary is adopted whose basic oppositions are between being higher and lower, inside or outside a given sphere. Semantic zones, boundaries between them, and an oriented movement into or out of a zone are as basic. These formal categories can be interpreted in spatial, temporal, cosmological, or axiological terms, and different cultures obviously satisfy them differently.

MTS assumes that all the semiotic systems of a culture serve as means of modeling (i.e., cognizing and explaining) the world. The primary modeling system is natural language, while all others are secondary. Some secondary modeling systems (literature, myth) use natural language as their material, adding to it further structures, and all of them are constructed on the analogy of natural language (elements, rules of selection and combination, levels), which also serves as the universal metalanguage for their interpretation. Modeling systems can be regarded as sign systems, as sets of rules (codes, instructions, programs) for the production of texts in the wide, semiotic sense, and as a totality of texts and their correlated functions. In fact, underlying codes can be manifested only through individual texts, and the category of text thus serves as the intermediary link between general semiotics and individual studies.

A cultural text may be in any semiotic medium: a painting, silent movie, ballet, or verbal utterance. It is a cohesive unit with overall differential features, an organized semantic unity, a macrosign with global meaning. It possesses fixity, having been set down via the use of signs; it is bounded or demarcated from other texts and nontexts via beginning and end signals. It further manifests internal articulation: texts are multileveled and possess an inner structuration on each level. The structures on different levels (e.g., sound and lexicon) interact, giving rise to a second-order structure of structures. These structures are the textual invariants. One can often extrapolate an invariant structure underlying a whole corpus of texts and regard it as the archetext of this corpus. This method is most fruitful in the study of folklore and mythology but may also be applied to the *oeuvre* of an author or the total literary production of a movement or school. In general, only those utterances considered worth conserving are considered as texts at a given cultural state. Texts belong to defined genres or types, are means for the transmission of messages, and are assigned an interpretation according to senders' and receivers' codes. Since the typologies and codes held by senders and receivers are often different, texts may be assigned to different types and acquire different interpretations over time or interculturally. Texts also possess cultural functions, but once again, the correlation between text types and functions is variable in space and time, and the same holds for the cultural prestige and value of any text type.

For Jurij Lotman, art is a functional category, based on a special mode of textual reception that consists of a hesitation between ludic and real world behavior. In his view, a work of art or artistic text in any medium is an analogue of reality in which reality is translated into the language of the given sign system. Any art is based on a set of semantic conventions that are arbitrary with regard to the objects portrayed, although to participants in the system they may look like the single, natural way of doing things. In fact, to understand any art is to understand its conventions. Some periods in the history of all Western arts (medieval, neoclassical) are based on an aesthetics of identity in which works are expected to satisfy preexistent familiar rules. Other periods (baroque, modernism) are governed by the aesthetics of opposition, where new works embody as a rule new, unfamiliar methods of modeling reality that are in opposition to the prevalent, preexistent ones.

Although MTS has contributed much to the study of visual, filmic, and mythological texts, we must limit our discussion to verbal ones. Verbal art is both a communicative and a modeling system, conveying information and constructing an image of reality. Verbal artistic texts are encoded and decoded according to semantic norms that differ from those of ordinary language communication, and so these texts are unique in their ability to condense information. Their degree of semantic saturation exceeds that of any other kind of discourse due to the complexity of their internal structure. They manifest more patterns of interrelation of elements on each level and among levels—from sound to architectonics—and it is in these texts alone that formal (expression) patterns are semanticized and transformed into the bearers of information.

In fact, the content or "message" of an artistic text is embodied precisely in its formal structures and their interrelations, in its total labyrinth of interconnections. Through their formal patterns, artistic texts create relations of equivalence or opposition between semantic units that are not related in this way in ordinary language, for example, *love = death* or *love vs. death*. This gives rise in succession to a secondary, occasional semantics, to a new system of relations between the denotations of these units, and ultimately to a secondary model of reality that is different from that embodied in ordinary language. Literature provides a wide array of such mimetic and conceptual world models, all different from one another and from the standard one. It thus expands and liberates our field of consciousness by formulating alternative views of reality.

So far we have discussed mechanisms of literary meaning-formation that are based on inner textual patterns of interrelation on each level and between levels. The information content of the artistic text is further enhanced by the multiple encoding and decoding relations in which it and each of its levels stand to the extratextual context, consisting of other texts, text models, literary norms and conventions, and communicative situations. We may term the immanent textual information "textual meaning" *(znachenie)* and the extratextual one "textual significance" *(znachimost')*. Textual significance is obviously polyvalent and historically variable. Artistic texts display a heterogeneity of governing norms and a resultant interplay of underlying codes. Any given level of the text may be patterned alternately according to two different competing principles or codes, for example, tragic and comic or natural intonation and regular meter. Different levels of the text may be governed by norms stemming from different codes, for example, romantic characters and realistic style. Another important component of literary significance is the minus device, that is, the absence of an element or pattern that is expected relative to a preceding dominant norm, for example, the absence of lyricisms and elevated style in Aleksandr Pushkin's "Belkin Stories."

All of the foregoing creates additional information through the confrontation between underlying textual codes. Still more information is engendered by the communicative context. The producer of an artistic text always has at his or her disposal a plurality of alternative literary codes to choose from; thus, any selection he or she makes is informative. What is more, the text producer may formulate his or her individual message according to an innovative, unfamiliar code that the reader needs to elicit from this very text, and innovation is always information. The receiver of a literary text does not know in advance which code(s) underlie the text being confronted, so that their very identification is informative. Like authors, readers too have several codes available to them, codes that change radically in the course of time and that may be very dissimilar from those employed by the author. This ensures that in literary diachrony new and different significances will be ascribed to the same text, rendering it semantically inexhaustible in this respect.

The secondary semantic organization of artistic texts is most evident in lyric poetry. As we know, the constructive principle of poetic texts is repetition or parallelism. Such repetition on the expression level of phonological, prosodic, morpho-syntactic, and graphic (position in the line) features creates formal equivalence between the corresponding text segments. But in the secondary language of art, these formal patterns also have semantic significance. Whenever words, parts of words, or word groups are juxtaposed into a pattern because of formal equivalence, we presume a semantic relation between them that often does not exist in ordinary language. An occasional, ad hoc semantic paradigm is created, and the reader is called upon to establish a relation of equivalence and opposition *(so-protivopostavlenie)* between its terms and to define a semantic common denominator (invariant) for them. Such invariants then function as terms in pairs of opposites on the next higher level, and so on. Opposites on the highest textual level define the polarities of the textual world model.

Several consequences follow from this view: occasional semantic paradigms take precedence over the standard language syntagmatic patterns existing in the poetic text and sometimes replace them altogether, as in many modernist texts. Lyric poetry is the only kind of text in which the content level is crucially organized and determined by properties or patterns on the expression level. In this sense, the linguistic sign becomes iconic in poetry. Since the secondary, poetic semantics is determined by features and patterns on the expression level, and since these are text- and language-bound, lyric poetry can be neither paraphrased nor translated without loss of meaning. The grid of formal equivalences that forms the backbone of the semantic organization of the poetic text is, by its very nature, spatial and regressive, not temporal and progressive. Poetic decoding involves constant reference back *(vozvrashchenie)* to earlier text segments, since parallelism can be perceived in retrospect only. Strictly speaking, a lyric poem can only be reread. A confrontation is inevitably created between the spatial occasional meaning system provided by the poetic code and the standard, successive semantic network ascribed to the text by ordinary language. This engenders dual perception and dialectical tension between the two, thereby enhancing the semantic density and overall informativeness of the text.

MTS work on narrative is based on cultural semiotics as well as folklore and mythology and bears little resemblance to Western NARRATOLOGY, with the exception of the study of point of view. Thus, Toporov and Lotman, respectively, are interested in the reconstruction of archaic, mythological world patterns in modern narrative and the emergence of plot, character, and point of view from myth. Lotman contrasts the cyclical time of myth, with its eternal typological recurrence, with the linear, directed time of narrative, with its unique events and agents. In his view, the most basic element of narrative is physical space, whose zones (e.g., home and forest) and boundaries model basic conceptual patterns. The originary space is divided into at least two areas, representing two semantic or axiological fields in binary opposition, such as life and death, riches and poverty, or one's own and alien. Each of these areas contains one or more inhabitants, who are identified by the bundle of differential features that define their area. The basic event of narrative is the shifting of a figure *(personazh)* across the boundary of a semantic field, typically the hero who goes out into the world and returns home with a boon (bride, riches). The static, classificatory conceptual structure of the narrative universe is thus dynamized through the mobile agent. The character of a literary figure is the paradigm of all the binary oppositions between it and other figures in the text. For Lotman, then, as for Bakhtin, action and character are anthropomorphizations of conceptual features, opposites, and transitions, and not full-fledged mimetic or psychological units.

Both Lotman and Uspenskij discuss point of view in great detail, and in both clear echoes of Bakhtin are discernible. Lotman defines point of view as an orientation or relation between a subject (a consciousness) and a domain that results in the construction of a model or image of the world, or part of it, for this consciousness. Uspenskij defines point of view as the relation between representation and that which is represented and distinguishes four basic aspects or planes on which this relation manifests itself: the spatio-temporal, psychological (especially perceptual), phraseological (stylistic), and ideological (axiological). The communicative structure of the narrative text defines three basic, hierarchically ordered communicative or representational positions: author (either global impersonal narrative voice or implied author), marked narrator, and characters. Since each of these three positions can be manifested on all four planes, a narrative yields up to twelve varieties of point of view. Uspenskij's book *Poetics of Composition* provides a comprehensive typology or calculus of the functioning and the possible interrelations, especially combinations and shifts, among these varieties in the course of the narrative text. From the perspective of an author, all of these varieties are compositional options, to be selected and combined according to particular artistic goals. Uspenskij singles out several artistically significant combinations, such as the association in a narrative of different planes with different communicative positions (e.g., perception from character, ideological evaluation from author) or the association of particular objects in the text's world with one communicative position in terms of one or more planes. Conversely, the information on a given plane may come alternately from two or three positions, while planes (e.g., perception and style) may not concur within an utterance coming technically from the same speech position, as in free indirect discourse or irony.

Lotman is primarily interested in the connection between the ideological and stylistic planes. To him, each stylistic variety (key, idiom, register) chosen by an author for a particular speech position is correlated with a specific world-view or axiological stance, especially when such a variety is associated with an antecedent literary tradition, school, or genre. Each stylistic-ideological position, together with the narrative speaker associated with it, claims to convey *the* truth about what happened in the narrative world, as well as about human nature and the ways of society. Narratives created by some schools are such that within their artistic worlds there is one authoritative world model, one full objective truth that is normally associated with the implied author's position. If the text presents several ideological perspectives, they are all seen as partial and subjective and are ranked according to their degree of coincidence with the dominant authorial standard of truth. When different ideological stances, embodied by different nar-

rative voices, are juxtaposed in a narrative, a process of multiple internal transcoding takes place, as in Mikhail Lermontov's *A Hero of Our Time*. The same event, character, or situation will be encoded by different speakers in different idioms, each embodying his or her modeling of this element, based in its turn on his or her own modeling system. All these partial idioms are translatable into the implied author's superior code in order to reveal their relative truthfulness or error. In some works, though, such as Pushkin's *Eugene Onegin,* multiple internal transcoding constantly occurs, but there is no longer a superior authorial idiom, a second-order ideological system, or standard of truth. Each of the ideological styles and stances in the text conditions and relativizes the others, and a complex game of juxtaposition and interaction among them ensues. Truth now resides in this dynamic interplay of partial, sometimes contradictory, perspectives, and not in any of them in isolation. One can thus no longer single out and absolutize any one position; there is no singular, ultimate truth, and no perspective can be ruled out.

Lotman's views on literature and literary criticism as dynamic systems reveal a historical relativism based on MTS general theories of cultural systems. The literary system is defined in terms of the aesthetic function—with its twin presumptions that the text is multiply encoded and that all of its expression elements are also content elements—as well as in terms of textual forms (signals and patterns). At each period, different text types are canonically associated with the aesthetic function, so that texts originally associated with it may lose their literary status over time, and vice versa. The boundary between literature and nonliterature is hence historically mobile. In different periods, the position of literary texts in the general cultural hierarchy of values is quite different, ranging from low in the Middle Ages to supreme in the context of art for art's sake. Within the literary system there are permanent binary oppositions between written and oral texts, high and popular kinds of writing, native and alien texts, and prose and verse ones. These subsystems represent heterogeneous factors standing in relations of conflict and tension. But the nature of the literary-historical process is such that textual elements and forms always move between the two poles of each oppositional pair.

Literary criticism and literary historiography are metatexts of the literary system. They constitute its self-defining, self-organizing mechanism and embody its self-description and procedures of interpretation and evaluation at a given time. The critical component consists of normative texts that set out rules of literary production, define the boundary between literature and nonliterature, and rank existing types of literary texts and establish one of them as the very essence of literature. Literary criticism thus formulates essential, closed definitions of literature that regulate literary production and reception alike. The criteria formulated in these metatexts are subsequently applied to past texts as well, leading to the exclusion from the literary canon of those that do not satisfy them. Each phase of the literary system thus creates a tendentious image, mythology, or legend of its own past, where one part of the past literary production is canonized as the only representation of this past. Both literary criticism and its resultant literary historiography change radically in the course of time, so that the collective literary memory is not an inert form of conservation but rather a mechanism of active and ever new modeling of past facts. Finally, literary criticism and historiography are themselves objects of study for the literary theorist, on a par with literature itself. The observing scholar may not adopt either the vocabulary or the norms of these metatexts, on pain of confusing his or her theory and its object, theoretical metalanguage and object language.

Uri Margolin

Henryk Baran, ed., *Semiotics and Structuralism* (1976); Karl Eimermacher, ed., *Semiotica Sovietica (1962–1973)* (2 vols., 1986); Reno Faccani and Umberto Eco, eds., *Semiotica della letteratura in URSS* (1969); Jurij Lotman, *Analysis of the Poetic Text* (ed. D. Barton Johnson, 1976), *Aufsätze zur Theorie und Methodologie der Literatur und Kultur* (ed. Karl Eimermacher, 1974), *La Semiosfera* (ed. Simonetta Salvestroni, 1985), *The Structure of the Artistic Text* (ed. Ronald Vroon, 1977), *Testo e contesto* (ed. Simonetta Salvestroni, 1980), *Universe of the Mind* (ed. and trans. Ann Shukman, 1990), *Vorlesungen zu einer strukturalen Poetik* (ed. Karl Eimermacher, 1972); Jurij Lotman and Boris Uspenskij, *Semiotica e cultura* (ed. Donatella Ferrari-Bravo, 1975), *The Semiotics of Russian Culture* (ed. Ann Shukman, 1984); Jurij Lotman et al., *Semiotica de la cultura* (ed. Jorge Lozano, 1979), *Theses on the Semiotic Study of Culture* (1975); Jurij Lotman and Boris Uspenskij, eds., *Travaux sur les systèmes de signes* (1976); Daniel Lucid, ed., *Soviet Semiotics* (1977, 2d ed., 1988); *Russian Poetics in Translation*, vol. 2, *Poetry and Prose* (1976), vol. 3, *General Semiotics* (ed. M. O'Toole and Ann Shukman, 1976); *Soviet Semiotics and Criticism: An Anthology,* special issue, *New Literary History* 9 (1978); *Soviet Semiotics of Literature and Culture,* special issue, *PTL: A Journal for Descriptive Poetics and Theory of Literature* 3 (1978); Boris Uspenskij, *A Poetics of Composition* (ed. Valentina Zavarin and Susan Wittig, 1973).

Henri Broms and Rebecca Kaufman, *Semiotics of Culture* (1988); Karl Eimermacher and Serge Shishkoff, *Subject Bibliography of Soviet Semiotics: The Moscow-Tartu School* (1977); Stephen Rudy, "Semiotics in the U.S.S.R.," *The Semiotic Sphere* (ed. Thomas A. Sebeok and Jean Umiker-Sebeok, 1986); *Russian Literature* 5 (1977, special issue on Jurij Lotman); A. Scheffcyzyk, "Moscow-Tartu School," *Encyclopedic Dictionary of Semiotics*, vol. 1 (ed. Thomas A. Sebeok, 1986); Dmitri Segal, *Aspects of Structuralism in Soviet Philology* (1974); Peter Seyffert, *Soviet Literary Structuralism* (1985); Ann Shukman, *Literature and Semiotics* (1977); Dolf Sörensen, *Theory Formation and the Study of Literature* (1987).

MYTH THEORY AND CRITICISM

Myth criticism designates not so much a critical approach in literary studies as the convergence of several methods and forms of inquiry about the complex relations between literature and myth. So heterogeneous are these inquiries, connecting with so many disciplines and interdisciplinary issues, that it is perhaps best to think of myth criticism as the locus for a series of complex, if powerfully suggestive, questions. Is myth embedded in literature, or are myth and literature somehow coextensive? Is myth (from Greek *mythos,* "tale," "story") inescapably narrative in form? Is all literature susceptible of myth criticism? How self-conscious are literary artists in the use or incorporation of myth? How does myth in, or as, literature evolve historically? Does a single governing myth, a "monomyth," organize disparate mythic narratives and dominate literary form? What tasks, besides a simple cataloging of putative mythic components, fall to the myth critic? And most fundamentally, what does "myth" mean in the context of literary criticism? The divergence in answers to this last question has been so great, recourse to different disciplines (philosophy, anthropology, psychology, folklore) so various, that the question becomes an inevitable *terminus a quo* for a survey of myth criticism.

A characteristic Romantic and post-Romantic tendency in defining myth is the denial of euhemerism, the theory that myths can be explained historically or by identifying their special objects or motives. The resistance to such reductionism is perhaps strongest in the work of the philosopher Ernst Cassirer, whose monumental *Philosophy of Symbolic Forms* is given over in its second volume (1925) to the proposition that "myth is a form of thought." By this Cassirer means to insist that myth is a fundamental "symbolic form" that, like language, is a means of responding to, and hence creating, our world. But unlike language, or at least the language of philosophy, myth is nonintellectual, nondiscursive, typically imagistic. It is the primal, emotion-laden, unmediated "language" of experience. As a consequence, for mythic consciousness there is no reflective separation of the real and the ideal; the mythic " 'image' does not represent the 'thing'; it *is* the thing" (2:38). This literal, as opposed to representational, quality of myth suggests that literature that taps into the recesses of mythic consciousness will reveal in powerful fashion the "dynamic of the life feeling" (2:38), which gives meaning and intelligibility to our world.

Myth, understood in this honorific rather than pejorative sense, has profoundly influenced numerous literary critics and theorists. Isabel MacCaffrey, for example, insists in her study of *Paradise Lost* that the Christian myth at the center of the epic is not for Milton an oblique *representation* but rather the "direct rendering of certain stupendous realities now known only indirectly in the symbolic signatures of earthly life" (30). It was for this reason, she feels, that Milton was obliged to give up earlier allegorical plans for the poem: mythic material is simply inaccessible to allegory or metaphor, because it is itself their "cause." A poetic method that emphasizes the separation of "idea" and "image" runs exactly counter to a mythic conception, which insists on their identity.

Two other highly influential, nonreductionist theories of myth come from the fields of anthropology and psychology (see ANTHROPOLOGICAL THEORY AND CRITICISM). The French anthropologist CLAUDE LÉVI-STRAUSS, whose extensive work with South American tribal societies has yielded extraordinary analyses, argues that the meaning of myths lies not in their manifest content but rather in their underlying structure of relations, which typically works to mediate between polar extremes (raw and cooked, agriculture and warfare, life and death). In other words, the purpose of myth is to provide a logical model capable of overcoming a contradiction. Ultimately this leads Lévi-Strauss to the notion that the structure of myths is identical with that of the human mind. Thus the mythopoeic (mythmaking) imagination, its structure and operations, is reflected in the structure and symbols of actual myths.

The very power of Lévi-Strauss's argument about the nature and function of myth has made it difficult for literary critics and theorists to incorporate or utilize his accounts in a sustained fashion. His abstract notion of "structure" (derived by analogy from FERDINAND DE SAUSSURE's enormously suggestive conception of linguistic structure), while appealing to the more systematic semioticians and structuralists, is difficult to accommodate to what are typically more labile definitions of literary form and structure in "mature" or sophisticated literary traditions. (See SEMIOTICS and STRUCTURALISM.) Eric Gould presents in *Mythical Intentions in Modern Literature* an intelligent and sympathetic account of Lévi-Strauss's thought about myth and its relation to literature but finally can do little more than point to the anthropologist's rather dispiriting conclusion that myth survives only tenuously in modern fictional forms and that the novel is a literary genre that "tells a story that ends badly, and . . . now, as a genre [is] itself coming to a bad end" (95). Gould's more optimistic conclusion—that literary studies can have in common with Lévi-Strauss's mythography a self-conscious interpretive posture—seems only vaguely useful.

For literary criticism perhaps the most productive anti-euhemerist has been the psychologist and one-time disciple of SIGMUND FREUD, C. G. Jung. Although he is usually associated with archetypes (see ARCHETYPAL THEORY AND CRITICISM), the distinction between archetype and myth has often been blurred, and Jung's theories have been appropriated, *mutatis mutandis,* by myth critics and archetypal critics alike. Jung's most influential idea is that of a "collective unconscious," a racial memory, consisting of "primordial images" or archetypes. These find expression in characteristic forms—the Earth Mother, the divine child, the wise old man, the sacrificial death of the god, the mandala, the satyr or man-animal monster, the cross, the number 4—which provide the primordial elements in the myths and narrative constructions of widely different cultures. Although Jean Piaget and others have expressed skepticism about the universality or "racial" quality of Jung's archetypes, the archetypal vocabulary is now widespread in the discourse of those who might be called myth critics, including the most influential member of that group, NORTHROP FRYE.

Frye and others are attracted to Jung's theories not only because of the richness of imagery and narrative elements (what Jung and his collaborator Carl Kerényi came to call "mythologems") but because these theories, like those of Cassirer and Lévi-Strauss, command for myth a central cultural position, unassailable by reductive intellectual methods or procedures. By entitling the third essay of *Anatomy of Criticism* "Archetypal Criticism: Theory of Myths," Frye suggests a conceptual means of drawing individual and apparently unrelated archetypal images—the fundaments of psyche and culture—into a coherent and ultimately hierarchical framework of "mythoi," one organizing not only individual literary works but the entire system of literary works, that is, literature. Thus, for example, works in the "realistic," or representational, mode (the ill-fated "modern" novel Lévi-Strauss speaks of) stand (nonpejoratively) at the opposite end of the spectrum from those in the "mythical mode," which, because they are about characters having the greatest possible powers and who act "near or at the conceivable limits of desire" (136), are the "most abstract and conventionalized" (134). The abstract and conventional qualities Frye attributes to the mythic mode in literature are ultimately reflective of the irreducible and inescapable place of myth itself; so conceived, Western literature, massively funded by the powerful myths of the Bible and classical culture, might be thought of as having a "grammar" or coherent structural principles basic to any critical organization or account of historical development. That Frye ultimately identifies the "quest-myth" in its various forms as the central myth (mono-myth) of literature and the source of literary genres is at once the logical conclusion of his approach to myth criticism and the source of ongoing debate.

No brief account can begin to do justice to the massive conceptual power and richly varied suggestiveness of Frye's theory of myths. If occasionally the schematization seems excessive or arbitrary, Frye's efforts nonetheless suggest how powerfully myth can organize our thinking about literature and about culture. His four "mythoi," or "generic narratives" (spring: comedy; summer: romance; autumn: tragedy; winter: irony and satire), have proved central in the ongoing project of rehabilitating genre theory. And his conviction that the "total mythopoeic structure of concern" extends beyond literature to religion, philosophy, political theory, and history suggests how myth criticism may ultimately connect with a larger theory of culture.

Frye's particular critical and theoretical project has stimulated enormous scholarly activity, but he has had considerable company in defining the possibilities for literary myth criticism. Leslie Fiedler argues that contemporary criticism has lost its way by failing to see how PLATO's "ancient quarrel between poetry and philosophy" is really a dispute between logos and mythos "as to which was the primal word" ("No! In Thunder" 1:518). Answering predictably and claiming that "*mythos* created poetry," Fiedler appropriates Jung's archetypes and Crocean intuitionism to define myth and thereby free poetry from the enervating embrace of logos (science,

rationalism, logic) (see BENEDETTO CROCE). Having succeeded so well in opposing mythos to logos, however, Fiedler comes perilously close to paralyzing criticism. His own critical project survives chiefly with his notion that literature comes into being only with the imposition of a "Signature" upon mythic materials, a "Signature" being the "sum total of individuating factors in a work" (1:537), the sign of the Persona. The insistence on both signature and myth, or archetype, with the predominance of each varying in individual literary works, creates a useful critical spectrum.

Many other modern myth critics and theorists, from the CAMBRIDGE RITUALISTS down to the present, have suggested productive ways of speaking about myth in literature and the connections between literary mythopoeia and the materials explored by other disciplines in our intellectual culture. C. L. Barber, for example, has explored the ways Shakespearean comedy achieves a characteristic "release" leading to social clarification; this "release" is related in turn to a ceremonial, ritualistic, finally mythic conception of human life that was evolving rapidly into a historical, psychological conception among the educated classes of Shakespeare's society. More recently, RENÉ GIRARD has taken up a wide-ranging investigation of the central cultural role of ritual sacrifice and its relation to myths, especially those prominent in Greek tragedy. Arguing that this ritual is society's effort to deflect upon a relatively indifferent or "sacrificeable" victim the violence that would otherwise be vented on its own members, Girard offers deeply suggestive commentary on such plays as *Ajax, Medea,* and, most impressively, *Oedipus Tyrannos.* Even in so effectively establishing connections between ritual and myth on the one hand and tragic drama on the other, however, Girard is at pains to acknowledge the distinctively literary qualities of the plays, what he calls the "essentially antimythical and antiritualistic inspiration of the drama" (95). Girard's most important critical claim is that the depiction of the ritual victim, or "scapegoat," must be seen in drama not as simple superstition, a crude mythic holdover, but as the metamorphosis of earlier "reciprocal violence," a communal violence "more deeply rooted in the human condition than we are willing to admit" (96).

Although "myth criticism" no longer enjoys its earlier vogue, its legacy is powerful. Frye's work remains deeply influential; critics of Shakespearean comedy or *Paradise Lost* must still come to terms with the arguments of Barber's and MacCaffrey's studies; Girard continues to be a striking presence on the contemporary critical scene; and many individual critical studies concentrating on mythic themes, as well as on the formal or generic consequences of those themes, form an important part of the exegetical tradition. This seems to be particularly true for studies of modernist and American literature. It is likely that the future of literary myth criticism will be determined by the vitality of mythography as a concern in other related or allied fields, as well as by the heuristic power of the questions such criticism can generate. One of the most important of these questions asks about the degree of mythic "self-consciousness" in literary texts. Is literature mythopoeia or mythology? the creation or reflective use of mythic materials? The nineteenth-century philologist and student of myth F. Max Müller proposed a distinction between the "mythic" and the "mythical" that gave early form to precisely this issue. And subsequently many critics have insisted on the very different ways in which myth is conceived and appropriated by Homer and Sophocles; Virgil and Milton; T. S. Eliot, Ezra Pound, James Joyce, Thomas Mann, and Gabriel García Márquez. (The peculiarly self-conscious and individual myth systems of poets such as William Blake and W. B. Yeats also point up the critical question sharply.) In turn, other critics have asked how the Western myth tradition has underwritten canon formation and how, for example, black and feminist literatures are to be understood in relation to, and in conscious rebellion against, this tradition. If one accepts that the proposition "myth *is* literature" is itself an aesthetic creation and hence defines further creative possibilities (as does, for example, the Americanist and myth critic Richard Chase), then the question of mythic self-consciousness becomes particularly exigent.

In short, complex critical and theoretical questions about myth and literature continue to be asked. The susceptibility of literature to forms of myth criticism depends upon the persuasiveness of answers to such questions, as well as upon the success of literary theorists in appropriating the empirical and conceptual investigations of myth by other disciplines.

Charles Eric Reeves

See also ANTHROPOLOGICAL THEORY AND CRITICISM, ARCHETYPAL THEORY AND CRITICISM, NORTHROP FRYE, and CLAUDE LÉVI-STRAUSS.

C. L. Barber, *Shakespeare's Festive Comedy: A Study of Dramatic Form and Its Relation to Social Custom* (1959); Douglas Bush, *Mythology and the Romantic Tradition in English Poetry* (1937); Joseph Campbell, *The Hero with a Thousand Faces* (1949); Ernst Cassirer, *Sprache und Mythos: Ein Beitrag zum Problem der Götternamen* (1925, *Language and Myth,* trans. Susanne K. Langer, 1946); *Philosophie der symbolischen Formen,* vol. 2 (1925, *The Philosophy of Symbolic Forms,* trans. Ralph Manheim, 1955), Richard Chase, *Quest for Myth* (1946); Joseph Duncan, "Archetypal Criticism in English, 1946–1980," *Bulletin of Bibliography* 40 (1983); Mircea Eliade, *Le Mythe de l'éternel retour: Archétypes et répétition* (1949, *The Myth of the Eternal Return,* trans. Willard Trask, 1954); Leslie A. Fiedler, *The Collected Essays of Leslie Fiedler* (2 vols., 1971); Sigmund Freud, *Totem und Tabu* (1913, *Totem and Taboo,* trans. A. A. Brill, 1918); Northrop Frye, *Anatomy of Criticism: Four Essays* (1957); René Girard, *La Violence et le sacré* (1972, *Violence and the Sacred,* trans. Patrick Gregory, 1977); Eric Gould, *Mythical Intentions in Modern Literature* (1981); C. G. Jung and C. Kerényi, *Einführung in das Wesen der Mythologie* (1941, *Essays on a Science of Mythology,* trans. R. F. C. Hull, 1949, rev. ed., 1963); G. S. Kirk, *Myth: Its Meaning and Functions in Ancient and Other Cultures* (1970); Claude Lévi-Strauss, *Anthropologie structurale* (1958, *Structural Anthropology,* trans. Claire Jacobson and Brooke Grundfest Schoepf, 1963), *La Pensée sauvage* (1962, *The Savage Mind,* 1962, trans. anon., 1966); Isabel MacCaffrey, *Paradise Lost as "Myth"* (1959); Marjorie McCune, Tucker Orbison, and Philip Withim, eds., *The Binding of Proteus: Perspectives on Myth and the Literary Process* (1980); Paul Ricoeur, *Le Symbolique du mal* (pt. 2 of *Philosophie de la volanté,* vol. 2, *Finitude et culpabilité,* 1960, *The Symbolism of Evil,* trans. Emerson Buchanan, 1967); John Vickery, ed., *Myth and Literature: Contemporary Theory and Practice* (1966).

NARRATOLOGY

Narratology is a theory of narrative. It examines what all narratives, and only narratives, have in common as well as what enables them to differ from one another qua narratives, and it aims to describe the narrative-specific system of rules presiding over narrative production and processing. The term "narratology" is a translation of the French term *narratologie*—introduced by Tzvetan Todorov in *Grammaire du Décaméron* (1969)—and the theory historically falls into the tradition of RUSSIAN FORMALISM and French STRUCTURALISM. Narratology exemplifies the structuralist tendency to consider texts (in the broad sense of signifying matter) as rule-governed ways in which human beings (re)fashion their universe. It also exemplifies the structuralist ambition to isolate the necessary and optional components of textual types and to characterize the modes of their articulation. As such, it constitutes a subset of SEMIOTICS, the study of the factors operative in signifying systems and practices.

One important starting point in the development of narratology was the observation that narratives are found, and stories told, in a variety of media: oral and written language (in prose or in verse), of course, but also sign languages, still or moving pictures (as in narrative paintings, stained-glass windows, or films), gestures, (programmatic) music, or a combination of vehicles (as in comic strips). Furthermore, a folktale can be transposed into a ballet, a comic strip turned into a pantomime, a novel brought to the screen, and vice versa. This arguably means that narrative, or more specifically, the narrative component of a narrative text, can and should be studied without reference to the medium in which it occurs.

Now, within the medium—say, written language—a given set of events can be presented in different ways, in the order of their (supposed) occurrence, for example, or in a different order. The narratologist should therefore be able to examine the narrated, the story presented, independently not only of the medium used but also of the narrating, the discourse, the *way* in which the me-

dium is used to present the *what*. In *Grammaire du Décaméron*, Todorov does not explicitly eliminate the study of narrating from the "science of narrative" he envisions; but his examination of Giovanni Boccaccio's tales focuses on the narrated, and his goal is to develop a grammar to account for it. Similarly, most of ROLAND BARTHES's influential "Introduction to the Structural Analysis of Narrative" is devoted to story rather than to discourse structure.

In concentrating on the *what* instead of the *way*, Barthes and Todorov were following a path taken by CLAUDE LÉVI-STRAUSS and Vladimir Propp. Lévi-Strauss had characterized the logic of myth by focusing on semantic structure: in *Structural Anthropology*, he contended that myth always involves the transformation of one set of semantic oppositions into another, less radical one through a mediation or a series of mediations. In *Morphology of the Folktale*, which has proven to be perhaps the most fertile modern account of story structure, Propp disregarded the narrating in Russian fairy tales and described them in terms of the component parts of the narrated. Propp developed the notion of function or category of actions considered from the point of view of their basic meaning in the tale where they appear; he isolated 31 functions that constitute the fundamental elements of (Russian) fairy tales; he maintained that no function excludes any other and that however many of them appear in a single tale, they always appear in the same order; and he argued that tales—and perhaps all stories—always contain the function *lack* or *villainy* and proceed from it to another function usable as a denouement (e.g., liquidation of the *lack* or *villainy*, *rescue*, or *wedding*). Propp also isolated seven basic roles assumed by characters in (fairy) tales, seven dramatis personae each of which corresponds to a particular sphere of action or set of functions: the hero (seeker or victim), the villain, the princess (a sought-for person) and her father, the dispatcher, the donor, the helper, and the false hero. The same character can play more than one role, and the same role can be played by more than one character.

Many narratologists besides Barthes and Todorov were inspired by Propp (and, to a lesser extent, by Lévi-

Strauss) in trying to account for the specificity of narrative by focusing on the narrated. In *Logique du récit*, Claude Bremond defined the elementary narrative sequence as a series of three functions corresponding to the three basic stages in the unfolding of any process: virtuality (a situation opening a possibility); actualization or nonactualization of the possibility; achievement or nonachievement. Moreover, Bremond developed an intricate typology of roles based on a fundamental distinction between patients (affected by processes and constituting victims or beneficiaries) and agents (initiating the processes and influencing the patients, modifying their situation, or maintaining it). Similarly, Algirdas Julien Greimas refined Propp's notion of dramatis personae and arrived at an "actantial" model, originally comprising six "actants," which has been very influential: Subject (looking for the Object), Object (looked for by the Subject), Sender (of the Subject on its quest for the Object), Receiver (of the Object to be secured by the Subject), Helper (of the Subject), and Opponent (of the Subject). According to Greimas, narrative is a signifying whole because it can be grasped in terms of the structure of relations between the actants. More generally, drawing on both Propp and Lévi-Strauss, Greimas argued that (canonical) narrative is organized according to a schema or frame whereby after a given order of things is disturbed, a contract is established between Sender and Subject to bring about a new order or reinstate the old one; the Subject, who becomes competent along the axes of desire, obligation, knowledge, and/or ability, goes on a quest and, as a result of (three basic) tests, fulfills or fails to fulfill its part of the contract and is (justly) rewarded or (unjustly) punished.

Although much of the early work on narratology thus centered on the narrated and characterized narrative in terms of it, some narratologists considered narrative to be essentially a mode of (verbal) presentation—the recounting of events by a narrator as opposed to, say, the enacting of them on a stage—and they defined their task as the study of narrative discourses rather than the study of the story. They had tradition on their side. Furthermore, they could argue that focusing on the structure of the narrated results in a failure to account for the many ways in which the same set of events can be recounted. Finally, in pursuing their task, they could profit from the extensive work on literary narration and such topics as distance or point of view that Anglo-Saxon critics (from HENRY JAMES to Wayne C. Booth), Germanic scholars (e.g., Eberhard Lämmert, Günther Müller, Franz Stanzel) and the Russian Formalists had performed. Gérard Genette is perhaps the most eminent representative of this narratological tendency. In *Narrative Discourse* and *Narrative Discourse Revisited,* he analyzed the temporal relations that can obtain between the narrative text and the story it recounts, the factors regulating narrative text and the story it recounts, the factors regulating narrative information, and the narrating instance (the producing narrative act inscribed in the text, as well as the situation in which that act occurs).

Defining narrative by its mode of presentation (and insisting on the role of a narrator) instead of defining it by its object (events) leads to a neglect of narratorless stories. In addition, it disregards the fact that the story, too, makes narrative whatever it is—without a story there can be no narrative. A number of narratologists consider both the events presented and their presentation pertinent to the exploration of its possibilities. Mieke Bal, Seymour Chatman, Michel Mathieu-Colas, and Gerald Prince, for example, have attempted to integrate the study of the *what* and the *way;* and Greimas's most recent model of narrative makes room for the story as well as for discourse. This "generalized" or "mixed" narratology can be said to correspond to the "science" that Roland Barthes evoked in his "Introduction" and to the practice manifested in the other articles making up the well-known 1966 number of *Communications* devoted to narrative. It can also be said to conform to the present scope of narratological activity.

It is perhaps the area of narrative discourse that narratologists have explored most thoroughly. Genette, Todorov (in *Introduction to Poetics*), Bal, Chatman, Dorrit Cohn, Shlomith Rimmon-Kenan, and others have described the kinds of order a narrative text can follow, the various speeds it can adopt (ellipsis, summary, scene, stretch, pause), the types of focalization and detailing of events it can feature, the relations that can obtain between the number of times an event happens and the number of times it is recounted (elliptical, singulative, iterative, or repeating narrative), the basic modes of depicting characters' thoughts and utterances, and the possible links between narrators, acts of narration, narratees, and events narrated.

The investigation of story structure has also yielded notable results. Narratologists have examined the minimal constituents of the narrated (actions and happenings, states and processes), and following the insight of the Russian Formalists, they have distinguished those constituents that are essential to the causal-chronological coherence of the story from those constituents that are not. They have studied the links (temporal, spatial, logical, functional, transformational) between the minimal constituents, and they have drawn attention to the *post hoc, ergo propter hoc* fallacy as a powerful motor of narrativity. They have also demonstrated that narrative sequences can be said to consist of a series of minimal constituents, the last of which in time is a (partial) repetition or transformation of the first; and they have proved that ever more complex sequences can be said to result from the conjoining of two simpler ones, from the alternation of units in one sequence with units in another one, or from an ordered mixture of these modes of combination. Moreover, apart from showing that actions and processes can be grouped into basic (functional) classes and that participants in them can be categorized according to fundamental roles, they have explored the techniques through which characters are established and settings described (Chatman, Hamon). Finally, they have analyzed how a story can be characterized semantically as a world consisting of domains (sets of *moves* or actions pertaining to a given character, called for by a *problem,* and representing an effort toward a *solution*), each of which is governed by (alethic, epistemic, axiological, or deontic) modal constraints that determine what "happens" (Pavel).

As for the integration of the study of story and the study of discourse, it usually follows the direction indicated by the Russian Formalists' work on the relations between *fabula* ("basic story material") and *sjužet* ("plot"), and it sometimes assumes a grammatical shape (Prince, *Narratology*): just as linguists aim to establish the grammar of language, narratologists aim to establish the grammar of narrative. Ultimately, such a grammar might consist of the following four interrelated parts: a syntactic component whereby a finite number of rules generate the macro- and microstructures of all stories, and only stories; a semantic component interpreting these structures, characterizing both the global macrostructural and the local microstructural narrative content; a "discoursive" component whereby a finite number of rules operate on the interpreted structures and account for narrative discourse (order of presentation, speed, narratorial mediation, etc.); and a pragmatic component specifying the basic cognitive and communicative factors affecting the production, processing, and narrativity of the output of the first three parts. These components, which constitute the narrative grammar proper, would be articulated with a textual component allowing for the translation of the grammatical data provided into a given medium (say, written English).

Of the criticisms directed against narratology and its assumptions, claims, and ambitions, at least four deserve attention. It is sometimes argued that narratological models are reductive and that they fail to capture many (important) aspects of narrative texts. But perhaps this overly general charge of reductiveness does not take into consideration the fact that narratology endeavors to account for all narratives, and only narratives, *to the extent that they are narrative:* narratologists have often made it clear that there are many elements other than narrative ones in a narrative text (e.g., pathos, philosophical force, psychological insight).

It is more pointedly argued that narratological models are too static and unable to characterize the very engine that drives a narrative forward to its end, the very dynamics that dictate its shape. It is of course true that Lévi-Strauss's analyses of myth disregarded the syntactic dimension entirely, that the seminal Proppian model, with its fixed order of functions, was static, and that grammars of narrative have frequently concentrated on isolating minimal story units rather than on capturing the dynamism of story configurations. On the other hand, it should be noted that Lévi-Strauss never was, nor did he ever claim to be, a narratologist, that Bremond criticized early on the static aspects of Propp's *Morphology,* and that his own model of the narrated emphasized the progressive logic of stories. Moreover, recent attempts to describe story structure have been explicitly concerned with its dynamic dimension. Thomas Pavel's grammar of plot, for instance, underlines the primacy of action and transformation and sketches the system of energies, tensions, and resistances that plot constitutes. Similarly, Marie-Laure Ryan has been developing a model inspired by artificial intelligence that gives their due to the moments of suspense and surprises, advance and delay, trickery and illumination—to the sambalike movement emblematic of plots.

It is also argued that narratology neglects the context in which narratives occur, the situation that partly determines their shape and contributes to their point, the pragmatic factors that partly govern their functioning. This criticism is not unjustified. The allegiance of narratology to strategies imported from structural or transformational linguistics, the concern for capturing the specificity of narrative (a lyric poem, a syllogism, or an essay can, after all, occur in the same context as a tale), the difficulty of incorporating contextual factors into a systematic description, and the "scientific" ambitions of the discipline (its desire to characterize universals of narrative) resulted in the narratologists' reluctance to make pragmatics part of their domain of inquiry. Still, even in the early years of narratology, pragmatically based notions (e.g., the role of the confusion of *post hoc* with *propter hoc*) were not entirely ignored. More recently, perhaps because of the repeated sociolinguistic reminders about the importance of communicative contexts, because of the growing interest in decoding practices, and because of the increasing awareness that narrative should be viewed not only as a product but also as a process, narratologists have begun to address more explicitly questions pertaining to pragmatics. Thus, Susan Lanser has sketched the foundations for a socially sensitive, feminist narratology; Ryan has argued that some configurations of events make better stories than others; and proposals have been made to consider narrative context as part narrative text (Prince, "Narrative Pragmatics").

Finally, the very possibility of a coherent narratology, one that successfully integrates the study of the *what* and the *way,* has been put into question by poststructuralist theorists and critics invoking the so-called double logic of narrative. This double logic consists of the two organizing principles in terms of which every narrative presumably operates. One principle emphasizes the primacy of event over meaning, that is, insists upon event as the origin of meaning; the other stresses the primacy of meaning and its requirements, that is, insists upon event as the effect of a will to meaning. The first principle emphasizes the logical priority of story over discourse; the second stresses the reverse and makes story the product of discourse. Each principle functions to the exclusion of the other, but, paradoxically, both are valid and necessary to the deployment of narrative, its impact, its force. This means that narratology, however much it is developed and refined, will always be deficient: neither principle by itself can lead to a satisfactory account of narrative, and the two principles cannot be synthesized. The argument is interesting but not entirely persuasive, for it conflates problems that should perhaps not be conflated: that of the evaluation of narrative veracity, for instance (is there a difference between historical and fictional narrative? is narrative a consequence of the events it presents, or vice versa?), that of hermeneutic practices (from text to event and from event to text), and that of narrative dynamics.

Whatever the deficiencies of narratology, its influence has been considerable, so much so that critical and theoretical work dealing with narrative corpuses is often called narratological even if it does not focus on traits that are narrative-specific and even when it has few links with or little regard of the narratologist's methods. Narratology can help to account for the distinctiveness of any given narrative, to compare any number of narratives and institute narrative classes according to narratively pertinent features, to illuminate certain reactions to certain texts (if *Madame Bovary* is esthetically pleasing, perhaps it is partly because of the way Gustave Flaubert uses scene in the midst of summary and summary in the midst of scene), to support certain interpretive conclusions (the privileging of iterative narration in *Remembrance of Things Past* underlines Proust's quest for essences), and even—by providing certain points of departure—to devise (new) interpretations (so-called narratological criticism starts with and is based upon narratological description).

Yet narratology is not primarily an adjunct to interpretation. In fact, through its concern for the governing principles of narrative and through its attempt to characterize not so much the particular meanings of particular narratives but rather what allows narratives to have meanings, narratology has proven to be an important participant in the assault against viewing literary studies as devoted above all to the interpretation of texts. Narratology has also played a significant role in another battle affecting the shape of literary studies. Through its investigation of the factors operating in all possible narratives (and not just great, fictional, or extant ones), it has helped to put into question the very nature of the canon by showing that many noncanonical narratives are just as sophisticated, narratively speaking, as canonical ones.

More generally, narratological tools and arguments have been used in domains exceeding the bounds of "literary studies proper": in cultural analysis, for example, to trace the ways various forms of knowledge legitimate themselves through narrative; in philosophy, to analyze the structure of action; in psychology, to study memory and comprehension. Indeed, narratology has important implications for our understanding of human beings. To explore the nature of all and only possible narratives, to account for the infinity of forms that they can take, to consider how it is that we construct them, paraphrase them, summarize them, or expand them, is to explore one of the fundamental ways, and a singularly human one at that, in which we *make* sense.

Gerald Prince

See also FICTION THEORY AND CRITICISM, RUSSIAN FORMALISM, and STRUCTURALISM.

Jean-Michel Adam, *Le Texte narratif* (1985); Mieke Bal, *De Theorie van vertellen en verhalen* (2d ed., 1980, *Narratology: Introduction to the Theory of Narrative,* trans. Christine van Boheemen, 1983); Roland Barthes, "Introduction à l'analyse structurale des récits" (1966, "Introduction to the Structural Analysis of Narrative," *Image-Music-Text,* ed. and trans. Stephen Heath, 1977); Claude

Bremond, *Logique du récit* (1973); Seymour Chatman, *Story and Discourse: Narrative Structure in Fiction and Film* (1978); Dorrit Cohn, *Transparent Minds: Narrative Modes for Presenting Consciousness in Fiction* (1978); Jonathan Culler, *The Pursuit of Signs: Semiotics, Literature, Deconstruction* (1981), *Structuralist Poetics: Structuralism, Linguistics, and the Study of Literature* (1975); Gérard Genette, *Figures III* (1972, partial trans., *Narrative Discourse: An Essay in Method*, trans. Jane E. Lewin, 1980), *Nouveau discours du récit* (1983, *Narrative Discourse Revisited*, trans. Jane E. Lewin, 1988); A. J. Greimas, *Sémantique structurale: Recherche de méthode* (1966, *Structural Semantics: An Attempt at Method*, trans. Daniele McDowell, Ronald Schleifer, and Alan Velie, 1983); A. J. Greimas and J. Courtés, *Sémiotique: Dictionnaire raisonné de la théorie du langage*, vol. 1 (1979, *Semiotics and Language: An Analytical Dictionary*, trans. Larry Crist et al., 1982); Philippe Hamon, *Introduction à l'analyse du descriptif* (1981), *Le Personel du roman: Le Système des personnages dans les Rougon-Macquart d'Émile Zola* (1983); Susan Sniader Lanser, "Toward a Feminist Narratology," *Style* 20 (1986); Claude Lévi-Strauss, *Anthropologie structurale* (1958, *Structural Anthropology*, trans. Claire Jacobson and Brooke Grundfest Schoepf, 1963); Wallace Martin, *Recent Theories of Narrative* (1986); Michel Mathieu-Colas, "Frontières de la narratologie," *Poétique* 17 (1986); W. J. T. Mitchell, ed., *On Narrative* (1981); Thomas Pavel, *The Poetics of Plot: The Case of English Renaissance Drama* (1985); Gerald Prince, *A Dictionary of Narratology* (1987), "Narrative Pragmatics, Message, and Point," *Poetics* 12 (1983), *Narratology: The Form and Functioning of Narrative* (1982); Vladimir Propp, *Morfologiia skazki* (1928, *Morphology of the Folktale*, trans. Laurence Scott, 1958, 2d ed., ed. Louis A. Wagner, 1968); Paul Ricoeur, *Temps et récit*, vol. 2 (1984, *Time and Narrative*, vol. 2, trans. Kathleen McLaughlin and David Pellauer, 1985); Shlomith Rimmon-Kenan, *Narrative Fiction: Contemporary Poetics* (1983); Marie-Laure Ryan, "Embedded Narratives and Tellability," *Style* 20 (1986), "Linguistic Models in Narratology," *Semiotica* 28 (1979); Robert Scholes, *Structuralism in Literature: An Introduction* (1974); Tzvetan Todorov, *Grammaire du Décaméron* (1969), *Poétique* (1973, *Introduction to Poetics*, trans. Richard Howard, 1981).

NEW CRITICISM

New Criticism is a name applied to a varied and extremely energetic effort among Anglo-American writers to focus critical attention on literature itself. Like RUSSIAN FORMALISM, following Boris Eikhenbaum and Victor Shklovskii, the New Critics developed speculative positions and techniques of reading that provide a vital complement to the literary and artistic emergence of modernism. Like many other movements in modern criticism, New Criticism was in part a reaction against the genteel cultivation of taste and sentiment that marked late-nineteenth- and early twentieth-century criticism and against the prevalence of traditional philological and antiquarian study of literature in the academy. In its later stages, New Criticism displayed some resemblances to STRUCTURALISM, just as it had an impact on the development of the French *nouvelle critique* as exemplified in the early work of ROLAND BARTHES.

The far-reaching influence of New Criticism stems less from theoretical or programmatic coherence than from the practical (and pedagogical) appeal of a characteristic way of reading. The theoretical differences among the critics commonly described as New Critics (not necessarily by themselves)— I. A. RICHARDS, WILLIAM EMPSON, F. R. LEAVIS, KENNETH BURKE, John Crowe Ransom, Allen Tate, YVOR WINTERS, Cleanth Brooks, R. P. BLACKMUR, W. K. Wimsatt, Jr., RENÉ WELLEK—are sometimes so great as to leave little ground for agreement. The New Critics tended to be eclectic on matters of theory, concentrating instead on what Blackmur called the critic's "job of work."

For most of the New Critics that job is PRACTICAL CRITICISM or "close reading," in which the poem or literary text is treated as a self-sufficient verbal artifact. By careful attention to language, the text is presumed to be a unique and privileged source of meaning and value, sharply distinguished from other texts or other uses of language (particularly scientific language). Accordingly, the meaning of the poem is not conveyed by any prose paraphrase and is valued as the source of an experience (for the reader) available in no other way. For this among other reasons, opponents of the New Critics have frequently charged that they ignore history, ideology, politics, philosophy, or other factors that shape literary experience. While such charges are not entirely fair, they arise because New Criticism in practice came to focus almost exclusively on problems of interpreting individual texts.

Partly for this reason, New Criticism can still be considered a movement, beginning after World War I with the critical work of modern poets and critics, especially T. S. ELIOT, Richards, and somewhat later John Crowe Ransom, culminating some 30 years later in the work of explicitly academic critics, such as Wellek, Wimsatt, and Brooks. Since these decades coincide with the institutional rise of English departments and the development of academic literary criticism in the United States, New

Criticism has exerted a complex and lasting influence on the shaping of educational programs in literature and, more generally, on the literary culture of the English-speaking world.

The debt of the New Critics to Eliot was pervasive, but two germinal ideas from his essays shaped both New Critical theory and practice. In "Tradition and the Individual Talent" (1917), Eliot argued that the literature of Western Europe could be viewed as a "simultaneous order" of works (3), where the value of any new work depended on its relation to the order of the tradition. Thus, the work of the "individual talent" does not so much express a personality as it affects and is affected by the literature of the past. Eliot was responding in part to complaints that modern poetry was too hard to understand, too austere, metaphysical, or unfamiliar. Eliot's essay asserts that difficult language reflects an equally difficult modern historical and psychological predicament. The point, however, is general: poetry as a historical process and a response to human predicaments *is* difficult, especially as the literature of any age is also a response to previous literature as a whole.

In "Hamlet and His Problems" (1919) Eliot further proposed that the effects of poetry stem from a relation between the words of the text and events, states of mind, or experiences that offer an "objective correlative" (124). Eliot suggests that there is a unique experience to which the language of the poem corresponds: the poem means just what it says, but it is the "objective correlative" in experience that makes the intellectual and emotional value of the poem intelligible. Ironically, Eliot propounds this idea while arguing that *Hamlet* is a less than satisfactory play because no sufficient correlative (or too many correlatives) can be found. A more encompassing irony is that both the origin and the collapse of New Criticism are contained in this point, where the precision of language demanded of the poem cannot be shown to determine a correlative meaning, "objective" or otherwise.

In suggesting that literature could be treated as a simultaneous order, a system, Eliot opened the way to more explicitly speculative and theoretical studies of literature, while in focusing attention on the fundamental operations by which literary works create intelligible structure, he provided an analytical example for critics that went well beyond traditional protocols for assigning critical praise or blame. While Eliot himself evinces no strong inclination to pursue either explicit theory or critical technique, Richards pursued both, partly in an attempt to appraise the value of modern poets such as Eliot in explicitly theoretical terms. Other critics, notably Leavis, pursued the questions as opportunities to reevaluate literary history, explicitly as a "great tradition," continuing into the modern age.

Richards's *Principles of Literary Criticism* (1924) is arguably the first book in English that attempted to develop a comprehensive theory of criticism, a view Richards himself took in describing all previous speculation about literature as a "chaos" consisting of "random aperçues" and "brilliant guesses" (6). According to Richards, a theory in criticism must offer both a theory of value and a theory of communication, on the assumption that poems communicate value, grounded on the reconciliation of conflicting "impulses" in the experience of the poet.

In *Science and Poetry* (1926) Richards elaborated his theory as it applied to the modern crisis of values. Following MATTHEW ARNOLD, Richards presumed that poetry could be an intellectually respectable substitute for religion in an emerging age of science. As an advocate for such a substitution, Richards urged that poetry should be regarded as presenting, not statements, but rather "pseudo-statements" valued for an "emotive" meaning (58–59) that could change our attitudes without requiring us to believe in what he called the "Magical View" (50 ff.) as found in myth or traditional religion.

For the New Critics, however, Richards's most influential book was *Practical Criticism* (1929). The book reports in detail an experiment in critical reading in which students were presented with the texts of poems without their titles or the names of their authors. Put simply, this experiment represents a severe complication for Richards's theory of poetic communication, which he had assumed in his previous work to be relatively unproblematic and based almost entirely on "emotive" effects. In the experiment, students were given the texts of the poems and asked to write brief commentaries on them. For the most part, the experiment showed that poetry (as typically read or misread) did not reconcile conflicts but induced them, that instead of communicating valuable experience it provoked confusion and incomprehension. The student responses, or "protocols," show a wide, sometimes bewildering range of irrelevant associations, "doctrinal adhesions," and confusions or uncertainties about sense, feeling, tone, and intent. *Practical Criticism* turned attention to the importance of teaching as it disclosed a problem that had largely escaped critical investigation: how do readers actually read? What do they actually understand, or fail to understand, and why?

This work also crystallized what would become, for the New Critics, the central problems of poetic language and form. One of Richards's students, the poet William Empson, pursued these problems with stunning effect in *Seven Types of Ambiguity* (1930), introducing many of the techniques of close reading that later became the hallmark of New Criticism. The book does not develop a systematic taxonomy of "types" but, rather, gives seven illustrations of increasingly complex ways in which poetry can be ambiguous or polysemous. In sometimes uncanny readings, Empson points out semantic relationships that a reader might miss habitually or systematically.

In the United States, Richards's work prior to *Practical Criticism* (and prior to Empson's *Seven Types*) had relatively little effect. But as Allen Tate later remarked (in *Essays of Four Decades,* 1970), "Nobody who read I. A. Richards' *Practical Criticism* when it appeared in 1929 could read any poem as he had read it before" (xi). For a group of critics generally associated with the Agrarian Revival in the southern United States, many of whom taught at the University of the South, Vanderbilt University, and later Kenyon College, *Practical Criticism* offered a technical example that could be adapted to a quite different concern with the value of poetry in the modern world.

Tate, John Crowe Ransom, and other agrarians viewed science not as a way out of mystification but as a direct threat to human values. While Richards saw poetry as a way to reconcile us to a brave new world, these critics recommended a conservative return to religion and, more particularly, a return to an agrarian style of life that set itself in deliberate opposition to industrialization. Similar concerns were expressed by critics who did not share the ideological views of the agrarians, critics whom MURRAY KRIEGER has called "apologists for poetry" (*New Apologists for Poetry,* 1956). Yvor Winters, for example, argued for reading poetry as moral statement (especially in *In Defense of Reason,* 1949), while Kenneth Burke, in some ways following Richards, viewed literature as "equipment for living" (*The Philosophy of Literary Form,* 1941).

In one of his most influential essays, "Poetry: A Note in Ontology" (in *The World's Body,* 1934), Ransom insisted on the priority in poetry of attention to the concrete image as natural object, in opposition to what he called "Platonism," or the impulse to render the world in terms of abstract ideas. This Platonism, for Ransom, is "always sciencing and devouring" and thereby represents both the force of scientific reason and the threat of industrialism. While this distinction recalls Richards's distinction between scientific and emotive uses of language, the difference of attitude is profound. Where Richards viewed the rise of science and "modernity" as generally beneficial, it represented for Ransom and many

of his associates (especially Allen Tate) a form of oppression to be vigorously opposed. Tate, however, insisted that the field of knowledge must not be so easily surrendered—as it appears to be in the work of both Richards and Ransom (Tate 72–105). To see poetry as a form of knowledge, however, requires renewed attention to the meaning of poetry and its relation to poetic language.

In later essays, Ransom modified his position so far as to admit that poetic language was the union of "logical structure" and "local texture," without compromising his insistence on the "rich contingent materiality" of poetry (Stauffer 92 ff.). As he later said in his essay "The Literary Criticism of Aristotle," "the critic never ceases to be impressed with his fine object" and, as a literary man himself, "starts with a spontaneous surge of piety, and is inducted by the contagion of art into a composition of his own" (Coleman 17). But Ransom also saw the value of academic criticism and the virtues of more precise abstract argument and literary scholarship. Increasingly, he moved away from the conservative ideology of his earlier essays to a position of mediation and acceptance of a wider range of critical practice by other critics who did not share his political or cultural views but were nevertheless encouraged by him and published in journals with which he was associated, such as the *Southern Review,* the *Sewanee Review,* and the *Kenyon Review.*

An important factor in the reputation of New Criticism as a movement is that it was, especially in the period just before and after World War II, a phenomenon of periodical journals, such as those just mentioned, together with Leavis's *Scrutiny* in England. Thriving in a climate of vitality for "little magazines," prevalent in the cultural scene in both America and England since the 1920s, New Criticism attracted younger critics by the example of distinctive essays with at least a rhetorical and thematic family resemblance, in which a concentration on literary form made a wide range of cultural and aesthetic topics available for treatment in shorter critical articles. While the variations are as rich as the literature examined, the New Critical essay is generally characterized by a close attention to the language of the text, to show a pattern of formal and thematic features that the critic commonly argues are fundamental to understanding the meaning of the work as a whole but that are expressed in terms that foreground the formal unity or balance of the work.

Essays by Blackmur in particular reflect an increasing degree of sophisticated concentration on matters of poetic form, technique, and value. Blackmur's criticism (like his poetry) reflects his conviction that "literature is the bearer . . . of all the modes of understanding of which *words* are capable; and not only that: it also bears, sets in motion or life, certain modes which words merely initiate and symbolize" (*The Lion and the Honeycomb: Essays in Solicitude and Critique*, 1955, 213). Although resolutely independent, and not a follower of any group, Blackmur is in many ways the paradigmatic New Critic as essayist. He approached criticism as the necessary expression of the man of letters contemplating the modes of words and their value. Although extremely influential in the academy, he did not generally conceive of criticism as a professional specialty, nor as a subject that either required or could sustain systematic theory, since literature itself, for him, was "always specific and unique; never general and repeated" (213).

In contrast, the impact of one of Ransom's later students, Cleanth Brooks, on academic criticism has been a good deal more specific, both in practice and in theory. Brooks's influential textbook *Understanding Poetry* (1939, written with Robert Penn Warren) provided practical and teachable examples. *The Well Wrought Urn* (1947) presented both exemplary instances of New Critical practice and a central account of New Critical doctrines that in many ways appears as a synthesis of ideas from Ransom, Eliot, Richards, and Empson. Following arguments begun in *Modern Poetry and the Tradition* (1939), Brooks set out to demonstrate that the tension, paradox, and ambiguity of much modern (and metaphysical) poetry—of just the sort exemplified by Eliot's poetry and explicated by Empson—was fundamental to the nature of poetry. In *The Well Wrought Urn* Brooks showed that in every age, in diverse styles, a quality of dramatic tension or paradox was essential to poetic meaning, so much so as to warrant the claim that poetry and paradox are all but identical. In Brooks's lucid arguments New Critical postulates are enacted, while explicit theoretical speculation is deferred to a series of appendices.

For Brooks, the term "paradox" calls attention to the contingent density of poetic language and metaphor, while evoking the practice of close reading that traces out the various elements that may be discerned in poetic paradoxes. It also reinforces the claim that no easy distinction between "form" and "content" can be maintained without distorting the overall meaning of the poem: the form of the poem uniquely embodies its meaning, which may itself seem "paradoxical" within a commonsense notion of "meaning." More particularly, Brooks asserted that the language of the poem itself effects the reconciliation of opposites or contraries and that the result *is* the meaning of the poem. In this way, Brooks replaced the psychologism of Richards's theory of reconciling and balancing experiential "impulses" by

claiming that the effect was embodied in poetic language itself.

Brooks concluded *The Well Wrought Urn* by describing what he called the "Heresy of Paraphrase," arguing that any attempt to reduce poetic meaning to a prose statement of a theme or a description of a plot was a betrayal of the poem as a poem. While it is often difficult to disentangle theory from polemic, by using the term "heresy" when in truth there was no proper orthodoxy of interpretation from which to depart, Brooks virtually guaranteed polemical replies to his position, just as he called attention to a pervasive perplexity about how to construct a viable theory. While critics such as Blackmur had regarded explicit theory as either redundant or irrelevant, the increasingly vigorous practice of critical interpretation led to frequently irresolvable conflicts over rival interpretations that seemed mutually exclusive. Thus, the very success of New Critical practice called attention to theoretical problems that had never been adequately addressed, just as its practical strength in producing intelligible readings is the source of a persistent anomaly of incompatible readings that no available postulates appear able to resolve.

A similar mixture of theory and polemic is evident in two influential essays by W. K. Wimsatt, Jr., and Monroe Beardsley, "The Intentional Fallacy" and "The Affective Fallacy" (Wimsatt 3–39), which argued, respectively, that reports of an author's original intention are not germane to judging a work of art, which either succeeds or fails according to what is actually expressed in its words, and that the meaning of a poem cannot be equated with how it affects a reader. A "heresy" may be more damning than a "fallacy," but both imply that there is a correct position and that it is in some way securely sanctioned. In this case, however, the supposition that one could accurately interpret texts without reference to authorial intention presents so severe a test of the reader that a strict avoidance of the intentional fallacy almost forces the reader into the affective fallacy, since the reader of the text is, by default, the only judge—as post–New Critical theorists, such as Norman Holland, David Bleich, or STANLEY FISH, advocating different versions of READER-RESPONSE THEORY AND CRITICISM, have not hesitated to assert (see PSYCHOANALYTIC THEORY AND CRITICISM: 2. RECONCEPTUALIZING FREUD). In perhaps the most ambitious (and least polemical) attempt to articulate a theory for New Criticism, *Theory of Literature* (1949), René Wellek and Austin Warren distinguish between the "intrinsic" and "extrinsic" study of literature. The former concentrates on the work as a "stratified system of norms," whereas the latter relegates literary biography, history, psychology, and sociology to the "extrinsic" domain, a move that incurred the ire of literary historians, scholars, sociologists, and so on.

In all of these major postwar efforts to consolidate theoretical gains, the same general problem persists: there is no well-grounded way to ascertain the validity of any particular interpretation. Thus, E. D. Hirsch argued in *Validity in Interpretation* (1967) that the proliferation of incommensurable interpretations required a return to historical evidence ("extrinsic," according to Wellek and Warren) to buttress appeals to the author's intention (pronounced a "fallacy" by Wimsatt and Beardsley). Unfortunately, the historical documents from which Hirsch presumed authorial intention could be ascertained are themselves subject to a similar interpretive dilemma.

While most of the early New Critics were no strangers to controversy, one of the most serious attacks came from R. S. Crane, who had earlier been welcomed by John Crowe Ransom as one of the most important "new critics." In the late 1940s, Crane and his colleagues at the University of Chicago had been included in Robert Stallman's very influential anthology, *Critiques and Essays in Criticism* (1949), which defined New Criticism as what contemporary critics were actually doing. Crane and his colleagues at Chicago had argued strenuously for making criticism central in the English curriculum, and with Ransom, Tate, and Brooks, they had emphasized the issue of poetic form, but the CHICAGO CRITICS followed ARISTOTLE and Richard McKeon instead of SAMUEL TAYLOR COLERIDGE, Arnold, Eliot, and Richards. Crane edited a collection of essays by various hands, *Critics and Criticism: Ancient and Modern* (1952), which, like Brooks's *The Well Wrought Urn,* sought to demonstrate the coherence of an approach to poetic form across a broad range of periods and styles. But included within the volume were a series of highly polemical attacks on Richards, Empson, and Brooks, who had, according to the Chicago critics, impoverished criticism by concentrating on only one element of form, its language, or "diction."

In "The Critical Monism of Cleanth Brooks" Crane argues that Brooks and other New Critics impoverish theory by making irony or paradox a unique principle of structure, and he points out with sharp effect that the balancing and reconciliation of opposites that Brooks held to be the sole differentia of "poetic" language was in fact the characteristic of all connected discourse. By Brooks's own criteria, the best example of a modern "ironic" poem was Einstein's formula $E = mc^2$, asserting the paradoxical identity of matter and energy (104).

While Crane's objection resembles later critiques of New Criticism as being unduly preoccupied with ques-

tions of interpreting poetic language, Crane himself treated this result as a *reductio ad absurdum,* implying the failure of Brooks and the New Critics to differentiate poetry from science by looking in the wrong place and by beginning "to theorize about poetry from the wrong end," just as he criticized their "morbid obsession . . . with the problem of justifying and preserving poetry in an age of science." In Crane's view, the proper place to start was with "concrete poetic wholes of various kinds" (105), ignoring the fact that a poetic whole is not in any meaningful way "concrete," but verbal, and that any idea of its wholeness required some interpretation of its language.

Perhaps inadvertently, however, Crane's polemic locates a fundamental problem in formalism and structuralism of all varieties, including his own and that of the logical positivists, whom the New Critics since Ransom had regarded as irreconcilable enemies. In this sense, what might have been a family quarrel among American academic critics turns out to be especially helpful for understanding the demise of New Criticism as well as its genetic relation to the archetypal structuralism of NORTHROP FRYE and to later, poststructuralist criticism.

Central to this dispute is the idea that literature (or literariness) could be defined (and therefore be distinguished from science) in an essential way by concentrating on formal properties of language, an assumption shared by all parties to this dispute, including the logical positivists, who had sought a guarantee of validity in the linguistic form of scientific theories. In a striking example of Coleridge's favorite maxim, "Extremes meet," the New Critics and the logical positivists appeared to be in irreconcilable opposition because of a proposition that both groups accepted—significantly, borrowed on both sides from I. A. Richards: that there is a fundamental opposition between the referential language of science and the expressive, "emotive" language of poetry.

Rudolph Carnap embraced this distinction in his first English publication, *Philosophy and Logical Syntax* (1935), which appeared in the Psyche Miniatures series edited by Richards's colleague and frequent collaborator, C. K. Ogden. Carnap used the distinction, however, as a grounds for rejecting metaphysical propositions because they assert nothing verifiable but have, like lyric poems, "no assertorial sense, no theoretical sense . . . [and do] not contain knowledge" (29). In the same work, for similar reasons, he adopts Richards's notion of the "pseudo-statement" in order to guard against any unwary acceptance of abstract entities (e.g., numbers) as if they existed in a material mode (78 ff.).

When Crane called for a "newer criticism" in his attack on Brooks in *The Languages of Criticism and the*

Structure of Poetry (1953, 106), he pressed his case for an Aristotelian formalism, while advocating a radical pluralism in critical theory, passing over any problem of the modality of poetic language. According to Crane, the kinds of questions one poses about literature determine what answers will be appropriate or valid, and the abstract or theoretical structure of such questions will make up the "framework" for the critic's practice. With what appears to be deliberate irony, however, Crane borrows the idea of a "framework" for theory from a classic essay of Carnap's, "Empiricism, Semantics, and Ontology" (1950, reprinted in *Naming and Necessity,* 1956). In that essay, in many ways a last-ditch effort to save logical positivism from "metaphysical" entities, Carnap had argued that one introduces and accepts a "framework" in order to be able to speak about such "entities" as numbers, space-time coordinates, and so on, without having to commit to a belief in their existence. The artifice of the "framework" then protects statements made within it, allowing them to be construed and evaluated for truth and theoretical cogency, without metaphysical compromises.

Crane, however, deflects the argument into a defense of theoretical pluralism, in which there may be many "incommensurable" frameworks for discussing poetry. In this vision of critical laissez faire, it is up to the critic to persuade others to accept one framework rather than another, on the practical basis of what a given framework will allow one to say and do. Quite obviously, a "framework" in this sense is not what Carnap proposed, for the existence of incommensurable frameworks for literary works, like the existence of incommensurable frameworks for numbers, would only indicate that no framework, in fact, had yet been accepted, perhaps because there was no general agreement about why or whether it was useful to be able to talk about literature, and if so, whether it was desirable to talk consistently.

Given the increasing evidence that New Critical readings of texts could proliferate indefinitely without the prospect of resolving mutually exclusive readings of the same poem, critical pluralism may have existed by default. Crane's argument did not succeed either in quelling the errors he had found in New Criticism or in establishing a new Aristotelian criticism. On the contrary, it led to yet another round of polemical argument, now led by Wimsatt. In his essay "The Chicago Critics: The Fallacy of the Neoclassic Species" (1953, reprinted in *The Verbal Icon*) Wimsatt imagines

> a stage on which stands the contemporary critic, a composite, let us say, of Richards, Eliot, Empson, Brooks and Warren, and Tate. He is wearing the mask of his role in the drama to be enacted, a tolerably good,

clean, bright critic's mask, though, let us say, it has some smudges on it (the psychologism of Richards, for instance, the excessive ingenuities of Empson). Enter: Professor Crane. He walks up to the critic and, taking a piece of burnt cork from his pocket, proceeds to blacken the mask all over. "There now," he says, "that is what you really look like."

The scene concludes with Crane reclaiming the mask, partially cleaning it, then writing "Aristotle" on the forehead to announce, "This looks a lot better on me than it did on you" (45–46). Pluralism in this guise is hard to distinguish from bickering, and one could say that by the mid-1950s, while New Critical practice was still thriving in journal articles and classrooms, New Critical theorizing had come to an impasse.

Literary historians such as Douglas Bush and Frederick Pottle continued the complaint that New Critical practice impoverished literary understanding by giving inadequate attention to historical specificity. Critics such as Murray Krieger and Philip Wheelwright sought a way beyond the impasse by a more systematic and intensive alignment of criticism with aesthetic theory and with philosophical studies of language and metaphor, while attempting to preserve the characteristic qualities of New Critical practice. Clearly the boldest theorist to emerge in the aftermath of the polemical quarrels of the late 1950s was Northrop Frye, whose *Anatomy of Criticism* (1957) turned back to Eliot and to an inductive survey of the literary field to view the "masterpieces of literature" as "phenomena to be explained in terms of a conceptual framework which criticism alone possesses" (16). In using Carnap's metaphor (quite probably drawn from Crane), Frye attempted to articulate a framework of precisely the kind Carnap had recommended. In place of Eliot's "simultaneous order" of works, Frye proposed a total "order of words" in which literature "imitates the total dream of man" (118–19), structured in and through literary archetypes.

In writing an anatomy of *criticism,* Frye set out explicitly to integrate all of his more or less contentious critical ancestors, including Aristotle, WILLIAM BLAKE, Coleridge and Arnold, Eliot and Richards, Brooks and Crane, into a theory of literature as cultural communication drawing from Romantic theories of symbolism and the medieval fourfold theory of interpretation. The result is a syncretic and encyclopedic survey that marks a passage from formalism to an indigenous Anglo-American literary structuralism. Where CLAUDE LÉVI-STRAUSS focused on myth, Frye focused on the archetype; where Lévi-Strauss drew upon FERDINAND DE SAUSSURE, Frye exploited T. S. Eliot's idea of a total order of words.

From this point of view, Frye can be seen as both the point of highest achievement of the modern tradition of New Criticism and the point of its irreversible collapse. For "myth" and "structure" in Lévi-Strauss, like the "archetype" and "anagogy" in Frye, are both subject to the same radical critique. The "myth" or the "archetype" appears to posit a form of transcendental agency that brings it into being, without having any way to explain that agency or to explain how it is that semantic or semiological differences arise. To see Frye as the culmination of New Criticism, however, is to see in his work both what is of enduring value in the movement and what is most vulnerable on theoretical grounds.

New Criticism, from Eliot to Frye, sponsored a project in the reformation of critical reading that first called attention to the radical specificity of poetic language and dramatically widened the scope for poetic interpretation. Its theoretical frustrations represent less a failure than a gradual realization that a radical rethinking would be required, on a wide range of philosophical and metaphysical issues, and thus prepared the way for a more general pursuit of theory by later critics. If the common belief of the New Critics in a fundamental linguistic opposition between poetry and science is untenable, and all uses of language reflect an intrinsic degree of freedom in the production of meaning, then the history of New Criticism may mark at once the end of a philosophical epoch and the beginning of a brave new world of speculative criticism. However that may be, New Criticism has left an indelible mark on the shaping of professional literary study and thereby on the reading habits, practices, and preferences of the last three generations of readers and critics.

Leroy F. Searle

See bibliographies in R. P. BLACKMUR, KENNETH BURKE, T. S. ELIOT, WILLIAM EMPSON, NORTHROP FRYE, MURRAY KRIEGER, F. R. LEAVIS, I. A. RICHARDS, RENÉ WELLEK, and YVOR WINTERS; for R. S. Crane see bibliography in CHICAGO CRITICS.

Cleanth Brooks, *Modern Poetry and the Tradition* (1939), *The Well Wrought Urn* (1947); Cleanth Brooks and Robert Penn Warren, *Understanding Poetry* (1938); Elliott Coleman, ed., *Lectures in Criticism* (1949); John Crowe Ransom, *The New Criticism* (1941), *Selected Essays* (1984), *The World's Body* (1938); John Crowe Ransom, ed., *The Kenyon Critics* (1951); Robert W. Stallman, ed., *Critiques and Essays in Criticism: 1920–1948* (1949); D. A. Stauffer, ed., *The Intent of the Critic* (1941); Allen Tate, *Essays of Four Decades* (1968); René Wellek and Austin Warren, *Theory of*

Literature (1949); Philip Wheelwright, *The Burning Fountain* (1954), *Metaphor and Reality* (1962); W. K. Wimsatt, Jr., *The Verbal Icon: Studies in the Meaning of Poetry* (1954); W. K. Wimsatt, Jr., and Cleanth Brooks, *Literary Criticism: A Short History* (1957).

M. H. Abrams, *The Mirror and The Lamp: Romantic Theory and the Critical Tradition* (1953); Jonathan Arac, *Critical Genealogies: Historical Situations for Postmodern Literary Studies* (1987); Paul Bové, *Intellectuals in Power: A Genealogy of Critical Humanism* (1986); John M. Bradbury, *The Fugitives: A Critical Account* (1958); Edward T. Cone, ed., *The Legacy of R. P. Blackmur* (1987); Louise Cowan, *The Fugitive Group* (1959); Paul de Man, "Form and Intent in the American New Criticism," *Blindness and Insight* (1971); Wallace Douglas, "Deliberate Exiles: The Social Roots of Agrarian Poetics," *Aspects of American Poetry* (ed. R. Ludwig Columbus, 1962); Geoffrey H. Hartman, *Beyond Formalism: Literary Essays, 1958–1970* (1970); C. Hugh Holman, "Literature and Culture: The Fugitive Agrarians," *Social Forces* 37 (1958); W. H. N. Hotopf, *Language, Thought, and Comprehension: A Case Study of the Writing of I. A. Richards* (1965); Vincent B. Leitch, *American Literary Criticism from the Thirties to the Eighties* (1988); Lee T. Lemon, *The Partial Critics* (1965); Frank Lentricchia, *After the New Criticism* (1980); John Paul Russo, *I. A. Richards: His Life and Work* (1989); Lewis P. Simpson, *The Possibilities of Order: Cleanth Brooks and His Works* (1976); Josef Szili, "The New Criticism," *Literature and Its Interpretations* (1979); E. M. Thompson, *Russian Formalism and Anglo-American New Criticism* (1971); Twelve Southerners, *I'll Take My Stand: The South and Agrarian Tradition* (1930); Kermit Vanderbilt, *American Literature and the Academy* (1986); Eliseo Vivas, "The Neo-Aristotelians of Chicago," *Sewanee Review* 61 (1953); Grant Webster, *The Republic of Letters: A History of Postwar American Criticism* (1979); René Wellek, *A History of Modern Criticism: 1750–1950*, vol. 6, *American Criticism, 1900–1950* (1986).

NEW HISTORICISM

In 1982 Stephen Greenblatt edited a special issue of *Genre* on Renaissance writing, and in his introduction to this volume he claimed that the articles he had solicited were engaged in a joint enterprise, namely, an effort to rethink the ways that early modern texts were situated within the larger spectrum of discourses and practices that organized sixteenth- and seventeenth-century English culture. This reconsideration had become necessary because many contemporary Renaissance critics had developed misgivings about two sets of assumptions that informed much of the scholarship of previous decades. Unlike the New Critics, Greenblatt and his colleagues were reluctant to consign texts to an autonomous aesthetic realm that dissociated Renaissance writing from other forms of cultural production (see NEW CRITICISM); and unlike the prewar historicists, they refused to assume that Renaissance texts mirrored, from a safe distance, a unified and coherent world-view that was held by a whole population, or at least by an entire literate class. Rejecting both of these perspectives, Greenblatt announced that a new historicism had appeared in the academy and that it would work from its own set of premises: that Elizabethan and Jacobean society was a site where occasionally antagonistic institutions sponsored a diverse and perhaps even contradictory assortment of beliefs, codes, and customs; that authors who were positioned within this terrain experienced a complex array of subversive and orthodox impulses and registered these complicated attitudes toward authority in their texts; and that critics who wish to understand sixteenth- and seventeenth-century writing must delineate the ways the texts they study were linked to the network of institutions, practices, and beliefs that constituted Renaissance culture in its entirety (see RENAISSANCE THEORY AND CRITICISM).

In some ways, Greenblatt's declaration of New Historicism's existence was a problematic gesture, for while his title quickly garnered considerable prestige for critics working in this area, it also created expectations that the New Historicists could not satisfy. Specifically, the scholars who encountered Greenblatt's term tended to conceive of New Historicism as a doctrine or movement, and their inference led them to anticipate that Greenblatt and his colleagues would soon articulate a coherent theoretical program and delineate a set of methodological procedures that would govern their interpretive efforts. When the New Historicists failed to produce such position papers, critics began to accuse them of having a disingenuous relation to literary theory. In response to such objections, Greenblatt published an essay entitled "Towards a Poetics of Culture" (1987), which has had a profound impact on the way academics understand the phenomenon of New Historicism today. In this piece, Greenblatt attempted to show, by way of a shrewd juxtaposition of JEAN-FRANÇOIS LYOTARD's and FREDRIC JAMESON's paradigms for conceptualizing capitalism, that the general question they address, namely, how art and society are interrelated, cannot be answered by appealing to a single theoretical stance. And since the question both Lyotard and Jameson pose is one that New Historicism also raises, its proponents should see the

failure of Marxist and poststructuralist attempts to understand the contradictory character of capitalist aesthetics as a warning against any attempt to convert New Historicism into a doctrine or a method (see MARXIST THEORY AND CRITICISM). From Greenblatt's perspective, New Historicism never was and never should be a theory; it is an array of reading practices that investigate a series of issues that emerge when critics seek to chart the ways texts, in dialectical fashion, both represent a society's behavior patterns and perpetuate, shape, or alter that culture's dominant codes.

In part because his argument was so effective, and in part because his colleagues developed similar positions independently, most of the critics working in the field of cultural poetics agree that New Historicism is organized by a series of questions and problems, not by a systematic paradigm for the interpretation of literary works. Louis Montrose, for instance, has described some of these issues at length, and in his essay "The Poetics and Politics of Culture" (1986) he provides a list of concerns shared by New Historicists that agrees with and extends Greenblatt's commentary. Like Greenblatt, Montrose insists that one aim of New Historicism is to refigure the relationship between texts and the cultural system in which they were produced, and he indicates that as a first step in such an undertaking, critics must problematize or reject both the formalist conception of literature as an autonomous aesthetic order that transcends needs and interests and the reflectionist notion that writing simply mirrors a stable and coherent ideology that is endorsed by all members of a society. Having abandoned these paradigms, the New Historicist, he argues, must explain how texts not only represent culturally constructed forms of knowledge and authority but actually instantiate or reproduce in readers the very practices and codes they embody.

Montrose also suggests that if New Historicism calls for a rethinking of the relationship between writing and culture, it also initiates a reconsideration of the ways authors specifically and human agents generally interact with social and linguistic systems. This second New Historicist concern is an extension of the first, for if the idea that every human activity is embedded in a cultural field raises questions about the autonomy of literary texts, it also implies that individuals may be inscribed more fully in a network of social practices than many critics tend to believe. But as Montrose goes on to suggest, the New Historicist hostility toward humanist models of freely functioning subjectivity does not imply that he and his colleagues are social determinists. Instead, Montrose argues that individual agency is constituted by a process he calls "subjectification," which he describes as follows: on the one hand, culture produces individuals who are endowed with subjectivity and the capacity of agency; on the other, it positions them within social networks and subjects them to cultural codes that ultimately exceed their comprehension and control.

In another section of his essay, Montrose adds a third concern to define New Historicism: to what extent can a literary text offer a genuinely radical critique of authority, or articulate views that threaten political orthodoxy? New Historicists have to confront this issue because they are interested in delineating the full range of social work that writing can perform, but as Montrose suggests, they have not yet arrived at a consensus regarding whether literature can generate effective resistance. On one side, critics such as Jonathan Dollimore and Alan Sinfield claim that Renaissance texts contest the dominant religious and political ideologies of their time; on the other, some critics argue that the hegemonic powers of the Tudor and Stuart governments are so great that the state can neutralize all dissident behavior. Although Montrose offers his own distinctive response to the containment-subversion problem, he insists that a willingness to explore the political potential of writing is a distinguishing mark of New Historicism.

A final problem Montrose expects his New Historicist colleagues to engage might be called "the question of theory." Even as he insists that cultural poetics is not itself a systematic paradigm for producing knowledge, he argues that the New Historicists must be well versed in literary and social theory and be prepared to deploy various modes of analysis in their study of writing and culture. Montrose finds notions of textuality from DE-CONSTRUCTION and poststructuralism to be particularly useful for the practice of historical criticism, for their emphasis on the discursive character of all experience and their position that every human act is embedded in an arbitrary system of signification that social agents use to make sense of their world allow him and his colleagues to think of events from the past as texts that must be deciphered. In fact, these poststructuralist theories often underlie the cryptically chiastic formulations, such as "the historicity of texts and the textuality of history," that appeal so much to the practitioners of cultural poetics. Other New Historicists invoke different interpretive perspectives, especially those found in the writings of MICHEL FOUCAULT and Clifford Geertz (see ANTHROPOLOGICAL THEORY AND CRITICISM), to aid their interpretive endeavors. The crucial point here is that virtually every New Historicist finds theory to be a potential ally.

Such, then, are the issues that shape the terrain of New Historicism. In what remains, I will comment in some detail upon the writings of three exemplary New Historicists, Stephen Greenblatt, Jonathan Goldberg, and Walter Benn Michaels. As a result, many significant contributors to this field will go undiscussed (writings by some of these contributors, however, are listed in the bibliography), but I think it is especially important to gain a sense of how these practitioners of cultural poetics actually interpret texts.

In his introduction to *Renaissance Self-Fashioning* (1980), Greenblatt indicates that his book aims to chart the ways identity was constituted in sixteenth-century English culture. He argues that the scene in which his authors lived was controlled by a variety of authorities—institutions such as the church, court, family, and colonial administration, as well as agencies such as God or a sacred book—and that these powers came into conflict because they endorsed competing patterns for organizing social experience. From Greenblatt's New Historicist perspective, the rival codes and practices that these authorities sponsored were cultural constructions, collective fictions that communities created to regulate behavior and make sense of their world; however, the powers themselves tended to view their customs as natural imperatives, and they sought to represent their enemies as aliens or demonic parodists of genuine order. Because human agents were constituted as selves at the moment they submitted to one of these cultural authorities, their behavior was shaped by the codes that were sponsored by the institution with which they identified, and they learned to fear or hate the Other that threatened their very existence.

Since authors were fully situated within this cultural system, Greenblatt contends that their writings both comment generally upon the political struggles that emerged within the Tudor state and register their complicated encounters with authorities and aliens. To prove his thesis, he analyzes self-fashioning in a number of significant Renaissance works, and he shows that these texts record sophisticated responses to a series of cultural problems. Greenblatt demonstrates that Thomas More's late writings are the culmination of his engagement with theological controversy, for these letters reiterate his sense that his identity is shaped by his participation in the Catholic community, and they restate his belief that Protestant theology is an alien threat that should be rooted out of England. Edmund Spenser's Bower of Bliss scene in *The Faerie Queene* encodes and relieves anxieties about the ways sexuality challenges the state's legitimate authority, and Thomas Wyatt's satires explore whether an aristocrat can detach himself from a court society that has become wholly corrupt.

By consistently situating the texts he studies in relation to sixteenth-century political problems, Greenblatt avoids the formalist error of consigning writing to an autonomous aesthetic realm and produces analyses that accord with the New Historicist premise that critics can understand Renaissance works only by linking them to the network of institutions, practices, and beliefs that constituted Tudor culture in its entirety. And if one of the aims of cultural poetics is to explain how texts are both socially produced and socially productive, Greenblatt addresses this question directly in his chapter on William Tyndale. He argues there that the invention of the printing press converted books into a form of power that could control, guide, and discipline, and he proves that texts fashioned acceptable versions of the self by narrating the story of James Bainham, that ultimate creation of the written word. Following John Foxe, Greenblatt recounts that when Bainham publicly declared his Protestant faith, he spoke with "the New Testament in his hand in English and the Obedience of a Christian Man in his bosom," and since the "Obedience" is the title of one of Tyndale's most influential moral tracts, Greenblatt concludes that Bainham's identity has been constituted by a text.

While Greenblatt's book distinctly advances the New Historicist project of rethinking the relationship between literature and society, it also investigates the other questions that Montrose uses to define cultural poetics. Since self-fashioning is a close analogue to Montrose's own idea of subjectification, it is clear that much of Greenblatt's attention is focused on the social processes by which identity is constituted. In his chapter on Christopher Marlowe's plays, Greenblatt also offers his views on the question whether literature can generate effective resistance, and he concludes that the political ideologies and economic practices that both Marlowe and his characters seek to contest are ultimately too powerful to subvert.

Finally, concerning Greenblatt's response to the question of theory, it seems fair to conclude that at the time he wrote *Renaissance Self-Fashioning* he had already decided that no single interpretive model could explain the full complexity of the cultural process New Historicism investigates. Although he invokes a vast array of approaches from a considerable number of disciplines, three of his theoretical borrowings are especially significant. Following Geertz, Greenblatt argues that every social action is embedded in a system of public signification, and this premise is responsible for one of the most

spectacular features of his reading practice, namely, his ability to trace in seemingly trivial anecdotes the codes, beliefs, and strategies that organize an entire society. If cultural anthropology supplies Greenblatt with the techniques of thick description that he uses to interpret letters from colonial outposts, then Foucault offers him the theory of power that informs much of his work, for as his chapters on More and Tyndale demonstrate, Greenblatt views disciplinary mechanisms such as shaming, surveillance, and confession as productive of Renaissance culture, not as repressive of innate human potential. Lastly, in poststructuralist criticism from the 1970s and 1980s, Greenblatt finds corroboration of his idea that the self is a vulnerable construction, not a fixed and coherent substance, though he deviates somewhat from deconstructive analyses when he argues that culture, rather than language, creates the subject's instability. Frankly, when considering his ability to forge these potentially contradictory theories into a powerful critical stance, one wonders who is more adept at self-fashioning, he or the writers he discusses.

In his introduction to *James I and the Politics of Literature* (1983), Jonathan Goldberg commends Greenblatt's study of the relationship between Renaissance texts and society, and he claims that his book, like Greenblatt's, will reveal "the social presence to the world of the literary text and the social presence of the world in the literary text" (Goldberg, *James* xv, quoting Greenblatt, *Renaissance* 5). But unlike Greenblatt, who analyzes the techniques that a number of competing institutions use to discipline behavior, Goldberg tends to focus on the ways political discourses circulate around a single authority, James I. According to Goldberg, James's Roman rhetoric is filled with contradictions, two of which are especially important. First, while James wishes to maintain the integrity of the royal line from which he descends, he also claims that he is both self-originating and the world's secret animating force. Second, while James refers to kingship as a kind of performance in which his thoughts are fully revealed, he also characterizes public display as necessarily obfuscating and opaque.

In a characteristically New Historicist manner, Goldberg offers a political interpretation of these inconsistencies, and he then proceeds to demonstrate that artistic productions replicate the structures of royal authority. Goldberg claims that James's emphasis on self-origination is an effort to mystify his body, to free himself from his dubious family history and to derive his sovereignty from a transcendent and eternal world. This strategy allows the king to claim that all life springs from his spiritual substance, but it also enables him to argue that he is unaccountable to the social world he governs. While the king used this doctrine of mystery and state secrecy to protect his political power, Renaissance writers appropriated his language to make sense of their own activities and experiences. BEN JONSON appeals to the theory of *arcana imperii* in his masques because he wants them to point beyond themselves to the royal patron who is responsible for their existence. John Donne uses James's terms to represent the undiagnosable disease that festers within him as an undisclosed policy that governs a newly founded kingdom. If the discourse of the state secret infiltrates the body here, it also pervades the Renaissance conception of the family, for in an astonishing analysis of domestic portraits, Goldberg shows that the father, modeled on royal authority, generates his lineage but remains distant and unaccountable as he dreamily gazes away from his wife and children.

From even this brief summary, we see that Goldberg shares many of the enabling assumptions of *Renaissance Self-Fashioning:* he senses that all human activity is inevitably inscribed in a system of signification that organizes the ways agents understand their world; he views Renaissance literature as being inextricably related to sixteenth- and seventeenth-century social practices; and he conceives of the self as a culturally constituted entity that is shaped by structures of authority. The above account also hints that Goldberg's theoretical orientation is heavily Foucauldian, for his description of the ways the body is inscribed within discourse echoes Foucault's notion that disciplinary mechanisms swarm and produce their subtle effects even in the domains of human experience that seem intensely private and personal.

But how does Goldberg respond to the containment-subversion problem, which is consistently investigated in New Historicist writing? We can answer this question by briefly summarizing the argument of his chapter "The Theatre of Conscience." Goldberg here examines the ways Renaissance texts replicate the second contradiction inherent in James's discourse, and he begins by suggesting that George Chapman's *Bussy D'Ambois* and William Shakespeare's *Henry V* both depict characters who gain authority by using performative arts to conceal their plans and desires. But if these works concur with James's sense that power can only be maintained through opaque self-dramatization, other texts invoke the royal rhetoric of obfuscating theatricality to challenge the king's policies. Writers such as Jonson and Donne confidently satirize the tolerated licentiousness of James's court because they recognize that if the monarch is aloof, unknowable, and unaccountable, then poets can never

say anything that intentionally questions royal motives. And if the censor or the king himself raises doubts about an author's loyalty, that writer can always cloak himself in the language of regal inscrutability and claim that his works, like James's acts, were constantly being misread. Goldberg's point, then, is that subversive behavior emerges *from within* absolutist discourse itself, and he implies that while such a structure allows writers to express feelings of disgust and contempt, it also ultimately contains the threat posed by gestures of dissent and rebellion.

Goldberg's work has helped to convince many Renaissance scholars that they should become practitioners of cultural poetics, and as a result New Historicism thrives in the field of sixteenth- and seventeenth-century English criticism. Since academics who work in other areas of literary studies have also found this reading strategy congenial, we should now briefly consider the way one of these figures has used New Historicist assumptions to interpret texts drawn from a later culture. In his introduction to *The Gold Standard and the Logic of Naturalism* (1987), Walter Benn Michaels states that his aim is to study how American writing is shaped by changes in economic production, distribution, and consumption that occurred after the Civil War, and his thesis is that the literary mode commonly called naturalism participates in and exemplifies a capitalist discursive system that is structured by a series of internal divisions. Each significant element of American economic practice—corporations, money, commodities, and identities—is intrinsically differentiated from itself, and since writing too is a part of this massive political formation, it must also display the logic of contradiction that drives mercantile culture.

Perhaps the chapter that most clearly illustrates Michaels's powers as a reader is the one from which he borrows his book's title. There Michaels discusses the late nineteenth-century debates between the goldbugs and the advocates of paper currency, and he shows that the controversy between these groups stems from competing assumptions about the nature of money itself: while the defenders of precious metals sense that the value of gold resides in its innate beauty, their opponents think that gold is only desirable because it is a *representation* of money. Having delineated these opposing views, Michaels shows that both of these positions are illustrated in Frank Norris's *McTeague,* for the narrative's two misers are motivated by these contradictory models of wealth. Trina's hoarding of gold enacts her society's presumption that metal is the money itself, and her act encodes her culture's fear that should precious metals stop circulating, civilization will be undone. Zerkow's collecting of junk embodies his world's recognition that if wealth is an effect of representation, then anything can be converted into money, and his behavior demonstrates that a discrepancy between material and value is the enabling condition of capital. Michaels's point in producing this analysis is not that either of these theories of wealth is truer than the other but that the tension between them is a constitutive element of the discourse of naturalism and that any literary text produced at this time will display both views toward money.

By demonstrating that the logic of naturalism informs both the gold-standard debate and Norris's text, Michaels performs the first task expected of the New Historicist, namely, explaining how writing is a part of the culture in which it was produced. In the same chapter, he turns to Norris's *Vandover and the Brute* to consider the ways that subjectivity is constructed. By means of an intricate reading operation, he shows that Vandover's consciousness is deeply divided, for while the character sometimes conceives of his self as an extension of his own animal being, at other times he discovers that his identity is a product of textual representation. But since this split neatly replicates the contradictions inherent in the nineteenth-century understanding of money, Michaels concludes that Vandover's subjectivity is fully inscribed in the discourse of naturalism. Michaels's understanding of selfhood shapes his response to the third question that Montrose claims New Historicists should address, for Michaels strongly insists that the socially constituted character of human identity prevents individuals from imagining progressive alternatives to the society in which they live. Indeed, in a particularly memorable passage, he dismisses utopian visions as fantasies of transcendence that have haunted cultural criticism from the time of Jeremiah. Finally, on the question of method, one must acknowledge that Michaels not only borrows from other scholars but actually offers insights that complicate existing theories. Although his use of Foucault's model of discourse is fairly predictable, his discussion of the ways capitalist practices conform to a structure of internal difference is innovative because, as Brook Thomas has noted, this idea indicates that the poststructuralist dismantling of the autonomous subject may be more complicit with mercantile economic systems than has often been recognized.

While few would deny the brilliance of Greenblatt's, Goldberg's, or Michaels's analyses, some critics have developed misgivings about various aspects of their reading practices. A number of critics have argued that despite the New Historicists' professed interest in cultural difference, many of them speak of societies as if they were monolithic entities and thereby suppress the fact that in a given political formation different paradigms for organizing economic or aesthetic activity exist simultaneously. Some feminists have claimed that the New Historicists have appropriated their assumptions and interpretive strategies but have not contributed much to the study of gender relations. While it is not yet apparent whether these and other criticisms will lead to the demise of cultural poetics in the foreseeable future, it is clear that the emergence of New Historicism has reminded scholars that they will not be able to understand texts unless they study the links between writing and other social practices, and this contribution alone is an honorable legacy.

Hunter Cadzow

See also MICHEL FOUCAULT.

Caroline Walker Bynum, *Holy Feast and Holy Fast: The Religious Significance of Food to Medieval Women* (1987); Walter Cohen, "Political Criticism of Shakespeare," *Shakespeare Reproduced: The Text in History and Ideology* (ed. Jean E. Howard and Marion F. O'Connor, 1987); Jonathan Goldberg, *James I and the Politics of Literature* (1983), "The Politics of Renaissance Literature: A Review Essay," *ELH* 49 (1982), "Recent Studies in the English Renaissance," *Studies in English Literature* (1984); Stephen Greenblatt, Introduction to *The Forms of Power and the Power of Forms,* special issue, *Genre* 15 (1992), "Invisible Bullets: Renaissance Authority and Its Subversion," *Political Shakespeare* (ed. Jonathan Dollimore and Alan Sinfield, 1985), *Renaissance Self-Fashioning* (1980), *Shakespearean Negotiations* (1988), "Towards a Poetics of Culture" (Veeser); Richard Helgerson, "The Land Speaks: Cartography, Chorography, and Subversion in Renaissance England," *Representations* 16 (1986), *Self-Crowned Laureates: Spenser, Jonson, Milton, and the Literary System* (1983); Jean E. Howard, "The New Historicism in Renaissance Studies," *English Literary Renaissance* 16 (1986); Walter Benn Michaels, *The Gold Standard and the Logic of Naturalism* (1987); Louis A. Montrose, "Of Gentlemen and Shepherds: The Politics of Elizabethan Pastoral Form" *ELH* 50 (1983), "The Poetics and Politics of Culture" (Veeser), "The Purpose of Playing: Reflections on a Shakespearean Anthropology," *Helios* 7 (1980), "Shaping Fantasies: Figurations of Gender and Power in Elizabethan Culture," *Representations* 2 (1983); Edward Pechter, "The New Historicism and Its Discontents: Politicizing Renaissance Drama,"

PMLA 101 (1987); Christopher Pye, *The Regal Phantasm: Shakespeare and the Politics of Spectacle* (1990); Leonard Tennenhouse, *Power on Display: The Politics of Shakespeare's Genres* (1986); Brook Thomas, *The New Historicism and Other Old-Fashioned Topics* (1991); H. Aram Veeser, ed., *The New Historicism* (1989); Don E. Wayne, "Power, Politics, and the Shakespearean Text: Recent Criticism in England and the United States," *Shakespeare Reproduced: The Text in History and Ideology* (ed. Jean E. Howard and Marion F. O'Connor, 1987).

NEW HUMANISM

Largely a reaction to modern relativism and determinism, New Humanism was a critical and cultural movement that affirmed freedom of the will and the necessity of standards in life and art. Although the New Humanists were not professional philosophers, their literary and social criticism was informed by "a working philosophy mediating between dogma and skepticism and devoid of revelation and ecclesiastical organization" (Foerster, *Towards Standards* 203). The movement came to brief prominence in the late 1920s because it offered to cure America's spiritual malaise and to check its fatal drift into materialism, hedonism, and demagoguery. However, Irving Babbitt (1865–1933) and Paul Elmer More (1864–1937) had been propounding humanism (they disliked the adjective "new") almost since their meeting as Harvard graduate students in 1892. Both were midwesterners who found a usable past in New England culture but who also read widely in the literature and philosophy of East and West to find "a law of life" (Babbitt, *Literature* 119) transcending time and place. In the great ethical teachers—Erasmus, Jesus, ARISTOTLE, Confucius, Buddha—they found versions of the same truth, that happiness results only from spiritual effort, the "civil war in the cave" between the will and natural impulse. While the country was entering an era of expanding democracy and humanitarian social reform, Babbitt and More were arguing for reform in the inner life and for an ethical aristocracy to exemplify the virtues of moderation.

The old liberal arts college had existed to produce such an aristocracy; New Humanism was born as the college became absorbed in the modern university devoted to social progress through original research. Like MATTHEW ARNOLD, whom they much admired, Babbitt, More, and their mostly academic followers sought to make literary study once more a "criticism of life" and a rigorous discipline for developing character. Often isolated within literature departments dominated by professors of PHILOLOGY and by "dilettantes," they considered themselves a scattered community of true scholars, civilization's "saving remnant."

Babbitt, a teacher of French and comparative literature at Harvard, was the group's chief theoretician and spiritual leader; More, a journalist and, after 1915, a reclusive scholar at Princeton, was its chief literary critic. Babbitt's *Literature and the American College,* published in 1908, presented the first full exposition of New Humanist principles and dialectic, defining humanism in opposition to humanitarianism and naturalism, classicism in opposition to romanticism. In defending the liberal arts college as the proving ground for the nation's future leaders, the book laid the foundation of New Humanist social thought; in deriding romantic individualism, it also established the characteristic tone of most later exchanges between the New Humanists and their modernist enemies. By 1908, however, More had already published four volumes of *Shelburne Essays,* which would eventually fill 11 volumes covering a wide range of political and philosophical topics and containing the most extensive body of New Humanist literary criticism.

In his Harvard classroom, Babbitt recruited a number of young men to the cause, notably Stuart Pratt Sherman (1881–1926) and Norman Foerster (1887–1972). Before turning apostate in the early 1920s, Sherman took on writers that Babbitt and More seldom read, his *On Contemporary Literature* (1917) applying New Humanist literary standards to such writers as Mark Twain, H. G. Wells, and Theodore Dreiser. In the late 1920s, when the New Humanists fought an often acrimonious "battle of the books" in popular magazines and literary journals, Foerster very nearly took Babbitt's place as leader. He lucidly explained New Humanist critical method in *Towards Standards* (1929) and edited the highly polemical *Humanism and America: Essays on the Outlook of Modern Civilization* (1930), provoking a counterattack, *The Critique of Humanism* (1930), from thirteen opponents, including Allen Tate. G. R. Elliott (1883–1963) completed the group's inner circle, arguing in *The Cycle of Modern Poetry* (1929) that Imagism merely carried on the old Romantic revolt against convention. Other important figures were Frank Jewett Mather (1868–1953), who wrote a New Humanist critique of modern painting, and Robert Shafer (1889–1956), who attacked the cult of science and wrote a book on More. Support also came from several journal editors, including T. S. ELIOT (1888–1965), a former student of Babbitt who gave New Humanism a hearing in the *Criterion* even while considering humanism parasitic on established religion. After 1930, interest in New Humanism waned. By 1942 Babbitt and More were both dead, and Alfred Kazin was dismissing them as "merely . . . the twin elder saints of the old school" (78).

Kazin's term "saints" is to the point, for the New Humanists were promoting something very like a non-theistic religion. Life, they argued, could be lived on three planes: the religious, the human, and the natural. The goal of the religious, or meditative, life is nirvanic peace, an extinction of desire. As the discipline of a "spiritual athlete," Babbitt argued, humanism itself can be a stage on the path to the same goal, and in some of his accounts it resembles the primitive Buddhism he admired. At the same time, the New Humanists offered a virtual equivalent for Christian grace and humility, an individual discipline leading "not to blank isolation but to some inexpressible communion of all spirits" (More, *Drift* 282). Modern skepticism, however, had made life on the religious plane impossible for most people, and history since the Renaissance had revealed the evil of life on the natural plane. The villains of history were FRANCIS BACON and JEAN-JACQUES ROUSSEAU, the founders of the two modern naturalistic movements—science and Romanticism—which denied the supernatural element in humanity and led to modern barbarism, the Great War presaging the fall of civilization as Romantic overreachers employed an amoral science with murderous efficiency.

Civilization might yet survive if the majority could be made to live somewhere within the middle, human plane, characterized not by meditation but by the "mediation" of opposing drives or the moderation rather than the extinction of desire, hence the group's veneration for the Greek ideal of the Golden Mean. All but the most debased individuals can restrain desire because they are innately dualistic, possessing both a natural self driven by impulse and a supernatural self with the power to resist those impulses, a power termed variously the "inner check," the "will to refrain," the *frein vital* (as opposed to Henri Bergson's *élan vital*), or the "higher will."

Humanity's dualism is the central tenet of New Humanism. The inner check, like grace, is a gift that raises people above nature, yet it requires no speculation about God, though some of the New Humanists, including More and Elliott, eventually embraced Christianity. The fact of a negative power to resist some impulses means freedom to act positively on others, to choose one's goals; it thus makes individuals responsible for their own happiness and reveals the inadequacy of all deterministic theories—Darwinism, Marxism, Freudianism, Behaviorism.

To choose goals wisely, one must have standards, which a skeptical humanist cannot accept on divine or human authority or take as absolute. Driven by what

More called the "Demon of the Absolute," individuals often take a half-truth—either some metaphysical unity or the Heraclitean flux—as the whole of reality. The New Humanists mediated between the One and the Many and departed from the Western rationalist tradition by giving the imagination primacy over reason in sustaining civilization. The highest form of imagination, the "moral imagination," is anything but an ability to escape into realms of fantasy; it is the power to glimpse the universal behind Maya, the veil of illusion. The spiritual leaders who founded enduring civilizations all perceived "something that abides in the midst of the phenomenal and transitory" (Babbitt, *On Being Creative* 142), and they all worked humbly to conform themselves to their vision of a "normal" human life, one fully expressing human nature. Most persons lack such insight but fortunately possess an innate capacity for imitating those on a higher plane. Jesus, Confucius, Buddha—all became the standard of human life, the "Word made flesh," for entire civilizations. Ethical leaders, traditional symbols, and social institutions appeal to the imagination in the same way and are especially important restraints on impulse where religious ideals have lost their power, as they had in the modern West.

While granting a crucial role to the imagination, the New Humanists were yet "consecrated to the service of a high, impersonal reason" (Babbitt, *Literature* 174), usually treated as the capacity for making judicious distinctions. Babbitt conceived himself and his followers to be a "Socratic remnant" (*Democracy* 281) protecting society against the sophistical manipulation of such abstract terms as "justice," once defined as the distribution of wealth and prestige according to an individual's moral worth but increasingly identified with the arbitrary redistribution of wealth that led to class wars such as the French and Russian revolutions.

In their distrust of absolutes, the New Humanists also employed reason in a typically American way, asserting a kind of moral pragmatism and claiming to apply it with more than scientific objectivity. Humanism was timeless and thoroughly modern, a "positive and critical" belief founded on direct observation of the inner check as one of the "immediate data of consciousness" (Babbitt, *Rousseau* xxiii) and on the pragmatic "experiments" of history. These experiments reveal that when the "moral imagination" of a Buddha or an Aristotle provides a norm of moderation and humility the "fruits" are invariably peace, happiness, and social convention, literally a "coming together" on the human plane. When the "idyllic imagination" of a Rousseau idealizes life on the natural plane, those caught in the delusion become spiritually restless and miserable; society disintegrates in the clash of warring egoists driven by the will to power. These sequences of cause and effect reveal moral laws that operate as certainly as natural laws. Although they were wary of RALPH WALDO EMERSON's reliance on natural impulse, the New Humanists found an epitome of their own philosophy in his "Ode" to W. H. Channing. There are two "laws discrete," Emerson asserts, a "law for man" and a "law for thing," and when the latter runs wild, it "doth the man unking" (*Complete Works of Ralph Waldo Emerson,* ed. Edward Waldo Emerson, vol. 9: *Poems,* 1904, 78).

As critics, the New Humanists were primarily concerned with judging the moral value of institutions, ideas, and literary works by the degree to which they recognized humanity's dualism and embodied the eternal human law. Although they valued formal excellence, they lacked the critical tools for formal analysis and reserved their highest regard for works in which artistic control serves a high moral intention. They found little in modern literature that measured up to the classics, to Dante Alighieri, or to John Milton. They especially scorned critical theories based on naturalistic premises, the determinism of HIPPOLYTE TAINE, or any form of "impressionism," the term they loosely applied to theories, such as those of WALTER PATER and BENEDETTO CROCE, that accepted IMMANUEL KANT's separation of aesthetic experience from practical life.

Still, the New Humanists were not the moralistic dogmatists their critics made them out to be. People need standards, Babbitt argued in *The New Laokoon,* yet because the truth will always "overflow" them, these standards "must be flexible" (35). Standards are fictions representing an imaginative, and thus incomplete, apprehension of the eternally human. When what should be flexible standards become rules, as in eighteenth-century France, the true humanist will speak out for freedom and originality. In life and art, Babbitt called for the Greeks' "creative imitation," a careful mediation "between the forces of tradition and the claims of originality" (*Literature* 135). Although More asserted that a literary work's moral value increases as "the immediate consciousness of dualism enters into expression" (*Drift* 265), he did not mean to promote didactic moralizing. The consciousness of dualism informs an author's entire vision of life and often reveals itself indirectly, as in the sense of repose More felt when reading some of Henry Wadsworth Longfellow and John Greenleaf Whittier. Sherman found it in George Meredith's tragicomic stance and in those characters of Henry James who make style a moral principle. Elliott saw it in Robert Frost's "poetry of true neighbourliness"

(112). At their best, then, New Humanist literary critics were more than judgmental, for their standard revealed the original as well as the traditional in an author's work.

History, the New Humanists thought, always changes but goes nowhere; tending to extremes, it resembles "the old story of Luther's drunken man on horseback: prop him up on one side and over he flops on the other" (More, *Demon* 30). Believing the world was leaning dangerously left, they pushed to the right and so were often called Puritans and reactionaries. According to their own logic, what was "new" in New Humanism sprang out of particular historical circumstances and belongs to the flux—terms like the "inner check" and *frein vital,* the insistence on a "positive and critical" method, the narrowly defined moral standard.

What was not new has remained an important element in American intellectual life—the Arnoldian belief that reading the best that has been thought and said unites individuals in a timeless human community. Most recently, heirs of the New Humanists have formed a National Association of Scholars to resist what they take to be a new "Demon of the Absolute," a "politically correct" relativism that would decenter the Western intellectual tradition and challenge received standards for determining the literary canon. Members of the new saving remnant consider themselves the necessary check on innovation that ensures the vitality of tradition. They should not be surprised at being called fascists. From the extremes, as Babbitt was fond of noting, the middle always looks like another extreme.

Stephen C. Brennan

Irving Babbitt, *Democracy and Leadership* (1924, reprint, 1979), *Literature and the American College: Essays in Defense of the Humanities* (1908, reprint, 1986), *The New Laokoon: An Essay on the Confusion of the Arts* (1910), *On Being Creative and Other Essays* (1932, reprint, 1968), *Representative Writings* (ed. George A. Panichas, 1981), *Rousseau and Romanticism* (1919, reprint, 1991); G. R. Elliott, *The Cycle of Modern Poetry: A Series of Essays toward Clearing Our Present Poetic Dilemma* (1929, reprint, 1965); Norman Foerster, ed., *Humanism and America* (1930, reprint, 1967), *Towards Standards: A Study of the Present Critical Movement in American Letters* (1930, reprint, 1966); Paul Elmer More, *The Demon of the Absolute* (1928, reprint, 1968), *The Drift of Romanticism* (1915, reprint, 1967), *Selected Shelburne Essays* (1935, reprint, 1977), *Shelburne Essays on American Literature* (ed. Daniel Aaron, 1963); Stuart Pratt Sherman, *On Contemporary Literature* (1917).

A. Owen Aldridge, "Irving Babbitt and the Standards

of Aesthetic Judgment," *Neohelicon* 14 (1987); Stephen C. Brennan and Stephen R. Yarbrough, *Irving Babbitt* (1987); Arthur Hazard Dakin, *Paul Elmer More* (1960); Robert M. Davies, *The Humanism of Paul Elmer More* (1958); Francis X. Duggan, *Paul Elmer More* (1967); J. David Hoeveler, Jr., *The New Humanism: A Critique of Modern America, 1900–1940* (1977); Alfred Kazin, "Liberals and New Humanists," *On Native Grounds* (1942); Thomas R. Nevin, *Irving Babbitt: An Intellectual Study* (1984); George A. Panichas and Claes Ryn, ed., *Irving Babbitt in Our Time* (1986); Michael A. Weinstein, *The Wilderness and the City: American Classical Philosophy as a Moral Quest* (1982).

NEW YORK INTELLECTUALS

The revival of *Partisan Review* in 1937 (the magazine had been founded four years earlier within the orbit of the Communist party) was one of those galvanizing moments in American intellectual life, important not so much for its discrediting effect on the Party as for its liberating and empowering effect on a group whose defiance of *partinost* conceptions of art and ideas was made in the name of a purer, more subtly dialectical Marxism. The critics and imaginative writers who grouped themselves around *Partisan Review* at this time (LIONEL TRILLING, Philip Rahv, Alfred Kazin, Delmore Schwartz, William Phillips, Clement Greenberg, Harold Rosenberg, Dwight Macdonald, Mary McCarthy, F. W. Dupee, Diana Trilling, Paul Goodman, Lionel Abel) were soon to be joined by a second generation (Irving Howe, Saul Bellow, Leslie Fiedler, Elizabeth Hardwick, Richard Chase, William Barrett, Daniel Bell, Hannah Arendt, Isaac Rosenfeld), and in the 1950s by a third generation (SUSAN SONTAG, Stephen Marcus, Norman Podhoretz, Hilton Kramer). That the Marxism of those New York writers who had come of age in the 1930s "was essentially accidental, sentimental, absurd," as Kazin once put it (*Contemporaries* 403), that it coexisted rather too comfortably with a more profound enthusiasm for Fyodor Dostoevsky, FRIEDRICH NIETZSCHE, SIGMUND FREUD, James Joyce, Franz Kafka, and other European moderns, has often been suggested. Yet for all their haste to turn their backs on the engagé 1930s, the New York writers never embraced the "formalist" tendencies of their friendly rivals, the New Critics (see NEW CRITICISM). And while they were hardly the first to champion writers such as Joyce, T. S. ELIOT, and HENRY JAMES, their insights into the rich and problematic relations of art to experience in the modernist canon were particularly attuned to the mood of intellectual pessimism and passivity that had

begun in the late 1930s and was to last through the McCarthy and Eisenhower eras.

In an Age of Criticism, as Randall Jarrell glumly dubbed the literary 1940s and 1950s, the *Partisan* critics were able to outdo everyone else, it seems, in evoking all that was extreme and exigent about the times. The typical *Partisan Review* article or review, whether it appeared in Rahv and Phillips's journal itself or in the *Kenyon Review*, say, or even in the American Jewish Committee's *Commentary*, was aphoristic, allusive, polemical, prone to ironic syntheses of the high and the low, the refined and the vulgar, and passionately engaged in making discoveries and registering judgments that went beyond the particular books or authors under discussion. That their views on modernism, capitalism, their own Jewishness and Americanness, and much else were to turn inside out over the years is a fact of considerable historical and even sociological interest. But no less interesting is the constancy of their focus on the socially and historically conditioned nature of the authorial self revealed in works of fiction and nonfiction (the distinction was not important) and also on the collective fate of the intelligentsia, especially in America (whence the numerous symposia in *Partisan Review* and other family publications).

Lionel Trilling wrote in 1946: "Dreiser and James: with that juxtaposition we are immediately at the dark and bloody crossroads where literature and politics meet. One does not go there gladly, but nowadays it is not exactly a matter of free choice whether one goes or does not go" (*Liberal* 8). Over the years, however much their circumstances changed and their youthful beliefs ruptured, these outsiders turned insiders were rarely to stray very far from Trilling's "dark and bloody crossroads." Nevertheless, their problem in the beginning was not so much political (once they were determined to challenge the programmatic literary nationalism of the Popular Front period) as it was intellectual: a matter of fixing on the American literary heritage in ways that would place in relief the distinct qualities of their own demotic cosmopolitanism. Hence *Partisan Review*'s extension of its opposition to the Party's "new Americanism" of the late 1930s into a wartime campaign against the cultural patrioteering of Van Wyck Brooks, Bernard DeVoto, and Archibald MacLeish. Even more significant was this group's paradigmatic insistence on a radical dissociation of mind and experience in American literature. Trilling's memorable essays on Sherwood Anderson (1941) and on V. L. Parrington and his disciples (1940 and 1946), all of which appear in *The Liberal Imagination*, are in this vein—though there is little of the demotic in

Trilling's Arnoldian manner. So is Kazin's overwrought portrait of William Faulkner in *On Native Grounds,* which he later tacitly corrected. To Philip Rahv, *Partisan Review*'s most imposing editor, the essential issue was the insubstantial personal culture of so many twentieth-century American novelists, what he liked to refer to as their typical "redskin" inability to transform ideas into actual dramatic motives or to provide perspective on the national experience. "Everything is contained in the American novel except ideas" (Rahv 1–6, 24).

Even EDMUND WILSON, admired though he was around *Partisan Review,* was felt to have a little too much of the shallow-thinking, popularizing side of the 1920s about him—an assessment that one can find tactfully adumbrated in a 1942 discussion of *Axel's Castle* by Delmore Schwartz (361–63). What particularly repelled "young would-be writers growing up in a Jewish slum in New York or Chicago during the 'twenties and 'thirties," Irving Howe (one of those writers) was later to write in a 1970s update of this general theme, was "the whole complex of Emersonian individualism" prevalent in American literature, an outlook that "seemed not only strange but sometimes even a version of that brutality which our parents had warned us was intrinsic to gentile life": "Then, too, Jewish would-be writers found the classical Americans, especially Emerson and Thoreau, a little wan and frail, deficient in those historical entanglements we felt to be essential to literature because inescapable in life" (*Celebrations* 12, 14–15).

That their own historical entanglements, most notably with Nazism and Stalinism, had provided Jews with a redemptive affinity for modern art and ideas was an unexamined assumption around *Partisan Review* in the 1940s. The Jewish writer, quipped Isaac Rosenfeld, "is a specialist in alienation (the one international banking system the Jews actually control)" (69). But as the themes associated with Jewish existence—uprootedness and vulnerability, the social fluidity of the urban landscape, ironic minglings of the streetwise and the erudite—became the very idiom by which America's increasingly pluralistic, postwar literary culture spoke to itself and the world, a surprising reversal took place. Was it not true, the editors asked in their introduction to *Partisan*'s well-known "Our Country and Our Culture" symposium of 1952, that power in the United States now comported itself with more maturity and that the needs of writers and artists were better understood? Most of the 25 contributors were inclined to agree. A year later the acclaim, both critical and popular, that greeted *The Adventures of Augie March,* Saul Bellow's exuberant 1953 celebration of urban-immigrant life in Chicago, seemed

to confirm the rather more tentative symposium judgments regarding the inappropriateness of literary angst and alienation, as did, in a very different way, the publication in 1954 of *A Treasury of Yiddish Stories,* co-edited by Irving Howe, which offered a literature rich in sweetness and human affirmation as an antidote to the nihilism and experimental imperatives of modernist writing.

Still, Howe was not about to dissociate himself from modernism at this point, as his evoking of such names as Eliot and Bertolt Brecht in his introduction to the *Treasury* attests. In the 1950s it remained possible for the New York critics to write about Bellow, Bernard Malamud, Isaac Bashevis Singer, and other American-Jewish novelists as if they were part of a continuous line stretching back to Isaak Babel and Kafka. In 1958, Richard Chase even published *The Democratic Vista,* evoking those commonplaces of New York criticism—highbrow, middlebrow, and lowbrow—in an effort to demonstrate that a continued loyalty to avant-garde experimentation, combined with a readiness to think of modern life in extreme terms, could coexist with a politics of acceptance. Praised by some New York writers as a blow against complacency, Chase's book was soon overtaken by events. "We must get it out of our heads that this is a doomed time, that we are waiting for the end, and the rest of it," declared Bellow in his 1964 *Herzog.* "Things are grim enough without these shivery games. . . . We love apocalypses too much" (316–17).

Affronted by apocalyptic students and by the protests and turmoil occasioned by the war in Vietnam, many New York writers were indeed ready to rethink what Bellow derisively called "the Wasteland outlook." In such works as Trilling's *Beyond Culture* and *Sincerity and Authenticity,* Howe's *Decline of the New,* Daniel Bell's *Cultural Contradictions of Capitalism,* and Hilton Kramer's *The Age of the Avant-Garde,* a wide-ranging critique was bodied forth. Modernism in this view was a spent force, an artistic and critical dead end; it represented a new orthodoxy of dissent, the indurated ideology of a smug and established "adversary culture" (Trilling, *Beyond* ix–xviii). None of the authors of these works was about to deny the intuitions of reality vouchsafed to the classic avant-garde, but literary modernism had a way of cavalierly dismissing both liberal values and the world of daily existence that made several New York writers especially uneasy in their former allegiance.

Modernism stood indicted, then, both because of the illiberalism of its pioneers (W. B. Yeats, Ezra Pound, Eliot, et al.) and because of the glib nihilism and apocalypticism of its post-1945 epigones. But its cardinal liability, Trilling, Bell, Howe, and even Sontag *(On Photography)* all suggested in their different ways, was the divorce it posited between mind and external reality. This "disruption of *mimesis*" not only marginalized and depoliticized literature (Bell 110), it ruled out the very notion of shared historical experience. With the ascendancy, in the 1980s, of SEMIOTICS, DECONSTRUCTION, and other forms of textually centered rejections of high art and the authorial self, these warnings about the eclipse of narrative mimesis and the "cultural criticism" logical to it resonated widely among academic traditionalists. Indeed, the very careers of Howe, Bell, Trilling, Kazin, Dwight Macdonald, and other New York intellectuals took on a kind of emblematic significance in the 1980s (Jacoby 72 ff.). Of course, there is always the danger of confusing the genuine critical and historical insights of the New York writers' "dissent from modernism" and, by extension, POSTMODERNISM with the vulgarization of these insights in neoconservative diatribes against "the new class" and its literary representatives. Nevertheless, I am confident that the fundamental reevaluations that events forced on this group in the 1960s and the 1970s will be found as liberating to literary study as were their battles against the socialist realists and hard-line nativists of an earlier day.

S. A. Longstaff

See also LIONEL TRILLING.

Daniel Bell, *The Cultural Contradictions of Capitalism* (1986); Richard Chase, *The Democratic Vista: A Dialogue on Life and Letters in Contemporary America* (1958); Irving Howe, *Celebrations and Attacks: Thirty Years of Literary and Cultural Commentary* (1979), *Decline of the New* (1970); Irving Howe and Eliezer Greenberg, eds., *A Treasury of Yiddish Stories* (1954); Alfred Kazin, *Contemporaries* (1962), *On Native Grounds: An Interpretation of Modern American Prose Literature* (1942); Hilton Kramer, *The Age of the Avant-Garde* (1973); "Our Country and Our Culture," symposium in *Partisan Review* 19 (1952); Philip Rahv, *Literature and the Sixth Sense* (1969); Isaac Rosenfeld, *An Age of Enormity: Life and Writing in the Forties and Fifties* (ed. Theodore Solotaroff, 1962); Delmore Schwartz, *Selected Essays* (ed. Donald A. Dike and David H. Zucker, 1970); Susan Sontag, *On Photography* (1977); Lionel Trilling, *Beyond Culture: Essays on Literature and Learning* (1965), *The Liberal Imagination: Essays on Literature and Society* (1950), *Sincerity and Authenticity* (1972).

Robert Alter, *After the Tradition: Essays on Modern Jewish Writing* (1969); Alexander Bloom, *Prodigal Sons: The New York Intellectuals and Their World* (1986); Frederick Crews, "The 'Partisan' Intellectuals," *New York Review of Books* (November 23, 1978); James Burkhart Gilbert, *Writers and Partisans: A History of Literary Partisans in America* (1968); Russell Jacoby, *The Last Intellectuals: American Culture in the Age of Academe* (1987); Mark Krupnick, *Lionel Trilling and the Fate of Cultural Criticism* (1986); S. A. Longstaff, "Ivy League Gentiles and Inner-City Jews: Class and Ethnicity around *Partisan Review* in the Thirties and the Forties," *American Jewish History* 81 (1991), "The New York Family," *Queen's Quarterly* 83 (1976); Mark Shechner, *After the Revolution: Studies in the Contemporary Jewish-American Imagination* (1987); Alan M. Wald, *The New York Intellectuals: The Rise and Decline of the Anti-Stalinist Left from the 1930s to the 1980s* (1987).

NIETZSCHE, FRIEDRICH

Friedrich Nietzsche (1844–1900) was a German philosopher of uncommon gifts and profound influence. His productive life was very short, lasting roughly from 1872 until he collapsed in Turin in 1889. During this brief span he composed 14 books, numerous shorter works, a prodigious mass of notes, and a huge number of letters. Totally incapacitated after his collapse, which may have been due to syphilis, he lived for 11 more years under the care of his sister, who had exclusive control of his papers and rigidly controlled access to them. Nietzsche's reputation as an anti-Semitic proto-Nazi thinker was in large part due to her activities. Generally unknown and not appreciated while he could still enjoy his status, Nietzsche, who once wrote of himself, "Only the day after tomorrow belongs to me. Some are born posthumously" (preface to *The Antichrist*), is now one of the most widely read philosophers in the world.

Part of the reason for Nietzsche's broad appeal is that he produced some of the greatest writing in the history of German letters. His works are extremely intense and passionate, do not at all depend on the technical terms and unwieldy syntax often characteristic of German philosophy, and—though Nietzsche's views themselves are often elusive—are accessible and engaging to a vast range of readers. Nietzsche was a master of the aphorism, and his extraordinarily personal style gave him an unusual place within the history of philosophy. It also made him attractive to a number of literary authors (W. B. Yeats, Henry James, and Thomas Mann, among others), painters (Pablo Picasso and the German Expressionists), and literary critics (ROLAND BARTHES and PAUL DE MAN), as well as to many philosophical writers (MARTIN HEIDEGGER, JEAN-PAUL SARTRE, JACQUES DERRIDA, MICHEL FOUCAULT, and many others).

Nietzsche was trained as a classical philologist, and at the unusually early age of 24 he was appointed to the chair of philology at the University of Basel. Already under the influence of ARTHUR SCHOPENHAUER, he there came to know Richard Wagner, who was living nearby. His first book, *The Birth of Tragedy,* was partly written in vindication of the thought and art of his early mentors.

The Birth of Tragedy offers a stunningly revisionary account of the nature of classical Greek drama. It calls for the regeneration of German culture through Wagnerian opera, which Nietzsche considered at the time to be the modern equivalent of the art of Aeschylus. The work depends essentially on Nietzsche's distinction between the "Apollonian" spirit of the plastic arts, of measure and moderation, and the "Dionysian" spirit of music, of intoxication, excess, loss of self, and total immersion in the underlying reality concealed by the Apollonian appearance of the world.

According to Nietzsche, tragedy began in the musical, undifferentiated Dionysian chorus and only later developed the discursive and discrete Apollonian action and characters in which ARISTOTLE had located the essence of the genre. Real tragedy, according to Nietzsche, depicts the doomed efforts of the Apollonian heroes to rise above the constraints of their individuality. It celebrates those efforts as a characteristic human gesture in the face of the ultimate irrationality of the world, and in the chorus, which always remains on stage after the hero's destruction, it offers, as he states in section 7 of *The Birth of Tragedy,* the "metaphysical comfort . . . that life is at the bottom of things, despite all the changes of appearances, indestructibly powerful and pleasurable" (*Basic* 59).

Tragedy died, Nietzsche shockingly claimed, because Euripides ("the most tragic of the poets," according to Aristotle in the *Poetics*), expressing the views of Socrates, refused to concede that the world had any irrational aspects and thereby robbed tragedy of all its Dionysian elements. Since that time, in Nietzsche's view, Europe has lived under the Socratic illusion that "science," the rational investigation of the world, is capable of answering all questions and solving all problems. But this exclusively intellectual approach is bound to fail, since rational investigation always finally reveals its own limits.

Nietzsche resigned from the university in 1879 and devoted the rest of his life to writing. And though Schopenhauer and Wagner ceased to be the dominant influences on his thought, many of the questions addressed in *The Birth of Tragedy* continued to occupy him throughout his

life; the book itself, despite its many problems, has remained one of his most popular and well-known works.

Nietzsche came to connect the Socratic-Platonic faith in reason with the Christian faith in God, who constitutes and guarantees the ultimate truth about the world ("Christianity," he wrote in the preface to *Beyond Good and Evil,* "is Platonism for the 'people'" [*Basic* 193]). He claimed that most people need to believe in values that exist independently as a matter of objective fact, values that are binding on everyone and adherence to which is a matter purely of obligation and not of choice.

To such "dogmatic" or "metaphysical" thought Nietzsche opposed his "perspectivism," a view he once expressed by writing that "facts are precisely what there is not, only interpretations" (*Will* 267). And he believed that the emergence of the possibility of perspectivism was due in part to the fact that Christianity had provided its very own undermining. This is the sense of his notorious dictum, "God is dead" (*Gay* 181). By this he meant that faith in God, which involves a total commitment to truthfulness, finally has led to the gradually emerging realization that God does not exist after all and that therefore there can be no objective, absolute values.

What we take as facts or absolute values, Nietzsche believes, are in reality earlier interpretations that have succeeded in effacing their interpretive, and therefore partial and nonbinding, character. This is particularly true of the moral values associated with Christianity. Such values make universal demands, but they were in fact created through what, in essay 1, section 7, of *The Genealogy of Morals,* Nietzsche calls "the slave revolt in morality" (*Basic* 47) and have been designed to make life tolerable for the large mass of people, to whom he often refers as "the herd."

Obnoxious as Nietzsche found the specific values of Christian morality, he reacted even more negatively to its universalism. Christian morality, he believed, prevents the few people who do not belong to "the herd" from going in good conscience against the majority's values and from fashioning their own way of life—a way of life that will differ from one type of person to another and will make no claim to universal validity. Nietzsche constantly praised such creativity and claimed that the only difference between the Christian and the type of character he praises as the *Übermensch,* the "free spirit" or "new philosopher," is that while both are creators of values, only the latter remains aware of this fact and actually takes pleasure in it.

Nietzsche therefore urged the proliferation of different approaches to life and value; he believed that there can be no single, overarching approach by which everyone can live and flourish. Dogmatic approaches, insofar as they are designed to be followed by all, only succeed in establishing values addressed to the lowest common denominator among people. Such values are therefore detrimental to the interests of those few who could, had their conscience not already been "poisoned" by the many, fashion their own, unusual modes of life.

What Nietzsche believes about life he also believes about interpretation—hence his immense importance for literary theory and criticism. As certain values come to appear binding, so many interpretations cease to display their interpretive status and begin to appear as fact about the texts they concern, which means that they no longer appear as interpretations at all. And just as Nietzsche's "genealogical" method aims to show how the particular interpretations of life that created the moral values of Christianity came about, so literary criticism must turn to an unmasking of what we take for granted in connection with every text. Such "facts" are the products of earlier, accepted, and therefore unacknowledged interpretations. And just as there is not a single mode of life, good for all people, so it is not clear that there can ever be a single, overarching interpretation of a particular text that everyone will have to accept. "The" world and "the" text are equally indeterminate.

The problem with this approach, in morality as well as in literature, is that every unmasking must itself proceed from a particular point of view, which it must take for granted while it is depending upon it. Thus, every revelation of the partiality of a previous point of view will contain within it an unquestioned commitment to some further point of view. The genealogical enterprise therefore cannot ever be fully completed. Even the claim that there is no truth, that the world and the text are equally indeterminate, in being claimed, is claimed to be true. And though *Thus Spoke Zarathustra* is probably Nietzsche's best-known book, some of his most engaging writing, addressing just this last problem, can be found in such texts as the third essay of *The Genealogy of Morals* and the fifth book of *The Gay Science*.

All interpretation, moral or literary, is an expression of what Nietzsche calls "the will to power." Much that he wrote about this idea sounds as if he believed in some sort of crude overpowering of "the weak" by "the strong" and has seemed to many to align him with fascist theories of political power. But the idea that interpretations manifest the will to power is the idea that no interpretation is a pure objective mirroring of the facts, since there are no facts to be mirrored in the first place. Rather, it is an effort to fashion a mode of life, or a reading of a text, through which the type of character each interpreter constitutes can best be manifested: "One seeks a picture of the world in that philosophy in which we feel freest, i.e., in which our most powerful drive feels free to function. This will also be the case with me!" (*Will* 224–25).

But given that Nietzsche denies the existence of any objective standards, how can we ever decide that a mode of life is worthwhile? The only answer to this question, according to him, is provided by the thought of "the eternal recurrence." This view is most often interpreted as a cosmological theory to the effect that the history of the world has been and will be repeated an infinite number of times, in exactly the same order, down to its smallest detail. A much more fruitful interpretation of the eternal recurrence, however, is to take it not as the assertion of a cosmology but rather as the hypothesis that if one were to have another life (though no one ever will), then that life—if it is to be the life of the *same* person—would have to be exactly the same, down to its smallest detail, as the life one has already had. And the question to ask is whether one would be willing to have this life, exactly as it has already been, down to its smallest detail, all over again. If the answer is affirmative, then one's life is justified, even though one may have failed to be good by moral standards.

Nietzsche therefore urges those who are able to do so not to remain in the grip of dogmatism and to fashion instead interpretations and lives of their own. In his view, it is much more important to be important than to be good. And even if the interpretation of life we are in the process of fashioning cannot but seem binding to us—because it is impossible, at that time, to conceive of another—he still urges that we retain the generalized awareness that there is nothing necessary about it. Any such construct is our own creation. Nietzsche, furthermore, wants his readers to revel in their difference from everyone else, if they are, of course, capable of being different in the first place. But he cannot possibly *convince* his readers to be different: one either is or is not capable of that. Accordingly, the nature of his intended audience and the mode of address appropriate to them remain for him questionable throughout his writings.

Nietzsche's perspectivism, therefore, is the view that all views are interpretations. Can this view be communicated without undermining itself? Is it a true view or not? If it is true, then at least that view itself is not simply an interpretation. If it is not true, then it need not be true that all views are simply interpretations. This is also a problem Nietzsche addressed repeatedly. His solution was to avoid asserting the perspectivist position—a project that is not, in any case, productive—and to present instead, through his writings, in all their remarkable stylistic multiplicity, the outline of a character—Nietzsche himself—who made out of the accidental events of his life a mode of life that was truly his own and that no one else should, or even could, imitate.

In doing so, Nietzsche also made the form of his writing essential to its content and thus raised profound questions about the relationship between philosophy and literature. The consequences of his views and of his overall project are still being pursued in philosophy, literature, and criticism. And if his perspectivism is, after all, true, then, in appropriately paradoxical fashion, this pursuit will never be finally over.

Alexander Nehamas

Friedrich Nietzsche, *Basic Writings of Nietzsche* (ed. and trans. Walter Kaufmann, 1968, including *The Birth of Tragedy, Beyond Good and Evil, The Genealogy of Morals, The Case of Wagner,* and *Ecce Homo*), *Briefwechsel: Kritische Gesamtausgabe* (ed. G. Colli and M. Montinari, 20 vols. to date, 1975–), *Die fröhliche Wissenschaft* (1887, *The Gay Science,* ed. and trans. Walter Kaufmann, 1974), *Menschliches, allzumenschliches* (1878, *Human, All-Too-Human,* trans. R. J. Hollingdale, 1986), *Morgenröte* (1881, *Daybreak,* trans. R. J. Hollingdale, 1986), *Philosophy and Truth: Selections from Nietzsche's Notebooks from the 1870s* (ed. and trans. Daniel Breazeale, 1979), *Unzeitgemässe Betrachtungen* (4 vols., 1873–76, *Untimely Meditations,* trans. R. J. Hollingdale, 1983), *The Viking Portable Nietzsche* (ed. and trans. Walter Kaufmann, 1954, including *Thus Spoke Zarathustra, Twilight of the Idols, Nietzsche contra Wagner,* and *The Antichrist*), *Werke: Kritische Gesamtausgabe* (ed. G. Colli and M. Montinari, 8 vols., 1967–91), *Der Wille zur Macht* (1901, *The Will to Power,* trans. Walter Kaufmann and R. J. Hollingdale, 1968).

Arthur Danto, *Nietzsche as Philosopher* (1965); Paul de Man, *Allegories of Reading: Figural Language in Rousseau, Nietzsche, Rilke, and Proust* (1979); Jacques Derrida, *Eperons: Les Styles du Nietzsche* (1978, *Spurs: Nietzsche's Styles,* trans. Barbara Harlow, 1979); Stephen Donadio, *Nietzsche, Henry James, and the Artistic Will* (1978); John Burt Foster, Jr., *Heirs to Dionysus: A Nietzschean Current in Literary Modernism* (1981); Allan Megill, *Prophets of Extremity: Nietzsche, Heidegger, Foucault, Derrida* (1985); Alexander Nehamas, *Nietzsche: Life as Literature* (1985); Alan Schrift, *Nietzsche and the Question of Interpretation* (1990); M. S. Silk and J. P. Stern, *Nietzsche on Tragedy* (1981).

O

ORALITY AND LITERACY

To a generally unacknowledged extent, issues raised by orality and literacy have always been important for literary criticism, especially in relation to three major areas of concern. First, there are questions about the medium in which literary texts exist. While literature is usually taken to involve books (though theatrical works are problematic for this conception, as are lyrics, if considered historically), "oral literature" seems to contradict this idea, given the meaning of "oral" (to do with the spoken) and the etymology of "literature" in *litterae* (Latin, meaning "letters"). Also, since many of the constituent elements of literature feature prominently in contemporary cultural forms in media other than "letters" (narrative occurs in film and television, lyricism is found in pop song lyrics, etc.), many of literature's apparently defining properties can be seen to exist outside "writing"; this problematizes literature's generally assumed close connection with "literate" forms and "literate" cultures (as has been shown, for example, by Ruth Finnegan).

Second, there are issues concerning ideas of authors and authorship. In oral societies—including not only those that have what are typically thought of as oral "literatures" but also (following work by Milman Parry and Albert Lord) the classical Greek culture of Homer—the notion of an author does not exist in anything like the form that gives it its importance in most traditional literary criticism. Rather, "authorship" exists in such societies, if at all, within conventions of communal improvisation and formulaic composition; and it is only with a transition to literate societies, especially with print literacy (see Eisenstein), that the modern category of an author fully emerges.

Third, there are issues of readerships. Reading is not simply a matter of interpretation based on a presumable physical and cognitive process but a socially formed and very unevenly distributed set of skills and conventions. Limits on the historically constituted readerships for literature—crucial for any socially based theory of reader response—are set by social patterns of literacy, differing massively between societies and periods. It is the main contribution made by ideas of orality and literacy to consideration of these three unresolved questions of literary criticism and theory that the terms connect works of "literature" with their broadest contexts of production and reception. Yet it is only recently, and in a relatively small number of critical works, that orality and literacy have been acknowledged as important structuring concepts in literary and cultural history (for a survey, see Ong).

At its simplest, the term "orality" describes a condition of society in which speaking and listening form the only or principal channel through which communication in language takes place. By far the majority of languages in the history of the world, and most languages in use today, are used primarily "orally" in this sense. (It has been estimated, for example, that only about 3 percent of all extant languages have "literatures," in even the most general sense.) The term "literacy," by contrast, describes the condition of societies in which reading and writing, based on the technology of a given writing system and possibly linked to technical modes of storage, transmission, and reproduction such as printing, postal systems, telegrams, and so on, form a channel through which communication in language takes place alongside speaking and listening. When used to describe individuals, as the term commonly is, "literacy" describes a set of skills of reading and writing (and so contrasts in this sense not with "orality" but with "illiteracy"). Notice immediately that orality and literacy do not form a symmetrical binary opposition. Orality exists very often without literacy; but wherever there is individual or collective literacy, there is also orality—literate societies involve a mix of the written and read with the spoken and heard; and the term "functional penetration" is used to characterize the range of roles or tasks generally performed in a society or period through reading and writing (e.g., for receipts, diaries, checks, etc.). The two realizations of language (speech and writing) are also acquired differently. Orality is the result, except in pathological cases, of a universal process of language acquisition in humans that requires little or no formal instruction—though it can be trained toward specialized, conventional capabilities in oral societies, such as memorization and formulaic narration (as has been shown in detail by Finnegan, Goody and Watt, Lord, Ong, Parry, and others). Literacy, on the other hand, is only acquired through a conscious, deliberate process of learning to read and write, usually in formal, educational situations.

Given an idea of literacy as a scale of skills that are progressively developed, the question immediately arises how much you need to be able to read and write to be described as literate. In historical studies, mere signatures have often been taken as an index of literacy. In contemporary educational programs, on the other hand, specially constructed tasks (often based on an essay-text principle rather than on signs, lists, business records, signatures, or labels) are widely used to define "functional literacy," which is characterized in turn, by literacy-promoting organizations such as UNESCO, with regard to one or more of the following considerations: some estimate of a desirable degree of democratic participation in a given society's political processes; some idea of employability, within increasingly technical and complex industrial processes; or some concept of educated consumerism or reachability by complex legal and administrative procedures. Calculating on the basis of definitions of functional literacy such as these, C. A. Anderson has suggested (influentially but also controversially) that 40 percent literacy in a population signals a readiness for economic take-off in development terms (though Anderson does not make clear what level of "literacy" is required or what precisely "economic take-off" means). More generally, definitions of functional literacy are abstracted from educational processes as a whole and are used to shape more specialized literacy programs, as well as being used in other areas of economic and political planning.

Major consequences have been claimed to follow from the distinction between orality and literacy (though critical commentators such as Levine and Street have challenged the theoretical bases of work along these lines). Stylistically, for example, there are evident contrasts between communications in speech and ones in writing. In spoken texts, there is likely to be less syntactic embedding, less use of explicit connectives, greater dependence on nonverbal contextual clues, and more use of fillers and repetition than in written texts. Extrapolating from such stylistic contrasts to speculate about the psychodynamics of members of cultures with access to *only* spoken traditions (though again, there is some doubt about how much idealization is involved in finding a purely "oral" culture today), the anthropologist Jack

Goody and others have suggested that the distinction between orality and literacy should replace earlier cultural "great divide" distinctions such as those between primitive and civilized, or prelogical and logical, societies. Goody and Ian Watt propose, in fact, that the distinction between oral and literate should mark the boundary between the fields of anthropology (which would study oral societies) and sociology (which would study literate societies), taking this view from the idea that literacy creates a new relationship for any individual to language and *determines* modes of thought and social organization (rather than taking cognitive differences, as was commonly done in earlier, more evidently ethnocentric anthropology, to be the result of innate differences between ethnic groups). For Goody and Watt, written language (unlike spoken language) can be kept stable for scrutiny on the page and scanned forward and backward, so facilitating large-scale arguments and discussion, including complex logical derivations such as sequences of syllogisms (hence, for many commentators, the significance of the emergence of logic in Greece roughly coincidentally with the earliest use of a phonetic-alphabetic script that, unlike its Semitic antecedents, defined vowel values as well as consonants).

Relatedly, it has been claimed that literacy removes the magic or ritualistic properties of language characteristic of oral societies and makes possible a new degree of abstraction and objectivity, as well as greater historical accuracy (compared with oral histories and genealogies, which place less emphasis on historical record than on current relevance). More generally, literacy is taken to encourage skepticism, in the sense of doubt about and disagreement with the established, communal wisdoms of a culture, and is therefore believed to promote social change. From the perspective of literate societies, literate forms (as well as literate people) are consequently assumed to be of higher cultural status than oral ones (a social prestige contrasting with the different privileges JACQUES DERRIDA claims are attributed to speech: that of being closer to thought and images of immediate self-presence and, since writing is a largely secondary system modeled on speech, that of being taken, in the twentieth century at least, as the proper subject of linguistic investigation).

Underlying such arguments over how far it is reasonable to assume that the distinction between orality and literacy determines individual modes of thought and directions of social change is a contrast between two viewpoints: an "autonomous" view of literacy (see Goody), which describes literacy as a complex of skills that do not carry any particular ideological load and are isolable from political structures and social formations, *causing* kinds of social change; and an "ideological" view of literacy (see Street), which suggests that the skills and applications of literacy always exist within a particular social matrix of goals, ideologies, and distributions of social roles, such that "literacy" itself is only an *instrument* of other, determining social and political forces and is never an autonomous agent. (These two views are usefully compared in Street and Levine.) Developing, in both theory and practice, one of the most influential versions so far of an "ideological" view of literacy, the Brazilian educationalist Paolo Freire has rejected any distinction in a given social situation between communicative means (reading and writing) and the content of the material to be communicated. Instead, he connects reading the word with reading the world, to create programs directed toward "emancipatory literacy," that is, programs that emphasize using vernacular languages rather than imposing colonial "standard" languages in postcolonial countries and that seek to develop critical skills of analysis of the political formations in which reading and writing are required. As a further objective, such programs seek also to stimulate cultural development, through affirmation of local and class history and cultural forms. In linking the reading of texts with the reading of social and political values in this way, literacy programs such as Freire's have something in common with much structuralist pedagogy and with critical discourse analysis, which both also focus on enlarged definitions of "literacy" in which it is used to mean a capability to decode texts closely linked to an ability to form critical perspectives not only on sign systems but also on the social structures that give rise to them.

In recent years, arguments over orality and literacy have been recognized to have taken on an added importance, as a result of the changing shapes of literacy and massive extensions in the use of modern communications media. Ong, for example (in *Orality and Literacy* and elsewhere), has proposed the term "secondary orality"—by contrast with his "primary orality"—to describe skills needed to cope with such transitions: a new kind of communications literacy that involves, in a changing mix with established literate modes, new and specialized understanding of the adapted, "oral" systems used in radio, telephones, audio recording, television, and film. The large-scale social consequences of such a transition into "secondary oral" societies have been widely discussed, not only by Ong but also, more celebratedly, by MARSHALL MCLUHAN, especially in *Understanding Media* (see McLuhan's concept of "rear-mirrorism," or the tendency of new communications media to carry over

forms initially from established communications systems until specific, new forms develop).

What emerges most clearly from current discussions of this contemporary transition, apart from the increasingly metaphorical way in which the term "literacy" is used, is a breakup within traditional ideas of literacy from one, supposedly isolable and autonomous set of reading and writing skills into a range of more specialized and contextually determined understanding and communications skills that suggest a range of new kinds of literacy: television literacy, computer literacy, political literacy, and so on. Some combination of these skills is recognized to be necessary for life in "information societies" of the future. But current argument is still entangled, not only over the extent to which what Goody has called "technologies of the intellect" can *cause* kinds of social change but also over what kind of participation in societies of the future is being contemplated in any given practical initiative regarding the new literacies: more active democratic participation; subjection to increasingly remote and technically governed bureaucratic procedures; suitability for new kinds of employment; or passive accessibility, as consumers, to new modes of commercial advertising and publicity.

Alan Durant

C. A. Anderson, "Literacy and Schooling on the Development Threshold: Some Historical Cases," *Education and Economic Development* (ed. C. A. Anderson and Mary Jean Bowman, 1966); Jacques Derrida, *De la grammatologie* (1967, *Of Grammatology*, trans. Gayatri Chakravorty Spivak, 1976); Elizabeth Eisenstein, *The Printing Press as an Agent of Social Change: Communications and Cultural Transformations in Early Modern Europe* (2 vols., 1979); Ruth Finnegan, *Oral Poetry: Its Nature, Significance, and Social Context* (1977); Paolo Freire, *Pedagogy of the Oppressed* (trans. Myra Bergman Ramos, 1972); Paolo Freire and Donaldo Macedo, *Literacy: Reading the Word and the World* (1987); Jack Goody, *The Domestication of the Savage Mind* (1977); Jack Goody and Ian Watt, "The Consequences of Literacy," *Literacy in Traditional Societies* (by Jack Goody, 1968); Harvey Graff, *Literacy and Social Development in the West: A Reader* (1982); Eric Havelock, *Origins of Western Literacy* (1976); Harold A. Innis, *Empire and Communications* (1972); Kenneth Levine, *The Social Context of Literacy* (1986); Albert Lord, *The Singer of Tales* (1968); Marshall McLuhan, *The Gutenberg Galaxy: The Making of Typographic Man* (1962), *Understanding Media: The Extensions of Man* (1964); Walter J. Ong, *Orality and Literacy: The Technologizing of the Word* (1982); Milman

Parry, *The Making of Homeric Verse* (1971); Neil Postman, "The Politics of Reading," *Harvard Educational Review* 4 (1970); Brian Street, *Literacy in Theory and Practice* (1984); UNESCO, "Literacy in the World: Shortcomings, Achievements, and Tendencies," *Reading: From Process to Practice* (ed. John Chapman and Pam Czerniewska, 1978); Frances A. Yates, *The Art of Memory* (1966); Paul Zumthor, *Introduction à la poésie orale* (1983, *Oral Poetry: An Introduction,* trans. Kathryn Murphy-Judy, 1990).

ORTEGA Y GASSET, JOSÉ

In the English-speaking world, the reputation of José Ortega y Gasset (1883-1955) has rested primarily upon his prophetic sociological treatise *The Revolt of the Masses* (1930) and his celebrated essay "The Dehumanization of Art" (1925). But within his own culture, Ortega is best known for guiding the tradition-oriented intelligentsia of Spain toward the modern age. This is no small accomplishment given the fact that until his arrival upon the scene Spain possessed the dubious distinction of having successfully resisted many of the intellectual consequences of the Enlightenment. Ortega was educated in German universities, and he viewed his lifelong mission as that of neutralizing a centuries-old archconservative national identity and of educating Spaniards for the European adventure. Ortega's interest in literature, which initially embraced literary criticism per se but more characteristically cultivated a philosophical aesthetics, was always part and parcel of this larger, more ambitious project. Gradually, the philosophical project was expanded to include a reform of all of Europe, but the point is that Ortega always saw literature not as autonomous or self-validating but rather as a cultural activity that was subordinated to and made to serve more important social and political ends. This attitude places Ortega in a well-defined posture with respect to the Romantic roots of modernism and the powerful aestheticism that has been so prominent in the twentieth century.

Moreover, Ortega's literary ideas can be properly understood only if they are recognized as directly connected with philosophical views that changed dramatically during his long career. As Ciriaco Morón Arroyo has shown in definitive fashion, Ortega did not have one philosophy, but four. Thus, the early forays into literary criticism (1907-13)—which will not concern us here—reflect a classicism associated with neo-Kantian premises; the essays of a second period (1914-20) develop from a world-view that blends earlier views with a novel perspectivism and with attempts to create a "worldly"

phenomenology; the essays of a third period (1921-27) spring from a quasi-Nietzschean vitalism that rejects the excessive rationalism of Western culture; and the infrequent literary essays of a fourth period (1927-55) emerge against the background of an original "philosophy of historical reason" indebted to MARTIN HEIDEGGER and Wilhelm Dilthey. For our purpose here, the second and third periods are the crucial ones, since they contain most of Ortega's contributions to literary theory. But I will refer as well to an important essay from the last period because of the perspective it provides concerning the development of Ortega's aesthetic ideas.

Finally, a word about the unusual nature of Ortega's discourse. He was a gifted writer in the best European belletrist tradition, and when he decided to address his thought to a larger public beyond specialists—today we would call what he did CULTURAL STUDIES—the result was a genre that was at once unconventional and a delight to read. His work has been compared to an iceberg because it hides the critical mass of its erudition beneath the surface and because it is deceptive, appearing to be more spontaneous and informal than it really is. Rhetorical clarity for its own sake is often subordinated to literary effect. Consequently Ortega's essays are not only illuminating in the substance they provide but eminently readable in an age when much literary theory is willfully esoteric and self-indulgent.

Meditations on Quixote (1914) is at once an eclectic philosophical masterpiece that sets out in programmatic fashion Ortega's doctrine of "vital reason" and a complex and brilliantly argued apology for the relevance of literature for liberal reform in Spain. The most valuable lesson Miguel de Cervantes made available to his compatriots when he created the modern novel had to do with the perennial difficulty of transforming illusions into reality, of bringing about significant change in a world that fiercely resists change. As the prototype of the modern novel, *Don Quixote* juxtaposes a desire for justice and limitless adventure on the one hand against a corrosive realism and a pitiless irony on the other. If the novel resolves the conflict in favor of the former, it lapses back into the epic mode; if it resolves it in favor of the latter, it anticipates the misanthropic critique of Gustave Flaubert. But when the novel is authentic and respects the mold created by Cervantes, it invites the reader into a tragicomedy where the protagonist appears at once ridiculous and noble, foolish and heroic. We should not minimize the profound ambiguity of the first great novel but recognize that the question whether its relentless mockery is always and necessarily a negation remains unanswered. Ortega left his book incomplete and thus intimated that the ambiguity was irresolvable. But at the same time he also contradicted that view and repeatedly suggested that Cervantes somehow came to grips with the problem by transforming it into art. Given all this, it comes as no surprise that Ortega insisted that "in one way or another, man is always the essential theme of art" (*Meditations* 113) or that he declared in this study that the artist does not "produce verses the way an almond tree blooms in March [but instead] has risen above his vital spontaneity . . . [and demonstrated] a strong power of reflection, of meditation" (100). The understanding of the artist as one who embodies a needed "serenity in the midst of the storm" (100) is consistent with Ortega's parallel emphasis on a "vital reason" that respects life and wants to engage the real instead of mere abstractions. Finally, it also reveals Ortega's characteristic impatience with any form of irrationalism and with Romantic theories of art as inspiration.

"The Dehumanization of Art" (1925) belongs to the quasi-vitalistic period of Ortega's thought when he reacted against the tyranny of the masses and championed a theory of elites. The scope is no longer the novel but a broader cultural movement that incorporates literature, the arts, and music. And the social framework is no longer limited to Spain but includes European civilization in the period between the world wars. No work of Ortega's has been more frequently cited, admired, or criticized than this one. In it he elaborated a perspective on nonrepresentational literature and art that sought to reveal their unconventional essence and make them more understandable to a public that was confused about their meaning. The essay was embraced as a manifesto extolling the virtues of the so-called vanguard movements, one that enthusiastically promoted the value of the newest generation's efforts to abandon both the realism and the Romanticism of the nineteenth century and the whole project of mimesis in general. The "dehumanization" mentioned in the title referred to a combination of qualities—a strident unpopularity, an unprecedented irony, an indifference to the past, an iconoclasm, and a "higher algebra of metaphors" (32)—all designed to effect a quantum leap beyond everything that preceded it. The essay is often cited as a defense of a subjectivistic, anything-goes kind of aesthetics and a Romantic exaltation of art for art's sake. And in contrast to the earlier, humanistic view of literature, the author now seems to reverse his course and maintain that the less human a work is, the more valuable it becomes. This is misleading, though, because the central contradiction of the new art is that it wanted to be completely liberated from previous definitions of art at the same time that its des-

tiny was to become a symptom of humanity's push toward a new and higher form of civilization. In the end Ortega viewed the real value of the new aesthetic as serving a well-defined cultural politics whose goal was still the transformation and renewal of society. And while he showed how the new art abandoned a familiar human pathos and any pretension to transcendence, he also emphasized in quasi-Nietzschean and Spenglerian tones that all of this belonged to a larger biological rhythm that was part of civilization's attempt to revitalize itself and become youthful again as a reaction to a decadent rationalism.

After 1927 Ortega became involved in the elaboration of what he called a "philosophy of historical reason" and entered actively into the political arena, serving as a deputy in the Spanish republic. Ultimately, however, he renounced politics in the face of the anarchy and the conservative backlash that subsequently doomed Spain's liberal hopes. The last period of Ortega's thought includes, then, in dramatic juxtaposition, the experience of freedom that came with the republic and the experience of exile and oppression that brutally descended upon Spain with the fundamentalist Franco regime. It is impossible to convey here how devastating this violent transition must have been for the intellectual whose entire career had been focused on liberal reform. He wrote no literary criticism during the republican period, probably owing to his political activism, and almost none during the decade of the 1940s, when he preferred to elaborate the philosophical and sociological intuitions he had reached during the 1930s. There is nevertheless an important piece called "The Idea of a Theater" (1946), which eloquently demonstrates what happened to the reformist optimism that inspired all his earlier literary work. It is a provocative and bittersweet investigation of the philosophical essence of theater, and by extension of all literature, one that seeks to isolate and examine the "being" of this genre, that is, the latent structure that endures beneath the genre's concrete and changing manifestations. Ortega finds that essence to be the ubiquitous human need to escape from the traumatic seriousness of a life that makes happiness in this world—one of civil and world wars—largely unattainable. In contrast to everything he said in his earlier works, where literature was a form of consciousness that promoted and even guaranteed social transformations, Ortega now portrays literature as legitimate escape and deep solace in the face of the failures that have exhausted the modern age. Theater is the supreme farce in which humanity contemplates an unreality that is more satisfying than what lies outside its walls; it is a liberation from the prison of historical reality and the destructive impulses of a humanity that refuses to be educated by beauty or by truth. Ortega's philosophy of historical reason, on balance, was more optimistic than this, and some relevant essays on art history—studies of Velásquez and Goya—are certainly more hopeful than what we see here. Even in this essay, he mentions that "man is the great builder," that we cannot rest content with a philosophy of ruins, and that the human being is a builder as well as a destroyer. At the same time, however, it is also clear that the culmination of decades of work in literary theory turns out to be a poignant reflection on the tremendous tragedy that he and his civilization lived through, one that we in retrospect can ignore only at our peril.

Patrick H. Dust

See also SPANISH THEORY AND CRITICISM.

José Ortega y Gasset, *"La Deshumanización del arte" e ideas sobre la novela* (1925, *"The Dehumanization of Art" and Other Essays on Art, Culture, and Literature,* trans. Helene Weyl et al., 1968, including "Notes on the Novel" and "On the Point of View in the Arts"), *Meditaciones del Quijote* (1914, *Meditations on Quixote,* trans. Evelyn Rugg and Diego Marín, 1961), *Phenomenology and Art* (trans. Philip W. Silver, 1975, including "An Essay in Esthetics by way of a Preface" and "The Idea of a Theater").

Joseph Frank, *The Widening Gyre: Crisis and Mastery in Modern Literature* (1963); Rockwell Gray, *The Imperative of Modernity: An Intellectual Biography of José Ortega y Gasset* (1989); Leon Livingston, "Ortega y Gasset's Philosophy of Art," *PMLA* 67 (1952); Angel Medina, "Hermeneutics and Reason: Dilthey, Ortega, and the Future of Hermeneutics," *Ortega y Gasset and the Question of Modernity* (ed. Patrick H. Dust, 1989); Ciriaco Morón Arroyo, *El sistema de Ortega y Gasset* (1968), "Ortega: La deshumanización del arte," *Studies in Honor of Sumner M. Greenfield* (ed. H. L. Boudreau and Luis T. Gonzalez del Valle, 1985); Nelson Orringer, *Ortega y sus fuentes germánicas* (1979); Philip W. Silver, *Ortega as Phenomenologist: The Genesis of "Meditations on Quixote"* (1978).

ORWELL, GEORGE

The critical essays and reviews that George Orwell (pen name of Eric Arthur Blair) (1903–50) began to publish in the 1930s are not "literary" in the familiar, narrow sense. Part of the politically committed, "semi-sociological" criticism (Orwell's phrase) that rose up in response to fascism and the Great Depression, they posed from the outset the question whether there *is* anything strictly "aesthetic" in literature that evades social explanation and moral or political evaluation. Moreover, writing for a livelihood in the periodical press, rather than occupying an academic post (he never attended university), Orwell largely wrote about books as they appeared on the market. To him "literary" thus referred to works on many subjects, not just to "imaginative" or "creative" literature. It did not indicate a canon of long-dead masterpieces to be revered and transmitted, but new and revived texts whose current usefulness was always in doubt. Without the institutional commitment to the past as such, a commitment that MATTHEW ARNOLD bequeathed to university-based criticism, Orwell could become, paradoxically, just the sort of critic Arnold had imagined, ranging over many fields in order to intervene in the most urgent public debates of his time.

One such debate concerned "high" versus "mass" culture. Unaffected by academic elitism, Orwell wrote generous appreciations of children's literature ("Boys' Weeklies"), humorous postcards ("The Art of Donald McGill"), detective novels ("Raffles and Miss Blandish"), and the journalistic murder story ("The Decline of the English Murder"). In the latter, he showed that the domestic murder story, which seemed a naive representation of brutal actuality, in fact obeyed the rules of a consistent form, which was also the bearer of a defensible set of values (see CULTURAL STUDIES). Like the Romantics, however, Orwell could celebrate popular culture only by locating it within a narrative of historical decline. His habit in these essays is to contrast the fallen postwar present, whose genres are characterized by sensationalism, power worship, and Americanization, with the period of his own birth—the first decade of the twentieth century—which becomes popular culture's lost paradise, an image of community that contains and moderates violence and conflict. In "Politics and the English Language," to take another example, his oft-cited plea for a purification of our political commonplaces is based on the questionable premise that the English language as a whole has declined in clarity and vigor.

Orwell's most characteristic critical act is the unexpected evaluation. One might expect his criteria to be referential, but they are not. If his journalism assumes a stance of unflinching, unbiased objectivity, his critical writing tends to override realism, resolving British criticism's chronic contradiction between moral instruction and the imitation of nature in favor of the former. "Charles Dickens," his longest and perhaps finest essay, transforms a monument of historical realism into a voice of righteous indignation. The unexpectedness of Orwell's evaluations emerges directly from his moral and political categories, in particular, from a charity toward political enemies that sometimes verges on self-hatred. When T. S. Eliot is accused of writing for the few, Orwell remarks that he is one of the few contemporary poets to reproduce spoken English. Toward leftists like himself, on the other hand, he is merciless. They are hypocrites, he fumes, for to be a writer at all is to be a bourgeois. The modernist separation of work from author protects authors of the Right but not of the Left.

The other side of Orwell's visceral disgust with, say, Jonathan Swift's misanthropy or Salvador Dali's "perversions"—the critical attitude that he calls, apropos of Leo Tolstoy, "anti-aesthetic"—is a strange willingness to withdraw from moral judgment altogether, or at least to bend over backwards to anti-activist anti-selves. In "Inside the Whale," for example, he praises Henry Miller's posture of quietistic aloofness in an incomprehensible world, the choice to accept, endure, record. What Orwell appreciates in Tobias Smollett, again, is a refusal to award points to virtue and vice that became conventional in later novelists. Often, respite from strenuous moral conscientiousness is embodied for Orwell not in art itself—he vacillates endlessly on the issue of art's autonomy from propaganda—but specifically in the pastness of past art. Pre-fascistic, Edwardian out-of-dateness is the key to his defense of both P. G. Wodehouse (about whom he uses the phrase "beyond good and evil") and Rudyard Kipling against charges from the Left.

If the price of consensus is quietism, Orwell seems to say, then so be it, even if the "decency" around which he gathers that consensus must exclude, say, what the Kipling essay calls the "pansy-left." The struggle against fascism put a premium on national unity, thus encouraging a merciful and even myopically appreciative revaluation of the British cultural heritage. In his wartime broadcasts to India, where the independence movement was far from eager to join Britain in its anti-German war effort, Orwell participated in this revaluation and also (since he favored Indian independence) experienced its contradictions. Infused with the neoclassical attempt to construct a new national norm that would both draw in former outsiders and block leftist impulses to divide and decenter, Orwell's criticism made itself, as he said about Dickens, "a national institution." Its uneffaced marks of self-division only add to its instructiveness.

Bruce Robbins

George Orwell, *The Collected Essays, Journalism and Letters of George Orwell* (ed. Sonia Orwell and Ian Angus, 4 vols., 1968), *The Lost Writings* (ed. W. J. West, 1985).

Harold Bloom, ed., *George Orwell: Modern Critical Views* (1987); Carl Freedman, "Writing, Ideology, and Politics: Orwell's 'Politics and the English Language' and English Composition," *College English* 43 (1981); Graham Good, "Ideology and Personality in Orwell's Criticism," *College Literature* 3 (1984); John Gross, *The Rise and Fall of the Man of Letters* (1970); J. R. Hammond, "The Essays of George Orwell," *Critical Essays on George Orwell* (ed. Bernard Oldsey and Joseph Browne, 1986); Jeffrey Myers, ed., *George Orwell: The Critical Heritage* (1975); Christopher Norris, ed., *Inside the Myth: Orwell, Views from the Left* (1984); Daphne Patai, *The Orwell Mystique: A Study in Male Ideology* (1984); Alan Sinfield, *Literature, Politics, and Culture in Postwar Britain* (1989); Raymond Williams, *Culture and Society, 1780–1950* (1958), *George Orwell: A Collection of Critical Essays* (1974), *Orwell* (1971); Alex Zwerdling, *Orwell and the Left* (1974).

PATER, WALTER

Walter Pater (1839–94) has an important place in a line that leads from WILLIAM WORDSWORTH and SAMUEL TAYLOR COLERIDGE, G. W. F. HEGEL and Friedrich Schlegel, through JOHN RUSKIN to Pater himself, then on to OSCAR WILDE, W. B. Yeats, Marcel Proust, and ultimately to certain vital movements in mid-twentieth-century literary criticism. Behind the Romantics the line extends from Pater by way of the Renaissance philosopher Giordano Bruno back through Lucretius to Epicurus and the pre-Socratics. Pater has had a strong though sometimes unacknowledged influence on three major ways of doing criticism in our own day. Through his essay "Style," his respect for the *mot juste,* and his belief that good literature will be organically unified, he was a somewhat oblique source for NEW CRITICISM, for the tradition of "close reading." By way of his (again hidden) influence on Proust and then through the influence of Proust's ideas about literary criticism, especially in his essays on Ruskin, Pater is a source at second remove of Georges Poulet's "criticism of consciousness" (see FRENCH THEORY AND CRITICISM: 4. EARLY TWENTIETH CENTURY and GENEVA SCHOOL). By way of Proust's influence on WALTER BENJAMIN and Benjamin's on PAUL DE MAN, Pater is one route by which a conception of allegory has become important in so-called DECONSTRUCTION. One empirical evidence of this filiation is the fact that Ruskin, Pater, and Proust all use as an example of the allegorical mode Giotto's frescoes in Padua, the *Allegory of the Virtues and Vices.* De Man, in an important essay working out his conception of allegory, cites the passage in Proust about Giotto that echoes Pater as well as Ruskin. For Pater already, as for de Man in our own day, allegory is a temporal mode of sign-to-sign relation based on distance and difference, as opposed to symbolism, which is a spatial sign-to-thing relation based on participatory similarity. For all three of these kinds of criticism Walter Pater is a grandfather of whom his grandchildren are not always entirely proud. HAROLD BLOOM is unusual among distinguished present-day critics in acknowledging his admiration for Pater.

Pater's relation to his precursors and successors is complex. It is often a matter of suppressed influence or of what might be called "creative misinterpretation" in both directions. Nevertheless, Pater's current significance for the theory of criticism and for its practice has hardly been fully appreciated. The term "impressionist criticism" as it is usually understood does not do justice either to Pater's theory or to his practice. In freeing Ruskin's conception of criticism from its ultimately misleading moralism; in his understanding of the historical imagination; in his insight into the role of myth in literature; in his focus on what actually happens in reading as the proper subject of literary criticism; in a theory of style, of figurative language, and of "repetition" that rivals FRIEDRICH NIETZSCHE in insight; in his refinement of a method of the "portrait" in criticism that connects, in one direction, with CHARLES AUGUSTIN SAINTE-BEUVE's criticism and Robert Browning's dramatic monologues and, in the other, with the critical mode of Poulet, Pater is, with Coleridge, Ruskin, and perhaps MATTHEW ARNOLD, one of the three or four greatest critics of nineteenth-century England. For us today, Pater is perhaps even more important than the others, by reason of his more evident consonance with what is most active in the criticism of today. His non-English analogues are RALPH WALDO EMERSON in Amerca and Nietzsche on the Continent. If the latter two have in our day been revived and reinterpreted, Pater too may also come to receive his due as their equal in insight if not in abundance.

Born in 1839 in East London, Pater entered Queen's College, Oxford, in 1858. In 1864 he obtained, on the basis of his knowledge of German philosophy, a fellowship at Brasenose College, Oxford. The story of the rest of his life is primarily the story of the sequence of his books. Though all contain material important to understanding his critical and theoretical position, the most important are *Studies in the History of the Renaissance* (1873), *Imaginary Portraits* (1887), *Appreciations* (1889), and the posthumous *Greek Studies* (1895).

It is possible to distill from all Pater's writings a single pattern of thought, a configuration that underlies all his criticism. For Pater, the beginning of spiritual life is the moment, the intense and wholly individual moment of experience. In this he has more in common with a phenomenological critic such as Poulet than with a rhetorical critic such as de Man, for whom language is the constitutive category. As Pater describes the moment in the well-known passage in the "Conclusion" to *The Renaissance,* each instant of experience, each "impression," is cut off by virtue of its uniqueness from all other moments before and after. It is also entirely private: "Every one of those impressions is the impression of the individual in his isolation, each mind keeping as a solitary prisoner its own dream of a world" (*Works* 1:235). Moreover, each moment lasts but a moment, the blink of an eye, and then is gone. Time is a flux, an endless stream of "impressions, unstable, flickering, inconsistent, which burn and are extinguished with our consciousness of them" (1:235). The inevitable end of each such sequence is death, a final end anticipated and rehearsed in the little death of each moment as it flies. For Pater, death and intensity of experience are always but two sides of the same coin, "the sense of death and the desire of beauty: the desire of beauty quickened by the sense of death," as he puts it in the essay on William Morris, "Aesthetic Poetry" (*Sketches* 19).

It would seem that the entire program of Paterian criticism follows from these solipsistic premises. Each person must concentrate full attention on each moment as it passes. That moment is all there is and all anyone has. Each person must purge away by an effort of refinement or askesis all impurities in the moment, all irrelevant associations, all false idealisms such as those that, in Pater's understanding of Coleridge, weakened that great poet-critic's force. This askesis is a crucial element in Pater's procedures as a critic and in the lives of those whose portraits he sketches. The person experiencing the unique moment may, when all dross has been shed, burn with the "hard, gemlike flame" (*Works* 1:236). Criticism is the exact recording of what Pater calls the unique "virtue" of each moment, meaning by "virtue" the power or energy specific to the elements concentrated in that moment. Reading a work of literature is therefore only one among many forms of intense experience. Virtue is "the property each [moment] has of affecting one with a special, a unique, impression of pleasure" (1:ix). This last phrase is from *The Renaissance,* where such a program for criticism is most exactly stated and exemplified.

The critic's effort, however, to identify precisely the unique virtue of a single impression, as he or she "experiences" a painting by Leonardo da Vinci or Sandro Botticelli, a poem by Wordsworth or Dante Gabriel Rossetti,

leads to an unexpected discovery. This discovery makes Pater's criticism something quite different from what it at first seems to be. It turns out that for Pater, the moment, though unique, is not single. Each "impression" is "infinitely divisible." It is hyperbolically divisible because it is self-divided, an "Anders-Streben" (1:134), as he calls it in "The School of Giorgione." The moment is in battle against itself in a way that recalls the Heraclitean flux, the Parmenidean or Empedoclean battle of opposites. Perhaps this inner conflict is even to be associated with that sadomasochistic element so evident in Pater's sense of human life and of the relations among persons.

The flame produced by the purification of an askesis is kindled by the bringing together of divided forces that burst into flame by their antagonistic proximity. That flame is "the focus where the greatest number of vital forces unite in their purest energy" (1:236). The first example Pater gives in the "Conclusion" to *The Renaissance* of the intense instant of sensation is "the moment . . . of delicious recoil from the flood of water in summer heat" (1:233). He speaks of the moment as the locus "of forces parting sooner or later on their ways" (1:234), or of brilliancy of gifts in a vital individual as arising from "some tragic dividing of forces on their ways" (1:237).

The uniqueness of the momentary impression is a result not of its singleness but of its special combination of antagonistic forces flowing into it from the past and destined to divide again, each to go its separate way into the future. This means that the moment, at first seemingly so isolated, is connected by multiple strands to past and future. Pater sometimes speaks of this according to a metaphor of streams meeting and dividing, sometimes according to a metaphor of weaving and unweaving. The concomitants of the unique moment's connection to past and future are Pater's versions of the theories of symbolism, figuration, allegory, myth, and repetition already present in Ruskin and worked out again in a somewhat different way in Proust. If the moment is the meeting place of divided forces, the forces of a single life, of an age, or of all the ages in their sequence, then that moment, in all its particular sensory vividness, can stand for a life, an age, or an aspect of all history. It can stand for these by a strange relation of likeness based on literalism, discontinuity, and dissimilarity that might better be called "allegorical" rather than "symbolic," according to the distinction between the two as defined by Paul de Man in "The Rhetoric of Temporality" (*Blindness and Insight: Essays in the Rhetoric of Contemporary Criticism,* 2d ed., 1983, 187 ff.). The relation in question is called by Pater, in the crucial passage on Giotto's *Allegory of the Virtues and Vices* in "The Myth of Demeter and Persephone," "something more than mere symbolism" (*Works* 7:98). "Symbolism intense as this," says Pater, "is the creation of a special temper, in which a certain simplicity, taking all things literally, *au pied de la lettre,* is united to a vivid preoccupation with the aesthetic beauty of the image itself, the *figured* side of figurative expression, the *form* of the metaphor" (7:99).

This conception of the moment as both individual and representative underlies a passage in "The School of Giorgione" notable for its anticipation of the Joycean notion of "epiphany" or of an eloquent passage in T. S. ELIOT's late criticism about "profoundly significant and animated instants . . . into which . . . all the motives, all the interests and effects of a long history, have condensed themselves." A similar allegorical theory of the moment is presupposed in Pater's conception of the "portrait" as a method in criticism. A portrait concentrates in a series of intense images the complexities of a whole life or of an elaborate *oeuvre.* A similar idea lies behind Pater's theory of myth in two crucial essays in *Greek Studies,* "The Myth of Demeter and Persephone" and "A Study of Dionysus." For Pater, as for Ruskin, a mythological figure or narrative is a focus of a multitude of motifs or cultural forces. The interpretation of a myth is the disentangling of these forces from their knotted concentration.

Pater's allegorical conception of the moment, finally, underlies the implicit theory of repetition, so Viconian or Nietzschean in its resonances, that so often functions in his work (see GIAMBATTISTA VICO). This idea of repetition is operative, for example, in Pater's concept of history. A great figure such as PLATO is unique, in Pater's view, only in being a special combination of ideas and images already present long before his time. The life of Marius, in *Marius the Epicurean,* to give another example of Pater's idea of recurrence, organizes itself into a series of episodes that repeat with a difference elements present from the beginning. Another application of his insight into repetition is his idea that a myth may reenact itself in a new form in a later age. This idea is presupposed in such "imaginary portraits" as "Apollo in Picardy" and "Denys l'Auxerrois." In one, Apollo is reincarnated in medieval Picardy. In the other, Dionysus reappears in France. Apollo and Dionysus are of course also the perpetually recurring figures in Nietzsche's nearly contemporary *The Birth of Tragedy* (1872). A final example is the way the Mona Lisa, in Pater's most celebrated mythological image, concentrates in herself the experience of all the ages in a perpetual repetition of the whole sequence. The "virtue" of a given moment does not die with that

moment. It divides again into the various elemental forces that have entered into it. Those forces are always potentially able to combine again in a repetition of the earlier flame, a reincarnation that will be no less unique and no less "wholly concrete" for being a recurrence. Criticism, for Pater, is the scrupulous discrimination of the particular elements that are configured in a painting, a poem, a work of philosophy, a personality.

J. Hillis Miller

Walter Pater, *Sketches and Reviews* (ed. Albert Mordell, 1919), *Works* (10 vols., 1910).

Harold Bloom, ed., *The Selected Writings of Walter Pater* (1974), *Walter Pater: Modern Critical Views* (1985); Jay Fellows, *Tombs, Despoiled and Haunted: 'Under-textures' and 'After-thoughts' in Walter Pater* (1991); Ian Fletcher, *Walter Pater* (rev. ed., 1972); Graham Hough, *The Last Romantics* (1949); Wolfgang Iser, *Walter Pater: Die Autonomie des Ästhetichen* (1960, *Walter Pater: The Aesthetic Moment,* trans. David Henry Wilson, 1987); Perry Meisel, *The Absent Father: Virginia Woolf and Walter Pater* (1980); J. Hillis Miller, "Walter Pater: A Partial Portrait," *Daedalus* 105 (1975); Gerald Monsman, *Pater's Portraits: Mythic Pattern in the Fiction of Walter Pater* (1967), *Walter Pater's Art of Autobiography* (1980); Thomas Wright, *The Life of Walter Pater* (2 vols., 1907).

PEIRCE, CHARLES SANDERS

Charles Sanders Peirce, pronounced "purse" (1839–1914), the founder of pragmatism and a pioneering theorist of SEMIOTICS, was one of America's most important and most original philosophers. His scope and range are perhaps wider than that of any philosopher since Gottfried Wilhelm Leibniz. He made fundamental contributions to probability theory, symbolic logic, the philosophy of science, mathematics, and semiotics, while publishing numerous papers on astronomy, physics, chemistry, and scientific method. Peirce generally described himself as an experimentalist and a "logician," a term that expanded in scope from his earliest papers to encompass virtually the whole enterprise of organized thought and inquiry.

Despite being frequently recommended for university appointments, Peirce served only as a part-time lecturer in logic at Johns Hopkins University from 1879 to 1884 and for three years as a special lecturer in the philosophy of science at Harvard. Although he was a prolific writer, only two books appeared during his lifetime:

Photometric Researches (1878), which established him as one of the leading astrophysicists of his day, and *Studies in Logic* (1883), a collection of essays by Peirce and his students at Johns Hopkins. A selection of his work *(Collected Papers)* was published between 1931 and 1935, with additional volumes in 1958; a new chronological edition published by Indiana University Press had, by 1992, produced 4 of a proposed 30 volumes. Peirce's main employment was with the U. S. Coast and Geodetic Survey, from his graduation from Harvard in 1859 until he retired to Milford, Pennsylvania, in 1887. From that time until his death Peirce lived in severe poverty, illness, and isolation, though his work on philosophical papers and essays continued.

In recent years Peirce has attracted considerable interest among literary critics and theorists for his contributions in three areas, sometimes treated separately: for his role in the development of pragmaticism, his pioneering work on semiotics and the sign, and his contributions to philosophical method. Examination of Peirce's papers shows clearly, however, that there is no plausible way to separate these interests without serious distortion of his thought. Partly for this reason, literary theorists with strong interests in American pragmatism have frequently found Peirce less congenial than JOHN DEWEY and William James, while others more concerned with semiotic questions have tended to rely more heavily upon FERDINAND DE SAUSSURE and later Continental linguists influenced by him. This is particularly so because Peirce's evolving project of articulating his philosophy in the form of a comprehensive theory of signs sometimes makes it difficult to fashion usable analytical tools that seem appropriate to a literary critic's concern with texts.

The general tendency in recent literary criticism to move from the explication of single texts toward more general theoretical concerns, however, puts Peirce in a singularly interesting light. In many varieties of contemporary critical theory, a dominant concern has been the critique of metaphysics, particularly in the light of linguistic analysis and speculation, just as the speculative questions that arise from efforts to relate literature to other disciplines, to society, and to history create a considerable pressure to rethink fundamental philosophical problems.

Christine Ladd-Franklin, one of Peirce's students, noted ironically that Peirce in his lectures had defined metaphysics as "the science of unclear thinking," though he went on to propose that "we should form . . . a Metaphysical Club" (quoted in Bosco 345). The anecdote neatly captures one of the most salient features of Peirce's

philosophical commitments: to bring logical clarity to traditional metaphysical issues. Although he was both drawn to and repelled by G. W. F. HEGEL, Peirce cites IMMANUEL KANT's critiques and the scholastic realism of Duns Scotus as major influences (see *Collected* 1, secs. 3–6).

While philosophical commentators may wish to "ignore the metaphysical side of Peirce's thought" (Nauta 121), it was crucial for Peirce, whose persistent complaint about metaphysics since RENÉ DESCARTES was that it was unclear, self-contradictory, or confused—not that one could get rid of it or otherwise deconstruct it. His turn to Duns Scotus, the subtlest medieval defender of realism, combined with his study of Kant, led to a version of critical realism in which he rejects the nominalism he finds in virtually all modern philosophers since Descartes (1, secs. 18–19).

In general, Peirce took the view that "nominalism" involves a metaphysical reduction of modes of reality to the existence of individual entities (1, sec. 21), thereby hopelessly obscuring the dependence of thought and inquiry on diverse forms of representation and so ensuring in all intellectual pursuits, but especially in experimental science, a chronic state of crisis or confusion over the status of truth claims, as well as the proliferation of destructive and not merely critical forms of skepticism. In Peirce's view, reality cannot be characterized without recourse to three modes of being, on grounds examined briefly below. As John Sheriff has pointed out, in this Peirce anticipates JACQUES DERRIDA's thoroughgoing deconstructive critique of the binary signifier-signified relation in structuralist linguistics, without himself being forced to inhabit it or endlessly reiterate it (Sheriff 53–62).

Also like Derrida, however, Peirce can induce a feeling resembling cognitive vertigo, because his triadic thinking generates more consequences than one can readily take into account. Perhaps the greatest difficulty for readers of Peirce, aside from the probability that they are born and bred nominalists, is that most will bring to Peirce's writing assumptions about "logic," "metaphysics," and "semiotics" or about the idea of the "sign" that may be fundamentally incompatible with the position Peirce elaborates. "Logic" for Peirce expands to cover the whole range of intelligent inquiry or associative thought for any "intelligence capable of learning by experience" (*Collected* 2, sec. 227) without losing the precision that made Peirce one of the fathers of modern formal logic. Similarly, "metaphysics" for Peirce does not issue in a simple ontology, nor does it lead to radical skepticism because the crucial (and subtle) question hinges on the character and function of representability, not being or existence. Thus, when Peirce argues for the "reality" of his categories, reality is already conceived as a process that can (and must) be indefinitely extended, even at the risk of infinite series (Boler, "Habits" 382–87). The problem for Peirce is not indeterminacy but multiplicity in the ways any phenomenon can be represented. That is, any particular thought or argument comes to a determinate end, but no argument could possibly exhaust its subject or claim its ground to be absolute. Thus, determinable meaning coincides with a potentially indefinite determinability in which every proposition, sign, or thought is part of an endless continuum (*Collected* 1, secs. 339, 447, 464, 548).

Particularly for readers who come to Peirce with an interest in the "sign" or "semiotics," the multiplicity of kinds or classifications of signs may be, to quote Jonathan Culler, "too much for all but the most masochistic theorists" (23), among whom Culler does not, evidently, count himself. If one presupposes a notion of the "sign," following either ST. AUGUSTINE or Saussure, as a twofold relation between a signifier (usually a word) and a signified (by default an object, thing, or concept), one is already likely to suppose that the privileged relation of representation is simple naming. While Augustine grounded his own doctrine of signs and their interpretation on divine charity, Saussure points out the obvious fact that the relation between signifier and signified is arbitrary (in the case of a word designating an object), since there is nothing in the word to necessarily attach it to the object, while the entire system of a language operates by differences among signifiers. Saussure's view of linguistics, then, posits "semiology" as a theoretical necessity in order to avoid the naiveté of a view of the sign as just a name, by examining signifiers synchronically (in the relation of elements of a language to each other) and diachronically (in the relation of a language to its own social history).

While Peirce's "semiotics" may appear intriguingly similar to Saussure's proposed discipline of "semiology" (Saussure 16), it should not be overlooked that the first of many fundamental differences is that Peirce's semiotics is not based on the *word* as "sign" but on the *proposition* as that which unifies consciousness and creates intelligibility or comprehension. In this sense, Peirce's semiotics is not a theory of language but a theory of the production of meaning. As the "interpretant," the experience of intelligibility is not itself a "signified" but the result of an act of signification. It might therefore be suggested that Peirce's account of the sign offers a very powerful way by which to represent and analyze literature *as* argument, always concerned with and embedded in a real historical context, aware of consequences, without becoming systematically entangled in linguistic issues that are always indeterminate when considered apart from pragmatics.

As these considerations suggest, despite the attenuated state of his papers, Peirce's logical, metaphysical, and semiotic doctrines are three aspects of an evolving, comprehensive philosophical outlook. When they are considered together, as "pragmatism," the same caveat applies for readers whose notions of pragmatism have been shaped by the pragmatism of William James and John Dewey, where Peirce's logic is replaced with psychology in the first instance and social action in the second (the logic of which Peirce singled out, in a 1904 letter to Dewey, as evincing a "debauch of loose reasoning" [*Collected* 8, sec. 240]). Peirce's own discomfort with what pragmatism had become after it took shape in the 1870s led him in 1905 to call his version of it "pragmaticism," a word, he said, "ugly enough to be safe from kidnappers" (5, sec. 414). As "pragmatism" has entered the vernacular, one can well imagine Peirce, James, and Dewey all uneasy with definitions that take "pragmatic" to mean "concerned with actual practice, not with theory or speculation." In the case of Peirce's pragmatism—or pragmaticism—the theory, and its relation to speculation, is the heart of the matter.

Peirce's concepts of "sign," "interpretant," and pragmaticism all arise from his conception of the categories Firstness, Secondness, and Thirdness, first described in print in "On a New List of Categories" (1867, *Collected* 1, secs. 545–67). While Peirce's theory of the categories evolved throughout his career (Esposito), his 1867 paper articulates brilliantly both the metaphysical implications of the categories and Peirce's own critical relation to past philosophers. The paper, written from a generally Kantian point of view, is explicitly modeled on ARISTOTLE's *Categories*, which elaborates the conception of substance as the subject or bearer of predicates—of quality, quantity, relation, position, possession, action, or affection—which in turn are related to Kant's categories of the understanding, as the pure a priori concepts intrinsic to the faculty of understanding itself (Kant 113), and Hegel's triad of thesis, antithesis, and synthesis (Peirce, *Collected* 8, sec. 267). Peirce begins from Kant's notion of the function of a conception to "reduce the manifold of sensuous impressions to unity" (1, sec. 545), not by a transcendental deduction, but as a pure act of attention within which the most universal conception is "the present, in general," or a consciousness of some "IT," which he designates "substance."

Where Kant had argued that the deduction of the categories relied only on our capacity for comparison and discrimination, Peirce points out that the "IT" is prior to any possible comparison and "cannot itself be made a predicate" because it is the subject to which any and all predicates apply. The "IT," however, is available to cognition only on the condition that the impressions that present it can be reduced to the unity of a *proposition*, requiring the logical (and grammatical) function of the copula, which, according to Peirce, "means either *actually is* or *would be,* as in the two propositions, 'There *is* no griffin,' and 'A griffin *is* a winged quadruped'" (1, sec. 548).

In Peirce's example, saying "The stove is black" indicates the stove as "*substance,* from which its blackness has not been discriminated, and the *is,* while it leaves the substance just as it was seen" (1, sec. 548), functions in applying *blackness* to it as a predicate. In this sense, "*being* implies an indefinite determinability of the predicate." The stove, for example, might also be iron, heavy, hot, in the corner, and so on. Peirce concludes, "Thus substance and being are the beginning and end of all conception." In this context, clearly the two terms are also the beginning and end of all predication. As Peirce puts it, "Substance is inapplicable to a predicate, and being is equally so to a subject" (1, sec. 548).

This conclusion may be startling because it makes inescapably clear that the condition of cognition is predication, just as it asserts that being is not the same as substantive existence. When we imagine there to be, beyond or behind "appearances," some thing in itself, we have merely fallen into the trap of collapsing being and substance. The thing in itself is precisely what we *do* see, and since it is substance, its reality is not ever in question, only its intelligibility: we bring it into being by understanding it in some light. Peirce goes on to show that our ability to discriminate (and therefore to compare), like our ability to abstract, or prescind (1, sec. 549n), and dissociate, is not all symmetrical. Only in those cases where a conception actually does reduce the manifold sensations to unity can we abstract or prescind, and by this test Peirce is able to eliminate entirely the need for a Kantian transcendental analysis or the pursuit of a hierarchical Hegelian dialectic. The quality abstracted, that is, is not Hegelian *Aufhebung* but retains its character in any occurrence and is the first step toward ensuring that one can provide a real explanation for a truth claim.

Peirce uses the example of the proposition "The stove is black" to show that blackness is a *quality* that can be abstracted (prescinded) from the stove, as the (precise)

respect in which the experience of seeing it is available to thought. Peirce then analyzes this experience into two distinct moments: first, reference to a "ground," as in this instance singling out the color rather than, say, the weight or temperature of the stove; and second, reference to a "correlate," indicating that the specific quality is abstractable so as to be applicable to other things, such as black shoes or black pots, as comparable to what is seen in the stove (1, sec. 551).

Thus our ability to make comparisons requires, in addition to the related thing, the ground and the correlate, a "mediating representation" or "interpretant" (1, sec. 553) that can be addressed to someone (including, in the limiting case, ourselves). This analysis provides a basis both for Peirce's theory of semiotic and for his distinctive version of pragmatism. As he later elaborated his theory of the categories, a "first" is a quality, a feeling, a possibility; a "second" is an individual, discerned by its resistance to and interaction with an environment, embodying or exemplifying a possibility as actual; while a "third" is a general term, a rule, a law, or a "habit" that represents the fallible but still determinate knowledge of a regularity or principle (8, secs. 264–69).

Semiotically, one can then say that as signs or representations, a first may be an "icon," based on resemblance; a second may be an "index," based on correspondence to fact; and a third may be a general sign or "symbol" (4, secs. 55 ff.; Peirce, *Semiotic* 22–36). As Peirce developed these three terms (especially in his letters to Lady Welby), they appear as the basis for a much fuller and more specific way of using Peirce's semiotic analytically, in reference to specific texts or other signifying elements. Thus, an "icon" is a semiotic function that invites attention to some character contained in or expressed by an instance, while an "index" depends on some existential relation into which the instance enters, as smoke is an index of fire. The "symbol," then, is not connected merely to a ground or a relation to the object but is a relation to an "interpretant." "Symbol" in this sense is general, because it presupposes both the quality (in a reference to a ground) and the existential relations of a particular case, but specific in that it refers to an interpretant, a cognitive state, determined by a first and a second but not confined to either (Sheriff 67).

Peirce's pragmaticism develops as the continuous elaboration of consequences from this account of logic-metaphysic-semiotic because it does not presume in any way that "meaning" can be determined in a binary relation. The requirement that a "first" be accessible by reference to a ground only ensures that one will note explicitly what particular aspect of a phenomenon one is noticing or representing. Peirce's pragmaticist maxim (restated to distance himself from James and Dewey) is that "the entire intellectual purport of any symbol consists in the total of all general modes of rational conduct that, conditionally upon all the possible different circumstances and desires, would ensue upon the acceptance of the symbol" (*Collected* 5, sec. 438).

While this maxim appears to leave meaning infinitely deferred, it would be more accurate to say that it accepts meaning (as it does thought and reality itself) as a continuous process, which we determine, with arbitrary precision (depending on "different circumstances and desires"), in communities of inquiry. Finally, Peirce's pragmaticism, with its debt to Duns Scotus, reflects Peirce's sense that thinking is normative and in its deepest reaches ethical and aesthetic; it must be these if it is to be scientific (5, sec. 36; 8, sec. 242). According to the title phrase of one of his most widely read essays, it is by inquiry and experiment that we seek the "fixation of belief" (5, secs. 358 ff.), while the ethics of the process is profoundly summarized in the slogan that Peirce would have on "every wall of the city of philosophy: Do not block the way of inquiry" (1, sec. 135)—which is to say, no belief is ever ultimate, and no one ever gets the last word.

Leroy F. Searle

See also SEMIOTICS.

Charles Sanders Peirce, *Collected Papers* (ed. Charles Hartshorne and Paul Weiss, 8 vols., 1931–58, reprint in 4 vols., 1960–66), *Semiotic and Significs: The Correspondence between Charles S. Peirce and Victoria Lady Welby* (ed. Charles S. Hardwick, 1977), *Writings of Charles S. Peirce: A Chronological Edition* (ed. Max Fisch et al., 4 vols. to date, 1982–).

Robert F. Almeder, *The Philosophy of Charles S. Peirce: A Critical Introduction* (1980); John Boler, *Charles Peirce and Scholastic Realism: A Study of Peirce's Relation to John Duns Scotus* (1963), "Habits of Thought" (Moore and Robin); Nynfa Bosco, "Peirce and Metaphysics" (Moore and Robin); Joseph Brent, *Charles Sanders Peirce: A Life* (1992); Jonathan Culler, *The Pursuit of Signs: Semiotics, Literature, Deconstruction* (1981); Joseph L. Esposito, *Evolutionary Metaphysics: The Development of Peirce's Theory of Categories* (1980); Max Harold Fisch, *Peirce, Semiotic, and Pragmaticism: Essays by Max H. Fisch* (ed. Kenneth Laine Ketner and Christian J. W. Kloesel, 1986); J. Fisette, *Introduction à la sémiotique de C. S. Peirce* (1990); Jürgen Habermas, *Erkenntnis und Interesse* (1968, *Knowledge and Human Interests,* trans. Jeremy J. Shapiro, 1972); Immanuel Kant, *The Critique of Pure Reason* (trans. Norman Kemp Smith, 1965); Edward C. Moore and Richard S. Robin, eds., *Studies in the Philosophy of Charles Sanders Peirce, Second Series* (1964); M. G. Murphey, *The Development of Peirce's Philosophy* (1961); Doede Nauta, "Peirce's Three Categories Regained: Toward an Interdisciplinary Reconstruction of Peircean Frameworks," *Proceedings of the C. S. Peirce Bicentennial International Congress* (1981); Sandra B. Rosenthal, *Pragmatism and Phenomenology: A Philosophic Encounter* (1980); Ferdinand de Saussure, *Cours de linguistique générale* (1916, *Course in General Linguistics,* trans. Wade Baskin, 1959); David Savan, *An Introduction to C. S. Peirce's Full System of Semeiotic* (1987); John K. Sheriff, *The Fate of Meaning: Charles Peirce, Structuralism, and Literature* (1989); Peter Skagestad, *The Road of Inquiry: Charles Peirce's Pragmatic Realism* (1981); Philip P. Wiener and Frederic H. Young, eds., *Studies in the Philosophy of Charles Sanders Peirce* (1952).

PHENOMENOLOGY

Phenomenology is a philosophy of experience. For phenomenology the ultimate source of all meaning and value is the lived experience of human beings. All philosophical systems, scientific theories, or aesthetic judgments have the status of abstractions from the ebb and flow of the lived world. The task of the philosopher, according to phenomenology, is to describe the structures of experience, in particular consciousness, the imagination, relations with other persons, and the situatedness of the human subject in society and history. Phenomenological theories of literature regard works of art as mediators between the consciousnesses of the author and the reader or as attempts to disclose aspects of the being of humans and their worlds.

The modern founder of phenomenology is the German philosopher Edmund Husserl (1859–1938), who sought to make philosophy "a rigorous science" by returning its attention "to the things themselves" *(zu den Sachen selbst).* He does not mean by this that philosophy should become empirical, as if "facts" could be determined objectively and absolutely. Rather, searching for foundations on which philosophers could ground their knowledge with certainty, Husserl proposes that reflection put out of play all unprovable assumptions (about the existence of objects, for example, or about ideal or metaphysical entities) and describe what is given in experience. The road to a presupposition-less philosophy, he argues, begins by suspending the "natural attitude" of everyday knowing, which assumes that things are simply there in the external world. Philosophers should "bracket" the object-world and, in a process he calls *epoché*, or "reduction," focus their attention on what is immanent in consciousness itself, without presupposing anything about its origins or supports. Pure description of the phenomena given in consciousness would, Husserl believes, give philosophers a foundation of necessary, certain knowledge and would thereby justify the claim of philosophy to be more radical and all-encompassing than other disciplines (see *Ideas* 95–105 and *Meditations* 11–23).

Later phenomenologists have been skeptical of Husserl's contention that description can occur without presuppositions, in part because of Husserl's own analysis of the structure of knowledge. According to Husserl, consciousness is made up of "intentional acts" correlated to "intentional objects." The "intentionality" of consciousness is its directedness toward objects, which it helps to constitute. Objects are always grasped partially and incompletely, in "aspects" *(Abschattungen)* that are filled out and synthesized according to the attitudes, interests, and expectations of the perceiver. Every perception includes a "horizon" of potentialities that the observer assumes, on the basis of past experiences with or beliefs about such entities, will be fulfilled by subsequent perceptions (see *Meditations* 39–46).

Extrapolating from Husserl's description of consciousness, MARTIN HEIDEGGER (1889–1976) argues that understanding is always "ahead of itself" *(sich vorweg)*, projecting expectations that interpretation then makes explicit. In the section "Understanding and Interpretation" in *Being and Time* (1927), Heidegger argues that inherent in understanding is a "forestructure" *(Vorstruktur)* of assumptions and beliefs that guide interpretation. Heidegger's account of the interdependence of understanding and expectations is in part a reformulation of the classic idea that interpretation of texts is fundamentally circular, inasmuch as in interpretation the construal of a textual detail is always necessarily based on assumptions about the whole to which it belongs (see Palmer and HERMENEUTICS). His theory of understanding also reflects his own assumptions about human existence, which he describes as a process of projection whereby we are always outside of and beyond ourselves as we direct ourselves toward the future. Heidegger's conception of the anticipatory structure of understanding is important for later versions of phenomenology that focus on interpretation and reading. Hermeneutic phenomenology (especially as developed by Hans-Georg Gadamer and PAUL RICOEUR) explores further the role of presuppositions in understanding, and phenome-

nological theories of textual reception (especially the "Constance school," led by Hans Robert Jauss and Wolfgang Iser) investigate how literary works are understood differently by audiences with different interpretive conventions (see READER-RESPONSE THEORY AND CRITICISM and RECEPTION THEORY).

Heidegger extends Husserl's concern with epistemology into the domain of ontology and in the process, according to some critics, departs from phenomenology's original methodological rigor and cautious avoidance of speculation. *Being and Time* provides a description of the structures of human existence *(Dasein,* or "being-there"), which can be seen as an application of Husserl's investigations of consciousness to other regions of experience, including relations with others, the meaning of death, and history. Heidegger's descriptions of existence as a "thrown project" *(geworfener Entwurf)* and of "care" *(Sorge)* as the founding structure of human being are the basis of the theories of such existential phenomenologists as the Swiss psychiatrist Ludwig Binswanger and the French philosophers JEAN-PAUL SARTRE and Maurice Merleau-Ponty. Heidegger's own conception of human existence is guided by his concern with the "ontological difference," the relation between "beings" and "Being." He defines human being as that being for which Being is an issue, although he also finds that for the most part in everyday life the question of Being is neglected or forgotten. In *Being and Time* he explores everyday existence for indirect evidence of Being. In his later work, Heidegger turns to the study of language, which he regards as the "home of Being," and especially to poetry, which has in his view special powers to disclose Being (see "Origin").

Merleau-Ponty (1908–61) retains many of Heidegger's existential analyses while rejecting his metaphysical speculations. He also corrects the early Husserl's tendency toward idealism by insisting on the primacy of perceptual experience and the ambiguities of the lived world. In his most important work, *Phenomenology of Perception* (1945), Merleau-Ponty situates consciousness in the body. His notion of "perception" as the situated, embodied, unreflected knowledge of the world rejects splitting the mind off from the body or treating the body mechanistically as a mere object. Consciousness is always incarnate, he argues, or else it would lack a situation through which to engage the world, and Merleau-Ponty's awareness of the necessary situatedness of existence makes him emphasize the inescapability of social and political entanglements in the constitution of subjects. The experience of embodied consciousness is also inherently obscure and ambiguous, he finds, and he consequently rejects the philosopher's dream of fully transparent understanding. Reflection cannot hope for a complete, certain knowledge that transcends the confusion and indeterminacy of unreflective experience. The activity of reflecting on the ambiguities of lived experience is always outstripped by and can never ultimately catch up with the fund of preexisting life it seeks to understand. For Merleau-Ponty, the primacy of perception makes philosophy an endless endeavor to clarify the meaning of experience without denying its density and obscurity.

Roman Ingarden (1893–1970), the founding father of phenomenological aesthetics, also rejects idealism, and he wrote his pioneering studies of *The Literary Work of Art* (1931) and *The Cognition of the Literary Work of Art* (1937) as contributions to resolving the opposition of the real and the ideal. Works of art originally attracted his attention because they seemed to belong to neither realm. Unlike autonomous, fully determinate objects, literary works depend for their existence, he argues, on the intentional acts of their creators and of their readers. But they are not mere figments or private dream-images, because they have an intersubjective "life." Yet their apparent ideal status as structures of consciousness does not make them like triangles or other mathematical figures, which are truly ideal objects, without a specific moment of birth or a history of subsequent transformations (see *Work* 331–55).

Ingarden describes a literary work as "an intersubjective intentional object" (*Cognition* 14). It has its origin in the acts of consciousness of its creator that are preserved in writing or through other physical means, and these acts are then reanimated (although not precisely duplicated) by the consciousness of the reader. The work is not reducible to the psychology of either the author or the reader, however. It has a history that goes beyond the consciousness that originated it or the consciousness of any individual reader. The existence of a work transcends any particular, momentary experience of it, even though it came into being and continues to exist only through various acts of consciousness. Ingarden argues that the work has an *"ontically heteronomous* mode of existence" (*Work* 362), because it is neither autonomous of nor completely dependent on the consciousnesses of the author and the reader; rather, it is paradoxically based on them even as it transcends them.

Ingarden finds that the literary work is a stratified formation. It consists of four related strata, each of which has its own characteristic "value qualities": (1) word sounds, (2) meaning units, (3) "schematized aspects" (the perspectives through which states of affairs are

viewed), and (4) represented objectivities. The work as a whole is "schematic," he argues, because the strata (especially the last two) have "places of indeterminacy" that readers may fill in differently. In a successful work, Ingarden argues, the strata combine to form a unified whole that provides a "polyphonic harmony of value qualities" (369–72).

Ingarden distinguishes the reader's "concretization" of the work from the work itself. The "aesthetic object" the reader produces is correlated to the "artistic object" the author created but necessarily differs from it. Not only will readers with different experiences respond differently to the possibilities left open by the work's indeterminacies or to the value qualities available in the various strata but the cognition of a work is an inherently temporal process, so that "the literary work is never *fully* grasped in *all* its strata and components but always only partially," in "foreshortenings" that "may change constantly" (334). Like other objects that present themselves through aspects *(Abschattungen),* the work itself is available only "horizontally," through an array of incomplete and perspectival views—in various experiences over the duration of a single reading, or in the variety of different ways in which it may be "concretized" over its history. Ingarden maintains, however, that "certain limits of variability" constrain a correct or adequate concretization, and he claims that these limits are predetermined by the structure of the work (352).

Ingarden has been extremely influential in the development of phenomenological reader-response theories, but his views have also been subjected to extensive criticisms and revisions, particularly by Wolfgang Iser (b. 1926). Iser faults Ingarden for limiting excessively the variability of permissible concretizations. According to Iser, Ingarden posits "a one-way incline from text to reader and not . . . a two-way relationship," which can take many unpredictable, possibly irreconcilable forms (*Act* 173). Reading is a more variable and dynamic activity than merely filling in blanks, Iser argues, and as a result "a work may be concretized in different, equally valid, ways" (178). Iser also faults Ingarden for holding a limited, "classical" aesthetics of value, which privileges "harmony" and fails to appreciate the disruptions and dissonances through which many (especially modern and postmodern) works achieve their effects. For Iser, reading is a process of discovery in which the surprises, frustrations, and reversals brought about by the disjunctions in a work have the power to provoke reflection about the reader's presuppositions.

Iser's appreciation of disjunction also leads him to criticize Georges Poulet's description of reading as a process of identification. For Poulet (1902–91), the mystery of reading is that the barriers ordinarily dividing selves are overcome: "My consciousness behaves as though it were the consciousness of another" (56; see also GENEVA SCHOOL). According to Iser, however, reading is more paradoxical than Poulet suggests, because "the real, virtual 'me'" never completely disappears even as "the alien 'me'" governing the text's world emerges (*Implied* 293). Reading therefore entails a duplication of consciousnesses, which can give rise to new self-understanding as a result of the juxtaposition of my habitual ways of thinking with those required by the text. Hans Robert Jauss (b. 1921) goes so far as to equate the "aesthetic value" of a text with its demand for a "change of horizons" in the reader due to the disparity between the audience's "horizon of expectations" and the horizon of the work (25). Jauss suggests that as literary works become familiar (e.g., through canonization), their value may decrease, because they lose their ability to shock, surprise, and challenge the reader.

Phenomenology has produced many studies of the imagination, and among the most original of these are the works of Gaston Bachelard (1884–1962). Bachelard regards the poetic image as a privileged place in which new meaning emerges and through which being discloses itself. "The poet speaks on the threshold of being," Bachelard claims, and the originality of the poetic imagination testifies to human freedom by displaying "the unforeseeable nature of speech" (xii, xxiii). Bachelard asks that readers, in order to open themselves up to the revelations of the image, lay aside preconceptions and cultivate a capacity for wonder. "One must be receptive," he says, and "reverberate" with the poem in order to experience "the very ecstasy of the newness of the image" (xi). In works like *The Poetics of Space* (1957), Bachelard attempts to exemplify the practice he advocates by playfully allowing his own imagination to resonate in response to images of various kinds. He is particularly drawn to images of "*felicitous* space," which suggest the "human value" of places and objects (xxxi). Bachelard's attitude toward images can be contradictory, however. At his best he regards images as evidence of the lived meaning of space, but at times he descends beneath experience and seeks the origins of images in the timeless, unconscious archetypes of Jungian psychology (see ARCHETYPAL THEORY AND CRITICISM). In any case, Bachelard's reveries about images of place are themselves lyrical demonstrations of the creative possibilities of speech.

Interpretation and language have been the central themes of the most recent phase of phenomenology. In order to prevent its reflections from becoming solipsistic and ahistorical, Paul Ricoeur (b. 1913) calls on phenomenology to take a hermeneutic turn and to direct its attention, not toward individual consciousness, but toward cultural objects, which provide social, historical evidence of existence. Because "the *cogito* can be recovered only by the detour of a decipherment of the documents of its life," reflection must become interpretation, that is, "the appropriation of our effort to exist and of our desire 'to be' by means of the works which testify to this effort and this desire" (102). Hermeneutic phenomenology must also explore the conflict of interpretations, because the possibility of "very different, even opposing, methods" of understanding is a fundamental aspect of our experience as interpreting beings (99). A concern with how new, different modes of understanding and expression emerge leads Ricoeur to pay special attention to creativity in language, especially the semantic innovations of metaphor. Phenomenology denies that structure alone can adequately explain language, because new ways of meaning can only be introduced through events of speech, which may extend or overturn the limits of existing conventions. Phenomenology also denies that language is self-enclosed. As Ricoeur argues, "Texts speak of possible worlds and of possible ways of orientating oneself in those worlds" (144). Language and interpretation are not stable, closed systems for phenomenology, because meaning, like experience, is endlessly open to new developments.

The inherent incompleteness of any moment of experience is the basis of JACQUES DERRIDA's influential critique of Husserl's version of phenomenology. Questioning Husserl's dream of a presupposition-less philosophy, Derrida (b. 1930) finds "a metaphysical presupposition" in the very assumption that a realm of "original self-giving evidence" can be found, a "self-presence" that is simple, self-contained, and prior to signification (4–5). Using Husserl's own theories about time and intersubjectivity, Derrida demonstrates that "nonpresence and otherness are internal to presence" (66). Because knowledge is always perspectival and incomplete, the present depends on memory and expectation (the no-more and the not-yet) to make sense of the world; elements of absence must consequently be part of presence for it to be meaningful. Furthermore, my assurance that my self-reflections reveal generally shared structures of knowledge and existence rests on the tacit assumption that another consciousness would experience this moment as I do, but this assumption is yet again evidence that the presence of the self to itself lacks the self-sufficiency Husserl sought in his quest for a solid foundation for philosophy. According to Derrida, Husserl's commitment to a view of knowledge as necessary, certain, and guaranteed by indubitable intuitions prevented him from recognizing the falsity of this ideal even though his own theories about consciousness and experience implicitly contradict it. Derrida concludes: "Sense, being temporal in nature, as Husserl recognized, is never simply present; it is always already engaged in the 'movement' of the trace, that is, in the order of 'signification'" (85). There is no getting beneath the repetitive, re-presentational structure of signification, Derrida argues, because supplementarity—the replacement of one sign or "trace" by another—is the structure of self-presence.

Contemporary phenomenology has for the most part abandoned Husserl's dream of finding indubitable foundations for knowledge. His quest for a presuppositionless philosophy now seems an example of what Hans-Georg Gadamer (b. 1900) calls "the fundamental prejudice of the enlightenment," namely, "the prejudice against prejudice itself, which deprives tradition of its power" (239–40). Although some prejudices may be misleading, constricting, and oppressive, understanding is impossible without pre-judgments *(Vor-urteile)* of the sort provided by cultural conventions and inherited beliefs. According to Gadamer, "The overcoming of all prejudices, this global demand of the enlightenment, will prove to be itself a prejudice, the removal of which opens the way to an appropriate understanding of our finitude" (244), including our belonging to history, culture, and language. Largely due to the influence of Gadamer, hermeneutic phenomenology and reader-response theory have turned their attention to the role of customs, conventions, and presuppositions in the constitution of the human subject and its understanding of the world. What remains distinctive about phenomenology is its focus on human experience, but recent phenomenologists have stressed the inherent entanglement of experience in language, history, and cultural traditions.

Paul B. Armstrong

Gaston Bachelard, *The Poetics of Space* (1958, trans. Maria Jolas, 1969); Ludwig Binswanger, *Being-in-the-World* (ed. Jacob Needleman, 1965); Jacques Derrida, *La Voix et la phénomène: Introduction au problème du signe dans la phénoménologie* (1967, *Speech and Phenomena, and Other Essays on Husserl's Theory of Signs,* trans. David B. Allison, 1973); Hans-Georg Gadamer, *Wahrheit und Methode: Grundzüge einer philosophischen Hermeneutik* (1960, 5th ed., *Gesammelte Werke,* vol. 1, ed. J. C. B. Mohr, 1986, *Truth and Method,* trans. Garrett Barden and John Cum-

ming, 1975, 2d ed., trans. rev. Joel Weinsheimer and Donald G. Marshall, 1989); Martin Heidegger, "The Origin of the Work of Art" (1936, *Martin Heidegger: Basic Writings,* ed. David Farrell Krell, 1977), *Sein und Zeit* (1927, *Being and Time,* trans. John Macquarrie and Edward Robinson, 1962); Edmund Husserl, *Cartesian Meditations: An Introduction to Phenomenology* (1950, trans. Dorian Cairns, 1960), *Ideas: General Introduction to Pure Phenomenology* (1913, trans. W. R. Boyce Gibson, 1962); Roman Ingarden, *Das literarische Kunstwerk* (1931, *The Literary Work of Art,* trans. George G. Grabowicz, 1973), *Vom Erkennen des literarischen Kunstwerks* (1968, *The Cognition of the Literary Work of Art,* trans. Ruth Ann Crowley and Kenneth R. Olson, 1973); Wolfgang Iser, *Der Akt des Lesens: Theorie ästhetischer Wirkung* (1976, *The Act of Reading: A Theory of Aesthetic Response,* trans. Iser, 1974), *Der implizite Leser: Kommunikationsformen des Romans von Bunyan bis Beckett* (1972, *The Implied Reader: Patterns of Communication in Prose Fiction from Bunyan to Beckett,* trans. Iser, 1974); Hans Robert Jauss, *Toward an Aesthetic of Reception* (trans. Timothy Bahti, 1982); Maurice Merleau-Ponty, *Phenomenology of Perception* (1945, trans. Colin Smith, 1962); Georges Poulet, "Phenomenology of Reading," *New Literary History* 1 (1969); Paul Ricoeur, *The Philosophy of Paul Ricoeur* (ed. Charles E. Reagan and David Stewart, 1978).

Robert Detweiler, *Story, Sign, and Self: Phenomenology and Structuralism as Literary Critical Methods* (1978); Eugene H. Falk, *The Poetics of Roman Ingarden* (1981); David Halliburton, *Poetic Thinking: An Approach to Heidegger* (1981); Don Ihde, *Hermeneutic Phenomenology: The Philosophy of Paul Ricoeur* (1971); Don Ihde and Hugh J. Silverman, eds., *Descriptions* (1986); Joseph J. Kockelmans, ed., *Phenomenology: The Philosophy of Edmund Husserl and Its Interpretation* (1967); Ludwig Landgrebe, *The Phenomenology of Edmund Husserl* (ed. Donn Welton, 1981); Edward N. Lee and Maurice Mandelbaum, eds., *Phenomenology and Existentialism* (1967); Gary Brent Madison, *The Phenomenology of Merleau-Ponty: A Search for the Limits of Consciousness* (1981); Robert R. Magliola, *Phenomenology and Literature: An Introduction* (1977); Michael Murray, ed., *Heidegger and Modern Philosophy: Critical Essays* (1978); Richard E. Palmer, *Hermeneutics: Interpretation Theory in Schleiermacher, Dilthey, Heidegger, and Gadamer* (1969); Paul Ricoeur, *Husserl: An Analysis of His Phenomenology* (1967); Herbert Spiegelberg, *The Phenomenological Movement: A Historical Introduction* (2 vols., 2d ed., 1976); Pierre Thévenaz, *"What Is Phenomenology?" and Other Essays* (ed. James M. Edie, 1962).

PHILOLOGY

Few terms associated with Western literature and language are as old as "philology." Tracing over time the meanings attributed to it, however necessary, is not easy, nor does the term command agreement today. The eighteenth-century coinage of "literature" (in roughly our present-day sense, combining the two notions of a corpus of texts and an activity) has added to the confusion. For Romans of the Augustan age *litteratura* meant a form of writing composed of letters (e.g., as opposed to hieroglyphics); somewhat later, around the time of Nero, it acquired the extended meaning "letters," as in "A schoolboy learns his letters," with slight overtones of our own "literature," in the sense of a school canon. It was with this meaning that "literature" continued to be used both in Latin and in the European vernaculars throughout the later Middle Ages until the second half of the eighteenth century. Up to that time a person well versed in "literature" was deemed to possess qualities of refinement and politeness valued by the upper echelons of society. These qualities were also frequently ascribed to "philology," and thus the two terms occasionally overlapped.

Historically, "philology," deriving from the Greek φιλολογία, meaning "love of words," has rather consistently retained a sense of "activity," of "discipline." Not only was the *philologus* viewed as versed in history, antiquities, and literature, he was a person engaged in learned pursuits and as such superior to a mere *litterator*. One of Petronius's characters in the *Satyricon* (c. C.E. 60) complains that in order to be invited to fashionable dinner parties, one must shine in *philologia,* that is, in tasteful and witty literary talk. Cicero describes some "noblemen" who do not deserve to be called *philologi;* he also identified Homer as the "leader" *(dux)* of "philology." However, already in classical antiquity a rivalry had sprung up between the "philologist" and the "philosopher," the practitioner of the activity known as *philosophia* ("love of wisdom"). Seneca lamented that in his own time what once was "philosophy" has turned into "philology" *(quae philosophia fuit, facta est philologia),* a complaint often repeated by those who find humane letters and their study insufficiently rigorous and even dilettantish. *The New Columbia Encyclopedia* (1975) devotes a column and a half of fine print to "philosophy," but "philology" goes unmentioned.

One of the most influential works bequeathed by antiquity to the Middle Ages was a curious Menippean satire, or *prosimetrum,* entitled *The Marriage of Mercury and Philology (De Nuptiis Mercurii et Philologiae)* by Martianus Capella (early fifth century). In it an aged narrator tells his bemused son the tale of Mercury's search for a suitable bride. All eligible immortals having been spoken for, Mercury decides to wed Philology, a mortal maiden, who spends her sleepless nights in the study of books. Philology, accorded immortality, is received by Juno and Jupiter on Olympus, and the wedding is celebrated. Apollo, Mercury's brother, presents the couple with seven gifts, each representing an intellectual activity and allegorically personified as a maiden: the "arts" (i.e., the verbal arts: Grammar, Rhetoric, and Dialectic); and the "Greek arts, now Latinized" (Arithmetic, Geometry, Astronomy, and Harmony). Together with her husband Mercury, Philology became the custodian of the Seven Liberal Arts—the entirety of learning as well as the means of acquiring it. Copied, translated, and otherwise transformed into a broad spectrum of texts, *De Nuptiis* remained canonical up to the end of the fifteenth century. The basis of the early medieval curriculum, its indirect influence on our own curricular values has been substantial.

The golden age of *De Nuptiis* in Europe lasted from about 1050 to 1230—to more or less the date of the first part of *The Romance of the Rose.* It was this period that witnessed the establishment of the arts curriculum, first in the cathedral schools, later in the universities. Prevailing then was the study of the *auctores,* the corpus of canonical writers of Classical Latinity: Virgil, Statius, Ovid, HORACE, Cicero, and so on. Such "philological" study involved grammar, of course, and literary analysis; it also led to the belief that moderns could imitate their classical forebears and in turn become models for posterity. This twelfth-century "renaissance" saw the emergence, primarily in France and England, but soon elsewhere as well, of learned literary activity in the vernacular. The French *clergie* corresponded fairly closely to Classical Latin *philologia.* Thus, as the modern philologist restores a corrupt text to its pristine original state, so the medieval cleric, first in glossing, then in commenting upon or translating or otherwise imitating a past work, endeavored to articulate meanings hidden or otherwise obscured in the text he imitates and to demonstrate the significance of that text to his own audience. With the tools provided by Apollo's gifts to Mercury and Philology, the cleric participated in the ongoing activity symbolized by this now immortal earth maiden. The writings of a twelfth- or thirteenth-century romancer constitute essentially the glossing, the recasting, and the translating of what he or she has read.

For much of this two-century period philosophy and philology lived in harmony. For John of Salisbury (c. 1115–80), the greatest representative of humane letters in his time, a distinction between the two would have made little sense. However, already in the logical works of St. Anselm (later eleventh century) one detects the seeds of future discord. The linguistic categories of the sixth-century grammarian Priscian, whose *Institutiones* had been composed in defense of *Latinitas,* no longer satisfied the requirements of the new logicians, and as these came to dominate teaching in the thirteenth-century universities the belletristic study of the ancient *auctores* fell into disfavor. By the time of his *De vulgari Eloquentia* (c. 1302), what DANTE ALIGHIERI called *gram-(m)atica* referred purely and simply to the "logical" Latin of the scholastic dialecticians. "Literature" came to be identified with the vernacular. It was in a French poem, titled *The Battle of the Seven Arts* (c. 1225), that Henri d'Andelis recounted a struggle in which Parisian Dialectic routs the Latin *auctores* and their leader, Grammar, from Orléans. (See MEDIEVAL THEORY AND CRITICISM.)

Vernacular *clergie* thus inherited the mantle of the old arts curriculum based on the study and the imitation of the ancient *auctores.* Eventually, certain highly regarded vernacular writers earned a status hitherto reserved for the ancients. Thus, Eustache Deschamps bestowed the title *poète,* formerly restricted to the ancients, upon his great teacher Guillaume de Machaut, a contemporary of Petrarch (who was, himself, crowned *poeta laureatus,* though principally as a modern master of Latin verse). Little by little, reading of the ancients by the vernacular moderns became an *indirect* reading, refracted through the "philology" of vernacular composition. *The Romance of the Rose* owes more to the conventions of vernacular lyric and romance narrative than it does to a direct perusal of Ovid or Catullus. Similarly, the *Rose* played a key role in literary production throughout Western Europe—Dante, Geoffrey Chaucer, François Villon, and Clément Marot, who provided a printed edition of it. This was the situation in northern Europe until the Reformation; in Italy and Spain matters took a different course.

The "manuscript culture" of the Middle Ages helped to determine *clergie* as a "creatively philological" enterprise. Writers, scribes, and patrons jointly participated in the production of hand-made books. With the exception of a few canonical texts, bookish transmission was epitomized by variation, not exact copying. Only after around 1350 did certain moderns begin to oversee the manufacture of codices containing their works, thereby according them traits we associate with printed books.

In complementary fashion both the Reformation and the Renaissance utilized printing in order to redefine and to stabilize the relationship between modern reader and ancient text. Textual traditions came to be viewed as raw material for the expert in the effort to restore "lost originals." Whether sacred or profane—an Ovidian poem or the Gospels—the text had to be stripped of whatever previous generations had added to it, or egregiously reconstructed ("corruptions"). A philology of textual establishment and criticism came into its own, sometimes, however, with ambiguous consequences. By applying rigorous criteria of philological analysis, the fifteenth-century humanist Lorenzo Valla exposed the fraudulence of *The Donation of Constantine,* a document utilized by the papacy in support of its claims to temporal power. Learning Greek and Hebrew, reforming humanists were able to apply criteria of equal rigor to sacred texts. Even the post-Tridentine church was affected. Jean Bolland (1596–1665), a Jesuit, founded the critical study of hagiographic traditions; the *Acta Sanctorum,* continued in our day by the Bollandist Order, would eventually inflict severe damage on numerous popular saintly cults (St. Christopher disappeared from the canon just a generation ago). Critical philology has served to underpin the skepticism still pervading our intellectual outlook.

Yet, reshaping the poetical works of a Virgil in the form of a critically defensible modern book with appropriate scholarly apparatus did not result merely in an easily accessible, widely diffused, and valuable product, available to other scholars and their students. It also helped to distance the ancient from the modern, a distancing to be bridged solely by a new literary, or cultural, historiography and/or by the development of a community of taste and values thanks to the mediating and foundational presence of philological expertise. This, in turn, led to the creation of a new social and cultural ideal: the educated man. It fell to him to gain a degree of familiarity with a remarkably stable canon; he was trained to view himself *historically* as heir to the Augustans. He might aspire to surpass them not only by virtue of his Christianity but also by outdoing them on their own intellectual terrain—literature, science, philosophy, and governance. Had he and his peers not discovered worlds—America, the movement of the planets—unknown to the ancients or badly understood by them? Reformatted in the shape of printed books, the ancients underwent a process of neutralization, as did, more slowly over the years, the authority they had enjoyed.

During the Renaissance one notes an increasing professionalization of textual philology. The careers of the two Scaligers—Julius Caesar (1484–1558) and, especially, Joseph Justus (1540–1609)—illustrate the point. Julius, Italian-born, was a philologist and scientist. For him, carefully edited books constituted a starting point for his own critical *oeuvre* as he applied methods gleaned from textual establishment to medicine and botany (arguing for more rational methods of classifying plants), to language (the stylistic and linguistic deficiencies of Cicero), and to literary theory (his *Poetics* extol Virgil and Seneca and would exert considerable influence on the development of neoclassicism in Europe). Meanwhile, Joseph, his son, first dwelled in France, then held a chair of philosophy at Geneva, and later accepted a professorship at Leiden. Several of his works deal with the theory and practice of textual establishment, such as *De Emendatione temporum* (1583), in which he placed the study of ancient calendars and dating on a rational basis; he found, and restored, the text of book 2 of Eusebius's *Chronicle*. His *Thesaurus temporum* (1606) provides the chronological basis for the study of ancient history. For historians of philological techniques and values Joseph Scaliger ranks as a founding father of the discipline.

A second trend concerns the application of the new critical perspectives in textual establishment and historiography to vernacular matters. Like Julius Scaliger a disciple of Jacques Cujas, Étienne Pasquier (1529–1615), a jurist and lover of belles-lettres, began publishing his *Recherches de la France* in 1560 in response to increased interest in the historical and literary past of his native land—an interest not unrelated to the rise of the national and centralized monarchy and probably corresponding to certain largely religious, decentralizing tendencies within the kingdom. Rather than focusing on such hoary myths as that of the Trojan origins of the French, Pasquier unearthed old documents, including chansons de geste, medieval romances, and the lyric; he studied French proverbs and other folk sayings, taking pains to establish parallels between the past and the France of his own day.

Pasquier was not an isolated case, nor was his style of work confined to France. Antonio de Nebrixa's (1444?–1522) ground-breaking grammar of Castilian was presented to Queen Isabella in 1492; in the *Diálogo de la lengua* Juan de Valdés (c. 1500–1540) based his affirmation of the "purity" and particular excellence of Spanish on the speech contained in Spanish proverbs. In tonesetting Italy debates surrounding the status of the literary *volgare* raged on: ought the literary vernacular be based on Tuscan, or should, as Dante had advised in *De vulgari Eloquentia* (but had not practiced in his own vernacular writings), the literary language be composed of elements taken from many, or all, the Italian dialects? Today these matters remain unresolved.

Finally, translations—biblical, classical, and so on—strove to incorporate the translated work into the literature of the target language. Thus, the truth, say, of the Gospels was not only more accessible to German-speakers in Martin Luther's translation; in its very accessibility this truth was "truer," more manifest. Jacques Amyot's Plutarch quite literally made the *Lives* French; the King James translators "Englished" the Bible. Luther, Amyot, and the King James Bible would exert decisive influence on the subsequent fate of the languages involved. Translation constituted the natural outcome of the philological activity we have been describing. It has been important to review these matters because Romantic and post-Romantic developments in historiography and in philology—the very grounding of these and of our own procedures today—would have been impossible had the tendencies just sketched out not been established within the European intellectual purview, even though the activities associated with them were at times marginalized.

It fell to GIAMBATTISTA VICO (1668–1744), professor of rhetoric and law at the University of Naples and historiographer to the king, to provide systematic theoretical underpinnings to the various trends so far summarized. Although his *New Science,* or *Scienza nuova* (1725, rev. ed., 1730, 1744), entered the mainstream of European thought only after the turbulence of the French Revolution— Vico's first major French disciple was the historian Jules Michelet (1798–1874)—its impact in Germany, whose intelligentsia denounced a French imperialism operating in the name of the principles of Enlightenment and Revolutionary universalism, was decisive.

Breaking with Eusebian Christian historiography as well as with the Roman tradition of emphasis upon the biographies of "great men," Vico understood history to be the creation of Man, in essence a kind of *text*. Its study was to consist in the analysis of the origins and development of human institutions in their "textual" specificity, for, as Vico explained, the universal resides in the specific. Keys to historical understanding lie in the careful study of languages, texts, and specific traditions (myths, rituals, legal practices, poetic forms). Although he retained a cyclical view of historical evolution ("corsi e ricorsi") from earlier doctrines, he argued that cycles never recurred in exactly the same form. Whereas Vico's *Scienza nuova* offers a general philosophy of history, its emphasis is on the particular, on the factual. It is in this emphasis that it runs counter to the prevailing philosophical (and scientific) rationalism of the time, particularly in its Cartesian garb (see RENÉ DESCARTES). Vico restored to philology its central role within the framework of his overall recuperation of history as fundamental to the truth of the human sciences.

Vico also provided philological activity with its raison d'être, namely, that the well-conducted examination of human creations—of texts and of other artifacts of the spirit—offers a priceless vantage point for the study of human creativity. He accorded primary importance to the "surface structures" disparaged by some philosophers and linguists in the late twentieth century. Only with regard to the law did Vico concede a certain innateness of ideas.

Vico's justification of philology as the study of documents in terms of their historical meaning combined with certain conditions prevailing in Romantic Germany to transform the philological disciplines into one of the pillars of the new European university. Philological faculties and institutes devoted to classical and medieval languages (and certain more or less exotic folk speeches or now-defunct "Indo-European" forebears), as well as to the documents and other surviving forms of evidence pertaining to them, began to take on a central role in Western intellectual life.

The success of these new establishments was due largely to contemporary politics and cultural values. The Romantics, weary of Enlightenment rationalism and in open rebellion against the "out-dated" practices of neoclassical rhetoric, proclaimed the higher truth of "naïve popular poetry" and of the *Volksgeist,* just as many also proclaimed the superiority of Shakespeare over Racine. The École Nationale des Chartes, a uniquely French institution devoted to the study of archival material, was founded by the restored monarchy in 1821 as a reply to the Revolutionary and Napoleonic *grandes écoles* (whose outlook had been largely antihistorical).

These various biases—nationalism, in particular—were reflected in the studies undertaken by their practitioners. The French chansons de geste, or medieval epics, were interpreted by German philologists as the latter-day Romance-language expression of fundamentally Germanic values and as "derived" from long-lost oral works praising the great deeds of a Carolingian past. Evidence of nationalist bickering lasts well into our own century, alas, with the Nazi identification of "Indo-European" racial "preeminence" with "Germanic" (or "Aryan") purity and, less tragically, in nevertheless acerbic scholarly squabbling such as that between the German Romance linguist Wilhelm Meyer-Lübke and Amado Alonso, the Spanish scholar, concerning whether Catalan "belongs" to the Ibero-Romance or to the Gallo-Romance "family" of dialects. Despite these aberrations, however, the practice of philological inquiry came to acquire new cultural values of its own as well as, along with other university-based disciplines, a certain self-reflective quality. No less

a personage than JOHANN WOLFGANG VON GOETHE himself counseled a young visitor, Friedrich Diez, to devote his career to the study of the Romance languages, their cultures, and their literatures. Diez went on to found the serious university-level discipline we know as Romance philology. Here, too, the university climate prompted methodological reflection and service to disciplinary principles.

By the end of the nineteenth century the very term "philology" had come to mean—and in British usage this lasted until at least World War II—all university-standard activity related specifically to the study of language; the term covered TEXTUAL CRITICISM, general linguistics, historical reconstruction of texts and languages (as well as the genetic and formal relationships between languages), lexicography, sociolinguistics, and language geography. The subdisciplines tended to be structured genetically, according to language "families." Romance philology coexisted with Germanic, Slavic, Oriental, Semitic, and classical counterparts, often organized into departmental "seminars" or other units. Detailed linguistic commentary often accompanied the edition of old texts, along with rich glossaries, and, of course, competently edited texts furnished important documentation for historical research and linguistic reconstruction—for grammars as well as for etymological and conventional dictionaries. The most prestigious fields of study were Indo-European and, in textual criticism, Greek and Roman literature, to the virtual exclusion, even, of the modern languages in Britain and America, where emulation of the German university began in earnest at the very close of the century.

Such "modern" European literary history and analysis as was practiced under the aegis of the nineteenth-century philological seminars and departments was mostly confined to late antiquity and to the Middle Ages. Meanwhile, in response to new political outlooks and intellectual concerns (e.g., the "laicization" of humanistic study in the French school system under the Third Republic), new areas and specializations were opened up to study and research in the university. One might cite, for example, the HISTORY OF IDEAS or inquiries into the emergence of modernity. Consequently, in practice "philology" became almost exclusively associated with textual and linguistic study of the earlier epochs. Literary historians concerned with postmedieval developments, such as Abel Lefranc and Gustave Lanson in France or their English counterparts (one thinks of Sir Walter Raleigh), evinced little interest in Old French or in Old English, and their disciples came to resent having to waste valuable time on these recondite subjects, for which they felt little ideological sympathy. The situation in Germany, where philology was culturally more firmly entrenched, as well as in Italy and Spain, differed from what prevailed in France and England. However, after World War I the association of philology with German *Wissenschaft* contributed even further to its marginalization.

Meanwhile, simply to glance at, say, Gustav Gröber's magnificent *Grundri der romanischen Philologie* (1888–93, trans., 1902–6), a survey of research accomplished to date and a presentation of vast amounts of data in the field of Romance philology, proves that by the turn of the century the field, even when confined to later antiquity and the Middle Ages, had generated so many subdisciplines and specializations that it was no longer reasonable for one scholar creatively to work with them all. Around this time also Indo-European studies were, so to speak, in the process of "creating" a new general (and theoretically oriented) linguistics, with FERDINAND DE SAUSSURE in Geneva, Baudouin de Courtenay in imperial Russia, William D. Whitney and the Germanist Leonard Bloomfield in America, and others; Romance linguistic geography (as practiced by Jules Gilliéron and his pupils) constituted a point of departure for socio- and for anthropological linguistics. Pressures on the unity of the activities gathered under the label "philology" became more intense and stemmed from a variety of sources. By around the third decade of the twentieth century it would no longer be possible for a scholar to present himself as both a linguist and a literary specialist.

It is something of a paradox, then, that the activities generally accepted throughout the period extending, roughly, from 1800 to 1950 as pertaining to "philology" were seen to be intellectually central, particularly within the university framework, at the same time that they remained entirely open to influences stemming from other, often antiphilological, concerns. One discerns, say, little influence exerted by philologists on the development of nineteenth-century biology, yet this discipline fascinated students of language and of linguistic change. The biological and medical metaphors employed by historical grammarians are legion and have come to sound ludicrous. Gilliéron, for one, spoke of "verbal pathology" and "therapeutics"; others, we noted, saw relationships between languages in terms of "family trees," and so on. More or less regular phonetic change over time (e.g., stressed Vulgar Latin *-A-* > French *-e-*, as in *PATREM* > *père*) was labeled "sound law" by the neogrammarians, who claimed that "phonetic laws" are "exceptionless laws of nature." Race also entered the picture. An English-language grammar of Swahili pub-

lished during the 1880s speaks of the correlation between "negroid" mouth configurations and the sounds of that language.

Similarly "scientific" procedures and vocabulary were applied in textual criticism, especially in such cases as involved recuperating in modern book form the "lost original" (Urtext) from which a variety of manuscripts were considered to have "derived." (Little heed was paid to the fact that a medieval work preserved in codicological form is something qualitatively different from a printed book.) In order to reduce as much as possible the factor of an "unscientific" editorial subjectivity, methods were devised to ensure the rational production of authentic texts. The name most frequently cited in this enterprise is that of Karl Lachmann (1798–1851), who applied the method of "the common error" in his work on Lucretius, the New Testament, and medieval German. The method consists of the rather mechanical process of, first, discovering which of the surviving manuscripts share the same misreadings; second, grouping these manuscripts as all deriving from a common lost model; third, establishing a *stemma codicum,* or "family tree," of manuscripts, with each branch possessing approximately the same weight; and fourth, accepting automatically in given instances the reading offered by the majority of the branches. The resulting text would be "scientifically" sound. It remained for the philologist to restore the language (or dialect) in which the author presumably composed his work. Thus, if the author was known to hail from Champagne, the editor would proceed to rewrite the text according to the dialectal characteristic of *champenois* (as the editor and/or others had reconstructed them).

Our paradox continues, then, for nineteenth-century philology's readiness to accept procedures and goals prized by other fields of intellectual inquiry not only demonstrated its receptiveness but also betrayed its insecurity and its disciplinary vulnerability. Lachmannian editors berated their "subjective" predecessors for their lack of scientific rigor, for, in other words, their theoretical inadequacy—the ancient charge philosophers brought against their dilettantish philologist confreres. Thus, an Italian savant, while admitting that A. E. Housman's edition of Manilius could scarcely be improved upon as a text, claimed the edition to be flawed because the editor did not say how he had arrived at his text. In other words, conformity to a "scientific" ideal took primacy over what, in practice, was achieved, and by appearing to condone this primacy, "positivist" philology undermined the discipline's age-old commitment to factualness. Small wonder, then, that twentieth-century antipositivists felt justified in introducing myriad sub-versions into their own activities. One thinks of Leo Spitzer, railing against Meyer-Lübke and the aesthetic intuitionism of his "philological click" (*Linguistics and Literary History*, 1949), or the rise of *Geistesgeschichte* so decried by Ernst Robert Curtius. One grasps why Joseph Bédier wittily derided Lachmannian principles in Old French textual criticism, but his replacement of this sci-entism by other, equally arbitrary criteria (i.e., the "edit-ing" with virtually no editorial intervention of a chosen "best manuscript" within the tradition at hand) led inev-itably to the production of fraudulently "authentic" edi-tions—the works of individual scribes—and to a refusal to consider the wider implications of textual criticism. The vulnerability of philology is at issue in all these positions.

No critic more cogently understood this vulnerability and the paradox it reflects than the philologically trained FRIEDRICH NIETZSCHE (1844–1900). Deploring those practitioners who sold their birthright in order to acquire the status of technicians, he proclaimed that neither the "mushroom specialist" nor the "good philologist" is "*characterized* by becoming this or that." Yet, as this pas-sage from *Beyond Good and Evil* attests, he relied on phi-lological values in damning the scientism of his day:

> Let me be pardoned, as an old philologist who cannot desist from the mischief of putting his finger on bad modes of interpretation, but "Nature's conformity to law," of which you physicists talk so proudly, as though—why, it exists only owing to your interpreta-tion and bad "philology." It is no matter of fact, no "text," but rather just a naïvely humanitarian adjust-ment and perversion of meaning, with which you make abundant concessions to the democratic in-stincts of the modern soul! "Everywhere equality before the law—Nature is not different in that re-spect, nor better than we": a fine instance of secret motive, in which the vulgar antagonism to every-thing privileged and autocratic—likewise a second and more refined atheism—is once more disguised. "*Ni Dieu, ni maître*"—that, also, is what you want; and therefore "Cheers for natural law?"—is it not so? But, as has been said, that is interpretation, not text; and somebody might come along, who, with opposite intentions and modes of interpretation, could read out of the same "Nature," and with re-gard to the same phenomenon, just the tyran-nically inconsiderate and relentless enforcement of the claims of power . . . as being too human; and who should, nevertheless, end by asserting the same about this world as you do, namely, that it has a "necessary" and "calculable" course, *not*,

> however, because laws obtain in it, but because they are absolutely *lacking,* and every power effects its ulti-mate consequences every moment. (*Beyond* 24–25)

This paragraph, I believe, exemplifies philological acu-ity at its most penetrating. Theories and philosophies have come and gone over the past couple centuries; in-tellectual totalitarianisms have risen and been toppled, usually leaving their clients with unfulfilled promises, as the intellectual media have scurried to bring us the latest news. The recent past has witnessed vertiginous activity of this sort. Yet, one detects nowadays the pres-ence of a new skepticism with regard to whoever offers us the next New Wave. Indeed, mistrust mitigates the welcome given by students of literature to recent devel-opments in, say, cognitive psychology or the philosophy of mind. A conscious text-centeredness, in literature and also other disciplines (e.g., anthropology, sociology), seems to be replacing the emphasis in DECONSTRUC-TION upon the reader and his or her neuroses, and texts themselves, even twentieth-century texts (e.g., those of James Joyce, W. B. Yeats, or Marcel Proust), are no longer simply taken for granted. (It is far easier to proclaim the "death" of the Author, or, for that matter, of the novel, than it is to declare the demise of *À la recherche du temps perdu* .) Fascination with what might be called the "fabu-lous"—stories purporting to serve truth—is general today, present in Latin American "magical realism" as well as in much historiography. Few scholars today would agree with a nineteenth-century editor's dis-missal of Martianus Capella as "insane," or, for that mat-ter, with Curtius's denunciation of his fable *De Nuptiis,* as "vapid."

Many now believe, with Vico, that veracity is located in specific human creations, that specific human truths provide the surest avenue to a more genuine understand-ing of general human truth. This belief, to be sure, is re-lated to the spirit of liberal tolerance and respect for law that we have inherited from the Enlightenment; it also de-rives, in equal measure, from one's own passionate com-mitments and those of others. It is impossible to translate values into watertight categories because, like Edward Sapir's "grammar," such categories inevitably leak. It would appear to be better to approach these values as facts, and as directly as possible; they are to be "read."

As Nietzsche and the philological tradition have con-sistently stated, the act of reading necessarily implies bringing one's learning, talents, and limitations to what one reads. Nietzsche was driving at something along these lines when he wrote of being "*characterized* by becoming this or that." This gift of self was also perhaps what Cicero understood by the superior nobility he conferred upon *philologi,* and what was meant in the past by certain aristocratic notions of taste.

The tyranny of the "definitive," whether as applied to an edition or to a view of history, has, at least provisionally, been consigned to the dustbin. At our own particular juncture in time what happened during the period we call late antiquity is of interest and significance; this was not true fifty years ago. Few knowledgeable Europeans or Americans at present are willing to dismiss as a period of obscurantism and religious bigotry the centuries comprising what we call the Middle Ages. Consequently, how we now read François Rabelais, Michel de Montaigne, William Shakespeare, or Lope de Vega has undergone a singular enrichment. Philology, let me suggest, is the human activity that makes change and enrichment possible. Curtius, in "The Author's Foreword to the English Translation" of *European Literature and the Latin Middle Ages* (1948, trans., 1953), has described this succinctly. Speaking of the circumstances that surrounded his decision to compose his masterpiece (Hitler's assumption of power in Germany), he writes:

My book . . . is not the product of purely scholarly interests. It grew out of vital urges and under the pressure of a concrete historical situation. But in order to convince, I had to use the scientific technique which is the foundation of all historical investigation: philology. For the intellectual sciences it has the same significance as mathematics has for the natural sciences. As Leibniz taught, there are two kinds of truths: on the one hand, those which are only arrived at by reason and which neither need nor are capable of empirical confirmation; on the other hand, those which are recognized through experience and which are logically indemonstrable; necessary truths and accidental truths, or, as Leibniz also puts it, *vérités éternelles et vérités de fait.* The accidental truths of fact can only be established by philology. Philology is the handmaid of the historical disciplines. I have attempted to employ it with something of the precision with which the natural sciences employ their methods. Geometry demonstrates with figures, philology with texts. But philology too ought to give results which are verifiable.

But if the subject of this book is approached through philological technique, it is nevertheless clear, I hope, that philology is not an end in itself. What we are dealing with is literature—that is, the great intellectual and spiritual tradition of Western culture as given form in language. (*European* x)

"Vital [personal] urges," "concrete historical situation," "science," "historical investigation," "factual truths,"

"texts," "philology" not being an end in itself—to us, these are recognizable terms and concepts. Curtius's "intellectual science" *(intellektuelle Wissenschaft)* requires some explanation. It implies familiarity with philological traditions on the part of the present-day practitioner, with what has been achieved by those working philologically. (One learns, Curtius admits, even from bad philologists.) And, in turn, this familiarity entails one's willingness to abjure the definitive. Philology possesses a history. One corrects the misconstruals of the past, and, by the same token, one understands that one's own work will undergo emendation. Philological activity is cumulative. An uninformed philology is a contradiction in terms.

Without denying the efficacy of Ockham's razor, the philologist necessarily realizes that his or her activity rarely permits shortcuts. Difficult languages have to be learned; mistakes have to be appreciated in order that they may be put right. To correct a bad reading can entail the questioning of the entire rationale supporting a structure of editorial practice or, at the very least, the manner in which the error first occurred. The sometimes painful acquisition of learning and experience and the humbling awareness of our limitations can lead to proper satisfactions and even joy. It is surely within the university, heir to the *studium* of the past, where different generations constantly confront one another, where resources in books, equipment, and respect for the varieties of human intelligence are concentrated, that the labor of Martianus's Philology can nowadays most gratifyingly be carried on to fruition.

Karl D. Uitti

See also HISTORICAL THEORY AND CRITICISM, MEDIEVAL THEORY AND CRITICISM, RENAISSANCE THEORY AND CRITICISM, and TEXTUAL CRITICISM.

Ernst Robert Curtius, *Europäische Literatur und lateinisches Mittelalter* (1948, *European Literature and the Latin Middle Ages,* trans. Willard Trask, 1953); Dante Alighieri, *Dante in Hell: The De vulgari Eloquentia* (ed. and trans. Warman Welliver, 1981); Alfred Foulet and Mary B. Speer, *On Editing Old French Texts* (1979); Anthony Grafton, *Defenders of the Text: The Traditions of Scholarship in an Age of Science, 1450–1800* (1991); Edward B. Ham, "Textual Criticism and Common Sense," *Romance Philology* 12 (1958–59); James Harris, *Hermes; or, A Philosophical Inquiry concerning Universal Grammar* (6th ed., 1806); A. E. Housman, *Selected Prose* (ed. John Carter, 1961); Martianus Capella, *De Nuptiis Philologiae et Mercurii* (ed. Adolfus Dick and

Jean Préaux, 1978); Friedrich Nietzsche, *Jenseits von Gut und Böse* (1885, *Beyond Good and Evil,* trans. Helen Zimmern, 1917); Lucius Annæus Seneca, *Epistulæ morales ad Lucilium* (ed. and trans. C. D. N. Costa, 1988); Leo Spitzer, *Linguistics and Literary History: Essays in Stylistics* (1948); Karl D. Uitti, Introduction to *Trends in Romance Linguistics and Philology,* vol. 3, *Language and Philology in Romance* (ed. Rebecca Posner and John N. Green, 1982), "Philology: Factualness and History," *Literary Style: A Symposium* (ed. Seymour Chatman, 1971); Giambattista Vico, *Opere* (ed. Andrea Battistini, 1990), *The New Science of Giambattista Vico,* trans. Thomas Goddard Bergin and Max Harold Fisch, 1984).

PLATO

Plato (c. 427–347 B.C.E.) was born into an aristocratic Athenian family. He is said to have practiced as a poet when young, but in maturity his main activity was as a philosopher and educator. His extensive writings in general philosophy (which he conceived in effect as the theory of education, believing all political institutions to be fundamentally educational in nature) established the fundamental direction of Western philosophy, and his works remain a permanent reference point for later discussions. Influenced by the philosophical critiques of Socrates (c. 469–439 B.C.E.), who was concerned with conceptual analysis and the relation between abstract thought and rational action, and by the followers of Pythagoras (sixth century B.C.E.), who were preoccupied with mathematics as a postulated common ground between cosmic and social realities, he mounted a sustained and radical critique of Athenian public life, which he presented as dominated by the rhetorical and poetical uses of language in the formation of policies and attitudes. (Members of his family were politically active in the antidemocratic movement, but he himself took no part in Athenian politics, though his writings are often taken to express the interests of his supposed party or his class.) The development and use of language in concept formation, in persuasion and conversation, and in literary composition are among his recurrent concerns. Thus, although neither the concept of literature nor that of literary criticism is part of his intellectual armory, he addresses those topics repeatedly, and anyone who writes on literary criticism is still expected to know what Plato had to say. In the *Republic,* books 2 and 3, and the *Laws,* book 2, poetry as song is treated as an integral part of more comprehensive practices of music and dance; but the poetic component is treated as autonomous, so that this important complication can be ignored here.

Most of Plato's writings are dialogues, in the majority of which Socrates is the central figure. It seems obvious that Socrates is Plato's spokesman, but caution is advisable. Socrates is consistently presented as an ironist, and there are hints that the dialogues are meant for a popular audience and differ accordingly from what Plato might say to colleagues and students. The course of discussion within a dialogue may in itself be as instructive as what its participants say. It is thus hazardous to impute doctrines to Plato himself, as opposed to identifying opinions and arguments that are sympathetically presented. Similar caution is advisable in relying on second-hand reports of what Plato "said." The pervasive ironies and the nuances of Plato's verbal artifice are such that one should also beware of trusting a single translation.

Despite these difficulties, Plato's work is a major influence in literary theory and literary criticism. Not only are the works themselves subtle, complex, and provocative but no comparable body of theorizing by his contemporaries and predecessors has survived. Plato thus stands as the original voice from the period to which our civilization looks back as formative. It appears, too, that one of his works (the *Republic*) provoked ARISTOTLE to write his *Poetics,* which long served as the charter of European literary theory.

Plato's aphorisms and images, powerfully evocative, have been as influential as his arguments, passing into our common heritage. Together with the systematic ironies already mentioned, this fact makes it inappropriate to essay a summary of his "doctrines." Themes dealt with or touched on include the following: the relation between technique and spontaneity in literary work, with its epistemological implications (*Apology, Ion, Phaedrus, Republic*); the relations between speech and writing and between text and discussion (*Phaedrus, Protagoras*); the extent to which the formation of languages is conventional or natural (*Cratylus*); the uses and dangers of fiction, and especially of drama, as an educational instrument (*Republic, Laws*); the relation between tragedy and comedy (*Symposium, Philebus*); the folly and danger of separating linguistic technique from cognitive content (*Gorgias, Phaedrus*); the proper basis of literary criticism and its use as an educational tool (*Protagoras*); the social origins and functions of myth (*Republic, Protagoras*); and the political control of literature (*Republic, Laws*). Less directly discussed are the nature of aesthetic value (*Greater Hippias*) and the motivation of literary creation (*Symposium*). Of the foregoing works, the *Republic* is most often cited, followed by the *Phaedrus* and the brief

Ion; the *Laws* is acknowledged to be a major text but is seldom cited.

Plato's mature writings express (and argue for) the conviction that the true referents of the words in any language are not the perceptible individuals in the world but an unchanging, intelligible reality of some sort, provisionally identified with entities ("Forms" or "Ideas") that would be the bearers of names in an ideal language. It is unclear whether the most detailed versions of this view (expounded in *Phaedo* and the *Republic*) represent a settled conviction of the author, but what seems constant and decisive is the view that what is intelligible in the world is a separate order of reality to which only philosophers have unimpeded access, from which it follows that truth in important matters is to be decided by trained experts, and not by ordinary people or by those whose education is based on literature.

Let us proceed to brief accounts of the relevant passages in (some of) the writings named, in what seems likely today to have been their approximate order of composition: *Apology, Ion, Greater Hippias, Protagoras, Gorgias, Symposium, Republic, Phaedrus, Cratylus, Philebus, Laws.* (References in parentheses are to page numbers and divisions from Stephanus's edition, which are reproduced in most modern editions.)

In the *Apology,* Socrates as spokesman for the philosophical life describes himself as having examined the credentials of the typical representatives of received wisdom: politicians, poets, technicians. The politicians understood nothing; the technicians had technical knowledge and could expound it but foolishly thought that this ability gave them authority on matters beyond their competence. The poets held an intermediate position: however excellent their poems, they could not explain what they meant: "Then I knew that not by wisdom do poets write poetry, but by a sort of genius and inspiration; they are like diviners or soothsayers who also say many fine things, but do not understand the meaning of them" (22c), and (like the technicians) "upon the strength of their poetry they believed themselves to be the wisest of men in other things in which they were not wise" (22d). The themes here mooted but not developed—the insufficiency of unreasoned convictions, the epistemologically puzzling status of inspiration, the danger of unwarranted extensions of influence—recur in Plato's writing. These few sentences in the *Apology* acquire from the familiarity and the programmatic importance of their context a historic significance disproportionate to their length.

The *Ion* elaborates the first two of the *Apology* themes and glances at the third. Ion, a prizewinning "rhapsode"

(i.e., a professional reciter of, and lecturer on, poetry), specializes in Homer: he professes to be uninterested in, and incompetent to expound, any other poet. Socrates says that this is odd, because all poets treat the same topics and all practice the same art, so that an expert on one should be an expert on all, just as a good critic of painting, or sculpture, or music is equally competent to discuss any practitioner of those arts. Since poets are no more expert on the matters they write about than rhapsodes are, Socrates infers that the Muses inspire poets, who inspire rhapsodes, who in turn inspire their audiences, in a way analogous to that in which attractive force is imparted by a magnet to successive bits of metal. The way rhapsodes are moved by poetry and in turn move their audiences suggests to Socrates that poets and their publics alike are out of their minds. Commentators wonder whether this talk of inspiration (repeated in later dialogues but nowhere explained) is meant literally or is a metaphorical way of talking about psychological causality as opposed to rational conviction. The *Ion* does not consider the possibility that interpreting a poet might involve some form of understanding other than that required to assess the accuracy of the poet's information. Readers may note that Socrates commits himself to the view that Homer is the best of poets (530b), a judgment his avowed principles should inhibit him from making otherwise than on the basis of a perfect mastery of every topic Homer deals with.

In the *Greater Hippias* (often suspected, as the *Ion* sometimes is, of being a pastiche in which an unknown author played with Platonic methods and themes), the eponymous protagonist claims to be an expert on literary excellence in general. Socrates nudges him to the conclusion that such excellence always results from the presence of a single property, *to kalon*—the Greek word is more obviously appropriate than its closest English equivalent, "beauty"—and asks him to define the property. Little of relevant interest emerges; most space is devoted to the inadequacies of the formula "what gives pleasure through sight or hearing."

The *Protagoras* is relatively little discussed by students of literary theory, perhaps because the dialogue is focused elsewhere. Protagoras is a professional educator (a "sophist"); his subject is civic excellence. He is relevant here because his preferred method is the criticism of literary texts. In a sample lesson, in which Socrates serves as interlocutor, criticism is directed at a fragment of a poem by Simonides; it is assumed that the criterion of literary excellence is the moral tenability of the lesson conveyed, and the poem cited is said to be self-contradictory, hence not true and therefore not good. But the discussion, in which other sophists join, turns on the problem of establishing what the poem means: by close analysis of the text, by postulating singularities in the author's dialect, by imputing to the author a set of unavowed intentions, and by constructing a moral theory within which the apparent discrepancies may be reconciled, a theory that is plainly that of the critic himself (Socrates) rather than of the author criticized.

Socrates' comment on these proceedings is that quoting poetry in a serious discussion is like having musicians at a party, a vulgar substitute for serious conversation (347c–e). The meaning of a literary text can never be ascertained, since the author is not present to be interrogated, so that such a debate (and the corresponding education) substitutes mere entertainment for a searching investigation of one's own and one's interlocutors' thoughts on the matter at hand. Also of significance for literary theory is a passage in which Protagoras offers his hearers a choice between a reasoned exposition of his views on a certain topic and a story, a myth, in fact, embodying them. In the event, he tells the story and then proceeds to something that is partly an exposition of what the myth is meant to show and partly a development of its themes (320c–324c). It is left to the reader to determine what is conveyed by the story and what is not and to assess, in the light of the ensuing conversation between Socrates and Protagoras, what sorts of lessons can be taught in the form of myth and what sorts cannot. We are also invited, a little later (334c–336e), to reflect on the relative effectiveness of continuous exposition and mutual cross-questioning as means of exposition and clarification. The interest of the dialogue lies in the questions raised and in what the course of the discussion suggests at least as much as in the opinions Socrates expresses.

Like the *Protagoras,* the *Gorgias* examines the rationale of the practice of a public educator, Gorgias. He says he teaches rhetoric as a literary and forensic skill without concern for issues of morality or public policy. This limitation is denounced by Socrates as sinister, a judgment supported by the opinions and character traits that Plato assigns to Gorgias's professed disciples in the dialogue. Socrates also argues that rhetoric as thus taught cannot be dignified as an art (which, like medicine, must proceed on the basis of an objectively identified and systematically pursued benefit), but can only amount to a knack (like cookery) with no other basis than perceived effectiveness and the hope that one can repeat an inexplicable success—success being identifiable in such cases only as the winning of approbation (500e–501c). This argument is parallel to that which is urged against

Ion. Together with the objection to an amoral concern for literary technique, it is repeated and elaborated in the *Phaedrus.* In that dialogue, however, the difference between an art and a knack is affirmed but not expounded, so that students of Plato's literary theory cannot ignore the *Gorgias* altogether.

The *Symposium* is an elaborate literary artifact concerned with love, idealism, creativity, sex, and the effects of alcohol. A small part of the dialogue is very important to our topic, though indirectly so. Socrates, obliged to deliver an encomium on (sexual) love, does so by recounting what he was taught by a (real or imaginary) wise woman (201d–212a). Love is the intermediary between the mortal and the immortal, between want and plenitude; its object is the beautiful (the external manifestation of the good), and its aim is to "give birth in beauty," physically or psychically, to achieve perpetual possession of the desired good by generation of a good of the same kind. Men beget children to perpetuate their stock and to keep their memories green; poets and other creative artists produce works to preserve their conceptions of "wisdom and virtue in general" (209a) and to immortalize themselves in the public mind as parents do in the private memories of their families. Statesmanship, science, and philosophy are more advanced manifestations of the same impulse, culminating in the vision of beauty itself, which somehow bestows some form of immortality. Our interest in this celebrated passage centers on two factors: first, the assimilation of sexuality and creativity to a common complex of aspiration and desire; and second, the attribution of poetry to a double motivation, the wish to avoid oblivion and the wish to perpetuate one's abstract ideals, the underlying implications, one might say, of one's vision of life. The mere submission to and exercise of psychic power (as in the *Ion*) and the bare desire to win applause (as in the *Gorgias*) yield to a more specific and more plausible account of the part played by poetry in the dynamics of human life. Poetry (*poiesis,* "making") itself is taken to be the paradigm of art, making something exist that did not exist before (205b–c). As in the *Apology,* however, the cognitive claims of poetry are judged by its ability to do what philosophical discussion also does, that is, to clarify general ideas.

The *Symposium* leaves us to wonder what, if any, the cognitive or educational function of fictional literature may be. The *Republic* offers an answer. Children and unintellectuals, the former of whom are unable, and the latter at least unwilling, to reason about abstract general ideas, can absorb such notions in an uncritical way if they are embodied in works of fiction, such as stories or plays. Ostensibly, the presentation of this theme in the *Republic* is part of the description of an imaginary city constructed, in effect, to embody the value of "justice" (right and wrong) without explicit regard for other values. It is not argued that value is all-embracing, and it is admitted that the imaginary constitution has no immediate practical bearing. Socrates nowhere says that the principles he applies to literary questions in this special case are universally applicable, but he nowhere says that they are not. In the *Laws* it seems that they are.

The relevant material in the *Republic* is in three sections. The first (374b–412b) is concerned with the upbringing of children chosen for their promise of aptitude for the public service (i.e., displaying exceptional disinterestedness, acuity, and tenacity) and destined for such service. All education of children should take the form of play, and the principal tool of their teaching is stories and songs, in the first instance nursery tales (337a–c). Such fictions are of two kinds: stories of gods and the afterlife, not realistic but presenting ideals (337e–392a), and stories about human beings, not idealizing but realistic (392a–c). For this special group of children, fictions of the former kind must be chosen to present the gods as wholly beneficent and death as benign; fictions of the latter kind are to show actions and characters having such consequences as they really do have (specifically, wickedness must be shown to be incompatible with true happiness, provided, of course, that that is true, as Socrates is sure it is). Thus fiction has a double function: to implant values by presenting ideals and to implant a sense of reality by presenting realistic cases. Socrates then makes a second fundamental distinction, between description and impersonation: the latter induces imaginative identification; the former does not (392c–398b). The children are not to take part in plays or dialogues (or, presumably, read or hear stories using direct speech) in which they impersonate people morally inferior to themselves, since one's sense of who one really is is not to be impaired, though *description* of bad characters is all right. Socrates says that the literature forbidden to these children should not be allowed within the imaginary society at all (398a–b), but he presents no argument to that effect. Nothing is said here about what functions, if any, literature may perform among adults or in other segments of the imaginary city or, a fortiori, in real societies. Nor is any argument adduced to show that any control at all should be exercised by government over literature in real societies—since Socrates and his companions are imagining the whole society, they control it in a way that might not be appropriate to real people legislating for other real people.

Socrates complains, however, that Homer (the keystone of Greek literary curricula) violates the prescriptions for treatment of the gods and the afterlife, and he leaves most readers convinced that he and, by implication, Plato think Homer really is a bad influence on his actual public.

In the second relevant passage in the *Republic* (414b–415d) Socrates proposes that his imaginary society be provided with a myth of its origins, a story that is known to be false but that even its inventors must convince themselves is true. The story is to consist of a metaphorical version of the principles on which the society is indeed founded, since the stability of a society rests on its principles being accepted even by those who cannot grasp the reason for them. This provides us with a new rationale for fiction, though not for the free creation of fiction. The implication is clearly that the founding myths of extant societies perform the same function and were originally devised to that end. Some later literary theorists argue that the entire literature of a nation serves the same purpose.

The other relevant passage in the *Republic* is in its tenth and last book and may represent an afterthought (595a–608b). It purports to reinforce the earlier treatment of drama but does not: it is a general argument against the public performance of any drama in any society and has usually been seen as a polemic against the value assigned to dramatic festivals in Athenian public life. The argument is that plays do not reliably convey truth to their audiences. If (as the *Symposium* argues) the function of poetry is to convey general concepts to its public, then drama is at a third remove from reality (595c–602c): it conveys, not moral qualities themselves, but individual humans in whom those qualities are (presumably imperfectly) embodied; and it presents, not actual people doing actual things, but actors pretending to be people they are not and to do things they are not really doing. The "actions" we seem to see have neither real causes nor real effects. Socrates adds that drama also systematically distorts social reality, in that its characters (typically kings and such) cannot act as such people really do. They have to explain themselves by talking, and reveal their feelings by emoting, in order to maintain the interest of the audience, thus conveying the impression that rational policymaking is a much more volatile and emotional matter than it really is (603c–606e). The only poetry really exempt from this charge would be something like praise poems, such as Pindar's odes. Socrates says he likes poetry but has nothing to set against the objections he has raised other than the pure pleasure that poetry gives; the ball is in the court of the defenders of poetry, who will have to explain what real benefits poetry conveys (606e–607e).

Complex and enigmatic, the *Phaedrus* demands attention but defies summary. In the dialogue, Phaedrus (the addressee of Socrates' speech on love in the *Symposium*, a dialogue of which the reader is constantly reminded) has borrowed a copy of a speech about "love" (in effect, seduction) from its author, Lysias, and is captivated by its prose style, especially by its wording. Socrates responds, directly and by offering two sample speeches of his own, by attacking the implicit approach to prose composition (of which the displacement of love by seduction is a metaphorical equivalent). The lexical virtuosity is conceded but is dismissed as trivial. Lysias's technical method supposes that one can cover a topic in its known completeness, as manifested in extant literature, much as a seducer coldly runs through his repertoire of moves. A true orator lets himself be inspired; the question is, by whom. Lovers and inspired writers are mad, but not all madness is sick and bad: a madness from the Muses "taking hold of a delicate and virgin soul, and there inspiring frenzy, awakens lyrical and all other numbers; with these adorning the myriad actions of ancient heroes for the instruction of posterity" (245a). Technique without this madness is ineffective. As in the *Symposium* love inspires many kinds of creation, so in the *Phaedrus* different forms of madness carry the (immortal) soul up to different visions of reality; and the progeny resulting from impregnation by beauty in the former dialogue are here described as different forms of *writing* (257b–258d).

In the sequel, two themes are developed, both derived from the identification of rhetoric as an "art of influencing the soul through words" (261a): first, that deception is impossible without knowledge of the truth (262a–b), and second, that the construction of a piece of persuasive prose should be determined by the logic of the situation and the topic, not by external features of paragraphing and phrasing (263b–264c). To fulfill these requirements, the speaker must know how to marshal his subject matter into a single system and how to classify it according to its natural articulations (265d–266b)—a summary reference to the methodological preoccupations of Plato's later years. Such a procedure cannot be effectively carried out without a habit of general reflection (269d–270a). The current textbook division of speeches into prologue, narrative, testimony, and so on, mistakes the preconditions of rhetorical practice for the practice itself, as though one were to practice medicine on the basis of one's reading of a textbook without learning how to diagnose actual ailments and treat actual

patients (268a–269c). The true art of rhetoric requires understanding the nature of the soul; knowing what sorts of considerations appeal to what sorts of people, and why; and being able to recognize and exploit the situations to which such knowledge applies. (The idea of general literature, of a text addressed to no one in particular on no particular occasion, is thus downgraded.) "Probability" should be construed, not as conformity to stereotyped expectations, but as what approximates to reality (272e–274a).

Socrates ends by considering the conditions under which writing (as opposed to the interchange of speech) is appropriate, attributing his views to figures from Egyptian mythology. Writing is not an aid to memory (in Plato's writings, "memory" stands for access to the deepest layers of one's mental resources) but a mere reminder; writing cuts words off from thought (274c–275e), from the discourse internal to the mind that recognizes occasions for speech and occasions for silence (276a–e). (A written text never speaks but is never silent.) Writing is fundamentally unserious, like the production of forced, infertile hothouse flowers by contrast with real gardening (276b–277a). Everyone sees that this conclusion is an apology for the written text of the *Phaedrus* itself; commentators add that the *Phaedrus* is a text that yields the structures of its meaning only to repeated readings, an aspect of the written word to which the dialogue does not directly refer.

The *Cratylus* extends the demand for appropriateness in language to the domain of word formation. An appropriate name must correctly combine its minimal meaningful components, but can that principle be applied to the formation of those components themselves? And are some languages better than others, or are imperfect names not names at all? Can a semantic system be internally consistent but erroneous? One can hardly discuss such questions without using a language, but to use a language in discussing them seems to beg the question. This dialogue does not belong to what we think of as the theory of literature, but it is an integral part of Plato's undifferentiated treatment of language use.

In the *Philebus*, a late dialogue concerned with the relation between understanding and enjoyment, there is an incidental comment to the effect that comedy, like tragedy, affords a mixed pleasure: the latter pleases us with distressing events, but in comedy the pleasure of laughing at follies like our own must be partly painful (47d–50e). The affinity of the two dramatic forms (institutionally separate at Athens and written by different people) is not discussed elsewhere in Plato's writings, though the end of the *Symposium* leaves Socrates arguing that the technique for writing both forms should be the same.

Plato's last work, the *Laws,* adds nothing new but reaffirms much and extends the project of controlling literature from the fanciful *Republic* to practical politics. The leading speaker, an "Athenian stranger," is giving advice on the constitution of a proposed new city. We read once more that poets are out of their minds—"like a fountain, he allows to flow out freely whatever comes in" (4.719c)—and it is not suggested that this can be changed. It follows that poets must not show their works to private citizens until they have shown them to the proper authorities (7.801b–d), who are best selected from elderly performers (2.670c–671b). Poetry is meant to give pleasure, certainly, but most people take pleasure in the wrong things (2.658d–660a), and education is a matter of getting people to take pleasure in the right things. The same censorship is imposed on tragedians from out of town, for the lawgivers will not accept competition, and their constitution is itself an "imitation of the best and noblest life," which is what a tragedy really is (7.817a–d).

In general, Plato emphasizes the fascination of poetry, but nowhere does he examine the basis of that charm. He insists on the use of poetry as an educational means but thinks that the conditions of successful creation preclude the poet's use of critical reasoning. It follows that poetry must be subject to control in the public interest. The criterion used, however, is correctness in the exposition of general ideas. The possibility that there might be other cognitive values realizable only in imaginative writing is nowhere mooted, though Plato's own writings exemplify them to the full.

Francis Sparshott

Plato, *The Collected Dialogues of Plato, including the Letters* (ed. Edith Hamilton and Huntington Cairns, 1961), *The Dialogues of Plato* (trans. Benjamin Jowett, 4 vols., 4th ed., 1953), *Oeuvres complètes* (14 vols., 1920–64), *Platonis Opera* (ed. John Burnet, 6 vols., 1899), *Plato's Hippias Major* (ed. and trans. Paul Woodruff, 1982), *Plato's Phaedrus* (ed. and trans. Reginald Hackforth, 1952), *Plato's Protagoras* (ed. and trans. C. C. W. Taylor, 1976), *Plato's Republic* (trans. G. M. A. Grube, 1974), *Plato: The Laws* (trans. Trevor J. Saunders, 1970).

Julia Annas, *An Introduction to Plato's Republic* (1981); J. W. H. Atkins, *Literary Criticism in Antiquity: A Sketch of Its Development* (2 vols., 1934); Gerald F. Else, *Plato and Aristotle on Poetry* (1986); G. R. F. Ferrari, *Listening to the Cicadas: A Study of Plato's Phaedrus* (1987); Hellmut Flashar, *Der Dialog Ion als Zeugnis platonischer Philosophie* (1958); G. M. A. Grube, *The Greek and Roman Critics* (1965); W. K. C. Guthrie, *A History of Greek Philosophy,* vols. 4 and 5 (1975–78); Eric A. Havelock, *Preface to Plato* (1963); R. F. Stalley, *An Introduction to Plato's Laws* (1983); E. N. Tigerstedt, *Plato's Idea of Poetical Inspiration* (1969).

POE, EDGAR ALLAN

Edgar Allan Poe (1809–49), poet, critic, and short-story writer, was a controversial figure in the literary world of antebellum America. He worked as an editor and contributor to magazines in several American cities, including Richmond, New York, and Philadelphia. His lifelong ambition was to found and edit his own magazine, an outlet that would have granted him financial security and artistic control in what he deemed an antagonistic literary marketplace. Poe's challenge to moralistic strictures against literature, his confrontations with the New England literary establishment, and his caustic critical style won him many enemies. Some readers too easily identified Poe with his deranged narrators, a tendency that made plausible the misrepresentations of the Reverend Rufus Griswold, his literary executor. Griswold's stinging memoir, published just after Poe's death, launched the "Poe legend." A combination of half-truths and outright fabrications about Poe's personal habits and conduct, Griswold's portrait almost irrevocably damaged his reputation. Rediscovery by French authors—CHARLES BAUDELAIRE, Stéphane Mallarmé, PAUL VALÉRY—partially rehabilitated his image, a process that preceded his acceptance in American literary circles.

Nearly all Poe's criticism was written as essays and reviews for the magazines for which he toiled. Despite their occasional nature, these pieces contributed significantly to the history of American literary criticism in a number of genres, most notably the short story. His exploration of the formal nature of the short prose tale, drawing upon ARISTOTLE's theory of plot and structure, stressed unity of tone. His comments on poetry asserted less influence, largely because Poe seemed to diminish the importance of all poetic forms except for the short lyric. In all genres, Poe applied the tools of the analytic critic by subjecting individual passages and specific works to rational scrutiny.

That mode of close analysis appealed to Poe's own self-conscious, deliberate view of art and the creative process. "The Philosophy of Composition" (1846), written to explain how he composed "The Raven" (1845), counters the Romantic assumption that the poet works in a "fine frenzy" of "ecstatic intuition" (*Essays* 14). Poe offers instead a painstaking and procedural account of poetic creation. Whatever sleight of hand he uses in his highly rational rehearsal of the steps followed by the practicing poet, the essay is noteworthy for the centrality of the theory of unified effect, the conscious choice of a consistent emotional atmosphere that takes primacy over incident, character, and versification. In this essay and in "The Poetic Principle" (1850), he refined ideas that he had previously presented in a review of Longfellow's *Ballads and Other Poems* (1842), the germ of his evolving notion that aesthetic appreciation, rather than didactic purpose, was a chief literary value. He also offered his oft-quoted pronouncement that the death of a beautiful woman is "the most poetical topic in the world" (*Essays* 19). Stressing in "The Poetic Principle" the emotional effect the literary text has on the reader, Poe elaborated ideas implicit in the Longfellow review: the aspiration for pure forms of beauty, embodied in the feminine ideal, reflects the spiritual yearnings of mortal human nature. He claimed that poetry works to achieve "an elevating excitement of the Soul" (93), a transport, similar to one's response to the sublime, that could not be long sustained or satisfied through the imperfection of earthly forms. Thus, he further asserted that a long poem is "a flat contradiction in terms" (71). His insistence that a poem's affective impact was enhanced by music or "sweet sound" led him to address unique forms of versification in theory and in practice, as his essay "The Rationale of Verse" (1848) indicates.

Poe's pronouncements on prose fiction remain scattered in a range of magazine pieces. His review of Robert Montgomery Bird's *Sheppard Lee* (1836) offers penetrating comments on supernatural fiction, on the artful combination of verisimilitude and improbability required of a skilled practitioner in that genre. His review of *The Old Curiosity Shop* (1841), drawing upon a standard eighteenth-century distinction between genius and talent, praised the apparent ease with which Dickens fashioned plot and setting without recourse to contrivances of plot. The smooth melding of character and setting, the adaptation of human figures to their fictional environment, was important to Poe, as is evident in his review of James Fenimore Cooper's *Wyandotte* (1843), which takes issue with American authors for their facile portrayals of American scenery.

His reviews of Nathaniel Hawthorne's tales offer, however, his most sustained views of the genre of prose fiction. Approaching the tale as a painter or a landscape architect might approach his craft, Poe discusses the importance of "design," the accommodation of heterogeneous elements into a "unity of effect or impression"

(*Essays* 571). Poe celebrates the short prose tale as much as his New England contemporary's artistry. His essay "Tale Writing—Nathaniel Hawthorne" (1847), in contrast, scores his subject's lack of originality and his penchant for allegory. Only when allegory is suggestive, that is, when it ceases "to enforce a truth" (582) and offers an unobtrusive "under-current" of meaning, are the "proper uses" of prose fiction served. Like many Romantic authors, Poe objected to allegory, especially when characters and events seemed to function in subservience to a system of abstract ideas.

Whatever the origins of Poe's critical principles—probably a combination of English and German sources (SAMUEL TAYLOR COLERIDGE, the common-sense philosophers, A. W. Schlegel, perhaps IMMANUEL KANT and FRIEDRICH SCHILLER)—his influence has been immense. His reviews of Hawthorne mark him as the first significant theorist of the modern short story; indeed, his notions that every word or phrase in a story is crucial to its impact and that the brevity of the short story could concentrate "the immense force derivable from *totality*" of effect (*Essays* 572), are overt or latent principles in many twentieth-century examples of the form. His influence on theories of poetry has been less powerful, although his celebration of pure forms of beauty and his opposition to the "heresy of *The Didactic*" (*Essays* 75) laid a foundation for champions of aestheticism and symbolism. His citation and close reading of key passages from works he reviewed suggest some affinity with the New Critics. These various strands of influence, affirming that a work of art is a rational construct, suggest an image of Poe as a conscious craftsman far different from that in Griswold's caricature.

It is thus paradoxical that the principle of authorial control, apparently championed in Poe's critical *oeuvre,* has been so vigorously challenged by theorists who cite Poe as an important precursor of postmodern tendencies. Apparently echoing nineteenth-century Continental interest in Poe, his name has been once again returned to contemporary critical discourse through French mediation, most notably through JACQUES LACAN's "Seminar on 'The Purloined Letter.'" Together with JACQUES DERRIDA's response, this essay initiated a series of theoretical readings that explore Poe's use of doubling and his implicit meditations on the nature of signification. From a deconstructionist perspective, the detective tales, *The Narrative of Arthur Gordon Pym,* and other stories are metafictional texts that disclose the problematic nature of writing and authorship.

Current theoretical approaches have brought renewed attention to issues in Poe's writings that had been consigned to the margins of his critical discourse. His comments on plagiarism and originality, his "tomahawking" critical style, his wordplay and parodic tendencies, his interest in secret writing and handwriting, and his compilation of periodical "filler" items for the "Pinakidia" (1836) and "Marginalia" (1844–46, 1848–49) reflect characteristics of a writer deeply immersed in the critical practices and controversies of his own time. In direct response to his immediate concerns as a reviewer and critic, William Carlos Williams asserts, Poe developed a firm sense of literary construction and method: "His concern, the apex of his immaculate attack, was to detach a 'method' from the smear of common usage—it is the work of nine tenths of his criticism" (221).

Kent P. Ljungquist

See also AMERICAN THEORY AND CRITICISM: NINETEENTH CENTURY.

Edgar Allan Poe, *The Complete Works of Edgar Allan Poe* (ed. James A. Harrison, 17 vols., 1902), *Essays and Reviews* (ed. G. Richard Thompson, 1984), *Selections from the Critical Writings of Edgar Allan Poe* (ed. F. C. Prescott, 1909).

Michael Allen, *Poe and the British Magazine Tradition* (1969); Margaret Alterton, *The Origins of Poe's Critical Theory* (1925); Robert D. Jacobs, *Poe: Journalist and Critic* (1969); George Kelly, "Poe's Theory of Beauty," *American Literature* 27 (1956), "Poe's Theory of Unity," *Philological Quarterly* 37 (1958); Sidney P. Moss, *Poe's Literary Battles: The Critic in the Context of His Literary Milieu* (1963); John P. Muller and William J. Richardson, eds., *The Purloined Poe: Lacan, Derrida, and Psychoanalytic Reading* (1988); Edd Winfield Parks, *Edgar Allan Poe as a Literary Critic* (1964); William Carlos Williams, *In the American Grain* (1956).

POSTCOLONIAL CULTURAL STUDIES

Postcolonial (cultural) studies (PCS) constitutes a major intervention in the widespread revisionist project that has impacted academia since the 1960s—together with such other counterdiscourses that are gaining academic and disciplinary recognition as CULTURAL STUDIES, women's studies, Chicano studies, African-American studies, gender studies, and ethnic studies. Postcolonial (mostly literary) studies is one of the latest "tempests" in a postist world replacing *Prospero's Books* (the title of Peter Greenaway's 1991 film) with a Calibanic viewpoint.

The beginning of this new project can be approximately located in the year 1952, when the academy was still more attendant to works such as Samuel Beckett's *En attendant Godot (Waiting for Godot)* and in anticipation of Roland Barthes's *Le Degré zéro de l'écriture* (1953, *Writing Degree Zero*). In other words, the project of validating modernism, a project so heavily indebted to "primitive" (other) cultures and, directly or indirectly, to colonialism, was on the verge of being institutionalized. In the meantime, the connection between colonialism, modernism, and STRUCTURALISM has been fairly well established and has provoked a similar awareness of the considerably more problematic correlation between the postmodern, poststructural, and postcolonial.

It was precisely during this decade of the 1950s that a great shift occurred. This was the period of the end of France's involvement in Indochina (Dien Bien Phu), the Algerian war, the Mau Mau uprisings in Kenya, the dethroning of King Farouk in Egypt. It was the time when JEAN-PAUL SARTRE broke with Albert Camus for reasons intrinsic to colonial studies, namely, opposing attitudes toward Algeria. In 1950 Aimé Césaire's pamphlet on colonialism, *Discours sur le colonialisme,* appeared. Two years later, Fidel Castro gave his speech "History Shall Absolve Me," and FRANTZ FANON published *Black Skin, White Masks*. In London the Faber and Faber publishing house, for which T. S. Eliot was a reader at the time, issued Nigerian Amos Tutuola's *The Palm Wine Drinker,* which led to "curiosity" about Anglo-African writing. It was the year the French demographer Alfred Sauvy coined the term "Third World," a term scrutinized ever since. Some see this term as derogative (mainly in the English-speaking world), while the term has become a staple in the French-, German-, and Spanish-speaking worlds.

Also in the 1950s, the founders of colonialist discourse, Fanon, Césaire, and Albert Memmi, published their works, which became foundational texts of colonialist discourse some decades later. In 1958 the Western narrative paradigm in which an author-anthropologist fabricates the other was seriously questioned in Chinua Achebe's novel *Things Fall Apart,* which clearly illustrates the sensationalism and inaccuracy of Western anthropology and history. The 1960s then saw major developments in the critical formulation of the problematic, with the appearance of Fanon's *The Wretched of the Earth* (1961), including Sartre's preface, which legitimized for many the issues raised and postulated the Western "Manichean delirium" (good versus bad, black versus white, etc.). In Fanon's book Western racism is seen as a form of scapegoating that permits the West to cling to its power and leads to violent reaction by the colonized. A year before, the Caribbean novelist George Lamming had given us his Calibanic reading of a classical text, William Shakespeare's *The Tempest,* in *The Pleasures of Exile* (1960). The 1970s then saw further increases in colonialist studies with Roberto Fernández Retamar's "Caliban" essays (1971 and 1986) and EDWARD W. SAID's *Orientalism* (1978), which most likely is the central text in the establishment of PCS. While Said could still deplore that the literary establishment had declared the serious study of imperialism off limits, the 1980s established the centrality of the colonialist debate with its focus on how imperialism affected the colonies and how the former colonies then wrote back in an attempt to correct Western views.

"To be colonized," according to Walter Rodney, "is to be removed from history." And Memmi, defining the situation of the colonized, claims that "the most serious blow suffered by the colonized is being removed from history" (*Colonizer* 91). Postcolonial writing, then, is the slow, painful, and highly complex means of fighting one's way into European-made history, in other words, a process of dialogue and necessary correction. That this writing back into history becomes institutionalized precisely at the moment when POSTMODERNISM questions the category of history should make us think about the implications of postmodernism in relation to the postcolonial.

The designation "postcolonial" has been used to describe writing and reading practices grounded in colonial experience occurring outside of Europe but as a consequence of European expansion and exploitation of "other" worlds. Postcolonial literature is constituted in counterdiscursive practices. Postcolonial writing is also related to other concepts that have resulted from internal colonialization, such as the repression of minority groups: Chicanos in the United States, *Gastarbeiter* in Germany, Beurs in France, and so on. It is similarly related to women voicing concern and frustration over colonialization by men, or a "double" colonialization when women of color are concerned. Among the large nomenclature, which includes so-called Third World literature, minority discourse, resistance literature, response literature (writing back or rewriting the Western "classics"), subaltern studies, othering discourse, colonialist discourse, and so on, the term "postcolonial" (sometimes hyphenated, sometimes not) has gained notoriety in recent years and clearly has replaced "Commonwealth literature" or "Commonwealth studies." It may even be on its way toward replacing "Third World literature" or "studies."

PCS is not a discipline but a distinctive problematic that can be described as an abstract combination of all the problems inherent in such newly emerging fields as minority discourse, Latin American studies, African studies, Caribbean studies, Third World studies (as the comparative umbrella term), *Gastarbeiterliteratur,* Chicano studies, and so on, all of which participated in the significant and overdue recognition that "minority" cultures are actually "majority" cultures and that hegemonized Western (Euro-American) studies have been unduly overprivileged for political reasons. The Australians Bill Ashcroft, Gareth Griffiths, and Helen Tiffin in their influential *The Empire Writes Back: Theory and Practice in Post-Colonial Literatures* (1989) define "postcolonial" "to cover all the culture affected by the imperial process from the moment of colonization to the present day" (2). This undoubtedly makes PCS an enormously large field, particularly since these critics see literature as offering one of the most important ways to express these new perceptions. In other words, PCS is the study of the totality of "texts" (in the largest sense of "text") that participate in hegemonizing other cultures and the study of texts that write back to correct or undo Western hegemony, or what GAYATRI CHAKRAVORTY SPIVAK has called "our ideological acceptance of error as truth" (*In Other* 109). The emphasis, therefore, is bound to be on the political and ideological rather than the aesthetic. By no means, however, does this exclude the aesthetic, but it links definitions of aesthetics with the ideology of the aesthetic, with hegemony, with what Louis Althusser has termed the Ideological State Apparatus, and connected with these issues, it obviously has to question the genesis of the Western canon. In other words, PCS is instrumental in curricular debates and demands a multicultural curriculum. It also perceives the former disciplines as participating in the colonizing process and is therefore bound to cross borders and be interdisciplinary. We cannot disconnect postcolonial studies from previous disciplines, nor can we attribute a definable core to such a "field." Cultural and postcolonial studies are deliberately not disciplinary but rather inquisitive activities that question the inherent problems of disciplinary studies; they "discipline the disciplines," as Patrick Brantlinger said about cultural studies.

In a way, cultural and postcolonial studies are what comparative literature always wanted or claimed to be but in reality never was, due to a deliberate and almost desperate clinging to Eurocentric values, canons, cultures, and languages. The closest parallels in the many debates within the field of comparative literature from the 1950s and 1960s are those involving the French comparatist René Etiemble, who pleaded for an open and planetary comparativism that would address questions of coloniality and examine literatures outside the Euro-American center. No discipline is unaffected by the colonialist paradigm, and every discipline, from anthropology to cartography, needs to be decolonized.

The word "postcolonial" shows up in a variety of journal titles since the mid-1980s but is used as a full title in a collection of interviews with a leading Indo-American critic, Gayatri Chakravorty Spivak, *The Post-Colonial Critic* (1990), as a subtitle to the book by Ashcroft, Griffiths, and Tiffin, *The Empire Writes Back: Theory and Practice in Post-Colonial Literatures* (1989), and again in a subtitle by the Canadian and Australian critics Ian Adam and Helen Tiffin, *Past the Last Post: Theorizing Post-Colonialism and Post-Modernism* (1990), thus showing clearly the preoccupation with the term in discourse from British Commonwealth countries. Benita Parry, one of the leading critics of the various attempts to come to terms with the colonialist formation, still speaks of colonial discourse. The term was probably used for the first time by Australian Simon During in his 1985 *Landfall* essay. Max Dorsinville had used "post-European" already in 1974, while Helen Tiffin used "commonwealth literature" still in 1984 but switched to the new term by 1987. By now, and largely due to Australian efforts, the terms "postcolonial literature" and "postcolonial culture" are well established.

This shift in terminology clearly is due to a wave of various postist constructions, such as "postindustrial," "poststructuralism," "postmodernism," "post-Marxism," and even "postfeminism." However, it hardly can make sense to speak of, say, South African literature as postcolonial, even though it has many or most of the characteristics we associate with postcolonial literature. Needless to say, the term has a jargonizing quality and lacks precision. Postist terminology in general is to be understood as a signpost for new emphases in literary and cultural studies, indicative of the long-felt move from the margin (minorities) to the center that is also the major contribution of Derridean DECONSTRUCTION. Both came into being in the wake of developments since Charles de Gaulle's referendum and the new emphasis on countries that had gained flag-independence in the 1960s. Robert Young points out that it is significant that Sartre, Althusser, JACQUES DERRIDA, JEAN-FRANÇOIS LYOTARD, and HÉLÈNE CIXOUS were all either born in Algeria or personally involved with the events of the war (1).

Though seldom identical with the other "post"—postmodernism—PCS is nevertheless involved in a broad network of conflicting attempts at intervention into the master narrative of Western discourse. It is part of postal politics and a series of inventions and interventions that the Western post(al) network suddenly seems to be assimilating. The urge of postmodernism is to incorporate or coopt almost everything, including its oppositional other. Even the postcolonial paradigm is not free of such absorption, so that one can already speak of the postmodern colonialization of the postcolonial. To preserve in this multifarious network some unitary sense without falling prey to homogenizing tendencies that underlie most theories, one may assume that the postcolonial critics and writers basically claim that the term "postcolonial" covers the cultures affected by the imperial process; in other words, postcolonial critics inevitably homogenize as "imperialist" critics did before them. The difference is that they typically profess an awareness of the problematics to a degree the others did not.

We can single out various schools of postcolonial criticism, those who homogenize and see postcolonial writing as resistance (Said, Barbara Harlow, Abdul JanMohamed, Spivak) and those who point out that there is no unitary quality to postcolonial writing (Homi Bhabha, Arun P. Mukherjee, Parry). Among the key terms and main figures associated with postcolonial discourse one often finds the following: "Orientalism" (Said); "minority discourse" (JanMohamed); "subaltern studies" (Spivak and Ranajit Guha); "resistance literature" (Harlow); "The Empire Writes Back" (Tiffin, Ashcroft, Stephen Slemon, During); "Third World literature" (Peter Nazareth, FREDRIC JAMESON, Georg M. Gugelberger); "hybridity," "mimicry," and "civility" (Bhabha). Generally speaking, the term "postcolonial" is used when texts in various forms of English are explored and when Canada and Australia are brought into the debate, while "Third World literature" is used more by those who approach the problem from a comparative point of view. Marxists also tend to use the term "Third World," while non-Marxists often accuse them of using pejorative language.

Diana Bryden (*Past the Last Post* 193) distinguishes postcolonial criticism by such writers as Ashcroft, Griffiths, and Tiffin (*Empire Writes Back*) from that developed by the U.S.-based Jameson, Henry Louis Gates, and Spivak. The main dividing line at present appears to be a postcolonial discourse by those who come from a Euro-American literary and critical background (Jameson, Harlow, Gugelberger), those who come originally from so-called Third World places but reside in the West (Spivak, Said, JanMohamed, Bhabha, Nazareth), and those from Third World countries adamantly opposed to the homogenizing tendencies of some of these critics (Mukherjee, Aija Ahmad).

Another way of ordering this manifold discourse could be via reference to the foundational texts: Fanonists such as JanMohamed, Said, Bhabha, and Parry; Calibanic critics such as Retamar and José David Saldívar founding their discursive practices on José Marti's concept of "Our America"; empire-ists such as Tiffin and Ashcroft; and Marxist deconstructionists such as Spivak.

PCS is foremost a shift in emphasis, a strategy of reading, an attempt to point out what was missing in previous analyses, and an attempt to rewrite and to correct. Any account of PCS will have to come to terms with the (equally problematical) concept of postcoloniality. Kwame Anthony Appiah has said that "postcoloniality is the condition of what we might ungenerously call a *comprador* intelligentsia: a relatively small, Western-style, Western-trained group of writers and thinkers, who mediate the trade in cultural commodities of world capitalism at the periphery" (348). In other words, PCS is not really performed by those who have been colonized and gained problematical flag-independence, nor is it the discourse that pushes former marginalized subjects into the center, as is often assumed in the many canon debates. PCS is a dialogue leading to the significant insight that the Western paradigm (Manichean and binary) is highly problematical. In other words, PCS does not necessarily imply the change that Western and non-Western intellectuals foresee but remains constituted in a particular class of well-educated people who should not confuse their theoretical insights with change. Though it is a correcting instrument that believes in facilitating change, no change is likely to occur with academic debates. Postcolonial discourse problematizes one face of the response to former Western hegemonic discourse paradigms, but it does not abolish anything; rather, it replaces one problematic with another. As Parry states, "The labour of producing a counter-discourse displacing imperialism's dominative system of knowledge rests with those engaged in developing a critique from outside its cultural hegemony" (55).

While postmodern literature tends to postulate the death of history, postcolonial writing insists on the historical as the foundational and all-embracing. Similarly, postmodernism refuses any representational quality, though the representational mandate remains strong in postcolonial writing and at times even relies on the topological. Postcolonial critical activity is "the de-imperialization of apparently monolithic European forms, ontologies, and epistemologies" (Ashcroft, Griffiths, and Tiffin 153). If postmodernism is identified with the "cultural logic of late capitalism" (Jameson), postcolonialism can be conceptualized as the last bulwark against an encroaching total capitalism. In a sense it is the only true counterdiscourse we are left with, truly "past the last post."

In conclusion, we must reemphasize that despite apparent similarities between postmodern and postcolonial modes of writing (particularly in cross-cultural texts by, for example, Salman Rushdie, J. M. Coetzee, Wilson Harris, and Gabriel García Márquez), the postmodern aestheticization of politics only appears radical (a kind of radical chic-ism) but is essentially conservative and tends to prolong the imperial, while the postcolonial frequently appears conservative or is bound to use a conventional mimetic mode (related to realism and its many debates) but is essentially radical in the sense of demanding change.

Georg M. Gugelberger

See also FRANTZ FANON, POSTMODERNISM, EDWARD W. SAID, and GAYATRI CHAKRAVORTY SPIVAK.

Ian Adam and Helen Tiffin, eds., *Past the Last Post: Theorizing Post-Colonialism and Post-Modernism* (1990); Aija Ahmad, "Jameson's Rhetoric of Otherness and the 'National Allegory,'" *Social Text* 17 (1987); Malek Alloula, *The Colonial Harem* (1986); Kwame Anthony Appiah, "Is the Post- in Postmodernism the Post- in Postcolonial?" *Critical Inquiry* 17 (1991); Bill Ashcroft, Gareth Griffiths, and Helen Tiffin, *The Empire Writes Back: Theory and Practice in Post-Colonial Literatures* (1989); Homi K. Bhabha, "Of Mimicry and Man: The Ambivalence of Colonial Discourse," *October* 28 (1984), "The Other Question," *Screen* 24 (1983); Patrick Brantlinger, *Crusoe's Footprints: Cultural Studies in Britain and America* (1990); Max Dorsinville, *Caliban Without Prospero* (1974); Simon During, "Postmodernism or Postcolonialism," *Landfall* 39 (1985); Terry Eagleton, Fredric Jameson, and Edward W. Said, *Nationalism, Colonialism, and Literature* (1990); Frantz Fanon, *Les Damnés de la terre* (1961, *The Wretched of the Earth*, trans. Constance Farrington, 1968), *Peau noire, masques blancs* (1952, *Black Skin, White Masks,* trans. Charles Lam Markmann, 1967); Roberto Fernández Retamar, *"Caliban" and Other Essays* (trans. Edward Baker, 1989); Henry Louis Gates, ed., *Race, Writing, and Difference* (1986); Georg M. Gugelberger, "Decolonizing the Canon: Considerations of Third World Literature," *New Literary History* 22 (1991); Ranajit Guha and Gayatri Chakravorty Spivak, *Selected Subaltern Studies* (1988); Dorothy Hammond and Alta Jablow, *The Africa That Never Was: Four Centuries of British Writing about Africa* (1970); Barbara Harlow, *Resistance Literature* (1987); Fredric Jameson, "Third World Literature in the Era of Multinational

Capitalism," *Social Text* 15 (1986); Abdul JanMohamed, "Humanism and Minority Literature: Toward a Definition of Counter-hegemonic Discourse," *Boundary 2* 12–13 (1984), *Manichean Aesthetics: The Politics of Literature in Colonial Africa* (1983); Albert Memmi, *The Colonizer and the Colonized* (1965); Arun P. Mukherjee, "Whose Post-Colonialism and Whose Postmodernism?" *World Literature Written in English* 30 (1990); Peter Nazareth, *The Third World Writer: His Social Responsibility* (1978); Benita Parry, "Problems in Current Theories of Colonial Discourse," *Oxford Literary Review* 9 (1987); Edward W. Said, *Orientalism* (1978), "Orientalism Reconsidered," *Cultural Critique* 1 (1985), "Representing the Colonized: Anthropology's Interlocutors," *Critical Inquiry* 15 (1989); José David Saldívar, *The Dialectics of Our America: Genealogy, Cultural Critique, and Literary History* (1991); Stephen Slemon and Helen Tiffin, eds., *After Europe: Critical Theory and Post-Colonial Writing* (1989); Gayatri Chakravorty Spivak, *In Other Worlds: Essays in Cultural Politics* (1987), *The Post-Colonial Critic: Interviews, Strategies, Dialogues* (ed. Sarah Harasym, 1990); Helen Tiffin, "Post-Colonial Literatures and Counter-Discourse," *Critical Approaches to the New Literatures in English* (ed. Dieter Riemenschneider, 1989); Robert Young, *White Mythologies: Writing History and the West* (1990).

POSTMODERNISM

The term "postmodernism" was first used in reference to architecture as early as 1947, spurring a fruitful debate among architects that has not disappeared (Jencks). Literary critics, most notably Harry Levin, Irving Howe, Leslie Fiedler, Frank Kermode, and Ihab Hassan, began to use the term in the 1960s to distinguish the post–World War II experimental fiction of Samuel Beckett, Jorge Luis Borges, John Barth, Donald Barthelme, Thomas Pynchon, and others from the classics of high modernism. From the start, postmodernism spurred skepticism (had not James Joyce, Franz Kafka, and the various avant-gardes already performed all the tricks now called postmodern?) and antagonistic evaluation. The Old Left (Howe) and the critical establishment (Levin) deplored the new writers' lack of high seriousness; their apparent contempt for the well-made, unified literary work; and their addiction to popular culture. The linchpin of modernism, according to critics of the 1950s and 1960s, was art's autonomy from the sordid daily concerns of a bourgeois, commercial culture. The artist (almost always male in this modernist vision of heroic alienation) exiled himself from ordinary life to create a useless, disin-

terested art object. This art was potentially revolutionary in the purity of its contempt for the given and in its creation of alternative worlds *ex nihilo*. Only the distance afforded by exile and autonomy maintained art's critical and oppositional edge. Postmodern art seemed to capitulate to the dominant culture, which was itself now designated postindustrial or postmodern by various writers. Thus, discussions of postmodernism considered not only changes in artistic style but also the extent to which society itself had changed and the fact that the contemporary artwork's relation to politics was problematic in new ways.

Fiedler's slogan "Cross the border, close the gap" (17) exemplified the determination of postmodernism's champions to pull art back into the maelstrom of daily life. Literary criticism, as well as its new colleague literary theory, began to explore the complex relations between the artwork and its social contexts. Generally speaking, the formal analysis of the artwork in isolation yielded to an exploration of the social determinants of the work and to the ideological impact the work had on its audience. (This shift took some twenty years, with 1965–85 the key period of transition.) The postmodernists argue that the belief that intellectuals and artists can enjoy an autonomy from capitalism is both illusionary and sterile artistically and politically: illusionary because the very materials of their work (language, images) come from the culture and because, even more radically, the individual creator is permeated with, even constituted by, that culture; sterile because the purity of the alienated artist forecloses access to the energies and disputes that are lived in the culture while also severing any connection to an audience beyond the artistic elite. The modernist artist is left high and dry.

A cultural politics accompanied this shift in critical paradigms. Against the traditional Marxist emphasis on economic issues and the liberal concern with legally guaranteed equality, the New Left and the liberation movements it inspired (feminism, gay and lesbian activism, post–Civil Rights racial politics) insisted that cultural practices—common linguistic usage, media images, educational curricula and techniques, for example— were crucial sites of oppression and of potentially transformative struggle. The playful and anarchistic "street theater" of May 1968 in Paris and of the Yippies in America was linked to similar antics (parody, hyperbole, disruptive narrative techniques) in postmodern novelists. The exuberant valuing of heterogeneity over unity in 1960s radicalism foreshadowed postmodern theory's later concern with "difference." The new art and the new politics ignored the old distinction between high and low art. (The universal love of rock music by the young contributed greatly to this embrace of the popular.) Postmodern art aspired to use the affective power of images much as popular culture does. And this postmodern populism opened the door to heterogeneous voices, mixed genres, and other breaches of decorum.

The rise of literary theory, particularly of theory inspired by JACQUES DERRIDA, ROLAND BARTHES, JACQUES LACAN, JULIA KRISTEVA, and MICHEL FOUCAULT, brought postmodernism from the streets and from the novel into the academy. At first, these French theorists were not associated with postmodernism, but the publication of JEAN-FRANÇOIS LYOTARD's *Postmodern Condition* (1979) made the two nearly synonymous. (The accuracy of this labeling is still a matter of dispute.) Lyotard emphasizes the antifoundational and antiholistic aspects of French theory, as well as its hostility to eternal, metaphysical truths or realities and to grand narratives (theories that provide totalizing explanations). "I define *postmodern* as incredulity toward metanarratives," Lyotard writes (xxiv). He proposes a postmodern world in which decisions are made on the basis of local conditions and are applicable only in that limited context. Individuals participate in a multitude of such localities and the lessons, beliefs, and practices of one site are not transferable to any other. Lyotard celebrates this multiplicity of "language games" (xxiv) and offers ceaseless experimentation in all these games as the highest good.

JÜRGEN HABERMAS and FREDRIC JAMESON led the counterattack against Lyotard's celebration of postmodernism in ways reminiscent of Levin's and Howe's earlier worries. Habermas insists that a complete immersion in the local gives us no way to judge it and is thus doomed to accommodation with the given. (He offers "the model of unconstrained consensus formation in a communication community" [295] as the normative criterion for such judging.) Jameson similarly laments a lack of distance between postmodern art and theory and the late capitalist society that generates it. While Habermas believes we must retain modernity's (the Enlightenment's) dream of emancipation through reason, Jameson argues that we need an art capable of representing the complex realities of a global economic order that exploits the vast majority. The debate here focuses on the political consequences of French theory, whether it actually disrupts Western society by advocating local, varied, heterogeneous "difference" against the unifying, identity-obsessed practices of the massive states and bureaucracies that characterize the contemporary West. What the French writers and their leftist critics (ED-WARD W. SAID and Terry Eagleton, as well as Jameson and Habermas) share in common is a conviction that language, images, and other cultural phenomena are as central, if not more central, to the production and maintenance of contemporary social order as economic or political processes. The French sociologist Jean Baudrillard has argued that we enter a postmodern world once it is the production of images and information, not the production of material goods, that determines who holds power. This "linguistic turn" in social and literary theory explains the centrality of art to all current versions of an oppositional politics. But the leftist critics of French theory almost always accuse it of having no model of political action beyond anarchistic linguistic play, and their work continues to struggle with the Brechtian question how to move from art to collective action.

Given this contested relation of postmodern (French) theory to politics, relations between feminism and postmodernism have been wary. The male theorists have paid little explicit attention to the issues raised by feminist theory. Many feminists have been impatient with the abstruse philosophical arguments surrounding epistemological foundations and have concentrated instead on more historically informed studies of the social conditions and biases of particular knowledge claims. Yet such work ultimately derives from French theory, as does feminism's appropriation of Derrida's account of Western thought's hostility to and fascination with the other, Foucault's work on the social constitution and discipline of sexual identity, and Lacan's account of female sexuality. However, feminists, like members of the Left, usually want to preserve some kind of distance from the dominant culture, a distance that French theory often denies is achievable.

Discussion during the 1980s of postmodernism in the arts focused on issues of style and of periodization. Critics such as Ihab Hassan, Hal Foster, Charles Jencks, Linda Hutcheon, and Brian McHale attempt to describe the stylistic hallmarks of postmodernism. Artists and critics influenced by Baudrillard show a concern with the images in circulation in the culture and their recoding, reuse, and recycling in art. Unlike the heroic modernist, who created works out of pure imagination, the postmodern artist works with cultural givens, trying to manipulate them in various ways (parody, pastiche, collage, juxtaposition) for various ends. The ultimate aim is to appropriate these materials in such a way as to avoid being utterly dominated by them. The photographer Sherrie Levine's "appropriations" exemplify this art most vividly, but these terms have also proved useful in criticism of such novelists as Salman Rushdie, Gabriel García Márquez, Kathy Acker, and Angela Carter.

Jameson and David Harvey try to link these stylistic features of contemporary art to a more general account of the current social order, adopting a fairly traditional Marxist notion that art reflects the material realities of the day. But as Jameson acknowledges and as Andreas Huyssen's work makes dramatically clear, the widespread use of the term "postmodern" has led to a crisis in the whole notion of historical and artistic periods. Every distinguishing feature of postmodernism can be located in an era prior to our own. Periodization begins to seem a rhetorical creation, a way of constructing a historical "other" that allows us to define a desirable present by contrasting it to a past (or to denigrate the present for being inferior to a past). Within such a view, what is distinctive about postmodernism is not something new but our attention to and interest in features of the past that until recently were most often ignored. Postmodernism, then, is just part of the very complex rereading of history taking place in the current climate of a critical questioning of the Western tradition. Paradoxically, most of the materials for a radical questioning can be found in the tradition itself if we look in different places (noncanonical works) or with new eyes at familiar places. But there is also a concomitant interest in non-Western voices that offer different perspectives on the West's image of itself and its past.

In sum, postmodernism is best understood as marking the site of several related, but not identical, debates among intellectuals in the last four decades of the twentieth century. These debates revolve around the relation of artworks to social context, the relation of art and of theory to political action and to the dominant social order, the relation of cultural practices to the transformation or maintenance of society in all its aspects, the relation of the collapse of traditional philosophical foundations to the possibility of critical distance from and effective critique of the status quo, the relation of an image-dominated consumer society to artistic practice, and the future of a Western tradition that now appears more heterogeneous than previously thought even while it appears insufficiently tolerant of (open to) multiplicity. At the very least, postmodernism highlights the multiplication of voices, questions, and conflicts that has shattered what once seemed to be (although it never really was) the placid unanimity of the great tradition and of the West that gloried in it.

John McGowan

See also FRENCH THEORY AND CRITICISM: 5. 1945–1968 and 6. 1968 AND AFTER, JÜRGEN HABERMAS, FREDRIC JAMESON, JEAN-FRANÇOIS LYOTARD, and MARXIST THEORY AND CRITICISM: 2. STRUCTURALIST MARXISM.

Jean Baudrillard, *Simulacres et simulation* (1980, *Simulacra and Simulations,* trans. Paul Foss, Paul Patton, and Philip Beitchman, 1983); Leslie A. Fiedler, *What Was Literature? Class Culture and Mass Society* (1982); Hal Foster, ed., *The Anti-Aesthetic: Essays on Postmodern Culture* (1983), *Recodings: Art, Spectacle, Cultural Politics* (1985); Jürgen Habermas, *Der Philosophische Diskurs der Moderne* (1985, *The Philosophical Discourse of Modernity,* trans. Frederick G. Lawrence, 1987); David Harvey, *The Condition of Postmodernity: An Inquiry Into the Origins of Cultural Change* (1989); Ihab Hassan, *The Postmodern Turn: Essays in Postmodern Theory and Culture* (1987); Susan J. Hekman, *Gender and Knowledge: Elements of a Postmodern Feminism* (1990); Linda Hutcheon, *A Poetics of Postmodernism: History, Theory, Fiction* (1988), *The Politics of Postmodernism* (1989); Andreas Huyssen, *After The Great Divide: Modernism, Mass Culture, Postmodernism* (1986); Fredric Jameson, *Postmodernism, or The Cultural Logic of Late Capitalism* (1991); Charles Jencks, *The Language of Post-Modern Architecture* (1977, 4th ed., 1984); Jean-François Lyotard, *La Condition postmoderne: Rapport sur le savoir* (1979, *The Postmodern Condition: A Report on Knowledge,* trans. Geoff Bennington and Brian Massumi, 1984); John McGowan, *Postmodernism and Its Critics* (1991); Brian McHale, *Postmodernist Fiction* (1987); Linda J. Nicholson, ed., *Feminism/Postmodernism* (1990); Christopher Norris, *What's Wrong with Postmodernism? Critical Theory and the Ends of Philosophy* (1990).

POUND, EZRA

Ezra Pound (1885–1972) was born in the frontier town of Hailey, Idaho, and reared in Philadelphia. He attended Hamilton College and the University of Pennsylvania, where he did graduate work in Romance languages. In 1908 he traveled to Europe and settled in London, which was to be his home until 1920, when he moved to Paris and later (1924) to Italy. During the 1930s his economic and political obsessions caused him to support the fascist regime of Mussolini, and in 1941–43 he gave a number of talks on Radio Rome criticizing the U.S. role in World War II. In 1945 he was arrested for treason and jailed for several months at Pisa before being flown to the United States, where he was declared "mentally unfit for trial" and remanded to St. Elizabeths Hospital for 12 years. In 1958 he was released from St. Elizabeths, after a number of prominent writers had intervened on his behalf; he returned to Italy, where he spent most of his last years in penitential silence.

Pound was the central figure in early modern literature, and his poems of 1909–22 reflect his search for a contemporary idiom. His long poem *The Cantos,* written over a period of nearly a half-century, is a record of personal struggle that mirrors the life of his time: it could only be ended by his death.

Criticism, Pound once said, is written in the hope of better things, and in the history of Anglo-American criticism Pound stands out as the quintessential poet-critic. He believed that "the man who formulates any forward reach of co-ordinating principle is the man who produces the demonstration" (*Literary Essays* 75), and when Pound's life's work is seen in this perspective it becomes a continuous act of literary criticism. His letters, his conversation, his essays, and his poetry flow together to form a single commentary on the literary tradition and the accomplishments of his own time.

In "Date Line" (1934, *Literary Essays* 74–75) Pound described the various "kinds" of criticism, ranking them in an ascending order of importance; and his categories provide a neat overview of his critical life:

1. *Criticism by discussion.* The range of this category, from occasional reviewing to literary theory, is immense. Pound wrote literally thousands of reviews and essays, but he considered these writings the least important part of his "criticism." Under this heading would fall his many reviews, generously written in the service of contemporary letters (one thinks of his role as the promoter of Robert Frost, James Joyce, T. S. ELIOT, and a host of other important figures), as well as his more general essays on critical procedure and the poetic language. All these writings reveal Pound as a critic of the "moment," alive to the immediate needs of English and American poetry. One example would be his deliberate decision (along with Eliot) to champion more formal verse as an antidote to the excesses of vers libre. Most of Pound's conventional criticism, such as his essays on Imagism and Vorticism, was part of a campaign to revitalize and redirect the language of poetry; it must be read against the background of a particular literary scene and in the context of a desire to reshape literature according to his notion of tradition.

2. *Criticism by translation.* Under this heading would come Pound's evocative rendering of the Anglo-Saxon "Seafarer," his adaptations from the Chinese in *Cathay,* his translations and adaptations from the Latin and Provençal languages, and his versions of Greek tragedy.

Appearing at crucial turns in his poetic life, these "translations" from one culture to another are just as much a part of his literary criticism as his conventional essays and have had at least an equal impact on the development of modern literature. Frost once said that poetry is what is lost in translation. Pound took the opposite view; he believed that the essential "virtue" of a poem could be preserved and even enhanced in translation.

3. *Criticism by exercise in the style of a given period.* According to Pound, the final test of the poet is his ability to recognize and recreate various traditional "styles," since this is an essential device for bringing past and present into alignment. *Hugh Selwyn Mauberly* (1920), for example, is a museum of imitated styles, each playing a crucial role in Pound's criticism of the immediate foreground and background of English poetry. Stretching from echoes of the poets of the 1890s and the Pre-Raphaelites to a marvelous pastiche of Elizabethan songs in "Envoi," *Mauberley* gives us Pound's view of the tradition in a form far more subtle than that of his discursive criticism.

4. *Criticism via music.* Whatever one may think of Pound's musical theories and his excursions in composition, these activities were part of his emphasis on the musical aspect of language (melopoeia), "wherein the words are charged, over and above their plain meaning, with some musical property, which directs the bearing or trend of that meaning" ("How to Read," *Literary Essays* 25).

5. *Criticism in new composition.* The most important of Pound's works would fall under this category of ultimate criticism. One example is Canto I, which provides a masterly synthesis of "criticism by translation" and "criticism by exercise in the style of a given period." Here the account of Odysseus's descent into the underworld (from book II of *The Odyssey*) is retold in a compressed form inherited from a Renaissance translator and styled in imitated Anglo-Saxon meter (since Pound felt the Old English epics had many of the qualities of the *Odyssey*). The result is a series of "overlays" that gives us a critical perspective on the quest of the modern artist and actually recreates a tradition.

In all his work Pound placed special emphasis on invention and discovery, taking from the Chinese his motto "Make It New." After he had collaborated with Eliot in what was a virtual rewriting of *The Waste Land,* Eliot affixed this dedication to the poem: "For Ezra Pound, *il miglior fabbro*" ("the better craftsman"). The phrase is DANTE ALIGHIERI's tribute (through Guido) to his precursor Arnaut Daniel, and Eliot knew it would please Pound to be cast in the role of someone who has invented a new style. The value Pound placed on invention or discovery is evident in his selective view of the literary tradition, where the inventors have pride of place because they are of most use to contemporary writers. In the preface to *The Spirit of Romance* (1910) Pound anticipated the argument of Eliot's "Tradition and the Individual Talent" (1919): "All ages are contemporaneous. . . . What we need is a literary scholarship, which will weigh Theocritus and Yeats with one balance, and . . . give praise to beauty before referring to an almanack" (6). And in 1933 he commented, retrospectively: "Mr. Eliot and I are in agreement, or 'belong to the same school of critics,' in so far as we both believe that existing works form a complete order which is changed by the introduction of the 'really new' work" (*Selected Prose* 389). Like Eliot, Pound had a view of our transactions with the past in which Joyce's *Ulysses* changes our reading of the *Odyssey* to the same extent that the *Odyssey* determines our response to *Ulysses*. But unlike Eliot, Pound did not feel an "academic" responsibility to take a balanced view of the tradition. He singled out those writers and styles that he felt were alive and useful to the modern poet and discarded the rest. Hence his "tradition" is much more idiosyncratic than Eliot's, omitting whole centuries (such as the eighteenth), major figures (William Shakespeare and the Renaissance dramatists), and important tendencies (Romanticism). Instead, he emphasized the poets, translators, and novelists who had, in his opinion, refashioned language and sensibility in ways available to the contemporary writer. The heroes of Pound's tradition, figures such as Catullus and François Villon and Gustave Flaubert, are the shapers of his own verse. For example, Pound cherished Flaubert as the model for the "prose tradition" in poetry, and it was the example of Flaubert that led him to his dictum "Poetry must be *as well written as prose*" (*Selected Letters* 48), by which he meant that most contemporary verse was loose and vague in comparison with the precise density of Flaubert and Joyce.

If we look for a key to Pound's criticism, the method of WALTER PATER comes immediately to mind, since Pater believed that the most effective criticism was that "which is itself a kind of construction, or creation, as it penetrates, through the given literary or artistic product, into the mental and inner constitution of the producer, shaping his work" (*Essays from The Guardian, Works,* 1910, 10:29). In his essay "Cavalcanti" Pound laments that modern men and women have lost the gift for seeing the forms of the past in the life of the present; when a magnet draws the steel filings on a sheet of paper into a pattern, few of us see in it the rose of courtly love (*Literary Essays* 154–55). Later this image was translated into Canto 74, where it sums up Pound's critical enterprise, his desire to make the past live through the present:

> Hast 'ou seen the rose in the steel dust
> (or swansdown ever?)
> so light is the urging, so ordered the dark petals of iron
> we who have passed over Lethe.
> (*Cantos of Ezra Pound,* 1972, 449)

A. Walton Litz

See also T. S. ELIOT and MODERNIST THEORY AND CRITICISM.

Ezra Pound, *ABC of Reading* (1934), *Guide to Kulchur* (1938), *Literary Essays of Ezra Pound* (ed. T. S. Eliot, 1954), *Selected Letters of Ezra Pound, 1907–1941* (ed. D. D. Paige, 1950), *Selected Prose, 1909–1965* (ed. William Cookson, 1973), *The Spirit of Romance* (1910).

Ian F. A. Bell, *Critic as Scientist: The Modernist Poetics of Ezra Pound* (1981); Donald Gallup, *Ezra Pound: A Bibliography* (1983); Lawrence I. Lipking and A. Walton Litz, eds., *Modern Literary Criticism, 1900–1970* (1972); K. K. Ruthven, *Ezra Pound as Literary Critic* (1990); Richard Sieburth, *Instigations: Ezra Pound and Remy De Gourmont* (1978).

PRACTICAL CRITICISM

Practical criticism is commonly contrasted to theoretical criticism and is defined as an "applied" criticism in which theoretical principles are assumed or implied. (In this loose sense of the term, JOHN DRYDEN and SAMUEL JOHNSON, for example, would be considered practical critics.) But practical criticism also has a distinctive history and a theoretical evolution. It is most frequently associated with the Cambridge lecturer and scholar I. A. RICHARDS, who formulated it as a pedagogy and as a text-reading practice in his 1929 book of that title. But an earlier attempt to develop a systematic "practical criticism" by which "the specific symptoms of poetic power" would be "elucidated" from the "critical analysis" of literary works is to be found in the *Biographia Literaria* of SAMUEL TAYLOR COLERIDGE (2:19), whose writing greatly influenced Richards's own. (Coleridge appears, in fact, to have been the originator of this term.) After developing a general set of philosophical principles throughout the first book of the *Biographia,* he then moved to specific and literary cases: the term "practical criticism" is inaugurated in the discussion of Shakespeare's poetry in chapter 15. "In the application of these principles to purposes of practical criticism as employed in the appraisal of works more or less imperfect," wrote Coleridge, "I have endeavoured to discover what the qualities in a poem are, which may be deemed promises and specific symptoms of poetic power" (2:19). While Shakespeare's virtues are many—musicality of verse, range of topic, depth and energy of thought—his "power for reducing multitude into unity of effect" is centrally important (2:20); for without this, Shakespeare's work would be excellent in parts but not in the whole. Thus, at its inception practical criticism took the form of a demonstration of poetic synthesis.

I. A. Richards's work in practical criticism bears many resemblances to that of Coleridge. Like his predecessor, he aimed to ground a theory of poetic affect in an account of the ordering operations of the mind, and his work also applies general principles to specific examples. But it is also "practical" in ways that are more or less absent from the *Biographia*. First, Richards wished to provide students with practice in reading by way of poetry response exercises designed to increase their analytical skills. And this was thought to be further "practical" (in the sense of having social utility), since good judgment was seen by Richards to provide the foundation for a good citizenry. Also, the book *Practical Criticism* was intended to be practical in categorizing sources of misunderstanding and unclear thinking and in using this typology to make suggestions for educational reform.

If we take "practical criticism" in this extended sense, as describing a criticism that is applicable or useful for literary or social functions, then a number of critical projects may be seen as "practical" although they are not given that name (Baldick 4). Although MATTHEW ARNOLD specifically contrasted his ideal "disinterested" criticism to a "practical" criticism directly tied to social affairs and vested interests, this very disinterestedness was itself "practical" as an intrinsic element of the Arnoldian project for social reform (Baldick 232). F. R. LEAVIS was to lament how the term "practical criticism" had become equated with "a specialized kind of gymnastic skill to be cultivated and practiced as something apart" and was no longer available to describe "criticism in practice," a socially engaged exercise of judgment and analysis (*Living* 19). Although practical criticism courses, as they are offered in many English programs, are ostensibly practical in the sense of an application of a specific theory or set of principles, the other notions of practicality persist. Students are trained in the techniques of close reading, and this is seen to outfit them both for further literary study and for life.

This compounding of literary and life skills is effected in Richards's *Practical Criticism,* a work that provides not only many of the existent methods of literary study but also its rationales. Training in psychology outfitted Richards well to work in the fledgling discipline of En-

glish studies, his approach seeming fresh, serious, and systematic. In earlier works, he had been concerned to distinguish scientific from emotive language, in the interests of communicative accuracy, and he had begun to view poetry as an antidote to the social disintegration he blamed on the rise of mass culture. *Practical Criticism,* written in 1929, provides a programmatic statement of the place of the literary and language critic in the fight against this perceived tendency toward confused thought and ideational erosion. Its founding premise could well be located in Coleridge's summary of the salutary effect of Shakespeare; faced with great poetry, Coleridge writes, "the reader is forced into too much action to sympathize with the merely passive of our nature" (2:22).

Practical Criticism draws on Richards's experiences and experiments in teaching. In his very popular Cambridge classes, Richards would distribute sets of poems from which the author's name, the title, and other identifying marks had been removed. Student responses ("protocols," to use Richards's term) were then collected and analyzed, with Richards's insightful, sarcastic, or suggestive commentary providing the next lectures. These were lessons designed less to demonstrate the specific sources of poetic power than to identify the specific sources of readerly weakness; in other words, it was the protocols, rather than the poems, that were examined. The book gives excerpts from the responses to thirteen poems and details the students' errors of literal or figurative understanding, their "stock" responses and "irrelevant associations." This is followed by a section of "analysis"—the psychoanalytic connotation is fully justified—where the sources of misunderstanding are located and categorized. Only occasionally is poetic obscurity targeted as the cause of the communicative breakdown. Typically, Richards sees the responsibility as lying in readerly inadequacy or immaturity. This he proceeds to conceive, more precisely, as the inability to differentiate sense, feeling, tone, and intention, a distinction necessary for good reading. Good reading becomes, in turn, the basis for a psychological integration or self-completion; thus Richards, in closing, recommends the study of interpretation at all schooling levels.

Whatever its title might indicate, in *Practical Criticism* no attempt is made to measure these student responses against a full reading put forward by the instructor (although it is assumed that the instructor has a more proximate understanding); nor does the book attempt to formulate the principles and procedures on which satisfactory readings could be based (although in other contexts Richards does develop more detailed recommendations for close reading). The ostensible explanation is that Richards was not primarily interested in literary elucidation; he considered the practical criticism project a "fieldwork in comparative ideology" (6). But the point could also be made that an alternate reading is unnecessary, since it is against the poem itself that readings will be measured, not necessarily as an interpretation per se but as an adjudication of a complex multiplicity for which the poem provides a standard.

Practical criticism, both narrowly and broadly defined, was to be adopted and amended in several significant ways. F. R. Leavis, a student of Richards's and often closely associated with practical criticism, was also skeptical of some aspects, as implied in his comparison of the two modern critics he considered most important. While Richards had "improved the instruments of analysis," T. S. ELIOT had not only refined the "conception and methods" of criticism but also "put into currency decisive re-organising and re-orienting ideas and valuations" (Leavis, *Continuity* 68–69). Such a "re-orientating" describes as well the goal of Leavis and other members of the *Scrutiny* project; this would involve, in part, a restoration of the element of personal discernment and evaluation somewhat occluded by Richards's methods. "Analysis is not a dissection of something that is already and passively there," wrote Leavis in another context. "It is a re-creation in which, by a considering attentiveness, we ensure a more than ordinary faithfulness and completeness." Leavis contrasted a "laboratory-method" analysis to this "constructive or creative process" (*Education* 70). Practitioners of NEW CRITICISM would also have substantive disagreements with Richards (and would leave behind issues, such as affect, that were central to him) while accepting other innovations. Taking as a point of reference Coleridgean assumptions of textual organicity, they also drew from Richards the emphasis on tone, tensions, and ironic and paradoxical structures as cohering principles. Many adopted, as well, the technique of close reading he espoused, seeing it as the counterpart to a prevailing historical scholarship they considered generally outmoded and particularly unsuited to modern texts. And the "practicality" of practical criticism for lecture-hall teaching ensured its pedagogic institutionalization in the large classes of the post–World War II period, especially in the United States, as did its seemingly "scientific" rigor. GEOFFREY H. HARTMAN has blamed this crude drawing out of the utilitarian strands of Richards's *Practical Criticism* project for a continuing antiphilosophical critical prejudice.

Thus, while Richards's *Practical Criticism* is not a systematic approach to literature or literary criticism, its recommendations and procedures were to be conse-

quential; and the book not only is of significant theoretical interest in its own right but has some status as a document in the history of the discipline. For while Richards himself and his eclectic later work moved increasingly to the periphery of mainstream literary study, certain aspects of practical criticism have become so ingrained as to form part of the Kuhnian "normal science" of English. E. M. W. Tillyard, chronicler of the controversial revisions to the English tripos at Cambridge, considered the school's "greatest single achievement" to be the introduction "into the more advanced of the two purely literary sections [of] a whole, compulsory paper on practical criticism," since "here at last we could confront the men with the actual texts and test their ultimate literary insight, making them use their own resources entirely" (82–83). Tillyard's account neatly summarizes both the express goals and the hidden implications of the practical criticism paper. The exercise is the "ultimate" and "advanced" test of a rigorous disciplinary training, yet it operates from the student's "own resources." The very term "resources" assumes an interpretive variability, yet these are responses to arrangements effected a priori in the text. It is perhaps because of this portmanteau capacity of practical criticism—its perceived ability to satisfy personal, social, disciplinary, and professional mandates—that many universities still offer a required or recommended course in practical criticism (usually of poetry).

While the term "practical criticism" has become somewhat detached from its earlier project, often operating as a synonym for "close reading" conceived in a general way, many earlier assumptions persist, and the "passage," as used by Richards, remains a common test question for students in a wide variety of courses and examination circumstances. Students are trained to detect what is already "there" in the poetry at the same time as they are (somewhat contradictorily) encouraged to develop their minds and senses in integrated yet independent ways. Thus, the "reading" resulting from the close reading is itself read as an index to the student's competencies or even qualities, and it will be judged, in many cases, for its perceived resemblance to the poem under examination—both poem and essay, under practical criticism criteria, valued for their balance, energy, synergy, complexity, self-containedness, and aesthetic completion. In its most extreme form, the "passage" question takes the form of the "sight passage." In this case, the removal of identifying data serves less to challenge students than to signal an appropriate critical approach, in a staging of an assumed textual self-sufficiency that in turn indicates that it is "internal" relations that are to be discerned. Thus, practical criticism and organic unity remain intertwined as they were in Coleridge's first formulation. How to develop a practical criticism based on other theoretical assumptions—how to put the textual "practice" back into "practical criticism"—is a problem occupying many in the academy today.

Heather Murray

See also F. R. LEAVIS, NEW CRITICISM, and I. A. RICHARDS.

Samuel Taylor Coleridge, *Biographia Literaria* (1817, ed. James Engell and W. Jackson Bate, 2 vols., 1983); F. R. Leavis, *Education and the University* (1943), *For Continuity* (1933), *The Living Principle: "English" as a Discipline of Thought* (1975); I. A. Richards, *Practical Criticism: A Study of Literary Judgment* (1929).

Chris Baldick, *The Social Mission of English Criticism, 1848–1932* (1983); John Fekete, *The Critical Twilight: Explorations in the Ideology of Anglo-American Literary Theory from Eliot to McLuhan* (1977); Geoffrey H. Hartman, "A Short History of Practical Criticism," *Criticism in the Wilderness: The Study of Literature Today* (1980); Pamela McCallum, *Literature and Method: Towards a Critique of I. A. Richards, T. S. Eliot, and F. R. Leavis* (1983); Francis Mulhern, *The Moment of "Scrutiny"* (1979); E. M. W. Tillyard, *The Muse Unchained: An Intimate Account of the Revolution in English Studies in Cambridge* (1958).

PRAGUE SCHOOL STRUCTURALISM

Twentieth-century SEMIOTICS and STRUCTURALISM emerged simultaneously from the same source: the postpositivistic paradigm initiated by FERDINAND DE SAUSSURE and RUSSIAN FORMALISM. The first systematic formulation of semiotic structuralism came from scholars of the Prague Linguistic Circle (PLC), who are now known as the Prague school. The PLC was inaugurated in 1926 by Vilém Mathesius, director of the English seminar at Charles University, and his colleagues ROMAN JAKOBSON, Bohuslav Havránek, Bohumil Trnka, and Jan Rypka. Mathesius gave the group an organized form and a clear theoretical direction. The PLC counted among its members such prominent scholars as Jan Mukařovský, Nikolaj Trubeckoj, Sergej Karcevskij, Petr Bogatyrjov, and Dmitrij Čyževskyj. Russian scholars, former members of the formalist groups, represented a substantial contingent. In the 1930s younger scholars joined, especially RENÉ

WELLEK, Felix Vodička, Jiří Veltruský, Jaroslav Průšek, and Josef Vachek. Many visitors (Edmund Husserl, Rudolf Carnap, Boris Tomaševskij, ÉMILE BENVENISTE, and others) presented papers in the Circle.

Travaux du Cercle linguistique de Prague (TCLP) contains in eight volumes (1929–39) pivotal contributions by members and "fellow travelers" in English, French, and German. In 1928 the Prague participants of the First International Congress of Linguists in The Hague drafted a program for structural linguistics with the Geneva school scholars (not to be confused with the later GENEVA SCHOOL phenomenological critics). The *Thèses du Cercle linguistique de Prague* (vol. 1 of *Travaux*) set out not only the principles of the new linguistics but also a theory of standard and poetic language. In 1929 Jakobson coined the term "structuralism."

In the 1930s the PLC became a force in Czech culture. Its first important Czech publication was a tribute to the philosopher president of the Czechoslovak republic, T. G. Masaryk. The volume *Spisovná čeština a jazyková kultura* [Standard Czech and language culture] (1932) resulted from a polemic with conservative purists; in alliance with avant-garde writers, the PLC formulated principles of language culture and planning that remain significant to the 1990s. In 1935 the PLC launched its Czech journal *Slovo a slovesnost* [The word and verbal art], exploiting in its title the etymological connection that in Slavic languages links the terms for "language" and "literature." The PLC maintained its eminent cultural position in rapidly changing political conditions: a jubilee volume, *Torso a tajemství Máchova díla* [Torso and mystery of Mácha's work] (1938), a popularizing work, *Čtení o jazyce a poesii* [Readings on language and poetry] (1942), and a cycle of radio broadcasts, *O básnickém jazyce* [On poetic language] (1947), were widely known. As the PLC's influence grew, so did the voices of the critics, coming from both the traditional academics and the Marxists. The polemic with Marxist publicists (1930–34) is probably the first confrontation between structuralism and Marxism in the twentieth century.

When Czech universities were closed by the Nazis in November 1939, the meetings of the PLC continued in private dwellings. Public activities were resumed in June 1945. A few leaders were lost to natural death (Trubeckoj, Mathesius) or to exile (Jakobson, Wellek). But the brief spell of democracy in postwar Czechoslovakia, from May 1945 to February 1948, was a very productive time for the Prague school. The standard, three-volume edition of Mukařovský's selected works, *Kapitoly z české poetiky* [Chapters from Czech poetics], and the school's last representative work, Vodička's monograph *Počátky krásné prózy novočeské* [The beginnings of Czech artistic prose], were published in 1948. The last lecture in the Circle took place in December 1948. After more than forty years, the PLC resumed its activities in February 1990.

In 1946 Jan Mukařovský presented a lecture on Prague school structuralism at the Institut d'Études Slaves in Paris. The lecture was never published in French and had no impact on the Parisian intellectual scene. This incident indicates a discontinuity in twentieth-century structuralism, reinforced by most of its Western historians, analysts, and critics. (This is especially true of structuralist poetics, aesthetics, and semiotics. Prague linguistics has fared better, but even its reception in the West has been hesitant.) Jonathan Culler's well-known *Structuralist Poetics: Structuralism, Linguistics, and the Study of Literature* (1975) set the pattern: the "structuralist poetics" is exclusively French. The subtitle of FREDRIC JAMESON's *The Prison-House of Language* (1972) promised to give "a critical account of structuralism and Russian Formalism," but from the Prague school only the concept of "foregrounding" is mentioned. Terence Hawkes's *Structuralism and Semiotics* (1977) provides a brief account of the Prague theory of poetic language but ignores all other achievements. Jan Broekman's *Structuralism: Moscow—Prague—Paris* (1971) and D. W. Fokkema and Elrud Kunne-Ibsch's *Theories of Literature in the Twentieth Century* (1977) should be singled out as exceptions. J. G. Merquior acknowledges that "the foundations of structuralism in criticism and aesthetics were laid down in Eastern Europe" (19) but treats the Prague school as mere "strategic background" to the Parisian "story" (x). He knows that Mukařovský's ideas "had no discernible influence on structuralist literary theory of the 1960s" (27). (To be sure, Jakobson was a strong influence in Paris, but it was Jakobson the Russian Formalist rather than the Prague structuralist.)

Without the Prague school, the image of twentieth-century structuralism is incomplete both historically and theoretically. Prague scholars took a broad view of the tasks and methods of aesthetics and poetics and developed an epistemology that preempts much of the poststructuralist critique:

1. Prague structuralism is functionalistic. All signs, including aesthetic signs, fulfill certain needs of their users. The functionalism inspired by Karl Bühler (Mukařovský, Jakobson) derived the functions from the factors of the speech act, Havránek's from the social channels of communication (see Doležel 149–55). In functionalism the Prague theory receives a pragmatic underpinning without sacrificing to pragmatics the sign's formal and seman-

tic dimensions. Prague epistemology's most prominent feature—its synthesizing character, its preferring dialectic to reductionism—can be discerned here.

2. The Prague theory of structure is located within an interdisciplinary mereology. In 1929 Jakobson already recognized the interdisciplinarity of structuralism:

> Were we to comprise the leading idea of present-day science in its most various manifestations, we could hardly find a more appropriate designation than structuralism. Any set of phenomena examined by contemporary science is treated not as a mechanical agglomeration but as a structural whole, and the basic task is to reveal the inner, whether static or developmental, laws of this system. (*Selected* 2:711)

For Mukařovský, structuralism was "an epistemological stance," the manner by which concepts are formed and put into operation: "The conceptual system of every particular discipline is a web of internal correlations. Every concept is determined by all the others and in turn determines them. Thus a concept is defined unequivocally by the place it occupies in its conceptual system rather than by the enumeration of its contents" (*Kapitoly* 1:13). Interdisciplinarity requires that aesthetics and poetics keep in touch with the advancement of human and social sciences: Mukařovský examined the links between structuralism and Jan Smuts's "biological holism" (*Kapitoly* 1:129); Trnka pointed to Russell's relational logic as one of the inspirations of structuralism (159).

3. The Prague epistemology distinguished between the activities of ordinary readers and those of expert students of literature. In a late evaluation of the structuralist position, Jakobson maintained that the poem, like a musical composition, "affords the ordinary reader the possibility of an artistic perception, but produces neither the need nor the competence to effect a scientific analysis" (*Dialogues* 116–17). He emphasized, however, that the student of human communication is not an engineer of signals but rather deals with cultural phenomena endowed with meaning, history, and value. Jakobson distinguished a "preliminary stage" of enquiry, where the researcher is "the most detached and external onlooker," a "cryptanalyst," and a stage of "internal approach," when he or she becomes "a potential or actual partner in the exchange of verbal messages among the members of the speech community, a passive or even active fellow member of that community" (*Selected* 3:574). Such flexibility satisfies the diverse needs of the student of literature without confusing the practical literary activities of writing and reading with cognitive activities aimed at theoretical understanding.

4. Prague school epistemology reconciled Saussure's opposition of synchrony and diachrony, of structural and historical study. Jakobson summed up the divergence from the father of structuralism: Saussure

> attempted to suppress the tie between the system of a language and its modifications by considering the system as the exclusive domain of synchrony and assigning modifications to the sphere of diachrony alone. In actuality, as indicated in the different social sciences, the concepts of a system and its change are not only compatible but indissolubly tied. (*Dialogues* 58)

The evolution of language is no less "systemic and goal-oriented" than its synchronic functioning (64).

In Prague, a comprehensive theory of literary history was developed: "What most sharply distinguishes Czech structuralism from the other twentieth-century literary theories is its commitment to literary history" (Galan 2). The PLC scholars unanimously claimed that literary history has to be based on literary theory. Even so, Mukařovský's first formulation of the principles of structuralist literary history in 1934 led to a polemic with traditionalists (see Galan 56–77). In 1936, Wellek published the penetrating essay "The Theory of Literary History," while perhaps the most significant contributions to literary history are Vodička's 1942 paper "Literární historie, Její problémy a úkoly" (reprinted in *Strucktura*) and his 1948 monograph. The PLC model of literary history was derived from the model of literary communication, with its three factors: writer, literary work, reader. Genetic history reconstructs the origins of literary works, structural history, and transformations in the "literary series"; and reception history, successive concretizations and interpretations (*Struktura* 16). In accepting genetic and reception history, the Prague scholars transcended their original historical "immanentism," recognizing that "literary works are made by people, they are facts of social culture and exist in numerous relationships to other phenomena of cultural life" (25).

5. The Prague epistemology is empirical: the problems, concepts, and metalanguage of theory are rooted in the praxis of literary analysis. "Today," according to Červenka,

> there is much speculation about the relationship between Marxism and structuralism, existentialism and structuralism, etc., as if we were dealing with a confrontation of contradictory philosophical trends. However, structuralism as conceived by Mukařovský, Jakobson, Vodička and their disciples . . . is not a philosophy, but a methodological trend in certain sciences, especially those concerned with sign systems and their concrete uses. (331–32)

Thanks to its empirical character, Prague school epistemology was able to overcome the postpositivistic split between sciences of nature *(Naturwissenschaften)* and human sciences *(Geisteswissenschaften)*. Because of the repeatability and regularity of the phenomena of nature, natural sciences are nomothetic; they aim at formulating universal laws. The *Geisteswissenschaften,* dealing with individualized and unrepeatable phenomena (historical events, human actions and personalities, works of art and of literature, etc.), are ideographic; they try to understand the uniqueness of form, meaning, relevance, and value (see Doležel). Some structuralists restricted literary theory (poetics) to the nomothetic study of categories and regularities, but the Prague epistemology is synthetic. It combines an abstract poetics of universal categories and general laws with an analytical poetics of individual literary works. Mukařovský's 1928 monograph (reprinted in *Kapitoly,* vol. 3) already demonstrated this synthesis. A theoretical system is developed in the introduction and then used to describe a particular poem (Mácha's *May*) in the uniqueness of its sound patterning, its semantic organization, and its thematic structure. Later Mukařovský proposed and explored the concept of semantic gesture, a poet's idiosyncratic "constructional principle," "which is applied in every segment of the work, even the most minute, and which results in a unified and unifying systematization of all the constituents" (3:239). Both in its name and in its sense, semantic gesture ties the literary structure to the creative subject; the organizational principle of the work's semantics has a pragmatic base.

In the same spirit, Jakobson's well-known poetological studies explore the role of abstract grammatical categories in the patterning of particular poems. Diverse works, such as the Hussite battle song, Aleksandr Pushkin's love poetry, and a political poem by Bertolt Brecht, are idiosyncratic in their use of personal pronouns. Even each of Pushkin's poems is "unique and unrepeatable in its artistic choice and use of grammatical material" (*Language* 136). Jakobson's method, as Pomorska noted, "allows us both to generalize and individualize the phenomena under investigation" (*Dialogues* 230).

The combination of nomothetic and ideographic poetics was perfected by Vodička in his most significant work, *Počátky krásné prózy novočeské* (1948). The monograph adopted an appropriate compositional pattern alternating analytical segments with theoretical reflections, a pattern invented by Wilhelm von Humboldt in his 1799 monograph on Johann Wolfgang von Goethe's *Hermann und Dorothea* (see Doležel 66–68); ROLAND BARTHES's *S/Z* (1970) is a more recent, and more celebrated, example of this pattern. For instance, Vodička reformulated the traditional system of narrative thematics by defining action, character, and setting in terms of elementary narrative units, motifs; then he demonstrated how in François-René de Chateaubriand's *Atala* the motifs of setting (of nature, human habitats, social and cultural customs, etc.) become polyfunctional, taking part in the structuring of character or action. Overall, Vodička developed a systematic theory of narrative on both the thematic and the discourse levels and analyzed in its terms a unique historical event: the rise of modern Czech prose fiction.

Lubomír Doležel

See also ROMAN JAKOBSON, RUSSIAN FORMALISM, SEMIOTICS, STRUCTURALISM, and RENÉ WELLEK.

Petr Bogatyrjov, *The Functions of Folk Costume in Moravian Slovakia* (trans. Richard G. Crum, 1971); Miroslav Červenka, "O Vodičkově metodologii literárních dějin" [On Vodička's methodology of literary history] (Vodička, *Struktura*); Paul L. Garvin, ed. and trans., *A Prague School Reader on Esthetics, Literary Structure, and Style* (1964); Roman Jakobson, *The Framework of Language* (1980), *Language in Literature* (ed. Krystyna Pomorska and Stephen Rudy, 1987), *Selected Writings* (8 vols., 1966–88); Roman Jakobson and Krystyna Pomorska, *Dialogues* (trans. Christian Hubert, 1983); Ladislav Matejka and Irwin R. Titunik, eds., *Semiotics of Art: Prague School Contributions* (1976); Jan Mukařovský, *Aesthetic Function, Norm, and Value as Social Facts* (trans. Mark E. Suino, 1970), *Kapitoly z české poetiky* [Chapters from Czech poetics] (3 vols., 1948, partial trans. in *The Word and Verbal Art*, 1977), *Structure, Sign, and Function: Selected Essays* (ed. and trans. Peter Steiner and John Burbank, 1978), *The Word and Verbal Art: Selected Essays* (ed. and trans. Peter Steiner and John Burbank, 1977); Peter Steiner, ed., *The Prague School: Selected Writings, 1929–1946* (trans. John Burbank et al., 1982); Josef V. Vachek, ed., *A Prague School Reader in Linguistics* (1964); Josef V. Vachek and Libuše Dušková, eds., *Praguiana: Some Basic and Less Known Aspects of the Prague Linguistics* (1983); Felix Vodička, *Počátky krásné prózy novočeské* [The beginnings of Czech artistic prose] (1948), *Struktura vývoje* [Structure of evolution] (1966, partial trans., Matejka and Titunik); René Wellek, "The Theory of Literary History," *Travaux du Cercle linguistique de Prague*, vol. 6 (1936).

Jan Broekman, *Structuralism: Moscow—Prague—Paris* (trans. Jan F. Beekman and Brunhilde Helm, 1974); Květoslav Chvatík, "Semiotics of a Literary Work of Art: Dedicated to the 90th Birthday of Jan Mukařovský (1891–1975)," *Semiotica* 37 (1981); Lubomír Doležel, *Occidental Poetics: Tradition and Progress* (1990); Victor Erlich, *Russian Formalism: History-Doctrine* (3d ed., 1981); D. W. Fokkema and Elrud Kunne-Ibsch, *Theories of Literature in the Twentieth Century* (1977); F. W. Galan, *Historic Structures: The Prague School Project, 1928–1946* (1985); Milan Jankovič, "Perspectives of Semantic Gesture," *Poetics* 4 (1972); Ladislav Matejka, ed., *Sound, Sign, and Meaning: Quinquagenary of the Prague Linguistic Circle* (1978); J. G. Merquior, *From Prague to Paris: A Critique of Structuralist and Post-structuralist Thought* (1986); Peter Steiner, M. Červenka, and R. Vroon, eds., *The Structure of the Literary Process: Studies Dedicated to the Memory of Felix Vodička* (1982); Jurij Striedter, *Literary Structure, Evolution, and Value: Russian Formalism and Czech Structuralism Reconsidered* (1989); Yishai Tobin, ed., *The Prague School and Its Legacy* (1988); Bohumil Trnka, "Linguistics and the Ideological Structure of the Period" (Vachek, *Linguistic School*); Josef Vachek, *The Linguistic School of Prague: An Introduction to Its Theory and Practice* (1966); Jiří Veltruský, "Jan Mukařovský's Structural Poetics and Esthetics," *Poetics Today* 2 (1980–81); Felix Vodička, "The Integrity of the Literary Process: Notes on the Development of Theoretical Thought in J. Mukařovský's Work," *Poetics* 4 (1972); René Wellek, *The Literary Theory and Aesthetics of the Prague School* (1969, reprint in *Discriminations: Further Concepts of Criticism*, 1970).

PSYCHOANALYTIC THEORY AND CRITICISM

1. Traditional Freudian Criticism

Along the lines of SIGMUND FREUD's own forays into literary criticism, such as his remarks on the Oedipal scheme in *Hamlet* (1899), his theoretical essay "Creative Writers and Day-dreaming" (1908), and his psychobiographical essay "Dostoevsky and Parricide" (1928), several of Freud's contemporaries as well as later writers produced studies of literary figures and literary works that established elementary models of psychoanalytic criticism. Such models typically assumed relative transparency between the fictional product and the creative artist: read psychoanalytically, the literary work disclosed the author's unconscious fantasies. The aim of this criticism was typically psychobiographical; the exact, manifest terms of the narrative were subordinated to those patterns of wish and defense revealed by analytic discovery of "latent content." The best examples of this style of criticism (still in practice) refuse to subordinate art to neurosis and deploy the tools of psycho-analysis to explore precise terms of language, metaphor, and character.

After Freud, the best-known pioneer of traditional psychoanalytic criticism is probably Ernest Jones (1879–1958). Jones was the author of almost 200 essays in theory and applied psychoanalysis, including articles on dreams, literature, religion, war neuroses, female sexuality, Ireland, chess, ice-skating, and the common cold. He was instrumental in introducing Freud to the English-speaking world and presided over the origins of the British psychoanalytic establishment. He was the author of the first full biography of Freud (1957), the standard account until more recent biographies were produced by Ronald W. Clark (1980) and Peter Gay (1988).

Jones's early monograph *On the Nightmare* (1910) demonstrates a bold effort to apply psychoanalytic perspectives to history and legend, sketching analyses of witches, vampires, Druids, and speculative etymology (mares, horses, and the linguistic *m[a]r* root). (Jones himself suffered throughout his life from vivid nightmares [see Brome].) His essay on "The Theory of Symbolism" (1916) is an energetic and shrewd effort to regularize Freud's ideas as stated in *The Interpretation of Dreams* and elsewhere: to articulate elementary structures of symbolic representation in dream and literature. Jones connected symbols with primitive sensorial residues of "primary process" mentation anchored in repressed, unconscious representations of the body, sexual life, family relations, and death: a reservoir of images common to human development and liable to regressive attention during periods of stress, dreaming, or creative activity. The potent puppet, *Punchinello,* for instance, is a phallic symbol (93)—the most common. Although Jones, like Freud, resisted the impulse, ultimately his argument implies a "dictionary of symbols," albeit highly overdetermined (97–98); there are about 100 commonly symbolized concepts (102–3). He is especially attentive to the linguistic, etymological origins of symbols. (JACQUES LACAN, in his insistence on the *letter* rather than the *corpus* in symbolism, still gives a substantial nod to Jones's essay ["Function" 81].)

Hamlet and Oedipus (1948), developed from an essay Jones originally wrote in 1910 into a slim book, is an elaboration of Freud's very brief remarks in *The Interpretation of Dreams* (1900, 264–66) on Oedipal motivations behind the prince's delay in avenging his father's foul murder. Whereas Freud used the example of Hamlet to support the Oedipus complex (Hamlet cannot punish Claudius, who has effected the patricide devoutly wished), Jones implicitly extends the psychoanalytic

reading into a clinical analysis of deep ambivalence toward the mother. For some literary critics, Jones's reading is vitiated by his speculations about Hamlet as a child: one chapter is titled "Tragedy and the Mind of the Infant." But Jones is candid about his assumptions: "No dramatic criticism of the personae in a play is possible except under the pretence that they are living people, and surely one is well aware of this pretence" (18).

Although Jones's work on *Hamlet* made him the best-known of early Freudian literary critics (Laurence Olivier consulted him for the 1950 film version), another of Freud's first-generation followers covered more literary and theoretical ground. Otto Rank (1884–1939) was one of Freud's brightest disciples. He eventually left over theoretical and personal disputes; for example, he favored "birth trauma" over castration as the originary model of personal deprivation. Author of an essay entitled "The Artist," which he presented to Freud in 1905, Rank maintained his interest in art throughout his life. *The Myth of the Birth of the Hero* (1909) is a remarkably erudite compilation of core motifs in cultural myths: the hero, the double, and the theme of incest. His vast mythological and literary research was in the service of grounding the Oedipus complex for psychoanalysis—although he eventually unsettled this ground with his ideas about birth trauma and pre-Oedipal separation anxiety.

Rank's essay on the *Doppelgänger* (1914, *The Double*) uses literary examples from E. T. A. Hoffman, Fyodor Dostoevsky, Robert Louis Stevenson, Oscar Wilde, Guy de Maupassant, and Edgar Allan Poe, aligning brief biographical sketches with theoretical emphasis on narcissism and projection: the double is both a reflection of self-love and a rival. His massive work on the incest-motif, *Das Inzest-Motiv in Dichtung und Sage* (1912, *The Incest Theme in Literature and Legend*), is a broad survey of Oedipal dynamics in European and world literature and mythology.

Less well known than Jones or Rank, Ella Freeman Sharpe (1875–1947) deserves mention because of her unique attention to language, especially metaphor. Sharpe came to psychoanalysis from literature, which she had been teaching. Many of her literary analyses follow Freud's: her essay "The Impatience of Hamlet" (1929) continues Jones's study (the early version published in 1910) and deepens it to consider pre-Oedipal issues, as well as the therapeutic functions of art: "The poet is not Hamlet. Hamlet is what he might have been if he had not written the play of *Hamlet*" (205). At her death she was working on a large treatment of Shakespeare's late career, a portion of which was published as "From *King Lear* to *The Tempest*" (1946). This fragmented essay is full of brilliant speculations and amplifies Freud's identification of the tripartite mother-imago in *Lear* (see Freud, "The Theme of the Three Caskets," 1913). Sharpe's literalism opens her to charges that she writes the worst sort of psychoanalytic criticism, as when she writes of "child Lear" howling in rage at his mother's pregnancy, or the King's retinue of knights as a symbol for feces, or the Bard himself as an angry, defecating infant (246). Yet her criticism was sharper than its reductions. She was well aware of the problem of treating characters as people or patients. At its best her own critical language marries the metaphors of Shakespeare and psychoanalysis to construct provocative readings of particular passages. Such analyses proceed from a deeply Freudian appreciation of metaphor and add a crucial developmental element to Jones's (1916) theoretical account in "Psycho-Physical Problems Revealed in Language: An Examination of Metaphor." "My theory," she stated, "is that metaphor can only evolve in language or in the arts when the bodily orifices become controlled. . . . A subterranean passage between mind and body underlies all analogy" (156). Later enthusiastic iterations of this concept may be found in Norman O. Brown's *Love's Body* (1966).

One of the fullest early developments of Freudian analysis of a single author was produced by Marie Bonaparte (1882–1962). Perhaps best known for her largess in helping Freud and his family escape the Nazis in 1938, Princess Bonaparte wrote an immense study of Edgar Allan Poe (1933). Freud wrote a brief preface to the work, which is a thorough effort to relate biographical details to all aspects of the artist's literary production. Bonaparte relied heavily on Freud's theoretical relation of the poet to the dreamer ("Creative Writers and Day-dreaming," 1908) and translated backwards from literature to unconscious wishes and fears, producing reductive psychosexual allegories. Hers is a primary-process criticism that seeks to collapse conventional forms of literary representation in favor of regressive translations to unconscious origins. She views Poe as a writer who transformed private traumata into fiction, principally the death of his mother when he was two. His artistic goal was to resurrect a living bond to a dead woman, a project simultaneously thrilling and terrifying. Bonaparte was especially attentive to characters, creatures, landscapes, and architecture as split or overdetermined representations of obsessive figures and themes. Her book is an extensive elaboration of Freud's dreamwork (condensation, displacement, symbolism): for example, maternal images appear in "The Black Cat" split into wife, cats, and the house itself; and Montresor's vaults in "A Cask of Amon-

tillado" are corporeal avenues of the maternal body. Bonaparte's Poe is a pathological, "sadonecrophilist" genius haunted by obsessive fantasies he could not comprehend but only repeat. More recent psychoanalytic approaches to the mystery of Poe, studies that essentially rely on Bonaparte even as they deride her apparent crudeness, are Daniel Hoffman's *Poe Poe Poe Poe Poe Poe Poe* (1972) and Lacan's "Seminar on 'The Purloined Letter'" (1972). This style of psychobiography achieved more sophisticated application in such works as Phyllis Greenacre on Jonathan Swift and Lewis Carroll and Leon Edel on Henry James.

Probably the best contemporary illustration of traditional Freudian criticism is the early work of Frederick Crews (b. 1938). Along with HAROLD BLOOM and Norman Holland, Crews encouraged by instruction and example much of the psychoanalytic criticism practiced in America since the mid-1960s. His seminal book on Nathaniel Hawthorne (1966) rescued that writer from conventional moralistic allegory and attended seriously to the dark landscape of sexual ambivalence that energizes his fiction. "The form of [Hawthorne's] plots," writes Crews, "often constitutes a return of the repressed" (17). Hawthorne's fascination with Puritans and the cultural history of guilt reflects his own unconscious impulses, which tend primarily to be Oedipal (79). In "Young Goodman Brown," for instance, Brown flees his wife's arms into a demonic forest full of sexual symbols and barely disguised primal-scene fantasies, a site that figures his own incestuous desires and fears of retribution (99–106). Crews offers finely tuned analyses of metaphor, image, and character, pressed toward psychobiographical conclusions about Hawthorne's "incomplete resolution of early Oedipal feelings" (241). For the most part, Crews's Hawthorne is carried by his fantasies rather than being the master of them: in "Rappaccini's Daughter," which allegorizes deep anxieties about genital sexuality into botanical imagery, "we can *almost* credit Hawthorne with a pitiless symbolic anatomy of an adolescent mind" (134). The critic judges the author's artistry to be ultimately hobbled by the obsessive power of his regressive fantasies. "All Hawthorne's serious fiction," Crews concludes, "amounts to a version of the same unconscious challenge; not one of his characters stands apart from the endless and finally suffocating debate about the gratification of forbidden wishes. . . . We must admire the art and separately regret the life. And yet it is a fact that the two are inextricable" (270–71).

Beginning in the mid-1970s, Crews developed a radical disaffection with psychoanalysis: see his critical reviews of Norman Holland's *Dynamics of Literary Response* (in *Out of My System*), Erik Erikson's *History and the Historical Moment* (in *Skeptical Engagements*), and the vigorous repudiations in several other essays in *Skeptical Engagements*. Although he came to reject the claims of psychoanalysis to scientific or interpretive validity, Crews retained a relatively generous attitude toward his book on Hawthorne. Instead of using Freud to explain Hawthorne's sexual fascinations, however, Crews later pointed to similar themes in both writers and located each in a *Zeitgeist* of "the psychological atmosphere of Romanticism" (*Skeptical* xiii–xiv).

David Willbern

Marie Bonaparte, *Edgar Poe, étude psychanalytique* (1933, 2 vols., *The Life and Works of Edgar Allan Poe: A Psychoanalytic Interpretation,* trans. John Rodker, 1971); Victor Brome, *Ernest Jones: A Biography* (1983); Norman O. Brown, *Love's Body* (1966); Ronald W. Clark, *Sigmund Freud: The Man and the Cause* (1980); Frederick Crews, *Out of My System: Psychoanalysis, Ideology, and Critical Method* (1975), *Psychoanalysis and Literary Process* (1970), *The Sins of the Fathers: Hawthorne's Literary Themes* (1966), *Skeptical Engagements* (1986); Leon Edel, *Henry James* (5 vols., 1953–72); Anton Ehrenzweig, *The Hidden Order of Art: A Study in the Psychology of Artistic Imagination* (1967); Otto Fenichel, *The Psychoanalytic Theory of Neurosis* (1945); Peter Gay, *Freud: A Life for Our Time* (1988); Phyllis Greenacre, *Swift and Carroll: A Psychoanalytic Study of Two Lives* (1955); Daniel Hoffman, *Poe Poe Poe Poe Poe Poe Poe* (1972); Frederick J. Hoffman, *Freudianism and the Literary Mind* (1945); Ernest Jones, *Hamlet and Oedipus* (1949), *The Life and Work of Sigmund Freud* (3 vols., 1957), *On the Nightmare* (1931), *Psycho-Myth, Psycho-History [Essays in Applied Psycho-Analysis]* (1974), "The Theory of Symbolism," *Papers on Psycho-Analysis* (5th ed., 1916); Ernst Kris, *Psychoanalytic Explorations in Art* (1952); Jacques Lacan, "The Function and Field of Speech and Language in Psychoanalysis" ("The Rome Discourse"), *Écrits: A Selection* (1953, trans. Alan Sheridan, 1977), "Seminar on 'The Purloined Letter,'" *The Purloined Poe* (ed. Muller and Richardson, trans. Jeffrey Mehlman, 1988); John Muller and William Richardson, eds., *The Purloined Poe: Lacan, Derrida, and Psychoanalytic Reading* (1988); Otto Rank, *Art and Artist: Creative Urge and Personality Development* (1932), *Der Doppelgänger* (1914, *The Double: A Psychoanalytic Study,* trans. Harry Tucker, Jr., 1925), *Das Inzest-Motiv in Dichtung und Sage* (1912, *The Incest Theme in Literature and Legend: Fundamentals of a Psychology of Literary Creation,* trans. Gregory C. Richter, 1992), *The Myth of the Birth of the Hero* (1909, trans. F. Robbins and Smith Ely

Jelliffe, 1914); Ella Freeman Sharpe, *Collected Papers on Psycho-Analysis* (ed. Marjorie Brierley, 1950).

2. Reconceptualizing Freud

Classical Freudianism was reconceptualized by four literary theorists who argued that the content of psychic fantasy was relevant to literary study as well as to therapy. Because they derived from SIGMUND FREUD evidence for extralinguistic ontologies, they are distinguishable, too, from strict Lacanian theorists. For Melanie Klein, literature and fantasy reflect the drive; for Simon O. Lesser and Norman N. Holland, texts evoke in readers intrapsychic struggles characterized chiefly by strategies of defense; for Norman O. Brown, such struggles are also observable in history. The impact of these theorists' writings challenged the postwar hegemony of NEW CRITICISM; their work continues to be invoked in contemporary literary debates, including those that concern DECONSTRUCTION.

Melanie Klein (1882–1960) was a prominent member of the interwar "English school" of psychoanalysis in London, which modified Freudian theory in significant ways. Following her intuition of a parallel between dreams and children at play, Klein undertook the first serious and extensive analyses of young children, work which culminated in *The Psycho-Analysis of Children* (1932). There Klein hypothesized the existence of a pre-Oedipal phase (or "position" in her terminology) in which children introject their first object, the breast, splitting it into ideal and persecutory (or "good" and "bad") modes, an action that corresponds to the genesis of ego and superego. This introjection and splitting presupposes the existence of a nonlibidinous aggressive drive. Children later experience "the depressive position," in which the final loss of the good object becomes the prototype of all subsequent mourning. Psychic life consists of symbiotic anxieties (at the prospect of annihilation or loss) and defenses (expressed in mature love as alternations between guilt and reparation).

Aside from a posthumously published essay on *The Oresteia*, Klein wrote no literary interpretation; however, her modifications of Freudian theory have been of interest to contemporary critics. In challenging the supremacy of the Oedipus complex, Klein presented an alternative psychoanalytic account of feminine sexuality. Rather than conceiving girls as arriving at sexuality through deprivation or lack, Klein redefined penis envy as a defense against a more primordial fear, the attack from either parent (as introjected in the nascent superego). In *Revolution in Poetic Language,* JULIA KRISTEVA draws on the Kleinian theory of the drive to argue that such pre-Oedipal processes correspond to the semiotic (27, 151–52). Toril Moi argues that HÉLÈNE CIXOUS's mother figure may be based in part on Klein's "Good Mother" (115). Kleinian theory is invoked by Margery Durham in her explication of Coleridge's "Christabel," and Simon Stuart applies Klein's theories to Romantic poets, especially William Blake and William Wordsworth.

Like Klein, whom he cites with approval, Simon O. Lesser (1909–79) found in the developmental aspects of Freudianism its greatest explanatory power. Lesser was one of the first American critics to argue that the experience of reading and interpreting literature should be understood psychoanalytically, as a function of the ego's defenses against prohibited impulses, especially as these impulses are stimulated by fantasies evoked by the text. Relying on the work of Klein, Ernst Kris, and Otto Fenichel, Lesser advanced this thesis in articles written between 1952 and 1976, collected in *Fiction and the Unconscious* (1957) and in *Whispered Meanings* (1977). There he argued the superiority of his psychoanalytic approach over the methods of New Criticism on the grounds that formalist criticism (e.g., that of Cleanth Brooks and Robert Penn Warren) was naive in its misunderstanding of the source of the reader's identification with the narrators and protagonists of fiction. Lesser's best-known demonstration of his case is his reading of Nathaniel Hawthorne's "My Kinsman, Major Molineux," which he sees as depicting unacknowledged Oedipal and aggressive forces in its hero, Robin. Lesser contends that readers implicitly identify with Robin's unconscious quest for sexual adventure and his fantasy of escape from authority even while consciously denying any such identification. Lesser finds similar dyads of fantasy and defense in works by Sherwood Anderson, T. S. Eliot, and Herman Melville. Following Klein, he sees literary form as functioning to enable the ego to contemplate otherwise repugnant or offensive material. Hence, Lesser accuses New Criticism and other formalisms of evading the powerful instinctual drives expressed in literature at the latent level. For example, Lesser repudiates Elder Olson's interpretation of Yeats's "Sailing to Byzantium," which he faults for ignoring the speaker's duplicity and ambivalence about sexuality.

Lesser's influence on Norman N. Holland (b. 1927) has been explicitly acknowledged: the younger critic recognized his predecessor's innovation in using the tenets of psychoanalysis to understand the act of reading literature. Holland developed his strategy with diverse, increasingly sophisticated tactics. He began his career

as a student of the drama—Reformation comedy and Shakespeare—in books that analyzed the function of costume, disguise, and role in the metamorphosis of identity. With *Psychoanalysis and Shakespeare* his criticism became overtly Freudian, although his objectives were still text-centered. But in *The Dynamics of Literary Response* and afterwards, Holland developed a reader-response criticism that drew upon psychoanalytic and psychological traditions of ego development (see READER-RESPONSE THEORY AND CRITICISM). The continuity between his earliest and latest work is in his concern to elaborate some fundamental human identity in and through the study of literature.

Holland's argument in *Dynamics* was close to Lesser's in *Fiction and the Unconscious:* readers experience literature as a transformation of unconscious fantasy materials. However, in later works Holland denied that the text actually "contained" as a totality the core of fantasies that would induce readers' individual, partial transformations of them. In works since *Five Readers Reading* he exchanged his earlier text-centered model for a wholly interactive one that defines text as promptuary and the experience of reading as part of infinitely recursive feedback loops in which readers are located. In *Five Readers Reading* Holland saw his interactive model as part of a twentieth-century tradition that includes Ernst Cassirer, Edmund Husserl, and JOHN DEWEY, and "bridged the gap" of Cartesian dualism (see RENÉ DESCARTES); in *The I,* identity as theme-and-variation is viewed less epistemologically, more as the construct of an interpreter and interpretee.

Holland's goal is to unify and synthesize reader-response criticism by articulating its affinities with psychiatry, psychology, phenomenology, and aesthetics. At the same time, his work has accorded increasing importance to individual variations in interpretation. In "The Delphi Seminar" and in later works, Holland advocates a pedagogy according to which diversity of interpretation is never divorced from individual psychology. He advocates and exemplifies the view that critics must acknowledge their own anxieties, defenses, and even sociopolitical biases in dealing with texts. In his most recent work he calls for reader-response criticism to become conscious of such unacknowledged presuppositions by learning from questions raised by feminist, Third World, and gay critics. One example of his engagement with feminist discourses is his dialogue with Leona Sherman on the nature of Gothic fiction. On the other hand, Elizabeth Flynn and Patrocinio Schweickart suggest that his reader-response criticism may embody inherently male approaches to the text (xxi–xxv). His position has also been criticized at length by David Bleich (111–21), who sees it as an attempt to reinstate objectivism. Holland distinguishes his own work from the reception criticism of Hans Robert Jauss or the reader-response criticism of Wolfgang Iser by arguing that those theorists seek to define a more generalized receiver of texts, created by culture or even by the text itself, whereas Holland's "reader" is irreducibly individual and idiosyncratic (see RECEPTION THEORY). A complete account of his critical position, together with his assessment of related ones, is available in *Holland's Guide to Psychoanalytic Psychology and Literature and Psychology*.

Of the works discussed in this group, Norman O. Brown's is the most idiosyncratic, but his vigorous interpretation of Freud remains influential. Brown (b. 1913) wrote two principal contributions to contemporary criticism: *Life Against Death* (1959) and *Love's Body* (1966). In *Life Against Death* he offered a radical interpretation of Freud drawing on classical literature, RALPH WALDO EMERSON, FRIEDRICH NIETZSCHE, and Continental writers of the Freudian Left, especially Wilhelm Reich and Geza Roheim. Brown argued that Freud's importance lay in his depiction, in *Civilization and Its Discontents* (1930), of a universal neurosis; that the institution of repression implied the seemingly permanent human subjugation to a life of illusion and sublimation; that repression was evidenced in the fall from the polymorphous perversity of infantile sexuality through oral, anal, and phallic stages to the tyranny of genital organization; that orthodox academic or clinical interpretations of Freud colluded with the forces of repression by emphasizing the necessity to adapt to societal norms that were by definition sick; and that the only chance for some "way out" of this dilemma was to be found in Freud's metapsychological speculations on Eros and Thanatos, the life and death drives (or libido and *Todestrieb*).

The "way out" that Brown adumbrates is set forth in *Life Against Death*'s last chapter, "The Resurrection of the Body." There he argues that psychoanalysis must situate itself inside the larger tradition of Occidental and Oriental mysticism, which he valorizes in works of Christian gnosticism, Jewish cabalism, Taoism, Boehme, Blake, Rilke, and dissident psychoanalytic theorists. Such a reconceptualization will disclose that the dual drives Freud postulated can themselves be subsumed into one unity; Brown interprets Freud's "oceanic feeling"—from *The Future of an Illusion* (1928)—to denote a desire for union between self and world that, once recovered, can heal the divisions created by repression. (Brown sees repression itself as equiprimordial with the separation of the

infant from the mother; hence, the "resurrection of the body" would imply the restoration of that time "before the fall" into repression. In this way he links his "way out" with Christian eschatology.)

One of the most influential sections of *Life Against Death* has been its fifth part, "Studies in Anality," in which Brown analyzes Protestantism, the scatological poems of Jonathan Swift, and the representation of money in literature. He argues that poetry dramatizes the horror of sublimation and repression. Regarding Protestantism, he holds that the Lutheran equation of the world with the devil, born of the link between money and excrement, anticipates his own indictment of a world given over to the death instinct. He finds support for both theses in the recurrent theme of "filthy lucre" in literature.

Brown's intent in *Love's Body* is to pursue to its logical conclusion the "way out" briefly sketched at the end of *Life Against Death*. The path to the realization of his hypostasized absolute unity is traced through psychological, historical, and social stages, beginning with a perception of separateness and the repression of political society, through intellectual rebellion to the achievement of fulfillment, freedom, and—perhaps ominously—nothingness. The book exemplifies and urges such an inner journey or quest, but its advocacy (based loosely on the fugitive anthropology of Freud's *Totem and Taboo* and *Moses and Monotheism*) is no less idiosyncratic than its composition and style: Brown paraphrases and quotes directly from more than 300 works in the mystical tradition he celebrates, but apart from free association and a general relevance to his chapters' broad rubrics, these excerpts are not otherwise connected. The result is a mosaic in which the intellectual affinities of various authors are asserted through juxtaposition. Brown's mosaic technique is a consequence of his attack on sequential logic and rationality, in both books, as exacerbations of repression and sublimation.

Since *Love's Body* Brown has persevered in the critical trajectory he has always followed. *Closing Time* continues the mosaic technique of *Love's Body*, this time juxtaposing the life and work of GIAMBATTISTA VICO with James Joyce's *Finnegans Wake* in an effort to disclose in each writer a cyclical eschatology that aims at the saying of some ultimate word. (It is likely that Brown was drawn to Vico in part by virtue of the latter's ambivalent relations with the academy, a constant motif in all of Brown's writings.) Most recently he has argued that the Western prophetic tradition must be defined as including Islamic as well as more conventional Judeo-Christian texts and movements, in order to locate the

Blakean unity—Brown's grail—under its apparently diverse surfaces.

Christopher D. Morris

See also SIGMUND FREUD and READER-RESPONSE THEORY AND CRITICISM.

David Bleich, *Subjective Criticism* (1978); Norman O. Brown, *Apocalypse and/or Metamorphosis* (1993), "Apocalypse: The Place of Mystery in the Life of the Mind," *Harper's* (May 1961), *Closing Time* (1973), "Daphne, or Metamorphosis," *Myths, Dreams, and Religion* (ed. Joseph Campbell, 1970), *Hermes, The Thief* (1947), *Hesiod's Theogeny* (1953), *Life Against Death* (1959), *Love's Body* (1966); Margery Durham, "The Mother Tongue: Christabel and the Language of Love," *The (M)other Tongue: Essays in Feminist Psychoanalytic Interpretation* (ed. Shirley N. Garner, Claire Kahane, and Madelon Sprengnether, 1986); Elizabeth A. Flynn and Patrocinio P. Schweickart, eds., *Gender and Reading: Essays on Readers, Texts, and Contexts* (1986); Phyllis Grosskurth, *Melanie Klein: Her World and Her Work* (1986); Norman N. Holland, *The Dynamics of Literary Response* (1968), *Five Readers Reading* (1975), *Holland's Guide to Psychoanalytic Psychology and Literature and Psychology* (1990), *The I* (1985), *Laughing: A Psychology of Humor* (1982), "The Nature of Psychoanalytic Criticism," *Literature and Psychology* 12 (1962), "The New Paradigm: Subjective or Transactive?" *New Literary History* 7 (1976), "The Prophetic Tradition," *Studies in Romanticism* 21 (1982), *Psychoanalysis and Shakespeare* (1966), "Twenty-five Years and Thirty Days," *Psychoanalytic Quarterly* 55 (1986), "Unity Identity Text Self," *PMLA* 90 (1975); Norman N. Holland and Murray Schwartz, "The Delphi Seminar," *College English* 36 (1975); Norman N. Holland and Leona F. Sherman, "Gothic Possibilities" (Flynn and Schweickart); Melanie Klein, *The Writings of Melanie Klein*, 4 vols. (1984, vol. 1, *Love, Guilt, and Reparation and Other Works, 1921–45*; vol. 2, *The Psycho-Analysis of Children*; vol. 3, *Envy and Gratitude and Other Works, 1946–1963*; vol. 4, *Narrative of a Child Analysis*); Julia Kristeva, *La Révolution du langage poétique: L'Avant-garde à la fin du XIXe siècle, Lautréamont et Mallarmé* (1974, *Revolution in Poetic Language,* trans. Margaret Waller, 1984); Simon O. Lesser, *Fiction and the Unconscious* (1957), "The Image of the Father," *Five Approaches of Literary Criticism* (ed. Wilbur Scott, 1963), "The Language of Fiction," *A College Book of Modern Fiction* (ed. Walter B. Rideout and James K. Robinson, 1961), "Some Unconscious Elements in Response to Fiction," *Literature and Psychology* 3 (1953), *The Whispered Meanings: Selected Essays of Simon O. Lesser* (ed. Robert Sprich and Richard Nolan, 1977); Toril Moi, *Sexual/Textual Politics: Feminist Literary Theory* (1985); Simon Stuart, *New Phoenix Wings: Reparation in Literature* (1979).

3. The Post-Lacanians

In the late 1930s JACQUES LACAN began challenging a number of conclusions long advanced by many psychoanalytic theorists and analysts. Lacan not only inveighed against the approach of American ego psychologists and its emphasis on the stability of the ego as a betrayal of Freudian thought but redefined the ego in relation to the "subject" of structural linguistics and SEMIOTICS. In his "return to Freud," Lacan attempted to find rigorously psychoanalytic explanations for the ego's relation to the most important of psychoanalytic concepts, the unconscious, the psychic agency Lacan reconceived in semiotic terms and claimed was "structured like a language." Consistent with the poststructuralist reconception of the "subject," this line of thought eventually led to far-reaching changes in psychoanalytic practice in France and beyond regarding how therapy is conducted and how it effects cures.

This new thinking, characteristic of post–World War II anti-Hegelianism among French intellectuals, also engendered widespread reconsideration of psychoanalysis's institutional function to the point that many in France took Lacan to be a prime instigator (because he was challenging established institutions) of the May 1968 uprisings by French students and workers. In the 1970s and 1980s a new wave of French theorists and critics trained or influenced by Lacan began to extend or revise psychoanalysis even further to address institutional and ideological issues more directly. They argued that Lacan did not go far enough in probing precisely the areas characterizing his discourse: the psychoanalytic dimensions of the "subject"; psychoanalysis as both a clinical practice and a cultural institution; and psychoanalysis as ideologically committed and engaged.

These post-Lacanians included contributors in the late 1960s and 1970s to the French journal *Tel Quel*, feminists influenced by DECONSTRUCTION, and Continental critics of the political Left. Some tended to *combine* Lacan's insights with other perspectives as an attempt to galvanize both sides but made no fundamental changes in Lacan's precepts. HÉLÈNE CIXOUS's criticism belongs in this category in that she incorporated Lacanian strategies in feminism and deconstruction but did not challenge psychoanalytic discourse. This "additive" approach includes the ongoing work of Shoshana Felman, JULIA KRISTEVA, Stephen Heath, and Colin MacCabe, among others. More demanding of concessions from psychoanalysis is the theoretical orientation of LUCE IRIGARAY. In yet another group are Gilles Deleuze and Félix Guattari, who have moved beyond psychoanalysis to challenge and recast its theoretical concerns and its function as an institutional representation of culture.

Kristeva, for example, has followed Lacan in her conception of the subject and in her problematic approach to the woman question: "A woman cannot 'be'; it is something which does not even belong in the order of *being*" (Marks and de Courtivron 137). As for writing, Kristeva sees women as facing two alternatives: either valorizing "phallic dominance, associated with the privileged father-daughter relationship, which gives rise to the tendency toward mastery," or valorizing "a silent underwater body," which entails the choice of marginalization (Marks and de Courtivron 166). The alternative she proposes is that women assume a negative function, one that would reject whole structures and explode social codes.

Likewise, Michèle Montrelay, who sees her writing as a contribution to a better understanding of the laws, structure, and dynamic of the unconscious, is convinced that "in our civilization, psychoanalysis, as theory and as treatment, is one of the most precious, highest, most symbolic forms of freedom" (Jardine and Menke 254) and emphasizes the political aspect of her work. In *L'Ombre et le nom* (1977), she attempts to probe psychoanalytic concepts, such as the assumption of woman as a "dark continent" and others concerning gender relations that continue to function within Freudian discourse. Often close to representing femininity in traditional terms—the feminine as the shadow and the outside that supports culture—Montrelay is also concerned with exposing the phallocentric bias in the Lacanian ethical hierarchy that privileges the Symbolic over the Imaginary. Rather than attempting to reverse the hierarchy, she proposes to shift the emphasis away from a hierarchy of values and to regard the Imaginary not as "the poor relative" but as necessary to give consistency to the Symbolic (Montrelay 155–56).

Naturally, many of these thinkers have been concerned with the problematic nature of the question of feminine subjectivity in Lacan. By discussing the subject solely in masculine terms, Lacan canceled out woman, and only too often he has reaffirmed that it is in the phallus that we find "the signifier intended to designate as a whole the effects of the signified, in that the signifier conditions them by its presence as signifier" (*Écrits: A Selection* 285). Many have agreed with Lacan's notion that "there is no woman but excluded by the nature of things which is the nature of words" (*Séminaire* 68) but have objected to what follows: "and it has to be said that if there is one thing about which women themselves are complaining at the moment, it is well and truly that—it is just that they don't know what they are saying, which is all the difference between them and me" (68). Indeed, much effort has been spent turning this lack to the advantage of women by devising strategies that, by revealing the ways in which femininity disrupts symbolic structures, also indicate the ways in which it circulates and inscribes itself. Woman's language, according to many feminists, will be found by returning to the pre-Oedipal union with the mother.

Committed to a more radical strategy, many critics of psychoanalysis do accept primary semiotic and structuralist advances of Lacan's thought and have worked in light of these assumptions to displace the traditional idea of a subject (as an ego) and to deconstruct the traditional Freudian idea of desire. This is the direction of the transformative psychoanalytic critiques of Nicholas Abraham, Maria Torok, Gilles Deleuze, and Félix Guattari—Deleuze and Guattari, in particular, influencing those who wanted to go "beyond" primary Freudian concepts and Lacanian innovations such as the subject, the Imaginary, the Symbolic, and the Real. They focus mainly on "Oedipus," Freud's master plot for familial and social organization, the narrative that evokes, first, fantasies of unity expressing infantile idealizations of parental care; second, fantasies of alienation, rupture, and "morcellation" associated with the assertion of paternal and cultural authority; and third, the partial reclamation of childhood fantasies in conjunction with adult responsibility and maturity. Likewise, several French feminists of the 1960s, Hélène Cixous among them, sought to meld psychoanalytic procedures with feminist projects for the reclamation of women's culture.

Shoshana Felman's work belongs in this area. Authoritative, wide-ranging, and always lucid, she has helped to shape Lacanian studies since the mid-1970s. And along with Anthony Wilden, Jane Gallop, and Ellie Ragland-Sullivan, she has been committed to exploring literary and cultural criticism in relation to what she frequently calls the force of his teaching, his "revolutionary" pedagogy. Her work indicates, moreover, the movement of Lacanian studies in the 1980s toward an appreciation of Lacanian *practice* as actively engaged with postmodern and avant-garde modes of thought.

For Felman, Lacan's great contribution to contemporary culture is his teaching about rhetorical "performance" and "cognition," doing and knowing. She draws on speech-act philosopher J. L. Austin's definition of the "performative" as rhetorical enactment, language use as much as possible as separate from what it conveys, a pure doing. The "constative," or cognitive, is what rhetoric creates, meaning as pure sense conveyed apart from how it came to be. The "revolutionary" dimension of Lacan's pedagogy for Felman is the dialogism of the performative and constative, how in practice they undermine, deconstruct, and yet inform each other. The interactions of doing and undoing form the dynamic basis, Felman says, of psychoanalysis's "ineradicable newness" (12), its evergreen vitality and unceasing "revolutionary" nature. Building on this insight, Lacan has shown experience, largely unconscious, to be structured like a language, since human behavior manifests the dialectical interaction of conscious and unconscious experience, the double writing of that which is *enacted* beyond what can ever be *known* at any one moment.

In *Jacques Lacan and the Adventure of Insight* Felman wants to bring pedagogy into psychoanalysis, which Lacan conceived to be fundamentally and *already* a teaching anyway, and to show that a pedagogue should teach in relation to the student's "unmeant knowledge" (77), the unconscious as it is inscribed but at the same time hidden in teaching as a kind of text. The "unmeant" is of paramount importance because "teaching, like analysis has to deal not so much with lack of knowledge as with resistances to knowledge" (79), unmeant knowledge being significant because its lapses and breaks are unconsciously motivated. In a reversal of priorities, Felman virtually promotes "ignorance" and decenters "learning" as the primary preoccupation of teaching. Felman's rendition of Lacan is an implicit plea for adoption of a complex and subtle response to pedagogical discourse: respect for the "Other" conceived as the unconscious within language, respect given through the performative enactment of reading the unconscious text by actively recognizing resistances and absences and "unmeant" knowledge. Felman argues in her discussions of literature, criticism, and education that humans must read and interpret psychoanalytically so as to respond to the radical alterity of the impossibilities posed by the Other. In actual practice, her reading of literature focuses on the rhetorical dimension of hiddenness in texts, that which emerges when one reads the patterns of rhetorical strategy in a text as well as the achieved effects of rhetoric.

Gilles Deleuze and Félix Guattari have moved in their own work from avant-garde experiments and probings of contemporary discourse to radical discursive practices. As an academic philosopher, for example, Deleuze began his career with typically "modern" topics such as

Empiricism and Subjectivity: An Essay on Hume's Theory of Human Nature (1953, trans., 1991), and *Kant's Critical Philosophy: The Doctrine of the Faculties* (1963, trans., 1984). Guattari began his work as a psychoanalyst trained in Lacan's school in Paris, and beginning in 1953 he also practiced at La Borde clinic, a radical experiment in providing noninstitutionalized versions of therapy. In different ways, in other words, both theorists performed early "immanent" critiques of contemporary psychoanalytic and other discourses. When they began working together, they moved toward radically "transformative" critique of the sort that Cixous and Irigaray call for.

Deleuze and Guattari, in short, seek to critique psychoanalysis to transform it altogether, ultimately to *destroy* it by unmasking its ideological foundation in the values of bourgeois culture. Accordingly, their move in this area is aimed at psychoanalytic "theory" but just as intently at psychoanalysis as an institutional representation of culture in its bourgeois and patriarchal dimensions. *Anti-Oedipus: Capitalism and Schizophrenia* (1977, trans., 1983) and *A Thousand Plateaus: Capitalism and Schizophrenia* (1980, trans., 1987) try to dissect psychoanalysis so as to institute truly new understandings and discourses for contemporary culture on the ashes of the old along three lines. First, they try to expose the nature of repression and castration as fundamental to psychoanalytic machinery. Second, they critique the psychoanalytic characterization of the unconscious as an ideal of static being rather than active production. And third, they try to expose the situating of discourse within the hegemonic constraints of the Oedipal narrative.

Deleuze and Guattari reject this notion of repression and castration as "molar"—blanket conceptions, a cluster of suppressed assumptions united in an ideologically motivated pattern that is taken mistakenly to be "scientific" and "naturally" the way humans function. The buried supposition behind the term "castration," as Deleuze and Guattari show, is "that there is finally only one sex, the masculine, in relation to which the woman, the feminine, is [also] defined as a lack, an absence" (*Anti-Oedipus* 294). Deleuze and Guattari challenge this hegemonic version of cultural regulation as promulgated to advance a "molar" (and essentialist) conception of males. By contrast, the "molecular," nonessentialist conception of the unconscious, like the repression that engenders it, "knows nothing of castration," precisely because castration as such is an ideologically motivated construct not attributable to the operation of repression (295). Deleuze and Guattari seek to explode the concept of castration as a form-giving and unifying concept and speak, instead, of the unconscious producing positive "multiplicities" and "flows" (295), potentially not just "two sexes, but *n* sexes," perhaps "a hundred thousand" (296).

What allows the constitution of such "molar" conceptions of castration to begin with is Freud's conception of the unconscious as a static *representation*. The fact of the unconscious as such is not objectionable, and to a certain point Freud conceived of the unconscious as the site of the "production of desire." Deleuze and Guattari, without irony, call this conception the "great discovery of psychoanalysis" (*Anti-Oedipus* 24). The problem comes, rather, in Freud's attempt to bury the unconscious "beneath a new brand of idealism" and to associate it with the *representation* (rather than *production*) of "a classical theater" of "myth, tragedy, [and] dreams" (24). In short, Freud, and Lacan after him, connects the unconscious, in a detour through Greek myth, inextricably with the family and the ideological investments inherent to the West.

The final target of Deleuze and Guattari's attack on psychoanalysis and patriarchal culture in general is Oedipus. The three areas of their attack are interrelated, and certainly the attack on Oedipus recapitulates that on the "familial" version of the unconscious. But Oedipus is an even broader concept and must be seen not merely as an ideological interpretation of psychological functions but in a broader, political sense, as Mark Seem asserts, "the [very] figurehead of imperialism [and] 'colonization'" (*Anti-Oedipus* xx). Oedipus is a construct "more powerful . . . than psychoanalysis, than the family, than ideology, even joined together" (122), and encompasses the whole of the hegemonic regime that is "Western culture"; it is "Oedipus" at this encompassing level that Deleuze and Guattari oppose in their fervor to be "anti-Oedipal."

Deleuze and Guattari project the "post-Oedipal" as a world without the genital and Oedipal organization characteristic of Western culture. The loss of this traditional genital economy will yet produce, among many other things, a radically liberated human body, a "body without organs" (*Thousand* 285), a body of energy "flows" and "excesses" that is capable of "becoming an animal" (259) in the specific sense that psychoanalysis, with its Western belief in castration and Oedipal commitments, "doesn't understand becoming an animal" (259). However one may understand "becoming an animal" or the a-linear logic and irrationality of the "rhizome" (or a-paternal) economy of culture as discussed in *A Thousand Plateaus*, it is clear that Deleuze and Guattari want to violate and suspend Western ideology as they find it figured in the schemata of psychoanalysis. They advo-

cate the pursuit of ratios and economies of experience *other than* those Freud could conceive in his own recapitulation of the values and commitments already evident in Western culture from the ancient Greeks forward. As literary critics, they tend to be deconstructive readers who challenge and dismantle the unities of realism and its metonymic effects of familiarity in a text. Ultimately, they wish to deconstruct the textual authority of the paternal metaphor that is at the heart of Oedipus.

Chiara Briganti and Robert Con Davis

See also HÉLÈNE CIXOUS, FRENCH THEORY AND CRITICISM: 5. 1945–1968 and 6. 1968 AND AFTER, LUCE IRIGARAY, JULIA KRISTEVA, and JACQUES LACAN.

Hélène Cixous, *Angst* (1977, *Angst,* trans. Jo Levy, 1985), "Castration or Decapitation?" (trans. Annette Kuhn, *Signs* 7 [1981]); Hélène Cixous and Catherine Clément, *La Jeune née* (1975, *The Newly Born Woman,* trans. Betsy Wing, 1986); Gilles Deleuze, *The Deleuze Reader* (ed. Constantin V. Boundas, 1992), *Empirisme et subjectivité* (1953, *Empiricism and Subjectivity: An Essay on Hume's Theory of Human Nature,* trans. Constantin V. Boundas, 1991), *La Philosophie critique de Kant* (1963, *Kant's Critical Philosophy: The Doctrine of the Faculties,* trans. Hugh Tomlinson and Barbara Habberjam, 1984); Gilles Deleuze and Félix Guattari, *L'Anti-Oedipe: Capitalisme et schizophrénie* (1972, *Anti-Oedipus: Capitalism and Schizophrenia,* trans. Robert Hurley, Mark Seem, and Helen R. Lane, 1983), *Mille Plateaux* (1980, *A Thousand Plateaus: Capitalism and Schizophrenia,* trans. Brian Massumi, 1987); Shoshana Felman, *Jacques Lacan and the Adventure of Insight: Psychoanalysis in Contemporary Culture* (1987), *The Literary Speech Act: Don Juan with J. L. Austin, or Seduction in Two Languages* (1980, trans. Catherine Porter, 1983); Félix Guattari, *La Révolution moléculaire* (1977, *Molecular Revolution: Psychiatry and Politics,* trans. Rosemary Sheed, 1984); Luce Irigaray, *Amante marine de Friedrich Nietzsche* (1979), *Ce Sexe qui n'en est pas un* (1977, *This Sex Which Is Not One,* trans. Catherine Porter with Carolyn Burke, 1985), *Speculum de l'autre femme* (1974, *Speculum of the Other Woman,* trans. Gillian C. Gill, 1985); Julia Kristeva, *Desire in Language: A Semiotic Approach to Literature and Art* (trans. Thomas Gora, Alice Jardine, and Leon S. Roudiez, 1980), *Pouvoirs de l'horreur: Essay sur l'adjection* (1980, *Powers of Horror: An Essay on Abjection,* trans. Leon S. Roudiez, 1982), *La Révolution du langage poétique: L'Avant-garde à la fin du XIXe siècle, Lautréamont et Mallarmé* (1974, *Revolution in Poetic Language,* trans. Margaret Waller, 1984); Jacques Lacan, *Écrits* (1966, *Écrits: A Selection,* trans. Alan Sheridan, 1977), *Le Séminaire livre XX: Encore* (ed. Jacques-

Alain Miller, 1975); Elaine Marks and Isabelle de Courtivron, eds., *New French Feminisms: An Anthology* (1980);
Michèle Montrelay, *L'Ombre et le nom: Sur la féminité*
(1977).

Shari Benstock, "Signifying the Body Feminine," *Tex-
tualizing the Feminine: On the Limits of Genre* (1991); Teresa
Brennan, ed., *Between Feminism and Psychoanalysis* (1989);
Judith Butler, *Gender Trouble: Feminism and the Subver-
sion of Identity* (1990); Teresa de Lauretis, *Alice Doesn't:
Feminism, Semiotics, Cinema* (1984); Jean-Joseph Goux,
Freud, Marx: Économie et symbolique (1973, *Symbolic Econ-
omies: After Marx and Freud,* trans. Jennifer Curtiss Gage,
1990); Elizabeth A. Grosz, *Jacques Lacan: A Feminist Intro-*
duction (1990); Alice Jardine, *Gynesis: Configurations of
Woman and Modernity* (1985); Alice Jardine and Anne
Menke, "The Politics of Tradition: Placing Women in
French Literature," *Yale French Studies* 75 (1988); Sarah
Kofman, *L'Enfance de l'art: Une Interprétation de l'esthé-
tique freudienne* (1970, *The Childhood of Art: An Interpreta-
tion of Freud's Aesthetic,* trans. Winifred Woodhull, 1988);
John Lechte, *Julia Kristeva* (1990); James M. Mellard,
Using Lacan: Reading Fiction (1991); Toril Moi, *Sexual/Tex-
tual Politics: Feminist Literary Theory* (1985); Toril Moi, ed.,
French Feminist Thought: A Reader (1987); Elaine Sho-
walter, ed., *The New Feminist Criticism: Essays on Women,
Literature, and Theory* (1985).

R

READER-RESPONSE THEORY AND CRITICISM

Reader-response criticism can be traced as far back as ARISTOTLE and PLATO, both of whom based their critical arguments at least partly on literature's effect on the reader. It has more immediate sources in the writings of the French structuralists (who stress the role of the perceiver as a maker of reality), the semioticians, and such American critics as KENNETH BURKE (esp. his "Psychology and Form," which defined "form" in terms of the audience's appetite), Louise Rosenblatt, Walker Gibson (who developed the notion of a "mock reader"), and Wayne Booth. But reader criticism became recognized as a distinct critical movement only in the 1970s, when it found a particularly congenial political climate in the growing anti-authoritarianism within the academy.

Calling it a movement, however, is misleading, for reader-response criticism is less a unified critical school than a vague collection of disparate critics with a common point of departure. That is, reader-response critics share neither a body of critical principles (as Marxist critics, for instance, do), nor a subject matter (as Renaissance critics do). Indeed, they barely share a name. "Reader theory" and "audience theory" are perhaps the most neutral general terms, since the more popular term "reader-response theory" most accurately refers to more subjective kinds of reader criticism, and "RECEPTION THEORY" most accurately refers to the German school of *Receptionkritik* represented by Hans Robert Jauss. But these and other terms are often used indiscriminately, and the boundaries separating them are cloudy at best.

What affinity there is among reader-critics comes from their rejection of the New Critical principle (most clearly enunciated in W. K. Wimsatt and Monroe Beardsley's pivotal essay, "The Affective Fallacy") that severs the work itself from its effect and strongly privileges the former, treated in formal terms. Refusing to accept this banning of the reader, reader-critics take the existence of the reader as a decisive component of any meaningful literary analysis, assuming, as Michael Riffaterre puts it, that "readers make the literary event" (116). But once

past that first step, there is little unanimity. Indeed, even the meaning of that first step has generated considerable debate, for different critics mean different things when they talk about "the reader."

For some critics, readers are abstract or hypothetical entities, and even these are of various sorts. The category of hypothetical readers is often thought, for instance, to take in what Gerald Prince calls the "narratee," the person to whom the narrator is addressing his or her narration (e.g., the "you" to whom Huckleberry Finn directs his opening sentence). For as Prince himself insists, the narratee, like the narrator, is really a character (even if sometimes only implicitly present in the text) and should therefore not be conflated with readers who are outside the text. Also included among hypothetical readers are readers who are *implied by* the text, that is, readers whose moves are charted out by (and hence more or less controlled by) the work in question. This is the kind of reader referred to, for instance, when one says, "The reader is surprised by the end of an Agatha Christie novel." Wolfgang Iser describes the implied reader's progress in phenomenological terms: although he pays particular attention to the indeterminacies in the texts—the gaps that the reader has to fill in on his or her own—his reader remains very much controlled by the author, since those gaps are part of the strategy of the text. On a more general level, some reader-critics examine the hypothetical reader who is implied, not by any specific text, but rather by the broader culture. In *Structuralist Poetics,* for instance, Jonathan Culler, influenced by French STRUCTURALISM and especially by SEMIOTICS, develops the notion of "literary competence," highlighting the ways in which the reader's knowledge of conventions allows him or her to make sense of literary texts.

Narratees and implied readers need to be distinguished, however, from at least two other types of hypothetical reader. Since they are in principle the product of textual features, narratees and implied readers both differ from the intended reader (what Rabinowitz calls the "authorial audience"). The intended reader is *presumed by* rather than marked in the text and therefore can be discovered only by looking at the text in terms of the context in which it arose. In addition, there are postulated readers. Such readers' characteristics do not emerge from a study of the text or its context; rather, the text's meaning emerges from perceiving it through the eyes of a reader whose characteristics are assumed by the critic to begin with. Thus, in his early and influential "Literature in the Reader: Affective Stylistics," Stanley Fish follows the experiences of a "reader" word by word, insisting, in a self-conscious reversal of the Wimsatt-Beardsley position, that what "*happens* to, and with the participation of, the reader" is in fact "the *meaning*" of a text (*Is There* 25). But that is not the implied reader; it is, rather, an abstraction Fish calls the "informed reader." He argues that real readers can become informed readers by developing linguistic, semantic, and literary competence, by making their minds "the repository of the (potential) responses a given text might call out" and by "suppressing, in so far as that is possible, . . . what is personal and idiosyncratic" (49). As is often the case with postulated readers, Fish's informed reader is presented as an ideal, the best reader of the text. The distinctions among narratees, implied readers, intended readers, and postulated readers are significant, but they are subtle and not always recognized. As a consequence, they are sometimes blurred as critics (including Fish and Iser) fuse them or move from one to another without notice.

In contrast to those who write about hypothetical readers are those critics who focus on the activities of *real* readers. In *Readings and Feelings,* for instance, David Bleich, starting from the assumption that "the role of personality in response is the most fundamental fact of criticism" (4), talks about the specific students in his classes and uses the actual interpretations they have presented in papers they have written, in order to learn where they originate and how the classroom, as a community, can negotiate among them. Janice Radway moves further from the academic center by studying the ways nonacademic women interpret popular romances.

Reader-critics not only differ with respect to what entity they mean by "reader"; they also differ with regard to the perspective from which they treat it. To put it in different terms, most reader-critics admit, to some extent, the necessity of "contextualizing" the act of reading. Stanley Fish, in essays written after "Affective Stylistics," has made some of the strongest arguments along these lines, claiming that meaning is entirely context-dependent and that there is consequently no such thing as literal meaning. Even audience critics who do not take this extreme position recognize the close relationship between meaning and interpretation on the one hand and context on the other. But readers are not simply in a

single context; they are always in several. And there is no more agreement about what constitutes the most appropriate context to study than there is about what the term "reader" means.

For example, one can look at what might loosely be called the cultural context of the reader. Culler, in his discussions of literary conventions, examines the process of reading in the context of the shared cultural practices of the academic community. Fish takes a related but more radical position, rejecting the notion of a generalized literary competence and arguing instead for the study of literature in terms of disparate "interpretive communities" united by shared "article[s] of faith" (e.g., commitment to authorial intention) and "repertoire[s] of [interpretive] strategies." According to Fish, these strategies do not decode some preexisting meaning, for the meaning of a literary work is not in the text at all. Rather, the very "properties" of the text are in fact "constituted" by whatever strategies the reader happens to bring to bear on the text: "These strategies exist prior to the act of reading and therefore determine the shape of what is read rather than, as is usually assumed, the other way around" (*Is There* 171). More recently, Steven Mailloux has expanded on this notion by developing a "rhetorical hermeneutics" that examines, with particular attention to institutional politics, the ways in which interpretations become accepted by given groups.

Alternatively, one can look at the psychological context of the reader. In *Dynamics of Literary Response* Norman Holland deals primarily with hypothetical readers; in *Five Readers Reading* he turns his attention to actual students. In both cases, he tries to make sense of interpretive activity by passing it through the lens of Freudian psychoanalysis. Still other critics look at the historical context of the reader. This is one of the distinguishing characteristics of *Receptionkritik,* most familiar through the writings of Hans Robert Jauss, who argues that the reader makes sense of literature in part through a "horizon of expectations." Since that horizon varies with history, the literary work offers different "views" at different times (Jauss 21–22). Jane Tompkins, following Fish, pushes the idea further, claiming in her study of American literature (*Sensational Designs*) that the reader's historical situation does not simply affect our view of the work but actually produces whatever it is that we call the text in the first place: "The circumstances in which a text is read . . . are what make the text available . . . [and] define the work 'as it really is'—under those circumstances" (7).

Tompkins is a feminist as well as a historian, and her work reminds us that yet another perspective is offered when the act of reading is studied in the context of gender. Like other forms of reader criticism, feminist reader criticism has moved in several different directions. In *The Resisting Reader,* for example, Judith Fetterley talks about the effects that reading particular texts can have on women. Radway, more willing to credit the reader's power to "make" the meaning of the text, asks instead how women (especially women of a particular socioeconomic class) read differently from men (especially male academic critics).

There is disagreement among reader-critics not only about the subject of inquiry but also about the whole purpose of critical activity. It is here that debates can become especially acrimonious. In particular, there is disagreement about the proper relation between the critic and interpretation, and consequently about the descriptive/prescriptive nature of the critical enterprise. Granted, most audience critics agree that to some extent, readers produce literary meaning; but since there are such widespread disagreements about who that "reader" is and what that production consists of, this apparent agreement yields no unity whatever on the issue of the reader's ultimate freedom to interpret as he or she wishes.

At one extreme, there are critics who start with the text and use the concept of the reader as an analytic tool to perfect traditional interpretive practices. As Mary Louise Pratt has argued, the study of many types of hypothetical readers is consistent with formalism. In traditional formalist interpretive practice, certain textual details are foregrounded, and an interpretation explaining those details is posited as "the" interpretation of the text. To the extent that the implied reader is simply a mirror of those textual features, an implied-reader analysis is often a formalist analysis in different language. Thus, for instance, Wolfgang Iser's interpretations, despite their heavy reliance on descriptions of "the reader's" activities, could in many cases be translated into formalist terms.

Problems become more acute when we come to analyses based on postulated readers whose activities serve as models for correct behavior. In practice, such readers often turn out to be the critic himself or herself, and the readerly terminology serves primarily as a rhetorical device to persuade us of the general validity of individual interpretations. Riffaterre's semiotic analyses in *Semiotics of Poetry* rely heavily on notions of what activities the text requires the reader to perform; readers are forced or compelled by the text, and individuals who, for one reason or another, wander in the wrong direction simply cannot find "the true reading" (142). For all the brilliance of his analyses, Riffaterre (as Culler has argued in *Pursuit*

of Signs) tells us less about what readers do or have done than about the way he himself reads; in fact, he often explicitly notes that no previous readers have followed what he sees as the dictates of the text. In the end, his use of reader terminology gives his prescriptions of how we ought to read the appearance of objective descriptions of what readers actually do.

Other critics, in contrast, use the concept of the reader not to engage in the act of interpretation but rather to explain how interpretations come about. Culler, for instance, like Riffaterre, describes much of his work as semiotic. But his actual practice is quite different. Arguing that "the interpretation of individual works is only tangentially related to the understanding of literature," Culler strives to construct a criticism "which seeks to identify the conventions and operations by which any signifying practice (such as literature) produces its observable effects of meaning" (*Pursuit* 5, 48). In contrast to Riffaterre, he builds his arguments not on the text but on interpretations already produced; and he aims not to persuade his own readers of the rightness or wrongness of those interpretations but rather to describe the practices that allowed them to come into being.

Culler's work in this line is not, strictly speaking, concerned with evaluating interpretations. Indeed, he explicitly claims that the semiotic "project is disrupted whenever one slips back into the position of judge" (*Pursuit* 67). Nonetheless, there is a sense in which his work tends to justify those interpretations he discusses. This is especially true because, as Pratt suggests, his arguments are frequently based on his notion of literary competence, and that notion is not really interrogated in terms of who determines competence or under what cultural and political circumstances. Since he tends to start with interpretations produced by professionally trained critics (rather than, as Bleich does, with students' readings), academic practices are implicitly valorized.

Other reader-critics, therefore, use the notion of reader in yet a different way, neither to persuade nor to explain but to question interpretations. In *The Resisting Reader,* for instance, Fetterley, without giving up the notion that there are more or less correct intended interpretations of the classical American texts she reads, argues that those interpretations are harmful because they "immasculate" women (i.e., train them to identify with male needs and desires). She therefore calls upon readers to recognize them and resist them. Radway questions interpretations in an even more fundamental way. She criticizes those who use traditional academic interpretive practices to determine the cultural meaning of mass-market romances. Starting with a position fairly close to Fish's, she insists that the cultural importance of those romances depends on the meaning they have for the actual women who consume them. She goes on to demonstrate, through ethnographic study, that since those women use different interpretive strategies than academic critics do, the texts for them have substantially different meanings.

Given the wide variety of interests and concerns exhibited by various reader-critics, it should not be surprising that audience criticism, as a whole, has not taken any definitive stands, except a negative attitude toward NEW CRITICISM, an attitude shared by virtually all other critical schools that have developed since the 1960s. Nonetheless, the very raising of certain questions (even unanswered questions) has had profound consequences for the commonplaces of the literary-critical profession and has, in conjunction with such movements as DECONSTRUCTION and feminism, encouraged general shifts in the direction of literary studies. In the first place, talk of the reader opens up talk of psychology, sociology, and history, and reader criticism has helped break down the boundaries separating literary study from other disciplines. In addition, by highlighting the reader's interpretive practice, even such prescriptive critics as Riffaterre have clarified the degree to which meaning is dependent upon the reader's performance. Even if one does not agree with such critics as Robert Crosman (who claims that "'validity' is a matter of individual conscience" [381]) or Bleich (who argues that "reading is a wholly subjective process" [*Readings* 3]), reader criticism has made it increasingly difficult to support the notion of definitive meaning in its most straightforward form. One can hardly claim that no critics, not even audience critics, continue to support the notion of "right" and "wrong" readings, but it is safe to say that the position is being increasingly discarded, and even critics who do argue for it have become ever more wary of how precarious interpretation is as a procedure and how little we can depend on the texts themselves to provide proper interpretive guidance.

What is most important, perhaps, as definitive meaning is undermined, so is the notion of definitive evaluation, since value is even more contextually determined than meaning. Statements of value are increasingly being put under pressure by the question, Value for whom? and value is increasingly being viewed not as a quality inherent in texts but rather as a function of particular social, historical, and cultural circumstances. By helping to throw into question the belief that texts have determinable, unvarying literary quality, reader-critics have helped fuel the attacks on the canon that have been launched from a number of other quarters, most notably, in the 1970s and 1980s, from feminist critics.

Peter J. Rabinowitz

See also STANLEY FISH and RECEPTION THEORY.

David Bleich, *Readings and Feelings: An Introduction to Subjective Criticism* (1975), *Subjective Criticism* (1978); Robert Crosman, "Some Doubts about 'The Reader of Paradise Lost,'" *College English* 37 (1975); Jonathan Culler, *The Pursuit of Signs: Semiotics, Literature, Deconstruction* (1981), *Structuralist Poetics: Structuralism, Linguistics, and the Study of Literature* (1975); Umberto Eco, *The Role of the Reader: Explorations in the Semiotics of Texts* (1979); Judith Fetterley, *The Resisting Reader: A Feminist Approach to American Fiction* (1978); Stanley Fish, *Doing What Comes Naturally: Change, Rhetoric, and the Practice of Theory in Literary and Legal Studies* (1989), *Is There a Text in This Class? The Authority of Interpretive Communities* (1980); Elizabeth Freund, *The Return of the Reader: Reader-Response Criticism* (1987); Norman N. Holland, *Five Readers Reading* (1975); Wolfgang Iser, *Der Akt des Lesens: Theorie ästhetischer Wirkung* (1976, *The Act of Reading: A Theory of Aesthetic Response,* trans. Iser, 1978), *Der implizite Leser: Kommunikationsformen des Romans von Bunyan bis Beckett* (1972, *The Implied Reader: Patterns of Communication in Prose Fiction from Bunyan to Beckett,* trans. Iser, 1974); Hans Robert Jauss, *Toward an Aesthetic of Reception* (trans. Timothy Bahti, 1982); Steven Mailloux, *Interpretive Conventions: The Reader in the Study of American Fiction* (1982), *Rhetorical Power* (1989); James Phelan, *Reading People, Reading Plots: Character, Progression, and the Interpretation of Narrative* (1989); Mary Louise Pratt, "Interpretive Strategies / Strategic Interpretations: On Anglo-American Reader Response Criticism," *Boundary 2* 11 (1981–82); Gerald Prince, "Introduction to the Study of the Narratee" (Tompkins, *Reader-Response Criticism*); Peter J. Rabinowitz, *Before Reading: Narrative Conventions and the Politics of Interpretation* (1987); Janice Radway, *Reading the Romance: Women, Patriarchy, and Popular Literature* (1984); Michael Riffaterre, *Semiotics of Poetry* (1978); Louise Rosenblatt, *The Reader, the Text, the Poem: The Transactional Theory of the Literary Work* (1978); Michael Steig, *Stories of Reading: Subjectivity and Literary Understanding* (1989); Susan R. Suleiman and Inge Crosman, eds., *The Reader in the Text: Essays on Audience and Interpretation* (1980); Jane P. Tompkins, *Sensational Designs: The Cultural Work of American Fiction, 1790–1860* (1985); Jane P. Tompkins, ed., *Reader-Response Criticism: From Formalism to Post-Structuralism* (1980).

RECEPTION THEORY

Reception theory, the approach to literature that concerns itself first and foremost with one or more readers' actualization of the text, is based on a collective enterprise that has had far-reaching institutional consequences. Hans Robert Jauss, with his University of Constance colleagues Manfred Fuhrmann and Wolfgang Iser and with philosophers, historians, and critics such as Rainer Warning, Karlheinz Stierle, Dieter Henrich, Günther Buck, JÜRGEN HABERMAS, Peter Szondi, and Hans Blumenberg, is part of a loosely organized group that gathers regularly at colloquia, the proceedings of which are published in the multivolume *Poetik und Hermeneutik.*

The group's first and most provocative pronouncements were two inaugural addresses at the University of Constance, Jauss's in 1967, later published as *Literaturgeschichte als Provokation für die Literaturwissenschaft* ("Literary History as a Challenge to Literary Theory"), and Iser's, "Die Appellstruktur der Texte," in 1970, published in English as "Indeterminacy and the Reader's Response in Prose Fiction" (in J. Hillis Miller, ed., *Aspects of Narrative,* 1971). Whereas Iser's work was based more on the works of Roman Ingarden and Hans-Georg Gadamer (see HERMENEUTICS: 2. TWENTIETH CENTURY and PHENOMENOLOGY) and on the German phenomenological tradition, Jauss's explicit aim was to reintroduce the issue of history into the study of literature (see GERMAN THEORY AND CRITICISM: 5. CONTEMPORARY). Jauss reacted against three different ways of referring to history in literary studies: an idealist conception of history as a teleology; the positivist bias of nineteenth-century historicism, which has to forgo questions of relevance in order to save objectivity; and *Geistesgeschichte,* a history of ideas based on an irrationalist aesthetic. The two last alternatives both have to abandon the question of aesthetic value judgments, and Jauss sees MARXIST THEORY AND CRITICISM and RUSSIAN FORMALISM as the two most influential methodologies that attempt to come to terms with the relationship between history and aesthetics. The two schools react strongly against the blind empiricism of positivism and against an aesthetic metaphysics, but they attempt to solve the problem in opposite ways.

Jauss criticizes Marxist thinkers such as GEORG LUKÁCS both for their naive view of literature as a passive reflection of the real world and for the classical contours of the canon on which their aesthetic is based. But he retains their insistence on the historicity of the work. From the Formalists he adopts the idea that in art the process of perception is a means in itself, an idea that originally implied a refusal to include a historical dimension but later was introduced in Iurri Tynianov and Boris Eikhenbaum's work on the evolution of literary forms. Jauss regrets the absence of a link between these literary evolutions and developments in nonliterary history. A new and more valid history of literature must take into account both the Marxist insistence on mediation and the Formalist findings about how literary works are perceived. This alternative is an aesthetics of reception, which shifts the critic's attention away from the producer of the text and from the text itself toward a dialectic of production and consumption. The history of literature becomes a crucial element in literary criticism because it allows us to comprehend the historical determiners of our understanding. The central notion Jauss uses to accomplish this task is the "horizon of expectations," or *Erwartungshorizont,* a term that derives from a number of German philosophical and historical traditions, indicating, in general, the set of expectations against which readers perceive the text (see HERMENEUTICS: 2. TWENTIETH CENTURY). This structure is objectified ideally in works such as *Don Quixote,* which provoke expectations and then proceed to destroy them, and Jauss in fact follows the Formalists in defining aesthetic value as a function of the distance between these expectations and their destruction in the work itself.

In 1969 Jauss published an essay in which he used THOMAS S. KUHN's *Structure of Scientific Revolutions* to show that a shift in paradigms had occurred that was based on three methodological novelties: a relationship between aesthetics and history, an attempt to combine structural and hermeneutical methods, and an aesthetics of effect that could deal equally well with canonized as with popular kinds of literature. The institutional consequences of this paradigm have been realized in the structure and curriculum of the University of Constance. Jauss does not overdramatize the effect of the works of the *Poetik und Hermeneutik* group. The impact of his own inaugural lecture was immediate though not always positive, and in the early 1970s he repeatedly defended and adjusted his theories, whether in a confrontation with the aesthetics of the FRANKFURT SCHOOL, especially the posthumously published work of THEODOR W. ADORNO, or in response to the criticism on reception aesthetics formulated by leading critics in the German Democratic Republic.

Unlike Adorno in his *Ästhetische Theorie,* Jauss believes that literature and art can play a role in our society that is both progressive and affirmative, and he points to the elitist consequences of positing an autonomy of art that cannot do justice to the role of art in the pre-autonomous period. To Adorno's negative aesthetics Jauss opposes the aesthetic experience itself, the pleasure involved in our enjoyment and use of art and literature. Inspired partly by IMMANUEL KANT, partly by JEAN-PAUL SARTRE, and partly by the work of the German phenomenologist Moritz Geiger, Jauss replaces the horizon of expectations as the cornerstone of his theory by the aesthetic experience as a dialectic of "Selbstgenuß im Fremdgenuß," of self-enjoyment in the enjoyment of something other. Reception theory came under attack from critics in the German Democratic Republic in the early 1970s, when influential theoreticians such as Robert Weimann diagnosed it as the logical result of a refusal to confront the Marxist answers to contradictions inherent in a bourgeois society. Jauss was singled out as the target of these attacks because he had attempted to reintroduce a non-Marxist and subjective concept of history in literary studies.

Jauss's work in the late seventies, gathered in his *Ästhetische Erfahrung und literarische Hermeneutik* in 1982 (the first part was issued in 1977 and translated into English as *Aesthetic Experience and Literary Hermeneutics* in 1982), moved toward a more hermeneutical interest in the aesthetic experience itself. Jauss distinguishes three basic experiences: a productive aesthetic praxis *(poiesis),* a receptive praxis *(aisthesis),* and a communicative praxis *(katharsis),* and he claims that a detailed study of these three elements can help literary history steer a course between an exclusively aesthetic and an exclusively sociological perspective. Central in this new phase of Jauss's thinking is the third, communicative aesthetic praxis, which is defined as "the enjoyment of the affects as stirred by speech or poetry which can bring about both a change in belief and the liberation of his mind in the listener or the spectator" (92). Important here is both the active part of the recipient of the aesthetic object and the two opposites this definition avoids: the unmediated losing oneself in the object and the sentimental self-indulgence by the subject in itself. The aesthetic experience can have three functions in society: it can create norms, simply pass on existing norms, or refuse to conform to the existing norms. Both bourgeois and (neo-)Marxist literary theories have failed to see the continuum between a progressive change of horizons and the adaptation to existing norms.

Whereas Jauss seems to have moved closer to Iser's insistence on the role of the individual reader, quite a number of his younger colleagues in Germany have concentrated on the sociological and empirical considerations of his early essays. On the basis of a "constructive functionalism" not unrelated to Habermas's commu-

nicative rationalism and to Imre Lakatos's critical rationalism, Norbert Groeben and Siegfried J. Schmidt have developed a theory of literature that opposes to the hermeneutical schools an empirical and functional view of literature. Hermeneutics can at best have a heuristic function: its findings must be tested intersubjectively and empirically before they can claim any validity. Work in this field is truly interdisciplinary and employs concepts and methods from social psychology, text theory, pragmatics, communication theory, linguistics, and philosophy.

Reception theory has initiated a new interest in the historical dimension and the communicative aspects of the literary text and has been very influential in the empirical and sociological study of literary phenomena in the 1970s and early 1980s, but its impact seems to have been limited for the most part to Germany and Western Europe.

Geert Lernout

See also GERMAN THEORY AND CRITICISM: 5. CONTEMPORARY and READER-RESPONSE THEORY AND CRITICISM.

Norbert Groeben, *Rezeptionsforschung als empirische Literaturwissenschaft: Paradigma- durch Methodendiskussion an Untersuchungsbeispielen* (1977); Hans Robert Jauss, *Ästhetische Erfahrung und literarische Hermeneutik* (1982; pt. 1, *Ästhetische Erfahrung und literarische Hermeneutik. Band I: Versuch im Feld der ästhetischen Erfahrung,* 1977, trans. Michael Shaw, *Aesthetic Experience and Literary Hermeneutics,* 1982; other essays appear in *Question and Answer: Forms of Dialogic Understanding,* trans. Michael Hays, 1989), "Der Leser als Instanz einer neuen Geschichte der Literatur," *Poetica* 7 (1975), *Literaturgeschichte als Provokation der Literaturwissenschaft* (1967, "Literary History as a Challenge to Literary Theory," in *Toward an Aesthetic of Reception*), *Die Theorie der Rezeption: Ruckschau auf ihre unerkannte Vorgeschichte* (1987), *Toward an Aesthetic of Reception* (trans. Timothy Bahti, 1982); Manfred Naumann et al., *Gesellschaft, Literatur, Lesen: Literaturrezeption in theoretischen Sicht* (1973); Siegfried Schmidt, *Grundriss der empirischen Literaturwissenschaft* (2 vols., 1980–82).

Elizabeth Freund, *The Return of the Reader: Reader-Reception Criticism* (1987); Gunter Grimm, *Rezeptionsgeschichte: Grundlegung einer Theorie* (1977); Robert C. Holub, *Reception Theory: A Critical Introduction* (1984).

RENAISSANCE THEORY AND CRITICISM

For its contribution to Renaissance literary culture at large, Renaissance literary criticism is a tentative and often unsatisfying body of work, shedding less light on that culture than might be hoped. The most durably interesting texts have proven to be manifestoes by working poets, notably Joachim DuBellay's *Défense et illustration de la langue française* (1549) and SIR PHILIP SIDNEY's *Defence of Poetry* (1595 [wr. 1579–83]), which can be read as glosses on the literary programs of, respectively, the Pléiade and the so-called golden age of Elizabethan poetry. But these are brief documents, shaped by immediate polemical needs, and notoriously slippery bases for generalization. Elsewhere, commentary on literary topics is dominated by humanist Latinity, within which contemporary vernacular literature is at an obvious and severe disadvantage. (Few contemporary readers of the work that Marco Girolamo Vida entitled *De arte poetica* [1527] would have been surprised to discover that it was essentially a training guide for the composition of a Neo-Latin epic along Virgilian lines.)

Even for the revered classics, moreover, we have very little in the way of sustained and coherent interpretation; for ancient authors—and for those few Renaissance writers, such as Petrarch, who attained comparable standing—the major vehicle for commentary is the humanist annotated edition, atomistic in its form and for the most part philological or antiquarian in its interests (see also PHILOLOGY). On what is now perhaps the most prestigious single corpus of Renaissance literary achievement, English popular drama, the record of contemporary response is spectacularly meager; the results of assiduous scholarly searches for fugitive remarks in published and unpublished sources serve for the most part to illustrate the age's inarticulateness in the face of its own most impressive works. Sidney's *Defence* appears to tell us that he would have found Shakespeare's plays distasteful; an apparently typical seventeenth-century commentator (Abraham Wright) calls *Hamlet* "an indifferent play, the lines but mean," though he praises the lead role as "an indifferent good part for a madman" (*Shakespeare: The Critical Heritage,* ed. Brian Vickers, 4 vols., 1974–76, I:29).

The desire for some extraliterary guidance to the literary sensibility of the time has accordingly involved a certain amount of conjecture and creative scholarship. Modern critics of Renaissance literature have asked their questions of various kinds of extraliterary materials:

rhetorical and mythographic treatises, numerological tracts, handbooks of courtly etiquette, theological debates, and so on. Such sources, skillfully handled, can give a far better sense than Renaissance literary criticism itself can of what contemporary writers had in mind when they wrote and of what contemporary readers would have been looking for; they can orient us as well to the age's aesthetic ambience, its identifying sense of the artificial. (Erasmus's modest composition manual *De copia* [1514, with several subsequent versions] has proved to be a particularly fruitful starting point.) They also sometimes reveal the roots of precisely the modern questions that they help answer: the most vehement, indeed bloody, religious controversy of the age centers on a question of signification—the exact linguistic status of the Eucharistic host—and indeed establishes some of the vocabulary of modern SEMIOTICS in the course of fiery and technical debates about idolatry and sacramentality.

Perhaps the most commonly employed supplement to the corpus of Renaissance literary criticism is the humanist version of Neoplatonism, as initiated by Marsilio Ficino in the late fifteenth century. This philosophical movement, bearing PLATO's name but also owing much to Plotinus and late classical hermetic texts, asserts an especially radical assimilation of physical into mental reality; and though Ficino himself has little directly to say on the matter, this assimilation is achieved in a way that promises to make art the firm ally rather than, as Plato himself would have it, the enemy of the higher truth. The philosophy is indeed used by some Renaissance writers to elucidate particular literary works. Giordano Bruno's *De gli eroici furori* (1585), a tumultuously intellectualized reading of a series of Italian love sonnets, is perhaps the most extravagant example; Cristoforo Landino's *Disputationes camaldulenses* (published in 1480), on the philosophic content of the *Aeneid,* had the cachet of Ficino's Florentine circle and is probably the most influential; George Chapman's annotated translation of Homer (completed in 1616), setting out the Neoplatonic message encrypted in the very origins of Western literature, is now the best-known.

A significant tradition in modern criticism has sought to expand on such efforts in a systematic way. The life's work of Frances Yates is an attempt to excavate in historically objective terms a vast intellectual synthesis in which Neoplatonism merges with a wide range of occult, magical, and scientific thought and to read some of the most valued artifacts of Renaissance culture, including Shakespearean drama, in the context of that synthesis. Even commentators skeptical of the results can find in the Neoplatonic focus on the mind and its theoretically limitless powers a way to do justice to an intuited sense of the sweep and power of the Renaissance imagination. When Julius Caesar Scaliger writes of the poet as another god, creating another nature, or when Sidney celebrates the poet for confecting a golden world such as nature herself could never provide, or when any number of critics locate poetry's origin in a divinely inspired *furor poeticus,* we seem to hear an almost Romantic faith in the preemptive authority of poetic invention, and it seems only helpful to take the remarks out of context and set them beside passages from Plotinus and Ficino.

In context, however, the Neoplatonic intimations of Renaissance literary critics are usually transient and entangled in other agendas, the unraveling of which requires other kinds of patience. As a specific body of texts, Renaissance criticism is best studied as its own enterprise, at most points less mature than that of contemporary literature, but developing on its own schedule. So considered, its integrity comes from its being part of the history of literary criticism as an intellectual discipline; indeed, something like the modern sense of that discipline first takes form in sixteenth-century Italy, where a newly amplified body of knowledge about literary history is codified and promulgated and where an identifiable tradition of commentary and debate on certain specific questions of literary theory arises and sustains itself. The effort continues earlier efforts to classify literary discourse within the medieval schema of the arts, in particular to specify its exact relation to history and moral philosophy, and also gears with the humanist revival of classical rhetoric to yield a new interest in the systematic classification of literary genres and their rules. But the real momentum, characteristically, seems to come from two major classical texts, both of them known but not intensively studied during the Middle Ages: HORACE's *Ars Poetica* and ARISTOTLE's *Poetics.* Their joint impact derives both from the specific opinions on literature that they advance (harmonizing them, like harmonizing the Gospels, becomes a common endeavor) and from the model they offer for literary criticism as an intellectual activity; what there is of a Platonic tradition in the field clearly suffers from the lack of a comparable text on which to build.

Aristotle's work is especially momentous and novel in its impact. A fresh Latin translation by Giorgio Valla was published in 1498; the Greek *editio princeps* was printed by Aldus Manutius in 1508; and Bernardo Segni's Italian translation, the first into any European vernacular, appeared in 1549. The key date seems to have been 1536,

when Alessandro de' Pazzi published a bilingual Greek and Latin edition; in that form the work quickly became a major focus of intellectual attention. Some of the most important critical works of the sixteenth century are specifically in the form of commentaries on Aristotle; the century sees at least a half-dozen of major stature, including particularly significant ones by Francesco Robortelli (1548), Pier Vettori (1560), and Lodovico Castelvetro (1570). An eclipse in certain circles of his prestige as a philosopher—it was in 1536 that Peter Ramus earned his master's degree in Paris by defending the proposition that all Aristotle's teachings are false—coincides with a powerful respect for this effectively new discovery. All its concepts and conclusions are worked over in detail, though the most important point of interest is unquestionably mimesis. A Latin equivalent—*imitatio*—is settled on early, but the meaning attached to it goes through some remarkable changes, prompted both by contemporary agendas and by problems in Aristotle's own text. *Imitatio* is variously taken to concern the truth value of poetry, its artful verisimilitude, a particular mode of representation (i.e., dramatization rather than narration), or even, in one tortuous but not uncommon train of thought, the story being told (*imitatio* as synonymous with *mythos* or *fabula*). These and other usages jostle the only meaning that is universally agreed upon, though the only one that unmistakably does not derive from Aristotle: *imitatio* as one writer's mimicking of another writer or group of writers, in particular, as the key humanist enterprise of imitating classical antiquity. The irresolutions of usage themselves measure the urgency of the issues being gathered for attention.

The dogmatic uniformity of the criticism that results is sometimes exaggerated; both the troublesomeness of the material and the combative style of Renaissance scholarship ensure that its history is a history of unresolved controversy in which even Aristotle's own authority is not beyond question. It has sometimes seemed convenient, though, to let Julius Caesar Scaliger's *Poetics* stand as a synthetic, or at least typical, statement. The work's flamboyantly named author (1484–1558), an Italian adventurer and claimant to princely ancestry who turned to literature after marrying and settling in southern France, first made a name for himself in the 1530s with two virulent attacks on Erasmus's *Ciceronianus. Ad hominem* arguments aside, the encounter located Scaliger as a defender of classical *imitatio* of a fairly narrow sort.

Scaliger's posthumously published *Poetics* (1561) is in one of its dimensions a massive codification of such a program for poetry. After an opening glance at Aristotle's incompleteness (and Horace's and Vida's inadequacy), the general topic is systematically organized into seven books, containing a very large number of chapters. The first four books identify and analyze traditional genres, meters, subject matter, sentiments, styles, and figures of speech and provide detailed illustrations from classical and occasionally Neo-Latin verse (including Scaliger's own). Two final books catalogue and evaluate the classical and Neo-Latin poets themselves. (Bilingual poets, such as Poliziano, are reviewed for their Latin verse alone.) Prominence is given to the concept of *imitatio* in a sense that affirms poetry's obligation and power to represent external reality; but Scaliger also makes clear that the reality he has in mind is already so perfectly captured in the best classical poetry—most especially by Virgil, whom in an extended syncrisis he judges easily superior to Homer—that the poet can best go about his business practicing *imitatio* in the specifically Renaissance sense of the term. In his opening section he traces the history of poetry back to the origins of speech— "the soul's ferryman" (*portitor amini* [*Poetices* I])—in the need to transmit information and provoke response; he regards this need as more fundamental than imitation as such, and his often quoted remark about the divine character of the poet's power comes in the context of an assertion of poetry's fundamentally suasive purpose.

That didactic dimension is almost universally affirmed in the Renaissance, but Italian criticism does provide one extended and rigorous dissent. In the most explicitly innovative of the Aristotelian commentaries, which announces the "discovery" that the text of the *Poetics* is a collection of rough notes put aside in expectation of further revision and hence calling not so much for explication as for rethinking, Castelvetro (1505–71), an excommunicated heretic no less contentious by nature than Scaliger, argues with remarkable consistency that pleasure, the first half of the Horatian *dulce et utile*, is the sole end of poetry of all sorts. This intent is also linked to an overt denial to the poet of any divine power or authority to create his own reality; to that end, Castelvetro propounds a doctrine of *imitatio* that is essentially a stern standard of verisimilitude that ties poetry very closely to history and on the basis of which he is willing to criticize even Virgil. These principles lead him to what proves to be the most influential feature of his commentary, the extrapolation of a few brief remarks from Aristotle into the firm doctrine of the three unities of dramatic composition: the requirement of a single action, transpiring at a single location, during a period of fictional time that Castelvetro specifies as no more than 12 hours. This tripartite rule becomes notorious for its legislative dogmatism, though Castelvetro urges it

with constant reference to the needs and expectations of an actual theatrical audience. He may have drawn on personal experience—he is very possibly the author of *Gl'ingannati* (1531), the comedy that supplied Shakespeare the main plot of *Twelfth Night*—and in the next century Castelvetro's doctrine (generally cited as Aristotle's doctrine) does in fact play a useful role in theatrical history, helping the French classical stage achieve its special kind of austere focus.

For all their differences, Scaliger and Castelvetro nevertheless resemble each other and most of their fellow critics in being what Bruno sarcastically calls *regolisti di Poesia*, "poetry's rule-mongers" (*Scritti scelti di Giordano Bruno e di Tommaso Campanella*, ed. Luigi Firpo, 2d ed., 1968, 185); the generic rules they seek are supposed to have an a priori rationality and to be essentially timeless and unchanging. Rarer but in some ways more interesting are occasional accounts of literary history as a history of deliberate experiment and change; it is in these accounts, indeed, that Renaissance criticism comes closest to dealing successfully with Renaissance literature.

The most consequential figure in this regard is Giambattista Giraldi Cinthio (1504–73), an author of *novelle* (including the source for *Othello*) and neo-Senecan tragedies, who in 1554 published his *Discorsi* on narrative poetry, drama, and satire. The essay on drama proceeds in constant reference to Aristotle, but its most striking arguments are for conscious generic innovation against the classical grid; in particular, Giraldi proposes a *tragedia di lieto fin*, "tragedy with a happy ending," as the best dramatic type for contemporary practice. He is of course defending his own productions in this line; and both his arguments and his plays look forward to an important debate toward the end of the century— precipitated by Giambattista Guarini's *Il pastor fido* (1589)—concerning the viability of tragicomedy as a distinctly modern theatrical genre. The essay on narrative poetry is concerned with the relation of the neo-chivalric *romanzo*, in particular *Orlando furioso*, to the classical epic tradition. Against complaints that Ariosto had written a work too sprawling and unruly to meet classical standards, Giraldi argues that precisely by showing how such diversity could be effectively linked together within a single poem—by showing how a narrative could achieve distinction with an aesthetic of variety rather than one of unity—the writers of *romanzi* had established a new genre that is in fact superior to classical epic. He suggests that a movement in this direction can be detected within the classical epic tradition itself. The controversy prompted Torquato Tasso (1544–95) to attempt a somewhat different reconciliation of the two genres in a series of writings over the course of almost 30 years. The theory achieves final if somewhat uneven form in his influential *Discorsi del poema eroico* (1594); they may be read in connection with his own romantic epic, *Gerusalemme liberata* (1581), which is, among other things, a practical illustration of how narrative form may embody unity precisely through diversity.

Perhaps the most surprising theorist, and the object of a good deal of fresh interest and respect in the twentieth century (he is singled out for praise by BENEDETTO CROCE and George Saintsbury), is Francesco Patrizi (1529–97), sometimes called da Cherso to distinguish him from the fifteenth-century bishop of the same name, who also wrote on literary matters. He participates briefly, on behalf of Ariosto, in the dispute over the *romanzi;* in his *Della poetica* (of which two books were published in 1586 and five more were discovered in manuscript in 1949) he sets out an extended critique of the prevailing way in which the rules of poetry were being sought. A professor of philosophy at Ferrara and then Rome, Patrizi starts with a comprehensively anti-Aristotelian agenda, which he applies to literary criticism with vehemence and thoroughness; the second book of his treatise is an emphatic, extended rejection of *imitatio* (in any sense of the term) as essential to poetry. His alternative program shows traces of Platonism—he is fully committed to the doctrine of the *furor poeticus*—but in many ways now seems even more innovative. He is even less interested than Giraldi Cinthio in uncovering transhistorical regulations for poetic form; the only indispensable requirement that Patrizi acknowledges for poetry is that it be written in verse, and his extensive and often laborious use of evidence from literary history is perhaps the least prescriptive of any Renaissance theorist's. His main aesthetic criterion, the subject of his third book, is in fact a species of surprise, the poet's ability to provoke *maraviglia,* "astonished admiration." The criterion is not new; its pedigree reaches back to Ciceronian rhetorical theory, and several sixteenth-century critics had sought to add it in one way or another to the Horatian list. But Patrizi makes the concept unprecedentedly emphatic and central. In support of his position, he repeatedly cites LONGINUS's *On the Sublime,* which in effect takes the place of Aristotle's *Poetics;* Patrizi is the first to make extensive use of what becomes one of the key critical texts for the seventeenth and eighteenth centuries, just as he is among the first to give voice to the aesthetic ambitions of Marinismo and analogous movements in seventeenth-century literature.

Gordon Braden

See also PHILOLOGY and SIR PHILIP SIDNEY.

Lodovico Castelvetro, *Castelvetro on the Art of Poetry* (ed. and trans. Andrew Bongiorno, 1984), *Poetica d'Aristotele vulgarizzata e sposta* (ed. Werther Romani, 2 vols., 1978–79); Giambattista Giraldi Cinzio, *Giraldi Cinthio on Romances* (trans. Henry L. Snuggs, 1968), *Scritti critici* (ed. Camillo Guerreri Crocetti, 1973); Francesco Patrizi da Cherso, *Della poetica* (ed. Danilo Aguzzi Barbagli, 3 vols., 1969–71); Julius Caesar Scaliger, *Poetices libri septem* (1561, facs. reprint, 1964), *Select Translations from Scaliger's Poetics* (ed. and trans. Frederick Morgan Padelford, 1905); G. Gregory Smith, ed., *Elizabethan Critical Essays* (2 vols., 1904); J. E. Spingarn, ed., *Critical Essays of the Seventeenth Century* (3 vols., 1908–9); Torquato Tasso, *Discourses on the Heroic Poem* (trans. Mariella Cavalchini and Irene Samuel, 1973); Marco Girolamo Vida, *The De Arte Poetica* (ed. and trans. Ralph G. Williams, 1976).

J. W. H. Atkins, *English Literary Criticism: The Renascence* (1947); Terence Cave, *The Cornucopian Text* (1979); Vernon Hall, Jr., *Renaissance Literary Criticism: A Study of Its Social Context* (1945); Baxter Hathaway, *The Age of Criticism: The Late Renaissance in Italy* (1962); Arthur F. Kinney, *Continental Humanist Poetics* (1989), *Humanist Poetics* (1986); George Saintsbury, *A History of Criticism and Literary Taste in Europe,* vol. 2 (1900); J. E. Spingarn, *A History of Literary Criticism in the Renaissance* (1899); Bernard Weinberg, *A History of Literary Criticism in the Italian Renaissance* (2 vols., 1961); Frances A. Yates, *Giordano Bruno and the Hermetic Tradition* (1964).

RHETORIC

Scholars have traditionally defined rhetoric either as the study of schemes and tropes (verbal artifice) or as the study of persuasion. Literary critics have been understandably eager to see rhetoric as heightening awareness of richness and shapeliness of language and have welcomed it as an ally in the struggle against certain notions of scientific, expository, or philosophic language as the language of seriousness and truth. In the faculty psychology of the Renaissance, rhetoric, like poetry, appealed to the imagination (and hence the passions); modern literary theorists, however, have repeatedly challenged the rest of the Renaissance legacy, which insisted on the proper subordination and governance of imagination by reason (see RENAISSANCE THEORY AND CRITICISM). John Locke, after all, had inveighed against using any of the arts of rhetoric other than those of order and clearness when discoursing upon "things as they are" (*Essay* 2:146), and if the new discourses of "truth and knowledge" had no use for rhetoric, it was welcomed by the emerging study soon to be called literature. There then ensued what is widely known as the death of rhetoric, or its "degeneration" into the study of schemes and tropes in the nineteenth century. Recently, as various "new rhetorics" have tried to establish themselves independent of the study of literature, the definition in terms of schemes and tropes has been denounced as a narrowed, uninformed, belletristic conception that reduces rhetoric to an adjunct of the study of style. Literary theorists, somewhat baffled and chagrined at the rebuff, might reply that their offer of merger was an attempt to formulate a theory of linguistic expression, or textuality as such, which they were gracious enough to call by the despised term "rhetoric," and that their forays into the realm of persuasion were necessarily limited by their strong heritage defining art as that which has no designs upon us. This dance of alignments has been repeated in the literary theory of the twentieth century, as exemplified in I. A. RICHARDS's *Philosophy of Rhetoric* (1936), NORTHROP FRYE's *Anatomy of Criticism* (1957), and more recently, PAUL DE MAN's "Semiology and Rhetoric" (1973, reprint, 1979).

At the beginning of *The Philosophy of Rhetoric,* Richards accepts the Lockean notion of a pure discourse for learned contemplation. "Exposition," persuasion, and poetry are distinct, legitimately different deployments of language ("Aims of Discourse"). Richards does not question these distinctions and in fact affirms them (defining exposition, for example, as "concerned to state a view, not to persuade people to agree or to do anything more than examine it" [24]), but he touches so frequently on the historical novelty of exposition, the narrowness of the domains in which it rules ("It is a relatively rare occurrence outside the routine of train services and the tamer, more settled parts of the sciences" [41]), and its vulnerability to "poaching" by persuasion (a.k.a. rhetoric) that he seems to have little invested in the distinction. On the other hand, this poaching, which he says we may observe in "the review and correspondence columns of learned and scientific journals" (24), is troubling to him, for it contaminates the pure (or at least relatively pure) motives of scientific discussion with combativeness and partisanship, and Richards constantly makes gestures of goodwill, geniality, and fair play to secure an equally charitable and generous reading from his audience and readers. The fault, Richards seems to say, is not in the signifier but in ourselves. Accordingly, he opposes what one might call the Lockean semiotic hygiene of fixing One True Meaning for each word.

For Richards, the need for charity in interpretation arises from the fact that outside of technical exposition, texts do not determine their readings. He goes on to describe a scale of the fixity of word meanings, which is to say, their independence of context: technical exposition anchors the most rigid end of the scale, and poetry the opposite, most fluid end, where words most "interanimate" and draw in echoes and associations from contexts extending even beyond the immediate poem at hand to include, in masterly uses, the entirety of the language. He cites as one example of heightened fluidity and interanimation Octavius Caesar's remark over Cleopatra's body in *Antony and Cleopatra:* "She looks like sleep, / As she would catch another Antony / In her strong toil of grace." Richards exclaims, "Where, in terms of what entries in what possible dictionary, do the meanings here of *toil* and *grace* come to rest?" (49). Rhetoric, however, he places lower on the scale, toward the rigid end, illustrating how attention to the context of words can dampen many associations that words taken singly might have, associations that would be irrelevant, distracting, overingenious, or just plain contrary to the author's intent. He cites a triad of metaphors from FRANCIS BACON that, if taken apart from their "service" in the passage, would "begin at once to fight against his intention" (57). It would be quite easy, based on what Richards says, to give a deconstructive reading to the passage by refusing to stop the interpretive process at Bacon's declared intention—which is that the pursuit of learning should be unselfish—instead pointing out that the passage, along with many other Royal Society pronouncements, attempts to deny and suppress the "other" of personal and national aggrandizement, which ultimately returned in a fierce eruption in the early eighteenth century (see Gross). Perhaps Richards places rhetoric closer to the fixed end because intention is easier to make out—it is the design that rhetoric has upon us. In any case, Richards argues that rhetoric can join hands with poetic in resisting the philosopher's hygiene and engage instead in a systematic study of how transfers, shifts, and displacements of meanings occur. He is pleased to call this new endeavor "rhetoric," now that the bad associations of manipulation and malice have been tagged as the bad manners of controversialists.

In *Anatomy of Criticism,* perhaps the most widely read and cited book of theory for his generation, Northrop Frye reworks the distinction between language in the service of truly describing the world (descriptive, scientific "exposition") and language turned in upon its own experience and form (literature). The traditional dual definition of "rhetoric" makes it unstable in relation to this opposition: insofar as it directs attention to the form of utterance, it is the study of ornament ("the articulation of emotion"), with an orientation toward contemplation of beauty and elegance that allies it with literature; but insofar as it studies persuasion ("the manipulation of emotion"), it turns toward the world of interest and action. As Frye describes things, however, the union of grammar and logic (a version of the semiotic hygiene) appears to serve the needs of the world best; wit, pregnant metaphors, and the well-turned phrase no longer have the power to seduce and delude the discourses of knowledge and truth, and the spirit of rhetoric becomes the spirit of literature: "Literature may be described as the rhetorical use of grammar and logic. Most of the features of literary form, such as rhyme, alliteration, metre, antithetical balance, the use of exempla, are also rhetorical schemata" (245).

Frye's argument does not end here, however, but has one final shift, which is to undermine the distinction between exposition ruled by logic and grammar and rhetoric/literature. The tactics of the discourses of truth and knowledge, Frye suggests, "impress the literary critic as being themselves rhetorical devices" (329), parts of a "conceptual rhetoric" aimed at persuading the understanding as "persuasive rhetoric" aims at action or emotional response. It quickly follows that there is no direct union of grammar and logic that excludes rhetoric, that connotative association and ambiguity cannot ever be wholly purged from discourse, and "that nothing built out of words can transcend the nature of words and that the nature and condition of *ratio,* in so far as *ratio* is verbal, are contained by *oratio*" (337). So rhetoric joined with literature becomes the study of words in all deployments.

Richards's opposition of grammar-logic and rhetoric appears again in Paul de Man's widely cited and reprinted "Semiology and Rhetoric." De Man is concerned that grammar-logic, still conceived as a stabilizing, normalizing apparatus (hygiene), has undertaken to annex rhetoric as persuasion via the development of speech-act theory and to annex rhetoric as figuration via the French semiological work of Tzvetan Todorov, Gérard Genette, Algirdas Julien Greimas, and ROLAND BARTHES (see also SEMIOTICS and SPEECH ACTS). He resists these moves by citing CHARLES SANDERS PEIRCE on infinite semiosis (the interpretation of a sign is another sign is . . .) and KENNETH BURKE on deflection (or "swerve"), which for Burke is the endless, ungovernable way that signs or gestures begin to mean more than they say, at the same time signifying something else. This constant potential for polyvalence is very close to what Richards means by

fluidity, and Frye by ambiguity and metaphor. And since de Man unhesitatingly equates "the rhetorical, figural potentiality of language with literature itself" (10), it is evident that his underlying opposition is to a grammaticization of literature. Hence, he does not conclude by advocating a systematic study of the ways words take on meanings in texts—à la Richards and Frye—perhaps because the spirit of system too readily precipitates one into grammar-logic. Rhetoric becomes the name of the unsystematizable, of the experience of undecidability or indetermination of meaning. This conclusion, STANLEY FISH notes in an otherwise sympathetic tracing of de Man's argument, paints the literary critic into the rather narrow corner of having to demonstrate over and over the "referential aberration" whereby rhetoric-literature resists the systematizing efforts of grammar-logic (493).

It is a primary axiom of power that weaker parties should beware of mergers, and it is clear in the present instance that literary theorists have made use of certain elements in the heritage of rhetoric for their own purposes, which broadly are to isolate, surround, and then ingest the discourses of truth and knowledge. The greatest omission in this selective view of rhetoric is the considerable body of work on argumentation, practical reason, and natural logic associated with Chaim Perelman and Lucie Olbrechts-Tyteca and with Stephen Toulmin, along with the burgeoning work in the rhetorics of science, legal discourse, policy deliberation, and the academic disciplines.

George L. Dillon

See also LINGUISTICS AND LANGUAGE and I. A. RICHARDS.

Charles Bazerman, *Shaping Written Knowledge: The Genre and Activity of the Experimental Article in Science* (1988); Charles Bazerman and James Paradis, eds., *Textual Dynamics of the Professions: Historical and Contemporary Studies of Writing in Professional Communities* (1991); Kenneth Burke, "Rhetoric—Old and New," *New Rhetorics* (ed. Martin Steinmann, Jr., 1967); Paul De Man, "Semiology and Rhetoric," *Allegories of Reading* (1979); George L. Dillon, *Contending Rhetorics: Writing in Academic Disciplines* (1991); Stanley E. Fish, "Rhetoric," *Doing What Comes Naturally* (1989); Northrop Frye, *Anatomy of Criticism* (1957); Alan G. Gross, "The Rhetorical Invention of Scientific Invention: The Emergence and Transformation of a Social Norm" (Simons, rev. in *The Rhetoric of Science,* 1990); John Locke, *An Essay concerning Human Understanding* (1689–91, 2 vols., 1959); Greg Myers, *Writing Biology: Texts in the Social Construction of Scientific*

Knowledge (1990); Walter Nash, ed., *The Writing Scholar: Studies in Academic Discourse* (1990); John S. Nelson, Alan Megill, and Donald N. McCloskey, eds., *The Rhetoric of the Human Sciences: Language and Argument in Scholarship and Public Affairs* (1987); Chaim Perelman, *The New Rhetoric and the Humanities* (1979), *The Realm of Rhetoric* (1982); Chaim Perelman and Lucie Olbrechts-Tyteca, *The New Rhetoric: A Treatise on Argumentation* (trans. John Wilkinson and Purcell Weaver, 1969); Michael J. Shapiro, *The Politics of Representation: Writing Practices in Biography, Photography, and Policy Analysis* (1988); Herbert Simons, ed., *Rhetoric in the Human Sciences* (1989); Stephen Toulmin, *Human Understanding* (1972), *The Uses of Argument* (1958); James Boyd White, *Justice as Translation* (1990).

RICH, ADRIENNE

Adrienne Rich (b. 1929), poet and theorist, represents an important voice in contemporary feminist criticism; her work has grown and developed with the women's movement, in which she has played an active role since 1970. Two collections, *On Lies, Secrets, and Silence* (1979) and *Blood, Bread, and Poetry* (1986), contain many of her significant essays; in addition to these and her many volumes of poetry, she published a pioneering feminist text, *Of Woman Born: Motherhood as Experience and Institution* (1976). Her publishing career well epitomizes a dualism in the way feminist thought has been communicated—both inside and outside the university, both inside and outside of major publishing houses. Her poems and essays often appeared first in small, experimental journals (and Rich is on the board of one such, *Sinister Wisdom*), but they have been collected and reissued by W. W. Norton.

Poets have played a conspicuous role in contemporary feminism, in part because of the movement's recognition of the crucial significance of language in defining and creating a reality. Realizing that oppressed groups tend to have their world named for them, the women's movement in the 1970s and 1980s placed importance on acts of re-naming and re-vision, to use Rich's phrase in "When We Dead Awaken: Writing as Re-Vision" (1971): "The dynamic between a political vision and the demand for a fresh vision of literature is clear: without a growing feminist movement, the first inroads of feminist scholarship could not have been made" (*Lies* 34). Rich has consistently worked to strengthen ties between literary feminism and activist feminism because she sees feminist criticism as intrinsically connected to politics:

she locates its beginnings not in a literary school but in a political agenda. Part of her project has been to keep feminist criticism radical; not content to rest with a white heterosexual women's tradition, Rich draws attention to the effects of race and sexuality. In her view feminist criticism is equivalent to unlearning assumptions of universal whiteness and universal heterosexuality, and for Rich it should be informed by the work being done in women's studies or feminist politics, not rarefied literary theory. Feminist criticism is part of a movement of real women and is accountable to that movement ("Towards a More Feminist Criticism," *Blood* 88–89).

Although her poetry was not always feminist, and although she, indeed, for a time resisted identification with womanhood (see "Writing as Re-Vision" in *On Lies* for her account of the change), Rich was nonetheless a prominent member of the early radical feminists, who identified patriarchy as the force oppressing women. *Of Woman Born* and "Compulsory Heterosexuality and Lesbian Existence" are good examples of her work in this mode; they contain sweeping insights, although they are susceptible of the charge of too readily grouping all women together. Her poetry and prose have been taken to task for their polemical tone, as well. Her writings move from that tendency to generalize about all women to an increasing emphasis on specifics—of race, class, national origin, sexuality, history. Although Rich has been crucial in articulating the significance of lesbian sexuality and its cultural invisibility, and although she was conscious of race early on, having taught in an open admissions program at the City College of the City University of New York, her awareness of race and class has deepened and become more subtle over time.

Given this development, it is not surprising that Rich increasingly draws attention to *her* position, recognizing that it is significant and must be taken into account; as she says in her foreword to *Blood, Bread, and Poetry,* "These essays were not written in an ivory tower. But neither were they written on the edges of a political organizer's daily life, or a nine-to-five manual or clerical job, or in prison" (vii). In short, she acknowledges the impact of material reality on her view of the world. She names herself not only woman but lesbian and Jew, white and southern. She is also inescapably North American: a poet attentive to variations, she emphasizes situational differences. Thus, she is particularly aware of herself as a North American when she is in Nicaragua or in Europe.

Such a subjectivity opens her to self-conscious change and growth, which we can see in her varying references to VIRGINIA WOOLF's *Three Guineas,* a feminist work linking fascism, professionalism, and patriarchy. Having, in "Disloyal to Civilization" (1978), used Woolf's statement that as a woman she has no country, she later rethinks it, for although women may not have men's loyalties, they cannot be simply separate from the place and time in which they find themselves (see "Notes toward a Politics of Location," 1984). Her more recent position is a considered form of "identity politics": "the white radical feminist is confronted by the analysis by women of color of simultaneity of oppressions" (*Blood* xii). The radical feminist's voice is still raised when Rich asserts her purpose "to write directly and overtly as a woman, out of a woman's body and experience, to take women's existence seriously as theme and source for art" (182). But distinctions between women are represented in a new way in her articulation of purpose: the feminist critic needs "a clear understanding of power: of how culture, as meted out in the university, works to empower some and disempower others; of how she herself may be writing out of a situation of unexamined privilege, whether of skin color, heterosexuality, economic and educational background, or other" (94).

A poetry or theory of location also implies a poetry or theory of history. Rich calls for a feminist attentiveness to history, necessary for a vision of the future. Feminist history would be political and engaged by definition, looking for ordinary women and their resistance of patriarchy. Rich has much in common with a writer such as Tillie Olsen and shares the mission of rescuing women's past from silence; in particular, she would resurrect women's bonds to other women from the obscurity surrounding them. By retracing the historical links, the modern critic provides a context for the reception of other feminist work, so that it will not seem "sporadic, errant, orphaned of any tradition of its own" (*Lies* 11).

Rich's writing is a critique of the teaching she received about the universal (male) nature of great art, about the effect of politics on poetry; she finds that all art and history are political—not just those works written from an oppositional perspective. Feminism also recreates the reader, making her no longer a passive recipient of art but rather an individual with a political interest in cracking the codes, reading between the lines, to find the messages left by women in the past. Rich's criticism forges connections between the past and the future, between the university or intellectual and the rest of society, between women of different identities, between feminist critic and woman reader. Her concerns inform her recent poetry as well as the criticism; in fact, negative reviews of the poetry tend to focus on the politics, while positive considerations often intersperse ref-

erences to the essays. Her theoretical work, while often taught in women's studies courses, has not, however, received sustained critical attention.

Nancy Sorkin Rabinowitz

See also FEMINIST THEORY AND CRITICISM: 1. 1963–1972 and 2. ANGLO-AMERICAN FEMINISMS.

Adrienne Rich, *Blood, Bread, and Poetry: Selected Prose, 1979–1985* (1986), "Compulsory Heterosexuality and Lesbian Existence" (1980, *The Signs Reader: Women, Gender, and Scholarship,* ed. Elizabeth Abel and Emily K. Abel, 1983), *Of Woman Born: Motherhood as Experience and Institution* (1976), *On Lies, Secrets, and Silence: Selected Prose, 1966–1987* (1979), *Women and Honor: Some Notes on Lying* (1977), "Words out of the Whirlwind," *Bridges* (1990).

Jane Roberta Cooper, ed., *Reading Adrienne Rich: Reviews and Re-Visions, 1951–81* (1984); Myriam Diaz-Diocaretz, *Translating Poetic Discourse: Questions about Feminist Strategies in Adrienne Rich* (1985); Wendy Martin, *An American Triptych: Anne Bradstreet, Emily Dickinson, Adrienne Rich* (1984).

RICHARDS, I. A.

Ivor Armstrong Richards (1893–1979), one of the founders of modern literary criticism, exerted an immense influence on the study of literature. Beginning with *The Meaning of Meaning* (co-authored with C. K. Ogden in 1923) and *Principles of Literary Criticism* (1924) and continuing with *Science and Poetry* (1926) and *Practical Criticism* (1929), Richards led the "age of analysis" into literary theory and practice. He attacked dogma in criticism; repudiated biography, historicism, and idealist metaphysics; and distanced himself from both *fin de siècle* aestheticism and the formalism of Clive Bell and Roger Fry (see BLOOMSBURY GROUP). The elements of reconstruction were gathered from psychology, Cambridge philosophical realism, and the linguistics of CHARLES SANDERS PEIRCE and Continental schools. His principal achievement was the invention of a method for analyzing language, particularly literary language. He broke down linguistic structures into smaller and smaller units, which could then be examined with regard to one another and to the context of the discourse at large, including speaker, situation, and audience. "Close reading" (or contextualism, as the method also came to be known) had its precursors, but no one had ever proceeded so systematically with a micrological approach to language, nor endowed the method with such incisive theoretical depth, nor applied it so broadly and with such revolutionary results. The method was shown to be capable of probing high modernist texts, some of the most difficult literature ever written. Through his influence on WILLIAM EMPSON (his student at Cambridge in 1928–29) and on the American New Critics, of whom he is the acknowledged "father," his method became the standard first-level approach to literary analysis in the English-speaking classroom, and eventually the standard elsewhere (see NEW CRITICISM).

Born in Sandbach, Cheshire, Richards attended Magdalene College, Cambridge, where he received first-class honors in moral sciences in 1915. Among his teachers were the Hegelian idealist J. M. E. McTaggart, the logician W. E. Johnson, and the realist G. E. Moore. The strongest influence was indubitably Moore's, whose problems (if not his solutions) he made his own: a reconstituted empiricism, theories of meaning and definition, common sense, intuition, and sincerity. After recuperating from tuberculosis, he returned to Cambridge to pursue medicine but was soon invited to teach in the newly founded English school. In 1919 he began lecturing on the contemporary novel and theory of criticism, subsequently adding courses on PRACTICAL CRITICISM (the method of "close reading"), SAMUEL TAYLOR COLERIDGE, rhetorical theory, and British moralists. He remained at Cambridge until 1939.

By all accounts he was a spellbinding lecturer—at Cambridge in the 1920s he was so popular that at times lectures had to be held in the streets, something that had not happened, it was said, since the Middle Ages. The inventor of close reading believed that theory was for books, textual analysis for the classroom. Lectures gave prominence to the subtleties of voice, allowed for a constant sifting of meanings, and permitted quick qualification and rereading.

In his first books, Richards constructed a model of mental functioning that he hoped would shed light on the effects of good and bad literature and the prevalence of inappropriate responses in reading. A testing structure was required to delineate mental action, "an energy system of prodigious complexity and extreme delicacy of organisation which has an indefinitely large number of stable poises" (*Principles* 104). From the writings of the neurophysiologist C. S. Sherrington, from William James, from the behaviorist J. B. Watson, from James Ward, G. F. Stout, and the Würzburg school, he devised a model patterned after a posited feature of the human nervous system, its integrative action. Whenever more impulses, of more varied kinds, are involved and "mutually modified" in mental action, fewer are suppressed. In

ideal poetic experience, no single set of impulses predominates. The whole complex of ideas, feelings, and impulses resolves into mental "attitudes," which are "imaginal and incipient activities" or "tendencies to action" but not action itself (112). The formation of attitudes allows a person the time to test a poetic experience, to develop flexible strategies of organization, and, by extension, to maneuver within the complexity of the modern world.

Not simply the specific attitudes but their processes of development and interaction are crucial in poetic experience. Richards's ideal "equilibrium of opposed opposites," or "synaesthesis," is no ordinary concept of wholeness. From the start he draws a distinction between an end-state of equilibrium (where the mind, in a state of heightened tension, experiences the varied attitudes before it) and a mere oscillation of just two sides, or a deadlock, or an inflexible order. He insists on an ever "wider" equilibrium, challenging readers to discover the fathomless complexity of great literature. The poet's mind "outwits the force of habit" and presents "conciliations of impulses which in most minds are still confused, intertrammelled, and conflicting"; it has gone furthest in these temporary conciliations—temporary because a fresh reading might result in a newly balanced poise—and exemplifies one central principle: a "growing order is the principle of the mind" (244, 61, 50). Richards's goal includes greater clarity of perception, alertness, emotional intensity, self-possession, and freedom.

The main theme of *The Meaning of Meaning,* called the best-known book ever written on semantics, is the significance of context. Richards and Ogden crossed pragmatism and linguistic theory to analyze the role of language in determining thought and to define words and things. As for the determination of thought, Richards's reliance on Watson and Pavlov, both behaviorists, led to a form of nominalism. He treats a stimulus as a sign that links two contexts: an external one, in which the stimulus-sign is found at the moment of stimulation, and a mental one, with which it has been associated in the past. In either case, interpretation of a sign ends in a spatiotemporal particular, an empiricist assumption that Richards does not seriously question. He takes issue with FERDINAND DE SAUSSURE and LUDWIG WITTGENSTEIN on the relations between thought, sign, and thing. These disputes prefigure the split between critics who argue the endlessly proliferating textual significations and those who would still link the text to empirical reality.

With regard to defining words and things, *The Meaning of Meaning* considers abstractions, universals, con-

RICHARDS 621

cepts, as so much symbolic machinery. Some could be useful for analysis; the rest are verbiage, or "word magic." In Richards's view, most philosophy, theology, and criticism fell in the latter category. His corrective starts with a "Triangle of Interpretation," which soon became a common item in linguistics textbooks: symbol (e.g., a noun), reference (or thought), and referent. According to his instrumentalist theory, words carry out jobs, duties, functions *in context*. One function is referential, the pointing to objective reality; a second is emotive, the conveyance of feeling; a third, the expression of a sense of relation to an audience; a fourth, the attitude of the speaker toward the object under discussion; a fifth, the overall intention of the utterance. By 1955, in a mature formulation, Richards had enumerated eight linguistic functions that were more or less simultaneously present within the stream of any given speech act. In addition to the functions, however, Richards sometimes speaks more simply of two broad uses of language: "referential" language, exemplified by the strictest scientific or expository prose (purely rational, functional language, the mark of specialization and technological society), and "emotive" language, which conveys or stimulates feeling and attitude.

Despite his attempts at clarification, critics attacked Richards's division of emotive and referential language on grounds that it divorces reference (knowledge, truth) from poetry. Actually, Richards's emphasis on the emotive function and poetic form in his first books stemmed from his effort to rid criticism of the then excessively message-oriented approach to literature. As the battle was won, more of his attention went to referential factors, though he had never dismissed them and called truth the "decisive notion" in his earliest publication (1919). In any case, a selective reading of Richards on this issue, as on others, is dangerous, since he is given to strong, epigrammatic assertion; local qualification, though normally present, may be extremely subtle and nuanced. Essentially he believes that if the multiple functions of language could be separated by analysis, one could diagnose errors in reading and plot strategies to avoid them. One could check emotive interference in what purported to be objective prose. One might at least get agreement on what was in dispute. Some problems might be found to be merely a matter of words, and not things.

In 1926 Richards published *Science and Poetry,* a popular compendium of his ideas. An optimist by nature, he put great faith in science (and a science of criticism) and a guarded belief in progress at a time when the sciences were in deep theoretical crisis and humanity had emerged

from a catastrophic war. His hope was to extend the range of criticism by bringing it into contact with disciplines that were impacting on the modern world. But while this and other early books give the impression that scientific concepts can deliver more than they possibly can and that solutions to ancient problems are just around the corner, Richards was neither captured nor controlled by his models. If some, mistakenly, labeled him a behaviorist, he had merely employed behaviorist themes and played off one psychological concept against another: behaviorism was not taken so seriously as to eliminate consciousness and introspection. The application of multiple models is a strong theme in his later writings, where he invokes Niels Bohr's principle of complementarity. The complementarity theme originates in his earliest "multiple definitions" (of "beauty" and "meaning") and builds steadily through his career.

Principles of Literary Criticism and *Practical Criticism* adapt psychological concepts to the analysis of literature. The highly valued "poetry of inclusion" wins its unity by embracing the broadest oppositions within its formal boundaries; contrary attitudes are not scarecrows or stalking horses but real, menacing alternatives. In the lesser "poetry of exclusion" a writer eliminates the heterogeneous elements for the sake of a more easily won wholeness and closure. Thus, irony is prized because it can be used to widen the scope of a poem; it "consists in the bringing in of the opposite, the complementary impulses." Tragedy, the greatest of the poetries of inclusion, is Richards's paradigmatic genre because it is "perhaps the most general, all-accepting, all-ordering experience known" and can "take anything into its organisation, modifying it so that it finds a place" (*Principles* 250, 247). (Next is "universal" satire, such as Falstaff and *Candide*.) Eliot's *Waste Land* and Joyce's *Ulysses* are praised in similar terms. Richards's early and effective championing of high modernism speeded its acceptance in the academy. Through the mid-1920s he explored the nature of poetic ambiguity, which opens linguistic depths in a poem and prevents premature closure.

Practical Criticism sums up Richards's best thought of the 1920s. More "scientific" in its sifting of evidence than the earlier books, with all their borrowed models, striking a finer balance between empiricism and creative intelligence, treating both subjective response and the objective work of art, this book is rightly considered his masterpiece. It is often seen as one of the fountainheads of READER-RESPONSE THEORY AND CRITICISM, while New Critics point to it as a main source of objectivist poetics. For his experiment in reading, Richards enlisted hundreds of Cambridge students to interpret 13 poems, some good, some bad, none especially cryptic. In the book he analyses nearly 400 responses (many shockingly bad), then details 10 main obstacles in reading: stock responses, irrelevant associations, doctrinal adhesion, inhibition, sentimentality, and so on. Although some of the terminology defining mental responses enters his discussion of the work of art ("wholeness," "tension," "doctrine"), he also proposes new strategies and terms for literary analysis. A work of art allows for variant readings, while it defends itself from misreading by contextual checks and controls. A poem is a blend of many meanings and linguistic functions, categorized under the headings of sense, feeling, tone, and intention. Tone, for example, includes the author and the narrator and also includes their separate attitudes toward each other, toward the audience (real or fictitious), and toward the subject matter.

Practical Criticism is also concerned with the aftereffects of poetry on mind and character, as well as the deleterious effects of the new communications media and "bad" art (a strong theme throughout his career). In studies on "doctrine in poetry" and "sincerity," Richards questions how readers "translate" the import of great writers whose beliefs and systems of thought have passed into history. This was a problem that MATTHEW ARNOLD addressed in "Literature and Science" (1882), and Richards writes in the spirit of Arnoldian humanism. One must not deny the problem by diverting attention to formalist matters or mere historical reconstruction. "There is something a little ridiculous, at least, in admiring only the rhythms and 'word harmonies' of an author who is writing about the salvation of his soul" (*Complementarities* 31). Nor is suspension of disbelief (as commonly understood) a solution: pretending, say, to believe for a moment in Homer's gods or DANTE ALIGHIERI's devils, then to drop the belief. What great writers communicate ought to be assimilated by and ought to modify the structure of the mind. In Richards's theory, the acceptance of the artistic import depends not on the object of belief, which may be disproved or superseded, but on the value of the feelings and attitudes associated with the belief. A supreme virtue of the critic and reader, "sincerity" is the feeling that comes from speaking the truth, the deepening sense of inner coherence and stability. While Richards expects preparatory work of "unremitting research and reflection," which in themselves may settle the question of value, there remains the "technique" or "ritual" of sincerity (*Practical* 287, 290), as well as a pragmatic "backwash" effect of the poem over the long term. His analysis is supported by a commentary on Confucius in which he wishes to take as wide a view of the subject of sincerity as possible and thereby to encompass the values of East and West.

Theoretical contributions of the 1930s elaborate his system. In *Mencius on the Mind* (1932) he defines key words in Mencius's psychological vocabulary (Richards's favorite book was the dictionary, and in his lifetime he made a "multiple definition" of about 250 key words). *Coleridge on Imagination* (1934), which refounded Coleridge studies in the modern period, interprets Coleridge's transcendental metaphysics as disguised psychology and reconstructs the theory of poetry accordingly. *Interpretation in Teaching* (1938) attempts to do for expository prose what *Practical Criticism* did for poetry.

The most significant work of this period lay in a highly original theory of metaphor, best set forth in *The Philosophy of Rhetoric* (1936). Traditionally, the two halves of a metaphor (the "image" and the "idea") were given unequal value: one side was ornamental, while the other contained the meaning. Richards, in contrast, grants parity to the two halves: the metaphor is the whole double unit whose meaning is generated by the interaction of its "tenor" ("underlying idea" or "principal subject") and a "vehicle" (the "figure"); the term "ground" names what the tenor and vehicle share in common. Tenor and vehicle bring their own contexts, not all parts of which become active in the exchange that creates an effective metaphor (more often, it is what is *not* shared in common that determines the effectiveness of the metaphor): his commonly cited definition of metaphor is "a transaction between contexts" (*Philosophy* 95). The theory is grounded in contextualism. Not regarding the meaning of a sentence as a result of the meaning of individual words, Richards begins the other way around, with the meaning of the sentence or discourse, and works backward, separating it into its elements. At issue is the extent of a speaker's context. He did not look far beyond the immediate context into social or historical causation, but nothing inherent in the theory bars doing so.

Through the 1930s Richards became increasingly involved in Ogden's Basic English movement. Basic English is a simplified version of English, "based on" 850 key words and rules of grammar. It was never meant to be a complete English, but rather a beginner's first, spacious plateau. Having spent years on the upper level of education, Richards turned to developing approaches to reading at the beginning levels. World literacy became his highest priority, and he spent several years in China, where he wrote a manual on learning English. In 1939 he accepted a position at Harvard, where he taught until 1963. There he pioneered (with Christine M. Gibson) the use of the media for both learning how to read and second-language instruction. Beginning with Basic English and cartoonlike drawings in the *Language through Pictures* series, he adapted his method to advances in media technology, from film and recording to tape, television, videotape, and cassette.

In 1974 Richards published *Beyond,* his humanistic testament, which contains close readings of the dialogues between central human figures and their gods in Homer, the Book of Job, Psalms, PLATO, Dante, and PERCY BYSSHE SHELLEY. Images of godhead and the self-images of the questioners stand in a mirrored or dialectical relation to one another. The book proposes a kind of inwardness that is anchored in experience, requires a fidelity to texts, and is essentially its own reward.

Richards eventually returned to Cambridge, England, in 1974. In his later career he published several collections of poems and plays. Even in retirement he never abandoned his hope of furthering world literacy, and his death was hastened by a strenuous lecture tour of China in his eighty-seventh year.

John Paul Russo

See also NEW CRITICISM, PRACTICAL CRITICISM, and RHETORIC.

I. A. Richards, *Beyond* (1973), *Coleridge on Imagination* (1934), *Complementarities: Uncollected Essays* (ed. John Paul Russo, 1976), *How to Read a Page* (1942), *Internal Colloquies: Poems and Plays* (1971), *Interpretation in Teaching* (1938), *Mencius on the Mind: Experiments in Multiple Definition* (1932), *New and Selected Poems* (1978), *The Philosophy of Rhetoric* (1936), *Practical Criticism: A Study of Literary Judgment* (1929), *Principles of Literary Criticism* (1924), *Richards on Rhetoric: I. A. Richards: Selected Essays (1929–1974)* (ed. Ann E. Berthoff, 1990), *Science and Poetry* (1926), *So Much Nearer: Essays toward a World English* (1968), *Speculative Instruments* (1955); I. A. Richards and C. K. Ogden, *The Meaning of Meaning* (1923).

Paul A. Bové, *Intellectuals in Power: A Genealogy of Critical Humanism* (1986); Reuben Brower, Helen Vendler, and John Hollander, eds., *I. A. Richards: Essays in His Honor* (1973); Giovanni Cianci, *La scuola di Cambridge: La critica letteraria di I. A. Richards, W. Empson, F. R. Leavis* (1970); Gerald Graff, *Poetic Statement and Critical Dogma* (1970, 2d ed., 1980); W. H. N. Hotopf, *Language, Thought, and Comprehension: A Case Study of the Writings of I. A. Richards* (1965); Pamela McCallum, *Literature and Method: Towards a Critique of I. A. Richards, T. S. Eliot, and F. R. Leavis* (1983); John Needham, *"The Completest Mode": I. A. Richards and the Continuity of English Criticism* (1982); John Crowe Ransom, *The New Criticism* (1941); John Paul Russo, "A Bibliography of . . . I. A. Richards (1919–1973)," *I. A. Richards: Essays in His Honor* (ed. Brower et al., suppl. 1973–79 in Russo, *I. A. Richards: His Life and Work*), *I. A. Richards: His Life and Work* (1989); Jerome P. Schiller, *I. A. Richards' Theory of Literature* (1969); Ronald Shusterman, *Critique et poésie selon I. A. Richards: De la confiance au relativisme naissant* (1988).

RICOEUR, PAUL

Paul Ricoeur (b. 1913), who has been professor of philosophy at the University of Paris and the University of Chicago, has had extraordinary influence in such disparate fields as theology, psychoanalysis, historiography, political economy, and literary theory. Only MICHEL FOUCAULT and JACQUES DERRIDA among contemporary French philosophers have had such an impact outside their domain. But in contrast to Foucault and Derrida, Ricoeur has never departed from the professional concerns of his discipline. All of his work has been written within the philosophical paradigm of the two traditions he has merged: PHENOMENOLOGY, as it developed from Edmund Husserl and MARTIN HEIDEGGER, and HERMENEUTICS, as revised by Hans-Georg Gadamer.

Beginning with *Interpretation Theory: Discourse and the Surplus of Meaning* (1976) and culminating with volume 3 of *Time and Narrative* (1986), Ricoeur has addressed every major theoretical issue of literary criticism. During these ten years he wrote five books and numerous articles, selections from which have been collected and edited by John B. Thompson in *Hermeneutics and the Human Sciences* (1981), by George H. Taylor in *Lectures on Ideology and Utopia* (1986), and by Mario J. Valdés in *A Ricoeur Reader* (1991).

In the introduction to *Interpretation Theory* Ricoeur sets as his goal nothing less than a systematic examination of the concept of textual unity as a construct of language, the necessary background for his literary theory. The philosophical means used in the pursuit of this goal are phenomenological dialectic and hermeneutic exegesis. His larger argument involves the examination of language as discourse, the separation of written from spoken discourse, the establishment of a theory of text (which includes a recognition of the polysemy of words and the ambiguity of sentences), and the development of a textual theory of interpretation based on a dialectic of explanation and understanding.

This project hinges upon a fundamental distinction Ricoeur makes between semiotics and semantics. Semiotics is the science of signs and relies on the dissociative capacity of language to be broken into constitutive parts, but it cannot deal with meaning, since meaning is produced at a discursive rather than a lexical level of language. Semantics, as the science of the sentence, is concerned with making sense, that is, with the communication of meaning, and thus responds to the integrative capacity of language. Discourse, for Ricoeur, is a dialectic of event and meaning. The event is experience as expression, but it is also the intersubjective exchange itself and communication with the recipient. What is communicated to the recipient in the event of the speech act is not the experience of the speaker as experienced but its meaning. The lived experience remains private, but its sense, its meaning, becomes public through discourse. Thus the literary author's private feelings must remain part of his or her psychological world, but the literary work as expression relates some sense of the author's lived experience. The point is crucial for Ricoeur, especially in his dialogue with Derridean deconstruction.

In the introduction to *Interpretation Theory* Ricoeur goes on to say:

> Only this dialectic [sense and reference] says something about the relation between language and the ontological condition of being in the world. Language is not a world of its own. It is not even a world. But because we are in the world, because we are affected by situations . . . we have something to say, we have experience to bring to language. (20–21)

Discourse "cannot fail to be about something"; "poetic texts speak about the world. But not in a descriptive way . . . the reference here is not abolished, but divided or split" (36–37). For Ricoeur, then, literature redescribes the world for its readers. The direct consequence of this text-reader relationship for literary criticism is the transformation of interpretation into a dynamic dialectic between the distanciation of the text and the appropriation of the reader. "Reading is the *pharmakon,* the remedy, by which the meaning of the text is rescued from the estrangement of distanciation and put in a new proximity which suppresses and preserves the cultural distance and includes the otherness within the ownness" (43). Literary criticism thus is reformed from a search for absolutes into a dynamic encounter of continuous refiguration within a tradition of commentary.

Ricoeur's tensional theory of metaphor (which is also extended to a consideration of the symbol) plays an important role in this interpretive process, granting fundamental control to the need for making sense as the basis for all meaning. This is the cornerstone of his larger theory of interpretation, which has given relational literary criticism a contemporary philosophical argument in the tradition of GIAMBATTISTA VICO, Wilhelm von Humboldt, and BENEDETTO CROCE. "As in metaphor theory," Ricoeur states, the "excess of signification in a symbol can be opposed to the literal signification, but only on the condition that we also oppose two interpretations at the same time" (55). Metaphor and symbolic signification is two-leveled and so constituted that we can attain the secondary signification only by way of the primary signification.

The Rule of Metaphor (1975) works together with *Interpretation Theory* in a project devoted to an intensive examination of metaphorical meaning. In chapter 7 of the former work, "Metaphor and Reference," Ricoeur brings his philosophy of language to bear explicitly on the concerns of literary criticism:

> The postulate of reference requires a separate discussion when it touches on those particular entities of discourse called texts, that is, more complex compositions than the sentence. The question henceforth arises in the context of hermeneutics rather than semantics, for which the sentence is at once the first and the last entity. (219)

In other words, the disciplines have been matched to their corresponding problematics: semiotics is concerned with the lexical level of language, semantics with the sentence, and hermeneutics considers the text as a unique construct. But texts that are "singularly complex," literary texts, seem to "constitute an exception" to the standard "reference requirement" of language (219). These highly figured texts—produced as works, as totalities irreducible to simple sums of sentences—are organized not as language but as discourse, and the question of their split reference is located not at the semantic level of the sentence but rather at the hermeneutic level of the work. The particular task of literary interpretation demands an understanding of literary meaning grounded in the obscured literal meaning. The referential power of literary discourse is thus linked to the eclipse of ordinary meaning, to the creation of a heuristic fiction, and to the redescribed reality brought to the reader.

Time and Narrative began in 1981 as a seminar at the University of Toronto and culminated in a four-part study published in three volumes, from 1983 to 1985. The first volume of *Time and Narrative* takes up the discussion of *The Rule of Metaphor* on semantic innovation and split reference in literary language and enlarges it considerably in order to address the full spectrum of creative linguistic invention. The heart of Ricoeur's philosophical argument here concerns the dialectical relationship of understanding and explanation—the process of grasping the text and transmitting this understanding to someone else. This is the operation that unifies into a whole the multiplicity of circumstances, human aims and plans, initiatives, intentions, and interaction, as well as the rise and fall of personal and collective fortunes attended by all the unforeseen and unintended consequences of human life in the world of action. The epistemological problem lies in the creation of a unique synthesis from an acquired familiarity and use of language that is both personal and collective and common to all. Ricoeur's answer is that time as human time exists only because of narrative expression—narrativity—which is the primary mode of knowing and therefore explaining the world to ourselves and to others.

To deal with the intricacies of the historical, ontological, and epistemological questions surrounding narrativity and human time, Ricoeur introduced a concept of threefold mimesis that keeps the focus on textual hermeneutics. Ricoeur's concept does not confine itself to setting mimesis$_2$ (the configuration of the text, i.e., the reader's organization of written language into a work) between mimesis$_1$ (the prefigured basis for language use) and mimesis$_3$ (the reader's refiguration of the text into the world of action). Hermeneutics, as Ricoeur says, "wants to characterize mimesis$_2$ by its mediating function. What is at stake, therefore, is the concrete process by which the textual configuration [mimesis$_2$] mediates between the prefiguration of the practical field and its refiguration through the reception of the work." The reader, Ricoeur goes on to say, "is that operator *par excellence* who takes up through doing something—the act of reading—the unity of the traversal from mimesis$_1$ to mimesis$_3$ by way of mimesis$_2$" (*Time* 1:53). Perhaps the most significant consequence of this project for contemporary literary criticism is that Ricoeur's philosophy moves poststructuralist theory into the camp of cultural hermeneutics.

Putting a text into play is an experience that transforms those who participate in it—critics and their readers. The subject of the aesthetic experience is not the critic but rather what takes place in the activity. Ricoeur puts it this way:

> The threshold separating these problematics [configuration and refiguration] is, in fact, crossed only when the world of the text is confronted with the world of the reader. *Only then does the literary work acquire a meaning in the full sense of the term, at the intersection of the world projected by the text and the life-world of the reader.* (*Time* 2:160, emphasis added)

In criticism inspired by Ricoeur the critic does not project the a priori of his or her own understanding, nor does he or she interpolate this a priori into the text. Quite the contrary: appropriation is the process by which the revelation of new modes of being in the experience of reading the text gives the critic a new capacity for self-knowledge. If the power of a text is to be found in its capacity to project a redescription of the world, then it is not the critic who projects herself or himself; rather, the text projects the discovery of refiguration upon the critic. Appropriation is not a remaking of the text in our own perspective but a response to the text that can become a commentary rooted in self-understanding. Because absolute knowledge is an illusion, the conflict of interpretations is inescapable. Ricoeur's philosophy, however, gives us the means to transcend the finite character of being-in-the-world and to celebrate the participation of text and readers in the community of commentary.

Mario J. Valdés

Paul Ricoeur, *Hermeneutics and Human Sciences: Essays on Language, Acts, and Interpretation* (ed. and trans. John B. Thompson, 1981), *Interpretation Theory: Discourse and the Surplus of Meaning* (1976), *La Métaphore vive* (1975, *The Rule of Metaphor: Multi-Disciplinary Studies of the Creation of Meaning in Language,* trans. Robert Czerny et al., 1977), *A Ricoeur Reader: Reflection and Imagination* (ed. Mario J. Valdés, 1991), *Soi-même: Comme un autre* (1990, *Oneself as Another,* trans. Katherine Blamey, 1992), *Temps et récit* (3 vols., 1983–85, *Time and Narrative,* vols. 1–2, trans. Kathleen McLaughlin and David Pellauer, 1984–85, vol. 3, trans. Kathleen Blamey and David Pellauer, 1988).

Steven H. Clark, *Paul Ricoeur* (1990); Theodore F. Geraets, ed., *À la recherche du sens / In Search of Meaning,* special issue, *Revue de l'Université d'Ottawa / University of Ottawa Quarterly* 55 (1985); Peter T. Kemp and David Rasmussen, eds., *The Narrative Path: The Later Works of Paul Ricoeur* (1989); G. B. Madison, *The Hermeneutics of Postmodernity* (1990); Oliver Mongin and Joël Roman, eds., *Paul Ricoeur,* special issue, *Esprit* 7–8 (1988); Charles E. Reagan, ed., *Studies in the Philosophy of Paul Ricoeur* (1979); John B. Thompson, *Critical Hermeneutics: A Study in the Thought of Paul Ricoeur and Jürgen Habermas* (1981); Mario J. Valdés, *Phenomenological Hermeneutics and the Study of Literature* (1987); Frans D. Vansina, *Paul Ricoeur: Bibliographie systématique de ses écrits et des publications consacrées a sa pensée (1935–1984) / A Primary and Secondary Systematic Bibliography (1935–1984)* (1985).

RORTY, RICHARD

Richard Rorty (b. 1931) is probably the most influential contemporary American philosopher on literary theory. After a long training and practice in the tradition of analytic philosophy, where he was well respected for his work in philosophy of mind and language, Rorty became important for literary theory when he repudiated that tradition to embrace a neopragmatism that converges with contemporary Continental theory on many major issues. Perhaps chief among these are anti-essentialism and antifoundationalism, the history of human thought and "truth," and the ineluctable hermeneutic and linguistic dimension of experience. Rorty's sympathetic readings of MARTIN HEIDEGGER, Hans-Georg Gadamer, JACQUES DERRIDA, JEAN-FRANÇOIS LYOTARD, JÜRGEN HABERMAS, and MICHEL FOUCAULT have been very influential in engendering a fruitful dialogue between the Continental and Anglo-American philosophical traditions and between philosophy and literary theory.

Rorty's concern with language as the constitutive core of all experience is evident already in his analytic period in the influential collection he edited, *The Linguistic Turn* (1967). Analytic philosophy regarded language as the foundational datum whose structure could be analyzed to provide the best account both of the nature of the world, which language represented, and of the human mind, which employed language and was structured by it. As such, analytic philosophy was but a linguistic turn to earlier foundational approaches (e.g., those of RENÉ DESCARTES, John Locke, IMMANUEL KANT) that tried to ground our knowledge of the world on the structure of our minds and mental processes.

Rorty's second book, *Philosophy and the Mirror of Nature* (1979), was a radical and enormously influential revolt against this traditional idea and ideal of knowledge as faithful representation of reality, where the mind is compared to a mirror that reflects the real and where philosophy's central task is the epistemological one of testing and repairing the mirror so that the propositions we assert will reflect the given realities with greater accuracy. In this way the language that structures our thought will more closely correspond to the real, ultimate structure of the world. Rorty's attack on the traditional representational project of philosophy was extremely persuasive not only because of its impressive historical sweep and rigorous argumentation but especially because it employed the very best methods and results of contemporary analytic philosophy to deconstruct the analytic project.

For Rorty, one of the central problems with founda-

tional philosophy is its pretensions to be ahistorical, to fix the basic and necessary conditions for human knowledge independent of changing social practices, language games, or world-pictures. In contrast to the traditional pantheon of "systematic" foundational philosophers, Rorty hailed LUDWIG WITTGENSTEIN, Heidegger, and JOHN DEWEY as the most important philosophers of the twentieth century because they are "edifying" rather than systematic, philosophers whose "common message . . . is a historicist one" and "whose aim is to edify—to help their readers, or society as a whole, break free from outworn vocabularies and attitudes, rather than to provide 'grounding' for the intuitions and customs of the present" (9, 11–12).

Wittgenstein, Heidegger, and Dewey share not only the theme of historicism but a strong emphasis on practice, on the priority of action to epistemological reflection. Rorty's next book, *Consequences of Pragmatism* (1982), which contains essays on these thinkers and on Derrida, builds on their pragmatist ideas to develop Rorty's own neopragmatism. This is concisely defined in "Pragmatism, Relativism, and Irrationalism" in terms of three basic features: first, "anti-essentialism applied to notions like 'truth,' 'knowledge,' 'language,' 'morality,' and similar objects of philosophical theorizing" (162); second, the substitution of *phronesis* (practical wisdom) for *theoria* as the philosophical model of knowledge. Traditional epistemology was wrong to look for a pure essence of truth or an absolute method of knowledge beyond what is good or useful in the way of belief. "For the pragmatists, the pattern of all inquiry—scientific as well as moral—is deliberation concerning the relative attractions of various concrete alternatives" (164). Rorty's third defining feature of pragmatism is its recognition of "the contingent character" and inalienable sociohistorical aspects of the context of inquiry. The starting points and criteria of our quest for knowledge are always a function of the history of our community and intellectual tradition. Our language, truths, and objects of inquiry are not simply dictated by nature but shaped by human interests; they are more made than found.

For Rorty the upshot of pragmatism's anti-essentialist, historicist constructivism is that since we create both language and truth about the world (for truth, as propositional, is only given in language), we should be constantly interested in reconstructing language to make it more useful and rewarding and to make our experienced world more satisfying to our desires. This privileging of creation and construction over discovery and objective description, together with the crucial role of imaginative new language in such efforts of creation and construction, formed a dominant theme of Rorty's important *Contingency, Irony, and Solidarity* (1989), which takes a distinctive aesthetic turn, privileging imaginative literature over "rationalist" philosophy and including chapters on the writings of Vladimir Nabokov and GEORGE ORWELL. In this book Rorty develops an aestheticized "private" ethics of personal self-enrichment and self-creation that is combined with (and in a sense also protected and held in check by) a "public" political morality of liberalism as procedural justice and the desire to avoid giving pain to others so that each may pursue his or her private vision of perfection in peace.

Language remains the prime material of philosophy, but it no longer represents the incarnation of reason, the expression of our shared human essence, nor does it function as a ground for foundationalist metaphysics or epistemology. Instead, Rorty sees language as primarily an aesthetic tool for self-fashioning; we reconstitute ourselves and our society by redescription, by retelling our histories through different "vocabularies." He urges that our highest cultural role of hero should be "the strong poet" (in a general sense of "poet" that can include both philosopher and scientist) as forger of new vocabularies and new narratives that redescribe and thus reconstitute our selves and world, rather than the traditional role of philosopher as seer into the timeless and necessary truths about the essence of humanity and reality. This involves passing from our traditional metaphysical culture based on reason and necessity to a (postmodern) "ironist" culture based on contingency and poetic imagination, one that convinces by narrative rhetoric rather than by strict logical argumentation. "Ironist theory must be narrative in form because the ironist's nominalism and historicism will not permit him to think of his work as establishing a relation to real essence; he can only establish a relation to the past" (101).

Rorty's own tendentious narrative of our path to ironist culture is sustained in this book through a philosophical genealogy that begins with G. W. F. HEGEL and continues through FRIEDRICH NIETZSCHE, Heidegger, Derrida, and Foucault, with the help of some pragmatists; some analytical philosophers, such as Wittgenstein and Donald Davidson; and some literary figures, such as Marcel Proust and HAROLD BLOOM. The triumphant tale of progress toward ironist culture is structured on a series of parallel binary oppositions that flesh out the central contrast of reason versus the aesthetic: necessity/contingency, universal/particular, public/private, philosophy/poetry, truth/metaphor, inference/narrative, logic/rhetoric, discovery/creation, metaphysics/

ironists. Freedom and progress are a function of reversing the representative privilege of the former terms.

A large part of Rorty's ironist message is a warning against the traditional philosophical error of universalizing one's vocabulary and narrative as authoritative for all, of assuming that private and public must be united by reason and foundational truth. The idea that private ideals are truly valid only if publicly validated and that validity implies universality is seen by Rorty as a pernicious remnant of the metaphysical claims of reason. The aestheticist liberal ironist should instead be satisfied with the contingency and particularity of the personal ideals he or she pursues for the private autonomy of "self-creation" and self-perfection. The ironist should give up the attempt "to unite the private and the public" and should try "to overcome authority without claiming authority" (125, 105), overcoming the authority of inherited narratives and vocabularies by creating a self and history in his or her own linguistic terms without claiming authority over the language and self-fashioning of others. Rejecting the idea of language in general as a fixed universal essence "intervening between self and reality" (14), Rorty advocates the idea of particular, historicized, and contingent linguistic practices or vocabularies whose highest function is not the Habermassian one of cooperative problem-solving to promote consensus of belief but rather the aesthetic one of individual, original creation, to "make things new" by redescribing them in new terms. Here Rorty's theory of textual interpretation as recontextualizing reconstitutive rewriting converges with Continental poststructuralist theories such as those of ROLAND BARTHES and Derrida as well as with American pragmatist theories such as those of STANLEY FISH and Harold Bloom.

This aesthetic view of language as a tool for constant change as novel personal creation is balanced by Rorty's recognition that there is also the use of stable shared "public" language for our common practical purposes and our political concerns of justice. Rorty's theory thus depends on a deep and ramified "public-private split" (85), which sharply separates the language of consensus from the language of creation, the realm of social life from the aesthetic realm of the quest for individual autonomy and self-creation. Rorty privileges the private and aesthetic as what gives content to life. Even his ideal of liberal polity is advocated for providing the needed framework for private aestheticism; the prime value and aim of such a liberal society is precisely "letting its citizens be as privatistic, 'irrationalist,' and aestheticist as they please so long as they do it on their own time— causing no harm to others" (xiv). This sharp dualism of the public and private has been criticized, since the private self and its language are always already socially constituted and since the success and power of innovative vocabularies are also dependent on the public. Moreover, the reduction of the self to language and self-creation to linguistic innovation seems to court a reductive linguistic essentialism with respect to human nature and praxis that is inconsistent with pragmatism's anti-essentialism and materialist sociohistoricism as advocated by Dewey. Finally, the ideal of an aesthetic life as radically innovative self-creation can be criticized as excessively elitist and constrained by romantic notions of art, as reflective of both the cult of superior genius and the selfishly privatized consumerist values of contemporary capitalist liberalism. (All of these criticisms can be found in Shusterman.)

Rorty elaborates and defends his views on ethics, bourgeois liberal democracy, POSTMODERNISM, and cultural politics in the two volumes of his *Philosophical Papers—Objectivity, Relativism, and Truth* and *Essays on Heidegger and Others*—written between 1980 and 1989, which also include articles defending pragmatist views of interpretation and scientific inquiry against varieties of representationalism, as well as articles connecting pragmatism with Heidegger and others in the Continental tradition of philosophy and literary theory.

Richard Shusterman

Richard Rorty, *Consequences of Pragmatism: Essays, 1972–1980* (1982), *Contingency, Irony, and Solidarity* (1989), *Essays on Heidegger and Others* (*Philosophical Papers*, vol. 1, 1991), *Objectivity, Relativism, and Truth* (*Philosophical Papers*, vol. 2, 1991), *Philosophy and The Mirror of Nature* (1979); Richard Rorty, ed., *The Linguistic Turn: Recent Essays in Philosophical Method* (1967).

Jean-Pierre Cometti, *Lire Rorty* (1992); Konstantin Kolenda, *Rorty's Humanistic Pragmatism* (1990); Alan Malachowski and Jo Burrows, eds., *Reading Rorty: Critical Responses to "Philosophy and the Mirror of Nature"* (1990); Richard Shusterman, *Pragmatist Aesthetics: Living Beauty, Rethinking Art* (1992).

ROUSSEAU, JEAN-JACQUES

The influence of Jean-Jacques Rousseau (1712–78) on literary theory is hard to estimate. That is not just because his thought has been closely woven into the fabric of our modernity and widely disseminated into the most diverse of spheres. It is rather more because from the very

first, Rousseau's work has transgressed the boundaries that allow critics to stand outside the work to assess it. This least academic of philosophers did not leave as his inheritance a systematic doctrine that can be taught to budding young disciples as a set of principles, concepts, methods, and formulae. Nor can Rousseau's inheritance be understood as purely literary, as the case of entrusting a formally perfect work of art intact to the future, like a sacred, empty vessel into which each generation can pour its concerns. This is not to say that Rousseau did not have an impact on the political and literary movements of his time, or that his work has not continued to have an effect. But to look at his work in this light is to misjudge it, to misunderstand the source of its revolutionary impact.

Rousseau's contribution is, first and foremost, a theory and practice of writing, of textual undecidability, of figurative language. These are all terms that have been excluded from philosophical discussion and sublimated in aesthetics as problems of style or ornament. Rousseau not only developed a theory of this forgotten corner of the Western tradition but pursued the ramifications of his theory of textuality into many of the domains onto which it impinged: into fiction (*Julie, ou la nouvelle Héloïse* [*Julie, or the New Heloïse*]), autobiography (*Les Confessions* [*The Confessions*]; *Rousseau juge de Jean-Jacques* [*Rousseau Judge of Jean-Jacques*]; *Les Rêveries du promeneur solitaire* [*Reveries of a Solitary Walker*]), the political sphere (*Discours sur les sciences et les arts* [*Discourse on the Sciences and the Arts*]; *Discours sur les origines et les fondements de l'inégalité parmi les hommes* [*Discourse on the Origin and Foundation of Inequality among Men*]; *Du contrat social* [*The Social Contract*]), education (*Émile*), religion (*Émile, Lettres écrites de la montagne* [*Letters Written from the Mountain*]), and so on. The result was paradoxical: what Rousseau was explaining as a general trend was the exclusion of writing by conceptual reason or its sublimation by the imagination; as if in demonstration of his theory, his readers have long proved at once enthusiastic about his uncovering of reason's blind spots and repressive of the textuality he brought to their attention.

Nowhere has Rousseau's theory of writing as the "unthought" of thought historically proven so open to this double, paradoxical reading than around the question of the proper—be it in the political realm as property, the ethical as propriety, or the literary as proper meaning. Readers early felt the revolutionary political force of Rousseau's statement in the *Discourse on Inequality* that the drawing of property lines is at once both an act of unparalleled violence, which snatches away a terrain hitherto open to all, and an act synonymous with the creation of society, which lays down a distinction between public and private spheres. Rousseau questioned the very ground on which people stood by reminding us that society was contractual and that the contract reposed on a violent forgetfulness. As for his ethics, IMMANUEL KANT, who called Rousseau the Newton of the moral universe, found that he criticized conventional propriety in the name of freedom, which served both as the origin of moral law (by way of man's natural goodness) and as the principle of its transgression. In aesthetics, Rousseau's analysis of proper meaning as grounded on forgotten figural exchanges challenged the classical aesthetic according to which figures were ornaments superadded to a God-given language of proper, referential meanings. In Rousseau, nature itself was synonymous with fiction. For him, there can be no concept of a tree, and thus no proper, referential term for it, without a prior metaphor comparing tree A to the very different tree B, and similarly no concept of man as natural entity without the violent forgetting of a prior figure. But at the same time that readers welcomed Rousseau's critique of the proper as liberating, they also found excesses in the work that, most often, they would have liked to delete. In a new attempt to redefine the proper, they found themselves repeating the violent gesture of exclusion Rousseau had analyzed.

Take his influence in the realm of political philosophy. He is credited as one of the leading inspirations for the French Revolution by virtue of his sweeping critique of property, his premise of man's goodness in the fictional state of nature, and his accompanying argument that human beings are not subjected to rule by might or by divine decree but rather freely contract with one another for the law, agreeing to obey as citizens the laws that bind them. Rousseau's political philosophy has continued to have an influence. Modern political philosophers on the left—from Karl Marx to Louis Althusser—have inherited much from the legacy of Rousseau's critique of property (see MARXIST THEORY AND CRITICISM). Those on the right have been struck rather more by the ideal state of nature, interpreted as leading from natural right to civic values such as republican virtue and to transcendent ones such as justice.

In both cases, however, there has been general agreement among philosophers that Rousseau's political treatises are not only compromised by his unsystematic and flowery presentation but actually contradicted by his imaginative fictions. For the conservative Leo Strauss, to accord each individual in the fictional state of nature rights and freedoms is to make a double gesture. As a premise in a philosophy, it places Rousseau's thought in line with the classical tradition concerned with natural law, but as an imaginative fiction, the state of nature shows Rousseau's work to be a critical stage in the breakdown of the classical ideal set forth in PLATO's *Republic*. For Strauss, such fictions justify the passions and so drive humanity further into a modernity synonymous— in its lack of concern for civic virtue and its hedonistic cult of individual happiness—with decadence. Marxists generally agree that Rousseau's critique of property is finally made in the name of bourgeois values and find that Rousseau proposes literary solutions (moral reform and a nostalgic return to preindustrial society) to real-life economic problems. They find Rousseau's critique of property to be compromised by his failure to respect the property lines dividing political philosophy from literature. If political philosophers so far apart can agree, it is because—as this intrepid traverser of boundaries has shown—literature poses a threat to the very ground of political thinking. It destabilizes terms such as "man," "property," and so on, which political and legal texts must take for granted as referential.

Rousseau has also been credited with having almost single-handedly brought about the literary revolution that was Romanticism, discovering the possibilities of the first-person imaginative subject, giving the public a taste for tales of passionate error and equally passionate repentance, exploring what would become Romanticism's dominant themes and literary devices. The most important texts of Rousseau's in this literary revolution were the epistolary novel *Julie, ou la nouvelle Heloïse* and the autobiographical works, the narrative *Confessions* and the introspective *Les Rêveries du promeneur solitaire*. The influence of Rousseau's literary theories and innovations in genre survived the end of the period called Romanticism. His forays into autobiographical writing can be seen as the distant ancestors of many a work by those invested in the construction and legitimation of a self, from the eighteenth-century citizen of revolutionary France, to the nineteenth-century ex-slave, factory worker, or petit bourgeois, to the late-twentieth-century feminist or Third World autobiographer. His theory of metaphor had a nineteenth-century inheritor in the Symbolists (see BRITISH THEORY AND CRITICISM: 5. SYMBOLISM and STÉPHANE MALLARMÉ AND FRENCH SYMBOLISM). His *Rêveries* were one model for CHARLES BAUDELAIRE's invention of the prose poem.

But both the autobiographical works and *Julie* have also made readers uneasy from the beginning because of their disregard for the property lines separating the self-referential, fictional function of language from its referential function. Take *Julie*, a work that is difficult to reduce to the beautiful product of the creative process of the sensuous imagination. The tale opens with St. Preux's confession of his passionate love for Julie and exploits in detail all the resources of the Romantic plot of frustrated passion—a metaphorical relation is established between the description of a natural landscape and the soul it symbolizes; the stages of St. Preux's wayward imagination as it endows Julie with all perfections are taken to stand for the stages of the artist's creative process, and so on. But there are signs that the book is not chiefly about the Romantic imagination at all. From the outset, St. Preux and Julie are budding moralists, young Enlightenment philosophers, whose letters are filled with their opinions on everything from the Valaisan peasant to the Parisian beau monde. By the middle of the book, the Romantic love plot has been interrupted: Julie not only accedes to her father's wishes in marrying an older man but undergoes a kind of conversion that has her firmly renouncing her earlier passion and all the figments of the imagination associated with it, including virtue, as error. All pretense to fictional verisimilitude is lost, as the book waxes didactic and turns to a series of philosophical treatises on such themes as household economy, religion, the education of children, suicide, friendship, and so on.

Rousseau was aware that *Julie* was an admixture. In the dialogued preface to the work he has one of his interlocutors say that it seems to be "two different books that the same people ought not to read" (*Oeuvres* 2:17). The interlocutor lists the various aesthetic mistakes and in so doing puts his finger on the chief source of uneasiness, the uncertain status of the work: "This collection is full of maladroit things that the least scribbler would have avoided: harangues, repetitions, contradictions, eternal harpings. . . . *if* all of this is a fiction, you have made a bad book" (2:28). *Julie* turns from a fiction revelatory of the self, whose language is self-referential, to a work that takes for granted as referential entities things such as virtue, whose existence was problematical in the first part. From an aesthetic standpoint, we like our fictions to be unalloyed by matters of fact; and from an epistemological and ethical standpoint, we want facts and fictions to come in separate parcels, because we want evidence and knowledge of their difference. When, as in *Julie,* the line between fictional and referential language starts to oscillate, readers would prefer that—if the referential language cannot be excluded in the name of taste—at the very least the lesson about the undecidability of language be exempted from the general oscillation and uncertainty. A similar problem haunts the autobiographical works, in which the two incompatible

truth claims of historical veracity and fictional verisimilitude vie for supremacy. The resultant hybrid makes readers wonder suspiciously whether Rousseau has not, when convenient, substituted one kind of truth for the other, to the detriment of both.

In earlier receptions of Rousseau's work, the presence in the philosophical texts of a fictional, rhetorical surplus, and in the fictional texts of philosophical or historical leftovers, was judged evidence of contradictions in the political theory, of bad art in the novel, of outright lying and delirious self-obsession in the autobiographical works—and that at the very moment when it was recognized that Rousseau had shaken the grounds of the state as of the literary world.

The third revolution in part owed to Rousseau is the one taking place in the university, reshaping departments and canons of study and transforming the disciplines themselves, so that departments of literature, for instance, conceive of literary criticism as less a historical than a theoretical discipline. Feminist and postcolonial attacks on the canon, such as on the use of terms such as "man," which mask ideological fictions under a presumed neutrality, owe much to Rousseau's critique of proper meaning, for example, to his insistence in the *Confessions* that "at bottom, everything is political" (1:404)—this debt existing despite their objection, in line with the early polemics of MARY WOLLSTONECRAFT, that Rousseau's view of woman is idealized and, as such, oppressive.

The Rousseau of recent feminism does not come to us directly, but is filtered through the deconstructionist readings of JACQUES DERRIDA and PAUL DE MAN, who concentrated very precisely on the leftovers, the "trash" excluded whenever politics or literature claimed to be able to determine the status of the language of a Rousseauian text. They saw that these leftovers never could be expunged from Rousseau's text. They were the places where Rousseau's theory of textual undecidability was being elaborated and instantiated. They were hyperbolic representations where the general problem of textuality was being theorized.

Derrida made Rousseau a linchpin in his critique of Western philosophy because he saw in Rousseau's work a thoroughgoing analysis of the forgotten term "writing," another name for textual undecidability. In his discussion of speech and writing in ". . . ce dangereux supplément" in *De la grammatologie (Of Grammatology),* Derrida shows first that for Rousseau, writing always arrives in the absence of a determinate referent. Even where a preface or a title page tries to define contractually the mode of reading of the text that follows, we still have to read the contract, to ask after the status of *its* language. Because writing hesitates between being signs that refer and symbols that signify, it does not so much further human communication and knowledge as get in its way. Derrida shows that for Rousseau, writing substitutes for speech by its likeness to speech and adds its deadly absence of determination to that for which it substitutes. But Derrida also shows that for Rousseau, speech is no more a transparent language of pure presence than writing. Spoken language does not give immediate access to the speaker's thought. It is a constitutive possibility of any code that it mean even in the absence of a subject's intention. Spoken language, too, is inhabited by a deadly indeterminacy.

The speech situation, however, assumes that language can serve as a transparent mode of communication. It covers over the absence of determination constitutive of language, not only lying about its own status but preventing any further consideration of language's reliability. Writing thus supplements for speech in another sense: it adds the reflective space missing from the speech situation. It brings the undecidability of language to the attention as an object of theory. In so doing, it enables the critique of the assumption of transparency and presence of speech, as well as of the concepts, oppositions, theories of knowledge, and so on, that rely on that assumption.

But according to Derrida, Rousseau incompletely theorizes the situation he describes so acutely. Derrida finds Rousseau to be nostalgic for a transparent language that eludes his grasp, so that his fiction making remains—as it does for Althusser—proof of a wish to escape from the conclusions imposed by his own analysis. It was Paul de Man who, in a review of Derrida's work reprinted in *Blindness and Insight,* saw the implications of Derrida's analysis of Rousseau for theory. He gave Rousseau credit for having opened the way to a theory of textuality, by way of his interest in the epistemology of reading and his general *parti pris* for knowledge. Rousseau knew texts to be at once idealized spaces wherein theory can be constituted and also the forgotten remainder whereby those theories can be undone as ideologies. His fictions were always already theoretical fictions, as his elaborated theory of figurative language shows. Probably the most important contribution de Man made to the reading of Rousseau was establishing that, for Rousseau, undecidability does *not* end in the aesthetician's hypothesis of a suspended, formal play of meanings. Rather, a "referential coercion" operates that makes even the statements in the work of art about undecidability liable to verification in the referential terms of truth and false-

hood. For de Man, then, Rousseau does not long for a return to the state of nature, advocate irrationalism, or retreat into a universal skepticism or nihilism. In his project, which was through and through a theoretical project, Rousseau saw with great clarity the operation of a referential coerciveness—synonymous with the political as well as with the practice of freedom—that made him rather more of a historical thinker than is commonly believed, and considerably less of a visionary dreamer.

In a word, then, Rousseau's work has proven to be the problematic site of the founding and contestation of idealisms and ideologies. It has been shown to provide a theory of such problematic sites, that is, of textuality.

E. S. Burt

See also BRITISH THEORY AND CRITICISM: 2. LATE EIGHTEENTH CENTURY and 3. ROMANTIC PERIOD AND EARLY NINETEENTH CENTURY, FRENCH THEORY AND CRITICISM: 2. EIGHTEENTH CENTURY and 3. NINETEENTH CENTURY, GERMAN THEORY AND CRITICISM: 2. ROMANTICISM, and ITALIAN THEORY AND CRITICISM: 1. ROMANTICISM.

Jean-Jacques Rousseau, *The Confessions of Jean-Jacques Rousseau* (1782–89, trans. J. M. Cohen, 1953), *A Discourse on Inequality* (1755, trans. Maurice Cranston, 1984), *Eloisa, or a Series of Original Letters* (1761, trans. William Kenrick, 1803), *Émile; or, on Education* (1762, trans. Allan Bloom, 1979), *Essai sur l'origine des langues, où il est parlé de la mélodie et de l'imitation musicale* (1817, ed. Charles Porset, 1970, *Essay on the Origin of Languages, On the Origin of Language,* ed. and trans. John H. Moran, 1966), *Oeuvres complètes* (ed. Marcel Raymond and Bernard Gagnebin, 4 vols., 1959–69), *The Reveries of a Solitary Walker* (1789, trans. Charles E. Butterworth, 1979), *Rousseau Judge of Jean-Jacques: Dialogues* (1782, ed. Roger D. Masters and Christopher Kelly, trans. Judith R. Bush, Christopher Kelly, and Roger D. Masters, 1989), *The Social Contract* (1762, trans. Maurice Cranston, 1968).

Louis Althusser, "Sur le *Contrat social* (les décalages)," *L'Impensé de Jean-Jacques Rousseau* (*Cahiers pour l'analyse,* vol. 8, 1972); Bronislaw Baczko, *Rousseau: Solitude et communauté* (1974); Maurice Blanchot, "Rousseau," *Le Livre à venir* (1959); Ernst Cassirer, "Das Problem Jean Jacques Rousseau" (1932, *The Question of Jean-Jacques Rousseau,* ed. and trans. Peter Gay, 1963); Paul de Man, *Allegories of Reading: Figural Language in Rousseau, Nietzsche, Rilke, and Proust* (1979), "The Rhetoric of Blindness: Jacques Derrida's Reading of Rousseau" and "The Rhetoric of Temporality," *Blindness and Insight: Essays in the Rhetoric of Contemporary Criticism* (1971); Jacques Derrida, *De la grammatologie* (1967, *Of Grammatology,* trans. Gayatri Chakravorty Spivak, 1976); Émile Durkheim, *Montesquieu and Rousseau: Forerunners of Sociology* (trans. Ralph Manheim, 1960); Sarah Kofman, "L'Ombre de la clôture: Rousseau," *Le Respect des femmes* (1982); Marcel Raymond, *Jean-Jacques Rousseau: La Quête de soi et la Rêverie* (1962); Jean Starobinski, *Jean-Jacques Rousseau: Transparency and Obstruction* (trans. A. Goldhammer, 1988), *L'Oeil vivant* (1961), *La Relation critique* (1970); Leo Strauss, "The Crisis of Modern Natural Right," *Natural Right and History* (1950); Samuel Weber, "In the Name of the Law," *Cardoza Law Review* 11 (1990).

RUSKIN, JOHN

John Ruskin (1819–1900), a lifelong experimenter with genre, is best known as an art critic whose theories of beauty and the imagination were formed by his evangelical training, his attention to detail, and the early poetry of WILLIAM WORDSWORTH. Ruskin's literary criticism, dispersed throughout *Modern Painters* (1843–60) and concentrated in his studies of myth, *The Queen of the Air* (1869), and of Romantic poetry and the novel, *Fiction Fair and Foul* (1880–81), reflects his sustained concern for art as a visible sign of an abstract quality, particularly the moral temper of the artist. His dramatic verbal translations of J. M. W. Turner's canvases in volume 1 of *Modern Painters* (1843), his highly wrought visual associations, and his allegorical readings of painting, sculpture, and landscape in later works such as *Modern Painters* 5 (1860) and *The Bible of Amiens* (1880–85) influenced George Eliot, Thomas Hardy, and Marcel Proust, among other writers.

Ruskin's aesthetic judgments were based on the link between beauty and morality made during daily Bible readings with his mother, who required him to recite passages from memory and enforced what he called in his autobiography accuracy of sensation and precision of feeling. In the habit of observing everything around him (including patterns in the carpet and bricks in the wall) and of searching the Bible for types and antitypes, Ruskin believed that physical qualities manifest divine attributes. In *Modern Painters* 2 (1846), he labels this relation "typical" after biblical typology, although the connection he makes between light, for example, and purity is actually allegorical, since it juxtaposes an abstraction with a phenomenon. Ruskin's "vital beauty," defined as "the appearance of felicitous fulfilment of function in living things" (4:146), is more akin to evangelical typol-

ogy; an object displaying vital beauty reenacts "a moral purpose and achievement" (4:147) that arouses the sympathy of the virtuous beholder. By claiming that beauty was in effect purposive and inherent in objects, Ruskin was able to dissociate aesthetics from utility and invest art with a divine pattern or order. His position allied him with the eighteenth-century sensationists, notably EDMUND BURKE, and opposed him to associationists such as Archibald Alison, who in *Essays on the Nature and Principles of Taste* (1790) described beauty by its concomitants and lodged its source in the mind. Ruskin did distinguish between "rational" association, the use of a fixed set of cultural symbols that furnished his iconography, and "accidental" association, a process of perceiving and imagining that he learned from SAMUEL TAYLOR COLERIDGE and particularly from Wordsworth's "Tintern Abbey." Though Ruskin insisted that an absolute standard of beauty exists, he was in practice an associationist; his own writings are tissues of accidental associations, and his discussion of imagination contemplative (in *Modern Painters* 2) derives from William Wordsworth's "Preface" to the *Poems* of 1815, which examines the way the mind endows images with extrinsic properties.

Yet Ruskin was never comfortable with the notion of the imagination as a half-creating, half-perceiving faculty; he thought it obscured the ultimate truth toward which every inventive mind worked. Further, by 1883 he felt he had neglected to discuss the popular imagination, which lacked traditional cultural information and needed discipline and restraint. For this reason, he tried to rely on historical, religious, and natural—or rational—associations in his criticism. In addition, he combined the Romantic basis of his aesthetic principles, or what he called his "theoretic" principles, with selective standards about the objects of representation. In *Modern Painters* 3, he declares that the power of poetry lies in the expression of what is "singular and particular" (5:27) produced by men who "feel *strongly* and *nobly*" (5:32). He did not, however, find poetic greatness in a mere proliferation of ideas, which he likened to the domestic scenes of seventeenth-century Dutch painters. The particular details rendered must themselves be great. Ruskin never abandoned his earliest declaration (made in *Modern Painters* 1) that great art conveys the greatest number of the greatest ideas, but he describes these ideas as emotional, not intellectual; his is an expressive theory of art applied to painting and literature.

Ruskin could transfer Wordsworth's views about poetry to the fine arts because he believed in the then-moribund eighteenth-century principle of *ut pictura poesis,* as did J. M. W. Turner, in defense of whose work he had begun *Modern Painters*. In order to claim that Turner's paintings were true to life, Ruskin traced the course of the artist's mind through the epigraphs that accompanied each canvas, then treated the pairing of words and images as an expression of emotional truth. Thus, the moral aesthetic applied to Turner throughout Ruskin's work and to the Gothic workman in *The Stones of Venice* describes a relation between art and a nation's or artist's psychological condition. But the moral sense he finds in great art has less to do with conventional morality than with an emotional state of humble, sincere inspiration that checks the power of the will over the imagination. Poets who lack this emotional restraint often commit what Ruskin calls in *Modern Painters* 3 the pathetic fallacy, a use of metaphor that anthropomorphizes nature and thereby betrays the artist's uncontrolled feelings, displayed in subjective impressions. Always the sign to Ruskin of a morbid and weak mind, the pathetic fallacy signals a poet's self-indulgence, a violation of the object's "power" of producing a sensation by the sensation itself. His examples, from Wordsworth, John Keats, Coleridge, and Alfred, Lord Tennyson, constitute a criticism of Romanticism from a writer who owed much to the Romantics but doubted their metaphysics. Thus, classical animism, illustrated in Homer's phrase "life-giving earth," conveys high poetical truth because the Greeks believed that nature harbored gods (5:212–13), but Romantic subjectivity arrogates all reality to the beholder and ignores any sort of transcendent truth.

In 1852 Ruskin wrote his father that he no longer believed in the literal truth of the Bible and had decided to treat it as metaphor, but he remained critical of any evidence of agnosticism in art. However, nature and myth gradually replaced the Bible as the storehouse of his types. *The Queen of the Air* (1869), Ruskin's study of Athena, reflects contemporary interest in comparative mythology, the study of Greek legends as linguistic distortions of natural occurrences. In this work, Ruskin continues to find essentially allegorical meanings for the representations of the goddess in the verbal and visual arts, as well as in nature, but his readings of the language are now polysemous. As in his earlier discussion of the symbolic grotesque in *The Stones of Venice* (1853), he detects a reversal and recoil of meaning in every myth. *The Queen of the Air* reflects his wish to recapture the Greek faith in chthonic deities, yet when he admits that Athena herself is a metaphor, the work becomes a great pathetic fallacy and, as many have noted, one of the first phenomenological studies.

In formulating the pathetic fallacy and then using it

himself, Ruskin was first deriding, then trying to reshape, the cultural values that, along with nature and myth, became the referents that art embodied. After *Unto This Last* (1860), an eloquent warning that no great art could be produced by an industrialized country with a "mercantile economy," based on the accumulation of capital and signifying a "legal or moral claim upon, or power over, the labour of others" (17:44–45), he reworked his typology of beauty into cultural emblems and perceived a nation's deteriorating moral and intellectual condition in its art. In *Fiction Fair and Foul* (1880–81), he denounced the modern novel for its depictions of what to its audience would be the familiar evils of city life. His derision of this popular literary response to the landscape, which satisfied urban readers' conditioned love of violence and death, reveals the extent to which Ruskin's religious typology had developed into cultural determinism based on physical conditions. This moral sociology of the novel prompted Ruskin to condemn Dickens, at the novelist's death, for catering to "the pit" (37:7) and, in *Sesame and Lilies* (1865), to prescribe for children "healthy" reading of the Greek classics, Shakespeare, and Walter Scott from strongly bound books.

Although starting with *The Stones of Venice*, Ruskin studied and often attacked the economic and social underpinnings of art, his conclusions about national ethics now seem both portentous and conservative. In his last work, the autobiography *Praeterita* (1885–89), he characterizes himself in the first sentence as a "violent Tory of the old school" (35:13). His criticism of mass production and the middle-class consumer, who in buying manufactured objects supported alienating factory labor and therefore engaged, he said, in the slave trade, never led to his condemning class lines. Rather, his disenchantment with industrialized society made Ruskin long for an agrarian society, celebrate a feudal economy, and remain loyal to allegorical interpretation even when the referent had changed to national ethics and he himself had become a pantheist-Catholic. His sustained idea of the artist as a visionary, and his own reputation in the late nineteenth century as a sage, are traceable to the Romantic notion of the poet. They also show that he continued to espouse (if not believe in) language as revelation and criticism as scriptural exegesis.

Linda Austin

John Ruskin, *The Works of John Ruskin* (ed. E. T. Cook and Alexander Wedderburn, 39 vols., 1903–12).

Peter D. Anthony, *John Ruskin's Labour: A Study of Ruskin's Social Theory* (1983); Patricia M. Ball, *The Science*

of Aspects: The Changing Role of Fact in the Work of Coleridge, Ruskin, and Hopkins (1971); Dinah Birch, Ruskin's
Myths (1988); Van Akin Burd, "Background to Modern
Painters: The Tradition and the Turner Controversy,"
PMLA 74 (1959); Raymond E. Fitch, The Poison Sky: Myth
and Apocalypse in Ruskin (1982); Kristine Ottesen Garrigan, "Bearding the Competition: John Ruskin's Academy Notes," Victorian Periodicals Review 22 (1989), " 'The
splendidest May number of the Graphic': John Ruskin
and the Royal Academy Exhibition of 1875," Victorian
Periodicals Review 24 (1991); Elizabeth K. Helsinger, Rus-
kin and the Art of the Beholder (1982); George L. Hersey,
"Ruskin as an Optical Thinker," The Ruskin Polygon: Es-
says on the Imagination of John Ruskin (ed. John Dixon
Hunt and Faith M. Holland, 1982); Robert Hewison, John
Ruskin: The Argument of the Eye (1976); Tim Hilton, John
Ruskin: The Early Years, 1819–1859 (1985); George P. Landow,
The Aesthetic and Critical Theories of John Ruskin (1971); J.
Hillis Miller, "Myth as 'Hieroglyph' in Ruskin," Studies in
the Literary Imagination 8 (1975); Paul L. Sawyer, Ruskin's
Poetic Argument: The Design of the Major Works (1985);
James Clark Sherburne, John Ruskin or the Ambiguities of
Abundance: A Study in Social and Economic Criticism (1972);
Jeffrey L. Spear, Dreams of an English Eden: Ruskin and His
Tradition in Social Criticism (1984); Richard L. Stein, The
Ritual of Interpretation: The Fine Arts as Literature in Rus-
kin, Rossetti, and Pater (1975).

RUSSIAN FORMALISM

Russian Formalism, a movement of literary criticism and
interpretation, emerged in Russia during the second decade of the twentieth century and remained active until
about 1930. Members of what can be loosely referred to
as the Formalist school emphasized first and foremost
the autonomous nature of literature and consequently
the proper study of literature as neither a reflection of the
life of its author nor as byproduct of the historical or
cultural milieu in which it was created. In this respect,
proponents of a formalist approach to literature attempted not only to isolate and define the "formal"
properties of poetic language (in both poetry and prose)
but also to study the way in which certain aesthetically
motivated devices (e.g., defamiliarization [ostranenie])
determined the literariness or artfulness of an object.

From its inception, the Russian Formalist movement
consisted of two distinct scholarly groups, both outside
the academy: the Moscow Linguistic Circle, which was
founded by the linguist ROMAN JAKOBSON in 1915 and
included Grigorii Vinokur and Petr Bogatyrev, and the

Petersburg OPOIaZ, or Society for the Study of Poetic
Language, which came into existence a year later and
was known for scholars such as Victor Shklovskii, Iurii
Tynianov, Boris Eikhenbaum, Boris Tomashevskii, and
Victor Vinogradov. (It should be noted that the term
"formalist" was initially applied pejoratively to the
Moscow Linguistic Circle and OPOIaZ.) Although the
leading figures in the Russian Formalist movement tended
to disagree with one another on what constituted formalism, they were united in their attempt to move beyond the psychologism and biographism that pervaded
nineteenth-century Russian literary scholarship. Although the Symbolists had partially succeeded in redressing the imbalance of content over form (see Andrei
Bely's studies in Symbolism [1910] on meter and rhyme),
they "could not rid themselves of the notorious theory
of the 'harmony of form and content' even though it
clearly contradicted their bent for formal experimentation and discredited it by making it seem mere 'aestheticism' " (Eikhenbaum, "Theory" 112).

In many ways, however, the Formalists remained indebted to two leading nineteenth-century literary and
linguistic theoreticians, Aleksandr Veselovskii (1838–
1906) and Aleksander Potebnia (1835–81). Veselovskii's
work in comparative studies of literature and folklore as
well as in the theory of literary evolution attracted the
attention of the Formalists (particularly Shklovskii, Eikhenbaum, and Vladimir Propp), who found much of
interest in his positivist notions of literary history and
the evolution of poetic forms. More specifically, as Peter
Steiner argues, "mechanistic Formalism was in some
respects a mirror image of Veselovskii's poetics" insofar
as both stressed the "genetic" aspect in their theories of
literary evolution.

Like the Formalists, Potebnia made a careful distinction between practical and poetic language. But his well-
known maxim that "art is thinking in images" (an idea,
it should be noted, that was promoted earlier by mid-
nineteenth-century literary critics Vissarion Belinskii
and Nikolai Chernyshevskii) made him an object of derision in Formalist writings. Shklovskii categorically objected to Potebnia's notion of the image, arguing that
since the same image could be found in various writers'
works, the image itself was less important than the techniques used by poets to arrange images. Shklovskii further noted that images were common in both prosaic
(common, everyday language) and poetic language;
hence, the image could not be considered uniquely essential to verbal art. Potebnia's theories led to "far-fetched
interpretations" and, what is more important, knowledge about the object itself rather than the poetic de-

vice(s) that enabled one to *perceive* the object (Shklovskii, "Art" 6). Above all, it was "literariness," rather than either image or referent, that the Formalists pursued in their studies of poetry and prose. With slight variations, literariness in Formalism denoted a particular *essential* function present in the relationship or system of poetic works called literature.

The personal and intellectual cooperation of the Moscow Linguistic Circle and OPOIaZ yielded several volumes of essays (*Sborniki po teorii poeticheskogo iazyka* [Studies in the theory of poetic language], 6 vols., 1916–23). Given that many of the Formalists had been students of the Polish linguist Jan Baudoin de Courtenay and were well apprised of the latest developments made in linguistics by the Swiss linguist FERDINAND DE SAUSSURE, it is not surprising that most of the essays in these volumes reflect a predominant interest in linguistics (see Jakubinskii, "O zvukakh stikhotvornago iazyka" [On the sounds of poetic language], 1916; and Brik, "Zvukovye povtory" [Sound repetitions], 1917). But while members of the Moscow Linguistic Circle considered the study of poetics to fall under the broader category of linguistics, OPOIaZ Formalists (such as Eikhenbaum or Viktor Zhirmunskii in "Zadachi poètiki" [The tasks of poetics], *Nachala*, 1921) insisted that the two be kept distinct. Shklovskii, for instance, remained predominantly concerned with literary theory (the laws of expenditure and economy in poetic language, general laws of plots and general laws of perception) rather than with linguistics, while Eikhenbaum and Tynianov are best known for their work as literary historians. Other Formalists, such as Tomashevskii (who was also interested in prose) and Jakobson, approached meter and rhythm in verse with a statistical approach and attempted to isolate the metrical laws in operation.

More specifically, the Formalists understood poetic language as operating both synchronically and, as Tzvetan Todorov notes, in an autonomous or "autotelic" fashion. The Formalists consistently stressed the internal mechanics of the poetic work over the semantics of extraliterary *systems*, that is, politics, ideology, economics, psychology, and so on. Thus, Roman Jakobson's 1921 analysis of futurist poet Velemir Khlebnikov, and especially his notion of the *samovitoe slovo* ("self-made word") and *zaum* ("transrational language"), serves essentially to illustrate the proposition that poetry is an utterance directed toward "expression" (*Noveishaia russkaia poèziia* [Recent Russian poetry]). Indeed, the futurist exploration of the exotic realm of *zaum* parallels the Formalist preoccupation with sound in poetic language at the phonemic level. In a similar way, essays such as Eikhenbaum's "How Gogol's 'Overcoat' Is Made" (1919, trans., 1978), which examined narrative devices and acoustic wordplay in the text without drawing any extraliterary, sociocultural conclusions, emphasized the autonomous, self-referential nature of verbal art. One of the most important of the devices Eikhenbaum described in that essay was *skaz*. *Skaz*, which in Russian is the root of the verb *skazat'*, "to tell," may be compared to "free indirect discourse" (in German, *erlebte Rede*), which is marked by the grammar of third-person narration and the style, tone, and syntax of direct speech on the part of the character.

Certain Formalists were not quite so eager to dismiss issues of content, however: Zhirmunskii maintained an interest in the thematic level of the poetic work; Tynianov considered an understanding of *byt*, the content of everyday, common language and experience as opposed to consciously poetic language, essential to any analysis of a poetic work. Rather than resolving the issue of form versus content, the Formalists tended instead to downplay it or to reframe it in new terms. For example, Eikhenbaum asserted the need to "destroy these traditional correlatives [form and content] and so to enrich the idea of form with new significance" (Eikhenbaum, "Theory" 115). "Technique," continued Eikhenbaum in the same essay, is "much more significant in the long-range evolution of formalism than is the notion of 'form'" (115). In his defense of the primacy of form, Shklovskii explained that "a new form appears not in order to express a new content, but in order to replace an old form, which has already lost its artistic value" ("Connection" 33).

Rejecting the subjectivism of nineteenth-century literary scholarship, the Formalists insisted that the study of literature be approached by means of a scientific and objective methodology. Their emphasis upon the scientific study of poetic language may be viewed in four ways. First, it may be traced to the more general nineteenth-century West European turn toward classification, genealogy, and evolution in the human sciences. In his best-known work, *Morphology of the Folktale* (1928, trans., 1958), Propp, a somewhat more peripheral yet not unimportant figure in the Formalist movement, employed the rhetoric and methodology of JOHANN WOLFGANG VON GOETHE and Georges Cuvier in his attempt to isolate certain regularly recurring features of the folktale. Second, the Russian Formalists viewed their work as a direct challenge to what they perceived as the subjectivism and mysticism inherent in the Symbolist movement (i.e., the literature and criticism of Aleksander Blok, Bely, and Viacheslav Ivanov, among others). Tomashevskii went so far as to denounce the futurists as well as the

Symbolists, claiming that it was futurism, especially, that "intensified to a hyperbolic clarity those features which had previously appeared only in hidden, mystically masked forms of Symbolism" ("Literature" 54). Third, Formalism sought to create a professional discipline independent of nineteenth-century configurations of university scholarship. And fourth, the Formalist shift toward science may also be considered as a response to the broader (and more radical) social, economic, and political transformations that the influx of industry and new technology helped to precipitate throughout early twentieth-century Russia. Not surprisingly, the poetic fetishization of the machine found in futurist poetics and avant-garde aesthetics quickly made its way into Formalist thought. Shklovskii's analyses of poetic works are distinguished by his reliance upon the metaphor of the machine (Steiner 44–67) and the rhetoric of technology to account for such poetic devices and formal laws as automatization and defamiliarization. Ironically, objectives of scientificity in Formalist literary study were held up as an ideal, but only insofar as the Formalists believed scientificity would shield their theory from external influences, since everything outside the poetic system could only corrupt and obfuscate data extrapolated from the text. By 1930 it was clear that this was not to be the case.

For Shklovskii, "literariness" is a function of the process of defamiliarization, which involves "estranging," "slowing down," or "prolonging" perception and thereby impeding the reader's habitual, automatic relation to objects, situations, and poetic form itself (see "Art" 12). According to Shklovskii, the difficulty involved in the process is an aesthetic end in itself, because it provides a heightened sensation of life. Indeed, the process of "laying bare" the poetic device, such as the narrative self-reflexiveness of Laurence Sterne's *Tristram Shandy* and its emphasis on the distinction between story and plot (see *Theory of Prose*), remained for Shklovskii one of the primary signs of artistic self-consciousness.

The notion that new literary production always involves a series of deliberate, self-conscious deviations from the poetic norms of the preceding genre and/or literary movement remained fundamental to Shklovskii's and other Formalists' theories of literary evolution. Tynianov's and Jakobson's notion of the "dominant" approximates Shklovskii's emphasis on defamiliarization, albeit as a feature of the diachronic system, inasmuch as it demands that other devices in the poetic text be "transformed" or pushed to the background to allow for the "foregrounding" of the dominant device. The function of the dominant in the service of literary evolu-

tion included the replacement of canonical forms and genres by new forms, which in turn would become canonized and, likewise, replaced by still newer forms (see esp. Tynianov, "Literary," and Jakobson, "Dominant").

Toward the end of the Formalist period, the emphasis on the synchronic nature of poetic devices was gradually mediated by a growing realization that literature and language should be considered within their diachronic contexts as well (see Tynianov and Jakobson). Some critics—Krystyna Pomorska, FREDRIC JAMESON, Jurij Striedter—regard this later shift in Formalist theory (as described particularly in the works of Tynianov) toward establishing a set of systemic relations between the internal and external organization of the poetic work as proto-structuralist. However, newly emerging literary groups such as the Bakhtin Linguistic Circle (M. M. BAKHTIN, Pavel Medvedev, Valentin Voloshinov) and PRAGUE SCHOOL STRUCTURALISM (Jan Mukarovsky) found the Formalists' attempts to incorporate a diachronic view of the literary work insufficient. Critics (e.g., Medvedev) attacked the Formalists for refusing to address social and ideological concerns in poetic language. The same criticism, of course, was leveled at the Formalists by the Soviet state (especially by Anatolii Lunacharskii and Lev Trotskii), and with much more serious consequences. Various individuals and groups advocating or at least incorporating a Marxist perspective on literature, including members of the "sociological school" as well as the Bakhtin school in the 1920s, attacked the Formalists for neglecting the social and ideological discourses impinging upon the structure and function of the poetic work. In *The Formal Method in Literary Scholarship* (1928), Medvedev dismisses the Formalists primarily for failing to provide an adequate sociological and philosophical justification for their theories. While many critics (e.g., Victor Erlich) approach Bakhtin's work as distinct from that of the Formalist school, others (e.g., Gary Saul Morson and Striedter) view Bakhtin's work as historically connected to the broader aims and implications of the Russian Formalist movement. Despite Tynianov and Jakobson's attempt to connect the aims of Formalism to the broader issues of culture (as an entire complex of systems), Russian Formalism remained committed to the idea that "literariness" alone, rather than the referent and its various contingencies, historical and otherwise, was the proper focus of literary scholarship.

Perhaps the ongoing, seemingly irresoluble debate over what constitutes Formalism (both then and now) arises in part from what Jurij Striedter describes as the "dialogic" nature of Formalism itself. The Formalists, especially Tynianov, based their theories of literary evolution (and their own role therein) largely upon G. W. F. HEGEL's dialectical method. In his summary of the contributions of the Formalist movement, Eikhenbaum ironically concluded that "when we have a theory that explains everything, a ready-made theory explaining all past and future events and therefore needing neither evolution nor anything like it—then we must recognize that the formal method has come to an end" ("Theory" 139). Eikhenbaum's vision of a type of Formalist dialectics suggests the dynamic character of the movement as a whole, though external political pressure was surely also a factor by the time Eikhenbaum wrote his essay in 1926.

Shklovskii's 1930 denunciation of Formalism signaled not just that political pressures had worsened but that the de facto end of the Formalist movement had arrived. Even before Shklovskii was forced to abandon Formalism to political exigencies, the Moscow Linguistic Circle and OPOIaZ had already dissolved in the early 1920s, the former in 1920 with the departure of its founder, Roman Jakobson, for Czechoslovakia, the latter in 1923. With the banning of all artistic organizations (including the various associations of proletarian writers) and the introduction of "socialist realism" as the new, official socialist literature of the Soviet Union in 1932, the Russian Formalist movement came to an official close.

The Formalist approach continued to make itself felt, however, in European and, later, American literary scholarship (though, it should be noted, the formalism of NEW CRITICISM possessed no direct relation to Russian Formalism). The immediate heirs to the Formalist legacy were the Prague Linguistic Circle (founded in 1926 by Jakobson and a group of Czech linguists) and the Bakhtin Linguistic Circle. The contributions of the Prague Linguistic Circle (especially of Mukarovsky) eventually made their way into the literary discourses of French structuralism. The work of French structural anthropologist CLAUDE LÉVI-STRAUSS echoes and acknowledges the work of Propp and, to a lesser extent, Tynianov's interest in cultural and literary systems. The Bakhtin Linguistic Circle's work (which first attracted the attention of Western scholars in the 1970s) extends several Formalist concerns, not the least of which deal with narrative theory and discourse in the novel. The development of structural-semiotic research and the emergence of the MOSCOW-TARTU SCHOOL of semiotics in the 1960s (see the writings of such scholars as Viacheslav Ivanov, Iurii Lotman, Vladimir Toporov, Boris Gasparov, and Boris Uspenskii, to name just a few) may also be viewed as an extension of the aims and interests of both formalism and structuralism. Specifically, semiotic re-

search continues to renew in various ways the Formalist emphasis upon language and the devices therein that function to generate meaning as sign systems.

In the United States, the Formalist approach found a sympathetic cousin in New Criticism, which emphasized, though in organic forms actually reminiscent of Russian Symbolism, the literary text as a discrete entity whose meaning and interpretation need not be contaminated by authorial intention, historical conditions, or ideological demands. Poststructuralism (and DECONSTRUCTION) in the 1970s and 1980s, though a partial critique of the organic notions of form in much American New Criticism, nevertheless extended certain Formalist assumptions. Figures as diverse as ROLAND BARTHES, PAUL DE MAN, JULIA KRISTEVA, and Fredric Jameson are all heavily indebted to the aims and strategies of Russian Formalism.

Karen A. McCauley

See also M. M. BAKHTIN, PRAGUE SCHOOL STRUCTURALISM, RUSSIAN THEORY AND CRITICISM: NINETEENTH CENTURY, and STRUCTURALISM.

Stephen Bann and John E. Bowlt, eds., *Russian Formalism: A Collection of Articles and Texts in Translation* (1973); Osip Brik, "Zvukovye povtory" [Sound repetitions], *Sborniki po teorii poeticheskago iazyka* 2 (1917); Boris Eikhenbaum, "Kak sdelana 'Shinel'' Gogolia" (1919, "How Gogol's 'Overcoat' Is Made," *Gogol from the Twentieth Century: Eleven Essays,* ed. and trans. Robert A. Maguire, 1974), "Teoriia 'formalnogo metoda'" (1927, "The Theory of the 'Formal Method,'" Lemon and Reis [appeared first in Ukrainian in 1926]); Roman Jakobson, "The Dominant" (Matejka and Pomorska), *Noveishaia russkaia poèziia* [Recent Russian poetry] (1921, *Selected Writings,* vol. 5, 1979); Lev Jakubinskii, "O zvukakh stikhotvornago iazyka" [On the sounds of poetic language], *Sborniki po teorii poeticheskago iazyka* 1 (1916); Lee T. Lemon and Marion J. Reis, eds. and trans., *Russian Formalist Criticism: Four Essays* (1965); Ladislav Matejka and Krystyna Pomorska, eds., *Readings in Russian Poetics: Formalist and Structuralist Views* (1978); P. N. Medvedev, *Formal'nyi metod v literaturovedenii (Kriticheskoe vvedenie v sotsiologicheskuiu poetiku)* (1928, *The Formal Method in Literary Scholarship: A Critical Introduction to Sociological Poetics,* trans. Albert J. Wehrle, 1978 [sometimes attributed also to M. M. Bakhtin]); Christopher Pike, ed. and trans., *The Futurists, the Formalists, and the Marxist Critique* (1979); Vladimir Propp, *Morfologiia skazki* (1928, *Morphology of the Folktale,* trans. Laurence Scott, 1958, 2d ed., ed. Louis A. Wagner, 1968); Victor Shklovskii, "Iskusstvo kak priem" (1917,

"Art as Technique," Lemon and Reis), "On the Connection between Devices of Siuzhet Construction and General Stylistic Devices" (1919, Bann and Bowlt), *O teorii prozy* (1927, *Theory of Prose,* trans. Benjamin Sher, 1990), "*Tristram Shendi:* Sterna i teoriia romana" [Sterne's *Tristram Shandy* and the theory of the novel] (1921, "Sterne's *Tristram Shandy:* Stylistic Commentary," Lemon and Reis); B. V. Tomashevskii, "Literatura i biografiia" (1923, "Literature and Biography," Matejka and Pomorska), *Teoriia Literatury* [Theory of literature] (1928); Iurii Tynianov, "O literaturnoi evoliucii" (1929, "On Literary Evolution," Matejka and Pomorska), *The Problem of Verse Language* (1924, ed. and trans. Michael Sosa and Brent Harvey, 1981); Iurii Tynianov and Roman Jakobson, "Problemy izucheniia literatury i iazyka" (1928, "Problems in the Study of Literature and Language," Matejka and Pomorska).

Victor Erlich, *Russian Formalism: History-Doctrine* (1955, 3d ed., 1981); Aage A. Hansen-Löve, *Der russische Formalismus* (1978); Robert Louis Jackson and Stephen Rudy, eds., *Russian Formalism: A Retrospective Glance* (1985); Fredric Jameson, *The Prison-House of Language: A Critical Account of Structuralism and Russian Formalism* (1972); Daniel P. Lucid, ed., *Soviet Semiotics: An Anthology* (1977); L. M. O'Toole and Ann Shukman, eds., *Formalism: History, Comparison, Genre* (1978), *Formalist Theory* (1977); Krystyna Pomorska, *Russian Formalist Theory and Its Poetic Ambience* (1968); Peter Steiner, *Russian Formalism: A Metapoetics* (1984); Jurij Striedter, *Literary Structure, Evolution, and Value* (1989); Ewa M. Thompson, *Russian Formalism and Anglo-American New Criticism* (1971); Tzvetan Todorov, *Critique de la critique* (1984, *Literature and Its Theorists: A Personal View of Twentieth-Century Criticism,* trans. Catherine Porter, 1987); Leon Trotsky, *Literature and Revolution* (trans. Rose Strunsky, 1975).

RUSSIAN THEORY AND CRITICISM: NINETEENTH CENTURY

The eighteenth century bequeathed to early nineteenth-century Russian culture both a dearth of creative writers and a predilection for literary theory derived from French neoclassicism's attempts at intellectually rigorous genre definitions. This situation was one that the author, critic, and journalist Nikolay Karamzin (1766–1826) recognized quite early. Writing in 1803 for the journal *Vestnik Evropy* [Herald of Europe], which he himself had founded in order to bring Russian culture into closer contact with

that of Western Europe, he attributed the lack of writing talent in his country to the "circumstances of Russian civil life" (*Selected* 192): until society became capable of appreciating literature, he held, at best only individual literary geniuses could appear. But then he was also certain that the situation would eventually change for the better (*Ot chego v Rossii malo avtorskikh talantov?* [Why is there so little writing talent in Russia?]). Still, if there was little original literature in the early nineteenth century, then it was very unlikely there could be much original literary criticism either.

A writer who dabbled in criticism, Karamzin set the pattern for his successor as editor of *Vestnik Evropy,* the poet Vasily Zhukovsky (1783–1852), who five years later, in 1808, himself took up the subject of the writer and society. Although as a poet he was a skilled translator and interpreter of recent developments in German Romanticism (he was especially famed for his versions of ballads by Burger), as a critic Zhukovsky held steadfastly to the neoclassical traditions. Thus in 1809 he published a substantial article on the genre of the fable and Ivan Krylov as a fabulist, and in 1810 he published another on poetic satire and the work of the eighteenth-century satirist Antiokh Kantemir.

This division between Romantic practice and neoclassical theory in the minds of writers functioning incidentally as critics continued for years. Even as the brief Romantic era in Russia (c. 1820–40) saw masterpieces of Romanticism coming from the pens of Alexander Pushkin and others, the critics staunchly defended the neoclassical theoretical approach. Pushkin's classmate Wilhelm Küchelbecker (1797–1846) in 1824 published a well-known article, *O napravlenii nashei poezii, osobenno liricheskoi, v poslednee desiatiletie* ("On the Trend of Our Poetry, Particularly Lyric, in the Past Decade" [Leighton]), in which he defended the values of the neoclassical ode against those embodied in such Romantic genres as the elegy and the epistle. Romantic writings, he proclaimed, were boringly similar. In almost all of them one found fog— "fog over a pine forest, fog over the field, fog in the writer's head" (Leighton 58). Küchelbecker's viewpoint found support six years later in a dissertation published as a book by Nikolay Nadezhdin (1804–56), primarily a critic and journalist, who linked Romantic poetry to the Middle Ages and called for Russian society to defend itself against what he called a "pseudoromantic plague" through the "study of classical antiquity" (*Literaturnaia* 253).

Such broadsides against regnant literary fashion eventually subsided, and at roughly the time Russian literary criticism began to come into its own as a cultural force with the appearance of Russia's first important professional critic—and still no doubt its greatest critical mind—Vissarion Belinsky (1811–48). Although in his early writings, of the mid-1830s, Belinsky was still influenced to a degree by neoclassical thought (see, e.g., his article on the genre of the *povest,* or "tale"), he soon turned to contemporary German aesthetics and brought Russian critical thought abreast of what was transpiring in Western Europe at the time. A man of intense but shifting enthusiasms, in his brief career he passed through several intellectual phases, including one of Hegelian "reconciliation with reality," before concluding that literature must contribute to social betterment without at the same time ceasing to be artistic.

Lacking literary ambitions of his own, Belinsky functioned as a first-rate critic through all his intellectual sea changes. He gave valuable pre- and postpublication advice to such writers as Ivan Turgenev, Ivan Goncharov, and Fyodor Dostoevsky; he published critical article after critical article; he was the very personification of the spirit of the "marvellous decade" (Pavel Annenkov's phrase) of the 1840s, that golden age of the Russian intelligentsia that followed close upon the golden age of Russian poetry during Pushkin's lifetime.

Belinsky's published criticism was extremely broad in scope to begin with and has since proven extraordinarily influential. In form his works range from genre studies through detailed treatments of individual works by his contemporaries (his interpretations of which have by now acquired almost canonical standing), investigations of the entire work of a single author (especially his book-length set of articles on Pushkin, whom he greatly admired), down to a series of annual surveys of Russian literature that he undertook in the final years of his life, beginning each with a sweeping summary of its history since the eighteenth century. In short, it is no exaggeration to say that all nineteenth-century Russian literary criticism pivots on Belinsky.

One sign of Belinsky's standing is the fact that virtually all the critics who came after him, although disparate in their critical approach, claimed to be his heirs. One who established that claim successfully was Nikolay Chernyshevsky (1828–89), who in 1855 brought out a remarkably influential theoretical treatise entitled *Esteticheskoe otnosheniia iskusstva k deistvitelnosti* [The aesthetic relations of art to reality]. In this essay the philosophical materialist Chernyshevsky demolished, at least to his own satisfaction, the foundations of Hegelian aesthetics and replaced it with a "realist" aesthetic equating the beautiful with the real, or else with reality as it should be according to our conceptions of it. In other words, he

argued that literature embodies, not a metaphysical ideal, but rather an ideal necessarily drawn from reality. In literature there could be no theoretical dichotomy between the real and the ideal.

On a more practical level, Chernyshevsky maintained that literature should be socially useful, a viewpoint he advocated vigorously in a series of articles on Nikolay Gogol. Gogol, as Chernyshevsky read him, believed that social reality could and should be altered for the better through the instrumentality of art.

Chernyshevsky fought in the critical arena for but a few years before he was arrested (in 1862) and later exiled for revolutionary activity. During that time, however, he had the good fortune to find a remarkable disciple, Nikolay Dobrolyubov (1836–61), whose career was also cut tragically short, by tuberculosis. As a theoretician Dobrolyubov seconded Chernyshevsky's view that aesthetic requirements should be subordinated to social or even political demands. Literature, he wrote, "is an auxiliary force, the importance of which lies in propaganda, and the merit of which is determined by what it propagates, and how it propagates it" ("A Ray of Light in the Realm of Darkness," *Selected* 570). In accordance with this approach to literature, Dobrolyubov read contemporary works as commentaries on the culture within which they were created. Thus, in his well-known article "Chto takoe oblomovshchina?" (1859, "What Is Oblomovism?") he analyzed the hero of Goncharov's novel *Oblomov* not in psychological but in social terms: Oblomov had been unfitted for normal mature life by the conditioning he had received within his family, whose attitudes had been in turn molded by the serf-owning society within which it existed. Such a literary character as Oblomov was emblematic of an entire society. Dobrolyubov's interpretation of Oblomov was so powerful that it must still be taken into account today, even by those who reject it. In the course of his brief career Dobrolyubov formulated similarly influential readings of works by the leading playwright Alexander Ostrovsky and the early post-exile Dostoevsky *(The Insulted and Injured)*. His best articles were extensive pieces, written apropos of a contemporary literary work, which amounted to social commentary.

The third great figure in the triumvirate of "radical critics" who succeeded Belinsky was Dmitry Pisarev (1840–68), who wrote many of his articles in a prison cell to which he was dispatched for revolutionary activity. Pisarev, who came to prominence only about 1862—after Dobrolyubov's death and Chernyshevsky's arrest—was an excellent stylist with an innate bent for literature. Intellectually he was an extremist, but an honest one.

Thus when Chernyshevsky and his immediate allies vigorously condemned Turgenev's *Fathers and Sons* (1862) as a slander upon radical youth, Pisarev not only recognized the sincerity of Turgenev's depiction of his hero Bazarov but even modeled himself on Bazarov to a degree ("Bazarov," 1862). At the same time, Pisarev criticized Chernyshevsky for intellectual timidity and developed the latter's ideas to their logical extreme. Thus, in marking the tenth anniversary of the publication of Chernyshevsky's *Esteticheskoe otnosheniia* [Aesthetic relations], Pisarev wrote that if the beautiful is life, as Chernyshevsky argued, then "esthetics, to our great satisfaction, vanishes in physiology and hygiene" (*Razrushenie estetiki* [Destruction of aesthetics], 1865, *Sochineniia* 3:423). To Pisarev's mind, a well-ordered society should have no need at all for literature, which would simply merge with journalism and scholarly investigation as descriptions of reality as it actually existed.

Recognizing that Pushkin's achievement was the strongest weapon available to those who believed in art's independent standing, in "Pushkin e Belinsky" [Pushkin and Belinsky] (1865) Pisarev mounted a massive assault on the poet's reputation. He argued that Pushkin's work was not merely useless but actually harmful to the cause of social progress and that therefore his writings should be consigned to the dustbin of history.

The critical disputes of the mid-nineteenth century centered on Gogol as the apostle of socially engaged literature and Pushkin as the model of the writer who stood above the political wars. The first extensive edition of Pushkin's works was brought out in 1855 by Pavel Annenkov (1811 [1813?]–87), friend of Belinsky's, literary commentator, memoirist, and critic, a man who managed to be present at a surprising number of the outstanding literary events of his lifetime and who also served as a personal literary advisor to many, especially Turgenev. Annenkov left a considerable body of critical writing in which he defended both the autonomy of art and the dualistic nature of the aesthetic ideal against the monistic doctrines of the radical critics. However, as a participant in the critical controversies of 1855–70 he was influenced by radical ideas, and that only intensified his natural inclination to indulge in vague generalities when formulating his critical opinions. His intellectual ally Alexander Druzhinin (1824–64), journalist and prose writer, was more straightforward than Annenkov in his attacks upon socially engaged art—literature could have a socially beneficial effect, he maintained, but only if that were not its principal objective—and his defense of literature's autonomy. Annenkov, Druzhinin, and their associates are often labeled the "aesthetic" critics to distinguish them from such "radical democrats" as Chernyshevsky, Dobrolyubov, and Pisarev.

Apollon Grigorev (1822–64), probably the most gifted nineteenth-century Russian critic after Belinsky, remained outside both the aesthetic and radical traditions by developing a third way of "organic criticism" drawn in large measure from F. W. J. Schelling and Thomas Carlyle. Endowed with a fine critical sense, Grigorev left many enduring critical evaluations, especially of Ostrovsky, whom he promoted actively and interpreted with sensitivity, and of Pushkin, whose central niche in Russian culture he helped to establish in the teeth of radical opposition. He also had a talent for critical phrase-making, and several of his coinages have entered the standard Russian critical vocabulary. In the early 1860s he was close to Dostoevsky, who derived many of his own critical approaches from him. But Grigorev was disorganized and verbose; he usually began his articles with no notion of how he would conclude them. Thus it is appropriately ironic that the two major attempts made to publish his collected works since his death have not been completed.

Leo Tolstoy (1828–1910) is not usually thought of as an intellectual offspring of the 1860s, but the publication in 1897 of his essay *What Is Art?* occasioned a scandal whose roots in fact reached back that far. In this disquisition Tolstoy denounced much of contemporary literature—quite as Pisarev had done, and as Tolstoy had done for his own writings during his spiritual crisis of 1879–80—as harmful for society's spiritual development. To be sure, unlike Pisarev, Tolstoy did reserve a place for literature in society, but only literature capable of "infecting" readers with Christian values, by which Tolstoy meant ideas and emotions uniting people rather than dividing them. And that was reminiscent of Dobrolyubov's call for politically committed literature promoting a society in which "everyone will be well off." Tolstoy's notion of the social good differed in some important respects from Dobrolyubov's, but both agreed that art should promote that good.

When the heated controversies between radical and aesthetic critics subsided, as they had by 1870, literary criticism fell into the doldrums. At this juncture it became extensively politicized, for it moved into the hands of the populists, who expected the peasantry to institute a revolutionary transformation of Russian society and wished literature to advance their political program. The most outstanding critic among this group was Nikolay Konstantinovich Mikhaylovsky (1842–1904), though he was in the first instance a social commentator and political thinker. Still, from the 1870s to the 1890s he published a number of lengthy articles on major writers—Tolstoy, Turgenev, Dostoevsky, Vsevolod Garshin, Mikhail Saltykov-Shchedrin, Chekhov. Perhaps his best-known critical article, *Zhestoky talant* (1882, "A Cruel Talent"), analyzes Dostoevsky in terms of a single idea. Although Mikhaylovsky claimed to consider Dostoevsky a "great and original writer" (*Dostoevsky* 11), he also maintained that Dostoevsky suffered from the "lack of a social ideal" (26) and that in his works he was above all dedicated to examining the psychological ramifications of "unnecessary, causeless and resultless suffering" (32), to investigating the "sensations of a wolf devouring a sheep" (12). Thus Mikhaylovsky applied an acutely reductivist yardstick to a complex writer and emerged with a distorted understanding of his achievement. On the other hand, Mikhaylovsky could offer sensible and stimulating observations on writers such as Turgenev, with whose view of the world he sympathized more fully.

In the final decades of the nineteenth century, literary criticism tended to coalesce with literary scholarship and literary history and thus to become more academic and less journalistic. It was in such a context that there appeared, in 1893, a long essay by Dmitry Merezhkovsky (1865–1941), *O prichinakh upadka i o novykh techeniiakh sovremennoi russkoi literatury* [On the causes of the present decline and the new currents of contemporary Russian literature]. Not a work of literary criticism or history as such, Merezhkovsky's piece was rather a discussion of the Russian cultural mood, with special reference to literature. Literature, Merezhkovsky said, had reached a nadir in the 1890s partly because of the low estate of literary criticism, but he saw a "new idealism" beginning to emerge, a development rooted in the works of Turgenev, Goncharov, Dostoevsky, and Tolstoy, one that revolved about a very broad conception of a "symbol" (Merezhkovsky held that even a literary character could be a symbol). He concluded by summoning his contemporaries to "pass from a poetic era which was creative, direct and unstructured into a period which is critical, conscious and cultured" (*Izbrannye* 304).

At the beginning of the nineteenth century, shortly before the Romantic golden age of Russian poetry began, Karamzin and Zhukovsky had complained of a dearth of Russian writers. Now, after the efflorescence of Russian realism at mid-century, Merezhkovsky complained of something similar. He was the harbinger of modernism and Symbolism, a new birth of Russian culture, literature, and criticism, the silver age of the turn of the century, which would emphasize literary values rather different from those dominant throughout most of the nineteenth century.

Charles A. Moser

Vissarion Belinskii [Belinsky], *Polnoe sobranie sochinenii* (13 vols., 1953–59), *Selected Philosophical Works* (1948); Vissarion Belinsky, Nikolay Chernyshevsky, and Nikolay Dobrolyubov, *Selected Criticism* (ed. Ralph Matlaw, 1962); Nikolai Chernyshevskii [Nikolay Chernyshevsky], *Polnoe sobranie sochinenii* (16 vols., 1939–53), *Selected Philosophical Essays* (1953); Nikolai Dobroliubov [Nikolay Dobrolyubov], *Selected Philosophical Essays* (1948), *Sobranie sochinenii* (9 vols., 1961–64); Aleksandr Druzhinin, *Prekrasnoe i vechnoe* (1988); Apollon Grigorev, *Literaturnaia kritika* (1967); Nikolai Karamzin, *Izbrannye sochineniia* (2 vols., 1964), *Selected Prose of N. M. Karamzin* (trans. Henry Nebel, Jr., 1969); Vilgelm Kiukhelbeker [Wilhelm Küchelbecker], *Puteshestvie. Dnevnik. Stati* (1979); Lauren Leighton, ed., *Russian Romantic Criticism: An Anthology* (1987); Dmitrii Merezhkovskii, *Izbrannye stati: Simvolizm, Gogol, Lermontov* (1911–12, reprint, 1972); Nikolai Konstantinovich Mikhailovskii [Nikolay Mikhaylovsky], *Dostoevsky: A Cruel Talent* (trans. S. Cadmus, 1978), *Literaturnaia kritika. Stati o russkoi literature XIX–nachala XX veka* (1989); Nikolai Nadezhdin, *Literaturnaia kritika. Estetika* (1972); Dmitrii Pisarev, *Sochineniia* (4 vols., 1955–56); Leo Tolstoy, *What Is Art?* (trans. Aylmer Maude, 1960).

Armand Coquart, *Dmitrii Pisarev (1840–1868) et l'idéologie du nihilisme russe* (1946); Boris Egorov, *O masterstve literaturnoi kritiki: Zhanry. Kompozitsiia. Stil* (1980); Charles Moser, *Esthetics as Nightmare: Russian Literary Theory, 1855–1870* (1989); Norman Pereira, *The Thought and Teachings of N. G. Cernysevskij* (1975); Robert H. Stacy, *Russian Literary Criticism: A Short History* (1974); Victor Terras, *Belinskij and Russian Literary Criticism* (1974).

S

SAID, EDWARD W.

In *The World, The Text, and the Critic,* Edward W. Said (b. 1935) writes that "texts have ways of existing that even in the most rarefied form are always enmeshed in circumstance, time, place, and society—in short, they are in the world, and hence worldly" (35). This idea, variously articulated as a motif in his work, marks a return to and repetition of the "beginning intention" of his career. "The writer's life, his career, and his text," Said remarks in *Beginnings,* "form a system of relationships whose configuration *in real human time* becomes progressively stronger (i.e., more distinct, more individualized and exacerbated). In fact, these relationships gradually become the writer's all-encompassing subject" (227). Said's work as a critic emerges from his life as a dislocated Palestinian. Such "engagements," which he calls "worldly," have characterized his career and have set him apart from other critics. Few other critics have been so often interviewed as partisan political commentators in the public media. By refusing to divorce his work from his life, Said has made his life's work relevant to the public.

Born in Palestinian Jerusalem, Said studied there and in Cairo before moving to the United States. Although he is a Palestinian by birth, his education has been "Western" (B.A., Princeton, 1957; M.A. and Ph.D., Harvard, 1960, 1964). Since 1963 he has taught at Columbia University, where he is now Old Dominion Professor in the Humanities. He is also a music critic for the *Nation* (see his *Musical Elaborations*). As a displaced Arab studying European literature in America, Said has fashioned a career out of the fabric of his own dislocation. From this singular perspective he has developed an influential type of cultural criticism. His importance to contemporary critics is that in refusing to accept the cloak of neutrality that most scholars wear he has shown how literary criticism can be applied to the most volatile and current of struggles for cultural hegemony.

Were it not for Said's own admonitions about attributing beginnings from which supposed continuities follow, one might be tempted to say of his career that his most recent views on the question of Palestine were already implicit in his dissertation on Joseph Conrad, a novelist of Western imperialism. Instead, applying his "postnarrative" (*Beginnings* 282) or nonlinear conception of a career to his own, it is more appropriate to say that three "configurations" appear as "beginning intentions" in his criticism: a desire to make critical work out of the fabric of life, a refusal to separate the imperialism of mind from that of nations, and a will to forge literary criticism into an act of political intervention in the production of cultures. These themes in Said's thought reconfigure correlative themes in the thought of GIAMBATTISTA VICO, GEORG LUKÁCS, ANTONIO GRAMSCI, THEODOR W. ADORNO, FRANTZ FANON, RAYMOND WILLIAMS, and MICHEL FOUCAULT—the thinkers who most influenced him.

Said's first book, *Joseph Conrad and the Fiction of Autobiography,* is a study of Conrad's letters (as autobiographical fictions) in relation to his work (as fictionalized autobiography). This study, informed by the reading strategies of the GENEVA SCHOOL of phenomenological criticism, correlates the process of self-definition apparent in Conrad's letters to the development of his fiction. Said shows how the past was always being renarrated in Conrad's writing as a remedy for his ongoing fear of personal disintegration. In *Beginnings* Said continues his study of the narrativization of experience, tracing the changes that culminate in the modern novel. Combining SIGMUND FREUD's nonlinear interpretation of texts with Foucault's and Vico's methods of analysis leads Said to an understanding of the novel as a complex of authority and molestation (83 ff., 169 ff.). His study of narrativization takes a political turn in *Orientalism,* which is a history of the characterizations through which Western scholars have fictionalized the Orient in unconscious collusion with governmental agencies. This work leads directly to his rewriting of contemporary history in *The Question of Palestine* and *Covering Islam* in order to protest fictions such as "Arabs" and "Islam." He theorizes that affiliations to cultural institutions replace the filiations of birthright. Throughout his writing the history of cultures and personal histories are inseparable.

The main topic of Said's work is Eurocentrism, especially as it manifests itself in imperialism. In his earliest work, Said shows that Conrad's identification with "Europeanism" was an act of secular salvation by which he rescued himself from "the heart of darkness." Then, a shift in Said's thinking occurs in *Beginnings*. Although implicitly a history of the modern novel, the book is also about the imperialism of the mind, which, in acts of linear narrativizing, reduces human subjects to functions of systems. In it, Said rejects the "linguacentrism" of structuralists. Undertaking in this work the development of a postnarrative mode of history-telling leads him in his subsequent work to retell the history of the orient. *Orientalism* explores, for example, relations between the imperialism that results from the production of knowledge and that which results from the invasion of territories. Imperialist history is the precondition of imperialism. Orientalism is the precursor of European empires in the Orient. In linking such discursive formations as "Arabs," "Islam," and "the Orient" with current political situations as he does so forcefully in his writings on Palestine, Said practices a committed form of cultural criticism.

Intervention in the formation of cultures is a goal of Said's work. The question of taking responsibility broached in his study of Conrad as a problem of authorship and in *Beginnings* as a problem of the authority of a "beginning intention" becomes in his later work the problem of political agency. Whether an author is a force of cultural production or a mere refraction of a cultural system is a question that permeates *Beginnings*. The issue is resolved in his practice, for example in *Orientalism*. The critic's responsibility is to analyze the prevailing cultural system of representation and to intervene in this discursive formation by retelling its history. In *Orientalism*, Said retells the history of Orientalism and in so doing intercedes decisively in its discursive formation. Similarly, he writes a history of Palestine to arbitrate *The Question of Palestine*. Again, explicitly using the techniques of literary criticism developed in his previous work, he disrupts the media's *Covering Islam*. In each case, like Foucault before him, Said intervenes to show how a particular discourse is formed.

In *The World, the Text, and the Critic*, he theorizes his view of cultural criticism. Critics, Said argues, should be "oppositional." As intellectuals, they have a responsibility to intervene in the formation of cultures, which are ensembles of pretexts, texts, and paratexts. "In the first place," he writes,

> culture is used to designate not merely something to which one belongs but something that one possesses and, along with that proprietary process, culture also

designates a boundary by which the concepts of what is extrinsic or intrinsic to the culture come into forceful play. . . . But, in the second place, there is a more interesting dimension to this idea of culture . . . by virtue of its elevated or superior position to authorize, to dominate, to legitimate, demote, interdict, and validate: in short, the power of culture to be an agent of, and perhaps the main agency for, powerful differentiation within its domain and beyond it too. (8–9)

The critic's responsibility is to challenge the hegemonic power of cultural formations. This cannot be accomplished by the deconstructive strategies of Derrideans, Said argues, because of "Derrida's elimination of voluntarism and intention in the interests of what he calls infinite substitution" (191). Moreover, these strategies are "based on a theory of undecideability and desemanticization [that] provides a new semantic horizon, and hence a new interpretive opportunity" (191) that replaces one orthodoxy with another. In brief, deconstructive interpretive strategies characteristically intervene in cultural formations in *unworldly* ways practiced with "nihilistic radicality" in pursuit of "the traces of writing that shimmers just a hair beyond utter blankness" (*Beginnings* 343). For Said, deconstructive practices ultimately relinquish responsibility for texts and therefore for what the culture becomes.

As his work amply testifies, Said is a critic who accepts the responsibilities of being a critic of cultures. "Were I to use one word consistently along with *criticism*," he writes,

> it would be *oppositional*. If criticism is reducible neither to a doctrine nor to a political position on a particular question, and if it is to be in the world and self-aware simultaneously, then its identity is its difference from other cultural activities and from systems of thought or of method. In its suspicion of totalizing concepts, in its discontent with reified objects, in its impatience with guilds, special interests, imperialized fiefdoms, and orthodox habits of mind, criticism is most itself and, if the paradox can be tolerated, most unlike itself at the moment it starts turning into organized dogma. (*World* 29)

James J. Sosnoski

See also POSTCOLONIAL CULTURAL STUDIES.

Edward W. Said, *Beginnings: Intention and Method* (1975), "Contemporary Fiction and Criticism," *Tri Quarterly* 33 (1975), *Covering Islam: How the Media and the Experts Determine How We See the Rest of the World* (1981), *Culture and Imperialism* (1993), "An Ethics of Language," diacritics 4 (1974), "An Ideology of Difference," *Critical Inquiry* 12 (1985), "Interview / Edward W. Said," *diacritics* 6 (1976), *Joseph Conrad and the Fiction of Autobiography* (1966), "Michel Foucault as an Intellectual Imagination," *Boundary 2* 1 (1972), "Michel Foucault, 1927–1984," *Raritan* 4 (1984), *Musical Elaborations* (1991), *Orientalism* (1978), "Orientalism Reconsidered," *Cultural Critique* 1 (1985), *The Question of Palestine: A Political Essay* (1979), "The Totalitarianism of Mind," *Kenyon Review* 29 (1967), "Vico on the Discipline of Bodies and Texts," *MLN* 91 (1976), "What Is Beyond Formalism?" *MLN* 86 (1971), *The World, the Text, and the Critic* (1983).

William E. Cain, "Edward W. Said, *Orientalism*," *The Crisis in Criticism: Theory, Literature, and Reform in English Studies* (1984); James Clifford, Review of *Orientalism, History and Theory* 19 (1980); Eugenio Donato, " 'Here, Now' / 'Always, Already,' " *diacritics* 6 (1976); Stanley Fish, "Profession Despise Thyself: Fear and Self-Loathing in Literary Studies," *Critical Inquiry* 10 (1983); A. R. Louch, Review of *The World, the Text, and the Critic, Philosophy and Literature* 8 (1984); J. Hillis Miller, "Beginning with a Text," *diacritics* 6 (1976); Daniel O'Hara, "Criticism Worldly and Otherworldly: Edward W. Said and the Cult of Theory," *Boundary 2* 12–13 (1984); Amal Rassam and Ross Chambers, "Comments on *Orientalism*," *Comparative Studies in Society and History* 22 (1980); Joseph N. Riddel, "Scriptive Fate / Scriptive Hope," *diacritics* 6 (1976); Imre Salusinszky, *Criticism in Society: Interviews with Jacques Derrida, Northrop Frye, Harold Bloom, Geoffrey Hartman, Frank Kermode, Edward Said, Barbara Johnson, Frank Lentricchia, and J. Hillis Miller* (1987); Michael Sprinker, ed., *Edward Said: A Critical Reader* (1993); *Symposium on "Orientalism,"* special issue, *Journal of Asian Studies* 39 (1980); Hayden White, "Criticism as Cultural Politics," *diacritics* 6 (1976).

SAINTE-BEUVE, CHARLES AUGUSTIN

In an essay considered crucial to the conceptualization of *Remembrance of Things Past*, Marcel Proust faulted Charles Augustin Sainte-Beuve (1804–69) for failing to understand that the literary work was created by a writer's inner self and thus was not explainable through aspects of an author's social persona. "A book," Proust explained, "is the product of a different *self* than the one we manifest in our habits, in our social life, in our vices" (*On Art* 99–100). Applying this viewpoint to Sainte-Beuve's own work, Proust concluded that the critic's poetry was

more interesting than the "chatter" of his literary articles. Early in his career, Sainte-Beuve published several collections of verse, *Vie, poésies et pensées de Joseph Delorme* (1829), *Les Consolations* (1830), *Pensées d'août* (1837), *Le Livre d'amour* (1843), as well as a novel, *Volupté* (1834), and a short story, *Madame de Pontivy* (1837). Sainte-Beuve's poetry and fiction are listed as minor works in the French literary canon, particularly when compared with his influential and voluminous literary studies. Proust's judgment puts an ironic twist on Sainte-Beuve's legacy: not only does it replay the tug of war between writers and critics concerning the supremacy of creativity over commentary but given Proust's own creative process, it recasts that traditional rivalry in a new causal relationship. Criticism is no longer solely a derivative product of the literary work; it can be its originating source. Proust's aesthetic framework for *Remembrance of Things Past* was elaborated in opposition to the critic's psychological method, as the novelist makes clear in a collection of his early essays published with the title *Contre Sainte-Beuve*.

Sainte-Beuve's voluminous critical writings include several books of articles from the 1820s, 1830s, and 1840s—*Critiques et portraits littéraires* (5 vols., 1832–39), *Portraits littéraires* (1844), *Portraits de femmes* (1844), *Portraits contemporains* (1846); his study of the seventeenth-century Jansenist retreat Port-Royal and its distinguished guests (*Port-Royal*, 3 vols., 1840–49); a two-volume *Chateaubriand et son groupe littéraire sous l'Empire* (1860); 15 volumes of essays from his weekly column in *Le Constitutionnel* published as *Causeries du lundi;* and another 13 volumes of essays from *Le Moniteur* and *Le Temps*, covering the years 1861 to 1870, published as the *Nouveaux lundi*. He taught briefly at the Universities of Lausanne and Liège, the Collège de France, and the École Normale, and in 1865 he was rewarded for his staunch support of the government of Napoleon III by being named a senator. After his death his notebooks were published as *Cahiers de Sainte-Beuve* and *Mes Poisons*.

"I am only the image maker [*imagier*] of great personalities," he confides in *Mes Poisons* (128). Composing his articles meticulously, Sainte-Beuve delineates the main features of an author's character, adding touches to bring out details, often proceeding by allusion to create an intricate psychological portrait. Between an author and the literary work, Sainte-Beuve establishes a network of subtle interconnections to explain the characteristic aspects of the latter in terms of the life and temperament of the former. As a reader, Sainte-Beuve was particularly sensitive to obsessive themes, repetitive devices and recurring phrases. As if foretelling psychoanalytical criticism, Sainte-Beuve noted in an essay on Étienne de

Senancour included in his *Portraits contemporains* that "every writer has his favorite word [*mot de prédilection*] which occurs frequently in his speech and inadvertently betrays a secret wish or partiality" (Chadbourne 97–98). Himself an elegant writer, Sainte-Beuve was fond of elaborate metaphors. For example, assessing his career as a critic, Sainte-Beuve describes himself as a topographer of the literary landscape: "In literature," he writes, "I am a great identifier [*reconnaisseur*] of new territories. I keep them in sight, I point them out, sometimes I set foot on them, but rarely do I dwell there" (*Mes Poisons* 13).

If the notion of the literary critic as explorer reflects the Romantic vision that writers have a guiding mission, on other literary matters Sainte-Beuve did not always embrace the values of the French Romantic movement. At first a supporter of his contemporaries Victor Hugo, Honoré de Balzac, George Sand, and Alfred de Musset, who were associated with French Romanticism, he later abandoned them to favor instead the aesthetics of French classicism represented by Jean Racine, Jacques Bénigne Bossuet, Madame de Sévigné, and François La Rochefoucauld. In opposition to what he considered "romantic exuberance," distinguished by its penchant for emotionality, bucolic landscapes, and realistic details, Sainte-Beuve praised instead French seventeenth-century writers for their concern with moral dilemmas, their appreciation of rationality and moderation, their belief in aesthetic codes and artistic hierarchies, as well as their reverence for Greek and Roman authors and literary genres. In turn attracted to the writers of his modernity, then to the authors of the past, alternating between the pleasures provided by the innovative and the satisfactions presented by the conventional, Saint-Beuve seems to have been both a humanist who believed in unbound creativity and at the same time a frustrated scientist who dreamed of standardized models to help classify literary phenomena. Less a man battling internal contradictions than a mind of insatiable curiosity, Sainte-Beuve spent his life engrossed in one book after another, imagining the lives and personalities of their authors, leaving behind a monumental corpus of literary studies as a testimony to his unabashed bibliophilia. More than a century before feminist critics would focus on the female literary tradition, Sainte-Beuve devoted a volume to women writers, *Portraits de femmes* (1844). But many of his judgments, particularly those he bestowed on his contemporaries, were on occasion disproved by posterity: Balzac, Gustave Flaubert, Charles Baudelaire, and Émile Zola fared a great deal better than he predicted. Neither his opinions nor his predictions have been his lasting legacy

to the literary world; rather, his extraordinary influence is to be found in the manner in which he approached the study of literature, that is to say, his method.

Port-Royal and *Chateaubriand et son groupe littéraire sous l'Empire* are prime examples of a critical praxis that for over a century set the standard of French literary studies. Bringing together a vast array of information, including the historical background of an era, the social settings, the individual talents of authors, their psychological profiles, and the characters of those in their entourage, Sainte-Beuve paints a richly detailed tableau of a cultural moment built around specific literary events, with their major and minor participants. Although neither Pierre Corneille nor Molière belonged to the abbey of Port-Royal, whose luminaries were Racine and Blaise Pascal, Sainte-Beuve included them in his study because they were contemporaries. On the other hand, Michel de Montaigne, who predates Pascal by a century, was also included because his philosophical interests anticipate those of Pascal. For Sainte-Beuve, authors belonged to a specific time and place, and in spite of discrete individual differences, they could still be classified as kindred minds in a generational grouping. His *Chateaubriand* could thus be described as a study of the literary movement of 1800. But whether focused on a book, an author, or a group in the present or in the past, Sainte-Beuve's method entails exhaustive historical research. Sainte-Beuve is said to have taken some 600 books with him to Lausanne to prepare his study of *Port-Royal*. Essentially, as the recurring word in the titles of his first volumes of criticism suggests, Sainte-Beuve's approach consists of a series of "portraits," a mixture of biographical disclosures and depiction of psychological traits designed to explain the character of a literary work in terms of the personality of its author in an attempt to unveil the part played by human behavior in the mystery of creativity.

> For me, literature, the production of an author, is not distinct or at any rate not separable from the rest of the man and his make-up. I can relish a work by itself, but I find it hard to judge it apart from a knowledge of the man who wrote it; I am quite willing to say, "As the tree is, so is its fruit." Quite naturally, therefore, literary study leads me to moral study. (*Literary Criticism* 1)

As readers of Sainte-Beuve's essays soon detect, the portrayals of others are also most revealing of the biographer's own subjectivity and moral stance, a fact not lost on the critic himself. "If I had to judge myself," he writes, "pursuing self-love in all its disguises, I would say: 'S.-B. paints no portrait without reflecting himself in it; on the pretext of depicting someone else, it is always his own profile which he describes'" (*Mes Poisons* 123).

For this former medical student turned literary critic, the portraiture of the author was not simply an exercise in evocative description; it had an analytical function as well. Features of character traits could be used to set the framework of a physiological system that would potentially lead to the classification of individuals.

> I conceive that in the course of time the science of the moralist will be established on broader foundations; at present it has reached the point where botany was before Jussieu, or comparative anatomy before Cuvier, the anecdotal stage, so to speak. We are simply compiling monographs, recording the details of observation; but I begin to make out links and relationships, and a more enlightened and comprehensive intellect with an acute sense for details will one day succeed in discovering the great natural divisions that correspond to the families of minds. (*Literary Criticism* 2–3)

Sainte-Beuve's organicist predictions fostered the search for formulas best capable of accounting for the specificity of a literary work. HIPPOLYTE TAINE's theory that a literary work is the product of "la race, le milieu et le moment" of its author owes much to Sainte-Beuve's scientific concerns. Since Sainte-Beuve, the relevance or irrelevance of biography has been a regularly debated topic among literary scholars. Critics of the latter part of the nineteenth century—Hippolyte Taine, Ferdinand Brunetière, Edmond Scherer, Ernest Renan, Émile Hennequin—each in his own way, were all influenced by Sainte-Beuve. In the first half of the twentieth century, Gustave Lanson (1857–1934) established literary history as *the* accredited model for literary studies in French universities. In his approach, Lanson incorporated many aspects of Sainte-Beuve's method: sources of inspiration and literary influences, cultural milieus and generational interests, biographical features and textual data. Not until the second half of the twentieth century would new modes of textual analyses—SEMIOTICS, NARRATOLOGY, STRUCTURALISM, PSYCHOANALYSIS, DECONSTRUCTION—challenge the supremacy of literary history in French higher education.

Nelly Furman

See also FRENCH THEORY AND CRITICISM: 2. EIGHTEENTH CENTURY, 3. NINETEENTH CENTURY, and 4. EARLY TWENTIETH CENTURY.

Charles Augustin Sainte-Beuve, *Cahiers I. Le Cahier vert (1834–1847)* (ed. Raphaël Molho, 1973), *Chateaubriand et son groupe littéraire sous l'Empire* (ed. Maurice Allem, 2 vols., 1948), *Literary Criticism of Sainte-Beuve* (ed. and trans. E. R. Marks, 1971), *Mes Poisons* (1965), *Oeuvres: Premiers lundis, Portraits littéraires, Portraits de femmes* (ed. Maxime Leroy, 2 vols., 1956–60), *Port-Royal* (ed. Maxime Leroy, 3 vols., 1953–55), *Sainte-Beuve: Selected Essays* (ed. and trans. F. Steegmuller and N. Guterman, 1963).

Irving Babbitt, *The Masters of Modern French Criticism* (1963); André Billy, *Sainte-Beuve, sa vie et son temps* (2 vols., 1952); Jean Bonnerot, *Un Demi-siècle d'études sur Sainte-Beuve, 1904–1954* (1957); Richard M. Chadbourne, *Charles-Augustin Sainte-Beuve* (1977); Pierre Moreau, *La Critique selon Sainte-Beuve* (1964); Harold Nicolson, *Sainte-Beuve* (1957); Marcel Proust, *Contre Sainte-Beuve: Suivi de nouveaux mélanges* (1954), *On Art and Literature, 1896–1919* (ed. and trans. Sylvia Townsend Warner, 1958); Maurice Regard, *Sainte-Beuve* (1959); René Wellek, "Sainte-Beuve," *A History of Modern Criticism: 1750–1950*, vol. 3, *The Age of Transition* (1965).

SANTAYANA, GEORGE

A philosopher, poet, critic of culture, and best-selling novelist, George Santayana (1863–1952) was also a major literary critic and theorist. Born in Spain and always a Spanish citizen, he lived in the United States from 1872 until 1912. Educated first at the Boston Latin School and then at Harvard University, Santayana eventually served as a faculty member at Harvard, building with William James and Josiah Royce one of the great eras in the Department of Philosophy. At the age of 48, he retired from Harvard to pursue his long-established desire to be a full-time writer, publishing 27 books and numerous articles during his lifetime.

Santayana's contributions to literary criticism are inextricably linked to his naturalistic philosophy, in which skepticism and relativism are foundational tenets. He casts his naturalism in a festive and celebrational form following the tradition of Lucretius, whom Santayana considered, along with DANTE ALIGHIERI and JOHANN WOLFGANG VON GOETHE, one of the major philosophical poets. The contingent, material world blindly interacts without vision or ideals, but consciousness and the resultant awareness of values are created in an arational evolutionary march. The "spirit" (Santayana's chosen term for awareness or consciousness) is a commemorative by-product of the material world. Religion, art, literature, and music are gala events that reconcile the human spirit to its impotence and make possible its liberation.

This naturalistic perspective was often misunderstood as morose or pessimistic by his mentors and colleagues at Harvard. William James's and Josiah Royce's confidence in the authority and command of the human intellect was countered by Santayana's skepticism about the mind's ability to master the material undercurrents structuring human society and the natural environment. For Santayana, romantic cant may cause one to believe that the arabesques of imagination are powerful allies in a hostile world, but ontologically the conscious realm is spiritual in nature, a celebration of existence that is powerless to alter it. Conscious life and its values are relative to the physical structures generating them, and the most cherished of human knowledge is merely "normal madness," accepted for its pragmatic value but with no guarantee of certainty.

Santayana's early works reveal his developing naturalism. His verse was written primarily from the 1880s through the turn of the century. His earliest books include *Sonnets and Other Verses* (1894), *The Sense of Beauty* (1896), *Lucifer: A Theological Tragedy* (1899), and *Interpretations of Poetry and Religion* (1900). *Interpretations* reveals Santayana to be a frank and unorthodox thinker regarding the nexus of poetry and religion. Poetry or expressive creativity and not the specificities of religion meant most to Santayana, who delighted in perspectives that he regarded as fictions.

The five-volume *Life of Reason* (1905–6) is the formal harbinger of Santayana's efforts to affirm the character and reality of the aesthetic, the moral, and the spiritual while at the same time asserting that only the material flux of nature exists and explains all events. The full development of his naturalism is seen in the four-volume *The Realms of Being* (1927–40), introduced in 1923 by *Scepticism and Animal Faith*.

Santayana views naturalism as a call, not to resignation, but to order and structure and, finally, to the spiritual life. Christianity and naturalism may appear to be antagonists, but from Santayana's perspective they embody historical wisdom often missing in the traditions of American thought. Structuring the environment in accord with our individual natures, which is the wisdom of naturalism, enables us to achieve the eminence of the conscious or spiritual life. For Christianity, this wisdom is conceived as willing what God wills. In both naturalism and Christianity, there is a willingness to affirm ultimate impotence and to structure one's life accordingly while celebrating conscious life.

Santayana's theory of poetry was given succinct expression in "The Elements and Functions of Poetry," the tenth chapter of *Interpretations*. Here he divides poetry

into four elements or functions: "euphony," attached to the tune, or measure, or rhythm of speech; "euphuism," a verbal quality often manifested in the choice of colored words and rare and elliptical phrases; "immediate experience," the breaking up of trite conceptions marked by current words into the "sensuous qualities out of which those conceptions were originally put together"; and a type of rational imagination, the power to seize hold of the "reality of sensation and fancy beneath the surface of conventional ideas, and then out of that living but indefinite material to build new structures, richer, finer, fitter to the primary tendencies of our nature, truer to the ultimate possibilities of the soul" (152, 154–55, 161). The highest poetry is that of prophets or of those who render verbally the visions the prophets felt or enacted. At their most powerful, poetry and religion are identical: then "poetry loses its frivolity and ceases to demoralise, while religion surrenders its illusions and ceases to deceive" (172).

Santayana's practical criticism is noteworthy also. His "Poetry of Barbarism" (in *Interpretations*) offers a brilliant though extreme assessment of Robert Browning and Walt Whitman colored by Santayana's more general indictment of Romanticism. Another essay from *Interpretations*, "The Absence of Religion in Shakespeare," is equally irreverent, faulting the dramatist for lack of religious sensibility. Perhaps Santayana's most insightful critical essay is his fine appreciation of Charles Dickens in *Soliloquies in England* (1923).

Santayana may have had his greatest impact as a critic in connection with the transformation of the American canon. He was among the Harvard intellectuals who helped displace the dominant canon of Henry Wadsworth Longfellow, James Russell Lowell, John Greenleaf Whittier, Oliver Wendell Holmes, William Cullen Bryant, and others. His essay "The Genteel Tradition in American Philosophy" (eventually part of *Winds of Doctrine*, 1913) was crucial in this regard, largely because of its shaping effect on Van Wyck Brooks's *America's Coming-of-Age*, a book that set the tone for modernism. Brooks drew directly on his predecessor's vision of an American culture split between what Santayana called "American Will" and "American Intellect" or between "aggressive enterprise" and "genteel tradition" (188) to fit his own notion of an America divided between highbrow and lowbrow culture.

Santayana's emphasis on the constructive imagination and his naturalistic outlook influenced both T. S. ELIOT and WALLACE STEVENS. It is widely agreed that Eliot's notion of the "objective correlative" (*Selected Essays*, 1932, 3d ed., 1950, 124–25) was drawn from Santayana. Stevens, too, follows the lead of Santayana in his refined naturalism, which incorporates both Platonism and Christianity, without any nostalgia for God or dogma. Stevens's poem "To an Old Philosopher in Rome," published, coincidentally, in the month of Santayana's death, describes Santayana as "an inquisitor of structures" who "stops upon this threshold, / As if the design of all his words takes form / And frame from thinking and is realized" (*Collected Poems*, 1954, 510–11). Although Santayana cannot be considered a modernist in poetry or literature (see MODERNIST THEORY AND CRITICISM), he was clearly one of the principal figures who made modernism possible.

Herman J. Saatkamp, Jr., and Kenneth M. Price

George Santayana, *Character and Opinion in the United States: With Reminiscences of William James and Josiah Royce and Academic Life in America* (1922), *The Genteel Tradition at Bay* (1934), *The Last Puritan: A Memoir in the Form of a Novel* (1936), *The Life of Reason, or, The Phases of Human Progress* (5 vols., 1905–6), *Realms of Being* (4 vols., 1927–40), *Scepticism and Animal Faith: Introduction to a System of Philosophy* (1923), *Soliloquies in England and Later Soliloquies* (1923), *Three Philosophical Poets: Lucretius, Dante, and Goethe* (1910), *Winds of Doctrine: Studies in Contemporary Opinion* (1913), *The Works of George Santayana* (gen. ed. Herman J. Saatkamp, Jr., textual ed. William G. Holzberger, 20 vols. to date, 1986–: vol. 1, *Persons and Places: Fragments of Autobiography*, 1986; vol. 2, *The Sense of Beauty: Being the Outlines of Aesthetic Theory*, 1988; vol. 3, *Interpretations of Poetry and Religion*, 1990).

Van Wyck Brooks, *America's Coming-of-Age* (1915); Daniel Cory, *Santayana, The Later Years: A Portrait with Letters* (1963); Jacques Duron, *La Pensée de George Santayana: Santayana en Amérique* (1950); Lois Hughson, *Thresholds of Reality: George Santayana and Modernist Poetics* (1977); John McCormick, *George Santayana: A Biography* (1987); *Overheard in Seville: The Bulletin of the Santayana Society* (ed. Angus Kerr-Lawson and Herman J. Saatkamp, Jr., 1983–); Herman J. Saatkamp, Jr., and John Jones, *George Santayana: A Bibliographical Checklist, 1880–1980* (1982); Irving Singer, *Santayana's Aesthetics: A Critical Introduction* (1957); Timothy L. S. Sprigge, *Santayana: An Examination of His Philosophy* (1974).

SARTRE, JEAN-PAUL

More than any other cultural figure of his generation, Jean-Paul Sartre (1905–80) set the tone of intellectual activity within—and often outside—postwar France. For the better part of a quarter-century, his novels and plays set crises of identity within the contexts of moral and historical action associated with the literature of postwar existentialism in France. Where *Nausea* (1938) was the anguished self-portrait of an alienated writer, *The Flies* (1943) reforged a Greek myth in order to stage resistance against unjust authority in contemporary terms. Sartre's creative writings should not be seen apart from a substantial engagement with literary criticism and theory, extending from reviews in the interwar *Nouvelle revue française* to the monumental—and ultimately unfinished—study of GUSTAVE FLAUBERT that obsessed him over the last two decades of his life.

After first experimenting with fiction, Sartre came to literary criticism and theory via philosophy. In particular, he came to it through an exposure to the PHENOMENOLOGY of Edmund Husserl and MARTIN HEIDEGGER in 1933–34 while studying at the Institut Français in Berlin. The strong associations linking Sartre to existentialism in postwar France often fail to account for critical writings that supplement his creative works well before 1945. *Nausea* is often read as the fictional account of an identity crisis brought on by a would-be novelist's reluctance to contend with the freedom that life imposes on him. But the novel also illustrates many of the concerns for description and narration that Sartre addressed in the interwar and wartime reviews republished in 1947 under the title of *Situations I*.

Sartre's early concerns as a literary critic are focused on fictional technique, with emphasis on point of view. At the same time, elements of an emerging philosophical vision direct his critical remarks toward representations of temporality and human freedom. The creative use of the diary form in *Nausea* should be seen in conjunction with Sartre's critical remarks on the relation between narrative technique and fictional worlds. In a 1938 review of John Dos Passos's *1919*, he argued that the presentation of seemingly pure events yielded to a perpetual sliding within and outside the novel's characters that the reader can hardly fail to notice. The effect was that of a contradictory world of inaction, which Sartre saw as a negative moment in the dialectic of human freedom that all novels ought to portray.

The moral imperative contained in Sartre's remarks on Dos Passos was intentional. It pointed in critical terms to the openness of human reality that is portrayed in *Nausea* and that he would recast, in the philosophical idiom of *Being and Nothingness* (1943), as the priority of existence over essence. Likewise, Sartre's notorious dismissal of François Mauriac—"God is not an artist; neither is Mr. Mauriac"—derived from an implicit thesis that successful fiction narrated from a variety of perspectives in order to simulate the temporal and physical immediacy of things, actions, and events. Because Mauriac forged the essence of his characters to a point where their actions were openly predetermined, his authorial perspective implied a claim to omniscience and omnipotence that Sartre refused to tolerate. This same combination of aesthetic and moral criteria allowed Sartre to conclude, in regard to William Faulkner's *Sound and the Fury,* that he liked Faulkner's art but did not believe in the closed fictional world it portrayed.

A decade later, this interplay of aesthetic and moral criteria grounded the argument of *What Is Literature?* (1947), the manifesto for the program of committed writing *(littérature engagée)* Sartre sought to implement via his postwar monthly, *Les Temps modernes. What Is Literature?* revised Sartre's prewar concerns with narrative technique in view of an urgency acquired as a result of the occupation period, during which communication under the Germans was often achieved at the expense of human lives. After the liberation, Sartre wanted to mobilize the wartime sense of solidarity in order to promote an open that is, classless society of total and reciprocal communication. As a result, the priority of aesthetics in Sartre's prewar criticism yielded to social concerns that were openly politicized. This change was expressed first in a distinction between prose and poetry that resulted less from conventions of form and genre than from divergent attitudes toward language. Prose denoted a utilitarian sense of language as a more or less transparent system of signs to be used, rightly or wrongly, in order to act in and on the world of things and people. For the postwar Sartre, the writer used prose to reveal the world as the site of human freedom. When and where such freedom was denied, the writer's responsibility was to disclose and to denounce the conditions that promoted such denial.

Where the prose writer used language to disclose the world to his or her reader, the poet contemplated language in its materiality as an end in itself. To the extent that the poetic attitude placed language between the writer and the world, Sartre saw it as an obstacle to the action in and on history that committed writing was meant to promote. Despite statements that in *littérature engagée,* engagement must in no way lead to a forgetting of *littérature,* the priority of prose over poetry in Sartre's postwar program ultimately turned literature against itself. This occurred because the qualities prescribed for committed writing were closer to journalism than to the fiction, poetry, and theater whose peculiarities of form and style illustrated the poetic attitude Sartre felt obliged to dismiss. Even the ideological novel and the didactic play had to suppress those literary—that is, "poetic"— qualities that interfered with their capacity to disclose the world as a site of human freedom.

The unresolved problems associated with the distinction between prose and poetry in *What Is Literature?* resurfaced in two separate projects over the following decade. The first was "Black Orpheus" (1948), the preface Léopold Sedar Senghor asked Sartre to write for his anthology of black African Francophone poetry. "Black Orpheus" redirected the distinction between prose and poetry toward circumstances in which *littérature engagée* could effectively promote political and social change. The resistance Sartre saw at work in the Senghor anthology rehabilitated poetry as an anti-prose that asserted difference by rejecting the instrumental usage of the French language imposed by the dominant colonialist culture. Under certain circumstances, poetry could fulfill the liberatory function of disclosing freedom that Sartre had formerly restricted to prose.

Sartre's second rehabilitation of poetry involved an interest in literary biography first announced in *Being and Nothingness* in relation to Gustave Flaubert and Fyodor Dostoevsky. In 1946, Sartre brought out a book-length introduction to CHARLES BAUDELAIRE's *Écrits intimes,* in which he studied the poet's decision *(choix originel)*—brought on by his mother's remarriage—to see himself as other. Intended as an experiment in existential psychoanalysis on the figure of the poet rather than on his writings, Sartre's *Baudelaire* was harshly received by critics who mistook it for a judgment against Baudelaire's literary standing. *Saint Genet, Actor and Martyr* (1952) expanded Sartre's hybrid of biography and literary criticism in the form of a 700-page introduction to the writings of Jean Genet. For the first time, Sartre also tried to reconcile psychoanalytic interpretation and Marxist analysis in order to relate literary style and form to the identity that an individual chose to build under conditions imposed by the circumstances of his or her life. As in "Black Orpheus," Sartre integrated the poetic attitude formerly dismissed in *What Is Literature?* within the process of what he referred to as the narrative of Genet's liberation. (See also Sartre's passionate 1961 preface to FRANTZ FANON's *Wretched of the Earth.*)

The three volumes of *The Family Idiot: Gustave Flaubert from 1821 to 1857* (1971–72) completed the trajectory of

Sartre's involvement with literary biography. The choice of biographical subject was telling, since Sartre had invoked Flaubert in *What Is Literature?* as a prime example of the uncommitted writer. Why, then, did he choose Flaubert in seeking to answer the question what can be known about a man? At a moment when Sartre claimed to be a bourgeois writer in solidarity with the working class, why did he devote some twenty years to a work that was likely to be read only by bourgeois intellectuals like himself? By the mid-1960s his original antipathy had changed, at least tentatively, into empathy, and he could write without irony of Flaubert's literary commitment. He portrayed Flaubert as an unstable synthesis of passive and aggressive behavior. Like Baudelaire, Flaubert was seen as never having recovered from the effects of an early trauma—the 1844 "fall" at Pont-L'Evêque—that, for Sartre, coincided with a decision to make literature the expression of passivity. In retrospect, the irony and self-destruction that Sartre saw in Flaubert pointed to his own ambivalence concerning the value of literature. The terms of this ambivalence recalled the distinction between prose and poetry in *What Is Literature?* but with the notable revision of poetry as a continual and necessary presence within fictional prose.

For all its more than 3,000 pages, *The Family Idiot* failed both to contain its ostensible subject and to reconcile the synthesis of psychoanalytic and Marxist elements of method that Sartre sought to implement. His open concern with critical method did not simply regress to the existential psychoanalysis of his earlier studies on Baudelaire and Genet. Instead, it asserted the high ambitions that Sartre held for a total understanding of literary practice that remained to the end as self-critical as it was critical. In more personal terms, *The Family Idiot* also illustrated the extent to which Sartre's interest in Flaubert bordered on the obsessional. As Sartre confessed on the first page of *What Is Literature?* Flaubert—who did not commit himself—haunted him "like remorse itself." But if *The Family Idiot* failed, its failure was authentic in that it pointed to the self-critical elements at work in what might otherwise be taken for an objective and disinterested analysis.

Littérature engagée remains the primary point of reference for measuring Sartre's impact on postwar literary criticism and theory. At the same time, his interwar essays should be seen in conjunction with phenomenology and the GENEVA SCHOOL surrounding such critics as Gaston Bachelard, Albert Béguin, and Marcel Raymond. A curious recycling has tied *littérature engagée* to the dynamics of writing as communication, from Robert Weimann's author-function and Wolfgang Iser's implied reader to the recent turn by literary critics to CULTURAL STUDIES and the NEW HISTORICISM. From another perspective, current attempts to revise critical understanding of minority, gender-specific, and non-Western practices extend many of Sartre's calls to make committed writing integral to social and political change. In this sense, the importance of the Sartrean program described by Frantz Fanon in *The Wretched of the Earth* as a tool to resist colonialism returns, with notable differences, in the critical practices of postcolonial and subaltern writings set forth by GAYATRI CHAKRAVORTY SPIVAK, Homi Bhabha, and Henry Louis Gates. Regis Debray asked recently what it might be like if we all decided to become Sartreans again ("Si nous redevenions tous sartriens?"). While any serious "return to Sartre" would be tenuous because it would oppose the Sartrean imperative to write for one's age, there is little doubt that Debray's rhetorical question asserts the ongoing relevance of Sartre's postwar program to contemporary critical debate.

Steven Ungar

See also ROLAND BARTHES, SIMONE DE BEAUVOIR, GUSTAVE FLAUBERT, and FRENCH THEORY AND CRITICISM: 5. 1945–1968.

Jean-Paul Sartre, *Baudelaire* (1947, *Baudelaire*, trans. Martin Turnell, 1950), "Black Orpheus," *Situations III* (1949, "Black Orpheus," trans. John MacCombie, *"What Is Literature?" and Other Essays,* 1988), *L'Idiot de la famille: Gustave Flaubert de 1821 à 1857* (3 vols., 1971–72, *The Family Idiot: Gustave Flaubert from 1821 to 1857,* trans. Carol Cosman, 1981–88), *Les Mots* (1964, *The Words,* trans. Bernard Frechtman, 1964), *Notebooks for an Ethics* (trans. David Pellauer, 1993), "Préface" to *Les Damnés de la terre,* by Frantz Fanon (1961, "Preface" to *The Wretched of the Earth,* trans. Constance Farrington, 1968), *Saint-Genet: Comédien et martyr* (1952, *Saint Genet: Actor and Martyr,* trans. Bernard Frechtman, 1964), "Sartre's Notes for the Fourth Volume of *The Family Idiot,*" *Yale French Studies* 68 (1985), *Situations I* (1947, *Literary and Philosophical Essays,* trans. Annette Michelson, 1962 [selections]), *Situations II* (1948, *"What Is Literature?" and Other Essays,* trans. Bernard Frechtman, 1988), *Situations IV* (1964, *Situations,* trans. Benita Eisler, 1965 [selections on literature], *Essays in Aesthetics,* trans. Wade Baskin, 1966 [selections on the arts]).

Anna Boschetti, *The Intellectual Enterprise: Sartre and "Les Temps Modernes"* (trans. Richard C. McCleary, 1988); Michel Contat and Michel Rybalka, *The Writings of Jean-Paul Sartre* (trans. Richard C. McCleary, 1974); Rhiannon Goldthorpe, *Sartre: Literature and Theory* (1984); Joseph

Halpern, *Critical Fictions: The Literary Criticism of Jean-Paul Sartre* (1976); Fredric Jameson, "Three Methods in Sartre's Literary Criticism," *Modern French Criticism: From Proust and Valéry to Structuralism* (ed. John K. Simon, 1972); Steven Ungar, "Introduction" to Sartre's *"What Is Literature?" and Other Essays* (1988).

SAUSSURE, FERDINAND DE

The Swiss linguist Ferdinand de Saussure (1857–1913) is widely considered to be the founder of modern linguistics in its attempts to describe the structure of language rather than the history of particular languages and language forms. In fact, the method of STRUCTURALISM in linguistics and literary studies and a significant branch of SEMIOTICS find their major starting point in his work at the turn of the twentieth century. It has even been argued that the complex of strategies and conceptions that has come to be called "poststructuralism"—the work of JACQUES DERRIDA, MICHEL FOUCAULT, JACQUES LACAN, JULIA KRISTEVA, ROLAND BARTHES, and others—is suggested by Saussure's work in linguistics and anagrammatic readings of late Latin poetry. If this is so, it can be seen most clearly in the way that Saussure's work in linguistics and interpretation participates in transformations in modes of understanding across a wide range of intellectual disciplines from physics to literary modernism to psychoanalysis and philosophy in the early twentieth century. As Algirdas Julien Greimas and Joseph Courtés argue in *Semiotics and Language: An Analytic Dictionary,* under the heading "Interpretation," a new mode of interpretation arose in the early twentieth century which they identify with Saussurean linguistics, Husserlian PHENOMENOLOGY, and Freudian psychoanalysis. In this mode, "interpretation is no longer a matter of attributing a given content to a form which would otherwise lack one; rather, it is a paraphrase which formulates in another fashion the equivalent content of a signifying element within a given semiotic system" (159). In this understanding of "interpretation," form and content are not distinct; rather, every "form" is, alternatively, a semantic "content" as well, a "signifying form," so that interpretation offers an analogical paraphrase of something that *already* signifies within some other system of signification.

Such a reinterpretation of form and understanding—which CLAUDE LÉVI-STRAUSS describes in one of his most programmatic articulations of the concept of structuralism, in "Structure and Form: Reflections on a Work by Vladimir Propp"—is implicit in Saussure's posthu-

mous *Course in General Linguistics* (1916, trans., 1959, 1983). In his lifetime, Saussure published relatively little, and his major work, the *Course,* was the transcription by his students of several courses in general linguistics he offered in 1907–11. In the *Course* Saussure called for the "scientific" study of language as opposed to the work in historical linguistics that had been done in the nineteenth century. That work is one of the great achievements of Western intellect: taking particular words as the building blocks of language, historical (or "diachronic") linguistics traced the origin and development of Western languages from a putative common language source, first an "Indo-European" language and then an earlier "proto-Indo-European" language.

It is precisely this study of the unique occurrences of words, with the concomitant assumption that the basic "unit" of language is, in fact, the *positive* existence of these "word-elements," that Saussure questioned. His work was an attempt to reduce the mass of facts about language, studied so minutely by historical linguistics, to a manageable number of propositions. The "comparative school" of nineteenth-century PHILOLOGY, Saussure says in the *Course,* "did not succeed in setting up the true science of linguistics" because "it failed to seek out the nature of its object of study" ([1959] 3). That "nature," he argues, is to be found not simply in the "elemental" words that a language comprises—the seeming "positive" facts (or "substances") of language—but in the *formal* relationships that give rise to those "substances."

Saussure's systematic reexamination of language is based upon three assumptions. The first is that the scientific study of language needs to develop and study the *system* rather than the history of linguistic phenomena. For this reason, he distinguishes between the particular occurrences of language—its particular "speech-events," which he designates as *parole*—and the proper object of linguistics, the system (or "code") governing those events, which he designates as *langue.* Such a systematic study, moreover, calls for a "synchronic" conception of the relationship among the elements of language at a particular instant rather than the "diachronic" study of the development of language through history.

This assumption gave rise to what ROMAN JAKOBSON in 1929 came to designate as "structuralism," in which "any set of phenomena examined by contemporary science is treated not as a mechanical agglomeration but as a structural whole [in which] the mechanical conception of processes yields to the question of their function" ("Romantic" 711). In this passage Jakobson is articulating Saussure's intention to define linguistics as a scientific system as opposed to a simple, "mechanical" accounting of historical accidents. Along with this, more-over, Jakobson is also describing the second founda-tional assumption in Saussurean—we can now call it "structural"—linguistics: that the basic elements of lan-guage can only be studied in relation to their *functions* rather than in relation to their *causes*. Instead of study-ing particular and unique events and entities (i.e., the history of particular Indo-European "words"), those events and entities have to be *situated* within a systemic framework in which they are related to other so-called events and entities. This is a radical reorientation in conceiving of experience and phenomena, one whose importance the philosopher Ernst Cassirer has com-pared to "the new science of Galileo which in the seven-teenth century changed our whole concept of the phys-ical world" (cited in Culler, *Pursuit* 24). This change, as Greimas and Courtés note, reconceives "interpretation" and thus reconceives explanation and understanding themselves. Instead of explanation's being in terms of a phenomenon's causes, so that, as an "effect," it is in some ways subordinate to its causes, explanation here consists in subordinating a phenomenon to its future-oriented "function" or "purpose." Explanation is no longer independent of human intentions or purposes (even though those intentions can be impersonal, com-munal, or, in Freudian terms, "unconscious").

In his linguistics Saussure accomplishes this transfor-mation specifically in the redefinition of the linguistic "word," which he describes as the linguistic "sign" and defines in functionalist terms. The sign, he argues, is the union of "a concept and a sound image," which he called "*signified* [*signifié*] and *signifier* [*signifiant*]" (66–67; Roy Harris's 1983 translation offers the terms "signification" and "signal" [67]). The nature of their "combination" is "functional" in that neither the signified nor the sig-nifier is the "cause" of the other; rather, "each [derives] its values from the other" (8). In this way, Saussure de-fines the basic element of language, the sign, *relationally* and makes the basic assumption of historical linguistics, namely, the *identity* of the elemental units of language and signification (i.e., "words"), subject to rigorous anal-ysis. The reason we can recognize different occurrences of the word "tree" as the "same" word is not because the word is defined by inherent qualities—it is not a "me-chanical agglomeration" of such qualities—but because it is defined as an element in a system, the "structural whole," of language.

Such a relational (or "diacritical") definition of an entity governs the conception of all the elements of lan-guage in structural linguistics. This is clearest in the most impressive achievement of Saussurean linguistics,

the development of the concepts of the "phonemes" and "distinctive features" of language. Phonemes are the smallest articulated and signifying units of a language. They are not the sounds that occur in language but the "sound images" Saussure mentions, which are appre-hended by speakers—*phenomenally* apprehended—as conveying meaning. (Thus, Elmar Holenstein describes Jakobson's linguistics, which follows Saussure in impor-tant ways, as "phenomenological structuralism.") It is for this reason that the leading spokesperson for PRAGUE SCHOOL STRUCTURALISM, Jan Mukarovsky, noted in 1937 that "structure . . . is a phenomenological and not an empirical reality; it is not the work itself, but a set of functional relationships which are located in the con-sciousness of a collective (generation, milieu, etc.)" (cited in Galan 35). Similarly, Lévi-Strauss, the leading spokesperson for French structuralism, noted in 1960 that "*structure* has no distinct content; it is content itself, and the logical organization in which it is arrested [or apprehended] is conceived as a property of the real" (167; see also Jakobson, *Fundamentals* 27–28).

Phonemes, then, the smallest perceptible elements of language, are not *positive* objects but a "phenomeno-logical reality." In English, for instance, the phoneme /t/ can be pronounced in many different ways, but in all cases an English speaker will recognize it as *functioning* as a /t/. An aspirated *t* (i.e., a *t* pronounced with an *h*-like breath after it), a high-pitched or low-pitched *t* sound, an extended *t* sound, and so on, will all function in the same manner in distinguishing the meaning of "to" and "do" in English. Moreover, the differences between lan-guages are such that phonological variations in one lan-guage can constitute distinct phonemes in another; thus, English distinguishes between /l/ and /r/, whereas other languages are so structured that these articulations are considered variations of the same phoneme (like the aspirated and unaspirated *t* in English). In every natural language, the vast number of possible words is a com-bination of a small number of phonemes. English, for instance, possesses less than 40 phonemes that combine to form over a million different words.

The phonemes of language are themselves systemat-ically organized *structures* of features. In the 1920s and 1930s, following Saussure's lead, Jakobson and N. S. Tru-betzkoy isolated the "distinctive features" of phonemes. These features are based upon the physiological struc-ture of the speech organs—tongue, teeth, vocal chords, and so on—that Saussure mentions in the *Course* and that Harris describes as "physiological phonetics" ([1983] 39; Baskin's earlier translation uses the term "phonol-ogy" [(1959) 38])—and they combine in "bundles" of binary oppositions to form phonemes. For instance, in English the difference between /t/ and /d/ is the presence or absence of "voice" (the engagement of the vocal chords), and on the level of voicing these phonemes reciprocally define one another. In this way, phonology is a specific example of a general rule of language described by Saussure:

> In language there are only differences. Even more important: a difference generally implies positive terms between which the difference is set up; but in language there are only differences *without positive terms.* Whether we take the signified or the signifier, language has neither ideas nor sounds that existed before the linguistic system. ([1959] 120)

In this framework, linguistic identities are determined not by inherent qualities but by systemic ("structural") relationships.

I have said that phonology "followed the lead" of Saussure, because even though his analysis of the physiology of language production "would nowadays," as Harris says, "be called 'physical,' as opposed to either 'psychological' or 'functional'" (*Reading* 49), nevertheless in the *Course* he articulated the direction and outlines of a functional analysis of language. Similarly, his only extended published work, *Mémoire sur le système primitif des voyelles dans les langues indo-européennes* (Memoir on the primitive system of vowels in Indo-European languages), which appeared in 1878, was fully situated within the project of nineteenth-century historical linguistics. Nevertheless, within this work, as Jonathan Culler has argued, Saussure demonstrated "the fecundity of thinking of language as a system of purely relational items, even when working at the task of historical reconstruction" (*Saussure* 66). By analyzing the systematic structural relationships among phonemes to account for patterns of vowel alternation in existing Indo-European languages, Saussure suggested that in addition to several different phonemes /a/, there must have been another phoneme that could be described formally. "What makes Saussure's work so very impressive," Culler concludes, "is the fact that nearly fifty years later, when cuneiform Hittite was discovered and deciphered, it was found to contain a phoneme, written *h*, which behaved as Saussure had predicted. He had discovered, by a purely formal analysis, what are now known as the laryngeals of Indo-European" (66).

This conception of the relational or diacritical determination of the elements of signification, which is both implicit and explicit in the *Course,* suggests a third assumption governing structural linguistics, what Saussure calls "the arbitrary nature of the sign." By this he means that the relationship between the signifier and signified in language is never necessary (or "motivated"): one could just as easily find the sound signifier *arbre* as the signifier *tree* to unite with the concept 'tree'. But more than this, it means that the signified is arbitrary as well: one could as easily define the concept 'tree' by its woody quality (which would exclude palm trees) as by its size (which excludes the "low woody plants" we call *shrubs*). This should make clear that the numbering of assumptions I have been presenting does not represent an order of priority: each assumption—the systemic nature of signification (best apprehended by studying language "synchronically"), the relational or "diacritical" nature of the elements of signification, the arbitrary nature of signs—derives its value from the others.

That is, Saussurean linguistics understands the phenomena it studies in overarching relationships of *combination* and *contrast* in language. In this conception, language is both the *process* of articulating meaning (signification) and its *product* (communication), and these two functions of language are neither identical nor fully congruent (see Schleifer, "Deconstruction"). Here, we can see the alternation between form and content that Greimas and Courtés describe in modernist interpretation: language presents contrasts that *formally* define its units, and these units combine on succeeding levels to create the signifying *content*. Since the elements of language are arbitrary, moreover, neither contrast nor combination can be said to be basic. Thus, in language distinctive features combine to form contrasting phonemes on another *level* of apprehension, phonemes combine to form contrasting morphemes, morphemes combine to form words, words combine to form sentences, and so on. In each instance, the whole phoneme, or word, or sentence, and so on, is greater than the sum of its parts (just as water, H_2O, in Saussure's example [(1959) 103] is more than the mechanical agglomeration of hydrogen and oxygen).

The three assumptions of the *Course in General Linguistics* led Saussure to call for a new science of the twentieth century that would go beyond linguistic science to study "the life of signs within society." Saussure named this science "*semiology* (from Greek *semeîon* 'sign')" (16). The "science" of semiotics, as it came to be practiced in Eastern Europe in the 1920s and 1930s and Paris in the 1950s and 1960s, widened the study of language and linguistic structures to literary artifacts constituted (or articulated) by those structures. Throughout the late part of his career, moreover, even while he was offering the courses in general linguistics, Saussure pursued his own "semiotic" analysis of late Latin poetry in an attempt to discover deliberately concealed anagrams of proper names. The method of study was in many ways the opposite of the functional rationalism of his linguistic analyses: it attempted, as Saussure mentions in one of the 99 notebooks in which he pursued this study, to examine systematically the problem of "chance," which "becomes the inevitable foundation of everything" (cited in Starobinski 101). Such a study, as Saussure himself says, focuses on "the material fact" of chance and meaning (cited 101), so that the "theme-word" whose anagram Saussure is seeking, as Jean Starobinski argues, "is, for the poet, an *instrument,* and not a vital germ of the poem. The poem is obliged to *re-employ* the phonic materials of the theme-word" (45). In this analysis, Starobinski says, "Saussure did not lose himself in a search for hidden meanings." Instead, his work seems to demonstrate a desire to evade all the problems arising from *consciousness:* "Since poetry is not only realized *in* words but is something born *from* words, it escapes the arbitrary control of consciousness to depend solely on a kind of linguistic legality" (121).

That is, Saussure's attempt to discover proper names in late Latin poetry—what Tzvetan Todorov calls the reduction of a "word . . . to its signifier" (266)—emphasizes one of the elements that governed his linguistic analysis, the arbitrary nature of the sign. (It also emphasizes the *formal* nature of Saussurean linguistics—"Language," he asserts, "is a form and not a substance" [*Course* (1959) 122]—which effectively eliminates semantics as a major object of analysis.) As Todorov concludes,

> Saussure's work appears remarkably homogeneous today in its refusal to accept symbolic phenomena [phenomena that have *intentional* meaning]. . . . In his research on anagrams, he pays attention only to the phenomena of repetition, not to those of evocation. . . . In his studies of the *Nibelungen,* he recognizes symbols only in order to attribute them to mistaken readings: since they are not intentional, symbols do not exist. Finally in his courses on general linguistics, he contemplates the existence of semiology, and thus of signs other than linguistic ones; but this affirmation is at once limited by the fact that semiology is devoted to a single type of sign: those which are arbitrary. (269–70)

If this is true, it is because Saussure could not conceive of "intention" without a subject; he could not quite escape the opposition between form and content his work did so much to call into question. Instead, he resorted to "linguistic legality." Situated between, on the one hand, nineteenth-century conceptions of history, subjectivity, and the mode of causal interpretation governed by these

conceptions and, on the other hand, twentieth-century "structuralist" conceptions of what Lévi-Strauss called "Kantianism without a transcendental subject" (cited in Connerton 23)—conceptions that erase the opposition between form and content (or subject and object) and the hierarchy of foreground and background in full-blown structuralism, psychoanalysis, and even quantum mechanics—the work of Ferdinand de Saussure in linguistics and semiotics circumscribes a signal moment in the study of meaning and culture.

Ronald Schleifer

See also LINGUISTICS AND LANGUAGE and STRUCTURALISM.

Émile Benveniste, *Problèmes de linguistique générale,* vol. 1 (1966, *Problems in General Linguistics,* trans. Mary Elizabeth Meek, 1971); Jacques Derrida, *De la grammatologie* (1967, *Of Grammatology,* trans. Gayatri Chakravorty Spivak, 1976), *Marges de la philosophie* (1972, *Margins of Philosophy,* trans. Alan Bass, 1982); A. J. Greimas and J. Courtés, *Sémiotique: Dictionnaire raisonné de la théorie du langage,* vol. 1 (1979, *Semiotics and Language: An Analytical Dictionary,* trans. Larry Crist et al., 1982); Louis Hjelmslev, *Omkring Sprogteoriens Grundlæggelse* (1943, *Prolegomena to a Theory of Language,* trans. Francis Whitfield, 1961); Roman Jakobson, "Romantic Panslavism—New Slavic Studies," *Selected Writings,* vol. 2 (1971); Roman Jakobson, with Morris Halle, *Fundamentals of Language* (1956); Claude Lévi-Strauss, "Structure and Form: Reflections on a Work by Vladimir Propp" (1960, trans. Monique Layton, rev. Anatoly Liberman, *Theory and History of Folklore,* by Vladimir Propp, 1984); Richard Macksey and Eugenio Donato, eds., *The Structuralist Controversy: The Languages of Criticism and the Sciences of Man* (1970); Ferdinand de Saussure, *Cours de linguistique générale* (1916, *Course in General Linguistics,* trans. Wade Baskin, 1959, trans. Roy Harris, 1983); Jean Starobinski, *Les Mots sous les mots: Les Anagrammes de Ferdinand de Saussure* (1971, *Words upon Words: The Anagrams of Ferdinand de Saussure,* trans. Olivia Emmett, 1979).

Paul Connerton, *The Tragedy of Enlightenment: An Essay on the Frankfurt School* (1980); Jonathan Culler, *The Pursuit of Signs: Semiotics, Literature, Deconstruction* (1981), *Saussure* (1976), *Structuralist Poetics: Structuralism, Linguistics, and the Study of Literature* (1975); Robert Con Davis and Ronald Schleifer, *Criticism and Culture: The Role of Critique in Modern Literary Theory* (1992); F. W. Galan, *Historical Structures: The Prague School Project, 1928–1946* (1985); Roy Harris, *Reading Saussure* (1987); Elmar Holenstein, *Roman Jakobson's Approach to Language* (trans. Catherine Schelbert and Tarcisius Schelbert, 1976); E. F. K. Koerner, *Ferdinand de Saussure: The Origin and Development of His Linguistic Thought in Western Studies of Language* (1973); Timothy J. Reiss, *The Uncertainty of Analysis: Problems in Truth, Meaning, and Culture* (1988); Geoffrey Sampson, *Schools of Linguistics* (1980); Ronald Schleifer, *A. J. Greimas and the Nature of Meaning: Linguistics, Semiotics, and Discourse Theory* (1987), "Analogy and Example: Heisenberg and the Language of Quantum Physics," *Criticism* 33 (1991), "Deconstruction and Linguistic Analysis," *College English* 49 (1987); Tzvetan Todorov, *Théories du symbole* (1977, *Theories of the Symbol,* trans. Catherine Porter, 1982); V. N. Volosinov, *Marksizm i filosofiia iazyka* (1929, *Marxism and the Philosophy of Language,* trans. Ladislav Matejka and I. R. Titunik, 1973).

SCHILLER, FRIEDRICH

Friedrich Schiller (1759–1805), German dramatist and poet, is best known for his early drama of political revolt, *Die Räuber* (1781); for his classical masterpiece, the *Wallenstein* trilogy (1798–99); and for *Wilhelm Tell* (1804)—in all of which he exhibits his fervent concern for freedom and the ideals of humanity. In German literary history Schiller and JOHANN WOLFGANG VON GOETHE are considered the major representatives of German classicism, which lasted from 1786 until Goethe's death in 1832. The majority of Schiller's aesthetic essays, which for a considerable time were barely recognized as part of his principal literary achievement, were conceived between 1793 and 1795 and are steeped in the language of IMMANUEL KANT's critical writings, especially the *Critique of Aesthetic Judgement.* Besides "Über Anmut und Würde" (1793, "On Grace and Dignity"), Schiller's two most influential essays, "Über die ästhetische Erziehung des Menschen" (1795, "On the Aesthetic Education of Man") and "Über naive und sentimentalische Dichtung" (1795–96, "On Naive and Sentimental Poetry"), have been instrumental in the germination of many Romantic and modern theories of art, and together with Johann Joachim Winckelmann's *Thoughts on the Imitation of Greek Works in Painting and Sculpture,* G. E. LESSING's *Laocoon,* and Kant's *Critique of Aesthetic Judgement,* they constitute the core of German aesthetic criticism of the mid- and late eighteenth century.

In his first major aesthetic treatise, "On Grace and Dignity," Schiller endeavored to establish, in opposition to Kant's definition of taste as subjective, an understanding of art based on principles. Here, as in his later essays, beauty is a function of the harmony of the physical and moral sense, of duty *(Pflicht)* and inclination *(Neigung);* this harmony culminates in "the beautiful soul" *(schöne Seele),* which expresses itself through graceful appearance and which may well be classified as a cornerstone concept of German classicism.

"On the Aesthetic Education of Man," with which Schiller undertook to further investigate the relationship between the beautiful and art, opens with a political analysis of contemporary society and in particular of the French Revolution and its failure to implement universal freedom. Since human beings cannot rise above the fetters of their time without education, and since the means of education can be art and art only, Schiller concedes that beauty must precede freedom. He conceives of art therefore as a vehicle, one that over time will improve humankind and set the individual free from the constraints and excesses of either pure nature or pure mind. The function of art must be to educate and elevate the human race toward this new and ideal, if in essence unattainable, position, one in which human beings, through aesthetic experience, have reconciled the antagonism within themselves between sense and intellect, nature and reason.

Schiller's argument operates simultaneously on at least two distinct planes of thought, diachronic and synchronic; hence his continued and at times confusing oscillation between positions and vocabulary. On the first plane Schiller constructs a philosophy of history in which humankind progresses from the physical through the aesthetic to the moral. On the second plane the aesthetic is the medium in which the physical and the moral are reconciled. In both models the function of art is to educate human beings, to synthesize the conflicting natures within us, animal and spiritual, the material drive *(Stofftrieb)* and the formal drive *(Formtrieb),* change on the outside *(Zustand)* and continuity on the inside *(Person),* by means of a third drive, play *(Spieltrieb),* which merges the dualistic categories of material and form, becoming and being, into living form *(lebende Gestalt)*— Schiller's ultimate definition of beauty. His treatise thus prefigures not only G. W. F. HEGEL's concept of art as the idea rendered sensible *(sinnliches Scheinen der Idee),* his three styles of art (symbolic, classical, Romantic), and his triadic model of historical progress (thesis-antithesis-synthesis) but also SIGMUND FREUD's second topographical model of id, superego, and their reconciliation in the ego.

"On Naive and Sentimental Poetry," Schiller's most important contribution to the theory of criticism, brings to fruition many of the arguments outlined earlier in "On the Aesthetic Education of Man" and marks a turning point in poetics and genre theory. In it Schiller repositions the century-old dispute over the superiority of antique or modern poetry, the *Querelle des anciens et des modernes*. Antique poetry now is equated with the naive mode of perception *(naive Empfindungsweise)*. Naive poets live in inner harmony and unity with nature, and their works of art are produced spontaneously and in the absence of poetic self-consciousness. The poetry of modernity, on the other hand, is sentimental in outlook (Schiller's German term is *sentimentalisch* rather than *sentimental*). Sentimental poets are self-reflective and skeptical of inspiration, they are apprehensive of the psychological abyss that dissociates their own age from antiquity, and they feel their cultural and moral self cut off from the harmony of senses and from the union with nature that they ascribe to the writers of antiquity. Schiller contends that it is impossible to recover that nature; as moderns we no longer live in, nor shall we ever regain, that state of naive, or unconscious, communion with nature that for him is so characteristic of Greek culture. Thus, in contrast to JEAN-JACQUES ROUSSEAU, Schiller does not champion a return to Arcadia; out of historical necessity, we must proceed toward what he calls Elysium, a state in which the ideal of beautiful humanity is realized through a fusion of the naive and sentimental characters.

In consequence, Schiller challenges the denigration of modern poetry by prescriptive neoclassicism, which deduced its criteria from ancient poetry alone. He asserts two distinct and incompatible modes of writing, equal in value, that dominate in but are not restricted to either antiquity or modernity. While naive poetry imitates reality, sentimental poetry aspires to present the ideal. Thus, while naive poets live in harmony with nature and reality and their mode of perception is unified, sentimental poets must assume one of three modes of perception that proceed from the ratio between the real and the ideal and must consequently employ in poetry one of three possible genres: the satiric, the elegiac, or the idyllic. Although the distinction between naive and sentimental poetry initially appears to be a diachronic antagonism equating antique and modern with naive and sentimental, the dichotomy soon evolves into a systematic one. The naive and sentimental then become an antagonism of the human mind and are incorporated into a psychological typology. Hence, the naive in poetry is merged with an objective style, an unconscious mode of production, and ultimately with realism (the prototype of which is Goethe, according to Schiller the naive and modern author per se); by contrast, the sentimental is fused with a subjective style, with a conscious and conscientious mode of writing, and with idealism (represented by Schiller himself). With this partitioning of stylistic modes, Schiller was, by and large, the first theorist to advance a distinctly psychological typology of literature.

The generic tandem of naive and sentimental has, ever since its introduction in 1795, remained a potent formula of historical poetics and critical practice. The terms have been used to develop or critique various isotopical antinomies of literary-historical periodization and classification, such as classicism and Romanticism, realism and idealism, FRIEDRICH NIETZSCHE's Apollonian and Dionysian, or even STRUCTURALISM and Poststructuralism (see Sychrava). With his conceptualization of the sentimental as a willful swerving away from a strong predecessor, whether author or movement (modernity from antiquity, idealism from classicism, Schiller from Goethe), Schiller has given us the late-eighteenth-century blueprint of what HAROLD BLOOM has termed the anxiety of influence. His notion of self-conscious, reflexive artistry was taken up, refined, and disseminated through German Romanticism into most brands of nineteenth- and twentieth-century literary practice and poetics. In particular by way of his adversary Friedrich von Schlegel (himself a strong poet whose influential definition of Romantic literature took shape in part as a revisionary rewriting of Schiller's aesthetic principles) and by way of his elder brother August Wilhelm von Schlegel's liaison with GERMAINE DE STAËL, as well as through the notorious influence of Goethe on European literature and of Hegel on European philosophy, Schiller's ideas and concepts have become, either directly or covertly, commonplaces of the European aesthetic and critical tradition.

Robert Weninger

See also GERMAN THEORY AND CRITICISM: 1. STURM UND DRANG / WEIMAR CLASSICISM and 2. ROMANTICISM, and JOHANN WOLFGANG VON GOETHE.

H. B. Nisbet, ed., *German Aesthetic and Literary Criticism: Winckelmann, Lessing, Hamann, Herder, Schiller, Goethe* (1986); Friedrich Schiller, *"Naive and Sentimental Poetry" and "On The Sublime": Two Essays* (trans. Julius A. Elias, 1966), *On the Aesthetic Education of Man in a Series of Letters* (ed. and trans. Elizabeth M. Wilkinson and L. A. Willoughby, 1967), *Sämtliche Werke*, vol. 5 (ed. Gerhard Fricke and Herbert G. Göpfert, 1960), *Schillers Werke: Nationalausgabe*, vol. 20, *Philosophische Schriften, Erster Teil* (ed. Benno von Wiese, 1962), *Über naive und sentimentalische Dichtung* (1795, ed. William F. Mainland, 1957).

Wilhelm Böhm, *Schillers "Briefe über die ästhetische Erziehung des Menschen"* (1927); Wolfgang Düsing, *Friedrich Schiller: Über die ästhetische Erziehung des Menschen* (1981); Hans Robert Jauss, "Schlegels und Schillers Replik auf die 'Querelle des Anciens et des Modernes,'" *Literaturgeschichte als Provokation* (1970); S. S. Kerry, *Schiller's Writings on Aesthetics* (1961); Wolfgang Ranke, "Schiller," *Klassiker der Literaturtheorie: Von Boileau bis Barthes* (ed. Horst Turk, 1979); Juliet Sychrava, *Schiller to Derrida: Idealism in Aesthetics* (1989); Peter Szondi, "Das Naive ist das Sentimentalische: Zur Begriffsdialektik in Schillers Abhandlung," *Lektüren und Lektionen: Versuche über Literatur, Literaturtheorie und Literatursoziologie* (1973); Gert Ueding, *Schillers Rhetorik: Idealistische Wirkungsästhetik und rhetorische Tradition* (1971); René Wellek, *A History of Modern Criticism: 1750–1950*, vol. I, *The Later Eighteenth Century* (1955).

SCHOPENHAUER, ARTHUR

Arthur Schopenhauer (1788–1860) was born in Danzig, the son of a merchant who left him wealthy enough to survive the collapse of a brief academic career at the University of Berlin, during which he failed to draw students away from his intellectual opponent G .W. F. HEGEL. His aesthetic theory can be found in the aphoristic *Parerga und Paralipomena* (1851) and more systematically in the third book of *The World as Will and Representation* (1818, rev. ed., 1844). Ignored until the latter was reissued, Schopenhauer's pessimistic metaphysics influenced such writers as Thomas Hardy and Joseph Conrad, while his aesthetics had a significant impact on the Symbolists and encapsulated some of the problems within Romanticism, in which he had read widely. What is equally important, his turning of metaphysics toward psychology anticipated SIGMUND FREUD and Freud's awareness of the unconscious motivations underlying conscious representations. Later in the century Schopenhauer's reputation eclipsed that of Hegel, but in the twentieth century his contribution has again been largely neglected.

Schopenhauer's aesthetics reflect certain tensions in the reluctant post-Kantian nihilism of his metaphysics. IMMANUEL KANT had argued that the "categories" we use to organize experience (space, time, causality) are "regulative" rather than "constitutive" and order rather than describe ultimate reality, which is unknowable. But although the categories lack the transcendent authority of PLATO's Ideas, as mental forms they are universal, and

we can act as if they were true. Schopenhauer agrees that the world is our construction but denies the disinterested objectivity of the forms by which we represent it, declaring that the world is purely a representation of the will. Ultimate reality, moreover, is not safely unknowable, nor is it the immanently developing Spirit of post-Kantian idealism. It is precisely the irrational substratum of "will," a desublimated version of Hegel's Spirit. Crucial to Schopenhauer is his construction and dismantling of a tempting opposition between will and representation.

The will, which is distinct from and even opposed to "free will," is a force operating both in humans and in nature: a self-perpetuating desire that is finally aimless, because the satisfaction of its immediate goals leads only to the substitution of further goals. Inchoate and at odds with herself or himself, the willing subject is described as bound to Ixion's wheel. The world as representation is our attempt to produce the stable forms that facilitate objective knowledge, because they are outside the self, and because as representations they can be seen rather than amorphously felt. Representations offer a saving entry into a world of Platonic or at least Kantian universals. But this escape is already debarred because the world as representation is only an expression of the will it tries to flee. Literally representation (*Vorstellung*), which used to be mistranslated by the Platonic term "Idea," is a picture produced in the brain by a neurophysiological impulse, an image on the boundary between objective and subjective.

Art is the will's first (and unsuccessful) attempt to abolish itself, the second being death. As part of his affiliation of art with the world as representation, Schopenhauer develops a Platonic aesthetics, which he then repudiates as a representation of his own will. He begins by defining "genius" as a state of "pure perception" emancipated from the will and proceeds to describe the arts both as expressions of this genius and in terms of their effect on the respondent. Beginning with architecture and continuing through painting and sculpture to literature, the arts form a scale that represents the Ideas in successively higher grades of objectification. Literature itself proceeds from lyric (which is subjective enough to contain an admixture of the will) through ballad, romance, and epic to drama, which reveals the "Idea of mankind." Schopenhauer follows Plato's adaptors in associating art with the representation of what is permanent and unaffected by the contingency of the will. He follows ARISTOTLE in seeing poetry as closer to the Ideas than history is and in associating art with the purgation or catharsis of the will. Yet one form does not find a place in his hierarchy: music. The only medium that is nonrepresentational, music copies not the Ideas in their objectivity but the will itself.

At the same time, because the Ideas are only epiphenomena of the will, a form that expresses the will must be more authentic than the various forms that sublimate it. We can best understand the third book of Schopenhauer's *World as Will and Representation* if we see it as staging the agonistic relationship between Romanticism and classicism. Beginning with a classical aesthetic that values objective representation, he concludes by developing in connection with music a theory that legitimizes the expression of the subjective will. This aesthetic is Romantic in being organized around expression rather than mimesis, but it also discloses a darker side of Romantic expressionism unexplored by his contemporaries. By the end of the third book the sublimatory nature of Schopenhauer's classicism is apparent, and he renounces art to avoid a Romanticism that would see art (in the form of music) as undoing the purgation of the will that it is supposed to effect as a representation of the "ideas."

Schopenhauer has an obvious historical importance for Romantic aesthetic theory (see BRITISH THEORY AND CRITICISM: 3. ROMANTIC PERIOD AND EARLY NINETEENTH CENTURY and GERMAN THEORY AND CRITICISM: 2. ROMANTICISM). In contemporary terms, because of his profound influence on FRIEDRICH NIETZSCHE, he anticipates certain aspects of DECONSTRUCTION. Will and representation become the Dionysus and Apollo of *The Birth of Tragedy*, which may introduce to literary criticism the method of constructing and collapsing binary oppositions. The will itself, as a self-differing and deferring process incapable of representation, anticipates JACQUES DERRIDA's *différance*, JACQUES LACAN's unconscious, and JULIA KRISTEVA's notions of the "semiotic" and the "chora," but without their emphasis on language as the site of difference. Perhaps most intriguing of all are Schopenhauer's comments on representation as ultimately self-referential rather than mimetic: representations point to something that is not an "object" but rather the will that generates them. What they refer to is not a reality outside them but the process by which they are produced. As the only art that has no signified, music, which is "the depiction" rather than "the thing depicted," may provide the first theoretical description of an art that refers only to the play of its own signifiers.

Tilottama Rajan

Arthur Schopenhauer, *Die Welt als Wille und Vorstellung* (1818, rev. ed., 1844, *Sämtliche Werke,* vols. 2–3, ed. Arthur Hübscher, 1948–61, *The World as Will and Representation,* trans. E. F. J. Payne, 2 vols., 1969).

William Desmond, "Schopenhauer, Art, and the Dark Origin," *Schopenhauer: New Essays in Honor of His Two Hundredth Birthday* (ed. Erich von der Luft, 1988); Terry Eagleton, "The Death of Desire: Arthur Schopenhauer," *The Ideology of the Aesthetic* (1990); Israel Knox, *The Aesthetic Theories of Kant, Hegel, and Schopenhauer* (1958); Georg Lukács, "The Bourgeois Irrationalism of Schopenhauer's Metaphysics," *Schopenhauer: His Philosophical Achievement* (ed. Michael Fox, 1980); Alexis Philonenko, "Métaphysique du Beau," *Schopenhauer: Une Philosophie de la tragédie* (1980); Tilottama Rajan, "Schiller, Schopenhauer, and Nietzsche: The Theoretical Background," *Dark Interpreter: The Discourse of Romanticism* (1980); Julian Young, "Art," *Willing and Unwilling: A Study in the Philosophy of Arthur Schopenhauer* (1987).

SEMIOTICS

Semiotics can be defined broadly as a domain of investigation that explores the nature and function of signs as well as the systems and processes underlying signification, expression, representation, and communication. As can be demonstrated from numerous cultural traces (verbal, pictorial, plastic, spatial artifacts, etc.), the role of signs in human life has been an ongoing concern over the ages whenever questions have been asked about what constitutes signs and what laws govern them. As noted by John Deely *(Frontiers of Semiotics)* and Thomas Sebeok *(Contributions to the Doctrine of Signs, The Sign and Its Masters),* the history of investigation into the nature of signs is an important aspect in the history of philosophy in general, and contributions to the theory can be traced back to the Greeks—from Heraclitus to the Stoics, from PLATO to ARISTOTLE—to the Hellenistic and Roman periods; the early Christian thinkers and church fathers (e.g., ST. AUGUSTINE); medieval authors; humanists such as DANTE ALIGHIERI and philosophers such as FRANCIS BACON; seventeenth-, eighteenth-, nineteenth-, and early twentieth-century philosophers, grammarians, and scientists such as John Locke, Gottfried Wilhelm Leibniz, George Berkeley, Étienne Bonnot de Condillac, Antoine Louis Claude Destutt de Tracy, Jean François Champollion, and Edmund Husserl, to name but a few of the many important contributors to the doctrine of signs. The twentieth century has witnessed a revival of interest in the principles of sign systems and processes inherited from this long tradition of intellectual activity, mainly because of the pioneering work of FERDINAND DE SAUSSURE and CHARLES SANDERS PEIRCE, who are recognized as the founders of the modern European and Anglo-American traditions of semiotics. An overview of some of the main contributors to the history of semiotics is provided by Tzvetan Todorov *(Theories of the Symbol),* Thomas Sebeok *(Encyclopedic Dictionary of Semiotics),* and John Deely *(Introducing Semiotic).*

Literary semiotics can be seen as a branch of the general science of signs that studies a particular group of texts within verbal texts in general. Although the task of literary semiotics is to describe what is characteristic of literary texts or discourse, it is founded on the same principles and analytical procedures as the semiotics of verbal discourse. However, for two fundamental reasons, there exists no generally accepted definition of the scope and object of literary semiotics. First, the boundaries of literary discourse seem to have been established more by tradition than by objective, formal criteria. Contrary to other semiotic discourses, for example, legal discourse, literary discourse cannot be characterized by a specifically distinctive content. For instance, the literariness of a text (in the framework of the intrinsic structure of the text) varies according to culture and epoch; as Yuri Lotman and others have shown, a text identified as being religious in the Middle Ages is seen as literary today. Second, there is still a wide-ranging, continuing debate regarding the status of the verbal sign and the nature of the signifying process, as underscored in the entry "Sign" in Thomas Sebeok's *Encyclopedic Dictionary* (936–47). The fundamental differences between opposing semioticians are related mainly to whether they adopt an intentional, or meaning-oriented, description of a sign system or the codes correlating a given expression with a given content or a more extensional, truth-condition-oriented one that concentrates on the processes of communication by which signs are used to designate, to refer to "things or states of the real or of some possible world" (937).

To review even the major contributions to literary semiotics in the twentieth century is beyond the scope of this survey. However, Charles Morris, who drew his inspiration from Peirce, can provide us with a conceptual framework that makes it possible to situate various approaches that have furthered the development of the semiotics of literature in relationship to one another. Starting with the definition of "semiosis" as a process in which signs function as vehicles, interpretants, and interpreters, Morris determines three areas of comple-

mentary investigation: syntactics, which studies the relation of sign-vehicles within sign systems; semantics, the relation of signs to objects they represent; and pragmatics, the relation of signs to interpreters. Hence, if one considers literary texts in terms of semiosis, they can be defined as syncretic sign systems encompassing a syntactic dimension that can be analyzed on the phonological level (e.g., the specific sound patterns organizing the text) and on the level of narrative syntax; the semantic level (the content elements of the text); and the pragmatic or communicative context (addresser and addressee). In short, the first two dimensions stress the structural features of texts and are concerned with their expression and content forms, whereas the other dimension stresses the signifying process and concentrates on analyzing their generative processes and interrelations with other texts (Sebeok, *Encyclopedic* 453–54). Far from being exclusive, the different methodological approaches to each of these domains of investigation mapped out by Morris are complementary.

Contrary to Peirce, who adopted a philosophical and logical perspective to the study of signs and proposed a general theory of semiotics in which linguistic signs had an important but by no means essential role, Saussure worked out the foundations of a general linguistic theory in which he considered language as a system of signs. Linguistics was considered to be part of the general science of semiology, which he defined as "a *science that studies the life of signs within society. . . . It* would be part of social psychology and consequently of general psychology; I shall call it *semiology* (from the Greek *semeîon* 'sign'). Semiology would show what constitutes signs, what laws govern them" (16).

Although Saussure himself did not make major contributions to the semiotics of literature before his death in 1916, his writings were instrumental in the development of literary semiotics in Europe, especially with respect to the study of the syntactic and semantic dimensions of texts. Yuri Tynianov and ROMAN JAKOBSON openly acknowledge the impact Saussurean linguistics had on the theoretical work undertaken by the RUSSIAN FORMALISTS during the first three decades of the century: the heuristic value of the synchronic/diachronic opposition, of the notion of system, of the speech and language distinction.

> For linguistics as well as for literary history, the clear opposition between the synchronic (static) aspect and the diachronic aspect was a rich working hypothesis because it demonstrated the systematic character of language (or literature) at each particular period of life. . . . The establishment of two different notions—

parole and *langue*—and the analysis of their relation (the Geneva School) were extremely fruitful for linguistics. To apply these two categories (the existing norm and individual utterances) to literature and to study their relation, is a problem that must be examined in detail. ("Problems" 101–2)

In his major review of the Formalists' goals and accomplishments, Boris Eikhenbaum stressed the importance of theory in uncovering the systematic nature of literary facts and, in the words of Roman Jakobson in "On Realism in Art," of focusing not on literature but on "literariness," that is to say, on the pertinent features of literary texts that distinguish them from other discourse. Contemporary linguistic theory was used by the Formalists to compare spoken language with literary language and to consolidate the principle of specification. Victor Shklovsky (*Theory of Prose*) made great progress in analyzing the short story and the novel when he linked processes inherent to composition with general stylistic processes and related the variable and permanent aspects of the artistic form of a work with other works, thereby setting out the possibilities for a history of forms, one that still remains to be written. Other fundamental concepts, such as motivation, basically concerned with plot construction (circular construction; composition by steps, or the breaking down of action into episodes, frame, and the rhetorical procedures that are built into this; parallelism; enumeration; oxymoron), led to the distinction between elements in the construction of a work (subject) and those that make up its material (fable) and laid the groundwork for Vladimir Propp's discovery of function in the plot analysis of folktales, one of the most important innovations of the Russian Formalists. Recent Soviet semioticians, such as M. M. BAKHTIN, who wrote major works on Rabelais, Fyodor Dostoevsky, and the dialogical principles governing communication, were influential in extending the boundaries of literary semiotics and reorienting the domain from a more scientist bent to a semiotics of culture (Todorov).

Whether imported directly from America and Geneva or indirectly via Russia or Vienna, both Peirce's "semiotic" and Saussure's "semiology" were influential in the studies of the verbal arts undertaken by the members of the Prague Linguistic Circle, as demonstrated by Ladislav Matejka and Irwin R. Titunik in the preface to their anthology, *Semiotics of Art*. In his programmatic article "Art as Semiotic Fact" (1934), Jan Mukařovský established the semiotic framework for the study of art and suggested that the work of art should be considered as a sign composed of "(1) a perceivable signifier, created

by the artist, (2) a 'signification' /= aesthetic object/ registered in the collective consciousness and (3) a relationship with that which is signified, a relationship which refers to the total context of social phenomena" (Matejka and Titunik 6). Other critics, such as Petr Bogatyrev and Jiri Veltrusky (in Matejka and Titunik), made important advances in the study of visual semiotics as applied to folk art, songs, and theater. Theater as a medium is considered by these critics as transforming its constituent elements into a semiotic structure (visual signs, such as decor, costume, body, etc., and acoustic signs, such as voice, dialogue, music, etc.), and an attempt is made to lay bare the rules underlying these systems. In other essays in *Semiotics of Art*, Roman Jakobson ("What Is Poetry?") and Jan Mukařovský ("Poetic Reference") further the study of poetic language by investigating the problem of poetic reference from the point of view of internal reference and its oblique but essential relationship to the extralinguistic context. Jakobson concludes that art is an integral part of social structure and that although the "concept of the content of *poetry* is unstable and temporally conditioned . . . the poetic function, *poeticity* is an element sui generis, one that cannot be mechanically reduced to other elements" (174). (See PRAGUE SCHOOL STRUCTURALISM.)

French semiotics, which developed directly from Russian Formalism and Prague structuralism and arrived in Paris via New York thanks to Roman Jakobson's influence on CLAUDE LÉVI-STRAUSS during World War II, made a critical contribution to the study of literary texts during the mid-1960s. A special issue of *Communications*, edited by ROLAND BARTHES in 1966 and devoted to the structural analysis of narrative, contains articles by the leading European semioticians who had a profound impact on the future and evolution of literary semiotics. In his introduction, which owes a great deal to Louis Hjelmslev's rethinking and development of Saussure's concepts of sign, system, and process, Barthes ascertains that narrative analysis must be based on deductive procedures and must construct hypothetical models patterned on structural linguistics. He proposes a multilevel model of analysis in which each level is in a hierarchical relationship to the others and narrative elements have both distributional (if relations are situated at the same level) and integrative relationships (if situated at different levels). In turn, levels are defined as operations or systems of symbols and rules. Barthes then delimits three linked levels of description—"functions," "actions," and "narration"—in which a function has meaning only within the field of action of an actant, and action is meaningful only when narrated.

The other authors in this volume propose alternate and complementary solutions to some of the problems raised by Barthes. Claude Bremond's contribution, on the logic of narrative possibilities, is situated at the most abstract level and examines the logical constraints (sequences of functions) of the organized events of any narrative. Algirdas Julien Greimas's text focuses on the more anthropomorphic level of representation, actions, where primary logical functions take on meaning. These actants, or agents, are described in terms not of what they are but of what they do and by their participation in a limited number of classifiable spheres of action, inasmuch as they partake of three major semantic axes: communication, desire (quest), and test. Moreover, agents are arranged in pairs, and the large number of characters in a narrative is reduced to a structure (Subject/Object, Addresser/Addressee, Helper/Opponent) that is projected along the entire narrative. As an object of communication, narrative is dependent upon an Addresser (narrator) and Addressee (narratee), and formal marks of both narrator and narratee are considered as being immanent to the text (see Denis Bertrand in Perron and Collins and *Greimassian Semiotics* for a more up-to-date elaboration of Greimas's theory of narrativity). UMBERTO ECO's paper, which analyzes Ian Fleming's James Bond novels, deals with narrative combinatories, whereas Tzvetan Todorov, in his study of the categories of literary texts, proposes a more global and more integrated theory of narrative that not only takes into account functions and actions but also concentrates heavily on the level of narration. The volume closes with an important article by Gérard Genette on the boundaries of narrative that establishes distinctions between diegesis and mimesis, narration and description, and narrative and discourse and lays the groundwork for his influential work on the structure of time (i.e., the relation between the form of expression and the form of content of time) in Proust's *À la recherche du temps perdu.*

It is possible to trace two major tendencies in France that evolve from the intellectual activity of the mid-1960s. The first, founded on the Saussurean-Hjelmslevian legacy, best represented by work done by Greimas, has become known as the "Paris school" of semiotics. This school, which concentrates more on syntactic and semantic domains of the discipline, adopts an immanentist attitude to texts, as pointed out by Herman Parret in his introduction to *Paris School Semiotics* (Perron and Collins). Greimas's own monumental *Maupassant,* in which he examines a short story from the perspective of his theoretical transpositional model of signification,

whereby complex procedures of textual production are identified and thematic readings are linked up with semantic analysis, is the most exemplary of these studies. (See also Greimas's *On Meaning* for an overview of his semiotic theory.) In his two most recent books, *De l'imperfection* and *Sémiotique des passions,* the latter co-authored with Jacques Fontanille, Greimas, having in his prior works set in place a modal syntax, explores the possibility of constructing a discursive syntax based on aspectualities (states of a temporal process—inchoateness, duration, termination—that allow for the representation of temporality *as* process). This final stage, which builds on the actional and cognitive dimensions of analysis worked out from the 1960s to the 1980s, attempts to give a semiotic interpretation to traditional theories of passions. Greimas and Fontanille seek to establish a coherent methodology that articulates the relationship between semiotic theory and philosophy, and they also endeavor to rethink semiotic theory in general, founded on the actional and the cognitive, by introducing the concept of passion. The study of the passional dimension of numerous literary texts is accompanied by a disengagement with Peirce's semiotic and an engagement with phenomenology and catastrophe theory, notably as represented by Maurice Merleau-Ponty (proprioception) and René Thom (perception, saliency/ *pregnanz*).

The second tendency is represented by the large number of works that draw their inspiration from a radical questioning of the structural principles defining semiosis. JULIA KRISTEVA and especially Roland Barthes were instrumental in this respect. Indeed, the latter begins his study *S/Z* by challenging the very possibility of structural analysis to account for the specificity or individuality of any text. He then shifts the problematics from that of science and ideology to that of writing and rewriting, in short to a semiotics of addressers and addressees, of signs and interpreters. In so doing he also substitutes a semiotics of codes for a semiotics of signs and processes and, without structuring or hierarchizing them, determines five codes under which all the textual signifiers can be grouped: hermeneutic (enigma), semic, symbolic, proairetic (actions), and cultural (references to a science or body of knowledge).

In his innovative work, Umberto Eco attempts to overcome some of the dramatic oppositions that exist between the Saussurean (Hjelmslevian-Greimassian) and Peircean theories of semiosis, which originate from very different epistemological contexts and traditions (see Perron, "Introduction," in *Greimassian Semiotics*). In *The Role of the Reader,* Eco integrates the three domains of semiotics identified by Morris and works out an elaborate theory of the reader as an active principle of interpretation in the generative process of text. He begins with the hypothesis that an author must form a model of a possible reader and must also assume that the set of codes relied upon is shared by the reader. He rewrites the standard communication model (Addresser-Message-Addressee) to better take into account the semantic-pragmatic processes at work within texts and examines the various codes and subcodes in which a message is emitted and by which an author organizes and communicates a text to a reader. Eco introduces operative notions such as model reader and closed and open texts, and he integrates concepts dealing with discursive and narrative structures, topics, isotopies, textual levels, and intertextual competence into a general semiotic theory of narrative.

Robert Scholes, whose work deals with particular texts and ways in which they may be read and interpreted, does not concentrate on the syntactic or semantic dimension of narrative per se but adopts a semiotic approach based on the study of codes. He shows how the literary work, far from being a closed system "free of authorial intention, free of historical necessity, and free of the readers' projection of value and meaning" (15), as NEW CRITICISM would have us believe, is, on the contrary, an open text linked to history, to cultural, semantic, and literary codes, and to other texts. Other critics, for example, Terence Hawkes (*Structuralism and Semiotics*, 1977), Jonathan Culler (*Structuralist Poetics: Structuralism, Linguistics, and the Study of Literature*, 1975, and *The Pursuit of Signs: Semiotics, Literature, Deconstruction*, 1981), Terry Eagleton (*Literary Theory: An Introduction*, 1983), and FREDRIC JAMESON (*The Prison-House of Language: A Critical Account of Structuralism and Russian Formalism*, 1972), have offered both a critique and discussion on the limits of the semiotic project.

Semiotic theory has been refined and modified progressively through the investigation of various literary genres and specific domains. Paul Zumthor, Donald Maddox, and Eugene Vance, among others, have been instrumental in reshaping a "new kind of linguistically informed medievalism that is as much oriented toward studying the discursive consciousness of medieval intellectual life as it is toward the documentation of events" (Vance, "Chaucer's" 725). James Burke considers the authorship of *Cantar de Mio Cid*, one of the great works of Spanish literature, by examining its key structural components and shows that the text was produced in a manner typical for the Middle Ages by an author who followed procedures very specific to the period,

whereas Stephen Nimis has contributed to the study of narrative semiotics in the epic tradition from Homer to Milton.

Michael Riffaterre has played a central role in advancing poetic theory by integrating a theory of intertextuality with semiotic theory and by providing a flexible definition of the notion of intertext. He begins by defining the semiotic process within the context of the reader and the act of reading and then distinguishes two levels or stages of reading: "heuristic reading," where meaning is apprehended and the reader's competence comes into play, followed by "retroactive reading," whereby the reader performs a structural decoding as a variant of the same structural matrix. Riffaterre defines and makes operational notions such as matrix, the minimal and literal sentence transformed into a longer, complex, and nonliteral periphrasis that results in the poem; model, the form of the variants actualized; descriptive systems, networks of words associated with one another around a kernel work; clichés, set phrases actualizing the semes of a matrix or of a descriptive system; and hypograms, formed out of a word's semes and/or presuppositions.

Numerous monographs and articles have been published on the semiotics of the theater and the novel. Anne Ubersfeld, Thomas Pavel, Keir Elam, Mark Kobernick, Patrice Pavis, Fernando de Toro, Jean Alter, Marvin Carlson, and André Helbo and his collaborators have written pioneering and seminal works on the semiotics of drama. While recognizing that a semiotics of theater must consider all aspects of dramatic discourse as parts of a signifying whole, Ubersfeld concentrates on the text itself and studies the relationships between its two distinct but inseparable parts, "dialogue" and "didascalia" (stage and production directions). Pavel proposes an original theory and methodology of plot analysis drawn from literary structuralism and generative grammar and applies his model to a group of English Renaissance tragedies. De Toro ("Toward a Specification") attempts to give a comprehensive and systematic approach to theater discourse that links its various components. He examines the process of communication-reception—in binaries such as enunciative situation and utterance, deixis and anaphora, the functions of theater language and actors' discourse—in order to furnish us with a base on which to establish the specificity of discourse at the linguistic level. Elam's work, the first full-length study of theater semiotics in English, provides both an exhaustive survey of all that has been done in the field beforehand and a personal theory of theater semiotics, illustrated by analysis of texts from classical (*Hamlet*) to modern drama *(Endgame),* whereas Kobernick undertakes a detailed study of the semiotics of drama and the style of Eugene O'Neill.

A second wave of critics, more interactive and contextual, examines theater from the point of view of performance, the sociosemiotic dimension, theater structures, and audience improvisation. Patrice Pavis goes beyond the first wave of theater semiology, which aspired to global coverage and "scientific" rigor, and concentrates on various aspects of semiological theory and stage practice—gesture, body language, reception, the discourse of drama criticism, systems of notation of theatrical performance—before concluding with the semiological analysis of two avant-garde theatrical performances. In another study, de Toro ("Toward a Socio-Semiotics") attempts to link the semiotic approach to theater to a possible sociosemiotics; that is, he tries to connect two theoretical and epistemological levels of the theater phenomenon, the formal and the contextual. He explores three major areas where semiotics and sociology could come together: the tasks of the sociosemiotics of the theater, the dramatic/performance text, and the process of reception in the theater. Alter's work tackles the sociosemiotic dimension of theater from a different point of view. He proposes to begin entirely anew by reexamining the basic notions about theater and semiotics, elucidating their problematic concepts, and proposing a new theory that would not give in to prevailing opinion. Working within the Saussurean framework that postulated the need to define the function of signs within a social context, Alter examines a number of plays and performances from various perspectives—reference and performance, a grammar of theater referentiality, transformational processes (production/reception and playwrights, directors, actors and their works). In so doing he reviews most of the current literature in the area in an attempt to give his theory an anthropological foundation. Carlson also examines a representative number of plays from a sociosemiotic perspective by analyzing the way theatrical signs are produced and the ways they are received and interpreted by an audience. First he studies how audiences develop interpretative strategies from sources both within and outside the production system itself, then he focuses on the semiotics of space and its relationship to interpretation of the theater event, and finally he deals with the creative contribution of the audience. In brief, this work envisions the theater not only as a signifying textual system but also as a much vaster phenomenon inscribed in a physical surrounding and a society that maintains a permanent relationship with an

audience. A final collaborative work by Helbo and his collaborators analyzes the theatrical event and the numerous elements that make up a performance—text, actor, space, spectator, social circumstances—from a variety of directions and using different methodologies, but mainly semiotic analysis. The seven sections of this work provide an overview of current theory as well as new tools for analyzing performances.

A great deal has been written on the semiotics of the novel, but much of it has concentrated on synchronic semiotic structures, for example, Claude Bremond *(Logique du récit),* who studies the logic of possibilities; Seymour Chatman *(Story and Discourse: Narrative Structure in Fiction and Film,* 1978); Roland Le Huenen and Paul Perron, who examine in detail the semiotics of character in Honoré de Balzac's *Eugénie Grandet;* and Shlomith Rimmon-Kenan, who gives an overview of narrative structures. Little has been written on the diachronic structuration and the dialectical process of production of narrative texts, and Wladimir Krysinski seeks to fill this void. In his work, theory and practice confront and sustain one another in an attempt to understand the novel as a historically motivated semiotic process. Not only does Krysinski attempt to work out a general semiotic theory, but his analysis also focuses on modern texts by writers from Dostoevsky to Roa Bastos, including HENRY JAMES, André Gide, Thomas Mann, John Dos Passos, Claude Simon, and Hubert Aquin.

Recent theoretical work by Teresa De Lauretis and Kaja Silverman makes important contributions to the semiotic analysis of texts, especially of film texts. De Lauretis problematizes the earlier structural models that consider desire as a type of thematic investment and reexamines the relations of narratives to genres and to epistemological frameworks. She shows how the productivity of the text engages the reader as subject in, and for, its process and places the reader in certain positions of plot space. Narrative is considered as obeying an Oedipal logic that constrains and defines each reader within the position of a sexual difference conceived as follows: male-hero-human on the side of the subject, and female-obstacle-boundary-space on the other side. The critique of poststructuralist semiotics is furthered by Silverman, who maintains the centrality of psychoanalysis to semiotics and also emphasizes "sexual difference as an organizing principle not only of the symbolic order and its 'contents' (signification, discourse, subjectivity), but of the semiotic account of those things" (viii). Both of these important studies extend the theoretical boundaries of literary semiotics into a domain of sociosemiotics and contribute to the redefinition of an important area of CULTURAL STUDIES focusing on current feminist theory and practice.

A number of studies attempt to focus and refocus semiotics on the literary work in general and its apprehension through the reading process. Literary semiotics is currently exploring two major areas of investigation, the first related to working out a semiotic theory of reading and the second examining the mediating function of the literary sign between symbolic forms and the materiality of the world. Although these two areas deal with what Charles Morris identified as the pragmatic dimension of semiosis, or the relation of signs to their interpreters, both build on prior theoretical work carried out by numerous semioticians in syntactics and semantics. Under the impetus of PAUL RICOEUR's *Time and Narrative (I, II, III)* and relying on a multidisciplinary approach, Bertrand Gervais focuses on the activity of reading, or what he calls the "reading contract." Gervais studies the structural features of the conceptual network of actions, their reception from the theoretical perspective of semiotics, the logic of actions, artificial intelligence, and the cognitive sciences. By isolating the discursive representation of action and considering it as a nodal component both of the narrative and of reading, and hence by instituting a cognitive level of reading, Gervais frees semiotic theory and analysis from the narrow confines of the structuralist and poststructuralist paradigm, opening up a very promising area of further inquiry.

If a major school of semiotics represented by Greimas and his collaborators seems to be disengaging its work from Peirce and embracing phenomenology and catastrophe theory, numerous other semioticians are reexamining Peircean theory and demonstrating its heuristic value in the study of literary texts. Julio C. M. Pinto's semantico-semiotic approach to the reading of time is also an attempt to develop an approach that goes beyond structuralism, which concentrated on how time was organized in a text. Pinto sets out to study the reader's behavior with respect to temporal relations and to explain reading strategies within semantic and semiotic theory. He adapts Peirce's categories of Firstness, Secondness, and Thirdness, and he equates them with perception, apprehension, and interpretation of the reading process before applying the model to the study of a play by Harold Pinter and a novel by Lêdo Ivo.

Michael Cabot Haley, in his study of the semiosis of poetic metaphor, examines the trope in light of Peirce's definitions of the sign. He deals successively with metaphor as symbol, index, and icon; metaphor as image, diagram, and metaicon; metaphor as firstness; Peircean hypoicons in poetry; the Peircean index in poetic metaphor; the index of figural displacement; and metaphoric semantic growth. John Sheriff proposes, first, a radical critique of semiotic studies stemming from Saussurean or structuralist theory that describe a literary work only as a closed formal network (Morris's syntactics and semantics), thereby negating its signification, that is, negating the relation of the text to its interpreters, to being and possibility. Second, Sheriff reexamines Peirce's triadic theory of signs and studies what he considers to be the three aspects of a literary text: the text not actualized through the act of reading is seen as a virtual signifier, corresponding to Peirce's eighth category of legisigns (rheme); the act of reading actualizes meaning by giving an interpretation related to the lived experience, and here the text corresponds to the ninth category of legisigns (dicisign); and the text as sign of autorepresentation, the most abstract level, corresponds to the tenth category (argument).

Most of the semioticians currently working in the Peircean paradigm to some degree or other adhere to Sheriff's critique of the limits of Saussurean- or structuralist-inspired semiotic theory and support the need, through the dynamics of semiosis, to open up the study of text onto the social environment. As Jean Fisette notes, these works, which raise important epistemological questions about the concept of texts, their mode of existence in a given culture, and also their contribution to the issue of symbolic productions in general, could herald a "renewal of studies in literary semiotics which, this time, would be free of all the canons inherited from structuralism" (184).

Paul Perron

See also ROLAND BARTHES, UMBERTO ECO, JULIA KRISTEVA, NARRATOLOGY, CHARLES SANDERS PEIRCE, PRAGUE SCHOOL STRUCTURALISM, RUSSIAN FORMALISM, FERDINAND DE SAUSSURE, and STRUCTURALISM.

See bibliographies in M. M. BAKHTIN, ROLAND BARTHES, UMBERTO ECO, FREDRIC JAMESON, JULIA KRISTEVA, PAUL RICOEUR, RUSSIAN FORMALISM, and FERDINAND DE SAUSSURE for texts on those writers and topics.

Jean Alter, *A Sociosemiotic Theory of Theatre* (1990); Roland Barthes, ed., *Communications* 8 (1966, special issue on structural analysis of narrative); Claude Bremond, *Logique du récit* (1973); James Burke, *Structures from the Trivium in the "Cantar de Mio Cid"* (1991); Marvin Carlson, *Theatre Semiotics: Signs of Life* (1990); John Deely, *Introducing Semiotic: Its History and Doctrine* (1982); John

Deely et al., eds., *Frontiers in Semiotics* (1986); Teresa de Lauretis, *Alice Doesn't: Feminism, Semiotics, Cinema* (1984); Fernando de Toro, "Toward a Socio-Semiotics of the Theatre," *Semiotica* 72 (1988), "Toward a Specification of Theatre Discourse," *Versus* 54 (1989); Keir Elam, *The Semiotics of Theatre and Drama* (1980); Jean Fisette, "Compte rendu," *RS/SI (Canadian Journal of Semiotics)* 11 (1991); Bertrand Gervais, *Récits et actions: Pour une théorie de la lecture* (1990); Algirdas Julien Greimas, *De l'imperfection* (1987), *Maupassant: La Sémiotique du texte* (1976, *Maupassant: The Semiotics of Text*, trans. Paul J. Perron, 1988), *On Meaning: Selected Writings in Semiotic Theory* (trans. Paul J. Perron and Frank H. Collins, 1987); Algirdas Julien Greimas and Jacques Fontanille, *Sémiotique des passions* (1991, *The Semiotics of Passions,* trans. Paul J. Perron and Frank H. Collins, 1992); *Greimassian Semiotics,* special issue, *New Literary History* 20 (1989); Michael Cabot Haley, *The Semiosis of Poetic Metaphor* (1988); André Helbo et al., *Approaching Theatre* (1991); Roman Jakobson, "On Realism in Art" (1921, *Readings in Russian Poetics: Formalist and Structuralist Views,* ed. Ladislav Matejka and Krystyna Pomorska, 1962); Mark Kobernick, *Semiotics of the Drama and the Style of Eugene O'Neill* (1989); Wladimir Krysinski, *Carrefours de signes: Essais sur le roman moderne* (1981); Roland Le Huenen and Paul Perron, *Balzac. Sémiotique du personnage romanesque: L'Exemple d' "Eugénie Grandet"* (1980); Donald Maddox, *The Semiotics of Deceit: The Pathelin Era* (1984), "Veridiction, Verification, Verifactions: Reflections on Methodology," *New Literary History* 20 (1989); Ladislav Matejka and Irwin R. Titunik, eds., *Semiotics of Art: Prague School Contributions* (1976); Charles Morris, "Foundations of the Theory of Signs," *Foundations of the Unity of Science* 1 (1938); Stephen Nimis, *Narrative Semiotics in the Epic Tradition: The Simile* (1987); Thomas Pavel, *The Poetics of Plot: The Case of English Renaissance Drama* (1985); Patrice Pavis, *Languages of the Stage: Essays in the Semiology of the Theatre* (1982); Paul J. Perron and Frank H. Collins, eds., *Paris School Semiotics* (2 vols.: vol. 1, *Theory,* 1988; vol. 2, *Practice,* 1989); Julio C. M. Pinto, *The Reading of Time: A Semantico-Semiotic Approach* (1988); Michael Riffaterre, *Semiotics of Poetry* (1978); Shlomith Rimmon-Kenan, *Narrative Fiction: Contemporary Poetics* (1983); Robert Scholes, *Semiotics and Interpretation* (1982); Thomas Sebeok, *Contributions to the Doctrine of Signs* (1976), *The Sign and Its Masters* (1979); Thomas Sebeok, ed., *Encyclopedic Dictionary of Semiotics* (3 vols., 1986); John Sheriff, *The Fate of Meaning: Charles Peirce, Structuralism, and Literature* (1989); Kaja Silverman, *The Subject of Semiotics* (1983); Tzvetan Todorov, *Mikhail Bakhtine: Le Principe dialogique* (1981, *Mikhail Bakhtin: The Dialogical Principle,* trans. Wlad Godzich,

1984), *Théories du symbole* (1977, *Theories of the Symbol,* trans. Catherine Porter, 1982); Yuri Tynianov and Roman Jakobson, "Problems in the Study of Literature and Language" (1928, *Readings in Russian Poetics: Formalist and Structuralist Views,* ed. Lasislav Matejka and Krystyna Pomorska, 1962); Anne Ubersfeld, *Lire le théâtre* (1978); Eugene Vance, "Chaucer's Pardoner, Relics, Discourse and Frames of Propriety," *New Literary History* 20 (1989), *Mervelous Signals: Poetics and Sign Theory in the Middle Ages* (1986); Paul Zumthor, *Essai de poétique médiévale* (1972).

SHELLEY, PERCY BYSSHE

While Percy Bysshe Shelley's (1792–1822) theoretical reflections on literature are metaphorically and unsystematically set forth in his *Defence of Poetry* (1821), written to defend poetry against Thomas Love Peacock's attack in *The Four Ages of Poetry* (1820), many of his major visionary poems also metaphorically thematize these reflections. The distinction, that is, between the poetry and the prose defense, is tenuous, HAROLD BLOOM going so far as to argue that the *Defence* "is more a visionary poem about poetry than it is a reasoned argument" (206). Bloom, however, may be misreading Shelley's distinction in the first paragraph of his *Defence* between "those two classes of mental action, which are called reason and imagination" (480). Both classes, for Shelley, are grounded in metaphor understood as "the relations borne by one thought to another, however produced." Reason, he argues, "may be considered as mind contemplating the relations," and imagination as mind coloring them "with its own light" so as to compose from them "as from elements, other thoughts" (480). Imagination, then, creates new metaphors or "other thoughts," which reason continues as "relations" to contemplate. Imagination does not, therefore, abandon reason in its discovery of what Shelley calls "before unapprehended relations of things" (482). On the contrary, it offers them to reason for its contemplation in order that their apprehension may be absorbed and perpetuated. Once absorbed and perpetuated, however, these relations tend to become canonized, fixed, and dead, so that if no new poets arise to liberate what has become fixed through contemplative absorption, poetry loses its capacity to redeem from decay what Shelley calls "the visitations of the divinity in man" (505). And here again, Shelley's notion of "visitations," of poetry acting "in a divine and unapprehended manner, beyond and above consciousness" (486), must not be understood as a flight from reason in a state of divine madness such as PLATO ironically describes with reference to the Bacchantes in the frenzy of the sacred dance in *Ion*. The intuition of what is "before unapprehended" is in poetry apprehended, which is to say, comprehended by the reason to extend thereby, rather than abrogate or abandon, the range of human consciousness. Precisely because acts of imagination are directly amenable to reasoned contemplation, poets are for Shelley "the unacknowledged legislators of the world" (508). What was "before unapprehended" in being apprehended has the power, as Shelley put it in "Mont Blanc," "to repeal / Large codes of fraud and woe" (91). "Mont Blanc" thus thematizes Shelley's view of poetry by rationally contemplating the action of the imagination that it directly presents.

While directing the reader's attention in his *Defence* to the manner in which reason necessarily mediates the action of the imagination in order to fulfill poetry's social function, upon which Shelley insists, he is equally insistent, as he writes in the preface to *Prometheus Unbound*, that "didactic poetry is my abhorrence" (135). And the cause is clear: "Until the mind can love, and admire, and trust, and hope, and endure, reasoned principles of moral conduct are seeds cast upon the highway of life which the unconscious passenger tramples into dust, although they would bear the harvest of his happiness" (135). Here "reasoned principles" are related to the "unconscious," while poetry itself is related to consciousness. Unless, then, we can "imagine that which we know"—what Shelley calls the "poetry of life"—we, as "unconscious passengers," trample upon "reasoned principles," because there is no creative, nonsystematic treatment of them that alone can awaken "the generous impulse to act" (502).

Because Shelley, unlike Peacock, affirms the interdependent rather than divided nature of the poet's "mental action," the poet's Promethean ascent "to bring light and fire from those eternal regions where the owl-winged faculty of calculation dare not ever soar" (503) remains answerable, as it does in Shelley's lyrical drama, to the demands of social and political reform. The measure of transcendence is the efficacy of its imminence. Only when the soul clasps "the pendulous Earth" can the "spirit's light" dart "Beyond all world's, until its spacious might / Satiate the void circumference," as Shelley puts it in *Adonais* (404). This dangerous acrobatic aerial act again metaphorically thematizes Shelley's view of poetry as paradoxically earthbound, the transcendental strategically serving to liberate the poem from the historical confines of the spatiotemporal accidents of its composition.

Arguing a binary opposition between imagination and reason, the one characterizing the child, the other characterizing the mature adult, Peacock satirically declares that it is absurd for "the maturity of mind to make a serious business of the playthings of childhood" (18). Without rejecting the association of the poet with childhood and play, Shelley in his *Defence,* following in the footsteps of SIR PHILIP SIDNEY, advances a very different notion of both. Because Sidney in his *Defence of Poetry* (1595) set out, as Shelley did, to defend a poetry that had fallen "from almost the highest estimation of learning . . . to be the laughing-stock of children" (74), Shelley found in Sidney's essay a chief support for his own argument. Shelley's *Defence* may therefore be partially described as an intertextual reading of Sidney's essay, just as that reading is in turn influenced by the accounts of childhood and play in JEAN-JACQUES ROUSSEAU and WILLIAM WORDSWORTH. Thus, Shelley's largely metaphorical approach carries within the metaphors themselves a carefully reasoned understanding of the origin and nature of language itself as it relates to thoughts alone. "For language," he writes, "is arbitrarily produced by the imagination and has relations to thoughts alone" (483).

"A child at play by itself," Shelley writes, "will express its delight by its voice and motions; and every inflexion of tone and every gesture will bear exact relation to a corresponding antitype in the pleasurable impressions which awakened it" (480). By internalizing the external world in this manner to construct what he calls a "vitally metaphorical" (482) enactment of it, the child at play unconsciously lays the foundation for all human progress, poetry becoming in Sidney's words "the first lightgiver to ignorance, and first nurse, whose milk by little and little enabled [the learned] to feed afterwards of tougher knowledges" (74). Beginning in "the infancy of art" (481), poetry for Shelley is propelled by an increasingly refined vision of a cosmic dance binding humanity and nature together in a single community of life. He thus postulates a single "great poem, which all poets, like the cooperating thoughts of one great mind, have built up since the beginning of the world" (493).

The poet's task is to prevent this "great poem" from hardening into a fixed system of belief. Drawing upon Sidney, Shelley argues that the poet creates by "feigning"; the poet is, Sidney says, like the child, free to play, "freely ranging only in the zodiac of his own wit" (78). By substituting a phenomenological approach focusing upon process for a metaphysical or religious system focusing upon product, Shelley argues that the poetic imagination restores language to its origins in metaphor by perceiving the "before unapprehended relations of things and perpetuat[ing the] apprehension" (482). The imagination, working with metaphors, prevents vision from hardening into a fixed system of belief. Shaping ever-new relationships, it dissolves whatever becomes fixed into "before unapprehended" combinations of thoughts. Shelley thus reaffirms in a radical manner Sidney's conviction that the poet who creates by "feigning" (a word Shelley uses with reference to DANTE ALIGHIERI) "nothing affirms" (Sidney 102) in a religious or metaphysical sense. Feigning as the action proper to the imagination (Sidney's "wit"), with its connotations of play, constellates a romance world of gratified desire grounded in "poetic faith," which, so long as it remains uncodified, has a redemptive or transformative power. SAMUEL TAYLOR COLERIDGE's "willing suspension of disbelief for the moment" (*Biographia Literaria,* ed. James Engell and W. Jackson Bate, 2 vols., 1983, 2:6) is thus for the deliberately nonsystematic and skeptical Shelley the creative aspect of "awful doubt," which, paradoxically, is at the same time a "faith so mild" (91). Thus, Shelley's faith resides in the creative power of doubt.

Shelley intended to write a second part to his *Defence,* applying the principles enunciated in the first to what he calls "the present state of the cultivation of Poetry, and a defence of the attempt to idealize the modern forms of manners and opinion, and compel them into a subordination to the imaginative and creative faculty" (507). He wrote instead *Adonais,* an elegy on the death of Keats, in which he thematizes his understanding of the power of poetry to mediate between transcendence and imminence by means of "interpenetration" (504). In addition, however, by describing Keats in *Adonais* as the "nursling" of Urania's "widowhood," her "youngest, dearest one," sired in *Hyperion* by Milton (393), Shelley, having abandoned the second part of his *Defence,* begins to come to terms with what he increasingly recognized to be the fate of Romanticism itself: a potentiality robbed of its realization. By 1821 Shelley was at least half-persuaded that his fellow Romantics, like Keats, had "died on the promise of the fruit" (393). Far from compelling "the modern forms of manners and opinion" into "a subordination to the imaginative and creative faculty," they had become reconciled to those manners and opinion to repeat the "feeble" catastrophe of the reconciliation of Prometheus and Jupiter in Aeschylus's lost drama, which Shelley in *Prometheus Unbound* rejected. They had betrayed their prophetic function as "the *unacknowledged* legislators of the World" (508, emphasis added). The Promethean Wordsworth who stood for Shelley as "a rock-built refuge . . . / Above the blind and battling

multitude" weaving "Songs consecrate to truth and liberty" had in *The Excursion* (1814) "cease[d] to be" (88). The claims made for his contemporaries on a theoretical level Shelley could not in practice support. Thus in some larger context than the one the poem in and of itself provides, *Adonais* becomes an elegy on the death of that version of Romanticism that ascribes to the imagination the power directly to reform the world, as distinct from a power that keeps the desire to reform alive.

Shelley, as a consequence, had some difficulty arriving at the right tone for his deliberately unsystematic and undogmatic *Defence*. He was by no means immune to the thrust of Peacock's satirical attack and was tempted in his reply to view himself in his defense as a Don Quixote striking at windmills, preferring that metaphor of himself as a poet to the more solemn and superstitious one of a priest, which the first generation of Romantic poets in his view came more and more to assume. "At the same time," he wrote to Peacock on February 15, 1821, after receiving a copy of *The Four Ages of Poetry* (agreeing with Peacock's criticism of particular poems),

> your anathemas against poetry itself excited me to a sacred rage, or *caloëthes scribendi* of vindicating the insulted Muses. I had the greatest possible desire to break a lance with you, within the lists of a magazine, in honour of my mistress Urania; but . . . an easy conquest would have remained to you in me, the knight of the shield of shadow and the lance of gossamere. (*Letters* 2:261)

Shelley's account of his fragile armor is written not only in the spirit of Peacock's mocking attack but equally in the ironic spirit of Plato's *Ion* (which Shelley translated), a dialogue in which poets such as Homer are described as divinely possessed and, like the Bacchantes in the frenzy of the sacred dance, drawing honey and milk from the rivers only to discover when they return to their senses that it is simple water. "Besides, I was at the moment reading Plato's 'Ion,' which I recommend you to reconsider," he tells Peacock (261). In inviting him to reconsider it as a way of reading his *Defence,* Shelley is, again as in the *Defence* and in his poetry, inviting Peacock to rationally consider the meaning of Plato's metaphors as the agents not of transcendence but of a social and political reform that the systematic (as opposed to poetic) Plato rejected as a threat to the stability of his ideal city- state.

Crucial, therefore, to an understanding of Shelley's critical, sometimes ironic, reflections is his phenomenological understanding of the "mind in creation" (503–4), for which he was unable to provide—nor did he wish to provide—any critically objective account. He remained persuaded, as he wrote in *Prometheus Unbound,* that the "Abysm" cannot "vomit forth its secrets" (175). Human beings are limited to their own fictions, to their metaphorical inventions of themselves. These fictions are not "pavilioned" upon any certain metaphysical or scientific foundation; they are, rather, as he wrote in *Hellas,* "pavilioned upon chaos" (431). They are "spells" wrought, as he put it in "Ode to the West Wind," by the "incantation of . . . verse" (223).

The danger for Shelley, as later for FRIEDRICH NIETZSCHE, was the conversion of these spells into false metaphysical systems that become, as in Christianity, binding or canonical. By virtue of its perpetual recreation of itself, poetry as "that great poem" is forever new because it is forever in the process of being written, just as Dante is being rewritten in Shelley's *Epipsychidion* and Milton is being rewritten in *Prometheus Unbound.* By maintaining the vitality of metaphor through the endless discovery of "before unapprehended relations," succeeding poets prevent the works of earlier poets from collapsing into what WILLIAM BLAKE calls in the *Marriage of Heaven and Hell* "forms of worship" (38). The danger of moral reformers' copying the "sketches" of poets (as opposed to the finished creation, which cannot be copied) into "the book of common life" lay in the hardening of those creations in the public mind into what JACQUES DERRIDA calls "white mythology." "Metaphysics," Derrida writes, "has erased within itself the fabulous scene that has produced it, the scene that nevertheless remains, active and stirring, inscribed in white ink, an invisible design covered over in the palimpsest" (*Marges de la philosophie,* 1972, *Margins of Philosophy,* trans. Alan Bass, 1982, 213). The poet's task, Shelley argues, is to recover what "nevertheless remains, active and stirring, inscribed in white ink," which is to say, what is active and stirring in what is otherwise "imageless" (175).

Shelley's mobilized reflections on poetry, like the poetry in which they are brilliantly thematized, engage a terrifying "Abyss" the "secrets" of which remain to his skeptical frame of mind forever sealed. Poetry thus becomes for him a form of magic, which he images in *Alastor* as the dream

> Of dark magician in his visioned cave,
> Raking the cinders of a crucible
> For life and power, even when his feeble hand
> Shakes in its last decay.
> (*Shelley's Poetry and Prose* 86)

This same thematizing metaphor is present in *Adonais,* where Shelley describes his "weak hand" holding the thyrsus, which vibrates under the influence of his "ever-

beating heart" (400). It is also present in his identification of poetry in his *Defence* with a "secret alchemy" that "turns to potable gold the poisonous waters which flow from death through life" (505). The "more select classes of poetical readers" (135), whom Shelley would initiate into the art of alchemy, have, in his speculative account, no illusions about the nature of metaphor. They know themselves, as Shelley himself warns in his preface to *Alastor,* to be momentarily "deluded" by "a generous error," "duped" by an "illustrious superstition" (69). In the absence of anything more certain, they also know that human civilization is precariously founded upon illusion, or maya (a notion encountered by Shelley in his study of the Hindu zodiac, described in his notes to *Queen Mab*). That illusion is the vitality of metaphor endlessly inventing new relationships, the stability of which forever threatens its vitality.

Metaphors, then, must not be allowed to incarnate in the manner decreed by Shelley's Jupiter. When and if this happens, poetry as the instrument of freedom becomes the means of tyranny. Poetry for Shelley is not a substitute for religion; it is the restoration of religion to its source in the "mind in creation." Abstracted from its own activity through loss of contact with itself, the human mind becomes a demonic parody of itself: the tyrannical mind of a nonexistent God. Against that tyranny, which Blake calls "Priesthood" (38), Shelley wrote his defense of poetry as a defense of freedom itself. His defense of poetry is in essence a defense of perpetual metamorphosis, which, translated into social and political terms, becomes a defense of perpetual revolution against the hardening and tyrannical influence of man's institutional life.

Because of its emphasis upon metaphoricity as opposed to system or dogma, Shelley's *Defence of Poetry,* as Tilottama Rajan writes, "contains so many voices its theoretical position is no where embodied in it" (296). The very nature of Shelley's defense rejects the very notion of system. Because mobility rather than stability characterizes for Shelley the life of poetry, his *Defence* may perhaps best be read and metaphorically understood in terms of Shelley's own carefully considered, rationally responsible metaphor of poetry as "a sword of lightning, ever unsheathed, which consumes the scabbard that would contain it" (491). Shelley in his *Defence,* as in the thematizing consciousness ceaselessly at work in his major poems, is careful not to construct a "scabbard" or theoretical container for a poetry that must, as "a sword of lightning," remain "ever unsheathed."

Ross G. Woodman

See also BRITISH THEORY AND CRITICISM: 3. RO-
MANTIC PERIOD AND EARLY NINETEENTH CENTURY
and SIR PHILIP SIDNEY.

Percy Bysshe Shelley, *Letters* (ed. Frederick L. Jones,
2 vols., 1964), *Shelley's Poetry and Prose* (ed. Donald H.
Reiman and Sharon B. Powers, 1977).

M. H. Abrams, *The Mirror and the Lamp: Romantic
Theory and the Critical Tradition* (1958), *Natural Supernaturalism: Tradition and Revolution in Romantic Literature* (1971); William Blake, *The Complete Poetry and Prose
of William Blake* (ed. David Erdman, rev. ed., 1982);
G. Kim Blank, ed., *The New Shelley: Later Twentieth-Century Views* (1991); Harold Bloom, *Shelley's Mythmaking*
(1959); James Engell, *The Creative Imagination: Enlightenment to Romanticism* (1981); Paul Fry, *The Reach of Criticism:
Method and Perception in Literary Theory* (1983); Jerrold E.
Hogle, *Shelley's Process: Radical Transference and the Development of His Major Works* (1988); Thomas Love Peacock, *The Four Ages of Poetry* (ed. John E. Jordan, 1965);
C. E. Pulos, *The Deep Truth: A Study of Shelley's Scepticism*
(1954); Tilottama Rajan, *The Supplement of Reading: Figures of Understanding in Romantic Theory and Practice*
(1990); Earl J. Schulze, *Shelley's Theory of Poetry* (1966); Sir
Philip Sidney, *Miscellaneous Prose of Sir Philip Sidney* (ed.
Katherine Duncan-Jones and Jan Van Dorsten, 1973); Earl
R. Wasserman, *Shelley: A Critical Reading* (1971); Ross G.
Woodman, *The Apocalyptic Vision in the Poetry of Shelley*
(1964), "Nietzsche, Blake, Keats, and Shelley: The Making
of a Metaphorical Body," *Studies in Romanticism* 29 (1990);
John Wright, *Shelley's Myth of Metaphor* (1970).

SIDNEY, SIR PHILIP

Sir Philip Sidney (1554–86) was the first in a line of English
poet-critics, and although his poetic writings (*Astrophil
and Stella* and the *Arcadia*) exhibit a reflexivity about
both the craft and function of poetry, his importance to
the history of literary theory rests on a single work, the
Apology for Poetry. Written early in the 1580s and published simultaneously in two slightly different posthumous editions of 1595 (*The Defence of Poesie* and *An Apology
for Poetry*), Sidney's *Defence* provides a brilliant synthesis
of classical and Renaissance poetic theory. It is notable
for its harmonious eclecticism, for it exhibits the influence of PLATO, ARISTOTLE, and HORACE, received both
directly and through the mediation of such Italian Renaissance critics as Antonio Sebastiano Minturno, Lodovico
Castelvetro, and Julius Caesar Scaliger. While the *Defence*
has traditionally and condescendingly been seen as an
elegant but derivative work, recent analyses have per-

suasively revealed the political and theoretical issues at
stake (Ferguson) and the subtle rhetorical dimensions
that project an authorial persona and—in an anticipation of modern reader-response theory—engage the
response of its audience (Barnes).

Sidney came from an aristocratic family and was
closely associated with the Elizabethan court through
his relationship to his uncle, Robert Dudley, earl of
Leicester. As befitted a man of his rank, Sidney received a
humanist education, both in England, where he studied
at Oxford, and on the Continent, where he spent three
years, perfecting his considerable skill in foreign languages and increasing his knowledge of culture and politics. The humanism in which he was schooled entailed
a strong emphasis on and imitation of classical texts, a
revived recognition of the importance of rhetoric, and a
belief that literature could teach a faculty of judgment
that would in turn be exemplified by virtuous behavior.
Where philosophy and rhetoric had traditionally been
antagonistic, in the Renaissance wisdom or truth was
seen as demanding exemplification and as manifested
in the complexity of experience rather than as abstract
concepts. Eloquence and wisdom thus were no longer
mutually exclusive but rather supportive; rhetoric was
not just ornamental of philosophy, as it had been, but
constitutive of it. These humanistic precepts determined
the language and structure of Sidney's defense, as well as
the impact the *Defence* was to have on subsequent theories of literature, since its linkage of the rhetorical with
the civic virtue of prudence produced a legacy that valued praxis (evident in action) over gnosis (abstract knowledge). Yet while Sidney sought the authority and prestige
that rhetoric could give, he distinguished poetry as having a freedom and inventiveness that was not characteristic of rhetoric.

It is still the subject of scholarly debate whether the
Defence was provoked by Stephen Gosson's 1579 puritan-
ical attack on poets, *The School of Abuse,* which was dedicated to Sidney. In fact, Sidney agreed with some of
Gosson's points, and he did not defend Gosson's main
target, the stage. Nevertheless, Gosson's diatribe was
symptomatic of a general antipathy to poetry and indicative of the need for a theoretical defense that would
justify it. Such a treatise did not exist in English; the
writings on poetry consisted mainly of guides to rhetoric, such as Thomas Wilson's *Arte of Rhetorique* (1553),
or classifications of genre, verse forms, and rhetorical
figures, such as George Puttenham's *Arte of English Poesie*
(1589), although a utilitarian defense of poetry is presented in Thomas Elyot's *Boke of the Governour* (1530).
Sidney's *Defence* furnished England with its first philo-

sophical defense; in it, he describes poetry's ancient and indispensable place in society, its mimetic nature, and its ethical function. His arguments respond to contemporary objections as well as to Plato's influential gesture when he banished the poets from his Republic.

The *Defence* is cast in the form of a judicial oration, a defense of a client that employs forensic rhetoric to make its argument. Because Sidney's defense of poetry is structured as a trial, its form thematizes the larger issue of the poet's relationship to political power, a situation that points not only to Plato's *Republic* but also to the court context for which Sidney wrote. Language was of crucial concern to the poet, and because plain speaking often carried the threat of retaliation or censorship, indirect language—allegory, fiction, dissimulation—provided a necessary protection for the poet. As a classical oration, the *Defence* is divided into the seven sections that Thomas Wilson had prescribed in his *Arte of Rhetorique:* exordium, narration, proposition, partition or division, confirmation, refutation, and peroration. As an argument, however, the *Defence* can be broken into three parts: the description of the history of poetry and the analysis of its nature, the refutation of the charges leveled against poetry, and the characterization of the current state of poetry in England.

Sidney defines poetry as fundamentally mimetic in character. His conception of imitation is, however, complex. On the one hand, like Horace, as well as many Renaissance humanists, Sidney believed that imitation meant copying other authors, creating a "world" whose authority derived from its inscription in tradition, especially a classical tradition. On the other hand, like Aristotle, Sidney saw poetry as imitating a reality that was not represented in books, a world unmediated by a prior tradition. This Aristotelian doctrine of mimesis was, however, a theory of idealized representation, since it emphasized not actuality but an idea of potential. Thus, a poet does not portray actual people, but a generalized version of them, a portrait of exemplarity. True poets are those who "imitate to teach and delight" and in order to imitate "borrow nothing of what is, hath been, or shall be; but range, only reined with learned discretion, into the divine consideration of what may be and should be" (81). While the other arts and sciences depend on nature, poetry alone surpasses its model, fashioning works through the power of the poet's invention. Where nature's world is "brazen," poetry creates a "golden" world (78). This definition allows Sidney to construct a hierarchy in which poetry is seen to be superior both to history (because poetry is not tethered to a description of actual events, as history is) and to philosophy (because poetry

is accessible in its presentation, and its wisdom has practical effects, as philosophy's does not).

Sidney's description of poetry as creating a separate reality is crucial both to his defense and to subsequent theoretical understandings of poetic discourse. Because poetry is linked to counterfeiting and feigning, it cannot be held accountable for its failure accurately to represent the world. Poetry is thus defined as a special discourse to which the rules of truth and falsity cannot apply: "The poet, he nothing affirms, and therefore never lieth" (102). Yet the impetus of poetry is not fundamentally formalist, according to Sidney, since its purpose is always moral and didactic. Sidney's defense of poetry, particularly as it argues against Plato's charges, involves a powerful theorization of pleasure and desire. Far from denying poetry's seductive aspects, Sidney sees pleasure as the lure that permits moral teaching. Like love, poetry contains the possibility for evil as well as for good; what readers glean depends upon their faculties of judgment and perception rather than on the work itself. The readers' knowledge that poetry is not a truthful medium arms them with an "aesthetic shield" (Ferguson 149), an intrinsic distrust that forms the basis for critical judgment.

Part of poetry's pleasure is its metaphorical nature, its capacity to produce "a speaking picture" (80). Sidney's reference to the visual arts as analog is derived from the Horatian *ut pictura poesis,* a precept that remained important to literary and aesthetic theory until the nineteenth century. While Sidney is not arguing for the interchangeability of the verbal and visual arts, he does see metaphorical language as central to poetry's power. The *Defence* makes frequent use of such speaking pictures, especially in prosopopeia (representing, e.g., philosophy, history, and poetry). Indeed, Sidney claims that Plato's own writing employs such poetical devices (107). Sidney's idea of poetic composition relies on the notion of the fore-conceit (101), a conception of the work that exists in the poet's mind. This emphasis upon a world within the mind can be seen as an anticipation of RENÉ DESCARTES's more developed belief in a mental sphere parallel with and independent of exterior matter (Shepherd 60). Sidney's process of poetic creation is thus *eikastike,* figuring forth good things, rather than *phantastike,* which is an infection of fancy (104). Crucial to this distinction is the poet's faculty of reason, which allows the poet to apprehend God's pictures or concepts and translate them into a language that will convey both their beauty and their moral import.

Although Sidney laments the abuse of poetry by its detractors, he celebrates some of England's poetic achievements, most notably Geoffrey Chaucer's *Troilus and*

Criseyde, sections of the *Mirror for Magistrates,* the earl of Surrey's lyrics, and Edmund Spenser's *Shepherd's Calendar,* though he disapproves of the antique rusticity of Spenser's language. His most severe censure, however, is reserved for the violation of the three unities in drama, a prescription Sidney attributes erroneously to Aristotle. In his criticism of English drama, Sidney epitomizes what O. B. Hardison has called an incipient neoclassicism (Hardison 59). Yet despite Sidney's reverence for classical models, he judged the English language to be equal as a poetic medium to Latin or Greek, and in fact he satirized the slavish imitation of Ciceronian eloquence (Sidney 117). It is difficult, nonetheless, to reconcile the theoretical doctrine of the three unities, with their emphasis on verisimilitude, and Sidney's earlier pronouncements on the poet's capacity to create a reality that diverges from nature. Hardison argues that there are actually two voices represented in the *Defence,* the voice of the humanist and Neoplatonist and the voice that, with Aristotle, anticipates neoclassical poetics (59). He hypothesizes that Sidney's description of English poetry may well be a later addition, inserted by the author when he revised the *Defence.*

There is, however, no direct evidence of these revisions. Moreover, a number of other critics have seen the contradictions in the *Defence*—verisimilitude versus the feigning nature of poetry is only one such example—as integral to its rhetorical strategies. Recent interpretations of the *Defence* have recognized that Sidney does not just describe an ethical practice of reading poetry, he enacts it. While persuasion is central to his purpose, he also recognizes the potential abuse of power such interpretive coercion entails. His defense of poetry against Plato's charges of immorality rests on the idea that the appropriate use of poetry (or love) will always be contingent on the exercise of prudential judgment. In order to test his own readers, Sidney playfully contradicts himself a number of times, asserting in the peroration, for instance (121), that poetry is defined by meter (in contradistinction to his assertion that poetry is a discourse characterized by its mimetic nature). He cautions against the excessive power ascribed to poetry in the peroration by the very hyperbole of his language, and whereas earlier he had flattered his readers, here the outrageous claims seem to pander to his audience's narcissism: he conjures them to believe the poets' claims when they tell their readers that poetry will make its readers immortal (121). Some critics have argued that in moments like these, as well as in the monitory exordium, where Pugliano's excessive love of horses almost causes his listeners to desire to be transformed into

horses, Sidney is putting his own theory into practice. The best defense against poetry's seductions resides, finally, not in an ethical poetry, but in the judiciousness of the reader. True to the Horatian principle of didacticism, the subtle rhetorical strategies of the *Defence* form a meditation on the abuse of power, instructing its readers to beware of the very persuasions that most convince them.

Elizabeth D. Harvey

See also RENAISSANCE THEORY AND CRITICISM.

Philip Sidney, *The Defence of Poetry: Miscellaneous Prose of Sir Philip Sidney* (ed. Katherine Duncan-Jones and Jan Van Dorsten, 1973).

Catherine Barnes, "The Complex Speaking Voice of Sidney's *Defence of Poetry*," *PMLA* 86 (1971); B. D. Cheadle, " 'The Truest Poetry Is the Most Feigning': Sidney on the Poet as Maker," *Theoria* 52 (1979); Margaret W. Ferguson, *Trials of Desire: Renaissance Defenses of Poetry* (1983); A. C. Hamilton, *Sir Philip Sidney: A Study of His Life and Works* (1977); O. B. Hardison, Jr., "The Two Voices of Sidney's *Apology for Poetry*," *Sidney in Retrospect* (ed. Arthur F. Kinney, 1988); Ronald Levao, "Sidney's Feigned *Apology*," *PMLA* 94 (1979); Kenneth Myrick, *Sir Philip Sidney as a Literary Craftsman* (1935, 2d ed., 1965); Martin Raitiere, "The Unity of Sidney's *Apology for Poetry*," *Studies in English Literature* 21 (1981); Neil L. Rudenstine, *Sidney's Poetic Development* (1967); Phillips Salman, "Instruction and Delight in Medieval and Renaissance Criticism," *Renaissance Quarterly* 32 (1979); Geoffrey Shepherd, "Introduction," *An Apology for Poetry: or The Defence of Poetry* (ed. Shepherd 1965); Gerald Snare, "Dissociation of Sensibility and the *Apology for Poetry* in the Twentieth Century," *Studies in the Literary Imagination* 15 (1982).

SONTAG, SUSAN

Susan Sontag (b. 1933) began her career as something of an academic prodigy throughout the 1950s and emerged as a productive author in the early 1960s, publishing a first experimental novel, *The Benefactor* (1963), and several critical pieces in such journals as *Partisan Review,* the *New York Review of Books,* and *Film Quarterly.* In the late 1960s and 1970s she advanced her avant-garde aesthetics in two more creative works, *Death Kit* (1967) and *I, Etcetera* (1978), as well as three experimental films, *Duet for Cannibals* (1969), *Brother Carl* (1972), and *Promised Lands* (1974). As a critic, Sontag struck a provocative stance in the 1960s by repudiating modernist hermeneutics—whether

New Critical, Marxist, or psychoanalytic—in favor of celebrating art's "sensuous surface" (see MARXIST THEORY AND CRITICISM, NEW CRITICISM, and PSYCHOANALYTIC THEORY AND CRITICISM). She drove home her critique with memorable one-liners, polemically contending, in *Against Interpretation* (1966), that "in place of a hermeneutics we need an erotics of art" (14). Such trenchant slogans appealed to a lay readership that she exploited in popularizing Continental cultural life and such American avant-garde figures as John Cage, Merce Cunningham, and Jasper Johns.

Opening critical rhetoric to the formal techniques of her creative fiction—assemblage, collage, inventory, and other disjunctive stylistics—Sontag sought in *Against Interpretation* to displace criticism's theoretical rigor in favor of a more ludic, subversive, and performative critical discourse. In her preface to this volume she asserted, "What I have been writing is not criticism at all, strictly speaking, but case studies for an aesthetic, a theory of my own sensibility" (viii). Often, as in "Notes on Camp," Sontag's writing subverted conventional boundary lines separating canonical from marginal texts, valorizing artworks that were "serious about the frivolous" and vice versa. Such camp fusions of elite and popular cultural references underpinned her critical readings throughout the next two decades.

In *Styles of Radical Will* (1969), Sontag advanced the aesthetic sensibility of *Against Interpretation* in such controversial pieces as "The Aesthetics of Silence" and "The Pornographic Imagination." Parting company with art's expressive and mimetic roles, she instead theorized an austere aesthetic, one that jettisoned culture's humanistic, and finally commercial, limits, what she described as the "patron, client, consumer" network (6). Her widespread consideration of aesthetic "silence"—her rubric for art's power to *negate* its media, audience, consciousness, and communicative meaning—took into account the "exemplary suicides" (9) of Heinrich von Kleist and the comte de Lautréamont, the "self-punishing" madness of Friedrich Hölderlin and Antonin Artaud (9), Samuel Beckett's "ontological stammer" (9), Ingmar Bergman's "spiritual vertigo" (17), Marcel Duchamp's readymades, and Cage's aleatory performances. Writing in the wake of such FRANKFURT SCHOOL theorists as THEODOR W. ADORNO and Herbert Marcuse, Sontag sought to deploy the aesthetic dimension as a powerful negation of advanced consumer society. Moreover, like WALTER BENJAMIN, she investigated how twentieth-century artists worked within the new media and technologies of mechanical reproduction to subvert the spreading signs of lowbrow culture, discussing the eloquent silence of

Harpo Marx and the "brutal nominalism" of Andy Warhol's pop art (25).

Sontag's award-winning volume *On Photography* (1977) advanced her aesthetic criticism, reflecting on the cinematic representation, or "acquisition," of life by "The Image-World" of contemporary photography, film, and the spectacle of popular media. Similarly, *Illness as Metaphor* (1978) broke new ground in cultural criticism by using her own survival of cancer to examine the discursive representation of disease. Collecting seven essays of the 1970s, Sontag's *Under the Sign of Saturn* (1980) comprised personal reflections on Paul Goodman and ROLAND BARTHES, notable cinematic essays on Leni Riefenstahl and Hans-Jürgen Syberberg, and literary appreciations of Artaud, Benjamin, and Elias Canetti. While this volume stands as the culmination of Sontag's critical powers, it also foregrounds the central impasse and theoretical limit of her project.

In the 1980s, Sontag's divided persona as at once vanguard intellectual and popular broker for the avant-garde became unbalanced. Even as she touted the subversive, "writerly" practice of such figures as Artaud, Barthes, and Benjamin, she domesticated the radically textual character of their verbal styles. While granting, for example, Barthes's concern for "writing itself," she largely ignored his heralding of the "death of the author" and instead valorized the artist's more traditional and humanizing role as a *promeneur solitaire,* writing at an elite remove from the vexed issues of textuality, history, and social change. Such aesthetic conservatism was dramatically underscored at a 1982 New York rally in support of Poland's Solidarnosc, where, like many other NEW YORK INTELLECTUALS during the Reagan years, Sontag renounced her earlier roots in radicalism. Here she attacked the *Nation* and the *New Statesman* as having less journalistic integrity than *Reader's Digest,* lodging the blunt charge that communism is merely "Fascism with a human face." Despite Sontag's polemical posturing for the new wave of aesthetic and intellectual currents of the 1960s, in the 1980s critics such as Walter Kendrick and Frank Kermode pointed with suspicion to her telling resistance to theory, with Kendrick dubbing her "our greatest living Victorian writer" (46). In 1992 she published a more conventional, historical novel, *The Volcano Lover.*

After the theoretical revolution of the 1980s, what Sohnya Sayres has described as Sontag's "elegiac modernism" appeared even more dated, especially so in her controversial 1989 study *AIDS and Its Metaphors.* However discerning in her cultural study of the discourse surrounding AIDS, Sontag paid scant attention to the specific historicity, micropolitics, and reception of AIDS both as a disease and a social justice issue. Her swerve from the lived experience of AIDS victims and their advocates points up the political limits of her late modernism. While cultural criticism of the post-Vietnam era has advanced apace in considering the sociohistorical and institutional foundations of aesthetic forms, Sontag's writing has remained noticeably silent about the representation of gender, race, and class in the expanded social field.

Walter B. Kalaidjian

Susan Sontag, *Against Interpretation and Other Essays* (1966), *AIDS and Its Metaphors* (1989), *Illness as Metaphor* (1978), *On Photography* (1977), *Styles of Radical Will* (1969), *A Susan Sontag Reader* (ed. Elizabeth Hardwick, 1982), *Trip to Hanoi* (1968), *Under the Sign of Saturn* (1980).

Robert Boyers, "Women, the Arts, and the Politics of Culture: An Interview with Susan Sontag," *Salmagundi* 31–32 (1975); Elizabeth W. Bruss, "Susan Sontag," *Beautiful Theories: The Spectacle of Discourse in Contemporary Criticism* (1982); Roger Copeland, "The Habits of Consciousness," *Commonweal* 108.3 (1981); Walter Kendrick, "Eminent Victorian," *Village Voice* 25 (1980); Frank Kermode, "Alien Sages," *New York Review of Books* 27.17 (1980); Cary Nelson, "Soliciting Self-Knowledge: The Rhetoric of Susan Sontag's Criticism," *Critical Inquiry* 6 (1980); Léon S. Roudiez, "Susan Sontag: Against the Ideological Grain," *World Literature Today* 57 (1983); Sohnya Sayres, *Susan Sontag: The Elegiac Modernist* (1990).

SOYINKA, WOLE

Wole Soyinka (b. 1934) was the first African writer to receive the Nobel prize in literature, in 1986. Apart from his stature as a pioneer in African drama in the English language and in professionalizing English-language theater in Nigeria, Soyinka is also significant among English-language writers in the world as a poet, theater director, autobiographer, critic, and theorist. His theoretical productions make a significant contribution to postcolonial discourse on issues of language, ideology, and cultural politics. His essays provide a writer's perspective on intellectual and sociopolitical issues significant in contemporary literary and cultural theory in general, and in African literature in particular.

Just as Soyinka's creative work evokes the Nigerian sociopolitical scene at different historical times, his essays delineate the history of criticism of modern African literature. In the 1950s and 1960s he notes the predominant

voice of European critics of African literature; in the 1970s and 1980s, that of African critics. His critical perceptiveness deals as effectively with the limitations of a Eurocentric interpretation of African texts as with the dangers of a "superficial traditionalism" prescribed by nativists in favor of local imagery and a simpleminded rejection of European influences. The consistency of Soyinka's vision—a commitment to social justice, to freedom, to human dignity—from his earliest to his most recent output, in his creative as well as his critical, journalistic, and theoretical work, is a mark of his integrity and courage in refining and deepening the same basic concerns from the 1960s into the 1990s.

In Soyinka's work there is an integral interrelatedness among the categories of aesthetic discourse, political ideology, and theoretical analyses. Although Soyinka resists being categorized, politically or theoretically, within any particular party or school of thought, his commitment is broadly socialist. In his essays, the sociopolitical and literary-theoretical do not belong to watertight compartments. An evaluation of his commitment must take into account the totality of his diverse and prolific output—in literary work as well as in journalistic articles in Nigerian newspapers on matters ranging from university administration to the condition of roads. Whenever his basic ideal of human freedom has been threatened, academically or otherwise, Soyinka has been characteristically outspoken, has taken risks, and has acted. He speaks openly as the conscience of his nation. The sense of communal responsibility that is at the root of his literary universe also engages his social activism.

Soyinka recognizes the politics of theory even as he acknowledges the theoretical bases of political action. As he remarks in his preface to *Myth, Literature, and the African World,* the kind of indigenous "progressive" position that denies one a "self-apprehension" of one's own world-view is "not merely culturally but politically hostile" (xi). Soyinka has the unique capacity to express his social commitment in explorations of Yoruba metaphysics, cosmology, and myth (often revised to resonate a contemporary reality), as well as in his involvement with concrete social action toward a humane and just society.

In his collection of essays *Myth, Literature, and the African World* (1976) Soyinka explores Yoruba ritual, religion, and myth in "Morality and Aesthetic in the Ritual Archetype" and in "Drama and the African World View." The appendix reprints "The Fourth Stage: From the Mysteries of Ogun to the Origins of Yoruba Tragedy" (originally published in a collection of essays for G. Wilson Knight, who had been Soyinka's teacher at the University of Leeds), where Soyinka draws centrally upon the

Ogun (the Yoruba god of war, iron, and creativity) in an abstruse formulation of a theory of tragedy. Soyinka is a pioneer in proposing a theory of Yoruba tragedy. The depth and breadth of his vision encompass the traditions of Greek and Shakespearean tragedy and FRIEDRICH NIETZSCHE's *Birth of Tragedy*. Figures such as Dionysus and Apollo are Yoruba-ized in Ogun and Obatala. Soyinka's theory of Yoruba tragedy can be analyzed in four broad categories: the origins of tragic feeling; the components of tragic action; the centrality of the human will in undergoing what Soyinka calls "the transitional gulf"; and what is most significant, the outcome of tragic drama, that is, communal benefit, new knowledge for the onlookers on and off stage. Yoruba tragedy does not end necessarily with the protagonist's death; in fact, the greater challenge is to stay alive, to endure the transitional gulf and to bring new knowledge from that experience to the community.

A more recent volume, *Art, Dialogue, and Outrage: Essays on Literature and Culture* (1988), brings together several of Soyinka's essays from the 1960s to the late 1980s. As Biodun Jeyifo remarks in his introduction, the emphasis in Soyinka's essays in those three decades remains on "distinctively *African* cultural, paradigmatic matrices for literature and a sense of history, for literature and freedom and dignity in an epoch of unfreedom and alienation for the vast majority of Africans and the rest of the human race" (xi). This collection includes such previously unpublished essays as "Between Self and System: The Artist in Search of Liberation" (lecture delivered at Cornell University, 1986), "The External Encounter: Ambivalence in African Arts and Literature" (the Herbert Read Memorial Lecture, at the Institute of Contemporary Arts, London, 1985), and "The Autistic Hunt; or How to Marximise Mediocrity."

Three important essays in this volume present Soyinka's engagement with, and his intellectually rigorous and at times strident responses to, prescriptive criticism that objects both to his uses of Yoruba ritual and mythology and to his concern with European figures. Although Soyinka's satiric voice takes on critics particularly of the "prescriptive" variety, his overall theoretical contributions go beyond the reactive and are significant for their discussions of social ideology and aesthetic vision, as well as the social responsibility of writer and critic.

Soyinka's response to the "Neo-Tarzanists," who practice "a form of criticism which actually presumes to re-write original poetry in the critic's own design" (*Art* 326), becomes more strident in "Who's Afraid of Elesin Oba?" (first delivered at the University of Ibadan, 1977), where he declares "literary warfare" on the type of criti-

cism that "has gone beyond its competence and has dared to enlarge upon the 'legitimate' purlieu of imaginative projection, sealing off areas of uncomfortable (for the ideologue) verities." And in "The Critic and Society: Barthes, Leftocracy, and Other Mythologies" (1981) his tone becomes even more urgent and serious:

> It is my view that literary infanticide is being committed right now, and by a fanatic minority of Leftocrats. . . . In Nigeria, the millipedes of a future literature are no sooner hatched than they are made to begin to count their feet. Naturally, they never walk. (165)

"The Critic and Society" is a fine example of Soyinka's engagement with global literary debates as these are relevant to an African context. He admires ROLAND BARTHES as the type of "honest intellectual" who recognizes the boundaries of his own bourgeois preoccupations (154). Soyinka finds such honesty to be lacking among Nigerian "radical chic critics."

Soyinka's theoretical work continues to respond keenly to contemporary issues of African and world politics. In his response as writer and responsible citizen of a human community, he optimally directed his Nobel prize acceptance speech, "This Present Must Address Its Past," to the continuance of apartheid South Africa, a blot on the world's humanity. In another recent essay, "Twice-Bitten: The Fate of Africa's Culture Producers," he severely indicts the many brutal regimes on the African continent that have driven culture producers such as writers into prison or exile. This "internal brain drain," as he puts it succinctly, is extremely grave and needs urgent recognition and action. Even as he would acknowledge the devastation by European colonizers, Soyinka's is, as one has come to recognize and respect, the voice of honesty in recognizing Africa's own internal monsters (some of whom he has satirized in plays such as *Kongi's Harvest* and more recently in the parade of such monsters as Idi Amin and Bokassa in his drama *A Play of Giants*).

Soyinka's theoretical production, "a sustained, vigorous reflection," in Jeyifo's words, "on the being and becoming of Modern African Literature" (introduction to *Art* xxx), belongs in the significant traditions of African aesthetics, philosophy, and politics; his is a voice that at times echoes, and takes further, FRANTZ FANON's and Amilcar Cabral's in their contributions to a continuing struggle toward decolonization. Soyinka's creative energy is equally at home with Yoruba cosmology and Ifa divination as it is with Shakespearean tragedy and Eastern philosophies. Amilcar Cabral's remark that "if imperialist domination has the virtual need to practise cultural oppression, national liberation is necessarily an act of culture" is echoed in Soyinka's stridency against dishonesty and injustice, academic and social, in his contemplativeness on culture and the complexities of "tradition" and in his powerful encapsulation of a distinctly African presence in the literature and cultural matrix of a much maligned continent.

Ketu H. Katrak

See also AFRICAN THEORY AND CRITICISM.

Wole Soyinka, "And After the Narcissist?" *African Forum* 4 (1966), *A Play of Giants* (1984), *Art, Dialogue, and Outrage: Essays on Literature and Culture* (ed. Biodun Jeyifo, 1988), *Collected Plays* (2 vols., 1973–74), "Drama and the Revolutionary Ideal," *In Person: Achebe, Awoonor, Soyinka* (ed. Karen L. Morell, 1975), *Myth, Literature, and the African World* (1976), "This Past Must Address Its Present" (Nobel lecture 1986), *PMLA* 102 (1987), "Triple Tropes of Trickery," *Transition* 54 (1991), "Twice-Bitten: The Fate of Africa's Culture Producers," *PMLA* 105 (1990), "The Writer in an African State," *Transition* 31 (1967).

John Agetua, *Interviews with Six Nigerian Writers* (1975); Una Cockshott, "A Dance of the Forests," *Ibadan* 10 (1960); Ann B. Davis, "Dramatic Theory of Wole Soyinka," *Ba Shiru* 7 (1976); Henry Louis Gates, Jr., ed., *Black American Literature Forum* 22 (1988, special issue on Soyinka); James Gibbs, ed., *Critical Perspectives on Wole Soyinka* (1980); James Gibbs, ed., *Research in African Literatures* 14 (1983, special issue on Soyinka); James Gibbs, Ketu H. Katrak, and Henry Louis Gates, Jr., eds., *Wole Soyinka: A Bibliography of Primary and Secondary Sources* (1986); Anthony Graham-White, *The Drama of Black Africa* (1974); Abiola Irele, *The African Experience in Literature and Ideology* (1981); Ketu H. Katrak, *Wole Soyinka and Modern Tragedy: A Study of Dramatic Theory and Practice* (1986); Gerald Moore, *Wole Soyinka* (1971); Oyin Ogunba, *The Movement of Transition: A Study of the Plays of Wole Soyinka* (1975); Oyin Ogunba and Irele Abiola, eds., *Theatre in Africa* (1978); Kolawole Ogungbesan, ed., *New West African Literature* (1979).

SPANISH THEORY AND CRITICISM

The well-publicized and largely unexamined belatedness of cultural formations in Spain cannot be traced to a weaker intellectual pulse, as deterministic and decadence theories would have it, but rather to the elitism and rigid institutionalism pervading intellectual Span-

ish culture down to the twentieth century. JOSÉ ORTEGA Y GASSET's quasi-hysterical pleas for the constitution of select minorities as a measure of national salvation against the "shapelessness" of a decentered or, to use his own term, "invertebrate" culture *(Invertebrate Spain)* should not be taken at face value as an indication of the absence of the *spirit* of such minorities. Rather, it is indicative of the retrenching of a progressively unsustainable attitude behind the redefinition of the traditional opposition between vulgus and the cultured elite according to modern class divisions. It is the gulf between evolving and institutionalized culture, and the defensive outlook exacted by the latter's system of allegiance, that accounts for the survival of old forms and the reluctant acceptance of new ones after they have acquired the obstinacy of hardened facts and gained a posthumous currency. The renewal of forms is thus related to the assimilation of models already invested with prestige, a largely indeterminate value often spilling over the entire genetic area of the canonized phenomenon, which would also explain the paradoxical influential preeminence, for Spanish culture at certain historical junctures, of models derived from the periphery of their own axiological systems.

In the Renaissance and in the field of literary thought the gulf between institution and literary pragmatics appears in the lack of a poetics in the vernacular until the last two decades of the sixteenth century. Side by side with an abundance of Latin treatises on poetics and rhetoric by humanists such as Antonio Nebrija, Juan Luis Vives, Arias Montano, Francisco Sánchez el Brocense, and others, who studied exclusively the models of classical antiquity, literary production in the Castilian language developed without influence or conceptual orientation from contemporary theoretical treatises. The turning point in the generalized disregard for contemporary vernacular literature was the ascendancy of the Italian stanzaic and metric models, whose reception among poets was facilitated by the prestige attributed to Renaissance Italian culture and whose later acceptance by humanists was not altogether unrelated to the fact that they originated in the same culture from which the humanists themselves had received the cult of antiquity.

Half a century after its innovative introduction by Juan Boscán, the active Petrarchan current in sixteenth-century Spanish poetry attracts the critical attention of preceptors, whose works served less to support and guide an Italianate school, which by then had firmly established its reputation, than to add a critical apparatus as a frame to an object assumed in its absolute, no longer disputable and thus no longer creative aesthetic value. The *Anotaciones y enmiendas* [Annotations and amendments] to Garcilaso de la Vega by Francisco Sánchez el Brocense (1577), an erudite study on the sources for Garcilaso's poetry, was in effect an attempt to assimilate the conception of the modern vernacular poet to that of the humanist, whose cult of the model, codified in the doctrine of the *imitatio,* and whose penchant for erudition were henceforth to be the measure of poetic value. Garcilaso became the first classic among the modern poets only after he could be shown to have masterfully imitated the classics of Greek and Latin antiquity.

This method of legitimation by reference to the dominant institutional doctrine and practice is explicit in the *Anotaciones* by Fernando de Herrera to the *Obras de Garcilaso de la Vega* [Works by Garcilaso de la Vega] (1580), where the author declares that he has applied to Garcilaso's poetry the same approach that Renaissance humanists applied to the poets of antiquity (1:77). The *Anotaciones,* however, reach beyond Herrera's stated intention, and the initial purpose to trace Garcilaso's sources and to comment on his poems devolves into a multifaceted exposition of aesthetic, philosophical, and linguistic ideas steeped in Platonic idealism. Herrera's concept of the supernatural origin of poetic inspiration is necessarily at odds with the doctrine of radical *imitatio* proposed by Julius Caesar Scaliger in the *Poetices libri septem* (1561) and submitted to by Alonso López Pinciano, Spain's greatest Renaissance theoretical figure, in his *Philosofía antigua poética* [Ancient poetic philosophy] (1596). Herrera's influence, however, is bound with his doctrine of poetic erudition, which he expounded in his response to the pamphlet by a writer known only as Prete Jacopín (c. 1580), and with hermeticism, which anticipated and was in fact the manifesto for the baroque aesthetics of Luis de Góngora and his school.

Herrera's defense of hermeticism and difficulty is, however, restricted to the concepts expressed, whereas from a formal point of view he bows to classical rhetoric in demanding clarity of expression. The opposition between content and form, resulting from Herrera's double allegiance to classical rhetorical doctrine and Platonic idealism (whose arcane representations in Renaissance symbology must be counted among the sources of poetic erudition), announces the double aesthetic current of the baroque: the formal and stylistic complexity of *culteranismo* and the tendency exemplified by Francisco de Quevedo and known as *conceptismo.* Clarity of expression as a classical ideal is not tantamount to universal intelligibility or to a narrowing of the distance between the literati and the vulgus. Herrera's admission of the popular as a legitimate source of poetic inspiration is conditioned to its assumption into a difficult and complicated

expression. The stakes in the literary skirmishes rending Spanish poets into two irreconcilable groups identified by their attitude toward the formal complexity of Góngora's poetry were neither the legitimation of elitism (Góngora's "I wish to do something; not for the many") nor the renewal of poetry from the popular sources that had proved decisive for the conquests of prose. The dispute was, rather, about degrees of accessibility, a theoretical drawing of lines in which even those who, like Francisco Cascales, were most radically opposed to hermeticism conceded that obscurity arising from the concepts and soluble by erudition was legitimate and imputable to the reader's ignorance (see CLASSICAL THEORY AND CRITICISM: 2. RHETORIC, PLATO, and RENAISSANCE THEORY AND CRITICISM).

In Alonso López Pinciano's *Philosophía antigua poética,* elements derived from ARISTOTLE's *Poetics* are organized and brought up to date in a unity meaningful for the Renaissance *episteme.* Aspiring to ground his aesthetic ideas in a system, Pinciano begins his work with an analysis of the human faculties as the base of all intellectual phenomena. Following the *Examen de ingenios para las ciencias* [The examinaton of men's wits] (1575), by Juan Huarte de San Juan, Pinciano, himself a medical doctor, attributes the poetic faculty to specific physiological conditions. His scientific approach contrasts with Herrera's idealism by its refusal to discuss metaphysical causes, restricting the compass of the imagination by tracing it to its origin in perception. Literature thus becomes both the product of observed reality and the object of observation in the mode of scientific scrutiny proper to it. The premise of a literary science appears in the affirmation of literary (aesthetic) criteria as the only adequate means to discriminate the qualities of the work, thus setting the doctrinal presupposition for the concept of artistic autonomy.

Pinciano's adaptation of the Aristotelian principle of verisimilitude, related to the concept of mimesis, is of the greatest importance for the development of the novel. His slighting of the marvelous and of the fantasies that appealed to Renaissance readers in books of chivalry had an unmistakable influence on Miguel de Cervantes's conception of narrativity and on the development of the novel. The ascendancy of reason over fantasy in the Renaissance finds a temporary balance in Pinciano's conjugation of literature's hedonistic appeal and didactic application. This balance between Pinciano's demand for an encyclopedic dimension of the literary work and his concession to the aesthetic experience was assumed by Cervantes as the critical measure of literary worth. Pinciano's resolution of the dispute about the essentiality of versification for poetry was to dismiss this formal definition in favor of the concept of mimesis, which, following Aristotle, he considered the touchstone for poetic discourse. Similarly, the epic need not be restricted to historical matter, since the criterion for poetry is not factual truth but plausibility. These theses were pregnant with consequences waiting to be embodied in an innovative work. Their critical appropriation by Cervantes was perhaps the greatest instance of theory's productivity in the Renaissance.

Although Pinciano did not consider critical judgment to be the province of the specialist, but one of the educated gentleman's abilities, his extension of this faculty to the lay individual does not amount to an admission of popular standards. It represents the application of the aristocratic norms of decorum to the cultural dimension of the literary work. The force of the *odi profanum vulgus,* to which even Lope de Vega, the most popular dramatic author in the seventeenth century, felt compelled to submit—"It is just to speak to him [the *vulgu*] in a stupid fashion in order to please him" (*Arte nuevo de hacer comedias en este tiempo* [New art for writing comedies in this time], 1609)—culminated in the *Libro de la erudición poética* [Book of poetic erudition] (1611) by Luis Carrillo y Sotomayor. Because of its emphasis on hermeticism and erudition and its defense of a formally inaccessible poetry and a language removed from ordinary discourse, this work stands as the representative poetic manifesto of the baroque. In addition to the formal difficulty corresponding to the program of the Góngorist school, Carrillo proposed a conceptual difficulty and sophistication of wit that pointed to Quevedo's virtuosity with conceit and verbal juggling and further on to Baltasar Gracián's aesthetics. Gracián's *Agudeza y arte de ingenio* [Sharpness and art of wit] (1648) responded to the need for a baroque rhetoric, attempting to systematize the forms and applications of conceit by means of a typology exemplified with what amounts to an anthology of wit in various languages. Gracián sums up the ideological nature of Renaissance and baroque literary theory in his characterization of a modality of truth privileged over other forms of evidence: "Truth is more pleasing the more difficult it is, and knowledge that is hard to obtain is more appreciated" (266).

The extreme political and economic decomposition of Spain at the beginning of the eighteenth century engendered a concern for the country's development and a search for solutions to the crisis. The reflection of such attitudes in literature often appeared as an attack against an idle aristocracy coupled at times with egalitarian ideals. But just as the practical measures undertaken to bring about reform were exclusively the initiative of the wealthy minority supported by the government, so in the field of literature an alliance came about between the writing minority, of noble or *hidalgo* composition, and the government, leading to the formation of a centralizing network of academies, much as economic reform was institutionalized in the economic societies organized by the wealthy for the promotion of commerce. One of the aims of these academies (the Real Academia Española was founded in 1714) was to implant a standardized language that responded to the notion of purity inherited and abstracted from the previous century's obsession with genealogical purity. Correspondingly, the method adopted was to suppress idiomatic multiplicity and competing national languages. Literature was subjected to normative measures of literary style and to the cleansing operations of censorship, conditions that found a theoretical support in the doctrines of neoclassicism.

The reform of style led to the condemnation of baroque diction and to the demand for a natural expression that paved the way for the linguistic organicism of the Romantic period. Ignacio de Luzán in his *Poética* [Poetics] (1737), Benito Jerónimo Feijóo in his *Teatro crítico universal* [Universal critical theater] (1726–40), and José Francisco de Isla in his novel *Fray Gerundio de Campazas* (1758–70) all attacked the high-flown rhetoric derived from baroque models, identifying it with the irrationalism that stood for the Enlightenment's nonironic, moralistic transvaluation of the baroque's meaning-endowed obscurity. Clarity of expression, as Luzán asserted in his *Retórica de las conversaciones* [Rhetoric of conversations] (1729), was the reflection in discourse of the natural, internal order of the soul. Typical of the timorous progressiveness of eighteenth-century authors and theoreticians is the contradiction between their call for naturalism of expression and their qualified adherence to the classical doctrine of styles, a stance that owed less to the often exaggerated influence of French poetics than to the persistence of classical literary theory and its adaptations by sixteenth- and seventeenth-century Spanish preceptors.

The conditioning of renewal by institutionalized culture, a situation defining the enlightened despotism characteristic of social and cultural initiative in this century, can be seen in the fact that Latin was still the scholarly language of the century's foremost literary historians, Gregorio Mayans y Siscar (1699–1781) and Francisco Cerdá y Rico (1730–92). Their reappraisal of the literary heritage from a historical point of view, like that in Antonio de Capmany's *Teatro histórico crítico de la elocuencia castellana* [Historico-critical theater of Castilian eloquence] (1786–

94), an anthology of stylistic prose samples according to evolutionary criteria, was not founded on aesthetic-philosophical principles that, reacting to neoclassical ahistoricism, could be considered an anticipation of Romantic theory. Their avowed aim was to counter the adverse opinions on Spanish culture that had gained currency in Europe after Père Bouhours's notorious attack on the excesses, that is, on the anticlassicism of Spanish writers. This apologetic intent led, however, through the revaluation of concreteness and a corresponding deemphasis of the conventional universality of classicism to an early emergence of the idea of folklore, associated by Capmany with the distinctiveness of national character. The class nature of the opposition between the normative production of the neoclassicists and the "badly polished tongues" of the peasants, hinted at by Capmany's explicit coupling of writers, professors, and rulers, assumes the form of another opposition that, crucial throughout the nineteenth century, will maintain a residual force in the social and cultural conflicts of the twentieth century. The opposition between "courtiers" and peasants is also one of center to periphery, or in the now outmoded ideological terminology of the eighteenth century, of capital to provinces. The authenticity intuited in the people, who thus become the differential source of value by which nations must be judged, is contrasted with the uniformity exhibited by writers and governing minorities who conform to conventions, and the *translatio preti* is accomplished the more decisively by endowing the people with the aristocratic capital dweller's legitimating idea: "only in [the people] are reason and manners constant, uniform and common" (Sáinz 144).

The problem engendered by the seventeenth-century theorists' inability to break through Aristotelian doctrine to meet the theoretical needs of contemporary Spanish drama traverses the eighteenth century, ostensibly as a dispute about the worth of art unlegitimated by theory, and persists in the nineteenth century, albeit in inverted form, following the support given to baroque Spanish drama by German Romanticism (see GERMAN THEORY AND CRITICISM: 2. ROMANTICISM). In 1828 Agustín Durán published his *Discurso sobre el influjo que ha tenido la crítica moderna en la decadencia del teatro antiguo español y sobre el modo con que debe ser considerado para juzgar convenientemente de su mérito peculiar* [Discourse on the influence of modern criticism on the decadence of ancient Spanish drama and on the way in which it must be considered for its peculiar merit to be judged appropriately]. Faithful to its programmatic title, this Romantic manifesto pits the enthusiasm communicated by "national interest" in seventeenth-century drama against the "pedantic moralism" of "reasoning critics," effectively condemning neoclassical doctrine by the very standards with which it had sought to measure baroque drama, now declared incommensurable with French-created paradigms and elevated to the category of "national drama."

The critical foundation of Romantic historicism in Spain was not, however, the by-product of a defensiveness touched off by wounded patriotism. As was the case with other movements of international scope, the assimilation and systematic application of A. W. Schlegel's theories was carried out by Catalan artists and intellectuals, traditionally less inclined to reflect on worn-out Spanish glories. Manuel Milà i Fontanals (1810–84) was originally attracted to Romanticism through the liberal tenet of literature's social function. He accepted the opposition between classicism and Romanticism, rejecting the mediation of a "monstrous middle term" equivalent to the contemporary "moderate" political model. In this first stage of his career, Milà conceived of Romanticism as a cosmopolitan movement, and as the only genuinely modern movement. Later, coinciding with the dismantling of the revolutionary impulse as a consequence of the strength gained by the moderationist party at the end of the civil war, he would reject literary radicalism in favor of the historicism artistically represented by Walter Scott. With the publication in 1857 of *Principios de estética* [Principles of aesthetics], Milà proposed to establish aesthetics as the basis for literary studies, substituting allegedly permanent philosophical principles for the arbitrary norms of neoclassic treatises. The turn toward historicism is related to his interest in traditional popular poetry as well as to his fundamental research on the poetry of the troubadours, an interest linked to the emergence of romance studies. In time Milà's early advocacy of the (progressive) social function of art became a plea for a socially conservative instrumentalization of art in the subordination of consciousness to a harmony that was the subjective constitution of public order and morality. Such ideological subsuming of aesthetics within an ethics historically grounded in tradition was to exert enormous influence among Spanish critics well into the twentieth century. It was through one of Milà's disciples, Marcelino Menéndez Pelayo (1856–1912), that this confusion of criticism with morality, now exacerbated by the disciple's frankly reactionary national Catholicism, would be transmitted to a school of literary historiographers and critics.

The appropriation of Menéndez Pelayo's criticism by the ideological establishment of the Franco dictatorship (1939–75) with a view to the definition of a politics of national affirmation is reminiscent of eighteenth-century attempts to turn criticism into a crusade for national dignity. In Menéndez Pelayo's case, criticism's investment in polemics was invited by the author's self-styled vocation as keeper of the national values, and in this sense it was inevitable once the reactionary forces he had contributed to legitimate found themselves confronted with the negative image of their exclusionary zeal. In claiming him as their own, they acknowledged their status as temporal fugitives in an axiological eternity presided over by Menéndez Pelayo's consecration as Spain's patron-critic. The generalized attribution to him of the paternity of modern Spanish criticism seems odd in light of the fact that Menéndez Pelayo's battles were fought against long-vanished enemies, images of the past (the encyclopedists, among others) whose "nefarious" influence on the social scene had long been superseded by other scientific and literary paradigms. Conversely, to contemporary theory incompatible with his staunch Catholicism he opposed not alternative theories but monuments, images of eternity. Miguel de Cervantes, William Shakespeare, and Diego Velázquez suffice to dismiss French naturalism as a modern profanation of true naturalism (*Discurso sobre la poesía mística* [Discourse on mystical poetry], 1881).

The measure of Menéndez Pelayo's antimodernism is indicated by his felt need to rectify modernity at its source, in an attempt to derail Spain's dangerous approach to a shared historical time. His search for a single, unitary line of spiritual progress in Spanish history (a concept that resounded in the Francoist postulate that Spain was "a unity of destiny in things eternal") resulted in the positing of a national consciousness shaped by traditional Catholicism, a conjunction reaching its highest level during the sixteenth century. With a naive, nondialectical idea of the realization of the national spirit, clearly indebted to Johann Gottfried Herder's philosophy of history in its preference for the earlier stages of the genetic process (see GERMAN THEORY AND CRITICISM: 1. STURM UND DRANG / WEIMAR CLASSICISM and 2. ROMANTICISM and HISTORICAL THEORY AND CRITICISM), Menéndez Pelayo attempted to trace a continuity of national consciousness originating in the peninsular Latin authors and traversing even those periods when, as in the eighteenth century, the line seemed to be interrupted by foreign influence. It is style, he claims, not language, that shows the unity of authors from the Latin Seneca to contemporary Castilian writers, and it is style, consequently, that he declares to be the principle of unity in the literary work (*Programa de literatura española* [Program of Spanish literature], *Obras* 1:9). Formulated

as early as 1878, these ideas did not so much anticipate STYLISTICS as provide a link for some practitioners of the later school of criticism, in whose work a conjunction can be found between the formal techniques associated with the notion of the autonomy of the literary work of art, accepted in principle by Menéndez Pelayo, and a nationalistic consciousness indebted to his apologetics.

The doctrine of continuity was taken over by Ramón Menéndez Pidal (1869–1968), whose own doctrine of traditionalism postulated the gradual appropriation and transformation of the individually produced literary work by the collectivity. A contemporary of the group of writers known as the Generation of 1898, Menéndez Pidal, who displayed no interest in contemporary literature, shared their project to discover the "soul of the Spanish people" with a view to tracing the necessary orientation in the present. Not only was his concept of "Spanishness" narrowly restricted to the Castilian language and cultural forms but his deployment of a vast erudition in the service of Castilian nationalism contributed decisively to the creation of myths such as that of the Cid, the epic hero derived from a historical warrior of the eleventh century, whose poetic representation Menéndez Pidal held up as a faithful historical portrait bearing the archetypal Castilian virtues, now promoted to those of the Spanish national genius.

Working also within the historico-cultural approach to literary studies, Américo Castro (1885–1972) is the Spanish scholar and critic whose influence has been most pervasive in the United States. Through his teaching he contributed to the formation of a school of criticism giving a recognizable orientation to the study of Spanish literature in American academia. This pervasive influence, now ironically on the wane at a time when NEW HISTORICISM, unconcerned with immediate precursors, is rehashing some of its tenets, weathered the years of nearly totalitarian rule by NEW CRITICISM and STRUCTURALISM. To those currents Castro opposed the thesis that the literary work cannot be properly understood divorced from its cultural circumstances and its author's historical and literary horizon. The nature of the literary text is a unity composed with different materials; it is in no case reducible to the linguistic component. To stylistics, the other major influence in Spanish literary criticism in the second half of the twentieth century, Castro opposed the principle that styles must be considered in connection with their life context, since literary forms do not sprout unrelated to human circumstances. Prominent in his insistence on the mutual dependence between the literary work and its vital context are Ortega y Gasset's (1883–1955) doctrines of "vital reason" and of the coexistence of subject and world. Ortega's phenomenological centering of history in human consciousness, in "man installed in a particular world, as in a house which he has made to shelter himself from the elements" (*Man and Crisis* 36), reappears in Castro's central concept of "life dwelling."

Ortega's reputation among literary and art theorists rests on *The Dehumanization of Art* (1925), one of the earliest attempts at a theory of the avant-garde. It is possible to speculate that Ortega's sensitivity to a contemporary phenomenon involving a generation younger than his own proceeded far less from an intimate appreciation for the experimental forms of the avant-garde than from his own imperative to be at the level of one's historical time. Ortega's historicizing of aesthetic values prompted him to identify in contemporary art a novelty that, in his own account, resided in the new art's exclusive preoccupation with aesthetic values. There appears to be a contradiction between Ortega's temporalization of aesthetic values (a precondition of novelty) and his distinction between traditional (nineteenth-century) art and the avant-garde in terms of the latter's "suspension" of all but aesthetic factors. The novelty involved in "new art" would seem to be, paradoxically, an intensification and concentration of timeless values rather than their destruction, advertised as a programmatic enterprise in so many manifestos of the period's isms.

This position approximates Ortega's concept of the avant-garde to his earlier definition of classicism as the permanent sense of all culture, that is, as a supra-historical concept ("Teoría del clasicismo" [Theory of classicism], *Obras* 1:71), a parallel born out by his speculation, in *The Dehumanization of Art,* that the new art's attack on the artistic past masked a hatred against culture itself. His sociological characterization of the avant-garde as intrinsically a minority phenomenon offers another clue to Ortega's analysis of its general form. His ambiguously sympathetic approach to the new movements ignored their extra-aesthetic goals and means, a far from accidental suspension allowing him to preempt the analyzed phenomenon's social significance by incorporating it into his longstanding opposition of select groups and uncomprehending, resentful majorities. Significantly, it was this opposition, as well as his reduction of the historical avant-garde to its alleged exacerbation of art's autonomy, that provided the theoretical guidelines for the younger writers and poets, many of whom belonged, as did Ortega himself, to a liberal bourgeoisie convinced of its salvational, mediative role between traditionalism's dead weight and the unkindlier, more aggressive forms of the avant-garde, assimilated only in

their technical aspect through a confusion (invited by Ortega's definition of the avant-garde as "artistic art") with the ideal of aesthetic purity. A defense of literary minorities owing much to Ortega's origination of value in the select group was undertaken as late as 1945, by Pedro Salinas (1891–1951). His acclaim for the minority's salvational role not only reflects Ortega's location of historical dynamics in the individual consciousness but betrays a more explicit naturalization of socially determined positions in his definition of the minority as "a psychological condition natural to the artist," who owes his situation neither to whim nor to effort, but to a birthright (see "La gran cabeza de turco o la minoría literaria" [The great scapegoat or the literary minority]).

Ortega's theory transpires also in Guillermo de Torre's (1900–1971) ambitious project to chronicle the appearance and development of the European avant-garde in his *Literaturas europeas de vanguardia* [European avant-garde literatures] (1925). One of the founders, in the previous decade, of Ultraísmo, a Spanish avant-garde movement, Torre substitutes now the principle of selection for that of militancy, with a consequent loss in belligerence in favor of a constructive project based on the artists' definition as "men of their time" and (again Ortega's trace) on the worship of life. As a historian of the avant-garde, Torre found himself sharing the point of view of an earlier, institutionally oriented movement founded by the Catalan Eugeni d'Ors (1881–1954). The central aesthetic normativism of Noucentisme ("Novecentismo" in its Castilian translation) has displaced avant-garde subversion in Torre's assertion that Guillaume Apollinaire anticipated the new classicist tendencies, a classicism, in Ortega's and d'Ors's supra-historical sense of the perfect, precise structuration of the new aesthetic norms. Such a *rappel à l'ordre* was all the more significant in that the *Primer manifiesto ultraísta* [First Ultraísta Manifesto] had proposed the supersession of Novecentismo as its artistic goal.

D'Ors's aesthetic doctrine, "arbitrarism," first defined in 1905, proposed the liberation of art from naturalism and Romantic organicism. Its principle was the imposition of human norms on the empirical material of art and of society. His sense of a European cultural unity, whose initial impulse and continuity he attributed to classicism, determined his unequivocal European orientation and his role in the Spanish reception of contemporary French culture, parallel to Ortega's mediation of German thought. Like Ortega, he believed in cultural intervention "from above," using institutions to further a cultural politics in a spirit reminiscent of the Enlightenment, whose epistemological metaphor reemerged drenched in baroque Neoplatonism in d'Ors's *helioma-quia,* or "battle for the sun."

While Ortega and d'Ors decisively influenced literary and artistic practice through intellectual positions ultimately dependent on philosophical and social speculations, contemporary academic literary criticism continued the philological tradition of Menéndez Pidal's school, now modified by the incorporation of stylistics. Amado Alonso (1896–1952) and, above all, Dámaso Alonso (1898–1990) were the most representative exponents of Spanish stylistics. The former substituted for FERDINAND DE SAUSSURE's components of the linguistic sign the double nature of poetic expression. This results from the integration of feeling and intuition, the first being the subjective impulse that seeks its form through an intuitive grasp of reality. This idealism, not entirely independent from the doctrine of empathy, opposed to an objective structure of things "a structure of sense in which the structural elements are the emotional sense of things and not the things themselves" (*Poesía y estilo de Pablo Neruda* [Poetry and style in Pablo Neruda] 29). Thus, it affirmed the intentional horizon of meaning and the need to supplement analysis with knowledge of the author's personality, the ultimate source of literary expression.

Dámaso Alonso's own amendment to Saussure's definition of the sign replicates Amado Alonso's conjunction of self and world in the distinction between outer and inner form. The outer form corresponds to the level of the signifier, while the inner form is related to the psychological movement toward the conception and expression of meaning. The latter is inseparable from the linguistic material in which it is formed and thus cannot be accessed except through detailed linguistic analysis. Dámaso Alonso upheld the intentional principle in the most radical way. Considering the work of art to be ahistorical, he conceived the history of its reception as a history of critical shortcomings due to the insufficiency or unavailability of a literary science. There is nothing in the impression (caused by a literary work) that was not already present in its expression. The critic's interpretive horizon is the author's original totalizing intuition formalized in the literary work. At the center of its program to found a literary science, Spanish stylistics placed the transcendental subject, both as the origin of the interpretive act (the initial critical movement is an intuition dependent on the critic's own expressive talent) and as its limiting epistemological goal. Stylistics' alleged scientific procedure is thus linked to a canonizing enterprise, and its method restricted in its applications to a predetermined selection of worthy literary works whose expressive excellence is supposedly guaranteed by the critic's pre-theoretical, intuitive appraisal. In Dámaso Alonso's radical hierarchization of reader, critic, and literary scientist, stylistics reveals itself as an institutional venture, both in method and object.

At the other end of the spectrum, the Catalan Josep Maria Castellet (b. 1926) was the first critic in post–Civil War Spain to consider the literary work in terms of its social function and historical dimension. Itself arising from a repudiation of its immediate social constraints, and in opposition to the ahistorical forces in the service of oppressive institutions, Castellet's notion of culture is dynamic. Social practices, among them writing and reading, are foregrounded, and in contrast to Dámaso Alonso's assertion of absolute expression, emphasis is placed on the necessarily schematic, unfinished nature of the literary work and the reader's productive role in its constitution. By an ideological displacement from the intuitive transparencies of official culture, the praise of obscurity serves, as in the seventeenth century, to legitimate literary practice. This time, however, its purpose is not to draw a line between the author's erudition and the reader's ignorance but to bring both to the same level in the common task of finding a shared truth. "The reader has become, therefore, an active protagonist in literary creation. And our time the time of the reader" (*L'hora del lector* [The time of the reader] 53). This theoretical positioning of reception at the level of production does not remain abstract. The contemporary author's "lonely failure" to fulfill his social function, related to the low cultural level of a potential readership abducted by mass culture for the celebration of a "literature of consumption," is traced to extraliterary conditions whose recognition ceases to support hierarchically naturalized divisions in a detached cultural sphere. Instead, the reader's distance from the "literature of production" must be reduced by an elevation of the economic level, allowing energies now consumed in survival to be redirected toward the processes of cultural creation. Castellet's awareness of the historical ground of literary production and the historical bounds of meaning alerts him to the emergence of literary difference and the constellation of new themes and forms. Although in practice the cultural establishment has tended to institutionalize as substitutive values those authors who were selected to illustrate historical trends, his critical intervention has, in principle, no canonizing purpose. His influential anthologies—*Veinte años de poesía española: Antología (1939–1959)* [Twenty years of Spanish poetry: an anthology (1939–1959)] (1960) and *Nueve novísimos poetas españoles* [Nine very new Spanish poets] (1970)—transgressed the conventions of the anthological mode by explicitly discarding the criterion of literary excellence in favor of difference and the historical implications of the samples organized according to strict chronology.

The political marginalization of Catalonia within the Spanish state, extreme during the period of the Franco dictatorship, strengthened the repudiation of institutional Spanish culture on the part of Catalan intellectuals. These intensified the assimilation of European, and now also American, cultural models, which had distinguished Catalan cultural formations from those of the rest of Spain ever more markedly since the second half of the nineteenth century. It is among the members of a generation that experienced the highest inflation of the modern idea of the state and the transformation of objective culture into rigid systems of domination that the most interesting and alert theoretical tendencies in contemporary Spain are to be found. Philosophers by training and method, although with an agenda surpassing academicism's restrictive concerns, writers such as Xavier Rubert de Ventós (b. 1939) and Eugenio Trías (b. 1942), founders of the para-institutional Col·legi de Filosofia in Barcelona, and Eduardo Subirats (b. 1947) have surveyed with great sensitivity significant cultural developments in their metaphysical, aesthetic, social, and historical dimensions. Although their intellectual scope ranges over the entire history of Western culture, their privileged domain has been modernity and its current exhaustion in the intensified empowerment of social and political institutions. Even when they have repeated Ortega's and d'Ors's attempt to affect institutions from within (e.g., Rubert de Ventós's short-lived political career in the Spanish Parliament and his continued post as deputy in the European Parliament), their critical independence has resisted cooption, reinforcing their sense of a task that Trías characterized as a *radical ontological politics*. To institutional politics and philosophy, to the profession in the Calvinistic sense of the word, Trías opposes a Weberian sense of vocation, the call originating in Being. For this reason, he says, "philosophy, today, is immediately politics" (*La Catalunya Ciutat i altres assaigs* [Catalonia as city and other essays] 128).

Having witnessed the stertorous avant-gardes of the 1960s, these thinkers lucidly took stock of the failure exemplified by the revolutionary utopianism of styles in the arts and its situationist translation into what Rubert de Ventós called the "mannerisms" of daily-life resistance to the total-control society (*Heresies* 216–18). But all the same, they remain aware of the bankruptcy the new conformity advertises in the banal formalism of the postmodern, whose cult of technology and bureaucratic professionalism links the "new non-style" of its accomplishments to the "non-politics of a techno-economic development with an aggressive value" (Subirats, *El final de las vanguardias* [The end of the avant-gardes] 157). The articulation of a critical dimension of intellectual life is doomed by the incommensurable competition from the communication systems and the organized academic and knowledge industry. Incapable of transcending the alternative between bureaucratic cultural efficiency and intellectual dysfunction, and aware of the schism over which critical consciousness hovers perhaps for the last time, these thinkers constituted their task in the paradox of a criticism to be engaged from modernity's horizon. Theirs aims to be a criticism poised between an obsolete intellectual independence and the dissolution of subjectivity in the expansion of anonymous power founded on the unlimited development of knowledge and indistinguishable from a nameless, supra-individual, yet not collectively administrated, intelligence. They have come, in Trías's expression, to inhabit the frontier of historical sense, the limits of a world whose last horizon "can be named critical modernity in crisis" (*Els habitants de la frontera* [Denizens of the frontier] 101).

In this vanishing perspective modernity's critical enterprise can still be perceived, not so much as an enlightened program whose ideals have, in fact, been too rigorously embodied in institutions (thus abdicating from their ideality), but as "a last refuge" in face of the wasted landscape of power (Subirats, *Metamorfosis de la cultura moderna* [Metamorphosis of modern culture] 155). This last refuge between knowledge and power, at the historical frontier beyond which both become indistinguishable, is the equivalent of a sensibility that, not above or beyond its own world, feels and finds itself *next to it, elsewhere,* perhaps only slightly displaced—in Catalonia for example." Thus, concrete political and cultural marginality, based on a concrete geographic and historical frontier existence, is understood as the privileged lookout for the paradox of late modernity, as the place where marginality constituted itself as a distinct experience and became conscious of itself as such. From this vantage point it became possible to undertake the difficult task that Rubert de Ventós defined as "to describe the milieu and its myths without thereby idealizing and making a myth out of one's own juncture or situation; without making out of its eccentricity or alienation a particular counterculture or antipsychiatry which would constitute them in a new 'orthodox discourse'" (*De la modernidad* [On modernity] 288).

Joan Ramon Resina

Amado Alonso, *Materia y forma en poesía* (1965), *Poesía y estilo de Pablo Neruda: Interpretación de una poesía hermética* (2d ed., 1951); Dámaso Alonso, *Poesía española: Ensayo de métodos y límites estilísticos* (1950); Josep Maria Castellet, *L'hora del lector* (1987); Benito Jerónimo Feijóo, *Teatro crítico universal* (9 vols., 1726–40, reprint, 1985); Baltasar Gracián, *Agudeza y arte de ingenio, Obras completas* (ed. Arturo del Hoyo, 1960); Fernando de Herrera, *Obras de Garcilaso de la Vega con anotaciones de Fernando de Herrera* (1580, ed. Antonio Gallego Morell, 7 vols., 1973); Alonso López Pinciano, *Philosophía antigua poética* (ed. Alfredo Carballo Picazo, 1953); Ignacio de Luzán, *Arte de hablar, o sea, retórica de las conversaciones* (ed. Manuel Béjar Hurtado, 1991); Marcelino Menéndez Pelayo, *Obras completas* (67 vols. to date, ed. Miguel Artigas, 1940–); José Ortega y Gasset, *"The Dehumanization of Art" and Other Essays on Art, Culture, and Literature* (trans. Helene Weyl et al., 1968), *En torno a Galileo* (1933, *Man and Crisis,* trans. Mildred Adams, 1958), *España invertebrada* (1922, *Invertebrate Spain,* trans. Mildred Adams, 1937), *Obras completas* (11 vols., 1957–69); Xavier Rubert de Ventós, *De la modernidad* (1980), *La estética y sus herejías* (1980, *Heresies of Modern Art,* trans. J. S. Bernstein, 1980); Pedro Salinas, "La gran cabeza de turco o la minoría literaria," *La responsabilidad del escritor y otros ensayos* (1961); Eduardo Subirats, *El final de las vanguardias* (1989), *Metamorfosis de la cultura moderna* (1991); Eugenio Trías, *Els habitants de la frontera: Sobre mètode, modernitat i crisi* (1985), *La Catalunya Ciutat i altres assaigs* (1984).

José Almeida, *La crítica literaria de Fernando de Herrera* (1976); Guillermo Díaz-Plaja, *Lo social en Eugenio d'Ors y otros estudios* (1982); Nigel Glendinning, *A Literary History of Spain: The Eighteenth Century* (1972); Graham Hough, *Style and Stylistics* (1969); Enric Jardí, *Eugenio d'Ors: Obra y vida* (1967); Manuel Jorba, *L'obra crítica i erudita de Manuel Milà i Fontanals* (1989); Oreste Macrí, *Fernando de Herrera* (1959); Pedro Sáinz Rodríguez, *Historia de la crítica literaria en España* (1989); Sanford Shepard, *El Pinciano y las teorías literarias del Siglo de Oro* (1962); Andrés Soria Olmedo, *Vanguardismo y crítica literaria en España (1910–1930)* (1988); Antonio Vilanova, "Preceptistas españoles de los siglos XVI y XVII," *Historia general de las literaturas hispánicas,* vol. 3 (ed. Guillermo Díaz-Plaja, 1953).

SPEECH ACTS

In its current form, speech-act theory is associated with a series of lectures given at Harvard in 1955 by the Oxford philosopher of language J. L. Austin (1911–60) and published posthumously in 1962 as *How to Do Things with Words*. The ideological and methodological roots of speech-act theory in Western thought go back, however, to the pre-Socratic philosophers and the Old Testament and have remained a peripheralized but still powerful force in the margins of the dominant Platonic-Christian-scientific intellectual tradition.

At issue in the debate over speech acts is whether language is to be conceived as essentially a system of structures and meanings or as a set of acts and practices. As such, the debate replicates the ancient Western debates between logic and RHETORIC, transcendence and immanence, description and persuasion; between PLATO and the Sophists (and the sixth-century Greek poets); between the rabbinical tradition and the Kabbalists; and between ST. AUGUSTINE and the Gnostics. It might even be thematized, as HAROLD BLOOM suggests in *A Map of Misreading* (42), as a clash between the Greek *logos* ("word"), with its associations of static visual structure, and the Hebrew *davhar* ("word"), with its associations of dynamic human action. Goethe's retranslation in *Faust* of the opening line to John's Gospel, from "In the beginning was the word" *(das Wort)* to "In the beginning was the deed" *(die Tat),* is patently an attempt to recover the peripheralized rhetorical tradition and to ground language not in inert transcendental structure but in creative human actions. The German Romantic tradition since Goethe has insisted on this revisionism, in fact, from G. W. F. HEGEL through KARL MARX AND FRIEDRICH ENGELS, FRIEDRICH NIETZSCHE, and MARTIN HEIDEGGER to Hans-Georg Gadamer, who in *Truth and Method* (sec. 3.2.A) rereads the history of medieval Christianity so as to find a dynamic, creative, active *logos* in St. Augustine and St. Thomas Aquinas. LUDWIG WITTGENSTEIN's insistence in *Philosophical Investigations* that "the meaning of a word is its use in the language" (remark 43) should probably be read as part of this same tradition.

In the study of literature, speech-act theory similarly moves the focus of the critic's attention from the "text," conceived formalistically as a stable object with certain intrinsic characteristics, to what we *do* with texts—as writers, readers, editors, publishers, and so on. In the broadest sense, every literary text is a speech act, an utterance in an ongoing speech situation ("literary tradition," dialogically conceived) that is shaped not only by a static authorial intention dwelling somehow hypostatically inside the text but by interpretation, by the writer's directedness toward interpretation, the reader's anticipation of that directedness, and various background factors that affect all speech situations, such as purpose (what drives the writer to write and the reader to read? what brings them together?) and medium (the technologies of voice, print, digital storage and transmission; the economics of acquisition, production, and distribution). From this perspective, a speech-act approach to literature shades into sociology and cultural critique. Looked at more narrowly, every reading of a text is a speech situation in which the reader constitutes the text as speech act and responds with his or her own speech act; here a speech-act approach shades into psychology, phenomenology, and READER-RESPONSE THEORY AND CRITICISM. From a still narrower perspective, every utterance within a literary text is a speech act, analyzable along Bakhtinian lines, say, in terms of who is speaking it to whom (character to character, narrator to narratee, implied author to implied reader, etc.) and how many (and whose) voices it polyphonically transforms; this shades speech-act theory back toward Formalism (see M. M. BAKHTIN).

Austin's specific formulation of speech-act theory opens with a distinction between what he calls the "constative," an utterance used for "stating" things, for conveying information, and the "performative," an utterance used for "doing" things, for performing actions. The phrases "I now pronounce you man and wife" (when uttered by the presiding minister at a wedding), "I christen this ship the *Joseph Stalin*," "I promise I'll be there," and "I bet you five dollars" convey no information, Austin notes, and therefore are neither true nor false: they perform the action referred to in the phrase (marrying, christening, promising, betting) *by* saying it.

Later, in *How to Do Things with Words*, Austin grows disenchanted with the constative-performative distinction, saying that it is finally impossible to make the distinction stick in linguistic analyses of specific utterances—all constatives perform actions too, and performatives convey information—and so he suggests a new framework for the study of utterances. He proposes that we call the utterance "itself"—the words artificially divorced from their social context—a "locution" and then explore the locution in context, as a complexly relational speech act; as an illocution, what we intend to do *in* saying something; and as a perlocution, the effect on our listener that we want to have *by* saying something. Thus, for example, the adult who says to a child, "I'd love to see your drawing," might be describing (or "constating") a state of mind (locution), promising to look at the drawing (illocutionary force), and attempting to make the child feel good, building the child's self-esteem (perlocutionary effect). This allows the linguist to explore the operation of language not in the abstract, in laboratory conditions of the mind, but in the give-and-take of real interpersonal speech-use situations.

This approach to language is ideologically deviant in the West, where the transcendental logos (linguistic structure in the mind of God) has always taken precedence over fallen human speech, what people actually say with their carnal lips and hear with their carnal ears. It is important to note this deviance, because the next stage of speech-act theory entailed an attempt to assimilate Austin's exciting insights to the dominant logical tradition of linguistic philosophy. In 1969 the American philosopher of language John Searle published *Speech Acts*, an analytical systematization of Austin's lectures in terms of a single speech act, promising. Searle worried that his dealing with speech acts would be seen as dealing with what FERDINAND DE SAUSSURE called *parole*, actual speech, the tabooed black hole of mainstream Western linguistics at least since Augustine's *On Christian Doctrine*. "I am arguing, however," Searle wrote, "that an adequate study of speech acts is a study of *langue*" (17), which is to say, transcendental structure. He states explicitly what an "adequate study of speech acts" must consist of in order to qualify as a study of *langue*:

> But this insight into the looseness of our concepts, and its attendant jargon of "family resemblance" should not lead us into a rejection of the very enterprise of philosophical analysis; rather the conclusion to be drawn is that certain forms of analysis, especially into necessary and sufficient conditions, are likely to involve (in varying degrees) idealization of the concept analyzed. In the present case, our analysis will be directed at the center of the concept of promising. I am ignoring marginal, fringe, and partially defective promises. (55)

This attempt to abstract ("idealize") out of actual speech acts a conceptual "center" of promising recuperates speech-act theory for transcendental linguistics by eliminating the dangerous variability of interpersonal communication in the real world (see also Searle, "Logical Status," on literary speech acts). Eight years later, the Chomskyan linguist Jerrold Katz went further and recuperated the constative-performative distinction for analytical philosophy, again by explicitly invoking the normative powers of idealization, but specifically in terms of NOAM CHOMSKY's distinction between competence (our possession of an idealized transformational system) and performance (our actual speech) (184–85). Rather than linking the performative with performance, however, Katz set performance to one side—just as the logical tradition had always set performatives aside and focused on language as a vehicle for the communication of information—and argued that it should be possible to analyze performatives and constatives in the "null context," in terms of a decontextualized competence.

This formalistic revision of Austin speaks strongly of the continuing ideological dominance of logic in Western thought. Austin broke the rules of logic (or of analytical philosophy), played with the rules, asked more questions than he could answer, proliferated real-life counterexamples even (or especially) when their effect was to undermine his own classifications. Searle and Katz assume that this was simply a mistake, a personal failing, and that Austin really meant to adhere to the rules of logic but, for whatever reason, was unable to. Their self-appointed task, then, becomes that of rescuing Austin's valuable insights for linguistic philosophy by pruning off the excess foliage and discovering the logical "core" or "center" of his work. They assume that there is only one game in town—logic—and that Austin tried but failed to play it by the rules.

In another reading, however, such as is offered powerfully by the French (particularly Shoshana Felman, JACQUES DERRIDA, and Gilles Deleuze and Félix Guattari), what Austin was in fact doing was playing a different game, a game that Felman associates with Don Juan, Derrida with DECONSTRUCTION, and Deleuze and Guattari with a nomadic stammering or "becoming-minoritarian" (*Thousand* 77 ff., 104–6). In traditional terms, Austin was doing rhetoric rather than logic; in an expansion of his own terms that Felman and Derrida hint at, he was attempting to displace "constative linguistics" (the mainstream tradition) with a new (or age-old but ideologically repressed) "performative linguistics," a concern with language as performance (or, as KENNETH BURKE would say in a similar vein, as drama).

As Derrida shows in his deconstruction of Austin, however ("Signature Event Context"), there is a "constative" or logical exclusion in Austin's own argument that undermines the explanatory power of speech-act theory. Like his constative forebears, Austin did not know what to do with "figurative" or "poetic" language and so split it off as extrinsic to his concerns:

> A performative utterance will, for example, be *in a peculiar way* hollow or void if said by an actor on the stage, or if introduced in a poem, or spoken in a soliloquy. . . . Language in such circumstances is in special ways—intelligibly—used not seriously, but in many ways *parasitic* upon its normal use—ways which fall under the doctrine of the *etiolations* of language. All this we are *excluding* from consideration. (22)

"Walt Whitman," Austin says later, "does not seriously incite the eagle of liberty to soar" (104).

This issue of parasitic language became one of the turning points of the Searle-Derrida debate. In the late 1970s Searle wrote a "reply" to Derrida's deconstruction of Austin, assuming that Derrida was attacking Austin and rushing to the master's defense. Derrida then wrote a hundred-page deconstruction of Searle's reply, more or less savaging Searle and demonstrating both that philosophically Searle is way out of his league and that methodologically Searle and Derrida are not so very far apart. Both Searle and Derrida are analytical philosophers who believe in rational, logical thought; Derrida is merely better at it than Searle, more sensitive to the mind-numbing complexity of analytical issues.

In his "Limited Inc" discussion of parasitic language, Derrida shows that "serious" speech acts are in fact and by rights grounded in the very possibility of linguistic parasitism, or, as Derrida prefers to say, "iterability": "A standard act depends as much upon the possibility of being repeated, and thus potentially [*éventuellement*] of being mimed, feigned, cited, played, simulated, parasited, etc., as the latter possibility depends upon the possibility said to be opposed to it" (91–92). Modifying Austin's terms again, we might say that a "serious" speech act *as* an act depends upon the possibility of being performed, that the stable or static ("constative") form of a "serious" (nonmarginal, nondefective, etc.) act of promising, say, only exists as a fictive construct generated by the speaker/actor in the act of performing it. This would suggest that there is no substantial difference between promising on stage and promising in "real life": both are performances of speech acts that the speaker/actor has witnessed and internalized as the ways other speakers/actors have of saying/doing a thing (promising, say), but which are realized as *acts* only in the performing or "iterating" of them. This suggests Bakhtin's theory of internal dialogism: every word we hear and speak is a repetition or reenactment of previous uses that is both saturated with earlier dialogues (Derrida would again say "iterability") and inclined toward a specific situational response from a real listener, and thus always both the "same" (dialogization as imaginary "essence") and "different" (dialogization as contextual act).

To put that simply, we are always acting, in both senses of the word, whether we have memorized our lines from a specific script for a specific play or, more generally, from "life," from previous speech encounters; and our acting always relies on that "script," a socially regulated pattern for our behavior, but in dynamic, situationally contingent ways. We roughly follow the script, but because the script never quite specifies every detail in every scene, we also constantly ad-lib, and in some sense, because the script is multiple and our memories are bad, we ad-lib the script itself.

Persuasive as Derrida's deconstruction of Austin on parasitic language is, however, he does not offer a methodological alternative to Austin's serious-parasitic distinction. Probably the most influential speech-act solution to Austin's problem is offered by H. Paul Grice in his 1975 article "Logic and Conversation." Grice poses the question, How is it possible for us to imply things, to convey intended meanings that we do not make explicit? This has been a recurrent problem for "constative" linguists, since their transcendental (systemic, rule-governed) model requires that communication be possible only if it obeys the rules, but various evasive speech acts fail to do so and yet succeed as speech acts.

Grice argues that implied speech acts do in fact break the rules, but in a controlled fashion. We all bring certain assumptions and expectations to speech situations, Grice says, and it is possible for us to manipulate those assumptions and expectations so as to make ourselves understood indirectly. By breaking the rules on one rather superficial level, we signal to our listeners that we are in fact obeying them on a deeper level, and thus we are understood.

Grice wants to formalize these assumptions (tacit "rules" or "maxims") for all human speech, and that really does not work. He assumes, for example, that all human conversation will naturally strive to be both rational and cooperative and that within this overriding "cooperative principle," we all know that we are supposed to provide all sufficient but no excess information and to be truthful, relevant, and perspicuous. These are manifestly ideological norms that have been programmed into the white middle class for the past century or two, especially the male members of that class. They can be conceived as conversational universals only by surrendering to that inner voice of ideology that whispers to us that "we" (the socially dominant "we") alone are normal. To accept Grice's model as universal, as his "constative" followers (linguistic pragmaticians, notably Deirdre Wilson and Dan Sperber) have done, also requires that we ignore all our own "irrational" speech acts, blind rages, oneiric discourse (sleep and dream talk), "uncooperative" speech acts, deliberate attempts to disrupt conversations, lies and cons, and pouting silences.

Still, Grice's model opens up exciting new methodological avenues. It can explain the operation of what Austin and Searle call parasitic speech acts, such as metaphorical and literary language, or jokes: In one of Grice's examples, the general wires back to headquarters, "Peccavi," and the commander realizes that he cannot possibly mean the literal translation, "I have sinned," since

that would be irrelevant to the battle being fought. Because the general in the field is a good, classically trained military man (the best schools, long training in military discipline—rationalism and cooperation—and, needless to say, ideologically "normal" masculinity), the commander assumes that he must be adhering to the cooperative principle and its maxims; he must, therefore, be implying something that he is not saying outright. Since the commander too went to all the best schools, he makes the translation quickly and interprets the telegram to mean "I have Sind," that is, "I have conquered the town."

Within ideologically "normal" discourse, in other words—as long as we agree to analyze the rationally cooperative speech of white middle-class males and ignore that of everyone else—Grice's theory of "conversational implicature" is an effective analytical tool. This limitation is a serious one, especially since the theory is founded on the universality of those ideological norms, but it is not an absolutely debilitating one. One could proliferate maxims, for example—maxims for urban working-class American black men, say, or for Marxist feminists, or for the gay community—or what would be more interesting, one could follow Derrida and make all "maxims" situationally and interpretively dependent on "implicature." We construct maxims, in this reading, in specific speech-use situations, as shifting interpretive fictions that help us to make tentative (never perfectly reliable) guesses at what the other person is trying to say.

Even with that modification, Grice's theory is too narrow. Charles Altieri, for example, shows that the very choice to speak indirectly has implications for interpretation: "What B says is fairly clear; why he puts his statement this way and what the choice itself may *mean* is tantalizing. Is B calling attention to his own perspicuity, making a joke, or trying to convince A that he can maintain a balanced judgment in which suspicion is tempered by ironic self-awareness?" (86). Altieri offers the term "expressive implicature" to describe speech acts "where aspects of tenor or mode are foregrounded" (88), especially acts of expressive self-referentiality that guide the listener (or the reader) to an interpretation of emotional motivation or what V. N. Voloshinov calls "evaluative accent" (80–81). This modification of Grice is particularly useful, Altieri argues, in the stylistic analysis of literature: it allows the critic to explore the significance of the writer's stylistic self-presentation. (For other speech-act approaches to literature, and extensive bibliographies of the field, see Pratt and Petrey.)

A similar modification of Grice is the conflation of his theory of implicature with Austin's theory of illocutionary force and perlocutionary effect as suggested by Douglas Robinson. All of Grice's examples deal with implicit constatives, or what might be called "locutionary implicature": conveying information in a roundabout way. But when Walt Whitman incites the eagle of liberty to soar, in Austin's example, he is not conveying implicit information; he is *doing* something, attempting to sway his readers in certain ways. He might be thought of as urging his readers to carry the banner of democracy, for example (illocutionary implicature), and attempting to goad those readers into action (perlocutionary implicature). This would be a reading sympathetic to Whitman's liberalism; a demystificatory Marxist reading might see Whitman as urging his readers to have a certain aesthetic experience of liberty through the image of the soaring eagle (illocutionary implicature), which has the effect of passivizing those readers, making them uncritical citizens, rendering them "tolerant" of the actual infractions of liberty all around them (perlocutionary implicature).

Speech-act theory is an inroad into the problematic of language not as transcendental structure but as human social behavior. As such, it offers one of the twentieth century's most persuasive methodological alternatives to the mainstream linguistic tradition from Plato and Augustine to Saussure and Chomsky. Despite numerous attempts to assimilate it back into that tradition, it continues to inspire oppositional—social, situational, detranscendentalized, deterritorialized—approaches to language.

Douglas Robinson

See also LINGUISTICS AND LANGUAGE.

Charles Altieri, *Act and Quality: A Theory of Literary Meaning and Humanistic Understanding* (1981); J. L. Austin, *How to Do Things with Words* (ed. J. O. Urmson and Marina Sbisà, 1962, 2d ed., 1975); Harold Bloom, *A Map of Misreading* (1975); Kenneth Burke, *A Grammar of Motives* (1945); Gilles Deleuze and Félix Guattari, *Mille plateaux* (1980, *A Thousand Plateaus: Capitalism and Schizophrenia*, trans. Brian Massumi, 1987); Jacques Derrida, "Limited Inc abc . . ." (1977, trans. Samuel Weber, *Glyph 2* [1977], reprint, *Limited Inc.*, 1988), "Signature Event Context" (1971, trans. Samuel Weber and Jeffrey Mehlman, *Glyph 1* [1977], reprint, *Limited Inc.*, 1988); Shoshana Felman, *The Literary Speech Act: Don Juan With J. L. Austin, or Seduction in Two Languages* (1980, trans. Catherine Porter, 1983);

Hans-Georg Gadamer, *Wahrheit und Methode: Grundzüge einer philosophischen Hermeneutik* (1960, 5th ed., *Gesammelte Werke*, vol. 1, ed. J. C. B. Mohr, 1986, *Truth and Method,* trans. Garrett Barden and John Cumming, 1975, 2d ed., trans. rev. Joel Weinsheimer and Donald G. Marshall, 1989); H. Paul Grice, "Logic and Conversation," *Speech Acts* (*Syntax and Semantics,* vol. 3, ed. Peter Cole and Jerry L. Morgan, 1975); Jerrold Katz, *Propositional Structure and Illocutionary Force* (1977); Mary Louise Pratt, *Toward a Speech Act Theory of Literary Discourse* (1977); Sandy Petrey, *Speech Acts and Literary Theory* (1990); Douglas Robinson, "Metapragmatics and Its Discontents," *Journal of Pragmatics* 10 (1986); John R. Searle, "The Logical Status of Fictional Discourse," *New Literary History* 6 (1975), "Reiterating the Differences: A Reply to Jacques Derrida," *Glyph 2* (1977), *Speech Acts: An Essay in the Philosophy of Language* (1969); V. N. Voloshinov, *Marksizm i filosofiia iazyka* (1929, *Marxism and the Philosophy of Language,* trans. Ladislav Matejka and I. R. Titunik, 1973); Deirdre Wilson and Dan Sperber, *Relevance: Communication and Cognition* (1986); Ludwig Wittgenstein, *Philosophical Investigations* (trans. G. E. M. Anscombe, 1953, 3d ed., 1967).

SPIVAK, GAYATRI CHAKRAVORTY

Gayatri Chakravorty Spivak (b. 1942) was born in Calcutta and grew up in a highly charged political atmosphere at a time of complex political dissension in India. As a young, active Bengali intellectual, she attended Presidency College in Calcutta, itself a highly politicized institution. She received a degree in English and spent two years in graduate school in Calcutta prior to her arrival in the United States in 1962 as a Ph.D. student of comparative literature at Cornell University. Her first book was *Myself, I Must Remake* (1974), a historical-biographical study of W. B. Yeats's poetry. The publication in 1976 of her introduction to and translation of JACQUES DERRIDA's *Of Grammatology* signed her *carte d'entrée* into the elite theoretical ateliers in France. Throughout the 1970s she also published a number of essays concerning feminist strategies of reading, Marxism, the politics of interpretation, and the place of the institution of literary studies within the politico-socio-economic text. The publication in 1980 of three seminal essays—"Draupadi," "French Feminism in an International Frame," and "Displacement and the Discourse of Woman"—marks an important transitional moment in Spivak's work, as questions concerning the problematics of race and gender; the historical antagonisms between Marxism, feminism, and DECONSTRUCTION; the critique of imperialism; subaltern history; and, finally, the position she occupies as a highly commodified so-called Third World Marxist-feminist-deconstructionist critic working in the United States enter her work.

The organization of the essays in the collection *In Other Worlds* (1987) into three chronological sections—"Literature," "Into the World," and "Entering the Third World"—accentuates these changes. The first group of essays focuses on developing counterideological feminist strategies of reading canonical texts that will render visible the ethico-political itineraries that constitute the "Great Tradition" and the discipline of literary studies. The second section includes a deliberation on what the question of value becomes when determined from a materialist predication such as Karl Marx's; a critique of the ideological implications operating in the 1981 Chicago conference "The Politics of Interpretation"; a critical review of the limits and the limitations of French feminism; and two essays that deal explicitly with the ideological production of knowledge in "First World" universities. The concluding section turns toward "Third World" texts and problematics and includes a translation and interpretation of Mashasweta Devi's "Draupadi"; a critical review of work by the subaltern historians; and a translation and powerful reading of Devi's "Stanadayini" (Breast-giver) in "A Literary Representation of the Subaltern: A Woman's Text from the Third World."

In all these essays, Spivak's indebtedness to and politicization of the strategies of deconstruction is evident. For example, she uses a deconstructive method of reading to call attention to the necessity of feminism to "negotiate" with—to inhabit and reinscribe—the "structures of violence" that make their practices possible. In "A Literary Representation of the Subaltern," this strategy of negotiating provides a method to illustrate the limits and limitations of using French/liberal/Marxist-feminist, deconstructive, and psychoanalytic arguments concerning women's work, women's reproductive and productive rights, value, and regulative psychobiographies to write the history of the "Third World" gendered subaltern subject. By reading against the grain Devi's allegorical reading of "Stanadayini" (Devi reads the story as a parable of India after decolonization) and by both using and bringing to crisis the analytic strategies of these heterogeneous discourses, Spivak emphasizes the extent and the politics of attempting to find a solution to the problems of the "Third World" gendered subject and of attempting to unravel her history. Many of the key issues that have been a substantive concern for Spivak for some time are reassembled in this essay. The critique of native informants and native information; the critique of allegorical, nationalist readings of "Third World" texts by "First World" and "Third World" critics; a concern with reading noncanonical and "other worldly" texts in a rigorous and theoretical way; and the discontinuity between feminism, Marxism, deconstruction, and critiques of imperialism—all of these issues find their way into this *tour de force* essay.

Sarah Harasym

See also POSTCOLONIAL CULTURAL STUDIES.

Jacques Derrida, *De la grammatologie* (1967, *Of Grammatology,* trans. Gayatri Chakravorty Spivak, 1976); Gayatri Chakravorty Spivak, "Can the Subaltern Speak?" *Marxism and the Interpretation of Culture* (ed. Cary Nelson and Larry Grossberg, 1988), "Displacement and the Discourse of Woman," *Displacement: Derrida and After* (ed. Mark Krupnick, 1983), "Feminism and Deconstruction, Again," *Between Feminism and Psychoanalysis* (ed. Teresa Brennan, 1989), *In Other Worlds: Essays in Cultural Politics* (1987), "Love Me, Love My Ombre Elle," *diacritics* 14 (1984), "The Making of Americans, the Teaching of English, and the Future of Cultural Studies," *New Literary History* 21 (1990), *Myself, I Must Remake: The Life and Poetry of W. B. Yeats* (1974), *Outside the Teaching Machine* (1992), *The Post-Colonial Critic: Interviews, Strategies, Dialogues* (ed. Sarah Harasym, 1990), "Poststructuralism, Marginality, Postcoloniality, and Value," *Literary Theory Today* (ed. Peter Collier and Helga Geyer-Ryan, 1990), "Versions of the Margin: J. M. Coetzee's *Foe* reading Defoe's *Crusoe/Roxana*," *Theory and Its Consequences* (ed. Jonathan Arac and Barbara Johnson, 1990), "Who Claims Alterity?" *Remaking History* (ed. Barbara Kruger and Phil Mariani, 1989); Gayatri Chakravorty Spivak and Ranajit Guha, eds., *Selected Subaltern Studies* (1988).

Eva Corredor, "Sociocritical and Marxist Literary Theory," *Tracing Literary Theory* (ed. Joseph Natoli, 1987); Barbara Foley, "The Politics of Deconstruction," *Rhetoric and Form: Deconstruction at Yale* (ed. Robert Con Davis and Ronald Schleifer, 1985); Toril Moi, "Feminism, Postmodernism, and Style: Recent Feminist Criticism in the United States," *Cultural Critique* 9 (1988); Benita Perry, "Problems in Current Theories of Colonial Discourse," *Oxford Literary Review* 9 (1987); Tobin Siebers, *The Ethics of Criticism* (1988).

STAËL, GERMAINE DE

The posthumous reputation of Germaine de Staël (1766–1817) as a canonical critic has in all likelihood been sustained by the brief but influential chapter from *De l'Allemagne* (1810–13, *On Germany*) entitled "On Classical Poetry and on Romantic Poetry." In its outspoken critique of classicism as a dead form and its celebration of the living spirit of Romanticism, the chapter certainly animated interest in the new art in France and in other places where it had not yet taken root. However, this text is but a segment of a far more extensive critical output.

Staël's career, until the French Revolution, was one of extraordinary opportunity for a woman. Born into wealth to the banker Jacques Necker, who would become finance minister to Louis XVI in 1789, and his bluestocking Genevan wife Suzanne Curchod, Germaine was, as the legend goes, virtually raised in a *salon*. Surrounded by such critical intelligences as Denis Diderot, abbé Antoine-Léonard Thomas, and Jean François Marmontel, she became accustomed from childhood to verbal intellectual challenges and acquired early on a sense of literary vocation as well as a permanent desire for *salon* interaction. Married in the turbulent 1780s to the Swedish ambassador to Paris, she pursued her Parisian career until the fall of the Bastille and then in its aftermath.

Her first critical essay, written before the Revolution, was *Lettres sur les ouvrages et le caractère J.-J. Rousseau* (1788, *Letters on the Writings and the Character of Jean-Jacques Rousseau*). As Georges Poulet has seen, this work already exhibits her critical stance, that of transmuting her own emotional response to reading into knowledge available to others. Identifying with JEAN-JACQUES ROUSSEAU, her generation's idol, she believed that she could become a medium of propagation for his thought. But as Poulet observes, this belief was at odds with a critical practice in which she herself became the feeling and mediating site of reflection. Her "appreciation" of Rousseau is mottled by unacknowledged differences with him. Thus, reading her criticism, indeed all her texts, is a task of hermeneutic dissection.

Even before the Revolution, Staël was striving to cope with the alterations to the Old Regime's mental structures wrought by the elite of her own generation, bred on Rousseau and Plutarch. The Terror would call a fatal halt to the cult of freedom to which Staël had given her allegiance. In its wake, in lieu of participation in politics, from which she would be disbarred by successive consular and Napoleonic regimes, she would turn to criticism as a mode of advocacy for individual (*De la littérature* [1800, *On Literature*]) and national (*On Germany*) rebirth.

For Staël's thought, the primary axis of scrutiny lies in the dichotomy between stasis and movement, the former, neoclassical value being systematically devalued in favor of the latter. As she puts a split between literatures of northern and southern Europe into play in *On Literature*, she utilizes the poetics of Marmontel and Jean-François de La Harpe, her sources, but adopts a more inclusive method. Uninterested in following these mentors in setting forth the rules governing art, as a proto-Romantic theorist she was to be the first influential critic to saturate literature in its historical, political, social, and even geographical settings and yet to insist on its impact upon the individual.

On Literature exalts the literatures of northern Europe and the present against those of southern Europe, with its ancient precedents. It admits the views of such technocrats as Jacques Turgot and Jean-Antoine-Nicolas de Caritat, marquis de Condorcet, as it praises science and the merits of demonstrable truth against static systems. And yet it illustrates a preference for Ossianic mists, for vagueness over what it sees as a false classical clarity. In a passionate espousal of the idea of progress that she had borrowed from Condorcet and William Godwin, Staël argues for the benefits to be derived from the catharsis of pain induced vicariously by art as enlightening and meliorative to human consciousness. She also reasons that the new republican taste must be simpler and yet more encompassing of a gamut of experience than the rules of classical art had permitted. As in her earlier *Essai sur les fictions* (1795, *Essay on Fiction*), she finds the novel to be the art form of the future because of its capacity to embrace all the passions, and not love alone. A text for an era of expanding liberation, Staël's *On Literature* deals with questions of women's freedom as well, if only secondarily and elliptically, as in her probing discussion "On Women who Cultivate Letters."

Freed by her own criticism to attempt large-scale fictions in *Delphine* (1802) and *Corinne* (1807), Staël would thunderously return to the first mode with *On Germany*. Napoleon ordered its first edition to be turned into pulp as he exiled its author even from her Swiss home at Coppet, near Geneva. This house, which had become a place of ingathering for Europe's intellectuals, was now under the emperor's sway. It was in a previous episode of exile that Staël had first gone to Germany, there to discover not only IMMANUEL KANT, JOHANN WOLFGANG VON GOETHE, Adam Müller, and FRIEDRICH SCHILLER but also the Schlegel brothers, that nation's eminent literary critics (see GERMAN THEORY AND CRITICISM:

1. STURM UND DRANG / WEIMAR CLASSICISM and 2. ROMANTICISM). Invigorated by their notion of criticism as the locus of legislation of literature and thought, Staël composed in *On Germany* a vast and various introduction to German literature, language, and society for her French readers, vaunting once more the suggestive mysteries of the northernness of its poetry and drama. But *On Germany* must be seen, at least in part, as constituting a political protest against the narrowing of French intellectual and artistic perspectives by Napoleonic reaction. In the book, Germany is frequently displaced from the center, as Staël abandons discussion of its religion or philosophy for a consideration of English or French philosophy, or scientific ethics, or nature in general. Exemplifying her Romantic mutation of criticism into prophecy, she ends her work with a paean to enthusiasm, the spiritual force in devotion to an ideal.

Staël thus strove to provide a bridge between the Enlightenment, which she read as a positive evolution arrested by the Revolution's failure, and the spiritual renewal she felt to be implicit in Romantic art. A path had to be found to enable France and Europe to emerge from the aridity and cynicism of the post-Terror ethos. That path was to be through the realm of an art of transcendent signification that she, as one of the new species of self-anointed artist-critics, like Alphonse de Lamartine, George Sand, and Victor Hugo after her, would have pointed to in her texts. Germaine de Staël's critical stance may be viewed as advocacy of the permanence of a revolution in the realm of the mind and the imagination directed toward the perfecting of humankind.

This imperative to a belief in mutability and hope was the call to which figures as various as the Frenchman Pierre Simon Ballanche and the American transcendentalists (see AMERICAN THEORY AND CRITICISM: NINETEENTH CENTURY) would respond, as Staël's critical texts continued to find resonance with readers throughout the nineteenth century.

Madelyn Gutwirth

See also ITALIAN THEORY AND CRITICISM: 1. ROMANTICISM.

Germaine de Staël, *Madame de Staël, an Extraordinary Woman: Selected Writings of Germaine de Staël* (ed. and trans. Vivian Folkenflik, 1987), *Madame de Staël on Politics, Literature, and National Character* (ed. and trans. Morroe Berger, 1964), *Oeuvres complètes* (17 vols., 1820–21, reprint, 1967).

Simone Balayé, *Madame de Staël: Lumières et liberté* (1979), "Le Système critique de Mme de Staël: Théorie et

sensibilité," *Revue de l'université d'Ottawa* 41 (1971); Paul de Man, "Madame de Staël and Jean-Jacques Rousseau" (1966, trans. Richard Howard, *Critical Writings, 1953–1978*, ed. Lindsay Waters, 1989); Béatrice Durand-Sendrail, "Madame de Staël et la condition post-révolutionnaire," *Romantic Review* 82 (1991); Madelyn Gutwirth, "Forging a Vocation: Germaine de Staël on Fiction, Power, and Passion," *Bulletin of Research in the Humanities* 86 (1983–85); Gruffed E. Gwynne, *Madame de Staël et la révolution française. Politique, philosophie, littérature* (1969); Charlotte Hogsett, *The Literary Existence of Germaine de Staël* (1987); Robert de Luppé, *Les Idées littéraires de Madame de Staël et l'héritage des lumières (1795–1800)* (1969); Haydn Mason, "The Way Forward: Madame de Staël, *De la littérature*," *French Writers and Their Society, 1715–1800* (1982); Roland Mortier, "Philosophie et religion dans la pensée de Madame de Staël," *Rivista di letteratura moderne e comparate* 20 (1967); Kurt Mueller-Vollmer, "Staël's *Germany* and the Beginnings of an American National Literature," *Germaine de Staël: Crossing the Borders* (ed. Madelyn Gutwirth, Avriel Goldberger, and Karyna Szmurlo, 1991); Laurence M. Porter, "The Emergence of a Romantic Style from *De la littérature* to *De l'Allemagne*," *Lettres françaises* 1 (1974); Georges Poulet, "La Pensée critique de Mme de Staël," *La Conscience critique* (1971); Jean Roussel, "La Critique de Madame de Staël," *Jean-Jacques Rousseau en France après la révolution, 1795–1830* (1972); Jean Starobinski, "Mme de Staël et la définition de la littérature," *Nouvelle revue française* 28 (1966); Susan Tenenbaum, "The Coppet Circle: Literary Criticism as Political Discourse," *History of Political Thought* 1 (1980).

STAROBINSKI, JEAN

Jean Starobinski (b. 1920) studied literature at the University of Geneva as a pupil of Marcel Raymond, one of the founders of the GENEVA SCHOOL. He also studied medicine, specializing in psychiatry. Until his retirement, in 1985, he was professor of French literature and of history of medicine in Geneva. He has written on the history of medicine and of psychology, particularly on melancholy, which has remained a concern throughout his career: melancholy in its relations to philosophy, medicine, fine arts, and literature was the theme of his 1988 Leçons du Collège de France, published under the evocative title *La Mélancolie au miroir: Trois lectures de Baudelaire*. It had also been the subject of his medical dissertation, *Histoire du traitement de la mélancolie des origines à 1900*, which appeared in 1960. Starobinski is known above all for his literary criticism, but from his training in psychiatry he has retained, it seems, an enduring interest in the phenomena of the mind (his criticism addresses prominently the question of the sensations, perceptions, and ideas of the self as represented in the literary text) and an unusual ability to decipher in a text the specific marks of a mind, an imagination, and a desire.

If the name of Starobinski remains associated with that of JEAN-JACQUES ROUSSEAU, as it has been for the last 30 years (ever since Starobinski's remarkable thesis *Rousseau, la transparence et l'obstacle*), it is no doubt because the critic found in this author the exemplary subject for his unremitting inquiry into the history and the phenomenology of subjectivity and consciousness. Starobinski's works on Rousseau (his book as well as numerous articles), on forms of representation in European art at the time of the French Revolution *(1789: The Emblems of Reason)*, and on the Enlightenment *(The Invention of Liberty)* have had a decisive influence on eighteenth-century studies. He has contributed also a number of important studies on Montaigne, Racine, Corneille, and La Rochefoucauld, as well as on Montesquieu, Diderot and Voltaire, Stendhal, CHARLES BAUDELAIRE, PAUL VALÉRY, and contemporary poets such as Yves Bonnefoy and Pierre-Jean Jouve. His more theoretical writings include a book on the anagrams of the linguist FERDINAND DE SAUSSURE, an important piece on the STYLISTICS of Leo Spitzer, a number of penetrating essays on SIGMUND FREUD, and several articles reflecting on the meaning of criticism and of literary history.

Starobinski's critical approach entails an attempt to recover as much as possible of the writer's work and to apply to it as much breadth of reference as necessary—history, history of ideas, psychology, medical science, philosophy. The act of interpretation thus ranges over the totality of an author's writings—published texts, letters, diaries, fragments—relying on a mode of close reading that is informed by an intimate knowledge of the philology, the stylistics, and the aesthetics of a particular period. There is no single critical method, for what determines his critical approach is the desire to create the best conditions for the observation and understanding of his object and to establish the most faithful possible relation to its reality. Starobinski uses the image of a panoramic look from above *(un regard surplombant)*: too much proximity blurs the lines, whereas by standing too far from the work, one ends up seeking an impossible totality. Yet, while defending the need for a critical distance, he also recognizes in this act of distanciation the threat of an irony that can turn into negation or of a theory devoid of ethics. The critic can never presume to

know but must listen to the virtualities of the text. As the interpretive act is never given in advance—there is no methodology, no school, no science—it will engender itself in the act of writing. Originating in a rigorously analytical spirit, Starobinski's writing is yet infused with a creative gesture and a questioning, introspective mood: it constitutes a literary performance in its own right.

An impressive monograph as well as a reflection on critical methods, his book on Rousseau sketches *l'imaginaire* of the author as it traces the "symbols and ideas in which the thought of a writer organizes itself" *(Rousseau* 10). Examining the autobiographical and the theoretical writings as well as the existential patterns that emerge from Rousseau's life, Starobinski discovers a binary organization: a withdrawal from society combined with a rejection of civilization in an attempt to recover a lost purity *(la transparence)* and a movement of return to the world through writing, which becomes a form of justification. But Rousseau's enterprise of recovery must fail: with the loss of the original purity, communication is always marred and the revelation of a true self is impossible. Hence the need for him to endlessly write, for writing is where "man will have to *invent* the forms of his desire" (205). In a later text, "Le Remède dans le mal: La Pensée de Rousseau," Starobinski shows how Rousseau's philosophical and literary enterprise develops as the remedy offered by the mind and the imagination to an originary fall into history and into reflexivity. He highlights the emergence of an inner world where "the soul, having cut off all outer ties, converses innerly with itself" (197) and where "suffering has become the mark of a difference that privileges the individual" (199). Starobinski thus makes of the writings of Rousseau the exemplary text of a revolution grounded in "the dangerous pact of the self with language" *(Transparence* 239); it inaugurates the birth of a modern subjectivity.

In *Montaigne in Motion* Starobinski pursues in the *Essais* the issues that were at the center of his reflection on Rousseau: appearance versus essence, the constitution of the subject, and the importance of writing in this process. He traces in Montaigne a phenomenology of the mind organized in a triadic pattern: the rejection of a world of illusory appearance, a quest for the essence in an attempt to seize the self, and the final recognition of the necessity and legitimacy of appearances. Montaigne's work shows the impossibility of seizing the essence and of achieving consciousness without representation. The critic thus identifies in Montaigne an imperative (defining humanism?) that requires each individual to create his or her relation to the world and find the rational and critical stance *(le regard vigilant)* bespeaking an awareness and a freedom in the world. The literary text bears testimony to a consciousness as it becomes the locus of a transference where the melancholy mind (for Starobinski, the quintessentially poetic and reflective mind) can make up through writing for the sense of a loss of the self and of the world.

"Melancholy is nothing but the consciousness of the state of the body," wrote one of the physicians quoted in his *Histoire du traitement de la mélancolie* (90). In his pursuit of the melancholy mind, Starobinski is interested not only in the history of modern subjectivity but also in the phenomenology of the subject in its relations to writing. Focusing on the triangulation body-mind-language that constitutes the thinking and writing subject, he traces as carefully as possible in the literary text the move from bodily sensation to form, and from form to signification. Thus, in an early preface to Rousseau's autobiographical writings he asks that "we join with the writer in the unformulated, at the level of the inner source, where the truth of the heart appears only as a mute sign" ("Préface" to Rousseau viii). His work on GUSTAVE FLAUBERT and Valéry in the late 1980s evidences more clearly the crucial question he addresses to writing: If the language of the body and the senses, "so close to the mute truth of objects," constitutes the most authentic expression of the self, what form can embody this truth and communicate it outside, "beyond the boundaries of a particular body"? ("L'Échelle" 183). And further, how can the critic not only retrieve but analyze this move from "interiority" to the expression of the self? Indeed, Starobinski wants us to read in the gaps and silences of the text neither the violence of repression nor the evidence of negativity but rather the inception, the inaugural moment of a subjectivity and a consciousness. One of the tasks of the critic is, then, to analyze this move from silence into writing and being; Starobinski fulfills it with the highest critical intelligence and sensibility.

But his concerns are also with the history and meaning of the European cultural tradition. For instance, in a brilliant introduction to the French translation of Ernest Jones's *Hamlet and Oedipus* and in "Acheronta Movebo," a study of the classical motives that shaped *The Interpretation of Dreams,* he studies the metaphors and narratives that informed Freud's thought and demonstrates how metalanguage and substructure converge in Freud's search for a totalizing discourse. The mind thinks itself in language and its representations, and as language is always a borrowing, a citation, our attempts to know are always relative, their authority deriving from other authorities. "L'Auteur et son autorité" is indeed the subtitle of Starobinski's most recent collection of essays, *Tables*

d'orientation, where his critical reflections (on Rousseau, GERMAINE DE STAËL, Marcel Raymond, Albert Béguin, and Denis de Rougemont) center on the ethical impulse that informs the works of these thinkers.

Writing about the powerful influence of Denis de Rougemont's *L'Amour et l'Occident,* Starobinski associates this book with those written in the 1930s by Marcel Raymond, Béguin, Roger Caillois, and Gaston Bachelard, and concludes:

> I have gathered the names of those works which have had an exceptional power of awakening and which are, I believe, landmarks in the intellectual life of this century: as they changed the relationship between literature, philosophy (or theology) and the *sciences humaines,* bringing together domains that had been separate, they have opened a fresh field. (173)

This no doubt is true as well of all of Starobinski's own books (beginning with *La Transparence et l'obstacle,* published two decades later): each of them has brought about a renewal of such an "awakening" and has widened the field of literary studies. It may be, however, that Starobinski's essays, if more discrete, give yet a richer picture of his abilities (they won him in 1985 the prestigious Prix Balzan): this more tentative and introspective genre seems to offer the ideal space for critical explorations that open, characteristically, onto the existential and ontological as well as the ethical and political domains. To read Jean Starobinski forces us to recognize the unexpected freedom and responsibility given to literary criticism. He shows us that reading in its fullest sense, far from being a secondary, mimetic and determined activity, is the "invention of [our] freedom."

Evelyne Ender

See also GENEVA SCHOOL.

Jean Starobinski, "Acheronta Movebo," *Critical Inquiry* 13 (1987), *Claude Garache* (1988), "L'Échelle des températures," *Le Temps de la réflexion* 1 (1980), *Histoire de la médecine* (1963, *A History of Medicine,* 1968), *Histoire du traitement de la mélancolie des origines à 1900* (1961), *L'Invention de la liberté* (1964, *The Invention of Liberty,* trans. Bernard C. Swift, 1987), *Jean-Jacques Rousseau: La Transparence et l'obstacle* (1957, 3d ed. with *Sept essais sur Rousseau,* 1976, *Jean-Jacques Rousseau: Transparency and Obstruction,* trans. Arthur Goldhammer, 1988), *La Mélancolie au miroir: Trois lectures de Baudelaire* (1989), "Monsieur Teste face à la douleur," *Valéry pour quoi?* (1987), *Montaigne en mouvement* (1982, *Montaigne in Motion,* trans. Arthur Goldhammer, 1985), *Montesquieu par lui-même* (1953), *Les Mots sous les mots: Les Anagrammes de Ferdinand de Saus-*

sure (1971, *Words upon Words,* trans. Olivia Emmet, 1979), "The Natural and Literary History of Bodily Sensation" (trans. Sarah Matthews and Lydia Davis, *Zone 4: Fragments for a History of the Human Body,* pt. 2, ed. Michel Feher, 1989), *L'Oeil vivant* (1961, *The Living Eye,* trans. Arthur Goldhammer, 1989), *Portrait de l'artiste en saltimbanque* (1970), "Préface" to Ernest Jones, *Hamlet and Oedipus* (1967), "Préface" to J.-J. Rousseau, *Oeuvres autobiographiques* (1962), "Préface" to Leo Spitzer, *Études de style* (1967), *La Relation critique* (1970), *Le Remède dans le mal: Critique et légitimation de l'artifice à l'âge des lumières* (1989), *1789: Les Emblèmes de la raison* (1973, *1789: The Emblems of Reason,* trans. Barbara Bray, 1982), *Table d'orientation: L'Auteur et son autorité* (1989).

Jacques Bonnet, ed., *Pour un temps: Jean Starobinski* (1985); Sarah Lawall, *Critics of Consciousness: The Existential Structures of Literature* (1968); Robert R. Magliola, *Phenomenology and Literature: An Introduction* (1977); J. Hillis Miller, "The Geneva School: The Criticism of Marcel Raymond, Albert Béguin, Georges Poulet, Jean Rousset, Jean-Pierre Richard, and Jean Starobinski" (1972, *Theory Then and Now,* 1991); Georges Poulet, *La Conscience critique* (1971).

STEIN, GERTRUDE

Born in Allegheny, Pennsylvania, raised in Oakland, California, educated at Harvard University and the Johns Hopkins Medical School, Gertrude Stein (1874–1946) spent most of her adult life in Paris, France. There she composed most of her expansive *oeuvre*—the novels *Fernhurst* (1902, reprint, 1971) and *Q.E.D.* (1903, reprint, 1950); the well-received collection of stories *Three Lives* (1909); the playful portraits of Cézanne, Matisse, and Picasso (1912); the equally playful yet controversial *Tender Buttons* (1914); the epic novel of family, *The Making of Americans* (1925); the delightful memoir of the Parisian art colony, *The Autobiography of Alice B. Toklas* (1933); and a concluding series of novels (e.g., *Lucy Church Amiably,* 1930; *Ida: A Novel,* 1941; and *Mrs. Reynolds,* 1941), plays (e.g., *Doctor Faustus Lights the Lights,* 1938, and *The Mother of Us All,* 1945), memoirs (e.g., *Everybody's Autobiography,* 1937), aesthetic treatises (e.g., *Lectures in America,* 1935; *Picasso,* 1938; and *The Geographical History of America,* 1936), and miscellanea (e.g., the children's book *The World Is Round,* 1938, and the detective story *Blood on the Dining-Room Floor,* 1934).

Stein's influence has followed as much from her literary experiments as from her critical writings. While she has always garnered attention, both favorable and other-

wise, her influence has lately been more and more on the rise, particularly among those interested in POSTMODERNISM and FEMINIST THEORY AND CRITICISM. In the first instance, her appeal stems from the fact that like Stéphane Mallarmé, Stein radically questioned the covenant between word and world and increasingly pushed her own work away from mimesis and toward autotelism. In *Lectures in America,* she expressed her growing annoyance with those who would require the artist (in this instance, the painter) to predicate the work upon things outside it: "The annoyance comes from the fact that the oil painting exists [for others] by reason of these things the oil painting represents . . . and profoundly it should not be so. . . . An oil painting is an oil painting" (84).

John Ashbery, praising Stein's aestheticism, notes that she creates a "counterfeit of reality more real than reality," something that he acknowledges cannot be done but nevertheless leaves us "with the conviction that it is the only thing worth trying" (107). Stein herself would welcome such praise, particularly as applied to the latter half of her career, when her work grew emphatically more self-reflexive. Still, she seems not to have begun here—in a mode of high aestheticism—but more in the nineteenth-century mode of scientism and the "innocent eye." For instance, the early works, such as *Q.E.D., Three Lives, A Long Gay Book* (1932), and *The Making of Americans,* are couched in the language of social typology. In *How Writing Is Written* she discussed the composition of *The Making of Americans:*

> I made enormous charts, and I tried to carry these charts out. You start in and you take everyone that you know, and then when you see anybody who has a certain expression or turn of the face that reminds you of some one, you find out where he agrees or disagrees with the character, until you build up the whole scheme. (156)

This kind of exercise, meanwhile, was followed by the attempt, in the portraits and particularly in *Tender Buttons,* to escape all influence, including remembrance, and make the word portrait be the thing. In *Lectures in America* she wrote that she had wanted, in this phase, to look "at anything until something that was not the name of that thing but was in a way that actual thing would come to be written" (256). Further theoretical statements about this and later phases of her work can be found in the volumes *The Geographical History of America* and *Picasso.* The first particularly evinces Stein's interest in typology and the distinction between "human nature," wherein perception is always colored by identity and memory, and "human mind," wherein perception "has nothing to do with identity or time or enough" (157). The second evinces Stein's interest in the innocent eye. Arguing that "related things are things remembered and for a creator . . . remembered things are not things seen, therefore they are not things known" (35), Stein proposes "to express things seen not as one knows them but as they are when one sees them without remembering having looked at them" (15).

Throughout her career, Stein seemed to wish to go against the grain of convention. And although she did not appear to take an interest in feminist politics—in *The Autobiography of Alice B. Toklas* she writes that she did not mind "the cause of women or any other cause but it does not happen to be her business" (83)—over the years her work has come to acquire a feminist resonance. Here again she is refusing to play by the rules, rules that in her day would have been, more often than not, man-made. In any event, recent feminist critics have been extremely interested in Stein's work and have put forward two strong contentions. First, Stein's experimental work, beginning, roughly, with *Tender Buttons,* should be understood as a kind of encoded language wherein meaning is not so much absent as "it is multiplied, fragmented, unresolved" (De Koven 172). Stein, as a lesbian in a society still shaking off its Victorian prudery, was forced to disguise her most important thoughts and emotions. Catharine Stimpson writes: "In the first decade of the twentieth century, she was fearful of what she might say, of what she might confess—to herself and others. She disguised her own lesbian experiences through projecting them onto others or through devising . . . her 'protective language'" (188). Secondly, this "coding of sexual activities" led Stein, artistically, into a kind of "anti-language," a language notable for its refusal to conform to traditional ("patriarchal") conceptions of meaning. Stein's language is deliberately playful, deliberately oppositional. In this way, De Koven writes, Stein "substitutes for coherent meaning and referentiality the primacy of surface—the ascendency of the signifier" (172).

There may be no statements by Stein to confirm the opinion that her work represents a kind of *écriture féminine.* Perhaps such statements are unnecessary. What is clear, however, is that through the offices of postmodernists and feminists, Stein's work has been recuperated and made meaningful to a present generation of readers. As she wrote in *The Geographical History of America,* "And so in this epoch the important literary thinking is done by a woman" (183).

Christopher J. Knight

Gertrude Stein, *The Geographical History of America* (1936), *How Writing Is Written* (1974), *Lectures in America* (1935), *Picasso* (1938).

John Ashbery, "The Impossible" (Hoffman); Marianne De Koven, "Gertrude Stein and Modern Painting: Beyond Literary Cubism" (Hoffman); Michael J. Hoffman, ed., *Critical Essays on Gertrude Stein* (1986); Catharine R. Stimpson, "The Somagrams of Gertrude Stein" (Hoffman).

STEVENS, WALLACE

One of the most important American poets of the twentieth century, Wallace Stevens (1879–1955) was also a successful insurance executive, so it is not surprising that his work questions the relation between "imagination" and "reality," placing him in the tradition of William Wordsworth, Samuel Taylor Coleridge, and Ralph Waldo Emerson, as well as Robert Frost, Marianne Moore, Hart Crane, and John Ashbery. Supremely among American poets, Stevens made his poetry an occasion for theorizing about poetry: it is deeply involved in the celebrated and lamented "turn" to theory in the recent history of criticism. Theories of language and literature, politics and letters, are resolutely *in* the texts of Stevens's poetry, more obsessively and explicitly than in any other American poet of this century. With such titles as "Theory," "The Ultimate Poem Is Abstract," "Of Modern Poetry," "The Motive for Metaphor," and "The Pure Good of Theory," as well as a self-reflexive, meditative attitude in his writing, Stevens became the champion, in criticism of the 1970s, of what has been called the deconstructive turn, the turn toward a questioning of the ontological and epistemological foundations of philosophy, literary theory, and criticism. Stevens's poetry foregrounds a skeptical view of language, the notion that reference in language itself is arbitrary. What some have called Stevens's indulgence in the pure sound of language beyond semantics and beyond syntax—the inclusion of exotic terms or nonsense, the disruption of grammatical forms—is a mark of his firm place in the avant-garde of literary theory, those theories that privilege a hermeneutical openness, a sliding of signification among words exploited for their etymological riches and musical beauties. Stevens's work collects the culmination of tendencies inherent in Western thinking since PLATO, for example, the tendency to semantic dispersal and undecidability that attends even "normal" language acts. In addition, the problem of metaphor, central to Stevens's poetic (how do we know reality when the language we use to name reality forever mediates us from it?), suggests also why Stevens's work is important for literary theory.

In "The Noble Rider and the Sound of Words" Stevens calls upon the sound of words to function as his way toward newness, toward a poetry capable of creating the balance between imagination and reality. He writes that only the poet can find the perfection lodged in the sound of words, finding "all the truth that we shall ever experience" (*Necessary* 32). Whereas the poetics of EZRA POUND gives us a kind of visual objectivism, Stevens attaches to the sound of words the power to give us reality imagined with vividness and clarity, more in the manner of Robert Frost, with his "sound of sense" and "sentence sounds," or Hart Crane, with his poem as a "new *word,* never before spoken." In both theories, the poet seeks to recover some lost but primal moment of power and nobility.

Similarly, another of Stevens's talks, "Effects of Analogy," leads to the proposition that poets "dwell" in metaphors and analogies, composing them from the particulars of reality itself. The essay also puts forth two theories of poetry and the poet. The first is that poets try to insert themselves into a general and powerful imagination in order to write good poetry. The second is that poets rely on their own wits, imagination, and power within in order to articulate in the work the center of poetic consciousness. If the poet accomplishes this second goal, it results in a central poetry for Stevens, and it would seem that Stevens's theory of poetry in fact depends upon the meeting of these two imaginations.

What is more important, however, for a theory of the autonomy of the art work, this essay also includes an important passage in response to proletarian writers and other leftists who argued that the poet writes on behalf of the community or nothing and on behalf of social change. Stevens evades this requirement—which apparently would have the poet write from a social view rather than from within his or her own imagination—by suggesting that the poet may have as his or her subject the community and other people by virtue of something internal to the poet. It may be, in other words, "congenital" to the poet's view of the world. Stevens slyly suggests that the most self-reflexive of poetries can (and ought to) be at the same time the most social of poetries, in that it concerns itself with the subject of the community and the individual's relation to it. There can be no notion of personality, temperament, or individuality without the context of the community to give it significance.

This recapitulation of the social in the midst of a most hermetic, self-reflective of poetries is an important irony of modernism. Stevens claimed that his concept of

the first idea in "Notes toward a Supreme Fiction" meant simply the world stripped of "varnish and dirt": "If you take the varnish and dirt of generations off a picture, you see it in its first idea" (*Letters* 426–27). The metaphor of the restoration of painting here suggests that the poet goes about removing all of the dead accumulations of history in order to give us the poem at its earliest offering. In other words, the poem's theory calls for the poem's own destruction. Pushed to its extreme, this poem would be utterly unreadable, totally sealed off from human experience and intelligibility. However, the poem instead merely rehearses the way *toward* such a sweeping denial of history. In this sense, Stevens's poetry enacts a theory of cultural renewal not as disorderly apocalypse or social crisis but as transformation of the canvas of modern life through imaginative scouring. As it turns out, then, aesthetic autonomy—as a central tenet of modernism—seems to be more complicated in Stevens than the term would at first suggest: what is outside the work of art, the social order as well as the literary past, is already inside the poem, and what is inside is another form of the outside (see MODERNIST THEORY AND CRITICISM).

> The poem is the cry of its occasion,
> Part of the res itself and not about it.
>   (*Collected* 473)

As Stevens knew from his Latin, "res" refers to thing or matter or object and is a root for "real." This is the moment of the uncanny in Stevens's work, the moment when the real, the everyday life of New Haven, the banal suburbs of Oxidia, are transformed into something strange. If Stevens is a poet that matters, it is because he was able to explore in poetry—as a theory of life—the fact of the autonomy of the work of art and to resist the reality that made that autonomy a necessity, theorizing the rapprochement of the aesthetic with the social realms.

Stevens shared with other modernists the belief in the autonomy of the aesthetic sphere—and in its value as autonomous—but he also spent a good deal of his energy trying to understand the consequences of that breach between the society and the work of art. There are moments in his writing when he is perfectly jubilant and broodingly meditative about the isolation of the poem: "Poetry is a purging of the world's poverty and change and evil and death. It is a present perfecting, a satisfaction in the irremediable poverty of life" (*Opus* 193). Stevens here ends with history read as the arena of death and decay, yet he begins with a sense of the power of the poem to perfect. His reference to the "present perfecting" of grammar as the poem's major tense recognizes the complexity of his claims for a theory of poetry: on the one hand, the poem gives us images of perfection; on the other hand, it gives us a vehicle that articulates the process of perfection. Stevens recognized the recalcitrance of the base, of reality, yet fashioned a theory of poetry in which the real was always in a state of transformation into his "intricate evasions of as." This phrase, from an important passage in "An Ordinary Evening in New Haven," in its context gives a precise sense of the ambivalence Stevens had for this definition of the poetic: "This endlessly elaborating poem / Displays the theory of poetry, / As the life of poetry" (*Collected* 486). These lines articulate precisely what poetry can and cannot do in Stevens's mode: the poem elaborates the conjunction between a theory of fiction and the fiction itself, but what it cannot do—which is why it imagines a "more harassing master"—is elaborate the conjunction between the fiction and life outside, the real world. Even so, the very language of the outside, the real—"as it is, in the intricate evasions of as"—gives us not philosophy's thing-in-itself, matter, substance, or history, but rather a real world as figured by the imagination. The imagination turns back upon itself, as the poet makes his endless elaborations the ground for a kind of reality posited by the imagination.

Stevens joins with RALPH WALDO EMERSON, FRIEDRICH NIETZSCHE, James Joyce, MARTIN HEIDEGGER, and other modernists in a project to deny or master or refigure the historical spirit. In this sense, Stevens writes a poetry that takes its place among the varieties of modernism available to him, though unlike Pound's or T. S. Eliot's, his modernism does not take the form of a retrospective recapitulation of some shining moment or figure of the past. His theory is more dangerous in that it asserts the necessity of always beginning anew, always reinventing the figures that had allowed those of the past to live. In this way, Stevens is one of our most Emersonian poets, one profoundly skeptical of history, one deeply invested in the renewing powers of language, and, finally, one who in his skepticism sought to confront history and the real and thus fulfill what he understood was a poet's major responsibility.

Andrew Lakritz

Wallace Stevens, *The Collected Poems of Wallace Stevens* (1954), *Letters of Wallace Stevens* (ed. Holly Stevens, 1966), *The Necessary Angel: Essays on Reality and the Imagination* (1951), *Opus Posthumous: Poems, Plays, Prose* (rev. Milton J. Bates, 1989), *The Palm at the End of the Mind: Selected Poems and a Play by Wallace Stevens* (ed. Holly Stevens, 1971), *Souvenirs and Prophecies: The Young Wallace Stevens* (ed. Holly Stevens, 1977).

Milton J. Bates, *Wallace Stevens: A Mythology of Self* (1985); Charles Berger, *Forms of Farewell: The Late Poetry of Wallace Stevens* (1985); Harold Bloom, *Wallace Stevens: The Poems of Our Climate* (1976); Peter Brazeau, *Parts of a World: Wallace Stevens Remembered* (1983); Margaret Dickie, *Lyric Contingencies: Emily Dickinson and Wallace Stevens* (1991); Frank Doggett and Robert Buttel, eds., *Wallace Stevens: A Celebration* (1980); Alan Filreis, *Wallace Stevens and the Actual World* (1991); Barbara M. Fisher, *Wallace Stevens: The Intensest Rendezvous* (1990); Albert Gelpi, ed., *Wallace Stevens: The Poetics of Modernism* (1985); B. J. Leggett, *Wallace Stevens and Poetic Theory: Conceiving the Supreme Fiction* (1987); Frank Lentricchia, *After the New Criticism* (1980), *Ariel and the Police: Michel Foucault, William James, Wallace Stevens* (1987); James Longenbach, *Wallace Stevens: The Plain Sense of Things* (1991); J. Hillis Miller, "Stevens' Rock and Criticism as Cure," *Georgia Review* 30 (1976); Roy Harvey Pearce and J. Hillis Miller, eds., *The Act of the Mind: Essays on the Poetry of Wallace Stevens* (1965); Richard Poirier, *The Renewal of Literature: Emersonian Reflections* (1987); Joan Richardson, *Wallace Stevens: The Early Years, 1879–1923* (1986), *Wallace Stevens: The Later Years, 1923–1955* (1988); Joseph N. Riddel, *The Clairvoyant Eye: The Poetry and Poetics of Wallace Stevens* (1965); Helen Vendler, *On Extended Wings: Wallace Stevens' Longer Poems* (1969).

STRUCTURALISM

Structuralism in linguistics and literary studies found its major starting point in the work of the Swiss linguist FERDINAND DE SAUSSURE, at the turn of the twentieth century. But it was more fully realized—in fact, the term "structuralism" was coined—in the ongoing work in linguistics, SEMIOTICS, and literary analysis of ROMAN JAKOBSON. (In this development, structuralism should be seen as a subdivision or a methodological field in the larger area of semiotics that finds its origins in the work of CHARLES SANDERS PEIRCE as well as in that of Saussure.) In the *Course in General Linguistics* (1916, trans., 1959, 1983), the transcription by his students of several courses in general linguistics he offered in 1907–11, Saussure called for the "scientific" study of language as opposed to the work in historical linguistics done in the nineteenth century. His work was an attempt to reduce the huge number of facts about language discovered by nineteenth-century historical linguistics to a manageable number of propositions based upon the *formal* relationships defining and existing between the elements of language.

Saussure's systematic reexamination of language is based upon three assumptions: the *systematic* nature of language, where the whole is greater than the sum of its parts; the *relational* conception of the elements of language, where linguistic "entities" are defined in relationships of combination and contrast to one another; and the *arbitrary nature* of linguistic elements, where they are defined in terms of the function and purpose they serve rather than in terms of their inherent qualities. All three of these assumptions gave rise to what Roman Jakobson came to designate as "structuralism" in 1929:

> Were we to comprise the leading idea of present-day science in its most various manifestations, we could hardly find a more appropriate designation than *structuralism*. Any set of phenomena examined by contemporary science is treated not as a mechanical agglomeration but as a structural whole, and the basic task is to reveal the inner . . . laws of this system. What appears to be the focus of scientific preoccupations is no longer the outer stimulus, but the internal premises of the development: now the mechanical conception of processes yields to the question of their function. ("Romantic" 711)

In this dense passage Jakobson is articulating the scientific aim of linguistics as opposed to simple, "mechanical" accounting. By focusing on the "structural whole," he is articulating all three of Saussure's assumptions. First of all, he is asserting that the scientific study of language needs to examine the system, or "code," of language rather than its particular "speech-events." Such a systematic study calls for a "synchronic" conception of the relationships among the elements of language at a particular moment of time rather than the "diachronic" study of the development of language through history. Finally, he is also describing the assumption that the basic elements of language are arbitrary and can only be studied in relation to their functions rather than their causes.

Such a structural analysis governs the conception of all the elements of language in linguistics, from the "distinctive features" that combine to form phonemes to sentences, paragraphs, and more extended segments of language that combine to form discourse insofar as discourse, in the words of Algirdas Julien Greimas, creates a "meaningful whole" (*Structural* 59). Perhaps this is clearest in the development of the concepts of the "phonemes" and "distinctive features" of language. But the aim of literary structuralism was to extend the method of struc-

tural analysis, focusing rigorously on binary oppositions to discover overarching relationships of *combination* and *contrast* in language, to discourses beyond the limit of the sentence—poetry, narratives (including the anonymous narratives of folktales studied in Vladimir Propp's *Morphology of the Folktale* and the anonymous narratives of myth studied in CLAUDE LÉVI-STRAUSS's "structural anthropology"), film, social formations (including gender and class relations), and wider areas of "semantics" and meaning. Such analyses are based on what Jakobson describes as the fact that language and systems of signification are structured as "both *energeia* and *ergon*—in other words, language (or any other social value) as creation and as oeuvre" ("Signum" 179). In this formulation, language is both the *process* of articulating meaning (signification) and its *product* (communication), and these two functions of language are neither identical nor fully congruent. Since the elements of language are arbitrary, moreover, neither contrast nor combination can be said to be "basic." Thus, in language distinctive features combine to form contrasting phonemes on another *level* of apprehension, phonemes combine to form contrasting morphemes, morphemes combine to form words, words combine to form sentences, sentences form paragraphs, paragraphs form (or are) discourses, and so forth. In each instance, the "structural whole" of the phoneme or word or sentence or general signification is greater than the sum of its parts (just as water, H_2O, in Saussure's example [*Course* (1959) 103; (1983) 102] is more than the mechanical agglomeration of hydrogen and oxygen).

The three assumptions of structural linguistics I have traced led Saussure to call for a new science that would go beyond linguistic science to study "the life of signs within society." Saussure named this science "*semiology* (from Greek *semeîon* 'sign')" ([1959] 16). The "science" of semiotics, as it came to be practiced in Eastern Europe in the 1920s and 1930s and Paris in the 1950s and 1960s, widened the study of language and linguistic structures to literary artifacts constituted (or articulated) by those structures. In this, PRAGUE SCHOOL STRUCTURALISM and French structuralism came to examine *meaningful* cultural phenomena from the viewpoint of the conditions that make such meaningful phenomena possible, including the structures that give rise to that meaning. But even before the term "structuralism" was coined, many of the principles of structural linguistics (if not the rigorous definitions of structure articulated by Jakobson, Jan Mukarovsky in Prague, and Lévi-Strauss in Paris) influenced RUSSIAN FORMALISM in its study of the particular "effects" of literature produced by the "elements" of literature and narrative. In all these areas,

Jakobson is a central figure: as a member of the Moscow Linguistic Circle, he participated in Russian formalism; as an exile in Prague, he helped organize the Prague Linguistic Circle; as an exile in the United States during World War II, he introduced Lévi-Strauss to structural linguistics, which allowed the latter to initiate the structural study of myth and cultural anthropology.

An understanding of Russian formalism is important for an understanding of the development of literary structuralism in Prague and Paris, because in focusing on the formal "devices" that create *literary* effects, it attempted to produce a "science" of literature, in the same way that Saussure attempted to produce a "science" of linguistics. However, Russian formalism assumed that "literature" could be legitimately—that is, "scientifically"—isolated from other cultural phenomena. This assumption led Jakobson, Mukarovsky, and Lévi-Strauss to oppose "structure" to "form" as the central concept of understanding. That is, the opposition, implicit in formalism, between form and content does not allow for a conception of literature as a *cultural* as well as an aesthetic phenomenon.

Structuralism, in contrast, offers a framework of understanding in which what is structured in not simply "content" but rather phenomena *already structured* on a different "level" of apprehension, so that the isolated content implicit in literary "formalism"—in New Critical formalism as well as in Russian formalism—betrays the dynamic *relational* nature of meaning. This can be seen, as F. W. Galan has argued, in contrasting Jakobson's 1921 description of the object of study in scientific formalism to his later description as a member of the Prague Linguistic Circle. In 1921 Jakobson claimed that literary study should study "literariness," those isolated forms that make an utterance characteristically "literary," and avoid anything "extraliterary" (such as psychology, politics, or philosophy). In 1933 in Prague, Jakobson modified this position in arguing that the poetic function, or "poeticity," can be viewed as only one constituent part of the complex structure of poetry. "According to Jakobson's structural view, in contrast to his formalist stance," Galan writes, "the difference between art and non-art, or between literary and nonliterary language, is one not of kind but of degree" (107–8). In other words, "poeticity" (unlike "literariness") is a *relational* rather than an absolute element of a poetic work. When the poetic function is dominant, Jakobson says, "the word is *felt* as a word and not a mere representation of the object being named or an outburst of emotion, when words and their composition, their meaning, their external and internal form, acquire a weight and value of

their own instead of referring to reality" ("What?" 378, emphasis added).

In other words, Jakobson, and Prague semiotics more generally, emphasizes the global *cultural* existence of literary discourse in emphasizing the existence of "literature" within configurations of cultural significance. In a similar way, French structuralism in the 1950s and 1960s, growing out of the work of Lévi-Strauss in cultural anthropology, also emphasizes the relationship between structuralism and cultural institutions. Lévi-Strauss studied a wide range of myths, mostly Amerindian myths, and attempted to discover the structure—or what might be called the grammar—of mythological narrative. In this work Lévi-Strauss applied the methods of structural linguistics to narrative, so that structural anthropology analyzes narrative discourse in just the way linguistics analyzes sentences. In this endeavor, he articulated the highest ambition of structuralism and semiotics. "I have tried," he says in *The Raw and the Cooked*, "to transcend the contrast between the tangible and the intelligible by operating from the outset at the sign level. The function of signs is, precisely, to express the one by means of the other" (14). Like Prague structuralism, he attempted to isolate and define the conditions of meaning in culture, to articulate the relationship between the tangible entities of nature and the intelligible meanings of culture.

Lévi-Strauss, in his important methodological essays such as "The Structural Study of Myth" and "Structure and Form: Reflections on the Work of Vladimir Propp," as well as in his extensive anthropological work, attempted, as Edmund Leach has noted, to describe the nature of the "human mind" through a kind of structural "algebraic matrix of possible permutations and combinations" (40). This work initiated a literary movement in the 1960s and early 1970s that has proved to be a watershed in modern criticism, causing a major reorientation in literary studies, marked most notably in the United States when Jonathan Culler's *Structuralist Poetics* won the annual award for an outstanding book of criticism from the Modern Language Association of America in 1975. (The work of Prague structuralism has only reappeared in Western Europe and America after the work of French structuralism [see Steiner x]. In "Structure and Form," for instance, Lévi-Strauss goes back to Propp's contribution to Russian formalism, which antedates the work at Prague.) As a school of literary criticism, French structuralism attempted to explain literature as a system of signs and codes and the conditions that allow that system to function in a way that emphasizes more than Prague structuralism the essential *intelligibility,* as Lévi-Strauss says, of the phenomena it studies. For instance,

Greimas's *Structural Semantics,* a book that enlarges the scope of Lévi-Strauss's *Structural Anthropology* to analyze meaning in general, asserts that "the phenomenon of language as such [may be] mysterious, but there are no mysteries in language" (65). In this, Greimas attempted to "account for" meaning (including literary meaning) as fully and objectively as Saussure's linguistic science attempted to account for the phenomenon of language.

The power of structuralism derived, as ROLAND BARTHES said, from its being "essentially an *activity*" that could "reconstruct an 'object' in such a way as to manifest thereby the rules of functioning" ("Structuralist" 214). By this, Barthes meant that structuralism focused on the *synchronic* dimension of a text (the system of *langue* as opposed to its individual speech events, *parole*), the specific ways in which a text is like other texts. The structural comparison of texts is based on similarities of function (character development, plot, theme, and so forth, as well as the functional definitions of linguistic elements such as finite verbs, pronouns, tenses, and so forth), relationships that Lévi-Strauss called "homologies." The predominantly synchronic analysis of homologies "recreates" the text as a "paradigm," a system of structural possibilities. Following these precepts, Greimas, for example, attempts to reduce the 31 functions of Propp's *Morphology of the Folktale* to axes of knowledge, desire, and power. In more specific studies of literature, Tzvetan Todorov attempts to describe the "grammar" of narratives *(The Poetics of Prose)* and to position *relationally* the "Fantastic" as a genre within a configuration of other literary genres *(The Fantastic).* The genre of the fantastic in his analysis, like the linguistic elements in Saussure's discussion, is an "entity" of literature precisely because it relates to other so-called entities of literature (which are themselves functions of other relationships).

Perhaps the clearest examples of structuralist analyses of literary texts—examples that in their pretense to scientific objectivity most fully seem to avoid the social and temporal contexts of discourse—are the series of analyses of poems that Roman Jakobson published, analyses of such poems as a Shakespeare sonnet and short lyrics by W. B. Yeats, Aleksandr Pushkin, Andrew Marvell, Edgar Allan Poe, and others. (Roland Barthes's structuralist analysis of a biblical narrative, "Introduction to the Structural Analysis of Narratives," and Greimas's book-length study of a single short story by Guy de Maupassant, *Maupassant: The Semiotics of Text,* could also stand as examples of structural analyses of anonymous and non-anonymous narratives.) In these analyses, Jakobson uses technical linguistic terminology—

"finite verbal forms," "coordinate clauses," "grammatical subject," and so forth—to perform a rigorous analysis of the semantics and syntax of each poem, so that it "emerges," as Victor Erlich has said, "as a system of systems, an intricate web of binary oppositions" (7).

These binary oppositions, as Jakobson and Lévi-Strauss note in their structuralist analysis of Charles Baudelaire's "Les Chats," demonstrate that "phenomena of formal distribution obviously have a semantic foundation" (218). In fact, in his headnote to this article, Lévi-Strauss notes that the "superimposed levels" of analysis of the poem—"phonological, phonetic, syntactic, prosodic, semantic, etc."—repeated in his ethnographic analysis of myths insofar as the structuralist *method* of analysis is repeated, while myths, he argues, "can be interpreted only on the semantic level, the system of variables (always an indispensable part of structural analysis) supplied by the multiplicity of versions of the same myth, that is to say, a cross-section through a body of myths at the semantic level only" (202). Similarly, Jakobson notes in "Poetry of Grammar and Grammar of Poetry" that

> any unbiased, attentive, exhaustive, total description of the selection, distribution and interrelation of the diverse morphological classes and syntactic constructions in a given poem surprises the examiner himself by unexpected, striking symmetries and antisymmetries, balanced structures, efficient accumulations of equivalent forms and salient contrasts . . . [which] permit us to follow the masterly interplay of the actualized constituents. (127)

In their analysis of "Les Chats," for example, Lévi-Strauss and Jakobson closely examine the structural oppositions of parts of speech, poetic forms, semantic features (e.g., animate versus inanimate nouns), and so forth, in order to demonstrate that "the different levels on which we touched blend, complement each other or combine to give the poem the value of an absolute object" (217). Such an "absolute" object is what Greimas calls "the still very vague, yet necessary concept of the *meaningful whole [totalité de signification]* set forth by a message" *(Structural* 59). It is the phenomenologically *given* of meaning that is the object of knowledge for all structuralist analyses. (This can be seen in Jakobson's definition of poeticity in terms of a word being "*felt* as a word" ["What?" 378].) That given, assumed by Jakobson and Lévi-Strauss, is that meaning is present, unified, and reasonably the object of scientific analysis. The very "effects" of a poem—or, as Lévi-Strauss says, the "profound aesthetic emotions" that myth and, by extension, discourse in general give rise to (Jakobson and Lévi-Strauss 202)—can be subject to rational scientific analysis. Thus, at the end of their analysis they present (in narrative form) the "experience" of the poem, the appearance of "Les Chats" as "a closed system" of grammatical forms and semantic meanings and, simultaneously, "the appearance of an open system in dynamic progression" aiming at "resolving" the felt grammatical/semantic oppositions of the poem between metaphors and metonymies (218–19). In more general terms, Lévi-Strauss argues elsewhere (in "The Story of Asdiwal") that the function of mythic discourse is to create the illusory resolution of real cultural contradictions.

Such general terms suggest that along with literary studies like those of Jakobson, structuralism expanded the areas subject to rigorous discursive analysis. Barthes's work, for example, charting a course through the early and late stages of structuralism, illuminated semiotic theory, the system of fashion, narrative structure, textuality, and many other topics. Claude Bremond has attempted to trace the "logic" of narrative. Paris school semiotics, following Greimas, has expanded structural analysis to such divergent areas as gestural language, legal discourse, and social science. Further, in semiotic approaches to semantic theory, closely allied to structuralism, there is significant work by Michael Riffaterre, UMBERTO ECO, Jonathan Culler, and others. In these kinds of analysis, as in Jakobson's linguistic analyses of poetry, structuralism tended to focus on the fixity of relations within synchronic paradigms at the expense of temporality, or the "diachronic" dimension, which involves history. This tendency to avoid dealing with time and social change, a tendency that is much less pronounced in Prague structuralism, concerned many critics of structuralism from its beginning and ultimately became a main component of the "poststructuralist" critique of the scientific goals of structuralism.

In this critique, structuralism's strength as an analytical technique is connected to what many conceive to be its major weakness. Its self-imposed limitations, most notable in French structuralism, and especially its lack of concern with diachronic change and its focus on general systems rather than on individual cases, became increasingly evident in the late 1960s. The French philosopher JACQUES DERRIDA offered a particularly decisive critique of Lévi-Strauss in "Structure, Sign, and Play in the Discourse of the Human Sciences" (1966, in *Writing and Difference*) and *On Grammatology*. Derrida points out that the attempt to investigate structure implies the ability to stand outside and apart from it, which is similar to the methods of formalism that both Prague and French structuralism criticized. In specific terms, Derrida critiqued the privileging in Lévi-Strauss of the opposition

between "nature" and "culture." Derrida argues that since one never transcends culture, one can never examine it from the "outside"; there is no standing free of structure, no so-called natural state free of the structural interplay that, in the structuralist analysis, constitutes meaning. For this reason, there is no objective examination of structure, and the attempt to "read" and "interpret" cultural structures cannot be adequately translated into exacting scientific models.

Structuralism and semiotics have come to learn from the critique of the structuralist enterprise and its enabling assumption of the opposition between the tangible and the intelligible, nature and culture. The work of JULIA KRISTEVA, like that of Barthes (see, e.g., *S/Z* [1970, trans., 1974]), both utilizes and goes beyond "structuralism." In such works as *Séméiotiké: Recherches pour une sémanalyse* (1969), *Revolution in Poetic Language* (1974, trans., 1984), *Powers of Horror* (1980, trans., 1982), and *Tales of Love* (1983, trans., 1987), Kristeva combines the "poststructural" work of JACQUES LACAN and Barthes and the earlier critiques of formalism and structural linguistics by M. M. BAKHTIN with the achievements of structuralism and semiotics. In fact, the poststructuralist critique of structuralism can be "accounted for" within the methodological framework of structuralism first fully articulated by Saussure. The *relational* and *arbitrary* nature of signifying phenomena both call for and also breach the third assumption of structuralism, its *systematicity*. That is, since the elements of meaning are relationally defined and arbitrary, they demand a *structural* system for their realization. But those very features of relationality and arbitrariness also continually unweave the structural system. Since language can use *anything* to articulate its meanings, any "structure" can be recontextualized (relationally and arbitrarily). As Greimas notes in *Structural Semantics* (which is among the most rigorous and *systematic* expressions of structuralism), the "edifice" of language "appears like a construction without plan or clear aim" (133). This is because "discourse, conceived as a hierarchy of units of communication fitting into one another, contains in itself the negation of that hierarchy by the fact that the units of communication with different dimensions can be at the same time recognized as equivalent" (82). Another way of seeing this is to note that the two global aims of language described by Saussure—the "articulation" and "communication" of meaning ([1959] 10–14), the structural "processes" and "products" of language that Jakobson mentions—are not fully congruent or compatible (see Schleifer, "Deconstruction"). In this way, then, structuralism, in its scientific study of language and meaning, anticipates and articulates the terms of its own "poststructuralist" critique.

Ronald Schleifer

See also FRENCH THEORY AND CRITICISM: 5. 1945–1968, ROMAN JAKOBSON, CLAUDE LÉVI-STRAUSS, NARRATOLOGY, RUSSIAN FORMALISM, FERDINAND DE SAUSSURE, and SEMIOTICS.

Roland Barthes, "Éléments de sémiologie" (1964, *Elements of Semiology,* trans. Annette Lavers and Colin Smith, 1967), "Introduction to the Structural Analysis of Narratives" (1966, *Image-Music-Text,* ed. and trans. Stephen Heath, 1977), "The Structuralist Activity" (1963, *Critical Essays,* trans. Richard Howard, 1972); Claude Bremond, *Logique du récit* (1973); Jacques Derrida, *De la grammatologie* (1967, *Of Grammatology,* trans. Gayatri Chakravorty Spivak, 1976), *L'Écriture et la différence* (1967, *Writing and Difference,* trans. Alan Bass, 1978); A. J. Greimas, *Maupassant: The Semiotics of Text: Practical Exercises* (1976, trans., 1988), *On Meaning: Selected Writings in Semiotic Theory* (trans. Paul Perron and Frank Collins, 1987), *Sémantique structurale: Recherche de méthode* (1966, *Structural Semantics: An Attempt at Method,* trans. Daniele McDowell, Ronald Schleifer, and Alan Velie, 1983); A. J. Greimas and J. Courtés, *Sémiotique: Dictionnaire raisonné de la théorie du langage,* vol. 1 (1979, *Semiotics and Language: An Analytical Dictionary,* trans. Larry Crist et al., 1982); Roman Jakobson, "Poetry of Grammar and Grammar of Poetry," *Language and Literature* (by Roman Jakobson, ed. Krystyna Pomorska and Stephen Rudy, 1968), "Romantic Panslavism—New Slavic Studies" (1929, *Selected Writings,* vol. 2, 1971), "Signum et Signatum" (1936, trans. M. Heim, *Semiotics of Art: Prague School Contributions,* ed. Ladislav Matejka and Irwin R. Titunik, 1976), "What Is Poetry?" (1934, trans. M. Heim, *Language and Literature*); Roman Jakobson and Claude Lévi-Strauss, "Charles Baudelaire's 'Les Chats'" (1962, trans. Katie Furness-Lane, *Introduction to Structuralism,* ed. Michael Lane, 1970); Claude Lévi-Strauss, *Anthropologie structurale* (1958, *Structural Anthropology,* trans. Clair Jacobson and Brooke Grundfest Schoepf, 1963), *Mythologiques I: Le Cru et la cuit* (1964, *The Raw and the Cooked,* trans. John Weightman and Doreen Weightman, 1975), "The Story of Asdiwal" (1962, trans. N. Mann, rev. Monique Layton, *Structural Anthropology,* vol. 2, 1976), "The Structural Study of Myth" (1955, *Structural Anthropology*), "Structure and Form: Reflections on a Work by Vladimir Propp" (1960, trans. Monique Layton, rev. Anatoly Liberman, *Theory and History of Folklore,* by Vladimir Propp, 1984); Richard Macksey and Eugenio Donato, eds., *The Structuralist Controversy: The Languages of Criticism and the Sciences of Man* (1970); Ferdinand de Saussure, *Cours de linguistique générale* (1916, *Course in General Linguistics,* trans. Wade Baskin, 1959, trans. Roy Harris, 1983); Tzvetan Todorov, *Introduction à la littérature fantastique* (1970, *The Fantastic: A Structural Approach to a Literary Genre,* trans. Richard Howard, 1973), *Poétique de la prose* (1971, *The Poetics of Prose,* trans. Richard Howard, 1977).

Art Berman, *From the New Criticism to Deconstruction: The Reception of Structuralism and Post-Structuralism* (1988); Jonathan Culler, *The Pursuit of Signs: Semiotics, Literature, Deconstruction* (1981), *Structuralist Poetics: Structuralism, Linguistics, and the Study of Literature* (1974); Robert Con Davis and Ronald Schleifer, *Criticism and Culture: The Role of Critique in Modern Literary Theory* (1992); Alan Dundes, "From Etic to Emic in the Structural Study of Myth," *Journal of American Folklore* 75 (1962); Terry Eagleton, *Literary Theory: An Introduction* (1983); Victor Erlich, "Roman Jakobson: Grammar of Poetry and Poetry of Grammar," *Approaches to Poetics* (ed. Seymour Chatman, 1973); F. W. Galan, *Historical Structures: The Prague School Project, 1928–1946* (1985); Terence Hawkes, *Structuralism and Semiotics* (1977); Fredric Jameson, *The Prison-House of Language: A Critical Account of Structuralism and Russian Formalism* (1972); Edmund Leach, *Lévi-Strauss* (1970, rev. ed., 1974); Ronald Schleifer, *A. J. Greimas and the Nature of Meaning: Linguistics, Semiotics, and Discourse Theory* (1987), "Analogy and Example: Heisenberg and the Language of Quantum Physics," *Criticism* 33 (1991), "Deconstruction and Linguistic Analysis," *College English* 49 (1987), *Rhetoric and Death: The Language of Modernism and Postmodern Discourse Theory* (1990); Robert Scholes, *Structuralism in Literature: An Introduction* (1974); Peter Steiner, ed., *The Prague School: Selected Writings, 1929–1946* (trans. John Burbank et al., 1982); John Sturrock, ed., *Structuralism and Since: From Lévi-Strauss to Derrida* (1979).

STYLISTICS

Treatises devoted to the study of style can be found as early as Demetrius's *On Style* (C.E. 100). But most pre-twentieth-century discussions appear as secondary components of rhetorical and grammatical analyses or in general studies of literature and literary language. The appearance of stylistics as a semiautonomous discipline is a modern phenomenon, an ongoing development in linguistic description that is closely tied to the similar rise of literary criticism and linguistics as academic subjects and departments. Modern stylistics, in general, draws much of its analytical power from the analytical methods and descriptive intentions of linguistics, while modern literary stylistics, in particular, draws upon that area and adds to it the interpretive goals of modern literary criticism. In both cases, the use of linguistic methodology has allowed stylistics to move beyond earlier normative and prescriptive descriptions of "correct" styles to a fuller analysis of language itself and the purposes to which language regularly is put.

Whatever the limits of previous approaches to style, or the difficulties that have arisen from the practical application of linguistic methods to stylistic analysis, the desire to begin with a set of well-defined terms and procedures lies at the core of the initial formation of stylistics as a discipline. While all versions of literary stylistics have dedicated themselves to the study and interpretation of literary texts, it was the growing importance of European historical linguistics during the mid-nineteenth century that produced the most easily recognized component of early modern stylistics: a deeply rooted concern with formal linguistic description of literary language. The methodological benefits that stylistics gained by uniting literary interpretation and linguistic analysis were matched by institutional gains as well. Historical and general linguistics were well-established academic disciplines at the turn of the twentieth century, and stylistics could expect to benefit from that status. The use of linguistic procedures thus offered stylistics both an affinity with an established discipline and the possibility of founding the description and interpretation of style upon the bedrock of science.

While its air of scientific analysis made linguistics attractive, linguistic science was not itself a monolithic entity. During the latter half of the nineteenth century, linguistic study oscillated between a desire to define language through efficient analytical methods (often requiring a-contextual descriptions) and another, competing desire to define language as a social and cultural phenomenon. The work of the neogrammarians, key figures in the formation of linguistics as a modern scientific discipline, displays the tension well. Although the neogrammarians began their work with the intention of reintroducing behavior into linguistic description, the attractiveness of scientific method dictated the slow elimination of the user as a complex part of the description. The result for some linguists, notably the philologians, was a sacrificing of the real heart of linguistics to a sterile formalism; for many, however, the shift was the logical result of a move into the modern scientific age. It was in terms of these separate views of the proper role of linguistic description that the predominant approaches

to modern stylistics developed, and because of the strong Continental influence of Romance PHILOLOGY on historical linguistics, modern stylistics usually is seen as having begun there.

The roots of modern stylistics can be uncovered in the work of Charles Bally (1865–1947) and Leo Spitzer (1887–1960). Bally's *Précis de stylistique* (1905) stresses the description and analysis of a language's generally available stylistic properties. Literary texts, in Bally's formulation, are particular examples of language use, and the analysis of their style is not a central part of the general stylistics he emphasizes. Nevertheless, Bally's work, and its later realization in the work of Jules Marouzeau (*Précis de stylistique française,* 1946) and Marcel Cressot (*Le Style et ses techniques,* 1947), strongly influenced the formation of literary stylistics. Such analytical work offered literary critics a relatively precise methodology for describing the components and features of a text. In place of an open-ended and evaluative interpretive process, linguistics both underwrote the need for a more precise analytical attitude toward language study and provided specific categories for characterizing sound, rhythm, and eventually syntax, as well as points of comparison and contrast between registers, forms, and functions within genres and literary periods.

In contrast to the *stylistique* of Bally and his proponents, Leo Spitzer insisted upon following the more philologically based tradition of textual (and often literary-textual) analysis. Such work, while using the analytical techniques of modern linguistics, strives to unite the analytical description with a critical interpretation that relates the style to a larger conceptual or situational frame (e.g., *Linguistics and Literary History* 1–39). Style is seen as an expression of a particular psychological, social, or historical sensibility or moment rather than as a general property of a particular language. In undertaking these wider interpretations, critics such as Spitzer did not, however, assume that they were defining their stylistics as separate from, or even as a subset of, linguistic analysis. In both his etymological studies and his more specifically literary-critical interpretations (*Stilstudien,* 1928, and *Romanische Stil- und Literaturstudien,* 1931), Spitzer insisted that he was promulgating a general program of linguistic study, offering his stylistics in opposition to what he saw as the more reductionist analyses of general, scientific linguistics. Spitzer himself emphasized the split until the end of his career, regularly referring to his work as *Stilforschung* (literary, cultural interpretation of style—philology in his eyes) to set it apart from that of *Stilistik,* or Bally's *stylistique* (e.g., "Les Études de style et les différents pays" 23–39). At the same time, he assumed—as did fellow critics of style such as Ernst Robert Curtius, Karl Vossler, and Helmut Hatzfeld—that he was not reducing the scientific aspect of linguistics but only offsetting a false, positivistic tone that was becoming increasingly predominant in the field. The tension in linguistics between general linguistic description and less formal sociocultural interpretation thus was mirrored in this early separation in stylistics between linguistic stylistic description and literary stylistic interpretation. It is a separation, and a tension, that remains at the heart of modern stylistics.

This tension, Spitzer's and Bally's position as Continental rather than Anglo-American linguists, and the popularity of PRACTICAL CRITICISM and NEW CRITICISM in England and the United States all lay behind the relative lack of an organized, Anglo-American literary stylistics during the first half of the twentieth century. Literary stylistic analyses were occurring in England and in the United States at this time, but they often did not contain the formal linguistic orientation that characterizes the modern discipline of stylistics. Instead, they drew support and procedures from the basic but less analytically structured orientation of New Criticism and practical criticism. And while the influence of Romance language study grew during the mid-twentieth century (due in no small part to the presence in England and in the United States of many expatriated scholars), the established strength of other, more empirical linguistic methodologies reduced possible exchanges between linguistics and literary criticism.

The eventual appearance of modern stylistics in Anglo-American work repeated the earlier Continental process, appearing most clearly when united with an interest in linguistic analysis at mid-century and with the related interest in literary STRUCTURALISM somewhat later. By the late 1950s, the general critical ambience provided by the rise and fall of New Criticism and practical criticism, in combination with a growing interest in comparative literary studies and a new awareness of the increasing importance of linguistic science, provided the needed impetus for a strong appearance of literary stylistics outside the European continent. The processes behind the formation of American stylistics are exemplified by work done by Michael Riffaterre on Romance languages. Riffaterre's published dissertation, *Le Style des Pléiades de Gobineau* (1957), is a self-described attempt to blend Spitzer's work with that of contemporary structural linguistics, while the later, even more formal stylistic methodology set forth in "Criteria for Style Analysis" (1959) and "Stylistic Context" (1960) shifts away from interpretive description and toward the general

linguistic analysis that was beginning to dominate academic study.

Such work in stylistics reflected a larger trend occurring within literary criticism as a whole during this period. Riffaterre's particular interest in a systematic, formal description of literary style mirrored a growing awareness among literary critics in general of the possibilities provided to literary study by trends and theories available from formal linguistic study. The discovery of linguistic work by FERDINAND DE SAUSSURE, ROMAN JAKOBSON, and structural linguistic theory in general all formed part of the rapid flowering of critical work closely related to, if not directly based upon, particular methods of linguistic analysis. It was not a link between literary stylistics and structural linguistic analysis that marked the real establishment of stylistics as a discipline within the United States, however. It was the transformational-generative grammar of NOAM CHOMSKY (*Syntactic Structures*, 1957) that signaled the arrival of stylistics as a discipline with independent, self-defined goals, if not yet a real autonomy from either linguistic or literary-critical approaches to language analysis.

The rapidly established importance of Chomsky's linguistics within his own discipline provided a strong argument for the importance of transformational-generative grammar within literary stylistics as well. But beneath that academic, institutional cause lay particular features of the theory that explain further the explosion of stylistic work using transformational-generative grammar. The grammar's focus on syntax, its distinction between deep and surface structures, and the resulting dynamism in its descriptive procedures all contributed to a methodology that allowed for a much wider discussion of the possible forms (and by implication styles) available to the user of language. At the same time, the declared mentalism of Chomsky's grammar was seen by many as providing literary stylistics with a means of uniting a still lingering Romantic sense of creativity with the formal linguistic description needed to provide the analysis with a now-requisite air of scientific study. Many critics found not only an implied linkage between language and mind within Chomsky's grammar but an actual justification for tying intention to structure. Whichever aspect of Chomsky's grammar provided the impetus for a particular study, the general influence was huge, and the numerous studies that appeared during the years 1965-75 testify to the boost that Chomsky's thinking on language gave to the era, one of the most hectic and dramatic in the formation and growth of stylistics.

The founding of the field's major Anglo-American

journals—*Style* (1967) and *Language and Style* (1968)—provides one convenient benchmark for the full arrival of stylistics as an academic discipline in Britain and the United States, while a plethora of studies and editions from 1970 and later provides another, more wide-ranging view. Representative texts, which display not only a sense of the myriad volumes available on the two continents but also a sampling of other methods either related or opposed to Chomsky's work, include Donald Freeman, ed., *Linguistics and Literary Style* (1970); Pierre Guiraud, *Essais de stylistique* (1970); Guiraud and Pierre Kuentz, eds., *La Stylistique: Lectures* (1970); Seymour Chatman, ed., *Literary Style: A Symposium* (1971); Roger Fowler, ed., *Style and Structure in Literature: Essays in the New Stylistics* (1975); Helmut Hatzfeld, ed., *Romanistische Stilforschung* (1975); and Freeman, ed., *Essays in Modern Stylistics* (1981). The last text in this list, Freeman's second collection, argued for the gradual cementing of transformational-generative grammar's position within much of American stylistics, an argument made clear by comparing this collection's announced focus on transformational-generative grammar with the eclecticism of Freeman's first text. But the position of transformational-generative grammar had become decidedly less dominating by 1980, as the rest of the collections demonstrate.

The differing models and methodologies found in a text such as Chatman and Samuel R. Levin's *Essays on the Language of Literature* (1967), which is not devoted to stylistics alone, serve to demonstrate that other methods were equally popular elsewhere, even before the eager pursuit of Chomsky's linguistics had faded. In England, interest in describing not only the structure of language but also the properties of discourse and its functions gathered around the work of J. R. Firth, in general, and in the union between linguistics and literary criticism that appears in the work of M. A. K. Halliday, in particular, while the work of Stephen Ullman provided yet another example of stylistic analysis brought to fruition by an expatriated Continental Romance scholar. At the same time, philologically oriented work similar to that of Spitzer continued to be available, especially in Italy, while other work, such as that of Richard W. Bailey and Lubomír Doležel in statistical analysis, argued for yet another method within what was already a very eclectic field. In fact, while linguistic formalism applied to literary language remained the basis of modern stylistic procedure, the field continued to build upon what was historically a large variety of possible stylistic approaches.

Numerous descriptive categories have been created to provide some order among the resulting variety of approaches to style, but the most common and useful taxonomies are those designed around a communication model such as that of Jakobson ("Linguistics and Poetics," in Sebeok). Some approaches are essentially concerned with describing style as a habitual form of expression particular to an author or authorial psyche, while other formats begin with style as an affective response generated in the reader. Similar to these alternatively expressive and receptive approaches are definitions that see style as indicative of a larger context: a cultural sensibility, a historical period, or a national feeling. More textually focused approaches define style in terms of a particular genre, or in relation to other linguistic registers, or simply as a web of relations between the elements of the text itself. In all this work, whatever its variety, the main attraction for stylistics remains that of formal descriptive power.

That interest eventually began to come under increasing censure for what was perceived as its sacrificing of interpretive complexity for scientific efficiency. The swinging back of the critical pendulum is most clearly apparent in STANLEY FISH's pointed attack, "What Is Stylistics and Why Are They Saying Such Terrible Things about It?" issued in two parts, in 1973 and 1980. The main thrust of such arguments was not simply that stylistic analyses were misguided or misinterpretive but that the very foundation of scientific analysis on which stylistics based itself was inherently flawed. In essence, the arguments stated that there was no way to link the empirically defined features of the text with the rest of the critical analysis except through the subjective, interpretive framework of the critic. In fact, the arguments declared, even the stylistic features described in the analysis were themselves subject to the interpretive choices of the reader/critic.

In attacking this aspect of stylistic analysis, these discussions were taking aim at one of the specific reasons for the rise of stylistics as an academic discipline during the twentieth century. The depth and cogency of arguments such as those put forth by Fish, Barbara Herrnstein Smith, and others were a clear signal of shifting trends in literary criticism—and in its attitude toward linguistic analysis. By 1980 it was impossible to argue for any stylistic model without addressing these trends, although by then the issue already had been partially settled by an increasing concern with discourse in the field of linguistics. Speech-act theory was providing cogent arguments in favor of a return to the speech situation and the context of production, and those discussions merged nicely in literary circles with an increased interest in historical and contextual analysis.

The question for stylistics became one of how to blend this increased desire for social, cultural, and contextual critical analyses with the discipline's foundation in formal linguistics. (See DISCOURSE and SPEECH ACTS.)

Although the problem came to the forefront of stylistics by 1980, it had been looming on the horizon for a while. The value of efficient description began to fade before a renewed desire for social and contextual analysis in the study of language and of its situation of production and reception, and the basic movement under way in linguistics displayed itself in a variety of ways and works in literary stylistics. Roger Fowler, for example, issued *Essays on Style and Language* (1966) and *Style and Structure in Literature* (1975) but shifted to *Literature as Social Discourse* (1981). Halliday, who also had been working on discourse issues for some time in Great Britain, produced *Language as Social Semiotic* (1978), while the positive reception given to Mary Louise Pratt's *Toward a Speech Act Theory of Literary Discourse* (1977) demonstrated the degree to which such concerns were taking root in critical discussions within the United States. Finally, the growing influence of feminism and psychoanalysis on linguistics and literary criticism, exemplified by Robin Lakoff's *Language and Woman's Place* (1975), Cheris Kramarae's *Women and Men Speaking* (1981), Deborah Cameron's *Feminism and Linguistic Theory* (1985), and John Forrester's *Language and the Origins of Psychoanalysis* (1980), reinforced the need to adopt a new stance toward contextually rooted discussions in both stylistics and linguistics. The resulting shift away from strict formalism and toward a greater concern with function and context, together with a rebirth of interest in interpretive as well as descriptive analysis, once again forcefully brought forward the issue of what constituted the proper degree (or non-degree) of methodological rigor in stylistics.

At the turn of the twentieth century, allegiance to linguistic procedures was the primary defining element of stylistics as a discipline, and it remains so in the last quarter of the century. The major question facing stylistics is whether movement away from that defining characteristic, no matter how slight, will result not only in a loss of self-definition but also in a shifting back of the entire field into the related disciplines of literary criticism, linguistics, or more probably RHETORIC, which is enjoying a strong rebirth. In addressing that question, stylistics continues to face its status as a discipline operating among all these disciplines, from which it historically has drawn both its goals and its methods. Work being done in the last quarter of the century on historical and contextual readings of literary and nonliterary texts suggests that stylistic models can be expanded sufficiently to allow the discipline to continue to draw upon all related fields adequately for its own purposes while maintaining its own autonomy.

James V. Catano

See also NOAM CHOMSKY and LINGUISTICS AND LANGUAGE.

Charles Bally, *Précis de stylistique* (1905); Deborah Cameron, *Feminism and Linguistic Theory* (1985); James Catano, *Language, History, Style: Leo Spitzer and the Critical Tradition* (1988); Seymour Chatman, ed., *Literary Style: A Symposium* (1971); Seymour Chatman and Samuel R. Levin, eds., *Essays on the Language of Literature* (1967); Noam Chomsky, *Syntactic Structures* (1957); Marcel Cressot, *Le Style et ses techniques* (1947); Lubomír Doležel and Richard W. Bailey, eds., *Statistics and Style* (1969); John Rupert Firth, *Selected Papers of J. R. Firth: 1952–59* (1968); Stanley Fish, "What Is Stylistics and Why Are They Saying Such Terrible Things about It?" (1973, pt. 2, 1980, *Is There a Text in This Class?* 1980); John Forrester, *Language and the Origins of Psychoanalysis* (1980); Roger Fowler, *Essays on Style and Language: Linguistic and Critical Approaches to Literary Style* (1966), *Literature as Social Discourse: The Practice of Linguistic Criticism* (1981); Roger Fowler, ed., *Style and Structure in Literature: Essays in the New Stylistics* (1975); Donald C. Freeman, ed., *Essays in Modern Stylistics* (1981), *Linguistics and Literary Style* (1970); Pierre Guiraud, *Essais de stylistique* (1970); Pierre Guiraud and Pierre Kuentz, eds., *La Stylistique: Lectures* (1970); M. A. K. Halliday, *Language as Social Semiotic: The Social Interpretation of Language and Meaning* (1978); Helmut Hatzfeld, ed., *Romanistische Stilforschung* (1975); Roman Jakobson, "Linguistics and Poetics" (Sebeok); Cheris Kramarae, *Women and Men Speaking* (1981); Robin T. Lakoff, *Language and Woman's Place* (1975); *Language and Style* (1968–); Jules Marouzeau, *Précis de stylistique française* (1946); Mary Louise Pratt, *Toward a Speech Act Theory of Literary Discourse* (1977); Michael Riffaterre, "Criteria for Style Analysis," *Word* 16 (1959), *Essais de stylistique structurale* (1971), *Le Style des Pléiades de Gobineau* (1957), "Stylistic Context," *Word* 16 (1960); Thomas Sebeok, ed., *Style in Language* (1960); Herbert Seidler, *Allgemeine Stilistik* (2d ed., 1963); Barbara Herrnstein Smith, *On the Margins of Discourse: The Relation of Literature to Language* (1978); Leo Spitzer, "Les Études de style et les différents pays," *Langue et littérature: Actes du VIII Congrès de la Fédération Internationale des Langues et Littératures Modernes* (1961), *Linguistics and Literary History: Essays in Stylistics* (1948), *Leo Spitzer on Language and Literature: A*

Descriptive Bibliography (ed. E. Kristina Baer and Daisy E. Shenholm, 1991), *Romanische Stil- und Literaturstudien* (2 vols., 1931), *Stilstudien* (2 vols., 1928); *Style* (1967–); Stephen Ullman, *Meaning and Style: Collected Papers* (1973).

Richard W. Bailey and Dolores M. Burton, *English Stylistics: A Bibliography* (1968); James R. Bennett, *A Bibliography of Stylistics and Related Criticism, 1967–83* (1986); Helmut Hatzfeld, *A Critical Bibliography of the New Stylistics Applied to the Romance Literatures, 1900–1952* (1953) and *1953–1965* (1966); Louis T. Milic, *Style and Stylistics: An Analytical Bibliography* (1967).

TAINE, HIPPOLYTE

Hippolyte Taine (1828–93) is best known for his theory that literature is the product of "la race, le milieu et le moment" (*Histoire* xxiii), a proposition that places him squarely in the positivist camp of Auguste Comte and other nineteenth-century French thinkers. Yet Taine's view of the essential nature of an author's surroundings is not as limiting as it appears, and in fact Taine often found himself at odds with prevailing positivist and naturalist theories. He was a prolific writer who explored history, literature, metaphysics, and psychology, all the while scorning Comte for his restricted vision of the world. Yet despite Taine's considerable influence in various disciplines, his principal interest to modern scholars can be resumed in the words "race," "milieu," and "moment."

Taine was born in the Ardennes mountains to a middle-class family of modest means. When his father died in 1840, Taine was sent to Paris to study, eventually attending the École Normale. Although he was clearly the outstanding student of his class, he failed his final examination for the *agrégation* because the conservative examiners disapproved of his lesson on Spinoza's moral system. This episode would have a profound effect upon Taine's career and on his attitude toward the dominant philosophers of his day. Forced to abandon his goal of university teaching, he taught secondary classes and gave private lessons, which allowed him time to produce such important works as *Les Philosophes classiques du dix-neuvième siècle en France* (1857, *The Nineteenth-Century French Philosophers*), *Essais de critique et d'histoire* (1858, *Critical and Historical Essays*), *History of English Literature* (1864), and *On Intelligence* (1870). He devoted much of the last 20 years of his life to his *Origins of Contemporary France*. For all his influential work and his active entry into the social life of the Parisian intellectuals, Taine was mistrusted by positivists, naturalists, and Romantics alike. It was not until his election to the Académie française in 1878, on his third attempt, that he was accepted by his contemporaries as a major force in nineteenth-century French thought.

While Taine's first love was psychology, his lasting contribution has been as a critic of literature and art. His studies in psychology, history, and philosophy have been relegated to the realm of minor works, but his literary criticism, and particularly his work on Honoré de Balzac, has stood the test of time, for it is here that he incorporates the scientific, naturalistic, and even Romantic views that shape his critical thought. His scientific side remained predominant, however, and resulted in the formulation of his theory of literary production.

In the introduction to *History of English Literature* Taine presents his view of the forces that determine the nature of a particular society. In this deterministic outlook, "race," "milieu," and "moment" are the sources of what he calls the master faculties, the "soul" of a nation (*Histoire* xxxiv). For Taine, race is defined as the innate and hereditary dispositions we bring with us into the world. It is a distinct force that can always be recognized despite the vast deviations the other two forces produce in us. As an example, Taine uses the Aryan race, spread throughout the world but retaining many similarities. Milieu is seen as the accidental and secondary tendencies that overlie our primitive traits, the physical or social circumstances that disturb or confirm our character. It includes all external powers that mold human character. Moment, finally, is what Taine calls the "acquired momentum" (xxix). It is indeed the accumulation of all past experiences, but as critics such as RENÉ WELLEK have pointed out, it is more importantly the situation of a particular time of the history of a nation or a race, the *Zeitgeist*.

Taine, like G. W. F. HEGEL, whom he greatly admired, believed that "all great change has its roots in the soul" and that the "psychological state is the cause of the social state" (quoted in Wellek 36). Taine does not, however, follow logical causal sequences but instead reduces a phenomenon to its logical precedence, its law, its essence. Like Hegel, he sees history as the development of large forces, nations, races, philosophies, literatures, and arts. These collective forces are expressed and represented by great individuals, who can be divided into two groups: those men of the classical ages and Latin races (scientists, orators, men of letters) and those of the Romantic ages and Germanic races (poets, prophets, inventors). It is precisely this division between the classical and the Romantic that we find within Taine himself and that accounts for much of his inconsistency.

Taine applies his ideas about society to literature in the same introduction to *History of English Literature*. For him a work of literature is a transcript of contemporary manners, a representation of a certain kind of mind. Behind each document there was a "man." One studies the document in order to know the man. But Taine is not a biographer; when he writes "man," he means not the individual author but the author as a representative of his race, surroundings, and epoch.

For twentieth-century critics, Taine's view of literature is oversimplified, naive, and limited. They point to Taine's disregard for the written document as an entity having its own life and significance. At the same time, they fail to recognize his Romantic side, which is less visible in the enunciation of the theory than is the influence of scientific positivism. Yet, Taine is very much a product of his time, divided between Romantic idealism, visible in his melancholy and in his sometimes violent style, and positivistic determinism. He eventually repudiated many of the Romantic writers he had once admired, but he retained a Romantic sensibility as well as a respect for the power of nature.

Taine's essay on Balzac is generally considered his most successful transposition of his theory to literary criticism. Although it was written in 1858, five years before *History of English Literature*, this essay contains all the elements found in the better-known introduction. In the analysis of Balzac, we also see the same contradiction between Romantic and realist that existed in Taine himself. Despite such opposing forces, there is a unity in Balzac's works. He is representative of his time, but he looks beyond contemporary mores to try to depict the hidden meaning in contemporary history. It is this hidden meaning, this amalgam of symbols, types, and characters, that constitutes the unity of Balzac's work and gives it its force. Taine links the man—his greed for money, his sensuality, his ambition, and his capacity for hard work—with his society, the imaginary world of his characters, his style, and his philosophy. The unity in contradiction, the interconnections, are developed effectively. Taine convincingly presents the sensation of the totality of the writer, his work, and the civilization he represents.

Despite the truth of much of his theory and his skill in applying it to Balzac, Taine is most often criticized for his lack of rigor in the development of a scientific theory. He deals only in generalities, leaving us dissatisfied with the lack of system, order, and evidence in his method. He either did not understand or rejected the work of literature as a text that could be considered a totality, isolated from its creator. Rather, he saw literature as indicative of an age, a nation, or individual mind. Taine's limitations thus render him less useful for those twentieth-century critics whose major concern is the text itself.

William VanderWolk

See also FRENCH THEORY AND CRITICISM: 3. NINETEENTH CENTURY.

Hippolyte Taine, *Balzac: A Critical Study* (1858, trans. Lorenzo O'Rourke, 1906), *De l'intelligence* (1870), *Essais de critique et d'histoire* (1858), *Histoire de la littérature anglaise* (1864, *History of English Literature*, trans. H. van Laun, 1872), *Les Origines de la France contemporaine* (1875–93, *The Origins of Contemporary France: The Ancient Regime, The Revolution, The Modern Regime: Selected Chapters*, ed. Edward T. Gargan, 1974), *Les Philosophes classiques du dix-neuvième siècle en France* (1857), *Philosophie de l'art* (1865).

André Chevrillon, *Taine: Formation de sa pensée* (1932); Alvin Eustis, *Hippolyte Taine and the Classical Genius* (1951); Colin Evans, "Taine and His Fate," *Nineteenth-Century French Studies* 6 (1977–78); Simon Jeune, "Taine, le romantisme et la nature," *Romantisme* 30 (1980); Sholom J. Kahn, *Science and Aesthetic Judgment: A Study in Taine's Critical Method* (1953); *Philosophies,* special issue, *Romantisme* 32 (1981); K. de Schaepdryver, *Hippolyte Taine: Essai sur l'unité de sa pensée* (1938); Leo Weinstein, *Hippolyte Taine* (1972); René Wellek, *A History of Modern Criticism, 1750–1950,* vol. 4, *The Later Nineteenth Century* (1965).

TEXTUAL CRITICISM

Textual criticism provides the principles for the scholarly editing of the texts of the cultural heritage. In the Western world, the tradition and practice of collecting, tending, and preserving records was first instituted in the Hellenistic period. The great library at Alexandria, before it was destroyed by fire, was the foremost treasury of manuscripts in classical antiquity. At the library, a school of textual scholarship established itself, with a strict fidelity to the letter in editing, but its systematic principles in the works of the librarian Aristarchus of Samothrace have for the most part not survived. The subsequent Christian ages were long oblivious of the

Hellenistic textual discipline. Instead, the scriptoria of the proliferating centers of medieval learning were ruled by the pragmatics of the copyist. Scribes interpreted texts as they copied them, and as they did so they often compared variant source document exemplars and, in the process, altered texts in transmission.

Such interpretive criticism of variant readings remained the mode of procedure for the humanist philologists who laid the early foundations of modern textual scholarship. Their first care was the classical and medieval texts in Latin and Greek, but by the eighteenth century scholarly editing was equally practiced on vernacular texts. In England during this period, it was typically men of letters and of the church—from Nicholas Rowe via Alexander Pope, Lewis Theobald, Bishop Warburton, and SAMUEL JOHNSON, among others, to Edward Capell—who turned to the editing of Shakespeare's plays and those of his fellow dramatists. Capell collected Shakespeare first editions to evaluate them in historical terms, thus paving the way for twentieth-century Shakespearean bibliography.

The epitome of this age of amateur learning was a type of edition designed to collocate the commentary on every variant reading from the accumulated editorial tradition—the edition *cum notibus variorum,* or "variorum edition" for short. As a mode of the scholarly edition, the variorum edition was revived in the era of positivism, the era of fact-finding in all sciences, and has, albeit with significant extensions and shifts of emphasis from the textual to the interpretive, survived to this day. Its revival in the late nineteenth century in the United States was the consequence of the professionalization of textual criticism that, beginning in Germany, set in under the auspices of historicity in the earlier nineteenth century. The seminal innovations in method were an evaluation of the documents as sources and their arrangement in a family tree, or stemma, of textual descent.

The heredity model of the stemma generated procedures of combinatory logic to ascertain and evaluate textual authority and from authority to establish critical texts. Stemmatology marked the beginnings of textual criticism as an articulation of principles and rules for editing. It was at first manuscript-oriented and again, initially, the domain of textual criticism in the classics. Deemed valid equally for medieval vernacular texts by Karl Lachmann and his followers, it was adopted, similarly, in biblical studies once rationalism had questioned the belief in Scripture as literally God-given and had opened ways to understanding the historicity of the words of the Bible through textual scholarship. For medieval textual studies, Paul Bédier in France early in the

twentieth century challenged the validity of textual decisions arrived at by way of logically schematized document relationships. He proposed instead a hermeneutics of editing pivoting on the critical evaluation of a "best text" to serve as the basis for a scholarly edition.

Neither stemmatology nor "best-text" editing appeared fully applicable, however, to texts of the eras since the invention of the printing press. The earliest orientation here was toward the text of the author's final redaction. The text as last overseen by the author was to provide the edition base text of a scholarly edition. Hence, over and above the text and its transmission, the author and authorial intention became important determinants for editorial rationale. A textual scholarship specific to the modern philologies began to emerge. Distinct in theory and methodology, it was, however, as gradual in forming as modern literary criticism was in gaining independence from the inherited modes of studying the ancients. The principle of the author's final redaction did not as such and by itself carry sufficient strength to oust eclectic editing by subjective choices grounded in taste and sensibility.

In the twentieth century, it was in England that modern textual criticism was first put on methodological foundations to counteract such subjectivity in editing. The material study of the book—bibliography—was reshaped into a virtual science of editing. As traditionally understood, bibliography was an auxiliary branch of historical study for book collectors, archivists, and librarians. Listing books by authentic date and place required systematic conventions of description. These in turn demanded precise analytical investigations of the physical characteristics of books. Springing from the recognition that the findings of such analytical bibliography not only spoke of books as material objects but held information also about the texts the books contained, the New Bibliography inaugurated by A. W. Pollard, R. B. McKerrow, and W. W. Greg in England was textual bibliography. It became the supreme methodology of textual criticism in England and America for the first two-thirds of the twentieth century. The claims for its status as a science grew from a conviction that bibliographical analysis was capable of revealing the patterns of textual transmission entirely through the black marks on paper, in total disregard of the sense and meanings that these marks carried. The goal of determining the history of a text according to the formal patterns of its transmission was to assess textual authority without the intervention of critically interpretive judgment, let alone of subjective taste, and to establish in editing the text of highest authority. Establishing this text meant retrieving it in a pristine state from extant documents in which it had become corrupted in transmission.

Despite the objectifying innovations of its analytical procedures, thinking in bibliography-based textual criticism remained structured as in the inherited approaches. Transmission was a priori defined as corruptive. Texts commonly survived in documents of transmission alone. To assess their relative authority, a distinction was made between authorized and nonauthorized documents. The texts that were substantive for editing resided in the authorized documents, referred to as witnesses, that is, those documents over which the author had exerted direct or indirect control. Where no authorized document survived, the extant derivative witness nearest the lost source was declared to be a substantive document carrying the relevant substantive text. (Substantive texts of this description are all that survive, for example, for the plays of Shakespeare, and it is from the textual problems of Shakespeare's plays that Anglo-American textual criticism in the twentieth century has derived its paradigms.) Authorization conferred presumptive authority, a quality assumed by analogy for substantive texts in nonauthorized documents. Yet, since at the same time transmissional corruption was always assumed, it was the obligation of textual criticism and editing to isolate and undo it. The pure text of unalloyed authority to be retrieved had its imagined existence before and behind the textual reality in the extant transmission. It was an ideal text.

The inherited perspective of textual criticism on the ideal text was thus rearward-directed, upstream against the lines of descent in textual transmission. The logical crunch came when revision carried texts forward and authoritative changes of text in derivative documents of transmission had to be dealt with. At this juncture, historically and systematically, the question of copy-text became a main focus of editorial theory in Anglo-American textual criticism. A copy-text is a material base and heuristic foundation for certain types of scholarly critical editions. It may be understood as a base text provided in an extant document that editorial labor by controlled alterations transforms into an edited text. A copy-text is not an absolute requirement for scholarly editing. In editorial modes that strictly equate document and text, such as the editing of draft manuscripts or the editing, severally, of different versions of a work, the base text is not treated, and especially not altered, in the manner of a copy-text. It is specifically when the editing aims to produce an ideal text that a copy-text is chosen, as the text from which to depart, from among the extant document texts.

The choice of copy-text is basically a practical matter. It did not loom large as a problem where no revision in transmission complicated the picture. The copy-text was simply the primary authorized text, or else the substantive text nearest the lost source. But with authorization being thought of as conferred upon the document, document and text were tied up together. R. B. McKerrow, in the course of his preparations in the 1930s for an old-spelling critical Shakespeare edition, encountered revisions in printings after the first editions. Because they were reprints, these were by definition nonsubstantive witnesses. Yet McKerrow saw no choice but, on the strength of the revisions, to nominate such derivative document texts as the copy-texts for his proposed edition. This entailed accepting all readings not manifestly corrupt from the copy-text, and it meant taking certain unidentifiable accretions of corruption into the bargain. It was only W. W. Greg, after McKerrow's death, who saw a way out of such a "tyranny of the copy-text" (Greg 382).

Greg's 1949 lecture "The Rationale of Copy-Text" became the focal text for Anglo-American textual criticism at mid-century. Empirically, based on his bibliographical and editorial experience with medieval and Renaissance texts, Greg pleaded for the earliest substantive text as copy-text even when revisions were found in an otherwise nonsubstantive witness. With respect to what he termed the accidentals of the text, that is, its orthography and punctuation, an edition would thereby remain as close to the primary authority as the transmissional situation allowed. Only in the extant witness closest to the lost original—deemed to be least overlaid by the preferential spellings and punctuation of scribes and compositors—would there be an appreciable chance that the accidentals were the author's own.

The same held true for the substantives, the words of the text themselves. Greg suggested that the copy-text closest to original authority should rule, too, in all instances of indifferent variation in substantives, that is, wherever it was critically undecidable whether a later variant was due to corruption or revision. Revision was conceded only where it was critically recognizable. Admitting that critical recognition was required implied abandoning the erstwhile claim that bibliography-grounded textual criticism could operate on the basis of the black marks on paper alone. Owing to the pragmatic situation with books of the period of hand printing, moreover, when authors could not or did not read proof or otherwise influence the compositors' choice of orthography and punctuation, only verbal variants were considered authorial revisions. A derivative witness thus was considered authoritative only where it contained substantive changes likely to be revisions and therefore superseding their respective antecedents in the copy-text. These revisions were emended into the copy-text as replacements for the corresponding original readings. The procedure amounted to a mode of critical eclecticism governed no longer by taste but by bibliographically controlled method. The text of composite authority that resulted was again an ideal text.

Greg's proposals advanced the practice of editing Renaissance texts. They proved seminal, moreover, beyond their original scope and purpose. In giving new respectability to eclecticism, they acknowledged the pragmatic nature of editing. (Embracing eclecticism, it is true, entails conceiving of a text as a heterogeneity of readings. That this is a theoretically doubtful proposition is a fact slow to be recognized even after 40 years of consideration.) Furthermore, Greg's "Rationale" made an implicit logical distinction between text and document, from which conceptions of virtual copy-texts have been derived for later non-Renaissance editions, such as editions of Henry Fielding, Nathaniel Hawthorne, Stephen Crane, or James Joyce. What is most important, the "Rationale" provided a theoretical place for taking authorial intention systematically into account in scholarly editing. As advanced argumentatively by Fredson T. Bowers, G. Thomas Tanselle, and others to provide, first, the foundations for the editorial projects of the Center for Editions of American Authors (CEAA) and, subsequently, the advisory principles of the Center for Scholarly Editions (CSE) of the Modern Language Association of America, Greg's pragmatics were developed into a full-scale theory of copy-text editing to yield critically edited texts of the author's final intention. Anglo-American scholarly editing became, as Peter Schillingsburg has maintained, essentially author-oriented.

The reformulation of Greg's pragmatics for Renaissance texts as general principles for editing modern literature was a triumph of the movement for grounding Anglo-American textual criticism in bibliography. At the same time, the application of the principles to nineteenth-century texts, as in the CEAA editions of Hawthorne (1963–) or Crane (1969–75), sparked controversies that have led to an intense theoretical debate over models, methods, concepts, and aims of textual criticism and editing that has not abated. Copy-text editing as codified following Greg's "Rationale," conceived as it was for texts surviving mainly in print, sought to integrate the aspect of revision—of authentic, and generally authorial, textual changes—within a methodology designed to undo errors that normally occur in copying or reprinting texts. The omnipresence of evidence for authorial

composition and revision in manuscripts and prints of recent times necessitates broadening the focus. To organize textual criticism and editing, however, around compositional and revisional processes would require significant reconsiderations of what texts are or may be considered to be. Late-twentieth-century literary theory, to be sure, entertains notions of text variously emphasizing textual stability, instability, or indeterminacy, yet none of these notions has had a marked impact on Anglo-American textual criticism and its editorial models. The editorial model of the ideal text, in particular—be it that of the text of archetypal purity or, as its mirror image, that of the text of authorial final intentions—has, it is true, a notional stability. Yet it is conceived of as stable in pre-theoretical terms, realized as it is under the pragmatics of copy-text eclecticism.

For theoretical foundations of an editorial model of textual stability, by contrast, the orientation for textual criticism may be suggested to lie in the tenets of STRUCTURALISM. (This is exemplified, for instance, in present-day German text-critical thought.) Also, correlative to the notion in modern literary theory of textual instability, one may envisage text-critical and editorial models answering to the processes of text composition and revision. Privileging textual fluidity over final stability, such models may be expected, in particular, to reconsider whether it is valid to grant overriding status to intention among the determinants by which texts (in writing as in editing) take shape. From one position, questionings of these determinants, as in the writings of Jerome McGann, focus on the social factors accompanying the publication and dissemination of the written word. From another angle, considerations of the implications for textual criticism of a psychology of the creative act have entered the debate, as in the writings of Hershel Parker. Such an approach may lead, thirdly, to a correlation of theories of textual indeterminacy with, specifically, the textuality of unresolved alternatives in draft manuscript texts.

Textual criticism and editing in the nineteenth and early twentieth centuries owed much of the impetus for its development in thought and method to German scholarship. The exhaustive *historisch-kritische Edition* of an author's complete works is essentially a German concept. As such, it was realized, for example, for JOHANN WOLFGANG VON GOETHE and FRIEDRICH SCHILLER in the late nineteenth century, that is, within decades of their deaths. This type of edition has continued to command allegiance as a scholarly ideal. German textual scholarship did not experience the urge for scientific objectivity by which bibliography became the focus of the discipline's orientation in England. In editing, the inherited modes of text constitution persisted almost to mid-century in Germany. Yet subjective eclecticism, or *Intuitionsphilologie,* as it came derogatorily to be called, was always tempered, in full-scale scholarly editions at least, by the element *historisch* in the double-barreled adjective. The specific sense of historicity fostered in German textual criticism has provided distinct orientations for the German direction of the discipline.

Innovation of stance and method came with Friedrich Beissner's edition of the works of FRIEDRICH HÖLDERLIN, which began publication in 1943. Endeavoring to present Hölderlin's poems through all their stages of development, from notes to drafts to publication (or abandonment), Beissner devised an apparatus to display what he saw as the organic growth of the poetic texts toward unity and superior aesthetic integrity. His teleological and intention-oriented assumptions were traditional, yet the edition's focus on composition and revision was unprecedented. In its wake, the German-speaking countries have seen an indigenous debate regarding principles of textual criticism and critical editing. In theoretical terms, its movement has been from Beissner's focus on the author, recognizably akin to the author-orientation of Anglo-American textual criticism, toward a focus on the text. Its points of perspective have been the historic integrity of the text version, on the one hand, and the dynamic progression in time of composition and revision, on the other. Under the structuralist tenet of the contextual referentiality of all elements of a text, and hence of the essential context relationship of textual variants, this double perspective has emphasized the distinct nature of the variance resulting from writing and rewriting, as opposed to that accumulating as errors in the transmission.

Following Beissner's lead, the demand for editorial representation of the textual developments of composition and revision has inspired in-depth reflections on the status and functions of the textual apparatus in critical editions and elicited new forms of design of the apparatus. The traditional editorial obligation to eliminate textual corruption, by contrast, has become a distinct side issue. Yet in the traditional field, concepts such as that of the textual error *(Textfehler)* have been seen to require special attention. "Textual error" has been restrictively defined in terms of both quality (as confined, e.g., to the "obvious misprint") and duration, the latter aspect admitting of the possibility that a textual error became incorporated in acts of revision (i.e., a reading may originate in the transmission as a corruption but end up as authenticated in the authorized text). Such

definitional reasoning with regard to the textual error may be seen as a special instance of an overall assessment of the extent to which the textual critic's and editor's interaction with the text requires, and depends on, critical interpretation. Critical interpretation, moreover, is recognized to interact with the text rather than with the author. Present-day German textual criticism, therefore, unlike author-oriented Anglo-American textual criticism, focuses on the integrity of the textual history, on the structural contextuality of texts and their variants, and on the role of critical interpretation to balance and neutralize, if not to eliminate outright, authorial intention as a principle guiding editorial procedures.

German text-critical thought today is characterized throughout by complementaries of opposites. Thus, the version is both extrinsically and intrinsically defined. Its extrinsic determinants guide editorial pragmatics, while its intrinsic determinants govern text-critical theory. The extrinsic determinants are mainly historical. Versions of a work are historical states of the text, such as the finished draft or any given published text, with all the social ramifications of its collaborative production or contemporary reception. In the extrinsic realm an editor decides which version to edit. The choice is as pragmatic in its way as is that of a copy-text. Yet with a version as base text, editing is strictly confined to emending manifest textual error. The edited text establishes not an ideality but the essential historicity of the version text. The editorial labor invested in the establishment of the edited text under the premises of copy-text editing is in the German mode of version editing expended on correlating text and apparatus. The correlation arises from the intrinsic definition of the version in terms of textual variance. As authorial variants of composition and revision, superseded and superseding readings stand in a relational context, and every antecedent text, like every succeeding text of a work, must be regarded as a structural system of language for that work: a version. These versions are successive synchronic structures, and the work as a whole appears structured as a diachronic succession of synchronic versions. The invariance of the versions provides the structural base, while their variance indicates the relational complexity in time of the work's texts. From a structuralist understanding of text, Hans Zeller has declared a single variant to be sufficient to differentiate versions, since by a single variant a text attains a new interrelationship of its elements. For all its editorial impracticability, this is a sound enough theoretical proposition. Anglo-American respondents have voiced empirical objections. In German editorial theory, one may say that it has been balanced from within the system through a reconception of the complementarity of text and apparatus reached by way of a critique of the role of interpretation in textual criticism and editing.

Critical interpretation has, in the German debate, been recognized as relevant again in two senses. First, text-critical and editorial activity begins from the given—documents, the black marks of ink on paper—but the moment it engages with that given, it enters upon interpretation. By accepting the implications of subjectivity, critical editions may attain a controlled objectivity. The interpretive demands of the very data that a textual critic and editor encounters make editorial judgment integral to a critical edition. Signaling through the apparatus the conditions of its controlled objectivity, a critical edition in turn calls upon the critical judgment of the reader. In the second sense, then, the reader's and user's interpretation engages with the critical edition to unlock the text. Critical editions in their specific formatting—established texts correlated to a multilevel system of apparatus—are seen to have a key function for interpretive discourse. Especially the transformation into apparatus of textual genesis and textual history has established the integral apparatus, displaying variance in context, as categorically opposed to the conventional apparatus, which isolates the edition's individual reading (or lemma) from its variants in footnotes or appendixes keyed to the edited text by page and line reference.

An integral apparatus lays out works to be read in the diachronic depth of their texts. In a sense, the acts of reading made possible for the user of a critical edition reenact the author's acts of reading in the writing process that shaped the text under his or her pen. While the author in writing is seen to be the originator of the text, it is the text itself that, for the author as reader, becomes the originator of its own continued revision. By such dynamic interplay of forces, authorial intention is effectively neutralized. The text is not so much what the author intends to achieve as it is what he or she does, or fails to, achieve. To the dynamism of the text, the integral apparatus is the logical answer. Consequently, the dynamic text in the shape of an integral apparatus, incorporating every act and stage of composition and revision in one continuous presentation, has in German textual criticism been theoretically proposed as the ultimate object of editing.

The proposition entails the notion that an edited clear, or reading, text might be dispensed with as being but a concession to the general reader. For unachieved texts, such as unfinished and unpublished drafts, the presentation of the integral apparatus presentation in itself would indeed seem to constitute the adequate editorial response. Clear texts abstracted from the given textual materials may in this case be considered not merely concessions but properly falsifications of their textual state. For works that have attained achieved, and mostly published, versions, on the other hand, the pragmatic choice of a version as the text-to-be-edited prevents the relentless realization of apparatus-only editions. Nevertheless, it follows from the thorough reconception of the functionalities of the apparatus that it is not the clear text but the integral apparatus of critical editions that provides the foundations for critical interpretive reading.

Essentially, the theories and practices reflected and developed in German textual scholarship over the past decades have persisted in conceiving of textual criticism as a hermeneutic discipline. At this point, German textual criticism encounters French *critique génétique,* as does Anglo-American textual criticism in pursuit of its incipient concern for the creative acts of writing. *Critique génétique* is, properly speaking, not a mode of textual criticism setting out principles for scholarly editing. It defines itself as a tributary to literary criticism, developing the critical discourse directly from the materials of authorial writing. It engages with notes, sketches, drafts, proofs—the *avant-texte*—not as raw materials for editing. Its perspective is trained on the critical implications of the writing processes to which the immediacy of the *avant-texte* alone holds the key. Concerned with the *différence* of all writing as it materializes in variants and in the advancing and receding of textual states, *critique génétique* lays claim to opening up a "third dimension of literature." As a scholarly approach to texts in their states of writing, it acknowledges its origins in the fundamental propositions of structural linguistics and modern literary theory and recognizes its existence and operation in reciprocity with historical, social, aesthetic, narratological, or psychoanalytic literary criticism. Defining its domain as one of exploring manuscripts systematically in their capacity to document the genesis of writing, it offers in the interchange an unlocking of the heuristic potential of the *avant-texte* for linguistics, literary theory, and literary criticism. Where it does so quite specifically by technically making the *avant-texte* readable, it overlaps with the domains of traditional textual scholarship. The end of even its technical methodology, however, is not the formal presentation but the critical reading of text in the entirety of its writing. (See also de Biasi.)

From an overview, then, of the directions of thought and the tendencies of practice in textual scholarship in England, the United States, Germany, and France, it may be said in conclusion that textual criticism at the end of the twentieth century is bringing its conservational traditions to bear on innovative redefinitions of its role among the modes of scholarship and criticism by which the written heritage of the culture lives and is continually reappropriated from its foundations.

Hans Walter Gabler

See also PHILOLOGY.

George Bornstein, ed., *Representing Modernist Texts: Editing as Interpretation* (1991); George Bornstein and Ralph Williams, eds., *Palimpsest: Editorial Theory in the Humanities* (1993); Fredson Bowers, *Bibliography and Textual Criticism* (1964), *Essays in Bibliography, Text, and Editing* (1975), *Textual and Literary Criticism* (1966); O. M. Brack, Jr., and Warner Barnes, eds., *Bibliography and Textual Criticism: English and American Literature, 1700 to the Present* (1969); Philip Cohen, ed., *Devils and Angels: Literary Theory and Textual Scholarship* (1991); P. M. de Biasi, "Vers une science de la littérature: L'Analyse des manuscrits et la genèse de l'oeuvre," *Encyclopedia Universalis* (1988); Philip Gaskell, *From Writer to Reader: Studies in Editorial Method* (1978), *New Introduction to Bibliography* (1972); Ronald Gottesman and Scott Bennett, eds., *Art and Error: Modern Textual Editing* (1970); D. C. Greetham, *Textual Scholarship: An Introduction* (1992), *Theories of the Text* (1993); D. C. Greetham, ed., *Scholarly Editing: A Guide to Research* (1993); W. W. Greg, "The Rationale of Copy-Text" (1950–51, *Collected Papers,* ed. J. C. Maxwell, 1966); Jerome J. McGann, *A Critique of Modern Textual Criticism* (1983), *The Textual Condition* (1991); Jerome J. McGann, ed., *Textual Criticism and Literary Interpretation* (1985); D. F. McKenzie, *Bibliography and the Sociology of Texts* (1986); R. B. McKerrow, *Prolegomena for the Oxford Shakespeare* (1939); Hershel Parker, *Flawed Texts and Verbal Icons: Literary Authority in American Fiction* (1984); Peter L. Shillingsburg, *Scholarly Editing in the Computer Age: Theory and Practice* (1986); G. Thomas Tanselle, *A Rationale of Textual Criticism* (1989), *Selected Studies in Bibliography* (1979); James Thorpe, *Principles of Textual Criticism* (1972); William Proctor Williams and Craig S. Abbott, *An Introduction to Bibliographical and Textual Studies* (1985, 2d ed., 1989); Hans Zeller, "A New Approach to the Critical Constitution of Literary Texts," *Studies in Bibliography* 28 (1975); Hans Zeller and Gunter Martens, eds., *Texte und Varianten: Probleme ihrer Edition und Interpretation* (1971).

TRILLING, LIONEL

Lionel Trilling (1905–75) was born in New York City and educated at Columbia University, where he spent almost his entire teaching career. (When he received a tenured appointment in 1939, he was the first Jew in the history of the Department of English to gain such security of employment.) He dedicated his career as a teacher, writer of fiction, essayist, and social critic to an attempt at integrating the worlds of Marxism, Freudianism, traditional moralism, and literary realism (see MARXIST THEORY AND CRITICISM). In so doing, he developed a manner prompted by his self-conscious awareness of the intricate complexities of his project. His prose, a dense and sinuous tissue of introspective deliberation and reflection, is testimony to the capaciousness of mind he thought literary criticism demanded. His prose style is also implicitly a product of his belief that significant literature possesses the same complexity, irony, and, to use a term he favored, "variousness."

Although he is the author of two very good short stories, "Of This Time, of That Place" (1943) and "The Other Margaret" (1945), and one admirable novel, *The Middle of the Journey* (1947), and although he apparently aspired to a greater career as a fiction writer, Trilling found his métier in the reflective essay. Beginning in the explication of a text (usually fiction rather than poetry), the essay would characteristically become a meditation on the condition of the contemporary American readers of that text, a class of intellectuals whom Trilling, for some 40 years, sought to represent in such journals as *Partisan Review*. A contemporary of his, the poet and short-story writer Delmore Schwartz, rightly said of him: "Mr. Trilling is interested in the ideas and attitudes and interests of the educated class, such as it is and such as it may become: it is of this class that he is, at heart, the guardian and the critic" (212). Trilling did not interpret literature so much as he sought to interpret the culture that, surrounding him, read literature in ways that revealed its own moral condition.

In this respect, he tried to sustain in the United States the tradition of literary criticism brought to a synthesis in England in the nineteenth century by MATTHEW ARNOLD. His detailed and able study of Arnold (1939), as well as his shorter study of E. M. Forster (1943), was written, as he said, under the aegis of a concern with "the tradition of humanistic thought and in the intellectual middle class which believes it continues this tradition" ("Situation" 111). However, these two books were also stalking-horses against another tradition, that of Marxism, a tradition gaining vitality among intellectuals after the worldwide economic depression of the 1930s.

Trilling set himself against that tradition, allying himself instead with the enlightened middle class of educated readers who considered themselves removed from partisan ideologies (Forster's elaborate sense of passivity had considerable appeal to Trilling). But Trilling also felt kinship with fellow writers and critics who had, after an earlier engagement with the radical Left and even with Soviet communism, broken with such affiliations: Philip Rahv, William Phillips (of *Partisan Review*), Sidney Hook, Lionel Abel, James Burnham, Dwight Macdonald, Max Eastman, and James T. Farrell. Arnold had said that "the great work to be done in this country, and at this hour, is not with the lower class, but with the middle" (*Essays Religious and Mixed,* ed. R. H. Super, 1992, 346). Echoing this idea, Trilling said that "however much I may acknowledge the historic role of the working class and the validity of Marxism, it would be *only* piety for me to say that my chief literary interest lay in this class [the middle class] and this tradition" ("Situation" 111).

More important to Trilling than Karl Marx, however, was SIGMUND FREUD (see also KARL MARX AND FRIEDRICH ENGELS). While Marx had recognized that all of life is struggle, and can be understood as a history of dialectical oppositions, and while he had understood that reality is hard, material, and substantial, he had not fully appreciated, Trilling believed, the weight that must be given to the intricacies of the private and individual human *sensibility*. The synthesis of that sensibility, modulated by the imagination, with the given circumstantiality of life, makes for literature. In "Freud and Literature," Trilling says that Freud gives us a way of thinking "which makes poetry indigenous to the very constitution of the mind" (*Liberal* 49).

Trilling's devotion to Freud is unstinting for his entire career, but it is not based on an interest in the technical nomenclature and dynamics of psychoanalysis. Neither the "scientific" Freud nor the constructive and therapeutic Freud attracted Trilling. Rather, it was the "tragic" Freud, the prophet who in *Civilization and Its Discontents* (1930) declared that "there are difficulties attaching to the nature of civilization which will not yield to any attempt at reform" (ed. James Strachey, 1961, 62).

Using this declaration as the background for his most important collection of essays, *The Liberal Imagination* (1950), Trilling castigated American liberals for the fatuity of their social and political optimism. He argued that such an ill-grounded belief had prevented them from coming to terms with the most important literary achievements of their century: "Proust, Joyce, Lawrence, Eliot, Yeats, Mann (in his creative work), Kafka, Rilke, Gide—all have their own love of justice and the good life, but in not one of them does it take the form of a love of the ideas and emotions which liberal democracy, as known by our educated class, has declared respectable" (*Liberal* 94). The conservative Freud, who had grasped the inherent limitations and disabilities of life, could open up the somber qualities of modern literature where American liberalism would prove inadequate.

In the 1950s, Trilling's two collections of essays, *The Opposing Self* (1955) and *A Gathering of Fugitives* (1956), revealed both his satisfaction with the relatively benign politics of the time (Eisenhower middle-of-the-roadism) and his belief that those politics promoted the kind of stability congenial to good literature. In an important 1950s symposium, "Our Country and Our Culture," sponsored by *Partisan Review,* Trilling championed the argument that the "party of mind" and "the party of money," previously at odds in American history, had now joined forces and could generate a middle-class cultural life freed of disfiguring political hostilities (*Gathering* 65). In previous times, the "party of mind" had been represented by the etiolated RALPH WALDO EMERSON and by twentieth-century "progressives." The "party of money" had been represented by Theodore Dreiser, whose prose Trilling had always seen as a touchstone of American vulgarity. Only HENRY JAMES had been able to find a balance between such extremes. Now other writers and critics would be able to do the same. In this period, Trilling gives his readers other examples of cultural strength and heroism to admire: John Keats (particularly in his letters), William Dean Howells, John O'Hara, GEORGE ORWELL, William Wordsworth, and Edith Wharton.

But out of this relatively optimistic period in his writing, during which time Trilling gained great eminence and authority among American critics and book reviewers, came two phrases that dominated, and then darkened, the rest of his career: the "morality of inertia" and the "sentiment of being." The first, employed in the Wharton essay, denotes "the morality imposed by brute circumstance, by biology, by habit." It is at the root, Trilling argues, of much of human life: "moral inertia, the *not* making of moral decisions, constitutes a large part of the moral life of humanity" (*Gathering* 37). The second, drawn from Wordsworth's *Prelude, Book Two* (and also from JEAN-JACQUES ROUSSEAU's "sentiment of existence"), denotes for Trilling "the common routine" and "the elemental *given* of biology" (*Opposing* 148).

With these two profoundly conservative assumptions governing his writing, Trilling brought his career to an end by criticizing a strain of thinking that he believed had become dominant in American intellectual life: the "adversary culture." In *Beyond Culture* (1965) and *Sincerity and Authenticity* (1972), he maintained that American intellectuals had wrongly become hostile and negative toward the culture that had nourished them. The bleakness, violence, and menace of much of modern literature (which Trilling argues is most tellingly manifested by Fyodor Dostoevsky, D. H. Lawrence, and Franz Kafka) has been internalized by its readers, and all of traditional society is thereafter exposed to attack. The avant-garde had triumphed, and tension no longer existed between the "shock" of art and the society that is to be shocked; the "anti-social" had been "socialized" (*Beyond* 26).

Stung and saddened by the student revolts at Columbia in the late 1960s, and grown enamored of an England (he lectured at Oxford) that seemed to him free of the grimmer and more turbulent realities of the United States, Trilling argued in *Sincerity and Authenticity* that the virtue of being sincere (Shakespeare's Horatio) had deteriorated, while the modern compulsion to become authentic (Joseph Conrad's Kurtz) had grown like a virus. Against this destructive tendency, which evoked for him lengthy and melancholy disquisitions on death and its power of ultimate conditioning and definition, Trilling opposed the figure of Jane Austen, who represented for him a kind of placid honesty, comfort, single-mindedness, and sincerity now lost to the cultural world.

Trilling founded no school of literary criticism; his ideas and judgments form no system. He abjured all narrowly technical methods of literary analysis, including the one most widespread during his life—NEW CRITICISM. He is rightly seen as essentially conservative in his assumptions and judgments. He wrote gracefully, meditated deeply, and left no successors. He nonetheless secured for himself and for his approach to literature a permanent place in American literary criticism. He deepened and broadened the moral and psychological perspectives through which literature can and will, despite changes in fashion and taste, be seen.

William M. Chace

See also NEW YORK INTELLECTUALS and PSYCHOANALYTIC THEORY AND CRITICISM.

Lionel Trilling, *Beyond Culture: Essays on Literature and Learning* (1965), *E. M. Forster* (1943), *The Experience of Literature: A Reader with Commentaries* (1967), *Freud and the Crisis of Our Culture* (1965), *A Gathering of Fugitives* (1956), *The Last Decade: Essays and Reviews, 1965–1975* (ed. Diana Trilling, 1979), *The Liberal Imagination: Essays on Literature and Society* (1950), *Matthew Arnold* (1939), *Mind in the Modern World* (1973), *The Opposing Self: Nine Essays in Criticism* (1955), *Sincerity and Authenticity* (1972), *Speaking of Literature and Society* (ed. Diana Trilling, 1980); Lionel Trilling, ed., *The Portable Matthew Arnold* (1949); Lionel Trilling et al., "The Situation in American Writing: A Symposium," *Partisan Review* 6.5 (1939).

Robert Boyers, *Lionel Trilling: Negative Capability and the Wisdom of Avoidance* (1977); William M. Chace, *Lionel Trilling: Criticism and Politics* (1980); Joseph Frank, "Lionel Trilling and the Conservative Imagination," *The Widening Gyre: Crisis and Mastery in Modern Literature* (1963); Thomas M. Leitch, *Lionel Trilling: An Annotated Bibliography* (1993); Daniel T. O'Hara, *Lionel Trilling: The Work of Liberation* (1988); Delmore Schwartz, "The Duchess' Red Shoes," *Selected Essays of Delmore Schwartz* (ed. Donald A. Dike and David H. Zucker, 1970); Nathan A. Scott, *Three American Moralists: Mailer, Bellow, Trilling* (1973); Edward Joseph Shoben, *Lionel Trilling* (1981); Stephen L. Tanner, *Lionel Trilling* (1988).

VALÉRY, PAUL

Paul Valéry (1871–1945), one of the preeminent poets of the twentieth century, was also a literary critic and theorist of great distinction. A founding writer of *La Nouvelle revue française,* begun by André Gide in 1908 and continued under the direction of Jacques Rivière after World War I as an organ for the expression of modernism, his criticism bears the mark of the originality, intense personal commitment, and intellectual resistance typical of that journal. With the publication of "La Jeune Parque" (1917), *L'Album de vers anciens* (1920), and *Charmes* (1922), Valéry became the poet laureate of France; in 1927 he was elected to the Académie Française, and he was awarded the poetry chair at the Collège de France in 1937. Although he wrote very little poetry after 1922, he was frequently called upon to speak at official occasions, address learned societies, or write prefatory comments to new editions. These occasional texts were published along with his journalistic criticism and lectures on poetics at the Collège de France in five volumes entitled *Variété* between 1924 and 1944. Despite the haphazard nature of the assignments, each of these texts provided Valéry with the opportunity to reconsider and represent the subject of his lifelong preoccupation: the nature and functioning of creative thought, by which, he held, culture is transformed and renewed. Together, the essays on Leonardo da Vinci, RENÉ DESCARTES, Voltaire, Stendhal, Victor Hugo, Edgar Allan Poe, Charles Baudelaire, and Stéphane Mallarmé, among others, constitute the outlines of the "Comédie de l'Intellect" (*Oeuvres* 1:518) that Valéry dreamed of writing about the handful of individuals who, by breaking with the cultural commonplaces of their times, changed the parameters of what it is possible to think (i.e., Baudelaire's break with Romanticism through his reading of Poe; Joris Karl Huysman's break with the naturalist novel ["Durtal"]; Mallarmé's reinvention of syntax and creation of a public). He referred to such seminal writers as "stars" or planets (583, 688), whose works constituted their own worlds and together gave shape to the cultural constellation that is "France." As literary critic he searched for the "principles of duration" (584) in their works that gave them a life beyond that of their authors' personal or cultural histories.

Certain of these "stars" (Leonardo, Descartes, Poe, Mallarmé) preoccupy Valéry more than others because they provide models for his own experience of discovery and invention. In this sense, the structures of their work constitute an ethics as well as a poetics. What attaches Valéry to Descartes, about whom he wrote five important essays between 1925 and 1944, for example, is not his search for a method (Valéry often warned against the dangers to creativity of overly rigid methodology) but the notion of the *cogito* that places the origin of thought in self-consciousness. For the first time, the voice of the "I" and the "me" enters philosophy; the self becomes the "foyer of reforms" (807) opposed to the inchoate multiplicity of the world. Only human beings can doubt; only human beings can break the equilibrium they maintain with their environment to begin the process by which the world can be considered and represented in a new light.

Leonardo—mathematician, physicist, artist, architect—was a model for the universal principle of which every individual contains the germ. He emerges as a kind of Nietzschean figure (Valéry began reading FRIEDRICH NIETZSCHE in 1899) whose activity possessed all the characteristics Valéry considered necessary for the inventive activity of the mind: intense observation of phenomena, not as ready-made concepts, but as discrete, unrelated entities; classification, with the aid of analogy, into abstract ensembles or *figura;* and finally, out of the incomplete evidence of the psycho-mechanical world, the articulation or fabrication of entirely new orders of being—Christs, angels, monsters—that possess an internal necessity of their own and bear the unique imprint of their maker. Valéry's Leonardo texts—"Introduction à la méthode de Léonard de Vinci" (1894), "Notes et digression" (1919), "Léonard et les philosophes" (1928), and the marginalia added to the "Introduction" in 1930—together constitute the ongoing dialogue of a mind imagining another mind that is emblematic of Valéry's criticism in general.

The genuinely creative self is paradoxically both universal and intensely solitary, capable, for this reason, of creative substitutions with a vast array of alter egos. In the many essays Valéry wrote on Mallarmé, the beloved friend and writer whose work influenced him most directly (reading him in 1892 was like discovering a new asterism, he says, and caused him to break with all the "old idols" [637]), Valéry admires the profundity of the older poet's understanding of the scientific structures of language. More than any other's, Mallarmé's work exemplifies the kind of resistant writing and reading a genuinely creative experience of influence requires. Valéry describes it as the effect of a crystal on a ray of light, altering its trajectory in a direction independent of the crystal itself.

The style of Valéry's essays—intimate, often passionate, unpredictable, rigorous, unsentimental—reflects the kind of resistant reading he believes great art demands. Any facile relationship of "bonhomie" (475) is forestalled from the outset by his rejection of the cultural commonplaces surrounding a writer's name—the anguish of Blaise Pascal's faith, the naiveté and nonchalance of Jean de La Fontaine's verse, Stendhal's tone of sincerity—for the discovery of a different, often opposing kind of intentionality in the individual works' structures. The essays, which tend to illuminate and deepen each other, are studded with aphorisms, distilled, often paradoxical expressions of analysis that can be heard, in a sense, as warnings both to the writer himself and to the reader who might try to simplify Valéry's position. It is a commonplace, for example, to speak of Valéry's rejection of mysticism and the antirationalist tendencies in modernism, yet his essays on Gérard de Nerval, Huysman's Catholic novels, or the "Cantiques spirituelles" of Saint John of the Cross are admiring and deeply moving. It is a commonplace to say that Valéry did not like or understand the novel, yet his essay on Stendhal is one of the richest, most sympathetic, and most insightful in *Variété*. What is more, there is a note of profound pessimism, even despair, that can be heard in certain texts at various moments in Valéry's career—e.g., "La Crise de l'esprit" (1918), "Propos sur l'intelligence" (1925), or "Voltaire" (1944)—regarding the relevance of his belief in the shaping powers of the intellectual for a world that is increasingly controlled by the "machinism" (1045) of fashion, technology, and corporate power. Rather than a potential Leonardo or the composer of an "opera of the mind," Valéry sees himself in these texts as Hamlet-like, interrogating the skulls of the dead in an empty landscape: "Adieu, fantomes! The world no longer needs you. Nor me" (994).

Valéry's skepticism, his withdrawal from contemporary politics, his disdain for popular culture, his cult of the totalizing powers of the intellect, and his intense formalism have earned him the label "nihilist" by many of his critics, yet the resistance of mind he championed as humankind's only guarantee of freedom, the necessity for risk-taking and self-sacrifice such resistance involved, belie a rejection of humanist ideals. If he saw his own poetry as merely an "exercise" (643, 1469) in the understanding and control of language, it is an exercise that is meant to inspire a condition of creativity in others. If he desacralizes poetry as an aesthetic object, he believes in a distinctly aesthetic experience produced by the compositional integrity of a form that can continuously incorporate the unexpected into an unfinished dialogue with itself.

Valéry, who proves his aphorism "Every true poet is a critic of the highest order" (587, 1335), rejects free verse in favor of the poetry *savante* of fixed forms, because these heaviest of "chains" (455, 477) more tellingly imply the freedom of the maker to disengage from the determinations of his life and produce an autonomous new order out of the severest of constraints. As he puts it, "The tighter the shoe, the more original the dance" (1305). Like a snake eating its own tail, poetry as a form represents the most concentrated expression of the mind's grasp of the structures of language that underlie its own ability to think, a *figura* or language within a language whose substitutions conserve a plenitude, a "charme" beyond time. In one of his greatest and best-known essays, "Poésie et pensée abstraite" (1939), Valéry uses the conjunction "and" in his title to show that poetry is not *opposed to* but is *more than* abstract thought because it is both body and mind, voice and image, presence and absence. As he puts it in the essay on Poe, "An implicit extension into the past, the secret structure of this sensuous combinatory machine affirms itself constantly in the present" (865). In his first lesson on poetics at the Collège de France, Valéry defines "poetics" as the *poiein*, the "making or forms of action" (1342) by which a writer constructs his work. He proposes a new history of literature, very different from those of CHARLES AUGUSTIN SAINTE-BEUVE or HIPPOLYTE TAINE, which would be a study of forms, detached from the life of the poets, a history of agency that could conceivably contain no names of writers at all.

Valéry's interest in the genesis of works, in the "secrets" of their formation, and in agency has much in common with the criticism of consciousness of the so-called GENEVA SCHOOL represented by Georges Poulet, Jean-Pierre Richard, and JEAN STAROBINSKI, for example. His focus on the linguistic aspects of the literary object detached from the life of the maker has, on the other hand, alienated him from existentialist critics who would connect agency to historical context and made his work interesting to structuralist and poststructuralist critics such as Gérard Genette and JACQUES DERRIDA. Current reviews dedicated to literature as a form of metalanguage, such as *Poétique* and *Tel Quel,* actually take their titles from Valéry's work and perform the kinds of analyses called for by his proposal of a new, purely formalist history of literature.

Suzanne Nash

Paul Valéry, *Aesthetics* (trans. R. Manheim, 1964), *Cahiers* (29 vols., facsim. ed., 1957–61), *Leonardo, Poe, Mallarmé* (trans. M. Cowley and J. R. Lawler, 1972), *Oeuvres* (ed. Jean Hytier, 2 vols., 1957–60), *Paul Valéry: An Anthology* (ed. James R. Lawler, 1977).

Jean Bucher, *La Situation de Paul Valéry, Critique* (1976); Steven Cassedy, *Flight from Eden: The Origins of Modern Literary Criticism and Theory* (1990); Jacques Derrida, "Les Sources de Valéry: Qual, quelle," *MLN* 87 (1972); Ralph Freedman, "Paul Valéry: Protean Critic," *Modern French Criticism* (ed. John K. Simon, 1972); Edouard Gaède, *Nietzsche et Valéry* (1962); Gérard Genette, "Valéry et la poétique du langage," *MLN* 87 (1972); Jean Hytier, *La Poétique de Valéry* (2d ed., 1970); Michel Jarrety, *Valéry devant la littérature: Mesure de la limite* (1991); Suzanne Nash, *Paul Valéry's "Album de vers anciens": A Past Transfigured* (1983).

VALUE THEORY

The study of value, called axiology, has three main branches: ethics, concerning the morally good; political theory, concerning the social good; and aesthetics, concerning the beautiful, or taste. One might perhaps add another branch, pragmatics, which concerns the utilitarian good or instrumental efficiency of means toward some specific end. Modern value theory may be said to have arisen with modern science, which distinguished between fact and value. For PLATO, there was no discord between the Good, the True, and the Beautiful. If the Good seemed to take precedence over the True or the Beautiful, it was because it was impossible to conceive the highest perfection as inactive and heartless, because the Good added the dimension of action to that of contemplation. In contrast, modern science separated morals, aesthetics, and science, banning from the True all

qualities to which decisive (i.e., intersubjectively verifiable) empirical observation was not applicable and relegating them to the domain of value. Thus was human value distinguished from natural fact, and subjectivity from objectivity. This distinction between fact and value, between qualities that by general consensus inhere in objects themselves and our preference for one object over another, has been challenged by recent critical theory.

The historical road to contemporary value theory in literary studies may be mapped upon an axiological continuum. Extrapolating from a Platonic notion of the objectivity of the Beautiful on one pole, we might continue through the more subjectivist theories of the great Enlightenment axiologists and finally conclude with our contemporary notions of value-contingency, in which all dualistic axiologies (both subjectivist and objectivist) are rejected and in which "contingency" replaces universality and naturalness. For Plato, beauty inhered in the object, was a *fact* of the object's existence, insofar as it reflected the objective Form of the Beautiful (*Phaedo* 100c ff., *Symposium* 211 ff.). By the time of DAVID HUME's essay "Of the Standard of Taste" (1757) the distinction between science and value had commenced. Beginning with the "obvious" observation of "the great variety of Taste, as well as of opinion, which prevails in the world" (226), the empiricist Hume recognizes diversity in matters of taste. Yet because he is also committed to a simplistic deterministic account of human psychology, his recognition of the relativity of value is checked and compromised. The psychological argument is, briefly, that certain "forms or qualities" of objects naturally produce feelings of pleasure or displeasure in us by virtue of our physiological constitution, and these feelings are the foundation of all general aesthetics (233). Consequently, for Hume, there are universal "objective" forms of beauty that are rarely recognized or appreciated due to what he calls "diversity in the internal frame or external situation" (244)—or contingent personal and social factors. These latter explain the varieties of taste that, as Hume says, are "too obvious not to have fallen under every one's observation."

In the *Critique of Judgment* (1790), IMMANUEL KANT is at pains to distinguish objective judgments, which are predicated upon objects (the table is brown), and subjective judgments, which are predicated upon subjective agreeableness (the wine is pleasant, it gives me pleasure, I like it), from judgments of taste, which are neither objective nor subjective in these senses but are rather both subjective and objective. They are subjective in that they express experiences I have alone, and they are objective in that everyone will agree with them *as if* they concerned objective properties of things. The experience I have, which is the "free play" of imagination synthesizing perception and concept (the phenomenology of which we find in book 1, "The Analytic"), however, is quite independent of our "demand" for universal assent to our liking, which Kant explicates in "The Dialectic." There he brings the phenomenological experience into alignment with his larger, logical project. We bestow upon our subjective experience the universality that accords it objective status by establishing the beautiful as the symbol of the morally good. It may be said that what has dropped out of aesthetics in the 200 years since Kant is the perceived connection between the beautiful and the morally good.

But Kantian aesthetics has not declined without a trace. By subsuming the beautiful to the morally good, Kant made it clear that humankind had no pressing need for the beautiful: the rational progress of history could occur without it. From FRIEDRICH SCHILLER through the present, Kant's notion of "free play" has been applied beyond the aesthetic arena proper, as a criticism, as it were, of life under modern conditions. Karl Marx and Marxists have echoed, more or less loudly, Schiller's insistence upon the need for the aesthetic "free play of the imagination" as an objective condition of the rational progress of history (the liberation of all human potentialities from the roles and hierarchies of modern life) and as a corrective to the instrumentalization and rationalization of the human faculties under modernity. All such critics have correspondingly resisted the division or rationalization of knowledge in the separation of fact and value, or science, politics, and art. In addition to KARL MARX AND FRIEDRICH ENGELS in *The German Ideology* (1846) and Leon Trotsky in "Revolutionary and Socialist Art" (1924), one might refer to the European Decadents of the late nineteenth century (e.g., OSCAR WILDE's "Soul of Man under Socialism," 1892), the FRANKFURT SCHOOL of the early twentieth, and certain tendencies in critical legal studies and CULTURAL STUDIES. In MICHEL FOUCAULT's last interviews he considered a less politicized and more individualistic (rather than socialist) version of "the idea of a self which had to be created as a work of art" (362-70).

With contemporary critical theory in the Left or progressive tradition, it is necessary to introduce FRIEDRICH NIETZSCHE, who in *The Genealogy of Morals* (1887) and elsewhere revealed value as a con, a tool of domination of some over others, and urged a "transvaluation of values" in the name of personal liberation. The fork that divides two major developments in contemporary value

theory—the progressive branch, which includes cultural studies, critiques of science and objectivity in feminist theory, Marxism, critical legal studies, and so on, and the skeptical branch, which includes value relativists and the so-called neopragmatists—was present in Nietzsche's critique of domination and his radical perspectivism or skepticism.

An influential tendency within the progressive critique of value is the critical legal studies movement (CLS). Although it is often confused with the recent area of study called "law and literature," which is concerned with epistemological and interpretive problems common to both legal texts (constitutions, statutes, judicial decisions) and literary texts, the group of legal scholars that first met in 1977 under the rubric CLS were driven not by philosophical hermeneutics but by the perception, historically shared by both political economists and Marxists, that legal theory had come to justify the status quo. Attacking the dualistic foundations of liberal thought, distinctions between the state of nature and the social order, subjective and objective, private and public, CLS saw no distinctive mode of legal reasoning that could be contrasted with political dialogue and accordingly asserted that law *was* politics. CLS's first task was to criticize objectivist legal theory for this rationalization of inequality, which it did in a form called "trashing" or "delegitimating," what in literary studies is called DECONSTRUCTION. This entailed a full-scale critique of liberal economic and political theory, which occupied the first decade of the movement. CLS's second task, uncompleted at the beginning of the 1990s, was to propose something else, to transform the institution of the law.

In aesthetics, CLS's attack upon dualistic formulations of fact and value, subjective and objective, private and public, has taken a more progressive turn than similar attacks in "law and literature." An important and prolific, if idiosyncratic, CLS writer, Roberto Mangabeira Unger, has proposed a reintegration of the extraordinary or art and the everyday. He urges us to transform the modern realms of private life and ideals—art, romantic love, religion—from their mystifications under current conditions into tools for the enrichment of ordinary life, so that imaginative literature, for example, would not be the realm of artistic alienation (say no to society) and sublimation (a dream of freedom, autonomy, personality) but rather a window upon possibilities of other social relations, a view that has much in common with Schiller's liberation of human potentialities as derived from Kantian "free play." "The extraordinary," Unger writes, makes it possible to grasp the ideal, and to contrast it with one's ordinary experience of the world. In this sense, the extraordinary is the starting point for the critique and transformation of social life. It poses the task of actualizing in the world of commonplace things and situations what has already been encountered as a divine liberation from the everyday. . . . In the course of this actualization both the extraordinary and the everyday must be changed. The final and most important change would be the disappearance of the distinction between them. (*Knowledge* 232)

Yet Unger's awareness of the double-edged value of art—its alternate function as haven or escape—also has much in common with Nietzsche's critique of value as domination, or a fraud.

The extraordinary representation of the ideal in art, religion, and love has a two-faced significance for everyday life. On the one hand, it can offer the self temporary refuge. In this sense, the extraordinary is a mystification, the aroma that sweetens the air of the established order. Its very availability makes the absence of the ideal from everyday life seem tolerable and even necessary. Because the sacred, art, and love are separated out from banal events, everything in the ordinary world can become all the more relentlessly profane, prosaic, and self-regarding. (232)

In other forms than Unger's, the critical practice of CLS, lying somewhere between the progressive project and that of the pragmatists, to whom we shall presently turn, is allied with cultural studies. Like CLS, in its assertion that law is politics (rather than "above" or "outside of" politics), cultural studies considers that the production of the literary canon, the consumption, or *meaning,* of imaginative literature, and the status of the literary community's cultural capital are within the realm of politics (see the discussion of Bourdieu below). Like CLS, in its various "trashings," cultural studies has deconstructed such knots of ideology in literature as subjective/objective, self/other, public/private, and extraordinary/everyday; and like CLS, it has argued that deconstruction that merely works on the status quo is ultimately a conservative practice. Like CLS, in its positive program to transform the law by reintegrating it with everyday life, cultural studies wants to reintegrate the extraordinary (called art or literature) with the ordinary (called popular culture). Like CLS, in its critique of the liberal subject as autonomous agent in pursuit of self-interest derived from the social position of dominant males, cultural studies reevaluates subjectivity and situates the "literary subject" in relation to other past, present, and even future forms as a product of culture rather

than nature. Like CLS, in its assault on hierarchy, cultural studies replaces Culture with a capital *C* as an elite cultural capital with a pluralistic, diverse conception of cultures.

These last goals bring us to the other major branch of contemporary value theory, to those who see progressive aesthetics as ultimately misguided, oppressive, or insufficiently pluralistic. These are the contemporary skeptics or value relativists or, in a weaker form, pragmatists. Following upon structuralist and poststructuralist critiques, this branch denies that value, including literary value, is a property of objects, subjects, or psychological processes between subjects and objects, arguing that it is instead a product of the dynamics of cultural systems. Although his own work is often more overtly political ("overtly" because relativists would deny the distinction between political and other practices), value relativists and pragmatists often cite Pierre Bourdieu to illustrate the contingency of value.

In contradistinction to Kant, Bourdieu considers that aesthetics has functioned as a negative force in human progress. Accusing the French educational establishment of merely reproducing bourgeois ideology and therefore reproducing the status quo, in *Distinction: A Social Critique of the Judgment of Taste* (1979, trans., 1984) Bourdieu argues that aesthetic "distinction," or taste, is solely a product of education, family, and the social trajectories of economic class and status. He has traced the establishment's aesthetic preference for form and style to its distance from economic necessity and the blue-collar taste for content ("realism") and moral or recreative agreeableness to engagement with material conditions. For Bourdieu, who provides a sociology of the institution of the art world, rather than the symbol of a freedom that *can be* (in Kant, *ought to be*) shared universally, taste has come to be institutionalized in a manner that excludes and oppresses. The "disinterested" aesthetic no longer refers to freedom but is reduced to a class-based preference for form. Contrasting Bourdieu, whom she calls "postaxiological," with earlier axiologists, Barbara Herrnstein Smith writes,

He emphasizes that, because these learned patterns of cultural consumption tend to be experienced as internal preferences and interpreted as evidence of different *natural* inclinations and competences, taste also functions to legitimate the power of the socially dominant. Specifically, the cultural objects and practices favored by the dominant classes . . . are legitimated as intrinsically superior by the normative institutions controlled by those very classes; at the same time, the tastes of the dominant *for* those objects and practices are interpreted as evidence of their own natural superiority and cultural enlightenment and thus also their right to social and cultural power. Moreover, this doubly legitimating interpretation is accepted and reproduced not only by those who benefit most directly from it but by everyone, including those whose subordination it implicitly justifies. (76)

Such analyses of value as institutional hegemony, whether called postaxiological or post-Nietzschean, make up the greater efforts of the new value relativists, whose project is to question and critique objectivist, or dualistic, thought. Thus, Smith sees literary value as neither objective (a property of objects and commanding universal assent) nor subjective (personally whimsical, locked into the consciousness of individual subjects, or without interest or value to others) but rather as a changing function of multiple contingent variables. For her, when we make an explicit judgment of a literary work, we articulate an estimate of how well the work will serve certain implicitly defined functions for a specific implicitly defined audience that is conceived of as experiencing the work under certain implicitly defined conditions. The project of cultural criticism, then, is not some universalist progressive trajectory but the examination of how literary values are formed, sustained, and exercised.

Similarly, in his debates with legal and "law and literature" theorists, STANLEY FISH hoped to redirect the inquiry into interpretation away from the self-conscious deliberation of the individual judge or critic and toward the battlefield of institutional practice, thus revealing the politics of legal or literary interpretation and, again, destabilizing the fact/value dichotomy. Fish contends that arguments based upon higher moral principles or theories, or even rationality per se, are the means by which institutional actors ply their trade and advance their interests. Each institutional faction will try to establish its own governing rules as the supposedly neutral principles that constrain interpretation. Fish insists that there are "no principles above interest, only principled interests" ("Interpretation" 501). Heretofore feminist and cultural critics have differed with Fish upon his notion of interpretive community, which, they claim, is typically based upon some monolithic or idealized version of "the profession" and is insufficiently differentiated or pluralistic. It may be said that Fish has had little to say about the ways in which institutional practices in law or literature change. Here, feminist and cultural critics have been most sensitive to the subtle articulations of pluralism, difference, and institutional change.

There are, then, three main areas of debate in the academy on the question of literary value. The first area centers on the humanistic attempt, following MATTHEW ARNOLD, to *use* literature to supply transcendent values to unify a pluralistic culture, the crudest recent attempt being Allan Bloom's. The second involves the leftist attempts to promote progressive culture through the traditions of critical theory and expansion of the curriculum beyond national, gendered, and generic boundaries. The third includes analyses of the institutionalization of literary value, as in Herbert Lindenberger's historical account of the "Great Books" or "Western Culture" courses in U.S. undergraduate curricula or Fish's long-standing preoccupation with interpretive communities, especially professional communities, that constrain interpretation by "deep" standards of rationality that determine such issues as what constitutes a good argument or what counts as evidence.

Regenia Gagnier

See also CULTURAL STUDIES and STANLEY FISH.

Andrew Arato and Eike Gebhardt, eds., *The Essential Frankfurt School Reader* (1978); Matthew Arnold, *Lectures and Essays in Criticism: The Complete Prose Works of Matthew Arnold,* vol. 4 (ed. R. H. Super, 1962); Pierre Bourdieu, *La Distinction: Critique sociale du jugement* (1979, *Distinction: A Social Critique of the Judgement of Taste,* trans. Richard Nice, 1984); Drucilla Cornell, "The Poststructuralist Challenge to the Ideal of Community," *Cardozo Law Review* 8 (1987), "Toward a Modern/Postmodern Reconstruction of Ethics," *University of Pennsylvania Law Review* 133 (1985); Louis Dumont, "On Value, Modern and Nonmodern," *Essays on Individualism: Modern Ideology in Anthropological Perspective* (1986); Stanley Fish, *Doing What Comes Naturally: Change, Rhetoric, and the Practice of Theory in Literary and Legal Studies* (1989), "Interpretation and the Pluralist Vision," *Texas Law Review* 60 (1982); Michel Foucault, *The Foucault Reader* (ed. Paul Rabinow, 1984); Regenia Gagnier, *Subjectivities: A History of Self-Representation in Britain, 1832–1920* (1991); Sandra Harding, *The Science Question in Feminism* (1986); *Harvard Law Review* 99 (1986, special issue on CLS); David Hume, "Of the Standard of Taste," *Essays Moral, Political, and Literary* (ed. Eugene F. Miller, 1963); David Kairys, *The Politics of Law: A Progressive Critique* (1982); Immanuel Kant, *Critique of Judgement* (1790, trans. Werner S. Pluhar, 1987); Mark Kelman, *A Guide to Critical Legal Studies* (1987); Duncan Kennedy and Karl E. Klare, "A Bibliography of Critical Legal Studies," *Yale Law Journal* 94 (1984); Herbert Lindenberger, "On the Sacrality of Reading Lists: The Western Culture Debate at Stanford

University," *Comparative Criticism* 2 (1989); Herbert Marcuse, *One-Dimensional Man: Studies in the Ideology of Advanced Industrial Society* (1964); Friedrich Nietzsche, *Das Geburt der Tragödie aus dem Geiste der Musik* and *Zur Genealogie der Moral* (1871 and 1887, *The Birth of Tragedy and The Genealogy of Morals,* trans. F. Golffing, 1956); Plato, *The Collected Dialogues including the Letters* (ed. E. Hamilton and H. Cairns, 1973); Richard Rorty, *Contingency, Irony, and Solidarity* (1989); Friedrich Schiller, *Über die ästhelische Erziehung des Menschen* (1795, *On the Aesthetic Education of Man, in a Series of Letters,* trans. Reginald Snell, 1965); Barbara Herrnstein Smith, *Contingencies of Value: Alternative Perspectives for Critical Theory* (1988); *Stanford Law Review* 36 (1984, special issues on CLS); Leon Trotsky, *Literature and Revolution* (trans. Rose Strunsky, 1975); Roberto Mangabeira Unger, *Knowledge and Politics* (1976), *Passion: An Essay on Personality* (1984); Oscar Wilde, "The Soul of Man under Socialism," *The Artist as Critic: The Critical Writings of Oscar Wilde* (ed. Richard Ellmann, 1969).

VICO, GIAMBATTISTA

Giambattista Vico (1668-1744) is one of the first modern thinkers to formulate a philosophy of mythology and to base both philosophical and historical knowledge on a conception of narration. Vico lived and taught in Naples throughout his life except for a nine-year period at the beginning of his career, when he served as tutor to the Rocca family on their estate a distance from Naples. Vico was professor of Latin eloquence, or what in modern terms would be understood as RHETORIC, at the University of Naples. In the last part of his career he was appointed royal historiographer.

Vico's major work is the *Scienza nuova (New Science),* which he published first in 1725 and then in a fully rewritten version in 1730. This second version, along with revisions he was making in the text for a third edition in the year of his death, 1744, has come to be known as the *Scienza nuova seconda.* Vico maintained that in the text of this second version he had placed practically all his ideas of any importance. His conception of his *New Science* and its leading ideas are developed in several prior works. In *De antiquissima Italorum sapientia* (*On the Most Ancient Wisdom of the Italians,* 1710) he states his principle *verum ipsum factum,* that the true is the same as the made, that is, "convertible" with the made, as part of a criticism of the metaphysics of RENÉ DESCARTES (ch. 1, sec. 1). In two Latin works and a set of notes on them which Vico grouped under the Italian title *Il diritto universale* [Universal law] (1720-22) he offers a first sketch of his conception of the new science, in a chapter entitled "Nova scientia tentatur" [A new science is essayed], and also states a principle of jurisprudence that may have shaped his conception of the method of the *New Science—certum est pars veri,* or, the certain is part of the true (bk. 1, ch. 82).

Vico says in his *Autobiography* (1725-28) and in the *New Science* itself that his "new science" is based on a *nuova'arte critica.* This "new critical art" is a means to elicit the "common nature of nations" (*New Science,* par. 348). In the *De antiquissima* Vico explains his principle the "true is the made" as applicable to mathematics; mathematical trues ("intelligibles") are such because they are made in accordance with the principles of mathematics, not because they correspond to some rational order of nature (ch. 1, sec. 2). Vico does not discuss this principle directly in the *New Science,* but he alludes to it, and his views generally presuppose it (par. 349). In the *New Science* it becomes a principle of history: that history is made by humans. In their creation of the things of the civil world humans make the trues or intelligibilities of history. The historical life of nations follows a common pattern in each nation. Because humans make history, a science that uncovers and expresses the principles of this making is possible. It can demonstrate the ways in which humans achieve trues or intelligibilities in their acts of making history.

This new science of history requires a new critical art of interpretation in which philosophy is joined with philology, in which the true *(verum)* is joined with the certain *(certum)* (pars. 338-60). Philosophy has by its nature always aimed at stating the forms of intelligibility common to all experience. PHILOLOGY presents the "certains" of the human world, by which Vico means all the things that depend upon human choice, that is, the histories of the languages, customs, and deeds of peoples in war and in peace. This new critical art must apply itself to the philology of these certains in order to show how they involve various principles of intelligibility ordinarily understood only in abstract terms by philosophical analysis. Vico discusses the conception of the certain *(il certo)* and the true *(il vero)* in the *New Science,* but his thought is likely guided by his jurisprudential principle *certum est pars veri,* the sense that a certain instance of positive law formed by human choice is valid and can truly be regarded as law only when understood as part of universal or natural law, and the reverse, that law in a universal sense is forever abstract unless embodied in positive systems of law. Even more specifically, Vico's notion of the connection between the universally true and the individually certain may be grounded in the Roman conception of *ius gentium,* that part of *ius naturale* that is understood to be actually present in the civil laws of all nations and thus to be in fact common to them all.

Vico turns this jurisprudential principle of the true and the certain into a metaphysics of history such that, as he holds in the *New Science,* it shows what providence has wrought in history (par. 342). The new critical art of the philosophical examination of philology shows, in Vico's view, that all nations follow a common pattern of development. This pattern shows the providential structure of human events. A further dimension to the new critical art is Vico's axiom that "doctrines must take their beginning from that of the matters of which they treat" (par. 314). He says that the first science to be learned must be mythology (par. 51) and that the "master key" to his new science is the discovery that the first humans thought in "poetic characters" or "imaginative universals" *(universali fantastici)* (par. 34). All nations begin in the same way by the power of the imagination *(fantasia)* to *make* the world intelligible in terms of gods. This age of gods gives way to a second age, in which *fantasia* is used to form social institutions and types of character or virtues in terms of heroes. Finally, these two ages, in which the world is ordered through the power of *fantasia,* decline into an age of rationality, in which the world is ordered in purely conceptual and logical terms and in which mental acting is finally dominated by what Vico calls a barbarism of reflection *(barbarie della riflessione)* (par. 1106).

This cycle of ages of gods, heroes, and humans repeats itself within the world of nations, forming what Vico calls ideal eternal history *(storia ideale eterna)* (par. 349). The world of nations is typified by the *corsi* and *ricorsi* of these three ages. From the standpoint of Vico's conception of the metaphysics of history, the divine attempts to reveal itself over and over again in human affairs, but history never takes on this sense of progress typical of eighteenth-century thought.

Vico's *New Science* is a large and varied work that treats many subjects, of which only a few can be touched on here. Of particular interest to the scholar of literary criticism, in addition to Vico's conception of a "new critical art," are two products of this art: *sapienza poetica,* or "poetic wisdom," which is the title of the second and largest book of the *New Science,* and his "discovery of the true Homer," the subject of the third book. Put in modern terms, Vico's "poetic wisdom" is a conception of a science of mythology. He regards mythic narrative as having a logic of its own that is achieved through the power of imagination, or *fantasia. Fantasia* is a primordial power of the mind through which the world and human experience are first given order. In Vico's view, *fantasia* is an active power through which the things of the civil world are first made. *Fantasia* is a type of learning that precedes reason in the history of human affairs. It is this original form of the mythic that literature later attempts to recover. Vico's conception of myth as a primordial form of thought has affinities with various and diverse modern theories of myth, such as those of CLAUDE LÉVI-STRAUSS and Mircea Eliade.

Vico believes that one of the verifications of his *New Science* is his discovery of the true Homer, namely, the ancient Greek people themselves (par. 806). Through his new critical art Vico claims to prove that Homer's works should be regarded not as containing a hidden philosophical wisdom but as commanding a form of wisdom of their own, a poetic or mythic wisdom that is a summation of the *fantasia* of the ancient Greeks. Implied in this conception of Homer is a solution to PLATO's ancient quarrel with the poets. Unlike Plato, Vico regards Homer not as in contest with philosophical thought but as embodying a form of thought that precedes philosophy and is required as a precursor to philosophy.

Vico's influence during his lifetime was not great, and it did not extend to the thinkers of northern Europe. He greatly desired their attention to his work, but it remained largely unknown to them. In Italy, there was a fairly continuous Vico tradition in criticism and literary criticism influencing, for example, the essays of Ugo Foscolo and, later, FRANCESCO DE SANCTIS and BENEDETTO CROCE. In Germany, J. G. von Herder knew something of Vico's ideas, but Vico did not directly influence Herder's work, although as Isaiah Berlin has shown, Vico and Herder taken together make a suggestive chapter in the history of ideas.

The first great revival of Vico's ideas occurred in France with Jules Michelet's discovery of the *New Science* in 1824 and his subsequent publication of his abridged translation and an exposition of Vico's ideas. It was from Michelet's translation that Victor Cousin derived his interest in Vico. The earliest English promoter of Vichian ideas was SAMUEL TAYLOR COLERIDGE, who was responsible for much of the interest in Vico among English writers in the latter nineteenth century. In a long and important footnote in *Capital,* Karl Marx discusses the possibility of applying Vico's conception of history to a history of human technology. Croce and Fausto Nicolini compiled the modern standard edition of Vico's works, the so-called Laterza edition, and Croce was the one philosopher in the contemporary period to base his conception of aesthetics and culture on Vico, merging Vico with Hegelian idealism. The most prominent figure to introduce Vico to twentieth-century readers was James Joyce, who used the *New Science* as the grid for *Finnegans Wake*. Joyce was especially interested in Vico's notion that "memory is the same as imagination" *(la memoria e la stessa che la fantasia)* and with Vico's notion of the cycle of the three ages of history. In the last two decades Vico's thought has undergone a renaissance of critical interpretation and application to various fields of literature and the humanities, largely among English-speaking scholars.

Donald Phillip Verene

See also BENEDETTO CROCE.

Giambattista Vico, *The Autobiography of Giambattista Vico* (1725–28, trans. Max Harold Fisch and Thomas Goddard Bergin, 1944), *The New Science of Giambattista Vico* (1725, 3d ed., 1744, trans. Thomas Goddard Bergin and Max Harold Fisch, 1948, rev. ed., 1968), *On the Most Ancient Wisdom of the Italians* (1710, trans. Lucia Marchetti Palmer, 1988), *On the Study Methods of Our Time* (1709, trans. Elio Gianturco, including "The Academies and the Relation between Philosophy and Eloquence," trans. Donald Phillip Verene, 1990); *Opere di G. B. Vico* (ed. Fausto Nicolini, 8 vols. in 11, 1911–41), *Vico: Selected Writings* (ed. and trans. Leon Pompa, 1982).

Isaiah Berlin, *Vico and Herder: Two Studies in the History of Ideas* (1976); Benedetto Croce, *Bibliografia vichiana* (rev. and enlarged Fausto Nicolini, 2 vols., 1947–48); Ernesto Grassi, *Vico and Humanism: Essays on Vico, Heidegger, and Rhetoric* (1990); Michael Mooney, *Vico in the Tradition of Rhetoric* (1984); *New Vico Studies* (ed. Giorgio Tagliacozzo and Donald Phillip Verene, 1983–); Leon Pompa, *Vico: A Study of the "New Science"* (1975, 2d ed., 1990); John D. Schaeffer, *Sensus Communis: Vico, Rhetoric, and the Limits of Relativism* (1990); Giorgio Tagliacozzo and Donald Phillip Verene, *Giambattista Vico's Science of Humanity* (1976); Giorgio Tagliacozzo, Donald Phillip Verene, and Vanessa Rumble, *A Bibliography of Vico in English, 1884–1984* (1986); Giorgio Tagliacozzo and Hayden V. White, eds., *Giambattista Vico: An International Symposium* (1969); Donald Phillip Verene, *The New Art of Autobiography: An Essay on the "Life of Giambattista Vico Written by Himself"* (1991), *Vico's Science of Imagination* (1981); Donald Phillip Verene, ed., *Vico and Joyce* (1987).

WELLEK, RENÉ

René Wellek (b. 1903), born in Vienna and educated in Prague, is the twentieth century's most influential scholar in comparative literature. As literary theorist and historian of literary criticism, he brought a philosophical and historiographical perspective to modern literary studies. His rejection of nineteenth-century mechanistic and positivist methods helped shape modern approaches that are text-centered, conceptually oriented, and international in scope. Wellek has spent his professional career almost entirely in the United States, where he moved in 1939 and quickly took part in academic debates about the nature of literary study. Upholding the Kantian tradition of the literary work as an autonomous aesthetic phenomenon but emphasizing concurrently that each work is embedded in a historical system of norms and values, he describes a dialectics of literary theory and literary history that is illustrated in his massive history of modern literary criticism. "There are no neutral facts in literature," he asserts ("Concept" 4). Literature as such is rooted in history, and critics must also be aware of the implications of their own methodology. While Wellek's approach suggests elements of later dialectical or self-reflexive theories, it is set apart by its humanistic focus, its emphasis on the autonomy of art, and the importance of qualitative distinctions and aesthetic value. His later work sharply attacks DECONSTRUCTION for concentrating on rhetorical structures and a regressive textuality rather than seeing the book as "a qualitative whole, a value-charged totality."

Wellek studied English and Germanic philology at Charles University in Prague, spent the years 1924–25 in England, and received his doctorate in 1926 with a thesis on Carlyle and Romanticism. The next year, he came to the United States for postgraduate study in English at Princeton University, where he was struck by the fact that there were no courses in modern literature or criticism and that literary scholarship was "dominated by literary history, understood largely as a study of facts: biographical, bibliographical, sources, parallels, and influences" ("Respect" 1356). In 1930 he returned to Charles

University, where he taught English literature until 1935 and joined the Prague Linguistic Circle. From Jan Mukarovsky and ROMAN JAKOBSON he learned to think of literary works as linguistic sign systems related to historical norms and values; from the Polish phenomenologist philosopher Roman Ingarden, whose *Literary Work of Art* he read in 1931, he adapted the concept of the work as a stratified system of norms, a concept he would extend from its original linguistic definition to a larger social context. His first book, *Immanuel Kant in England, 1793–1838,* appeared in 1931.

In 1935 Wellek took a position teaching Czech language and literature at the School of Slavonic Studies in London, a position whose funding was withdrawn by the Nazis after their invasion of Czechoslovakia. He moved in June 1939 to the University of Iowa, where he found acrimonious debates between literary critics and conservative literary historians. It was a time of great ferment in literary studies nationwide, with symposia on "Literature and the Professors" and polemical statements in favor of criticism from such figures as Norman Foerster, R. S. Crane, John Crowe Ransom, and Allen Tate. Cleanth Brooks and Robert Penn Warren's influential teaching anthology, *Understanding Poetry,* appeared in 1938. On the basis of a future book, *Theory of Literature* (1949, co-authored with Austin Warren), Wellek was to be associated with the American New Critics and even considered their philosopher, but at the time he was still preoccupied with broader questions of literary history. In 1941 he published *The Rise of English Literary History,* as well as a version of a 1936 Prague Circle essay, "Theory of Literary History," in Foerster's revisionary *Literary Scholarship: Its Aims and Methods.* In 1946 he became director of comparative literature at Yale University, a position he held until his retirement in 1972.

Wellek is best known for *Theory of Literature,* which has been translated into 23 languages and used as a textbook around the world. Historical coincidence, as well as shared beliefs, led to the book's being taken as a philosophical argument for NEW CRITICISM, despite Wellek's insistence that he was primarily concerned with questions of literary historiography. The central essay, "The

Mode of Existence of the Literary Work of Art," encouraged readers to use commonsense distinctions in order to see the work of art as a specific object of study; Wellek ended by adapting Ingarden's description of the work as a "stratified system of norms" (e.g., *Theory* 153), layers that interacted but could be studied in themselves. Immediately popular was the distinction between *extrinsic* approaches (evaluating literature in terms of another discipline) and *intrinsic* ones (focusing on the work's aesthetic structure), as well as the emphasis on studying works as autonomous aesthetic wholes ("monuments") rather than as historical "documents" or collections of facts. The final chapter in the first edition, "The Study of Literature in the Graduate School" (dropped in the second and third editions), argued against overspecialization and urged the reform of graduate literary study toward a more philosophical, interdisciplinary understanding of literature. Such concepts, which corresponded to the antihistorical and Kantian views of contemporary New Criticism, defined the book for most readers, who ignored the later editions' concluding essay, "Literary History," which set out Wellek's Prague-inspired historical aesthetics. *Theory of Literature* became ensconced as a standard reference work and the philosophical foundation for New Critical methods. When a later generation of critics attacked it in their turn, they also ignored its historical aspect and generally focused on the distinction between extrinsic and intrinsic categories, noting that the "extrinsic" disciplines (e.g., sociology and psychology) had evolved concepts and methodologies that went far beyond the limited examples of 1949.

Wellek's historiographical side, ironically, is less recognized, although it constitutes the bulk of his work. A series of essays on literary-historical concepts (e.g., *Concepts of Criticism*, 1963; *Confrontations*, 1965; and *Discriminations*, 1970) ranges from studies of periods and movements to inquiries into terms and critical categories. Throughout, Wellek attempts to grasp systems and regulative concepts, while recognizing the aesthetic identity of individual texts. A typical strategy is to inquire into the actual usage of a term or concept in history and then to explore its implications. Essays such as "The Concept of Romanticism in Literary History," "The Concept of Realism in Literary Scholarship," and "The Name and Nature of Comparative Literature" have been fundamental reference works for generations of scholars. Wellek's monumental eight-volume *History of Modern Criticism: 1750–1950* (1955–93) was intended to demonstrate the evolution of critical theory in the work of major Western literary critics after 1750, but after 1973 he

abandoned the notion of evolution and described the history of criticism as a series of debates on recurrent or "essentially contested concepts" ("The Fall of Literary History," *Attack* 77). The *History* portrays a dialectical relationship between individual works and historical systems of norms. In addition, it expresses Wellek's belief in what he calls "perspectivism," a combination of history, theory, and criticism, as well as of absolute and relative points of view, that alone can grasp the work's stratified system of meanings.

Modern comparative literature studies have been crucially shaped, if not defined, by Wellek's insistence on the conceptual nature of literary studies. In 1958, conservative European scholars were defining comparative literature as the documentable study of literary influence and warning against "encroaching" on national literatures. Speaking at the second International Comparative Literature Association Congress that year, Wellek rejected the idea of "artificial fences" (*Concepts* 284) and suggested that comparative literature should use its international scope to study "the problem of 'literariness,' the central issue of aesthetics," without regard to national boundaries (293). His attack on "the dead hand of nineteenth-century factualism, scientism, and historical relativism" (282) provoked a running debate between what were called the "French" and "American" schools of comparative literature (a nationalist interpretation that was not his intention). It is paradoxical that Wellek, who introduced Slavic phenomenological theory to American literary studies, should be classified as the leader of an "American" school. Yet the range of his publications and professional activity—he was president of the American Comparative Literature Association and of the International Comparative Literature Association, editor, lecturer, and co-founder of the widely taught *Norton Anthology of World Masterpieces*—gave him for decades a central position in literary studies in the United States as well as considerable influence abroad. The strength and impact of his work is attested by the fact that he remains an indispensable reference point, even for later critics who challenge his aesthetic and work-centered approach as part of an earlier humanistic world-view.

Sarah Lawall

See also NEW CRITICISM.

René Wellek, *The Attack on Literature* (1982), "Collaborating with Austin Warren on Theory of Literature," *Teacher and Critic: Essays by and about Austin Warren* (ed. Myron Simon and Harvey Gross, 1976), "The Concept of Comparative Literature," *Yearbook of Comparative and*

General Literature 2 (1953), *Concepts of Criticism* (ed. Stephen G. Nichols, Jr., 1963), *Confrontations: Studies in the Intellectual and Literary Relations between Germany, England, and the United States during the Nineteenth Century* (1965), *Discriminations: Further Concepts of Criticism* (1970), *Four Critics: Croce, Valéry, Lukács, and Ingarden* (1981), *A History of Modern Criticism: 1750–1950* (8 vols.: vol. 1, *The Later Eighteenth Century*, 1955; vol. 2, *The Romantic Age*, 1955; vol. 3, *The Age of Transition*, 1965; vol. 4, *The Later Nineteenth Century*, 1965; vol. 5, *English Criticism, 1900–1950*, 1986; vol. 6, *American Criticism, 1900–1950*, 1986; vol. 7, *German, Russian, and Eastern European Criticism, 1900–1950*, 1991; vol. 8, *French, Italian, and Spanish Criticism, 1900–1950*, 1993), "My Early Life," *Contemporary Authors Autobiography Series*, vol. 7 (ed. Adele Sarkissian, 1988), "Respect for Tradition," *TLS* (December 10, 1982), *The Rise of English Literary History* (1941); René Wellek and Austin Warren, *Theory of Literature* (1949, 3d ed., 1962).

Martin Bucco, *René Wellek* (1981); Walter G. Creed, "René Wellek and Karl Popper on the Mode of Existence of Ideas in Literature and Science," *Journal of the History of Ideas* 44 (1983); Péter Dávidházi, "René Wellek and the Originality of American Criticism," *The Origins and Originality of American Culture* (ed. Tibor Frank, 1984); Peter Demetz, "Interview with René Wellek," *Cross Currents* 9 (1990); Lothar Fietz, "René Welleks Literaturtheorie und der Prager Strukturalismus," *Englische und amerikanische Literaturtheorie* (ed. Rüdiger Ahrens and Erwin Wolff, 2 vols., 1978–79); Sarah Lawall, "René Wellek: Phenomenological Literary Historian," *Literary Theory and Criticism: Festschrift in Honor of René Wellek* (ed. Joseph Strelka, 1984), "René Wellek and Modern Literary Criticism," *Comparative Literature* 40 (1988); Thomas G. Winner and John P. Kasik, "René Wellek's Contribution to American Literary Scholarship," *Forum* 2 (1977).

WHITE, HAYDEN

Hayden White (b. 1928), University Professor and Professor of the History of Consciousness at the University of California, Santa Cruz, is the most prominent American scholar to unite historiography and literary criticism into a broader reflection on narrative and cultural understanding. In his essay "The Burden of History" (1965, in *Tropics*) White noted that the traditional description of history as *both* an art and a science has prevented history from confronting recent developments in either area and has justified an antagonism to "theory," an antagonism many historians have taken to be the mark of the truly historical mind. Aimed at overcoming this

hostility, White's *Metahistory: The Historical Imagination in Nineteenth-Century Europe* (1973) offers an ambitious schema of the "poetics of history," describing four structures of emplotment, four argumentative models, and four ideological strategies. He adds to this a fourth, deeper category of analysis, also comprising four modes—the theory of tropes. Adapted from GIAMBATTISTA VICO and KENNETH BURKE, the theory of tropes defines the "deep structural forms" of historical thought as the four literary figures metaphor, metonymy, synecdoche, and irony, each possessing its characteristic means of organizing parts into wholes. White asserts that the vision of a given historian derives not from the evidence, since the vision decides in advance what will constitute the relevant evidence, but rather from conscious and unconscious choices made among the possibilities offered by the categories of his historical poetics. Thus, given a basic honesty and competence on the part of the historian studied, White can find no reason to prefer one account over another *on historical grounds alone*. The version of the past we choose depends rather *on moral and aesthetic values*, which ground both the historian and the audience and are beyond the call of historical evidence.

White has been influenced by existentialism's emphasis on freedom and responsibility in the world; his writings consistently promote the Kantian notion that the choices among forms of historical representation are in fact choices among possible futures. STRUCTURALISM has been a second influence on White's critical method, which typically assumes a mediating stance. White strives to get "above" the question at hand in order to discern the system of thought that authorizes the terms of the debate. He sees the tropology described in *Metahistory* and in *Tropics of Discourse: Essays in Cultural Criticism* (1978) as a powerful tool for distinguishing modes of thought because it describes how discursive choices are *pre*-figured by one dominant trope. Nevertheless, White does not claim that tropes are laws of discourse; they are instead "conventional" models in Western discourse.

All interpretation is fundamentally rhetorical because interpreting is what we do when we are uncertain how to describe or explain something. This uncertainty leads the interpreter to search for the available means of persuasion, which are figural in form and which can be successfully invoked only by working through the range of tropes. "In a word, in the sequence of tropological modes which leads from an original metaphorical characterization of an *interpretandum*, through a metonymic reduction and a synecdochic identification, to an ironic apprehension of the figurality of the whole sequence, we have something like the plot of all possible emplot-ments—the meaning of which is nothing but the process of linguistic figuration itself" ("The Rhetoric of Interpretation" 271). In this comment, which accompanies a discussion of Proust's *Sodome et Gomorrhe* from *À la recherche du temps perdu* (*Cities of the Plain,* vol. 4 of *Remembrance of Things Past*), White characteristically situates his own rhetorical position at the highest level of metacommentary. He discusses a paragraph in which Proust describes a fountain by Hubert Robert from the changing perspectives offered by the four tropes as the tropological summation of the novel, which has up to that point proceeded through a metaphoric discourse on male homosexuality, a metonymic reflection on certain marginal characters, and a synecdochic depiction of nobility. Elsewhere White extends his claims for the tropological essence of literary interpretation to encompass both style and narrative.

Because the four tropes describe the logically possible relationships between part and whole, tropology forms a basic component in the study of narrative, which fashions a unity from the diverse elements of language. In *The Content of the Form: Narrative Discourse and Historical Representation* (1987) White maintains that the decision to narrativize real events as history serves the ideological function of asserting the "beautiful," meaningful nature of the past (and present) and repressing any possible choice of encoding a "sublime," chaotic, terrifying meaninglessness as reality. This "de-sublimation" made possible the professionalization of nineteenth-century history by cutting its traditional ties to rhetoric, which emphasizes choices among possible forms of representation. Thus, history makes the past into an object of desire by giving it the same kind of coherence found in stories. In asking how a non-narrative history is possible, White does not examine the analytic, socioeconomic historiography of recent decades (which he considers fundamentally narrative) but rather pre-narrative forms—the medieval annals and chronicles. These forms could be replaced by proper historical narrative only when a sense of public order in the modern state prevailed, providing a "subject" for narrative representation. The "content" of the narrative "form" asserts the rationality of any social order dominated by centralized hierarchies and state power; the authority of narrative as a representation of "reality" depends upon its putative "realism" and its condemnation of all utopian choices as politically and artistically *un*realistic.

Although White believes that historical texts are an ideal place to study narrative realism because historians traditionally claim to represent reality itself rather than fictional simulacra, his inquiry into the ideology of narrative forms and his use of tropology extend to all narrative forms. White's work also serves as a warning to any criticism or would-be NEW HISTORICISM that would ground readings of texts in given historical contexts. History cannot serve as a neutral, factual support for their interpretations, because it has the same hermeneutic foundations as other humanistic studies. Any image of a historical context is itself, taken as a whole, a prior interpretation chosen for a particular purpose and is in no way less problematic than the literary text that constitutes its part.

Hans Kellner

Hayden White, *The Content of the Form: Narrative Discourse and Historical Representation* (1987), "Conventional Conflicts: Authority and the Profession of Criticism," *New Literary History* 13 (1981), "The Discourse of History," *Humanities in Society* 2 (1979), "Ethnological 'Lie' and Mythical 'Truth,'" *diacritics* 8 (1978), "The Limits of Relativism in the Arts," *Relativism in the Arts* (ed. Betty Jean Craige, 1983), "Literary History: The Point of It All," *New Literary History* 2 (1970), "Literature and Social Action: Reflections on the Reflection Theory of Literary Art," *New Literary History* 11 (1980), *Metahistory: The Historical Imagination in Nineteenth-Century Europe* (1973), "The New Historicism: A Comment," *The New Historicism* (ed. H. Aram Veeser, 1989), "The Problem of Change in Literary History," *New Literary History* 7 (1975), "The Problem of Style in Realistic Representation: Marx and Flaubert," *The Concept of Style* (ed. Berel Lang, 1979), "The Rhetoric of Interpretation," *Poetics Today* 9 (1988), "Structuralism and Popular Culture," *Journal of Popular Culture* 7 (1974), *Tropics of Discourse: Essays in Cultural Criticism* (1978).

David Carroll, "On Tropology: The Forms of History," *diacritics* 6 (1976); Fredric Jameson, "Figural Relativism, or the Poetics of Historiography," *diacritics* 6 (1976); Hans Kellner, "Hayden White and the Kantian Discourse: Tropology, Narrative, Freedom," *The Philosophy of Discourse* (ed. C. Sills and G. Jensen, forthcoming), *Language and Historical Representation: Getting the Story Crooked* (1989); Dominick LaCapra, "A Poetics of Historiography: Hayden White's *Tropics of Discourse,*" *Rethinking Intellectual History: Texts, Contexts, Language* (1983); James M. Mellard, *Doing Tropology: Analysis of Narrative Discourse* (1987); "*Metahistory*: Six Critiques," *History and Theory* 19 (*Beiheft 19*, 1980).

WILDE, OSCAR

Oscar Wilde (1854–1900), an Irishman who was educated at Oxford and lived in London, was a dominant and controversial figure in British cultural life from his undergraduate days until his imprisonment for "acts of gross indecency" in 1895. His views on literature, art, and criticism and their relation to conduct are implicit or explicit in almost everything he wrote and in his public demeanor and his celebrated table talk as well. The scandalous nature of Wilde's peripeteia contributed to a swift and severe reaction against the view of art he represented; and although his reputation has enjoyed a gradual rehabilitation, he is still sometimes narrowly identified with a kind of amoral aestheticism that many people associate, invidiously or not, with a stereotyped conception of male homosexuality. Wilde's habit of expressing himself epigrammatically has made his ideas seem to be essentially clever paradoxes and inversions, designed to amuse and *épater,* and this has led to a tendency (which Wilde did little enough to discourage) to reduce his critical position to a list of slogans snipped from their contexts: "Life imitates Art" (*Artist* 311), "A Truth in art is that whose contradictory is also true" (432), "All art is quite useless" (236).

Nearly all Wilde's criticism was written between 1885, when he stopped making his living as a lecturer, and 1891, when he started making his living as a dramatist. It consists of about a hundred book reviews and brief articles; the preface to his novel, *The Picture of Dorian Gray* (1891); and six essays: "The Portrait of Mr. W. H." (1889), an interpretation of Shakespeare's sonnets presented in the form of a short story; "The Soul of Man under Socialism" (1891), an argument against private property in the name of individualism and artistic freedom; "The Truth of Masks" (1885), on the use of costumes in the staging of Shakespeare's plays; "Pen, Pencil and Poison" (1889), on the nineteenth-century litterateur and murderer Thomas Griffiths Wainewright; and two imaginary dialogues on art and criticism, "The Decay of Lying" (1889) and "The Critic as Artist" (1890). The last four of these essays were revised and published in 1891 in a volume called *Intentions.*

In Wilde's reviews and shorter pieces, he praised Elizabeth Barrett Browning for her sincerity, Whitman for his "fine ethical purpose" (*Artist* 125), and Honoré de Balzac and Fyodor Dostoevsky for their realism; he criticized Robert Browning for failing to write poetry that "create[s] a desire to lead a higher, a holier, and a more useful life" (45); and he took other critics to task for scholarly inaccuracies. In his longer essays, he declared

that a "little sincerity is a dangerous thing, and a great deal of it is absolutely fatal" (393); that "the sphere of Art and the sphere of Ethics are absolutely distinct" (393); that "as a method, realism is a complete failure" (303); that "the State is to make what is useful. The individual is to make what is beautiful" (268); and that "the primary aim of the critic is to see the object as in itself it really is not" (369).

The appearance of inconsistency has sometimes been explained by the hypothesis that Wilde possessed a divided critical temperament, part moralistic and part aesthetical, reflecting the legacies of his two masters, JOHN RUSKIN and WALTER PATER (both of whom he knew at Oxford). An alternative explanation is that Wilde's longer essays, particularly the dialogues "The Decay of Lying" and "The Critic as Artist," examine art and criticism from a theoretical or philosophical, rather than a practical, standpoint—much as the dialogues in PLATO's *Republic* consider art and other matters in the light of a theory of knowledge without regard to practicality.

The philosophical foundation of Wilde's theoretical essays is the one that underwrites Pater's *Renaissance* (1873), a work Wilde admired almost unreservedly. It combines the skepticism of empirical philosophy, the materialism of nineteenth-century science, and the determinism of evolutionary theory. Its moral, as Pater expressed it in his essay on Johann Joachim Winckelmann, is that "natural laws we shall never modify, embarrass us as they may; but there is still something in the nobler or less noble attitude with which we watch their fatal combinations." Pater called this state of affairs "the tragic situation," but Wilde put it to the comedic service of turning conventional notions of art and value upside down. The traditional aesthetic virtues of sincerity, originality, morality, and truth to life, he explained, presuppose a world in which the self is an autonomous entity, in which ethical standards have transcendent status, in which "life" and "nature" are things that can be known apart from our representations of them. This was not the world nineteenth-century science described.

Wilde's protagonists in "The Decay of Lying" and "The Critic as Artist" propose that epistemological skepticism liberates the critic from the impossible task of measuring the work of art against the real and that "the principle of Heredity" (evolutionary theory) relieves him or her of the responsibility to produce an objective interpretation. The individual subject is the product of all previous subjectivities—"The imagination is the result of heredity. It is simply concentrated race experience"—and cultural history is thus a series of creative misinterpretations. Because it makes no claim to objec-

tivity, art is the supreme record of human experience—
"We look back on the ages entirely through the medium
of Art, and Art, very fortunately, has never once told us
the truth"—and the "duty" of the critic (a term Wilde
expands to include the artist and "any man of . . . culture") is therefore to add a fresh misinterpretation to the
series. The critic can know the past only by remaining
true to his or her subjectivity, itself a product of the past;
and, correlatively, "he to whom the present is the only
thing that is present, knows nothing of the age in which
he lives." Thus Wilde's insistence on the absolute freedom of the artist: art's usefulness and truthfulness can
only be realized if the artist, in his or her pursuit of
beauty, is unfettered by the requirement that art be
useful or true.

Wilde's championship of art's autonomy, his separation of art and ethics, and his critique of conventional
morality belong to the history of aestheticism. They are
themes that, expressed in a different vocabulary and in
support of different cultural tastes, reemerge in the criticism of twentieth-century modernism. Wilde's historicism, though, with its ties to the thought of FRIEDRICH
NIETZSCHE, Wilhelm Dilthey and nineteenth-century
hermeneutics, and BENEDETTO CROCE, resonates with
the critical discourse of poststructuralism—or with any
intellectual dispensation in which value is understood
to be an unstable and constructed affair.

Louis Menand

See also WALTER PATER.

Oscar Wilde, *The Artist as Critic: Critical Writings of
Oscar Wilde* (ed. Richard Ellmann, 1969), *The Letters
of Oscar Wilde* (ed. Rupert Hart-Davis, 1962), *More Letters of
Oscar Wilde* (ed. Rupert Hart-Davis, 1988), *Oscar Wilde's
Oxford Notebooks: A Portrait of Mind in the Making* (ed.
Philip E. Smith II and Michael S. Helfand, 1989).

Bruce Bashford, "Oscar Wilde and Subjectivist Criticism," *English Literature in Transition* 21 (1978), "Oscar
Wilde, His Criticism and His Critics," *English Literature
in Transition* 20 (1977); Richard Ellmann, *Oscar Wilde*
(1988); Richard Ellmann, ed., *Oscar Wilde: A Collection of
Critical Essays* (1969); Stuart Mason, *Oscar Wilde: A Bibliography* (1914, reprint, 1972); Rodney Shewan, *Oscar Wilde:
Art and Egotism* (1977); Susan Sontag, "Notes on 'Camp,' "
"Against Interpretation" and Other Essays (1966).

WILLIAMS, RAYMOND

The most important legacy of Raymond Williams (1921–
88) is the emergent interdisciplinary field of CULTURAL
STUDIES—a field that he, more than anyone else in the
English-speaking world since the late 1940s, pioneered
and consolidated. Above all, Williams exemplified the
social figure of the politically committed writer. Confident that "all kinds of writing produce meaning and
value" (*Politics* 326), he wrote in a multiplicity of modes
and discourses (as critic, theorist, historian, journalist,
political commentator, pamphleteer, dramatist, and
novelist) and in a variety of styles (conversational, high
academic, technically condensed, literary, and polemical). At his death in 1988, after a career of 40 years, he left
behind more than 650 publications, including 27 academic books, 5 novels, 3 plays, 7 pamphlets, 60 columns
on television in *The Listener,* and more than 500 articles
and reviews, among them his regular book reviews for
the *Guardian* and *New Society.*

Williams was born into a working-class family in
Pandy, a village in the parish of Llanfihangel, in Mon-
mouthshire, Wales, and was educated at Abergavenny
Grammar School and Trinity College, Cambridge. The
foundations of his prolific intellectual career were set
down after World War II, during a period of employment with the Oxford University Extra-Mural Delegacy
(1946 61) and active involvement with the Workers Educational Association. Williams taught drama and fiction
with increasing emphasis on their political and social
contexts and also stressed the theme of a democratic and
permanent education. His important books of this period
move from criticism (*Reading and Criticism,* 1950) and
drama (*Drama from Ibsen to Eliot,* 1952; *Drama in Performance,* 1954) to film (*Preface to Film,* 1954) and culture
and communications (*Culture and Society, 1780–1950,*
1958; *The Long Revolution,* 1961). The last two, in particular, formed his contributions to the radical cultural milieu that was emerging in postwar England through such
political initiatives as the Campaign for Nuclear Disarmament and the New Left clubs, such publications in
cultural studies as Richard Hoggart's seminal *Uses of Literacy,* and such enterprises in radical journalism as the
successful merger of *New Reasoner* and *Universities and
Left Review* into the still eminent *New Left Review.*

In *Culture and Society,* through a close reading of ED-
MUND BURKE, JOHN STUART MILL, MATTHEW ARNOLD,
and other such writers from the late eighteenth to the
mid-twentieth century, Williams breaches the narrow
confines of the prevailing definitions that separate literature, culture, and politics. He reconstructs the newly

active sense of "culture" that emerged around the time of the Industrial Revolution as a critique of industrialization and mechanization. This book, now a humanities classic, found warm response in the cultural politics of the 1960s. By studying culture in the context of its relationships with the four terms ("class," "industry," "democracy," and "art") with which it had been associated structurally in the "culture and society" tradition that he was organizing and making visible, Williams breaks further new ground. He initiates a historical semantics that stresses connection and interaction in support of the claim that important social and historical processes occur *within* language and, indeed, that the active meanings and values embodied in language and in the changing patterns of language exert a formative social force. *Keywords* (1976), first developed as an appendix to this earlier text but not published until nearly two decades later, offers a selective vocabulary of culture and society within this theoretical framework. A recognizable trademark of Williams's own writings is a continual recourse to keyword analysis.

The Long Revolution, one of Williams's two or three most important and most enduring works, provides evidence that the changes and conflicts of a whole way of life are deeply implicated in its systems of learning and communication, with the result that cultural history is far from being a mere province of idle aesthetic interest. The theoretical work and the historical scholarship combine to restore both conceptual terms ("creativity," "culture," "individual," "society") and instituted forms (education, literacy, the press, standardization of the language, the conventions of drama and fiction) to the actual historical networks of active social relationships that give them meaning. *The Long Revolution* made a substantial contribution to the production of modern cultural studies in general but also to the advance of a politically committed current within it. For Williams's argument weds together culture and democracy. Where *Culture and Society* looks backward, *The Long Revolution* looks forward to the next decade and, in contrast with the cultural conservatism of F. R. LEAVIS and T. S. ELIOT, offers a program for the radical democratic reform of cultural institutions. Its theoretical perspective meanwhile is also one of the most generous political creeds of our times: that we are living through a long revolution that is simultaneously and in connected ways economic, political, and cultural and that transforms people and institutions in the process of extending the transformation of nature, the forms of democratic self-governance, and the modes of education and communication. Uneven and conflicted as this process may be, enhancing its

development is the main criterion of intellectual, moral, and political value.

In *Communications* (1962), consolidating the argument of *The Long Revolution,* Williams deepens his fieldwork in cultural studies, reviewing the contents and methods of cultural media and finding supports for the contention that relationships of power, property, and production are no more fundamental to a society than relationships in describing, learning, modifying, exchanging, and preserving experiences. He asserts that these latter, far from being secondary communications about some other primary reality, are "a central and necessary part of our humanity" (*Communications* 11). Later, in *Television* (1974), Williams investigates one particular cultural institution in historical depth, with the intention of refuting MARSHALL MCLUHAN's arguments of technological determinism and instead situating television and its effects within a critical sociology of society as a totality, analyzing both its achievements in extending public education and its falling short of the possibilities for democratic broadcasting controlled by the cultural producers. Williams's intuition, as advanced in his inaugural lecture as professor of drama (1974), is that "we have never as a society acted so much or watched so many others acting." Drama is built into the rhythms of everyday life; the flow of representation and performance, complemented by the romance of advertising, becomes a new convention and a new need. The study of culture is called to embrace with urgency the study of such transfers and transformations between minority forms, media effects, and popular experience.

From 1961 to his early retirement in 1983, Williams worked at Cambridge University, housed in Jesus College in a room once occupied by SAMUEL TAYLOR COLERIDGE. During the first half of the 1960s, he was active on the left of the Labour party and then in the extraparliamentary New Left, indicting capitalism in the *May Day Manifesto* (1967–68), co-edited with E. P. Thompson and Stuart Hall. Meanwhile, cultural studies was finding its first institutionalized form as a graduate unit of the English department at the University of Birmingham, with Richard Hoggart as the founding director of the Centre for Contemporary Cultural Studies (1964), Stuart Hall as his successor (1969–79), and Williams as a major intellectual influence during the first decade.

During this same period, in such books as *Modern Tragedy* (1966), *Drama from Ibsen to Brecht* (1968), *The English Novel from Dickens to Lawrence* (1970), and *The Country and the City* (1973), Williams produced major revaluations of both the dramatic and the fictional traditions by reading texts as the scenes of historical meanings and transformations. In these texts, where Williams is most actively concerned with the aesthetic access to historical (lived) form and with the latter's relationships with recorded forms and their conventions, he also most fully works two of his best-known categories: "the knowable community" (contrasting with both the unknowable and the known and thus incorporating a certain dynamic potentiality that links the object-community and the subject-observer) and "structure of feeling" (the distilled residue of the organization of the lived experience of a community over and above the institutional and ideological organization of the society).

In the 1970s a widely increasing international theoretical sophistication, converging with a period of renaissance of intellectual Western Marxism, offered Williams new opportunities, audiences, and confirmations, both validating, however indirectly, his own longstanding efforts to argue for a more complex world of relationships between literature, criticism, and other forms of writing and social practice and also inviting him, as a longtime critic of the crude anticultural Marxism of the received orthodox traditions, to take up residence as a respected innovator in the renewed house of Marxism. By the end of the decade, most of Williams's writing refers itself to Marxism, testifying to a change of address if not of opinion, although he never ceases to engage oppositionally with the established culture. His works now appear as initiatives within the development of a general Marxist theoretical culture. The remarkable *Politics and Letters* (1979) comprises an innovation in form: through hundreds of pages of exacting interview, Williams reviews with four editors of *New Left Review* the frames and details of his life's work and repeatedly tests himself against that journal's view of Marxism. In the earlier "Notes on Marxism in Britain since 1945" (1976, in *Problems in Materialism and Culture*), he defines his current position—by which many will want to identify his legacy—as "cultural materialism"; this is a theory of culture as a productive process and a theory of specific cultural practices or "arts" as social uses of the material means of production (including language and the technologies of writing and other communications media).

This position is elaborated further in *Contact: Communication and Culture* (1981) and in *Culture* (1981). Against the anthropological sense of culture as a whole way of life that had been prominent in Williams's earlier formulations, he now delimits culture within modern society; that is, he delimits manifestly signifying institutions, practices, and works (including language, fashion, and advertising) from others in which signification, though present, is "more or less completely" dissolved

into other substantial needs and actions (just as these latter, in turn, are reciprocally in solution in manifestly signifying activities). "Thus the social organization of culture, as a realized signifying system, is embedded in a whole range of activities, relations and institutions, of which only some are manifestly 'cultural'" (*Culture* 13, 208–9).

Marxism and Literature (1977), though rather schematic and compressed, is perhaps the best and most fully coherent of this Marxist theoretical series. On the one hand, it conducts a characteristically coded struggle against French STRUCTURALISM and poststructuralism, taking issue with the language paradigm and the notion of the arbitrary sign. On the other hand, the text is a rewarding encounter with all the elements of a Marxist cultural and literary theory, on which numerous improvements are convincingly worked. The most important single contributions here may be the revisions in the categories of "hegemony" and "structure of feeling." The concept of hegemonic cultural domination, based in *selective* systems of inclusion and exclusion, provides for both social reproduction and resistance and for both connectedness and a determinate order among social practices. In the 1980s, Williams's refinements have provided renewed points of contact between his work and the program of cultural studies at Birmingham (which became an independent department in 1988). "Structure of feeling," now redefined with greater categorial precision to mark the generative border country between the lived and the fully articulated as a structured social experience in solution, effective but still semantically pre-emergent, may be considered Williams's important contribution to that striving in contemporary cultural thought that has produced a family of undefinable yet operative categories, among which should be included Pierre Bourdieu's "habitus," JACQUES DERRIDA's *différance*, MICHEL FOUCAULT's "procedures," JULIA KRISTEVA's *chora*, and Gilles Deleuze and Félix Guattari's "plane of consistence."

In all his cultural work, Williams was writing against two traditions: "one which has totally spiritualized cultural production, the other which has relegated it to secondary status" (*Politics* 352–53). He was committed to the view that "the categories of literature and criticism were so deeply compromised that they had to be challenged *in toto*" (326). In the 1980s, his concern with "the general crisis now developing" (*Towards* 105) led him to issues of feminism, ecology, and North-South relations. The possibilities of democratic cultural innovation and an alternative social order continued to win his confidence far more readily than the cultural pessimism in the light of which only the past is to be won and a high culture is to be preserved and extended. He opted for "making hope practical, rather than despair convincing" (240).

So far, very few books and only a small body of articles and reviews have been addressed specifically to his work. Meanwhile, nearly everything in the increasingly voluminous literature emerging on cultural studies makes some kind of reference to Williams. At present, in the sharpening struggles for a definition of cultural studies, there is some risk that Williams's legacy may be diminished to a narrow political sociology, cut to a measure that ill suits the richer dimensions both of his own concerns and of the potentialities of the field. At the same time, his pronounced *parti pris* with Marxism and modernism is bound to bring the paradigm-bound aspects of his work under increasingly sharp scrutiny and criticism from a post-Marxist or postmodernist site of inquiry. Stock-taking, like the long revolution for which Williams struggled, is yet at an early stage.

John Fekete

See also CULTURAL STUDIES and MARXIST THEORY AND CRITICISM.

Raymond Williams, *Communications* (1962, 3d ed., 1976), *The Country and the City* (1973), *Culture* (1981), *Culture and Society, 1780–1950* (1958), *Drama from Ibsen to Brecht* (1952, rev. ed., 1968), *The English Novel from Dickens to Lawrence* (1970), *Keywords: A Vocabulary of Culture and Society* (1976, rev. ed., 1983), *The Long Revolution* (1961, rev. ed., 1966), *Marxism and Literature* (1977), *Modern Tragedy* (1966), *Politics and Letters: Interview with "New Left Review"* (1979), *Problems in Materialism and Culture: Selected Essays* (1980), *Television: Technology and Cultural Form* (1974), *Towards 2000* (1983).

Terry Eagleton, ed., *Raymond Williams: Critical Perspectives* (1989); Jan Gorak, *The Alien Mind of Raymond Williams* (1988); Stephen Heath and Gillian Skirrow, "An Interview with Raymond Williams," *Studies in Entertainment: Critical Approaches to Mass Culture* (ed. Tania Modleski, 1986); Lesley Johnson, *The Cultural Critics: From Matthew Arnold to Raymond Williams* (1979); Alan O'Connor, *Raymond Williams: Writing, Culture, Politics* (1989); J. P. Ward, *Raymond Williams* (1981).

WILSON, EDMUND

Edmund Wilson (1895–1972) was an American journalist whose interests included American, British, French, and Russian literature of all periods; nineteenth- and twentieth-century political thought; and a variety of minority literatures and cultures. His importance in the history of criticism can be described under three heads: the establishment of American studies, the canonization of the modernist writers, and the changing status of literary journalism in American intellectual life.

Wilson belonged to the generation of writers who came of age in the 1920s. He shared with many of his contemporaries the hope that the postwar years would see American culture emerge from the shadow of Europe— a hope reflected, for example, in Van Wyck Brooks's reconstruction of the American literary tradition, in H. L. Mencken's work on the American language, and in Gilbert Seldes's studies of the popular arts. Wilson's contribution to that project began with his own writing. In his reviews and essays for such magazines as *Vanity Fair,* the *New Republic,* and the *New Yorker* (he was an editor at the first two and for many years the regular book critic for the third), he undertook to provide American letters with the equivalent of the work of two nineteenth-century critics he admired, CHARLES AUGUSTIN SAINTE-BEUVE and HIPPOLYTE TAINE. He produced informed judgments on contemporary literary developments, and he wrote studies that tried to present, as he put it, "a history of man's ideas and imaginings in the setting of the conditions which have shaped them" (*Axel's Castle,* dedication).

Three works of Wilson's have particular importance in the history of American studies: *The Shock of Recognition* (1943), an anthology of criticism by writers from Edgar Allan Poe to Sherwood Anderson that "attempt[s] to present a chronicle of the progress of literature in the United States as one finds it recorded by those who had some part in creating that literature" (vii); *Patriotic Gore* (1962), an extensive survey of the literature of the American Civil War and its aftermath; and "The Fruits of the MLA" (1968), an attack on professional textual editing that led, after Wilson's death, to the Library of America, a series of inexpensive editions of the classics of American literature.

But writers of Wilson's generation tempered their enthusiasm for the American century with doubts about the susceptibility of American culture to leavening and with an attraction to European traditions—an ambivalence reflected in Wilson's first critical book. *Axel's Castle* (1931) is a study of W. B. Yeats, Paul Valéry, T. S. Eliot,

Marcel Proust, James Joyce, and Gertrude Stein. Wilson's intention was to critique the aestheticism of the Symbolist tradition (to which, he argued, those writers belonged) and to clear the ground for the major American writing he predicted for the years ahead. But the critique was obscured by Wilson's admiration for the boldness and difficulty of the literature he discussed, and the book's effect was to make accessible and to help canonize the writers it criticized.

In the decade that followed, Wilson produced two collections of essays on literary subjects, *The Triple Thinkers* (1938) and *The Wound and the Bow* (1941), and a history of socialist thought in the form of a series of interlocked essays on major figures, *To the Finland Station* (1940). *The Triple Thinkers* includes essays on Aleksandr Pushkin, Gustave Flaubert, A. E. Housman, John Jay Chapman, George Bernard Shaw, and Ben Jonson and an influential discussion of "The Ambiguity of Henry James"—all given a loose methodological unity by an essay entitled "The Historical Interpretation of Literature." *The Wound and the Bow* contains essays on Rudyard Kipling, Casanova, Edith Wharton, Ernest Hemingway, and Joyce's *Finnegans Wake* and an important reconsideration of Charles Dickens—all tied together by an essay explaining art as compensation for some psychic "wound" of the artist.

The typical Wilsonian essay is a profile of a single writer that is constructed from literary and biographical evidence and gives some attention to historical context. The entire *oeuvre* is usually considered—diachronically, to indicate development as well as consistency—and emphasis is frequently placed on works less well known or less well regarded, reflecting Wilson's journalistic cast of mind: he considered it his business to introduce readers to works they might otherwise neglect rather than to offer fresh readings to those already initiated.

There is not enough history in Wilson's work for him to be called a Marxist critic, or even a historical or materialist one, and his interest is not psychoanalytic enough for his criticism to be called Freudian. His interpretive formulas tend to be either schematic, as in the case of the cyclical model of literary history used to explain the emergence of symbolism in *Axel's Castle* (Wilson adapted it from Alfred North Whitehead's *Science and the Modern World* [1925]), or reductive, as in the case of the "seaslug" theory of history proposed in *Patriotic Gore* (that war is the result of the instinct of the larger organism to ingest the smaller).

By the early 1940s Wilson felt that his style of criticism had become anachronistic, displaced (as he wrote in 1943) by the criticism of the professional journalist and of "the literary man in college, incorporated in that quite different organism, the academic profession, with its quite other hierarchies of value and competitions for status" (*Classics* 109). He took no part in the academic debates surrounding the rise of NEW CRITICISM in the 1940s and 1950s and its displacement by other critical ideologies in the 1960s.

Wilson's interest in canonical literature waned after the 1940s, and he became a student of the popular (in much of *Patriotic Gore*), the marginal (in his writings on Haitian and Canadian literature), the obscure (in his study of the Essenes, the sect that produced the Dead Sea scrolls), and the nearly extinct (in his essays on the Iroquois and Zuni tribes). In some respects this turn in Wilson's work reflects the ascendancy of the academic critic as the figure responsible for the maintenance and interpretation of the canon. But it represents as well a reaction against the formalism and the exclusivity of academic literary studies, and it is in that sense proleptic of a reaction that took place in the academy itself after Wilson's death.

Louis Menand

Edmund Wilson, *Apologies to the Iroquois* (1960), *Axel's Castle: A Study in the Imaginative Literature of 1870–1930* (1931), *The Bit between My Teeth: A Literary Chronicle of 1950–1965* (1965), *Classics and Commercials: A Literary Chronicle of the Forties* (1950), *The Devils and Canon Barham: Ten Essays on Poets, Novelists, and Monsters* (1973), *Letters on Literature and Politics, 1912–1972* (ed. Elena Wilson, 1977), *O Canada: An American's Notes on Canadian Culture* (1965), *Patriotic Gore: Studies in the Literature of the American Civil War* (1962), *Red, Black, Blond, and Olive: Studies in Four Civilizations: Zuni, Haiti, Soviet Russia, Israel* (1956), *The Scrolls from the Dead Sea* (1955), *The Shock of Recognition: The Development of Literature in the United States Recorded by the Men Who Made It* (1943), *The Shores of Light: A Literary Chronicle of the Twenties and Thirties* (1952), *To the Finland Station: A Study in the Writing and Acting of History* (1940), *The Triple Thinkers: Twelve Essays on Literary Subjects* (1938, rev. ed., 1948), *The Wound and the Bow: Seven Studies in Literature* (1941).

Warner Berthoff, "Edmund Wilson," *American Writers*, vol. 4 (ed. Leonard Unger, 1974); David Castronovo, *Edmund Wilson* (1984); Charles Frank, *Edmund Wilson* (1970); Janet Groth, *Edmund Wilson: A Critic for Our Time* (1989); Leonard Kriegel, *Edmund Wilson* (1971); Sherman Paul, *Edmund Wilson* (1965); Richard David Ramsey, *Edmund Wilson: A Bibliography* (1971); John Wain, ed., *Edmund Wilson: The Man and His Work* (1978).

WINTERS, YVOR

Yvor Winters (1900–1968) grew up in Chicago at the very center of the incipient American modernism fostered by Harriet Monroe's *Poetry* magazine. But in 1918 he contracted tuberculosis and was removed to New Mexico for his health; subsequently (in 1927) he went to Stanford as a graduate student, and he remained there as a professor until his death. Winters's sense of isolation from his peers was compounded in the 1930s by his rejection, as a poet and as a critic, of what he came to see as the dangerous irresponsibility and "obscurantism" of the writers he had most admired in his youth (William Carlos Williams, WALLACE STEVENS, Hart Crane, Allen Tate). The violence and irrationality of the southwestern landscape and the "darkness" to which it seemed to solicit the solitary mind had become the pervasive themes of his own verse; they were, as well, the crucial subtext of his evolving "defense of reason" as a critic.

Winters differed most fundamentally from the other New Critics of his generation in his estimate of the nature and function of literary language (*In Defense* 3–14, 361–73) (see NEW CRITICISM). He refused to accord it an "autotelic" status, a being distinct from the language of everyday transactions with the world. The urgency of his experience as a poet made it impossible for him to regard poems as merely self-referential structures, aloof from moral or political concern. Poems are not "structures" at all, Winters contended, not "aesthetic objects." They are statements, acts of predication, exercises of prudence. The poet's practice is distinguished from the other communicative practices that make up a culture only by its special capacity for organizing otherwise slippery and unfathomable nuances or intensities of feeling. A poem is "what one should say" (*Collected Poems*, 1978, 146).

Winters's theoretical position (there is little significant change after *Primitivism and Decadence,* 1937) was worked out in opposition not only to the New Critics but also to the "didacticism" of New Humanists such as Irving Babbitt (see NEW HUMANISM). "Moral intelligence," Winters insisted, is to be located not in the subject matter of poetry but in those discursive strategies by which the power of its language—the scope and intensity of its "saying"—is either enhanced or vitiated (*In Defense* 17–35). The "fallacy of expressive, or imitative, form" (chaotic poems about chaos) codifies Winters's objection to language employed at less than full capacity (41): he saw drama, with its implication in incomplete and shifting perspectives, as a sort of generic institutionalization of this fallacy (*Function* 51–58). Perhaps Winters's most striking and durable achievement is his account of the

morality of poetic meter (*In Defense* 103–52, *Function* 81–100). The identity of a poetic line or of a whole poem, its "soul," inheres not primarily in ideas or images but in the way it moves. Rhythm sounds at once in the "sensual ear" and in the "mind's ear" and in itself constitutes a mode of consciousness that facilitates certain mental operations and precludes others. T. S. Eliot's "spiritual limpness" is a matter less of the nihilism of his opinions than of the slackness of his meters. Winters's disillusionment with modernism was not based, as were Babbitt's objections, on a recoil from the unorthodoxy of its ideas. Rather, he came to believe that a whole range of formal devices ("pseudo reference," Romantic irony, "qualitative progression") designed to circumvent the need for conceptual content—devices with which Winters himself had come of age as a poet—impoverish the poet's language, rather than "making it new," and leave him the victim of his own ungrounded perceptions (*In Defense* 30–102). Ezra Pound, Winters remarked, is a sensibility without a mind. Not that ideas are ever irrelevant, but in poetry, as in life, they are properly judged by what Winters (following Henry Bamford Parkes) called "the pragmatic test": in terms, not of dogma, but of the kind of behavior they authorize, the quality of consciousness for which they provide occasion. Winters's most striking essays in PRACTICAL CRITICISM are based on this testing of the stylistic consequences of moral or aesthetic ideas (and vice versa): his account of Hart Crane's tragic attempt to fathom, in his life as well as in his verse, the behavioral meaning of Emersonianism (*In Defense* 577–603); or the essays on American literature in *Maule's Curse* (1938), the first systematic attempt to demonstrate continuities between the "obscurantism" of the American Romantics, with their feverish groping toward "the intense inane" (*Maule's* 175), and the Symbolist traditions of the twentieth century (see also AMERICAN THEORY AND CRITICISM: NINETEENTH CENTURY and RALPH WALDO EMERSON).

Winters's "absolutism" has often seemed as troublesome as his moralism. But if one believes, as Winters did, that "it is in our language that we live the life of human beings, and only in our language" (*Forms* xviii)—that human "reality" is constituted in language—then one will be unlikely to dismiss literary judgments as matters only of taste or convenience. A failure of language is quite literally, for individuals or for a whole society, a diminishment of being. The critic cannot afford the luxury of "philosophical speculation and learned paraphrasing" in a genteelly value-free atmosphere. If it was imperative that Winters anatomize the dangerous inanity he saw all about him, then he also felt called upon to sift out from the detritus of literary history a stylistic tradition that would make possible a more adequate humanity than he found in the aftermath of modernism.

Winters's judgments are grounded not in some privileged access to transcendent value but in a collection of Arnoldian touchstones that define, collectively and cumulatively, what counts in our culture as being human. No doubt his canon often seems eccentric, and a good deal of harmless merriment has been inspired by his enthusiasm for little-read (and oddly named) poets such as Barnabe Googe, Elizabeth Daryush, or Adelaide Crapsey. But it should be remembered that he was not engaged in a history of taste or reputation and that for the task he set himself (the final version of his canon is an anthology called *Quest for Reality*) a single poem or even a single line will do as well as an extended corpus. And if he purges, as tainted with "associationism" and related irrationalities, most of the eighteenth, nineteenth, and early twentieth centuries, the intensity of his interrogation of received ideas and the keenness of his ear do succeed in making audible as a distinct voice—where earlier accounts detected only stumbling approximations of the Petrarchan mode—the "plain style" of the sixteenth and seventeenth centuries. At its best, Winters's criticism, like the poems he admires, becomes a "form of discovery."

Terry Comito

Yvor Winters, *Edward Arlington Robinson* (1946, rev. ed., 1971), *Forms of Discovery: Critical and Historical Essays on the Short Poem in English* (1967), *The Function of Criticism: Problems and Exercises* (1957), *In Defense of Reason* (1947, includes *Primitivism and Decadence*, 1937; *Maule's Curse: Seven Studies in American Obscurantism*, 1938; and *The Anatomy of Nonsense*, 1943), *Uncollected Essays and Reviews* (ed. Frances Murphy, 1973); Yvor Winters and Kenneth Fields, eds., *Quest for Reality* (1969).

Jonas Barish, "Yvor Winters and the Antimimetic Prejudice," *New Literary History* 2 (1971); R. P. Blackmur, *The Expense of Greatness* (1940); Terry Comito, *In Defense of Winters: The Poetry and Prose of Yvor Winters* (1986); Donald Davie, "Yvor Winters and the History of Ideas," *Southern Review,* n.s. 17 (1981); Dick Davis, *Wisdom and Wilderness: The Achievement of Yvor Winters* (1983); John Fraser, "Leavis, Winters, and Tradition," *Southern Review,* n.s. 7 (1971), "Winters' *Summa*," Review of *Forms of Discovery, Southern Review,* n.s. 5 (1969), "Yvor Winters: The Perils of Mind," *Centennial Review* 14 (1970); John Holloway, "The Critical Theory of Yvor Winters," *Critical Quarterly* 7 (1965); Stanley Edgar Hyman, "Yvor Winters and Evaluation in Criticism," *The Armed Vision: A Study in the Methods of Modern Literary Criticism* (1948, rev. ed., 1955); David Levin, "A Historical Reconsideration of *Maule's Curse," Southern Review,* n.s. 17 (1981); Grosvenor Powell, *Language as Being in the Poetry of Yvor Winters* (1980); John Crowe Ransom, "Yvor Winters: The Logical Critic," *The New Criticism* (1941); Marshall Van Deusen, "In Defense of Yvor Winters," *Thought* 32 (1957); René Wellek, "Yvor Winters," *A History of Modern Criticism: 1750–1950,* vol. 6, *American Criticism, 1900–1950* (1986).

WITTGENSTEIN, LUDWIG

Ludwig Josef Johann Wittgenstein (1889–1951) is generally considered to be the most influential thinker in modern Anglo-American language philosophy—a leading, if not founding, figure in the history of ordinary-language philosophy, speech-act theory (see SPEECH ACTS), logical positivism, and analytic linguistic philosophy and an important contributor to the philosophy of perceptual psychology and the tradition of moral realism. Although Wittgenstein's influence has been less persistent and direct in the realm of literary criticism and theory than in academic philosophy, there is a diverse and growing body of "Wittgensteinian" writing on literary issues, including certain brands of psychological and ethical criticism (e.g., Stanley Cavell), numerous writings concerning the nature of the literary "image" (W. J. T. Mitchell in *Wittgenstein and Literary Theory*), "ordinary language" critiques of "theory" (W. J. T. Mitchell, ed., *Against Theory*; John M. Ellis in *Wittgenstein and Literary Theory*), "speech act" criticism focusing on the contextual understanding of literary expression (Charles Altieri), and a small body of work concerning the relationship between rhetoric and what Wittgenstein called "forms of life" (Cavell; Henry Staten; Frank Cioffi in *Wittgenstein and Literary Theory*).

Born and raised in Vienna, Wittgenstein moved to England in 1908 in order to pursue his secondary education, enrolling at Cambridge in 1912 on the advice of Gottlob Frege. For the remainder of his life he moved back and forth between Cambridge, where he taught intermittently, and a number of European locales, where he tried to escape deep ambivalences both about his professional academic philosophy and about his personal and sexual relationships. Allan Janik and Stephen Toulmin examine Wittgenstein's relationship to the intellectual culture of turn-of-the-century Vienna, and Ray Monk has argued for a deep continuity between Wittgenstein's philosophy and the personal and spiritual crises that constantly beset him. Wittgenstein's intellectual relationships with his Cambridge colleagues such as Bertrand Russell, G. E. Moore, John Maynard Keynes, F. R. LEAVIS, and F. P. Ramsey have been chronicled in numerous memoirs, "recollections," "conversations," and letters published by his contemporaries. Many of Wittgenstein's most interesting meditations on aesthetic and literary issues are to be found scattered throughout these documents.

The most fundamental division in Wittgenstein's intellectual career lies between the *Tractatus Logico-Philosophicus* (1922) and the "later work," of which *Philosophical Investigations* (1953) is the principal document. These are the only of his extensive philosophical writings that Wittgenstein himself prepared for publication. (Wittgenstein did all his writing in German, but he saw only one book to press in his lifetime, and many of his "books" in print are posthumous collections—and translations—of his notebooks and file cards. These range from collections that he himself actually arranged and titled to those that he neither collected nor titled. Thus at one end of the spectrum we have the *Tractatus,* a straightforward bibliographical case of an English translation from a work written, titled, and previously published in German by Wittgenstein himself, while at the other end we have *Culture and Value,* an English book that translates German notes neither collected, titled, nor published by Wittgenstein. Somewhere in between lie works such as *Remarks on Colour,* which, despite the pretentious German title page in the facing-page translation edition, was never published in German; or *The Blue and Brown Books,* first published in a facing-page dual language edition.)

The *Tractatus* is one of the classic statements of logical positivism, though it is complicated considerably by Wittgenstein's almost mystical idealism. Through a series of simple but highly condensed propositions, the *Tractatus* elaborates a complex argument relating the "logical form" of "the world" to the "logic of language." It is Wittgenstein's contention that "the world" consists fundamentally of "facts" pertaining to the location and relationship of "objects" and that it is thus possible to give a *complete description* of the world independent of all questions of "sense" and "value."

Three aspects of Wittgenstein's argument in the *Tractatus* are of particular interest for literary criticism and theory. First is the project of reducing "everyday language" to its underlying logical form. The legacy of Frege's and Russell's philosophy of logical analysis, it has found its way into "literary" discussion via the contemporary philosophical work of John Searle, RICHARD RORTY, and others on the logical status of "fictional discourse." Here, Wittgenstein's contribution was to claim, not that the problems of aesthetics and ethics are pseudoproblems (as later logical positivists asserted), but rather that such problems pertain to the relationship *between* language and the "world," a relationship that cannot be represented *in* language. The second important aspect of the *Tractatus* is its vision of a world of immanent "structure" and "form," reflected endlessly, if not always perfectly, in language. This obsession with order and form aligns the *Tractatus* not only with STRUCTURALISM but also with a central impulse in literary modernism: the encyclopedic and totalitarian or mock-totalitarian fantasies of James Joyce, Samuel Beckett, Thomas Pynchon, and Jorge Luis Borges, among others. Finally, the *Tractatus* is of interest for what has come to be called the "picture-theory" of the early Wittgenstein. In the *Tractatus* Wittgenstein states that "a proposition is a picture of reality." By this he means that our comprehension of a sentence depends, not on our performing a set of translations from individual signs to individual referents, but on our immediate, intuitive perception of the *relationship* among the "constituent" parts of the sentence, as represented or displayed by the sentence in its concrete appearance. This picture-theory, which has affinities with both traditional and contemporary theories of RHETORIC, is subjected to criticism in the *Investigations,* where Wittgenstein emphasizes the potentially misleading nature of the analogy between visual and linguistic representations.

There is some debate among professional philosophers whether *Philosophical Investigations* constitutes an absolute rejection or only a modification of the position represented by the *Tractatus.* Literary theorists by and large have not contributed to this debate but have tended to take for granted that the *Investigations* constitutes a definitive rejection of the abstract and totalizing theoretical idealism of the *Tractatus* and a correlative recognition of the diverse forms of "ordinary" linguistic practice and social context. In fact, the anti-idealist impulse of the *Investigations* has encouraged many literary critics to offer Wittgenstein as a foil to literary theory generally and to poststructuralism specifically. However, since Rorty's *Philosophy and the Mirror of Nature* (1979), a small body of work has developed emphasizing the complex blend of skepticism, idealism, and pragmatism in the late Wittgenstein, a blend that makes Wittgenstein an uneasy ally for critics of "theory" (Staten, Dasenbrock).

Philosophical Investigations, written between 1935 and 1949, departs from the *Tractatus* not only in its conclusions; what is just as important, it differs in its philosophical method and style. It is composed of sequences of "remarks," less deductive in both tone and logical arrangement than the propositions of the *Tractatus*. Where the *Tractatus* makes abstract generalizations about the nature and status of "language" without ever giving examples, the *Investigations* argues by way of comparison between apposite phenomena or cases, often "quoting" hypothetical interlocutors or conventional turns of phrase. Part 1 of the *Investigations* opens (remarks 1–64) with an extended critique of the idea that a coherent language must have an underlying logical *form* or *function*. Wittgenstein begins by examining whether we are always thinking of the same thing when we say that a particular word has a "reference," a "purpose," a "meaning," or is "understood." This leads him to criticize the assumption that a language must have "simple," elementary units of signification that are unambiguously recognizable and can be unproblematically *taught, named,* and *pointed to.* Wittgenstein next (89–133) proposes to replace the concept of language as a logical system with the concept of "language-games" possessing "family resemblances." Games are learned partly by imitation and partly by "following rules," and this leads Wittgenstein to a discussion of the usefulness and limits of *approximation* in the formulation of rules, definitions, and descriptions. The discussion of games culminates in a provisional distinction between the demands of "ordinary language" and the demands of "philosophy" or "theory." Wittgenstein then proceeds (139–202) to examine the role of "rules" and "examples" in the learning and use of language and the implications of these practices for the activity of interpretation. This section includes incipient formulations of the question that will loom much larger in the latter half of part 1, namely, In what ways are "thinking," "meaning," and "intending" to be regarded as *mental states,* and to what extent are they *linguistic practices?*

Remarks 202–363 contain the argument denying the possibility of a "private language" or "private" sensations; here Wittgenstein speculates on the role of the figurative distinction between "inner" and "outer" in our ideas about what is mental, private, shared, public, linguistic, and so on. Wittgenstein then relates the distinction between "sense" and "nonsense" to our criteria for metaphor, fiction, and "imagination." Central to this discussion is Wittgenstein's concept of "grammar": the family of overlapping but ultimately unassimilable uses we make of a word in different contexts or expressions. The grammar of the word "inner," for example, includes the apparent interiority of sense in relation to expression, of pain to the body, of the brain to the skull, of a word to a sentence, and of a moment to its surrounding

moments. None of these uses provides a regulative analogy by which we might understand the others, and yet at the same time we cannot help but conceive of the various uses of the term primarily *through analogy*.

Part 2 of the *Investigations* is somewhat narrower in focus than part 1, and here Wittgenstein discusses problems in the psychology of perception, with particular reference to the concepts "atmosphere" and "aspect." In the well-known section 11 Wittgenstein examines the distinction between what we call "seeing" and "seeing something *as.*" This leads back to Wittgenstein's most insistent question throughout the *Investigations:* how is our comprehension of the various "aspects" (or "associations") of words both *determined* and yet in some way *not fully determined* by our language games?

Aside from the *Tractatus* and the *Investigations,* Wittgenstein wrote several manuscripts and countless notes on a variety of philosophical topics. Published only posthumously, these works, like the *Investigations,* were composed by sifting, polishing, and rearranging collections of short "remarks" written on a particular topic or set of topics over a course of time. Although none of the posthumous publications have the range or intricate organization of the *Investigations*—and cannot demonstrate as clearly the complex relationships Wittgenstein took pains to draw among his various philosophical topics—they often contain more sustained reflections upon specific topics, or more striking and illuminating examples and anecdotes, than the *Investigations* and thus may in some cases be more accessible than the latter. The collections known as *The Blue and Brown Books* and *Zettel* have been particularly helpful for readers trying to come to grasp with the *Investigations;* the former collection occasionally offers more extended examples and analogies than the *Investigations* and is somewhat less compressed and aphoristic in style, while the latter offers a more focused look at Wittgenstein's philosophy of mind.

Several posthumously published collections are concerned explicitly with aesthetic topics. *Culture and Value* contains aphorisms and remarks that appear scattered, and for the most part bracketed or set aside, throughout the posthumous manuscripts. These remarks on such figures as William Shakespeare, Ludwig von Beethoven, Wolfgang Amadeus Mozart, and JOHANN WOLFGANG VON GOETHE attempt to shed light on the shifting relationship between critical and creative activity across a broad range of media and genres. *Lectures and Conversations* contains some of Wittgenstein's most fascinating meditations on the conflicting roles of "appreciation," "judgment," "comparison," "explanation," and "interpretation" in cultural life. *Remarks on Colour* consists of a series of speculations on the relationship between the "sciences" of color perception (e.g., physics, optics, psychology) and our conventions for describing and representing colors; these remarks probe the limits of the analogy between linguistic and visual representation.

Finally, the collection published as *On Certainty* contains Wittgenstein's most sustained treatment of the relationship between ordinary language and skepticism. This volume has taken on an important role in recent debates over the cognitive claims and limits of both literature and literary theory.

Jules David Law

Ludwig Wittgenstein, "Bemerkungen über Frazers 'Golden Bough'" (1967, "Remarks on Frazer's *Golden Bough*," trans. A. C. Miles, rev. Rush Rhees, *Wittgenstein: Sources and Perspectives*, ed. C. G. Luckhardt, 1979), *The Blue and Brown Books: Preliminary Studies for the "Philosophical Investigations"* (1958), *Lectures and Conversations on Aesthetics, Psychology, and Religious Belief* (ed. Cyril Barrett, 1967), *Logisch-philosophische Abhandlung* (1921, *Tractatus Logico-Philosophicus,* trans. D. F. Pears and B. F. McGuinness, 1961), *On Certainty / Über Gewissheit* (ed. G. E. M. Anscombe and G. H. von Wright, trans. Denis Paul and Anscombe, 1969), *Philosophical Grammar* (ed. Rush Rhees, trans. Anthony Kenny, 1974), *Philosophical Investigations / Philosophische Untersuchungen* (trans. G. E. M. Anscombe, 1953, 3d ed., 1967), *Remarks on Colour / Bemerkungen über die Farben* (ed. G. E. M. Anscombe, trans. Linda L. McAlister and Margarete Schättle, 1977), *Vermischte Bemerkungen* (1977, *Culture and Value,* ed. G. H. von Wright with Keikki Nyman, trans. Peter Winch, 1980), *Zettel* (ed. G. E. M. Anscombe and G. H. von Wright, trans. Anscombe, 1967).

Charles Altieri, *Act and Quality: A Theory of Literary Meaning and Humanistic Understanding* (1981); Stanley Cavell, *The Claim of Reason: Wittgenstein, Skepticism, Morality, and Tragedy* (1979); Reed Way Dasenbrock, ed., *Redrawing the Lines: Analytic Philosophy, Deconstruction, and Literary Theory* (1989); Allan Janik and Stephen Toulmin, *Wittgenstein's Vienna* (1973); Anthony Kenny, *Wittgenstein* (1973); Saul A. Kripke, *Wittgenstein on Rules and Private Language: An Elementary Exposition* (1982); Norman Malcolm, *Ludwig Wittgenstein: A Memoir* (2d ed., 1984); W. J. T. Mitchell, ed., *Against Theory: Literary Studies and the New Pragmatism* (1985); Ray Monk, *Ludwig Wittgenstein: The Duty of Genius* (1990); Richard Rorty, *Philosophy and the Mirror of Nature* (1979); Henry Staten, *Wittgenstein and Derrida* (1984); *Wittgenstein and Literary Theory,* special issue, *New Literary History* 19 (1988).

WOLLSTONECRAFT, MARY

Feminist, radical, social theorist, educator, journalist, travel writer, and novelist, Mary Wollstonecraft (1759–97) was born in London. Her work and her life, her theory and her practice, were all turbulent and experimental. After a middle-class childhood fraught with poverty, family illness, and domestic violence, her early career evinced a bold independence of mind and action. She started a school for girls at Newington Green, where she came to know the radical, Dissenting minister Richard Price and a community of reformers and intellectuals. Always passionate in her attachments, Wollstonecraft sailed to Lisbon in 1785 to attend her beloved friend Fanny Blood, who died in childbirth. On returning in 1786, she wrote *Thoughts on the Education of Daughters,* which advocates a wide range of occupations for women and the necessity of quality education as preparation for motherhood. Afterwards, her brief stint as governess with the aristocratic and scandal-ridden Kingsborough family in Ireland bred in her a lifelong contempt for aristocracy, made palpable in both her novels: *Mary, a Fiction* (1788) and the unfinished *Wrongs of Woman; or, Maria* (1798). On returning to London in 1787, she was chosen by Joseph Johnson, the radical publisher, to edit the *Analytical Review.*

During the early days of the French Revolution, Wollstonecraft wrote *A Vindication of the Rights of Men* (1790), a withering reply to EDMUND BURKE's *Reflections on the Revolution in France.* A year later she called for a "revolution in female manners" in her most original and most influential book, *A Vindication of the Rights of Woman.* From 1792 to 1795 she lived in France, where she wrote about the Revolution and fell in love with an American entrepreneur, Gilbert Imlay. After Imlay abandoned her and their infant daughter, Fanny, she returned to London, where she met the philosopher William Godwin, whom she lived with and later married. She died in 1797 after complications resulting from childbirth; her surviving infant would become the writer Mary Wollstonecraft Shelley.

Wollstonecraft's most enduring insight in *A Vindication of the Rights of Woman* is that the condition of women in a given culture is not natural but is produced and replicated by that culture. The prevailing focus on gender in women's studies and in FEMINIST THEORY AND CRITICISM—on a culturally, rather than naturally, produced female identity—owes a profound debt to Wollstonecraft's analysis of the debasement of women in her own culture. Basing her arguments on the "first principles" of the Enlightenment—the natural capacity for reason, virtue, and knowledge—as well as on the immortality of the soul, she steers a bold course between the Scylla of Burkean "prejudice" and the Charybdis of Rousseauvian "nature" (see JEAN-JACQUES ROUSSEAU). While attacking the prejudices that have "clouded" the Enlightenment's attitudes toward both women and women's minds, she also refuses the intellectual temptations of a "state of nature." Her frank analysis of sensibility, of its sublimity as well as its dangers, would resonate in the novels of such writers as Jane Austen, Mary Shelley, Emily Brontë, Charlotte Brontë, and George Eliot. Rather than advising young women against reading sentimental novels, Wollstonecraft in the *Vindication* urges the use of literary criticism as a pedagogical, political, and moral instrument: "The best method, I believe, that can be adopted to correct a fondness for novels is to ridicule them" (185). Her own sentimental novels, particularly *The Wrongs of Woman,* are cut through with sharp social commentary and remarkable descriptions of life within the prison and the madhouse.

If the *Vindication* does not advocate a sentimental education, it advocates several other types: intellectual, spiritual, moral, physical, marital, maternal, and professional. Revising her early writing on education, Wollstonecraft argues that women should be taught not what to know but "how to begin to think" (163), that they should be educated not for marriage but for a life of self-respect, moral virtue, and "a civil existence within the state" (149). She urges teaching methods still regarded as progressive (including coeducation and government-sponsored education) and advocates female representation and women's suffrage. A hybrid of reasoned analysis, provocative metaphors (women are compared to soldiers, slaves, and aristocrats), sharp indictments, and cogent proposals, the *Vindication* addresses itself to the rich complexity of female experience. Wollstonecraft's admonition to women to "effect a revolution in female manners" and to "labour by reforming themselves to reform the world" (45) remains the manifesto of modern feminism.

Esther H. Schor

Mary Wollstonecraft, *Collected Letters of Mary Wollstonecraft* (ed. Ralph M. Wardle, 1979), *Letters Written During a Short Residence in Sweden, Norway, and Denmark* (1796, ed. Carol H. Poston, 1976), *Mary, A Fiction* (1788, ed. Gary Kelly, 1976), *A Vindication of the Rights of Woman* (1792, ed. Carol H. Poston, 1975), *Works of Mary Wollstonecraft* (ed. Janet Todd and Marilyn Butler, 7 vols., 1989), *The Wrongs of Woman; or, Maria* (1798, ed. Gary Kelly, 1976; also called *Maria, or the Wrongs of Woman*).

Julie Ellison, "Politics, Sentiment, and the Sublime in Williams and Wollstonecraft," *Studies in Eighteenth-Century Culture* 20 (1990); Moira Ferguson, "The Discovery of Mary Wollstonecraft's *The Female Reader,*" *Signs* 3 (1978); William Godwin, *Memoirs of the Author of A Vindication of the Rights of Woman* (1798); Cora Kaplan, "Wild Nights: Pleasure/Sexuality/Feminism," *Sea Changes: Culture and Feminism* (1986); Laurie Langbauer, "An Early Romance: Motherhood and Women's Writing in Mary Wollstonecraft's Novels," *Romanticism and Feminism* (ed. Anne K. Mellor, 1988); Mitzi Myers, "Mary Wollstonecraft's *Letters Written . . . in Sweden:* Toward Romantic Autobiography," *Studies in Eighteenth-Century Culture* 8 (1978), "Pedagogy as Self-Expression in Mary Wollstonecraft: Exorcising the Past, Finding a Voice," *The Private Self* (ed. Shari Benstock, 1988); Mary Poovey, *The Proper Lady and the Woman Writer* (1984); Tilottama Rajan, "Wollstonecraft and Godwin: Reading the Secrets of the Political Novel," *Studies in Romanticism* 27 (1988); William St. Clair, *The Godwins and the Shelleys* (1989); Harrison R. Steeves, *Mary Wollstonecraft: A Bibliography* (1976); Emily W. Sunstein, *A Different Face: The Life of Mary Wollstonecraft* (1975); Claire Tomalin, *The Life and Death of Mary Wollstonecraft* (1974); Anna Wilson, "Mary Wollstonecraft and the Search for the Radical Woman," *Genders* 6 (1989); Virginia Woolf, "Mary Wollstonecraft," *The Second Common Reader* (1932).

WOOLF, VIRGINIA

Virginia Woolf (1882–1941) is a critic whose theoretical strengths have been retrospectively identified and revised by successive generations of readers and critics. First, her call for fiction whose "stuff . . . is a little other than custom would have us believe it" (*Collected* 2:106) and the example of her nine novels were seen as defining her as a major British high modernist. Then she was reconstructed as one of the founders of contemporary feminism. Her emphases in her novels on the experiences and inner lives of her female characters, her discussions in her criticism and reviews of women authors, and especially her essay on women and writing, *A Room of One's Own* (1929), led to her elevation as a literary "mother" as an alternative to the many "fathers" available to male writers. Finally, the 1980s saw an increased emphasis on Woolf's subversive strategies as a writer and especially as an instance of feminist writing and on the politics of her writings.

Much of Woolf's strictly literary criticism appeared in journal articles and reviews, which she published from December 1904, when her first review appeared in the women's pages of the *Guardian,* a weekly newspaper for the clergy, to March 1941, when three weeks before her death her last review appeared in the *New Statesman & Nation.* Her long and fruitful relationship with the *Times Literary Supplement* began in 1905; as her work became better known, she published in other journals as well, among them the *Athenaeum* (later the *Nation & Athenaeum*), the *New Statesman* (later the *New Statesman & Nation*), the *London Mercury,* and the *Criterion* in England and the *New Republic, Vogue, Dial,* the *New York Herald Tribune,* and the *Yale Review* in the United States.

In 1925 and 1932 Woolf published revised versions of some of her reviews and articles, along with new pieces, in *The Common Reader* and *The Second Common Reader* (edited as *The Common Reader: First Series* in 1984 and *The Second Common Reader* in 1986). After her death, Leonard Woolf released four collections—*The Death of the Moth* (1942), *The Moment* (1947), *The Captain's Death Bed* (1950), and *Granite and Rainbow* (1958)—and then in 1966 and 1967 assembled all the essays published in these six books in a four-volume edition of the *Collected Essays.* He arranged the essays according to subject matter, putting, he explained in a note, the "literary and critical" essays in volumes 1 and 2 and those that were "mainly biographical" into volumes 3 and 4. Other collections appearing in the late 1960s and 1970s brought together additional reviews and articles: *Contemporary Writers* (1965), *Books and Portraits* (1977), and *Women and Writing* (1979). A complete edition of Woolf's essays, projected to comprise six volumes and containing many previously uncollected pieces, began to appear in 1986.

Woolf's critical writings have received less scholarly attention than have her fiction and autobiographical writings. Some commentators have assumed her to be an impressionistic critic whose essays are of interest mainly as graceful footnotes to her fictional works, but others have questioned this limited assessment. She has been praised, for example, for her contribution to biographical criticism, for her emphasis on the importance of a writer's historical and social context, and for the ways in which she explores the art of writing itself, not only in the content of her essays but also in their form and language.

More broadly, she has been "credited with changing the literary canon" (Caughie 180) through her attempts to redefine the important elements in literature and her notices of writers whose work includes those elements. The form of her critical writing, mixing as it often does imaginative, fictional construction with more traditional discursive prose, has received increased attention in the 1980s and 1990s. One prominent example of Woolf's mingling of fiction with social criticism is in the first draft of *The Years,* the early chapters of which were edited by Mitchell A. Leaska and published as *The Pargiters* in 1977. (The social-criticism chapters grew out of a lecture Woolf gave in 1931, a much-reduced version of which was published the same year as "Professions for Women.")

Besides the critical essays, Woolf also wrote many biographical sketches (e.g., her "Lives of the Obscure" series); personal essays in the tradition of WILLIAM HAZLITT, Thomas De Quincey, and WALTER PATER; as well as sketches that border on short fiction. Her lifelong interest in the writing of lives is reflected in her numerous reviews of biographies and memoirs; her interest in other art forms can be seen in her essays on painting and cinema. Her sense of the importance of the historical and social context in which a work was written is, as many feminist literary critics have noted, central to her extended essays on the conditions in which women live and work, *A Room of One's Own* (1929) and *Three Guineas* (1938), as well as to her shorter feminist essays, including "Women and Fiction" (1929) and "Professions for Women." Her historical perspective is also reflected in the prominent essays in which she assessed the contemporary literary scene: "Modern Fiction" (1919), "How It Strikes a Contemporary" (1923), "Mr. Bennett and Mrs. Brown" (1924), "The Narrow Bridge of Art" (1927), "The Art of Fiction" (1927), and "The Leaning Tower" (1940), among others.

Woolf wrote her essays and reviews not only *for* but *as* a "common reader." Thus her comments about reading offer fascinating insights into her own methods as a critic. In "How Should One Read a Book?" (1926), for example, she describes "the true complexity of reading." The reader must "receive impressions with the utmost understanding," she writes, but this "is only half the process of reading." For the reader must also "pass judgment upon these multitudinous impressions." We must let the book "as a whole" return in our mind after we have finished it and then compare that book with others. We are no longer the writer's friend, she adds, "but his judges; and just as we cannot be too sympathetic as friends, so as judges we cannot be too severe" (*Collected* 2: 8). The "process of measurement," she writes in "An Essay in Criticism" (1927), "is one of the most difficult of a critic's tasks" (2:255).

The sympathetic perspective she recommends for the reader is one Woolf habitually adopts as a critic. "Our first task," she says in her review of *Robinson Crusoe*

(1926), "and it is often formidable enough, is to master" the writer's "perspective" (*Collected* 1:70). This assumption underlies the open-mindedness that characterizes her reviews, a generosity that, for one thing, leads her to seek something good to say about works that she must finally judge to be failures. Woolf will often enact in a critical essay the process of her effort to master the writer's perspective. This process is characteristically heuristic: she asks questions as she reads, tests possible answers, and then considers the new questions her tentative conclusions give rise to. "Our first impressions of Tchekov are not of simplicity but of bewilderment," she writes in "The Russian Point of View." "What is the point of it, and why does he make a story out of this? we ask as we read story after story" (1:240). The process of assessment is less tentative, although here too Woolf tends to avoid dogmatism.

As some of the best analyses of Woolf's critical writings have shown, one of her primary and consistent concerns in these (as in her fiction) is with language. Her concern with words is reflected in numerous essays, including "Impassioned Prose" (1926), "The Art of Fiction" (1927), "A Letter to a Young Poet" (1932), "Craftsmanship" (1937), and the extended essay "Phases of Fiction" (1929), where she concludes:

> It is the gift of style, arrangement, construction, to put us at a distance from the special life and to obliterate its features; while it is the gift of the novel to bring us into close touch with life. The two powers fight if they are brought into combination. The most complete novelist must be the novelist who can balance the two powers so that the one enhances the other. (2:101)

One can see Woolf also balancing the two "powers" in her critical essays. They are vividly concrete, filled with images and details that bring us close to the person, works, or period she is discussing. But what is equally important, they also express in their shape and style the remarkable sense of language that enabled her to present the complex fabric of "life." "I feel in my fingers the weight of every word," she acknowledged late in her life, "even of a review" (*Diary* 5:335).

If Woolf did indeed help to change the literary canon, the accomplishment is tied to her tireless attempts to redirect the content and form of fiction and to open up possibilities for the writing and appreciation of writing by women. Two of her best-known essays—"Modern Fiction" (a 1919 *TLS* article, revised in *The Common Reader;* the original article has been reprinted as "Modern Novels" in *Essays,* vol. 3) and "Mr. Bennett and Mrs. Brown" (1924)—articulate her conception of modernist fiction.

Both essays contrast the group of writers she calls the Edwardians—H. G. Wells, Arnold Bennett, John Galsworthy—with those she calls the Georgians—E. M. Forster, D. H. Lawrence, Lytton Strachey, James Joyce, T. S. Eliot, and, by implication, herself ("Mr. Bennett," 1:320). Faced with the Edwardian "materialists" (2:104), who concentrate on superficial external details rather than on the more important inner experience, Woolf asks in "Modern Fiction," "Is life like this? Must novels be like this?" (2:106) and argues memorably that

> Life is not a series of gig-lamps symmetrically arranged; life is a luminous halo, a semi-transparent envelope surrounding us from the beginning of consciousness to the end. Is it not the task of the novelist to convey this varying, this unknown and uncircumscribed spirit, whatever aberration or complexity it may display, with as little mixture of the alien and external as possible? (2:106)

Central to the attempt to convey this "spirit" is a willingness to depict "the dark places of psychology" (2:108), as already evident in Russian writers such as Chekhov. In "Mr. Bennett and Mrs. Brown," Woolf focuses more directly on characterization. Claiming provocatively that "in or about December, 1910, human character changed" (1:320), she accuses Arnold Bennett and the other Edwardians of ignoring the change. Were Bennett to write a novel about an elderly couple—named by Woolf Mrs. Brown and Mr. Smith—whom she observed on a train, he would present only external details about clothing and property: "He is trying to hypnotize us into the belief that, because he has made a house, there must be a person living there" (1:330). The Edwardians have not looked at Mrs. Brown, "never at her, never at life, never at human nature" (1:330). Modern art will be possible only "if we are determined never, never to desert Mrs. Brown" (1:337).

Woolf's concerns for the development of fiction led her to take issue with some of the main critics and theorists of fiction of her day. She criticized E. M. Forster's *Aspects of the Novel* for too easily assuming that fiction simply imitates and is parasitic on life ("What is this 'Life' that keeps on cropping up so mysteriously and complacently in books about fiction?" ["The Art of Fiction," 2:53]) and for ignoring the language of fiction ("Almost nothing is said about words" [2:54]). On the other hand, she berated Percy Lubbock for, as she saw it, assuming equally easily in *The Craft of Fiction* that a book is equivalent to its form; for her, a book's form involves the novelist's ability to place emotions "in right relations to each other" and to find, modify, or invent methods to do this, and also the reader's emotions and feelings while reading ("On Re-reading Novels," 2:125–26, 129–30).

An important part of Woolf's passionate concern for the art of her day, but moving far beyond it, is her attention to the question of women and writing. Her 1905 review of W. L. Courtney's *The Feminine Note in Fiction,* in which she asked, "Is it not too soon after all to criticise the 'feminine note' in anything? And will not the adequate critic of women be a woman?" (*Essays* 1:15), shows her already asking questions that will be central to her own critical discussions of works by and about women. She addressed these issues most forcefully and influentially in her books *A Room of One's Own* (1929) and *Three Guineas* (1938) and in essays such as the published lecture "Professions for Women" (1931). *A Room of One's Own,* the published version of two lectures given at Oxford University in 1928, claims that "a woman must have money and a room of her own if she is to write fiction" (4). The "money" is eventually specified at five hundred pounds a year, and Woolf later explains that "five hundred a year stands for the power to contemplate" and "a lock on the door means the power to think for oneself" (106). Reflecting often calmly, sometimes angrily, on the exclusion of women over the centuries from such patriarchal educational institutions as Oxford and Cambridge, Woolf shows how the creative impulses of women have been continually stifled, leading her to speculate about the inevitable suicide of Judith Shakespeare, William's imagined, equally gifted sister, who lacked any outlets for her talents (46 ff.), and about the fictional Mary Carmichael, a potentially talented contemporary novelist who, because she lacks models and a tradition to draw on, is still a hundred years away from being able to develop her gifts fully, to "be a poet" (94).

Along with "Professions for Women," which argues that "killing the Angel in the House was part of the occupation of a woman writer" of her generation (*Collected* 2:286), and with the more controversial *Three Guineas,* which attempts to bridge the gap between literature and politics and satirically to expose male authority figures, linking patriarchy and fascism, *A Room of One's Own* has been enormously influential for Anglo-American FEMINIST THEORY AND CRITICISM. For one thing, it inspired many subsequent writers to look for literary ancestors in both well-known and lost women writers from the past. It led to a process of "thinking back through our mothers," as Jane Marcus titled an article on Woolf (in *Art and Anger*), and writers like Alice Walker (in her 1983 *In Search of Our Mothers' Gardens*) credit *Room* as inspirational. Second, along similar lines, it helped to redirect critical receptiveness to "private" as well as "public"

subject matter in fiction and to find historical authority figures not only in the public sphere but also in the private and domestic ones. Third, *Room* introduced the concept of "the androgynous mind" as a model for the artist. Attributing the idea to SAMUEL TAYLOR COLERIDGE (98), Woolf describes the androgynous mind as "resonant and porous; . . . it transmits emotion without impediment; . . . it is naturally creative, incandescent and undivided" (98). Androgyny is necessary because "it is fatal to be a man or woman pure and simple; one must be woman-manly or man-womanly" (104). The androgynous ideal has been both fruitful and controversial, championed most prominently by Carolyn G. Heilbrun in *Toward a Recognition of Androgyny* (1973) and attacked by Elaine Showalter in *A Literature of Their Own* (1977). Fourth, *Room* (and *Three Guineas* even more strongly) positions women as outsiders in patriarchal society, denied opportunities in education and limited in the kinds of available life experiences. Finally, *Room* is striking in its tone, described by Hermione Lee as one of "ease and urbanity" (ix) and by Mary Gordon as "exalted" but also "conversational" (xiii). Only recently, with the publication of Woolf's complete diary, has it become obvious how hard Woolf worked to suppress her anger in order to construct that tone (*Diary* 3:242, 262; Lee ix).

Changes since the mid-1980s in Virginia Woolf criticism have affected the perception of Woolf's critical and theoretical writings in several ways. For one thing, Woolf's idea of the "common reader" has received renewed and increased attention. What she meant by the term is more puzzling and more provocative, shifting as it does from a casual reader to one like Woolf herself to a contemporary reader to a transhistorical one (Caughie 184–85). At times, it anticipates readers such as those posited by Wayne C. Booth, whose reader picks up the cues supplied by the novel's "implied author," and Wolfgang Iser, whose reader fills in gaps in a text (181; see also FICTION THEORY AND CRITICISM: 3. EARLY TWENTIETH-CENTURY BRITISH AND AMERICAN, GERMAN THEORY AND CRITICISM: 5. CONTEMPORARY, and RECEPTION THEORY). Reading for Woolf can be seen as more a process than a product (12–13).

Second, Woolf's self-conscious use, especially in *A Room of One's Own,* of the first-person pronoun (the obsession of modern men, she declares) has been linked to DECONSTRUCTION's attack on the Western idea of the unified self. Woolf states at the beginning of *Room* that she will be "making use of all the liberties and licences of a novelist" in her lectures and that the "'I' is only a convenient term for somebody who has no real being" (4). She notes "a straight, dark bar, a shadow shaped something like the letter 'I'," which makes it hard "to catch a glimpse of the landscape behind it" (99), and she continues, "One began to be tired of 'I.' Not but what this 'I' was a most respectable 'I'; honest and logical; as hard as a nut, and polished for centuries by good teaching and good feeding. . . . But . . . the worst of it is that in the shadow of the letter 'I' all is shapeless as mist" (100).

Third, her critical and theoretical writings blend, and subvert distinctions between, traditional genres, mixing as they do discursive prose and imaginative creation. Major examples are the creation of the "character" Mrs. Brown in her essay on characterization, "Mr. Bennett and Mrs. Brown," and the novelist Mary Carmichael and especially Shakespeare's sister Judith in *A Room of One's Own*. There is also *The Pargiters,* part of the early "novel-essay" sections of the first draft of *The Years,* which in its original conception was a book interspersing essay chapters with fictional ones. Finally, the materialist aspect of Woolf's thinking has received renewed attention. She emphasizes "the importance of material things" in *Room* and *Three Guineas* (Lee vii), arguing that a woman can write only if she has enough money for privacy, adequate food, and so on. Attention to this aspect of Woolf's thought has also led to renewals of old charges that her thinking is class-bound, since she makes claims like the one in *Room* that "genius like Shakespeare's is not born among labouring, uneducated, servile people" (48; Gordon viii). Likewise, the charge brought by Q. D. Leavis against *Three Guineas* in 1938—that Woolf had no experience with working-class people and their experiences ("Caterpillars of the World, Unite," *Scrutiny,* September 1938)—has been raised again in a more contemporary context by Elaine Showalter (295–96).

Susan Dick (revised by the editors)

See also FEMINIST THEORY AND CRITICISM: 2. ANGLO-AMERICAN FEMINISMS and FICTION THEORY AND CRITICISM: 3. EARLY TWENTIETH-CENTURY BRITISH AND AMERICAN.

Virginia Woolf, " 'Anon' and 'The Reader': Virginia Woolf's Last Essays" (ed. Brenda Silver, *Twentieth Century Literature* 25 [1979]), *Books and Portraits: Some Further Selections from the Literary and Biographical Writings of Virginia Woolf* (ed. Mary Lyon, 1977), *Collected Essays* (ed. Leonard Woolf, 4 vols., 1966–67), *The Common Reader: First Series* (1925, ed. Andrew McNeillie, 1984), *Contemporary Writers* (ed. Jean Guiguet, 1965), *The Diary of Virginia Woolf* (ed. Anne Olivier Bell, 5 vols., 1977–84), *The Essays of Virginia Woolf* (ed. Andrew McNeillie, 3 vols. to date, 1986–), *The Pargiters: The Novel-Essay Portion of "The*

Years" (ed. Mitchell A. Leaska, 1977), *A Room of One's Own* (1929, reprint, 1981), *The Second Common Reader* (1932, ed. Andrew McNeillie, 1986), *Three Guineas* (1938), *Women and Writing* (ed. Michèle Barrett, 1979).

Pamela L. Caughie, *Virginia Woolf and Postmodernism: Literature In Quest and Question of Itself* (1991); Mark Goldman, *The Reader's Art: Virginia Woolf as Literary Critic* (1976); Mary Gordon, Foreword to *A Room of One's Own* (by Virginia Woolf, 1981); Suzette Henke, "Virginia Woolf: The Modern Tradition," *The Gender of Modernism* (ed. Bonnie Kime Scott, 1990); B. J. Kirkpatrick, *A Bibliography of Virginia Woolf* (1980); Hermione Lee, Introduction to *A Room of One's Own / Three Guineas* (by Virginia Woolf, 1984); Jane Marcus, *Art and Anger: Reading Like a Woman* (1988); Perry Meisel, *The Absent Father: Virginia Woolf and Walter Pater* (1980); Toril Moi, *Sexual/Textual Politics: Feminist Literary Theory* (1985); Elaine Showalter, *A Literature of Their Own: British Women Novelists from Brontë to Lessing* (1977); Brenda Silver, *Virginia Woolf's Reading Notebooks* (1983); Elizabeth Steele, *Virginia Woolf's Literary Sources and Allusions: A Guide to the Essays* (1983), *Virginia Woolf's Rediscovered Essays: Sources and Allusions* (1986); René Wellek, *A History of Modern Criticism: 1750–1950,* vol. 5, *English Criticism, 1900–1950* (1986).

WORDSWORTH, WILLIAM

"Wordsworth," MATTHEW ARNOLD wrote in 1864, "was himself a great critic, and it is to be sincerely regretted that he has not left us more criticism" (238). Twentieth-century opinion has tended to agree with Arnold's statement, both in its assessment of Wordsworth's importance as a literary critic and in its recognition of the relatively small body of work on which his critical reputation stands. Although Wordsworth made numerous critical observations on literature in his letters, in his notes on his poems dictated to Isabella Fenwick, and even in his poetry itself (especially his 14-book epic *The Prelude*), his contribution to critical theory resides primarily in the preface to *Lyrical Ballads* (1800) and the preface to *Poems* (1815) and in the *Essays Upon Epitaphs* (1810).

Wordsworth is generally regarded as the central English Romantic poet, distinguished for his radical innovations in poetic theory and practice, which have been seen as anticipating modernism. To the second edition (1800) of his *Lyrical Ballads* (originally a collaboration with SAMUEL TAYLOR COLERIDGE), Wordsworth added a preface in which he explained the poetics of his sometimes unconventional verses. The poems were written as an "experiment," he said, to determine to what extent "a selection of the real language of men in a state of vivid sensation" might be suitable for poetry (*Prose* 1:119). Aware of conventional late-eighteenth-century literary taste, Wordsworth in the 1798 advertisement to *Lyrical Ballads* had already anticipated objections to the volume because of its stylistic "strangeness and awkwardness" or its use of language "too familiar, and not of sufficient dignity" to be acceptable as poetry (1:116). His achievement in both his criticism and his poetry is to have reoriented literary taste toward a new language.

The two main ideas of Wordsworth's preface to *Lyrical Ballads* center on the related issues of style and psychology, or as he put it, on the manner in which "language and the human mind act and re-act on each other" (1:121). The first part of the argument concerns what sort of language—diction, rhetorical figures, syntax—is proper to poetry. Repudiating the "gaudiness and inane phraseology of many modern writers" (1:123), Wordsworth strives for what Coleridge later calls "an austere purity of language" (*Biographia* 2:142). The emphasis on simplicity of poetic language, which Wordsworth continues to urge in the 1802 appendix to the preface, derives from his contention that "humble and rustic life" provides "a more permanent, and a far more philosophical language, than that which is frequently substituted for it by Poets" (*Prose* 1:125). The radical nature of Wordsworth's declared swerve from conventional poetic diction, especially stock "poetic" vocabularies, cannot be overemphasized. Such a literary revolution, in which common life was described in common language, ordinary incidents were presented in an extraordinary aspect, and poetry sought nothing less than to reinvent its medium of words, was sometimes charged with banality and triviality; yet it was this new style in English poetry, claiming to be based on "a selection of the language really spoken by men" (1:137) and self-consciously defining itself against previous "extravagant and absurd" styles (1:162), that paved the way for the modern idiom in poetry. In conjunction with his stress on purity of diction Wordsworth argues for simplicity of rhetoric and syntax. His statement that "there neither is, nor can be, any *essential* difference between the language of prose and metrical composition" (1:135) affirms a desire for natural word order, grammar, and sentence structure in poetry, as distinct from the corrupt style of earlier poets; and his aversion to certain rhetorical figures, especially "personifications of abstract ideas" in the eighteenth-century manner (1:131), shows his deliberate move away from what he perceived to be another mechanical artifice.

The other main concern of the preface is the process of the poet's mind in creation and the reader's mind in the act of reading. By defining good poetry as "the spontaneous overflow of powerful feelings" arising from "emotion recollected in tranquillity" (1:149), Wordsworth participates in what M. H. ABRAMS calls an "expressive" aesthetics (*Mirror* 21), that is, a conception of poetry as the expression or manifestation of a psyche. Certainly it could be said that Romanticism generally is "expressive" in its theoretical underpinnings, and Wordsworth most clearly so in his extensive autobiographical poetry; but it should also be said that Wordsworth balances his theoretical emphasis on the "spontaneous overflow" of the poet's soul with what Abrams would call a "pragmatic" (*Mirror* 14) awareness of the reader. To the question "What is a Poet?" Wordsworth replies: "He is a man speaking to men" (*Prose* 1:138)—a definition that combines both the sender and the receiver in the poetic speech act. This double focus, on both the character of the poet (i.e., superior sensibility, greater knowledge of human nature, more immediate sympathy, and more spontaneous expressiveness), on the one hand, and the mind of the informed, sympathetic, and imaginative reader, on the other, is implicit in many of the poems in *Lyrical Ballads,* in which "the feeling therein developed gives importance to the action and situation, and not the action and situation to the feeling" (1:129). As the hybrid genre of the "lyrical ballad" itself suggests, external incident (ballad) is subordinated to internal feeling (lyric), in polemical contrast to what Wordsworth sees as the "degrading thirst after outrageous stimulation" in contemporary literature (1:129–31). The neoclassical belief that poetry should give both pleasure and knowledge still stands in Wordsworth's theory, but with a new emphasis on the interaction of language and the human mind, on the way that a common style can express "the manner in which we associate ideas in a state of excitement" (1:123–25).

The 1815 preface to *Poems,* though not as widely read today as Wordsworth's earlier preface, is crucial to an understanding of his theory of imagination and fancy. After explaining the classification of his poems according to their psychological motivation, literary form, or subject, Wordsworth devotes the remainder of the 1815 preface to a discussion of the relation between the "divine" faculty imagination and the less creative faculty fancy. The distinction, by no means absolute in either his theory or his practice, involves different processes of poetic selection and combination and different rhetorical or psychological effects. The "processes of imagination," Wordsworth writes, "are carried on either by conferring additional properties upon an object, or abstracting from it some of those which it actually possesses, and thus enabling it to re-act upon the mind which hath performed the process, like a new existence" (3:32). To illustrate "the conferring, the abstracting, and the modifying powers of the Imagination" (3:33), Wordsworth quotes examples from Virgil, William Shakespeare, and John Milton, as well as from his own poetry, that involve either metaphor or metonymy. Metaphor "confers" qualities on the basis of identity or similarity; metonymy "abstracts" qualities on the basis of property or association. His example from *King Lear*—"half way down / Hangs one who gathers samphire"—seizes on the metaphor "hangs" as "a slight exertion of . . . imagination, in the use of one word" (3:31), while his self-quotation from "To the Cuckoo"—"O, Cuckoo! shall I call thee Bird, / Or but a wandering Voice?"—illustrates an abstraction or displacement (from the bird to its voice) which is metonymic or synecdochic in its effect. Rejecting seventeenth- and eighteenth-century empirical definitions of imagination as merely "a mode of memory" (3:30), an ability to image absent external objects in the mind, Wordsworth argues for imagination as "a word of higher import, denoting operations of the mind upon those objects, and processes of creation or of composition" (3:31). Chief among these creative processes is the act of "consolidating numbers into unity, and dissolving and separating unity into number" (3:33).

While the imagination operates on "the plastic, the pliant, and the indefinite" (3:36), fancy works with what Coleridge in the *Biographia Literaria* calls "fixities and definites" (1:305). Here Wordsworth and Coleridge agree, but Wordsworth gives more credit to fancy than Coleridge does, claiming that "Fancy, as she is an active, is also, under her own laws and in her own spirit, a creative faculty" (*Prose* 3:37). In his note to "The Thorn" (1800), Wordsworth puts it somewhat differently: the imagination is "the faculty which produces impressive effects out of simple elements," while the fancy is "the power by which pleasure and surprise are excited by sudden varieties of situation and by accumulated imagery" (*Wordsworth's Literary* 96). Coleridge outlines his disagreement with Wordsworth in chapter 12 of the *Biographia,* arguing that what Wordsworth thinks is fancy alone is really fancy and imagination blended. For Wordsworth, however, the materials, the processes, and the rhetorical or psychological effects of the fancy differ from those of the imagination in that they are merely capricious, transient, only temporarily surprising; the imagination, by contrast, deals with infinitude: it is, as Wordsworth writes in *The Prelude,* "another name for absolute power / And clearest insight, amplitude of mind, / And Reason in her most exalted mood" (14.190–92).

The three *Essays Upon Epitaphs* (only the first of which

was published in Wordsworth's lifetime, in 1810) have come into prominence recently as major theoretical texts both because of their focus on a central Wordsworthian genre, the epitaph, and because of their implications for a theory of figurative language. As a minor literary genre, the epitaph has a long tradition stretching back to classical times and rising in interest in the eighteenth century. For Wordsworth the epitaph becomes a literary form that permeates his poetry, often in radically transfigured and unexpected ways: the recurrent Wordsworthian encounter with seemingly or actually dead figures—the Boy of Winander, the blind beggar, the drowned man, the Maid of Buttermere, and the discharged soldier, to name some examples from *The Prelude*—frequently draws on an epitaphic rhetoric to bring the poet into relation with a metaphysical absence or loss that is proleptically his own. Wordsworth's interest in the *Essays,* however, is primarily in the style and decorum of verse epitaphs, that is, in both their proper sentiments and the corresponding language in which those sentiments are to be expressed. As in the preface to *Lyrical Ballads,* Wordsworth's aim here is to separate "truth and sincerity from falsehood and affectation" (*Prose* 2:82), and by way of illustration, not least, to condemn Alexander Pope's epitaphs as "little better than a tissue of false thoughts, languid and vague expression, unmeaning antithesis, and laborious attempts at discrimination" (2:80). The necessary "criterion of sincerity" (2:70) for the poet is consistent with Wordsworth's "expressive" orientation; hence the extravagant and hyperbolic style of many eighteenth-century epitaphs must be rejected in favor of simple, passionate, and permanent language.

The importance of the *Essays* to a theory of language, as understood by rhetorical and deconstructive critics, stems from Wordsworth's discussion of the figure of personification, or prosopopoeia. While in the preface to *Lyrical Ballads* Wordsworth wishes to avoid "personifications of abstract ideas" intended only "to elevate the style, and raise it above prose" (1:131), here he confronts the reason "why epitaphs so often personate the deceased, and represent him as speaking from his own tomb-stone" (2:60). Wordsworth regards this rhetorical device as a "tender fiction" (2:60), consistent with human intimations of immortality, but still less preferable than epitaphs "in which the survivors speak in their own persons" (2:61). Even this latter mode, however, can make use of prosopopoeia through addresses or apostrophes to the deceased. What is at issue, in poststructuralist terms, is the relation between epitaph and (auto)biography and the rhetorical function of personification in giving voice to a dead figure, either character or author.

On the larger question of proper epitaphic style, Wordsworth makes his greatest claim for the power of language: "Words are too awful an instrument for good and evil to be trifled with: they hold above all other external powers a dominion over thoughts. If words be not . . . an incarnation of the thought but only a clothing for it, then surely will they prove an ill gift" (2:84). Rewriting the neoclassical commonplace that words are the dress of thought, Wordsworth substitutes a supremely logocentric or incarnationist conception of language, implicit in which is the possibility that words might be "a counter-spirit, unremittingly and noiselessly at work to derange, to subvert, to lay waste, to vitiate, and to dissolve" meaning as much as to incarnate it (2:85). The *Essays Upon Epitaphs* thus pose questions of a hermeneutic or interpretive nature that are of considerable interest to literary theorists today.

While Wordsworth's literary criticism may be, as W. J. B. Owen has said, "almost invariably an exposition or a defence of his own poetry" (*Wordsworth's Literary* 1), it nevertheless expresses ideas, values, and precepts applicable beyond his own *oeuvre,* beyond the particular literary context or historical occasion that prompted a preface, essay, or appendix. Wordsworth's "Conversations with Klopstock" (*Prose* 1:91–95), "Reply to 'Mathetes'" (2:8–25), "Letter to a Friend of Robert Burns" (3:117–29), his fragmentary essay on "The Sublime and the Beautiful" (2:349–60), and numerous letters to Coleridge, the Beaumonts, John Wilson, Charles James Fox, and Alexander Dyce (see *Letters of William and Dorothy Wordsworth*), not to mention his social and political criticism, stand as widely ranging examples of his theorizing on literature and aesthetics. But it is mainly the two prefaces, and more recently the *Essays Upon Epitaphs,* that secure Wordsworth's reputation as a critic. Whether read in the immediate context of his theory and practice or taken to represent the poetics of Romanticism generally, Wordsworth's literary criticism continues to be of central importance in the history of criticism and theory.

J. Douglas Kneale

See also BRITISH THEORY AND CRITICISM: 3. ROMANTIC PERIOD AND EARLY NINETEENTH CENTURY and SAMUEL TAYLOR COLERIDGE.

William Wordsworth, *The Letters of William and Dorothy Wordsworth* (2d ed., ed. Ernest de Selincourt, rev. Chester L. Shaver, Mary Moorman, and Alan G. Hill, 7 vols., 1967–88), *Literary Criticism of William Wordsworth* (ed. Paul M. Zall, 1966), *The Poetical Works of William Wordsworth* (ed. Ernest de Selincourt, rev. Helen Darbishire, 5 vols., 1952–63), *The Prelude: 1799, 1805, 1850* (ed. Jonathan Wordsworth, M. H. Abrams, and Stephen Gill, 1979), *The Prose Works of William Wordsworth* (ed. W. J. B. Owen and Jane Worthington Smyser, 3 vols., 1974), *Wordsworth's Literary Criticism* (ed. W. J. B. Owen, 1974).

M. H. Abrams, *The Mirror and the Lamp: Romantic Theory and the Critical Tradition* (1953); Matthew Arnold, "The Function of Criticism at the Present Time," *Poetry and Criticism of Matthew Arnold* (ed. A. Dwight Culler, 1961); Samuel Taylor Coleridge, *Biographia Literaria* (1817, ed. James Engell and W. Jackson Bate, 2 vols., 1983); Paul de Man, "Autobiography as De-Facement," *The Rhetoric of Romanticism* (1984); Frances Ferguson, *Wordsworth: Language as Counter-Spirit* (1977); Geoffrey H. Hartman, *The Unremarkable Wordsworth* (1987), *Wordsworth's Poetry, 1787–1814* (1964, 3d ed., 1971); J. Douglas Kneale, *Monumental Writing: Aspects of Rhetoric in Wordsworth's Poetry* (1988); W. J. B. Owen, *Wordsworth as Critic* (1969); Markham L. Peacock, Jr., *The Critical Opinions of William Wordsworth* (1950).

ZOLA, ÉMILE

Émile Zola (1840–1902) achieved notoriety and renown in a number of fields, as art critic, political journalist, novelist, literary critic and theorist, dramatist, and defender of Alfred Dreyfus. As the supposed originator and principal advocate of literary naturalism, he also enjoyed extensive influence in a number of countries, even in the English-speaking world. Despite his claims of scientific objectivity and disinterestedness, the provocative nature of his literary works and ideas and his readiness to engage in polemics made him a controversial figure for most of his career and have led to widely divergent assessments of his achievements. Zola's creative works have undergone thorough and extensive scrutiny, interpretation, and reevaluation in the last three decades. But his critical and theoretical writings still suffer from the discredit attached to his unconvincing theory of the "experimental novel."

Born in Paris, the son of an Italian engineer, Zola spent his early years in Aix-en-Provence. This period of his life was clouded by his father's death in 1847 and by ensuing financial hardship but provided the consolations of a deep friendship with Paul Cézanne and their shared love of the Provençal landscape. Impelled to Paris in 1858, Zola lived in penurious bohemia for a number of years, giving himself an unconventional yet thorough literary education. Eventually he obtained modest employ with the publisher Hachette, where he became imbued with the positivist, scientific, encyclopedist spirit of his age, turning to new literary and intellectual models, notably Honoré de Balzac and HIPPOLYTE TAINE. During the last few years of the Second Empire Zola launched into an independent career as a journalist, causing stirs not only for his political opposition to the imperial regime but also for his defense of Manet and the pre-Impressionist painters. In 1868 he embarked upon what would become his major literary achievement, a 20-volume series of novels, *Les Rougon-Macquart*, that took him 25 years to complete. Yet, before very long, he would find himself more reviled and extolled than ever, not for the didactic novels and lyrical

dramas to which he turned in his later years but for his courageous intervention in the Dreyfus affair. There are still those who believe that his death by asphyxiation from a blocked chimney in his Paris apartment in 1902 was not the accident that it was officially declared to be.

Zola's critical writings, which occupy three substantial volumes of his complete works, fall roughly into two phases. The first comprises a series of texts belonging to the period 1865–69, mostly book reviews published in the Parisian and provincial press, some of which were collected together in 1866 under the forbidding title *Mes Haines* ("My Hates"). Though less audacious than his art criticism of this period, his early literary studies do establish basic principles of what he came at this time to call "naturalism," a body of convictions that derived from the realist literary tradition, the visual arts, positivist philosophy, and the natural sciences. These articles contain pleas for the freedom of artistic expression; for the rejection of traditional dogmatic formulas; for a respect for the truth, however brutal and unpleasant it might be; and for modern subjects. In a study of Taine, whose disciple he proudly proclaimed himself to be, Zola summarizes with approval his mentor's view that a mind is "a plant that he examines as a naturalist" (*Oeuvres complètes* 10:563). The lexicon of the natural sciences would become an integral part of his critical vocabulary.

A second and more substantial body of writings belongs to the period 1875–80, when a further spate of journalistic activity was prompted by the urgent need to defend, justify, explain, and theorize upon the fiction that he and certain fellow naturalist writers had been recently publishing in the face of virulent critical reactions. A number of these studies first appeared in a Russian periodical *Vestnik Evropy* [Herald of Europe] before being published in French, along with many others, in *Le Voltaire* and *Le Bien public,* then in a series of volumes: *Le Roman expérimental* (1880), *Les Romanciers naturalistes* (1881), *Le Naturalisme au théâtre* (1881), *Nos Auteurs dramatiques* (1881), and *Documents littéraires* (1881), to which should be added the articles of Zola's *Le Figaro* "campaign" of 1880–81 collected together as *Une Campagne*

(1882). *Le Roman expérimental,* for example, contains, in addition to the controversial essay on "The Experimental Novel," a variety of studies of contemporary writers and critics, of naturalism in the theater, and of the place of literature in the French republic. Even though these articles do contain an abundance of sound critical judgments and sensible comments on individual writers and works, they are in general marked and marred by a disarming dogmatism. Zola employs all the strategies of the propagandist, incessantly repeating certain catch phrases, inveighing against his opponents, ruthlessly dividing writers into two camps: the naturalist depicters of the truth and the vain rhetoricians, recuperating all realist writers into an imaginary, longstanding naturalist tradition. Zola privately called himself at this time a *critique de combat,* and clearly, even his most theoretical statements can only be judged or understood in relation to the polemical context in which they were uttered.

Obscured by the more strident scientism of his better-known theories, there are, however, frequent assertions of Zola's fundamental belief in the mimetic purpose of literature, wrought from a constant struggle against literary conventions and endowed with a compelling "sense of the real." But Zola's reputation as a theoretician has depended almost exclusively upon the attention aroused by his essay "The Experimental Novel," first published in *Vestnik Evropy* in September 1879. On the basis of a reading of Claude Bernard's *Introduction à l'étude de la médecine expérimentale* (1865), Zola argues that just as the experimental method had been successfully adapted from chemistry and physics to apply to physiology and medicine, so it could be brought to apply to the novel. The novelist should therefore become not only an observer, as Zola had previously asserted, but also an experimenter, directing his characters in a particular situation to demonstrate that a succession of events is rigorously ordered by the "determinism of phenomena." "Finally", he claimed, "you possess knowledge of [the] man, scientific knowledge of him, in both his individual and social relations" (*Naturalist Novel* 5).

Critics have summarily dismissed Zola's theory as naive and untenable. Yet the essay itself does deserve the more sympathetic explanations and more careful scrutiny that it is beginning to receive. Zola's scheme may be viewed, for example, as an elaborate motivating sys-

tem of fictional representation, one that is perfectly logical and understandable in the age of the prestigious biological *episteme* on which it is based. The scientifically verified laws of nature provided established, guiding sequences of consequentiality to motivate naturalist fictions, whose domain remained, as Zola was careful to insist, not the realm of the sciences themselves but the world of the novelist, of the individual in society. Furthermore, a closer study of the essay suggests that Zola's views are no more than an emphatic version of the aesthetics of the 1860s, with Taine's principles remaining as a subtext of this apparently wholesale appropriation of Claude Bernard's theories. Thus the essay may be considered less as a theoretical essay than as a strategic text, issued within the context of the relentless battle of prefaces, manifestoes, critical reviews, pamphlets, and articles that characterized the Parisian literary scene, belonging therefore to the process of challenge, conflict, and renewal by which new styles, forms, and genres need to be forcibly imposed on literary institutions and on the reading public. Finally, the text of Zola's essay itself bears witness to the author's polemical intentions in the use of more than 50 quotations from Claude Bernard's book, for the quotation is, of course, a common rhetorical strategy, a feature of authoritarian forms of discourse and of forms of discourse that seek to be authoritative. Thus Zola's *compilation de textes,* as he called it, through the very otherness of its citational devices, still allows him indirectly to preserve the integrity of his own more flexible views.

David Baguley

See also FRENCH THEORY AND CRITICISM: 3. NINETEENTH CENTURY and HIPPOLYTE TAINE.

Émile Zola, *The Experimental Novel, and Other Essays* (trans. Belle M. Sherman, 1893), *The Naturalist Novel* (ed. Maxwell Geismar, 1964), *Oeuvres critiques I–III* (vols. 10–12 of *Oeuvres complètes,* ed. Henri Mitterand, 1968–69).

Aimé Guedj, "Diderot et Zola," *Europe* 46 (1968); F. W. J. Hemmings, *Émile Zola* (2d ed., 1966); Alain de Lattre, *Le Réalisme selon Zola: Archéologie d'une intelligence* (1975); Henri Mitterand, *Zola journaliste* (1962), *Zola et le naturalisme* (1986); Guy Robert, "Zola et le classicisme," *Revue des sciences humaines* 49–50 (1948); Michel Serres, *Feux et signaux de brume, Zola* (1975).

ENTRIES

CONTRIBUTORS

John Allison, Eastern Illinois University: American Theory and Criticism: Nineteenth Century

Charles Altieri, University of Washington: G. W. F. Hegel

Frederick Amrine, University of Michigan: Johann Wolfgang von Goethe

Paul B. Armstrong, University of Oregon: Phenomenology

Evelyn W. Asher: German Theory and Criticism: 4. Twentieth Century to 1968, 5. Contemporary

G. Douglas Atkins, University of Kansas: Geoffrey H. Hartman

Linda Austin, Oklahoma State University: John Ruskin

David Baguley, University of Western Ontario: Émile Zola

Ian Balfour, York University: Walter Benjamin

Eve Tavor Bannet: Georg Lukács

Zygmunt G. Barański, University of Reading: Dante Alighieri

Robert de Beaugrande, University of Vienna: Discourse: 1. Discourse Analysis

Russell A. Berman, Stanford University: German Theory and Criticism: 3. Nineteenth Century

Don Bialostosky, University of Toledo: M. H. Abrams; Francis Bacon

James A. Boon, Princeton University: Claude Lévi-Strauss

Gordon Braden, University of Virginia: Renaissance Theory and Criticism

Stephen C. Brennan, Louisiana State University, Shreveport: New Humanism

Chiara Briganti, Carleton College: Hélène Cixous; Luce Irigaray; Psychoanalytic Theory and Criticism: 3. The Post-Lacanians

Gerald L. Bruns, University of Notre Dame: Martin Heidegger

E. S. Burt, University of California, Irvine: Jean-Jacques Rousseau

Hunter Cadzow, University of Oklahoma: New Historicism

Jay L. Caplan, Amherst College: French Theory and Criticism: 2. Eighteenth Century

Marvin Carlson, City University of New York Graduate Center: Drama Theory

Susan R. Carlton, University of Michigan: Simone de Beauvoir

W. B. Carnochan, Stanford University: David Hume

Peter Carravetta, Queens College, City University of New York: Italian Theory and Criticism: 2. Twentieth Century

Joseph Carroll, University of Missouri—St. Louis: Matthew Arnold

Anthony J. Cascardi, University of California, Berkeley: Immanuel Kant

Robert L. Caserio, University of Utah: Fiction Theory and Criticism: 2. Nineteenth-Century British and American

James V. Catano, Louisiana State University, Baton Rouge: Stylistics

Mary Ann Caws, City University of New York Graduate Center: Charles Baudelaire; French Theory and Criticism: 4. Early Twentieth Century

William M. Chace, Wesleyan University: Lionel Trilling

James K. Chandler, University of Chicago: William Hazlitt

Cynthia Chase, Cornell University: Paul de Man

Michael P. Clark, University of California, Irvine: Jacques Lacan

Clare Colquitt, San Diego State University: Margaret Fuller

Terry Comito, George Mason University: Yvor Winters

Rita Copeland, University of Minnesota: Medieval Theory and Criticism

Brian Corman, University of Toronto: Chicago Critics

Reed Way Dasenbrock, New Mexico State University: Stanley Fish

Frank Davey, University of Western Ontario: Canadian Theory and Criticism: 1. English

Robert Con Davis, University of Oklahoma: Hélène Cixous; Luce Irigaray; Psychoanalytic Theory and Criticism: 3. The Post-Lacanians

Frank Day, Clemson University: William Empson

Patrick Deane, University of Western Ontario: W. H. Auden

Richard Dellamora, Trent University: Gay Theory and Criticism: 1. Gay Male

Susan Dick, Queen's University: Virginia Woolf

George L. Dillon, University of Washington: Discourse: 2. Discourse Theory; Rhetoric

Lubomír Doležel, University of Toronto: Prague School Structuralism

Milena Doleželová-Velingerová, University of Toronto: Chinese Theory and Criticism: 2. Pre-modern Theories of Fiction and Drama

Alan Durant, University of London: Orality and Literacy

Patrick H. Dust, Carleton College: José Ortega y Gasset

Antony Easthope, Manchester Metropolitan University: Cultural Studies: 1. United Kingdom

Kathy Eden, Columbia University: Classical Theory and Criticism: 2. Rhetoric

Mark Edmundson, University of Virginia: Samuel Taylor Coleridge

Diane Elam, Indiana University: Feminist Theory and Criticism: 3. Poststructuralist Feminisms

John M. Ellis, University of California, Santa Cruz: German Theory and Criticism: 4. Twentieth Century to 1968, 5. Contemporary

Caryl Emerson, Princeton University: M. M. Bakhtin

Evelyne Ender, University of Geneva: Geneva School; Jean Starobinski

Mark W. Epstein, Princeton University: Galvano della Volpe

Angela Esterhammer, University of Western Ontario: Friedrich Hölderlin

Michèle Longino Farrell, Duke University: Nicolas Boileau-Despréaux

John Fekete, Trent University: Raymond Williams

Peter Fenves, Northwestern University: Søren Kierkegaard

Nelly Furman, Cornell University: Charles Augustin Sainte-Beuve

Hans Walter Gabler, University of Munich: Textual Criticism

Regenia Gagnier, Stanford University: Value Theory

Steven Gillies: German Theory and Criticism: 1. Sturm und Drang / Weimar Classicism, 2. Romanticism

Gîtahi Gîtîtî, University of Rhode Island: African Theory and Criticism

Leon Golden, Florida State University: Aristotle; Classical Theory and Criticism: 1. Greek

Sandor Goodhart, Cornell University: Biblical Theory and Criticism: 2. Modern Criticism; René Girard

Paul Gordon, University of Colorado at Boulder: J. Hillis Miller

Vernon Gras, George Mason University: Cambridge Ritualists

Michael Groden, University of Western Ontario: Fiction Theory and Criticism: 3. Early Twentieth-Century British and American

Georg M. Gugelburger, University of California, Riverside: Postcolonial Cultural Studies

Madelyn Gutwirth, University of Pennsylvania: Germaine de Staël

M. A. R. Habib, Rutgers University, Camden: Marxist Theory and Criticism: 1. Classical Marxism

Walid Hamarneh, Yale University: Arabic Theory and Criticism

Sarah Harasym, University of Western Ontario: Gayatri Chakravorty Spivak

Elizabeth D. Harvey, University of Western Ontario: Sir Philip Sidney

Bruce Henricksen, Loyola University, New Orleans: Murray Krieger

Judith Scherer Herz, Concordia University: Bloomsbury Group

Nelson Hilton, University of Georgia: William Blake

Michael Ann Holly, University of Rochester: Art Theory

Renate Holub, University of California, Berkeley: Francesco De Sanctis

Robert C. Holub, University of California, Berkeley: Jürgen Habermas; Hermeneutics: 2. Twentieth Century

Linda Hutcheon, University of Toronto: Sigmund Freud

Theodore Huters, University of California, Irvine: Chinese Theory and Criticism: 3. Twentieth Century

Michael Issacharoff, University of Western Ontario: Émile Benveniste; Roman Jakobson

Robin Jarvis, University of the West of England, Bristol: F. R. Leavis

Paul Jay, Loyola University, Chicago: Kenneth Burke

Biodun Jeyifo, Cornell University: Frantz Fanon

Michael T. Jones, University of Kentucky: Theodor W. Adorno

Verina R. Jones, University of Reading: Italian Theory and Criticism: 1. Romanticism

Feroza Jussawalla, University of Texas at El Paso: Indian Theory and Criticism

Walter B. Kalaidjian, St. Cloud State University: Susan Sontag

Ketu H. Katrak, University of Massachusetts, Amherst: Wole Soyinka

Thomas Keenan, Princeton University: Walter Benjamin

Douglas Kellner, University of Texas at Austin: Fredric Jameson

Hans Kellner, University of Texas at Arlington: Hayden White

R. L. Kesler, Oregon State University: Ben Jonson

Jon Klancher, Boston University: British Theory and Criticism: 3. Romantic Period and Early Nineteenth Century

J. Douglas Kneale, University of Western Ontario: Deconstruction; William Wordsworth

Christopher J. Knight, Miami University: Gertrude Stein

Ira Konigsberg, University of Michigan: Film Theory

Martin Kreiswirth, University of Western Ontario: Henry James

Vera M. Kutzinski, Yale University: Caribbean Theory and Criticism

Andrew Lakritz, Miami University: Wallace Stevens

Donna Landry, Wayne State University: Feminist Theory and Criticism: 4. Materialist Feminisms

Jules David Law, Northwestern University: Ludwig Wittgenstein

Sarah Lawall, University of Massachusetts, Amherst: René Wellek

Roland Le Huenen, University of Toronto: French Theory and Criticism: 3. Nineteenth Century

Mónica Lebron, University of Western Ontario: Latin American Theory and Criticism

Vincent B. Leitch, Purdue University: Cultural Studies: 2. United States

Seth Lerer, Stanford University: Erich Auerbach

Geert Lernout, University of Antwerp: Reception Theory

Robert Leventhal, University of Virginia: G. E. Lessing

A. Walton Litz, Princeton University: R. P. Blackmur; Ezra Pound

Kent P. Ljungquist, Worcester Polytechnic Institute: Edgar Allan Poe

S. A. Longstaff, York University: New York Intellectuals

Nigel Love, University of Cape Town: Noam Chomsky

Gregory L. Lucente, University of Michigan: Antonio Gramsci

Murray McArthur, University of Waterloo: British Theory and Criticism: 5. Symbolism

Karen A. McCauley, University of California, Los Angeles: Russian Formalism

John McGowan, University of North Carolina, Chapel Hill: Postmodernism

Richard Macksey, Johns Hopkins University: History of Ideas; Longinus

Gerald MacLean, Wayne State University: Feminist Theory and Criticism: 4. Materialist Feminisms

Vicki Mahaffey, University of Pennsylvania: Modernist Theory and Criticism

Marc Manganaro, Rutgers University: Anthropological Theory and Criticism

Uri Margolin, University of Alberta: Moscow-Tartu School

Robert Markley, University of Washington: British Theory and Criticism: 1. Early Eighteenth Century

Jean I. Marsden, University of Connecticut: British Theory and Criticism: 2. Late Eighteenth Century

Theodore O. Mason, Jr., Kenyon College: African-American Theory and Criticism: 1. Harlem Renaissance to the Black Arts Movement, 2. 1977 and After

Louis Menand, Queens College and Graduate Center, City University of New York: Oscar Wilde; Edmund Wilson

Ellen Messer-Davidow, University of Minnesota: Feminist Theory and Criticism: 1. 1963—1972

J. Hillis Miller, University of California, Irvine: Walter Pater

Christopher D. Morris, Norwich University: Psychoanalytic Theory and Criticism: 2. Reconceptualizing Freud

Gary Saul Morson, Northwestern University: M. M. Bakhtin

Charles A. Moser, George Washington University: Russian Theory and Criticism: Nineteenth Century

Gabriel Moyal, McMaster University: René Descartes

Heather Murray, University of Toronto: Practical Criticism

Suzanne Nash, Princeton University: Paul Valéry

Alexander Nehamas, Princeton University: Friedrich Nietzsche

Margot Norris, University of California, Irvine: D. H. Lawrence

Kelly Oliver, University of Texas at Austin: Julia Kristeva

Deborah Parker, University of Virginia: Umberto Eco

Donald E. Pease, Dartmouth College: Harold Bloom

Vincent P. Pecora, University of California, Los Angeles: Frankfurt School

Paul Perron, University of Toronto: Semiotics

Mark Poster, University of California, Irvine: Michel Foucault

Kenneth M. Price, Texas A&M University: George Santayana

Gerald Prince, University of Pennsylvania: Narratology

Anthony Purdy, University of Alberta: Canadian Theory and Criticism: 2. French

Jean-Michel Rabaté, University of Pennsylvania: Roland Barthes; Jacques Derrida

Nancy Sorkin Rabinowitz, Hamilton College: Adrienne Rich

Peter J. Rabinowitz, Hamilton College: Reader-Response Theory and Criticism

Balachandra Rajan, University of Western Ontario: T. S. Eliot

Tilottama Rajan, University of Western Ontario: Hermeneutics: 1. Nineteenth Century; Arthur Schopenhauer

Herman Rapaport, University of Iowa: French Theory and Criticism: 5. 1945—1968, 6. 1968 and After

Bill Readings, University of Montreal: John Dryden; Jean-François Lyotard

Marc Redfield, Claremont Graduate School: Georges Bataille; Maurice Blanchot

Charles Eric Reeves, Smith College: Myth Theory and Criticism

Joan Ramon Resina, Northwestern University: Spanish Theory and Criticism

John J. Richetti, University of Pennsylvania: Fiction Theory and Criticism: 1. Seventeenth- and Eighteenth-Century British

David H. Richter, Queens College, City University of New York: Benedetto Croce

Bruce Robbins, Rutgers University: George Orwell

Douglas Robinson, University of Mississippi: Linguistics and Language; Speech Acts

Robert Ross, University of Texas at Austin: Australian Theory and Criticism

Carol Schreier Rupprecht, Hamilton College: Archetypal Theory and Criticism

John Paul Russo, University of Miami: Historical Theory and Criticism; I. A. Richards

Herman J. Saatkamp, Jr., Texas A&M University: George Santayana

R. G. Saisselin, University of Rochester: French Theory and Criticism: 1. Seventeenth Century

Ronald Schleifer, University of Oklahoma: Ferdinand de Saussure; Structuralism

Esther H. Schor, Princeton University: Mary Wollstonecraft

Bonnie Kime Scott, University of Delaware: Feminist Theory and Criticism: 2. Anglo-American Feminisms

Leroy F. Searle, University of Washington: New Criticism; Charles Sanders Peirce

Giuseppe Sertoli, University of Genoa: Edmund Burke

W. David Shaw, University of Toronto: British Theory and Criticism: 4. Victorian; John Stuart Mill

Richard Shusterman, Temple University: John Dewey; Richard Rorty

James J. Sosnoski, Miami University: Edward W. Said

Francis Sparshott, University of Toronto: Plato

Richard Stingle, University of Western Ontario: Northrop Frye

Leon Surette, University of Western Ontario: Thomas S. Kuhn, Marshall McLuhan

Neal Tolchin, Hunter College, City University of New York: Ralph Waldo Emerson

Makoto Ueda, Stanford University: Japanese Theory and Criticism

Karl D. Uitti, Princeton University: Philology

Steven Ungar, University of Iowa: Jean-Paul Sartre

Mario J. Valdés, University of Toronto: Paul Ricoeur

William VanderWolk, Bowdoin College: Gustave Flaubert; Hippolyte Taine

Steven Van Zoeren, Stanford University: Chinese Theory and Criticism: 1. Pre-modern Theories of Poetry

Donald Phillip Verene, Emory University: Giambattista Vico

David Wallace, University of Minnesota: Giovanni Boccaccio

Robert Weninger, Washington University: Friedrich Schiller

Gary Wihl, McGill University: Marxist Theory and Criticism: 2. Structuralist Marxism

David Willbern, State University of New York at Buffalo: Psychoanalytic Theory and Criticism: 1. Traditional Freudian Criticism

James A. Winders, Appalachian State University: Stéphane Mallarmé and French Symbolism; Karl Marx and Friedrich Engels

Dolora Wojciehowski, University of Texas at Austin: St. Augustine

Ross G. Woodman, University of Western Ontario: Percy Bysshe Shelley

James Woodruff, University of Western Ontario: Samuel Johnson

Tzvee Zahavy, University of Minnesota: Biblical Theory and Criticism: 1. Midrash and Medieval Commentary

Bonnie Zimmerman, San Diego State University: Gay Theory and Criticism: 2. Lesbian

Sheldon Zitner, University of Toronto: Horace

INDEX OF NAMES

Darío, Rubénz: Latin American

Defoe, Daniel: Fiction 1

De Laurctis, Teresa: Feminist 3; Gay 1; Semiotics

Deleuze, Gilles: Film; French 6; Psychoanalytic 3

DELLA VOLPE, GALVANO: Italian 2

DE MAN, PAUL: Bloom; British 5; Chicago; Deconstruction; French 6; Miller; Pater; Rhetoric; Rousseau

Demosthenes: Longinus

Dennis, John: British 1; Edmund Burke

DERRIDA, JACQUES: Art; Deconstruction; French 4, 5, 6; Linguistics; Mallarmé; McLuhan; Phenomenology; Rousseau; Speech Acts; Structuralism

DE SANCTIS, FRANCESCO: Italian 2

DESCARTES, RENÉ: Hegel; Kant; Valéry

Deschamps, Eustache: Medieval

Descombes, Vincent: French 6

Devi, Mashasweta: Spivak

Devoto, Giacomo: Italian 2

Dewart, Edward Hartley: Canadian 1

DEWEY, JOHN: Peirce

Dickens, Charles: Fiction 2; Miller

Diderot, Denis: French 2

Dilthey, Wilhelm: German 4; Hermeneutics 1; Historical

Dobell, Sydney: British 4

Dobrolyubov, Nikolay: Russian: Nineteenth

Donovan, Josephine: Feminist 1

D'Ors, Eugeni: Spanish

Dos Passos, John: Sartre

Dostoevsky, Fyodor: Bakhtin; Russian: Nineteenth

Droysen, Johann Gustav: Historical

Druzhinin, Alexander: Russian: Nineteenth

DuBois, W. E. B.: African-American 1

Dudek, Louis: Canadian 1

Duff, William: British 2

Eagleton, Terry: Marxist 2

Echeverría, Esteban: Latin American

ECO, UMBERTO: Semiotics

Eikhenbaum, Boris: Russian Formalism

Eisenstein, Sergei: Film

Eliot, George: Fiction 2

ELIOT, T. S.: Anthropological; Arnold; Blackmur; Modernist; New Criticism; Pound

Elliott, G. R.: New Humanism

Ellison, Ralph: African-American 1, 2

Ellmann, Mary: Feminist 1

Else, Gerald: Aristotle

EMERSON, RALPH WALDO: American

EMPSON, WILLIAM: New Criticism

Euripides: Classical 1

Faderman, Lillian: Gay 2

FANON, FRANTZ: Postcolonial

Fauriel, Claude: French 3

Faye, Jean Pierre: French 6

Felman, Shoshana: Deconstruction; Psychoanalytic 3

Feng Menglong: Chinese 2

Fetterley, Judith: Feminist 2; Reader

Fichte, Johann Gottlieb: Hegel

Ficino, Marsilio: Renaissance

Fiedler, Leslie: Myth

Fielding, Henry: Fiction 1

Figes, Eva: Feminist 1

Firestone, Shulamith: Feminist 1

FISH, STANLEY: Reader; Stylistics; Value

FLAUBERT, GUSTAVE: Fiction 2; Pound; Sartre

Foerster, Norman: New Humanism

Ford, Ford Madox: Fiction 3

Forster, E. M.: Bloomsbury; Fiction 3

FOUCAULT, MICHEL: Discourse 2; French 5; Gay 1; History of Ideas; Linguistics; New Historicism

Fox, W. J.: British 4

Frank, Joseph: Fiction 3

Frank, Manfred: Hermeneutics 2

Frazer, James G.: Anthropological; Cambridge

Freire, Paolo: Orality

FREUD, SIGMUND: Auden; Bloom; Feminist 2; Frankfurt; French 5, 6; German 3; Irigaray; Lacan; Psychoanalytic 1, 2, 3; Trilling

Friedan, Betty: Feminist 1

Friedemann, Käthe: German 4

Fromm, Erich: Frankfurt

Fry, Roger: Bloomsbury

FRYE, NORTHROP: Anthropological; Archetypal; Arnold; Canadian 1; Myth; New Criticism; Rhetoric

Fu Sinian: Chinese 3

Fulgentius: Medieval

Fumaroli, Marc: French 1

Furetière, Antoine: French 1

TRILLING, LIONEL: Arnold; Fiction 3; New York
    Intellectuals
Trinh T. Minh-ha: Feminist 3
Trotsky, Leon: Marxist 1
Truffaut, François: Film
Turgenev, Ivan: Fiction 2; Russian: Nineteenth
Turim, Maureen: Film
Turner, J. M. W.: Ruskin
Turner, Victor: Anthropological
Tyndale, William: New Historicism
Tynianov, Iurii: Russian Formalism

Unger, Roberto Mangabeira: Value
Uspenskij, Boris: Moscow-Tartu

VALÉRY, PAUL: French 4; Mallarmé
Valmiki: Indian
Van Ghent, Dorothy: Fiction 3
Van Meurs, Jos: Archetypal
Ventós, Xavier Rubert de: Spanish
VICO, GIAMBATTISTA: Auerbach; Historical; Philology
Villiers De l'Isle-Adam, Philippe Auguste: British 5
Virgil: Medieval
Voloshinov, Valentin: Bakhtin; Linguistics
Voltaire: French 2
Von Fritz, Kurt: Aristotle

Wagner, Christian: Aristotle
Wagner, Richard: Drama; Nietzsche
Walcott, Derek: Caribbean
Walker, Alice: African-American 2
Walpole, Horace: Fiction 1
Walzel, Oskar: German 4
Wang Guowei: Chinese 2
Warburg, Aby: Art
Warren, Robert Penn: Fiction 3
Warton, Joseph: British 2
Warton, Thomas: British 2
Watt, Ian: Fiction 3

Weber, Max: Frankfurt
Weimann, Robert: German 5
WELLEK, RENÉ: Goethe; Historical
Wells, H. G.: Fiction 2
White, Patrick: Australian
Whiter, Walter: British 2
Whitman, Walt: American; Gay 1
WILDE, OSCAR: Arnold; British 4; Fiction 2
WILLIAMS, RAYMOND: Bloomsbury; Fiction 3; Marx and
    Engels
Wimsatt, W. K., Jr.: New Criticism
Winckelmann, Johann Joachim: Historical
WITTGENSTEIN, LUDWIG: Linguistics
Wittig, Monique: Feminist 3
Wölfflin, Heinrich: Art
Woolf, Leonard: Bloomsbury
WOOLF, VIRGINIA: Bloomsbury; Cixous; Feminist 2; Fiction 3; Modernist
WORDSWORTH, WILLIAM: Abrams; British 3; Coleridge;
    Mill; Ruskin
Wright, Richard: African-American 1, 2
Wycherley, William: British 1
Wynter, Sylvia: Caribbean

Xiao Gang: Chinese 1
Xiao Tong: Chinese 1

Yan Yu: Chinese 1
Yeats, William Butler: Bloom; British 5; Modernist
Young, Edward: British 2
Yuan Hongdao: Chinese 1

Zeami: Japanese
Zhang Zhupo: Chinese 2
Zhdanov, A. A.: Marxist 1
Zhong Hong: Chinese 1
Zhou Deqing: Chinese 2
Zhou Zuoren: Chinese 3
ZOLA, ÉMILE: Fiction 2

INDEX OF TOPICS

Designed by Edward D. King.

Text composed by Connell Zeko Type & Graphics in Stone Serif developed
by Sumner Stone with Carol Twombly's Trajan Display.

Printed on 60-pound Glatfelter Offset and bound in ICG Arrestox C 62000 with
Rainbow Ivory Felt endsheets by the Maple Press Company.